# OFFICIAL BASEBALL GUIDE for 1976

•

PUBLISHER
## C. C. JOHNSON SPINK

EDITORS
## JOE MARCIN
## CHRIS ROEWE
## LARRY WIGGE
## LARRY VICKREY

•

PUBLISHED BY
## The Sporting News
1212 North Lindbergh Boulevard
St. Louis, Missouri 63166

Copyright © 1976
The Sporting News Publishing Company

ISBN 0-89204-007-6

# Government of Organized Baseball

⊖✖⊖

## MAJOR LEAGUES

COMMISSIONER—Bowie K. Kuhn

SECRETARY-TREASURER—Alexander H. Hadden

HEADQUARTERS—75 Rockefeller Plaza
New York, N. Y. 10019

Telephone—586-7400 (area code 212)

Teletype—710-581-4279

EXECUTIVE COUNCIL—Bowie K. Kuhn, Commissioner; Leland S. Mac-Phail, Jr., President of American League; Charles S. Feeney, President of National League; John E. Fetzer and Edmund D. Fitzgerald, representatives of American League, and Walter F. O'Malley and John J. McHale, representatives of National League.

ADMINISTRATIVE OFFICER—John Johnson

SPECIAL ASSISTANT TO THE COMMISSIONER—Joseph L. Reichler

DIRECTOR OF INFORMATION—Robert A. Wirz

CO-ORDINATOR OF INTER-AMERICAN BASEBALL—Roberto Maduro

DIRECTOR OF SECURITY—Henry A. Fitzgibbon

NATIONAL ASSOCIATION REPRESENTATIVES—Robert R. Bragan, President of the National Association, and members of National Association Executive Committee.

⊖✖⊖

## NATIONAL ASSOCIATION
## OF PROFESSIONAL BASEBALL LEAGUES

PRESIDENT-TREASURER—Robert R. Bragan

VICE-PRESIDENT—P. Patrick McKernan

ASSISTANT TO PRESIDENT—William J. Wood

DIRECTOR OF RESEARCH AND RECORDS—Don Avery

SECRETARY TO PRESIDENT—Karen Stencil

FIELD REPRESENTATIVES—Robert L. Freitas, Jim Mills

HEADQUARTERS—225 Fourth Street South, P. O. Box A,
St. Petersburg, Fla. 33731

Telephone—813-822-6937

Teletype—810-863-0361

EXECUTIVE COMMITTEE—P. Patrick McKernan, Chairman, President of the Eastern League; George H. Sisler, Jr., President of the International League; Wallace McKenna, President of the Carolina League.

# TABLE OF CONTENTS

*For Complete Index See Pages 533 & 534*

---

ON THE COVER: Top left, Tom Seaver, New York—THE SPORTING NEWS N.L. Pitcher of the Year, 1975; top right, Joe Morgan, Cincinnati—THE SPORTING NEWS N.L. Player of the Year, 1975; bottom left, Jim Palmer, Baltimore—THE SPORTING NEWS A.L. Pitcher of the Year, 1975; bottom right, Fred Lynn, Boston—THE SPORTING NEWS A.L. Player of the Year, 1975.

**CHARLES S. FEENEY**
President of the National League

# NATIONAL LEAGUE

### Including

**Club Directories**

**Club Reviews of 1975 Season**

**Club Day-By-Day Scores**

**N. L. Team Pictures**

**1975 League Leaders**

**1975 Official N. L. Averages**

**All-Time N. L. Player Performance Tables**

# National League

### Organized 1876

**CHARLES S. FEENEY**
President

**WARREN C. GILES**
President Emeritus

**JOHN J. McHALE**
Vice-President

**FRED G. FLEIG**
Secretary-Treasurer

**BLAKE CULLEN**
Director of Public Relations

**LOUIS H. KREMS**
Business Manager

Headquarters—Mills Building, 220 Montgomery St., San Francisco, Calif. 94104

Telephone—986-1300 (area code 415)

UMPIRES—Nick Colosi, Jerry Dale, David Davidson, Robert Engel, Bruce Froemming, Thomas Gorman, H. Douglas Harvey, John Kibler, John McSherry, Andy Olsen, Paul Pryor, Frank Pulli, Laurence (Dutch) Rennert, Paul Runge, Dick Stello, Ed Sudol, Terry Tata, Ed Vargo, Harry Wendelstedt, Lee Weyer, Art Williams, William G. Williams, Ed Montague, Jim Quick.

OFFICIAL STATISTICIANS—Elias Sports Bureau, Inc., 500 5th Ave., Suite 2114, New York, N. Y. 10036. Telephone (212) 869-1530.

Players cannot be transferred from one major league club to another after June 15 to the close of the championship season except through regular waiver channels.

WAIVER PRICE, $20,000. Interleague waivers, $20,000, except for selected players and draft-excluded players.

# ATLANTA BRAVES

Chairman of the Board—William C. Bartholomay

President—R. E. (Ted) Turner III
Executive Vice-President—Eddie Robinson
Special Assistant to the General Manager—Connie Ryan
Secretary—Phyllis Collins
Assistant to the Chairman and Traveling Secretary—Don Davidson
Minor League Administrator—Bill Lucas
Assistant Minor League Administrator—Paul Snyder
Manager of Broadcast Sales—Wayne Long
Director of Broadcasting—Ernie Johnson
Controller—Charles Sanders
Chief Accountant—Michael Warren
Ticket Distribution Manager—Lamar Vernon
Director of Public Relations, Promotions and Ticket Sales—
Bob Hope
Publicity Manager—Randy Donaldson
Ticket Sales Manager—Frank Spence
Group Sales Manager—Jon Richardson
Director of Stadium Operations—Joe Shirley
Manager—Dave Bristol
Club Physician—Dr. David T. Watson
Executive Offices — P. O. Box 4064, Atlanta, Ga. 30302
Telephone—522-7630 (area code 404)

SCOUTS — Sam Berry, Ted. Cabrall, Pedro Gonzales, Phil Holmes, Al LaMacchia, Burney R. (Dickey) Martin, Tom Morgan, Bob Turzilli, William R. Wight, H. F. (Red) Wooten.

PARK LOCATION—Atlanta-Fulton County Stadium, on Capitol Avenue at the junction of Interstate Highway 20, 75 and 85.

Seating capacity—51,556

FIELD DIMENSIONS—Home plate to left field at foul line, 330 feet; to center field, 402 feet; to right field at foul line, 330 feet.

# CHICAGO CUBS

President—Philip K. Wrigley

Executive Vice-President—John Holland

Vice-President-General Manager—E. R. Saltwell

Vice-President-Administration, Secretary-Treasurer—
William Heymans

Vice-President-Director of Player Development—
Carroll Lockman

Honorary Vice-President—Charles J. Grimm

Assistant to the General Manager—John Cox

Director of Scouting and Procurement—Vedie Himsl

Director, Park Operations—Charles S. Feeney, Jr.

Traveling Secretary—Dennis Beyreuther

Assistant Traveling Secretary—G. A. Settergren

Home Secretary—Howard Roberts

Manager, Information and Services—Buck Peden

Manager, Group Sales—David Lamont

Director, Ticket Services—Jerome Foran

Manager—Jim Marshall

Club Physician—Dr. Jacob Suker

Executive Offices—Wrigley Field, N. Clark and Addison Streets,
Chicago, Ill. 60613

Telephone—281-5050 (area code 312)

SCOUTS—William T. Capps, Frank DeMoss, Walt Dixon, Eugene L. Handley, John Hennessy, Roy Johnson, Lou Klein, Frank Obregon, John J. O'Neil, H. D. Wilson.

PARK LOCATION—Wrigley Field, Addison Street, N. Clark Street, Waveland Avenue and Sheffield Avenue.

Seating capacity—37,741

FIELD DIMENSIONS—Home plate to left field at foul line, 355 feet; to center field, 400 feet; to right field at foul line, 353 feet.

# CINCINNATI REDS

President & Chief Executive Officer—Robert L. Howsam

Chairman of the Board—Louis P. Nippert
Vice-President—William J. Williams
Treasurer—James R. Williams
Secretary—Andrew Hopple
Assistant Secretary—Henry Hobson, Jr.
Vice-President, Administrative—Dick Wagner
Director of Player Personnel—Sheldon (Chief) Bender
Director of Scouting—Joe Bowen
Special Assistant—Rex Bowen
Director of Publicity—Jim Ferguson
Special Assignment Scout—Ray Shore
Director of Publications—Bob Rathgeber
Director Speakers' Bureau—Gordon Coleman
Traveling Secretary—Paul Campbell
Controller—D. L. Porco
Director of Broadcasting—Jim Winters
Director of Ticket Services—Dale Stoeber
Director of Ticket Department—Craig Dissinger
Director Group Sales—Jeff Odenwald
Director Promotions and Sales—Roger Ruhl
Director Stadium Operations—Terry Barthelmas
Director of Season Tickets—Ann Mansfield
Director of Advertising—Fred Khammar, Jr.
Manager—George (Sparky) Anderson
Club Physician—Dr. George Ballou

Executive Offices—100 Riverfront Stadium, Cincinnati, O. 45202
Telephone—421-4510 (area code 513)

SCOUTS—Larry Barton, Sr., Larry Barton, Jr., Gene Bennett, Porter Blinn, Joseph Caputo, Bill Clark, Larry D'Amato, Reno DeBenedetti, Larry Doughty, Elmer Gray, Edwin Howsam, Chester Montgomery, Tony Robello, Neil Summers, Fred Uhlman, George Zuraw.

PARK LOCATION—Riverfront Stadium, downtown Cincinnati, bounded by Second Street to Ohio River & from Walnut Street to Broadway.

Seating capacity—51,786

FIELD DIMENSIONS—Home plate to left field at foul line, 330 feet; to center field, 404 feet; to right field at foul line, 330 feet.

# HOUSTON ASTROS

Chairman of the Board—Judge Roy Hofheinz

President—Sidney L. Shlenker
Vice-President—Earl Allen
Executive Vice-President and General Manager—Tal Smith
Financial Vice-President, Treasurer and Secretary—John Easter
Vice-President Sales-Marketing-Broadcasting—Dean Borba
Assistant Secretary—Mary Frances Hofheinz
Assistant to the General Manager—John W. Mullen
Director of Scouting and Minor League Clubs—Lynwood Stallings
Traveling Secretary—Arthur V. Perkins
Comptroller—Adam Richards
Director of Promotions and Broadcast Operations—Art Elliott
Director of Ticket Sales—Buddy Hancken
Ticket Manager—Ralph Stolarski
Group Ticket Sales—Loel Passe
Director of Public Relations & Publicity for
Houston Astros—Bobby Risinger
Director of Public Relations & Publicity for
Astrodome—Mack Newberry
Manager—Bill Virdon
Club Physicians—Drs. Harold J. Brelsford,
Hatch Cummings and Joe W. King

## ASTRODOME-ASTROHALL STADIUM CORPORATION

Chairman of the Board—Judge Roy Hofheinz
President—T. H. Neyland
Executive Vice-President—Jimmie Fore
Financial Vice-President, Treasurer and Secretary—John Easter
Vice-President and Director of Operations—Tom Martin
Stadium Engineering and Maintenance—James R. Garner
Executive Offices—Astrodome, P. O. Box, 288, Astrodome,
Houston, Tex. 77001
Telephone—748-4500 (area code 713)
Teletype—910 881-1740

SCOUTS — Harry Craft, Paul Florence, Stan Hollmig, Walt
Matthews, John Quinn, Earl Rapp, Billy Smith.

PARK LOCATION—Astrodome, Kirby Drive and Interstate
Loop 610.

Seating capacity—45,000

FIELD DIMENSIONS—Home plate to left field at foul line, 330
feet; to center field, 400 feet; to right field at foul line, 330 feet.

# LOS ANGELES DODGERS

### BOARD OF DIRECTORS

Walter F. O'Malley, Chairman of the Board; Peter O'Malley, President; Harry M. Bardt, Treasurer; Roland Seidler, Jr., Secretary; Sylvan Oestreicher, H. C McClellan, Robert L. Gordon.

President—Peter O'Malley

Vice-President, Player Personnel—Al Campanis

Vice-President, Minor League Operations—William P. Schweppe

Vice-President, Marketing—Merritt Willey

Vice-President, Public Relations and Promotions—Fred Claire

Controller and Assistant Treasurer—Ken Hasemann

Assistant Secretary—Irene Tanji

Director, Advertising, Novelties and Souvenirs—Danny Goodman

Director, Dodgertown—Charles Blaney

Director, Stadium Operations—Bob Smith

Director, Ticket Operations—Walter Nash

Director, Stadium Club and Transportation—Bob Schenz

Director, Dodger Network—David Van de Walker

Director, Scouting—Ben Wade

Director, Publicity—Steve Brener

Director, Community Relations—Don Newcombe

Director, Speakers' Bureau—Tuck Stainback

Executive Pilot, Dodger 720-B Fan Jet—Captain Lewis G. Carlisle

Administrative Assistant—Ike Ikuhara

Traveling Secretary—Lee Scott

Auditor—Michael Strange

Manager—Walter E. Alston

Club Physicians—Dr. Frank Jobe, Dr. Robert Woods

Executive Offices—Dodger Stadium, 1000 Elysian Park Avenue, Los Angeles, Calif. 90012.

Telephone—224-1500 (area code 213)

SCOUTS — Rafael Avila, Boyd Bartley, Bill Brenzel, Jerry Cunningham, Mel Didier, Dick Hager, Gail Henley, Goldie Holt, Tony John, Dale Jones, John Keenan, Ron King, Ed Liberatore, Dick McLaughlin, Dale McReynolds, Tommy Mixon, Lew Morton, Greg Mulleavy, Mel Nelson, George Noga, John O'Neil, Regie Otero, Ed Roebuck, Rudy Rufer, Jerry Stephenson, Guy Wellman, Bert Wells.

PARK LOCATION—Dodger Stadium, 1000 Elysian Park Avenue.

Seating capacity—56,000

FIELD DIMENSIONS—Home plate to left field at foul line, 330 feet; to center field, 395 feet; to right field at foul line, 330 feet.

# MONTREAL EXPOS

BOARD OF DIRECTORS—Charles R. Bronfman, Chairman; Paul Beaudry, Vice - Chairman; Lorne C. Webster, Vice - Chairman; Charlemagne Beaudry, M. W. Griffin, Hugh Hallward, E. Leo Kolber, Arnold Ludwick, John J. McHale, Sydney Maislin.

President—John J. McHale

Vice-President & Secretary-Treasurer—Harry J. Renaud

Vice-President & Director of Player Personnel—James Fanning

Director of Scouting—Danny Menendez

Director of Public Relations—Larry Chiasson

Director of Merchandising and Broadcasting—Ron Millichamp

Business Manager, Minor League Clubs—Kevin McHale

Field Director, Minor League Clubs—Bob Gebhard

Co-ordinator of Canadian Scouting—Bill MacKenzie

Traveling Secretary—Dick Rock

Controller—Gerry Trudeau

Manager, Tickets—Lucien Geoffrion

Manager, Group Sales—Roger Savard

Co-ordinator of Game Services—Claude St. Vincent

Assistant Director of Public Relations—Rodger Brulotte

Administrative Assistant, Public Relations—Monique Giroux

Assistants, Marketing—Normand Martin, Paul Shubin

Manager—Karl Kuehl

Club Physician—Dr. Robert (Bob) Brodrick

Mailing Address—P. O. Box 500, Station R, Montreal, Quebec H2S 3G7, Canada

Telephone: 273-0433 (area code 514)

SCOUTS (special assignment)—Charlie Fox, Ed Lopat, Bobby Mattick; (full time)—John (Red) Murff, Robert Oldis, Patrick J. Mullin, Robert Zuk; (Canadian)—Wayne Norton, Andre Pratte; (part-time) — Gilbert Bodet, Bob Guess, Steve Hill, Georges Hughes, Gary Kretz, Harry Postove, Chester Reese, Tony Rivas, Luis Rosa.

Park Location—Jarry Park, 285 Faillon Street West, Montreal, Quebec H2R 2W1, Canada

Seating Capacity—28,000

FIELD DIMENSIONS—Home plate to left field at foul line, 340 feet; to center field, 420 feet; to right field at foul line, 340 feet.

# NEW YORK METS

Chairman of the Board—M. Donald Grant

President—Mrs. Lorinda de Roulet
Executive Vice-President-Treasurer—G. Herbert Walker, Jr.
Vice-President-Business Manager—James K. Thomson
Secretary—John W. Payson
Assistant Secretary—Robert M. Riggs
Assistant Secretary and Assistant Treasurer—Francis M. Ellis
Directors—Mrs. Lorinda de Roulet, M. Donald Grant, G. Herbert Walker, Jr., John W. Payson, Frederick K. Trask, James K. Thompson, Joseph A. McDonald.

General Manager—Joseph A. McDonald
Director of Minor League Operations—Pete Gebrian
Director of Player Development—Nelson Burbrink
Special Consultant—Robert B. Scheffing
Controller—William Murray
Ticket Manager—Bob Mandt
Director of Public Relations—Harold Weissman
Promotion Director—Arthur Richman
Traveling Secretary—Lou Niss
Manager—Joe Frazier
Club Physician—Dr. James C. Parkes II
Executive Offices — William A. Shea Stadium, Roosevelt Avenue and 126th Street, Flushing, N. Y. 11368.

Telephone—672-2000 (area code 212)

SCOUTS—Bob Bishop, Wayne Britton, Jocko Collins, Buck Elliott, Nino Escalera, Al Harper, Jim Hughes, Roger Jongewaard, Hank Kelly, Buddy Kerr, Dave Madison, Hershel Martin, Walter Millies, Harry Minor, Julian Morgan, Roy Partee, Warren (Sheriff) Robinson, Marvin Scott, Russ Sehon, Paul Tretiak, Ollie Vanek, Len Zanke.

PARK LOCATION—William A. Shea Stadium, Roosevelt Avenue and 126th Street, Flushing, N. Y. 11368.

Ticket Information—672-3000 (area code 212)

Seating capacity—55,300

FIELD DIMENSIONS—Home plate to left field at foul line, 341 feet; to center field, 410 feet; to right field at foul line, 341 feet.

# PHILADELPHIA PHILLIES

Chairman of the Board—R. R. M. Carpenter, Jr.

President—R. R. M. Carpenter III
Executive Vice-President—William Y. Giles
Vice-President-Director of Player Personnel—Paul Owens
Vice-President-Director of Finance—George F. H. Harrison
Secretary-Treasurer—G. Theodore Harrison
Director of Minor Leagues and Scouting—G. Dallas Green
Director of Publicity and Public Relations—Larry Shenk
Director of Ticket Sales—Thomas T. Hudson
Director of Promotions—Frank H. Sullivan
Ticket Manager—Raymond B. Krise
Traveling Secretary—Edward G. Ferenz
Director of Stadium Operations—Patrick J. Cassidy
Director of Group Sales—Richard Deats
Director of Sales and Advertising—David P. Montgomery
Executive Secretary, Minor Leagues—William V. Gargano
Assistant Director of Stadium Operations—Andrew J. Clarke
Assistant Director of Publicity and Public Relations—Chris Wheeler
Public Relations Assistant—Dennis Lehman
Scouting Administrator—Jack Pastore
Administrator, Minor Leagues—Howie Bedell
National Scouting Supervisor—Brandy Davis
Manager—Danny Ozark
Club Physician—Dr. Phillip Marone
Executive Offices — Philadelphia Veterans Stadium, Broad
Street and Pattison Avenue, Philadelphia, Pa. 19148.
Telephone—463-6000 (area code 215)

SCOUTS—Herb Anderson, Hugh Alexander, Ruben Amaro,
Edward Bockman, George Bradley, Brandy Davis, Paul Duval,
Doug Gassaway, Gordon Goldsberry, Fred Goodman, Carl Greene,
Bill Harper, Wilbur Johnson, John Jorgensen, Lou Kahn, Dick
LeMay, Wes Livengood, Anthony Lucadello, Gene Martin, Gary
Nickels, Tom Oliver, Gust Poulos, Joe Reilly, Ernie Schuerman,
A. C. Swails, Dick Teed, Elmer Valo, Carlton Willey.

PARK LOCATION — Philadelphia Veterans Stadium, Broad
Street and Pattison Avenue.

Seating capacity—56,581

FIELD DIMENSIONS—Home plate to left field at foul line, 330
feet; to center field, 408 feet; to right field at foul line, 330 feet.

# PITTSBURGH PIRATES

Chairman of the Board—John W. Galbreath

President—Daniel M. Galbreath
Vice-President-Secretary—Thomas P. Johnson
Vice-President—Harry L. (Bing) Crosby
Director—Edwin Gott (Emeritus)
Frank R. Denton (Emeritus)
Leslie Worthington (Emeritus)
Director—James M. Johnson
Director—Thomas P. Johnson, Jr.
Director—John A. Mayer
Director—James W. Phillips
Director—Edgar B. Speer
Director—Willard F. Rockwell, Jr.
General Manager—Joe L. Brown
Assistant to General Manager—Joseph M. O'Toole
Treasurer—Arthur C. Routzong
Special Assistant to the General Manager and Director of
Public Relations—William Guilfoile
Assistant Director of Public Relations—Edward Routzong
Director of Group Sales and Promotions—Jack Berger
Assistant Director of Group Sales and Promotions—Michael Baldy
Traveling Secretary—Milt Graff
Director of Advertising—Olin J. DePolo
Auditor—Douglas McCormick
Assistant Auditor—Kenneth C. Curcio
Ticket Manager—Richard C. Holland
Director of Scouting and Minor League Clubs—Harding Peterson
Assistant Director of Scouting—Merrill S. Hess
Assistant Directors of Minor League Clubs—
William G. Turner, Murray Cook
Assistant Director Minor League Clubs and Scouting—
Branch B. Rickey
Special Assignments—Howie Haak, Gene Baker, Lenny Yochim,
Jerry Gardner, Jim Maxwell
Manager—Danny Murtaugh
Club Physician—Dr. Joseph Finegold

Executive Offices—Three Rivers Stadium, 600 Stadium Circle, Pittsburgh, Pa. 15212.

Telephone—323-1000 (area code 412)

Scouting Assistants — Roy Ammoscato, Bard Baukol, Bud Baurle, Carmen Beatrice, Calvin Biron, Antonio Bojos, Paul Bordi, Bill Bryan, F. "Kid" Carr, Dom Cirrito, Frank Coimbre, Cecil Cole, Dick Coury, Pablo Cruz, Bill Darden, Paul Eldredge, Ed Farnum, Ben Fiore, Lou Fitzgerald, Jim Frail, Jack Heimbuecher, LeRoy Hill, Bud Hoff, Bob Johnson, Joe Lacko, Walter (Bucky) Lucas, Julio Martinez, Rudolf Mauriello, Luis Mayorel, Andy Moynihan, Luis Olave, Steve Oleschuk, Hank Pavlik, Dick Probola, Harold Ray, Herb Raybourne, George Schmidt, Jesse Smith, Lloyd Sorrells, Tom Venditelli, Bill White.

PARK LOCATION—Three Rivers Stadium, 600 Stadium Circle.

Seating capacity—50,235

FIELD DIMENSIONS—Home plate to left field at foul line, 335 feet; to center field, 400 feet; to right field at foul line, 335 feet.

# ST. LOUIS CARDINALS

Chairman of the Board, President and Chief Executive Officer—
August A. Busch, Jr.

Vice-President—August A. Busch, III
Vice-President—Fred L. Kuhlmann
Vice-President—Margaret M. Snyder
Secretary and Treasurer—John L. Hayward
Controller—Bob Dilliard
Assistant Secretary—Richard Schwartz
Assistant Treasurer—H. F. Suellentrop
Executive Vice-President & General Manager—V. P. (Bing) Devine
Senior Vice-President—Stan Musial
Special Assistant to General Manager—George Kissell
Vice-President-Administration—Jim Toomey
Vice-President-Operations—Joe McShane
Director of Public Relations—Jerry Lovelace
Traveling Secretary—Lee Thomas
Director of Player Procurement—George Silvey
Administrative Director of Player Development & Scouting—
Jim Bayens
Field Co-ordinator for Player Development—Harry Walker
Ticket Director—Mike Bertani
Director of Promotions—Ken Daust
Director of Sales—Joe Cunningham
Director of Season and Group Ticket Sales—Paul Fauks
Assistant Director of Public Relations—Marty Hendin
Assistant to Director of Player Development & Scouting—
Mike Kavanaugh
Manager—Albert (Red) Schoendienst
Club Physician—Dr. Stan London
Executive Offices — Busch Memorial Stadium, 250 Stadium
Plaza, St. Louis, Mo. 63102.
Telephone—421-3060 (area code 314)

SCOUTS—Dave Bartosch, James Belz, Piper Davis, Roberto
Diaz, Tom DuFour, Angel Figueroa, John Groth, Robert Harrison,
James Johnston, Bob Kennedy, Thornton Lee, Joe Mathes, Fred
McAlister, Jr., Virgil Melvin, Maurice (Mo) Mozzali, Carlos Ne-
gron, Charles (Chase) Riddle, William Sayles, Danny Simons, Roy
Smith, Charles (Tim) Thompson, Norman Trasolini.

PARK LOCATION — Busch Memorial Stadium, Broadway,
Walnut Street, Stadium Plaza and Spruce Street.

Seating capacity—50,126

FIELD DIMENSIONS—Home plate to left field at foul line, 330
feet; to center field, 404 feet; to right field at foul line, 330 feet.

# SAN DIEGO PADRES

### BOARD OF DIRECTORS

Ray A. Kroc, Chairman and Treasurer; Joan Kroc, E. J Bavasi, Donald G. Lubin, Dr. Robert K. Kerlan.

President—E. J. Bavasi

Vice-President and General Manager—Peter Bavasi

Vice-President and Secretary—Donald G. Lubin

Assistant Secretary—Robert N. Grant

Director of Player Personnel—Robert Fontaine

Minor League Administrator—Mike Port

Director of Business Operations—Elten Schiller

Director of Public Relations—Mike Ryan

Director of Promotions—Jim Wiegel

Director of Group Sales—Tom Mulcahy

Director of Season Ticket Sales—Andy Strasberg

Controller—Jan Willis

Traveling Secretary and Trainer—John Mattei

Manager—John McNamara

Club Physician—Dr. Paul Bauer

Executive Offices—P. O. Box 2000, San Diego, Calif. 92120

Telephone—283-4494 (area code 714)

SCOUTS—Ken Bracey, Cliff Ditto, Bobby Fontaine, Warren Hacker, Al Heist, Billy Herman, Mark Just, Marty Keough, Gus Lombardo, Jim Marshall, Richard Schlenker, Don Williams.

PARK LOCATION—San Diego Stadium, 9449 Friars Road.

Seating capacity—47,491

FIELD DIMENSIONS—Home plate to left field at foul line, 330 feet; to center field, 410 feet; to right field at foul line, 330 feet.

# SAN FRANCISCO GIANTS

Co-owners—Robert Lurie and Arthur Herseth

Director of Baseball Operations—Spec Richardson
Coordinator of Baseball Operations—Jerry Donovan
Director of Player Development—Carl Hubbell
Farm Director and Scouting Coordinator—Jack Schwarz
Traveling Secretary—Frank Bergonzi
Ticket Manager—Arthur Schulze
Public Relations Director—John Taddeucci
Promotions Director—Sam Spear
Publicity Director—Stu Smith
Group Sales Director—Mike Beacom
Speakers' Bureau—Joe Orengo
Manager—Bill Rigney

Executive Offices—Candlestick Park, San Francisco, Calif. 94124.

Telephone—467-8000 (area code 415)

SCOUTS — John D. Anderson, Milt Axt, Ellsworth Brown, Walker Cress, Larry DeHaven, Dutch Deutsch, Hugh East, Jack Fulmer, Thomas Futch, Frank Genovese, George Genovese, Edward Hallauer, Herman Hannah, Red Hayworth, Joe Henderson, Thomas J. Hull, Richard Klaus, Jim Lyke, Sal Margaglione, Horacio Martinez, Edward F. Montague, Herbert Newberry, John Piurek, Evo M. Pusich, Hugh Poland, Ron Reynolds, Henry Sauer, Jack Shafer, Nick Shinkoff, Herman Strutz, Gene Thompson, Michael Trbovich, Dick Wilson, Pedro Zorrilla.

PARK LOCATION—Candlestick Park, Bayshore.

Seating capacity—58,000

FIELD DIMENSIONS—Home plate to left field at foul line, 335 feet; to center field, 410 feet; to right field at foul line, 335 feet.

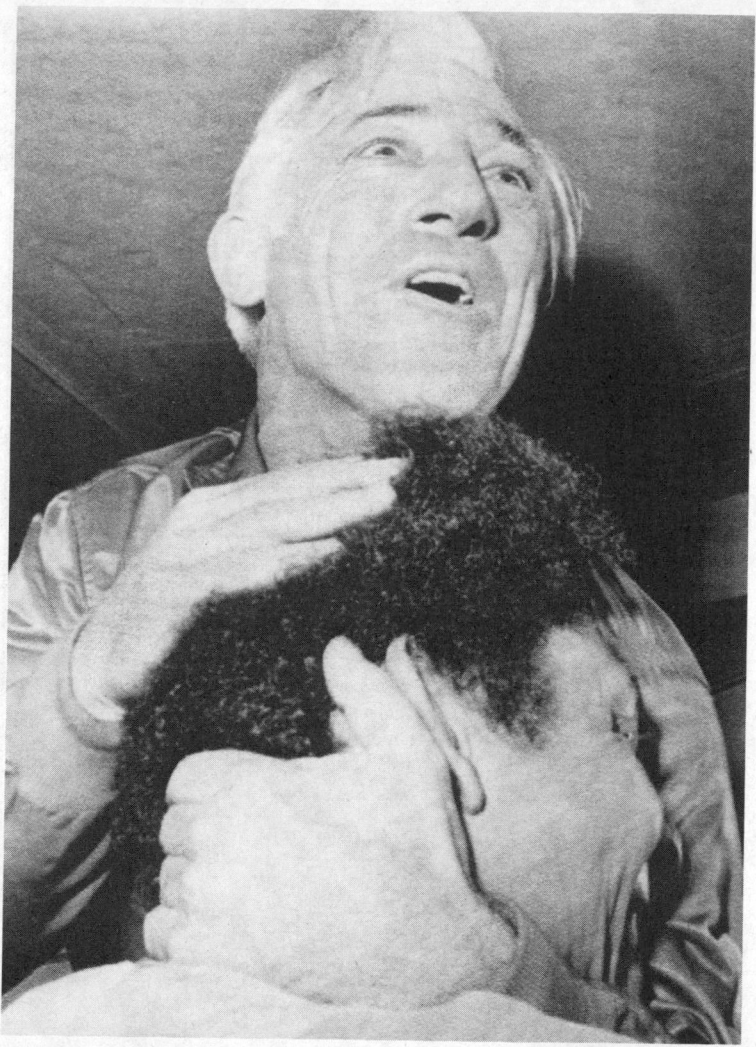

**THE JOY OF VICTORY**—Cincinnati Manager Sparky Anderson hugs first baseman Tony Perez after the Reds won their first World Series since 1940.

# WEST DIVISION

## Reds Raise Series Flag—First Since '40

### By EARL LAWSON

The Cincinnati Reds piled up a club record 108 victories, swept the National League playoffs from the Pittsburgh Pirates in three games and then gave the city its first World Championship since 1940, beating the Boston Red Sox in a thrill-packed seven-game series.

And, what's more, in doing so, the Reds of 1975 stamped itself as the best team in the history of a club which is the oldest in professional baseball.

Appropriately enough, it was Joe Morgan, voted the National League's most valuable player by a panel of 24 writers, two from each city, who delivered the game-winning ninth-inning single in the seventh game of the World Series.

The Reds' 108 victories rated as the third highest total in the league's history, topped only by the 1906 Chicago Cubs (116) and the 1909 Pittsburgh Pirates (110).

Forty-one of those 108 victories came during a 50-game stretch extending from May 21 to July 13 when the Reds, after floundering during the first six weeks of the season, made a runaway of the West Division race.

It was on September 7 that the Reds defeated the San Francisco Giants, 8-4, at Riverfront Stadium to become the earliest National League team in history to clinch a title.

Two weeks later the Reds blanked the Atlanta Braves, 3-0, for their 103rd victory, topping by one the old club record set by the pennant-winning team of 1970.

This, though, was just one of several records, club and individual, which toppled during that almost unbelievable 1975 season.

Others were:

* The Reds won a National League record number of home victories (64), topping the old mark of 61 set by the San Francisco Giants in 1962.

* They set a major league record by playing 15 consecutive games without making an error.

* The pitching staff set a major league record by going 45 consecutive games without a complete-game performance.

("That's one record I'm not too proud of," Red Manager Sparky Anderson remarked after rookie righthander Pat Darcy ended the string.)

* Morgan broke his old club record for walks by drawing 132.

* The Reds drew a club record 2,315,603 in home attendance. A record, too, was the road attendance of 1,694,160.

* Tony Perez became the all-time Reds' run producer, raising his career total to 1,024 RBIs. He passed former record holder Frank Robinson when he singled home Morgan September 2 at San Diego with RBI No. 1,010.

* Relief pitcher Clay Carroll appeared in 56 games boosting his career total with the Reds to 486, two more than the old club record previ-

CINCINNATI REDS—1975

Front row—Rose, Morgan, Kluszewski, coach; Grammas, coach; Anderson, manager; Scherger, coach; Shepard, coach; Norman, Flynn, Rettenmund. Second row—Stowe, equipment manager; Campbell, traveling secretary; Bench, Plummer, Kirby, Foster, Billingham, T. Carroll, Darcy, Eastwick, Perez, Borbon, Starr, trainer. Third row—Driessen, Chaney, Griffey, Nolan, Concepcion, Armbrister, C. Carroll, McEnaney, Crowley, Geronimo, Gullett. Front—McGinn, batboy.

ously held by Joe Nuxhall, a member of the club's broadcasting team.

* Morgan, in addition to setting a club record for walks, also drove home 94 runs, eclipsing by one the team record for second basemen set by Tony Cuccinello in 1931.

* Johnny Bench tied Vada Pinson for the club record for grand-slam homers by hitting No. 6.

* The Reds stole 168 bases while setting a major league record for the best percentage mark in history—.8235 compared to the Los Angeles Dodgers' .8215 in 1962.

* Red pitchers set a major league mark by yielding the fewest number of unearned runs in a season—40.

* Pete Rose, a three-time league batting champ, passed the 2,500th-hit milestone with an August 17 single off the Pirates' Bruce Kison en route to his 10th .300 or better season in the past 11 years.

The Reds owned a 20-20 record, were in second place and trailed the Dodgers by five games in the West Division before wiping out a 3-0 deficit in rolling to an 11-4 victory over the New York Mets' Tom Seaver May 21.

That victory was the first of the 41 the Reds were to win over a 50-game span.

By the All-Star Game break the Reds owned a 61-29 record and held a comfortable 12½-game bulge over the second-place Dodgers. And, at season's end the Reds had stretched that lead to 20 games.

One of the prime reasons for the Reds' almost unbelievable season of 1975 was the switching of Rose from left field to third base on May 3 by Anderson.

Rose, moving to third, replaced the weak-hitting John Vukovich, who was outrighted to the Indianapolis farm club and later involved in a minor league trade with the Phillies.

More important, perhaps, was the fact that the switch enabled Anderson to utilize the potent bat of George Foster, who replaced Rose in left field.

Foster, given a chance to play regularly for the first time since his acquisition from the Giants in 1972, finished the season with an even .300 batting average. His 23 homers ranked second only to the 28 hit by Bench, the Reds' all-star catcher.

Johnny topped the club in homers and RBIs with 110 and batted .283, even though he was plagued throughout the season by a painful left shoulder injury sustained in a home plate collision with the Giants' Gary Matthews April 27.

Minor surgery was performed on Bench a month after the World Series to correct the ailment.

Surprisingly, perhaps, the Reds racked up their record total of 108 victories even though no starter on the club won more than 15 games.

The 15-game winners were Jack Billingham, Don Gullett and Gary Nolan.

Gullett finished the season with a 15-4 mark even though he was sidelined for two months after suffering a fractured left thumb when struck by a smash off the bat of Atlanta's Larvell Blanks.

Nolan's 15 victories came after the veteran righthander had been idled for two years by a shoulder injury. The remarkable comeback by Gary, who underwent shoulder surgery in May, 1974, earned him the coveted "Hutch Award," named in honor of Red Manager Fred Hutchinson, who died of cancer in the winter of 1964.

One of baseball's strongest bullpens played a prominent role in the Reds' fantastic success. And the two most effective members of the relief corps were the two youngest, Rawly Eastwick, a 24-year-old rookie righthander, and Will McEnaney, a 23-year-old lefty.

Eastwick, recalled from the Indianapolis farm club late in May, had a 5-3 won-and-lost record accompanied by a 2.60 earned-run average and a team high 22 saves.

McEnaney's 5-2 won-lost mark was accompanied by a 2.47 earned-run average and 15 saves. Veterans Clay Carroll and Pedro Borbon rounded out the relief corps. Darcy, a rookie righthander who doubled as a starter and relief pitcher, chimed in with an impressive 11-5 mark. Fred Norman (12-4), Clay Kirby (10-6) and Clay Carroll (7-5) also doubled as starters and relievers.

Just as in 1974, the Reds in 1975 also had four players—Bench, shortstop Dave Concepcion, center fielder Cesar Geronimo and second baseman Morgan—voted Gold Gloves.

Concepcion again proved himself a respectable hitter by batting .276.

But, perhaps, one of the most pleasant surprises for Anderson was the all-round performance of Ken Griffey.

The young outfielder from Donora, Pa., playing his first full season for the Reds, responded with a .305 batting average and displayed marked improvement in his defensive play and his throwing.

After 1975, what can the Reds do for an encore?

"We'll think of something," is the answer of Morgan, who'd like to see the Reds duplicate the feat of the Oakland A's three straight world titles.

## SCORES OF CINCINNATI REDS' 1975 GAMES

**APRIL**

| | | | | Winner | Loser |
|---|---|---|---|---|---|
| 7—Los Ang. | W | 2-1§ | | Darcy | Hough |
| 9—Los Ang. | W | 4-3 | | Borbon | Marshall |
| 10—Los Ang. | W | 7-6 | | C. Carroll | Hough |
| 11—At S. D. | L | 2-5 | | Spillner | Norman |
| 12—At S. D. | L | 2-3 | | McIntosh | Nolan |
| 13—At S. D. | W | 10-0 | | Gullett | Freisleben |
| 14—At L. A. | L | 2-5 | | Rau | Billingham |
| 15—At L. A. | L | 1-3 | | Sutton | Kirby |
| 16—At L. A. | L | 6-7 | | Marshall | C. Carroll |
| 17—At L. A. | L | 4-5† | | Marshall | C. Carroll |
| 18—Houston | W | 5-2 | | Gullett | Griffin |
| 19—Houston | W | 9-8 | | C. Carroll | Forsch |
| 20—Houston | W | 5-3 | | C. Carroll | Scherman |
| 20—Houston | L | 6-7 | | Richard | Kirby |
| 21—S. Fran. | L | 3-4* | | Lavelle | Borbon |
| 22—S. Fran. | W | 5-4 | | Kirby | Williams |
| 23—At Atl. | L | 4-5† | | Reed | Gullett |
| 24—At Atl. | W | 11-3 | | Billingham | Niekro |
| 25—At Hous. | L | 4-6 | | Dierker | Darcy |
| 26—At Hous. | W | 9-3 | | Norman | Griffin |
| 27—At Hous. | W | 6-2* | | Borbon | Konieczny |
| 29—At S. F. | L | 3-4 | | Moffitt | C. Carroll |
| 30—At S. F. | W | 4-1 | | Billingham | Barr |
| | | Won 12, Lost 11 | | | |

**MAY**

| | | | | | |
|---|---|---|---|---|---|
| 2—Atlanta | L | 5-6 | | Gentry | Kirby |
| 3—Atlanta | W | 6-1 | | Nolan | Harrison |
| 4—Atlanta | W | 3-2 | | Gullett | Niekro |

**MAY**

| | | | | Winner | Loser |
|---|---|---|---|---|---|
| 6—S. Diego | W | 7-3 | | Billingham | Siebert |
| 7—S. Diego | W | 10-2 | | Norman | Spillner |
| 8—S. Diego | L | 0-3 | | Jones | Nolan |
| 9—At N. Y. | W | 4-3 | | Gullett | Tate |
| 10—At N. Y. | W | 7-1 | | Kirby | Webb |
| 11—At N. Y. | L | 2-3 | | Seaver | Billingham |
| 13—At Phila. | L | 0-4 | | Underwood | Nolan |
| 14—At Phila. | L | 0-4 | | Carlton | Darcy |
| 15—At Phila. | L | 3-6 | | McGraw | Gullett |
| 15—At Phila. | L | 3-5 | | Garber | C. Carroll |
| 16—At Mon. | L | 2-4 | | Blair | Billingham |
| 17—At Mon. | W | 5-3* | | McEnaney | Montague |
| 18—At Mon. | W | 6-1 | | Nolan | McNally |
| 20—N. York | L | 2-6 | | Koosman | Gullett |
| 21—N. York | W | 11-4 | | Billingham | Seaver |
| 23—Phila. | W | 5-2 | | Nolan | Christenson |
| 24—Phila. | W | 3-2† | | C. Carroll | McGraw |
| 25—Phila. | W | 4-3 | | Kirby | Lonborg |
| 26—Montreal | W | 4-3 | | C. Carroll | Fryman |
| 26—Montreal | W | 5-4 | | Gullett | Renko |
| 28—Montreal | W | 6-0 | | Nolan | Blair |
| 30—At St. L. | W | 4-5 | | Hrabosky | Eastwick |
| 31—At St. L. | W | 6-0 | | Gullett | Gibson |
| | | Won 16, Lost 10 | | | |

**JUNE**

| | | | | | |
|---|---|---|---|---|---|
| 1—At St. L. | W | 5-1 | | Billingham | Forsch |
| 3—At Pitts. | W | 8-4 | | Nolan | Moose |
| 4—At Pitts. | L | 1-2 | | Reuss | Norman |

| JUNE | | | Winner | Loser |
|---|---|---|---|---|
| 6—Chicago | W | 5-1 | Gullett | Bonham |
| 7—Chicago | W | 8-1 | Billingham | Burris |
| 8—Chicago | W | 2-1 | Nolan | R. Reuschel |
| 8—Chicago | W | 8-5 | Borbon | Zahn |
| 9—Pitts. | L | 2-9 | Reuss | Norman |
| 10—Pitts. | L | 5-9 | McDowell | Darcy |
| 11—St. Louis | W | 3-1 | Gullett | Forsch |
| 12—St. Louis | W | 10-1 | Nolan | McGlothen |
| 13—At Chi. | W | 18-11 | Borbon | Zamora |
| 14—At Chi. | W | 11-3y | Kirby | Stone |
| 15—At Chi. | L | 3-4 | Bonham | Darcy |
| 16—Atlanta | W | 9-2 | Gullett | Niekro |
| 17—Atlanta | L | 1-5 | Morton | Nolan |
| 18—Atlanta | W | 6-1 | Billingham | Odom |
| 20—At Hous. | W | 7-3 | T. Carroll | Konieczny |
| 21—At Hous. | W | 7-6§ | Norman | Niekro |
| 22—At Hous. | L | 4-8 | Dierker | Nolan |
| 23—At Atl. | W | 8-4 | Billingham | Easterly |
| 24—At Atl. | W | 3-0 | Darcy | Niekro |
| 25—At Atl. | W | 2-0 | T. Carroll | Morton |
| 27—S. Diego | W | 5-2† | McEnaney | Frisella |
| 28—S. Diego | W | 6-4* | McEnaney | Tomlin |
| 29—S. Diego | W | 4-1 | Billingham | Jones |
| 29—S. Diego | L | 3-4 | Strom | Darcy |
| 30—Houston | W | 9-6‡ | Kirby | Niekro |

Won 21, Lost 7

| JULY | | | | |
|---|---|---|---|---|
| 1—Houston | W | 8-7x | Darcy | Niekro |
| 2—Houston | W | 4-3 | Eastwick | Dierker |
| 3—At S. D. | L | 1-2 | Jones | McEnaney |
| 4—At S. D. | W | 7-6 | Billingham | Folkers |
| 5—At S. D. | W | 6-3 | Norman | Strom |
| 6—At S. D. | W | 13-2 | Kirby | McIntosh |
| 7—Phila. | W | 7-3 | Darcy | Carlton |
| 8—Phila. | W | 2-1 | Nolan | Underwood |
| 9—Phila. | W | 9-7 | Borbon | Garber |
| 11—N. York | W | 4-3 | Norman | Matlack |
| 11—N. York | W | 4-1 | Kirby | Tate |
| 12—N. York | W | 3-2 | T. Carroll | Koosman |
| 13—N. York | W | 5-3 | McEnaney | Seaver |
| 17—At Mon. | L | 0-3 | Rogers | Billingham |
| 18—At Mon. | W | 10-3 | Nolan | Blair |
| 19—At Mon. | L | 2-4 | Murray | Borbon |
| 20—At Phila. | L | 4-11 | Underwood | Kirby |
| 21—At Phila. | W | 10-4 | Darcy | Schueler |
| 22—At N. Y. | L | 1-3 | Koosman | Billingham |
| 23—At N. Y. | L | 2-5 | Matlack | Nolan |
| 24—At N. Y. | W | 2-1 | Norman | Seaver |
| 25—Los Ang. | L | 3-4 | Messersmith | C. Carroll |
| 25—Los Ang. | W | 6-3 | Darcy | Marshall |
| 26—Los Ang. | W | 5-3 | Billingham | Rau |
| 27—Los Ang. | L | 3-5 | Sutton | T. Carroll |
| 28—S. Fran. | W | 8-4 | Borbon | Halicki |
| 29—S. Fran. | L | 2-4 | Barr | Eastwick |
| 30—S. Fran. | W | 6-1 | Darcy | Falcone |
| 31—S. Fran. | W | 11-6 | Kirby | Montefusco |

Won 20, Lost 9

| AUGUST | | | Winner | Loser |
|---|---|---|---|---|
| 1—At L. A. | L | 3-5* | Hough | Borbon |
| 2—At L. A. | W | 1-0 | T. Carroll | Messersmith |
| 3—At L. A. | W | 3-1 | Darcy | Rau |
| 4—At S. F. | W | 7-5 | C. Carroll | Caldwell |
| 5—At S. F. | W | 6-3 | Borbon | Halicki |
| 6—At S. F. | W | 12-5 | Billingham | Barr |
| 8—Montreal | L | 7-8 | Fryman | Borbon |
| 9—Montreal | W | 9-1 | Nolan | Blair |
| 10—Montreal | W | 11-3 | Norman | Carrithers |
| 11—Chicago | W | 9-3 | Billingham | R. Reuschel |
| 12—Chicago | W | 12-8 | Eastwick | Knowles |
| 14—Pitts. | W | 6-1 | Nolan | Reuss |
| 15—Pitts. | W | 8-3 | Norman | Rooker |
| 16—Pitts. | W | 5-3 | Billingham | Candelaria |
| 17—Pitts. | W | 3-1 | Darcy | Kison |
| 18—At St. L. | W | 3-2 | Gullett | Forsch |
| 19—At St. L. | L | 1-2 | McGlothen | Nolan |
| 20—At St. L. | L | 0-4 | Reed | Norman |
| 22—At Pitts. | L | 2-7 | Demery | Billingham |
| 22—At Pitts. | L | 2-4 | Candelaria | McEnaney |
| 23—At Pitts. | W | 12-7 | Kirby | Kison |
| 24—At Pitts. | L | 1-5 | Reuss | Nolan |
| 25—At Chi. | W | 11-4 | Norman | R. Reuschel |
| 26—At Chi. | W | 6-5 | Eastwick | Stone |
| 27—At Chi. | W | 6-5 | Borbon | Bonham |
| 28—St. Louis | W | 4-0 | Gullett | Garman |
| 29—St. Louis | W | 6-2 | Nolan | McGlothen |
| 30—St. Louis | W | 3-2* | Eastwick | Garman |
| 31—St. Louis | L | 3-5 | Rasmussen | Billingham |

Won 21, Lost 8

| SEPTEMBER | | | | |
|---|---|---|---|---|
| 1—S. Diego | L | 1-2 | Jones | Borbon |
| 2—S. Diego | W | 10-4 | Gullett | Spillner |
| 3—Los Ang. | W | 13-2 | Nolan | Messersmith |
| 4—Los Ang. | L | 2-3 | Rau | Kirby |
| 5—S. Frun. | W | 4-3 | Eastwick | Heaverlo |
| 6—S. Fran. | W | 3-2 | Billingham | Halicki |
| 7—S. Fran. | W | 8-4 | Gullett | Falcone |
| 8—At S. D. | W | 3-2 | C. Carroll | Greif |
| 9—At S. D. | L | 2-11 | Folkers | Kirby |
| 10—At L. A. | L | 2-3 | Hooton | Eastwick |
| 11—At L. A. | L | 2-5 | Rhoden | Billingham |
| 12—At S. F. | W | 6-3 | Norman | Montefusco |
| 13—At S. F. | L | 2-9 | Barr | Gullett |
| 14—At S. F. | L | 2-4 | Heaverlo | Nolan |
| 14—At S. F. | W | 8-3 | Darcy | Minton |
| 16—Houston | L | 1-5 | Dierker | Billingham |
| 17—Houston | W | 10-1 | Norman | Stanton |
| 18—At Atl. | W | 4-3* | Borbon | Torrealba |
| 19—At Atl. | W | 7-6 | Darcy | LaCorte |
| 20—At Atl. | W | 9-2 | Nolan | Easterly |
| 21—At Atl. | W | 3-0 | Gullett | Niekro |
| 22—At Hous. | L | 1-5 | Niekro | Billingham |
| 23—At Hous. | W | 5-3 | Norman | Cosgrove |
| 24—At Hous. | W | 6-4 | Kirby | Dierker |
| 26—Atlanta | W | 12-5 | Nolan | Niekro |
| 27—Atlanta | W | 7-6 | Gullett | Odom |
| 28—Atlanta | W | 7-6 | McEnaney | Dal Canton |

Won 18, Lost 9

* 10 innings.   † 11 innings.   ‡ 12 innings.   § 14 innings.   x 15 innings.   y Suspended game, completed June 15.

# Injuries Stifle Dodger Pennant Repeat

## By GORDON VERRELL

The Dodgers didn't suffer their first costly injury until the first week of the 1975 season.

It was the start of a succession of injuries that would strip the defending National League champions of a half a dozen key regulars for various lengths of time during the season.

LOS ANGELES DODGERS—1975

Front row—Buhler, trainer; Mota, Powell, Basgall, coach; Adams, coach; Alston, manager; Gilliam, coach; Lasorda, coach; Wynn, Paciorek, Lee, Crawford, Scott, traveling secretary. Second row—Woods, team physician; Jobe, team physician; Lacy, Mc-Mullen, Yeager, Auerbach, Cey, Russell, Lopes, Hale, Buckner, Garvey, Vernon, batting instructor; Ferguson, Homel, assistant trainer. Third row—Downing, Marshall, Wall, Messersmith, Sutton, Rhoden, Hooton, Rau, Hough, John, Cresse, bullpen catcher. Front—Wetton and Evans, batboys.

But once, when the subject of injuries was broached, Cincinnati's Pete Rose noted: "The worst injury the Dodgers had was when we won 41 out of 50 games."

It was during that incredible stretch by the Reds that the Dodgers' lead in the National League West, a lead that was once 5½ games, first dwindled, then disappeared entirely and then for nearly three months the only question was whether the Dodgers could hold on for second.

They did, quite handily, but the 20 games that separated them from first place Cincinnati was the club's poorest finish since they wound up 21 games back of St. Louis in 1968.

"There are three reasons," Alston replied when asked why the Dodgers, who won 102 games and the pennant in 1974, won only 88 games and were scarcely a factor after the first week of July.

"First, there were the injuries. Then, quite a few of our players didn't have the year this season they had in 1974, a year when we put everything together. And, finally, the Reds. I doubt if anyone could have beaten them the way they played."

No one, including club president Peter O'Malley, vice-president Al Campanis and manager Alston, wanted to use the injuries as an alibi.

But it is a fact, that for various extended periods, the Dodgers were without shortstop Bill Russell, Bill Buckner, Cy Young Award winner of 1974 Mike Marshall who missed 10 weeks because of a recurring injury to his left side, and Joe Ferguson, who went out for the season with a broken arm following a brawl with the San Diego Padres on July 1.

"Our lineup was hardly the same this year as it was the year we won," said Jimmy Wynn, who sat out himself with a bad arm early in the year but was bothered more by an ailing bat.

"It was as if he was trying to make up for everything himself," said Alston, attempting to explain why Wynn, who slugged 32 homers, drove in 108 runs and batted .271 in 1974, would fall off to 18 homers, 58 RBIs and a .248 average in 1975.

On the other hand, three Dodgers not stricken with any serious injuries—first baseman Steve Garvey, second baseman Dave Lopes and third baseman Ron Cey—had excellent seasons.

Garvey, the league's Most Valuable Player in 1974, collected 210 hits —the first Dodger in more than 50 years to have 200 or more hits two straight seasons—and finished at .319, tops on the club. He also drove in 95 runs.

Lopes led the league in stolen bases with 77, becoming only the ninth player in history to steal 70 or more bases in a single season. He batted .262 and continued marked improvement at second base.

Cey's play at third base at times bordered on sensational and he continued to assert himself as one of the league's most feared sluggers. He drove in 101 runs, the first time he's topped the 100-RBI plateau, and he led the club in home runs with 25.

Pitching, however, remained the Dodgers' No. 1 strength.

The Dodgers led the league in earned-run average for the fourth straight year, posting a collective 2.92 and ended the season with a rock-solid starting staff of Andy Messersmith (19-14, 2.29 ERA), Don Sutton

(16-13, 2.87), Burt Hooton (18-9, 3.06) and Doug Rau (15-9, 3.10).

It was the acquisition of Hooton from the Chicago Cubs on May 2 that provided the brightest note all season.

The 25-year-old Hooton not only hit his career high for victories with 18, but won a staggering 12 straight decisions to close the season, a Los Angeles record for starting pitchers previously shared at 11 by Sandy Koufax (twice) and Don Drysdale. Hooton was 0-2 when he joined the Dodgers.

Steve Yeager, who took over the No. 1 catching job when Ferguson was injured, rapped out 12 homers and 54 RBIs, both career highs, and knuckleballer Charlie Hough assumed an iron man role in the bullpen after Marshall departed, winding up with a 2.95 ERA.

Lee Lacy played both in the infield and outfield and batted a fine .314. However, at season's end the Dodgers, in an effort to secure long-term insurance in the outfield, traded Lacy and Wynn along with Tom Paciorek and Jerry Royster to Atlanta for Dusty Baker and Ed Goodson. The Dodger brass pointed to Baker as their center fielder for years to come.

Sidelined midway through the 1974 season with an elbow injury, left-handed pitcher Tommy John also fell short of expectations. It wasn't until late in '75 that John even tried his injured arm in an Instructional League game.

Attendance again was astounding, however. The Dodgers drew 2,539,349, tops in the majors.

Prior to the season, Peter O'Malley had startled the baseball society by predicting the Dodgers might draw three million fans if (a) the weatherman cooperated, (b) there was no rationing of gasoline and (c) the club stayed in the race.

Two out of three isn't bad.

## SCORES OF LOS ANGELES DODGERS' 1975 GAMES

| APRIL | | | Winner | Loser | | MAY | | | | Winner | Loser |
|---|---|---|---|---|---|---|---|---|---|---|---|
| 7—At Cinn. | L | 1-2x | Darcy | Hough | | 6—Houston | W | 3-1 | | Sutton | Konieczny |
| 9—At Cinn. | L | 3-4 | Borbon | Marshall | | 7—Houston | W | 5-1 | | Messersmith | Griffin |
| 10—At Cinn. | L | 6-7 | C. Carroll | Hough | | 9—At Pitts. | L | 3-11 | | Ellis | Marshall |
| 11—At Hous. | W | 7-0 | Sutton | Griffin | | 10—At Pitts. | W | 6-2 | | Rau | Rooker |
| 12—At Hous. | L | 5-7 | Dierker | Marichal | | 11—At Pitts. | W | 7-0 | | Sutton | Brett |
| 13—At Hous. | W | 7-4 | Messersmith | Konieczny | | 12—At St. L. | W | 6-4* | | Brewer | Garman |
| 14—Cinn. | W | 5-2 | Rau | Billingham | | 13—At St. L. | W | 5-0 | | Hooton | McGlothen |
| 15—Cinn. | W | 3-1 | Sutton | Kirby | | 14—At St. L. | L | 4-7 | | Curtis | Rau |
| 16—Cinn. | W | 7-6 | Marshall | C. Carroll | | 16—Pitts. | L | 2-3 | | Giusti | Sutton |
| 17—Cinn. | W | 5-4† | Marshall | C. Carroll | | 17—Pitts. | W | 4-3* | | Messersmith | Hernandez |
| 18—S. Fran. | L | 1-3 | Montefusco | Rau | | 18—Pitts. | L | 2-7 | | Brett | Hooton |
| 19—S. Fran. | L | 3-2 | Sutton | Falcone | | 19—Chicago | W | 3-2 | | Brewer | Knowles |
| 20—S. Fran. | L | 3-6§ | Moffitt | Zahn | | 20—Chicago | L | 1-2 | | Bonham | Sutton |
| 21—At Atl. | W | 2-1 | Messersmith | Capra | | 21—Chicago | W | 10-0 | | Messersmith | Zahn |
| 22—At Atl. | L | 2-3 | Morton | Hough | | 22—Chicago | W | 8-3 | | Hooton | Burris |
| 23—At S. D. | L | 1-7 | McIntosh | Sutton | | 23—St. Louis | L | 3-4 | | Hrabosky | Hough |
| 24—At S. D. | W | 11-6 | Rhoden | Freisleben | | 24—St. Louis | L | 2-6 | | McGlothen | Rau |
| 25—At S. F. | W | 6-5 | Messersmith | Caldwell | | 25—St. Louis | W | 7-3 | | Sutton | Curtis |
| 26—At S. F. | W | 13-3 | Rau | D'Acquisto | | 26—At N. Y. | L | 3-6 | | Seaver | Messersmith |
| 27—At S. F. | W | 7-3 | Sutton | Montefusco | | 27—At N. Y. | W | 10-4 | | Hooton | Parker |
| 28—Atlanta | W | 4-3 | Brewer | House | | 28—At N. Y. | L | 4-5 | | Matlack | Rau |
| 29—Atlanta | W | 8-0 | Messersmith | Capra | | 30—At Chi. | W | 3-1z | | Sutton | Burris |
| 30—Atlanta | W | 5-2 | Rau | Morton | | 31—At Chi. | L | 1-2 | | R. Reuschel | Messersmith |
| | | | **Won 15, Lost 8** | | | | | | **Won 15, Lost 12** | | |

| MAY | | | Winner | Loser | | JUNE | | | | Winner | Loser |
|---|---|---|---|---|---|---|---|---|---|---|---|
| 2—S. Diego | W | 3-0 | Sutton | Spillner | | 1—At Chi. | L | 2-7 | | Bonham | Hooton |
| 3—S. Diego | W | 1-3y | Foster | Brewer | | 2—At Mon. | L | 3-5 | | Fryman | Rau |
| 4—S. Diego | L | 7-10 | Jones | Hooton | | 3—At Mon. | W | 6-5 | | Sutton | Renko |
| 5—Houston | W | 2-0 | Rau | Dierker | | 4—At Mon. | W | 3-0 | | Messersmith | Blair |

| JUNE | | | Winner | Loser |
|---|---|---|---|---|
| 6—At Phila. | W | 3-2 | Hooton | Underwood |
| 7—At Phila. | L | 0-4 | Carlton | Rau |
| 8—At Phila. | L | 2-4 | Lonborg | Sutton |
| 9—Montreal | W | 4-0 | Messersmith | Fryman |
| 10—Montreal | L | 4-5 | Renko | Marshall |
| 11—N. York | L | 1-2 | Apodaca | Marshall |
| 12—N. York | L | 0-2 | Matlack | Sutton |
| 13—Phila. | L | 1-5 | Lonborg | Messersmith |
| 14—Phila. | W | 4-3 | Hooton | McGraw |
| 15—Phila. | L | 3-4 | Garber | Marshall |
| 16—Houston | W | 4-2 | Sutton | Dierker |
| 17—Houston | W | 6-1 | Messersmith | Roberts |
| 18—Houston | W | 4-0 | Hooton | Griffin |
| 19—At S. D. | W | 4-1 | Rau | Jones |
| 20—At S. D. | L | 1-2 | Strom | Sutton |
| 21—At S. D. | W | 4-3 | Messersmith | Folkers |
| 22—At S. D. | W | 3-2 | Marshall | Frisella |
| 23—At Hous. | L | 5-6 | Roberts | Hooton |
| 24—At Hous. | W | 8-3 | Rau | Griffin |
| 25—At Hous. | L | 4-5 | Granger | Sutton |
| 26—At S. F. | L | 0-2 | Halicki | Messersmith |
| 27—At S. F. | L | 5-10 | Williams | Hooton |
| 28—At S. F. | L | 1-2 | Montefusco | Rau |
| 29—At S. F. | L | 2-5 | Bradley | Sutton |
| 30—S. Diego | W | 4-1 | Messersmith | Folkers |

Won 13, Lost 16

| JULY | | | | |
|---|---|---|---|---|
| 1—S. Diego | L | 1-10 | Spillner | Hooton |
| 2—S. Diego | W | 6-5x | Downing | McIntosh |
| 3—S. Fran. | W | 7-1 | Sutton | Falcone |
| 4—S. Fran. | L | 0-1 | Montefusco | Messersmith |
| 5—S. Fran. | W | 5-4 | Downing | Halicki |
| 6—S. Fran. | W | 5-1 | Rau | Bradley |
| 8—At Pitts. | W | 3-0 | Sutton | Ellis |
| 9—At Pitts. | L | 2-3 | Kison | Messersmith |
| 10—At Pitts. | L | 1-4 | Reuss | Hooton |
| 11—At St. L. | W | 6-5 | Marshall | Garman |
| 12—At St. L. | L | 1-2* | Hrabosky | Rhoden |
| 13—At St. L. | L | 1-2 | Hrabosky | Marshall |
| 17—Pitts. | L | 2-5 | Kison | Messersmith |
| 18—Pitts. | W | 4-3 | Marshall | Demery |
| 19—Pitts. | L | 3-5 | Giusti | Marshall |
| 20—Chicago | W | 5-3‡ | Marshall | Dettore |
| 21—Chicago | L | 0-1 | R. Reuschel | Messersmith |
| 22—St. Louis | L | 3-4† | Hrabosky | Marshall |
| 23—St. Louis | L | 4-5 | Forsch | Sutton |
| 24—St. Louis | W | 8-2 | Hooton | McGlothen |
| 25—At Cinn. | W | 4-3 | Messersmith | C. Carroll |
| 25—At Cinn. | L | 3-6 | Darcy | Rau |
| 26—At Cinn. | L | 3-5 | Billingham | Rau |
| 27—At Cinn. | W | 5-3 | Sutton | T. Carroll |
| 28—At Atl. | L | 3-5 | Niekro | Marshall |
| 29—At Atl. | L | 2-4 | Odom | Messersmith |
| 30—At Atl. | W | 8-2 | Rau | Morton |
| 31—At Atl. | L | 10-11 | House | Marshall |

Won 12, Lost 16

| AUGUST | | | Winner | Loser |
|---|---|---|---|---|
| 1—Cinn. | W | 5-3* | Hough | Borbon |
| 2—Cinn. | L | 0-1 | T. Carroll | Messersmith |
| 3—Cinn. | L | 1-3 | Darcy | Rau |
| 4—Atlanta | W | 9-1 | Hooton | Dal Canton |
| 5—Atlanta | W | 5-0 | Sutton | Niekro |
| 6—Atlanta | L | 4-5 | House | Messersmith |
| 8—At N. Y. | W | 4-3 | Marshall | Sanders |
| 9—At N. Y. | W | 2-0 | Hooton | Koosman |
| 10—At N. Y. | W | 2-1 | Sutton | Webb |
| 11—At Phila. | W | 7-1 | Messersmith | Christenson |
| 12—At Phila. | W | 7-6* | Marshall | Garber |
| 13—At Phila. | W | 5-4 | Hooton | Carlton |
| 15—At Mon. | L | 4-8 | Rogers | Sutton |
| 16—At Mon. | L | 2-3* | Murray | Marshall |
| 17—At Mon. | W | 5-3 | Rau | Renko |
| 18—At Chi. | W | 3-1 | Hooton | Stone |
| 19—At Chi. | W | 2-1 | Marshall | Bonham |
| 21—At Chi. | L | 0-7 | R. Reuschel | Messersmith |
| 22—Montreal | L | 1-3‡ | Murray | Downing |
| 23—Montreal | W | 3-1 | Hooton | Rogers |
| 23—Montreal | L | 2-5 | Murray | Marshall |
| 24—Montreal | L | 3-5x | Murray | Marshall |
| 25—Phila. | L | 2-4 | Christenson | Messersmith |
| 26—Phila. | W | 8-1 | Rau | Underwood |
| 27—Phila. | W | 10-0 | Hooton | Carlton |
| 28—N. York | L | 1-4 | Koosman | Rhoden |
| 29—N. York | L | 1-6 | Matlack | Sutton |
| 30—N. York | W | 7-0 | Messersmith | Webb |
| 31—N. York | W | 5-2 | Rau | Swan |

Won 17, Lost 12

| SEPTEMBER | | | | |
|---|---|---|---|---|
| 1—At S. F. | W | 3-1 | Hooton | Williams |
| 2—At S. F. | L | 3-7 | Halicki | Sutton |
| 3—At Cinn. | L | 2-13 | Nolan | Messersmith |
| 4—At Cinn. | W | 3-2 | Rau | Kirby |
| 5—At Atl. | W | 5-2 | Hooton | Thompson |
| 6—At Atl. | L | 2-3 | Morton | Hough |
| 7—At Atl. | L | 4-5 | Dal Canton | Hough |
| 8—S. Fran. | W | 4-0 | Messersmith | Montefusco |
| 9—S. Fran. | W | 8-3 | Hough | Barr |
| 10—Cinn. | W | 3-2 | Hooton | Eastwick |
| 11—Cinn. | W | 5-2 | Rhoden | Billingham |
| 12—Atlanta | L | 1-2 | Niekro | Sutton |
| 13—Atlanta | W | 6-0 | Messersmith | LaCorte |
| 14—Atlanta | W | 3-2 | Rau | Morton |
| 15—S. Diego | W | 5-4 | Hooton | McIntosh |
| 16—S. Diego | W | 5-2 | Rhoden | Strom |
| 17—S. Diego | W | 7-1 | Messersmith | Spillner |
| 19—At Hous. | L | 5-6‡ | Roberts | Sells |
| 20—At Hous. | W | 5-4§ | Hough | Siebert |
| 21—At Hous. | L | 1-4 | Richard | Rhoden |
| 22—At S. D. | L | 5-6† | Metzger | Sells |
| 23—At S. D. | L | 4-6 | Jones | Wall |
| 24—At S. D. | W | 14-0 | Rau | Folkers |
| 26—Houston | W | 3-2 | Hooton | Richard |
| 27—Houston | W | 5-1 | Messersmith | Stanton |
| 28—Houston | L | 2-4 | York | Hough |

Won 16, Lost 10

\* 10 innings.  † 11 innings.  ‡ 12 innings.  § 13 innings.  s 14 innings.  y 15 innings.  z Suspended game, completed May 31.

# Giants Play Well in Privacy

## By ART SPANDER

At the conclusion of one of the more bizarre journeys across the calendar and the country by any athletic franchise, the 1975 Giants managed to end up in third place and in San Francisco. Considering the alternatives, this is to be considered an accomplishment.

So the Giants finished a couple of miles behind the Cincinnati Reds in

SAN FRANCISCO GIANTS—1975

Front row—Heaverlo, Lavelle, Murcer, Virgil, coach; Amalfitano, coach; Westrum, manager; Gilbert, coach; McMahon, coach; Montefusco, Sadek, Rader. Second row—Logan, equipment manager; Murphy, assistant equipment manager; Bradley, Barr, Oniveros, Robinson, Matthews, Miller, Speier, Thomasson, Brinson, clubhouse man; Wylder, trainer. Third row—Williams, Hill, Falcone, Halicki, Montanez, Brown, Caldwell, Moffitt, D'Acquisto, Thomas. Front—McCormack and Dudum, bat boys.

National League West? So they drew only a half-million spectators? So, mocking the tradition of a club long known for its power, no one hit more than a dozen home runs? You have to accentuate the positive.

The manner in which the Giants figuratively were being shuttled to every American city big enough to have paved streets—and some foreign ones too. The way the team seemed in bigger financial trouble than stock brokers in 1929. The way players were dropping like front line troops at Chateau-Thierry. Well, some people said they were lucky to have a season at all.

But they did have a season, a season that if not successful—since success in baseball, as in all sports means winning a championship—at least was eventful. And an improvement over 1974, when San Francisco finished in fifth place with a record of 72-90.

Last season the Giants missed only by the whimsy of the weatherman of finishing at .500. They ended 80-81, the missing game having been washed away in Atlanta the final week of the season.

Actually, the way things went off the playing field, it's a wonder the Giants did that well.

From the day the season began, the major subject concerning the Giants was not strikeouts or the hit-and-run. It was money. Owner Horace Stoneham was running out of it. Rumors were soaring like pop flies in the Candlestick Park wind that Stoneham was going to sell the Giants. Every day brought another buyer—and story. And locale.

Horace couldn't pay the rent. Horace was borrowing money. Horace was going to sell the team by July. Horace wasn't going to sell the team by July—or ever. The Japanese would buy the Giants. The Canadians would buy the Giants. The Giants would be moved to Seattle, New Orleans, Tokyo, Toronto, Upper Darby, Lower Slobovia, _____ (The reader is asked to fill in the region of his choice).

Somehow, despite the rumors, despite enough injuries to wipe out a military platoon, despite crowds that occasionally never got to four figures, the Giants, with manager Wes Westrum making decisions and a few waves, made themselves presentable.

For a while they looked as if first might be within reach. Then the Reds locked up the pennant by Mother's Day. After that, it seemed San Francisco could wrest second place away from the Dodgers. But a late-season tumble placed the Giants squarely in third.

Streaks were commonplace. The Giants won seven in a row, later lost six in a row. Then came an eight-game winning streak. And a losing streak in which runs were more difficult to get than an honest political speech—San Francisco scoring only 11 in seven games. A few months later the Giants were rolling box cars, losing six, winning six, losing six.

To make up that scoring drought in June, the Giants got 35 runs during a five-game win streak in August.

During May they got one of the men responsible for their improvement, first baseman Willie Montanez. He came from the Phillies in trade for outfielder Garry Maddox, and the deal proved to be an excellent one for San Francisco. Montanez ended up with 182 hits, a .302 batting average and 101 runs batted in.

Two earlier transactions also proved beneficial. During the off-season the Giants traded Bobby Bonds to the Yankees for Bobby Murcer, and then—in the biggest steal since Brinks—picked up Von Joshua on waivers from the Dodgers. Murcer batted .298 and drove in 91 runs, Joshua batted a team-leading .318. Chris Speier hit a solid .271 and led N. L. shortstops in fielding.

The problem was Murcer, Joshua, Speier and Gary Matthews—the Giants' only righthanded power hitter—missed numerous games with injuries. To make matters worse, Matthews' came when he was goofing around with infielder Derrel Thomas. Shadow boxing, he broke his thumb and missed more than 40 games.

Near the close of the season, Jim Barr, supposed to be the team's key pitcher, had a public argument with Westrum, calling him gutless. Eventually, everybody became friends again.

Most of the news made by the other Giant pitchers was only good. On August 24, Ed Halicki pitched a no-hitter, first in the National League in two years, beating the New York Mets 6-0. Within the next 11 days, Halicki, John Montefusco and Pete Falcone combined to strike out 93 batters.

Montefusco, who had come up at the end of the 1974 season and pitched a shutout against the Dodgers, picked up the tempo in 1975—and in the process THE SPORTING NEWS NL Rookie Pitcher of the Year Award.

Making promises he certainly could keep, the 25-year-old Montefusco set a team rookie record of 215 strikeouts. He had a 15-9 record that could have easily been much better. Twice Montefusco pitched nine innings of shutout baseball and had nothing to show for it but a loss and a no decision.

The Giants' only major trade at the winter meetings sent Falcone to St. Louis for third baseman Ken Reitz.

However, as the calendar moved to spring training 1976, there still hung a cloud of mystery over the future of the club in San Francisco.

### SCORES OF SAN FRANCISCO GIANTS' 1975 GAMES

| APRIL | | | Winner | Loser | MAY | | | Winner | Loser |
|---|---|---|---|---|---|---|---|---|---|
| 10—At S. D. | W | 2-0* | Barr | Folkers | 6—At Atl. | W | 7-1 | Falcone | Capra |
| 11—Atlanta | L | 2-4 | Capra | Caldwell | 7—At Atl. | W | 6-2 | Barr | Morton |
| 12—Atlanta | L | 4-7 | Morton | D'Acquisto | 8—At Atl. | L | 2-3 | Reed | Caldwell |
| 13—Atlanta | W | 5-0 | Montefusco | Reed | 9—At St. L. | L | 4-6 | McGlothen | D'Acquisto |
| 13—Atlanta | W | 4-2 | Falcone | House | 10—At St. L. | L | 2-9 | Curtis | Williams |
| 14—S. Diego | L | 1-3 | Siebert | Barr | 11—At St. L. | L | 3-4 | Forsch | Falcone |
| 15—S. Diego | L | 1-2 | Jones | Caldwell | 12—At N. Y. | L | 2-3 | Matlack | Barr |
| 16—S. Diego | W | 7-1 | D'Acquisto | Spillner | 14—At N. Y. | L | 1-5 | Koosman | Caldwell |
| 18—At L. A. | W | 3-1 | Montefusco | Rau | 16—St. Louis | W | 4-3* | Lavelle | Sosa |
| 19—At L. A. | L | 2-3 | Sutton | Falcone | 17—St. Louis | L | 2-17 | Forsch | Falcone |
| 20—At L. A. | W | 6-3§ | Moffitt | Zahn | 18—St. Louis | W | 2-0 | Barr | McGlothen |
| 21—At Cinn. | W | 4-3* | Lavelle | Borbon | 19—Pitts. | W | 6-4 | Caldwell | Reuss |
| 22—At Cinn. | L | 4-5 | Kirby | Williams | 20—Pitts. | W | 12-4 | Halicki | Ellis |
| 23—At Hous. | L | 2-3 | Konieczny | Montefusco | 21—Pitts. | W | 2-1† | Barr | Giusti |
| 23—At Hous. | W | 9-2 | Falcone | Roberts | 23—Chicago | W | 3-2 | Falcone | R. Reuschel |
| 24—At Hous. | W | 6-5 | Lavelle | Forsch | 24—Chicago | W | 10-3 | Barr | Bonham |
| 25—Los Ang. | L | 5-6 | Messersmith | Caldwell | 25—Chicago | W | 9-7 | Williams | Frailing |
| 26—Los Ang. | L | 3-13 | Rau | D'Acquisto | 26—At Phila. | L | 0-1† | McGraw | Halicki |
| 27—Los Ang. | L | 3-7 | Sutton | Montefusco | 27—At Phila. | W | 1-0* | Montefusco | Garber |
| 29—Cinn. | W | 4-3 | Moffitt | C. Carroll | 28—At Phila. | L | 6-8 | Carlton | Falcone |
| 30—Cinn. | L | 1-4 | Billingham | Barr | 31—At Mon. | L | 2-3 | Warthen | Lavelle |
| | | | **Won 10, Lost 11** | | | | | **Won 13, Lost 11** | |

| MAY | | | | | JUNE | | | | |
|---|---|---|---|---|---|---|---|---|---|
| 2—Houston | W | 5-4 | Moffitt | York | 1—At Mon. | W | 13-5 | Caldwell | Warthen |
| 4—Houston | W | 8-6 | Barr | York | 3—At Chi. | L | 5-6* | Zahn | Moffitt |
| 4—Houston | L | 8-12 | Richard | D'Acquisto | 4—At Chi. | W | 10-8 | Williams | Zamora |

| JUNE | | | Winner | Loser |
|---|---|---|---|---|
| 5—At Chi. | L | 4-8 | Knowles | Moffitt |
| 6—At Pitts. | L | 2-7 | Kison | Barr |
| 7—At Pitts. | L | 6-7 | Hernandez | Toms |
| 8—At Pitts. | W | 3-1 | Halicki | Candelaria |
| 8—At Pitts. | W | 4-2 | Lavelle | Demery |
| 9—N. York | W | 5-4 | Heaverlo | Koosman |
| 10—N. York | L | 0-5 | Seaver | Barr |
| 11—Phila. | W | 8-3 | Caldwell | Underwood |
| 12—Phila. | L | 1-4 | Carlton | Halicki |
| 13—Montreal | L | 2-4 | Warthen | Falcone |
| 14—Montreal | L | 1-3 | Fryman | Montefusco |
| 15—Montreal | L | 1-2 | Renko | Barr |
| 15—Montreal | L | 2-5 | Blair | Caldwell |
| 16—S. Diego | L | 1-7 | Folkers | Halicki |
| 17—S. Diego | W | 3-1 | Falcone | Freisleben |
| 18—S. Diego | W | 8-1 | Montefusco | McIntosh |
| 20—At Atl. | L | 2-4 | Niekro | Barr |
| 21—At Atl. | W | 4-3 | Caldwell | Morton |
| 22—At Atl. | L | 2-8 | Beard | Halicki |
| 22—At Atl. | W | 5-2 | Falcone | Odom |
| 23—At S. D. | L | 6-7 | Tomlin | Lavelle |
| 24—At S. D. | L | 1-2* | Jones | Lavelle |
| 24—At S. D. | L | 0-3 | Strom | Bradley |
| 25—At S. D. | L | 2-6 | Folkers | Caldwell |
| 26—Los Ang. | W | 2-0 | Halicki | Messersmith |
| 27—Los Ang. | W | 10-5 | Williams | Hooton |
| 28—Los Ang. | W | 2-1 | Montefusco | Rau |
| 29—Los Ang. | W | 5-2 | Bradley | Sutton |
| **Won 14, Lost 17** | | | | |

| JULY | | | | |
|---|---|---|---|---|
| 1—Atlanta | W | 9-1 | Caldwell | Easterly |
| 2—Atlanta | L | 0-6 | Niekro | Halicki |
| 3—At L. A. | L | 1-7 | Sutton | Falcone |
| 4—At L. A. | W | 1-0 | Montefusco | Messersmith |
| 5—At L. A. | W | 4-5 | Downing | Halicki |
| 6—At L. A. | L | 1-5 | Rau | Bradley |
| 7—At St. L. | L | 6-8 | Reed | Caldwell |
| 8—At St. L. | W | 6-4 | Falcone | Gibson |
| 9—At St. L. | L | 0-9 | Denny | Montefusco |
| 11—At Chi. | L | 6-8 | Dettore | Moffitt |
| 12—At Chi. | L | 4-6 | Stone | Caldwell |
| 13—At Chi. | W | 4-1 | Montefusco | Zahn |
| 17—St. Louis | L | 0-1 | Hrabosky | Barr |
| 18—St. Louis | W | 2-1* | Lavelle | Terlecky |
| 19—St. Louis | W | 5-2 | Montefusco | McGlothen |
| 20—Pitts. | W | 2-1 | Halicki | Rooker |
| 20—Pitts. | L | 1-7 | Brett | Caldwell |
| 21—Pitts. | W | 7-2 | Barr | Candelaria |
| 22—Chicago | W | 9-5 | Williams | Burris |
| 23—Chicago | W | 10-2 | Montefusco | Stone |
| 24—Chicago | L | 3-4 | Bonham | Halicki |
| 25—At Hous. | W | 8-1 | Barr | Roberts |
| 26—At Hous. | W | 3-2 | Moffitt | Forsch |
| 26—At Hous. | W | 9-3 | Bradley | Konieczny |
| 27—At Hous. | W | 3-1 | Montefusco | Richard |
| 28—At Cinn. | L | 4-8 | Borbon | Halicki |
| 29—At Cinn. | L | 2-4 | Barr | Eastwick |
| 30—At Cinn. | L | 1-6 | Darcy | Falcone |
| 31—At Cinn. | L | 6-11 | Kirby | Montefusco |
| **Won 15, Lost 14** | | | | |

| AUGUST | | | Winner | Loser |
|---|---|---|---|---|
| 1—Houston | W | 3-2 | Halicki | Richard |
| 2—Houston | W | 8-7* | Heaverlo | Crawford |
| 3—Houston | W | 5-4 | Falcone | Roberts |
| 3—Houston | L | 9-10 | Crawford | Caldwell |
| 4—Cinn. | L | 5-7 | C. Carroll | Caldwell |
| 5—Cinn. | L | 3-6 | Borbon | Halicki |
| 6—Cinn. | L | 5-12 | Billingham | Barr |
| 8—At Phila. | L | 4-6 | Garber | Moffitt |
| 9—At Phila. | L | 4-11 | Carlton | Montefusco |
| 10—At Phila. | W | 8-1 | Barr | Ruthven |
| 11—At Mon. | W | 9-2 | Halicki | Rogers |
| 12—At Mon. | W | 5-2† | Caldwell | Murray |
| 13—At Mon. | W | 4-3‡ | Williams | Fryman |
| 14—At Mon. | W | 9-2 | Barr | Blair |
| 15—At N. Y. | W | 6-2 | Halicki | Koosman |
| 15—At N. Y. | L | 4-9 | Webb | Bradley |
| 16—At N. Y. | L | 2-4 | Swan | Falcone |
| 17—At N. Y. | L | 0-3 | Seaver | Montefusco |
| 19—At Pitts. | L | 0-4 | Reuss | Barr |
| 20—At Pitts. | L | 1-3 | Rooker | Halicki |
| 22—N. York | L | 4-6 | Seaver | Falcone |
| 23—N. York | W | 2-1 | Lavelle | Lockwood |
| 24—N. York | L | 5-9 | Matlack | Barr |
| 24—N. York | W | 6-0 | Halicki | Swan |
| 26—Montreal | W | 4-3 | Falcone | Warthen |
| 27—Montreal | W | 9-1 | Montefusco | Fryman |
| 28—Phila. | L | 5-8 | Hilgendorf | Barr |
| 29—Phila. | L | 4-1 | Christenson | Barr |
| 30—Phila. | W | 4-1 | Falcone | Underwood |
| 31—Phila. | W | 5-4 | Montefusco | Carlton |
| **Won 15, Lost 15** | | | | |

| SEPTEMBER | | | | |
|---|---|---|---|---|
| 1—Los Ang. | L | 1-3 | Hooton | Williams |
| 2—Los Ang. | W | 7-3 | Halicki | Sutton |
| 3—At Hous. | W | 9-4 | Falcone | Richard |
| 4—At Hous. | W | 2-1 | Montefusco | Dierker |
| 5—At Cinn. | L | 3-6 | Eastwick | Heaverlo |
| 6—At Cinn. | L | 2-3 | Billingham | Halicki |
| 7—At Cinn. | L | 4-8 | Gullett | Falcone |
| 8—At L. A. | L | 0-4 | Messersmith | Montefusco |
| 9—At L. A. | L | 3-8 | Hough | Barr |
| 10—Houston | L | 3-6 | Cosgrove | Halicki |
| 11—Houston | L | 3-4‡ | Niekro | Moffitt |
| 12—Cinn. | L | 3-6 | Norman | Montefusco |
| 13—Cinn. | W | 9-2 | Barr | Gullett |
| 14—Cinn. | W | 4-2 | Heaverlo | Nolan |
| 14—Cinn. | L | 3-8 | Darcy | Minton |
| 15—Atlanta | L | 0-12 | Easterly | Falcone |
| 16—Atlanta | W | 7-6 | D'Acquisto | House |
| 17—Atlanta | W | 4-1 | Barr | Niekro |
| 19—S. Diego | W | 3-1 | Caldwell | Jones |
| 20—S. Diego | W | 4-2 | Falcone | Folkers |
| 21—S. Diego | W | 2-1 | Montefusco | Strom |
| 24—At Atl. | L | 6-7† | Sosa | Barr |
| 25—At S. D. | L | 6-8 | Tomlin | Caldwell |
| 26—At S. D. | W | 5-0 | Montefusco | Strom |
| 27—At S. D. | W | 4-1 | Dressler | McIntosh |
| 28—At S. D. | W | 5-3 | Minton | Jones |
| **Won 13, Lost 13** | | | | |

* 10 innings.   † 11 innings.   ‡ 12 innings.   § 13 innings.

# Padres Desert Cellar, Move Up to Fourth

### By PHIL COLLIER

It was a banner seventh season for the San Diego Padres—who set records for victories (71) and home attendance (1,281,747) in addition to finishing fourth in the National League West and escaping the cellar for the first time.

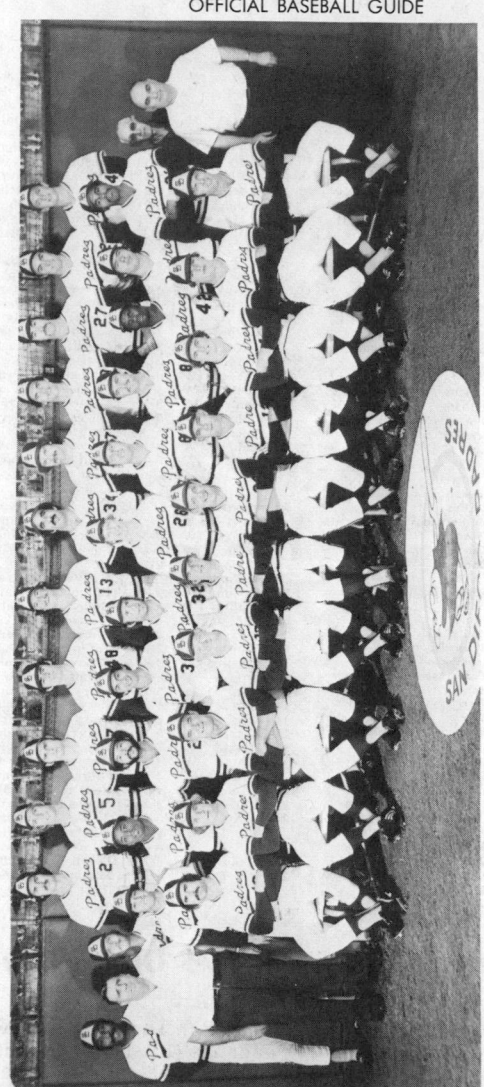

SAN DIEGO PADRES—1975

Front row—Kendall, Jones, Sisler, coach; Wietelmann, coach; McNamara, manager; Morgan, coach; Davenport, coach; Freisleben, Johnson, Hundley. Second row—McCovey, Tunis, assistant trainer; Ivie, Hernandez, Fuentes, Tolan, Torres, Locklear, Folkers, Hahn, Kubiak, Turner, Metzger, Winfield, Peralta, equipment manager; Mattei, trainer and traveling secretary. Third row—Grubb, Almon, Davis, Spillner, Sharon, Frisella, Tomlin, Roberts, Greif, Strom, McIntosh. Missing—Foster.

They led their division for 13 of the 15 days from April 12 through April 26 and were as high as a tie for third place (with San Francisco) as late as July 9.

In addition to finishing ahead of Atlanta and Houston in their division, the Padres finally developed a player of national reputation. Randy Jones, their 25-year-old lefthander, went from an 8-22 record in 1974 to 20-12 in 1975, led the N. L. with a 2.24 earned-run average, was second with six shutouts, finished second to the Mets' Tom Seaver in the Cy Young balloting and was 10th in the N. L. in most valuable player voting.

"Our goal was to get out of last place, which we did, but our big objective was to play .500 ball and we might have made it if it hadn't been for injuries," said manager John McNamara, who will enter his third term at the San Diego helm in 1976.

Last in the majors in pitching in 1974, the Padres led both leagues in earned-run percentages into late June and that was a tribute to first-year pitching coach Tom Morgan. Surprisingly Morgan's contract wasn't renewed at the end of the season. The team finished sixth in the N. L. in ERA and eighth in the majors, despite a second-half collapse.

For the second year in a row, the Padres were last in the majors in runs scored. They hit only 78 home runs and led the N. L. in errors with 188.

However, their home attendance was 206,000 ahead of 1974, their first season under the ownership of hamburger king Ray Kroc.

Jones pitched two one-hitters, two two-hitters, one three-hitter and three four-hitters. The sinkerball specialist was the Padres' lone representative on the National League All-Star squad and pitched a scoreless ninth inning of relief in the midseason classic.

Thirty-seven-year-old first baseman Willie McCovey again led the club in homers, clouting 23 for the second time in as many seasons here, while veteran second baseman Tito Fuentes, a San Diego newcomer, led the club with a .280 average and helped the Padres reel off a record 163 double plays.

The Padres had a lot of surprises. Veteran utility infielder Hector Torres, invited to camp on a tryout, batted .259, fielded expertly at three positions and won the regular shortstop job away from Enzo Hernandez. Enzo stole 20 bases. Ted Kubiak, picked up in a trade with Oakland, combined with Torres to give the Padres the finest infield depth in their brief history.

Lefthander Brent Strom, called up from Hawaii after Alan Foster (3-1) was laid low for the season with a shoulder ailment, compiled an 8-8 record and a 2.55 ERA to establish himself as the No. 2 man in the starting rotation.

Newcomers Rich Folkers and Danny Frisella combined with Bill Greif and Dave Tomlin to give the Padres the deepest and strongest bullpen they've ever had.

However, the Padres had many disappointments. Dave Winfield, the right fielder with super star potential, was tied for the league lead in homers and was near the top in runs batted in until two wrist injuries just before the All-Star break limited his ability. He never fully recovered, winding up at .267 with 15 homers and 76 RBI.

Stylish center fielder John Grubb faltered to .269, after compiling a .299 average in his first two big league seasons.

The San Diego catchers—Fred Kendall, Randy Hundley, Jerry Moses and Bob Davis—hit only one homer and none hit for an average. The bench was weak, offensively, except for outfielder Gene Locklear, who averaged .321.

Sophomore righthanders Dave Freisleben (5-14) and Dan Spillner (5-13) and rookie righthander Joe McIntosh (8-15) were disappointments and outfielder Bobby Tolan (.255 with five homers) didn't live up to expectations.

The injury jinx that hit Winfield, Foster, Grubb and several others also struck first baseman-third baseman Mike Ivie (.249 with eight homers and 46 RBIs) but he still managed to win a spot in Topps' All-Star Major League Rookie Team.

McNamara philosophized: "We improved and we proved to ourselves and to the rest of the league that we are competitive."

## SCORES OF SAN DIEGO PADRES' 1975 GAMES

| APRIL | | | Winner | Loser |
|---|---|---|---|---|
| 10—S. Fran. | L | 0-2* | Barr | Folkers |
| 11—Cinn. | W | 5-2 | Spillner | Norman |
| 12—Cinn. | W | 3-2 | McIntosh | Nolan |
| 13—Cinn. | L | 0-10 | Gullett | Freisleben |
| 14—At S. F. | W | 3-1 | Siebert | Barr |
| 15—At S. F. | W | 2-1 | Jones | Caldwell |
| 16—At S. F. | L | 1-7 | D'Acquisto | Spillner |
| 18—At Atl. | W | 3-1 | McIntosh | Reed |
| 19—At Atl. | W | 8-2 | Freisleben | Gentry |
| 20—At Atl. | L | 3-4 | House | Folkers |
| 21—At Hous. | W | 4-0 | Jones | Crawford |
| 22—At Hous. | W | 2-1 | Spillner | Griffin |
| 23—Los Ang. | W | 7-1 | McIntosh | Sutton |
| 24—Los Ang. | L | 6-11 | Rhoden | Freisleben |
| 25—Atlanta | W | 5-3 | Siebert | Capra |
| 26—Atlanta | L | 4-6 | Morton | Jones |
| 27—Atlanta | L | 8-12 | Reed | Folkers |
| 27—Atlanta | L | 1-4 | Harrison | Foster |
| 28—Houston | L | 1-4 | Roberts | McIntosh |
| 29—Houston | L | 2-8 | Richard | Freisleben |
| 30—Houston | W | 4-2 | Siebert | Dierker |
| | | **Won 11, Lost 10** | | |
| MAY | | | | |
| 1—Houston | L | 3-6 | Forsch | Jones |
| 2—At L. A. | L | 0-3 | Sutton | Spillner |
| 3—At L. A. | W | 3-1x | Foster | Brewer |
| 4—At L. A. | L | 10-7 | Jones | Hooton |
| 6—At Cinn. | L | 3-7 | Billingham | Siebert |
| 7—At Cinn. | L | 2-10 | Norman | Spillner |
| 8—At Cinn. | W | 3-0 | Jones | Nolan |
| 9—At Chi. | L | 2-5 | Burris | McIntosh |
| 10—At Chi. | L | 1-5 | R. Reuschel | Siebert |
| 11—At Chi. | W | 2-1 | Freisleben | Bonham |
| 13—At Pitts. | L | 0-2 | Reuss | Spillner |
| 14—At Pitts. | L | 4-5† | McDowell | Greif |
| 16—Chicago | W | 8-2 | McIntosh | Bonham |
| 17—Chicago | W | 4-1 | Freisleben | Knowles |
| 18—Chicago | L | 2-3 | Burris | Spillner |
| 19—St. Louis | W | 1-0* | Jones | Curtis |
| 20—St. Louis | W | 3-2 | Foster | Sosa |
| 21—St. Louis | W | 1-0 | McIntosh | Gibson |
| 22—Pitts. | L | 2-4 | Rooker | Freisleben |
| 23—Pitts. | W | 4-3 | Frisella | Giusti |
| 24—Pitts. | W | 5-0 | Jones | Reuss |
| 25—Pitts. | L | 5-6† | Hernandez | Frisella |
| 26—At St. L. | W | 9-6 | Greif | Hrabosky |

| MAY | | | Winner | Loser |
|---|---|---|---|---|
| 27—At St. L. | L | 1-7 | Forsch | Freisleben |
| 28—At St. L. | L | 5-6* | Garman | Greif |
| 30—At N. Y. | W | 6-2 | Jones | Koosman |
| 31—At N. Y. | L | 2-7 | Seaver | McIntosh |
| | | **Won 13, Lost 14** | | |
| JUNE | | | | |
| 1—At N. Y. | W | 4-0 | Foster | Tate |
| 2—At Phila. | L | 1-5 | Carlton | Freisleben |
| 3—At Phila. | L | 1-12 | Lonborg | Spillner |
| 4—At Phila. | L | 2-7 | Twitchell | Jones |
| 8—At Mon. | W | 5-2 | McIntosh | McNally |
| 8—At Mon. | L | 1-3 | Rogers | Freisleben |
| 9—Phila. | W | 8-3 | Jones | Twitchell |
| 10—Phila. | L | 0-7 | Christenson | Spillner |
| 11—Montreal | W | 3-1 | Folkers | Blair |
| 12—Montreal | L | 2-3x | DeMola | Frisella |
| 13—N. York | L | 2-7 | Stone | McIntosh |
| 14—N. York | W | 7-1 | Jones | Koosman |
| 15—N. York | L | 0-6 | Seaver | Strom |
| 16—At S. F. | W | 7-1 | Folkers | Halicki |
| 17—At S. F. | L | 1-3 | Falcone | Freisleben |
| 18—At S. F. | L | 1-8 | Montefusco | McIntosh |
| 19—Los Ang. | L | 1-4 | Rau | Jones |
| 20—Los Ang. | W | 2-1 | Strom | Sutton |
| 21—Los Ang. | L | 3-4 | Messersmith | Folkers |
| 22—Los Ang. | L | 2-3 | Marshall | Frisella |
| 23—S. Fran. | W | 7-6 | Tomlin | Lavelle |
| 24—S. Fran. | W | 2-1* | Jones | Lavelle |
| 24—S. Fran. | W | 3-0 | Strom | Bradley |
| 25—S. Fran. | W | 6-2 | Folkers | Caldwell |
| 27—At Cinn. | L | 2-5† | McEnaney | Frisella |
| 28—At Cinn. | L | 4-6* | McEnaney | Tomlin |
| 29—At Cinn. | L | 1-4 | Billingham | Jones |
| 29—At Cinn. | W | 4-3 | Strom | Darcy |
| 30—At L. A. | L | 1-4 | Messersmith | Folkers |
| | | **Won 12, Lost 17** | | |
| JULY | | | | |
| 1—At L. A. | W | 10-1 | Spillner | Hooton |
| 2—At L. A. | L | 5-6§ | Downing | McIntosh |
| 3—Cinn. | W | 2-1 | Jones | McEnaney |
| 4—Cinn. | L | 6-7 | Billingham | Folkers |
| 5—Cinn. | L | 3-6 | Norman | Strom |
| 6—Cinn. | L | 2-13 | Kirby | McIntosh |
| 8—At Chi. | W | 8-6x | McIntosh | Dettore |
| 9—At Chi. | W | 3-2 | Strom | Zahn |

| JULY | | | Winner | Loser |
|---|---|---|---|---|
| 10—At Chi. | L | 1-3 | Burris | Freisleben |
| 11—At Pitts. | L | 2-6 | Rooker | Folkers |
| 11—At Pitts. | L | 0-5 | Candelaria | McIntosh |
| 12—At Pitts. | L | 4-6 | Hernandez | Jones |
| 13—At Pitts. | W | 7-5 | Strom | Ellis |
| 17—Chicago | L | 5-6 | R. Reuschel | Strom |
| 18—Chicago | W | 4-2 | Greif | Wilcox |
| 19—Chicago | W | 2-1 | Freisleben | Stone |
| 20—St. Louis | L | 1-3† | Hrabosky | Greif |
| 20—St. Louis | L | 2-10 | Curtis | Folkers |
| 21—St. Louis | L | 0-4 | Rasmussen | Strom |
| 22—Pitts. | W | 1-0 | Jones | Kison |
| 23—Pitts. | L | 1-8 | Ellis | Freisleben |
| 25—At Atl. | W | 7-3 | McIntosh | Sadecki |
| 25—At Atl. | W | 8-1 | Spillner | Thompson |
| 26—At Atl. | W | 4-2 | Johnson | Morton |
| 27—At Atl. | W | 3-1 | Jones | Dal Canton |
| 28—At Hous. | W | 2-0 | Freisleben | Dierker |
| 29—At Hous. | L | 2-6 | Roberts | Spillner |
| 30—At Hous. | L | 4-8 | Konieczny | McIntosh |
| 31—At Hous. | W | 5-3 | Tomlin | Granger |
| | | | **Won 14, Lost 15** | |

| AUGUST | | | | |
|---|---|---|---|---|
| 1—Atlanta | W | 4-0 | Jones | Niekro |
| 2—Atlanta | L | 6-8x | Beard | McIntosh |
| 3—Atlanta | L | 1-5 | Morton | Spillner |
| 4—Houston | L | 3-5 | Niekro | Freisleben |
| 5—Houston | W | 6-5* | Greif | Granger |
| 6—Houston | W | 6-1 | Jones | Dierker |
| 8—At St. L. | L | 6-10 | Forsch | Spillner |
| 9—At St. L. | L | 1-6 | McGlothen | Freisleben |
| 10—At St. L. | L | 2-3* | Hrabosky | Greif |
| 11—At N. Y. | L | 4-8 | Lockwood | Jones |
| 12—At N. Y. | L | 4-9 | Seaver | Johnson |
| 13—At N. Y. | W | 8-5 | Folkers | Tate |
| 15—At Phila. | L | 3-4 | Hilgendorf | McIntosh |
| 16—At Phila. | W | 5-1 | Jones | McGraw |
| 17—At Phila. | L | 4-10 | Underwood | Freisleben |
| 18—At Mon. | L | 1-4 | Warthen | Tomlin |
| 18—At Mon. | W | 5-2 | Folkers | Fryman |
| 19—At Mon. | L | 0-5 | Rogers | McIntosh |

| AUGUST | | | Winner | Loser |
|---|---|---|---|---|
| 20—At Mon. | W | 8-6 | Johnson | Fryman |
| 22—Phila. | L | 5-6 | Hilgendorf | Greif |
| 23—Phila. | W | 8-3 | Spillner | Carlton |
| 24—Phila. | W | 7-2 | Jones | Ruthven |
| 24—Phila. | W | 7-6‡ | Greif | Schueler |
| 25—N. York | L | 0-4 | Webb | Strom |
| 26—N. York | L | 2-7 | Tate | Freisleben |
| 27—N. York | L | 0-7 | Seaver | Spillner |
| 28—Montreal | L | 8-10 | Scherman | Jones |
| 29—Montreal | L | 0-4 | Carrithers | McIntosh |
| 30—Montreal | L | 1-5 | Renko | Folkers |
| 31—Montreal | W | 6-0 | Strom | Warthen |
| | | | **Won 11, Lost 19** | |

| SEPTEMBER | | | | |
|---|---|---|---|---|
| 1—At Cinn. | W | 2-1 | Jones | Borbon |
| 2—At Cinn. | L | 4-10 | Gullett | Spillner |
| 3—At Atl. | W | 10-9 | Johnson | House |
| 4—At Atl. | L | 1-2 | Dal Canton | Frisella |
| 5—At Hous. | L | 1-2 | Richard | Jones |
| 6—At Hous. | W | 2-1 | Strom | Konieczny |
| 7—At Hous. | L | 2-3 | York | Frisella |
| 8—Cinn. | L | 2-3 | C. Carroll | Greif |
| 9—Cinn. | W | 11-2 | Folkers | Kirby |
| 10—Atlanta | W | 2-1 | Jones | Dal Canton |
| 11—Atlanta | W | 4-3 | Strom | House |
| 12—Houston | W | 1-0 | Tomlin | York |
| 14—Houston | L | 2-4 | Richard | Jones |
| 15—At L. A. | L | 4-5 | Hooton | McIntosh |
| 16—At L. A. | L | 2-5 | Rhoden | Strom |
| 17—At L. A. | L | 1-3 | Messersmith | Spillner |
| 19—At S. F. | L | 1-3 | Caldwell | Jones |
| 20—At S. F. | L | 2-4 | Falcone | Folkers |
| 21—At S. F. | L | 1-2 | Montefusco | Strom |
| 22—Los Ang. | W | 6-5† | Metzger | Sells |
| 23—Los Ang. | W | 6-4 | Jones | Wall |
| 24—Los Ang. | L | 0-14 | Rau | Folkers |
| 25—S. Fran. | W | 8-6 | Tomlin | Caldwell |
| 26—S. Fran. | L | 0-5 | Montefusco | Strom |
| 27—S. Fran. | L | 1-4 | Dressler | McIntosh |
| 28—S. Fran. | L | 3-5 | Minton | Jones |
| | | | **Won 10, Lost 16** | |

* 10 innings.  † 11 innings.  ‡ 12 innings.  § 14 innings.  x 15 innings.

# Too Slow Braves Stumble to Fifth

## By WAYNE MINSHEW

The Braves, who appeared in 1974 to be ready to emerge as one of the National League's most improved teams, took a giant step backward last season, revealing themselves to be too slow afoot and too awkward defensively to escape the depths of fifth place in the West Division standings.

There were few positive happenings concerning the Braves. They fired another manager, Clyde King, a stand-pat sort of leader who made little use of his full 25-player roster and, according to his critics, wasn't there soon enough, often enough with moves of strategy during games. King was the fifth managerial victim for the Braves since they moved here 10 years ago.

The team's leading hitter was outfielder Rowland Office, who batted a modest .290. Darrell Evans belted 22 homers and knocked in 73 runs to lead the club in those departments, and his figures would also have to be labeled less than imposing. Righthander Carl Morton had a 17-16 record as the team's top pitcher, but that could have been better had Morton been supported with more offense from his teammates.

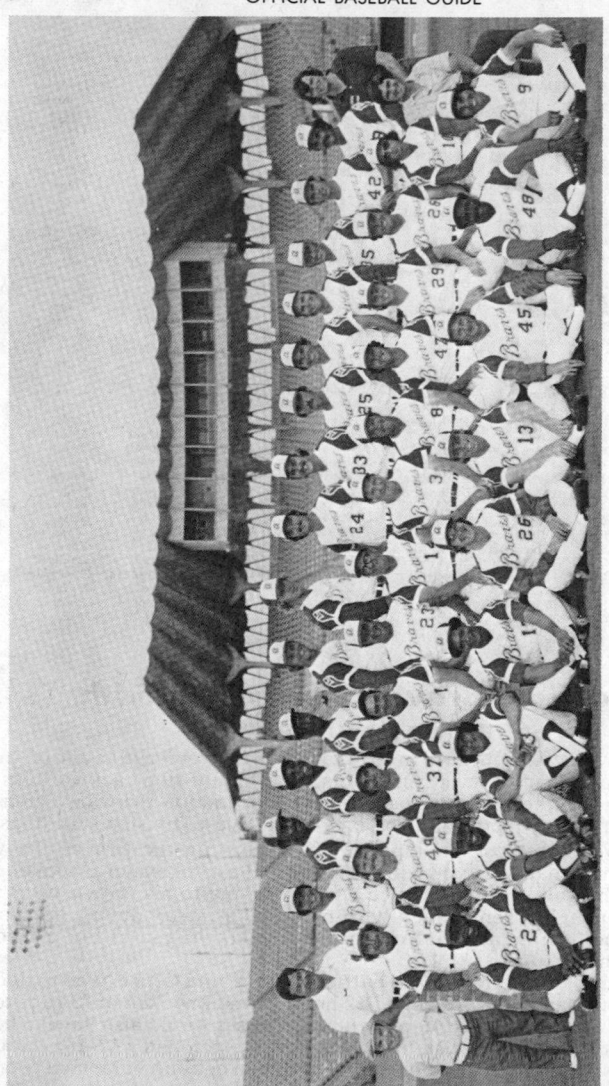

ATLANTA BRAVES—1975

Front row—May, Blanks, Leon, Foster, House, Beall, Easterly, Garr, Perez. Second row—Davidson, traveling secretary; Oates, Morton, Beard, Haas, coach; Starrette, coach; King, manager; Silvestri, coach; Busby, coach; Capra, Correll, Lum, Robinson, Acree, equipment manager. Third row—Pursley, trainer; Tepedino, Gaston, Baker, Office, Nordhagen, Reed, Harrison, Thompson, Gentry, Evans, Gilbreath, Niekro, Pocoroba, Torrealba, Holland, assistant equipment manager.

There were performances that lent hope for the future. Besides Office, Marty Perez batted .275 and played second base in adequate fashion, while the Braves' relief corps of Tom House, Mike Beard, Bruce Dal Canton and Elias Sosa had their moments in the sun.

The Braves played well for a month, but on May 16 dropped a 12-8 decision to the Phillies at Philadelphia, making their record 18-19 at the time and were never to see the sunny side of .500 again.

Chief culprit was the defense, which committed 175 errors, 36 by third baseman Evans and 25 by shortstop Larvell Blanks. Catchers had difficulty throwing out baserunners on steal attempts, even when Braves' pitchers managed to hold them close. The outfield was a little better over all, but it could not be said they played intelligently, throwing many times over the heads of cutoff men and to wrong bases.

The club lacked offensive firepower, especially in clutch situations, although they thought perhaps that problem was solved with the acquisition of Richie Allen's contract during the off-season. Allen never showed. He made it clear he wouldn't from the start and finally was dealt to the Phillies for outfielder Barry Bonnell, catcher Jim Essian and cash.

At season's beginning, it was thought that the pitching staff was strong enough to overcome other weaknesses. However, the 1974 earned-run average leader, Buzz Capra, suffered from a bad shoulder and had to be sent home for prescribed rest in June with a 4-7 record. Phil Niekro (15-15) labored through the campaign with recurring back trouble, and reliever Max Leon could never quite shake a sore shoulder. Ron Reed and Roric Harrison were in the starting rotation early, but were traded away before mid-season.

It might also be pointed out that the Braves, who finished the year under an interim manager, Connie Ryan, played less than enthusiastically at times. One night, in a nationally televised game, announcer Tony Kubek, a former major league player, wondered aloud if some of the players were giving an honest effort.

And so it went, loss following loss, and once again the Braves were never in serious contention for the West Division title, a situation in which they were not alone on this occasion as the Reds ran away with the championship. At any rate, it showed at the gate, where only 534,672 came to watch. It marked the lowest attendance total for the team since it moved here in 1966.

Whether the Braves will emerge to their 1975 expectations is still a question, but there will be a new look to the Atlanta nine in '76.

Dave Bristol, who has had flings as skipper for Cincinnati and Milwaukee, was named the new manager. The Braves obtained among others Jim Wynn, Tom Paciorek, Lee Lacy and Jerry Royster from the Dodgers, Ken Henderson and Dick Ruthven from the White Sox, Roger Moret from Boston and Darrel Chaney from Cincinnati. They gave up Dusty Baker, Ed Goodson, Ralph Garr, Larvell Blanks, Tom House and Mike Lum.

Bristol forecast aggressiveness and a positive attitude for a sometimes lackadaisical atmosphere on the club.

Perhaps the brightest look, however, came when R. E. (Ted) Turner, an Atlanta television station owner and millionaire sportsman and yachtsman, purchased the Braves. "I thought if the team was to be sold," said Turner, "that somebody who cares should be the owner. I care."

## SCORES OF ATLANTA BRAVES' 1975 GAMES

### APRIL

| Date | | Score | Winner | Loser |
|---|---|---|---|---|
| 7—At Hous. | L | 2-6 | Dierker | Niekro |
| 8—At Hous. | W | 2-0 | Morton | Konieczny |
| 9—At Hous. | L | 2-14 | Roberts | Reed |
| 11—At S. F. | W | 4-2 | Capra | Caldwell |
| 12—At S. F. | W | 7-4 | Morton | D'Acquisto |
| 13—At S. F. | L | 0-5 | Montefusco | Reed |
| 13—At S. F. | L | 2-4 | Falcone | House |
| 15—Houston | W | 6-1 | Niekro | Richard |
| 16—Houston | W | 5-2 | Capra | Dierker |
| 17—Houston | W | 2-1* | Morton | Roberts |
| 18—S. Diego | L | 1-3 | McIntosh | Reed |
| 19—S. Diego | L | 2-8 | Freisleben | Gentry |
| 20—S. Diego | W | 4-3 | House | Folkers |
| 21—Los Ang. | L | 1-2 | Messersmith | Capra |
| 22—Los Ang. | W | 3-2 | Morton | Hough |
| 23—Cinn. | L | 5-4† | Reed | Gullett |
| 24—Cinn. | L | 3-11 | Billingham | Niekro |
| 25—At S. D. | L | 3-5 | Siebert | Capra |
| 26—At S. D. | W | 6-4 | Morton | Jones |
| 27—At S. D. | W | 12-8 | Reed | Folkers |
| 27—At S. D. | W | 4-1 | Harrison | Foster |
| 28—At L. A. | L | 3-4 | Brewer | House |
| 29—At L. A. | L | 0-8 | Messersmith | Capra |
| 30—At L. A. | L | 2-5 | Rau | Morton |

**Won 12, Lost 12**

### MAY

| Date | | Score | Winner | Loser |
|---|---|---|---|---|
| 2—At Cinn. | W | 6-5 | Gentry | Kirby |
| 3—At Cinn. | L | 1-6 | Nolan | Harrison |
| 4—At Cinn. | L | 2-3 | Gullett | Niekro |
| 6—S. Fran. | L | 1-7 | Falcone | Capra |
| 7—S. Fran. | L | 2-6 | Barr | Morton |
| 8—S. Fran. | W | 3-2 | Reed | Caldwell |
| 9—Phila. | L | 3-1 | Harrison | Underwood |
| 10—Phila. | W | 2-1† | Niekro | Garber |
| 11—Phila. | W | 7-3 | Capra | Twitchell |
| 12—At Mon. | L | 1-11 | Rogers | Morton |
| 13—At Mon. | W | 9-4 | Reed | McNally |
| 14—At Mon. | L | 4-5 | Fryman | Harrison |
| 15—At Mon. | W | 5-4x | Niekro | Renko |
| 16—At Phila. | L | 8-12 | Garber | Capra |
| 17—At Phila. | L | 8-9 | Garber | Niekro |
| 18—At Phila. | L | 1-5 | Underwood | Reed |
| 20—Montreal | W | 9-4 | Harrison | Fryman |
| 21—Montreal | W | 6-3 | Niekro | Renko |
| 23—N. York | L | 1-3 | Matlack | Morton |
| 24—N. York | L | 1-5 | Tate | Reed |
| 25—N. York | W | 6-3 | Capra | Koosman |
| 26—At Chi. | L | 0-6 | Burris | Harrison |
| 27—At Chi. | W | 7-2 | Niekro | R. Reuschel |
| 28—At Chi. | L | 4-5 | Zamora | Morton |
| 30—At Pitts. | L | 1-2 | Reuss | Capra |
| 31—At Pitts. | L | 4-11 | Kison | Harrison |

**Won 11, Lost 15**

### JUNE

| Date | | Score | Winner | Loser |
|---|---|---|---|---|
| 1—At Pitts. | W | 5-2 | Niekro | Rooker |
| 2—At St. L. | L | 0-1 | McGlothen | Morton |
| 3—At St. L. | L | 2-4 | Reed | Capra |
| 4—At St. L. | L | 2-5 | Curtis | Sadecki |
| 6—At N. Y. | W | 4-1 | Niekro | Tate |
| 7—At N. Y. | W | 7-3 | Morton | Matlack |
| 8—At N. Y. | W | 6-7‡ | Webb | Sosa |
| 9—St. Louis | W | 4-5 | Curtis | Odom |
| 12—Chicago | W | 5-4 | House | Frailing |
| 12—Chicago | W | 6-2y | Morton | Zahn |
| 13—Pitts. | L | 3-8 | Rooker | Odom |
| 14—Pitts. | L | 1-2 | Reuss | Thompson |
| 15—Pitts. | L | 6-8 | Demery | Sosa |

### JUNE

| Date | | Score | Winner | Loser |
|---|---|---|---|---|
| 16—At Cinn. | L | 2-9 | Gullett | Niekro |
| 17—At Cinn. | W | 2-1 | Morton | Nolan |
| 18—At Cinn. | L | 1-6 | Billingham | Odom |
| 20—S. Fran. | W | 4-2 | Niekro | Barr |
| 21—S. Fran. | L | 3-4 | Caldwell | Morton |
| 22—S. Fran. | W | 8-2 | Beard | Halicki |
| 22—S. Fran. | L | 2-5 | Falcone | Odom |
| 23—Cinn. | L | 4-8 | Billingham | Easterly |
| 24—Cinn. | L | 0-3 | Darcy | Niekro |
| 25—Cinn. | L | 0-2 | T. Carroll | Morton |
| 26—At Hous. | L | 4-8 | Richard | Thompson |
| 27—At Hous. | W | 7-4 | Easterly | Dierker |
| 28—At Hous. | W | 6-3 | Beard | Roberts |
| 29—At Hous. | W | 3-1 | Morton | Forsch |

**Won 11, Lost 16**

### JULY

| Date | | Score | Winner | Loser |
|---|---|---|---|---|
| 1—At S. F. | L | 1-9 | Caldwell | Easterly |
| 2—At S. F. | W | 6-0 | Niekro | Halicki |
| 4—Houston | W | 5-4 | Morton | Granger |
| 5—Houston | W | 4-3 | Sadecki | Forsch |
| 5—Houston | W | 8-4 | Leon | Konieczny |
| 6—Houston | L | 2-6 | Richard | Niekro |
| 7—N. York | L | 1-3 | Webb | Easterly |
| 8—N. York | L | 3-4 | Koosman | Morton |
| 9—N. York | L | 1-2* | Seaver | Leon |
| 11—Montreal | W | 2-1* | House | Murray |
| 12—Montreal | W | 9-4 | Morton | Scherman |
| 12—Montreal | L | 3-7 | Fryman | Easterly |
| 13—Montreal | W | 5-4‡ | Sadecki | DeMola |
| 17—At N. Y. | L | 3-4 | Baldwin | House |
| 18—At N. Y. | W | 4-3 | Morton | Matlack |
| 19—At N. Y. | L | 4-5 | Seaver | Dal Canton |
| 20—At Mon. | L | 5-6† | Scherman | House |
| 21—At Mon. | W | 4-1 | Beard | Warthen |
| 22—At Phila. | L | 0-1 | Carlton | Morton |
| 23—At Phila. | L | 2-3 | Lonborg | Dal Canton |
| 24—At Phila. | W | 5-4 | Niekro | Christenson |
| 25—S. Diego | L | 3-7 | McIntosh | Sadecki |
| 25—S. Diego | L | 1-8 | Spillner | Thompson |
| 26—S. Diego | L | 2-4 | Johnson | Morton |
| 27—S. Diego | L | 1-3 | Jones | Dal Canton |
| 28—Los Ang. | W | 5-3 | Niekro | Marshall |
| 29—Los Ang. | W | 4-2 | Odom | Messersmith |
| 30—Los Ang. | L | 2-8 | Rau | Morton |
| 31—Los Ang. | W | 11-10 | House | Marshall |

**Won 13, Lost 16**

### AUGUST

| Date | | Score | Winner | Loser |
|---|---|---|---|---|
| 1—At S. D. | L | 0-4 | Jones | Niekro |
| 2—At S. D. | W | 8-6§ | Beard | McIntosh |
| 3—At S. D. | W | 5-1 | Morton | Spillner |
| 4—At L. A. | L | 1-9 | Hooton | Dal Canton |
| 5—At L. A. | L | 0-5 | Sutton | Niekro |
| 6—At L. A. | W | 5-4 | House | Messersmith |
| 8—Chicago | W | 1-0 | Morton | Dettore |
| 8—Chicago | L | 1-3 | Burris | Dal Canton |
| 9—Chicago | L | 2-8 | Stone | Niekro |
| 10—Chicago | L | 1-9 | Bonham | Odom |
| 11—Pitts. | L | 1-6 | Candelaria | Easterly |
| 12—Pitts. | W | 3-2 | Morton | Kison |
| 13—Pitts. | W | 4-3 | House | Brett |
| 14—St. Louis | W | 6-4 | Niekro | McGlothen |
| 15—St. Louis | L | 1-4 | Reed | Easterly |
| 15—St. Louis | L | 1-2 | Rasmussen | Thompson |
| 16—St. Louis | W | 8-7 | House | Gibson |
| 17—St. Louis | L | 1-8 | Denny | Odom |
| 18—Phila. | L | 3-6 | Hilgendorf | Niekro |
| 19—Phila. | W | 6-4 | Leon | Garber |

| AUGUST | | | Winner | Loser |
|---|---|---|---|---|
| 20—Phila. | L | 1-4 | Christenson | Morton |
| 22—At St. L. | W | 9-5 | Sosa | Parker |
| 23—At St. L. | L | 2-7 | Denny | Niekro |
| 24—At St. L. | L | 2-6 | Forsch | Morton |
| 25—At Pitts. | L | 0-4 | Rooker | Thompson |
| 26—At Pitts. | L | 2-8 | Demery | Easterly |
| 27—At Pitts. | W | 6-2 | Niekro | Candelaria |
| 29—At Chi. | L | 3-8 | Burris | Morton |
| 31—At Chi. | W | 3-1 | Niekro | R. Reuschel |
| 31—At Chi. | L | 8-9* | Dettore | Sadecki |
| | | Won 12, Lost 18 | | |

| SEPTEMBER | | | | |
|---|---|---|---|---|
| 1—At Hous. | L | 3-5 | Konieczny | Easterly |
| 2—At Hous. | W | 4-1 | Morton | York |
| 3—S. Diego | W | 9-10 | Johnson | House |
| 4—S. Diego | W | 2-1 | Dal Canton | Frisella |
| 5—Los Ang. | L | 2-5 | Hooton | Thompson |
| 6—Los Ang. | W | 3-2 | Morton | Hough |
| 7—Los Ang. | W | 5-4 | Dal Canton | Hough |

| SEPTEMBER | | | Winner | Loser |
|---|---|---|---|---|
| 8—Houston | L | 6-9 | Sosa | LaCorte |
| 9—Houston | W | 4-1 | Devine | Dierker |
| 10—At S. D. | L | 1-2 | Jones | Dal Canton |
| 11—At S. D. | L | 3-4 | Strom | House |
| 12—At L. A. | W | 2-1 | Niekro | Sutton |
| 13—At L. A. | L | 0-6 | Messersmith | LaCorte |
| 14—At L. A. | L | 2-3 | Rau | Morton |
| 15—At S. F. | W | 12-0 | Easterly | Falcone |
| 16—At S. F. | L | 6-7 | D'Acquisto | House |
| 17—At S. F. | L | 1-4 | Barr | Niekro |
| 18—Cinn. | L | 3-4* | Borbon | Torrealba |
| 19—Cinn. | L | 6-7 | Darcy | LaCorte |
| 20—Cinn. | L | 2-9 | Nolan | Easterly |
| 21—Cinn. | L | 0-3 | Gullett | Niekro |
| 24—S. Fran. | W | 7-6† | Sosa | Barr |
| 26—At Cinn. | L | 5-12 | Nolan | Niekro |
| 27—At Cinn. | L | 6-7 | Gullett | Odom |
| 28—At Cinn. | L | 6-7 | McEnaney | Dal Canton |
| | | Won 8, Lost 17 | | |

* 10 innings.   † 11 innings.   ‡ 14 innings.   § 15 innings.   x Protested game, completed July 20.   y Suspended game, completed August 9.

# Astro Promises Still Unfulfilled

## By HARRY SHATTUCK

Houston Astro management, which had preceded the previous three years with predictions of a pennant contender, took a more cautious approach in 1975.

"We're not promising any championships," a team spokesman said in February. "All we're promising is that fans who come to the Astrodome will see good major league baseball."

As it turned out, the Astro brass was still too optimistic. This year's Houston team posted the worst record (64-97) in the club's 14-year history. The Orange finished a distant last in the National League West Division and most of the good baseball in the Astrodome was played by opponents.

The year began tragically with the accidental January death of veteran pitcher Don Wilson. His absence was deeply felt as the club compiled an over-all earned-run average of 4.04.

But the Astros' demise could not be traced solely to ineffective pitching. The team batting average of .254, while respectable, was not what club officials expected and the season home run total was only 84. Defensively Houston committed 137 errors, not bad but far above its league-leading pace of 1974.

The unexpectedly bad on-the-field performances, coupled with internal developments in the parent Houston Sports Association, took their toll during the summer.

The Roy Hofheinz family, primary owners of the Astros, were beset by massive debts and lost control of the baseball operation to creditors near midseason. Sidney Shlenker and T. H. Neyland were named with Hofheinz to a three-man board to run the Astrodomain empire. And since Schlenker and Neyland were responsible to creditors, their voices were the ones that counted.

It was only a matter of time then before Spec Richardson, the Houston general manager for eight years and a Hofheinz loyalist, was fired by

## HOUSTON ASTROS—1975

Front row—Rader, Johnson, Jutze, Lillis, coach; Craig, coach; Gomez, manager; Kittle, coach; Williams, coach; Watson. Second row—Arriaga, assistant trainer; Perkins, traveling secretary; Andrews, Boswell, Cabell, Helms, Milbourne, Metzger, Howard, Cruz, May, Cedeno, Lake, equipment manager; Ewell, trainer. Third row—Niekro, Granger, Griffin, Konieczny, Richard, Dierker, Forsch, Roberts, Crawford, Scherman, Gross. Front—Walker and Newsome, batboys.

the new powers-that-be. Richardson was replaced by John Mullen, his assistant, and Mullen in turn was replaced in early August by Tal Smith, a former Astro official who had been in the New York Yankees' front office for two seasons.

Smith soon fired Manager Preston Gomez, who was nearing the end of his second season, and deposed Yankee field boss Bill Virdon was imported to manage the Astros.

All this had an obvious negative effect upon players, coaches and managers. As Gomez said at midseason, "Every time I turn around I hear a different rumor about me being fired, about my coaches, about the front office's troubles. It is difficult to keep your mind on baseball."

Still, some Astros provided productive seasons. Bob Watson batted .324 and drove home a team-high 85 runs. Cliff Johnson clubbed 20 homers, despite only 340 at-bats and owning no set fielding position. Greg Gross followed his .300-plus rookie season with a .294 sophomore year. Willie Howard was a pleasant surprise, batting .283 and stealing 32 bases although he did not enter the starting lineup until midseason. Cesar Cedeno experienced a horrible beginning but rallied for a .288 average, stole 50 bases and excelled defensively.

A prime trouble spot offensively was the infield. Rookie Rob Andrews finished strong but batted only .238 and shortstop Roger Metzger (.227) and third baseman Doug Rader (.223) were far below expectations. Catcher Milt May also disappointed at the plate with a .241 mark.

Larry Dierker led pitchers with a 14-16 record. James Rodney Richard, troubled in the early season by wildness, rebounded to finish at 12-10. But no other moundsman won more than eight games. And no regular starter had an ERA of under 4.00.

Injuries didn't help. Tom Griffin, the top winner in 1974, developed a circulation problem in his pitching hand in June and was lost for the remainder of the year. Ken Forsch, whose 70 appearances in '74 were a club record and who made an impressive transition from relief to starting in midseason, missed most of August and September with an ankle sprain.

The season left Virdon and Smith knowing their rebuilding task was no easy project.

"We do have some talent here and we are not going to give it away," Virdon said. "This team can score runs. What we mainly need is pitching help."

The Astros disposed of May and pitchers Dave Roberts and Jim Crawford to Detroit for four young ballplayers, including young hurlers Gene Pentz and Mark Lemongello. Tommy Helms went to Pittsburgh and Rader to San Diego for pitchers Joe McIntosh and Larry Hardy.

"Pitching depth and quality," Smith described Houston's biggest need. "We are not going to be able to build a winner overnight. It will take time and I hope our fans are patient. We cannot reasonably expect to make up 40 games in one season on a team as good as Cincinnati."

## SCORES OF HOUSTON ASTROS' 1975 GAMES

| APRIL | | | Winner | Loser | APRIL | | | Winner | Loser |
|---|---|---|---|---|---|---|---|---|---|
| 7—Atlanta | W | 6-2 | Dierker | Niekro | 12—Los Ang. | W | 7-5 | Dierker | Marichal |
| 8—Atlanta | L | 0-2 | Morton | Konieczny | 13—Los Ang. | L | 4-7 | Messersmith | Konieczny |
| 9—Atlanta | W | 14-2 | Roberts | Reed | 15—At Atl. | L | 1-6 | Niekro | Richard |
| 11—Los Ang. | L | 0-7 | Sutton | Griffin | 16—At Atl. | L | 2-5 | Capra | Dierker |

**APRIL**

| | | | | Winner | Loser |
|---|---|---|---|---|---|
| 17—At Atl. | L | 1-2* | | Morton | Roberts |
| 18—At Cinn. | L | 2-5 | | Gullett | Griffin |
| 19—At Cinn. | L | 8-9 | | C. Carroll | Forsch |
| 20—At Cinn. | L | 3-5 | | C. Carroll | Scherman |
| 20—At Cinn. | W | 7-6 | | Richard | Kirby |
| 21—S. Diego | L | 0-4 | | Jones | Crawford |
| 22—S. Diego | L | 1-2 | | Spillner | Griffin |
| 23—S. Fran. | W | 3-2 | | Konieczny | Montefusco |
| 23—S. Fran. | L | 0-3 | | Falcone | Roberts |
| 24—S. Fran. | L | 5-6 | | Lavelle | Forsch |
| 25—Cinn. | W | 6-4 | | Dierker | Darcy |
| 26—Cinn. | L | 3-9 | | Norman | Griffin |
| 27—Cinn. | L | 2-6* | | Borbon | Konieczny |
| 28—At S. D. | W | 4-1 | | Roberts | McIntosh |
| 29—At S. D. | W | 8-2 | | Richard | Freisleben |
| 30—At S. D. | L | 2-4 | | Siebert | Dierker |

Won 8, Lost 16

**MAY**

| | | | | Winner | Loser |
|---|---|---|---|---|---|
| 1—At S. D. | W | 6-3 | | Forsch | Jones |
| 2—At S. F. | L | 4-5 | | Moffitt | York |
| 4—At S. F. | L | 6-8 | | Barr | York |
| 4—At S. F. | W | 12-8 | | Richard | D'Acquisto |
| 5—At L. A. | L | 0-2 | | Rau | Dierker |
| 6—At L. A. | L | 1-3 | | Sutton | Konieczny |
| 7—At L. A. | L | 1-5 | | Messersmith | Griffin |
| 9—At Mon. | L | 4-5 | | DeMola | Roberts |
| 10—At Mon. | L | 7-8 | | Murray | Crawford |
| 11—At Mon. | W | 6-0 | | Dierker | Blair |
| 13—At Chi. | L | 1-2 | | Stone | Konieczny |
| 14—At Chi. | W | 11-7 | | Griffin | Burris |
| 15—At Chi. | L | 2-4 | | R. Reuschel | Richard |
| 16—N. York | L | 2-10 | | Seaver | Dierker |
| 17—N. York | L | 4-6 | | Matlack | Roberts |
| 18—N. York | W | 12-7 | | Konieczny | Tate |
| 19—Phila. | W | 4-2 | | Griffin | Carlton |
| 20—Phila. | W | 4-2 | | Forsch | McGraw |
| 21—Phila. | W | 4-0 | | Dierker | Twitchell |
| 23—Montreal | W | 4-2 | | Roberts | Blair |
| 24—Montreal | L | 1-2 | | Rogers | Konieczny |
| 25—Montreal | W | 8-7‡ | | Niekro | DeMola |
| 26—At Pitts. | L | 2-10 | | Kison | Richard |
| 27—At Pitts. | L | 5-6 | | Demery | Niekro |
| 28—At Pitts. | L | 0-3 | | Brett | Roberts |
| 30—At Phila. | W | 5-0 | | Konieczny | Lonborg |
| 31—At Phila. | W | 15-3 | | Richard | Twitchell |

Won 12, Lost 15

**JUNE**

| | | | | Winner | Loser |
|---|---|---|---|---|---|
| 1—At Phila. | L | 4-5 | | Underwood | Dierker |
| 2—At N. Y. | L | 0-2 | | Matlack | Roberts |
| 3—At N. Y. | L | 3-4 | | Hall | Forsch |
| 4—At N. Y. | L | 0-1 | | Koosman | Konieczny |
| 5—At N. Y. | L | 1-2 | | Seaver | Griffin |
| 6—St. Louis | L | 0-6 | | Forsch | Dierker |
| 7—St. Louis | L | 1-5 | | McGlothen | Roberts |
| 8—St. Louis | L | 1-5 | | Reed | Forsch |
| 9—Chicago | L | 3-4* | | Zamora | Granger |
| 10—Chicago | W | 4-3 | | Konieczny | Watt |
| 11—Pitts. | W | 5-1 | | Dierker | Kison |
| 12—Pitts. | L | 2-4 | | Ellis | Roberts |
| 13—At St. L. | L | 2-6 | | Reed | Siebert |
| 14—At St. L. | W | 9-0 | | Griffin | Curtis |
| 15—At St. L. | W | 8-7 | | Niekro | Garman |
| 16—At L. A. | L | 2-4 | | Sutton | Dierker |
| 17—At L. A. | L | 1-6 | | Messersmith | Roberts |
| 18—At L. A. | L | 0-4 | | Hooton | Griffin |
| 20—Cinn. | L | 3-7 | | T. Carroll | Konieczny |
| 21—Cinn. | L | 6-7x | | Norman | Niekro |
| 22—Cinn. | W | 8-4 | | Dierker | Nolan |
| 23—Los Ang. | W | 6-5 | | Roberts | Hooton |
| 24—Los Ang. | L | 3-8 | | Rau | Griffin |
| 25—Los Ang. | W | 5-4 | | Granger | Sutton |
| 26—Atlanta | W | 8-4 | | Richard | Thompson |
| 27—Atlanta | L | 4-7 | | Easterly | Dierker |
| 28—Atlanta | L | 3-6 | | Beard | Roberts |

**JUNE**

| | | | | Winner | Loser |
|---|---|---|---|---|---|
| 29—Atlanta | L | 1-3 | | Morton | Forsch |
| 30—At Cinn. | L | 6-9‡ | | Kirby | Niekro |

Won 8, Lost 21

**JULY**

| | | | | Winner | Loser |
|---|---|---|---|---|---|
| 1—At Cinn. | L | 7-8y | | Darcy | Niekro |
| 2—At Cinn. | L | 3-4 | | Eastwick | Dierker |
| 4—At Atl. | L | 4-5 | | Morton | Granger |
| 5—At Atl. | L | 3-4 | | Sadecki | Forsch |
| 5—At Atl. | L | 4-8 | | Leon | Konieczny |
| 6—At Atl. | W | 6-2 | | Richard | Niekro |
| 7—Montreal | W | 5-1 | | Dierker | Rogers |
| 8—Montreal | W | 5-1 | | Roberts | Renko |
| 9—Montreal | W | 4-3* | | Granger | DeMola |
| 11—Phila. | L | 1-2 | | Christenson | Konieczny |
| 12—Phila. | L | 2-14 | | Carlton | Richard |
| 13—Phila. | W | 9-5 | | Forsch | Underwood |
| 17—At Phila. | L | 5-6† | | McGraw | Forsch |
| 18—At Phila. | L | 4-7 | | Hilgendorf | Richard |
| 19—At Phila. | L | 0-1 | | Christenson | Dierker |
| 20—At N. Y. | L | 9-10 | | Hall | Granger |
| 21—At N. Y. | W | 6-2 | | Forsch | Stone |
| 22—At Mon. | L | 1-2† | | Murray | Sosa |
| 23—At Mon. | W | 2-1 | | Richard | Blair |
| 24—At Mon. | W | 6-5 | | Dierker | Renko |
| 25—S. Fran. | L | 1-8 | | Barr | Roberts |
| 26—S. Fran. | L | 2-3 | | Moffitt | Forsch |
| 26—S. Fran. | L | 3-9 | | Bradley | Konieczny |
| 27—S. Fran. | L | 1-3 | | Montefusco | Richard |
| 28—S. Diego | L | 0-2 | | Freisleben | Dierker |
| 29—S. Diego | W | 6-2 | | Roberts | Spillner |
| 30—S. Diego | W | 8-4 | | Konieczny | McIntosh |
| 31—S. Diego | L | 3-5 | | Tomlin | Granger |

Won 10, Lost 18

**AUGUST**

| | | | | Winner | Loser |
|---|---|---|---|---|---|
| 1—At S. F. | L | 2-3 | | Halicki | Richard |
| 2—At S. F. | L | 7-8* | | Heaverlo | Crawford |
| 3—At S. F. | L | 4-5 | | Falcone | Roberts |
| 3—At S. F. | W | 10-9 | | Crawford | Caldwell |
| 4—At S. D. | W | 5-3 | | Niekro | Freisleben |
| 5—At S. D. | L | 5-6* | | Greif | Granger |
| 6—At S. D. | L | 1-6 | | Jones | Dierker |
| 7—Pitts. | W | 6-1 | | Roberts | Kison |
| 8—Pitts. | W | 5-3 | | Crawford | Tekulve |
| 9—Pitts. | W | 5-0 | | Niekro | Reuss |
| 10—Pitts. | W | 5-3 | | Richard | Rooker |
| 11—St. Louis | W | 7-2 | | Dierker | Curtis |
| 12—St. Louis | L | 4-5 | | Denny | Roberts |
| 13—St. Louis | L | 3-4† | | Garman | Cosgrove |
| 14—Chicago | L | 3-5 | | Stone | Richard |
| 15—Chicago | W | 4-1 | | Dierker | Bonham |
| 16—Chicago | L | 2-3 | | R. Reuschel | Roberts |
| 17—Chicago | L | 7-11 | | Burris | Crawford |
| 18—N. York | W | 4-0 | | Richard | Tate |
| 19—N. York | L | 3-6 | | Matlack | Dierker |
| 20—N. York | W | 5-4* | | Crawford | Baldwin |
| 22—At Chi. | L | 5-6† | | Knowles | Crawford |
| 23—At Chi. | W | 14-12 | | York | Bonham |
| 24—At Chi. | W | 8-4 | | Dierker | Burris |
| 25—At St. L. | T | 3-3* | | ........ | ........ |
| 26—At St. L. | L | 9-10‡ | | Hrabosky | Sosa |
| 26—At St. L. | L | 1-2 | | Rasmussen | Konieczny |
| 27—At St. L. | W | 5-1 | | York | Denny |
| 30—At Pitts. | W | 7-4 | | Dierker | Reuss |
| 31—At Pitts. | L | 6-9 | | Kison | Sosa |

Won 14, Lost 15, Tied 1

**SEPTEMBER**

| | | | | Winner | Loser |
|---|---|---|---|---|---|
| 1—Atlanta | W | 5-3 | | Konieczny | Easterly |
| 2—Atlanta | L | 1-4 | | Morton | York |
| 3—S. Fran. | L | 4-9 | | Falcone | Richard |
| 4—S. Fran. | L | 1-2 | | Montefusco | Dierker |
| 5—S. Diego | W | 2-1 | | Richard | Jones |
| 6—S. Diego | L | 1-2 | | Strom | Konieczny |
| 7—S. Diego | W | 3-2 | | York | Frisella |
| 8—At Atl. | W | 9-6 | | Sosa | LaCorte |

| SEPTEMBER | | | Winner | Loser | SEPTEMBER | | | Winner | Loser |
|---|---|---|---|---|---|---|---|---|---|
| 9—At Atl. | L | 1-4 | Devine | Dierker | 21—Los Ang. | W | 4-1 | Richard | Rhoden |
| 10—At S. F. | W | 6-3 | Cosgrove | Halicki | 22—Cinn. | W | 5-1 | Niekro | Billingham |
| 11—At S. F. | W | 4-3‡ | Niekro | Moffitt | 23—Cinn. | L | 3-5 | Norman | Cosgrove |
| 12—At S. D. | L | 0-1 | Tomlin | York | 24—Cinn. | L | 4-6 | Kirby | Dierker |
| 14—At S. D. | W | 4-2 | Richard | Jones | 26—At L. A. | L | 2-3 | Hooton | Richard |
| 16—At Cinn. | W | 5-1 | Dierker | Billingham | 27—At L. A. | L | 1-5 | Messersmith | Stanton |
| 17—At Cinn. | L | 1-10 | Norman | Stanton | 28—At L. A. | W | 4-2 | York | Hough |
| 19—Los Ang. | W | 6-5‡ | Roberts | Sells | | | | | |
| 20—Los Ang. | L | 4-5§ | Hough | Siebert | **Won 12, Lost 12** | | | | |

* 10 innings.   † 11 innings.   ‡ 12 innings.   § 13 innings.   x 14 innings.   y 15 innings.

# EAST DIVISION

## Division Success Not Enough for Pirates

### By CHARLEY FEENEY

When the Championship Series ended it was another disappointing season for the Pirates. And yet there was success before they lost three straight to the Reds.

The Pirates are the champions of the East Division. They've been East Division champions for five of the last six seasons. That's success, isn't it?

The Galbreaths—Danny and John—aren't so sure. Danny Galbreath is president of the Pirates and his father, John, is chairman of the board.

"We're disappointed that we didn't go beyond the playoffs," John Galbreath said.

"Maybe next year," said Manager Danny Murtaugh.

"Next year, I think I heard that before," said John Galbreath whose Pirates have won one world championship while winning five division titles.

Only the Mets in 1969 and '73 have interrupted the Pirates' string of division championships. The Pirates never do things the easy way. The 1975 season was no exception.

Defense was a problem all year. The team's overall lack of speed showed up often. Yet when the Pirates had to win, they won.

Their pitching was vastly underrated because it had to overcome the defensive shortcomings. Their hitters didn't remain consistent all year, but when it was over, the Bucs led the league with 138 home runs.

Dave Parker, the right fielder, emerged as a bright new star. Parker's big season was vital because most of the other hitters didn't duplicate their performances in 1974.

Manny Sanguillen batted .328 and was among the top five hitters in the league most of the season. But defensively, Sanguillen's play was poor. He not only failed to throw out many base stealers, he seemed to lose some of his agility behind the plate.

The Bucs were not without their inner problems. Dock Ellis refused to work in relief in August. Later he agreed. Later, he called a clubhouse meeting. Murtaugh didn't like Ellis' remarks and suspended him for insubordination. Two weeks later, the suspension was lifted.

The Pirates overcame injuries. Ken Brett, a nine-game winner, was on the disabled list twice because of a sore elbow.

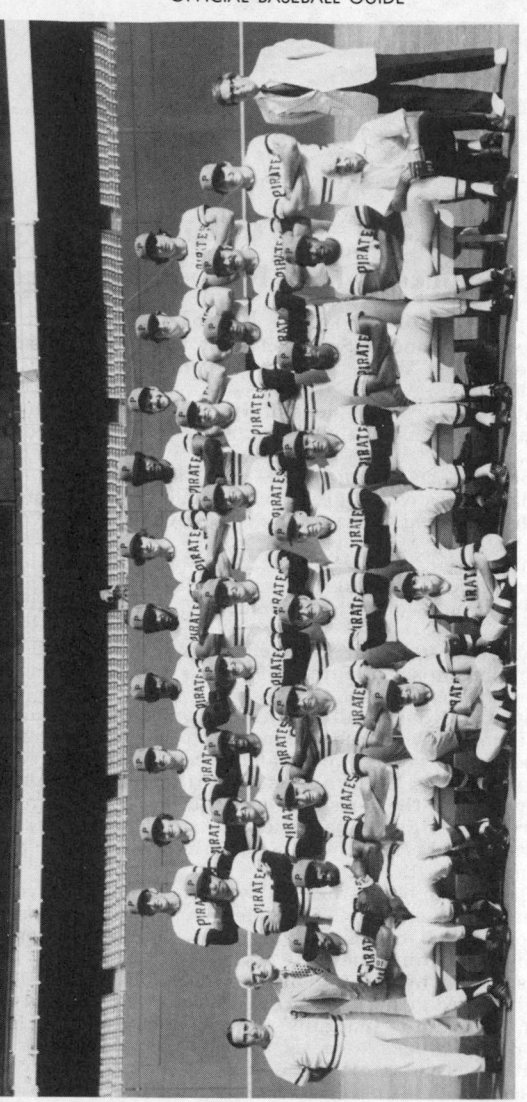

PITTSBURGH PIRATES—1975

Front row—Taveras, Sanguillen, Skinner, coach; Murtaugh, manager; Osborn, coach; Pagan, coach; Randolph, Oliver, J. Hallahan, equipment manager. Second row—Bartirome, trainer; Finegold, team physician; Candelaria, Giusti, Stennett, Brett, Dyer, Rooker, Reuss, Demery, Hernandez, Kirkpatrick, Fitzpatrick, traveling secretary. Third row—Tekulve, Reynolds, Howe, Robinson, Stargell, Kison, Parker, Zisk, Robertson, Hebner. Front—Briercheck and G. Hallahan, bat boys.

Bob Moose was disabled for a severely bruised thumb and, after spending some time on the disabled list, Moose agreed to go to Charleston, W. Va., in the International League where he pitched himself back into shape.

Moose returned in September—too late to be eligible for post-season play—but he showed that he had regained the form that made him a winning pitcher a few years ago.

For pitching consistency, Jerry Reuss was the man. He finished with a personal high 18 victories and won many key games, especially after June 6 when the Pirates took over first place.

Bruce Kison was a big winner early. Jim Rooker was a big winner late. Kison, who finished 12-11, won seven of his first nine decisions.

Larry Demery, Mr. Everything on Murtaugh's staff, was 7-5. His record doesn't show his true value to the club. Demery, only 22, worked in long relief, short relief, and started eight games.

Dave Giusti and Ramon Hernandez have had better seasons. Yet they did their job more often than they failed.

The starting corps was picked up by John Candelaria, a 21-year-old lefthander, who after joining the club in early June posted an 8-6 record.

Kent Tekulve, a righthander brought up in late June, was a big help in relief especially during the last two months of the season.

The Pirates appeared ready to blow it all in August. They lost 12 out of 14 on a road trip and on the night of August 18, the Phillies won while the Bucs were playing an exhibition game in Charleston. The East Division race was tied.

The Pirates were the cold club. The Phillies were the hot club. But the Pirates had returned home where they played their best baseball. Responding to the challenge of the Phillies, the Pirates, in their remaining 39 games, won 25 of them. They finished 52-28 at home, offsetting a 40-41 road record. They were a team supposedly that could be handled by left-handed pitching. The Bucs, off to a poor start against southpaws, finished 34-29 against them.

Through it all, the Pirates must have been doing something right. Parker drove in 101 runs. Richie Zisk, who didn't sign his contract until the season ended, was sluggish until August. He batted well over .300 the last three months of the season and finished with .290 and 75 RBIs.

The club pro, Willie Stargell, was steady. He missed several weeks in the summer because of a broken rib. But Stargell kept his average near .300 most of the year. He ended with .295 with 90 RBIs and 22 homers—three less than Parker, the club leader.

Rennie Stennett, who went 7-for-7 in a 22-0 plastering of the Cubs on September 16 in Chicago, was the Bucs' best defensive man. His play at second base was eye-catching. He struggled at the plate for half the season, but finished strong to wind up .286.

The left side of the infield caused Pirate pitchers problems. Frank Taveras, showing improvement in the field in September, made 28 errors. Richie Hebner made 19 at third base.

At the plate, Taveras batted .212. Hebner, whose only hot month was

June when he hit 10 of his 15 homers, skidded to .246. Hebner was bothered by a bad back most of the year, but he never offered it as an excuse for his worst bat season.

Al Oliver, in center field, didn't throw well. That's the only negative thing that can be said about him. True his average dropped from .321 in 1974 to .280, but Oliver remained a productive Pirate. He drove in 84 runs and he led the club in runs scored with 90.

The Buc bench was an asset to the team. Bill Robinson, acquired from the Phillies in April for pitcher Wayne Simpson, helped defensively and offensively.

Ed Kirkpatrick, a first baseman-outfielder, led the club as a pinch-hitter. He was 13-for-42 for .310.

Art Howe, a weak sticker, played well at third base when he subbed for Hebner. Duffy Dyer, obtained from the Mets for outfielder Gene Clines, proved a valuable backup man to Sanguillen.

Willie Randolph, a second baseman, and Craig Reynolds, a shortstop, were called from Charleston in late July. Reynolds platooned with Taveras at short in August, but Taveras won his job back in September. Randolph got little chance to play because Stennett was too much of a key man to be rested in the stretch.

When it was over, the pitching staff had an excellent 3.01 earned-run average. The hitters, as per custom, received most of the publicity, and the Pirates had their fifth Eastern Division title in six years.

Was it enough?

Apparently not, because the Pirates unloaded Dock Ellis, Ken Brett and Willie Randolph to the Yankees for righthander Doc Medich (16-16) and they secured veteran infielder Tommy Helms from the Astros for Art Howe.

The Galbreaths won't be satisfied until the Bucs can whip the West in the playoffs and go on to the World Series.

### SCORES OF PITTSBURGH PIRATES' 1975 GAMES

| APRIL | | | Winner | Loser | MAY | | | Winner | Loser |
|---|---|---|---|---|---|---|---|---|---|
| 10—At Chi. | W | 8-4 | Giusti | Frailing | 13—S. Diego | W | 2-0 | Reuss | Spillner |
| 11—N. York | W | 4-3 | Demery | Baldwin | 14—S. Diego | W | 5-4‡ | McDowell | Greif |
| 13—N. York | W | 5-3 | Kison | Seaver | 16—At L. A. | W | 3-2 | Giusti | Sutton |
| 14—Chicago | L | 2-4 | R. Reuschel | Moose | 17—At L. A. | L | 3-4† | Messersmith | Hernandez |
| 16—Montreal | L | 0-5 | Fryman | Ellis | 18—At L. A. | W | 7-2 | Brett | Hooton |
| 17—Montreal | L | 4-7 | McNally | Reuss | 19—At S. F. | L | 4-6 | Caldwell | Reuss |
| 18—At St. L. | L | 4-5§ | Sadecki | McDowell | 20—At S. F. | L | 4-12 | Halicki | Ellis |
| 19—At St. L. | W | 7-1 | Rooker | Forsch | 21—At S. F. | L | 1-2‡ | Barr | Giusti |
| 20—At St. L. | W | 5-0 | Brett | Denny | 22—At S. D. | W | 4-2 | Rooker | Freisleben |
| 22—At Mon. | L | 3-4 | McNally | Ellis | 23—At S. D. | L | 3-4 | Frisella | Giusti |
| 23—At Mon. | L | 0-5 | Fryman | Reuss | 24—At S. D. | L | 2-1 | Jones | Reuss |
| 25—Phila. | W | 3-2 | Kison | Carlton | 25—At S. D. | W | 6-5‡ | Hernandez | Frisella |
| 26—Phila. | W | 7-3 | Rooker | Twitchell | 26—Houston | W | 10-2 | Kison | Richard |
| 27—Phila. | W | 2-0 | Ellis | Underwood | 27—Houston | W | 6-5 | Demery | Niekro |
| 29—St. Louis | L | 0-3 | McGlothen | Brett | 28—Houston | W | 3-0 | Brett | Roberts |
| 30—St. Louis | W | 5-0 | Reuss | Gibson | 30—Atlanta | W | 2-1 | Reuss | Capra |
| | | | **Won 9, Lost 7** | | 31—Atlanta | W | 11-4 | Kison | Harrison |
| **MAY** | | | | | | | | **Won 15, Lost 11** | |
| 2—At Phila. | L | 5-9 | Twitchell | Kison | | | | | |
| 3—At Phila. | L | 2-6 | Underwood | Rooker | **JUNE** | | | | |
| 3—At Phila. | L | 3-4‡ | McGraw | Hernandez | 1—Atlanta | L | 2-5 | Niekro | Rooker |
| 6—At N. Y. | W | 2-1* | Brett | Seaver | 3—Cinn. | L | 4-8 | Nolan | Moose |
| 7—At N. Y. | W | 6-1 | Reuss | Matlack | 4—Cinn. | W | 2-1 | Reuss | Norman |
| 8—At N. Y. | W | 4-2 | Kison | Koosman | 6—S. Fran. | W | 7-2 | Kison | Barr |
| 9—Los Ang. | W | 11-3 | Ellis | Marshall | 7—S. Fran. | W | 7-6 | Hernandez | Toms |
| 10—Los Ang. | L | 2-6 | Rau | Rooker | 8—S. Fran. | L | 1-3 | Halicki | Candelaria |
| 11—Los Ang. | L | 0-7 | Sutton | Brett | 8—S. Fran. | L | 2-4 | Lavelle | Demery |
| | | | | | 9—At Cinn. | W | 9-2 | Reuss | Norman |

| JUNE | | | Winner | Loser |
|---|---|---|---|---|
| 10—At Cinn. | W | 9-5 | McDowell | Darcy |
| 11—At Hous. | L | 1-5 | Dierker | Kison |
| 12—At Hous. | W | 4-2 | Ellis | Roberts |
| 13—At Atl. | W | 8-3 | Rooker | Odom |
| 14—At Atl. | W | 2-1 | Reuss | Thompson |
| 15—At Atl. | W | 8-6 | Demery | Sosa |
| 16—St. Louis | W | 10-4 | Kison | Bryant |
| 17—St. Louis | L | 4-7 | McGlothen | Ellis |
| 18—St. Louis | W | 9-3 | Rooker | Reed |
| 19—St. Louis | W | 5-0 | Reuss | Curtis |
| 20—At N. Y. | W | 5-1 | Candelaria | Hall |
| 21—At N. Y. | W | 7-3 | Hernandez | Parker |
| 22—At N. Y. | W | 2-0 | Ellis | Tate |
| 23—At Phila. | L | 5-6 | Hilgendorf | Demery |
| 24—At Phila. | L | 3-6 | Christenson | Reuss |
| 24—At Phila. | L | 1-8 | Underwood | Kison |
| 25—At Phila. | L | 6-7§ | Schueler | Giusti |
| 26—Chicago | W | 5-2 | Candelaria | Frailing |
| 27—Chicago | W | 5-1 | Ellis | Zahn |
| 27—Chicago | W | 5-3 | Hernandez | Knowles |
| 28—Chicago | L | 0-1 | Bonham | Rooker |
| 29—Chicago | W | 4-3 | Giusti | R. Reuschel |
| 29—Chicago | W | 7-0 | Reuss | Dettore |
| 30—At Mon. | W | 5-3 | Demery | Blair |
| Won 21, Lost 11 | | | | |

| JULY | | | | |
|---|---|---|---|---|
| 1—At Mon. | W | 10-4 | Candelaria | Fryman |
| 3—At Mon. | W | 5-1 | Ellis | Rogers |
| 4—At Chi. | L | 1-6 | Stone | Kison |
| 4—At Chi. | L | 1-2‡ | Knowles | Reuss |
| 5—At Chi. | W | 5-4 | Rooker | Burris |
| 6—At Chi. | W | 18-12 | Hernandez | Frailing |
| 7—At Chi. | W | 5-0 | Brett | R. Reuschel |
| 8—Los Ang. | L | 0-3 | Sutton | Ellis |
| 9—Los Ang. | W | 3-2 | Kison | Messersmith |
| 10—Los Ang. | W | 4-1 | Reuss | Hooton |
| 11—S. Diego | W | 6-2 | Rooker | Folkers |
| 11—S. Diego | W | 5-0 | Candelaria | McIntosh |
| 12—S. Diego | W | 6-4 | Hernandez | Jones |
| 13—S. Diego | L | 5-7 | Strom | Ellis |
| 17—At L. A. | W | 5-2 | Kison | Messersmith |
| 18—At L. A. | L | 3-4 | Marshall | Demery |
| 19—At L. A. | W | 5-3 | Giusti | Marshall |
| 20—At S. F. | L | 1-2 | Halicki | Rooker |
| 20—At S. F. | W | 7-1 | Brett | Caldwell |
| 21—At S. F. | L | 2-7 | Barr | Candelaria |
| 22—At S. D. | L | 0-1 | Jones | Kison |
| 23—At S. D. | W | 8-1 | Ellis | Freisleben |
| 25—Montreal | W | 6-1 | Reuss | DeMola |
| 26—Montreal | L | 2-5 | Rogers | Rooker |
| 27—Montreal | W | 4-1 | Brett | Scherman |
| 27—Montreal | W | 5-3 | Giusti | Warthen |
| 28—Phila. | L | 2-5 | Christenson | Kison |
| 29—Phila. | L | 1-5 | Underwood | Ellis |
| 30—Phila. | W | 8-1 | Reuss | Carlton |
| 31—N. York | L | 2-6 | Koosman | Rooker |
| Won 18, Lost 12 | | | | |

| AUGUST | | | Winner | Loser |
|---|---|---|---|---|
| 1—N. York | L | 2-4 | Stone | Brett |
| 2—N. York | L | 0-6 | Matlack | Kison |
| 3—N. York | W | 5-4x | Demery | Apodaca |
| 3—N. York | W | 4-3 | Candelaria | Webb |
| 4—At St. L. | L | 4-5 | Curtis | Reuss |
| 5—At St. L. | W | 6-1 | Rooker | Rasmussen |
| 6—At St. L. | L | 2-4 | Denny | Brett |
| 7—At Hous. | L | 1-6 | Roberts | Kison |
| 8—At Hous. | L | 3-5 | Crawford | Tekulve |
| 9—At Hous. | L | 0-5 | Niekro | Reuss |
| 10—At Hous. | L | 3-5 | Richard | Rooker |
| 11—At Atl. | W | 8-1 | Candelaria | Easterly |
| 12—At Atl. | L | 2-3 | Morton | Kison |
| 13—At Atl. | L | 3-4 | House | Brett |
| 14—At Cinn. | L | 1-6 | Nolan | Reuss |
| 15—At Cinn. | L | 3-8 | Norman | Rooker |
| 16—At Cinn. | L | 3-5 | Billingham | Candelaria |
| 17—At Cinn. | L | 1-3 | Darcy | Kison |
| 19—S. Fran. | W | 4-0 | Reuss | Barr |
| 20—S. Fran. | W | 3-1 | Rooker | Halicki |
| 22—Cinn. | W | 7-2 | Demery | Billingham |
| 22—Cinn. | W | 4-2 | Candelaria | McEnaney |
| 23—Cinn. | L | 7-12 | Kirby | Kison |
| 24—Cinn. | W | 5-1 | Reuss | Nolan |
| 25—Atlanta | W | 4-0 | Rooker | Thompson |
| 26—Atlanta | W | 8-2 | Demery | Easterly |
| 27—Atlanta | L | 2-6 | Niekro | Candelaria |
| 30—Houston | L | 4-7 | Dierker | Reuss |
| 31—Houston | W | 9-6 | Kison | Sosa |
| Won 12, Lost 17 | | | | |

| SEPTEMBER | | | Winner | Loser |
|---|---|---|---|---|
| 1—At N. Y. | L | 0-3 | Seaver | Candelaria |
| 2—At N. Y. | W | 8-4 | Tekulve | Koosman |
| 3—At N. Y. | W | 3-1 | Reuss | Matlack |
| 5—At Mon. | L | 3-4† | Taylor | Tekulve |
| 5—At Mon. | W | 5-2 | Rooker | Renko |
| 6—At Mon. | W | 12-5‡ | Brett | Murray |
| 7—At Mon. | W | 6-0 | Reuss | Blair |
| 8—Chicago | W | 4-1 | Ellis | Prall |
| 9—Chicago | L | 5-6 | Bonham | Demery |
| 10—N. York | W | 8-4 | Rooker | Seaver |
| 11—N. York | L | 0-7 | Koosman | Reuss |
| 12—Montreal | W | 6-3 | Moose | Carrithers |
| 13—Montreal | L | 2-5 | Warthen | Ellis |
| 14—Montreal | W | 4-3 | Hernandez | Fryman |
| 15—At Chi. | L | 5-6 | Knowles | Giusti |
| 16—At Chi. | W | 9-1 | Rooker | Prall |
| 16—At Chi. | W | 22-0 | Candelaria | R. Reuschel |
| 17—At Phila. | W | 9-1 | Kison | Underwood |
| 18—At Phila. | L | 1-4 | Carlton | Ellis |
| 19—St. Louis | W | 7-1 | Brett | Denny |
| 20—St. Louis | L | 2-8 | Rasmussen | Rooker |
| 21—St. Louis | W | 5-3 | Reuss | Garman |
| 22—Phila. | W | 11-3 | Kison | Underwood |
| 23—Phila. | W | 3-1 | Moose | Carlton |
| 24—Phila. | L | 1-8 | Christenson | Demery |
| 26—At St. L. | L | 0-1 | Forsch | Rooker |
| 27—At St. L. | W | 4-2 | Reuss | McGlothen |
| 28—At St. L. | L | 2-6 | Reed | Candelaria |
| Won 17, Lost 11 | | | | |

* 8 innings.   † 10 innings.   ‡ 11 innings.   § 13 innings.   x 15 innings.

# Flag Miss a Puzzle To Phillies

## By RAY KELLY

The Phillies had such a great season in so many respects that when it was all over they couldn't quite figure out why they didn't win the National League's East Division title.

After all, Mike Schmidt was the major leagues' homer champion,

PHILADELPHIA PHILLIES—1975

Front row—Garber, McGraw, Rogodzinski, Martin, Underwood, Bowa, Cox, Oates, K. Bush, Jr., bat boy. Second row—Cera, clubhouse attendant; Madrack, bat boy; Taylor, DeMars, coach; Beringer, coach; Ozark, manager; Rippelmeyer, coach; Wine, coach; Cash, Seger, trainer. Third row—Ferenz, traveling secretary; Schmidt, Allen, Luzinski, Hilgendorf, Maddox, Brown, Harmon, Hutton, K. Bush, Sr., equipment manager. Fourth row—Johnstone, Boone, Hoerner, Twitchell, Lonborg, Schueler, Christenson, Carlton, Anderson.

Greg Luzinski drove in more runs (120) than any other player in either league and Dave Cash had more hits (213) than anybody else.

In addition, Larry Bowa had his greatest season at the plate. The shortstop batted .305 and teamed with Cash (.305) to be the first keystone combination with plus .300 averages since Luke Appling and Cass Michaels did it with the White Sox in 1949.

There were lots of other things for the Phillies to feel good about. Tom Underwood won 14 games as a lefthanded rookie and Larry Christenson, who came on strong at the end, was hailed as a top righthanded pitching prospect.

Johnny Oates, a throw-in in the Richie Allen deal, became the Phillies' first-string catcher and hit .295, while Garry Maddox, obtained from the Giants in a swap for first baseman Willie Montanez, was hailed as the finest defensive center fielder the Phillies ever owned.

"What happened?" people kept asking Manager Danny Ozark.

Danny isn't sure he really knows the answer, but he agrees that the Phillies' chances went down the drain when southpaw Steve Carlton came up with a tender elbow and Jim Lonborg, the veteran righthander, pulled a groin muscle.

Carlton spent most of the season trying to be a finesse pitcher and it was a struggle all the way. Then with six weeks to go, Steve started throwing "pain free" and was his overpowering self again. Lonborg just sat around for almost two months after he tried to pitch with an injury and made things that much worse.

Relief pitchers Tug McGraw, with a 9-6 mark, 2.97 ERA and 14 saves, Gene Garber with 10 wins and 14 saves and Tom Hilgendorf (7-3, 2.13) were used often.

At the same time, no review on the Phillies would be complete without mention of Richie Allen, the world's highest salaried first baseman.

It was the Phillies' players who prodded club President Ruly Carpenter into making a deal with the Braves for the Wampum (Pa.) Walloper. The Phillies' players claimed that Allen's presence would assure the division title. Richie Ashburn, writing in the Philadelphia Bulletin, said that with Allen, the team would win by 15 games.

Anyhow, General Manager Paul Owens finally negotiated the deal with the Braves and Allen joined the Phillies in mid-May. He hit a line single his first trip to the plate and the fans went wild.

Allen kept swinging his 41-ounce bat, but he wasn't swinging it with his accustomed abandon. For him, the season was a struggle (.233 and 12 homers), even though he insisted "I've never been happier."

Allen said he was going to make sure he was ready next season, adding, "I owe this team something."

The Phillies had a brief fling with glory on August 18. They beat the Braves in Atlanta and went into a first-place tie with the slumping Pirates. But that was the last gasp. They lost the next night and stayed behind the Bucs the rest of the campaign, finishing second with an 86-76 record.

During 1975 pitching ineffectiveness hurt the Phillies, so they went out and obtained Jim Kaat (20-14) from the White Sox for Alan Bannister, Dick Ruthven and Roy Thomas, and Ron Reed (13-13) from the Cardinals for Mike Anderson.

"Everybody else is going to be picking us to win the division and I'll have to go along with them," Ozark said after the two deals were consummated. "We've got the players to do it."

### SCORES OF PHILADELPHIA PHILLIES' 1975 GAMES

| APRIL | | | Winner | Loser |
|---|---|---|---|---|
| 8—At N.Y. | L | 1-2 | Seaver | Carlton |
| 10—At N.Y. | W | 3-2‡ | Schueler | Parker |
| 11—St. Louis | L | 3-6 | McGlothen | Twitchell |
| 12—St. Louis | L | 5-7 | Garman | Garber |
| 13—St. Louis | W | 2-0 | Underwood | Forsch |
| 14—N. York | W | 4-3 | Garber | Cram |
| 16—Chicago | L | 3-9 | Bonham | Carlton |
| 17—Chicago | W | 9-10 | Frailing | Twitchell |
| 18—At Mon. | W | 6-3 | Underwood | Renko |
| 19—At Mon. | W | 3-0 | Lonborg | Blair |
| 22—At Chi. | W | 7-5 | Twitchell | Bonham |
| 23—At Chi. | L | 3-9 | Burris | Underwood |
| 24—At Chi. | L | 1-4 | Stone | Lonborg |
| 25—At Pitts. | L | 2-3 | Kison | Carlton |
| 26—At Pitts. | L | 3-7 | Rooker | Twitchell |
| 27—At Pitts. | L | 0-2 | Ellis | Underwood |
| 29—Montreal | W | 5-0 | Lonborg | Blair |
| 30—Montreal | W | 2-1 | Carlton | Rogers |
| | | **Won 8, Lost 10** | | |

| MAY | | | | |
|---|---|---|---|---|
| 2—Pitts. | W | 9-5 | Twitchell | Kison |
| 3—Pitts. | W | 6-2 | Underwood | Rooker |
| 3—Pitts. | W | 4-3‡ | McGraw | Hernandez |
| 5—At St.L. | L | 3-11 | Gibson | Carlton |
| 7—At St.L. | W | 4-1 | Twitchell | Forsch |
| 8—At St.L. | W | 6-2 | Lonborg | Denny |
| 9—At Atl. | L | 1-3 | Harrison | Underwood |
| 10—At Atl. | L | 1-2‡ | Niekro | Garber |
| 11—At Atl. | L | 3-7 | Capra | Twitchell |
| 13—Cinn. | W | 4-0 | Underwood | Nolan |
| 14—Cinn. | W | 4-0 | Carlton | Darcy |
| 15—Cinn. | W | 6-3 | McGraw | Gullett |
| 15—Cinn. | W | 5-3 | Garber | C. Carroll |
| 16—Atlanta | W | 12-8 | Garber | Capra |
| 17—Atlanta | W | 9-8 | Garber | Niekro |
| 18—Atlanta | W | 5-1 | Underwood | Reed |
| 19—At Hous. | L | 2-4 | Griffin | Carlton |
| 20—At Hous. | L | 2-4 | Forsch | McGraw |
| 21—At Hous. | L | 0-4 | Dierker | Twitchell |
| 23—At Cinn. | L | 2-5 | Nolan | Christenson |
| 24—At Cinn. | L | 2-3‡ | C. Carroll | McGraw |
| 25—At Cinn. | L | 3-4 | Kirby | Lonborg |
| 26—S. Fran. | W | 1-0‡ | McGraw | Halicki |
| 27—S. Fran. | L | 0-1† | Montefusco | Garber |
| 28—S. Fran. | W | 8-6 | Carlton | Falcone |
| 30—Houston | L | 0-5 | Konieczny | Lonborg |
| 31—Houston | L | 3-15 | Richard | Twitchell |
| | | **Won 14, Lost 13** | | |

| JUNE | | | | |
|---|---|---|---|---|
| 1—Houston | W | 5-4 | Underwood | Dierker |
| 2—S. Diego | W | 5-1 | Carlton | Freisleben |
| 3—S. Diego | W | 12-1 | Lonborg | Spillner |
| 4—S. Diego | W | 7-2 | Twitchell | Jones |
| 6—Los Ang. | L | 2-3 | Hooton | Underwood |
| 7—Los Ang. | W | 4-0 | Carlton | Rau |
| 8—Los Ang. | W | 4-2 | Lonborg | Sutton |
| 9—At S. D. | L | 3-8 | Jones | Twitchell |
| 10—At S. D. | W | 7-0 | Christenson | Spillner |
| 11—At S. F. | L | 3-8 | Caldwell | Underwood |
| 12—At S. F. | W | 4-1 | Carlton | Halicki |
| 13—At L. A. | W | 5-1 | Lonborg | Messersmith |
| 14—At L. A. | L | 3-4 | Hooton | McGraw |
| 15—At L. A. | W | 4-3 | Garber | Marshall |
| 16—At Chi. | L | 7-9 | Zahn | Garber |

| JUNE | | | Winner | Loser |
|---|---|---|---|---|
| 17—At Chi. | L | 5-9 | Dettore | Lonborg |
| 18—At Chi. | W | 9-7 | Garber | Locker |
| 19—At Chi. | W | 6-3y | McGraw | Knowles |
| 20—Montreal | W | 7-4 | Underwood | Renko |
| 21—Montreal | L | 1-5 | Blair | Lonborg |
| 22—Montreal | L | 0-4 | Rogers | Schueler |
| 22—Montreal | W | 4-3 | Garber | Taylor |
| 23—Pitts. | W | 6-5 | Hilgendorf | Demery |
| 24—Pitts. | W | 6-3 | Christenson | Reuss |
| 24—Pitts. | W | 8-1 | Underwood | Kison |
| 25—Pitts. | W | 7-6x | Schueler | Guisti |
| 27—At N. Y. | L | 2-4 | Matlack | Twitchell |
| 28—At N. Y. | L | 2-5 | Tate | Carlton |
| 29—At N. Y. | W | 9-6 | Christenson | Koosman |
| 29—At N. Y. | W | 4-3§ | McGraw | Hall |
| 30—St. Louis | L | 5-6 | Forsch | Lonborg |
| | | **Won 20, Lost 11** | | |

| JULY | | | | |
|---|---|---|---|---|
| 1—St. Louis | L | 5-6 | McGlothen | Twitchell |
| 2—St. Louis | W | 5-3 | Carlton | Reed |
| 3—St. Louis | W | 7-4 | Underwood | Gibson |
| 4—N. York | L | 3-4 | Seaver | McGraw |
| 5—N. York | W | 8-2 | Schueler | Tate |
| 5—N. York | W | 10-7 | Lonborg | Espinosa |
| 6—N. York | W | 8-6 | Twitchell | Matlack |
| 7—At Cinn. | L | 3-7 | Darcy | Carlton |
| 8—At Cinn. | L | 1-2 | Nolan | Underwood |
| 9—At Cinn. | L | 7-9 | Borbon | Garber |
| 11—At Hous. | W | 2-1 | Christenson | Konieczny |
| 12—At Hous. | L | 14-2 | Carlton | Richard |
| 13—At Hous. | L | 5-9 | Forsch | Underwood |
| 17—Houston | W, | 6-5‡ | McGraw | Forsch |
| 18—Houston | W | 7-4 | Hilgendorf | Richard |
| 19—Houston | W | 1-0 | Christenson | Dierker |
| 20—Cinn. | W | 11-4 | Underwood | Kirby |
| 21—Cinn. | L | 4-10 | Darcy | Schueler |
| 22—Atlanta | W | 1-0 | Carlton | Morton |
| 23—Atlanta | W | 3-2 | Lonborg | Dal Canton |
| 24—Atlanta | L | 4-5 | Niekro | Christenson |
| 25—At St. L. | L | 3-4 | Hrabosky | Garber |
| 25—At St. L. | W | 5-2 | Schueler | Curtis |
| 26—At St. L. | W | 9-4 | Carlton | Rasmussen |
| 27—At St. L. | L | 6-9 | Gibson | Hilgendorf |
| 28—At Pitts. | W | 5-2 | Christenson | Kison |
| 29—At Pitts. | W | 5-1 | Underwood | Ellis |
| 30—At Pitts. | L | 1-8 | Reuss | Carlton |
| 31—At Mon. | L | 4-7 | Warthen | Schueler |
| | | **Won 17, Lost 12** | | |

| AUGUST | | | | |
|---|---|---|---|---|
| 1—At Mon. | W | 8-6† | Garber | Murray |
| 1—At Mon. | L | 4-6 | Scherman | Hilgendorf |
| 2—At Mon. | L | 3-4 | Murray | Underwood |
| 3—At Mon. | W | 5-4† | McGraw | Murray |
| 4—Chicago | L | 2-3 | Stone | Hilgendorf |
| 5—Chicago | W | 13-5 | Ruthven | Bonham |
| 7—Chicago | L | 3-5 | R. Reuschel | Christenson |
| 8—S. Fran. | W | 5-4 | Garber | Moffitt |
| 9—S. Fran. | W | 11-4 | Carlton | Montefusco |
| 10—S. Fran. | L | 1-8 | Barr | Ruthven |
| 11—Los Ang. | L | 1-7 | Messersmith | Christenson |
| 12—Los Ang. | L | 6-7† | Marshall | Garber |
| 13—Los Ang. | W | 4-5 | Hooton | Carlton |
| 15—S. Diego | W | 4-3 | Hilgendorf | McIntosh |
| 16—S. Diego | L | 1-5 | Jones | McGraw |

| AUGUST | | | Winner | Loser |
|---|---|---|---|---|
| 17—S. Diego | W | 10-4 | Underwood | Freisleben |
| 18—At Atl. | W | 6-3 | Hilgendorf | Niekro |
| 19—At Atl. | L | 4-6 | Leon | Garber |
| 20—At Atl. | W | 4-1 | Christenson | Morton |
| 22—At S. D. | W | 6-5 | Hilgendorf | Greif |
| 23—At S. D. | L | 3-8 | Spillner | Carlton |
| 24—At S. D. | L | 2-7 | Jones | Ruthven |
| 24—At S. D. | L | 6-7§ | Greif | Schueler |
| 25—At L. A. | W | 4-2 | Christenson | Messersmith |
| 26—At L. A. | L | 1-8 | Rau | Underwood |
| 27—At L. A. | L | 0-10 | Hooton | Carlton |
| 28—At S. F. | W | 8-5 | Hilgendorf | Barr |
| 29—At S. F. | W | 3-1 | Christenson | Halicki |
| 30—At S. F. | L | 1-4 | Falcone | Underwood |
| 31—At S. F. | L | 4-5 | Montefusco | Carlton |
| **Won 13, Lost 17** | | | | |
| | | | | |
| SEPTEMBER | | | | |
| 1—Montreal | L | 5-6 | Murray | Garber |
| 2—Montreal | L | 3-4 | Blair | Christenson |
| 3—Montreal | L | 6-3 | Underwood | Carrithers |
| 5—Chicago | L | 3-4 | Bonham | Carlton |
| 5—Chicago | W | 6-3 | McGraw | P. Reuschel |

| SEPTEMBER | | | Winner | Loser |
|---|---|---|---|---|
| 6—Chicago | L | 6-7 | Stone | Garber |
| 7—Chicago | L | 4-6 | Burris | Twitchell |
| 8—St. Louis | W | 6-3 | Underwood | Reed |
| 9—St. Louis | W | 6-2 | Carlton | Denny |
| 10—At Mon. | W | 5-1 | Simpson | Renko |
| 11—At Mon. | W | 5-0* | Christenson | Rogers |
| 13—At Chi. | L | 1-4 | Burris | Underwood |
| 14—At Chi. | W | 13-7 | Carlton | Stone |
| 15—At St. L. | L | 6-7 | Hrabosky | Garber |
| 16—At St.L. | W | 4-3x | Hilgendorf | Garman |
| 17—Pitts. | L | 1-9 | Kison | Underwood |
| 18—Pitts. | W | 4-1 | Carlton | Ellis |
| 19—At N. Y. | W | 4-3 | McGraw | Lockwood |
| 20—At N. Y. | L | 7-9‡ | Apodaca | Garber |
| 21—At N. Y. | W | 4-2 | Ruthven | Matlack |
| 22—At Pitts. | L | 3-11 | Kison | Underwood |
| 23—At Pitts. | L | 1-3 | Moose | Carlton |
| 24—At Pitts. | W | 8-1 | Christenson | Demery |
| 26—N. York | W | 4-3§ | Garber | Apodaca |
| 26—N. York | L | 2-3§ | Koosman | McGraw |
| 27—N. York | W | 8-1 | Carlton | Tate |
| 28—N. York | L | 4-5 | Seaver | Christenson |
| **Won 14, Lost 13** | | | | |

* 6½ innings.   † 10 innings.   ‡ 11 innings.   § 12 innings.   x 13 innin gs.   y 14 innings.

# Mets Finish In Left Field

### By JACK LANG

In a year when Tom Seaver won 22 games and the Cy Young Award, when Dave Kingman set a club home run record with 36 and when Rusty Staub became the first in the club's history to knock in 100 runs, it is difficult to conceive the New York Mets had as many problems as they did or were as bad as their final third place tie in the standings reveals.

But troubles they had by the bundle in a season full of turmoil that saw them dump a manager in mid-season for the first time and also unconditionally release one of the team's all-time stars . . . also in mid-season. That one move was related to the other caused considerable speculation in the Gotham press.

Yogi Berra, the gnomish figure who has long been one of the most popular sports personalities on the New York scene, was the victim of the axing on August 6th when Mets' board chairman M. Donald Grant announced "we are trying to salvage something from the season."

Roy McMillan, the club's first base coach since 1973, was named as interim manager replacing Berra and Grant said at the time he felt Roy had all the makings of another Gil Hodges. But under McMillan's uninspirational leadership the Mets continued to flounder and actually had a worse record for him than they did for Berra.

On the final day of the season, when Seaver cemented his third Cy Young Award with his 22nd victory, the Mets beat the Phillies to tie with the Cardinals for third place. But they were 10½ games in arrears of the division-champion Pittsburgh Pirates who they almost caught four weeks earlier.

While the Mets finished the season without Yogi Berra, who had led them to a pennant two years earlier, they also were without Cleon Jones, their regular left fielder for so many years. Eleven days prior to Berra's canning, Jones was released by the Mets following a suspension resulting

NEW YORK METS—1975

Front row—Cavarretta, coach; Yost, coach; Walker, coach; McMillan, manager; Pignatano, coach; Mays, coach. Second row—Clines, Baldwin, Unser, Seaver, Millan, Lockwood, Grote, Garrett, Phillips, Torre. Third row—Niss, traveling secretary; McKenna, trainer; Kingman, Hall, Heidemann, Milner, Apodaca, Stearns, Sanders, Deer, trainer. Fourth row—Norman, equipment manager; Harrelson, Alou, Kranepool, Webb, Matlack, Stone, Staub, Koosman, Tate, Vail, Swan.

from his refusal to follow Berra's order.

There was considerable conflict over that issue. After appearing in a pinch-hitting role the night of July 18, Jones was told to finish the game in left field and refused. The Mets did not suspend him until four days later and then only after Berra rebuffed Grant's pleas and refused to reinstate his recalcitrant outfielder. Grant even made phone calls to Berra's coaches in Chicago imploring them to have Yogi reconsider. Berra could not be moved.

Grant insisted August 6th when Berra was relieved of his reins that the Jones incident had nothing to do with it. He stated the floundering of the club was the only issue. A few days earlier the Mets had made a move by taking three in a row from the Pirates but then dropped a doubleheader to the Bucs to start a five-game losing streak. Grant said Berra's inability to rouse the team after that double loss was the main reason a change was made.

Jones was gone by then but the memories of all the problems he caused during the year continued to linger. Jones had started the season recuperating from a knee operation. Observers of the club in spring training, including many of the players, felt the batboy exerted greater effort than Cleon. On opening day of the season, Jones was placed on the disabled list and sent back to Florida to work on his own.

With no supervision, Cleon could come and go as he pleased. And he pleased. One night long past midnight St. Petersburg police arrested him for what the blotter listed as "indecent exposure." He was caught sleeping nude in a van with a young lady on a main street in St. Petersburg. The case was eventually dismissed but Grant did not overlook the indiscretion. He fined Jones $2,000 for breaking training rules and in a press room conference with Jones' wife, Angela, standing alongside him, he made Cleon read a public apology. Grant was severely criticized for this action.

Jones' knee wasn't the one that caused the Mets the most trouble. It was Bud Harrelson's knee. The little shortstop, who has always been regarded as the guts of the New York infield, was continually seeing a doctor to have fluid drained from his right knee and was getting as many shots of cortisone as allowed. Finally, on May 27, he was placed on the disabled list and underwent surgery for removal of a loose piece in his cartilage.

The Mets had fortunately claimed Mike Phillips from the Giants on waivers on May 4 with the intention of sending him to Tidewater but Mike stayed around all year and played 115 games at shortstop. While his throwing was erratic and he was no Bud Harrelson, the young man at least gave the Mets a major league shortstop and salvaged something for them at that position.

Several new faces made their debuts in Met uniforms in 1975 as general manager Joe McDonald, in his first year on the job, sought to increase the club's run production. Two of the deals helped, another did not.

Joe Torre, former Most Valuable player with the Cards, was obtained to play third base but at 35, The Godfather was not the answer. Joe's range at third was limited and at bat his average was a disappointing .247. He also hit into an excruciating number (22) of double plays.

But two big deals that did keep the Mets in the race were the acquisition of Del Unser from the Phillies and the purchase of Dave Kingman from the Giants in spring training. That deal for $200,000 was a steal.

Kingman, despite his 153 strikeouts and .231 average, became the darling of the Shea fans with his king-sized homers. He walloped 36 in all, setting a club record and finishing just two round-trippers behind big league leader Mike Schmidt.

Unser proved a class center fielder, something the Mets have lacked for years. Del also batted a respectable .294.

Shea fans discovered another favorite in September when the Mets purchased Mike Vail from the Tidewater farm. He had been a gift from the Cardinals in a minor deal. Vail came on like gangbusters, tying a rookie record by hitting safely in 23 consecutive games and batting .302 for 38 contests.

The Mets' bullpen was not what it once was in the good Tug McGraw days but Bob Apodaca still managed to rack up 13 saves, despite being on the disabled list twice. Ken Sanders and Skip Lockwood were valuable additions during the season.

On August 7th the Mets held third place alone, their high spot of the season. But on September 1st, Labor Day, they pulled to within four games of Pittsburgh after Tom Seaver shut out the Bucs, 3-0. On that day he also registered his 200th strikeout, the eighth consecutive year with 200 or more for a major league record.

But the Mets stumbled after that. Jerry Koosman lost to the Pirates the following night and Jon Matlack the next night. What chance the Mets had to catch the Pirates had escaped them. Seaver, with 22 wins, doubled his 1974 total when a sciatic hip problem reduced his effectiveness. Matlack won a personal high of 16 but failed to record a victory in his last six starts. He went the entire month of September without a win. Veteran Koosman, a gutty competitor, was pleased to finish over .500 with a 14-13 record but the Mets found that they were sorely short in second line pitching and went hunting for help at the season's end.

The Mets acquired veteran lefty Mickey Lolich from Detroit for Rusty Staub in December and summoned stern Joe Frazier from their Tidewater affiliate as their full-time field general.

### SCORES OF NEW YORK METS' 1975 GAMES

| APRIL | | | Winner | Loser | MAY | | | Winner | Loser |
|---|---|---|---|---|---|---|---|---|---|
| 8—Phila. | W | 2-1 | Seaver | Carlton | 1—At Chi. | L | 2-5 | Stone | Tate |
| 10—Phila. | L | 2-3‡ | Schueler | Parker | 2—Montreal | W | 3-0 | Koosman | McNally |
| 11—At Pitts. | L | 3-4 | Demery | Baldwin | 3—Montreal | L | 0-3 | Fryman | Webb |
| 13—At Pitts. | L | 3-5 | Kison | Seaver | 6—Pitts. | L | 1-2* | Brett | Seaver |
| 14—At Phila. | L | 3-4 | Garber | Cram | 7—Pitts. | L | 1-6 | Reuss | Matlack |
| 16—At St. L. | L | 2-3 | Denny | Matlack | 8—Pitts. | L | 2-4 | Kison | Koosman |
| 17—At St. L. | W | 14-7 | Baldwin | Sosa | 9—Cinn. | L | 3-4 | Gullett | Tate |
| 19—Chicago | L | 2-4 | Stone | Seaver | 10—Cinn. | L | 1-7 | Kirby | Webb |
| 20—Chicago | W | 8-6 | Matlack | R. Reuschel | 11—Cinn. | W | 3-2 | Seaver | Billingham |
| 20—Chicago | W | 4-3 | Tate | Hooton | 12—S. Fran. | W | 3-2 | Matlack | Barr |
| 22—St. Louis | W | 9-5 | Koosman | McGlothen | 14—S. Fran. | W | 5-1 | Koosman | Caldwell |
| 23—St. Louis | W | 7-1 | Seaver | Gibson | 16—At Hous. | W | 10-2 | Seaver | Dierker |
| 25—At Mon. | W | 5-3 | Matlack | Rogers | 17—At Hous. | W | 6-4 | Matlack | Roberts |
| 27—At Mon. | W | 7-6 | Parker | McNally | 18—At Hous. | L | 7-12 | Konieczny | Tate |
| 29—At Chi. | W | 9-1 | Seaver | Hooton | 20—At Cinn. | W | 6-2 | Koosman | Gullett |
| 30—At Chi. | L | 4-7 | Burris | Matlack | 21—At Cinn. | L | 4-11 | Billingham | Seaver |
| | | | **Won 9, Lost 7** | | 23—At Atl. | W | 3-1 | Matlack | Morton |

**MAY**

| Date | | Score | Winner | Loser |
|---|---|---|---|---|
| 24—At Atl. | W | 5-1 | Tate | Reed |
| 25—At Atl. | L | 3-6 | Capra | Koosman |
| 26—Los Ang. | W | 6-3 | Seaver | Messersmith |
| 27—Los Ang. | L | 4-10 | Hooton | Parker |
| 28—Los Ang. | W | 4-3 | Matlack | Rau |
| 30—S. Diego | L | 2-6 | Jones | Koosman |
| 31—S. Diego | W | 7-2 | Seaver | McIntosh |

Won 12, Lost 12

**JUNE**

| Date | | Score | Winner | Loser |
|---|---|---|---|---|
| 1—S. Diego | L | 0-4 | Foster | Tate |
| 2—Houston | W | 2-0 | Matlack | Roberts |
| 3—Houston | W | 4-3 | Hall | Forsch |
| 4—Houston | W | 1-0 | Koosman | Konieczny |
| 5—Houston | W | 2-1 | Seaver | Griffin |
| 6—Atlanta | L | 1-4 | Niekro | Tate |
| 7—Atlanta | L | 3-7 | Morton | Matlack |
| 8—Atlanta | W | 7-6y | Webb | Sosa |
| 9—At S. F. | L | 4-5 | Heaverlo | Koosman |
| 10—At S. F. | W | 5-0 | Seaver | Barr |
| 11—At L. A. | W | 2-1 | Apodaca | Marshall |
| 12—At L. A. | W | 2-0 | Matlack | Sutton |
| 13—At S. D. | W | 7-2 | Stone | McIntosh |
| 14—At S. D. | L | 1-7 | Jones | Koosman |
| 15—At S. D. | W | 6-0 | Seaver | Strom |
| 17—At Mon. | L | 5-6 | Warthen | Matlack |
| 17—At Mon. | W | 5-2‡ | Parker | Taylor |
| 18—At Mon. | L | 6-7† | Taylor | Apodaca |
| 19—At Mon. | L | 2-3x | Murray | Baldwin |
| 20—Pitts. | L | 1-5 | Candelaria | Hall |
| 21—Pitts. | L | 3-7 | Hernandez | Parker |
| 22—Pitts. | L | 0-2 | Ellis | Tate |
| 23—St. Louis | L | 0-1 | Reed | Webb |
| 23—St. Louis | L | 0-4 | Denny | Stone |
| 24—St. Louis | W | 5-1 | Koosman | Curtis |
| 25—St. Louis | W | 2-1 | Seaver | Forsch |
| 27—Phila. | W | 4-2 | Matlack | Twitchell |
| 28—Phila. | W | 5-2 | Tate | Carlton |
| 29—Phila. | L | 6-9 | Christenson | Koosman |
| 29—Phila. | L | 3-4§ | McGraw | Hall |
| 30—Chicago | W | 5-1 | G. Stone | S. Stone |

Won 16, Lost 15

**JULY**

| Date | | Score | Winner | Loser |
|---|---|---|---|---|
| 1—Chicago | L | 4-5† | Dettore | Baldwin |
| 2—Chicago | W | 7-2 | Matlack | Bonham |
| 3—Chicago | W | 4-0 | Koosman | R. Reuschel |
| 4—At Phila. | W | 4-3 | Seaver | McGraw |
| 5—At Phila. | L | 2-8 | Schueler | Tate |
| 5—At Phila. | L | 7-10 | Lonborg | Espinosa |
| 6—At Phila. | W | 6-8 | Twitchell | Matlack |
| 7—At Atl. | W | 3-1 | Webb | Easterly |
| 8—At Atl. | W | 4-3 | Koosman | Morton |
| 9—At Atl. | W | 2-1† | Seaver | Leon |
| 11—At Cinn. | L | 3-4 | Norman | Matlack |
| 11—At Cinn. | L | 1-4 | Kirby | Tate |
| 12—At Cinn. | L | 2-3 | T. Carroll | Koosman |
| 13—At Cinn. | L | 3-5 | McEnaney | Seaver |
| 17—Atlanta | W | 4-3 | Baldwin | House |
| 18—Atlanta | L | 3-4 | Morton | Matlack |
| 19—Atlanta | W | 5-4 | Seaver | Dal Canton |
| 20—Houston | W | 10-9 | Hall | Granger |
| 21—Houston | L | 2-6 | Forsch | Stone |
| 22—Cinn. | W | 3-1 | Koosman | Billingham |
| 23—Cinn. | W | 5-2 | Matlack | Nolan |
| 24—Cinn. | L | 1-2 | Norman | Seaver |
| 25—At Chi. | W | 6-3 | Tate | R. Reuschel |
| 26—At Chi. | W | 9-8† | Hall | Knowles |
| 27—At Chi. | L | 2-4 | Stone | Koosman |
| 27—At Chi. | W | 4-1† | Webb | P. Reuschel |
| 28—At St. L. | W | 11-7 | Matlack | Forsch |

**JULY**

| Date | | Score | Winner | Loser |
|---|---|---|---|---|
| 29—At St. L. | L | 3-5 | McGlothen | Seaver |
| 29—At St. L. | W | 11-6 | Hall | Reed |
| 30—At St. L. | L | 2-5 | Curtis | Tate |
| 31—At Pitts. | W | 6-2 | Koosman | Rooker |

Won 17, Lost 14

**AUGUST**

| Date | | Score | Winner | Loser |
|---|---|---|---|---|
| 1—At Pitts. | W | 4-2 | Stone | Brett |
| 2—At Pitts. | W | 6-0 | Matlack | Kison |
| 3—At Pitts. | L | 4-5z | Demery | Apodaca |
| 3—At Pitts. | L | 3-4 | Candelaria | Webb |
| 4—Montreal | L | 3-4 | DeMola | Tate |
| 5—Montreal | L | 0-7 | Carrithers | Koosman |
| 5—Montreal | L | 0-7 | Blair | Hall |
| 6—Montreal | W | 9-6* | Webb | Renko |
| 7—Montreal | W | 7-0 | Seaver | Rogers |
| 8—Los Ang. | L | 3-4 | Marshall | Sanders |
| 9—Los Ang. | L | 0-2 | Hooton | Koosman |
| 10—Los Ang. | L | 1-2 | Sutton | Webb |
| 11—S. Diego | W | 8-4 | Lockwood | Jones |
| 12—S. Diego | W | 9-4 | Seaver | Johnson |
| 13—S. Diego | L | 5-8 | Folkers | Tate |
| 15—S. Fran. | L | 2-6 | Halicki | Koosman |
| 15—S. Fran. | W | 9-4 | Webb | Bradley |
| 16—S. Fran. | W | 4-2 | Swan | Falcone |
| 17—S. Fran. | W | 3-0 | Seaver | Montefusco |
| 18—At Hous. | L | 0-4 | Richard | Tate |
| 19—At Hous. | W | 6-3 | Matlack | Dierker |
| 20—At Hous. | L | 4-5† | Crawford | Baldwin |
| 22—At S. F. | W | 6-4 | Seaver | Falcone |
| 23—At S. F. | L | 1-2 | Lavelle | Lockwood |
| 24—At S. F. | W | 9-5 | Matlack | Barr |
| 24—At S. F. | L | 0-6 | Halicki | Swan |
| 25—At S. D. | W | 4-0 | Webb | Strom |
| 26—At S. D. | W | 7-2 | Tate | Freisleben |
| 27—At S. D. | W | 7-0 | Seaver | Spillner |
| 28—At L. A. | W | 4-1 | Koosman | Rhoden |
| 29—At L. A. | W | 6-1 | Matlack | Sutton |
| 30—At L. A. | L | 0-7 | Messersmith | Webb |
| 31—At L. A. | L | 2-5 | Rau | Swan |

Won 17, Lost 16

**SEPTEMBER**

| Date | | Score | Winner | Loser |
|---|---|---|---|---|
| 1—Pitts. | W | 3-0 | Seaver | Candelaria |
| 2—Pitts. | L | 4-8 | Tekulve | Koosman |
| 3—Pitts. | L | 1-3 | Reuss | Matlack |
| 5—St. Louis | W | 5-2 | Seaver | Rasmussen |
| 6—St. Louis | L | 3-6 | Forsch | Koosman |
| 7—St. Louis | L | 4-12 | McGlothen | Matlack |
| 8—At Mon. | L | 5-6 | Murray | Baldwin |
| 8—At Mon. | L | 1-6 | Carrithers | Stone |
| 9—At Mon. | L | 1-2† | Murray | Apodaca |
| 10—At Pitts. | L | 4-8 | Rooker | Seaver |
| 11—At Pitts. | W | 7-0 | Koosman | Reuss |
| 12—At St. L. | L | 1-5 | McGlothen | Matlack |
| 13—At St. L. | W | 6-2 | Webb | Reed |
| 14—At St. L. | L | 2-6 | Denny | Seaver |
| 15—Montreal | W | 3-2 | Koosman | Rogers |
| 16—Montreal | W | 4-3a | Baldwin | DeMola |
| 17—Chicago | L | 2-5 | Burris | Swan |
| 18—Chicago | W | 7-5 | Sanders | Knowles |
| 19—Phila. | L | 3-4 | McGraw | Lockwood |
| 20—Phila. | W | 9-7‡ | Apodaca | Garber |
| 21—Phila. | L | 2-4 | Ruthven | Matlack |
| 23—At Chi. | W | 8-6 | Apodaca | Knowles |
| 24—At Chi. | L | 0-1‡ | Crosby | Lockwood |
| 26—At Phila. | L | 3-4§ | Garber | Apodaca |
| 26—At Phila. | W | 3-2§ | Koosman | McGraw |
| 27—At Phila. | L | 1-8 | Carlton | Tate |
| 28—At Phila. | W | 5-4 | Seaver | Christenson |

Won 11, Lost 16

* 8 innings. † 10 innings. ‡ 11 innings. § 12 innings. x 13 innings. y 14 innings. z 15 innings. a 18 innings.

ST. LOUIS CARDINALS—1975

Front row—Denny, Dwyer, Herndon, Forsch, Mumphrey, Cruz, Osteen, Melendez, Godby. Second row—Sosa, Sizemore, Kissell, coach; Benson, coach; Schultz, coach; Schoendienst, manager; Ricketts, manager; Lewis, coach; Hernandez, Reitz, Tyson, Yakeman, equipment manager. Third row—Bauman, trainer; Martinez, Lindsey, Rudolph, Brinkman, Capilla, Fairly, Billings, Brock, Curtis, Hunt, Gibson, Gieselmann, trainer. Fourth row—Parsons, Simmons, Smith, Sadecki, Terlecky, Covert, McBride, Gonzalez, Garman, Hrabosky, McGlothen, Moore, Bare.

# Cards Short of Bing's Flag Prophecy

## By NEAL RUSSO

It was after a game in Atlanta on August 17, and many of the Cardinal players were in a happy mood. Why not? An 8-1 laugher over the Braves behind young John Denny had lifted the rebounding Redbirds within two games of the faltering Pirates, leaders of the East Division.

The Cardinals had been in fourth place, 13 big games from the top perch, as late as July 19 after bowing to rookie John Montefusco in San Francisco. But now it appeared that the Birds were jelling into the kind of club that General Manager Bing Devine had envisioned in his state of the union message on his birthday March 1 at the Florida training camp.

Bing had said then, "I think we've got a heckuva club that could have won the last two years, but should win now." Devine pointed to some deals that looked good, at least on paper, and to the expected improvement of some young players as a result of that invaluable asset, experience.

But the Cardinals, who had finished just 1½ games from the top each of the last two previous seasons, then went into a swoon, a long, long swoon that would find them tied for third place, 10½ games behind the Pirates, at season's end.

As was the case in 1974, many of the players had good years—but not quite enough. It was a most frustrating 1975. The club led the league in batting average with a .273 mark. For the second successive season, the Birds could boast of an excellent-hitting outfield, with Willie Davis joining Lou Brock and Bake McBride this time around—Reggie Smith moving to first base, even to third for one game.

Ted Simmons not only reached a personal peak with his .332 mark, but he showed about as much balance any anyone could expect of a switch-hitter. Ted, who had become so discouraged a few years back that he seriously considered batting lefthanded exclusively, finished at .336 righthanded and .329 lefthanded. Twelve of his 18 home runs came while swinging righthanded, and he had 81 fewer at-bats righthanded.

Ron Fairly (.301) was a most welcome addition as a clutch swinger, whether pinch-hitting or handling starting assignments at first base.

Ken Reitz got off to another blazing start at bat and checked in with a respectable .269 finish.

Mike Tyson, again consigned to a reserve role at the outset of the season, came through admirably when newcomer veteran Eddie Brinkman was found wanting. Mike not only fielded well at shortstop, though second base is his natural position, but he helped out much more than expected at bat. He batted .266.

Luis Melendez, the club's best pinch-hitter in 1974, did a good job of filling in as the center fielder during McBride's long absence. Luis batted .265. Buddy Bradford turned out to be a good pickup as another right-handed-hitting reserve, nailing lefties at a .347 clip.

Before faltering in September, the young pitching did its job in keeping the Redbirds afloat. Bob Forsch deserved to finish better than 15-10 (he had a 2.86 earned-run average). Denny (10-7) earned his way on the varsity with an excellent showing in spring training. He stumbled after a good start, but came back strong following a stint with the Tulsa (American Association) farm club.

Harry Rasmussen showed promise as soon as he was called up. He closed out at 5-5. Lynn McGlothen was 15-13 in his second season as a Cardinal. Like Forsch a frequent victim of anemic offensive support, Ron Reed had to settle for a 9-8 record despite a glittering 3.22 ERA as a Redbird after coming from the Braves where he had been 4-5.

Reed's pitching gave Al Hrabosky plenty of chances of fattening up his record, and the Mad Hungarian took advantage of the opportunities as he became the league's premier relief pitcher.

Hrabosky, quite a crowd pleaser with his self-psyching routines behind the mound, turned in a 13-3 record and collected 22 saves in earning THE SPORTING NEWS Fireman of the Year award. The Hungarian, who made 65 appearances totaling 97⅓ innings, could boast of a 1.67 earned-run mark.

But, of course, there had to be many negative happenings to bring the club down to an 82-80 record.

The defense was far too erratic. All too often the hitting was far from timely. Bob Gibson's farewell was a sore disappointment. Mike Garman had an off year in the bullpen. Ted Sizemore, who had a good year in 1974 as he supplemented Lou Brock on his way to a record-setting total of 118 stolen bases, had his worst year at bat, tumbling to .240.

Besides Simmons' .332, there was Brock's .309, along with Reggie Smith's .302, Bake McBride's .300 and Davis was a .291 hitter as a Cardinal despite a late sag. But the runs just didn't come often enough. In fact, even though the '75 Cardinals played two more games than in '74, they scored 15 fewer runs, 662 to 677.

Gibson wound up his illustrious career with a 3-10 mark, that might well have been 3-11. Rain saved him once after Houston's Cliff Johnson had homered in the top of an inning to shatter a tie. Gibby sparkled a few times in relief after being dropped from the starting rotation, but he also failed a few times. The bottom seemed to have been reached when he yielded a grand-slam pinch homer to the Cubs' Pete LaCock. That cost a key ball game.

Some changes were made after the World Series. The Redbirds dispatched Reitz to the Giants for promising lefty Pete Falcone, 12-11 in his first season out of Class A ball. Reed went to the Phillies for Mike Anderson and Garman was traded to the Cubs for Don Kessinger.

### SCORES OF ST. LOUIS CARDINALS' 1975 GAMES

| APRIL | | | Winner | Loser | APRIL | | | Winner | Loser |
|---|---|---|---|---|---|---|---|---|---|
| 7—Montreal | L | 4-8 | McNally | Gibson | 26—At Chi. | L | 6-8 | Frailing | Curtis |
| 9—Montreal | W | 4-0 | Forsch | Rogers | 29—At Pitts. | W | 3-0 | McGlothen | Brett |
| 10—Montreal | W | 7-2 | Denny | Murray | 30—At Pitts. | L | 0-5 | Reuss | Gibson |
| 11—At Phila. | W | 6-3 | McGlothen | Twitchell | | | | **Won 7, Lost 10** | |
| 12—At Phila. | W | 7-5 | Garman | Garber | | | | | |
| 13—At Phila. | L | 0-2 | Underwood | Forsch | MAY | | | | |
| 16—N. York | W | 3-2 | Denny | Matlack | 2—Chicago | W | 5-1 | Forsch | R. Reuschel |
| 17—N. York | L | 7-14 | Baldwin | Sosa | 3—Chicago | L | 3-7 | Bonham | Garman |
| 18—Pitts. | W | 5-4§ | Sadecki | McDowell | 4—Chicago | W | 6-8 | Zamora | McGlothen |
| 19—Pitts. | L | 1-7 | Rooker | Forsch | 5—Phila. | W | 11-3 | Gibson | Carlton |
| 20—Pitts. | L | 0-5 | Brett | Denny | 7—Phila. | L | 1-4 | Twitchell | Forsch |
| 22—At N. Y. | L | 5-9 | Koosman | McGlothen | 8—Phila. | L | 2-6 | Lonborg | Denny |
| 23—At N. Y. | L | 1-7 | Seaver | Gibson | 9—S. Fran. | W | 6-4 | McGlothen | D'Acquisto |
| 25—At Chi. | L | 3-4 | Knowles | Hrabosky | 10—S. Fran. | W | 9-2 | Curtis | Williams |
| | | | | | 11—S. Fran. | W | 4-3 | Forsch | Falcone |

## MAY

| Date | | | Winner | Loser |
|---|---|---|---|---|
| 12—Los Ang. | L | 4-6* | Brewer | Garman |
| 13—Los Ang. | L | 0-5 | Hooton | McGlothen |
| 14—Los Ang. | W | 7-4 | Curtis | Rau |
| 16—At S. F. | L | 3-4* | Lavelle | Sosa |
| 17—At S. F. | W | 17-2 | Forsch | Falcone |
| 18—At S. F. | L | 0-2 | Barr | McGlothen |
| 19—At S. D. | L | 0-1* | Jones | Curtis |
| 20—At S. D. | L | 2-5 | Foster | Sosa |
| 21—At S. D. | L | 0-1 | McIntosh | Gibson |
| 23—At L. A. | W | 4-3 | Hrabosky | Hough |
| 24—At L. A. | W | 6-2 | McGlothen | Rau |
| 25—At L. A. | L | 3-7 | Sutton | Curtis |
| 26—S. Diego | L | 6-9 | Greif | Hrabosky |
| 27—S. Diego | W | 7-1 | Forsch | Freisleben |
| 28—S. Diego | W | 6-5* | Garman | Greif |
| 30—Cinn. | W | 5-4 | Hrabosky | Eastwick |
| 31—Cinn. | L | 0-6 | Gullett | Gibson |

**Won 12, Lost 14**

## JUNE

| Date | | | Winner | Loser |
|---|---|---|---|---|
| 1—Cinn. | L | 1-5 | Billingham | Forsch |
| 2—Atlanta | W | 1-0 | McGlothen | Morton |
| 3—Atlanta | W | 4-2 | Reed | Capra |
| 4—Atlanta | W | 5-2 | Curtis | Sadecki |
| 6—At Hous. | W | 6-0 | Forsch | Dierker |
| 7—At Hous. | W | 5-1 | McGlothen | Roberts |
| 8—At Hous. | W | 5-1 | Reed | Forsch |
| 9—At Atl. | W | 5-4 | Curtis | Odom |
| 11—At Cinn. | L | 1-3 | Gullett | Forsch |
| 12—At Cinn. | L | 1-10 | Nolan | McGlothen |
| 13—Houston | W | 6-2 | Reed | Siebert |
| 14—Houston | L | 0-9 | Griffin | Curtis |
| 15—Houston | L | 7-8 | Niekro | Garman |
| 16—At Pitts. | L | 4-10 | Kison | Bryant |
| 17—At Pitts. | W | 7-4 | McGlothen | Ellis |
| 18—At Pitts. | L | 3-9 | Rooker | Reed |
| 19—At Pitts. | L | 0-5 | Reuss | Curtis |
| 20—Chicago | W | 8-3 | Forsch | Zahn |
| 21—Chicago | L | 1-6 | R. Reuschel | Gibson |
| 22—Chicago | W | 7-2 | McGlothen | Stone |
| 23—At N. Y. | W | 1-0 | Reed | Webb |
| 23—At N. Y. | W | 4-0 | Denny | Stone |
| 24—At N. Y. | L | 1-5 | Koosman | Curtis |
| 25—At N. Y. | L | 1-2 | Seaver | Forsch |
| 26—At Mon. | W | 4-3 | McGlothen | Fryman |
| 27—At Mon. | W | 6-4 | Gibson | Rogers |
| 27—At Mon. | L | 4-5 | Warthen | Reed |
| 28—At Mon. | W | 3-2* | Hrabosky | DeMola |
| 29—At Mon. | L | 3-7 | Renko | Curtis |
| 30 At Phila. | W | 4-2 | Forsch | Lonborg |

**Won 17, Lost 13**

## JULY

| Date | | | Winner | Loser |
|---|---|---|---|---|
| 1—At Phila. | W | 6-5 | McGlothen | Twitchell |
| 2—At Phila. | L | 3-5 | Carlton | Reed |
| 3—At Phila. | L | 4-7 | Underwood | Gibson |
| 4—Montreal | L | 1-5 | Renko | Denny |
| 5—Montreal | L | 0-3 | Blair | Forsch |
| 5—Montreal | W | 1-0 | Curtis | Fryman |
| 6—Montreal | L | 3-4 | DeMola | McGlothen |
| 7—S. Fran. | W | 8-6 | Reed | Caldwell |
| 8—S. Fran. | L | 4-6 | Falcone | Gibson |
| 9—S. Fran. | W | 9-0 | Denny | Montefusco |
| 11—Los Ang. | L | 5-6 | Marshall | Garman |
| 12—Los Ang. | W | 2-1* | Hrabosky | Rhoden |
| 13—Los Ang. | W | 2-1 | Hrabosky | Marshall |
| 17—At S. F. | W | 1-0 | Hrabosky | Barr |
| 18—At S. F. | L | 1-2* | Lavelle | Terlecky |
| 19—At S. F. | L | 2-5 | Montefusco | McGlothen |
| 20—At S. D. | W | 3-1† | Hrabosky | Greif |
| 20—At S. D. | W | 10-2 | Curtis | Folkers |
| 21—At S. D. | W | 4-0 | Rasmussen | Strom |
| 22—At L. A. | W | 4-3† | Hrabosky | Marshall |
| 23—At L. A. | W | 5-4 | Forsch | Sutton |
| 24—At L. A. | L | 2-8 | Hooton | McGlothen |

## JULY

| Date | | | Winner | Loser |
|---|---|---|---|---|
| 25—Phila. | W | 4-3 | Hrabosky | Garber |
| 25—Phila. | L | 2-5 | Schueler | Curtis |
| 26—Phila. | L | 4-9 | Carlton | Rasmussen |
| 27—Phila. | W | 9-6 | Gibson | Hilgendorf |
| 28—N. York | L | 7-11 | Matlack | Forsch |
| 29—N. York | W | 5-3 | McGlothen | Seaver |
| 29—N. York | L | 6-11 | Hall | Reed |
| 30—N. York | W | 5-2 | Curtis | Tate |
| 31—At Chi. | L | 3-5 | P. Reuschel | Reynolds |

**Won 16, Lost 15**

## AUGUST

| Date | | | Winner | Loser |
|---|---|---|---|---|
| 1—At Chi. | W | 9-4 | Denny | Bonham |
| 2—At Chi. | W | 4-0 | Forsch | R. Reuschel |
| 3—At Chi. | L | 3-6 | Dettore | Hrabosky |
| 3—At Chi. | W | 7-4 | Reed | Burris |
| 4—Pitts. | W | 5-4 | Curtis | Reuss |
| 5—Pitts. | L | 1-6 | Rooker | Rasmussen |
| 6—Pitts. | W | 4-2 | Denny | Brett |
| 8—S. Diego | W | 10-6 | Forsch | Spillner |
| 9—S. Diego | W | 6-1 | McGlothen | Freisleben |
| 10—S. Diego | W | 3-2* | Hrabosky | Greif |
| 11—At Hous. | L | 2-7 | Dierker | Curtis |
| 12—At Hous. | W | 5-4 | Denny | Roberts |
| 13—At Hous. | W | 4-3† | Garman | Cosgrove |
| 14—At Atl. | L | 4-6 | Niekro | McGlothen |
| 15—At Atl. | W | 4-1 | Reed | Easterly |
| 15—At Atl. | W | 2-1 | Rasmussen | Thompson |
| 16—At Atl. | L | 7-8 | House | Gibson |
| 17—At Atl. | W | 8-1 | Denny | Odom |
| 18—Cinn. | L | 2-3 | Gullett | Forsch |
| 19—Cinn. | W | 2-1 | McGlothen | Nolan |
| 20—Cinn. | W | 4-0 | Reed | Norman |
| 22—Atlanta | L | 5-9 | Sosa | Parker |
| 23—Atlanta | W | 7-2 | Denny | Niekro |
| 24—Atlanta | W | 6-2 | Forsch | Morton |
| 25—Houston | T | 3-3* | ------ | ------ |
| 26—Houston | W | 10-9‡ | Hrabosky | Sosa |
| 26—Houston | W | 2-1 | Rasmussen | Konieczny |
| 27—Houston | L | 1-5 | York | Denny |
| 28—At Cinn. | L | 0-4 | Gullett | Garman |
| 29—At Cinn. | L | 2-6 | Nolan | McGlothen |
| 30—At Cinn. | L | 2-3* | Eastwick | Garman |
| 31—At Cinn. | W | 5-3 | Rasmussen | Billingham |

**Won 20, Lost 11, Tied 1**

## SEPTEMBER

| Date | | | Winner | Loser |
|---|---|---|---|---|
| 1—Chicago | W | 6-3 | Forsch | Bonham |
| 2—Chicago | L | 3-5 | Burris | McGlothen |
| 3—Chicago | L | 6-11 | Schultz | Gibson |
| 5—At N. Y. | L | 2-5 | Seaver | Rasmussen |
| 6—At N. Y. | W | 6-3 | Forsch | Koosman |
| 7—At N. Y. | W | 12-4 | McGlothen | Matiack |
| 8—At Phila. | L | 3-6 | Underwood | Reed |
| 9—At Phila. | L | 2-6 | Carlton | Denny |
| 10—At Chi. | L | 5-7 | Schultz | Rasmussen |
| 11—At Chi. | L | 6-12 | Zamora | Forsch |
| 12—N. York | W | 5-1 | McGlothen | Matlack |
| 13—N. York | L | 2-6 | Webb | Reed |
| 14—N. York | W | 6-2 | Denny | Seaver |
| 15—Phila. | W | 7-6 | Hrabosky | Garber |
| 16—Phila. | L | 3-4§ | Hilgendorf | Garman |
| 17—Montreal | L | 3-6 | Warthen | McGlothen |
| 18—Montreal | L | 0-5 | Renko | Reed |
| 19—At Pitts. | L | 1-7 | Brett | Denny |
| 20—At Pitts. | W | 8-2 | Rasmussen | Rooker |
| 21—At Pitts. | L | 3-5 | Reuss | Garman |
| 22—At Mon. | W | 6-4‡ | Hrabosky | Fryman |
| 22—At Mon. | L | 5-8 | Scherman | Reed |
| 23—At Mon. | L | 0-7 | Rogers | Denny |
| 24—At Mon. | L | 2-6 | Carrithers | Rasmussen |
| 26—Pitts. | W | 1-0 | Forsch | Rooker |
| 27—Pitts. | L | 2-4 | Reuss | McGlothen |
| 28—Pitts. | W | 6-2 | Reed | Candelaria |

**Won 10, Lost 17**

* 10 innings.   † 11 innings.   ‡ 12 innings.   § 13 innings.

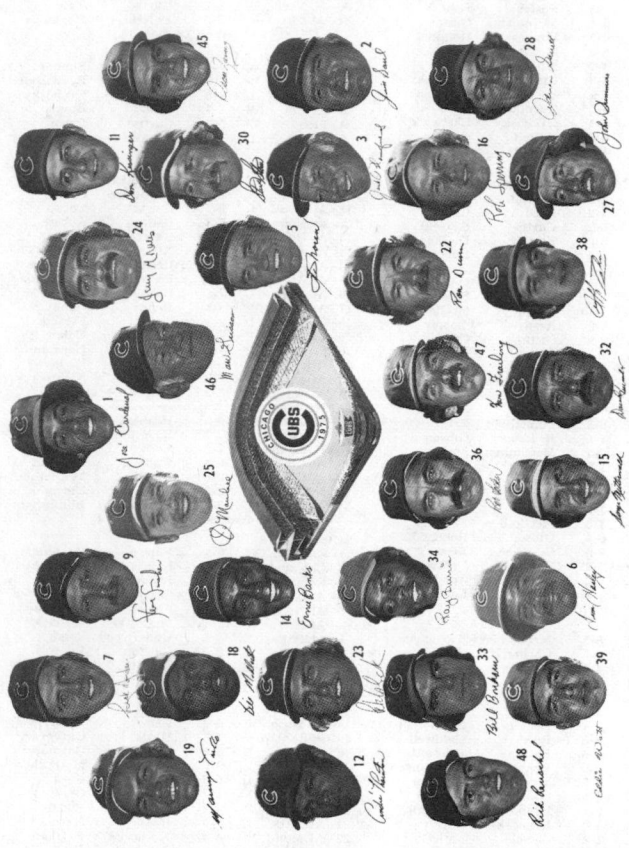

## CHICAGO CUBS—1975

Bottom row—Watt, Hosley, Mitterwald, Knowles, Zahn, Summers. Second row—Rick Reuschel, Bonham, Burris, Locker, Frailing, Dunn, Sperring, Garrett. Third row—Thornton, LaCock, Banks, coach; Noren, coach; Bloomfield, coach; Saul, coach. Fourth row—Trillo, Madlock, Marshall, manager; Grissom, coach; Stone, Zamora. Fifth row—Monday, Swisher, Cardenal, Morales, Kessinger.

# Early-Foot Cubs Trapped by Pitching

## By RICHARD DOZER

Manager Jim Marshall called it improvement. The Cubs won nine more games in 1975 than they did in '74, and instead of finishing dead last in the National League East, they wound up sharing the dungeon with the Montreal Expos. It's a matter of momentum apparently. Marshall got a new contract and a pat on the back; Montreal's Gene Mauch was fired.

There were, indeed, some good signs with the Cubs. They had the National League batting champion in Bill (.354) Madlock. They had another among the league's top ten hitters in Jose Cardenal, who played a steady .317 tune and stole 34 bases. Manny Trillo was a pleasant surprise at second base, and once Andy Thornton recovered from a broken wrist he gave more promise of power than any young player since Billy Williams came on the scene in 1961.

Jerry Morales led the club in runs batted in for the second year in a row, knocking in 91 this time as the housecleaning deals of the last two years continued to bear fruit. Morales batted .270, Thornton came on strong at the end, batting .293 and belting half of his 18 homers in the final six weeks of the campaign.

"I'd like to think Thornton can start where he left off," said Marshall in projecting his thoughts to a happy Bicentennial '76.

"I said in spring training that Madlock would bat .300, but with him leading the league . . . well, that was a 50-point bonus. And I surely didn't dream that Trillo would drive in 70 runs for us while playing so well at second base. He was just super."

When Marshall finished looking back over the season, he could honestly say that the Cubs put a highly-representative club on the field day-by-day and night-by-night. But it was their pitching that did them in.

At the outset, they were getting some good starts out of Steve Stone and aid from the bullpen headed by Oscar Zamora and Darold Knowles. The Cubs enjoyed a great start. They led the league well into the month of May and had some observers excited about their chances throughout a good portion of the first half.

Then realism set in, and the great tailspin began—predictable, of course, because the pitching just wasn't there. Stone, who won five before he lost, wound up at 12-8 but never really was the same after missing a month with a back injury. Of the regulars, Ray Burris finished impressively and burst from the ranks of the .500 hurlers to wind up at 15-10 but couldn't get his earned-run average down to 4.00

The entire staff had only two men with earned-run marks under that figure—the brothers Reuschel. Rick Reuschel, two years younger than brother Paul, had an 11-17 record that was better than that. His 3.73 ERA was best among the starters. Paul, summoned from Wichita in August, saved five and won one, but by the end of the season the hitters were catching up to him, too. Paul's ERA was 3.50, and together with the earlier relief mainstays, Zamora and Knowles, this trio recorded 42 saves among the Cubs' 75 victories.

But if this sounds like bullpen success, it wasn't. The failures were more frequent than the good news. Zamora's ERA was 5.07 and Knowles' 5.83.

The Cub staff's mark was a rotund 4.49, and Marshall said it will have to be under 4.00 for something better in '76, although he did lay a portion of the trouble at the doorstep of Wrigley Field, where the confines are scarcely regarded as a pitcher's paradise. Bill Bonham suffered perhaps more than the rest. Inconsistency was his chief enemy. On August 5 in Philadelphia he gave up seven hits for 15 total bases without retiring a batter. Five days later, he pitched a 9-1 five-hitter in Atlanta.

Bonham hurled two of the Cubs' eight shutouts. Rich Reuschel got none on his own but was part of three of them, including one which Paul finished against the Dodgers August 21—the majors' first brother shutout in history.

Mike Garman, who had a 2.39 ERA in 66 games with the Cardinals, was obtained at the expense of dealing the final member of a once highly regarded Cub infield, Don Kessinger. Don was a fixture at shortstop in Chicago for 11 seasons.

The other end of the battery was something less than sensational for the 1975 Cubs, too. Their catchers hit only a composite .225. They were not very prohibitive defensively either. Steve Swisher, the youngster Marshall hopes will take charge of the job one day, did show signs of living up to expectations, and Lew Fonseca, the club's special batting coach, predicts an upturn at the plate for Swisher, who batted .213.

The club chiefly responsible for keeping the Cubs 12 games under .500 was world champion Cincinnati. The Chicagoans managed to beat the Reds only once in 12 games. Against the rest they were respectable, finishing 45-45 in their own division and handling arch-rival St. Louis 11 out of 18.

## SCORES OF CHICAGO CUBS' 1975 GAMES

| APRIL | | | Winner | Loser |
|---|---|---|---|---|
| 10—Pitts. | L | 4-8 | Giusti | Frailing |
| 11—Montreal | W | 2-1 | Burris | Blair |
| 12—Montreal | W | 6-3 | Zamora | Murray |
| 13—Montreal | W | 7-0 | Stone | Rogers |
| 14—At Pitts. | W | 4-2 | R. Reuschel | Moose |
| 16—At Phila. | W | 9-3 | Bonham | Carlton |
| 17—At Phila. | W | 10-9 | Frailing | Twitchell |
| 19—At N. Y. | W | 4-2 | Stone | Seaver |
| 20—At N. Y. | L | 6-8 | Matlack | R. Reuschel |
| 20—At N. Y. | L | 3-4 | Tate | Hooton |
| 22—Phila. | L | 5-7 | Twitchell | Bonham |
| 23—Phila. | W | 9-3 | Burris | Underwood |
| 24—Phila. | W | 4-1 | Stone | Lonborg |
| 25—St. Louis | W | 4-3 | Knowles | Hrabosky |
| 26—St. Louis | W | 8-6 | Frailing | Curtis |
| 29—N. York | L | 1-9 | Seaver | Hooton |
| 30—N. York | W | 7-4 | Burris | Matlack |
| | | **Won 12, Lost 5** | | |

| MAY | | | | |
|---|---|---|---|---|
| 1—N. York | W | 5-2 | Stone | Tate |
| 2—At St. L. | L | 1-5 | Forsch | R. Reuschel |
| 3—At St. L. | W | 7-3 | Bonham | Garman |
| 4—At St. L. | W | 8-6 | Zamora | McGlothen |
| 5—At Mon. | L | 2-3 | Blair | Burris |
| 6—At Mon. | L | 4-9 | Rogers | R. Reuschel |
| 7—At Mon. | W | 7-0 | Bonham | McNally |
| 9—S. Diego | W | 5-2 | Burris | McIntosh |
| 10—S. Diego | W | 5-1 | R. Reuschel | Siebert |

| MAY | | | Winner | Loser |
|---|---|---|---|---|
| 11—S. Diego | L | 1-2 | Freisleben | Bonham |
| 13—Houston | W | 2-1 | Stone | Konieczny |
| 14—Houston | L | 7-11 | Griffin | Burris |
| 15—Houston | W | 4-2 | R. Reuschel | Richard |
| 16—At S. D. | L | 2-8 | McIntosh | Bonham |
| 17—At S. D. | L | 1-4 | Freisleben | Knowles |
| 18—At S. D. | W | 3-2 | Burris | Spillner |
| 19—At L. A. | L | 2-3 | Brewer | Knowles |
| 20—At L. A. | W | 2-1 | Bonham | Sutton |
| 21—At L. A. | L | 0-10 | Messersmith | Zahn |
| 22—At L. A. | L | 3-8 | Hooton | Burris |
| 23—At S. F. | L | 2-3 | Falcone | R. Reuschel |
| 24—At S. F. | L | 3-10 | Barr | Bonham |
| 25—At S. F. | L | 7-9 | Williams | Frailing |
| 26—Atlanta | W | 6-0 | Burris | Harrison |
| 27—Atlanta | L | 2-7 | Niekro | R. Reuschel |
| 28—Atlanta | W | 5-4 | Zamora | Morton |
| 30—Los Ang. | L | 1-3y | Sutton | Burris |
| 31—Los Ang. | W | 2-1 | R. Reuschel | Messersmith |
| | | **Won 13, Lost 15** | | |

| JUNE | | | | |
|---|---|---|---|---|
| 1—Los Ang. | W | 7-2 | Bonham | Hooton |
| 3—S. Fran. | W | 6-5* | Zahn | Moffitt |
| 4—S. Fran. | L | 8-10 | Williams | Zamora |
| 5—S. Fran. | W | 8-4 | Knowles | Moffitt |
| 6—At Cinn. | L | 1-5 | Gullett | Bonham |
| 7—At Cinn. | L | 1-8 | Billingham | Burris |
| 8—At Cinn. | L | 1-2 | Nolan | R. Reuschel |

| JUNE | | | Winner | Loser |
|---|---|---|---|---|
| 8—At Cinn. | L | 5-8 | Borbon | Zahn |
| 9—At Hous. | W | 4-3* | Zamora | Granger |
| 10—At Hous. | L | 3-4 | Konieczny | Watt |
| 12—At Atl. | L | 4-5 | House | Frailing |
| 12—At Atl. | L | 2-6z | Morton | Zahn |
| 13—Cinn. | L | 11-18 | Borbon | Zamora |
| 14—Cinn. | L | 3-11a | Kirby | Stone |
| 15—Cinn. | W | 4-3 | Bonham | Darcy |
| 16—Phila. | W | 9-7 | Zahn | Garber |
| 17—Phila. | W | 9-5 | Dettore | Lonborg |
| 18—Phila. | L | 7-9 | Garber | Locker |
| 19—Phila. | L | 3-6§ | McGraw | Knowles |
| 20—At St. L. | L | 3-8 | Forsch | Zahn |
| 21—At St. L. | W | 6-1 | R. Reuschel | Gibson |
| 22—At St. L. | L | 2-7 | McGlothen | Stone |
| 23—At Mon. | W | 6-0 | Burris | Scherman |
| 24—At Mon. | W | 13-6 | Bonham | Warthen |
| 25—At Mon. | L | 6-12 | Blair | R. Reuschel |
| 26—At Pitts. | L | 2-5 | Candelaria | Frailing |
| 27—At Pitts. | L | 1-5 | Ellis | Zahn |
| 27—At Pitts. | L | 3-5 | Hernandez | Knowles |
| 28—At Pitts. | W | 1-0 | Bonham | Rooker |
| 29—At Pitts. | L | 3-4 | Giusti | R. Reuschel |
| 29—At Pitts. | L | 0-7 | Reuss | Dettore |
| 30—At N. Y. | L | 1-5 | G. Stone | S. Stone |
| | | | Won 11, Lost 21 | |

| JULY | | | | |
|---|---|---|---|---|
| 1—At N. Y. | W | 5-4* | Dettore | Baldwin |
| 2—At N. Y. | L | 2-7 | Matlack | Bonham |
| 3—At N. Y. | L | 0-4 | Koosman | R. Reuschel |
| 4—Pitts. | W | 6-1 | Stone | Kison |
| 4—Pitts. | W | 2-1† | Knowles | Reuss |
| 5—Pitts. | L | 4-5 | Rooker | Burris |
| 6—Pitts. | L | 12-18 | Hernandez | Frailing |
| 7—Pitts. | L | 0-5 | Brett | R. Reuschel |
| 8—S. Diego | W | 6-8x | McIntosh | Dettore |
| 9—S. Diego | L | 2-3 | Strom | Zahn |
| 10—S. Diego | W | 3-1 | Burris | Freisleben |
| 11—S. Fran. | W | 8-6 | Dettore | Moffitt |
| 12—S. Fran. | W | 6-4 | Stone | Caldwell |
| 13—S. Fran. | L | 1-4 | Montefusco | Zahn |
| 17—At S. D. | W | 6-5 | R. Reuschel | Strom |
| 18—At S. D. | L | 2-4 | Greif | Wilcox |
| 19—At S. D. | L | 1-2 | Freisleben | Stone |
| 20—At L. A. | L | 3-5‡ | Marshall | Dettore |
| 21—At L. A. | L | 1-0 | R. Reuschel | Messersmith |
| 22—At S. F. | L | 5-9 | Williams | Burris |
| 23—At S. F. | L | 2-10 | Montefusco | Stone |
| 24—At S. F. | W | 4-3 | Bonham | Halicki |
| 25—N. York | L | 3-6 | Tate | R. Reuschel |
| 26—N. York | W | 8-9* | Hall | Knowles |
| 27—N. York | W | 4-2 | Stone | Koosman |
| 27—N. York | W | 1-4* | Webb | P. Reuschel |
| 28—Montreal | W | 4-2 | Bonham | Blair |
| 29—Montreal | W | 4-3 | Knowles | Murray |
| 30—Montreal | L | 1-6 | Rogers | Burris |
| 31—St. Louis | W | 5-3 | P. Reuschel | Reynolds |
| | | | Won 13, Lost 17 | |

| AUGUST | | | Winner | Loser |
|---|---|---|---|---|
| 1—St. Louis | L | 4-9 | Denny | Bonham |
| 2—St. Louis | L | 0-4 | Forsch | R. Reuschel |
| 3—St. Louis | W | 6-3 | Dettore | Hrabosky |
| 3—St. Louis | L | 4-7 | Reed | Burris |
| 4—At Phila. | W | 3-2 | Stone | Hilgendorf |
| 5—At Phila. | L | 5-13 | Ruthven | Bonham |
| 7—At Phila. | W | 5-3 | R. Reuschel | Christenson |
| 8—At Atl. | L | 0-1 | Morton | Dettore |
| 8—At Atl. | W | 3-1 | Burris | Dal Canton |
| 9—At Atl. | W | 8-2 | Stone | Niekro |
| 10—At Atl. | W | 9-1 | Bonham | Odom |
| 11—At Cinn. | L | 3-9 | Billingham | R. Reuschel |
| 12—At Cinn. | L | 8-12 | Eastwick | Knowles |
| 14—At Hous. | W | 5-3 | Stone | Richard |
| 15—At Hous. | L | 1-4 | Dierker | Bonham |
| 16—At Hous. | W | 3-2 | R. Reuschel | Roberts |
| 17—At Hous. | W | 11-7 | Burris | Crawford |
| 18—Los Ang. | L | 1-3 | Hooton | Stone |
| 19—Los Ang. | L | 1-2 | Marshall | Bonham |
| 21—Los Ang. | W | 7-0 | R. Reuschel | Messersmith |
| 22—Houston | W | 6-5† | Knowles | Crawford |
| 23—Houston | L | 12-14 | York | Bonham |
| 24—Houston | L | 4-8 | Dierker | Burris |
| 25—Cinn. | L | 4-11 | Norman | R. Reuschel |
| 26—Cinn. | L | 5-6 | Eastwick | Stone |
| 27—Cinn. | L | 5-6 | Borbon | Bonham |
| 29—Atlanta | W | 8-3 | Burris | Morton |
| 31—Atlanta | L | 1-3 | Niekro | R. Reuschel |
| 31—Atlanta | W | 9-8* | Dettore | Sadecki |
| | | | Won 13, Lost 16 | |

| SEPTEMBER | | | | |
|---|---|---|---|---|
| 1—At St. L. | L | 3-6 | Forsch | Bonham |
| 2—At St. L. | W | 5-3 | Burris | McGlothen |
| 3—At St. L. | W | 11-6 | Schultz | Gibson |
| 5—At Phila. | W | 4-3 | Bonham | Carlton |
| 5—At Phila. | L | 3-6 | McGraw | P. Reuschel |
| 6—At Phila. | W | 7-6 | Stone | Garber |
| 7—At Phila. | W | 6-4 | Burris | Twitchell |
| 8—At Pitts. | L | 1-4 | Ellis | Prall |
| 9—At Pitts. | W | 6-5 | Bonham | Demery |
| 10—St. Louis | W | 7-5 | Schultz | Rasmussen |
| 11—St. Louis | W | 12-6 | Zamora | Forsch |
| 13—Phila. | W | 4-1 | Burris | Underwood |
| 14—Phila. | L | 7-13 | Carlton | Stone |
| 15—Pitts. | W | 6-5 | Knowles | Giusti |
| 15—Pitts. | L | 1-9 | Rooker | Prall |
| 16—Pitts. | L | 0-22 | Candelaria | R. Reuschel |
| 17—At N. Y. | W | 5-2 | Burris | Swan |
| 18—At N. Y. | L | 5-7 | Sanders | Knowles |
| 19—At Mon. | L | 6-9 | Murray | Bonham |
| 20—At Mon. | L | 1-3 | Carrithers | R. Reuschel |
| 21—At Mon. | L | 4-5 | Murray | P. Reuschel |
| 23—N. York | L | 6-8 | Apodaca | Knowles |
| 24—N. York | W | 1-0† | Crosby | Lockwood |
| 26—Montreal | L | 2-3‡ | Murray | Knowles |
| 27—Montreal | L | 3-5† | Fryman | Bonham |
| 28—Montreal | W | 9-6 | R. Reuschel | DeMola |
| | | | Won 13, Lost 13 | |

* 10 innings.  † 11 innings.  ‡ 12 innings.  § 14 innings.  x 15 innings.  y Suspended game, completed May 31.  z Suspended game, completed August 9.  a Suspended game, completed June 15.

# Phase Two Expos Have Phase One Results

## By BOB DUNN

The Expos called it Phase Two. Their critics called it Fizz Two. But they agree that whatever it was, it was necessary.

After six years in the National League, the Expos found themselves going nowhere. After seven years and one housecleaning, they still found

MONTREAL EXPOS—1975

Front row—Rock, traveling secretary; Mackanin, Scanlon, Foli, Zimmerman, coach; Bristol, coach; Mauch, manager; McLish, coach; Snider, coach; Hriniak, coach; Plamondon, ball boy. Second row—Colbert, Bailey, Parrish, Carter, Biittner, White, Cox, Frias, Dwyer, Breeden, Stone, equipment manager. Third row—Blair, Rogers, Carrithers, Jorgensen, Fryman, Scherman, Scott, Mangual, Morales, Belanger, trainer. Fourth row—Warthen, McAnally, Renko, DeMola, Taylor, Lang, Murray, Roenicke, Valentine, Johnson. Missing—Foote, Lyttle.

themselves going nowhere. The difference was the promise.

The '75 Expos, as things turned out, weren't that much worse than their predecessors. They won 75 games, justifying the slogan manager Gene Mauch didn't make for a change—75 in '75. It was only four wins off their all-time high.

They finished in a dead heat for fifth, or sixth, with the Chicago Cubs and, realistically, nobody should have expected much better at spring training. Nor should anybody have expected much better out of the young kids, the children of Phase Two. Primarily, Gary Carter and Larry Parrish and Pete Mackanin.

Carter hit .270, led the team in runs batted in with 68 and slammed 17 home runs, one off the club record for rookies. He played a strange position, right field, for much of the year and didn't get to catch regularly until Barry Foote hurt his knee in September.

Parrish was perhaps the year's biggest surprise, at least offensively. He hit, after never having played a game of Triple A ball, .274, with 10 homers and 65 RBIs in a performance that was tarnished only by his club-record 35 errors.

Mackanin won the second-base job from Larry Lintz before mid-season, and Lintz was traded. A late-season slump dragged Mackanin's average down to .225, but he did hit a dozen homers and drove in 44 runs, fair figures for a middle infielder.

A couple of surprises were in store for the Phase Two Expos as well. Dan Warthen, a chunky lefthander who fits the youth movement mold, was promoted from Memphis in June, was a regular starter by July and finished the season 8-6 and with the club's best earned-run average, 3.11. Outfielder Larry Biittner, who doesn't fit the Phase Two philosophy because he's 30, slow and just adequate defensively, hit .315 to lead all Expos' hitters. Biittner played predominantly against righthanded pitchers.

Righthanded relief specialist Dale Murray, who battled early-season ineffectiveness and then infectious hepatitis that cost him six weeks, finished strongly and became the first Expos' reliever to win 15 games. He was 15-8 with nine saves and, generally, lived up to the potential he'd shown in late 1974, when he had 10 saves and one win in the final six weeks.

Those were the brightest spots. Behind that came the outstanding hitting of pinch-hitter Jose Morales (.294 and 15 pinch hits), the consistency of outfielder Jim Dwyer's bat (.286) after he was acquired from St. Louis for Lintz, the late-season flurry that carried Mike Jorgensen to a career-high 18 homers, the way rookie Jerry White played center field in September and the pitching of Don Carrithers, briefly, and Woodie Fryman, over the whole season.

The silver clouds, however, had their dark linings.

Catcher Barry Foote, the team's outstanding rookie in 1974, hit only .194 and was over .200 only once all year. While Foote didn't suffer defensively, his season came to a merciful conclusion in September when he tore a knee cartilage.

Southpaw Dave McNally, the principal return in the trade that cost the Expos .300 hitter Ken Singleton and 20-game winner (at Baltimore) Mike Torrez, struggled through two months of the season without a contract and went home. Rather than fault the contractual problems, McNally faulted 3-6, which was his record, the six losses coming in succession and leading to his retirement.

Outfielder Rich Coggins, the secondary figure in the Baltimore trade, left spring training with a thyroid condition and spent weeks in the hospital. But Coggins was unimpressive, before and after his sickness, and was ultimately unloaded to the New York Yankees.

Righthander Dennis Blair, another sophomore, went from 11-7 in '74 to 8-15 in '75 and was only a spot starter through the final two months.

Bob Bailey fell from a 20-homer season to just five, the lowest home run total of his career, before being traded to Cincinnati for pitcher Clay Kirby. Tim Foli hit only .238. Righthander Steve Rogers finished with an 11-12 record.

The Expos committed far too many errors, 181, three short of their club record, and the running speed supposedly evident in spring training was gone with the trade of Lintz and Pepe Mangual's subsequent removal from the starting lineup.

Playing 40-39 baseball after the All-Star break and 10-2 in the final two weeks, the Expos plunged below the 1 million mark (908,292) in attendance for the first time in seven seasons.

Manager Gene Mauch was fired and Karl Kuehl, who managed the Expos' top affiliate at Memphis in '74, was named to replace the man who had been Montreal's only manager through Phase One and Phase Two.

### SCORES OF MONTREAL EXPOS' 1975 GAMES

| APRIL | | | Winner | Loser |
|---|---|---|---|---|
| 7—At St. L. | W | 8-4 | McNally | Gibson |
| 9—At St. L. | L | 0-4 | Forsch | Rogers |
| 10—At St. L. | L | 2-1 | Denny | Murray |
| 11—At Chi. | L | 1-2 | Burris | Blair |
| 12—At Chi. | L | 3-6 | Zamora | Murray |
| 13—At Chi. | L | 0-7 | Stone | Rogers |
| 16—At Pitts. | W | 5-0 | Fryman | Ellis |
| 17—At Pitts. | W | 7-4 | McNally | Reuss |
| 18—Phila. | L | 3-6 | Underwood | Renko |
| 19—Phila. | L | 0-3 | Lonborg | Blair |
| 22—Pitts. | W | 4-3 | McNally | Ellis |
| 23—Pitts. | W | 5-0 | Fryman | Reuss |
| 25—N. York | L | 3-5 | Matlack | Rogers |
| 27—N. York | L | 6-7 | Parker | McNally |
| 29—At Phila. | L | 0-5 | Lonborg | Blair |
| 30—At Phila. | L | 1-2 | Carlton | Rogers |
| | | | Won 5, Lost 11 | |
| **MAY** | | | | |
| 2—At N. Y. | L | 0-3 | Koosman | McNally |
| 3—At N. Y. | W | 3-0 | Fryman | Webb |
| 5—Chicago | W | 3-2 | Blair | Burris |
| 6—Chicago | W | 9-4 | Rogers | R. Reuschel |
| 7—Chicago | L | 2-7 | Bonham | McNally |
| 9—Houston | W | 5-4 | DeMola | Roberts |
| 10—Houston | W | 8-7 | Murray | Crawford |
| 11—Houston | L | 0-6 | Dierker | Blair |
| 12—Atlanta | W | 11-1 | Rogers | Morton |
| 13—Atlanta | L | 4-9 | Reed | McNally |
| 14—Atlanta | W | 5-4 | Fryman | Harrison |
| 15—Atlanta | L | 4-5c | Niekro | Renko |
| 16—Cinn. | W | 4-2 | Blair | Billingham |
| 17—Cinn. | L | 3-5‡ | McEnaney | Montague |
| 18—Cinn. | L | 1-6 | Nolan | McNally |
| 20—At Atl. | L | 4-9 | Harrison | Fryman |

| MAY | | | Winner | Loser |
|---|---|---|---|---|
| 21—At Atl. | L | 3-6 | Niekro | Renko |
| 23—At Hous. | L | 2-4 | Roberts | Blair |
| 24—At Hous. | W | 2-1 | Rogers | Konieczny |
| 25—At Hous. | L | 7-8x | Niekro | DeMola |
| 26—At Cinn. | L | 3-4 | C. Carroll | Fryman |
| 26—At Cinn. | L | 4-5 | Gullett | Renko |
| 28—At Cinn. | L | 0-6 | Nolan | Blair |
| 31—S. Fran. | W | 3-2 | Warthen | Lavelle |
| | | | Won 10, Lost 14 | |
| **JUNE** | | | | |
| 1—S. Fran. | L | 5-13 | Caldwell | Warthen |
| 2—Los Ang. | W | 5-3 | Fryman | Rau |
| 3—Los Ang. | L | 5-6 | Sutton | Renko |
| 4—Los Ang. | L | 0-3 | Messersmith | Blair |
| 8—S. Diego | L | 2-5 | McIntosh | McNally |
| 8—S. Diego | W | 3-1 | Rogers | Freisleben |
| 9—At L. A. | L | 0-4 | Messersmith | Fryman |
| 10—At L. A. | W | 5-4 | Renko | Marshall |
| 11—At S. D. | L | 1-3 | Folkers | Blair |
| 12—At S. D. | W | 3-2a | DeMola | Frisella |
| 13—At S. F. | W | 4-2 | Warthen | Falcone |
| 14—At S. F. | W | 3-1 | Fryman | Montefusco |
| 15—At S. F. | W | 2-1 | Renko | Barr |
| 15—At S. F. | W | 5-2 | Blair | Caldwell |
| 17—N. York | W | 6-5 | Warthen | Matlack |
| 17—N. York | L | 2-5§ | Parker | Taylor |
| 18—N. York | W | 7-6‡ | Taylor | Apodaca |
| 19—N. York | W | 3-2y | Murray | Baldwin |
| 20—At Phila. | L | 4-7 | Underwood | Renko |
| 21—At Phila. | W | 5-1 | Blair | Lonborg |
| 22—At Phila. | W | 4-0 | Rogers | Schueler |
| 22—At Phila. | L | 3-4 | Garber | Taylor |
| 23—Chicago | L | 0-6 | Burris | Scherman |
| 24—Chicago | L | 6-13 | Bonham | Warthen |

| JUNE | | | Winner | Loser |
|---|---|---|---|---|
| 25—Chicago | W | 12-6 | Blair | R. Reuschel |
| 26—St. Louis | L | 3-4 | McGlothen | Fryman |
| 27—St. Louis | L | 4-6 | Gibson | Rogers |
| 27—St. Louis | W | 5-4 | Warthen | Reed |
| 28—St. Louis | L | 2-3‡ | Hrabosky | DeMola |
| 29—St. Louis | W | 7-3 | Renko | Curtis |
| 30—Pitts. | L | 3-5 | Demery | Blair |
| | | | Won 16, Lost 15 | |

| JULY | | | | |
|---|---|---|---|---|
| 1—Pitts. | L | 4-10 | Candelaria | Fryman |
| 3—Pitts. | L | 1-5 | Ellis | Rogers |
| 4—At St. L. | W | 5-1 | Renko | Denny |
| 5—At St. L. | W | 3-0 | Blair | Forsch |
| 5—At St. L. | L | 0-1 | Curtis | Fryman |
| 6—At St. L. | W | 4-3 | DeMola | McGlothen |
| 7—At Hous. | L | 1-5 | Dierker | Rogers |
| 8—At Hous. | L | 1-5 | Roberts | Renko |
| 9—At Hous. | L | 3-4‡ | Granger | DeMola |
| 11—At Atl. | L | 1-2† | House | Murray |
| 12—At Atl. | L | 4-9 | Morton | Scherman |
| 12—At Atl. | W | 7-3 | Fryman | Easterly |
| 13—At Atl. | L | 4-5z | Sadecki | DeMola |
| 17—Cinn. | W | 3-0 | Rogers | Billingham |
| 18—Cinn. | L | 3-10 | Nolan | Blair |
| 19—Cinn. | W | 4-2 | Murray | Borbon |
| 20—Atlanta | W | 6-5§ | Scherman | House |
| 21—Atlanta | L | 1-4 | Beard | Warthen |
| 22—Houston | W | 2-1§ | Murray | Sosa |
| 23—Houston | L | 1-2 | Richard | Blair |
| 24—Houston | L | 5-6 | Dierker | Renko |
| 25—At Pitts. | L | 1-6 | Reuss | DeMola |
| 26—At Pitts. | W | 5-2 | Rogers | Rooker |
| 27—At Pitts. | L | 1-4 | Brett | Scherman |
| 27—At Pitts. | L | 3-5 | Giusti | Warthen |
| 28—At Chi. | L | 2-4 | Bonham | Blair |
| 29—At Chi. | L | 3-4 | Knowles | Murray |
| 30—At Chi. | W | 6-1 | Rogers | Burris |
| 31—Phila. | W | 7-4 | Warthen | Schueler |
| | | | Won 11, Lost 18 | |

| AUGUST | | | | |
|---|---|---|---|---|
| 1—Phila. | L | 6-8‡ | Garber | Murray |
| 1—Phila. | W | 6-4 | Scherman | Hilgendorf |
| 2—Phila. | W | 4-3 | Murray | Underwood |
| 3—Phila. | L | 4-5‡ | McGraw | Murray |
| 4—At N. Y. | W | 4-3 | DeMola | Tate |
| 5—At N. Y. | W | 7-0 | Carrithers | Koosman |
| 5—At N. Y. | W | 7-0 | Blair | Hall |
| 6—At N. Y. | L | 6-9† | Webb | Renko |
| 7—At N. Y. | L | 0-7 | Seaver | Rogers |
| 8—At Cinn. | W | 8-7 | Fryman | Borbon |
| 9—At Cinn. | L | 1-9 | Nolan | Blair |
| 10—At Cinn. | L | 3-11 | Norman | Carrithers |

| AUGUST | | | Winner | Loser |
|---|---|---|---|---|
| 11—S. Fran. | L | 2-9 | Halicki | Rogers |
| 12—S. Fran. | L | 2-5§ | Caldwell | Murray |
| 13—S. Fran. | L | 3-4x | Williams | Fryman |
| 14—S. Fran. | L | 2-9 | Barr | Blair |
| 15—Los Ang. | W | 8-4 | Rogers | Sutton |
| 16—Los Ang. | W | 3-2‡ | Murray | Marshall |
| 17—Los Ang. | L | 3-5 | Rau | Renko |
| 18—S. Diego | W | 4-1 | Warthen | Tomlin |
| 18—S. Diego | L | 2-5 | Folkers | Fryman |
| 19—S. Diego | W | 5-0 | Rogers | McIntosh |
| 20—S. Diego | L | 6-8 | Johnson | Fryman |
| 22—At L. A. | W | 3-1x | Murray | Downing |
| 23—At L. A. | L | 1-3 | Hooton | Rogers |
| 23—At L. A. | W | 5-2 | Murray | Marshall |
| 24—At L. A. | W | 5-3z | Murray | Marshall |
| 26—At S. F. | L | 3-4 | Falcone | Warthen |
| 27—At S. F. | L | 1-9 | Montefusco | Fryman |
| 28—At S. D. | W | 10-8 | Scherman | Jones |
| 29—At S. D. | W | 4-0 | Carrithers | McIntosh |
| 30—At S. D. | W | 5-1 | Renko | Folkers |
| 31—At S. D. | L | 0-6 | Strom | Warthen |
| | | | Won 16, Lost 17 | |

| SEPTEMBER | | | | |
|---|---|---|---|---|
| 1—At Phila. | W | 6-5 | Murray | Garber |
| 2—At Phila. | W | 4-3 | Blair | Christenson |
| 3—At Phila. | W | 3-6 | Underwood | Carrithers |
| 5—Pitts. | W | 4-3‡ | Taylor | Tekulve |
| 5—Pitts. | L | 2-5 | Rooker | Renko |
| 6—Pitts. | L | 5-12§ | Brett | Murray |
| 7—Pitts. | L | 0-6 | Reuss | Blair |
| 8—N. York | W | 6-5 | Murray | Baldwin |
| 8—N. York | W | 6-1 | Carrithers | Stone |
| 9—N. York | W | 2-1‡ | Murray | Apodaca |
| 10—Phila. | L | 1-5 | Simpson | Renko |
| 11—Phila. | L | 0-5* | Christenson | Rogers |
| 12—At Pitts. | L | 3-6 | Moose | Carrithers |
| 13—At Pitts. | W | 5-2 | Warthen | Ellis |
| 14—At Pitts. | L | 3-4 | Hernandez | Fryman |
| 15—At N. Y. | L | 2-3 | Koosman | Rogers |
| 16—At N. Y. | L | 3-4b | Baldwin | DeMola |
| 17—At St. L. | W | 6-3 | Warthen | McGlothen |
| 18—At St. L. | W | 5-0 | Renko | Reed |
| 19—Chicago | W | 9-6 | Murray | Bonham |
| 20—Chicago | W | 3-1 | Carrithers | R. Reuschel |
| 21—Chicago | W | 5-4 | Murray | P. Reuschel |
| 22—St. Louis | L | 4-6x | Hrabosky | Fryman |
| 22—St. Louis | W | 8-5 | Scherman | Reed |
| 23—St. Louis | W | 7-0 | Rogers | Denny |
| 24—St. Louis | W | 6-2 | Carrithers | Rasmussen |
| 26—At Chi. | W | 3-2x | Murray | Knowles |
| 27—At Chi. | W | 5-3§ | Fryman | Bonham |
| 28—At Chi. | L | 6-9 | R. Reuschel | DeMola |
| | | | Won 17, Lost 12 | |

* 6½ innings.  † 8 innings.  ‡ 10 innings.  § 11 innings.  x 12 innings.  y 13 innings.  z 14 innings.  a 15 innings.  b 18 innings.  c Protested game, completed July 20.

**BILL MADLOCK**
• CUBS •
BATTING CHAMPION (.354)

**DAVE LOPES**
• DODGERS •
STOLEN BASES (77)

**MIKE SCHMIDT**
• PHILLIES •
HOMERS (38)

# 1975 NATIONAL LEAGUE LEADERS

**TOM SEAVER**
• METS •
WINS (22)
STRIKEOUTS (243)

**RANDY JONES**
• PADRES •
ERA (2.24)

**ANDY MESSERSMITH**
• DODGERS •
GAMES STARTED (40)
COMPLETE GAMES (19)
INNINGS (322)
SHUTOUTS (7)

# National League Averages for 1975

## CHAMPIONSHIP WINNERS IN PREVIOUS YEARS

| | | |
|---|---|---|
| 1876—Chicago ....................... .788 | 1909—Pittsburgh ................. .724 | 1942—St. Louis .................... .688 |
| 1877—Boston .......................... .646 | 1910—Chicago ..................... .675 | 1943—St. Louis .................... .682 |
| 1878—Boston .......................... .683 | 1911—New York .................. .647 | 1944—St. Louis .................... .682 |
| 1879—Providence ................. .705 | 1912—New York .................. .682 | 1945—Chicago ..................... .636 |
| 1880—Chicago ....................... .798 | 1913—New York .................. .664 | 1946—St. Louis* ................. .628 |
| 1881—Chicago ....................... .667 | 1914—Boston ....................... .614 | 1947—Brooklyn .................. .610 |
| 1882—Chicago ....................... .655 | 1915—Philadelphia ............ .592 | 1948—Boston ....................... .595 |
| 1883—Boston .......................... .643 | 1916—Brooklyn .................. .610 | 1949—Brooklyn .................. .630 |
| 1884—Providence ................. .750 | 1917—New York .................. .636 | 1950—Philadelphia ........... .591 |
| 1885—Chicago ....................... .777 | 1918—Chicago ..................... .651 | 1951—New York† ............... .624 |
| 1886—Chicago ....................... .726 | 1919—Cincinnati ............... .686 | 1952—Brooklyn .................. .627 |
| 1887—Detroit ........................ .637 | 1920—Brooklyn .................. .604 | 1953—Brooklyn .................. .682 |
| 1888—New York .................... .641 | 1921—New York .................. .614 | 1954—New York .................. .630 |
| 1889—New York .................... .659 | 1922—New York .................. .604 | 1955—Brooklyn .................. .641 |
| 1890—Brooklyn ..................... .667 | 1923—New York .................. .621 | 1956—Brooklyn .................. .604 |
| 1891—Boston .......................... .630 | 1924—New York .................. .608 | 1957—Milwaukee ............... .617 |
| 1892—Boston .......................... .680 | 1925—Pittsburgh ............... .621 | 1958—Milwaukee ............... .597 |
| 1893—Boston .......................... .662 | 1926—St. Louis .................. .578 | 1959—Los Angeles‡ ........... .564 |
| 1894—Baltimore ................... .695 | 1927—Pittsburgh ............... .610 | 1960—Pittsburgh ............... .617 |
| 1895—Baltimore ................... .669 | 1928—St. Louis .................. .617 | 1961—Cincinnati ............... .604 |
| 1896—Baltimore ................... .698 | 1929—Chicago ..................... .645 | 1962—San Francisco§ ....... .624 |
| 1897—Boston .......................... .705 | 1930—St. Louis .................. .597 | 1963—Los Angeles ............ .611 |
| 1898—Boston .......................... .685 | 1931—St. Louis .................. .656 | 1964—St. Louis .................. .574 |
| 1899—Brooklyn ..................... .677 | 1932—Chicago ..................... .584 | 1965—Los Angeles ............ .599 |
| 1900—Brooklyn ..................... .603 | 1933—New York .................. .599 | 1966—Los Angeles ............ .586 |
| 1901—Pittsburgh ................. .647 | 1934—St. Louis .................. .621 | 1967—St. Louis .................. .627 |
| 1902—Pittsburgh ................. .741 | 1935—Chicago ..................... .649 | 1968—St. Louis .................. .599 |
| 1903—Pittsburgh ................. .650 | 1936—New York .................. .597 | 1969—New York (East)a..... .617 |
| 1904—New York .................... .693 | 1937—New York .................. .625 | 1970—Cincinnati (West)b .... .630 |
| 1905—New York .................... .686 | 1938—Chicago ..................... .586 | 1971—Pittsburgh (East)c .... .599 |
| 1906—Chicago ....................... .763 | 1939—Cincinnati ............... .630 | 1972—Cincinnati (West)b .... .617 |
| 1907—Chicago ....................... .704 | 1940—Cincinnati ............... .654 | 1973—New York (East)d .... .509 |
| 1908—Chicago ....................... .643 | 1941—Brooklyn .................. .649 | 1974—Los Angeles (West)b .. .630 |

*Defeated Brooklyn, two games to none, in playoff for pennant. †Defeated Brooklyn, two games to one, in play-off for pennant. ‡Defeated Milwaukee, two games to none, in playoff for pennant. §Defeated Los Angeles, two games to one, in playoff for pennant. aDefeated Atlanta (West) in Championship Series. bDefeated Pittsburgh (East) in Championship Series. cDefeated San Francisco (West) in Championship Series. dDefeated Cincinnati (West) in Championship Series

## STANDING OF CLUBS AT CLOSE OF SEASON

### EAST DIVISION

| Club | Pitt. | Phil. | N.Y. | St.L. | Chi. | Mon. | Atl. | Cin. | Hou. | L.A. | S.D. | S.F. | W. | L. | Pct. | G.B. |
|---|---|---|---|---|---|---|---|---|---|---|---|---|---|---|---|---|
| Pittsburgh | .. | 7 | 13 | 10 | 12 | 11 | 8 | 6 | 5 | 7 | 8 | 5 | 92 | 69 | .571 | ...... |
| Philadelphia | 11 | .. | 11 | 10 | 6 | 11 | 7 | 5 | 6 | 5 | 7 | 6 | 86 | 76 | .531 | 6½ |
| New York | 5 | 7 | .. | 9 | 11 | 8 | 8 | 4 | 8 | 6 | 8 | 8 | 82 | 80 | .506 | 10½ |
| St. Louis | 8 | 8 | 9 | .. | 7 | 7 | 9 | 4 | 8 | 7 | 8 | 7 | 82 | 80 | .506 | 10½ |
| Chicago | 6 | 12 | 7 | 11 | .. | 9 | 7 | 1 | 7 | 5 | 5 | 5 | 75 | 87 | .463 | 17½ |
| Montreal | 7 | 7 | 10 | 11 | 9 | .. | 4 | 4 | 4 | 7 | 7 | 5 | 75 | 87 | .463 | 17½ |

### WEST DIVISION

| Club | Cin. | L.A. | S.F. | S.D. | Atl. | Hou. | Chi. | Mon. | N.Y. | Phil. | Pitt. | St.L. | W. | L. | Pct. | G.B. |
|---|---|---|---|---|---|---|---|---|---|---|---|---|---|---|---|---|
| Cincinnati | .. | 8 | 13 | 11 | 15 | 13 | 11 | 8 | 8 | 7 | 6 | 8 | 108 | 54 | .667 | ...... |
| Los Angeles | 10 | .. | 10 | 11 | 10 | 12 | 7 | 5 | 6 | 7 | 5 | 5 | 88 | 74 | .543 | 20 |
| San Francisco | 5 | 8 | .. | 10 | 9 | 13 | 7 | 7 | 4 | 5 | 7 | 5 | 80 | 81 | .497 | 27½ |
| San Diego | 7 | 7 | 8 | .. | 11 | 9 | 7 | 5 | 4 | 5 | 4 | 4 | 71 | 91 | .438 | 37 |
| Atlanta | 3 | 8 | 8 | 7 | .. | 12 | 5 | 8 | 4 | 5 | 4 | 3 | 67 | 94 | .416 | 40½ |
| Houston | 6 | 6 | 5 | 9 | 6 | .. | 5 | 8 | 4 | 6 | 6 | 4 | 64 | 97 | .398 | 43½ |

CANCELED GAMES—San Francisco at Atlanta; Houston at Pittsburgh.

TIE GAME—Houston at St. Louis, August 25, ten innings (3-3).

CHAMPIONSHIP SERIES—Cincinnati defeated Pittsburgh, three games to none.

## RECORD AT HOME

### EAST DIVISION

| Club | Pitt. | Phil. | St.L. | Chi. | N.Y. | Mon. | Cin. | L.A. | S.F. | S.D. | Atl. | Hou. | W. | L. | Pct. |
|---|---|---|---|---|---|---|---|---|---|---|---|---|---|---|---|
| Pittsburgh | ..... | 6-3 | 6-3 | 6-3 | 5-4 | 5-4 | 4-2 | 3-3 | 4-2 | 5-1 | 4-2 | 4-1 | 52 | 28 | .650 |
| Philadelphia | 8-1 | ..... | 5-4 | 2-7 | 6-3 | 5-4 | 5-1 | 2-4 | 4-2 | 5-1 | 5-1 | 4-2 | 51 | 30 | .630 |
| St. Louis | 5-4 | 4-5 | ..... | 4-5 | 5-4 | 3-6 | 3-3 | 3-3 | 5-1 | 5-1 | 5-1 | 3-3 | 45 | 36 | .556 |
| Chicago | 5-4 | 6-3 | 6-3 | ..... | 4-5 | 6-3 | 1-5 | 3-3 | 4-2 | 3-3 | 4-2 | 3-3 | 42 | 39 | .519 |
| New York | 1-8 | 4-5 | 5-4 | 6-3 | ..... | 5-4 | 3-3 | 2-4 | 5-1 | 3-3 | 3-3 | 5-1 | 42 | 39 | .519 |
| Montreal | 3-6 | 3-6 | 5-4 | 6-3 | 6-3 | ..... | 3-3 | 3-3 | 1-5 | 3-3 | 3-3 | 3-3 | 39 | 42 | .481 |

### WEST DIVISION

| Club | Cin. | L.A. | S.F. | S.D. | Atl. | Hou. | Pitt. | Phil. | St.L. | Chi. | N.Y. | Mon. | W. | L. | Pct. |
|---|---|---|---|---|---|---|---|---|---|---|---|---|---|---|---|
| Cincinnati | ..... | 6-3 | 7-2 | 6-3 | 7-2 | 7-2 | 4-2 | 6-0 | 5-1 | 6-0 | 5-1 | 5-1 | 64 | 17 | .790 |
| Los Angeles | 7-2 | ..... | 6-3 | 6-3 | 7-2 | 8-1 | 2-4 | 2-4 | 2-4 | 4-2 | 2-4 | 4-2 | 49 | 32 | .605 |
| San Francisco | 3-6 | 5-4 | ..... | 6-3 | 5-4 | 5-4 | 5-1 | 3-3 | 4-2 | 5-1 | 3-3 | 2-4 | 46 | 35 | .568 |
| San Diego | 4-5 | 4-5 | 5-4 | ..... | 4-5 | 5-4 | 3-3 | 4-2 | 3-3 | 4-2 | 1-5 | 2-4 | 38 | 43 | .469 |
| Atlanta | 1-8 | 6-3 | 4-4 | 2-7 | ..... | 7-2 | 2-4 | 4-2 | 2-4 | 3-3 | 1-5 | 5-1 | 37 | 43 | .463 |
| Houston | 3-6 | 5-4 | 1-8 | 4-5 | 4-5 | ..... | 5-1 | 4-2 | 1-5 | 2-4 | 3-3 | 5-1 | 37 | 44 | .457 |

## RECORD ABROAD

### EAST DIVISION

| Club | N.Y. | Pitt. | St.L. | Mon. | Phil. | Chi. | Cin. | L.A. | S.F. | S.D. | Atl. | Hou. | W. | L. | Pct. |
|---|---|---|---|---|---|---|---|---|---|---|---|---|---|---|---|
| New York | ..... | 4-5 | 4-5 | 3-6 | 3-6 | 5-4 | 1-5 | 4-2 | 3-3 | 5-1 | 5-1 | 3-3 | 40 | 41 | .494 |
| Pittsburgh | 8-1 | ..... | 4-5 | 3-6 | 1-8 | 6-3 | 2-4 | 4-2 | 1-5 | 3-3 | 4-2 | 1-5 | 40 | 41 | .494 |
| St. Louis | 4-5 | 3-6 | ..... | 4-5 | 3-6 | 3-6 | 1-5 | 4-2 | 2-4 | 3-3 | 4-2 | 5-1 | 37 | 44 | .457 |
| Montreal | 4-5 | 4-5 | 6-3 | ..... | 4-5 | 3-6 | 1-5 | 4-2 | 4-2 | 4-2 | 1-5 | 1-5 | 36 | 45 | .444 |
| Philadelphia | 5-4 | 3-6 | 5-4 | 6-3 | ..... | 4-5 | 0-6 | 3-3 | 3-3 | 2-4 | 2-4 | 2-4 | 35 | 46 | .432 |
| Chicago | 3-6 | 3-6 | 5-4 | 3-6 | 7-2 | ..... | 0-6 | 2-4 | 1-5 | 2-4 | 3-3 | 4-2 | 33 | 48 | .407 |

### WEST DIVISION

| Club | Cin. | L.A. | S.F. | S.D. | Atl. | Hou. | N.Y. | Pitt. | St.L. | Mon. | Phil. | Chi. | W. | L. | Pct. |
|---|---|---|---|---|---|---|---|---|---|---|---|---|---|---|---|
| Cincinnati | ..... | 2-7 | 6-3 | 5-4 | 8-1 | 6-3 | 3-3 | 2-4 | 3-3 | 3-3 | 1-5 | 5-1 | 44 | 37 | .543 |
| Los Angeles | 3-6 | ..... | 4-5 | 5-4 | 3-6 | 4-5 | 4-2 | 3-3 | 3-3 | 4-2 | 3-3 | 3-3 | 39 | 42 | .481 |
| San Francisco | 2-7 | 3-6 | ..... | 4-5 | 4-4 | 8-1 | 1-5 | 2-4 | 1-5 | 5-1 | 2-4 | 2-4 | 34 | 46 | .425 |
| San Diego | 3-6 | 3-6 | 3-6 | ..... | 7-2 | 5-4 | 3-3 | 1-5 | 1-5 | 3-3 | 1-5 | 3-3 | 33 | 48 | .407 |
| Atlanta | 2-7 | 2-7 | 4-5 | 5-4 | ..... | 5-4 | 3-3 | 2-4 | 1-5 | 3-3 | 1-5 | 2-4 | 30 | 51 | .370 |
| Houston | 2-7 | 1-8 | 4-5 | 5-4 | 2-7 | ..... | 1-5 | 1-4 | 3-3 | 3-3 | 2-4 | 3-3 | 27 | 53 | .338 |

## SHUTOUT GAMES

| Club | L.A. | Phil. | Cinn. | N.Y. | Chi. | Pitt. | St.L. | S.F. | S.D. | Mon. | Hou. | Atl. | W. | L. | Pct. |
|---|---|---|---|---|---|---|---|---|---|---|---|---|---|---|---|
| Los Angeles | .. | 1 | 0 | 2 | 1 | 2 | 1 | 1 | 2 | 2 | 3 | 3 | 18 | 7 | .720 |
| Philadelphia | 1 | .. | 2 | 0 | 0 | 0 | 1 | 1 | 1 | 3 | 1 | 1 | 11 | 6 | .647 |
| Cincinnati | 1 | 0 | .. | 0 | 0 | 0 | 2 | 0 | 1 | 1 | 0 | 3 | 8 | 5 | .615 |
| New York | 1 | 0 | 0 | .. | 1 | 3 | 0 | 2 | 3 | 2 | 2 | 0 | 14 | 12 | .538 |
| Chicago | 2 | 0 | 0 | 1 | .. | 1 | 0 | 0 | 0 | 3 | 0 | 1 | 8 | 7 | .533 |
| Pittsburgh | 0 | 1 | 0 | 1 | 3 | .. | 3 | 1 | 2 | 1 | 1 | 1 | 14 | 13 | .519 |
| St. Louis | 0 | 0 | 1 | 2 | 1 | 2 | .. | 2 | 1 | 2 | 1 | 1 | 13 | 14 | .481 |
| San Francisco | 2 | 1 | 0 | 1 | 0 | 0 | 1 | .. | 2 | 0 | 1 | 1 | 9 | 10 | .474 |
| San Diego | 0 | 0 | 1 | 1 | 0 | 2 | 2 | 1 | .. | 1 | 3 | 1 | 12 | 14 | .462 |
| Montreal | 0 | 1 | 1 | 3 | 0 | 2 | 3 | 0 | 2 | .. | 0 | 0 | 12 | 16 | .429 |
| Houston | 0 | 2 | 0 | 1 | 0 | 1 | 1 | 0 | 0 | 1 | .. | 0 | 6 | 13 | .316 |
| Atlanta | 0 | 0 | 0 | 0 | 1 | 0 | 0 | 0 | 2 | 0 | 1 | .. | 4 | 12 | .250 |

# OFFICIAL NATIONAL LEAGUE BATTING AVERAGES

Compiled by Elias Sports Bureau, New York, N. Y.

## CLUB BATTING

| Club | Pct. | G. | AB. | R. | OR. | H. | TB. | 2B. | 3B. | HR. | RBI. | SH. | SF. | SB. | CS. | LOB. |
|------|------|----|-----|-----|-----|-----|-----|-----|-----|-----|------|-----|-----|-----|-----|------|
| St. Louis | .273 | 163 | 5597 | 662 | 689 | 1527 | 2101 | 239 | 46 | 81 | 619 | 92 | 45 | 116 | 49 | 1183 |
| Cinci. | .271 | 162 | 5581 | 840 | 586 | 1515 | 2239 | 278 | 37 | 124 | 779 | 66 | 45 | 168 | 36 | 1271 |
| Phila. | .269 | 162 | 5592 | 735 | 694 | 1506 | 2248 | 283 | 42 | 125 | 687 | 88 | 42 | 126 | 57 | 1272 |
| Pitts. | .263 | 162 | 5489 | 712 | 565 | 1444 | 2207 | 255 | 47 | 138 | 669 | 76 | 40 | 49 | 28 | 1120 |
| Chicago | .259 | 162 | 5470 | 712 | 671 | 1419 | 2015 | 229 | 41 | 95 | 645 | 107 | 66 | 67 | 55 | 1262 |
| S. Fran. | .259 | 161 | 5447 | 659 | 671 | 1412 | 1989 | 235 | 45 | 84 | 606 | 62 | 51 | 99 | 47 | 1233 |
| N. York | .256 | 162 | 5587 | 646 | 625 | 1430 | 2018 | 217 | 34 | 101 | 604 | 75 | 37 | 32 | 26 | 1200 |
| Houston | .254 | 162 | 5515 | 664 | 711 | 1401 | 1979 | 218 | 54 | 84 | 606 | 97 | 44 | 133 | 62 | 1142 |
| Los Ang. | .248 | 162 | 5453 | 648 | 534 | 1355 | 1988 | 217 | 31 | 118 | 606 | 104 | 47 | 138 | 52 | 1208 |
| Montreal | .244 | 162 | 5518 | 601 | 690 | 1346 | 1918 | 216 | 31 | 98 | 542 | 110 | 38 | 108 | 58 | 1221 |
| Atlanta | .244 | 161 | 5424 | 583 | 739 | 1323 | 1879 | 179 | 28 | 107 | 541 | 72 | 35 | 55 | 38 | 1170 |
| S. Diego | .244 | 162 | 5429 | 552 | 683 | 1324 | 1817 | 215 | 22 | 78 | 505 | 133 | 46 | 85 | 50 | 1186 |
| Totals | .257 | | 66102 | 8014 | 8014 | 17002 | 24398 | 2781 | 458 | 1233 | 7409 | 1082 | 536 | 1176 | 558 | 14468 |

## INDIVIDUAL BATTING

(Top Fifteen Qualifiers for Batting Championship—502 or More Plate Appearances)

°Bats lefthanded.  †Switch-hitter.

| Player and Club | Pct. | G. | AB. | R. | H. | TB. | 2B. | 3B. | HR. | RBI. | SH. | SF. | SB. | CS. |
|-----------------|------|----|-----|-----|----|-----|-----|-----|-----|------|-----|-----|-----|-----|
| Madlock, Bill, Chicago | .354 | 130 | 514 | 77 | 182 | 246 | 29 | 7 | 7 | 64 | 1 | 5 | 9 | 7 |
| Simmons, Ted, St. Louis† | .332 | 157 | 581 | 80 | 193 | 285 | 32 | 3 | 18 | 100 | 0 | 4 | 1 | 3 |
| Sanguillen, Manuel, Pittsburgh | .328 | 133 | 481 | 60 | 158 | 217 | 24 | 4 | 9 | 58 | 2 | 3 | 5 | 4 |
| Morgan, Joe, Cincinnati° | .327 | 146 | 498 | 107 | 163 | 253 | 27 | 6 | 17 | 94 | 0 | 6 | 67 | 10 |
| Watson, Robert, Houston | .324 | 132 | 485 | 67 | 157 | 240 | 27 | 1 | 18 | 85 | 0 | 5 | 3 | 5 |
| Garvey, Steven, Los Angeles | .319 | 160 | 659 | 85 | 210 | 314 | 38 | 6 | 18 | 95 | 3 | 6 | 11 | 2 |
| Joshua, Von, San Francisco° | .318 | 129 | 507 | 75 | 161 | 227 | 25 | 10 | 7 | 43 | 4 | 1 | 20 | 10 |
| Rose, Peter, Cincinnati† | .317 | 162 | 662 | 112 | 210 | 286 | 47 | 4 | 7 | 74 | 1 | 0 | 0 | 1 |
| Cardenal, Jose, Chicago | .317 | 154 | 574 | 85 | 182 | 243 | 30 | 2 | 9 | 68 | 4 | 7 | 34 | 12 |
| Brock, Louis, St. Louis° | .309 | 136 | 528 | 78 | 163 | 211 | 27 | 6 | 3 | 47 | 3 | 0 | 56 | 16 |
| Parker, David, Pittsburgh° | .308 | 148 | 558 | 75 | 172 | 302 | 35 | 10 | 25 | 101 | 0 | 1 | 8 | 6 |
| Bowa, Lawrence, Philadelphia† | .305 | 162 | 699 | 111 | 213 | 271 | 40 | 3 | 4 | 57 | 0 | 7 | 13 | 6 |
| Cash, David, Philadelphia | .305 | 162 | 699 | 111 | 213 | 271 | 40 | 3 | 4 | 57 | 0 | 7 | 13 | 6 |
| Griffey, G. Kenneth, Cincinnati° | .305 | 132 | 463 | 95 | 141 | 186 | 15 | 9 | 4 | 46 | 6 | 3 | 16 | 7 |
| Montanez, Guillermo, Phil-SF° | .302 | 156 | 602 | 61 | 182 | 250 | 34 | 2 | 10 | 101 | 2 | 10 | 6 | 6 |

DEPARTMENTAL LEADERS: G—Cash, Millan, Rose, 162; AB—Cash, 699; R—Rose, 112; H—Cash, 213; TB—Luzinski, 322; 2B—Rose, 47; 3B—Garr, 11; HR—Schmidt, 38; RBI—Luzinski, 120; SH—E. Hernandez, 24; SF—Murcer, 12; SB—Lopes, 77; CS—Cedeno, 17.

### (All Players—Listed Alphabetically)

| Player and Club | Pct. | G. | AB. | R. | H. | TB. | 2B. | 3B. | HR. | RBI. | SH. | SF. | SB. | CS. |
|-----------------|------|----|-----|-----|----|-----|-----|-----|-----|------|-----|-----|-----|-----|
| Acosta, Cecilio, Philadelphia | .000 | 6 | 0 | 0 | 0 | 0 | 0 | 0 | 0 | 0 | 0 | 0 | 0 | 0 |
| Adams, Glenn, San Francisco° | .300 | 61 | 90 | 10 | 27 | 43 | 2 | 1 | 4 | 15 | 0 | 1 | 1 | 0 |
| Alexander, Gary, San Francisco | .000 | 3 | 3 | 1 | 0 | 0 | 0 | 0 | 0 | 0 | 0 | 0 | 0 | 0 |
| Allen, Richard, Philadelphia | .233 | 119 | 416 | 54 | 97 | 160 | 21 | 3 | 12 | 62 | 1 | 4 | 11 | 2 |
| Almon, William, San Diego | .400 | 6 | 10 | 0 | 4 | 4 | 0 | 0 | 0 | 0 | 0 | 0 | 0 | 0 |
| Alou, Jesus, New York | .265 | 62 | 102 | 8 | 27 | 30 | 3 | 0 | 0 | 11 | 1 | 0 | 0 | 1 |
| Alvarez, J. Orlando, Los Angeles | .000 | 4 | 4 | 0 | 0 | 0 | 0 | 0 | 0 | 0 | 0 | 0 | 0 | 0 |
| Anderson, Michael A., Phila. | .259 | 115 | 247 | 24 | 64 | 92 | 10 | 3 | 4 | 28 | 1 | 4 | 1 | 2 |
| Andrews, Robert, Houston | .238 | 103 | 277 | 29 | 66 | 79 | 5 | 4 | 0 | 19 | 8 | 5 | 12 | 5 |
| Apodaca, Robert, New York | .364 | 46 | 11 | 2 | 4 | 4 | 0 | 0 | 0 | 0 | 4 | 0 | 0 | 0 |
| Armbrister, Edison, Cincinnati | .185 | 59 | 65 | 9 | 12 | 13 | 1 | 0 | 0 | 2 | 1 | 0 | 3 | 1 |
| Arnold, Christopher, San Fran | .195 | 29 | 41 | 4 | 8 | 8 | 0 | 0 | 0 | 0 | 0 | 0 | 0 | 0 |
| Auerbach, Frederick, Los Angeles | .224 | 85 | 170 | 18 | 38 | 47 | 9 | 0 | 0 | 12 | 0 | 0 | 3 | 2 |
| Bailey, Robert, Montreal | .273 | 106 | 227 | 23 | 62 | 82 | 5 | 0 | 5 | 30 | 1 | 4 | 4 | 4 |
| Baker, Johnnie, Atlanta | .261 | 142 | 494 | 63 | 129 | 208 | 18 | 2 | 19 | 72 | 1 | 5 | 12 | 7 |
| Baldwin, Rick, New York° | .200 | 54 | 15 | 1 | 3 | 3 | 0 | 0 | 0 | 1 | 0 | 0 | 2 | 0 |
| Bannister, Alan, Philadelphia | .262 | 24 | 61 | 10 | 16 | 21 | 3 | 1 | 0 | 0 | 0 | 0 | 2 | 0 |
| Barlow, Michael, St. Louis | .000 | 9 | 0 | 0 | 0 | 0 | 0 | 0 | 0 | 0 | 0 | 0 | 0 | 0 |
| Barr, James, San Francisco | .118 | 38 | 76 | 5 | 9 | 10 | 1 | 0 | 0 | 2 | 12 | 0 | 0 | 0 |
| Batista, Rafael, Houston° | .300 | 10 | 10 | 0 | 3 | 4 | 1 | 0 | 0 | 0 | 0 | 0 | 0 | 0 |
| Beall, Robert, Atlanta† | .226 | 20 | 31 | 2 | 7 | 9 | 2 | 0 | 0 | 1 | 1 | 0 | 0 | 0 |
| Beard, Michael, Atlanta° | .111 | 34 | 9 | 0 | 1 | 1 | 0 | 0 | 0 | 0 | 1 | 0 | 0 | 0 |

| Player and Club | Pct. | G | AB | R | H | TB. | 2B. | 3B. | HR. | RBI. | SH. | SF. | SB. | CS. |
|---|---|---|---|---|---|---|---|---|---|---|---|---|---|---|
| Beckert, Glenn, San Diego | .375 | 9 | 16 | 2 | 6 | 7 | 1 | 0 | 0 | 0 | 0 | 0 | 0 | 0 |
| Belloir, Robert, Atlanta | .219 | 43 | 105 | 11 | 23 | 27 | 2 | 1 | 0 | 9 | 6 | 0 | 0 | 0 |
| Bench, Johnny, Cincinnati | .283 | 142 | 530 | 83 | 150 | 275 | 39 | 1 | 28 | 110 | 0 | 8 | 11 | 0 |
| Biittner, Larry, Montreal° | .315 | 121 | 346 | 34 | 109 | 141 | 13 | 5 | 3 | 28 | 4 | 0 | 1 | 0 |
| Billingham, John, Cincinnati | .108 | 33 | 65 | 5 | 7 | 7 | 0 | 0 | 0 | 4 | 10 | 0 | 2 | 1 |
| Billings, Richard, St. Louis | .000 | 3 | 3 | 0 | 0 | 0 | 0 | 0 | 0 | 0 | 0 | 0 | 0 | 0 |
| Blair, Dennis, Montreal | .143 | 30 | 49 | 0 | 7 | 7 | 0 | 0 | 0 | 0 | 0 | 0 | 0 | 0 |
| Blanks, Larvell, Atlanta | .234 | 141 | 471 | 49 | 110 | 138 | 13 | 3 | 3 | 38 | 1 | 2 | 0 | 0 |
| Bonham, William, Chicago | .183 | 40 | 82 | 8 | 15 | 18 | 1 | 3 | 3 | 38 | 3 | 3 | 4 | 3 |
| Boone, Robert, Philadelphia | .246 | 97 | 289 | 28 | 71 | 95 | 14 | 1 | 0 | 6 | 8 | 1 | 0 | 0 |
| Borbon, Pedro, Cincinnati | .292 | 67 | 24 | 4 | 7 | 8 | 2 | 2 | 2 | 20 | 6 | 1 | 1 | 3 |
| Boswell, Kenneth, Houston° | .242 | 86 | 178 | 16 | 43 | 55 | 8 | 1 | 0 | 2 | 3 | 0 | 0 | 0 |
| Bowa, Lawrence, Philadelphia† | .305 | 136 | 583 | 79 | 178 | 220 | 18 | 2 | 0 | 21 | 0 | 3 | 0 | 3 |
| Bradford, Charles, St. Louis | .272 | 50 | 81 | 12 | 22 | 35 | 1 | 9 | 2 | 38 | 17 | 2 | 24 | 6 |
| Bradley, Thomas, San Francisco | .000 | 13 | 10 | 0 | 0 | 0 | 0 | 0 | 4 | 15 | 0 | 0 | 0 | 2 |
| Breeden, Harold, Montreal | .135 | 24 | 37 | 4 | 5 | 7 | 2 | 0 | 0 | 1 | 1 | 0 | 0 | 0 |
| Brett, Kenneth, Pittsburgh° | .231 | 26 | 52 | 5 | 12 | 19 | 4 | 0 | 1 | 0 | 0 | 0 | 0 | 0 |
| Brewer, James, Los Angeles° | .000 | 21 | 3 | 0 | 0 | 0 | 0 | 1 | 4 | 1 | 0 | 0 | 0 | 0 |
| Brinkman, Edwin, St. Louis | .240 | 28 | 75 | 6 | 18 | 25 | 4 | 0 | 0 | 0 | 0 | 0 | 0 | 0 |
| Brock, Louis, St. Louis° | .309 | 136 | 528 | 78 | 163 | 211 | 27 | 6 | 1 | 6 | 0 | 2 | 0 | 0 |
| Brown, Jerald, San Francisco | .209 | 41 | 43 | 6 | 9 | 12 | 3 | 3 | 3 | 47 | 3 | 0 | 56 | 16 |
| Brown, Ollie, Philadelphia | .303 | 84 | 145 | 19 | 44 | 74 | 12 | 0 | 0 | 4 | 0 | 0 | 0 | 0 |
| Bryant, Ronald, St. Louis† | .000 | 10 | 1 | 0 | 0 | 0 | 0 | 0 | 6 | 26 | 1 | 0 | 1 | 1 |
| Buckner, William, Los Angeles° | .243 | 92 | 288 | 30 | 70 | 103 | 11 | 0 | 0 | 1 | 0 | 0 | 0 | 0 |
| Burris, B. Ray, Chicago | .183 | 38 | 82 | 10 | 15 | 17 | 2 | 2 | 6 | 31 | 4 | 8 | 3 | 5 |
| Cabell, Enos, Houston | .264 | 117 | 348 | 43 | 92 | 127 | 17 | 0 | 0 | 4 | 7 | 0 | 0 | 1 |
| Caldwell, R. Michael, San Fran | .159 | 38 | 44 | 2 | 7 | 10 | 3 | 6 | 2 | 43 | 1 | 4 | 12 | 3 |
| Candelaria, John, Pittsburgh° | .140 | 18 | 43 | 2 | 6 | 6 | 0 | 0 | 0 | 3 | 7 | 0 | 0 | 0 |
| Capra, Lee, Atlanta | .043 | 12 | 23 | 2 | 1 | 2 | 0 | 0 | 0 | 2 | 0 | 0 | 0 | 0 |
| Cardenal, Jose, Chicago | .317 | 154 | 574 | 85 | 182 | 243 | 30 | 2 | 9 | 68 | 4 | 7 | 34 | 12 |
| Carlton, Steven, Philadelphia° | .156 | 37 | 90 | 8 | 14 | 16 | 2 | 0 | 9 | 68 | 7 | 0 | 0 | 0 |
| Carrithers, Donald, Montreal | .176 | 19 | 34 | 3 | 6 | 9 | 3 | 0 | 0 | 3 | 1 | 1 | 0 | 0 |
| Carroll, Clay, Cincinnati | .000 | 56 | 19 | 1 | 0 | 0 | 0 | 0 | 0 | 0 | 2 | 0 | 0 | 0 |
| Carroll, Thomas, Cincinnati° | .000 | 12 | 14 | 0 | 0 | 0 | 0 | 0 | 0 | 0 | 0 | 0 | 0 | 0 |
| Carter, Gary, Montreal | .270 | 144 | 503 | 58 | 136 | 209 | 20 | 1 | 17 | 68 | 10 | 4 | 5 | 2 |
| Cash, David, Philadelphia | .305 | 162 | 699 | 111 | 213 | 271 | 40 | 3 | 4 | 57 | 0 | 7 | 13 | 6 |
| Cater, Danny, St. Louis | .229 | 22 | 35 | 3 | 8 | 10 | 2 | 0 | 2 | 0 | 0 | 0 | 0 | 0 |
| Cedeno, Cesar, Houston | .288 | 131 | 500 | 93 | 144 | 220 | 31 | 3 | 13 | 63 | 2 | 5 | 50 | 17 |
| Cey, Ronald, Los Angeles | .283 | 158 | 566 | 72 | 160 | 268 | 29 | 2 | 25 | 101 | 3 | 8 | 5 | 2 |
| Chaney, Darrel, Cincinnati° | .219 | 71 | 160 | 18 | 35 | 47 | 6 | 0 | 2 | 26 | 0 | 1 | 3 | 0 |
| Christenson, Larry, Philadelphia | .246 | 29 | 57 | 3 | 14 | 24 | 2 | 1 | 2 | 6 | 8 | 0 | 0 | 0 |
| Clark, Ronald B., Philadelphia | .000 | 1 | 1 | 0 | 0 | 0 | 0 | 0 | 0 | 0 | 0 | 0 | 0 | 0 |
| Clark, Jack, San Francisco | .235 | 8 | 17 | 3 | 4 | 4 | 0 | 0 | 0 | 2 | 0 | 1 | 1 | 0 |
| Clines, Eugene, New York | .227 | 82 | 203 | 25 | 46 | 58 | 6 | 3 | 0 | 10 | 0 | 1 | 4 | 4 |
| Coggins, Richard, Montreal° | .270 | 13 | 37 | 1 | 10 | 15 | 3 | 1 | 0 | 4 | 2 | 0 | 4 | 4 |
| Colbert, Nathan, Montreal | .173 | 38 | 81 | 10 | 14 | 32 | 4 | 1 | 4 | 11 | 0 | 0 | 0 | 0 |
| Concepcion, David, Cincinnati | .274 | 140 | 507 | 62 | 139 | 179 | 23 | 1 | 5 | 49 | 6 | 4 | 33 | 6 |
| Correll, Victor, Atlanta | .215 | 103 | 325 | 37 | 70 | 117 | 12 | 1 | 11 | 39 | 5 | 2 | 0 | 2 |
| Cosgrove, Michael, Houston° | .154 | 32 | 13 | 0 | 2 | 3 | 1 | 0 | 0 | 0 | 2 | 0 | 0 | 0 |
| Cox, James, Montreal | .259 | 11 | 27 | 1 | 7 | 11 | 1 | 0 | 1 | 5 | 0 | 1 | 1 | 0 |
| Cox, Larry, Philadelphia | .200 | 11 | 5 | 0 | 1 | 1 | 0 | 0 | 0 | 0 | 1 | 1 | 0 | 0 |
| Cram, Gerald, New York | .000 | 4 | 0 | 0 | 0 | 0 | 0 | 0 | 0 | 0 | 0 | 0 | 0 | 0 |
| Crawford, James, Houston° | .294 | 44 | 17 | 1 | 5 | 6 | 1 | 0 | 0 | 2 | 1 | 0 | 0 | 0 |
| Crawford, Willie, Los Angeles° | .263 | 124 | 373 | 46 | 98 | 144 | 15 | 2 | 9 | 46 | 6 | 4 | 5 | 5 |
| Crosby, Kenneth, Chicago | .000 | 9 | 0 | 1 | 0 | 0 | 0 | 0 | 0 | 0 | 0 | 0 | 0 | 0 |
| Crowley, Terrence, Cincinnati° | .268 | 66 | 71 | 8 | 19 | 28 | 6 | 0 | 1 | 11 | 0 | 0 | 0 | 0 |
| Cruz, Hector, St. Louis | .146 | 23 | 48 | 7 | 7 | 13 | 2 | 0 | 6 | 50 | 1 | 1 | 0 | 0 |
| Cruz, Henry, Los Angeles° | .266 | 53 | 94 | 8 | 25 | 30 | 3 | 1 | 0 | 5 | 0 | 0 | 1 | 1 |
| Cruz, Jose, Houston° | .257 | 120 | 315 | 44 | 81 | 127 | 15 | 2 | 9 | 49 | 3 | 6 | 6 | 3 |
| Curtis, John, St. Louis° | .211 | 39 | 38 | 6 | 8 | 8 | 0 | 0 | 0 | 1 | 5 | 0 | 0 | 0 |
| D'Acquisto, John, San Francisco | .000 | 10 | 7 | 2 | 0 | 0 | 0 | 0 | 0 | 0 | 0 | 0 | 0 | 0 |
| Dal Canton, J. Bruce, Atlanta | .105 | 26 | 19 | 0 | 2 | 2 | 0 | 0 | 0 | 0 | 0 | 0 | 0 | 0 |
| Darcy, Patrick, Cincinnati | .085 | 27 | 47 | 1 | 4 | 5 | 1 | 0 | 0 | 1 | 2 | 0 | 0 | 0 |
| DaVanon, F. Gerald, Houston | .278 | 32 | 97 | 15 | 27 | 38 | 4 | 2 | 1 | 10 | 0 | 0 | 2 | 2 |
| Davis, Robert, San Diego | .234 | 43 | 128 | 6 | 30 | 37 | 3 | 2 | 0 | 7 | 1 | 0 | 0 | 0 |
| Davis, William, St. Louis° | .291 | 98 | 350 | 41 | 102 | 151 | 19 | 6 | 6 | 50 | 0 | 8 | 10 | 1 |
| DeJesus, Ivan, Los Angeles | .184 | 63 | 87 | 10 | 16 | 20 | 2 | 1 | 0 | 2 | 1 | 0 | 0 | 2 |
| de la Rosa, Jesus, Houston | .333 | 3 | 3 | 1 | 1 | 2 | 1 | 0 | 0 | 0 | 0 | 0 | 0 | 0 |
| Demery, Lawrence, Pittsburgh | .125 | 49 | 24 | 3 | 3 | 5 | 0 | 1 | 0 | 0 | 2 | 0 | 0 | 0 |

| Player and Club | Pct. | G. | AB. | R. | H. | TB. | 2B. | 3B. | HR. | RBI. | SH. | SF. | SB. | CS. |
|---|---|---|---|---|---|---|---|---|---|---|---|---|---|---|
| DeMola, Donald, Montreal | .000 | 60 | 8 | 0 | 0 | 0 | 0 | 0 | 0 | 0 | 0 | 0 | 0 | 0 |
| Denny, John, St. Louis | .227 | 26 | 44 | 4 | 10 | 10 | 0 | 0 | 0 | 3 | 6 | 0 | 0 | 0 |
| Dettore, Thomas, Chicago° | .250 | 36 | 24 | 2 | 6 | 6 | 0 | 0 | 0 | 2 | 0 | 0 | 0 | 0 |
| Devine, P. Adrian, Atlanta | .000 | 5 | 5 | 0 | 0 | 0 | 0 | 0 | 0 | 0 | 0 | 0 | 0 | 0 |
| Dierker, Lawrence, Houston | .092 | 34 | 76 | 0 | 7 | 7 | 0 | 0 | 0 | 5 | 13 | 0 | 0 | 0 |
| Dilone, Miguel, Pittsburgh† | .000 | 18 | 6 | 8 | 0 | 0 | 0 | 0 | 0 | 0 | 0 | 0 | 2 | 2 |
| Downing, Alphonso, Los Angeles | .000 | 22 | 16 | 0 | 0 | 0 | 0 | 0 | 0 | 1 | 0 | 1 | 0 | 0 |
| Dressler, Robert, San Francisco | .000 | 3 | 4 | 1 | 0 | 0 | 0 | 0 | 0 | 0 | 0 | 0 | 0 | 0 |
| Driessen, Daniel, Cincinnati° | .281 | 88 | 210 | 38 | 59 | 90 | 8 | 1 | 7 | 38 | 0 | 2 | 10 | 3 |
| Dunn, Ronald, Chicago | .159 | 32 | 44 | 2 | 7 | 13 | 3 | 0 | 1 | 6 | 0 | 2 | 0 | 0 |
| Dwyer, James, StL-Mtl° | .272 | 81 | 206 | 26 | 56 | 75 | 8 | 1 | 3 | 21 | 12 | 2 | 4 | 1 |
| Dyer, Don, Pittsburgh | .227 | 48 | 132 | 8 | 30 | 48 | 5 | 2 | 3 | 16 | 1 | 0 | 0 | 0 |
| Easler, Michael, Houston° | .000 | 5 | 5 | 0 | 0 | 0 | 0 | 0 | 0 | 0 | 0 | 0 | 0 | 0 |
| Easterly, James, Atlanta† | .056 | 21 | 18 | 1 | 1 | 1 | 0 | 0 | 0 | 1 | 3 | 0 | 0 | 0 |
| Eastwick, Rawlins, Cincinnati | .067 | 58 | 15 | 0 | 1 | 1 | 0 | 0 | 0 | 0 | 1 | 0 | 0 | .0 |
| Ellis, Dock, Pittsburgh† | .111 | 30 | 36 | 3 | 4 | 5 | 1 | 0 | 0 | 1 | 7 | 0 | 0 | 0 |
| Espinosa, Arnulfo, New York | .000 | 2 | 0 | 0 | 0 | 0 | 0 | 0 | 0 | 0 | 0 | 0 | 0 | 0 |
| Essian, James, Philadelphia | 1.000 | 2 | 1 | 1 | 1 | 1 | 0 | 0 | 0 | 1 | 0 | 0 | 0 | 0 |
| Evans, Darrell, Atlanta° | .243 | 156 | 567 | 82 | 138 | 230 | 22 | 2 | 22 | 73 | 2 | 5 | 12 | 3 |
| Fairly, Ronald, St. Louis° | .301 | 107 | 229 | 32 | 69 | 107 | 13 | 2 | 7 | 37 | 1 | 1 | 0 | 1 |
| Falcone, Peter, San Francisco° | .062 | 34 | 65 | 2 | 4 | 4 | 0 | 0 | 0 | 0 | 4 | 0 | 1 | 0 |
| Ferguson, Joseph, Los Angeles | .208 | 66 | 202 | 15 | 42 | 61 | 2 | 1 | 5 | 23 | 1 | 2 | 2 | 1 |
| Flynn, R. Douglas, Cincinnati | .268 | 89 | 127 | 17 | 34 | 44 | 7 | 0 | 1 | 20 | 4 | 1 | 3 | 0 |
| Foli, Timothy, Montreal | .238 | 152 | 572 | 64 | 136 | 168 | 25 | 2 | 1 | 29 | 17 | 3 | 13 | 3 |
| Folkers, Richard, San Diego° | .167 | 45 | 36 | 2 | 6 | 7 | 1 | 0 | 0 | 4 | 4 | 0 | 0 | 1 |
| Foote, Barry, Montreal | .194 | 118 | 387 | 25 | 75 | 114 | 16 | 1 | 7 | 30 | 4 | 1 | 0 | 1 |
| Forsch, Kenneth, Houston | .045 | 34 | 22 | 1 | 1 | 1 | 0 | 0 | 0 | 0 | 3 | 0 | 0 | 0 |
| Forsch, Robert, St. Louis | .308 | 35 | 78 | 9 | 24 | 36 | 3 | 3 | 1 | 5 | 6 | 0 | 0 | 0 |
| Foster, Alan, San Diego | .091 | 19 | 11 | 1 | 1 | 1 | 0 | 0 | 0 | 2 | 0 | 0 | 0 | 0 |
| Foster, George, Cincinnati | .300 | 134 | 463 | 71 | 139 | 240 | 24 | 4 | 23 | 78 | 0 | 5 | 2 | 1 |
| Frailing, Kenneth, Chicago° | .143 | 41 | 7 | 2 | 1 | 1 | 0 | 0 | 0 | 0 | 1 | 0 | 0 | 0 |
| Freisleben, David, San Diego | .083 | 36 | 48 | 2 | 4 | 4 | 0 | 0 | 0 | 2 | 6 | 0 | 0 | 0 |
| Frias, Jesus, Montreal | .125 | 51 | 64 | 4 | 8 | 10 | 2 | 0 | 0 | 4 | 2 | 1 | 0 | 1 |
| Frisella, Daniel, San Diego° | .200 | 65 | 5 | 1 | 1 | 1 | 0 | 0 | 0 | 0 | 0 | 0 | 0 | 0 |
| Fritz, Lawrence, Philadelphia° | .000 | 1 | 1 | 0 | 0 | 0 | 0 | 0 | 0 | 0 | 0 | 0 | 0 | 0 |
| Fryman, Woodrow, Montreal | .204 | 38 | 49 | 4 | 10 | 12 | 2 | 0 | 0 | 2 | 5 | 0 | 0 | 0 |
| Fuentes, Rigoberto, San Diego† | .280 | 146 | 565 | 57 | 158 | 197 | 21 | 3 | 4 | 43 | 12 | 8 | 8 | 8 |
| Gallagher, Robert, New York° | .133 | 33 | 15 | 5 | 2 | 3 | 1 | 0 | 0 | 0 | 0 | 0 | 0 | 0 |
| Garber, H. Eugene, Philadelphia | .167 | 71 | 12 | 0 | 2 | 2 | 0 | 0 | 0 | 1 | 1 | 0 | 0 | 0 |
| Gardner, Arthur, Houston° | .194 | 13 | 31 | 3 | 6 | 6 | 0 | 0 | 0 | 2 | 0 | 0 | 1 | 0 |
| Garman, Michael, St. Louis | .000 | 66 | 2 | 0 | 0 | 0 | 0 | 0 | 0 | 0 | 0 | 0 | 0 | 0 |
| Garr, Ralph, Atlanta° | .278 | 151 | 625 | 74 | 174 | 240 | 26 | 11 | 6 | 31 | 3 | 3 | 14 | 9 |
| Garrett, H. Adrian, Chicago° | .095 | 16 | 21 | 1 | 2 | 5 | 0 | 0 | 1 | 6 | 0 | 1 | 0 | 0 |
| Garrett, R. Wayne, New York° | .266 | 107 | 274 | 49 | 73 | 105 | 8 | 3 | 6 | 34 | 1 | 2 | 3 | 2 |
| Garvey, Steven, Los Angeles | .319 | 160 | 659 | 85 | 210 | 314 | 38 | 6 | 18 | 95 | 3 | 6 | 11 | 2 |
| Gaston, Clarence, Atlanta | .241 | 64 | 141 | 17 | 34 | 56 | 4 | 0 | 6 | 15 | 0 | 1 | 1 | 0 |
| Gentry, Gary, Atlanta | .000 | 7 | 5 | 0 | 0 | 0 | 0 | 0 | 0 | 1 | 0 | 0 | 0 | 0 |
| Geronimo, Cesar, Cincinnati° | .257 | 148 | 501 | 69 | 129 | 182 | 25 | 5 | 6 | 53 | 3 | 1 | 13 | 5 |
| Gibson, Robert, St. Louis | .179 | 22 | 28 | 1 | 5 | 5 | 0 | 0 | 0 | 4 | 4 | 2 | 0 | 0 |
| Gilbreath, Rodney, Atlanta | .243 | 90 | 202 | 24 | 49 | 60 | 3 | 1 | 2 | 16 | 8 | 2 | 5 | 5 |
| Giusti, David, Pittsburgh | .300 | 61 | 10 | 2 | 3 | 3 | 0 | 0 | 0 | 1 | 4 | 0 | 0 | 0 |
| Goodson, J. Edward, SF-Atl° | .208 | 86 | 197 | 15 | 41 | 56 | 9 | 0 | 2 | 16 | 1 | 2 | 0 | 1 |
| Granger, Wayne, Houston | .000 | 55 | 9 | 0 | 0 | 0 | 0 | 0 | 0 | 0 | 0 | 0 | 0 | 0 |
| Greif, William, San Diego | .000 | 59 | 1 | 0 | 0 | 0 | 0 | 0 | 0 | 0 | 1 | 0 | 0 | 0 |
| Griffey, G. Kenneth, Cincinnati° | .305 | 132 | 463 | 95 | 141 | 186 | 15 | 9 | 4 | 46 | 6 | 3 | 16 | 7 |
| Griffin, Thomas, Houston | .136 | 17 | 22 | 2 | 3 | 3 | 0 | 0 | 0 | 0 | 2 | 0 | 0 | 0 |
| Gross, Gregory, Houston° | .294 | 132 | 483 | 67 | 142 | 176 | 14 | 10 | 0 | 41 | 9 | 3 | 2 | 2 |
| Grote, Gerald, New York | .295 | 119 | 386 | 28 | 114 | 144 | 14 | 5 | 2 | 39 | 0 | 3 | 0 | 1 |
| Grubb, John, San Diego° | .269 | 144 | 553 | 72 | 149 | 201 | 36 | 2 | 4 | 38 | 3 | 5 | 2 | 7 |
| Guerrero, Mario, St. Louis | .239 | 64 | 184 | 17 | 44 | 53 | 9 | 0 | 0 | 11 | 1 | 3 | 0 | 0 |
| Gullett, Donald, Cincinnati | .226 | 22 | 62 | 5 | 14 | 17 | 1 | 1 | 0 | 9 | 3 | 1 | 0 | 0 |
| Hahn, Donald, Phil-StL-SD | .179 | 50 | 39 | 10 | 7 | 12 | 1 | 2 | 0 | 3 | 1 | 0 | 1 | 0 |
| Hale, John, Los Angeles° | .211 | 71 | 204 | 20 | 43 | 68 | 7 | 0 | 6 | 22 | 4 | 2 | 1 | 2 |
| Halicki, Edward, San Francisco | .113 | 24 | 53 | 2 | 6 | 7 | 1 | 0 | 0 | 3 | 5 | 0 | 0 | 0 |
| Hall, Tom, Cin-NY° | .400 | 37 | 5 | 2 | 2 | 2 | 0 | 0 | 0 | 1 | 0 | 0 | 0 | 0 |
| Hanna, Preston, Atlanta | .000 | 4 | 0 | 0 | 0 | 0 | 0 | 0 | 0 | 0 | 0 | 0 | 0 | 0 |
| Hardy, H. Lawrence, San Diego | .000 | 3 | 0 | 0 | 0 | 0 | 0 | 0 | 0 | 0 | 0 | 0 | 0 | 0 |
| Harmon, Terry, Philadelphia | .181 | 48 | 72 | 14 | 13 | 18 | 1 | 2 | 0 | 5 | 3 | 0 | 0 | 0 |
| Harrelson, Derrel, New York† | .219 | 34 | 73 | 5 | 16 | 18 | 2 | 0 | 0 | 3 | 2 | 0 | 0 | 0 |

| Player and Club | Pct. | G. | AB. | R. | H. | TB. | 2B. | 3B. | HR. | RBI. | SH. | SF. | SB. | CS. |
|---|---|---|---|---|---|---|---|---|---|---|---|---|---|---|
| Harris, Victor, Chicago† | .179 | 51 | 56 | 6 | 10 | 10 | 0 | 0 | 0 | 5 | 1 | 1 | 0 | 0 |
| Harrison, Roric, Atlanta | .200 | 15 | 15 | 1 | 3 | 4 | 1 | 0 | 0 | 1 | 0 | 0 | 0 | 0 |
| Heaverlo, David, San Francisco | .500 | 42 | 4 | 0 | 2 | 2 | 0 | 0 | 0 | 0 | 0 | 0 | 0 | 0 |
| Hebner, Richard, Pittsburgh° | .246 | 128 | 472 | 65 | 116 | 185 | 16 | 4 | 15 | 57 | 3 | 5 | 0 | 1 |
| Heidemann, Jack, New York | .214 | 61 | 145 | 12 | 31 | 42 | 4 | 2 | 1 | 16 | 2 | 3 | 1 | 0 |
| Helms, Tommy, Houston | .207 | 64 | 135 | 7 | 28 | 30 | 2 | 0 | 0 | 14 | 0 | 1 | 0 | 0 |
| Hernandez, Enzo, San Diego | .218 | 116 | 344 | 37 | 75 | 91 | 12 | 2 | 0 | 19 | 24 | 3 | 20 | 4 |
| Hernandez, Keith, St. Louis° | .250 | 64 | 188 | 20 | 47 | 68 | 8 | 2 | 3 | 20 | 0 | 2 | 0 | 1 |
| Hernandez, Ramon, Pittsburgh† | .000 | 46 | 6 | 0 | 0 | 0 | 0 | 0 | 0 | 0 | 0 | 0 | 0 | 0 |
| Hilgendorf, Thomas, Philadelphia† | .250 | 53 | 12 | 0 | 3 | 4 | 1 | 0 | 0 | 3 | 2 | 0 | 0 | 0 |
| Hill, Marc, San Francisco | .214 | 72 | 182 | 14 | 39 | 58 | 4 | 0 | 5 | 23 | 1 | 3 | 0 | 0 |
| Hilton, J. David, San Diego | .000 | 4 | 8 | 0 | 0 | 0 | 0 | 0 | 0 | 0 | 0 | 0 | 0 | 0 |
| Hiser, Gene, Chicago° | .242 | 45 | 62 | 11 | 15 | 18 | 3 | 0 | 0 | 6 | 2 | 1 | 0 | 1 |
| Hodges, Ronald, New York° | .206 | 9 | 34 | 3 | 7 | 14 | 1 | 0 | 2 | 4 | 2 | 0 | 0 | 0 |
| Hoerner, Joseph, Philadelphia | .000 | 25 | 2 | 0 | 0 | 0 | 0 | 0 | 0 | 0 | 0 | 0 | 0 | 0 |
| Hooton, Burt, Chi-LA | .123 | 34 | 73 | 6 | 9 | 15 | 3 | 0 | 1 | 7 | 13 | 0 | 0 | 0 |
| Hosley, Timothy, Chicago | .255 | 62 | 141 | 22 | 36 | 61 | 7 | 0 | 6 | 20 | 1 | 0 | 1 | 1 |
| Hough, Charles, Los Angeles | .333 | 38 | 6 | 1 | 2 | 2 | 0 | 0 | 0 | 0 | 0 | 0 | 0 | 0 |
| House, Thomas, Atlanta° | .111 | 58 | 9 | 0 | 1 | 1 | 0 | 0 | 0 | 1 | 0 | 0 | 0 | 0 |
| Howard, Douglas, St. Louis | .207 | 17 | 29 | 1 | 6 | 9 | 0 | 0 | 1 | 1 | 0 | 0 | 0 | 0 |
| Howard, Wilbur, Houston† | .283 | 121 | 392 | 62 | 111 | 143 | 16 | 8 | 0 | 21 | 2 | 1 | 32 | 11 |
| Howe, Arthur, Pittsburgh | .171 | 63 | 146 | 13 | 25 | 37 | 9 | 0 | 1 | 10 | 1 | 0 | 1 | 0 |
| Hrabosky, Alan, St. Louis | .200 | 65 | 15 | 2 | 3 | 3 | 0 | 0 | 0 | 4 | 3 | 0 | 0 | 0 |
| Hundley, C. Randolph, San Diego | .206 | 74 | 180 | 7 | 37 | 50 | 5 | 1 | 2 | 14 | 0 | 1 | 0 | 0 |
| Huntz, Stephen, San Diego† | .151 | 22 | 53 | 3 | 8 | 12 | 4 | 0 | 0 | 4 | 2 | 0 | 0 | 0 |
| Hutton, Thomas, Philadelphia° | .248 | 113 | 165 | 24 | 41 | 56 | 6 | 0 | 3 | 24 | 1 | 1 | 2 | 5 |
| Ivie, Michael, San Diego | .249 | 111 | 377 | 36 | 94 | 138 | 16 | 2 | 8 | 46 | 5 | 4 | 4 | 4 |
| Johnson, Clifford, Houston | .276 | 122 | 340 | 52 | 94 | 172 | 16 | 1 | 20 | 65 | 1 | 1 | 0 | 0 |
| Johnson, David, Atlanta | 1.000 | 1 | 1 | 0 | 1 | 2 | 1 | 0 | 0 | 1 | 0 | 0 | 0 | 0 |
| Johnson, Jerry, San Diego | .083 | 21 | 12 | 1 | 1 | 2 | 1 | 0 | 0 | 0 | 0 | 0 | 0 | 0 |
| Johnson, Larry Doby, Montreal | .333 | 1 | 3 | 0 | 1 | 2 | 1 | 0 | 0 | 1 | 0 | 0 | 0 | 0 |
| Johnstone, John, Philadelphia° | .329 | 122 | 350 | 50 | 115 | 159 | 19 | 2 | 7 | 54 | 3 | 3 | 7 | 3 |
| Jones, Cleon, New York | .240 | 21 | 50 | 2 | 12 | 13 | 1 | 0 | 0 | 2 | 0 | 0 | 0 | 0 |
| Jones, Odell, Pittsburgh | .000 | 2 | 0 | 0 | 0 | 0 | 0 | 0 | 0 | 0 | 0 | 0 | 0 | 0 |
| Jones, Randall, San Diego | .133 | 40 | 83 | 7 | 11 | 13 | 2 | 0 | 0 | 4 | 5 | 0 | 0 | 0 |
| Jorgensen, Michael, Montreal° | .261 | 144 | 445 | 58 | 116 | 188 | 18 | 0 | 18 | 67 | 1 | 4 | 17 | 0 |
| Joshua, Von, San Francisco° | .318 | 129 | 507 | 75 | 161 | 227 | 25 | 10 | 7 | 43 | 4 | 1 | 20 | 10 |
| Jutze, Alfred, Houston | .226 | 51 | 93 | 9 | 21 | 23 | 2 | 0 | 0 | 6 | 3 | 0 | 1 | 0 |
| Kelleher, Michael, St. Louis | .000 | 7 | 4 | 0 | 0 | 0 | 0 | 0 | 0 | 0 | 0 | 0 | 0 | 0 |
| Kendall, Fred, San Diego | .199 | 103 | 286 | 16 | 57 | 71 | 12 | 1 | 0 | 24 | 1 | 1 | 0 | 1 |
| Kessinger, Donald, Chicago† | .243 | 154 | 601 | 77 | 146 | 192 | 26 | 10 | 0 | 46 | 14 | 9 | 4 | 7 |
| Kingman, David, New York | .231 | 134 | 502 | 65 | 116 | 248 | 22 | 1 | 36 | 88 | 1 | 2 | 7 | 5 |
| Kirby, Clayton, Cincinnati† | .188 | 26 | 32 | 3 | 6 | 7 | 1 | 0 | 0 | 2 | 4 | 0 | 0 | 0 |
| Kirkpatrick, Edgar, Pittsburgh° | .236 | 89 | 144 | 15 | 34 | 54 | 5 | 0 | 5 | 16 | 1 | 1 | 1 | 0 |
| Kison, Bruce, Pittsburgh | .119 | 35 | 59 | 4 | 7 | 7 | 0 | 0 | 0 | 3 | 10 | 1 | 1 | 0 |
| Knowles, Darold, Chicago° | .067 | 58 | 15 | 0 | 1 | 1 | 0 | 0 | 0 | 1 | 2 | 0 | 0 | 0 |
| Konieczny, Douglas, Houston | .160 | 32 | 50 | 2 | 8 | 10 | 2 | 0 | 0 | 4 | 5 | 0 | 0 | 0 |
| Koosman, Jerry, New York | .179 | 36 | 78 | 4 | 14 | 16 | 2 | 0 | 0 | 6 | 7 | 0 | 1 | 0 |
| Kranepool, Edward, New York° | .323 | 106 | 325 | 42 | 105 | 133 | 16 | 0 | 4 | 43 | 0 | 5 | 1 | 1 |
| Kubiak, Theodore, San Diego† | .224 | 87 | 196 | 13 | 44 | 49 | 5 | 0 | 0 | 14 | 2 | 1 | 3 | 1 |
| Kurosaki, Ryan, St. Louis | .000 | 7 | 1 | 0 | 0 | 0 | 0 | 0 | 0 | 0 | 0 | 0 | 0 | 0 |
| LaCock, R. Pierre, Chicago° | .229 | 106 | 249 | 30 | 57 | 85 | 8 | 1 | 6 | 30 | 2 | 4 | 0 | 2 |
| LaCorte, Frank, Atlanta | .000 | 3 | 5 | 0 | 0 | 0 | 0 | 0 | 0 | 0 | 0 | 0 | 0 | 0 |
| Lacy, Leondaus, Los Angeles | .314 | 101 | 306 | 44 | 96 | 138 | 11 | 5 | 7 | 40 | 5 | 3 | 5 | 9 |
| Lang, Robert, Montreal | .000 | 1 | 0 | 0 | 0 | 0 | 0 | 0 | 0 | 0 | 0 | 0 | 0 | 0 |
| Lavelle, Gary, San Francisco† | .111 | 65 | 9 | 0 | 1 | 1 | 0 | 0 | 0 | 0 | 1 | 0 | 0 | 0 |
| Lee, Leron, Los Angeles° | .256 | 48 | 43 | 2 | 11 | 15 | 4 | 0 | 0 | 2 | 0 | 1 | 0 | 0 |
| LeMaster, Johnnie, San Fran | .189 | 22 | 74 | 4 | 14 | 24 | 4 | 0 | 2 | 9 | 0 | 0 | 2 | 1 |
| Leon, Maximino, Atlanta | .333 | 50 | 9 | 0 | 3 | 3 | 0 | 0 | 0 | 1 | 0 | 0 | 0 | 0 |
| Lerch, Randy, Philadelphia° | .000 | 3 | 0 | 0 | 0 | 0 | 0 | 0 | 0 | 0 | 0 | 0 | 0 | 0 |
| Lewallyn, Dennis, Los Angeles° | .000 | 2 | 0 | 0 | 0 | 0 | 0 | 0 | 0 | 0 | 0 | 0 | 0 | 0 |
| Lintz, Larry, Mtl-StL† | .207 | 73 | 150 | 24 | 31 | 32 | 1 | 0 | 0 | 4 | 7 | 0 | 21 | 9 |
| Locker, Robert, Chicago | .000 | 22 | 0 | 0 | 0 | 0 | 0 | 0 | 0 | 0 | 0 | 0 | 0 | 0 |
| Locklear, Gene, San Diego° | .321 | 100 | 237 | 31 | 76 | 104 | 11 | 1 | 5 | 27 | 1 | 2 | 4 | 2 |
| Lockwood, Claude, New York | .167 | 24 | 6 | 0 | 1 | 1 | 0 | 0 | 0 | 1 | 1 | 0 | 0 | 0 |
| Lonborg, James, Philadelphia | .023 | 27 | 44 | 2 | 1 | 1 | 0 | 0 | 0 | 1 | 6 | 0 | 0 | 0 |
| Lopes, David, Los Angeles | .262 | 155 | 618 | 108 | 162 | 222 | 24 | 6 | 8 | 41 | 13 | 2 | 77 | 12 |
| Lum, Michael, Atlanta° | .228 | 124 | 364 | 32 | 83 | 119 | 8 | 2 | 8 | 36 | 2 | 1 | 2 | 4 |
| Luzinski, Gregory, Philadelphia | .300 | 161 | 596 | 85 | 179 | 322 | 35 | 3 | 34 | 120 | 0 | 8 | 3 | 6 |

| Player and Club | Pct. | G. | AB. | R. | H. | TB. | 2B. | 3B. | HR. | RBI. | SH. | SF. | SB. | CS. |
|---|---|---|---|---|---|---|---|---|---|---|---|---|---|---|
| Lyttle, James, Montreal° | .273 | 44 | 55 | 7 | 15 | 19 | 4 | 0 | 0 | 6 | 1 | 1 | 0 | 1 |
| Mackanin, Peter, Montreal | .225 | 130 | 448 | 59 | 101 | 168 | 19 | 6 | 12 | 44 | 10 | 4 | 11 | 5 |
| Maddox, Garry, SF-Phila | .272 | 116 | 426 | 54 | 116 | 173 | 26 | 8 | 5 | 50 | 1 | 3 | 25 | 4 |
| Madlock, Bill, Chicago | .354 | 130 | 514 | 77 | 182 | 246 | 29 | 7 | 7 | 64 | 1 | 5 | 9 | 7 |
| Mangual, Jose, Montreal | .245 | 140 | 514 | 84 | 126 | 173 | 16 | 2 | 9 | 45 | 9 | 8 | 33 | 11 |
| Manuel, Charles, Los Angeles° | .133 | 15 | 15 | 0 | 2 | 2 | 0 | 0 | 0 | 2 | 0 | 0 | 0 | 0 |
| Marichal, Juan, Los Angeles | .000 | 2 | 2 | 0 | 0 | 0 | 0 | 0 | 0 | 0 | 0 | 0 | 0 | 0 |
| Marshall, Michael, Los Angeles | .067 | 58 | 15 | 0 | 1 | 1 | 0 | 0 | 0 | 0 | 4 | 0 | 0 | 0 |
| Martin, Jerry, Philadelphia | .212 | 57 | 113 | 15 | 24 | 39 | 7 | 1 | 2 | 11 | 3 | 0 | 2 | 2 |
| Martinez, Teodoro, St. Louis | .190 | 16 | 21 | 1 | 4 | 6 | 2 | 0 | 0 | 2 | 2 | 0 | 0 | 0 |
| Matlack, Jonathan, New York° | .100 | 33 | 70 | 6 | 7 | 7 | 0 | 0 | 0 | 2 | 5 | 0 | 0 | 0 |
| Matthews, Gary, San Francisco | .280 | 116 | 425 | 67 | 119 | 183 | 22 | 3 | 12 | 58 | 0 | 2 | 13 | 4 |
| May, David, Atlanta° | .276 | 82 | 203 | 28 | 56 | 100 | 8 | 0 | 12 | 40 | 0 | 0 | 1 | 1 |
| May, Milton, Houston° | .241 | 111 | 386 | 29 | 93 | 122 | 15 | 1 | 4 | 52 | 4 | 3 | 1 | 2 |
| McBride, Arnold, St. Louis° | .300 | 116 | 413 | 70 | 124 | 167 | 10 | 9 | 5 | 36 | 6 | 1 | 26 | 8 |
| McCarver, J. Timothy, Phila° | .254 | 47 | 59 | 6 | 15 | 20 | 2 | 0 | 1 | 7 | 0 | 0 | 0 | 0 |
| McCovey, Willie, San Diego° | .252 | 122 | 413 | 43 | 104 | 190 | 17 | 0 | 23 | 68 | 0 | 2 | 1 | 0 |
| McDowell, Samuel, Pittsburgh° | .000 | 14 | 8 | 0 | 0 | 0 | 0 | 0 | 0 | 0 | 0 | 0 | 0 | 0 |
| McEnaney, William, Cincinnati° | .000 | 70 | 14 | 0 | 0 | 0 | 0 | 0 | 0 | 0 | 0 | 0 | 0 | 0 |
| McGlothen, Lynn, St. Louis° | .088 | 35 | 80 | 3 | 7 | 7 | 0 | 0 | 0 | 0 | 10 | 0 | 0 | 0 |
| McGraw, Frank, Philadelphia | .154 | 56 | 13 | 0 | 2 | 2 | 0 | 0 | 0 | 0 | 1 | 0 | 0 | 0 |
| McIntosh, Joseph, San Diego† | .188 | 38 | 48 | 6 | 9 | 11 | 2 | 0 | 0 | 5 | 5 | 3 | 0 | 0 |
| McMullen, Kenneth, Los Angeles° | .239 | 39 | 46 | 4 | 11 | 20 | 1 | 1 | 2 | 14 | 0 | 0 | 0 | 0 |
| McNally, David, Montreal° | .190 | 12 | 21 | 1 | 4 | 4 | 0 | 0 | 0 | 1 | 1 | 0 | 0 | 0 |
| Melendez, Luis, St. Louis | .265 | 110 | 291 | 33 | 77 | 101 | 8 | 5 | 2 | 27 | 7 | 2 | 3 | 2 |
| Mendoza, Mario, Pittsburgh | .180 | 56 | 50 | 8 | 9 | 10 | 1 | 0 | 0 | 2 | 3 | 0 | 0 | 0 |
| Messersmith, John, Los Angeles | .157 | 44 | 108 | 8 | 17 | 21 | 4 | 0 | 0 | 9 | 5 | 2 | 0 | 0 |
| Metzger, Clarence, San Diego | .000 | 4 | 0 | 0 | 0 | 0 | 0 | 0 | 0 | 0 | 0 | 0 | 0 | 0 |
| Metzger, Roger, Houston† | .227 | 127 | 450 | 54 | 102 | 133 | 7 | 9 | 2 | 26 | 15 | 4 | 4 | 5 |
| Milbourne, Lawrence, Houston | .212 | 73 | 151 | 17 | 32 | 40 | 1 | 2 | 1 | 9 | 4 | 1 | 1 | 2 |
| Millan, Felix, New York | .283 | 162 | 676 | 81 | 191 | 235 | 37 | 2 | 1 | 56 | 17 | 2 | 1 | 6 |
| Miller, C. Bruce, San Francisco | .239 | 99 | 309 | 22 | 74 | 89 | 6 | 3 | 1 | 31 | 1 | 2 | 0 | 1 |
| Milner, John, New York° | .191 | 91 | 220 | 24 | 42 | 74 | 11 | 0 | 7 | 29 | 0 | 0 | 1 | 1 |
| Minshall, James, Pittsburgh† | .000 | 1 | 0 | 0 | 0 | 0 | 0 | 0 | 0 | 0 | 0 | 0 | 0 | 0 |
| Minton, Gregory, San Francisco† | .000 | 4 | 6 | 0 | 0 | 0 | 0 | 0 | 0 | 0 | 1 | 0 | 0 | 0 |
| Mitterwald, George, Chicago | .220 | 84 | 200 | 19 | 44 | 69 | 4 | 3 | 5 | 26 | 1 | 2 | 0 | 0 |
| Moffitt, Randall, San Francisco | .214 | 55 | 14 | 2 | 3 | 5 | 0 | 1 | 0 | 0 | 0 | 0 | 0 | 0 |
| Monday, Robert, Chicago° | .267 | 136 | 491 | 89 | 131 | 219 | 29 | 4 | 17 | 60 | 7 | 1 | 8 | 3 |
| Montague, John, Mtl-Phila | .000 | 16 | 1 | 0 | 0 | 0 | 0 | 0 | 0 | 0 | 0 | 0 | 0 | 0 |
| Montanez, Guillermo, Phila-SF° | .302 | 156 | 602 | 61 | 182 | 250 | 34 | 2 | 10 | 101 | 2 | 10 | 6 | 3 |
| Montefusco, John, San Francisco | .088 | 35 | 80 | 4 | 7 | 12 | 0 | 1 | 1 | 2 | 9 | 0 | 0 | 0 |
| Moore, Donnie, Chicago° | .000 | 4 | 3 | 0 | 0 | 0 | 0 | 0 | 0 | 0 | 0 | 0 | 0 | 0 |
| Moore, Tommy, St. Louis | .500 | 10 | 2 | 0 | 1 | 1 | 0 | 0 | 0 | 0 | 0 | 0 | 0 | 0 |
| Moose, Robert, Pittsburgh | .167 | 23 | 18 | 1 | 3 | 3 | 0 | 0 | 0 | 0 | 1 | 0 | 0 | 0 |
| Morales, Jose, Montreal | .301 | 93 | 163 | 18 | 49 | 63 | 6 | 1 | 2 | 24 | 0 | 1 | 0 | 2 |
| Morales, Julio, Chicago | .270 | 153 | 578 | 62 | 156 | 213 | 21 | 0 | 12 | 91 | 0 | 11 | 3 | 7 |
| Moreno, Omar, Pittsburgh° | .167 | 6 | 6 | 1 | 1 | 1 | 0 | 0 | 0 | 0 | 0 | 0 | 1 | 0 |
| Morgan, Joe, Cincinnati° | .327 | 146 | 498 | 107 | 163 | 253 | 27 | 6 | 17 | 94 | 0 | 6 | 67 | 10 |
| Morton, Carl, Atlanta | .160 | 39 | 94 | 9 | 15 | 17 | 2 | 0 | 0 | 5 | 5 | 0 | 0 | 0 |
| Moses, Gerald, San Diego | .158 | 13 | 19 | 1 | 3 | 5 | 2 | 0 | 0 | 1 | 0 | 0 | 0 | 0 |
| Mota, Manuel, Los Angeles | .265 | 52 | 49 | 3 | 13 | 14 | 1 | 0 | 0 | 10 | 3 | 0 | 0 | 0 |
| Mumphrey, Jerry, St. Louis† | .375 | 11 | 16 | 2 | 6 | 8 | 2 | 0 | 0 | 1 | 0 | 0 | 0 | 0 |
| Murcer, Bobby, San Francisco° | .298 | 147 | 526 | 80 | 157 | 227 | 29 | 4 | 11 | 91 | 1 | 12 | 9 | 5 |
| Murray, Dale, Montreal | .214 | 63 | 14 | 1 | 3 | 3 | 0 | 0 | 0 | 1 | 0 | 0 | 0 | 0 |
| Niekro, Joseph, Houston | .214 | 40 | 14 | 1 | 3 | 3 | 0 | 0 | 0 | 0 | 2 | 0 | 0 | 0 |
| Niekro, Philip, Atlanta | .172 | 39 | 99 | 5 | 17 | 21 | 2 | 1 | 0 | 10 | 4 | 2 | 0 | 0 |
| Nolan, Gary, Cincinnati | .176 | 32 | 68 | 10 | 12 | 15 | 1 | 1 | 0 | 7 | 6 | 0 | 0 | 0 |
| Nolan, Joseph, Atlanta° | .250 | 4 | 4 | 0 | 1 | 1 | 0 | 0 | 0 | 0 | 0 | 0 | 0 | 0 |
| Norman, Fredie, Cincinnati† | .117 | 34 | 60 | 3 | 7 | 8 | 1 | 0 | 0 | 4 | 9 | 0 | 0 | 0 |
| Oates, Johnny, Atl-Phila° | .282 | 98 | 287 | 28 | 81 | 99 | 15 | 0 | 1 | 25 | 4 | 4 | 1 | 0 |
| Odom, Johnny, Atlanta | .077 | 15 | 13 | 0 | 1 | 2 | 1 | 0 | 0 | 1 | 1 | 0 | 0 | 0 |
| Office, Rowland, Atlanta° | .290 | 126 | 355 | 30 | 103 | 128 | 14 | 1 | 3 | 30 | 5 | 2 | 2 | 2 |
| Oliver, Albert, Pittsburgh° | .280 | 155 | 628 | 90 | 176 | 285 | 39 | 8 | 18 | 84 | 0 | 8 | 4 | 2 |
| Ontiveros, Steven, San Fran† | .289 | 108 | 325 | 21 | 94 | 119 | 16 | 0 | 3 | 31 | 2 | 4 | 2 | 0 |
| Ott, N. Edward, Pittsburgh° | .200 | 5 | 5 | 0 | 1 | 1 | 0 | 0 | 0 | 0 | 0 | 0 | 0 | 0 |
| Paciorek, Thomas, Los Angeles | .193 | 62 | 145 | 14 | 28 | 39 | 8 | 0 | 1 | 5 | 1 | 0 | 4 | 3 |
| Parker, David, Pittsburgh° | .308 | 148 | 558 | 75 | 172 | 302 | 35 | 10 | 25 | 101 | 0 | 1 | 8 | 6 |
| Parker, Harry, NY-StL | .000 | 32 | 3 | 0 | 0 | 0 | 0 | 0 | 0 | 1 | 2 | 0 | 0 | 0 |
| Parrish, Larry, Montreal | .274 | 145 | 532 | 50 | 146 | 218 | 32 | 5 | 10 | 65 | 7 | 2 | 4 | 5 |

| Player and Club | Pct. | G. | AB | R. | H. | TB. | 2B. | 3B. | HR. | RBI. | SH. | SF. | SB. | CS. |
|---|---|---|---|---|---|---|---|---|---|---|---|---|---|---|
| Pemberton, Brock, New York† | .000 | 2 | 2 | 0 | 0 | 0 | 0 | 0 | 0 | 0 | 0 | 0 | 0 | 0 |
| Perez, Atanasio, Cincinnati | .282 | 137 | 511 | 74 | 144 | 238 | 28 | 3 | 20 | 109 | 0 | 6 | 1 | 2 |
| Perez, Martin, Atlanta | .275 | 120 | 461 | 50 | 127 | 151 | 14 | 2 | 2 | 34 | 7 | 3 | 2 | 2 |
| Phillips, Michael, SF-NY° | .251 | 126 | 414 | 34 | 104 | 131 | 10 | 7 | 1 | 29 | 2 | 4 | 4 | 0 |
| Plummer, William, Cincinnati | .182 | 65 | 159 | 17 | 29 | 39 | 7 | 0 | 1 | 19 | 2 | 4 | 0 | 0 |
| Pocoroba, Biff, Atlanta† | .255 | 67 | 188 | 15 | 48 | 60 | 7 | 1 | 1 | 22 | 2 | 1 | 0 | 0 |
| Popovich, Paul, Pittsburgh† | .200 | 25 | 40 | 5 | 8 | 9 | 1 | 0 | 0 | 1 | 0 | 0 | 0 | 0 |
| Powell, Paul, Los Angeles | .200 | 8 | 10 | 2 | 2 | 3 | 1 | 0 | 0 | 0 | 0 | 0 | 0 | 0 |
| Prall, Wilfred, Chicago° | .000 | 3 | 4 | 1 | 0 | 0 | 0 | 0 | 0 | 1 | 2 | 0 | 0 | 0 |
| Rader, David, San Francisco° | .291 | 98 | 292 | 39 | 85 | 115 | 15 | 0 | 5 | 31 | 0 | 3 | 1 | 0 |
| Rader, Douglas, Houston | .223 | 129 | 448 | 41 | 100 | 163 | 23 | 2 | 12 | 48 | 2 | 2 | 5 | 4 |
| Randolph, Willie, Pittsburgh | .164 | 30 | 61 | 9 | 10 | 11 | 1 | 0 | 0 | 3 | 1 | 1 | 1 | 0 |
| Rasmussen, Harold, St. Louis | .154 | 14 | 26 | 1 | 4 | 4 | 0 | 0 | 0 | 3 | 1 | 0 | 0 | 0 |
| Rau, Douglas, Los Angeles° | .195 | 38 | 87 | 5 | 17 | 17 | 0 | 0 | 0 | 6 | 10 | 0 | 0 | 0 |
| Reed, Ronald, Atl-StL | .183 | 34 | 82 | 7 | 15 | 20 | 5 | 0 | 0 | 6 | 10 | 0 | 0 | 0 |
| Reitz, Kenneth, St. Louis | .269 | 161 | 592 | 43 | 159 | 201 | 25 | 1 | 5 | 63 | 2 | 6 | 1 | 1 |
| Renko, Steve, Montreal | .278 | 33 | 54 | 5 | 15 | 19 | 1 | 0 | 1 | 7 | 5 | 0 | 1 | 0 |
| Rettenmund, Mervin, Cincinnati | .239 | 93 | 188 | 24 | 45 | 59 | 6 | 1 | 2 | 19 | 1 | 2 | 5 | 0 |
| Reuschel, Paul, Chicago | .000 | 28 | 4 | 0 | 0 | 0 | 0 | 0 | 0 | 0 | 1 | 0 | 0 | 0 |
| Reuschel, Ricky, Chicago | .208 | 38 | 77 | 3 | 16 | 21 | 2 | 0 | 1 | 7 | 6 | 0 | 0 | 1 |
| Reuss, Jerry, Pittsburgh° | .197 | 32 | 71 | 6 | 14 | 16 | 2 | 0 | 0 | 2 | 10 | 0 | 0 | 0 |
| Reynolds, G. Craig, Pittsburgh° | .224 | 31 | 76 | 8 | 17 | 20 | 3 | 0 | 0 | 4 | 0 | 0 | 0 | 1 |
| Reynolds, Kenneth, St. Louis° | .000 | 10 | 2 | 0 | 0 | 0 | 0 | 0 | 0 | 0 | 0 | 0 | 0 | 1 |
| Rhoden, Richard, Los Angeles | .071 | 26 | 28 | 0 | 2 | 2 | 0 | 0 | 0 | 1 | 1 | 0 | 0 | 0 |
| Richard, James, Houston | .203 | 33 | 74 | 4 | 15 | 24 | 6 | 0 | 1 | 13 | 5 | 0 | 0 | 0 |
| Rivera, Jesus, Montreal | .111 | 5 | 9 | 1 | 1 | 1 | 0 | 0 | 0 | 0 | 0 | 0 | 0 | 0 |
| Roberts, David A., Houston° | .143 | 32 | 63 | 2 | 9 | 13 | 2 | 1 | 0 | 5 | 10 | 0 | 0 | 0 |
| Roberts, David W., San Diego | .283 | 33 | 113 | 7 | 32 | 40 | 2 | 0 | 2 | 12 | 4 | 0 | 3 | 1 |
| Robertson, Robert, Pittsburgh | .274 | 75 | 124 | 17 | 34 | 56 | 4 | 0 | 6 | 18 | 0 | 3 | 0 | 0 |
| Robinson, Craig, Atl-SF | .065 | 39 | 46 | 5 | 3 | 4 | 1 | 0 | 0 | 1 | 0 | 0 | 0 | 0 |
| Robinson, William, Pittsburgh | .280 | 92 | 200 | 26 | 56 | 90 | 12 | 2 | 6 | 33 | 3 | 3 | 3 | 1 |
| Rogers, Stephen, Montreal | .169 | 35 | 77 | 4 | 13 | 15 | 0 | 1 | 0 | 5 | 6 | 0 | 3 | 1 |
| Rogodzinski, Michael, Phila° | .263 | 16 | 19 | 3 | 5 | 6 | 1 | 0 | 0 | 6 | 1 | 0 | 0 | 0 |
| Rooker, James, Pittsburgh | .095 | 28 | 63 | 4 | 6 | 6 | 0 | 0 | 0 | 4 | 0 | 0 | 0 | 0 |
| Rose, Peter, Cincinnati† | .317 | 162 | 662 | 112 | 210 | 286 | 47 | 4 | 7 | 74 | 1 | 1 | 0 | 1 |
| Rosello, David, Chicago | .259 | 19 | 58 | 7 | 15 | 20 | 2 | 0 | 1 | 8 | 2 | 0 | 0 | 1 |
| Royster, Jeron, Los Angeles | .250 | 13 | 36 | 2 | 9 | 13 | 2 | 1 | 0 | 1 | 0 | 0 | 1 | 0 |
| Rudolph, Kenneth, St. Louis | .200 | 44 | 80 | 5 | 16 | 21 | 2 | 0 | 1 | 6 | 0 | 0 | 0 | 0 |
| Russell, William, Los Angeles | .206 | 84 | 252 | 24 | 52 | 65 | 9 | 2 | 0 | 14 | 4 | 1 | 5 | 0 |
| Ruthven, Richard, Philadelphia | .154 | 12 | 13 | 1 | 2 | 2 | 0 | 0 | 0 | 1 | 2 | 0 | 0 | 0 |
| Sadecki, Raymond, StL-Atl° | .200 | 33 | 15 | 0 | 3 | 4 | 1 | 0 | 0 | 2 | 1 | 0 | 0 | 0 |
| Sadek, Michael, San Francisco | .236 | 42 | 106 | 14 | 25 | 34 | 5 | 2 | 0 | 9 | 0 | 3 | 0 | 0 |
| Sanders, Kenneth, New York | .000 | 30 | 2 | 0 | 0 | 0 | 0 | 0 | 0 | 0 | 1 | 0 | 0 | 0 |
| Sanguillen, Manuel, Pittsburgh | .328 | 133 | 481 | 60 | 158 | 217 | 24 | 4 | 9 | 58 | 2 | 3 | 5 | 4 |
| Scanlon, J. Patrick, Montreal° | .183 | 60 | 109 | 5 | 20 | 31 | 3 | 1 | 2 | 15 | 0 | 0 | 0 | 1 |
| Scarce, G. McCurdy, New York° | .000 | 1 | 0 | 0 | 0 | 0 | 0 | 0 | 0 | 0 | 0 | 0 | 0 | 0 |
| Scherman, Frederick, Hou-Mtl° | .059 | 50 | 17 | 0 | 1 | 2 | 1 | 0 | 0 | 0 | 0 | 0 | 0 | 0 |
| Schmidt, Michael, Philadelphia | .249 | 158 | 562 | 93 | 140 | 294 | 34 | 3 | 38 | 95 | 6 | 1 | 29 | 12 |
| Schueler, Ronald, Philadelphia | .154 | 46 | 13 | 0 | 2 | 2 | 0 | 0 | 0 | 1 | 6 | 0 | 0 | 0 |
| Schultz, C. Budd, Chicago | .000 | 6 | 0 | 0 | 0 | 0 | 0 | 0 | 0 | 0 | 1 | 0 | 0 | 0 |
| Scott, Anthony, Montreal† | .182 | 92 | 143 | 19 | 26 | 34 | 4 | 2 | 0 | 11 | 0 | 1 | 5 | 6 |
| Scott, John, San Diego | .000 | 25 | 9 | 6 | 0 | 0 | 0 | 0 | 0 | 0 | 0 | 1 | 5 | 6 |
| Seaver, G. Thomas, New York | .179 | 37 | 95 | 7 | 17 | 18 | 1 | 0 | 0 | 5 | 7 | 0 | 2 | 0 |
| Sells, David, Los Angeles | 1.000 | 5 | 1 | 0 | 1 | 1 | 0 | 0 | 0 | 1 | 0 | 0 | 0 | 0 |
| Sharon, Richard, San Diego | .194 | 91 | 160 | 14 | 31 | 50 | 7 | 0 | 4 | 20 | 5 | 0 | 0 | 2 |
| Siebert, Paul, Houston° | .000 | 7 | 3 | 0 | 0 | 0 | 0 | 0 | 0 | 0 | 1 | 0 | 0 | 0 |
| Siebert, Wilfred, San Diego | .375 | 7 | 8 | 1 | 3 | 4 | 1 | 0 | 0 | 1 | 1 | 0 | 0 | 0 |
| Simmons, Ted, St. Louis† | .332 | 157 | 581 | 80 | 193 | 285 | 32 | 3 | 18 | 100 | 0 | 4 | 1 | 3 |
| Simpson, Joe, Los Angeles° | .333 | 9 | 6 | 3 | 2 | 2 | 0 | 0 | 0 | 0 | 0 | 0 | 0 | 0 |
| Simpson, Wayne, Philadelphia | .222 | 7 | 9 | 0 | 2 | 2 | 0 | 0 | 0 | 0 | 0 | 0 | 0 | 0 |
| Sizemore, Ted, St. Louis | .240 | 153 | 562 | 56 | 135 | 169 | 23 | 1 | 3 | 49 | 21 | 5 | 1 | 5 |
| Smith, C. Reginald, St. Louis† | .302 | 135 | 477 | 67 | 144 | 233 | 26 | 3 | 19 | 76 | 0 | 7 | 9 | 7 |
| Solomon, Eddie, Chicago | .000 | 6 | 0 | 0 | 0 | 0 | 0 | 0 | 0 | 0 | 0 | 0 | 0 | 0 |
| Sosa, Elias, StL-Atl | .133 | 57 | 15 | 0 | 2 | 2 | 0 | 0 | 0 | 1 | 1 | 0 | 0 | 0 |
| Sosa, Jose, Houston | .333 | 26 | 9 | 2 | 3 | 3 | 0 | 0 | 0 | 0 | 1 | 0 | 0 | 0 |
| Speed, Horace, San Francisco | .133 | 17 | 15 | 2 | 2 | 3 | 1 | 0 | 0 | 1 | 0 | 0 | 0 | 0 |
| Speier, Chris, San Francisco | .271 | 141 | 487 | 60 | 132 | 202 | 30 | 5 | 10 | 69 | 3 | 3 | 4 | 5 |
| Sperring, Robert, Chicago | .208 | 65 | 144 | 25 | 30 | 39 | 4 | 1 | 1 | 9 | 3 | 2 | 0 | 2 |
| Spillner, Daniel, San Diego | .133 | 37 | 45 | 4 | 6 | 7 | 1 | 0 | 0 | 6 | 0 | 0 | 0 | 0 |

| Player and Club | Pct. | G. | AB. | R. | H. | TB. | 2B. | 3B. | HR. | RBI. | SH. | SF. | SB. | CS. |
|---|---|---|---|---|---|---|---|---|---|---|---|---|---|---|
| Staiger, Roy, New York | .158 | 13 | 19 | 2 | 3 | 4 | 1 | 0 | 0 | 0 | 0 | 0 | 0 | 0 |
| Stanhouse, Donald, Montreal | .333 | 4 | 3 | 0 | 1 | 1 | 0 | 0 | 0 | 0 | 0 | 0 | 0 | 0 |
| Stanton, Michael, Houston | .250 | 7 | 4 | 0 | 1 | 1 | 0 | 0 | 0 | 0 | 0 | 0 | 0 | 0 |
| Stargell, Wilver, Pittsburgh° | .295 | 124 | 461 | 71 | 136 | 238 | 32 | 2 | 22 | 90 | 0 | 4 | 0 | 0 |
| Staub, Daniel, New York° | .282 | 155 | 574 | 93 | 162 | 257 | 30 | 4 | 19 | 105 | 1 | 9 | 2 | 0 |
| Stearns, John, New York | .189 | 59 | 169 | 25 | 32 | 48 | 5 | 1 | 3 | 10 | 3 | 2 | 4 | 1 |
| Stennett, Renaldo, Pittsburgh | .286 | 148 | 616 | 89 | 176 | 236 | 25 | 7 | 7 | 62 | 6 | 5 | 5 | 4 |
| Stone, George, New York° | .167 | 13 | 18 | 2 | 3 | 3 | 0 | 0 | 0 | 2 | 2 | 0 | 0 | 0 |
| Stone, Steven, Chicago | .111 | 34 | 72 | 3 | 8 | 10 | 2 | 0 | 0 | 3 | 7 | 0 | 0 | 0 |
| Strom, Brent, San Diego | .100 | 18 | 30 | 3 | 3 | 4 | 1 | 0 | 0 | 1 | 6 | 0 | 0 | 0 |
| Summers, John, Chicago* | .231 | 76 | 91 | 14 | 21 | 31 | 5 | 1 | 1 | 16 | 0 | 1 | 0 | 0 |
| Sutton, Donald, Los Angeles | .138 | 35 | 80 | 4 | 11 | 12 | 1 | 0 | 0 | 3 | 12 | 0 | 0 | 0 |
| Swan, Craig, New York | .000 | 6 | 7 | 0 | 0 | 0 | 0 | 0 | 0 | 0 | 1 | 2 | 0 | 0 |
| Swisher, Steven, Chicago | .213 | 93 | 254 | 20 | 54 | 77 | 16 | 2 | 1 | 22 | 6 | 4 | 1 | 0 |
| Tate, Randall, New York | .000 | 26 | 41 | 2 | 0 | 0 | 0 | 0 | 0 | 0 | 5 | 5 | 0 | 1 |
| Taveras, Franklin, Pittsburgh | .212 | 134 | 378 | 44 | 80 | 97 | 9 | 4 | 0 | 23 | 8 | 2 | 17 | 6 |
| Taylor, Antonio, Philadelphia | .243 | 79 | 103 | 13 | 25 | 35 | 5 | 1 | 1 | 17 | 1 | 2 | 3 | 3 |
| Taylor, Charles G., Montreal | .000 | 54 | 2 | 0 | 0 | 0 | 0 | 0 | 0 | 0 | 0 | 0 | 0 | 0 |
| Tekulve, Kenton, Pittsburgh | .091 | 34 | 11 | 1 | 1 | 1 | 0 | 0 | 0 | 1 | 0 | 0 | 0 | 0 |
| Tepedino, Francis, Atlanta° | .000 | 8 | 7 | 0 | 0 | 0 | 0 | 0 | 0 | 0 | 0 | 0 | 0 | 0 |
| Terlecky, Gregory, St. Louis | .333 | 20 | 3 | 0 | 1 | 1 | 0 | 0 | 0 | 0 | 0 | 0 | 0 | 0 |
| Thomas, Derrel, San Francisco† | .276 | 144 | 540 | 99 | 149 | 206 | 21 | 9 | 6 | 48 | 8 | 3 | 28 | 13 |
| Thomasson, Gary, San Francisco° | .227 | 114 | 326 | 44 | 74 | 113 | 12 | 3 | 7 | 32 | 0 | 5 | 9 | 3 |
| Thompson, Michael, Atlanta | .071 | 16 | 14 | 0 | 1 | 1 | 0 | 0 | 0 | 0 | 2 | 0 | 0 | 0 |
| Thornton, Andre, Chicago | .293 | 120 | 372 | 70 | 109 | 192 | 21 | 4 | 18 | 60 | 3 | 6 | 3 | 2 |
| Tolan, Robert, San Diego° | .255 | 147 | 506 | 58 | 129 | 171 | 19 | 4 | 5 | 43 | 14 | 2 | 11 | 13 |
| Tomlin, David, San Diego° | .200 | 67 | 5 | 1 | 1 | 1 | 0 | 0 | 0 | 0 | 2 | 0 | 0 | 0 |
| Toms, Thomas, San Francisco | .000 | 7 | 0 | 0 | 0 | 0 | 0 | 0 | 0 | 0 | 0 | 0 | 0 | 0 |
| Torre, Joseph, New York | .247 | 114 | 361 | 33 | 89 | 129 | 16 | 3 | 6 | 35 | 2 | 0 | 0 | 0 |
| Torrealba, Pablo, Atlanta° | 1.000 | 6 | 1 | 0 | 1 | 1 | 0 | 0 | 0 | 0 | 0 | 0 | 0 | 0 |
| Torres, Hector, San Diego | .259 | 112 | 352 | 31 | 91 | 118 | 12 | 0 | 5 | 26 | 7 | 6 | 2 | 3 |
| Trillo, J. Manuel (Marcano), Chi | .248 | 154 | 545 | 55 | 135 | 172 | 12 | 2 | 7 | 70 | 15 | 5 | 1 | 7 |
| Turner, J. Jerry, San Diego° | .273 | 11 | 22 | 1 | 6 | 6 | 0 | 0 | 0 | 0 | 0 | 0 | 0 | 0 |
| Twitchell, Wayne, Philadelphia | .088 | 36 | 34 | 1 | 3 | 5 | 2 | 0 | 0 | 1 | 3 | 0 | 0 | 0 |
| Tyrone, James, Chicago | .227 | 11 | 22 | 0 | 5 | 7 | 0 | 1 | 0 | 3 | 0 | 1 | 1 | 1 |
| Tyson, Michael, St. Louis | .266 | 122 | 368 | 45 | 98 | 126 | 16 | 3 | 2 | 37 | 6 | 1 | 5 | 2 |
| Underwood, Thomas, Philadelphia | .122 | 35 | 74 | 4 | 9 | 10 | 1 | 0 | 0 | 8 | 7 | 0 | 0 | 0 |
| Unser, Delbert, New York° | .294 | 147 | 531 | 65 | 156 | 208 | 18 | 2 | 10 | 53 | 8 | 4 | 4 | 3 |
| Vail, Michael, New York | .302 | 38 | 162 | 17 | 49 | 68 | 8 | 1 | 3 | 17 | 0 | 0 | 0 | 0 |
| Valentine, Ellis, Montreal | .364 | 12 | 33 | 2 | 12 | 19 | 4 | 0 | 1 | 3 | 0 | 0 | 0 | 0 |
| Valentine, Robert, San Diego | .133 | 7 | 15 | 1 | 2 | 5 | 0 | 0 | 1 | 1 | 1 | 0 | 1 | 0 |
| Vukovich, John, Cincinnati | .211 | 31 | 38 | 4 | 8 | 11 | 3 | 0 | 0 | 2 | 4 | 0 | 0 | 0 |
| Wall, Stanley, Los Angeles° | .000 | 10 | 0 | 0 | 0 | 0 | 0 | 0 | 0 | 0 | 0 | 0 | 0 | 0 |
| Wallace, Michael, St. Louis° | .000 | 9 | 0 | 0 | 0 | 0 | 0 | 0 | 0 | 0 | 0 | 0 | 0 | 0 |
| Wallis, H. Joseph, Chicago° | .286 | 16 | 56 | 9 | 16 | 25 | 2 | 2 | 1 | 4 | 0 | 0 | 2 | 0 |
| Warthen, Daniel, Montreal† | .118 | 40 | 51 | 2 | 6 | 6 | 0 | 0 | 0 | 1 | 4 | 0 | 0 | 0 |
| Watson, Robert, Houston | .324 | 132 | 485 | 67 | 157 | 240 | 27 | 1 | 18 | 85 | 0 | 5 | 3 | 5 |
| Watt, Eddie, Chicago | .000 | 6 | 0 | 0 | 0 | 0 | 0 | 0 | 0 | 0 | 0 | 0 | 0 | 0 |
| Webb, Henry, New York | .258 | 31 | 31 | 5 | 8 | 8 | 0 | 0 | 0 | 3 | 0 | 0 | 0 | 0 |
| Werner, Donald, Cincinnati | .125 | 7 | 8 | 0 | 1 | 1 | 0 | 0 | 0 | 0 | 0 | 0 | 0 | 0 |
| White, Jerome, Montreal† | .299 | 39 | 97 | 14 | 29 | 41 | 4 | 1 | 2 | 7 | 0 | 0 | 5 | 2 |
| Wilcox, Milton, Chicago | .333 | 25 | 3 | 0 | 1 | 1 | 0 | 0 | 0 | 0 | 1 | 0 | 0 | 0 |
| Williams, Charles, San Francisco | .125 | 55 | 16 | 1 | 2 | 4 | 0 | 1 | 0 | 0 | 0 | 0 | 0 | 0 |
| Williams, Earl, Atlanta | .240 | 111 | 383 | 42 | 92 | 138 | 13 | 0 | 11 | 50 | 1 | 3 | 0 | 0 |
| Winfield, David, San Diego | .267 | 143 | 509 | 74 | 136 | 205 | 20 | 2 | 15 | 76 | 3 | 7 | 23 | 4 |
| Wynn, James, Los Angeles | .248 | 130 | 412 | 80 | 102 | 172 | 16 | 0 | 18 | 58 | 1 | 5 | 7 | 3 |
| Yeager, Stephen, Los Angeles | .228 | 135 | 452 | 34 | 103 | 157 | 16 | 1 | 12 | 54 | 9 | 6 | 2 | 5 |
| York, James, Houston | .091 | 19 | 11 | 0 | 1 | 1 | 0 | 0 | 0 | 0 | 0 | 0 | 0 | 0 |
| Zahn, Geoffrey, LA-Chi° | .133 | 18 | 15 | 1 | 2 | 2 | 0 | 0 | 0 | 1 | 7 | 0 | 0 | 0 |
| Zamora, Oscar, Chicago | .167 | 52 | 6 | 0 | 1 | 1 | 0 | 0 | 0 | 0 | 4 | 0 | 0 | 0 |
| Zisk, Richard, Pittsburgh | .290 | 147 | 504 | 69 | 146 | 239 | 27 | 3 | 20 | 75 | 0 | 4 | 0 | 1 |

AWARDED FIRST BASE ON INTERFERENCE: Brock, St.L. 2 (C. Johnson, Carter); Luzinski, Phila. 2 (Simmons 2); Phillips, N.Y. 2 (M. May, Foote); Torres, S.D. 2 (Hosley, M. May); Bench, Cin. (Foote); Bowa, Phila. (Swisher); Capra, Atl. (Boone); Hebner, Pitts. (Boone); Hundley, S.D. (Simmons); Hutton, Phila. (Simmons); May, Hous. (Correll); Perez, Atl. (Simmons).

## PLAYERS WITH TWO OR MORE CLUBS
### (Alphabetically Arranged With Player's First Club on Top)

| Player and Club | Pct. | G. | AB. | R. | H. | TB. | 2B. | 3B. | HR. | RBI. | SH. | SF. | Tot. BB. | Int. BB. | HP. | SO. | SB. | CS. | GI DP. |
|---|---|---|---|---|---|---|---|---|---|---|---|---|---|---|---|---|---|---|---|
| Dwyer, StL | .194 | 21 | 31 | 4 | 6 | 7 | 1 | 0 | 0 | 1 | 1 | 0 | 4 | 0 | 0 | 6 | 0 | 0 | 1 |
| Dwyer, Mtl | .286 | 60 | 175 | 22 | 50 | 68 | 7 | 1 | 3 | 20 | 11 | 2 | 23 | 0 | 0 | 30 | 4 | 1 | 0 |
| Goodson, SF | .207 | 39 | 121 | 10 | 25 | 35 | 7 | 0 | 1 | 8 | 0 | 1 | 7 | 2 | 0 | 14 | 0 | 1 | 4 |
| Goodson, Atl | .211 | 47 | 76 | 5 | 16 | 21 | 2 | 0 | 1 | 8 | 1 | 1 | 2 | 0 | 0 | 8 | 0 | 0 | 5 |
| Hahn, Phil | .000 | 9 | 5 | 0 | 0 | 0 | 0 | 0 | 0 | 0 | 1 | 0 | 0 | 0 | 0 | 2 | 0 | 0 | 0 |
| Hahn, StL | .125 | 7 | 8 | 3 | 1 | 1 | 0 | 0 | 0 | 0 | 0 | 0 | 1 | 0 | 0 | 1 | 0 | 0 | 1 |
| Hahn, SD | .231 | 34 | 26 | 7 | 6 | 11 | 1 | 2 | 0 | 3 | 0 | 0 | 10 | 0 | 0 | 2 | 1 | 0 | 2 |
| Hall, Cin | .000 | 2 | 0 | 0 | 0 | 0 | 0 | 0 | 0 | 0 | 0 | 0 | 0 | 0 | 0 | 0 | 0 | 0 | 0 |
| Hall, NY | .400 | 35 | 5 | 2 | 2 | 2 | 0 | 0 | 0 | 0 | 1 | 0 | 0 | 0 | 0 | 1 | 0 | 0 | 0 |
| Hooton, Chi | .000 | 3 | 3 | 0 | 0 | 0 | 0 | 0 | 0 | 0 | 0 | 0 | 0 | 0 | 0 | 0 | 0 | 0 | 0 |
| Hooton, LA | .129 | 31 | 70 | 6 | 9 | 15 | 3 | 0 | 1 | 7 | 13 | 0 | 4 | 0 | 0 | 27 | 0 | 0 | 1 |
| Lintz, Mtl | .197 | 46 | 132 | 18 | 26 | 26 | 0 | 0 | 0 | 3 | 7 | 0 | 23 | 0 | 0 | 18 | 17 | 9 | 3 |
| Lintz, StL | .278 | 27 | 18 | 6 | 5 | 6 | 1 | 0 | 0 | 1 | 0 | 0 | 3 | 0 | 0 | 2 | 4 | 0 | 0 |
| Maddox, SF | .135 | 17 | 52 | 4 | 7 | 11 | 1 | 0 | 1 | 4 | 1 | 0 | 6 | 1 | 1 | 3 | 1 | 1 | 0 |
| Maddox, Phil. | .291 | 99 | 374 | 50 | 109 | 162 | 25 | 8 | 4 | 46 | 0 | 3 | 36 | 5 | 5 | 54 | 24 | 3 | 3 |
| Montague, Mtl | .000 | 13 | 1 | 0 | 0 | 0 | 0 | 0 | 0 | 0 | 0 | 0 | 0 | 0 | 0 | 1 | 0 | 0 | 0 |
| Montague, Phil | .000 | 3 | 0 | 0 | 0 | 0 | 0 | 0 | 0 | 0 | 0 | 0 | 0 | 0 | 0 | 0 | 0 | 0 | 0 |
| Montanez, Phil | .286 | 21 | 84 | 9 | 24 | 38 | 8 | 0 | 2 | 16 | 1 | 1 | 4 | 0 | 0 | 12 | 1 | 0 | 3 |
| Montanez, SF | .305 | 135 | 518 | 52 | 158 | 212 | 26 | 2 | 8 | 85 | 1 | 9 | 45 | 8 | 4 | 50 | 5 | 3 | 23 |
| Oates, Atl | .222 | 8 | 18 | 0 | 4 | 5 | 1 | 0 | 0 | 0 | 0 | 0 | 1 | 0 | 0 | 4 | 0 | 0 | 0 |
| Oates, Phil | .286 | 90 | 269 | 28 | 77 | 94 | 14 | 0 | 1 | 25 | 4 | 4 | 33 | 10 | 0 | 29 | 1 | 0 | 6 |
| Parker, NY | .000 | 18 | 2 | 0 | 0 | 0 | 0 | 0 | 0 | 0 | 1 | 1 | 0 | 0 | 0 | 2 | 0 | 0 | 0 |
| Parker, StL | .000 | 14 | 1 | 0 | 0 | 0 | 0 | 0 | 0 | 0 | 1 | 0 | 1 | 0 | 0 | 0 | 0 | 0 | 0 |
| Phillips, SF | .194 | 10 | 31 | 3 | 6 | 6 | 0 | 0 | 0 | 1 | 0 | 0 | 6 | 0 | 0 | 11 | 4 | 1 | 0 |
| Phillips, NY | .256 | 116 | 383 | 31 | 98 | 125 | 10 | 7 | 1 | 28 | 2 | 4 | 25 | 5 | 1 | 47 | 3 | 0 | 8 |
| Reed, Atl | .231 | 10 | 26 | 3 | 6 | 8 | 2 | 0 | 0 | 4 | 0 | 0 | 1 | 0 | 0 | 11 | 0 | 0 | 0 |
| Reed, StL | .161 | 24 | 56 | 4 | 9 | 12 | 3 | 0 | 0 | 3 | 5 | 0 | 1 | 0 | 0 | 19 | 0 | 0 | 0 |
| Robinson, Atl | .059 | 10 | 17 | 1 | 1 | 1 | 0 | 0 | 0 | 0 | 0 | 0 | 0 | 0 | 0 | 5 | 0 | 0 | 1 |
| Robinson, SF | .069 | 29 | 29 | 4 | 2 | 3 | 1 | 0 | 0 | 0 | 1 | 0 | 2 | 0 | 0 | 6 | 0 | 0 | 1 |
| Sadecki, StL | .000 | 8 | 0 | 0 | 0 | 0 | 0 | 0 | 0 | 0 | 0 | 0 | 0 | 0 | 0 | 0 | 0 | 0 | 0 |
| Sadecki, Atl | .200 | 25 | 15 | 0 | 3 | 4 | 1 | 0 | 0 | 2 | 1 | 0 | 0 | 0 | 0 | 4 | 0 | 0 | 1 |
| Scherman, Hou | .000 | 16 | 1 | 0 | 0 | 0 | 0 | 0 | 0 | 0 | 0 | 0 | 0 | 0 | 0 | 1 | 0 | 0 | 0 |
| Scherman, Mtl | .063 | 34 | 16 | 0 | 1 | 2 | 1 | 0 | 0 | 0 | 0 | 0 | 1 | 0 | 0 | 2 | 0 | 0 | 0 |
| Sosa, StL | .125 | 14 | 8 | 0 | 1 | 1 | 0 | 0 | 0 | 0 | 1 | 0 | 0 | 0 | 0 | 4 | 0 | 0 | 0 |
| Sosa, Atl | .143 | 43 | 7 | 0 | 1 | 1 | 0 | 0 | 0 | 0 | 1 | 0 | 0 | 0 | 0 | 1 | 0 | 0 | 0 |
| Zahn, LA | .000 | 2 | 0 | 0 | 0 | 0 | 0 | 0 | 0 | 0 | 0 | 0 | 0 | 0 | 0 | 0 | 0 | 0 | 0 |
| Zahn, Chi | .133 | 16 | 15 | 1 | 2 | 2 | 0 | 0 | 0 | 1 | 7 | 0 | 0 | 0 | 0 | 3 | 0 | 0 | 1 |

# OFFICIAL MISCELLANEOUS NATIONAL LEAGUE BATTING RECORDS

## CLUB MISCELLANEOUS BATTING RECORDS

| Club | Slg. Pct. | G. | Tot. BB. | Int. BB. | HP. | SO. | GIDP. | ShO. |
|---|---|---|---|---|---|---|---|---|
| Pittsburgh | .402 | 161 | 468 | 55 | 38 | 832 | 124 | 13 |
| Philadelphia | .402 | 162 | 610 | 78 | 31 | 960 | 114 | 6 |
| Cincinnati | .401 | 162 | 691 | 67 | 35 | 916 | 122 | 5 |
| St. Louis | .375 | 163 | 444 | 66 | 29 | 649 | 137 | 14 |
| Chicago | .368 | 162 | 650 | 78 | 30 | 802 | 112 | 7 |
| San Francisco | .365 | 161 | 604 | 52 | 22 | 775 | 139 | 10 |
| Los Angeles | .365 | 162 | 611 | 72 | 31 | 825 | 123 | 7 |
| New York | .361 | 162 | 501 | 70 | 37 | 805 | 143 | 12 |
| Houston | .359 | 162 | 523 | 66 | 32 | 762 | 118 | 13 |
| Montreal | .348 | 162 | 579 | 73 | 27 | 954 | 110 | 16 |
| Atlanta | .346 | 161 | 543 | 58 | 18 | 759 | 139 | 12 |
| San Diego | .335 | 162 | 506 | 60 | 37 | 754 | 128 | 14 |
| Totals | .369 | | 6730 | 795 | 367 | 9793 | 1509 | 129 |

## INDIVIDUAL MISCELLANEOUS BATTING RECORDS

(Top Fifteen Qualifiers for Slugging Championship—502 or More Plate Appearances)

| Player—Club | Slg. Pct. | Tot. BB. | Int. BB. | HP. | SO. | GI DP. |
|---|---|---|---|---|---|---|
| Parker, Pitt | .541 | 38 | 4 | 5 | 89 | 18 |
| Luzinski, Phil | .540 | 89 | 17 | 8 | 151 | 12 |
| Schmidt, Phil | .523 | 101 | 10 | 4 | 180 | 7 |
| Bench, Cin | .519 | 65 | 12 | 2 | 108 | 12 |
| Foster, Cin | .518 | 40 | 11 | 3 | 73 | 14 |
| Stargell, Pitt | .516 | 58 | 6 | 3 | 109 | 9 |
| Morgan, Cin | .508 | 132 | 3 | 3 | 52 | 3 |
| Watson, Hou | .495 | 40 | 10 | 3 | 50 | 11 |
| Kingman, NY | .494 | 34 | 5 | 4 | 153 | 13 |
| Simmons, StL | .491 | 63 | 16 | 1 | 35 | 20 |
| Smith, StL | .488 | 63 | 9 | 3 | 59 | 16 |
| Madlock, Chi | .479 | 42 | 5 | 3 | 34 | 11 |
| Garvey, LA | .476 | 33 | 6 | 3 | 66 | 19 |
| Zisk, Pitt | .474 | 68 | 9 | 2 | 109 | 12 |
| Cey, LA | .473 | 78 | 15 | 7 | 74 | 15 |

DEPARTMENTAL LEADERS: Tot. BB—Morgan, 132; Int. BB—Garr, Luzinski, 17; HP—Millan 12; SO—Schmidt, 180; GIDP—Montanez, 26.

### (All Players—Listed Alphabetically)

| Player—Club | Slg. Pct. | Tot. BB. | Int. BB. | HP. | SO. | GI DP. |
|---|---|---|---|---|---|---|
| Acosta, Phil | .000 | 0 | 0 | 0 | 0 | 0 |
| Adams, SF | .478 | 11 | 0 | 1 | 25 | 1 |
| Alexander, SF | .000 | 1 | 0 | 0 | 2 | 0 |
| Allen, Phil | .385 | 58 | 4 | 2 | 109 | 19 |
| Almon, SD | .400 | 0 | 0 | 0 | 1 | 0 |
| Alou, NY | .294 | 4 | 2 | 1 | 5 | 4 |
| Alvarez, LA | .000 | 0 | 0 | 0 | 1 | 0 |
| Anderson, Phil | .372 | 17 | 3 | 2 | 66 | 6 |
| Andrews, Hou | .285 | 31 | 4 | 0 | 34 | 6 |
| Apodaca, NY | .364 | 1 | 0 | 0 | 5 | 0 |
| Armbrister, Cin | .200 | 5 | 0 | 1 | 19 | 1 |
| Arnold, SF | .195 | 4 | 0 | 0 | 8 | 3 |
| Auerbach, LA | .276 | 18 | 3 | 0 | 22 | 8 |
| Bailey, Mtl | .361 | 46 | 3 | 1 | 38 | 8 |
| Baker, Atl | .421 | 67 | 7 | 0 | 57 | 10 |
| Baldwin, NY | .200 | 0 | 0 | 0 | 5 | 0 |
| Bannister, Phil | .344 | 1 | 0 | 0 | 9 | 1 |
| Barlow, StL | .000 | 0 | 0 | 0 | 0 | 0 |
| Barr, SF | .132 | 3 | 0 | 0 | 24 | 2 |
| Batista, Hou | .400 | 0 | 0 | 0 | 4 | 1 |
| Beall, Atl | .290 | 6 | 0 | 0 | 9 | 0 |
| Beard, Atl | .111 | 1 | 0 | 0 | 5 | 0 |
| Beckert, SD | .438 | 1 | 0 | 0 | 0 | 0 |
| Belloir, Atl | .257 | 7 | 0 | 0 | 8 | 5 |
| Bench, Cin | .519 | 65 | 12 | 2 | 108 | 12 |
| Biittner, Mtl | .408 | 34 | 8 | 0 | 33 | 12 |
| Billingham, Cin | .108 | 8 | 0 | 0 | 22 | 0 |
| Billings, StL | .000 | 0 | 0 | 0 | 2 | 0 |
| Blair, Mtl | .143 | 2 | 0 | 0 | 22 | 0 |
| Blanks, Atl | .293 | 38 | 1 | 2 | 43 | 11 |
| Bonham, Chi | .220 | 1 | 0 | 0 | 19 | 1 |
| Boone, Phil | .329 | 32 | 6 | 1 | 14 | 8 |
| Borbon, Cin | .333 | 0 | 0 | 0 | 4 | 0 |
| Boswell, Hou | .309 | 30 | 7 | 1 | 12 | 7 |
| Bowa, Phil | .377 | 24 | 0 | 2 | 32 | 9 |
| Bradford, StL | .432 | 12 | 0 | 0 | 24 | 3 |
| Bradley, SF | .000 | 1 | 0 | 0 | 4 | 0 |
| Breeden, Mtl. | .189 | 7 | 3 | 0 | 5 | 1 |
| Brett, Pitt | .365 | 1 | 0 | 0 | 7 | 1 |
| Brewer, Phil | .000 | 0 | 0 | 0 | 0 | 0 |
| Brinkman, StL | .333 | 7 | 2 | 1 | 10 | 3 |
| Brock, StL | .400 | 38 | 6 | 3 | 64 | 7 |
| Brown, SF | .279 | 5 | 0 | 0 | 13 | 0 |
| Brown, Phil | .510 | 15 | 1 | 0 | 29 | 1 |
| Bryant, StL | .000 | 0 | 0 | 0 | 0 | 0 |
| Buckner, LA | .358 | 17 | 7 | 2 | 15 | 11 |
| Burris, Chi | .207 | 7 | 0 | 0 | 24 | 1 |
| Cabell, Hou | .365 | 18 | 1 | 3 | 53 | 9 |
| Caldwell, SF | .227 | 0 | 0 | 0 | 11 | 2 |
| Candelaria, Pitt | .140 | 3 | 0 | 0 | 12 | 0 |
| Capra, Atl | .043 | 1 | 0 | 0 | 5 | 0 |
| Cardenal, Chi | .423 | 77 | 5 | 4 | 50 | 11 |
| Carlton, Phil | .178 | 5 | 0 | 0 | 24 | 3 |
| Carrithers, Mtl | .265 | 0 | 0 | 0 | 10 | 0 |
| C. Carroll, Cin | .000 | 0 | 0 | 0 | 6 | 0 |
| T. Carroll, Cin. | .000 | 0 | 0 | 0 | 6 | 0 |
| Carter, Mtl | .416 | 72 | 8 | 1 | 83 | 7 |
| Cash, Phil | .388 | 56 | 5 | 4 | 34 | 8 |
| Cater, StL | .286 | 1 | 1 | 0 | 3 | 0 |
| Cedeno, Hou | .440 | 62 | 9 | 7 | 52 | 12 |
| Cey, LA | .473 | 78 | 15 | 7 | 74 | 15 |
| Chaney, Cin | .294 | 14 | 2 | 0 | 38 | 3 |
| Christenson, Phil. | .421 | 3 | 0 | 0 | 27 | 0 |
| Clark, Phil | .000 | 0 | 0 | 0 | 1 | 0 |
| Clark, SF | .235 | 1 | 0 | 0 | 2 | 0 |
| Clines, NY | .286 | 11 | 1 | 1 | 21 | 4 |
| Coggins, Mtl | .405 | 1 | 0 | 0 | 7 | 0 |
| Colbert, Mtl | .395 | 5 | 3 | 1 | 31 | 1 |
| Concepcion, Cin. | .353 | 39 | 4 | 2 | 51 | 17 |
| Correll, Atl | .360 | 42 | 5 | 1 | 66 | 13 |
| Cosgrove, Hou | .231 | 0 | 0 | 0 | 1 | 1 |
| Cox, Mtl | .407 | 1 | 1 | 0 | 2 | 2 |
| Cox, Phil | .200 | 1 | 0 | 0 | 0 | 1 |
| Cram, NY | .000 | 0 | 0 | 0 | 0 | 0 |
| Crawford, Hou | .353 | 2 | 0 | 0 | 3 | 1 |
| Crawford, LA | .386 | 49 | 11 | 0 | 43 | 2 |
| Crosby, Chi | .000 | 1 | 0 | 0 | 0 | 0 |
| Crowley, Cin | .394 | 7 | 1 | 0 | 6 | 6 |
| Cruz, StL | .271 | 2 | 0 | 0 | 4 | 1 |
| Cruz, LA | .319 | 7 | 0 | 0 | 6 | 0 |
| Cruz, Hou | .403 | 52 | 6 | 1 | 44 | 6 |
| Curtis, StL | .211 | 5 | 0 | 0 | 16 | 1 |
| D'Acquisto, SF | .000 | 2 | 0 | 0 | 6 | 0 |
| Dal Canton, Atl | .105 | 0 | 0 | 0 | 8 | 0 |
| Darcy, Cin | .106 | 0 | 0 | 0 | 27 | 0 |
| DaVanon, Hou | .392 | 16 | 1 | 1 | 7 | 3 |
| Davis, SD | .289 | 11 | 3 | 3 | 31 | 3 |
| Davis, StL | .431 | 14 | 1 | 4 | 27 | 5 |
| DeJesus, LA | .230 | 11 | 0 | 0 | 15 | 0 |
| de la Rosa, Hou | .667 | 0 | 0 | 0 | 0 | 0 |
| Demery, Pitt | .208 | 4 | 0 | 0 | 10 | 0 |
| DeMola, Mtl | .000 | 0 | 0 | 0 | 6 | 0 |
| Denny, StL | .227 | 0 | 0 | 0 | 17 | 0 |
| Dettore, Chi | .250 | 1 | 0 | 0 | 7 | 0 |
| Devine, Atl | .000 | 0 | 0 | 0 | 2 | 0 |
| Dierker, Hou | .092 | 0 | 0 | 0 | 21 | 1 |
| Dilone, Pitt | .000 | 0 | 0 | 0 | 1 | 0 |
| Downing, LA | .000 | 2 | 0 | 0 | 8 | 0 |

| Player—Club | Slg. Pct. | Tot. BB. | Int. BB. | HP. | SO. | GI DP. |
|---|---|---|---|---|---|---|
| Dressler, SF | .000 | 1 | 0 | 0 | 2 | 0 |
| Driessen, Cin | .429 | 35 | 2 | 2 | 30 | 8 |
| Dunn, Chi | .295 | 6 | 0 | 0 | 17 | 0 |
| Dwyer, StL-Mtl | .364 | 27 | 0 | 0 | 36 | 1 |
| Dyer, Pitt | .364 | 6 | 0 | 1 | 22 | 4 |
| Easler, Hou | .000 | 0 | 0 | 0 | 1 | 0 |
| Easterly, Atl | .056 | 0 | 0 | 0 | 6 | 1 |
| Eastwick, Cin | .067 | 0 | 0 | 0 | 8 | 0 |
| Ellis, Pitt | .139 | 5 | 0 | 0 | 8 | 1 |
| Espinosa, NY | .000 | 0 | 0 | 0 | 0 | 0 |
| Essian, Phil | 1.000 | 1 | 0 | 0 | 0 | 0 |
| Evans, Atl | .406 | 105 | 5 | 2 | 106 | 10 |
| Fairly, StL | .467 | 45 | 9 | 3 | 22 | 8 |
| Falcone, SF | .062 | 1 | 0 | 0 | 26 | 2 |
| Ferguson, LA | .302 | 35 | 5 | 1 | 47 | 4 |
| Flynn, Cin | .346 | 11 | 2 | 0 | 13 | 5 |
| Foli, Mtl | .294 | 36 | 5 | 2 | 49 | 11 |
| Folkers, SD | .194 | 4 | 0 | 0 | 14 | 0 |
| Foote, Mtl | .295 | 17 | 6 | 1 | 48 | 9 |
| Forsch, Hou | .045 | 4 | 0 | 0 | 7 | 0 |
| Forsch, StL | .462 | 3 | 0 | 1 | 20 | 0 |
| Foster, SD | .091 | 0 | 0 | 0 | 3 | 1 |
| Foster, Cin | .518 | 40 | 11 | 3 | 73 | 14 |
| Frailing, Chi | .143 | 1 | 0 | 0 | 1 | 0 |
| Freisleben, SD | .083 | 6 | 0 | 0 | 17 | 0 |
| Frias, Mtl | .156 | 3 | 0 | 0 | 13 | 1 |
| Frisella, SD | .200 | 0 | 0 | 0 | 2 | 0 |
| Fritz, Phil | .000 | 0 | 0 | 0 | 0 | 0 |
| Fryman, Mtl | .245 | 2 | 0 | 1 | 12 | 0 |
| Fuentes, SD | .349 | 25 | 2 | 3 | 51 | 15 |
| Gallagher, NY | .200 | 1 | 0 | 0 | 3 | 1 |
| Garber, Phil | .167 | 0 | 0 | 0 | 2 | 0 |
| Gardner, Hou | .194 | 1 | 1 | 1 | 8 | 2 |
| Garman, StL | .000 | 0 | 0 | 0 | 1 | 0 |
| Garr, Atl | .384 | 44 | 17 | 3 | 50 | 8 |
| Garrett, Chi | .238 | 1 | 0 | 0 | 8 | 0 |
| Garrett, NY | .383 | 50 | 4 | 1 | 45 | 3 |
| Garvey, LA | .476 | 33 | 6 | 3 | 66 | 19 |
| Gaston, Atl | .397 | 17 | 3 | 0 | 33 | 5 |
| Gentry, NY | .000 | 0 | 0 | 0 | 4 | 0 |
| Geronimo, Cin | .363 | 48 | 8 | 4 | 97 | 7 |
| Gibson, StL | .179 | 3 | 0 | 0 | 9 | 0 |
| Gilbreath, Atl | .297 | 24 | 0 | 1 | 26 | 2 |
| Giusti, Pitt | .300 | 1 | 0 | 0 | 2 | 0 |
| Goodson, SF-Atl | .284 | 9 | 2 | 0 | 22 | 9 |
| Granger, Hou | .000 | 1 | 0 | 0 | 5 | 1 |
| Greif, SD | .000 | 0 | 0 | 0 | 0 | 0 |
| Griffey, Cin | .402 | 67 | 2 | 1 | 67 | 10 |
| Griffin, Hou | .136 | 1 | 0 | 0 | 6 | 1 |
| Gross, Hou | .364 | 63 | 1 | 0 | 37 | 11 |
| Grote, NY | .373 | 38 | 8 | 1 | 23 | 11 |
| Grubb, SD | .363 | 59 | 4 | 5 | 59 | 7 |
| Guerrero, StL | .288 | 10 | 1 | 2 | 7 | 9 |
| Gullett, Cin | .274 | 2 | 0 | 0 | 15 | 2 |
| Hahn, Phil-StL-SD | .308 | 11 | 0 | 0 | 5 | 3 |
| Hale, LA | .333 | 26 | 4 | 2 | 51 | 1 |
| Halicki, SF | .132 | 3 | 0 | 0 | 21 | 0 |
| Hall, Cin-NY | .400 | 0 | 0 | 0 | 1 | 0 |
| Hanna, Atl | .000 | 0 | 0 | 0 | 0 | 0 |
| Hardy, SD | .000 | 0 | 0 | 0 | 0 | 0 |
| Harmon, Phil | .250 | 9 | 0 | 1 | 13 | 3 |
| Harrelson, NY | .247 | 12 | 2 | 0 | 13 | 1 |
| Harris, Chi | .179 | 6 | 0 | 0 | 7 | 0 |
| Harrison, Atl | .267 | 0 | 0 | 1 | 5 | 1 |
| Heaverlo, SF | .500 | 0 | 0 | 0 | 1 | 0 |
| Hebner, Pitt | .392 | 43 | 6 | 10 | 48 | 7 |
| Heidemann, NY | .290 | 17 | 3 | 0 | 28 | 2 |
| Helms, Hou | .222 | 10 | 1 | 1 | 8 | 3 |
| Hernandez, SD | .265 | 26 | 0 | 2 | 25 | 7 |
| Hernandez, StL | .362 | 17 | 2 | 0 | 26 | 5 |
| Hernandez, Pitt | .000 | 2 | 0 | 0 | 2 | 0 |
| Hilgendorf, Phil | .333 | 1 | 0 | 0 | 4 | 0 |
| Hill, SF | .319 | 25 | 5 | 0 | 27 | 7 |
| Hilton, SD | .000 | 0 | 0 | 0 | 0 | 1 |
| Hiser, Chi | .290 | 11 | 1 | 0 | 7 | 1 |
| Hodges, NY | .412 | 1 | 0 | 0 | 6 | 1 |
| Hoerner, Phil | .000 | 0 | 0 | 0 | 0 | 0 |
| Hooton, Chi-LA | .205 | 4 | 0 | 0 | 27 | 1 |
| Hosley, Chi | .433 | 27 | 3 | 2 | 25 | 5 |
| Hough, LA | .333 | 0 | 0 | 0 | 1 | 0 |
| House, Atl | .111 | 1 | 0 | 0 | 2 | 1 |
| Howard, StL | .310 | 0 | 0 | 0 | 7 | 0 |
| Howard, Hou | .365 | 21 | 3 | 3 | 67 | 2 |
| Howe, Pitt | .253 | 15 | 3 | 0 | 15 | 5 |
| Hrabosky, StL | .200 | 2 | 0 | 0 | 5 | 0 |
| Hundley, SD | .278 | 19 | 1 | 1 | 29 | 5 |
| Huntz, SD | .226 | 7 | 2 | 0 | 8 | 1 |
| Hutton, Phil | .339 | 27 | 1 | 0 | 10 | 7 |
| Ivie, SD | .366 | 20 | 2 | 4 | 63 | 12 |
| Johnson, Hou | .506 | 46 | 5 | 5 | 64 | 7 |
| Johnson, Atl | 2.000 | 0 | 0 | 0 | 0 | 0 |
| Johnson, SD | .167 | 0 | 0 | 0 | 4 | 1 |
| Johnson, Mtl | .667 | 1 | 0 | 0 | 1 | 0 |
| Johnstone, Phil | .454 | 42 | 7 | 0 | 39 | 8 |
| Jones, NY | .260 | 3 | 0 | 0 | 6 | 0 |
| Jones, Pitt | .000 | 0 | 0 | 0 | 0 | 0 |
| Jones, SD | .157 | 5 | 0 | 0 | 30 | 1 |
| Jorgensen, Mtl | .422 | 79 | 8 | 7 | 75 | 8 |
| Joshua, SF | .448 | 32 | 0 | 1 | 75 | 6 |
| Jutze, Hou | .247 | 2 | 0 | 0 | 4 | 1 |
| Kelleher, StL | .000 | 0 | 0 | 0 | 1 | 0 |
| Kendall, SD | .248 | 26 | 5 | 0 | 28 | 10 |
| Kessinger, Chi | .319 | 68 | 2 | 1 | 47 | 4 |
| Kingman, NY | .494 | 34 | 5 | 4 | 153 | 13 |
| Kirby, Cin | .219 | 2 | 0 | 0 | 15 | 1 |
| Kirkpatrick, Pitt | .375 | 18 | 2 | 0 | 22 | 5 |
| Kison, Pitt | .119 | 2 | 0 | 0 | 29 | 0 |
| Knowles, Chi | .067 | 1 | 0 | 0 | 8 | 0 |
| Konieczny, Hou | .200 | 3 | 0 | 0 | 24 | 2 |
| Koosman, NY | .205 | 4 | 0 | 0 | 31 | 0 |
| Kranepool, NY | .409 | 27 | 6 | 0 | 21 | 12 |
| Kubiak, SD | .250 | 24 | 5 | 0 | 18 | 5 |
| Kurosaki, StL | .000 | 0 | 0 | 0 | 0 | 0 |
| LaCock, Chi | .341 | 37 | 7 | 0 | 27 | 10 |
| LaCorte, Atl | .000 | 0 | 0 | 0 | 1 | 0 |
| Lacy, LA | .451 | 22 | 1 | 0 | 29 | 10 |
| Lang, Mtl | .000 | 0 | 0 | 0 | 0 | 0 |
| Lavelle, SF | .111 | 1 | 0 | 0 | 4 | 1 |
| Lee, LA | .349 | 3 | 1 | 0 | 9 | 0 |
| LeMaster, SF | .324 | 4 | 0 | 1 | 15 | 0 |
| Leon, Atl | .333 | 1 | 0 | 0 | 1 | 0 |
| Lerch, Phila | .000 | 0 | 0 | 0 | 0 | 0 |
| Lewallyn, LA | .000 | 0 | 0 | 0 | 0 | 0 |
| Lintz, Mtl-StL | .213 | 26 | 0 | 0 | 20 | 3 |
| Locker, Chi | .000 | 0 | 0 | 0 | 0 | 0 |
| Locklear, SD | .439 | 22 | 4 | 1 | 26 | 4 |
| Lockwood, NY | .167 | 0 | 0 | 0 | 0 | 0 |
| Lonborg, Phila | .023 | 6 | 0 | 0 | 17 | 1 |
| Lopes, LA | .359 | 91 | 3 | 2 | 93 | 4 |
| Lum, Atl | .327 | 39 | 7 | 0 | 38 | 11 |
| Luzinski, Phila | .540 | 89 | 17 | 8 | 151 | 12 |
| Lyttle, Mtl | .345 | 13 | 3 | 0 | 6 | 0 |
| Mackanin, Mtl | .375 | 31 | 4 | 2 | 99 | 8 |
| Maddox, SF-Phila | .406 | 42 | 6 | 6 | 57 | 3 |
| Madlock, Chi | .479 | 42 | 5 | 3 | 34 | 11 |
| Mangual, Mtl | .337 | 74 | 1 | 4 | 115 | 11 |

| Player—Club | Slg. Pct. | Tot. BB. | Int. BB. | HP. | SO. | GI DP. |
|---|---|---|---|---|---|---|
| Manuel, LA | .133 | 0 | 0 | 0 | 3 | 2 |
| Marichal, LA | .000 | 0 | 0 | 0 | 1 | 0 |
| Marshall, LA | .067 | 0 | 0 | 0 | 6 | 0 |
| Martin, Phila | .345 | 11 | 4 | 1 | 16 | 1 |
| Martinez, StL | .286 | 0 | 0 | 0 | 2 | 2 |
| Matlack, NY | .100 | 13 | 0 | 0 | 33 | 0 |
| Matthews, SF | .431 | 65 | 5 | 2 | 53 | 13 |
| May, Atl | .493 | 25 | 3 | 2 | 27 | 4 |
| May, Hou | .316 | 26 | 3 | 0 | 41 | 7 |
| McBride, StL | .404 | 34 | 1 | 1 | 52 | 6 |
| McCarver, Phila | .339 | 14 | 3 | 0 | 7 | 0 |
| McCovey, SD | .460 | 57 | 8 | 3 | 80 | 10 |
| McDowell, Pitt | .000 | 0 | 0 | 0 | 5 | 0 |
| McEnaney, Cin | .000 | 0 | 0 | 0 | 5 | 1 |
| McGlothen, StL | .088 | 0 | 0 | 0 | 25 | 0 |
| McGraw, Phila | .154 | 0 | 0 | 0 | 4 | 0 |
| McIntosh, SD | .229 | 4 | 0 | 0 | 10 | 0 |
| McMullen, LA | .435 | 7 | 0 | 0 | 12 | 1 |
| McNally, Mtl | .190 | 7 | 0 | 0 | 9 | 0 |
| Melendez, StL | .347 | 16 | 3 | 0 | 25 | 10 |
| Mendoza, Pitt | .200 | 3 | 0 | 0 | 17 | 1 |
| Messersmith, LA | .194 | 7 | 0 | 1 | 25 | 2 |
| Metzger, SD | .000 | 0 | 0 | 0 | 0 | 0 |
| Metzger, Hou | .296 | 41 | 10 | 0 | 39 | 6 |
| Milbourne, Hou | .265 | 6 | 1 | 1 | 14 | 4 |
| Millan, NY | .348 | 36 | 2 | 12 | 28 | 17 |
| Miller, SF | .288 | 15 | 0 | 1 | 26 | 15 |
| Milner, NY | .336 | 33 | 4 | 2 | 22 | 5 |
| Minshall, Pitt | .000 | 0 | 0 | 0 | 0 | 0 |
| Minton, SF | .000 | 0 | 0 | 0 | 3 | 0 |
| Mitterwald, Chi | .345 | 19 | 7 | 0 | 42 | 3 |
| Moffitt, SF | .357 | 0 | 0 | 0 | 4 | 0 |
| Monday, Chi | .446 | 83 | 12 | 1 | 95 | 8 |
| Montague, Mtl-Phila | .000 | 0 | 0 | 0 | 1 | 0 |
| Montanez, Phila-SF | .415 | 49 | 8 | 4 | 62 | 26 |
| Montefusco, SF | .150 | 5 | 0 | 0 | 44 | 1 |
| Moore, Chi | .000 | 0 | 0 | 0 | 3 | 0 |
| Moore, StL | .500 | 0 | 0 | 0 | 1 | 0 |
| Moose, Pitt | .167 | 1 | 0 | 0 | 8 | 2 |
| Morales, Mtl | .387 | 14 | 9 | 0 | 21 | 6 |
| Morales, Chi | .369 | 50 | 9 | 5 | 65 | 14 |
| Moreno, Pitt | .167 | 1 | 0 | 0 | 1 | 0 |
| Morgan, Cin | .508 | 132 | 3 | 3 | 52 | 3 |
| Morton, Atl | .181 | 4 | 0 | 0 | 30 | 0 |
| Moses, SD | .263 | 2 | 0 | 0 | 3 | 1 |
| Mota, LA | .286 | 5 | 0 | 2 | 1 | 3 |
| Mumphrey, StL | .500 | 4 | 0 | 0 | 3 | 0 |
| Murcer, SF | .432 | 91 | 6 | 2 | 45 | 11 |
| Murray, Mtl | .214 | 2 | 0 | 0 | 5 | 0 |
| Niekro, Hou | .214 | 2 | 0 | 0 | 2 | 0 |
| Niekro, Atl | .212 | 1 | 0 | 0 | 18 | 1 |
| Nolan, Cin | .221 | 7 | 0 | 0 | 29 | 1 |
| Nolan, Atl | .250 | 1 | 0 | 0 | 0 | 0 |
| Norman, Cin | .133 | 3 | 0 | 0 | 19 | 0 |
| Oates, Atl-Phila | .345 | 34 | 10 | 0 | 33 | 6 |
| Odom, Atl | .154 | 0 | 0 | 0 | 5 | 0 |
| Office, Atl | .361 | 23 | 4 | 3 | 41 | 10 |
| Oliver, Pitt | .454 | 25 | 3 | 5 | 73 | 19 |
| Ontiveros, SF | .366 | 55 | 4 | 2 | 44 | 9 |
| Ott, Pitt | .200 | 0 | 0 | 0 | 0 | 0 |
| Paciorek, LA | .269 | 11 | 1 | 0 | 29 | 3 |
| Parker, Pitt | .541 | 38 | 4 | 5 | 89 | 18 |
| Parker, NY-StL | .000 | 5 | 0 | 0 | 2 | 0 |
| Parrish, Mtl | .410 | 28 | 5 | 4 | 74 | 14 |
| Pemberton, NY | .000 | 0 | 0 | 0 | 1 | 0 |
| Perez, Cin | .466 | 54 | 6 | 3 | 101 | 12 |
| Perez, Atl | .328 | 37 | 2 | 0 | 44 | 16 |
| Phillips, SF-NY | .316 | 31 | 5 | 1 | 51 | 9 |
| Plummer, Cin | .245 | 24 | 2 | 2 | 28 | 0 |
| Pocoroba, Atl | .319 | 20 | 2 | 0 | 11 | 5 |
| Popovich, Pitt | .225 | 3 | 0 | 1 | 2 | 0 |
| Powell, LA | .300 | 1 | 0 | 0 | 2 | 1 |
| Prall, Chi | .000 | 0 | 0 | 0 | 3 | 0 |
| Rader, SF | .394 | 32 | 12 | 1 | 30 | 9 |
| Rader, Hou | .364 | 42 | 3 | 5 | 101 | 11 |
| Randolph, Pitt | .180 | 7 | 1 | 0 | 6 | 3 |
| Rasmussen, StL | .154 | 1 | 0 | 0 | 8 | 0 |
| Rau, LA | .195 | 5 | 0 | 0 | 28 | 3 |
| Reed, Atl.-StL | .244 | 2 | 0 | 0 | 30 | 0 |
| Reitz, StL | .340 | 22 | 9 | 5 | 54 | 18 |
| Renko, Mtl | .352 | 5 | 0 | 0 | 13 | 0 |
| Rettenmund, Cin | .314 | 35 | 3 | 0 | 22 | 6 |
| P. Reuschel, Chi | .000 | 1 | 0 | 0 | 2 | 0 |
| R. Reuschel, Chi | .273 | 3 | 0 | 0 | 11 | 2 |
| Reuss, Pitt | .225 | 5 | 0 | 0 | 27 | 0 |
| Reynolds, Pitt | .263 | 3 | 1 | 0 | 5 | 1 |
| Reynolds, StL | .000 | 0 | 0 | 0 | 0 | 0 |
| Rhoden, LA | .071 | 1 | 0 | 0 | 6 | 0 |
| Richard, Hou | .324 | 1 | 0 | 0 | 29 | 2 |
| Rivera, Mtl | .111 | 2 | 0 | 0 | 3 | 1 |
| Roberts, Hou | .206 | 1 | 0 | 0 | 12 | 0 |
| Roberts, SD | .354 | 13 | 3 | 2 | 19 | 1 |
| Robertson, Pitt | .452 | 23 | 0 | 2 | 25 | 0 |
| Robinson, Atl-SF | .087 | 2 | 0 | 0 | 11 | 2 |
| Robinson, Pitt | .450 | 11 | 4 | 0 | 36 | 6 |
| Rogers, Mtl | .195 | 8 | 0 | 0 | 24 | 0 |
| Rogodzinski, Phila | .316 | 3 | 0 | 0 | 2 | 0 |
| Rooker, Pitt | .095 | 3 | 0 | 0 | 20 | 1 |
| Rose, Cin | .432 | 89 | 8 | 11 | 50 | 13 |
| Rosello, Chi | .345 | 9 | 2 | 0 | 8 | 1 |
| Royster, LA | .361 | 1 | 0 | 0 | 3 | 1 |
| Rudolph, StL | .263 | 3 | 0 | 0 | 10 | 4 |
| Russell, LA | .258 | 23 | 6 | 2 | 28 | 6 |
| Ruthven, Phila | .154 | 0 | 0 | 0 | 3 | 0 |
| Sadecki, StL-Atl | .267 | 0 | 0 | 0 | 4 | 1 |
| Sadek, SF | .321 | 14 | 1 | 0 | 14 | 6 |
| Sanders, NY | .000 | 0 | 0 | 0 | 1 | 0 |
| Sanguillen, Pitt | .451 | 48 | 15 | 3 | 31 | 12 |
| Scanlon, Mtl | .284 | 17 | 3 | 0 | 25 | 2 |
| Scarce, NY | .000 | 0 | 0 | 0 | 0 | 0 |
| Scherman, Hou-Mtl | .118 | 1 | 0 | 0 | 3 | 0 |
| Schmidt, Phila | .523 | 101 | 10 | 4 | 180 | 7 |
| Schueler, Phila | .154 | 0 | 0 | 0 | 3 | 0 |
| Schultz, Chi | .000 | 0 | 0 | 0 | 0 | 0 |
| Scott, Mtl | .238 | 12 | 2 | 3 | 38 | 4 |
| Scott, SD | .000 | 0 | 0 | 0 | 2 | 0 |
| Seaver, NY | .189 | 8 | 0 | 1 | 24 | 2 |
| Sells, LA | 1.000 | 0 | 0 | 0 | 0 | 0 |
| Sharon, SD | .313 | 26 | 0 | 0 | 35 | 6 |
| Siebert, Hou | .000 | 0 | 0 | 0 | 2 | 0 |
| Siebert, SD | .500 | 2 | 0 | 0 | 2 | 0 |
| Simmons, StL | .491 | 63 | 16 | 1 | 35 | 20 |
| Simpson, LA | .333 | 0 | 0 | 0 | 2 | 0 |
| Simpson, Phila | .222 | 1 | 0 | 0 | 6 | 0 |
| Sizemore, StL | .301 | 45 | 2 | 2 | 37 | 10 |
| Smith, StL | .488 | 63 | 9 | 3 | 59 | 16 |
| Solomon, Chi | .000 | 0 | 0 | 0 | 0 | 0 |
| Sosa, StL-Atl | .133 | 0 | 0 | 0 | 5 | 0 |
| Sosa, Hou | .778 | 0 | 0 | 0 | 3 | 0 |
| Speed, SF | .200 | 1 | 0 | 1 | 8 | 0 |
| Speier, SF | .415 | 70 | 7 | 1 | 50 | 13 |
| Sperring, Chi | .271 | 16 | 3 | 1 | 31 | 3 |
| Spillner, SD | .156 | 8 | 0 | 0 | 25 | 0 |
| Staiger, NY | .211 | 0 | 0 | 0 | 4 | 2 |
| Stanhouse, Mtl | .333 | 0 | 0 | 0 | 0 | 0 |
| Stanton, Hou | .250 | 0 | 0 | 0 | 1 | 0 |

| Player—Club | Slg. Pct. | Tot. BB | Int. BB | HP | SO | GI DP | Player—Club | Slg. Pct. | Tot. BB | Int. BB | HP | SO | GI DP |
|---|---|---|---|---|---|---|---|---|---|---|---|---|---|
| Stargell, Pitt | .516 | 58 | 6 | 3 | 109 | 9 | Turner, SD | .273 | 2 | 1 | 0 | 1 | 1 |
| Staub, NY | .448 | 77 | 14 | 9 | 55 | 18 | Twitchell, Phila | .147 | 0 | 0 | 0 | 24 | 0 |
| Stearns, NY | .284 | 17 | 4 | 2 | 15 | 6 | Tyrone, Chi | .318 | 1 | 0 | 0 | 4 | 0 |
| Stennett, Pitt | .383 | 33 | 1 | 4 | 42 | 15 | Tyson, StL | .342 | 24 | 4 | 3 | 39 | 7 |
| Stone, NY | .167 | 1 | 0 | 0 | 5 | 0 | Underwood, Phila | .135 | 3 | 0 | 0 | 19 | 3 |
| Stone, Chi | .139 | 3 | 0 | 1 | 29 | 1 | Unser, NY | .392 | 37 | 6 | 0 | 76 | 8 |
| Strom, SD | .133 | 2 | 0 | 0 | 6 | 0 | Vail, NY | .420 | 9 | 1 | 0 | 37 | 3 |
| Summers, Chi | .341 | 10 | 0 | 1 | 13 | 3 | Valentine, Mtl | .576 | 2 | 0 | 0 | 4 | 1 |
| Sutton, LA | .150 | 4 | 0 | 0 | 20 | 3 | Valentine, SD | .333 | 4 | 0 | 0 | 0 | 0 |
| Swan, NY | .000 | 0 | 0 | 0 | 5 | 0 | Vukovich, Cin | .289 | 4 | 1 | 0 | 5 | 0 |
| Swisher, Chi | .303 | 30 | 7 | 4 | 57 | 15 | Wall, LA | .000 | 0 | 0 | 0 | 0 | 0 |
| Tate, NY | .000 | 1 | 0 | 0 | 22 | 0 | Wallace, StL | .000 | 0 | 0 | 0 | 0 | 0 |
| Taveras, Pitt | .257 | 37 | 0 | 2 | 42 | 2 | Wallis, Chi | .446 | 5 | 0 | 0 | 14 | 1 |
| Taylor, Phil | .340 | 17 | 2 | 1 | 18 | 4 | Warthen, Mtl | .118 | 1 | 0 | 0 | 24 | 0 |
| Taylor, Mtl | .000 | 0 | 0 | 0 | 1 | 0 | Watson, Hou | .495 | 40 | 10 | 3 | 50 | 11 |
| Tekulve, Pitt | .091 | 1 | 0 | 0 | 7 | 0 | Watt, Chi | .000 | 0 | 0 | 0 | 0 | 0 |
| Tepedino, Atl | .000 | 1 | 0 | 0 | 2 | 1 | Webb, NY | .258 | 2 | 0 | 0 | 7 | 0 |
| Terlecky, StL | .333 | 0 | 0 | 0 | 2 | 0 | Werner, Cin | .125 | 0 | 0 | 1 | 0 | 0 |
| Thomas, SF | .381 | 57 | 0 | 3 | 56 | 7 | White, Mtl | .423 | 10 | 1 | 0 | 7 | 0 |
| Thomasson, SF | .347 | 37 | 1 | 1 | 48 | 1 | Wilcox, Chi | .333 | 0 | 0 | 0 | 0 | 0 |
| Thompson, Atl | .071 | 0 | 0 | 0 | 10 | 1 | Williams, SF | .250 | 1 | 0 | 0 | 7 | 1 |
| Thornton, Chi | .516 | 88 | 12 | 4 | 63 | 6 | Williams, Atl | .360 | 34 | 2 | 3 | 63 | 16 |
| Tolan, SD | .338 | 28 | 3 | 10 | 45 | 15 | Winfield, SD | .403 | 69 | 14 | 3 | 82 | 11 |
| Tomlin, SD | .200 | 2 | 0 | 0 | 1 | 0 | Wynn, LA | .417 | 110 | 2 | 1 | 77 | 8 |
| Toms, SF | .000 | 0 | 0 | 0 | 0 | 0 | Yeager, LA | .347 | 40 | 7 | 8 | 75 | 15 |
| Torre, NY | .357 | 35 | 3 | 2 | 55 | 22 | York, Hou | .091 | 1 | 0 | 0 | 5 | 0 |
| Torrealba, Atl | 1.000 | 0 | 0 | 0 | 0 | 0 | Zahn, LA-Chi | .133 | 0 | 0 | 0 | 3 | 1 |
| Torres, SD | .335 | 22 | 3 | 0 | 32 | 8 | Zamora, Chi | .167 | 0 | 0 | 0 | 0 | 0 |
| Trillo, Chi | .316 | 45 | 3 | 3 | 78 | 10 | Zisk, Pitt | .474 | 68 | 9 | 2 | 109 | 12 |

# OFFICIAL NATIONAL LEAGUE FIELDING AVERAGES

## CLUB FIELDING

| Club | Pct. | G. | PO. | A. | E. | TC. | DP. | TP. | PB. |
|---|---|---|---|---|---|---|---|---|---|
| Cincinnati | .984 | 162 | 4377 | 1782 | 102 | 6261 | 173 | 0 | 3 |
| Los Angeles | .979 | 162 | 4409 | 1654 | 127 | 6190 | 106 | 0 | 17 |
| Houston | .979 | 162 | 4375 | 1880 | 137 | 6392 | 166 | 0 | 30 |
| San Francisco | .976 | 161 | 4298 | 1768 | 146 | 6212 | 164 | 0 | 13 |
| New York | .976 | 162 | 4398 | 1736 | 151 | 6285 | 144 | 0 | 8 |
| Philadelphia | .976 | 162 | 4365 | 1795 | 152 | 6312 | 156 | 0 | 10 |
| Pittsburgh | .976 | 161 | 4312 | 1802 | 151 | 6265 | 147 | 0 | 19 |
| St. Louis | .973 | 163 | 4364 | 1723 | 171 | 6258 | 140 | 0 | 31 |
| Montreal | .973 | 162 | 4440 | 1953 | 180 | 6573 | 179 | 1 | 20 |
| Atlanta | .972 | 161 | 4290 | 1877 | 175 | 6342 | 147 | 0 | 35 |
| Chicago | .972 | 162 | 4333 | 1907 | 179 | 6419 | 152 | 0 | 15 |
| San Diego | .971 | 162 | 4390 | 1930 | 188 | 6508 | 163 | 0 | 7 |
| Totals | .976 | | 52351 | 21807 | 1859 | 76017 | 1837 | 1 | 208 |

## INDIVIDUAL FIELDING

(Position Leader in Capitals)

°Throws lefthanded.

### FIRST BASEMEN

| Player—Club | Pct. | G. | PO. | A. | E. | DP. | Player—Club | Pct. | G. | PO. | A. | E. | DP. |
|---|---|---|---|---|---|---|---|---|---|---|---|---|---|
| Kirkpatrick, Pitt | 1.000 | 28 | 141 | 9 | 0 | 10 | Watson, Hou | .993 | 118 | 1077 | 69 | 8 | 106 |
| Tolan, SD° | 1.000 | 27 | 106 | 15 | 0 | 7 | Montanez, 21 Phil-134 SF° | .993 | 155 | 1333 | 98 | 10 | 134 |
| Kranepool, NY° | .997 | 82 | 666 | 46 | 2 | 51 | Goodson, 16 SF-13 Atl | .992 | 29 | 230 | 20 | 2 | 21 |
| Hernandez, StL° | .996 | 56 | 469 | 36 | 2 | 34 | Lum, Atl° | .992 | 60 | 562 | 34 | 5 | 41 |
| Robertson, Pitt | .996 | 27 | 209 | 18 | 1 | 10 | Stargell, Pitt° | .992 | 122 | 1121 | 54 | 10 | 112 |
| GARVEY, LA | .995 | 160 | 1500 | 77 | 8 | 96 | Milner, NY° | .991 | 29 | 204 | 25 | 2 | 21 |
| Jorgensen, Mtl° | .994 | 133 | 1150 | 91 | 7 | 123 | Johnson, Hou | .991 | 47 | 407 | 21 | 4 | 33 |
| Hutton, Phil° | .994 | 71 | 307 | 32 | 2 | 37 | | | | | | | |
| Perez, Cin | .993 | 132 | 1192 | 72 | 9 | 113 | | | | | | | |

## FIRST BASEMEN (Continued)

| Player—Club | Pct. | G. | PO. | A. | E. | DP. | Player—Club | Pct. | G. | PO. | A. | E. | DP. |
|---|---|---|---|---|---|---|---|---|---|---|---|---|---|
| Williams, Atl | .989 | 90 | 844 | 50 | 10 | 77 | McCovey, SD° | .986 | 115 | 979 | 73 | 15 | 94 |
| Breeden, Mtl° | .989 | 12 | 84 | 4 | 1 | 5 | Morales, Mtl | .983 | 27 | 201 | 26 | 4 | 19 |
| Ivie, SD | .989 | 78 | 490 | 36 | 6 | 47 | Smith, StL | .982 | 66 | 524 | 33 | 10 | 51 |
| Kingman, NY | .988 | 58 | 386 | 38 | 5 | 36 | Allen, Phila | .982 | 113 | 900 | 70 | 18 | 79 |
| LaCock, Chi° | .988 | 53 | 453 | 43 | 6 | 39 | Cater, StL | .981 | 12 | 49 | 4 | 1 | 4 |
| Thornton, Chi | .988 | 113 | 982 | 77 | 13 | 88 | Fairly, StL° | .980 | 56 | 351 | 33 | 8 | 33 |
| Colbert, Mtl | .988 | 22 | 151 | 9 | 2 | 18 | Thomasson, SF° | .977 | 17 | 121 | 9 | 3 | 12 |
| Mitterwald, Chi | .987 | 10 | 68 | 6 | 1 | 6 | Cabell, Hou | .976 | 25 | 75 | 5 | 2 | 12 |
| Driessen, Cin | .986 | 41 | 268 | 20 | 4 | 34 | Torre, NY | .968 | 24 | 111 | 9 | 4 | 12 |

### (Fewer Than Ten Games)

| Player—Club | Pct. | G. | PO. | A. | E. | DP. | Player—Club | Pct. | G. | PO. | A. | E. | DP. |
|---|---|---|---|---|---|---|---|---|---|---|---|---|---|
| Howard, StL | 1.000 | 7 | 60 | 6 | 0 | 5 | McCarver, Phila | 1.000 | 1 | 4 | 0 | 0 | 0 |
| Crowley, Cin° | 1.000 | 4 | 35 | 3 | 0 | 4 | Hiser, Chi° | 1.000 | 1 | 3 | 0 | 0 | 1 |
| Oliver, Pitt° | 1.000 | 4 | 29 | 1 | 0 | 3 | Kubiak, SD | 1.000 | 1 | 1 | 1 | 0 | 0 |
| Garrett, Chi | 1.000 | 4 | 22 | 4 | 0 | 4 | Scanlon, SD | 1.000 | 1 | 2 | 0 | 0 | 0 |
| Taylor, Phila | 1.000 | 4 | 22 | 1 | 0 | 0 | Beall, Atl° | .984 | 8 | 57 | 4 | 1 | 6 |
| McMullen, LA | 1.000 | 3 | 19 | 4 | 0 | 1 | Bench, Cin | .978 | 9 | 45 | 0 | 1 | 2 |
| Simmons, StL | 1.000 | 2 | 10 | 2 | 0 | 0 | Gaston, Atl | .889 | 1 | 8 | 0 | 1 | 1 |
| Ontiveros, SF | 1.000 | 4 | 9 | 1 | 0 | 1 | Foster, Cin | .000 | 1 | 0 | 0 | 0 | 0 |
| Anderson, Phila | 1.000 | 3 | 9 | 0 | 0 | 1 | TRIPLE PLAY: Morales. | | | | | | |
| Evans, Atl | 1.000 | 3 | 3 | 1 | 0 | 0 | | | | | | | |

## SECOND BASEMEN

| Player—Club | Pct. | G. | PO. | A. | E. | DP. | Player—Club | Pct. | G. | PO. | A. | E. | DP. |
|---|---|---|---|---|---|---|---|---|---|---|---|---|---|
| Flynn, Cin | 1.000 | 30 | 33 | 59 | 0 | 10 | Thomas, SF | .974 | 141 | 348 | 372 | 19 | 100 |
| Chaney, Cin | 1.000 | 23 | 28 | 44 | 0 | 9 | Sizemore, StL | .972 | 153 | 329 | 405 | 21 | 82 |
| Kubiak, SD | 1.000 | 11 | 14 | 15 | 0 | 3 | Millan, NY | .972 | 162 | 379 | 419 | 23 | 95 |
| Boswell, Hou | .991 | 31 | 40 | 65 | 1 | 11 | Fuentes, SD | .970 | 142 | 389 | 448 | 26 | 105 |
| Helms, Hou | .988 | 42 | 58 | 109 | 2 | 19 | Milbourne, Hou | .968 | 43 | 67 | 85 | 5 | 27 |
| MORGAN, Cin | .986 | 142 | 356 | 425 | 11 | 96 | Trillo, Chi | .967 | 153 | 350 | 509 | 29 | 103 |
| Perez, Atl | .985 | 116 | 259 | 341 | 9 | 74 | Tyson, StL | .966 | 24 | 29 | 57 | 3 | 8 |
| Torres, SD | .984 | 16 | 24 | 36 | 1 | 10 | Mackanin, Mtl | .966 | 127 | 300 | 410 | 25 | 100 |
| Sperring, Chi | .982 | 17 | 22 | 32 | 1 | 4 | Blanks, Atl | .964 | 12 | 29 | 24 | 2 | 7 |
| Andrews, Hou | .982 | 94 | 191 | 237 | 8 | 65 | Lintz, | | | | | | |
| Cash, Phila | .981 | 162 | 400 | 481 | 17 | 126 | 39 Mtl-6 StL | .963 | 45 | 93 | 116 | 8 | 18 |
| Gilbreath, Atl | .980 | 52 | 121 | 125 | 5 | 29 | Miller, StL | .963 | 21 | 44 | 59 | 4 | 17 |
| Stennett, Pitt | .979 | 144 | 379 | 463 | 18 | 98 | Randolph, Pitt | .962 | 14 | 34 | 42 | 3 | 8 |
| Lopes, LA | .979 | 137 | 307 | 377 | 15 | 58 | Lacy, LA | .935 | 43 | 62 | 68 | 9 | 10 |

### (Fewer Than Ten Games)

| Player—Club | Pct. | G. | PO. | A. | E. | DP. | Player—Club | Pct. | G. | PO. | A. | E. | DP. |
|---|---|---|---|---|---|---|---|---|---|---|---|---|---|
| Cox, Mtl | 1.000 | 8 | 10 | 21 | 0 | 7 | DaVanon, Hou | .976 | 9 | 16 | 24 | 1 | 3 |
| Popovich, Pitt | 1.000 | 8 | 16 | 14 | 0 | 2 | Phillips, | | | | | | |
| Royster, LA | 1.000 | 4 | 5 | 11 | 0 | 3 | 6 SF-1 NY | .971 | 7 | 15 | 18 | 1 | 4 |
| Harmon, Phila | 1.000 | 7 | 2 | 7 | 0 | 1 | Roberts, SD | .950 | 5 | 14 | 5 | 1 | 2 |
| Auerbach, LA | 1.000 | 1 | 5 | 0 | 0 | 1 | Harris, Chi | .933 | 5 | 6 | 8 | 1 | 2 |
| Frias, Mtl | 1.000 | 7 | 2 | 2 | 0 | 0 | Arnold, SF | .923 | 4 | 5 | 7 | 1 | 4 |
| Huntz, SD | 1.000 | 2 | 2 | 0 | 0 | 0 | Robinson, SF | .867 | 9 | 7 | 6 | 2 | 2 |
| Martinez, StL | 1.000 | 2 | 1 | 0 | 0 | 0 | Taylor, Phila | .800 | 3 | 2 | 2 | 1 | 1 |
| Bannister, Phila | 1.000 | 1 | 1 | 0 | 0 | 0 | Belloir, Atl | .800 | 1 | 0 | 4 | 1 | 0 |
| Dunn, Chi | 1.000 | 1 | 0 | 1 | 0 | 0 | Heidemann, NY | .500 | 1 | 1 | 0 | 1 | 0 |
| Foli, Mtl | 1.000 | 1 | 1 | 0 | 0 | 0 | Parrish, Mtl | .000 | 1 | 0 | 0 | 0 | 0 |
| Garrett, NY | 1.000 | 1 | 0 | 1 | 0 | 0 | TRIPLE PLAY: Mackanin. | | | | | | |

## THIRD BASEMEN

| Player—Club | Pct. | G. | PO. | A. | E. | DP. | Player—Club | Pct. | G. | PO. | A. | E. | DP. |
|---|---|---|---|---|---|---|---|---|---|---|---|---|---|
| Staiger, NY | 1.000 | 13 | 5 | 11 | 0 | 0 | Rose, Cin | .963 | 137 | 106 | 230 | 13 | 21 |
| McMullen, LA | 1.000 | 11 | 7 | 8 | 0 | 0 | Flynn, Cin | .962 | 40 | 6 | 19 | 1 | 1 |
| Frias, Mtl | 1.000 | 11 | 7 | 6 | 0 | 2 | Cey, LA | .960 | 158 | 144 | 309 | 19 | 23 |
| Cabell, Hou | .985 | 22 | 23 | 43 | 1 | 5 | Scanlon, Mtl | .957 | 28 | 10 | 57 | 3 | 4 |
| Torres, SD | .974 | 42 | 7 | 30 | 1 | 0 | Dunn, Chi | .957 | 11 | 6 | 16 | 1 | 0 |
| RADER, Hou | .971 | 124 | 111 | 257 | 11 | 24 | Kubiak, SD | .954 | 64 | 36 | 110 | 7 | 9 |
| Garrett, NY | .966 | 94 | 64 | 160 | 8 | 24 | Schmidt, Phila | .954 | 151 | 132 | 368 | 24 | 30 |

### THIRD BASEMEN (Continued)

| Player—Club | Pct. | G. | PO. | A. | E. | DP. | Player—Club | Pct. | G. | PO. | A. | E. | DP. |
|---|---|---|---|---|---|---|---|---|---|---|---|---|---|
| Chaney, Cin | .952 | 13 | 6 | 14 | 1 | 0 | Roberts, SD | .925 | 30 | 23 | 63 | 7 | 5 |
| Gilbreath, Atl | .952 | 10 | 5 | 15 | 1 | 0 | Vukovich, Cin | .925 | 31 | 12 | 37 | 4 | 4 |
| Torre, NY | .950 | 83 | 61 | 148 | 11 | 14 | Ontiveros, SF | .923 | 89 | 64 | 188 | 21 | 14 |
| Miller, SF | .949 | 68 | 66 | 120 | 10 | 11 | Kingman, NY | .919 | 12 | 6 | 28 | 3 | 1 |
| Sperring, Chi | .946 | 22 | 10 | 43 | 3 | 2 | Parrish, Mtl | .919 | 143 | 105 | 291 | 35 | 33 |
| Reitz, StL | .946 | 160 | 124 | 279 | 23 | 21 | Taylor, Phila | .913 | 16 | 10 | 32 | 4 | 1 |
| Hebner, Pitt | .946 | 126 | 86 | 244 | 19 | 17 | Goodson, | | | | | | |
| Kessinger, Chi | .943 | 13 | 5 | 28 | 2 | 3 | 13 SF-1 Atl. | .913 | 14 | 10 | 32 | 4 | 2 |
| Madlock, Chi | .943 | 128 | 79 | 250 | 20 | 14 | Boswell, Hou | .912 | 23 | 14 | 38 | 5 | 2 |
| Huntz, SD | .939 | 16 | 13 | 33 | 3 | 6 | Ivie, SD | .899 | 61 | 49 | 102 | 17 | 7 |
| Howe, Pitt | .938 | 42 | 17 | 89 | 7 | 4 | Cruz, StL | .800 | 12 | 4 | 4 | 2 | 0 |
| Evans, Atl | .938 | 156 | 161 | 381 | 36 | 41 | | | | | | | |

#### (Fewer Than Ten Games)

| Player—Club | Pct. | G. | PO. | A. | E. | DP. | Player—Club | Pct. | G. | PO. | A. | E. | DP. |
|---|---|---|---|---|---|---|---|---|---|---|---|---|---|
| Phillips, SF | 1.000 | 6 | 3 | 12 | 0 | 0 | Speier, SF | 1.000 | 1 | 0 | 1 | 0 | 0 |
| Bailey, Mtl | 1.000 | 3 | 1 | 6 | 0 | 1 | Hilton, SD | .900 | 4 | 2 | 7 | 1 | 0 |
| Boone, Phila | 1.000 | 3 | 3 | 4 | 0 | 0 | Heidemann, NY | .857 | 4 | 1 | 5 | 1 | 0 |
| Harris, Chi | 1.000 | 7 | 0 | 6 | 0 | 0 | Royster, LA | .714 | 3 | 1 | 4 | 2 | 1 |
| Tyson, StL | 1.000 | 5 | 1 | 5 | 0 | 0 | Randolph, Pitt | .500 | 1 | 0 | 3 | 3 | 0 |
| Beckert, SD | 1.000 | 4 | 0 | 6 | 0 | 0 | Mackanin, Mtl | .500 | 1 | 0 | 1 | 1 | 0 |
| DaVanon, Hou | 1.000 | 3 | 1 | 5 | 0 | 0 | Helms, Hou | .000 | 3 | 0 | 0 | 0 | 0 |
| Concepcion, Cin | 1.000 | 6 | 3 | 1 | 0 | 0 | Auerbach, LA | .000 | 1 | 0 | 0 | 0 | 0 |
| Martinez, StL | 1.000 | 1 | 1 | 2 | 0 | 0 | Carter, Mtl | .000 | 1 | 0 | 0 | 0 | 0 |
| Smith, StL | 1.000 | 1 | 0 | 3 | 0 | 0 | Harmon, Phil | .000 | 1 | 0 | 0 | 0 | 0 |
| Clark, SF | 1.000 | 2 | 1 | 1 | 0 | 0 | Hill, SF | .000 | 1 | 0 | 0 | 0 | 0 |
| Thornton, Chi | 1.000 | 2 | 2 | 0 | 0 | 0 | Mendoza, Pitt | .000 | 1 | 0 | 0 | 0 | 0 |
| Rettenmund, Cin | 1.000 | 1 | 0 | 1 | 0 | 0 | | | | | | | |

## SHORTSTOPS

| Player—Club | Pct. | G. | PO. | A. | E. | DP. | Player—Club | Pct. | G. | PO. | A. | E. | DP. |
|---|---|---|---|---|---|---|---|---|---|---|---|---|---|
| Harmon, Phila | .989 | 25 | 30 | 58 | 1 | 8 | Blanks, Atl | .960 | 129 | 183 | 414 | 25 | 68 |
| Flynn, Cin | .983 | 17 | 18 | 40 | 1 | 9 | Auerbach, LA | .960 | 81 | 77 | 137 | 9 | 17 |
| SPEIER, SF | .982 | 136 | 247 | 420 | 12 | 81 | Guerrero, StL | .955 | 64 | 76 | 198 | 13 | 29 |
| Concepcion, Cin | .977 | 130 | 238 | 445 | 16 | 102 | Taveras, Pitt | .953 | 132 | 200 | 369 | 28 | 74 |
| Metzger, Hou | .977 | 126 | 186 | 441 | 15 | 83 | Rosello, Chi | .952 | 19 | 27 | 53 | 4 | 7 |
| DeJesus, LA | .974 | 63 | 45 | 107 | 4 | 18 | Mendoza, Pitt | .952 | 53 | 29 | 70 | 5 | 10 |
| Foli, Mtl | .973 | 151 | 260 | 497 | 21 | 104 | Heidemann, NY | .951 | 44 | 70 | 84 | 8 | 14 |
| Torres, SD | .971 | 75 | 97 | 272 | 11 | 45 | Brinkman, StL | .948 | 24 | 40 | 69 | 6 | 15 |
| Tyson, StL | .971 | 95 | 154 | 246 | 12 | 44 | DaVanon, Hou | .944 | 21 | 37 | 65 | 6 | 13 |
| Reynolds, Pitt | .969 | 30 | 43 | 82 | 4 | 12 | Phillips, NY | .944 | 115 | 185 | 334 | 31 | 52 |
| Russell, LA | .967 | 83 | 94 | 230 | 11 | 27 | Harrelson, NY | .941 | 34 | 44 | 67 | 7 | 18 |
| LeMaster, SF | .967 | 22 | 26 | 62 | 3 | 12 | Milbourne, Hou | .940 | 22 | 28 | 51 | 5 | 8 |
| Kessinger, Chi | .967 | 140 | 205 | 436 | 22 | 100 | Frias, Mtl | .938 | 29 | 46 | 59 | 7 | 14 |
| Robinson, | | | | | | | Schmidt, Phila | .935 | 10 | 7 | 22 | 2 | 2 |
| 7 Atl-12 SF | .967 | 19 | 27 | 31 | 2 | 7 | Lopes, LA | .933 | 14 | 8 | 6 | 1 | 1 |
| Hernandez, SD | .965 | 111 | 168 | 327 | 18 | 70 | Belloir, Atl | .922 | 38 | 39 | 102 | 12 | 17 |
| Bowa, Phila | .962 | 135 | 227 | 403 | 25 | 82 | Sperring, Chi | .905 | 16 | 27 | 40 | 7 | 12 |
| Chaney, Cin | .961 | 34 | 43 | 106 | 6 | 18 | | | | | | | |

#### (Fewer Than Ten Games)

| Player—Club | Pct. | G. | PO. | A. | E. | DP. | Player—Club | Pct. | G. | PO. | A. | E. | DP. |
|---|---|---|---|---|---|---|---|---|---|---|---|---|---|
| Almon, SD | 1.000 | 2 | 6 | 5 | 0 | 0 | Popovich, Pitt | .889 | 8 | 1 | 7 | 1 | 1 |
| Rader, Hou | 1.000 | 2 | 3 | 2 | 0 | 1 | Andrews, Hou | .875 | 6 | 2 | 12 | 2 | 2 |
| Garrett, NY | 1.000 | 3 | 1 | 1 | 0 | 0 | Bannister, Phila | .750 | 1 | 2 | 4 | 2 | 0 |
| Howe, Pitt | 1.000 | 3 | 2 | 0 | 0 | 0 | Martinez, StL | .500 | 1 | 0 | 1 | 1 | 0 |
| Gilbreath, Atl | 1.000 | 1 | 1 | 1 | 0 | 0 | Helms, Hou | .000 | 1 | 0 | 0 | 0 | 0 |
| Lacy, LA | 1.000 | 1 | 1 | 0 | 0 | 0 | Mackanin, Mtl | .000 | 1 | 0 | 0 | 0 | 0 |
| Lintz, 2 Mtl-6 StL | .960 | 8 | 8 | 16 | 1 | 3 | Parrish, Mtl | .000 | 1 | 0 | 0 | 0 | 0 |
| Perez, Atl | .917 | 7 | 3 | 8 | 1 | 1 | Royster, LA | .000 | 1 | 0 | 0 | 0 | 0 |
| Miller, SF | .917 | 6 | 4 | 7 | 1 | 3 | Trillo, Chi | .000 | 1 | 0 | 0 | 0 | 0 |
| Kelleher, StL | .909 | 7 | 3 | 7 | 1 | 1 | TRIPLE PLAY: Foli. | | | | | | |

## OUTFIELDERS

| Player—Club | Pct. | G. | PO. | A. | E. | DP. |
|---|---|---|---|---|---|---|
| Rettenmund, Cin..... | 1.000 | 61 | 99 | 1 | 0 | 1 |
| Lum, Atl° | 1.000 | 38 | 95 | 0 | 0 | 0 |
| Brown, Phil | 1.000 | 63 | 67 | 0 | 0 | 0 |
| Bannister, Phila | 1.000 | 18 | 51 | 0 | 0 | 0 |
| Lopes, LA | 1.000 | 24 | 45 | 3 | 0 | 1 |
| Hahn, 7 Phila- 4 StL-26 SD | 1.000 | 37 | 32 | 2 | 0 | 0 |
| Bench, Cin | 1.000 | 19 | 33 | 1 | 0 | 0 |
| Fairly, StL° | 1.000 | 20 | 32 | 0 | 0 | 0 |
| Wallis, Chi | 1.000 | 15 | 31 | 1 | 0 | 0 |
| LaCock, Chi° | 1.000 | 26 | 26 | 2 | 0 | 0 |
| Kirkpatrick, Pitt | 1.000 | 14 | 26 | 0 | 0 | 0 |
| Hiser, Chi° | 1.000 | 18 | 25 | 0 | 0 | 0 |
| Lyttle, Mtl | 1.000 | 16 | 17 | 1 | 0 | 0 |
| Coggins, Mtl° | 1.000 | 10 | 16 | 0 | 0 | 0 |
| Jones, NY° | 1.000 | 12 | 9 | 0 | 0 | 0 |
| Howard, Hou | .995 | 95 | 194 | 7 | 1 | 0 |
| JOSHUA, SF° | .9931 | 117 | 279 | 10 | 2 | 3 |
| Geronimo, Cin°..... | .9929 | 148 | 408 | 12 | 3 | 5 |
| Grubb, SD | .991 | 139 | 334 | 3 | 3 | 0 |
| Robinson, Pitt | .991 | 57 | 107 | 3 | 1 | 1 |
| Foster, Cin | .990 | 125 | 299 | 11 | 3 | 3 |
| Crawford, LA° | .990 | 113 | 201 | 2 | 2 | 0 |
| Baker, Atl | .990 | 136 | 287 | 10 | 3 | 0 |
| McBride, StL | .990 | 107 | 289 | 4 | 3 | 1 |
| Oliver, Pitt° | .987 | 153 | 380 | 5 | 5 | 3 |
| Unser, NY° | .987 | 144 | 362 | 13 | 5 | 2 |
| Buckner, LA° | .986 | 72 | 138 | 4 | 2 | 0 |
| Staub, NY | .986 | 153 | 267 | 15 | 4 | 3 |
| Maddox, 13 SF-97 Phil | .985 | 110 | 325 | 13 | 5 | 4 |
| Milner, NY° | .985 | 31 | 63 | 2 | 1 | 0 |
| Ferguson, LA | .984 | 34 | 57 | 4 | 1 | 3 |
| Wynn, LA | .983 | 120 | 282 | 6 | 5 | 2 |
| Melendez, StL | .983 | 89 | 169 | 3 | 3 | 1 |
| Cedeno, Hou | .982 | 131 | 322 | 8 | 6 | 2 |
| Rose, Cin | .982 | 35 | 55 | 0 | 1 | 0 |
| Clines, NY | .982 | 60 | 98 | 9 | 2 | 2 |
| Murcer, SF | .981 | 144 | 201 | 10 | 4 | 3 |
| Cruz, Hou° | .980 | 94 | 187 | 6 | 4 | 0 |
| Morales, Chi | .979 | 151 | 273 | 11 | 6 | 1 |
| Martin, Phila | .979 | 49 | 90 | 3 | 2 | 1 |
| Bailey, Mtl | .979 | 61 | 88 | 4 | 2 | 1 |
| Thomasson, SF° | .978 | 74 | 172 | 9 | 4 | 2 |
| Hale, LA | .977 | 68 | 128 | 2 | 3 | 0 |
| Anderson, Phila | .977 | 105 | 161 | 6 | 4 | 0 |
| White, Mtl | .976 | 30 | 81 | 1 | 2 | 1 |
| Driessen, Cin | .976 | 29 | 41 | 0 | 1 | 0 |
| Cardenal, Chi | .976 | 151 | 313 | 14 | 8 | 3 |
| Johnstone, Phila | .976 | 101 | 152 | 10 | 4 | 3 |
| Zisk, Pitt | .975 | 140 | 264 | 7 | 7 | 1 |
| Carter, Mtl | .974 | 92 | 150 | 1 | 4 | 1 |
| Gaston, Atl | .974 | 35 | 72 | 2 | 2 | 0 |
| Cabell, Hou | .973 | 67 | 99 | 10 | 3 | 0 |
| Monday, Chi° | .973 | 131 | 315 | 6 | 9 | 0 |
| Parker, Pitt | .972 | 141 | 311 | 7 | 9 | 2 |
| Mangual, Mtl | .972 | 138 | 308 | 8 | 9 | 2 |
| Biittner, Mtl° | .972 | 93 | 166 | 8 | 5 | 0 |
| Winfield, SD | .972 | 138 | 302 | 9 | 9 | 1 |
| Paciorek, LA | .972 | 54 | 69 | 0 | 2 | 0 |
| Vail, NY | .971 | 36 | 92 | 9 | 3 | 1 |
| Tolan, SD° | .971 | 120 | 230 | 5 | 7 | 1 |
| Davis, StL° | .970 | 89 | 187 | 5 | 6 | 2 |
| Locklear, SD | .970 | 51 | 92 | 4 | 3 | 1 |
| Griffey, Cin° | .967 | 119 | 202 | 6 | 7 | 0 |
| Matthews, SF | .967 | 113 | 225 | 11 | 8 | 2 |
| Office, Atl° | .967 | 107 | 229 | 6 | 8 | 0 |
| Luzinski, Phila | .966 | 159 | 248 | 10 | 9 | 0 |
| Garr, Atl | .966 | 148 | 298 | 12 | 11 | 2 |
| Brock, StL° | .966 | 128 | 247 | 5 | 9 | 0 |
| Dwyer, 9 StL- 52 Mtl° | .966 | 61 | 104 | 8 | 4 | 1 |
| May, Atl | .964 | 53 | 103 | 3 | 4 | 2 |
| Alou, NY | .963 | 20 | 23 | 3 | 1 | 0 |
| Smith, StL | .963 | 69 | 126 | 3 | 5 | 0 |
| Scott, Mtl | .962 | 71 | 94 | 6 | 4 | 0 |
| Lacy, NY | .960 | 43 | 89 | 7 | 4 | 1 |
| Cruz, LA° | .960 | 41 | 48 | 0 | 2 | 0 |
| Gross, Hou° | .958 | 121 | 216 | 14 | 10 | 2 |
| Kingman, NY | .958 | 71 | 134 | 3 | 6 | 0 |
| Sharon, SD | .948 | 57 | 91 | 1 | 5 | 0 |
| Adams, SF | .941 | 25 | 31 | 1 | 2 | 0 |
| Bradford, StL | .935 | 25 | 42 | 1 | 3 | 0 |
| Hutton, Phila° | .909 | 12 | 9 | 1 | 1 | 1 |
| Gallagher, NY° | .900 | 16 | 9 | 0 | 1 | 0 |
| Harris, Chi | .900 | 11 | 9 | 0 | 1 | 0 |
| Summers, Chi | .889 | 18 | 16 | 0 | 2 | 0 |
| Armbrister, Cin..... | .867 | 19 | 13 | 0 | 2 | 0 |
| Valentine, Mtl | .867 | 11 | 12 | 1 | 2 | 1 |
| Brown, SF | .857 | 14 | 11 | 1 | 2 | 0 |

### (Fewer Than Ten Games)

| Player—Club | Pct. | G. | PO. | A. | E. | DP. |
|---|---|---|---|---|---|---|
| Gardner, Hou° | 1.000 | 8 | 14 | 0 | 0 | 0 |
| Watson, Hou | 1.000 | 9 | 12 | 1 | 0 | 0 |
| Morales, Mtl | 1.000 | 6 | 11 | 0 | 0 | 0 |
| Martinez, StL | 1.000 | 7 | 9 | 0 | 0 | 0 |
| Mota, LA | 1.000 | 5 | 9 | 0 | 0 | 0 |
| Crowley, Cin° | 1.000 | 4 | 8 | 1 | 0 | 0 |
| Mumphrey, StL | 1.000 | 3 | 9 | 0 | 0 | 0 |
| Tyrone, Chi | 1.000 | 8 | 7 | 1 | 0 | 0 |
| Ontiveros, SF | 1.000 | 8 | 7 | 0 | 0 | 0 |
| Clark, SF | 1.000 | 3 | 7 | 0 | 0 | 0 |
| Royster, LA | 1.000 | 7 | 6 | 0 | 0 | 0 |
| Arnold, SF | 1.000 | 4 | 5 | 1 | 0 | 1 |
| Simpson, LA° | 1.000 | 6 | 5 | 0 | 0 | 0 |
| Kranepool, NY° | 1.000 | 4 | 5 | 0 | 0 | 0 |
| Simmons, StL | 1.000 | 2 | 5 | 0 | 0 | 0 |
| Valentine, SD | 1.000 | 4 | 4 | 0 | 0 | 0 |
| Jorgensen, Mtl° | 1.000 | 6 | 3 | 0 | 0 | 0 |
| Dilone, Pitt | 1.000 | 2 | 3 | 0 | 0 | 0 |
| Johnson, Hou | 1.000 | 1 | 2 | 1 | 0 | 0 |
| Lee, LA | 1.000 | 4 | 1 | 0 | 0 | 0 |
| Thomas, SF | 1.000 | 1 | 1 | 0 | 0 | 0 |
| Cruz, StL | .941 | 6 | 16 | 0 | 1 | 0 |
| Sperring, Chi | .917 | 8 | 11 | 0 | 1 | 0 |
| Turner, SD° | .909 | 4 | 10 | 0 | 1 | 0 |
| Speed, SF | .900 | 9 | 9 | 0 | 1 | 0 |
| Rivera, Mtl | .889 | 5 | 8 | 0 | 1 | 0 |
| Rogodzinski, Phila .. | .667 | 2 | 2 | 0 | 1 | 0 |
| Moreno, Pitt° | .000 | 1 | 0 | 0 | 1 | 0 |
| Dunn, Chi | .000 | 2 | 0 | 0 | 0 | 0 |
| Powell, LA | .000 | 1 | 0 | 0 | 0 | 0 |
| Scott, SF | .000 | 1 | 0 | 0 | 0 | 0 |

## CATCHERS

| Player—Club | Pct. | G. | PO. | A. | E. | DP. | PB. |
|---|---|---|---|---|---|---|---|
| Cox, Phila | 1.000 | 10 | 10 | 0 | 0 | 0 | 1 |
| Sadek, SF | .995 | 38 | 207 | 10 | 1 | 3 | 1 |
| GROTE, NY | .995 | 111 | 706 | 55 | 4 | 8 | 6 |
| Ferguson, LA | .994 | 35 | 158 | 16 | 1 | 1 | 5 |
| Stearns, NY | .994 | 54 | 297 | 40 | 2 | 9 | 2 |
| Hill, SF | .994 | 60 | 282 | 27 | 2 | 7 | 2 |
| Yeager, LA | .992 | 135 | 806 | 62 | 7 | 4 | 11 |
| Dyer, Pitt | .990 | 36 | 187 | 14 | 2 | 0 | 2 |
| Boone, Phil | .990 | 92 | 456 | 44 | 5 | 7 | 5 |
| Plummer, Cin | .990 | 63 | 186 | 14 | 2 | 5 | 2 |
| Oates, 6 Atl-82 Phila | .990 | 88 | 450 | 45 | 5 | 10 | 4 |
| Bench, Cin | .989 | 121 | 568 | 51 | 7 | 9 | 0 |
| Jutze, Hou | .988 | 47 | 147 | 15 | 2 | 3 | 4 |
| Sanguillen, Pitt | .987 | 132 | 650 | 53 | 9 | 4 | 16 |
| Davis, SD | .986 | 43 | 195 | 18 | 3 | 4 | 3 |
| May, Hou | .986 | 102 | 568 | 70 | 9 | 8 | 18 |
| Foote, Mtl | .985 | 115 | 590 | 50 | 10 | 10 | 10 |
| Carter, Mtl | .984 | 66 | 280 | 37 | 5 | 6 | 6 |
| McCarver, Phila | .984 | 10 | 58 | 5 | 1 | 1 | 1 |
| Rader, SF | .984 | 94 | 457 | 37 | 8 | 7 | 10 |
| Simmons, StL | .983 | 154 | 803 | 62 | 15 | 5 | 28 |
| Swisher, Chi | .979 | 93 | 426 | 36 | 10 | 5 | 7 |
| Kendall, SD | .977 | 85 | 337 | 38 | 9 | 6 | 3 |
| Mitterwald, Chi | .976 | 59 | 247 | 32 | 7 | 4 | 1 |
| Correll, Atl | .973 | 97 | 413 | 63 | 13 | 2 | 16 |
| Rudolph, StL | .972 | 31 | 93 | 11 | 3 | 1 | 3 |
| Pocoroba, Atl | .970 | 62 | 237 | 25 | 8 | 2 | 13 |
| Hundley, SD | .970 | 51 | 237 | 20 | 8 | 3 | 1 |
| Hosley, Chi | .968 | 53 | 254 | 16 | 9 | 3 | 7 |
| Williams, Atl | .967 | 11 | 52 | 6 | 2 | 3 | 5 |
| Johnson, Hou | .963 | 41 | 195 | 16 | 8 | 4 | 8 |

### (Fewer Than Ten Games)

| Player—Club | Pct. | G. | PO. | A. | E. | DP. | PB. |
|---|---|---|---|---|---|---|---|
| Hodges, NY | 1.000 | 9 | 69 | 1 | 0 | 0 | 0 |
| Morales, Mtl | 1.000 | 5 | 22 | 2 | 0 | 0 | 4 |
| Johnson, Mtl | 1.000 | 1 | 4 | 1 | 0 | 0 | 0 |
| Alexander, SF | 1.000 | 2 | 2 | 0 | 0 | 0 | 0 |
| Essian, Phil | 1.000 | 2 | 1 | 1 | 0 | 0 | 0 |
| Ott, Pitt | 1.000 | 2 | 2 | 0 | 0 | 0 | 0 |
| Nolan, Atl | 1.000 | 1 | 2 | 0 | 0 | 0 | 0 |
| Ivie, SD | 1.000 | 1 | 1 | 0 | 0 | 0 | 0 |
| Powell, LA | .955 | 7 | 18 | 3 | 1 | 1 | 1 |
| Werner, Cin | .923 | 7 | 10 | 2 | 1 | 0 | 1 |
| Moses, SD | .900 | 5 | 17 | 1 | 2 | 0 | 0 |

## PITCHERS

| Player—Club | Pct. | G. | PO. | A. | E. | DP. |
|---|---|---|---|---|---|---|
| NIEKRO, Atl | 1.000 | 39 | 21 | 41 | 0 | 2 |
| R. REUSCHEL, Chi° | 1.000 | 38 | 23 | 39 | 0 | 5 |
| Reuss, Pitt° | 1.000 | 32 | 6 | 48 | 0 | 1 |
| Roberts, Hou° | 1.000 | 32 | 13 | 36 | 0 | 0 |
| McIntosh, SD | 1.000 | 37 | 12 | 26 | 0 | 1 |
| Nolan, Cin | 1.000 | 32 | 12 | 22 | 0 | 1 |
| Knowles, Chi° | 1.000 | 58 | 6 | 26 | 0 | 1 |
| Fryman, Mtl° | 1.000 | 38 | 6 | 26 | 0 | 4 |
| Billingham, Cin | 1.000 | 33 | 8 | 24 | 0 | 5 |
| Carrithers, Mtl | 1.000 | 19 | 7 | 24 | 0 | 2 |
| Garber, Phila | 1.000 | 71 | 13 | 12 | 0 | 0 |
| Gullett, Cin° | 1.000 | 22 | 2 | 22 | 0 | 0 |
| Hilgendorf, Phila° | 1.000 | 53 | 5 | 18 | 0 | 1 |
| Frailing, Chi° | 1.000 | 41 | 7 | 15 | 0 | 0 |
| Scherman, 16 Hou-34 Mtl° | 1.000 | 50 | 5 | 16 | 0 | 2 |
| Webb, NY | 1.000 | 29 | 11 | 10 | 0 | 2 |
| Downing, LA° | 1.000 | 22 | 4 | 17 | 0 | 0 |
| Niekro, Hou | 1.000 | 40 | 7 | 13 | 0 | 0 |
| Capra, Atl | 1.000 | 12 | 6 | 13 | 0 | 1 |
| Taylor, Mtl | 1.000 | 54 | 6 | 11 | 0 | 0 |
| Dal Canton, Atl | 1.000 | 26 | 6 | 11 | 0 | 1 |
| C. Carroll, Cin | 1.000 | 56 | 2 | 14 | 0 | 0 |
| Stone, NY° | 1.000 | 13 | 1 | 15 | 0 | 1 |
| McEnaney, Cin° | 1.000 | 70 | 6 | 8 | 0 | 0 |
| Hernandez, Pitt° | 1.000 | 46 | 1 | 13 | 0 | 0 |
| Rasmussen, StL | 1.000 | 14 | 2 | 11 | 0 | 0 |
| Sanders, NY | 1.000 | 29 | 7 | 5 | 0 | 0 |
| Thompson, Atl | 1.000 | 16 | 3 | 9 | 0 | 0 |
| Parker, 18 NY-14 StL | 1.000 | 32 | 0 | 11 | 0 | 0 |
| Locker, Chi. | 1.000 | 22 | 5 | 6 | 0 | 0 |
| Harrison, Atl | 1.000 | 15 | 1 | 10 | 0 | 0 |
| Eastwick, Cin | 1.000 | 58 | 5 | 5 | 0 | 1 |
| Easterly, Atl° | 1.000 | 21 | 1 | 9 | 0 | 1 |
| Bradley, SF | 1.000 | 13 | 1 | 9 | 0 | 0 |
| Reynolds, StL° | 1.000 | 10 | 4 | 6 | 0 | 0 |
| Hall, 2 Cin-34 NY° | 1.000 | 36 | 2 | 7 | 0 | 0 |
| Brewer, LA° | 1.000 | 21 | 0 | 7 | 0 | 1 |
| Terlecky, StL | 1.000 | 20 | 2 | 5 | 0 | 0 |
| Hrabosky, StL° | 1.000 | 65 | 0 | 6 | 0 | 0 |
| McDowell, Pitt° | 1.000 | 14 | 1 | 5 | 0 | 2 |
| Moore, StL | 1.000 | 10 | 2 | 4 | 0 | 1 |
| T. Carroll, Cin | 1.000 | 12 | 1 | 4 | 0 | 1 |
| Bryant, StL° | 1.000 | 10 | 1 | 2 | 0 | 0 |
| Wall, LA° | 1.000 | 10 | 0 | 3 | 0 | 0 |
| Sosa, Hou | 1.000 | 25 | 1 | 1 | 0 | 0 |
| Forsch, StL | .982 | 34 | 18 | 37 | 1 | 7 |
| Kison, Pitt | .980 | 33 | 11 | 39 | 1 | 5 |
| Reed, 10 Atl-24 StL. | .979 | 34 | 15 | 31 | 1 | 0 |
| Caldwell, SF° | .977 | 38 | 10 | 33 | 1 | 2 |
| Carlton, Phila° | .977 | 37 | 10 | 32 | 1 | 4 |
| Hooton, 3 Chi-31 LA | .977 | 34 | 13 | 29 | 1 | 0 |
| Lonborg, Phila | .977 | 27 | 24 | 18 | 1 | 0 |
| Freisleben, SD | .976 | 36 | 15 | 26 | 1 | 2 |
| Curtis, StL° | .974 | 39 | 7 | 31 | 1 | 3 |
| Montefusco, SF | .973 | 35 | 11 | 25 | 1 | 0 |
| Morton, Atl | .972 | 39 | 29 | 40 | 2 | 3 |
| Warthen, Mtl° | .970 | 40 | 6 | 26 | 1 | 3 |
| Brett, Pitt° | .969 | 23 | 13 | 18 | 1 | 0 |
| Williams, SF | .968 | 55 | 12 | 18 | 1 | 5 |
| Apodaca, NY | .968 | 46 | 8 | 22 | 1 | 1 |
| Blair, Mtl | .967 | 30 | 8 | 21 | 1 | 2 |
| Richard, Hou | .964 | 33 | 8 | 19 | 1 | 0 |
| Strom, SD° | .964 | 18 | 8 | 19 | 1 | 2 |
| Barr, SF | .962 | 35 | 28 | 48 | 3 | 2 |
| Borbon, Cin | .962 | 67 | 6 | 19 | 1 | 1 |
| Sutton, LA | .961 | 35 | 24 | 25 | 2 | 0 |
| Tekulve, Pitt | .957 | 34 | 5 | 17 | 1 | 1 |
| Moose, Pitt | .957 | 23 | 6 | 16 | 1 | 2 |
| Jones, SD° | .955 | 37 | 14 | 70 | 4 | 5 |
| Rhoden, LA | .955 | 26 | 5 | 16 | 1 | 1 |
| Demery, Pitt | .952 | 45 | 7 | 13 | 1 | 1 |
| McGraw, Phila° | .950 | 56 | 4 | 15 | 1 | 2 |

## PITCHERS (Continued)

| Player—Club | Pct. | G. | PO. | A. | E. | DP. | Player—Club | Pct. | G. | PO. | A. | E. | DP. |
|---|---|---|---|---|---|---|---|---|---|---|---|---|---|
| Griffin, Hou | .950 | 17 | 5 | 14 | 1 | 2 | Sadecki, | | | | | | |
| McGlothen, StL | .946 | 35 | 10 | 25 | 2 | 3 | 8 StL-25 Atl° | .909 | 33 | 2 | 8 | 1 | 0 |
| Lavelle, SF° | .944 | 65 | 6 | 11 | 1 | 2 | Marshall, LA | .906 | 57 | 6 | 23 | 3 | 6 |
| Heaverlo, SF | .944 | 42 | 7 | 10 | 1 | 1 | Frisella, SD | .905 | 65 | 6 | 13 | 2 | 0 |
| Odom, Atl | .944 | 15 | 11 | 6 | 1 | 0 | Rau, LA° | .902 | 38 | 6 | 40 | 5 | 1 |
| Seaver, NY | .941 | 36 | 21 | 43 | 4 | 6 | Sosa, | | | | | | |
| Stone, Chi | .941 | 33 | 21 | 27 | 3 | 1 | 14 StL-43 Atl | .895 | 57 | 3 | 14 | 2 | 1 |
| Burris, Chi | .941 | 36 | 16 | 16 | 2 | 0 | Rogers, Mtl | .894 | 35 | 18 | 41 | 7 | 2 |
| Falcone, SF° | .939 | 34 | 2 | 29 | 2 | 0 | P. Reuschel, Chi | .889 | 28 | 1 | 7 | 1 | 0 |
| Dierker, Hou | .939 | 34 | 15 | 31 | 3 | 1 | Wilcox, Chi | .889 | 25 | 0 | 8 | 1 | 0 |
| Tate, NY | .938 | 26 | 11 | 19 | 2 | 0 | Leon, Atl | .880 | 50 | 3 | 19 | 3 | 0 |
| Beard, Atl° | .938 | 34 | 2 | 13 | 1 | 1 | Konieczny, Hou | .875 | 32 | 7 | 21 | 4 | 1 |
| Darcy, Cin | .935 | 27 | 8 | 21 | 2 | 0 | Giusti, Pitt | .875 | 61 | 4 | 17 | 3 | 0 |
| Koosman, NY° | .933 | 36 | 10 | 32 | 3 | 3 | Gibson, StL | .875 | 22 | 6 | 15 | 3 | 2 |
| Norman, Cin° | .933 | 34 | 9 | 19 | 2 | 2 | Granger, Hou | .870 | 55 | 2 | 18 | 3 | 1 |
| Cosgrove, Hou° | .933 | 32 | 2 | 12 | 1 | 1 | Foster, SD | .857 | 17 | 4 | 8 | 2 | 0 |
| Bonham, Chi | .929 | 38 | 15 | 37 | 4 | 3 | House, Atl° | .852 | 58 | 7 | 16 | 4 | 0 |
| Murray, Mtl | .929 | 63 | 9 | 30 | 3 | 1 | Underwood, Phila° | .852 | 35 | 2 | 21 | 4 | 1 |
| Christenson, Phila | .929 | 29 | 14 | 12 | 2 | 1 | Hough, LA | .846 | 38 | 4 | 7 | 2 | 0 |
| Zamora, Chi | .929 | 52 | 3 | 10 | 1 | 0 | Halicki, SF | .844 | 24 | 7 | 20 | 5 | 0 |
| Schueler, Phila | .926 | 46 | 11 | 14 | 2 | 3 | Kirby, Cin | .842 | 26 | 7 | 9 | 3 | 0 |
| Renko, Mtl | .925 | 31 | 13 | 24 | 3 | 0 | McNally, Mtl° | .833 | 12 | 3 | 12 | 3 | 0 |
| Ellis, Pitt | .923 | 27 | 8 | 16 | 2 | 4 | Greif, SD | .833 | 59 | 0 | 5 | 1 | 0 |
| Tomlin, SD° | .919 | 67 | 7 | 27 | 3 | 3 | York, Hou | .833 | 19 | 3 | 2 | 1 | 0 |
| Spillner, SD | .919 | 37 | 13 | 21 | 3 | 2 | Montague, | | | | | | |
| Zahn, 2 LA-16Chi° | .917 | 18 | 6 | 16 | 2 | 0 | 12 Mtl-3 Phila | .833 | 15 | 0 | 5 | 1 | 1 |
| Johnson, SD | .917 | 21 | 6 | 5 | 1 | 0 | Moffitt, SF° | .824 | 55 | 4 | 10 | 3 | 1 |
| Messersmith, LA° | .915 | 42 | 11 | 43 | 5 | 1 | Candelaria, Pitt° | .800 | 18 | 3 | 13 | 4 | 0 |
| Rooker, Pitt° | .913 | 28 | 10 | 32 | 4 | 1 | DeMola, Mtl | .800 | 60 | 1 | 3 | 1 | 0 |
| Baldwin, NY | .913 | 54 | 3 | 18 | 2 | 2 | Lockwood, NY | .800 | 24 | 1 | 3 | 1 | 0 |
| Crawford, Hou° | .913 | 44 | 8 | 13 | 2 | 2 | Ruthven, Phila | .778 | 11 | 2 | 5 | 2 | 1 |
| Matlack, NY° | .912 | 33 | 3 | 28 | 3 | 1 | Twitchell, Phila | .765 | 36 | 7 | 6 | 4 | 0 |
| Denny, StL | .911 | 25 | 11 | 30 | 4 | 2 | Garman, StL | .750 | 66 | 3 | 9 | 4 | 0 |
| Folkers, SD° | .909 | 45 | 10 | 20 | 3 | 0 | D'Acquisto, SF | .600 | 10 | 1 | 2 | 2 | 1 |
| Dettore, Chi | .909 | 36 | 6 | 14 | 2 | 2 | Hoerner, Phil° | .000 | 25 | 0 | 0 | 0 | 0 |
| Forsch, Hou | .909 | 34 | 6 | 14 | 2 | 3 | | | | | | | |

### (Fewer Than Ten Games)

| Player—Club | Pct. | G. | PO. | A. | E. | DP. | Player—Club | Pct. | G. | PO. | A. | E. | DP. |
|---|---|---|---|---|---|---|---|---|---|---|---|---|---|
| Simpson, Phila | 1.000 | 7 | 6 | 4 | 0 | 0 | Marichal, LA | 1.000 | 2 | 0 | 2 | 0 | 0 |
| Siebert, Hou° | 1.000 | 7 | 3 | 4 | 0 | 0 | Kurosaki, StL | 1.000 | 7 | 0 | 1 | 0 | 0 |
| Minton, SF | 1.000 | 4 | 2 | 4 | 0 | 1 | Schultz, Chi° | 1.000 | 6 | 1 | 0 | 0 | 0 |
| Dressler, SF | 1.000 | 3 | 2 | 4 | 0 | 0 | Watt, Chi | 1.000 | 6 | 0 | 1 | 0 | 0 |
| Stanton, Hou | 1.000 | 7 | 2 | 3 | 0 | 0 | Cram, NY | 1.000 | 4 | 0 | 1 | 0 | 0 |
| Gentry, Atl | 1.000 | 7 | 0 | 4 | 0 | 1 | Metzger, SD | 1.000 | 4 | 0 | 1 | 0 | 0 |
| Torrealba, Atl° | 1.000 | 6 | 1 | 3 | 0 | 0 | Jones, Pitt | 1.000 | 2 | 0 | 1 | 0 | 0 |
| Crosby, Chi | 1.000 | 9 | 0 | 3 | 0 | 0 | Lewallyn, LA | 1.000 | 2 | 1 | 0 | 0 | 0 |
| Wallace, StL° | 1.000 | 9 | 2 | 1 | 0 | 0 | Siebert, SD | .750 | 6 | 1 | 5 | 2 | 1 |
| Stanhouse, Mtl | 1.000 | 4 | 2 | 1 | 0 | 0 | Barlow, StL | .500 | 9 | 0 | 1 | 1 | 0 |
| Prall, Chi° | 1.000 | 3 | 0 | 3 | 0 | 0 | Hardy, SD | .000 | 3 | 0 | 0 | 1 | 0 |
| Toms, SF | 1.000 | 7 | 2 | 0 | 0 | 0 | Acosta, Phila | .000 | 6 | 0 | 0 | 0 | 0 |
| Solomon, Chi | 1.000 | 6 | 0 | 2 | 0 | 0 | Hanna, Atl | .000 | 4 | 0 | 0 | 0 | 0 |
| Swan, NY | 1.000 | 6 | 1 | 1 | 0 | 0 | Lerch, Phila° | .000 | 3 | 0 | 0 | 0 | 0 |
| Devine, Atl | 1.000 | 5 | 1 | 1 | 0 | 0 | Espinosa, NY | .000 | 2 | 0 | 0 | 0 | 0 |
| Sells, LA | 1.000 | 5 | 1 | 1 | 0 | 0 | Lang, Mtl | .000 | 1 | 0 | 0 | 0 | 0 |
| Moore, Chi | 1.000 | 4 | 2 | 0 | 0 | 0 | Minshall, Pitt | .000 | 1 | 0 | 0 | 0 | 0 |
| LaCorte, Atl | 1.000 | 3 | 0 | 2 | 0 | 1 | Scarce, NY° | .000 | 1 | 0 | 0 | 0 | 0 |

# OFFICIAL NATIONAL LEAGUE PITCHING AVERAGES

Compiled by Elias Sports Bureau, New York, N. Y.

## CLUB PITCHING

| Club | ERA. | G. | CG. | Sv. | ShO. | IP. | H. | BFP. | R. | ER. | HR. | SH. | SF. | Tot. BB. | Int. BB. | HB. | SO. | WP. | Bk. |
|---|---|---|---|---|---|---|---|---|---|---|---|---|---|---|---|---|---|---|---|
| Los Angeles | 2.92 | 162 | 51 | 21 | 18 | 1469⅔ | 1215 | 6015 | 534 | 477 | 104 | 89 | 39 | 448 | 81 | 28 | 894 | 34 | 10 |
| Pittsburgh | 3.01 | 161 | 51 | 31 | 14 | 1437⅓ | 1302 | 6072 | 565 | 480 | 79 | 92 | 37 | 551 | 102 | 20 | 768 | 37 | 11 |
| Cincinnati | 3.37 | 162 | 43 | 50 | 8 | 1459 | 1422 | 6158 | 586 | 546 | 112 | 79 | 37 | 487 | 63 | 29 | 663 | 49 | 10 |
| New York | 3.39 | 162 | 22 | 41 | 12 | 1466 | 1344 | 6190 | 625 | 552 | 99 | 87 | 32 | 580 | 64 | 24 | 989 | 48 | 20 |
| San Diego | 3.48 | 162 | 40 | 20 | 11 | 1463⅓ | 1494 | 6314 | 683 | 566 | 99 | 112 | 49 | 521 | 94 | 24 | 713 | 44 | 9 |
| St. Louis | 3.57 | 163 | 40 | 36 | 12 | 1454⅔ | 1452 | 6304 | 689 | 577 | 98 | 70 | 43 | 571 | 94 | 24 | 824 | 44 | 5 |
| Montreal | 3.72 | 162 | 30 | 24 | 13 | 1480 | 1448 | 6430 | 690 | 612 | 102 | 87 | 43 | 665 | 63 | 37 | 831 | 55 | 12 |
| San Francisco | 3.74 | 161 | 37 | 25 | 12 | 1432⅔ | 1406 | 6211 | 671 | 595 | 92 | 99 | 40 | 612 | 93 | 38 | 856 | 65 | 15 |
| Philadelphia | 3.82 | 162 | 33 | 30 | 9 | 1455 | 1353 | 6140 | 694 | 618 | 111 | 79 | 47 | 546 | 49 | 25 | 897 | 51 | 15 |
| Atlanta | 3.91 | 161 | 32 | 24 | 11 | 1430 | 1543 | 6279 | 739 | 622 | 101 | 107 | 51 | 519 | 50 | 44 | 669 | 50 | 20 |
| Houston | 4.04 | 162 | 39 | 25 | 6 | 1458⅓ | 1436 | 6337 | 711 | 654 | 106 | 80 | 56 | 679 | 44 | 34 | 839 | 55 | 17 |
| Chicago | 4.49 | 162 | 27 | 33 | 8 | 1444⅓ | 1587 | 6383 | 827 | 721 | 130 | 101 | 49 | 551 | 59 | 40 | 850 | 35 | 9 |
| Totals | 3.62 | | 427 | 350 | 129 | 17450⅓ | 17002 | 74833 | 8014 | 7020 | 1233 | 1082 | 536 | 6730 | 795 | 367 | 9793 | 606 | 153 |

(BFP total includes 16 batsmen awarded first base because of interference or obstruction).

Note—Totals for earned runs for several clubs do not agree with the composite totals for all pitchers of each respective club due to instances in which provisions of Section 10:18 (i) of the Scoring Rules were applied. The following differences are to be noted: Atlanta pitchers add to 624; Chicago, 732; Houston, 656; Montreal, 614; Pittsburgh, 482; St. Louis, 578; San Diego, 570.

## PITCHERS' RECORDS

(Top Fifteen Qualifiers for Earned-Run Average Leadership—162 or More Innings)

*Throws lefthanded.

| Pitcher and Club | ERA. | W. | L. | Pct. | G. | GS. | CG. | GF. | Sv. | ShO. | IP. | H. | BFP. | R. | ER. | HR. | SH. | SF. | Tot. BB. | Int. BB. | HB. | SO. | WP. | Bk. |
|---|---|---|---|---|---|---|---|---|---|---|---|---|---|---|---|---|---|---|---|---|---|---|---|---|
| Jones, Randall, San Diego* | 2.24 | 20 | 12 | .625 | 37 | 36 | 18 | 1 | 0 | 1 | 285 | 242 | 1124 | 94 | 71 | 17 | 15 | 9 | 86 | 9 | 6 | 103 | 3 | 0 |
| Messersmith, John, Los Angeles | 2.29 | 19 | 14 | .576 | 42 | 40 | 19 | 2 | 1 | 0 | 322 | 244 | 1276 | 92 | 82 | 22 | 20 | 7 | 96 | 8 | 5 | 213 | 8 | 1 |
| Seaver, G. Thomas, New York | 2.38 | 22 | 9 | .710 | 36 | 36 | 15 | 0 | 0 | 4 | 280 | 217 | 1115 | 81 | 74 | 11 | 9 | 10 | 88 | 6 | 4 | 243 | 7 | 1 |
| Reuss, Jerry, Pittsburgh* | 2.54 | 18 | 11 | .621 | 32 | 32 | 15 | 0 | 0 | 4 | 237 | 224 | 984 | 73 | 67 | 10 | 18 | 3 | 78 | 8 | 3 | 131 | 4 | 0 |
| Forsch, Robert, St. Louis | 2.86 | 15 | 10 | .600 | 34 | 34 | 11 | 0 | 0 | 4 | 230 | 213 | 958 | 89 | 73 | 14 | 6 | 7 | 70 | 8 | 3 | 108 | 10 | 1 |
| Sutton, Donald, Los Angeles | 2.87 | 16 | 13 | .552 | 35 | 34 | 11 | 1 | 0 | 4 | 254 | 202 | 1031 | 87 | 81 | 13 | 14 | 6 | 62 | 8 | 8 | 175 | 7 | 0 |
| Montefusco, John, San Francisco | 2.88 | 15 | 9 | .625 | 35 | 34 | 10 | 1 | 0 | 2 | 244 | 210 | 1018 | 80 | 78 | 14 | 11 | 5 | 86 | 12 | 8 | 215 | 6 | 2 |
| Rooker, James, Pittsburgh* | 2.97 | 13 | 11 | .542 | 28 | 28 | 7 | 0 | 0 | 2 | 197 | 177 | 839 | 80 | 65 | 16 | 11 | 4 | 76 | 13 | 13 | 102 | 6 | 1 |
| Barr, James, San Francisco | 3.06 | 13 | 14 | .481 | 35 | 33 | 12 | 0 | 0 | 4 | 244 | 244 | 1004 | 94 | 83 | 13 | 17 | 5 | 58 | 10 | 3 | 77 | 3 | 1 |
| Hooton, Burt, Chi-LA | 3.06 | 18 | 9 | .667 | 34 | 33 | 12 | 1 | 0 | 2 | 235 | 190 | 949 | 96 | 80 | 17 | 18 | 8 | 68 | 10 | 8 | 153 | 5 | 1 |
| Rau, Douglas, Los Angeles* | 3.10 | 15 | 9 | .625 | 40 | 38 | 8 | 0 | 0 | 1 | 258 | 227 | 1046 | 89 | 89 | 18 | 8 | 1 | 61 | 8 | 1 | 128 | 3 | 4 |
| Warthen, Daniel, Montreal* | 3.11 | 8 | 6 | .571 | 40 | 18 | 2 | 12 | 0 | 3 | 168 | 130 | 700 | 62 | 58 | 8 | 15 | 7 | 87 | 4 | 7 | 74 | 1 | 5 |
| Nolan, Gary, Cincinnati | 3.16 | 15 | 9 | .625 | 32 | 32 | 13 | 0 | 0 | 1 | 211 | 202 | 852 | 75 | 74 | 18 | 9 | 5 | 29 | 5 | 3 | 74 | 3 | 2 |
| Niekro, Philip, Atlanta | 3.20 | 15 | 15 | .500 | 39 | 37 | 13 | 2 | 0 | 0 | 276 | 285 | 1160 | 115 | 98 | 29 | 14 | 11 | 72 | 3 | 11 | 144 | 15 | 2 |
| Kison, Bruce, Pittsburgh | 3.23 | 12 | 11 | .522 | 33 | 29 | 6 | 2 | 0 | 0 | 192 | 160 | 819 | 89 | 69 | 9 | 11 | 4 | 92 | 9 | 4 | 89 | 9 | 2 |

DEPARTMENTAL LEADERS: W—Seaver, 22; L—R. Reuschel, 17; Pct.—Gullett, .789; G—Garber, 71; GS—Messersmith, 40; CG—Messersmith, 19; GF—Garber, 47; Sv—Eastwick, Hrabosky, 22; ShO—Messersmith, 7; IP—Messersmith, 322; H—Morton, 302; BFP—Messersmith, 1,276; R—Bonham, 133; ER—Bonham, 120; HR—P. Niekro, 29; SH—Messersmith, R. Reuschel, 20; SF—Carlton, 12; Tot. BB—Richard, 138; Int. BB—Garman, 23; HB—P. Niekro, 11; SO—Seaver, 243; WP—Richard, 20; Bk—Carlton, Koosman, 7.

°Throws lefthanded.

(All Pitchers—Listed Alphabetically)

| Pitcher and Club | ERA | W | L | Pct. | G | GS | CG | GF | Sv | ShO | IP | H | BFP | R | ER | HR | SH | SF | Tot. BB | Int. BB | HB | SO | WP | Bk |
|---|---|---|---|---|---|---|---|---|---|---|---|---|---|---|---|---|---|---|---|---|---|---|---|---|
| Acosta, Cecilio, Philadelphia | 6.00 | 0 | 0 | .000 | 6 | 0 | 0 | 4 | 0 | 0 | 9 | 9 | 36 | 7 | 6 | 1 | 4 | 0 | 3 | 0 | 0 | 2 | 0 | 0 |
| Apodaca, Robert, New York | 1.48 | 3 | 4 | .429 | 46 | 0 | 0 | 36 | 13 | 0 | 85 | 66 | 338 | 18 | 14 | 4 | 4 | 2 | 28 | 9 | 1 | 45 | 5 | 0 |
| Baldwin, Rick, New York | 3.34 | 3 | 5 | .375 | 54 | 0 | 0 | 29 | 6 | 0 | 97 | 97 | 418 | 39 | 36 | 4 | 8 | 3 | 34 | 4 | 1 | 54 | 2 | 2 |
| Barlow, Michael, St. Louis | 4.50 | 0 | 0 | .000 | 8 | 0 | 0 | 2 | 0 | 0 | 8 | 11 | 37 | 6 | 4 | 0 | 1 | 2 | 3 | 1 | 0 | 5 | 0 | 0 |
| Barr, James, San Francisco | 3.06 | 13 | 14 | .481 | 35 | 33 | 12 | 2 | 0 | 2 | 244 | 244 | 1004 | 94 | 83 | 17 | 17 | 6 | 58 | 10 | 3 | 77 | 2 | 1 |
| Beard, Michael, Atlanta | 3.21 | 4 | 0 | 1.000 | 34 | 3 | 0 | 8 | 0 | 0 | 70 | 71 | 309 | 31 | 25 | 4 | 6 | 2 | 28 | 5 | 1 | 27 | 3 | 2 |
| Billingham, John, Cincinnati | 4.11 | 15 | 10 | .600 | 33 | 32 | 5 | 0 | 1 | 0 | 208 | 222 | 893 | 100 | 95 | 22 | 7 | 8 | 76 | 12 | 3 | 79 | 8 | 1 |
| Blair, Dennis, Montreal | 3.81 | 8 | 15 | .348 | 30 | 27 | 7 | 1 | 0 | 0 | 163 | 150 | 718 | 77 | 69 | 14 | 3 | 1 | 106 | 6 | 3 | 82 | 8 | 1 |
| Bonham, William, Chicago | 4.72 | 13 | 15 | .464 | 38 | 36 | 11 | 1 | 0 | 2 | 229 | 254 | 1035 | 133 | 120 | 15 | 11 | 6 | 109 | 6 | 6 | 165 | 12 | 1 |
| Borbon, Pedro, Cincinnati | 2.95 | 9 | 5 | .643 | 67 | 0 | 0 | 25 | 5 | 0 | 125 | 145 | 523 | 47 | 41 | 14 | 16 | 6 | 21 | 6 | 1 | 29 | 0 | 0 |
| Bradley, Thomas, San Francisco | 6.21 | 2 | 9 | .182 | 13 | 6 | 0 | 0 | 0 | 0 | 42 | 57 | 199 | 33 | 29 | 6 | 1 | 1 | 18 | 0 | 4 | 13 | 6 | 0 |
| Brett, Kenneth, Pittsburgh° | 3.36 | 9 | 5 | .643 | 23 | 16 | 4 | 4 | 0 | 1 | 118 | 110 | 492 | 47 | 44 | 10 | 16 | 5 | 43 | 5 | 2 | 47 | 2 | 1 |
| Brewer, James, Los Angeles° | 5.18 | 3 | 1 | .750 | 22 | 0 | 0 | 14 | 2 | 0 | 33 | 44 | 152 | 20 | 19 | 1 | 2 | 5 | 12 | 4 | 0 | 21 | 1 | 0 |
| Burris, B. Ray, Chicago | 4.12 | 15 | 10 | .600 | 38 | 35 | 8 | 0 | 1 | 1 | 238 | 259 | 1020 | 121 | 109 | 25 | 13 | 0 | 73 | 6 | 2 | 108 | 2 | 2 |
| Bryant, Ronald, St. Louis° | 16.00 | 0 | 1 | .000 | 10 | 1 | 0 | 1 | 0 | 0 | 8 | 20 | 55 | 16 | 15 | 2 | 1 | 0 | 7 | 0 | 0 | 7 | 1 | 0 |
| Caldwell, R. Michael, San Fran° | 4.80 | 7 | 13 | .350 | 38 | 21 | 4 | 4 | 0 | 0 | 163 | 194 | 723 | 102 | 87 | 16 | 10 | 4 | 48 | 7 | 5 | 57 | 5 | 0 |
| Candelaria, John, Pittsburgh° | 2.75 | 8 | 6 | .571 | 18 | 18 | 1 | 0 | 0 | 0 | 121 | 95 | 492 | 41 | 37 | 8 | 6 | 6 | 36 | 5 | 0 | 95 | 1 | 0 |
| Capra, Lee, Atlanta | 4.27 | 4 | 7 | .364 | 12 | 12 | 2 | 0 | 0 | 0 | 78 | 77 | 336 | 41 | 37 | 8 | 5 | 2 | 28 | 7 | 1 | 35 | 0 | 0 |
| Carlton, Steven, Philadelphia° | 3.56 | 15 | 14 | .517 | 37 | 37 | 14 | 0 | 0 | 2 | 255 | 217 | 1063 | 116 | 101 | 24 | 15 | 12 | 104 | 8 | 1 | 192 | 5 | 7 |
| Carrithers, Donald, Montreal | 3.30 | 5 | 4 | .556 | 37 | 14 | 2 | 7 | 0 | 1 | 101 | 93 | 424 | 39 | 37 | 4 | 8 | 3 | 38 | 8 | 3 | 44 | 3 | 0 |
| Carroll, Clay, Cincinnati | 2.63 | 7 | 5 | .583 | 56 | 0 | 0 | 27 | 7 | 0 | 96 | 96 | 407 | 30 | 28 | 2 | 6 | 3 | 32 | 8 | 2 | 26 | 0 | 0 |
| Carroll, Thomas, Cincinnati | 4.98 | 4 | 1 | .800 | 29 | 2 | 0 | 13 | 2 | 0 | 47 | 52 | 212 | 28 | 26 | 1 | 2 | 1 | 26 | 4 | 0 | 22 | 0 | 0 |
| Christenson, Larry, Philadelphia | 3.66 | 11 | 6 | .647 | 32 | 26 | 6 | 3 | 0 | 1 | 172 | 149 | 689 | 73 | 70 | 12 | 5 | 7 | 45 | 3 | 1 | 88 | 6 | 0 |
| Cosgrove, Michael, Houston° | 3.04 | 2 | 5 | .286 | 44 | 3 | 0 | 13 | 1 | 0 | 71 | 62 | 300 | 24 | 24 | 7 | 3 | 5 | 37 | 4 | 0 | 32 | 0 | 1 |
| Cram, Gerald, New York | 5.40 | 0 | 0 | .000 | 9 | 0 | 0 | 4 | 0 | 0 | 8 | 10 | 42 | 5 | 3 | 0 | 0 | 2 | 7 | 0 | 0 | 6 | 0 | 0 |
| Crawford, James, Houston° | 3.62 | 2 | 6 | .250 | 39 | 0 | 0 | 19 | 6 | 0 | 87 | 92 | 377 | 40 | 35 | 3 | 7 | 4 | 37 | 6 | 0 | 37 | 7 | 0 |
| Crosby, Kenneth, Chicago | 3.38 | 1 | 0 | 1.000 | 18 | 0 | 0 | 8 | 1 | 0 | 10 | 10 | 42 | 5 | 3 | 0 | 0 | 0 | 7 | 0 | 0 | 6 | 0 | 0 |
| Curtis, John, St. Louis° | 3.43 | 8 | 9 | .471 | 26 | 22 | 3 | 1 | 0 | 0 | 131 | 147 | 645 | 70 | 56 | 13 | 8 | 7 | 65 | 6 | 0 | 67 | 7 | 0 |
| D'Acquisto, John, San Francisco | 10.29 | 0 | 0 | .000 | 3 | 0 | 0 | 0 | 0 | 0 | 8 | 10 | 42 | 10 | 9 | 1 | 0 | 0 | 6 | 0 | 0 | 6 | 0 | 0 |
| Dal Canton, J. Bruce, Atlanta | 3.36 | 2 | 7 | .222 | 26 | 9 | 1 | 3 | 0 | 0 | 67 | 63 | 297 | 35 | 32 | 2 | 1 | 6 | 24 | 4 | 0 | 14 | 2 | 0 |
| Darcy, Patrick, Cincinnati | 3.57 | 11 | 5 | .688 | 27 | 22 | 1 | 2 | 0 | 1 | 131 | 134 | 572 | 54 | 52 | 11 | 11 | 4 | 59 | 9 | 3 | 63 | 4 | 2 |
| Demery, Lawrence, Pittsburgh | 2.90 | 7 | 5 | .583 | 45 | 8 | 0 | 12 | 1 | 1 | 115 | 95 | 468 | 40 | 37 | 8 | 10 | 2 | 42 | 9 | 6 | 59 | 2 | 1 |
| DeMola, Donald, Montreal | 3.97 | 4 | 7 | .364 | 45 | 0 | 0 | 27 | 2 | 0 | 98 | 92 | 424 | 47 | 45 | 8 | 5 | 3 | 51 | 4 | 1 | 63 | 4 | 2 |
| Denny, John, St. Louis | 5.40 | 10 | 7 | .588 | 25 | 24 | 3 | 0 | 0 | 1 | 136 | 149 | 591 | 73 | 60 | 5 | 1 | 3 | 51 | 6 | 4 | 72 | 8 | 0 |
| Dettore, Thomas, Chicago | 4.50 | 5 | 4 | .556 | 36 | 5 | 2 | 13 | 0 | 0 | 85 | 88 | 373 | 57 | 51 | 8 | 5 | 5 | 31 | 3 | 6 | 46 | 5 | 1 |
| Devine, P. Adrian, Atlanta | 4.00 | 2 | 0 | 1.000 | 32 | 2 | 0 | 13 | 3 | 0 | 16 | 19 | 76 | 9 | 8 | 1 | 1 | 0 | 7 | 1 | 0 | 8 | 1 | 0 |
| Dierker, Lawrence, Houston. | 2.88 | 14 | 16 | .467 | 34 | 34 | 14 | 0 | 0 | 0 | 232 | 225 | 982 | 109 | 103 | 24 | 7 | 10 | 91 | 6 | 1 | 127 | 13 | 1 |
| Downing, Alphonso, Los Angeles° | 1.13 | 1 | 1 | .667 | 21 | 13 | 0 | 4 | 0 | 0 | 75 | 59 | 311 | 31 | 24 | 6 | 6 | 0 | 28 | 2 | 2 | 39 | 2 | 2 |
| Dressler, Robert, San Francisco | 1.13 | 2 | 1 | 1.000 | 13 | 0 | 0 | 4 | 0 | 0 | 16 | 17 | 67 | 3 | 2 | 0 | 1 | 0 | 7 | 1 | 0 | 6 | 2 | 0 |
| Easterly, James, Atlanta° | 4.96 | 2 | 9 | .182 | 21 | 13 | 0 | 4 | 0 | 0 | 69 | 73 | 319 | 47 | 38 | 5 | 7 | 3 | 42 | 2 | 2 | 34 | 8 | 1 |

°Throws lefthanded

| Pitcher and Club | ERA | W. | L. | Pct. | G. | GS. | CG. | GF. | Sv. | ShO. | IP. | H. | BFP. | R. | ER. | HR. | SH. | SF. | Tot. BB. | Int. BB. | HB. | SO. | WP. | Bk. |
|---|---|---|---|---|---|---|---|---|---|---|---|---|---|---|---|---|---|---|---|---|---|---|---|---|
| Eastwick, Rawlins, Cincinnati | 2.60 | 5 | 3 | .625 | 58 | 0 | 0 | 40 | 22 | 0 | 90 | 77 | 367 | 26 | 26 | 9 | 4 | 0 | 25 | 4 | 3 | 61 | 1 | 0 |
| Ellis, Dock, Pittsburgh | 3.79 | 8 | 9 | .471 | 27 | 24 | 5 | 1 | 0 | 2 | 140 | 163 | 621 | 69 | 59 | 6 | 9 | 7 | 43 | 9 | 4 | 69 | 0 | 2 |
| Espinosa, Arnulfo, New York | 18.00 | 0 | 1 | .000 | 2 | 0 | 0 | 1 | 0 | 0 | 3 | 8 | 18 | 6 | 6 | 0 | 0 | 0 | 2 | 1 | 0 | 1 | 0 | 0 |
| Falcone, Peter, San Francisco° | 4.17 | 12 | 11 | .522 | 34 | 32 | 4 | 1 | 0 | 2 | 190 | 171 | 836 | 97 | 88 | 16 | 13 | 6 | 111 | 7 | 4 | 131 | 5 | 0 |
| Folkers, Richard, San Diego° | 4.18 | 6 | 11 | .353 | 45 | 15 | 1 | 7 | 1 | 0 | 142 | 155 | 614 | 70 | 66 | 8 | 11 | 6 | 39 | 1 | 1 | 87 | 1 | 1 |
| Forsch, Kenneth, Houston | 3.22 | 4 | 8 | .333 | 34 | 9 | 1 | 12 | 2 | 0 | 114 | 114 | 451 | 42 | 39 | 14 | 2 | 6 | 30 | 8 | 3 | 54 | 0 | 1 |
| Forsch, Robert, St. Louis | 2.86 | 15 | 10 | .600 | 34 | 34 | 8 | 0 | 0 | 3 | 230 | 213 | 958 | 89 | 73 | 9 | 9 | 2 | 70 | 5 | 4 | 108 | 0 | 0 |
| Foster, Alan, San Diego° | 2.40 | 3 | 1 | .750 | 17 | 4 | 1 | 4 | 0 | 0 | 45 | 41 | 193 | 14 | 12 | 2 | 1 | 2 | 21 | 2 | 0 | 10 | 0 | 1 |
| Frailing, Kenneth, Chicago° | 5.43 | 2 | 5 | .286 | 41 | 0 | 0 | 10 | 2 | 0 | 53 | 61 | 244 | 37 | 32 | 11 | 6 | 1 | 26 | 5 | 1 | 29 | 1 | 0 |
| Freisleben, David, San Diego | 4.28 | 5 | 14 | .263 | 65 | 20 | 7 | 0 | 0 | 2 | 181 | 206 | 825 | 102 | 86 | 13 | 6 | 4 | 82 | 16 | 6 | 77 | 3 | 1 |
| Frisella, Daniel, San Diego | 3.12 | 1 | 6 | .143 | 38 | 0 | 0 | 39 | 9 | 0 | 98 | 86 | 421 | 36 | 34 | 10 | 8 | 4 | 51 | 17 | 2 | 67 | 2 | 0 |
| Fryman, Woodrow, Montreal° | 3.32 | 9 | 12 | .429 | 38 | 20 | 7 | 0 | 3 | 3 | 157 | 141 | 671 | 69 | 58 | 13 | 10 | 5 | 68 | 11 | 5 | 118 | 7 | 1 |
| Garber, H. Eugene, Philadelphia | 3.60 | 10 | 12 | .455 | 71 | 0 | 0 | 47 | 14 | 0 | 110 | 104 | 448 | 48 | 44 | 13 | 8 | 4 | 27 | 23 | 2 | 69 | 2 | 0 |
| Garman, Michael, St. Louis | 2.39 | 3 | 8 | .273 | 66 | 0 | 0 | 36 | 7 | 0 | 79 | 73 | 358 | 31 | 21 | 3 | 6 | 5 | 48 | 5 | 3 | 48 | 1 | 1 |
| Gentry, Gary, Atlanta | 4.95 | 1 | 1 | .500 | 2 | 2 | 1 | 0 | 0 | 0 | 24 | 25 | 90 | 14 | 11 | 0 | 0 | 0 | 8 | 0 | 0 | 10 | 0 | 0 |
| Gibson, Robert, St. Louis | 5.04 | 3 | 10 | .231 | 22 | 14 | 2 | 0 | 0 | 3 | 109 | 120 | 499 | 66 | 61 | 11 | 3 | 2 | 62 | 3 | 4 | 60 | 4 | 2 |
| Giusti, David, Pittsburgh | 2.93 | 5 | 4 | .556 | 61 | 0 | 0 | 43 | 17 | 0 | 92 | 79 | 389 | 38 | 30 | 10 | 11 | 7 | 42 | 6 | 1 | 52 | 2 | 1 |
| Granger, Wayne, Houston | 3.65 | 2 | 5 | .286 | 59 | 0 | 0 | 17 | 9 | 0 | 74 | 76 | 323 | 39 | 30 | 3 | 11 | 5 | 23 | 17 | 1 | 35 | 3 | 1 |
| Greif, William, San Diego | 3.88 | 4 | 6 | .400 | 17 | 13 | 2 | 0 | 0 | 1 | 72 | 74 | 331 | 44 | 31 | 7 | 4 | 2 | 38 | 5 | 1 | 45 | 3 | 0 |
| Griffin, Thomas, Houston | 5.35 | 3 | 8 | .273 | 25 | 23 | 8 | 0 | 0 | 2 | 160 | 143 | 363 | 49 | 47 | 11 | 4 | 2 | 46 | 4 | 1 | 56 | 5 | 0 |
| Gullett, Donald, Cincinnati° | 2.42 | 15 | 4 | .789 | 24 | 24 | 12 | 0 | 0 | 4 | 160 | 127 | 648 | 49 | 43 | 11 | 5 | 4 | 56 | 7 | 5 | 98 | 1 | 1 |
| Halicki, Edward, San Francisco | 3.49 | 9 | 13 | .409 | 24 | 23 | 7 | 0 | 0 | 0 | 160 | 143 | 679 | 76 | 62 | 12 | 7 | 7 | 59 | 3 | 4 | 153 | 2 | 2 |
| Hall, Tom, Cin-NY° | 4.57 | 4 | 3 | .571 | 36 | 0 | 0 | 16 | 1 | 0 | 63 | 60 | 282 | 39 | 32 | 10 | 11 | 2 | 33 | 5 | 1 | 51 | 1 | 1 |
| Hanna, Preston, Atlanta | 1.50 | 0 | 0 | .000 | 4 | 4 | 1 | 0 | 0 | 0 | 6 | 8 | 30 | 1 | 1 | 0 | 0 | 0 | 5 | 0 | 0 | 2 | 0 | 0 |
| Hardy, H. Lawrence, San Diego | 12.00 | 0 | 0 | .000 | 2 | 0 | 0 | 2 | 0 | 0 | 3 | 8 | 18 | 6 | 6 | 3 | 0 | 0 | 4 | 0 | 0 | 1 | 1 | 0 |
| Harrison, Roric, Atlanta | 4.75 | 3 | 4 | .429 | 15 | 7 | 1 | 5 | 0 | 0 | 55 | 58 | 240 | 33 | 29 | 6 | 4 | 5 | 19 | 4 | 0 | 22 | 3 | 0 |
| Heaverlo, David, San Francisco | 2.39 | 3 | 1 | .750 | 42 | 0 | 0 | 23 | 1 | 0 | 64 | 62 | 275 | 18 | 17 | 3 | 5 | 2 | 28 | 14 | 2 | 35 | 3 | 1 |
| Hernandez, Ramon, Pittsburgh° | 2.95 | 7 | 2 | .778 | 46 | 0 | 0 | 27 | 5 | 0 | 64 | 62 | 280 | 22 | 21 | 6 | 3 | 5 | 38 | 10 | 0 | 45 | 2 | 2 |
| Hilgendorf, Thomas, Philadelphia° | 2.13 | 7 | 3 | .700 | 53 | 0 | 0 | 14 | 1 | 0 | 97 | 81 | 403 | 32 | 23 | 6 | 1 | 5 | 38 | 3 | 1 | 52 | 0 | 2 |
| Hoerner, Joseph, Philadelphia° | 2.57 | 0 | 0 | .000 | 25 | 0 | 0 | 14 | 2 | 0 | 21 | 25 | 96 | 7 | 6 | 1 | 2 | 1 | 5 | 3 | 0 | 5 | 0 | 1 |
| Hooton, Burt, Chi-LA | 3.06 | 18 | 9 | .667 | 34 | 33 | 12 | 0 | 0 | 6 | 235 | 190 | 949 | 88 | 80 | 18 | 8 | 8 | 68 | 6 | 3 | 153 | 1 | 2 |
| Hough, Charles, Los Angeles | 2.95 | 3 | 7 | .300 | 38 | 0 | 0 | 24 | 4 | 0 | 79 | 43 | 266 | 25 | 28 | 2 | 8 | 3 | 34 | 10 | 2 | 48 | 3 | 1 |
| House, Thomas, Atlanta° | 3.19 | 7 | 7 | .500 | 58 | 0 | 0 | 45 | 11 | 0 | 72 | 72 | 351 | 27 | 28 | 3 | 9 | 3 | 33 | 10 | 1 | 36 | 4 | 0 |
| Hrabosky, Alan, St. Louis° | 1.67 | 13 | 3 | .813 | 65 | 0 | 0 | 41 | 22 | 0 | 97 | 73 | 393 | 27 | 18 | 9 | 3 | 3 | 31 | 12 | 0 | 82 | 2 | 3 |
| Johnson, Jerry, San Diego | 5.17 | 3 | 1 | .750 | 21 | 0 | 0 | 4 | 0 | 0 | 54 | 61 | 250 | 37 | 31 | 9 | 3 | 1 | 30 | 8 | 0 | 18 | 1 | 0 |
| Jones, Odell, Pittsburgh | 0.00 | 0 | 2 | .000 | 2 | 2 | 0 | 0 | 0 | 0 | 6 | 1 | 30 | 0 | 0 | 0 | 0 | 0 | 2 | 0 | 0 | 2 | 0 | 0 |
| Jones, Randall, San Diego° | 2.24 | 20 | 12 | .625 | 37 | 36 | 18 | 1 | 0 | 6 | 285 | 242 | 1124 | 94 | 71 | 17 | 15 | 9 | 56 | 8 | 1 | 103 | 2 | 0 |
| Kirby, Clayton, Cincinnati | 4.70 | 10 | 11 | .476 | 26 | 19 | 6 | 3 | 1 | 0 | 113 | 113 | 499 | 63 | 58 | 13 | 11 | 5 | 54 | 9 | 5 | 48 | 3 | 1 |
| Kison, Bruce, Pittsburgh | 3.23 | 12 | 11 | .522 | 32 | 29 | 11 | 0 | 0 | 0 | 192 | 160 | 819 | 89 | 69 | 15 | 11 | 7 | 89 | 6 | 3 | 89 | 6 | 1 |
| Konieczny, Douglas, Houston | 4.47 | 6 | 13 | .316 | 32 | 29 | 4 | 0 | 0 | 0 | 171 | 184 | 762 | 93 | 85 | 15 | 9 | 8 | 87 | 1 | 1 | 89 | 2 | 7 |
| Knowles, Darold, Chicago° | 5.83 | 6 | 9 | .400 | 58 | 0 | 0 | 36 | 15 | 0 | 88 | 107 | 410 | 61 | 57 | 8 | 14 | 7 | 36 | 9 | 3 | 63 | 7 | 1 |
| Koosman, Jerry, New York° | 3.41 | 14 | 13 | .519 | 36 | 36 | 11 | 0 | 0 | 5 | 240 | 234 | 1018 | 106 | 91 | 19 | 7 | 6 | 98 | 6 | 1 | 173 | 0 | 0 |
| Kurosaki, Ryan, St. Louis | 7.62 | 0 | 0 | .000 | 7 | 0 | 0 | 2 | 0 | 0 | 13 | 15 | 61 | 11 | 11 | 0 | 1 | 0 | 7 | 1 | 0 | 6 | 0 | 0 |
| Lang, Robert, Montreal | 9.00 | 0 | 0 | .000 | 1 | 0 | 0 | 0 | 0 | 0 | 2 | 2 | 10 | 2 | 2 | 1 | 0 | 0 | 3 | 0 | 0 | 2 | 0 | 0 |
| LaCorte, Frank, Atlanta | 5.14 | 0 | 3 | .000 | 3 | 2 | 0 | 0 | 0 | 0 | 14 | 13 | 59 | 9 | 8 | 2 | 0 | 1 | 6 | 0 | 0 | 10 | 0 | 0 |
| Lavelle, Gary, San Francisco° | 2.96 | 6 | 3 | .667 | 65 | 0 | 0 | 29 | 8 | 0 | 82 | 80 | 370 | 30 | 27 | 3 | 10 | 3 | 48 | 12 | 3 | 51 | 2 | 3 |

*Throws lefthanded.

| Pitcher and Club | ERA | W. | L. | Pct. | G. | GS. | CG. | GF. | Sv. | ShO | IP. | H. | BFP. | R. | ER. | HR. | SH. | SF. | Tot. BB. | Int. BB. | SO. | WP. | Bk. |
|---|---|---|---|---|---|---|---|---|---|---|---|---|---|---|---|---|---|---|---|---|---|---|---|
| Leon, Maximino, Atlanta | 4.13 | 2 | 1 | .667 | 50 | 1 | 0 | 20 | 6 | 0 | 85 | 90 | 381 | 52 | 39 | 5 | 8 | 4 | 33 | 8 | 53 | 2 | 0 |
| Lerch, Randy, Philadelphia* | 6.43 | 0 | 0 | .000 | 3 | 0 | 0 | 2 | 0 | 0 | 7 | 6 | 27 | 5 | 5 | 1 | 0 | 0 | 1 | 0 | 8 | 0 | 0 |
| Lewallyn, Dennis, Los Angeles | 0.00 | 0 | 0 | .000 | 3 | 0 | 0 | 2 | 0 | 0 | 3 | 1 | 10 | 0 | 0 | 0 | 0 | 0 | 0 | 0 | 1 | 1 | 0 |
| Locker, Robert, Chicago | 4.91 | 0 | 1 | .000 | 22 | 0 | 0 | 8 | 2 | 0 | 33 | 38 | 148 | 21 | 18 | 3 | 5 | 1 | 16 | 6 | 14 | 1 | 0 |
| Lockwood, Claude, New York | 1.50 | 1 | 3 | .250 | 24 | 0 | 0 | 6 | 1 | 0 | 48 | 28 | 192 | 9 | 8 | 3 | 2 | 1 | 25 | 2 | 61 | 5 | 1 |
| Lonborg, James, Philadelphia | 4.13 | 8 | 6 | .571 | 27 | 26 | 6 | 0 | 0 | 0 | 159 | 161 | 683 | 84 | 73 | 12 | 5 | 3 | 45 | 1 | 72 | 3 | 0 |
| Marichal, Juan, Los Angeles | 13.50 | 0 | 1 | .000 | 2 | 2 | 0 | 0 | 0 | 0 | 6 | 11 | 34 | 9 | 9 | 2 | 2 | 0 | 5 | 0 | 5 | 0 | 0 |
| Marshall, Michael, Los Angeles | 3.30 | 9 | 14 | .391 | 57 | 0 | 0 | 46 | 13 | 0 | 109 | 98 | 469 | 46 | 40 | 8 | 16 | 4 | 39 | 11 | 64 | 4 | 1 |
| Matlack, Jonathan, New York* | 3.38 | 16 | 12 | .571 | 33 | 32 | 8 | 0 | 0 | 3 | 229 | 224 | 949 | 105 | 86 | 15 | 7 | 4 | 58 | 5 | 154 | 7 | 1 |
| McDowell, Samuel, Pittsburgh* | 2.83 | 2 | 2 | .500 | 14 | 14 | 8 | 0 | 0 | 0 | 92 | 30 | 149 | 11 | 11 | 1 | 4 | 1 | 20 | 3 | 29 | 5 | 1 |
| McEnaney, William, Cincinnati* | 2.47 | 2 | 2 | .500 | 70 | 0 | 0 | 38 | 15 | 0 | 91 | 92 | 380 | 29 | 25 | 6 | 9 | 1 | 23 | 7 | 48 | 1 | 2 |
| McGlothen, Lynn, St. Louis | 3.92 | 15 | 13 | .536 | 35 | 34 | 9 | 0 | 0 | 0 | 239 | 231 | 1046 | 110 | 104 | 21 | 10 | 7 | 97 | 11 | 146 | 5 | 1 |
| McGraw, Frank, Philadelphia* | 2.97 | 9 | 6 | .600 | 56 | 0 | 0 | 37 | 14 | 0 | 103 | 84 | 419 | 38 | 34 | 4 | 7 | 1 | 36 | 9 | 55 | 5 | 1 |
| McIntosh, Joseph, San Diego | 3.69 | 8 | 15 | .348 | 37 | 28 | 4 | 5 | 0 | 0 | 183 | 195 | 789 | 88 | 75 | 14 | 10 | 4 | 60 | 6 | 71 | 5 | 1 |
| McNally, David, Montreal* | 5.26 | 3 | 6 | .333 | 12 | 12 | 0 | 0 | 0 | 0 | 77 | 88 | 358 | 50 | 45 | 8 | 0 | 2 | 36 | 4 | 36 | 3 | 1 |
| Messersmith, John, Los Angeles | 2.29 | 19 | 14 | .576 | 42 | 40 | 19 | 0 | 0 | 7 | 322 | 244 | 1276 | 92 | 82 | 22 | 20 | 7 | 96 | 21 | 213 | 8 | 0 |
| Metzger, Clarence, San Diego | 7.20 | 0 | 0 | .000 | 4 | 0 | 0 | 3 | 0 | 0 | 5 | 9 | 24 | 4 | 4 | 0 | 1 | 0 | 4 | 1 | 6 | 0 | 0 |
| Minshall, James, Pittsburgh | 0.00 | 0 | 0 | 1.000 | 1 | 0 | 0 | 0 | 0 | 0 | 1 | 0 | 2 | 0 | 0 | 0 | 0 | 0 | 0 | 0 | 0 | 0 | 0 |
| Minton, Gregory, San Francisco | 6.88 | 0 | 1 | .000 | 4 | 2 | 0 | 1 | 0 | 0 | 17 | 19 | 79 | 14 | 13 | 0 | 6 | 1 | 11 | 3 | 6 | 2 | 0 |
| Moffitt, Randall, San Francisco | 3.89 | 4 | 5 | .444 | 55 | 0 | 0 | 33 | 11 | 0 | 73 | 73 | 327 | 35 | 32 | 6 | 6 | 6 | 32 | 6 | 39 | 2 | 1 |
| Montague, John, Mtl-Phila | 6.26 | 0 | 0 | .000 | 15 | 0 | 0 | 5 | 4 | 0 | 23 | 31 | 106 | 16 | 16 | 5 | 0 | 0 | 10 | 2 | 10 | 2 | 0 |
| Montefusco, John, San Francisco | 2.88 | 15 | 9 | .625 | 35 | 34 | 10 | 1 | 0 | 4 | 244 | 210 | 1018 | 92 | 78 | 11 | 15 | 6 | 86 | 12 | 215 | 6 | 2 |
| Moore, Donnie, Chicago | 4.00 | 0 | 0 | .000 | 10 | 0 | 0 | 3 | 0 | 0 | 9 | 12 | 42 | 4 | 4 | 2 | 0 | 0 | 4 | 0 | 6 | 0 | 0 |
| Moore, Tommy, St. Louis | 3.79 | 0 | 0 | .000 | 23 | 5 | 0 | 5 | 0 | 0 | 68 | 63 | 287 | 30 | 28 | 4 | 9 | 0 | 25 | 3 | 34 | 2 | 1 |
| Moose, Robert, Pittsburgh | 3.71 | 0 | 2 | .000 | 39 | 0 | 1 | 40 | 7 | 0 | 68 | 63 | 287 | 32 | 28 | 4 | 3 | 0 | 25 | 3 | 34 | 3 | 1 |
| Morton, Carl, Atlanta | 3.50 | 17 | 16 | .515 | 39 | 39 | 11 | 0 | 0 | 2 | 278 | 302 | 1199 | 122 | 108 | 19 | 19 | 5 | 82 | 10 | 78 | 1 | 2 |
| Murray, Dale, Montreal | 3.97 | 15 | 8 | .652 | 63 | 0 | 0 | 40 | 14 | 0 | 113 | 134 | 499 | 59 | 49 | 3 | 12 | 2 | 39 | 7 | 43 | 4 | 2 |
| Niekro, Joseph, Houston | 3.07 | 6 | 15 | .286 | 34 | 4 | 1 | 21 | 4 | 0 | 88 | 79 | 378 | 32 | 30 | 9 | 14 | 5 | 39 | 3 | 54 | 2 | 2 |
| Niekro, Philip, Atlanta | 3.20 | 15 | 15 | .500 | 39 | 37 | 13 | 2 | 0 | 2 | 276 | 285 | 1160 | 115 | 98 | 28 | 14 | 3 | 72 | 5 | 144 | 15 | 1 |
| Nolan, Gary, Cincinnati | 3.16 | 15 | 9 | .625 | 34 | 37 | 2 | 0 | 0 | 1 | 211 | 202 | 852 | 75 | 74 | 20 | 7 | 4 | 29 | 5 | 74 | 4 | 0 |
| Norman, Fredie, Cincinnati* | 3.73 | 12 | 7 | .632 | 32 | 26 | 2 | 1 | 0 | 0 | 188 | 163 | 795 | 85 | 78 | 23 | 4 | 2 | 84 | 5 | 119 | 4 | 0 |
| Odom, Johnny, Atlanta | 7.07 | 2 | 1 | .667 | 14 | 1 | 0 | 9 | 3 | 0 | 56 | 78 | 263 | 46 | 44 | 5 | 4 | 2 | 28 | 0 | 30 | 6 | 0 |
| Parker, Harry, NY-StL | 5.09 | 1 | 2 | .333 | 38 | 13 | 2 | 0 | 1 | 0 | 53 | 58 | 246 | 30 | 30 | 6 | 3 | 0 | 29 | 2 | 35 | 0 | 0 |
| Prall, Wilfred, Chicago* | 8.40 | 0 | 0 | .000 | 34 | 0 | 0 | 0 | 3 | 0 | 15 | 21 | 71 | 15 | 14 | 5 | 0 | 0 | 8 | 1 | 6 | 0 | 0 |
| Rasmussen, Harold, St. Louis | 3.78 | 5 | 9 | .357 | 31 | 13 | 2 | 2 | 0 | 0 | 81 | 86 | 348 | 44 | 34 | 8 | 15 | 2 | 20 | 0 | 59 | 5 | 0 |
| Rau, Douglas, Los Angeles* | 3.10 | 15 | 9 | .625 | 38 | 34 | 8 | 0 | 1 | 6 | 258 | 227 | 1046 | 96 | 89 | 18 | 11 | 6 | 61 | 7 | 151 | 1 | 1 |
| Reed, Ronald, Atl-StL | 3.53 | 13 | 13 | .500 | 38 | 34 | 8 | 0 | 1 | 2 | 250 | 274 | 1067 | 118 | 98 | 20 | 11 | 6 | 53 | 11 | 139 | 6 | 1 |
| Renko, Steve, Montreal | 4.08 | 6 | 13 | .316 | 28 | 25 | 0 | 0 | 0 | 0 | 170 | 175 | 751 | 89 | 77 | 13 | 9 | 1 | 76 | 7 | 99 | 8 | 0 |
| Reuschel, Paul, Chicago | 3.50 | 1 | 3 | .250 | 10 | 0 | 0 | 18 | 5 | 0 | 36 | 44 | 160 | 15 | 14 | 4 | 0 | 4 | 13 | 1 | 12 | 1 | 0 |
| Reuschel, Ricky, Chicago | 3.73 | 11 | 17 | .393 | 38 | 37 | 9 | 0 | 0 | 0 | 234 | 244 | 1007 | 116 | 97 | 10 | 20 | 3 | 67 | 7 | 155 | 4 | 2 |
| Reuss, Jerry, Pittsburgh* | 2.54 | 18 | 11 | .621 | 32 | 32 | 15 | 0 | 0 | 6 | 237 | 224 | 984 | 73 | 67 | 7 | 18 | 8 | 78 | 8 | 131 | 4 | 1 |
| Reynolds, Kenneth, St. Louis* | 1.59 | 3 | 11 | .214 | 10 | 0 | 0 | 5 | 1 | 0 | 17 | 12 | 68 | 4 | 3 | 0 | 2 | 1 | 11 | 2 | 6 | 0 | 2 |
| Rhoden, Richard, Los Angeles | 3.09 | 3 | 3 | .500 | 26 | 11 | 1 | 7 | 0 | 0 | 99 | 94 | 415 | 40 | 34 | 8 | 5 | 5 | 32 | 1 | 40 | 2 | 0 |
| Richard, James, Houston | 4.39 | 12 | 10 | .545 | 33 | 31 | 7 | 1 | 0 | 1 | 203 | 178 | 905 | 107 | 99 | 8 | 5 | 5 | 138 | 0 | 176 | 20 | 5 |
| Roberts, David, Houston* | 4.27 | 8 | 14 | .364 | 32 | 27 | 7 | 3 | 0 | 0 | 198 | 182 | 841 | 98 | 94 | 16 | 12 | 8 | 73 | 4 | 101 | 8 | 0 |

°Throws lefthanded.

| Pitcher and Club | ERA | W. | L. | Pct. | G. | GS. | CG. | GF. | Sv. | ShO. | IP. | H. | BFP. | R. | ER. | HR. | SH. | SF. | Tot. BB. | Int. BB. | HB. | SO. | WP. | Bk. |
|---|---|---|---|---|---|---|---|---|---|---|---|---|---|---|---|---|---|---|---|---|---|---|---|---|
| Rogers, Stephen, Montreal | 3.29 | 11 | 12 | .478 | 35 | 35 | 12 | 0 | 0 | 3 | 252 | 248 | 1068 | 104 | 92 | 13 | 18 | 4 | 88 | 8 | 4 | 137 | 13 | 1 |
| Rooker, James, Pittsburgh° | 2.97 | 13 | 11 | .542 | 28 | 28 | 7 | 0 | 0 | 0 | 197 | 177 | 839 | 80 | 65 | 16 | 11 | 4 | 76 | 13 | 3 | 102 | 5 | 1 |
| Ruthven, Richard, Philadelphia | 4.17 | 2 | 2 | .500 | 11 | 5 | 0 | 3 | 0 | 0 | 41 | 37 | 177 | 22 | 19 | 3 | 2 | 2 | 22 | 6 | 1 | 26 | 2 | 1 |
| Sadecki, Raymond, StL-Atl° | 4.09 | 3 | 3 | .500 | 33 | 5 | 1 | 9 | 2 | 0 | 77 | 86 | 346 | 46 | 35 | 5 | 5 | 0 | 28 | 7 | 1 | 32 | 4 | 0 |
| Sanders, Kenneth, New York | 2.30 | 1 | 3 | .250 | 29 | 0 | 0 | 18 | 5 | 0 | 43 | 31 | 172 | 11 | 11 | 2 | 6 | 2 | 14 | 0 | 0 | 22 | 0 | 0 |
| Scarce, G. McCurdy, New York° | 0.00 | 0 | 0 | .000 | 1 | 0 | 0 | 1 | 0 | 0 | 1 | 1 |  | 0 | 0 | 0 | 0 | 0 | 0 | 0 | 0 | 1 | 0 | 0 |
| Scherman, Frederick, Hou-Mtl° | 3.77 | 0 | 4 | .000 | 50 | 0 | 0 | 14 | 5 | 0 | 93 | 105 | 426 | 48 | 39 | 11 | 9 | 1 | 45 | 8 | 0 | 56 | 4 | 2 |
| Schueler, Ronald, Philadelphia | 5.23 | 4 | 4 | .500 | 46 | 6 | 0 | 17 | 0 | 0 | 93 | 88 | 391 | 55 | 54 | 6 | 7 | 2 | 40 | 1 | 1 | 69 | 7 | 0 |
| Schultz, C. Budd, Chicago° | 6.00 | 2 | 0 | 1.000 | 6 | 0 | 0 | 0 | 0 | 0 | 6 | 11 | 35 | 4 | 4 | 0 | 0 | 0 | 4 | 0 | 0 | 4 | 1 | 0 |
| Seaver, G. Thomas, New York | 2.38 | 22 | 9 | .710 | 36 | 36 | 15 | 0 | 0 | 5 | 280 | 217 | 1115 | 81 | 74 | 11 | 11 | 6 | 88 | 6 | 1 | 243 | 7 | 0 |
| Sells, David, Los Angeles | 3.86 | 0 | 0 | .000 | 5 | 0 | 0 | 5 | 0 | 0 | 7 | 6 | 30 | 3 | 3 | 0 | 0 | 1 | 6 | 1 | 0 | 6 | 1 | 0 |
| Siebert, Paul, Houston° | 3.00 | 0 | 2 | .000 | 5 | 2 | 0 | 0 | 0 | 0 | 18 | 20 | 77 | 7 | 6 | 1 | 2 | 0 | 10 | 1 | 0 | 10 | 0 | 0 |
| Siebert, Wilfred, San Diego | 4.33 | 0 | 0 | .000 | 6 | 2 | 0 | 2 | 1 | 0 | 27 | 37 | 126 | 15 | 13 | 3 | 1 | 1 | 11 | 1 | 0 | 19 | 2 | 0 |
| Simpson, Wayne, Philadelphia | 3.19 | 1 | 1 | .500 | 7 | 5 | 0 | 0 | 0 | 0 | 31 | 31 | 132 | 11 | 11 | 1 | 0 | 1 | 11 | 0 | 0 | 10 | 0 | 0 |
| Solomon, Eddie, Chicago | 1.29 | 0 | 1 | .000 | 6 | 1 | 0 | 3 | 0 | 0 | 7 | 7 | 34 | 6 | 1 | 0 | 1 | 0 | 6 | 2 | 0 | 3 | 1 | 0 |
| Sosa, Elias, StL-Atl | 4.30 | 2 | 5 | .286 | 57 | 0 | 0 | 25 | 6 | 0 | 90 | 92 | 395 | 49 | 43 | 6 | 8 | 4 | 43 | 9 | 2 | 46 | 4 | 0 |
| Sosa, Jose, Houston | 4.02 | 3 | 3 | .500 | 25 | 1 | 0 | 9 | 1 | 0 | 47 | 51 | 206 | 21 | 21 | 4 | 1 | 0 | 23 | 2 | 0 | 31 | 5 | 2 |
| Spillner, Daniel, San Diego | 4.26 | 5 | 13 | .278 | 25 | 25 | 3 | 0 | 0 | 1 | 167 | 194 | 746 | 79 | 79 | 14 | 7 | 3 | 63 | 4 | 1 | 104 | 5 | 2 |
| Stanhouse, Donald, Montreal | 8.31 | 0 | 2 | .000 | 3 | 3 | 0 | 0 | 0 | 0 | 13 | 19 | 67 | 12 | 12 | 1 | 2 | 0 | 11 | 0 | 0 | 5 | 1 | 0 |
| Stanton, Michael, Houston | 7.41 | 0 | 0 | .000 | 4 | 2 | 0 | 1 | 0 | 0 | 17 | 20 | 89 | 14 | 14 | 2 | 1 | 0 | 20 | 0 | 0 | 16 | 4 | 0 |
| Stone, George, New York° | 5.05 | 3 | 3 | .500 | 13 | 11 | 2 | 1 | 0 | 0 | 57 | 75 | 261 | 38 | 32 | 6 | 7 | 1 | 21 | 3 | 2 | 21 | 2 | 0 |
| Stone, Steven, Chicago | 3.95 | 12 | 8 | .600 | 33 | 32 | 6 | 0 | 0 | 1 | 214 | 198 | 911 | 103 | 94 | 14 | 11 | 8 | 80 | 5 | 2 | 139 | 2 | 2 |
| Strom, Brent, San Diego° | 2.55 | 8 | 8 | .500 | 18 | 16 | 6 | 0 | 0 | 2 | 120 | 103 | 488 | 42 | 34 | 2 | 10 | 0 | 33 | 1 | 1 | 56 | 2 | 0 |
| Sutton, Donald, Los Angeles | 2.87 | 16 | 13 | .552 | 35 | 35 | 11 | 0 | 0 | 4 | 254 | 202 | 1031 | 87 | 81 | 17 | 14 | 7 | 62 | 3 | 1 | 175 | 2 | 2 |
| Swan, Craig, New York | 6.39 | 1 | 3 | .250 | 6 | 4 | 0 | 1 | 0 | 0 | 31 | 38 | 142 | 22 | 22 | 4 | 0 | 0 | 22 | 1 | 1 | 19 | 0 | 2 |
| Taylor, Randall, New York | 4.43 | 5 | 4 | .556 | 26 | 23 | 2 | 0 | 0 | 0 | 138 | 121 | 605 | 73 | 68 | 8 | 7 | 2 | 86 | 5 | 3 | 99 | 6 | 0 |
| Taylor, Charles G., Montreal | 3.53 | 0 | 0 | .000 | 54 | 0 | 0 | 28 | 6 | 0 | 72 | 72 | 308 | 32 | 29 | 6 | 6 | 2 | 24 | 11 | 0 | 27 | 3 | 2 |
| Tekulve, Kenton, Pittsburgh | 2.25 | 5 | 3 | .625 | 34 | 0 | 0 | 9 | 5 | 0 | 56 | 43 | 232 | 14 | 14 | 2 | 5 | 3 | 23 | 6 | 2 | 28 | 0 | 0 |
| Terlecky, Gregory, St. Louis | 4.67 | 0 | 2 | .000 | 16 | 0 | 0 | 10 | 0 | 0 | 52 | 60 | 240 | 32 | 27 | 2 | 1 | 0 | 32 | 5 | 0 | 13 | 5 | 0 |
| Thompson, Michael, Atlanta | 3.25 | 4 | 6 | .400 | 20 | 10 | 2 | 3 | 0 | 0 | 83 | 87 | 365 | 38 | 30 | 5 | 8 | 2 | 31 | 2 | 0 | 48 | 0 | 0 |
| Tomlin, David, San Diego° | 6.30 | 0 | 0 | .000 | 7 | 0 | 0 | 5 | 0 | 0 | 10 | 13 | 48 | 8 | 7 | 1 | 1 | 0 | 3 | 1 | 0 | 6 | 0 | 0 |
| Toms, Thomas, San Francisco | 1.29 | 0 | 1 | .000 | 6 | 0 | 0 | 2 | 0 | 0 | 7 | 7 | 31 | 2 | 1 | 1 | 0 | 0 | 3 | 0 | 0 | 3 | 0 | 0 |
| Torrealba, Pablo, Atlanta° | 4.43 | 0 | 0 | .000 | 36 | 0 | 0 | 12 | 6 | 0 | 61 | 66 | 261 | 33 | 30 | 6 | 2 | 3 | 31 | 3 | 1 | 48 | 2 | 0 |
| Twitchell, Wayne, Philadelphia | 4.15 | 5 | 10 | .333 | 36 | 20 | 7 | 3 | 1 | 0 | 132 | 132 | 578 | 66 | 61 | 10 | 12 | 6 | 78 | 3 | 1 | 101 | 10 | 4 |
| Underwood, Thomas, Philadelphia° | 4.15 | 14 | 13 | .519 | 35 | 35 | 7 | 0 | 0 | 1 | 219 | 221 | 949 | 110 | 101 | 12 | 9 | 6 | 84 | 6 | 3 | 123 | 9 | 4 |
| Wall, Stanley, Los Angeles° | 1.69 | 0 | 1 | .000 | 40 | 0 | 0 | 21 | 3 | 0 | 66 | 39 | 257 | 16 | 12 | 2 | 5 | 2 | 30 | 6 | 0 | 38 | 1 | 0 |
| Wallace, Michael, St. Louis° | 2.00 | 1 | 0 | 1.000 | 6 | 0 | 0 | 2 | 0 | 0 | 18 | 12 | 66 | 3 | 2 | 0 | 1 | 0 | 7 | 2 | 0 | 6 | 1 | 0 |
| Warthen, Daniel, Montreal° | 3.11 | 8 | 6 | .571 | 29 | 25 | 2 | 2 | 0 | 0 | 168 | 130 | 700 | 62 | 58 | 8 | 6 | 4 | 87 | 4 | 2 | 128 | 5 | 0 |
| Watt, Eddie, Chicago | 13.50 | 0 | 1 | .000 | 6 | 0 | 0 | 2 | 0 | 0 | 10 | 14 | 41 | 9 | 8 | 1 | 0 | 0 | 8 | 4 | 0 | 6 | 0 | 0 |
| Webb, Henry, New York | 4.07 | 7 | 6 | .538 | 29 | 15 | 3 | 6 | 2 | 1 | 115 | 102 | 502 | 52 | 52 | 10 | 12 | 4 | 62 | 4 | 2 | 38 | 5 | 3 |
| Wilcox, Milton, Chicago | 5.68 | 0 | 1 | .000 | 25 | 2 | 0 | 2 | 0 | 0 | 38 | 50 | 178 | 24 | 24 | 2 | 6 | 2 | 17 | 2 | 1 | 21 | 1 | 0 |
| Williams, Charles, S. F. | 3.49 | 5 | 3 | .625 | 55 | 4 | 0 | 21 | 6 | 0 | 98 | 94 | 438 | 40 | 38 | 4 | 5 | 1 | 66 | 14 | 4 | 45 | 7 | 1 |
| York, James, Houston | 3.83 | 4 | 4 | .500 | 19 | 10 | 2 | 5 | 1 | 0 | 47 | 43 | 209 | 22 | 20 | 2 | 3 | 5 | 25 | 2 | 1 | 17 | 1 | 0 |
| Zahn, Geoffrey, LA-Chi° | 4.64 | 2 | 8 | .200 | 18 | 10 | 1 | 2 | 0 | 0 | 66 | 69 | 286 | 40 | 34 | 7 | 2 | 4 | 31 | 1 | 2 | 22 | 2 | 1 |
| Zamora, Oscar, Chicago | 5.07 | 5 | 2 | .714 | 52 | 0 | 0 | 31 | 10 | 0 | 71 | 84 | 306 | 42 | 40 | 17 | 7 | 5 | 15 | 5 | 0 | 28 | 1 | 0 |

NOTE.—Following pitchers combined to pitch shutout games: Atlanta (1)—Easterly and Hanna; Chicago (3)—R. Reuschel and Zamora, R. Reuschel and P. Reuschel, R. Reuschel and Crosby; Cincinnati (4)—Darcy, Norman and Borbon, T. Carroll and McEnaney, T. Carroll and C. Carroll, Gullett and Eastwick; Los Angeles (1)—Sutton and Marshall; Montreal (3)—Blair and Warthen, Rogers and Murray;

Blair and Fryman; New York (1)—Seaver and Koosman; Philadelphia (2)—Twitchell and McGraw, Christenson and McGraw; Pittsburgh (3)—Brett and Giusti, Brett, Hernandez and Giusti, Candelaria and Brett; St. Louis (2)—Curtis and Hrabosky, Denny and Hrabosky; San Diego (1)—Foster and Frisella.

## PITCHERS WITH TWO OR MORE CLUBS

(Alphabetically Arranged With Pitcher's First Club on Top)

| Pitcher and Club | ERA | W. | L. | Pct. | G. | GS. | CG. | GF. | Sv. | ShO. | IP. | H. | BFP. | R. | ER. | HR. | SH. | SF. | BB. | Tot. Int. BB. | HB. | SO. | WP. | Bk. |
|---|---|---|---|---|---|---|---|---|---|---|---|---|---|---|---|---|---|---|---|---|---|---|---|---|
| Hall, Cincinnati | 0.00 | 0 | 0 | .000 | 2 | 0 | 0 | 1 | 0 | 0 | 60⅔ | 2 | 10 | 2 | 0 | 0 | 0 | 0 | 2 | 0 | 0 | 2 | 0 | 0 |
| Hall, New York | 4.75 | 4 | 3 | .571 | 34 | 4 | 0 | 15 | 1 | 0 |  | 58 | 272 | 39 | 32 | 10 | 8 | 2 | 31 | 3 | 0 | 48 | 2 | 0 |
| Hooton, Chicago | 8.18 | 0 | 2 | .000 | 3 | 3 | 0 | 0 | 0 | 0 | 11 | 18 | 54 | 12 | 10 | 2 | 3 | 0 | 4 | 0 | 0 | 5 | 0 | 1 |
| Hooton, Los Angeles | 2.82 | 18 | 7 | .720 | 31 | 30 | 12 | 0 | 0 | 4 | 223⅔ | 172 | 895 | 76 | 70 | 16 | 5 | 6 | 64 | 2 | 0 | 148 | 3 | 1 |
| Montague, Montreal | 5.60 | 0 | 0 | .000 | 12 | 0 | 0 | 7 | 0 | 0 | 17⅓ | 23 | 81 | 11 | 11 | 4 | 0 | 1 | 6 | 1 | 0 | 9 | 2 | 0 |
| Montague, Philadelphia | 9.00 | 0 | 0 | .000 | 3 | 0 | 0 | 1 | 0 | 0 | 5 | 8 | 25 | 5 | 5 | 1 | 1 | 0 | 4 | 1 | 0 | 1 | 0 | 0 |
| Parker, New York | 4.41 | 2 | 3 | .400 | 18 | 1 | 0 | 5 | 2 | 0 | 34⅓ | 37 | 159 | 17 | 17 | 2 | 4 | 0 | 19 | 5 | 0 | 22 | 4 | 0 |
| Parker, St. Louis | 6.27 | 1 | 1 | 1.000 | 14 | 0 | 0 | 4 | 1 | 0 | 18⅓ | 21 | 87 | 13 | 13 | 4 | 2 | 2 | 10 | 2 | 0 | 13 | 2 | 0 |
| Reed, Atlanta | 4.22 | 4 | 5 | .444 | 10 | 10 | 1 | 0 | 0 | 0 | 74⅓ | 93 | 328 | 39 | 35 | 4 | 1 | 3 | 16 | 5 | 2 | 40 | 9 | 0 |
| Reed, St. Louis | 3.23 | 9 | 8 | .529 | 24 | 24 | 7 | 0 | 0 | 2 | 175⅓ | 181 | 739 | 79 | 63 | 8 | 3 | 8 | 37 | 5 | 4 | 99 | 4 | 0 |
| Sadecki, St. Louis | 3.27 | 1 | 2 | .333 | 8 | 5 | 0 | 4 | 0 | 1 | 11 | 13 | 55 | 7 | 4 | 0 | 1 | 2 | 7 | 2 | 0 | 8 | 0 | 0 |
| Sadecki, Atlanta | 4.21 | 2 | 3 | .400 | 25 | 5 | 0 | 9 | 0 | 0 | 66⅓ | 73 | 291 | 39 | 31 | 3 | 4 | 5 | 21 | 5 | 4 | 24 | 4 | 0 |
| Scherman, Houston | 4.96 | 0 | 1 | .000 | 16 | 0 | 0 | 9 | 0 | 0 | 16⅓ | 21 | 74 | 11 | 9 | 0 | 4 | 1 | 14 | 1 | 1 | 13 | 1 | 0 |
| Scherman, Montreal | 3.54 | 4 | 3 | .571 | 34 | 7 | 0 | 5 | 0 | 0 | 76⅓ | 84 | 352 | 37 | 30 | 3 | 4 | 5 | 41 | 7 | 5 | 43 | 3 | 6 |
| Sosa, St. Louis | 3.95 | 0 | 3 | .000 | 14 | 1 | 0 | 4 | 0 | 0 | 27⅓ | 22 | 116 | 14 | 12 | 3 | 0 | 8 | 14 | 2 | 1 | 15 | 3 | 1 |
| Sosa, Atlanta | 4.48 | 2 | 2 | .500 | 43 | 0 | 0 | 21 | 4 | 0 | 62⅓ | 70 | 279 | 35 | 31 | 5 | 8 | 1 | 29 | 7 | 3 | 11 | 3 | 3 |
| Zahn, Los Angeles | 9.00 | 0 | 1 | .000 | 2 | 0 | 0 | 2 | 0 | 0 | 3 | 2 | 14 | 3 | 3 | 0 | 0 | 0 | 5 | 1 | 0 | 1 | 1 | 0 |
| Zahn, Chicago | 4.45 | 0 | 2 | .222 | 16 | 10 | 0 | 3 | 0 | 0 | 62⅔ | 67 | 272 | 37 | 31 | 2 | 5 | 3 | 26 | 3 | 0 | 21 | 0 | 0 |

## MAJOR LEAGUE UMPIRES ASSOCIATION

### BOARD OF DIRECTORS

Dave Phillips, American League
Marty Springstead, American League
Don Denkinger, American League
Bruce Froemming, National League
Bob Engel, National League
John McSherry, National League
Paul Runge, National League

President—Bob Engel, National League
Vice-President—Dave Phillips, American League
Secretary-Treasurer—Billy Williams, National League

John L. Cifelli, Attorney-Negotiator
Citizens Federal Building
Chicago Heights, Ill. 60411
754-5311 (312)

# 1975 N. L. Pitching Against Each Club

## ATLANTA—67-94

| Pitcher | Chi. W—L | Cin. W—L | Hou. W—L | L.A. W—L | Mont. W—L | N.Y. W—L | Phila. W—L | Pitts. W—L | St.L. W—L | S.D. W—L | S.F. W—L | Totals W—L |
|---|---|---|---|---|---|---|---|---|---|---|---|---|
| Beard | 0—0 | 0—0 | 1—0 | 0—0 | 1—0 | 0—0 | 0—0 | 0—0 | 1—0 | 1—0 | 0—0 | 4— 0 |
| Capra | 0—0 | 0—0 | 1—0 | 0—2 | 0—0 | 1—0 | 1—1 | 0—1 | 0—1 | 0—1 | 1—1 | 4— 7 |
| Dal Canton | 0—0 | 0—1 | 0—0 | 1—1 | 0—0 | 0—1 | 0—1 | 0—0 | 1—2 | 0—0 | 0—0 | 2— 7 |
| Devine | 0—0 | 0—0 | 1—0 | 0—0 | 0—0 | 0—0 | 0—0 | 0—0 | 0—0 | 0—0 | 0—0 | 1— 0 |
| Easterly | 0—0 | 0—2 | 1—1 | 0—0 | 0—1 | 0—1 | 0—0 | 0—2 | 0—1 | 0—0 | 1—1 | 2— 9 |
| Gentry | 0—0 | 1—0 | 0—0 | 0—0 | 0—0 | 0—0 | 0—0 | 0—0 | 0—0 | 0—1 | 0—0 | 1— 1 |
| Harrison | 0—1 | 0—1 | 0—0 | 0—0 | 1—1 | 0—0 | 1—0 | 0—1 | 0—0 | 1—0 | 0—0 | 3— 4 |
| House | 1—0 | 0—0 | 0—0 | 2—1 | 1—1 | 0—1 | 0—0 | 1—0 | 1—0 | 1—2 | 0—2 | 7— 7 |
| LaCorte | 0—0 | 0—1 | 0—1 | 0—1 | 0—0 | 0—0 | 0—0 | 0—0 | 0—0 | 0—0 | 0—0 | 0— 3 |
| Leon | 0—0 | 0—0 | 1—0 | 0—0 | 0—0 | 0—1 | 1—0 | 0—0 | 0—0 | 0—0 | 0—0 | 2— 1 |
| Morton | 2—2 | 1—1 | 5—0 | 2—3 | 1—1 | 2—2 | 0—2 | 1—0 | 0—2 | 2—1 | 1—2 | 17—16 |
| Niekro | 2—1 | 0—6 | 1—2 | 2—1 | 2—0 | 1—0 | 2—2 | 2—0 | 1—1 | 0—1 | 2—1 | 15—15 |
| Odom | 0—1 | 0—2 | 0—0 | 1—0 | 0—0 | 0—0 | 0—0 | 0—1 | 0—2 | 0—0 | 0—1 | 1— 7 |
| Reed | 0—0 | 1—0 | 0—1 | 0—0 | 1—0 | 0—1 | 0—1 | 0—0 | 0—0 | 1—1 | 1—1 | 4— 5 |
| Sadecki | 0—1 | 1—0 | 1—0 | 0—0 | 1—0 | 0—0 | 0—0 | 0—0 | 0—1 | 0—0 | 0—0 | **2— 3** |
| Sosa | 0—0 | 0—0 | 0—0 | 0—0 | 0—0 | 0—1 | 0—0 | 0—1 | 1—0 | 0—0 | 1—0 | 2— 2 |
| Thompson | 0—0 | 0—0 | 0—1 | 0—1 | 0—0 | 0—0 | 0—0 | 0—2 | 0—1 | 0—1 | 0—0 | 0— 6 |
| Torrealba | 0—0 | 0—1 | 0—0 | 0—0 | 0—0 | 0—0 | 0—0 | 0—0 | 0—0 | 0—0 | 0—0 | 0— 1 |
| Totals | 5—7 | 3—15 | 12—6 | 8—10 | 8—4 | 4—8 | 5—7 | 4—8 | 3—9 | 7—11 | 8—9 | 67—94 |

No Decisions—Hanna.

## CHICAGO—75-87

| Pitcher | Atl. W—L | Cin. W—L | Hou. W—L | L.A. W—L | Mont. W—L | N.Y. W—L | Phila. W—L | Pitts. W—L | St.L. W—L | S.D. W—L | S.F. W—L | Totals W—L |
|---|---|---|---|---|---|---|---|---|---|---|---|---|
| Bonham | 1—0 | 1—2 | 0—2 | 2—1 | 3—2 | 0—1 | 2—2 | 2—0 | 1—2 | 0—2 | 1—1 | 13—15 |
| Burris | 3—0 | 0—1 | 1—2 | 0—2 | 2—2 | 2—0 | 3—0 | 0—1 | 1—1 | 3—0 | 0—1 | 15—10 |
| Crosby | 0—0 | 0—0 | 0—0 | 0—0 | 0—0 | 1—0 | 0—0 | 0—0 | 0—0 | 0—0 | 0—0 | 1— 0 |
| Dettore | 1—1 | 0—0 | 0—0 | 0—1 | 0—0 | 1—0 | 0—0 | 0—1 | 1—0 | 0—1 | 1—0 | 5— 4 |
| Frailing | 0—1 | 0—0 | 0—0 | 0—0 | 0—0 | 0—0 | 1—0 | 0—3 | 1—0 | 0—0 | 0—1 | 2— 5 |
| Hooton | 0—0 | 0—0 | 0—0 | 0—0 | 0—0 | 0—2 | 0—0 | 0—0 | 0—0 | 0—0 | 0—0 | 0— 2 |
| Knowles | 0—0 | 0—1 | 1—0 | 0—1 | 1—1 | 0—3 | 0—1 | 2—1 | 1—0 | 0—1 | 1—0 | 6— 9 |
| Locker | 0—0 | 0—0 | 0—0 | 0—0 | 0—0 | 0—0 | 0—1 | 0—0 | 0—0 | 0—0 | 0—0 | 0— 1 |
| Prall | 0—0 | 0—0 | 0—0 | 0—0 | 0—0 | 0—0 | 0—0 | 0—2 | 0—0 | 0—0 | 0—0 | 0— 2 |
| P. Reuschel | 0—0 | 0—0 | 0—0 | 0—0 | 0—0 | 0—1 | 0—1 | 0—0 | 1—0 | 0—0 | 0—0 | 1— 3 |
| R. Reuschel | 0—2 | 0—3 | 2—0 | 3—0 | 1—3 | 0—3 | 1—0 | 1—3 | 1—2 | 2—0 | 0—1 | 11—17 |
| Schultz | 0—0 | 0—0 | 0—0 | 0—0 | 0—0 | 0—0 | 0—0 | 2—0 | 0—0 | 0—0 | 0—0 | 2— 0 |
| Stone | 1—0 | 0—2 | 2—0 | 0—1 | 1—0 | 3—1 | 3—1 | 1—0 | 0—1 | 0—1 | 1—1 | 12— 8 |
| Watt | 0—0 | 0—0 | 0—1 | 0—0 | 0—0 | 0—0 | 0—0 | 0—0 | 0—0 | 0—0 | 0—0 | 0— 1 |
| Wilcox | 0—0 | 0—0 | 0—0 | 0—0 | 0—0 | 0—0 | 0—0 | 0—0 | 0—1 | 0—0 | 0—0 | 0— 1 |
| Zahn | 0—1 | 0—1 | 0—0 | 0—0 | 0—0 | 1—0 | 0—0 | 0—1 | 0—1 | 0—1 | 1—1 | 2— 7 |
| Zamora | 1—0 | 0—1 | 1—0 | 0—0 | 1—0 | 0—0 | 0—0 | 0—0 | 2—0 | 0—0 | 0—0 | 5— 2 |
| Totals | 7—5 | 1—11 | 7—5 | 5—7 | 9—9 | 7—11 | 12—6 | 6—12 | 11—7 | 5—7 | 5—7 | 75—87 |

No Decisions—Moore, Solomon.

## CINCINNATI—108-54

| Pitcher | Atl. W—L | Chi. W—L | Hou. W—L | L.A. W—L | Mont. W—L | N.Y. W—L | Phila. W—L | Pitts. W—L | St.L. W—L | S.D. W—L | S.F. W—L | Totals W—L |
|---|---|---|---|---|---|---|---|---|---|---|---|---|
| Billingham | 3—0 | 2—0 | 0—2 | 1—2 | 0—2 | 1—2 | 0—0 | 1—1 | 1—1 | 3—0 | 3—0 | 15—10 |
| Borbon | 1—0 | 3—0 | 1—0 | 1—1 | 0—2 | 0—0 | 1—0 | 0—0 | 0—0 | 0—1 | 2—1 | 9— 5 |
| C. Carroll | 0—0 | 0—0 | 2—0 | 1—3 | 1—0 | 0—0 | 1—1 | 0—0 | 0—0 | 1—1 | 1—1 | 7— 5 |
| T. Carroll | 1—0 | 0—0 | 1—0 | 1—1 | 0—0 | 0—0 | 0—0 | 0—0 | 0—0 | 0—0 | 0—0 | 4— 1 |
| Darcy | 2—0 | 0—1 | 1—1 | 3—0 | 0—0 | 0—0 | 2—1 | 1—1 | 0—0 | 0—1 | 2—0 | 11— 5 |
| Eastwick | 0—0 | 2—0 | 1—0 | 0—1 | 0—0 | 0—0 | 0—0 | 0—0 | 1—1 | 0—0 | 1—1 | 5— 3 |
| Gullett | 4—1 | 1—0 | 1—0 | 0—0 | 1—0 | 1—1 | 0—1 | 0—0 | 4—0 | 2—0 | 1—1 | 15— 4 |
| Kirby | 0—1 | 1—0 | 2—1 | 0—2 | 0—0 | 2—0 | 1—1 | 1—0 | 0—0 | 1—1 | 2—0 | 10— 6 |
| McEnaney | 1—0 | 0—0 | 0—0 | 0—0 | 1—0 | 1—0 | 0—0 | 0—0 | 0—0 | 2—1 | 0—0 | 5— 2 |
| Nolan | 3—1 | 1—0 | 0—1 | 1—0 | 4—0 | 0—1 | 2—1 | 2—1 | 2—1 | 0—2 | 0—1 | 15— 9 |
| Norman | 0—0 | 1—0 | 4—0 | 0—0 | 1—0 | 2—0 | 0—0 | 1—2 | 0—1 | 2—1 | 1—0 | 12— 4 |
| Totals | 15—3 | 11—1 | 13—5 | 8—10 | 8—4 | 8—4 | 7—5 | 6—6 | 8—4 | 11—7 | 13—5 | 108—54 |

No Decisions—Hall.

## HOUSTON—64-97

| Pitcher | Atl. W—L | Chi. W—L | Cin. W—L | L.A. W—L | Mont. W—L | N.Y. W—L | Phila. W—L | Pitts. W—L | St.L. W—L | S.D. W—L | S.F. W—L | Totals W—L |
|---|---|---|---|---|---|---|---|---|---|---|---|---|
| Cosgrove ... | 0—0 | 0—0 | 0—1 | 0—0 | 0—0 | 0—6 | 0—0 | 0—0 | 0—1 | 0—0 | 1—0 | 1— 2 |
| Crawford ... | 0—0 | 0—2 | 0—0 | 0—0 | 0—0 | 0—0 | 1—0 | 0—0 | 0—0 | 0—1 | 1—1 | 3— 5 |
| Dierker .... | 1—3 | 2—0 | 3—2 | 1—2 | 3—0 | 0—2 | 1—2 | 2—0 | 1—1 | 0—3 | 0—1 | 14—16 |
| Forsch ..... | 0—2 | 0—0 | 0—1 | 0—0 | 0—0 | 1—1 | 2—1 | 0—0 | 0—1 | 1—0 | 0—2 | 4— 8 |
| Granger .... | 0—1 | 0—0 | 1—0 | 1—0 | 1—0 | 0—1 | 0—0 | 0—0 | 0—0 | 0—2 | 0—0 | 2— 5 |
| Griffin ..... | 0—0 | 1—0 | 0—2 | 0—4 | 0—0 | 0—1 | 1—0 | 0—0 | 1—0 | 0—1 | 0—0 | 3— 8 |
| Konieczny .. | 1—2 | 1—1 | 0—2 | 0—2 | 0—1 | 1—1 | 1—1 | 0—0 | 0—1 | 1—1 | 1—1 | 6—13 |
| Niekro ..... | 0—0 | 0—0 | 1—3 | 0—0 | 1—0 | 0—0 | 0—0 | 1—1 | 1—0 | 1—0 | 1—0 | 6— 4 |
| Richard .... | 2—1 | 0—2 | 1—0 | 1—1 | 1—0 | 1—0 | 1—2 | 1—1 | 0—0 | 3—0 | 1—3 | 12—10 |
| Roberts .... | 1—2 | 0—1 | 0—0 | 2—1 | 2—1 | 0—2 | 0—0 | 1—2 | 0—2 | 2—0 | 0—3 | 8—14 |
| Scherman .. | 0—0 | 0—0 | 0—1 | 0—0 | 0—0 | 0—0 | 0—0 | 0—0 | 0—0 | 0—0 | 0—0 | 0— 1 |
| Siebert .... | 0—0 | 0—0 | 0—0 | 0—1 | 0—0 | 0—0 | 0—0 | 0—0 | 0—1 | 0—0 | 0—0 | 0— 2 |
| Sosa ....... | 1—0 | 0—0 | 0—0 | 0—0 | 0—0 | 0—1 | 0—0 | 0—1 | 0—1 | 0—0 | 0—0 | 1— 3 |
| Stanton .... | 0—0 | 0—0 | 0—1 | 0—1 | 0—0 | 0—0 | 0—0 | 0—0 | 0—0 | 0—0 | 0—0 | 0— 2 |
| York ...... | 0—1 | 1—0 | 0—0 | 1—0 | 0—0 | 0—0 | 0—0 | 0—0 | 1—0 | 1—1 | 0—2 | 4— 4 |
| **Totals ..** | 6—12 | 5—7 | 5—13 | 6—12 | 8—4 | 4—8 | 6—6 | 6—5 | 4—8 | 9—9 | 5—13 | 64—97 |

No Decisions—None.

## LOS ANGELES—88-74

| Pitcher | Atl. W—L | Chi. W—L | Cin. W—L | Hou. W—L | Mont. W—L | N.Y. W—L | Phila. W—L | Pitts. W—L | St.L. W—L | S.D. W—L | S.F. W—L | Totals W—L |
|---|---|---|---|---|---|---|---|---|---|---|---|---|
| Brewer ..... | 1—0 | 1—0 | 0—0 | 0—0 | 0—0 | 0—0 | 0—0 | 0—0 | 1—0 | 0—1 | 0—0 | 3— 1 |
| Downing ... | 0—0 | 0—0 | 0—0 | 0—0 | 0—1 | 0—0 | 0—0 | 0—0 | 0—0 | 1—0 | 1—0 | 2— 1 |
| Hooton .... | 2—0 | 2—1 | 1—0 | 2—1 | 1—0 | 2—0 | 4—0 | 0—2 | 2—0 | 1—2 | 1—1 | 18— 7 |
| Hough ..... | 0—3 | 0—0 | 1—2 | 1—1 | 0—0 | 0—0 | 0—0 | 0—0 | 0—1 | 0—0 | 1—0 | 3— 7 |
| Marichal ... | 0—0 | 0—0 | 0—1 | 0—0 | 0—0 | 0—0 | 0—0 | 0—0 | 0—0 | 0—0 | 0—0 | 0— 1 |
| Marshall ... | 0—2 | 2—0 | 2—2 | 0—0 | 0—4 | 1—1 | 1—1 | 1—2 | 1—2 | 1—0 | 0—0 | 9—14 |
| Messersmith. | 3—2 | 1—3 | 1—2 | 4—0 | 2—0 | 1—1 | 1—2 | 1—2 | 0—0 | 3—0 | 2—2 | 19—14 |
| Rau ........ | 3—0 | 0—0 | 2—2 | 2—0 | 1—1 | 1—1 | 1—1 | 1—0 | 0—2 | 2—2 | 2—2 | 15— 9 |
| Rhoden .... | 0—0 | 0—0 | 1—0 | 0—1 | 0—0 | 0—1 | 0—0 | 0—0 | 0—1 | 2—0 | 0—0 | 3— 3 |
| Sells ...... | 0—0 | 0—0 | 0—0 | 0—1 | 0—0 | 0—0 | 0—0 | 0—0 | 0—0 | 0—1 | 0—0 | 0— 2 |
| Sutton .... | 1—1 | 1—1 | 2—0 | 3—1 | 1—1 | 1—2 | 0—1 | 2—1 | 1—1 | 1—2 | 3—2 | 16—13 |
| Wall ...... | 0—0 | 0—0 | 0—0 | 0—0 | 0—0 | 0—0 | 0—0 | 0—0 | 0—1 | 0—0 | 0—0 | 0— 1 |
| Zahn ...... | 0—0 | 0—0 | 0—0 | 0—0 | 0—0 | 0—0 | 0—0 | 0—0 | 0—0 | 0—0 | 0—1 | 0— 1 |
| **Totals ..** | 10—8 | 7—5 | 10—8 | 12—6 | 5—7 | 6—6 | 7—5 | 5—7 | 5—7 | 11—7 | 10—8 | 88—74 |

No Decisions—Lewallyn.

## MONTREAL—75-87

| Pitcher | Atl. W—L | Chi. W—L | Cin. W—L | Hou. W—L | L.A. W—L | N.Y. W—L | Phila. W—L | Pitts. W—L | St.L. W—L | S.D. W—L | S.F. W—L | Totals W—L |
|---|---|---|---|---|---|---|---|---|---|---|---|---|
| Blair ...... | 0—0 | 2—2 | 1—3 | 0—3 | 0—1 | 1—0 | 2—2 | 0—2 | 1—0 | 0—1 | 1—1 | 8—15 |
| Carrithers .. | 0—0 | 1—0 | 0—1 | 0—0 | 0—0 | 2—0 | 0—1 | 0—1 | 1—0 | 1—0 | 0—0 | 5— 3 |
| DeMola .... | 0—1 | 0—1 | 0—0 | 1—2 | 0—0 | 1—1 | 0—0 | 0—1 | 1—1 | 1—0 | 0—0 | 4— 7 |
| Fryman .... | 2—1 | 1—0 | 1—1 | 0—0 | 1—1 | 1—0 | 0—0 | 2—2 | 0—3 | 0—2 | 1—2 | 9—12 |
| McNally .... | 0—1 | 0—1 | 0—1 | 0—0 | 0—0 | 0—2 | 0—0 | 2—0 | 1—0 | 0—1 | 0—0 | 3— 6 |
| Montague .. | 0—0 | 0—0 | 0—1 | 0—0 | 0—0 | 0—0 | 0—0 | 0—0 | 0—0 | 0—0 | 0—0 | 0— 1 |
| Murray .... | 0—1 | 3—2 | 1—0 | 2—0 | 4—0 | 3—0 | 2—2 | 0—1 | 0—1 | 0—0 | 0—1 | 15— 8 |
| Renko ..... | 0—2 | 0—0 | 0—1 | 0—2 | 1—2 | 0—1 | 0—3 | 0—1 | 3—0 | 1—0 | 1—0 | 6—12 |
| Rogers ..... | 1—0 | 2—1 | 1—0 | 1—1 | 1—1 | 0—3 | 1—2 | 1—1 | 1—2 | 2—0 | 0—1 | 11—12 |
| Scherman ... | 1—1 | 0—1 | 0—0 | 0—0 | 0—0 | 0—0 | 1—0 | 0—1 | 1—0 | 1—0 | 0—0 | 2— 2 |
| Taylor ..... | 0—0 | 0—0 | 0—0 | 0—0 | 0—0 | 1—1 | 0—0 | 1—0 | 0—0 | 0—0 | 0—0 | 2— 2 |
| Warthen ... | 0—1 | 0—1 | 0—0 | 0—0 | 0—0 | 1—0 | 1—0 | 1—1 | 2—0 | 1—1 | 2—2 | 8— 6 |
| **Totals ..** | 4—8 | 9—9 | 4—8 | 4—8 | 7—5 | 10—8 | 7—11 | 7—11 | 11—7 | 7—5 | 5—7 | 75—87 |

No Decisions—Lang, Stanhouse.

### NEW YORK—82-80

| Pitcher | Atl. W—L | Chi. W—L | Cin. W—L | Hou. W—L | L.A. W—L | Mont. W—L | Phila. W—L | Pitts. W—L | St.L. W—L | S.D. W—L | S.F. W—L | Totals W—L |
|---|---|---|---|---|---|---|---|---|---|---|---|---|
| Apodaca | 0—0 | 1—0 | 0—0 | 0—0 | 1—0 | 0—2 | 1—1 | 0—1 | 0—0 | 0—0 | 0—0 | 3—4 |
| Baldwin | 1—0 | 0—1 | 0—0 | 0—1 | 0—0 | 1—2 | 0—0 | 0—1 | 1—0 | 0—0 | 0—0 | 3—5 |
| Cram | 0—0 | 0—0 | 0—0 | 0—0 | 0—0 | 0—0 | 0—1 | 0—0 | 0—0 | 0—0 | 0—0 | 0—1 |
| Espinosa | 0—0 | 0—0 | 0—0 | 0—0 | 0—0 | 0—0 | 0—1 | 0—0 | 0—0 | 0—0 | 0—0 | 0—1 |
| Hall | 0—0 | 1—0 | 0—0 | 2—0 | 0—0 | 0—1 | 0—1 | 0—1 | 1—0 | 0—0 | 0—0 | 4—3 |
| Koosman | 1—1 | 1—1 | 2—1 | 1—0 | 1—1 | 2—1 | 1—1 | 2—2 | 2—1 | 0—2 | 1—2 | 14—13 |
| Lockwood | 0—0 | 0—1 | 0—0 | 0—0 | 0—0 | 0—0 | 0—1 | 0—0 | 0—0 | 1—0 | 0—1 | 1—3 |
| Matlack | 1—2 | 2—1 | 1—1 | 3—0 | 3—0 | 1—1 | 1—2 | 1—2 | 1—3 | 0—0 | 2—0 | 16—12 |
| Parker | 0—0 | 0—0 | 0—0 | 0—0 | 0—1 | 2—0 | 0—1 | 0—1 | 0—0 | 0—0 | 0—0 | 2—3 |
| Sanders | 0—0 | 1—0 | 0—0 | 0—0 | 0—1 | 0—0 | 0—0 | 0—0 | 0—0 | 0—0 | 0—0 | 1—1 |
| Seaver | 2—0 | 1—1 | 1—3 | 2—0 | 1—0 | 1—0 | 3—0 | 1—3 | 3—2 | 4—0 | 3—0 | 22—9 |
| Stone | 0—0 | 1—0 | 0—0 | 0—1 | 0—0 | 0—1 | 0—0 | 1—0 | 0—1 | 1—0 | 0—0 | 3—3 |
| Swan | 0—0 | 0—1 | 0—0 | 0—0 | 0—1 | 0—0 | 0—0 | 0—0 | 0—0 | 0—0 | 1—1 | 1—3 |
| Tate | 1—1 | 2—1 | 0—2 | 0—2 | 0—0 | 0—1 | 1—2 | 0—1 | 0—1 | 1—2 | 0—0 | 5—13 |
| Webb | 2—0 | 1—0 | 0—1 | 0—0 | 0—2 | 1—1 | 0—0 | 0—1 | 1—1 | 1—0 | 1—0 | 7—6 |
| Totals | 8—4 | 11—7 | 4—8 | 8—4 | 6—6 | 8—10 | 7—11 | 5—13 | 9—9 | 8—4 | 8—4 | 82—80 |

No Decisions—Scarce.

### PHILADELPHIA—86-76

| Pitcher | Atl. W—L | Chi. W—L | Cin. W—L | Hou. W—L | L.A. W—L | Mont. W—L | N.Y. W—L | Pitts. W—L | St.L. W—L | S.D. W—L | S.F. W—L | Totals W—L |
|---|---|---|---|---|---|---|---|---|---|---|---|---|
| Carlton | 1—0 | 1—2 | 1—1 | 1—1 | 1—2 | 1—0 | 1—2 | 1—3 | 3—1 | 1—1 | 3—1 | 15—14 |
| Christenson | 1—1 | 0—1 | 0—1 | 2—0 | 1—1 | 1—1 | 1—1 | 3—0 | 0—0 | 1—0 | 1—0 | 11—6 |
| Garber | 2—2 | 1—2 | 1—1 | 0—0 | 1—1 | 2—1 | 2—1 | 0—0 | 0—3 | 0—0 | 1—1 | 10—12 |
| Hilgendorf | 1—0 | 0—1 | 0—0 | 1—0 | 0—0 | 0—1 | 0—0 | 1—0 | 1—1 | 2—0 | 1—0 | 7—3 |
| Lonborg | 1—0 | 0—2 | 0—1 | 0—1 | 2—0 | 2—1 | 1—0 | 0—0 | 1—1 | 1—0 | 0—0 | 8—6 |
| McGraw | 0—0 | 2—0 | 1—1 | 1—1 | 0—1 | 1—0 | 2—2 | 1—0 | 0—0 | 0—1 | 1—0 | 9—6 |
| Ruthven | 0—0 | 1—0 | 0—0 | 0—0 | 0—0 | 0—0 | 0—0 | 0—0 | 0—0 | 0—1 | 0—1 | 2—2 |
| Schueler | 0—0 | 0—0 | 0—1 | 0—0 | 0—0 | 0—2 | 2—0 | 1—0 | 1—0 | 0—1 | 0—0 | 4—4 |
| Simpson | 0—0 | 0—0 | 0—0 | 0—0 | 0—0 | 1—0 | 0—0 | 0—0 | 0—0 | 0—0 | 0—0 | 1—0 |
| Twitchell | 0—1 | 1—2 | 0—0 | 0—2 | 0—0 | 0—0 | 1—1 | 1—1 | 1—2 | 1—0 | 0—0 | 5—10 |
| Underwood | 1—1 | 0—2 | 2—1 | 1—1 | 2—2 | 3—1 | 0—0 | 3—3 | 2—0 | 1—0 | 0—2 | 14—13 |
| Totals | 7—5 | 6—12 | 5—7 | 6—6 | 5—7 | 11—7 | 11—7 | 11—7 | 10—8 | 7—5 | 7—5 | 86—76 |

No Decisions—Acosta, Hoerner, Lerch, Montague.

### PITTSBURGH—92-69

| Pitcher | Atl. W—L | Chi. W—L | Cin. W—L | Hou. W—L | L.A. W—L | Mont. W—L | N.Y. W—L | Phila. W—L | St.L. W—L | S.D. W—L | S.F. W—L | Totals W—L |
|---|---|---|---|---|---|---|---|---|---|---|---|---|
| Brett | 0—1 | 1—0 | 0—0 | 1—0 | 1—1 | 2—0 | 1—1 | 0—0 | 2—2 | 0—0 | 1—0 | 9—5 |
| Candelaria | 1—1 | 2—0 | 1—1 | 0—0 | 0—0 | 1—0 | 2—1 | 0—0 | 0—1 | 1—0 | 0—2 | 8—6 |
| Demery | 2—0 | 0—1 | 1—0 | 1—0 | 0—1 | 1—0 | 2—0 | 0—2 | 0—0 | 0—0 | 0—1 | 7—5 |
| Ellis | 0—0 | 2—0 | 0—0 | 1—0 | 1—1 | 1—3 | 1—0 | 1—2 | 0—1 | 1—1 | 0—1 | 8—9 |
| Giusti | 0—0 | 2—1 | 0—0 | 0—0 | 2—0 | 1—0 | 0—3 | 0—1 | 0—0 | 0—1 | 0—1 | 5—4 |
| Hernandez | 0—0 | 2—0 | 0—0 | 0—0 | 1—0 | 1—0 | 1—0 | 0—0 | 2—0 | 1—0 | 0—0 | 7—2 |
| Kison | 1—1 | 0—1 | 0—2 | 2—2 | 2—0 | 0—0 | 2—1 | 3—3 | 1—0 | 0—1 | 1—0 | 12—11 |
| McDowell | 0—0 | 0—0 | 1—0 | 0—0 | 0—0 | 0—0 | 0—0 | 0—0 | 0—1 | 1—0 | 0—0 | 2—1 |
| Moose | 0—0 | 0—1 | 0—1 | 0—0 | 0—0 | 1—0 | 0—0 | 1—0 | 0—0 | 0—0 | 0—0 | 2—2 |
| Reuss | 2—0 | 1—1 | 3—1 | 0—2 | 1—0 | 2—2 | 2—1 | 1—1 | 4—1 | 1—1 | 1—1 | 18—11 |
| Rooker | 2—1 | 2—1 | 0—1 | 0—1 | 0—1 | 1—1 | 1—1 | 1—1 | 3—2 | 2—0 | 1—1 | 13—11 |
| Tekulve | 0—0 | 0—0 | 0—0 | 0—0 | 0—0 | 0—1 | 1—0 | 0—0 | 0—0 | 0—0 | 0—0 | 1—2 |
| Totals | 8—4 | 12—6 | 6—6 | 5—6 | 7—5 | 11—7 | 13—5 | 7—11 | 10—8 | 8—4 | 5—7 | 92—69 |

No Decisions—Jones, Minshall.

### ST. LOUIS—82-80

| Pitcher | Atl. W—L | Chi. W—L | Cin. W—L | Hou. W—L | L.A. W—L | Mont. W—L | N.Y. W—L | Phila. W—L | Pitts. W—L | S.D. W—L | S.F. W—L | Totals W—L |
|---|---|---|---|---|---|---|---|---|---|---|---|---|
| Bryant | 0—0 | 0—0 | 0—0 | 0—0 | 0—0 | 0—0 | 0—0 | 0—0 | 0—1 | 0—0 | 0—0 | 0—1 |
| Curtis | 2—0 | 0—1 | 0—0 | 0—2 | 1—1 | 1—1 | 1—1 | 0—1 | 1—1 | 1—1 | 1—0 | 8—9 |
| Denny | 2—0 | 1—0 | 0—0 | 1—1 | 0—0 | 1—2 | 3—0 | 0—2 | 1—2 | 0—0 | 1—0 | 10—7 |
| Forsch | 1—0 | 4—1 | 0—3 | 1—0 | 1—0 | 1—1 | 1—2 | 1—2 | 0—1 | 2—0 | 2—0 | 15—10 |
| Garman | 0—0 | 0—1 | 0—2 | 1—1 | 0—2 | 0—0 | 0—0 | 1—1 | 0—1 | 1—0 | 0—0 | 3—8 |
| Gibson | 0—1 | 0—2 | 0—1 | 0—0 | 0—0 | 1—1 | 0—1 | 2—1 | 0—1 | 0—1 | 0—1 | 3—10 |
| Hrabosky | 0—0 | 0—2 | 1—0 | 1—0 | 4—0 | 2—0 | 0—0 | 2—0 | 0—0 | 2—1 | 1—0 | 13—3 |
| McGlothen | 1—1 | 1—2 | 1—2 | 1—0 | 1—2 | 1—2 | 3—1 | 2—0 | 2—1 | 1—0 | 1—2 | 15—13 |
| Parker | 0—1 | 0—0 | 0—0 | 0—0 | 0—0 | 0—0 | 0—0 | 0—0 | 0—0 | 0—0 | 0—0 | 0—1 |
| Rasmussen | 1—0 | 0—1 | 1—0 | 1—0 | 0—0 | 0—1 | 0—1 | 0—1 | 1—1 | 1—0 | 0—0 | 5—5 |
| Reed | 2—0 | 1—0 | 1—0 | 2—0 | 0—0 | 0—3 | 1—2 | 0—2 | 1—1 | 0—0 | 1—0 | 9—8 |
| Reynolds | 0—0 | 0—1 | 0—0 | 0—0 | 0—0 | 0—0 | 0—0 | 0—0 | 0—0 | 0—0 | 0—0 | 0—1 |
| Sadecki | 0—0 | 0—0 | 0—0 | 0—0 | 0—0 | 0—0 | 0—0 | 0—0 | 1—0 | 0—0 | 0—0 | 1—0 |
| Sosa | 0—0 | 0—0 | 0—0 | 0—0 | 0—0 | 0—0 | 0—0 | 0—1 | 0—0 | 0—1 | 0—1 | 0—3 |
| Terlecky | 0—0 | 0—0 | 0—0 | 0—0 | 0—0 | 0—0 | 0—0 | 0—0 | 0—0 | 0—0 | 0—1 | 0—1 |
| **Totals** | 9—3 | 7—11 | 4—8 | 8—4 | 7—5 | 7—11 | 9—9 | 8—10 | 8—10 | 8—4 | 7—5 | 82—80 |

No Decisions—Barlow, Kurosaki, Moore, Wallace.

### SAN DIEGO—71-91

| Pitcher | Atl W—L | Chi. W—L | Cin. W—L | Hou. W—L | L.A. W—L | Mont. W—L | N.Y. W—L | Phila. W—L | Pitts. W—L | St.L. W—L | S.F. W—L | Totals W—L |
|---|---|---|---|---|---|---|---|---|---|---|---|---|
| Folkers | 0—2 | 0—0 | 1—1 | 0—0 | 0—3 | 2—1 | 1—0 | 0—0 | 0—1 | 0—1 | 2—2 | 6—11 |
| Foster | 0—1 | 0—0 | 0—0 | 0—0 | 1—0 | 0—0 | 1—0 | 0—9 | 0—0 | 1—0 | 0—0 | 3—1 |
| Freisleben | 1—0 | 3—1 | 0—1 | 1—2 | 0—1 | 0—1 | 0—1 | 0—2 | 0—2 | 0—2 | 0—0 | 5—14 |
| Frisella | 0—1 | 0—0 | 0—1 | 0—1 | 0—1 | 0—1 | 0—0 | 0—0 | 1—1 | 0—0 | 0—0 | 1—6 |
| Greif | 0—0 | 1—0 | 0—1 | 1—0 | 0—0 | 0—0 | 0—0 | 1—1 | 0—1 | 1—3 | 0—0 | 4—6 |
| Johnson | 2—0 | 0—0 | 0—0 | 0—6 | 0—0 | 1—0 | 0—1 | 0—0 | 0—0 | 0—0 | 0—0 | 3—1 |
| Jones | 3—1 | 0—0 | 3—1 | 2—3 | 2—1 | 0—1 | 2—1 | 3—1 | 2—1 | 1—0 | 2—2 | 20—12 |
| McIntosh | 2—1 | 2—1 | 1—1 | 0—2 | 1—2 | 1—2 | 0—2 | 0—1 | 0—1 | 0—0 | 0—2 | 8—15 |
| Metzger | 0—0 | 0—0 | 0—0 | 0—0 | 0—0 | 0—0 | 0—0 | 0—0 | 0—0 | 0—0 | 1—0 | 1—0 |
| Siebert | 1—0 | 0—1 | 0—1 | 1—0 | 0—0 | 0—0 | 0—0 | 0—0 | 0—0 | 0—0 | 1—0 | 3—2 |
| Spillner | 1—1 | 0—1 | 1—2 | 1—1 | 1—2 | 0—0 | 0—1 | 1—2 | 0—1 | 0—1 | 0—1 | 5—13 |
| Strom | 1—0 | 1—1 | 1—1 | 0—0 | 1—1 | 1—0 | 0—2 | 0—0 | 1—0 | 0—1 | 1—2 | 8—8 |
| Tomlin | 0—0 | 0—0 | 0—1 | 2—0 | 0—0 | 0—1 | 0—0 | 0—0 | 0—0 | 0—0 | 2—0 | 4—2 |
| **Totals** | 11—7 | 7—5 | 7—11 | 9—9 | 7—11 | 5—7 | 4—8 | 5—7 | 4—8 | 4—8 | 8—10 | 71—91 |

No Decisions—Hardy.

### SAN FRANCISCO—80-81

| Pitcher | Atl. W—L | Chi. W—L | Cin. W—L | Hou. W—L | L.A. W—L | Mont. W—L | N.Y. W—L | Phila. W—L | Pitts. W—L | St.L. W—L | S.D. W—L | Totals W—L |
|---|---|---|---|---|---|---|---|---|---|---|---|---|
| Barr | 2—2 | 1—0 | 2—2 | 2—0 | 0—1 | 1—1 | 0—3 | 1—1 | 2—2 | 1—1 | 1—1 | 13—14 |
| Bradley | 0—0 | 0—0 | 0—0 | 1—0 | 1—1 | 0—0 | 0—1 | 0—0 | 0—0 | 0—0 | 0—1 | 2—3 |
| Ca'dwell | 2—2 | 0—1 | 0—1 | 0—1 | 0—1 | 2—1 | 0—1 | 1—0 | 1—1 | 0—1 | 1—3 | 7—13 |
| D'Acquisto | 1—1 | 0—0 | 0—0 | 0—1 | 0—1 | 0—0 | 0—0 | 0—0 | 0—0 | 0—0 | 1—0 | 2—4 |
| Dressler | 0—0 | 0—0 | 0—0 | 0—0 | 0—0 | 0—0 | 0—0 | 0—0 | 0—0 | 0—0 | 1—0 | 1—0 |
| Falcone | 3—1 | 1—0 | 0—2 | 3—0 | 0—2 | 1—1 | 0—2 | 1—1 | 0—0 | 1—2 | 2—0 | 12—11 |
| Halicki | 0—2 | 0—1 | 0—3 | 1—1 | 2—1 | 1—6 | 2—0 | 0—3 | 3—1 | 0—0 | 0—0 | 9—13 |
| Heaverlo | 0—0 | 0—0 | 1—1 | 1—0 | 0—0 | 0—0 | 1—0 | 0—0 | 0—0 | 0—0 | 0—0 | 3—1 |
| Lavelle | 0—0 | 0—0 | 1—0 | 1—0 | 0—0 | 0—1 | 1—0 | 0—0 | 1—0 | 2—0 | 0—2 | 6—3 |
| Minton | 0—0 | 0—0 | 0—1 | 0—0 | 0—0 | 0—0 | 0—0 | 0—0 | 0—0 | 0—0 | 0—0 | 1—1 |
| Moffitt | 0—0 | 0—3 | 1—0 | 2—1 | 1—0 | 0—0 | 0—0 | 0—1 | 1—0 | 0—0 | 0—0 | 4—5 |
| Montefusco | 1—0 | 2—0 | 0—2 | 2—1 | 3—2 | 1—1 | 0—1 | 2—1 | 0—0 | 1—1 | 3—0 | 15—9 |
| Toms | 0—0 | 0—0 | 0—0 | 0—0 | 0—0 | 0—0 | 0—0 | 0—0 | 0—1 | 0—0 | 0—0 | 0—1 |
| Williams | 0—0 | 3—0 | 0—1 | 0—0 | 1—1 | 1—0 | 0—0 | 0—0 | 0—0 | 0—1 | 0—0 | 5—3 |
| **Totals** | 9—8 | 7—5 | 5—13 | 13—5 | 8—10 | 7—5 | 4—8 | 5—7 | 7—5 | 5—7 | 10—8 | 80—81 |

No Decisions—None.

# NATIONAL LEAGUE

## PENNANT WINNERS

| Year | Club | Manager | W. | L. | Pct. | °G.A. |
|------|------|---------|----|----|------|-------|
| 1900 | Brooklyn | Edward (Ned) Hanlon | 82 | 54 | .603 | 4½ |
| 1901 | Pittsburgh | Frederick Clarke | 90 | 49 | .647 | 7½ |
| 1902 | Pittsburgh | Frederick Clarke | 103 | 36 | .741 | 27½ |
| 1903 | Pittsburgh | Frederick Clarke | 91 | 49 | .650 | 6½ |
| 1904 | New York | John McGraw | 106 | 47 | .693 | 13 |
| 1905 | New York | John McGraw | 105 | 48 | .686 | 9 |
| 1906 | Chicago | Frank Chance | 116 | 36 | .763 | 20 |
| 1907 | Chicago | Frank Chance | 107 | 45 | .704 | 17 |
| 1908 | Chicago | Frank Chance | 99 | 55 | .643 | 1 |
| 1909 | Pittsburgh | Frederick Clarke | 110 | 42 | .724 | 6½ |
| 1910 | Chicago | Frank Chance | 104 | 50 | .675 | 13 |
| 1911 | New York | John McGraw | 99 | 54 | .647 | 7½ |
| 1912 | New York | John McGraw | 103 | 48 | .682 | 10 |
| 1913 | New York | John McGraw | 101 | 51 | .664 | 12½ |
| 1914 | Boston | George Stallings | 94 | 59 | .614 | 10½ |
| 1915 | Philadelphia | Patrick Moran | 90 | 62 | .592 | 7 |
| 1916 | Brooklyn | Wilbert Robinson | 94 | 60 | .610 | 2½ |
| 1917 | New York | John McGraw | 98 | 56 | .636 | 10 |
| 1918 | Chicago | Fred Mitchell | 84 | 45 | .651 | 10½ |
| 1919 | Cincinnati | Patrick Moran | 96 | 44 | .686 | 9 |
| 1920 | Brooklyn | Wilbert Robinson | 93 | 61 | .604 | 7 |
| 1921 | New York | John McGraw | 94 | 59 | .614 | 4 |
| 1922 | New York | John McGraw | 93 | 61 | .604 | 7 |
| 1923 | New York | John McGraw | 95 | 58 | .621 | 4½ |
| 1924 | New York | John McGraw | 93 | 60 | .608 | 1½ |
| 1925 | Pittsburgh | William McKechnie | 95 | 58 | .621 | 8½ |
| 1926 | St. Louis | Rogers Hornsby | 89 | 65 | .578 | 2 |
| 1927 | Pittsburgh | Owen (Donie) Bush | 94 | 60 | .610 | 1½ |
| 1928 | St. Louis | William McKechnie | 95 | 59 | .617 | 2 |
| 1929 | Chicago | Joseph McCarthy | 98 | 54 | .645 | 10½ |
| 1930 | St. Louis | Charles (Gabby) Street | 92 | 62 | .597 | 2 |
| 1931 | St. Louis | Charles (Gabby) Street | 101 | 53 | .656 | 13 |
| 1932 | Chicago | Charles Grimm | 90 | 64 | .584 | 4 |
| 1933 | New York | William Terry | 91 | 61 | .599 | 5 |
| 1934 | St. Louis | Frank Frisch | 95 | 58 | .621 | 2 |
| 1935 | Chicago | Charles Grimm | 100 | 54 | .649 | 4 |
| 1936 | New York | William Terry | 92 | 62 | .597 | 5 |
| 1937 | New York | William Terry | 95 | 57 | .625 | 3 |
| 1938 | Chicago | Charles (Gabby) Hartnett | 89 | 63 | .586 | 2 |
| 1939 | Cincinnati | William McKechnie | 97 | 57 | .630 | 4½ |
| 1940 | Cincinnati | William McKechnie | 100 | 53 | .654 | 12 |
| 1941 | Brooklyn | Leo Durocher | 100 | 54 | .649 | 2½ |
| 1942 | St. Louis | William Southworth | 106 | 48 | .688 | 2 |
| 1943 | St. Louis | William Southworth | 105 | 49 | .682 | 18 |
| 1944 | St. Louis | William Southworth | 105 | 49 | .682 | 14½ |
| 1945 | Chicago | Charles Grimm | 98 | 56 | .636 | 3 |
| 1946 | St. Louis† | Edwin Dyer | 98 | 58 | .628 | 2 |
| 1947 | Brooklyn | Burton Shotton | 94 | 60 | .610 | 5 |
| 1948 | Boston | William Southworth | 91 | 62 | .595 | 6½ |
| 1949 | Brooklyn | Burton Shotton | 97 | 57 | .630 | 1 |
| 1950 | Philadelphia | Edwin Sawyer | 91 | 63 | .591 | 2 |
| 1951 | New York‡ | Leo Durocher | 98 | 59 | .624 | 1 |
| 1952 | Brooklyn | Charles Dressen | 96 | 57 | .627 | 4½ |
| 1953 | Brooklyn | Charles Dressen | 105 | 49 | .682 | 13 |
| 1954 | New York | Leo Durocher | 97 | 57 | .630 | 5 |
| 1955 | Brooklyn | Walter Alston | 98 | 55 | .641 | 13½ |
| 1956 | Brooklyn | Wlater Alston | 93 | 61 | .604 | 1 |
| 1957 | Milwaukee | Fred Haney | 95 | 59 | .617 | 8 |
| 1958 | Milwaukee | Fred Haney | 92 | 62 | .597 | 8 |
| 1959 | Los Angeles§ | Walter Alston | 88 | 68 | .564 | 2 |

## PENNANT WINNERS—Continued

| Year | Club | Manager | W. | L. | Pct. | °G.A. |
|------|------|---------|----|----|------|-------|
| 1960—Pittsburgh | | Daniel Murtaugh | 95 | 59 | .617 | 7 |
| 1961—Cincinnati | | Frederick Hutchinson | 93 | 61 | .604 | 4 |
| 1962—San Francisco x | | Alvin Dark | 103 | 62 | .624 | 1 |
| 1963—Los Angeles | | Walter Alston | 99 | 63 | .611 | 6 |
| 1964—St. Louis | | John Keane | 93 | 69 | .574 | 1 |
| 1065—Los Angeles | | Walter Alston | 97 | 65 | .599 | 2 |
| 1966—Los Angeles | | Walter Alston | 95 | 67 | .586 | 1½ |
| 1967—St. Louis | | Albert (Red) Schoendienst | 101 | 60 | .627 | 10½ |
| 1968—St. Louis | | Albert (Red) Schoendienst | 97 | 65 | .599 | 9 |
| 1969—New York (E)°° | | Gilbert Hodges | 100 | 62 | .617 | 8 |
| 1970—Cincinnati (W)°° | | George (Sparky) Anderson | 102 | 60 | .630 | 14½ |
| 1971—Pittsburgh (E)°° | | Daniel Murtaugh | 97 | 65 | .599 | 7 |
| 1972—Cincinnati (W)°° | | George (Sparky) Anderson | 95 | 59 | .617 | 10½ |
| 1973—New York (E)°° | | Lawrence (Yogi) Berra | 82 | 79 | .509 | 1½ |
| 1974—Los Angeles (W)°° | | Walter Alston | 102 | 60 | .630 | 4 |
| 1975—Cincinnati (W)°° | | George (Sparky) Anderson | 108 | 54 | .667 | 20 |

°Games ahead of second-place club. †Defeated Brooklyn, two games to none, in playoff for pennant. ‡Defeated Brooklyn, two games to one, in playoff for pennant. §Defeated Milwaukee, two games to none, in playoff for pennant. xDefeated Los Angeles, two games to one, in playoff for pennant. °°Won Championship Series.

## YEARLY FINISHES

| Year | Atl. | Chi. | Cin. | Hou. | L.A. | N.Y. | Phil. | Pitt. | St.L. | S.F. |
|------|------|------|------|------|------|------|-------|-------|-------|------|
| 1900 | °4 | x5 | 7 | .... | †1 | .... | 3 | 2 | x5 | ‡8 |
| 1901 | °5 | 6 | 8 | .... | †3 | .... | 2 | 1 | 4 | ‡7 |
| 1902 | °3 | 5 | 4 | .... | †2 | .... | 7 | 1 | 6 | ‡8 |
| 1903 | °6 | 3 | 4 | .... | †5 | .... | 7 | 1 | 8 | ‡2 |
| 1904 | °7 | 2 | 3 | .... | †6 | .... | 8 | 4 | 5 | ‡1 |
| 1905 | °7 | 3 | 5 | .... | †8 | .... | 4 | 2 | 6 | ‡1 |
| 1906 | °8 | 1 | 6 | .... | †5 | .... | 3 | 2 | 7 | ‡2 |
| 1907 | °7 | 1 | 6 | .... | †5 | .... | 3 | 2 | 8 | ‡4 |
| 1908 | °6 | 1 | 5 | .... | †7 | .... | 4 | x2 | 8 | x‡2 |
| 1909 | °8 | 2 | 4 | .... | †6 | .... | 5 | 1 | 7 | ‡3 |
| 1910 | °8 | 1 | 5 | .... | †6 | .... | 4 | 3 | 7 | ‡2 |
| 1911 | °8 | 2 | 6 | .... | †7 | .... | 4 | 3 | 5 | ‡1 |
| 1912 | °8 | 3 | 4 | .... | †7 | .... | 5 | 2 | 6 | ‡1 |
| 1913 | °5 | 3 | 7 | .... | †6 | .... | 2 | 4 | 8 | ‡1 |
| 1914 | °1 | 4 | 8 | .... | †5 | .... | 6 | 7 | 3 | ‡2 |
| 1915 | °2 | 4 | 7 | .... | †3 | .... | 1 | 5 | 6 | ‡8 |
| 1916 | °3 | 5 | x7 | .... | †1 | .... | 2 | 6 | x7 | ‡4 |
| 1917 | °6 | 5 | 4 | .... | †7 | .... | 2 | 8 | 3 | ‡1 |
| 1918 | °7 | 1 | 3 | .... | †5 | .... | 6 | 4 | 8 | ‡2 |
| 1919 | °6 | 3 | 1 | .... | †5 | .... | 8 | 4 | 7 | ‡2 |
| 1920 | °7 | x5 | 3 | .... | †1 | .... | 8 | 4 | x5 | ‡2 |
| 1921 | °4 | 7 | 6 | .... | †5 | .... | 8 | 2 | 3 | ‡1 |
| 1922 | °8 | 5 | 2 | .... | †6 | .... | 7 | x3 | x3 | ‡1 |
| 1923 | °7 | 4 | 2 | .... | †7 | .... | 8 | 3 | 5 | ‡1 |
| 1924 | °8 | 5 | 4 | .... | †2 | .... | 7 | 3 | 6 | ‡1 |
| 1925 | °5 | 8 | 3 | .... | x†6 | .... | x6 | 1 | 4 | ‡2 |
| 1926 | °7 | 4 | 2 | .... | †6 | .... | 8 | 3 | 1 | ‡5 |
| 1927 | °7 | 4 | 5 | .... | †6 | .... | 8 | 1 | 2 | ‡3 |
| 1928 | °7 | 3 | 5 | .... | †6 | .... | 8 | 4 | 1 | ‡2 |
| 1929 | °8 | 1 | 7 | .... | †6 | .... | 5 | 2 | 4 | ‡3 |
| 1930 | °6 | 2 | 7 | .... | †4 | .... | 8 | 5 | 1 | ‡3 |
| 1931 | °7 | 3 | 8 | .... | †4 | .... | 6 | 5 | x6 | x‡6 |
| 1932 | °5 | 1 | 8 | .... | †3 | .... | 4 | 2 | 5 | ‡1 |
| 1933 | °4 | 3 | 8 | .... | †6 | .... | 7 | 2 | 5 | ‡1 |
| 1934 | °4 | 3 | 8 | .... | †6 | .... | 7 | 5 | 1 | ‡2 |
| 1935 | °8 | 1 | 6 | .... | †5 | .... | 7 | 4 | 2 | ‡3 |
| 1936 | °6 | x2 | 5 | ... | †7 | .... | 8 | 4 | x2 | ‡1 |

## YEARLY FINISHES—Continued

| Year | Atl. | Chi. | Cin. | Hous. | L.A. | N.Y. | Phil. | Pitt. | St.L. | S.F. |
|---|---|---|---|---|---|---|---|---|---|---|
| 1937 | *5 | 2 | 8 | .... | †6 | .... | 7 | 3 | 4 | ‡1 |
| 1938 | *5 | 1 | 4 | .... | †7 | .... | 8 | 2 | 6 | ‡3 |
| 1939 | *7 | 4 | 1 | .... | †3 | .... | 8 | 6 | 2 | ‡5 |
| 1940 | *7 | 5 | 1 | .... | †2 | .... | 8 | 4 | 3 | ‡6 |
| 1941 | *7 | 6 | 3 | .... | †1 | .... | 8 | 4 | 2 | ‡5 |
| 1942 | *7 | 6 | 4 | .... | †2 | .... | 8 | 5 | 1 | ‡3 |
| 1943 | *6 | 5 | 2 | .... | †3 | .... | 7 | 4 | 1 | ‡8 |
| 1944 | *6 | 4 | 3 | .... | †7 | .... | 8 | 2 | 1 | ‡5 |
| 1945 | *6 | 1 | 7 | .... | †2 | .... | 8 | 4 | 2 | ‡5 |
| 1946 | *4 | 3 | 6 | .... | †2 | .... | 5 | 7 | 1 | ‡8 |
| 1947 | *3 | 6 | 5 | .... | †1 | .... | x7 | x7 | 2 | ‡4 |
| 1948 | *1 | 8 | 7 | .... | †3 | .... | 6 | 4 | 2 | ‡5 |
| 1949 | *4 | 8 | 7 | .... | †1 | .... | 3 | 6 | 2 | ‡5 |
| 1950 | *4 | 7 | 6 | .... | †2 | .... | 1 | 8 | 5 | ‡3 |
| 1951 | *4 | 8 | 6 | .... | †2 | .... | 5 | 7 | 3 | ‡1 |
| 1952 | *7 | 5 | 6 | .... | †1 | .... | 4' | 8 | 3 | ‡2 |
| 1953 | *2 | 7 | 6 | .... | †1 | .... | x3 | 8 | x3 | ‡5 |
| 1954 | *3 | 7 | 5 | .... | †2 | .... | 4 | 8 | 6 | ‡1 |
| 1955 | *2 | 6 | 5 | .... | †1 | .... | 4 | 8 | 7 | ‡3 |
| 1956 | *2 | 8 | 3 | .... | †1 | .... | 5 | 7 | 4 | ‡6 |
| 1957 | *1 | x7 | 4 | .... | †3 | .... | 7 | x7 | 2 | ‡6 |
| 1958 | *1 | x5 | 4 | .... | 7 | .... | 8 | 2 | x5 | 3 |
| 1959 | *2 | x5 | x5 | .... | 1 | .... | 8 | 4 | 7 | 3 |
| 1960 | *2 | 7 | 6 | .... | 4 | .... | 8 | 1 | 3 | 5 |
| 1961 | *4 | 7 | 1 | .... | 2 | .... | 8 | 6 | 5 | 3 |
| 1962 | *5 | 9 | 3 | 8 | 2 | 10 | 7 | 4 | 6 | 1 |
| 1963 | *6 | 7 | 5 | 9 | 1 | 10 | 4 | 8 | 2 | 3 |
| 1964 | *5 | 8 | x2 | 9 | x6 | 10 | x2 | x6 | 1 | 4 |
| 1965 | *5 | 8 | 4 | 9 | 1 | 10 | 6 | 3 | 7 | 2 |
| 1966 | 5 | 10 | 7 | 8 | 1 | 9 | 4 | 3 | 6 | 2 |
| 1967 | 7 | 3 | 4 | 9 | 8 | 10 | 5 | 6 | 1 | 2 |
| 1968 | 5 | 3 | 4 | 10 | x7 | 9 | x7 | 6 | 1 | 2 |

| | EAST DIVISION | | | | | | WEST DIVISION | | | | | |
|---|---|---|---|---|---|---|---|---|---|---|---|---|
| Year | Chi. | Mon. | N.Y. | Phila. | Pitt. | St.L. | Atl. | Cin. | Hous. | L.A. | S.D. | S.F. |
| 1969 | 2 | 6 | 1 | 5 | 3 | 4 | 1 | 3 | 5 | 4 | 6 | 2 |
| 1970 | 2 | 6 | 3 | 5 | 1 | 4 | 5 | 1 | 4 | 2 | 6 | 3 |
| 1971 | x3 | 5 | x3 | 6 | 1 | 2 | 3 | x4 | x4 | 2 | 6 | 1 |
| 1972 | 2 | 5 | 3 | 6 | 1 | 4 | 4 | 1 | 2 | 3 | 6 | 5 |
| 1973 | 5 | 4 | 1 | 6 | 3 | 2 | 5 | 1 | 4 | 2 | 6 | 3 |
| 1974 | 6 | 4 | 5 | 3 | 1 | 2 | 3 | 2 | 4 | 1 | 6 | 5 |
| 1975 | x5 | x5 | x3 | 2 | 1 | x3 | 5 | 1 | 6 | 2 | 4 | 3 |

*Record of predecessor Boston (1900-1952) and Milwaukee (1953-1965) clubs; †Brooklyn club; ‡New York Giants. xTied for position.

## LEADING BATSMEN

| Year Player and Club | G. | AB. | R. | H. | TB. | 2B. | 3B. | HR. | RBI. | B.A. |
|---|---|---|---|---|---|---|---|---|---|---|
| 1900—John (Honus) Wagner, Pittsburgh | 134 | 528 | 107 | 201 | 302 | 45 | 22 | 4 | .... | .381 |
| 1901—Jesse Burkett, St. Louis | 142 | 597 | 139 | 228 | 313 | 21 | 17 | 10 | .... | .382 |
| 1902—Clarence Beaumont, Pittsburgh | 131 | 544 | 101 | 194 | 227 | 21 | 6 | 0 | .... | .357 |
| 1903—John (Honus) Wagner, Pittsburgh | 129 | 512 | 97 | 182 | 265 | 30 | 19 | 5 | .... | .355 |
| 1904—John (Honus) Wagner, Pittsburgh | 132 | 490 | 97 | 171 | 255 | 44 | 14 | 4 | .... | .349 |
| 1905—J. Bentley Seymour, Cincinnati | 149 | 581 | 95 | 219 | 325 | 40 | 21 | 8 | .... | .377 |
| 1906—John (Honus) Wagner, Pittsburgh | 140 | 516 | 103 | 175 | 237 | 38 | 9 | 2 | .... | .339 |
| 1907—John (Honus) Wagner, Pittsburgh | 142 | 515 | 98 | 180 | 264 | 38 | 14 | 6 | 91 | .350 |
| 1908—John (Honus) Wagner, Pittsburgh | 151 | 568 | 100 | 201 | 308 | 39 | 19 | 10 | 106 | .354 |
| 1909—John (Honus) Wagner, Pittsburgh | 137 | 495 | 92 | 168 | 242 | 39 | 10 | 5 | 102 | .339 |
| 1910—Sherwood Magee, Philadelphia | 154 | 519 | 110 | 172 | 263 | 39 | 17 | 6 | 116 | .331 |
| 1911—John (Honus) Wagner, Pittsburgh | 130 | 473 | 87 | 158 | 240 | 23 | 16 | 9 | 108 | .334 |
| 1912—Henry Zimmerman, Chicago | 145 | 557 | 95 | 207 | 318 | 41 | 14 | 14 | 98 | .372 |
| 1913—Jacob Daubert, Brooklyn | 139 | 508 | 76 | 178 | 215 | 17 | 7 | 2 | 46 | 3.50 |

# LEADING BATSMEN—Continued

| Year | Player and Club | G. | AB. | R. | H. | TB. | 2B. | 3B. | HR. | RBI. | B.A. |
|------|----------------|-----|-----|-----|-----|-----|-----|-----|-----|------|------|
| 1914—Jacob Daubert, Brooklyn | | 126 | 474 | 89 | 156 | 205 | 17 | 7 | 6 | 44 | .329 |
| 1915—Lawrence Doyle, New York | | 150 | 591 | 86 | 189 | 261 | 40 | 10 | 4 | 68 | .320 |
| 1916—Harold Chase, Cincinnati | | 142 | 542 | 66 | 184 | 249 | 29 | 12 | 4 | 84 | .339 |
| 1917—Edd Roush, Cincinnati | | 136 | 522 | 82 | 178 | 237 | 19 | 14 | 4 | 62 | .341 |
| 1918—Zachariah Wheat, Brooklyn | | 105 | 409 | 39 | 137 | 158 | 15 | 3 | 0 | 48 | .335 |
| 1919—Edd Roush, Cincinnati | | 133 | 504 | 73 | 162 | 216 | 19 | 13 | 3 | 69 | .321 |
| 1920—Rogers Hornsby, St. Louis | | 149 | 589 | 96 | 218 | 329 | 44 | 20 | 9 | 94 | .370 |
| 1921—Rogers Hornsby, St. Louis | | 154 | 592 | 131 | 235 | 378 | 44 | 18 | 21 | 126 | .397 |
| 1922—Rogers Hornsby, St. Louis | | 154 | 623 | 141 | 250 | 450 | 46 | 14 | 42 | 152 | .401 |
| 1923—Rogers Hornsby, St. Louis | | 107 | 424 | 89 | 163 | 266 | 32 | 10 | 17 | 83 | .384 |
| 1924—Rogers Hornsby, St. Louis | | 143 | 536 | 121 | 227 | 373 | 43 | 14 | 25 | 94 | .424 |
| 1925—Rogers Hornsby, St. Louis | | 138 | 504 | 133 | 203 | 381 | 41 | 10 | 39 | 143 | .403 |
| 1926—Eugene Hargrave, Cincinnati | | 105 | 326 | 42 | 115 | 171 | 22 | 8 | 6 | 62 | .353 |
| 1927—Paul Waner, Pittsburgh | | 155 | 623 | 113 | 237 | 338 | 40 | 17 | 9 | 131 | .380 |
| 1928—Rogers Hornsby, Boston | | 140 | 486 | 99 | 188 | 307 | 42 | 7 | 21 | 94 | .387 |
| 1929—Frank O'Doul, Philadelphia | | 154 | 638 | 152 | 254 | 397 | 35 | 6 | 32 | 122 | .398 |
| 1930—William Terry, New York | | 154 | 633 | 139 | 254 | 392 | 39 | 15 | 23 | 129 | .401 |
| 1931—Chas. (Chick) Hafey, St. Louis | | 122 | 450 | 94 | 157 | 256 | 35 | 8 | 16 | 95 | .349 |
| 1932—Frank O'Doul, Brooklyn | | 148 | 595 | 120 | 219 | 330 | 32 | 8 | 21 | 90 | .368 |
| 1933—Charles Klein, Philadelphia | | 152 | 606 | 101 | 223 | 365 | 44 | 7 | 28 | 120 | .368 |
| 1934—Paul Waner, Pittsburgh | | 146 | 599 | 122 | 217 | 323 | 32 | 16 | 14 | 90 | .362 |
| 1935—J. Floyd (Arky) Vaughn, Pitt. | | 137 | 499 | 108 | 192 | 303 | 34 | 10 | 19 | 99 | .385 |
| 1936—Paul Waner, Pittsburgh | | 148 | 585 | 107 | 218 | 304 | 53 | 9 | 5 | 94 | .373 |
| 1937—Joseph Medwick, St. Louis | | 156 | 633 | 111 | 237 | 406 | 56 | 10 | 31 | 154 | .374 |
| 1938—Ernest Lombardi, Cincinnati | | 129 | 489 | 60 | 167 | 256 | 30 | 1 | 19 | 95 | .342 |
| 1939—John Mize, St. Louis | | 153 | 564 | 104 | 197 | 353 | 44 | 14 | 28 | 108 | .349 |
| 1940—Debs Garms, Pittsburgh | | 103 | 358 | 76 | 127 | 179 | 23 | 7 | 5 | 57 | .355 |
| 1941—Harold (Pete) Reiser, Brooklyn | | 137 | 536 | 117 | 184 | 299 | 39 | 17 | 14 | 76 | .343 |
| 1942—Ernest Lombardi, Boston | | 105 | 309 | 32 | 102 | 149 | 14 | 0 | 11 | 46 | .330 |
| 1943—Stanley Musial, St. Louis | | 157 | 617 | 108 | 220 | 347 | 48 | 20 | 13 | 81 | .357 |
| 1944—Fred (Dixie) Walker, Brooklyn | | 147 | 535 | 77 | 191 | 283 | 37 | 8 | 13 | 91 | .357 |
| 1945—Philip Cavarretta, Chicago | | 132 | 498 | 94 | 177 | 249 | 34 | 10 | 6 | 97 | .355 |
| 1946—Stanley Musial, St. Louis | | 156 | 624 | 124 | 228 | 366 | 50 | 20 | 16 | 103 | .365 |
| 1947—Harry Walker, St. Louis-Phila. | | 140 | 513 | 81 | 186 | 250 | 29 | 16 | 1 | 41 | .363 |
| 1948—Stanley Musial, St. Louis | | 155 | 611 | 135 | 230 | 429 | 46 | 18 | 39 | 131 | .376 |
| 1949—Jack Robinson, Brooklyn | | 156 | 593 | 122 | 203 | 313 | 38 | 12 | 16 | 124 | .342 |
| 1950—Stanley Musial, St. Louis | | 146 | 555 | 105 | 192 | 331 | 41 | 7 | 28 | 109 | .346 |
| 1951—Stanley Musial, St. Louis | | 152 | 578 | 124 | 205 | 355 | 30 | 12 | 32 | 108 | .355 |
| 1952—Stanley Musial, St. Louis | | 154 | 578 | 105 | 194 | 311 | 42 | 6 | 21 | 91 | .336 |
| 1953—Carl Furillo, Brooklyn | | 132 | 479 | 82 | 165 | 278 | 38 | 6 | 21 | 92 | .344 |
| 1954—Willie Mays, New York | | 151 | 565 | 119 | 195 | 377 | 33 | 13 | 41 | 110 | .345 |
| 1955—Richie Ashburn, Philadelphia | | 140 | 533 | 91 | 180 | 239 | 32 | 9 | 3 | 42 | .338 |
| 1956—Henry Aaron, Milwaukee | | 153 | 609 | 106 | 200 | 340 | 34 | 14 | 26 | 92 | .328 |
| 1957—Stanley Musial, St. Louis | | 134 | 502 | 82 | 176 | 307 | 38 | 3 | 29 | 102 | .351 |
| 1958—Richie Ashburn, Philadelphia | | 152 | 615 | 98 | 215 | 271 | 24 | 13 | 2 | 33 | .350 |
| 1959—Henry Aaron, Milwaukee | | 154 | 629 | 116 | 223 | 400 | 46 | 7 | 39 | 123 | .355 |
| 1960—Richard Groat, Pittsburgh | | 138 | 573 | 85 | 186 | 226 | 26 | 4 | 2 | 50 | .325 |
| 1961—Roberto Clemente, Pittsburgh | | 146 | 572 | 100 | 201 | 320 | 30 | 10 | 23 | 89 | .351 |
| 1962—H. Thomas Davis, Los Angeles | | 163 | 665 | 120 | 230 | 356 | 27 | 9 | 27 | 153 | .346 |
| 1963—H. Thomas Davis, Los Angeles | | 146 | 556 | 69 | 101 | 254 | 19 | 3 | 16 | 88 | .326 |
| 1964—Roberto Clemente, Pittsburgh | | 155 | 622 | 95 | 211 | 301 | 40 | 7 | 12 | 87 | .339 |
| 1965—Roberto Clemente, Pittsburgh | | 152 | 589 | 91 | 194 | 273 | 21 | 14 | 10 | 65 | .329 |
| 1966—Mateo Alou, Pittsburgh | | 141 | 535 | 86 | 183 | 225 | 18 | 9 | 2 | 27 | .342 |
| 1967—Roberto Clemente, Pittsburgh | | 147 | 585 | 103 | 209 | 324 | 26 | 10 | 23 | 110 | .357 |
| 1968—Peter Rose, Cincinnati | | 149 | 626 | 94 | 210 | 294 | 42 | 6 | 10 | 49 | .335 |
| 1969—Peter Rose, Cincinnati | | 156 | 627 | 120 | 218 | 321 | 33 | 11 | 16 | 82 | .348 |
| 1970—Ricardo Carty, Atlanta | | 136 | 478 | 84 | 175 | 279 | 23 | 3 | 25 | 101 | .366 |
| 1971—Joseph Torre, St. Louis | | 161 | 634 | 97 | 230 | 352 | 34 | 8 | 24 | 137 | .363 |
| 1972—Billy L. Williams, Chicago | | 150 | 574 | 95 | 191 | 348 | 34 | 6 | 37 | 122 | .333 |
| 1973—Peter Rose, Cincinnati | | 160 | 680 | 115 | 230 | 297 | 36 | 8 | 5 | 64 | .338 |
| 1974—Ralph Garr, Atlanta | | 143 | 606 | 87 | 214 | 305 | 24 | 17 | 11 | 54 | .353 |
| 1975—Bill Madlock, Chicago | | 130 | 514 | 77 | 182 | 246 | 29 | 7 | 7 | 64 | .354 |

## LEADERS IN RUNS SCORED

| Year | Player and Club | Runs |
|---|---|---|
| 1900— | Roy Thomas, Philadelphia | 131 |
| 1901— | Jesse Burkett, St. Louis | 139 |
| 1902— | John (Honus) Wagner, Pittsburgh | 105 |
| 1903— | Clarence Beaumont, Pittsburgh | 137 |
| 1904— | George Browne, New York | 99 |
| 1905— | Michael Donlin, New York | 124 |
| 1906— | John (Honus) Wagner, Pittsburgh | 103 |
|  | Frank Chance, Chicago | 103 |
| 1907— | W. Porter Shannon, New York | 104 |
| 1908— | Frederick Tenney, New York | 101 |
| 1909— | Thomas Leach, Pittsburgh | 126 |
| 1910— | Sherwood Magee, Philadelphia | 110 |
| 1911— | James Sheckard, Chicago | 121 |
| 1912— | Robert Bescher, Cincihnati | 120 |
| 1913— | Thomas Leach, Chicago | 99 |
|  | Max Carey, Pittsburgh | 99 |
| 1914— | George Burns, New York | 100 |
| 1915— | Cliff. (Gavvy) Cravath, Philadelphia | 89 |
| 1916— | George Burns, New York | 105 |
| 1917— | George Burns, New York | 103 |
| 1918— | Henry Groh, Cincinnati | 88 |
| 1919— | George Burns, New York | 86 |
| 1920— | George Burns, New York | 115 |
| 1921— | Rogers Hornsby, St. Louis | 131 |
| 1922— | Rogers Hornsby, St. Louis | 141 |
| 1923— | Ross Youngs, New York | 121 |
| 1924— | Frank Frisch, New York | 121 |
|  | Rogers Hornsby, St. Louis | 121 |
| 1925— | Hazen (Kiki) Cuyler, Pittsburgh | 144 |
| 1926— | Hazen (Kiki) Cuyler, Pittsburgh | 113 |
| 1927— | Lloyd Waner, Pittsburgh | 133 |
|  | Rogers Hornsby, New York | 133 |
| 1928— | Paul Waner, Pittsburgh | 142 |
| 1929— | Rogers Hornsby, Chicago | 156 |
| 1930— | Charles (Chuck) Klein, Philadelphia | 158 |
| 1931— | Terry, New York-Klein, Philadelphia | 121 |
| 1932— | Charles (Chuck) Klein, Philadelphia | 152 |
| 1933— | John (Pepper) Martin, St. Louis | 122 |
| 1934— | Paul Waner, Pittsburgh | 122 |
| 1935— | August Galan, Chicago | 133 |
| 1936— | J. Floyd (Arky) Vaughan, Pittsburgh | 122 |
| 1937— | Joseph Medwick, St. Louis | 111 |
| 1938— | Melvin Ott, New York | 116 |
| 1939— | William Werber, Cincinnati | 115 |
| 1940— | J. Floyd (Arky) Vaughan, Pittsburgh | 113 |
| 1941— | Harold (Pete) Reiser, Brooklyn | 117 |
| 1942— | Melvin Ott, New York | 118 |
| 1943— | J. Floyd (Arky) Vaughan, Brooklyn | 112 |
| 1944— | William Nicholson, Chicago | 116 |
| 1945— | Edward Stanky, Brooklyn | 128 |
| 1946— | Stanley Musial, St. Louis | 124 |
| 1947— | John Mize, New York | 137 |
| 1948— | Stanley Musial, St. Louis | 135 |
| 1949— | Harold (Pee Wee) Reese, Brooklyn | 132 |
| 1950— | C. Earl Torgeson, Boston | 120 |
| 1951— | Musial, St. Louis-Kiner, Pittsburgh | 124 |
| 1952— | Musial, St. Louis-Hemus, St. Louis | 105 |
| 1953— | Edwin (Duke) Snider, Brooklyn | 132 |
| 1954— | Musial, St. Louis-Snider, Brooklyn | 120 |
| 1955— | Edwin (Duke) Snider, Brooklyn | 126 |
| 1956— | Frank Robinson, Cincinnati | 122 |
| 1957— | Henry Aaron, Milwaukee | 118 |
| 1958— | Willie Mays, San Francisco | 121 |
| 1959— | Vada Pinson, Cincinnati | 131 |
| 1960— | William Bruton, Milwaukee | 112 |
| 1961— | Willie Mays, San Francisco | 129 |
| 1962— | Frank Robinson, Cincinnati | 134 |
| 1963— | Henry Aaron, Milwaukee | 121 |
| 1964— | Richard Allen, Philadelphia | 125 |
| 1965— | Tommy Harper, Cincinnati | 126 |
| 1966— | Felipe Alou, Atlanta | 122 |
| 1967— | Henry Aaron, Atlanta | 113 |
|  | Louis Brock, St. Louis | 113 |
| 1968— | Glenn Beckert, Chicago | 98 |
| 1969— | Bobby Bonds, San Francisco | 120 |
|  | Peter Rose, Cincinnati | 120 |
| 1970— | Billy Williams, Chicago | 137 |
| 1971— | Louis Brock, St. Louis | 126 |
| 1972— | Joe Morgan, Cincinnati | 122 |
| 1973— | Bobby Bonds, San Francisco | 131 |
| 1974— | Peter Rose, Cincinnati | 110 |
| 1975— | Peter Rose, Cincinnati | 112 |

## LEADERS IN HITS

| Year | Player and Club | Hits |
|---|---|---|
| 1900— | William Keeler, Brooklyn | 208 |
| 1901— | Jesse Burkett, St. Louis | 228 |
| 1902— | Clarence Beaumont, Pittsburgh | 194 |
| 1903— | Clarence Beaumont, Pittsburgh | 209 |
| 1904— | Clarence Beaumont, Pittsburgh | 185 |
| 1905— | J. Bentley Seymour, Cincinnati | 219 |
| 1906— | Harry Steinfeldt, Chicago | 176 |
| 1907— | Clarence Beaumont, Boston | 187 |
| 1908— | John (Honus) Wagner, Pittsburgh | 201 |
| 1909— | Lawrence Doyle, New York | 172 |
| 1910— | John (Honus) Wagner, Pittsburgh | 178 |
|  | Robert Bryne, Pittsburgh | 178 |
| 1911— | Roy Miller, Boston | 192 |
| 1912— | Henry Zimmerman, Chicago | 207 |
| 1913— | Cliff. (Gavvy) Cravath, Philadelphia | 179 |
| 1914— | Sherwood Magee, Philadelphia | 171 |
| 1915— | Lawrence Doyle, New York | 189 |
| 1916— | Harold Chase, Cincinnati | 184 |
| 1917— | Henry Groh, Cincinnati | 182 |
| 1918— | Charles Hollocher, Chicago | 161 |
| 1919— | Ivy Olson, Brooklyn | 164 |
| 1920— | Rogers Hornsby, St. Louis | 218 |
| 1921— | Rogers Hornsby, St. Louis | 235 |
| 1922— | Rogers Hornsby, St. Louis | 250 |
| 1923— | Frank Frisch, New York | 223 |
| 1924— | Rogers Hornsby, St. Louis | 227 |
| 1925— | James Bottomley, St. Louis | 227 |
| 1926— | Edward Brown, Boston | 201 |
| 1927— | Paul Waner, Pittsburgh | 237 |
| 1928— | Fred Lindstrom, New York | 231 |

## LEADERS IN HITS—Continued

| Year | Player and Club | Hits |
|------|-----------------|------|
| 1929 | Frank O'Doul, Philadelphia | 254 |
| 1930 | William Terry, New York | 254 |
| 1931 | Lloyd Waner, Pittsburgh | 214 |
| 1932 | Charles Klein, Philadelphia | 226 |
| 1933 | Charles Klein, Philadelphia | 223 |
| 1934 | Paul Waner, Pittsburgh | 217 |
| 1935 | William Herman, Chicago | 227 |
| 1936 | Joseph Medwick, St. Louis | 223 |
| 1937 | Joseph Medwick, St. Louis | 237 |
| 1938 | Frank McCormick, Cincinnati | 209 |
| 1939 | Frank McCormick, Cincinnati | 209 |
| 1940 | Stanley Hack, Chicago | 191 |
|      | Frank McCormick, Cincinnati | 191 |
| 1941 | Stanley Hack, Chicago | 186 |
| 1942 | Enos Slaughter, St. Louis | 188 |
| 1943 | Stanley Musial, St. Louis | 220 |
| 1944 | Musial, St. Louis-Cavarretta, Chicago | 197 |
| 1945 | Thomas Holmes, Boston | 224 |
| 1946 | Stanley Musial, St. Louis | 228 |
| 1947 | Thomas Holmes, Boston | 191 |
| 1948 | Stanley Musial, St. Louis | 230 |
| 1949 | Stanley Musial, St. Louis | 207 |
| 1950 | Edwin (Duke) Snider, Brooklyn | 199 |
| 1951 | Richie Ashburn, Philadelphia | 221 |
| 1952 | Stanley Musial, St. Louis | 194 |
| 1953 | Richie Ashburn, Philadelphia | 205 |
| 1954 | Donald Mueller, New York | 212 |
| 1955 | Theodore Kluszewski, Cincinnati | 192 |
| 1956 | Henry Aaron, Milwaukee | 200 |
| 1957 | Al (Red) Schoendienst, N.Y.-Mil. | 200 |
| 1958 | Richie Ashburn, Philadelphia | 215 |
| 1959 | Henry Aaron, Milwaukee | 223 |
| 1960 | Willie Mays, San Francisco | 190 |
| 1961 | Vada Pinson, Cincinnati | 208 |
| 1962 | H. Thomas Davis, Los Angeles | 230 |
| 1963 | Vada Pinson, Cincinnati | 204 |
| 1964 | Clemente, Pittsburgh-Flood, St. Louis | 211 |
| 1965 | Peter Rose, Cincinnati | 209 |
| 1966 | Felipe Alou, Atlanta | 218 |
| 1967 | Roberto Clemente, Pittsburgh | 209 |
| 1968 | Felipe Alou, Atlanta | 210 |
|      | Peter Rose, Cincinnati | 210 |
| 1969 | Mateo Alou, Pittsburgh | 231 |
| 1970 | Peter Rose, Cincinnati | 205 |
|      | Billy Williams, Chicago | 205 |
| 1971 | Joseph Torre, St. Louis | 230 |
| 1972 | Peter Rose, Cincinnati | 198 |
| 1973 | Peter Rose, Cincinnati | 230 |
| 1974 | Ralph Garr, Atlanta | 214 |
| 1975 | David Cash, Philadelphia | 213 |

## ONE-BASE HIT LEADERS

| Year | Player and Club | 1B. |
|------|-----------------|-----|
| 1900 | William H. Keeler, Brooklyn | 179 |
| 1901 | Jesse L. Burkett, St. Louis | 180 |
| 1902 | Clarence H. Beaumont, Pittsburgh | 167 |
| 1903 | Clarence H. Beaumont, Pittsburgh | 166 |
| 1904 | Clarence H. Beaumont, Pittsburgh | 158 |
| 1905 | Michael J. Donlin, New York | 162 |
| 1906 | Miller J. Huggins, Cincinnati | 141 |
|      | William P. Shannon, St. Louis-NY | 141 |
| 1907 | Clarence H. Beaumont, Pittsburgh | 150 |
| 1908 | Michael J. Donlin, New York | 153 |
| 1909 | Edward L. Grant, Philadelphia | 147 |
| 1910 | Edward L. Grant, Philadelphia | 134 |
| 1911 | Jacob E. Daubert, Brooklyn | 146 |
|      | Roy O. Miller, Boston | 146 |
| 1912 | William J. Sweeney, Boston | 159 |
| 1913 | Jacob E. Daubert, Brooklyn | 152 |
| 1914 | Beals Becker, Philadelphia | 128 |
| 1915 | Lawrence J. Doyle, New York | 135 |
| 1916 | David A. Robertson, New York | 142 |
| 1917 | Benjamin M. Kauff, New York | 141 |
|      | Edd J. Roush, Cincinnati | 141 |
| 1918 | Charles J. Hollocher, Chicago | 130 |
| 1919 | Ivan M. Olson, Brooklyn | 140 |
| 1920 | Milton J. Stock, St. Louis | 170 |
| 1921 | Carson L. Bigbee, Pittsburgh | 161 |
| 1922 | Carson L. Bigbee, Pittsburgh | 166 |
| 1923 | Frank F. Frisch, New York | 169 |
| 1924 | Zachary D. Wheat, Brooklyn | 149 |
| 1925 | Milton J. Stock, Brooklyn | 164 |
| 1926 | Edward W. Brown, Boston | 160 |
| 1927 | Lloyd J. Waner, Pittsburgh | 198 |
| 1928 | Lloyd J. Waner, Pittsburgh | 180 |
| 1929 | Frank J. O'Doul, Philadelphia | 181 |
|      | Lloyd J. Waner, Pittsburgh | 181 |
| 1930 | William H. Terry, New York | 177 |
| 1931 | Lloyd J. Waner, Pittsburgh | 172 |
| 1932 | Frank J. O'Doul, Brooklyn | 158 |
| 1933 | Charles P. Fullis, Philadelphia | 162 |
| 1934 | William H. Terry, New York | 169 |
| 1935 | Forrest D. Jensen, Pittsburgh | 160 |
| 1936 | Joseph G. Moore, New York | 160 |
| 1937 | Paul G. Waner, Pittsburgh | 178 |
| 1938 | Frank A. McCormick, Cincinnati | 160 |
| 1939 | John A. Hassett, Boston | 162 |
| 1940 | Burgess U. Whitehead, New York | 141 |
| 1941 | Stanley C. Hack, Chicago | 141 |
| 1942 | Enos B. Slaughter, St. Louis | 127 |
| 1943 | Nicholas J. Witek, New York | 172 |
| 1944 | Philip J. Cavaretta, Chicago | 142 |
| 1945 | Stanley C. Hack, Chicago | 155 |
| 1946 | Stanley F. Musial, St. Louis | 142 |
| 1947 | Thomas F. Holmes, Boston | 146 |
| 1948 | Stanley A. Rojek, Pittsburgh | 150 |
| 1949 | Albert F. Schoendienst, St. Louis | 160 |
| 1950 | Edward S. Waitkus, Philadelphia | 143 |
| 1951 | Richie Ashburn, Philadelphia | 181 |
| 1952 | Robert H. Adams, Cincinnati | 145 |
| 1953 | Richie Ashburn, Philadelphia | 169 |
| 1954 | Donald F. Mueller, New York | 165 |
| 1955 | Donald F. Mueller, New York | 152 |
| 1956 | John E. Temole, Cincinnati | 157 |
| 1957 | Richie Ashburn, Philadelphia | 152 |
| 1958 | Richie Ashburn, Philadelphia | 176 |
| 1959 | Don L. Blasingame, St. Louis | 144 |

## ONE-BASE HIT LEADERS—Continued

| Year | Player and Club | 1B. |
|------|-----------------|-----|
| 1960— | Richard M. Groat, Pittsburgh | 154 |
| 1961— | Vada E. Pinson, Cincinnati | 150 |
| | Maurice M. Wills, Los Angeles | 150 |
| 1962— | Maurice M. Wills, Los Angeles | 179 |
| 1963— | Curtis C. Flood, St. Louis | 152 |
| 1964— | Curtis C. Flood, St. Louis | 178 |
| 1965— | Maurice M. Wills, Los Angeles | 165 |
| 1966— | Roland T. Jackson, Houston | 160 |
| 1967— | Maurice M. Wills, Pittsburgh | 162 |

| Year | Player and Club | 1B. |
|------|-----------------|-----|
| 1968— | Curtis C. Flood, St. Louis | 160 |
| 1969— | Mateo R. Alou, Pittsburgh | 183 |
| 1970— | Mateo R. Alou, Pittsburgh | 171 |
| 1971— | Ralph A. Garr, Atlanta | 180 |
| 1972— | Louis C. Brock, St. Louis | 156 |
| 1973— | Peter E. Rose, Cincinnati | 181 |
| 1974— | David Cash, Philadelphia | 167 |
| 1975— | David Cash, Philadelphia | 166 |

## TWO-BASE HIT LEADERS

| Year | Player and Club | 2B. |
|------|-----------------|-----|
| 1900— | John (Honus) Wagner, Pittsburgh | 45 |
| 1901— | Wagner, Pitts-Beckley, Cinn | 39 |
| 1902— | John (Honus) Wagner, Pittsburgh | 33 |
| 1903— | Clarke, Pittsburgh-Mertes, New York-Steinfeldt, Cincinnati | 32 |
| 1904— | John (Honus) Wagner, Pittsburgh | 44 |
| 1905— | J. Bentley Seymour, Cincinnati | 40 |
| 1906— | John (Honus) Wagner, Pittsburgh | 38 |
| 1907— | John (Honus) Wagner, Pittsburgh | 38 |
| 1908— | John (Honus) Wagner, Pittsburgh | 39 |
| 1909— | John (Honus) Wagner, Pittsburgh | 39 |
| 1910— | Robert Byrne, Pittsburgh | 43 |
| 1911— | Edward Konetchy, St. Louis | 38 |
| 1912— | Henry Zimmerman, Chicago | 41 |
| 1913— | J. Carlisle Smith, Brooklyn | 40 |
| 1914— | Sherwood Magee, Philadelphia | 39 |
| 1915— | Lawrence Doyle, New York | 40 |
| 1916— | O. Albert Niehoff, Philadelphia | 42 |
| 1917— | Henry Groh, Cincinnati | 39 |
| 1918— | Henry Groh, Cincinnati | 28 |
| 1919— | Ross Youngs, New York | 31 |
| 1920— | Rogers Hornsby, St. Louis | 44 |
| 1921— | Rogers Hornsby, St. Louis | 44 |
| 1922— | Rogers Hornsby, St. Louis | 46 |
| 1923— | Edd Roush, Cincinnati | 41 |
| 1924— | Rogers Hornsby, St. Louis | 43 |
| 1925— | James Bottomley, St. Louis | 44 |
| 1926— | James Bottomley, St. Louis | 40 |
| 1927— | J. Riggs Stephenson, Chicago | 46 |
| 1928— | Paul Waner, Pittsburgh | 50 |
| 1929— | John Frederick, Brooklyn | 52 |
| 1930— | Charles Klein, Philadelphia | 59 |
| 1931— | Earl (Sparky) Adams, St. Louis | 46 |
| 1932— | Paul Waner, Pittsburgh | 62 |
| 1933— | Charles Klein, Philadelphia | 44 |
| 1934— | Cuyler, Chicago-Allen, Philadelphia | 42 |
| 1935— | William Herman, Chicago | 57 |
| 1936— | Joseph Medwick, St. Louis | 64 |
| 1937— | Joseph Medwick, St. Louis | 56 |

| Year | Player and Club | 2B. |
|------|-----------------|-----|
| 1938— | Joseph Medwick, St. Louis | 47 |
| 1939— | Enos Slaughter, St. Louis | 52 |
| 1940— | Frank McCormick, Cincinnati | 44 |
| 1941— | Reiser, Brooklyn-Mize, St. Louis | 39 |
| 1942— | Martin Marion, St. Louis | 38 |
| 1943— | Stanley Musial, St. Louis | 48 |
| 1944— | Stanley Musial, St. Louis | 51 |
| 1945— | Thomas Holmes, Boston | 47 |
| 1946— | Stanley Musial, St. Louis | 50 |
| 1947— | Edward Miller, Cincinnati | 38 |
| 1948— | Stanley Musial, St. Louis | 46 |
| 1949— | Stanley Musial, St. Louis | 41 |
| 1950— | Al (Red) Schoendienst, St. Louis | 43 |
| 1951— | Alvin Dark, New York | 41 |
| 1952— | Stanley Musial, St. Louis | 42 |
| 1953— | Stanley Musial, St. Louis | 53 |
| 1954— | Stanley Musial, St. Louis | 41 |
| 1955— | Logan, Milwaukee-Aaron, Milwaukee | 37 |
| 1956— | Henry Aaron, Milwaukee | 34 |
| 1957— | Donald Hoak, Cincinnati | 39 |
| 1958— | Orlando Cepeda, San Francisco | 38 |
| 1959— | Vada Pinson, Cincinnati | 47 |
| 1960— | Vada Pinson, Cincinnati | 37 |
| 1961— | Henry Aaron, Milwaukee | 39 |
| 1962— | Frank Robinson, Cincinnati | 51 |
| 1963— | Richard Groat, St. Louis | 43 |
| 1964— | A. Lee Maye, Milwaukee | 44 |
| 1965— | Henry Aaron, Milwaukee | 40 |
| 1966— | John Callison, Philadelphia | 40 |
| 1967— | Daniel Staub, Houston | 44 |
| 1968— | Louis Brock, St. Louis | 46 |
| 1969— | Mateo Alou, Pittsburgh | 41 |
| 1970— | M. Wesley Parker, Los Angeles | 47 |
| 1971— | Cesar Cedeno, Houston | 40 |
| 1972— | Cesar Cedeno, Houston | 39 |
| | Guillermo Montanez, Philadelphia | 39 |
| 1973— | Wilver Stargell, Pittsburgh | 43 |
| 1974— | Peter Rose, Cincinnati | 45 |
| 1975— | Peter Rose, Cincinnati | 47 |

## THREE-BASE HIT LEADERS

| Year | Player and Club | 3B. |
|------|-----------------|-----|
| 1900— | John (Honus) Wagner, Pittsburgh | 22 |
| 1901— | James Sheckard, Brooklyn | 21 |
| 1902— | Samuel Crawford, Cincinnati | 23 |
| 1903— | John (Honus) Wagner, Pittsburgh | 19 |
| 1904— | Harry Lumley, Brooklyn | 18 |
| 1905— | J. Bentley Seymour, Cincinnati | 21 |

| Year | Player and Club | 3B. |
|------|-----------------|-----|
| 1906— | Clarke, Pittsburgh-Schulte, Chicago | 13 |
| 1907— | Ganzel, Cincinnati-Alperman, Brooklyn | 16 |
| 1908— | John (Honus) Wagner, Pittsburgh | 19 |
| 1909— | Michael Mitchell, Cincinnati | 17 |
| 1910— | Michael Mitchell, Cincinnati | 18 |
| 1911— | Lawrence Doyle, New York | 25 |

# THREE-BASE HIT LEADERS—Continued

| Year | Player and Club | 3B. | Year | Player and Club | 3B. |
|---|---|---|---|---|---|
| 1912— | John (Chief) Wilson, Pittsburgh | 36 | 1945— | Luis Olmo, Brooklyn | 13 |
| 1913— | Victor Saier, Chicago | 21 | 1946— | Stanley Musial, St. Louis | 20 |
| 1914— | Max Carey, Pittsburgh | 17 | 1947— | Harry Walker, St. Louis-Philadelphia | 16 |
| 1915— | Thomas Long, St. Louis | 25 | 1948— | Stanley Musial, St. Louis | 18 |
| 1916— | William Hinchman, Pittsburgh | 16 | 1949— | Musial, St. Louis-Slaughter, St. Louis | 13 |
| 1917— | Rogers Hornsby, St. Louis | 17 | 1950— | Richie Ashburn, Philadelphia | 14 |
| 1918— | Jacob Daubert, Brooklyn | 15 | 1951— | Musial, St. Louis-Bell, Pittsburgh | 12 |
| 1919— | Hi Myers, Brooklyn-Southworth, Pitt. | 14 | 1952— | Robert Thomson, New York | 14 |
| 1920— | Henry (Hi) Myers, Brooklyn | 22 | 1953— | James Gilliam, Brooklyn | 17 |
| 1921— | Hornsby, St. Louis-Powell, Boston | 18 | 1954— | Willie Mays, New York | 13 |
| 1922— | Jacob Daubert, Cincinnati | 22 | 1955— | Mays, New York-Long, Pittsburgh | 13 |
| 1923— | Carey, Pittsburgh-Traynor, Pittsburgh. | 19 | 1956— | William Bruton, Milwaukee | 15 |
| 1924— | Edd Roush, Cincinnati | 21 | 1957— | Willie Mays, New York | 20 |
| 1925— | Hazen (Kiki) Cuyler, Pittsburgh | 26 | 1958— | Richie Ashburn, Philadelphia | 13 |
| 1926— | Paul Waner, Pittsburgh | 22 | 1959— | Moon, Los Angeles-Neal, Los Angeles | 11 |
| 1927— | Paul Waner, Pittsburgh | 17 | 1960— | William Bruton, Milwaukee | 13 |
| 1928— | James Bottomley, St. Louis | 20 | 1961— | George Altman, Chicago | 12 |
| 1929— | Lloyd Waner, Pittsburgh | 20 | 1962— | Callison, Philadelphia-Virdon, Pitt. | 10 |
| 1930— | Adam Comorosky, Pittsburgh | 23 | | W. Davis, Wills, Los Angeles | 10 |
| 1931— | William Terry, New York | 20 | 1963— | Vada Pinson, Cincinnati | 14 |
| 1932— | Floyd (Babe) Herman, Cincinnati | 19 | 1964— | Allen, Philadelphia-Santo, Chicago | 13 |
| 1933— | J. Floyd (Arky) Vaughan, Pittsburgh | 19 | 1965— | John Callison, Philadelphia | 16 |
| 1934— | Joseph Medwick, St. Louis | 18 | 1966— | J. Timothy McCarver, St. Louis | 13 |
| 1935— | Ival Goodman, Cincinnati | 18 | 1967— | Vada Pinson, Cincinnati | 13 |
| 1936— | Ival Goodman, Cincinnati | 14 | 1968— | Louis Brock, St. Louis | 14 |
| 1937— | J. Floyd (Arky) Vaughan, Pittsburgh. | 17 | 1969— | Roberto Clemente, Pittsburgh | 12 |
| 1938— | John Mize, St. Louis | 16 | 1970— | William Davis, Los Angeles | 16 |
| 1939— | William Herman, Chicago | 18 | 1971— | Joe Morgan, Houston | 11 |
| 1940— | J. Floyd (Arky) Vaughan, Pittsburgh. | 15 | | Roger Metzger, Houston | 11 |
| 1941— | Harold (Pete) Reiser, Brooklyn | 17 | 1972— | Lawrence Bowa, Philadelphia | 13 |
| 1942— | Enos Slaughter, St. Louis | 17 | 1973— | Roger Metzger, Houston | 14 |
| 1943— | Stanley Musial, St. Louis | 20 | 1974— | Ralph Garr, Atlanta | 17 |
| 1944— | John Barrett, Pittsburgh | 19 | 1975— | Ralph Garr, Atlanta | 11 |

# HOME RUN LEADERS

| Year | Player and Club | HR. | Year | Player and Club | HR. |
|---|---|---|---|---|---|
| 1900— | Herman Long, Boston | 12 | 1923— | Fred (Cy) Williams, Philadelphia | 41 |
| 1901— | Samuel Crawford, Cincinnati | 16 | 1924— | Jacques Fournier, Brooklyn | 27 |
| 1902— | Thomas Leach, Pittsburgh | 6 | 1925— | Rogers Hornsby, St. Louis | 39 |
| 1903— | James Sheckard, Brooklyn | 9 | 1926— | Lewis (Hack) Wilson, Chicago | 21 |
| 1904— | Harry Lumley, Brooklyn | 9 | 1927— | Wilson, Chicago-Williams, Philadelphia | 30 |
| 1905— | Fred Odwell, Cincinnati | 9 | 1928— | Wilson, Chicago-Bottomley, St. Louis | 31 |
| 1906— | Timothy Jordan, Brooklyn | 12 | 1929— | Charles Klein, Philadelphia | 43 |
| 1907— | David Brian, Boston | 10 | 1930— | Lewis (Hack) Wilson, Chicago | 56 |
| 1908— | Timothy Jordan, Brooklyn | 12 | 1931— | Charles Klein, Philadelphia | 31 |
| 1909— | John (Red) Murray, New York | 7 | 1932— | Klein, Philadelphia-Ott, New York | 38 |
| 1910— | Fred Beck, Bos.-F. Schulte, Chi. | 10 | 1933— | Charles Klein, Philadelphia | 28 |
| 1911— | Frank Schulte, Chicago | 21 | 1934— | Collins, St. Louis-Ott, New York | 35 |
| 1912— | Henry Zimmerman, Chicago | 14 | 1935— | Walter Berger, Boston | 34 |
| 1913— | Cliff. (Gavvy) Cravath, Philadelphia | 19 | 1936— | Melvin Ott, New York | 33 |
| 1914— | Cliff. (Gavvy) Cravath, Philadelphia | 19 | 1937— | Ott, New York-Medwick, St. Louis | 31 |
| 1915— | Cliff. (Gavvy) Cravath, Philadelphia | 24 | 1938— | Melvin Ott, New York | 36 |
| 1916— | Robertson, New York-Williams, Chi. | 12 | 1939— | John Mize, St. Louis | 28 |
| 1917— | Robertson, New York-Cravath, Phila. | 12 | 1940— | John Mize, St. Louis | 43 |
| 1918— | Cliff. (Gavvy) Cravath, Philadelphia | 8 | 1941— | Adolph Camilli, Brooklyn | 34 |
| 1919— | Cliff. (Gavvy) Cravath, Philadelphia | 12 | 1942— | Melvin Ott, New York | 30 |
| 1920— | Fred (Cy) Williams, Philadelphia | 15 | 1943— | William Nicholson, Chicago | 29 |
| 1921— | George Kelly, New York | 23 | 1944— | William Nicholson, Chicago | 33 |
| 1922— | Rogers Hornsby, St. Louis | 42 | 1945— | Thomas Holmes, Boston | 28 |

## HOME RUN LEADERS—Continued

| Year | Player and Club | HR. |
|---|---|---|
| 1946— | Ralph Kiner, Pittsburgh | 23 |
| 1947— | Kiner, Pittsburgh-Mize, New York | 51 |
| 1948— | Kiner, Pittsburgh-Mize, New York | 40 |
| 1949— | Ralph Kiner, Pittsburgh | 54 |
| 1950— | Ralph Kiner, Pittsburgh | 47 |
| 1951— | Ralph Kiner, Pittsburgh | 42 |
| 1952— | Kiner, Pittsburgh-Sauer, Chicago | 37 |
| 1953— | Edwin Mathews, Milwaukee | 47 |
| 1954— | Theodore Kluszewski, Cincinnati | 49 |
| 1955— | Willie Mays, New York | 51 |
| 1956— | Edwin (Duke) Snider, Brooklyn | 23 |
| 1957— | Henry Aaron, Milwaukee | 44 |
| 1958— | Ernest Banks, Chicago | 47 |
| 1959— | Edwin Mathews, Milwaukee | 46 |
| 1960— | Ernest Banks, Chicago | 41 |

| Year | Player and Club | HR. |
|---|---|---|
| 1961— | Orlando Cepeda, San Francisco | 46 |
| 1962— | Willie Mays, San Francisco | 49 |
| 1963— | H. Aaron, Milw.-McCovey, San Fran. | 44 |
| 1964— | Willie Mays, San Francisco | 47 |
| 1965— | Willie Mays, San Francisco | 52 |
| 1966— | Henry Aaron, Atlanta | 44 |
| 1967— | Henry Aaron, Atlanta | 39 |
| 1968— | Willie McCovey, San Francisco | 36 |
| 1969— | Willie McCovey, San Francisco | 45 |
| 1970— | Johnny Bench, Cincinnati | 45 |
| 1971— | Wilver Stargell, Pittsburgh | 48 |
| 1972— | Johnny Bench, Cincinnati | 40 |
| 1973— | Wilver Stargell, Pittsburgh | 44 |
| 1974— | Michael Schmidt, Philadelphia | 36 |
| 1975— | Michael Schmidt, Philadelphia | 38 |

## LEADERS IN TOTAL BASES

| Year | Player and Club | T.B. |
|---|---|---|
| 1900— | John (Honus) Wagner, Pittsburgh | 302 |
| | Elmer Flick, Philadelphia | 302 |
| 1901— | Jesse Burkett, St. Louis | 314 |
| 1902— | Samuel Crawford, Cincinnati | 256 |
| 1903— | Clarence Beaumont, Pittsburgh | 272 |
| 1904— | John (Honus) Wagner, Pittsburgh | 255 |
| 1905— | J. Bentley Seymour, Cincinnati | 325 |
| 1906— | John (Honus) Wagner, Pittsburgh | 237 |
| 1907— | John (Honus) Wagner, Pittsburgh | 264 |
| 1908— | John (Honus) Wagner, Pittsburgh | 308 |
| 1909— | John (Honus) Wagner, Pittsburgh | 242 |
| 1910— | Sherwood Magee, Philadelphia | 263 |
| 1911— | Frank Schulte, Chicago | 308 |
| 1912— | Henry Zimmerman, Chicago | 318 |
| 1913— | Cliff (Gavvy) Cravath, Philadelphia | 298 |
| 1914— | Sherwood Magee, Philadelphia | 277 |
| 1915— | Cliff (Gavvy) Cravath, Philadelphia | 266 |
| 1916— | Zachariah Wheat, Brooklyn | 262 |
| 1917— | Rogers Hornsby, St. Louis | 253 |
| 1918— | Charles Hollocher, Chicago | 202 |
| 1919— | Henry (Hi) Myers, Brooklyn | 223 |
| 1920— | Rogers Hornsby, St. Louis | 329 |
| 1921— | Rogers Hornsby, St. Louis | 378 |
| 1922— | Rogers Hornsby, St. Louis | 450 |
| 1923— | Frank Frisch, New York | 311 |
| 1924— | Rogers Hornsby, St. Louis | 373 |
| 1925— | Rogers Hornsby, St. Louis | 381 |
| 1926— | James Bottomley, St. Louis | 305 |
| 1927— | Paul Waner, Pittsburgh | 338 |
| 1928— | James Bottomley, St. Louis | 362 |
| 1929— | Rogers Hornsby, Chicago | 410 |
| 1930— | Charles Klein, Philadelphia | 445 |
| 1931— | Charles Klein, Philadelphia | 347 |
| 1932— | Charles Klein, Philadelphia | 420 |
| 1933— | Charles Klein, Philadelphia | 365 |
| 1934— | James (Rip) Collins, St. Louis | 369 |
| 1935— | Joseph Medwick, St. Louis | 365 |
| 1936— | Joseph Medwick, St. Louis | 367 |
| 1937— | Joseph Medwick, St. Louis | 406 |

| Year | Player and Club | T.B. |
|---|---|---|
| 1938— | John Mize, St. Louis | 326 |
| 1939— | John Mize, St. Louis | 353 |
| 1940— | John Mize, St. Louis | 368 |
| 1941— | Harold (Pete) Reiser, Brooklyn | 299 |
| 1942— | Enos Slaughter, St. Louis | 292 |
| 1943— | Stanley Musial, St. Louis | 347 |
| 1944— | William Nicholson, Chicago | 317 |
| 1945— | Thomas Holmes, Boston | 367 |
| 1946— | Stanley Musial, St. Louis | 366 |
| 1947— | Ralph Kiner, Pittsburgh | 361 |
| 1948— | Stanley Musial, St. Louis | 429 |
| 1949— | Stanley Musial, St. Louis | 382 |
| 1950— | Edwin (Duke) Snider, Brooklyn | 343 |
| 1951— | Stanley Musial, St. Louis | 355 |
| 1952— | Stanley Musial, St. Louis | 311 |
| 1953— | Edwin (Duke) Snider, Brooklyn | 370 |
| 1954— | Edwin (Duke) Snider, Brooklyn | 378 |
| 1955— | Willie Mays, New York | 382 |
| 1956— | Henry Aaron, Milwaukee | 340 |
| 1957— | Henry Aaron, Milwaukee | 369 |
| 1958— | Ernest Banks, Chicago | 379 |
| 1959— | Henry Aaron, Milwaukee | 400 |
| 1960— | Henry Aaron, Milwaukee | 334 |
| 1961— | Henry Aaron, Milwaukee | 358 |
| 1962— | Willie Mays, San Francisco | 382 |
| 1963— | Henry Aaron, Milwaukee | 370 |
| 1964— | Richard Allen, Philadelphia | 352 |
| 1965— | Willie Mays, San Francisco | 360 |
| 1966— | Felipe Alou, Atlanta | 355 |
| 1967— | Henry Aaron, Atlanta | 344 |
| 1968— | Billy Williams, Chicago | 321 |
| 1969— | Henry Aaron, Atlanta | 332 |
| 1970— | Billy Williams, Chicago | 373 |
| 1971— | Joseph Torre, St. Louis | 352 |
| 1972— | Billy Williams, Chicago | 348 |
| 1973— | Bobby Bonds, San Francisco | 341 |
| 1974— | Johnny Bench, Cincinnati | 315 |
| 1975— | Gregory Luzinski, Philadelphia | 322 |

# RUNS BATTED IN LEADERS

| Year | Player and Club | RBI |
|------|-----------------|-----|
| 1907— | John (Honus) Wagner, Pittsburgh | 91 |
| 1908— | John (Honus) Wagner, Pittsburgh | 106 |
| 1909— | John (Honus) Wagner, Pittsburgh | 102 |
| 1910— | Sherwood Magee, Philadelphia | 116 |
| 1911— | Frank Schulte, Chicago | 121 |
| 1912— | Henry Zimmerman, Chicago | 98 |
| 1913— | Cliff (Gavvy) Cravath, Philadelphia | 118 |
| 1914— | Sherwood Magee, Philadelphia | 101 |
| 1915— | Cliff (Gavvy) Cravath, Philadelphia | 118 |
| 1916— | Harold Chase, Cincinatti | 84 |
| 1917— | Henry Zimmerman, New York | 100 |
| 1918— | Frederick Merkle, Chicago | 71 |
| 1919— | Henry (Hi) Myers, Brooklyn | 72 |
| 1920— | George Kelly, New York | 94 |
|  | Rogers Hornsby, St. Louis | 94 |
| 1921— | Rogers Hornsby, St. Louis | 126 |
| 1922— | Rogers Hornsby, St. Louis | 152 |
| 1923 | Emil Meusel, New York | 125 |
| 1924— | George Kelly, New York | 136 |
| 1925— | Rogers Hornsby, St. Louis | 143 |
| 1926— | James Bottomley, St. Louis | 120 |
| 1927— | Paul Waner, Pittsburgh | 131 |
| 1928— | James Bottomley, St. Louis | 136 |
| 1929— | Lewis (Hack) Wilson, Chicago | 159 |
| 1930— | Lewis (Hack) Wilson, Chicago | 190 |
| 1931— | Charles Klein, Philadelphia | 121 |
| 1932— | Frank (Don) Hurst, Philadelphia | 143 |
| 1933— | Charles Klein, Philadelphia | 120 |
| 1934— | Melvin Ott, New York | 135 |
| 1935— | Walter Berger, Boston | 130 |
| 1936— | Joseph Medwick, St. Louis | 138 |
| 1937— | Joseph Medwick, St. Louis | 154 |
| 1938— | Joseph Medwick, St. Louis | 122 |
| 1939— | Frank McCormick, Cincinnati | 128 |
| 1940— | John Mize, St. Louis | 137 |
| 1941— | Adolph Camilli, Brooklyn | 120 |
| 1942— | John Mize, New York | 110 |
| 1943— | William Nicholson, Chicago | 128 |
| 1944— | William Nicholson, Chicago | 122 |
| 1945— | Fred (Dixie) Walker, Brooklyn | 124 |
| 1946— | Enos Slaughter, St. Louis | 130 |
| 1947— | John Mize, New York | 138 |
| 1948— | Stanley Musial, St. Louis | 131 |
| 1949— | Ralph Kiner, Pittsburgh | 127 |
| 1950— | Delmer Ennis, Philadelphia | 126 |
| 1951— | Monford Irvin, New York | 121 |
| 1952— | Henry Sauer, Chicago | 121 |
| 1953— | Roy Campanella, Brooklyn | 142 |
| 1954— | Theodore Kluszewski, Cincinnati | 141 |
| 1955— | Edwin (Duke) Snider, Brooklyn | 136 |
| 1956— | Stanley Musial, St. Louis | 109 |
| 1957— | Henry Aaron, Milwaukee | 132 |
| 1958— | Ernest Banks, Chicago | 129 |
| 1959— | Ernest Banks, Chicago | 143 |
| 1960— | Henry Aaron, Milwaukee | 126 |
| 1961— | Orlando Cepeda, San Francisco | 142 |
| 1962— | H. Thomas Davis, Los Angeles | 153 |
| 1963— | Henry Aaron, Milwaukee | 130 |
| 1964— | Kenton Boyer, St. Louis | 119 |
| 1965— | Deron Johnson, Cincinnati | 130 |
| 1966— | Henry Aaron, Atlanta | 127 |
| 1967— | Orlando Cepeda, St. Louis | 111 |
| 1968— | Willie McCovey, San Francisco | 105 |
| 1969— | Willie McCovey, San Francisco | 126 |
| 1970— | Johnny Bench, Cincinnati | 148 |
| 1971— | Joseph Torre, St. Louis | 137 |
| 1972— | Johnny Bench, Cincinnati | 125 |
| 1973— | Wilver Stargell, Pittsburgh | 119 |
| 1974— | Johnny Bench, Cincinnati | 129 |
| 1975— | Gregory Luzinski, Philadelphia | 120 |

Note—Runs batted in not compiled prior to 1907; officially adopted in 1920.

# BATTERS LEADING IN BASES ON BALLS

| Year | Player and Club | BB. |
|------|-----------------|-----|
| 1910— | Miller Huggins, St. Louis | 116 |
| 1911— | James Sheckard, Chicago | 147 |
| 1912— | James Sheckard, Chicago | 122 |
| 1913— | Robert Bescher, Cincinnati | 94 |
| 1914— | Miller Huggins, St. Louis | 105 |
| 1915— | Cliff. (Gavvy) Cravath, Philadelphia | 86 |
| 1916— | Henry Groh, Cincinatti | 84 |
| 1917— | George Burns, New York | 75 |
| 1918— | Max Carey, Pittsburgh | 62 |
| 1919— | George Burns, New York | 82 |
| 1920— | George Burns, New York | 76 |
| 1921— | George Burns, New York | 80 |
| 1922— | Max Carey, Pittsburgh | 80 |
| 1923— | George Burns, New York | 101 |
| 1924— | Rogers Hornsby, St. Louis | 89 |
| 1925— | Jacques Fournier, Brooklyn | 86 |
| 1926— | Lewis (Hack) Wilson, Chicago | 69 |
| 1927— | Rogers Hornsby, New York | 86 |
| 1928— | Rogers Hornsby, Boston | 107 |
| 1929— | Melvin Ott, New York | 113 |
| 1930— | Lewis (Hack) Wilson, Chicago | 105 |
| 1931— | Melvin Ott, New York | 80 |
| 1932— | Melvin Ott, New York | 100 |
| 1933— | Melvin Ott, New York | 75 |
| 1934— | J. Floyd (Arky) Vaughan, Pittsburgh | 94 |
| 1935— | J. Floyd (Arky) Vaughan, Pittsburgh | 97 |
| 1936— | J. Floyd (Arky) Vaughan, Pittsburgh | 118 |
| 1937— | Melvin Ott, New York | 102 |
| 1938— | Adolph Camilli, Brooklyn | 119 |
| 1939— | Adolph Camilli, Brooklyn | 110 |
| 1940— | Elburt Fletcher, Pittsburgh | 119 |
| 1941— | Elburt Fletcher, Pittsburgh | 118 |
| 1942— | Melvin Ott, New York | 109 |
| 1943— | August Galan, Brooklyn | 103 |
| 1944— | August Galan, Brooklyn | 101 |
| 1945— | Edward Stanky, Brooklyn | 148 |
| 1946— | Edward Stanky, Brooklyn | 137 |
| 1947— | Henry Greenberg, Pittsburgh | 104 |
|  | Harold (Pee Wee) Reese, Brooklyn | 104 |
| 1948— | Robert Elliott, Boston | 131 |
| 1949— | Ralph Kiner, Pittsburgh | 117 |
| 1950— | Edward Stanky, New York | 144 |
| 1951— | Ralph Kiner, Pittsburgh | 137 |
| 1952— | Ralph Kiner, Pittsburgh | 110 |
| 1953— | Stanley Musial, St. Louis | 105 |
| 1954— | Richie Ashburn, Philadelphia | 125 |

# BATTERS LEADING IN BASES ON
# BALLS—Continued

| Year | Player and Club | BB. | Year | Player and Club | BB. |
|------|-----------------|-----|------|-----------------|-----|
| 1955— | Edwin Mathews, Milwaukee | 109 | 1965— | Joe Morgan, Houston | 97 |
| 1956— | Edwin (Duke) Snider, Brooklyn | 99 | 1966— | Ronald Santo, Chicago | 95 |
| 1957— | Richie Ashburn, Philadelphia | 94 | 1967— | Ronald Santo, Chicago | 96 |
| | John Temple, Cincinnati | 94 | 1968— | Ronald Santo, Chicago | 96 |
| 1958— | Richie Ashburn, Philadelphia | 97 | 1969— | James Wynn, Houston | 148 |
| 1959— | James Gilliam, Los Angeles | 96 | 1970— | Willie McCovey, San Francisco | 137 |
| 1960— | Richie Ashburn, Chicago | 116 | 1971— | Willie Mays, San Francisco | 112 |
| 1961— | Edwin Mathews, Milwaukee | 93 | 1972— | Joe Morgan, Cincinnati | 115 |
| 1962— | Edwin Mathews, Milwaukee | 101 | 1973— | Darrell Evans, Atlanta | 124 |
| 1963— | Edwin Mathews, Milwaukee | 124 | 1974— | Darrell Evans, Atlanta | 126 |
| 1964— | Ronald Santo, Chicago | 86 | 1975— | Joe Morgan, Cincinnati | 132 |

Note—Bases on balls not included in batting records in National League prior to 1910.

# BATTERS LEADING IN STRIKEOUTS

| Year | Player and Club | SO. | Year | Player and Club | SO. |
|------|-----------------|-----|------|-----------------|-----|
| 1910— | John Hummell, Brooklyn | 81 | 1942— | Vincent DiMaggio, Pittsburgh | 87 |
| 1911— | Robert Coulson, Brooklyn | 78 | 1943— | Vincent DiMaggio, Pittsburgh | 126 |
| | Robert Bescher, Cincinnati | 78 | 1944— | Vincent DiMaggio, Pittsburgh | 83 |
| 1912— | Edward McDonald, Boston | 91 | 1945— | Vincent DiMaggio, Philadelphia | 91 |
| 1913— | George Burns, New York | 74 | 1946— | Ralph Kiner, Pittsburgh | 109 |
| 1914— | Frederick, Merkle, New York | 80 | 1947— | William Nicholson, Chicago | 83 |
| 1915— | H. Douglas Baird, Pittsburgh | 88 | 1948— | Henry Sauer, Cincinnati | 85 |
| 1916— | Cliff. (Gavvy) Cravath, Philadelphia | 89 | 1949— | Edwin (Duke) Snider, Brooklyn | 92 |
| 1917— | Fred Williams, Chicago | 78 | 1950— | Roy Smalley, Chicago | 114 |
| 1918— | Ross Youngs, New York | 49 | 1951— | Gilbert Hodges, Brooklyn | 99 |
| | George Paskert, Chicago | 49 | 1952— | Edwin Mathews, Boston | 115 |
| 1919— | Raymond Powell, Boston | 79 | 1953— | Stephen Bilko, St. Louis | 125 |
| 1920— | George Kelly, New York | 92 | 1954— | Edwin (Duke) Snider, Brooklyn | 96 |
| 1921— | Raymond Powell, Boston | 85 | 1955— | Walter Post, Cincinnati | 102 |
| 1922— | Frank Parkinson, Philadelphia | 93 | 1956— | Walter Post, Cincinnati | 124 |
| 1923— | George Grantham, Chicago | 92 | 1957— | Edwin (Duke) Snider, Brooklyn | 104 |
| 1924— | George Grantham, Chicago | 63 | 1958— | Harry Anderson, Philadelphia | 95 |
| 1925— | Chas. (Gabby) Hartnett, Chicago | 77 | 1959— | Walter Post, Philadelphia | 101 |
| 1926— | Bernard Friberg, Philadelphia | 77 | 1960— | J. Francisco Herrera, Philadelphia | 136 |
| 1927— | Lewis (Hack) Wilson, Chicago | 70 | 1961— | Richard Stuart, Pittsburgh | 121 |
| 1928— | Lewis (Hack) Wilson, Chicago | 94 | 1962— | Kenneth Hubbs, Chicago | 129 |
| 1929— | Lewis (Hack) Wilson, Chicago | 83 | 1963— | Donn Clendenon, Pittsburgh | 136 |
| 1930— | Lewis (Hack) Wilson, Chicago | 84 | 1964— | Richard Allen, Philadelphia | 138 |
| 1931— | H. Nicholas Cullop, Cincinnati | 86 | 1965— | Richard Allen, Philadelphia | 150 |
| 1932— | Lewis (Hack) Wilson, Brooklyn | 85 | 1966— | Byron Browne, Chicago | 143 |
| 1933— | Walter Berger, Boston | 77 | 1967— | James Wynn, Houston | 137 |
| 1934— | Adolph Camilli, Chicago-Philadelphia | 94 | 1968— | Donn Clendenon, Pittsburgh | 163 |
| 1935— | Adolph Camilli, Philadelphia | 113 | 1969— | Bobby Bonds, San Francisco | 187 |
| 1936— | Wilbur Brubaker, Pittsburgh | 96 | 1970— | Bobby Bonds, San Francisco | 189 |
| 1937— | Vincent DiMaggio, Boston | 111 | 1971— | Wilver Stargell, Pittsburgh | 154 |
| 1938— | Vincent DiMaggio, Boston | 134 | 1972— | Lee May, Houston | 145 |
| 1939— | Adolph Camilli, Brooklyn | 107 | 1973— | Bobby Bonds, San Francisco | 148 |
| 1940— | Chester Ross, Boston | 128 | 1974— | Michael Schmidt, Philadelphia | 138 |
| 1941— | Adolph Camilli, Brooklyn | 115 | 1975— | Michael Schmidt, Philadelphia | 180 |

Note—Strikeouts not included in batting records in National League prior to 1910.

# LEADING BASE STEALERS

| Year | Player and Club | SB. | Year | Player and Club | SB. |
|------|-----------------|-----|------|-----------------|-----|
| 1900— | James Barrett, Cincinnati | 46 | 1906— | Frank Chance, Chicago | 57 |
| 1901— | John (Honus) Wagner, Pittsburgh | 48 | 1907— | John (Honus) Wagner, Pittsburgh | 61 |
| 1902— | John (Honus) Wagner, Pittsburgh | 43 | 1908— | John (Honus) Wagner, Pittsburgh | 53 |
| 1903— | Sheckard, Brooklyn-Chance, Chicago | 67 | 1909— | Robert Bescher, Cincinnati | 54 |
| 1904— | John (Honus) Wagner, Pittsburgh | 58 | 1910— | Robert Bescher, Cincinnati | 70 |
| 1905— | Maloney, Chicago-Devlin, New York | 59 | 1911— | Robert Bescher, Cincinnati | 80 |

# LEADING BASE STEALERS—Continued

| Year | Player and Club | SB. |
|------|-----------------|-----|
| 1912— | Robert Bescher, Cincinnati | 67 |
| 1913— | Max Carey, Pittsburgh | 61 |
| 1914— | George Burns, New York | 62 |
| 1915— | Max Carey, Pittsburgh | 36 |
| 1916— | Max Carey, Pittsburgh | 63 |
| 1917— | Max Carey, Pittsburgh | 46 |
| 1918— | Max Carey, Pittsburgh | 58 |
| 1919— | George Burns, New York | 40 |
| 1920— | Max Carey, Pittsburgh | 52 |
| 1921— | Frank Frisch, New York | 49 |
| 1922— | Max Carey, Pittsburgh | 51 |
| 1923— | Max Carey, Pittsburgh | 51 |
| 1924— | Max Carey, Pittsburgh | 49 |
| 1925— | Max Carey, Pittsburgh | 46 |
| 1926— | Hazen (Kiki) Cuyler, Pittsburgh | 35 |
| 1927— | Frank Frisch, St. Louis | 48 |
| 1928— | Hazen (Kiki) Cuyler, Chicago | 37 |
| 1929— | Hazen (Kiki) Cuyler, Chicago | 43 |
| 1930— | Hazen (Kiki) Cuyler, Chicago | 37 |
| 1931— | Frank Frisch, St. Louis | 28 |
| 1932— | Charles Klein, Philadelphia | 20 |
| 1933— | John (Pepper) Martin, St. Louis | 26 |
| 1934— | John (Pepper) Martin, St. Louis | 23 |
| 1935— | August Galan, Chicago | 22 |
| 1936— | John (Pepper) Martin, St. Louis | 23 |
| 1937— | August Galan, Chicago | 23 |
| 1938— | Stanley Hack, Chicago | 16 |
| 1939— | Hack, Chicago-Handley, Pittsburgh | 17 |
| 1940— | Linus Frey, Cincinnati | 22 |
| 1941— | Daniel Murtaugh, Philadelphia | 18 |
| 1942— | Harold (Pete) Reiser, Brooklyn | 20 |
| 1943— | J. Floyd (Arky) Vaughan, Brooklyn | 20 |
| 1944— | John Barrett, Pittsburgh | 28 |
| 1945— | Al. (Red) Schoendienst, St. Louis | 26 |
| 1946— | Harold (Pete) Reiser, Brooklyn | 34 |
| 1947— | Jack Robinson, Brooklyn | 29 |
| 1948— | Richie Ashburn, Philadelphia | 32 |
| 1949— | Jack Robinson, Brooklyn | 37 |
| 1950— | Samuel Jethroe, Boston | 35 |
| 1951— | Samuel Jethroe, Boston | 35 |
| 1952— | Harold (Pee Wee) Reese, Brooklyn | 30 |
| 1953— | William Bruton, Milwaukee | 26 |
| 1954— | William Bruton, Milwaukee | 34 |
| 1955— | William Bruton, Milwaukee | 35 |
| 1956— | Willie Mays, New York | 40 |
| 1957— | Willie Mays, New York | 38 |
| 1958— | Willie Mays, San Francisco | 31 |
| 1959— | Willie Mays, San Francisco | 27 |
| 1960— | Maurice Wills, Los Angeles | 50 |
| 1961— | Maurice Wills, Los Angeles | 35 |
| 1962— | Maurice Wills, Los Angeles | 104 |
| 1963— | Maurice Wills, Los Angeles | 40 |
| 1964— | Maurice Wills, Los Angeles | 53 |
| 1965— | Maurice Wills, Los Angeles | 94 |
| 1966— | Louis Brock, St. Louis | 74 |
| 1967— | Louis Brock, St. Louis | 52 |
| 1968— | Louis Brock, St. Louis | 62 |
| 1969— | Louis Brock, St. Louis | 53 |
| 1970— | Robert Tolan, Cincinnati | 57 |
| 1971— | Louis Brock, St. Louis | 64 |
| 1972— | Louis Brock, St. Louis | 63 |
| 1973— | Louis Brock, St. Louis | 70 |
| 1974— | Louis Brock, St. Louis | 118 |
| 1975— | David Lopes, Los Angeles | 77 |

# SLUGGING LEADERS

| Year | Player and Club | Slug. Avg. |
|------|-----------------|------------|
| 1900— | John (Honus) Wagner, Pittsburgh | .572 |
| 1901— | James Sheckard, Brooklyn | .536 |
| 1902— | John (Honus) Wagner, Pittsburgh | .467 |
| 1903— | Fred Clarke, Pittsburgh | .532 |
| 1904— | John (Honus) Wagner, Pittsburgh | .520 |
| 1905— | J. Bentley Seymour, Cincinnati | .559 |
| 1906— | Harry Lumley, Brooklyn | .477 |
| 1907— | John (Honus) Wagner, Pittsburgh | .513 |
| 1908— | John (Honus) Wagner, Pittsburgh | .542 |
| 1909— | John (Honus) Wagner, Pittsburgh | .489 |
| 1910— | Sherwood Magee, Philadelphia | .507 |
| 1911— | Frank Schulte, Chicago | .534 |
| 1912— | Henry Zimmerman, Chicago | .571 |
| 1913— | Cliff. (Gavvy) Cravath, Philadelphia | .568 |
| 1914— | Sherwood Magee, Philadelphia | .501 |
| 1915— | Cliff. (Gavvy) Cravath, Philadelphia | .510 |
| 1916— | Zachariah Wheat, Brooklyn | .461 |
| 1917— | Rogers Hornsby, St. Louis | .484 |
| 1918— | Edd Roush, Cincinnati | .455 |
| 1919— | Henry (Hi) Myers, Brooklyn | .436 |
| 1920— | Rogers Hornsby, St. Louis | .559 |
| 1921— | Rogers Hornsby, St. Louis | .659 |
| 1922— | Rogers Hornsby, St. Louis | .722 |
| 1923— | Rogers Hornsby, St. Louis | .627 |
| 1924— | Rogers Hornsby, St. Louis | .696 |
| 1925— | Rogers Hornsby, St. Louis | .756 |
| 1926— | Fred Williams, Philadelphia | .569 |
| 1927— | Charles Hafey, St. Louis | .590 |
| 1928— | Rogers Hornsby, Boston | .632 |
| 1929— | Rogers Hornsby, Chicago | .681 |
| 1930— | Lewis (Hack) Wilson, Chicago | .723 |
| 1931— | Charles Klein, Philadelphia | .584 |
| 1932— | Charles Klein, Philadelphia | .646 |
| 1933— | Charles Klein, Philadelphia | .602 |
| 1934— | James (Rip) Collins, St. Louis | .615 |
| 1935— | J. Floyd (Arky) Vaughan, Pittsburgh | .607 |
| 1936— | Melvin Ott, New York | .588 |
| 1937— | Joseph Medwick, St. Louis | .641 |
| 1938— | John Mize, St. Louis | .614 |
| 1939— | John Mize, St. Louis | .626 |
| 1940— | John Mize, St. Louis | .636 |
| 1941— | Harold (Pete) Reiser, Brooklyn | .558 |
| 1942— | John Mize, New York | .521 |
| 1943— | Stanley Musial, St. Louis | .562 |
| 1944— | Stanley Musial, St. Louis | .549 |
| 1945— | Tommy Holmes, Boston | .577 |
| 1946— | Stanley Musial, St. Louis | .587 |
| 1947— | Ralph Kiner, Pittsburgh | .639 |
| 1948— | Stanley Musial, St. Louis | .702 |
| 1949— | Ralph Kiner, Pittsburgh | .658 |

## SLUGGING LEADERS—Continued

| Year | Player and Club | Slug. Avg. | Year | Player and Club | Slug. Avg. |
|------|-----------------|-----------|------|-----------------|-----------|
| 1950— | Stanley Musial, St. Louis | .596 | 1963— | Henry Aaron, Milwaukee | .586 |
| 1951— | Ralph Kiner, Pittsburgh | .627 | 1964— | Willie Mays, San Francisco | .607 |
| 1952— | Stanley Musial, St. Louis | .538 | 1965— | Willie Mays, San Francisco | .645 |
| 1953— | Edwin (Duke) Snider, Brooklyn | .6271 | 1966— | Richard Allen, Philadelphia | .632 |
| 1954— | Willie Mays, New York | .667 | 1967— | Henry Aaron, Atlanta | .573 |
| 1955— | Willie Mays, New York | .659 | 1968— | Willie McCovey, San Francisco | .545 |
| 1956— | Edwin (Duke) Snider, Brooklyn | .598 | 1969— | Willie McCovey, San Francisco | .656 |
| 1957— | Willie Mays, New York | .626 | 1970— | Willie McCovey, San Francisco | .612 |
| 1958— | Ernest Banks, Chicago | .614 | 1971— | Henry Aaron, Atanta | .669 |
| 1959— | Henry Aaron, Milwaukee | .636 | 1972— | Billy Williams, Chicago | .606 |
| 1960— | Frank Robinson, Cincinnati | .595 | 1973— | Wilver Stargell, Pittsburgh | .646 |
| 1961— | Frank Robinson, Cincinnati | .611 | 1974— | Michael Schmidt, Philadelphia | .546 |
| 1962— | Frank Robinson, Cincinnati | .624 | 1975— | David Parker, Pittsburgh | .541 |

# LEADING PITCHERS IN WINNING PERCENTAGE
## (15 OR MORE VICTORIES)

| Year | Pitcher | Club | Won | Lost | Pct. |
|------|---------|------|-----|------|------|
| 1900— | Joseph McGinnity | Brooklyn | 29 | 9 | .763 |
| 1901— | John Chesbro | Pittsburgh | 21 | 9 | .700 |
| 1902— | John Chesbro | Pittsburgh | 28 | 6 | .824 |
| 1903— | Samuel Leever | Pittsburgh | 25 | 7 | .781 |
| 1904— | Joseph McGinnity | New York | 35 | 8 | .814 |
| 1905— | Samuel Leever | Pittsburgh | 20 | 5 | .800 |
| 1906— | Edward Reulbach | Chicago | 19 | 4 | .826 |
| 1907— | Edward Reulbach | Chicago | 17 | 4 | .810 |
| 1908— | Edward Reulbach | Chicago | 24 | 7 | .774 |
| 1909— | Christy Mathewson | New York | 25 | 6 | .806 |
| | Howard Camnitz | Pittsburgh | 25 | 6 | .806 |
| 1910— | Leonard Cole | Chicago | 20 | 4 | .833 |
| 1911— | Richard (Rube) Marquard | New York | 24 | 7 | .774 |
| 1912— | Claude Hendrix | Pittsburgh | 24 | 9 | .727 |
| 1913— | Albert Humphries | Chicago | 16 | 4 | .800 |
| 1914— | Williams James | Boston | 26 | 7 | .788 |
| 1915— | Grover Alexander | Philadelphia | 31 | 10 | .756 |
| 1916— | Thomas Hughes | Boston | 16 | 3 | .842 |
| 1917— | Ferdinand Schupp | New York | 21 | 7 | .750 |
| 1918— | Claude Hendrix | Chicago | 20 | 7 | .741 |
| 1919— | Walter Ruether | Cincinnati | 19 | 6 | .760 |
| 1920— | Burleigh Grimes | Brooklyn | 23 | 11 | .676 |
| 1921— | William L. Doak | St. Louis | 15 | 6 | .714 |
| 1922— | Peter Donohue | Cincinnati | 18 | 9 | .667 |
| 1923— | Adolfo Luque | Cincinnati | 27 | 8 | .771 |
| 1924— | Emil Yde | Pittsburgh | 16 | 3 | .842 |
| 1925— | William Sherdel | St. Louis | 15 | 6 | .714 |
| 1926— | Ray Kremer | Pittsburgh | 20 | 6 | .769 |
| 1927— | Lawrence Benton | Boston-New York | 17 | 7 | .708 |
| 1928— | Lawrence Benton | New York | 25 | 9 | .735 |
| 1929— | Charles Root | Chicago | 19 | 6 | .760 |
| 1930— | Fred Fitzsimmons | New York | 19 | 7 | .731 |
| 1931— | Paul Derringer | St. Louis | 18 | 8 | .692 |
| 1932— | Lonnie Warneke | Chicago | 22 | 6 | .786 |
| 1933— | Benjamin Cantwell | Boston | 20 | 10 | .667 |
| 1934— | Jerome (Dizzy) Dean | St. Louis | 30 | 7 | .811 |
| 1935— | William Lee | Chicago | 20 | 6 | .769 |
| 1936— | Carl Hubbell | New York | 26 | 6 | .813 |
| 1937— | Carl Hubbell | New York | 22 | 8 | .733 |
| 1938— | William Lee | Chicago | 22 | 9 | .710 |
| 1939— | Paul Derringer | Cincinnati | 25 | 7 | .781 |
| 1940— | Fred Fitzsimmons | Brooklyn | 16 | 2 | .889 |

# LEADING PITCHERS IN WINNING PERCENTAGE—Continued

## (15 or MORE VICTORIES)

| Year | Pitcher | Club | Won | Lost | Pct. |
|------|---------|------|-----|------|------|
| 1941— | Elmer Riddle | Cincinnati | 19 | 4 | .826 |
| 1942— | Lawrence French | Brooklyn | 15 | 4 | .789 |
| 1943— | Morton Cooper | St. Louis | 21 | 8 | .724 |
| 1944— | Theodore Wilks | St. Louis | 17 | 4 | .810 |
| 1945— | Harry Breechen | St. Louis | 15 | 4 | .789 |
| 1946— | Murry Dickson | St. Louis | 15 | 6 | .714 |
| 1947— | Lawrence Jansen | New York | 21 | 5 | .808 |
| 1948— | Harry Brecheen | St. Louis | 20 | 7 | .741 |
| 1949— | Elwin (Preacher) Roe | Brooklyn | 15 | 6 | .714 |
| 1950— | Salvatore Maglie | New York | 18 | 4 | .818 |
| 1951— | Elwin (Preacher) Roe | Brooklyn | 22 | 3 | .880 |
| 1952— | J. Hoyt Wilhelm | New York | 15 | 3 | .833 |
| 1953— | Carl Erskine | Brooklyn | 20 | 6 | .769 |
| 1954— | John Antonelli | New York | 21 | 7 | .750 |
| 1955— | Donald Newcombe | Brooklyn | 20 | 5 | .800 |
| 1956— | Donald Newcombe | Brooklyn | 27 | 7 | .794 |
| 1957— | Robert Buhl | Milwaukee | 18 | 7 | .720 |
| 1958— | Warren E. Spahn | Milwaukee | 22 | 11 | .667 |
|  | S. Lewis Burdette | Milwaukee | 20 | 10 | .667 |
| 1959— | ElRoy Face | Pittsburgh | 18 | 1 | .947 |
| 1960— | Ernest Broglio | St. Louis | 21 | 9 | .700 |
| 1961— | John Podres | Los Angeles | 18 | 5 | .783 |
| 1962— | Robert Purkey | Cincinnati | 23 | 5 | .821 |
| 1963— | Ronald Perranoski | Los Angeles | 16 | 3 | .842 |
| 1964— | Sanford Koufax | Los Angeles | 19 | 5 | .792 |
| 1965— | Sanford Koufax | Los Angeles | 26 | 8 | .765 |
| 1966— | Juan Marichal | San Francisco | 25 | 6 | .806 |
| 1967— | Richard Hughes | St. Louis | 16 | 6 | .727 |
| 1968— | Stephen R. Blass | Pittsburgh | 18 | 6 | .750 |
| 1969— | G. Thomas Seaver | New York | 25 | 7 | .781 |
| 1970— | Robert Gibson | St. Louis | 23 | 7 | .767 |
| 1971— | Donald E. Gullett | Cincinnati | 16 | 6 | .727 |
| 1972— | Gary L. Nolan | Cincinnati | 15 | 5 | .750 |
| 1973— | Thomas E. John | Los Angeles | 16 | 7 | .696 |
| 1974— | John (Andy) Messersmith | Los Angeles | 20 | 6 | .769 |
| 1975— | Donald E. Gullett | Cincinnati | 15 | 4 | .789 |

# LEADING PITCHERS—EARNED-RUN AVERAGE

## (Based on Ten Complete Games Through 1950, Then 154 Innings Until N. L. Expanded in 1962, When It Became 162 Innings)

| Year | Pitcher and Club | G. | IP. | ERA. | Year | Pitcher and Club | G. | IP. | ERA. |
|------|------------------|-----|-----|------|------|------------------|-----|-----|------|
| 1912— | Tesreau, New York | 36 | 243 | 1.96 | 1929— | Walker, New York | 29 | 178 | 3.08 |
| 1913— | Mathewson, New York | 40 | 306 | 2.06 | 1930— | Vance, Brooklyn | 35 | 259 | 2.61 |
| 1914— | Doak, St. Louis | 36 | 256 | 1.72 | 1931— | Walker, New York | 37 | 239 | 2.26 |
| 1915— | Alexander, Philadelphia | 49 | 376 | 1.22 | 1932— | Warneke, Chicago | 35 | 277 | 2.37 |
| 1916— | Alexander, Philadelphia | 48 | 390 | 1.55 | 1933— | Hubbell, New York | 45 | 309 | 1.66 |
| 1917— | Alexander, Philadelphia | 45 | 388 | 1.83 | 1934— | Hubbell, New York | 49 | 313 | 2.30 |
| 1918— | Vaughn, Chicago | 35 | 290 | 1.74 | 1935— | Blanton, Pittsburgh | 35 | 254 | 2.59 |
| 1919— | Alexander, Chicago | 30 | 235 | 1.72 | 1936— | Hubbell, New York | 42 | 304 | 2.31 |
| 1920— | Alexander, Chicago | 46 | 363 | 1.91 | 1937— | Turner, Boston | 33 | 257 | 2.38 |
| 1921— | Doak, St. Louis | 32 | 209 | 2.58 | 1938— | W. Lee, Chicago | 44 | 291 | 2.66 |
| 1922— | Ryan, New York | 46 | 192 | 3.00 | 1939— | Walters, Cincinnati | 39 | 319 | 2.29 |
| 1923— | Luque, Cincinnati | 41 | 322 | 1.93 | 1940— | Walters, Cincinnati | 36 | 305 | 2.48 |
| 1924— | Vance, Brooklyn | 35 | 309 | 2.16 | 1941— | E. Riddle, Cincinnati | 33 | 217 | 2.24 |
| 1925— | Luque, Cincinnati | 36 | 291 | 2.63 | 1942— | M. Cooper, St. Louis | 37 | 279 | 1.77 |
| 1926— | Kremer, Pittsburgh | 37 | 231 | 2.61 | 1943— | Pollett, St. Louis | 16 | 118 | 1.75 |
| 1927— | Kremer, Pittsburgh | 35 | 226 | 2.47 | 1944— | Heusser, Cincinnati | 30 | 193 | 2.38 |
| 1928— | Vance, Brooklyn | 38 | 280 | 2.09 | 1945— | Borowy, Chicago | 15 | 122 | 2.14 |

# LEADING PITCHERS—EARNED-RUN
## AVERAGE—Continued

| Year | Pitcher and Club | G. | IP. | ERA. | Year | Pitcher and Club | G. | IP. | ERA. |
|------|------------------|-----|------|------|------|------------------|-----|------|------|
| 1946 | Pollet, St. Louis | 40 | 266 | 2.10 | 1961 | Spahn, Milwaukee | 38 | 263 | 3.01 |
| 1947 | Spahn, Boston | 40 | 290 | 2.33 | 1962 | Koufax, Los Angeles | 28 | 184 | 2.54 |
| 1948 | Brecheen, St. Louis | 33 | 233 | 2.24 | 1963 | Koufax, Los Angeles | 40 | 311 | 1.88 |
| 1949 | Koslo, New York | 38 | 212 | 2.50 | 1964 | Koufax, Los Angeles | 29 | 223 | 1.74 |
| 1950 | Hearn, St. Louis-New York | 22 | 134 | 2.49 | 1965 | Koufax, Los Angeles | 43 | 336 | 2.04 |
| 1951 | Nichols, Boston | 33 | 156 | 2.88 | 1966 | Koufax, Los Angeles | 41 | 323 | 1.73 |
| 1952 | Wilhelm, New York | 71 | 159 | 2.43 | 1967 | P. Niekro, Atlanta | 46 | 207 | 1.87 |
| 1953 | Spahn, Milwaukee | 35 | 266 | 2.10 | 1968 | Gibson, St. Louis | 34 | 305 | 1.12 |
| 1954 | Antonelli, New York | 39 | 259 | 2.29 | 1969 | Marichal, San Francisco | 37 | 300 | 2.10 |
| 1955 | Friend, Pittsburgh | 44 | 200 | 2.84 | 1970 | Seaver, New York | 37 | 291 | 2.81 |
| 1956 | Burdette, Milwaukee | 39 | 256 | 2.71 | 1971 | Seaver, New York | 36 | 286 | 1.76 |
| 1957 | Podres, Brooklyn | 31 | 196 | 2.66 | 1972 | Carlton, Philadelphia | 41 | 346 | 1.98 |
| 1958 | Miller, San Francisco | 41 | 182 | 2.47 | 1973 | Seaver, New York | 36 | 290 | 2.08 |
| 1959 | S. Jones, San Francisco | 50 | 271 | 2.82 | 1974 | Capra, Atlanta | 39 | 217 | 2.28 |
| 1960 | McCormick, San Francisco | 40 | 253 | 2.70 | 1975 | Jones, San Diego | 37 | 285 | 2.24 |

Note—Earned-run records not tabulated in National League prior to 1912.

# STRIKEOUT LEADERS—PITCHING

| Year | Pitcher and Club | SO. | Year | Pitcher and Club | SO. |
|------|------------------|-----|------|------------------|-----|
| 1900 | George (Rube) Waddell, Pittsburgh | 133 | 1939 | Claude Passeau, Philadelphia-Chicago | 137 |
| 1901 | Frank (Noodles) Hahn, Cincinnati | 233 |  | William (Bucky) Walters, Cincinnati | 137 |
| 1902 | Victor Willis, Boston | 226 | 1940 | W. Kirby Higbe, Philadelphia | 137 |
| 1903 | Christopher Mathewson, New York | 267 | 1941 | John Vander Meer, Cincinnati | 202 |
| 1904 | Christopher Mathewson, New York | 212 | 1942 | John Vander Meer, Cincinnati | 186 |
| 1905 | Christopher Mathewson, New York | 206 | 1943 | John Vander Meer, Cincinnati | 174 |
| 1906 | Frederick Beebe, Chicago-St. Louis | 171 | 1944 | William Voiselle, New York | 161 |
| 1907 | Christopher Mathewson, New York | 178 | 1945 | Elwin (Preacher) Roe, Pittsburgh | 148 |
| 1908 | Christopher Mathewson, New York | 259 | 1946 | John Schmitz, Chicago | 135 |
| 1909 | Orval Overall, Chicago | 205 | 1947 | Ewell Blackwell, Cincinnati | 193 |
| 1910 | Christopher Mathewson, New York | 190 | 1948 | Harry Brecheen, St. Louis | 149 |
| 1911 | Richard (Rube) Marquard, New York | 237 | 1949 | Warren Spahn, Boston | 151 |
| 1912 | Grover Alexander, Philadelphia | 195 | 1950 | Warren Spahn, Boston | 191 |
| 1913 | Thomas Seaton, Philadelphia | 168 | 1951 | Warren Spahn, Boston | 164 |
| 1914 | Grover Alexander, Philadelphia | 214 |  | Donald Newcombe, Brooklyn | 164 |
| 1915 | Grover Alexander, Philadelphia | 241 | 1952 | Warren Spahn, Boston | 183 |
| 1916 | Grover Alexander, Philadelphia | 167 | 1953 | Robin Roberts, Philadelphia | 198 |
| 1917 | Grover Alexander, Philadelphia | 200 | 1954 | Robin Roberts, Philadelphia | 185 |
| 1918 | James (Hippo) Vaughn, Chicago | 148 | 1955 | Samuel Jones, Chicago | 198 |
| 1919 | James (Hippo) Vaughn, Chicago | 141 | 1956 | Samuel Jones, Chicago | 176 |
| 1920 | Grover Alexander, Chicago | 173 | 1957 | John Sanford, Philadelphia | 188 |
| 1921 | Burleigh Grimes, Brooklyn | 136 | 1958 | Samuel Jones, St. Louis | 225 |
| 1922 | Arthur (Dazzy) Vance, Brooklyn | 134 | 1959 | Donald Drysdale, Los Angeles | 242 |
| 1923 | Arthur (Dazzy) Vance, Brooklyn | 197 | 1960 | Donald Drysdale, Los Angeles | 246 |
| 1924 | Arthur (Dazzy) Vance, Brooklyn | 262 | 1961 | Sanford Koufax, Los Angeles | 269 |
| 1925 | Arthur (Dazzy) Vance, Brooklyn | 221 | 1962 | Donald Drysdale, Los Angeles | 232 |
| 1926 | Arthur (Dazzy) Vance, Brooklyn | 140 | 1963 | Sanford Koufax, Los Angeles | 306 |
| 1927 | Arthur (Dazzy) Vance, Brooklyn | 184 | 1964 | Robert Veale, Pittsburgh | 250 |
| 1928 | Arthur (Dazzy) Vance, Brooklyn | 200 | 1965 | Sanford Koufax, Los Angeles | 382 |
| 1929 | Perce (Pat) Malone, Chicago | 166 | 1966 | Sanford Koufax, Los Angeles | 317 |
| 1930 | William Hallahan, St. Louis | 177 | 1967 | James Bunning, Philadelphia | 253 |
| 1931 | William Hallahan, St. Louis | 159 | 1968 | Robert Gibson, St. Louis | 268 |
| 1932 | Jerome (Dizzy) Dean, St. Louis | 191 | 1969 | Ferguson Jenkins, Chicago | 273 |
| 1933 | Jerome (Dizzy) Dean, St. Louis | 199 | 1970 | G. Thomas Seaver, New York | 283 |
| 1934 | Jerome (Dizzy) Dean, St. Louis | 195 | 1971 | G. Thomas Seaver, New York | 289 |
| 1935 | Jerome (Dizzy) Dean, St. Louis | 182 | 1972 | Steven Carlton, Philadelphia | 310 |
| 1936 | Van Lingle Mungo, Brooklyn | 238 | 1973 | G. Thomas Seaver, New York | 251 |
| 1937 | Carl Hubbell, New York | 159 | 1974 | Steven Carlton, Philadelphia | 240 |
| 1938 | Claiborne Bryant, Chicago | 135 | 1975 | G. Thomas Seaver, New York | 243 |

# SHUTOUT LEADERS

| Year | Pitcher and Club | ShO. |
|------|------------------|------|
| 1900— | Clark C. Griffith, Chicago | 4 |
| | Frank G. Hahn, Cincinnati | 4 |
| | Charles A. Nichols, Boston | 4 |
| 1952— | Ken D. Raffensberger, Cincinnati | 6 |
| | Albert L. Orth, Philadelphia | 6 |
| | Victor G. Willis, Boston | 6 |
| 1902— | John D. Chesbro, Pittsburgh | 8 |
| | Christopher Mathewson, New York | 8 |
| 1903— | Samuel W. Leever, Pittsburgh | 7 |
| 1904— | Joseph J. McGinnity, New York | 9 |
| 1905— | Christopher Mathewson, New York | 9 |
| 1906— | Mordecai P. Brown, Chicago | 9 |
| 1907— | Orval Overall, Chicago | 9 |
| | Christopher Mathewson, New York | 9 |
| 1908— | Christopher Mathewson, New York | 12 |
| 1909— | Orval Overall, Chicago | 9 |
| 1910— | Earl L. Moore, Philadelphia | 7 |
| 1911— | Charles B. Adams, Pittsburgh | 7 |
| | Grover C. Alexander, Philadelphia | 7 |
| 1912— | George N. Rucker, Brooklyn | 6 |
| 1913— | Grover C. Alexander, Philadelphia | 9 |
| 1914— | Charles M. Tesreau, New York | 8 |
| 1915— | Grover C. Alexander, Philadelphia | 12 |
| 1916— | Grover C. Alexander, Philadelphia | 16 |
| 1917— | Grover C. Alexander, Philadelphia | 8 |
| 1918— | George A. Tyler, Chicago | 8 |
| | James L. Vaughn, Chicago | 8 |
| 1919— | Grover C. Alexander, Chicago | 9 |
| 1920— | Charles B. Adams, Pittsburgh | 8 |
| 1921— | Grover C. Alexander, Chicago | 3 |
| | Philip B. Douglas, New York | 3 |
| | Dana Filligim, Boston | 3 |
| | Adolph Luque, Cincinnati | 3 |
| | Clarence E. Mitchell, Brooklyn | 3 |
| | John D. Morrison, Pittsburgh | 3 |
| | Joseph C. Oeschger, Boston | 3 |
| | Jesse J. Haines, St. Louis | 3 |
| 1922— | Arthur C. Vance, Brooklyn | 6 |
| 1923— | Adolfo Luque, Cincinnati | 6 |
| 1924— | Jesse L. Barnes, Boston | 4 |
| | A. Wilbur Cooper, Pittsburgh | 4 |
| | Remey Kremer, Pittsburgh | 4 |
| | Eppa Rixey, Cincinnati | 4 |
| | Allen S. Sothoron, St. Louis | 4 |
| | Emil O. Yde, Pittsburgh | 4 |
| 1925— | Harold G. Carlson, Philadelphia | 4 |
| | Arthur C. Vance, Brooklyn | 4 |
| 1926— | Peter J. Donohue, Cincinnati | 5 |
| 1927— | Jesse J. Haines, St. Louis | 6 |
| 1928— | John F. Blake, Chicago | 4 |
| | Burleigh A. Grimes, Pittsburgh | 4 |
| | Charles F. Lucas, Cincinnati | 4 |
| | Douglas L. McWeeney, Brooklyn | 4 |
| | Arthur C. Vance, Brooklyn | 4 |
| 1929— | Perce L. Malone, Chicago | 5 |
| 1930— | Charles H. Root, Chicago | 4 |
| | Arthur C. Vance, Brooklyn | 4 |
| 1931— | William H. Walker, New York | 6 |
| 1932— | Lonnie Warneke, Chicago | 4 |
| | Jerome H. Dean, St. Louis | 4 |
| | Stephen A. Swetonic, Pittsburgh | 4 |
| 1933— | Carl O. Hubbell, New York | 10 |
| 1934— | Jerome H. Dean, St. Louis | 7 |

| Year | Pitcher and Club | ShO |
|------|------------------|-----|
| 1935— | Darrell E. Blanton, Pittsburgh | 4 |
| | Freddie L. Fitzsimmons, New York | 4 |
| | Lawrence H. French, Chicago | 4 |
| | Van L. Mungo, Brooklyn | 4 |
| | James D. Weaver, Pittsburgh | 4 |
| 1936— | Darrell E. Blanton, Pittsburgh | 4 |
| | James O. Carleton, Chicago | 4 |
| | Lawrence H. French, Chicago | 4 |
| | William C. Lee, Chicago | 4 |
| | Alfred J. Smith, New York | 4 |
| | Williams H. Walters, Philadelphia | 4 |
| | Lonnie Warneke, Chicago | 4 |
| 1937— | Louis H. Fette, Boston | 5 |
| | Leo T. Grissom, Cincinnati | 5 |
| | James R. Turner, Boston | 5 |
| 1938— | William C. Lee, Chicago | 9 |
| 1939— | Louis H. Fette, Boston | 6 |
| 1940— | William L. Lohrman, New York | 5 |
| | Manuel L. Salvo, Boston | 5 |
| | J. Whitlow Wyatt, Brooklyn | 5 |
| 1941— | J. Whitlow Wyatt, Brooklyn | 7 |
| 1942— | Morton C. Cooper, St. Louis | 10 |
| 1943— | Hiram G. Bithorn, Chicago | 7 |
| 1944— | Morton C. Cooper, St. Louis | 7 |
| 1945— | Claude W. Passeau, Chicago | 5 |
| 1946— | Ewell Blackwell, Cincinnati | 6 |
| 1947— | Warren E. Spahn, Boston | 7 |
| 1948— | Harry D. Brecheen, St. Louis | 7 |
| 1949— | Kenneth A. Heintzelman, Philadelphia | 5 |
| | Donald Newcombe, Brooklyn | 5 |
| | Howard J. Pollett, St. Louis | 5 |
| | Kenneth D. Raffensberger, Cincinnati | 5 |
| 1950— | James T. Hearn, New York | 5 |
| | Lawrence H. Jansen, New York | 5 |
| | Salvatore A. Maglie, New York | 5 |
| | Robin E. Roberts, Philadelphia | 5 |
| 1951— | Warren E. Spahn, Boston | 7 |
| 1952— | Ken D. Raffensberger, Cincinnati | 6 |
| | Curtis T. Simmons, Philadelphia | 6 |
| 1953— | Harvey Haddix, St. Louis | 6 |
| 1954— | John A. Antonelli, New York | 6 |
| 1955— | Joseph H. Nuxhall, Cincinnati | 5 |
| 1956— | John A. Antonelli, New York | 6 |
| | S. Lewis Brudette, Milwaukee | 6 |
| 1957— | John L. Podres, Brooklyn | 6 |
| 1958— | Carlton F. Willey, Milwaukee | 4 |
| 1959— | John A. Antonelli, San Francisco | 4 |
| | Robert R. Buhl, Milwaukee | 4 |
| | S. Lewis Burdette, Milwaukee | 4 |
| | Roger L. Craig, Los Angeles | 4 |
| | Donald S. Drysdale, Los Angeles | 4 |
| | Sam Jones, San Francisco | 4 |
| | Warren E. Spahn, Milwaukee | 4 |
| 1960— | John S. Sanford, San Francisco | 6 |
| 1961— | Joseph R. Jay, Cincinnati | 4 |
| | Warren E. Spahn, Milwaukee | 4 |
| 1962— | Robert B. Friend, Pittsburgh | 5 |
| | Robert Gibson, St. Louis | 5 |
| 1963— | Sanford Koufax, Los Angeles | 11 |
| 1964— | Sanford Koufax, Los Angeles | 7 |
| 1965— | Juan A. Marichal, San Francisco | 10 |

## SHUTOUT LEADERS—Continued

| Year | Pitcher and Club | ShO. |
|---|---|---|
| 1966— | James P. Bunning, Philadelphia | 5 |
| | Robert Gibson, St. Louis | 5 |
| | Lawrence C. Jackson, Philadelphia | 5 |
| | Larry E. Jaster, St. Louis | 5 |
| | Sanford Koufax, Los Angeles | 5 |
| | James W. Maloney, Cincinnati | 5 |
| 1967— | James P. Bunning, Philadelphia | 6 |
| 1968— | Robert Gibson, St. Louis | 13 |
| 1969— | Juan A. Marichal, San Francisco | 8 |
| 1970— | Gaylord J. Perry, San Francisco | 5 |
| 1971— | Stephen R. Blass, Pittsburgh | 5 |
| | Alphonso E. Downing, Los Angeles | 5 |
| | Robert Gibson, St. Louis | 5 |
| | Milton S. Pappas, Chicago | 5 |
| 1972— | Donald H. Sutton, Los Angeles | 9 |
| 1973— | John E. Billingham, Cincinnati | 7 |
| 1974— | Jonathan T. Matlack, New York | 7 |
| 1975— | John A. Messersmith, Los Angeles | 7 |

## PRE-1900 PENNANT WINNERS

| Year | Club | Manager | W | L | Pct. |
|---|---|---|---|---|---|
| 1876— | Chicago | Albert Spalding | 52 | 14 | .788 |
| 1877— | Boston | Harry Wright | 31 | 17 | .646 |
| 1878— | Boston | Harry Wright | 41 | 19 | .683 |
| 1879— | Providence | George Wright | 55 | 23 | .705 |
| 1880— | Chicago | Adrian Anson | 67 | 17 | .798 |
| 1881— | Chicago | Adrian Anson | 56 | 28 | .667 |
| 1882— | Chicago | Adrian Anson | 55 | 29 | .655 |
| 1883— | Boston | John Morrill | 63 | 35 | .643 |
| 1884— | Providence | Frank Bancroft | 84 | 28 | .750 |
| 1885— | Chicago | Adrian Anson | 87 | 25 | .777 |
| 1886— | Chicago | Adrian Anson | 90 | 34 | .726 |
| 1887— | Detroit | Wm. Watkins | 79 | 45 | .637 |
| 1888— | New York | James Mutrie | 84 | 47 | .641 |
| 1889— | New York | James Mutrie | 83 | 43 | .659 |
| 1890— | Brooklyn | Wm. McGunnigle | 86 | 43 | .667 |
| 1891— | Boston | Frank Selee | 87 | 51 | .630 |
| 1892— | Boston | Frank Selee | 102 | 48 | .680 |
| 1893— | Boston | Frank Selee | 86 | 44 | .662 |
| 1894— | Baltimore | Edward Hanlon | 89 | 39 | .695 |
| 1895— | Baltimore | Edward Hanlon | 87 | 43 | .669 |
| 1896— | Baltimore | Edward Hanlon | 90 | 39 | .698 |
| 1897— | Boston | Frank Selee | 93 | 39 | .705 |
| 1898— | Boston | Frank Selee | 102 | 47 | .685 |
| 1899— | Brooklyn | Edward Hanlon | 88 | 42 | .677 |

## PRE-1900 YEARLY FINISHES

| Year | Bos. | Bkn. | Chi. | Cin. | N.Y. | Phil. | Pitt. | St.L. | Balt. | Buf. | Clev. |
|---|---|---|---|---|---|---|---|---|---|---|---|
| 1876 | 4 | .... | 1 | 8 | 6 | 7 | .... | 3 | .... | .... | .... |
| 1877 | 1 | .... | 5 | 6 | .... | .... | .... | 4 | .... | .... | .... |
| 1878 | 1 | .... | 4 | 2 | .... | .... | .... | .... | .... | .... | .... |
| 1879 | 2 | .... | 4 | 5 | .... | .... | .... | .... | .... | 3 | 6 |
| 1880 | 6 | .... | 1 | 8 | .... | .... | .... | .... | .... | 7 | 3 |
| 1881 | 6 | .... | 1 | .... | .... | .... | .... | .... | .... | 3 | 7 |
| 1882 | *3 | .... | 1 | .... | .... | .... | .... | .... | .... | *3 | 5 |
| 1883 | 1 | .... | 2 | .... | 6 | 8 | .... | .... | .... | 5 | 4 |
| 1884 | 2 | .... | *4 | .... | *4 | 6 | .... | .... | .... | 3 | 7 |
| 1885 | 5 | .... | 1 | .... | 2 | 3 | .... | 8 | .... | 7 | .... |
| 1886 | 5 | .... | 1 | .... | 3 | 4 | .... | 6 | .... | .... | .... |
| 1887 | 5 | .... | 3 | .... | 4 | 2 | 6 | .... | .... | .... | .... |
| 1888 | 4 | .... | 2 | .... | 1 | 3 | 6 | .... | .... | .... | .... |
| 1889 | 2 | .... | 3 | .... | 1 | 4 | 5 | .... | .... | .... | 6 |
| 1890 | 5 | 1 | 2 | 4 | 6 | 3 | 8 | .... | .... | .... | 7 |
| 1891 | 1 | 6 | 2 | 7 | 3 | 4 | 8 | .... | .... | .... | 5 |
| 1892 | 1 | 3 | 7 | 5 | 8 | 4 | 6 | 11 | 12 | .... | 2 |
| 1893 | 1 | *6 | 9 | *6 | 5 | 4 | 2 | 10 | 8 | .... | 3 |
| 1894 | 3 | 5 | 8 | 10 | 2 | 4 | 7 | 9 | 1 | .... | 6 |
| 1895 | *5 | *5 | 4 | 8 | 9 | 3 | 7 | 11 | 1 | .... | 2 |
| 1896 | 4 | *9 | 5 | 3 | 7 | 8 | 6 | 11 | 1 | .... | 2 |
| 1897 | 1 | *6 | 9 | 4 | 3 | 10 | 8 | 12 | 2 | .... | 5 |
| 1898 | 1 | 10 | 4 | 3 | 7 | 6 | 8 | 12 | 2 | .... | 5 |
| 1899 | 2 | 1 | 8 | 6 | 10 | 3 | 7 | 5 | 4 | .... | 12 |

# PRE-1900 YEARLY FINISHES—Continued

| Year | Det. | Hart. | Ind. | K.C. | Lou. | Mil. | Prov. | Syr. | Troy | Wash. | Wor. |
|------|------|-------|------|------|------|------|-------|------|------|-------|------|
| 1876 | .... | 2 | .... | .... | 5 | .... | .... | .... | .... | .... | .... |
| 1877 | .... | 3 | .... | .... | 2 | .... | .... | .... | .... | .... | .... |
| 1878 | .... | .... | 5 | .... | .... | 6 | 3 | .... | .... | .... | .... |
| 1879 | .... | .... | .... | .... | .... | .... | 1 | 8 | 7 | .... | .... |
| 1880 | .... | .... | .... | .... | .... | .... | 2 | .... | 4 | .... | 5 |
| 1881 | 4 | .... | .... | .... | .... | .... | 2 | .... | 5 | .... | 8 |
| 1882 | 6 | .... | .... | .... | .... | .... | 3 | .... | 7 | .... | 8 |
| 1883 | 7 | .... | .... | .... | .... | .... | 1 | .... | .... | .... | .... |
| 1884 | 8 | .... | .... | .... | .... | .... | 4 | .... | .... | .... | .... |
| 1885 | 6 | .... | .... | .... | .... | .... | .... | .... | .... | 8 | .... |
| 1886 | 2 | .... | .... | 7 | .... | .... | .... | .... | .... | 7 | .... |
| 1887 | 1 | .... | 8 | .... | .... | .... | .... | .... | .... | 8 | .... |
| 1888 | 5 | .... | 7 | .... | .... | .... | .... | .... | .... | 8 | .... |
| 1889 | .... | .... | 7 | .... | .... | .... | .... | .... | .... | .... | .... |
| 1890 | .... | .... | .... | .... | .... | .... | .... | .... | .... | .... | .... |
| 1891 | .... | .... | .... | .... | .... | .... | .... | .... | .... | 10 | .... |
| 1892 | .... | .... | .... | .... | 9 | .... | .... | .... | .... | 12 | .... |
| 1893 | .... | .... | .... | .... | 11 | .... | .... | .... | .... | 11 | .... |
| 1894 | .... | .... | .... | .... | 12 | .... | .... | .... | .... | 10 | .... |
| 1895 | .... | .... | .... | .... | 12 | .... | .... | .... | .... | *9 | .... |
| 1896 | .... | .... | .... | .... | 12 | .... | .... | .... | .... | *6 | .... |
| 1897 | .... | .... | .... | .... | 11 | .... | .... | .... | .... | 11 | .... |
| 1898 | .... | .... | .... | .... | 9 | .... | .... | .... | .... | 11 | .... |
| 1899 | .... | .... | .... | .... | 9 | .... | .... | .... | .... | .... | .... |

*Tied for position

# PRE-1900 LEADERS

## LEADING BATSMEN

| Year | Player and Club | G. | H. | Pct. |
|------|-----------------|-----|-----|------|
| 1876 | Barnes, Chicago | 66 | 138 | .404 |
| 1877 | White, Boston | 48 | 82 | .385 |
| 1878 | Dalrymple, Milwaukee | 60 | 95 | .356 |
| 1879 | Anson, Chicago | 49 | 90 | .407 |
| 1880 | Gore, Chicago | 75 | 114 | .365 |
| 1881 | Anson, Chicago | 84 | 137 | .399 |
| 1882 | Brouthers, Buffalo | 84 | 129 | .367 |
| 1883 | Brouthers, Buffalo | 97 | 156 | .371 |
| 1884 | O'Rourke, Buffalo | 104 | 157 | .350 |
| 1885 | Connor, New York | 110 | 169 | .371 |
| 1886 | Kelly, Chicago | 118 | 175 | .388 |
| 1887 | Anson, Chicago | 122 | *224 | .421 |
| 1888 | Anson, Chicago | 134 | 177 | .343 |
| 1889 | Brouthers, Boston | 126 | 181 | .373 |
| 1890 | Glasscock, New York | 124 | 172 | .336 |
| 1891 | Hamilton, Philadelphia | 133 | 179 | .338 |
| 1892 | Brouthers, Brooklyn | 152 | 197 | .335 |
| | Childs, Cleveland | 144 | 185 | .335 |
| 1893 | Duffy, Boston | 131 | 203 | .378 |
| 1894 | Duffy, Boston | 124 | 236 | .438 |
| 1895 | Burkett, Cleveland | 132 | 235 | .423 |
| 1896 | Burkett, Cleveland | 133 | 240 | .410 |
| 1897 | Keeler, Baltimore | 128 | 243 | .432 |
| 1898 | Keeler, Baltimore | 128 | 214 | .379 |
| 1899 | Delahanty, Philadelphia | 145 | 234 | .408 |

*Bases on balls counted as hits.

## TWO-BASE HIT LEADERS

| Year | Player and Club | 2B. |
|------|-----------------|-----|
| 1876 | Roscoe Barnes, Chicago | 23 |
| 1877 | Adrian (Cap) Anson, Chicago | 20 |
| 1878 | Lewis Brown, Providence | 18 |
| 1879 | Charles Eden, Cleveland | 31 |
| 1880 | Fred Dunlap, Cleveland | 27 |
| 1881 | Michael (King) Kelly, Chicago | 28 |
| 1882 | Michael (King) Kelly, Chicago | 36 |
| 1883 | Edward Williamson, Chicago | 50 |
| 1884 | Paul Hines, Providence | 34 |
| 1885 | Adrian (Cap) Anson, Chicago | 35 |
| 1886 | Dennis (Dan) Brouthers, Detroit | 41 |
| 1887 | Dennis (Dan) Brouthers, Detroit | 35 |
| 1888 | James Ryan, Chicago | 37 |
| 1889 | John Glasscock, Indianapolis | 39 |
| 1890 | Samuel Thompson, Philadelphia | 38 |
| 1891 | Michael Griffin, Brooklyn | 36 |
| 1892 | Brouthers, Bkn.-Delahanty, Phil | 33 |
| 1893 | Oliver (Pat) Tebeau, Cleveland | 35 |
| 1894 | Hugh Duffy, Boston | 50 |
| 1895 | Edward Delahanty, Philadelphia | 47 |
| 1896 | Edward Delahanty, Philadelphia | 42 |
| 1897 | Jacob Stenzel, Baltimore | 40 |
| 1898 | Napoleon Lajoie, Philadelphia | 40 |
| 1899 | Edward Delahanty, Philadelphia | 56 |

## PRE-1900 LEADERS—Continued

### THREE-BASE HIT LEADERS

| Year | Player and Club | 3B. |
|------|-----------------|-----|
| 1876 | George Hall, Athletics | 12 |
| 1877 | Brown, Bos.-McVey, Chi.-White, Bos | 9 |
| 1878 | Thomas York, Providence | 9 |
| 1879 | L. Dickerson, Cin.-M. Kelly, Cin | 14 |
| 1880 | Harry Stovey, Worcester | 14 |
| 1881 | John Rowe, Buffalo | 11 |
| 1882 | Roger Connor, Troy | 17 |
| 1883 | Dennis (Dan) Brouthers, Buffalo | 17 |
| 1884 | William (Buck) Ewing, New York | 18 |
| 1885 | R. Connor, N.Y.-J. O'Rourke, N.Y. | 15 |
| 1886 | Roger Connor, New York | 19 |
| 1887 | Samuel Thompson, Detroit | 23 |

| Year | Player and Club | 3B. |
|------|-----------------|-----|
| 1888 | R. Connor, N.Y.-R. Johnson, Bos | 17 |
| 1889 | Connor, N.Y.-Fogarty, Ph.-Wilmot, W. | 17 |
| 1890 | John McPhee, Cincinnati | 25 |
| 1891 | Jacob Beckley, Pittsburgh | 20 |
| 1892 | Dennis (Dan) Brouthers, Brooklyn | 20 |
| 1893 | Perry Werden, St. Louis | 33 |
| 1894 | Henry Reitz, Baltimore | 29 |
| 1895 | A. Selbach, Wash.-S. Thompson, Phil | 22 |
| 1896 | McCreery, Lou.-G. Van Haltren, N.Y. | 21 |
| 1897 | Harry Davis, Pittsburgh | 28 |
| 1898 | John Anderson, Bkn.-Wash. | 19 |
| 1899 | James Williams, Pittsburgh | 27 |

### HOME RUN LEADERS

| Year | Player and Club | HR. |
|------|-----------------|-----|
| 1876 | George Hall, Athletics | 5 |
| 1877 | George Shaffer, Louisville | 3 |
| 1878 | Paul Hines, Providence | 4 |
| 1879 | Charles Jones, Boston | 9 |
| 1880 | J. O'Rourke, Bos.-H. Stovey, Wor. | 6 |
| 1881 | Dennis (Dan) Brouthers, Buffalo | 8 |
| 1882 | George Wood, Detroit | 7 |
| 1883 | William (Buck) Ewing, New York | 10 |
| 1884 | Edward Williamson, Chicago | 27 |
| 1885 | Abner Dalrymple, Chicago | 11 |
| 1886 | Harding Richardson, Detroit | 11 |
| 1887 | R. Connor, N.Y.-T. O'Brien, Wash | 17 |

| Year | Player and Club | HR. |
|------|-----------------|-----|
| 1888 | Roger Connor, New York | 14 |
| 1889 | Samuel Thompson, Philadelphia | 20 |
| 1890 | T. Burns, Bkn.-M. Tiernan, N.Y. | 13 |
| 1891 | H. Stovey, Bos.-M. Tiernan, N.Y. | 16 |
| 1892 | James Holliday, Cincinnati | 13 |
| 1893 | Edward Delahanty, Philadelphia | 19 |
| 1894 | H. Duffy, Boston-R. Lowe, Boston | 18 |
| 1895 | William Joyce, Washington | 17 |
| 1896 | Delahanty, Phil.-S. Thompson, Phil | 13 |
| 1897 | Napoleon Lajoie, Philadelphia | 10 |
| 1896 | James Collins, Boston | 14 |
| 1899 | John (Buck) Freeman, Washington | 25 |

### STOLEN BASE LEADERS

| Year | Player and Club | SB. |
|------|-----------------|-----|
| 1886 | George Andrews, Philadelphia | 56 |
| 1887 | John M. Ward, New York | 111 |
| 1888 | William (Dummy) Hoy, Washington | 82 |
| 1889 | James Fogarty, Philadelphia | 99 |
| 1890 | William Hamilton, Philadelphia | 102 |
| 1891 | William Hamilton, Philadelphia | 115 |
| 1892 | John M. Ward, Brooklyn | 94 |

| Year | Player and Club | SB. |
|------|-----------------|-----|
| 1893 | John M. Ward, New York | 72 |
| 1894 | William Hamilton, Philadelphia | 99 |
| 1895 | William Hamilton, Philadelphia | 95 |
| 1896 | William Lange, Chicago | 100 |
| 1897 | William Lange, Chicago | 83 |
| 1898 | Frederick Clarke, Louisville | 66 |
| 1899 | James Sheckard, Baltimore | 78 |

## LEADING PITCHERS IN WINNING PERCENTAGE
### (15 OR MORE VICTORIES)

| Year | Pitcher and Club | W. | L. | Pct. |
|------|------------------|----|----|------|
| 1876 | Albert Spalding, Chicago | 47 | 13 | .783 |
| 1877 | Thomas Bond, Boston | 31 | 17 | .646 |
| 1878 | Thomas Bond, Boston | 40 | 19 | .678 |
| 1879 | Jom M. Ward, Providence | 44 | 18 | .710 |
| 1880 | Fred Goldsmith, Chicago | 22 | 3 | .880 |
| 1881 | Chas. Radbourn, Providence | 25 | 11 | .694 |
| 1882 | Lawrence Corcoran, Chicago | 27 | 13 | .675 |
| 1883 | James McCormick, Cleveland | 27 | 13 | .675 |
| 1884 | Chas. Radbourn, Providence | 60 | 12 | .833 |
| 1885 | Michael Welch, New York | 44 | 11 | .800 |
| 1886 | John Flynn, Chicago | 24 | 6 | .800 |
| 1887 | Charles Getzein, Detroit | 29 | 13 | .690 |

| Year | Pitcher and Club | W. | L. | Pct. |
|------|------------------|----|----|------|
| 1888 | Timothy Keefe, New York | 35 | 12 | .745 |
| 1889 | John Clarkson, Boston | 49 | 19 | .721 |
| 1890 | Thomas Lovett, Brooklyn | 32 | 11 | .744 |
| 1891 | John Ewing, New York | 22 | 8 | .733 |
| 1892 | Denton (Cy) Young, Cleve | 36 | 11 | .766 |
| 1893 | Frank Killen, Pittsburgh | 34 | 10 | .773 |
| 1894 | Jouett Meekin, New York | 34 | 9 | .791 |
| 1895 | William Hoffer, Baltimore | 30 | 7 | .811 |
| 1896 | William Hoffer, Baltimore | 26 | 7 | .788 |
| 1897 | Amos Rusie, New York | 29 | 8 | .784 |
| 1898 | Edward Lewis, Boston | 25 | 8 | .758 |
| 1899 | James Hughes, Brooklyn | 28 | 6 | .824 |

# AMERICAN LEAGUE

### Including

**Club Directories**

**Club Reviews of 1975 Season**

**Club Day-By-Day Scores**

**A. L. Team Pictures**

**1975 League Leaders**

**1975 Official A. L. Averages**

**All-Time A. L. Player Performance Tables**

LELAND S. MacPHAIL, JR.
President of the American League

# American League

Organized 1900

**LELAND S. MacPHAIL, Jr.**
President

**JOSEPH E. CRONIN**
Chairman

**THOMAS A. YAWKEY**
Vice-President Emeritus

**CALVIN R. GRIFFITH**
Vice-President

**ROBERT F. HOLBROOK**
Secretary

**ROBERT O. FISHEL**
Assistant to the President

**DONALD C. MARR, Jr.**
Controller

**DICK BUTLER**
Supervisor of Umpires

Headquarters—280 Park Avenue, New York, N. Y. 10017

Telephone—682-7000 (area code 212)

UMPIRES—Lawrence Barnett, Nicholas Bremigan, Joseph Brinkman, Nestor Chylak, Terry Cooney, Bill Deegan, Donald Denkinger, Louis DiMuro, James Evans, Dale Ford, Arthur Frantz, Rich Garcia, Russell Goetz, William Haller, William Kunkel, Ronald Luciano, George Maloney. Larry McCoy, James McKean, Jerome Neudecker, David Phillips, Martin Springstead, Alan Clark, Gregory Kosc.

OFFICIAL STATISTICIANS—Sports Information Center, 1776 Heritage Drive, No. Quincy, Mass. 02171.

Players cannot be transferred from one major league club to another after June 15 to the close of the championship season except through regular waiver channels.

WAIVER PRICE, $20,000. Interleague waivers, $20,000, except for selected players and draft-excluded players.

# BALTIMORE ORIOLES

Chairman of the Board—Jerold C. Hoffberger

Chairman of Executive Committee and Treasurer—Zanvyl Krieger
Executive Vice-President-General Manager—Henry J. Peters
Vice-President for Business Affairs—Jack Dunn, III
Vice-President-Secretary—Joseph P. Hamper, Jr.
Vice-President—J. Frank Cashen
Public Relations Director—Robert W. Brown
Traveling Secretary—Philip E. Itzoe
Director of Business Affairs—Alan E. Harazin
Special Assistant to the General Manager—James J. Russo
Coordinator of Player Development and Scouting—
James M. McLaughlin
Director of Player Development—Clyde Kluttz
Director of Scouting—Thomas A. Giordano
Sales Manager—Don B. Shaver
Ticket Manager—Walter R. Freeman, Jr.
Assistant Ticket Manager—Joseph B. Codd
Consultant-President, Oriole Foundation—Herbert E. Armstrong
Manager—Earl S. Weaver
Club Physician—Dr. Leonard Wallenstein
Executive Offices—Memorial Stadium, Baltimore, Md. 21218
Telephone—243-9800 (area code 301)

SCOUTS—Jack Baker, Julio Blanco-Herrera, Dick Bowie, Joe Bowman, Rafael Cabrera, Arthur Ehlers, Robert Engle, Tom Gamboa, Charles Hum, Frank McGowan, Joe McIlvaine, Don McShane, Ray Poitevint, John Stokoe, Ramon Vargas, Bill Werle.

PARK LOCATION—Memorial Stadium, 33rd Street, Ellerslie Avenue, 36th Street and Ednor Road.

Seating capacity—52,137

FIELD DIMENSIONS—Home plate to left field at foul line, 309 feet; to center field, 405 feet; to right field at foul line, 309 feet.

# BOSTON RED SOX

President—Thomas A. Yawkey

Executive Vice-President-General Manager—Richard H. O'Connell
Assistant General Manager—John W. Claiborne
Vice-President—Gene Kirby
Vice-President—Haywood C. Sullivan
Treasurer—John L. Harrington
Secretary—Joseph LaCour
Director, Minor League Clubs—Edward F. Kenney
Traveling Secretary—John J. Rogers
Director of Public Relations—William C. Crowley
Statistician-Assistant Director of Public Relations—
Richard L. Bresciani
Manager—Darrell D. Johnson
Club Physician—Dr. Thomas M. Tierney
Executive Offices—24 Jersey Street, Boston, Mass. 02215
Telephone—267-9440 (area code 617)

SCOUTS—Milton Bolling, Ray Boone, Mace Brown, George Digby, Howard (Danny) Doyle, Bill Enos, Earl Johnson, Eddie Kasko, Charles Koney, Donald Lee, Wi'fred Lefebvre, Don Lenhardt, Tommy McDonald, Felix Maldonado. Frank Malzone, Sam Mele, Frank (Bots) Nekola, Willie Paffen, Edward Scott, Matt Sczesny, Joe Stephenson, Larry Thomas, Charlie Wagner.

PARK LOCATION—Fenway Park, Jersey Street, Lansdowne Street and Ipswich Street.

Seating capacity—33,437

FIELD DIMENSIONS—Home plate to left field at foul line, 315 feet; to center field, 420 feet; to right field at foul line, 302 feet; average right field distance, 382 feet.

# CALIFORNIA ANGELS

### BOARD OF DIRECTORS

Gene Autry, Chairman of the Board; Harry Dalton, Arthur E. Patterson, Walton S. Reid, Forrest Shumway, A. Ray Smith, Clair L. Stout.

President—Arthur E. (Red) Patterson

Executive Vice-President-General Manager—Harry Dalton

Vice-President, Treasurer—Francis X. Leary

Consultant—Fred Haney

Assistant to President, Public Relations—Tom Seeberg

Stadium Operations Director—Dick Foster

Scouting Director—Walter Shannon

Minor League Director—Tom Sommers

Promotions, Season Sales Director—George Lederer

Ticket Manager—Carl Gordon

Sales and Marketing Director—Ed Munson

Traveling Secretary and Trainer—Freddie Frederico

Group Sales Director—Lynn Kirchmann

Publications Director—Mel Franks

Advertising Director—Tim Reilly

Administrative Asst., Minor Leagues—Chuck Franklin

Film Coordinator, Special Statistics—George Goodale

Special Assignment Scouts— Del Rice, Frank Lane

Manager—Richard H. Williams

Club Physician—Dr. Jules Rasinski

Executive Offices—Anaheim Stadium, 2000 State College Blvd., Anaheim, Calif. 92806

Telephone—634-2000 (area code 714)

SCOUTS—Loyd Christopher, E. R. (Bob) Clear, Larry Himes, Al Hollingsworth, Nicholas Kamzic, Gene Kerns, Al Kubski, Frank Lane, Johnny Neun, Del Rice, Ray Scarborough, Roy (Red) Smith, Jim Terrell, E. E. Whitsett, Walter Youse.

PARK LOCATION — Anaheim Stadium, 2000 State College Boulevard.

### Seating capacity—43,204

FIELD DIMENSIONS—Home plate to left field at foul line, 333 feet; to center field, 404 feet; to right field at foul line, 333 feet.

# CHICAGO WHITE SOX

Chairman of the Board—Wm. O. DeWitt

President—Bill Veeck
Vice-President—Roland Hemond
Treasurer—Leo Breen
Secretary—Newton P. Frye, Jr.
Business Manager—Rudie Schaffer
Director of Public Relations—Don Unferth
Traveling Secretary—Glen Rosenbaum
Farm Director—C. V. Davis
General Sales Manager for TV—Marshall Black
Manager—Paul Richards
Club Physicians—Drs. Edwin Feldman, William Meltzer,
and Sid J. Shafer
Executive Offices—Comiskey Park, Dan Ryan at 35th Street,
Chicago, Ill. 60616
Telephone—924-1000 (area code 312)

SCOUTS — Carl Ackerman, Bruce Andrew, Joe Begani, Al Brown, Sam Hairston, Bennie Huffman, Gary Johnson, Bill Kimball, Leo Labossiere, Bill Lentini, Dario Lodigiana, Al Lynch, Pete Milito, Mel Preibisch, Steve Vrablik, Walter Widmayer.

PARK LOCATION — Comiskey Park, Dan Ryan at 35th Street, Chicago, Ill. 60616.

Seating capacity—44,492

FIELD DIMENSIONS—Home plate to left field at foul line, 352 feet; to center field, 440 feet; to right field at foul line, 352 feet.

# CLEVELAND INDIANS

President—Alva T. Bonda
General Partner—Nick Mileti

General Manager—Phil Seghi
Director of Scouting and Minor League Operations—Bob Quinn
Secretary—Brooks M. Jones
Assistant Secretary—Theodore M. Garver
Vice-President and Treasurer—Dudley S. Blossom, III
Director of Stadium Operations—Daniel W. Zerbey
Public Relations Director—Randy Adamack
Traveling Secretary—Mike Seghi
Promotions Director—Jackie York
Director of Sales & Marketing—Carl Fazio, Jr.
Group Sales Director—Rich Rollins
Office Manager—Art Pease
Manager—Frank Robinson
Club Physician—Dr. Walter O. Lewin
Executive Offices—Cleveland Stadium, Cleveland, Ohio 44114
Telephone—861-1200 (area code 216)

SCOUTS — Willie Calvino, Daniel Carnevale, Jack Cassini, Merrill Combs, Harry Dorish, Red Gaskill, Leon Hamilton, Paul O'Dea, Dr. Bob Shupala.

PARK LOCATION—Cleveland Stadium, foot of West Third Street.

Seating capacity—76,713

FIELD DIMENSIONS—Home plate to left field at foul line, 320 feet; to center field, 400 feet; to right field at foul line, 320 feet.

# DETROIT TIGERS

Owner—John E. Fetzer

Executive Vice-President-General Manager—James A. Campbell
Consultant—Richard B. (Rick) Ferrell
Secretary-Treasurer—Alex Callam
Director of Public Relations—Hal Middlesworth
Director of Player Development—Walter A. (Hoot) Evers
Director of Player Procurement—William R. Lajoie
Coordinator of Scouting—Edward G. Katalinas
Director of Ticket Sales—William H. Willis
Director of Stadium Operations—Ralph Snyder
Auditor—William E. Haase
Traveling Secretary—Vince Desmond
Assistant Director of Public Relations—Bill A. Brown
Assistant Director Public Relations, Special Events—Lew Matlin
Assistant Director of Player Development—Dave Miller
Assistant Director Stadium Operations, Administration—
George Minnis
Assistant Directors Stadium Operations, Grounds & Maintenance—
Mike Fenell and Frank Feneck
Manager—Ralph Houk
Club Physician—Clarence Livingood, M. D.
Executive Offices—Tiger Stadium, Detroit, Mich. 48216
Telephone—962-4000 (area code 313)

SCOUTS—Wayne Blackburn, Gates Brown, James Miller, Frank Overmire, Bob Prentice, Frank Skaff, Jack Tighe, Richard Wiencek.

PARK LOCATION—Tiger Stadium, Michigan Avenue, Cochrane Avenue, Kaline Drive and Trumbull Avenue.

Seating capacity—54,226

FIELD DIMENSIONS—Home plate to left field at foul line, 340 feet; to center field, 440 feet; to right field at foul line, 325 feet.

# KANSAS CITY ROYALS

BOARD OF DIRECTORS—Joe Burke, William Deramus III, Charles Hughes, Ewing Kauffman, Mrs. Ewing Kauffman, Les Milgram, Earl Smith.

President—Ewing Kauffman
Executive Vice-President and General Manager—Joe Burke
Vice-President and Assistant General Manager—
James "Lou" Gorman
Vice-President for Operations—Spencer "Herk" Robinson
Vice-President and Legal Counsel—Phil Koury
Controller—Dale Rohr
Director of Public Relations—Dean Vogelaar
Director of Promotions and Assistant Public Relations Director—
Bryan Burns
Traveling Secretary—Bill Beck
Advertising/Group Sales—Bruce Carnahan
Ticket Manager—Al Marcum
Farm Director—John Schuerholz
Assistant Ticket Manager—Joe Grigoli
Manager—Whitey Herzog
Club Physician—Dr. Paul Meyer
Executive Offices—Royals Stadium, Harry S. Truman Sports
Complex
Mailing Address—P. O. Box 1969, Kansas City, Mo. 64141
Telephone—921-8000 (area code 816)

SCOUTS—Gary Blaylock, Al Diez, Tom Ferrick, Bill Fischer, Rosey Gilhousen, Art Lilly, Art Stewart.

PARK LOCATION—Royals Stadium, Harry S. Truman Sports Complex.

Seating capacity—40,762

FIELD DIMENSIONS—Home plate to left field at foul line, 330 feet; to center field, 410 feet; to right field at foul line, 330 feet.

# MILWAUKEE BREWERS

President, Chief Executive Officer—Allan H. (Bud) Selig

Chairman of the Board—Edmund B. Fitzgerald
DIRECTORS—Edmund B. Fitzgerald, Al'an H. Selig, Everett G. Smith, Roswell N. Stearns, Carlton P. Wilson.
Secretary—Bernard S. Kubale
Vice-President, Director of Baseball Operations—James S. Baumer
Vice-President, Administraton—Thomas J. Ferguson
Vice-President, Stadium & Broadcast Operations—Gabe Paul, Jr.
Vice-President, Marketing & Director of Public Relations—Richard Hackett
Treasurer, Controller, Assistant Secretary—Richard R. Hoffmann
Farm Director & Administrator of Scouting—Anthony C. Siegle
Director of Scouting—Dee Fondy
Director of Player Development—Al J. Widmar
Director of Information & Services—Tom Skibosh
Assistant Director of Stadium Operations—Jack Hutchinson
Advance and Group Sales—Steve Comte
Manager—Alex Grammas
Club Physician—Dr. Gary N. Guten

Executive Offices—Milwaukee Brewers Baseball Club, Inc., Milwaukee County Stadium, Milwaukee, Wis. 53214
Telephone—933-8650 (area code 414)

SCOUTS—Dick Bogard, Felix Delgado, Roland LeBlanc, Anton A. Roig.

PARK LOCATION — Milwaukee County Stadium, S. 44th Street off Bluemound Road.

Seating capacity—52,293

FIELD DIMENSIONS—Home plate to left field at foul line, 320 feet; to center field, 402 feet; to right field at foul line, 315 feet.

# MINNESOTA TWINS

Chairman of Board, President—Calvin R. Griffith

Vice-President-Assistant Treasurer—Mrs. Thelma Griffith Haynes
Vice-President, Secretary, Treasurer—Clark Griffith
Director—Eugene V. Young
Director—Wheelock Whitney
Vice-President—William S. Robertson
Vice-President—James K. Robertson
Vice-President-Farm Director—George Brophy
Vice-President-Traveling Secretary—Howard T. Fox, Jr.
Assistant Farm Director—Jim Rantz
Farm System Coordinator—Bruce Haynes
Controller—Jack Alexander
Director of Public Relations—Tom Mee
Director of Sales—Don Cassidy
Stadium Superintendent—Richard Ericson
Manager—Gene Mauch
Club Physicians—Dr. Leonard J. Michienzi and Dr. Harvey O'Phelan
Executive Offices—Metropolitan Stadium, 8001 Cedar Avenue
Bloomington, Minn. 55420
Telephone—854-4040 (area code 612)

SCOUTS—Floyd Baker, Zinn Beck, Otto Bluege, Ellis Clary, Edward Dunn, Jesse Flores, Jesse Flores, Jr., Angelo Giuliani, Lee Irwin, William Messmann, Marvin Olson, Carlos Pascual, Spencer (Red) Robbins, Stanley Rogers, Walter Via.

PARK LOCATION—Metropolitan Stadium, 8001 Cedar Avenue, Bloomington, Minn. 55420.

Seating capacity—45,919

FIELD DIMENSIONS—Home plate to left field at foul line, 330 feet; to center field, 410 feet; to right field at foul line, 330 feet.

# NEW YORK YANKEES

General Partner—George M. Steinbrenner II

Limited Partners—Harold Bowman, Michael Burke, Lester Crown, John Z. DeLorean, Thomas Evans, Michael Friedman, Edward Greenwald, Joseph A. W. Iglehart, Daniel McCarthy, John J. McMullen, James Nederlander, Francis J. "Steve" O'Neill, Gabe Paul, Albert L. Rosen, Edward Rosenthal, Marvin Warner, Charlotte Witkind.

President—Gabe Paul

Vice-President, Operations—Cedric Tallis

Controller—Eugene J. McHale

Special Assistant to the President and In-House Counsel—Joseph Garagiola, Jr.

Director, Minor League Operations—Patrick Nugent

Coordinator, Player Development and Scouting—Pat Gillick

Major League and Special Assignment Scouting—Birdie Tebbetts

Special Assignments—Whitey Ford

Stadium Manager—Patrick Kelly

Director of Publicity—Martin Appel

Director of Sales and Promotions—Barry M. Landers

Traveling Secretary and Statistician—Bill Kane

Ticket Director—Michael Rendine

Assistant Ticket Director—Jerry Waring

Director of Accounting—David Weidler

Director, Yankee Alumni Association—Judy Serra

Assistant to Director, Minor League Operations—Elliott Wahle

Director Emeritus, Speakers' Bureau—Jackie Farrell

Manager—Billy Martin

Club Physician—Dr. Edward Crane

Executive Offices—Yankee Stadium, Bronx, New York 10451

Telephone—293-4300 (area code 212)

SCOUTS—Al Cuccinello, Gustavo Escobar, Tom Greenwade, Eppy Guerrero, Roy Hamey, Lou Maguolo, Wayne Morgan, Frank O'Rourke, Jose Seda, Jerry Walker, Jack Warner, Dave Yoakum.

PARK LOCATION—Yankee Stadium, E. 161 St. and River Ave., Bronx, N. Y. 10451.

Ticket Information—293-6000 (area code 212)

Seating capacity—54,028

FIELD DIMENSIONS—Home plate to left field at foul line, 312 feet; to center field, 417 feet; to right field at foul line, 310 feet.

# OAKLAND A's

President—Charles O. Finley

Secretary and Treasurer—Charles O. Finley, Jr.
Controller—Chuck Cottonaro
Director of Minor League Operations—Syd Thrift
Director of Public Relations and Promotions—Carl Finley
Minor League Department—Norman Koselke
Ticket Manager—Lorraine Paulus
Traveling Secretary and Public Relations—Jim Bank
Manager—Chuck Tanner
Club Physician—Dr. Charles Hudson
Executive Offices—Oakland-Alameda County Coliseum, Oakland, Calif. 94621

Telephone—762-3100 (area code 415)

SCOUTS—Jim Guinn, Robert Nieman, Phil Pote, Fred J. Shaffer, Caesar Sinibaldi.

PARK LOCATION — Oakland-Alameda County Coliseum, Nimitz Freeway and Hegenberger Road.

Seating capacity—50,000.

FIELD DIMENSIONS—Home plate to left field at foul line, 330 feet; to center field, 400 feet; to right field at foul line, 330 feet.

# TEXAS RANGERS

Chairman of the Board—Bradford G. Corbett

Vice-President—Amon G. Carter, Jr.
Vice-President-Treasurer—Raymond D. Nasher
Vice-President-Secretary—William H. Seay
General Manager—Daniel F. O'Brien
Farm Director—Hal Keller
Assistant Farm Director—Joseph Klein
Assistant Treasurer-Business Affairs—Charles F. Wangner
Traveling Secretary-News Media Director—Burton S. Hawkins
Marketing Director, Promotions Director—Kip Horsburgh
Stadium Operations Director—John L. Welaj
Special Assignments—Del Wilber
Ticket Manager—Joseph L. Sullivan
Equipment and Clubhouse Manager—Joseph Macko
Manager—Frank Lucchesi
Club Physician—Dr. B. J. Mycoskie
Executive Offices—Arlington Stadium, P. O. Box 1111, 1500 Copeland Road, Arlington, Tex. 76010
Telephone—265-9101 (area code 817)

SCOUTS—Harley Anderson, Lee Ballanfant, Joseph Branzell, Paddy Cottrell, Joseph Lewis, Joseph Marchese.

PARK LOCATION—Arlington Stadium, 1500 Copeland Road, Arlington, Tex.

Seating capacity—35,698

FIELD DIMENSIONS—Home plate to left field, at foul line, 330 feet; to center field, 400 feet; to right field at foul line, 330 feet.

## BOSTON RED SOX—1975

Front row—Rice, Fisk, Petrocelli, Pesky, coach; Johnson, manager; Williams, coach; Zimmer, coach; Yastrzemski, Burleson, Lynn. Second row—Cerrone, equipment manager; Moss, trainer; Griffin, Heise, Doyle, Blackwell, Cooper, Montgomery, Evans, Beniquez, Carbo, Segui, Orlando, equipment manager. Third row—Miller, Drago, Tiant, Wise, Lee, Burton, Moret, Pole, Cleveland. In front—Naticchioni and Krall, batboys. Insert—Willoughby.

# EAST DIVISION

## Bosox Are Surprising Winners in East

### By PETER GAMMONS

It was a season woven from the fantasies of a madman.

Back on March 31, think where so many of the central characters were: Jim Rice, in the throes of a .133 spring training, wasn't wondering about playing regularly, only making the Red Sox; Fred Lynn, hitting .230, was apparently the opening day left fielder, with Rick Miller in center. Carlton Fisk was sitting at a house six blocks from Winter Haven's Chain O'Lakes Park, wondering, with his knee still unproven and a broken arm, if he might not just be "another Randy Hundley." Rick Wise's shoulder, which had kept him out most of 1974, still wasn't completely certain. That day the news had been Tony Conigliaro's big day against the Dodgers. Tony C would be returning to Fenway as the designated hitter.

Over in St. Petersburg, Jim Willoughby languished with the Cardinals' Tulsa farm club because the Cardinals wouldn't let him come to spring training with the major league club. In Palm Springs, Denny Doyle, knowing he was being replaced by rookie Jerry Remy, was asking to be traded by the Angels.

And the Red Sox? As the writers prepared their Sunday predictions, this was a team assigned to at best third place. A team, that in this mad, fantastic season, came very close to being world champions.

The story of this team is one of pieces coming together, of Doyle and Willoughby being acquired, Fisk's comeback at the right time and Wise's return as the staff leader, but more than anything it is one of an organization which has completely rebuilt its system in the last decade. The story revolved around Lynn and Rice, two young outfielders who may have put together the most memorable rookie duet in history.

Lynn very simply did what no one had ever done before him. In batting .331 with 21 homers, 105 RBIs and a league-leading 103 runs scored, he became the first player ever to be named Rookie of the Year and Most Valuable Player. This loping, sculptured 23-year-old center fielder from the University of Southern California was a class major league player from the day the previous September he first stepped on a major league field.

Rice was the basher, a huge, raw talent who may well be the game's next great righthanded power hitter. Unfortunately cast in Lynn's shadow, Rice batted .309, drove in 102 runs, scored 92 and once he moved from the DH spot to left field worked hard to become a good outfielder; in fact, he didn't make an error. Unfortunately the Red Sox had to play without him in the World Series; the 22-year-old slugger had broken his arm in Detroit September 21 and was out the rest of the way.

Lynn and Rice were the headliners, but many others that came from Ed Kenney and Haywood Sullivan's farm system developed: Rick Burleson, into the team's most indispensible player and a first-rate shortstop; Dwight Evans, from a nervous and injury-ridden first few months to a strong finish and fine effort in the Series; Cecil Cooper, who forced his way into the lineup in June and proceeded to hit .311.

Doyle, who came from the Angels June 13 to platoon with Doug Griffin and hit .310 in a Boston uniform, gave Boston a much-needed No. 2 hitter. Bernie Carbo went on his annual two-month tear in which he reached base more than 50 percent of the time and slugged at an .850 percentage.

The club struggled into June, but went through an important 9-4 road trip during which they acquired Doyle. In key series with their then-rival Yankees, the Red Sox took three out of four in each of two tough series the end of June and July, highlighted on July 27 in Shea Stadium with a 1-0 Bill Lee victory over Catfish Hunter.

After a two-week, 9-5 trip in August, what was left was holding off Baltimore, and when Wise, on Cooper's 10th-inning homer, beat Jim Palmer, 3-2, September 3, in Baltimore and Luis Tiant did the same to the Cy Young winner, 2-0, in Boston September 16, Boston's first divisional championship was assured. Which brings up the pitching. Statistically it wasn't much, but the trademark of this Red Sox team was that it won the games it had to win. Wise, the steadiest of the staff, Tiant, Lee, Rogelio Moret, Dick Pole, Reggie Cleveland and relievers Dick Drago and Willoughby always rose to the occasion.

The divisional crown was finally clinched September 27, as the Red Sox lost to Cleveland and the Orioles lost two to the Yankees. Then came the playoffs. Once again the Sox were the underdogs. El Tiante had recovered from back problems to come on in September, and he hurled a three-hitter in beating the A's, 7-1. In the second game, the Sox beat Rollie Fingers, 6-3, and when Wise and Drago had finished it, 5-3, in Oakland two days later, the Red Sox had won their eighth American League pennant.

Two veterans also made contributions—Rico Petrocelli and Carl Yastrzemski. Rico was bothered into late August by balance problems caused by a beaning the previous September. He had an outstanding final month and played well in the World Series.

Yastrzemski, now 36 years old, had shoulder problems and finished at .269 but starred in the field and at bat in the divisional playoffs and World Series.

The World Series then provided this basically young team with a stage for the world to see just how good they were. Again they were underdogs, and they almost won. Almost. . .

### SCORES OF BOSTON RED SOX' 1975 GAMES

| APRIL | | | Winner | Loser | APRIL | | | Winner | Loser |
|---|---|---|---|---|---|---|---|---|---|
| 8—Milw. | W | 5-2 | Tiant | Slaton | 26—At Det. | L | 2-3* | Hiller | Lee |
| 9—Milw. | L | 4-7 | Broberg | Lee | 27—At Det. | L | 4-5 | LaGrow | Wise |
| 11—At Balt. | W | 6-5† | Segui | Alexander | 30—Cleve. | L | 1-8 | G. Perry | Tiant |
| 12—At Balt. | W | 3-2§ | Cleveland | Jefferson | | | | Won 7, Lost 9 | |
| 13—At Balt. | L | 3-11 | Torrez | Tiant | | | | | |
| 15—At N. Y. | W | 5-3 | Lee | Hunter | MAY | | | | |
| 16—At N. Y. | W | 4-2 | Wise | Dobson | 1—Cleve. | W | 7-6 | Lee | J. Perry |
| 18—Balt. | L | 7-9 | Alexander | Cleveland | 3—Detroit | W | 12-2 | Wise | LaGrow |
| 20—Balt. | W | 10-2 | Tiant | Torrez | 5—At Cleve. | W | 7-5 | Tiant | J. Perry |
| 21—N. York | L | 1-12 | Dobson | Lee | 6—At Cleve. | W | 4-1 | Lee | Bosman |
| 22—N. York | L | 0-5 | Medich | Wise | 7—At Cleve. | W | 4-2 | Cleveland | Peterson |
| 23—N. York | W | 11-7 | Moret | Lyle | 9—At Calif. | W | 4-1 | Wise | Hassler |
| 25—At Det. | L | 0-1 | Lolich | Tiant | 10—At Calif. | L | 0-2 | Tanana | Tiant |

| MAY | | | Winner | Loser |
|---|---|---|---|---|
| 11—At Calif. | W | 5-2 | Lee | Singer |
| 12—At Oak. | L | 3-5 | Fingers | Segui |
| 13—At Oak. | L | 5-9 | Holtzman | Wise |
| 15—Kan. C. | L | 0-3 | Busby | Tiant |
| 16—Kan. C. | L | 2-5 | Leonard | Lee |
| 17—Kan. C. | L | 3-5 | Fitzmorris | Cleveland |
| 18—Kan. C. | W | 4-2 | Wise | Briles |
| 19—Oakland | W | 10-5 | Tiant | Odom |
| 20—Oakland | W | 7-0 | Lee | Blue |
| 21—Oakland | W | 7-3 | Cleveland | Holtzman |
| 22—Calif. | L | 3-6 | Singer | Wise |
| 23—Calif. | W | 6-1 | Tiant | Ryan |
| 24—Calif. | W | 6-0 | Lee | Hassler |
| 25—Calif. | L | 1-6 | Figueroa | Cleveland |
| 26—At Texas | W | 7-5 | Wise | Foucault |
| 28—At Texas | W | 4-1 | Lee | Jenkins |
| 30—At Minn. | L | 3-4 | Goltz | Segui |
| 31—At Minn. | W | 12-8 | Moret | Burgmeier |
| | | | **Won 16, Lost 9** | |

| JUNE | | | | |
|---|---|---|---|---|
| 1—At Minn. | W | 11-9 | Tiant | Hughes |
| 2—Chicago | L | 2-9 | Bahnsen | Lee |
| 3—Chicago | W | 4-0 | Pole | Allen |
| 4—Chicago | W | 7-6 | Moret | Gossage |
| 6—Minn. | W | 13-10 | Tiant | Pazik |
| 7—Minn. | W | 3-1 | Lee | Corbin |
| 8—Minn. | L | 5-7 | Goltz | Pole |
| 9—Texas | L | 4-12 | Brown | Wise |
| 10—Texas | L | 3-8 | Jenkins | Tiant |
| 11—At Chi. | W | 9-7x | Moret | Gossage |
| 12—At Chi. | L | 2-9 | Kaat | Burton |
| 13—At K. C. | W | 10-4 | Wise | Fitzmorris |
| 13—At K C | L | 5-6 | Bird | Pole |
| 14—At K. C. | W | 4-3 | Tiant | Pattin |
| 15—At K. C. | W | 8-7 | Lee | McDaniel |
| 16—At Det. | W | 6-2‡ | Cleveland | Walker |
| 17—At Det. | W | 7-6 | Wise | LaGrow |
| 18—At Det. | W | 15-1 | Tiant | Coleman |
| 20—At Balt. | W | 4-3‡ | Drago | Miller |
| 21—At Balt. | L | 0-3 | Palmer | Pole |
| 22—At Balt. | L | 0-3 | Cuellar | Wise |
| 22—At Balt. | W | 5-1 | Tiant | Alexander |
| 23—Cleve. | L | 3-11 | Raich | Burton |
| 24—Cleve. | L | 6-8 | Buskey | Drago |
| 25—Cleve. | L | 5-8 | Harrison | Pole |
| 26—N. York | W | 6-1 | Tiant | Dobson |
| 27—N. York | W | 9-1 | Wise | Gura |
| 28—N. York | L | 6-8 | Tidrow | Cleveland |
| 29—N. York | W | 3-2 | Moret | Hunter |
| 30—Balt. | W | 5-2 | Pole | Palmer |
| 30—Balt. | L | 2-8 | Alexander | Tiant |
| | | | **Won 18, Lost 13** | |

| JULY | | | | |
|---|---|---|---|---|
| 1—Balt. | L | 6-10 | Jackson | Cleveland |
| 2—At Milw. | W | 6-3 | Wise | Castro |
| 2—At Milw. | L | 3-4 | Broberg | Lee |
| 3—At Milw. | L | 2-3* | Austin | Segui |
| 4—At Cleve. | L | 2-3 | Raich | Tiant |
| 5—At Cleve. | L | 2-12 | Harrison | Barr |
| 6—At Cleve. | W | 5-3 | Lee | Bibby |
| 6—At Cleve. | L | 10-11 | Beene | Cleveland |
| 7—Minn. | W | 6-3 | Wise | Hughes |
| 8—Minn. | W | 6-5 | Cleveland | Johnson |
| 9—Minn. | W | 9-8 | Segui | Burgmeier |
| 10—Texas | W | 8-7 | Cleveland | Perry |
| 11—Texas | W | 11-8 | Burton | Thomas |
| 12—Texas | W | 10-4 | Tiant | Jenkins |
| 13—Texas | W | 7-5 | Wise | Hargan |
| 17—Kan. C. | W | 8-3 | Tiant | Fitzmorris |
| 18—Kan. C. | W | 9-3 | Lee | Busby |
| 19—At Texas | W | 8-0 | Wise | Hands |
| 20—At Texas | L | 5-10 | Wright | Moret |
| 20—At Texas | W | 3-2 | Cleveland | Hargan |

| JULY | | | Winner | Loser |
|---|---|---|---|---|
| 21—At Texas | L | 0-6 | Jenkins | Tiant |
| 22—At Minn. | W | 5-4 | Lee | Goltz |
| 23—At Minn. | W | 4-2 | Moret | Hughes |
| 24—At Minn. | W | 6-2 | Wise | Decker |
| 25—At N. Y. | L | 6-8 | May | Tiant |
| 26—At N. Y. | W | 4-2 | Cleveland | Dobson |
| 27—At N. Y. | W | 1-0 | Lee | Hunter |
| 27—At N. Y. | W | 6-0 | Moret | Martinez |
| 28—Milw. | W | 7-6 | Willoughby | Murphy |
| 29—Milw. | L | 0-4 | Colborn | Segui |
| 30—Milw. | L | 2-6 | Slaton | Cleveland |
| 31—Detroit | W | 3-2* | Lee | Reynolds |
| 31—Detroit | W | 6-1 | Moret | Lemanczyk |
| | | | **Won 22, Lost 11** | |

| AUGUST | | | | |
|---|---|---|---|---|
| 1—Detroit | W | 8-7 | Willoughby | Pentz |
| 2—Detroit | W | 7-2 | Wise | Ruhle |
| 3—Detroit | W | 6-4 | Cleveland | Walker |
| 4—Balt. | L | 8-12 | Alexander | Willoughby |
| 5—Balt. | L | 0-3 | Palmer | Tiant |
| 6—At Milw. | W | 5-2 | Willoughby | Murphy |
| 7—At Milw. | W | 4-2 | Wise | Slaton |
| 8—At Oak. | L | 2-3 | Holtzman | Cleveland |
| 9—At Oak. | W | 7-2 | Lee | Siebert |
| 10—At Oak. | W | 5-3 | Tiant | Bosman |
| 11—At Oak. | L | 3-4 | Blue | Moret |
| 12—At Calif. | W | 8-2 | Wise | Hockenbery |
| 13—At Calif. | L | 3-8 | Figueroa | Cleveland |
| 14—At Calif. | L | 3-5 | Singer | Lee |
| 15—At Chi. | W | 3-2 | Tiant | Jefferson |
| 16—At Chi. | W | 5-0 | Moret | Wood |
| 17—At Chi. | L | 2-6 | Hamilton | Wise |
| 17—At Chi. | W | 4-3† | Willoughby | Gossage |
| 19—At K. C. | W | 5-0 | Lee | Fitzmorris |
| 20—At K. C. | L | 1-3 | Leonard | Tiant |
| 22—Chicago | W | 2-1 | Moret | Osteen |
| 23—Chicago | L | 4-6 | Jefferson | Wise |
| 24—Chicago | W | 6-1 | Lee | Wood |
| 26—Calif. | L | 2-8 | Figueroa | Tiant |
| 27—Calif. | W | 6-2 | Moret | Singer |
| 29—Oakland | W | 6-1 | Wise | Bahnsen |
| 30—Oakland | L | 6-7* | Fingers | Drago |
| 31—Oakland | L | 6-8 | Fingers | Segui |
| | | | **Won 16, Lost 12** | |

| SEPTEMBER | | | | |
|---|---|---|---|---|
| 1—N. York | L | 2-4 | Medich | Moret |
| 2—N. York | W | 7-4 | Cleveland | Dobson |
| 3—At Balt. | W | 3-2* | Wise | Palmer |
| 4—At Balt. | W | 3-1 | Pole | Torrez |
| 5—At Milw. | L | 2-4 | Broberg | Lee |
| 6—At Milw. | W | 20-6 | Moret | Travers |
| 7—At Milw. | W | 6-3 | Cleveland | Colborn |
| 7—At Milw. | L | 3-7 | Travers | Pole |
| 8—At Cleve. | L | 1-4 | Hood | Wise |
| 9—At Cleve. | L | 2-3* | Waits | Lee |
| 10—Detroit | W | 7-4 | Moret | Ruhle |
| 10—Detroit | L | 3-5 | Arroyo | Willoughby |
| 11—Detroit | W | 3-1 | Tiant | Lemanczyk |
| 13—Milw. | L | 6-9 | Broberg | Wise |
| 13—Milw. | W | 6-3 | Cleveland | Travers |
| 14—Milw. | W | 8-6 | Willoughby | Murphy |
| 15—Milw. | W | 9-7 | Moret | Colborn |
| 16—Balt. | W | 2-0 | Tiant | Palmer |
| 17—Balt. | L | 2-5 | Torrez | Wise |
| 19—At Det. | W | 7-5 | Pole | Glynn |
| 20—At Det. | L | 1-5 | Lolich | Tiant |
| 21—At Det. | W | 6-5 | Drago | Pentz |
| 22—At N. Y. | W | 6-4 | Wise | Guidry |
| 26—Cleve. | W | 4-0 | Tiant | Eckersley |
| 26—Cleve. | W | 4-0 | Cleveland | Hood |
| 27—Cleve. | L | 2-5 | Waits | Wise |
| 28—Cleve. | L | 4-11 | Raich | Pole |
| | | | **Won 16, Lost 11** | |

* 10 innings.  † 11 innings.  ‡ 12 innings.  § 13 innings.  x 14 innings.

BALTIMORE ORIOLES—1975

Front row—Bumbry, Shopay, Frey, coach; Hunter, coach; Weaver, manager; Bamberger, coach; Staller, coach; Davis, May. Second row—Reid, equipment manager; Jackson, Singleton, Torrez, Grimsley, Garland, Northrup, Duncan, Robinson, Palmer, Hendricks, Salvon, trainer. Third row—Miller, Nordbrook, Cuellar, Belanger, Jefferson, Grich, Baylor, DeCinces, Alexander, Blair. In front—Cashen, batboy.

# Orioles Stumble at Wire

### By JIM HENNEMAN

Coming from off the pace was getting to be an Oriole trademark. In 1973, they marked time until mid-August then went on a 14-game winning streak that disposed of all pretenders to the American League's East Division title by September 1.

A year later they dragged anchor even longer, falling two games under .500 on August 28, then ripped off 10 straight wins and finished with 28 victories in the last 34 games to claim their fifth divisional title in six years.

Little wonder then that most of the American League remained cautious and the Orioles remained optimistic right up to the bitter end of the 1975 race.

It was deemed too early to worry when Earl Weaver's club lost 11 out of 12 in May and fell into last place.

And when they were 9½ games out in early August, the memories of the previous two years remained vivid.

But it wasn't to be this time. They went to the well once too often, and when the season finally ended in the midst of the East Coast monsoon season, the Orioles were relegated to second place.

Despite another furious rush to the wire (they won 15 of 18 at one point), the Orioles were unable to overtake Boston for two reasons—their inability to win early in the season, and their failure in head-to-head combat with the Red Sox in September.

When the bell tolled for the last time on the next-to-last day of the season, Weaver preferred to give the Red Sox credit rather than fault his club, which rode a trail of peaks and valleys all season long.

"We did what we had to do in order to win," Weaver said, citing the Orioles' effort after the All-Star Game, when they had the best won-lost record in baseball (49-25, .662). "But the Red Sox also did what they had to do. The time has come to give them some credit. Their pitching staff did a great job down the stretch."

However, it must be pointed out that the Orioles simply dug too deep a hole early in the season.

Despite several outstanding individual performances, most notably by Jim Palmer, who won his second Cy Young Award in three years; Mike Torrez, who became a 20-game winner for the first time; Ken Singleton, whose .300 average reflected his consistency; Lee May and Don Baylor, the Orioles rarely combined solid hitting with good pitching.

When the final statistics came out, Baltimore showed the best ERA in the league (3.17), but pitching failures as much as anything else accounted for the early slump. Most of the problems centered around the bullpen, which had a 1-9 record (with no saves) and a 5.25 ERA nearly two months into the campaign.

It wasn't until the arrival of Dyar Miller, recalled from Rochester in mid-July, that the bullpen provided adequate late-inning relief.

May, acquired in the off-season from Houston, performed as expected, with 20 home runs and 99 runs batted in and Baylor produced 25 home runs and 76 RBIs, both personal highs, to key, along with Singleton, an attack that struggled throughout.

Palmer was brilliant as he rubbed out the memory of an injury-plagued 1974 season, rebounding from a 7-12 record to post a 23-11 mark and lead the major leagues in ERA (2.09) and shutouts (10). He broke numerous club records enroute and set several personal highs while winning 20 games for the fifth time in six years, and maintaining a lifetime percentage of .655 (152-80).

Torrez, who was acquired with Singleton from Montreal, more than lived up to expectations with a 20-9 record and a 3.06 ERA. His won-lost percentage of .690 was the best in the league as he solidified himself behind Palmer to give the Orioles the best 1-2 punch in the circuit.

There were, of course, some major disappointments. Brooks Robinson, as gilt-edged as ever defensively, had the worst year of his career at the plate, hitting .201.

Paul Blair started and finished strong, but hit only .144 in the middle three months to finish with a .218 mark.

Ross Grimsley lost eight of his first nine decisions and despite a 9-5 finish he fell far below his 18-13 mark of 1974, and ended the season in the bullpen. With righthander Paul Mitchell virtually assured a starting spot in the 1976 rotation, it could be that the Orioles will groom Grimsley for bullpen duty.

The keystone combination of Mark Belanger and Bobby Grich helped the Orioles lead the league in fielding (.983) and double plays (175). Along with Robinson and Blair they gave the Orioles four Golden Glove winners for the third straight year, a feat unmatched in the history of the awards.

Grich's final offensive totals of .260, 13 home runs and 57 runs batted in did not reach expectations, but he became the first second baseman in history to successfully handle over 900 chances for three straight years.

Despite their deficiencies in 1975, the Orioles still have a lot of talent. They could use more lefthanded hitting and the bullpen could stand bolstering, but overall the nucleus is there for the Orioles to bounce back in 1976. Their pitching and defense almost guarantee them contending status.

But they'll need comebacks by Robinson and Blair, or help via off-season trades, if they have any thoughts of dethroning the Red Sox.

### SCORES OF BALTIMORE ORIOLES' 1975 GAMES

| APRIL | | | Winner | Loser | APRIL | | | Winner | Loser |
|---|---|---|---|---|---|---|---|---|---|
| 10—At Det. | W | 10-0 | Palmer | Coleman | 29—Detroit | L | 2-4* | Walker | Grimsley |
| 11—Boston | L | 5-6‡ | Segui | Alexander | 30—At N.Y. | L | 4-6 | Lyle | Jackson |
| 12—Boston | L | 2-3§ | Cleveland | Jefferson | | | **Won 7, Lost 9** | | |
| 13—Boston | W | 11-3 | Torrez | Tiant | **MAY** | | | | |
| 15—Milw. | L | 1-7 | Champion | Palmer | 1—At N.Y. | L | 0-5 | Hunter | Palmer |
| 16—Milw. | W | 2-0 | Cuellar | Slaton | 2—At Cleve. | L | 3-4 | Eckersley | Johnson |
| 18—At Bos. | W | 9-7 | Alexander | Cleveland | 3—At Cleve. | L | 1-6 | Peterson | Grimsley |
| 20—At Bos. | L | 2-10 | Tiant | Torrez | 4—At Cleve. | W | 11-1 | Torrez | G. Perry |
| 22—At Milw. | W | 1-0 | Palmer | Broberg | 4—At Cleve. | L | 3-4† | Buskey | Jefferson |
| 23—At Milw. | L | 5-8 | Rodriguez | Reynolds | 5—N. York | W | 3-1 | Palmer | Hunter |
| 26—Cleve. | L | 0-3 | G. Perry | Grimsley | 7—N. York | W | 4-3 | Cuellar | Medich |
| 26—Cleve. | W | 3-2 | Torrez | Bosman | 9—Minn. | L | 2-5 | Hughes | Grimsley |
| 27—Cleve. | W | 6-1 | Palmer | J. Perry | 10—Minn. | W | 8-6 | Torrez | Corbin |
| 28—Detroit | L | 3-5 | Coleman | Cuellar | 11—Minn. | L | 4-6 | Blyleven | Cuellar |

**MAY**

| Date | | Score | Winner | Loser |
|---|---|---|---|---|
| 11—Minn. | W | 9-3 | Palmer | Pazik |
| 13—Chicago | W | 3-2 | Grimsley | Kaat |
| 14—Chicago | W | 3-2 | Torrez | Forster |
| 16—Calif. | W | 1-0 | Palmer | Tanana |
| 16—Calif. | L | 2-3 | Figueroa | Cuellar |
| 17—Calif. | L | 3-6 | Singer | Garland |
| 18—Calif. | L | 1-5 | Ryan | Torrez |
| 19—At Chi. | L | 1-2 | Bahnsen | Alexander |
| 21—At Chi. | W | 6-2 | Palmer | Osteen |
| 22—At Chi. | L | 1-2 | Kaat | Cuellar |
| 23—At K. C. | L | 1-2 | Fitzmorris | Grimsley |
| 24—At K. C. | L | 4-5 | Pattin | Garland |
| 25—At K. C. | L | 1-9 | Busby | Palmer |
| 26—At Oak. | L | 5-6† | Fingers | Alexander |
| 27—At Oak. | L | 2-4 | Todd | Grimsley |
| 28—At Oak. | L | 0-5 | Blue | Torrez |
| 30—At Calif. | W | 5-0 | Palmer | Figueroa |
| 31—At Calif. | W | 1-0 | Cuellar | Singer |

Won 11, Lost 17

**JUNE**

| Date | | Score | Winner | Loser |
|---|---|---|---|---|
| 1—At Calif. | L | 0-1 | Ryan | Grimsley |
| 3—Texas | W | 6-3 | Torrez | Hargan |
| 4—Texas | L | 2-3‡ | Brown | Jackson |
| 6—Kan. C. | W | 3-2† | Jackson | Pattin |
| 7—Kan. C. | W | 7-3 | Torrez | Leonard |
| 8—Kan. C. | W | 1-0 | Palmer | Busby |
| 9—Oakland | L | 3-4z | Lindblad | Miller |
| 10—Oakland | L | 0-3 | Perry | Grimsley |
| 11—At Texas | W | 9-8* | Miller | Thomas |
| 12—At Texas | W | 7-1 | Palmer | Bibby |
| 13—At Minn. | L | 3-7 | Goltz | Cuellar |
| 14—At Minn. | W | 7-0 | Grimsley | Hughes |
| 15—At Minn. | L | 4-5 | Corbin | Torrez |
| 16—At Cleve. | W | 8-3 | Palmer | Bibby |
| 17 At Cleve. | W | 5-3 | Cuellar | Raich |
| 18—At Cleve. | W | 13-6 | Grimsley | Peterson |
| 20—Boston | L | 3-4‡ | Drago | Miller |
| 21—Boston | W | 3-0 | Palmer | Pole |
| 22—Boston | W | 3-0 | Cuellar | Wise |
| 22—Boston | L | 1-5 | Tiant | Alexander |
| 23—N. York | L | 1-6 | Medich | Grimsley |
| 24—N. York | L | 1-3 | Hunter | Torrez |
| 25—N. York | L | 1-2 | Lyle | Palmer |
| 26—Detroit | L | 5-6 | Lolich | Alexander |
| 27—Detroit | W | 3-2 | Grimsley | Hiller |
| 28—Detroit | W | 7-4 | Torrez | Coleman |
| 29—Detroit | W | 2-1 | Cuellar | Bare |
| 30—At Bos. | L | 2-5 | Pole | Palmer |
| 30—At Bos. | W | 8-2 | Alexander | Tiant |

Won 16, Lost 13

**JULY**

| Date | | Score | Winner | Loser |
|---|---|---|---|---|
| 1—At Bos. | W | 10-6 | Jackson | Cleveland |
| 2—At Det. | W | 13-5 | Torrez | Walker |
| 3—At Det. | L | 5-9 | Coleman | Garland |
| 4—At N. Y. | W | 5-4 | Palmer | Hunter |
| 5—At N. Y. | W | 5-2 | Grimsley | May |
| 6—At N. Y. | L | 1-6 | Dobson | Cuellar |
| 8—At Calif. | W | 8-5* | Alexander | Ryan |
| 9—At Calif. | L | 2-3 | Tanana | Grimsley |
| 10—At Calif. | W | 7-3 | Cuellar | Figueroa |
| 11—At Oak. | W | 4-0 | Torrez | Blue |
| 12—At Oak. | L | 1-7 | Perry | Palmer |
| 13—At Oak. | L | 3-4 | Holtzman | Grimsley |
| 17—Minn. | W | 6-3‡ | Jackson | Campbell |
| 18—Minn. | W | 9-6 | Cuellar | Goltz |
| 19—Oakland | W | 3-2 | Mitchell | Blue |
| 19—Oakland | W | 5-1 | Grimsley | Perry |
| 20—Oakland | L | 2-5 | Fingers | Alexander |
| 21—Oakland | W | 6-2 | Torrez | Holtzman |
| 22—Calif. | W | 8-3 | Cuellar | Ryan |
| 23—Calif. | L | 0-1 | Tanana | Palmer |

**JULY**

| Date | | Score | Winner | Loser |
|---|---|---|---|---|
| 24—At Milw. | W | 10-7 | Garland | Broberg |
| 25—At Milw. | L | 2-5 | Colborn | Torrez |
| 26—At Milw. | W | 4-0 | Cuellar | Slaton |
| 27—At Milw. | W | 7-4 | Palmer | Currence |
| 27—At Milw. | W | 11-6* | Miller | Austin |
| 28—Cleve. | L | 5-7* | Waits | Alexander |
| 29—Cleve. | W | 7-1 | Torrez | Hood |
| 30—Cleve. | L | 1-3 | Eckersley | Cuellar. |

Won 18, Lost 10

**AUGUST**

| Date | | Score | Winner | Loser |
|---|---|---|---|---|
| 1—Milw. | W | 6-4 | Palmer | Champion |
| 1—Milw. | W | 3-1 | Grimsley | Hausman |
| 2—Milw. | W | 6-1 | Torrez | Colborn |
| 3—Milw. | L | 1-4 | Slaton | Cuellar |
| 4—At Bos. | W | 12-8 | Alexander | Willoughby |
| 5—At Bos. | W | 3-0 | Palmer | Tiant |
| 6—At Det. | W | 4-2 | Torrez | LaGrow |
| 6—At Det. | W | 8-2 | Grimsley | Lemanczyk |
| 7—At Det. | W | 7-6* | Miller | Reynolds |
| 8—At Chi. | W | 7-4 | Alexander | Wood |
| 9—At Chi. | W | 12-6 | Palmer | Osteen |
| 10—At Chi. | L | 2-3 | Gossage | Jackson |
| 11—Kan. C. | W | 4-0 | Cuellar | Busby |
| 12—Kan. C. | L | 2-4* | Bird | Miller |
| 13—Kan. C. | W | 3-0 | Palmer | Pattin |
| 15—Texas | L | 6-10 | Foucault | Garland |
| 15—Texas | W | 13-1 | Cuellar | Wright |
| 16—Texas | L | 1-5 | Perry | Grimsley |
| 17—Texas | W | 4-0 | Palmer | Perzanowski |
| 18—At Minn. | L | 1-6 | Goltz | Torrez |
| 19—At Minn. | L | 2-5 | Blyleven | Cuellar |
| 20—At Minn. | W | 3-2 | Grimsley | Hughes |
| 21—At Texas | W | 4-2y | Miller | Foucault |
| 22—At Texas | W | 8-5 | Torrez | Perzanowski |
| 23—At Texas | L | 0-1 | Jenkins | Cuellar |
| 24—At Texas | L | 7-8 | Foucault | Palmer |
| 26—At K. C. | L | 3-4 | Leonard | Palmer |
| 26—At K. C. | W | 3-2 | Alexander | Busby |
| 27—At K. C. | W | 4-2 | Torrez | Splittorff |
| 28—Chicago | W | 2-1 | Cuellar | Wood |
| 29—Chicago | L | 2-4 | Kaat | Grimsley |
| 30—Chicago | W | 4-2 | Palmer | Jefferson |

Won 21, Lost 11

**SEPTEMBER**

| Date | | Score | Winner | Loser |
|---|---|---|---|---|
| 2—Cleve. | W | 3-2* | Cuellar | Reynolds |
| 2—Cleve. | L | 1-2 | Bibby | Alexander |
| 3—Boston | L | 2-3* | Wise | Palmer |
| 4—Boston | L | 1-3 | Pole | Torrez |
| 5—N. York | W | 5-4 | Mitchell | Medich |
| 5—N. York | W | 2-1 | Grimsley | Gura |
| 6—N. York | W | 7-6§ | Jackson | Lyle |
| 7—N. York | L | 0-2 | Hunter | Palmer |
| 8—At Milw. | W | 6-2 | Torrez | Slaton |
| 9—At Milw. | W | 9-1 | Alexander | Broberg |
| 10—At Cleve. | L | 1-7 | Eckersley | Cuellar |
| 10—At Cleve. | W | 6-5x | Miller | Reynolds |
| 11—At Cleve. | W | 10-2 | Palmer | Harrison |
| 12—At Det. | W | 6-4† | Torrez | Coleman |
| 13—At Det. | W | 8-0 | Alexander | Lolich |
| 14—At Det. | W | 9-3 | Mitchell | Bare |
| 16—At Bos. | L | 0-2 | Tiant | Palmer |
| 17—At Bos. | W | 5-2 | Torrez | Wise |
| 19—Milw. | W | 6-5 | Miller | Murphy |
| 20—Milw. | W | 5-4 | Garland | Colborn |
| 21—Milw. | W | 3-0 | Torrez | Broberg |
| 24—Detroit | W | 8-1 | Palmer | Coleman |
| 27—At N. Y. | L | 2-3* | Hunter | Torrez |
| 27—At N. Y. | L | 3-7 | Medich | Cuellar |
| 28—At N. Y. | W | 3-0 | Palmer | May |
| 28—At N. Y. | L | 2-3 | Gura | Flanagan |

Won 17, Lost 9

* 10 innings.  † 11 innings.  ‡ 12 innings.  § 13 innings.  x September 1 game (part of doubleheader) at Baltimore transferred to Cleveland (13 innings).  y 14 innings.  z 15 innings.

**1975 NEW YORK YANKEES**

NEW YORK YANKEES—1975

Front row—Williams, Dempsey, Munson, Wright, coach; Howser, coach; Virdon, manager; Howard, coach; Ford, coach; Boyer, coach; Alomar, White, Mason. Second row—Monahan, trainer; Whitfield, Dineen, Maddox, Pagan, Nettles, Gura, Hunter, Brinkman, Stanley, Bonds, Sheehy, equipment manager. Third row—Dobson, Chambliss, Blomberg, Lyle, Medich, Tidrow, Oliver, Herrmann, Johnson, Kane, traveling secretary. Front—Bunch and Maldarelli, batboys. Missing—May, Piniella.

# Hunter Wins, Yankees Don't

### By PHIL PEPE

To tell the story of the Yankees' disappointing season, one needs to focus on three terrible days in June that will live in infamy for Yankee fans.

This was to have been the year the Yankees recaptured the glory days of the 1950s and 1960s. The signing of Catfish Hunter after the biggest manhunt in baseball history and the acquisition of Bobby Bonds in one of the biggest one-for-one trades in baseball history promised to provide the impetus for another Yankee championship.

The season turned out, instead, to be one of the most disappointing in Yankee history; and the sad story can be told by events of those three days in June.

June 7—Bobby Bonds falls down in the outfield making a game-saving catch against the White Sox in Chicago. The injury, not considered serious at the time, proved to be disastrous. At the time of his injury, in the Yankees' 51st game, Bonds was leading the American League in home runs (15) and RBIs (45). He would play hurt the remainder of the year, never again getting to the top of the list in either category.

June 13—Elliott Maddox falls in the wet Shea Stadium outfield and tears the cartilage in his knee. At the time of his injury, he was batting .307 in 55 games, had scored 36 runs, driven in 23, stolen nine bases. He would not play again for the remainder of the season, and the Yankees would not only miss his bat, but his defense.

June 27—Rick Wise beats the Yankees, 9-1, in Fenway Park, knocking New York out of first place, never to return.

In microcosm, that was the Yankee season. Toss in injuries to Ron Blomberg (shoulder) and Lou Piniella (inner ear infection) and the picture is complete. Maddox, Blomberg and Piniella were the Yankees' three top hitters in 1974. Each a .300 hitter, they had combined to play in 367 games, get 381 hits, score 185 runs, hit 22 homers, drive in 163 runs. In 1975, they played in 163 games, got 133 hits, scored 61 runs, hit five homers, drove in 62 runs. It was too much to lose.

Perhaps the most frustrating part of it all is that three Yankees, Thurman Munson, Graig Nettles and Chris Chambliss, had their best years in '75.

Munson was superb as the team's cleanup hitter, his .318 average being his highest in six years as a Yankee regular and placing him third in the league's batting race. He was also among the leaders with 102 RBIs, his first time over the century mark.

Nettles had personal highs in batting (.267) and RBIs (91), while belting 21 homers.

Chambliss was a .300 hitter (.304) for the first time, had career highs in doubles (38) and RBIs (72), and slammed nine home runs.

Bobby Bonds, playing on one leg most of the year, had creditable marks of 85 RBIs, 93 runs, a .270 average, 32 homers and 30 stolen bases, the first player in baseball history to have three 30-30 seasons in homers and steals.

And there were no regrets over the $3.2 million the Yankees shelled out for Catfish Hunter.

"He was worth every penny," said club president Gabe Paul. "If he went on the open market again this year, he would bring the same amount he brought a year ago. When we got him, we said he would be worth it if he won 20 games. Well, he did that and more."

Hunter won 23 and lost 14, just two games poorer than his Cy Young Award-winning season with Oakland the year before. He completed 30 games, the most by any AL pitcher since Bob Feller's 36 in 1946, and he beat his former Oakland teammates four times in four starts, completing all four games, holding them to three runs and without an extra base hit.

"There is no doubt in my mind," said Reggie Jackson. "Hunter is the best pitcher in baseball."

Still, there were too many negatives. As a team, the Yankees hit only 110 homers and had only 20 saves from the bullpen. Doc Medich and Pat Dobson, who won 38 games between them in '74, won only 27 in '75. And Sparky Lyle, with nine wins and 15 saves in '74, slipped to five and six in '75.

A season that began with promise and hope and Bill Virdon as manager, ended with despair and disappointment and Billy Martin as manager. Hired on August 2, with the Yankees showing a 53-51 record, Martin won 30 and lost 26, but in fairness to him, the race was over by then. Billy watched and learned and promised things would be different in 1976.

They will for two reasons. The Yankees return home to remodeled Yankee Stadium. The new park will help, but reconstruction and a paint job satisfies fans for just so long.

There will be new faces in pinstripes in '76. Three major trades were made after the season ended. Dobson went to Cleveland for outfielder Oscar Gamble, Medich was dealt to the Pirates for pitchers Dock Ellis and Ken Brett and infielder Willie Randolph and, in a shocker, Bonds was traded to the Angels for outfielder Mickey Rivers and pitcher Ed Figueroa.

The season will start again with hope and promise, but it also starts with impatient Yankee fans wondering when hope will turn to reality.

### SCORES OF NEW YORK YANKEES' 1975 GAMES

| APRIL | | | Winner | Loser | APRIL | | | Winner | Loser |
|---|---|---|---|---|---|---|---|---|---|
| 8—At Cleve. | L | 3-5 | G. Perry | Medich | 29—Cleve. | L | 1-3 | Hood | Gura |
| 11—Detroit | L | 3-5 | Lolich | Hunter | 30—Balt. | W | 6-4 | Lyle | Jackson |
| 12—Detroit | L | 2-7 | Ruhle | Dobson | | | **Won 9, Lost 10** | | |
| 13—Detroit | W | 6-0 | Medich | Walker | | | | | |
| 13—Detroit | L | 2-5 | LaGrow | May | **MAY** | | | | |
| 15—Boston | L | 3-5 | Lee | Hunter | 1—Balt. | W | 5-0 | Hunter | Palmer |
| 16—Boston | L | 2-4 | Wise | Dobson | 2—At Milw. | L | 2-4 | Champion | Medich |
| 18—At Det. | W | 11-3 | Medich | Coleman | 3—At Milw. | L | 3-4 | Murphy | Lyle |
| 19—At Det. | L | 3-8 | Lolich | Hunter | 4—At Milw. | L | 4-11 | Slaton | Dobson |
| 20—At Det. | W. | 7-1 | May | Ruhle | 5—At Balt. | L | 1-3 | Palmer | Hunter |
| 21—At Bos. | W | 12-1 | Dobson | Lee | 7—At Balt. | L | 3-4 | Cuellar | Medich |
| 22—At Bos. | W | 5-0 | Medich | Wise | 9—At Oak. | L | 3-4 | Fingers | Dobson |
| 23—At Bos. | L | 7-11 | Moret | Lyle | 10—At Oak. | W | 3-0 | Hunter | Holtzman |
| 26—Milw. | W | 10-1 | Dobson | Slaton | 11—At Oak. | L | 5-7 | Blue | May |
| 27—Milw. | L | 0-7 | Broberg | Medich | 13—At Calif. | L | 0-5 | Ryan | Medich |
| 27—Milw. | W | 10-1 | Hunter | Champion | 14—At Calif. | W | 4-3* | Hunter | Hassler |
| 28—Cleve. | W | 6-1 | May | Peterson | 16—Oakland | L | 2-4 | Blue | Dobson |
| | | | | | 17—Oakland | L | 1-6 | Holtzman | Medich |

| | | | Winner | Loser |
|---|---|---|---|---|
| **MAY** | | | | |
| 18—Oakland | W | 9-1 | Hunter | Abbott |
| 19—Kan. C. | W | 5-1 | May | Busby |
| 20—Kan. C. | W | 6-0 | Dobson | Splittorff |
| 21—Kan. C. | L | 1-4* | Bird | Medich |
| 23—Texas | W | 11-7 | Hunter | Jenkins |
| 24—Texas | W | 9-5 | Tidrow | Wright |
| 25—Texas | W | 5-4 | Dobson | Bibby |
| 26—At K. C. | L | 5-6† | Pattin | Lyle |
| 27—At K. C. | L | 0-3 | Fitzmorris | Hunter |
| 28—At K. C. | W | 6-2 | May | Briles |
| 29—At Texas | W | 7-5 | Tidrow | Umbarger |
| 30—At Texas | L | 5-6 | Brown | Lyle |
| 31—At Texas | W | 6-0 | Hunter | Hands |
| | | **Won 12, Lost 14** | | |
| | | | | |
| **JUNE** | | | | |
| 1—At Texas | W | 8-4 | May | Jenkins |
| 3—At Minn. | W | 5-4 | Dobson | Goltz |
| 4—At Minn. | W | 6-3 | Medich | Blyleven |
| 5—At Minn. | W | 7-4 | Hunter | Hughes |
| 6—At Chi. | W | 5-1 | May | Wood |
| 7—At Chi. | W | 6-3 | Dobson | Bahnsen |
| 8—At Chi. | W | 4-1 | Medich | Kaat |
| 9—Calif. | L | 3-5 | Singer | Hunter |
| 10—Calif. | W | 6-4 | Gura | Ryan |
| 11—Minn. | W | 5-1 | May | Pazik |
| 13—Chicago | W | 2-1 | Dobson | Osteen |
| 14—Chicago | L | 2-7 | Wood | Medich |
| 15—Chicago | W | 3-0 | Hunter | Bahnsen |
| 16—Milw. | W | 10-7 | Tidrow | Sprague |
| 17—Milw. | L | 3-4 | Castro | Lyle |
| 17—Milw. | W | 4-2 | Tidrow | Colborn |
| 18—Milw. | L | 3-5 | Travers | Medich |
| 19—At Det. | W | 9-2 | Hunter | Bare |
| 20—At Det. | L | 9-10 | Ruhle | May |
| 21—At Det. | W | 4-1 | Dobson | Lolich |
| 22—At Det. | W | 5-3 | Gura | Walker |
| 23—At Balt. | W | 6-1 | Medich | Grimsley |
| 24—At Balt. | W | 3-1 | Hunter | Torrez |
| 25—At Balt. | W | 2-1 | Lyle | Palmer |
| 26—At Bos. | L | 1-6 | Tiant | Dobson |
| 27—At Bos. | L | 1-9 | Wise | Gura |
| 28—At Bos. | W | 8-6 | Tidrow | Cleveland |
| 29—At Bos. | L | 2-3 | Moret | Hunter |
| 30—At Milw. | L | 4-5 | Travers | May |
| | | **Won 20, Lost 9** | | |
| | | | | |
| **JULY** | | | | |
| 1—At Milw. | L | 3-6 | Colborn | Dobson |
| 2—At Cleve. | L | 2-3 | LaRoche | Tidrow |
| 3—At Cleve. | L | 2-3 | Hood | Medich |
| 4—Balt. | L | 4-5 | Palmer | Hunter |
| 5—Balt. | L | 2-5 | Grimsley | May |
| 6—Balt. | W | 6-1 | Dobson | Cuellar |
| 7—Texas | W | 5-2 | Medich | Hands |
| 8—Texas | W | 4-0 | Hunter | Hargan |
| 9—Texas | L | 0-4 | Jenkins | May |
| 10—Minn. | L | 3-6 | Corbin | Dobson |
| 11—Minn. | L | 1-11 | Blyleven | Medich |
| 11—Minn. | W | 4-3 | Gura | Wiley |
| 12—Minn. | W | 8-7§ | Martinez | Burgmeier |
| 17—At Texas | L | 2-7 | Jenkins | Dobson |
| 18—At Texas | L | 0-1 | Perry | Hunter |
| 19—At Minn. | L | 1-2 | Hughes | Medich |
| 20—At Minn. | W | 14-2 | May | Corbin |
| 20—At Minn. | W | 5-4x | Tidrow | Campbell |
| 21—At Minn. | L | 0-3 | Blyleven | Dobson |
| 22—At Chi. | W | 11-6 | Hunter | Kaat |
| 24—At Chi. | L | 3-4† | Gossage | Tidrow |
| 24—At Chi. | L | 0-1 | Hamilton | Gura |
| 25—Boston | W | 8-6 | May | Tiant |

| | | | Winner | Loser |
|---|---|---|---|---|
| **JULY** | | | | |
| 26—Boston | L | 2-4 | Cleveland | Dobson |
| 27—Boston | L | 0-1 | Lee | Hunter |
| 27—Boston | L | 0-6 | Moret | Martinez |
| 28—Detroit | L | 0-3 | Ruhle | Gura |
| 29—Detroit | W | 4-2 | Medich | Coleman |
| 30—Detroit | W | 2-1 | May | Lolich |
| | | **Won 11, Lost 18** | | |
| | | | | |
| **AUGUST** | | | | |
| 1—Cleve. | W | 5-4 | Hunter | Raich |
| 2—Cleve. | W | 5-3 | Lyle | Bibby |
| 3—Cleve. | W | 12-1 | Medich | Harrison |
| 3—Cleve. | L. | 2-3 | Hood | Tidrow |
| 4—At Milw. | W | 2-1 | May | Travers |
| 5—At Milw. | W | 4-3 | Hunter | Murphy |
| 6—At Cleve. | L | 3-5 | Peterson | Dobson |
| 7—At Cleve. | W | 6-3 | Medich | Hood |
| 8—At Calif. | W | 4-3 | Gura | Ryan |
| 9—At Calif. | L | 1-8 | Figueroa | Hunter |
| 10—At Calif. | L | 0-1 | Scott | May |
| 11—At Calif. | L | 1-8 | Tanana | Dobson |
| 12—At Oak. | W | 7-2 | Medich | Holtzman |
| 13—At Oak. | W | 3-1 | Hunter | Bahnsen |
| 14—At Oak. | L | 1-5 | Bosman | May |
| 15—At K. C. | W | 5-4 | Dobson | Bird |
| 16—At K. C. | L | 3-4 | Briles | Medich |
| 17—At K. C. | L | 3-5 | Splittorff | Hunter |
| 19—Chicago | L | 6-7† | Hamilton | Lyle |
| 20—Chicago | L | 3-5 | Wood | May |
| 21—Chicago | L | 1-2 | Kaat | Medich |
| 22—Calif. | W. | 5-2 | Hunter | Figueroa |
| 23—Calif. | W | 12-4 | Gura | Singer |
| 24—Calif. | L | 0-9 | Tanana | May |
| 24—Calif. | L | 3-4 | Ryan | Martinez |
| 26—Oakland | W | 7-1 | Hunter | Siebert |
| 27—Oakland | L | 2-3 | Blue | Medich |
| 28—Oakland | W | 3-2 | Dobson | Holtzman |
| 29—Kan. C. | W | 6-5* | Lyle | Pattin |
| 30—Kan. C. | L | 2-5 | Leonard | Hunter |
| 31—Kan. C. | L | 0-7 | Splittorff | Gura |
| | | **Won 15, Lost 16** | | |
| | | | | |
| **SEPTEMBER** | | | | |
| 1—At Bos. | W | 4-2 | Medich | Moret |
| 2—At Bos. | L | 4-7 | Cleveland | Dobson |
| 3—At Det. | W | 8-0 | Hunter | Lolich |
| 4—At Det. | W | 8-1 | May | Bare |
| 5—At Balt. | L | 4-5 | Mitchell | Medich |
| 5—At Balt. | L | 1-2 | Grimsley | Gura |
| 6—At Balt. | L | 6-7‡ | Jackson | Lyle |
| 7—At Balt. | W | 2-0 | Hunter | Palmer |
| 8—Detroit | W | 3-0 | May | Lolich |
| 9—Detroit | W | 9-6 | Medich | Bare |
| 10—Milw. | W | 8-2 | Gura | Osburn |
| 11—Milw. | W | 10-2 | Hunter | Colborn |
| 13—Cleve. | L | 1-7 | Peterson | May |
| 13—Cleve. | W | 4-3 | Medich | Bibby |
| 14—Cleve. | W | 6-2 | Hunter | Waits |
| 16—At Milw. | L | 2-5 | Augustine | Gura |
| 17—At Milw. | W | 6-5† | Lyle | Broberg |
| 19—At Cleve. | L | 2-3 | Peterson | Hunter |
| 20—At Cleve. | W | 4-1 | May | Hood |
| 21—At Cleve. | L | 2-3 | Waits | Gura |
| 21—At Cleve. | W | 11-5 | Medich | Eckersley |
| 22—Boston | L | 4-6 | Wise | Guidry |
| 27—Balt. | W | 3-2* | Hunter | Torrez |
| 27—Balt. | W | 7-3 | Medich | Cuellar |
| 28—Balt. | L | 0-3 | Palmer | May |
| 28—Balt. | W | 3-2 | Gura | Flanagan |
| | | **Won 16, Lost 10** | | |

* 10 innings.　† 11 innings.　‡ 13 innings.　§ Suspended game, completed July 19 (16 innings).　x July 13 game at New York transferred to Minnesota.

CLEVELAND INDIANS—1975

Front row—Buynak, equipment manager; Warfield, trainer; Haddix, coach; McCraw, player-coach; Bonda, club president; Robinson, player-manager; P. Seghi, general manager; M. Seghi, traveling secretary; Torborg, coach; Garcia, coach; Moulder, bat-boy. Second row—Beene, Lowenstein, Gamble, Crosby, Brohamer, Ashby, LaRoche, Ellis, Brown, Peterson, Manning, Duffy, Kuiper. Third row—Bell, Hendrick, Hood, Eckersley, Bibby, Powell, Raich, Spikes, Buskey, Carty, Harrison. Missing—Kern.

# Tribe on the Rise in '75

## By RUSSELL SCHNEIDER

For a change, the 1975 baseball season wasn't too long in Cleveland.

In fact, it wasn't long enough, in the opinion of many, including Frank Robinson, who distinguished himself as major league baseball's first black manager, piloting the Tribe to a fourth-place finish with a final spurt that almost overtook the third-place Yankees.

In the middle of September, Robinson, elated with his team's excellent play, remarked, "I wish the season had two months to go instead of only two weeks."

Little wonder. At the time the Indians were in the midst of a success streak that produced 27 victories in their final 42 games, including two over the champion Boston Red Sox on the last two days.

One of those two triumphs, a six-hitter (5-2) by Rick Waits, established him as the only opposing southpaw to hurl a complete-game victory over the Red Sox in Fenway Park in 1975.

Consequently, the Indians were the only American League team to win a season series against the Red Sox, doing so with 11 victories in their 18 meetings.

Many believe the turning point in the Indians' campaign occurred on August 16, following an embarrassing 9-1 loss to the Twins in Minnesota.

After that debacle, Robinson lost his patience—and his temper.

"I've never seen Frank so mad," confirmed one of the Tribesmen, and he was right.

After castigating the Indians in a 15-minute clubhouse meeting that day in Minnesota, things went much better and, by the end of the season, nobody—not the Red Sox or the Orioles or the Yankees— played any better than Cleveland.

Later, Robinson chuckled about the tongue-lashing. "If I'd known it would have produced such positive results, I would have done it sooner, like last spring training—or last winter," he said, half-seriously.

That late six-week spurt produced a final 79-80 record for the Indians (three home games against the Twins were cancelled by bad weather), best for a Cleveland team since 1968 when the record was 86-75.

Robinson's avowed pre-season goal was "at least a .500 record," so he didn't fall much short of the mark. In fact, if those three games against the Twins had been played, chances are good the Indians would have achieved Robinson's objective.

There was, however, considerable frustration early in the season before Robinson and General Manager Phil Seghi traded three veteran pitchers, Gaylord and Jim Perry, and Dick Bosman, and released two outfielders, Leron Lee and Ken Berry, making room for four rookies who infused new spirit into the team.

Those rookies were pitchers Dennis Eckersley and Eric Raich, center fielder Rick Manning, and second baseman Duane Kuiper.

Until the emphasis was changed to youth during the period from late-May until mid-June, the Indians floundered, compiling records of 7-8 in April, 12-16 in May, and 13-17 in June.

Jim Perry and Bosman were traded to Oakland on May 20 when Raich was recalled from Oklahoma City and inserted into the regular pitching rotation. The Indians received Blue Moon Odom for Perry and Bosman, and Odom subsequently (June 7) was dealt to Atlanta for another pitcher, Roric Harrison, who also made some major contributions.

Gaylord Perry was swapped to the Texas Rangers on June 13 for pitchers Jim Bibby, Jackie Brown, and Waits. The latter initially was assigned to Oklahoma City, but was promoted to the varsity on July 25 (when Tom Buskey was placed on the disabled list), and also came on to pitch splendidly.

Lee was released and Manning called up from Oklahoma City on May 22. Berry was dropped and Kuiper promoted from Oklahoma City on June 5.

Eckersley, a 20-year-old righthander who made the jump from Double-A (San Antonio, Texas League) to win a job as a reliever in spring training, made his first start on May 25 and responded with a 6-0 three-hitter over Oakland. Eckersley went on to become the ace of the Tribe staff, compiling a 13-7 won-lost mark, and a 2.60 earned-run average. He subsequently was voted the winner of THE SPORTING NEWS American League Rookie Pitcher of the Year Award.

Raich won seven and lost eight, and Waits, who became a starter in September, was 6-2.

Manning, who is compared to Pete Rose because of their style of play, hit .285 and stole 19 bases in 120 games and was an excellent defensive center fielder.

Kuiper, winning the second base job from Jack Brohamer, batted .292 and also swiped 19 bases in 90 games.

"Those kids turned it around for us," Robinson said often of the contributions of the rookies, particularly Manning, Kuiper and Eckersley.

The "turn around" wasn't spontaneous, however, as the Indians hit what Seghi called "the low point of the season" on June 21. Then their record was only 24-39, 15 below .500. At the time they had lost 13 of 15 games, including five in a row, and were in last place, 13 lengths behind Boston and three in arrears of the fifth-place Detroit Tigers.

July was better, as the Tribe won 14 and lost 14, the record in August was 15-13, and jumped to 18-12 in September. Following the All-Star Game, in which outfielder George Hendrick was the Indians' only representative, the team won 39 and lost 34.

Robinson was rehired on September 23, strictly as a manager, with a one-year contract at a salary estimated at $80,000.

At the time, he said, "A year ago, when I first was hired, I expected we'd do better, I really did. Realistically, I thought we had a chance of finishing second in our division, and if things broke right, like they did for the Red Sox, I thought we could sneak away with the championship.

"Anytime you don't finish first, you've got to be disappointed. But the way we played the last couple of months, I'm happy," added Robinson.

As a player in 1975, his 20th season in the big leagues, Robinson suffered an injury to his left shoulder—a torn tendon—on May 1 which hampered his ability. He appeared in 49 games, all as a designated or pinch-hitter, and batted .237 with nine homers and 24 RBIs.

Thus, Robinson finished his career with 2,928 hits and 583 homers, short of the two goals—3,000 hits and 600 homers—he had striven to reach.

A few days after the World Series ended, Robinson underwent surgery to correct the torn tendon in his left shoulder, but it isn't expected to change his mind about playing again.

For the record, Robinson's active career ended on September 20, in two at-bats against southpaw Rudy May of the Yankees. In his first trip to the plate, Robinson sent a long fly to center that was caught a few feet in front of the fence by Rick Bladt. He was called out on strikes in the fifth inning, and Boog Powell batted for him in the seventh.

Powell was one of two key player acquisitions by Seghi in spring training that helped immeasurably. The other was reliever Dave La-Roche, who was elected by Cleveland baseball writers at the end of the season as the Indians' Man of the Year. Powell also was nominated for that award.

Powell came to the Wigwam (with pitcher Don Hood) on February 25 in a trade with the Baltimore Orioles for catcher Dave Duncan and minor league outfielder Alvin McGrew. Big Boog made a startling comeback under Robinson, hitting .297 with 27 homers and 86 RBIs.

LaRoche, a southpaw, was obtained in a waiver deal with the Chicago Cubs for pitcher Milt Wilcox on February 28 and proceeded to register 17 saves and five victories in 61 appearances.

Other performances of note were by southpaw Fritz Peterson, who won 14 games (including 10 in a row) and lost eight with a 3.95 ERA; veteran first baseman-designated hitter Rico Carty, who led the team with a .308 average with 18 homers and 64 RBIs; and Hendrick, who compiled a .258 mark with 24 homers and 86 RBIs.

Robinson's first homer seemed to be an omen of good things to come, being struck in his first at-bat on Opening Day against George Medich of the Yankees in a 5-3 Cleveland victory on April 8, electrifying 56,715 fans. Nearly three months later, on July 6, a crowd of 59,161 in the Stadium for a doubleheader against Boston comprised the largest American League crowd of the season.

Attendance went on to suffer some, however, as the Indians struggled, and the final turnstile count was 977,039 (though it certainly would have reached the million mark if those aforementioned three games against the Twins had not been rained out and cancelled).

For Robinson, it was a good debut, though he was involved in several controversies, all of which were highly-publicized.

The first was a spring training squabble with Gaylord Perry which, many believe, led to the trading of the veteran pitcher, whose record for the Indians was only 6-9 (3.55 ERA) at the time he was sent to Texas.

On May 17 in Chicago, Robinson became embroiled in a complaint with umpire Jerry Neudecker in which he pushed the arbiter, costing him a three-day suspension and a $250 fine. It led to the Indians volunteering to sit out Robinson's suspension with him, so strongly did they feel their manager was not totally at fault.

In Oakland, on July 7, Robinson was ejected for the third time in the season (he also was thrown out of a game on June 11 by Ron Luciano). The latter ejection was by Larry Barnett, and Robinson lashed back, accusing the umpires in the American League of discriminating against him and his team. That story also was headlined across the country.

Finally, on July 18 in Cleveland, Robinson and catcher John Ellis nearly came to blows in an argument in the Indians' dugout. It, too, was bannered in the newspapers and relations between the two men never were the same.

Ellis was traded to the Rangers for pitcher Stan Thomas and catcher Ron Pruitt, December 9.

However, all things considered, it was a good year—for a change—in Cleveland, even if the season didn't last quite long enough (again, for a change).

## SCORES OF CLEVELAND INDIANS' 1975 GAMES

| APRIL | | | Winner | Loser | JUNE | | | Winner | Loser |
|---|---|---|---|---|---|---|---|---|---|
| 8—N. York | W | 5-3 | G. Perry | Medich | 7—Texas | L | 4-5‡ | Thomas | G. Perry |
| 11—At Milw. | L | 2-6 | Champion | J. Perry | 8—Texas | W | 3-2 | Raich | Bibby |
| 12—At Milw. | L | 5-6 | Slaton | Peterson | 8—Texas | L | 6-7y | Thomas | Buskey |
| 13—At Milw. | W | 3-1 | G. Perry | Broberg | 9—Minn. | L | 10-11† | Albury | Buskey |
| 18—Milw. | L | 1-5 | Broberg | G. Perry | 10—Minn. | L | 3-5‡ | Burgmeier | LaRoche |
| 19—Milw. | L | 0-3 | Champion | J. Perry | 11—At K. C. | L | 1-7 | Leonard | G. Perry |
| 20—Milw. | W | 7-4 | Peterson | Slaton | 12—At K. C. | L | 1-2* | Busby | Raich |
| 22—At Det. | L | 2-6 | LaGrow | G. Perry | 13—At Texas | L | 1-2 | Umbarger | Peterson |
| 23—At Det. | W | 4-3 | J. Perry | Coleman | 14—At Texas | L | 1-2 | Jenkins | Harrison |
| 26—At Balt. | W | 3-0 | G. Perry | Grimsley | 15—At Texas | W | 5-1 | Eckersley | G. Perry |
| 26—At Balt. | L | 2-3 | Torrez | Bosman | 16—Balt. | L | 3-8 | Palmer | Bibby |
| 27—At Balt. | L | 1-6 | Palmer | J. Perry | 17—Balt. | L | 3-5 | Cuellar | Raich |
| 28—At N. Y. | L | 1-6 | May | Peterson | 18—Balt. | L | 6-13 | Grimsley | Peterson |
| 29—At N. Y. | W | 3-1 | Hood | Gura | 20—Milw. | L | 0-6 | Slaton | Harrison |
| 30—At Bos. | W | 8-1 | G. Perry | Tiant | 21—Milw. | L | 9-11 | Broberg | Eckersley |
| | | **Won 7, Lost 8** | | | 22—Milw. | W | 3-2* | Buskey | Sprague |
| | | | | | 23—At Bos. | W | 11-3 | Raich | Burton |
| MAY | | | | | 24—At Bos. | W | 8-6 | Buskey | Drago |
| 1—At Bos. | L | 6-7 | Lee | J. Perry | 25—At Bos. | W | 8-5 | Harrison | Pole |
| 2—Balt. | W | 4-3 | Eckersley | Johnson | 26—At Milw. | W | 9-2 | Eckersley | Colborn |
| 3—Balt. | L | 6-1 | Peterson | Grimsley | 27—At Milw. | W | 6-1 | Bibby | Sprague |
| 4—Balt. | L | 1-11 | Torrez | G. Perry | 28—At Milw. | L | 6-10 | Austin | Brown |
| 4—Balt. | W | 4-3† | Buskey | Jefferson | 29—At Milw. | L | 3-4 | Rodriguez | Hood |
| 5—Boston | L | 5-7 | Tiant | J. Perry | 30—Detroit | W | 4-1 | Harrison | Ruhle |
| 6—Boston | L | 1-4 | Lee | Bosman | 30—Detroit | W | 3-2 | Raich | LaGrow |
| 7—Boston | L | 2-4 | Cleveland | Peterson | | | **Won 13, Lost 17** | | |
| 9—Chicago | L | 0-2 | Kaat | G. Perry | | | | | |
| 10—Chicago | L | 3-8 | Wood | Hood | JULY | | | | |
| 11—Chicago | W | 4-3† | Buskey | Forster | 1—Detroit | L | 2-6 | Lolich | Bibby |
| 13—At Minn. | W | 3-2 | Peterson | Albury | 2—N. York | W | 3-2 | LaRoche | Tidrow |
| 14—At Minn. | L | 0-3 | Hughes | G. Perry | 3—N. York | W | 3-2 | Hood | Medich |
| 15—At Minn. | L | 6-7 | Burgmeier | J. Perry | 4—Boston | W | 3-2 | Raich | Tiant |
| 16—At Chi. | L | 2-3 | Gossage | Buskey | 5—Boston | W | 12-2 | Harrison | Barr |
| 17—At Chi. | L | 1-10 | Kaat | Peterson | 6—Boston | L | 3-5 | Lee | Bibby |
| 18—At Chi. | W | 7-6 | G. Perry | Wood | 6—Boston | W | 11-10 | Beene | Cleveland |
| 19—Calif. | L | 5-12 | Lange | Hood | 7—At Oak. | L | 3-7 | Perry | Eckersley |
| 21—Calif. | W | 3-2 | Kern | Tanana | 8—At Oak. | L | 5-15 | Holtzman | Hood |
| 23—Oakland | L | 0-3 | Siebert | G. Perry | 9—At Oak. | L | 1-3 | Bosman | Raich |
| 24—Oakland | L | 5-10 | Fingers | Hood | 11—At Calif. | W | 5-3 | Harrison | Lange |
| 25—Oakland | W | 6-0 | Eckersley | J. Perry | 12—At Calif. | W | 9-1 | Eckersley | Ryan |
| 25—Oakland | L | 3-6 | Bosman | Kern | 13—At Calif. | W | 8-7 | Bibby | Kirkwood |
| 26—At Calif. | W | 9-3 | Peterson | Tanana | 17—Oakland | L | 3-6 | Holtzman | Raich |
| 27—At Calif. | W | 6-3 | G. Perry | Singer | 18—Oakland | L | 6-7 | Abbott | Bibby |
| 28—At Calif. | W | 9-2 | Raich | Ryan | 19—Calif. | L | 0-8 | Tanana | Eckersley |
| 30—At Oak. | L | 2-6 | Bosman | Kern | 19—Calif. | L | 2-3* | Kirkwood | LaRoche |
| 31—At Oak. | W | 4-1 | Eckersley | Holtzman | 20—Calif. | W | 10-4 | Hood | Lange |
| | | **Won 12, Lost 16** | | | 21—Calif. | W | 2-1† | LaRoche | Figueroa |
| | | | | | 22—At Texas | L | 0-4 | Perry | Raich |
| JUNE | | | | | 23—At Texas | L | 8-9§ | Foucault | Brown |
| 1—At Oak. | L | 3-6 | Siebert | G. Perry | 25—At Det. | L | 3-4 | Bare | Hood |
| 3—Kan. C. | L | 2-5 | Leonard | Peterson | 26—At Det. | W | 6-0 | Eckersley | Lolich |
| 4—Kan. C. | W | 4-0 | Odom | Busby | 27—At Det. | L | 7-8 | Arroyo | LaRoche |
| 5—Kan. C. | W | 8-7† | LaRoche | Pattin | 27—At Det. | W | 7-2 | Peterson | LaGrow |
| 6—Texas | W | 7-5 | LaRoche | Jenkins | 28—At Balt. | W | 7-5* | Waits | Alexander |

| JULY | | | Winner | Loser | SEPTEMBER | | | Winner | Loser |
|---|---|---|---|---|---|---|---|---|---|
| 29—At Balt. | L | 1-7 | Torrez | Hood | 2—At Balt. | L | 2-3* | Cuellar | Reynolds |
| 30—At Balt. | W | 3-1 | Eckersley | Cuellar | 2—At Balt. | W | 2-1 | Bibby | Alexander |
| | | **Won 14, Lost 14** | | | 3—At Milw. | W | 11-3 | Peterson | Slaton |
| **AUGUST** | | | | | 4—At Milw. | W | 10-5 | Harrison | Currence |
| 1—At N. Y. | L | 4-5 | Hunter | Raich | 5—Detroit | L | 2-11 | Ruhle | Waits |
| 2—At N. Y. | L | 3-5 | Lyle | Bibby | 6—Detroit | W | 4-2 | Eckersley | Lemanczyk |
| 3—At N. Y. | L | 1-12 | Medich | Harrison | 7—Detroit | W | 7-2 | Bibby | Coleman |
| 3—At N. Y. | W | 3-2 | Hood | Tidrow | 7—Detroit | W | 9-0 | Peterson | LaGrow |
| 4—Detroit | W | 6-4 | Eckersley | Lolich | 8—Boston | W | 4-1 | Hood | Wise |
| 5—Detroit | W | 8-4 | Raich | Bare | 9—Boston | W | 3-2* | Waits | Lee |
| 6—N. York | W | 5-3 | Peterson | Dobson | 10—Balt. | W | 7-1 | Eckersley | Cuellar |
| 7—N. York | L | 3-6 | Medich | Hood | 10—Balt. | L | 5-6x | Miller | Reynolds |
| 8—Kan. C. | W | 4-3 | Harrison | Pattin | 11—Balt. | L | 2-10 | Palmer | Harrison |
| 9—Kan. C. | L | 4-6 | McDaniel | Bibby | 13—At N. Y. | W | 7-1 | Peterson | May |
| 10—Kan. C. | L | 1-5 | Fitzmorris | Raich | 13—At N. Y. | L | 3-4 | Medich | Bibby |
| 12—At Chi. | W | 6-3 | Peterson | Wood | 14—At N. Y. | L | 2-6 | Hunter | Waits |
| 13—At Chi. | W | 3-4‡ | Gossage | Bibby | 16—At Det. | W | 9-2 | Eckersley | Arroyo |
| 14—At Chi. | L | 4-6 | Kaat | Harrison | 17—At Det. | L | 0-4 | Coleman | Harrison |
| 15—At Minn. | L | 4-8 | Blyleven | Eckersley | 18—At Det. | W | 2-1 | Bibby | Lemanczyk |
| 16—At Minn. | L | 1-9 | Hughes | Raich | 19—N. York | W | 3-2 | Peterson | Hunter |
| 17—At Minn. | W | 14-5 | Peterson | Butler | 20—N. York | L | 1-4 | May | Hood |
| 18—Texas | W | 4-3 | Waits | Hargan | 21—N. York | W | 3-2 | Waits | Gura |
| 18—Texas | W | 4-2z | Harrison | Jenkins | 21—N. York | L | 5-11 | Medich | Eckersley |
| 19—Texas | L | 1-2 | Umbarger | Eckersley | 22—Milw. | W | 7-6 | Buskey | Murphy |
| 21—At K. C. | W | 7-3 | Brown | Littell | 23—Milw. | W | 4-3 | LaRoche | Travers |
| 22—At K. C. | W | 9-5 | Peterson | Splittorff | 24—Milw. | L | 3-10 | Colborn | Peterson |
| 23—At K. C. | W | 7-1 | Waits | Briles | 26—At Bos. | L | 0-4 | Tiant | Eckersley |
| 24—At K. C. | L | 2-5 | Fitzmorris | Harrison | 26—At Bos. | L | 0-4 | Cleveland | Hood |
| 25—Chicago | W | 5-1 | Eckersley | Kaat | 27—At Bos. | W | 5-2 | Waits | Wise |
| 27—Chicago | L | 0-2 | Osteen | Bibby | 28—At Bos. | W | 11-4 | Raich | Pole |
| 27—Chicago | W | 5-0 | Peterson | Jefferson | | | **Won 18, Lost 12** | | |
| 29—Minn. | W | 9-6 | Hood | Hughes | | | | | |
| | | **Won 15, Lost 13** | | | | | | | |

* 10 innings.   † 11 innings.   ‡ 12 innings.   § 13 innings.   x September 1 game (part of doubleheader) at Baltimore transferred to Cleveland (13 innings).   y 17 innings.   z July 24 games at Texas transferred to Cleveland.

# Brewers Start Fast, Stop Fast

## By LOU CHAPMAN

MILWAUKEE—A glorious dream in the middle of May turned into a horrendous nightmare for the Brewers in September.

Visions of pennant turned into a scene of disaster as the Brewers dropped 59 of their last 84 games and, in the process, became the worst club in baseball for that stretch.

What happened between that beautiful day in May and that last day of the 1975 season, when the Brewers finished fifth in the American League East?

It depends on how much time a listener—or a reader has—but for starters, the Brewers lost half of their starting pitching staff by the time the last month of the season rolled around.

For example, Ed Sprague underwent knee surgery; Billy Champion had bone chips in his elbow and also was due to go under the knife; Ed Rodriguez and Bill Castro had shoulder and elbow trouble, respectively; Rookie righthander Tom Hausman had back trouble and was in traction in a hospital for a while.

To top it all off, Brewer Fireman of the Year, Tom Murphy, their bread and butter man in relief, had shoulder trouble and was never the same when he returned to action.

It's true that when he was hurt, the Brewers had dropped out of con-

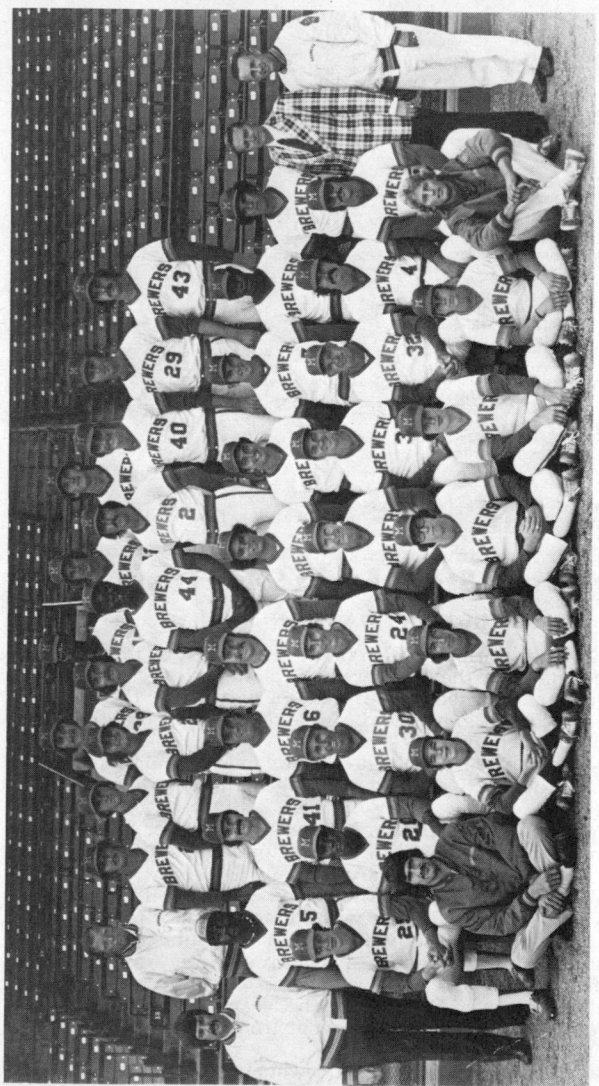

MILWAUKEE BREWERS—1975

Front row—P. McBride, clubhouse man; Stoller, batboy; Logan, batboy; Scanlon, batboy; Filbert, batboy; Reuteman, batboy; Napholz, clubhouse man. Second row—Travers, Currence, Walton, coach; Nossek, coach; Crandall, manager; K. McBride, money; Kuenn, coach; Johnson, Porter. Third row—Ksicinski, clubhouse man; Scott, Slaton, Hegan, Colborn, Lezcano, Sharp, Money, Darwin, Castro, Ferguson, traveling secretary; Rayer, trainer. Fourth row—Sullivan, equipment manager; Rodriguez, Yount, Moore, Thomas, Aaron, Bevacqua, Broberg, Sprague, Austin. Fifth row—Champion, Mitchell, Murphy, Hausman.

tention, but then his absence hurt when they were trying to fight their way back.

That's only part of the injury story for the Brewers. Third baseman Don Money had an operation for a hernia and was out for six weeks. He was absent when the Brewers really needed him. When he finally returned, he, too, wasn't the same.

Bobby Darwin, obtained from Minnesota in a trade for Johnny Briggs, also was hurt and out of the lineup for at least a month. He broke his hand and the Brewers missed his big bat.

Robin Yount, the kid shortstop, also hurt his foot after a spectacular start. He never got back in the groove after coming back and was particularly unsteady in the field.

Henry Aaron, the home run king, frankly didn't have a good year as expected as the club's designated hitter.

The club also had morale problems. Del Crandall, the manager who received his walking papers the last day of the season, found himself in personality clashes with second baseman Pedro Garcia practically all year and with rookie outfielder Sixto Lezcano toward the end of the season.

Players confided they lost respect for Crandall the way he handled Garcia and his failure to properly discipline him.

Both Garcia and Lezcano drew fines—Pedro at one time for flagrantly showing up Crandall publicly paid a fine of $200, in addition to apologizing to his teammates and the manager. It happened after Garcia defiantly stood out at second base during batting drill and refused to field balls hit in his direction.

The second baseman was benched by Crandall, but, after the club's failure to get waivers on him, he returned to the lineup. Crandall and he had problems behind the scenes the rest of the year.

General Manager Jim Baumer accused Crandall in effect of not motivating his young players and the manager walked a tightrope late in July after the Brewers dropped a doubleheader in Milwaukee to Baltimore. The brass became disenchanted with Crandall when the Brewers blew a six run lead in the ninth inning on the way to an 11-6 defeat in extra innings to the Orioles.

The club really nose dived the last two months and the Brewer top officials even offered the job to Aaron. He refused, however, because of his long friendship with Crandall.

Crandall lasted the year and finally, Selig painfully announced his manager had been fired. They had been friends for years.

About the only bright spot in the Brewers' dismal finish was the performance of first baseman George Scott. The Boomer tied with Reggie Jackson for the American League homer crown with 36 and led everybody in runs batted in with 109. Of course, he won his seventh Gold Glove award from THE SPORTING NEWS.

Scott will be the first to admit that Aaron, hitting behind him, enabled the first baseman to get better pitches to hit. Aaron's reputation was such that rival pitchers still hesitated to walk Scott and pitch to the all-time home run king.

Then, too, Scott listens to a different drummer. He's a man of moods and what is known as a loner in the trade. Aaron was Scott's adviser and kept his morale high.

Morale on the Brewer club frankly wasn't too high—about as low as their final standing. But then what is it they say about wait until next year?

## SCORES OF MILWAUKEE BREWERS' 1975 GAMES

| APRIL | | | Winner | Loser |
|---|---|---|---|---|
| 8—At Bos. | L | 2-5 | Tiant | Slaton |
| 9—At Bos. | W | 7-4 | Broberg | Lee |
| 11—Cleve. | W | 6-2 | Champion | J. Perry |
| 12—Cleve. | W | 6-5 | Slaton | Peterson |
| 13—Cleve. | L | 1-3 | G. Perry | Broberg |
| 15—At Balt. | W | 7-1 | Champion | Palmer |
| 16—At Balt. | L | 0-2 | Cuellar | Slaton |
| 18—At Cleve. | W | 5-1 | Broberg | G. Perry |
| 19—At Cleve. | W | 3-0 | Champion | J. Perry |
| 20—At Cleve. | L | 4-7 | Peterson | Slaton |
| 22—Balt. | L | 0-1 | Palmer | Broberg |
| 23—Balt. | W | 8-5 | Rodriguez | Reynolds |
| 26—At N.Y. | L | 1-10 | Dobson | Slaton |
| 27—At N.Y. | W | 7-0 | Broberg | Medich |
| 27—At N.Y. | L | 1-10 | Hunter | Champion |
| 30—Detroit | W | 6-2 | Slaton | Lemanczyk |
| **Won 9, Lost 7** | | | | |

| MAY | | | | |
|---|---|---|---|---|
| 1—Detroit | W | 17-3 | Broberg | Bare |
| 2—N. York | W | 4-2 | Champion | Medich |
| 3—N. York | W | 4-3 | Murphy | Lyle |
| 4—N. York | W | 11-4 | Slaton | Dobson |
| 6—At Det. | L | 2-4 | Coleman | Broberg |
| 7—At Det. | W | 7-5 | Rodriguez | Lolich |
| 8—At Det. | L | 4-6 | Bare | Colborn |
| 9—At K. C. | W | 7-1 | Sprague | Fitzmorris |
| 10—At K. C. | W | 3-0 | Broberg | Briles |
| 11—At K. C. | L | 0-4 | Busby | Champion |
| 13—At Texas | L | 0-5* | Bibby | Slaton |
| 14—At Texas | W | 3-2x | Rodriguez | Brown |
| 15—At Texas | W | 8-5 | Broberg | Hargan |
| 16—At Minn. | W | 3-1 | Champion | Goltz |
| 17—At Minn. | L | 7-8 | Corbin | Murphy |
| 18—At Minn. | L | 0-6 | Hughes | Sprague |
| 20—Texas | W | 7-6† | Rodriguez | Brown |
| 21—Texas | L | 4-5 | Hargan | Champion |
| 22—Texas | L | 0-6 | Hands | Colborn |
| 23—Minn. | L | 1-2 | Blyleven | Sprague |
| 24—Minn. | L | 2-3 | Hughes | Broberg |
| 25—Minn. | L | 2-7 | Goltz | Champion |
| 26—Chicago | L | 2-4 | Kaat | Colborn |
| 27—Chicago | W | 9-8 | Hausman | Wood |
| 28—Chicago | L | 3-9 | Bahnsen | Slaton |
| 31—Kan. C. | L | 5-7 | McDaniel | Broberg |
| **Won 12, Lost 14** | | | | |

| JUNE | | | | |
|---|---|---|---|---|
| 1—Kan. C. | L | 6-13 | Pattin | Hausman |
| 1—Kan. C. | L | 5-11 | Fitzmorris | Colborn |
| 2—At Oak. | W | 6-3 | Castro | Blue |
| 3—At Oak. | L | 5-4 | Champion | Todd |
| 4—At Oak. | L | 3-11 | Holtzman | Broberg |
| 6—At Calif. | L | 0-6 | Ryan | Slaton |
| 7—At Calif. | L | 2-5 | Tanana | Castro |
| 8—At Calif. | W | 4-3 | Colborn | Figueroa |
| 9—At Chi. | W | 1-0 | Rodriguez | Gossage |
| 10—At Chi. | L | 2-9 | Wood | Broberg |
| 11—Oakland | L | 3-5 | Bosman | Slaton |
| 12—Oakland | W | 9-7 | Castro | Blue |
| 13—Calif. | W | 10-2 | Colborn | Singer |
| 14—Calif. | W | 6-4 | Travers | Ryan |
| 15—Calif. | L | 7-8‡ | Kirkwood | Champion |
| 15—Calif. | W | 4-2 | Slaton | Hassler |
| 16—At N.Y. | L | 7-10 | Tidrow | Sprague |

| JUNE | | | Winner | Loser |
|---|---|---|---|---|
| 17—At N. Y. | W | 4-3 | Castro | Lyle |
| 17—At N. Y. | L | 2-4 | Tidrow | Colborn |
| 18—At N. Y. | W | 5-3 | Travers | Medich |
| 20—At Cleve. | W | 6-0 | Slaton | Harrison |
| 21—At Cleve. | W | 11-9 | Broberg | Eckersley |
| 22—At Cleve. | L | 2-3† | Buskey | Sprague |
| 23—Detroit | W | 8-4 | Hausman | Coleman |
| 24—Detroit | W | 5-0 | Slaton | Bare |
| 24—Detroit | W | 4-2 | Travers | LaGrow |
| 25—Detroit | W | 7-6 | Broberg | Ruhle |
| 26—Cleve. | L | 2-9 | Eckersley | Colborn |
| 27—Cleve. | L | 1-6 | Bibby | Sprague |
| 28—Cleve. | W | 10-6 | Austin | Brown |
| 29—Cleve. | W | 4-3 | Rodriguez | Hood |
| 30—N. York | W | 5-4 | Travers | May |
| **Won 19, Lost 13** | | | | |

| JULY | | | | |
|---|---|---|---|---|
| 1—N. York | W | 6-3 | Colborn | Dobson |
| 2—Boston | L | 3-6 | Wise | Castro |
| 2—Boston | W | 4-3 | Broberg | Lee |
| 3—Boston | L | 3-2† | Austin | Segui |
| 4—At Det. | L | 2-8 | Bare | Travers |
| 5—At Det. | L | 2-3 | Ruhle | Colborn |
| 6—At Det. | L | 5-7 | Lolich | Hausman |
| 6—At Det. | L | 2-11 | LaGrow | Broberg |
| 7—At K. C. | W | 4-3 | Slaton | Fitzmorris |
| 8—At K. C. | L | 1-9 | Leonard | Travers |
| 9—At K. C. | W | 6-4 | Colborn | Briles |
| 11—Chicago | L | 3-5 | Osteen | Sprague |
| 12—Chicago | W | 5-4 | Slaton | Kaat |
| 13—Chicago | L | 0-5 | Wood | Travers |
| 17—Calif. | L | 1-6 | Figueroa | Colborn |
| 18—Calif. | W | 2-0 | Slaton | Ryan |
| 19—At Chi. | L | 2-4 | Jefferson | Travers |
| 20—At Chi. | L | 2-9 | Wood | Sprague |
| 20—At Chi. | L | 5-10 | Osborn | Broberg |
| 21—At Chi. | W | 7-4 | Colborn | Osteen |
| 22—Kan. C. | L | 2-3 | Busby | Slaton |
| 22—Kan. C. | W | 6-3 | Hausman | Fitzmorris |
| 23—Kan. C. | L | 1-4 | Pattin | Travers |
| 24—Balt. | L | 7-10 | Garland | Broberg |
| 25—Balt. | W | 5-2 | Colborn | Torrez |
| 26—Balt. | L | 0-4 | Cuellar | Slaton |
| 27—Balt. | L | 4-7 | Palmer | Currence |
| 27—Balt. | L | 6-11 | Miller | Austin |
| 28—At Bos. | L | 6-7 | Willoughby | Murphy |
| 29—At Bos. | W | 4-0 | Colborn | Segui |
| 30—At Bos. | W | 5-2 | Slaton | Cleveland |
| **Won 12, Lost 19** | | | | |

| AUGUST | | | | |
|---|---|---|---|---|
| 1—At Balt. | L | 4-6 | Palmer | Champion |
| 1—At Balt. | L | 1-3 | Grimsley | Hausman |
| 2—At Balt. | L | 1-6 | Torrez | Colborn |
| 3—At Balt. | W | 4-1 | Slaton | Cuellar |
| 4—N. York | L | 1-2 | May | Travers |
| 5—N. York | L | 3-4 | Hunter | Murphy |
| 6—Boston | L | 2-5 | Willoughby | Murphy |
| 7—Boston | L | 2-4 | Wise | Slaton |
| 8—Texas | L | 4-6 | Hargan | Travers |
| 9—Texas | L | 2-4 | Jenkins | Hausman |
| 10—Texas | W | 7-4 | Broberg | Hands |
| 11—At Minn. | L | 7-8 | Johnson | Slaton |
| 12—At Minn. | W | 7-4 | Travers | Hughes |

| AUGUST | | | Winner | Loser | SEPTEMBER | | | | Winner | Loser |
|---|---|---|---|---|---|---|---|---|---|---|
| 13—At Minn. | L | 2-5 | Goltz | Hausman | 5—Boston | W | | 4-2 | Broberg | Lee |
| 15—At Oak. | W | 8-4 | Colborn | Blue | 6—Boston | L | | 6-20 | Moret | Travers |
| 16—At Oak. | L | 1-2 | Fingers | Slaton | 7—Boston | L | | 3-6 | Cleveland | Colborn |
| 17—At Oak. | L | 1-3 | Bahnsen | Broberg | 7—Boston | W | | 7-3 | Travers | Pole |
| 18—At Calif. | L | 4-5 | Kirkwood | Murphy | 8—Balt. | L | | 2-6 | Torrez | Slaton |
| 19—At Calif. | L | 4-5§ | Scott | Austin | 9—Balt. | L | | 1-9 | Alexander | Broberg |
| 20—At Calif. | L | 1-6 | Ryan | Slaton | 10—At N. Y. | L | | 2-8 | Gura | Osburn |
| 21—Oakland | L | 2-5 | Holtzman | Broberg | 11—At N. Y. | L | | 2-10 | Hunter | Colborn |
| 23—Oakland | L | 3-6 | Todd | Murphy | 13—At Bos. | W | | 9-6 | Broberg | Wise |
| 23—Oakland | L | 3-9 | Bahnsen | Hausman | 13—At Bos. | L | | 3-6 | Cleveland | Travers |
| 24—Oakland | W | 7-6 | Rodriguez | Fingers | 14—At Bos. | L | | 6-8 | Willoughby | Murphy |
| 25—Minn. | L | 3-6 | Butler | Slaton | 15—At Bos. | L | | 7-9 | Moret | Colborn |
| 26—Minn. | L | 1-2 | Goltz | Broberg | 16—N. York | W | | 5-2 | Augustine | Gura |
| 27—Minn. | L | 0-1‡ | Blyleven | Travers | 17—N. York | L | | 5-6‡ | Lyle | Broberg |
| 29—At Texas | W | 13-1 | Colborn | Hargan | 19—At Balt. | L | | 5-6 | Miller | Murphy |
| 30—At Texas | L | 3-8 | Umbarger | Slaton | 20—At Balt. | L | | 4-5 | Garland | Colborn |
| 31—At Texas | W | 4-1 | Broberg | Perry | 21—At Balt. | L | | 0-3 | Torrez | Broberg |
| | | **Won 7, Lost 23** | | | 22—At Cleve. | L | | 6-7 | Buskey | Murphy |
| | | | | | 23—At Cleve. | L | | 3-4 | LaRoche | Travers |
| SEPTEMBER | | | | | 24—At Cleve. | W | | 10-3 | Colborn | Peterson |
| 1—At Det. | L | 4-5 | Lemanczyk | Austin | 26—Detroit | W | | 3-0 | Broberg | Bare |
| 2—At Det. | W | 6-5 | Colborn | Coleman | 27—Detroit | W | | 5-2 | Augustine | Ruhle |
| 3—Cleve. | L | 3-11 | Peterson | Slaton | 28—Detroit | W | | 7-0 | Anderson | Glynn |
| 4—Cleve. | L | 5-10 | Harrison | Currence | | | **Won 9, Lost 18** | | | |

* 5 innings.   † 10 innings.   ‡ 11 innings.   § 15 innings.   x Suspended game, completed May 15 (15 innings).

# Defeat Becomes Habit for Docile Tigers

## By JIM HAWKINS

All spring, Ralph Houk shrugged off the Tigers' daily shortcomings, admonishing the club's corps of critics to "Wait until the bell rings." If he said it once, he surely must have said it a thousand times.

But when the bell rang, it tolled a death knell for the tabby Tigers.

In finishing dead last for the second year in a row—and only the third time in three-quarters of a century—they managed to lose more often than anyone else in the big leagues.

In 75 years, only one Tiger team was ever more consistently unsuccessful. And if they hadn't had three games cancelled because of the elements, the sad sack 1975 Tigers might have broken the all-time club record of 104 losses, set in 1952, instead of settling for a mere 102.

Despite Houk's initial optimism, the Tigers did little right all year. The defense made more errors than any Tiger team since 1944. . . . The pitchers permitted more earned runs than any Detroit staff since '53. . . . And the offense scored fewer runs, stole fewer bases and drew fewer walks than anyone else in the American League.

Along the way, they obliterated the all-time Tiger record for consecutive failures, losing 19 in a row before finally winning—just one setback shy of the American League record for uninterrupted futility.

The nondescript Tigers couldn't even distinguish themselves in defeat.

After a surprising start that actually had them in front of the American League East for a few days in April, they got progressively worse, particularly after the All-Star break.

They won just six games during the entire month of August, and only five in all of September, dropping 47 of their last 58 decisions.

Perhaps more than any other single factor, the failure of first base-

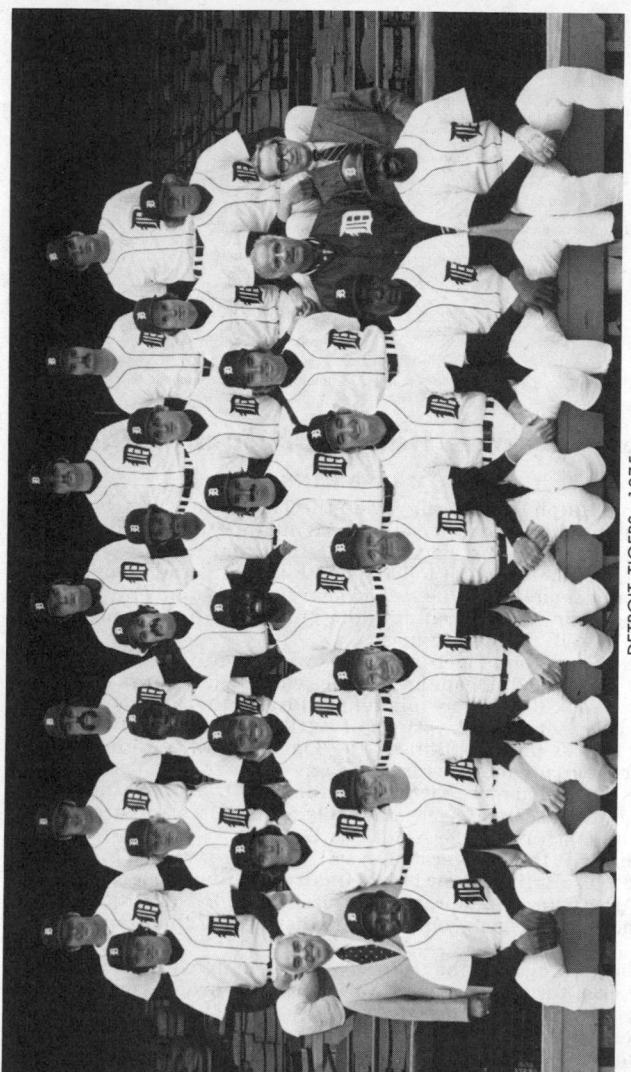

DETROIT TIGERS—1975

Front row—LeFlore, Ruhle, Schultz, coach; Houk, manager; Hamilton, coach; Brown, Horton. Second row—Desmond, traveling secretary; Veryzer, Freehan, Colbert, Humphrey, Walker, Behm, trainer; Livingood, team physician. Third row—Roberts, Meyer, Oglivie, Rodriguez, James, Lamont, Knox, Sutherland. Fourth row—Lolich, Coleman, Hiller, LaGrow, Lemanczyk, Bare, Stanley. Missing—Michael, Hegan, coach; Tracewski, coach.

man Nate Colbert to produce at all proved fatal to the Tigers.

And the loss of ace John Hiller for the final two months of the season helped to assure them of a most miserable finish.

Only Willie Horton—the only player in the A. L. to appear in every game—came through with the kind of season that was expected of him.

As the Tigers' full-time designated hitter, Horton enjoyed his most productive summer in a decade, knocking in 92 runs and hammering 25 homers. But even he did little during the second half.

The Tigers' hottest player as they faded in the stretch was Ben Oglivie, who came off the bench after rookie Danny Meyer was transferred to first base and won himself a job in left field.

Though none of them enjoyed an outstanding season, the kids—Tom Veryzer, Meyer, Vern Ruhle, Ron LeFlore and Leon Roberts—all at least proved that they can play in the big leagues.

LeFlore in particular, found his first full season in the majors most frustrating as he stole a mere 28 bases—a far cry from the 50 or 60 he expected to swipe.

Joe Coleman remained an enigma, piling up an atrocious 5.55 ERA while losing 18 and winning only 10. Mickey Lolich, likewise, had another off-year—although the veteran Tiger pitcher, who surpassed Warren Spahn to become baseball's all-time lefthanded strikeout king, did pitch far better than his 12-18 record would suggest. In a surprising deal made at the winter meetings, Lolich and rookie outfielder Billy Baldwin were traded to the Mets for outfielder Rusty Staub and pitcher Bill Laxton.

In the end even Houk, ever the optimist, readily admitted it was not a summer the Tigers would look back upon with pride.

## SCORES OF DETROIT TIGERS' 1975 GAMES

| APRIL | | | Winner | Loser |
|---|---|---|---|---|
| 10—Balt. | L | 0-10 | Palmer | Coleman |
| 11—At N. Y. | W | 5-3 | Lolich | Hunter |
| 12—At N. Y. | W | 7-2 | Ruhle | Dobson |
| 13—At N. Y. | L | 0-6 | Medich | Walker |
| 13—At N. Y. | L | 5-2 | LaGrow | May |
| 18—N. York | L | 3-11 | Medich | Coleman |
| 19—N. York | W | 8-3 | Lolich | Hunter |
| 20—N. York | L | 1-7 | May | Ruhle |
| 22—Cleve. | W | 6-2 | LaGrow | G. Perry |
| 23—Cleve. | L | 3-4 | J. Perry | Coleman |
| 25—Boston | W | 1-0 | Lolich | Tiant |
| 26—Boston | W | 3-2† | Hiller | Lee |
| 27—Boston | W | 5-4 | LaGrow | Wise |
| 28—At Balt. | W | 5-3 | Coleman | Cuellar |
| 29—At Balt. | W | 4-2† | Walker | Grimsley |
| 30—At Milw. | L | 2-6 | Slaton | Lemanczyk |
| | | | **Won 10, Lost 6** | |

| MAY | | | Winner | Loser |
|---|---|---|---|---|
| 1—At Milw. | L | 3-17 | Broberg | Bare |
| 3—At Bos. | L | 2-12 | Wise | LaGrow |
| 6—Milw. | W | 4-2 | Coleman | Broberg |
| 7—Milw. | L | 5-7 | Rodriguez | Lolich |
| 8—Milw. | W | 6-4 | Bare | Colborn |
| 9—Texas | L | 1-3 | Brown | LaGrow |
| 10—Texas | L | 2-5 | Hands | Coleman |
| 11—Texas | L | 7-11 | Jenkins | Lolich |
| 12—Kan. C. | W | 5-0 | Ruhle | Leonard |
| 13—Kan. C. | L | 7-8 | Fitzmorris | LaGrow |
| 14—Kan. C. | L | 1-4 | Briles | Coleman |
| 16—At Texas | L | 3-10 | Hands | Lolich |
| 17—At Texas | W | 6-4 | Ruhle | Brown |
| 18—At Texas | L | 6-7‡ | Thomas | Lemanczyk |

| MAY | | | Winner | Loser |
|---|---|---|---|---|
| 19—At Minn. | W | 6-3 | Coleman | Pazik |
| 20—At Minn. | W | 5-3 | Lolich | Goltz |
| 21—At Minn. | L | 5-6‡ | Corbin | Hiller |
| 23—At Chi. | L | 1-6 | Forster | LaGrow |
| 24—At Chi. | L | 8-10 | Bahnsen | Coleman |
| 25—At Chi. | W | 4-1* | Lolich | Osteen |
| 26—Minn. | W | 6-2 | Ruhle | Campbell |
| 27—Minn. | L | 5-6 | Albury | Hiller |
| 28—Minn. | L | 2-5 | Hughes | Coleman |
| 31—Chicago | W | 2-0 | Ruhle | Kaat |
| | | | **Won 9, Lost 15** | |

| JUNE | | | Winner | Loser |
|---|---|---|---|---|
| 1—Chicago | W | 5-1 | Lolich | Wood |
| 1—Chicago | L | 2-3 | Gossage | Walker |
| 3—At Calif. | W | 8-5 | Hiller | Tanana |
| 4—At Calif. | L | 1-2 | Figueroa | Bare |
| 5—At Calif. | L | 3-8 | Singer | Ruhle |
| 6—At Oak. | W | 11-2 | Lolich | Bosman |
| 7—At Oak. | W | 3-0 | LaGrow | Blue |
| 8—At Oak. | L | 0-4 | Holtzman | Coleman |
| 9—At K. C. | L | 2-5 | McDaniel | Walker |
| 10—At K. C. | L | 3-4 | Pattin | Ruhle |
| 11—Calif. | L | 7-14 | Tanana | Lolich |
| 11—Calif. | W | 5-3x | Bare | Hassler |
| 12—Calif. | L | 1-7 | Figueroa | LaGrow |
| 13—Oakland | L | 5-7 | Lindblad | Coleman |
| 14—Oakland | W | 3-2 | Walker | Siebert |
| 16—Boston | L | 2-6§ | Cleveland | Walker |
| 17—Boston | L | 6-7 | Wise | LaGrow |
| 18—Boston | L | 1-15 | Tiant | Coleman |
| 19—N. York | L | 2-9 | Hunter | Bare |
| 20—N. York | W | 10-9 | Ruhle | May |

| JUNE | | | Winner | Loser |
|---|---|---|---|---|
| 21—N. York | L | 1-4 | Dobson | Lolich |
| 22—N. York | L | 3-5 | Gura | Walker |
| 23—At Milw. | L | 4-8 | Hausman | Coleman |
| 24—At Milw. | L | 0-5 | Slaton | Bare |
| 24—At Milw. | L | 2-4 | Travers | LaGrow |
| 25—At Milw. | L | 6-7 | Broberg | Ruhle |
| 26—At Balt. | W | 6-5 | Lolich | Alexander |
| 27—At Balt. | L | 2-3 | Grimsley | Hiller |
| 28—At Balt. | L | 4-7 | Torrez | Coleman |
| 29—At Balt. | L | 1-2 | Cuellar | Bare |
| 30—At Cleve. | L | 1-4 | Harrison | Ruhle |
| 30—At Cleve. | L | 2-3 | Raich | LaGrow |
| | | | **Won 8, Lost 24** | |

| JULY | | | | |
|---|---|---|---|---|
| 1—At Cleve. | W | 6-2 | Lolich | Bibby |
| 2—Balt. | L | 5-13 | Torrez | Walker |
| 3—Balt. | W | 9-5 | Coleman | Garland |
| 4—Milw. | W | 8-2 | Bare | Travers |
| 5—Milw. | W | 3-2 | Ruhle | Colborn |
| 6—Milw. | W | 7-5 | Lolich | Hausman |
| 6—Milw. | W | 11-2 | LaGrow | Broberg |
| 7—Chicago | W | 2-1 | Walker | Kaat |
| 8—Chicago | W | 3-0 | Coleman | Wood |
| 9—Chicago | W | 6-2 | Bare | Jefferson |
| 10—At K. C. | W | 3-2 | Ruhle | Busby |
| 11—At K. C. | L | 2-5 | Pattin | Lolich |
| 12—At K. C. | W | 2-0 | LaGrow | Fitzmorris |
| 13—At K. C. | W | 8-4 | Coleman | Leonard |
| 17—At Chi. | L | 0-4 | Wood | Lolich |
| 17—At Chi. | W | 9-1 | LaGrow | Osteen |
| 18—At Chi. | L | 0-4 | Kaat | Ruhle |
| 19—Kan. C. | W | 10-8 | Coleman | Pattin |
| 20—Kan. C. | W | 7-3 | Bare | Briles |
| 21—Kan. C. | L | 2-3 | Leonard | Lolich |
| 22—Oakland | L | 0-11 | Abbott | Walker |
| 22—Oakland | L | 4-16 | Bahnsen | LaGrow |
| 23—Oakland | L | 0-3 | Blue | Ruhle |
| 24—Oakland | W | 5-2 | Coleman | Perry |
| 25—Cleve. | W | 4-3 | Bare | Hood |
| 26—Cleve. | L | 0-6 | Eckersley | Lolich |
| 27—Cleve. | W | 8-7 | Arroyo | LaRoche |
| 27—Cleve. | L | 2-7 | Peterson | LaGrow |
| 28—At N. Y. | W | 3-0 | Ruhle | Gura |
| 29—At N. Y. | L | 2-4 | Medich | Coleman |
| 30—At N. Y. | L | 1-2 | May | Lolich |
| 31—At Bos. | L | 2-3† | Lee | Reynolds |
| 31—At Bos. | L | 1-6 | Moret | Lemanczyk |
| | | | **Won 19, Lost 14** | |

| AUGUST | | | | |
|---|---|---|---|---|
| 1—At Bos. | L | 7-8 | Willoughby | Pentz |
| 2—At Bos. | L | 2-7 | Wise | Ruhle |
| 3—At Bos. | L | 4-6 | Cleveland | Walker |
| 4—At Cleve. | L | 4-6 | Eckersley | Lolich |

| AUGUST | | | Winner | Loser |
|---|---|---|---|---|
| 5—At Cleve. | L | 4-8 | Raich | Bare |
| 6—Balt. | L | 2-4 | Torrez | LaGrow |
| 6—Balt. | L | 2-8 | Grimsley | Lemanczyk |
| 7—Balt. | L | 6-7† | Miller | Reynolds |
| 8—Minn. | L | 1-3 | Hughes | Coleman |
| 9—Minn. | L | 0-1 | Goltz | Lolich |
| 10—Minn. | L | 0-4 | Blyleven | Bare |
| 11—Texas | L | 0-7 | Perry | LaGrow |
| 12—Texas | L | 3-4 | Perzanowski | Ruhle |
| 13—Texas | L | 5-6‡ | Foucault | Pentz |
| 15—At Calif. | L | 0-8 | Tanana | Lolich |
| 16—At Calif. | W | 8-0 | Bare | Hockenbery |
| 17—At Calif. | W | 7-0 | Ruhle | Figueroa |
| 18—At Oak. | W | 5-3 | Coleman | Blue |
| 19—At Oak. | W | 3-1 | Lolich | Bosman |
| 20—At Oak. | L | 1-2 | Siebert | Bare |
| 22—At Minn. | L | 4-8 | Goltz | Ruhle |
| 23—At Minn. | W | 6-5§ | Lemanczyk | Burgmeier |
| 24—At Minn. | L | 1-3 | Hughes | Lolich |
| 25—At Texas | L | 0-1 | Umbarger | Bare |
| 26—At Texas | L | 2-3† | Perry | Pentz |
| 27—At Texas | L | 2-8 | Jenkins | LaGrow |
| 29—Calif. | L | 1-8 | Tanana | Lolich |
| 30—Calif. | W | 9-2 | Bare | Hockenbery |
| | | | **Won 6, Lost 22** | |

| SEPTEMBER | | | | |
|---|---|---|---|---|
| 1—Milw. | W | 5-4 | Lemanczyk | Austin |
| 2—Milw. | L | 5-6 | Colborn | Coleman |
| 3—N. York | L | 0-8 | Hunter | Lolich |
| 4—N. York | L | 1-8 | May | Bare |
| 5—At Cleve. | W | 11-2 | Ruhle | Waits |
| 6—At Cleve. | L | 2-4 | Eckersley | Lemanczyk |
| 7—At Cleve. | L | 2-7 | Bibby | Coleman |
| 7—At Cleve. | L | 0-9 | Peterson | LaGrow |
| 8—At N. Y. | L | 0-3 | May | Lolich |
| 9—At N. Y. | L | 6-9 | Medich | Bare |
| 10—At Bos. | L | 4-7 | Moret | Ruhle |
| 10—At Bos. | W | 5-3 | Arroyo | Willoughby |
| 11—At Bos. | L | 1-3 | Tiant | Lemanczyk |
| 12—Balt. | L | 4-6‡ | Torrez | Coleman |
| 13—Balt. | L | 0-8 | Alexander | Lolich |
| 14—Balt. | L | 3-9 | Mitchell | Bare |
| 16—Cleve. | L | 2-9 | Eckersley | Arroyo |
| 17—Cleve. | W | 4-0 | Coleman | Harrison |
| 18—Cleve. | L | 1-2 | Bibby | Lemanczyk |
| 19—Boston | L | 5-7 | Pole | Glynn |
| 20—Boston | W | 5-1 | Lolich | Tiant |
| 21—Boston | L | 5-6 | Drago | Pentz |
| 24—At Balt. | L | 1-8 | Palmer | Coleman |
| 26—At Milw. | L | 0-3 | Broberg | Bare |
| 27—At Milw. | L | 2-5 | Augustine | Ruhle |
| 28—At Milw. | L | 0-7 | Anderson | Glynn |
| | | | **Won 5, Lost 21** | |

\* 8 innings.   † 10 innings.   ‡ 11 innings.   § 12 innings.   x Suspended game, completed June 12.

# WEST DIVISION

## Finley and Dark Part Company

### By RON BERGMAN

After three years in a row as world champions, the Athletics' reign ended in 1975. They breezed to a fifth straight title in the West Division, finishing seven in front of the Royals, but were wiped out, three games to none, by the Red Sox in the American League Championship Series.

And so ended the second term of Alvin Dark as manager when owner

Charlie Finley didn't invite him back for a third year. At least Dark lasted two full seasons this time. Finley first hired him as manager in 1966 and fired him in August of 1967, re-hiring him in 1974.

Actually, Dark did a better job in 1975 than he had in 1974. Between seasons, Catfish Hunter had wriggled out of his contract and signed on with the Yankees for more than $3 million. He was no help at all to the A's, beating them all four times he pitched against them while losing all three times he faced the Royals.

At first, it didn't seem that the A's would miss their Cy Young Award winner. A 20-year-old rookie named Mike Norris popped up from nowhere. He followed a great exhibition season by shutting out the White Sox on three hits in his first outing of the regular campaign, and had a one-hitter through seven innings in his second start before being removed for a reliever. But an old elbow injury flared up in his third appearance, and he had to undergo surgery on his right arm which ended his season, except for two-thirds of an inning in relief on September 25.

Young hurlers Glenn Abbott and Dave Hamilton couldn't take up the slack and Finley looked around for help. In three separate deals, he picked up four veteran pitchers over 30 years old.

The best of the bunch was Dick Bosman, who posted an 11-4 record for the A's after coming from the Indians on May 20 along with Jim Perry for pitcher Blue Moon Odom and $15,000 in cash. Perry was 3-4 with the A's before he was released on August 13.

Sonny Siebert, obtained from the Padres, was 4-4, and Stan Bahnsen, who came from the White Sox just before the trading deadline on June 15, was 6-7 for the A's.

What made the Over-30 Gang so effective was Dark's astute use of a three-man bullpen that compiled impressive statistics. Once again, Rollie Fingers led the way, saving 24 victories and winning 10 outright while appearing in 75 games, high in the majors.

Fingers never tired because of help from Jim Todd, a righthanded refugee from the Cubs who saved 12, won eight, lost only three and finished with a 2.29 ERA in 58 games. Paul Lindblad (9-1 with seven saves and a 2.73 ERA) appeared 68 times as the lefthander of the bullpen.

Fingers, Todd and Lindblad became the Big Three of the A's pitching staff. In the championship years, it had been Hunter, Vida Blue and Ken Holtzman. The two surviving starters again did well.

Blue was 22-11, his third 20-victory season in five years. Holtzman was 18-14. He missed a no-hitter in Oakland on June 8 when the Tigers' Tom Veryzer, batting with two outs in the ninth inning, hit a fly to center that landed for a double when Billy North misjudged it and could not make the catch.

Hunter wasn't the only missing player. Second baseman Dick Green, after threatening to do so for many years, finally retired for good. His spot was assumed by rookie Phil Garner, previously a third baseman exclusively. Garner responded by making all the necessary routine plays and drove in 54 runs as a bonus.

Another new player in the lineup was Claudell Washington, who had broken in sensationally in the middle of 1974. He was placed in left field,

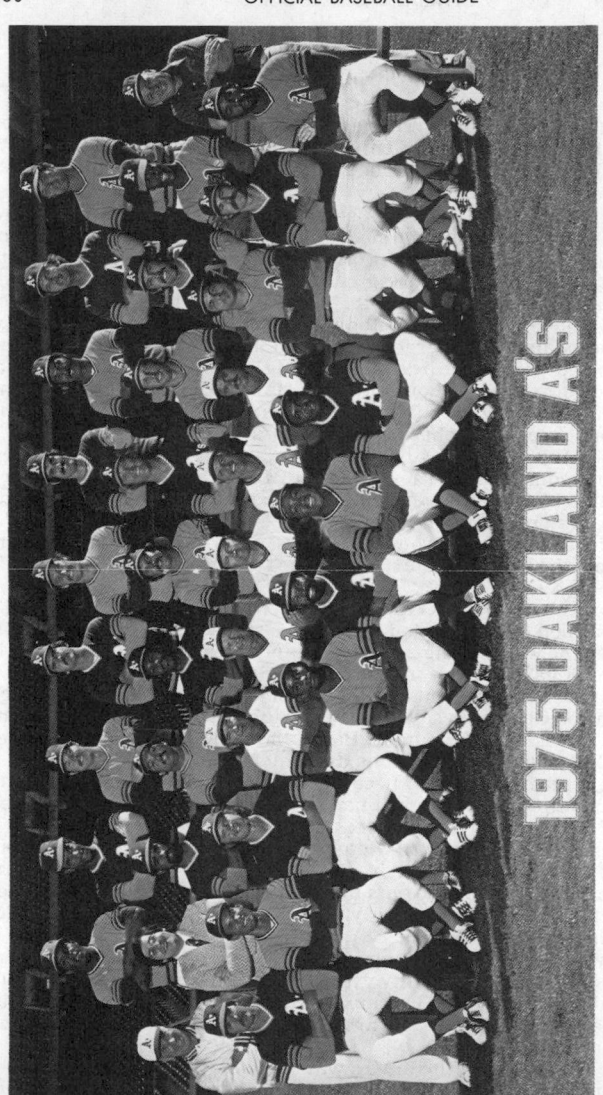

OAKLAND A's—1975

Front row—Alexander, Harper, Tovar, Holt. Second row—Lindblad, Campaneris, Bosman, Hofman, coach; Winkles, coach; Dark, manager; Stock, coach; Maxvill, coach; Bando, Garner, North. Third row—Romo, trainer; Bank, traveling secretary; Martinez, Jackson, Hopkins, Todd, Abbott, Rudi, Fosse, Norris, Ciensczyk, equipment manager. Fourth row—Blue, Washington, Tenace, Haney, Holtzman, Fingers, Williams, Bahnsen, Siebert.

supplanting Gold Glove winner Joe Rudi, who was moved to first base. Washington had problems defensively, but was the league's fifth-leading batter at .308 and was second in stolen bases with 40.

Billy Williams, a mainstay with the Cubs for 14 years, became the A's designated hitter and batted only .244, but hit 23 homers and drove in 81 runs.

The A's were out of first place only 11 days all season and took over the top spot for good on June 4. They accomplished all this without the fights and controversies that had marked their progress in the three previous years.

On September 8, the second-place Royals, only five back, roared into the Oakland Coliseum riding an eight-game winning streak. The A's ended the race right there with a three-game sweep over the Royals, who lost eight of nine in Oakland.

On September 24 the A's clinched the division title by beating the White Sox in the 158th game of the season.

The 162nd, and last contest, proved the most interesting. Dark was trying to give a number of pitchers a tuneup for the Championship Series. Instead, he unintentionally came up with the first four-way no-hitter in major league history.

Blue blanked the Angels over the first five innings, allowing three baserunners, two on walks and one because of an error. The next three pitchers were perfect. Abbott and Lindblad worked one inning each, and Rollie Fingers handled the final two.

In that unusual game, Reggie Jackson hit two homers and tied the Brewers' George Scott for the league title with 36. Jackson's 104 RBIs was the fourth-best total in the league.

Gene Tenace also enjoyed a good year for the A's, slamming 29 homers and driving in 87 runs, both career highs.

Finley's unique pinch-runner experiment ended May 5 with the release of Herb Washington, a world-class sprinter with no previous baseball experience before 1974. In his brief career, Herbie stole 31 bases in 48 attempts. He never appeared at the plate or in the field.

His place was taken by two new rabbits, Matt Alexander and Don Hopkins. Although neither was on a major league roster when the season began, they at least could bat or field without risking injury. They helped the A's steal 183 bases.

The A's set an Oakland attendance record with 1,075,518 in 77 dates, the second-highest home attendance in the 75-year history of the franchise, going back to its beginnings in Philadelphia. Road attendance was 1,436,383 in 72 dates.

## SCORES OF OAKLAND ATHLETICS' 1975 GAMES

| APRIL | | | Winner | Loser | APRIL | | | Winner | Loser |
|---|---|---|---|---|---|---|---|---|---|
| 8—Chicago | W | 3-2 | Blue | Wood | 19—Minn. | W | 4-1 | Blue | Corbin |
| 9—Chicago | L | 5-7 | Kaat | Fingers | 20—Minn. | W | 4-1 | Abbott | Blyleven |
| 10—Chicago | W | 9-0 | Norris | Bahnsen | 20—Minn. | W | 5-1 | Hamilton | Hughes |
| 11—At Texas | W | 7-5 | Lindblad | Hands | 21—Texas | W | 11-6 | Lindblad | Bibby |
| 12—At Texas | W | 5-4 | Blue | Jenkins | 22—Texas | L | 1-2 | Jenkins | Holtzman |
| 14—At K.C. | W | 3-2 | Holtzman | Splittorff | 23—Kan. C. | W | 3-2 | Blue | Busby |
| 15—At K.C. | L | 3-4 | Fitzmorris | Fingers | 24—Kan. C. | W | 3-2 | Abbott | Splittorff |
| 16—At K.C. | L | 2-6 | Briles | Blue | 25—At Calif. | L | 0-2 | Hassler | Hamilton |
| 18—Minn. | L | 4-5 | Albury | Holtzman | 26—At Calif. | L | 0-1 | Tanana | Holtzman |

**APRIL**

| | | | Winner | Loser |
|---|---|---|---|---|
| 27—At Calif. | W | 7-1 | Blue | Singer |
| 27—At Calif. | L | 1-9 | Figueroa | Odom |
| | | | Won 12, Lost 8 | |

**MAY**

| | | | | |
|---|---|---|---|---|
| 2—At Chi. | W | 4-3‡ | Fingers | Forster |
| 3—At Chi. | L | 3-4* | Gossage | Todd |
| 4—At Chi. | L | 2-5 | Kaat | Abbott |
| 6—Calif. | W | 5-3 | Lindblad | Kirkwood |
| 7—Calif. | W | 9-1 | Blue | Singer |
| 8—Calif. | L | 0-5 | Ryan | Hamilton |
| 9—N. York | W | 4-3 | Fingers | Dobson |
| 10—N. York | L | 0-3 | Hunter | Holtzman |
| 11—N. York | W | 7-5 | Blue | May |
| 12—Boston | W | 5-3 | Fingers | Segui |
| 13—Boston | W | 9-5 | Holtzman | Wise |
| 16—At N. Y. | W | 4-2 | Blue | Dobson |
| 17—At N. Y. | W | 6-1 | Holtzman | Medich |
| 18—At N. Y. | L | 1-9 | Hunter | Abbott |
| 19—At Bos. | L | 5-10 | Tiant | Odom |
| 20—At Bos. | L | 0-7 | Lee | Blue |
| 21—At Bos. | L | 3-7 | Cleveland | Holtzman |
| 23—At Cleve. | W | 3-0 | Siebert | G. Perry |
| 24—At Cleve. | W | 10-5 | Fingers | Hood |
| 25—At Cleve. | L | 0-6 | Eckersley | G. Perry |
| 25—At Cleve. | W | 6-3 | Bosman | Kern |
| 26—Balt. | W | 6-5† | Fingers | Alexander |
| 27—Balt. | W | 4-2 | Todd | Grimsley |
| 28—Balt. | W | 5-0 | Blue | Torrez |
| 30—Cleve. | W | 6-2 | Bosman | Kern |
| 31—Cleve. | L | 1-4 | Eckersley | Holtzman |
| | | | Won 16, Lost 10 | |

**JUNE**

| | | | | |
|---|---|---|---|---|
| 1—Cleve. | W | 6-3 | Siebert | G. Perry |
| 2—Milw. | L | 3-6 | Castro | Blue |
| 3—Milw. | L | 4-5 | Champion | Todd |
| 4—Milw. | W | 11-3 | Holtzman | Broberg |
| 6—Detroit | L | 2-11 | Lolich | Bosman |
| 7—Detroit | L | 0-3 | LaGrow | Blue |
| 8—Detroit | W | 4-0 | Holtzman | Coleman |
| 9—At Balt. | W | 4-3y | Lindblad | Miller |
| 10—At Balt. | W | 3-0 | Perry | Grimsley |
| 11—At Milw. | W | 5-3 | Bosman | Slaton |
| 12—At Milw. | L | 7-9 | Castro | Blue |
| 13—At Det. | W | 7-5 | Lindblad | Coleman |
| 14—At Det. | L | 2-3 | Walker | Siebert |
| 16—At Minn. | L | 6-7 | Burgmeier | Fingers |
| 17—At Minn. | W | 4-2 | Blue | Goltz |
| 17—At Minn. | W | 8-7 | Holtzman | Butler |
| 18—At Minn. | W | 7-6 | Todd | Albury |
| 19—At Minn. | W | 5-2* | Abbott | Hughes |
| 20—Kan. C. | W | 3-1 | Bahnsen | Leonard |
| 21—Kan. C. | L | 1-4 | Busby | Holtzman |
| 22—Kan. C. | W | 7-6‡ | Todd | Mingori |
| 22—Kan. C. | W | 8-1 | Bosman | Pattin |
| 23—Minn. | W | 5-2 | Lindblad | Hughes |
| 24—Minn. | W | 6-4 | Todd | Decker |
| 25—Minn. | W | 7-1 | Holtzman | Corbin |
| 27—At Calif. | W | 12-4 | Blue | Hassler |
| 28—At Calif. | W | 10-4 | Bosman | Singer |
| 29—At Calif. | W | 7-1 | Holtzman | Ryan |
| 30—At Chi. | L | 1-6 | Wood | Bahnsen |
| | | | Won 20, Lost 9 | |

**JULY**

| | | | | |
|---|---|---|---|---|
| 1—At Chi. | W | 10-1 | Blue | Jefferson |
| 2—At Chi. | L | 4-5 | Gossage | Fingers |
| 3—At Chi. | L | 2-3 | Kaat | Todd |
| 4—Calif. | W | 6-0 | Holtzman | Tanana |
| 5—Calif. | L | 0-2 | Figueroa | Bahnsen |
| 6—Calif. | L | 0-2 | Lange | Blue |
| 7—Cleve. | W | 7-3 | Perry | Eckersley |
| 8—Cleve. | W | 15-5 | Holtzman | Hood |
| 9—Cleve. | W | 3-1 | Bosman | Raich |
| 11—Balt. | L | 0-4 | Torrez | Blue |

**JULY**

| | | | Winner | Loser |
|---|---|---|---|---|
| 12—Balt. | W | 7-1 | Perry | Palmer |
| 13—Balt. | W | 4-3 | Holtzman | Grimsley |
| 17—At Cleve. | W | 6-3 | Holtzman | Raich |
| 18—At Cleve. | W | 7-6 | Abbott | Bibby |
| 19—At Balt. | L | 2-3 | Mitchell | Blue |
| 19—At Balt. | L | 1-5 | Grimsley | Perry |
| 20—At Balt. | W | 5-2 | Fingers | Alexander |
| 21—At Balt. | L | 2-6 | Torrez | Holtzman |
| 22—At Det. | W | 11-0 | Abbott | Walker |
| 22—At Det. | W | 16-4 | Bahnsen | LaGrow |
| 23—At Det. | W | 3-0 | Blue | Ruhle |
| 24—At Det. | L | 2-5 | Coleman | Perry |
| 25—Chicago | W | 8-6§ | Lindblad | Upshaw |
| 26—Chicago | L | 2-5 | Kaat | Fingers |
| 27—Chicago | W | 10-1 | Blue | Jefferson |
| 27—Chicago | W | 7-1 | Bahnsen | Allen |
| 28—Texas | W | 12-6 | Lindblad | Moore |
| 29—Texas | L | 1-6 | Hargan | Perry |
| 30—Texas | W | 1-0 | Holtzman | Jenkins |
| | | | Won 18, Lost 11 | |

**AUGUST**

| | | | | |
|---|---|---|---|---|
| 1—At K. C. | L | 0-6 | Busby | Bahnsen |
| 2—At K. C. | W | 6-5 | Fingers | Mingori |
| 3—At K. C. | L | 0-5 | Splittorff | Abbott |
| 4—At Texas | L | 0-12 | Jenkins | Holtzman |
| 5—At Texas | W | 3-2 | Bosman | Perzanowski |
| 5—At Texas | L | 2-15 | Wright | Siebert |
| 6—At Texas | L | 2-5 | Perry | Bahnsen |
| 7—At Texas | W | 10-1 | Blue | Umbarger |
| 8—Boston | W | 3-2 | Holtzman | Cleveland |
| 9—Boston | L | 2-7 | Lee | Siebert |
| 10—Boston | L | 3-5 | Tiant | Bosman |
| 11—Boston | W | 4-3 | Blue | Moret |
| 12—N. York | L | 2-7 | Medich | Holtzman |
| 13—N. York | L | 1-3 | Hunter | Bahnsen |
| 14—N. York | W | 5-1 | Bosman | May |
| 15—Milw. | L | 4-8 | Colborn | Blue |
| 16—Milw. | W | 2-1 | Fingers | Slaton |
| 17—Milw. | W | 3-1 | Bahnsen | Broberg |
| 18—Detroit | L | 3-5 | Coleman | Blue |
| 19—Detroit | L | 1-3 | Lolich | Bosman |
| 20—Detroit | W | 2-1 | Siebert | Bare |
| 21—At Milw. | W | 5-2 | Holtzman | Broberg |
| 23—At Milw. | W | 6-3 | Todd | Murphy |
| 23—At Milw. | W | 9-3 | Bahnsen | Hausman |
| 24—At Milw. | L | 6-7 | Rodriguez | Fingers |
| 26—At N. Y. | L | 1-7 | Hunter | Siebert |
| 27—At N. Y. | W | 3-2 | Blue | Medich |
| 28—At N. Y. | L | 2-3 | Dobson | Holtzman |
| 29—At Bos. | L | 1-6 | Wise | Bahnsen |
| 30—At Bos. | W | 7-6* | Fingers | Drago |
| 31—At Bos. | W | 8-6 | Fingers | Segui |
| | | | Won 15, Lost 16 | |

**SEPTEMBER**

| | | | | |
|---|---|---|---|---|
| 1—At Calif. | W | 6-3 | Blue | Figueroa |
| 2—At Calif. | L | 1-4 | Tanana | Holtzman |
| 5—Texas | L | 2-4 | Perry | Blue |
| 6—Texas | W | 2-1 | Lindblad | Jenkins |
| 7—Texas | W | 4-1 | Bosman | Wright |
| 7—Texas | W | 7-3 | Siebert | Hargan |
| 8—Kan. C. | W | 8-2 | Holtzman | Leonard |
| 9—Kan. C. | W | 2-1x | Todd | Pattin |
| 10—Kan. C. | W | 9-1 | Blue | Busby |
| 12—At Minn. | W | 11-4 | Bosman | Hughes |
| 12—At Minn. | L | 6-7 | Bane | Lindblad |
| 13—At Minn. | W | 8-5 | Holtzman | Goltz |
| 14—At Minn. | L | 8-10 | Butler | Abbott |
| 16—At Texas | W | 11-5 | Todd | Perry |
| 16—At Texas | W | 6-4 | Bahnsen | Jenkins |
| 17—At Chi. | L | 2-3 | Wood | Holtzman |
| 18—At Chi. | W | 7-6 | Todd | Kaat |
| 19—At K. C. | L | 4-5 | Busby | Abbott |
| 20—At K. C. | W | 16-4 | Blue | Splittorff |
| 21—At K. C. | L | 1-2 | Leonard | Bosman |

| SEPTEMBER | | | Winner | Loser | SEPTEMBER | | | Winner | Loser |
|---|---|---|---|---|---|---|---|---|---|
| 22—Minn. | L | 1-2 | Bane | Holtzman | 26—Calif. | W | 4-2 | Bosman | Figueroa |
| 23—Minn. | L | 3-4 | Blyleven | Bahnsen | 27—Calif. | W | 6-3 | Holtzman | Tanana |
| 24—Chicago | W | 13-2 | Blue | Jefferson | 28—Calif. | W | 5-0 | Blue | Ross |
| 25—Chicago | L | 2-8 | Wood | Mitchell | | | Won 17, Lost 10 | | |

* 10 innings.   † 11 innings.   ‡ 12 innings.   § 13 innings.   x 14 innings.   y 15 innings.

# Royals Are Bridesmaids—Again

## By JOE McGUFF

The Royals' 1975 season can best be described as a mixed bag of success and failure, hope and disappointment. The year produced an unusual amount of turmoil, but in the end stability was restored and the future seemed promising.

The Royals won 91 games, making 1975 the best season in Kansas City's major league history. Even so it was less than an unqualified success because the Royals were never able to seriously challenge the A's, who won their fourth straight West Division title.

The turmoil started early and did not subside until Jack McKeon was fired as manager on July 24. He was replaced by Whitey Herzog, who proved to be popular with the players and fans.

The outstanding individual accomplishments of the year were turned in by John Mayberry, the club's slugging first baseman, and youthful George Brett, who appears to be a likely successor to Brooks Robinson as the American League's best third baseman. Mayberry started slowly, but had a sizzling July and August. He drove in 106 runs, an all-time high by a Royal and set a Royals' record for home runs with 34. Mayberry batted .291.

Brett led the club in hitting with an average of .308, the sixth highest in the American League. He led the league in hits with 195, three more than Rod Carew. He broke the all-time Kansas City record of 193 set by Jerry Lumpe in 1962. Brett had 11 homers, 89 RBIs and tied for the league lead in triples with 13.

The Royals, who suffered an embarrassing collapse in the final month of the 1974 season and finished fifth, broke camp in spring training vowing that they could win the pennant and for a time they seemed to mean what they said. They won nine of their first 11 games and for once Oakland was chasing Kansas City.

At this point the Royals suffered a sinking spell. They won only five times in their next 18 starts and through games of May 10 they were one game under .500.

On May 18 the Royals flew from Boston to New York. After the flight arrived, Steve Busby, the club's best pitcher, informed McKeon that he was leaving the team and returning home. Busby later changed his mind and took his regular pitching turn, but the story was in the papers and speculation spread that his action was directed against McKeon.

After the club returned home, Joe Burke, the executive vice-president and general manager, met with Owner Ewing Kauffman amid rumors that McKeon would be fired. Instead Burke appeared before the players and gave McKeon a vote of confidence.

KANSAS CITY ROYALS—1975

Front row—White, Splittorff, Boros, coach; Cisco, coach; McKeon, manager; Dunlop, coach; Brett, Fitzmorris, Healy, Solaita. Second row—Dudley, trainer; McRae, Pattin, Busby, Mayberry, Paepke, Martinez, Mingori, Wohlford, Briles, Pinson, Zych, equipment manager; Cobb, organization trainer. Third row—Rojas, Patek, Killebrew, Bird, Dal Canton, Scott, McDaniel, Leonard, Mallory, Cowens, Otis, Quirk.

By June 4 the Royals had moved back to nine games over .500. At the All-Star break they had a 47-41 record and were eight and a half games behind Oakland. The Royals were hoping to narrow the gap between themselves and Oakland when the season resumed, but instead they lost their first four games to Boston and Detroit and found themselves caught up in a six-game losing streak.

At this point they were 11 games behind Oakland and rumors of McKeon's dismissal were rekindled. Burke joined the club in Detroit and went on to Milwaukee. On the flight home from Milwaukee he told McKeon that he was going to have to make a change in managers.

The following morning a press conference was called and Herzog, who had been a coach for the Angels, was presented as the fifth manager of the Royals. The others, in addition to McKeon, were Bob Lemon, Charlie Metro and Joe Gordon.

Herzog's first move was to announce the rehiring of Charlie Lau, the hitting instructor McKeon dismissed at the end of the 1974 season. The move was popular with the players and the Royals settled down and began to play well.

In early September the Royals put together an eight-game winning streak, the longest in Royals' history. When the Royals arrived in Oakland September 8 for a three-game series they were five games behind the A's, but they still had a chance to get back in the race. However, they lost all three games and the pennant race was over.

The middle game of the series was decisive. The Royals had a runner on third with no one out in the eighth and the score tied, but were unable to score. They finally lost in the 14th inning when the A's scored on an error, a stolen base and a broken bat single.

The Royals finished with a 41-25 record under Herzog for a .621 percentage. They were 24-12 at home and 17-13 on the road. The Royals raised their team batting average 13 points under Herzog and lowered their staff earned-run average from 3.75 to 3.06. The bullpen had seven saves when Herzog took over, but recorded 18 the rest of the season.

Hal McRae finished the year with a .306 batting average, his second straight year in the .300-plus category. He was out with a injury the final month of the season and his loss proved costly. Al Cowens, a young outfielder, came on strong the last two months. Dennis Leonard, a rookie pitcher, finished with an impressive 15-7 record and Paul Splittorff finished well after a poor start. Steve Busby had a shoulder problem late in the season, but still won 18 games.

When the season began most managers in the A. L. West were predicting that 91 or 92 victories would win the division pennant. Actually the Royals did as well as anyone could reasonably expect, but Oakland exceeded expectations and the Royals again were forced to wait until next year.

## SCORES OF KANSAS CITY ROYALS' 1975 GAMES

| APRIL | | | Winner | Loser | APRIL | | | Winner | Loser |
|---|---|---|---|---|---|---|---|---|---|
| 7—At Calif. | L | 2-3 | Ryan | Mingori | 14—Oakland | L | 2-3 | Holtzman | Splittorff |
| 9—At Calif. | W | 7-6 | McDaniel | Dobson | 15—Oakland | W | 4-3 | Fitzmorris | Fingers |
| 11—Minn. | W | 8-3 | Fitzmorris | Butler | 16—Oakland | W | 6-2 | Briles | Blue |
| 12—Minn. | W | 2-1* | Bird | Campbell | 18—At Texas | W | 5-3 | Busby | Brown |
| 13—Minn. | W | 5-3 | Busby | Decker | 19—At Texas | W | 5-2 | Splittorff | Hands |

## APRIL

| Date | | Score | Winner | Loser |
|---|---|---|---|---|
| 20—At Texas | W | 2-0 | Fitzmorris | Hargan |
| 22—At Chi. | L | 3-7 | Kaat | Dal Canton |
| 23—At Oak. | L | 2-3 | Blue | Busby |
| 24—At Oak. | L | 2-3 | Abbott | Splittorff |
| 25—Chicago | L | 2-5 | Osteen | Fitzmorris |
| 26—Chicago | W | 8-6 | Briles | Bahnsen |
| 27—Chicago | L | 6-8 | Kaat | Dal Canton |
| 28—Chicago | W | 7-5 | Busby | Wood |
| 29—Calif. | L | 1-12 | Hassler | Splittorff |
| 30—Calif. | L | 6-7 | Scott | Bird |

Won 11, Lost 9

## MAY

| Date | | Score | Winner | Loser |
|---|---|---|---|---|
| 1—Calif. | W | 11-10§ | Bird | Pena |
| 2—At Minn. | L | 1-4 | Goltz | Busby |
| 3—At Minn. | L | 5-14 | Blyleven | Splittorff |
| 4—At Minn. | L | 3-6 | Hughes | Fitzmorris |
| 6—Texas | W | 6-2 | Briles | Bibby |
| 7—Texas | W | 6-5 | Busby | Wright |
| 8—Texas | L | 3-5 | Hargan | Bird |
| 9—Milw. | L | 1-7 | Sprague | Fitzmorris |
| 10—Milw. | L | 0-3 | Broberg | Briles |
| 11—Milw. | W | 4-0 | Busby | Champion |
| 12—At Det. | L | 0-5 | Ruhle | Leonard |
| 13—At Det. | W | 8-7 | Fitzmorris | LaGrow |
| 14—At Det. | W | 4-1 | Briles | Coleman |
| 15—At Bos. | W | 3-0 | Busby | Tiant |
| 16—At Bos. | W | 5-2 | Leonard | Lee |
| 17—At Bos. | W | 5-3 | Fitzmorris | Cleveland |
| 18—At Bos. | L | 2-4 | Wise | Briles |
| 19—At N. Y. | L | 1-5 | May | Busby |
| 20—At N. Y. | L | 0-6 | Dobson | Splittorff |
| 21—At N. Y. | W | 4-1* | Bird | Medich |
| 23—Balt. | W | 10-1 | Fitzmorris | Grimsley |
| 24—Balt. | W | 5-4 | Pattin | Garland |
| 25—Balt. | W | 9-1 | Busby | Palmer |
| 26—N. York | W | 6-5† | Pattin | Lyle |
| 27—N. York | W | 3-0 | Fitzmorris | Hunter |
| 28—N. York | L | 2-6 | May | Briles |
| 31—At Milw. | W | 7-5 | McDaniel | Broberg |

Won 16, Lost 11

## JUNE

| Date | | Score | Winner | Loser |
|---|---|---|---|---|
| 1—At Milw. | W | 13-6 | Pattin | Hausman |
| 1—At Milw. | W | 11-5 | Fitzmorris | Colborn |
| 3—At Cleve. | W | 5-2 | Leonard | Peterson |
| 4—At Cleve. | L | 0-4 | Odom | Busby |
| 5—At Cleve. | L | 7-8† | LaRoche | Pattin |
| 6—At Balt. | L | 2-3† | Jackson | Pattin |
| 7—At Balt. | L | 3-7 | Torrez | Leonard |
| 8—At Balt. | L | 0-1 | Palmer | Busby |
| 9—Detroit | W | 5-2 | McDaniel | Walker |
| 10—Detroit | W | 4-3 | Pattin | Ruhle |
| 11—Cleve. | W | 7-1 | Leonard | G. Perry |
| 12—Cleve. | W | 2-1* | Busby | Raich |
| 13—Boston | L | 4-10 | Wise | Fitzmorris |
| 13—Boston | W | 6-5 | Bird | Pole |
| 14—Boston | L | 3-4 | Tiant | Pattin |
| 15—Boston | L | 7-8 | Lee | McDaniel |
| 17—Calif. | W | 3-2 | Busby | Figueroa |
| 18—Calif. | W | 13-0 | Pattin | Ryan |
| 20—At Oak. | L | 1-3 | Bahnsen | Leonard |
| 21—At Oak. | W | 4-1 | Busby | Holtzman |
| 22—At Oak. | L | 6-7‡ | Todd | Mingori |
| 22—At Oak. | L | 1-8 | Bosman | Pattin |
| 24—At Calif. | W | 5-3† | Bird | Scott |
| 25—At Calif. | W | 6-2‡ | Busby | Quintana |
| 26—At Calif. | W | 7-1 | Pattin | Figueroa |
| 27—At Chi. | L | 3-4 | Hamilton | Bird |
| 28—At Chi. | L | 3-5 | Osteen | Leonard |
| 29—At Chi. | L | 1-3 | Kaat | Splittorff |

Won 14, Lost 14

## JULY

| Date | | Score | Winner | Loser |
|---|---|---|---|---|
| 1—At Texas | L | 4-5 | Jenkins | Busby |
| 2—At Texas | W | 7-5* | Bird | Perry |
| 3—At Texas | W | 10-5 | Fitzmorris | Hands |
| 4—Chicago | W | 3-2 | Leonard | Wood |
| 5—Chicago | W | 6-4 | Splittorff | Hamilton |
| 6—Chicago | L | 3-9 | Osteen | Pattin |
| 7—Milw. | L | 3-4 | Slaton | Fitzmorris |
| 8—Milw. | W | 9-1 | Leonard | Travers |
| 9—Milw. | L | 4-6 | Colborn | Briles |
| 10—Detroit | L | 2-3 | Ruhle | Busby |
| 11—Detroit | W | 5-2 | Pattin | Lolich |
| 12—Detroit | L | 0-2 | LaGrow | Fitzmorris |
| 13—Detroit | L | 4-8 | Coleman | Leonard |
| 17—At Bos. | L | 3-8 | Tiant | Fitzmorris |
| 18—At Bos. | L | 3-9 | Lee | Busby |
| 19—At Det. | L | 8-10 | Coleman | Pattin |
| 20—At Det. | L | 3-7 | Bare | Briles |
| 21—At Det. | W | 3-2 | Leonard | Lolich |
| 22—At Milw. | W | 3-2 | Busby | Slaton |
| 22—At Milw. | L | 3-6 | Hausman | Fitzmorris |
| 23—At Milw. | W | 4-1 | Pattin | Travers |
| 25—Texas | W | 6-3 | Briles | Wright |
| 25—Texas | W | 6-1 | Leonard | Thomas |
| 26—Texas | W | 7-0 | Fitzmorris | Jenkins |
| 27—Texas | W | 2-1 | Busby | Perry |
| 28—At Minn. | L | 8-9 | Burgmeier | Bird |
| 29—At Minn. | W | 5-2 | Splittorff | Blyleven |
| 30—At Minn. | W | 6-4 | Leonard | Albury |
| 31—At Minn. | L | 2-7 | Hughes | Fitzmorris |

Won 15, Lost 14

## AUGUST

| Date | | Score | Winner | Loser |
|---|---|---|---|---|
| 1—Oakland | W | 6-0 | Busby | Bahnsen |
| 2—Oakland | L | 5-6 | Fingers | Mingori |
| 3—Oakland | W | 5-0 | Splittorff | Abbott |
| 4—Minn. | W | 6-5* | Bird | Wiley |
| 5—Minn. | W | 6-1 | Fitzmorris | Goltz |
| 6—Minn. | W | 4-3 | Busby | Blyleven |
| 7—Minn. | W | 10-2 | Splittorff | Albury |
| 8—At Cleve. | L | 3-4 | Harrison | Pattin |
| 9—At Cleve. | W | 6-4 | McDaniel | Bibby |
| 10—At Cleve. | W | 5-1 | Fitzmorris | Raich |
| 11—At Balt. | L | 0-4 | Cuellar | Busby |
| 12—At Balt. | W | 4-2* | Bird | Miller |
| 13—At Balt. | L | 0-3 | Palmer | Pattin |
| 15—N. York | L | 4-5 | Dobson | Bird |
| 16—N. York | W | 4-3 | Briles | Medich |
| 17—N. York | W | 5-3 | Splittorff | Hunter |
| 19—Boston | L | 0-5 | Lee | Fitzmorris |
| 20—Boston | W | 3-1 | Leonard | Tiant |
| 21—Cleve. | L | 3-7 | Brown | Littell |
| 22—Cleve. | L | 5-9 | Peterson | Splittorff |
| 23—Cleve. | L | 1-7 | Waits | Briles |
| 24—Cleve. | W | 5-2 | Fitzmorris | Harrison |
| 26—Balt. | W | 4-3 | Leonard | Palmer |
| 26—Balt. | L | 2-3 | Alexander | Busby |
| 27—Balt. | L | 2-4 | Torrez | Splittorff |
| 29—At N. Y. | L | 5-6* | Lyle | Pattin |
| 30—At N. Y. | W | 5-2 | Leonard | Hunter |
| 31—At N. Y. | W | 7-0 | Splittorff | Gura |

Won 16, Lost 12

## SEPTEMBER

| Date | | Score | Winner | Loser |
|---|---|---|---|---|
| 1—At Chi. | L | 8-10 | Gossage | Busby |
| 1—At Chi. | W | 3-1 | Bird | Osteen |
| 2—At Chi. | W | 4-1‡ | Fitzmorris | Kaat |
| 3—At Chi. | W | 5-4* | Leonard | Hamilton |
| 4—At Chi. | W | 7-0 | Splittorff | Kravec |
| 5—At Calif. | W | 5-2 | Busby | Figueroa |
| 6—At Calif. | W | 4-3 | McDaniel | Tanana |
| 6—At Calif. | W | 6-3 | Pattin | Singer |
| 7—At Calif. | W | 8-7† | Littell | Scott |
| 8—At Oak. | L | 2-8 | Holtzman | Leonard |
| 9—At Oak. | L | 1-2x | Todd | Pattin |
| 10—At Oak. | L | 1-9 | Blue | Busby |
| 12—Calif. | W | 10-2 | Leonard | Singer |
| 12—Calif. | W | 7-2 | Fitzmorris | Kirkwood |
| 13—Calif. | L | 2-6 | Figueroa | Bird |

| SEPTEMBER | | | Winner | Loser | SEPTEMBER | | | Winner | Loser |
|---|---|---|---|---|---|---|---|---|---|
| 14—Calif. | W | 10-4 | Busby | Tanana | 22—Texas | W | 2-1 | Fitzmorris | Foucault |
| 15—Chicago | W | 3-2 | Splittorff | Osteen | 23—Texas | W | 4-0 | McClure | Umbarger |
| 16—Chicago | L | 5-6 | Jefferson | Leonard | 24—Minn. | W | 4-2 | Pattin | Hughes |
| 17—At Minn. | L | 1-2 | Goltz | Fitzmorris | 25—Minn. | L | 2-5 | Butler | Splittorff |
| 18—At Minn. | W | 4-3 | Sadecki | Bane | 26—At Texas | W | 8-6 | Leonard | Jenkins |
| 19—Oakland | W | 5-4 | Busby | Abbott | 27—At Texas | L | 4-5 | Perry | Fitzmorris |
| 20—Oakland | L | 4-16 | Blue | Splittorff | 28—At Texas | L | 1-3 | Perzanowski | Littell |
| 21—Oakland | W | 2-1 | Leonard | Bosman | | | | Won 19, Lost 11 | |

* 10 innings.    † 11 innings.    ‡ 12 innings.    § 13 innings.    x 14 innings.

# Lucchesi to the Rescue

### By MERLE HERYFORD

If 1974 was a year for the Texas Rangers to remember, 1975 was one to forget.

The club won only five fewer games, but, instead of finishing only five games behind Oakland in the American League West, had to hang on by its fingernails to salvage third, 19 games off the pace.

The pill was made less palatable by the fact that Billy Martin, who was fired as manager on July 21, had confidently predicted a pennant and expressed complete confidence in a mound staff which intermittently bombed and blossomed—usually in unexpected places.

Biggest disappointments, of course, were the bellwethers of the 1974 climb from obscurity to false security: Ferguson Jenkins and Jeff Burroughs.

Jenkins, despite occasional flashes of his old brilliance, plummeted from a 25-12 year to 17-18, only the second time in 10 years he had failed to win 20 or more games.

And Burroughs, coming off a .301, 118 RBIs performance which had netted him the Most Valuable Player Award, skidded to .226 and 94 RBIs, figures made more impressive than their actual contribution by a strong September during which he hit seven homers for a total of 29.

Overall, the team batting average was down 16 points to .256, as Mike Hargrove, Rookie of the Year in 1974, was the only one of three .300 hitters to repeat. Hargrove dropped from .323 to .303, and Len Randle, as well as Burroughs, fell—from .302 to .276 while battling the handicap of playing at six positions.

That was the story—and to a large extent the fallacy—of 1975. The players occupied so many positions even they needed programs.

It started with Martin's insatiable passion for platooning, intensified after Willie Davis, who had been hailed as the savior in center field, failed to deliver both at bat and afield, and, after several altercations with Martin, was traded to the St. Louis Cardinals.

It continued somewhat after Frank Lucchesi, third base coach for a year and a half, was elevated to the managerial post and used the remainder of a lost season to evaluate his personnel.

Martin departed with a 44-51 record, leaving behind a club which had exhibited an almost pathological inability to win at home. Lucchesi took over on an interim basis and a week later had his contract extended through 1976.

TEXAS RANGERS—1975

Front row—Harrah, Sundberg, Cubbage, Gernert, coach; Hudson, coach; Lucchesi, manager; J. Moore, coach; Pruitt, Moates, Nelson. Second row—Zeigler, trainer; Umbarger, Thomas, Cardenas, Wright, Burroughs, Lovitto, Fahey, Hargrove, T. Moore, Foucault, Howell, Tovar. Third row—Fregosi, Hands, Grieve, Spencer, Perry, Robson, Perzanowski, Jones, Hargan, Jenkins.

The Rangers did an immediate turnabout, going 35-32 the rest of the way despite the experiments.

Earlier, on June 13, the Rangers had made their biggest roster change by trading pitchers Jim Bibby, Jackie Brown and Rick Waits, latter with Spokane, to Cleveland for 36-year-old Gaylord Perry. Bibby, a 19-game winner in '74, had only a 2-6 record and Brown had been inconsistent.

Perry brought with him a 6-9 record and lost four more before returning to form. He was 12-4 in the stretch for a gutty 18-17 overall.

One of Lucchesi's earliest moves was to install 21-year-old rookie Roy Howell at third base and make Tom Grieve, for three seasons an uncomplaining bridesmaid, a starter.

Grieve zoomed to .276, and Howell, improving steadily on defense, batted a creditable .251.

Lucchesi made rookie lefthander Jim Umbarger a starter and he won four straight to finish 8-7.

Among the undenied reclamation projects were catcher Jim Sundberg and ace reliever Steve Foucault, both of whom had lost confidence.

Foucault bounced back, wound up 8-4 with 10 saves, and was the old fireman in the last two months.

Another late season experiment is expected to bear fruit next season. Rookie Roy Smalley, the No. 1 draft choice a year ago, failed early to dislodge Toby Harrah at shortstop, was returned to AAA Spokane and came back in September to play a flashy second base.

Randle, who played second, third, all the outfield positions and even caught a few innings, will go to center field in '76, backed by Dave Moates. Dave Nelson, who underwent an ankle operation in May and missed most of the season, was traded to the Royals for pitcher Nelson Briles after the World Series.

Real bright spot of the season was Harrah, in his fifth major league campaign. Toby jumped from .260 to .293 and led the club in most offensive departments while playing three positions, frequently two in one game.

He hit 20 homers, drove in 93 runs, walked 98 times and stole 23 bases, impressive credentials for a shortstop.

Also impressive was the fact that, despite constant rain interference, the Rangers topped the million mark in attendance for the second straight year, finishing with 1,127,924.

The Rangers made the headlines on November 17 when Jenkins was traded to Boston for outfielder Juan Beniquez and young pitchers Steve Barr and Craig Skok.

### SCORES OF TEXAS RANGERS' 1975 GAMES

| APRIL | | | Winner | Loser | APRIL | | | Winner | Loser |
|-------|---|-----|--------|-------|-------|---|------|--------|-------|
| 8—Minn. | L | 4-11 | Blyleven | Jenkins | 18—Kan. C. | L | 3-5 | Busby | Brown |
| 9—Minn. | L | 2-3 | Decker | Bibby | 19—Kan. C. | L | 2-5 | Splittorff | Hands |
| 10—Minn. | W | 5-4 | Foucault | Goltz | 20—Kan. C. | L | 0-2 | Fitzmorris | Hargan |
| 11—Oakland | L | 5-7 | Lindblad | Hands | 21—At Oak. | L | 6-11 | Lindblad | Bibby |
| 12—Oakland | L | 4-5 | Blue | Jenkins | 22—At Oak. | W | 2-1 | Jenkins | Holtzman |
| 15—At Chi. | W | 6-5x | Hargan | Gossage | 23—At Calif. | L | 1-4 | Singer | Wright |
| 16—At Chi. | W | 14-4 | Umbarger | Wood | 24—At Calif. | W | 5-0 | Brown | Ryan |
| 17—At Chi. | W | 7-3 | Jenkins | Bahnsen | 26—At Minn. | W | 7-2 | Hands | Albury |

**APRIL**

| | | | Winner | Loser |
|---|---|---|---|---|
| 29—Chicago | W | 3-2 | Jenkins | Osteen |
| 30—Chicago | W | 8-2 | Bibby | Bahnsen |

**Won 9, Lost 9**

**MAY**

| | | | Winner | Loser |
|---|---|---|---|---|
| 1—Chicago | W | 2-1 | Foucault | Gossage |
| 2—Calif. | W | 4-3 | Hargan | Singer |
| 3—Calif. | L | 2-4 | Ryan | Brown |
| 4—Calif. | W | 1-0 | Hands | Hassler |
| 5—Calif. | W | 4-3 | Jenkins | Lange |
| 6—At K. C. | L | 2-6 | Briles | Bibby |
| 7—At K. C. | L | 5-6 | Busby | Wright |
| 8—At K. C. | W | 5-3 | Hargan | Bird |
| 9—At Det. | W | 3-1 | Brown | LaGrow |
| 10—At Det. | W | 5-2 | Hands | Coleman |
| 11—At Det. | W | 11-7 | Jenkins | Lolich |
| 13—Milw. | W | 5-0* | Bibby | Slaton |
| 14—Milw. | L | 2-3z | Rodriguez | Brown |
| 15—Milw. | L | 5-8 | Broberg | Hargan |
| 16—Detroit | W | 10-3 | Hands | Lolich |
| 17—Detroit | L | 4-6 | Ruhle | Brown |
| 18—Detroit | W | 7-6‡ | Thomas | Lemanczyk |
| 20—At Milw. | L | 6-7† | Rodriguez | Brown |
| 21—At Milw. | W | 5-4 | Hargan | Champion |
| 22—At Milw. | W | 6-0 | Hands | Colborn |
| 23—At N. Y. | L | 7-11 | Hunter | Jenkins |
| 24—At N. Y. | L | 5-9 | Tidrow | Wright |
| 25—At N. Y. | L | 4-5 | Dobson | Bibby |
| 26—Boston | L | 5-7 | Wise | Foucault |
| 28—Boston | L | 1-4 | Lee | Jenkins |
| 29—N. York | L | 5-7 | Tidrow | Umbarger |
| 30—N. York | W | 6-5 | Brown | Lyle |
| 31—N. York | L | 0-6 | Hunter | Hands |

**Won 14, Lost 14**

**JUNE**

| | | | Winner | Loser |
|---|---|---|---|---|
| 1—N. York | L | 4-8 | May | Jenkins |
| 3—At Balt. | L | 3-6 | Torrez | Hargan |
| 4—At Balt. | W | 3-2§ | Brown | Jackson |
| 6—At Cleve. | L | 5-7 | LaRoche | Jenkins |
| 7—At Cleve. | W | 5-4§ | Thomas | G. Perry |
| 8—At Cleve. | L | 2-3 | Raich | Bibby |
| 8—At Cleve. | W | 7-6a | Thomas | Buskey |
| 9—At Bos. | W | 12-4 | Brown | Wise |
| 10—At Bos. | W | 8-3 | Jenkins | Tiant |
| 11—Balt. | L | 8-9† | Miller | Thomas |
| 12—Balt. | L | 1-7 | Palmer | Bibby |
| 13—Cleve. | W | 2-1 | Umbarger | Peterson |
| 14—Cleve. | W | 2-1 | Jenkins | Harrison |
| 15—Cleve. | L | 1-5 | Eckersley | Perry |
| 17—Chicago | L | 3-13 | Kaat | Umbarger |
| 18—Chicago | W | 10-3 | Jenkins | Wood |
| 19—Chicago | W | 5-3 | Thomas | Gossage |
| 20—At Calif. | L | 11-12‡ | Kirkwood | Foucault |
| 21—At Calif. | L | 2-4 | Tanana | Umbarger |
| 21—At Calif. | W | 6-5 | Umbarger | Quintana |
| 22—At Calif. | L | 0-1 | Figueroa | Jenkins |
| 23—At Calif. | L | 0-x | Umbarger | Kirkwood |
| 24—At Chi. | L | 5-7 | Osteen | Perry |
| 25—At Chi. | L | 2-5 | Kaat | Bacsik |
| 26—At Chi. | L | 3-8 | Wood | Jenkins |
| 27—Minn. | W | 2-0 | Hargan | Blyleven |
| 27—Minn. | L | 5-8 | Albury | Umbarger |
| 28—Minn. | L | 3-5 | Hughes | Perry |
| 29—Minn. | W | 9-7 | Bacsik | Campbell |

**Won 13, Lost 16**

**JULY**

| | | | Winner | Loser |
|---|---|---|---|---|
| 1—Kan. C. | W | 5-4 | Jenkins | Busby |
| 2—Kan. C. | L | 2-5 | Bird | Perry |
| 3—Kan. C. | L | 5-10 | Fitzmorris | Hands |
| 4—At Minn. | L | 0-8 | Campbell | Bacsik |
| 4—At Minn. | W | 4-2 | Hargan | Corbin |
| 5—At Minn. | L | 4-5 | Goltz | Jenkins |
| 6—At Minn. | W | 4-2 | Wright | Blyleven |
| 6—At Minn. | W | 7-0 | Perry | Wiley |

**JULY**

| | | | Winner | Loser |
|---|---|---|---|---|
| 7—At N. Y. | L | 2-5 | Medich | Hands |
| 8—At N. Y. | L | 0-4 | Hunter | Hargan |
| 9—At N. Y. | W | 4-0 | Jenkins | May |
| 10—At Bos. | L | 7-8 | Cleveland | Perry |
| 11—At Bos. | L | 8-11 | Burton | Thomas |
| 12—At Bos. | L | 4-10 | Tiant | Jenkins |
| 13—At Bos. | L | 5-7 | Wise | Hargan |
| 17—N. York | W | 7-2 | Jenkins | Dobson |
| 18—N. York | W | 1-0 | Perry | Hunter |
| 19—Boston | L | 0-8 | Wise | Hands |
| 20—Boston | W | 10-5 | Jenkins | Moret |
| 20—Boston | L | 2-3 | Cleveland | Hargan |
| 21—Boston | W | 6-0 | Jenkins | Tiant |
| 22—Cleve. | W | 4-0 | Perry | Raich |
| 23—Cleve. | W | 9-8x | Foucault | Brown |
| 25—At K. C. | L | 3-6 | Briles | Wright |
| 25—At K. C. | L | 1-6 | Leonard | Thomas |
| 26—At K. C. | L | 0-7 | Fitzmorris | Jenkins |
| 27—At K. C. | L | 1-2 | Busby | Perry |
| 28—At Oak. | L | 6-12 | Lindblad | Moore |
| 29—At Oak. | W | 6-1 | Hargan | Perry |
| 30—At Oak. | L | 0-1 | Holtzman | Jenkins |

**Won 12, Lost 18**

**AUGUST**

| | | | Winner | Loser |
|---|---|---|---|---|
| 1—Calif. | W | 2-1 | Perry | Figueroa |
| 2—Calif. | W | 8-2 | Hands | Lange |
| 3—Calif. | L | 4-6 | Kirkwood | Moore |
| 4—Oakland | W | 12-0 | Jenkins | Holtzman |
| 5—Oakland | L | 2-3 | Bosman | Perzanowski |
| 5—Oakland | W | 15-2 | Wright | Siebert |
| 6—Oakland | W | 5-2 | Perry | Bahnsen |
| 7—Oakland | L | 1-10 | Blue | Umbarger |
| 8—At Milw. | W | 6-4 | Hargan | Travers |
| 9—At Milw. | W | 4-2 | Jenkins | Hausman |
| 10—At Milw. | L | 4-7 | Broberg | Hands |
| 11—At Det. | W | 7-0 | Perry | LaGrow |
| 12—At Det. | W | 4-3 | Perzanowski | Ruhle |
| 13—At Det. | W | 6-5‡ | Foucault | Pentz |
| 15—At Balt. | W | 10-6 | Foucault | Garland |
| 15—At Balt. | L | 1-13 | Cuellar | Wright |
| 16—At Balt. | W | 5-1 | Perry | Grimsley |
| 17—At Balt. | L | 0-4 | Palmer | Perzanowski |
| 18—At Cleve. | L | 3-4 | Waits | Hargan |
| 18—At Cleve. | L | 2-4b | Harrison | Jenkins |
| 19—At Cleve. | W | 2-1 | Umbarger | Eckersley |
| 21—Balt. | L | 2-4y | Miller | Foucault |
| 22—Balt. | L | 5-8 | Torrez | Perzanowski |
| 23—Balt. | W | 1-0 | Jenkins | Cuellar |
| 24—Balt. | W | 8-7 | Foucault | Garland |
| 25—Detroit | W | 1-0 | Umbarger | Bare |
| 26—Detroit | W | 3-2† | Perry | Pentz |
| 27—Detroit | W | 8-2 | Jenkins | LaGrow |
| 29—Milw. | L | 1-13 | Colborn | Hargan |
| 30—Milw. | W | 8-3 | Umbarger | Slaton |
| 31—Milw. | L | 1-4 | Broberg | Perry |

**Won 19, Lost 12**

**SEPTEMBER**

| | | | Winner | Loser |
|---|---|---|---|---|
| 1—Minn. | L | 4-5 | Butler | Jenkins |
| 2—Minn. | L | 3-5 | Hughes | Hargan |
| 3—At Calif. | W | 5-4 | Wright | Hassler |
| 4—At Calif. | L | 4-6 | Brewer | Thomas |
| 5—At Oak. | W | 4-2 | Perry | Blue |
| 6—At Oak. | L | 1-2 | Lindblad | Jenkins |
| 7—At Oak. | L | 1-4 | Bosman | Wright |
| 7—At Oak. | L | 3-7 | Siebert | Hargan |
| 9—At Minn. | W | 3-0 | Umbarger | Goltz |
| 9—At Minn. | W | 4-2 | Perzanowski | Johnson |
| 10—At Minn. | W | 9-4 | Perry | Blyleven |
| 12—Chicago | L | 2-5 | Hinton | Jenkins |
| 13—Chicago | W | 8-7† | Foucault | Hamilton |
| 14—Chicago | W | 9-8x | Foucault | Hamilton |
| 16—Oakland | L | 5-11 | Todd | Perry |
| 16—Oakland | L | 4-6 | Bahnsen | Jenkins |
| 17—Calif. | L | 2-3 | Figueroa | Clyde |

| SEPTEMBER | | | | Winner | Loser |
|---|---|---|---|---|---|
| 18—Calif. | L | 3-5 | | Tanana | Umbarger |
| 19—At Chi. | W | 10-6 | | Hargan | Osteen |
| 20—At Chi. | W | 5-3 | | Jenkins | Jefferson |
| 21—At Chi. | W | 8-2 | | Perry | Wood |
| 22—At K. C. | L | 1-2 | | Fitzmorris | Foucault |

| SEPTEMBER | | | | Winner | Loser |
|---|---|---|---|---|---|
| 23—At K. C. | L | 0-4 | | McClure | Umbarger |
| 26—Kan. C. | L | 6-8 | | Leonard | Jenkins |
| 27—Kan. C. | W | 5-4 | | Perry | Fitzmorris |
| 28—Kan. C. | W | 3-1 | | Perzanowski | Littell |
| | | | **Won 12, Lost 14** | | |

* 5 innings.  † 10 innings.  ‡ 11 innings.  § 12 innings.  x 13 innings.  y 14 innings.  z Suspended game, completed May 15 (15 innings).  a 17 innings.  b July 24 game at Texas transferred to Cleveland.

# Poor Pitching Plagues Twins

## By BOB FOWLER

Minnesota, like the other 23 major league baseball teams, started the 1975 season optimistically. When it ended, the Twins were downcast and disorganized. Not only did they finish fourth in the American League West, their manager, Frank Quilici, and his coaching staff were fired before the season finale started.

Yes, Quilici became the sixth manager Calvin Griffith hired and fired in the 15 years he has had the franchise in Minnesota. But Frank wouldn't tell his players of his fate before that season-ending game because, he said, he didn't want that announcement to effect their possible third-place finish and a chance to receive some playoff money.

It didn't. The Twins lost that game to Chicago and finished fourth, 1½ games behind Texas, with a 76-83 record.

Yet there they were in April, leaving Florida with enthusiasm for after a 5-22 spring training record in 1974, they had compiled a 17-13 exhibition mark. And they opened the campaign with two straight wins in Texas.

Then, after losing the final game of that series, they went to Kansas City where they lost three straight on the Royals' artificial turf. Worse, in the final game, they lost starting pitcher Joe Decker, who completed the game, but suffered a virus that would keep him out of action for two months.

Decker won 16 games in 1974, but he never regained his control or confidence after recovering from the virus and finished the season with a 1-3 record in a mere 10 games.

He exemplified Minnesota's basic problem—ineffective pitching.

Yes, Bert Blyleven was 15-10 with a 3.00 ERA, 20 complete games and 233 strikeouts. Yes, Dave Goltz was 14-14 and righthander Jim Hughes posted a 16-14 record to become the majors' winningest rookie pitcher.

But there never was a consistent fourth starter, the staff combined for a club-record 617 walks and the overall ERA was a whopping 4.05—10th in the league.

A woefully weak bullpen helped up that ERA. Tom Burgmeier was the top reliever with 11 saves and five wins while Bill Campbell, the top reliever in 1974, was shuffled between starting and relieving and didn't do well in either with a mere five saves and four wins.

To further illustrate the point, consider that the Twins were shut out only seven times all year, the league's best showing in that category.

MINNESOTA TWINS—1975

Front row—Ferrer, Gomez, Braun, Rowe, coach; Stange, coach; Quilici, manager; Morgan, coach; Thompson, Soderholm, Burgmeier. Second row—Jarzyna, clubhouse attendant; Wiesner, clubhouse attendant; Albury, Brye, Walton, Carew, Butler, Bostock, Decker, Martin, trainer; Crump, equipment manager. Third row—Oliva, Hisle, Borgmann, Corbin, Blyleven, Goltz, Roof, Campbell, Kusick, Darwin, Hughes, Ford.

As usual, the Twins had no problems offensively. They finished second only to Boston in team batting with a .271 mark—the third straight year they ranked first or second in that department. And, while they ranked eighth in home runs with 121 despite moving Metropolitan Stadium's left field fence in 16 feet, they were third in runs scored behind only Boston and Oakland.

Minnesota had three regulars with .300 batting averages. Rod Carew hit .359, Larry Hisle .314 and Steve Braun .302 while reserve catcher Phil Roof also hit .302.

Add to those the averages of third baseman Eric Soderholm (.286), utilityman Jerry Terrell (.286), designated hitter Tony Oliva (.270) and shortstop Danny Thompson (.270) plus the .282 and .280 marks of rookie outfielders Lyman Bostock and Dan Ford, and you can see why the Twins had a potent attack.

To illustrate how potent, consider six games played between May 31 and June 6 against Boston and New York when the Twins scored 38 runs and posted an 0-6 record because their opponents got 54.

In mid-June, Bobby Darwin was traded to Milwaukee for John Briggs. That appeared to be a wise deal until Hisle suffered an arm injury and eventually was placed on the disabled list until mid-September. Then Steve Brye (.252) suffered a broken hand July 3 when he was hit by a Nolan Ryan fastball and missed two months of the season.

Without those three righthanded hitters, the Twins became vulnerable to southpaws—they finished the year with a 48-45 mark against righthanded pitchers but were 28-38 against lefthanders.

Plus, without Darwin and Hisle to drive in runs, Carew had to become a virtual one-man gang.

He won a fifth batting title that was his fourth straight—a feat last accomplished by Ty Cobb. But more remarkably, he maintained that high average while hitting a career-high 14 homers with 80 RBIs.

In addition, the team had only 81 stolen bases and Carew had 35 of them. And in mid-September he made a successful defensive switch to first base—a position he may play full-time in 1976 after nine years at second base on the league's All-Star Game squad.

Carew was, simply, Minnesota's superstar—an argument he failed to win in 1975 when he lost his pre-season arbitration case.

But even his best-ever season wasn't enough to save the Twins from a losing season, or Quilici's job. Thus, Quilici, who replaced Bill Rigney in mid-season 1972 at age 33, bowed out as the big leagues' youngest manager with a 280-287 record.

Not bad, considering that this 3½-year period saw the Twins in a rebuilding era.

Yet, not good enough for home attendance totaled only 737,156—an increase of about 75,000 over the all-time low reached in 1974. It wasn't enough to prevent the Griffith organization from losing money for a fifth straight year, but it was encouraging enough for it to sign another lease for Metropolitan Stadium.

However, it's only a one-year lease. In other words, if the new manager doesn't produce a team that pulls in big crowds, the Twins could be in another area in 1977—like Toronto, Seattle or New Orleans.

That new manager was unveiled, November 24, when Gene Mauch, fired by Montreal after seven years at the Expo helm, was signed to a three-year pact, longest contract given a Twins' manager in their 15-year history.

## SCORES OF MINNESOTA TWINS' 1975 GAMES

### APRIL

| Date | W/L | Score | Winner | Loser |
|---|---|---|---|---|
| 8—At Texas | W | 11-4 | Blyleven | Jenkins |
| 9—At Texas | W | 3-2 | Decker | Bibby |
| 10—At Texas | L | 4-5 | Foucault | Goltz |
| 11—At K. C. | L | 3-8 | Fitzmorris | Butler |
| 12—At K. C. | L | 1-2† | Bird | Campbell |
| 13—At K. C. | L | 3-5 | Busby | Decker |
| 15—Calif. | L | 3-7 | Ryan | Goltz |
| 16—Calif. | W | 10-4 | Blyleven | Hassler |
| 18—At Oak. | W | 5-4 | Albury | Holtzman |
| 19—At Oak. | L | 1-4 | Blue | Corbin |
| 20—At Oak. | L | 1-4 | Abbott | Blyleven |
| 20—At Oak. | L | 1-5 | Hamilton | Hughes |
| 21—At Calif. | W | 8-6 | Burgmeier | Pena |
| 22—At Calif. | W | 7-1 | Albury | Dobson |
| 24—Chicago | L | 3-4 | Wood | Burgmeier |
| 26—Texas | L | 2-7 | Hands | Albury |

Won 6, Lost 10

### MAY

| Date | W/L | Score | Winner | Loser |
|---|---|---|---|---|
| 2—Kan. C. | W | 4-1 | Goltz | Busby |
| 3—Kan. C. | W | 14-5 | Blyleven | Splittorff |
| 4—Kan. C. | W | 6-3 | Hughes | Fitzmorris |
| 6—At Chi. | W | 4-1 | Goltz | Wood |
| 7—At Chi. | L | 2-3 | Forster | Campbell |
| 9—At Balt. | L | 5-7 | Hughes | Grimsley |
| 10—At Balt. | L | 6-8 | Torrez | Corbin |
| 11—At Balt. | W | 6-4 | Blyleven | Cuellar |
| 11—At Balt. | L | 3-9 | Palmer | Pazik |
| 13—Cleve. | L | 2-3 | Peterson | Albury |
| 14—Cleve. | W | 3-0 | Hughes | G. Perry |
| 15—Cleve. | W | 7-6 | Burgmeier | J. Perry |
| 16—Milw. | L | 1-3 | Champion | Goltz |
| 17—Milw. | W | 8-7 | Corbin | Murphy |
| 18—Milw. | W | 6-0 | Hughes | Sprague |
| 19—Detroit | L | 3-6 | Coleman | Pazik |
| 20—Detroit | L | 3-5 | Lolich | Goltz |
| 21—Detroit | W | 6-5† | Corbin | Hiller |
| 23—At Milw. | W | 2-1 | Blyleven | Sprague |
| 24—At Milw. | W | 3-2 | Hughes | Broberg |
| 25—At Milw. | W | 7-2 | Goltz | Champion |
| 26—At Det. | L | 2-6 | Ruhle | Campbell |
| 27—At Det. | W | 6-5 | Albury | Hiller |
| 28—At Det. | W | 5-2 | Hughes | Coleman |
| 30—Boston | W | 4-3 | Goltz | Segui |
| 31—Boston | L | 8-12 | Moret | Burgmeier |

Won 17, Lost 9

### JUNE

| Date | W/L | Score | Winner | Loser |
|---|---|---|---|---|
| 1—Boston | L | 9-11 | Tiant | Hughes |
| 3—N. York | L | 4-5 | Dobson | Goltz |
| 4—N. York | L | 3-6 | Medich | Blyleven |
| 5—N. York | L | 4-7 | Hunter | Hughes |
| 6—At Bos. | L | 10-13 | Tiant | Pazik |
| 7—At Bos. | L | 1-3 | Lee | Corbin |
| 8—At Bos. | W | 7-5 | Goltz | Pole |
| 9—At Cleve. | W | 11-10‡ | Albury | Buskey |
| 10—At Cleve. | W | 5-3§ | Burgmeier | LaRoche |
| 11—At N. Y. | L | 1-5 | May | Pazik |
| 13—Balt. | W | 7-3 | Goltz | Cuellar |
| 14—Balt. | L | 0-7 | Grimsley | Hughes |
| 15—Balt. | W | 5-4 | Corbin | Torrez |
| 16—Oakland | W | 7-6 | Burgmeier | Fingers |
| 17—Oakland | L | 2-4 | Blue | Goltz |
| 17—Oakland | L | 7-8 | Holtzman | Butler |
| 18—Oakland | L | 6-7 | Todd | Albury |
| 19—Oakland | L | 2-5† | Abbott | Hughes |
| 20—At Chi. | W | 5-3 | Corbin | Hamilton |
| 21—At Chi. | W | 8-3 | Campbell | Kaat |
| 22—At Chi. | L | 5-6† | Osborn | Burgmeier |
| 22—At Chi. | L | 2-9 | Jefferson | Albury |
| 23—At Oak. | L | 2-5 | Lindblad | Hughes |
| 24—At Oak. | L | 4-6 | Todd | Decker |
| 25—At Oak. | L | 1-7 | Holtzman | Corbin |
| 27—At Texas | L | 0-2 | Hargan | Blyleven |
| 27—At Texas | W | 8-5 | Albury | Umbarger |
| 28—At Texas | W | 5-3 | Hughes | Perry |
| 29—At Texas | L | 7-9 | Bacsik | Campbell |
| 30—Calif. | L | 3-10 | Tanana | Corbin |

Won 10, Lost 20

### JULY

| Date | W/L | Score | Winner | Loser |
|---|---|---|---|---|
| 1—Calif. | L | 3-4† | Lange | Burgmeier |
| 1—Calif. | W | 12-3 | Wiley | Hassler |
| 2—Calif. | W | 9-4 | Blyleven | Hudson |
| 3—Calif. | L | 6-7 | Scott | Butler |
| 4—Texas | W | 8-0 | Campbell | Bacsik |
| 5—Texas | L | 2-4 | Hargan | Corbin |
| 5—Texas | W | 5-4 | Goltz | Jenkins |
| 6—Texas | L | 2-4 | Wright | Blyleven |
| 6—Texas | L | 0-7 | Perry | Wiley |
| 7—At Bos. | L | 3-6 | Wise | Hughes |
| 8—At Bos. | L | 5-6 | Cleveland | Johnson |
| 9—At Bos. | L | 8-9 | Segui | Burgmeier |
| 10—At N. Y. | W | 6-3 | Corbin | Dobson |
| 11—At N. Y. | W | 11-1 | Blyleven | Medich |
| 11—At N. Y. | L | 3-4 | Gura | Wiley |
| 12—At N. Y. | L | 7-8x | Martinez | Burgmeier |
| 17—At Balt. | L | 3-6§ | Jackson | Campbell |
| 18—At Balt. | L | 6-9 | Cuellar | Goltz |
| 19—N. York | W | 2-1 | Hughes | Medich |
| 20—N. York | L | 2-14 | May | Corbin |
| 20—N. York | L | 4-5y | Tidrow | Campbell |
| 21—N. York | W | 3-0 | Blyleven | Dobson |
| 22—Boston | L | 4-5 | Lee | Goltz |
| 23—Boston | L | 2-4 | Moret | Hughes |
| 24—Boston | L | 2-6 | Wise | Decker |
| 25—At Calif. | W | 12-1 | Blyleven | Singer |
| 26—At Calif. | W | 9-4 | Goltz | Figueroa |
| 26—At Calif. | L | 0-5 | Ryan | Albury |
| 27—At Calif. | L | 1-6 | Lange | Hughes |
| 28—Kan. C. | W | 9-8 | Burgmeier | Bird |
| 29—Kan. C. | L | 2-5 | Splittorff | Blyleven |
| 30—Kan. C. | L | 4-6 | Leonard | Albury |
| 31—Kan. C. | W | 7-2 | Hughes | Fitzmorris |

Won 12, Lost 21

### AUGUST

| Date | W/L | Score | Winner | Loser |
|---|---|---|---|---|
| 1—Chicago | L | 1-5* | Wood | Goltz |
| 2—Chicago | W | 4-1 | Blyleven | Osteen |
| 2—Chicago | W | 8-3 | Butler | Jefferson |
| 3—Chicago | W | 7-4 | Albury | Kaat |
| 3—Chicago | W | 12-9 | Campbell | Vuckovich |
| 4—At K. C. | L | 5-6† | Bird | Wiley |
| 5—At K. C. | L | 1-6 | Fitzmorris | Goltz |
| 6—At K. C. | L | 3-4 | Busby | Blyleven |
| 7—At K. C. | L | 2-10 | Splittorff | Albury |
| 8—At Det. | W | 3-1 | Hughes | Coleman |
| 9—At Det. | W | 1-0 | Goltz | Lolich |
| 10—At Det. | W | 4-0 | Blyleven | Bare |
| 11—Milw. | W | 8-7 | Johnson | Slaton |
| 12—Milw. | L | 4-7 | Travers | Hughes |

| AUGUST | | | Winner | Loser |
|---|---|---|---|---|
| 13—Milw. | W | 5-2 | Goltz | Hausman |
| 15—Cleve. | W | 8-4 | Blyleven | Eckersley |
| 16—Cleve. | W | 9-1 | Hughes | Raich |
| 17—Cleve. | L | 5-14 | Peterson | Butler |
| 18—Balt. | W | 6-1 | Goltz | Torrez |
| 19—Balt. | W | 5-2 | Blyleven | Cuellar |
| 20—Balt. | L | 2-3 | Grimsley | Hughes |
| 22—Detroit | W | 8-4 | Goltz | Ruhle |
| 23—Detroit | L | 5-6§ | Lemanczyk | Burgmeier |
| 24—Detroit | W | 3-1 | Hughes | Lolich |
| 25—At Milw. | W | 6-3 | Butler | Slaton |
| 26—At Milw. | W | 2-1 | Goltz | Broberg |
| 27—At Milw. | W | 1-0‡ | Blyleven | Travers |
| 29—At Cleve. | L | 6-9 | Hood | Hughes |
| **Won 18, Lost 10** | | | | |

| SEPTEMBER | | | | |
|---|---|---|---|---|
| 1—At Texas | W | 5-4 | Butler | Jenkins |
| 2—At Texas | W | 5-3 | Hughes | Hargan |
| 5—At Chi. | L | 2-3 | Wood | Goltz |
| 6—At Chi. | L | 2-5 | Kaat | Blyleven |
| 7—At Chi. | W | 9-1 | Hughes | Osteen |

| SEPTEMBER | | | Winner | Loser |
|---|---|---|---|---|
| 9—Texas | L | 0-3 | Umbarger | Goltz |
| 9—Texas | L | 2-4 | Perzanowski | Johnson |
| 10—Texas | L | 4-9 | Perry | Blyleven |
| 12—Oakland | L | 4-11 | Bosman | Hughes |
| 12—Oakland | W | 7-6 | Bane | Lindblad |
| 13—Oakland | L | 5-8 | Holtzman | Goltz |
| 14—Oakland | W | 10-8 | Butler | Abbott |
| 15—Calif. | W | 7-6§ | Campbell | Hockenbery |
| 16—Calif. | W | 4-3 | Hughes | Monge |
| 17—Kan. C. | W | 2-1 | Goltz | Fitzmorris |
| 18—Kan. C. | L | 3-4 | Sadecki | Bane |
| 19—At Calif. | L | 0-1 | Pactwa | Blyleven |
| 20—At Calif. | W | 3-2 | Hughes | Monge |
| 21—At Calif. | L | 2-5 | Figueroa | Goltz |
| 22—At Oak. | W | 2-1 | Bane | Holtzman |
| 23—At Oak. | W | 4-3 | Blyleven | Bahnsen |
| 24—At K. C. | L | 2-4 | Pattin | Hughes |
| 25—At K. C. | W | 5-2 | Butler | Splittorff |
| 26—Chicago | W | 2-1 | Bane | Kaat |
| 27—Chicago | L | 0-1 | Gossage | Blyleven |
| 28—Chicago | L | 4-6† | Hamilton | Burgmeier |
| **Won 13, Lost 13** | | | | |

* 6 innings.   † 10 innings.   ‡ 11 innings.   § 12 innings.   x Suspended game, completed July 19 (16 innings). y July 13 at New York transferred to Minnesota.

# Disappointing White Sox Make Changes

## By JEROME HOLTZMAN

The Chicago White Sox, still in a rebuilding posture, staggered home in fifth place, their third successive second division finish in the American League West. Though expected to be competitive, the Sox were never in contention and won only 75 games, five less than the previous year. More remarkable, perhaps, was that, after splitting their first two games, they were never able to climb back to the .500 mark.

The disappointment of the season was reflected at the gate with 750,802 paid home admissions, down almost 400,000 from 1974, a dip that hastened the sale of the club. It was the smallest home gate in the last five years and the lowest in the five-year managerial reign of Chuck Tanner who, once the club was sold, was immediately replaced as field manager by Paul Richards, the original architect, two decades earlier, of the Go-Go White Sox.

The club suffered financial losses in 1975 estimated at $2 million, a situation that plunged owner John Allyn into financial agony and forced him to sell 80 percent of the Sox to a group headed by Bill Veeck. It was a highly-publicized and somewhat melodramatic sale and when consummated in mid-December prevented the franchise from being transferred to Seattle. Allyn remained as a 20 percent shareholder.

The Sox had four players selected on the American League's All-Star Game squad and among them was Rich Gossage, a hard-throwing right-hander who was, by far, the club's most outstanding performer. Unsuccessful in previous trials as a spot starter, Gossage operated exclusively out of the bullpen in 1975, appeared in 37 of the club's 75 victories and won the league's Fireman Trophy awarded by THE SPORTING NEWS with 35 points, on the basis of 26 saves and nine victories.

The club's other standouts were veteran lefthander Jim Kaat, a 20-

## CHICAGO WHITE SOX—1975

Bottom row—Rosenbaum, coach; Saad, trainer; Bradford, Hairston, May, Osteen, Wood. Second row—Mahoney, coach; Unferth, traveling secretary; Bahnsen, Gossage, Kelly, Osborn, Varney. Third row—Lonnett, coach; Gogolewski, Kaat, Orta, Upshaw. Fourth row—Monchak, coach; Forster, D. Johnson, Nyman, Stein. Fifth row—Sain, coach; Downing, B. Johnson, Muser, Sharp. Sixth row—Tanner, manager; Dent, Henderson, Melton, Richard.

game winner, and infielders Jorge Orta and Bucky Dent. Orta, for the second year in a row, led the club in batting with a .304 average, eighth best in the league, and also led in runs batted in with 83. Dent led A. L. shortstops in fielding with a .981 percentage and also had the most total chances, putouts and assists. A late slump pulled his batting average, which had been near .300 most of the season, down to .264.

It was the second consecutive 20-victory season for the 36-year-old Kaat who quickened his no-windup delivery to such an extent that he often took only about eight seconds between pitches, a strategem which though perfectly legal, sometimes brought angry words from opposing batsmen. The bullpen was also of considerable help to Kaat who had only six complete-game triumphs.

Veteran knuckleballer Wilbur Wood, a 20-game winner in each of the previous four seasons, was second to Kaat in victories with 16 but lost 20 games to join Ted Lyons as the only pitcher in club history to lose 20 or more games in two different seasons. None of the club's other starters— Claude Osteen, Jesse Jefferson and Dave Hamilton—was able to win more than seven games.

Bart Johnson, who figured to be the club's No. 3 starter behind Wood and Kaat, sprained his back in spring training, an injury which idled him for the entire season. Bullpen star Terry Forster, effective early, hurt his left elbow while pitching on May 23 and worked only two innings thereafter.

The White Sox were weak at the plate and ranked 10th in the league in runs and 11th in home runs. Their leading power hitter was the veteran Deron Johnson, a spring training pick-up who had been given his free agency by the Boston Red Sox. Johnson was used at first base and as a designated hitter and led the club in home runs with 18 and was second to Orta in RBIs with 72.

Ed Herrmann, long-time Sox catcher, was sent to the Yankees in a spring training deal and was replaced by Brian Downing who had a good season and showed signs of maturing into an outstanding receiver. But two veterans, center fielder Ken Henderson and third baseman Bill Melton, had disappointing seasons.

Henderson batted only .251 with 53 RBIs, losing 41 points from his 1974 average, with a companion drop of 42 RBIs. Melton was in the low .200s most of the season but had a strong September that lifted him from .213 to .240. Veterans Carlos May and Pat Kelly finished in the .270s but, together, drove in less than 100 runs.

Melton and Henderson engaged in what was almost a running feud with Harry Caray, the team's principal and popular broadcaster. They insisted that Caray, in describing the games, was constantly belittling their efforts, that this turned the fans against them and was among the reasons for their poor production. Manager Tanner, no Caray fan, either, supported his players and 72 hours after the season ended owner Allyn fired Caray, claiming he was a "disruptive influence."

Caray countered by calling Allyn "stupid," said that Allyn was constantly being manipulated by Tanner and general manager Roland Hemond, and then added: "The best thing that could happen for the White

Sox would be if John Allyn sold the team."

Allyn did just that and consummated his deal with Veeck on December 16, after five months of negotiation and after Veeck's purchase had twice been rejected by the American League owners. The owners originally vetoed Veeck's bid at a league meeting on December 3 in Cleveland. Needing nine votes for approval, Veeck only received three votes in this ballot but the owners relented several hours later and passed a resolution to approve his deal if he raised an additional $1.2 million in capital and substituted $4,080,000 he had sold in debentures into preferred stock.

Veeck was given seven days to make these changes and appeared before the owners again a week later at the winter convention in Hollywood, Fla. Though he had met most of the conditions, he only received eight votes, one short of approval, but at the urging of Detroit owner John Fetzer, a second vote was taken and Veeck was accepted by a 10-2 margin.

Veeck immediately began re-tooling the White Sox and in the next 53 hours made six trades. Veterans Henderson, Melton and Kaat were used in these deals. Tanner, who had three years remaining on his contract, was dismissed on December 17 and replaced by Paul Richards who had been the White Sox manager two decades earlier. The next day, while still in Chicago, Tanner signed a three-year contract to manage the Oakland A's.

### SCORES OF CHICAGO WHITE SOX' 1975 GAMES

| APRIL | | | Winner | Loser | MAY | | | Winner | Loser |
|---|---|---|---|---|---|---|---|---|---|
| 8—At Oak. | L | 2-3 | Blue | Wood | 23—Detroit | W | 6-1 | Forster | LaGrow |
| 9—At Oak. | W | 7-5 | Kaat | Fingers | 24—Detroit | W | 10-8 | Bahnsen | Coleman |
| 10—At Oak. | L | 0-9 | Norris | Bahnsen | 25—Detroit | L | 1-4† | Lolich | Osteen |
| 11—At Calif. | L | 0-5 | Ryan | Osteen | 26—At Milw. | W | 4-2 | Kaat | Colborn |
| 12—At Calif. | L | 3-4‡ | Hassler | Wood | 27—At Milw. | L | 8-9 | Hausman | Wood |
| 13—At Calif. | W | 7-5x | Forster | Kirkwood | 28—At Milw. | W | 9-3 | Bahnsen | Slaton |
| 13—At Calif. | W | 5-4 | Upshaw | Singer | 31—At Det. | L | 0-2 | Ruhle | Kaat |
| 15—Texas | L | 5-6y | Hargan | Gossage | | | | Won 13, Lost 11 | |
| 16—Texas | L | 4-14 | Umbarger | Wood | | | | | |
| 17—Texas | L | 3-7 | Jenkins | Bahnsen | JUNE | | | | |
| 19—Calif. | L | 5-6 | Singer | Wood | 1—At Det. | L | 1-5 | Lolich | Wood |
| 20—Calif. | L | 4-8 | Ryan | Osteen | 1—At Det. | W | 3-2 | Gossage | Walker |
| 22—Kan. C. | W | 7-3 | Kaat | Dal Canton | 2—At Bos. | W | 9-2 | Bahnsen | Lee |
| 24—At Minn. | W | 4-3 | Wood | Burgmeier | 3—At Bos. | L | 0-4 | Pole | Allen |
| 25—At K. C. | W | 5-2 | Osteen | Fitzmorris | 4—At Bos. | L | 6-7 | Moret | Gossage |
| 26—At K. C. | L | 6-8 | Briles | Bahnsen | 6—N. York | L | 1-5 | May | Wood |
| 27—At K. C. | W | 8-6 | Kaat | Dal Canton | 7—N. York | L | 3-6 | Dobson | Bahnsen |
| 28—At K. C. | L | 5-7 | Busby | Wood | 8—N. York | L | 1-4 | Medich | Kaat |
| 29—At Texas | L | 2-3 | Jenkins | Osteen | 9—Milw. | L | 0-1 | Rodriguez | Gossage |
| 30—At Texas | L | 2-8 | Bibby | Bahnsen | 10—Milw. | W | 9-2 | Wood | Broberg |
| | | | Won 7, Lost 13 | | 11—Boston | L | 7-9z | Moret | Gossage |
| | | | | | 12—Boston | W | 9-2 | Kaat | Burton |
| MAY | | | | | 13—At N. Y. | L | 1-2 | Dobson | Osteen |
| 1—At Texas | L | 1-2 | Foucault | Gossage | 14—At N. Y. | W | 7-2 | Wood | Medich |
| 2—Oakland | L | 3-4x | Fingers | Forster | 15—At N. Y. | L | 0-3 | Hunter | Bahnsen |
| 3—Oakland | W | 4-3‡ | Gossage | Todd | 17—At Texas | W | 13-3 | Kaat | Umbarger |
| 4—Oakland | W | 5-2 | Kaat | Abbott | 18—At Texas | L | 3-10 | Jenkins | Wood |
| 6—Minn. | L | 1-4 | Goltz | Wood | 19—At Texas | L | 3-5 | Thomas | Gossage |
| 7—Minn. | W | 3-2 | Forster | Campbell | 20—Minn. | L | 3-5 | Corbin | Hamilton |
| 9—At Cleve. | W | 2-0 | Kaat | G. Perry | 21—Minn. | L | 3-8 | Campbell | Kaat |
| 10—At Cleve. | W | 8-3 | Wood | Hood | 22—Minn. | W | 6-5‡ | Osborn | Burgmeier |
| 11—At Cleve. | L | 3-4§ | Buskey | Forster | 22—Minn. | W | 9-2 | Jefferson | Albury |
| 13—At Balt. | L | 2-3 | Grimsley | Kaat | 24—Texas | W | 7-5 | Osteen | Perry |
| 14—At Balt. | L | 2-3 | Torrez | Forster | 25—Texas | W | 5-2 | Kaat | Bacsik |
| 16—Cleve. | W | 3-2 | Gossage | Buskey | 26—Texas | W | 8-3 | Wood | Jenkins |
| 17—Cleve. | W | 10-1 | Kaat | Peterson | 27—Kan. C. | W | 4-3 | Hamilton | Bird |
| 18—Cleve. | L | 6-7 | G. Perry | Wood | 28—Kan. C. | W | 5-3 | Osteen | Leonard |
| 19—Balt. | W | 2-1 | Bahnsen | Alexander | 29—Kan. C. | W | 3-1 | Kaat | Splittorff |
| 21—Balt. | L | 2-6 | Palmer | Osteen | 30—Oakland | W | 6-1 | Wood | Bahnsen |
| 22—Balt. | W | 2-1 | Kaat | Cuellar | | | | Won 15, Lost 14 | |

| JULY | | | Winner | Loser |
|---|---|---|---|---|
| 1—Oakland | L | 1-10 | Blue | Jefferson |
| 2—Oakland | W | 5-4 | Gossage | Fingers |
| 3—Oakland | W | 3-2 | Kaat | Todd |
| 4—At K. C. | L | 2-3 | Leonard | Wood |
| 5—At K. C. | L | 4-6 | Splittorff | Hamilton |
| 6—At K. C. | W | 9-3 | Osteen | Pattin |
| 7—At Det. | L | 1-2 | Walker | Kaat |
| 8—At Det. | L | 0-3 | Coleman | Wood |
| 9—At Det. | L | 2-6 | Bare | Jefferson |
| 11—At Milw. | W | 5-3 | Osteen | Sprague |
| 12—At Milw. | L | 4-5 | Slaton | Kaat |
| 13—At Milw. | W | 5-0 | Wood | Travers |
| 17—Detroit | W | 4-0 | Wood | Lolich |
| 17—Detroit | L | 1-9 | LaGrow | Osteen |
| 18—Detroit | W | 4-0 | Kaat | Ruhle |
| 19—Milw. | W | 4-2 | Jefferson | Travers |
| 20—Milw. | W | 9-2 | Wood | Sprague |
| 20—Milw. | W | 10-5 | Osborn | Broberg |
| 21—Milw. | L | 4-7 | Colborn | Osteen |
| 22—N. York | L | 6-11 | Hunter | Kaat |
| 24—N. York | W | 4-3§ | Gossage | Tidrow |
| 24—N. York | W | 1-0 | Hamilton | Gura |
| 25—At Oak. | L | 6-8y | Lindblad | Upshaw |
| 26—At Oak. | W | 5-2 | Kaat | Fingers |
| 27—At Oak. | L | 1-10 | Blue | Jefferson |
| 27—At Oak. | L | 1-7 | Bahnsen | Allen |
| 28—At Calif. | W | 3-2 | Wood | Tanana |
| 29—At Calif. | W | 7-4 | Osteen | Hassler |
| 30—At Calif. | W | 4-5 | Ryan | Kaat |
| | | **Won 15, Lost 14** | | |

| AUGUST | | | | |
|---|---|---|---|---|
| 1—At Minn. | W | 5-1* | Wood | Goltz |
| 2—At Minn. | L | 1-4 | Blyleven | Osteen |
| 2—At Minn. | L | 3-8 | Butler | Jefferson |
| 3—At Minn. | L | 4-7 | Albury | Kaat |
| 3—At Minn. | L | 9-12 | Campbell | Vuckovich |
| 4—Calif. | W | 4-2 | Wood | Hockenbery |
| 5—Calif. | L | 4-10 | Figueroa | Osteen |
| 5—Calif. | W | 4-1 | Jefferson | Singer |
| 6—Calif. | W | 11-1 | Kaat | Lange |
| 7—Calif. | W | 8-4 | Hamilton | Hassler |
| 8—Balt. | L | 4-7 | Alexander | Wood |
| 9—Balt. | L | 6-12 | Palmer | Osteen |
| 10—Balt. | W | 3-2 | Gossage | Jackson |
| 12—Cleve. | L | 3-6 | Peterson | Wood |
| 13—Cleve. | W | 4-3x | Gossage | Bibby |

| AUGUST | | | Winner | Loser |
|---|---|---|---|---|
| 14—Cleve. | W | 6-4 | Kaat | Harrison |
| 15—Boston | L | 2-3 | Tiant | Jefferson |
| 16—Boston | L | 0-5 | Moret | Wood |
| 17—Boston | W | 6-2 | Hamilton | Wise |
| 17—Boston | L | 3-4§ | Willoughby | Gossage |
| 19—At N. Y. | W | 7-6§ | Hamilton | Lyle |
| 20—At N. Y. | W | 5-3 | Wood | May |
| 21—At N. Y. | W | 2-1 | Kaat | Medich |
| 22—At Bos. | L | 1-2 | Moret | Osteen |
| 23—At Bos. | W | 6-4 | Jefferson | Wise |
| 24—At Bos. | L | 1-6 | Lee | Wood |
| 25—At Cleve. | L | 1-5 | Eckersley | Kaat |
| 27—At Cleve. | W | 2-0 | Osteen | Bibby |
| 27—At Cleve. | L | 0-5 | Peterson | Jefferson |
| 28—At Balt. | L | 1-2 | Cuellar | Wood |
| 29—At Balt. | W | 4-2 | Kaat | Grimsley |
| 30—At Balt. | L | 2-4 | Palmer | Jefferson |
| | | **Won 15, Lost 17** | | |

| SEPTEMBER | | | | |
|---|---|---|---|---|
| 1—Kan. C. | W | 10-8 | Gossage | Busby |
| 1—Kan. C. | L | 1-3 | Bird | Osteen |
| 2—Kan. C. | L | 1-4x | Fitzmorris | Kaat |
| 3—Kan. C. | L | 4-5‡ | Leonard | Hamilton |
| 4—Kan. C. | L | 0-7 | Splittorff | Kravec |
| 5—Minn. | W | 3-2 | Wood | Goltz |
| 6—Minn. | W | 5-2 | Kaat | Blyleven |
| 7—Minn. | L | 1-9 | Hughes | Osteen |
| 9—Calif. | L | 4-5 | Figueroa | Wood |
| 10—Calif. | L | 2-4 | Tanana | Kaat |
| 12—At Texas | W | 5-2 | Hinton | Jenkins |
| 13—At Texas | L | 7-8‡ | Foucault | Hamilton |
| 14—At Texas | L | 8-9y | Foucault | Hamilton |
| 15—At K. C. | L | 2-3 | Splittorff | Osteen |
| 16—At K. C. | W | 6-5 | Jefferson | Leonard |
| 17—Oakland | W | 3-2 | Wood | Holtzman |
| 18—Oakland | L | 6-7 | Todd | Kaat |
| 19—Texas | W | 6-10 | Hargan | Osteen |
| 20—Texas | L | 3-5 | Jenkins | Jefferson |
| 21—Texas | L | 2-8 | Perry | Wood |
| 22—At Calif. | L | 0-3a | Kirkwood | Gossage |
| 23—At Calif. | W | 5-4 | Osborn | Lange |
| 24—At Oak. | L | 2-13 | Blue | Jefferson |
| 25—At Oak. | W | 8-2 | Wood | Mitchell |
| 26—At Minn. | L | 1-2 | Bane | Kaat |
| 27—At Minn. | L | 1-0 | Gossage | Blyleven |
| 28—At Minn. | W | 6-4‡ | Hamilton | Burgmeier |
| | | **Won 10, Lost 17** | | |

* 6 innings.  † 8 innings.  ‡ 10 innings.  § 11 innings.  x 12 innings.  y 13 innings.  z 14 innings.  a 16 innings.

# Angels First in Steals—Last in Standings

## By DICK MILLER

As a team, the Angels were unable to catch Roger Maris, Babe Ruth, Jimmy Foxx, Hank Greenberg and Hack Wilson.

As a result, the Angels were unable to catch Oakland, Kansas City, Texas, Minnesota and Chicago in the American League West.

While the nation recovered from the energy crisis, a severe power shortage hit the Orange County area in the summer of '75, resulting in another sixth place finish in Dick Williams' first full season as manager.

It was the Year of the Hare on the Chinese calendar and the Angels ran the bases like rabbits: Their 220 stolen bases were the most in the majors since the 1916 St. Louis Browns had 234. The Angels were the first major league team to steal 200 bases since 1918, when the Pittsburgh Pirates had 200.

CALIFORNIA ANGELS—1975

Front row—Triggs, club physician; Goldman, batboy; Adair, coach; Muffett, coach; Williams, manager; Resinger, coach; Reese, coach; Rivers, Remy, Rasinski, club physician. Second row—Atkinson, assistant trainer; Llenas, Collins, Miley, Garrett, Balaz, Hampton, Meoli, Lange, Brewer, Dunn, ballboy; Buzbee, ballboy; Frederico, trainer. Third row—Munson, traveling secretary; Singer, Hassler, Kirkwood, Tanana, Bochte, Etchebarren, Chalk, Stanton, Schneider, assistant equipment manager. Fourth row—Shishido, equipment manager; Rodriguez, Allietta, Hockenbery, Scott, Valentine, Ryan, Figueroa.

Richard's Rabbits were unable to steal their way out of the cellar. A team total of 55 home runs was the reason as the rabbits were unable to match the season individual totals of Maris, Ruth, Foxx, Greenberg and Wilson.

Nolan Ryan appeared on his way to a 30-victory season with a no-hitter against Baltimore and a 10-3 record through June 6. But a series of injuries forced The Express to finish with a 14-12 record, sitting out September at his home in Alvin, Texas.

Four bone chips were removed from his pitching arm in October to cloud the future of one of the most brilliant performers in the game. Twenty-game winner Bill Singer also was beset with injuries and had to submit to off-season surgery on his pitching arm.

Representing the city made famous by Disneyland, the Angels put the capper on a Mickey Mouse season by being shut out without a hit by four Oakland pitchers in their final game of the season.

Despite the team performance, there were a number of individual efforts of note. Frank Tanana developed into one of the best pitchers in the majors in his second season. The 22-year-old lefthander led the majors in strikeouts with 269 and set an American League record for lefthanders by striking out 17 Texas batters at Anaheim on June 21.

He tied Sam McDowell's A. L. record for lefthanders with 40 strikeouts in three games en route to a 16-9 record. His ERA (2.63) was the best for a lefthanded starter in the A. L.

Mickey Rivers was the American League stolen base champion with 70.

Rivers led the Angels in games (155), at bats (616), hits (175), tied Kaycee's George Brett for the major league lead in triples (13), and was caught stealing only 14 times.

In addition to Tanana, the youngest major league strikeout king since Herb Score in 1955, the Angels had a 16-game winner in Ed Figueroa. Although hard-hit by injuries (Ryan, Singer and Tanana missed 32 starts and were ailing in others), the pitching staff led the majors in strikeouts and tied for the lead in shutouts.

Other plusses included the performance of Jerry Remy at second base, the emergence of outfielder Lee Stanton as an all-round player and the fielding of third baseman Dave Chalk.

Minuses? There were many. Pitcher Andy Hassler lost 11 games in succession and finished with a 3-12 record. Four shortstops were given the opportunity to play. Among them, Orlando Ramirez, Mike Miley, Rudy Meoli and Billy Smith combined for an incredible 50 errors.

Injuries hurt. In addition to the starting pitchers, described by Williams prior to the season as "the best starting rotation in baseball," catcher Andy Etchebarren and first baseman Bruce Bochte both missed eight weeks of the season with broken thumbs. Etchebarren was acquired from Baltimore on waivers just before the trading deadline.

The lack of power was evident in the fact Adrian Garrett tied for second on the club in home runs. The veteran infielder-outfielder wasn't acquired until August, yet his six home runs in 37 games tied him with Joe Lahoud behind Stanton's 14. Stanton also paced the club with 82 runs batted in.

Stanton also led the Angels in game-winning hits with 20 and produced the club's first grand-slam home runs in four seasons with a pair against Detroit and Milwaukee. Both were delivered in the same week.

Building for the future—again—the Angels fielded an Incubator Infield, the youngest in the majors, for most of the season. First baseman Bochte was 24, second baseman Remy 23, shortstop Miley 22 and third baseman Chalk 23. At the start of the season Chalk was the only one of the quartet with a full year in the majors under his belt.

In an effort to add to the woefully weak home run punch, the Angels dealt for two long-ball hitters at the major league meetings in December. Singer was traded to the Rangers for first baseman Jim Spencer and cash and Spencer and outfielder Morris Nettles then went to the White Sox for third baseman Bill Melton and pitcher Steve Dunning. The Angels packaged two of their best performers of 1975—Rivers and Figueroa—and traded them to the Yankees for outfield star Bobby Bonds. Between them, Bonds and Melton, a former A. L. home run champion, should hit more homers than the entire Angel club did in '75.

Despite the club's 11th losing season in the 15 years of its existence, attendance was up 140,000 to 1,058,163. It was the sixth time in the Angels' 10 years in Anaheim that the one million barrier had been broken.

## SCORES OF CALIFORNIA ANGELS' 1975 GAMES

**APRIL**

| | | | Winner | Loser |
|---|---|---|---|---|
| 7—Kan. C. | W | 3-2 | Ryan | Mingori |
| 9—Kan. C. | L | 6-7 | McDaniel | Dobson |
| 11—Chicago | W | 5-0 | Ryan | Osteen |
| 12—Chicago | W | 4-3* | Hassler | Wood |
| 13—Chicago | L | 5-7† | Forster | Kirkwood |
| 13—Chicago | L | 4-5 | Upshaw | Singer |
| 15—At Minn. | W | 7-3 | Ryan | Goltz |
| 16—At Minn. | L | 4-10 | Blyleven | Hassler |
| 19—At Chi. | W | 6-5 | Singer | Wood |
| 20—At Chi. | W | 8-4 | Ryan | Osteen |
| 21—Minn. | L | 6-8 | Burgmeier | Pena |
| 22—Minn. | L | 1-7 | Albury | Dobson |
| 23—Texas | W | 4-1 | Singer | Wright |
| 24—Texas | L | 0-5 | Brown | Ryan |
| 25—Oakland | W | 2-0 | Hassler | Hamilton |
| 26—Oakland | W | 1-0 | Tanana | Holtzman |
| 27—Oakland | L | 1-7 | Blue | Singer |
| 27—Oakland | W | 9-1 | Figueroa | Odom |
| 29—At K.C. | W | 12-1 | Hassler | Splittorff |
| 30—At K.C. | W | 7-6 | Scott | Bird |
| | | **Won 12, Lost 8** | | |

**MAY**

| | | | Winner | Loser |
|---|---|---|---|---|
| 1—At K.C. | L | 10-11§ | Bird | Pena |
| 2—At Texas | L | 3-4 | Hargan | Singer |
| 3—At Texas | W | 4-2 | Ryan | Brown |
| 4—At Texas | L | 0-1 | Hands | Hassler |
| 5—At Texas | L | 3-4 | Jenkins | Lange |
| 6—At Oak. | L | 3-5 | Lindblad | Kirkwood |
| 7—At Oak. | L | 1-9 | Blue | Singer |
| 8—At Oak. | W | 5-0 | Ryan | Hamilton |
| 9—Boston | L | 1-4 | Wise | Hassler |
| 10—Boston | W | 2-0 | Tanana | Tiant |
| 11—Boston | L | 2-5 | Lee | Singer |
| 13—N. York | W | 5-0 | Ryan | Medich |
| 14—N. York | W | 3-4* | Hunter | Hassler |
| 16—At Balt. | L | 0-1 | Palmer | Tanana |
| 16—At Balt. | W | 3-2 | Figueroa | Cuellar |
| 17—At Balt. | W | 6-3 | Singer | Garland |
| 18—At Balt. | W | 5-1 | Ryan | Torrez |
| 19—At Cleve. | W | 12-5 | Lange | Hood |

**MAY**

| | | | Winner | Loser |
|---|---|---|---|---|
| 21—At Cleve. | L | 2-3 | Kern | Tanana |
| 22—At Bos. | W | 6-3 | Singer | Wise |
| 23—At Bos. | L | 1-6 | Tiant | Ryan |
| 24—At Bos. | L | 0-6 | Lee | Hassler |
| 25—At Bos. | W | 6-1 | Figueroa | Cleveland |
| 26—Cleve. | L | 3-9 | Peterson | Tanana |
| 27—Cleve. | L | 3-6 | G. Perry | Singer |
| 28—Cleve. | L | 2-9 | Raich | Ryan |
| 30—Balt. | L | 0-5 | Palmer | Figueroa |
| 31—Balt. | L | 0-1 | Cuellar | Singer |
| | | **Won 10, Lost 18** | | |

**JUNE**

| | | | Winner | Loser |
|---|---|---|---|---|
| 1—Balt. | W | 1-0 | Ryan | Grimsley |
| 3—Detroit | L | 5-8 | Hiller | Tanana |
| 4—Detroit | W | 2-1 | Figueroa | Bare |
| 5—Detroit | W | 8-3 | Singer | Ruhle |
| 6—Milw. | W | 6-0 | Ryan | Slaton |
| 7—Milw. | W | 5-2 | Tanana | Castro |
| 8—Milw. | L | 3-4 | Colborn | Figueroa |
| 9—At N. Y. | W | 5-3 | Singer | Hunter |
| 10—At N. Y. | L | 4-6 | Gura | Ryan |
| 11—At Det. | W | 14-7 | Tanana | Lolich |
| 11—At Det. | L | 3-5z | Bare | Hassler |
| 12—At Det. | W | 7-1 | Figueroa | LaGrow |
| 13—At Milw. | L | 2-10 | Colborn | Singer |
| 14—At Milw. | L | 4-6 | Travers | Ryan |
| 15—At Milw. | W | 8-7† | Kirkwood | Champion |
| 15—At Milw. | L | 2-4 | Slaton | Hassler |
| 17—At K.C. | L | 2-3 | Busby | Figueroa |
| 18—At K.C. | L | 0-13 | Pattin | Ryan |
| 20—Texas | W | 12-11† | Kirkwood | Foucault |
| 21—Texas | W | 4-2 | Tanana | Umbarger |
| 21—Texas | L | 5-6 | Umbarger | Quintana |
| 22—Texas | W | 1-0 | Figueroa | Jenkins |
| 23—Texas | L | 0-1§ | Umbarger | Kirkwood |
| 24—Kan. C. | L | 3-5† | Bird | Scott |
| 25—Kan. C. | L | 2-6‡ | Busby | Quintana |
| 26—Kan. C. | L | 1-7 | Pattin | Figueroa |
| 27—Oakland | L | 4-12 | Blue | Hassler |

**JUNE**

| | | | Winner | Loser |
|---|---|---|---|---|
| 28—Oakland | L | 4-10 | Bosman | Singer |
| 29—Oakland | L | 1-7 | Holtzman | Ryan |
| 30—At Minn. | W | 10-3 | Tanana | Corbin |
| | | **Won 13, Lost 17** | | |

**JULY**

| | | | Winner | Loser |
|---|---|---|---|---|
| 1—At Minn. | W | 4-3* | Lange | Burgmeier |
| 1—At Minn. | L | 3-12 | Wiley | Hassler |
| 2—At Minn. | L | 4-9 | Blyleven | Hudson |
| 3—At Minn. | W | 7-6 | Scott | Butler |
| 4—At Oak. | L | 0-6 | Holtzman | Tanana |
| 5—At Oak. | W | 2-0 | Figueroa | Bahnsen |
| 6—At Oak. | W | 2-0 | Lange | Blue |
| 8—Balt. | L | 5-8* | Alexander | Ryan |
| 9—Balt. | W | 3-2 | Tanana | Grimsley |
| 10—Balt. | L | 3-7 | Cuellar | Figueroa |
| 11—Cleve. | L | 3-5 | Harrison | Lange |
| 12—Cleve. | L | 1-9 | Eckersley | Ryan |
| 13—Cleve. | L | 7-8 | Bibby | Kirkwood |
| 17—At Milw. | W | 6-1 | Figueroa | Colborn |
| 18—At Milw. | L | 0-2 | Slaton | Ryan |
| 19—At Cleve. | W | 8-0 | Tanana | Eckersley |
| 19—At Cleve. | W | 3-2* | Kirkwood | LaRoche |
| 20—At Cleve. | L | 4-10 | Hood | Lange |
| 21—At Cleve. | L | 1-2† | LaRoche | Figueroa |
| 22—At Balt. | L | 3-8 | Cuellar | Ryan |
| 23—At Balt. | W | 1-0 | Tanana | Palmer |
| 25—Minn. | L | 1-12 | Blyleven | Singer |
| 26—Minn. | L | 4-9 | Goltz | Figueroa |
| 26—Minn. | W | 5-0 | Ryan | Albury |
| 27—Minn. | W | 6-1 | Lange | Hughes |
| 28—Chicago | L | 2-3 | Wood | Tanana |
| 29—Chicago | L | 4-7 | Osteen | Hassler |
| 30—Chicago | W | 5-4 | Ryan | Kaat |
| | | **Won 12, Lost 16** | | |

**AUGUST**

| | | | Winner | Loser |
|---|---|---|---|---|
| 1—At Texas | L | 1-2 | Perry | Figueroa |
| 2—At Texas | L | 2-8 | Hands | Lange |
| 3—At Texas | W | 6-4 | Kirkwood | Moore |
| 4—At Chi. | L | 2-4 | Wood | Hockenbery |
| 5—At Chi. | W | 10-4 | Figueroa | Osteen |
| 5—At Chi. | L | 1-4 | Jefferson | Singer |
| 6—At Chi. | L | 1-11 | Kaat | Lange |
| 7—At Chi. | L | 4-8 | Hamilton | Hassler |
| 8—N. York | L | 3-4 | Gura | Ryan |
| 9—N. York | W | 8-1 | Figueroa | Hunter |
| 10—N. York | W | 1-0 | Scott | May |

**AUGUST**

| | | | Winner | Loser |
|---|---|---|---|---|
| 11—N. York | W | 8-1 | Tanana | Dobson |
| 12—Boston | L | 2-8 | Wise | Hockenbery |
| 13—Boston | W | 8-3 | Figueroa | Cleveland |
| 14—Boston | W | 5-3 | Singer | Lee |
| 15—Detroit | W | 8-0 | Tanana | Lolich |
| 16—Detroit | L | 0-8 | Bare | Hockenbery |
| 17—Detroit | L | 0-7 | Ruhle | Figueroa |
| 18—Milw. | W | 5-4 | Kirkwood | Murphy |
| 19—Milw. | W | 5-4x | Scott | Austin |
| 20—Milw. | W | 6-1 | Ryan | Slaton |
| 22—At N. Y. | L | 2-5 | Hunter | Figueroa |
| 23—At N. Y. | L | 4-12 | Gura | Singer |
| 24—At N. Y. | W | 9-0 | Tanana | May |
| 24—At N. Y. | W | 4-3 | Ryan | Martinez |
| 26—At Bos. | W | 8-2 | Figueroa | Tiant |
| 27—At Bos. | L | 2-6 | Moret | Singer |
| 29—At Det. | W | 8-1 | Tanana | Lolich |
| 30—At Det. | L | 2-9 | Bare | Hockenbery |
| | | **Won 15, Lost 14** | | |

**SEPTEMBER**

| | | | Winner | Loser |
|---|---|---|---|---|
| 1—Oakland | L | 3-6 | Blue | Figueroa |
| 2—Oakland | W | 4-1 | Tanana | Holtzman |
| 3—Texas | L | 4-5 | Wright | Hassler |
| 4—Texas | W | 6-4 | Brewer | Thomas |
| 5—Kan. C. | L | 2-5 | Busby | Figueroa |
| 6—Kan. C. | L | 3-4 | McDaniel | Tanana |
| 6—Kan. C. | L | 3-6 | Pattin | Singer |
| 7—Kan. C. | L | 7-8† | Littell | Scott |
| 9—At Chi. | W | 5-4 | Figueroa | Wood |
| 10—At Chi. | W | 4-2 | Tanana | Kaat |
| 12—At K. C. | L | 2-10 | Leonard | Singer |
| 12—At K. C. | L | 2-7 | Fitzmorris | Kirkwood |
| 13—At K. C. | W | 6-2 | Figueroa | Bird |
| 14—At K. C. | L | 4-10 | Busby | Tanana |
| 15—At Minn. | L | 6-7‡ | Campbell | Hockenbery |
| 16—At Minn. | L | 3-4 | Hughes | Monge |
| 17—At Texas | W | 3-2 | Figueroa | Clyde |
| 18—At Texas | W | 5-3 | Tanana | Umbarger |
| 19—Minn. | W | 1-0 | Pactwa | Blyleven |
| 20—Minn. | L | 2-3 | Hughes | Monge |
| 21—Minn. | W | 5-2 | Figueroa | Goltz |
| 22—Chicago | W | 3-0y | Kirkwood | Gossage |
| 23—Chicago | L | 4-5 | Osborn | Lange |
| 26—At Oak. | L | 2-4 | Bosman | Figueroa |
| 27—At Oak. | L | 3-6 | Holtzman | Tanana |
| 28—At Oak. | L | 0-5 | Blue | Ross |
| | | **Won 10, Lost 16** | | |

* 10 innings.  † 11 innings.  ‡ 12 innings.  § 13 innings.  x 15 innings.  y 16 innings.  z Suspended game, completed June 12.

**ROD CAREW**
• TWINS •
BATTING CHAMPION (.359)

**GEORGE BRETT**
• ROYALS •
HITS (195)
TRIPLES (13) TIE

**GEORGE SCOTT**
• BREWERS •
RBIs (109)
HOMERS (36) TIE

# 1975 AMERICAN LEAGUE LEADERS

**FRANK TANANA**
• ANGELS •
STRIKEOUTS (269)

**JIM HUNTER**
• YANKEES •
WINS (23) TIE
INNINGS (328)
COMPLETE GAMES (30)

**JIM PALMER**
• ORIOLES •
ERA (2.09)
WINS (23) TIE
SHUTOUTS (10)

# American League Averages for 1975

## CHAMPIONSHIP WINNERS IN PREVIOUS YEARS

| | | |
|---|---|---|
| 1900—Chicago* .607 | 1925—Washington .636 | 1950—New York .636 |
| 1901—Chicago .610 | 1926—New York .591 | 1951—New York .636 |
| 1902—Philadelphia .610 | 1927—New York .714 | 1952—New York .617 |
| 1903—Boston .659 | 1928—New York .656 | 1953—New York .656 |
| 1904—Boston .617 | 1929—Philadelphia .693 | 1954—Cleveland .721 |
| 1905—Philadelphia .622 | 1930—Philadelphia .662 | 1955—New York .623 |
| 1906—Chicago .616 | 1931—Philadelphia .704 | 1956—New York .630 |
| 1907—Detroit .613 | 1932—New York .695 | 1957—New York .636 |
| 1908—Detroit .588 | 1933—Washington .651 | 1958—New York .597 |
| 1909—Detroit .645 | 1934—Detroit .656 | 1959—Chicago .610 |
| 1910—Philadelphia .680 | 1935—Detroit .616 | 1960—New York .630 |
| 1911—Philadelphia .669 | 1936—New York .667 | 1961—New York .673 |
| 1912—Boston .691 | 1937—New York .662 | 1962—New York .593 |
| 1913—Philadelphia .627 | 1938—New York .651 | 1963—New York .646 |
| 1914—Philadelphia .651 | 1939—New York .702 | 1964—New York .611 |
| 1915—Boston .669 | 1940—Detroit .584 | 1965—Minnesota .630 |
| 1916—Boston .591 | 1941—New York .656 | 1966—Baltimore .606 |
| 1917—Chicago .649 | 1942—New York .669 | 1967—Boston .568 |
| 1918—Boston .595 | 1943—New York .636 | 1968—Detroit .636 |
| 1919—Chicago .629 | 1944—St. Louis .578 | 1969—Baltimore (East)‡ .673 |
| 1920—Cleveland .636 | 1945—Detroit .575 | 1970—Baltimore (East)‡ .667 |
| 1921—New York .641 | 1946—Boston .675 | 1971—Baltimore (East)§ .639 |
| 1922—New York .610 | 1947—New York .630 | 1972—Oakland (West)a .600 |
| 1923—New York .645 | 1948—Cleveland† .626 | 1973—Oakland (West)b .580 |
| 1924—Washington .597 | 1949—New York .630 | 1974—Oakland (West)b .556 |

*Not recognized as major league in 1900.  †Defeated Boston in one-game playoff for pennant.  ‡Defeated Minnesota (West) in Championship Series.  §Defeated Oakland (West) in Championship Series.  aDefeated Detroit (East) in Championship Series.  bDefeated Baltimore (East) in Championship Series.

## STANDING OF CLUBS AT CLOSE OF SEASON

### EAST DIVISION

| Club | Bos. | Balt. | N.Y. | Clev. | Mil. | Det. | Cal. | Chi. | K.C. | Minn. | Oak. | Tex. | W. | L. | Pct. | G.B. |
|---|---|---|---|---|---|---|---|---|---|---|---|---|---|---|---|---|
| Boston | .. | 9 | 11 | 7 | 10 | 13 | 6 | 8 | 7 | 10 | 6 | 8 | 95 | 65 | .594 | ........ |
| Baltimore | 9 | .. | 8 | 10 | 14 | 12 | 6 | 7 | 6 | 4 | 7 | 8 | 90 | 69 | .566 | 4½ |
| New York | 5 | 10 | .. | 9 | 9 | 12 | 5 | 6 | 5 | 8 | 6 | 8 | 83 | 77 | .519 | 12 |
| Cleveland | 11 | 8 | 9 | .. | 9 | 12 | 9 | 5 | 6 | 3 | 2 | 5 | 79 | 80 | .497 | 15½ |
| Milwaukee | 8 | 4 | 9 | 9 | .. | 11 | 5 | 4 | 5 | 2 | 5 | 6 | 68 | 94 | .420 | 28 |
| Detroit | 5 | 4 | 6 | 6 | 7 | .. | 5 | 7 | 6 | 4 | 6 | 1 | 57 | 102 | .358 | 37½ |

### WEST DIVISION

| Club | Oak. | K.C. | Tex. | Minn. | Chi. | Cal. | Balt. | Bos. | Clev. | Det. | Mil. | N.Y. | W. | L. | Pct. | G.B. |
|---|---|---|---|---|---|---|---|---|---|---|---|---|---|---|---|---|
| Oakland | .. | 11 | 12 | 12 | 9 | 11 | 8 | 6 | 10 | 6 | 7 | 6 | 98 | 64 | .605 | ........ |
| Kansas City | 7 | .. | 14 | 11 | 9 | 14 | 5 | 5 | 6 | 7 | 7 | 7 | 91 | 71 | .562 | 7 |
| Texas | 6 | 4 | .. | 10 | 13 | 9 | 5 | 4 | 7 | 11 | 6 | 4 | 79 | 83 | .488 | 19 |
| Minnesota | 6 | 7 | 8 | .. | 9 | 10 | 6 | 2 | 6 | 8 | 10 | 4 | 76 | 83 | .478 | 20½ |
| Chicago | 9 | 9 | 5 | 9 | .. | 9 | 4 | 4 | 7 | 5 | 8 | 6 | 75 | 86 | .466 | 22½ |
| California | 7 | 4 | 9 | 8 | 9 | .. | 6 | 6 | 3 | 6 | 7 | 7 | 72 | 89 | .447 | 25½ |

CANCELED GAMES—Chicago at Baltimore; Detroit at Baltimore (2); Minnesota at Cleveland (3); California at Detroit; Boston at New York (2).

CHAMPIONSHIP SERIES—Boston defeated Oakland, three games to none.

## RECORD AT HOME

### EAST DIVISION

| Club | Bos. | Balt. | N.Y. | Clev. | Mil. | Det. | Oak. | K.C. | Chi. | Tex. | Minn. | Cal. | W. | L. | Pct. |
|---|---|---|---|---|---|---|---|---|---|---|---|---|---|---|---|
| Boston | .... | 3-6 | 5-4 | 3-6 | 5-4 | 8-1 | 4-2 | 3-3 | 4-2 | 4-2 | 5-1 | 3-3 | 47 | 34 | .580 |
| Baltimore | 3-6 | .... | 5-4 | 4-4 | 7-2 | 4-3 | 3-3 | 5-1 | 4-1 | 3-3 | 4-2 | 2-4 | 44 | 33 | .571 |
| New York | 1-6 | 6-3 | .... | 6-3 | 6-3 | 5-4 | 3-3 | 3-3 | 2-4 | 5-1 | 3-2 | 3-3 | 43 | 35 | .551 |
| Cleveland | 5-4 | 4-6 | 6-3 | .... | 4-5 | 7-2 | 1-5 | 3-3 | 3-3 | 4-3 | 1-2 | 3-3 | 41 | 39 | .513 |
| Milwaukee | 4-5 | 2-7 | 6-3 | 4-5 | .... | 9-0 | 2-4 | 1-5 | 2-4 | 2-4 | 0-6 | 4-2 | 36 | 45 | .444 |
| Detroit | 4-5 | 1-8 | 2-7 | 4-5 | 7-2 | .... | 2-4 | 3-3 | 5-1 | 0-6 | 1-5 | 2-3 | 31 | 49 | .388 |

### WEST DIVISION

| Club | Oak. | K.C. | Chi. | Tex. | Minn. | Cal. | Bos. | Balt. | N.Y. | Clev. | Mil. | Det. | W. | L. | Pct. |
|---|---|---|---|---|---|---|---|---|---|---|---|---|---|---|---|
| Oakland | .... | 8-1 | 6-3 | 6-3 | 6-3 | 4-5 | 4-2 | 5-1 | 3-3 | 5-1 | 3-3 | 2-4 | 54 | 27 | .667 |
| Kansas City | 6-3 | .... | 5-4 | 8-1 | 8-1 | 6-3 | 2-4 | 4-2 | 4-2 | 3-3 | 2-4 | 3-3 | 51 | 30 | .630 |
| Chicago | 6-3 | 5-4 | .... | 3-6 | 5-4 | 4-5 | 2-4 | 3-3 | 2-4 | 4-2 | 4-2 | 4-2 | 42 | 39 | .519 |
| Texas | 3-6 | 3-6 | 7-2 | .... | 3-6 | 5-4 | 2-4 | 2-4 | 3-3 | 4-1 | 2-4 | 5-1 | 39 | 41 | .488 |
| Minnesota | 3-6 | 6-3 | 5-4 | 2-7 | .... | 5-4 | 1-5 | 4-2 | 2-5 | 4-2 | 4-2 | 3-3 | 39 | 43 | .476 |
| California | 4-5 | 1-8 | 4-5 | 5-4 | 4-5 | .... | 3-3 | 2-4 | 4-2 | 0-6 | 5-1 | 3-3 | 35 | 46 | .432 |

## RECORD ABROAD

### EAST DIVISION

| Club | Bos. | Balt. | N.Y. | Clev. | Mil. | Det. | Oak. | K.C. | Tex. | Minn. | Cal. | Chi. | W. | L. | Pct. |
|---|---|---|---|---|---|---|---|---|---|---|---|---|---|---|---|
| Boston | .... | 6-3 | 6-1 | 4-5 | 5-4 | 5-4 | 2-4 | 4-2 | 4-2 | 5-1 | 3-3 | 4-2 | 48 | 31 | .608 |
| Baltimore | 6-3 | .... | 3-6 | 6-4 | 7-2 | 8-1 | 1-5 | 2-4 | 4-2 | 2-4 | 4-2 | 3-3 | 46 | 36 | .561 |
| New York | 4-5 | 4-5 | .... | 3-6 | 3-6 | 7-2 | 3-3 | 2-4 | 3-3 | 5-2 | 2-4 | 4-2 | 40 | 42 | .488 |
| Cleveland | 6-3 | 4-4 | 3-6 | .... | 5-4 | 5-4 | 1-5 | 3-3 | 1-4 | 2-4 | 6-0 | 2-4 | 38 | 41 | .481 |
| Milwaukee | 4-5 | 2-7 | 3-6 | 5-4 | .... | 2-7 | 3-3 | 4-2 | 4-2 | 2-4 | 1-5 | 2-4 | 32 | 49 | .395 |
| Detroit | 1-8 | 3-4 | 4-5 | 2-7 | 0-9 | .... | 4-2 | 3-3 | 1-5 | 3-3 | 3-3 | 2-4 | 26 | 53 | .329 |

### WEST DIVISION

| Club | Oak. | K.C. | Tex. | Minn. | Cal. | Chi. | Bos. | Balt. | N.Y. | Clev. | Mil. | Det. | W. | L. | Pct. |
|---|---|---|---|---|---|---|---|---|---|---|---|---|---|---|---|
| Oakland | .... | 3-6 | 6-3 | 6-3 | 5-4 | 3-6 | 2-4 | 3-3 | 3-3 | 4-2 | 4-2 | 3-3 | 44 | 37 | .543 |
| Kansas City | 1-8 | .... | 6-3 | 3-6 | 8-1 | 4-5 | 3-3 | 1-5 | 3-3 | 3-3 | 5-1 | 3-3 | 40 | 41 | .494 |
| Texas | 3-6 | 1-8 | .... | 7-2 | 4-5 | 6-3 | 2-4 | 3-3 | 1-5 | 3-4 | 4-2 | 6-0 | 40 | 42 | .488 |
| Minnesota | 3-6 | 1-8 | 6-3 | .... | 5-4 | 4-5 | 1-5 | 2-4 | 2-3 | 2-1 | 6-0 | 5-1 | 37 | 40 | .481 |
| California | 3-6 | 3-6 | 4-5 | 4-5 | .... | 5-4 | 3-3 | 4-2 | 3-3 | 3-3 | 3-2 | 3-1 | 37 | 43 | .463 |
| Chicago | 3-6 | 4-5 | 2-7 | 4-5 | 5-4 | .... | 2-4 | 1-4 | 4-2 | 3-3 | 4-2 | 1-5 | 33 | 47 | .413 |
| Club | Oak. | K.C. | Tex. | Minn. | Cal. | Chi. | Bos. | Balt. | N.Y. | Clev. | Mil. | Det. | W. | L. | Pct. |

## SHUTOUT GAMES

| Club | Balt. | Tex. | Calif. | Bos. | K.C. | Minn. | Mil. | N.Y. | Oak. | Chi. | Clev. | Det. | W. | L. | Pct. |
|---|---|---|---|---|---|---|---|---|---|---|---|---|---|---|---|
| Baltimore | .. | 1 | 3 | 3 | 3 | 1 | 4 | 1 | 1 | 0 | 0 | 2 | 19 | 9 | .679 |
| Texas | 1 | .. | 3 | 1 | 0 | 3 | 2 | 2 | 1 | 0 | 1 | 2 | 16 | 10 | .615 |
| California | 2 | 1 | .. | 1 | 0 | 2 | 1 | 3 | 5 | 2 | 1 | 1 | 19 | 13 | .594 |
| Boston | 1 | 1 | 1 | .. | 1 | 0 | 0 | 2 | 1 | 2 | 2 | 0 | 11 | 9 | .550 |
| Kansas City | 0 | 3 | 1 | 1 | .. | 0 | 1 | 2 | 2 | 1 | 0 | 0 | 11 | 9 | .550 |
| Minnesota | 0 | 1 | 0 | 0 | 0 | .. | 2 | 1 | 0 | 0 | 1 | 2 | 7 | 7 | .500 |
| Milwaukee | 0 | 0 | 1 | 1 | 1 | 0 | .. | 0 | 0 | 1 | 2 | 4 | 10 | 11 | .476 |
| New York | 2 | 2 | 0 | 1 | 1 | 0 | 0 | .. | 1 | 1 | 0 | 3 | 11 | 14 | .440 |
| Oakland | 2 | 1 | 2 | 0 | 0 | 0 | 0 | 0 | .. | 1 | 1 | 3 | 10 | 13 | .435 |
| Chicago | 0 | 0 | 0 | 0 | 0 | 1 | 1 | 1 | 0 | .. | 2 | 2 | 7 | 11 | .389 |
| Cleveland | 1 | 0 | 0 | 0 | 1 | 0 | 0 | 1 | 1 | 1 | .. | 1 | 6 | 11 | .353 |
| Detroit | 0 | 0 | 2 | 1 | 2 | 0 | 0 | 1 | 1 | 2 | 1 | .. | 10 | 20 | .333 |

# OFFICIAL AMERICAN LEAGUE BATTING AVERAGES

Compiled by Sports Information Center, No. Quincy, Mass.

## CLUB BATTING

| Club | Pct. | G. | AB. | R. | OR. | H. | TB. | 2B. | 3B. | HR. | RBI. | SH. | SF. | SB. | CS. | LOB. |
|------|------|----|-----|----|----|----|----|-----|-----|-----|------|-----|-----|-----|-----|------|
| Boston .. | .275 | 160 | 5448 | 796 | 709 | 1500 | 2274 | 284 | 44 | 134 | 756 | 75 | 53 | 66 | 58 | 1113 |
| Minn. .... | .271 | 159 | 5514 | 724 | 736 | 1497 | 2131 | 215 | 28 | 121 | 669 | 62 | 46 | 81 | 48 | 1238 |
| N. York.. | .264 | 160 | 5415 | 681 | 588 | 1430 | 2068 | 230 | 39 | 110 | 642 | 54 | 53 | 102 | 59 | 1083 |
| Cleve.... | .261 | 159 | 5404 | 688 | 703 | 1409 | 2119 | 201 | 25 | 153 | 643 | 64 | 40 | 106 | 89 | 1067 |
| Kan. C... | .261 | 162 | 5491 | 710 | 649 | 1431 | 2164 | 263 | 58 | 118 | 667 | 68 | 51 | 155 | 75 | 1180 |
| Texas ... | .256 | 162 | 5599 | 714 | 733 | 1431 | 2075 | 208 | 17 | 134 | 675 | 64 | 41 | 102 | 62 | 1213 |
| Chicago.. | .255 | 161 | 5490 | 655 | 703 | 1400 | 1967 | 209 | 38 | 94 | 604 | 50 | 52 | 101 | 54 | 1220 |
| Oakland | .254 | 162 | 5415 | 758 | 606 | 1376 | 2115 | 220 | 33 | 151 | 703 | 74 | 35 | 183 | 82 | 1127 |
| Balt. .... | .252 | 159 | 5474 | 682 | 553 | 1382 | 2044 | 224 | 33 | 124 | 635 | 73 | 46 | 104 | 55 | 1184 |
| Milw. .... | .250 | 162 | 5378 | 675 | 792 | 1343 | 2091 | 242 | 34 | 146 | 632 | 73 | 49 | 65 | 64 | 1080 |
| Detroit .. | .249 | 159 | 5366 | 570 | 786 | 1338 | 1962 | 171 | 39 | 125 | 546 | 37 | 38 | 63 | 57 | 1029 |
| Calif...... | .246 | 161 | 5377 | 628 | 723 | 1324 | 1766 | 195 | 41 | 55 | 572 | 97 | 47 | 220 | 108 | 1126 |
| Totals | .258 | | 65371 | 8281 | 8281 | 16861 | 24776 | 2662 | 429 | 1465 | 7744 | 791 | 551 | 1348 | 811 | 13660 |

## INDIVIDUAL BATTING

(Top Fifteen Qualifiers for Batting Championship—502 or More Plate Appearances)

°Bats lefthanded.    †Switch-hitter.

| Player and Club | Pct. | G. | AB. | R. | H. | TB. | 2B. | 3B. | HR. | RBI. | SH. | SF. | SB. | CS. |
|-----------------|------|----|-----|----|----|----|-----|-----|-----|------|-----|-----|-----|-----|
| Carew, Rodney, Minnesota° | .359 | 143 | 535 | 89 | 192 | 266 | 24 | 14 | 80 | 7 | 10 | 35 | 9 | |
| Lynn, Fredric, Boston° | .331 | 145 | 528 | 103 | 175 | 299 | 47 | 7 | 21 | 105 | 6 | 6 | 10 | 5 |
| Munson, Thurman, New York | .318 | 157 | 597 | 83 | 190 | 256 | 24 | 3 | 12 | 102 | 3 | 10 | 3 | 2 |
| Rice, James, Boston | .309 | 144 | 564 | 92 | 174 | 277 | 29 | 4 | 22 | 102 | 1 | 8 | 10 | 5 |
| Washington, Claudell, Oakland° | .308 | 148 | 590 | 86 | 182 | 250 | 24 | 7 | 10 | 77 | 1 | 7 | 40 | 15 |
| Brett, George, Kansas City° | .308 | 159 | 634 | 84 | 195 | 289 | 35 | 13 | 11 | 89 | 9 | 6 | 13 | 13 |
| McRae, Harold, Kansas City | .306 | 126 | 480 | 58 | 147 | 212 | 38 | 6 | 5 | 71 | 6 | 10 | 11 | 8 |
| Orta, Jorge, Chicago° | .304 | 140 | 542 | 64 | 165 | 244 | 26 | 10 | 11 | 83 | 4 | 4 | 16 | 9 |
| Chambliss, C. Christopher, NY° | .304 | 150 | 562 | 66 | 171 | 244 | 38 | 4 | 9 | 72 | 4 | 6 | 0 | 1 |
| Hargrove, D. Michael, Texas° | .303 | 145 | 519 | 82 | 157 | 216 | 22 | 2 | 11 | 62 | 2 | 5 | 4 | 3 |
| Braun, Stephen, Minnesota° | .302 | 136 | 453 | 70 | 137 | 194 | 18 | 3 | 11 | 45 | 2 | 4 | 0 | 2 |
| Singleton, Kenneth, Baltimore† | .300 | 155 | 586 | 88 | 176 | 266 | 37 | 4 | 15 | 55 | 3 | 6 | 3 | 5 |
| Powell, John, Cleveland° | .297 | 134 | 435 | 64 | 129 | 228 | 18 | 0 | 27 | 86 | 1 | 6 | 1 | 3 |
| Harrah, Colbert, Texas | .293 | 151 | 522 | 81 | 153 | 239 | 24 | 1 | 20 | 93 | 6 | 4 | 23 | 9 |
| Mayberry, John, Kansas City° | .291 | 156 | 554 | 95 | 161 | 303 | 38 | 1 | 34 | 106 | 1 | 5 | 5 | 3 |

DEPARTMENTAL LEADERS: G—Bando, Garner, 160; AB—Brett, 634; R—Lynn, 103; H—Brett, 195; TB—G. Scott, 318; 2B—Lynn, 47; 3B—Brett, Rivers, 13; HR—Re. Jackson, G. Scott, 36; RBI—G. Scott, 109; SH—Belanger, 23; SF—G. Nettles, 11; SB—Rivers, 70; CS—Remy, 21.

# EXPLANATION OF ABBREVIATION TERMS

G—Games Played. AB—At Bats. R—Runs. H—Hits. TB—Total Bases. 2B—Two-Base Hits. 3B—Three-Base Hits. HR—Home Runs. RBI—Runs Batted In. SH—Sacrifice Hits. SF—Sacrifice Flies. SB—Stolen Bases. CS—Caught Stealing. BB—Bases on Balls. IBB—Intentional Bases on Balls. HP—Hit by Pitcher. SO—Strikeouts. Pct.—Percentage. GIDP—Grounded Into Double Plays. Slg.Pct.—Slugging Percentage. OR—Opponents' Runs. LOB—Left on Bases. PO—Putouts. A—Assists. E—Errors. TC—Total Chances. DP—Double Plays. TP—Triple Plays. PB—Passed Balls. G—Games Pitched. GS—Games Started. CG—Complete Games. GF—Games Finished in Relief. ShO—Shutouts. W—Games Won. L—Games Lost. IP—Innings Pitched. BFP—Total Batters Facing Pitcher. ER—Earned Runs. HB—Hit Batsmen. WP—Wild Pitches. Bk—Balks. ERA—Earned-Run Average. Sv—Saves.

(All Players—Listed Alphabetically)

| Player and Club | Pct. | G. | AB. | R. | H. | TB. | 2B. | 3B. | HR. | RBI. | SH. | SF. | SB. | CS. |
|---|---|---|---|---|---|---|---|---|---|---|---|---|---|---|
| Aaron, Henry, Milwaukee | .234 | 137 | 465 | 45 | 109 | 165 | 16 | 2 | 12 | 60 | 1 | 6 | 0 | 1 |
| Albury, Victor, Minnesota° | .000 | 33 | 1 | 0 | 0 | 0 | 0 | 0 | 0 | 0 | 0 | 0 | 0 | 0 |
| Alexander, Matthew, Oakland† | .100 | 63 | 10 | 16 | 1 | 1 | 0 | 0 | 0 | 0 | 0 | 0 | 17 | 10 |
| Allietta, Robert, California | .178 | 21 | 45 | 4 | 8 | 12 | 1 | 0 | 1 | 2 | 1 | 0 | 0 | 0 |
| Alomar, Santos, New York† | .239 | 151 | 489 | 61 | 117 | 149 | 18 | 4 | 2 | 39 | 11 | 2 | 28 | 6 |
| Andrew, Kim, Boston | .500 | 2 | 2 | 0 | 1 | 1 | 0 | 0 | 0 | 0 | 0 | 0 | 0 | 0 |
| Ashby, Alan, Cleveland† | .224 | 90 | 254 | 32 | 57 | 84 | 10 | 1 | 5 | 32 | 16 | 0 | 3 | 2 |
| Bahnsen, Stanley, 12 Chi-21 Oak | .000 | 33 | 1 | 0 | 0 | 0 | 0 | 0 | 0 | 0 | 0 | 0 | 0 | 0 |
| Bailor, Robert, Baltimore | .143 | 5 | 7 | 0 | 1 | 1 | 0 | 0 | 0 | 0 | 0 | 0 | 0 | 0 |
| Balaz, John, California | .242 | 45 | 120 | 10 | 29 | 42 | 8 | 1 | 1 | 10 | 1 | 1 | 0 | 0 |
| Baldwin, Robert, Detroit° | .221 | 30 | 95 | 8 | 21 | 36 | 3 | 0 | 4 | 8 | 1 | 0 | 2 | 1 |
| Bando, Salvatore, Oakland | .230 | 160 | 562 | 64 | 129 | 200 | 24 | 1 | 15 | 78 | 2 | 2 | 7 | 1 |
| Baylor, Donald, Baltimore | .282 | 145 | 524 | 79 | 148 | 256 | 21 | 6 | 25 | 76 | 4 | 4 | 32 | 17 |
| Belanger, Mark, Baltimore | .226 | 152 | 442 | 44 | 100 | 122 | 11 | 1 | 3 | 27 | 23 | 0 | 16 | 4 |
| Bell, David, Cleveland | .271 | 153 | 553 | 66 | 150 | 208 | 20 | 4 | 10 | 59 | 10 | 4 | 6 | 5 |
| Beniquez, Juan, Boston | .291 | 78 | 254 | 43 | 74 | 102 | 14 | 4 | 2 | 17 | 6 | 1 | 7 | 10 |
| Bergman, David, New York° | .000 | 7 | 17 | 0 | 0 | 0 | 0 | 0 | 0 | 0 | 0 | 0 | 0 | 0 |
| Berry, A. Kent, Cleveland | .200 | 25 | 40 | 6 | 8 | 9 | 1 | 0 | 0 | 1 | 0 | 0 | 0 | 1 |
| Bevacqua, Kurt, Milwaukee | .229 | 104 | 258 | 30 | 59 | 79 | 14 | 0 | 2 | 24 | 7 | 2 | 3 | 4 |
| Bianco, Thomas, Milwaukee† | .176 | 18 | 34 | 6 | 6 | 7 | 1 | 0 | 0 | 0 | 0 | 0 | 0 | 0 |
| Blackwell, Timothy, Boston† | .197 | 59 | 132 | 15 | 26 | 33 | 3 | 2 | 0 | 6 | 5 | 0 | 0 | 0 |
| Bladt, Richard, New York | .222 | 52 | 117 | 13 | 26 | 34 | 3 | 1 | 1 | 11 | 3 | 1 | 6 | 2 |
| Blair, Paul, Baltimore | .218 | 140 | 440 | 51 | 96 | 132 | 13 | 4 | 5 | 31 | 17 | 5 | 17 | 11 |
| Blomberg, Ronald, New York° | .255 | 34 | 106 | 18 | 27 | 51 | 8 | 2 | 4 | 17 | 0 | 0 | 0 | 0 |
| Bochte, Bruce, California° | .285 | 107 | 375 | 41 | 107 | 141 | 19 | 3 | 3 | 48 | 3 | 3 | 3 | 4 |
| Bonds, Bobby, New York | .270 | 145 | 529 | 93 | 143 | 271 | 26 | 3 | 32 | 85 | 0 | 5 | 30 | 17 |
| Borgmann, Glenn, Minnesota | .207 | 125 | 352 | 34 | 73 | 98 | 15 | 2 | 2 | 33 | 10 | 2 | 0 | 1 |
| Bostock, Lyman, Minnesota° | .282 | 98 | 369 | 52 | 104 | 135 | 21 | 5 | 0 | 29 | 1 | 2 | 2 | 3 |
| Bradford, Charles, Chicago | .155 | 25 | 58 | 8 | 9 | 20 | 3 | 1 | 2 | 15 | 1 | 4 | 3 | 2 |
| Braun, Stephen, Minnesota° | .302 | 136 | 453 | 70 | 137 | 194 | 18 | 3 | 11 | 45 | 2 | 4 | 0 | 2 |
| Brett, George, Kansas City° | .308 | 159 | 634 | 84 | 195 | 289 | 35 | 13 | 11 | 89 | 9 | 6 | 13 | 10 |
| Briggs, Daniel, California° | .226 | 13 | 31 | 3 | 7 | 11 | 1 | 0 | 1 | 3 | 1 | 0 | 0 | 2 |
| Briggs, John, 28 Milw-87 Minn.° | .246 | 115 | 338 | 56 | 83 | 127 | 10 | 2 | 10 | 44 | 1 | 2 | 6 | 4 |
| Brinkman, Edwin, 1 Tex-44 NY | .169 | 45 | 65 | 2 | 11 | 17 | 4 | 1 | 0 | 2 | 1 | 0 | 0 | 0 |
| Brohamer, John, Cleveland° | .244 | 69 | 217 | 15 | 53 | 76 | 5 | 0 | 6 | 16 | 2 | 1 | 2 | 2 |
| Brown, W. Gates, Detroit° | .171 | 47 | 35 | 1 | 6 | 11 | 2 | 0 | 1 | 3 | 0 | 0 | 0 | 0 |
| Brye, Stephen, Minnesota | .252 | 86 | 246 | 41 | 62 | 104 | 13 | 1 | 9 | 34 | 2 | 1 | 2 | 1 |
| Bumbry, Alonza, Baltimore° | .269 | 114 | 349 | 47 | 94 | 127 | 19 | 4 | 2 | 32 | 3 | 2 | 16 | 3 |
| Burleson, Richard, Boston | .252 | 158 | 580 | 66 | 146 | 191 | 25 | 1 | 6 | 62 | 17 | 9 | 8 | 5 |
| Burroughs, Jeffrey, Texas | .226 | 152 | 585 | 81 | 132 | 239 | 20 | 0 | 29 | 94 | 0 | 7 | 4 | 4 |
| Campaneris, Dagoberto, Oakland | .265 | 137 | 509 | 69 | 135 | 168 | 15 | 3 | 4 | 46 | 19 | 3 | 24 | 12 |
| Campbell, William, Minnesota | .000 | 47 | 1 | 0 | 0 | 0 | 0 | 0 | 0 | 0 | 0 | 0 | 0 | 0 |
| Carbo, Bernardo, Boston° | .257 | 107 | 319 | 64 | 82 | 154 | 21 | 3 | 15 | 50 | 1 | 3 | 2 | 4 |
| Cardenas, Leonardo, Texas | .235 | 55 | 102 | 15 | 24 | 29 | 2 | 0 | 1 | 5 | 3 | 0 | 0 | 0 |
| Carew, Rodney, Minnesota° | .359 | 143 | 535 | 89 | 192 | 266 | 24 | 4 | 14 | 80 | 7 | 10 | 35 | 9 |
| Carty, Ricardo, Cleveland | .308 | 118 | 383 | 57 | 118 | 193 | 19 | 1 | 18 | 64 | 0 | 6 | 2 | 2 |
| Cerone, Richard, Cleveland | .250 | 7 | 12 | 1 | 3 | 4 | 1 | 0 | 0 | 1 | 0 | 0 | 0 | 0 |
| Chalk, David, California | .273 | 149 | 513 | 59 | 140 | 177 | 24 | 2 | 3 | 56 | 11 | 9 | 6 | 9 |
| Chambliss, C. Christopher, NY° | .304 | 150 | 562 | 66 | 171 | 244 | 38 | 4 | 9 | 72 | 4 | 6 | 0 | 1 |
| Chant, Charles, Oakland | .000 | 5 | 5 | 1 | 0 | 0 | 0 | 0 | 0 | 0 | 0 | 0 | 0 | 0 |
| Coggins, Richard, New York° | .224 | 51 | 107 | 7 | 24 | 28 | 1 | 0 | 1 | 6 | 5 | 0 | 3 | 3 |
| Colbert, Nathan, Detroit | .147 | 45 | 156 | 16 | 23 | 43 | 4 | 2 | 4 | 18 | 0 | 0 | 0 | 2 |
| Collins, David, California† | .266 | 93 | 319 | 41 | 85 | 115 | 13 | 4 | 3 | 29 | 3 | 3 | 24 | 10 |
| Coluccio, Robert, 22 Milw-61 Chi | .202 | 83 | 223 | 30 | 45 | 70 | 4 | 3 | 5 | 18 | 6 | 1 | 5 | 4 |
| Congiliaro, Anthony, Boston | .123 | 21 | 57 | 8 | 7 | 14 | 1 | 0 | 2 | 9 | 1 | 3 | 1 | 0 |
| Cooper, Cecil, Boston° | .311 | 106 | 305 | 49 | 95 | 166 | 17 | 6 | 14 | 44 | 3 | 3 | 1 | 4 |
| Cowens, Alfred, Kansas City | .277 | 120 | 328 | 44 | 91 | 132 | 13 | 8 | 4 | 42 | 5 | 2 | 12 | 7 |
| Crosby, Edward, Cleveland° | .234 | 61 | 128 | 12 | 30 | 33 | 3 | 0 | 0 | 7 | 4 | 0 | 0 | 4 |
| Cubbage, Michael, Texas° | .224 | 58 | 143 | 12 | 32 | 50 | 6 | 0 | 4 | 21 | 4 | 3 | 0 | 0 |
| Dade, L. Paul, California | .200 | 11 | 30 | 5 | 6 | 10 | 4 | 0 | 0 | 1 | 0 | 0 | 0 | 0 |
| Darwin, A. Bobby, 48 Min-55 Mil | .234 | 103 | 355 | 45 | 83 | 138 | 12 | 2 | 13 | 41 | 1 | 1 | 6 | 1 |
| Davis, H. Thomas, Baltimore | .283 | 116 | 460 | 43 | 130 | 164 | 14 | 1 | 6 | 57 | 2 | 3 | 2 | 0 |
| Davis, William, Texas° | .249 | 42 | 169 | 16 | 42 | 69 | 8 | 2 | 5 | 17 | 0 | 0 | 13 | 5 |
| DeCinces, Douglas, Baltimore | .251 | 61 | 167 | 20 | 42 | 66 | 6 | 3 | 4 | 23 | 0 | 2 | 0 | 1 |
| Dempsey, J. Rikard, New York | .262 | 71 | 145 | 18 | 38 | 49 | 8 | 0 | 1 | 11 | 3 | 1 | 0 | 0 |
| Dent, Russell, Chicago | .264 | 157 | 602 | 52 | 159 | 205 | 29 | 4 | 3 | 58 | 15 | 9 | 2 | 4 |
| Dillard, Stephen, Boston | .400 | 1 | 5 | 2 | 2 | 2 | 0 | 0 | 0 | 0 | 0 | 0 | 1 | 0 |

| Player and Club | Pct. | G. | AB. | R. | H. | TB. | 2B. | 3B. | HR. | RBI. | SH. | SF. | SB. | CS. |
|---|---|---|---|---|---|---|---|---|---|---|---|---|---|---|
| Dineen, Kerry, New York° | .364 | 7 | 22 | 3 | 8 | 9 | 1 | 0 | 0 | 1 | 0 | 0 | 0 | 0 |
| Doherty, John, California° | .202 | 30 | 94 | 7 | 19 | 25 | 3 | 0 | 1 | 12 | 2 | 1 | 1 | 1 |
| Downing, Brian, Chicago | .240 | 138 | 420 | 58 | 101 | 136 | 12 | 1 | 7 | 41 | 11 | 6 | 13 | 4 |
| Doyle, R. Dennis, 8 Calif-89 Bos° | .298 | 97 | 325 | 50 | 97 | 134 | 21 | 2 | 4 | 36 | 10 | 2 | 5 | 7 |
| Duffy, Frank, Cleveland | .243 | 146 | 482 | 44 | 117 | 146 | 22 | 2 | 1 | 47 | 6 | 4 | 10 | 10 |
| Duncan, David, Baltimore | .205 | 96 | 307 | 30 | 63 | 106 | 7 | 0 | 12 | 41 | 0 | 2 | 0 | 0 |
| Egan, Thomas, California† | .229 | 28 | 70 | 7 | 16 | 21 | 3 | 1 | 0 | 3 | 4 | 0 | 0 | 0 |
| Ellis, John, Cleveland | .230 | 92 | 296 | 22 | 68 | 102 | 11 | 1 | 7 | 32 | 0 | 4 | 0 | 1 |
| Ellis, Robert, Milwaukee | .286 | 6 | 7 | 3 | 2 | 2 | 0 | 0 | 0 | 0 | 1 | 0 | 0 | 0 |
| Etchebarren, Andrew, 8 Ba-31 Ca .. | .267 | 39 | 128 | 10 | 32 | 44 | 1 | 1 | 3 | 20 | 1 | 1 | 1 | 0 |
| Evans, Dwight, Boston | .274 | 128 | 412 | 61 | 113 | 188 | 24 | 6 | 13 | 56 | 5 | 2 | 3 | 4 |
| Fahey, William, Texas° | .297 | 21 | 37 | 3 | 11 | 14 | 1 | 1 | 0 | 3 | 1 | 0 | 0 | 0 |
| Ferrer, Sergio, Minnesota† | .247 | 32 | 81 | 14 | 20 | 25 | 3 | 1 | 0 | 2 | 3 | 1 | 3 | 4 |
| Fingers, Roland, Oakland | .000 | 76 | 1 | 0 | 0 | 0 | 0 | 0 | 0 | 0 | 0 | 0 | 0 | 0 |
| Fisk, Carlton, Boston | .331 | 79 | 263 | 47 | 87 | 139 | 14 | 4 | 10 | 52 | 0 | 2 | 4 | 3 |
| Ford, Darnell, Minnesota | .280 | 130 | 440 | 72 | 123 | 191 | 21 | 1 | 15 | 59 | 3 | 0 | 6 | 7 |
| Fosse, Raymond, Oakland | .140 | 82 | 136 | 14 | 19 | 26 | 3 | 2 | 0 | 12 | 1 | 1 | 0 | 1 |
| Freehan, William, Detroit | .246 | 120 | 427 | 42 | 105 | 170 | 17 | 3 | 14 | 47 | 1 | 2 | 2 | 0 |
| Fregosi, James, Texas | .262 | 77 | 191 | 25 | 50 | 76 | 5 | 0 | 7 | 33 | 1 | 4 | 0 | 1 |
| Gamble, Oscar, Cleveland° | .261 | 121 | 348 | 60 | 91 | 158 | 16 | 3 | 15 | 45 | 1 | 1 | 11 | 5 |
| Garcia, Pedro, Milwaukee | .225 | 98 | 302 | 40 | 68 | 105 | 15 | 2 | 6 | 38 | 10 | 3 | 12 | 6 |
| Garner, Philip, Oakland | .246 | 160 | 488 | 46 | 120 | 169 | 21 | 5 | 6 | 54 | 21 | 3 | 4 | 6 |
| Garrett, H. Adrian, California° | .262 | 37 | 107 | 17 | 28 | 51 | 5 | 0 | 6 | 18 | 1 | 1 | 3 | 0 |
| Gomez, Luis, Minnesota | .139 | 89 | 72 | 7 | 10 | 10 | 0 | 0 | 0 | 5 | 4 | 1 | 0 | 2 |
| Goodwin, Danny, California° | .100 | 4 | 10 | 0 | 1 | 1 | 0 | 0 | 0 | 0 | 0 | 0 | 0 | 0 |
| Grabarkewitz, Billy, Oakland | .000 | 6 | 2 | 0 | 0 | 0 | 0 | 0 | 0 | 0 | 0 | 0 | 0 | 0 |
| Grich, Robert, Baltimore | .260 | 150 | 524 | 81 | 136 | 209 | 26 | 4 | 13 | 57 | 9 | 7 | 14 | 10 |
| Grieve, Thomas, Texas | .276 | 118 | 369 | 46 | 102 | 163 | 17 | 1 | 14 | 61 | 4 | 1 | 0 | 2 |
| Griffin, Douglas, Boston | .240 | 100 | 287 | 21 | 69 | 78 | 6 | 0 | 1 | 29 | 7 | 2 | 2 | 2 |
| Hairston, Jerry, Chicago† | .283 | 69 | 219 | 26 | 62 | 70 | 8 | 0 | 0 | 23 | 6 | 2 | 1 | 0 |
| Hampton, Isaac, California† | .152 | 31 | 66 | 8 | 10 | 13 | 3 | 0 | 0 | 4 | 3 | 0 | 0 | 0 |
| Haney, W. Larry, Oakland | .192 | 47 | 26 | 3 | 5 | 8 | 0 | 0 | 1 | 2 | 0 | 0 | 0 | 0 |
| Hargrove, D. Michael, Texas° | .303 | 145 | 519 | 82 | 157 | 216 | 22 | 2 | 11 | 62 | 2 | 5 | 4 | 3 |
| Harlow, Larry, Baltimore° | .333 | 4 | 3 | 1 | 1 | 1 | 0 | 0 | 0 | 0 | 0 | 0 | 0 | 0 |
| Harper, Tommy, 89 Calif.-34 Oak. .. | .254 | 123 | 354 | 55 | 90 | 121 | 14 | 1 | 5 | 38 | 4 | 3 | 26 | 8 |
| Harrah, Colbert, Texas | .293 | 151 | 522 | 81 | 153 | 239 | 24 | 1 | 20 | 93 | 6 | 4 | 23 | 9 |
| Healy, Francis, Kansas City | .255 | 56 | 188 | 16 | 48 | 63 | 5 | 2 | 2 | 18 | 1 | 0 | 4 | 3 |
| Hegan, J. Michael, Milwaukee° | .251 | 93 | 203 | 19 | 51 | 77 | 11 | 0 | 5 | 22 | 0 | 2 | 1 | 1 |
| Heise, Robert, Boston | .214 | 63 | 126 | 12 | 27 | 30 | 3 | 0 | 0 | 21 | 4 | 2 | 0 | 0 |
| Henderson, Kenneth, Chicago† | .251 | 140 | 513 | 65 | 129 | 182 | 20 | 3 | 9 | 53 | 1 | 5 | 5 | 3 |
| Hendrick, George, Cleveland | .258 | 145 | 561 | 82 | 145 | 242 | 21 | 2 | 24 | 86 | 4 | 8 | 6 | 7 |
| Hendricks, Elrod, Baltimore° | .215 | 85 | 223 | 32 | 48 | 84 | 8 | 2 | 8 | 38 | 2 | 2 | 0 | 1 |
| Herrmann, Edward, New York° | .255 | 80 | 200 | 16 | 51 | 82 | 9 | 2 | 6 | 30 | 0 | 1 | 0 | 0 |
| Hisle, Larry, Minnesota | .314 | 80 | 255 | 37 | 80 | 126 | 9 | 2 | 11 | 51 | 2 | 4 | 17 | 3 |
| Hobson, Clell, Boston | .250 | 2 | 4 | 0 | 1 | 1 | 0 | 0 | 0 | 0 | 0 | 0 | 0 | 0 |
| Holt, James, Oakland° | .220 | 102 | 123 | 7 | 27 | 36 | 3 | 0 | 2 | 16 | 0 | 1 | 0 | 0 |
| Holtzman, Kenneth, Oakland | .000 | 39 | 2 | 0 | 0 | 0 | 0 | 0 | 0 | 0 | 0 | 0 | 0 | 0 |
| Hood, Donald, Cleveland° | .000 | 35 | 0 | 1 | 0 | 0 | 0 | 0 | 0 | 0 | 0 | 0 | 0 | 0 |
| Hopkins, Donald, Oakland° | .167 | 82 | 6 | 25 | 1 | 1 | 0 | 0 | 0 | 0 | 0 | 0 | 21 | 9 |
| Horton, Willie, Detroit | .275 | 159 | 615 | 62 | 169 | 259 | 13 | 1 | 25 | 92 | 0 | 8 | 1 | 2 |
| Howell, Roy, Texas° | .251 | 125 | 383 | 43 | 96 | 145 | 15 | 2 | 10 | 51 | 2 | 3 | 2 | 2 |
| Humphrey, Terryal, Detroit | .244 | 18 | 41 | 0 | 10 | 10 | 0 | 0 | 0 | 1 | 1 | 0 | 0 | 0 |
| Hunter, Harold, Boston | .000 | 1 | 1 | 0 | 0 | 0 | 0 | 0 | 0 | 0 | 0 | 0 | 0 | 0 |
| Hutto, James, Baltimore | .000 | 4 | 5 | 0 | 0 | 0 | 0 | 0 | 0 | 0 | 0 | 0 | 0 | 0 |
| Jackson, Reginald, Oakland° | .253 | 157 | 593 | 91 | 150 | 303 | 39 | 3 | 36 | 104 | 0 | 6 | 17 | 8 |
| Jackson, Ronnie, California | .231 | 13 | 39 | 2 | 9 | 11 | 2 | 0 | 0 | 2 | 2 | 0 | 1 | 1 |
| James, Arthur, Detroit° | .225 | 11 | 40 | 2 | 9 | 11 | 2 | 0 | 0 | 1 | 0 | 0 | 1 | 2 |
| Johnson, Alexander, New York | .261 | 52 | 119 | 15 | 31 | 41 | 5 | 1 | 1 | 15 | 0 | 2 | 2 | 3 |
| Johnson, Deron, 148 Chi.-3 Bos. .... | .239 | 151 | 565 | 68 | 135 | 219 | 25 | 1 | 19 | 75 | 0 | 5 | 0 | 1 |
| Johnson, Lamar, Chicago | .200 | 8 | 30 | 2 | 6 | 12 | 3 | 0 | 1 | 1 | 0 | 0 | 0 | 0 |
| Johnson, Timothy, Milwaukee° | .141 | 38 | 85 | 6 | 12 | 13 | 1 | 0 | 0 | 2 | 3 | 0 | 3 | 0 |
| Jones, Robert O., Texas° | .091 | 9 | 11 | 2 | 1 | 1 | 0 | 0 | 0 | 0 | 0 | 0 | 0 | 0 |
| Kelly, H. Patrick, Chicago° | .274 | 133 | 471 | 73 | 129 | 191 | 21 | 7 | 9 | 45 | 3 | 4 | 18 | 10 |
| Kelly, J. Thomas, Minnesota° | .181 | 49 | 127 | 11 | 23 | 31 | 5 | 0 | 1 | 11 | 2 | 3 | 0 | 0 |
| Killebrew, Harmon, Kansas City | .199 | 106 | 312 | 25 | 62 | 117 | 13 | 0 | 14 | 44 | 0 | 2 | 1 | 2 |
| Knox, John, Detroit° | .267 | 43 | 86 | 8 | 23 | 24 | 1 | 0 | 0 | 2 | 0 | 0 | 1 | 2 |
| Kubiak, Theodore, Oakland† | .250 | 20 | 28 | 2 | 7 | 8 | 1 | 0 | 0 | 4 | 3 | 0 | 0 | 0 |
| Kuiper, Duane, Cleveland° | .292 | 90 | 346 | 42 | 101 | 114 | 11 | 1 | 0 | 25 | 4 | 0 | 19 | 18 |
| Kusick, Craig, Minnesota | .237 | 57 | 156 | 14 | 37 | 63 | 8 | 0 | 6 | 27 | 1 | 0 | 0 | 0 |

| Player and Club | Pct. | G. | AB. | R. | H. | TB. | 2B. | 3B. | HR. | RBI. | SH. | SF. | SB. | CS. |
|---|---|---|---|---|---|---|---|---|---|---|---|---|---|---|
| Lahoud, Joseph, California° | .214 | 76 | 192 | 21 | 41 | 69 | 6 | 2 | 6 | 33 | 2 | 1 | 2 | 1 |
| Lamont, Gene, Detroit° | .375 | 4 | 8 | 1 | 3 | 4 | 1 | 0 | 0 | 1 | 0 | 1 | 0 | 0 |
| Lee, Leron, Cleveland° | .130 | 13 | 23 | 3 | 3 | 4 | 1 | 0 | 0 | 0 | 0 | 0 | 1 | 0 |
| LeFlore, Ronald, Detroit | .258 | 136 | 550 | 66 | 142 | 191 | 13 | 6 | 8 | 37 | 4 | 2 | 28 | 20 |
| Lemon, Chester, Chicago | .257 | 9 | 35 | 2 | 9 | 11 | 2 | 0 | 0 | 1 | 1 | 0 | 1 | 0 |
| Leon, Eduardo, New York | .000 | 1 | 0 | 0 | 0 | 0 | 0 | 0 | 0 | 0 | 0 | 0 | 0 | 0 |
| Lezcano, Sixto, Milwaukee | .247 | 134 | 429 | 55 | 106 | 164 | 19 | 3 | 11 | 43 | 7 | 3 | 5 | 5 |
| Lind, Jackson, Milwaukee† | .050 | 17 | 20 | 1 | 1 | 1 | 0 | 0 | 0 | 0 | 0 | 0 | 0 | 0 |
| Lindblad, Paul, Oakland° | .000 | 68 | 1 | 0 | 0 | 0 | 0 | 0 | 0 | 0 | 0 | 0 | 1 | 0 |
| Lis, Joseph, Cleveland | .308 | 9 | 13 | 4 | 4 | 12 | 2 | 0 | 2 | 8 | 0 | 1 | 0 | 0 |
| Llenas, Winston, California | .186 | 56 | 113 | 6 | 21 | 25 | 4 | 0 | 0 | 11 | 4 | 1 | 0 | 1 |
| Lovitto, Joseph, Texas† | .208 | 50 | 106 | 17 | 22 | 28 | 3 | 0 | 1 | 8 | 2 | 2 | 2 | 2 |
| Lowenstein, John, Cleveland° | .242 | 91 | 265 | 37 | 64 | 107 | 5 | 1 | 12 | 33 | 3 | 1 | 15 | 10 |
| Lundstedt, Thomas, Minnesota† | .107 | 18 | 28 | 2 | 3 | 3 | 0 | 0 | 0 | 1 | 0 | 0 | 0 | 0 |
| Lynn, Fredric, Boston° | .331 | 145 | 528 | 103 | 175 | 299 | 47 | 7 | 21 | 105 | 6 | 6 | 10 | 5 |
| Maddox, Elliott, New York | .307 | 55 | 218 | 36 | 67 | 86 | 10 | 3 | 1 | 23 | 2 | 3 | 9 | 3 |
| Mangual, Angel, Oakland | .220 | 62 | 109 | 13 | 24 | 30 | 3 | 0 | 1 | 6 | 0 | 0 | 0 | 1 |
| Manning, Richard, Cleveland° | .285 | 120 | 480 | 69 | 137 | 172 | 16 | 5 | 3 | 35 | 7 | 2 | 19 | 11 |
| Manuel, Jerry, Detroit† | .056 | 6 | 18 | 0 | 1 | 1 | 0 | 0 | 0 | 0 | 0 | 0 | 0 | 0 |
| Martinez, John, Kansas City | .226 | 80 | 226 | 15 | 51 | 73 | 9 | 2 | 3 | 23 | 6 | 1 | 1 | 0 |
| Martinez, Teodoro, Oakland | .172 | 86 | 87 | 7 | 15 | 15 | 0 | 0 | 0 | 3 | 7 | 0 | 1 | 1 |
| Martz, Gary, Kansas City | .000 | 1 | 1 | 0 | 0 | 0 | 0 | 0 | 0 | 0 | 0 | 0 | 0 | 0 |
| Mason, James, New York° | .152 | 94 | 223 | 17 | 34 | 47 | 3 | 2 | 2 | 16 | 5 | 1 | 0 | 2 |
| Maxvill, C. Dallan, Oakland | .200 | 20 | 10 | 1 | 2 | 2 | 0 | 0 | 0 | 0 | 0 | 0 | 0 | 0 |
| May, Carlos, Chicago° | .271 | 128 | 454 | 55 | 123 | 170 | 19 | 2 | 8 | 53 | 0 | 4 | 12 | 7 |
| May, Lee, Baltimore | .262 | 146 | 580 | 67 | 152 | 246 | 28 | 3 | 20 | 99 | 0 | 5 | 1 | 2 |
| Mayberry, John, Kansas City° | .291 | 156 | 554 | 95 | 161 | 303 | 38 | 1 | 34 | 106 | 1 | 5 | 5 | 3 |
| McAuliffe, Richard, Boston° | .133 | 7 | 15 | 0 | 2 | 2 | 0 | 0 | 0 | 1 | 1 | 0 | 0 | 0 |
| McCarver, J. Timothy, Boston° | .381 | 12 | 21 | 1 | 8 | 12 | 2 | 1 | 0 | 3 | 0 | 0 | 0 | 0 |
| McCraw, Tommy, Cleveland° | .275 | 23 | 51 | 7 | 14 | 23 | 1 | 1 | 2 | 5 | 1 | 0 | 4 | 1 |
| McKay, David, Minnesota | .256 | 33 | 125 | 8 | 32 | 44 | 4 | 1 | 2 | 16 | 1 | 2 | 1 | 1 |
| McKinney, C. Richard, Oakland | .143 | 8 | 7 | 0 | 1 | 1 | 0 | 0 | 0 | 2 | 0 | 2 | 0 | 0 |
| McRae, Harold, Kansas City | .306 | 126 | 480 | 58 | 147 | 212 | 38 | 6 | 5 | 71 | 6 | 10 | 11 | 8 |
| Melton, William, Chicago | .240 | 149 | 512 | 62 | 123 | 184 | 16 | 0 | 15 | 70 | 3 | 6 | 5 | 4 |
| Meoli, Rudolph, California° | .214 | 70 | 126 | 12 | 27 | 31 | 2 | 1 | 0 | 6 | 2 | 0 | 3 | 0 |
| Merchant, J. Anderson, Boston° | .500 | 1 | 4 | 1 | 2 | 2 | 0 | 0 | 0 | 0 | 0 | 0 | 0 | 0 |
| Meyer, Daniel, Detroit° | .236 | 122 | 470 | 56 | 111 | 158 | 17 | 3 | 8 | 47 | 2 | 3 | 8 | 3 |
| Michael, Eugene, Detroit† | .214 | 56 | 145 | 15 | 31 | 42 | 2 | 0 | 3 | 13 | 4 | 1 | 0 | 0 |
| Miley, Michael, California† | .174 | 70 | 224 | 17 | 39 | 58 | 3 | 2 | 4 | 26 | 7 | 2 | 0 | 1 |
| Miller, Richard, Boston° | .194 | 77 | 108 | 21 | 21 | 25 | 2 | 1 | 0 | 3 | 0 | 0 | 3 | 2 |
| Mingori, Stephen, Kansas City° | .000 | 36 | 1 | 0 | 0 | 0 | 0 | 0 | 0 | 0 | 0 | 0 | 0 | 0 |
| Mitchell, Robert, Milwaukee | .249 | 93 | 229 | 39 | 57 | 104 | 14 | 3 | 9 | 41 | 3 | 2 | 3 | 4 |
| Moates, David, Texas° | .274 | 54 | 175 | 21 | 48 | 66 | 9 | 0 | 3 | 14 | 3 | 2 | 9 | 2 |
| Molinaro, Robert, Detroit† | .263 | 6 | 19 | 2 | 5 | 7 | 0 | 1 | 0 | 1 | 1 | 0 | 0 | 0 |
| Money, Donald, Milwaukee | .277 | 109 | 405 | 58 | 112 | 175 | 16 | 1 | 15 | 43 | 4 | 2 | 7 | 9 |
| Montgomery, Robert, Boston | .226 | 62 | 195 | 16 | 44 | 62 | 10 | 1 | 2 | 26 | 3 | 3 | 1 | 1 |
| Moore, Charles, Milwaukee | .290 | 73 | 241 | 26 | 70 | 95 | 20 | 1 | 1 | 29 | 3 | 1 | 1 | 5 |
| Moore, Tommy, Texas | .000 | 14 | 0 | 1 | 0 | 0 | 0 | 0 | 0 | 0 | 0 | 0 | 0 | 0 |
| Moses, Gerald, Chicago | .500 | 2 | 2 | 1 | 1 | 3 | 0 | 1 | 0 | 0 | 0 | 0 | 0 | 0 |
| Munson, Thurman, New York | .318 | 157 | 597 | 83 | 190 | 256 | 24 | 3 | 12 | 102 | 3 | 10 | 3 | 2 |
| Murphy, Thomas, Milwaukee | .000 | 53 | 0 | 0 | 0 | 0 | 0 | 0 | 0 | 0 | 0 | 0 | 0 | 0 |
| Murray, Larry, New York† | .000 | 6 | 1 | 1 | 0 | 0 | 0 | 0 | 0 | 0 | 0 | 0 | 0 | 0 |
| Muser, Anthony, 43 Chi.-80 Balt.° | .275 | 123 | 193 | 22 | 53 | 59 | 6 | 0 | 0 | 17 | 2 | 2 | 2 | 1 |
| Nelson, David, Texas | .213 | 28 | 80 | 9 | 17 | 24 | 1 | 0 | 2 | 10 | 2 | 1 | 6 | 0 |
| Nettles, Graig, New York° | .267 | 157 | 581 | 71 | 155 | 250 | 24 | 4 | 21 | 91 | 2 | 11 | 1 | 3 |
| Nettles, Morris, California° | .231 | 112 | 294 | 50 | 68 | 79 | 11 | 0 | 0 | 23 | 3 | 1 | 22 | 15 |
| Nordbrook, Timothy, Baltimore | .118 | 40 | 34 | 6 | 4 | 5 | 1 | 0 | 0 | 0 | 0 | 0 | 0 | 0 |
| North, William, Oakland† | .273 | 140 | 524 | 74 | 143 | 173 | 17 | 5 | 1 | 43 | 13 | 2 | 30 | 12 |
| Northrup, James, Baltimore° | .273 | 84 | 194 | 27 | 53 | 81 | 13 | 0 | 5 | 29 | 0 | 3 | 0 | 1 |
| Nyman, Nyls, Chicago° | .226 | 106 | 327 | 36 | 74 | 92 | 6 | 3 | 2 | 28 | 1 | 1 | 10 | 4 |
| Odom, Johnny, 8 Oak.-3 Clev. | .000 | 11 | 0 | 1 | 0 | 0 | 0 | 0 | 0 | 0 | 0 | 0 | 0 | 0 |
| Oglivie, Benjamin, Detroit° | .286 | 100 | 332 | 45 | 95 | 138 | 14 | 1 | 9 | 36 | 3 | 4 | 11 | 8 |
| Oliva, Pedro (Tony), Minnesota° | .270 | 131 | 455 | 46 | 123 | 172 | 10 | 0 | 13 | 58 | 0 | 6 | 0 | 1 |
| Oliver, Robert, New York | .132 | 18 | 38 | 3 | 5 | 6 | 1 | 0 | 0 | 1 | 0 | 0 | 0 | 0 |
| Orta, Jorge, Chicago° | .304 | 140 | 542 | 64 | 165 | 244 | 26 | 10 | 11 | 83 | 4 | 4 | 16 | 9 |
| Otis, Amos, Kansas City | .247 | 132 | 470 | 87 | 116 | 181 | 26 | 6 | 9 | 46 | 4 | 4 | 39 | 11 |
| Patek, Freddie, Kansas City | .228 | 136 | 483 | 58 | 110 | 149 | 14 | 5 | 5 | 45 | 11 | 3 | 32 | 7 |
| Petrocelli, Americo, Boston | .239 | 115 | 402 | 31 | 96 | 134 | 15 | 1 | 7 | 59 | 3 | 5 | 0 | 2 |
| Pierce, L. Jack, Detroit° | .235 | 53 | 170 | 19 | 40 | 72 | 6 | 1 | 8 | 22 | 0 | 2 | 0 | 0 |

| Player and Club | Pct. | G. | AB. | R. | H. | TB. | 2B. | 3B. | HR. | RBI. | SH. | SF. | SB. | CS. |
|---|---|---|---|---|---|---|---|---|---|---|---|---|---|---|
| Piniella, Louis, New York | .196 | 74 | 199 | 7 | 39 | 45 | 4 | 1 | 0 | 22 | 0 | 3 | 0 | 0 |
| Pinson, Vada, Kansas City° | .223 | 103 | 319 | 38 | 71 | 107 | 14 | 5 | 4 | 22 | 1 | 4 | 5 | 6 |
| Pitts, Gaylen, Oakland | .333 | 10 | 3 | 1 | 1 | 2 | 1 | 0 | 0 | 1 | 0 | 0 | 0 | 0 |
| Poepping, Michael, Minnesota | .135 | 14 | 37 | 0 | 5 | 6 | 1 | 0 | 0 | 1 | 0 | 0 | 0 | 0 |
| Porter, Darrell, Milwaukee° | .232 | 130 | 409 | 66 | 95 | 171 | 12 | 5 | 18 | 60 | 1 | 7 | 2 | 5 |
| Powell, John, Cleveland° | .297 | 134 | 435 | 64 | 129 | 228 | 18 | 0 | 27 | 86 | 1 | 6 | 1 | 3 |
| Pruitt, Ronald, Texas | .176 | 14 | 17 | 2 | 3 | 3 | 0 | 0 | 0 | 0 | 0 | 0 | 0 | 0 |
| Quirk, James, Kansas City° | .256 | 14 | 39 | 2 | 10 | 13 | 0 | 0 | 1 | 5 | 0 | 0 | 0 | 0 |
| Ramirez, Orlando, California | .240 | 44 | 100 | 10 | 24 | 30 | 4 | 1 | 0 | 4 | 2 | 0 | 9 | 6 |
| Randle, Leonard, Texas† | .276 | 156 | 601 | 85 | 166 | 216 | 24 | 7 | 4 | 57 | 10 | 4 | 16 | 19 |
| Remy, Gerald, California° | .258 | 147 | 569 | 82 | 147 | 177 | 17 | 5 | 1 | 46 | 12 | 3 | 34 | 21 |
| Rice, James, Boston | .309 | 144 | 564 | 92 | 174 | 277 | 29 | 4 | 22 | 102 | 1 | 8 | 10 | 5 |
| Richard, Lee, Chicago | .200 | 43 | 45 | 11 | 9 | 11 | 0 | 1 | 0 | 5 | 0 | 0 | 2 | 3 |
| Rivers, John, California° | .284 | 155 | 616 | 70 | 175 | 221 | 17 | 13 | 1 | 53 | 7 | 4 | 70 | 14 |
| Roberts, Leon, Detroit | .257 | 129 | 447 | 51 | 115 | 172 | 17 | 5 | 10 | 38 | 5 | 4 | 3 | 7 |
| Robinson, Brooks, Baltimore | .201 | 144 | 482 | 50 | 97 | 132 | 15 | 1 | 6 | 53 | 8 | 4 | 0 | 0 |
| Robinson, Frank, Cleveland | .237 | 49 | 118 | 19 | 28 | 60 | 5 | 0 | 9 | 24 | 1 | 1 | 0 | 0 |
| Robson, Thomas, Texas | .200 | 17 | 35 | 3 | 7 | 7 | 0 | 0 | 0 | 2 | 0 | 1 | 0 | 0 |
| Rodriguez, Aurelio, Detroit | .245 | 151 | 507 | 47 | 124 | 195 | 20 | 6 | 13 | 60 | 8 | 1 | 1 | 1 |
| Rodriguez, Eliseo, California | .235 | 90 | 226 | 20 | 53 | 68 | 6 | 0 | 3 | 27 | 9 | 3 | 2 | 2 |
| Rojas, Octavio, Kansas City | .254 | 120 | 406 | 34 | 103 | 131 | 18 | 2 | 2 | 37 | 7 | 2 | 4 | 5 |
| Roof, Philip, Minnesota | .302 | 63 | 126 | 18 | 38 | 61 | 2 | 0 | 7 | 21 | 6 | 0 | 0 | 0 |
| Rudi, Joseph, Oakland | .278 | 126 | 468 | 66 | 130 | 231 | 26 | 6 | 21 | 75 | 3 | 1 | 2 | 1 |
| Sands, Charlie, Oakland° | .500 | 3 | 2 | 0 | 1 | 1 | 0 | 0 | 0 | 0 | 0 | 0 | 0 | 0 |
| Sandt, Thomas, Oakland | .000 | 1 | 0 | 0 | 0 | 0 | 0 | 0 | 0 | 0 | 0 | 0 | 0 | 0 |
| Scott, George, Milwaukee | .285 | 158 | 617 | 86 | 176 | 318 | 26 | 4 | 36 | 109 | 1 | 3 | 6 | 5 |
| Scott, Rodney, Kansas City | .067 | 48 | 15 | 13 | 1 | 1 | 0 | 0 | 0 | 0 | 2 | 0 | 4 | 2 |
| Scrivener, Wayne, Detroit° | .250 | 4 | 16 | 0 | 4 | 5 | 1 | 0 | 0 | 0 | 0 | 0 | 1 | 0 |
| Sharp, William, 18 Chi.-125 Mil.° | .250 | 143 | 408 | 38 | 102 | 138 | 27 | 3 | 1 | 38 | 10 | 5 | 0 | 3 |
| Sheldon, Bob, Milwaukee° | .287 | 53 | 181 | 17 | 52 | 61 | 3 | 3 | 0 | 14 | 2 | 2 | 0 | 3 |
| Shopay, Thomas, Baltimore° | .161 | 40 | 31 | 4 | 5 | 6 | 1 | 0 | 0 | 2 | 1 | 0 | 3 | 0 |
| Siebert, Wilfred, Oakland | .000 | 17 | 1 | 0 | 0 | 0 | 0 | 0 | 0 | 0 | 0 | 0 | 0 | 0 |
| Singleton, Kenneth, Baltimore† | .300 | 155 | 586 | 88 | 176 | 266 | 37 | 4 | 15 | 55 | 3 | 6 | 3 | 5 |
| Smalley, Roy, Texas† | .228 | 78 | 250 | 22 | 57 | 74 | 8 | 0 | 3 | 33 | 4 | 2 | 4 | 0 |
| Smith, Billy E., California† | .203 | 59 | 143 | 10 | 29 | 36 | 5 | 1 | 0 | 14 | 3 | 1 | 1 | 3 |
| Smith, Tommy A., Cleveland | .125 | 8 | 8 | 0 | 1 | 1 | 0 | 0 | 0 | 2 | 0 | 1 | 0 | 0 |
| Soderholm, Eric, Minnesota | .286 | 117 | 419 | 62 | 120 | 174 | 17 | 2 | 11 | 58 | 1 | 2 | 3 | 5 |
| Solaita, Tolia, Kansas City° | .260 | 93 | 231 | 35 | 60 | 119 | 11 | 0 | 16 | 44 | 1 | 2 | 0 | 1 |
| Spencer, James, Texas° | .266 | 132 | 403 | 50 | 107 | 160 | 18 | 1 | 11 | 47 | 2 | 1 | 0 | 1 |
| Spikes, L. Charles, Cleveland | .229 | 111 | 345 | 41 | 79 | 131 | 13 | 3 | 11 | 33 | 3 | 0 | 7 | 6 |
| Squires, Michael, Chicago° | .231 | 20 | 65 | 5 | 15 | 15 | 0 | 0 | 0 | 4 | 0 | 1 | 3 | 0 |
| Stanley, Frederick, New York | .222 | 117 | 252 | 34 | 56 | 63 | 5 | 1 | 0 | 15 | 8 | 2 | 3 | 1 |
| Stanley, Mitchell, Detroit | .256 | 52 | 164 | 26 | 42 | 64 | 7 | 3 | 3 | 19 | 0 | 1 | 1 | 1 |
| Stanton, Leroy, California | .261 | 137 | 440 | 67 | 115 | 183 | 20 | 3 | 14 | 82 | 8 | 4 | 18 | 6 |
| Stein, William, Chicago | .270 | 76 | 226 | 23 | 61 | 79 | 7 | 1 | 3 | 21 | 2 | 0 | 2 | 2 |
| Stillman, Royle, Baltimore° | .429 | 13 | 14 | 1 | 6 | 6 | 0 | 0 | 0 | 1 | 0 | 0 | 0 | 0 |
| Stinson, G. Robert, Kansas City† | .265 | 63 | 147 | 18 | 39 | 53 | 9 | 1 | 1 | 9 | 4 | 2 | 1 | 0 |
| Sudakis, William, 30 Cal.-20 Cle.† | .154 | 50 | 104 | 8 | 16 | 24 | 2 | 0 | 2 | 9 | 0 | 2 | 1 | 2 |
| Sundberg, James, Texas | .199 | 155 | 472 | 45 | 94 | 121 | 9 | 0 | 6 | 36 | 13 | 0 | 3 | 1 |
| Sutherland, Gary, Detroit | .258 | 129 | 503 | 51 | 130 | 166 | 12 | 3 | 6 | 39 | 4 | 4 | 0 | 2 |
| Tenace, F. Gene, Oakland | .255 | 158 | 498 | 83 | 127 | 231 | 17 | 0 | 29 | 87 | 3 | 4 | 7 | 4 |
| Terrell, Jerry, Minnesota† | .286 | 108 | 385 | 48 | 110 | 133 | 16 | 2 | 1 | 36 | 9 | 1 | 4 | 4 |
| Thomas, J. Gorman, Milwaukee | .179 | 121 | 240 | 34 | 43 | 89 | 12 | 2 | 10 | 28 | 4 | 5 | 4 | 2 |
| Thompson, Danny, Minnesota | .270 | 112 | 355 | 25 | 96 | 126 | 11 | 2 | 5 | 37 | 7 | 4 | 0 | 3 |
| Tiant, Luis, Boston | .000 | 35 | 1 | 0 | 0 | 0 | 0 | 0 | 0 | 0 | 0 | 0 | 0 | 0 |
| Tovar, Cesar, 102 Tex.-19 Oak. | .256 | 121 | 453 | 58 | 116 | 142 | 17 | 0 | 3 | 31 | 5 | 1 | 20 | 11 |
| Valentine, Robert, California | .281 | 26 | 57 | 5 | 16 | 18 | 2 | 0 | 0 | 5 | 1 | 3 | 0 | 2 |
| Varney, Richard, Chicago | .271 | 36 | 107 | 12 | 29 | 42 | 5 | 1 | 2 | 8 | 0 | 0 | 2 | 0 |
| Velez, Otoniel, New York | .250 | 6 | 48 | 0 | 2 | 2 | 0 | 0 | 0 | 1 | 0 | 0 | 0 | 0 |
| Veryzer, Thomas, Detroit | .252 | 128 | 404 | 37 | 102 | 132 | 13 | 1 | 5 | 48 | 2 | 5 | 2 | 6 |
| Walling, Dennis, Oakland° | .125 | 6 | 8 | 0 | 1 | 2 | 1 | 0 | 0 | 2 | 0 | 0 | 0 | 0 |
| Walton, Daniel, Minnesota† | .175 | 42 | 63 | 4 | 11 | 16 | 2 | 0 | 1 | 8 | 0 | 0 | 0 | 0 |
| Washington, Claudell, Oakland° | .308 | 148 | 590 | 86 | 182 | 250 | 24 | 7 | 10 | 77 | 1 | 7 | 40 | 15 |
| Washington, Herbert, Oakland | .000 | 13 | 0 | 4 | 0 | 0 | 0 | 0 | 0 | 0 | 0 | 0 | 2 | 1 |
| White, Frank, Kansas City | .250 | 111 | 304 | 43 | 76 | 111 | 10 | 2 | 7 | 36 | 2 | 2 | 11 | 3 |
| White, Roy, New York† | .290 | 148 | 556 | 81 | 161 | 239 | 32 | 5 | 12 | 59 | 4 | 2 | 16 | 15 |
| Whitfield, Terry, New York° | .272 | 28 | 81 | 9 | 22 | 25 | 1 | 1 | 0 | 7 | 0 | 2 | 1 | 0 |
| Williams, Billy, Oakland° | .244 | 155 | 520 | 68 | 127 | 218 | 20 | 1 | 23 | 81 | 1 | 3 | 0 | 0 |
| Williams, Walter, New York | .281 | 82 | 185 | 27 | 52 | 74 | 5 | 1 | 5 | 16 | 3 | 1 | 0 | 1 |

| Player and Club | Pct. | G. | AB. | R. | H. | TB. | 2B. | 3B. | HR. | RBI. | SH. | SF. | SB. | CS. |
|---|---|---|---|---|---|---|---|---|---|---|---|---|---|---|
| Wockenfuss, Johnny, Detroit | .229 | 35 | 118 | 15 | 27 | 51 | 6 | 3 | 4 | 13 | 1 | 1 | 0 | 0 |
| Wohlford, James, Kansas City | .255 | 116 | 353 | 45 | 90 | 110 | 10 | 5 | 0 | 30 | 8 | 6 | 12 | 7 |
| Yastrzemski, Carl, Boston° | .269 | 149 | 543 | 91 | 146 | 220 | 30 | 1 | 14 | 60 | 0 | 2 | 8 | 4 |
| Yount, Robin, Milwaukee | .267 | 147 | 558 | 67 | 149 | 205 | 28 | 2 | 8 | 52 | 10 | 5 | 12 | 4 |

The following pitchers had no plate appearances primarily because of use of designated hitters; they are listed alphabetically by club with number of games, including pinch-running appearances, in parentheses:

BALTIMORE—Alexander, Doyle (32), Cuellar, Miguel (36), Flanagan, Michael K. (2), Garland, Wayne (29), Grimsley, Ross (35), Jackson, Grant (41), Johnson, David C. (6), Miller, Dyar (30), Mitchell, Paul (11), Palmer, James (39), Torrez, Michael (36).

BOSTON—Barr, Steven (3), Burton, James (29), Cleveland, Reginald (31), Drago, Richard (40), Kreuger, Richard (2), Lee, William (41), Moret, Rogelio (37), Pole, Richard (18), Segui, Diego (33), Willoughby, James (24), Wise, Richard (35).

CALIFORNIA—Blateric, Stephen (2), Brewer, James (21), Dobson, Charles (9), Figueroa, Eduardo (33), Hassler, Andrew (30), Hockenbery, Charles (16), Hudson, Charles (3), Kirkwood, Donald (45), Lange, Richard (30), Monge, Isidro (4), Pactwa, Joseph (4), Pena, Orlando (7), Quintana, Luis (4), Ross, Gary (1), Ryan, L. Nolan (28), Scott, Ralph (50), Sells, David (4), Singer, William (29), Tanana, Frank (34).

CHICAGO—Allen, Lloyd (3), Forster, Terry (17), Gogolewski, William (19), Gossage, Richard (62), Hamilton, David (41—includes 11 with Oakland), Hinton, Richard (15), Jefferson, Jesse (26—includes 4 with Baltimore), Kaat, James (43), Knapp, R. Christian (2), Kravec, Kenneth (2), Kucek, John (2), Osborn, Danny (24), Osten, Claude (37), Otten, James (2), Pitlock, Lee (1), Stoddard, Timothy (1), Upshaw, Cecil (29), Vuckovich, Peter (4), Wood, Wilbur (43).

CLEVELAND—Andersen, Larry (3), Beene, Fred (20), Bibby, James (36—includes 12 with Texas), Brown, Jackie (42—includes 17 with Texas), Buskey, Thomas (50), Eckersley, Dennis (34), Harrison, Roric (19), Kern, James (13), LaRoche, David (61), Peterson, Fred (25), Raich, Eric (18), Reynolds, Robert (33—includes 7 with Baltimore and 21 with Detroit), Strickland, James (4), Waits, M. Richard (16).

DETROIT—Arroyo, Fernando (4), Bare, Raymond (29), Brookens, Edward (3), Coleman, Joseph (31), Glynn, Edward (3), Grilli, Stephen (3), Hiller, John (36), LaGrow, Lerrin (32), Lemanczyk, David (26), Lolich, Michael (32), Makowski, Thomas (3), Pentz, Eugene (13), Ruhle, Vernon (32), Walker, R. Thomas (36).

KANSAS CITY—Bird, J. Douglas (51), Briles, Nelson (24), Busby, Steven (34), Dal Canton, J. Bruce (4), Fitzmorris, Alan (35), Leonard, Dennis (32), Littell, Mark (7), McClure, Robert (12), McDaniel, Lyndall (40), Pattin, Martin (45), Sadecki, Raymond (5), Splittorff, Paul (35), Throop, George (7).

MILWAUKEE—Anderson, Lawrence (8), Augustine, Gerald (5), Austin, Rick (32), Broberg, Peter (38), Castro, William (18), Champion, B. Billy (27), Colborn, James (36), Currence, D. Lafayette (8), Hausman, Thomas (29), Osburn, L. Patrick (6), Rodriguez, Eduardo (43), Slaton, James (37), Sprague, Edward (18), Travers, William (28).

MINNESOTA—Bane, Edward (4), Blyleven, Rikalbert (35), Burgmeier, Thomas (47), Butler, William (23), Corbin, A. Ray (18), Decker, George (10), Goltz, David (32), Hughes, James (37), Johnson, Thomas R. (18), Pazik, Michael (4), Wiley, Mark (15).

NEW YORK—Dobson, Patrick (33), Guidry, Ronald (10), Gura, Lawrence (26), Hunter, James (39), Lyle, Albert (49), Martinez, Felix (23), May, Rudolph (32), Medich, George (38), Pagan, David (13), Sawyer, Richard (4), Tidrow, Richard (37), Wallace, Michael (3).

OAKLAND—Abbott, W. Glenn (30), Blue, Vida (39), Bosman, Richard (28—includes 6 with Cleveland), Mitchell, Craig (1), Norris, Michael (4), Perry, James (23—includes 8 with Cleveland), Todd, James (58).

TEXAS—Bacsik, Michael (7), Clyde, David (1), Foucault, Steven (59), Gideon, James (1), Hands, William (18), Hargan, Steven (33), Jenkins, Ferguson (37), Kekich, Michael (23), Merritt, James (5), Perry, Gaylord (37—includes 15 with Cleveland), Perzanowski, Stanley (12), Thomas, Stanley (46), Umbarger, James (56), Wright, Clyde (25).

AWARDED FIRST BASE ON INTERFERENCE: Ashby, Cleve. (Fisk), Chambliss, N.Y. (Hampton), Garner, Oak. (Freehan), Hargrove, Tex. (J. Ellis), Hegan, Milw. (Munson), Hendrick, Cleve. (Munson), Lahoud, Calif. (C. Moore), A. Rodriguez, Det. (Munson), Stinson, K.C. (Fosse).

## PLAYERS WITH TWO OR MORE CLUBS
### (Alphabetically Arranged, With Player's First Club on Top)

| Player and Club | Pct. | G. | AB. | R. | H. | TB. | 2B. | 3B. | HR. | RBI. | SH. | SF. | Tot. BB. | Int. BB. | HP. | SO. | SB. | CS. | GI DP. |
|---|---|---|---|---|---|---|---|---|---|---|---|---|---|---|---|---|---|---|---|
| Bahnsen, Chi | .000 | 12 | 0 | 0 | 0 | 0 | 0 | 0 | 0 | 0 | 0 | 0 | 0 | 0 | 0 | 0 | 0 | 0 | 0 |
| Bahnsen, Oak | .000 | 21 | 1 | 0 | 0 | 0 | 0 | 0 | 0 | 0 | 0 | 0 | 0 | 0 | 0 | 1 | 0 | 0 | 0 |
| Briggs, Milw | .297 | 28 | 74 | 12 | 22 | 32 | 1 | 0 | 3 | 5 | 0 | 0 | 20 | 0 | 0 | 13 | 0 | 2 | 1 |
| Briggs, Minn | .231 | 87 | 264 | 44 | 61 | 95 | 9 | 2 | 7 | 39 | 1 | 2 | 60 | 10 | 0 | 41 | 6 | 2 | 1 |
| Brinkman, Tex | .000 | 1 | 2 | 0 | 0 | 0 | 0 | 0 | 0 | 0 | 0 | 0 | 0 | 0 | 0 | 1 | 0 | 0 | 0 |
| Brinkman, NY | .175 | 44 | 63 | 2 | 11 | 17 | 4 | 1 | 0 | 2 | 1 | 0 | 3 | 0 | 1 | 6 | 0 | 0 | 3 |
| Coluccio, Milw | .194 | 22 | 62 | 8 | 12 | 17 | 0 | 1 | 1 | 5 | 6 | 1 | 11 | 0 | 1 | 11 | 1 | 4 | 2 |
| Coluccio, Chi | .205 | 61 | 161 | 22 | 33 | 53 | 4 | 2 | 4 | 13 | 0 | 0 | 13 | 1 | 1 | 34 | 4 | 0 | 3 |

| Player and Club | Pct. | G. | AB. | R. | H. | TB. | 2B. | 3B. | HR. | RBI. | SH. | SF. | Tot. BB. | Int. BB. | HP. | SO. | SB. | CS. | GI DP. |
|---|---|---|---|---|---|---|---|---|---|---|---|---|---|---|---|---|---|---|---|
| Darwin, Minn | .219 | 48 | 169 | 26 | 37 | 58 | 6 | 0 | 5 | 18 | 0 | 1 | 18 | 1 | 4 | 44 | 2 | 0 | 8 |
| Darwin, Milw | .247 | 55 | 186 | 19 | 46 | 80 | 6 | 2 | 8 | 23 | 1 | 0 | 11 | 0 | 3 | 54 | 4 | 1 | 4 |
| Doyle, Calif | .067 | 8 | 15 | 0 | 1 | 1 | 0 | 0 | 0 | 0 | 0 | 0 | 1 | 0 | 0 | 1 | 0 | 0 | 0 |
| Doyle, Bos | .310 | 89 | 310 | 50 | 96 | 133 | 21 | 2 | 4 | 36 | 10 | 2 | 14 | 0 | 1 | 11 | 5 | 7 | 5 |
| Etchebarren, Balt | .200 | 8 | 20 | 0 | 4 | 5 | 1 | 0 | 0 | 3 | 0 | 0 | 0 | 0 | 0 | 3 | 0 | 0 | 0 |
| Etchebarren, Calif | .280 | 31 | 100 | 10 | 28 | 39 | 0 | 1 | 3 | 17 | 1 | 1 | 14 | 1 | 0 | 19 | 1 | 0 | 3 |
| Harper, Calif | .239 | 89 | 285 | 40 | 68 | 89 | 10 | 1 | 3 | 31 | 4 | 3 | 38 | 5 | 2 | 51 | 19 | 8 | 6 |
| Harper, Oak | .319 | 34 | 69 | 11 | 22 | 32 | 4 | 0 | 2 | 7 | 0 | 0 | 5 | 0 | 1 | 9 | 7 | 0 | 3 |
| D. Johnson, Chi | .232 | 148 | 555 | 66 | 129 | 210 | 25 | 1 | 18 | 72 | 0 | 5 | 48 | 0 | 1 | 117 | 0 | 1 | 19 |
| D. Johnson, Bos | .600 | 3 | 10 | 2 | 6 | 9 | 0 | 0 | 1 | 3 | 0 | 0 | 2 | 0 | 0 | 0 | 0 | 0 | 0 |
| Muser, Chi | .243 | 43 | 111 | 11 | 27 | 30 | 3 | 0 | 0 | 6 | 1 | 1 | 7 | 1 | 0 | 8 | 2 | 1 | 5 |
| Muser, Balt | .317 | 80 | 82 | 11 | 26 | 29 | 3 | 0 | 0 | 11 | 1 | 1 | 8 | 0 | 0 | 9 | 0 | 0 | 3 |
| Odom, Oak | .000 | 8 | 0 | 1 | 0 | 0 | 0 | 0 | 0 | 0 | 0 | 0 | 0 | 0 | 0 | 0 | 0 | 0 | 0 |
| Odom, Cleve | .000 | 3 | 0 | 0 | 0 | 0 | 0 | 0 | 0 | 0 | 0 | 0 | 0 | 0 | 0 | 0 | 0 | 0 | 0 |
| Sharp, Chi | .200 | 18 | 35 | 1 | 7 | 7 | 0 | 0 | 0 | 4 | 1 | 0 | 2 | 0 | 0 | 3 | 0 | 0 | 0 |
| Sharp, Milw | .255 | 125 | 373 | 37 | 95 | 131 | 27 | 3 | 1 | 34 | 9 | 5 | 19 | 2 | 1 | 26 | 0 | 3 | 9 |
| Sudakis, Calif | .121 | 30 | 58 | 4 | 7 | 12 | 2 | 0 | 1 | 6 | 0 | 2 | 12 | 3 | 1 | 15 | 1 | 1 | 0 |
| Sudakis, Clev | .196 | 20 | 46 | 4 | 9 | 12 | 0 | 0 | 1 | 3 | 0 | 0 | 4 | 1 | 0 | 7 | 0 | 1 | 0 |
| Tovar, Tex | .258 | 102 | 427 | 53 | 110 | 135 | 16 | 0 | 3 | 28 | 5 | 1 | 27 | 0 | 3 | 25 | 16 | 11 | 8 |
| Tovar, Oak | .231 | 19 | 26 | 5 | 6 | 7 | 1 | 0 | 0 | 3 | 0 | 0 | 3 | 0 | 0 | 3 | 4 | 0 | 0 |

## OFFICIAL MISCELLANEOUS AMERICAN LEAGUE BATTING RECORDS

### CLUB MISCELLANEOUS BATTING RECORDS

| Club | Slg. Pct. | G. | Tot. BB. | Int. BB. | HP. | SO. | GIDP. | ShO. |
|---|---|---|---|---|---|---|---|---|
| Boston | .417 | 160 | 565 | 57 | 34 | 741 | 137 | 9 |
| Kansas City | .394 | 162 | 591 | 47 | 29 | 675 | 109 | 9 |
| Cleveland | .392 | 159 | 525 | 36 | 24 | 667 | 145 | 11 |
| Oakland | .391 | 162 | 609 | 45 | 51 | 846 | 107 | 13 |
| Milwaukee | .389 | 162 | 553 | 33 | 28 | 922 | 131 | 11 |
| Minnesota | .386 | 159 | 563 | 67 | 40 | 746 | 127 | 7 |
| New York | .382 | 160 | 486 | 41 | 30 | 710 | 142 | 14 |
| Baltimore | .373 | 159 | 580 | 55 | 38 | 834 | 114 | 9 |
| Texas | .371 | 162 | 613 | 48 | 25 | 863 | 125 | 10 |
| Detroit | .366 | 159 | 383 | 26 | 28 | 872 | 120 | 20 |
| Chicago | .358 | 161 | 611 | 53 | 40 | 800 | 150 | 11 |
| California | .328 | 161 | 593 | 35 | 27 | 811 | 98 | 13 |
| Totals | .379 | | 6672 | 543 | 394 | 9487 | 1505 | 137 |

### INDIVIDUAL MISCELLANEOUS BATTING RECORDS
(Top Fifteen Qualifiers for Slugging Championship—502 or More Plate Appearances)

| Player—Club | Slg. Pct. | Tot. BB. | Int. BB. | HP. | SO. | GI DP. | Player—Club | Slg. Pct. | Tot. BB. | Int. BB. | HP. | SO. | GI DP. |
|---|---|---|---|---|---|---|---|---|---|---|---|---|---|
| Lynn, Bos | .566 | 62 | 10 | 3 | 90 | 11 | Rice, Bos | .491 | 36 | 7 | 4 | 122 | 19 |
| Mayberry, KC | .547 | 119 | 16 | 4 | 73 | 8 | Baylor, Balt | .489 | 53 | 8 | 13 | 64 | 12 |
| Powell, Clev | .524 | 59 | 5 | 1 | 72 | 5 | Tenace, Oak | .464 | 106 | 2 | 12 | 127 | 8 |
| Scott, Milw | .515 | 51 | 7 | 3 | 97 | 26 | Harrah, Tex | .458 | 98 | 3 | 1 | 71 | 7 |
| Bonds, NY | .512 | 89 | 8 | 3 | 137 | 10 | Brett, KC | .456 | 46 | 6 | 2 | 49 | 8 |
| Jackson, Oak | .511 | 67 | 5 | 3 | 133 | 10 | Singleton, Balt | .454 | 118 | 12 | 1 | 82 | 9 |
| Carew, Minn | .497 | 64 | 18 | 1 | 40 | 10 | Orta, Chi | .450 | 48 | 7 | 4 | 67 | 17 |
| Rudi, Oak | .494 | 40 | 12 | 3 | 56 | 11 | | | | | | | |

DEPARTMENTAL LEADERS: Tot. BB—Mayberry, 119; Int. BB—Carew, 18; HP—Baylor, Oliva, 13; SO—Burroughs, 155; GIDP—L. May, G. Scott, 26.

### (All Players—Listed Alphabetically)

| Player—Club | Slg. Pct. | Tot. BB. | Int. BB. | HP. | SO. | GI DP. | Player—Club | Slg. Pct. | Tot. BB. | Int. BB. | HP. | SO. | GI DP. |
|---|---|---|---|---|---|---|---|---|---|---|---|---|---|
| Aaron, Milw | .355 | 70 | 3 | 1 | 51 | 15 | Dineen, NY | .409 | 2 | 0 | 0 | 1 | 0 |
| Albury, Minn | .000 | 0 | 0 | 0 | 1 | 0 | Doherty, Calif | .266 | 8 | 1 | 0 | 12 | 2 |
| Alexander, Oak | .100 | 1 | 0 | 0 | 1 | 0 | Downing, Chi | .324 | 76 | 5 | 3 | 75 | 12 |
| Allietta, Calif | .267 | 1 | 1 | 0 | 6 | 1 | Doyle, Calif-Bos | .412 | 15 | 0 | 1 | 12 | 5 |
| Alomar, NY | .305 | 26 | 0 | 0 | 58 | 6 | Duffy, Clev | .303 | 27 | 0 | 2 | 60 | 12 |
| Andrew, Bos | .500 | 0 | 0 | 0 | 0 | 0 | Duncan, Balt | .345 | 16 | 0 | 1 | 82 | 8 |
| Ashby, Clev | .331 | 30 | 1 | 1 | 42 | 10 | Egan, Calif | .300 | 5 | 0 | 0 | 14 | 3 |
| Bahnsen, Chi-Oak | .000 | 0 | 0 | 0 | 1 | 0 | Ellis, Clev | .345 | 14 | 2 | 2 | 33 | 13 |
| Bailor, Balt | .143 | 1 | 0 | 0 | 0 | 0 | Ellis, Milw | .286 | 0 | 0 | 0 | 0 | 1 |
| Balaz, Calif | .350 | 5 | 0 | 0 | 25 | 1 | Etchebarren, Balt-Cal | .367 | 14 | 1 | 0 | 22 | 3 |
| Baldwin, Det. | .379 | 5 | 0 | 0 | 14 | 0 | Evans, Bos | .456 | 47 | 3 | 4 | 60 | 10 |
| Bando, Oak | .356 | 87 | 2 | 5 | 80 | 10 | Fahey, Tex | .378 | 1 | 0 | 0 | 10 | 1 |
| Baylor, Balt | .489 | 53 | 8 | 13 | 64 | 12 | Ferrer, Minn | .309 | 3 | 0 | 1 | 11 | 0 |
| Belanger, Balt | .276 | 36 | 0 | 1 | 53 | 2 | Fingers, Oak | .000 | 0 | 0 | 0 | 0 | 0 |
| Bell, Clev | .376 | 51 | 6 | 1 | 72 | 11 | Fisk, Bos | .529 | 27 | 4 | 2 | 32 | 7 |
| Beniquez, Bos | .402 | 25 | 1 | 2 | 26 | 7 | Ford, Minn. | .434 | 30 | 2 | 5 | 79 | 10 |
| Bergman, NY | .000 | 2 | 0 | 0 | 4 | 0 | Fosse, Clev | .191 | 8 | 0 | 1 | 19 | 5 |
| Berry, Clev | .225 | 1 | 0 | 1 | 7 | 1 | Freehan, Det | .398 | 32 | 3 | 6 | 56 | 11 |
| Bevacqua, Milw | .306 | 26 | 1 | 1 | 45 | 6 | Fregosi, Tex | .398 | 20 | 4 | 1 | 39 | 6 |
| Bianco, Milw | .206 | 3 | 0 | 1 | 7 | 1 | Gamble, Clev | .454 | 53 | 4 | 2 | 39 | 8 |
| Blackwell, Bos | .250 | 19 | 0 | 1 | 13 | 3 | Garcia, Milw | .348 | 18 | 1 | 2 | 59 | 9 |
| Bladt, NY | .291 | 11 | 0 | 1 | 8 | 1 | Garner, Oak | .346 | 30 | 1 | 5 | 65 | 12 |
| Blair, Balt | .300 | 25 | 0 | 0 | 82 | 7 | Garrett, Calif | .477 | 14 | 0 | 0 | 28 | 0 |
| Blomberg, NY | .481 | 13 | 1 | 0 | 10 | 3 | Gomez, Minn | .139 | 4 | 0 | 0 | 12 | 1 |
| Bochte, Calif | .376 | 45 | 5 | 2 | 43 | 6 | Goodwin, Calif | .100 | 0 | 0 | 0 | 5 | 2 |
| Bonds, NY | .512 | 89 | 8 | 3 | 137 | 10 | Grabarkewitz, Oak | .000 | 0 | 0 | 0 | 1 | 0 |
| Borgmann, Minn | .278 | 47 | 1 | 2 | 59 | 10 | Grich, Balt | .399 | 107 | 4 | 8 | 88 | 9 |
| Bostock, Minn | .366 | 28 | 2 | 0 | 42 | 7 | Grieve, Tex | .442 | 22 | 0 | 0 | 74 | 11 |
| Bradford, Chi | .345 | 8 | 0 | 3 | 22 | 1 | Griffin, Bos | .272 | 18 | 0 | 2 | 29 | 8 |
| Braun, Milw | .428 | 66 | 5 | 1 | 55 | 8 | Hairston, Chi | .320 | 46 | 3 | 1 | 23 | 4 |
| Brett, KC | .456 | 46 | 6 | 2 | 49 | 8 | Hampton, Calif | .197 | 7 | 0 | 1 | 19 | 1 |
| Briggs, Calif | .355 | 2 | 0 | 0 | 6 | 0 | Haney, Oak | .308 | 1 | 0 | 0 | 4 | 0 |
| Briggs, Milw-Minn | .376 | 80 | 10 | 0 | 54 | 2 | Hargrove, Tex | .416 | 79 | 10 | 4 | 66 | 14 |
| Brinkman, NY-Tex | .262 | 3 | 0 | 1 | 7 | 3 | Harlow, Tex | .333 | 0 | 0 | 0 | 1 | 0 |
| Brohamer, Clev | .350 | 14 | 0 | 0 | 14 | 5 | Harper, Calif-Oak | .342 | 43 | 5 | 3 | 60 | 9 |
| Brown, Det | .314 | 9 | 1 | 1 | 6 | 2 | Harrah, Tex | .458 | 98 | 3 | 1 | 71 | 7 |
| Brye, Minn | .423 | 21 | 2 | 2 | 37 | 6 | Healy, KC | .335 | 14 | 1 | 0 | 19 | 5 |
| Bumbry, Balt | .364 | 32 | 3 | 4 | 81 | 2 | Hegan, Milw | .379 | 31 | 3 | 0 | 42 | 3 |
| Burleson, Bos | .329 | 45 | 1 | 3 | 44 | 18 | Heise, Bos | .238 | 4 | 0 | 2 | 6 | 1 |
| Burroughs, Tex | .409 | 79 | 11 | 1 | 155 | 13 | Henderson, Chi | .355 | 74 | 14 | 4 | 65 | 18 |
| Campaneris, Oak | .330 | 50 | 2 | 7 | 71 | 9 | Hendrick, Clev | .431 | 40 | 2 | 0 | 78 | 25 |
| Campbell, Minn | .000 | 0 | 0 | 0 | 1 | 0 | Hendricks, Balt. | .377 | 34 | 5 | 1 | 40 | 3 |
| Carbo, Bos | .483 | 83 | 5 | 1 | 69 | 6 | Herrmann, NY | .410 | 16 | 5 | 0 | 23 | 6 |
| Cardenas, Tex | .284 | 14 | 0 | 0 | 12 | 0 | Hisle, Minn | .494 | 27 | 3 | 1 | 39 | 5 |
| Carew, Minn | .497 | 64 | 18 | 1 | 40 | 10 | Hobson, Bos | .250 | 0 | 0 | 0 | 2 | 0 |
| Carty, Clev | .504 | 45 | 3 | 2 | 31 | 16 | Holt, Oak | .293 | 11 | 2 | 2 | 11 | 5 |
| Cerone, Clev | .333 | 1 | 0 | 0 | 0 | 0 | Holtzman, Oak | .000 | 0 | 0 | 0 | 0 | 0 |
| Chalk, Calif | .345 | 66 | 4 | 2 | 49 | 13 | Hood, Clev | .000 | 0 | 0 | 0 | 0 | 0 |
| Chambliss, NY | .434 | 29 | 9 | 1 | 50 | 19 | Hopkins, Oak | .167 | 2 | 0 | 0 | 0 | 0 |
| Chant, Oak | .000 | 0 | 0 | 0 | 0 | 0 | Horton, Det | .421 | 44 | 11 | 0 | 109 | 18 |
| Coggins, NY | .262 | 7 | 0 | 0 | 16 | 1 | Howell, Tex | .379 | 39 | 6 | 3 | 79 | 5 |
| Colbert, Det | .276 | 17 | 0 | 0 | 52 | 4 | Humphrey, Det | .244 | 2 | 0 | 0 | 6 | 1 |
| Collins, Calif | .361 | 36 | 1 | 1 | 55 | 4 | Hunter, Bos | .000 | 0 | 0 | 0 | 0 | 0 |
| Coluccio, Milw-Chi | .314 | 24 | 1 | 2 | 45 | 5 | Hutto, Balt | .000 | 0 | 0 | 0 | 2 | 0 |
| Conigliaro, Bos | .246 | 8 | 0 | 0 | 9 | 2 | Jackson, Oak | .511 | 67 | 5 | 3 | 133 | 10 |
| Cooper, Bos | .544 | 19 | 6 | 3 | 33 | 3 | Jackson, Calif | .282 | 2 | 0 | 0 | 10 | 0 |
| Cowens, KC | .402 | 28 | 1 | 4 | 36 | 9 | James, Det | .275 | 1 | 0 | 0 | 3 | 1 |
| Crosby, Clev | .258 | 13 | 0 | 0 | 14 | 4 | Johnson, NY | .345 | 7 | 1 | 0 | 21 | 4 |
| Cubbage, Tex | .350 | 18 | 2 | 0 | 14 | 2 | D. Johnson, Chi-Bos | .388 | 50 | 0 | 1 | 117 | 19 |
| Dade, Calif | .333 | 6 | 0 | 0 | 7 | 0 | L. Johnson, Chi | .400 | 1 | 0 | 0 | 5 | 0 |
| Darwin, Minn-Milw | .389 | 29 | 1 | 7 | 98 | 12 | Johnson, Milw | .153 | 6 | 0 | 0 | 17 | 2 |
| Davis, Balt | .357 | 23 | 2 | 0 | 52 | 14 | Jones, Tex | .091 | 3 | 0 | 0 | 3 | 0 |
| Davis, Tex | .408 | 4 | 0 | 1 | 25 | 2 | Kelly, Chi | .406 | 58 | 2 | 2 | 69 | 15 |
| DeCinces, Balt | .395 | 13 | 2 | 1 | 32 | 3 | Kelly, Minn | .244 | 15 | 0 | 0 | 22 | 3 |
| Dempsey, NY | .338 | 21 | 1 | 0 | 15 | 5 | Killebrew, KC | .375 | 54 | 4 | 0 | 70 | 5 |
| Dent, Chi | .341 | 36 | 3 | 0 | 48 | 16 | Knox, Det | .279 | 10 | 0 | 0 | 9 | 4 |
| Dillard, Bos | .400 | 0 | 0 | 0 | 0 | 0 | Kubiak, Oak | .286 | 2 | 0 | 0 | 2 | 1 |

| Player—Club | Slg. Pct. | Tot. BB. | Int. BB. | HP. | SO. | GI DP. |
|---|---|---|---|---|---|---|
| Kuiper, Clev | .329 | 30 | 0 | 8 | 26 | 9 |
| Kusick, Minn | .404 | 21 | 1 | 5 | 23 | 3 |
| Lahoud, Calif | .359 | 48 | 2 | 1 | 33 | 1 |
| Lamont, Det | .500 | 0 | 0 | 0 | 2 | 0 |
| Lee, Clev | .174 | 2 | 0 | 1 | 5 | 0 |
| LeFlore, Det | .347 | 33 | 1 | 2 | 139 | 3 |
| Lemon, Chi | .314 | 2 | 0 | 0 | 6 | 0 |
| Leon, NY | .000 | 0 | 0 | 0 | 0 | 0 |
| Lezcano, Milw | .382 | 46 | 1 | 4 | 93 | 15 |
| Lind, Milw | .050 | 2 | 0 | 0 | 12 | 0 |
| Lindblad, Oak | .000 | 0 | 0 | 0 | 0 | 0 |
| Lis, Clev | .923 | 3 | 0 | 1 | 3 | 0 |
| Llenas, Clev | .221 | 10 | 0 | 0 | 11 | 6 |
| Lovitto, Tex | .264 | 13 | 1 | 0 | 16 | 2 |
| Lowenstein, Clev | .404 | 28 | 2 | 0 | 28 | 4 |
| Lundstedt, Minn | .107 | 4 | 1 | 0 | 5 | 1 |
| Lynn, Bos | .566 | 62 | 10 | 3 | 90 | 11 |
| Maddox, NY | .394 | 21 | 0 | 7 | 24 | 9 |
| Mangual, Oak | .275 | 3 | 0 | 0 | 18 | 2 |
| Manning, Milw | .358 | 44 | 2 | 2 | 62 | 9 |
| Manuel, Det | .056 | 0 | 0 | 0 | 4 | 1 |
| Martinez, KC | .323 | 21 | 0 | 1 | 28 | 4 |
| Martinez, Oak | .172 | 2 | 0 | 1 | 9 | 0 |
| Martz, KC | .000 | 0 | 0 | 0 | 0 | 0 |
| Mason, NY | .211 | 22 | 0 | 0 | 49 | 10 |
| Maxvill, Oak | .200 | 0 | 0 | 0 | 0 | 1 |
| May, Chi | .374 | 67 | 13 | 9 | 46 | 12 |
| May, Balt | .424 | 36 | 8 | 5 | 91 | 26 |
| Mayberry, KC | .547 | 119 | 16 | 4 | 73 | 8 |
| McAuliffe, Bos | .133 | 1 | 0 | 0 | 2 | 1 |
| McCarver, Bos | .571 | 1 | 1 | 0 | 3 | 0 |
| McCraw, Clev | .451 | 7 | 2 | 0 | 7 | 0 |
| McKay, Minn | .352 | 6 | 0 | 1 | 14 | 4 |
| McKinney, Oak | .143 | 1 | 0 | 0 | 2 | 0 |
| McRae, KC | .442 | 47 | 7 | 4 | 47 | 18 |
| Melton, Chi | .359 | 78 | 1 | 8 | 106 | 13 |
| Meoli, Calif | .246 | 15 | 0 | 0 | 20 | 2 |
| Merchant, Bos | .500 | 1 | 0 | 0 | 0 | 0 |
| Meyer, Det | .336 | 26 | 1 | 2 | 25 | 16 |
| Michael, Det | .290 | 8 | 0 | 0 | 28 | 3 |
| Miley, Calif | .259 | 16 | 1 | 0 | 54 | 6 |
| Miller, Bos | .231 | 21 | 6 | 0 | 20 | 3 |
| Mingori, KC | .000 | 0 | 0 | 0 | 1 | 0 |
| Mitchell, Milw | .454 | 25 | 1 | 0 | 69 | 5 |
| Moates, Tex | .377 | 13 | 0 | 0 | 15 | 9 |
| Molinaro, Det | .368 | 1 | 0 | 0 | 0 | 0 |
| Money, Milw | .432 | 31 | 1 | 3 | 51 | 1 |
| Montgomery, Bos | .318 | 4 | 0 | 1 | 37 | 3 |
| Moore, Milw | .394 | 17 | 0 | 0 | 31 | 6 |
| Moore, Tex | .000 | 0 | 0 | 0 | 0 | 0 |
| Moses, Chi | 1.500 | 0 | 0 | 0 | 0 | 0 |
| Munson, NY | .429 | 45 | 8 | 6 | 52 | 23 |
| Murphy, Milw | .000 | 0 | 0 | 0 | 0 | 0 |
| Murray, NY | .000 | 0 | 0 | 0 | 0 | 0 |
| Muser, Chi-Balt | .306 | 15 | 1 | 0 | 17 | 8 |
| Nelson, Tex | .300 | 8 | 1 | 1 | 10 | 3 |
| Nettles, NY | .430 | 51 | 3 | 2 | 88 | 8 |
| Nettles, Calif | .269 | 26 | 2 | 1 | 57 | 2 |
| Nordbrook, Balt | .147 | 7 | 0 | 0 | 7 | 0 |
| North, Oak | .330 | 81 | 3 | 4 | 80 | 8 |
| Northrup, Balt | .418 | 22 | 1 | 2 | 22 | 8 |
| Nyman, Chi | .281 | 11 | 0 | 2 | 34 | 5 |
| Odom, Oak-Clev | .000 | 0 | 0 | 0 | 0 | 0 |
| Oglivie, Det | .416 | 16 | 0 | 2 | 62 | 10 |
| Oliva, Minn | .378 | 41 | 15 | 13 | 45 | 10 |
| Oliver, NY | .158 | 1 | 0 | 0 | 9 | 2 |
| Orta, Chi | .450 | 48 | 7 | 4 | 67 | 17 |
| Otis, KC | .385 | 66 | 1 | 4 | 48 | 8 |
| Patek, KC | .308 | 42 | 0 | 2 | 65 | 9 |
| Petrocelli, Bos | .333 | 41 | 1 | 3 | 66 | 16 |
| Pierce, Det | .424 | 20 | 1 | 2 | 40 | 2 |
| Piniella, NY | .226 | 16 | 3 | 3 | 22 | 13 |
| Pinson, KC | .335 | 10 | 4 | 2 | 21 | 5 |
| Pitts, Oak | .667 | 0 | 0 | 0 | 0 | 1 |
| Poepping, Minn | .162 | 5 | 0 | 0 | 7 | 2 |
| Porter, Milw | .418 | 89 | 10 | 5 | 77 | 8 |
| Powell, Milw | .524 | 59 | 5 | 1 | 72 | 5 |
| Pruitt, Tex | .176 | 1 | 0 | 0 | 3 | 1 |
| Quirk, KC | .333 | 2 | 1 | 0 | 7 | 1 |
| Ramirez, Calif | .300 | 11 | 0 | 0 | 22 | 2 |
| Randle, Tex | .359 | 57 | 3 | 4 | 80 | 8 |
| Remy, Calif | .311 | 45 | 1 | 0 | 55 | 15 |
| Rice, Bos | .491 | 36 | 7 | 4 | 122 | 19 |
| Richard, Chi | .244 | 4 | 0 | 0 | 7 | 0 |
| Rivers, Calif | .359 | 43 | 5 | 2 | 42 | 6 |
| Roberts, Det | .385 | 36 | 1 | 4 | 94 | 9 |
| Robinson, Balt | .274 | 44 | 10 | 1 | 33 | 6 |
| Robinson, Clev | .508 | 29 | 3 | 0 | 15 | 2 |
| Robson, Tex | .200 | 1 | 0 | 0 | 3 | 2 |
| Rodriguez, Det | .385 | 30 | 1 | 0 | 63 | 8 |
| Rodriguez, Calif | .301 | 49 | 0 | 6 | 37 | 7 |
| Rojas, KC | .323 | 30 | 2 | 0 | 24 | 15 |
| Roof, Minn | .484 | 9 | 1 | 1 | 28 | 2 |
| Rudi, Oak | .494 | 40 | 12 | 3 | 56 | 11 |
| Sands, Oak | .500 | 1 | 0 | 0 | 1 | 0 |
| Sandt, Oak | .000 | 0 | 0 | 0 | 0 | 0 |
| Scott, Milw | .515 | 51 | 7 | 3 | 97 | 26 |
| Scott, KC | .067 | 1 | 0 | 0 | 3 | 0 |
| Scrivener, Det | .313 | 0 | 0 | 0 | 1 | 0 |
| Sharp, Chi-Milw | .338 | 21 | 2 | 1 | 29 | 9 |
| Sheldon, Milw | .337 | 13 | 0 | 2 | 14 | 5 |
| Shopay, Balt | .194 | 4 | 0 | 0 | 7 | 2 |
| Siebert, Oak | .000 | 0 | 0 | 0 | 1 | 0 |
| Singleton, Balt | .454 | 118 | 12 | 1 | 82 | 9 |
| Smalley, Tex | .296 | 30 | 1 | 0 | 42 | 6 |
| Smith, Calif | .252 | 12 | 0 | 0 | 27 | 0 |
| Smith, Clev | .125 | 0 | 0 | 0 | 1 | 0 |
| Soderholm, Minn | .415 | 53 | 1 | 0 | 66 | 14 |
| Solaita, KC | .515 | 39 | 1 | 2 | 79 | 6 |
| Spencer, Tex | .397 | 35 | 6 | 2 | 43 | 9 |
| Spikes, Clev | .380 | 30 | 3 | 0 | 51 | 11 |
| Squires, Chi | .231 | 8 | 2 | 0 | 5 | 2 |
| Stanley, NY | .250 | 21 | 0 | 1 | 27 | 8 |
| Stanley, Det | .390 | 15 | 2 | 1 | 27 | 2 |
| Stanton, Calif | .416 | 52 | 4 | 6 | 85 | 8 |
| Stein, Chi | .350 | 18 | 0 | 1 | 32 | 6 |
| Stillman, Balt | .429 | 1 | 0 | 0 | 3 | 0 |
| Stinson, KC | .361 | 18 | 1 | 1 | 29 | 1 |
| Sudakis, Calif-Clev | .231 | 16 | 4 | 1 | 22 | 0 |
| Sundberg, Tex | .256 | 51 | 0 | 4 | 77 | 16 |
| Sutherland, Det | .330 | 45 | 3 | 3 | 41 | 13 |
| Tenace, Oak | .464 | 106 | 2 | 12 | 127 | 8 |
| Terrell, Minn | .345 | 19 | 0 | 3 | 27 | 12 |
| Thomas, Milw | .371 | 31 | 0 | 0 | 84 | 4 |
| Thompson, Minn | .355 | 18 | 2 | 0 | 30 | 7 |
| Tiant, Bos | .000 | 0 | 0 | 0 | 0 | 0 |
| Tovar, Tex-Oak | .313 | 30 | 0 | 3 | 28 | 8 |
| Valentine, Calif | .316 | 4 | 0 | 1 | 3 | 1 |
| Varney, Chi | .393 | 6 | 1 | 1 | 28 | 1 |
| Velez, NY | .250 | 2 | 0 | 0 | 0 | 0 |
| Veryzer, Det | .327 | 23 | 1 | 5 | 76 | 7 |
| Walling, Oak | .250 | 0 | 0 | 0 | 4 | 0 |
| Walton, Minn | .254 | 4 | 2 | 0 | 18 | 3 |
| C. Washington, Oak | .424 | 32 | 9 | 5 | 80 | 12 |
| H. Washington, Oak | .000 | 0 | 0 | 0 | 0 | 0 |
| White, KC | .365 | 20 | 0 | 1 | 39 | 4 |

| Player—Club | Slg. Pct. | Tot. BB. | Int. BB. | HP. | SO. | GI DP. | Player—Club | Slg. Pct. | Tot. BB. | Int. BB. | HP. | SO. | GI DP. |
|---|---|---|---|---|---|---|---|---|---|---|---|---|---|
| White, NY | .430 | 72 | 1 | 2 | 50 | 5 | Wockenfuss, Det | .432 | 10 | 0 | 0 | 15 | 5 |
| Whitfield, NY | .309 | 1 | 0 | 0 | 17 | 2 | Wohlford, KC | .312 | 34 | 2 | 1 | 37 | 3 |
| Williams, Oak | .419 | 76 | 7 | 2 | 68 | 9 | Yastrzemski, Bos | .405 | 87 | 12 | 2 | 67 | 14 |
| Williams, NY | .400 | 8 | 1 | 3 | 23 | 4 | Yount, Milw | .367 | 33 | 3 | 1 | 69 | 8 |

# OFFICIAL AMERICAN LEAGUE DESIGNATED HITTING

## CLUB DESIGNATED HITTING

| Club | Pct. | AB. | R. | H. | TB. | 2B. | 3B. | HR. | RBI. | SH. | SF. | BB. | HP. | SO. | SB. | CS. | GI DP. |
|---|---|---|---|---|---|---|---|---|---|---|---|---|---|---|---|---|---|
| Baltimore | .278 | 670 | 73 | 186 | 239 | 27 | 4 | 6 | 76 | 3 | 5 | 43 | 4 | 95 | 20 | 3 | 15 |
| Texas | .277 | 671 | 78 | 186 | 263 | 27 | 1 | 16 | 75 | 2 | 4 | 48 | 2 | 94 | 9 | 8 | 16 |
| Detroit | .274 | 620 | 62 | 170 | 261 | 14 | 1 | 25 | 93 | 0 | 8 | 45 | 0 | 110 | 1 | 2 | 18 |
| Boston | .271 | 632 | 97 | 171 | 283 | 38 | 7 | 20 | 76 | 7 | 7 | 50 | 2 | 119 | 7 | 6 | 9 |
| Minnesota | .256 | 610 | 78 | 156 | 219 | 13 | 1 | 16 | 70 | 1 | 8 | 62 | 13 | 77 | 1 | 2 | 15 |
| Cleveland | .255 | 591 | 86 | 151 | 268 | 23 | 2 | 30 | 91 | 3 | 6 | 79 | 2 | 68 | 8 | 8 | 17 |
| New York | .247 | 603 | 69 | 149 | 232 | 26 | 6 | 15 | 69 | 5 | 5 | 60 | 2 | 86 | 2 | 5 | 21 |
| Oakland | .247 | 587 | 93 | 145 | 243 | 21 | 1 | 25 | 92 | 1 | 4 | 84 | 3 | 83 | 18 | 5 | 9 |
| Chicago | .240 | 630 | 60 | 151 | 218 | 29 | 1 | 12 | 74 | 3 | 7 | 52 | 2 | 131 | 6 | 3 | 19 |
| Kansas City | .240 | 572 | 73 | 137 | 243 | 26 | 1 | 26 | 89 | 3 | 4 | 101 | 1 | 127 | 8 | 3 | 8 |
| Milwaukee | .232 | 591 | 72 | 137 | 218 | 23 | 2 | 18 | 75 | 1 | 8 | 85 | 5 | 74 | 1 | 3 | 17 |
| California | .225 | 579 | 75 | 130 | 195 | 22 | 2 | 13 | 80 | 6 | 13 | 90 | 3 | 102 | 24 | 9 | 7 |
| Totals | .254 | 7356 | 916 | 1869 | 2882 | 289 | 29 | 222 | 960 | 35 | 79 | 799 | 39 | 1166 | 105 | 57 | 171 |

## INDIVIDUAL DESIGNATED HITTING
(Listed According to Number of Official Times at Bat)

| Player and Club | Pct. | G. | AB. | R. | H. | TB. | 2B. | 3B. | HR. | RBI. | SH. | SF. | BB. | HP. | SO. | SB. | CS. | GI DP. |
|---|---|---|---|---|---|---|---|---|---|---|---|---|---|---|---|---|---|---|
| Horton, Det | .275 | 159 | 615 | 62 | 169 | 259 | 13 | 1 | 25 | 92 | 0 | 8 | 44 | 0 | 109 | 1 | 2 | 18 |
| Williams, Oak | .244 | 145 | 500 | 64 | 122 | 209 | 19 | 1 | 22 | 77 | 1 | 3 | 72 | 2 | 67 | 0 | 0 | 9 |
| Davis, Balt | .283 | 111 | 456 | 43 | 129 | 163 | 14 | 1 | 6 | 56 | 2 | 3 | 22 | 0 | 51 | 2 | 0 | 14 |
| Aaron, Milw | .238 | 128 | 450 | 44 | 107 | 163 | 16 | 2 | 12 | 55 | 1 | 6 | 68 | 1 | 48 | 0 | 1 | 15 |
| Oliva, Minn | .265 | 120 | 445 | 45 | 118 | 164 | 10 | 0 | 12 | 51 | 0 | 6 | 40 | 13 | 44 | 0 | 1 | 10 |
| D. Johnson, Chi-Bos | .241 | 94 | 365 | 38 | 88 | 138 | 17 | 0 | 11 | 53 | 0 | 5 | 25 | 1 | 79 | 0 | 0 | 11 |
| Tovar, Tex-Oak | .264 | 73 | 307 | 34 | 81 | 95 | 11 | 0 | 1 | 20 | 1 | 1 | 19 | 0 | 21 | 13 | 7 | 6 |
| Killebrew, KC | .197 | 92 | 289 | 23 | 57 | 108 | 12 | 0 | 13 | 41 | 0 | 2 | 51 | 1 | 66 | 1 | 1 | 5 |
| Carty, Clev | .277 | 72 | 249 | 36 | 69 | 116 | 9 | 1 | 12 | 42 | 0 | 5 | 28 | 2 | 23 | 1 | 1 | 8 |
| Rice, Bos | .287 | 54 | 216 | 36 | 62 | 101 | 13 | 1 | 8 | 39 | 0 | 4 | 12 | 0 | 57 | 4 | 1 | 6 |
| Harper, Calif-Oak | .251 | 60 | 207 | 27 | 52 | 73 | 7 | 1 | 4 | 26 | 2 | 3 | 23 | 1 | 38 | 17 | 6 | 2 |
| Cooper, Bos | .318 | 54 | 201 | 32 | 64 | 115 | 13 | 4 | 10 | 25 | 3 | 1 | 12 | 2 | 19 | 1 | 2 | 2 |
| Bumbry, Balt | .258 | 48 | 182 | 25 | 47 | 62 | 9 | 3 | 0 | 16 | 1 | 1 | 20 | 4 | 37 | 14 | 2 | 1 |
| Grieve, Tex | .284 | 45 | 162 | 17 | 46 | 73 | 6 | 0 | 7 | 29 | 1 | 1 | 6 | 0 | 39 | 0 | 0 | 5 |
| Robinson, Clev | .232 | 42 | 112 | 17 | 26 | 58 | 5 | 0 | 9 | 22 | 1 | 1 | 28 | 0 | 14 | 0 | 0 | 2 |
| Solaita, KC | .259 | 37 | 112 | 10 | 29 | 46 | 5 | 0 | 4 | 15 | 1 | 1 | 19 | 0 | 34 | 0 | 0 | 1 |
| Herrmann, NY | .286 | 35 | 105 | 7 | 30 | 45 | 4 | 1 | 3 | 13 | 0 | 1 | 12 | 0 | 12 | 0 | 0 | 4 |
| Lahoud, Calif | .223 | 35 | 103 | 16 | 23 | 39 | 5 | 1 | 3 | 19 | 1 | 1 | 30 | 0 | 15 | 1 | 0 | 0 |
| Lowenstein, Clev | .238 | 31 | 101 | 14 | 24 | 41 | 2 | 0 | 5 | 15 | 2 | 0 | 9 | 0 | 12 | 4 | 4 | 2 |
| Darwin, Minn-Milw | .253 | 28 | 99 | 17 | 25 | 47 | 4 | 0 | 6 | 14 | 0 | 0 | 7 | 2 | 26 | 0 | 0 | 3 |
| Blomberg, NY | .237 | 27 | 97 | 17 | 23 | 46 | 7 | 2 | 4 | 14 | 0 | 0 | 12 | 0 | 10 | 0 | 0 | 3 |
| Mayberry, KC | .247 | 27 | 89 | 14 | 22 | 47 | 4 | 0 | 7 | 25 | 0 | 1 | 25 | 0 | 17 | 3 | 0 | 1 |
| Munson, NY | .279 | 22 | 86 | 9 | 24 | 36 | 4 | 1 | 2 | 13 | 1 | 1 | 6 | 0 | 9 | 0 | 1 | 2 |
| Gamble, Clev | .282 | 29 | 85 | 13 | 24 | 42 | 7 | 1 | 3 | 9 | 0 | 0 | 11 | 0 | 10 | 2 | 2 | 3 |
| Johnson, NY | .247 | 28 | 81 | 10 | 20 | 25 | 3 | 1 | 0 | 10 | 0 | 2 | 5 | 0 | 14 | 2 | 3 | 4 |
| Spencer, Tex | .320 | 25 | 75 | 9 | 24 | 40 | 5 | 1 | 3 | 15 | 0 | 0 | 8 | 1 | 6 | 0 | 1 | 3 |
| Garrett, Calif | .265 | 23 | 68 | 10 | 18 | 33 | 3 | 0 | 4 | 10 | 1 | 1 | 9 | 0 | 14 | 3 | 0 | 0 |
| May, Chi | .227 | 19 | 66 | 4 | 15 | 19 | 1 | 0 | 1 | 7 | 0 | 0 | 7 | 1 | 12 | 2 | 0 | 1 |
| Beniquez, Bos | .200 | 20 | 60 | 7 | 12 | 18 | 4 | 1 | 0 | 0 | 2 | 0 | 7 | 0 | 10 | 1 | 2 | 0 |
| Dempsey, NY | .233 | 18 | 60 | 6 | 14 | 16 | 2 | 0 | 0 | 2 | 1 | 0 | 7 | 0 | 8 | 0 | 0 | 3 |
| Stein, Chi | .222 | 18 | 54 | 3 | 12 | 15 | 3 | 0 | 0 | 2 | 1 | 0 | 4 | 0 | 6 | 0 | 0 | 2 |
| Conigliaro, Bos | .135 | 15 | 52 | 8 | 7 | 14 | 1 | 0 | 2 | 7 | 1 | 2 | 8 | 0 | 8 | 1 | 0 | 1 |
| Williams, NY | .294 | 17 | 51 | 7 | 15 | 23 | 2 | 0 | 2 | 2 | 0 | 0 | 2 | 1 | 6 | 0 | 1 | 2 |
| McRae, KC | .432 | 12 | 44 | 8 | 19 | 31 | 4 | 1 | 2 | 7 | 0 | 0 | 5 | 0 | 6 | 3 | 0 | 1 |
| Kelly, Chi | .326 | 14 | 43 | 7 | 14 | 19 | 3 | 1 | 0 | 4 | 0 | 0 | 4 | 0 | 6 | 1 | 0 | 1 |
| Bonds, NY | .262 | 12 | 42 | 9 | 11 | 27 | 2 | 1 | 4 | 10 | 0 | 1 | 11 | 0 | 17 | 0 | 0 | 1 |
| Scott, Milw | .225 | 12 | 40 | 6 | 9 | 18 | 3 | 0 | 2 | 7 | 0 | 1 | 4 | 1 | 7 | 1 | 1 | 2 |

| Player and Club | Pct. | G. | AB. | R. | H. | TB. | 2B. | 3B. | HR. | RBI. | SH. | SF. | BB. | HP. | SO. | SB. | CS. | GI DP. |
|---|---|---|---|---|---|---|---|---|---|---|---|---|---|---|---|---|---|---|
| Hargrove, Tex | .325 | 12 | 40 | 7 | 13 | 23 | 1 | 0 | 3 | 5 | 0 | 0 | 6 | 1 | 5 | 0 | 0 | 1 |
| Carbo, Bos | .167 | 13 | 36 | 4 | 6 | 8 | 2 | 0 | 0 | 3 | 0 | 0 | 7 | 0 | 12 | 0 | 0 | 0 |
| Collins, Calif | .222 | 12 | 36 | 4 | 8 | 14 | 0 | 0 | 2 | 9 | 0 | 1 | 6 | 0 | 5 | 1 | 0 | 0 |
| Melton, Chi | .306 | 11 | 36 | 3 | 11 | 13 | 2 | 0 | 0 | 3 | 0 | 1 | 4 | 0 | 11 | 0 | 1 | 2 |
| Valentine, Calif | .294 | 13 | 34 | 3 | 10 | 11 | 1 | 0 | 0 | 4 | 1 | 3 | 3 | 1 | 2 | 0 | 2 | 1 |
| Sudakis, Calif-Cleve | .118 | 13 | 34 | 3 | 4 | 8 | 1 | 0 | 1 | 4 | 0 | 2 | 11 | 1 | 8 | 1 | 1 | 0 |
| Jackson, Oak | .294 | 9 | 34 | 6 | 10 | 17 | 1 | 0 | 2 | 5 | 0 | 1 | 5 | 0 | 7 | 0 | 0 | 0 |
| Fregosi, Tex | .382 | 13 | 34 | 6 | 13 | 19 | 0 | 0 | 2 | 6 | 0 | 1 | 4 | 0 | 7 | 0 | 0 | 0 |
| Piniella, NY | .152 | 12 | 33 | 1 | 5 | 6 | 1 | 0 | 0 | 3 | 0 | 0 | 3 | 1 | 3 | 0 | 0 | 2 |
| Balaz, Calif | .188 | 11 | 32 | 2 | 6 | 8 | 2 | 0 | 0 | 3 | 0 | 1 | 0 | 0 | 2 | 0 | 0 | 0 |
| Braun, Minn | .286 | 9 | 28 | 5 | 8 | 13 | 0 | 1 | 1 | 5 | 0 | 0 | 6 | 0 | 4 | 0 | 0 | 0 |
| Hisle, Minn | .269 | 14 | 26 | 2 | 7 | 7 | 0 | 0 | 0 | 4 | 1 | 1 | 8 | 0 | 3 | 0 | 1 | 0 |
| Coggins, NY | .167 | 9 | 24 | 1 | 4 | 5 | 1 | 0 | 0 | 2 | 3 | 0 | 1 | 0 | 3 | 0 | 0 | 0 |
| Evans, Bos | .261 | 7 | 23 | 2 | 6 | 8 | 2 | 0 | 0 | 0 | 1 | 0 | 2 | 0 | 3 | 0 | 1 | 0 |
| Sheldon, Milw | .217 | 6 | 23 | 3 | 5 | 5 | 0 | 0 | 0 | 4 | 0 | 1 | 2 | 1 | 2 | 0 | 0 | 0 |
| Walton, Minn | .182 | 6 | 22 | 2 | 4 | 4 | 0 | 0 | 0 | 1 | 0 | 0 | 1 | 0 | 4 | 0 | 0 | 1 |
| Fisk, Bos | .250 | 6 | 20 | 3 | 5 | 5 | 0 | 0 | 0 | 0 | 0 | 0 | 1 | 0 | 3 | 0 | 0 | 0 |
| Dade, Calif | .100 | 7 | 20 | 2 | 2 | 3 | 1 | 0 | 0 | 0 | 0 | 0 | 4 | 0 | 6 | 0 | 0 | 0 |
| Mangual, Oak | .263 | 15 | 19 | 2 | 5 | 6 | 1 | 0 | 0 | 2 | 0 | 0 | 1 | 0 | 3 | 0 | 0 | 0 |
| Llenas, Calif | .176 | 6 | 17 | 0 | 3 | 4 | 1 | 0 | 0 | 1 | 0 | 0 | 2 | 0 | 1 | 0 | 0 | 1 |
| Howell, Tex | .294 | 5 | 17 | 3 | 5 | 8 | 3 | 0 | 0 | 2 | 0 | 0 | 1 | 0 | 6 | 0 | 0 | 1 |
| Baylor, Balt | .313 | 7 | 16 | 2 | 5 | 7 | 2 | 0 | 0 | 2 | 0 | 0 | 0 | 0 | 4 | 3 | 1 | 0 |
| Hairston, Chi | .313 | 8 | 16 | 0 | 5 | 6 | 1 | 0 | 0 | 2 | 1 | 1 | 3 | 0 | 2 | 0 | 0 | 0 |
| Powell, Clev | .375 | 5 | 16 | 4 | 6 | 9 | 0 | 0 | 1 | 2 | 0 | 0 | 3 | 0 | 2 | 0 | 0 | 0 |
| Mitchell, Milw | .200 | 11 | 15 | 7 | 3 | 8 | 2 | 0 | 1 | 3 | 0 | 0 | 4 | 0 | 4 | 0 | 1 | 0 |
| Pinson, KC | .286 | 5 | 14 | 1 | 4 | 5 | 1 | 0 | 0 | 1 | 1 | 0 | 0 | 0 | 0 | 0 | 0 | 0 |
| Healy, KC | .250 | 4 | 12 | 2 | 3 | 3 | 0 | 0 | 0 | 0 | 0 | 0 | 0 | 0 | 3 | 0 | 0 | 0 |
| Hegan, Milw | .167 | 5 | 12 | 1 | 2 | 3 | 1 | 0 | 0 | 0 | 0 | 0 | 3 | 0 | 1 | 0 | 0 | 0 |
| Oliver, NY | .167 | 3 | 12 | 1 | 2 | 2 | 0 | 0 | 0 | 0 | 0 | 0 | 1 | 0 | 2 | 0 | 0 | 0 |
| Burroughs, Tex | .083 | 3 | 12 | 1 | 1 | 2 | 1 | 0 | 0 | 0 | 0 | 0 | 2 | 0 | 5 | 0 | 0 | 0 |
| Robson, Tex | .333 | 4 | 12 | 2 | 4 | 4 | 0 | 0 | 0 | 1 | 0 | 1 | 0 | 0 | 1 | 0 | 0 | 0 |
| Bradford, Chi | .091 | 4 | 11 | 0 | 1 | 2 | 1 | 0 | 0 | 2 | 0 | 0 | 1 | 0 | 7 | 1 | 1 | 1 |
| Northrup, Balt | .444 | 3 | 9 | 2 | 4 | 5 | 1 | 0 | 0 | 1 | 0 | 0 | 0 | 0 | 1 | 0 | 0 | 0 |
| Goodwin, Calif | .111 | 3 | 9 | 0 | 1 | 1 | 0 | 0 | 0 | 0 | 0 | 0 | 0 | 0 | 4 | 0 | 0 | 2 |
| Lemon, Chi | .333 | 2 | 9 | 0 | 3 | 4 | 1 | 0 | 0 | 0 | 1 | 0 | 1 | 0 | 1 | 0 | 0 | 0 |
| L. Johnson, Chi | .000 | 2 | 9 | 0 | 0 | 0 | 0 | 0 | 0 | 0 | 0 | 0 | 0 | 0 | 3 | 0 | 0 | 0 |
| Ellis, Clev | .111 | 3 | 9 | 0 | 1 | 1 | 0 | 0 | 0 | 0 | 0 | 0 | 0 | 0 | 1 | 0 | 0 | 2 |
| Montgomery, Bos | .250 | 3 | 8 | 1 | 2 | 3 | 1 | 0 | 0 | 0 | 0 | 0 | 0 | 0 | 2 | 0 | 0 | 0 |
| Nettles, Calif | .375 | 9 | 8 | 5 | 3 | 4 | 1 | 0 | 0 | 3 | 1 | 1 | 2 | 0 | 1 | 1 | 0 | 0 |
| Orta, Chi | .125 | 2 | 8 | 0 | 1 | 1 | 0 | 0 | 0 | 0 | 0 | 0 | 0 | 0 | 2 | 0 | 0 | 0 |
| Randle, Tex | .125 | 3 | 8 | 0 | 1 | 1 | 0 | 0 | 0 | 0 | 0 | 0 | 2 | 0 | 2 | 0 | 0 | 0 |
| May, Balt | .143 | 2 | 7 | 0 | 1 | 2 | 1 | 0 | 0 | 1 | 0 | 1 | 0 | 0 | 2 | 0 | 0 | 0 |
| Richard, Chi | .286 | 5 | 7 | 2 | 2 | 2 | 0 | 0 | 0 | 1 | 0 | 0 | 2 | 0 | 1 | 0 | 1 | 0 |
| Rudi, Oak | .143 | 2 | 7 | 1 | 1 | 1 | 0 | 0 | 0 | 1 | 0 | 0 | 0 | 0 | 2 | 0 | 0 | 0 |
| Yastrzemski, Bos | .500 | 2 | 6 | 3 | 3 | 5 | 2 | 0 | 0 | 1 | 0 | 0 | 0 | 0 | 2 | 0 | 0 | 0 |
| Lee, Clev | .000 | 3 | 6 | 1 | 0 | 0 | 0 | 0 | 0 | 0 | 0 | 0 | 0 | 0 | 2 | 0 | 0 | 0 |
| Porter, Milw | .000 | 2 | 6 | 0 | 0 | 0 | 0 | 0 | 0 | 0 | 0 | 0 | 2 | 0 | 1 | 0 | 0 | 0 |
| Bianco, Milw | .167 | 2 | 6 | 0 | 1 | 1 | 0 | 0 | 0 | 0 | 0 | 0 | 0 | 0 | 0 | 0 | 0 | 0 |
| Carew, Minn | .333 | 2 | 6 | 1 | 2 | 2 | 0 | 0 | 0 | 0 | 0 | 0 | 0 | 0 | 3 | 0 | 0 | 0 |
| Cubbage, Tex | .167 | 2 | 6 | 1 | 1 | 1 | 0 | 0 | 0 | 0 | 0 | 0 | 1 | 0 | 0 | 0 | 0 | 0 |
| Blackwell, Bos | .200 | 2 | 5 | 0 | 1 | 3 | 0 | 1 | 0 | 0 | 0 | 0 | 0 | 0 | 3 | 0 | 0 | 0 |
| Bochte, Calif | .200 | 1 | 5 | 0 | 1 | 1 | 0 | 0 | 0 | 2 | 0 | 0 | 0 | 0 | 2 | 0 | 0 | 1 |
| Spikes, Clev | .000 | 2 | 5 | 0 | 0 | 0 | 0 | 0 | 0 | 0 | 0 | 0 | 0 | 0 | 2 | 0 | 0 | 0 |
| Thompson, Minn | .000 | 3 | 5 | 0 | 0 | 0 | 0 | 0 | 0 | 0 | 0 | 0 | 0 | 0 | 1 | 0 | 0 | 0 |
| Whitfield, NY | .000 | 1 | 5 | 1 | 0 | 0 | 0 | 0 | 0 | 0 | 0 | 0 | 0 | 0 | 1 | 0 | 0 | 0 |
| Henderson, Chi | .250 | 4 | 4 | 1 | 1 | 1 | 0 | 0 | 0 | 0 | 0 | 0 | 0 | 0 | 0 | 0 | 0 | 0 |
| Lezcano, Milw | .000 | 2 | 4 | 0 | 0 | 0 | 0 | 0 | 0 | 0 | 0 | 0 | 0 | 0 | 1 | 0 | 0 | 0 |
| Moore, Milw | .250 | 1 | 4 | 0 | 1 | 1 | 0 | 0 | 0 | 0 | 0 | 0 | 0 | 0 | 0 | 0 | 0 | 0 |
| White, NY | .000 | 2 | 4 | 0 | 0 | 0 | 0 | 0 | 0 | 0 | 0 | 0 | 0 | 0 | 1 | 0 | 0 | 0 |
| Tenace, Oak | .250 | 1 | 4 | 0 | 1 | 1 | 0 | 0 | 0 | 2 | 0 | 0 | 0 | 0 | 1 | 0 | 0 | 0 |
| Jones, Tex | .250 | 1 | 4 | 0 | 1 | 1 | 0 | 0 | 0 | 0 | 0 | 0 | 1 | 0 | 2 | 0 | 0 | 0 |
| Doherty, Calif | .000 | 1 | 3 | 0 | 0 | 0 | 0 | 0 | 0 | 0 | 0 | 0 | 0 | 0 | 2 | 0 | 0 | 0 |
| Downing, Chi | .000 | 1 | 3 | 0 | 0 | 0 | 0 | 0 | 0 | 0 | 0 | 0 | 1 | 0 | 1 | 0 | 0 | 0 |
| Berry, Clev | .000 | 5 | 3 | 0 | 0 | 0 | 0 | 0 | 0 | 0 | 0 | 0 | 0 | 0 | 1 | 0 | 0 | 0 |
| Stanley, Det | .333 | 1 | 3 | 0 | 1 | 2 | 1 | 0 | 0 | 1 | 0 | 0 | 0 | 0 | 0 | 0 | 0 | 0 |
| Cowens, KC | .333 | 2 | 3 | 1 | 1 | 1 | 0 | 0 | 0 | 0 | 0 | 0 | 0 | 0 | 0 | 0 | 0 | 0 |
| Scott, KC | .000 | 22 | 3 | 9 | 0 | 0 | 0 | 0 | 0 | 0 | 0 | 1 | 0 | 0 | 0 | 1 | 2 | 0 |
| Velez, NY | .333 | 1 | 3 | 0 | 1 | 1 | 0 | 0 | 0 | 0 | 0 | 0 | 0 | 0 | 0 | 0 | 0 | 0 |

| Player and Club | Pct. | G. | AB. | R. | H. | TB. | 2B. | 3B. | HR. | RBI. | SH. | SF. | BB. | HP. | SO. | SB. | CS. | GI DP. |
|---|---|---|---|---|---|---|---|---|---|---|---|---|---|---|---|---|---|---|
| McKinney, Oak | .333 | 2 | 3 | 0 | 1 | 1 | 0 | 0 | 0 | 0 | 0 | 0 | 1 | 0 | 2 | 0 | 0 | 0 |
| Lovitto, Tex | .000 | 2 | 3 | 1 | 0 | 0 | 0 | 0 | 0 | 0 | 0 | 0 | 1 | 0 | 0 | 0 | 0 | 0 |
| Briggs, Calif | .000 | 2 | 2 | 0 | 0 | 0 | 0 | 0 | 0 | 0 | 0 | 0 | 0 | 0 | 1 | 0 | 0 | 0 |
| Smith, Clev | .000 | 3 | 2 | 0 | 0 | 0 | 0 | 0 | 0 | 0 | 0 | 0 | 0 | 0 | 0 | 0 | 0 | 0 |
| Manning, Clev | .500 | 1 | 2 | 1 | 1 | 1 | 0 | 0 | 0 | 1 | 0 | 0 | 0 | 1 | 1 | 0 | 0 | 0 |
| Wohlford, KC | .500 | 4 | 2 | 2 | 1 | 1 | 0 | 0 | 0 | 0 | 0 | 0 | 1 | 0 | 0 | 0 | 0 | 0 |
| Quirk, KC | .500 | 1 | 2 | 0 | 1 | 1 | 0 | 0 | 0 | 0 | 0 | 0 | 0 | 0 | 1 | 0 | 0 | 0 |
| Soderholm, Minn | .000 | 3 | 2 | 3 | 0 | 0 | 0 | 0 | 0 | 0 | 0 | 0 | 1 | 0 | 1 | 0 | 0 | 0 |
| Lundstedt, Minn | .000 | 2 | 2 | 0 | 0 | 0 | 0 | 0 | 0 | 0 | 0 | 0 | 1 | 0 | 0 | 0 | 0 | 1 |
| Ford, Minn | .000 | 3 | 2 | 1 | 0 | 0 | 0 | 0 | 0 | 0 | 0 | 0 | 0 | 0 | 0 | 0 | 0 | 0 |
| Briggs, Milw–Minn | .500 | 3 | 2 | 2 | 1 | 1 | 0 | 0 | 0 | 0 | 0 | 0 | 0 | 1 | 0 | 0 | 0 | 0 |
| Hopkins, Oak | .000 | 20 | 2 | 8 | 0 | 0 | 0 | 0 | 0 | 0 | 0 | 0 | 0 | 0 | 0 | 3 | 2 | 0 |
| Chant, Oak | .000 | 1 | 2 | 0 | 0 | 0 | 0 | 0 | 0 | 0 | 0 | 0 | 0 | 0 | 0 | 0 | 0 | 0 |
| Holt, Oak | .000 | 4 | 2 | 0 | 0 | 0 | 0 | 0 | 0 | 0 | 0 | 0 | 1 | 0 | 0 | 0 | 0 | 0 |
| Nelson, Tex | .000 | 1 | 2 | 0 | 0 | 0 | 0 | 0 | 0 | 0 | 0 | 0 | 1 | 0 | 0 | 0 | 0 | 0 |
| Petrocelli, Bos | .000 | 1 | 1 | 0 | 0 | 0 | 0 | 0 | 0 | 0 | 0 | 0 | 0 | 0 | 0 | 0 | 0 | 0 |
| Rivers, Calif | .000 | 1 | 1 | 1 | 0 | 0 | 0 | 0 | 0 | 0 | 0 | 0 | 0 | 0 | 0 | 0 | 0 | 0 |
| Jackson, Calif | .000 | 1 | 1 | 0 | 0 | 0 | 0 | 0 | 0 | 0 | 0 | 0 | 0 | 0 | 1 | 0 | 0 | 0 |
| Varney, Chi | 1.000 | 2 | 1 | 0 | 1 | 1 | 0 | 0 | 0 | 1 | 0 | 0 | 1 | 0 | 0 | 0 | 0 | 0 |
| Moses, Chi | .000 | 1 | 1 | 0 | 0 | 0 | 0 | 0 | 0 | 0 | 0 | 0 | 0 | 0 | 0 | 0 | 0 | 0 |
| Nyman, Chi | .000 | 4 | 1 | 2 | 0 | 0 | 0 | 0 | 0 | 0 | 0 | 0 | 0 | 0 | 2 | 0 | 0 | 0 |
| Ashby, Clev | .000 | 1 | 1 | 0 | 0 | 0 | 0 | 0 | 0 | 0 | 0 | 0 | 0 | 0 | 0 | 0 | 0 | 0 |
| Colbert, Det | .000 | 1 | 1 | 0 | 0 | 0 | 0 | 0 | 0 | 0 | 0 | 0 | 1 | 0 | 1 | 0 | 0 | 0 |
| Roberts, Det | .000 | 1 | 1 | 0 | 0 | 0 | 0 | 0 | 0 | 0 | 0 | 0 | 0 | 0 | 0 | 0 | 0 | 0 |
| Stinson, KC | .000 | 1 | 1 | 1 | 0 | 0 | 0 | 0 | 0 | 0 | 0 | 0 | 0 | 0 | 0 | 0 | 0 | 0 |
| White, KC | .000 | 2 | 1 | 1 | 0 | 0 | 0 | 0 | 0 | 0 | 0 | 0 | 0 | 0 | 0 | 0 | 0 | 0 |
| Ferrer, Minn | .000 | 2 | 1 | 2 | 0 | 0 | 0 | 0 | 0 | 0 | 0 | 0 | 0 | 0 | 0 | 1 | 0 | 0 |
| Terrell, Minn | .000 | 2 | 1 | 1 | 0 | 0 | 0 | 0 | 0 | 1 | 0 | 1 | 0 | 0 | 0 | 0 | 0 | 0 |
| North, Oak | .000 | 1 | 1 | 2 | 0 | 0 | 0 | 0 | 0 | 1 | 0 | 0 | 1 | 0 | 0 | 0 | 0 | 0 |
| Moates, Tex | .000 | 1 | 1 | 0 | 0 | 0 | 0 | 0 | 0 | 0 | 0 | 0 | 0 | 0 | 0 | 0 | 0 | 0 |
| Blair, Balt | .000 | 1 | 0 | 0 | 0 | 0 | 0 | 0 | 0 | 0 | 0 | 0 | 0 | 0 | 0 | 0 | 0 | 0 |
| Shopay, Balt | .000 | 3 | 0 | 1 | 0 | 0 | 0 | 0 | 0 | 0 | 0 | 0 | 1 | 0 | 1 | 0 | 0 | 0 |
| Meoli, Calif | .000 | 3 | 0 | 1 | 0 | 0 | 0 | 0 | 0 | 0 | 0 | 0 | 0 | 0 | 1 | 0 | 0 | 0 |
| Smith, Calif | .000 | 4 | 0 | 2 | 0 | 0 | 0 | 0 | 0 | 0 | 0 | 0 | 0 | 0 | 0 | 0 | 0 | 0 |
| Stanton, Calif | .000 | 1 | 0 | 0 | 0 | 0 | 0 | 0 | 0 | 0 | 0 | 0 | 0 | 0 | 0 | 0 | 0 | 0 |
| Coluccio, Chi | .000 | 1 | 0 | 1 | 0 | 0 | 0 | 0 | 0 | 0 | 0 | 0 | 0 | 0 | 0 | 0 | 0 | 0 |
| Kuiper, Clev | .000 | 1 | 0 | 0 | 0 | 0 | 0 | 0 | 0 | 0 | 0 | 0 | 0 | 0 | 0 | 0 | 1 | 0 |
| Hood, Clev | .000 | 1 | 0 | 0 | 0 | 0 | 0 | 0 | 0 | 0 | 0 | 0 | 0 | 0 | 0 | 0 | 0 | 0 |
| Lis, Clev | .000 | 1 | 0 | 0 | 0 | 0 | 0 | 0 | 0 | 0 | 0 | 0 | 0 | 0 | 0 | 0 | 0 | 0 |
| Knox, Det | .000 | 3 | 0 | 0 | 0 | 0 | 0 | 0 | 0 | 0 | 0 | 0 | 0 | 0 | 0 | 0 | 0 | 0 |
| Oglivie, Det | .000 | 2 | 0 | 0 | 0 | 0 | 0 | 0 | 0 | 0 | 0 | 0 | 0 | 0 | 0 | 0 | 0 | 0 |
| Baldwin, Det | .000 | 1 | 0 | 0 | 0 | 0 | 0 | 0 | 0 | 0 | 0 | 0 | 0 | 0 | 0 | 0 | 0 | 0 |
| Rojas, KC | .000 | 1 | 0 | 0 | 0 | 0 | 0 | 0 | 0 | 0 | 0 | 0 | 0 | 0 | 0 | 0 | 0 | 0 |
| Patek, KC | .000 | 1 | 0 | 1 | 0 | 0 | 0 | 0 | 0 | 0 | 0 | 0 | 0 | 0 | 0 | 0 | 0 | 0 |
| Pattin, KC | .000 | 1 | 0 | 0 | 0 | 0 | 0 | 0 | 0 | 0 | 0 | 0 | 0 | 0 | 0 | 0 | 0 | 0 |
| Thomas, Milw | .000 | 6 | 0 | 2 | 0 | 0 | 0 | 0 | 0 | 0 | 0 | 0 | 0 | 0 | 0 | 0 | 0 | 0 |
| Johnson, Milw | .000 | 3 | 0 | 0 | 0 | 0 | 0 | 0 | 0 | 0 | 0 | 0 | 0 | 0 | 0 | 0 | 0 | 0 |
| Ellis, Milw | .000 | 1 | 0 | 1 | 0 | 0 | 0 | 0 | 0 | 0 | 0 | 0 | 0 | 0 | 0 | 0 | 0 | 0 |
| Garcia, Milw | .000 | 1 | 0 | 1 | 0 | 0 | 0 | 0 | 0 | 0 | 0 | 0 | 0 | 0 | 0 | 0 | 0 | 0 |
| Bevacqua, Milw | .000 | 1 | 0 | 0 | 0 | 0 | 0 | 0 | 0 | 0 | 0 | 0 | 0 | 0 | 0 | 0 | 0 | 0 |
| Murphy, Milw | .000 | 1 | 0 | 1 | 0 | 0 | 0 | 0 | 0 | 0 | 0 | 0 | 0 | 0 | 0 | 0 | 0 | 0 |
| Bostock, Minn | .000 | 1 | 0 | 1 | 0 | 0 | 0 | 0 | 0 | 0 | 0 | 0 | 0 | 0 | 0 | 0 | 0 | 0 |
| Brye, Minn | .000 | 6 | 0 | 0 | 0 | 0 | 0 | 0 | 0 | 0 | 0 | 0 | 0 | 0 | 0 | 0 | 0 | 0 |
| Albury, Minn | .000 | 1 | 0 | 0 | 0 | 0 | 0 | 0 | 0 | 0 | 0 | 0 | 0 | 0 | 0 | 0 | 0 | 0 |
| Gomez, Minn | .000 | 7 | 0 | 2 | 0 | 0 | 0 | 0 | 0 | 0 | 0 | 0 | 0 | 0 | 0 | 0 | 0 | 0 |
| H. Washington, Oak | .000 | 3 | 0 | 0 | 0 | 0 | 0 | 0 | 0 | 0 | 0 | 0 | 0 | 0 | 0 | 0 | 0 | 0 |
| Sands, Oak | .000 | 1 | 0 | 0 | 0 | 0 | 0 | 0 | 0 | 0 | 0 | 0 | 1 | 0 | 0 | 0 | 0 | 0 |
| Grabarkewitz, Oak | .000 | 1 | 0 | 0 | 0 | 0 | 0 | 0 | 0 | 0 | 0 | 0 | 0 | 0 | 0 | 0 | 0 | 0 |
| Alexander, Oak | .000 | 17 | 0 | 6 | 0 | 0 | 0 | 0 | 0 | 0 | 0 | 0 | 0 | 0 | 0 | 10 | 3 | 0 |

# OFFICIAL AMERICAN LEAGUE FIELDING AVERAGES

## CLUB FIELDING

| Club | Pct. | G. | PO. | A. | E. | TC. | DP. | TP. | PB. |
|------|------|-----|------|------|-----|------|------|-----|-----|
| Baltimore | .983 | 159 | 4353 | 1974 | 107 | 6434 | 175 | 0 | 5 |
| Cleveland | .978 | 159 | 4306 | 1754 | 134 | 6194 | 156 | 0 | 15 |
| Chicago | .978 | 161 | 4357 | 1859 | 140 | 6356 | 155 | 0 | 12 |
| New York | .978 | 160 | 4272 | 1698 | 135 | 6105 | 148 | 0 | 9 |
| Boston | .977 | 160 | 4310 | 1724 | 139 | 6173 | 142 | 0 | 3 |
| Oakland | .977 | 162 | 4344 | 1686 | 143 | 6173 | 140 | 0 | 13 |
| Kansas City | .976 | 162 | 4370 | 1831 | 155 | 6356 | 151 | 0 | 13 |
| Minnesota | .973 | 159 | 4269 | 1842 | 170 | 6281 | 147 | 0 | 9 |
| Detroit | .972 | 159 | 4188 | 1756 | 173 | 6117 | 141 | 0 | 11 |
| Milwaukee | .971 | 162 | 4295 | 1776 | 180 | 6251 | 162 | 0 | 20 |
| Texas | .971 | 162 | 4397 | 1980 | 191 | 6568 | 173 | 0 | 11 |
| California | .971 | 161 | 4360 | 1705 | 184 | 6249 | 164 | 0 | 12 |
| Totals | .975 | | 51821 | 21585 | 1851 | 75257 | 1854 | 0 | 133 |

# INDIVIDUAL FIELDING

(Position Leader in Capitals)

## FIRST BASEMEN

°Throws lefthanded.

| Player—Club | Pct. | G. | PO. | A. | E. | DP. |
|-------------|------|-----|------|-----|----|-----|
| Stanley, Det | 1.000 | 14 | 119 | 7 | 0 | 8 |
| McCraw, Clev° | 1.000 | 16 | 110 | 6 | 0 | 9 |
| Sudakis, 2 Calif-12 Clev | 1.000 | 14 | 91 | 4 | 0 | 10 |
| Garrett, Calif | 1.000 | 10 | 77 | 8 | 0 | 10 |
| Tenace, Oak | .998 | 68 | 401 | 21 | 1 | 27 |
| POWELL, Clev | .997 | 121 | 997 | 69 | 3 | 92 |
| Yastrzemski, Bos | .996 | 140 | 1202 | 87 | 5 | 103 |
| Cooper, Bos° | .995 | 35 | 197 | 20 | 1 | 20 |
| Hegan, Milw° | .995 | 27 | 182 | 20 | 1 | 19 |
| Spencer, Tex° | .995 | 99 | 844 | 70 | 5 | 92 |
| Muser, 41 Chi-62 Balt° | .994 | 103 | 476 | 37 | 3 | 58 |
| D. Johnson, 55 Chi-2 Bos | .994 | 57 | 475 | 24 | 3 | 40 |
| Solaita, KC° | .994 | 35 | 282 | 28 | 2 | 24 |
| May, Balt | .993 | 144 | 1312 | 106 | 10 | 138 |
| Chambliss, NY | .991 | 147 | 1222 | 106 | 12 | 113 |
| Rudi, Oak | .991 | 91 | 732 | 36 | 7 | 64 |
| Holt, Oak | .991 | 52 | 192 | 18 | 2 | 19 |
| Carty, KC | .990 | 26 | 189 | 15 | 2 | 21 |
| Kusick, Minn | .990 | 51 | 372 | 31 | 4 | 45 |
| Meyer, Det | .990 | 46 | 441 | 37 | 5 | 39 |
| Scott, Milw | .989 | 144 | 1202 | 109 | 14 | 118 |
| May, Chi | .989 | 63 | 508 | 46 | 6 | 54 |
| Squires, Chi° | .988 | 20 | 155 | 12 | 2 | 14 |
| Mayberry, KC° | .988 | 131 | 1199 | 100 | 16 | 105 |
| Bochte, Calif° | .987 | 105 | 850 | 51 | 12 | 90 |
| Terrell, Minn | .985 | 15 | 126 | 6 | 2 | 8 |
| Fregosi, Tex | .985 | 54 | 355 | 34 | 6 | 31 |
| Kelly, Minn° | .985 | 27 | 227 | 6 | 27 |  |
| Hargrove, Tex° | .984 | 48 | 326 | 43 | 6 | 24 |
| Briggs, Minn° | .983 | 49 | 420 | 53 | 8 | 38 |
| Doherty, Calif° | .983 | 26 | 216 | 14 | 4 | 20 |
| Colbert, Det | .982 | 44 | 407 | 22 | 8 | 31 |
| Harper, 19 Calif-16 Oak | .978 | 35 | 217 | 9 | 5 | 23 |
| Carew, Minn. | .978 | 14 | 123 | 8 | 3 | 10 |
| Pierce, Det | .971 | 49 | 407 | 26 | 13 | 38 |

### (Fewer Than Ten Games)

| Player—Club | Pct. | G. | PO. | A. | E. | DP. |
|-------------|------|----|-----|----|----|-----|
| Freehan, Det | 1.000 | 5 | 53 | 2 | 0 | 4 |
| Llenas, Calif | 1.000 | 6 | 44 | 2 | 0 | 10 |
| Oglivie, Det° | 1.000 | 5 | 40 | 4 | 0 | 4 |
| Lis, Clev | 1.000 | 8 | 39 | 2 | 0 | 2 |
| Oliver, NY | 1.000 | 8 | 39 | 2 | 0 | 9 |
| Robson, Tex | 1.000 | 5 | 38 | 2 | 0 | 6 |
| Killebrew, KC | 1.000 | 6 | 28 | 0 | 0 | 4 |
| DeCinces, Balt | 1.000 | 2 | 19 | 1 | 0 | 0 |
| Munson, NY | 1.000 | 2 | 20 | 0 | 0 | 1 |
| Baylor, Balt | 1.000 | 2 | 18 | 0 | 0 | 1 |
| Smith, Calif | 1.000 | 6 | 15 | 1 | 0 | 0 |
| Bianco, Milw | 1.000 | 5 | 12 | 1 | 0 | 0 |
| Velez, NY | 1.000 | 1 | 11 | 0 | 0 | 1 |
| Lind, Milw | 1.000 | 1 | 9 | 0 | 0 | 1 |
| Lovitto, Tex | 1.000 | 2 | 9 | 0 | 0 | 0 |
| Ashby, Clev | 1.000 | 2 | 8 | 0 | 0 | 1 |
| Pinson, KC° | 1.000 | 4 | 7 | 0 | 0 | 0 |
| Bevacqua, Milw | 1.000 | 3 | 4 | 2 | 0 | 0 |
| Fosse, Oak | 1.000 | 1 | 3 | 0 | 0 | 0 |
| McCarver, Bos | 1.000 | 1 | 3 | 0 | 0 | 0 |
| Heise, Bos | 1.000 | 1 | 1 | 0 | 0 | 0 |
| Johnson, Milw | 1.000 | 2 | 1 | 0 | 0 | 0 |
| McKinney, Oak | 1.000 | 1 | 1 | 0 | 0 | 0 |
| Moses, Chi | 1.000 | 1 | 1 | 0 | 0 | 0 |
| White, NY | .983 | 7 | 58 | 1 | 1 | 3 |
| Williams, Oak | .971 | 7 | 30 | 3 | 1 | 5 |
| Braun, Minn. | .964 | 9 | 75 | 5 | 3 | 3 |
| Walton, Minn | .962 | 7 | 24 | 1 | 1 | 4 |
| L. Johnson, Chi | .960 | 6 | 46 | 2 | 2 | 4 |
| Valentine, Calif | .958 | 3 | 23 | 0 | 1 | 2 |
| Briggs, Calif° | .953 | 6 | 40 | 1 | 2 | 4 |
| Montgomery, Bos | .939 | 6 | 29 | 2 | 2 | 1 |
| Ellis, Clev | .900 | 2 | 17 | 1 | 2 | 1 |
| Blair, Balt | .000 | 1 | 0 | 0 | 0 | 0 |
| Stinson, KC | .000 | 1 | 0 | 0 | 0 | 0 |

## SECOND BASEMEN

| Player—Club | Pct. | G. | PO. | A. | E. | DP. |
|---|---|---|---|---|---|---|
| DeCinces, Balt | 1.000 | 11 | 41 | 25 | 0 | 10 |
| Martinez, Oak | 1.000 | 31 | 23 | 21 | 0 | 7 |
| Johnson, Milw | 1.000 | 11 | 20 | 23 | 0 | 5 |
| Llenas, Calif | 1.000 | 12 | 16 | 24 | 0 | 5 |
| Terrell, Minn | .987 | 39 | 68 | 89 | 2 | 20 |
| White, KC | .987 | 67 | 124 | 179 | 4 | 35 |
| Garcia, Milw | .985 | 94 | 230 | 293 | 8 | 67 |
| ALOMAR, NY | .985 | 150 | 340 | 368 | 11 | 93 |
| Remy, Calif | .982 | 147 | 336 | 427 | 14 | 111 |
| Stanley, NY | .982 | 33 | 54 | 54 | 2 | 17 |
| Knox, Det | .980 | 23 | 38 | 61 | 2 | 10 |
| Rojas, KC | .980 | 117 | 233 | 303 | 11 | 65 |
| Orta, Chi | .978 | 135 | 354 | 354 | 16 | 95 |
| Grich, Balt | .977 | 150 | 423 | 484 | 21 | 122 |
| Sheldon, Milw | .977 | 44 | 87 | 122 | 5 | 33 |
| Brohamer, Clev | .976 | 66 | 166 | 162 | 8 | 52 |
| Bevacqua, Milw | .975 | 32 | 95 | 63 | 4 | 20 |
| Stein, Chi | .974 | 28 | 71 | 79 | 4 | 16 |
| Randle, Tex | .973 | 79 | 205 | 232 | 12 | 61 |
| Carew, Minn | .973 | 123 | 285 | 369 | 18 | 79 |
| Kuiper, Clev | .972 | 87 | 192 | 230 | 12 | 65 |
| Ferrer, Minn | .971 | 10 | 15 | 18 | 1 | 2 |
| Doyle, 6 Calif-84 Bos | .970 | 90 | 153 | 206 | 11 | 37 |
| Sutherland, Det | .968 | 128 | 278 | 365 | 21 | 83 |
| Garner, Oak | .968 | 160 | 354 | 426 | 26 | 93 |
| Griffin, Bos | .967 | 99 | 195 | 215 | 14 | 45 |
| Cubbage, Tex | .962 | 37 | 67 | 111 | 7 | 24 |
| Crosby, Clev | .961 | 19 | 25 | 49 | 3 | 5 |
| Nelson, Tex | .959 | 23 | 56 | 60 | 5 | 16 |
| Smalley, Minn | .955 | 19 | 28 | 57 | 4 | 14 |
| Heise, Bos | .955 | 14 | 11 | 10 | 1 | 3 |
| Harrah, Tex | .949 | 21 | 39 | 54 | 5 | 10 |
| Meoli, Calif | .933 | 11 | 11 | 17 | 2 | 3 |

### (Fewer Than Ten Games)

| Player—Club | Pct. | G. | PO. | A. | E. | DP. |
|---|---|---|---|---|---|---|
| Michael, Det | 1.000 | 7 | 9 | 23 | 0 | 5 |
| Gomez, Minn | 1.000 | 6 | 5 | 15 | 0 | 3 |
| Dillard, Bos | 1.000 | 1 | 5 | 4 | 0 | 1 |
| Kubiak, Oak | 1.000 | 6 | 3 | 5 | 0 | 1 |
| Scott, KC | 1.000 | 9 | 5 | 2 | 0 | 1 |
| Bailor, Balt | 1.000 | 1 | 2 | 4 | 0 | 1 |
| Nordbrook, Balt | 1.000 | 3 | 4 | 1 | 0 | 0 |
| Thompson, Minn | 1.000 | 1 | 5 | 0 | 0 | 0 |
| Tovar, 1 Tex-4 Oak | 1.000 | 5 | 2 | 3 | 0 | 0 |
| Williams, NY | 1.000 | 6 | 2 | 3 | 0 | 0 |
| Brinkman, NY | 1.000 | 3 | 0 | 4 | 0 | 0 |
| Pitts, Oak | 1.000 | 1 | 2 | 2 | 0 | 0 |
| Cardenas, Tex | 1.000 | 3 | 1 | 2 | 0 | 0 |
| Lowenstein, Clev | 1.000 | 2 | 0 | 3 | 0 | 0 |
| Andrew, Minn | 1.000 | 2 | 1 | 1 | 0 | 0 |
| Maxvill, Oak | 1.000 | 2 | 2 | 0 | 0 | 0 |
| Stinson, KC | 1.000 | 1 | 0 | 2 | 0 | 0 |
| Maddox, NY | 1.000 | 1 | 1 | 0 | 0 | 0 |
| Manuel, Det | .944 | 6 | 11 | 23 | 2 | 4 |
| Richard, Chi | .833 | 5 | 7 | 3 | 2 | 0 |
| Grabarkewitz, Oak | .833 | 4 | 4 | 1 | 1 | 0 |
| Braun, Minn | .800 | 1 | 1 | 3 | 1 | 0 |
| Hunter, Bos | .750 | 1 | 2 | 1 | 1 | 1 |
| Alexander, Oak | .667 | 3 | 0 | 2 | 1 | 1 |
| Mason, NY | .000 | 1 | 0 | 0 | 0 | 0 |
| Fosse, Oak | .000 | 1 | 0 | 0 | 0 | 0 |
| Sandt, Oak | .000 | 1 | 0 | 0 | 0 | 0 |

## THIRD BASEMEN

| Player—Club | Pct. | G. | PO. | A. | E. | DP. |
|---|---|---|---|---|---|---|
| Terrell, Minn | 1.000 | 12 | 7 | 29 | 0 | 3 |
| Beniquez, Bos | 1.000 | 14 | 6 | 14 | 0 | 0 |
| Richard, Chi | 1.000 | 12 | 5 | 11 | 0 | 0 |
| Martinez, Oak | 1.000 | 14 | 6 | 7 | 0 | 0 |
| ROBINSON, Balt | .979 | 143 | 96 | 326 | 9 | 30 |
| Chalk, Calif | .976 | 149 | 108 | 333 | 11 | 30 |
| Randle, Tex | .975 | 17 | 10 | 29 | 1 | 3 |
| Harrah, Tex | .971 | 28 | 16 | 52 | 2 | 4 |
| Soderholm, Minn | .969 | 113 | 94 | 277 | 12 | 14 |
| Bando, Oak | .967 | 160 | 122 | 314 | 15 | 36 |
| Nettles, NY | .964 | 157 | 135 | 379 | 19 | 31 |
| Petrocelli, Bos | .960 | 113 | 85 | 229 | 13 | 13 |
| Cardenas, Tex | .956 | 43 | 32 | 76 | 5 | 9 |
| Rodriguez, Det | .953 | 151 | 136 | 375 | 25 | 33 |
| Money, Milw | .951 | 99 | 95 | 179 | 14 | 22 |
| Bell, Clev | .950 | 153 | 146 | 330 | 25 | 29 |
| Brett, KC | .949 | 159 | 131 | 355 | 26 | 27 |
| Bevacqua, Milw | .948 | 60 | 50 | 96 | 8 | 12 |
| DeCinces, Balt | .947 | 34 | 19 | 71 | 5 | 7 |
| Melton, Chi | .945 | 138 | 131 | 313 | 26 | 23 |
| Heise, Bos | .940 | 45 | 36 | 90 | 8 | 7 |
| Howell, Tex | .933 | 115 | 80 | 214 | 21 | 32 |
| McKay, Minn | .923 | 33 | 38 | 70 | 9 | 12 |
| Stein, Chi | .917 | 24 | 16 | 39 | 5 | 5 |
| Crosby, Clev | .900 | 13 | 4 | 5 | 1 | 1 |
| Johnson, Milw | .857 | 11 | 7 | 17 | 4 | 0 |
| Meoli, Calif | .824 | 15 | 9 | 19 | 6 | 2 |

### (Fewer Than Ten Games)

| Player—Club | Pct. | G. | PO. | A. | E. | DP. |
|---|---|---|---|---|---|---|
| Kubiak, Oak | 1.000 | 7 | 1 | 8 | 0 | 0 |
| Stanley, NY | 1.000 | 1 | 2 | 6 | 0 | 0 |
| White, KC | 1.000 | 4 | 1 | 7 | 0 | 1 |
| Llenas, Calif | 1.000 | 3 | 1 | 6 | 0 | 1 |
| Michael, Det | 1.000 | 4 | 2 | 3 | 0 | 0 |
| Brinkman, 1 Tex-3 NY | 1.000 | 4 | 1 | 3 | 0 | 0 |
| Hobson, Bos | 1.000 | 1 | 1 | 3 | 0 | 0 |
| Scrivener, Det | 1.000 | 3 | 0 | 4 | 0 | 0 |
| Lind, Milw | 1.000 | 6 | 0 | 3 | 0 | 0 |
| Fregosi, Tex | 1.000 | 4 | 1 | 1 | 0 | 0 |
| Oliver, NY | 1.000 | 1 | 0 | 2 | 0 | 0 |
| Quirk, KC | 1.000 | 2 | 0 | 2 | 0 | 0 |
| Tovar, Oak | 1.000 | 3 | 1 | 1 | 0 | 1 |
| Dade, Calif | 1.000 | 1 | 0 | 1 | 0 | 0 |
| Haney, Oak | 1.000 | 4 | 1 | 0 | 0 | 0 |
| Stanley, Det | .952 | 7 | 6 | 14 | 1 | 1 |
| Lowenstein, Clev | .941 | 8 | 5 | 11 | 1 | 0 |
| Bianco, Milw | .941 | 7 | 4 | 12 | 1 | 0 |
| Lemon, Chi | .923 | 6 | 5 | 7 | 1 | 0 |
| Doyle, 1 Calif-6 Bos | .917 | 7 | 2 | 9 | 1 | 0 |
| Thompson, Minn | .909 | 7 | 4 | 16 | 2 | 1 |
| Scott, Milw | .909 | 5 | 3 | 7 | 1 | 1 |

### THIRD BASEMEN—Continued

| Player—Club | Pct. | G. | PO. | A. | E. | DP. | Player—Club | Pct. | G. | PO. | A. | E. | DP. |
|---|---|---|---|---|---|---|---|---|---|---|---|---|---|
| Jackson, Calif | .833 | 3 | 2 | 3 | 1 | 0 | Braun, Minn | .000 | 2 | 0 | 0 | 0 | 0 |
| Cubbage, Tex | .833 | 3 | 1 | 4 | 1 | 1 | Harper, Oak | .000 | 2 | 0 | 0 | 0 | 0 |
| Pitts, Oak | .800 | 6 | 1 | 3 | 1 | 0 | Hampton, Calif | .000 | 1 | 0 | 0 | 0 | 0 |
| McAuliffe, Bos | .769 | 7 | 2 | 8 | 3 | 1 | McRae, KC | .000 | 1 | 0 | 0 | 0 | 0 |
| Valentine, Calif | .750 | 2 | 2 | 1 | 1 | 0 | Alexander, Oak | .000 | 2 | 0 | 0 | 0 | 0 |
| Ashby, Clev | .500 | 1 | 1 | 0 | 1 | 0 | Bumbry, Balt | .000 | 1 | 0 | 0 | 0 | 0 |
| Knox, Det | .250 | 3 | 0 | 1 | 3 | 0 | Munson, NY | .000 | 1 | 0 | 0 | 0 | 0 |
| Smith, Calif | .000 | 2 | 0 | 0 | 1 | 0 | Dempsey, NY | .000 | 1 | 0 | 0 | 0 | 0 |

## SHORTSTOPS

| Player—Club | Pct. | G. | PO. | A. | E. | DP. | Player—Club | Pct. | G. | PO. | A. | E. | DP. |
|---|---|---|---|---|---|---|---|---|---|---|---|---|---|
| DENT, Chi | .981 | 157 | 279 | 543 | 16 | 105 | Martinez, Oak | .955 | 45 | 32 | 53 | 4 | 9 |
| Belanger, Balt | .978 | 152 | 259 | 508 | 17 | 105 | Maxvill, Oak | .955 | 20 | 8 | 13 | 1 | 1 |
| Duffy, Clev | .977 | 145 | 225 | 464 | 16 | 85 | White, KC | .953 | 42 | 55 | 86 | 7 | 20 |
| Stanley, NY | .977 | 83 | 105 | 189 | 7 | 36 | Terrell, Minn | .947 | 41 | 56 | 106 | 9 | 29 |
| Meoli, Calif | .976 | 28 | 19 | 61 | 2 | 8 | Thompson, Minn | .941 | 100 | 138 | 245 | 24 | 40 |
| Gomez, Minn | .975 | 70 | 50 | 65 | 3 | 17 | Smalley, Tex | .941 | 59 | 80 | 175 | 16 | 30 |
| Crosby, Clev | .974 | 30 | 40 | 72 | 3 | 12 | DeCinces, Balt | .939 | 13 | 13 | 18 | 2 | 3 |
| Johnson, Milw | .971 | 10 | 10 | 23 | 1 | 3 | Miley, Calif | .939 | 70 | 107 | 186 | 19 | 53 |
| Nordbrook, Balt | .970 | 37 | 15 | 50 | 2 | 7 | Yount, Milw | .939 | 145 | 273 | 402 | 44 | 80 |
| Burleson, Bos | .963 | 158 | 267 | 498 | 29 | 102 | Michael, Det | .938 | 44 | 52 | 99 | 10 | 23 |
| Harrah, Tex | .963 | 118 | 198 | 375 | 22 | 68 | Brinkman, NY | .933 | 39 | 30 | 53 | 6 | 13 |
| Campaneris, Oak | .962 | 137 | 199 | 378 | 23 | 58 | Smith, Calif | .932 | 50 | 80 | 98 | 13 | 19 |
| Veryzer, Det | .960 | 128 | 215 | 358 | 24 | 62 | Ferrer, Minn. | .924 | 18 | 17 | 44 | 5 | 10 |
| Patek, KC | .959 | 136 | 231 | 405 | 27 | 78 | Ramirez, Calif | .905 | 40 | 62 | 90 | 16 | 27 |
| Mason, NY | .955 | 93 | 134 | 209 | 16 | 45 | | | | | | | |

### (Fewer Than Ten Games)

| Player—Club | Pct. | G. | PO. | A. | E. | DP. | Player—Club | Pct. | G. | PO. | A. | E. | DP. |
|---|---|---|---|---|---|---|---|---|---|---|---|---|---|
| Kubiak, Oak | 1.000 | 7 | 8 | 18 | 0 | 4 | Money, Milw | .967 | 7 | 14 | 15 | 1 | 2 |
| Cardenas, Tex | 1.000 | 5 | 5 | 7 | 0 | 3 | Richard, Chi | .964 | 9 | 8 | 19 | 1 | 3 |
| Bailor, Balt | 1.000 | 2 | 3 | 5 | 0 | 0 | Bevacqua, Milw | .938 | 5 | 8 | 7 | 1 | 3 |
| Scrivener, Det | 1.000 | 2 | 2 | 4 | 0 | 0 | Lind, Milw | .919 | 9 | 10 | 24 | 3 | 2 |
| Doyle, Bos | 1.000 | 2 | 0 | 5 | 0 | 0 | Heise, Bos | .909 | 4 | 4 | 6 | 1 | 2 |
| Alomar, NY | 1.000 | 1 | 1 | 2 | 0 | 1 | Scott, KC | .867 | 8 | 3 | 10 | 2 | 1 |
| Brett, KC | 1.000 | 1 | 1 | 1 | 0 | 0 | Hampton, Calif | .750 | 2 | 2 | 1 | 1 | 0 |
| Garner, Oak | 1.000 | 1 | 1 | 1 | 0 | 1 | Griffin, Bos | .000 | 1 | 0 | 0 | 0 | 0 |
| Pitts, Oak | 1.000 | 2 | 1 | 1 | 0 | 1 | Leon, NY | .000 | 1 | 0 | 0 | 0 | 0 |
| Tovar, Oak | 1.000 | 1 | 0 | 1 | 0 | 0 | Randle, Tex | .000 | 1 | 0 | 0 | 0 | 0 |

## OUTFIELDERS

| Player—Club | Pct. | G. | PO. | A. | E. | DP. | Player—Club | Pct. | G. | PO. | A. | E. | DP. |
|---|---|---|---|---|---|---|---|---|---|---|---|---|---|
| Rice, Bos | 1.000 | 90 | 162 | 6 | 0 | 0 | Coluccio, | | | | | | |
| Maddox, NY | 1.000 | 55 | 157 | 5 | 0 | 3 | 22 Mil-59 Chi | .987 | 81 | 149 | 5 | 2 | 0 |
| Rudi, Oak | 1.000 | 44 | 72 | 1 | 0 | 1 | Gamble, Clev | .987 | 82 | 146 | 8 | 2 | 2 |
| Bumbry, Balt | 1.000 | 39 | 70 | 2 | 0 | 1 | Bonds, NY | .987 | 129 | 287 | 12 | 4 | 6 |
| Balaz, Calif | 1.000 | 27 | 40 | 3 | 0 | 1 | Evans, Bos | .987 | 115 | 281 | 15 | 4 | 8 |
| Lahoud, Calif° | 1.000 | 29 | 41 | 1 | 0 | 0 | McRae, KC | .986 | 114 | 207 | 7 | 3 | 2 |
| James, Det° | 1.000 | 11 | 33 | 0 | 0 | 0 | Piniella, NY | .986 | 46 | 65 | 5 | 1 | 0 |
| Llenas, Calif | 1.000 | 10 | 15 | 4 | 0 | 0 | Lovitto, Tex | .985 | 38 | 62 | 3 | 1 | 1 |
| Shopay, Balt | 1.000 | 13 | 12 | 0 | 0 | 0 | Bostock, Minn | .985 | 92 | 188 | 3 | 3 | 0 |
| Alexander, Oak | 1.000 | 11 | 7 | 0 | 0 | 0 | White, NY | .984 | 135 | 303 | 11 | 5 | 0 |
| Pinson, KC° | .993 | 82 | 144 | 6 | 1 | 0 | Moates, Tex° | .984 | 51 | 114 | 6 | 2 | 1 |
| Mitchell, Milw | .992 | 72 | 128 | 2 | 1 | 1 | Hegan, Milw° | .984 | 42 | 59 | 1 | 1 | 0 |
| KELLY, Chi° | .9912 | 115 | 222 | 4 | 2 | 1 | Brye, Minn | .983 | 72 | 112 | 7 | 2 | 0 |
| Blair, Balt | .9911 | 138 | 327 | 8 | 3 | 1 | Lynn, Bos° | .983 | 144 | 404 | 11 | 7 | 1 |
| Sharp, | | | | | | | Stanley, Det | .983 | 28 | 58 | 1 | 1 | 0 |
| 14 Chi-124 Mil° | .991 | 138 | 310 | 12 | 3 | 4 | Lowenstein, Clev | .983 | 36 | 56 | 2 | 1 | 1 |
| Beniquez, Bos | .991 | 44 | 104 | 3 | 1 | 2 | Briggs, | | | | | | |
| Davis, Tex° | .990 | 42 | 100 | 1 | 1 | 1 | 21 Mil-35 Minn° | .983 | 56 | 110 | 5 | 2 | 0 |
| Henderson, Chi | .990 | 137 | 394 | 7 | 4 | 0 | Hendrick, Clev | .983 | 143 | 338 | 4 | 6 | 1 |
| Singleton, Balt | .990 | 155 | 283 | 9 | 3 | 2 | Baldwin, Det° | .983 | 25 | 53 | 4 | 1 | 1 |
| Grieve, Tex | .990 | 63 | 93 | 3 | 1 | 0 | Randle, Tex | .982 | 66 | 160 | 8 | 3 | 4 |
| Ford, Minn | .988 | 120 | 246 | 3 | 3 | 2 | Williams, NY | .982 | 31 | 55 | 1 | 1 | 0 |
| Collins, Calif° | .988 | 75 | 159 | 3 | 2 | 2 | Roberts, Det. | .982 | 127 | 268 | 10 | 5 | 2 |
| Otis, KC | .988 | 130 | 310 | 9 | 4 | 3 | Baylor, Balt | .982 | 135 | 268 | 8 | 5 | 0 |

## OUTFIELDERS (Continued)

| Player—Club | Pct. | G. | PO. | A. | E. | DP. |
|---|---|---|---|---|---|---|
| Miller, Bos° | .981 | 65 | 101 | 2 | 2 | 1 |
| Northrup, Balt | .979 | 58 | 91 | 2 | 2 | 0 |
| Mangual, Oak | .978 | 39 | 44 | 1 | 1 | 0 |
| Whitfield, NY | .978 | 25 | 42 | 3 | 1 | 0 |
| C. Washington, Oak° | .978 | 148 | 305 | 8 | 7 | 1 |
| Cowens, KC | .978 | 113 | 214 | 4 | 5 | 2 |
| Rivers, Calif.° | .977 | 152 | 371 | 13 | 9 | 3 |
| Moore, Milw | .977 | 22 | 40 | 2 | 1 | 0 |
| Lezcano, Milw | .977 | 129 | 240 | 10 | 6 | 1 |
| Carbo, Bos | .976 | 85 | 157 | 7 | 4 | 1 |
| Hisle, Minn | .976 | 58 | 118 | 2 | 3 | 0 |
| Darwin, 27 Minn-43 Mil | .975 | 70 | 110 | 8 | 3 | 1 |
| Oglivie, Det° | .975 | 86 | 192 | 4 | 5 | 1 |
| North, Oak | .975 | 138 | 420 | 10 | 11 | 1 |
| May, Chi | .975 | 46 | 72 | 6 | 2 | 1 |
| Manning, Clev | .974 | 118 | 331 | 12 | 9 | 2 |
| Nettles, Calif° | .974 | 90 | 186 | 4 | 5 | 0 |
| Spikes, Clev | .974 | 103 | 176 | 13 | 5 | 5 |
| LeFlore, Det | .973 | 134 | 317 | 13 | 9 | 3 |
| Bladt, NY | .973 | 51 | 103 | 4 | 3 | 1 |
| Braun, Minn | .971 | 106 | 195 | 6 | 6 | 1 |
| Harper, 9 Cal-9 Oak | .971 | 18 | 32 | 1 | 1 | 0 |
| Coggins, NY° | .970 | 36 | 62 | 2 | 2 | 2 |
| Burroughs, Tex | .966 | 148 | 249 | 10 | 9 | 2 |
| Bradford, Chi | .966 | 18 | 27 | 1 | 1 | 0 |
| Jackson, Oak° | .965 | 147 | 315 | 13 | 12 | 5 |
| Hargrove, Tex° | .964 | 96 | 187 | 2 | 7 | 0 |
| Stanton, Calif | .961 | 131 | 230 | 16 | 10 | 2 |
| Thomas, Milw | .961 | 113 | 215 | 5 | 9 | 1 |
| Nyman, Chi° | .958 | 94 | 177 | 6 | 8 | 0 |
| Wohlford, KC | .953 | 102 | 175 | 9 | 9 | 1 |
| Carty, Clev | .952 | 12 | 20 | 0 | 1 | 0 |
| Hairston, Chi | .951 | 59 | 111 | 6 | 6 | 1 |
| Meyer, Det | .950 | 74 | 130 | 4 | 7 | 0 |
| Poepping, Minn | .950 | 13 | 18 | 1 | 1 | 0 |
| Berry, Clev | .926 | 18 | 24 | 1 | 2 | 0 |
| Tovar, Tex | .919 | 31 | 56 | 1 | 5 | 0 |
| Quirk, KC | .909 | 10 | 19 | 1 | 2 | 0 |

### (Fewer Than Ten Games)

| Player—Club | Pct. | G. | PO. | A. | E. | DP. |
|---|---|---|---|---|---|---|
| Dineen, NY | 1.000 | 7 | 19 | 0 | 0 | 0 |
| Yastrzemski, Bos | 1.000 | 8 | 15 | 1 | 0 | 0 |
| Briggs, Calif° | 1.000 | 5 | 9 | 0 | 0 | 0 |
| Johnson, NY | 1.000 | 7 | 9 | 0 | 0 | 0 |
| Molinaro, Det | 1.000 | 6 | 8 | 1 | 0 | 0 |
| Dade, Calif | 1.000 | 3 | 8 | 0 | 0 | 0 |
| Lee, Clev | 1.000 | 5 | 7 | 0 | 0 | 0 |
| Jones, Tex° | 1.000 | 5 | 6 | 0 | 0 | 0 |
| Munson, NY | 1.000 | 2 | 5 | 0 | 0 | 0 |
| Smith, Clev | 1.000 | 3 | 4 | 0 | 0 | 0 |
| Hopkins, Oak | 1.000 | 5 | 3 | 0 | 0 | 0 |
| Stillman, Balt° | 1.000 | 2 | 3 | 0 | 0 | 0 |
| Walling, Oak | 1.000 | 3 | 3 | 0 | 0 | 0 |
| Aaron, Milw | 1.000 | 3 | 2 | 0 | 0 | 0 |
| Blomberg, NY | 1.000 | 1 | 2 | 0 | 0 | 0 |
| Harlow, Balt | 1.000 | 4 | 2 | 0 | 0 | 0 |
| Kelly, Minn° | 1.000 | 2 | 1 | 1 | 0 | 0 |
| Valentine, Calif. | 1.000 | 2 | 2 | 0 | 0 | 0 |
| Chant, Oak | 1.000 | 5 | 1 | 0 | 0 | 0 |
| Ellis, Milw | 1.000 | 5 | 1 | 0 | 0 | 0 |
| Martz, KC | 1.000 | 1 | 1 | 0 | 0 | 0 |
| Murray, NY | 1.000 | 4 | 1 | 0 | 0 | 0 |
| Stinson, KC | 1.000 | 1 | 1 | 0 | 0 | 0 |
| Jackson, Calif | .947 | 9 | 17 | 1 | 1 | 0 |
| Dempsey, NY | .944 | 8 | 16 | 1 | 1 | 1 |
| Terrell, Minn | .923 | 6 | 10 | 2 | 1 | 0 |
| Bergman, NY° | .917 | 6 | 10 | 1 | 1 | 1 |
| McCraw, Clev° | .667 | 3 | 2 | 0 | 1 | 0 |
| Garrett, Calif | .500 | 2 | 1 | 0 | 1 | 0 |
| Holt, Oakland | .000 | 2 | 0 | 0 | 0 | 0 |
| Stein, Chi | .000 | 1 | 0 | 0 | 0 | 0 |
| Lemon, Chi | .000 | 1 | 0 | 0 | 0 | 0 |
| Pruitt, Tex | .000 | 1 | 0 | 0 | 0 | 0 |

## CATCHERS

| Player—Club | Pct. | G. | PO. | A. | E. | DP. | PB. |
|---|---|---|---|---|---|---|---|
| Allietta, Calif | 1.000 | 21 | 92 | 6 | 0 | 0 | 1 |
| Haney, Oak | 1.000 | 43 | 69 | 4 | 0 | 1 | 0 |
| Humphrey, Det | 1.000 | 18 | 61 | 9 | 0 | 1 | 0 |
| Lundstedt, Minn | 1.000 | 14 | 46 | 3 | 0 | 2 | 1 |
| Pruitt, Tex | 1.000 | 13 | 21 | 5 | 0 | 0 | 1 |
| HENDRICKS, Balt. | .995 | 83 | 332 | 36 | 2 | 3 | 2 |
| Stinson, KC | .993 | 59 | 256 | 31 | 2 | 4 | 3 |
| Freehan, Det | .991 | 113 | 582 | 64 | 6 | 8 | 4 |
| Rodriguez, Calif | .991 | 90 | 492 | 33 | 5 | 2 | 3 |
| Downing, Chi | .990 | 137 | 730 | 84 | 8 | 5 | 11 |
| Ashby, Clev | .990 | 87 | 441 | 43 | 5 | 6 | 6 |
| Roof, Minn | .989 | 63 | 245 | 30 | 3 | 4 | 6 |
| Borgmann, Minn | .989 | 125 | 618 | 81 | 8 | 6 | 2 |
| Varney, Chi | .988 | 34 | 151 | 14 | 2 | 1 | 1 |
| Montgomery, Bos | .987 | 53 | 210 | 23 | 3 | 6 | 1 |
| Blackwell, Bos | .984 | 57 | 230 | 23 | 4 | 3 | 2 |
| Tenace, Oak | .984 | 125 | 541 | 63 | 10 | 10 | 11 |
| Fahey, Tex | .983 | 21 | 54 | 5 | 1 | 1 | 1 |
| Etchebarren, 7 Balt-31 Cal | .983 | 38 | 216 | 17 | 4 | 2 | 3 |
| Healy, KC | .982 | 51 | 258 | 17 | 5 | 2 | 1 |
| Duncan, Balt | .982 | 95 | 397 | 41 | 8 | 5 | 3 |
| Wockenfuss, Det | .982 | 34 | 195 | 23 | 4 | 4 | 7 |
| Fosse, Oak | .981 | 82 | 250 | 15 | 5 | 1 | 2 |
| Sundberg, Tex | .981 | 155 | 791 | 101 | 17 | 11 | 9 |
| Martinez, KC | .980 | 79 | 361 | 39 | 8 | 4 | 9 |
| Porter, Milw | .979 | 124 | 532 | 82 | 13 | 10 | 15 |
| Fisk, Bos | .979 | 71 | 347 | 30 | 8 | 2 | 0 |
| Herrmann, NY | .979 | 24 | 121 | 18 | 3 | 5 | 0 |
| Dempsey, NY | .977 | 19 | 76 | 8 | 2 | 0 | 0 |
| Ellis, Clev | .976 | 84 | 396 | 44 | 11 | 3 | 6 |
| Munson, NY | .972 | 130 | 700 | 95 | 23 | 14 | 9 |
| Sudakis, 5 Cal-6 Clev | .971 | 11 | 30 | 3 | 1 | 0 | 0 |
| Egan, Calif | .965 | 28 | 145 | 19 | 6 | 4 | 2 |
| Moore, Milw | .960 | 47 | 194 | 21 | 9 | 2 | 5 |
| Hampton, Calif | .947 | 28 | 111 | 14 | 7 | 1 | 3 |

## CATCHERS (Continued)

### (Fewer Than Ten Games)

| Player—Club | Pct. | G. | PO. | A. | E. | DP. | PB. |
|---|---|---|---|---|---|---|---|
| Cerone, Clev | 1.000 | 7 | 18 | 1 | 0 | 0 | 3 |
| Shopay, Balt | 1.000 | 1 | 5 | 3 | 0 | 0 | 0 |
| Hutto, Balt | 1.000 | 3 | 6 | 0 | 0 | 0 | 0 |
| Merchant, Bos | 1.000 | 1 | 2 | 1 | 0 | 0 | 0 |
| Walton, Minn | 1.000 | 2 | 3 | 0 | 0 | 0 | 0 |
| Randle, Tex | 1.000 | 1 | 1 | 1 | 0 | 0 | 0 |
| McCarver, Bos | .957 | 7 | 18 | 4 | 1 | 1 | 0 |
| Lamont, Det | .944 | 4 | 14 | 3 | 1 | 0 | 0 |
| White, KC | .833 | 1 | 2 | 3 | 1 | 0 | 0 |
| Garrett, Calif | .000 | 1 | 0 | 0 | 0 | 0 | 0 |
| Holt, Oak | .000 | 1 | 0 | 0 | 0 | 0 | 0 |
| Lovitto, Tex | .000 | 1 | 0 | 0 | 0 | 0 | 0 |
| Smalley, Tex | .000 | 1 | 0 | 0 | 0 | 0 | 0 |

## PITCHERS

| Player—Club | Pct. | G. | PO. | A. | E. | DP. |
|---|---|---|---|---|---|---|
| GRIMSLEY, Balt° | 1.000 | 35 | 6 | 33 | 0 | 2 |
| Lolich, Det° | 1.000 | 32 | 2 | 32 | 0 | 0 |
| Gura, NY° | 1.000 | 26 | 8 | 21 | 0 | 2 |
| Hausman, Milw | 1.000 | 29 | 8 | 19 | 0 | 1 |
| Bosman, 6 Clev-22 Oak | 1.000 | 28 | 6 | 20 | 0 | 0 |
| Fingers, Oak | 1.000 | 75 | 8 | 14 | 0 | 0 |
| LaRoche, Clev° | 1.000 | 61 | 7 | 13 | 0 | 0 |
| Moret, Bos° | 1.000 | 36 | 2 | 18 | 0 | 1 |
| Lange, Calif | 1.000 | 30 | 6 | 13 | 0 | 2 |
| J. Perry, 8 Clev-15 Oak | 1.000 | 23 | 6 | 13 | 0 | 1 |
| Thomas, Tex | 1.000 | 46 | 6 | 13 | 0 | 1 |
| Burgmeier, Minn° | 1.000 | 46 | 6 | 12 | 0 | 1 |
| Hamilton, 11 Oak-30 Chi° | 1.000 | 41 | 3 | 15 | 0 | 3 |
| Arroyo, Det | 1.000 | 14 | 6 | 11 | 0 | 2 |
| Garland, Balt | 1.000 | 29 | 6 | 11 | 0 | 0 |
| Drago, Bos | 1.000 | 40 | 3 | 12 | 0 | 0 |
| Beene, Clev | 1.000 | 19 | 3 | 9 | 0 | 0 |
| Scott, Calif° | 1.000 | 50 | 2 | 9 | 0 | 0 |
| Hinton, Chi° | 1.000 | 15 | 1 | 9 | 0 | 1 |
| Reynolds, 7 Balt-21 Det-5 Clev | 1.000 | 33 | 4 | 6 | 0 | 0 |
| Segui, Bos | 1.000 | 33 | 2 | 8 | 0 | 1 |
| Willoughby, Bos | 1.000 | 24 | 3 | 7 | 0 | 0 |
| Burton, Bos° | 1.000 | 29 | 2 | 7 | 0 | 1 |
| Hiller, Det° | 1.000 | 36 | 1 | 8 | 0 | 0 |
| Kekich, Tex° | 1.000 | 23 | 0 | 9 | 0 | 0 |
| Tidrow, NY | 1.000 | 37 | 3 | 6 | 0 | 1 |
| Hockenbery, Calif | 1.000 | 16 | 1 | 6 | 0 | 1 |
| Mitchell, Balt | 1.000 | 11 | 2 | 5 | 0 | 0 |
| Siebert, Oak | 1.000 | 17 | 3 | 4 | 0 | 0 |
| Austin, Milw° | 1.000 | 32 | 1 | 3 | 0 | 0 |
| Decker, Minn | 1.000 | 10 | 1 | 3 | 0 | 0 |
| Brewer, Calif° | 1.000 | 21 | 0 | 3 | 0 | 1 |
| Holtzman, Oak° | .986 | 39 | 11 | 58 | 1 | 3 |
| Wood, Chi° | .984 | 43 | 8 | 53 | 1 | 3 |
| G. Perry, 15 Clev-22 Tex | .984 | 37 | 19 | 43 | 1 | 3 |
| Fitzmorris, KC | .984 | 35 | 26 | 37 | 1 | 1 |
| Kaat, Chi° | .982 | 43 | 15 | 39 | 1 | 2 |
| Splittorff, KC° | .977 | 35 | 10 | 33 | 1 | 4 |
| Dobson, NY | .976 | 33 | 14 | 27 | 1 | 0 |
| Blue, Oak° | .974 | 39 | 4 | 34 | 1 | 1 |
| Peterson, Clev° | .971 | 25 | 8 | 26 | 1 | 3 |
| Umbarger, Tex° | .971 | 56 | 8 | 26 | 1 | 2 |
| Cuellar, Balt° | .970 | 36 | 11 | 53 | 2 | 3 |
| Campbell, Minn | .968 | 47 | 12 | 18 | 1 | 2 |
| Hassler, Calif° | .967 | 30 | 6 | 23 | 1 | 1 |
| Buskey, Clev | .966 | 50 | 9 | 19 | 1 | 2 |
| Tanana, Calif° | .964 | 34 | 9 | 44 | 2 | 5 |
| Osteen, Chi° | .964 | 37 | 12 | 41 | 2 | 1 |
| Briles, KC | .963 | 24 | 11 | 15 | 1 | 1 |
| Colborn, Milw | .962 | 36 | 15 | 36 | 2 | 2 |
| Busby, KC | .961 | 34 | 22 | 52 | 3 | 2 |
| Lemanczyk, Det | .958 | 26 | 9 | 14 | 1 | 1 |
| Medich, NY | .957 | 38 | 18 | 27 | 2 | 1 |
| Alexander, Balt | .956 | 32 | 14 | 29 | 2 | 1 |
| Todd, Oak | .956 | 58 | 6 | 37 | 2 | 4 |
| Leonard, KC | .955 | 32 | 14 | 28 | 2 | 4 |
| Castro, Milw | .952 | 18 | 9 | 11 | 1 | 1 |
| Goltz, Minn | .951 | 32 | 20 | 38 | 3 | 4 |
| Bibby, 12 Tex-24 Clev | .950 | 36 | 11 | 27 | 2 | 3 |
| Coleman, Det | .950 | 31 | 6 | 32 | 2 | 1 |
| Eckersley, Clev | .950 | 34 | 7 | 12 | 1 | 0 |
| Pole, Bos | .950 | 18 | 4 | 15 | 1 | 1 |
| Cleveland, Bos | .949 | 31 | 12 | 25 | 2 | 1 |
| Bare, Det | .949 | 29 | 6 | 31 | 2 | 3 |
| Bahnsen, 12 Chi-21 Oak | .947 | 33 | 10 | 26 | 2 | 1 |
| Foucault, Tex | .947 | 59 | 5 | 13 | 1 | 3 |
| May, NY° | .944 | 32 | 9 | 25 | 2 | 0 |
| Waits, Clev° | .944 | 16 | 5 | 12 | 1 | 1 |
| Lindblad, Oak° | .943 | 68 | 10 | 23 | 2 | 3 |
| Hunter, NY | .942 | 39 | 23 | 26 | 3 | 0 |
| Forster, Chi° | .941 | 17 | 2 | 14 | 1 | 1 |
| Raich, Clev | .941 | 18 | 5 | 11 | 1 | 0 |
| Gogolewski, Chi | .938 | 19 | 4 | 11 | 1 | 2 |
| Wright, Tex° | .935 | 25 | 7 | 22 | 2 | 2 |
| Albury, Minn° | .933 | 32 | 4 | 24 | 2 | 3 |
| Palmer, Balt | .932 | 39 | 30 | 52 | 6 | 7 |
| Champion, Milw | .931 | 27 | 8 | 19 | 2 | 2 |
| Jenkins, Tex | .930 | 37 | 27 | 39 | 5 | 1 |
| Torrez, Balt | .929 | 36 | 19 | 46 | 5 | 3 |
| Lee, Bos° | .926 | 41 | 9 | 54 | 5 | 4 |
| Slaton, Milw | .926 | 37 | 16 | 34 | 4 | 3 |
| Wise, Bos | .923 | 35 | 16 | 32 | 4 | 3 |
| Abbott, Oak | .923 | 30 | 9 | 15 | 2 | 0 |
| Singer, Calif | .921 | 29 | 7 | 28 | 3 | 1 |
| Pattin, KC | .921 | 44 | 13 | 22 | 3 | 1 |
| Perzanowski, Tex | .920 | 12 | 6 | 17 | 2 | 0 |
| Hargan, Tex | .917 | 33 | 19 | 36 | 5 | 4 |
| Corbin, Minn | .917 | 18 | 6 | 16 | 2 | 2 |
| Broberg, Milw | .915 | 38 | 7 | 36 | 4 | 4 |
| Blyleven, Minn | .914 | 35 | 16 | 48 | 6 | 5 |
| Harrison, Clev | .913 | 19 | 9 | 12 | 2 | 2 |
| Travers, Milw° | .913 | 28 | 2 | 19 | 2 | 5 |
| Johnson, Minn | .909 | 18 | 5 | 5 | 1 | 0 |
| Hughes, Minn | .908 | 37 | 18 | 41 | 6 | 1 |
| Tiant, Bos | .905 | 35 | 16 | 22 | 4 | 2 |
| Gossage, Chi | .903 | 62 | 3 | 25 | 3 | 3 |
| Hands, Tex | .900 | 18 | 11 | 16 | 3 | 1 |
| Miller, Balt | .900 | 30 | 1 | 8 | 1 | 0 |
| Figueroa, Calif | .898 | 33 | 11 | 42 | 6 | 5 |
| Murphy, Milw | .895 | 52 | 6 | 11 | 2 | 1 |
| Jackson, Balt° | .889 | 41 | 2 | 6 | 1 | 1 |
| Osborn, Chi | .889 | 24 | 3 | 5 | 1 | 0 |
| Kern, Clev | .882 | 13 | 4 | 11 | 2 | 0 |

## PITCHERS (Continued)

| Player—Club | Pct. | G. | PO. | A. | E. | DP. | Player—Club | Pct. | G. | PO. | A. | E. | DP. |
|---|---|---|---|---|---|---|---|---|---|---|---|---|---|
| Walker, Det | .882 | 36 | 3 | 12 | 2 | 0 | Kirkwood, Calif | .833 | 44 | 3 | 12 | 3 | 1 |
| McDaniel, KC | .882 | 40 | 4 | 11 | 2 | 0 | Sprague, Milw | .833 | 18 | 7 | 8 | 3 | 0 |
| Butler, Minn° | .882 | 23 | 4 | 11 | 2 | 0 | Lyle, NY° | .818 | 49 | 2 | 16 | 4 | 1 |
| Hood, Clev° | .880 | 29 | 7 | 15 | 3 | 0 | Ryan, Calif | .811 | 28 | 12 | 18 | 7 | 3 |
| Ruhle, Det | .872 | 32 | 15 | 19 | 5 | 1 | Upshaw, Chi | .800 | 29 | 0 | 8 | 2 | 1 |
| Brown, | | | | | | | Odom, | | | | | | |
| 17 Tex-25 Clev | .870 | 42 | 8 | 12 | 3 | 1 | 7 Oak-3 Clev | .800 | 10 | 2 | 2 | 1 | 0 |
| Bird, KC | .870 | 51 | 12 | 8 | 3 | 2 | Martinez, NY° | .800 | 23 | 2 | 2 | 1 | 0 |
| Jefferson, | | | | | | | Moore, Tex | .778 | 12 | 3 | 4 | 2 | 0 |
| 4 Balt-22 Chi | .867 | 26 | 5 | 21 | 4 | 2 | Rodriguez, Milw | .769 | 43 | 4 | 6 | 3 | 0 |
| Mingori, KC° | .857 | 36 | 3 | 9 | 2 | 2 | Pentz, Det | .667 | 13 | 2 | 2 | 2 | 0 |
| Wiley, Minn | .857 | 15 | 3 | 3 | 1 | 1 | McClure, KC° | .000 | 12 | 0 | 0 | 0 | 0 |
| Pagan, NY | .857 | 13 | 5 | 1 | 1 | 0 | Guidry, NY° | .000 | 10 | 0 | 0 | 0 | 0 |
| LaGrow, Det | .852 | 32 | 6 | 17 | 4 | 3 | | | | | | | |

### (Fewer Than Ten Games)

| Player—Club | Pct. | G. | PO. | A. | E. | DP. | Player—Club | Pct. | G. | PO. | A. | E. | DP. |
|---|---|---|---|---|---|---|---|---|---|---|---|---|---|
| Anderson, Milw | 1.000 | 8 | 2 | 5 | 0 | 0 | Littell, KC | .909 | 7 | 4 | 6 | 1 | 0 |
| Bacsik, Tex | 1.000 | 7 | 2 | 3 | 0 | 0 | Norris, Oak | .833 | 4 | 1 | 4 | 1 | 0 |
| Osburn, Milw° | 1.000 | 6 | 2 | 3 | 0 | 0 | Makowski, Det° | .800 | 3 | 0 | 4 | 1 | 0 |
| Kravec, Chi° | 1.000 | 2 | 0 | 4 | 0 | 0 | Glynn, Det° | .800 | 3 | 1 | 3 | 1 | 1 |
| Dal Canton, KC | 1.000 | 4 | 1 | 2 | 0 | 0 | Augustine, Milw° | .800 | 5 | 1 | 3 | 1 | 0 |
| Kreuger, Bos° | 1.000 | 2 | 1 | 2 | 0 | 0 | Hudson, Calif° | .667 | 3 | 0 | 2 | 1 | 0 |
| Monge, Calif° | 1.000 | 4 | 1 | 2 | 0 | 0 | Bane, Minn° | .600 | 4 | 1 | 2 | 2 | 0 |
| Throop, KC | 1.000 | 7 | 1 | 2 | 0 | 0 | Barr, Bos° | .500 | 3 | 0 | 1 | 1 | 1 |
| Vuckovich, Chi | 1.000 | 4 | 1 | 2 | 0 | 0 | Sadecki, KC° | .500 | 5 | 1 | 0 | 1 | 0 |
| Andersen, Clev | 1.000 | 3 | 1 | 1 | 0 | 0 | Clyde, Tex° | .500 | 1 | 0 | 1 | 1 | 0 |
| Brookens, Det | 1.000 | 3 | 0 | 2 | 0 | 0 | Pena, Calif | .000 | 7 | 0 | 0 | 0 | 0 |
| Dobson, Calif | 1.000 | 9 | 0 | 2 | 0 | 0 | Quintana, Calif° | .000 | 4 | 0 | 0 | 0 | 0 |
| Flanagan, Balt° | 1.000 | 2 | 0 | 2 | 0 | 0 | Blateric, Calif | .000 | 2 | 0 | 0 | 0 | 0 |
| Johnson, Balt | 1.000 | 6 | 1 | 1 | 0 | 0 | Ross, Calif | .000 | 1 | 0 | 0 | 0 | 0 |
| Mitchell, Oak | 1.000 | 1 | 1 | 1 | 0 | 1 | Pitlock, Chi° | .000 | 1 | 0 | 0 | 0 | 0 |
| Pactwa, Calif° | 1.000 | 4 | 0 | 2 | 0 | 0 | Knapp, Chi | .000 | 2 | 0 | 0 | 0 | 0 |
| Sells, Calif | 1.000 | 4 | 0 | 2 | 0 | 0 | Kucek, Chi | .000 | 2 | 0 | 0 | 0 | 0 |
| Allen, Chi | 1.000 | 3 | 0 | 1 | 0 | 1 | Strickland, Clev° | .000 | 4 | 0 | 0 | 0 | 0 |
| Currence, Milw° | 1.000 | 8 | 0 | 1 | 0 | 0 | Pazik, Minn° | .000 | 5 | 0 | 0 | 0 | 0 |
| Grilli, Det | 1.000 | 3 | 1 | 0 | 0 | 1 | Sawyer, NY | .000 | 4 | 0 | 0 | 0 | 0 |
| Otten, Chi | 1.000 | 2 | 0 | 1 | 0 | 0 | Merritt, Tex° | .000 | 5 | 0 | 0 | 0 | 0 |
| Stoddard, Chi | 1.000 | 1 | 0 | 1 | 0 | 0 | Gideon, Tex | .000 | 1 | 0 | 0 | 0 | 0 |
| Wallace, NY° | 1.000 | 3 | 0 | 1 | 0 | 0 | | | | | | | |

# OFFICIAL AMERICAN LEAGUE PITCHING AVERAGES

Compiled by Sports Information Center, No. Quincy, Mass.

## CLUB PITCHING

| Club | ERA | G. | CG. | Sv. | ShO. | IP. | H. | BFP. | R. | ER. | HR. | SH. | SF. | Tot. BB. | Int. BB. | HB. | SO. | WP. | Bk. |
|---|---|---|---|---|---|---|---|---|---|---|---|---|---|---|---|---|---|---|---|
| Baltimore | 3.17 | 159 | 70 | 21 | 19 | 1451 | 1285 | 5943 | 553 | 511 | 110 | 74 | 37 | 500 | 46 | 12 | 717 | 42 | 3 |
| Oakland | 3.27 | 162 | 36 | 44 | 10 | 1448 | 1267 | 6039 | 606 | 526 | 102 | 64 | 51 | 523 | 41 | 37 | 784 | 47 | 3 |
| New York | 3.29 | 160 | 70 | 20 | 11 | 1424 | 1325 | 5937 | 588 | 520 | 104 | 50 | 53 | 502 | 41 | 21 | 809 | 39 | 3 |
| Kansas City | 3.47 | 162 | 52 | 25 | 11 | 1456⅔ | 1422 | 6156 | 649 | 561 | 108 | 66 | 40 | 498 | 52 | 30 | 815 | 40 | 2 |
| Cleveland | 3.84 | 159 | 37 | 33 | 6 | 1435⅓ | 1395 | 6156 | 703 | 613 | 136 | 67 | 40 | 599 | 78 | 35 | 800 | 51 | 9 |
| Texas | 3.86 | 162 | 60 | 17 | 16 | 1465⅔ | 1456 | 6252 | 733 | 629 | 123 | 75 | 45 | 518 | 60 | 43 | 792 | 49 | 7 |
| California | 3.89 | 161 | 59 | 16 | 19 | 1453⅓ | 1386 | 6242 | 723 | 628 | 123 | 62 | 59 | 613 | 34 | 39 | 975 | 62 | 5 |
| Chicago | 3.93 | 160 | 34 | 39 | 7 | 1452⅓ | 1489 | 6343 | 703 | 634 | 107 | 73 | 35 | 655 | 38 | 33 | 799 | 26 | 6 |
| Boston | 3.98 | 160 | 62 | 31 | 11 | 1436⅔ | 1463 | 6129 | 709 | 636 | 145 | 57 | 43 | 490 | 24 | 20 | 720 | 34 | 1 |
| Minnesota | 4.05 | 159 | 57 | 22 | 10 | 1423 | 1381 | 6146 | 736 | 640 | 137 | 75 | 43 | 617 | 22 | 36 | 846 | 49 | 6 |
| Detroit | 4.27 | 159 | 52 | 17 | 10 | 1396 | 1496 | 6127 | 786 | 663 | 137 | 66 | 57 | 533 | 47 | 30 | 787 | 48 | 3 |
| Milwaukee | 4.34 | 162 | 36 | 34 | 10 | 1431⅔ | 1496 | 6318 | 792 | 693 | 133 | 62 | 46 | 624 | 60 | 58 | 643 | 65 | 3 |
| Totals | 3.78 | | 625 | 319 | 137 | 17273⅔ | 16861 | 73788 | 8281 | 7251 | 1465 | 791 | 551 | 6672 | 543 | 394 | 9487 | 552 | 51 |

(BFP total includes nine batsmen awarded first base because of interference or obstruction).

Totals for earned runs for several clubs do not agree with the composite totals for all pitchers of each respective club due to instances in which provisions of Section 10.18 (i) of the Scoring Rules were applied. The following differences are to be noted: Boston pitchers add to 637; Detroit, 666; Kansas City, 565; Minnesota, 643; Oakland, 530; Texas, 635.

## PITCHERS' RECORDS

(Top Fifteen Qualifiers for Earned-Run Average Leadership—162 or More Innings)

| Pitcher and Club | ERA | W. | L. | Pct. | G. | GS. | CG. | GF. | Sv. | ShO. | IP. | H. | BFP. | R. | ER. | HR. | SH. | SF. | Tot. BB. | Int. BB. | HB. | SO. | WP. | Bk. |
|---|---|---|---|---|---|---|---|---|---|---|---|---|---|---|---|---|---|---|---|---|---|---|---|---|
| Palmer, James, Baltimore | 2.09 | 23 | 11 | .676 | 39 | 38 | 25 | 1 | 0 | 10 | 323 | 253 | 1268 | 87 | 75 | 20 | 10 | 7 | 80 | 4 | 5 | 193 | 4 | 0 |
| Hunter, James, New York | 2.58 | 23 | 14 | .622 | 39 | 39 | 30 | 0 | 0 | 7 | 328 | 248 | 1294 | 107 | 94 | 25 | 7 | 8 | 83 | 4 | 5 | 177 | 7 | 0 |
| Eckersley, Dennis, Cleveland | 2.60 | 13 | 7 | .650 | 34 | 24 | 6 | 5 | 1 | 2 | 187 | 147 | 794 | 61 | 54 | 16 | 13 | 4 | 90 | 8 | 7 | 152 | 4 | 2 |
| Tanana, Frank, California* | 2.63 | 16 | 9 | .640 | 34 | 33 | 16 | 1 | 0 | 6 | 257 | 211 | 1029 | 80 | 75 | 21 | 16 | 4 | 73 | 7 | 4 | 269 | 8 | 0 |
| Figueroa, Eduardo, California | 2.90 | 16 | 13 | .552 | 35 | 33 | 16 | 0 | 0 | 2 | 245 | 213 | 1014 | 96 | 79 | 24 | 14 | 10 | 84 | 6 | 6 | 139 | 5 | 1 |
| Blyleven, Rikalbert, Minnesota | 3.00 | 15 | 10 | .600 | 35 | 35 | 20 | 0 | 0 | 3 | 276 | 219 | 1104 | 104 | 92 | 25 | 10 | 15 | 84 | 6 | 4 | 233 | 5 | 2 |
| Blue, Vida, Oakland* | 3.01 | 22 | 11 | .667 | 38 | 38 | 20 | 0 | 0 | 3 | 278 | 243 | 1153 | 103 | 93 | 21 | 15 | 7 | 99 | 2 | 5 | 189 | 4 | 0 |
| Torrez, Michael, Baltimore* | 3.06 | 20 | 9 | .690 | 36 | 36 | 16 | 0 | 0 | 5 | 271 | 238 | 1144 | 103 | 92 | 15 | 7 | 5 | 133 | 4 | 5 | 119 | 0 | 2 |
| May, Rudolph, New York* | 3.06 | 14 | 12 | .538 | 32 | 31 | 13 | 0 | 0 | 3 | 212 | 179 | 894 | 87 | 72 | 18 | 11 | 4 | 99 | 4 | 4 | 145 | 10 | 1 |
| Busby, Steven, Kansas City | 3.08 | 18 | 12 | .600 | 34 | 34 | 18 | 0 | 0 | 2 | 260 | 233 | 1064 | 96 | 89 | 9 | 13 | 4 | 81 | 3 | 2 | 160 | 5 | 0 |
| Kaat, James, Chicago* | 3.11 | 20 | 14 | .588 | 43 | 41 | 12 | 1 | 0 | 0 | 304 | 321 | 1279 | 121 | 105 | 20 | 11 | 10 | 77 | 4 | 3 | 142 | 8 | 0 |
| Holtzman, Kenneth, Oakland* | 3.15 | 18 | 14 | .563 | 39 | 38 | 13 | 0 | 0 | 2 | 266 | 217 | 1110 | 111 | 93 | 16 | 8 | 8 | 108 | 1 | 7 | 122 | 6 | 0 |

*Throws lefthanded.

| Pitcher and Club | ERA | W. | L. | Pct. | G. | GS. | CG. | GF. | Sv. | ShO. | IP. | H. | BFP. | R. | ER. | HR. | SH. | SF. | Tot. BB. | Int. BB. | HB. | SO. | WP. | Bk. |
|---|---|---|---|---|---|---|---|---|---|---|---|---|---|---|---|---|---|---|---|---|---|---|---|---|
| Perry, Gaylord, 15 Clev.-22 Tex. | 3.24 | 18 | 17 | .514 | 37 | 37 | 25 | 0 | 0 | 5 | 306 | 277 | 1248 | 127 | 110 | 28 | 11 | 3 | 70 | 6 | 4 | 233 | 5 | 0 |
| Pattin, Martin, Kansas City | 3.25 | 10 | 10 | .500 | 44 | 15 | 5 | 16 | 5 | 0 | 177 | 173 | 739 | 90 | 64 | 13 | 2 | 6 | 45 | 0 | 7 | 89 | 0 | 0 |
| Ryan, L. Nolan, California | 3.45 | 14 | 12 | .538 | 28 | 28 | 10 | 0 | 5 | 1 | 198 | 152 | 864 | 90 | 76 | 13 | 6 | 7 | 132 | 0 | 7 | 186 | 12 | 0 |

DEPARTMENTAL LEADERS: W—Hunter, Palmer, 23; L—Wood, 20; Pct.—Torrez, 690; G—Fingers, 75; GS—Wood, 43; CG—Hunter, 30; GF—Fingers, 59; Sv—Gossage, 26; ShO—Palmer, 10; IP—Hunter, 328; H—Kaat, 321; BFP—Hunter, 1,294; R—Wood, 148; ER—Wood, 133; HR—Jenkins, 37; SH—Cuellar, 20; SF—Medich, 15; TBB—Torrez, 133; IBB—Foucault, Gossage, 15; HB—Broberg, 16; SO—Tanana, 269; WP—Coleman, 15; Bk—Hood, 5.

## INDIVIDUAL PITCHING
### (All Pitchers—Listed Alphabetically)

°Throws lefthanded.

| Pitcher and Club | ERA | W. | L. | Pct. | G. | GS. | CG. | GF. | Sv. | ShO. | IP. | H. | BFP. | R. | ER. | HR. | SH. | SF. | Tot. BB. | Int. BB. | HB. | SO. | WP. | Bk. |
|---|---|---|---|---|---|---|---|---|---|---|---|---|---|---|---|---|---|---|---|---|---|---|---|---|
| Abbott, Glenn, Oakland | 4.26 | 5 | 5 | .500 | 30 | 15 | 3 | 4 | 1 | 0 | 114 | 109 | 495 | 61 | 54 | 12 | 7 | 1 | 51 | 2 | 1 | 51 | 2 | 0 |
| Albury, Victor, Minnesota° | 4.53 | 6 | 8 | .462 | 32 | 15 | 2 | 11 | 1 | 0 | 135 | 115 | 606 | 82 | 68 | 16 | 12 | 1 | 97 | 1 | 4 | 72 | 8 | 0 |
| Alexander, Doyle, Baltimore | 3.05 | 8 | 8 | .500 | 32 | 21 | 6 | 3 | 1 | 0 | 133 | 127 | 561 | 47 | 45 | 7 | 7 | 0 | 47 | 1 | 4 | 46 | 6 | 0 |
| Allen, Lloyd, Chicago | 12.60 | 0 | 0 | .000 | 3 | 0 | 0 | 2 | 0 | 0 | 6 | 8 | 31 | 7 | 7 | 2 | 1 | 0 | 6 | 0 | 0 | 4 | 0 | 0 |
| Andersen, Larry, Cleveland | 5.10 | 0 | 0 | .000 | 3 | 0 | 0 | 1 | 0 | 0 | 6 | 4 | 23 | 3 | 3 | 0 | 0 | 0 | 2 | 0 | 0 | 4 | 0 | 0 |
| Anderson, Lawrence, Milwaukee | 4.58 | 2 | 1 | .667 | 8 | 1 | 0 | 6 | 0 | 0 | 30 | 36 | 128 | 18 | 27 | 5 | 0 | 0 | 22 | 2 | 0 | 13 | 6 | 0 |
| Arroyo, Fernando, Detroit | 3.00 | 2 | 2 | .500 | 14 | 5 | 1 | 1 | 0 | 0 | 53 | 56 | 232 | 28 | 27 | 5 | 2 | 1 | 12 | 1 | 1 | 25 | 1 | 0 |
| Augustine, Gerald, Milwaukee° | 4.05 | 2 | 3 | .400 | 5 | 3 | 0 | 1 | 0 | 0 | 27 | 26 | 111 | 19 | 18 | 3 | 2 | 0 | 12 | 1 | 0 | 8 | 1 | 0 |
| Austin, Rick, Milwaukee° | 3.67 | 1 | 2 | .333 | 32 | 7 | 3 | 21 | 0 | 0 | 40 | 28 | 179 | 17 | 11 | 3 | 1 | 3 | 32 | 2 | 4 | 30 | 4 | 0 |
| Bacsik, Michael, Texas | 4.37 | 10 | 13 | .435 | 33 | 28 | 4 | 4 | 0 | 0 | 167 | 166 | 734 | 91 | 81 | 11 | 10 | 1 | 77 | 1 | 6 | 80 | 10 | 0 |
| Bahnsen, Stanley, 12 Chi.-21 Oak. | 2.89 | 3 | 1 | .750 | 4 | 4 | 0 | 2 | 0 | 0 | 28 | 28 | 126 | 11 | 9 | 1 | 2 | 1 | 15 | 0 | 0 | 13 | 0 | 0 |
| Bane, Edward, Minnesota | 4.47 | 8 | 13 | .381 | 29 | 21 | 6 | 5 | 0 | 0 | 151 | 174 | 654 | 81 | 75 | 10 | 6 | 1 | 47 | 1 | 0 | 71 | 1 | 0 |
| Bare, Raymond, Detroit | 2.57 | 0 | 0 | 1.000 | 7 | 1 | 0 | 0 | 0 | 0 | 7 | 11 | 38 | 9 | 2 | 1 | 1 | 0 | 2 | 0 | 0 | 5 | 0 | 0 |
| Barr, Stephen, California | 6.89 | 1 | 0 | 1.000 | 19 | 4 | 0 | 6 | 1 | 0 | 47 | 63 | 227 | 42 | 36 | 4 | 3 | 1 | 25 | 3 | 0 | 20 | 6 | 0 |
| Beene, Fred, Cleveland | 3.88 | 7 | 15 | .318 | 36 | 24 | 6 | 5 | 0 | 0 | 181 | 172 | 781 | 89 | 78 | 7 | 9 | 0 | 83 | 3 | 2 | 93 | 8 | 0 |
| Bibby, James, 12 Tex.-24 Clev. | 3.26 | 9 | 6 | .600 | 36 | 24 | 6 | 10 | 0 | 3 | 219 | 219 | 1104 | 104 | 92 | 9 | 8 | 5 | 84 | 4 | 4 | 81 | 7 | 2 |
| Bird, J. Douglas, Kansas City | 6.75 | 0 | 0 | .000 | 51 | 0 | 0 | 36 | 11 | 0 | 4 | 11 | 24 | 4 | 3 | 0 | 0 | 0 | 5 | 0 | 0 | 5 | 0 | 0 |
| Blateric, Stephen, California | 3.01 | 0 | 0 | .000 | 2 | 0 | 0 | 1 | 0 | 0 | 7 | 9 | 38 | 3 | 2 | 1 | 0 | 1 | 3 | 0 | 0 | 4 | 0 | 0 |
| Blue, Vida, Oakland° | 3.01 | 22 | 11 | .667 | 39 | 38 | 13 | 0 | 0 | 2 | 278 | 243 | 1153 | 103 | 93 | 21 | 15 | 8 | 99 | 2 | 4 | 189 | 4 | 0 |
| Bosman, Richard, 6 Clev.-22 Oak. | 3.00 | 11 | 10 | .600 | 35 | 35 | 6 | 0 | 0 | 3 | 276 | 219 | 1104 | 104 | 92 | 19 | 10 | 5 | 84 | 2 | 4 | 233 | 7 | 0 |
| Brewer, James, California° | 3.64 | 6 | 6 | .647 | 21 | 24 | 2 | 3 | 0 | 0 | 151 | 145 | 627 | 67 | 61 | 15 | 8 | 5 | 61 | 4 | 6 | 53 | 2 | 0 |
| Briles, Nelson, Kansas City | 1.80 | 6 | 6 | .500 | 24 | 16 | 3 | 2 | 0 | 0 | 35 | 38 | 150 | 14 | 9 | 4 | 5 | 1 | 22 | 1 | 1 | 22 | 1 | 0 |
| Broberg, Peter, Milwaukee | 4.26 | 14 | 16 | .467 | 38 | 32 | 7 | 0 | 0 | 0 | 220 | 219 | 967 | 114 | 101 | 17 | 8 | 0 | 106 | 2 | 16 | 100 | 10 | 0 |
| Brookens, Edward, Detroit | 5.40 | 6 | 0 | .000 | 3 | 2 | 0 | 18 | 0 | 0 | 10 | 11 | 46 | 11 | 6 | 1 | 1 | 0 | 6 | 0 | 1 | 8 | 1 | 0 |
| Brown, Jackie, 17 Tex.-25 Clev. | 4.24 | 6 | 7 | .462 | 42 | 10 | 0 | 18 | 11 | 0 | 140 | 142 | 603 | 77 | 66 | 16 | 7 | 6 | 64 | 8 | 2 | 76 | 6 | 0 |
| Burgmeier, Thomas, Minnesota° | 3.08 | 5 | 8 | .385 | 46 | 4 | 0 | 37 | 11 | 0 | 76 | 76 | 318 | 32 | 26 | 7 | 4 | 1 | 23 | 2 | 1 | 41 | 1 | 0 |
| Burton, James, Boston° | 2.89 | 4 | 2 | .333 | 29 | 4 | 0 | 8 | 0 | 0 | 53 | 58 | 232 | 30 | 17 | 6 | 4 | 2 | 19 | 9 | 0 | 39 | 8 | 0 |
| Busby, Steven, Kansas City | 3.08 | 18 | 12 | .600 | 34 | 34 | 18 | 0 | 0 | 0 | 260 | 233 | 1064 | 96 | 89 | 18 | 13 | 4 | 81 | 3 | 3 | 160 | 8 | 0 |
| Buskey, Thomas, Cleveland | 2.57 | 5 | 3 | .625 | 50 | 0 | 0 | 34 | 7 | 0 | 77 | 69 | 316 | 27 | 22 | 7 | 10 | 4 | 29 | 9 | 0 | 29 | 0 | 0 |
| Butler, William, Minnesota° | 5.93 | 5 | 4 | .556 | 23 | 8 | 1 | 7 | 0 | 0 | 82 | 100 | 377 | 61 | 54 | 12 | 5 | 4 | 35 | 2 | 2 | 55 | 5 | 0 |
| Campbell, William, Minnesota | 3.79 | 4 | 6 | .400 | 47 | 7 | 2 | 28 | 5 | 1 | 121 | 119 | 512 | 58 | 51 | 6 | 6 | 4 | 58 | 7 | 2 | 76 | 2 | 0 |
| Castro, William, Milwaukee | 2.52 | 3 | 2 | .600 | 18 | 5 | 0 | 8 | 1 | 0 | 75 | 78 | 314 | 28 | 21 | 3 | 5 | 3 | 17 | 5 | 2 | 25 | 1 | 0 |

°Throws lefthanded.

| Pitcher and Club | ERA | W | L | Pct | G | GS | CG | GF | Sv | ShO | IP | H | BFP | R | ER | HR | SH | SF | Tot BB | Int BB | HB | SO | WP | Bk |
|---|---|---|---|---|---|---|---|---|---|---|---|---|---|---|---|---|---|---|---|---|---|---|---|---|
| Champion, B. Billy, Milwaukee | 5.89 | 6 | 6 | .500 | 27 | 13 | 3 | 2 | 0 | 1 | 110 | 125 | 496 | 77 | 72 | 11 | 5 | 5 | 55 | 8 | 1 | 40 | 3 | 1 |
| Cleveland, Reginald, Boston | 4.42 | 13 | 9 | .591 | 31 | 20 | 8 | 6 | 0 | 0 | 171 | 173 | 724 | 90 | 84 | 19 | 4 | 5 | 52 | 3 | 0 | 78 | 9 | 0 |
| Clyde, David, Texas° | 2.57 | 0 | 1 | .000 | 1 | 1 | 0 | 0 | 0 | 0 | 7 | 6 | 29 | 3 | 2 | 0 | 1 | 0 | 3 | 0 | 0 | 3 | 1 | 0 |
| Colborn, James, Milwaukee | 4.28 | 11 | 13 | .458 | 36 | 29 | 6 | 3 | 0 | 1 | 206 | 215 | 879 | 111 | 98 | 18 | 8 | 7 | 65 | 9 | 0 | 79 | 2 | 0 |
| Coleman, Joseph, Detroit | 5.55 | 10 | 18 | .357 | 31 | 31 | 8 | 0 | 0 | 0 | 201 | 234 | 915 | 124 | 124 | 27 | 11 | 5 | 85 | 6 | 5 | 125 | 15 | 1 |
| Corbin, A. Ray, Minnesota | 5.10 | 5 | 5 | .500 | 36 | 11 | 3 | 4 | 0 | 0 | 90 | 105 | 406 | 59 | 51 | 13 | 6 | 8 | 38 | 5 | 1 | 49 | 2 | 1 |
| Cuellar, Miguel, Baltimore° | 3.66 | 14 | 12 | .538 | 36 | 36 | 17 | 0 | 0 | 2 | 256 | 229 | 1034 | 112 | 104 | 17 | 20 | 4 | 84 | 1 | 0 | 105 | 1 | 0 |
| Currence, D. Lafayette, Milwaukee° | 7.58 | 0 | 2 | .000 | 4 | 0 | 0 | 2 | 0 | 0 | 19 | 25 | 94 | 17 | 16 | 1 | 1 | 0 | 14 | 1 | 0 | 7 | 1 | 0 |
| Dal Canton, J. Bruce, Kansas City | 15.00 | 0 | 1 | .000 | 10 | 7 | 0 | 1 | 0 | 0 | 26 | 25 | 56 | 18 | 15 | 2 | 1 | 0 | 7 | 0 | 0 | 8 | 1 | 0 |
| Decker, George, Minnesota | 8.65 | 0 | 3 | .000 | 9 | 2 | 0 | 2 | 0 | 0 | 28 | 30 | 135 | 23 | 25 | 5 | 1 | 0 | 13 | 0 | 0 | 5 | 1 | 0 |
| Dobson, Charles, California | 6.75 | 0 | 2 | .000 | 33 | 9 | 2 | 1 | 0 | 0 | 208 | 205 | 129 | 26 | 21 | 21 | 6 | 1 | 83 | 2 | 0 | 14 | 4 | 0 |
| Dobson, Patrick, New York | 4.07 | 11 | 14 | .440 | 30 | 7 | 7 | 3 | 0 | 0 | 208 | 205 | 886 | 110 | 94 | 21 | 10 | 8 | 83 | 10 | 3 | 129 | 2 | 0 |
| Drago, Richard, Boston | 3.82 | 5 | 7 | .417 | 40 | 2 | 0 | 34 | 15 | 0 | 73 | 69 | 313 | 31 | 31 | 6 | 5 | 2 | 31 | 7 | 1 | 43 | 4 | 2 |
| Eckersley, Dennis, Cleveland | 2.60 | 13 | 7 | .650 | 34 | 24 | 6 | 4 | 0 | 2 | 187 | 147 | 794 | 61 | 54 | 16 | 4 | 6 | 90 | 8 | 7 | 152 | 6 | 2 |
| Figueroa, Eduardo, California | 2.90 | 16 | 13 | .552 | 33 | 32 | 16 | 1 | 0 | 0 | 245 | 213 | 1014 | 96 | 79 | 14 | 5 | 5 | 84 | 6 | 1 | 139 | 2 | 0 |
| Fingers, Roland, Oakland | 2.98 | 10 | 6 | .625 | 75 | 0 | 0 | 59 | 24 | 0 | 127 | 111 | 493 | 57 | 42 | 4 | 11 | 5 | 33 | 6 | 0 | 115 | 6 | 0 |
| Fitzmorris, Alan, Kansas City | 3.57 | 16 | 12 | .571 | 35 | 35 | 11 | 0 | 0 | 1 | 242 | 239 | 1010 | 104 | 96 | 16 | 6 | 6 | 76 | 4 | 0 | 78 | 8 | 0 |
| Flanagan, Michael K., Baltimore° | 2.70 | 0 | 0 | .000 | 2 | 0 | 0 | 0 | 0 | 0 | 10 | 11 | 42 | 4 | 3 | 1 | 0 | 0 | 6 | 1 | 0 | 7 | 0 | 0 |
| Forster, Terry, Chicago° | 2.19 | 3 | 4 | .429 | 17 | 1 | 0 | 12 | 24 | 0 | 37 | 30 | 155 | 12 | 9 | 0 | 4 | 4 | 24 | 6 | 1 | 32 | 2 | 0 |
| Foucault, Steven, Texas | 4.12 | 8 | 5 | .615 | 59 | 0 | 0 | 40 | 10 | 0 | 96 | 96 | 463 | 57 | 49 | 10 | 12 | 3 | 55 | 14 | 3 | 56 | 2 | 0 |
| Garland, Wayne, Baltimore | 3.72 | 2 | 5 | .286 | 29 | 1 | 1 | 14 | 4 | 0 | 87 | 80 | 359 | 37 | 36 | 7 | 4 | 6 | 33 | 15 | 0 | 46 | 2 | 0 |
| Gideon, James, Texas | 7.50 | 0 | 2 | .000 | 1 | 1 | 0 | 0 | 0 | 0 | 6 | 11 | 29 | 8 | 5 | 1 | 0 | 0 | 5 | 0 | 0 | 2 | 1 | 0 |
| Glynn, Edward, Detroit° | 4.20 | 0 | 0 | .000 | 3 | 1 | 0 | 0 | 0 | 0 | 15 | 11 | 59 | 9 | 7 | 1 | 0 | 1 | 8 | 0 | 0 | 8 | 1 | 0 |
| Gogolewski, William, Chicago | 5.24 | 0 | 2 | .000 | 19 | 0 | 0 | 10 | 0 | 0 | 55 | 61 | 245 | 35 | 32 | 5 | 2 | 0 | 28 | 3 | 0 | 37 | 7 | 0 |
| Goltz, David, Minnesota | 3.67 | 14 | 14 | .500 | 32 | 32 | 15 | 0 | 0 | 0 | 243 | 235 | 1015 | 112 | 99 | 18 | 8 | 6 | 72 | 6 | 2 | 128 | 12 | 0 |
| Gossage, Richard, Chicago | 1.84 | 9 | 8 | .529 | 62 | 0 | 0 | 49 | 26 | 0 | 142 | 99 | 582 | 57 | 29 | 3 | 15 | 5 | 70 | 15 | 0 | 130 | 10 | 3 |
| Grilli, Stephen, Detroit | 1.29 | 0 | 0 | .000 | 3 | 0 | 0 | 3 | 0 | 0 | 7 | 3 | 29 | 2 | 1 | 1 | 0 | 0 | 6 | 0 | 0 | 3 | 1 | 0 |
| Grimsley, Ross, Baltimore° | 4.07 | 10 | 13 | .435 | 35 | 32 | 8 | 3 | 0 | 0 | 197 | 210 | 822 | 95 | 89 | 29 | 9 | 4 | 47 | 1 | 0 | 89 | 3 | 0 |
| Guidry, Ronald, New York° | 3.38 | 0 | 1 | .000 | 10 | 0 | 0 | 6 | 0 | 0 | 16 | 15 | 69 | 6 | 6 | 0 | 5 | 0 | 9 | 0 | 1 | 15 | 1 | 0 |
| Gura, Lawrence, New York° | 3.52 | 7 | 8 | .467 | 26 | 20 | 5 | 1 | 0 | 0 | 151 | 173 | 640 | 65 | 59 | 13 | 8 | 3 | 41 | 3 | 0 | 65 | 1 | 5 |
| Hamilton, David, 11 Oak-30 Chi° | 3.26 | 7 | 7 | .500 | 41 | 1 | 0 | 27 | 6 | 0 | 105 | 118 | 458 | 65 | 38 | 6 | 5 | 2 | 28 | 2 | 0 | 71 | 7 | 0 |
| Hands, William, Texas | 4.01 | 6 | 7 | .462 | 18 | 15 | 4 | 2 | 0 | 0 | 110 | 118 | 469 | 58 | 49 | 12 | 1 | 1 | 27 | 1 | 0 | 67 | 1 | 0 |
| Hargan, Steven, Texas | 3.81 | 9 | 10 | .474 | 33 | 26 | 8 | 0 | 0 | 0 | 189 | 203 | 822 | 96 | 80 | 17 | 11 | 5 | 62 | 7 | 6 | 93 | 12 | 0 |
| Harrison, Roric, Cleveland | 4.79 | 7 | 7 | .500 | 19 | 18 | 4 | 0 | 0 | 0 | 126 | 137 | 559 | 80 | 67 | 9 | 4 | 4 | 46 | 4 | 2 | 52 | 5 | 0 |
| Hassler, Andrew, California° | 5.95 | 3 | 12 | .200 | 30 | 18 | 3 | 6 | 0 | 0 | 133 | 158 | 597 | 94 | 88 | 12 | 10 | 5 | 53 | 7 | 0 | 46 | 10 | 0 |
| Hausman, Thomas, Milwaukee | 4.10 | 3 | 2 | .600 | 29 | 9 | 1 | 5 | 0 | 0 | 112 | 110 | 492 | 57 | 51 | 9 | 2 | 9 | 47 | 0 | 6 | 82 | 5 | 0 |
| Hiller, John, Detroit° | 2.15 | 1 | 0 | 1.000 | 36 | 0 | 0 | 34 | 14 | 0 | 71 | 52 | 295 | 20 | 17 | 6 | 7 | 1 | 36 | 6 | 0 | 87 | 1 | 0 |
| Hinton, Richard, Chicago° | 4.86 | 0 | 1 | .000 | 15 | 0 | 0 | 6 | 0 | 0 | 41 | 41 | 170 | 25 | 22 | 3 | 2 | 2 | 22 | 4 | 0 | 30 | 6 | 0 |
| Hockenbery, Charles, California | 5.27 | 1 | 0 | 1.000 | 16 | 4 | 0 | 6 | 0 | 0 | 41 | 48 | 185 | 27 | 24 | 16 | 1 | 1 | 19 | 1 | 0 | 15 | 2 | 0 |
| Holtzman, Kenneth, Oakland° | 3.15 | 18 | 14 | .563 | 39 | 38 | 13 | 0 | 0 | 2 | 266 | 217 | 1110 | 91 | 93 | 16 | 8 | 8 | 108 | 7 | 1 | 122 | 6 | 0 |
| Hood, Donald, Cleveland° | 4.40 | 6 | 10 | .375 | 29 | 19 | 2 | 2 | 0 | 0 | 135 | 136 | 572 | 76 | 66 | 16 | 5 | 0 | 57 | 6 | 0 | 51 | 6 | 0 |
| Hudson, Charles, California° | 9.00 | 0 | 2 | .000 | 3 | 3 | 0 | 0 | 0 | 0 | 6 | 6 | 29 | 6 | 6 | 0 | 3 | 0 | 4 | 0 | 0 | 0 | 5 | 0 |
| Hughes, James, Minnesota | 3.82 | 16 | 14 | .533 | 37 | 34 | 12 | 1 | 0 | 2 | 250 | 241 | 1100 | 119 | 106 | 17 | 11 | 7 | 127 | 13 | 0 | 130 | 10 | 2 |
| Hunter, James, New York | 2.58 | 23 | 14 | .622 | 39 | 39 | 30 | 0 | 0 | 7 | 328 | 248 | 1294 | 107 | 94 | 25 | 7 | 6 | 83 | 0 | 3 | 177 | 7 | 0 |
| Jackson, Grant, Baltimore° | 3.38 | 4 | 3 | .571 | 41 | 0 | 0 | 26 | 7 | 0 | 48 | 21 | 202 | 18 | 18 | 3 | 3 | 1 | 21 | 1 | 0 | 39 | 4 | 5 |
| Jefferson, Jesse, 4 Balt-22 Chi... | 4.93 | 5 | 11 | .313 | 26 | 21 | 1 | 4 | 0 | 0 | 115 | 105 | 538 | 72 | 63 | 10 | 7 | 4 | 102 | 2 | 2 | 71 | 5 | 2 |

*Throws lefthanded.

| Pitcher and Club | ERA | W | L | Pct. | G | GS | CG | GF | Sv | ShO | IP | H | BFP | R | ER | HR | SH | SF | Tot. BB | Int. BB | HB | SO | WP | Bk |
|---|---|---|---|---|---|---|---|---|---|---|---|---|---|---|---|---|---|---|---|---|---|---|---|---|
| Jenkins, Ferguson, Texas | 3.93 | 17 | 18 | .486 | 37 | 37 | 22 | 0 | 0 | 0 | 270 | 261 | 1119 | 130 | 118 | 37 | 9 | 2 | 56 | 7 | 9 | 157 | 3 | 0 |
| Johnson, David C., Baltimore | 4.00 | 1 | 1 | .000 | 6 | 0 | 0 | 3 | 0 | 0 | 9 | 8 | 41 | 4 | 4 | 0 | 2 | 2 | 7 | 1 | 1 | 4 | 1 | 0 |
| Johnson, Thomas R., Minnesota | 4.15 | 0 | 2 | .333 | 18 | 0 | 0 | 12 | 3 | 0 | 39 | 40 | 179 | 23 | 18 | 4 | 2 | 0 | 21 | 4 | 1 | 17 | 0 | 2 |
| Kaat, James, Chicago* | 3.11 | 20 | 14 | .588 | 43 | 41 | 12 | 0 | 0 | 1 | 304 | 321 | 1279 | 121 | 105 | 20 | 11 | 10 | 77 | 4 | 2 | 142 | 1 | 0 |
| Kekich, Michael, Texas* | 3.77 | 1 | 0 | .000 | 23 | 7 | 0 | 8 | 2 | 0 | 72 | 60 | 311 | 31 | 30 | 5 | 6 | 0 | 45 | 3 | 1 | 55 | 3 | 1 |
| Kern, James, Cleveland | 3.75 | 1 | 2 | .333 | 13 | 7 | 1 | 2 | 0 | 0 | 84 | 85 | 356 | 38 | 35 | 5 | 6 | 0 | 28 | 3 | 0 | 49 | 5 | 1 |
| Kirkwood, Donald, California | 4.50 | 6 | 5 | .545 | 44 | 2 | 0 | 27 | 7 | 0 | 84 | 84 | 359 | 38 | 38 | 5 | 6 | 0 | 28 | 3 | 0 | 49 | 0 | 0 |
| Knapp, R. Christian, Chicago | 3.11 | 1 | 0 | .000 | 2 | 2 | 0 | 0 | 0 | 0 | 4 | 1 | 12 | 2 | 1 | 0 | 0 | 0 | 4 | 0 | 0 | 3 | 0 | 0 |
| Kravec, Kenneth, Chicago* | 4.50 | 6 | 5 | .000 | 22 | 0 | 0 | 1 | 0 | 0 | 4 | 2 | 22 | 2 | 2 | 0 | 0 | 0 | 8 | 0 | 1 | 1 | 0 | 0 |
| Kreuger, Richard, Boston* | 6.75 | 0 | 0 | .000 | 2 | 0 | 0 | 0 | 0 | 0 | 4 | 4 | 16 | 3 | 3 | 0 | 0 | 0 | 4 | 0 | 0 | 1 | 0 | 0 |
| Kucek, John, Chicago | 4.50 | 0 | 0 | .000 | 2 | 2 | 0 | 0 | 0 | 0 | 4 | 9 | 22 | 3 | 2 | 0 | 0 | 0 | 4 | 0 | 1 | 1 | 1 | 0 |
| LaGrow, Lerrin, Detroit | 4.39 | 7 | 14 | .333 | 32 | 26 | 7 | 4 | 1 | 0 | 164 | 183 | 736 | 105 | 80 | 15 | 6 | 6 | 66 | 5 | 1 | 75 | 2 | 1 |
| Lange, Richard, California | 5.21 | 4 | 6 | .400 | 30 | 8 | 1 | 7 | 1 | 0 | 102 | 119 | 468 | 70 | 59 | 12 | 6 | 0 | 53 | 3 | 1 | 45 | 5 | 0 |
| LaRoche, David, Cleveland* | 2.20 | 5 | 3 | .625 | 61 | 0 | 0 | 41 | 17 | 0 | 82 | 61 | 359 | 26 | 20 | 2 | 10 | 4 | 57 | 8 | 0 | 94 | 3 | 1 |
| Lee, William, Boston* | 3.95 | 17 | 9 | .654 | 41 | 34 | 17 | 4 | 0 | 0 | 260 | 274 | 1093 | 123 | 114 | 20 | 7 | 7 | 69 | 1 | 3 | 78 | 1 | 1 |
| Lemanczyk, David, Detroit | 4.46 | 2 | 7 | .222 | 26 | 8 | 1 | 8 | 0 | 0 | 109 | 120 | 487 | 60 | 54 | 8 | 4 | 4 | 46 | 3 | 1 | 67 | 6 | 0 |
| Leonard, Dennis, Kansas City | 3.78 | 15 | 7 | .682 | 32 | 30 | 8 | 1 | 0 | 2 | 212 | 212 | 916 | 98 | 89 | 18 | 11 | 6 | 90 | 0 | 0 | 146 | 4 | 1 |
| Lindblad, Paul, Oakland* | 2.73 | 9 | 1 | .900 | 68 | 0 | 0 | 20 | 7 | 0 | 122 | 105 | 499 | 43 | 37 | 6 | 4 | 7 | 43 | 10 | 0 | 58 | 3 | 1 |
| Littell, Mark, Kansas City | 3.75 | 5 | 4 | .333 | 7 | 3 | 1 | 1 | 0 | 0 | 24 | 19 | 102 | 11 | 10 | 1 | 4 | 0 | 15 | 1 | 0 | 19 | 1 | 1 |
| Lolich, Michael, Detroit* | 3.77 | 12 | 18 | .400 | 32 | 32 | 19 | 0 | 0 | 0 | 241 | 260 | 1016 | 114 | 101 | 19 | 11 | 8 | 64 | 5 | 5 | 139 | 7 | 0 |
| Lyle, Albert, New York* | 3.13 | 7 | 7 | .417 | 49 | 0 | 0 | 37 | 6 | 0 | 89 | 94 | 387 | 34 | 31 | 1 | 4 | 3 | 36 | 5 | 5 | 65 | 5 | 0 |
| Makowski, Thomas, Detroit* | 5.00 | 1 | 0 | .000 | 3 | 0 | 0 | 0 | 0 | 0 | 9 | 10 | 48 | 5 | 5 | 2 | 2 | 0 | 9 | 0 | 0 | 3 | 0 | 0 |
| Martinez, Felix, New York* | 2.68 | 0 | 0 | .333 | 23 | 0 | 0 | 13 | 8 | 0 | 37 | 27 | 167 | 15 | 11 | 2 | 2 | 1 | 32 | 3 | 0 | 20 | 2 | 0 |
| May, Rudolph, New York* | 3.06 | 14 | 12 | .538 | 32 | 31 | 13 | 0 | 0 | 0 | 212 | 179 | 894 | 87 | 72 | 9 | 11 | 0 | 99 | 1 | 1 | 145 | 5 | 0 |
| McClure, Robert, Kansas City* | 0.00 | 1 | 0 | 1.000 | 12 | 0 | 0 | 4 | 0 | 0 | 15 | 4 | 66 | 0 | 0 | 0 | 8 | 0 | 14 | 1 | 3 | 15 | 0 | 0 |
| McDaniel, Lyndall, Kansas City | 4.15 | 1 | 0 | .833 | 40 | 0 | 0 | 21 | 1 | 0 | 66 | 66 | 333 | 40 | 36 | 25 | 0 | 3 | 24 | 8 | 1 | 40 | 0 | 0 |
| Medich, George, New York | 3.51 | 16 | 16 | 1.000 | 38 | 37 | 15 | 0 | 0 | 1 | 272 | 271 | 1121 | 115 | 106 | 3 | 6 | 4 | 72 | 4 | 3 | 132 | 7 | 0 |
| Merritt, James, Texas* | 0.00 | 6 | 3 | .000 | 5 | 0 | 0 | 4 | 0 | 0 | 15 | 12 | 15 | 14 | 0 | 0 | 0 | 0 | 0 | 0 | 0 | 3 | 2 | 0 |
| Miller, Dyar, Baltimore | 2.74 | 6 | 3 | .667 | 30 | 0 | 0 | 21 | 8 | 0 | 46 | 32 | 184 | 14 | 14 | 3 | 4 | 1 | 16 | 1 | 0 | 33 | 0 | 0 |
| Mingori, Stephen, Kansas City* | 2.52 | 3 | 0 | .000 | 36 | 0 | 0 | 15 | 2 | 0 | 50 | 42 | 212 | 21 | 14 | 2 | 2 | 0 | 20 | 4 | 0 | 25 | 2 | 0 |
| Mitchell, Craig, Oakland | 11.25 | 3 | 1 | 1.000 | 3 | 0 | 0 | 2 | 0 | 0 | 9 | 18 | 48 | 11 | 5 | 2 | 0 | 1 | 2 | 0 | 0 | 2 | 0 | 0 |
| Mitchell, Paul, Baltimore | 3.63 | 3 | 2 | .667 | 11 | 4 | 1 | 4 | 0 | 0 | 57 | 41 | 224 | 23 | 23 | 8 | 3 | 0 | 19 | 0 | 4 | 31 | 3 | 1 |
| Monge, Isidro, California* | 4.13 | 1 | 0 | .000 | 4 | 2 | 0 | 2 | 0 | 0 | 24 | 21 | 103 | 12 | 11 | 3 | 1 | 0 | 10 | 1 | 1 | 17 | 2 | 1 |
| Moore, Tommy, Texas | 8.14 | 0 | 0 | .000 | 12 | 1 | 0 | 6 | 0 | 0 | 21 | 31 | 103 | 21 | 19 | 1 | 2 | 0 | 12 | 1 | 1 | 15 | 1 | 2 |
| Moret, Rogelio, Boston* | 3.60 | 14 | 3 | .824 | 36 | 16 | 6 | 5 | 1 | 1 | 145 | 132 | 624 | 60 | 58 | 8 | 8 | 3 | 76 | 1 | 0 | 80 | 4 | 0 |
| Murphy, Thomas, Milwaukee | 4.63 | 1 | 9 | .100 | 52 | 0 | 0 | 43 | 20 | 0 | 72 | 85 | 327 | 43 | 37 | 5 | 4 | 1 | 27 | 6 | 0 | 32 | 1 | 0 |
| Norris, Michael, Oakland | 0.00 | 1 | 0 | 1.000 | 10 | 3 | 1 | 1 | 0 | 1 | 21 | 21 | 65 | 7 | 0 | 0 | 2 | 1 | 8 | 0 | 1 | 5 | 2 | 0 |
| Odom, Johnny, 7 Oak-3 Clev | 7.71 | 1 | 9 | .333 | 24 | 1 | 0 | 7 | 0 | 0 | 58 | 57 | 258 | 21 | 18 | 2 | 8 | 1 | 37 | 0 | 1 | 14 | 1 | 0 |
| Osburn, Danny, Chicago | 4.50 | 1 | 2 | 1.000 | 6 | 1 | 0 | 3 | 0 | 0 | 12 | 19 | 61 | 9 | 6 | 2 | 0 | 1 | 9 | 2 | 0 | 38 | 2 | 0 |
| Osburn, L. Patrick, Milwaukee* | 5.25 | 2 | 1 | .000 | 11 | 0 | 0 | 0 | 0 | 0 | 58 | 57 | 258 | 29 | 18 | 2 | 2 | 0 | 19 | 2 | 0 | 9 | 2 | 0 |
| Osteen, Claude, Chicago* | 4.37 | 7 | 16 | .304 | 37 | 37 | 7 | 0 | 0 | 1 | 204 | 237 | 919 | 110 | 99 | 16 | 11 | 7 | 92 | 1 | 0 | 63 | 3 | 1 |
| Otten, James, Chicago | 7.20 | 0 | 1 | 1.000 | 4 | 0 | 0 | 2 | 0 | 0 | 16 | 23 | 26 | 16 | 4 | 1 | 1 | 1 | 10 | 2 | 0 | 3 | 1 | 1 |
| Pactwa, Joseph, California* | 3.94 | 1 | 0 | .000 | 13 | 0 | 0 | 4 | 0 | 0 | 31 | 30 | 135 | 15 | 14 | 0 | 1 | 0 | 13 | 2 | 0 | 18 | 1 | 0 |
| Pagan, David, New York | 4.06 | 0 | 0 | .000 | 13 | 0 | 0 | 5 | 1 | 0 | 31 | 30 | 135 | 16 | 14 | 4 | 2 | 0 | 13 | 2 | 1 | 18 | 4 | 0 |
| Palmer, James, Baltimore | 2.09 | 23 | 11 | .676 | 39 | 38 | 25 | 0 | 1 | 10 | 323 | 268 | 1268 | 81 | 75 | 20 | 10 | 4 | 80 | 2 | 9 | 193 | 1 | 0 |
| Pattin, Martin, Kansas City | 3.25 | 10 | 10 | .500 | 44 | 15 | 5 | 16 | 5 | 1 | 177 | 173 | 739 | 77 | 64 | 13 | 2 | 5 | 45 | 6 | 3 | 89 | 0 | 0 |

| Pitcher and Club | Pct. | L. | W. | ERA. | G. | GS. | CG. | GF. | Sv. | ShO. | IP. | H. | BFP. | R. | ER. | HR. | SH. | SF. | Tot. BB. | Int. BB. | HB. | SO. | WP. | Bk. |
|---|---|---|---|---|---|---|---|---|---|---|---|---|---|---|---|---|---|---|---|---|---|---|---|---|
| Pazik, Michael, Minnesota° | .000 | 4 | 0 | 8.10 | 5 | 3 | 0 | 0 | 0 | 0 | 20 | 28 | 96 | 20 | 18 | 5 | 1 | 1 | 10 | 0 | 0 | 8 | 1 | 0 |
| Pena, Orlando, California° | .000 | 2 | 0 | 2.08 | 7 | 0 | 0 | 5 | 0 | 0 | 13 | 13 | 55 | 3 | 3 | 0 | 0 | 1 | 8 | 1 | 0 | 4 | 1 | 0 |
| Pentz, Eugene, Detroit | .000 | 2 | 0 | 3.24 | 13 | 0 | 0 | 11 | 0 | 0 | 25 | 27 | 118 | 14 | 9 | 0 | 4 | 2 | 20 | 4 | 0 | 21 | 1 | 0 |
| Perry, Gaylord, 15 Clev-22 Tex | .514 | 17 | 18 | 3.24 | 37 | 37 | 25 | 0 | 0 | 1 | 306 | 277 | 1248 | 127 | 110 | 28 | 11 | 5 | 70 | 8 | 6 | 233 | 5 | 0 |
| Perry, James, 8 Clev-15 Oak | .286 | 10 | 4 | 5.40 | 23 | 17 | 1 | 2 | 0 | 0 | 105 | 107 | 466 | 72 | 63 | 15 | 2 | 4 | 44 | 1 | 4 | 44 | 3 | 0 |
| Perzanowski, Stanley, Texas | .500 | 4 | 4 | 3.00 | 12 | 8 | 2 | 1 | 0 | 0 | 66 | 59 | 274 | 25 | 22 | 5 | 1 | 2 | 25 | 0 | 5 | 26 | 2 | 0 |
| Peterson, Fred, Cleveland° | .636 | 8 | 14 | 3.95 | 25 | 25 | 6 | 0 | 0 | 2 | 146 | 154 | 609 | 64 | 64 | 10 | 3 | 4 | 24 | 0 | 4 | 47 | 0 | 0 |
| Pitlock, Lee, Chicago° | .000 | 0 | 0 | 0.00 | 2 | 0 | 0 | 1 | 0 | 0 | 0 | 0 | 1 | 0 | 0 | 0 | 0 | 0 | 0 | 0 | 0 | 0 | 0 | 0 |
| Pole, Richard, Boston | .400 | 6 | 4 | 4.40 | 18 | 11 | 2 | 3 | 0 | 0 | 90 | 102 | 394 | 46 | 44 | 11 | 3 | 4 | 32 | 0 | 1 | 42 | 4 | 0 |
| Quintana, Luis, California° | .000 | 2 | 0 | 6.43 | 4 | 0 | 0 | 3 | 0 | 0 | 7 | 13 | 39 | 6 | 5 | 1 | 1 | 1 | 6 | 1 | 0 | 5 | 1 | 0 |
| Raich, Eric, Cleveland | .467 | 8 | 7 | 5.52 | 18 | 17 | 0 | 0 | 0 | 0 | 93 | 118 | 415 | 61 | 57 | 12 | 2 | 0 | 31 | 0 | 1 | 34 | 4 | 0 |
| Reynolds, Robert, 7 Bal-21 Det-5 Cle | .000 | 5 | 0 | 5.22 | 33 | 0 | 0 | 21 | 5 | 0 | 50 | 62 | 227 | 33 | 29 | 9 | 7 | 5 | 18 | 2 | 1 | 32 | 5 | 0 |
| Rodriguez, Eduardo, Milwaukee. | 1.000 | 0 | 7 | 3.48 | 43 | 1 | 0 | 24 | 7 | 0 | 88 | 77 | 384 | 37 | 34 | 9 | 9 | 2 | 44 | 7 | 0 | 65 | 2 | 1 |
| Ross, Gary, California | .000 | 1 | 0 | 5.40 | 1 | 1 | 0 | 0 | 0 | 0 | 5 | 5 | 23 | 3 | 3 | 1 | 0 | 0 | 4 | 0 | 0 | 4 | 0 | 0 |
| Ruhle, Vernon, Detroit | .478 | 12 | 11 | 4.03 | 32 | 31 | 8 | 1 | 0 | 1 | 190 | 199 | 830 | 104 | 85 | 17 | 6 | 5 | 65 | 0 | 0 | 67 | 2 | 0 |
| Ryan, L. Nolan, California. | .538 | 12 | 14 | 3.45 | 28 | 28 | 10 | 0 | 0 | 3 | 198 | 152 | 864 | 90 | 76 | 13 | 10 | 7 | 132 | 0 | 7 | 186 | 12 | 0 |
| Sadecki, Raymond, Kansas City° | .000 | 1 | 0 | 3.00 | 5 | 0 | 0 | 2 | 0 | 0 | 6 | 7 | 25 | 2 | 2 | 0 | 0 | 0 | 3 | 0 | 0 | 3 | 0 | 0 |
| Sawyer, Richard, New York° | .286 | 5 | 2 | 3.31 | 17 | 13 | 0 | 2 | 0 | 0 | 68 | 59 | 283 | 34 | 25 | 8 | 6 | 5 | 18 | 5 | 0 | 31 | 1 | 0 |
| Scott, Ralph, California° | .000 | 1 | 0 | 9.00 | 4 | 0 | 0 | 1 | 0 | 0 | 3 | 5 | 18 | 5 | 3 | 0 | 0 | 0 | 3 | 0 | 0 | 3 | 0 | 0 |
| Segui, Diego, Boston | .500 | 5 | 2 | 4.82 | 33 | 0 | 0 | 21 | 6 | 0 | 71 | 71 | 316 | 41 | 38 | 10 | 10 | 3 | 43 | 3 | 1 | 45 | 7 | 0 |
| Sells, David, California | .000 | 1 | 0 | 4.50 | 8 | 0 | 0 | 2 | 0 | 0 | 8 | 9 | 44 | 5 | 4 | 0 | 0 | 0 | 8 | 0 | 0 | 5 | 1 | 0 |
| Siebert, Wilfred, Oakland° | .500 | 4 | 4 | 3.69 | 29 | 13 | 0 | 8 | 0 | 0 | 61 | 60 | 275 | 34 | 25 | 8 | 8 | 2 | 31 | 6 | 1 | 44 | 2 | 0 |
| Singer, William, California | .318 | 15 | 7 | 4.98 | 37 | 33 | 6 | 0 | 0 | 0 | 179 | 171 | 770 | 107 | 99 | 18 | 9 | 5 | 81 | 1 | 6 | 78 | 6 | 1 |
| Slaton, James, Milwaukee | .379 | 18 | 11 | 4.52 | 37 | 35 | 8 | 0 | 0 | 3 | 217 | 238 | 970 | 129 | 109 | 28 | 9 | 5 | 90 | 6 | 2 | 119 | 6 | 0 |
| Splittorff, Paul, Kansas City° | .474 | 10 | 9 | 3.17 | 35 | 18 | 6 | 11 | 2 | 1 | 159 | 156 | 677 | 67 | 56 | 10 | 9 | 0 | 56 | 10 | 1 | 76 | 6 | 0 |
| Sprague, Edward, Milwaukee | .125 | 7 | 1 | 4.70 | 18 | 11 | 3 | 5 | 2 | 0 | 67 | 81 | 320 | 46 | 35 | 5 | 5 | 2 | 40 | 3 | 0 | 21 | 6 | 0 |
| Stoddard, Timothy, Chicago | .000 | 0 | 0 | 9.00 | 4 | 0 | 0 | 2 | 0 | 0 | 1 | 1 | 7 | 1 | 1 | 0 | 0 | 0 | 1 | 0 | 0 | 0 | 0 | 0 |
| Strickland, James, Cleveland° | .000 | 0 | 0 | 1.80 | 4 | 0 | 0 | 2 | 0 | 0 | 5 | 5 | 21 | 2 | 1 | 1 | 1 | 0 | 3 | 1 | 0 | 3 | 0 | 0 |
| Tanana, Frank, California° | .640 | 9 | 16 | 2.63 | 34 | 33 | 16 | 0 | 0 | 7 | 257 | 211 | 1029 | 80 | 75 | 21 | 13 | 4 | 73 | 6 | 7 | 269 | 8 | 1 |
| Thomas, Stanley, Texas | .500 | 4 | 4 | 3.11 | 46 | 0 | 0 | 19 | 3 | 0 | 81 | 72 | 341 | 36 | 28 | 6 | 2 | 1 | 34 | 6 | 0 | 46 | 1 | 0 |
| Throop, George, Kansas City | .000 | 0 | 0 | 4.00 | 7 | 0 | 0 | 3 | 0 | 0 | 9 | 8 | 36 | 8 | 4 | 1 | 1 | 1 | 8 | 2 | 0 | 8 | 0 | 0 |
| Tidrow, Richard, New York | .563 | 7 | 9 | 4.02 | 37 | 35 | 8 | 0 | 0 | 0 | 260 | 262 | 1080 | 126 | 116 | 25 | 7 | 5 | 72 | 4 | 4 | 142 | 4 | 0 |
| Todd, James, Oakland | .727 | 3 | 8 | 2.29 | 58 | 0 | 0 | 23 | 12 | 0 | 122 | 104 | 489 | 37 | 31 | 4 | 6 | 3 | 31 | 3 | 3 | 38 | 2 | 0 |
| Torrez, Michael, Baltimore | .690 | 9 | 20 | 3.06 | 36 | 36 | 16 | 0 | 0 | 5 | 271 | 238 | 1144 | 103 | 92 | 15 | 7 | 6 | 133 | 5 | 11 | 119 | 10 | 0 |
| Travers, William, Milwaukee° | .500 | 8 | 8 | 4.30 | 28 | 23 | 3 | 2 | 1 | 0 | 136 | 130 | 594 | 65 | 65 | 11 | 9 | 6 | 59 | 3 | 2 | 57 | 4 | 0 |
| Umbarger, James, Texas° | .533 | 7 | 8 | 4.12 | 28 | 16 | 2 | 3 | 1 | 0 | 131 | 134 | 561 | 63 | 60 | 15 | 9 | 0 | 59 | 9 | 1 | 50 | 2 | 0 |
| Upshaw, Cecil, Chicago° | .667 | 3 | 6 | 3.26 | 36 | 0 | 0 | 14 | 4 | 0 | 47 | 49 | 208 | 19 | 17 | 5 | 1 | 0 | 27 | 7 | 1 | 22 | 3 | 0 |
| Vuckovich, Peter, Chicago° | 1.000 | 0 | 1 | 13.50 | 4 | 2 | 0 | 1 | 0 | 0 | 10 | 17 | 52 | 15 | 15 | 0 | 1 | 0 | 7 | 0 | 1 | 5 | 0 | 0 |
| Waits, M. Richard, Cleveland° | .750 | 2 | 6 | 2.96 | 16 | 9 | 3 | 2 | 0 | 1 | 70 | 57 | 285 | 25 | 23 | 0 | 1 | 0 | 25 | 1 | 0 | 34 | 0 | 0 |
| Walker, R. Thomas, Detroit. | .273 | 8 | 3 | 4.46 | 36 | 9 | 1 | 17 | 6 | 0 | 115 | 116 | 505 | 69 | 57 | 16 | 9 | 0 | 40 | 0 | 1 | 60 | 4 | 0 |
| Wallace, Michael, New York° | .000 | 0 | 0 | 15.75 | 3 | 0 | 0 | 1 | 0 | 0 | 4 | 11 | 25 | 7 | 7 | 0 | 0 | 0 | 7 | 0 | 0 | 1 | 1 | 0 |
| Wiley, Mark, Minnesota. | .250 | 3 | 1 | 6.00 | 15 | 3 | 0 | 6 | 0 | 0 | 39 | 46 | 172 | 30 | 26 | 4 | 1 | 1 | 13 | 1 | 1 | 15 | 0 | 0 |
| Willoughby, James, Boston | .714 | 2 | 5 | 3.56 | 24 | 3 | 1 | 15 | 8 | 0 | 48 | 46 | 208 | 25 | 19 | 6 | 2 | 2 | 16 | 3 | 2 | 29 | 2 | 0 |

| Pitcher and Club | ERA | W | L | Pct. | G | GS | CG | GF | Sv. | ShO | IP | H | BFP | R | ER | HR | SH | SF | Tot.BB | Int.BB | HB | SO | WP | Bk. |
|---|---|---|---|---|---|---|---|---|---|---|---|---|---|---|---|---|---|---|---|---|---|---|---|---|
| Wise, Richard, Boston | 3.95 | 19 | 12 | .613 | 35 | 35 | 17 | 0 | 0 | 1 | 255 | 262 | 1091 | 126 | 112 | 34 | 10 | 9 | 72 | 1 | 4 | 141 | 1 | 1 |
| Wood, Wilbur, Chicago° | 4.11 | 16 | 20 | .444 | 43 | 43 | 14 | 5 | 0 | 2 | 291 | 309 | 1245 | 148 | 133 | 26 | 8 | 6 | 92 | 5 | 5 | 140 | 6 | 2 |
| Wright, Clyde, Texas° | 4.45 | 4 | 6 | .400 | 25 | 14 | 1 | 5 | 0 | 0 | 93 | 105 | 423 | 56 | 46 | 7 | 10 | 8 | 47 | 3 | 1 | 32 | 3 | 1 |

NOTE—Following pitchers combined to pitch shutout games: Boston (1)—Moret and Pattin; Milwaukee (2)—Broberg and Murphy, Travers, Rodriguez and Willoughby; California (6)—Tanana and Kirkwood 2, Lange, Hassler and Kirkwood, Ryan and Brewer, Singer and Scott, Pactwa and Brewer; Chicago (4)—Kaat, Gossage and Forster, Jefferson and Hamilton, Osteen and Gossage 2; Detroit (2)—Ruhle and Hiller, Coleman and Hiller; Kansas City (1)—Bird, McClure, Mingori and Pattin; Milwaukee (2)—Broberg and Murphy, Travers, Rodriguez and Murphy; Oakland (3)—Siebert and Todd, Holtzman, Fingers and Lindblad; Blue, Abbott, Lindblad and Fingers; Texas (2)—Hands, Umbarger and Foucault, Hargan and Umbarger.

## PITCHERS WITH TWO OR MORE CLUBS

(Alphabetically Arranged With Pitcher's First Club on Top)

| Pitcher and Club | ERA | W | L | Pct. | G | GS | CG | GF | Sv. | ShO | IP | H | BFP | R | ER | HR | SH | SF | Tot.BB | Int.BB | HB | SO | WP | Bk. |
|---|---|---|---|---|---|---|---|---|---|---|---|---|---|---|---|---|---|---|---|---|---|---|---|---|
| Bahnsen, Chi. | 6.01 | 2 | 3 | .400 | 12 | 12 | 2 | 0 | 0 | 0 | 67⅓ | 78 | 313 | 49 | 45 | 9 | 2 | 0 | 40 | 0 | 3 | 31 | 1 | 0 |
| Bahnsen, Oak. | 3.24 | 4 | 7 | .462 | 21 | 16 | 2 | 4 | 0 | 0 | 100 | 88 | 421 | 42 | 36 | 2 | 1 | 0 | 37 | 1 | 1 | 49 | 9 | 0 |
| Bibby, Tex. | 5.00 | 2 | 6 | .250 | 12 | 12 | 4 | 0 | 1 | 0 | 68⅓ | 73 | 302 | 41 | 38 | 2 | 1 | 5 | 28 | 0 | 1 | 31 | 5 | 0 |
| Bibby, Clev. | 3.20 | 5 | 9 | .357 | 24 | 24 | 2 | 5 | 1 | 0 | 112⅔ | 99 | 479 | 48 | 40 | 7 | 3 | 2 | 50 | 3 | 0 | 62 | 3 | 0 |
| Bosman, Clev. | 4.08 | 0 | 2 | .000 | 6 | 3 | 0 | 3 | 0 | 0 | 28⅔ | 33 | 127 | 17 | 13 | 3 | 1 | 3 | 8 | 1 | 3 | 11 | 0 | 0 |
| Bosman, Oak. | 3.52 | 11 | 4 | .733 | 22 | 21 | 2 | 0 | 0 | 0 | 122⅔ | 112 | 500 | 50 | 48 | 12 | 3 | 1 | 24 | 3 | 3 | 42 | 1 | 0 |
| Brown, Tex. | 4.22 | 5 | 5 | .500 | 17 | 7 | 3 | 4 | 1 | 0 | 70⅓ | 70 | 305 | 37 | 33 | 7 | 4 | 4 | 35 | 2 | 0 | 35 | 4 | 0 |
| Brown, Clev. | 4.28 | 1 | 2 | .333 | 25 | 3 | 1 | 14 | 0 | 0 | 69⅓ | 72 | 298 | 40 | 33 | 9 | 3 | 5 | 29 | 6 | 0 | 41 | 2 | 0 |
| Hamilton, Oak. | 4.04 | 1 | 2 | .333 | 11 | 4 | 0 | 4 | 0 | 0 | 35⅔ | 42 | 166 | 19 | 16 | 4 | 2 | 1 | 18 | 0 | 0 | 20 | 0 | 0 |
| Hamilton, Clev. | 2.84 | 6 | 5 | .545 | 30 | 1 | 0 | 23 | 6 | 0 | 69⅔ | 63 | 292 | 23 | 22 | 4 | 6 | 1 | 29 | 2 | 0 | 51 | 5 | 2 |
| Jefferson, Balt. | 2.35 | 0 | 2 | .000 | 4 | 2 | 1 | 1 | 0 | 0 | 7⅔ | 5 | 33 | 9 | 2 | 2 | 0 | 0 | 8 | 0 | 2 | 4 | 1 | 0 |
| Jefferson, Chi. | 5.10 | 5 | 9 | .357 | 22 | 21 | 1 | 0 | 0 | 0 | 107⅔ | 100 | 505 | 69 | 61 | 10 | 4 | 4 | 94 | 2 | 1 | 67 | 5 | 2 |
| Odom, Oak. | 12.27 | 0 | 2 | .000 | 7 | 2 | 0 | 1 | 0 | 0 | 11 | 19 | 59 | 15 | 15 | 1 | 1 | 0 | 11 | 1 | 1 | 4 | 1 | 0 |
| Odom, Clev. | 2.61 | 1 | 0 | 1.000 | 3 | 1 | 0 | 1 | 0 | 0 | 10⅓ | 4 | 42 | 4 | 3 | 1 | 0 | 0 | 8 | 0 | 0 | 10 | 0 | 0 |
| G. Perry, Clev. | 3.55 | 6 | 9 | .400 | 15 | 15 | 10 | 0 | 0 | 0 | 121⅔ | 120 | 509 | 57 | 48 | 16 | 5 | 1 | 34 | 5 | 3 | 85 | 2 | 0 |
| G. Perry, Tex. | 3.03 | 12 | 8 | .600 | 22 | 22 | 15 | 0 | 0 | 4 | 184 | 157 | 739 | 70 | 62 | 12 | 6 | 2 | 36 | 1 | 3 | 148 | 3 | 0 |
| J. Perry, Clev. | 6.69 | 1 | 6 | .143 | 8 | 6 | 0 | 0 | 0 | 0 | 37⅔ | 46 | 170 | 34 | 28 | 8 | 3 | 1 | 18 | 0 | 1 | 11 | 0 | 0 |
| J. Perry, Oak. | 4.66 | 3 | 4 | .429 | 15 | 11 | 2 | 2 | 0 | 0 | 67⅔ | 61 | 296 | 43 | 35 | 7 | 1 | 5 | 26 | 5 | 0 | 33 | 3 | 0 |
| Reynolds, Balt | 9.00 | 0 | 1 | .000 | 1 | 0 | 0 | 0 | 0 | 0 | 6 | 11 | 29 | 6 | 6 | 1 | 2 | 1 | 4 | 0 | 0 | 1 | 1 | 0 |
| Reynolds, Det | 4.67 | 0 | 2 | .000 | 21 | 0 | 0 | 14 | 3 | 0 | 34⅔ | 40 | 157 | 20 | 18 | 8 | 1 | 2 | 26 | 7 | 1 | 26 | 1 | 1 |
| Reynolds, Clev. | 4.66 | 0 | 2 | .000 | 5 | 0 | 0 | 3 | 2 | 0 | 9⅔ | 11 | 41 | 7 | 5 | 0 | 0 | 0 | 3 | 1 | 0 | 5 | 1 | 2 |

# 1975 A. L. Pitching Against Each Club

### BALTIMORE—90-69

| Pitcher | Bos. W—L | Cal. W—L | Chi. W—L | Clev. W—L | Det. W—L | K.C. W—L | Mil. W—L | Minn. W—L | N.Y. W—L | Oak. W—L | Tex. W—L | Totals W—L |
|---|---|---|---|---|---|---|---|---|---|---|---|---|
| Alexander .. | 3—2 | 1—0 | 1—1 | 0—2 | 1—1 | 1—0 | 1—0 | 0—0 | 0—0 | 0—2 | 0—0 | 8— 8 |
| Cuellar .... | 1—0 | 3—1 | 1—1 | 2—2 | 1—1 | 1—6 | 2—1 | 1—3 | 1—2 | 0—0 | 1—1 | 14—12 |
| Flanagan .. | 0—0 | 0—0 | 0—0 | 0—0 | 0—0 | 0—0 | 0—0 | 0—0 | 0—1 | 0—0 | 0—0 | 0— 1 |
| Garland ... | 0—0 | 0—1 | 0—0 | 0—0 | 0—1 | 0—1 | 2—0 | 0—0 | 0—0 | 0—0 | 0—2 | 2— 5 |
| Grimsley .. | 0—0 | 0—2 | 1—1 | 1—2 | 2—1 | 0—1 | 1—0 | 2—1 | 2—1 | 1—3 | 0—1 | 10—13 |
| Jackson .... | 1—0 | 0—0 | 0—3 | 0—0 | 0—0 | 1—0 | 0—0 | 1—0 | 1—1 | 0—0 | 0—1 | 4— 3 |
| Jefferson .. | 0—1 | 0—0 | 0—0 | 0—1 | 0—0 | 0—6 | 0—0 | 0—0 | 0—0 | 0—0 | 0—0 | 0— 2 |
| Johnson .... | 0—0 | 0—0 | 0—0 | 0—1 | 0—0 | 0—0 | 0—0 | 0—0 | 0—0 | 0—0 | 0—0 | 0— 1 |
| Miller ..... | 0—1 | 0—0 | 0—0 | 1—0 | 1—0 | 0—1 | 2—0 | 0—0 | 0—0 | 0—1 | 2—0 | 6— 3 |
| Mitchell ... | 0—0 | 0—0 | 0—0 | 0—0 | 1—0 | 0—0 | 0—0 | 0—0 | 1—0 | 1—0 | 0—0 | 3— 0 |
| Palmer .... | 2—3 | 2—1 | 3—0 | 3—0 | 2—0 | 2—2 | 3—1 | 1—0 | 3—3 | 0—1 | 2—0 | 23—11 |
| Reynolds ... | 0—0 | 0—0 | 0—0 | 0—0 | 0—0 | 0—0 | 0—1 | 0—0 | 0—0 | 0—0 | 0—0 | 0— 1 |
| Torrez ..... | 2—2 | 0—1 | 1—0 | 3—0 | 4—0 | 2—0 | 3—1 | 1—2 | 0—2 | 2—1 | 2—0 | 20— 9 |
| Totals .. | 9—9 | 6—6 | 7—4 | 10—8 | 12—4 | 7—5 | 14—4 | 6—6 | 8—10 | 4—8 | 7—5 | 90—69 |

No Decisions—None.

### BOSTON—95-65

| Pitcher | Balt. W—L | Cal. W—L | Chi. W—L | Clev. W—L | Det. W—L | K.C. W—L | Mil. W—L | Minn. W—L | N.Y. W—L | Oak. W—L | Tex. W—L | Totals W—L |
|---|---|---|---|---|---|---|---|---|---|---|---|---|
| Barr ....... | 0—0 | 0—0 | 0—0 | 0—1 | 0—0 | 0—0 | 0—0 | 0—0 | 0—0 | 0—0 | 0—0 | 0— 1 |
| Burton .... | 0—0 | 0—0 | 0—1 | 0—0 | 0—0 | 0—0 | 0—0 | 0—0 | 0—0 | 0—0 | 1—0 | 1— 2 |
| Cleveland .. | 1—2 | 0—2 | 0—0 | 2—1 | 2—0 | 0—1 | 2—1 | 1—0 | 2—1 | 1—1 | 2—0 | 13— 9 |
| Drago ..... | 1—0 | 0—0 | 0—0 | 0—1 | 1—0 | 0—0 | 0—0 | 0—0 | 0—0 | 0—1 | 0—0 | 2— 2 |
| Lee ........ | 0—0 | 2—1 | 1—1 | 3—1 | 1—1 | 3—1 | 0—3 | 2—0 | 2—1 | 2—0 | 1—0 | 17— 9 |
| Moret ...... | 0—0 | 1—0 | 4—0 | 0—0 | 2—0 | 0—0 | 2—0 | 2—0 | 3—1 | 0—1 | 0—1 | 14— 3 |
| Pole ....... | 2—1 | 0—0 | 1—0 | 0—2 | 1—0 | 0—1 | 0—1 | 0—1 | 0—0 | 0—0 | 0—0 | 4— 6 |
| Segui ...... | 0—0 | 0—0 | 0—0 | 0—0 | 0—0 | 0—0 | 0—2 | 1—1 | 0—0 | 0—2 | 0—0 | 2— 5 |
| Tiant ...... | 3—3 | 1—2 | 1—0 | 2—2 | 2—2 | 2—2 | 1—0 | 2—0 | 1—1 | 2—0 | 1—2 | 18—14 |
| Willoughby . | 0—1 | 0—0 | 1—0 | 0—0 | 1—1 | 0—0 | 3—0 | 0—0 | 0—0 | 0—0 | 0—0 | 5— 2 |
| Wise ....... | 1—2 | 2—1 | 0—2 | 0—0. | 3—1 | 2—0 | 2—1 | 2—0 | 3—1 | 1—1 | 3—1 | 19—12 |
| Totals .. | 9—9 | 6—6 | 8—4 | 7—11 | 13—5 | 7—5 | 10—8 | 10—2 | 11—5 | 6—6 | 8—4 | 95—65 |

### CALIFORNIA—72-89

| Pitcher | Balt. W—L | Bos. W—L | Chi. W—L | Clev. W—L | Det. W—L | K.C. W—L | Mil. W—L | Minn. W—L | N.Y. W—L | Oak. W—L | Tex. W—L | Totals W—L |
|---|---|---|---|---|---|---|---|---|---|---|---|---|
| Brewer ..... | 0—0 | 0—0 | 0—0 | 0—0 | 0—0 | 0—0 | 0—0 | 0—0 | 0—0 | 0—0 | 1—0 | 1— 0 |
| Dobson .... | 0—0 | 0—0 | 0—0 | 0—0 | 0—0 | 0—1 | 0—0 | 0—1 | 0—0 | 0—0 | 0—0 | 0— 2 |
| Figueroa ... | 1—2 | 3—0 | 2—0 | 0—1 | 2—1 | 1—3 | 1—1 | 1—1 | 1—1 | 2—2 | 2—1 | 16—13 |
| Hassler .... | 0—0 | 0—2 | 1—2 | 0—0 | 0—1 | 1—0 | 0—1 | 0—2 | 0—1 | 1—1 | 0—2 | 3—12 |
| Hockenbery . | 0—0 | 0—1 | 0—1 | 0—0 | 0—2 | 0—0 | 0—1 | 0—0 | 0—0 | 0—0 | 0—0 | 0— 5 |
| Hudson .... | 0—0 | 0—0 | 0—0 | 0—0 | 0—0 | 0—0 | 0—0 | 0—1 | 0—0 | 0—0 | 0—0 | 0— 1 |
| Kirkwood .. | 0—0 | 0—0 | 1—1 | 1—1 | 0—0 | 0—1 | 2—0 | 0—0 | 0—0 | 0—1 | 2—1 | 6— 5 |
| Lange ...... | 0—0 | 0—0 | 0—2 | 1—2 | 0—0 | 0—0 | 0—0 | 2—0 | 1—0 | 0—2 | 0—0 | 4— 6 |
| Monge ..... | 0—0 | 0—0 | 0—0 | 0—0 | 0—0 | 0—0 | 0—0 | 0—2 | 0—0 | 0—0 | 0—0 | 0— 2 |
| Pactwa .... | 0—0 | 0—0 | 0—0 | 0—0 | 0—0 | 0—0 | 0—0 | 1—0 | 0—0 | 0—0 | 0—0 | 1— 0 |
| Pena ....... | 0—0 | 0—0 | 0—0 | 0—0 | 0—0 | 0—1 | 0—0 | 0—1 | 0—0 | 0—0 | 0—0 | 0— 2 |
| Quintana .. | 0—0 | 0—0 | 0—0 | 0—0 | 0—0 | 0—0 | 0—0 | 0—0 | 0—0 | 0—1 | 0—0 | 0— 1 |
| Ross ....... | 0—0 | 0—6 | 0—0 | 0—0 | 0—0 | 0—0 | 0—0 | 0—0 | 0—0 | 0—1 | 0—0 | 0— 2 |
| Ryan ....... | 2—2 | 0—1 | 3—0 | 0—2 | 0—0 | 1—1 | 2—2 | 2—0 | 2—2 | 1—1 | 1—1 | 14—12 |
| Scott ...... | 0—0 | 0—0 | 0—0 | 0—0 | 0—0 | 1—2 | 1—0 | 1—0 | 0—0 | 0—0 | 0—0 | 4— 2 |
| Singer ..... | 1—1 | 2—2 | 1—2 | 0—1 | 1—0 | 0—2 | 0—2 | 0—1 | 1—1 | 0—3 | 1—1 | 7—15 |
| Tanana .... | 2—1 | 1—0 | 1—1 | 1—2 | 3—1 | 0—2 | 1—0 | 1—0 | 2—0 | 2—2 | 2—0 | 16— 9 |
| Totals .. | 6—6 | 6—6 | 9—9 | 3—9 | 6—5 | 4—14 | 7—5 | 8—10 | 7—5 | 7—11 | 9—9 | 72—89 |

No Decisions—Blateric, Sells.

## CHICAGO—75-86

| Pitcher | Balt. W–L | Bos. W–L | Cal. W–L | Clev. W–L | Det. W–L | K.C. W–L | Mil. W–L | Minn. W–L | N.Y. W–L | Oak. W–L | Tex. W–L | Totals W–L |
|---|---|---|---|---|---|---|---|---|---|---|---|---|
| Allen | 0—0 | 0—1 | 0—0 | 0—0 | 0—0 | 0—0 | 0—0 | 0—0 | 0—0 | 0—1 | 0—0 | 0— 2 |
| Bahnsen | 1—0 | 1—0 | 0—0 | 0—0 | 1—0 | 0—1 | 1—0 | 0—0 | 0—1 | 0—2 | 0—2 | 4— 6 |
| Forster | 0—1 | 0—0 | 1—0 | 0—1 | 1—0 | 0—0 | 0—0 | 1—0 | 0—0 | 0—1 | 0—0 | 3— 3 |
| Gossage | 0—0 | 0—3 | 0—1 | 2—0 | 1—0 | 1—0 | 0—1 | 1—0 | 1—0 | 2—0 | 0—3 | 9— 8 |
| Hamilton | 0—0 | 0—0 | 0—0 | 0—0 | 0—0 | 1—2 | 0—0 | 1—1 | 2—0 | 0—0 | 0—3 | 6— 5 |
| Hinton | 0—0 | 0—0 | 0—0 | 0—0 | 0—0 | 0—0 | 0—0 | 0—0 | 0—0 | 0—0 | 0—0 | 1— 0 |
| Jefferson | 0—1 | 1—1 | 1—0 | 0—1 | 0—0 | 1—0 | 1—0 | 0—0 | 0—0 | 1—0 | 0—0 | 5— 9 |
| Kaat | 2—1 | 1—0 | 1—2 | 3—1 | 1—2 | 3—1 | 1—1 | 1—3 | 1—2 | 4—1 | 2—0 | 20—14 |
| Kravec | 0—0 | 0—0 | 0—0 | 0—0 | 0—0 | 0—1 | 0—0 | 1—0 | 0—0 | 0—0 | 0—0 | 1— 1 |
| Osborn | 0—0 | 0—0 | 1—0 | 0—0 | 0—0 | 0—1 | 0—0 | 0—0 | 0—0 | 0—0 | 0—0 | 0— 1 |
| Osteen | 0—2 | 0—1 | 1—3 | 1—0 | 0—2 | 0—0 | 0—0 | 1—0 | 1—0 | 1—2 | 0—0 | 7—16 |
| Upshaw | 0—0 | 0—0 | 1—0 | 0—0 | 0—0 | 0—0 | 0—0 | 1—0 | 0—0 | 1—0 | 0—0 | 3— 0 |
| Vuckovich | 0—0 | 0—0 | 0—0 | 0—0 | 0—0 | 0—0 | 0—0 | 0—0 | 0—0 | 0—1 | 0—0 | 1— 1 |
| Wood | 0—2 | 0—2 | 2—3 | 1—2 | 1—2 | 0—0 | 0—2 | 3—1 | 3—1 | 3—1 | 1—3 | 16—20 |
| **Totals** | 4—7 | 4—8 | 9—9 | 7—5 | 5—7 | 9—9 | 8—4 | 9—9 | 6—6 | 9—9 | 5—13 | 75—86 |

No Decisions—Gogolewski, Knapp, Kucek, Otten, Pitlock, Stoddard.

## CLEVELAND—79-80

| Pitcher | Balt. W–L | Bos. W–L | Cal. W–L | Chi. W–L | Det. W–L | K.C. W–L | Mil. W–L | Minn. W–L | N.Y. W–L | Oak. W–L | Tex. W–L | Totals W–L |
|---|---|---|---|---|---|---|---|---|---|---|---|---|
| Beene | 0—0 | 1—0 | 0—0 | 0—0 | 0—0 | 0—0 | 0—0 | 0—0 | 0—0 | 0—0 | 0—0 | 1— 0 |
| Bibby | 1—1 | 0—1 | 1—0 | 0—2 | 2—1 | 0—1 | 1—0 | 0—0 | 0—2 | 0—1 | 0—0 | 5— 9 |
| Bosman | 0—1 | 0—1 | 0—0 | 0—0 | 0—0 | 0—0 | 0—0 | 0—0 | 0—0 | 0—0 | 0—0 | 1— 2 |
| Brown | 0—0 | 0—0 | 0—0 | 0—0 | 1—0 | 0—1 | 0—0 | 0—0 | 0—0 | 0—0 | 0—0 | 1— 2 |
| Buskey | 1—0 | 1—0 | 0—0 | 1—1 | 0—0 | 0—0 | 2—0 | 0—1 | 0—0 | 0—0 | 0—1 | 1— 2 |
| Eckersley | 3—0 | 0—1 | 1—1 | 1—0 | 4—0 | 0—0 | 1—1 | 0—1 | 2—1 | 1—1 | 0—1 | 13— 7 |
| Harrison | 0—1 | 1—0 | 0—1 | 0—1 | 1—1 | 1—1 | 1—1 | 0—0 | 1—1 | 1—0 | 1—0 | 7— 7 |
| Hood | 0—0 | 1—1 | 1—1 | 0—0 | 1—0 | 0—1 | 0—1 | 1—0 | 0—1 | 1—0 | 0—1 | 6—10 |
| Kern | 0—0 | 0—0 | 0—0 | 0—0 | 0—1 | 0—0 | 0—1 | 1—0 | 3—2 | 0—2 | 0—0 | 5—10 |
| LaRoche | 0—0 | 0—0 | 0—1 | 0—0 | 0—1 | 1—0 | 0—0 | 0—0 | 0—2 | 1—0 | 0—0 | 1— 0 |
| Odom | 0—0 | 0—0 | 0—0 | 0—0 | 0—1 | 1—0 | 1—0 | 0—1 | 1—0 | 1—0 | 0—0 | 5— 3 |
| G. Perry | 1—1 | 1—0 | 1—0 | 1—1 | 0—0 | 1—0 | 0—0 | 0—0 | 0—0 | 0—0 | 0—0 | 1— 0 |
| J. Perry | 0—1 | 0—2 | 1—0 | 0—0 | 1—0 | 0—0 | 0—2 | 0—1 | 0—0 | 0—0 | 0—0 | 6— 9 |
| Peterson | 0—1 | 0—1 | 1—0 | 2—1 | 2—0 | 1—1 | 2—2 | 2—0 | 3—1 | 0—0 | 1—1 | 14— 8 |
| Raich | 0—1 | 3—0 | 1—0 | 0—0 | 2—0 | 0—0 | 0—2 | 0—1 | 0—2 | 1—1 | 0—1 | 7— 8 |
| Reynolds | 0—0 | 0—0 | 0—0 | 0—0 | 0—0 | 0—0 | 0—0 | 0—0 | 0—0 | 0—0 | 0—2 | 0— 2 |
| Waits | 1—0 | 2—0 | 0—0 | 0—0 | 0—1 | 1—0 | 0—0 | 0—0 | 1—1 | 1—0 | 0—0 | 6— 2 |
| **Totals** | 8—10 | 11—7 | 9—3 | 5—7 | 12—6 | 6—6 | 9—9 | 3—6 | 9—9 | 2—10 | 5—7 | 79—80 |

No Decisions—Andersen, Strickland.

## DETROIT—57-102

| Pitcher | Balt. W–L | Bos. W–L | Cal. W–L | Chi. W–L | Clev. W–L | K.C. W–L | Mil. W–L | Minn. W–L | N.Y. W–L | Oak. W–L | Tex. W–L | Totals W–L |
|---|---|---|---|---|---|---|---|---|---|---|---|---|
| Arroyo | 0—0 | 1—0 | 0—0 | 0—0 | 1—1 | 0—0 | 0—0 | 0—0 | 0—0 | 0—0 | 0—0 | 2— 1 |
| Bare | 0—2 | 0—0 | 3—1 | 1—0 | 1—1 | 1—0 | 2—3 | 0—1 | 0—3 | 0—1 | 0—1 | 8—13 |
| Coleman | 2—4 | 0—1 | 0—0 | 1—1 | 1—2 | 2—1 | 1—2 | 1—2 | 0—2 | 2—2 | 0—1 | 10—18 |
| Glynn | 0—0 | 0—1 | 0—0 | 0—0 | 0—0 | 0—0 | 0—1 | 0—0 | 0—0 | 0—0 | 0—0 | 0— 2 |
| Hiller | 0—1 | 1—0 | 1—0 | 0—0 | 0—0 | 0—0 | 0—0 | 0—2 | 0—0 | 0—0 | 0—0 | 2— 3 |
| La Grow | 0—1 | 1—2 | 0—1 | 1—1 | 1—3 | 1—1 | 1—1 | 1—0 | 1—1 | 0—3 | 0—0 | 7—14 |
| Lemanczyk | 0—1 | 0—2 | 0—0 | 0—0 | 0—2 | 0—0 | 1—1 | 1—0 | 0—0 | 0—1 | 0—0 | 2— 7 |
| Lolich | 1—1 | 2—0 | 0—3 | 2—1 | 1—2 | 0—2 | 1—1 | 1—2 | 2—4 | 2—0 | 0—2 | 12—18 |
| Pentz | 0—0 | 0—2 | 0—0 | 0—0 | 0—0 | 0—0 | 0—0 | 0—0 | 0—0 | 0—2 | 0—0 | 0— 4 |
| Reynolds | 0—1 | 0—1 | 0—0 | 0—0 | 0—0 | 0—0 | 0—0 | 0—0 | 0—0 | 0—0 | 0—0 | 0— 2 |
| Ruhle | 0—0 | 0—2 | 1—1 | 1—1 | 1—1 | 2—1 | 1—2 | 1—1 | 3—1 | 0—1 | 1—1 | 11—12 |
| Walker | 1—1 | 0—2 | 0—1 | 0—0 | 1—1 | 0—0 | 1—0 | 0—0 | 0—2 | 1—1 | 0—0 | 3— 8 |
| **Totals** | 4—12 | 5—13 | 5—6 | 7—5 | 6—12 | 6—6 | 7—11 | 4—8 | 6—12 | 6—6 | 1—11 | 57—102 |

No Decisions—Brookens, Grilli, Makowski.

## KANSAS CITY—91-71

| Pitcher | Balt. W—L | Bos. W—L | Cal. W—L | Chi. W—L | Clev. W—L | Det. W—L | Mil. W—L | Minn. W—L | N.Y. W—L | Oak. W—L | Tex. W—L | Totals W—L |
|---|---|---|---|---|---|---|---|---|---|---|---|---|
| Bird | 1—0 | 1—0 | 2—2 | 1—1 | 0—0 | 0—0 | 0—0 | 2—1 | 1—1 | 0—0 | 1—1 | 9— 6 |
| Briles | 0—0 | 0—1 | 0—0 | 1—0 | 0—1 | 1—1 | 0—2 | 0—0 | 1—1 | 1—0 | 2—0 | 6— 6 |
| Busby | 1—3 | 1—1 | 4—0 | 1—1 | 1—1 | 0—1 | 2—0 | 2—1 | 0—1 | 3—2 | 3—1 | 18—12 |
| Dal Canton | 0—0 | 0—0 | 0—0 | 0—2 | 0—0 | 0—0 | 0—0 | 0—0 | 0—0 | 0—0 | 0—0 | 0— 2 |
| Fitzmorris | 1—0 | 1—3 | 1—0 | 1—1 | 2—0 | 1—1 | 1—3 | 2—3 | 1—0 | 1—0 | 4—1 | 16—12 |
| Leonard | 1—1 | 2—0 | 1—0 | 2—2 | 2—0 | 1—2 | 1—0 | 1—0 | 1—0 | 1—2 | 2—0 | 15— 7 |
| Littell | 0—0 | 0—0 | 1—0 | 0—0 | 0—1 | 0—0 | 0—0 | 0—0 | 0—0 | 0—0 | 0—1 | 1— 2 |
| McClure | 0—0 | 0—0 | 0—0 | 0—0 | 0—0 | 0—0 | 0—0 | 0—0 | 0—0 | 0—0 | 1—0 | 1— 0 |
| McDaniel | 0—0 | 0—1 | 2—0 | 0—0 | 1—0 | 1—0 | 1—0 | 0—0 | 0—0 | 0—0 | 0—0 | 5— 1 |
| Mingori | 0—0 | 0—0 | 0—1 | 0—0 | 0—0 | 0—0 | 0—0 | 0—0 | 0—0 | 0—2 | 0—0 | 0— 3 |
| Pattin | 1—2 | 0—1 | 3—0 | 0—1 | 0—2 | 2—1 | 2—0 | 1—0 | 1—1 | 0—2 | 0—0 | 10—10 |
| Sadecki | 0—0 | 0—0 | 0—0 | 0—0 | 0—0 | 0—0 | 0—0 | 1—0 | 0—0 | 0—0 | 0—0 | 1— 0 |
| Splittorff | 0—1 | 0—0 | 0—1 | 3—1 | 0—1 | 0—0 | 0—0 | 2—2 | 2—1 | 1—3 | 1—0 | 9—10 |
| Totals | 5—7 | 5—7 | 14—4 | 9—9 | 6—6 | 6—6 | 7—5 | 11—7 | 7—5 | 7—11 | 14—4 | 91—71 |

No Decisions—Throop.

## MILWAUKEE—68-94

| Pitcher | Balt. W—L | Bos. W—L | Cal. W—L | Chi. W—L | Clev. W—L | Det. W—L | K.C. W—L | Minn. W—L | N.Y. W—L | Oak. W—L | Tex. W—L | Totals W—L |
|---|---|---|---|---|---|---|---|---|---|---|---|---|
| Anderson | 0—0 | 0—0 | 0—0 | 0—0 | 0—0 | 1—0 | 0—0 | 0—0 | 0—0 | 0—0 | 0—0 | 1— 0 |
| Augustine | 0—0 | 0—0 | 0—0 | 0—0 | 0—0 | 1—0 | 0—0 | 0—0 | 1—0 | 0—0 | 0—0 | 2— 0 |
| Austin | 0—1 | 1—0 | 0—1 | 0—0 | 1—0 | 0—1 | 0—0 | 0—0 | 0—0 | 0—0 | 0—0 | 2— 3 |
| Broberg | 0—4 | 4—0 | 0—0 | 0—2 | 2—1 | 3—2 | 1—1 | 0—2 | 1—1 | 0—3 | 3—0 | 14—16 |
| Castro | 0—0 | 0—1 | 0—1 | 0—0 | 0—0 | 0—0 | 0—0 | 0—0 | 1—0 | 2—0 | 0—0 | 3— 2 |
| Champion | 0—0 | 0—0 | 0—1 | 0—0 | 2—0 | 0—0 | 0—1 | 1—1 | 1—1 | 1—0 | 0—1 | 6— 6 |
| Colborn | 1—2 | 1—2 | 2—1 | 1—1 | 1—1 | 1—2 | 1—1 | 0—0 | 1—2 | 1—0 | 1—1 | 11—13 |
| Currence | 0—1 | 0—0 | 0—0 | 0—0 | 0—1 | 0—0 | 0—0 | 0—0 | 0—0 | 0—0 | 0—0 | 0— 2 |
| Hausman | 0—1 | 0—0 | 0—0 | 1—0 | 0—0 | 1—1 | 1—1 | 0—1 | 0—0 | 0—1 | 0—1 | 3— 6 |
| Murphy | 0—1 | 0—3 | 0—1 | 0—0 | 0—1 | 0—0 | 0—0 | 0—1 | 1—1 | 0—1 | 0—0 | 1— 9 |
| Osburn | 0—0 | 0—0 | 0—0 | 0—0 | 0—0 | 0—0 | 0—0 | 0—0 | 0—1 | 0—0 | 0—0 | 0— 1 |
| Rodriguez | 1—0 | 0—0 | 0—0 | 1—0 | 1—0 | 1—0 | 0—0 | 0—0 | 0—0 | 0—0 | 0—0 | 7— 0 |
| Slaton | 1—3 | 1—2 | 2—2 | 1—1 | 2—2 | 2—0 | 1—1 | 0—2 | 1—1 | 0—2 | 0—2 | 11—18 |
| Sprague | 0—0 | 0—0 | 0—0 | 0—2 | 0—2 | 0—0 | 1—0 | 0—2 | 0—1 | 0—0 | 0—0 | 1— 7 |
| Travers | 0—0 | 1—2 | 1—0 | 0—2 | 0—1 | 1—1 | 1—1 | 0—2 | 1—1 | 2—1 | 0—1 | 6—11 |
| Totals | 4—14 | 8—10 | 5—7 | 4—8 | 9—9 | 11—7 | 5—7 | 2—10 | 9—9 | 5—7 | 6—6 | 68—94 |

Ne Decisions—None.

## MINNESOTA—76-83

| Pitcher | Balt. W—L | Bos. W—L | Cal. W—L | Chi. W—L | Clev. W—L | Det. W—L | K.C. W—L | Mil. W—L | N.Y. W—L | Oak. W—L | Tex. W—L | Totals W—L |
|---|---|---|---|---|---|---|---|---|---|---|---|---|
| Albury | 0—0 | 0—0 | 1—1 | 1—1 | 1—1 | 1—0 | 0—2 | 0—0 | 0—0 | 1—1 | 1—1 | 6— 7 |
| Bane | 0—0 | 0—0 | 0—0 | 1—0 | 0—0 | 0—0 | 0—1 | 0—0 | 0—0 | 2—0 | 0—0 | 3— 1 |
| Blyleven | 2—0 | 0—0 | 3—1 | 1—2 | 1—0 | 1—0 | 1—2 | 2—0 | 2—1 | 1—1 | 1—3 | 15—10 |
| Burgmeier | 0—0 | 0—2 | 1—1 | 0—3 | 2—0 | 0—1 | 1—0 | 0—0 | 0—1 | 1—0 | 0—0 | 5— 8 |
| Butler | 0—0 | 0—0 | 0—1 | 1—0 | 0—1 | 0—1 | 1—1 | 1—0 | 0—1 | 1—0 | 1—0 | 5— 4 |
| Campbell | 0—1 | 0—0 | 1—0 | 2—1 | 0—0 | 0—1 | 0—1 | 0—0 | 0—1 | 0—0 | 1—1 | 4— 6 |
| Corbin | 1—1 | 0—1 | 0—1 | 1—0 | 0—0 | 1—0 | 0—0 | 1—0 | 1—1 | 0—2 | 0—1 | 5— 7 |
| Decker | 0—0 | 0—1 | 0—0 | 0—0 | 0—0 | 0—0 | 0—1 | 0—0 | 0—0 | 0—1 | 1—0 | 1— 3 |
| Goltz | 2—1 | 2—1 | 1—2 | 1—2 | 0—0 | 2—1 | 2—1 | 3—1 | 0—1 | 0—2 | 1—2 | 14—14 |
| Hughes | 1—2 | 0—3 | 2—1 | 1—0 | 2—1 | 3—0 | 2—1 | 2—1 | 1—1 | 0—4 | 2—0 | 16—14 |
| Johnson | 0—0 | 0—1 | 0—0 | 0—0 | 0—0 | 0—0 | 0—0 | 1—0 | 0—0 | 0—0 | 0—1 | 1— 2 |
| Pazik | 0—1 | 0—1 | 0—0 | 0—0 | 0—0 | 0—0 | 0—1 | 0—0 | 0—0 | 0—0 | 0—0 | 0— 4 |
| Wiley | 0—0 | 0—0 | 1—0 | 0—0 | 0—0 | 0—0 | 0—1 | 0—0 | 0—1 | 0—0 | 0—1 | 1— 3 |
| Totals | 6—6 | 2—10 | 10—8 | 9—9 | 6—3 | 8—4 | 7—11 | 10—2 | 4—8 | 6—12 | 8—10 | 76—83 |

No Decisions—None.

### NEW YORK—83-77

| Pitcher | Balt. W—L | Bos. W—L | Cal. W—L | Chi. W—L | Clev. W—L | Det. W—L | K.C. W—L | Mil. W—L | Minn. W—L | Oak. W—L | Tex. W—L | Totals W—L |
|---|---|---|---|---|---|---|---|---|---|---|---|---|
| Dobson | 1—0 | 1—4 | 0—1 | 2—0 | 0—1 | 1—1 | 2—0 | 1—2 | 1—2 | 1—1 | | 11—14 |
| Hunter | 4—2 | 0—3 | 2—2 | 2—0 | 2—1 | 2—2 | 0—3 | 3—0 | 1—0 | 4—0 | 3—1 | 23—14 |
| Guidry | 0—0 | 0—1 | 0—0 | 0—0 | 0—0 | 0—0 | 0—0 | 0—0 | 0—0 | 0—0 | 0—0 | 0—1 |
| Gura | 1—1 | 0—1 | 3—0 | 0—1 | 0—2 | 1—1 | 1—1 | 1—0 | 0—0 | 0—0 | | 7—8 |
| Lyle | 2—1 | 0—1 | 0—0 | 0—1 | 1—0 | 0—0 | 1—1 | 1—2 | 0—0 | 0—0 | 0—1 | 5—7 |
| Martinez | 0—0 | 0—1 | 0—1 | 0—0 | 0—0 | 0—0 | 0—0 | 0—0 | 1—0 | 0—0 | 0—0 | 1—2 |
| May | 0—2 | 1—0 | 0—2 | 1—1 | 2—1 | 4—2 | 0—0 | 2—1 | 2—0 | 0—2 | 1—1 | 14—12 |
| Medich | 2—2 | 2—0 | 0—1 | 1—2 | 4—2 | 4—0 | 0—2 | 0—3 | 1—2 | 1—2 | 1—0 | 16—16 |
| Tidrow | 0—0 | 1—0 | 0—0 | 0—1 | 0—2 | 0—0 | 0—0 | 0—0 | 2—0 | 1—0 | 2—0 | 6—3 |
| Totals | 10—8 | 5—11 | 5—7 | 6—6 | 9—9 | 12—6 | 5—7 | 9—9 | 8—4 | 6—6 | 8—4 | 83—77 |

No Decisions—Pagan, Sawyer, Wallace.

### OAKLAND—98-64

| Pitcher | Balt. W—L | Bos. W—L | Cal. W—L | Chi. W—L | Clev. W—L | Det. W—L | K.C. W—L | Mil. W—L | Minn. W—L | N.Y. W—L | Tex. W—L | Totals W—L |
|---|---|---|---|---|---|---|---|---|---|---|---|---|
| Abbott | 0—0 | 0—0 | 0—0 | 0—1 | 1—0 | 1—0 | 1—2 | 0—0 | 2—1 | 0—1 | 0—0 | 5—5 |
| Bahnsen | 0—0 | 0—1 | 0—1 | 1—1 | 0—0 | 1—0 | 1—1 | 2—0 | 0—1 | 0—1 | 1—1 | 6—7 |
| Blue | 1—2 | 1—1 | 5—1 | 4—0 | 0—0 | 1—2 | 3—1 | 0—3 | 2—0 | 3—0 | 2—1 | 22—11 |
| Bosman | 0—0 | 0—1 | 2—0 | 0—0 | 3—0 | 0—2 | 1—1 | 1—0 | 1—0 | 1—0 | 2—0 | 11—4 |
| Fingers | 2—0 | 3—0 | 0—0 | 1—3 | 1—0 | 0—0 | 0—1 | 1—1 | 0—1 | 1—0 | 0—0 | 10—6 |
| Hamilton | 0—0 | 0—0 | 0—2 | 0—0 | 0—0 | 0—0 | 0—0 | 0—0 | 1—0 | 0—0 | 0—0 | 1—2 |
| Holtzman | 1—1 | 2—1 | 3—2 | 0—1 | 2—1 | 1—0 | 2—1 | 2—0 | 3—2 | 1—3 | 1—2 | 18—14 |
| Lindblad | 1—0 | 0—0 | 1—0 | 1—0 | 0—0 | 1—0 | 0—0 | 0—0 | 0—1 | 4—0 | 0—0 | 9—1 |
| Mitchell | 0—0 | 0—0 | 0—0 | 0—1 | 0—0 | 0—0 | 0—0 | 0—0 | 0—0 | 0—0 | 0—0 | 0—1 |
| Norris | 0—0 | 0—0 | 0—0 | 1—0 | 0—0 | 0—0 | 0—0 | 0—0 | 0—0 | 0—0 | 0—0 | 1—0 |
| Odom | 0—0 | 0—1 | 0—1 | 0—0 | 0—0 | 0—0 | 0—0 | 0—0 | 0—0 | 0—0 | 0—0 | 0—2 |
| J. Perry | 2—1 | 0—0 | 0—0 | 0—0 | 1—1 | 0—1 | 0—0 | 0—0 | 0—0 | 0—0 | 0—1 | 3—4 |
| Siebert | 0—0 | 0—1 | 0—0 | 0—2 | 2—0 | 1—1 | 0—0 | 0—0 | 0—0 | 0—1 | 1—1 | 4—4 |
| Todd | 1—0 | 0—0 | 0—0 | 1—2 | 0—0 | 0—0 | 2—0 | 1—1 | 2—0 | 0—0 | 1—0 | 8—3 |
| Totals | 8—4 | 6—6 | 11—7 | 9—9 | 10—2 | 6—6 | 11—7 | 7—5 | 12—6 | 6—6 | 12—6 | 98—64 |

No Decisions—None.

### TEXAS—79-83

| Pitcher | Balt. W—L | Bos. W—L | Cal. W—L | Chi. W—L | Clev. W—L | Det. W—L | K.C. W—L | Mil. W—L | Minn. W—L | N.Y. W—L | Oak. W—L | Totals W—L |
|---|---|---|---|---|---|---|---|---|---|---|---|---|
| Bacsik | 0—0 | 0—0 | 0—0 | 0—1 | 0—0 | 0—0 | 0—0 | 0—0 | 1—1 | 0—0 | 0—0 | 1—2 |
| Bibby | 0—1 | 0—0 | 0—0 | 1—0 | 0—1 | 0—0 | 0—0 | 1—0 | 0—1 | 0—1 | 0—1 | 2—6 |
| Brown | 1—0 | 1—0 | 1—1 | 0—0 | 0—0 | 1—1 | 0—1 | 0—2 | 0—0 | 1—0 | 0—0 | 5—5 |
| Clyde | 0—0 | 0—0 | 0—1 | 0—0 | 0—0 | 0—0 | 0—0 | 0—0 | 0—0 | 0—0 | 0—0 | 0—1 |
| Foucault | 2—1 | 0—1 | 0—1 | 3—0 | 1—0 | 0—0 | 0—0 | 0—0 | 1—0 | 0—0 | 0—0 | 8—4 |
| Hands | 0—0 | 0—1 | 2—0 | 0—0 | 0—0 | 2—0 | 0—2 | 1—1 | 1—0 | 0—2 | 0—1 | 6—7 |
| Hargan | 0—0 | 1—0 | 0—2 | 1—0 | 0—1 | 0—0 | 1—1 | 2—2 | 2—1 | 0—1 | 1—1 | 9—10 |
| Jenkins | 1—0 | 2—2 | 1—1 | 4—2 | 1—2 | 2—0 | 1—2 | 1—0 | 0—3 | 2—2 | 2—4 | 17—18 |
| Moore | 0—0 | 0—0 | 0—1 | 0—0 | 0—0 | 0—0 | 0—0 | 0—0 | 0—0 | 0—0 | 0—1 | 0—2 |
| G. Perry | 1—0 | 0—1 | 1—0 | 1—1 | 1—1 | 2—0 | 1—2 | 0—1 | 2—1 | 1—0 | 2—1 | 12—8 |
| Perzanowski | 0—2 | 0—0 | 0—0 | 0—0 | 0—0 | 0—0 | 1—0 | 0—1 | 2—1 | 1—0 | 2—1 | 3—3 |
| Thomas | 0—1 | 0—1 | 0—1 | 1—0 | 2—0 | 1—0 | 0—1 | 0—0 | 0—0 | 0—0 | 0—0 | 4—4 |
| Umbarger | 0—0 | 0—0 | 2—2 | 1—1 | 2—0 | 0—1 | 0—1 | 1—0 | 1—1 | 0—1 | 0—1 | 8—7 |
| Wright | 0—1 | 1—0 | 1—1 | 0—0 | 0—0 | 0—0 | 0—2 | 0—0 | 1—0 | 0—1 | 1—1 | 4—6 |
| Totals | 5—7 | 4—8 | 9—9 | 13—5 | 7—5 | 11—1 | 4—14 | 6—6 | 10—8 | 4—8 | 6—12 | 79—83 |

No Decisions—Gideon, Kekich, Merritt.

# AMERICAN LEAGUE

## PENNANT WINNERS

| Year — Club | Manager | W. | L. | Pct. | °G.A. |
|---|---|---|---|---|---|
| 1901—Chicago | Clark Griffith | 83 | 53 | .610 | 4 |
| 1902—Philadelphia | Connie Mack | 83 | 53 | .610 | 5 |
| 1903—Boston | James Collins | 91 | 47 | .659 | 14½ |
| 1904—Boston | James Collins | 95 | 59 | .617 | 1½ |
| 1905—Philadelphia | Connie Mack | 92 | 56 | .622 | 2 |
| 1906—Chicago | Fielder Jones | 93 | 58 | .616 | 3 |
| 1907—Detroit | Hugh Jennings | 92 | 58 | .613 | 1½ |
| 1908—Detroit | Hugh Jennings | 90 | 63 | .588 | ½ |
| 1909—Detroit | Hugh Jennings | 98 | 54 | .645 | 3½ |
| 1910—Philadelphia | Connie Mack | 102 | 48 | .682 | 14½ |
| 1911—Philadelphia | Connie Mack | 101 | 50 | .669 | 13½ |
| 1912—Boston | Garland Stahl | 105 | 47 | .691 | 14 |
| 1913—Philadelphia | Connie Mack | 96 | 57 | .627 | 6½ |
| 1914—Philadelphia | Connie Mack | 99 | 53 | .651 | 8½ |
| 1915—Boston | William Carrigan | 101 | 50 | .669 | 2½ |
| 1916—Boston | William Carrigan | 91 | 63 | .591 | 2 |
| 1917—Chicago | Clarence Rowland | 100 | 54 | .649 | 9 |
| 1918—Boston | Edward Barrow | 75 | 51 | .595 | 2½ |
| 1919—Chicago | William Gleason | 88 | 52 | .629 | 3½ |
| 1920—Cleveland | Tristram Speaker | 98 | 56 | .636 | 2 |
| 1921—New York | Miller Huggins | 98 | 55 | .641 | 4½ |
| 1922—New York | Miller Huggins | 94 | 60 | .610 | 1 |
| 1923—New York | Miller Huggins | 98 | 54 | .645 | 16 |
| 1924—Washington | Stanley (Bucky) Harris | 92 | 62 | .597 | 2 |
| 1925—Washington | Stanley (Bucky) Harris | 96 | 55 | .636 | 8½ |
| 1926—New York | Miller Huggins | 91 | 63 | .591 | 3 |
| 1927—New York | Miller Huggins | 110 | 44 | .714 | 19 |
| 1928—New York | Miller Huggins | 101 | 53 | .656 | 2½ |
| 1929—Philadelphia | Connie Mack | 104 | 46 | .693 | 18 |
| 1930—Philadelphia | Connie Mack | 102 | 52 | .662 | 8 |
| 1931—Philadelphia | Connie Mack | 107 | 45 | .704 | 13½ |
| 1632—New York | Joseph McCarthy | 107 | 47 | .695 | 13 |
| 1933—Washington | Joseph Cronin | 99 | 53 | .651 | 7 |
| 1934—Detroit | Gordon (Mickey) Cochrane | 101 | 53 | .656 | 7 |
| 1935—Detroit | Gordon (Mickey) Cochrane | 93 | 58 | .616 | 3 |
| 1936—New York | Joseph McCarthy | 102 | 51 | .667 | 19½ |
| 1937—New York | Joseph McCarthy | 102 | 52 | .662 | 13 |
| 1938—New York | Joseph McCarthy | 99 | 53 | .651 | 9½ |
| 1939—New York | Joseph McCarthy | 106 | 45 | .702 | 17 |
| 1940—Detroit | Delmer Baker | 90 | 64 | .584 | 1 |
| 1941—New York | Joseph McCarthy | 101 | 53 | .656 | 17 |
| 1942—New York | Joseph McCarthy | 103 | 51 | .669 | 9 |
| 1943—New York | Joseph McCarthy | 98 | 56 | .636 | 13½ |
| 1944—St. Louis | J. Luther Sewell | 89 | 65 | .578 | 1 |
| 1945—Detroit | Stephen O'Neill | 88 | 65 | .575 | 1½ |
| 1946—Boston | Joseph Cronin | 104 | 50 | .675 | 12 |
| 1947—New York† | Stanley (Bucky) Harris | 97 | 57 | .630 | 12 |
| 1948—Cleveland† | Louis Boudreau | 97 | 58 | .626 | 1 |
| 1949—New York | Charles (Casey) Stengel | 97 | 57 | .630 | 1 |
| 1950—New York | Charles (Casey) Stengel | 98 | 56 | .636 | 3 |
| 1951—New York | Charles (Casey) Stengel | 98 | 56 | .636 | 5 |
| 1952—New York | Charles (Casey) Stengel | 95 | 59 | .617 | 2 |
| 1953—New York | Charles (Casey) Stengel | 99 | 52 | .656 | 8½ |
| 1954—Cleveland | Alfonso Lopez | 111 | 43 | .721 | 8 |
| 1955—New York | Charles (Casey) Stengel | 96 | 58 | .623 | 3 |
| 1956—New York | Charles (Casey) Stengel | 97 | 57 | .630 | 9 |
| 1957—New York | Charles (Casey) Stengel | 98 | 56 | .636 | 8 |
| 1958—New York | Charles (Casey) Stengel | 92 | 62 | .597 | 10 |
| 1959—Chicago | Alfonso Lopez | 94 | 60 | .610 | 5 |
| 1960—New York | Charles (Casey) Stengel | 97 | 57 | .630 | 8 |

## PENNANT WINNERS—Continued

| Year | Club | Manager | W. | L. | Pct. | *G.A. |
|---|---|---|---|---|---|---|
| 1961—New York | | Ralph Houk | 109 | 53 | .673 | 8 |
| 1962—New York | | Ralph Houk | 96 | 66 | .593 | 5 |
| 1963—New York | | Ralph Houk | 104 | 57 | .646 | 10½ |
| 1964—New York | | Lawrence (Yogi) Berra | 99 | 63 | .611 | 1 |
| 1965—Minnesota | | Sabath (Sam) Mele | 102 | 60 | .630 | 7 |
| 1966—Baltimore | | Henry A. Bauer | 97 | 63 | .606 | 9 |
| 1967—Boston† | | Richard H. Williams | 92 | 70 | .568 | 1 |
| 1968—Detroit | | E. Mayo Smith | 103 | 59 | .636 | 12 |
| 1969—Baltimore (E)** | | Earl S. Weaver | 109 | 53 | .673 | 19 |
| 1970—Baltimore (E)** | | Earl S. Weaver | 108 | 54 | .667 | 15 |
| 1971—Baltimore (E)** | | Earl S. Weaver | 101 | 57 | .639 | 12 |
| 1972—Oakland (W)** | | Richard H. Williams | 93 | 62 | .600 | 5½ |
| 1973—Oakland (W)** | | Richard H. Williams | 94 | 68 | .580 | 6 |
| 1974—Oakland (W)** | | Alvin Ralph Dark | 90 | 72 | .556 | 5 |
| 1975—Boston (E)** | | Darrell D. Johnson | 95 | 65 | .594 | 4½ |

*Games ahead of second-place club.   †Defeated Boston in one-game playoff.
**Won Championship Series.

## YEARLY FINISHES

| Year | Balt. | Bos. | Calif. | Chi. | Cleve. | Det. | Minn. | N.Y. | Oak. | Wash. |
|---|---|---|---|---|---|---|---|---|---|---|
| 1901 | 5 | 2 | .... | 1 | 7 | 3 | ‡6 | .... | †4 | .... |
| 1902 | 8 | 3 | .... | 4 | 5 | 7 | ‡6 | .... | †1 | .... |
| 1903 | *6 | 1 | .... | 7 | 3 | 5 | ‡8 | 4 | †2 | .... |
| 1904 | *6 | 1 | .... | 3 | 4 | 7 | ‡8 | 2 | †5 | .... |
| 1905 | *8 | 4 | .... | 2 | 5 | 3 | ‡7 | 6 | †1 | .... |
| 1906 | *5 | 8 | .... | 1 | 3 | 6 | ‡7 | 2 | †4 | .... |
| 1907 | *6 | 7 | .... | 3 | 4 | 1 | ‡8 | 5 | †2 | .... |
| 1908 | *4 | 5 | .... | 3 | 2 | 1 | ‡7 | 8 | †6 | .... |
| 1909 | *7 | 3 | .... | 4 | 6 | 1 | ‡8 | 5 | †2 | .... |
| 1910 | *8 | 4 | .... | 6 | 5 | 3 | ‡7 | 2 | †1 | .... |
| 1911 | *8 | 5 | .... | 4 | 3 | 2 | ‡7 | 6 | †1 | .... |
| 1912 | *7 | 1 | .... | 4 | 5 | 3 | ‡2 | 8 | †3 | .... |
| 1913 | *8 | 4 | .... | 5 | 3 | 6 | ‡2 | 7 | †1 | .... |
| 1914 | *5 | 2 | .... | x6 | 8 | 4 | ‡3 | x6 | †1 | .... |
| 1915 | *6 | 1 | .... | 3 | 7 | 2 | ‡4 | 5 | †8 | .... |
| 1916 | *5 | 1 | .... | 2 | 6 | 3 | ‡7 | 4 | †8 | .... |
| 1917 | *7 | 2 | .... | 1 | 3 | 4 | ‡5 | 6 | †8 | .... |
| 1918 | *5 | 1 | .... | 6 | 2 | 7 | ‡3 | 4 | †8 | .... |
| 1919 | *5 | 6 | .... | 1 | 2 | 4 | ‡7 | 3 | †8 | .... |
| 1920 | *4 | 5 | .... | 2 | 1 | 7 | ‡6 | 3 | †8 | .... |
| 1921 | *3 | 5 | .... | 7 | 2 | 6 | ‡4 | 1 | †8 | .... |
| 1922 | *2 | 8 | .... | 5 | 4 | 3 | ‡6 | 1 | †7 | .... |
| 1923 | *5 | 8 | .... | 7 | 3 | 2 | ‡4 | 1 | †6 | .... |
| 1924 | *4 | 7 | .... | 8 | 6 | 3 | ‡1 | 2 | †5 | .... |
| 1925 | *3 | 8 | .... | 5 | 6 | 4 | ‡1 | 7 | †2 | .... |
| 1926 | *7 | 8 | .... | 5 | 2 | 6 | ‡4 | 1 | †3 | .... |
| 1927 | *7 | 8 | .... | 5 | 6 | 4 | ‡3 | 1 | †2 | .... |
| 1928 | *3 | 8 | .... | 5 | 7 | 3 | ‡4 | 1 | †2 | .... |
| 1929 | *4 | 8 | .... | 7 | 3 | 6 | ‡5 | 2 | †1 | .... |
| 1930 | *6 | 8 | .... | 7 | 4 | 5 | ‡2 | 3 | †1 | .... |
| 1931 | *5 | 6 | .... | 8 | 4 | 7 | ‡3 | 2 | †1 | .... |
| 1932 | *6 | 8 | .... | 7 | 4 | 5 | ‡3 | 1 | †2 | .... |
| 1933 | *8 | 7 | .... | 6 | 4 | 5 | ‡1 | 2 | †3 | .... |
| 1934 | *6 | 4 | .... | 8 | 3 | 1 | ‡7 | 2 | †5 | .... |
| 1935 | *7 | 4 | .... | 5 | 3 | 1 | ‡6 | 2 | †8 | .... |
| 1936 | *7 | 6 | .... | 3 | 5 | 2 | ‡4 | 1 | †8 | .... |
| 1937 | *8 | 5 | .... | 3 | 4 | 2 | ‡6 | 1 | †8 | .... |
| 1938 | *7 | 2 | .... | 6 | 3 | 4 | ‡5 | 1 | †8 | .... |
| 1939 | *8 | 2 | .... | 6 | 3 | 4 | ‡5 | 1 | †7 | .... |
| 1940 | *6 | x4 | .... | x4 | 2 | 1 | ‡7 | 3 | †8 | .... |
| 1941 | x*6 | x4 | .... | 3 | x4 | x4 | x‡6 | 1 | †8 | .... |

## YEARLY FINISHES—Continued

| Year | Balt. | Bos. | Calif. | Chi. | Cleve. | Det. | Minn. | N.Y. | Oak. | Wash. |
|---|---|---|---|---|---|---|---|---|---|---|
| 1942 | *3 | 2 | .... | 6 | 4 | 5 | ‡7 | 1 | †8 | .... |
| 1943 | *6 | 7 | .... | 4 | 3 | 5 | ‡2 | 1 | †8 | .... |
| 1944 | *1 | 4 | .... | 7 | x5 | 2 | ‡8 | 3 | x†5 | .... |
| 1945 | *3 | 7 | .... | 6 | 5 | 1 | ‡2 | 4 | †8 | .... |
| 1946 | *7 | 1 | .... | 5 | 6 | 2 | ‡4 | 3 | †8 | .... |
| 1947 | *8 | 3 | .... | 6 | 4 | 2 | ‡7 | 1 | †5 | .... |
| 1948 | *6 | 2 | .... | 8 | 1 | 5 | ‡7 | 3 | †4 | .... |
| 1949 | *7 | 2 | .... | 6 | 3 | 4 | ‡8 | 1 | †5 | .... |
| 1950 | *7 | 3 | .... | 6 | 4 | 2 | ‡5 | 1 | †8 | .... |
| 1951 | *8 | 3 | .... | 4 | 2 | 5 | ‡7 | 1 | †6 | .... |
| 1952 | *7 | 6 | .... | 3 | 2 | 8 | ‡5 | 1 | †4 | .... |
| 1953 | *8 | 4 | .... | 3 | 2 | 6 | ‡5 | 1 | †7 | .... |
| 1954 | 7 | 4 | .... | 3 | 1 | 5 | ‡6 | 2 | †8 | .... |
| 1955 | 7 | 4 | .... | 3 | 2 | 5 | ‡8 | 1 | †6 | .... |
| 1956 | 6 | 4 | .... | 3 | 2 | 5 | ‡7 | 1 | †8 | .... |
| 1957 | 5 | 3 | .... | 2 | 6 | 4 | ‡8 | 1 | †7 | .... |
| 1958 | 6 | 3 | .... | 2 | 4 | 5 | ‡8 | 1 | †7 | .... |
| 1959 | 6 | 5 | .... | 1 | 2 | 4 | ‡8 | 3 | †7 | .... |
| 1960 | 2 | 7 | .... | 3 | 4 | 6 | ‡5 | 1 | †8 | .... |
| 1961 | 3 | 6 | §8 | 4 | 5 | 2 | 7 | 1 | x†9 | x9 |
| 1962 | 7 | 8 | §3 | 5 | 6 | 4 | 2 | 1 | †9 | 10 |
| 1963 | 4 | 7 | §9 | 2 | x5 | x5 | 3 | 1 | †8 | 10 |
| 1964 | 3 | 8 | §5 | 2 | x6 | 4 | x6 | 1 | †10 | 9 |
| 1965 | 3 | 9 | §7 | 2 | 5 | 4 | 1 | 6 | †10 | 8 |
| 1966 | 1 | 9 | 6 | 4 | 5 | 3 | 2 | 10 | †7 | 8 |
| 1967 | x6 | 1 | 5 | 4 | 8 | x2 | x2 | 9 | †10 | x6 |
| 1968 | 2 | 4 | x8 | x8 | 3 | 1 | 7 | 5 | 6 | 10 |

| | EAST DIVISION | | | | | | | WEST DIVISION | | | | | | |
|---|---|---|---|---|---|---|---|---|---|---|---|---|---|---|
| Year | Balt. | Bos. | Cleve. | Det. | N.Y. | Wash. | Mil. | Calif. | Chi. | K.C. | Mil. | Minn. | Oak. | Tex. |
| 1969 | 1 | 3 | 6 | 2 | 5 | 4 | .... | 3 | 5 | 4 | y6 | 1 | 2 | .... |
| 1970 | 1 | 3 | 5 | 4 | 2 | 3 | .... | 3 | 6 | x4 | x4 | 1 | 2 | .... |
| 1971 | 1 | 3 | 6 | 2 | 4 | 5 | .... | 4 | 3 | 3 | 6 | 5 | 1 | .... |
| 1972 | 3 | 2 | 5 | 1 | 4 | .... | 6 | 5 | 2 | 4 | .... | 3 | 1 | 6 |
| 1973 | 1 | 2 | 6 | 3 | 4 | .... | 5 | 4 | 5 | 2 | .... | 3 | 1 | 2 |
| 1974 | 1 | 3 | 4 | 6 | 2 | .... | 5 | 6 | 4 | 5 | .... | 3 | 1 | 2 |
| 1975 | 2 | 1 | 4 | 6 | 3 | .... | 5 | 6 | 5 | 2 | .... | 4 | 1 | 3 |

*Record of predecessor St. Louis club. †Predecessor Philadelphia (1901-54), Kansas City (1955-67). ‡Predecessor Washington Club. §Known as Los Angeles Angels from 1961 to September 2, 1965. yPredecessor Seattle club. xTied for position.

Note—In 1901, Milwaukee was eighth. In 1902, St. Louis was second.

## LEADING BATSMEN

| Year Player and Club | G. | AB. | R. | H. | TB. | 2B. | 3B. | HR. | RBI. | B.A. |
|---|---|---|---|---|---|---|---|---|---|---|
| 1901— Napoleon Lajoie, Philadelphia | 131 | 543 | 145 | 229 | 342 | 48 | 13 | 13 | .... | .422 |
| 1902— Edward Delahanty, Washington | 123 | 474 | 103 | 178 | 279 | 41 | 15 | 10 | .... | .376 |
| 1903— Napoleon Lajoie, Cleveland | 126 | 488 | 90 | 173 | 260 | 40 | 13 | 7 | .... | .355 |
| 1904— Napoleon Lajoie, Cleveland | 140 | 554 | 92 | 211 | 304 | 50 | 14 | 5 | .... | .381 |
| 1905— Elmer Flick, Cleveland | 131 | 496 | 71 | 152 | 231 | 29 | 19 | 4 | .... | .306 |
| 1906— George Stone, St. Louis | 154 | 581 | 91 | 208 | 288 | 24 | 19 | 6 | .... | .358 |
| 1907— Tyrus Cobb, Detroit | 150 | 605 | 97 | 212 | 286 | 29 | 15 | 5 | 116 | .350 |
| 1908— Tyrus Cobb, Detroit | 150 | 581 | 88 | 188 | 276 | 36 | 20 | 4 | 101 | .324 |
| 1909— Tyrus Cobb, Detroit | 156 | 573 | 116 | 216 | 296 | 33 | 10 | 9 | 115 | .377 |
| 1910— Tyrus Cobb, Detroit | 140 | 509 | 106 | 196 | 282 | 36 | 13 | 8 | 88 | .385 |
| 1911— Tyrus Cobb, Detroit | 146 | 591 | 147 | 248 | 367 | 47 | 24 | 8 | 144 | .420 |
| 1912— Tyrus Cobb, Detroit | 140 | 553 | 119 | 227 | 324 | 30 | 23 | 7 | 90 | .410 |
| 1913— Tyrus Cobb, Detroit | 122 | 428 | 70 | 167 | 229 | 18 | 16 | 4 | 65 | .390 |
| 1914— Tyrus Cobb, Detroit | 97 | 345 | 69 | 127 | 177 | 22 | 11 | 2 | 57 | .368 |
| 1915— Tyrus Cobb, Detroit | 156 | 563 | 114 | 208 | 274 | 31 | 13 | 3 | 95 | .369 |
| 1916— Tristram Speaker, Cleveland | 151 | 546 | 102 | 211 | 274 | 41 | 8 | 2 | 83 | .386 |

# LEADING BATSMEN—Continued

| Year | Player and Club | G. | AB. | R. | H. | TB. | 2B. | 3B. | HR. | RBI. | B.A. |
|------|-----------------|-----|-----|-----|-----|-----|-----|-----|-----|------|------|
| 1917— | Tyrus Cobb, Detroit | 152 | 588 | 107 | 225 | 336 | 44 | 23 | 7 | 108 | .383 |
| 1978— | Tyrus Cobb, Detroit | 111 | 421 | 83 | 161 | 217 | 19 | 14 | 3 | 64 | .382 |
| 1919— | Tyrus Cobb, Detroit | 124 | 497 | 92 | 191 | 256 | 36 | 13 | 1 | 69 | .384 |
| 1920— | George Sisler, St. Louis | 154 | 631 | 137 | 257 | 399 | 49 | 18 | 19 | 122 | .407 |
| 1921— | Harry Heilmann, Detroit | 149 | 602 | 114 | 237 | 365 | 43 | 14 | 19 | 139 | .394 |
| 1922— | George Sisler, St. Louis | 142 | 586 | 134 | 246 | 348 | 42 | 18 | 8 | 105 | .420 |
| 1923— | Harry Heilmann, Detroit | 144 | 524 | 121 | 211 | 331 | 44 | 11 | 18 | 115 | .403 |
| 1924— | George (Babe) Ruth, New York | 153 | 529 | 143 | 200 | 391 | 39 | 7 | 46 | 121 | .378 |
| 1925— | Harry Heilmann, Detroit | 150 | 573 | 97 | 225 | 326 | 40 | 11 | 13 | 133 | .393 |
| 1926— | Henry Manush, Detroit | 136 | 498 | 95 | 188 | 281 | 35 | 8 | 14 | 86 | .378 |
| 1927— | Harry Heilmann, Detroit | 141 | 505 | 106 | 201 | 311 | 50 | 9 | 14 | 120 | .398 |
| 1928— | Leon (Goose) Goslin, Washington | 135 | 456 | 80 | 173 | 280 | 36 | 10 | 17 | 102 | .379 |
| 1929— | Lew Fonseca, Cleveland | 148 | 566 | 97 | 209 | 301 | 44 | 15 | 6 | 103 | .369 |
| 1930— | Aloysius Simmons, Philadelphia | 138 | 554 | 152 | 211 | 392 | 41 | 16 | 36 | 165 | .381 |
| 1931— | Aloysius Simmons, Philadelphia | 128 | 513 | 105 | 200 | 329 | 37 | 13 | 22 | 128 | .390 |
| 1932— | Dale Alexander, Detroit-Boston | 124 | 392 | 58 | 144 | 201 | 27 | 3 | 8 | 60 | .367 |
| 1933— | James Foxx, Philadelphia | 149 | 573 | 125 | 204 | 403 | 37 | 9 | 48 | 163 | .356 |
| 1934— | H. Louis Gehrig, New York | 154 | 579 | 128 | 210 | 409 | 40 | 6 | 49 | 165 | .363 |
| 1935— | Chas. (Buddy) Myer, Washington | 151 | 616 | 115 | 215 | 288 | 36 | 11 | 5 | 100 | .349 |
| 1936— | Lucius Appling, Chicago | 138 | 526 | 111 | 204 | 267 | 31 | 7 | 6 | 128 | .388 |
| 1937— | Charles Gehringer, Detroit | 144 | 564 | 133 | 209 | 293 | 40 | 1 | 14 | 96 | .371 |
| 1938— | James Foxx, Boston | 149 | 565 | 139 | 197 | 398 | 33 | 9 | 50 | 175 | .349 |
| 1939— | Joseph DiMaggio, New York | 120 | 462 | 108 | 176 | 310 | 32 | 6 | 30 | 126 | .381 |
| 1940— | Joseph DiMaggio, New York | 132 | 508 | 93 | 179 | 318 | 28 | 9 | 31 | 133 | .352 |
| 1941— | Theodore Williams, Boston | 143 | 456 | 135 | 185 | 335 | 33 | 3 | 37 | 120 | .406 |
| 1942— | Theodore Williams, Boston | 150 | 522 | 141 | 186 | 338 | 34 | 5 | 36 | 137 | .356 |
| 1943— | Lucius Appling, Chicago | 155 | 585 | 63 | 192 | 238 | 33 | 2 | 3 | 80 | .328 |
| 1944— | Louis Boudreau, Cleveland | 150 | 584 | 91 | 191 | 255 | 45 | 5 | 3 | 67 | .327 |
| 1945— | George Stirnweiss, New York | 152 | 632 | 107 | 195 | 301 | 32 | 22 | 10 | 64 | .309 |
| 1946— | Jas. (Mickey) Vernon, Washington | 148 | 587 | 88 | 207 | 298 | 51 | 8 | 8 | 85 | .353 |
| 1947— | Theodore Williams, Boston | 156 | 528 | 125 | 181 | 335 | 40 | 9 | 32 | 114 | .343 |
| 1948— | Theodore Williams, Boston | 137 | 509 | 124 | 188 | 313 | 44 | 3 | 25 | 127 | .369 |
| 1949— | George Kell, Detroit | 134 | 522 | 97 | 179 | 244 | 38 | 9 | 3 | 59 | .343 |
| 1950— | William Goodman, Boston | 110 | 424 | 91 | 150 | 193 | 25 | 3 | 4 | 68 | .354 |
| 1951— | Ferris Fain, Philadelphia | 117 | 425 | 63 | 146 | 200 | 30 | 3 | 6 | 57 | .344 |
| 1952— | Ferris Fain, Philadelphia | 145 | 538 | 82 | 176 | 231 | 43 | 3 | 2 | 59 | .327 |
| 1953— | Jas. (Mickey) Vernon, Washington | 152 | 608 | 101 | 205 | 315 | 43 | 11 | 15 | 115 | .337 |
| 1954— | Roberto Avila, Cleveland | 143 | 555 | 112 | 189 | 265 | 27 | 2 | 15 | 67 | .341 |
| 1955— | Albert Kaline, Detroit | 152 | 588 | 121 | 200 | 321 | 24 | 8 | 27 | 102 | .340 |
| 1956— | Mickey Mantle, New York | 150 | 533 | 132 | 188 | 376 | 22 | 5 | 52 | 130 | .353 |
| 1957— | Theodore Williams, Boston | 132 | 420 | 96 | 163 | 307 | 28 | 1 | 38 | 87 | .388 |
| 1958— | Theodore Williams, Boston | 129 | 411 | 81 | 135 | 240 | 23 | 2 | 26 | 85 | .328 |
| 1959— | Harvey Kuenn, Detroit | 139 | 561 | 99 | 198 | 281 | 42 | 7 | 9 | 71 | .353 |
| 1960— | James (Pete) Runnels, Boston | 143 | 528 | 80 | 169 | 208 | 29 | 2 | 2 | 35 | .320 |
| 1961— | Norman Cash, Detroit | 159 | 535 | 119 | 193 | 354 | 22 | 8 | 41 | 132 | .361 |
| 1962— | James (Pete) Runnels, Boston | 152 | 562 | 80 | 183 | 256 | 33 | 5 | 10 | 60 | .326 |
| 1963— | Carl Yastrzemski, Boston | 151 | 570 | 91 | 183 | 271 | 40 | 3 | 14 | 68 | .321 |
| 1964— | Pedro (Tony) Oliva, Minnesota | 161 | 672 | 109 | 217 | 374 | 43 | 9 | 32 | 94 | .323 |
| 1965— | Pedro (Tony) Oliva, Minnesota | 149 | 576 | 107 | 185 | 283 | 40 | 5 | 16 | 98 | .321 |
| 1966— | Frank Robinson, Baltimore | 155 | 576 | 122 | 182 | 367 | 34 | 2 | 49 | 122 | .316 |
| 1967— | Carl Yastrzemski, Boston | 161 | 579 | 112 | 189 | 360 | 31 | 4 | 44 | 121 | .326 |
| 1968— | Carl Yastrzemski, Boston | 157 | 539 | 90 | 162 | 267 | 32 | 2 | 23 | 74 | .301 |
| 1969— | Rodney Carew, Minnesota | 123 | 458 | 79 | 152 | 214 | 30 | 4 | 8 | 56 | .332 |
| 1970— | Alexander Johnson, California | 156 | 614 | 85 | 202 | 282 | 26 | 6 | 14 | 86 | .329 |
| 1971— | Pedro (Tony) Oliva, Minnesota | 126 | 487 | 73 | 164 | 266 | 30 | 3 | 22 | 81 | .337 |
| 1972— | Rodney Carew, Minnesota | 142 | 535 | 61 | 170 | 203 | 21 | 6 | 0 | 51 | .318 |
| 1973— | Rodney Carew, Minnesota | 149 | 580 | 98 | 203 | 273 | 30 | 11 | 6 | 62 | .350 |
| 1974— | Rodney Carew, Minnesota | 153 | 599 | 86 | 218 | 267 | 30 | 5 | 3 | 55 | .364 |
| 1975— | Rodney Carew, Minnesota | 143 | 535 | 89 | 192 | 266 | 24 | 4 | 14 | 80 | .359 |

# LEADERS IN RUNS SCORED

| Year | Player and Club | Runs |
|------|-----------------|------|
| 1900— | (Not classed as major) | |
| 1901— | Napoleon Lajoie, Philadelphia | 145 |
| 1902— | David Fultz, Philadelphia | 110 |
| 1903— | Patrick Dougherty, Boston | 108 |
| 1904— | Patrick Dougherty, Boston-New York | 113 |
| 1905— | Harry Davis, Philadelphia | 92 |
| 1906— | Elmer Flick, Cleveland | 98 |
| 1907— | Samuel Crawford, Detroit | 102 |
| 1908— | Matthew McIntyre, Detroit | 105 |
| 1909— | Tyrus Cobb, Detroit | 116 |
| 1910— | Tyrus Cobb, Detroit | 106 |
| 1911— | Tyrus Cobb, Detroit | 147 |
| 1912— | Edward Collins, Philadelphia | 137 |
| 1913— | Edward Collins, Philadelphia | 125 |
| 1914— | Edward Collins, Philadelphia | 122 |
| 1915— | Tyrus Cobb, Detroit | 144 |
| 1916— | Tyrus Cobb, Detroit | 113 |
| 1917— | Owen (Donie) Bush, Detroit | 112 |
| 1918— | Raymond Chapman, Cleveland | 84 |
| 1919— | George (Babe) Ruth, Boston | 103 |
| 1920— | George (Babe) Ruth, New York | 158 |
| 1921— | George (Babe) Ruth, New York | 177 |
| 1922— | George Sisler, St. Louis | 134 |
| 1923— | George (Babe) Ruth, New York | 151 |
| 1924— | George (Babe) Ruth, New York | 143 |
| 1925— | John Mostil, Chicago | 135 |
| 1926— | George (Babe) Ruth, New York | 139 |
| 1927— | George (Babe) Ruth, New York | 158 |
| 1928— | George (Babe) Ruth, New York | 163 |
| 1929— | Charles Gehringer, Detroit | 131 |
| 1930— | Aloysius Simmons, Philadelphia | 152 |
| 1931— | H. Louis Gehrig, New York | 163 |
| 1932— | James Foxx, Philadelphia | 151 |
| 1933— | H. Louis Gehrig, New York | 138 |
| 1934— | Charles Gehringer, Detroit | 134 |
| 1935— | H. Louis Gehrig, New York | 125 |
| 1936— | H. Louis Gehrig, New York | 167 |
| 1937— | Joseph DiMaggio, New York | 151 |
| 1938— | Henry Greenberg, Detroit | 144 |
| 1939— | Robert (Red) Rolfe, New York | 139 |
| 1940— | Theodore Williams, Boston | 134 |
| 1941— | Theodore Williams, Boston | 135 |
| 1942— | Theodore Williams, Boston | 141 |
| 1943— | George Case, Washington | 102 |
| 1944— | George Stirnweiss, New York | 125 |
| 1945— | George Stirnweiss, New York | 107 |
| 1946— | Theodore Williams, Boston | 142 |
| 1947— | Theodore Williams, Boston | 125 |
| 1948— | Thomas Henrich, New York | 138 |
| 1949— | Theodore Williams, Boston | 150 |
| 1950— | Dominic DiMaggio, Boston | 131 |
| 1951— | Dominic DiMaggio, Boston | 113 |
| 1952— | Lawrence Doby, Cleveland | 104 |
| 1953— | Albert Rosen, Cleveland | 115 |
| 1954— | Mickey Mantle, New York | 129 |
| 1955— | Alphonse Smith, Cleveland | 123 |
| 1956— | Mickey Mantle, New York | 132 |
| 1957— | Mickey Mantle, New York | 121 |
| 1958— | Mickey Mantle, New York | 127 |
| 1959— | Edward Yost, Detroit | 115 |
| 1960— | Mickey Mantle, New York | 119 |
| 1961— | Mantle, New York-Maris, New York | 132 |
| 1962— | Albert G. Pearson, Los Angeles | 115 |
| 1963— | W. Robert Allison, Minnesota | 99 |
| 1964— | Pedro (Tony) Oliva, Minnesota | 109 |
| 1965— | Zoilo Versalles, Minnesota | 126 |
| 1966— | Frank Robinson, Baltimore | 122 |
| 1967— | Carl Yastrzemski, Boston | 112 |
| 1968— | Richard McAuliffe, Detroit | 95 |
| 1969— | Reginald Jackson, Oakland | 123 |
| 1970— | Carl Yastrzemski, Boston | 125 |
| 1971— | Donald Buford, Baltimore | 99 |
| 1972— | Bobby Murcer, New York | 102 |
| 1973— | Reginald Jackson, Oakland | 99 |
| 1974— | Carl Yastrzemski, Boston | 93 |
| 1975— | Fred Lynn, Boston | 103 |

# LEADERS IN HITS

| Year | Player and Club | Hits |
|------|-----------------|------|
| 1900— | (Not classed as major) | |
| 1901— | Napoleon Lajoie, Philadelphia | 229 |
| 1902— | Charles Hickman, Cleveland | 194 |
| 1903— | Patrick Dougherty, Boston | 195 |
| 1904— | Napoleon Lajoie, Cleveland | 211 |
| 1905— | George Stone, St. Louis | 187 |
| 1906— | Napoleon Lajoie, Cleveland | 214 |
| 1907— | Tyrus Cobb, Detroit | 212 |
| 1908— | Tyrus Cobb, Detroit | 188 |
| 1909— | Tyrus Cobb, Detroit | 216 |
| 1910— | Napoleon Lajoie, Cleveland | 227 |
| 1911— | Tyrus Cobb, Detroit | 248 |
| 1912— | Tyrus Cobb, Detroit | 227 |
| 1913— | Joseph Jackson, Cleveland | 197 |
| 1914— | Tristram Speaker, Boston | 193 |
| 1915— | Tyrus Cobb, Detroit | 208 |
| 1916— | Tristram Speaker, Cleveland | 211 |
| 1917— | Tyrus Cobb, Detroit | 225 |
| 1918— | George Burns, Philadelphia | 178 |
| 1919— | Cobb, Detroit-Robert Veach, Detroit | 191 |
| 1920— | George Sisler, St. Louis | 257 |
| 1921— | Harry Heilmann, Detroit | 237 |
| 1922— | George Sisler, St. Louis | 246 |
| 1923— | Charles Jamieson, Cleveland | 222 |
| 1924— | Edgar (Sam) Rice, Washington | 216 |
| 1925— | Aloysius Simmons, Philadelphia | 253 |
| 1926— | George Burns, Cleveland | 216 |
| | Edgar (Sam) Rice, Washington | 216 |
| 1927— | Earle Combs, New York | 231 |
| 1928— | Henry Manush, St. Louis | 241 |
| 1929— | Dale Alexander, Detroit | 215 |
| | Charles Gehringer, Detroit | 215 |
| 1930— | U. John Hodapp, Cleveland | 225 |
| 1931— | H. Louis Gehrig, New York | 211 |
| 1932— | Aloysius Simmons, Philadelphia | 216 |
| 1933— | Henry Manush, Washington | 221 |
| 1934— | Charles Gehringer, Detroit | 214 |
| 1935— | Joseph Vosmik, Cleveland | 216 |
| 1936— | H. Earl Averill, Cleveland | 232 |
| 1937— | Roy (Beau) Bell, St. Louis | 218 |
| 1938— | Joseph Vosmik, Boston | 201 |
| 1939— | Robert (Red) Rolfe, New York | 213 |

## LEADERS IN HITS—Continued

| Year | Player and Club | Hits |
|---|---|---|
| 1940— | Raymond (Rip) Radcliff, St. Louis | 200 |
| | W. Barney McCosky, Detroit | 200 |
| | Roger (Doc) Cramer, Boston | 200 |
| 1941— | Cecil Travis, Washington | 218 |
| 1942— | John Pesky, Boston | 205 |
| 1943— | Richard Wakefield, Detroit | 200 |
| 1944— | George Stirnweiss, New York | 205 |
| 1945— | George Stirnweiss, New York | 195 |
| 1946— | John Pesky, Boston | 208 |
| 1947— | John Pesky, Boston | 207 |
| 1948— | Robert Dillinger, St. Louis | 207 |
| 1949— | L. Dale Mitchell, Cleveland | 203 |
| 1950— | George Kell, Detroit | 218 |
| 1951— | George Kell, Detroit | 191 |
| 1952— | J. Nelson Fox, Chicago | 192 |
| 1953— | Harvey Kuenn, Detroit | 209 |
| 1954— | Fox, Chicago-Kuenn, Detroit | 201 |
| 1955— | Albert Kaline, Detroit | 200 |
| 1956— | Harvey Kuenn, Detroit | 196 |

| Year | Player and Club | Hits |
|---|---|---|
| 1957— | J. Nelson Fox, Chicago | 196 |
| 1958— | J. Nelson Fox, Chicago | 187 |
| 1959— | Harvey Kuenn, Detroit | 198 |
| 1960— | Orestes (Minnie) Minoso, Chicago | 184 |
| 1961— | Norman Cash, Detroit | 193 |
| 1962— | Robert Richardson, New York | 209 |
| 1963— | Carl Yastrzemski, Boston | 183 |
| 1964— | Pedro (Tony) Oliva, Minnesota | 217 |
| 1965— | Pedro (Tony) Oliva, Minnesota | 185 |
| 1966— | Pedro (Tony) Oliva, Minnesota | 191 |
| 1967— | Carl Yastrzemski, Boston | 189 |
| 1968— | Dagoberto Campaneris, Oakland | 177 |
| 1969— | Pedro (Tony) Oliva, Minnesota | 197 |
| 1970— | Pedro (Tony) Oliva, Minnesota | 204 |
| 1971— | Cesar Tovar, Minnesota | 204 |
| 1972— | Joseph Rudi, Oakland | 181 |
| 1973— | Rodney Carew, Minnesota | 203 |
| 1974— | Rodney Carew, Minnesota | 218 |
| 1975— | George Brett, Kansas City | 195 |

## ONE-BASE HIT LEADERS

| Year | Player and Club | 1B. |
|---|---|---|
| 1900— | (Not classed as major) | |
| 1901— | Napoleon Lajoie, Philadelphia | 155 |
| 1902— | Fielder A. Jones, Chicago | 148 |
| 1903— | Patrick H. Dougherty, Boston | 161 |
| 1904— | William H. Keeler, New York | 164 |
| 1905— | William H. Keeler, New York | 147 |
| 1906— | William H. Keeler, New York | 166 |
| 1907— | Tyrus R. Cobb, Detroit | 163 |
| 1908— | Matthew W. McIntyre, Detroit | 131 |
| | George R. Stone, St. Louis | 131 |
| 1909— | Tyrus R. Cobb, Detroit | 164 |
| 1910— | Napoleon Lajoie, Cleveland | 165 |
| 1911— | Tyrus R. Cobb, Detroit | 169 |
| 1912— | Tyrus R. Cobb, Detroit | 167 |
| 1913— | Edward T. Collins, Philadelphia | 145 |
| 1914— | John P. McInnis, Philadelphia | 160 |
| 1915— | Tyrus R. Cobb, Detroit | 161 |
| 1916— | Tristram Speaker, Cleveland | 160 |
| 1917— | Tyrus R. Cobb, Detroit | 151 |
| | J. Clyde Milan, Washington | 151 |
| 1918— | George H. Burns, Philadelphia | 141 |
| 1919— | Edgar C. Rice, Washington | 144 |
| 1920— | George H. Sisler, St. Louis | 171 |
| 1921— | John T. Tobin, St. Louis | 179 |
| 1922— | George Sisler, St. Louis | 134 |
| 1923— | Charles D. Jamieson, Cleveland | 172 |
| 1924— | Charles D. Jamieson, Cleveland | 168 |
| 1925— | Edgar C. Rice, Washington | 182 |
| 1926— | Edgar C. Rice, Washington | 167 |
| 1927— | Earle B. Combs, New York | 166 |
| 1928— | Henry E. Manush, St. Louis | 161 |
| 1929— | Earle B. Combs, New York | 151 |
| 1930— | Edgar C. Rice, Washington | 158 |
| 1931— | Oscar D. Melillo, St. Louis | 142 |
| | Jonathan T. Stone, Detroit | 142 |
| 1932— | Henry E. Manush, Washington | 145 |
| 1933— | Henry E. Manush, Washington | 167 |
| 1934— | Roger M. Cramer, Philadelphia | 158 |
| 1935— | Roger M. Cramer, Philadelphia | 170 |
| 1936— | Raymond A. Radcliff, Chicago | 161 |

| Year | Player and Club | 1B. |
|---|---|---|
| 1937— | John K. Lewis, Washington | 162 |
| 1938— | Melo B. Almada, Wash.-St. Louis | 158 |
| 1939— | Roger M. Cramer, Boston | 147 |
| 1940— | Roger M. Cramer, Boston | 160 |
| 1941— | Cecil H. Travis, Washington | 153 |
| 1942— | John M. Pesky, Boston | 165 |
| 1943— | Roger M. Cramer, Detroit | 159 |
| 1944— | George H. Stirnweiss, New York | 146 |
| 1945— | Irvin G. Hall, Philadelphia | 139 |
| 1946— | John M. Pesky, Boston | 159 |
| 1947— | John M. Pesky, Boston | 172 |
| 1948— | L. Dale Mitchell, Cleveland | 162 |
| 1949— | L. Dale Mitchell, Cleveland | 161 |
| 1950— | Philip F. Rizzuto, New York | 150 |
| 1951— | George C. Kell, Detroit | 150 |
| 1952— | J. Nelson Fox, Chicago | 157 |
| 1953— | Harvey E. Kuenn, Detroit | 167 |
| 1954— | J. Nelson Fox, Chicago | 167 |
| 1955— | J. Nelson Fox, Chicago | 157 |
| 1956— | J. Nelson Fox, Chicago | 158 |
| 1957— | J. Nelson Fox, Chicago | 155 |
| 1958— | J. Nelson Fox, Chicago | 160 |
| 1959— | J. Nelson Fox, Chicago | 149 |
| 1960— | J. Nelson Fox, Chicago | 139 |
| 1961— | Robert C. Richardson, New York | 148 |
| 1962— | Robert C. Richardson, New York | 158 |
| 1963— | Albert G. Pearson, Los Angeles | 139 |
| 1964— | Robert C. Richardson, New York | 148 |
| 1965— | Donald A. Buford, Chicago | 129 |
| 1966— | Luis E. Aparicio, Baltimore | 143 |
| 1967— | Horace M. Clarke, New York | 140 |
| 1968— | Dagoberto B. Campaneris, Oakland | 139 |
| 1969— | Horace M. Clarke, New York | 146 |
| 1970— | Alexander Johnson, California | 156 |
| 1971— | Cesar L. Tovar, Minnesota | 171 |
| 1972— | Rodney C. Carew, Minnesota | 143 |
| 1973— | Rodney C. Carew, Minnesota | 156 |
| 1974— | Rodney C. Carew, Minnesota | 180 |
| 1975— | Thurman Munson, New York | 151 |

# TWO-BASE HIT LEADERS

| Year | Player and Club | 2B. |
|---|---|---|
| 1900— | (Not classed as major) | |
| 1901— | Napoleon Lajoie, Philadelphia | 48 |
| 1902— | Harry Davis, Philadelphia | 43 |
| 1903— | Ralph Seybold, Philadelphia | 43 |
| 1904— | Napoleon Lajoie, Cleveland | 50 |
| 1905— | Harry Davis, Philadelphia | 47 |
| 1906— | Napoleon Lajoie, Cleveland | 49 |
| 1907— | Harry Davis, Philadelphia | 37 |
| 1908— | Tyrus Cobb, Detroit | 36 |
| 1909— | Samuel Crawford, Detroit | 35 |
| 1910— | Napoleon Lajoie, Cleveland | 51 |
| 1911— | Tyrus Cobb, Detroit | 47 |
| 1912— | Tristram Speaker, Boston | 53 |
| 1913— | Joseph Jackson, Cleveland | 39 |
| 1914— | Tristram Speaker, Boston | 46 |
| 1915— | Robert Veach, Detroit | 40 |
| 1916— | Graney, Cleveland-Speaker, Cleveland | 41 |
| 1917— | Tyrus Cobb, Detroit | 44 |
| 1918— | Tristram Speaker, Cleveland | 33 |
| 1919— | Robert Veach, Detroit | 45 |
| 1920— | Tristram Speaker, Cleveland | 50 |
| 1921— | Tristram Speaker, Cleveland | 52 |
| 1922— | Tristram Speaker, Cleveland | 48 |
| 1923— | Tristram Speaker, Cleveland | 59 |
| 1924— | J. Sewell, Cleveland-Heilmann, Detroit | 45 |
| 1925— | Martin McManus, St. Louis | 44 |
| 1926— | George Burns, Cleveland | 64 |
| 1927— | H. Louis Gehrig, New York | 52 |
| 1928— | Manush, St. Louis-Gehrig, New York | 47 |
| 1929— | Manush, St. L.-R. Johnson, Detroit-Gehringer, Detroit | 45 |
| 1930— | U. John Hodapp, Cleveland | 51 |
| 1931— | Earl Webb, Boston | 67 |
| 1932— | Eric McNair, Philadelphia | 47 |
| 1933— | Joseph Cronin, Washington | 45 |
| 1934— | Henry Greenberg, Detroit | 63 |
| 1935— | Joseph Vosmik, Cleveland | 47 |
| 1936— | Charles Gehringer, Detroit | 60 |
| 1937— | Roy (Beau) Bell, St. Louis | 51 |
| 1938— | Joseph Cronin, Boston | 51 |
| 1939— | Robert (Red) Rolfe, New York | 46 |
| 1940— | Henry Greenberg, Detroit | 50 |
| 1941— | Louis Boudreau, Cleveland | 45 |
| 1942— | Donald Kolloway, Chicago | 40 |
| 1943— | Richard Wakefield, Detroit | 38 |
| 1944— | Louis Boudreau, Cleveland | 45 |
| 1945— | Wallace Moses, Chicago | 35 |
| 1946— | Jas. (Mickey) Vernon, Washington | 51 |
| 1947— | Louis Boudreau, Cleveland | 45 |
| 1948— | Theodore Williams, Boston | 44 |
| 1949— | Theodore Williams, Boston | 39 |
| 1950— | George Kell, Detroit | 56 |
| 1951— | Kell, Det.-Yost, Wash.-Mele, Wash. | 36 |
| 1952— | Ferris Fain, Philadelphia | 43 |
| 1953— | Jas. (Mickey) Vernon, Washington | 43 |
| 1954— | Jas. (Mickey) Vernon, Washington | 33 |
| 1955— | Harvey Kuenn, Detroit | 38 |
| 1956— | James Piersall, Boston | 40 |
| 1957— | Minoso, Chicago-Gardner, Baltimore | 36 |
| 1958— | Harvey Kuenn, Detroit | 39 |
| 1959— | Harvey Kuenn, Detroit | 42 |
| 1960— | John (Tito) Francona, Cleveland | 36 |
| 1961— | Albert Kaline, Detroit | 41 |
| 1962— | Floyd Robinson, Chicago | 45 |
| 1963— | Carl Yastrzemski, Boston | 40 |
| 1964— | Pedro (Tony) Oliva, Minnesota | 43 |
| 1965— | Zoilo Versalles, Minnesota | 45 |
| | Carl Yastrzemski, Boston | 45 |
| 1966— | Carl Yastrzemski, Boston | 39 |
| 1967— | Pedro (Tony) Oliva, Minnesota | 34 |
| 1968— | C. Reginald Smith, Boston | 37 |
| 1969— | Pedro (Tony) Oliva, Minnesota | 39 |
| 1970— | Pedro (Tony) Oliva, Minnesota | 36 |
| | Amos Otis, Kansas City | 36 |
| | Cesar Tovar, Minnesota | 36 |
| 1971— | C. Reginald Smith, Boston | 33 |
| 1972— | Louis Piniella, Kansas City | 33 |
| 1973— | Salvatore Bando, Oakland | 32 |
| | Pedro Garcia, Milwaukee | 32 |
| 1974— | Joseph Rudi, Oakland | 39 |
| 1975— | Fred Lynn, Boston | 47 |

# THREE-BASE HIT LEADERS

| Year | Player and Club | 3B. |
|---|---|---|
| 1900— | (Not classed as major) | |
| 1901— | James Williams, Baltimore | 22 |
| 1902— | James Williams, Baltimore | 23 |
| 1903— | Samuel Crawford, Detroit | 25 |
| 1904— | Charles (Chick) Stahl, Boston | 22 |
| 1905— | Elmer Flick, Cleveland | 19 |
| 1906— | Elmer Flick, Cleveland | 22 |
| 1907— | Elmer Flick, Cleveland | 18 |
| 1908— | Tyrus, Cobb, Detroit | 20 |
| 1909— | J. Franklin Baker, Philadelphia | 19 |
| 1910— | Samuel Crawford, Detroit | 19 |
| 1911— | Tyrus Cobb, Detroit | 24 |
| 1912— | Joseph Jackson, Cleveland | 26 |
| 1913— | Samuel Crawford, Detroit | 23 |
| 1914— | Samuel Crawford, Detroit | 26 |
| 1915— | Samuel Crawford, Detroit | 19 |
| 1916— | Joseph Jackson, Chicago | 21 |
| 1917— | Tyrus Cobb, Detroit | 23 |
| 1918— | Tyrus Cobb, Detroit | 14 |
| 1919— | Robert Veach, Detroit | 17 |
| 1920— | Joseph Jackson, Chicago | 20 |
| 1921— | Howard Shanks, Washington | 19 |
| 1922— | George Sisler, St. Louis | 18 |
| 1923— | Rice, Washington-Goslin, Washington | 18 |
| 1924— | Walter Pipp, New York | 19 |
| 1925— | Leon (Goose) Goslin, Washington | 20 |
| 1926— | H. Louis Gehrig, New York | 20 |
| 1927— | Earle Combs, New York | 23 |
| 1928— | Earle Combs, New York | 21 |
| 1929— | Charles Gehringer, Detroit | 19 |
| 1930— | Earle Combs, New York | 22 |
| 1931— | Roy Johnson, Detroit | 19 |
| 1932— | Joseph Cronin, Washington | 18 |
| 1933— | Henry Manush, Washington | 17 |
| 1934— | W. Benjamin Chapman, New York | 13 |
| 1935— | Joseph Vosmik, Cleveland | 20 |
| 1936— | Averill, Cleveland-J. MiMaggio, N.Y. | 15 |
| | Rolfe, New York | 15 |

## THREE-BASE LEADERS—Continued

| Year | Player and Club | 3B. |
|---|---|---|
| 1937— | F. Walker, Chicago-Kreevich, Chicago | 16 |
| 1938— | J. Geoffrey Heath, Cleveland | 18 |
| 1939— | John (Buddy) Lewis, Washington | 16 |
| 1940— | Barney McCosky, Detroit | 19 |
| 1941— | J. Geoffrey Heath, Cleveland | 20 |
| 1942— | Stanley Spencer, Washington | 15 |
| 1943— | Lindell, New York-Moses, Chicago | 12 |
| 1944— | Lindell, N. York-Stirnweiss, N. York | 16 |
| 1945— | George Stirnweiss, New York | 22 |
| 1946— | Henry Edwards, Cleveland | 16 |
| 1947— | Thomas Henrich, New York | 13 |
| 1948— | Thomas Henrich, New York | 14 |
| 1949— | L. Dale Mitchell, Cleveland | 23 |
| 1950— | D. DiMaggio, Doerr, Bos.-Evers, Det. | 11 |
| 1951— | Orestes (Minnie) Minoso, Clev.-Chi. | 14 |
| 1952— | Roberto Avila, Cleveland | 11 |
| 1953— | Manuel (Jim) Rivera, Chicago | 16 |
| 1954— | Orestes (Minnie) Minoso, Chicago | 18 |
| 1955— | Mantle, New York-Carey, New York | 11 |
| 1956— | Minoso, Chicago-Jensen, Boston-Simpson, Kansas City-Lemon, Wash. | 11 |
| 1957— | McDougald, Bauer, Simpson, New York | 9 |

| Year | Player and Club | 3B. |
|---|---|---|
| 1958— | Victor Power, Kansas City-Cleveland | 10 |
| 1959— | W. Robert Allison, Washington | 9 |
| 1960— | J. Nelson Fox, Chicago | 10 |
| 1961— | Jacob Wood, Detroit | 14 |
| 1962— | Gino Cimoli, Kansas City | 15 |
| 1963— | Zoilo Versalles, Minnesota | 13 |
| 1964— | Rich, Rollins, Versalles, Minnesota | 10 |
| 1965— | Dagoberto Campaneris, Kansas City | 12 |
| | Zoilo Versalles, Minnesota | 12 |
| 1966— | Robert Knoop, California | 11 |
| 1967— | Paul L. Blair, Baltimore | 12 |
| 1968— | James Fregosi, California | 13 |
| 1969— | Delbert Unser, Washington | 8 |
| 1970— | Cesar Tovar, Minnesota | 13 |
| 1971— | Freddie Patek, Kansas City | 11 |
| 1972— | Carlton Fisk, Boston | 9 |
| | Joseph Rudi, Oakland | 9 |
| 1973— | Alonza Bumbry, Baltimore | 11 |
| | Rodney Carew, Minnesota | 11 |
| 1974— | John (Mickey) Rivers, California | 11 |
| 1975— | George Brett, Kansas City | 13 |
| | John Rivers, California | 13 |

## HOME RUN LEADERS

| Year | Player and Club | HR. |
|---|---|---|
| 1900— | (Not classed as major) | |
| 1901— | Napoleon Lajoie, Philadelphia | 13 |
| 1902— | Ralph (Socks) Seybold, Philadelphia | 16 |
| 1903— | John (Buck) Freeman, Boston | 13 |
| 1904— | Harry Davis, Philadelphia | 10 |
| 1905— | Harry Davis, Philadelphia | 8 |
| 1906— | Harry Davis, Philadelphia | 12 |
| 1907— | Harry Davis, Philadelphia | 8 |
| 1908— | Samuel Crawford, Detroit | 7 |
| 1909— | Tyrus Cobb, Detroit | 9 |
| 1910— | J. Garland (Jake) Stahl, Boston | 10 |
| 1911— | J. Franklin Baker, Philadelphia | 9 |
| 1912— | J. Franklin Baker, Philadelphia | 10 |
| 1913— | J. Franklin Baker, Philadelphia | 12 |
| 1914— | Baker, Philadelphia-Crawford, Detroit | 8 |
| 1915— | Robert Roth, Chicago-Cleveland | 7 |
| 1916— | Walter Pipp, New York | 12 |
| 1917— | Walter Pipp, New York | 9 |
| 1918— | Ruth, Boston-Tilly Walker, Phila. | 11 |
| 1919— | George (Babe) Ruth, Boston | 29 |
| 1920— | George (Babe) Ruth, New York | 54 |
| 1921— | George (Babe) Ruth, New York | 59 |
| 1922— | Kenneth Williams, St. Louis | 39 |
| 1923— | George (Babe) Ruth, New York | 41 |
| 1924— | George (Babe) Ruth, New York | 46 |
| 1925— | Robert Meusel, New York | 33 |
| 1926— | George (Babe) Ruth, New York | 47 |
| 1927— | George (Babe) Ruth, New York | 60 |
| 1928— | George (Babe) Ruth, New York | 54 |
| 1929— | George (Babe) Ruth, New York | 46 |
| 1930— | George (Babe) Ruth, New York | 49 |
| 1931— | Ruth, New York-Gehrig, New York | 46 |
| 1932— | James Foxx, Philadelphia | 58 |
| 1933— | James Foxx, Philadelphia | 48 |
| 1934— | H. Louis Gehrig, New York | 49 |
| 1935— | Foxx, Philadelphia-Greenberg, Detroit | 36 |
| 1936— | H. Louis Gehrig, New York | 49 |
| 1937— | Joseph DiMaggio, New York | 46 |
| 1938— | Henry Greenberg, Detroit | 58 |

| Year | Player and Club | HR. |
|---|---|---|
| 1939— | James Foxx, Boston | 35 |
| 1940— | Henry Greenberg, Detroit | 41 |
| 1941— | Theodore Williams, Boston | 37 |
| 1942— | Theodore Williams, Boston | 36 |
| 1943— | Rudolph York, Detroit | 34 |
| 1944— | Nicholas Etten, New York | 22 |
| 1945— | Vernon Stephens, St. Louis | 24 |
| 1946— | Henry Greenberg, Detroit | 44 |
| 1947— | Theodore Williams, Boston | 32 |
| 1948— | Joseph DiMaggio, New York | 39 |
| 1949— | Theodore Williams, Boston | 43 |
| 1950— | Albert Rosen, Cleveland | 37 |
| 1951— | Gus Zernial, Chicago-Philadelphia | 33 |
| 1952— | Lawrence Doby, Cleveland | 32 |
| 1953— | Albert Rosen, Cleveland | 43 |
| 1954— | Lawrence Doby, Cleveland | 32 |
| 1955— | Mickey Mantle, New York | 37 |
| 1956— | Mickey Mantle, New York | 52 |
| 1957— | Roy Sievers, Washington | 42 |
| 1958— | Mickey Mantle, New York | 42 |
| 1959— | Colavito, Cleveland-Killebrew, Wash. | 42 |
| 1960— | Mickey Mantle, New York | 40 |
| 1961— | Roger Maris, New York | 61 |
| 1962— | Harmon Killebrew, Minnesota | 48 |
| 1963— | Harmon Killebrew, Minnesota | 45 |
| 1964— | Harmon Killebrew, Minnesota | 49 |
| 1965— | Anthony Conigilaro, Boston | 32 |
| 1966— | Frank Robinson, Baltimore | 49 |
| 1967— | Harmon Killebrew, Minnesota | 44 |
| | Carl Yastrzemski, Boston | 44 |
| 1968— | Frank Howard, Washington | 44 |
| 1969— | Harmon Killebrew, Minnesota | 49 |
| 1970— | Frank Howard, Washington | 44 |
| 1971— | William E. Melton, Chicago | 33 |
| 1972— | Richard Allen, Chicago | 37 |
| 1973— | Reginald Jackson, Oakland | 32 |
| 1974— | Richard Allen, Chicago | 32 |
| 1975— | Reginald Jackson, Oakland | 36 |
| | George Scott, Milwaukee | 36 |

## LEADERS IN TOTAL BASES

| Year | Player and Club | T.B. |
|---|---|---|
| 1900— | (Not classed as major) | |
| 1901— | Napoleon Lajoie, Philadelphia | 342 |
| 1902— | John (Buck) Freeman, Boston | 287 |
| 1903— | John (Buck) Freeman, Boston | 281 |
| 1904— | Napoleon Lajoie, Cleveland | 304 |
| 1905— | George Stone, St. Louis | 260 |
| 1906— | George Stone, St. Louis | 288 |
| 1907— | Tyrus Cobb, Detroit | 286 |
| 1908— | Tyrus Cobb, Detroit | 276 |
| 1909— | Tyrus Cobb, Detroit | 296 |
| 1910— | Napoleon Lajoie, Cleveland | 304 |
| 1911— | Tyrus Cobb, Detroit | 367 |
| 1912— | Joseph Jackson, Cleveland | 331 |
| 1913— | Samuel Crawford, Detroit | 298 |
| 1914— | Tristram Speaker, Boston | 287 |
| 1915— | Tyrus Cobb, Detroit | 274 |
| 1916— | Joseph Jackson, Chicago | 293 |
| 1917— | Tyrus Cobb, Detroit | 336 |
| 1918— | George Burns, Philadelphia | 236 |
| 1919— | George (Babe) Ruth, Boston | 284 |
| 1920— | George Sisler, St. Louis | 399 |
| 1921— | George (Babe) Ruth, New York | 457 |
| 1922— | Kenneth Williams, St. Louis | 367 |
| 1923— | George (Babe) Ruth, New York | 399 |
| 1924— | George (Babe) Ruth, New York | 391 |
| 1925— | Aloysius Simmons, Philadelphia | 392 |
| 1926— | George (Babe) Ruth, New York | 365 |
| 1927— | H. Louis Gehrig, New York | 447 |
| 1928— | George (Babe) Ruth, New York | 380 |
| 1929— | Aloysius Simmons, Philadelphia | 373 |
| 1930— | H. Louis Gehrig, New York | 419 |
| 1931— | H. Louis Gehrig, New York | 410 |
| 1932— | James Foxx, Philadelphia | 438 |
| 1933— | James Foxx, Philadelphia | 403 |
| 1934— | H. Louis Gehrig, New York | 409 |
| 1935— | Henry Greenberg, Detroit | 389 |
| 1936— | Harold Trosky, Cleveland | 405 |
| 1937— | Joseph DiMaggio, New York | 418 |
| 1938— | James Foxx, Boston | 398 |
| 1939— | Theodore Williams, Boston | 344 |
| 1940— | Henry Greenberg, Detroit | 384 |
| 1941— | Joseph DiMaggio, New York | 348 |
| 1942— | Theodore Williams, Boston | 338 |
| 1943— | Rudolph York, Detroit | 301 |
| 1944— | John Lindell, New York | 297 |
| 1945— | George Stirnweiss, New York | 301 |
| 1946— | Theodore Williams, Boston | 343 |
| 1947— | Theodore Williams, Boston | 335 |
| 1948— | Joseph DiMaggio, New York | 355 |
| 1949— | Theodore Williams, Boston | 368 |
| 1950— | Walter Dropo, Boston | 326 |
| 1951— | Theodore Williams, Boston | 295 |
| 1952— | Albert Rosen, Cleveland | 297 |
| 1953— | Albert Rosen, Cleveland | 367 |
| 1954— | Orestes (Minnie) Minoso, Chicago | 304 |
| 1955— | Albert Kaline, Detroit | 321 |
| 1956— | Mickey Mantle, New York | 376 |
| 1957— | Roy Sievers, Washington | 331 |
| 1958— | Mickey Mantle, New York | 307 |
| 1959— | Rocco Colavito, Cleveland | 301 |
| 1960— | Mickey Mantle, New York | 294 |
| 1961— | Roger Maris, New York | 366 |
| 1962— | Rocco Colavito, Detroit | 309 |
| 1963— | Richard Stuart, Boston | 319 |
| 1964— | Pedro (Tony) Oliva, Minnesota | 374 |
| 1965— | Zoilo Versalles, Minnesota | 308 |
| 1966— | Frank Robinson, Baltimore | 367 |
| 1967— | Carl Yastrzemski, Boston | 360 |
| 1968— | Frank Howard, Washington | 330 |
| 1969— | Frank Howard, Washington | 340 |
| 1970— | Carl Yastrzemski, Boston | 335 |
| 1971— | C. Reginald Smith, Boston | 302 |
| 1972— | Bobby Murcer, New York | 314 |
| 1973— | David L. May, Milwaukee | 295 |
| | George Scott, Milwaukee | 295 |
| | Salvatore L. Bando, Oakland | 295 |
| 1974— | Joseph Rudi, Oakland | 287 |
| 1975— | George Scott, Milwaukee | 318 |

## RUNS BATTED IN LEADERS

Note—Runs batted in not compiled prior to 1907; officially adopted in 1920.

| Year | Player and Club | RBI |
|---|---|---|
| 1907— | Tyrus Cobb, Detroit | 116 |
| 1908— | Tyrus Cobb, Detroit | 101 |
| 1909— | Tyrus Cobb, Detroit | 115 |
| 1910— | Samuel Crawford, Detroit | 115 |
| 1911— | Tyrus Cobb, Detroit | 144 |
| 1912— | J. Franklin Baker, Philadelphia | 133 |
| 1913— | J. Franklin Baker, Philadelphia | 126 |
| 1914— | Samuel Crawford, Detroit | 112 |
| 1915— | Samuel Crawford, Detroit | 116 |
| 1916— | Walter Pipp, New York | 99 |
| 1917— | Robert Veach, Detroit | 115 |
| 1918— | George Burns, Philadelphia | 74 |
| | Robert Veach, Detroit | 74 |
| 1919— | George (Babe) Ruth, Boston | 112 |
| 1920— | George (Babe) Ruth, New York | 137 |
| 1921— | George (Babe) Ruth, New York | 171 |
| 1922— | Kenneth Williams, St. Louis | 155 |
| 1923— | George (Babe) Ruth, New York | 131 |
| 1924— | Leon (Goose) Goslin, Washington | 129 |
| 1925— | Robert Meusel, New York | 138 |
| 1926— | George (Babe) Ruth, New York | 145 |
| 1927— | H. Louis Gehrig, New York | 175 |
| 1928— | George (Babe) Ruth, New York | 142 |
| | H. Louis Gehrig, New York | 142 |
| 1929— | Aloysius Simmons, Philadelphia | 157 |
| 1930— | H. Louis Gehrig, New York | 174 |
| 1931— | H. Louis Gehrig, New York | 184 |
| 1932— | James Foxx, Philadelphia | 169 |
| 1933— | James Foxx, Philadelphia | 163 |
| 1934— | H. Louis Gehrig, New York | 165 |
| 1935— | Henry Greenberg, Detroit | 170 |
| 1936— | Harold Trosky, Cleveland | 162 |

# RUNS BATTED IN LEADERS—Continued

| Year | Player and Club | RBI |
|---|---|---|
| 1937— | Henry Greenberg, Detroit | 183 |
| 1938— | James Foxx, Boston | 175 |
| 1939— | Theodore Williams, Boston | 145 |
| 1940— | Henry Greenberg, Detroit | 150 |
| 1941— | Joseph DiMaggio, New York | 125 |
| 1942— | Theodore Williams, Boston | 137 |
| 1943— | Rudolph York, Detroit | 118 |
| 1944— | Vernon Stephens, St. Louis | 109 |
| 1945— | Nicholas Etten, New York | 111 |
| 1946— | Henry Greenberg, Detroit | 127 |
| 1947— | Theodore Williams, Boston | 114 |
| 1948— | Joseph DiMaggio, New York | 155 |
| 1949— | Theodore Williams, Boston | 159 |
| | Vernon Stephens, Boston | 159 |
| 1950— | Walter Dropo, Boston | 144 |
| | Vernon Stephens, Boston | 144 |
| 1951— | Gus Zernial, Chicago-Philadelphia | 129 |
| 1952— | Albert Rosen, Cleveland | 105 |
| 1953— | Albert Rosen, Cleveland | 145 |
| 1954— | Lawrence Doby, Cleveland | 126 |
| 1955— | Raymond Boone, Detroit | 116 |
| | Jack Jensen, Boston | 116 |

| Year | Player and Club | RBI |
|---|---|---|
| 1956— | Mickey Mantle, New York | 130 |
| 1957— | Roy Sievers, Washington | 114 |
| 1958— | Jack Jensen, Boston | 122 |
| 1959— | Jack Jensen, Boston | 112 |
| 1960— | Roger Maris, New York | 112 |
| 1961— | Roger Maris, New York | 142 |
| 1962— | Harmon Killebrew, Minnesota | 126 |
| 1963— | Richard Stuart, Boston | 118 |
| 1964— | Brooks Robinson, Baltimore | 118 |
| 1965— | Rocco Colavito, Cleveland | 108 |
| 1966— | Frank Robinson, Baltimore | 122 |
| 1967— | Carl Yastrzemski, Boston | 121 |
| 1968— | Kenneth Harrelson, Boston | 109 |
| 1969— | Harmon Killebrew, Minnesota | 140 |
| 1970— | Frank Howard, Washington | 126 |
| 1971— | Harmon Killebrew, Minnesota | 119 |
| 1972— | Richard Allen, Chicago | 113 |
| 1973— | Reginald Jackson, Oakland | 117 |
| 1974— | Jeffrey Burroughs, Texas | 118 |
| 1975— | George Scott, Milwaukee | 109 |

# BATTERS LEADING IN BASES ON BALLS

Note—Bases on balls not included in batting records in American League prior to 1913.

| Year | Player and Club | BB. |
|---|---|---|
| 1913— | Burton Shotton, St. Louis | 102 |
| 1914— | Owen (Donie) Bush, Detroit | 112 |
| 1915— | Edward Collins, Chicago | 119 |
| 1916— | Burton Shotton, St. Louis | 111 |
| 1917— | John Graney, Cleveland | 94 |
| 1918— | Raymond Chapman, Cleveland | 84 |
| 1919— | John Graney, Cleveland | 105 |
| 1920— | George (Babe) Ruth, New York | 148 |
| 1921— | George (Babe) Ruth, New York | 144 |
| 1922— | L. W. (Whitey) Witt, New York | 89 |
| 1923— | George (Babe) Ruth, New York | 170 |
| 1924— | George (Babe) Ruth, New York | 142 |
| 1925— | William Kamm, Chicago | 90 |
| | John Mostil, Chicago | 90 |
| 1926— | George (Babe) Ruth, New York | 144 |
| 1927— | George (Babe) Ruth, New York | 138 |
| 1928— | George (Babe) Ruth, New York | 135 |
| 1929— | Max Bishop, Philadelphia | 128 |
| 1930— | George (Babe) Ruth, New York | 136 |
| 1931— | George (Babe) Ruth, New York | 128 |
| 1932— | George (Babe) Ruth, New York | 130 |
| 1933— | George (Babe) Ruth, New York | 114 |
| 1934— | James Foxx, Philadelphia | 111 |
| 1935— | H. Louis Gehrig, New York | 132 |
| 1936— | H. Louis Gehrig, New York | 130 |
| 1937— | H. Louis Gehrig, New York | 127 |
| 1938— | James Foxx, Boston | 119 |
| | Henry Greenberg, Detroit | 119 |
| 1939— | Harlond Clift, St. Louis | 111 |
| 1940— | Charles Keller, New York | 106 |
| 1941— | Theodore Williams, Boston | 145 |
| 1942— | Theodore Williams, Boston | 145 |
| 1943— | Charles Keller, New York | 106 |

| Year | Player and Club | BB. |
|---|---|---|
| 1944— | Nicholas Etten, New York | 97 |
| 1945— | Roy Cullenbine, Cleveland-Detroit | 112 |
| 1946— | Theodore Williams, Boston | 156 |
| 1947— | Theodore Williams, Boston | 162 |
| 1948— | Theodore Williams, Boston | 126 |
| 1949— | Theodore Williams, Boston | 162 |
| 1950— | Edward Yost, Washington | 141 |
| 1951— | Theodore Williams, Boston | 143 |
| 1952— | Edward Yost, Washington | 129 |
| 1953— | Edward Yost, Washington | 123 |
| 1954— | Theodore Williams, Boston | 136 |
| 1955— | Mickey Mantle, New York | 113 |
| 1956— | Edward Yost, Washington | 151 |
| 1957— | Mickey Mantle, New York | 146 |
| 1958— | Mickey Mantle, New York | 129 |
| 1959— | Edward Yost, Detroit | 135 |
| 1960— | Edward Yost, Detroit | 125 |
| 1961— | Mickey Mantle, New York | 126 |
| 1962— | Mickey Mantle, New York | 122 |
| 1963— | Carl Yastremski, Boston | 95 |
| 1964— | Norman Siebern, Baltimore | 106 |
| 1965— | Rocco Colavito, Cleveland | 93 |
| 1966— | Harmon Killebrew, Minnesota | 103 |
| 1967— | Harmon Killebrew, Minnesota | 131 |
| 1968— | Carl Yastrzemski, Boston | 119 |
| 1969— | Harmon Killebrew, Minnesota | 145 |
| 1970— | Frank Howard, Washington | 132 |
| 1971— | Harmon Killebrew, Minnesota | 114 |
| 1972— | Richard Allen, Chicago | 99 |
| | Roy White, New York | 99 |
| 1973— | John Mayberry, Kansas City | 122 |
| 1974— | F. Gene Tenace, Oakland | 110 |
| 1975— | John Mayberry, Kansas City | 119 |

# BATTERS LEADING IN STRIKEOUTS

Note—Strikeouts not included in batting records in American League prior to 1913.

| Year | Player and Club | SO. |
|------|-----------------|-----|
| 1913— | Daniel Moeller, Washington | 106 |
| 1914— | August Williams, St. Louis | 120 |
| 1915— | John Lavan, St. Louis | 83 |
| 1916— | Walter Pipp, New York | 82 |
| 1917— | Robert Roth, Cleveland | 73 |
| 1918— | George (Babe) Ruth, Boston | 58 |
| 1919— | Maurice Shannon, Philadelphia-Boston | 70 |
| 1920— | Aaron Ward, New York | 84 |
| 1921— | Robert Meusel, New York | 88 |
| 1922— | James Dykes, Philadelphia | 98 |
| 1923— | George (Babe) Ruth, New York | 93 |
| 1924— | George (Babe) Ruth, New York | 81 |
| 1925— | Martin McManus, St. Louis | 69 |
| 1926— | Anthony Lazzeri, New York | 96 |
| 1927— | George (Babe) Ruth, New York | 89 |
| 1928— | George (Babe) Ruth, New York | 87 |
| 1929— | James Foxx, Philadelphia | 70 |
| 1930— | James Foxx, Philadelphia | 66 |
|  | Edward Morgan, Cleveland | 66 |
| 1931— | James Foxx, Philadelphia | 84 |
| 1932— | Bruce Campbell, Chicago-St. Louis | 104 |
| 1933— | James Foxx, Philadelphia | 93 |
| 1934— | Harlond Cliff, St. Louis | 100 |
| 1935— | James Foxx, Philadelphia | 99 |
| 1936— | James Foxx, Boston | 119 |
| 1937— | Frank Crosetti, New York | 105 |
| 1938— | Frank Crosetti, New York | 97 |
| 1939— | Hank Greenberg, Detroit | 95 |
| 1940— | Samuel Chapman, Philadelphia | 96 |
| 1941— | James Foxx, Boston | 103 |
| 1942— | Joseph Gordon, New York | 95 |
| 1943— | Chester Laabs, St. Louis | 105 |
| 1944— | J. Patrick Seerey, Cleveland | 99 |
| 1945— | J. Patrick Seerey, Cleveland | 97 |

| Year | Player and Club | SO. |
|------|-----------------|-----|
| 1946— | Charles Keller, New York | 101 |
|  | J. Patrick Seerey, Cleveland | 101 |
| 1947— | Edwin Joost, Philadelphia | 110 |
| 1948— | J. Patrick Seerey, Cleveland-Chicago | 102 |
| 1949— | Richard Kokos, St. Louis | 91 |
| 1950— | Gus Zernial, Chicago | 110 |
| 1951— | Gus Zernial, Chicago-Philadelphia | 101 |
| 1952— | Lawrence Doby, Cleveland | 111 |
|  | Mickey Mantle, New York | 111 |
| 1953— | Lawrence Doby, Cleveland | 121 |
| 1954— | Mickey Mantle, New York | 107 |
| 1955— | Norbert Zauchin, Boston | 105 |
| 1956— | James Lemon, Washington | 138 |
| 1957— | James Lemon, Washington | 94 |
| 1958— | James Lemon, Washington | 120 |
|  | Mickey Mantle, New York | 120 |
| 1959— | Mickey Mantle, New York | 126 |
| 1960— | Mickey Mantle, New York | 125 |
| 1961— | Jacob Wood, Detroit | 141 |
| 1962— | Harmon Killebrew, Minnesota | 142 |
| 1963— | David Nicholson, Chicago | 175 |
| 1964— | Nelson Matthews, Kansas City | 143 |
| 1965— | Zoilo Versalles, Minnesota | 122 |
| 1966— | George Scott, Boston | 152 |
| 1967— | Frank Howard, Washington | 155 |
| 1968— | Reginald Jackson, Oakland | 171 |
| 1969— | Reginald Jackson, Oakland | 142 |
| 1970— | Reginald Jackson, Oakland | 135 |
| 1971— | Reginald Jackson, Oakland | 161 |
| 1972— | A. Bobby Darwin, Minnesota | 145 |
| 1973— | A. Bobby Darwin, Minnesota | 137 |
| 1974— | A. Bobby Darwin, Minnesota | 127 |
| 1975— | Jeffrey Burroughs, Texas | 155 |

# LEADING BASE STEALERS

| Year | Player and Club | SB. |
|------|-----------------|-----|
| 1900— | (Not classed as major) |  |
| 1901— | Frank Isbell Chicago | 48 |
| 1902— | Fred (Topsy) Hartsel, Philadelphia | 54 |
| 1903— | Harry Bay, Cleveland | 46 |
| 1904— | Elmer Flick, Clev-Harry Bay, Clev. | 42 |
| 1905— | Daniel Hoffman, Philadelphia | 46 |
| 1906— | Flick, Cleveland-Anderson, Washington | 39 |
| 1907— | Tyrus Cobb, Detroit | 49 |
| 1908— | Patrick Dougherty, Chicago | 47 |
| 1909— | Tyrus Cobb, Detroit | 76 |
| 1910— | Edward Collins, Philadelphia | 81 |
| 1911— | Tyrus Cobb, Detroit | 83 |
| 1912— | J. Clyde Milan, Washington | 88 |
| 1913— | J. Clyde Milan, Washington | 74 |
| 1914— | Frederick Maisel, New York | 74 |
| 1915— | Tyrus Cobb, Detroit | 96 |
| 1916— | Tyrus Cobb, Detroit | 68 |
| 1917— | Tyrus Cobb, Detroit | 55 |
| 1918— | George Sisler, St. Louis | 45 |
| 1919— | Edward Collins, Chicago | 33 |
| 1920— | Edgar (Sam) Rice, Washington | 63 |
| 1921— | George Sisler, St. Louis | 35 |

| Year | Player and Club | SB. |
|------|-----------------|-----|
| 1922— | George Sisler, St. Louis | 51 |
| 1923— | Edward Collins, Chicago | 49 |
| 1924— | Edward Collins, Chicago | 42 |
| 1925— | John Mostil, Chicago | 43 |
| 1926— | John Mostil, Chicago | 35 |
| 1927— | George Sisler, St. Louis | 27 |
| 1928— | Charles (Buddy) Myer, Boston | 30 |
| 1929— | Charles Gehringer, Detroit | 27 |
| 1930— | Martin McManus, Detroit | 23 |
| 1931— | W. Benjamin Chapman, New York | 61 |
| 1932— | W. Benjamin Chapman, New York | 38 |
| 1933— | W. Benjamin Chapman, New York | 27 |
| 1934— | William Werber, Boston | 40 |
| 1935— | William Werber, Boston | 29 |
| 1936— | Lynford Lary, St. Louis | 37 |
| 1937— | Werber, Phila-Chapman, Wash-Bos | 35 |
| 1938— | Frank Crosetti, New York | 27 |
| 1939— | George Case, Washington | 51 |
| 1940— | George Case, Washington | 35 |
| 1941— | George Case, Washington | 33 |
| 1942— | George Case, Washington | 44 |
| 1943— | George Case, Washington | 61 |

## LEADING BASE STEALERS—Continued

| Year — Player and Club | SB. | Year — Player and Club | SB. |
|---|---|---|---|
| 1944— George Stirnweiss, New York | 55 | 1960— Luis Aparicio, Chicago | 51 |
| 1945— George Stirnweiss, New York | 33 | 1961— Luis Aparicio, Chicago | 53 |
| 1946— George Case, Cleveland | 28 | 1962— Luis Aparicio, Chicago | 31 |
| 1947— Robert Dillinger, St. Louis | 34 | 1963— Luis Aparicio, Baltimore | 40 |
| 1948— Robert Dillinger, St. Louis | 28 | 1964— Luis Aparicio, Baltimore | 57 |
| 1949— Robert Dillinger, St. Louis | 20 | 1965— Dagoberto Campaneris, Kansas City | 51 |
| 1950— Dominic DiMaggio, Boston | 15 | 1966— Dagoberto Campaneris, Kansas City | 52 |
| 1951— Orestes (Minnie) Minoso, Clev-Chi | 31 | 1967— Dagoberto Campaneris, Kansas City | 55 |
| 1952— Orestes (Minnie) Minoso, Chicago | 22 | 1968— Dagoberto Campaneris, Kansas City | 62 |
| 1953— Orestes (Minnie) Minoso, Chicago | 25 | 1969— Tommy Harper, Seattle | 73 |
| 1954— Jack Jensen, Boston | 22 | 1970— Dagoberto Campaneris, Oakland | 42 |
| 1955— Manuel (Jim) Rivera, Chicago | 25 | 1971— Amos Otis, Kansas City | 52 |
| 1956— Luis Aparicio, Chicago | 21 | 1972— Dagoberto Campaneris, Oakland | 52 |
| 1957— Luis Aparicio, Chicago | 28 | 1973— Tommy Harper, Boston | 54 |
| 1958— Luis Aparicio, Chicago | 29 | 1974— William North, Oakland | 54 |
| 1959— Luis Aparicio, Chicago | 56 | 1975— John Rivers, California | 70 |

## SLUGGING LEADERS

| Year — Player and Club | Slug. Avg. | Year — Player and Club | Slug. Avg. |
|---|---|---|---|
| 1900— (Not classed as major) | | 1938— James Foxx, Boston | .704 |
| 1901— Napoleon Lajoie, Philadelphia | .630 | 1939— James Foxx, Boston | .694 |
| 1902— Edward Delahanty, Washington | .589 | 1940— Henry Greenberg, Detroit | .670 |
| 1903— Napoleon Lajoie, Cleveland | .533 | 1941— Theodore Williams, Boston | .735 |
| 1904— Napoleon Lajoie, Cleveland | .549 | 1942— Theodore Williams, Boston | .648 |
| 1905— Elmer Flick, Cleveland | .466 | 1943— Rudolph York, Detroit | .527 |
| 1906— George Stone, St. Louis | .496 | 1944— Robert Doerr, Boston | .5278 |
| 1907— Tyrus Cobb, Detroit | .473 | 1945— George Stirnweiss, New York | .476 |
| 1908— Tyrus Cobb, Detroit | .475 | 1946— Theodore Williams, Boston | .667 |
| 1909— Tyrus Cobb, Detroit | .517 | 1947— Theodore Williams, Boston | .634 |
| 1910— Tyrus Cobb, Detroit | .554 | 1948— Theodore Williams, Boston | .615 |
| 1911— Tyrus Cobb, Detroit | .621 | 1949— Theodore Williams, Boston | .650 |
| 1912— Tyrus Cobb, Detroit | .586 | 1950— Joseph DiMaggio, New York | .585 |
| 1913— Joseph Jackson, Cleveland | .551 | 1951— Theodore Williams, Boston | .556 |
| 1914— Tyrus Cobb, Detroit | .513 | 1952— Lawrence Doby, Cleveland | .541 |
| 1915— Jacques F. Fournier, Chicago | .491 | 1953— Albert Rosen, Cleveland | .613 |
| 1916— Tristram Speaker, Cleveland | .502 | 1954— Theodore Williams, Boston | .635 |
| 1917— Tyrus Cobb, Detroit | .571 | 1955— Mickey Mantle, New York | .611 |
| 1918— George (Babe) Ruth, Boston | .555 | 1956— Mickey Mantle, New York | .705 |
| 1919— George (Babe) Ruth, Boston | .657 | 1957— Theodore Williams, Boston | .731 |
| 1920— George (Babe) Ruth, New York | .847 | 1958— Rocco Colavito, Cleveland | .620 |
| 1921— George (Babe) Ruth, New York | .846 | 1959— Albert Kaline, Detroit | .530 |
| 1922— George (Babe) Ruth, New York | .672 | 1960— Roger Maris, New York | .581 |
| 1923— George (Babe) Ruth, New York | .764 | 1961— Mickey Mantle, New York | .687 |
| 1924— George (Babe) Ruth, New York | .739 | 1962— Mickey Mantle, New York | .605 |
| 1925— Kenneth Williams, St. Louis | .613 | 1963— Harmon Killebrew, Minnesota | .555 |
| 1926— George (Babe) Ruth, New York | .737 | 1964— John (Boog) Powell, Baltimore | .606 |
| 1927— George (Babe) Ruth, New York | .772 | 1965— Carl Yastrzemski, Boston | .536 |
| 1928— George (Babe) Ruth, New York | .709 | 1966— Frank Robinson, Baltimore | .637 |
| 1929— George (Babe) Ruth, New York | .697 | 1967— Carl Yastrzemski, Boston | .622 |
| 1930— George (Babe) Ruth, New York | .732 | 1968— Frank Howard, Washington | .552 |
| 1931— George (Babe) Ruth, New York | .700 | 1969— Reginald Jackson, Oakland | .608 |
| 1932— James Foxx, Philadelphia | .749 | 1970— Carl Yastrzemski, Boston | .592 |
| 1933— James Foxx, Philadelphia | .703 | 1971— Pedro (Tony) Oliva, Minnesota | .546 |
| 1934— H. Louis Gehrig, New York | .706 | 1972— Richard Allen, Chicago | .603 |
| 1935— James Foxx, Philadelphia | .636 | 1973— Reginald Jackson, Oakland | .531 |
| 1936— H. Louis Gehrig, New York | .696 | 1974— Richard Allen, Chicago | .563 |
| 1937— Joseph DiMaggio, New York | .673 | 1975— Fred Lynn, Boston | .566 |

# LEADING PITCHERS IN WINNING PERCENTAGE

## (15 OR MORE VICTORIES)

| Year | Pitcher | Club | Won | Lost | Pct. |
|---|---|---|---|---|---|
| 1901—Clark Griffith | | Chicago | 24 | 7 | .774 |
| 1902—William Bernhard | | Philadelphia-Cleveland | 18 | 5 | .783 |
| 1903—Earl Moore | | Cleveland | 22 | 7 | .759 |
| 1904—John Chesbro | | New York | 41 | 12 | .774 |
| 1905—Jess Tannehill | | Boston | 22 | 9 | .710 |
| 1906—Edward Plank | | Philadelphia | 19 | 6 | .760 |
| 1907—William Donovan | | Detroit | 25 | 4 | .862 |
| 1908—Edward Walsh | | Chicago | 40 | 15 | .727 |
| 1909—George Mullin | | Detroit | 29 | 8 | .784 |
| 1910—Albert (Chief) Bender | | Philadelphia | 23 | 5 | .821 |
| 1911—Albert (Chief) Bender | | Philadelphia | 17 | 5 | .773 |
| 1912—Joseph Wood | | Boston | 34 | 5 | .872 |
| 1913—Walter Johnson | | Washington | 36 | 7 | .837 |
| 1914—Albert (Chief) Bender | | Philadelphia | 17 | 3 | .850 |
| 1915—Ernest Shore | | Boston | 19 | 8 | .704 |
|        George Foster | | Boston | 19 | 8 | .704 |
| 1916—Edward V. Cicotte | | Chicago | 15 | 7 | .682 |
| 1917—Ewell (Reb) Russell | | Chicago | 15 | 5 | .750 |
| 1918—Samuel Jones | | Boston | 16 | 5 | .762 |
| 1919—Edeard V. Cicotte | | Chicago | 29 | 7 | .806 |
| 1920—James Bagby | | Cleveland | 31 | 12 | .721 |
| 1921—Carl Mays | | New York | 27 | 9 | .750 |
| 1922—Leslie (Joe) Bush | | New York | 26 | 7 | .788 |
| 1923—Herbert Pennock | | New York | 19 | 6 | .760 |
| 1924—Walter Johnson | | Washington | 23 | 7 | .767 |
| 1925—Stanley Coveleski | | Washington | 20 | 5 | .800 |
| 1926—George Uhle | | Cleveland | 27 | 11 | .711 |
| 1927—Waite Hoyt | | New York | 27 | 7 | .759 |
| 1928—Alvin Crowder | | St. Louis | 21 | 5 | .808 |
| 1929—Robert Grove | | Philadelphia | 20 | 6 | .769 |
| 1930—Robert Grove | | Philadelphia | 28 | 5 | .848 |
| 1931—Robert Grove | | Philadelphia | 31 | 4 | .886 |
| 1932—John Allen | | New York | 17 | 4 | .810 |
| 1933—Robert Grove | | Philadelphia | 24 | 8 | .750 |
| 1934—Vernon Gomez | | New York | 26 | 5 | .839 |
| 1935—Elden Auker | | Detroit | 18 | 7 | .720 |
| 1936—Monte Pearson | | New York | 19 | 7 | .731 |
| 1937—John Allen | | Cleveland | 15 | 1 | .938 |
| 1938—Charles (Red) Ruffing | | New York | 21 | 7 | .750 |
| 1939—Robert Grove | | Boston | 15 | 4 | .789 |
| 1940—Lynwood (Schoolboy) Rowe | | Detroit | 16 | 3 | .842 |
| 1941—Vernon Gomez | | New York | 15 | 5 | .750 |
| 1942—Ernest Bonham | | New York | 21 | 5 | .808 |
| 1943—Spurgeon (Spud) Chandler | | New York | 20 | 4 | .833 |
| 1944—Cecil (Tex) Hughson | | Boston | 18 | 5 | .783 |
| 1945—Harold Newhouser | | Detroit | 25 | 9 | .735 |
| 1946—David (Boo) Ferris | | Boston | 25 | 6 | .806 |
| 1947—Allie Reynolds | | New York | 19 | 8 | .704 |
| 1948—John Kramer | | Boston | 18 | 5 | .783 |
| 1949—Ellis Kinder | | Boston | 23 | 6 | .793 |
| 1950—Victor Raschi | | New York | 21 | 8 | .724 |
| 1951—Robert Feller | | Cleveland | 22 | 8 | .733 |
| 1952—Robert Shantz | | Philadelphia | 24 | 7 | .774 |
| 1953—Edmund Lopat | | New York | 16 | 4 | .800 |
| 1954—Sandalio Consuegra | | Chicago | 16 | 3 | .842 |
| 1955—Thomas Byrne | | New York | 16 | 5 | .762 |
| 1956—Edward (Whitey) Ford | | New York | 19 | 6 | .760 |
| 1957—Richard Donovan | | Chicago | 16 | 6 | .727 |
|        Thomas Sturdivant | | New York | 16 | 6 | .727 |
| 1958—Robert Turley | | New York | 21 | 7 | .750 |
| 1959—Robert Shaw | | Chicago | 18 | 6 | .750 |
| 1960—James Perry | | Cleveland | 18 | 10 | .643 |

# LEADING PITCHERS IN WINNING
## PERCENTAGE—Continued

| Year | Pitcher | Club | Won | Lost | Pct. |
|------|---------|------|-----|------|------|
| 1961—Edward (Whitey) Ford | | New York | 25 | 4 | .862 |
| 1962—Raymond Herbert | | Chicago | 20 | 9 | .690 |
| 1963—Edward (Whitey) Ford | | New York | 24 | 7 | .774 |
| 1964—Wallace Bunker | | Baltimore | 19 | 5 | .792 |
| 1965—James (Mudcat) Grant | | Minnesota | 21 | 7 | .750 |
| 1966—Wilfred (Sonny) Siebert | | Cleveland | 16 | 8 | .667 |
| 1967—Joel Horlen | | Chicago | 19 | 7 | .731 |
| 1968—Dennis McLain | | Detroit | 31 | 6 | .838 |
| 1969—James Palmer | | Baltimore | 16 | 4 | .800 |
| 1970—Miguel (Mike) Cuellar | | Baltimore | 24 | 8 | .750 |
| 1971—David McNally | | Baltimore | 21 | 5 | .808 |
| 1972—James A. Hunter | | Oakland | 21 | 7 | .750 |
| 1973—James A. Hunter | | Oakland | 21 | 5 | .808 |
| 1974—Miguel (Mike) Cuellar | | Baltimore | 22 | 10 | .688 |
| 1975—Michael A. Torrez | | Baltimore | 20 | 9 | .690 |

# LEADING PITCHERS—EARNED-RUN AVERAGE

## (Based on Ten Complete Games Through 1950, Then 154 Innings Until A. L. Expanded in 1961, When It Became 162 Innings)

| Year | Pitcher and Club | G. | IP. | ERA. | Year | Pitcher and Club | G. | IP. | ERA. |
|------|------------------|-----|-----|------|------|------------------|-----|-----|------|
| 1913— | Johnson, Washington | 48 | 346 | 1.14 | 1945— | Newhouser, Detroit | 40 | 313 | 1.81 |
| 1914— | Leonard, Boston | 35 | 222 | 1.01 | 1946— | Newhouser, Detroit | 37 | 293 | 1.94 |
| 1915— | Wood, Boston | 25 | 157 | 1.49 | 1947— | Chandler, New York | 17 | 128 | 2.46 |
| 1916— | Ruth, Boston | 44 | 324 | 1.75 | 1948— | Bearden, Cleveland | 37 | 230 | 2.43 |
| 1917— | Cicotte, Chicago | 49 | 346 | 1.53 | 1949— | Parnell, Boston | 39 | 295 | 2.78 |
| 1918— | Johnson, Washington | 39 | 325 | 1.27 | 1950— | Wynn, Cleveland | 32 | 214 | 3.20 |
| 1919— | Johnson, Washington | 39 | 290 | 1.49 | 1951— | Rogovin, Detroit-Chicago | 27 | 217 | 2.78 |
| 1920— | Shawkey, New York | 38 | 267 | 2.46 | 1952— | Reynolds, New York | 35 | 244 | 2.07 |
| 1921— | Faber, Chicago | 43 | 331 | 2.47 | 1953— | Lopat, New York | 25 | 178 | 2.43 |
| 1922— | Faber, Chicago | 43 | 353 | 2.80 | 1954— | Garcia, Cleveland | 45 | 259 | 2.64 |
| 1923— | S. Coveleski, Cleveland | 33 | 228 | 2.76 | 1955— | Pierce, Chicago | 33 | 206 | 1.97 |
| 1924— | Johnson, Washington | 38 | 278 | 2.72 | 1956— | Ford, New York | 31 | 226 | 2.47 |
| 1925— | S. Coveleski, Washington | 32 | 241 | 2.84 | 1957— | Shantz, New York | 30 | 173 | 2.45 |
| 1926— | Grove, Philadelphia | 45 | 258 | 2.51 | 1958— | Ford, New York | 30 | 219 | 2.01 |
| 1927— | Moore, New York | 50 | 213 | 2.28 | 1959— | Wilhelm, Baltimore | 32 | 226 | 2.19 |
| 1928— | Braxton, Washington | 38 | 218 | 2.52 | 1960— | Baumann, Chicago | 47 | 185 | 2.68 |
| 1929— | Grove, Philadelphia | 42 | 275 | 2.81 | 1961— | Donovan, Washington | 23 | 169 | 2.40 |
| 1930— | Grove, Philadelphia | 50 | 291 | 2.54 | 1962— | Aguirre, Detroit | 42 | 216 | 2.21 |
| 1931— | Grove, Philadelphia | 41 | 289 | 2.06 | 1963— | Peters, Chicago | 41 | 243 | 2.33 |
| 1932— | Grove, Philadelphia | 44 | 292 | 2.84 | 1964— | Chance, Los Angeles | 46 | 278 | 1.65 |
| 1933— | Pearson, New York | 19 | 135 | 2.33 | 1965— | McDowell, Cleveland | 42 | 273 | 2.18 |
| 1934— | Gomez, New York | 38 | 282 | 2.33 | 1966— | Peters, Chicago | 30 | 205 | 1.98 |
| 1935— | Grove, Boston | 35 | 273 | 2.70 | 1967— | Horlen, Chicago | 35 | 258 | 2.06 |
| 1936— | Grove, Boston | 35 | 253 | 2.81 | 1968— | Tiant, Cleveland | 34 | 258 | 1.60 |
| 1937— | Gomez, New York | 34 | 278 | 2.33 | 1969— | Bosman, Washington | 31 | 193 | 2.19 |
| 1938— | Grove, Boston | 24 | 164 | 3.07 | 1970— | Segui, Oakland | 47 | 162 | 2.56 |
| 1939— | Grove, Boston | 23 | 191 | 2.54 | 1971— | Blue, Oakland | 39 | 312 | 1.82 |
| 1940— | Feller, Cleveland | 43 | 320 | 2.62 | 1972— | Tiant, Boston | 43 | 179 | 1.91 |
| 1941— | T. Lee, Chicago | 35 | 300 | 2.37 | 1973— | Palmer, Baltimore | 38 | 296 | 2.40 |
| 1942— | Lyons, Chicago | 20 | 180 | 2.10 | 1974— | Hunter, Oakland | 41 | 318 | 2.49 |
| 1943— | Chandler, New York | 30 | 253 | 1.64 | 1975— | Palmer, Baltimore | 39 | 323 | 2.09 |
| 1944— | Trout, Detroit | 49 | 352 | 2.12 | | | | | |

Note—Wilcy Moore pitched only six complete games—he started 12—in 1927, but was recognized as leader because of 213 innings pitched; Ernie Bonham, New York, had 1.91 ERA and ten complete games in 1940, but appeared in only 12 games and 99 innings, and Bob Feller was recognized as leader.

Note—Earned-runs not tabulated in American League prior to 1913.

## STRIKEOUT LEADERS—PITCHING

| Year | Pitcher and Club | SO. |
|------|------------------|-----|
| 1900— | (Not classed as major) | |
| 1901— | Denton (Cy) Young, Boston | 159 |
| 1902— | George (Rube) Waddell, Philadelphia | 210 |
| 1903— | George (Rube) Waddell, Philadelphia | 301 |
| 1904— | George (Rube) Waddell, Philadelphia | 349 |
| 1905— | George (Rube) Waddell, Philadelphia | 286 |
| 1906— | George (Rube) Waddell, Philadelphia | 203 |
| 1907— | George (Rube) Waddell, Philadelphia | 226 |
| 1908— | Edward Walsh, Chicago | 269 |
| 1909— | Frank Smith, Chicago | 177 |
| 1910— | Walter Johnson, Washington | 313 |
| 1911— | Edward Walsh, Chicago | 255 |
| 1912— | Walter Johnson, Washington | 303 |
| 1913— | Walter Johnson, Washington | 243 |
| 1914— | Walter Johnson, Washington | 225 |
| 1915— | Walter Johnson, Washington | 203 |
| 1916— | Walter Johnson, Washington | 228 |
| 1917— | Walter Johnson, Washington | 188 |
| 1918— | Walter Johnson, Washington | 162 |
| 1919— | Walter Johnson, Washington | 147 |
| 1920— | Stanley Coveleski, Cleveland | 133 |
| 1921— | Walter Johnson, Washington | 143 |
| 1922— | Urban Shocker, St. Louis | 149 |
| 1923— | Walter Johnson, Washington | 130 |
| 1924— | Walter Johnson, Washington | 158 |
| 1925— | Robert Grove, Philadelphia | 116 |
| 1926— | Robert Grove, Philadelphia | 194 |
| 1927— | Robert Grove, Philadelphia | 174 |
| 1928— | Robert Grove, Philadelphia | 183 |
| 1929— | Robert Grove, Philadelphia | 170 |
| 1930— | Robert Grove, Philadelphia | 209 |
| 1931— | Robert Grove, Philadelphia | 175 |
| 1932— | Charles (Red) Ruffing, New York | 190 |
| 1933— | Vernon Gomez, New York | 163 |
| 1934— | Vernon Gomez, New York | 158 |
| 1935— | Thomas Bridges, Detroit | 163 |
| 1936— | Thomas Bridges, Detroit | 175 |
| 1937— | Vernon Gomez, New York | 194 |
| 1938— | Robert Feller, Cleveland | 240 |
| 1939— | Robert Feller, Cleveland | 246 |
| 1940— | Robert Feller, Cleveland | 261 |
| 1941— | Robert Feller, Cleveland | 260 |
| 1942— | Louis (Bobo) Newsom, Washington | 113 |
| | Cecil (Tex) Hughson, Boston | 113 |
| 1943— | Allie Reynolds, Cleveland | 151 |
| 1944— | Harold Newhouser, Detroit | 187 |
| 1945— | Harold Newhouser, Detroit | 212 |
| 1946— | Robert Feller, Cleveland | 348 |
| 1947— | Robert Feller, Cleveland | 196 |
| 1948— | Robert Feller, Cleveland | 164 |
| 1949— | Virgil Trucks, Detroit | 153 |
| 1950— | Robert Lemon, Cleveland | 170 |
| 1951— | Victor Raschi, New York | 164 |
| 1952— | Allie Reynolds, New York | 160 |
| 1953— | W. William Pierce, Chicago | 186 |
| 1954— | Robert Turley, Baltimore | 185 |
| 1955— | Herbert Score, Cleveland | 245 |
| 1956— | Herbert Score, Cleveland | 263 |
| 1957— | Early Wynn, Cleveland | 184 |
| 1958— | Early Wynn, Cleveland | 179 |
| 1959— | James Bunning, Detroit | 201 |
| 1960— | James Bunning, Detroit | 201 |
| 1961— | Camilo Pascual, Minnesota | 221 |
| 1962— | Camilo Pascual, Minnesota | 206 |
| 1963— | Camilo Pascual, Minnesota | 202 |
| 1964— | Alphonso Downing, New York | 217 |
| 1965— | Samuel McDowell, Cleveland | 325 |
| 1966— | Samuel McDowell, Cleveland | 225 |
| 1967— | James Lonborg, Boston | 246 |
| 1968— | Samuel McDowell, Cleveland | 283 |
| 1969— | Samuel McDowell, Cleveland | 279 |
| 1970— | Samuel McDowell, Cleveland | 304 |
| 1971— | Michael Lolich, Detroit | 308 |
| 1972— | L. Nolan Ryan, California | 329 |
| 1973— | L. Nolan Ryan, California | 383 |
| 1974— | L. Nolan Ryan, California | 367 |
| 1975— | Frank Tanana, California | 269 |

## SHUTOUT LEADERS

| Year | Pitcher and Club | ShO. |
|------|------------------|------|
| 1900— | (Not classed as major) | |
| 1901— | Clark C. Griffith, Chicago | 5 |
| | Denton T. Young, Boston | 5 |
| 1902— | Adrian Joss, Cleveland | 5 |
| 1903— | Denton T. Young, Boston | 7 |
| 1904— | Denton T. Young, Boston | 10 |
| 1905— | Edward H. Killian, Detroit | 8 |
| 1906— | Edward A. Walsh, Chicago | 10 |
| 1907— | Edward S. Plank, Philadelphia | 8 |
| 1908— | Edward A. Walsh, Chicago | 12 |
| 1909— | Edward A. Walsh, Chicago | 8 |
| 1910— | John W. Coombs, Philadelphia | 13 |
| 1911— | Walter P. Johnson, Washington | 6 |
| | Edward S. Plank, Philadelphia | 6 |
| 1912— | Joseph Wood, Boston | 10 |
| 1913— | Walter P. Johnson, Washington | 12 |
| 1914— | Walter P. Johnson, Washington | 10 |
| 1915— | Walter P. Johnson, Washington | 8 |
| 1916— | George H. Ruth, Boston | 9 |
| 1917— | Stanley Coveleski, Cleveland | 9 |
| 1918— | Walter P. Johnson, Washington | 8 |
| | Carl W. Mays, Boston | 8 |
| 1919— | Walter P. Johnson, Washington | 7 |
| 1920— | Carl W. Mays, New York | 6 |
| 1921— | Samuel P. Jones, Boston | 5 |
| 1922— | George E. Uhle, Cleveland | 5 |
| 1923— | Stanley Coveleski, Cleveland | 5 |
| 1924— | Walter P. Johnson, Washington | 6 |
| 1925— | Theodore A. Lyons, Chicago | 5 |
| 1926— | Edwin L. Wells, Detroit | 4 |
| 1927— | Horace M. Lisenbee, Washington | 4 |
| 1928— | Herbert J. Pennock, New York | 5 |
| 1929— | George F. Blaeholder, St. Louis | 4 |
| | Alvin F. Crowder, St. Louis | 4 |
| | Samuel D. Gray, St. Louis | 4 |
| | Daniel K. MacFayden, Boston | 4 |

# SHUTOUT LEADERS—Continued

| Year | Pitcher and Club | ShO. |
|---|---|---|
| 1930— | Clinton H. Brown, Cleveland | 3 |
| | George L. Earnshaw, Philadelphia | 3 |
| | George W. Pipgras, New York | 3 |
| 1931— | Robert M. Grove, Philadelphia | 4 |
| | Victor G. Sorrell, Detroit | 4 |
| 1932— | Thomas D. Bridges, Detroit | 4 |
| | Robert M. Grove, Philadelphia | 4 |
| 1933— | Oral C. Hildebrand, Cleveland | 6 |
| 1934— | Vernon L. Gomez, New York | 6 |
| | Melvin L. Harder, Cleveland | 6 |
| 1935— | Lynwood T. Rowe, Detroit | 6 |
| 1936— | Robert M. Grove, Boston | 6 |
| 1937— | Vernon L. Gomez, New York | 6 |
| 1938— | Vernon L. Gomez, New York | 4 |
| 1939— | Charles H. Ruffing, New York | 5 |
| 1940— | Robert W. Feller, Cleveland | 4 |
| | Theodore A. Lyons, Chicago | 4 |
| | Albert J. Milnar, Cleveland | 4 |
| 1941— | Robert W. Feller, Cleveland | 6 |
| 1942— | Ernest E. Bonham, New York | 6 |
| 1943— | Spurgeon F. Chandler, New York | 5 |
| | Paul H. Trout, Detroit | 5 |
| 1944— | Paul H. Trout, Detroit | 7 |
| 1945— | Harold Newhouser, Detroit | 8 |
| 1946— | Robert W. Feller, Cleveland | 10 |
| 1947— | Robert W. Feller, Cleveland | 5 |
| 1948— | Robert W. Feller, Cleveland | 10 |
| 1949— | Edward M. Garcia, Cleveland | 6 |
| | Ellis R. Kinder, Boston | 6 |
| | Virgil O. Trucks, Detroit | 6 |
| 1950— | Arthur J. Houtteman, Detroit | 4 |
| 1951— | Allie P. Reynolds, New York | 7 |
| 1952— | Edward M. Garcia, Cleveland | 6 |
| | Allie P. Reynolds, New York | 6 |
| 1953— | Erwin C. Porterfield, Washington | 9 |
| 1954— | Edward M. Garcia, Cleveland | 5 |
| | Virgil O. Trucks, Chicago | 5 |
| 1955— | William F. Hoeft, Detroit | 7 |
| 1956— | Herbert J. Score, Cleveland | 5 |
| 1957— | James A. Wilson, Chicago | 5 |
| 1958— | Edward C. Ford, New York | 7 |
| 1959— | Camilo A. Pascual, Washington | 6 |
| 1960— | Edward C. Ford, New York | 4 |
| | James E. Perry, Cleveland | 4 |
| | Early Wynn, Chicago | 4 |
| 1961— | Stephen D. Barber, Baltimore | 8 |
| | Camilo A. Pascual, Minnesota | 8 |
| 1962— | Richard E. Donovan, Cleveland | 5 |
| | James L. Kaat, Minnesota | 5 |
| | Camilo A. Pascual, Minnesota | 5 |
| 1963— | Raymond E. Herbert, Chicago | 7 |
| 1964— | W. Dean Chance, Los Angeles | 11 |
| 1965— | James T. Grant, Minnesota | 6 |
| 1966— | Thomas E. John, Chicago | 5 |
| | Samuel E. McDowell, Cleveland | 5 |
| | Luis C. Tiant, Cleveland | 5 |
| 1967— | Steven L. Hargan, Cleveland | 6 |
| | Joel E. Horlen, Chicago | 6 |
| | Thomas E. John, Chicago | 6 |
| | Michael S. Lolich, Detroit | 6 |
| | James E. McGlothlin, California | 6 |
| 1968— | Luis C. Tiant, Cleveland | 9 |
| 1969— | Dennis D. McLain, Detroit | 9 |
| 1970— | Charles T. Dobson, Oakland | 5 |
| | James A. Palmer, Baltimore | 5 |
| 1971— | Vida Blue, Oakland | 8 |
| 1972— | L. Nolan Ryan, California | 9 |
| 1973— | Rikalbert Blyleven, Minnesota | 9 |
| 1974— | Luis C. Tiant, Boston | 7 |
| 1975— | James A. Palmer, Baltimore | 10 |

# SEVENTH CHAMPIONSHIP SERIES

## Including

A. L. Playoff Review

A. L. Game Box Scores

A. L. Composite Box Score

N. L. Playoff Review

N. L. Game Box Scores

N. L. Composite Box Score

# Red Sox End Oakland Dynasty

## By JOE MARCIN

The Boston Red Sox captured their first pennant since 1967 and stopped the Oakland A's bid for their fourth straight American League title by sweeping the Championship Series in three straight games.

Many observers had felt before the playoffs that the A's might be at a disadvantage because the first two games of the set were slated for Boston's Fenway Park, a nightmare arena for lefthanders. But the A's were still rated favorites on the strength of their championship experience, despite their heavy reliance on southpaw starters.

In the opener, Luis Tiant pitched a three-hitter as the Bosox batted out lefty Ken Holtzman in less than seven innings. Holtzman's cause wasn't helped at all by four errors behind him, three of the miscues coming on two consecutive first-inning plays.

The tone of the series was set in the opening inning when, with two out and Carl Yastrzemski on first, Bando let Carlton Fisk's grounder go through him. A's outfielder Claudell Washington threw over the cutoff man's head, off Bando's glove. As Yastrzemski scored, Fisk moved to second from where he immediately scored on an error by second baseman Phil Garner.

The Sox added five more tallies in the seventh frame as a dropped fly by Bill North and Washington's problems at the wall added to the A's troubles.

### GAME OF SATURDAY, OCTOBER 4, AT BOSTON

| Oakland | AB. | R. | H. | RBI. | PO. | A. |
|---|---|---|---|---|---|---|
| North, cf | 3 | 0 | 0 | 1 | 2 | 0 |
| Washington, lf | 4 | 0 | 0 | 0 | 1 | 0 |
| Bando, 3b | 4 | 0 | 0 | 0 | 1 | 4 |
| Jackson, rf | 4 | 0 | 1 | 0 | 2 | 0 |
| Tenace, c | 3 | 0 | 0 | 0 | 4 | 0 |
| Rudi, 1b | 4 | 0 | 1 | 0 | 10 | 1 |
| Williams, dh | 3 | 0 | 0 | 0 | 0 | 0 |
| Hopkins, pr-dh | 0 | 0 | 0 | 0 | 0 | 0 |
| Campaneris, ss | 4 | 1 | 0 | 0 | 1 | 2 |
| Garner, 2b | 2 | 0 | 0 | 0 | 2 | 1 |
| Holt, ph | 1 | 0 | 1 | 0 | 0 | 0 |
| Martinez, pr-2b | 0 | 0 | 0 | 0 | 0 | 1 |
| Holtzman, p | 0 | 0 | 0 | 0 | 1 | 1 |
| Todd, p | 0 | 0 | 0 | 0 | 0 | 0 |
| Lindblad, p | 0 | 0 | 0 | 0 | 0 | 0 |
| Bosman, p | 0 | 0 | 0 | 0 | 0 | 0 |
| Abbott, p | 0 | 0 | 0 | 0 | 0 | 0 |
| Totals | 32 | 1 | 3 | 1 | 24 | 10 |

| Boston | AB. | R. | H. | RBI. | PO. | A. |
|---|---|---|---|---|---|---|
| Beniquez, dh | 4 | 1 | 2 | 1 | 0 | 0 |
| Doyle, 2b | 3 | 1 | 0 | 1 | 0 | 1 |
| Yastrzemski, lf | 4 | 1 | 1 | 0 | 3 | 0 |
| Fisk, c | 4 | 2 | 1 | 0 | 9 | 0 |
| Lynn, cf | 4 | 0 | 1 | 2 | 7 | 0 |
| Petrocelli, 3b | 4 | 0 | 0 | 0 | 1 | 0 |
| Evans, rf | 4 | 1 | 1 | 0 | 4 | 0 |
| Cooper, 1b | 3 | 0 | 1 | 0 | 2 | 0 |
| Burleson, ss | 3 | 1 | 1 | 1 | 1 | 0 |
| Tiant, p | 0 | 0 | 0 | 0 | 0 | 1 |
| Totals | 33 | 7 | 8 | 5 | 27 | 2 |

| | | | | | | | | | |
|---|---|---|---|---|---|---|---|---|---|
| Oakland | 0 | 0 | 0 | 0 | 0 | 0 | 0 | 1 | 0—1 |
| Boston | 2 | 0 | 0 | 0 | 0 | 0 | 0 | x—7 |

| Oakland | IP. | H. | R. | ER. | BB. | SO. |
|---|---|---|---|---|---|---|
| Holtzman (Loser) | 6⅓ | 5 | 4 | 2 | 1 | 4 |
| Todd | 0* | 1 | 1 | 1 | 0 | 0 |
| Lindblad | ⅓ | 2 | 2 | 0 | 0 | 0 |
| Bosman | ⅓ | 0 | 0 | 0 | 0 | 0 |
| Abbott | 1 | 0 | 0 | 0 | 0 | 0 |

| Boston | IP. | H. | R. | ER. | BB. | SO. |
|---|---|---|---|---|---|---|
| Tiant (Winner) | 9 | 3 | 1 | 0 | 3 | 8 |

*Pitched to one batter in seventh.

Errors—Bando, Washington, Garner, Lynn, North, Burleson, Cooper. Left on bases—Oakland 7, Boston 5. Two-base hits—Evans, Burleson, Lynn, Holt. Stolen bases—Beniquez 2. Sacrifice hit—Cooper. Sacrifice fly—Doyle. Umpires—Denkinger, DiMuro, Kunkel, Luciano, Evans and Morgenweck. Time—2:40. Attendance—35,578.

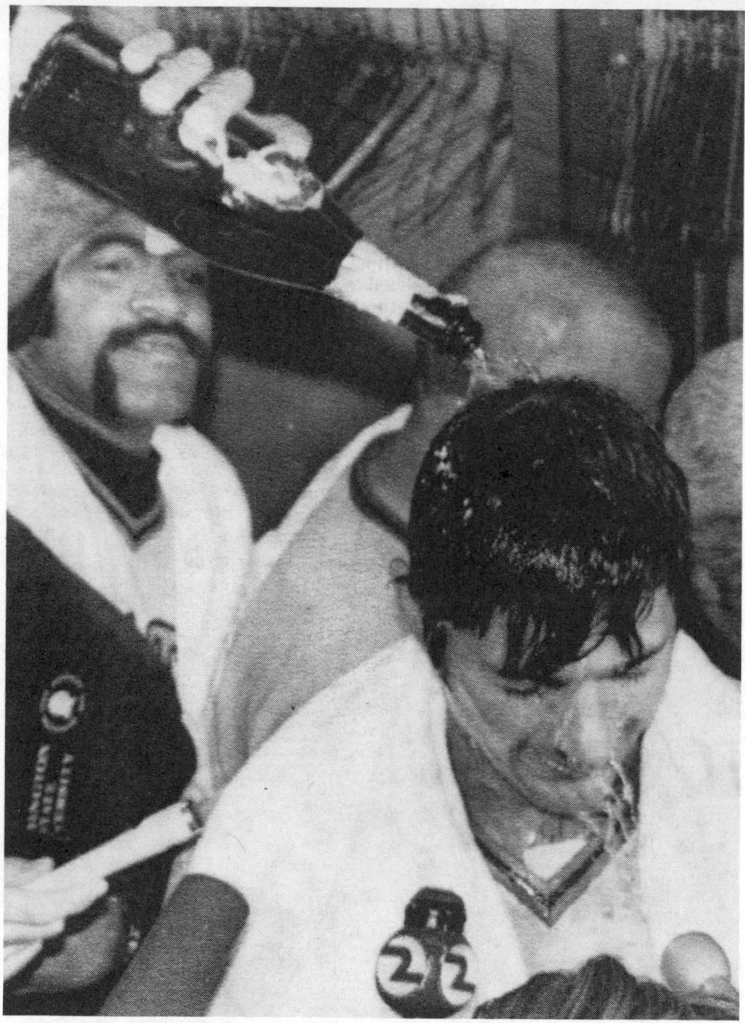

Boston outfielder Carl Yastrzemski has champagne poured over him in dressing room after Red Sox won third straight game, 5-3, over Oakland A's and became American League Champions. Pitcher Luis Tiant is in background, at left.

The A's jumped off to a three-run lead in the second game, Reggie Jackson's two-run homer in the first being the big blow. But the Sox chased lefty Vida Blue in the fourth inning on the strength of Yastrzemski's two-run homer, Fisk's double, Fred Lynn's single and a double play grounder.

Fisk's single plated Yastrzemski, who had doubled, with the go-ahead run in the sixth. Rico Petrocelli's homer in the seventh and an RBI single by Lynn in the eighth added to the margin.

The A's, going down to the wire with resolute obstinacy, tried in the third game with another lefthander. It was again Holtzman, this time with just two days' rest. The result was failure.

The lefty left the game in the fifth inning with four runs charged to him, enough for the Boston victory. Once more, Holtzman received less than decent support from his teammates, an error by Washington giving the Red Sox their first run of the game.

As a matter of fact, the difference in outfield play between the two clubs was startling. The Boston gardeners, especially Yastrzemski, time and again thwarted A's rallies with great catches and throws, while the A's outfielders behaved, for the most part, as if the whole thing was a strange new experience for them.

Charles O. Finley, the ebullient owner of the defeated team, found little sympathy for his woes. He was left to ponder through the winter what the outcome might have been had his club possessed a good right-handed starting pitcher. Someone like Catfish Hunter.

## GAME OF SUNDAY, OCTOBER 5. AT BOSTON

| Oakland | AB. | R. | H. | RBI. | PO. | A. |
|---|---|---|---|---|---|---|
| North, cf | 4 | 0 | 0 | 0 | 0 | 0 |
| Campaneris, ss | 3 | 0 | 0 | 0 | 1 | 6 |
| Bando, 3b | 4 | 1 | 4 | 0 | 0 | 3 |
| Jackson, rf | 4 | 1 | 2 | 2 | 1 | 1 |
| Tenace, 1b-c | 4 | 0 | 0 | 0 | 11 | 0 |
| Rudi, lf | 4 | 1 | 2 | 0 | 1 | 0 |
| Washington, dh | 4 | 0 | 2 | 1 | 0 | 0 |
| Garner, 2b | 2 | 0 | 0 | 0 | 4 | 2 |
| Harper, ph | 0 | 0 | 0 | 0 | 0 | 0 |
| Holt, 1b | 1 | 0 | 0 | 0 | 1 | 2 |
| Fosse, c | 2 | 0 | 0 | 0 | 3 | 0 |
| Williams, ph | 1 | 0 | 0 | 0 | 0 | 0 |
| Martinez, 2b | 0 | 0 | 0 | 0 | 1 | 0 |
| Tovar, ph | 1 | 0 | 0 | 0 | 0 | 0 |
| Blue, p | 0 | 0 | 0 | 0 | 0 | 0 |
| Todd, p | 0 | 0 | 0 | 0 | 0 | 0 |
| Fingers, p | 0 | 0 | 0 | 0 | 1 | 0 |
| Totals | 34 | 3 | 10 | 3 | 24 | 15 |

| Boston | AB. | R. | H. | RBI. | PO. | A. |
|---|---|---|---|---|---|---|
| Beniquez, dh | 4 | 1 | 1 | 0 | 0 | 0 |
| Doyle, 2b | 3 | 1 | 1 | 0 | 2 | 1 |
| Yastrzemski, lf | 3 | 2 | 2 | 2 | 2 | 0 |
| Fisk, c | 4 | 1 | 2 | 1 | 4 | 0 |
| Lynn, cf | 4 | 0 | 2 | 1 | 4 | 1 |
| Petrocelli, 3b | 4 | 1 | 1 | 1 | 2 | 3 |
| Evans, rf | 3 | 0 | 0 | 0 | 1 | 0 |
| Cooper, 1b | 3 | 0 | 2 | 0 | 11 | 0 |
| Burleson, ss | 2 | 0 | 1 | 0 | 1 | 6 |
| Cleveland, p | 0 | 0 | 0 | 0 | 0 | 1 |
| Moret, p | 0 | 0 | 0 | 0 | 0 | 0 |
| Drago, p | 0 | 0 | 0 | 0 | 0 | 0 |
| Totals | 30 | 6 | 12 | 5 | 27 | 13 |

```
Oakland .................... 2   0   0     1   0   0     0   0   0—3
Boston  .................... 0   0   0     3   0   1     1   1   x—6
```

| Oakland | IP. | H. | R. | ER. | BB. | SO. |
|---|---|---|---|---|---|---|
| Blue | 3* | 6 | 3 | 3 | 0 | 2 |
| Todd | 1† | 1 | 0 | 0 | 0 | 0 |
| Fingers (Loser) | 4 | 5 | 3 | 3 | 1 | 3 |

| Boston | IP. | H. | R. | ER. | BB. | SO. |
|---|---|---|---|---|---|---|
| Cleveland | 5‡ | 7 | 3 | 3 | 1 | 2 |
| Moret (Winner) | 1§ | 1 | 0 | 0 | 1 | 0 |
| Drago (Save) | 3 | 2 | 0 | 0 | 0 | 2 |

*Pitched to four batters in fourth.
†Pitched to one batter in fifth.
‡Pitched to one batter in sixth.
§Pitched to one batter in seventh.

Errors—None. Double plays—Oakland 4, Boston 2. Left on bases—Oakland 6, Boston 3. Two-base hits—Bando 2, Rudi 2, Washington. Fisk, Cooper 2, Yastrzemski. Home runs—Jackson, Yastrzemski, Petrocelli. Sacrifice hits—Burleson, Doyle. Wild pitch—Drago. Umpires—DiMuro, Kunkel, Luciano, Evans, Morgenweck and Denkinger. Time—2:27. Attendance—35,578.

Exultant Red Sox rush from field after winning third game.

## GAME OF TUESDAY, OCTOBER 7, AT OAKLAND

| Boston | AB. | R. | H. | RBI. | PO. | A. |
|---|---|---|---|---|---|---|
| Beniquez, dh | 4 | 0 | 0 | 0 | 0 | 0 |
| Doyle, 2b | 5 | 1 | 2 | 1 | 3 | 6 |
| Yastrzemski, lf | 4 | 1 | 2 | 0 | 2 | 1 |
| Fisk, c | 4 | 1 | 2 | 1 | 2 | 0 |
| Lynn, cf | 3 | 1 | 1 | 0 | 1 | 6 |
| Petrocelli, 3b | 4 | 0 | 1 | 1 | 1 | 0 |
| Evans, rf | 3 | 0 | 0 | 0 | 2 | 0 |
| Cooper, 1b | 4 | 0 | 1 | 1 | 11 | 1 |
| Burleson, ss | 4 | 1 | 2 | 0 | 2 | 6 |
| Wise, p | 0 | 0 | 0 | 0 | 2 | 3 |
| Drago, p | 0 | 0 | 0 | 0 | 1 | 1 |
| Totals | 35 | 5 | 11 | 4 | 27 | 18 |

| Oakland | AB. | R. | H. | RBI. | PO. | A. |
|---|---|---|---|---|---|---|
| Campaneris, ss | 4 | 0 | 0 | 0 | 0 | 2 |
| Washington, lf | 4 | 1 | 1 | 0 | 0 | 0 |
| Bando, 3b | 4 | 0 | 2 | 2 | 2 | 4 |
| Jackson, rf | 4 | 0 | 2 | 1 | 2 | 0 |
| Rudi, 1b | 4 | 0 | 0 | 0 | 11 | 1 |
| Williams, dh | 4 | 0 | 0 | 0 | 0 | 0 |
| Tenace, c | 2 | 0 | 0 | 0 | 4 | 0 |
| North, cf | 3 | 0 | 0 | 0 | 4 | 1 |
| Garner, 2b | 1 | 0 | 0 | 0 | 1 | 1 |
| Tovar, ph-2b | 2 | 1 | 1 | 0 | 2 | 2 |
| Martinez, 2b | 0 | 0 | 0 | 0 | 0 | 0 |
| Holt, ph | 1 | 0 | 0 | 0 | 0 | 0 |
| Holtzman, p | 0 | 0 | 0 | 0 | 0 | 0 |
| Todd, p | 0 | 0 | 0 | 0 | 0 | 0 |
| Lindblad, p | 0 | 0 | 0 | 0 | 1 | 4 |
| Totals | 32 | 3 | 6 | 3 | 27 | 15 |

| Boston | | | | | | | | |
|---|---|---|---|---|---|---|---|---|
| Boston | 0 | 0 | 0 | 1 | 3 | 0 | 0 | 1 | 0—5 |
| Oakland | 0 | 0 | 0 | 0 | 0 | 1 | 0 | 2 | 0—3 |

| Boston | IP. | H. | R. | ER. | BB. | SO. |
|---|---|---|---|---|---|---|
| Wise (Winner) | 7⅓ | 6 | 3 | 2 | 3 | 2 |
| Drago (Save) | 1⅔ | 0 | 0 | 0 | 1 | 0 |

| Oakland | IP. | H. | R. | ER. | BB. | SO. |
|---|---|---|---|---|---|---|
| Holtzman (Loser) | 4⅔ | 7 | 4 | 3 | 0 | 3 |
| Todd | 0* | 1 | 0 | 0 | 0 | 0 |
| Lindblad | 4⅓ | 3 | 1 | 0 | 1 | 0 |

*Pitched to one batter in fifth.

Errors—Washington, Tovar, Doyle. Double play—Boston 1. Left on bases—Boston 6, Oakland 6. Two-base hit—Burleson. Stolen base—Fisk. Sacrifice hits—Beniquez, Lynn. Wild pitch—Lindblad. Umpires—Kunkel, Luciano, Evans, Morgenweck, Denkinger and DiMuro. Time—2:30. Attendance—49,358.

## BOSTON RED SOX' BATTING AND FIELDING AVERAGES

| Player—Position | G. | AB. | R. | H. | TB. | 2B. | 3B. | HR. | RBI. | B.A. | PO. | A. | E. | F.A. |
|---|---|---|---|---|---|---|---|---|---|---|---|---|---|---|
| Yastrzemski, lf | 3 | 11 | 4 | 5 | 9 | 1 | 0 | 1 | 2 | .455 | 7 | 2 | 0 | 1.000 |
| Burleson, ss | 3 | 9 | 2 | 4 | 6 | 2 | 0 | 0 | 1 | .444 | 4 | 12 | 1 | .941 |
| Fisk, c | 3 | 12 | 4 | 5 | 6 | 1 | 0 | 0 | 2 | .417 | 15 | 0 | 0 | 1.000 |
| Cooper, 1b | 3 | 10 | 0 | 4 | 6 | 2 | 0 | 0 | 1 | .400 | 24 | 1 | 1 | .962 |
| Lynn, cf | 3 | 11 | 1 | 4 | 5 | 1 | 0 | 0 | 3 | .364 | 12 | 1 | 1 | .929 |
| Doyle, 2b | 3 | 11 | 3 | 3 | 3 | 0 | 0 | 0 | 2 | .273 | 5 | 8 | 1 | .929 |
| Beniquez, dh | 3 | 12 | 2 | 3 | 3 | 0 | 0 | 0 | 1 | .250 | 0 | 0 | 0 | .000 |
| Petrocelli, 3b | 3 | 12 | 1 | 2 | 5 | 0 | 0 | 1 | 2 | .167 | 4 | 3 | 0 | 1.000 |
| Evans, rf | 3 | 10 | 1 | 1 | 2 | 1 | 0 | 0 | 0 | .100 | 7 | 0 | 0 | 1.000 |
| Cleveland, p | 1 | 0 | 0 | 0 | 0 | 0 | 0 | 0 | 0 | .000 | 0 | 1 | 0 | 1.000 |
| Drago, p | 2 | 0 | 0 | 0 | 0 | 0 | 0 | 0 | 0 | .000 | 1 | 1 | 0 | 1.000 |
| Moret, p | 1 | 0 | 0 | 0 | 0 | 0 | 0 | 0 | 0 | .000 | 0 | 0 | 0 | .000 |
| Tiant, p | 1 | 0 | 0 | 0 | 0 | 0 | 0 | 0 | 0 | .000 | 1 | 0 | 0 | 1.000 |
| Wise, p | 1 | 0 | 0 | 0 | 0 | 0 | 0 | 0 | 0 | .000 | 2 | 3 | 0 | 1.000 |
| Totals | 3 | 98 | 18 | 31 | 45 | 8 | 0 | 2 | 14 | .316 | 81 | 33 | 4 | .966 |

## OAKLAND ATHLETICS' BATTING AND FIELDING AVERAGES

| Player—Position | G. | AB. | R. | H. | TB. | 2B. | 3B. | HR. | RBI. | B.A. | PO. | A. | E. | F.A. |
|---|---|---|---|---|---|---|---|---|---|---|---|---|---|---|
| Bando, 3b | 3 | 12 | 1 | 6 | 8 | 2 | 0 | 0 | 2 | .500 | 3 | 11 | 1 | .933 |
| Tovar, ph-2b | 2 | 2 | 1 | 1 | 1 | 0 | 0 | 0 | 0 | .500 | 2 | 2 | 1 | .800 |
| Jackson, rf | 3 | 12 | 1 | 5 | 8 | 0 | 0 | 1 | 3 | .417 | 5 | 1 | 0 | 1.000 |
| Holt, ph-1b | 3 | 3 | 0 | 1 | 8 | 1 | 0 | 0 | 0 | .333 | 1 | 2 | 0 | 1.000 |
| Rudi, 1b-lf | 3 | 12 | 1 | 3 | 5 | 2 | 0 | 0 | 0 | .250 | 22 | 2 | 0 | 1.000 |
| Washington, lf-dh | 3 | 12 | 1 | 3 | 4 | 1 | 0 | 0 | 1 | .250 | 1 | 0 | 2 | .333 |
| Fosse, c | 1 | 2 | 0 | 0 | 0 | 0 | 0 | 0 | 0 | .000 | 3 | 0 | 0 | 1.000 |
| Garner, 2b | 3 | 5 | 0 | 0 | 0 | 0 | 0 | 0 | 0 | .000 | 7 | 4 | 1 | .917 |
| Williams, dh-ph | 3 | 8 | 0 | 0 | 0 | 0 | 0 | 0 | 0 | .000 | 0 | 0 | 0 | .000 |
| Tenace, c-1b | 3 | 9 | 0 | 0 | 0 | 0 | 0 | 0 | 0 | .000 | 19 | 1 | 0 | 1.000 |
| North cf | 3 | 10 | 0 | 0 | 0 | 0 | 0 | 0 | 1 | .000 | 6 | 1 | 1 | .875 |
| Campaneris, ss | 3 | 11 | 1 | 0 | 0 | 0 | 0 | 0 | 0 | .000 | 2 | 10 | 0 | 1.000 |
| Abbott, p | 1 | 0 | 0 | 0 | 0 | 0 | 0 | 0 | 0 | .000 | 0 | 0 | 0 | .000 |
| Blue, p | 1 | 0 | 0 | 0 | 0 | 0 | 0 | 0 | 0 | .000 | 0 | 0 | 0 | .000 |
| Bosman, p | 1 | 0 | 0 | 0 | 0 | 0 | 0 | 0 | 0 | .000 | 1 | 0 | 0 | 1.000 |
| Fingers, p | 1 | 0 | 0 | 0 | 0 | 0 | 0 | 0 | 0 | .000 | 0 | 0 | 0 | .000 |
| Harper, ph | 1 | 0 | 0 | 0 | 0 | 0 | 0 | 0 | 0 | .000 | 0 | 0 | 0 | .000 |
| Holtzman, p | 2 | 0 | 0 | 0 | 0 | 0 | 0 | 0 | 0 | .000 | 1 | 1 | 0 | 1.000 |
| Hopkins, pr-dh | 1 | 0 | 0 | 0 | 0 | 0 | 0 | 0 | 0 | .000 | 0 | 0 | 0 | .000 |
| Lindblad, p | 2 | 0 | 0 | 0 | 0 | 0 | 0 | 0 | 0 | .000 | 1 | 4 | 0 | 1.000 |
| Martinez, pr-2b | 1 | 0 | 0 | 0 | 0 | 0 | 0 | 0 | 0 | .000 | 1 | 1 | 0 | 1.000 |
| Todd, p | 3 | 0 | 0 | 0 | 0 | 0 | 0 | 0 | 0 | .000 | 0 | 0 | 0 | .000 |
| Totals | 3 | 98 | 7 | 19 | 28 | 6 | 0 | 1 | 7 | .194 | 75 | 40 | 6 | .950 |

## BOSTON RED SOX' PITCHING RECORDS

| Pitcher | G. | GS. | CG. | IP. | H. | R. | ER. | BB. | SO. | HB. | WP. | W. | L. | Pct. | ERA. |
|---|---|---|---|---|---|---|---|---|---|---|---|---|---|---|---|
| Tiant | 1 | 1 | 1 | 9 | 3 | 1 | 0 | 3 | 8 | 0 | 1 | 1 | 0 | 1.000 | 0.00 |
| Drago | 2 | 0 | 0 | 4⅔ | 2 | 0 | 0 | 1 | 2 | 0 | 1 | 0 | 0 | .000 | 0.00 |
| Moret | 1 | 0 | 0 | 1 | 1 | 0 | 0 | 1 | 0 | 0 | 1 | 1 | 0 | 1.000 | 0.00 |
| Wise | 1 | 1 | 0 | 7⅓ | 6 | 3 | 2 | 3 | 2 | 0 | 0 | 1 | 0 | 1.000 | 2.45 |
| Cleveland | 1 | 1 | 0 | 5 | 7 | 3 | 3 | 1 | 2 | 0 | 0 | 0 | 0 | .000 | 5.40 |
| Totals | 3 | 3 | 1 | 27 | 19 | 7 | 5 | 9 | 14 | 0 | 1 | 3 | 0 | 1.000 | 1.67 |

No shutouts. Saves—Drago 2.

## OAKLAND ATHLETICS' PITCHING RECORDS

| Pitcher | G. | GS. | CG. | IP. | H. | R. | ER. | BB. | SO. | HB. | WP. | W. | L. | Pct. | ERA |
|---|---|---|---|---|---|---|---|---|---|---|---|---|---|---|---|
| Lindblad | 2 | 0 | 0 | 4⅔ | 5 | 3 | 0 | 1 | 0 | 0 | 1 | 0 | 0 | .000 | 0.00 |
| Abbott | 1 | 0 | 0 | 1 | 0 | 0 | 0 | 0 | 0 | 0 | 0 | 0 | 0 | .000 | 0.00 |
| Bosman | 1 | 0 | 0 | ⅓ | 0 | 0 | 0 | 0 | 0 | 0 | 0 | 0 | 0 | .000 | 0.00 |
| Holtzman | 2 | 2 | 0 | 11 | 12 | 8 | 5 | 1 | 7 | 0 | 0 | 0 | 2 | .000 | 4.09 |
| Fingers | 1 | 0 | 0 | 4 | 5 | 3 | 3 | 1 | 3 | 0 | 0 | 0 | 1 | .000 | 6.75 |
| Blue | 1 | 1 | 0 | 3 | 6 | 3 | 3 | 0 | 2 | 0 | 0 | 0 | 0 | .000 | 9.00 |
| Todd | 3 | 0 | 0 | 1 | 3 | 1 | 1 | 0 | 0 | 0 | 0 | 0 | 0 | .000 | 9.00 |
| Totals | 3 | 3 | 0 | 25 | 31 | 18 | 12 | 3 | 12 | 0 | 1 | 0 | 3 | .000 | 4.32 |

No shutouts or saves.

## COMPOSITE SCORE BY INNINGS

```
Boston .............................. 2 0 0    4 3 1    6 2 0—18
Oakland ............................. 2 0 0    1 0 1    0 3 0— 7
```

Sacrifice hits—Cooper, Doyle, Burleson, Beniquez, Lynn.

Sacrifice fly—Doyle.

Stolen bases—Beniquez 2, Fisk.

Caught stealing—None.

Double plays—Campaneris, Garner and Tenace 2; Jackson and Fosse; Tenace, Campaneris and Tenace; Petrocelli, Doyle and Cooper; Lynn and Cooper; Burleson, Doyle and Cooper.

Left on bases—Boston 14—5, 3, 6; Oakland 19—7, 6, 6.

Hit by pitcher—None.

Passed balls—None.

Time of games—First game, 2:40; second game, 2:27; third game, 2:30.

Attendance—First game, 35,578; second game, 35,578; third game, 49,358.

Umpires—Denkinger, DiMuro, Kunkel, Luciano, Evans and Morgenweck.

Official scorers—Glenn Schwarz, San Francisco Examiner; George Bankert, Quincy Patriot Ledger.

# Reds Have Easy Time With Pirates

## By JOE MARCIN

The Cincinnati Reds, easy winners of the National League's West Division, were expected to have little trouble with their Championship Series rivals, the Pittsburgh Pirates. And that's just the way things turned out.

The Cincinnati club swept the three-game series and only the third game provided any of the dramatics that one might expect from two clubs contesting for baseball's oldest title, the National League pennant.

The Rhinelanders cuffed four Bucco hurlers for 11 hits in the opener, breezing to an 8-3 triumph. Even Reds' pitcher Don Gullett got into the act, getting two hits, one a home run, and driving in three runs.

The Cincinnati regulars took batting practice in the second game, banging out 12 hits as four more Pirate hurlers trudged to the mound. Tony Perez was the big cannon in the Reds' artillery, getting three hits, one a homer, as he drove in three runs. The final score was 6-1.

The high drama of the series came in the third game, played at Pittsburgh's Three Rivers Stadium.

The home team sent an angular 6-foot, 5-inch lefthander, John Candelaria, to the hill to try and stem the Red tide and the 21-year-old rookie responded magnificently. He yielded a solo homer to Concepcion in the

### GAME OF SATURDAY, OCTOBER 4 AT CINCINNATI

| Pittsburgh | AB. | R. | H. | RBI. | PO. | A. |
|---|---|---|---|---|---|---|
| Stennett. 2b | 5 | 0 | 1 | 0 | 1 | 5 |
| Sanguillen, c | 4 | 0 | 1 | 0 | 5 | 1 |
| Oliver, cf | 4 | 0 | 1 | 0 | 3 | 0 |
| Stargell, 1b | 4 | 0 | 0 | 0 | 8 | 0 |
| Zisk, lf | 4 | 0 | 1 | 0 | 2 | 0 |
| Parker, rf | 2 | 2 | 0 | 0 | 4 | 0 |
| Hebner, 3b | 4 | 1 | 2 | 1 | 0 | 1 |
| Taveras, ss | 3 | 0 | 1 | 1 | 1 | 2 |
| Reuss, p | 1 | 0 | 0 | 0 | 0 | 1 |
| Brett, p | 0 | 0 | 0 | 0 | 0 | 0 |
| Robinson, ph | 1 | 0 | 0 | 0 | 0 | 0 |
| Demery, p | 0 | 0 | 0 | 0 | 0 | 0 |
| Randolph, ph | 1 | 0 | 0 | 0 | 0 | 0 |
| Ellis, p | 0 | 0 | 0 | 0 | 0 | 0 |
| Robertson, ph | 1 | 0 | 1 | 1 | 0 | 0 |
| Reynolds. pr | 0 | 0 | 0 | 0 | 0 | 0 |
| Totals | 34 | 3 | 8 | 3 | 24 | 10 |

| Cincinnati | AB. | R. | H. | RBI. | PO. | A. |
|---|---|---|---|---|---|---|
| Rose, 3b | 5 | 0 | 2 | 0 | 0 | 0 |
| Morgan, 2b | 3 | 1 | 0 | 0 | 1 | 2 |
| Bench, c | 4 | 1 | 1 | 0 | 5 | 0 |
| Perez, 1b | 4 | 2 | 2 | 1 | 6 | 3 |
| Foster, lf | 4 | 2 | 2 | 0 | 2 | 0 |
| Concepcion, ss | 3 | 0 | 1 | 0 | 0 | 3 |
| Griffey, rf | 4 | 1 | 1 | 3 | 2 | 1 |
| Geronimo, cf | 3 | 0 | 0 | 1 | 7 | 0 |
| Gullett, p | 4 | 1 | 2 | 3 | 4 | 1 |
| Totals | 34 | 8 | 11 | 8 | 27 | 10 |

| | | | | | | | | | |
|---|---|---|---|---|---|---|---|---|---|
| Pittsburgh | 0 | 2 | 0 | 0 | 0 | 0 | 0 | 0 | 1—3 |
| Cincinnati | 0 | 1 | 3 | 0 | 4 | 0 | 0 | 0 | x—8 |

| Pittsburgh | IP. | H. | R. | ER. | BB. | SO. |
|---|---|---|---|---|---|---|
| Reuss (Loser) | 2⅔ | 4 | 4 | 4 | 4 | 1 |
| Brett | 1⅓ | 1 | 0 | 0 | 0 | 1 |
| Demery | 2 | 4 | 4 | 4 | 1 | 1 |
| Ellis | 2 | 2 | 0 | 0 | 0 | 2 |

| Cincinnati | IP. | H. | R. | ER. | BB. | SO. |
|---|---|---|---|---|---|---|
| Gullett (Winner) | 9 | 8 | 3 | 3 | 2 | 5 |

Errors—None. Left on bases—Pittsburgh 7, Cincinnati 8. Two-base hits—Hebner, Griffey. Home run—Gullett. Stolen bases—Morgan 3. Sacrifice fly—Geronimo. Hit by pitch—By Gullett (Parker). Wild pitch—Gullett. Passed balls—Sanguillen 2. Umpires—Kibler, Olsen, Pulli, W. Williams, Gorman and A. Williams. Time—3:00. Attendance—54,633.

Reds' catcher Johnny Bench waves to a crowd of more than 5,000 on Fountain Square in downtown Cincinnati. The people waited until 3:45 A.M. to greet the players as they arrived from Pittsburgh where they won the National League pennant by beating the Pirates in three straight games.

## GAME OF SUNDAY, OCTOBER 5, AT CINCINNATI

| Pittsburgh | AB. | R. | H. | RBI. | PO. | A. |
|---|---|---|---|---|---|---|
| Stennett, 2b | 4 | 0 | 2 | 0 | 0 | 3 |
| Sanguillen, c | 4 | 0 | 0 | 0 | 9 | 0 |
| Oliver, cf | 2 | 0 | 0 | 0 | 0 | 0 |
| Stargell, 1b | 3 | 1 | 1 | 0 | 6 | 0 |
| Zisk, lf | 3 | 0 | 2 | 0 | 2 | 0 |
| Parker, rf | 4 | 0 | 0 | 0 | 4 | 1 |
| Hebner, 3b | 3 | 0 | 0 | 1 | 0 | 1 |
| Taveras, ss | 3 | 0 | 0 | 0 | 3 | 3 |
| Robertson, ph | 1 | 0 | 0 | 0 | 0 | 0 |
| Rooker, p | 1 | 0 | 0 | 0 | 0 | 0 |
| Robinson, ph | 1 | 0 | 0 | 0 | 0 | 0 |
| Tekulve, p | 0 | 0 | 0 | 0 | 0 | 0 |
| Brett, p | 0 | 0 | 0 | 0 | 0 | 0 |
| Kirkpatrick, ph | 1 | 0 | 0 | 0 | 0 | 0 |
| Kison, p | 0 | 0 | 0 | 0 | 0 | 0 |
| Totals | 30 | 1 | 5 | 1 | 24 | 8 |

| Cincinnati | AB. | R. | H. | RBI. | PO. | A. |
|---|---|---|---|---|---|---|
| Rose, 3b | 4 | 1 | 1 | 0 | 0 | 1 |
| Morgan, 2b | 3 | 1 | 1 | 0 | 1 | 2 |
| Bench, c | 4 | 0 | 0 | 0 | 5 | 3 |
| Perez, 1b | 4 | 1 | 3 | 3 | 12 | 2 |
| Foster, lf | 4 | 1 | 2 | 0 | 2 | 0 |
| Concepcion, ss | 4 | 1 | 3 | 0 | 5 | 4 |
| Griffey, rf | 4 | 1 | 2 | 1 | 0 | 0 |
| Geronimo, cf | 3 | 0 | 0 | 0 | 1 | 0 |
| Norman, p | 1 | 0 | 0 | 1 | 0 | 1 |
| Armbrister, ph | 1 | 0 | 0 | 0 | 0 | 0 |
| Crowley, ph | 0 | 0 | 0 | 0 | 0 | 0 |
| Rettenmund, ph | 1 | 0 | 0 | 0 | 0 | 0 |
| Eastwick, p | 0 | 0 | 0 | 0 | 1 | 0 |
| Totals | 32 | 6 | 12 | 5 | 27 | 13 |

| | | | | | | | | | | |
|---|---|---|---|---|---|---|---|---|---|---|
| Pittsburgh | 0 | 0 | 0 | 1 | 0 | 0 | 0 | 0 | 0—1 |
| Cincinnati | 2 | 0 | 0 | 0 | 2 | 0 | 1 | 1 | 0 | x—6 |

| Pittsburgh | IP. | H. | R. | ER. | BB. | SO. |
|---|---|---|---|---|---|---|
| Rooker (Loser) | 4 | 7 | 4 | 4 | 0 | 5 |
| Tekulve | 1* | 3 | 1 | 1 | 1 | 2 |
| Brett | 1 | 0 | 0 | 0 | 0 | 0 |
| Kison | 2 | 2 | 1 | 1 | 1 | 1 |

| Cincinnati | IP. | H. | R. | ER. | BB. | SO. |
|---|---|---|---|---|---|---|
| Norman (Winner) | 6 | 4 | 1 | 1 | 5 | 4 |
| Eastwick (Save) | 3 | 1 | 0 | 0 | 0 | 1 |

*Pitched to two batters in sixth.

Error—Concepcion. Double plays—Pittsburgh 3, Cincinnati 2. Left on bases—Pittsburgh 7, Cincinnati 5. Two-base hits—Stargell, Zisk, Morgan. Home run—Perez. Stolen bases—Foster, Concepcion 2, Griffey 3, Morgan. Sacrifice fly—Norman. Wild pitch—Norman. Balk—Brett. Umpires—Olsen, Pulli, W. Williams, Gorman, A. Williams and Kibler. Time—2:51. Attendance—54,752.

second inning, but going into the eighth had a 2-1 lead, the result of Al Oliver's two-run homer in the Pirate sixth.

Candelaria struck out the first two batters in the eighth. That gave him a total of 14 for the game, a new playoff record. Concepcion's circuit clout had been the only Red hit to that point.

### GAME OF TUESDAY, OCTOBER 7, AT PITTSBURGH

| Cincinnati | AB. | R. | H. | RBI. | PO. | A. |
|---|---|---|---|---|---|---|
| Rose, 3b | 5 | 2 | 2 | 2 | 2 | 0 |
| Morgan, 2b | 5 | 0 | 2 | 1 | 0 | 5 |
| Bench, c | 5 | 0 | 0 | 0 | 8 | 1 |
| Perez, 1b | 4 | 0 | 0 | 0 | 8 | 1 |
| Foster, lf | 3 | 0 | 0 | 0 | 9 | 0 |
| Concepcion, ss | 4 | 1 | 1 | 1 | 1 | 1 |
| Griffey, rf | 4 | 1 | 1 | 0 | 2 | 0 |
| Geronimo, cf | 4 | 0 | 0 | 0 | 5 | 0 |
| Nolan, p | 2 | 0 | 0 | 0 | 0 | 0 |
| C. Carroll, p | 0 | 0 | 0 | 0 | 0 | 1 |
| Rettenmund, ph | 0 | 1 | 0 | 0 | 0 | 0 |
| McEnaney, p | 0 | 0 | 0 | 0 | 0 | 0 |
| Eastwick, p | 0 | 0 | 0 | 0 | 0 | 0 |
| Armbrister, ph | 0 | 0 | 0 | 1 | 0 | 0 |
| Borbon, p | 0 | 0 | 0 | 0 | 0 | 0 |
| Totals | 36 | 5 | 6 | 5 | 30 | 8 |

| Pittsburgh | AB. | R. | H. | RBI. | PO. | A. |
|---|---|---|---|---|---|---|
| Stennett, 2b-ss | 5 | 0 | 0 | 0 | 2 | 0 |
| Hebner, 3b | 5 | 1 | 2 | 0 | 0 | 0 |
| Oliver, cf | 5 | 1 | 1 | 2 | 2 | 0 |
| Stargell, 1b | 4 | 0 | 1 | 0 | 1 | 0 |
| Randolph, pr-2b | 1 | 1 | 0 | 0 | 0 | 1 |
| Parker, rf | 4 | 0 | 0 | 0 | 5 | 0 |
| Zisk, lf | 3 | 0 | 2 | 0 | 4 | 0 |
| Sanguillen, c | 4 | 0 | 1 | 0 | 15 | 0 |
| Taveras, ss | 1 | 0 | 0 | 0 | 0 | 1 |
| Kirkpatrick, ph | 1 | 0 | 0 | 0 | 0 | 0 |
| Reynolds, ss | 1 | 0 | 0 | 0 | 0 | 0 |
| Robertson, ph-1b | 0 | 0 | 0 | 0 | 1 | 0 |
| Candelaria, p | 3 | 0 | 0 | 0 | 0 | 0 |
| Giusti, p | 0 | 0 | 0 | 0 | 0 | 0 |
| Dyer, ph | 0 | 0 | 0 | 1 | 0 | 0 |
| Hernandez, p | 0 | 0 | 0 | 0 | 0 | 0 |
| Tekulve, p | 0 | 0 | 0 | 0 | 0 | 0 |
| Totals | 37 | 3 | 7 | 3 | 30 | 2 |

| | | | | | | | | | | |
|---|---|---|---|---|---|---|---|---|---|---|
| Cincinnati | 0 | 1 | 0 | 0 | 0 | 0 | 0 | 2 | 0 | 2—5 |
| Pittsburgh | 0 | 0 | 0 | 0 | 2 | 0 | 0 | 1 | 0 | 0—3 |

| Cincinnati | IP. | H. | R. | ER. | BB. | SO. |
|---|---|---|---|---|---|---|
| Nolan | 6 | 5 | 2 | 2 | 0 | 5 |
| C. Carroll | 1 | 0 | 0 | 0 | 1 | 0 |
| McEnaney | 1⅓ | 1 | 1 | 1 | 0 | 1 |
| Eastwick (Winner) | ⅔ | 1 | 0 | 0 | 0 | 1 |
| Borbon (Save) | 1 | 0 | 0 | 0 | 2 | 0 |

| Pittsburgh | IP. | H. | R. | ER. | BB. | SO. |
|---|---|---|---|---|---|---|
| Candelaria | 7⅔ | 3 | 3 | 3 | 2 | 14 |
| Giusti | 1⅓ | 0 | 0 | 0 | 0 | 1 |
| Hernandez (Loser) | ⅔ | 3 | 2 | 2 | 0 | 0 |
| Tekulve | ⅓ | 0 | 0 | 0 | 0 | 0 |

Errors—Reynolds, Sanguillen. Left on bases—Cincinnati 4, Pittsburgh 7. Two-base hits—Morgan 2. Home runs—Concepcion, Oliver, Rose. Stolen base—Bench. Sacrifice fly—Armbrister. Balk—Hernandez. Umpires—Pulli, W. Williams, Gorman, A. Williams, Kibler and Olsen. Time—2:47. Attendance—46,355.

But, inexplicably, he lost his control and walked the weak-hitting Merv Rettenmund, a pinch-hitter. Pete Rose then blasted a home run to put the Reds ahead, 3-2. When Joe Morgan followed Rose's homer with a double, Candelaria left the game. He had hurled valiantly but it wasn't good enough to win.

The Pirates tied the game in the ninth when Reds' relief pitcher Rawly Eastwick walked in the tieing run with the bases loaded and two out.

But it all served to merely delay the inevitable.

The Reds got three hits and two runs off veteran Ramon Hernandez, the third Pittsburgh hurler, in the top of the 10th and so clinched the pennant.

If there was anything noteworthy about the series, except the Reds' complete superiority, it was the dazzling baserunning displayed by the victors. They stole 11 bases during the three games and the Pittsburgh team was simply unable to cope with this display of speed.

Pirate rookie pitcher John Candelaria sits dejectedly after third playoff game. He struck out 14 batters but failed to win.

### CINCINNATI REDS' BATTING AND FIELDING AVERAGES

| Player—Position | G. | AB. | R. | H. | TB. | 2B. | 3B. | HR. | RBI. | B.A. | PO. | A. | E. | F.A. |
|---|---|---|---|---|---|---|---|---|---|---|---|---|---|---|
| Gullett, p | 1 | 4 | 1 | 2 | 5 | 0 | 0 | 1 | 3 | .500 | 4 | 1 | 0 | 1.000 |
| Concepcion, ss | 3 | 11 | 2 | 5 | 8 | 0 | 0 | 1 | 1 | .455 | 6 | 8 | 1 | .933 |
| Perez, 1b | 3 | 12 | 3 | 5 | 8 | 0 | 1 | 4 | 4 | .417 | 27 | 5 | 0 | 1.000 |
| Foster, lf | 3 | 11 | 3 | 4 | 4 | 0 | 0 | 0 | 0 | .364 | 7 | 0 | 0 | 1.000 |
| Rose, 3b | 3 | 14 | 3 | 5 | 8 | 0 | 0 | 1 | 2 | .357 | 2 | 1 | 0 | 1.000 |
| Griffey, rf | 3 | 12 | 3 | 4 | 5 | 1 | 0 | 0 | 4 | .333 | 4 | 1 | 0 | 1.000 |
| Morgan, 2b | 3 | 11 | 2 | 3 | 6 | 3 | 0 | 0 | 1 | .273 | 2 | 9 | 0 | 1.000 |
| Bench, c | 3 | 13 | 1 | 1 | 1 | 0 | 0 | 0 | 0 | .077 | 18 | 4 | 0 | 1.000 |
| Norman, p | 1 | 1 | 0 | 0 | 0 | 0 | 0 | 0 | 1 | .000 | 0 | 1 | 0 | 1.000 |
| Rettenmund, ph | 2 | 1 | 1 | 0 | 0 | 0 | 0 | 0 | 0 | .000 | 0 | 0 | 0 | .000 |
| Nolan, p | 1 | 2 | 0 | 0 | 0 | 0 | 0 | 0 | 0 | .000 | 0 | 0 | 0 | .000 |
| Geronimo, cf | 3 | 10 | 0 | 0 | 0 | 0 | 0 | 0 | 1 | .000 | 13 | 0 | 0 | 1.000 |
| Armbrister, ph | 2 | 0 | 0 | 0 | 0 | 0 | 0 | 0 | 1 | .000 | 0 | 0 | 0 | .000 |
| Borbon, p | 1 | 0 | 0 | 0 | 0 | 0 | 0 | 0 | 0 | .000 | 0 | 0 | 0 | .000 |
| Carroll, p | 1 | 0 | 0 | 0 | 0 | 0 | 0 | 0 | 0 | .000 | 0 | 1 | 0 | 1.000 |
| Crowley, ph | 1 | 0 | 0 | 0 | 0 | 0 | 0 | 0 | 0 | .000 | 0 | 0 | 0 | .000 |
| Eastwick, p | 2 | 0 | 0 | 0 | 0 | 0 | 0 | 0 | 0 | .000 | 1 | 0 | 0 | 1.000 |
| McEnaney, p | 1 | 0 | 0 | 0 | 0 | 0 | 0 | 0 | 0 | .000 | 0 | 0 | 0 | .000 |
| Totals | 3 | 102 | 19 | 29 | 45 | 4 | 0 | 4 | 18 | .284 | 84 | 31 | 1 | .991 |

## PITTSBURGH PIRATES' BATTING AND FIELDING AVERAGES

| Player—Position | G. | AB. | R. | H. | TB. | 2B. | 3B. | HR. | RBI. | B.A. | PO. | A. | E. | F.A. |
|---|---|---|---|---|---|---|---|---|---|---|---|---|---|---|
| Zisk, lf | 3 | 10 | 0 | 5 | 6 | 1 | 0 | 0 | 0 | .500 | 8 | 0 | 0 | 1.000 |
| Robertson, ph-1b | 3 | 2 | 0 | 1 | 1 | 0 | 0 | 0 | 1 | .500 | 1 | 0 | 0 | 1.000 |
| Hebner, 3b | 3 | 12 | 2 | 4 | 5 | 1 | 0 | 0 | 2 | .333 | 0 | 2 | 0 | 1.000 |
| Stennett, 2b-ss | 3 | 14 | 0 | 3 | 3 | 0 | 0 | 0 | 0 | .214 | 3 | 8 | 0 | 1.000 |
| Oliver, cf | 3 | 11 | 1 | 2 | 5 | 0 | 0 | 1 | 2 | .182 | 5 | 0 | 0 | 1.000 |
| Stargell, 1b | 3 | 11 | 1 | 2 | 3 | 1 | 0 | 0 | 0 | .182 | 15 | 0 | 0 | 1.000 |
| Sanguillen, c | 3 | 12 | 0 | 2 | 2 | 0 | 0 | 0 | 0 | .167 | 29 | 1 | 1 | .968 |
| Taveras, ss | 3 | 7 | 0 | 1 | 1 | 0 | 0 | 0 | 1 | .143 | 4 | 6 | 0 | 1.000 |
| Reuss, p | 1 | 1 | 0 | 0 | 0 | 0 | 0 | 0 | 0 | .000 | 0 | 1 | 0 | 1.000 |
| Reynolds, pr-ss | 2 | 1 | 0 | 0 | 0 | 0 | 0 | 0 | 0 | .000 | 0 | 0 | 1 | .000 |
| Rooker, p | 1 | 1 | 0 | 0 | 0 | 0 | 0 | 0 | 0 | .000 | 0 | 0 | 0 | .000 |
| Kirkpatrick, ph | 2 | 2 | 0 | 0 | 0 | 0 | 0 | 0 | 0 | .000 | 0 | 0 | 0 | .000 |
| Randolph, ph-pr-2b | 2 | 2 | 1 | 0 | 0 | 0 | 0 | 0 | 0 | .000 | 0 | 1 | 0 | 1.000 |
| Robinson, ph | 2 | 2 | 0 | 0 | 0 | 0 | 0 | 0 | 0 | .000 | 0 | 0 | 0 | .000 |
| Candelaria, p | 1 | 3 | 0 | 0 | 0 | 0 | 0 | 0 | 0 | .000 | 0 | 0 | 0 | .000 |
| Parker, rf | 3 | 10 | 2 | 0 | 0 | 0 | 0 | 0 | 0 | .000 | 13 | 1 | 0 | 1.000 |
| Brett, p | 2 | 0 | 0 | 0 | 0 | 0 | 0 | 0 | 0 | .000 | 0 | 0 | 0 | .000 |
| Demery, p | 1 | 0 | 0 | 0 | 0 | 0 | 0 | 0 | 0 | .000 | 0 | 0 | 0 | .000 |
| Dyer, ph | 1 | 0 | 0 | 0 | 0 | 0 | 0 | 0 | 1 | .000 | 0 | 0 | 0 | .000 |
| Ellis, p | 1 | 0 | 0 | 0 | 0 | 0 | 0 | 0 | 0 | .000 | 0 | 0 | 0 | .000 |
| Giusti, p | 1 | 0 | 0 | 0 | 0 | 0 | 0 | 0 | 0 | .000 | 0 | 0 | 0 | .000 |
| Hernandez, p | 1 | 0 | 0 | 0 | 0 | 0 | 0 | 0 | 0 | .000 | 0 | 0 | 0 | .000 |
| Kison, p | 1 | 0 | 0 | 0 | 0 | 0 | 0 | 0 | 0 | .000 | 0 | 0 | 0 | .000 |
| Tekulve, p | 2 | 0 | 0 | 0 | 0 | 0 | 0 | 0 | 0 | .000 | 0 | 0 | 0 | .000 |
| Totals | 3 | 101 | 7 | 20 | 26 | 3 | 0 | 1 | 7 | .198 | 78 | 20 | 2 | .980 |

## CINCINNATI REDS' PITCHING RECORDS

| Pitcher | G. | GS. | CG. | IP. | H. | R. | ER. | BB. | SO. | HB. | WP. | W. | L. | Pct. | ERA. |
|---|---|---|---|---|---|---|---|---|---|---|---|---|---|---|---|
| Eastwick | 2 | 0 | 0 | 3⅔ | 2 | 0 | 0 | 2 | 1 | 0 | 0 | 1 | 0 | 1.000 | 0.00 |
| Borbon | 1 | 0 | 0 | 1 | 0 | 0 | 0 | 1 | 0 | 0 | 0 | 0 | 0 | .000 | 0.00 |
| Carroll | 1 | 0 | 0 | 1 | 0 | 0 | 0 | 1 | 1 | 0 | 0 | 0 | 0 | .000 | 0.00 |
| Norman | 1 | 1 | 0 | 6 | 4 | 1 | 1 | 5 | 4 | 0 | 1 | 1 | 0 | 1.000 | 1.50 |
| Gullett | 1 | 1 | 1 | 9 | 8 | 3 | 3 | 2 | 5 | 1 | 1 | 1 | 0 | 1.000 | 3.00 |
| Nolan | 1 | 1 | 0 | 6 | 5 | 2 | 2 | 0 | 5 | 0 | 0 | 0 | 0 | .000 | 3.00 |
| McEnaney | 1 | 0 | 0 | 1⅓ | 1 | 1 | 1 | 0 | 1 | 0 | 0 | 0 | 0 | .000 | 6.75 |
| Totals | 3 | 3 | 1 | 28 | 20 | 7 | 7 | 10 | 18 | 1 | 2 | 3 | 0 | 1.000 | 2.25 |

No shutouts. Saves—Eastwick, Borbon.

## PITTSBURGH PIRATES' PITCHING RECORDS

| Pitcher | G. | GS. | CG. | IP. | H. | R. | ER. | BB. | SO. | HB. | WP. | W. | L. | Pct. | ERA. |
|---|---|---|---|---|---|---|---|---|---|---|---|---|---|---|---|
| Brett | 2 | 0 | 0 | 2⅓ | 1 | 0 | 0 | 1 | 0 | 0 | 0 | 0 | 0 | .000 | 0.00 |
| Ellis | 1 | 0 | 0 | 2 | 2 | 0 | 0 | 2 | 0 | 0 | 0 | 0 | 0 | .000 | 0.00 |
| Giusti | 1 | 0 | 0 | 1½ | 0 | 0 | 0 | 1 | 0 | 0 | 0 | 0 | 0 | .000 | 0.00 |
| Candelaria | 1 | 1 | 0 | 7⅔ | 3 | 3 | 3 | 2 | 14 | 0 | 0 | 0 | 0 | .000 | 3.52 |
| Kison | 1 | 0 | 0 | 2 | 2 | 1 | 1 | 1 | 2 | 0 | 0 | 0 | 0 | .000 | 4.50 |
| Tekulve | 2 | 0 | 0 | 1⅓ | 3 | 1 | 1 | 1 | 2 | 0 | 0 | 0 | 0 | .000 | 6.75 |
| Rooker | 1 | 1 | 0 | 4 | 7 | 4 | 4 | 0 | 5 | 0 | 0 | 0 | 1 | .000 | 9.00 |
| Reuss | 1 | 1 | 0 | 2⅔ | 4 | 4 | 4 | 1 | 0 | 0 | 0 | 0 | 1 | .000 | 13.50 |
| Demery | 1 | 0 | 0 | 2 | 4 | 4 | 4 | 1 | 1 | 0 | 0 | 0 | 0 | .000 | 18.00 |
| Hernandez | 1 | 0 | 0 | ⅔ | 3 | 2 | 2 | 0 | 0 | 0 | 0 | 0 | 1 | .000 | 27.00 |
| Totals | 3 | 3 | 0 | 26 | 29 | 19 | 19 | 9 | 28 | 0 | 0 | 0 | 3 | .000 | 6.58 |

No shutouts or saves.

## COMPOSITE SCORE BY INNINGS

| | | | | | | | | | | |
|---|---|---|---|---|---|---|---|---|---|---|
| Cincinnati | 2 | 2 | 3 | 2 | 4 | 1 | 1 | 2 | 0 | 2—19 |
| Pittsburgh | 0 | 2 | 0 | 1 | 0 | 2 | 0 | 0 | 2 | 0— 7 |

Sacrifice hits—None.

Sacrifice flies—Armbrister, Geronimo, Norman.

Stolen bases—Morgan 4, Griffey 3, Concepcion 2, Bench, Foster.

Caught stealing—None.

Double plays—Concepcion and Perez; Morgan, Concepcion and Perez; Parker and Sanguillen; Stennett, Taveras and Stargell 2.

Left on bases—Cincinnati 17—8, 5, 4; Pittsburgh 21—7, 7, 7.

Hit by pitcher—By Gullett (Parker).

Passed balls—Sanguillen 2.

Balks—Brett, Hernandez.

Time of games—First game, 3:00; second game, 2:51; third game, 2:47.

Attendance—First game, 54,633; second game, 54,752; third game, 46,355.

Umpires Kibler, Olsen, Pulli, W. Williams, Gorman and A. Williams.

Official scorers—Earl Lawson, Cincinnati Post; Luke Quay, McKeesport Daily News.

# 1975 WORLD SERIES

### Including

**Review of '75 Series**

**Official Play-By-Play, Each Game**

**Official Composite Box Score**

**World Series Tables—Attendance, Money, Results**

The controversial play of the third game of the 1975 World Series. Boston catcher Carlton Fisk is going for the ball and collides with batter Ed Armbrister, who was attempting to lay down a sacrifice bunt. Umpire Larry Barnett ruled the collision wasn't intentional and called no interference.

# World Series

## WORLD SERIES CHAMPIONS, 1903-1975

| | | |
|---|---|---|
| New York, A. L. | 20 | 1923-27-28-32-36-37-38-39-41-43-47-49-50-51-52-53-56-58-61-62 |
| St. Louis, N. L. | 8 | 1926-31-34-42-44-46-64-67 |
| New York, N.L. | 6 | 1905-21-22-33-54 (Giants). 1969 (Mets) |
| Philadelphia, A.L. | 5 | 1910-11-13-29-30 |
| Boston, A. L. | 5 | 1903-12-15-16-18 |
| Pittsburgh, N.L. | 4 | 1909-25-60-71 |
| Los Angeles, N.L. | 3 | 1959-63-65 |
| Detroit, A. L. | 3 | 1935-45-68 |
| Oakland, A. L. | 3 | 1972-73-74 |
| Cincinnati, N. L. | 3 | 1919-40-75 |
| Chicago, A. L. | 2 | 1906-17 |
| Chicago, N. L. | 2 | 1907-08 |
| Cleveland, A. L. | 2 | 1920-48 |
| Baltimore, A.L. | 2 | 1966-70 |
| Boston, N. L. | 1 | 1914 |
| Washington, A.L. | 1 | 1924 |
| Brooklyn, N. L. | 1 | 1955 |
| Milwaukee, N.L. | 1 | 1957 |

American League has won 43, National League 29.

## RESULTS OF WORLD SERIES GAMES OF 1975

| Game | Where Played | Date | Winner | | Winner | Loser | Att. |
|---|---|---|---|---|---|---|---|
| First | Boston | Oct. 11 | Boston | 6-0 | Tiant | Gullett | 35,205 |
| Second | Boston | Oct. 12 | Cincinnati | 3-2 | Eastwick | Drago | 35,205 |
| Third | Cincinnati | Oct. 14 | Cincinnati | 6-5 | Eastwick | Willoughby | 55,392 |
| Fourth | Cincinnati | Oct. 15 | Boston | 5-4 | Tiant | Norman | 55,667 |
| Fifth | Cincinnati | Oct. 16 | Cincinnati | 6-2 | Gullett | Cleveland | 56,393 |
| Sixth | Boston | Oct. 21 | Boston | 7-6 | Wise | Darcy | 35,205 |
| Seventh | Boston | Oct. 22 | Cincinnati | 4-3 | Carroll | Burton | 35,205 |

## ROSTERS OF ELIGIBLES FOR WORLD SERIES

**Cincinnati Reds**—Edison R. Armbrister, Johnny L. Bench, John E. Billingham, Pedro Borbon, Clay P. Carroll, Darrel L. Chaney, David I. Concepcion, Terrence M. Crowley, Patrick L. Darcy, Daniel Driessen, Rawlins J. Eastwick, Robert D. Flynn, George A. Foster, Cesar F. Geronimo, G. Kenneth Griffey, Donald E. Gullett, Clayton L. Kirby, William H. McEnaney, Joe L. Morgan, Gary L. Nolan, Fredie H. Norman, Atanasio R. Perez, William F. Plummer, Mervin W. Rettenmund, Peter E. Rose, George L. (Sparky) Anderson, manager; Alexander P. Grammas, Theodore B. Kluszewski, George R. Scherger and Lawrence W. Shepard, coaches; Larry M. Starr, trainer.

**Boston Red Sox**—Juan J. Beniquez, Timothy P. Blackwell, Richard P. Burleson, James S. Burton, Bernardo Carbo, Reginald L. Cleveland, Cecil C. Cooper, R. Dennis Doyle, Richard A. Drago, Dwight M. Evans, Carlton E. Fisk, Douglas L. Griffin, Robert L. Heise, William F. Lee, Fredric M. Lynn, Richard A. Miller, Robert E. Montgomery, Rogelio Moret, Americo P. Petrocelli, Richard H. Pole, Diego P. Segui, Luis C. Tiant, James A. Willoughby, Richard C. Wise, Carl M. Yastrzemski, Darrell D. Johnson, manager; Donald R. Bryant, John M. Pesky, Edward J. Popowski, Stanley W. Williams and Donald W. Zimmer, coaches; Charles E. Moss, trainer.

## By JOE MARCIN

The 1975 World Series must go down in memory as one of the most exciting ever. It produced a play which baseball fans will argue about as long as the game itself is played.

More people saw the 1975 Series than ever before. It produced the highest television ratings ever attained by any American sporting event.

The Cincinnati Reds entered the Classic as heavy favorites with their admirers proclaiming them one of the great clubs of all time. The Boston Red Sox, basically a young team, played the Series with one of their best hitters, rookie outfielder Jim Rice, sidelined because of a late-season injury and were held by the majority to be easy prey for the National League champions.

But such was not to be the case.

The first game was played at a genuine baseball stadium, Boston's venerable Fenway Park, and turned into a personal triumph for Luis Tiant. The veteran Cuban righthander, with his parents coming on from their native country to see their son perform, shut out the Reds on five hits.

Don Gullett matched Tiant's string of goose eggs until the seventh inning, when a six-run explosion sent the Reds' lefty to the showers and locked up the contest for the home team. Tiant himself, who had batted only once all year under the American League's designated hitter rule, started the winning rally with a single. He later scored the run that broke the deadlock on Carl Yastrzemski's single. Rico Petrocelli drove in two runs during the inning, also with a single.

The second game was played with rain falling throughout much of the contest. In fact, there was a 27-minute rain delay after the Reds batted in the seventh inning. But the millions watching on Sunday television were not to be denied.

The Sox, with southpaw Bill Lee on the mound, carried a 2-1 lead into the top of the ninth. But Johnny Bench doubled to right to begin the frame. Lee was promptly excused and replaced by righthander Dick Drago. Drago almost closed out the game. He retired the next two batters but Dave Concepcion hit a ground single up the middle that scored Bench. Concepcion then stole second and scored on Ken Griffey's double.

Concepcion's steal emphasized the fact that the Reds' speed on the bases was to be a thorn in the side of the Red Sox throughout the Series.

The third game, played at Cincinnati's Riverfront Stadium after a day off for travel, produced a record-tying six home runs, but a 10th-inning bunt was the key play of the game and gave vent to one of the more controversial happenings in World Series history.

The Red Sox, down at one point 5-1, fought back and eventually tied the game, 5-5, in the top of the ninth, scoring two runs on Dwight Evans' one-out home run.

Cesar Geronimo opened the bottom of the 10th with a single to center. Ed Armbrister, sent up as a pinch-hitter for relief pitcher Rawly Eastwick, attempted to sacrifice the runner to second and laid down a bunt. The ball bounced just a few feet in front of the plate and catcher Carlton Fisk went to field it. There was a collision between Armbrister and Fisk before Fisk picked up the ball and threw wildly into center field trying to get Geronimo advancing from first to second. Armbrister and Geronimo wound up at second and third respectively.

The Red Sox claimed interference on the play and argued strenuously. Plate umpire Larry Barnett, an American League arbiter, stuck by his decision. Television replays definitely showed the collision and there was no dearth of commentary and opinions voiced on the air and in the press for several days after the game. Rules were quoted to prove interference or lack of interference. But the decision, of course, stood.

When the game furor had subsided, Pete Rose was given an intentional walk to load the bases. After pinch-hitter Merv Rettenmund struck out, Joe Morgan singled to center to end the game on a winning note for the Reds.

The Red Sox called on Tiant again for the fourth game and again he was equal to the occasion. Although not nearly as sharp as he was in the opener and requiring 163 pitches to do it, Tiant managed to notch a 5-4 verdict and evened the Series at two games apiece.

The Sox got all their runs in the fourth inning on singles by Fisk and Fred Lynn, a wild pitch by Reds' starter Fred Norman, Evans' triple, Rick Burleson's double, a single by Tiant, an error and Yastrzemski's single.

The Reds threatened in the late-going but Tiant managed to repulse all threats.

Cincinnati first baseman Tony Perez snapped out of an 0-for-15 slump with two home runs and lefty Gullett hurled brilliantly to enable the Reds to capture the fifth game. Gullett, who worked 8⅔ innings, had carried a two-hitter into the ninth and at one point retired 16 consecutive batters. Two-out singles by Yastrzemski and Fisk and a double by Lynn gave Boston a ninth-inning run. But Rawly Eastwick came on for the Reds and struck out Petrocelli for the final out.

The teams did not play again for four more days. One of those days was a travel day but the other three were caused by rainstorms which swept the New England coast. When the teams finally resumed, what resulted was one of the really exciting sporting events of modern times.

Lynn got the Sox off in front by blasting a three-run homer off Reds' starter Gary Nolan in the first inning. Tiant, trying for his third Series victory, sailed through the first four frames but started to come unglued in the fifth. In that stanza, a walk to Armbrister, Rose's single, a triple by Griffey that Lynn crashed into the center field wall attempting to catch, and Bench's single tied the score.

The Reds went ahead, 5-3, in the seventh when George Foster doubled off the center field wall to score Griffey and Morgan who had hit singles. They added another tally an inning later on Geronimo's homer.

The Sox tied the game in the eighth when pinch-hitter Bernie Carbo hit a two-out two-on homer.

It looked like the Boston club would win in the ninth when Doyle opened with a walk and took third on Yastrzemski's single. After an intentional walk to Fisk, Lynn hit a fly just barely foul to Foster in shallow left field, an estimated 180 feet from the plate. Doyle, against coaching instructions, tried to score after the catch and was thrown out.

A sensational catch by Evans of Morgan's bid for a homer stopped a Cincy bid in the top of the 11th.

In the bottom of the 12th, Fisk, first man up for Boston, hit a long blast that caromed off the left field foul pole for a home run to end the game and set up a climactic seventh game.

The sixth game lasted for one minute over four hours and ended at 12:33 a. m.

The opposing pitchers for the finale were the two lefties, Gullett and Lee. Gullett was plagued by control problems and the Sox appeared to be closing in on a great upset when they got three runs in the third inning, two of the tallies being forced home by bases-loaded walks.

The Reds got two back in the sixth. With one out and Rose on first as the result of a single, Bench hit a grounder to Burleson at shortstop for what might have been a double play. But Rose slid hard into second and Doyle threw the ball past first, Bench reaching second. Perez then hit a home run.

The Reds' base-running speed enabled them to tie the score in their next turn at bat. Griffey walked, stole second and scored on Rose's single.

The last run of the game and the Series and the one that won it all came in the Reds' ninth. Griffey walked, was sacrificed to second and advanced to third on an infield out. Rose walked and that left it up to Morgan. He responded with a single to center, scoring Griffey.

Boston went out in order in the ninth and the Series was over.

All observers agreed that the 1975 World Series was the best product that baseball had sold for many years and that the game called the nation's pastime was still No. 1.

## AT BOSTON   GAME 1   OCTOBER 11

| Cincinnati | AB. | R. | H. | PO. | A. | E. | Boston | AB. | R. | H. | PO. | A. | E. |
|---|---|---|---|---|---|---|---|---|---|---|---|---|---|
| Rose, 3b | 4 | 0 | 0 | 0 | 0 | 0 | Evans, rf | 4 | 1 | 1 | 4 | 0 | 0 |
| Morgan, 2b | 4 | 0 | 2 | 2 | 2 | 0 | Doyle, 2b | 3 | 1 | 2 | 3 | 3 | 0 |
| Bench, c | 4 | 0 | 0 | 6 | 1 | 0 | Yastrzemski, lf | 4 | 1 | 1 | 3 | 0 | 0 |
| Perez, 1b | 4 | 0 | 0 | 9 | 0 | 0 | Fisk, c | 3 | 1 | 0 | 4 | 1 | 0 |
| Foster, lf | 4 | 0 | 2 | 1 | 0 | 0 | Lynn, cf | 4 | 0 | 2 | 3 | 0 | 0 |
| Concepcion, ss | 4 | 0 | 0 | 2 | 3 | 0 | Petrocelli, 3b | 3 | 1 | 2 | 1 | 3 | 0 |
| Griffey, rf | 3 | 0 | 1 | 2 | 0 | 0 | Burleson, ss | 3 | 0 | 3 | 1 | 1 | 0 |
| Geronimo, cf | 1 | 0 | 0 | 2 | 1 | 0 | Cooper, 1b | 3 | 0 | 0 | 8 | 0 | 0 |
| Gullett, p | 3 | 0 | 0 | 0 | 0 | 0 | Tiant, p | 3 | 1 | 1 | 0 | 0 | 0 |
| Carroll, p | 0 | 0 | 0 | 0 | 0 | 0 | | | | | | | |
| McEnaney, p | 0 | 0 | 0 | 0 | 0 | 0 | | | | | | | |
| Totals | 31 | 0 | 5 | 24 | 7 | 0 | Totals | 30 | 6 | 12 | 27 | 8 | 0 |

```
Cincinnati ............  0   0   0      0   0   0      0   0   0—0
Boston ................  0   0   0      0   0   0      6   0   x—6
```

| Cincinnati | IP. | H. | R. | ER. | BB. | SO. |
|---|---|---|---|---|---|---|
| Gullett (Loser) | 6* | 10 | 4 | 4 | 4 | 3 |
| Carroll | 0† | 0 | 1 | 1 | 1 | 0 |
| McEnaney | 2 | 2 | 1 | 1 | 1 | 1 |
| Boston | IP. | H. | R. | ER. | BB. | SO. |
| Tiant (Winner) | 9 | 5 | 0 | 0 | 2 | 3 |

*Pitched to four batters in seventh.
†Pitched to one batter in seventh.

Bases on balls—Off Gullett 4 (Yastrzemski, Petrocelli, Tiant, Burleson), off Carroll 1 (Fisk), off McEnaney 1 (Doyle), off Tiant 2 (Geronimo 2).
Strikeouts—By Gullett 3 (Cooper 2, Tiant), by McEnaney 1 (Lynn), by Tiant 3 (Perez 2, Concepcion).
Runs batted in—Yastrzemski, Fisk, Petrocelli 2, Burleson, Cooper. Two-base hits—Morgan, Petrocelli, Griffey. Sacrifice hits—Doyle, Evans. Sacrifice fly—Cooper. Caught stealing—Burleson, Foster. Double plays—Geronimo and Bench; Perez unassisted. Balk—Tiant. Left on bases—Cincinnati 6, Boston 9. Umpires—Frantz (A.L.) plate, Colosi (N.L.) first base, Barnett (A.L.) second base, Stello (N.L.) third base, Maloney (A.L.) left field, Davidson (N.L.) right field. Time—2:27. Attendance 35,205.

### FIRST INNING

**Cincinnati**—Rose bounced to Doyle. Morgan lined to Doyle. Bench lined to Evans in short right. No runs, no hits, no errors, none left.

**Boston**—Evans grounded a single between third and short into left field. Doyle sacrificed, Perez unassisted. Yastrzemski walked on four pitches. Fisk popped to Morgan in short center. Lynn beat out a high hopper over Gullett's head but Evans was cut down at the plate when he attempted to score all the way from second, Concepcion to Bench. No runs, two hits, no errors, two left.

### SECOND INNING

**Cincinnati**—Perez lined to Evans. Foster lined to Cooper who made a leaping catch. Concepcion fouled to Yastrzemski. No runs, no hits, no errors, none left.

**Boston**—Petrocelli walked on four pitches. Burleson singled past the bag at third, Petrocelli going to third. Cooper struck out. Tiant also fanned. Evans fouled to Griffey. No runs, one hit, no errors, two left.

### THIRD INNING

**Cincinnati**—Griffey bounced to Doyle who made a backhanded stop and threw the runner out by a step. Geronimo flied to Lynn in deep right-center. Gullett flied to Yastrzemski. No runs, no hits, no errors, none left.

**Boston**—Doyle bounced sharply to Morgan. Yastrzemski grounded to Concepcion. Fisk flied to Foster in deep left-center. No runs, no hits, no errors, none left.

### FOURTH INNING

**Cincinnati**—Rose smashed a ground ball to Doyle who threw to Cooper for the out. Morgan lined a single to center. Morgan advanced to second on a balk. Bench fouled to Fisk. Perez was called out on strikes. No runs, one hit, no errors, one left.

**Boston**—Lynn popped to Concepcion. Petrocelli flied deep to Geronimo. Burleson lined a single to right. Burleson was out stealing, Bench to Concepcion. No runs, one hit, no errors, none left.

### FIFTH INNING

**Cincinnati**—Foster lined a single to left. Concepcion fanned. Attempting to check his swing, Griffey rolled out to Petrocelli, Foster moving to second. Geronimo was purposely passed. Gullett fouled to Petrocelli. No runs, one hit, no errors, two left.

**Boston**—Cooper struck out. Tiant walked. Evans popped to Morgan in short right. Doyle lined a single to right, Tiant stopping at second. Yastrzemski bounced out to Perez unassisted. No runs, one hit, no errors, two left.

### SIXTH INNING

**Cincinnati**—Rose lined to Evans. Morgan doubled just inside the first-base bag. Bench grounded to Petrocelli, Morgan holding second. Perez struck out. No runs, one hit, no errors, one left.

**Boston**—Fisk grounded sharply to Concepcion. Lynn grounded a single to center. Petrocelli doubled to right, Lynn racing to third. Burleson was walked intentionally, loading the bases. Cooper flied to Geronimo in short center and Lynn was cut down attempting to score after the catch, Geronimo to Bench. No runs, two hits, no errors, two left.

### SEVENTH INNING

**Cincinnati**—Foster grounded a single to left. Concepcion looped a fly to short left where Yastrzemski made a diving catch, Foster holding first. Foster was thrown out stealing, Fisk to Burleson. Griffey lined a double into the right field corner. Geronimo was intentionally passed. Gullett popped to Doyle who made a running grab in short right. No runs, two hits, no errors, two left.

**Boston**—Tiant smashed a single to left. Evans bunted to Gullett who threw the ball into center field trying for a force out on Tiant. Geronimo fielded the ball quickly, forcing Tiant to hold at second. It was ruled a sacrifice and fielder's choice. Doyle grounded a single to left, loading the bases. Yastrzemski lined a single to right, Tiant scoring. Evans going to third and Doyle to second. Carroll replaced Gullett on the mound for Cincinnati. Fisk walked, Evans scoring the second run. McEnaney replaced Carroll on the mound for Cincinnati. Lynn fanned. Petrocelli grounded a single between third and short, Doyle and Yastrzemski scoring and Fisk stopping at second. Burleson grounded a single in the same spot, Fisk scoring and Petrocelli going to third, and on the throw to the plate Burleson moved to second. Cooper flied deep to Griffey, Petrocelli scoring and Burleson advancing to third after the catch. Tiant fouled to Perez. Six runs, five hits, no errors, one left.

Dwight Evans of the Red Sox is out at home plate in the first inning of the first game when he tried to score from second on Fred Lynn's slow roller past the mound. Johnny Bench is making the tag.

### EIGHTH INNING

**Cincinnati**—Rose lined to Lynn. Morgan flied to Evans. Bench grounded to Burleson. No runs, no hits, no errors, none left.

**Boston**—Evans bounced to Morgan. Doyle walked. Yastrzemski lined to Perez who stepped on first, doubling Doyle. No runs, no hits, no errors, none left.

### NINTH INNING

**Cincinnati**—Perez lined to Lynn. Foster popped to Doyle in short center. Concepcion grounded to Petrocelli who made a diving stop to his left and threw to Cooper for the out. No runs, no hits, no errors, none left.

## AT BOSTON  GAME 2  OCTOBER 12

| Cincinnati | AB. | R. | H. | PO. | A. | E. | Boston | AB. | R. | H. | PO. | A. | E. |
|---|---|---|---|---|---|---|---|---|---|---|---|---|---|
| Rose, 3b | 4 | 0 | 2 | 1 | 1 | 0 | Cooper, 1b | 5 | 0 | 1 | 10 | 1 | 0 |
| Morgan, 2b | 3 | 1 | 0 | 0 | 4 | 0 | Doyle, 2b | 4 | 0 | 1 | 2 | 5 | 0 |
| Bench, c | 4 | 1 | 2 | 9 | 3 | 0 | Yastrzemski, lf | 3 | 2 | 1 | 1 | 0 | 0 |
| Perez, 1b | 3 | 0 | 0 | 8 | 0 | 0 | Fisk, c | 3 | 0 | 1 | 5 | 1 | 0 |
| Foster, lf | 4 | 0 | 1 | 2 | 0 | 0 | Lynn, cf | 4 | 0 | 0 | 5 | 0 | 0 |
| Concepcion, ss | 4 | 1 | 1 | 2 | 4 | 1 | Petrocelli, 3b | 4 | 0 | 2 | 0 | 0 | 0 |
| Griffey, rf | 4 | 0 | 1 | 2 | 0 | 0 | Evans, rf | 2 | 0 | 0 | 2 | 0 | 0 |
| Geronimo, cf | 3 | 0 | 0 | 3 | 0 | 0 | Burleson, ss | 4 | 0 | 1 | 2 | 4 | 0 |
| Billingham, p | 2 | 0 | 0 | 0 | 2 | 0 | Lee, p | 3 | 0 | 0 | 0 | 0 | 0 |
| Borbon, p | 0 | 0 | 0 | 0 | 0 | 0 | Drago, p | 0 | 0 | 0 | 0 | 0 | 0 |
| McEnaney, p | 0 | 0 | 0 | 0 | 0 | 0 | bCarbo | 1 | 0 | 0 | 0 | 0 | 0 |
| aRettenmund | 1 | 0 | 0 | 0 | 0 | 0 | | | | | | | |
| Eastwick, p | 1 | 0 | 0 | 0 | 0 | 0 | | | | | | | |
| | | | | | | | Totals | 33 | 2 | 7 | 27 | 11 | 0 |
| Totals | 33 | 3 | 7 | 27 | 14 | 1 | | | | | | | |

| | | | | | | | | | | |
|---|---|---|---|---|---|---|---|---|---|---|
| Cincinnati | 0 | 0 | 0 | | 1 | 0 | 0 | | 0 | 0 | 2—3 |
| Boston | 1 | 0 | 0 | | 0 | 0 | 1 | | 0 | 0 | 0—2 |

| Cincinnati | IP. | H. | R. | ER. | BB. | SO. |
|---|---|---|---|---|---|---|
| Billingham | 5⅔ | 6 | 2 | 1 | 2 | 5 |
| Borbon | ⅓ | 0 | 0 | 0 | 0 | 0 |
| McEnaney | 1 | 0 | 0 | 0 | 0 | 2 |
| Eastwick (Winner) | 2 | 1 | 0 | 0 | 1 | 1 |

| Boston | IP. | H. | R. | ER. | BB. | SO. |
|---|---|---|---|---|---|---|
| Lee | 8* | 5 | 2 | 2 | 2 | 5 |
| Drago (Loser) | 1 | 2 | 1 | 1 | 1 | 0 |

*Pitched to one batter in ninth.

Bases on balls—Off Billingham 2 (Yastrzemski, Evans), off Eastwick 1 (Fisk), off Lee 2 (Morgan, Perez), off Drago 1 (Geronimo). Strikeouts—By Billingham 5 (Petrocelli, Lee, Fisk, Evans, Burleson), by McEnaney 2 (Lee, Doyle), by Eastwick 1 (Evans), by Lee 5 (Rose, Perez, Foster, Geronimo, Griffey). aFouled out for McEnaney in eighth. bLined out for Drago in ninth. Runs batted in—Perez, Concepcion, Griffey, Fisk, Petrocelli. Two-base hits—Cooper, Bench, Griffey. Stolen base—Concepcion. Caught stealing—Evans, Morgan. Double play—Billingham, Concepcion, Bench, Rose and Bench. Hit by pitcher—By Billingham (Evans). Left on bases—Cincinnati 6, Boston 8. Umpires—Colosi (N.L.) plate, Barnett (A.L.) first base, Stello (N.L.) second base, Maloney (A.L.) third base, Davidson (N.L.) left field, Frantz (A.L.) right field. Time—2:38. Attendance—35,205.

### FIRST INNING

**Cincinnati**—Rose struck out. Morgan grounded to Doyle. Bench flied to Lynn. No runs, no hits, no errors, none left.

**Boston**—Cooper lined a double over the head of Foster who stumbled on the wet turf as he ran toward the line. Doyle singled off Billingham's glove, Cooper moving to third. Yastrzemski bounced to Billingham who threw to Concepcion covering second, forcing Doyle, and when Cooper made a belated break for the plate he was trapped and tagged out, Concepcion to Bench to Rose to Bench for a double play, Yastrzemski going to second. Fisk lined a single to right, Yastrzemski scoring. Lynn bounced to Morgan. One run, three hits, no errors, one left.

### SECOND INNING

**Cincinnati**—Perez struck out. Foster also struck out. Concepcion grounded to Burleson. No runs, no hits, no errors, none left.

**Boston**—Petrocelli fanned. Evans was hit by a pitched ball. Burleson grounded a single to center, Evans stopping at second. Attempting to bunt, Lee missed the pitch and Evans was trapped off second and tagged out attempting to go to third, Bench to Concepcion to Rose. Lee fanned. No runs, one hit, no errors, one left.

Rick Burleson argues with umpire Dick Stello when Dave Concepcion stole second in the 9th inning of the second game. Concepcion subsequently scored the game's winning run on a double by Ken Griffey.

### THIRD INNING

**Cincinnati**—Griffey bounced out to Cooper unassisted. Geronimo struck out. Billingham grounded to Burleson. No runs, no hits, no errors, none left.

**Boston**—Cooper rolled to Morgan. Doyle grounded to Morgan. Yastrzemski walked. Fisk struck out. No runs, no hits, no errors, one left.

### FOURTH INNING

**Cincinnati**—Rose bounced sharply to Doyle. Morgan walked. Bench lined a single to right-center, Morgan racing to third. Perez forced Bench, Burleson to Doyle, Morgan scoring. Foster looped a single to left, Perez stopping at second. Concepcion flied to Lynn in short center. One run, two hits, no errors, two left.

**Boston**—Lynn flied to Foster. Petrocelli bounced to Concepcion. Evans fanned. No runs, no hits, no errors, none left.

### FIFTH INNING

**Cincinnati**—Griffey grounded to Cooper who made the play unassisted, Geronimo flied to Evans. Billingham bounced sharply to Doyle. No runs, no hits, no errors, none left.

**Boston**—Burleson struck out. Lee bunted down the third base line and was out on a close play when Bench pounced on the ball and fired to Perez. Cooper bounced to Billingham who made a good play on the hard-hit ball. No runs, no hits, no errors, none left.

### SIXTH INNING

**Cincinnati**—Rose grounded a single to left. Morgan forced Rose, Cooper to Burleson. Morgan was out attempting to steal, Fisk to Doyle. Bench flied to Lynn who made a diving catch in short center. No runs, one hit, no errors, none left.

**Boston**—Doyle bounced to Morgan. Yastrzemski grounded a single to right. Fisk was safe when Concepcion fumbled his ground ball, Yastrzemski stopping at second. Lynn flied to Griffey in short right, both runners holding their bases. Petrocelli singled through the box into center field, Yastrzemski scoring and Fisk going to third. Evans walked, filling the bases. Borbon replaced Billingham on the mound for Cincinnati. Burleson flied to Geronimo. One run, two hits, one error, three left.

### SEVENTH INNING

**Cincinnati**—Perez walked. Foster flied to Lynn in left-center. Concepcion flied to Evans in short right. Griffey struck out. No runs, no hits, no errors, one left.

**Boston**—Play was resumed after a 27-minute delay because of rain. McEnaney was the new pitcher for Cincinnati. Lee struck out. Cooper grounded to Concepcion. Doyle was called out on strikes. No runs, no hits, no errors, none left.

### EIGHTH INNING

**Cincinnati**—Geronimo lined to Lynn. Rettenmund batted for McEnaney and fouled to Cooper. Rose looped a single to right. Morgan rolled to Doyle. No runs, one hit, no errors, one left.

**Boston**—Eastwick was the new pitcher for Cincinnati. Yastrzemski flied to Geronimo in left-center. Fisk walked. Lynn flied to Geronimo in short right-center. Petrocelli looped a single to right, Fisk stopping at second. Evans was called out on strikes. No runs, one hit, no errors, two left.

### NINTH INNING

**Cincinnati**—Bench lined a double to right. Drago replaced Lee on the mound for Boston. Perez bounced to Burleson who made a good play near second base. Bench moving to third. Foster flied to Yastrzemski in shallow left, Bench holding third. Concepcion beat out a high hopper over Drago's head, Bench scoring. Doyle fielded the ball behind second but had no play. Concepcion stole second as Burleson was late with the tag after taking a bouncing throw from Fisk. Griffey doubled to the wall in left-center scoring Concepcion. Geronimo was intentionally passed. Eastwick forced Geronimo, Doyle to Burleson. Two runs, three hits, no errors, two left.

**Boston**—Burleson fouled to Griffey in short right. Carbo batted for Drago and lined to Foster. Cooper popped to Concepcion. No runs, no hits, no errors, none left.

## AT CINCINNATI GAME 3 OCTOBER 14

| Boston | AB. | R. | H. | PO. | A. | E. |
|---|---|---|---|---|---|---|
| Cooper, 1b | 5 | 0 | 0 | 14 | 0 | 0 |
| Doyle, 2b | 5 | 0 | 1 | 0 | 6 | 0 |
| Yastrzemski, lf | 4 | 1 | 0 | 1 | 0 | 0 |
| Fisk, c | 3 | 1 | 1 | 5 | 0 | 2 |
| Lynn, cf | 3 | 0 | 1 | 6 | 0 | 0 |
| Petrocelli, 3b | 4 | 1 | 2 | 1 | 5 | 0 |
| Evans, rf | 4 | 1 | 2 | 1 | 0 | 0 |
| Burleson, ss | 4 | 0 | 2 | 0 | 1 | 0 |
| Wise, p | 2 | 0 | 0 | 0 | 0 | 0 |
| Burton, p | 0 | 0 | 0 | 0 | 0 | 0 |
| Cleveland, p | 0 | 0 | 0 | 0 | 0 | 0 |
| aCarbo | 1 | 1 | 1 | 0 | 0 | 0 |
| Willoughby, p | 0 | 0 | 0 | 0 | 0 | 0 |
| Moret, p | 0 | 0 | 0 | 0 | 0 | 0 |
| Totals | 35 | 5 | 10 | 28 | 12 | 2 |

| Cincinnati | AB. | R. | H. | PO. | A. | E. |
|---|---|---|---|---|---|---|
| Rose, 3b | 4 | 1 | 1 | 2 | 1 | 0 |
| Griffey, rf | 3 | 0 | 0 | 1 | 1 | 0 |
| cRettenmund | 1 | 0 | 0 | 0 | 0 | 0 |
| Morgan, 2b | 4 | 0 | 1 | 4 | 5 | 0 |
| Perez, 1b | 3 | 1 | 0 | 13 | 1 | 0 |
| Bench, c | 4 | 1 | 1 | 2 | 1 | 0 |
| Foster, lf | 3 | 0 | 0 | 3 | 0 | 0 |
| Concepcion, ss | 4 | 1 | 1 | 2 | 5 | 0 |
| Geronimo, cf | 4 | 2 | 2 | 3 | 0 | 0 |
| Nolan, p | 1 | 0 | 0 | 0 | 0 | 0 |
| Darcy, p | 1 | 0 | 0 | 0 | 0 | 0 |
| Carroll, p | 0 | 0 | 0 | 0 | 0 | 0 |
| McEnaney, p | 1 | 0 | 1 | 0 | 0 | 0 |
| Eastwick, p | 0 | 0 | 0 | 0 | 0 | 0 |
| bArmbrister | 1 | 0 | 0 | 0 | 0 | 0 |
| Totals | 34 | 6 | 7 | 30 | 14 | 0 |

| | | | | | | | | | | |
|---|---|---|---|---|---|---|---|---|---|---|
| Boston | 0 | 1 | 0 | 0 | 1 | 0 | 1 | 0 | 2 | 0-5 |
| Cincinnati | 0 | 0 | 0 | 2 | 3 | 0 | 0 | 0 | 1 | 1-6 |

One out when winning run scored.

| Boston | IP. | H. | R. | ER. | BB. | SO. |
|---|---|---|---|---|---|---|
| Wise | 4⅓ | 4 | 5 | 5 | 2 | 1 |
| Burton | ⅓ | 0 | 0 | 0 | 1 | 0 |
| Cleveland | 1½ | 0 | 0 | 0 | 0 | 2 |
| Willoughby (Loser) | 3† | 2 | 1 | 0 | 0 | 1 |
| Moret | ⅓ | 1 | 0 | 0 | 1 | 1 |

| Cincinnati | IP. | H. | R. | ER. | BB. | SO. |
|---|---|---|---|---|---|---|
| Nolan | 4 | 5 | 1 | 1 | 0 | 0 |
| Darcy | 2* | 2 | 1 | 1 | 2 | 0 |
| Carroll | ⅔ | 1 | 1 | 1 | 0 | 0 |
| McEnaney | 1⅔ | 1 | 1 | 1 | 0 | 2 |
| Eastwick (Winner) | 1⅔ | 3 | 1 | 1 | 0 | 0 |

*Pitched to one batter in seventh.
†Pitched to two batters in tenth.

Bases on balls—Off Wise 2 (Foster, Perez), off Burton 1 (Griffey), off Moret 1 (Rose), off Nolan 1 (Fisk), off Darcy 2 (Yastrzemski, Fisk).

Strikeouts—By Wise 1 (Darcy), by Cleveland 2 (Perez, Bench), by Willoughby 1 (Perez), by Moret 1 (Rettenmund), by McEnaney 2 (Yastrzemski, Lynn).

aHomered for Cleveland in seventh. bSafe on error for Eastwick in tenth. cCalled out on strikes for Griffey in tenth. Runs batted in—Fisk, Lynn, Carbo, Evans 2, Bench 2, Concepcion. Geronimo, Morgan 2. Three-base hit—Rose. Home runs—Fisk, Bench, Concepcion. Geronimo, Carbo, Evans. Stolen bases—Foster, Perez, Griffey. Sacrifice hit—Willoughby. Sacrifice flies—Morgan, Lynn. Double plays—Morgan, Concepcion and Perez; Petrocelli and Cooper; Morgan and Perez. Wild pitch—Darcy. Left on bases—Boston 5, Cincinnati 5. Umpires—Barnett (A.L.) plate, Stello (N.L.) first base, Maloney (A.L.) second base, Davidson (N.L.) third base, Frantz (A.L.) left field, Colosi (N.L.) right field. Time—3:03. Attendance—55,392.

### FIRST INNING

**Boston**—Cooper bounced to Perez unassisted. Doyle went out the same way. Yastrzemski grounded to Morgan. No runs, no hits, no errors, none left.

**Cincinnati**—Rose grounded to Doyle. Griffey grounded to Doyle. Morgan flied to Lynn in left-center. No runs, no hits, no errors, none left.

### SECOND INNING

**Boston**—Fisk drove a homer deep into the left field stands. Lynn flied to Geronimo in short left-center. Petrocelli grounded a single to left. Evans fouled to Griffey. Burleson forced Petrocelli, Concepcion to Morgan. One run, two hits, no errors, one left.

**Cincinnati**—Perez lined to Lynn. Bench grounded to Petrocelli who fielded the ball behind the bag and made a long throw to get the batter by a step. Foster walked. Foster stole second and continued on to third when Fisk's throw went into center field. Concepcion lined to Evans. No runs, no hits, one error, one left.

### THIRD INNING

**Boston**—Wise flied to Foster Cooper flied to Foster in short left-center. Doyle popped to Rose. No runs, no hits, no errors, none left.

**Cincinnati**—Geronimo bounced to Doyle. Rose grounded to Cooper unassisted. Nolan grounded to Cooper. No runs, no hits, no errors, none left.

### FOURTH INNING

**Boston**—Yastrzemski grounded to Perez unassisted. Fisk walked. Lynn lined a single to right sending Fisk to third. Griffey's throw to third was cut off by Concepcion who fired to Perez and Lynn, who had rounded first, was tagged out as he slid back. Petrocelli grounded to Morgan who made a good play behind second and threw to Perez for the out. No runs, one hit, no errors, one left.

**Cincinnati**—Griffey flied to Lynn in left-center. Morgan flied deep to Lynn. Perez walked. Perez stole second. Bench homered off the facade of the left field stands, Perez scoring ahead of him. Foster grounded to Petrocelli. Two runs, one hit, no errors, none left.

### FIFTH INNING

**Boston**—Darcy replaced Nolan on the mound for Cincinnati. Evans rolled to Concepcion. Burleson grounded a single to left. Wise forced Burleson, Rose to Morgan. Cooper smashed a ground ball to Morgan who knocked the ball down and threw out the batter. No runs, one hit, no errors, one left.

**Cincinnati**—Concepcion homered over the wall in left-center. Geronimo homered into the right field stands. Darcy fanned. Rose tripled over Lynn's head to the center field wall. Burton replaced Wise on the mound for Boston. Griffey walked. Morgan flied to Lynn, Rose scoring after the catch and Griffey holding first. Griffey stole second. Cleveland replaced Burton as the Boston pitcher. Perez struck out. Three runs, three hits, no errors, one left.

### SIXTH INNING

**Boston**—Doyle fouled to Rose behind third. Yastrzemski walked on four pitches. Fisk walked. Both runners advanced on a wild pitch. Lynn flied to Foster in left-center, Yastrzemski scoring after the catch and Fisk holding second. Petrocelli grounded to Concepcion. One run, no hits, no errors, one left.

**Cincinnati**—Bench struck out. Foster flied to Yastrzemski. Concepcion grounded to Cooper unassisted. No runs, no hits, no errors, none left.

### SEVENTH INNING

**Boston**—Evans grounded a single to center. Carroll replaced Darcy on the mound for Cincinnati. Burleson grounded into a double play, Morgan to Concepcion to Perez. Carbo batted for Cleveland and hit a home run over the

Carlton Fisk was so mad he could spit during argument with umpire Larry Barnett in 10th inning of the third game. Fisk claimed interference on the attempted sacrifice bunt by the Reds' Ed Armbrister but Barnett ruled against the Red Sox.

left field wall. McEnaney replaced Carroll as the Cincinnati pitcher. Cooper popped to Concepcion in short left. One run, two hits, no errors, none left.

Cincinnati—Willoughby was the new pitcher for Boston. Geronimo flied deep to Lynn. McEnaney beat out a hit to Doyle who made the stop behind second but made no throw. Rose lined to Petrocelli who threw to Cooper, doubling McEnaney. No runs, one hit, no errors, none left.

### EIGHTH INNING

Boston—Doyle grounded to Perez unassisted. Yastrzemski was called out on strikes. Fisk chopped a bouncer to the left of the plate and was thrown out by Bench. No runs, no hits, no errors, none left.

Cincinnati—Griffey grounded to Doyle. Morgan also grounded to Doyle. Perez fanned. No runs, no hits, no errors, none left.

### NINTH INNING

Boston—Lynn was called out on strikes. Petrocelli lined a single to center. Eastwick replaced McEnaney on the mound for Cincinnati. Evans homered into the left field stands, Petrocelli scoring ahead of him. Burleson looped a single to center. Willoughby sacrificed, Perez to Morgan covering first. Cooper flied to Geronimo in short center. Two runs, three hits, no errors, one left.

Cincinnati—Bench grounded to Petrocelli. Foster grounded to Burleson, Cooper making a good play on the one-bounce throw. Concepcion grounded to Petrocelli. No runs, no hits, no errors, none left.

### TENTH INNING

Boston—Doyle beat out a ground ball fielded behind second by Morgan who had no play. Yastrzemski flied to Geronimo who made the catch at the base of the center field wall. With the hit-and-run on, Fisk grounded to Morgan who made the stop near second base, tagged Doyle and threw to Perez for a double play. No runs, one hit, no errors, none left.

**Cincinnati**—Geronimo grounded a single to center just out of the reach of Doyle who dove for the ball. Attempting to sacrifice, Armbrister, batting for Eastwick, bunted in front of the plate. Fisk grabbed the ball and trying for a force play at second threw wildly into center field, Geronimo racing to third and Armbrister reaching second. The play was ruled an error all the way and no sacrifice was credited. Boston protested that Armbrister had interfered with Fisk on the play but Umpire Barnett ruled that no interference had occurred. Moret replaced Willoughby on the mound for Boston. Rose was purposely passed, loading the bases. Rettenmund batted for Griffey and was called out on strikes. Morgan drove a fly ball over the head of drawn-in center fielder Lynn for a single, Geronimo scoring the winning run. One run, two hits, one error, three left.

## AT CINCINNATI  GAME 4  OCTOBER 15

| Boston | AB. | R. | H. | PO. | A. | E. |
|---|---|---|---|---|---|---|
| Beniquez, lf | 4 | 0 | 1 | 4 | 0 | 0 |
| Miller, lf | 1 | 0 | 0 | 1 | 0 | 0 |
| Doyle, 2b | 5 | 0 | 1 | 2 | 3 | 1 |
| Yastrzemski, 1b | 4 | 0 | 2 | 8 | 0 | 0 |
| Fisk, c | 5 | 1 | 1 | 4 | 0 | 0 |
| Lynn, cf | 4 | 1 | 1 | 4 | 1 | 0 |
| Petrocelli, 3b | 4 | 0 | 1 | 1 | 2 | 0 |
| Evans, rf | 4 | 1 | 2 | 3 | 0 | 0 |
| Burleson, ss | 4 | 1 | 1 | 0 | 2 | 0 |
| Tiant, p | 3 | 1 | 1 | 0 | 2 | 0 |
| Totals | 38 | 5 | 11 | 27 | 10 | 1 |

| Cincinnati | AB. | R. | H. | PO. | A. | E. |
|---|---|---|---|---|---|---|
| Rose, 3b | 3 | 1 | 1 | 1 | 3 | 0 |
| Griffey, rf | 5 | 0 | 1 | 0 | 0 | 0 |
| Morgan, 2b | 3 | 1 | 0 | 2 | 7 | 0 |
| Perez, 1b | 4 | 0 | 0 | 12 | 1 | 1 |
| Bench, c | 4 | 0 | 1 | 4 | 0 | 0 |
| Foster, lf | 4 | 1 | 2 | 0 | 0 | 0 |
| Concepcion, ss | 4 | 1 | 1 | 3 | 4 | 0 |
| Geronimo, cf | 4 | 0 | 3 | 4 | 0 | 0 |
| Norman, p | 1 | 0 | 0 | 0 | 0 | 0 |
| Borbon, p | 0 | 0 | 0 | 0 | 0 | 0 |
| aCrowley | 1 | 0 | 0 | 0 | 0 | 0 |
| Carroll, p | 0 | 0 | 0 | 1 | 0 | 0 |
| bChaney | 1 | 0 | 0 | 0 | 0 | 0 |
| Eastwick, p | 0 | 0 | 0 | 0 | 0 | 0 |
| cArmbrister | 0 | 0 | 0 | 0 | 0 | 0 |
| Totals | 34 | 4 | 9 | 27 | 15 | 1 |

| Boston | | | | | | | | | |
|---|---|---|---|---|---|---|---|---|---|
| Boston | 0 | 0 | 0 | 5 | 0 | 0 | 0 | 0 | 0—5 |
| Cincinnati | 2 | 0 | 0 | 2 | 0 | 0 | 0 | 0 | 0—4 |

| Boston | IP. | H. | R. | ER. | BB. | SO. |
|---|---|---|---|---|---|---|
| Tiant (Winner) | 9 | 9 | 4 | 4 | 4 | 4 |

| Cincinnati | IP. | H. | R. | ER. | BB. | SO. |
|---|---|---|---|---|---|---|
| Norman (Loser) | 3⅓ | 7 | 4 | 4 | 1 | 2 |
| Borbon | ⅔ | 2 | 1 | 0 | 0 | 0 |
| Carroll | 2 | 2 | 0 | 0 | 0 | 2 |
| Eastwick | 3 | 0 | 0 | 0 | 1 | 0 |

Bases on balls—Off Tiant 4 (Morgan 2, Rose 2), off Norman 1 (Tiant), off Eastwick 1 (Yastrzemski).

Strikeouts—By Tiant 4 (Perez, Crowley, Chaney, Bench), by Norman 2 (Fisk, Lynn), by Carroll 2 (Petrocelli, Tiant).

aStruck out for Borbon in fourth. bStruck out for Carroll in sixth. cSacrificed for Eastwick in ninth. Runs batted in—Evans 2, Burleson, Beniquez, Yastrzemski, Griffey, Bench, Concepcion, Geronimo. Two-base hits—Griffey, Bench, Burleson, Concepcion. Three-base hits—Evans, Geronimo. Sacrifice hit—Armbrister. Double play—Morgan, Concepcion and Perez. Wild pitch—Norman. Left on bases—Boston 8, Cincinnati 8. Umpires—Stello (N.L.) plate, Maloney (A.L.) first base, Davidson (N.L.) second base, Frantz (A.L.) third base, Colosi (N.L.) left field, Barnett (A.L.) right field. Time—2:52. Attendance—55,667.

### FIRST INNING

**Boston**—Beniquez flied to Geronimo. Doyle grounded to Morgan. Yastrzemski lined a single to right. Fisk struck out. No runs, one hit, no errors, one left.

**Cincinnati**—Rose grounded a single to center. Griffey lined a double to left-center, Rose scoring, but Griffey was out trying to stretch his hit into a triple, Lynn to Burleson to Petrocelli. Morgan walked. Perez rolled softly to Burleson who threw him out on a close play, Morgan advancing to second. Bench's high drive to deep right-center fell between Lynn and Evans for a double, Morgan scoring. Foster grounded sharply to Petrocelli. Two runs, three hits, no errors, one left.

### SECOND INNING

**Boston**—Lynn struck out. Petrocelli looped a single to left. Evans forced Petrocelli, Concepcion to Morgan. Burleson grounded to Rose. No runs, one hit, no errors, one left.

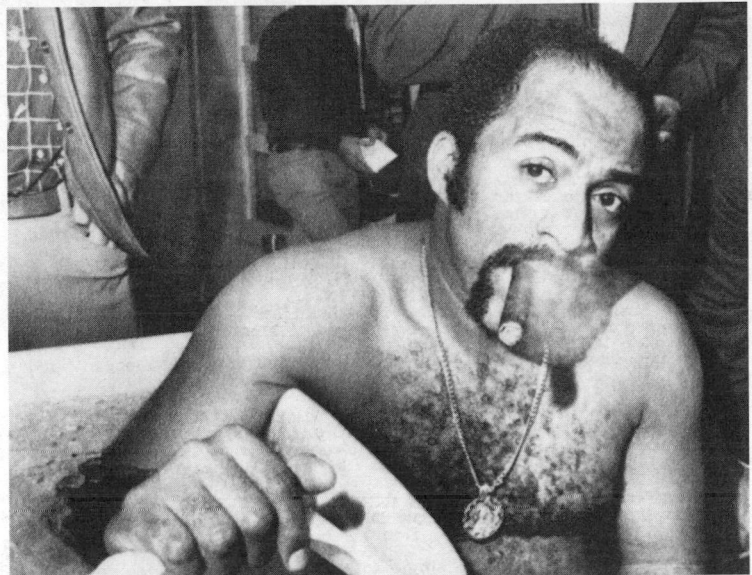

Luis Tiant soaks his arm in ice water after going nine innings to defeat the Reds, 5-4, in the fourth game.

Cincinnati—Concepcion grounded to Petrocelli. Geronimo grounded to Doyle. Norman flied to Beniquez. No runs, no hits, no errors, none left.

### THIRD INNING

Boston—Tiant walked. Beniquez grounded a single between Morgan and Perez into right, Tiant stopping at second. Doyle lined to Geronimo, both runners holding their bases. Yastrzemski grounded into a double play, Morgan to Concepcion to Perez. No runs, one hit, no errors, one left.

Cincinnati—Rose lined to Lynn. Griffey bounced to Tiant. Morgan lined to Beniquez in left-center. No runs, no hits, no errors, none left.

### FOURTH INNING

Boston—Fisk lined a single to left-center. Lynn lined a single to right, Fisk stopping at second. Petrocelli popped to Concepcion. Both runners advanced on a wild pitch. Evans lined a triple to the wall in right-center, Fisk and Lynn scoring. Burleson lined a double to left-center scoring Evans. Borbon replaced Norman on the mound for Cincinnati. Tiant grounded a single to center, Burleson stopping at third. Trying to check his swing, Beniquez tapped a roller to Perez who fumbled for an error, Burleson scoring and Tiant stopping at second. Doyle fouled to Rose. Yastrzemski looped a single to center, Tiant scoring and Beniquez racing to third. Fisk flied to Geronimo in short left-center. Five runs, six hits, one error, two left.

Cincinnati—Perez struck out. Bench lined to Beniquez. Foster beat out a hit to Doyle behind second and when Doyle's throw went into the Cincinnati dugout, Foster advanced to second. Concepcion's pop fly to left-center fell between Burleson, Beniquez and Lynn for a double, Foster scoring. Geronimo tripled into the left field corner scoring Concepcion. Crowley batted for Borbon and fanned. Two runs, three hits, no errors, one left.

### FIFTH INNING

**Boston**—Carroll was the new pitcher for Cincinnati. Lynn grounded to Morgan. Petrocelli was called out on strikes. Evans smashed a single off Carroll's hip. Burleson forced Evans, Concepcion to Morgan. No runs, one hit, no errors, one left.

**Cincinnati**—Rose walked. Griffey flied deep to Evans. Morgan walked. Perez grounded to Doyle who fielded the ball behind second base and threw the batter out by a step, both runners advancing. Bench flied to Beniquez. No runs, no hits, no errors, two left.

### SIXTH INNING

**Boston**—Tiant was called out on strikes. Beniquez bounced to Rose. Doyle grounded a single to center. Yastrzemski grounded to Perez who threw to Carroll covering first for the out. No runs, one hit, no errors, one left.

**Cincinnati**—Miller replaced Beniquez in left field for Boston. Foster flied to Lynn in left-center. Concepcion flied to Evans in short right. Geronimo looped a single to center. Chaney batted for Carroll and fanned. No runs, one hit, no errors, one left.

### SEVENTH INNING

**Boston**—Eastwick took the mound for Cincinnati. Fisk popped to Perez. Lynn grounded to Morgan. Petrocelli grounded to Morgan. No runs, no hits, no errors, none left.

**Cincinnati**—Rose lined to Doyle. Griffey grounded to Doyle. Morgan lined to Lynn in right-center. No runs, no hits, no errors, none left.

### EIGHTH INNING

**Boston**—Evans flied to Geronimo in deep left-center. Burleson grounded to Rose. Tiant grounded to Concepcion. No runs, no hits, no errors, none left.

**Cincinnati**—Perez flied to Miller in left-center. Bench struck out. Foster grounded a single to center. Concepcion flied to Evans in short right. No runs, one hit, no errors, one left.

### NINTH INNING

**Boston**—Miller grounded to Morgan. Doyle grounded to Morgan. Yastrzemski walked. Fisk popped to Concepcion in short left. No runs, no hits, no errors, one left.

**Cincinnati**—Geronimo lined a single to right. Armbrister batted for Eastwick and sacrificed, Tiant to Doyle covering first. Rose walked. Griffey lined deep to Lynn who made a running over-the-shoulder catch, both runners holding their bases. Morgan popped to Yastrzemski. No runs, one hit, no errors, two left.

## AT CINCINNATI    GAME 5    OCTOBER 16

| Boston | AB. | R. | H. | PO. | A. | E. |
|---|---|---|---|---|---|---|
| Beniquez, lf | 3 | 0 | 0 | 2 | 1 | 0 |
| Doyle, 2b | 4 | 1 | 1 | 1 | 1 | 0 |
| Yastrzemski, 1b | 3 | 1 | 1 | 6 | 0 | 0 |
| Fisk, c | 4 | 0 | 1 | 6 | 0 | 0 |
| Lynn, cf | 4 | 0 | 1 | 2 | 0 | 0 |
| Petrocelli, 3b | 4 | 0 | 0 | 2 | 1 | 0 |
| Evans, rf | 3 | 0 | 1 | 3 | 0 | 0 |
| Burleson, ss | 3 | 0 | 0 | 1 | 2 | 0 |
| Cleveland, p | 2 | 0 | 0 | 0 | 0 | 0 |
| Willoughby, p | 0 | 0 | 0 | 1 | 0 | 0 |
| aGriffin | 1 | 0 | 0 | 0 | 0 | 0 |
| Pole, p | 0 | 0 | 0 | 0 | 0 | 0 |
| Segui, p | 0 | 0 | 0 | 0 | 0 | 0 |
| **Totals** | **31** | **2** | **5** | **24** | **5** | **0** |

| Cincinnati | AB. | R. | H. | PO. | A. | E. |
|---|---|---|---|---|---|---|
| Rose, 3b | 3 | 0 | 2 | 1 | 0 | 0 |
| Griffey, rf | 4 | 0 | 1 | 2 | 0 | 0 |
| Morgan, 2b | 3 | 1 | 1 | 3 | 2 | 0 |
| Bench, c | 3 | 2 | 1 | 8 | 1 | 0 |
| Perez, 1b | 3 | 2 | 2 | 5 | 0 | 0 |
| Foster, lf | 4 | 0 | 0 | 2 | 0 | 0 |
| Concepcion, ss | 2 | 0 | 0 | 0 | 0 | 0 |
| Geronimo, cf | 4 | 0 | 0 | 6 | 0 | 0 |
| Gullett, p | 3 | 1 | 1 | 0 | 0 | 0 |
| Eastwick, p | 0 | 0 | 0 | 0 | 0 | 0 |
| **Totals** | **29** | **6** | **8** | **27** | **3** | **0** |

| | | | | | | | | | |
|---|---|---|---|---|---|---|---|---|---|
| Boston | | 1 | | 0 | 0 | 0 | 0 | 0 | 1—2 |
| Cincinnati | 0 | 0 | 0 | 1 | 1 | 3 | 0 | 1 | x—6 |

| Boston | IP. | H. | R. | ER. | BB. | SO. |
|---|---|---|---|---|---|---|
| Cleveland (Loser) | 5* | 7 | 5 | 5 | 2 | 3 |
| Willoughby | 2 | 1 | 0 | 0 | 0 | 1 |
| Pole | 0† | 0 | 1 | 1 | 2 | 0 |
| Segui | 1 | 0 | 0 | 0 | 0 | 0 |

| Cincinnati | IP. | H. | R. | ER. | BB. | SO. |
|---|---|---|---|---|---|---|
| Gullett (Winner) | 8⅔ | 5 | 2 | 2 | 1 | 7 |
| Eastwick (Save) | ⅓ | 0 | 0 | 0 | 0 | 1 |

*Pitched to three batters in sixth.
†Pitched to two batters in eighth.

Cincinnati second baseman Joe Morgan has a pat on the head for teammate Tony Perez as the Reds' first baseman crosses plate on his second home run of the fifth game of the World Series. Johnny Bench (5) also scored on the blast, which came off Red Sox starter Reggie Cleveland in the bottom of the sixth inning and gave the Reds a 5-1 lead in the game.

Bases on balls—Off Cleveland 2 (Rose, Morgan), off Pole 2 (Bench, Perez), off Gullett 1 (Beniquez).

Strikeouts—By Cleveland 3 (Griffey, Perez, Gullett), by Willoughby 1 (Gullett), by Gullett 7 (Fisk 2, Petrocelli, Cleveland 2, Lynn, Beniquez), by Eastwick 1 (Petrocelli).

Lined out for Willoughby in eighth. Runs batted in—Yastrzemski, Lynn, Perez 4, Rose, Concepcion. Two-base hits—Rose, Lynn. Three-base hit—Doyle. Home runs—Perez 2. Stolen bases—Morgan, Concepcion. Sacrifice flies—Yastrzemski, Concepcion. Double plays—Beniquez and Fisk; Burleson and Yastrzemski. Hit by pitcher—By Willoughby (Concepcion). Left on bases—Boston 4, Cincinnati 5. Umpires—Maloney (A.L.) plate, Davidson (N.L.) first base, Frantz (A.L.) second base. Colosi (N.L.) third base, Barnett (A.L.) left field. Stello (N.L.) right field. Time—2:23. Attendance—56,393.

### FIRST INNING

**Boston**—Beniquez grounded to Morgan. Doyle tripled down the right field line. Yastrzemski flied to Griffey, Doyle scoring after the catch. Fisk was called out on strikes. One run, one hit, no errors, none left.

**Cincinnati**—Rose lined a single to left. Griffey struck out. Morgan lined a single to right-center sending Rose to third. Morgan stole second. Bench lined to Beniquez and Rose was out at the plate trying to score after the catch, Beniquez to Fisk. No runs, two hits, no errors, one left.

## SECOND INNING

**Boston**—Lynn popped to Rose. Petrocelli fanned. Evans flied to Foster. No runs, no hits, no errors, none left.

**Cincinnati**—Perez struck out. Foster fouled to Fisk. Concepcion grounded to Burleson. No runs, no hits, no errors, none left.

## THIRD INNING

**Boston**—Burleson popped to Morgan near the pitcher's mound. Cleveland was called out on strikes. Beniquez popped to Morgan who made a running catch in short right. No runs, no hits, no errors, none left.

**Cincinnati**—Geronimo lined to Lynn. Gullett struck out. Rose walked. Griffey lined to Doyle who made a leaping catch. No runs, no hits, no errors, one left.

## FOURTH INNING

**Boston**—Doyle's high chop in front of the plate was grabbed by Bench who threw to Perez for the out. Yastrzemski lined to Geronimo in right-center. Fisk struck out. No runs, no hits, no errors, none left.

**Cincinnati**—Morgan flied to Evans in short right. Bench lined to Petrocelli who made a leaping catch. Perez homered into the stands in left-center. Foster popped to Yastrzemski. One run, one hit, no errors, none left.

## FIFTH INNING

**Boston**—Lynn struck out. Petrocelli flied to Geronimo in shallow right-center. Evans flied to Geronimo in deep left-center. No runs, no hits, no errors, none left.

**Cincinnati**—Concepcion bounced to Petrocelli. Geronimo rolled to Doyle. Gullett lined a single to center. Rose smashed a double into the left field corner, Gullett scoring. Griffey fouled to Petrocelli. One run, two hits, no errors, one left.

## SIXTH INNING

**Boston**—Burleson lined to Griffey. Cleveland struck out. Beniquez walked. Doyle bounced to Perez unassisted. No runs, no hits, no errors, one left.

**Cincinnati**—Morgan walked. Bench grounded a single past Doyle who was breaking toward second base, Morgan racing to third, and on the throw to third Bench took second. Perez lined a homer into the left-center field stands scoring Morgan and Bench ahead of him. Willoughby replaced Cleveland on the mound for Boston. Foster lined to Willoughby. Concepcion was hit by a pitched ball. Concepcion stole second. Geronimo was out, Yastrzemski unassisted. Concepcion advancing to third. Gullett fanned. Three runs, two hits, no errors, one left.

## SEVENTH INNING

**Boston**—Yastrzemski fouled to Perez. Fisk lined deep to Foster. Lynn flied to Geronimo in short center. No runs, no hits, no errors, none left.

**Cincinnati**—Rose lined deep to Beniquez. Griffey beat out a slow tap to Doyle. With the runner breaking, Morgan lined to Burleson who made the catch near second base and threw to Yastrzemski, doubling Griffey. No runs, one hit, no errors, none left.

## EIGHTH INNING

**Boston**—Petrocelli flied to Geronimo in front of the wall in left-center. Evans grounded a single to center. Burleson flied to Geronimo. Griffin batted for Willoughby and lined softly to Morgan. No runs, one hit, no errors, one left.

**Cincinnati**—Pole was the new pitcher for Boston. Bench walked on four pitches. Perez also walked on four pitches. Segui replaced Pole on the mound for Boston. Foster flied deep to Evans. Bench moving to third after the catch and Perez holding first. Concepcion flied to Evans, Bench scoring after the catch and Perez remaining at first. Geronimo lined to Lynn in deep right-center. One run, no hits, no errors, one left.

## NINTH INNING

**Boston**—Beniquez struck out. Doyle grounded to Morgan. Yastrzemski lined a single to center. Fisk grounded a single to left, Yastrzemski stopping at second. Lynn lined a double into the right field corner, Yastrzemski scoring and Fisk stopping at third. Eastwick replaced Gullett on the mound for Cincinnati. Petrocelli struck out on three pitches. One run, three hits, no errors, two left.

## AT BOSTON GAME 6 OCTOBER 21

| Cincinnati | AB. | R. | H. | PO. | A. | E. |
|---|---|---|---|---|---|---|
| Rose, 3b | 5 | 1 | 2 | 0 | 2 | 0 |
| Griffey, rf | 5 | 2 | 2 | 0 | 0 | 0 |
| Morgan, 2b | 6 | 1 | 1 | 4 | 4 | 0 |
| Bench, c | 6 | 0 | 1 | 8 | 0 | 0 |
| Perez, 1b | 6 | 0 | 2 | 11 | 2 | 0 |
| Foster, lf | 6 | 0 | 2 | 4 | 1 | 0 |
| Concepcion, ss | 6 | 0 | 1 | 3 | 4 | 0 |
| Geronimo, cf | 6 | 1 | 2 | 2 | 0 | 0 |
| Nolan, p | 0 | 0 | 0 | 1 | 0 | 0 |
| aChaney | 1 | 0 | 0 | 0 | 0 | 0 |
| Norman, p | 0 | 0 | 0 | 0 | 0 | 0 |
| Billingham, p | 0 | 0 | 0 | 0 | 0 | 0 |
| bArmbrister | 0 | 1 | 0 | 0 | 0 | 0 |
| Carroll, p | 0 | 0 | 0 | 0 | 0 | 0 |
| cCrowley | 1 | 0 | 1 | 0 | 0 | 0 |
| Borbon, p | 1 | 0 | 0 | 0 | 0 | 0 |
| Eastwick, p | 0 | 0 | 0 | 0 | 0 | 0 |
| McEnaney, p | 0 | 0 | 0 | 0 | 0 | 0 |
| eDriessen | 1 | 0 | 0 | 0 | 0 | 0 |
| Darcy, p | 0 | 0 | 0 | 0 | 1 | 0 |
| Totals | 50 | 6 | 14 | 33 | 14 | 0 |

| Boston | AB. | R. | H. | PO. | A. | E. |
|---|---|---|---|---|---|---|
| Cooper, 1b | 5 | 0 | 0 | 8 | 0 | 0 |
| Drago, p | 0 | 0 | 0 | 0 | 0 | 0 |
| fMiller | 0 | 0 | 0 | 0 | 0 | 0 |
| Wise, p | 0 | 0 | 0 | 0 | 0 | 0 |
| Doyle, 2b | 5 | 0 | 1 | 0 | 2 | 0 |
| Yastrzemski, lf-1b | 6 | 1 | 3 | 7 | 1 | 0 |
| Fisk, c | 4 | 2 | 2 | 9 | 1 | 0 |
| Lynn, cf | 4 | 2 | 2 | 2 | 0 | 0 |
| Petrocelli, 3b | 4 | 1 | 0 | 1 | 1 | 0 |
| Evans, rf | 5 | 0 | 1 | 5 | 1 | 0 |
| Burleson, ss | 3 | 0 | 0 | 3 | 2 | 1 |
| Tiant, p | 2 | 0 | 0 | 0 | 2 | 0 |
| Moret, p | 0 | 0 | 0 | 0 | 0 | 0 |
| dCarbo, lf | 2 | 1 | 1 | 1 | 0 | 0 |
| Totals | 41 | 7 | 10 | 36 | 11 | 1 |

```
Cincinnati ...  0  0  0   0  0  0   3   0  2  1  0   0  0  0—6
Boston      ...  3  0  0   0  0  0   0   3  0  0  1  0  0  1—7
```
None out when winning run scored.

| Cincinnati | IP. | H. | R. | ER. | BB. | SO. |
|---|---|---|---|---|---|---|
| Nolan | 2 | 3 | 3 | 3 | 0 | 2 |
| Norman | ⅔ | 1 | 0 | 0 | 2 | 0 |
| Billingham | 1⅓ | 1 | 0 | 0 | 1 | 1 |
| Carroll | 1 | 1 | 0 | 0 | 0 | 0 |
| Borbon | 2† | 1 | 2 | 2 | 2 | 1 |
| Eastwick | 1‡ | 2 | 1 | 1 | 1 | 2 |
| McEnaney | 1 | 0 | 0 | 0 | 1 | 0 |
| Darcy (Loser) | 2§ | 1 | 1 | 1 | 0 | 1 |
| Boston | IP. | H. | R. | ER. | BB. | SO. |
| Tiant | 7* | 11 | 6 | 6 | 2 | 5 |
| Moret | 1 | 0 | 0 | 0 | 0 | 0 |
| Drago | 3 | 1 | 0 | 0 | 0 | 1 |
| Wise (Winner) | 1 | 2 | 0 | 0 | 0 | 1 |

*Pitched to one batter in eighth.
†Pitched to two batters in eighth.
‡Pitched to two batters in ninth.
§Pitched to one batter in twelfth.

Bases on balls—Off Norman 2 (Fisk, Lynn), off Billingham 1 (Burleson), off Borbon 2 (Burleson, Petrocelli), off Eastwick 1 (Doyle), off McEnaney 1 (Fisk), off Tiant 2 (Griffey, Armbrister). Strikeouts—By Nolan 2 (Evans, Tiant), by Billingham 1 (Petrocelli), by Eastwick 2 (Evans. Cooper,), by Darcy 1 (Carbo), by Tiant 5 (Bench 2, Perez 2, Geronimo), by Drago 1 (Geronimo), by Wise 1 (Geronimo), by Borbon 1 (Tiant). aFlied out for Nolan in third. bWalked for Billingham in fifth. cSingled for Carroll in sixth. dHomered for Moret in eighth. eFlied out for McEnaney in tenth. fFlied out for Drago in eleventh. Runs batted in—Griffey 2, Bench, Foster 2. Geronimo, Lynn 3, Carbo 3, Fisk. Two-base hits—Doyle, Evans, Foster. Three-base hit—Griffey. Home runs—Lynn, Geronimo, Carbo, Fisk. Stolen base—Concepcion. Sacrifice hit—Tiant. Double plays—Foster and Bench; Evans, Yastrzemski and Burleson. Hit by pitcher—by Drago (Rose). Left on bases—Cincinnati 11, Boston 9. Umpires—Davidson (N.L.) plate, Frantz (A.L.) first base, Colosi (N.L.) second base, Barnett (A.L.) third base, Stello (N.L.) left field, Maloney (A.L.) right field. Time—4:01. Attendance—35,205.

### FIRST INNING
**Cincinnati**—Rose flied to Yastrzemski who made a sliding catch. Griffey walked. Morgan fouled to Fisk. Bench struck out on three pitches. No runs, no hits, no errors, one left.

**Boston**—Cooper flied to Geronimo. Doyle grounded to Perez who fumbled but recovered in time to throw to Nolan covering first for the out. Yastrzemski lined a single to right. Fisk grounded a single to left, Yastrzemski stopping at second. Lynn homered into the bleachers in right-center, Yastrzemski and Fisk scoring ahead of him. Petrocelli flied to Geronimo in deep left-center. Three runs, three hits, no errors, none left.

### SECOND INNING
**Cincinnati**—Perez struck out. Foster fouled to Cooper. Concepcion flied to Lynn. No runs, no hits, no errors, none left.

The two big guns responsible for the Red Sox winning the sixth game: Bernie Carbo (L.), who hit a three-run homer in 8th inning to tie the score at 6-6, and Carlton Fisk, whose 12th-inning homer ended the contest.

**Boston**—Evans was called out on strikes. Burleson grounded to Perez unassisted. Tiant was called out on strikes. No runs, no hits, no errors, none left.

### THIRD INNING

**Cincinnati**—Geronimo fanned. Chaney batted for Nolan and flied deep to Yastrzemski. Rose lined a single to center. Griffey's ground ball was deflected by Tiant to Doyle who threw to Cooper for the out. No runs, one hit, no errors, one left.

**Boston**—Norman was the new pitcher for Cincinnati. Cooper popped to Concepcion in short left. Doyle lined a double into the right field corner. Yastrzemski popped to Morgan. Fisk was purposely passed. Lynn walked, loading the bases. Billingham replaced Norman on the mound for Cincinnati. Petrocelli struck out. No runs, one hit, no errors, three left.

### FOURTH INNING

**Cincinnati**—Morgan bounced to Doy'e. Bench was called out on strikes. Perez lined a single past Doyle into right field. Trying to check his swing, Foster grounded to Burleson who threw badly to second trying for a force play, Perez reaching third and Foster holding at first. Concepcion fouled to Cooper. No runs, one hit, one error, two left.

**Boston**—Evans drove a liner to right that bounced into the stands for a ground-rule double. Burleson walked on four pitches. Tiant sacrificed, Perez to Morgan covering first. Cooper bounced slowly to Perez, both runners holding their bases. Doyle grounded to Morgan. No runs, one hit, no errors, two left.

### FIFTH INNING

**Cincinnati**—Geronimo lined to Evans. Armbrister batted for Billingham and walked. Rose lined a single to center, Armbrister racing to third. Griffey lined a triple off the wall in left-center scoring Armbrister and Rose. Lynn was hurt as he leaped against the wall but remained in the game after receiving attention from the trainer. Morgan popped to Petrocelli. Bench lined a single off the wall in left, Griffey scoring. Perez struck out. Three runs, three hits, no errors, one left.

Boston—Carroll was the new pitcher for Cincinnati. Yastrzemski lined a single to left. Fisk forced Yastrzemski, Rose to Morgan. Lynn flied to Foster in shallow left. Petrocelli forced Fisk, Concepcion to Morgan. No runs, one hit, no errors, one left.

## SIXTH INNING

Cincinnati—Foster attempted to check his swing but tapped to Tiant. Concepcion flied to Evans. Geronimo lined a single down the left field line. Crowley batted for Carroll and bounced softly to Burleson who started to throw to second for a force play but held the ball when Doyle could not get there in time. It was ruled a hit. Rose forced Crowley, Burleson unassisted. No runs, two hits, no errors, two left.

Boston—Borbon was the new pitcher for Cincinnati. Evans bounced to Morgan. Burleson walked. With two strikes, Tiant bunted foul for a strike-out. Cooper bounced to Morgan. No runs, no hits, no errors, one left.

## SEVENTH INNING

Cincinnati—Griffey bounced a single to right. Morgan lined a single to left, Griffey stopping at second. Bench lined to Yastrzemski, both runners holding their bases. Perez flied to Evans, Griffey going to third after the catch and Morgan holding first. Foster lined a double off the center field fence, Griffey and Morgan scoring. Concepcion grounded to Burleson. Two runs, three hits, no errors, one left.

Boston—Doyle popped to Concepcion. Yastrzemski rolled to Morgan. Fisk grounded to Concepcion who came in fast for the slowly-hit ball. No runs, no hits, no errors, none left.

## EIGHTH INNING

Cincinnati—Geronimo homered into the right field stands just inside the foul pole. Moret replaced Tiant on the mound for Boston. Borbon grounded to Cooper unassisted. Rose bounced to Moret. Griffey lined to Lynn. One run, one hit, no errors, none left.

Boston—Lynn smashed a single off the leg of Borbon who could not make a play. Petrocelli walked. Eastwick replaced Borbon on the mound for Cincinnati. Evans fanned. Burleson lined to Foster. Carbo batted for Moret and lined a homer into the center field bleachers, Lynn and Petrocelli scoring ahead of him. Cooper struck out. Three runs, two hits, no errors, none left.

## NINTH INNING

Cincinnati—Carbo remained in the game in left field. Yastrzemski moved to first base and Drago was the new pitcher for Boston. Morgan popped to Yastrzemski. Bench grounded to Petrocelli who made a good play to his left. Perez fouled to Yastrzemski. No runs, no hits, no errors, none left.

Boston—Doyle walked. Yastrzemski lined a single to right, Doyle moving to third. McEnaney replaced Eastwick on the mound for Cincinnati. Fisk drew an intentional pass, loading the bases. Lynn fouled to Foster in short left and Doyle was out at the plate attempting to score after the catch, Foster to Bench. Yastrzemski moved to third and Fisk remained at first on the play. Petrocelli grounded to Rose. No runs, one hit, no errors, two left.

## TENTH INNING

Cincinnati—Foster grounded to Burleson. Concepcion singled on the ground into center field. Concepcion stole second. Geronimo struck out. Driessen batted for McEnaney and flied to Carbo just inside the line in shallow left. No runs, one hit, no errors, one left.

Boston—Darcy was the eighth pitcher for Cincinnati. Evans' smash was knocked down by Darcy who threw to Perez for the out. Burleson popped to Concepcion. Carbo struck out. No runs, no hits, no errors, none left.

## ELEVENTH INNING

Cincinnati—Rose was hit by a pitched ball. Griffey attempted to sacrifice but forced Rose, Fisk to Burleson. Morgan drove a liner to deep right where Evans made a leaping one-handed catch and Griffey, who had rounded second, was easily doubled, Evans to Yastrzemski to Burleson who covered first. No runs, no hits, no errors, none left.

Boston—Miller batted for Drago and flied to Foster in short left. Doyle rolled to Concepcion. Yastrzemski grounded to Concepcion. No runs, no hits, no errors, none left.

### TWELFTH INNING

**Cincinnati**—Wise was the new pitcher for Boston. Bench fouled to Fisk. Perez grounded a single to center. Foster looped a single to left, Perez stopping at second. Concepcion flied to Evans, both runners holding their bases. Geronimo was called out on strikes. No runs, two hits, no errors, two left.

**Boston**—Fisk hit a home run that struck the foul pole high above the left field wall, winning the game. One run, one hit, no errors, none left.

## AT BOSTON GAME 7 OCTOBER 22

| Cincinnati | AB. | R. | H. | PO. | A. | E. | Boston | AB. | R. | H. | PO. | A. | E. |
|---|---|---|---|---|---|---|---|---|---|---|---|---|---|
| Rose. 3b | 4 | 0 | 2 | 2 | 2 | 0 | Carbo. lf | 3 | 1 | 1 | 0 | 1 | 0 |
| Morgan, 2b | 4 | 0 | 2 | 2 | 4 | 0 | Miller. lf | 0 | 0 | 0 | 0 | 0 | 0 |
| Bench, c | 4 | 1 | 0 | 7 | 0 | 0 | eBeniquez | 1 | 0 | 0 | 0 | 0 | 0 |
| Perez, 1b | 5 | 1 | 1 | 8 | 1 | 0 | Doyle, 2b | 4 | 1 | 1 | 5 | 3 | 2 |
| Foster, lf | 4 | 0 | 1 | 1 | 0 | 0 | fMontgomery | 1 | 0 | 0 | 0 | 0 | 0 |
| Concepcion, ss | 4 | 0 | 1 | 0 | 2 | 0 | Yastrzemski, 1b | 5 | 1 | 1 | 9 | 0 | 0 |
| Griffey, rf | 2 | 2 | 1 | 3 | 0 | 0 | Fisk, c | 3 | 0 | 4 | 0 | 0 | 0 |
| Geronimo, cf | 3 | 0 | 0 | 3 | 0 | 0 | Lynn, cf | 2 | 0 | 0 | 1 | 0 | 0 |
| Gullett, p | 1 | 0 | 1 | 0 | 0 | 0 | Petrocelli. 3b | 3 | 0 | 1 | 1 | 3 | 0 |
| aRettenmund | 1 | 0 | 0 | 0 | 0 | 0 | Evans. rf | 2 | 0 | 0 | 5 | 0 | 0 |
| Billingham, p | 0 | 0 | 0 | 0 | 0 | 0 | Burleson, ss | 3 | 0 | 0 | 2 | 7 | 0 |
| bArmbrister | 0 | 0 | 0 | 0 | 0 | 0 | Lee, p | 3 | 0 | 1 | 0 | 1 | 0 |
| Carroll, p | 0 | 0 | 0 | 1 | 0 | 0 | Moret, p | 0 | 0 | 0 | 0 | 0 | 0 |
| dDriessen | 1 | 0 | 0 | 0 | 0 | 0 | Willoughby, p | 0 | 0 | 0 | 0 | 0 | 0 |
| McEnaney, p | 0 | 0 | 0 | 0 | 0 | 0 | cCooper | 1 | 0 | 0 | 0 | 0 | 0 |
| | | | | | | | Burton, p | 0 | 0 | 0 | 0 | 0 | 0 |
| | | | | | | | Cleveland, p | 0 | 0 | 0 | 0 | 0 | 0 |
| Totals | 33 | 4 | 9 | 27 | 9 | 0 | Totals | 31 | 3 | 5 | 27 | 15 | 2 |

```
Cincinnati  ............  0  0  0    0  0  2    1  0  1—4
Boston  ...............  0  0  3    0  0  0    0  0  0—3
```

| Cincinnati | IP. | H. | R. | ER. | BB. | SO. |
|---|---|---|---|---|---|---|
| Gullett | 4 | 4 | 3 | 3 | 5 | 5 |
| Billingham | 2 | 1 | 0 | 0 | 2 | 1 |
| Carroll (Winner) | 2 | 0 | 0 | 0 | 1 | 1 |
| McEnaney (Save) | 1 | 0 | 0 | 0 | 0 | 0 |

| Boston | IP. | H. | R. | ER. | BB. | SO. |
|---|---|---|---|---|---|---|
| Lee | 6⅓ | 7 | 3 | 3 | 1 | 2 |
| Moret | ⅓ | 1 | 0 | 0 | 1 | 0 |
| Willoughby | 1⅓ | 0 | 0 | 0 | 2 | 0 |
| Burton (Loser) | 2⅔ | 1 | 1 | 1 | 2 | 0 |
| Cleveland | ⅓ | 0 | 0 | 1 | 0 | 0 |

Bases on balls—Off Gullett 5 (Lynn, Carbo, Fisk, Petrocelli, Evans), off Billingham 2 (Lynn, Burleson), off Carroll 1 (Evans), off Lee 1 (Griffey), off Moret 2 (Armbrister, Morgan), off Burton 2 (Griffey, Rose), off Cleveland 1 (Bench).

Strikeouts—By Gullett 5 (Fisk, Petrocelli, Lee, Lynn, Burleson), by Billingham 1 (Fisk), by Carroll 1 (Fisk), by Lee 2 (Morgan, Geronimo).

aHit into double play for Gullett in fifth. bWalked for Billingham in seventh. cFouled out for Willoughby in eighth. dGrounded out for Carroll in ninth. eFlied out for Miller in ninth. fGrounded out for Doyle in ninth. Runs batted in—Perez 2, Rose, Morgan, Yastrzemski, Petrocelli, Evans. Two-base hit—Carbo. Home run—Perez. Stolen bases—Morgan, Griffey. Sacrifice hit—Geronimo. Double plays—Doyle, Burleson and Yastrzemski; Burleson, Doyle and Yastrzemski; Rose, Morgan and Perez. Wild pitch—Gullett. Left on bases—Cincinnati 9, Boston 9. Umpires—Frantz (A.L.) plate, Colosi (N.L.) first base, Barnett (A.L.) second base, Stello (N.L.) third base, Maloney (A.L.) left field, Davidson (N.L.) right field. Time—2:52. Attendance—35,205.

### FIRST INNING

**Cincinnati**—Rose flied to Evans in short right. Morgan struck out. Bench grounded to Burleson. No runs, no hits, no errors, none left.

**Boston**—Carbo doubled off the wall in left-center. Doyle flied to Griffey, Carbo holding second. Yastrzemski grounded to Morgan, Carbo moving to third. Fisk struck out. No runs, one hit, no errors, one left.

### SECOND INNING

**Cincinnati**—Perez grounded to Petrocelli who made a good play to his left. Foster lined a hit off the wall in left-center but was out trying to stretch it into a double, Carbo to Doyle. Concepcion grounded to Burleson, whose throw was to the home plate side of first but Yastrzemski made the grab and tagged the runner. No runs, one hit, no errors, none left.

Cincinnati Reds jubilantly rush out on the field after they clinched the World Series by defeating the Boston Red Sox, 4-3, in the 7th game. Identifiable are Clay Kirby (31), Pete Rose (14), batting practice pitcher Art Siefert (62) and Tony Perez (24).

**Boston**—Lynn walked. Petrocelli struck out. Evans fouled to Rose. Burleson flied to Griffey. No runs, no hits, no errors, one left.

### THIRD INNING

**Cincinnati**—Griffey lined a single to right-center. Geronimo bounced into a double play, Doyle to Burleson to Yastrzemski. Gullett lined a single to right. Rose's sharp ground ball bounced off Lee's leg but the pitcher recovered in time to throw to Doyle, forcing Gullett. No runs, two hits, no errors, one left.

**Boston**—Lee bunted foul on the third strike. Carbo walked. Doyle lined a single to right, Carbo racing to third. Yastrzemski grounded a single to right, Carbo scoring and Doyle going to third, and on the throw to third Yastrzemski advanced to second. Fisk was intentionally passed, loading the bases. Lynn was called out on strikes. Petrocelli walked, forcing in Doyle.

Evans walked on four pitches, forcing in Yastrzemski. Burleson fanned. Three runs, two hits, no errors, three left.

### FOURTH INNING

**Cincinnati**—Morgan beat out a bunt down the first base line. Bench flied to Lynn in deep right-center, Morgan holding first. Morgan stole second. Perez flied to Evans in shallow right. Foster fouled to Fisk. No runs, one hit, no errors, one left.

**Boston**—Lee grounded a single to right. Lee advanced to second on a wild pitch. Carbo grounded to Morgan who made the play behind second, Lee moving to third. Doyle tried to check his swing but bounced to Rose, Lee holding third. Yastrzemski fouled to Morgan outside first base. No runs, one hit, no errors, one left.

### FIFTH INNING

**Cincinnati**—Concepcion tapped to Yastrzemski and beat it out for a hit when Lee was late covering the bag. Griffey was safe at first when his hot smash got through Doyle for an error, Concepcion racing to third. Geronimo was called out on strikes. Rettenmund batted for Gullett and grounded into a double play, Burleson to Doyle to Yastrzemski. No runs, one hit, one error, one left.

**Boston**—Billingham was the new Cincinnati pitcher. Fisk struck out. Lynn walked. Petrocelli grounded a single to left, Lynn stopping at second. Evans flied deep to Geronimo, Lynn moving to third after the catch and Petrocelli holding first. Burleson walked to load the bases. Lee flied deep to Geronimo. No runs, one hit, no errors, three left.

### SIXTH INNING

**Cincinnati**—Rose singled on the ground into right. Morgan flied to Evans in shallow right. Bench forced Rose, Burleson to Doyle, but Doyle's throw to first trying for the double play went into the Boston dugout, Bench reaching second. Perez hit a long home run over the screen in left, Bench scoring ahead of him. Foster flied to Evans. Two runs, two hits, one error, none left.

**Boston**—Carbo bounced to Perez unassisted. Doyle flied to Foster in short left. Yastrzemski bounced to Morgan. No runs, no hits, no errors, none left.

### SEVENTH INNING

**Cincinnati**—Miller replaced Carbo in left field for Boston. Concepcion grounded to Burleson. Griffey walked on four pitches. Moret replaced Lee on the mound for Boston. Geronimo popped to Burleson behind second base. Griffey stole second base. Armbrister batted for Billingham and walked. Rose lined a single to center, Griffey scoring and Armbrister going to third, and on the throw to the plate Rose advanced to second. Morgan walked, filling the bases. Willoughby replaced Moret on the mound for Boston. Bench fouled to Fisk who reached into the stands behind home plate to make the catch. One run, one hit, no errors, three left.

**Boston**—Carroll was the new Cincinnati pitcher. Fisk struck out. Lynn bounced to Perez who made a good play to his right and threw to Carroll covering first for the out. Petrocelli grounded to Concepcion. No runs, no hits, no errors, none left.

### EIGHTH INNING

**Cincinnati**—Perez popped to Petrocelli. Foster grounded to Burleson. Concepcion bounced to Petrocelli. No runs, no hits, no errors, none left.

**Boston**—Evans walked. After failing to sacrifice, Burleson grounded into a double play, Rose to Morgan to Perez. Cooper batted for Willoughby and fouled to Rose. No runs, no hits, no errors, none left.

### NINTH INNING

**Cincinnati**—Burton was the new pitcher for Boston. Griffey walked. Geronimo sacrificed, Petrocelli to Doyle covering first. Driessen batted for Carroll and grounded to Doyle, Griffey advancing to third. Rose walked. Morgan looped a single to center, Griffey scoring and Rose going to third, and on the throw to third Morgan moved to second. Cleveland replaced Burton on the mound for Boston. Bench walked, loading the bases. Perez flied to Evans. One run, one hit, no errors, three left.

**Boston**—McEnaney was the new pitcher for Cincinnati. Beniquez batted for Miller and flied to Griffey. Montgomery batted for Doyle and grounded to Concepcion. Yastrzemski flied to Geronimo in left-center. No runs, no hits, no errors, none left.

## CINCINNATI REDS' BATTING AND FIELDING AVERAGES

| Player—Position | G. | AB. | R. | H. | TB. | 2B. | 3B. | HR. | RBI. | BB. | IBB. | SO. | B.A. | PO. | A. | E. | F.A. |
|---|---|---|---|---|---|---|---|---|---|---|---|---|---|---|---|---|---|
| McEnaney, p | 5 | 1 | 0 | 1 | 1 | 0 | 0 | 0 | 0 | 0 | 0 | 0 | 1.000 | 0 | 0 | 0 | .000 |
| Crowley, ph | 2 | 2 | 0 | 1 | 1 | 0 | 0 | 0 | 0 | 0 | 0 | 0 | .500 | 0 | 0 | 0 | .000 |
| Rose, 3b | 7 | 27 | 3 | 10 | 13 | 1 | 1 | 0 | 2 | 5 | 1 | 1 | .370 | 7 | 9 | 0 | 1.000 |
| Gullett, p | 3 | 7 | 1 | 2 | 2 | 0 | 0 | 0 | 0 | 0 | 0 | 2 | .286 | 0 | 0 | 0 | .000 |
| Geronimo, cf | 7 | 25 | 3 | 7 | 15 | 0 | 1 | 2 | 3 | 3 | 3 | 5 | .280 | 23 | 1 | 0 | 1.000 |
| Foster, lf | 7 | 29 | 1 | 8 | 9 | 1 | 0 | 0 | 2 | 1 | 0 | 1 | .276 | 13 | 1 | 0 | 1.000 |
| Griffey, rf | 7 | 26 | 4 | 7 | 12 | 3 | 1 | 0 | 4 | 4 | 0 | 2 | .269 | 10 | 1 | 0 | 1.000 |
| Morgan, 2b | 7 | 27 | 4 | 7 | 8 | 1 | 0 | 0 | 3 | 5 | 0 | 1 | .259 | 17 | 28 | 0 | 1.000 |
| Bench, c | 7 | 29 | 5 | 6 | 11 | 2 | 0 | 1 | 4 | 2 | 0 | 4 | .207 | 44 | 6 | 0 | 1.000 |
| Concepcion, ss | 7 | 28 | 3 | 5 | 9 | 1 | 0 | 1 | 4 | 0 | 0 | 1 | .179 | 12 | 22 | 1 | .971 |
| Perez, 1b | 7 | 28 | 4 | 5 | 14 | 0 | 0 | 3 | 7 | 3 | 0 | 9 | .179 | 66 | 5 | 1 | .986 |
| Armbrister, ph | 4 | 1 | 1 | 0 | 0 | 0 | 0 | 0 | 0 | 2 | 0 | 0 | .000 | 0 | 0 | 0 | .000 |
| Eastwick, p | 5 | 1 | 0 | 0 | 0 | 0 | 0 | 0 | 0 | 0 | 0 | 0 | .000 | 0 | 0 | 0 | .000 |
| Borbon, p | 3 | 1 | 0 | 0 | 0 | 0 | 0 | 0 | 0 | 0 | 0 | 0 | .000 | 0 | 1 | 0 | 1.000 |
| Darcy, p | 2 | 1 | 0 | 0 | 0 | 0 | 0 | 0 | 0 | 0 | 0 | 0 | .000 | 1 | 0 | 0 | 1.000 |
| Nolan, p | 2 | 1 | 0 | 0 | 0 | 0 | 0 | 0 | 0 | 0 | 0 | 0 | .000 | 0 | 0 | 0 | .000 |
| Norman, p | 2 | 1 | 0 | 0 | 0 | 0 | 0 | 0 | 0 | 0 | 0 | 0 | .000 | 0 | 2 | 0 | 1.000 |
| Billingham, p | 2 | 2 | 0 | 0 | 0 | 0 | 0 | 0 | 0 | 0 | 0 | 0 | .000 | 0 | 0 | 0 | .000 |
| Chaney, ph | 2 | 2 | 0 | 0 | 0 | 0 | 0 | 0 | 0 | 0 | 0 | 1 | .000 | 0 | 0 | 0 | .000 |
| Driessen, ph | 2 | 2 | 0 | 0 | 0 | 0 | 0 | 0 | 0 | 0 | 0 | 0 | .000 | 0 | 0 | 0 | .000 |
| Rettenmund, ph | 3 | 3 | 0 | 0 | 0 | 0 | 0 | 0 | 0 | 0 | 1 | 0 | .000 | 0 | 0 | 0 | .000 |
| Carroll, p | 5 | 0 | 0 | 0 | 0 | 0 | 0 | 0 | 0 | 0 | 0 | 0 | .000 | 2 | 0 | 0 | 1.000 |
| Totals | 7 | 244 | 29 | 59 | 95 | 9 | 3 | 7 | 29 | 25 | 4 | 30 | .242 | 195 | 76 | 2 | .993 |

Rettenmund fouled out for McEnaney in eighth inning of second game; called out on strikes for Griffey in tenth inning of third game; hit into double play for Gullett in fifth inning of seventh game.

Armbrister safe on error for Eastwick in tenth inning of third game; sacrificed for Eastwick in ninth inning of fourth game; walked for Billingham in fifth inning of sixth game; walked for Billingham in seventh inning of seventh game.

Crowley struck out for Borbon in fourth inning of fourth game; singled for Carroll in sixth inning of sixth game.

Chaney struck out for Carroll in sixth inning of fourth game; flied out for Nolan in third inning of sixth game.

Driessen flied out for McEnaney in tenth inning of sixth game; grounded out for Carroll in ninth inning of seventh game.

## BOSTON RED SOX' BATTING AND FIELDING AVERAGES

| Player—Position | G. | AB. | R. | H. | TB. | 2B. | 3B. | HR. | RBI. | BB. | IBB. | SO. | B.A. | PO. | A. | E. | F.A. |
|---|---|---|---|---|---|---|---|---|---|---|---|---|---|---|---|---|---|
| Carbo, ph-lf | 4 | 7 | 3 | 3 | 10 | 1 | 0 | 2 | 4 | 1 | 0 | 1 | .429 | 1 | 1 | 0 | 1.000 |
| Yastrzemski, lf-1b | 7 | 29 | 7 | 9 | 9 | 0 | 0 | 0 | 4 | 4 | 0 | 1 | .310 | 35 | 1 | 0 | 1.000 |
| Petrocelli, 3b | 7 | 26 | 3 | 8 | 9 | 1 | 0 | 0 | 4 | 3 | 0 | 6 | .308 | 7 | 15 | 0 | 1.000 |
| Burleson, ss | 7 | 24 | 1 | 7 | 8 | 1 | 0 | 0 | 2 | 4 | 1 | 2 | .292 | 9 | 19 | 1 | .966 |
| Evans, rf | 7 | 24 | 3 | 7 | 13 | 1 | 1 | 1 | 5 | 3 | 0 | 4 | .292 | 23 | 1 | 0 | 1.000 |
| Lynn, cf | 7 | 25 | 3 | 7 | 11 | 1 | 0 | 1 | 5 | 3 | 0 | 5 | .280 | 23 | 1 | 0 | 1.000 |
| Doyle, 2b | 7 | 30 | 3 | 8 | 11 | 1 | 1 | 0 | 2 | 0 | 1 | | .267 | 13 | 23 | 3 | .923 |
| Tiant, p | 3 | 8 | 2 | 2 | 2 | 0 | 0 | 0 | 0 | 2 | 0 | 4 | .250 | 0 | 4 | 0 | 1.000 |
| Fisk, c | 7 | 25 | 5 | 6 | 12 | 0 | 0 | 2 | 4 | 7 | 3 | 7 | .240 | 37 | 3 | 2 | .952 |
| Lee, p | 2 | 6 | 0 | 1 | 1 | 0 | 0 | 0 | 0 | 0 | 0 | 3 | .167 | 0 | 1 | 0 | 1.000 |
| Beniquez, lf-ph | 3 | 8 | 0 | 1 | 1 | 0 | 0 | 0 | 1 | 1 | 0 | 1 | .125 | 6 | 1 | 0 | 1.000 |
| Cooper, 1b-ph | 5 | 19 | 0 | 1 | 2 | 1 | 0 | 0 | 1 | 0 | 0 | 3 | .053 | 40 | 1 | 0 | 1.000 |
| Griffin, ph | 1 | 1 | 0 | 0 | 0 | 0 | 0 | 0 | 0 | 0 | 0 | 0 | .000 | 0 | 0 | 0 | .000 |
| Montgomery, ph | 1 | 1 | 0 | 0 | 0 | 0 | 0 | 0 | 0 | 0 | 0 | 0 | .000 | 0 | 0 | 0 | .000 |
| Cleveland, p | 3 | 2 | 0 | 0 | 0 | 0 | 0 | 0 | 0 | 0 | 0 | 2 | .000 | 0 | 0 | 0 | .000 |
| Miller, lf-ph | 3 | 2 | 0 | 0 | 0 | 0 | 0 | 0 | 0 | 0 | 0 | 0 | .000 | 1 | 0 | 0 | 1.000 |
| Wise, p | 2 | 2 | 0 | 0 | 0 | 0 | 0 | 0 | 0 | 0 | 0 | 0 | .000 | 0 | 1 | 0 | 1.000 |
| Moret, p | 3 | 0 | 0 | 0 | 0 | 0 | 0 | 0 | 0 | 0 | 0 | 0 | .000 | 1 | 0 | 0 | 1.000 |
| Willoughby, p | 3 | 0 | 0 | 0 | 0 | 0 | 0 | 0 | 0 | 0 | 0 | 0 | .000 | 0 | 0 | 0 | .000 |
| Burton, p | 2 | 0 | 0 | 0 | 0 | 0 | 0 | 0 | 0 | 0 | 0 | 0 | .000 | 0 | 0 | 0 | .000 |
| Drago, p | 2 | 0 | 0 | 0 | 0 | 0 | 0 | 0 | 0 | 0 | 0 | 0 | .000 | 0 | 0 | 0 | .000 |
| Pole, p | 1 | 0 | 0 | 0 | 0 | 0 | 0 | 0 | 0 | 0 | 0 | 0 | .000 | 0 | 0 | 0 | .000 |
| Segui, p | 1 | 0 | 0 | 0 | 0 | 0 | 0 | 0 | 0 | 0 | 0 | 0 | .000 | 0 | 0 | 0 | .000 |
| Totals | 7 | 239 | 30 | 60 | 89 | 7 | 2 | 6 | 30 | 30 | 4 | 40 | .251 | 196 | 72 | 6 | .978 |

Carbo lined out for Drago in ninth inning of second game; homered for Cleveland in seventh inning of third game; homered for Moret in eighth inning of sixth game.

Griffin lined out for Willoughby in eighth inning of fifth game.

Miller flied out for Drago in eleventh inning of sixth game.

Cooper fouled out for Willoughby in eighth inning of seventh game.

Beniquez flied out for Miller in ninth inning of seventh game.

Montgomery grounded out for Doyle in ninth inning of seventh game.

## CINCINNATI REDS' PITCHING RECORDS

| Pitcher | G. | GS. | CG. | IP. | H. | R. | ER. | HR. | BB. | IBB. | SO. | HB. | WP. | W. | L. | Pct. | ERA. |
|---|---|---|---|---|---|---|---|---|---|---|---|---|---|---|---|---|---|
| Billingham | 3 | 1 | 0 | 9 | 8 | 2 | 1 | 0 | 5 | 0 | 7 | 1 | 0 | 0 | 0 | .000 | 1.00 |
| Eastwick | 5 | 0 | 0 | 8 | 6 | 2 | 2 | 2 | 3 | 0 | 4 | 0 | 0 | 2 | 0 | .000 | 2.25 |
| McEnaney | 5 | 0 | 0 | 6⅔ | 3 | 2 | 2 | 0 | 2 | 1 | 5 | 0 | 0 | 0 | 0 | .000 | 2.70 |
| Carroll | 5 | 0 | 0 | 5⅔ | 4 | 2 | 2 | 1 | 2 | 0 | 5 | 0 | 0 | 1 | 0 | 1.000 | 3.18 |
| Gullett | 3 | 3 | 0 | 18⅔ | 19 | 9 | 9 | 0 | 10 | 2 | 15 | 0 | 1 | 1 | 1 | .500 | 4.34 |
| Darcy | 2 | 0 | 0 | 4 | 3 | 2 | 2 | 1 | 2 | 0 | 1 | 0 | 1 | 0 | 1 | .000 | 4.50 |
| Nolan | 2 | 2 | 0 | 6 | 6 | 4 | 4 | 2 | 1 | 0 | 2 | 0 | 0 | 0 | 0 | .000 | 6.00 |
| Borbon | 3 | 0 | 0 | 3 | 3 | 2 | 2 | 0 | 2 | 0 | 1 | 0 | 0 | 0 | 0 | .000 | 6.00 |
| Norman | 2 | 1 | 0 | 4 | 8 | 4 | 4 | 0 | 3 | 1 | 2 | 0 | 1 | 0 | 1 | .000 | 9.00 |
| Totals | 7 | 7 | 0 | 65 | 60 | 30 | 28 | 6 | 30 | 4 | 40 | 1 | 3 | 4 | 3 | .571 | 3.88 |

Saves—Eastwick, McEnaney.

## BOSTON RED SOX' PITCHING RECORDS

| Pitcher | G. | GS. | CG. | IP. | H. | R. | ER. | HR. | BB. | IBB. | SO. | HB. | WP. | W. | L. | Pct. | ERA. |
|---|---|---|---|---|---|---|---|---|---|---|---|---|---|---|---|---|---|
| Willoughby | 3 | 0 | 0 | 6⅓ | 1 | 0 | 0 | 0 | 2 | 1 | 0 | 0 | 1 | 0 | 1 | .000 | 0.00 |
| Moret | 3 | 0 | 0 | 1⅔ | 2 | 0 | 0 | 0 | 3 | 1 | 1 | 0 | 0 | 0 | 0 | .000 | 0.00 |
| Segui | 1 | 0 | 0 | 1 | 0 | 0 | 0 | 0 | 0 | 0 | 0 | 0 | 0 | 0 | 0 | .000 | 0.00 |
| Drago | 2 | 0 | 0 | 4 | 3 | 1 | 1 | 0 | 1 | 0 | 0 | 0 | 0 | 0 | 1 | .000 | 2.25 |
| Lee | 2 | 2 | 0 | 14⅓ | 12 | 5 | 5 | 1 | 3 | 0 | 7 | 0 | 0 | 0 | 0 | .000 | 3.14 |
| Tiant | 3 | 3 | 2 | 25 | 25 | 10 | 10 | 1 | 8 | 2 | 12 | 0 | 0 | 2 | 0 | 1.000 | 3.60 |
| Cleveland | 3 | 1 | 0 | 6⅔ | 7 | 5 | 5 | 2 | 3 | 0 | 5 | 0 | 0 | 1 | 0 | 1.000 | 6.75 |
| Wise | 2 | 1 | 0 | 5⅓ | 6 | 5 | 5 | 3 | 2 | 0 | 2 | 0 | 0 | 1 | 0 | 1.000 | 8.44 |
| Burton | 2 | 0 | 0 | 1 | 1 | 1 | 1 | 0 | 3 | 0 | 0 | 0 | 0 | 0 | 1 | .000 | 9.00 |
| Pole | 1 | 0 | 0 | 0 | 0 | 1 | 1 | 0 | 2 | 0 | 0 | 0 | 0 | 0 | 0 | .000 | ... |
| Totals | 7 | 7 | 2 | 65⅓ | 59 | 29 | 28 | 7 | 25 | 4 | 30 | 2 | 0 | 3 | 4 | .429 | 3.86 |

Shutout—Tiant.

## COMPOSITE SCORE BY INNINGS

| | | | | | | | | | | | | | |
|---|---|---|---|---|---|---|---|---|---|---|---|---|---|
| Cincinnati | 2 | 0 | 0 | 6 | 7 | 5 | 3 | 2 | 3 | 1 | 0 | 0— | 29 |
| Boston | 5 | 1 | 3 | 5 | 0 | 2 | 7 | 3 | 3 | 0 | 0 | 1— | 30 |

Sacrifice hits—Doyle, Evans, Willoughby, Tiant, Armbrister, Geronimo.

Sacrifice flies—Cooper, Lynn, Yastrzemski, Morgan, Concepcion.

Stolen bases—Concepcion 3, Griffey 2, Morgan 2, Foster, Perez.

Caught stealing—Burleson, Evans, Foster, Morgan.

Double plays—Morgan, Concepcion and Perez 2; Geronimo and Bench; Perez unassisted; Billingham, Concepcion, Bench, Rose and Bench; Morgan and Perez; Foster and Bench; Rose, Morgan and Perez; Petrocelli and Cooper; Beniquez and Fisk; Burleson and Yastrzemski; Evans, Yastrzemski and Burleson; Doyle, Burleson and Yastrzemski; Burleson, Doyle and Yastrzemski.

Passed balls—None.

Hit by pitcher—By Billingham Evans), by Willoughby, (Concepcion), by Drago (Rose).

Balk—Tiant.

Bases on balls—By Gullett 10 (Petrocelli 2, Beniquez, Burleson, Carbo, Evans, Fisk, Lynn, Tiant, Yastrzemski), by Billingham 5 (Burleson 2, Evans, Lynn, Yastrzemski), by Eastwick 3 (Doyle, Fisk, Yastrzemski), by Norman 3 (Fisk, Lynn, Tiant), by Borbon 2 (Burleson, Petrocelli), by Carroll 2 (Evans, Fisk), by Darcy 2 (Fisk, Yastrzemski), by McEnaney 2 (Doyle, Fisk), by Nolan 1 (Fisk), by Tiant 8 (Geronimo 2, Morgan 2, Rose 2, Armbrister, Griffey), by Burton 3 (Griffey 2, Rose), by Cleveland 3 (Bench, Morgan, Rose), by Lee 3 (Griffey, Morgan, Perez), by Moret 3 (Armbrister, Morgan, Rose), by Pole 2 (Bench, Perez), by Wise 2 (Foster, Perez), by Drago 1 (Geronimo).

Strikeouts—By Gullett 15 (Fisk 3, Cleveland 2, Cooper 2, Lynn 2, Petrocelli 2, Beniquez, Burleson, Lee, Tiant), by Billingham 7 (Fisk 2, Petrocelli 2, Burleson, Evans, Lee), by McEnaney 5 (Lynn 2, Doyle, Lee, Yastrzemski), by Eastwick 4 (Evans 2, Cooper, Petrocelli), by Carroll 3 (Fisk, Petrocelli, Tiant), by Nolan 2 (Evans, Tiant), by Norman 2 (Fisk, Lynn), by Darcy 1 (Carbo), by Borbon 1 (Tiant), by Tiant 12 (Perez 5, Bench 3, Chaney, Concepcion, Crowley, Geronimo), by Lee 7 (Geronimo 2, Foster, Griffey, Morgan, Perez, Rose), by Cleveland 5 (Perez 2, Bench, Griffey, Gullett), by Willoughby 2 (Gullett, Perez), by Wise 2 (Darcy, Geronimo), by Drago 1 (Geronimo), by Moret 1 (Rettenmund).

Left on bases—Cincinnati 50—6, 6, 5, 8, 5, 11, 9; Boston 52—9, 8, 5, 8, 4, 9, 9.

Time of games—First game, 2:27; second game, 2:38; third game, 3:03; fourth game, 2:52; fifth game, 2:23; sixth game, 4:01; seventh game, 2:52.

Attendance—First game, 35,205; second game, 35,205; third game, 55,392; fourth game, 55,667; fifth game, 56,393; sixth game, 35,205; seventh game, 35,205. Total, 308,272.

Umpires—Frantz (A.L.), Colosi (N.L.), Barnett (A.L.), Stello (N.L.), Maloney (A.L.), Davidson, (N.L.).

Official scorers—Charley Feeney, Pittsburgh Post-Gazette; Bob Hertzel, Cincinnati Enquirer; Clif Keane, Boston Globe.

# WORLD SERIES RESULTS

Year—Winner                                    Loser
1903—Boston A. L., 5 games; Pittsburgh N. L., 3 games.
1904—No Series.
1905—New York N. L., 4 games; Philadelphia A. L., 1 game.
1906—Chicago A. L., 4 games; Chicago N. L., 2 games.
1907—Chicago N. L., 4 games; Detroit A. L., 0 games; 1 tie.
1908—Chicago N. L., 4 games; Detroit A. L., 1 game.
1909—Pittsburgh N. L., 4 games; Detroit A. L., 3 games
1910—Philadelphia A. L., 4 games; Chicago N. L., 1 game.
1911—Philadelphia A. L., 4 games; New York N. L., 2 games.
1912—Boston A. L., 4 games; New York N. L., 3 games; 1 tie.
1913—Philadelphia A. L., 4 games, New York N. L., 1 game.
1914—Boston N. L., 4 games; Philadelphia A. L., 0 games.
1915—Boston A. L., 4 games; Philadelphia N. L., 1 game.
1916—Boston A. L., 4 games; Brooklyn N. L., 1 game.
1917—Chicago A. L., 4 games; New York N. L., 2 games.
1918—Boston A. L., 4 games; Chicago N. L., 2 games.
1919—Cincinnati N. L., 5 games; Chicago A. L., 3 games.
1920—Cleveland A. L., 5 games; Brooklyn N. L., 2 games.
1921—New York N. L., 5 games; New York A. L., 3 games.
1922—New York N. L., 4 games; New York A. L., 0 games; 1 tie.
1923—New York A. L., 4 games; New York N. L., 2 games.
1924—Washington A. L., 4 games; New York N. L., 3 games.
1925—Pittsburgh N. L., 4 games; Washington A. L., 3 games.
1926—St. Louis N. L., 4 games; New York A. L., 3 games.
1927—New York A. L., 4 games; Pittsburgh N. L., 0 games.
1928—New York A. L., 4 games; St. Louis N. L., 0 games.
1929—Philadelphia A. L., 4 games; Chicago N. L., 1 game.
1930—Philadelphia A. L., 4 games; St. Louis N. L., 2 games.
1931—St. Louis N. L., 4 games; Philadelphia A. L., 3 games.
1932—New York A. L., 4 games; Chicago N. L., 0 games.
1933—New York N. L., 4 games; Washington A. L., 1 game.
1934—St. Louis N. L., 4 games; Detroit A. L., 3 games
1935—Detroit A. L., 4 games; Chicago N. L., 2 games.
1936—New York A. L., 4 games; New York N. L., 2 games.
1937—New York A. L., 4 games; New York N. L., 1 game.
1938—New York A. L., 4 games; Chicago N. L., 0 games.
1939—New York A. L., 4 games; Cincinnati N. L., 0 games.
1940—Cincinnati N. L., 4 games; Detroit A. L., 3 games.
1941—New York A. L., 4 games; Brooklyn N. L., 1 game.
1942—St. Louis N. L., 4 games; New York A. L., 1 game.
1943—New York A. L., 4 games; St. Louis N. L., 1 game.
1944—St. Louis N. L., 4 games; St. Louis A. L., 2 games.
1945—Detroit A. L., 4 games; Chicago N. L., 3 games.
1946—St. Louis N. L., 4 games; Boston A. L., 3 games.
1947—New York A. L., 4 games; Brooklyn N. L., 3 games.
1948—Cleveland A. L., 4 games; Boston N. L., 2 games.
1949—New York A. L., 4 games; Brooklyn N. L., 1 game.
1950—New York A. L., 4 games; Philadelphia N. L., 0 games.
1951—New York A. L., 4 games; New York N. L., 2 games.
1952—New York A. L., 4 games; Brooklyn N. L., 3 games.
1953—New York A. L., 4 games; Brooklyn N. L., 2 games.
1954—New York N. L., 4 games; Cleveland A. L., 0 games.
1955—Brooklyn N. L., 4 games; New York A. L., 3 games.
1956—New York A. L., 4 games; Brooklyn N. L., 3 games.
1957—Milwaukee N. L., 4 games; New York A. L., 3 games.
1958—New York A. L., 4 games; Milwaukee N. L., 3 games.
1959—Los Angeles N. L., 4 games; Chicago A. L., 2 games.
1960—Pittsburgh N. L., 4 games; New York A. L., 3 games.
1961—New York A. L., 4 games; Cincinnati N. L., 1 game.
1962—New York A. L., 4 games; San Francisco N. L., 3 games.
1963—Los Angeles N. L., 4 games; New York A. L., 0 games.
1964—St Louis N. L., 4 games; New York A. L., 3 games.
1965—Los Angeles N. L., 4 games; Minnesota A. L., 3 games.
1966—Baltimore A. L., 4 games; Los Angeles N. L., 0 games.
1967—St. Louis N. L., 4 games; Boston A. L., 3 games.
1968—Detroit A. L., 4 games; St. Louis N. L., 3 games.
1969—New York N. L., 4 games; Baltimore A. L., 1 game.
1970—Baltimore A. L., 4 games; Cincinnati N. L., 1 game.
1971—Pittsburgh N. L., 4 games; Baltimore A. L., 3 games.
1972—Oakland A. L., 4 games; Cincinnati N. L., 3 games.
1973—Oakland A. L., 4 games; New York N. L., 3 games.
1974—Oakland A. L., 4 games; Los Angeles N. L., 1 game.
1975—Cincinnati N. L., 4 games; Boston A. L., 3 games.

# WORLD SERIES ATTENDANCE, MONEY

| Year | Games | Attendance | Gate Receipts | Players' Tot. | W. Share | L. Share |
|---|---|---|---|---|---|---|
| 1903 | 8 | 100,429 | $ 50,000.00 | $ 32,612.00 | $ 1,182.00 | $1,316.25 |
| 1905 | 5 | 91,723 | 68,436.81 | 27,394.20 | 1,142.00 | 832.22 |
| 1906 | 6 | 99,845 | 106,550.00 | 33,401.70 | 1,874.63 | 439.50 |
| 1907 | 5 | 78,068 | 101,728.50 | 54,933.39 | 2,142.85 | 1,945.96 |
| 1908 | 5 | 62,232 | 94,975.50 | 46,114.92 | 1,317.58 | 870.00 |
| 1909 | 7 | 145,295 | 188,302.50 | 66,924.90 | 1,825.22 | 1,274.76 |
| 1910 | 5 | 124,222 | 173,980.00 | 79,071.93 | 2,062.79 | 1,375.16 |
| 1911 | 6 | 179,851 | 342,364.50 | 127,910.61 | 3,654.58 | 2,436.39 |
| 1912 | 8 | 252,037 | 490,833.00 | 147,572.28 | 4,024.68 | 2,566.47 |
| 1913 | 5 | 151,000 | 325,980.00 | 135,164.16 | 3,246.36 | 2,164.22 |
| 1914 | 4 | 111,009 | 225,739.00 | 121,898.94 | 2,812.28 | 2,031.65 |
| 1915 | 5 | 143,351 | 320,361.50 | 144,899.55 | 3,780.25 | 2,520.17 |
| 1916 | 5 | 162,859 | 385,590.50 | 162,927.45 | 3,910.26 | 2,834.82 |
| 1917 | 6 | 186,654 | 425,878.00 | 152,888.58 | 3,669.32 | 2,442.21 |
| 1918 | 6 | 128,483 | 179,619.00 | 69,527.70 | 1,102.51 | 671.09 |
| 1919 | 8 | 236,928 | 722,414.00 | 260,349.66 | 5,207.07 | 3,254.36 |
| 1920 | 7 | 178,737 | 564,800.00 | 214,882.74 | 4,168.00 | 2,419.60 |
| 1921 | 8 | 269,976 | 900,233.00 | 292,522.23 | 5,265.00 | 3,510.00 |
| 1922 | 5 | 185,947 | 605,475.00 | 247,309.71 | 4,545.71 | 2,842.86 |
| 1923 | 6 | 301,430 | 1,063,815.00 | 368,783.04 | 6,143.49 | 4,112.88 |
| 1924 | 7 | 283,665 | 1,093,104.00 | 331,092.51 | 5,959.64 | 3,820.29 |
| 1925 | 7 | 282,848 | 1,182,854.00 | 339,664.19 | 5,332.72 | 3,734.60 |
| 1926 | 7 | 328,051 | 1,207,864.00 | 372,390.51 | 5,584.51 | 3,417.75 |
| 1927 | 4 | 201,705 | 783,217.00 | 399,440.67 | 5,782.24 | 3,985.47 |
| 1928 | 4 | 199,072 | 777,290.00 | 419,736.60 | 5,813.20 | 4,181.30 |
| 1929 | 5 | 190,490 | 859,494.00 | 388,086.66 | 5,620.57 | 3,782.01 |
| 1930 | 6 | 212,619 | 953,772.00 | 323,865.00 | 5,038.07 | 3,536.68 |
| 1931 | 7 | 231,567 | 1,030,723.00 | 320,303.46 | 4,467.59 | 3,023.00 |
| 1932 | 4 | 191,998 | 713,377.00 | 363,822.27 | 5,231.77 | 4,244.60 |
| 1933 | 5 | 163,076 | 679,365.00 | 284,665.68 | 4,256.72 | 3,019.86 |
| 1934 | 7 | 281,510 | 1,031,341.00 | 287,050.46 | 5,389.57 | 3,354.68 |
| 1935 | 6 | 286,672 | 1,073,794.00 | 397,360.24 | 6,544.76 | 4,198.53 |
| 1936 | 6 | 302,924 | 1,204,399.00 | 460,002.66 | 6,430.55 | 4,655.58 |
| 1937 | 5 | 238,142 | 985,994.00 | 459,629.35 | 6,471.11 | 4,489.96 |
| 1938 | 4 | 200,833 | 851,166.00 | 434,094.66 | 5,728.76 | 4,674.87 |
| 1939 | 4 | 183,849 | 745,329.09 | 431,117.84 | 5,541.89 | 4,193.39 |
| 1940 | 7 | 281,927 | 1,222,328.21 | 404,414.04 | 5,803.62 | 3,531.81 |
| 1941 | 5 | 235,773 | 1,007,762.00 | 474,184.54 | 5,943.31 | 4,829.40 |
| 1942 | 5 | 277,101 | 1,105,249.00 | 427,579.41 | 6,192.53 | 3,351.77 |
| 1943 | 5 | 277,312 | 1,105,784.00 | 488,905.74 | 6,139.46 | 4,321.96 |
| 1944 | 6 | 206,708 | 906,122.00 | 309,590.91 | 4,626.01 | 2,743.79 |
| 1945 | 7 | 333,457 | 1,492,454.00 | 475,579.04 | 6,443.34 | 3,930.22 |
| 1946 | 7 | 250,071 | 1,052,900.00 | 304,141.05 | 3,742.34 | 2,140.89 |
| 1947 | 7 | 389,763 | 1,781,348.92 | 493,674.82 | 5,830.03 | 4,081.19 |
| 1948 | 6 | 358,362 | 1,633,685.56 | 548,214.99 | 6,772.07 | 4,570.73 |
| 1949 | 5 | 236,716 | 1,129,627.88 | 490,855.84 | 5,626.74 | 4,272.74 |
| 1950 | 4 | 196,009 | 953,669.03 | 486,371.21 | 5,737.95 | 4,081.34 |
| 1951 | 6 | 341,977 | 1,653,457.47 | 560,562.37 | 6,446.09 | 4,951.03 |
| 1952 | 7 | 340,706 | 1,622,753.01 | 500,003.28 | 5,082.65 | 4,200.64 |
| 1953 | 6 | 307,350 | 1,779,269.44 | 691,341.61 | 8,280.68 | 6,178.42 |
| 1954 | 4 | 251,507 | 1,566,203.38 | 881,763.72 | 11,147.90 | 6,712.50 |
| 1955 | 7 | 362,310 | 2,337,515.34 | 737,853.59 | 9,768.21 | 5,598.58 |
| 1956 | 7 | 345,903 | 2,183,254.59 | 758,561.63 | 8,714.76 | 6,934.34 |
| 1957 | 7 | 394,712 | 2,475,978.94 | 709,027.55 | 8,924.36 | 5,606.06 |
| 1958 | 7 | 393,909 | 2,397,223.03 | 726,044.55 | 8,759.10 | 5,896.08 |
| 1959 | 6 | 420,784 | 2,628,809.44 | 893,301.40 | 11,231.18 | 7,257.17 |
| 1960 | 7 | 349,813 | 2,230,627.88 | 682,144.82 | 8,417.94 | 5,214.64 |
| 1961 | 5 | 223,247 | 1,480,059.95 | 645,928.28 | 7,389.13 | 5,356.37 |
| 1962 | 7 | 376,864 | 2,878,891.11 | 893,281.71 | 9,882.74 | 7,291.49 |
| 1963 | 4 | 247,279 | 1,995,189.09 | 1,017,546.43 | 12,794.00 | 7,874.32 |
| 1964 | 7 | 321,807 | 2,243,187.96 | 696,520.15 | 8,622.19 | 5,309.29 |
| 1965 | 7 | 364,326 | 2,975,041.60 | 885,612.21 | 10,297.43 | 6,634.36 |
| 1966 | 4 | 220,791 | 2,047,142.46 | 1,044,042.65 | 11,683.04 | 8,189.36 |
| 1967 | 7 | 304,085 | 2,350,607.10 | 705,878.44 | 8,314.81 | 5,115.23 |
| 1968 | 7 | 379,6.0 | 3,018,113.40 | 879,761.08 | 10,936.66 | 7,078.71 |
| 1969 | 5 | 272,378 | 2,857,782.78 | *1,734,696.37 | *18,338.18 | *14,904.21 |
| 1970 | 6 | 253,183 | 2,599,170.26 | *1,714,305.14 | *18,215.78 | *13,687.59 |
| 1971 | 7 | 351,091 | 3,049,803.46 | *1,742,325.31 | *18,144.58 | *13,906.46 |
| 1972 | 7 | 363,149 | 3,954,542.99 | *1,882,178.15 | *20,705.01 | *15,080.25 |
| 1973 | 7 | 358,289 | 3,923,968.37 | *1,992,461.17 | *24,617.57 | *14,950.18 |
| 1974 | 5 | 260,004 | 3,007,194.00 | *2,045,442.79 | *22,219.09 | *15,703.97 |
| 1975 | 7 | 308,272 | 3,380,579.61 | 1,826,264.97 | *19,060.46 | *13,325.87 |

*Total combined figures for World Series and League Championship Series.

NOTE—Losers' shares in 1903-05-07 and winners' in 1906-07 include club owners' slices which were added to their teams' player pools.

# 1975 ALL-STAR GAME

### Including

### Review of '75 Game

### Official Box Score

### Official Play-By-Play

### Results of Previous Games

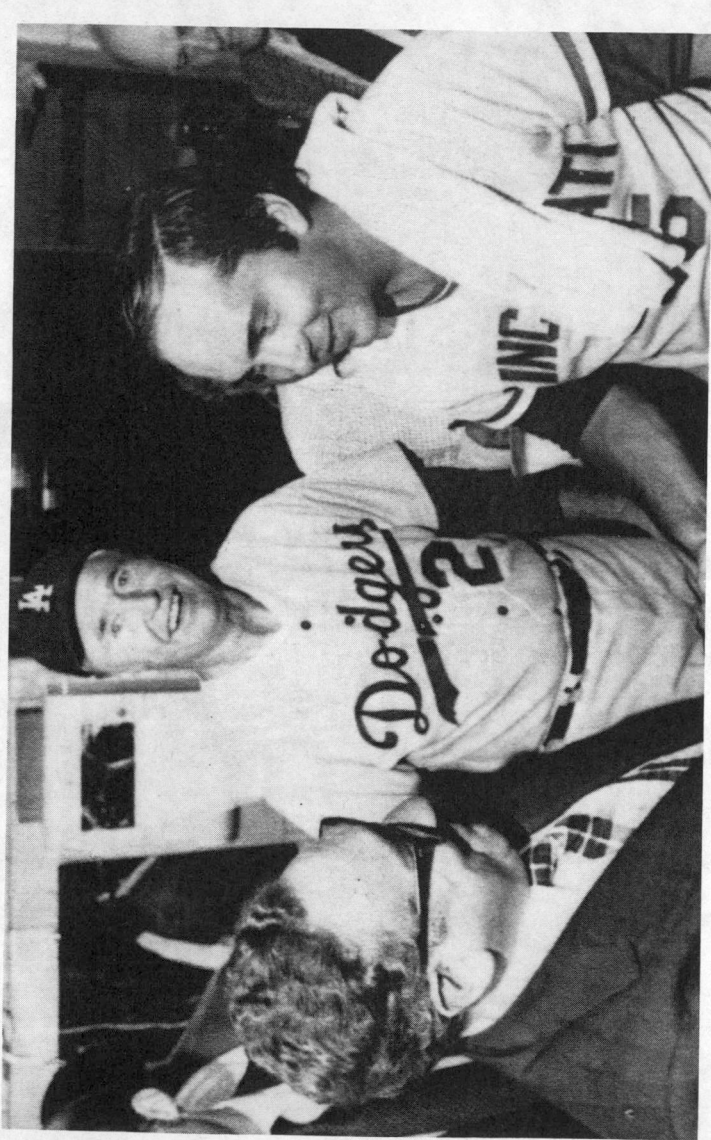

Secretary of State Henry Kissinger greets Johnny Bench of the Cincinnati Reds in dressing room after the All-Star Game. Los Angeles Dodgers' skipper Walt Alston, manager of the National League team, smilingly looks on.

# N.L. Wins All-Star Game. So What's New?

### By JOE MARCIN

The American League had its pitchers well-rested and ready for the 46th All-Star Game. It's a good thing, too. For 51,480 spectators at Milwaukee's County Stadium the evening of July 15 were left wondering what would have happened had the junior loop's hurlers not been well-rested. As it was, Manager Walter Alston's National Leaguers pounded out 13 hits en route to a 6-3 victory, their 12th triumph in the last 13 games in a series which has become an increasing embarrassment to the American League.

The overall standings now read Nationals 27, Americans 18, with one game ending in a tie.

The Oakland A's ace lefty, Vida Blue, the last American League hurler to be a winning pitcher in an All-Star Game—in 1971 at Detroit—was nominated by Manager Alvin Dark to be the starter for the Americans. Blue was tapped for five hits in the two innings he worked. Two of the five hits were back-to-back home runs in the second inning by the Los Angeles Dodgers' Steve Garvey and Jimmy Wynn.

With Kansas City's Steve Busby pitching in the third, the St. Louis Cardinals' base-stealing king, Lou Brock, singled and moved to second on a balk as Busby was apparently rattled by the spectre of Brock stealing. Once on second, Brock proved Busby's fears justified as he promptly stole third. He then scored on a single to left by Johnny Bench, the Cincinnati Reds' perennial All-Star catcher.

The Americans threatened several times in the early going but Pittsburgh's Jerry Reuss, the N.L. starter, and his immediate relief, the Dodgers' Don Sutton, held them at bay.

But in the sixth inning, the game took a dramatic turn. With the New York Mets' Tom Seaver on the mound, Cleveland's George Hendrick, running for Oakland's Joe Rudi who had opened the inning with a single, stole second as Seaver carelessly permitted him to get a big jump. The Yankees' Graig Nettles struck out but Oakland's Gene Tenace drew a walk. Boston's sensational rookie outfielder, Fred Lynn, flied out to right but his teammate, the veteran Carl Yastrzemski, pinch-hitting for the White Sox' Jim Kaat, propelled Seaver's first serve deep into the right field bullpen for a three-run homer, tieing the game at 3-3.

Kaat pitched two perfect innings for the Americans but Seaver's successor, his teammate, Jon Matlack, shut out the Americans for two cantos and the game went into the ninth still tied.

Catfish Hunter, the Yankees' expensive acquisition, who had pitched two scoreless innings, was still on the hill when the ninth began. The Cardinals' Reggie Smith dumped a fly into short left field. The A's Claudell Washington almost caught up with it but the ball went off his glove for a single. The Pirates' Al Oliver then doubled into the left field corner, Smith stopping at third. On both Smith's single and Oliver's double, Washington's fielding was somewhat short of All-Star calibre.

Hunter was replaced by the hard-throwing reliever of the Chicago White Sox, Rich Gossage. Gossage hit the Phillies' Larry Bowa with a pitch to load the bases. This brought to the plate the leading hitter in the National League, Chicago Cub third baseman Bill Madlock. Madlock singled past the drawn-in third baseman, Nettles, and two runs crossed the plate, Bowa racing to third. Cincinnati's Pete Rose scored Bowa with a long sacrifice fly to left-center field.

The fine young lefty of the San Diego Padres, Randy Jones, pitched the bottom of the ninth for the Nationals and retired the side in routine fashion, sealing the doom of the American Leaguers.

Among the highlights surrounding the game was the tremendous standing ovation given Henry Aaron by the fans during the pre-game introductions. Aaron equaled the record of Willie Mays and Stan Musial by appearing in his 24th All-Star Game. He was used as a pinch-hitter in the second inning and lined out to the shortstop.

Commissioner Bowie Kuhn named Mickey Mantle and Stan Musial as honorary captains of the teams and the two Hall of Famers were warmly received by the crowd. For Musial it was a return to a scene of past glory as he had hit a home run in the 12th inning to win the game for the National League back in 1955, the last time it had been played at Milwaukee.

Secretary of State Henry Kissinger, a guest of Commissioner Kuhn, threw out the first ball and confessed that he was a Yankee fan.

For the first time, there were two winners of the Arch Ward Memorial Trophy, emblematic of the game's most valuable player. Madlock, for his game-winning hit, and Matlack, for pitching two scoreless innings and striking out four, were named by the working press.

The All-Star Game continues to be truly America's mid-summer sports classic. No other all-star game in any sport can begin to compare in interest with baseball's. But it might be even better if the American League could get back into the competitive swim of a contest which it dominated in the early years.

### FIRST INNING

**Nationals**—Rose grounded a single to center. Brock lined to Rudi. Morgan looped a single to center and Rose was out attempting to go to third, Bonds to Nettles, Morgan moving to second on the throw to third. Bench fouled to Campaneris. No runs, two hits, no errors, one left.

**Americans**—Bonds lined to Rose. Carew lined to Brock. Munson was hit by a pitched ball. Jackson was called out on strikes. No runs, no hits, no errors, one left.

### SECOND INNING

**Nationals**—Garvey lined a homer into the left field stands. Wynn also homered into the stands in left. Cey lined a single to left. Concepcion was called out on strikes. Attempting to sacrifice, Reuss forced Cey, Blue to Campaneris. Rose flied to Jackson in the right field corner. Two runs, three hits, no errors, one left.

**Americans**—Rudi grounded sharply to Cey. Nettles flied to Rose in short right-center. Tenace was safe at first when Concepcion could not handle his ground ball. Campaneris grounded a single to right, Tenace stopping at second. Aaron batted for Blue and lined softly to Concepcion. No runs, one hit, one error, two left.

### THIRD INNING

**Nationals**—Busby took the mound for the Americans. Brock lined a single to left-center. Brock advanced to second on a balk. Morgan fou'ed to Tenace. Brock stole third. Bench grounded a single inside the third base bag scoring Brock. Garvey grounded a single to left, Bench moving to second. Wynn forced Garvey, Campaneris to Carew, Bench going to third. Cey lined to Rudi who made a backhanded catch. One run, three hits, no errors, two left.

Americans—Bonds struck out. Carew grounded a single to center. Munson flied to Wynn. Jackson beat out a hit to deep short, Carew stopping at second. Rudi grounded to Concepcion who made a strong throw from deep short to get the runner by a step. No runs, two hits, no errors, two left.

### FOURTH INNING

Nationals—Concepcion lined a single to left. Watson batted for Reuss. Concepcion was out stealing, Munson to Carew. Watson flied to Rudi. Rose lined to Campaneris. No runs, one hit, no errors, none left.

Americans—Sutton was the new pitcher for the Nationals. Nettles lined a single to right. Tenace flied to Brock. Campaneris smashed a hit off Sutton's glove, the ball rolling into short center, Nettles stopping at second. Hargrove batted for Busby and flied to Rose in deep right-center, Nettles moving to third after the catch. Campaneris was picked off first on a snap throw from Bench to Garvey. No runs, two hits, no errors, one left.

### FIFTH INNING

Nationals—Kaat came in to pitch for the Americans. Brock bounced to Campaneris. Morgan fouled to Nettles. Bench lined deep to Rudi. No runs, no hits, no errors, none left.

Americans—Murcer went to right field, Smith to center and Rose moved to left field for the Nationals. Bonds lined to Rose who made a tumbling catch. Carew bounced to Morgan. Munson lined a single to left. Washington ran for Munson. Washington stole second. Jackson looked at a called third strike. No runs, one hit, no errors, one left.

### SIXTH INNING

Nationals—Washington went to center field, Scott to first base and Tenace moved behind the plate for the Americans. Garvey flied to Jackson in right-center. Smith flied to Rudi. Cey grounded to Nettles. No runs, no hits, no errors, none left.

Americans—Madlock went to third base and Seaver was the new pitcher for the Nationals. Rudi lined a single to left. Hendrick ran for Rudi and stole second. Nettles struck out. Tenace walked. Lynn batted for Campaneris and flied to Murcer, both runners holding their bases. Yastrzemski batted for Kaat and lined the first pitch into the bullpen in right-center for a homer, scoring Hendrick and Tenace ahead of him. Scott fanned. Three runs, two hits, no errors, none left.

### SEVENTH INNING

Nationals—Hendrick went to right field, Lynn to center, Dent to shortstop, Washington moved from center to left and Hunter was the new pitcher for the Americans. Luzinski batted for Concepcion and struck out. Madlock flied to Lynn. Rose grounded a single to center. Murcer tapped to Nettles. No runs, one hit, no errors, one left.

Americans—Bowa went to shortstop and Matlack took the mound for the Nationals. Carew fanned. Washington singled on the ground into center. Washington was picked off first and tagged out, Matlack to Garvey to Bowa. Dent struck out. No runs, one hit, no errors, none left.

### EIGHTH INNING

Nationals—Morgan popped to Carew. Bench popped to Scott. Perez batted for Garvey and was called out on strikes. No runs, no hits, no errors, none left.

Americans—Perez went to first base and Cash to second base for the Nationals. Hendrick beat out a hit to Cash who fielded his grounder behind second but could not make a throw. Nettles forced Hendrick, Perez to Bowa. Tenace struck out. Nettles stole second and went on to third when the pitch eluded Bench who was charged with a passed ball. Lynn fanned. No runs, one hit, no errors, one left.

### NINTH INNING

Nationals—Smith was credited with a single when Washington could not hold his looping liner to left-center after a long run. Oliver batted for Matlack and doubled into the left field corner, Smith stopping at third. Gossage replaced Hunter on the mound for the Americans. Bowa was hit by a pitched ball, loading the bases. Madlock grounded a single between Nettles and the bag, scoring Smith and Oliver, Bowa racing to third, and when the throw to the plate got by Tenace, Madlock went to second. Tenace was charged with an error. Rose flied to Washington, Bowa scoring after the catch and Madlock going to third. Murcer bounced to Carew, Madlock holding third. Cash grounded to Dent. Three runs, three hits, one error, one left.

**Americans**—Oliver went to center field, Carter to left, Smith moved to right and Jones was the new pitcher for the Nationals. McRae batted for Gossage and tapped to Jones. Scott struck out. Carew flied to Carter. No runs, no hits, no errors, none left.

| NATIONALS | AB | R | H | RBI | PO | A |
|---|---|---|---|---|---|---|
| Rose (Reds), rf-lf | 4 | 0 | 2 | 1 | 4 | 0 |
| Carter (Expos), lf | 0 | 0 | 0 | 0 | 1 | 0 |
| Brock (Cardinals), lf | 3 | 1 | 1 | 0 | 2 | 0 |
| Murcer (Giants), rf | 2 | 0 | 0 | 0 | 1 | 0 |
| Jones (Padres), p | 0 | 0 | 0 | 0 | 0 | 1 |
| Morgan (Reds), 2b | 4 | 0 | 1 | 0 | 0 | 1 |
| Cash (Phillies), 2b | 1 | 0 | 0 | 0 | 0 | 0 |
| Bench (Reds), c | 4 | 0 | 1 | 1 | 10 | 1 |
| Garvey (Dodgers), 1b | 3 | 1 | 2 | 1 | 4 | 1 |
| iPerez (Reds), 1b | 1 | 0 | 0 | 1 | 1 | 1 |
| Wynn (Dodgers), cf | 2 | 1 | 1 | 1 | 1 | 0 |
| Smith (Cardinals), cf-rf | 2 | 1 | 1 | 0 | 0 | 0 |
| Cey (Dodgers), 3b | 3 | 0 | 1 | 0 | 0 | 1 |
| Seaver (Mets), p | 0 | 0 | 0 | 0 | 0 | 0 |
| Matlack (Mets), p | 0 | 0 | 0 | 0 | 0 | 1 |
| jOliver (Pirates), p | 1 | 1 | 1 | 1 | 0 | 0 |
| Concepcion (Reds), ss | 2 | 0 | 1 | 0 | 1 | 1 |
| hLuzinski (Phillies) | 1 | 0 | 0 | 0 | 0 | 0 |
| Bowa (Phillies), ss | 0 | 1 | 0 | 0 | 2 | 0 |
| Reuss (Pirates), p | 1 | 0 | 0 | 0 | 0 | 0 |
| bWatson (Astros) | 1 | 0 | 0 | 0 | 0 | 0 |
| Sutton (Dodgers), p | 0 | 0 | 0 | 0 | 0 | 0 |
| Madlock (Cubs), 3b | 2 | 0 | 1 | 2 | 0 | 0 |
| Totals | 37 | 6 | 13 | 6 | 27 | 8 |

| AMERICANS | AB | R | H | RBI | PO | A |
|---|---|---|---|---|---|---|
| Bonds (Yankees), cf | 3 | 0 | 0 | 0 | 0 | 1 |
| Scott (Brewers), 1b | 2 | 0 | 0 | 0 | 5 | 0 |
| Carew (Twins), 2b | 5 | 0 | 1 | 0 | 3 | 1 |
| Munson (Yankees), c | 2 | 0 | 1 | 0 | 1 | 1 |
| dWashington (Ath.), cf-lf | 1 | 0 | 1 | 0 | 1 | 0 |
| Jackson (Athletics), rf | 3 | 0 | 1 | 0 | 2 | 0 |
| Dent (White Sox), ss | 1 | 0 | 0 | 0 | 0 | 1 |
| Rudi (Athletics), lf | 3 | 0 | 1 | 0 | 5 | 0 |
| eHendrick (Indians), rf | 1 | 1 | 1 | 0 | 0 | 0 |
| Nettles (Yankees), 3b | 4 | 0 | 1 | 0 | 2 | 2 |
| Tenace (Athletics), 1b-c | 3 | 1 | 0 | 0 | 4 | 0 |
| Campaneris (Ath.), ss | 2 | 0 | 2 | 0 | 3 | 2 |
| fLynn (Red Sox), cf | 2 | 0 | 0 | 1 | 0 | 0 |
| Blue (Athletics), p | 0 | 0 | 0 | 0 | 1 | 0 |
| aAaron (Brewers) | 1 | 0 | 0 | 0 | 0 | 0 |
| Busby (Royals), p | 0 | 0 | 0 | 0 | 0 | 0 |
| cHargrove (Rangers) | 1 | 0 | 0 | 0 | 0 | 0 |
| Kaat (White Sox), p | 0 | 0 | 0 | 0 | 0 | 0 |
| gYastrzemski (Red Sox) | 1 | 1 | 1 | 3 | 0 | 0 |
| Hunter (Yankees), p | 0 | 0 | 0 | 0 | 0 | 0 |
| Gossage (White Sox), p. | 0 | 0 | 0 | 0 | 0 | 0 |
| kMcRae (Royals) | 1 | 0 | 0 | 0 | 0 | 0 |
| Totals | 36 | 3 | 10 | 3 | 27 | 9 |

| | | | | | | | | | | |
|---|---|---|---|---|---|---|---|---|---|---|
| Nationals | 0 | 2 | 1 | 0 | 0 | 0 | 0 | 0 | 3 | —6 |
| Americans | 0 | 0 | 0 | 0 | 3 | 0 | 0 | 0 | 0 | —3 |

| Nationals | IP | H | R | ER | BB | SO |
|---|---|---|---|---|---|---|
| Reuss (Pirates) | 3 | 3 | 0 | 0 | 0 | 2 |
| Sutton (Dodgers) | 2 | 3 | 0 | 0 | 0 | 1 |
| Seaver (Mets) | 1 | 2 | 3 | 3 | 1 | 2 |
| Matlack (Mets) | 2 | 2 | 0 | 0 | 0 | 4 |
| Jones (Padres) | 1 | 0 | 0 | 0 | 0 | 1 |

| Americans | IP | H | R | ER | BB | SO |
|---|---|---|---|---|---|---|
| Blue (Athletics) | 2 | 5 | 2 | 2 | 0 | 1 |
| Busby (Royals) | 2 | 4 | 1 | 1 | 0 | 0 |
| Kaat (White Sox) | 2 | 0 | 0 | 0 | 0 | 0 |
| Hunter (Yankees) | 2* | 3 | 2 | 2 | 0 | 2 |
| Gossage (White Sox) | 1 | 1 | 1 | 1 | 0 | 0 |

*Pitched to two batters in ninth.

Winning pitcher—Matlack. Losing pitcher—Hunter.

aLined out for Blue in second. bFlied out for Reuss in fourth. cFlied out for Busby in fourth. dRan for Munson in fifth. eRan for Rudi in sixth. fFlied out for Campaneris in sixth. gHomered for Kaat in sixth. hStruck out for Concepcion in seventh. iCalled out on strikes for Garvey in eighth. jDoubled for Matlack in ninth. kGrounded out for Gossage in ninth. Errors—Concepcion, Tenace. Double plays—None. Left on bases—Nationals 6, Americans 8. Double—Oliver. Home runs—Garvey, Wynn, Yastrzemski. Stolen bases—Brock, Washington, Hendrick, Nettles. Caught stealing—Concepcion, Washington. Sacrifice fly—Lynn. Hit by pitcher—By Reuss (Munson), by Gossage (Bowa). Balk—Busby. Passed ball—Bench. Bases on balls—Off Seaver 1 (Tenace). Strike-outs—By Blue 1 (Concepcion), by Hunter 2 (Luzinski, Perez), by Reuss 2 (Jackson, Bonds), by Sutton 1 (Jackson), by Seaver 2 (Nettles, Scott), by Matlack 4 (Carew, Dent, Tenace, Lynn), by Jones 1 (Scott). Umpires—Haller (AL) plate, Pelekoudas (NL) first base, Springstead (AL) second base, Froemming (NL) third base, Goetz (AL) left field, McSherry (NL) right field. Time—2:35. Attendance—51,480. Official scorers—Charley Feeney, Pittsburgh Post-Gazette; Jerome Holtzman, Chicago Sun-Times; Tom Briere, Minneapolis Tribune.

## RESULTS OF PREVIOUS GAMES

1933—At Comiskey Park, Chicago, July 6. Americans 4, Nationals 2. Managers—Connie Mack, John McGraw. Winning pitcher—Lefty Gomez. Losing pitcher—Bill Hallahan. Attendance—47,595.

1934—At Polo Grounds, New York, July 10. Americans 9, Nationals 7. Managers—Joe Cronin, Bill Terry. Winning pitcher—Mel Harder. Losing pitcher—Van Mungo. Attendance—48,363.

1935—At Municipal Stadium, Cleveland, July 8. Americans 4, Nationals 1. Managers—Mickey Cochrane, Frankie Frisch. Winning pitcher—Lefty Gomez. Losing pitcher—Bill Walker. Attendance—69,831.

1936—At Braves Field, Boston, July 7. Nationals 4, Americans 3. Managers—Charlie Grimm, Joe McCarthy. Winning pitcher—Dizzy Dean. Losing pitcher—Lefty Grove. Attendance—25,556.

1937—At Griffith Stadium, Washington, July 7. Americans 8, Nationals 3. Managers—Joe McCarthy, Bill Terry. Winning pitcher—Lefty Gomez. Losing pitcher—Dizzy Dean. Attendance—31,391.

1938—At Crosley Field, Cincinnati, July 6. Nationals 4, Americans 1. Managers—Bill Terry, Joe McCarthy. Winning pitcher—Johnny Vander Meer. Losing pitcher—Lefty Gomez. Attendance—27,067.

1939—At Yankee Stadium, New York, July 11. Americans 3, Nationals 1. Managers—Joe McCarthy, Gabby Hartnett. Winning pitcher—Tommy Bridges. Losing pitcher—Bill Lee. Attendance—62,892.

1940—At Sportsman's Park, St. Louis, July 9. Nationals 4, Americans 0. Managers—Bill McKechnie, Joe Cronin. Winning pitcher—Paul Derringer. Losing pitcher—Red Ruffing. Attendance—32,373.

1941—At Briggs Stadium, Detroit, July 8. Americans 7, Nationals 5. Managers—Del Baker, Bill McKechnie. Winning pitcher—Ed Smith. Losing pitcher—Claude Passeau. Attendance—54,674.

1942—At Polo Grounds, New York, July 6. Americans 3, Nationals 1. Managers—Joe Cronin, Leo Durocher. Winning pitcher—Spud Chandler. Losing pitcher—Mort Cooper. Attendance—34,178.

1943—At Shibe Park, Philadelphia, July 13 (night game). Americans 5, Nationals 3. Managers—Joe McCarthy, Billy Southworth. Winning pitcher—Dutch Leonard. Losing pitcher—Mort Cooper. Attendance—31,938.

1944—At Forbes Field, Pittsburgh, July 11 (night game). Nationals 7, Americans 1. Managers—Billy Southworth, Joe McCarthy. Winning pitcher—Ken Raffensberger. Losing pitcher—Tex Hughson. Attendance—29,589.

1945—No game played.

1946—At Fenway Park, Boston, July 9. Americans 12, Nationals 0. Managers—Steve O'Neill, Charlie Grimm. Winning pitcher—Bob Feller. Losing pitcher—Claude Passeau. Attendance—34,906.

1947—At Wrigley Field, Chicago, July 8. Americans 2, Nationals 1. Managers—Joe Cronin, Eddie Dyer. Winning pitcher—Frank Shea. Losing pitcher—Johnny Sain. Attendance—41,123.

1948—At Sportsman's Park, St. Louis, July 13. Americans 5, Nationals 2. Managers—Bucky Harris, Leo Durocher. Winning pitcher—Vic Raschi. Losing pitcher—Johnny Schmitz. Attendance—34,009.

1949—At Ebbets Field, Brooklyn, July 12. Americans 11, Nationals 7. Managers—Lou Boudreau, Billy Southworth. Winning pitcher—Virgil Trucks. Losing pitcher—Don Newcombe. Attendance—32,577.

1950—At Comiskey Park, Chicago, July 11. Nationals 4, Americans 3 (14 innings). Managers—Burt Shotton, Casey Stengel. Winning pitcher—Ewell Blackwell. Losing pitcher—Ted Gray. Attendance—46,127.

1951—At Briggs Stadium, Detroit, July 10. Nationals 8, Americans 3. Managers—Eddie Sawyer, Casey Stengel. Winning pitcher—Sal Maglie. Losing pitcher—Ed Lopat. Attendance—52,075.

1952—At Shibe Park, Philadelphia, July 8. Nationals 3, Americans 2 (five innings—rain). Managers—Leo Durocher, Casey Stengel. Winning pitcher—Bob Rush. Losing pitcher—Bob Lemon. Attendance—32,785.

1953—At Crosley Field, Cincinnati, July 14. Nationals 5, Americans 1. Managers—Chuck Dressen, Casey Stengel. Winning pitcher—Warren Spahn. Losing pitcher—Allie Reynolds. Attendance—30,846.

1954—At Municipal Stadium, Cleveland, July 13. Americans 11, Nationals 9. Managers—Casey Stengel, Walter Alston. Winning pitcher—Dean Stone. Losing pitcher—Gene Conley. Attendance—68,751.

1955—At Milwaukee County Stadium, Milwaukee, July 12. Nationals 6, Americans 5 (12 innings). Managers—Leo Durocher, Al Lopez. Winning pitcher—Gene Conley. Losing pitcher—Frank Sullivan. Attendance—45,643.

1956—At Griffith Stadium, Washington, July 10. Nationals 7, Americans 3. Managers—Walter Alston, Casey Stengel. Winning pitcher—Bob Friend. Losing pitcher—Billy Pierce. Attendance—28,843.

1957—At Busch Stadium, St. Louis, July 9. Americans 6, Nationals 5. Managers—Casey Stengel, Walter Alston. Winning pitcher—Jim Bunning. Losing pitcher—Curt Simmons. Attendance—30,693.

1958—At Memorial Stadium, Baltimore, July 8. Americans 4, Nationals 3. Managers—Casey Stengel, Fred Haney. Winning pitcher—Early Wynn. Losing pitcher—Bob Friend. Attendance—48,829.

1959 (first game)—At Forbes Field, Pittsburgh, July 7. Nationals 5, Americans 4. Managers—Fred Haney, Casey Stengel. Winning pitcher—Johnny Antonelli. Losing pitcher—Whitey Ford. Attendance—35,277.

1959 (second game)—At Memorial Coliseum, Los Angeles, August 3. Americans 5, Nationals 3. Managers—Casey Stengel, Fred Haney. Winning pitcher—Jerry Walker. Losing pitcher—Don Drysdale. Attendance—55,105.

1960 (first game)—At Municipal Stadium, Kansas City, July 11. Nationals 5, Americans 3. Managers—Walter Alston, Al Lopez. Winning pitcher—Bob Friend. Losing pitcher—Bill Monbouquette. Attendance—30,619.

1960 (second game)—At Yankee Stadium, New York, July 13. Nationals 6, Americans 0. Managers—Walter Alston, Al Lopez. Winning pitcher—Vern Law. Losing pitcher—Whitey Ford. Attendance—38,362.

1961 (first game)—At Candlestick Park, San Francisco, July 11. Nationals 5, Americans 4 (10 innings). Managers—Danny Murtaugh, Paul Richards. Winning pitcher—Stu Miller. Losing pitcher—Hoyt Wilhelm. Attendance—44,115.

1961 (second game)—At Fenway Park, Boston, July 31. Americans 1, Nationals 1 (nine-inning tie, stopped by rain). Managers—Paul Richards, Danny Murtaugh. Attendance—31,851.

1962 (first game)—At District of Columbia Stadium, Washington, July 10. Nationals 3, Americans 1. Managers—Fred Hutchinson, Ralph Houk. Winning pitcher—Juan Marichal. Losing pitcher—Camilo Pascual. Attendance—45,480.

1962 (second game)—At Wrigley Field, Chicago, July 30, Americans 9, Nationals 4. Managers—Ralph Houk, Fred Hutchinson. Winning pitcher—Ray Herbert. Losing pitcher—Art Mahaffey. Attendance—38,359.

1963—At Municipal Stadium, Cleveland, July 9. Nationals 5, Americans 3. Managers—Alvin Dark, Ralph Houk. Winning pitcher—Larry Jackson. Losing pitcher—Jim Bunning. Attendance—44,160.

1964—At Shea Stadium, New York, July 7. Nationals 7, Americans 4. Managers—Walter Alston, Al Lopez. Winning pitcher—Juan Marichal. Losing pitcher—Dick Radatz. Attendance—50,850.

1965—At Metropolitan Stadium, Bloomington (Minnesota), July 13. Nationals 6, Americans 5. Managers—Gene Mauch, Al Lopez. Winning pitcher—Sandy Koufax. Losing pitcher—Sam McDowell. Attendance—46,706.

1966—At Busch Memorial Stadium, St. Louis, July 12. Nationals 2, Americans 1 (10 innngs). Managers—Walter Alston, Sam Mele. Winning pitcher—Gaylord Perry. Losing pitcher—Pete Richert. Attendance—49,936.

1967—At Anaheim Stadium, Anaheim (California), July 11. Nationals 2, Americans 1 (15 innings). Managers—Walter Alston, Hank Bauer. Winning pitcher—Don Drysdale. Losing pitcher—Jim Hunter. Attendance—46,309.

1968—At Astrodome, Houston, July 9 (night). Nationals 1, Americans 0. Managers—Red Schoendienst, Dick Williams. Winning pitcher—Don Drysdale. Losing pitcher—Luis Tiant. Attendance—48,321.

1969—At Robert F. Kennedy Memorial Stadium, Washington, July 23. Nationals, 9, Americans 3. Managers—Red Schoendienst, Mayo Smith. Winning pitcher—Steve Carlton. Losing pitcher—Mel Stottlemyre. Attendance—45,259.

1970—At Riverfront Stadium, Cincinnati, July 14 (night). Nationals 5, Americans 4 (12 innings). Managers—Gil Hodges, Earl Weaver. Winning pitcher—Claude Osteen. Losing pitcher—Clyde Wright. Attendance—51,838.

1971—At Tiger Stadium, Detroit, July 13 (night). Americans 6, Nationals 4. Managers—Earl Weaver, George (Sparky) Anderson. Winning pitcher—Vida Blue. Losing pitcher—Dock Ellis. Attendance—53,559.

1972—At Atlanta Stadium, Atlanta, July 25 (night). Nationals 4, Americans 3 (10 innings). Managers—Danny Murtaugh, Earl Weaver. Winning pitcher—Tug McGraw. Losing pitcher—Dave McNally. Attendance—53,107.

1973—At Royals Stadium, Kansas City, July 24 (night). Nationals 7, Americans 1. Managers—George (Sparky) Anderson, Dick Williams. Winning pitcher—Rick Wise. Losing pitcher—Bert Blyleven. Attendance—40,849.

1974—At Three Rivers Stadium, Pittsburgh, July 23 (night). Nationals 7, Americans 2. Managers—Yogi Berra, Dick Williams. Winning pitcher—Ken Brett. Losing pitcher—Luis Tiant. Attendance—50,706.

**JOE MORGAN**
• CINCINNATI REDS •
PLAYER OF THE YEAR

**DICK O'CONNELL**
• BOSTON RED SOX •
MAJOR LEAGUE EXECUTIVE

**DARRELL JOHNSON**
• BOSTON RED SOX •
MAJOR LEAGUE MANAGER

**JOE FRAZIER**
• TIDEWATER •
MINOR LEAGUE MANAGER

**STAN NACCARATO**
• TACOMA •
MINOR LEAGUE EXECUTIVE
IN CLASS AAA

**HECTOR CRUZ**
• TULSA •
MINOR LEAGUE PLAYER

**JIM PAUL**
• EL PASO •
MINOR LEAGUE EXECUTIVE
IN CLASS AA

The Sporting News

NO. **1**

# MEN

OF

## 1975

**CORDY JENSEN**
• EUGENE •
MINOR LEAGUE EXECUTIVE
IN CLASS A

# REVIEW OF 1975

### Including

## Summation of Year's Activities

## MVP Tables, All-Star Teams

## Homers by Parks

## By JEROME HOLTZMAN

Major league baseball continued to endure and prosper in 1975, although a post-season arbitrator's decision, subsequently upheld in a federal court, struck at the centerpiece of the reserve clause and resulted in the apparent free agency of veteran pitchers Andy Messersmith of the Los Angeles Dodgers and Dave McNally of the Montreal Expos. This decision widened the gulf at the bargaining table between the owners and the players and was easily the most significant occurrence of the year off the field.

Attendance at the major league level remained firm at 29 million-plus for the regular league season, an impressive total considering the absence of pennant races in three of the four divisions and a generally depressed economy. Of the 24 clubs, 17 had home gates in excess of a million. The Los Angeles Dodgers went over the million mark on June 9, on their 27th home date, precisely one-third into the season, and led with a total of 2,539,349 paid admissions. The only other club to exceed two million was Cincinnati, a runaway winner over the Dodgers in the National League West.

## Baseball Still No. 1 Spectator Sport

Even more encouraging was an unmistakable and unexpected reconfirmation of baseball's long-time position as the nation's No. 1 spectator sport, a hold which in the last decade had been challenged by professional football. Many of the nation's sports columnists, including most of those who had been critical of baseball, contending the games were dull and overly long, were suddenly changing their views. They were now insisting that constant action, as offered in football, was often meaningless and that the leisurely pace of a baseball game was considerably more desirable. This thinking may have been influenced, to some extent, by Red Smith of the New York Times who, prior to the season, insisted, "Baseball becomes dull only to dull minds," a view that was to be repeated by other columnists.

That baseball was on the upbeat was reflected in the uncommonly large interest in the World Series. An estimated 76 million people watched the seventh and final game on television. Remarkably, 40 percent of the total TV sets in the country, including those not in use, were tuned to the seventh game. It was the largest audience for any single event ever televised exclusively by one network. Moon-walks, the assassination of President John F. Kennedy, presidential election results, etc., have attracted more viewers but could be seen simultaneously on more than one network.

## The First Black Major League Manager

Frank Robinson of the Cleveland Indians easily led both leagues in submitting to interviews. Baseball writers at every stop probed and pondered his psyche; in addition, F. Robby had to contend with two authors, both of whom were preparing full length books for presumed posterity on this, his pioneer season as major league baseball's first black manager. F. Robby opened the season with a home run as a designated hitter but there were no further miracles. The Indians finished fourth in the American League East, same as the previous year.

Bowie Kuhn, in one of the year's biggest stories, successfully withstood an anticipated "Dump Bowie" movement led by Owners Finley of Oakland and Jerold Hoffberger of Baltimore. Long-time Kuhn antagonists, Finley and Hoffberger made strange bedfellows. Never the best of friends, and sharing only a common dislike for Kuhn, they teamed up and sparked a revolt to unseat Kuhn from his $175,000 a year post as the commissioner of baseball.

It was a one-day rebellion and occurred in Milwaukee on July 15, at the owners' annual summer meeting. Four American League owners voted against renewing Kuhn's contract, precisely enough to unhorse him. But half of Kuhn's opposition melted overnight, while Finley and Hoffberger were asleep in their Pfister Hotel suites, joyful and confident of the success of their coup. Early the next morning, at a joint meeting, Kuhn was reelected for a second seven-year term, with Finley and Hoffberger still dissenting but harmless at the finish.

It was the National League which rode to Kuhn's defense. The N.L., for years the dominant league, in both influence and total attendance, also led in troubled franchises in 1975, a surprising paradox. Four clubs were in varying degrees of financial agony during the season and three of them— the Atlanta Braves, San Francisco Giants and the Houston Astros—were in the N.L. The fourth club in this group was the Chicago White Sox who in mid-December were sold to a 47-person group headed by Bill Veeck and dedicated to keeping the franchise in Chicago.

The White Sox were the only club to undergo a change of ownership during the calendar year. But the Braves, Giants and Astros were on the block in 1975 and had found, or were seeking buyers. Ted Turner, a wealthy Atlantan, acquired a tentative purchase agreement for 100 percent of the Braves on December 4, and this deal was consummated on January 14, 1976. At the same time, the Giants, who had become a ward of the league, were approaching an inevitable sale; and in Houston, Judge Roy Hofheinz, also in severe financial stress, had already publicly announced the Astros were on the block and that he was hunting for a buyer.

## Veeck Saves White Sox for Chicago

The White Sox sale to Veeck, who was returning to baseball after a 15-year absence, had a pivotal effect. Seattle purchasers had been eager and ready to buy the White Sox and carry the franchise to their city, which the American League had abandoned in 1970 after a one-year trial. Once Veeck saved the Sox for Chicago, the A.L. approved an expansion team for Seattle in 1977, a maneuver with two purposes: (1) to rid themselves of a $32.5 million suit brought against them by the City of Seattle, the State of Washington and King County; and (2) to force the National League to also expand to 13 teams, a premeditated schedule imbalance that would necessitate inter-league play.

That as many as four clubs required such financial infusions was regarded by the other owners as ominous. There seemed no question that spiraling costs, of which player salaries and player procurement and development were a part, were making ownership an uncertain investment.

## The Messersmith Case

This awareness of diminishing profits, real and potential, came into focus perhaps as never before on December 23 when Peter Seitz, the impartial chairman of baseball's three-man arbitration panel announced he had decided in favor of the Players Association in what was to become known in baseball circles as "No. 29." To the public it was the Messersmith decision, a ruling that struck at the center of the reserve rule and, if implemented, would give the players an even bigger slice of the economic pie.

The crux of the Messersmith decision was the interpretation of 10 A, the so-called renewal clause in the standard player's contract and which had been invoked by management perhaps as many as 100 times in the past, always without conclusive challenge. The section reads as follows:

"If prior to March 1, the Player and the Club have not agreed upon the terms of the contract, then on or before 10 days after said March 1, the Club shall have the right by written notice to the Player to renew this contract for the period of one year."

Only the year before, in 1974, the Players Association had filed grievances challenging 10 A in behalf of outfielder Bobby Tolan of San Diego who became the first player to go through a full season with a renewed contract. But Tolan, constantly wooed by the Padres, signed a two-year contract on December 9, 1974 which, in effect, was an ex-post facto agreement embracing the 1974 season and the challenge was dropped.

Prior to the opening of the 1975 season approximately nine players had their contracts similarly renewed. Included among these holdouts were veteran pitchers Messersmith of Los Angeles and McNally of Montreal, and Richie Zisk, young, heavy-hitting outfielder of the Pittsburgh Pirates.

Like Tolan before him, Zisk went the length of the regular league season before capitulating. Zisk signed prior to the National League playoffs, which involved the Pirates. Messersmith and McNally never did sign and the Players Association immediately filed grievances in their behalf and with their approval. But there now was a difference in the status of the petitioners. McNally had quit baseball on June 8, after losing the first game of a doubleheader, and though his case was heard, the decision in his favor was moot. Messersmith completed the season without incident; his challenge was free of encumbrance.

## The McNally Case

There appears to be no published evidence to indicate that McNally's contract squabble was, in any way, responsible for his unexpected retirement. A consistent winner with the Orioles, for whom he won 181 games in the 13 previous seasons, McNally didn't enjoy similar success with Montreal. He won his first three decisions, then lost his next six, his earned-run average rising to 5.26.

Before departing for his home in Billings, Mont., where he is a part-owner of an automobile agency, McNally was interviewed by Bob Dunn, Montreal correspondent for THE SPORTING NEWS and told him: "It got to the point where I almost was stealing money. I was being paid quite a bit. I knew what my job was supposed to be but I wasn't even coming close to doing it. I've been proud of the things I've accomplished in baseball. I didn't want to drag them down."

The Expos, in renewing McNally's contract, gave him a $10,000 salary boost, which increased his pay to $125,000. According to Montreal General Manager Jim Fanning, the club offered McNally a two-year salary package for $250,000, an offer that was rejected. Also rejected, Fanning said, was a single-season contract for $140,000. By retiring as he did, McNally forfeited more than a half season's pay, an indication that money was not his motive. The Expos made repeated but futile efforts to get him to return.

## Messersmith's Contract Dispute

Messersmith subsequently insisted that he, too, didn't do it for the money.

He conceded, however, that in the beginning his differences with the Dodgers "were more or less a contract dispute." The original disagreement apparently centered on his request for a "no-trade" clause. The Dodgers renewed him at a salary of $115,000, a $25,000 increase over his 1974 earnings. Moreover, at the season's end they not only agreed to a "no-trade" provision but offered him a three-year contract totalling $540,000—$150,000 for 1975; $170,000 for 1976, and $220,000 for 1977.

But by this time Messersmith said he felt morally committed to provide the Association with a test case. Explained Messersmith:

"I gave it a lot of thought. I am not a martyr, but I think it had to be done. I didn't do it necessarily for myself because I'm making a lot of money. I don't want everyone to think, 'Well, here's a guy in involuntary servitude at $115,000 a year.' That's a lot of bull and I know it.

"This isn't for a guy like myself, or an established player, unless he's having trouble with his owner or something like that. I did it for the guys sitting on the bench, the utility men who couldn't crack the lineup with us (the Dodgers), but who could make it elsewhere. These guys should have an opportunity to make a move and go to another club."

Dick Moss, attorney for the players, filed for Messersmith on October 7, contending that Messersmith, having completed his "renewal year," no longer had any relationship with the Los Angeles Dodgers and should now "become free to negotiate with any of the 24 Clubs with respect to his services for 1976." Two days later the Association entered a companion grievance for McNally which included the same allegations and "a prayer for relief similar to those contained in the Messersmith grievance."

The Clubs responded on October 24, through their Player Relations Committee which speaks and negotiates for management in player affairs. The Player Relations Committee insisted that "the claims made by the Association are not within the scope of the arbitration panel" and, in addition, stated, "it is our position that the substance of these claims is totally without merit and that both players remain properly reserved by their respective clubs."

## Ewing Kauffman Files Civil Action

The next voice was that of Ewing Kauffman, owner of the Kansas City Royals. Attorneys for Kauffman filed a civil action on October 28 asking for a preliminary injunction to restrain the Association from going ahead with its demand for the Messersmith and McNally grievances. The suit was instituted in the U.S. District Court for the Western District of Missouri and assigned to Judge John W. Oliver in Kansas City. The other 23 clubs followed with a motion to intervene as plaintiffs, putting themselves solidly in support of the litigation.

The Clubs' position, in essence, was that the issues raised were not subject to arbitration and that matters relating to the reserve system, according to Article XV of the Basic Agreement are "expressly exempted" from the Grievance Procedure. The Basic Agreement is the principal contract which binds the Association and the Clubs.

In a personal plea, Kauffman declared his purchase price of the Kansas

City franchise was in excess of $6 million, with approximately $5.5 million of the cost representing the value of the players acquired from the other clubs in a 1969 expansion draft. By 1972, Kauffman said, his stake in the club had increased to $9.5 million, not including an annual commitment, for 25 years, of $400,000 for a lease on the new Kansas City stadium. He emphasized that he entered into this venture in reliance on continuation of baseball's historic reserve system.

"Should the reserve system become the subject of arbitration," Kauffman said, in a prepared statement, "the investment which I have made could be substantially jeopardized. The investment depends upon the continued competitive balance of the American League and major league baseball. I have no doubt that this stability and balance would be severely impaired and perhaps destroyed by the scramble for talented players which would follow if the Major League Baseball Players Association were to succeed in persuading an arbitrator to limit the reserve system.

"A maintenance of the status quo will have a minimal effect upon the Association and its members since they will merely continue to operate during the pendency of this action as they have for many years in the past."

## Miller's Reply to Kauffman

Marvin Miller, in an interview with Oscar Kahan in THE SPORTING NEWS, issued an angry reply.

"They're trying to screw the players," Miller said. "The Basic Agreement provides for rapid adjudication of all grievances, but they're trying to cancel the arbitration hearings until they get a final and unappealable decision in the courts. That would take years.

"What we have is a dispute concerning an interpretation of the Basic Agreement. Such disputes are within the jurisdiction of an arbitrator. If the owners had any confidence in their position they would not be trying to avoid arbitration."

Attorney Moss described Kauffman's suit as "unmeritorious" and a delaying action and emphasized that 16 grievances, all involving interpretation and application relating to the reserve system, had been heard since 1970. Moss further emphasized that there was no threat or attempt made to enjoin the arbitration of the 1974 Bobby Tolan grievance which went through the preliminary phases of the Grievance Procedure before it was withdrawn.

Moss filed an affidavit asking the court to direct the parties to arbitrate the grievances "as scheduled." Judge Oliver then recommended that the Association and the Clubs agree to proceed with the arbitration, but with the understanding that the Clubs, if dissatisfied with the judgment, could subsequently contest the jurisdiction of the arbitration panel. Both parties agreed to this suggestion.

## Hearings Held in New York City

Hearings on both grievances were held in New York City on November 21 and 24 and December 1. The transcript ran 842 pages and included 97 documents, some of them quite lengthy, and marked as exhibits. The three-man arbitration panel also held executive sessions on December 5, 8, 13 and 20.

As in the celebrated Catfish Hunter case of the previous December, the panel consisted of Peter Seitz, the impartial chairman; John Gaherin, chairman of the owners' Player Relations Committee and Miller of the Players Association. Gaherin and Miller always cast opposite opinions and cancel each other out. Seitz' judgment is decisive.

Seitz found for the Association on December 23, though the news of his opinion was reported two days earlier by Bob Hunter of the Los Angeles Herald-Examiner, one of the few scribes who had an open line to Messersmith. The Seitz opinion ran 64 typewritten pages and was divided into four principal chapters; Procedural Background; The Issues; The Jurisdictional Question, and The Merits.

Aware that Seitz had ruled against them, the Clubs had prepared a statement advising him of his termination. Gaherin made this announcement several minutes after the Seitz opinion was notarized and signed by all three panel members.

Seitz likened this action to the dismissal of an umpire who, after calling a play at the plate, is fired by the losing team. But there was a significant difference. The Basic Agreement permits either side to terminate the impartial chairman but can do so only after a grievance, once initiated, is heard to conclusion and an opinion rendered. Seitz was baseball's fourth arbitrator and the first to be dismissed by either side.

## The Associated Press Report

The following is an Associated Press report, in part, that moved on the national wire several hours after the decision was announced:

NEW YORK—Peter Seitz, a gray-haired gentleman with a penchant for dark blue suits, is not a rock-tosser or a bomb-thrower. His lavish Central Park apartment is a testament to his belief in law and order.

But today the baseball establishment is calling this 70-year-old lawyer with 40 years in the arbitration business a wild-eyed radical and an assassin of the national pastime— all because his law has caused baseball's brass more disorder than it can handle.

"I decided it (the Messersmith-McNally case) as a lawyer and an arbitrator," said Seitz. "I hope it's a workmanlike job. I'm not always right. But I know I did my best."

Seitz said it wasn't his job to decide on the merits of the reserve system, which binds a player to one team until he is released, sold or traded. "The panel's sole duty is to interpret and apply the agreements and understandings of the parties. The free agents were created by the contract itself as seen by the majority of the panel.

"I'm not a new Abraham Lincoln freeing the slaves. I wasn't striking a blow at the reserve clause. This decision does not destroy baseball. My own feeling is that the problems of the reserve system ought to be worked out by the parties in collective bargaining."

"Every arbitrator is terminated," said Seitz, in referring to his dismissal. "It's part of the professional mortality. It's expected because somebody wins and somebody loses. But I've never been terminated this way—two minutes after I signed the order, I'm gone.

"It's a disappointment and a blow to my ego," said Seitz,

a pipe-smoking grandfather who refuses to regard himself as either a freedom fighter or a radical but instead considers himself a professional arbitrator, "but I'm as busy as I can be. I don't think it's the end of the line for me. I'll survive."

## Seitz' Reasoning

Significant portions of the Seitz decision follow:

"It deserves emphasis that this decision strikes no blow emancipating players from claimed serfdom or involuntary servitude such as was alleged in the Flood Case. It does not condemn the reserve system presently in force on constitutional or moral grounds. It does not counsel or require that the reserve system be changed to suit the predilections or preferences of an arbitrator acting as a Philosopher-King intent upon imposing his own personal brand of industrial justice on the parties. It does no more than seek to interpret and apply provisions that are in the agreements of the parties. To go beyond this would be an act of quasi-judicial arrogance.

"I am not unmindful of the testimony of the Commissioner of Baseball and the Presidents of the National and American Leagues given at the hearings as to the importance of maintaining the integrity of the reserve system. It was represented to me that any decision of the arbitration panel sustaining the Messersmith and McNally grievances would have dire results, wreak great harm to the reserve system and do serious damage to the sport of baseball.

"Thus, for example, it was stated that a decision favoring these grievants would encourage many other players to elect to become free agents at the end of renewal years; that this would encourage clubs with the largest monetary resources to engage free agents, thus unsettling the competitive balance between clubs, so essential to the sport; that it would increase enormously the already high costs of training and seasoning young players to achieve the level of skills required in professional baseball and such investments would be sacrificed if they became free agents at the end of a renewal year; that driven by the compulsion to win, owners of franchises would over-extend themselves financially in improvident bidding for players in an economic climate in which, today, some clubs are strained, financially; that investors will be discouraged from putting money in franchises in which several of the star players on the club team will become free agents at the end of a renewal year and no continuing control over the players' services can be exercised; and that even the integrity of the sport may be placed in hazard under certain circumstances.

"I do not purport to appraise these apprehensions. They are all based on speculations as to what may ensue. Some of the fears may be imaginary or exaggerated; but some may be reasonable, realistic and sound. After all, they were voiced by distinguished baseball officials with long experience in the sport and a background for judgment in such matters much superior to my own. However, it is not for the panel to determine what, if anything, is good or bad about the reserve system. The panel's sole duty is to interpret and apply the agreements and undertakings of the parties. If any of the expressed apprehensions and fears are soundly based, I am confident that the dislocations and damage to the reserve system can be avoided or minimized through good faith collective bargaining. There are numerous arrangements that can be made that will soften the blow—if this decision, indeed, should be regarded as a blow. This is not the end of the line by any means. The parties, jointly, are free to agree to disregard it and compose their differences as to the reserve system any way they see fit."

The last sentence in the above paragraph, the recommendation that "the parties, jointly, are free to disregard it (his decision) and compose their differences . . . any way they see fit" was central to Seitz' ruling and certainly indicates his eagerness that the Clubs and Players could and should resolve their dispute at the bargaining table.

## Seitz Claims Owners Forced Decision

Much later, after the owners had refused to open the spring training camps on schedule, Seitz told The Chicago Sun-Times he would have withheld judgment if the owners had expressed a desire to negotiate on the reserve system.

"I could have waited for months and months," Seitz said. "I had no deadline. I didn't have to issue a decision within five days, or five weeks. I told Gaherin (John Gaherin, the owners' negotiator), 'Look, take the case out of my hands. Negotiate with the Players and settle your differences.' But the owners rebuffed me completely and said, 'No, we want a decision now.' "

Why the Clubs forced Seitz to such an immediate decision is not clear. Certainly, the Clubs didn't expect to win, not at this level, on the narrow issue of 10A, which was the core of the disagreement; that Seitz had urged negotiation was a tip-off of impending defeat. It could be that the attorneys for the Clubs refused to recognize these signs and wanted a decision with the hope that they would win their appeal on the grounds that the reserve system was not arbitrable and the sooner the appeal the better.

## Owners Lose Appeal

But the owners also lost their first appeal. Federal Judge Oliver upheld Seitz in a 45-page memorandum opinion and order delivered on February 4, 1976. Moreover, Judge Oliver, in a footnote, praised Seitz and wrote that the arbitrator "discharged his duties with the highest sense of fidelity, intelligence and responsibility."

Wrote Judge Oliver:

"The grievances of Messersmith and McNally are sustained. There is no contractural bond between these players and the Los Angeles and Montreal clubs, respectively. Absent such a contract, their clubs had no right or power under the Basic Agreement, the uniform player's contract, or the major league rules to reserve their services for their exclusive use for any period beyond the 'renewal year' in the contracts, which these players had heretofore signed."

On the crucial point of jurisdiction, Judge Oliver maintained that once the owners signed their first collective bargaining contract with the Players, which was the 1968 Basic Agreement, "both parties immediately became subject to the Labor-Management Relations Act and its provisions favoring the arbitration of labor disputes . . . This court is convinced and therefore concludes that the award of the arbitration panel draws its essence from the collective bargaining agreement."

Interestingly, the owners also expected to lose this first appeal.

"It comes as no surprise to me," said Ruly Carpenter of the Phillies in a statement typical of owner reaction. "I think everyone realized there was a 90 percent chance the judge would sustain it."

Commented Joe Burke, the general manager of the Kansas City Royals: "If you sat in the courtroom and listened to the proceedings you would have expected it."

## Kuhn Deplores Decision

Commissioner Bowie Kuhn emphasized that "Baseball cannot function under the Messersmith decision" and predicted that "the economic consequences to the Clubs would be enormous."

Said Kuhn: "The 140 clubs in the minor leagues, which provided entertainment for 12 million people last season, if not erased completely could be seriously curtailed. I think you could expect bankruptcies, sharp retrenchment of franchises and great dissatisfaction among the players themselves as the money gravitates to the top—to the super stars—at the expense of the majority of the players."

As anticipated, the Clubs lodged a second appeal and the case progressed to the Eighth U.S. Circuit Court of Appeals, which subsequently upheld the original decision. Attorney Moss, who successfully fought the case for the players, said:

"The owners have been defending a phantom case. As every lawyer knows, if the law is against you, you argue the facts. If the facts are against you, you argue the law and if both are against you, you create confusion. The owners have been in the third class since this matter began."

Neither Messersmith nor McNally would have had a grievance had they elected to take their disputes to salary arbitration, a new wrinkle in player-management relations resulting from previous negotiations and available for the second consecutive year. A player, when agreeing to such arbitration, signs a blank contract prior to his hearing and must abide by the arbitrator's decision, which is binding.

Once again the method used was on the "either/and or" basis, somewhat common in industry. The club and player simultaneously submit salary figures, the club stating its offer and the player his demand. The arbitrator must choose one or the other. There can be no compromise.

## 1975 Salary Arbitrations

Slightly more than 30 players filed for salary arbitration in 1975 but approximately half of them settled at the 11th hour, prior to the scheduled hearings. A total of 16 players went the route, compared to 29 in 1974. Of these 16, only six succeeded in convincing the arbitrator that their demands were more equitable than the club offers and, as could be expected, the interpretation was that the owners won by a 10-6 score to increase their two-year edge to 26-19.

The owners seemed pleased with the results and emphasized that the 10-6 score demonstrated beyond doubt, that their salary dealings with the players had been fair across the board, and not only with those who went to arbitration. Some general managers voiced the opinion that the procedure be changed so that the clubs be extended the same privilege as the players and be permitted to initiate salary arbitration, a suggestion which did not meet with the approval of Marvin Miller.

Frank Cashen, the general manager of the Baltimore Orioles, was the most outspoken in this regard. Cashen pointed out that the Orioles had an uncommonly large number of holdouts. Faced with this impasse, Cashen advised eight of his players to go to arbitration but none did.

"If we have an honest disagreement, then why shouldn't I be able to say, 'Okay, I want arbitration,'" said Cashen. "Then if I'm wrong I have to pay what the player asks, and if he's wrong, he has to take my offer. If I'm forced to go to arbitration on the players' requests I think I should be entitled to the same consideration."

Oakland owner Charlie Finley, who lost five out of nine in 1974, did considerably better in 1975. Thirteen A's filed for arbitration but seven settled out of court, so to speak. Of the six A's who went the distance, the only winners were pitcher Rollie Fingers and infielder Ted Kubiak. The Oakland losers were pitcher Ken Holtzman, third baseman Sal Bando, outfielder Reggie Jackson and catcher Ray Fosse.

Unlike the previous year, the 1975 salary arbitrations didn't receive much publicity. In fact, no complete chart is available on the various offers and no lists were published showing precisely which players won, or lost. The biggest single winner, however, was outfielder Ralph Garr of Atlanta, the 1974 National League batting champion, who requested and won his salary request of $114,500, an increase of $59,500 from his previous season's pay. The Braves had offered Garr $85,000.

Player salaries, it was believed, rose 12 percent in 1975, an increase that was reflected in ticket prices. A total of 17 of the 24 major league clubs, including the Los Angeles Dodgers, raised their prices in 1975. In most instances the increases were modest and averaged about 50 cents per ticket.

## Dodgers Finally Raise Ticket Prices

Pricewise, the Dodgers have been a phenomenon and certainly one of the most profitable of all the enterprises embracing professional sports. It was the first time the Dodgers raised their prices since 1958, which is when they opened in Los Angeles. "We are sorry that rising costs have forced us to take this step," said President Peter O'Malley, "but we are proud that we were able to maintain our prices for so long." Two clubs, the Pittsburgh Pirates and Houston Astros, actually reduced prices in 1975, but only on certain tickets.

Despite the higher prices, the 24 major league teams, for their regular league season, had a combined gate of 29,789,913, third highest in history. This was achieved despite the absence of pennant races in three of the four divisions and terrible September weather, particularly on the East Coast. There were 17 weather postponements, including 10 cancellations in the last month of the season.

The total gate was 500,000 ahead of the '74 pace going into September and was 175,000 ahead until the final week. The final count was 235,695 less than the previous year, less than eight-tenths of one percent.

The return of Hank Aaron to Milwaukee enabled the Brewers to show the largest gain of any of the 24 clubs. The Brewers had 1,213,357 paid admissions, an increase of 257,616 over 1974. The only other clubs with a 200,000-plus gain were Oakland and San Diego.

The Los Angeles Dodgers, who led both leagues with a draw of 2,539,349, set one gate record and tied another. They reached the million mark in their 27th home game, breaking the record of the 1948 Cleveland Indians who reached a million in their 28th game. The Dodgers hit two million on their 55th date, tying a record set by the 1970 New York Mets.

It was a remarkable achievement for the Dodgers, considering that they fell out of first place in their division on June 7 and lost ground steadily thereafter. Going into August, they were 14½ games behind the front-running Cincinnati Reds but were still averaging 36,576 paid admissions after action of August 3.

The Atlanta Braves and the Chicago White Sox suffered the biggest losses from the previous season. The Braves were off by a whopping 446,413 and finished with a gate of 534,672, lowest in the majors with the exception of the San Francisco Giants, who drew 522,919. The White Sox attendance was 750,802, a one-season decline of 398,794. Cincinnati, Milwaukee, Oakland, San Diego and Philadelphia had record gates. The American League had a total attendance of 13,189,423; the National 16,600,490.

## Baseball's New Television Contracts

Further proof of baseball's rosy glow was the signing of new television contracts engineered chiefly by Commissioner Bowie Kuhn. Two networks, not one, were involved in the new four-year agreement which was to start in 1976 and continue through 1979.

The total cost to the networks was announced at $92,800,000, a remarkable 30 percent increase in revenue from the previous $72 million, four-year contract which had been the exclusive property of the National Broadcasting Company.

Under the new arrangement, the American Broadcasting Company was to televise 16 Monday night games in 1976 and 18 in each of the next three years. NBC, in the meantime, would continue telecasting one game every Saturday during the 25-week season, as it has done annually since 1966. Both networks agreed to alternate coverage of the All-Star Game, the leagues' championship playoffs and the World Series.

Commissioner Kuhn and Alexander (Sandy) Hadden, baseball's general counsel, also announced a separate deal with the CBS Radio Network which has some 250 affiliated stations. At a cost of $300,000, CBS Radio agreed to broadcast the All-Star Game, league playoffs and the World Series.

THE SPORTING NEWS, in a May 3 editorial, commended Kuhn and his staff for these new contracts: "Two television networks promoting baseball are better than one. Television revenue and exposure play a critical role in the health of spectator sports and baseball seems to be more than holding its own in this area. Commissioner Kuhn rates applause."

## The "Palace Revolt"

Despite these successes, Commissioner Kuhn was confronted with what The New York Times described as "a palace revolt." It was a brief, 24-hour rebellion and certainly didn't come as a surprise. The Chicago Sun-Times, in its June 10 editions, revealed the existence of a "Dump Bowie Club," identified its three charter members, predicted they would surface at the owners' summer meeting in Milwaukee on July 15, and also reported "they will succeed if they can find a fourth American League owner to join their club."

Arrayed against Kuhn were Finley of Oakland, Hoffberger of Baltimore and George Steinbrenner of the New York Yankees. At this time, Steinbrenner was in the midst of a two-year suspension from baseball, ordered by Kuhn. This disciplinary action was taken after Steinbrenner was indicted and convicted for illegal contributions to the 1972 political campaigns, a federal offense.

Finley refused to comment on the Sun-Times report. Hoffberger denied knowledge of a "Dump Bowie Club" and said he was unaware of a campaign to unseat Kuhn. Steinbrenner also pleaded innocent and insisted his suspension specifically prevented him from participating in club affairs. Said Steinbrenner: "I would never vote against the commissioner because of anything he did within the perimeter of his authority. People seem to think the Yankees will vote against him because of my suspension but that is not true. I will not enter into retaliatory attempts of any sort."

Kuhn's first seven-year term was to expire on August 12, 1976. According to baseball regulations, the contract of a commissioner must be a topic of discussion 12 to 18 months prior to renewal. Also, according to the rules, Kuhn needed a 9-3 majority in each of the two major leagues. Hence, a cabal of four owners, providing all were from the same league, could block his re-election.

## Kuhn Keeps Silent

For almost a month Kuhn maintained a public silence, refusing to comment on the Sun-Times report which he knew to be true. Privately, he asked American League President Lee MacPhail to make an informal telephone canvass in his behalf. MacPhail did so and reported that the vote would be in Kuhn's favor, 10-2. Encouraged, Kuhn promptly placed the issue of his contract on the agenda for the summer meeting. The press applauded the commissioner for his courage in challenging his antagonists, unaware of the MacPhail poll which revealed only two dissenters, Finley and Hoffberger.

But, as they say, a funny thing happened on the way to the forum. On the eve of the All-Star Game, Finley cornered Texas owner Brad Corbett in a Milwaukee bistro. Young and new to baseball, Corbett remained with Finley long past midnight. By dawn the "Dump Bowie Club" had the fourth vote it needed. Corbett didn't remain for the meeting but left instructions with club attorney Mel Snyder that the Texas vote should be against Kuhn. Later, Corbett said, in explanation, that he felt baseball needed "a more aggressive posture."

The National and American leagues met in separate sessions at the Pfister Hotel which the day before had been the festive headquarters for the All-Star Game. The Americans leaped into the matter of Kuhn's contract and took a straw vote which revealed four clubs against renewal—the Yankees and Rangers joining Finley and Hoffberger. The result was immediately passed on to the National League owners and also to Kuhn who had remained in seclusion, aloof and with an Olympian though disdainful view from his 22nd floor hotel suite.

Joe Reichler, one of Kuhn's aides, reported that the commissioner was "eager" to descend into the pit below. But Kuhn was persuaded to remain in seclusion. The National League, in the meantime, had also taken an informal vote which apparently was 11-1 in Kuhn's favor, with the San Diego Padres believed to be the dissenting club.

## Nationals Delay Vote

The Nationals, led by the persuasive Walter O'Malley of the Los Angeles Dodgers, successfully delayed an immediate joint, 24-club meeting necessary for a formal vote, a parliamentary procedure which delayed the action. Delighted with their success, Finley and Hoffberger retired believing their coup had succeeded.

But in the night, while Finley and Hoffberger slept, the National League owners, with the help of many of their American League brothers, convinced the Yankees and the Texas Rangers to change their votes. A joint meeting followed and was gaveled to order by Kuhn at 9 a.m. the next morning. Kuhn then left the room while each league took a formal vote. The Nationals voted for Kuhn 12-0. The Americans supported him 10-2.

Kuhn was called back into the meeting room and received a standing ovation. Finley and Hoffberger, though disappointed, joined in the applause. The commissioner, his term now extended through 1983, then said: "Thank you, gentlemen, especially those who voted for me." Kuhn then followed with a statement he was to regret. "It's too bad it took so long but it's not surprising, considering the quality of the opposition."

Unable to contain himself, Finley shouted, "What a joke."

## Finley-Kuhn Bitterness

The bitterness between Kuhn and Finley was publicly apparent several minutes later when Kuhn was making his final remarks at a press conference. Finley was in attendance at this press conference, along with most of the other owners. As soon as Kuhn finished with the press, Finley walked to the front of the room, saying that he, too, wanted to issue a statement.

Replied Kuhn, sharply, "Charlie, you may leave my room."

"Thank you, commissioner," Finley replied in sarcasm. "That just shows more class."

Reporters followed Finley into another, smaller room and Finley held court for the next five to 10 minutes during which time he explained he was not embarrassed to admit he had voted against Kuhn but that he had no malice toward any of the other 22 owners who voted for Kuhn.

Said Finley: "I would say that the commissioner hasn't been in baseball long enough. When you're in baseball, you realize you win a few and lose a few and when you lose, you have to lose as graciously as when you win."

## Hoffberger Expresses Disappointment

Hoffberger conducted no such press conference and did not linger, as Finley did. But Hoffberger did admit he was disappointed, expressed surprise that the Yankees and Texas had switched their votes and indicated he would continue boycotting league and joint meetings. The Milwaukee meeting was the first he had attended in several years.

Kuhn's re-election was generally applauded in the press which urged that the voting rules be changed to a simple majority, without regard to league lines. THE SPORTING NEWS, in an editorial, supported this view and said:

"Bowie Kuhn not only hung onto his job as baseball commissioner but in beating back the attempt to unseat him, he strengthened his hand considerably . . . They (the owners) were saying they want a strong commissioner, one who is willing to slap down a club owner when such action is called for."

There were some, though not many, changes at the executive level in 1975. Arthur (Red) Patterson, previously a vice-president with the Los Angeles Dodgers, became the president of the rival California Angels in a surprise move. In another top level change, Sidney Shlenker replaced Judge Roy Hofheinz as the chief operating officer of the Houston Astros who were having financial difficulty.

Almost immediately, Shlenker shook up the Astros' front office and gave the boot to Spec Richardson, who was in his 14th season as Houston's general manager. Tal Smith, who had spent 13 years with the Astros before switching to the Yankees, returned to the Houston organization as Richardson's replacement.

There were two other changes at the general manager level. John Holland, who had been the Cubs' G.M. for the last 19 years, went into semiretirement and was succeeded by E. R. Saltwell, long-time Cub organization man who had been in charge of park operations. Owner Philip Wrigley, in announcing the change, said he purposely selected Saltwell because he "is a tough individual." Said Wrigley: "To put it in simple terms, we ought to get a day's work (from the Cub players) for a day's wages and I don't think we've been getting it."

Hank Peters, another veteran baseball administrator, succeeded Frank Cashen as the general manager of the Baltimore Orioles. A one-time sportswriter, Cashen had been with the Orioles for 10 years and had had huge success in the G.M.'s chair but agreed to an executive post with a brewing company which was among the holdings of Baltimore owner Jerry Hoffberger. Peters had been the president of the National Association for four years and before that had been affiliated with four major league clubs.

## Twelve Managers Bite the Dust

As it usually does, the ax fell with considerably more rapidity on the field. Twelve field managers, precisely half of the major league total, were fired during or after the season. The first to go was Billy Martin, dismissed by the Texas Rangers on July 21. In departing, Martin blasted Texas owner Brad Corbett whom he said wanted "to call all the shots and wanted a yes man." Frank Lucchesi, Martin's third base coach, became the new Texas manager.

Three days later Jack McKeon got the bounce at Kansas City and was succeeded by Whitey Herzog, who had previous, though brief major league managing experience at Texas. Joe Burke, the Royals' general manager, said firing McKeon "was not a spur of the moment thing." The 43-year old Herzog was given a contract through the 1976 season. McKeon left without complaint. "Most times things work out for the best," he said.

## Billy Martin Succeeds Bill Virdon

Bill Virdon was dismissed as the Yankees' field boss on August 1 in a change inspired essentially because of Billy Martin's sudden availability. "This is in no way a criticism of Bill Virdon," said Yankee President Gabe Paul. "It's just that we think this move is in the best interest of the Yankees." Martin, fired by the Rangers 12 days earlier, expressed delight to be returning to the Yankees, for whom he had starred as a player.

The crosstown Mets then swung into action and on August 6 fired Yogi Berra, one of two managers in baseball history to win pennants in both leagues. Berra, who had been at the Met helm since April, 1972, was succeeded by Roy McMillan, one of his coaches who was appointed interim manager. McMillan, in turn, was succeeded by Joe Frazier who had won pennants with Met farm teams in each of the three previous years.

The game of musical chairs continued on August 19 when Virdon, fired by the Yankees three weeks earlier, replaced Preston Gomez at Houston. Gomez, who managed the Astros for approximately two full seasons, departed with a 144-167 won-and-lost record, which included the 22 games he handled in 1973 when Leo Durocher was ill. The Gomez firing occurred the day the Astros were eliminated from the flag race in the National League West.

## Clyde King Fired at Atlanta

Atlanta was next. Clyde King was fired on August 30 and replaced by Connie Ryan, who had been a special aide to general manager Eddie Robinson. King went back to his old job as Robinson's assistant. Ryan's appointment was on an interim basis and at the season's end he was succeeded by Dave Bristol. "I took my time and talked to a lot of people," Robinson said when he announced Bristol as his new choice, "and Dave's the best man I could get."

The Milwaukee Brewers and Minnesota Twins changed managers on September 28, the final day of the regular league season. Del Crandall exited at Milwaukee in favor of Alex Grammas, a third base coach in the National League for the previous 11 years, five years with Pittsburgh and six with Cincinnati. Hank Aaron, the home run star who spent the entire 1975 season with the Brewers, apparently was not given serious consideration as Crandall's successor.

Frank Quilici, characterized by Minnesota owner Calvin Griffith as "too fine a guy," was given the gate after three and a half years as the Twins' field boss. "It's been enjoyable," said Quilici who, at 36, had been the major league's youngest manager. Owner Griffith said he would try to find a manager with "more experience."

Griffith found his man in Gene Mauch, 50, the veteran Montreal pilot who was given the gate on October 1, after seven years at the Expos' helm. Charles Bronfman, the Expos' chief executive officer, thanked Mauch, expressed appropriate sorrow and then told him "We're all very grateful for the job you did for us." Karl Kuehl, who had been managing Montreal farm clubs, succeeded Mauch.

## Alvin Dark and Charlie Finley Part Company

Alvin Dark of Oakland said his farewell two and a half weeks later, on October 17, when Owner Charlie Finley gave him the pink slip. Dark's dismissal was believed to be the result of remarks he made while speaking at the Redwood Chapel Community Church in California's Castro Valley. While in the pulpit Dark told of an anecdote involving Finley and in the telling said, "But to God, Charlie Finley is just a very little, bitty thing. And if he (Finley) doesn't accept Jesus Christ as his personal saviour he's going to hell." Said Finley, in announcing the reason for Dark's departure: "I simply believe his many outside church activities interfered with his managing the club."

The final two managerial firings came as a result of changes at the ownership level. Horace Stoneham, who eventually sold the San Francisco Giants to a group headed by Bob Lurie, dismissed Wes Westrum, his field manager, on November 20. Lurie, after he bought the club, persuaded Bill Rigney to come out of retirement and lead the Giants in 1976. It was Rigney's second managerial term with the Giants.

Also returning for a second term was Paul Richards, 67, who replaced Chuck Tanner as manager of the Chicago White Sox. Tanner was dismissed after a 47-person syndicate headed by Bill Veeck bought 80 percent of the Sox from John Allyn. Veeck fired Tanner on December 17. Less than

24 hours later Charlie Finley gave Tanner a three-year contract to manage the Oakland A's.

Darrell Johnson of the American League champion Boston Red Sox was selected as the Manager of the Year in THE SPORTING NEWS poll of his peers, winning by a substantial margin over Sparky Anderson of Cincinnati. Johnson, who managed by the book and had fair-to-poor relations with the press, was only in his second season at the Boston helm. "He did a damn good job," said Boston Owner Tom Yawkey when advised of John-son's selection.

In its other major awards, THE SPORTING NEWS selected Boston rookie Fred Lynn as the American League Player of the Year and veteran Cincinnati in-fielder Joe Morgan the National League Player of the Year. Jim Palmer of the Baltimore Orioles and Tom Seaver of the New York Mets won THE SPORTING NEWS Pitcher of the Year awards. THE SPORTING NEWS Rookie awards were won by pitchers John Montefusco, San Francisco, and Dennis Eckers-ley, Cleveland; and by the aforementioned Lynn and Gary Carter, a catcher-outfielder with the Montreal Expos.

Lynn received the most post-season honors and was also a double winner in the annual awards presented by the Baseball Writers' Association of America. He was a landslide winner for the BBWAA's prestigious American League Most Valuable Player trophy and, in addition, was chosen as the A.L.'s Rookie of the Year.

A 23-year old outfielder who led the Red Sox to their first pennant since 1967, Lynn was the only player named on all 24 MVP ballots and the first rookie to ever win an MVP award. The only other rookie who came close was Pistol Pete Reiser of the 1941 Brooklyn Dodgers who finished second to teammate Dolph Camilli.

A Pair of MVPs: Joe Morgan and Fred Lynn

Lynn led the league in runs with 103, in doubles with 47, batted .331, second in the league to Minnesota's Rod Carew and was third in RBIs with 105. He received a total of 326 points, 169 more than runner-up John Mayberry of the Kansas City Royals, the biggest margin in MVP history. Jim Rice, like Lynn also a rookie outfielder with the Red Sox, was third in the MVP balloting with 154 points and relief pitcher Rollie Fingers of Oakland was fourth with 129.

The BBWAA balloting for American League MVP with 14 points awarded for a first-place vote, nine for a second-place vote, eight for a third-place vote, etc.:

| | 1 | 2 | 3 | 4 | 5 | 6 | 7 | 8 | 9 | 10 | Pts. |
|---|---|---|---|---|---|---|---|---|---|---|---|
| Fred Lynn | 22 | 2 | — | — | — | — | — | — | — | — | 326 |
| John Mayberry | — | 8 | 4 | 4 | 3 | — | — | 2 | — | 1 | 157 |
| Jim Rice | — | 4 | 6 | 4 | 3 | 1 | 4 | 1 | — | — | 154 |
| Rollie Fingers | 2 | 4 | 4 | 2 | — | 1 | 2 | 2 | — | — | 129 |
| Reggie Jackson | — | 2 | 3 | 3 | 2 | 5 | 2 | 2 | 2 | — | 118 |
| Jim Palmer | — | 2 | — | 1 | 5 | 3 | 2 | 1 | — | 1 | 82 |
| Thurman Munson | — | — | 3 | 1 | 1 | 3 | 1 | 2 | 3 | 1 | 69 |
| George Scott | — | 1 | 1 | 1 | 1 | 1 | 1 | 5 | 4 | 2½ | 64½ |
| Rod Carew | — | — | — | 2 | 2 | 1 | 1 | 3 | 2 | 6½ | 54½ |
| Ken Singleton | — | 1 | 1 | 1 | 1 | 1 | 2 | — | — | 1 | 44 |
| George Brett | — | — | 1 | — | 1 | 1 | 3 | 1 | 1 | 1½ | 37½ |
| Jim Hunter | — | — | 1 | 1 | — | 1 | — | 2 | 2 | 1 | 31 |
| Rick Burleson | — | — | — | — | 1 | 2 | 1 | 1 | 2 | 1 | 28 |
| Claudell Washington | — | — | — | 2 | 1 | — | — | — | 1 | — | 22 |
| Toby Harrah | — | — | — | — | — | 1 | 2 | — | 1 | 1 | 16 |
| Mike Torrez | — | — | — | 1 | — | 1 | — | — | — | — | 12 |
| Rich Gossage | — | — | — | — | 1 | — | — | — | 2 | 1 | 11 |
| Paul Lindblad | — | — | — | 1 | — | — | — | — | — | — | 7 |
| Gene Tenace | — | — | — | — | — | — | 1 | — | 1 | 1 | 7 |
| Boog Powell | — | — | — | — | — | — | — | 1 | 1 | 1½ | 6½ |
| Don Baylor | — | — | — | — | 1 | — | — | — | — | — | 6 |
| Bert Campaneris | — | — | — | — | 1 | — | — | — | — | — | 6 |
| Bill Lee | — | — | — | — | — | 1 | — | — | — | — | 5 |
| Jim Todd | — | — | — | — | — | 1 | — | — | — | — | 5 |
| Denny Doyle | — | — | — | — | — | — | 1 | — | — | 1 | 5 |
| Rick Wise | — | — | — | — | — | — | 1 | — | — | — | 4 |
| Joe Rudi | — | — | — | — | — | — | — | 1 | — | — | 3 |
| Jim Kaat | — | — | — | — | — | — | — | — | 1 | — | 2 |
| Lee May | — | — | — | — | — | — | — | — | 1 | — | 2 |
| Bobby Bonds | — | — | — | — | — | — | — | — | — | 1 | 1 |
| Carl Yastrzemski | — | — | — | — | — | — | — | — | — | 1 | 1 |

Cincinnati's Morgan was also a big winner in the balloting for the National League's MVP trophy and finished with 321½ points, 167½ more than runner-up Greg Luzinski of Philadelphia who received 154 points; this winning total, in fact, was the biggest margin in MVP history prior to Lynn's victory which was announced a week later.

Morgan received 21½ of the 24 first-place votes. Pete Rose, Morgan's Cincinnati teammate, was the only other player to receive first-place recognition in the N.L.'s MVP derby. Rose got the other 2½ votes. One of the selectors split his vote between Morgan and Rose.

Morgan hit .327, fourth best in the league, scored 107 runs and led the league in walks with 132. He also hit 17 home runs, drove in 94 runs, stole 67 bases and was the fielding leader among second basemen, making only 11 errors. Outfielder Dave Parker of Pittsburgh was third in the voting behind Morgan and Luzinski. Johnny Bench and Rose, both of Cincinnati, were fourth and fifth.

The BBWAA balloting for National League MVP:

| | 1 | 2 | 3 | 4 | 5 | 6 | 7 | 8 | 9 | 10 | Pts. |
|---|---|---|---|---|---|---|---|---|---|---|---|
| Joe Morgan | 21½ | — | 2 | — | — | — | — | — | — | — | 321½ |
| Greg Luzinski | — | 6 | 5 | 3 | 2 | 4 | — | 2 | — | 1 | 154 |
| Dave Parker | — | 3 | 2 | 5 | 2 | 2 | 2 | 2 | 2 | 2 | 120 |
| Johnny Bench | — | 3 | 4 | 2 | 2 | 4 | 1 | 2 | 1 | — | 117 |
| Pete Rose | 2½ | 1 | 2 | 2 | 2 | 1 | 1 | 2 | 4 | ½ | 114 |
| Ted Simmons | — | 4 | 2 | 1 | 3 | 3 | — | 1 | 3 | 2 | 103 |
| Willie Stargell | — | 2 | 1 | 3 | 3 | — | 1 | — | — | — | 69 |
| Al Hrabosky | — | 1 | 1 | 2 | 1 | 1 | 5 | 1 | — | 1 | 66 |
| Tom Seaver | — | 1 | 1 | 1 | 2 | — | 4 | 3 | 1 | 2 | 65 |
| Randy Jones | — | 1 | 2 | 3 | 1 | — | — | 1 | — | — | 54 |
| Steve Garvey | — | 1 | — | 1 | 2 | 1 | 2 | 1 | 2 | 2 | 50 |
| Bill Madlock | — | — | — | 1 | 1 | 1 | 4 | 1 | 2 | 4 | 45 |
| Dave Cash | — | — | — | — | 1 | 1 | 1 | 2 | 1 | 3 | 26 |
| Rusty Staub | — | — | — | — | — | 2 | 1 | 1 | 1 | 1 | 20 |
| Tony Perez | — | — | — | — | 1 | — | — | 3 | 1 | 1 | 18 |
| Mike Schmidt | — | — | 1 | — | — | 1 | — | 1 | — | — | 16 |
| Manny Sanguillen | — | — | 1 | — | — | 1 | — | — | 1 | 1 | 16 |
| Ron Cey | — | — | — | — | — | 1 | — | 1 | 1 | 1½ | 11½ |
| Dave Kingman | — | — | — | — | — | 1 | 1 | — | — | — | 9 |
| Bob Watson | — | — | — | — | — | — | 1 | — | 2 | — | 8 |
| Lou Brock | — | — | — | — | 1 | — | — | — | — | — | 6 |
| Larry Bowa | — | — | — | — | — | — | — | 1 | — | — | 3 |
| Jerry Reuss | — | — | — | — | — | — | — | 1 | — | — | 2 |
| Andy Messersmith | — | — | — | — | — | — | — | — | 1 | — | 1 |
| Willie Montanez | — | — | — | — | — | — | — | — | 1 | 1 | 1 |

*Note—One voter gave Morgan and Rose each one-half vote for first place and did not vote for second place. Both are credited with an additional 4½ points to account for the missing second-place vote.*

Two veteran pitchers, Tom Seaver of the New York Mets and Jim Palmer of the Baltimore Orioles, won the BBWAA's Cy Young awards, Palmer for the second time and Seaver for the third, joining Sandy Koufax as the only three-time Cy Young winners.

Palmer, who had a 7-12 won-and-lost record in 1974 when he was hindered by injuries, rebounded with a 23-11 season, led both leagues with a 2.09 earned-run average and in shutouts with 10. He received 15 first-place votes for a total of 98 points. Catfish Hunter of the Yankees, who was 23-14 for the season, had seven first-place votes and was second in the balloting with 74 points. Fingers of Oakland was third with 25.

The vote was closer in the National League, with Seaver holding an 18-point margin over Randy Jones of San Diego. Jones and Seaver were the N.L.'s only 20-game winners. Seaver got credit for his 22nd triumph in the Mets' finale whereas Jones lost his last start, finishing at 20-12. Seaver, who was 11-11 in 1974, finished with a 22-9 mark and a 2.38 ERA.

Lynn dominated the voting for the BBWAA's A.L. Rookie of the Year award and got 23½ of a maximum 24 first-place votes, one writer splitting his vote between Lynn and Jim Rice. The BBWAA voted the San Francisco Giants' Montefusco as N.L. Rookie of the Year.

THE SPORTING NEWS American League All-Star Team, picked by the players who were allowed to vote only for opponents, follows:

John Mayberry, Kansas City, first base; Rod Carew, Minnesota, second base; Graig Nettles, New York, third base; Toby Harrah, Texas, shortstop; Thurman Munson, New York, catcher; outfielders Fred Lynn and Jim Rice, Boston, and Reggie Jackson, Oakland; DH Willie Horton, Detroit and pitchers Jim Palmer, Baltimore, and Jim Kaat, Chicago.

## Additional Sporting News Awards

THE SPORTING NEWS National League All-Stars:

Steve Garvey, Los Angeles, first base; Joe Morgan, Cincinnati, second base; Bill Madlock, Chicago, third base; Larry Bowa, Philadelphia, shortstop; Johnny Bench, Cincinnati, catcher; outfielders Greg Luzinski, Philadelphia, and Dave Parker and Al Oliver, Pittsburgh; and pitchers Tom Seaver, New York, and Randy Jones, San Diego.

THE SPORTING NEWS All-Star Fielding Teams:

NATIONAL LEAGUE—Steve Garvey, Los Angeles, first base; Joe Morgan, Cincinnati, second base; Ken Reitz, St. Louis, third base; Dave Concepcion, Cincinnati, shortstop; Johnny Bench, Cincinnati, catcher; outfielders Cesar Geronimo, Cincinnati; Cesar Cedeno, Houston, and Garry Maddox, Philadelphia, and pitcher Andy Messersmith, Los Angeles.

AMERICAN LEAGUE—George Scott, Milwaukee, first base; Bobby Grich, second base, Brooks Robinson, third base, and Mark Belanger, shortstop, all of Baltimore; Thurman Munson, New York, catcher; outfielders Joe Rudi, Oakland, Paul Blair, Baltimore, and Fred Lynn, Boston, and pitcher Jim Kaat, Chicago.

THE SPORTING NEWS also honored Richard (Dick) O'Connell, vice-president and general manager of the Boston Red Sox, as the Major League Executive of the Year. Bob Howsam of Cincinnati was second in the balloting and Charlie Finley of Oakland was third.

Stan Naccarato, general manager of the Tacoma Twins of the Pacific Coast League, was selected as the winner of THE SPORTING NEWS award as the Triple A Executive of the Year. Jim Paul, owner-general manager of the El Paso Diablos in the Texas League, was acclaimed as the Class AA Executive of the Year, the second time in a row Paul won this award, and Cordy Jensen, general manager of Eugene in the Northwest League, was honored as top executive in Class A ball.

# Major League Attendance for 1975

| AMERICAN LEAGUE | Home | Away |
|---|---|---|
| Baltimore | 1,002,157 | 1,163,631 |
| Boston | 1,748,587 | 1,283,466 |
| California | 1,058,163 | 975,645 |
| Chicago | 750,802 | 990,254 |
| Cleveland | 977,039 | 1,037,030 |
| Detroit | 1,058,836 | 932,102 |
| Kansas City | 1,151,836 | 932,819 |
| Milwaukee | 1,213,357 | 1,136,428 |
| Minnesota | 737,156 | 892,629 |
| New York | 1,288,048 | 1,435,321 |
| Oakland | 1,075,518 | 1,436,383 |
| Texas | 1,127,924 | 973,715 |

A.L. 1975 Total—13,189,423

| NATIONAL LEAGUE | Home | Away |
|---|---|---|
| Atlanta | 534,672 | 1,375,454 |
| Chicago | 1,034,819 | 1,362,813 |
| Cincinnati | 2,315,603 | 1,694,160 |
| Houston | 858,002 | 1,161,573 |
| Los Angeles | 2,539,349 | 1,702,148 |
| Montreal | 908,292 | 1,080,782 |
| New York | 1,730,566 | 1,290,135 |
| Philadelphia | 1,909,233 | 1,323,919 |
| Pittsburgh | 1,270,018 | 1,682,182 |
| St. Louis | 1,695,270 | 1,352,658 |
| San Diego | 1,281,747 | 1,152,310 |
| San Francisco | 522,919 | 1,422,356 |

N.L. 1975 Total—16,600,490

# Homers by Parks for 1975

## NATIONAL LEAGUE

| Club | At Atl. | At Chi. | At Cin. | At Hou. | At L.A. | At Mon. | At N.Y. | At Phil. | At Pitt. | At St.L. | At S.D. | At S.F. | Totals 1975 | Totals 1974 |
|---|---|---|---|---|---|---|---|---|---|---|---|---|---|---|
| Atlanta | 58 | 3 | 10 | 2 | 5 | 6 | 3 | 7 | 2 | 1 | 5 | 5 | 107 | 120 |
| Chicago | 4 | 54 | 1 | 1 | 2 | 5 | 4 | 7 | 7 | 7 | 2 | 1 | 95 | 110 |
| Cincinnati | 11 | 6 | 70 | 5 | 8 | 6 | 2 | 2 | 2 | 5 | 3 | 4 | 124 | 135 |
| Houston | 6 | 10 | 5 | 40 | 4 | 1 | 1 | 3 | 5 | 3 | 3 | 3 | 84 | 110 |
| Los Angeles | 3 | 4 | 7 | 7 | 64 | 5 | 6 | 3 | 4 | 3 | 7 | 5 | 118 | 139 |
| Montreal | 4 | 4 | 2 | 4 | 7 | 53 | 6 | 2 | 3 | 7 | 2 | 4 | 98 | 86 |
| New York | 5 | 5 | 2 | 5 | 2 | 3 | 52 | 8 | 11 | 2 | 2 | 4 | 101 | 96 |
| Philadelphia | 5 | 9 | 3 | 3 | 4 | 10 | 9 | 72 | 1 | 3 | 5 | 1 | 125 | 95 |
| Pittsburgh | 6 | 14 | 7 | 2 | 6 | 9 | 7 | 6 | 67 | 5 | 4 | 5 | 138 | 114 |
| St. Louis | 5 | 6 | 3 | 3 | 3 | 4 | 3 | 4 | 1 | 46 | 0 | 3 | 81 | 83 |
| San Diego | 9 | 2 | 7 | 7 | 6 | 2 | 5 | 1 | 3 | 1 | 33 | 2 | 78 | 99 |
| San Francisco | 5 | 8 | 5 | 4 | 5 | 6 | 2 | 4 | 2 | 2 | 5 | 36 | 84 | 93 |
| 1975 Totals | 121 | 125 | 122 | 83 | 116 | 110 | 100 | 119 | 108 | 85 | 71 | 73 | 1233 | .... |
| 1974 Totals | 109 | 139 | 136 | 93 | 119 | 99 | 92 | 111 | 79 | 91 | 101 | 111 | .... | 1280 |

**AT ATLANTA (121): Atlanta (58)**—Evans 12, Baker 9, May 7, Williams 7, Correll 6, Lum 6, Garr 5, Gaston 2, Office 2, Blanks, Perez. **Chicago (4)**—Monday 2, Thornton 2. **Cincinnati (11)**—Bench 2, Driessen 2, Foster 2, Concepcion, Griffey, Morgan, Perez, Plummer. **Houston (6)**—Cedeno 4, Cruz, Johnson, Richard, Watson. **Los Angeles (3)**—Cey, Lacy, Yeager. **Montreal (4)**—Carter 4. **New York (5)**—Kingman 2, Staub 2, Garrett. **Philadelphia (5)**—Schmidt 2, Allen, Luzinski, Maddox. **Pittsburgh (6)**—Robertson 2, Hebner, Oliver, Parker, Zisk. **St. Louis (5)**—Smith 2, Bradford, Davis, Simmons. **San Diego (9)**—Winfield 3, Grubb 2, McCovey 2, Ivie, Torres. **San Francisco (5)**—Montanez, Ontiveros, Rader, Speier, Thomas.

**AT CHICAGO (125): Atlanta (3)**—Evans, Lum, May. **Chicago (54)**—Monday 12, Thornton 8, Morales 7, Madlock 6, Hosley 5, Cardenal 4, Trillo 3, LaCock 2, Mitterwald 2, Dunn, R. Reuschel, Rosello, Summers, Swisher. **Cincinnati (6)**—Bench 2, Chaney, Foster, Morgan, Rose. **Houston (10)**—Cruz 3, Johnson 3, Rader 2, Watson 2. **Los Angeles (4)**—Cey, Garvey, Hale, Wynn. **Montreal (4)**—Jorgensen 4. **New York (5)**—Kingman 3, Milner, Stearns. **Philadelphia (9)**—Schmidt 3, Allen 2, Hutton 2, Luzinski, Montanez. **Pittsburgh (14)**—Stargell 3, Zisk 3, Hebner 2, Parker 2, Oliver, Robertson, Sanguillen, Stennett. **St. Louis (6)**—Hernandez 2, Brock, Davis, Reitz, Smith. **San Diego (2)**—McCovey, Tolan. **San Francisco (8)**—Adams 2, Speier 2, Thomas 2, Hill, Murcer.

**AT CINCINNATI (122): Atlanta (10)**—Gaston 2, May 2, Williams 2, Baker, Blanks, Evans, Goodson. **Chicago (1)**—Morales. **Cincinnati (70)**—Bench 15, Foster 15, Perez 12, Morgan 10, Driessen 5, Geronimo 3, Rose 3, Concepcion 2, Rettenmund 2, Chaney, Flynn, Griffey. **Houston (5)**—Watson 2, Cedeno, Johnson, May. **Los Angeles (8)**—Buckner, Cey, Crawford, Garvey, Hale, Wynn, Yeager. **Montreal (2)**—Foote, Jorgensen. **New York (2)**—Staub, Torre. **Philadelphia (3)**—Boone, Luzinski, Schmidt. **Pittsburgh (7)**—Sanguillen 2, Kirkpatrick, Parker, Stargell, Stennett, Zisk. **St. Louis (3)**—Simmons 2, Davis. **San Diego (7)**—McCovey 2, Winfield 2, Ivie, Locklear, Roberts. **San Francisco (5)**—Joshua 2, LeMaster, Miller, Speier.

**AT HOUSTON (83): Atlanta (2)**—Gilbreath, Pocoroba. **Chicago (1)**—Cardenal. **Cincinnati (5)**—Perez 2, Bench, Geronimo, Morgan. **Houston (40)**—Johnson 10, Rader 10, Cedeno 6, Watson 6, Cruz 3, Cabell, DaVanon, May, Milbourne, Sosa. **Los Angeles (7)**—Wynn 2, Buckner, Cey, Garvey, Hooton, Yeager. **Montreal (4)**—Mangual 3, Parrish. **New York (5)**—Kingman 2, Garrett, Staub, Unser. **Philadelphia (3)**—Luzinski 2, Schmidt. **Pittsburgh (2)**—Parker, Robertson. **St. Louis (3)**—Reitz, Simmons, Smith. **San Diego (7)**—McCovey 3, Ivie, Sharon, Tolan, Winfield. **San Francisco (4)**—Speier 2, Rader, Thomasson.

**AT LOS ANGELES (116): Atlanta (5)**—Baker 2, Blanks, Evans, Garr. **Chicago (2)**—Cardenal, Madlock. **Cincinnati (8)**—Bench 2, Concepcion 2, Foster, Geronimo, Perez, Rose. **Houston (4)**—Johnson 2, Cedeno, Watson. **Los Angeles (64)**—Cey 18, Garvey 9, Wynn 9, Crawford 6, Yeager 6, Lacy 4, Buckner 3, Ferguson 3, Hale 3, Lopes 2, McMullen. **Montreal (7)**—Parrish 2, Bailey, Biittner, Colbert, Jorgensen, Mackanin. **New York (2)**—Kingman, Unser. **Philadelphia (4)**—Cash, Luzinski, Martin, Schmidt. **Pittsburgh (6)**—Oliver 2, Parker 2, Stargell, Zisk. **St. Louis (3)**—Hernandez, Howard, Melendez. **San Diego (6)**—Locklear 2, McCovey 2, Ivie, Torres. **San Francisco (5)**—Joshua, Maddox, Matthews, Murcer, Rader.

**AT MONTREAL (110): Atlanta (6)**—Williams 2, Correll, Evans, Gaston, May. **Chicago (5)**—Cardenal, Monday, Morales, Sperring, Trillo. **Cincinnati (6)**—Bench, Foster, Griffey, Morgan, Perez, Rose. **Houston (1)**—Metzger. **Los Angeles (5)**—Buckner, Garvey, Lacy, Lopes, Wynn. **Montreal (53)**—Carter 9, Jorgensen 8, Mackanin 7, Parrish 5, Mangual 4, Dwyer 3, Biittner 2, Colbert 2, Foote 2, Morales 2, Scanlon 2, White 2, Bailey, Cox, Foli, Renko, Valentine. **New York (3)**—Kingman 2, Vail. **Philadelphia (10)**—Schmidt 3, Luzinski 2, Anderson, Bowa, Johnstone, Montanez, Taylor. **Pittsburgh (9)**—Oliver 3, Parker 2, Stargell 2, Zisk 2. **St. Louis (4)**—Simmons 2, Sizemore 2. **San Diego (2)**—Locklear, Sharon. **San Francisco (6)**—Murcer 2, Adams, Matthews, Montanez, Rader.

**AT NEW YORK (100): Atlanta (3)**—Gaston, Gilbreath, Lum. **Chicago (4)**—Cardenal, LaCock, Thornton, Trillo. **Cincinnati (2)**—Foster, Rose. **Houston (1)**—Metzger. **Los Angeles (6)**—Wynn 3, Garvey, Hale, Lopes. **Montreal (6)**—Bailey 2, Foote, Jorgensen, Mackanin, Mangual. **New York (52)**—Kingman 14, Staub 11, Garrett 4, Kranepool 4, Torre 4, Unser 4, Milner 3, Hodges 2, Vail 2, Grote, Heidemann, Millan, Stearns. **Philadelphia (9)**—Luzinski 3, Allen, Boone, Brown, Christenson, Johnstone, Schmidt. **Pittsburgh (7)**—Robinson 3, Parker, Sanguillen, Stargell, Stennett. **St. Louis (3)**—Simmons, Smith, Tyson. **San Diego (5)**—Grubb, Hundley, Ivie, McCovey, Tolan. **San Francisco (2)**—Hill, Matthews.

**AT PHILADELPHIA (119): Atlanta (7)**—Correll 3, Baker 2, Evans, Office. **Chicago (7)**—Thornton 2, Cardenal, LaCock, Mitterwald, Monday, Trillo. **Cincinnati (2)**—Geronimo, Morgan.

Houston (3)—Cabell, Johnson, Watson. Los Angeles (3)—Crawford, Garvey, Yeager. Montreal (2)—Foote, Mackanin. New York (8)—Kingman 3, Grote, Milner, Phillips, Staub, Stearns. Philadelphia (72)—Schmidt 22, Luzinski 21, Allen 6, Johnstone 5, Brown 4, Anderson 3, Cash 3, Maddox 2, Bowa, Christenson, Hutton, Martin, McCarver, Oates. Pittsburgh (6)—Parker 3, Hebner, Robertson, Zisk. St. Louis (4)—Bradford 2, McBride, Sizemore. San Diego (1)—Winfield. San Francisco (4)—Matthews 2, Hill, Montanez.

AT PITTSBURGH (108): Atlanta (1)—Baker 2. Chicago (7)—Thornton 2, Hosley, Mitterwald, Morales, Trillo, Wallis. Cincinnati (2)—Bench, Perez. Houston (5)—Cedeno 3, Cruz, Watson. Los Angeles (4)—Garvey, Hale, Paciorek, Wynn. Montreal (3)—Carter, Foote, Parrish. New York (11)—Kingman 7, Milner, Staub, Torre, Unser. Philadelphia (1)—Brown. Pittsburgh (67)—Stargell 12, Hebner 11, Parker 10, Oliver 9, Zisk 8, Dyer 3, Kirkpatrick 3, Robinson 3, Sanguillen 3, Stennett 3, Howe, Robertson. St. Louis (1)—Melendez. San Diego (3)—Locklear, McCovey, Winfield. San Francisco (2)—Adams, Joshua.

AT ST. LOUIS (85): Atlanta (1)—Evans. Chicago (7)—Thornton 3, LaCock 2, Morales 2. Cincinnati (5)—Morgan 2, Bench, Foster, Griffey. Houston (3)—Johnson 2, Watson. Los Angeles (3)—Lopes 2, Wynn. Montreal (7)—Carter 3, Jorgensen 2, Mackanin, Parrish. New York (2)—Unser 2. Philadelphia (3)—Allen, Luzinski, Schmidt. Pittsburgh (5)—Oliver 2, Brett, Parker, Zisk. St. Louis (46)—Smith 14, Simmons 10, Fairly 7, McBride 4, Davis 3, Reitz 3, Bradford, Brock, Forsch, Rudolph, Tyson. San Diego (1)—Fuentes. San Francisco (2)—Matthews, Murcer.

AT SAN DIEGO (71): Atlanta (5)—Baker 2, Evans 2, May. Chicago (2)—Garrett, Monday. Cincinnati (3)—Bench 3. Houston (3)—Watson 3. Los Angeles (7)—Garvey 3, Cey 2, McMullen, Yeager. Montreal (2)—Colbert, Jorgensen. New York (2)—Kingman, Staub. Philadelphia (5)—Schmidt 3, Allen, Maddox. Pittsburgh (4)—Stargell 2, Kirkpatrick, Sanguillen. St. Louis (0). San Diego (33)—McCovey 11, Winfield 7, Fuentes 3, Torres 3, Ivie 2, Sharon 2, Tolan 2, Grubb, Hundley, Roberts. San Francisco (5)—Matthews 2, Murcer, Ontiveros, Thomasson.

AT SAN FRANCISCO (73): Atlanta (5)—Evans 2, Baker, Correll, Perez. Chicago (1)—Mitterwald. Cincinnati (4)—Perez 2, Crowley, Foster. Houston (3)—May 2, Cruz. Los Angeles (5)—Cey, Crawford, Ferguson, Lacy, Lopes. Montreal (4)—Bailey, Foote, Mackanin, Mangual. New York (4)—Kingman, Milner, Staub, Unser. Philadelphia (1)—Luzinski. Pittsburgh (5)—Zisk 2, Parker, Sanguillen, Stennett. St. Louis (3)—Brinkman, Brock, Simmons. San Diego (2)—Ivie, Valentine. San Francisco (36)—Montanez 5, Murcer 5, Thomasson 5, Matthews 4, Speier 4, Joshua 3, Thomas 3, Hill 2, Goodson, LeMaster, Montefusco, Ontiveros, Rader.

# AMERICAN LEAGUE

|  | At Balt. | At Bos. | At Calif. | At Chi. | At Clev. | At Det. | At K.C. | At Milw. | At Minn. | At N.Y. | At Oak. | At Tex. | Totals 1975 | 1974 |
|---|---|---|---|---|---|---|---|---|---|---|---|---|---|---|
| Baltimore | 46 | 11 | 3 | 7 | 12 | 12 | 4 | 7 | 4 | 4 | 6 | 8 | 124 | 116 |
| Boston | 5 | 74 | 1 | 4 | 4 | 8 | 5 | 8 | 8 | 4 | 8 | 5 | 134 | 109 |
| California | 2 | 1 | 24 | 1 | 6 | 5 | 3 | 3 | 5 | 1 | 0 | 4 | 55 | 95 |
| Chicago | 7 | 3 | 5 | 42 | 5 | 4 | 3 | 5 | 7 | 4 | 2 | 7 | 94 | 135 |
| Cleveland | 6 | 12 | 7 | 5 | 79 | 11 | 4 | 8 | 6 | 8 | 6 | 1 | 153 | 131 |
| Detroit | 6 | 11 | 3 | 1 | 8 | 63 | 3 | 3 | 11 | 9 | 3 | 4 | 125 | 131 |
| Kansas City | 2 | 5 | 13 | 4 | 4 | 7 | 46 | 9 | 3 | 4 | 6 | 15 | 118 | 89 |
| Milwaukee | 4 | 13 | 2 | 5 | 11 | 7 | 6 | 72 | 8 | 7 | 5 | 6 | 146 | 120 |
| Minnesota | 2 | 1 | 3 | 12 | 4 | 5 | 2 | 1 | 75 | 6 | 2 | 8 | 121 | 111 |
| New York | 2 | 9 | 1 | 3 | 13 | 10 | 3 | 5 | 7 | 50 | 4 | 3 | 110 | 101 |
| Oakland | 4 | 6 | 2 | 8 | 7 | 9 | 7 | 12 | 4 | 75 | 11 | 151 | 132 |
| Texas | 5 | 11 | 8 | 10 | 10 | 7 | 3 | 12 | 4 | 5 | 52 | 134 | 99 |
| 1975 Totals | 91 | 157 | 76 | 96 | 164 | 146 | 91 | 135 | 163 | 106 | 118 | 122 | 1465 | |
| 1974 Totals | 94 | 124 | 93 | 109 | 164 | 158 | 80 | 127 | 116 | 92 | 112 | 100 | | 1369 |

AT BALTIMORE (91): Baltimore (46)—Baylor 10, May 8, Singleton 6, Grich 5, Blair 4, DeCinces 3, Duncan 3, Hendricks 3, Davis 2, Belanger, Robinson. Boston (5)—Burleson, Conigliaro, Cooper, Evans, Yastrzemski. California (2)—Harper 2. Chicago (2)—Henderson 2, Coluccio, D. Johnson, Kelly, Orta, Varney. Cleveland (6)—Carty 2, Spikes 2, Brohamer, Ellis. Detroit (6)—Horton 2, Freehan, LeFlore, Michael, Rodriguez. Kansas City (2)—Brett 2. Milwaukee (4)—Hegan, Mitchell, Porter, Scott. Minnesota (2)—Ford, Hisle. New York (2)—Bonds, Munson. Oakland (4)—Campaneris, Jackson, Tenace, C. Washington. Texas (5)—Burroughs, Fregosi, Grieve, Hargrove, Sundberg.

AT BOSTON (157): Baltimore (11)—May 3, Baylor 2, Grich 2, Davis, Northrup, Robinson, Singleton. Boston (74)—Rice 12, Carbo 11, Lynn 9, Evans 8, Yastrzemski 8, Cooper 6, Fisk 6, Petrocelli 5, Burleson 3, Montgomery 2, Beniquez, Conigliaro, Doyle, Johnson. California (1)—Etchebarren. Chicago (3)—D. Johnson, Melton, Nyman. Cleveland (12)—Ashby 2, Hendrick 2, Powell 2, Spikes 2, Duffy, Ellis, Lis, Robinson. Detroit (11)—Horton 3, Freehan 2, Baldwin, Oglivie, Pierce, Roberts, Rodriguez, Sutherland. Kansas City (5)—Mayberry 2, Healy, Killebrew, White. Milwaukee (13)—Lezcano 2, Money 2, Porter 2, Scott 2, Yount 2, Aaron, Bevacqua, Darwin. Minnesota (1)—Oliva. New York (9)—White 3, Bonds 2, Chambliss 2, Johnson, Munson. Oakland (4)—Tenace 3, Jackson 2, Harper. Texas (11)—Burroughs 4, Harrah 2, Cubbage, Howell, Randle, Spencer, Sundberg.

AT CALIFORNIA (76): Baltimore (3)—Northrup, Robinson, Singleton. Boston (1)—Rice. California (24)—Stanton 9, Garrett 4, Bochte 2, Lahoud 2, Miley 2, Balaz, Chalk, Collins, Etchebarren, Rivers. Chicago (5)—Henderson 2, May 2, D. Johnson. Cleveland (7)—Lowenstein 2, Bell, Gamble, Manning, Powell, Spikes. Detroit (3)—Horton, Pierce, Veryzer. Kansas City (13)—Mayberry 4, Solaita 3, Brett, Cowens, McRae, Otis, Patek, White. Milwaukee (2)—Mitchell, Porter. Minnesota (3)—Darwin, Hisle, Oliva. New York (1)—Herrmann. Oakland (6)—Jackson 3, Garner, Tenace, Williams. Texas (8)—Grieve 3, Hargrove 2, Burroughs, Cubbage, Lovitto.

**AT CHICAGO (96)—Baltimore (7)**—Duncan 3, Baylor, Grich, May, Singleton. **Boston (4)**—Evans 2, Cooper, Yastrzemski. **California (1)**—Chalk. **Chicago (42)**—D. Johnson 8, Melton 8, Orta 6, Downing 5, Kelly 4, Henderson 3, Coluccio 2, May 2, Stein 2, Bradford, L. Johnson. **Cleveland (5)**—Hendrick 2, Carty, Ellis, Powell. **Detroit (1)**—Michael. **Kansas City (4)**—Mayberry 2, Brett, Killebrew. **Milwaukee (5)**—Scott 2, Darwin, Porter, Thomas. **Minnesota (12)**—Brye 4, Ford 3, Briggs 2, Carew, Darwin, Kusick. **New York (3)**—Bonds 3. **Oakland (2)**—Jackson, Tenace. **Texas (10)**—Burroughs 3, Grieve 2, Hargrove 2, Davis, Fregosi, Nelson.

**AT CLEVELAND (164): Baltimore (12)**—May 4, Hendricks 2, Baylor, Bumbry, DeCinces, Duncan, Robinson, Singleton. **Boston (4)**—Burleson, Fisk, Rice, Yastrzemski. **California (6)**—Stanton 2, Collins, Harper, Miley, Remy. **Chicago (5)**—Melton 2, Bradford, Kelly, Orta. **Cleveland (79)**—Hendrick 13, Powell 12, Carty 11, Gamble 10, Lowenstein 8, Robinson 8, Bell 6, Spikes 5, Manning 2, Ashby, Brohamer, Ellis, McCraw. **Detroit (8)**—Horton 2, LeFlore 2, Oglivie 2, Baldwin, Freehan. **Kansas City (4)**—Mayberry 3, Solaita. **Milwaukee (11)**—Scott 4, Darwin 2, Thomas 2, Aaron, Briggs, Porter. **Minnesota (4)**—Carew, Ford, Oliva, Walton. **New York (13)**—Bonds 6, White 2, Alomar, Chambliss, Dempsey, Munson, Nettles. **Oakland (8)**—Rudi 2, Bando, Campaneris, Garner, Jackson, Tenace, Williams. **Texas (10)**—Burroughs 3, Hargrove 2, Harrah 2, Fregosi, Randle, Spencer.

**AT DETROIT (146): Baltimore (12)**—Baylor 4, Hendricks 2, Northrup 2, Blair, Grich, May, Singleton. **Boston (8)**—Lynn 3, Carbo 2, Beniquez, Evans, Rice. **California (9)**—Lahoud 2, Bochte, Collins, Stanton. **Chicago (4)**—Downing, Henderson, May, Stein. **Cleveland (11)**—Ashby 2, Brohamer 2, Gamble 2, Powell 2, Carty, Ellis, Hendrick. **Detroit (63)**—Meyer 8, Roberts 7, Rodriguez 7, Freehan 6, Horton 6, Oglivie 6, LeFlore 4, Pierce 4, Veryzer 3, Wockenfuss 3, Baldwin 2, Colbert 2, Stanley 2, Sutherland 2, Brown. **Kansas City (7)**—Mayberry 2, Solaita 2, Cowens, Pinson, Stinson. **Milwaukee (7)**—Scott 3, Money 2, Aaron, Lezcano. **Minnesota (5)**—Braun, Carew, Hisle, Kelly, Roof. **New York (10)**—Bonds 3, Blomberg 2, Nettles 2, Munson, White, Williams. **Oakland (7)**—Jackson 3, Bando, Haney, Tenace, Williams. **Texas (7)**—Grieve 2, Burroughs, Cardenas, Harrah, Moates, Smalley.

**AT KANSAS CITY (91): Baltimore (4)**—Duncan 2, Baylor, Belanger. **Boston (5)**—Lynn 3, Carbo, Doyle. **California (3)**—Allietta, Briggs, Lahoud. **Chicago (3)**—D. Johnson, Melton, Orta. **Cleveland (4)**—Carty, Gamble, Hendrick, Powell. **Detroit (3)**—Freehan, Horton, Pierce. **Kansas City (46)**—Mayberry 11, Killebrew 8, Otis 6, Solaita 6, White 4, Brett 2, Cowens 2, McRae 2, Martinez, Patek, Pinson, Quirk, Rojas. **Milwaukee (6)**—Money 2, Aaron, Darwin, Scott, Thomas. **Minnesota (2)**—Kusick, Soderholm. **New York (3)**—Bonds 2, Munson. **Oakland (9)**—Rudi 2, Williams 2, Bando, Holt, Jackson, Tenace, C. Washington. **Texas (3)**—Davis 2, Harrah.

**AT MILWAUKEE (135): Baltimore (7)**—Grich 3, Davis 2, Bumbry, Duncan. **Boston (8)**—Rice 3, Cooper 2, Burleson, Fisk, Petrocelli. **California (3)**—Chalk, Rodriguez, Stanton. **Chicago (5)**—Dent, Downing, Kelly, Melton, Orta. **Cleveland (8)**—Bell 2, Powell 2, Hendrick, Lis, Lowenstein, Spikes. **Detroit (3)**—Freehan, Horton, Pierce. **Kansas City (9)**—Mayberry 3, Martinez 2, Pinson 2, Brett, Solaita. **Milwaukee (72)**—Scott 18, Porter 9, Money 8, Garcia 5, Mitchell 5, Thomas 5, Aaron 4, Hegan 4, Lezcano 4, Yount 4, Briggs 2, Darwin 2, Bevacqua, Sharp. **Minnesota (1)**—McKay. **New York (5)**—Chambliss 2, Bonds, Nettles, Williams. **Oakland (2)**—Williams 2, Tenace, Campaneris, Jackson. **Texas (7)**—Howell 2, Burroughs, Davis, Harrah, Spencer, Sundberg.

**AT MINNESOTA (163): Baltimore (4)**—Baylor 2, Grich, Singleton. **Boston (8)**—Rice 3, Lynn 2, Cooper, Griffin, Yastrzemski. **California (5)**—Rodriguez 2, Doherty, Lahoud, Stanton. **Chicago (7)**—D. Johnson 2, Henderson, Kelly, May, Melton, Nyman. **Cleveland (6)**—Powell 2, Bell, Brohamer, Gamble, Hendrick. **Detroit (11)**—Horton 3, Rodriguez 3, Sutherland 2, Michael, Roberts, Veryzer, Wockenfuss. **Kansas City (8)**—Killebrew 2, Brett, Mayberry, McRae, Otis, Rojas, Solaita. **Milwaukee (8)**—Aaron 2, Porter 2, Lezcano, Mitchell, Money, Scott. **Minnesota (75)**—Carew 10, Soderholm 10, Braun 9, Ford 8, Hisle 7, Brye 5, Roof 5, Kusick 4, Oliva 4, Thompson 4, Briggs 3, Borgmann 2, Darwin 2, McKay, Terrell. **New York (7)**—Munson 3, Bonds 2, Nettles, White. **Oakland (12)**—Rudi 3, Tenace 3, Bando 2, Jackson 2, Garner, C. Washington. **Texas (12)**—Burroughs 3, Harrah 3, Fregosi 2, Grieve, Howell, Randle, Sundberg.

**AT NEW YORK (106): Baltimore (8)**—Baylor 3, Singleton 2, Davis, May, Robinson. **Boston (4)**—Lynn 2, Yastrzemski 2. **California (1)**—Miley. **Chicago (2)**—D. Johnson 2, Dent, Varney. **Cleveland (8)**—Powell 3, Carty 2, Brohamer, Ellis, Lowenstein. **Detroit (9)**—Horton 4, Colbert 2, Freehan, LeFlore, Sutherland. **Kansas City (1)**—Healy. **Milwaukee (7)**—Lezcano 2, Aaron, Coluccio, Darwin, Thomas, Yount. **Minnesota (6)**—Oliva 3, Braun, Briggs, Ford. **New York (50)**—Nettles 14, Bonds 9, Herrmann 5, Chambliss 4, Munson 4, White 4, Blomberg 2, Mason 2, Williams 2, Alomar, Bladt, Coggins, Maddox. **Oakland (2)**—Williams 3, Jackson. **Texas (2)**—Spencer 2, Howell, Sundberg.

**AT OAKLAND (118): Baltimore (4)**—Belanger, May, Northrup, Robinson. **Boston (8)**—Cooper 2, Fisk 2, Doyle, Lynn, Petrocelli, Rice. **California (0)**. **Chicago (2)**—Dent, May. **Cleveland (6)**—Hendrick 3, McCraw, Powell, Sudakis. **Detroit (3)**—Freehan, Horton, Stanley. **Kansas City (4)**—Brett 2, McRae, Patek. **Milwaukee (5)**—Scott 4, Moore. **Minnesota (2)**—Darwin, Thompson. **New York (4)**—Bonds, Nettles, White, Williams. **Oakland (75)**—Jackson 18, Tenace 15, Rudi 12, Bando 8, Williams 8, C. Washington 7, Garner 3, Campaneris, Harper, Holt, North. **Texas (5)**—Harrah 2, Spencer 2, Burroughs.

**AT TEXAS (122): Baltimore (6)**—Duncan 2, Baylor, Hendricks, May, Singleton. **Boston (5)**—Carbo, Cooper, Doyle, Evans, Lynn. **California (4)**—Garrett 2, Etchebarren, Sudakis. **Chicago (7)**—D. Johnson 2, Coluccio, Kelly, May, Melton, Orta. **Cleveland (1)**—Ellis. **Detroit (4)**—Rodriguez 2, Horton, Roberts. **Kansas City (15)**—Mayberry 6, Killebrew 2, Patek 2, Solaita 2, Brett, Otis, White. **Milwaukee (6)**—Aaron, Garcia, Lezcano, Mitchell, Porter, Yount. **Minnesota (8)**—Oliva 3, Briggs, Carew, Ford, Hisle, Roof. **New York (3)**—Bonds 2, Nettles. **Oakland (11)**—Williams 4, Bando 2, Jackson 2, Rudi 2, Mangual. **Texas (52)**—Burroughs 11, Harrah 8, Grieve 5, Howell 5, Hargrove 4, Spencer 4, Tovar 3, Cubbage 2, Fregosi 2, Moates 2, Smalley 2, Davis, Nelson, Randle, Sundberg.

# NO-HITTERS

### Including

**Review of Three '75 No-Hitters**
**Official Box Score of Each**
**Picture of Each Game**

## BATTING, PITCHING FEATURES
## THE SPORTING NEWS AWARDS

### Including

### BBWAA Awards

## MAJOR LEAGUE FARM SYSTEMS
## HALL OF FAME ELECTION

### Including

**Feature on Electees**
**All Hall-of-Famers Listed According to Years Selected**

# No-Hitters Scarce in 1975

## By MIKE DOUCHANT

The 1975 major league season was the first campaign since 1966 not to have as many as three complete game no-hitters.

One route-going no-hit game was performed in each circuit. The spectacles were authored by Nolan Ryan of the California Angels and Ed Halicki of the San Francisco Giants.

Nolan Ryan is all smiles as he stands with his wife, Ruth, after he pitched the fourth no-hitter of his career against Baltimore.

A third no-hitter occurred, of the multi-pitcher variety, on the final day of the major league season. Four Oakland Athletic hurlers combined to achieve the whitewash.

Also, for the fourth consecutive year no lefthanded pitcher attained no-hit distinction. The last southpaw to record such a feat was Ken Holtzman of the Chicago Cubs against the Cincinnati Reds on June 3, 1971.

The initial no-hitter of the 1975 season was thrown by Nolan Ryan against the Baltimore Orioles, June 1, in Anaheim, Calif. In his 12th start of the campaign, Ryan tied Sandy Koufax for the major league record of four career no-hitters. The hard-throwing righthander hurled the gems in a span of 109 starts. Ryan surely has defied the law of averages which states that a no-hitter is thrown once approximately every 1,500 games in the majors.

The Alvin, Tex., resident threw the first no-hit game against Baltimore since Bo Belinsky blanked the Orioles, May 5, 1962. Ryan is the only righthanded pitcher in Los Angeles-California Angel history to turn the trick. The last righthander to no-hit the St. Louis Brown-Baltimore Oriole franchise was Dick Fowler, September 9, 1945.

Angel third baseman Dave Chalk drove in the only run of the contest in the third inning. Ryan, the majors' strikeout king, was placid about the historic occasion, giving credence to a post-season revelation that he actually tossed the no-hit game with an ailing arm. Surgery was eventually required for calcium deposits.

### AT ANAHEIM—JUNE 1

| Baltimore | AB. | R. | H. | RBI. | E. | California | AB. | R. | H. | RBI. | E. |
|---|---|---|---|---|---|---|---|---|---|---|---|
| Singleton, rf | 4 | 0 | 0 | 0 | 0 | Remy, 2b | 3 | 0 | 1 | 0 | 0 |
| Shopay, cf | 3 | 0 | 0 | 0 | 0 | Rivers, cf | 4 | 1 | 1 | 0 | 0 |
| Bumbry, lf | 4 | 0 | 0 | 0 | 0 | Harper, dh | 4 | 0 | 1 | 0 | 0 |
| Baylor, dh | 2 | 0 | 0 | 0 | 0 | Chalk, 3b | 3 | 0 | 2 | 1 | 0 |
| Davis, dh | 2 | 0 | 0 | 0 | 0 | Llenas, lf | 3 | 0 | 1 | 0 | 0 |
| Grich, 2b | 2 | 0 | 0 | 0 | 0 | Nettles, lf | 0 | 0 | 0 | 0 | 0 |
| May, 1b | 3 | 0 | 0 | 0 | 0 | Stanton, rf | 2 | 0 | 1 | 0 | 0 |
| Robinson, 3b | 3 | 0 | 0 | 0 | 0 | Bochte, 1b | 3 | 0 | 1 | 0 | 0 |
| Hendricks, c | 3 | 0 | 0 | 0 | 0 | Rodriguez, c | 3 | 0 | 0 | 0 | 0 |
| Belanger, ss | 2 | 0 | 0 | 0 | 0 | Smith, ss | 2 | 0 | 1 | 0 | 1 |
| Grimsley, p | 0 | 0 | 0 | 0 | 0 | RYAN, p | 0 | 0 | 0 | 0 | 0 |
| Garland, p | 0 | 0 | 0 | 0 | 0 | | | | | | |
| Totals | 28 | 0 | 0 | 0 | 0 | Totals | 27 | 1 | 9 | 1 | 1 |

```
Baltimore ....................... 0  0  0     0  0  0     0  0  0—0
California ...................... 1  0  0     0  0  0     0  0  x—1
```

| Baltimore | IP. | H. | R. | ER. | BB. | SO. |
|---|---|---|---|---|---|---|
| Grimsley (L. 1-7) | 3⅓ | 8 | 1 | 1 | 0 | 1 |
| Garland | 4⅔ | 1 | 0 | 0 | 1 | 1 |

| California | IP. | H. | R. | ER. | BB. | SO. |
|---|---|---|---|---|---|---|
| RYAN (W. 9-3) | 9 | 0 | 0 | 0 | 4 | 9 |

Double plays—Baltimore 2. Left on bases—Baltimore 5, California 5. Stolen base—Belanger. Sacrifice hits—Stanton, Remy. Umpires—Morgenweck, Soar, Denkinger and Barnett. Time—2:01. Attendance—18,492.

The first no-hitter in the National League in over two years was fashioned by rangy Ed Halicki. The 6-foot-7, 220-pound righthander zeroed the New York Mets, 6-0, on August 24 in the second game of a doubleheader at Candlestick Park. In his 36th major league appearance, Halicki experienced a pitcher's supreme accomplishment.

It was the Giants' first no-hitter since Gaylord Perry blanked the St. Louis Cardinals, 1-0, September 17, 1968. Gary Thomasson headed the

Ed Halicki in eighth-inning action of his no-hitter.

## AT SAN FRANCISCO—AUGUST 24

### Second Game

| New York | AB | R | H | RBI | E | | San Francisco | AB | R | H | RBI | E |
|---|---|---|---|---|---|---|---|---|---|---|---|---|
| Unser, cf | 3 | 0 | 0 | 0 | 0 | | Thomas, 2b | 2 | 2 | 0 | 0 | 1 |
| Millan, 2b | 4 | 0 | 0 | 0 | 0 | | Rader, c | 3 | 2 | 1 | 0 | 0 |
| Garrett, 3b | 4 | 0 | 0 | 0 | 0 | | Thomasson, cf | 4 | 2 | 3 | 2 | 0 |
| Staub, rf | 3 | 0 | 0 | 0 | 0 | | Matthews, lf | 3 | 0 | 0 | 0 | 0 |
| Kingman, 1b | 3 | 0 | 0 | 0 | 0 | | Montanez, 1b | 4 | 0 | 2 | 2 | 0 |
| Milner, lf | 3 | 0 | 0 | 0 | 0 | | Speier, ss | 4 | 0 | 1 | 0 | 0 |
| Phillips, ss | 3 | 0 | 0 | 0 | 0 | | Ontiveros, rf | 4 | 0 | 1 | 0 | 0 |
| Stearns, c | 3 | 0 | 0 | 0 | 0 | | Miller, 3b | 3 | 0 | 0 | 0 | 0 |
| Swan, p | 1 | 0 | 0 | 0 | 0 | | HALICKI, p | 4 | 0 | 0 | 0 | 0 |
| Vail, ph | 0 | 0 | 0 | 0 | 0 | | | | | | | |
| Baldwin, p | 0 | 0 | 0 | 0 | 0 | | | | | | | |
| Alou, ph | 1 | 0 | 0 | 0 | 0 | | | | | | | |
| Totals | 28 | 0 | 0 | 0 | | | Totals | 31 | 6 | 8 | 4 | 1 |

```
New York ...................... 0  0  0   0  0  0   0  0  0—0
San Francisco ................. 2  0  0   0  2  0   2  0  x—6
```

| New York | IP | H | R | ER | BB | SO |
|---|---|---|---|---|---|---|
| Swan (L. 1-1) | 5 | 4 | 4 | 3 | 5 | |
| Baldwin | 3 | 4 | 2 | 2 | 2 | 1 |

| San Francisco | IP | H | R | ER | BB | SO |
|---|---|---|---|---|---|---|
| HALICKI (W. 8-10) | 9 | 0 | 0 | 0 | 2 | 10 |

Double play—New York 1. Left on bases—New York 3. San Francisco 6. Two-base hit—Speier. Three-base hit—Thomasson. Stolen bases—Thomas 3, Thomasson, Rader. Wild pitch—Baldwin. Umpires—Froemming, A. Williams, Runge and Vargo. Time—2:15. Attendance—24,132.

offensive attack with a 3-for-4 performance as the Giants scored a pair of runs in the first, fifth and seventh innings.

After achieving the third no-hit game in San Francisco history, Halicki said, "I was very fortunate—it's gotta be luck. If a no-hitter takes skill, guys like Tom Seaver, Nolan Ryan, Bob Gibson and Sandy Koufax would have 20 apiece."

The last no-hit game suffered by the Mets was against Bill Stoneman and the Montreal Expos, October 2, 1972. That contest was also part of a twin bill.

When four Oakland A's pitchers—Vida Blue, Glenn Abbott, Paul Lindblad and Rollie Fingers—no-hit the California Angels on September 28, several milestones were established.

It was the first time in major league history that as many as four pitchers combined to hurl a no-hitter. The last contest in which two or more hurlers participated in a no-hit game was on April 30, 1967, when the Baltimore Orioles' Steve Barber and Stu Miller lost to the Detroit Tigers.

Oakland's 5-0 win was the initial multi-pitcher no-hit game victory in major league history.

Also, it was the first occasion in which the Angels were thwarted since Earl Wilson of the Boston Red Sox blanked the California club, June 26, 1962.

Vida Blue started and pitched five hitless frames for the Athletics. Among the three relievers, the last 12 Angel batters were retired in order. Outfielder Reggie Jackson supplied most of the offense by driving in three runs with two homers.

## AT OAKLAND—SEPTEMBER 28

| California | AB. | R. | H. | RBI. | E. |
|---|---|---|---|---|---|
| Remy, 2b | 4 | 0 | 0 | 0 | 0 |
| Chalk, 3b | 2 | 0 | 0 | 0 | 0 |
| Rivers, ph | 1 | 0 | 0 | 0 | 0 |
| Stanton, cf | 3 | 0 | 0 | 0 | 0 |
| Balaz, rf | 3 | 0 | 0 | 0 | 0 |
| Bochte, 1b | 3 | 0 | 0 | 0 | 0 |
| Ro. Jackson, lf | 2 | 0 | 0 | 0 | 0 |
| Nettles, ph-lf | 1 | 0 | 0 | 0 | 0 |
| Dade, dh | 1 | 0 | 0 | 0 | 0 |
| Briggs, dh | 1 | 0 | 0 | 0 | 0 |
| Allietta, c | 3 | 0 | 0 | 0 | 0 |
| Hampton, ss | 2 | 0 | 0 | 0 | 1 |
| Collins, ph | 1 | 0 | 0 | 0 | 0 |
| Ross, p | 0 | 0 | 0 | 0 | 0 |
| Monge, p | 0 | 0 | 0 | 0 | 0 |
| Pactwa, p | 0 | 0 | 0 | 0 | 0 |
| Totals | 27 | 0 | 0 | 0 | 1 |

| Oakland | AB. | R. | H. | RBI. | E. |
|---|---|---|---|---|---|
| North, cf | 4 | 0 | 1 | 0 | 0 |
| Washington, lf | 4 | 2 | 1 | 0 | 0 |
| Tenace, c-1b | 3 | 1 | 0 | 0 | 0 |
| Re. Jackson, rf | 4 | 2 | 3 | 0 | |
| Bando, 3b | 4 | 0 | 2 | 0 | 0 |
| Williams, dh | 4 | 0 | 0 | 0 | 0 |
| Rudi, 1b | 1 | 0 | 0 | 0 | 0 |
| Holt, ph-1b | 1 | 0 | 0 | 0 | 0 |
| Harper, ph | 1 | 0 | 0 | 0 | 0 |
| Fosse, c | 0 | 0 | 0 | 0 | 0 |
| Campaneris, ss | 3 | 0 | 1 | 0 | 1 |
| Hopkins, pr | 1 | 0 | 0 | 0 | 0 |
| Martinez, 2b | 1 | 0 | 0 | 0 | 0 |
| Garner, 2b | 3 | 0 | 1 | 0 | 0 |
| Maxvill, ss | 1 | 0 | 0 | 0 | 0 |
| BLUE, p | 0 | 0 | 0 | 0 | 0 |
| ABBOTT, p | 0 | 0 | 0 | 0 | 0 |
| LINDBLAD, p | 0 | 0 | 0 | 0 | 0 |
| FINGERS, p | 0 | 0 | 0 | 0 | 0 |
| Totals | 34 | 5 | 9 | 5 | 1 |

```
California ......... 0 0 0   0 0   0—0
Oakland ........... 2 0 0   1 0 0 0   2 0 x—5
```

| California | IP. | H. | R. | ER. | BB. | SO. |
|---|---|---|---|---|---|---|
| Ross (L. 0-1) | 5 | 6 | 3 | 3 | 1 | 4 |
| Monge | 2 | 2 | 2 | 1 | | |
| Pactwa | 1 | 1 | 0 | 0 | 1 | 0 |

| Oakland | IP. | H. | R. | ER. | BB. | SO. |
|---|---|---|---|---|---|---|
| BLUE (W. 22-11) | 5 | 0 | 0 | 0 | 2 | 2 |
| ABBOTT | 1 | 0 | 0 | 0 | 0 | 1 |
| LINDBLAD | 1 | 0 | 0 | 0 | 0 | 1 |
| FINGERS | 2 | 0 | 0 | 0 | 0 | 2 |

Double play—Oakland 1. Left on bases—California 2, Oakland 8. Two-base hit—Bando. Home runs—Re. Jackson 2 (36). Stolen bases—Stanton, Hopkins, Bando. Umpires—Kunkel, DiMuro and Phillips. Time—1:59. Attendance—22,131.

The four Oakland pitchers who combined on a no-hitter: L. to R.— Vida Blue, Glenn Abbott, Paul Lindblad and Rollie Fingers. It was the first time in major league history that four men combined to hurl a no-hitter.

# A. L. Pitchers Lead in Low-Hit Games

## By CHRIS ROEWE

Major league pitchers authored 73 artistic efforts in which the opposition was limited to no more than two hits in 1975. American League moundsmen led the way with two no-hit games, nine one-hitters and 32 two-hitters for a total of 43 low-hit gems. There were 30 low-hit games hurled in the National, including one no-hitter, six one-hit games and 23 two-hitters.

Randy Jones, young lefthander of the Padres, was the leader in this category with four low-hit games, all fashioned before the hometown fans at San Diego Stadium. Jones blanked the Cardinals 1-0 on May 19, permitting only one single in the 10-inning win; stopped the Reds 2-1 on one hit, July 3; held the Astros to two safeties in winning 6-1, August 6 and edged the Braves 2-1 in another two-hit effort, September 10.

Ken Holtzman of the Athletics came within one putout of registering his third no-hit game as he shut out the Tigers 4-0, at Oakland, June 8. With two out in the ninth Tom Veryzer lofted a long fly to left-center and was credited with the Tigers' only hit when center fielder Bill North misjudged the ball and was unable to make the catch.

A complete list of major league one-hit and two-hit games follows:

### AMERICAN LEAGUE
#### One-Hit Games

April 26—Tanana (six and one-third innings) and Kirkwood (two and two-thirds innings), California vs. Oakland, 1-0—Fosse, single in sixth.

May 6—Coleman, Detroit vs. Milwaukee, 4-2—Scott, homer in first.

May 31—Hunter, New York vs. Texas, 6-0—Tovar, single in sixth.

May 31—Cuellar, Baltimore vs. California, 1-0—Bochte, single in third.

June 8—Palmer, Baltimore vs. Kansas City, 1-0—McRae, single in fourth.

June 8—Holtzman, Oakland vs. Detroit, 4-0—Veryzer, double in ninth.

June 10—J. Perry, Oakland vs. Baltimore, 3-0—Bumbry, single in sixth.

July 26—Cuellar, Baltimore vs. Milwaukee, 4-0—Scott, single in seventh.

Aug. 3—Splittorff, Kansas City vs. Oakland, 5-0—C. Washington, single in first.

#### Two-Hit Games

April 13—Medich, New York vs. Detroit, 6-0 (first game)—Sutherland, single in first; James, single in third.

April 19—Champion, Milwaukee vs. Cleveland, 3-0—Spikes, double in fifth; McCraw, single in sixth.

April 22—Jenkins, Texas vs. Oakland, 2-1—Williams, homer in second and single in seventh.

April 25—Tiant, Boston vs. Detroit, lost, 1-0—Meyer, homer in fifth; LeFlore, single in sixth.

May 10—Hunter, New York vs. Oakland, 3-0—North, single in third; C. Washington, single in fourth.

May 10—Broberg (seven innings) and Murphy (two innings), Milwaukee vs. Kansas City, 3-0—Martinez, single in sixth; Mayberry, double in seventh.

May 13—Ryan, California vs. New York, 5-0—Bonds and Chambliss, singles in seventh.

May 13—Bibby, Texas vs. Milwaukee, 5-0 (five innings)—Money and Sharp, singles in first.

May 18—Ryan (eight and two-thirds innings) and Kirkwood (one-third inning), California vs. Baltimore, 5-1—Bumbry, single in sixth; Davis, double in ninth.

May 20—Lee, Boston vs. Oakland, 7-0—Bando, double in fifth; Mangual, single in ninth.

May 31—Ruhle, Detroit vs. Chicago, 2-0—Henderson, single in fourth; Downing, single in fifth.

June 4—Odom, Cleveland vs. Kansas City, 4-0—McRae and Mayberry, singles in sixth.

June 6—Ryan, California vs. Milwaukee, 6-0—Aaron, single in sixth; Scott, single in eighth.

June 22—Figueroa, California vs. Texas, 1-0—Randle, single in second; Smalley, single in ninth.

June 22—Jefferson (five and two-thirds innings) and Upshaw (three and one-third innings), Chicago vs. Minnesota, 9-2 (second game)—Soderholm, single in sixth; Briggs, homer in seventh.

June 29—Holtzman (six and two-thirds innings) and Fingers (two and one-third innings), Oakland vs. California, 7-1—Harper and Stanton, doubles in first.

July 2—Wise, Boston vs. Milwaukee, 6-3 (first game)—Scott and Darwin, homers in ninth.

July  3—Hood (eight and one-third innings) and LaRoche (two-thirds inning), Cleveland vs. New York, 3-2—Bonds, homers in fourth and ninth.

July 17—Wood, Chicago vs. Detroit, 4-0 (first game)—LeFlore, single in third; Pierce, single in eighth.

July 22—G. Perry, Texas vs. Cleveland, 4-0—Manning, single in first; Gamble, single in second.

Aug.  1—G. Perry, Texas vs. California 2-1—Remy, single in first; Nettles, single in third.

Aug.  5—Palmer, Baltimore vs. Boston, 3-0—Fisk, double in fifth; Burleson, double in ninth.

Aug.  5—Bosman (eight and one-third innings) and Fingers (two-thirds inning), Oakland vs. Texas, 3-2 (first game)—Harrah, homer in second; Moates, single in sixth.

Aug.  5—Fitzmorris, Kansas City vs. Minnesota, 6-1—Briggs, double, and Soderholm, single, in fifth.

Aug. 11—Cuellar, Baltimore vs. Kansas City, 4-0—Mayberry, double in fourth; Brett, single in fifth.

Aug. 13—Palmer, Baltimore vs. Kansas City, 3-0—Stinson, double in third; Pinson, single in ninth.

Aug. 16—Moret (seven innings) and Willoughby (two innings), Boston vs. Chicago, 5-0—Stein, single in third; Dent, single in seventh.

Aug. 16—Bare, Detroit vs. California, 8-0—Chalk, single in seventh; Miley, single in eighth.

Aug. 23—Jenkins, Texas vs. Baltimore, 1-0—Hendricks, double in sixth; Bumbry, single in ninth.

Sept.  5—G. Perry, Texas vs. Oakland, 4-2—Martinez, single in third; Harper, double in ninth.

Sept. 21—Torrez, Baltimore vs. Milwaukee, 3-0—Sharp, single in third; Porter, single in fifth.

Sept. 23—Bird (one and one-third innings), McClure (six innings), Mingori (two-thirds inning) and Pattin (one inning), Kansas City vs. Texas, 4-0—Smalley, single in eighth; Fregosi, single in ninth.

## NATIONAL LEAGUE
### One-Hit Games

April 15—Sutton, Los Angeles vs. Cincinnati, 3-1—Bench, homer in seventh.

May  3—Fryman, Montreal vs. New York, 3-0—Stearns, double in fifth.

May 19—Jones, San Diego vs. St. Louis, 1-0 (ten innings)—Melendez, single in seventh.

July  3—Jones, San Diego vs. Cincinnati, 2-1—Plummer, double in eighth.

July 19—Stone (six and two-thirds innings) and Dettore one and one-third innings), Chicago vs. San Diego, lost, 2-1—Grubb, single in seventh.

Sept. 27—Carlton, Philadelphia vs. New York, 8-1—Millan, double in sixth.

### Two-Hit Games

April  9—Forsch, St. Louis vs. Montreal, 4-0—Foote, single in second; Scott, single in seventh.

April 13—Gullett, Cincinnati vs. San Diego, 10-0—Hundley, single in third; Winfield, single in fourth.

May  5—Rau, Los Angeles vs. Houston, 2-0—Rader, single in second; Dierker, single in third.

May 13—Hooton, Los Angeles vs. St. Louis, 5-0—Sizemore, double in fourth; Melendez, single in ninth.

May 18—Barr, San Francisco vs. St. Louis, 2-0—Brock, singles in seventh and ninth.

May 18—Brett, Pittsburgh vs. Los Angeles, 7-2—Lopes, single in first and homer in ninth.

May 20—Bonham, Chicago vs. Los Angeles, 2-1—Cey, single in second; Lacy, homer in fourth.

May 28—Nolan, Cincinnati vs. Montreal, 6-0—Mangual, double in first; Coggins, double in sixth.

June  4—Reuss (six innings), Giusti (two and one-third innings) and Hernandez (two-thirds inning), Pittsburgh vs. Cincinnati, 2-1—Concepcion, single, and Griffey, triple, in seventh.

June  4—Blair (five innings), Carrithers (two innings) and DeMola (two innings), Montreal vs. Los Angeles, lost, 3-0—Crawford and Cey, singles in eighth.

June  6—Forsch, St. Louis vs. Houston, 6-0—Cedeno, single in first; Dierker, single in third.

June  7—Carlton, Philadelphia vs. Los Angeles, 4-0—Wynn, single in fourth; Mota, single in eighth.

June 13—Lonborg, Philadelphia vs. Los Angeles, 5-1—Wynn, doubles in first and ninth.

June 24—Strom, San Diego vs. San Francisco, 3-0 (second game)—Murcer, single in first; Speier, single in second.

July 20—Halicki, San Francisco vs. Pittsburgh, 2-1 (first game)—Stargell, double in fourth; Sanguillen, homer in ninth.

Aug.  6—Jones, San Diego vs. Houston, 6-1—Watson, triple in second; Gross, single in seventh.

Aug. 18—Tate (four innings), Lockwood (two innings) and Apodaca (two innings), New York vs. Houston, lost, 4-0—DaVanon double, and Richard, single, in fourth.

Aug. 19—Sutton (six innings) and Marshall (three innings), Los Angeles vs. Chicago, 2-1—Madlock, triple in fourth; Morales, single in seventh.

Aug. 23—Montefusco (eight innings) and Lavelle (one inning), San Francisco vs. New York, 2-1—Unser, homer in fourth; Phillips, single in eighth.

Sept. 10—Jones, San Diego vs. Atlanta, 2-1—Garr and Baker, singles in seventh.

Sept. 15—Rooker, Pittsburgh vs. Chicago, 9-1 (second game)—Tyrone, single in first; Trillo, single in fourth.

Sept. 21—Gullett (seven innings) and Eastwick (two innings), Cincinnati vs. Atlanta, 3-0—May, single in fourth; Blanks, single in fifth.

Sept. 26—Richard, Houston vs. Los Angeles, lost, 3-2—Garvey, single in second and homer in ninth.

# Tanana Is New Strikeout Leader

## By LARRY WIGGE

From THE SPORTING NEWS' Rookie Pitcher of the Year to major league strikeout leader in one season, California's Frank Tanana was the only big league hurler to post a 15-strikeout game in 1975. Within a period of nine days in June, Tanana struck out 17 Texas Rangers and 15 Minnesota Twins.

The stylish Angel southpaw replaced teammate Nolan Ryan as the majors' leading strikeout artist, with 269 in 257 innings. Ryan had reigned as major league strikeout king for three seasons.

Tanana fanned 17 Texas batters in the first game of a twi-night doubleheader, won by the Angels, 4-2, at Anaheim Stadium on June 21. The 21-year-old lefty whiffed every batter in the Ranger lineup at least once to finish just two shy of the nine-inning game strikeout mark held jointly by Steve Carlton, Tom Seaver and Ryan, plus two pre-1900 pitchers.

Nine days later Tanana snapped a seven-game California losing streak with 15 strikeouts in a 10-3 triumph over the Twins at Metropolitan Stadium.

A complete record of Tanana's 15-strikeout games follows:

| Date | Pitcher—Club—Opp. | Place | IP. | H. | R. | ER. | BB. | SO. | Result |
|------|-------------------|-------|-----|----|----|-----|-----|-----|--------|
| June 21*— | Tanana, Angels vs. Rangers.. | H | 9 | 9 | 2 | 2 | 0 | 17 | W 4-2 |
| June 30 — | Tanana, Angels vs. Twins...... | A | 9 | 8 | 3 | 3 | 2 | 15 | W 10-3 |

*First game of doubleheader.

John (The Count) Montefusco of San Francisco, who finished with 215 strikeouts, 12 short of Grover Cleveland Alexander's National League rookie mark set in 1911, paced N. L. pitchers with seven 10-strikeout efforts in 1975. He had the N. L. single-game tops with 14 strikeouts.

Tanana's eight games with 10 or more strikeouts also led the majors. All pitchers to accomplish this feat plus the number of times achieved follow:

AMERICAN LEAGUE: Baltimore (2)—Cuellar, Palmer. Boston (3)—Tiant 2, Segui. California (14)—Tanana 8, Ryan 4, Hassler, Singer. Chicago—None. Cleveland (2)—Eckersley 2. Detroit—None. Kansas City (2)—Briles, Littell. Milwaukee—None. Minnesota (5)—Blyleven 5. New York (2)—Hunter, May. Oakland (2)—Blue 2. Texas (5)—Perry 5.

NATIONAL LEAGUE: Atlanta—None. Chicago (2)—Bonham, R. Reuschel. Cincinnati (1)—Gullett. Houston—None. Los Angeles (6)—Hooton 3, Sutton 2, Messersmith. Montreal (1)—Fryman. New York (7)—Koosman 3, Seaver 3, Tate. Philadelphia (2)—Carlton 2. Pittsburgh (2)—Candelaria, Reuss. St. Louis (3)—McGlothen 2, Gibson. San Diego—None. San Francisco (13)—Montefusco 7, Halicki 5, Falcone.

# Gossage and Hrabosky Top Firemen

## By CHRIS ROEWE

Young fast-ballers Rich Gossage of the White Sox and Al Hrabosky of the Cardinals captured the 1975 Fireman of the Year awards. THE SPORTING NEWS makes the awards annually in recognition of the contributions made by major league relief pitchers.

One point is credited for each save and one for each win in relief. Both winners totaled 35 points. Gossage led all relievers in saves with 26 and won nine in relief while Hrabosky had 22 saves and picked up 13 victories in late-inning Cardinal rallies.

Hrabosky had no real competition for the N.L. title, winning by eight points over his closest pursuer, Rawly Eastwick of the pennant-winning Reds. Husky southpaw Hrabosky fashioned a gaudy 1.67 ERA in winning 13 while losing only three for a club that finished barely above the .500 mark.

Tied for third place with 24 points were Gene Garber of the Phillies, who appeared in 71 games, tops in the league, and the Expos' Dale Murray, who led all relievers in both circuits in wins with 15.

Gossage permitted only 99 hits and fanned 130 batters in 142 innings, compiling a 9-8 mark for the lowly White Sox. He succeeded his teammate, Terry Forster, as A.L. Fireman of the Year after a season-long battle with Rollie Fingers, veteran rescue ace of the defending world champion A's.

Fingers' 24 saves and 10 wins left him one point short of Gossage's winning total. Had the A's not scored twice in the seventh inning of their last game September 28, giving them a five-run lead prior to Fingers' entry into the game, his two scoreless innings would have earned him a save and a tie for the top rung.

Curiously, this was the game in which four Oakland pitchers combined to hurl a no-hitter against the Angels.

Dave LaRoche of the Indians finished a distant third with 22 points and the Brewers' Tom Murphy had 20 saves and one victory for fourth place.

The 1974 winners, Forster and Mike Marshall of the Dodgers, were both sidelined by arm injuries and had little chance to repeat. Marshall finished in a sixth-place tie with 13 saves and nine relief wins. Forster missed practically the last three months of the season and totaled only seven points.

The rules for earning saves were rewritten in 1975 for the second successive year, but there were no radical changes and individual totals were comparable to 1974 results.

A complete list of saves and wins in relief by major league hurlers in 1975 follows:

RICH GOSSAGE
Chicago, A.L.

AL HRABOSKY
St. Louis, N.L.

## AMERICAN LEAGUE

| Pitcher—Club | Saves | Relief Wins | Tot. Pts. | Pitcher—Club | Saves | Relief Wins | Tot. Pts. |
|---|---|---|---|---|---|---|---|
| Gossage, Chicago | 26 | 9 | 35 | Moret, Boston | 1 | 4 | 5 |
| Fingers, Oakland | 24 | 10 | 34 | Reynolds, Balt.-Det.-Cleve. | 5 | 0 | 5 |
| LaRoche, Cleveland | 17 | 5 | 22 | Scott, California | 1 | 4 | 5 |
| Murphy, Milwaukee | 20 | 1 | 21 | Umbarger, Texas | 2 | 3 | 5 |
| Bird, Kansas City | 11 | 9 | 20 | Albury, Minnesota | 1 | 3 | 4 |
| Todd, Oakland | 12 | 8 | 20 | Alexander, Baltimore | 1 | 3 | 4 |
| Foucault, Texas | 10 | 8 | 18 | Austin, Milwaukee | 2 | 2 | 4 |
| Drago, Boston | 15 | 2 | 17 | Brown, Texas-Cleveland | 1 | 3 | 4 |
| Burgmeier, Minnesota | 11 | 5 | 16 | Johnson, Minnesota | 3 | 1 | 4 |
| Hiller, Detroit | 14 | 2 | 16 | Briles, Kansas City | 2 | 1 | 3 |
| Lindblad, Oakland | 7 | 9 | 16 | Cleveland, Boston | 0 | 3 | 3 |
| Miller, Baltimore | 8 | 6 | 14 | Eckersley, Cleveland | 2 | 1 | 3 |
| Rodriguez, Milwaukee | 7 | 7 | 14 | Hausman, Milwaukee | 0 | 3 | 3 |
| Hamilton, Oakland-Chicago | 6 | 7 | 13 | Lange, California | 1 | 2 | 3 |
| Kirkwood, California | 7 | 6 | 13 | Osborn, Chicago | 0 | 3 | 3 |
| Willoughby, Boston | 8 | 5 | 13 | Waits, Cleveland | 1 | 2 | 3 |
| Buskey, Cleveland | 7 | 5 | 12 | Abbott, Oakland | 0 | 2 | 2 |
| Jackson, Baltimore | 7 | 4 | 11 | Beene, Cleveland | 1 | 1 | 2 |
| Lyle, New York | 6 | 5 | 11 | Bibby, Texas-Cleveland | 1 | 1 | 2 |
| Tidrow, New York | 5 | 6 | 11 | Broberg, Milwaukee | 0 | 2 | 2 |
| Pattin, Kansas City | 5 | 4 | 9 | Burton, Boston | 1 | 1 | 2 |
| Martinez, New York | 8 | 1 | 9 | Butler, Minnesota | 0 | 2 | 2 |
| Segui, Boston | 6 | 2 | 8 | Castro, Milwaukee | 1 | 1 | 2 |
| Forster, Chicago | 4 | 3 | 7 | Colborn, Milwaukee | 2 | 0 | 2 |
| Thomas, Texas | 3 | 4 | 7 | Corbin, Minnesota | 0 | 2 | 2 |
| Brewer, California | 5 | 1 | 6 | Gogolewski, Chicago | 2 | 0 | 2 |
| Campbell, Minnesota | 5 | 1 | 6 | Kekich, Texas | 2 | 0 | 2 |
| Garland, Baltimore | 4 | 2 | 6 | Lemanczyk, Detroit | 0 | 2 | 2 |
| McDaniel, Kansas City | 1 | 5 | 6 | McClure, Kansas City | 1 | 1 | 2 |

| Pitcher—Club | Saves | Relief Wins | Tot. Pts. | Pitcher—Club | Saves | Relief Wins | Tot. Pts. |
|---|---|---|---|---|---|---|---|
| Mingori, Kansas City | 2 | 0 | 2 | Throop, Kansas City | 2 | 0 | 2 |
| Mitchell, Baltimore | 0 | 2 | 2 | Upshaw, Chicago | 1 | 1 | 2 |
| Splittorff, Kansas City | 1 | 1 | 2 | Wiley, Minnesota | 2 | 0 | 2 |

One Save—Blue, Oakland; Hockenbery, California; Pagan, New York; Palmer, Baltimore; Singer, California; Sprague, Milwaukee; Strickland, Cleveland; Travers, Milwaukee.

One Relief Win—Arroyo, Detroit; Bare, Detroit; Champion, Milwaukee; Hargan, Texas; Hinton, Chicago; Holtzman, Oakland; Hood, Cleveland; Hughes, Minnesota; Leonard, Kansas City; Littell, Kansas City; Pole, Boston; Raich, Cleveland; Sadecki, Kansas City; Walker, Detroit; Wright, Texas.

## NATIONAL LEAGUE

| Pitcher—Club | Saves | Relief Wins | Tot. Pts. | Pitcher—Club | Saves | Relief Wins | Tot. Pts. |
|---|---|---|---|---|---|---|---|
| Hrabosky, St. Louis | 22 | 13 | 35 | Brewer, Los Angeles | 2 | 3 | 5 |
| Eastwick, Cincinnati | 22 | 5 | 27 | Cosgrove, Houston | 5 | 0 | 5 |
| Garber, Philadelphia | 14 | 10 | 24 | Dal Canton, Atlanta | 3 | 2 | 5 |
| Murray, Montreal | 9 | 15 | 24 | De Mola, Montreal | 1 | 4 | 5 |
| McGraw, Philadelphia | 14 | 9 | 23 | Fryman, Montreal | 3 | 2 | 5 |
| Giusti, Pittsburgh | 17 | 5 | 22 | Parker, New York-St. Louis | 3 | 2 | 5 |
| Marshall, Los Angeles | 13 | 9 | 22 | Tomlin, San Diego | 1 | 4 | 5 |
| Knowles, Chicago | 15 | 6 | 21 | Beard, Atlanta | 0 | 4 | 4 |
| McEnaney, Cincinnati | 15 | 5 | 20 | Dettore, Chicago | 0 | 4 | 4 |
| House, Atlanta | 11 | 7 | 18 | Forsch, Houston | 2 | 2 | 4 |
| Apodaca, New York | 13 | 3 | 16 | Heaverlo, San Francisco | 1 | 3 | 4 |
| Moffitt, San Francisco | 11 | 4 | 15 | Scherman, Houston-Montreal | 0 | 4 | 4 |
| Zamora, Chicago | 10 | 5 | 15 | E. Sosa, St. Louis-Atlanta | 2 | 2 | 4 |
| Borbon, Cincinnati | 5 | 9 | 14 | Darcy, Cincinnati | 1 | 2 | 3 |
| C. Carroll, Cincinnati | 7 | 7 | 14 | Downing, Los Angeles | 1 | 2 | 3 |
| Lavelle, San Francisco | 8 | 6 | 14 | Frailing, Chicago | 1 | 2 | 3 |
| Garman, St. Louis | 10 | 3 | 13 | Gibson, St. Louis | 2 | 1 | 3 |
| Greif, San Diego | 9 | 4 | 13 | Hall, Cincinnati-New York | 1 | 2 | 3 |
| Hernandez, Pittsburgh | 5 | 7 | 12 | Kirby, Cincinnati | 0 | 3 | 3 |
| Frisella, San Diego | 9 | 1 | 10 | Lockwood, New York | 2 | 1 | 3 |
| Baldwin, New York | 6 | 3 | 9 | Roberts, Houston | 1 | 2 | 3 |
| Demery, Pittsburgh | 4 | 4 | 8 | Sadecki, St. Louis-Atlanta | 1 | 2 | 3 |
| Taylor, Montreal | 6 | 2 | 8 | Zahn, Los Angeles-Chicago | 1 | 2 | 3 |
| Williams, San Francisco | 3 | 5 | 8 | Barr, San Francisco | 0 | 2 | 2 |
| Crawford, Houston | 4 | 3 | 7 | Caldwell, San Francisco | 1 | 1 | 2 |
| Granger, Houston | 5 | 2 | 7 | Johnson, San Diego | 0 | 2 | 2 |
| Hilgendorf, Philadelphia | 0 | 7 | 7 | Koosman, New York | 2 | 0 | 2 |
| Hough, Los Angeles | 4 | 3 | 7 | Montague, Montreal-Phila. | 2 | 0 | 2 |
| Leon, Atlanta | 6 | 1 | 7 | Schueler, Philadelphia | 0 | 2 | 2 |
| Niekro, Houston | 4 | 3 | 7 | Schultz, Chicago | 0 | 2 | 2 |
| Warthen, Montreal | 3 | 4 | 7 | Siebert, Houston | 2 | 0 | 2 |
| P. Reuschel, Chicago | 5 | 1 | 6 | J. Sosa, Houston | 1 | 1 | 2 |
| Sanders, New York | 5 | 1 | 6 | Webb, New York | 0 | 2 | 2 |
| Tekulve, Pittsburgh | 5 | 1 | 6 | | | | |

One Save—Acosta, Philadelphia; Christenson, Philadelphia; Curtis, St. Louis; Harrison, Atlanta; Messersmith, Los Angeles; Renko, Montreal; R. Reuschel, Chicago; Spillner, San Diego; Stanton, Houston.

One Relief Win—Brett, Pittsburgh; T. Carroll, Cincinnati; Crosby, Chicago; D'Acquisto, San Francisco; Folkers, San Diego; Foster, San Diego; Gentry, Atlanta; Jones, San Diego; Kison, Pittsburgh; McDowell, Pittsburgh; McIntosh, San Diego; Metzger, San Diego; Moose, Pittsburgh; Norman, Cincinnati; Richard, Houston; York, Houston.

# 1-0 Games Decline in 1975

## By CHRIS ROEWE

The 1975 major league season produced 43 games in which only one run scored, a decline of 20 from the previous year.

California was involved in the most 1-0 contests, winning six and losing four. San Diego had a perfect 4-0 record while the Rangers and Cardinals each had 5-2 marks.

Baltimore's Jim Palmer led in 1-0 victories with three. The Orioles' meal ticket blanked the Brewers at Milwaukee, April 22, stopped the Angels in the first game of a doubleheader at Baltimore, May 16, and hurled a one-hitter in victimizing the Royals at Memorial Stadium, June 8.

Randy Jones of the Padres, John Montefusco of the Giants, Frank Tanana of the Angels and Jim Umbarger of the Rangers each were credited with two 1-0 wins. The Dodgers' Andy Messersmith was the unfortunate loser in three minimum-score games.

Ten of these battles were decided by home runs, with Bobby Grich of the Orioles the only hitter to supply the clincher more than once. Grich homered on April 22 and May 16, each time providing the only run needed by Jim Palmer.

The complete list of 1-0 games, including the winning and losing pitchers and the innings in which the runs were scored, follows:

### AMERICAN LEAGUE (23)

**APRIL—**

| Date | Winner | Loser | Inning |
|---|---|---|---|
| 22 — | Palmer, Baltimore | *Broherg, Milwaukee | 8 |
| 25 — | Lolich, Detroit | Tiant, Boston | 5 |
| 26 —* | Tanana, California | Holtzman, Oakland | 3 |

**MAY—**

| | | | |
|---|---|---|---|
| 4 —* | Hands, Texas | Hassler, California | 4 |
| 16† — | Palmer, Baltimore | Tanana, California | 9 |
| 31 — | Cuellar, Baltimore | Singer, California | |

**JUNE—**

| | | | |
|---|---|---|---|
| 1 — | Ryan, California | *Grimsley, Baltimore | 3 |
| 8 — | Palmer, Baltimore | Busby, Kansas City | 7 |
| 9 —* | Rodriguez, Mil. | *Gossage, Chicago | 9 |
| 22 — | Figueroa, Calif. | Jenkins, Texas | 4 |
| 23 —* | Umbarger, Texas | *Kirkwood, Calif. | 13 |

**JULY—**

| | | | |
|---|---|---|---|
| 18 — | Perry, Texas | Hunter, New York | 7 |
| 23 — | Tanana, California | Palmer, Baltimore | 1 |
| 24‡ —* | Hamilton, Chicago | *Gura, New York | 8 |
| 27† — | Lee, Boston | Hunter, New York | 9 |
| 30 —* | Holtzman, Oakland | Jenkins, Texas | 3 |

**AUGUST—**

| | | | |
|---|---|---|---|
| 9 — | Goltz, Minnesota | Lolich, Detroit | 4 |
| 10 —* | Scott, California | May, New York | 9 |
| 23 — | Jenkins, Texas | Cuellar, Baltimore | 6 |
| 25 — | Umbarger, Texas | Bare, Detroit | 2 |
| 27 — | Blyleven, Minn. | *Travers, Milwaukee | 11 |

**SEPTEMBER—**

| | | | |
|---|---|---|---|
| 19 —* | Pactwa, California | Blyleven, Minnesota | 4 |
| 27 —* | Gossage, Chicago | Blyleven, Minnesota | 8 |

### NATIONAL LEAGUE (20)

**APRIL—**

| Date | Winner | Loser | Inning |
|---|---|---|---|
| | None. | | |

**MAY—**

| | | | |
|---|---|---|---|
| 19 — | Jones, San Diego | Curtis, St. Louis | 10 |
| 21 — | McIntosh, San D. | Gibson, St. Louis | 7 |
| 26 —* | McGraw, Phila. | Halicki, San Fran. | 11 |
| 27 — | Montefusco, S.F. | *Garber, Phila. | 10 |

**JUNE—**

| | | | |
|---|---|---|---|
| 2 — | McGlothen, St. L. | *Morton, Atlanta | 4 |
| 4 — | Koosman, N.Y. | *Konieczny, Houston | 1 |
| 23† — | Reed, St. Louis | *Webb, New York | 1 |
| 28 — | Bonham, Chicago | Rooker, Pittsburgh | 2 |

**JULY—**

| | | | |
|---|---|---|---|
| 4 — | Montefusco, S.F. | *Messersmith, Los. A. | 5 |
| 5† — | Curtis, St. Louis | *Fryman, Montreal | 4 |
| 17 —* | Hrabosky, St. L. | Barr, San Francisco | 9 |
| 19 — | Christenson, Phila. | *Dierker, Houston | 4 |
| 21 —* | R. Reuschel, Chi. | Messersmith, Los. A. | 9 |
| 22 — | Carlton, Phila. | Morton, Atlanta | 9 |
| 22 — | Jones, San Diego | *Kison, Pittsburgh | 6 |

**AUGUST—**

| | | | |
|---|---|---|---|
| 2 —* | T. Carroll, Cin. | *Messersmith, Los.A. | 5 |
| 8† — | Morton, Atlanta | *Dettore, Chicago | 1 |

**SEPTEMBER—**

| | | | |
|---|---|---|---|
| 12 —* | Tomlin, San Diego | *York, Houston | 9 |
| 24 —* | Crosby, Chicago | *Lockwood, N.Y. | 11 |
| 26 — | Forsch, St. Louis | *Rooker, Pittsburgh | 1 |

*Did not pitch complete game. †First game of doubleheader. ‡Second game of doubleheader.

# Texas Rangers Lead Majors in Grand-Slams

## By CHRIS ROEWE

Grand-slam home run production fell off in 1975. Major league hitters totaled only 52 boundary belts with the bases loaded as compared to 76 the previous season.

The Texas Rangers led all clubs in grand-slams with five while the Athletics, Reds and Dodgers each hit four.

Top individual total was two, achieved by five players: Tommy Davis of the Orioles, Lee Stanton of the Angels, Joe Rudi of the Athletics, Johnny Bench of the Reds and Ted Simmons of the Cardinals. Bench's two were hit on May 7 and May 26, tying the National League mark for most bases-loaded homers in one month.

Willie McCovey hit his 16th career grand-slam as a pinch-hitter against the Mets May 30, at Shea Stadium. The homer tied the veteran Padre first baseman with Hank Aaron for most National League grand-slams. The major league mark is 23 by the great Lou Gehrig.

The most dramatic blow was struck by Cliff Johnson of the Astros at St. Louis, June 15. With the Cardinals leading 7-4 in the ninth and the bases loaded with one out, Johnson came up as a pinch-hitter against Mike Garman and lined a homer into the center field stands to turn impending defeat into an 8-7 victory.

A complete list of grand-slam homers with the inning in which each was hit in parentheses, follows:

### AMERICAN LEAGUE (28)

**APRIL—**
9 —Tenace, Oakland vs. Kaat, Chicago... (3)
1/2 —Colbert, Detroit vs. Dobson, New York (7)

**MAY—**
7 —Bando, Oakland vs. Dobson, Calif.... (7)
21 —Yastrzemski, Boston vs. Holtzman, Oak. (7)

**JUNE—**
6 —Evans, Boston vs. Decker, Minn...... (1)
9 —Carbo, Boston vs. Brown, Texas...... (6)
9 —Sundberg, Texas vs. Wise, Boston.... (7)
11* —Stanton, Calif. vs. Reynolds, Det.... (8)
15* —Stanton, Calif. vs. Rodriguez, Mil... (3)
16 —Thomas, Milwaukee vs. May, N.Y.... (4)
18 —Rudi, Oakland vs. Albury, Minn..... (7)
18 —Smalley, Texas vs. Gogolewski, Chi... (8)
20 —Cubbage, Texas vs. Singer, Calif..... (1)
25 —White, K.C. vs. Quintana, Calif......(12)
26 —Melton, Chicago vs. Jenkins, Texas... (8)
29 —Oliva, Minnesota vs. Umbarger, Texas. (6)

**JULY—**
5 —Bell, Cleveland vs. Barr, Boston...... (2)
18 —Hendricks, Balt. vs. Goltz, Minn..... (4)
19 —Kelly, Chicago vs. Travers, Mil...... (2)
19 —Rodriguez, Det. vs. Bird, K.C........ (6)
20 —Stein, Chicago vs. Broberg, Mil...... (4)
27† —Davis, Baltimore vs. Austin, Mil.....(10)
29 —Harrah, Texas vs. Perry, Oakland.... (1)

**AUGUST—**
1* —Davis, Baltimore vs. Champion, Mil... (5)
5† —Howell, Texas vs. Todd, Oakland..... (6)
7 —Rudi, Oakland vs. Moore, Texas...... (7)
29 —Manning, Cleve. vs. Albury, Minn..... (8)

**SEPTEMBER—**
28 —Ashby, Cleveland vs. Pole, Boston.... (5)

### NATIONAL LEAGUE (24)

**APRIL—**
16 —Wynn, Los Angeles vs. Darcy, Cin.... (7)
23 —Staub, New York vs. Gibson, St. L.... (5)
24 —McMullen, L.A. vs. Tomlin, S.D..... (6)

**MAY—**
6 —Jorgensen, Mont. vs. R. Reuschel, Chi. (4)
7 —Bench, Cin. vs. Foster, San Diego.... (5)
20 —Correll, Atlanta vs. Montague, Mont... (8)
26† —Bench, Cin. vs. Renko, Montreal..... (5)
30 —McCovey, San Diego vs. Apodaca, N.Y. (8)

**JUNE—**
13 —Oliver, Pitts. vs. Beard, Atlanta..... (4)
13 —Martin, Phila. vs. Messersmith, L.A... (7)
15 —Johnson, Houston vs. Garman, St. L... (9)
17 —May, Atlanta vs. Nolan, Cincinnati... (8)
18 —Cey, Los Angeles vs. Griffin, Houston. (1)
23† —Simmons, St. Louis vs. Matlack, N.Y.. (8)

**JULY—**
1 —Ivie, San Diego vs. Brewer, L.A...... (5)
8 —Fairly, St. Louis vs. Falcone, San F.. (8)
18 —Perez, Cincinnati vs. Blair, Montreal. (3)

**AUGUST—**
4 —Foster, Cin. vs. Moffitt, San. F...... (8)
23 —Simmons, St. Louis vs. Niekro, Atl... (5)
23 —Summers, Chicago vs. York, Houston.. (7)
24* —Kingman, New York vs. Barr, San F... (5)

**SEPTEMBER—**
3 —LaCock, Chicago vs. Gibson, St. Louis. (7)
14 —Hosley, Chicago vs. Lerch, Phila...... (5)
27 —Yeager, Los Angeles vs. Forsch, Hous. (3)
*First game of doubleheader.
†Second game of doubleheader.

# Lynn Has 10 RBIs in 3-Homer Game

### By LARRY WIGGE

Two days after Boston outfielder Fred Lynn had a 20-game hitting streak snapped, the 23-year-old Bosox bopper banged out five hits good for 10 runs batted in. Included in the five-hit performance were a single, triple and three home runs. Lynn was one of four American Leaguers who achieved this home run-hitting feat in 1975.

Consistent and powerful, Lynn, only a rookie, belted a two-run homer in the first inning of a June 18 game at Detroit, won by Boston 15-1. He blasted a three-run clout in the second and, just missing another in the third, tripled for two more runs. He lined out in the fifth, singled in the eighth and capped an unforgettable night with another three-run bonanza in the ninth. Lynn's 10 RBIs were one short of Tony Lazzeri's A.L. record and two shy of Jim Bottomley's major mark.

Kansas City's John Mayberry had three solo homers in a 5-4 loss at Texas July 1. One day later, Baltimore's Don Baylor had a two-run homer and two solo shots at Detroit in a 13-5 victory. Samoan-born Tony Solaita accounted for Kansas City's second three-homer game with three solo homers and a game-winning single in an 8-7 11-inning triumph at Anaheim Stadium September 7.

A complete record of the three-homer games follows:

| Date | Player—Opposition | Place | AB. | R. | H. | 2B. | 3B. | HR. | RBI. | Result |
|---|---|---|---|---|---|---|---|---|---|---|
| June 18 | Lynn, Red Sox vs. Tigers | A | 6 | 4 | 5 | 0 | 1 | 3 | 10 | W 15-1 |
| July 1 | Mayberry, Roy'ls vs. Ran'rs | A | 4 | 3 | 3 | 0 | 0 | 3 | 3 | L 5-4 |
| July 2 | Baylor, Orioles vs. Tigers | A | 4 | 3 | 3 | 0 | 0 | 3 | 5 | W 13-5 |
| Sept. 7* | Solaita, Royals vs. Angels | A | 4 | 3 | 4 | 0 | 0 | 3 | 4 | W 8-7 |

*11-inning game.

Bobby Bonds of the Yankees, Milwaukee's George Scott and Philadelphia's Mike Schmidt paced hitters with four multiple-homer games in 1975. A listing of players with two or more homers in a game and the number of times achieved follows:

AMERICAN LEAGUE: Baltimore (6)—Duncan 2, May 2, Baylor, Grich. Boston (10)—Carbo 3, Lynn 2, Rice 2, Evans, Fisk, Yastrzemski. California (2)—Harper, Lahoud. Chicago (2)—Henderson, D. Johnson. Cleveland (7)—Hendrick 2, Powell 2, Robinson 2, Bell. Detroit (5)—Horton 2, Freehan, Rodriguez, Sutherland. Kansas City (7)—Mayberry 2, Solaita 2, Killebrew. Milwaukee (10)—Scott 4, Money 3, Hegan, Mitchell, Porter. Minnesota (6)—Ford 2, Soderholm 2, Brye, Carew. New York (8)—Bonds 4, Nettles 2, Chambliss, White. Oakland (11)—Jackson 3, Williams 3, Rudi 2, Bando, Tenace, C. Washington. Texas (2)—Burroughs, Howell.

NATIONAL LEAGUE: Atlanta (4)—Baker 2, Correll, Evans. Chicago (3)—Cardenal, Madlock, Thornton. Cincinnati (3)—Foster 2, Bench. Houston (5)—Cedeno 2, Rader 2, Cruz. Los Angeles (5)—Cey 2, Ferguson, Garvey, Wynn. Montreal (1)—Carter. New York (3)—Kingman 3. Philadelphia (7)—Schmidt 4, Luzinski 2, Allen. Pittsburgh (4)—Zisk 2, Parker, Stargell. St. Louis (4)—Bradford, McBride, Simmons, Smith. San Diego (1)—McCovey. San Francisco (3)—Adams, Matthews, Murcer.

# Stennett Hit Spree Shatters Marks

### By CHRIS ROEWE

Two National League infielders, Rennie Stennett of the Pirates and Bill Madlock of the Cubs, joined the exclusive ranks of major leaguers who have made more than five hits in one game in 1975.

Stennett re-wrote the record book as the Pirates slaughtered the Cubs September 16 at Chicago, 22-0. Rennie went seven-for-seven to become only the second player to get seven safeties in a nine-inning game. Wilbert Robinson of the old Baltimore Orioles set the mark, June 10, 1892. Stennett doubled and singled in the first inning, singled in the third, doubled and singled in the fifth, singled in the seventh and tripled in the eighth. His two hits in both the first and fifth tied the major league record for most times two hits in one inning in one game.

The next day in Philadelphia Stennett had three hits for a total of ten in two consecutive nine-inning games, establishing a modern (since 1900) major league mark. On September 18 Rennie made two more hits against the Phillies for a total of 12 in three consecutive nine-inning games, tying the modern National League record.

Batting champion Bill Madlock had six hits in six trips to the plate in a losing cause as the Cubs dropped a 10-inning slugfest to the Mets 9-8, at Wrigley Field, July 26. Madlock began his assault with a triple in the first and then delivered singles in the third, fourth, sixth, eighth and 10th ininngs off a quintet of New York pitchers.

Records of all players with five or more hits in one game follow:

| Date | Player—Opposition | Place | AB | R. | H. | 2B. | 3B. | HR | RBI. | Result |
|------|-------------------|-------|----|----|----|----|----|----|----|--------|
| April 17 | Garvey, Dodgers vs. Reds (11 innings) | H | 6 | 1 | 5 | 1 | 0 | 0 | 1 | W 5-4 |
| May 4 | Smith, Cardinals vs. Cubs | H | 5 | 2 | 5 | 1 | 0 | 2 | 5 | L 8-6 |
| May 25 | Rader, Astros vs. Expos (12 innings) | H | 6 | 3 | 5 | 3 | 0 | 0 | 1 | W 8-7 |
| June 13 | Geronimo, Reds vs. Cubs | A | 6 | 2 | 5 | 1 | 0 | 0 | 1 | W 18-11 |
| June 14* | Bench, Reds vs. Cubs | A | 5 | 2 | 5 | 2 | 0 | | 1 | W 11-3 |
| June 18 | Lynn, Red Sox vs. Tigers | A | 6 | 4 | 5 | 0 | 1 | 3 | 10 | W 15-1 |
| June 20 | Collins, Angels vs. Rangers (11 innings) | H | 6 | 1 | 5 | 1 | 1 | 0 | 2 | W 12-11 |
| July 13 | Yastrzemski, Red Sox vs. Rangers (10 innings) | H | 5 | 2 | 5 | 2 | 0 | 0 | 1 | 1 7-5 |
| July 26 | Madlock, Cubs vs. Mets | H | 6 | 1 | 6 | 0 | 1 | 0 | 3 | L 9-8 |
| July 30 | Sanguillen, Pirates vs. Phillies | H | 5 | 3 | 5 | 0 | 0 | 1 | 2 | W 8-1 |
| Aug. 1 | Rose, Reds vs. Dodgers (10 innings) | A | 5 | 1 | 5 | 2 | 0 | 0 | 0 | L 5-3 |
| Aug. 4 | Baylor, Orioles vs. Red Sox | A | 5 | 4 | 5 | 0 | 0 | 1 | 3 | W 12-8 |
| Aug. 11 | Foster, Reds vs. Cubs | H | 5 | 1 | 5 | 1 | 0 | 0 | 2 | W 9-3 |
| Sept. 2 | Scott, Brewers vs. Tigers | A | 5 | 1 | 5 | 2 | 0 | 0 | 2 | W 6-5 |
| Sept. 5 | Brett, Royals vs. Angels | A | 5 | 1 | 5 | 1 | 0 | 0 | 4 | W 5-2 |
| Sept. 6 | Evans, Red Sox vs. Brewers | A | 6 | 2 | 5 | 1 | 0 | 0 | 3 | W 20-6 |
| Sept. 9 | Chambliss, Yankees vs. Tigers | H | 5 | 2 | 5 | 1 | 0 | 0 | 3 | W 9-6 |
| Sept. 15 | Bochte, Angels vs. Twins (12 innings) | A | 5 | 2 | 5 | 1 | 1 | 0 | 2 | L 7-6 |
| Sept. 16 | Stennett, Pirates vs. Cubs | A | 7 | 5 | 7 | 2 | 1 | 0 | 2 | W 22-0 |
| Sept. 20 | Staub, Mets vs. Phillies (11 innings) | H | 6 | 1 | 5 | 1 | 0 | 1 | 1 | W 9-7 |
| Sept. 24 | Matthews, Giants vs. Braves (11 innings) | A | 6 | 1 | 5 | 0 | 0 | 0 | 1 | L 7-6 |

*Suspended after eight innings, completed June 15.

Mike Vail, rookie outfielder of the Mets, put together the longest batting streak of the year, a 23-game skein. The righthanded-hitting Vail began his streak on August 22 and was not stopped until September 16 when he went hitless in seven trips to the plate as the Mets defeated the Expos in an 18-inning marathon, 4-3. Mike batted .364 in this stretch with 36 hits in 99 at-bats. His streak tied the modern National League rookie record, last accomplished by Richie Ashburn of the Phillies in 1948.

The longest American League streak was compiled by Denny Doyle of the Red Sox who hit safely in 22 consecutive games from July 12 through August 4. Doyle's string was halted when he went 0-for-4 as Jim Palmer of the Orioles blanked the Red Sox 3-0, August 5. Denny had 31 hits in 79 times at bat for a sizzling .392 mark during his streak.

The folowing players also had streaks of 15 or more games: 20 games— Fred Lynn, Red Sox; 19 games—Felix Millan, Mets; Ted Simmons, Cardinals; 18 games—Tony Perez, Reds; Pepe Mangual, Expos; Ed Kranepool, Mets; 17 games—Leon Roberts, Tigers; Ted Sizemore, Cardinals; 16 games— Tommy Davis, Orioles; Carlton Fisk, Red Sox; John Mayberry, Royals; Dave McKay, Twins; Gene Tenace, Athletics; George Foster, Reds; Joe Torre, Mets; Larry Bowa, Phillies; Dave Parker, Pirates; 15 games—Dave Collins, Angels; Ron Cey, Dodgers; Manny Sanguillen, Pirates; Reggie Smith, Cardinals; Von Joshua, Giants.

George Brett of Kansas City was the leader in number of games with four or more hits. The Royals' third baseman had one five-hit game and made four safeties in one game on five occasions for a total of six in this department. Another third sacker, the Cubs' Bill Madlock, was the National League leader with five four-or-more-hit games.

The complete list of all players with four hits in one game follows:

AMERICAN LEAGUE: Baltimore (15)—Baylor 3, Bumbry 3, Grich 2, Singleton 2, Belanger, Davis, DeCinces, Duncan, Robinson. Boston (14)— Rice 4, Evans 2, Lynn 2, Petrocelli 2, Burleson, Cooper, Fisk, Yastrzemski. California (9)—Rivers 2, Bochte, Chalk, Collins, Harper, Nettles, Ramirez, Stanton. Chicago (7)—May 2, Coluccio, Hairston, Henderson, Orta, Stein. Cleveland (10)— Carty 3, Manning 2, Powell 2, Bell, Duffy, Hendrick. Detroit (6)—LeFlore 2, Sutherland 2, Freehan, Knox, Stanley, Wockenfuss. Kansas City (18)—Brett 6, Wohlford 3, Mayberry 2, McRae 2, Martinez, Otis, Patek, Pinson, Solaita. Milwaukee (10)—Scott 4, Aaron 2, Money 2, Lezcano, Mitchell. Minnesota (10)— Carew 2, Bostock, Brye, Ferrer, Ford, Hisle, Oliva, Soderholm, Terrell. New York (10)—White 3, Chambliss 2, Maddox 2, Bonds, Johnson, Munson. Oakland (12)—C. Washington 5, Williams 2, Campaneris, Garner, Jackson, North, Rudi. Texas (10)—Grieve 2, Hargrove 2, Randle 2, Davis, Harrah, Spencer, Tovar.

NATIONAL LEAGUE: Atlanta (8)—Office 3, Baker 2, Garr 2, Perez. Chicago (9)—Madlock 5, Cardenal 2, Morales, Trillo. Cincinnati (18)—Foster 4, Rose 4, Bench 3, Geronimo 2, Griffey 2, Perez 2, Concepcion. Houston (12)— Cedeno 3, Howard 2, Cabell, Cruz, Johnson, May, Metzger, Rader, Watson. Los Angeles (11)—Garvey 3, Lacy 2, Lopes 2, Yeager 2, Buckner, Wynn. Montreal (6)—Bailey, Carter, Jorgensen, Mangual, Morales, White. New York (11) —Millan 3, Kingman 2, Torre 2, Garrett, Staub, Unser, Vail. Philadelphia (16)— Luzinski 4, Bowa 3, Cash 3, Maddox 3, Allen, Brown, Montanez. Pittsburgh (16)—Stargell 4, Stennett 3, Hebner 2, Oliver 2, Sanguillen 2, Zisk 2, Kirkpatrick. St. Louis (17)—Reitz 4, Brock 3, Simmons 3, Davis 2, McBride 2, Smith 2, Sizemore. San Diego (8)—Fuentes 3, Grubb 2, Hernandez, Locklear, Winfield. San Francisco (10)—Thomas 3, Joshua 2, Matthews, Murcer, Ontiveros, Rader, Speier.

# Beniquez & Garrett Top Pinch-Hitters

The 1975 major league pinch-hitting leaders were Juan Beniquez of the Red Sox and Wayne Garrett of the Mets.

Beniquez hit safely in five of seven official at-bats to top the American League with a lofty .714 mark. Garrett led the National League pinch-hitters with six hits in 11 tries for a .545 average.

Champ Summers of the Cubs and the Phillies' Tony Taylor were the most frequently used pinch-hitters, each making 64 appearances. Summers led in RBIs with 14 and made 15 hits to tie for the lead in that category with Jose Morales of Montreal.

## NATIONAL LEAGUE PINCH-HITTING

(Compiled by Elias Sports Bureau)

### Club Pinch-Hitting

| Club | AB. | H. | HR. | RBI. | Pct. | Club | AB. | H. | HR. | RBI. | Pct. |
|------|-----|-----|-----|------|------|------|-----|-----|-----|------|------|
| St. Louis | 209 | 56 | 4 | 35 | .268 | Houston | 230 | 53 | 1 | 24 | .230 |
| Chicago | 215 | 54 | 6 | 43 | .251 | New York | 214 | 48 | 3 | 21 | .224 |
| Atlanta | 222 | 55 | 6 | 24 | .248 | San Diego | 205 | 44 | 2 | 20 | .215 |
| Philadelphia | 247 | 60 | 4 | 41 | .243 | Pittsburgh | 203 | 43 | 4 | 22 | .212 |
| Cincinnati | 190 | 45 | 1 | 30 | .237 | Los Angeles | 233 | 48 | 4 | 39 | .206 |
| Montreal | 272 | 64 | 3 | 30 | .235 | | | | | | |
| San Francisco | 182 | 42 | 3 | 23 | .231 | Totals | 2622 | 612 | 41 | 352 | .233 |

### Individual Pinch-Hitting (10 or More At-Bats)

| Player—Club | G. | AB. | H. | HR. | RBI. | Pct. | Player—Club | G. | AB. | H. | HR. | RBI. | Pct. |
|-------------|-----|-----|-----|-----|------|------|-------------|-----|-----|-----|-----|------|------|
| Garrett, New York | 14 | 11 | 6 | 2 | 4 | .545 | Torre, New York | 24 | 22 | 5 | 0 | 3 | .227 |
| Cabell, Houston | 21 | 17 | 7 | 0 | 4 | .412 | McCarver, Phil. | 38 | 31 | 7 | 0 | 2 | .226 |
| Gilbreath, Atlanta | 32 | 25 | 10 | 1 | 2 | .400 | Goodson, S.F.-Atl. | 44 | 40 | 9 | 0 | 4 | .225 |
| Johnstone, Phil. | 28 | 25 | 10 | 1 | 6 | .400 | Taylor, Philadelphia | 64 | 54 | 12 | 1 | 11 | .222 |
| Kranepool, New York | 22 | 20 | 8 | 0 | 3 | .400 | Howe, Pittsburgh | 19 | 18 | 4 | 0 | 0 | .222 |
| Adams, San Francisco | 38 | 33 | 12 | 1 | 8 | .364 | Hundley, San Diego | 23 | 18 | 4 | 0 | 2 | .222 |
| Joshua, San Francisco | 11 | 11 | 4 | 0 | 1 | .364 | Kendall, San Diego | 19 | 18 | 4 | 0 | 1 | .222 |
| Rogodzinski, Phil. | 13 | 11 | 4 | 0 | 2 | .364 | Mitterwald, Chicago | 21 | 18 | 4 | 1 | 6 | .222 |
| Melendez, St. Louis | 28 | 25 | 9 | 0 | 5 | .360 | Cruz, Houston | 33 | 28 | 6 | 0 | 2 | .214 |
| Alou, New York | 45 | 40 | 14 | 0 | 6 | .350 | Lyttle, Montreal | 30 | 19 | 4 | 0 | 3 | .211 |
| Office, Atlanta | 21 | 20 | 7 | 0 | 0 | .350 | Rettenmund, Cin. | 39 | 30 | 6 | 0 | 6 | .200 |
| Fairly, St. Louis | 45 | 35 | 12 | 0 | 6 | .343 | McMullen, Los Ang. | 28 | 25 | 5 | 2 | 10 | .200 |
| Helms, Houston | 30 | 27 | 9 | 0 | 5 | .333 | Hill, San Francisco | 17 | 15 | 3 | 1 | 3 | .200 |
| LaCock, Chicago | 32 | 27 | 9 | 1 | 8 | .333 | Popovich, Pittsburgh | 17 | 15 | 3 | 0 | 1 | .200 |
| Summers, Chicago | 64 | 48 | 15 | 1 | 14 | .313 | Concepcion, Cin. | 10 | 10 | 2 | 0 | 1 | .200 |
| Kirkpatrick, Pitt. | 52 | 42 | 13 | 1 | 6 | .310 | Griffey, Cincinnati | 14 | 10 | 2 | 0 | 0 | .200 |
| Hiser, Chicago | 29 | 26 | 8 | 0 | 2 | .308 | Hosley, Chicago | 13 | 10 | 2 | 2 | 5 | .200 |
| Batista, St. Louis | 10 | 10 | 3 | 0 | 0 | .300 | Paciorek, Los Ang. | 10 | 10 | 2 | 0 | 0 | .200 |
| Howard, St. Louis | 10 | 10 | 3 | 1 | 1 | .300 | Kubiak, San Diego | 12 | 11 | 2 | 0 | 0 | .182 |
| Hutton, Philadelphia | 42 | 37 | 11 | 1 | 9 | .297 | Ontiveros, San Fran. | 13 | 11 | 2 | 0 | 0 | .182 |
| Biittner, Montreal | 33 | 27 | 8 | 0 | 2 | .296 | Dunn, Chicago | 19 | 17 | 3 | 0 | 3 | .176 |
| Morales, Montreal | 60 | 51 | 15 | 1 | 11 | .294 | Robertson, Pitts. | 48 | 40 | 7 | 1 | 5 | .175 |
| Buckner, Los Angeles | 22 | 17 | 5 | 0 | 5 | .294 | Brown, San Fran. | 27 | 23 | 4 | 0 | 1 | .174 |
| Locklear, San Diego | 49 | 48 | 14 | 0 | 3 | .292 | Boswell, Houston | 44 | 35 | 6 | 0 | 3 | .171 |
| Dwyer, St.L.-Montreal | 26 | 21 | 6 | 0 | 1 | .286 | Harris, Chicago | 26 | 24 | 4 | 0 | 2 | .167 |
| Gaston, Atlanta | 30 | 25 | 7 | 1 | 4 | .280 | Oates, Atl.-Phil. | 14 | 12 | 2 | 0 | 0 | .167 |
| Bailey, Montreal | 46 | 40 | 11 | 0 | 3 | .275 | Colbert, Montreal | 21 | 19 | 3 | 2 | 5 | .158 |
| Dyer, Pittsburgh | 12 | 11 | 3 | 1 | 2 | .273 | Lum, Atlanta | 28 | 26 | 4 | 1 | 3 | .154 |
| McBride, St. Louis | 13 | 11 | 3 | 0 | 1 | .273 | Cater, St. Louis | 14 | 13 | 2 | 0 | 0 | .154 |
| May, Atlanta | 34 | 26 | 7 | 2 | 6 | .269 | Johnson, Houston | 40 | 33 | 5 | 1 | 8 | .152 |
| Brown, Philadelphia | 35 | 30 | 8 | 1 | 9 | .267 | Arnold, San Francisco | 23 | 20 | 3 | 0 | 0 | .150 |
| Anderson, Philadelphia | 15 | 15 | 4 | 0 | 1 | .267 | Cruz, Los Angeles | 17 | 14 | 2 | 0 | 1 | .143 |
| Crowley, Cincinnati | 58 | 49 | 13 | 0 | 4 | .265 | Tolan, San Diego | 15 | 14 | 2 | 0 | 1 | .143 |
| Howard, Houston | 23 | 23 | 6 | 0 | 0 | .261 | Crawford, Los Angeles | 20 | 15 | 2 | 1 | 3 | .133 |
| Lee, Los Angeles | 47 | 40 | 10 | 0 | 2 | .250 | Manuel, Los Angeles | 15 | 15 | 2 | 0 | 2 | .133 |
| Mota, Los Angeles | 49 | 40 | 10 | 0 | 10 | .250 | Robinson, Pittsburgh | 37 | 33 | 4 | 0 | 1 | .121 |
| Armbrister, Cincinnati | 36 | 28 | 7 | 0 | 2 | .250 | Scanlon, Montreal | 33 | 26 | 3 | 0 | 0 | .115 |
| Jorgensen, Montreal | 21 | 16 | 4 | 0 | 1 | .250 | Clines, New York | 19 | 18 | 2 | 0 | 0 | .111 |
| Breeden, Montreal | 15 | 12 | 3 | 0 | 0 | .250 | Gallagher, New York | 11 | 10 | 1 | 0 | 0 | .100 |
| Davis, St. Louis | 12 | 12 | 3 | 0 | 0 | .250 | Milner, New York | 37 | 32 | 3 | 0 | 1 | .094 |
| Sharon, San Diego | 38 | 33 | 8 | 0 | 4 | .242 | Miller, San Francisco | 13 | 12 | 1 | 0 | 0 | .083 |
| Bradford, St. Louis | 25 | 21 | 5 | 1 | 2 | .238 | Williams, Atlanta | 12 | 12 | 1 | 0 | 0 | .083 |
| Driessen, Cincinnati | 28 | 21 | 5 | 0 | 3 | .238 | Rudolph, St. Louis | 14 | 14 | 1 | 0 | 1 | .071 |
| Thomasson, San Fran. | 22 | 17 | 4 | 1 | 3 | .235 | Heidemann, New York | 18 | 17 | 1 | 0 | 1 | .059 |
| Lacy, Los Angeles | 26 | 22 | 5 | 1 | 1 | .227 | Wynn, Los Angeles | 13 | 10 | 0 | 0 | 1 | .000 |

Wayne Garrett

Juan Beniquez

## AMERICAN LEAGUE PINCH-HITTING
(Compiled by Sports Information Center)

### Club Pinch-Hitting

| Club | AB. | H. | HR. | RBI. | Pct. | Club | AB. | H. | HR. | RBI. | Pct. |
|---|---|---|---|---|---|---|---|---|---|---|---|
| Cleveland | 103 | 34 | 3 | 28 | .330 | California | 107 | 23 | 0 | 25 | .215 |
| Minnesota | 120 | 38 | 5 | 33 | .317 | Oakland | 108 | 23 | 0 | 13 | .213 |
| Boston | 93 | 27 | 1 | 22 | .290 | Texas | 120 | 22 | 2 | 14 | .183 |
| New York | 139 | 37 | 1 | 23 | .266 | Kansas City | 83 | 14 | 3 | 16 | .169 |
| Baltimore | 107 | 27 | 1 | 19 | .252 | Chicago | 51 | 8 | 1 | 8 | .157 |
| Detroit | 60 | 14 | 2 | 11 | .233 | | | | | | |
| Milwaukee | 91 | 20 | 2 | 18 | .220 | Totals | 1182 | 287 | 21 | 230 | .243 |

### Individual Pinch-Hitting (7 or More At-Bats)

| Player—Club | G. | AB. | H. | HR. | RBI. | Pct. | Player—Club | G. | AB. | H. | HR. | RBI. | Pct. |
|---|---|---|---|---|---|---|---|---|---|---|---|---|---|
| Beniquez, Boston | 8 | 7 | 5 | 0 | 2 | .714 | Walton, Minnesota | 36 | 32 | 7 | 1 | 7 | .219 |
| Carty, Cleveland | 13 | 9 | 6 | 0 | 7 | .667 | Dempsey, New York | 26 | 23 | 5 | 0 | 2 | .217 |
| Ellis, Cleveland | 9 | 9 | 5 | 0 | 3 | .556 | Piniella, New York | 20 | 19 | 4 | 0 | 2 | .211 |
| Braun, Minnesota | 15 | 11 | 6 | 1 | 4 | .545 | Solaita, Kansas City | 22 | 15 | 3 | 1 | 4 | .200 |
| Griffin, Boston | 17 | 16 | 8 | 0 | 7 | .500 | Gamble, Cleveland | 14 | 11 | 2 | 0 | 2 | .182 |
| Oliva, Minnesota | 11 | 10 | 5 | 1 | 7 | .500 | Shopay, Baltimore | 14 | 11 | 2 | 0 | 0 | .182 |
| Brye, Minnesota | 10 | 10 | 5 | 1 | 1 | .500 | Brown, Detroit | 47 | 35 | 6 | 1 | 3 | .171 |
| Hargrove, Texas | 8 | 8 | 4 | 0 | 1 | .500 | Bumbry, Baltimore | 23 | 18 | 3 | 0 | 0 | .167 |
| Harper, Calif.-Oak. | 12 | 7 | 3 | 0 | 1 | .429 | Hegan, Milwaukee | 28 | 18 | 3 | 0 | 3 | .167 |
| Moore, Milwaukee | 8 | 7 | 3 | 0 | 1 | .429 | Herrmann, New York | 23 | 19 | 3 | 0 | 5 | .158 |
| Spikes, Cleveland | 19 | 17 | 7 | 1 | 5 | .412 | Mitchell, Milwaukee | 15 | 13 | 2 | 0 | 2 | .154 |
| Spencer, Texas | 11 | 8 | 3 | 0 | 0 | .375 | DeCinces, Baltimore | 9 | 7 | 1 | 0 | 1 | .143 |
| McCarver, Boston | 8 | 8 | 3 | 0 | 1 | .375 | Lovitto, Texas | 8 | 7 | 1 | 0 | 0 | .143 |
| Northrup, Baltimore | 31 | 22 | 8 | 1 | 10 | .364 | Hendricks, Baltimore | 9 | 8 | 1 | 0 | 0 | .125 |
| Powell, Cleveland | 12 | 11 | 4 | 0 | 3 | .364 | Valentine, California | 8 | 8 | 1 | 0 | 0 | .125 |
| Johnson, New York | 14 | 14 | 5 | 0 | 3 | .357 | Pinson, Kansas City | 18 | 17 | 2 | 0 | 2 | .118 |
| Muser, Chi.-Balt. | 25 | 18 | 6 | 0 | 2 | .333 | Cardenas, Texas | 11 | 9 | 1 | 0 | 0 | .111 |
| Cooper, Boston | 20 | 18 | 6 | 1 | 4 | .333 | Miller, Boston | 11 | 9 | 1 | 0 | 1 | .111 |
| Howell, Texas | 12 | 12 | 4 | 2 | 5 | .333 | Briggs, Mil.-Minn. | 13 | 9 | 1 | 0 | 0 | .111 |
| Kusick, Minnesota | 11 | 9 | 3 | 1 | 4 | .333 | Killebrew, Kansas City | 10 | 9 | 1 | 0 | 1 | .111 |
| Rojas, Kansas City | 10 | 9 | 3 | 0 | 5 | .333 | Meoli, California | 10 | 9 | 1 | 0 | 0 | .111 |
| Williams, New York | 34 | 31 | 10 | 0 | 2 | .323 | Sharp, Chicago-Mil. | 12 | 10 | 1 | 0 | 0 | .100 |
| Llenas, California | 26 | 23 | 7 | 0 | 7 | .304 | Wohlford, Kansas City | 16 | 12 | 1 | 0 | 1 | .083 |
| Lowenstein, Cleveland | 15 | 14 | 4 | 1 | 4 | .286 | Tovar, Texas-Oakland | 13 | 12 | 1 | 0 | 0 | .083 |
| Balaz, California | 7 | 7 | 2 | 0 | 1 | .286 | Grieve, Texas | 15 | 14 | 1 | 0 | 0 | .071 |
| Carbo, Boston | 10 | 8 | 2 | 0 | 2 | .250 | Cubbage, Texas | 20 | 16 | 1 | 0 | 1 | .063 |
| Cowens, Kansas City | 10 | 8 | 2 | 1 | 2 | .250 | Sudakis, Calif.-Cleve. | 20 | 19 | 1 | 0 | 2 | .053 |
| Robson, Texas | 9 | 8 | 2 | 0 | 0 | .250 | Fregosi, Texas | 27 | 20 | 1 | 0 | 3 | .050 |
| Mangual, Oakland | 17 | 17 | 4 | 0 | 0 | .235 | Duncan, Baltimore | 7 | 7 | 0 | 0 | 1 | .000 |
| Holt, Oakland | 54 | 43 | 10 | 0 | 8 | .233 | Stein, Chicago | 7 | 7 | 0 | 0 | 0 | .000 |
| Lahoud, California | 15 | 9 | 2 | 0 | 5 | .222 | Stanton, California | 12 | 10 | 0 | 0 | 0 | .000 |

# The Sporting News AWARDS

## THE SPORTING NEWS MVP AWARDS

| AMERICAN LEAGUE | | | | NATIONAL LEAGUE | | |
|---|---|---|---|---|---|---|
| Year | Player Club | Points | | Player Club | Points | |
| 1929—Al Simmons, Philadelphia, of .. | 40 | | No selection | | |
| 1930—Joseph Cronin, Washington, ss | 52 | | William Terry, New York, 1b | 47 | |
| 1931—H. Louis Gehrig, New York, 1b | 40 | | Charles Klein, Philadelphia, of | 40 | |
| 1932—James Foxx, Philadelphia, 1b.... | 56 | | Charles Klein, Philadelphia, of | 46 | |
| 1933—James Foxx, Philadelphia, 1b ... | 49 | | Carl Hubbell, New York, p | 64 | |
| 1934—H. Louis Gehrig, New York, 1b | 51 | | Jerome Dean, St. Louis, p | 57 | |
| 1935—Henry Greenberg, Detroit, 1b .. | 64 | | J. Floyd Vaughan, Pitts., ss | 42 | |
| 1936—H. Louis Gehrig, New York, 1b | 55 | | Carl Hubbell, New York, p | 61 | |
| 1937—Charles Gehringer, Detroit, 2b | 78 | | Joseph Medwick, St. Louis, of | 70 | |
| 1938—James Foxx, Boston, 1b ..........| 305 | | Ernest Lombardi, Cincinnati, c | 229 | |
| 1939—Joseph DiMaggio, N. York, of | .280 | | William Walters, Cincinnati, p | 303 | |
| 1940—Henry Greenberg, Detroit, of | .292 | | Frank McCormick, Cinn., 1b | 274 | |
| 1941—Joseph DiMaggio, N. York, of | .291 | | Adolph Camilli, Brooklyn, 1b | 300 | |
| 1942—Joseph Gordon, New York, 2b | .270 | | Morton Cooper, St. Louis, p | 263 | |
| 1943—Spurgeon Chandler, N. Y., p | 246 | | Stanley Musial, St. Louis, of | 267 | |
| 1944—Robert Doerr, Boston, 2b ........| | | Martin Marion, St. Louis, ss | | |
| 1945—Edward J. Mayo, Detroit, 2b .... | | | Thomas Holmes, Boston, of | | |

## THE SPORTING NEWS PLAYER, PITCHER OF YEAR

1948—Louis Boudreau, Cleveland, ss
    Robert Lemon, Cleveland, p
1949—Theodore Williams, Boston, of
    Ellis Kinder, Boston, p
1950—Philip Rizzuto, New York, ss
    Robert Lemon, Cleveland, p
1951—Ferris Fain, Philadelphia, 1b
    Robert Feller, Cleveland, p
1952—Luscious Easter, Cleveland, 1b
    Robert Shantz, Philadelphia, p
1953—Albert Rosen, Cleveland, 3b
    Erv (Bob) Porterfield, Wash., p
1954—Roberto Avila, Cleveland, 2b
    Robert Lemon, Cleveland, p
1955—Albert Kaline, Detroit, of
    Edward Ford, New York, p
1956—Mickey Mantle, New York, of
    W. William Pierce, Chicago, p
1957—Theodore Williams, Boston, of
    W. William Pierce, Chicago, p
1958—Jack Jensen, Boston, of
    Robert Turley, New York, p
1959—J. Nelson Fox, Chicago, 2b
    Early Wynn, Chicago, p
1960—Roger Maris, New York, of
    Charles Estrada, Baltimore, p
1961—Roger Maris, New York, of
    Edward Ford, New York, p
1962—Mickey Mantle, New York, of
    Richard Donovan, Cleveland, p
1963—Albert Kaline, Detroit, of
    Edward Ford, New York, p
1964—Brooks Robinson, Baltimore, 3b
    Dean Chance, Los Angeles, p
1965—Pedro (Tony) Oliva, Minn., of
    James Grant, Minnesota, p
1966—Frank Robinson, Baltimore, of
    James Kaat, Minnesota, p
1967—Carl Yastrzemski, Boston, of
    Jim Lonborg, Boston, p

1948—Stanley Musial, St. Louis, of-1b
    John Sain, Boston, p
1949—Enos Slaughter, St. Louis, of
    Howard Pollet, St. Louis, p
1950—Ralph Kiner, Pittsburgh, of
    C. James Konstanty, Phila., p
1951—Stanley Musial, St. Louis, of
    Elwin Roe, Brooklyn, p
1952—Henry Sauer, Chicago, of
    Robin Roberts, Philadelphia, p
1953—Roy Campanella, Brooklyn, c
    Warren Spahn, Milwaukee, p
1954—Willie Mays, New York, of
    John Antonelli, New York, p
1955—Edwin Snider, Brooklyn, of
    Robin Roberts, Philadelphia, p
1956—Henry Aaron, Milwaukee, of
    Donald Newcombe, Brooklyn, p
1957—Stanley Musial, St. Louis, 1b
    Warren Spahn, Milwaukee, p
1958—Ernest Banks, Chicago, ss
    Warren Spahn, Milwaukee, p
1959—Ernest Banks, Chicago, ss
    Samuel Jones, San Francisco, p
1960—Richard Groat, Pittsburgh, ss
    Vernon Law, Pittsburgh, p
1961—Frank Robinson, Cincinnati, of
    Warren Spahn, Milwaukee, p
1962—Maurice Wills, Los Angeles, ss
    Donald Drysdale, Los Angeles, p
1963—Henry Aaron, Milwaukee, of
    Sanford Koufax, Los Angeles, p
1964—Kenton Boyer, St. Louis, 3b
    Sanford Koufax, Los Angeles, p
1965—Willie Mays, San Francisco, of
    Sanford Koufax, Los Angeles, p
1966—Roberto Clemente, Pittsburgh, of
    Sanford Koufax, Los Angeles, p
1967—Orlando Cepeda, St. Louis, 1b
    Mike McCormick, San Fran. p

## PLAYER, PITCHER OF YEAR—Continued

### AMERICAN LEAGUE

1968—Ken Harrelson, Boston, of
Denny McLain, Detroit, p
1969—Harmon Killebrew, Minn., 1b-3b
Denny McLain, Detroit, p
1970—Harmon Killebrew, Minn., 3b
Sam McDowell, Cleveland, p
1971—Tony Oliva, Minnesota, of
Vida Blue, Oakland, p
1972—Dick Allen, Chicago, 1b
Wilbur Wood, Chicago, p
1973—Reggie Jackson, Oakland, of
Jim Palmer, Baltimore, p
1974—Jeff Burroughs, Texas, of
Jim Hunter, Oakland, p
1975—Fred Lynn, Boston, of
Jim Palmer, Baltimore, p

### NATIONAL LEAGUE

1968—Pete Rose, Cincinnati, of
Bob Gibson, St. Louis, p
1969—Willie McCovey, San Fran., 1b
Tom Seaver, New York, p
1970—Johnny Bench, Cin., c
Bob Gibson, St. Louis, p
1971—Joe Torre, St. Louis, 3b
Ferguson Jenkins, Chicago, p
1972—Billy Williams, Chicago, of
Steve Carlton, Philadelphia, p
1973—Bobby Bonds, San Francisco, of
Ron Bryant, San Francisco, p
1974—Lou Brock, St. Louis, of
Mike Marshall, Los Angeles, p
1975—Joe Morgan, Cincinnati, 2b
Tom Seaver, New York, p

## FIREMAN (Relief Pitcher) OF THE YEAR

| Year | Player | Club |
|---|---|---|
| 1960 | Mike Fornieles, Boston | |
| 1961 | Luis Arroyo, New York | |
| 1962 | Dick Radatz, Boston | |
| 1963 | Stu Miller, Baltimore | |
| 1964 | Dick Radatz, Boston | |
| 1965 | Eddie Fisher, Chicago | |
| 1966 | Jack Aker, Kansas City | |
| 1967 | Minnie Rojas, California | |
| 1968 | Wilbur Wood, Chicago | |
| 1969 | Ron Perranoski, Minnesota | |
| 1970 | Ron Perranoski, Minnesota | |
| 1971 | Ken Sanders, Milwaukee | |
| 1972 | Sparky Lyle, New York | |
| 1973 | John Hiller, Detroit | |
| 1974 | Terry Forster, Chicago | |
| 1975 | Rich Gossage, Chicago | |

| Year | Player | Club |
|---|---|---|
| 1960 | Lindy McDaniel, St. Louis | |
| 1961 | Stu Miller, San Francisco | |
| 1962 | Roy Face, Pittsburgh | |
| 1963 | Lindy McDaniel, Chicago | |
| 1964 | Al McBean, Pittsburgh | |
| 1965 | Ted Abernathy, Chicago | |
| 1966 | Phil Regan, Los Angeles | |
| 1967 | Ted Abernathy, Cincinnati | |
| 1968 | Phil Regan, L.A.-Chicago | |
| 1969 | Wayne Granger, Cincinnati | |
| 1970 | Wayne Granger, Cincinnati | |
| 1971 | Dave Giusti, Pittsburgh | |
| 1972 | Clay Carroll, Cincinnati | |
| 1973 | Mike Marshall, Montreal | |
| 1974 | Mike Marshall, Los Angeles | |
| 1975 | Al Hrabosky, St. Louis | |

## THE SPORTING NEWS ROOKIE AWARDS

1946—Combined selection—Delmer Ennis, Philadelphia, N. L., of
1947—Combined selection—Jack Robinson, Brooklyn, 1b
1948—Combined selection—Richie Ashburn, Philadelphia, N. L., of

| Year | Player | Club | Player | Club |
|---|---|---|---|---|
| 1949 | Roy Sievers, St. Louis, of | | Donald Newcombe, Brooklyn, p | |
| 1950 | Combined selection—Edward Ford, New York, A. L., p | | | |
| 1951 | Orestes Minoso, Chicago, of | | Willie Mays, New York, of | |
| 1952 | Clinton Courtney, St. Louis, c | | Joseph Black, Brooklyn, p | |
| 1953 | Harvey Kuenn, Detroit, ss | | James Gilliam, Brooklyn, 2b | |
| 1954 | Robert Grim, New York, p | | Wallace Moon, St. Louis, of | |
| 1955 | Herbert Score, Cleveland, p | | William Virdon, St. Louis, of | |
| 1956 | Luis Aparicio, Chicago, ss | | Frank Robinson, Cincinnati, of | |
| 1957 | Anthony Kubek, New York, inf-of | | Edward Bouchee, Philadelphia, 1b | |
| | (No pitcher named) | | Jack Sanford, Philadelphia, p | |
| 1958 | Albert Pearson, Washington, of | | Orlando Cepeda, San Francisco, 1b | |
| | Ryne Duren, New York, p | | Carlton Willey, Milwaukee, p | |
| 1959 | W. Robert Allison, Washington, of | | Willie McCovey, San Francisco, 1b | |
| 1960 | Ronald Hansen, Baltimore, ss | | Frank Howard, Los Angeles, of | |
| 1961 | Richard Howser, Kansas City, ss | | Billy Williams, Chicago, of | |
| | Donald Schwall, Boston, p | | Kenneth Hunt, Cincinnati, p | |
| 1962 | Thomas Tresh, New York, of-ss | | Kenneth Hubbs, Chicago, 2b | |
| 1963 | Peter Ward, Chicago, 3b | | Peter Rose, Cincinnati, 2b | |
| | Gary Peters, Chicago, p | | Raymond Culp, Philadelphia, p | |
| 1964 | Pedro (Tony) Oliva, Minn., of | | Richard Allen, Philadelphia, 3b | |
| | Wallace Bunker, Baltimore, p | | William McCool, Cincinnati, p | |
| 1965 | Curtis Blefary, Baltimore, of | | Joseph Morgan, Houston, 2b | |
| | Marcelino Lopez, California, p | | Frank Linzy, San Francisco, p | |

## THE SPORTING NEWS ROOKIE AWARDS—Continued

### AMERICAN LEAGUE

| Year | Player | Club |
|---|---|---|
| 1966— | Tommie Agee, Chicago, of | |
| | James Nash, Kansas City, p | |
| 1967— | Rod Carew, Minnesota, 2b | |
| | Tom Phoebus, Baltimore, p | |
| 1968— | Del Unser, Washington, of | |
| | Stan Bahnsen. New York, p | |
| 1969— | Carlos May, Chicago, of | |
| | Mike Nagy, Boston, p | |
| 1970— | Roy Foster, Cleveland, of | |
| | Bert Blyleven, Minnesota, p | |
| 1971— | Chris Chambliss, Cleveland, 1b | |
| | Bill Parsons, Milwaukee, p | |
| 1972— | Carlton Fisk, Boston, c | |
| | Dick Tidrow, Cleveland, p | |
| 1973— | Al Bumbry, Baltimore, of | |
| | Steve Busby, Kansas City, p | |
| 1974— | Mike Hargrove, Texas, 1b | |
| | Frank Tanana, California, p | |
| 1975— | Fred Lynn, Boston, of | |
| | Dennis Eckersley, Cleveland, p | |

### NATIONAL LEAGUE

| Year | Player | Club |
|---|---|---|
| 1966— | Tommy Helms, Cincinnati, 3b | |
| | Donald Sutton, Los Angeles, p | |
| 1967— | Lee May, Cincinnati, 1b | |
| | Dick Hughes, St. Louis, p | |
| 1968— | Johnny Bench, Cincinnati, c | |
| | Jerry Koosman, New York, p | |
| 1969— | Coco Laboy, Montreal, 3b | |
| | Tom Griffin, Houston, p | |
| 1970— | Bernie Carbo, Cincinnati, of | |
| | Carl Morton, Montreal, p | |
| 1971— | Earl Williams, Atlanta, c | |
| | Reggie Cleveland, St. Louis, p | |
| 1972— | Dave Rader, San Francisco, c | |
| | Jon Matlack, New York, p | |
| 1973— | Gary Matthews, San Fran., of | |
| | Steve Rogers, Montreal, p | |
| 1974— | Greg Gross, Houston, of | |
| | John D'Acquisto, San Francisco, p | |
| 1975— | Gary Carter, Montreal, of-c | |
| | John Montefusco, San Francisco, p | |

## MAJOR LEAGUE EXECUTIVE

| Year | Executive | Club |
|---|---|---|
| 1936— | Branch Rickey, St. Louis NL | |
| 1937— | Edward Barrow, New York Al | |
| 1938— | Warren Giles, Cincinnati NL | |
| 1939— | Larry MacPhail, Brooklyn NL | |
| 1940— | W. O. Briggs, Sr., Detroit AL | |
| 1941— | Edward Barrow, New York AL | |
| 1942— | Branch Rickey, St. Louis NL | |
| 1943— | Clark Griffith, Washington | |
| 1944— | Wm. O. DeWitt, St. Louis AL | |
| 1945— | Philip K. Wrigley, Chicago NL | |
| 1946— | Thomas A. Yawkey, Boston AL | |
| 1947— | Branch Rickey, Brooklyn NL | |
| 1948— | Bill Veeck, Cleveland AL | |
| 1949— | Robt. Carpenter, Phila'phia NL | |
| 1950— | George Weiss, New York AL | |
| 1951— | George Weiss, New York AL | |
| 1952— | George Weiss, New York AL | |
| 1953— | Louis Perini, Milwaukee NL | |
| 1954— | Horace Stoneham, N. York NL | |
| 1955— | Walter O'Malley, Brooklyn NL | |
| 1956— | Gabe Paul, Cincinnati NL | |

| Year | Executive | Club |
|---|---|---|
| 1957— | Frank Lane, St. Louis NL | |
| 1958— | Joe L. Brown, Pittsburgh NL | |
| 1959— | E. J. (Buzzie) Bavasi, L. A. NL | |
| 1960— | George Weiss, New York AL | |
| 1961— | Dan Topping, New York AL | |
| 1962— | Fred Haney, Los Angeles AL | |
| 1963— | Vaughan (Bing) Devine, St. L. NL | |
| 1964— | Vaughan (Bing) Devine, St. L. NL | |
| 1965— | Calvin Griffith, Minnesota AL | |
| 1966— | Lee MacPhail, Commissioner's Office | |
| 1967— | Dick O'Connell, Boston AL | |
| 1968— | James Campbell, Detroit AL | |
| 1969— | John Murphy, New York NL | |
| 1970— | Harry Dalton, Baltimore AL | |
| 1971— | Cedric Tallis, Kansas City AL | |
| 1972— | Roland Hemond, Chicago AL | |
| 1973— | Bob Howsam, Cincinnati NL | |
| 1974— | Gabe Paul, New York AL | |
| 1975— | Dick O'Connell, Boston AL | |

## MAJOR LEAGUE MANAGER

| Year | Manager | Club |
|---|---|---|
| 1936— | Joe McCarthy, New York AL | |
| 1937— | Bill McKechnie, Boston NL | |
| 1938— | Joe McCarthy, New York AL | |
| 1939— | Leo Durocher, Brooklyn NL | |
| 1940— | Bill McKechnie, Cincinnati NL | |
| 1941— | Billy Southworth, St. Louis NL | |
| 1942— | Billy Southworth, St. Louis NL | |
| 1943— | Joe McCarthy, New York AL | |
| 1944— | Luke Sewell, St. Louis AL | |
| 1945— | Ossie Bluege, Washington AL | |
| 1946— | Eddie Dyer, St. Louis NL | |
| 1947— | Bucky Harris, New York AL | |
| 1948— | Bill Meyer, Pittsburgh NL | |
| 1949— | Casey Stengel, New York AL | |
| 1950— | Red Rolfe, Detroit AL | |
| 1951— | Leo Durocher, New York NL | |
| 1952— | Eddie Stanky, St. Louis NL | |

| Year | Manager | Club |
|---|---|---|
| 1953— | Casey Stengel, New York AL | |
| 1954— | Leo Durocher, New York NL | |
| 1955— | Walter Alston, Brooklyn NL | |
| 1956— | Birdie Tebbetts, Cincinnati NL | |
| 1957— | Fred Hutchinson, St. Louis NL | |
| 1958— | Casey Stengel, New York AL | |
| 1959— | Walter Alston, Los Angeles NL | |
| 1960— | Danny Murtaugh, Pitts. NL | |
| 1961— | Ralph Houk, New York AL | |
| 1962— | Bill Rigney, Los Angeles AL | |
| 1963— | Walter Alston, Los Angeles NL | |
| 1964— | Johnny Keane, St. Louis NL | |
| 1965— | Sam Mele, Minnesota AL | |
| 1966— | Hank Bauer, Baltimore AL | |
| 1967— | Dick Williams, Boston AL | |
| 1968— | Mayo Smith, Detroit AL | |
| 1969— | Gil Hodges, New York NL | |

## MAJOR LEAGUE MANAGER—Continued

| Year | Manager Club | Year | Manager Club |
|---|---|---|---|
| 1970 | Danny Murtaugh, Pittsburgh NL | 1973 | Gene Mauch, Montreal NL |
| 1971 | Charlie Fox, San Francisco NL | 1974 | Bill Virdon, New York AL |
| 1972 | Chuck Tanner, Chicago AL | 1975 | Darrell Johnson, Boston AL |

## MAJOR LEAGUE PLAYER

| Year | Player Club | Year | Player Club |
|---|---|---|---|
| 1936 | Carl Hubbell, New York NL | 1957 | Ted Williams, Boston AL |
| 1937 | Johnny Allen, Cleveland AL | 1958 | Bob Turley, New York AL |
| 1938 | Johnny Vander Meer, Cinn. NL | 1959 | Early Wynn, Chicago AL |
| 1939 | Joe DiMaggio, New York AL | 1960 | Bill Mazeroski, Pittsburgh NL |
| 1940 | Bob Feller, Cleveland AL | 1961 | Roger Maris, New York AL |
| 1941 | Ted Williams, Boston AL | 1962 | Maury Wills, Los Angeles NL |
| 1942 | Ted Williams, Boston AL | | Don Drysdale, Los Angeles NL |
| 1943 | Spud Chandler, New York AL | 1963 | Sandy Koufax, Los Angeles NL |
| 1944 | Marty Marion, St. Louis NL | 1964 | Ken Boyer, St. Louis NL |
| 1945 | Hal Newhouser, Detroit AL | 1965 | Sandy Koufax, Los Angeles NL |
| 1946 | Stan Musial, St. Louis NL | 1966 | Frank Robinson, Baltimore AL |
| 1947 | Ted Williams, Boston AL | 1967 | Carl Yastrzemski, Boston AL |
| 1948 | Lou Boudreau, Cleveland AL | 1968 | Denny McLain, Detroit AL |
| 1949 | Ted Williams, Boston AL | 1969 | Willie McCovey, San Fran. NL |
| 1950 | Phil Rizzuto, New York AL | 1970 | Johnny Bench, Cin. NL |
| 1951 | Stan Musial, St. Louis NL | 1971 | Joe Torre, St. Louis NL |
| 1952 | Robin Roberts, Philadelphia NL | 1972 | Billy Williams, Chicago NL |
| 1953 | Al Rosen, Cleveland AL | 1973 | Reggie Jackson, Oakland AL |
| 1954 | Willie Mays, New York NL | 1974 | Lou Brock, St. Louis NL |
| 1955 | Duke Snider, Brooklyn NL | 1975 | Joe Morgan, Cincinnati NL |
| 1956 | Mickey Mantle, New York AL | | |

## MINOR LEAGUE EXECUTIVE (HIGHER CLASSIFICATIONS)

### (Restricted to Class AAA Starting in 1963)

| Year | Executive Club | Year | Executive Club |
|---|---|---|---|
| 1936 | Earl Mann, Atlanta, Southern | 1956 | Robert Howsam, Denver, A.A. |
| 1937 | Robt. LaMotte, Savannah, Sally | 1957 | John Stiglmeier, Buffalo, Int. |
| 1938 | Louis McKenna, St. Paul, A.A. | 1958 | Ed. Glennon, Bir'ham, Southern |
| 1939 | Bruce Dudley, Louisville, A.A. | 1959 | Ed Leishman, Salt Lake, PCL |
| 1940 | Roy Hamey, Kansas City, A.A. | 1960 | Ray Winder, Little R., Southern |
| 1941 | Emil Sick, Seattle, PCL | 1961 | Elten Schiller, Omaha, A.A. |
| 1942 | Bill Veeck, Milwaukee, A.A. | 1962 | George Sisler, Rochester, Int. |
| 1943 | Clar. Rowland, Los Angeles, PCL | 1963 | Lewis Matlin, Hawaii, PCL |
| 1944 | William Mulligan, Seattle, PCL | 1964 | Ed. Leishman, San Diego, PCL |
| 1945 | Bruce Dudley, Louisville, A.A. | 1965 | Harold Cooper, Columbus, Int. |
| 1946 | Earl Mann, Atlanta, Southern | 1966 | John Quinn, Jr., Hawaii, PCL |
| 1947 | Wm. Purnhage, Waterloo, I.I.I. | 1967 | Hillman Lyons, Richmond, Int. |
| 1948 | Ed. Glennon, Bir'ham, Southern | 1968 | Gabe Paul, Jr., Tulsa, PCL |
| 1949 | Ted Sullivan, Indianapolis, A.A. | 1969 | Bill Gardner, Louisville, Int. |
| 1950 | Cl. (Brick) Laws, Oakland, PCL | 1970 | Dick King, Wichita, A.A. |
| 1951 | Robert Howsam, Denver, West. | 1971 | Carl Steinfeldt, Jr., Roch'ter, Int. |
| 1952 | Jack Cooke, Toronto. Int. | 1972 | Don Labbruzzo, Evansville, A.A. |
| 1953 | Richard Burnett, Dallas, Texas | 1973 | Merle Miller, Tucson, PCL |
| 1954 | Edward Stumpf, Indpls., A.A. | 1974 | John Carbray, Sacramento, PCL |
| 1955 | Dewey Soriano, Seattle, PCL | 1975 | Stan Naccarato, Tacoma, PCL |

## MINOR LEAGUE EXECUTIVE (LOWER CLASSIFICATIONS)

### (Separate Awards for Class AA and Class A Started in 1963)

| Year | Executive Club | Year | Executive Club |
|---|---|---|---|
| 1950 | H. Cooper, Hutch'son. West. A. | 1958 | Gerald Waring, Macon, Sally |
| 1951 | O. W. (Bill) Hayes, T'ple, B.S. | 1959 | Clay Dennis, Des Moines, III |
| 1952 | Hillman Lyons, Danville, MOV | 1960 | Hubert Kittle, Yakima, Northw. |
| 1953 | Carl Roth, Peoria, III | 1961 | David Steele, Fresno, California |
| 1954 | James Meaghan, Cedar R., III | 1962 | John Quinn, Jr., S. Jose, Calif. |
| 1955 | John Petrakis, Dubuque, MOV | 1963 | Hugh Finnerty, Tulsa, Texas |
| 1956 | Marvin Milkes, Fresno, Calif. | | Ben Jewell, M. Valley, Pioneer |
| 1957 | Richard Wagner, L'coln, West. | | |

# MINOR LEAGUE EXECUTIVE (LOWER CLASSIFICATIONS) (Continued)

### (Separate Awards for Class AA and Class A Started in 1963)

| Year | Executive — Club |
|---|---|
| 1964 | Glynn West, B'ham, Southern |
| | Jas. Bayens, Rock Hill, W. Car. |
| 1965 | Dick Butler, Dallas-Ft.W., Tex. |
| | Ken. Blackman, Quad C., Midw. |
| 1966 | Tom Fleming, Evansville, South. |
| | Cappy Harada, Lodi, California |
| 1967 | Robt. Quinn, Reading, East. |
| | Pat Williams, Spar'burg, W. C. |
| 1968 | Phil Howser, Charlotte, South. |
| | Merle Miller, Burlington, Midw. |
| 1969 | Charlie Blaney, Albuq., Tex. |
| | Bill Gorman, Visalia, Calif. |
| 1970 | Carl Sawatski, Arkansas, Tex. |
| | Bob Williams, Bakersfield, Calif. |
| 1971 | Miles Wolff, Savannah, Dixie A. |
| | Ed Holtz, Appleton, Midwest |
| 1972 | John Begzos, S. Antonio, Texas |
| | Bob Piccinini, Modesto, Calif. |
| 1973 | Dick Kravitz, Jacksonville, Sou. |
| | Fritz Colschen, Clinton, Midw. |
| 1974 | Jim Paul, El Paso, Texas |
| | Bing Russell, Portland, N'west |
| 1975 | Jim Paul, El Paso, Texas |
| | Cordy Jensen, Eugene, N'west |

## MINOR LEAGUE MANAGER

| Year | Manager — Club | Year | Manager — Club |
|---|---|---|---|
| 1936 | Al Sothoron, Milwaukee, A.A. | 1956 | Kerby Farrell, Indpls., A.A. |
| 1937 | Jake Flowers, Salis'y, East. Sh. | 1957 | Ben Geraghty, Wichita, A.A. |
| 1938 | Paul Richards, Atlanta, South. | 1958 | Cal Ermer, Birmingham, South. |
| 1939 | Bill Meyer, Kansas City, A.A. | 1959 | Pete Reiser, Victoria, Texas |
| 1940 | Larry Gilbert, Nashville, South. | 1960 | Mel McGaha, Toronto, Int. |
| 1941 | Burt Shotton, Columbus, A.A. | 1961 | Kerby Farrell, Buffalo, Int. |
| 1942 | Eddie Dyer, Columbus, A.A. | 1962 | Ben Geraghty, Jackson'le., Int. |
| 1943 | Nick Cullop, Columbus, A.A. | 1963 | Rollie Hemsley, Indpls., Int. |
| 1944 | Al Thomas, Baltimore, Int. | 1964 | Harry Walker, Jacks'vle., Int. |
| 1945 | Lefty O'Doul, San Fran., PCL | 1965 | Grady Hatton, Okla. City, PCL |
| 1946 | Clay Hopper, Montreal, Int. | 1966 | Bob Lemon, Seattle, PCL |
| 1947 | Nick Cullop, Milwaukee, A.A. | 1967 | Bob Skinner, San Diego, PCL |
| 1948 | Casey Stengel, Oakland, PCL | 1968 | Jack Tighe, Toledo, Int. |
| 1949 | Fred Haney, Hollywood, PCL | 1969 | Clyde McCullough, Tide., Int. |
| 1950 | Rollie Hemsley, Columbus, A.A. | 1970 | Tom Lasorda, Spokane, PCL |
| 1951 | Charlie Grimm, Milw., A.A. | 1971 | Del Rice, Salt Lake City, PCL |
| 1952 | Luke Appling, Memphis, South. | 1972 | Hank Bauer, Tidewater, Int. |
| 1953 | Bobby Bragan, Hollywood, PCL | 1973 | Joe Morgan, Charleston, Int. |
| 1954 | Kerby Farrell, Indpls., A.A. | 1974 | Joe Altobelli, Rochester, Int. |
| 1955 | Bill Rigney, Minneapolis, A.A. | 1975 | Joe Frazier, Tidewater, Int. |

## MINOR LEAGUE PLAYER

| Year | Player — Club | Year | Player — Club |
|---|---|---|---|
| 1936 | Jn. Vander Meer Durham, Pied. | 1956 | Steve Bilko, Los Angeles, PCL |
| 1937 | Charlie Keller, Newark, Int. | 1957 | Norm Siebern, Denver, A.A. |
| 1938 | Fred Hutchinson, Seattle, PCL | 1958 | Jim O'Toole, Nashville, South. |
| 1939 | Lou Novikoff, Tulsa-Los A'les. | 1959 | Frank Howard, Victoria-Spok. |
| 1940 | Phil Rizzuto, Kansas City, A.A. | 1960 | Willie Davis, Spokane, PCL |
| 1941 | John Lindell, Newark, Int. | 1961 | Howie Koplitz, Bir'ham, South. |
| 1942 | Dick Barrett, Seattle, PCL | 1962 | Bob Bailey, Columbus, Int. |
| 1943 | Chet Covington, Scranton, East. | 1963 | Don Buford, Indianapolis, Int. |
| 1944 | Rip Collins, Albany, Eastern | 1964 | Mel Stottlemyre, Richm'd., Int. |
| 1945 | Gil Coan, Chattanooga, South. | 1965 | Joe Foy, Toronto, International |
| 1946 | Sibby Sisti, Indianapolis, A. A. | 1966 | Mike Epstein, Rochester, Int. |
| 1947 | Hank Sauer, Syracuse, Int. | 1967 | John Bench, Buffalo, Int. |
| 1948 | Gene Woodling, S. F., PCL | 1968 | Merv Rettenmund, Roch'ter, Int. |
| 1949 | Orie Arntzen, Albany, Eastern | 1969 | Danny Walton, Okla. City, A.A. |
| 1950 | Frank Saucier. San Ant'o. Tex. | 1970 | Don Baylor, Rochester, Int. |
| 1951 | Gene Conley, Hartford, Eastern | 1971 | Bobby Grich, Rochester, Int. |
| 1952 | Bill Skowron, Kans. City, A.A. | 1972 | Tom Paciorek, Albuq'que, PCL |
| 1953 | Gene Conley, Toledo, A.A. | 1973 | Steve Ontiveros, Phoenix, PCL |
| 1954 | Herb Score, Indianapolis, A.A. | 1974 | Jim Rice, Pawtucket, Int. |
| 1955 | John Murff, Dallas, Texas | 1975 | Hector Cruz, Tulsa, A.A. |

# BASEBALL WRITERS' ASSOCIATION AWARDS
## Most Valuable Player Citations

### CHALMERS AWARD

| AMERICAN LEAGUE | | NATIONAL LEAGUE | |
|---|---|---|---|
| Year Player Club | Points | Player Club | Points |
| 1911—Tyrus Cobb, Detroit, of | 64 | Frank Schulte, Chicago, of | 29 |
| 1912—Tristram Speaker, Boston, of | 59 | Lawrence Doyle, N. Y., 2b | 48 |
| 1913—Walter Johnson, Washington, p | 54 | Jacob Daubert, Brooklyn, 1b | 50 |
| 1914—Edward Collins, Phila., 2b | 63 | John Evers, Boston, 2b | 50 |

### LEAGUE AWARDS

| AMERICAN LEAGUE | | NATIONAL LEAGUE | |
|---|---|---|---|
| Year Player Club | Points | Player Club | Points |
| 1922—George Sisler, St. Louis, 1b | 59 | No selection | |
| 1923—George Ruth, New York, of | 64 | No selection | |
| 1924—Walter Johnson, Washington, p | 55 | Arthur Vance, Brooklyn, p | 74 |
| 1925—Roger Peckinpaugh, Wash., ss | 45 | Rogers Hornsby, St. Louis, 2b | 73 |
| 1926—George Burns, Cleveland, 1b | 63 | Robert O'Farrell, St. Louis, c | 79 |
| 1927—H. Louis Gehrig, New York, 1b | 56 | Paul Waner, Pittsburgh, of | 72 |
| 1928—Gordon Cochrane, Phila., c | 53 | James Bottomley, St. Louis, 1b | 76 |
| 1929—No selection | | Rogers Hornsby, Chicago, 2b | 60 |

## BASEBALL WRITERS' ASSOCIATION MVP AWARDS

| AMERICAN LEAGUE | | NATIONAL LEAGUE | |
|---|---|---|---|
| Year Player Club | Points | Player Club | Points |
| 1931—Robert Grove, Philadelphia, p | 78 | Frank Frisch, St. Louis, 2b | 65 |
| 1932—James Foxx, Philadelphia, 1b | 75 | Charles Klein, Phila., of | 78 |
| 1933—James Foxx, Philadelphia, 1b | 74 | Carl Hubbell, New York, p | 77 |
| 1934—Gordon Cochrane, Detroit, c | 67 | Jerome Dean, St. Louis, p | 78 |
| 1935—Henry Greenberg, Detroit, 1b | *80 | Charles Hartnett, Chicago, c | 75 |
| 1936—H. Louis Gehrig, New York, 1b | 73 | Carl Hubbell, New York, p | 60 |
| 1937—Charles Gehringer, Detroit, 2b | 78 | Joseph Medwick, St. Louis, of | 70 |
| 1938—James Foxx, Boston, 1b | 305 | Ernest Lombardi, Cincinnati, c | 229 |
| 1939—Joseph DiMaggio, N. York, of | 280 | William Walters, Cincinnati, p | 303 |
| 1940—Henry Greenberg, Detroit, of | 292 | Frank McCormick, Cinn., 1b | 274 |
| 1941—Joseph DiMaggio, N. York, of | 291 | Adolph Camilli, Brooklyn, 1b | 300 |
| 1942—Joseph Gordon, New York, 2b | 270 | Morton Cooper, St. Louis, p | 263 |
| 1943—Spurgeon Chandler, N. Y., p | 246 | Stanley Musial, St. Louis, of | 267 |
| 1944—Harold Newhouser, Detroit, p | 236 | Martin Marion, St. Louis, ss | 190 |
| 1945—Harold Newhouser, Detroit, p | 236 | Philip Cavarretta, Chicago, 1B | 279 |
| 1946—Theodore Williams, Boston, of | 224 | Stanley Musial, St. Louis, 1b | 319 |
| 1947—Joseph DiMaggio, N. York, of | 202 | Robert Elliott, Boston, 3b | 205 |
| 1948—Louis Boudreau, Cleveland, ss | 324 | Stanley Musial, St. Louis, of | 303 |
| 1949—Theodore Williams, Boston, of | 272 | Jack Robinson, Brooklyn, 2b | 264 |
| 1950—Philip Rizzuto, New York, ss | 284 | C. James Konstanty, Phila., p | 286 |
| 1951—Lawrence Berra, New York, c | 184 | Roy Campanella, Brooklyn, c | 243 |
| 1952—Robert Shantz, Phila., p | 280 | Henry Sauer, Chicago, of | 226 |
| 1953—Albert Rosen, Cleveland, 3b | *336 | Roy Campanella, Brooklyn, c | 297 |
| 1954—Lawrence Berra, New York, c | 230 | Willie Mays, New York, of | 283 |
| 1955—Lawrence Berra, New York, c | 218 | Roy Campanella, Brooklyn, c | 226 |
| 1956—Mickey Mantle, N. Y., of | *336 | Donald Newcombe, Brkn., p | 223 |
| 1957—Mickey Mantle. New York, of | 233 | Henry Aaron, Milwaukee, of | 239 |
| 1958—Jack Jensen, Boston, of | 233 | Ernest Banks, Chicago, ss | 283 |
| 1959—J. Nelson Fox, Chicago, 2b | 295 | Ernest Banks, Chicago, ss | 232½ |
| 1960—Roger Maris, New York, of | 225 | Richard Groat, Pittsburgh, ss | 276 |
| 1961—Roger Maris, New York, of | 202 | Frank Robinson, Cincinnati, of | 219 |
| 1962—Mickey Mantle, New York, of | 234 | Maurice Wills, Los Angeles, ss | 209 |
| 1963—Elston Howard, New York, c | 248 | Sanford Koufax, Los Angeles, p | 237 |
| 1964—Brooks Robinson, Balti., 3b | 269 | Kenton Boyer, St. Louis, 3b | 243 |
| 1965—Zoilo Versalles, Minn., ss | 275 | Willie Mays, San Francisco, of | 224 |

# BASEBALL WRITERS' ASSOCIATION MVP AWARDS—Cont.

| AMERICAN LEAGUE | | | NATIONAL LEAGUE | | |
|---|---|---|---|---|---|
| Year Player Club | | Points | Player Club | | Points |
| 1966—Frank Robinson, Balti., of | | *280 | Roberto Clemente, Pitts., of | | 218 |
| 1967—Carl Yastrzemski, Boston, of | | .275 | Orlando Cepeda, St. Louis, 1b | | *280 |
| 1968—Dennis McLain, Detroit, p | | *280 | Robert Gibson, St. Louis, p | | 242 |
| 1969—Harmon Killebrew, Minn., 1-3b | | 294 | Willie McCovey, San Fran., 1b | | 265 |
| 1970—John (Boog) Powell, Balti., 1b | | 234 | Johnny Bench, Cincinnati, c | | 326 |
| 1971—Vida Blue, Oakland, p | | 268 | Joseph Torre, St. Louis, 3b | | 318 |
| 1972—Dick Allen, Chicago, 1b | | 321 | Johnny Bench, Cincinnati, c | | 263 |
| 1973—Reggie Jackson, Oak., of | | *336 | Pete Rose, Cincinnati, of | | 274 |
| 1974—Jeff Burroughs, Texas, of | | 248 | Steve Garvey, Los Angeles, 1b | | 270 |
| 1975—Fred Lynn, Boston, of | | 326 | Joe Morgan, Cincinnati, 2b | | 321½ |

*Unanimous selection.

# BASEBALL WRITERS' ASSOCIATION ROOKIE AWARDS

1947—Combined selection—Jack Robinson, Brooklyn, 1b.
1948—Combined selection—Alvin Dark, Boston, N. L., ss.

| Year Player Club | Votes | Player Club | Votes |
|---|---|---|---|
| 1949—Roy Sievers, St. Louis, of | 10 | Donald Newcombe, Brklyn., p | 21 |
| 1950—Walter Dropo, Boston, 1b | 15 | Samuel Jethroe, Boston, of | 11 |
| 1951—Gilbert McDougald, N. Y., 3b | 13 | Willie Mays, New York, of | 18 |
| 1952—Harry Byrd, Philadelphia, p | 9 | Joseph Black, Brooklyn, p | 19 |
| 1953—Harvey Kuenn, Detroit, ss | 23 | James Gilliam, Brooklyn, 2b | 11 |
| 1954—Robert Grim, New York, p | 15 | Wallace Moon, St. Louis, of | 17 |
| 1955—Herbert Score, Cleveland, p | 18 | William Virdon, St. Louis, of | 15 |
| 1956—Luis Aparicio, Chicago, ss | 22 | Frank Robinson, Cincinnati, of | *24 |
| 1957—Anthony Kubek, N. Y., inf-of | 23 | John Sanford, Philadelphia, p | 16 |
| 1958—Albert Pearson, Washington, of | 14 | Orlando Cepeda, San Fran., 1b | *†21 |
| 1959—W. Robert Allison, Wash., of | 18 | Willie McCovey, San Fran., 1b | *24 |
| 1960—Ronald Hansen, Baltimore, ss | 22 | Frank Howard, Los Angeles, of | 12 |
| 1961—Donald Schwall, Boston, p | 7 | Billy Williams, Chicago, of | 10 |
| 1962—Thomas Tresh, New York, of-ss | 13 | Kenneth Hubbs, Chicago, 2b | 19 |
| 1963—Gary Peters, Chicago, p | 10 | Peter Rose, Cincinnati, 2b | 17 |
| 1964—Pedro (Tony) Oliva, Minn., of | 19 | Richard Allen, Philadelphia, 3b | 18 |
| 1965—Curtis Blefary, Baltimore, of | 12 | James Lefebvre, Los Ang., 2b | 13 |
| 1966—Tommie Agee, Chicago, of | 16 | Tommy Helms, Cincinnati, 3b | 12 |
| 1967—Rod Carew, Minnesota, 2b | 19 | Tom Seaver New York, p | 11 |
| 1968—Stan Bahnsen, New York, p | 17 | Johnny Bench, Cincinnati, c | 10½ |
| 1969—Lou Piniella, Kansas City, of | 9 | Ted Sizemore, Los Angeles, 2b | 14 |
| 1970—Thurman Munson N. Y., c | 23 | Carl Morton, Montreal, p | 11 |
| 1971—Chris Chambliss, Cleveland, 1b | 11 | Earl Williams, Atlanta, c | 18 |
| 1972—Carlton Fisk, Boston, c | *24 | Jon Matlack, New York, p | 19 |
| 1973—Al Bumbry, Baltimore, of | 13½ | Gary Matthews, San Fran., of | 11 |
| 1974—Mike Hargrove, Texas, 1b | 16½ | Bake McBride, St. Louis, of | 16 |
| 1975—Fred Lynn, Boston, of | 23 | John Montefusco, San Fran., p | 12 |

*Unanimous selection. †Three writers did not vote.

# CY YOUNG MEMORIAL AWARD

| Year Pitcher Club | Votes | Year Pitcher Club | Votes |
|---|---|---|---|
| 1956—Donald Newcombe, Brooklyn | 10 | 1969—A. L.—Dennis McLain, Det. | 10 |
| 1957—Warren Spahn, Milwaukee | 15 | Mike Cuellar, Balt. | 10 |
| 1958—Robert Turley, N. Y., A. L. | 5 | N. L.—Tom Seaver, N. Y. | 23 |
| 1959—Early Wynn, Chicago, A. L. | 13 | 1970—A. L.—Jim Perry, Minn. | †55 |
| 1960—Vernon Law, Pittsburgh | 8 | N. L.—Bob Gibson, St. L. | †118 |
| 1961—Edward Ford, N. Y., A. L. | 9 | 1971—A. L.—Vida Blue, Oakland | †98 |
| 1962—Donald Drysdale, L. A., N. L. | 14 | N. L.—Ferguson Jenkins, Chi. | †97 |
| 1963—Sanford Koufax, L. A., N. L. | *20 | 1972—A. L.—Gaylord Perry, Cleve. | †64 |
| 1964—Dean Chance. L. A., A. L. | 17 | N. L.—Steve Carlton, Phil. | *†120 |
| 1965—Sanford Koufax, L. A., N. L. | *20 | 1973—A. L.—Jim Palmer, Balt. | †88 |
| 1966—Sanford Koufax, L. A., N. L. | *20 | N. L.—Tom Seaver, N. Y. | †70 |
| 1967—A. L.—Jim Lonborg, Boston | 18 | 1974—A. L.—Jim Hunter, Oakland | †90 |
| N. L.—M. McCormick, S. F. | 18 | N. L.—Mike Marshall, L.A. | †96 |
| 1968—A. L.—Dennis McLain, Det. | *20 | 1975—A. L.—Jim Palmer, Baltimore | †98 |
| N. L.—Robert Gibson, St. L. | *20 | N. L.—Tom Seaver, N.Y. | †98 |

*Unanimous selection. †Point system used.

# Major League Farm Systems for 1976

**\*Indicates working agreement. All other clubs owned outright.**

## AMERICAN LEAGUE

BALTIMORE (4): AAA—\*Rochester. AA—\*Charlotte. A—\*Miami. Rookie—Bluefield.

BOSTON (5): AAA—\*Rhode Island. AA—\*Bristol, Conn. A—\*Elmira, \*Winston-Salem, Winter Haven.

CALIFORNIA (5): AAA—\*Salt Lake City. AA—\*El Paso. A—\*Quad Cities, \*Salinas. Rookie—\*Idaho Falls.

CHICAGO (4): AAA—\*Iowa. AA—\*Knoxville. A—\*Appleton. Rookie—Sarasota.

CLEVELAND (4): AAA—\*Toledo. AA—\*Williamsport. A—\*San Jose, \*Batavia.

DETROIT (4): AAA — \*Evansville. AA — \*Montgomery. A — \*Lakeland. Rookie—\*Bristol, Va.

KANSAS CITY (4): AAA—Omaha. AA—\*Jacksonville. A—\*Waterloo. Rookie—Sarasota.

MILWAUKEE (4): AAA—\*Spokane. AA—\*Pittsfield. A—\*Burlington, Ia., \*Newark.

MINNESOTA (5): AAA—\*Tacoma. AA—Orlando. A—\*Reno (shares working agreement with San Diego), \*Wisconsin Rapids. Rookie—\*Elizabethton.

NEW YORK (4): AAA—\*Syracuse. AA—\*West Haven. A—\*Oneonta, Fort Lauderdale.

OAKLAND (4): AAA—\*Tucson. AA—\*Chattanooga. A—\*Modesto, \*Boise.

TEXAS (4): AAA — \*Sacramento. AA — \*San Antonio. A — \*Asheville. Rookie—Sarasota.

## NATIONAL LEAGUE

ATLANTA (4): AAA—Richmond. AA—Savannah. A—Greenwood. Rookie—Kingsport.

CHICAGO (4): AAA — \*Wichita. AA — Midland. A — \*Pompano Beach. Rookie—Bradenton.

CINCINNATI (5): AAA—\*Indianapolis. AA—\*Three Rivers. A—\*Tampa, \*Eugene. Rookie—Billings.

HOUSTON (4): AAA—\*Memphis. AA—\*Columbus. A—\*Dubuque. Rookie—Covington.

LOS ANGELES (5): AAA—Albuquerque. AA—\*Waterbury. A—\*Bellingham, \*Danville, \*Lodi.

MONTREAL (4): AAA—\*Denver. AA—\*Quebec City. A—\*West Palm Beach. Rookie—\*Lethbridge.

NEW YORK (5): AAA—\*Tidewater. AA—Jackson. A—\*Lynchburg, \*Wausau. Rookie—Marion.

PHILADELPHIA (5): AAA—\*Oklahoma City. AA—\*Reading. A—Peninsula, Spartanburg, \*Auburn.

PITTSBURGH (6): AAA—\*Charleston, W. Va. AA—\*Shreveport. A—\*Charleston, S. C., \*Salem, \*Niagara Falls. Rookie—Bradenton.

ST. LOUIS (5): AAA—\*Tulsa. AA—\*Arkansas. A—\*St. Petersburg. Rookie—Sarasota, \*Johnson City.

SAN DIEGO (4): AAA—\*Hawaii. AA—\*Amarillo. A—\*Walla Walla, \*Reno (shares working agreement with Minnesota).

SAN FRANCISCO (5): AAA—\*Phoenix. AA—\*Lafayette. A—\*Fresno, \*Cedar Rapids. Rookie—Great Falls.

**ROBIN ROBERTS**

**BOB LEMON**

**FRED LINDSTROM**

# HALL OF FAME
# FOR 1976

**ROGER CONNOR**

**CAL HUBBARD**

**OSCAR CHARLESTON**

# Roberts, Lemon Head Shrine Inductees

## By CHRIS ROEWE

The Hall of Fame honor list rose to 157 as six men were voted into Cooperstown in early 1976 in the annual elections. All three electing bodies selected honorees: pitchers Robin Roberts and Bob Lemon were named by the Baseball Writers' Association of America; the Committee on Veterans picked third baseman-outfielder Fred Lindstrom, first baseman Roger Connor and umpire Cal Hubbard, and the Special Committee on Negro Leagues named outfielder Oscar Charleston.

Roberts won election on his fourth try and Lemon on his 12th as 388 10-year members of the BBWAA cast ballots. Both won by comfortable margins. Roberts received 337 votes and Lemon 305, considerably more than the 75 per cent needed for election. The only other candidate to get 200 votes was the late Gil Hodges, for many years the slugging first baseman of the Brooklyn Dodgers who in 1969 managed the New York Mets to their first National League pennant and world championship. Gil was named on 233 ballots.

Possessed of a live fast ball and pinpoint control, Robin Evan Roberts joined the Phillies after only a half-season in the Interstate League in 1948 and led the Whiz Kids to a pennant in 1950. Roberts was 20-11 that year, his first of six consecutive 20-win seasons. His finest year was 1952 when he had a 28-7 mark for the fourth-place Phillies, leading the league in victories and innings pitched and walking only 45 in the 330 innings he toiled. The Phillies sold Robin to the Yankees after the 1961 season but he did not appear in a regular-season game with the Bombers who released him, April 30, 1962. Roberts then signed with Baltimore and pitched well for the Orioles from May, 1962 until he drew his release, July 31, 1965. He then returned to the National League, pitching for Houston and Chicago, winding up his major league career with the Cubs in 1966. Roberts finished with a won-and-lost mark of 286-245 in 19 major league campaigns. He walked only 902 batters in 4,689 innings, an average of 1.73 per nine-inning game. The 49-year-old Roberts makes his home in the Philadelphia area and works in the investment and brokerage field.

Robert Granville Lemon, a lefthanded-hitting outfielder and third baseman who seemed destined to spend most of his career in the minor leagues, switched in desperation to the mound and went on to become the mainstay of a Cleveland staff that led the Indians to two pennants and made them perennial flag contenders in the period from 1948 through 1956. Lemon won 20 games for the world champion Indians of 1948 and had six more 20-win seasons for the Tribe. His won-and-lost totals for 13 seasons, all with Cleveland, were 207-128. Bob led the league in victories with 23 in 1950 and tied for the lead in 1954-55. He hurled a no-hitter against Detroit in 1948. Retiring as an active player after the 1958 season, Lemon remained in Organized Ball, working as a coach for the Indians, Phillies and Angels and managing the Kansas City Royals in 1971-72. After managing in the minors in 1974-75, Bob, now 55, is returning to the majors as a coach for the Yankees in 1976.

A native of Chicago, Frederick Charles Lindstrom joined the pennant-winning New York Giants in 1924 when he was only 18. Regular Giant third baseman Heinie Groh was injured in late September and Lindstrom became the youngest player to ever appear in a World Series when he played in all seven games as the Giants were beaten by Washington. Lindy had 10 hits, including four off Walter Johnson in the fifth game and played errorless ball in the field. He became the regular third baseman the following year and remained with New York through the 1932 season. His greatest year was 1930 when he hit .379 with 22 homers and 106 RBIs. Switching to the outfield, Lindstrom was with Pittsburgh in 1933-34, Chicago Cubs in 1935 and finished his career with Brooklyn in 1936. His lifetime batting average in the majors was .311 with 1,747 hits and 103 homers. Now 70 years old, Lindstrom lives in retirement in Port Richey, Fla.

Roger Connor was a slugging first baseman whose major league career extended from 1880 through 1897. Roger played with Troy, New York, Philadelphia and St. Louis, all in the National League, and one season with New York's club in the short-lived Players' League. Connor made 2,535 hits in compiling a lifetime major league batting average of .325. His 131 home runs stood as the big league record until surpassed by Babe Ruth in 1921. Connor died at age 73 in 1931.

A former tackle in the National Football League, Robert Cal Hubbard is the only man to be named to the pro football Hall of Fame and the baseball Hall of Fame. At 6:02½ and 265 pounds, Cal permitted little argument with his decisions as he umpired in the American League from 1936 through 1951. From 1954 through 1969 Hubbard served as supervisor of umpires for the A.L. Now 75, Cal makes his home in Milan, Mo.

Oscar Charleston began his career in the Negro major leagues in 1915 when he was only 19 years old. A lefthanded batter and thrower, Charleston was rated by many as the finest outfielder in the history of the Negro major leagues. In later years he switched to first base and remained an active player until well into his 40s. He also managed various clubs in a career that extended into the 1950s. Oscar died in 1954 when he was 58.

The complete tabulation of the voting by the BBWAA follows: Robin Roberts, 337; Bob Lemon, 305; Gil Hodges, 233; Enos Slaughter, 197; Eddie Mathews, 189; Pee Wee Reese, 186; Nellie Fox, 174; Duke Snider, 159; Phil Rizzuto, 149; Red Schoendienst, 129; George Kell, 129; Don Drysdale, 114; Roger Maris, 87; Richie Ashburn, 85; Alvin Dark, 62; Walker Cooper, 56; Elston Howard, 55; Mickey Vernon, 52; Ted Kluszewski, 50; Don Larsen, 47; ElRoy Face, 23; Lew Burdette, 21; Don Newcombe, 21; Ken Boyer, 15; Del Crandall. 15; Bobby Thomson, 9; Vern Law, 9; Harvey Haddix, 8; Dick Groat, 7; Bill White, 7; Vic Wertz, 5; Johnny Podres, 2.

Following is a complete list of those enshrined in the Hall of Fame prior to 1976 with the vote by which each enrollee was elected:

1936—Tyrus Cobb (222), John (Honus) Wagner (215), George (Babe) Ruth (215), Christy Mathewson (205), Walter Johnson (189), named by Baseball Writers Association of America. Total ballots cast, 226.

1937—Napoleon Lajoie (168), Tristram Speaker (165). Denton (Cy) Young (153), named by the BBWAA. Total ballots cast, 201. George Wright, Morgan G. Bulkeley, Byron Bancroft Johnson, John J. McGraw, Cornelius McGillicuddy (Connie Mack), named by Centennial Commission.

1938—Grover C. Alexander (212), named by BBWAA. Total ballots, 262. Henry Chadwick, Alexander J. Cartwright, named by Centennial Commission.

1939—George Sisler (235), Edward Collins (213), William Keeler (207), Louis Gehrig, named by BBWAA. (Gehrig by special election after retirement from game was announced). Total ballots cast, 274. Albert G. Spalding, Adrian C. Anson, Charles A. Comiskey, William (Buck) Ewing, Charles Radbourn, William A. (Candy) Cummings named by committee of old-time players and writers.

1942—Rogers Hornsby (182) named by BBWAA. Total ballots cast, 233.

1944—Judge Kenesaw M. Landis, named by committee on old timers.

1945—Hugh Duffy, Jimmy Collins, Hugh Jennings, Ed Delahanty, Fred Clarke, Mike Kelly, Wilbert Robinson, Jim O'Rourke, Dennis (Dan) Brouthers and Roger Bresnahan, named by committee on old-timers.

1946—Jesse Burkett, Frank Chance, Jack Chesbro, Johnny Evers, Clark Griffith, Tom McCarthy, Joe McGinnity, Eddie Plank, Joe Tinker, Rube Waddell and Ed Walsh, named by committee on old timers.

1947—Carl Hubbell (140), Frank Frisch (136), Gordon (Mickey) Cochrane (128), and Robert (Lefty) Grove (123), named by BBWAA. Total ballots, 161.

1948—Herbert J. Pennock (94) and Harold (Pie) Traynor (93), named by BBWAA. Total ballots cast, 121.

1949—Charles Gehringer (159), named by BBWAA in runoff election. Total ballots cast, 187. Charles (Kid) Nichols and Mordecai (Three-Finger) Brown, named by committee on old-timers.

1951—Mel Ott (197) and Jimmie Foxx (179), named by BBWAA. Total ballots cast, 226.

1952—Harry Heilmann (203) and Paul Waner (195), named by BBWAA. Total ballots cast, 234.

1953—Jerome (Dizzy) Dean (209) and Al Simmons (199), named by BBWAA. Total ballots cast, 264. Charles Albert (Chief) Bender, Roderick (Bobby) Wallace, William Klem, Tom Connolly, Edward G. Barrow and William Henry (Harry) Wright, named by the new Committee on Veterans.

1954—Walter (Rabbit) Maranville (209), William Dickey (202) and William Terry (195), named by BBWAA. Total ballots cast, 252.

1955—Joe DiMaggio (223), Ted Lyons (217), Arthur (Dazzy) Vance (205) and Charles (Gabby) Hartnett (195), named by BBWAA. Total ballots cast, 251. J. Franklin (Home Run) Baker and Ray Schalk, named by Committee on Veterans.

1956—Hank Greenberg (164) and Joe Cronin (152), named by BBWAA. Total ballots cast, 193.

1957—Joseph V. McCarthy and Sam Crawford, named by Committee on Veterans.

1959—Zachariah (Zack) Wheat, named by Committee on Veterans.

1961—Max Carey and William Hamilton, named by Committee on Veterans.

1962—Bob Feller (150) and Jackie Robinson (124), named by BBWAA. Total ballots cast, 160. Bill McKechnie and Edd Roush, named by Committee on Veterans.

1963—Eppa Rixey, Edgar (Sam) Rice, Elmer Flick and John Clarkson, named by Committee on Veterans.

1964—Luke Appling (189), named by BBWAA in runoff election. Total ballots cast, 225. Urban (Red) Faber, Burleigh Grimes, Tim Keefe, Heinie Manush, Miller Huggins and John Montgomery Ward, named by Committee on Veterans.

1965—James (Pud) Galvin, named by Committee on Veterans.

1966—Ted Williams (282), named by BBWAA. Total ballots cast, 302. Casey Stengel, named by Committee on Veterans.

1967—Charles (Red) Ruffing (266), named by BBWAA in runoff election. Total ballots cast, 306. Branch Rickey and Lloyd Waner, named by Committee on Veterans.

1968—Joseph (Ducky) Medwick (240), named by BBWAA. Total ballots cast, 283. Leon (Goose) Goslin and Hazen (Kiki) Cuyler, named by Committee on Veterans.

1969—Stan (The Man) Musial (317) and Roy Campanella (270), named by BBWAA. Total ballots cast, 340. Stan Coveleski and Waite Hoyt, named by Committee on Veterans.

1970—Lou Boudreau (232), named by BBWAA. Total ballots cast, 300. Earle Combs, Jesse Haines and Ford Frick, named by Committee on Veterans.

1971—Chick Hafey, Rube Marquard, Joe Kelley, Dave Bancroft, Harry Hooper, Jake Beckley and George Weiss, named by Committee on Veterans. Satchel Paige, named by Special Committee on Negro Leagues.

1972—Sandy Koufax (344), Yogi Berra (339) and Early Wynn (301), named by BBWAA. Total ballots cast, 396. Lefty Gomez, Will Harridge and Ross Youngs, named by Committee on Veterans. Josh Gibson and Walter (Buck) Leonard, named by Special Committee on Negro Leagues.

1973—Warren Spahn (316), named by BBWAA. Total ballots cast, 380. Roberto Clemente (393), in special election by BBWAA in which 424 ballots were cast. Billy Evans, George Kelly and Mickey Welch, named by Committee on Veterans. Monte Irvin, named by Special Committee on Negro Leagues.

1974—Mickey Mantle (322) and Whitey Ford (284), named by BBWAA. Total ballots cast, 365. Jim Bottomley, Sam Thompson and Jocko Conlan, named by Committee on Veterans. James (Cool Papa) Bell, named by Special Committee on Negro Leagues.

1975—Ralph Kiner (273), named by BBWAA. Total ballots cast, 362. Earl Averill, Bucky Harris and Billy Herman, named by Committee on Veterans. William (Judy) Johnson, named by Special Committee on Negro Leagues.

**MAJOR LEAGUE HOTELS**

**MAJOR LEAGUE DEALS**

**NECROLOGY**

**MINOR LEAGUE PRESIDENTS**

# Hotels of Major League Teams

## AMERICAN LEAGUE

**AT BALTIMORE: Baltimore-Hilton**—California, Cleveland, Detroit, Minnesota, Oakland. **Baltimore Holiday Inn**—Milwaukee, Texas. **Cross Keys Inn**—Boston, Chicago. **Lord Baltimore**—Kansas City, New York.

**AT BOSTON: Parker House**—Chicago and Texas. **Sheraton-Boston**—All clubs except Chicago and Texas.

**AT CALIFORNIA: Grand**—Detroit. **Royal Inn**—All clubs except Detroit.

**AT CHICAGO: Executive House**—All clubs except California and Kansas City. **Sheraton Plaza**—Kansas City. **Water Tower**—California.

**AT CLEVELAND: Holiday Inn Lakeside**—Chicago and Kansas City. **Hollenden House**—All clubs except Chicago and Kansas City.

**AT DETROIT: Pontchartrain**—All clubs except Milwaukee and Oakland. **Sheraton-Cadillac**—Milwaukee. **Southfield Sheraton**—Oakland.

**AT KANSAS CITY: Muehlebach**—Baltimore. **Plaza Inn Downtown**—New York. **Sheraton-Royal**—All clubs except Baltimore and New York.

**AT MILWAUKEE: Downtowner Inn**—Minnesota. **Marc Plaza**—Chicago, Cleveland, Minnesota. **Marriott Inn**—Kansas City. **Pfister**—Baltimore, Boston, California, Detroit, New York, Oakland, Texas.

**AT MINNESOTA: Leamington (Minneapolis)**—All clubs.

**AT NEW YORK: Essex House**—Minnesota. **New York Sheraton**—All clubs except Minnesota and Detroit. **Roosevelt**—Detroit.

**AT OAKLAND: Edgewater**—All clubs except Texas. **Oakland-Hilton**—Texas.

**AT TEXAS: Inn of Six Flags**—California, New York, Kansas City. **Rodeway Inn**—Kansas City. **Sheraton-Dallas**—All clubs except California, Kansas City and New York.


## NATIONAL LEAGUE

**AT ATLANTA: Atlanta Hilton**—San Francisco. **Marriott**—All clubs except San Francisco.

**AT CHICAGO: Executive House**—All clubs except Montreal. **Hyatt Regency**—Montreal.

**AT CINCINNATI: Netherland Hilton**—Atlanta. **Stouffer's Inn**—Montreal, New York, Philadelphia, Pittsburgh, St. Louis, San Francisco. **Terrace Hilton**—Chicago, Houston, Los Angeles, San Diego.

**AT HOUSTON: Marriott**—Atlanta, Chicago, Cincinnati, Los Angeles, Montreal, San Diego. **Shamrock Hilton**—New York, Philadelphia, Pittsburgh, St. Louis, San Francisco.

**AT LOS ANGELES: Hyatt Regency**—Chicago, Houston, New York, Pittsburgh, St. Louis. **Los Angeles Hilton**—Cincinnati. **Sheraton West**—Atlanta, Montreal, San Diego. **Wilshire Hyatt House**—Philadelphia, San Francisco.

**AT MONTREAL: Queen Elizabeth**—Chicago, Philadelphia, Pittsburgh. **Sheraton Mt. Royal**—All clubs except Chicago, Philadelphia, Pittsburgh.

**AT NEW YORK: Americana**—Los Angeles. **New York Sheraton**—Cincinnati, Houston, Philadelphia, Pittsburgh, St. Louis, San Diego, San Francisco. **Roosevelt**—Atlanta. **Waldorf-Astoria**—Chicago, Montreal.

**AT PHILADELPHIA: Bellevue-Stratford**—Chicago, Houston, New York, St. Louis, San Diego, San Francisco. **Marriott**—Atlanta, Montreal. **Philadelphia Hilton**—Cincinnati, Los Angeles, Pittsburgh.

**AT PITTSBURGH: Carlton House**—Cincinnati, San Francisco. **Pittsburgh Hilton**—Chicago, Los Angeles, Montreal, New York, Philadelphia, St. Louis, San Diego. **William Penn**—Atlanta, Houston.

**AT ST. LOUIS: Chase-Park Plaza**—Atlanta, Chicago, Cincinnati, Houston, New York. **Stouffer's Riverfront Inn**—Los Angeles, Montreal, Philadelphia, Pittsburgh, San Diego, San Francisco.

**AT SAN DIEGO: Sheraton Harbor Island**—Atlanta, Chicago, Montreal, New York, Pittsburgh, St. Louis. **Town & Country**—Cincinnati, Houston, Los Angeles, Philadelphia, San Francisco.

**AT SAN FRANCISCO: Jack Tar**—Chicago, San Diego. **San Francisco Hilton**—Los Angeles, Montreal, Philadelphia, Pittsburgh. **Sheraton Palace**—Atlanta, Cincinnati, Houston, New York, St. Louis.

# Trade Mart Busy At Winter Meetings

## By CHRIS ROEWE

There were very few significant trades made while the 1975 major league season was in progress.

The Dodgers were the surprising beneficiaries of what appeared to be an unimportant deal with the Cubs, May 2. Los Angeles turned over young hurlers Geoff Zahn and Eddie Solomon in exchange for Burt Hooton, a righthander with an 0-2 mark. Hooton proceeded to become an 18-game winner and a regular starter on the National League's top pitching staff. Two days later the Giants traded center fielder Garry Maddox to the Phillies for first baseman-outfielder Willie Montanez, a deal that helped both clubs.

Brothers Gaylord and Jim Perry, both 200-game winners, were disposed of by the Indians. Jim was dealt to the Athletics, May 20 and drew his unconditional release on August 13. Gaylord was traded to the Rangers for three pitchers and a bundle of cash, June 13.

A flurry of trades occurred shortly after the World Series ended and there were many uniform changes made at the winter meetings. The Yankees figured in three major transactions, disposing of three mainstays of the club that failed to contend in 1975. In a controversial move the Bombers traded Bobby Bonds, the slugging outfielder and base stealer acquired only the year before, to the Angels for outfielder Mickey Rivers and righthander Ed Figueroa. Two Yankee starting pitchers also were involved in deals. Pat Dobson went to the Indians for outfielder Oscar Gamble and George Medich was traded to the Pirates for pitchers Dock Ellis and Ken Brett and young infielder Willie Randolph.

Veteran stars Harmon Killebrew and Juan Marichal have apparently come to the end of the line. Killebrew, 39, drew his unconditional release from the Royals, November 10. The long ball-hitting first baseman is fifth on the all-time major league homer list with 573. The 37-year-old Marichal was placed on the Voluntarily Retired List by the Dodgers, April 17. The high-kicking righthander finished his brilliant career with an impressive won-and-lost mark of 243-142.

A list of 1975 major league transactions follows:

January 13—Phillies signed pitcher Joe Hoerner, a free agent.

January 23—Rangers released catcher Duane (Duke) Sims.

January 24—Royals signed first baseman Harmon Killebrew, released by Twins.

January 28—Tigers signed shortstop Gene Michael, released by Yankees.

January 29—Giants purchased outfielder Von Joshua from Dodgers.

January 30—Mets purchased catcher Gerry Moses from Tigers.

February 1—Dodgers signed outfielder Norm Miller, a free agent.

February 11—Indians released outfielder John Jeter.

February 13—Indians signed outfielder Ken Berry, released by Brewers.

February 18—White Sox signed pitcher Bill Gogolewski, released by Indians, and assigned him to Denver.

February 25—Orioles traded first baseman John (Boog) Powell and pitcher Don Hood to Indians for catcher Dave Duncan and outfielder Al McGrew, latter assigned from Oklahoma City to Rochester.

February 25—Rangers traded pitcher Steve Dunning to White Sox for pitcher Stan Perzanowski, assigned from Denver to Spokane.

February 28—Cubs traded pitcher Dave LaRoche and outfielder Bryshear (Brock) Davis, latter assigned from Midland to San Antonio, to Indians for pitcher Milt Wilcox.

February 28—Mets purchased first baseman-outfielder Dave Kingman from Giants.

March 6—Athletics released second baseman Dick Green.

March 6—Brewers purchased infielder Kurt Bevacqua from Omaha, Royals' affiliate, and assigned him to Sacramento.

March 11—Phillies traded outfielder Nelson Garcia to Indians for pitcher Tom Hilgendorf.

March 15—Dodgers signed pitcher Juan Marichal, a free agent; placed on Voluntarily Retired List, April 17.

March 17—Phillies purchased pitcher Cecilio (Cy) Acosta from White Sox.

March 22—Mets traded catcher Isaac Hampton to Angels for pitcher Ken Sanders; Hampton was assigned to Salt Lake City and Sanders to Tidewater.

March 25—White Sox released pitcher Roger Nelson.

March 27—Braves released catcher Paul Casanova.

March 27—Pirates released pitcher Steve Blass.

March 27—Rangers released pitcher Robert D. Johnson.

March 27—Cardinals released infielder Ron Hunt.

March 28—Athletics purchased outfielder Don Hopkins from Expos.

March 28—Padres released pitcher Vicente Romo.

March 29—Braves traded first baseman Jack Pierce to Tigers for first baseman Reggie Sanders; Pierce was assigned to Evansville and Sanders to Richmond.

March 29—Red Sox traded first baseman Danny Cater to Cardinals for outfielder Danny Godby, assigned to Pawtucket.

March 29—Yankees released pitcher Mel Stottlemyre.

March 31—Angels released pitcher Horacio Pina.

March 31—Giants released pitcher John Morris.

March 31—Royals purchased catcher Bob Stinson from Expos.

April 1—White Sox traded catcher Ed Herrmann to Yankees for cash and four minor league players—outfielder Ken Bennett, catcher Terry Quinn, pitcher Fred Anyzeski and outfielder-first baseman John Narron.

April 3—Padres signed catcher Randy Hundley, a free agent.

April 4—Cardinals purchased shortstop Mario Guerrero from Red Sox and assigned him to Tulsa; Red Sox acquired pitcher Jim Willoughby from Tulsa, July 4, to complete deal.

April 4—Tigers purchased pitcher Ray Bare from Cardinals.

April 5—Phillies traded outfielder Bill Robinson to Pirates for pitcher Wayne Simpson, assigned to Toledo.

April 5—Dodgers released outfielder Norm Miller.

April 6—Astros purchased pitcher Joe Niekro from Braves and assigned him to Iowa.

April 6—Athletics purchased pitcher Jim Todd from Cubs and assigned him to Tucson; Athletics sent outfielder John Summers to Cubs to complete deal, April 29.

April 6—Tigers released pitcher Luke Walker.

April 7—Phillies released pitcher Eddie Watt.

April 8—Athletics signed infielder Billy Grabarkewitz, released by Cubs.

April 8—White Sox signed first baseman Deron Johnson, a free agent.

April 11—White Sox signed pitcher Claude Osteen, released by Cardinals.

April 11—Braves released infielder Dave Johnson.

April 12—Mets signed outfielder Jesus Alou, released by Athletics.

April 14—Athletics signed pitcher Claude (Skip) Lockwood, released by Yankees, and assigned him to Tucson.

April 15—Reds traded pitcher Tom Hall to Mets for pitcher Mac Scarce, assigned to Indianapolis.

April 17—Orioles traded first baseman-catcher Earl Williams to Braves for cash and pitcher Jimmy Freeman, assigned from Richmond to Rochester.

April 28—Cubs traded infielder-outfielder Matt Alexander, on Wichita roster, to Athletics for pitcher Howell Copeland, assigned to Wichita.

April 28—Padres released second baseman Glenn Beckert.

April 28—Padres purchased catcher Gerry Moses from Mets.

May 2—Cubs traded pitcher Burt Hooton to Dodgers for pitchers Geoff Zahn and Eddie Solomon, latter assigned from Albuquerque to Wichita.

May 3—Mets purchased shortstop Mike Phillips from Giants.

May 4—Giants traded outfielder Garry Maddox to Phillies for first baseman-outfielder Willie Montanez.

May 5—Angels released pitcher Orlando Pena.

May 5—Athletics released pinch-runner Herb Washington.

May 5—Yankees released infielder Eddie Leon.

May 7—Braves traded first baseman Richie Allen and catcher Johnny Oates to Phillies for catcher Jim Essian, outfielder Barry Bonnell, latter assigned from Spartanburg to Greenwood, and cash.

May 8—Brewers traded outfielder Bob Coluccio to White Sox for outfielder Bill Sharp.

May 8—Braves released pitcher Gary Gentry.

May 9—Giants traded pitcher Ron Bryant to Cardinals for outfielder Larry Herndon and pitcher Luis Gonzalez, both assigned to Phoenix.

May 15—White Sox acquired catcher Jim Essian and cash from Braves in completion of deal in which Braves acquired first baseman Richie Allen, December 3, 1974.

May 16—Padres traded pitcher Wilfred (Sonny) Siebert to Athletics for infielder Ted Kubiak.

May 18—Cardinals traded infielder Ted Martinez to Athletics for pitcher Steve Staniland, assigned from Modesto to St. Petersburg, and a player to be named later; pitcher Mike Barlow was assigned from Tucson to Tulsa, Cardinals' affiliate, to complete deal, May 23.

May 20—Indians traded pitchers Dick Bosman and Jim Perry to Athletics for pitcher Johnny Odom and cash.

May 21—Cardinals signed outfielder Don Hahn, released by Phillies.

May 28—Braves traded pitcher Ron Reed and a player to be named later to Cardinals for pitchers Elias Sosa and Ray Sadecki; Braves assigned outfielder Wayne Nordhagen from Richmond to Tulsa, Cardinals' affiliate, to complete deal, June 2.

May 29—Mets signed pitcher Gary Gentry, released by Braves, and assigned him to Jackson; released, June 19.

May 29—Orioles traded pitcher Bob Reynolds to Tigers for pitcher Fred Holdsworth, assigned to Rochester.

June 4—Rangers traded outfielder Willie Davis to Cardinals for shortstop Eddie Brinkman and pitcher Tommy Moore, latter assigned to Spokane.

June 7—Indians traded pitcher Johnny Odom and a player to be named later to Braves for pitcher Roric Harrison; Indians assigned shortstop Rob Belloir from San Antonio to Richmond, Braves' affiliate, to complete deal, June 16.

June 8—Expos purchased pitcher Fred Scherman from Astros.

June 8—Indians released outfielder Ken Berry.

June 11—Dodgers signed outfielder Leron Lee, released by Indians.

June 11—Giants traded first baseman Ed Goodson to Braves for shortstop Craig Robinson.

June 13—Cardinals purchased pitcher Mike Wallace from Yankees and assigned him to Tulsa.

June 13—Indians traded pitcher Gaylord Perry to Rangers for pitchers Jim Bibby, Jackie Brown and Rick Waits, latter recalled from Spokane, and an estimated $100,000 in cash.

June 13—Yankees purchased shortstop Eddie Brinkman from Rangers.

June 14—Brewers traded outfielder John Briggs to Twins for outfielder Bobby Darwin.

June 14—Red Sox purchased second baseman Denny Doyle from Angels.

June 15—White Sox traded pitchers Stan Bahnsen and Lee Pitlock, latter assigned from Denver to Tucson, to Athletics for pitcher Dave Hamilton and infielder Chester Lemon, latter assigned to Denver.

June 15—Angels purchased catcher Andy Etchebarren from Orioles.

June 15—Expos purchased first baseman Nate Colbert from Tigers.

June 15—White Sox traded first baseman Tony Muser to Orioles for pitcher Jesse Jefferson.

June 20—Yankees purchased outfielder Rich Coggins from Memphis, Expos' affiliate.

June 24—Padres purchased outfielder Don Hahn from Cardinals.

June 25—Cubs released pitcher Bob Locker.

June 26—Pirates released pitcher Sam McDowell.

June 30—White Sox traded outfielder Charles (Buddy) Bradford to Cardinals for cash and a player to be named later; Cardinals assigned pitcher Bill Parsons, on Tulsa roster, to Denver, White Sox' affiliate, July 7, to complete deal.

June 30—Indians signed first baseman-catcher Bill Sudakis, released by Angels.

June 30—Braves purchased pitcher Bruce Dal Canton from Royals; in completion of transaction Royals acquired pitcher Ray Sadecki from Braves and pitchers Norm Angelini and Al Autry were assigned from Omaha to Richmond, Braves' affiliate, September 4.

June 30—Angels released catcher Tom Egan.

June 30—Indians released first baseman-outfielder Tom McCraw as a player and signed him as a coach.

July 1—Phillies signed catcher Tim McCarver, released by Red Sox.

July 15—Angels purchased pitcher Jim Brewer from Dodgers.

July 15—Yankees released outfielder-first baseman Bob Oliver.

July 17—Rangers released pitcher Jim Merritt.

July 18—Expos purchased outfielder Jim Lyttle from Denver, White Sox' affiliate.

July 18—White Sox purchased catcher Gerry Moses from Padres.

July 25—Cardinals traded outfielder Jim Dwyer, on Tulsa roster, to Expos for infielder Larry Lintz.

July 27—Mets released outfielder Cleon Jones.

July 28—Mets purchased pitcher Claude (Skip) Lockwood from Tucson, Athletics' affiliate, and assigned him to Tidewater.

July 30—Pirates released infielder Paul Popovich.

July 31—Angels purchased outfielder-catcher Adrian Garrett from Wichita, Cubs' affiliate.

July 31—Cardinals released pitcher Ron Bryant.

August 1—Cardinals purchased pitcher Lloyd Allen from White Sox and assigned him to Tulsa.

August 4—Cardinals purchased pitcher Harry Parker from Mets.

August 11—Indians released first baseman-catcher Bill Sudakis.

August 13—Athletics released pitcher Jim Perry.

August 13—Athletics purchased outfielder-infielder Tommy Harper from Angels.

August 21—Red Sox signed infielder Dick McAuliffe who had been managing their farm club at Bristol, Conn., in the Eastern League.

August 26—Indians purchased pitcher Bob Reynolds from Tigers.

August 29—Athletics signed coach Dal Maxvill to an active player's contract.

August 31—Athletics purchased infielder-outfielder Cesar Tovar from Rangers.

September 2—Phillies purchased pitcher John Montague from Expos.

September 2—Red Sox released outfielder Tony Conigliaro, recalled from Pawtucket.

September 4—Yankees released outfielder Alex Johnson.

September 11—White Sox released catcher Gerry Moses.

September 17—Angels traded infielder-outfielder Bobby Valentine and a player to be named later to Padres for pitcher Gary Ross, on Hawaii roster; Angels assigned infielder Rudy Meoli to Padres to complete deal, November 4.

September 19—Cardinals signed pitcher John Sielicki, released by Giants, and assigned him to Tulsa.

September 22—Red Sox purchased first baseman Deron Johnson from White Sox for cash and a player to be named later; Red Sox assigned catcher Chuck Erickson to Denver, White Sox' affiliate, November 7, to complete deal.

September 29—Cardinals released catcher Rich Billings.

September 30—Cardinals traded pitcher Mike Barlow to Astros for outfielder Mike Easler who had been loaned to Tulsa, Cardinals' affiliate, June 25.

September 30—Cardinals assigned first baseman Doug Howard to Oklahoma City, Indians' affiliate, in completion of deal in which Tulsa, Cardinals' affiliate, acquired shortstop Luis Alvarado from Oklahoma City, May 27.

October 10—Athletics released shortstop Dal Maxvill.

October 20—Cardinals traded outfielder Willie Davis to Padres for outfielder Dick Sharon, assigned to Tulsa.

October 22—Tigers released shortstop Gene Michael.

October 24—Phillies traded catcher Larry Cox to Twins for shortstop Sergio Ferrer.

October 24—Reds traded pitcher Joaquin Andujar to Astros for two players to be named later; pitchers Luis Sanchez and Carlos Alfonso were assigned to Indianapolis, Reds' affiliate, to complete deal, December 12.

October 24—Phillies released pitcher Joe Hoerner.

October 24—Red Sox released infielder Dick McAuliffe.

October 28—Cubs traded shortstop Don Kessinger to Cardinals for pitcher Mike Garman and a player to be named later.

October 28—Athletics traded outfielder Charlie Chant to Cardinals for infielder Larry Lintz.

November 10—Royals released first baseman Harmon Killebrew.

November 12—Royals traded pitcher Nelson Briles to Rangers for second baseman Dave Nelson.

November 17—Rangers traded pitcher Ferguson Jenkins to Red Sox for outfielder Juan Beniquez, pitcher Steve Barr, cash and a player to be named later; Red Sox assigned pitcher Craig Skok to Sacramento, Rangers' affiliate, to complete deal, December 12.

November 17—Dodgers traded outfielders Jim Wynn and Tom Paciorek and infielders Lee Lacy and Jerry Royster to Braves for outfielder Johnnie (Dusty) Baker and first baseman Ed Goodson.

November 20—Athletics released outfielder-infielder Tommy Harper.

November 22—Yankees traded pitcher Pat Dobson to Indians for outfielder Oscar Gamble.

December 6—Astros traded catcher Milt May and pitchers Dave Roberts and Jim Crawford to Tigers for outfielder Leon Roberts, catcher Terry Humphrey and pitchers Gene Pentz and Mark Lemongello, latter assigned from Evansville to Memphis.

December 8—Giants traded pitcher Pete Falcone to Cardinals for third baseman Ken Reitz.

December 9—Phillies traded outfielder Mike Anderson to Cardinals for pitcher Ron Reed.

December 9—Astros released pitcher Wayne Granger.

December 9—Indians purchased catcher Ray Fosse from Athletics.

December 9—Indians traded catcher-first baseman John Ellis to Rangers for pitcher Stan Thomas and catcher Ron Pruitt.

December 10—Angels traded pitcher Bill Singer to Rangers for first baseman Jim Spencer and cash estimated at $100,000.

December 10—Phillies traded pitchers Dick Ruthven and Roy Thomas and outfielder Alan Bannister to White Sox for pitcher Jim Kaat and shortstop Mike Buskey, latter assigned from Denver to Oklahoma City.

December 11—Astros traded third baseman Doug Rader to Padres for pitchers Joe McIntosh and Larry Hardy, latter assigned to Memphis.

December 11—Yankees traded outfielder Bobby Bonds to Angels for outfielder John (Mickey) Rivers and pitcher Ed Figueroa.

December 11—Yankees traded pitcher George Medich to Pirates for pitchers Dock Ellis and Ken Brett and infielder Willie Randolph.

December 11—Angels traded first baseman Jim Spencer and outfielder Morris Nettles to White Sox for third baseman Bill Melton and pitcher Steve Dunning.

December 12—Red Sox traded pitcher Rogelio Moret to Braves for pitcher Tom House.

December 12—Reds traded shortstop Darrel Chaney to Braves for outfielder Mike Lum.

December 12—Reds traded pitcher Clay Kirby to Expos for infielder-outfielder Bob Bailey.

December 12—Expos purchased infielder Rodney Scott from Royals.

December 12—Astros traded second baseman Tommy Helms to Pirates for a player to be named later; third baseman Art Howe was assigned to Astros, January 6, 1976, to complete deal.

December 12—Rangers traded outfielder Joe Lovitto to Mets for outfielder Gene Clines.

December 12—Braves traded outfielder Ralph Garr and infielder Larvell Blanks to White Sox for outfielder Ken Henderson and pitchers Dick Ruthven and Danny Osborn, latter assigned to Richmond.

December 12—White Sox traded infielder Larvell Blanks to Indians for second baseman Jack Brohamer.

December 12—Mets traded outfielder Daniel (Rusty) Staub and pitcher Bill Laxton to Tigers for pitcher Mickey Lolich and outfielder Robert (Billy) Baldwin.

December 12—Cardinals traded outfielder Charles (Buddy) Bradford and pitcher Greg Terlecky to White Sox for infielder Lee Richard.

December 12—Reds traded pitcher Clay Carroll to White Sox for catcher Jeff Sovern and pitcher Rich Hinton, latter assigned to Indianapolis.

December 15—Royals released outfielder Vada Pinson.

December 17—Athletics released pitcher Wilfred (Sonny) Siebert.

December 18—Athletics released infielder Billy Grabarkewitz.

December 22—Cubs traded second baseman Vic Harris to Cardinals for shortstop Michael (Mick) Kelleher.

# Stengel Heads List of '75 Decedents

## By CHRIS ROEWE

The American League's most successful manager and baseball's long-time goodwill ambassador, Casey Stengel, died at 86 in Glendale, Calif., September 29.

Charles Dillon Stengel began his playing career in Organized Ball in 1910, reaching the majors in 1912. An outfielder, Casey played with Brooklyn, Pittsburgh, Philadelphia, New York and Boston in a National League career that extended from 1912 through 1925. He managed Brooklyn in 1934-35-36 and the Boston N.L. club from 1938 through 1943 with little success, none of his teams finishing higher than fifth. Stengel managed Oakland to the Pacific Coast League championship in 1948 and was named Yankee skipper in 1949. He proceeded to win five consecutive world championships and when he was dismissed after the 1960 season Casey had won 10 pennants and seven world titles. The New York Mets picked Stengel as manager when they entered the National League in 1962 and Casey suffered through four last-place finishes with the expansion club. Relieved of active duty in 1965 he maintained his ties with the Mets and was a familiar figure at baseball gatherings until his death. Stengel was named to the Hall of Fame in 1966.

Two other members of the Hall of Fame, outfielder Joe Medwick and pitcher Lefty Grove, passed away in 1975.

Joseph Michael Medwick compiled a .324 batting mark in 17 National League seasons. His greatest years were with St. Louis for whom he was a batting star from 1932 until he was traded to Brooklyn during the 1940 season. Joe had his finest year in 1937 when he won the Triple Crown, leading the league in batting average (.374), RBIs (154) and tying for the lead in homers (31). He was named Most Valuable Player that year. Medwick also played with the Giants and Braves and finished his big league career with the Cardinals again in 1947-48. Hall of Fame election came in 1968. Joe was only 63 when he died suddenly at St. Petersburg, Fla., March 21.

Robert Moses (Lefty) Grove, named to the Hall of Fame in 1947, is rated by many as the game's greatest lefthanded pitcher. An American League hurler from 1925 through 1941, Lefty compiled a lifetime won-and-lost record of 300-140 for the Philadelphia Athletics and Boston Red Sox. In 1931 Grove won 16 straight games, an American League record he shares with three other pitchers, and was named Most Valuable Player. He had a composite mark of 79-15 for the pennant-winning Athletics of 1929-30-31. Grove, 75, died at Norwalk, O., May 22.

Many other baseball luminaries died in 1975. They included Larry MacPhail, who served as chief executive of the Reds, Dodgers and Yankees and who introduced night ball to the majors in 1935; Joan Payson, principal owner of the New York Mets since their inception in 1961; Nellie Fox, major league second baseman for 19 seasons and the American League Most Valuable Player in 1959; Don Wilson, Houston Astros' pitcher from 1966 through 1974, who hurled two no-hit games; Sid Gordon, outfielder-third baseman, who hit 202 National League homers; Jeff Heath, slugging outfielder, who is the only American League player to get 20 or more doubles, triples and home runs in the same season and shortstop Charles

(Swede) Risberg, last survivor of the eight Chicago White Sox banned from Organized Ball for life in 1920 for conspiring to lose the 1919 World Series to Cincinnati.

An alphabetical listing of baseball deaths in 1975 follows:

**Clifford Allen Alexander,** 61, scout for the Brooklyn and Los Angeles Dodgers from 1950 through 1967 and for Cincinnati from 1968 until his death at Hamilton, O., June 30.

**Tracy Lee Baker,** 85, first baseman in one game with the Boston Red Sox in 1911, at Placerville, Calif., March 14.

**Edward Thomas Brannick,** 82, an employee of the New York and San Francisco Giants from 1905 through 1970 who served as traveling secretary for 40 years and later was named club secretary, at West Palm Beach, Fla., July 18.

**Sigmund Theodore Broskie,** 64, catcher with the Boston Braves in 1940, at Canton, O., May 17.

**Garland Maiers (Gob) Buckeye,** 78, pitcher with Washington briefly in 1918, Cleveland from 1925 through 1928 and New York Giants in 1928, at Stone Lake, Wis., November 14.

**Jess Robert Buckles,** 85, pitcher in two games with the New York Yankees in 1916, at Westminster, Calif., August 2.

**Leslie Kingston Burke,** 72, second baseman with Detroit from 1923 through 1926, at Danvers, Mass., May 6.

**Irving John (Jack) Burns,** 67, first baseman with the St. Louis Browns from 1930 through 1936 and Detroit in 1936, at Boston, Mass., April 18; scouted for Boston Red Sox in 1947-48, coached for Red Sox from 1955 through 1959 and again worked as a scout for the Red Sox from 1961 through 1973.

**Merritt Patrick (Sugar) Cain,** 66, pitcher with the Philadelphia Athletics from 1932 through 1935, St. Louis Browns in 1935-36 and Chicago White Sox in 1936-37-38, at Carrollton, Ga., April 3.

**Martin Francis Callaghan,** 75, outfielder with the Chicago Cubs in 1922-23 and Cincinnati in 1928 and 1930, at Norfolk, Mass., June 24; went to bat three times in the fourth inning, August 25, 1922, a modern major league record shared by five players.

**Owen Thomas (Ownie) Carroll,** 72, pitcher with Detroit from 1925 through 1930, New York Yankees in 1930, Cincinnati in 1930-31-32 and Brooklyn in 1933-34, at Orange, N. J., June 8; one of greatest col'ege pitchers in history, winning 50 games and losing only two in four years at Holy Cross College.

**Charles L. (Buster) Chatham,** 73, third baseman-shortstop with the Boston Braves in 1930-31, at Waco, Tex., December 15; associated with Organized Ball for more than 50 years as a player, minor league manager and club official, and scout for Pittsburgh, San Francisco, Detroit and Texas Rangers.

**Alan Thomas Clarke,** 79, pitcher in one game with Cincinnati in 1921, at Cheverly, Md., March 11.

**Albert George (Bert) Cole,** 76, pitcher with Detroit from 1921 through 1925, Cleveland in 1925 and Chicago White Sox in 1927, at San Mateo, Calif., May 30.

**Rollin Edward Cook,** 84, pitcher with the St. Louis Browns briefly in 1915, at Toledo, O., August 11.

**John Daniel Couch,** 84, pitcher with Detroit briefly in 1917, Cincinnati in 1922-23 and the Philadelphia Phillies in 1923-24-25, at Palo Alto, Calif., December 8.

**Clinton Dawdson Courtney,** 48, major league catcher from 1951 through 1961 and manager of Richmond in the International League from June 16, 1973 until his death at Rochester, N. Y., June 15; played with the New York Yankees in 1951, St. Louis Browns in 1952-53, Baltimore in 1954, Chicago White Sox in 1955, Washington from 1955 through 1959, Baltimore in 1960-61 and Kansas City in 1961.

**Walton Edwin Cruise,** 84, outfielder with the St. Louis Cardinals from 1914 through 1919 and Boston Braves from 1919 through 1924, at Sylacauga, Ala., January 9; played all 26 innings of longest game in major league history when Braves and Brooklyn Dodgers tied, 1-1, May 1, 1920.

**Astyanax Saunders Douglas,** 75, catcher with Cincinnati briefly in 1921 and 1925, January 26.

**Charles Bruce Edwards, 51,** catcher-infielder with Brooklyn from 1946 through 1951, Chicago Cubs in 1951-52-54, Washington in 1955 and Cincinnati in 1956, at Sacramento, Calif., April 25.

**Herrick Smith Emery, 76,** outfielder with the Philadelphia Phillies briefly in 1924, at Cape Canaveral, Fla., June 2.

**Major Kerby Farrell, 62,** active in Organized Ball for more than 40 years as a player, manager, coach and scout, at Nashville, Tenn., December 17; played first base for the Boston Braves in 1943 and Chicago White Sox in 1945; managed Cleveland in 1957; coached for the White Sox from 1966 through 1969 and Cleveland in 1970-71; scouted for Minnesota in 1974.

**Stephen Charles Filipowicz, 53,** outfielder with the New York Giants in 1944-45 and Cincinnati in 1948 and a halfback with New York in the National Football League in 1945-46, at Wilkes-Barre, Pa., February 21.

**Max John Flack, 85,** outfielder with the Chicago Cubs from 1916 through 1922 and St. Louis Cardinals from 1922 through 1925 and one of only two men to play for two major league clubs on the same day, at Belleville, Ill., July 31; between games of a morning and afternoon doubleheader at Chicago, May 30, 1922, Flack was traded by the Cubs to the Cardinals for outfielder Cliff Heathcote and both men played in each game.

**Jacob Nelson (Nellie) Fox, 47,** major league second baseman for 19 seasons and American League Most Valuable Player in 1959, at Baltimore, Md., December 1; played with the Philadelphia Athletics in 1947-48-49, Chicago White Sox from 1950 through 1963 and Houston in 1964-65; coached for Houston in 1965-66-67 and Washington from 1968 through 1971 and Texas Rangers in 1972; made 2,663 hits for a major league lifetime batting mark of .288; holds major league record for most consecutive games played at second base, 798; led American League second basemen in fielding percentage six times; holds major league record for most years leading second basemen in putouts (10), 1952 through 1961; led A.L. second basemen in assists six times and in double plays five times; led A.L. in hits in 1952-54-57-58.

**Joseph Frank Frisa, 63,** major league scout for the St. Louis Cardinals, Cincinnati, New York Yankees and Philadelphia Phillies from 1943 through 1973, at Buffalo, N. Y., March 5.

**Oscar Lawrence Fuhr, 78,** pitcher with the Chicago Cubs briefly in 1921 and Boston Red Sox in 1924-25, at Dallas, Tex., March 27.

**Curtis Hooper Fullerton, 76,** pitcher with the Boston Red Sox from 1921 through 1925 and in 1933, at Winthrop, Mass., January 2.

**Arthur P. Gaines, 57,** owner and operator of the Art Gaines Baseball Camp which has been in continuous operation since 1957, at St. Louis, Mo., November 13.

**John Beverly Gooch, 77,** catcher with Pittsburgh from 1921 through 1928, Brooklyn in 1928-29, Cincinnati in 1929-30 and Boston Red Sox in 1933 and a coach for Pittsburgh in 1939-40, at Nashville, Tenn., May 15.

**Sidney Gordon, 56,** outfielder-third baseman with the New York Giants from 1941 through 1949, Boston and Milwaukee Braves from 1950 through 1953, Pittsburgh in 1954-55 and the Giants in 1955, at New York City, June 17; hit 202 major league home runs and batted in more than 100 runs in 1948-50-51.

**Newton Michael (Mickey) Grasso, 55,** catcher with the New York Giants in 1946, Washington from 1950 through 1953, Cleveland in 1954 and the Giants in 1955, at Miami, Fla., October 15.

**Robert Moses (Lefty) Grove, 75,** generally considered the game's greatest lefthanded pitcher and a member of the Hall of Fame, at Norwalk, O., May 22; pitched for the Philadelphia Athletics from 1925 through 1933 and Boston Red Sox from 1934 through 1941; won 20 or more games eight times, including seven consecutive seasons, 1927 through 1933, in compiling a lifetime won-and-lost total of 300-140; won 16 straight games in 1931, an American League record he shares with three other pitchers; had marks of 20-6, 28-5 and 31-4 for the pennant-winning A's of 1929-30-31; led league in strikeouts seven straight years, 1925 through 1931; won four and lost two in World Series play with an earned-run average of 1.75 for 51⅓ innings; named to Hall of Fame in 1947.

**Hyland Gunning, 86,** first baseman with the Boston Red Sox briefly in 1911, at Togus, Me., March 28.

**Bruce Daniel Hartford, 83,** shortstop with Cleveland in 1914, at Los Angeles, Calif., May 25.

**John Geoffrey (Jeff) Heath, 60,** outfielder with Cleveland from 1936 through 1945, Washington in 1946, St. Louis Browns in 1946-47 and Boston Braves in 1948-49, at Seattle, Wash., December 9; had his greatest year in 1941 when he batted .340 with 32 doubles, 20 triples and 24 homers to become the first and only American League player to get 20 or more doubles, triples and homers in the same season.

**George Alvin (Al) Helfer, 63,** play-by-play broadcaster for Pittsburgh, Cincinnati, Brooklyn, New York Giants and Oakland and on the Mutual network's "Game of the Day" in the period from 1935 through 1970, at Sacramento, Calif., May 16.

**Thomas (Tommy) Holmes, 71,** New York sportswriter for many years, former correspondent for THE SPORTING NEWS and president of the Baseball Writers' Association in 1947, at Brooklyn, N. Y., March 25.

**Edwin Cyril Johnson, 76,** outfielder with Washington briefly in 1920, at Morganfield, Ky., July 3.

**Kenneth Peter (Curly) Jungels, 59,** pitcher with Cleveland in 1937-38 and 1940-41 and Pittsburgh in 1942, at West Bend, Wis., September 9.

**Horace Kent Kibbie, 72,** infielder with the Boston Braves in 1925, at Ft. Worth, Tex., October 19.

**Westcott William Kingdon, 74,** infielder with Washington in 1932, who played in the top minor leagues from 1919 through 1934, at Capistrano, Calif., April 19.

**Elmer Ellsworth Knetzer, 90,** pitcher with Brooklyn from 1909 through 1912, the Boston Braves in 1916 and Cincinnati in 1916-17, at Pittsburgh, Pa., October 3.

**George Bernard (Dave) Koslo, 55,** pitcher with the New York Giants in 1941-42 and from 1946 through 1953, Baltimore in 1954 and the Milwaukee Braves in 1954-55, at Menasha, Wis., December 1; led league in earned-run average in 1949 with a 2.50 mark; pitched a complete-game victory over the New York Yankees in the opening game of the 1951 World Series.

**George A. (Doc) Lentz, 72,** trainer for the Washington Senators and Minnesota Twins from 1947 through 1972, at Silver Spring. Md., November 11.

**Louis Bailey Lowdermilk, 88,** pitcher with the St. Louis Cardinals in 1911-12 and a brother of Grover Lowdermilk, also a major league pitcher, at Centralia, Ill., December 27.

**Leland Stanford (Larry) MacPhail, 85,** chief executive of three major league clubs at Miami, Fla., October 1; served as general manager at Cincinnati in 1934-35-36 where he introduced night ball to the major leagues on May 24, 1935; president and general manager at Brooklyn from 1938 through 1942; purchased the New York Yankees with Dan Topping and Del Webb in 1945 and served as president and general manager until October, 1947 when he sold his interest to his partners.

**John M. (Jack) Malaney, 83,** baseball writer for many years, long-time correspondent for THE SPORTING NEWS and a member of the public relations department of the Boston Red Sox from 1956 through 1960, at Boston, Mass., November 24.

**John Wyeth (Red) Marion, 59,** outfielder with Washington briefly in 1935 and again in 1943 and a brother of Marty Marion, star shortstop of the St. Louis Cardinals in the 1940s, at San Jose. Calif., March 13.

**James Milton McGlothlin, 32,** pitcher with the California Angels from 1965 through 1969, Cincinnati from 1970 through 1973 and Chicago White Sox in 1973, at Union, Ky., December 23; pitched in World Series of 1970 and 1972 with no decisions; tied for league lead in shutouts with six in 1967.

**Joseph Michael (Ducky) Medwick, 63,** National League outfielder for 17 seasons and a member of the Hall of Fame, at St. Petersburg, Fla., March 21; had greatest years for St. Louis Cardinals for whom he starred from 1932 until traded to Brooklyn, June 12, 1940; last National Leaguer to win Triple Crown, leading league in batting average (.374) and RBIs (154) and tying for lead in homers (31) in 1937; made 64 doubles in 1936, still an N. L. record; led league in RBIs in 1936-37-38, tying the major league mark for most consecutive years leading in runs batted in; named Most Valuable Player in

National League in 1937; played with Brooklyn from 1940 through 1943, New York Giants in 1944-45, Boston Braves in 1945, Brooklyn in 1946 and Cardinals in 1947-48; served as batting instructor for Cardinals from 1966 until his death; named to Hall of Fame in 1968.

**Albert Ernest (Dutch) Mele, 60,** outfielder with Cincinnati briefly in 1937 and a star in the high minors from 1939 through 1951, at Hollywood, Fla., February 12.

**Jacob Walter Miller, 77,** pitcher with Cleveland from 1924 through 1931 and the Chicago White Sox in 1933, at Venice, Fla., August 20.

**Arthur Grant Mills, 72,** pitcher with the Boston Braves briefly in 1927-28 and a coach for Detroit from 1944 through 1948, at Utica, N. Y., July 23.

**Vernon Thomas Morgan, 47,** third baseman with the Chicago Cubs briefly in 1954-55 and a coach for the Minnesota Twins from 1969 through 1975, at Minneapolis, Minn., November 8.

**Willard Blackmer Morrell, 75,** pitcher with Washington in 1926 and the New York Giants in 1930-31, at Birmingham, Ala., August 5.

**Eugene R. (Lefty) Morrison, 81,** scout for Washington in 1961-62 and the Philadelphia Phillies in 1936-67, at Indianapolis, Ind., March 21.

**Clarence Francis (Heinie) Mueller, 75,** outfielder with the St. Louis Cardinals from 1920 through 1926, New York Giants in 1926-27, Boston Braves in 1928-29 and St. Louis Browns in 1935, at DeSoto, Mo., January 23; brother of Walter Mueller, outfielder with Pittsburgh in the 1920s.

**Harold David Ock, 63,** catcher in one game with Brooklyn in 1935, at Mount Kisco, N. Y., March 18.

**Joan Whitney Payson, 72,** principal owner of the New York Mets since the club was formed in 1961 and a prominent figure in horse racing, at New York City, October 4.

**James Niels Peterson, 66,** pitcher with the Philadelphia Athletics in 1931 and 1933 and Brooklyn in 1937, at Palm Beach, Fla., April 8.

**James Ralph Poole, 79,** first baseman with the Philadelphia Athletics in 1925-26-27, at Hickory, N. C., January 2; played in major and minor leagues for 35 years, from 1912 through 1946, a record for Organized Ball; hit 50 homers and had 167 RBIs for Nashville of the Southern Association in 1930.

**Drew Leon Rader, 74,** pitcher in one game with Pittsburgh in 1921, June 5.

**Roderick Blan (Wog) Rice, 72,** scout for the Boston Red Sox from 1948 through 1973, at Norman, Okla., April 23.

**Lancelot Clayton (Lance) Richbourg, 77,** outfielder with the Philadelphia Phillies in 1921, Washington in 1924, Boston Braves from 1927 through 1931 and Chicago Cubs in 1932, at Crestview, Fla., September 10; made 206 hits and batted .337 in 1928.

**Lewis Sidney Riggs, 65,** third baseman with the St. Louis Cardinals in 1934, Cincinnati from 1935 through 1940, and Brooklyn in 1941-42 and 1946, at Durham, N. C., August 12; played in the World Series of 1940-41.

**Charles August (Swede) Risberg, 81,** shortstop with the Chicago White Sox from 1917 through 1920 and the last surviving member of the "Black Sox," a group of eight Chicago players who were barred from Organized Ball for life in 1920 for conspiring to lose the 1919 World Series to Cincinnati, at Red Bluff, Calif., October 13.

**Carlos Rubio, 65,** former president of the Mexican League who was associated with baseball in Mexico for almost 50 years as a player, club owner and league official, at Veracruz, Mex., July 7.

**Frederick Paul Schliebner, 80,** first baseman with Brooklyn and the St. Louis Browns in 1923 and a native of Berlin, Germany, at Toledo, O., April 15.

**John Herman Schulte, 93,** shortstop with the Boston Braves briefly in 1906, at Roseville, Mich., August 17.

**Raymond Francis Shepherdson, 78,** catcher with the St. Louis Cardinals briefly in 1924 at Little Falls, N. Y., November 8.

**Fred Peter Sherry, 86,** pitcher with Washington in 1911, at Honesdale, Pa., July 27.

**Julius Joseph (Moose) Solters, 69,** outfielder with the Boston Red Sox in 1934-35, St. Louis Browns in 1935-36, Cleveland in 1937-38-39, Browns in 1939 and Chicago White Sox in 1940-41 and 1943, at Pittsburgh, Pa., September 28;

had more than 100 runs batted in for three consecutive seasons, 1935-36-37, and hit three home runs in one game, July 7, 1935.

**Charles Dillon (Casey) Stengel, 86,** major league outfielder and manager who won 10 pennants and seven world championships as skipper of the New York Yankees and a member of the Hall of Fame, at Glendale, Calif., September 29; played with Brooklyn from 1912 through 1917, Pittsburgh in 1918-19, Philadelphia Phillies in 1920-21, New York Giants in 1921-22-23 and Boston Braves in 1924-25; had a composite batting average of .393 in the World Series of 1916-22-23; coached for Brooklyn in 1932-33 and managed the Dodgers in 1934-35-36; managed the Boston N. L. club from 1938 through 1943; managed the New York Yankees from 1949 through 1960, winning pennants in 1949-50-51-52-53-55-56-57-58-60 and world championships in 1949-50-51-52-53-56-58; managed the New York Mets from their inception in 1962 through the 1965 season; named to Hall of Fame in 1966.

**George Butler Storer, 75,** owner of the Miami Marlins of the International League in 1957-58-59 and head of the Storer Broadcasting Co., a radio and television chain, at Miami, Fla., November 4.

**Harry George Strohm, 74,** infielder, who spent more than 50 years in Organized Ball as a player, manager, club executive and league president in the minors and as a major league scout, at Lafayette, La., December 23.

**Adam William (Doc) Swigler, 79,** pitcher in one game with the New York Giants in 1917, at Philadelphia, Pa., February 5.

**Marion Brooks (Pat) Tobin, 58,** pitcher in one game with the Philadelphia Athletics in 1941, at Shreveport, La., January 21.

**Philip J. Troy, 78,** traveling secretary for the Boston Braves from 1919 through 1927 and for the Boston Red Sox from 1930 through 1945 and assistant to the general manager of the Red Sox from 1946 through 1948, at North Quincy, Mass., March 25.

**George Frederick Twombly, 82,** outfielder with Cincinnati in 1914-15-16, Boston Braves in 1917 and Washington in 1919, at Lexington, Mass., February 18.

**Leo Ward, 68,** traveling secretary for the St. Louis Cardinals from 1937 through 1972, at St. Louis, Mo., March 17.

**Frank Wayenburg, 75,** pitcher with Cleveland briefly in 1924, at Zanesville, O., April 16.

**Julian Valentine Wera, 73,** third baseman with the New York Yankees in 1927 and 1929, at Rochester, Minn., December 12.

**Stephen Vincent White, 90,** pitcher briefly with Washington and Boston Braves in 1912, at Braintree, Mass., January 29.

**Donald Edward Wilson, 29,** pitcher with Houston of the National League from 1966 through 1974, of carbon monoxide poisoning, at Houston, Tex., January 5; pitched two no-hit games in the majors—against Atlanta, June 18, 1967, and against Cincinnati, May 1, 1969.

**Frederick Davis (Ted) Wingfield, 75,** pitcher with Washington in 1923-24 and the Boston Red Sox from 1924 through 1927, at Johnson City, Tenn., July 18.

# Presidents of Minor Leagues for '76

## CLASS AAA

American Association—Joe Ryan, P. O. Box 382, Wichita, Kan. 67201

International League—George H. Sisler, Jr., 401 Times Square Building, Rochester, N. Y. 14604

Mexican League—Lic. Antonio Ramirez (Muro), Campos Eliseos 169-202, Mexico 5, D. F., Mexico

Pacific Coast League—Roy Jackson, P. O. Box 530, Paoli, Pa. 19301

## CLASS AA

Eastern League—P. Patrick McKernan, 26 Spadina Parkway, Pittsfield, Mass. 01201

Southern League—Billy Hitchcock, Box 528, Opelika, Ala. 36801

Texas League—Carl Sawatski, P. O. Box 5240, Little Rock, Ark. 72205

## CLASS A

California League—E. W. (Bill) Wickert, 677 Santa Barbara Road, Berkeley, Calif. 94707

Carolina League—Wallace McKenna, P. O. Box 1326, Lynchburg, Va. 24505

Florida State League—George MacDonald, Jr., P. O. Box 414, Lakeland, Fla. 33802

Gulf States League—Howard L. Green, 1244 Karla Drive, Hurst, Tex. 76053

Mexican Center League—Lic. Antonio Ramirez (Muro), Campos Eliseos 169-202, Mexico 5, D. F., Mexico

Mexican Pacific League—Horacio Lopez Diaz, Perimetral Oeste No. 171-A, Colonia Modelo, Hermosillo, Sonora, Mexico

Midwest League—William K. Walters, P. O. Box 444, Burlington, Ia. 52601

New York-Pennsylvania League—Vincent M. McNamara, 220 Brookside Drive, Buffalo, N. Y. 14220

Northwest League—Bob Richmond, P. O. Box 848, Eugene, Ore. 97401

Western Carolinas League—John H. Moss, P. O. Box 49, Kings Mountain, N. C. 28086

## ROOKIE CLASSIFICATION

Appalachian League—Chauncey DeVault, P. O. Box 927, Bristol, Va. 24201

Gulf Coast League—George MacDonald, Jr., P. O. Box 414, Lakeland, Fla. 33802

Pioneer League—Ralph C. Nelles, P. O. Box 570, Billings, Mont. 59103

Bobby Bragan—National Association President

# Official Minor League Averages

1975 Junior World Series

Official Averages Of All Triple A, Double A

and A Leagues, Plus Rookie Leagues

# Evansville Wins Junior World Series

## By ART VOELLINGER

Before the start of the 50th Junior World Series, Don Labbruzzo, President and General Manager of the Evansville Triplets, called his team "truly a Cinderella team."

In breezing to a four games to one title over Tidewater, Evansville completely supported Labbruzzo's description.

Unlike the 1972 Triplet edition which brought Evansville its first American Association pennant, the 1975 farm team of Detroit had no super stars and was not even represented on the A. A. all-star team.

Ironically, in 1972 when the Kodak World Classic at Honolulu replaced the JWS for one season, Evansville, then affiliated with Milwaukee, suffered a loss to Tidewater en route to a fourth-place finish behind the champion Caribbean All-Stars.

But in '75 the Triplets were as much a problem for the International League champion Tides, a farm club of the New York Mets, as for the A. A. teams that succumbed to a torrid Evansville drive.

From a second-place standing, 8½ games back on June 22 after losing 19 of 23 games, the Triplets roared by winning 49 of 72 games, including a 2-1 Eastern division clinching triumph August 27 at Omaha.

A post-season mark of 4-2 against Denver in the A. A. title series and a 4-1 record against Tidewater gave the Triplets a 59-29 record after their June swoon.

Tidewater also did not waltz to the JWS. The Tides were forced to win 22 of their final 33 regular season games for a .667 pace to finish in a tie with Rochester, which won 24 of its final 36 contests.

In a one-game playoff the Tides blanked Rochester, 1-0, on the four-hit pitching of Nino Espinosa, who set a precedent for a trek to the Governor's Cup championship.

Despite the mid-August call-ups of I. L. batting champion Mike Vail and team victory leader, pitcher Craig Swan, the Tides rolled.

First, Charleston fell as Bill Laxton and Gary Manderbach flipped 8-0 and 1-0 shutouts around a 10-2 romp sparked by the seven-hit pitching of rookie Jeff Grose and two home runs by Roy Staiger. Then, Syracuse slid as Randy Sterling, Laxton and Manderbach and reliever Bob Myrick permitted just a total of three runs in the triumphs of a 3-1 series edge.

But following the recall of Tide RBI leader Staiger and catcher Ron Hodges before the JWS, Evansville's hungry young hurlers prevailed.

The Triplets had advanced to the A. A. flag as 21-year-old Mark Fidrych, one of four hurlers called from Montgomery (Southern) during the season, led the way with two victories. Mark Lemongello, 20, and Frank MacCormack, 21, also triumphed with Ed Glynn, 22, gaining a save.

Little changed in the JWS as the Triplets permitted eight runs (four earned) and 27 hits in a pitching-dominated series . . . until home runs helped clinch the final game.

In the first game at Norfolk, Va., Lemongello fired a 4-0 four-hitter, struck out eight, walked two and allowed just one runner past second base.

The Triplets rallied for three runs in the seventh inning after Bob

Molinaro singled and raced to third when starting pitcher Sterling fielded a bunt by Ed Kurpiel but bobbled the ball and threw wildly to second base. Marv Lane followed with a two-run triple and scored when Chuck Scrivener singled.

Rain postponed the second game but did not cool Evansville which followed the seven-hit hurling of Bill Slayback and Steve Grilli to a 6-1 breather and a 2-0 series edge.

The Triplets' second run came in the fifth after Art James apparently had bunted foul on a third strike. With two out and a 1-2 count, James' bunt landed foul on the lip of the basepath, 45 feet from home plate, then squirted into fair territory to score John Gamble from third base.

Evansville plated three runs in the eighth when Bruce Kimm, Kurpiel and Gamble lashed clutch singles. Ron Diggle had two hits and an RBI for the Tides.

Tidewater's only series success came in game No. 3 when Laxton pitched a two-hitter, faced just 30 batters and permitted one runner to get as far as second base.

The Tides tallied against Fidrych in the sixth when Mark DeJohn singled, advanced to second on a sacrifice bunt by Bruce Boisclair and scored on a two-out single by Diggle.

MacCormack sparked the Triplets with 8⅔ innings of four-hit pitching in a 2-1 victory in game No. 4 at Evansville.

In the sixth inning the Triplets broke a 1-1 tie when Jerry Manuel reached first on an infield single, and took second on third baseman Randy Trapp's wild throw and scored on Molinaro's line drive single off the glove of first baseman Brock Pemberton.

Tidewater jumped to a 5-0 lead in the fifth game with the aid of four Triplet errors, but Evansville rallied with five in the fifth on a three-run homer by Lane off Myrick and a two-run homer by Kurpiel off reliever Espinosa.

While reliever Tom Makowski was in the process of retiring the final 13 Tidewater batters, Evansville waited until the seventh for its decisive run.

After singles by Kimm and Kurpiel and a wild pitch, Gamble singed for a 6-5 lead that grew when Kurpiel sprinted home on a squeeze bunt by Boots Day.

"I never saw a more deserving team," said Triplets' Manager Fred Hatfield, a pennant-winner for the fourth time in his last five seasons as a minor-league manager.

For their efforts the Triplets earned $363 per player with $242 going to the Tides.

### Game of September 11

| | | | | | | | | | | | | | | |
|---|---|---|---|---|---|---|---|---|---|---|---|---|---|---|
| Evansville | 0 | 0 | 0 | | 1 | 0 | 0 | | 3 | 0 | 0 | — | 4 | 9 | 1 |
| Tidewater | 0 | 0 | 0 | | 0 | 0 | 0 | | 0 | 0 | 0 | — | 0 | 4 | 1 |

Lemongello and Kimm; Sterling, Myrick (7), Wegener (8), Cram (9) and Kleven. W—Lemongello. L—Sterling. A—1,831.

### Game of September 13

| | | | | | | | | | | | | | | |
|---|---|---|---|---|---|---|---|---|---|---|---|---|---|---|
| Evansville | 0 | 0 | 1 | | 0 | 1 | 1 | | 0 | 3 | 0 | — | 6 | 7 | 0 |
| Tidewater | 0 | 0 | 0 | | 0 | 0 | 1 | | 0 | 0 | 0 | — | 1 | 7 | 3 |

Slayback, Grilli (6) and Lamont; Grose, Contreras (6), Wegener (9) and Kleven. W—Slayback. L—Grose. A—2,917.

### Game of September 14

| | | | | | | | | | | | | | |
|---|---|---|---|---|---|---|---|---|---|---|---|---|---|
| Evansville | 0 | 0 | 0 | 0 | 0 | 0 | 0 | 0 | 0 | — | 0 | 2 | 0 |
| Tidewater | 0 | 0 | 0 | 0 | 0 | 1 | 0 | 0 | x | — | 1 | 6 | 1 |

Fidrych and Kimm; Laxton and Kleven. W—Laxton. L—Fidrych. A—1,209.

### Game of September 15

| | | | | | | | | | | | | | |
|---|---|---|---|---|---|---|---|---|---|---|---|---|---|
| Tidewater | 0 | 0 | 0 | 0 | 1 | 0 | 0 | 0 | 0 | — | 1 | 5 | 1 |
| Evansville | 0 | 1 | 0 | 0 | 0 | 1 | 0 | 0 | x | — | 2 | 7 | 0 |

Manderbach and Kleven; MacCormack, Glynn (9), Brookens (9) and Kimm. W—MacCormack. L—Manderbach. HR—(Evansville) Lane. A—1,968.

### Game of September 16

| | | | | | | | | | | | | | |
|---|---|---|---|---|---|---|---|---|---|---|---|---|---|
| Tidewater | 3 | 0 | 0 | 0 | 2 | 0 | 0 | 0 | 0 | — | 5 | 5 | 2 |
| Evansville | 0 | 0 | 0 | 0 | 5 | 0 | 2 | 1 | x | — | 8 | 13 | 4 |

Myrick, Espinosa (5), Cram (8) and Kleven; Lemongello, Makowski (5) and Kimm. W—Makowski. L—Espinosa. HR—(Evansville) Lane, Kurpiel. A—2,261.

# American Association

## CLASS AAA

**Leading Batter**
**LAMAR JOHNSON**
Denver

**League President**
**JOE RYAN**

**Leading Pitcher**
**PAT ZACHRY**
Indianapolis

### CHAMPIONSHIP WINNERS IN PREVIOUS YEARS

| | |
|---|---|
| 1902—Indianapolis | .683 |
| 1903—St. Paul | .657 |
| 1904—St. Paul | .646 |
| 1905—Columbus | .658 |
| 1906—Columbus | .615 |
| 1907—Columbus | .584 |
| 1908—Indianapolis | .601 |
| 1909—Louisville | .554 |
| 1910—Minneapolis | .637 |
| 1911—Minneapolis | .600 |
| 1912—Minneapolis | .636 |
| 1913—Milwaukee | .599 |
| 1914—Milwaukee | .590 |
| 1915—Minneapolis | .597 |
| 1916—Louisville | .605 |
| 1917—Indianapolis | .588 |
| 1918—Kansas City | .589 |
| 1919—St. Paul | .610 |
| 1920—St. Paul | .701 |
| 1921—Louisville | .583 |
| 1922—St. Paul | .641 |
| 1923—Kansas City | .675 |
| 1924—St. Paul | .578 |
| 1925—Louisville | .635 |
| 1926—Louisville | .629 |
| 1927—Toledo | .601 |
| 1928—Indianapolis | .593 |
| 1929—Kansas City | .665 |
| 1930—Louisville | .608 |
| 1931—St. Paul | .623 |
| 1932—Minneapolis | .595 |
| 1933—Columbus* | .604 |

| | |
|---|---|
| Minneapolis | .562 |
| 1934—Minneapolis | .570 |
| Columbus* | .556 |
| 1935—Minneapolis | .591 |
| 1936—Milwaukee† | .584 |
| 1937—Columbus† | .584 |
| 1938—St. Paul | .596 |
| Kansas City (2nd)‡ | .556 |
| 1939—Kansas City | .695 |
| Louisville (4th)‡ | .490 |
| 1940—Kansas City | .625 |
| Louisville (4th)‡ | .500 |
| 1941—Columbus† | .621 |
| 1942—Kansas City | .549 |
| Columbus (3rd)‡ | .532 |
| 1943—Milwaukee | .596 |
| Columbus (3rd)‡ | .532 |
| 1944—Milwaukee | .667 |
| Louisville (3rd)‡ | .574 |
| 1945—Milwaukee | .604 |
| Louisville (3rd)‡ | .545 |
| 1946—Louisville† | .601 |
| 1947—Kansas City | .608 |
| Milwaukee (3rd)‡ | .513 |
| 1948—Indianapolis | .649 |
| St. Paul (3rd)†‡ | .558 |
| 1949—St. Paul | .608 |
| Indianapolis (2nd)‡ | .604 |
| 1950—Minneapolis | .584 |
| Columbus (3rd)‡ | .549 |
| 1951—Milwaukee† | .623 |
| 1952—Milwaukee | .656 |

| | |
|---|---|
| Kansas City (2nd)‡ | .578 |
| 1953—Toledo | .584 |
| Kansas City (2nd)‡ | .571 |
| 1954—Indianapolis | .625 |
| Louisville (2nd)‡ | .556 |
| 1955—Minneapolis† | .597 |
| 1956—Indianapolis† | .597 |
| 1957—Wichita | .604 |
| Denver (2nd)‡ | .584 |
| 1958—Charleston | .589 |
| Minneapolis (3rd)‡ | .536 |
| 1959 Louisville§ | .599 |
| Omaha§ | .516 |
| Minneapolis (2nd)‡ | .586 |
| 1960—Denver | .571 |
| Louisville (2nd)‡ | .556 |
| 1961—Indianapolis | .573 |
| Louisville (2nd)‡ | .533 |
| 1962—Indianapolis | .605 |
| Louisville (4th)‡ | .486 |
| 1963-68—Did not operate. | |
| 1969—Omaha | .607 |
| 1970—Omaha* | .529 |
| Denver | .504 |
| 1971—Indianapolis | .604 |
| Denver* | .521 |
| 1972—Wichita | .621 |
| Evansville* | .593 |
| 1973—Iowa | .610 |
| Tulsa* | .504 |
| 1974—Indianapolis | .578 |
| Tulsa* | .567 |

*Won playoff (East vs. West). †Won championship and four-team playoff. ‡Won four-team playoff. §Respective Eastern and Western Division winners.

## STANDING OF CLUBS AT CLOSE OF SEASON, SEPTEMBER 1

### EASTERN DIVISION

| Club | Evan. | Ind. | Omaha | Iowa | Den. | Tul. | Wich. | O.C. | W. | L. | T. | Pct. | G.B. |
|------|-------|------|-------|------|------|------|-------|------|----|----|----|------|------|
| Evansville (Tigers) ........ | .. | 14 | 16 | 14 | 9 | 5 | 9 | 10 | 77 | 59 | 1 | .566 | .... |
| Indianapolis (Reds) ........ | 10 | .. | 11 | 16 | 5 | 11 | 8 | 10 | 71 | 64 | 0 | .526 | 5½ |
| Omaha (Royals) ............ | 8 | 13 | .. | 19 | 8 | 5 | 5 | 9 | 67 | 69 | 0 | .493 | 10 |
| Iowa (Astros) ............. | 10 | 7 | 5 | .. | 5 | 10 | 9 | 10 | 56 | 79 | 0 | .415 | 20½ |

### WESTERN DIVISION

| Club | Evan. | Ind. | Omaha | Iowa | Den. | Tul. | Wich. | O.C. | W. | L. | T. | Pct. | G.B. |
|------|-------|------|-------|------|------|------|-------|------|----|----|----|------|------|
| Denver (White Sox) ...... | 7 | 11 | 8 | 11 | .. | 14 | 15 | 15 | 81 | 55 | 0 | .596 | .. |
| Tulsa (Cardinals) ......... | 11 | 5 | 11 | 6 | 10 | .. | 15 | 15 | 73 | 63 | 0 | .537 | 8 |
| Wichita (Cubs) .......... | 7 | 8 | 11 | 7 | 9 | 9 | .. | 17 | 68 | 68 | 1 | .500 | 13 |
| Oklahoma City (Indians).. | 6 | 6 | 7 | 6 | 9 | 9 | 7 | .. | 50 | 86 | 0 | .368 | 31 |

Iowa club represented Des Moines, Iowa.
Major league affiliations in parentheses.
Playoff—Evansville defeated Denver, four games to two.
Managers: Denver—Loren Babe; Evansville—Fred Hatfield; Indianapolis—Vern Rapp; Iowa—Joe Sparks; Oklahoma City—John (Red) Davis; Omaha—Billy Gardner; Tulsa—Ken Boyer; Wichita—Mike Roarke.
Regular-Season Attendance—Denver, 193,571; Evansville, 114,985; Indianapolis, 142,953; Iowa, 108,165; Oklahoma City, 46,752; Omaha, 107,988; Tulsa, 143,131; Wichita, 173,504. Total, 1,031,049. All-Star Game, 11,615. Playoffs, 13,699.
All-Star Team: 1B—Johnson, Denver; 2B—Estrada, Denver; 3B—Cruz, Tulsa; SS—Rosello, Wichita; Utility—Adams, Wichita; OF—Tyrone, Wichita; Smith, Oklahoma City; Easler, Tulsa; Molinaro, Evansville; DH—Ewing, Denver; C—Sovern, Denver; Wathan, Omaha; P—Dunning, Denver; Zachry, Indianapolis; Manager—Hatfield, Evansville.
(Compiled by Ed Williams, League Statistician, Shawnee, Okla.)

## CLUB BATTING

| Club | G. | AB. | R. | OR. | H. | TB. | 2B. | 3B. | HR. | RBI. | SH. | SF. | BB. | Int. BB. | HP. | SO. | LOB. | CS. | Pct. |
|------|----|----|----|----|----|----|----|----|----|----|----|----|----|----|----|----|----|----|----|
| Denver ......136 | 4460 | 728 | 635 | 1293 | 1949 | 257 | 39 | 107 | 665 | 50 | 48 | 570 | 47 | 24 | 650 | 71 | 993 | 53 | .290 |
| Tulsa .....136 | 4684 | 737 | 615 | 1354 | 2004 | 279 | 28 | 105 | 694 | 34 | 43 | 545 | 45 | 37 | 735 | 89 | 1049 | 66 | .289 |
| Wichita ...137 | 4561 | 708 | 719 | 1228 | 1838 | 226 | 39 | 102 | 657 | 38 | 45 | 637 | 41 | 40 | 724 | 61 | 1100 | 22 | .269 |
| Evansville .137 | 4407 | 617 | 545 | 1171 | 1678 | 194 | 35 | 81 | 561 | 58 | 41 | 528 | 41 | 41 | 687 | 110 | 934 | 52 | .266 |
| Iowa .....135 | 4342 | 516 | 599 | 1110 | 1549 | 190 | 24 | 67 | 455 | 48 | 38 | 473 | 50 | 36 | 693 | 108 | 1000 | 63 | .256 |
| Okla. City ..136 | 4316 | 513 | 764 | 1095 | 1412 | 162 | 31 | 31 | 457 | 59 | 38 | 500 | 45 | 21 | 644 | 135 | 980 | 62 | .254 |
| Omaha .....136 | 4343 | 555 | 536 | 1099 | 1644 | 176 | 36 | 99 | 515 | 33 | 26 | 473 | 38 | 27 | 864 | 71 | 924 | 27 | .253 |
| Indianapolis .135 | 4235 | 530 | 491 | 1017 | 1512 | 172 | 46 | 77 | 465 | 67 | 30 | 481 | 50 | 29 | 778 | 104 | 872 | 59 | .240 |

## INDIVIDUAL BATTING

(Leading Qualifiers for Batting Championship—367 or More Plate Appearances)

*Bats lefthanded.    †Switch-hitter.

| Player and Club | G. | AB. | R. | H. | TB. | 2B. | 3B. | HR. | RBI. | SH. | SF. | BB. | HP. | SO. | SB. | CS. | Pct. |
|------|----|----|----|----|----|----|----|----|----|----|----|----|----|----|----|----|----|
| Johnson, Lamar, Denver....129 | 485 | 73 | 163 | 262 | 35 | 2 | 20 | 101 | 0 | 5 | 53 | 0 | 67 | 5 | 3 | .336 |
| Hernandez, Keith, Tulsa*....85 | 324 | 70 | 107 | 172 | 29 | 3 | 10 | 48 | 0 | 2 | 62 | 3 | 48 | 3 | 1 | .330 |
| Leon, Richard, Tulsa*......106 | 342 | 53 | 109 | 151 | 22 | 1 | 6 | 59 | 2 | 6 | 47 | 0 | 57 | 2 | 1 | .319 |
| Ewing, Samuel, Denver*....119 | 377 | 62 | 120 | 182 | 27 | 4 | 9 | 71 | 0 | 6 | 76 | 2 | 45 | 5 | 1 | .318 |
| Easler, Michael, 46 Ia-67 Tul* | 113 | 415 | 69 | 130 | 218 | 31 | 6 | 15 | 69 | 1 | 6 | 43 | 4 | 78 | 5 | 6 | .313 |
| DaVanon, F. Gerald, Iowa.. | 90 | 309 | 53 | 96 | 119 | 17 | 3 | 0 | 34 | 3 | 4 | 57 | 5 | 27 | 18 | 8 | .311 |
| Adams, R. Michael, Wichita | 133 | 474 | 104 | 146 | 221 | 26 | 5 | 13 | 77 | 0 | 6 | 91 | 8 | 78 | 18 | 1 | .308 |
| Cruz, Hector, Tulsa.........115 | 435 | 84 | 133 | 252 | 30 | 1 | 29 | 116 | 2 | 2 | 63 | 2 | 76 | 6 | 4 | .306 |
| Wathan, John, Omaha......104 | 360 | 42 | 109 | 155 | 14 | 4 | 8 | 46 | 3 | 2 | 33 | 1 | 48 | 2 | 1 | .303 |
| Smith, Tommy, Okla City*..130 | 497 | 65 | 150 | 195 | 23 | 5 | 4 | 63 | 2 | 7 | 37 | 0 | 55 | 25 | 9 | .302 |

Departmental Leaders: G—Manuel, 137; AB—Rosello, 522; R—Adams, 104; H—L. Johnson, 163; TB—L. Johnson, 262; 2B—L. Johnson, 35; 3B—Buskey, Youngblood, 9; HR—Cruz, 29; RBI—Cruz, 116; SH—Taveras, 17; SF—DeFreites, 10; BB—Lis, 100; HP—Gardner, 9; SO—Washington, 145; SB—Mumphrey, 44; CS—Mumphrey, 21.

(All Players—Listed Alphabetically)

| Player and Club | G. | AB. | R. | H. | TB. | 2B. | 3B. | HR. | RBI. | SH. | SF. | BB. | HP. | SO. | SB. | CS. | Pct. |
|------|----|----|----|----|----|----|----|----|----|----|----|----|----|----|----|----|----|
| Adams, R. Michael, Wichita | 133 | 474 | 104 | 146 | 221 | 26 | 5 | 13 | 77 | 0 | 6 | 91 | 8 | 78 | 18 | 1 | .308 |
| Alcala, Santo, Indianapolis.. | 27 | 56 | 2 | 5 | 5 | 0 | 0 | 0 | 4 | 5 | 0 | 2 | 0 | 35 | 0 | 0 | .089 |
| Alexander, Matthew, Wichita† | 7 | 32 | 4 | 8 | 14 | 0 | 0 | 2 | 8 | 0 | 0 | 5 | 0 | 2 | 4 | 1 | .250 |
| Alvarado, Luis, OC 25-Tu 92 | 117 | 462 | 58 | 111 | 136 | 16 | 0 | 3 | 64 | 7 | 6 | 29 | 2 | 51 | 6 | 2 | .240 |
| Andersen, Larry, Okla City.. | 25 | 1 | 0 | 0 | 0 | 0 | 0 | 0 | 0 | 0 | 0 | 0 | 0 | 0 | 0 | 0 | .000 |
| Baldwin, Robert, Evansville† | 14 | 62 | 9 | 19 | 26 | 2 | 1 | 1 | 7 | 2 | 1 | 3 | 0 | 10 | 3 | 0 | .306 |
| Baney, Richard, Indianapolis | 16 | 9 | 1 | 3 | 3 | 0 | 0 | 0 | 0 | 0 | 0 | 0 | 0 | 1 | 0 | 0 | .333 |
| Barnes, Luther, Indianapolis | 78 | 174 | 23 | 35 | 45 | 7 | 0 | 1 | 10 | 3 | 1 | 25 | 4 | 20 | 7 | 1 | .201 |
| Bass, A. Earl, Tulsa........ | 14 | 0 | 1 | 0 | 0 | 0 | 0 | 0 | 0 | 0 | 0 | 1 | 0 | 0 | 0 | 0 | .000 |
| Batista, Rafael, Iowa*...... | 23 | 87 | 10 | 19 | 29 | 7 | 0 | 1 | 4 | 0 | 0 | 9 | 0 | 17 | 0 | 0 | .218 |
| Beach, Randolph, Denver ... | 46 | 134 | 16 | 31 | 39 | 6 | 1 | 0 | 10 | 5 | 1 | 18 | 0 | 24 | 1 | 3 | .231 |
| Bell, Jerry, Okla City†...... | 5 | 0 | 0 | 0 | 0 | 0 | 0 | 0 | 0 | 0 | 0 | 0 | 0 | 1 | 0 | 0 | .000 |
| Bennett, Kenneth, Denver*..119 | 359 | 47 | 96 | 122 | 16 | 2 | 2 | 32 | 5 | 2 | 33 | 1 | 37 | 6 | 3 | .267 |
| Billings, Richard, Tulsa..... | 44 | 126 | 21 | 37 | 50 | 8 | 1 | 1 | 12 | 0 | 0 | 27 | 2 | 23 | 2 | 1 | .294 |
| Boone, Rodney, Iowa........ | 16 | 46 | 6 | 9 | 14 | 2 | 0 | 1 | 4 | 0 | 1 | 6 | 0 | 13 | 0 | 0 | .191 |
| Brennan, Thomas, Okla City. | 25 | 2 | 0 | 0 | 0 | 0 | 0 | 0 | 0 | 0 | 0 | 0 | 0 | 0 | 0 | 0 | .000 |
| Brooks, Michael, Okla City.. | 54 | 167 | 12 | 38 | 50 | 2 | 2 | 2 | 15 | 1 | 1 | 20 | 0 | 39 | 1 | 2 | .228 |
| Buskey, Michael, Denver.... | 133 | 448 | 67 | 109 | 148 | 15 | 9 | 2 | 43 | 10 | 2 | 42 | 2 | 87 | 13 | 11 | .243 |
| Busse, Raymond, Ia 74-Om 58 | 132 | 473 | 52 | 117 | 188 | 24 | 4 | 13 | 66 | 2 | 3 | 33 | 0 | 117 | 4 | 3 | .247 |
| Carroll, Thomas, Indianapolis* | 20 | 36 | 5 | 8 | 12 | 2 | 1 | 0 | 3 | 0 | 1 | 0 | 0 | 8 | 0 | 0 | .222 |
| Cash, Ronald, Evansville.... | 73 | 203 | 26 | 55 | 74 | 10 | 3 | 1 | 20 | 1 | 0 | 31 | 0 | 27 | 3 | 1 | .271 |

| Player and Club | G. | AB. | R. | H. | TB. | 2B. | 3B. | HR. | RBI. | SH. | SF. | BB. | HP. | SO. | SB. | CS. | Pct. |
|---|---|---|---|---|---|---|---|---|---|---|---|---|---|---|---|---|---|
| Cater, Danny, Tulsa | 5 | 14 | 3 | 3 | 4 | 1 | 0 | 0 | 3 | 0 | 0 | 0 | 0 | 2 | 0 | 0 | .214 |
| Cerone, Richard, Okla City | 46 | 140 | 22 | 35 | 49 | 6 | 1 | 2 | 13 | 2 | 0 | 26 | 2 | 29 | 0 | 2 | .250 |
| Cleverly, Gary, Okla City* | 3 | 4 | 0 | 0 | 0 | 0 | 0 | 0 | 0 | 0 | 0 | 3 | 0 | 2 | 1 | 1 | .000 |
| Craig, Rockne, Om 48-Ia 52 | 100 | 286 | 44 | 68 | 82 | 14 | 0 | 0 | 18 | 4 | 3 | 58 | 2 | 49 | 9 | 4 | .238 |
| Cruz, Hector, Tulsa | 115 | 435 | 84 | 133 | 252 | 30 | 1 | 29 | 116 | 2 | 2 | 63 | 2 | 76 | 6 | 4 | .306 |
| DaVanon, F. Gerald, Iowa | 90 | 309 | 53 | 96 | 119 | 17 | 3 | 0 | 34 | 3 | 4 | 57 | 5 | 27 | 18 | 8 | .311 |
| Davis, Bryshear, Okla City* | 14 | 49 | 3 | 10 | 15 | 2 | 0 | 1 | 2 | 0 | 0 | 6 | 0 | 5 | 2 | 1 | .204 |
| Day, Charles, Evansville* | 96 | 294 | 39 | 73 | 97 | 14 | 2 | 2 | 33 | 9 | 3 | 43 | 1 | 30 | 2 | 4 | .248 |
| DeFreites, Arturo, Indpls | 126 | 446 | 40 | 102 | 170 | 20 | 3 | 14 | 70 | 1 | 10 | 17 | 0 | 78 | 6 | 4 | .229 |
| de la Rosa, Jesus, Iowa | 71 | 235 | 24 | 61 | 93 | 14 | 0 | 6 | 29 | 0 | 1 | 10 | 3 | 50 | 2 | 3 | .260 |
| Didier, Robert, Iowa | 109 | 354 | 30 | 89 | 110 | 12 | 0 | 3 | 39 | 5 | 2 | 27 | 4 | 29 | 1 | 3 | .251 |
| Driscoll, James, Iowa* | 75 | 210 | 23 | 43 | 59 | 8 | 1 | 2 | 10 | 5 | 2 | 42 | 1 | 38 | 4 | 8 | .205 |
| Droege, William, Wichita | 12 | 41 | 1 | 8 | 10 | 2 | 0 | 0 | 4 | 1 | 0 | 1 | 2 | 7 | 1 | 0 | .195 |
| Dunn, Ronald, Wichita | 37 | 125 | 16 | 34 | 61 | 8 | 2 | 5 | 28 | 0 | 0 | 9 | 1 | 26 | 1 | 0 | .272 |
| Dunning, Steven, Denver | 36 | 14 | 1 | 3 | 4 | 1 | 0 | 0 | 2 | 0 | 0 | 3 | 0 | 7 | 0 | 0 | .214 |
| Dusan, Gene, Okla City† | 93 | 266 | 26 | 54 | 67 | 13 | 0 | 0 | 25 | 4 | 0 | 40 | 0 | 38 | 0 | 0 | .203 |
| Dwyer, James, Tulsa* | 33 | 109 | 17 | 44 | 59 | 8 | 2 | 1 | 17 | 3 | 2 | 16 | 1 | 15 | 1 | 5 | .404 |
| Easler, Michael, Ia 46-Tu 67* | 113 | 415 | 69 | 130 | 218 | 31 | 6 | 15 | 69 | 1 | 6 | 43 | 4 | 78 | 5 | 6 | .313 |
| Eastwick, Rawlins, Indpls. | 13 | 3 | 0 | 0 | 0 | 0 | 0 | 0 | 0 | 0 | 0 | 0 | 0 | 1 | 0 | 0 | .000 |
| Enyart, Terry, Indianapolis | 15 | 1 | 0 | 1 | 1 | 0 | 0 | 0 | 0 | 0 | 0 | 0 | 0 | 0 | 0 | 0 | 1.000 |
| Estrada, Manuel, Denver | 126 | 487 | 89 | 146 | 210 | 30 | 5 | 8 | 68 | 9 | 5 | 54 | 1 | 47 | 5 | 6 | .300 |
| Ewing, Samuel, Denver* | 119 | 377 | 62 | 120 | 182 | 27 | 4 | 9 | 71 | 0 | 6 | 76 | 2 | 45 | 5 | 1 | .318 |
| Floyd, Robert, Omaha | 42 | 124 | 13 | 29 | 30 | 1 | 0 | 0 | 10 | 4 | 0 | 10 | 0 | 27 | 1 | 0 | .234 |
| Foster, Larry, Denver | 37 | 98 | 17 | 22 | 39 | 3 | 1 | 4 | 11 | 2 | 2 | 22 | 0 | 14 | 1 | 2 | .225 |
| Franklin, Anthony, Indpls† | 99 | 238 | 34 | 56 | 75 | 11 | 1 | 2 | 21 | 5 | 1 | 44 | 1 | 41 | 11 | 2 | .235 |
| Gallagher, Robert, Iowa* | 79 | 286 | 36 | 80 | 102 | 11 | 1 | 3 | 30 | 1 | 2 | 28 | 2 | 50 | 2 | 2 | .280 |
| Gamble, John, Evansville | 106 | 316 | 47 | 91 | 111 | 11 | 3 | 1 | 36 | 7 | 0 | 38 | 3 | 53 | 13 | 6 | .288 |
| Garcia, Nelson, Okla City† | 121 | 441 | 48 | 110 | 135 | 13 | 6 | 0 | 33 | 9 | 4 | 14 | 6 | 68 | 35 | 8 | .249 |
| Gardner, Arthur, Iowa* | 135 | 518 | 66 | 136 | 192 | 21 | 7 | 7 | 54 | 5 | 5 | 33 | 9 | 72 | 19 | 9 | .263 |
| Garrett, H. Adrian, Wichita* | 52 | 212 | 41 | 68 | 127 | 17 | 3 | 12 | 48 | 2 | 1 | 20 | 1 | 47 | 2 | 1 | .321 |
| Gonzales, Daniel, Evansville* | 7 | 27 | 4 | 10 | 10 | 0 | 0 | 0 | 2 | 0 | 0 | 0 | 0 | 2 | 0 | 0 | .370 |
| Gonzalez, Julio, Wichita | 56 | 171 | 13 | 35 | 40 | 5 | 0 | 0 | 11 | 2 | 2 | 13 | 2 | 17 | 2 | 0 | .205 |
| Gonzalez, Orlando, Okla City* | 85 | 297 | 40 | 91 | 112 | 15 | 3 | 0 | 29 | 6 | 2 | 30 | 0 | 23 | 11 | 6 | .306 |
| Gorinski, Robert, Denver | 35 | 114 | 14 | 37 | 66 | 8 | 0 | 7 | 24 | 0 | 3 | 7 | 0 | 31 | 0 | 0 | .325 |
| Green, Joel, Wichita | 50 | 114 | 19 | 33 | 39 | 3 | 0 | 1 | 11 | 1 | 1 | 21 | 1 | 14 | 0 | 0 | .289 |
| Grow, Lorin, Indianapolis* | 24 | 35 | 3 | 2 | 2 | 0 | 0 | 0 | 2 | 4 | 0 | 5 | 0 | 11 | 0 | 0 | .057 |
| Guerrero, Mario, Tulsa | 31 | 115 | 11 | 32 | 40 | 6 | 1 | 0 | 15 | 1 | 1 | 7 | 1 | 8 | 1 | 3 | .278 |
| Hairston, Jerry, Denver† | 40 | 139 | 28 | 51 | 69 | 9 | 0 | 3 | 31 | 0 | 3 | 35 | 3 | 15 | 3 | 2 | .367 |
| Hannah, James, Okla City | 17 | 49 | 5 | 9 | 11 | 2 | 0 | 0 | 8 | 0 | 0 | 11 | 0 | 11 | 1 | 1 | .184 |
| Harmon, Thomas, Tulsa* | 30 | 96 | 12 | 27 | 41 | 3 | 3 | 0 | 13 | 0 | 0 | 8 | 3 | 5 | 0 | 0 | .281 |
| Harris, Victor, Wichita† | 32 | 132 | 23 | 32 | 41 | 2 | 1 | 1 | 2 | 0 | 0 | 15 | 0 | 31 | 5 | 0 | .242 |
| Haug, Steven, Wichita | 50 | 119 | 10 | 19 | 23 | 2 | 1 | 0 | 7 | 7 | 0 | 12 | 0 | 28 | 0 | 1 | .160 |
| Heise, Benjamin, Okla City | 96 | 312 | 30 | 69 | 76 | 7 | 0 | 0 | 31 | 7 | 3 | 19 | 3 | 42 | 4 | 2 | .221 |
| Henderson, Joseph, Indpls* | 49 | 31 | 2 | 5 | 11 | 3 | 0 | 1 | 2 | 0 | 0 | 2 | 1 | 19 | 0 | 0 | .161 |
| Henninger, Richard, Okla City | 27 | 1 | 0 | 0 | 0 | 0 | 0 | 0 | 0 | 0 | 0 | 0 | 0 | 0 | 0 | 0 | .000 |
| Hernandez Keith, Tulsa* | 85 | 324 | 70 | 107 | 172 | 29 | 3 | 10 | 48 | 0 | 2 | 62 | 3 | 48 | 3 | 1 | .330 |
| Herndon, Larry, Tulsa | 22 | 96 | 13 | 23 | 31 | 5 | 0 | 1 | 5 | 0 | 0 | 10 | 0 | 22 | 12 | 4 | .240 |
| Hiatt, Jack, Wichita | 1 | 2 | 0 | 0 | 0 | 0 | 0 | 0 | 0 | 0 | 0 | 0 | 0 | 0 | 0 | 0 | .000 |
| Hinton, Richard, Denver* | 37 | 15 | 2 | 5 | 9 | 1 | 0 | 1 | 2 | 0 | 0 | 0 | 0 | 3 | 0 | 0 | .333 |
| Hiser, Gene, Wichita* | 72 | 272 | 50 | 87 | 120 | 10 | 4 | 5 | 32 | 3 | 6 | 36 | 1 | 36 | 2 | 1 | .320 |
| Howard, Douglas, Tulsa | 90 | 336 | 56 | 110 | 177 | 25 | 0 | 14 | 71 | 5 | 4 | 18 | 2 | 48 | 0 | 1 | .327 |
| Huisman, William, Wichita | 38 | 120 | 14 | 28 | 38 | 4 | 3 | 0 | 14 | 1 | 0 | 12 | 2 | 12 | 0 | 0 | .233 |
| Hume, Thomas, Indianapolis | 18 | 35 | 3 | 7 | 7 | 0 | 0 | 0 | 1 | 3 | 0 | 1 | 0 | 8 | 0 | 0 | .200 |
| Hutson, G. Herbert, Wichita | 30 | 1 | 0 | 0 | 0 | 0 | 0 | 0 | 0 | 0 | 0 | 0 | 0 | 0 | 0 | 0 | .000 |
| Isaac, Luis, Okla City | 41 | 128 | 3 | 27 | 33 | 4 | 1 | 0 | 15 | 4 | 2 | 7 | 0 | 28 | 0 | 0 | .211 |
| James, Arthur, Evansville* | 101 | 401 | 55 | 115 | 140 | 14 | 4 | 1 | 31 | 2 | 2 | 16 | 0 | 41 | 13 | 9 | .287 |
| Javier, I. Alfredo, Iowa | 13 | 45 | 5 | 12 | 19 | 4 | 0 | 1 | 10 | 1 | 1 | 2 | 0 | 5 | 0 | 0 | .267 |
| Johnson, John C., Tulsa | 4 | 3 | 0 | 0 | 0 | 0 | 0 | 0 | 0 | 0 | 0 | 1 | 0 | 2 | 0 | 0 | .000 |
| Johnson, Lamar, Denver | 129 | 485 | 73 | 163 | 262 | 35 | 2 | 20 | 101 | 0 | 5 | 53 | 0 | 67 | 5 | 3 | .336 |
| Jones, Ruppert, Omaha* | 119 | 403 | 62 | 98 | 172 | 25 | 5 | 13 | 54 | 2 | 3 | 56 | 3 | 86 | 12 | 1 | .243 |
| Kelleher, Michael, Tulsa | 127 | 420 | 48 | 100 | 117 | 17 | 0 | 0 | 27 | 8 | 3 | 29 | 8 | 50 | 2 | 4 | .238 |
| Kennedy, Junior, Indpls | 116 | 405 | 49 | 112 | 144 | 13 | 5 | 3 | 46 | 6 | 2 | 57 | 3 | 73 | 10 | 8 | .277 |
| Kimm, Bruce, Evansville | 92 | 268 | 35 | 63 | 81 | 11 | 2 | 1 | 21 | 8 | 1 | 28 | 3 | 35 | 7 | 6 | .235 |
| Knight, C. Ray, Indpls* | 123 | 434 | 58 | 118 | 156 | 16 | 5 | 4 | 48 | 8 | 4 | 40 | 2 | 51 | 3 | 2 | .272 |
| Kuiper, Duane, Okla City* | 40 | 164 | 18 | 40 | 48 | 5 | 0 | 1 | 12 | 0 | 1 | 15 | 1 | 12 | 4 | 6 | .244 |
| Kurpiel, Edward, Evansville | 94 | 296 | 42 | 85 | 137 | 15 | 2 | 11 | 57 | 2 | 3 | 59 | 2 | 40 | 3 | 4 | .287 |
| Lambe, Bryan, Evansville | 56 | 148 | 29 | 40 | 45 | 5 | 0 | 0 | 13 | 4 | 0 | 37 | 2 | 19 | 13 | 3 | .270 |
| Lamont, Gene, Evansville* | 49 | 130 | 15 | 40 | 58 | 9 | 3 | 1 | 20 | 1 | 1 | 20 | 0 | 20 | 1 | 0 | .308 |
| Lance, Gary, Omaha† | 29 | 2 | 0 | 0 | 0 | 0 | 0 | 0 | 0 | 0 | 0 | 1 | 0 | 0 | 0 | 0 | .000 |
| Lane, Marvin, Evansville* | 108 | 324 | 49 | 83 | 140 | 22 | 4 | 9 | 42 | 3 | 2 | 49 | 8 | 83 | 2 | 0 | .256 |
| Lanier, Harold, Tulsa | 21 | 74 | 11 | 15 | 21 | 1 | 1 | 1 | 7 | 0 | 1 | 5 | 0 | 16 | 0 | 0 | .203 |
| LaRussa, Anthony, Denver | 118 | 354 | 87 | 99 | 147 | 23 | 2 | 7 | 46 | 3 | 4 | 70 | 4 | 46 | 13 | 5 | .280 |
| Leaver, Alberto, Iowa | 1 | 0 | 1 | 0 | 0 | 0 | 0 | 0 | 0 | 0 | 0 | 0 | 0 | 0 | 0 | 0 | .000 |
| Lee, Leon, Tulsa | 31 | 112 | 10 | 35 | 49 | 8 | 0 | 2 | 13 | 0 | 0 | 18 | 0 | 21 | 0 | 0 | .313 |
| Lemon, Chester, Denver | 70 | 254 | 40 | 78 | 129 | 15 | 6 | 8 | 49 | 4 | 2 | 25 | 3 | 35 | 11 | 2 | .307 |
| Leon, Richard, Tulsa* | 106 | 342 | 53 | 109 | 151 | 22 | 1 | 6 | 59 | 2 | 6 | 47 | 0 | 57 | 2 | 1 | .319 |
| Lersch, Barry, Okla City* | 32 | 1 | 0 | 0 | 0 | 0 | 0 | 0 | 0 | 0 | 0 | 0 | 0 | 1 | 0 | 0 | .000 |
| Lindsey, Joseph, Tulsa* | 54 | 190 | 28 | 46 | 56 | 10 | 0 | 0 | 10 | 2 | 1 | 26 | 3 | 36 | 6 | 6 | .242 |
| Lis, Joseph, Oklahoma City | 130 | 423 | 69 | 116 | 195 | 25 | 0 | 18 | 69 | 1 | 4 | 100 | 6 | 73 | 5 | 2 | .274 |
| Lyttle, James, Denver* | 80 | 315 | 44 | 98 | 132 | 24 | 2 | 2 | 37 | 1 | 1 | 38 | 1 | 53 | 4 | 7 | .311 |

| Player and Club | G | AB | R | H | TB | 2B | 3B | HR | RBI | SH | SF | BB | HP | SO | SB | CS | Pct. |
|---|---|---|---|---|---|---|---|---|---|---|---|---|---|---|---|---|---|
| Manning, Richard, Okla City* | 30 | 117 | 18 | 37 | 46 | 5 | 2 | 0 | 15 | 1 | 0 | 12 | 0 | 16 | 9 | 1 | .316 |
| Manuel, Jerry, Evansville... | 137 | 501 | 63 | 115 | 145 | 10 | 4 | 4 | 43 | 9 | 3 | 44 | 7 | 101 | 20 | 5 | .230 |
| Marshall, Keith, Omaha... | 93 | 295 | 36 | 71 | 93 | 12 | 2 | 2 | 24 | 3 | 2 | 25 | 1 | 38 | 3 | 4 | .241 |
| Martz, Gary, Omaha........ | 119 | 435 | 67 | 121 | 194 | 12 | 2 | 19 | 73 | 1 | 4 | 45 | 7 | 108 | 4 | 2 | .278 |
| Matney, Ronnie, Wichita†... | 110 | 387 | 53 | 98 | 155 | 23 | 2 | 10 | 74 | 0 | 4 | 63 | 4 | 92 | 1 | 2 | .253 |
| McLaren, John, Iowa....... | 4 | 7 | 1 | 4 | 9 | 2 | 0 | 1 | 2 | 0 | 0 | 5 | 0 | 2 | 0 | 0 | .571 |
| McLaughlin, Donnie, Iowa... | 12 | 20 | 2 | 3 | 4 | 1 | 0 | 0 | 1 | 0 | 0 | 3 | 0 | 1 | 0 | 0 | .150 |
| McMillan, Thomas, Ok City | 136 | 503 | 66 | 125 | 155 | 14 | 5 | 2 | 58 | 4 | 6 | 42 | 2 | 94 | 14 | 10 | .249 |
| Meier, F. Calvin, Tulsa..... | 52 | 131 | 21 | 30 | 39 | 4 | 1 | 1 | 13 | 0 | 1 | 19 | 1 | 17 | 1 | 2 | .229 |
| Milbourne, Lawrence, Iowa†.. | 24 | 77 | 9 | 17 | 25 | 3 | 1 | 1 | 6 | 2 | 1 | 6 | 0 | 5 | 3 | 1 | .221 |
| Molinaro, Robert, Evansville* | 126 | 471 | 69 | 135 | 202 | 20 | 4 | 13 | 75 | 1 | 5 | 27 | 5 | 52 | 26 | 7 | .287 |
| Mumphrey, Jerry, Tulsa‡... | 127 | 495 | 87 | 141 | 196 | 19 | 6 | 8 | 59 | 1 | 5 | 81 | 0 | 106 | 44 | 21 | .285 |
| Nasif, Ralph, Evansville... | 8 | 9 | 0 | 1 | 1 | 0 | 0 | 0 | 2 | 0 | 1 | 1 | 2 | 0 | 0 | 0 | .111 |
| Nordhagen, Wayne, Tulsa ... | 74 | 268 | 40 | 94 | 156 | 19 | 2 | 13 | 60 | 0 | 1 | 19 | 3 | 60 | 1 | 4 | .351 |
| Norris, James, Okla City*... | 79 | 253 | 32 | 71 | 96 | 14 | 4 | 1 | 33 | 6 | 5 | 52 | 0 | 48 | 15 | 5 | .281 |
| Norton, Fred, Denver...... | 28 | 66 | 11 | 16 | 22 | 2 | 2 | 0 | 5 | 2 | 1 | 5 | 2 | 13 | 1 | 3 | .242 |
| Oliver, David J., Okla City | 65 | 249 | 36 | 64 | 75 | 9 | 1 | 0 | 18 | 5 | 1 | 22 | 0 | 17 | 7 | 4 | .257 |
| Oliver, Richard, Wichita.... | 75 | 240 | 21 | 55 | 85 | 10 | 1 | 6 | 30 | 3 | 2 | 26 | 2 | 48 | 1 | 0 | .229 |
| Ortenzio, Frank, Omaha..... | 115 | 414 | 48 | 100 | 166 | 17 | 2 | 15 | 72 | 1 | 4 | 51 | 2 | 101 | 1 | 0 | .242 |
| Ostrosser, Brian, Okla City* | 63 | 178 | 15 | 36 | 41 | 3 | 1 | 0 | 13 | 6 | 1 | 38 | 1 | 29 | 0 | 2 | .202 |
| Otten, James, Denver...... | 29 | 1 | 0 | 0 | 0 | 0 | 0 | 0 | 0 | 0 | 0 | 0 | 0 | 0 | 0 | 0 | .000 |
| Payne, Larry, Indianapolis.. | 27 | 49 | 4 | 4 | 4 | 0 | 0 | 0 | 3 | 2 | 0 | 5 | 0 | 17 | 0 | 0 | .082 |
| Pena, George, Iowa....... | 99 | 288 | 33 | 69 | 116 | 14 | 0 | 11 | 46 | 1 | 2 | 51 | 2 | 66 | 2 | 2 | .240 |
| Perez, Ramon, Iowa....... | 94 | 277 | 25 | 60 | 74 | 6 | 4 | 0 | 18 | 5 | 1 | 13 | 1 | 43 | 4 | 5 | .217 |
| Perkins, Craig, Omaha...... | 75 | 248 | 22 | 60 | 100 | 11 | 1 | 9 | 28 | 0 | 1 | 18 | 1 | 30 | 1 | 0 | .242 |
| Pierce, L. Jack, Evansville*.. | 36 | 132 | 26 | 37 | 71 | 7 | 0 | 9 | 25 | 0 | 3 | 17 | 4 | 33 | 0 | 1 | .280 |
| Proly, Michael, Tulsa...... | 55 | 1 | 0 | 0 | 0 | 0 | 0 | 0 | 0 | 0 | 0 | 0 | 0 | 1 | 0 | 0 | .000 |
| Quinn, Terrence, Denver.... | 72 | 207 | 26 | 50 | 85 | 13 | 2 | 6 | 27 | 4 | 2 | 24 | 0 | 40 | 1 | 1 | .242 |
| Quirk, James, Omaha*..... | 127 | 445 | 62 | 122 | 192 | 23 | 4 | 13 | 64 | 7 | 3 | 49 | 5 | 96 | 4 | 0 | .274 |
| Revering, David, Indpls*... | 120 | 382 | 53 | 97 | 185 | 15 | 5 | 21 | 71 | 1 | 1 | 59 | 3 | 80 | 1 | 3 | .254 |
| Rima, Thomas, Iowa*...... | 35 | 100 | 9 | 27 | 29 | 2 | 0 | 0 | 6 | 0 | 1 | 8 | 2 | 17 | 2 | 1 | .270 |
| Robinson, Robert, Evansville | 84 | 236 | 24 | 56 | 93 | 10 | 0 | 9 | 46 | 1 | 7 | 40 | 1 | 36 | 1 | 1 | .237 |
| Robles, Sergio, Tulsa...... | 45 | 152 | 25 | 33 | 51 | 7 | 1 | 3 | 17 | 1 | 1 | 6 | 2 | 17 | 1 | 0 | .217 |
| Rosello, David, Wichita.... | 135 | 522 | 100 | 134 | 188 | 29 | 2 | 7 | 46 | 6 | 4 | 77 | 4 | 73 | 15 | 6 | .257 |
| Rothermel, Russell, Iowa*... | 48 | 1 | 0 | 0 | 0 | 0 | 0 | 0 | 0 | 0 | 0 | 0 | 0 | 0 | 0 | 0 | .000 |
| Ruberto, John, Indianapolis.. | 90 | 260 | 27 | 68 | 100 | 12 | 1 | 6 | 25 | 3 | 2 | 19 | 2 | 52 | 3 | 5 | .262 |
| Scarce, G. McCurdy, Indpls* | 60 | 10 | 0 | 0 | 0 | 0 | 0 | 0 | 0 | 0 | 0 | 0 | 0 | 8 | 0 | 0 | .000 |
| Schlueter, Jay, Tulsa...... | 14 | 37 | 4 | 8 | 13 | 2 | 0 | 1 | 6 | 1 | 1 | 5 | 0 | 7 | 1 | 0 | .216 |
| Schneck, David, Indianapolis* | 23 | 76 | 11 | 19 | 27 | 3 | 1 | 1 | 5 | 1 | 0 | 6 | 0 | 5 | 5 | 2 | .250 |
| Scott, Rodney, Omaha...... | 12 | 37 | 6 | 10 | 13 | 1 | 1 | 0 | 1 | 1 | 0 | 6 | 0 | 3 | 5 | 1 | .270 |
| Scrivener, Wayne, Evansville | 131 | 447 | 65 | 112 | 177 | 23 | 6 | 10 | 62 | 5 | 7 | 47 | 3 | 86 | 3 | 5 | .251 |
| Shaffer, Duane, Denver.... | 27 | 1 | 0 | 0 | 0 | 0 | 0 | 0 | 0 | 0 | 0 | 0 | 0 | 1 | 0 | 0 | .000 |
| Sinatro, Gregory, Indpls.... | 89 | 265 | 36 | 60 | 83 | 11 | 3 | 2 | 21 | 1 | 1 | 25 | 5 | 49 | 5 | 6 | .226 |
| Skidmore, R. Roe, Iowa.... | 111 | 412 | 41 | 109 | 172 | 21 | 0 | 14 | 52 | 0 | 3 | 34 | 2 | 67 | 1 | 1 | .265 |
| Smith, Tommy, Okla City*... | 130 | 497 | 65 | 130 | 195 | 23 | 5 | 4 | 63 | 2 | 7 | 37 | 0 | 55 | 25 | 9 | .302 |
| Sovern, Jeffrey, Denver..... | 106 | 334 | 52 | 98 | 162 | 13 | 0 | 17 | 65 | 4 | 8 | 24 | 5 | 41 | 2 | | .293 |
| Spencer, H. Thomas, Indpls | 129 | 434 | 68 | 116 | 170 | 19 | 7 | 7 | 41 | 4 | 4 | 61 | 3 | 49 | 29 | 12 | .267 |
| Staggs, Stephen, Omaha.... | 122 | 428 | 64 | 108 | 151 | 17 | 3 | 7 | 39 | 1 | 1 | 81 | 3 | 60 | 5 | 2 | .252 |
| Stelmaszek, Richard, Wich* | 106 | 336 | 40 | 89 | 127 | 14 | 3 | 6 | 47 | 0 | 4 | 61 | 1 | 52 | 1 | 1 | .265 |
| Strickland, James, Okla City* | 50 | 1 | 0 | 0 | 0 | 0 | 0 | 0 | 0 | 0 | 0 | 2 | 0 | 0 | 0 | 0 | .000 |
| Swisher, Steven, Wichita.... | 7 | 21 | 8 | 6 | 18 | 0 | 0 | 4 | 9 | 1 | 0 | 8 | 2 | 8 | 1 | 0 | .286 |
| Tabb, Jerry, Wichita*..... | 97 | 355 | 57 | 86 | 127 | 18 | 1 | 7 | 48 | 2 | 2 | 50 | 3 | 48 | 2 | 2 | .242 |
| Talley, Joseph, Denver*... | 16 | 49 | 9 | 12 | 22 | 2 | 1 | 2 | 4 | 0 | 0 | 15 | 0 | 10 | 0 | 2 | .245 |
| Tamargo, John, Tulsa†..... | 53 | 164 | 27 | 47 | 74 | 12 | 0 | 5 | 23 | 0 | 4 | 30 | 1 | 17 | 0 | 1 | .287 |
| Taveras, Alejandro, Iowa... | 135 | 489 | 58 | 125 | 148 | 15 | 4 | 0 | 36 | 17 | 6 | 60 | 2 | 61 | 38 | 13 | .256 |
| Taylor, Bruce, Indianapolis.. | 51 | 15 | 0 | 2 | 2 | 0 | 0 | 0 | 1 | 1 | 0 | 5 | 0 | 0 | 3 | | .133 |
| Tyrone, James, Wichita.... | 120 | 449 | 71 | 135 | 199 | 21 | 2 | 13 | 73 | 4 | 9 | 50 | 3 | 53 | 4 | 2 | .301 |
| Vuckovich, Peter, Denver ... | 19 | 1 | 0 | 1 | 1 | 0 | 0 | 0 | 1 | 0 | 0 | 0 | 0 | 0 | 0 | 0 | 1.000 |
| Vukovich, John, Indianapolis | 49 | 152 | 6 | 21 | 28 | 7 | 0 | 0 | 12 | 3 | 0 | 9 | 0 | 20 | 1 | 1 | .138 |
| Walker, J. Luke, Iowa*..... | 20 | 1 | 0 | 0 | 0 | 0 | 0 | 0 | 0 | 0 | 0 | 0 | 0 | 1 | 0 | 0 | .000 |
| Wallis, H. Joseph, Wichita* | 34 | 120 | 22 | 40 | 71 | 15 | 5 | 2 | 24 | 1 | 1 | 15 | 1 | 19 | 0 | 3 | .333 |
| Ward, Chris, Wichita*..... | 86 | 316 | 41 | 87 | 134 | 17 | 3 | 8 | 55 | 2 | 3 | 52 | 2 | 33 | 1 | 1 | .275 |
| Washington, U. L., Omaha.. | 128 | 475 | 60 | 113 | 155 | 11 | 8 | 5 | 37 | 5 | 1 | 47 | 0 | 145 | 22 | 12 | .238 |
| Wathan, John, Omaha...... | 104 | 360 | 42 | 109 | 155 | 14 | 4 | 8 | 46 | 3 | 2 | 33 | 1 | 48 | 2 | 1 | .303 |
| Werner, Donald, Indianapolis | 86 | 228 | 39 | 64 | 112 | 11 | 5 | 9 | 34 | 1 | 0 | 41 | 3 | 67 | 5 | 1 | .281 |
| Williams, Mark, Omaha*... | 103 | 333 | 35 | 75 | 98 | 15 | 1 | 2 | 28 | 3 | 2 | 18 | 3 | 51 | 8 | 2 | .225 |
| Williams, Richard A., Iowa. | 9 | 0 | 0 | 0 | 0 | 0 | 0 | 0 | 0 | 0 | 0 | 0 | 0 | 0 | 0 | 0 | .000 |
| Willoughby, James, Tulsa... | 18 | 1 | 0 | 0 | 0 | 0 | 0 | 0 | 0 | 0 | 0 | 1 | 0 | 0 | 0 | 0 | .000 |
| Wockenfuss, Johnny, Evans. | 43 | 142 | 20 | 41 | 70 | 11 | 0 | 6 | 28 | 1 | 3 | 28 | 1 | 17 | 0 | 0 | .289 |
| Yancy, Hugh, Denver....... | 56 | 208 | 43 | 58 | 99 | 14 | 0 | 9 | 36 | 1 | 1 | 26 | 0 | 34 | 2 | 1 | .279 |
| York, James, Iowa....... | 31 | 4 | 1 | 2 | 2 | 0 | 0 | 0 | 0 | 0 | 1 | 0 | 0 | 0 | 1 | | .500 |
| Youngblood, Joel, Inpls.... | 123 | 418 | 65 | 110 | 167 | 21 | 9 | 6 | 51 | 5 | 4 | 55 | 2 | 63 | 18 | 12 | .263 |
| Zachry, Patrick, Indpls .... | 27 | 43 | 1 | 2 | 3 | 1 | 0 | 0 | 2 | 7 | 0 | 4 | 0 | 17 | 0 | 0 | .047 |

The following pitchers had no plate appearances primarily through use of designated-hitters, listed alphabetically by club, games in parentheses:

DENVER—Barrios, Francisco (3); Komadina, Tony (10); Kucek, John (6); Lehman, William (13); Lukevics, Mitchell (4); McClain, Harold (26); Moran, C. William (30); Pitlock, Lee (13); Ray, James F., (2).

EVANSVILLE—Arroyo, Fernando (11); Brookens, Edward (29); Christenson, Gary (2); DeBarr,

Dennis (11); Fidrych, Mark (6); Glynn, Edward (7); Grilli, Stephen (45); Holdsworth, Frederick, (7); Ignasiak, Gary (11); Lemongello, Mark (15); MacCormack, Frank (3); Makowski, Thomas (30); Motil, John (1); Newman, Raymond (12); Pentz, Eugene (16); Skok, Craig (13); Slayback, William (27); Swanson, Charles (25).

IOWA—Alfonso, Carlos (41); Cosgrove, Michael (18); Crawford, James (1); Cuen, Eleno (5); de los Santos, Ramon (15); Elenes, Larry (12); Larson, Daniel (12); Nagy, Michael (4); Niekro, Joseph (7); Roznovsky, Ronald (35); Selak, Ronald (16); Siebert, Paul (30); Spinks, Scipio (3); Sprinkle, Charles (28); Stanton, Michael (18).

OKLAHOMA CITY—Baldwin, Michael (11); Ellingsen, H. Bruce (27); Grossman, Robert (7); Kern, James (3); Linnert, Thomas (3); McAnally, Ernest (1); McCutchin, James (18); McGough, Thomas (18); O'Toole, Dennis (6); Raich, Eric (7); Strahler, Michael (10); Waits, M. Richard (9).

OMAHA—Angelini, Norman (54); Autry, Albert (23); Baird, Harry (39); Bernard, Edward (12); Bruno, Thomas (23); Chlan, Gregory (31); Hasbach, David (3); Leonard, Dennis (3); Littell, Mark (24); Meyring, Bradley (12); Throop, George (26).

TULSA—Barlow, Michael (20); Denny, John (8); Foor, James (31); Rasmussen, Harold (18); Reynolds, Kenneth (19); Staniland, Stephen (4); Terlecky, Gregory (14); Wallace, Michael (21); Waterbury, Steven (11); Wiles, Randall (11).

WICHITA—Beckman, Bernhard (16); Copeland, Howell (27); Dettore, Thomas (13); Junge, Gary (3); Kremmel, James (34); Manz, George (3); Prall, Wilfred (29); Reuschel, Paul (35); Schultz, Charles (47); Temple, V. James (18); Turner, Darrell (5); Watt, Edward (44); Weiss, Michael (2); Wilcox, Milton (8).

TWO CLUBS—Allen, Lloyd (8 Denver-6 Tulsa); Crosby, Kenneth (29 Tulsa-3 Wichita); Parsons, William (14 Tulsa-15 Denver); Solomon, Eddie (8 Wichita-7 Tulsa).

GRAND-SLAM HOME RUNS—Alvarado, Leon, Mumphrey, 2 each; Barnes, Busse, Cash, DeFreites, Estrada, Howard, Jones, Kurpiel, Manuel, Matney, McMillan, Molinaro, R. Oliver, Perkins, Quirk, Sovern, Stelmaszek, Werner, 1 each.

AWARDED FIRST BASE ON INTERFERENCE—Perez 2 (Ruberto 2); Barnes (Wockenfuss), Busse (Kimm), Droege (Werner), Green (Werner), Hiser (Ruberto), Quinn (Kimm).

## CLUB FIELDING

| Club | G. | PO. | A. | E. | DP. | PB. | Pct. | Club | G. | PO. | A. | E. | DP. | PB. | Pct. |
|---|---|---|---|---|---|---|---|---|---|---|---|---|---|---|---|
| Tulsa | 136 | 3582 | 1559 | 114 | 133 | 12 | .978 | Wichita | 137 | 3522 | 1481 | 159 | 151 | 13 | .969 |
| Indianapolis | 135 | 3447 | 1397 | 129 | 137 | 19 | .974 | Denver | 136 | 3460 | 1422 | 165 | 138 | 8 | .967 |
| Oklahoma City | 136 | 3391 | 1378 | 134 | 127 | 23 | .973 | Iowa | 135 | 3450 | 1459 | 169 | 106 | 21 | .967 |
| Evansville | 137 | 3480 | 1550 | 149 | 147 | 16 | .971 | Omaha | 136 | 3426 | 1432 | 177 | 116 | 6 | .965 |

Triple Plays—None.

## INDIVIDUAL FIELDING

*Throws lefthanded.

### FIRST BASEMEN

| Player and Club | G. | PO. | A. | E. | DP. | Pct. | Player and Club | G. | PO. | A. | E. | DP. | Pct. |
|---|---|---|---|---|---|---|---|---|---|---|---|---|---|
| Batista, Iowa* | 12 | 115 | 9 | 0 | 4 | 1.000 | Revering, Indpls | 117 | 959 | 91 | 12 | 98 | .989 |
| Norris, Okla City* | 11 | 82 | 9 | 0 | 10 | 1.000 | Lis, Okla City | 105 | 829 | 58 | 10 | 80 | .989 |
| Robinson, Evansville | 10 | 70 | 2 | 0 | 8 | 1.000 | Tabb, Wichita | 86 | 785 | 49 | 10 | 88 | .988 |
| Bennett, Denver* | 10 | 48 | 7 | 0 | 7 | 1.000 | DeFreites, Indpls | 25 | 152 | 7 | 2 | 13 | .988 |
| Howard, Tulsa | 63 | 578 | 59 | 1 | 49 | .998 | Johnson, Denver | 114 | 939 | 71 | 13 | 107 | .987 |
| Pierce, Evansville | 36 | 348 | 19 | 2 | 36 | .995 | Kurpiel, Evansville* | 91 | 784 | 41 | 11 | 80 | .987 |
| Gonzalez, Okla City* | 16 | 140 | 10 | 1 | 12 | .993 | Ewing, Denver | 18 | 139 | 11 | 2 | 9 | .987 |
| ORTENZIO, Omaha | 93 | 842 | 47 | 7 | 57 | .9921 | Martz, Omaha | 44 | 372 | 26 | 7 | 41 | .983 |
| Skidmore, Iowa | 108 | 918 | 72 | 8 | 71 | .9919 | Hernandez, Tulsa* | 72 | 581 | 53 | 13 | 63 | .980 |
| Matney, Wichita* | 56 | 414 | 15 | 4 | 55 | .991 | Busse, Iowa | 14 | 113 | 14 | 5 | 8 | .962 |

(Fewer Than Ten Games)

| Player and Club | G. | PO. | A. | E. | DP. | Pct. | Player and Club | G. | PO. | A. | E. | DP. | Pct. |
|---|---|---|---|---|---|---|---|---|---|---|---|---|---|
| Vukovich, Indpls | 5 | 34 | 0 | 0 | 4 | 1.000 | DaVanon, Iowa | 2 | 3 | 0 | 0 | 0 | 1.000 |
| Leon, Tulsa* | 4 | 24 | 2 | 0 | 0 | 1.000 | Pena, Iowa | 1 | 3 | 0 | 0 | 0 | 1.000 |
| Gallagher, Iowa* | 2 | 9 | 1 | 0 | 0 | 1.000 | Lane, Evansville | 1 | 2 | 0 | 0 | 0 | 1.000 |
| Billings, Tulsa | 1 | 10 | 0 | 0 | 2 | 1.000 | Garrett, Wichita | 1 | 2 | 0 | 0 | 0 | 1.000 |
| Foster, Denver | 1 | 8 | 0 | 0 | 2 | 1.000 | Haug, Wichita | 1 | 1 | 0 | 0 | 0 | 1.000 |
| Day, Evansville* | 2 | 6 | 0 | 0 | 1 | 1.000 | de la Rosa, Iowa | 1 | 1 | 0 | 0 | 0 | 1.000 |
| Sovern, Denver | 1 | 5 | 1 | 0 | 2 | 1.000 | Dusan, Okla City | 6 | 37 | 0 | 1 | 2 | .974 |
| Dunn, Wichita | 1 | 4 | 1 | 0 | 0 | 1.000 | Ostrosser, Okla City | 2 | 20 | 1 | 1 | 1 | .955 |
| Bass, Tulsa | 1 | 4 | 0 | 0 | 0 | 1.000 | Kimm, Evansville | 3 | 11 | 0 | 2 | 2 | .846 |
| LaRussa, Denver | 1 | 3 | 1 | 0 | 0 | 1.000 | | | | | | | |

### SECOND BASEMEN

| Player and Club | G. | PO. | A. | E. | DP. | Pct. | Player and Club | G. | PO. | A. | E. | DP. | Pct. |
|---|---|---|---|---|---|---|---|---|---|---|---|---|---|
| Vukovich, Indpls | 16 | 23 | 34 | 0 | 7 | 1.000 | Heise, Okla City | 83 | 188 | 219 | 12 | 61 | .971 |
| ALVARADO, Tulsa | 92 | 232 | 263 | 3 | 65 | .994 | LaRussa, Denver | 14 | 29 | 34 | 2 | 6 | .969 |
| Hisman, Wichita | 27 | 47 | 65 | 1 | 13 | .991 | Staggs, Omaha | 122 | 254 | 348 | 23 | 72 | .963 |
| Franklin, Indpls | 80 | 144 | 176 | 4 | 42 | .988 | Barnes, Indianapolis | 71 | 115 | 187 | 12 | 36 | .962 |
| Kuiper, Okla City | 110 | 94 | 3 | 23 | | .986 | Perez, Iowa | 79 | 159 | 184 | 15 | 36 | .958 |
| Manuel, Evansville | 137 | 348 | 394 | 16 | 108 | .979 | Estrada, Denver | 123 | 271 | 344 | 28 | 83 | .956 |
| Adams, Wichita | 79 | 172 | 250 | 10 | 57 | .977 | DaVanon, Iowa | 20 | 31 | 54 | 4 | 9 | .955 |
| Kelleher, Tulsa | 32 | 69 | 103 | 4 | 16 | .977 | Gonzalez, Wichita | 36 | 74 | 87 | 10 | 26 | .942 |
| Driscoll, Iowa | 28 | 52 | 69 | 3 | 14 | .976 | Milbourne, Iowa | 21 | 33 | 47 | 8 | 9 | .909 |

## SECOND BASEMEN
### (Fewer Than Ten Games)

| Player and Club | G. | PO. | A. | E. | DP. | Pct. | Player and Club | G. | PO. | A. | E. | DP. | Pct. |
|---|---|---|---|---|---|---|---|---|---|---|---|---|---|
| Lanier, Tulsa | 9 | 19 | 26 | 0 | 8 | 1.000 | Meier, Tulsa | 6 | 12 | 21 | 1 | 4 | .971 |
| Gamble, Evansville | 2 | 7 | 8 | 0 | 3 | 1.000 | Oliver, Okla City | 6 | 6 | 17 | 1 | 3 | .958 |
| Dunn, Wichita | 1 | 5 | 2 | 0 | 4 | 1.000 | Green, Wichita | 6 | 11 | 9 | 1 | 6 | .952 |
| McLaughlin, Iowa | 1 | 0 | 4 | 0 | 1 | 1.000 | Brooks, Okla City | 8 | 15 | 20 | 2 | 1 | .946 |
| Kennedy, Indpls | 1 | 0 | 3 | 0 | 1 | 1.000 | Yancy, Denver | 2 | 4 | 5 | 1 | 3 | .900 |
| Cater, Tulsa | 1 | 1 | 1 | 0 | 1 | 1.000 | Youngblood, Indpls | 2 | 5 | 3 | 1 | 1 | .889 |
| Floyd, Omaha | 8 | 19 | 24 | 1 | 8 | .977 | Scott, Omaha | 6 | 9 | 11 | 3 | 2 | .870 |

## THIRD BASEMEN

| Player and Club | G. | PO. | A. | E. | DP. | Pct. | Player and Club | G. | PO. | A. | E. | DP. | Pct. |
|---|---|---|---|---|---|---|---|---|---|---|---|---|---|
| Gonzalez, Wichita | 20 | 16 | 41 | 0 | 12 | 1.000 | Dunn, Wichita | 23 | 14 | 42 | 4 | 10 | .933 |
| Lanier, Tulsa | 10 | 7 | 24 | 0 | 2 | 1.000 | DaVanon, Iowa | 66 | 51 | 129 | 14 | 6 | .928 |
| Howard, Tulsa | 19 | 15 | 33 | 1 | 3 | .980 | Hannah, Okla City | 15 | 13 | 32 | 4 | 3 | .918 |
| Alvarado, Okla City | 13 | 7 | 24 | 1 | 2 | .969 | Adams, Wichita | 10 | 6 | 25 | 3 | 4 | .912 |
| Heise, Okla City | 10 | 6 | 21 | 1 | 1 | .964 | Yancy, Denver | 51 | 32 | 80 | 11 | 7 | .911 |
| Ostrosser, Okla City | 13 | 16 | 32 | 2 | 1 | .960 | LaRussa, Denver | 29 | 19 | 32 | 5 | 2 | .911 |
| QUIRK, Omaha | 126 | 109 | 254 | 16 | 31 | .958 | Busse, Iowa-Omaha | 33 | 26 | 65 | 9 | 4 | .910 |
| Meier, Tulsa | 12 | 6 | 16 | 1 | 2 | .957 | Brooks, Okla City | 28 | 28 | 47 | 8 | 6 | .904 |
| Knight, Indianapolis | 122 | 116 | 227 | 17 | 29 | .953 | Cash, Evansville | 47 | 23 | 70 | 10 | 10 | .903 |
| Cruz, Tulsa | 103 | 75 | 197 | 17 | 14 | .941 | Oliver, Wichita | 65 | 51 | 110 | 22 | 15 | .880 |
| Driscoll, Iowa | 41 | 23 | 68 | 6 | 9 | .938 | Tyrone, Wichita | 16 | 16 | 20 | 6 | 3 | .857 |
| Oliver, Okla City | 59 | 47 | 162 | 14 | 14 | .937 | Lemon, Denver | 55 | 33 | 76 | 19 | 5 | .852 |
| Gamble, Evansville | 93 | 69 | 238 | 22 | 24 | .933 | Green, Wichita | 13 | 14 | 17 | 7 | 2 | .816 |

### (Fewer Than Ten Games)

| Player and Club | G. | PO. | A. | E. | DP. | Pct. | Player and Club | G. | PO. | A. | E. | DP. | Pct. |
|---|---|---|---|---|---|---|---|---|---|---|---|---|---|
| Vukovich, Indpls | 6 | 3 | 7 | 0 | 1 | 1.000 | Estrada, Denver | 2 | 2 | 5 | 1 | 0 | .875 |
| Huisman, Wichita | 3 | 1 | 6 | 0 | 0 | 1.000 | Nasif, Evansville | 2 | 1 | 5 | 1 | 0 | .857 |
| Sovern, Denver | 1 | 1 | 3 | 0 | 1 | 1.000 | McLaughlin, Iowa | 7 | 0 | 10 | 2 | 0 | .833 |
| Johnson, Tulsa | 1 | 0 | 1 | 0 | 0 | 1.000 | Ruberto, Indpls | 5 | 3 | 12 | 3 | 0 | .833 |
| Floyd, Omaha | 7 | 4 | 16 | 1 | 1 | .952 | Franklin, Indianapolis | 4 | 1 | 3 | 1 | 0 | .800 |
| Perez, Iowa | 7 | 5 | 15 | 2 | 1 | .909 | Lis, Okla City | 2 | 3 | 4 | 2 | 1 | .778 |
| Dunning, Denver | 6 | 2 | 5 | 1 | 0 | .875 | Sinatro, Indianapolis | 5 | 3 | 3 | 2 | 1 | .750 |
| Ewing, Denver | 3 | 0 | 7 | 1 | 1 | .875 | Lambe, Evansville | 1 | 2 | 1 | 1 | 0 | .750 |

## SHORTSTOPS

| Player and Club | G. | PO. | A. | E. | DP. | Pct. | Player and Club | G. | PO. | A. | E. | DP. | Pct. |
|---|---|---|---|---|---|---|---|---|---|---|---|---|---|
| KELLEHER, Tulsa | 95 | 177 | 273 | 10 | 64 | .978 | McMillan, Okla City | 136 | 236 | 363 | 30 | 76 | .952 |
| Scrivener, Evansville | 130 | 208 | 427 | 17 | 98 | .974 | Meier, Tulsa | 21 | 23 | 52 | 4 | 8 | .949 |
| Kennedy, Indpls | 114 | 234 | 275 | 18 | 67 | .966 | Taveras, Iowa | 133 | 207 | 385 | 33 | 75 | .947 |
| Buskey, Denver | 132 | 245 | 395 | 24 | 90 | .964 | LaRussa, Denver | 17 | 15 | 23 | 3 | 10 | .927 |
| Guerrero, Tulsa | 31 | 44 | 83 | 5 | 17 | .962 | Vukovich, Indpls | 21 | 27 | 47 | 6 | 13 | .925 |
| Rosello, Wichita | 135 | 225 | 435 | 32 | 85 | .954 | Washington, Omaha | 127 | 195 | 367 | 46 | 68 | .924 |

### (Fewer Than Ten Games)

| Player and Club | G. | PO. | A. | E. | DP. | Pct. | Player and Club | G. | PO. | A. | E. | DP. | Pct. |
|---|---|---|---|---|---|---|---|---|---|---|---|---|---|
| Floyd, Omaha | 5 | 2 | 12 | 0 | 1 | 1.000 | DaVanon, Iowa | 3 | 7 | 9 | 1 | 0 | .941 |
| Green, Wichita | 6 | 2 | 8 | 0 | 1 | 1.000 | Gamble, Evansville | 8 | 18 | 19 | 3 | 4 | .925 |
| Johnson, Tulsa | 1 | 1 | 5 | 0 | 1 | 1.000 | Scott, Omaha | 5 | 4 | 7 | 2 | 1 | .846 |
| Alvarado, OC-Tul | 4 | 4 | 2 | 0 | 1 | 1.000 | Dunn, Wichita | 1 | 3 | 2 | 1 | 1 | .833 |
| Huisman, Wichita | 1 | 3 | 1 | 0 | 1 | 1.000 | | | | | | | |

## OUTFIELDERS

| Player and Club | G. | PO. | A. | E. | DP. | Pct. | Player and Club | G. | PO. | A. | E. | DP. | Pct. |
|---|---|---|---|---|---|---|---|---|---|---|---|---|---|
| Day, Evansville* | 71 | 137 | 4 | 0 | 0 | 1.000 | Gallagher, Iowa* | 78 | 138 | 4 | 3 | 0 | .979 |
| Manning, Okla City | 30 | 62 | 4 | 0 | 2 | 1.000 | Wallis, Wichita | 34 | 89 | 6 | 2 | 0 | .979 |
| Schneck, Indpls* | 21 | 34 | 3 | 0 | 0 | 1.000 | Hiser, Wichita* | 70 | 172 | 10 | 4 | 3 | .978 |
| Matney, Wichita* | 25 | 37 | 1 | 0 | 0 | 1.000 | de la Rosa, Iowa | 59 | 82 | 9 | 2 | 1 | .978 |
| Martz, Omaha | 19 | 36 | 2 | 0 | 0 | 1.000 | Mumphrey, Tulsa | 126 | 248 | 7 | 6 | 1 | .977 |
| Lee, Tulsa | 18 | 32 | 5 | 0 | 1 | 1.000 | Garcia, Okla City | 121 | 295 | 15 | 8 | 4 | .975 |
| LaRussa, Denver | 28 | 29 | 1 | 0 | 1 | 1.000 | Hairston, Denver | 40 | 72 | 3 | 2 | 1 | .974 |
| Droege, Wichita | 12 | 22 | 1 | 0 | 1 | 1.000 | Molinaro, Evansville | 121 | 174 | 2 | 5 | 1 | .972 |
| Cruz, Tulsa | 14 | 18 | 0 | 0 | 0 | 1.000 | Youngblood, Indpls | 118 | 196 | 10 | 6 | 2 | .972 |
| Hernandez, Tulsa* | 10 | 16 | 0 | 0 | 0 | 1.000 | Williams, Omaha* | 96 | 198 | 7 | 6 | 1 | .972 |
| Kimm, Evansville | 12 | 5 | 0 | 0 | 0 | 1.000 | Bennett, Denver* | 108 | 199 | 3 | 6 | 0 | .971 |
| SPENCER, Indpls | 125 | 265 | 16 | 2 | 4 | .9929 | Lyttle, Denver | 80 | 187 | 5 | 6 | 2 | .970 |
| Smith, Okla City | 129 | 251 | 15 | 2 | 0 | .9925 | Schlueter, Tulsa | 13 | 32 | 0 | 1 | 0 | .970 |
| Craig, Omaha-Iowa | 92 | 201 | 8 | 3 | 2 | .986 | Baldwin, Evansville* | 14 | 29 | 2 | 1 | 0 | .969 |
| Harris, Wichita | 27 | 63 | 7 | 1 | 0 | .986 | Gardner, Iowa* | 134 | 286 | 21 | 10 | 6 | .968 |
| Garrett, Wichita | 35 | 59 | 2 | 1 | 0 | .984 | Sinatro, Indpls | 69 | 121 | 1 | 4 | 0 | .968 |
| Ward, Wichita* | 64 | 115 | 4 | 2 | 0 | .983 | Green, Wichita | 29 | 1 | 1 | 0 | 0 | .968 |
| James, Evansville* | 98 | 196 | 6 | 4 | 0 | .981 | Lambe, Evansville | 48 | 54 | 5 | 2 | 1 | .967 |
| Marshall, Omaha | 89 | 152 | 3 | 3 | 1 | .981 | Gorinski, Denver | 31 | 54 | 2 | 2 | 1 | .966 |
| Lane, Evansville | 72 | 146 | 6 | 3 | 0 | .981 | Norris, Okla City* | 53 | 103 | 4 | 4 | 0 | .964 |
| Beach, Denver | 45 | 96 | 8 | 2 | 1 | .981 | Tyrone, Wichita | 93 | 164 | 17 | 7 | 2 | .963 |
| Gonzalez, Okla C* | 57 | 91 | 6 | 2 | 1 | .980 | Adams, Wichita | 38 | 74 | 3 | 3 | 0 | .963 |
| Norton, Denver | 25 | 45 | 3 | 1 | 0 | .980 | Dwyer, Tulsa* | 31 | 49 | 2 | 2 | 1 | .962 |

## OUTFIELDER—Continued

| Player and Club | G. | PO. | A. | E. | DP. | Pct. |
|---|---|---|---|---|---|---|
| Davis, Okla City* | 12 | 24 | 1 | 1 | 0 | .962 |
| Foster, Denver | 33 | 46 | 1 | 2 | 0 | .959 |
| Nordhagen, Tulsa | 67 | 102 | 7 | 5 | 3 | .956 |
| Lindsey, Tulsa | 53 | 82 | 3 | 4 | 0 | .955 |
| Rima, Iowa | 11 | 19 | 2 | 1 | 1 | .955 |
| Easler, Iowa-Tulsa | 101 | 161 | 6 | 8 | 1 | .954 |
| Busse, Iowa-Omaha | 89 | 155 | 12 | 8 | 4 | .954 |
| Talley, Denver | 16 | 20 | 0 | 1 | 0 | .952 |
| DeFreites, Indpls | 101 | 152 | 12 | 10 | 5 | .943 |
| Jones, Omaha | 119 | 171 | 15 | 13 | 5 | .935 |
| Ewing, Denver | 24 | 14 | 0 | 1 | 0 | .933 |
| Herndon, Tulsa | 19 | 35 | 2 | 3 | 0 | .925 |
| Javier, Iowa | 13 | 20 | 0 | 2 | 0 | .909 |

### (Fewer Than Ten Games)

| Player and Club | G. | PO. | A. | E. | DP. | Pct. |
|---|---|---|---|---|---|---|
| Alexander, Wichita | 7 | 25 | 1 | 0 | 0 | 1.000 |
| Dusan, Okla City | 6 | 14 | 0 | 0 | 0 | 1.000 |
| Gonzales, Evansville | 7 | 12 | 0 | 0 | 0 | 1.000 |
| Wockenfuss, Evansville | 3 | 4 | 3 | 0 | 0 | 1.000 |
| Lemon, Denver | 5 | 6 | 0 | 0 | 0 | 1.000 |
| Perez, Iowa | 2 | 6 | 0 | 0 | 0 | 1.000 |
| Brooks, Okla City | 6 | 4 | 1 | 0 | 0 | 1.000 |
| Wathan, Omaha | 3 | 4 | 0 | 0 | 0 | 1.000 |
| Hinton, Denver* | 3 | 4 | 0 | 0 | 0 | 1.000 |
| Howard, Tulsa | 2 | 4 | 0 | 0 | 0 | 1.000 |
| Estrada, Denver | 1 | 4 | 0 | 0 | 0 | 1.000 |
| Leon, Tulsa* | 2 | 2 | 0 | 0 | 0 | 1.000 |
| Vukovich, Indpls | 1 | 2 | 0 | 0 | 0 | 1.000 |
| Cater, Tulsa | 1 | 1 | 0 | 0 | 0 | 1.000 |
| Pena, Iowa | 6 | 10 | 0 | 2 | 0 | .833 |
| Stelmaszek, Wichita | 3 | 5 | 0 | 1 | 0 | .833 |
| Kurpiel, Evansville* | 3 | 3 | 0 | 1 | 0. | .750 |

## CATCHERS

| Player and Club | G. | PO. | A. | E. | DP. | PB. | Pct. |
|---|---|---|---|---|---|---|---|
| Isaac, Okla City | 39 | 224 | 34 | 0 | 8 | 5 | 1.000 |
| Haug, Wichita | 49 | 203 | 15 | 0 | 1 | 3 | 1.000 |
| McLaren, Iowa | 3 | 14 | 2 | 0 | 0 | 1 | 1.000 |
| Boone, Iowa | 1 | 5 | 0 | 0 | 0 | 0 | 1.000 |
| Hiatt, Wichita | 1 | 3 | 0 | 0 | 0 | 0 | 1.000 |
| Harmon, Tulsa | 27 | 158 | 12 | 1 | 2 | 1 | .994 |
| Tamargo, Tulsa | 40 | 231 | 19 | 2 | 3 | 5 | .992 |
| Quinn, Denver | 62 | 318 | 25 | 3 | 6 | 4 | .991 |
| Billings, Tulsa | 41 | 236 | 28 | 3 | 5 | 5 | .989 |
| Cerone, Okla City | 40 | 178 | 30 | 3 | 7 | 7 | .986 |
| WERNER, Indpls. | 75 | 423 | 51 | 7 | 7 | 9 | .985 |
| Wockenfuss, Evans | 33 | 170 | 23 | 3 | 2 | 7 | .985 |
| Dusan, Okla City | 61 | 270 | 36 | 5 | 1 | 11 | .984 |
| Wathan, Omaha | 97 | 528 | 45 | 10 | 7 | 5 | .983 |
| Didier, Iowa | 95 | 571 | 61 | 11 | 5 | 13 | .983 |
| Lamont, Evansville | 49 | 211 | 23 | 4 | 3 | 3 | .983 |
| Robles, Tulsa | 43 | 249 | 28 | 5 | 3 | 1 | .982 |
| Perkins, Omaha | 43 | 236 | 32 | 5 | 2 | 1 | .982 |
| Stelmaszek, Wchta | 99 | 469 | 35 | 10 | 6 | 10 | .981 |
| Sovern, Evansville | 86 | 467 | 68 | 11 | 4 | 4 | .980 |
| Ruberto, Indpls | 74 | 431 | 50 | 12 | 6 | 10 | .976 |
| Pena, Iowa | 52 | 258 | 19 | 7 | 7 | 7 | .975 |
| Kimm, Evansville | 67 | 353 | 43 | 12 | 4 | 6 | .971 |
| Swisher, Wichita | 6 | 27 | 4 | 1 | 0 | 0 | .969 |

## PITCHERS

| Player and Club | G. | PO. | A. | E. | DP. | Pct |
|---|---|---|---|---|---|---|
| Lersch, Okla City | 32 | 9 | 20 | 0 | 2 | 1.000 |
| Parsons, Tul-Den | 29 | 7 | 22 | 0 | 1 | 1.000 |
| Taylor, Indpls | 51 | 9 | 17 | 0 | 2 | 1.000 |
| Terlecky, Tulsa | 14 | 10 | 14 | 0 | 3 | 1.000 |
| Hume, Indianapolis | 17 | 3 | 20 | 0 | 1 | 1.000 |
| Crosby, Tulsa-Wchta | 32 | 4 | 10 | 0 | 1 | 1.000 |
| McCutchin, Okla City | 18 | 7 | 7 | 0 | 0 | 1.000 |
| Beckman, Wichita* | 16 | 0 | 14 | 0 | 1 | 1.000 |
| Elenes, Iowa | 12 | 5 | 9 | 0 | 0 | 1.000 |
| Schultz, Wichita* | 47 | 5 | 7 | 0 | 0 | 1.000 |
| York, Iowa | 31 | 5 | 7 | 0 | 2 | 1.000 |
| Foor, Tulsa* | 31 | 3 | 7 | 0 | 0 | 1.000 |
| Wallace, Tulsa* | 21 | 1 | 9 | 0 | 0 | 1.000 |
| McGough, Okla City | 18 | 4 | 6 | 0 | 0 | 1.000 |
| Brookens, Evansville | 29 | 0 | 9 | 0 | 0 | 1.000 |
| Sprinkle, Iowa | 28 | 1 | 8 | 0 | 0 | 1.000 |
| Baldwin, Okla City* | 11 | 3 | 6 | 0 | 0 | 1.000 |
| Chlan, Omaha | 31 | 2 | 6 | 0 | 0 | 1.000 |
| Eastwick, Indpls | 15 | 5 | 3 | 0 | 1 | 1.000 |
| Enyart, Indpls* | 15 | 2 | 5 | 0 | 0 | 1.000 |
| Baney, Indpls | 16 | 2 | 4 | 0 | 0 | 1.000 |
| Komadina, Denver* | 10 | 1 | 5 | 0 | 1 | 1.000 |
| Lehman, Denver | 12 | 2 | 3 | 0 | 0 | 1.000 |
| Pentz, Evansville | 18 | 1 | 3 | 0 | 0 | 1.000 |
| de los Santos, Iowa* | 15 | 0 | 3 | 0 | 0 | 1.000 |
| Bernard, Omaha | 12 | 0 | 3 | 0 | 0 | 1.000 |
| Strahler, Okla City | 10 | 0 | 3 | 0 | 1 | 1.000 |
| Newman, Evansville* | 12 | 0 | 2 | 0 | 0 | 1.000 |
| DUNNING, Denver | 28 | 13 | 43 | 1 | 4 | .982 |
| Slayback, Evansville | 27 | 9 | 40 | 1 | 4 | .980 |
| Willoughby, Tulsa | 15 | 13 | 34 | 1 | 3 | .979 |
| Reynolds, Tulsa* | 19 | 13 | 33 | 1 | 7 | .979 |
| Payne, Indianapolis | 26 | 15 | 27 | 1 | 0 | .977 |
| Siebert, Iowa* | 30 | 4 | 29 | 1 | 3 | .971 |
| Andersen, Okla City | 25 | 10 | 24 | 1 | 2 | .971 |
| Hutson, Wichita | 30 | 10 | 22 | 1 | 4 | .970 |
| Proly, Tulsa | 55 | 7 | 23 | 1 | 3 | .968 |
| Arroyo, Evansville | 11 | 4 | 24 | 1 | 1 | .966 |
| Selak, Iowa | 16 | 9 | 18 | 1 | 0 | .964 |
| Henderson, Indpls | 45 | 9 | 17 | 1 | 1 | .963 |
| Otten, Denver | 28 | 10 | 16 | 1 | 1 | .963 |
| Strickland, Ok City* | 50 | 5 | 19 | 1 | 1 | .960 |
| Baird, Omaha* | 39 | 4 | 20 | 1 | 0 | .960 |
| Watt, Wichita | 44 | 4 | 19 | 1 | 3 | .958 |
| Walker, Iowa* | 20 | 2 | 21 | 1 | 0 | .958 |
| Rasmussen, Tulsa | 18 | 9 | 14 | 1 | 0 | .958 |
| Prall, Wichita* | 29 | 6 | 16 | 1 | 2 | .957 |
| Littell, Omaha | 24 | 8 | 32 | 2 | 0 | .952 |
| Skok, Evansville* | 13 | 7 | 13 | 1 | 1 | .952 |
| Rothermel, Iowa* | 48 | 7 | 12 | 1 | 3 | .950 |
| Reuschel, Wichita | 35 | 7 | 12 | 1 | 1 | .950 |
| Throop, Omaha | 26 | 9 | 29 | 2 | 2 | .950 |
| Lemongello, Evansville | 15 | 6 | 13 | 1 | 0 | .950 |
| Henninger, Okla City | 27 | 6 | 12 | 1 | 0 | .947 |
| Dettore, Wichita | 13 | 3 | 15 | 1 | 0 | .947 |
| Waterbury, Tulsa | 11 | 9 | 9 | 1 | 0 | .947 |
| Scarce, Inpls* | 60 | 1 | 16 | 1 | 0 | .944 |
| McClain, Denver* | 26 | 9 | 37 | 3 | 3 | .939 |
| Grow, Indianapolis* | 24 | 10 | 18 | 2 | 2 | .933 |
| Larson, Iowa | 12 | 4 | 10 | 1 | 1 | .933 |
| Copeland, Wichita | 27 | 17 | 9 | 2 | 1 | .929 |
| Swanson, Evansville | 25 | 6 | 20 | 2 | 2 | .929 |
| DeBarr, Evansville* | 11 | 2 | 11 | 1 | 0 | .929 |
| Alcala, Indpls | 27 | 6 | 19 | 2 | 2 | .926 |
| Stanton, Iowa | 18 | 18 | 18 | 3 | 0 | .923 |
| Allen, Denver-Tulsa | 14 | 5 | 19 | 2 | 1 | .923 |
| Lance, Omaha | 28 | 26 | 32 | 5 | 0 | .921 |
| Kremmel, Wichita* | 34 | 3 | 19 | 2 | 3 | .917 |
| Hinton, Denver* | 30 | 5 | 17 | 2 | 2 | .917 |
| Grilli, Evansville | 44 | 4 | 17 | 2 | 1 | .913 |
| Moran, Denver | 30 | 6 | 15 | 2 | 0 | .913 |
| Barlow, Tulsa | 20 | 7 | 14 | 2 | 0 | .913 |
| Vukovich, Denver | 19 | 11 | 19 | 3 | 3 | .909 |
| Carroll, Indianapolis | 16 | 6 | 14 | 2 | 1 | .909 |
| Roznovsky, Iowa | 35 | 5 | 33 | 4 | 3 | .905 |
| Zachry, Indianapolis | 27 | 10 | 26 | 4 | 0 | .900 |
| Pitlock, Denver* | 13 | 4 | 5 | 1 | 1 | .900 |
| Alfonso, Iowa | 41 | 9 | 17 | 3 | 3 | .897 |
| Ellingsen, Okla City* | 27 | 8 | 16 | 3 | 2 | .889 |
| Brennan, Okla City | 25 | 12 | 15 | 4 | 2 | .871 |
| Shaffer, Denver | 27 | 7 | 6 | 2 | 0 | .867 |
| Angelini, Omaha* | 54 | 2 | 10 | 2 | 1 | .857 |
| Solomon, Wchta-Tul | 15 | 3 | 9 | 2 | 0 | .857 |
| Temple, Wichita | 18 | 3 | 8 | 2 | 1 | .846 |

### PITCHERS—Continued

| Player and Club | G. | PO. | A. | E. | DP. | Pct. |
|---|---|---|---|---|---|---|
| Bruno, Omaha | 23 | 3 | 18 | 4 | 0 | .840 |
| Wiles, Tulsa* | 11 | 1 | 4 | 1 | 0 | .833 |
| Makowski, Evans* | 30 | 2 | 12 | 3 | 1 | .824 |
| Autry, Omaha | 23 | 9 | 25 | 8 | 0 | .810 |
| Cosgrove, Iowa* | 17 | 3 | 1 | 1 | 1 | .800 |
| Meyring, Omaha | 12 | 0 | 4 | 1 | 0 | .800 |
| Bass, Tulsa | 12 | 3 | 2 | 2 | 1 | .714 |
| Ignasiak, Evansville* | 11 | 2 | 6 | 4 | 0 | .667 |

#### (Fewer Than Ten Games)

| Player and Club | G. | PO. | A. | E. | DP. | Pct. |
|---|---|---|---|---|---|---|
| Waits, Okla City* | 9 | 3 | 9 | 0 | 1 | 1.000 |
| Barrios, Denver | 3 | 4 | 6 | 0 | 1 | 1.000 |
| Holdsworth, Evans | 7 | 1 | 6 | 0 | 0 | 1.000 |
| Cuen, Iowa | 5 | 3 | 4 | 0 | 0 | 1.000 |
| Kucek, Denver | 6 | 2 | 3 | 0 | 0 | 1.000 |
| Matney, Wichita* | 5 | 1 | 3 | 0 | 1 | 1.000 |
| Kern, Okla City | 3 | 3 | 1 | 0 | 0 | 1.000 |
| Hasbach, Omaha | 3 | 1 | 3 | 0 | 1 | 1.000 |
| Niekro, Iowa | 7 | 1 | 2 | 0 | 0 | 1.000 |
| Manz, Wichita | 3 | 1 | 2 | 0 | 1 | 1.000 |
| Linnert, Okla City* | 3 | 0 | 3 | 0 | 0 | 1.000 |
| Bell, Okla City | 5 | 0 | 2 | 0 | 0 | 1.000 |
| Williams, Iowa | 4 | 1 | 1 | 0 | 0 | 1.000 |
| Staniland, Tulsa | 4 | 1 | 1 | 0 | 0 | 1.000 |
| Spinks, Iowa | 3 | 2 | 0 | 0 | 0 | 1.000 |
| Junge, Wichita | 3 | 1 | 1 | 0 | 1 | 1.000 |
| MacCormack, Evans | 3 | 0 | 1 | 0 | 0 | 1.000 |
| Christenson, Evans* | 2 | 0 | 1 | 0 | 0 | 1.000 |
| Weiss, Wichita | 2 | 0 | 1 | 0 | 0 | 1.000 |
| McAnally, Okla City | 1 | 0 | 1 | 0 | 0 | 1.000 |
| Denny, Tulsa | 7 | 7 | 12 | 1 | 2 | .950 |
| Wilcox, Wichita | 8 | 7 | 8 | 1 | 0 | .938 |
| Fidrych, Evansville | 6 | 3 | 6 | 1 | 1 | .900 |
| Turner, Wichita | 5 | 2 | 5 | 1 | 0 | .875 |
| Grossman, Okla City | 7 | 5 | 4 | 2 | 0 | .818 |
| Raich, Okla City | 7 | 2 | 10 | 3 | 0 | .800 |
| Nagy, Iowa | 4 | 1 | 3 | 1 | 0 | .800 |
| Leonard, Omaha | 3 | 0 | 7 | 2 | 1 | .778 |
| Lukevics, Denver | 4 | 2 | 1 | 1 | 0 | .750 |
| Glynn, Evansville* | 7 | 0 | 4 | 2 | 0 | .667 |
| Day, Evansville* | 9 | 1 | 0 | 1 | 0 | .500 |

The following players do not have any recorded accepted chances at the positions indicated; therefore, are not listed in the fielding averages for those particular positions: Brooks, p; Cerone, of; Cleverly, 3b; Crawford*, p; Driscoll, 1b; Dunn, of; Dunning, of; Franklin, of; Gamble, of; Knight, 1b; Lis, of; Motil*, p; Nasif, of; O'Toole, p; Ray, p; Ruberto, 2b. Leaver appeared as a pinch-runner only.

### CLUB PITCHING

| Club | G. | CG. | ShO. | Sv. | IP. | H. | R. | ER. | HR. | BB. | Int.BB. | HB. | SO. | WP. | Bk. | ERA. |
|---|---|---|---|---|---|---|---|---|---|---|---|---|---|---|---|---|
| Indianapolis | 135 | 28 | 20 | 19 | 1149 | 1013 | 491 | 412 | 71 | 515 | 44 | 33 | 724 | 45 | 5 | 3.23 |
| Omaha | 136 | 41 | 8 | 27 | 1142 | 1085 | 536 | 444 | 73 | 461 | 62 | 35 | 727 | 40 | 4 | 3.50 |
| Evansville | 137 | 32 | 8 | 28 | 1160 | 1121 | 545 | 470 | 71 | 483 | 41 | 23 | 695 | 48 | 6 | 3.65 |
| Iowa | 135 | 30 | 9 | 26 | 1150 | 1144 | 599 | 509 | 84 | 563 | 40 | 43 | 800 | 52 | 9 | 3.98 |
| Denver | 136 | 50 | 7 | 14 | 1153 | 1155 | 635 | 542 | 93 | 506 | 27 | 23 | 752 | 51 | 5 | 4.23 |
| Tulsa | 136 | 36 | 11 | 25 | 1194 | 1238 | 615 | 569 | 83 | 582 | 61 | 25 | 794 | 50 | 2 | 4.29 |
| Wichita | 137 | 29 | 9 | 24 | 1174 | 1339 | 719 | 582 | 101 | 490 | 44 | 31 | 665 | 51 | 1 | 4.46 |
| Oklahoma City | 136 | 35 | 4 | 14 | 1130 | 1272 | 764 | 652 | 93 | 607 | 44 | 42 | 618 | 80 | 11 | 5.19 |

### PITCHERS' RECORDS

#### (Leading Qualifiers for Earned-Run Average Leadership—109 or More Innings)
*Throws lefthanded.

| Pitcher—Club | G. | GS. | CG. | ShO. | W. | L. | Sv. | Pct. | IP. | H. | R. | ER. | HR. | BB. | Int.BB. | HB. | SO. | WP. | ERA. |
|---|---|---|---|---|---|---|---|---|---|---|---|---|---|---|---|---|---|---|---|
| Zachry, Indpls | 27 | 22 | 6 | 4 | 10 | 7 | 0 | .588 | 159 | 120 | 52 | 43 | 3 | 70 | 6 | 3 | 100 | 5 | 2.43 |
| Alcala, Ind | 27 | 26 | 7 | 2 | 13 | 12 | 0 | .520 | 173 | 144 | 61 | 53 | 15 | 64 | 1 | 6 | 118 | 8 | 2.76 |
| Throop, Omaha | 26 | 26 | 10 | 3 | 12 | 9 | 0 | .571 | 186 | 173 | 73 | 61 | 11 | 49 | 6 | 6 | 115 | 1 | 2.95 |
| Baird, Omaha* | 39 | 5 | 0 | 0 | 2 | 6 | 3 | .250 | 109 | 105 | 54 | 36 | 3 | 49 | 14 | 0 | 55 | 7 | 2.97 |
| Payne, Indpls | 26 | 25 | 4 | 2 | 9 | 12 | 0 | .429 | 154 | 136 | 67 | 54 | 13 | 64 | 4 | 5 | 105 | 2 | 3.16 |
| Lance, Omaha | 28 | 24 | 7 | 0 | 12 | 11 | 0 | .522 | 178 | 160 | 77 | 64 | 7 | 58 | 4 | 7 | 77 | 6 | 3.24 |
| Willoughby, Tulsa | 15 | 15 | 7 | 3 | 8 | 6 | 0 | .571 | 114 | 112 | 43 | 41 | 4 | 28 | 7 | 3 | 62 | 2 | 3.24 |
| Strickland, OC* | 50 | 3 | 0 | 0 | 7 | 4 | 12 | .636 | 110 | 98 | 51 | 40 | 2 | 73 | 10 | 4 | 114 | 12 | 3.27 |
| Slayback, Evans | 27 | 26 | 9 | 1 | 9 | 11 | 0 | .450 | 188 | 179 | 79 | 70 | 9 | 66 | 6 | 2 | 114 | 5 | 3.35 |
| Littell, Omaha | 24 | 24 | 8 | 1 | 13 | 6 | 0 | .684 | 168 | 160 | 81 | 65 | 17 | 74 | 3 | 5 | 128 | 4 | 3.48 |

Departmental Leaders: G—Scarce, 60; GS—Hutson, 29; CG—Dunning, 16; ShO—Siebert, 5; W—Dunning, 15; L—Brennan, 14; Sv—Angelini, 20; Pct.—Grilli, Vuckovich, .733; IP—Dunning, 196; H—Hutson, 218; R—Hutson, 126; ER—Hutson, 113; HR—Hutson, 27; BB—Brennan, 98; IBB—Angelini, 16; HB—Ellingsen, 9; SO—Dunning, 139; WP—Reynolds, 13.

#### (All Pitchers—Listed Alphabetically)

| Pitcher—Club | G. | GS. | CG. | ShO. | W. | L. | Sv. | Pct. | IP. | H. | R. | ER. | HR. | BB. | Int.BB. | HB. | SO. | WP. | ERA. |
|---|---|---|---|---|---|---|---|---|---|---|---|---|---|---|---|---|---|---|---|
| Alcala, Ind | 27 | 26 | 7 | 2 | 13 | 12 | 0 | .520 | 173 | 144 | 61 | 53 | 15 | 64 | 1 | 6 | 118 | 8 | 2.76 |
| Alfonso, Iowa | 41 | 1 | 1 | 0 | 3 | 4 | 3 | .429 | 89 | 88 | 42 | 36 | 4 | 39 | 6 | 3 | 53 | 11 | 3.64 |
| Allen, 8 Den-6 Tul | 14 | 14 | 4 | 0 | 9 | 2 | 0 | .818 | 108 | 99 | 44 | 41 | 9 | 46 | 3 | 2 | 81 | 8 | 3.42 |
| Andersen, Okla C. | 25 | 23 | 10 | 1 | 10 | 11 | 0 | .476 | 156 | 179 | 87 | 73 | 14 | 52 | 7 | 4 | 64 | 0 | 4.21 |
| Angelini, Omaha* | 54 | 0 | 0 | 0 | 3 | 8 | 20 | .273 | 69 | 58 | 35 | 34 | 2 | 43 | 16 | 4 | 71 | 3 | 4.43 |
| Arroyo, Evans | 11 | 11 | 3 | 0 | 5 | 4 | 0 | .556 | 86 | 82 | 37 | 25 | 4 | 18 | 2 | 0 | 44 | 5 | 2.62 |
| Autry, Omaha | 23 | 23 | 5 | 0 | 9 | 7 | 0 | .563 | 137 | 140 | 70 | 60 | 11 | 63 | 2 | 4 | 81 | 9 | 3.94 |
| Baird, Omaha* | 39 | 5 | 0 | 0 | 2 | 6 | 3 | .250 | 109 | 105 | 54 | 36 | 3 | 49 | 14 | 0 | 55 | 7 | 2.97 |
| Baldwin, Okla C* | 11 | 0 | 0 | 0 | 1 | 1 | 0 | .000 | 26 | 23 | 23 | 22 | 3 | 20 | 0 | 1 | 15 | 4 | 7.62 |
| Baney, Ind | 16 | 5 | 0 | 0 | 0 | 3 | 0 | .000 | 39 | 51 | 25 | 23 | 7 | 17 | 1 | 1 | 9 | 1 | 5.31 |
| Barlow, Tulsa | 20 | 7 | 1 | 0 | 4 | 4 | 2 | .500 | 73 | 62 | 32 | 32 | 6 | 47 | 4 | 5 | 56 | 4 | 3.95 |
| Barrios, Denver | 3 | 3 | 1 | 0 | 2 | 0 | 1 | 1.000 | 23 | 21 | 10 | 10 | 1 | 9 | 0 | 1 | 12 | 0 | 3.91 |
| Bass, Tulsa | 12 | 10 | 1 | 0 | 2 | 4 | 0 | .333 | 66 | 79 | 53 | 42 | 7 | 42 | 6 | 1 | 56 | 0 | 5.73 |

| Pitcher—Club | G. | GS. | CG. | ShO. | W. | L. | Sv. | Pct. | IP. | H. | R. | ER. | HR. | BB. | Int. BB. | HB. | SO. | WP. | ERA. |
|---|---|---|---|---|---|---|---|---|---|---|---|---|---|---|---|---|---|---|---|
| Beckman, Wichita* | 16 | 15 | 4 | 1 | 5 | 7 | 0 | .417 | 86 | 98 | 46 | 44 | 6 | 50 | 3 | 4 | 51 | 4 | 4.60 |
| Bell, Okla City .. | 5 | 5 | 1 | 0 | 1 | 4 | 0 | .200 | 28 | 38 | 22 | 20 | 1 | 10 | 2 | 2 | 11 | 3 | 6.43 |
| Bernard, Omaha | 12 | 0 | 0 | 0 | 0 | 1 | 2 | .000 | 10 | 17 | 10 | 9 | 1 | 15 | 5 | 2 | 9 | 1 | 8.10 |
| Brennan, Okla City | 25 | 25 | 3 | 0 | 5 | 14 | 0 | .263 | 122 | 149 | 103 | 96 | 21 | 98 | 2 | 2 | 52 | 11 | 7.08 |
| Brookens, Evans | 29 | 0 | 0 | 0 | 7 | 3 | 11 | .700 | 54 | 42 | 12 | 10 | 2 | 18 | 3 | 1 | 26 | 3 | 1.67 |
| Brooks, Okla City | 1 | 0 | 0 | 0 | 0 | 0 | 0 | .000 | 3 | 5 | 5 | 2 | 0 | 3 | 0 | 1 | 1 | 0 | 6.00 |
| Bruno, Omaha | 23 | 23 | 8 | 1 | 9 | 12 | 0 | .429 | 156 | 157 | 76 | 65 | 11 | 55 | 6 | 2 | 112 | 4 | 3.75 |
| Carroll, Ind ...... | 16 | 16 | 4 | 1 | 6 | 6 | 0 | .500 | 102 | 79 | 41 | 35 | 6 | 45 | 2 | 3 | 58 | 2 | 3.09 |
| Chlan, Omaha .. | 31 | 0 | 0 | 0 | 4 | 3 | 2 | .571 | 45 | 44 | 18 | 17 | 3 | 20 | 3 | 0 | 16 | 4 | 3.40 |
| Christenson, Ev* .. | 2 | 2 | 0 | 0 | 1 | 0 | 0 | 1.000 | 5 | 6 | 3 | 3 | 0 | 5 | 0 | 1 | 2 | 5 | 5.40 |
| Copeland, Wichita | 27 | 16 | 1 | 0 | 4 | 10 | 2 | .286 | 99 | 123 | 77 | 57 | 9 | 46 | 5 | 3 | 56 | 6 | 5.18 |
| Cosgrove, Iowa* .. | 17 | 6 | 0 | 0 | 2 | 6 | 3 | .250 | 43 | 49 | 40 | 35 | 5 | 30 | 1 | 4 | 27 | 2 | 7.33 |
| Crawford, Iowa* .. | 1 | 1 | 0 | 0 | 0 | 0 | 0 | .000 | 6 | 5 | 3 | 1 | 0 | 3 | 0 | 0 | 4 | 0 | 1.50 |
| Crosby, 29 Tu-3 Wic | 32 | 0 | 0 | 0 | 1 | 5 | 1 | .167 | 71 | 81 | 46 | 40 | 7 | 43 | 9 | 0 | 57 | 0 | 5.07 |
| Cuen, Iowa ........ | 5 | 5 | 1 | 0 | 1 | 3 | 0 | .250 | 33 | 29 | 13 | 12 | 4 | 13 | 0 | 1 | 16 | 0 | 3.27 |
| Day, Evansville* .. | 9 | 1 | 0 | 0 | 1 | 0 | 0 | 1.000 | 19 | 19 | 8 | 7 | 3 | 8 | 0 | 0 | 14 | 1 | 3.32 |
| DeBarr, Evans* .... | 11 | 11 | 2 | 0 | 2 | 4 | 0 | .333 | 64 | 69 | 30 | 29 | 4 | 30 | 1 | 2 | 36 | 1 | 4.08 |
| de los Santos, Ia* .. | 15 | 1 | 0 | 0 | 3 | 2 | 0 | .600 | 25 | 25 | 18 | 13 | 2 | 18 | 1 | 2 | 26 | 1 | 4.68 |
| Denny, Tulsa ..... | 7 | 7 | 3 | 1 | 3 | 1 | 0 | .750 | 60 | 47 | 12 | 12 | 1 | 32 | 1 | 1 | 44 | 3 | 1.80 |
| Dettore, Wichita .. | 13 | 8 | 3 | 1 | 7 | 1 | 1 | .875 | 70 | 67 | 24 | 22 | 5 | 28 | 3 | 4 | 50 | 1 | 2.83 |
| Dunning, Denver .. | 28 | 27 | 16 | 3 | 15 | 9 | 0 | .625 | 196 | 187 | 79 | 76 | 10 | 85 | 3 | 2 | 139 | 8 | 3.49 |
| Eastvick, Ind ..... | 13 | 0 | 0 | 0 | 1 | 0 | 2 | 1.000 | 20 | 11 | 8 | 3 | 0 | 8 | 0 | 0 | 14 | 0 | 1.35 |
| Elenes, Iowa ..... | 12 | 6 | 1 | 0 | 2 | 1 | 0 | .667 | 48 | 53 | 16 | 14 | 2 | 29 | 1 | 0 | 43 | 2 | 2.63 |
| Ellingsen, Okla C* | 27 | 19 | 3 | 1 | 4 | 12 | 0 | .250 | 119 | 158 | 103 | 85 | 9 | 82 | 6 | 9 | 67 | 8 | 6.43 |
| Enyart, Ind* ...... | 15 | 0 | 0 | 0 | 0 | 0 | 1 | .000 | 19 | 14 | 6 | 6 | 1 | 10 | 3 | 2 | 13 | 1 | 2.84 |
| Fidrych, Evans | 6 | 6 | 4 | 1 | 4 | 1 | 0 | .800 | 40 | 27 | 8 | 7 | 1 | 9 | 0 | 1 | 29 | 1 | 1.58 |
| Foor, Tulsa* ..... | 31 | 0 | 0 | 0 | 4 | 2 | 3 | .667 | 34 | 33 | 11 | 11 | 0 | 14 | 1 | 0 | 21 | 0 | 2.91 |
| Glynn, Evansville* | 7 | 7 | 1 | 0 | 1 | 2 | 0 | .333 | 40 | 40 | 18 | 11 | 0 | 19 | 1 | 1 | 23 | 2 | 2.48 |
| Grilli, Evansville.. | 44 | 1 | 0 | 0 | 11 | 4 | 12 | .733 | 102 | 84 | 40 | 34 | 0 | 63 | 5 | 4 | 66 | 6 | 3.00 |
| Grossman, Okla C | 8 | 7 | 1 | 0 | 1 | 5 | 0 | .167 | 23 | 33 | 30 | 32 | 28 | 5 | 24 | 1 | 3 | 14 | 5 | 10.96 |
| Grow, Ind* ...... | 24 | 23 | 3 | 2 | 8 | 10 | 0 | .444 | 120 | 122 | 76 | 65 | 9 | 47 | 2 | 0 | 42 | 7 | 4.88 |
| Hasbach, Omaha | 3 | 2 | 0 | 0 | 1 | 2 | 0 | .333 | 23 | 15 | 5 | 5 | 2 | 6 | 1 | 0 | 22 | 1 | 1.96 |
| Henderson, Indpls | 45 | 0 | 0 | 0 | 5 | 4 | 8 | .556 | 101 | 74 | 32 | 27 | 4 | 50 | 7 | 3 | 85 | 1 | 2.41 |
| Henninger, Okla C | 27 | 7 | 2 | 0 | 3 | 7 | 1 | .300 | 91 | 112 | 70 | 57 | 6 | 35 | 5 | 1 | 50 | 5 | 5.64 |
| Hinton, Denver* .. | 30 | 0 | 0 | 0 | 9 | 2 | 5 | .818 | 69 | 66 | 34 | 25 | 3 | 22 | 2 | 4 | 51 | 0 | 3.26 |
| Holdsworth, Evans | 7 | 7 | 0 | 0 | 2 | 4 | 0 | .333 | 46 | 47 | 25 | 22 | 5 | 10 | 0 | 2 | 39 | 1 | 4.30 |
| Hume, Ind ...... | 17 | 16 | 4 | 3 | 6 | 6 | 0 | .500 | 100 | 106 | 49 | 45 | 7 | 36 | 4 | 2 | 56 | 6 | 4.05 |
| Hutson, Wichita .. | 30 | 29 | 5 | 1 | 12 | 12 | 0 | .500 | 181 | 218 | 126 | 113 | 27 | 76 | 7 | 4 | 104 | 3 | 5.62 |
| Ignasiak, Evans* .. | 11 | 9 | 1 | 0 | 2 | 5 | 0 | .286 | 54 | 47 | 42 | 38 | 4 | 42 | 2 | 2 | 37 | 3 | 6.33 |
| Junge, Wichita .. | 3 | 0 | 0 | 0 | 0 | 0 | 0 | .000 | 8 | 13 | 12 | 8 | 2 | 4 | 1 | 1 | 6 | 3 | 9.00 |
| Kern, Okla City .. | 3 | 3 | 0 | 0 | 1 | 1 | 0 | .500 | 14 | 12 | 10 | 10 | 0 | 11 | 1 | 2 | 11 | 0 | 6.43 |
| Komadina, Denver* | 10 | 0 | 0 | 0 | 1 | 1 | 0 | .500 | 24 | 29 | 19 | 17 | 3 | 19 | 2 | 0 | 8 | 1 | 6.38 |
| Kremmel, Wichita* | 34 | 17 | 4 | 0 | 7 | 5 | 0 | .583 | 142 | 172 | 84 | 68 | 11 | 63 | 2 | 5 | 75 | 12 | 4.31 |
| Kucek, Denver .. | 6 | 2 | 1 | 0 | 1 | 2 | 1 | .333 | 17 | 24 | 13 | 13 | 4 | 3 | 0 | 0 | 17 | 2 | 6.88 |
| Lance, Omaha .. | 28 | 24 | 7 | 0 | 12 | 11 | 0 | .522 | 178 | 160 | 77 | 64 | 7 | 58 | 4 | 7 | 77 | 6 | 3.24 |
| Larson, Iowa ..... | 12 | 12 | 3 | 0 | 4 | 6 | 0 | .400 | 83 | 82 | 42 | 34 | 13 | 45 | 3 | 2 | 67 | 3 | 3.69 |
| Lehman, Denver .. | 13 | 3 | 1 | 0 | 0 | 2 | 0 | .000 | 39 | 39 | 26 | 22 | 3 | 19 | 0 | 0 | 21 | 4 | 5.08 |
| Lemongello, Evans | 15 | 15 | 4 | 1 | 7 | 4 | 0 | .636 | 100 | 111 | 49 | 43 | 6 | 25 | 2 | 2 | 63 | 3 | 3.87 |
| Leonard, Omaha .. | 3 | 3 | 0 | 0 | 0 | 2 | 0 | .000 | 19 | 19 | 11 | 9 | 2 | 10 | 1 | 0 | 14 | 0 | 4.26 |
| Lersch, Okla City. | 32 | 5 | 0 | 0 | 6 | 2 | 0 | .750 | 108 | 116 | 62 | 56 | 12 | 32 | 2 | 2 | 54 | 8 | 4.67 |
| Linnert, Okla C* .. | 3 | 0 | 0 | 0 | 0 | 0 | 0 | .000 | 10 | 11 | 10 | 9 | 0 | 6 | 0 | 1 | 7 | 2 | 8.10 |
| Littell, Omaha ... | 24 | 24 | 8 | 1 | 13 | 6 | 0 | .684 | 168 | 160 | 81 | 65 | 17 | 74 | 3 | 5 | 128 | 4 | 3.48 |
| Lukevics, Denver . | 4 | 4 | 0 | 0 | 0 | 3 | 0 | .000 | 15 | 21 | 17 | 15 | 5 | 9 | 0 | 0 | 9 | 1 | 9.00 |
| MacCormack, Evans | 3 | 1 | 0 | 3 | 0 | 0 | 1 | 1.000 | 19 | 12 | 3 | 3 | 0 | 9 | 0 | 0 | 21 | 0 | 1.42 |
| Makowski, Evans* | 30 | 2 | 0 | 0 | 4 | 4 | 1 | .500 | 78 | 82 | 42 | 33 | 6 | 52 | 3 | 5 | 49 | 4 | 3.81 |
| Manz, Wichita ... | 3 | 2 | 0 | 0 | 0 | 2 | 0 | .000 | 10 | 22 | 17 | 12 | 2 | 6 | 0 | 0 | 9 | 0 | 10.80 |
| Matney, Wichita* | 5 | 0 | 0 | 0 | 0 | 0 | 0 | .000 | 10 | 12 | 3 | 3 | 2 | 2 | 0 | 0 | 4 | 1 | 2.70 |
| McAnally, Okla .. | 1 | 1 | 0 | 0 | 0 | 1 | 0 | .000 | 2 | 5 | 7 | 7 | 0 | 1 | 0 | 1 | 0 | 0 | 31.50 |
| McClain, Denver* . | 26 | 23 | 9 | 3 | 10 | 9 | 0 | .526 | 154 | 162 | 86 | 72 | 13 | 48 | 3 | 0 | 56 | 7 | 4.21 |
| McCutchin, Okla C | 18 | 6 | 2 | 1 | 4 | 2 | 0 | .667 | 73 | 65 | 31 | 27 | 4 | 36 | 2 | 3 | 33 | 7 | 3.33 |
| McGough, Okla C | 18 | 18 | 6 | 1 | 4 | 11 | 0 | .267 | 97 | 113 | 67 | 54 | 11 | 48 | 3 | 3 | 51 | 9 | 5.01 |
| Meyring, Omaha | 12 | 5 | 1 | 0 | 2 | 2 | 0 | .500 | 41 | 37 | 23 | 19 | 3 | 19 | 1 | 5 | 27 | 0 | 4.17 |
| Moran, Denver ... | 30 | 20 | 5 | 0 | 7 | 8 | 0 | .467 | 127 | 149 | 103 | 86 | 14 | 79 | 4 | 2 | 91 | 7 | 6.09 |
| Motil, Evansville* | 1 | 0 | 0 | 0 | 0 | 0 | 0 | .000 | 2 | 1 | 2 | 1 | 0 | 1 | 0 | 0 | 4 | 0 | 4.50 |
| Nagy, Iowa ...... | 4 | 1 | 0 | 0 | 0 | 0 | 0 | .000 | 9 | 16 | 9 | 7 | 0 | 5 | 0 | 0 | 7 | 0 | 7.00 |
| Newman, Evans* .. | 12 | 0 | 0 | 0 | 0 | 1 | 0 | .000 | 19 | 21 | 10 | 7 | 0 | 9 | 4 | 0 | 9 | 1 | 3.32 |
| Niekro, Iowa ..... | 7 | 0 | 0 | 0 | 1 | 0 | 1 | 1.000 | 9 | 7 | 5 | 5 | 1 | 7 | 0 | 0 | 9 | 1 | 5.00 |
| O'Toole, Okla City | 6 | 0 | 0 | 0 | 1 | 0 | 1 | 1.000 | 11 | 18 | 13 | 13 | 1 | 7 | 0 | 2 | 6 | 1 | 10.64 |
| Otten, Denver ..... | 28 | 19 | 8 | 1 | 9 | 9 | 3 | .500 | 151 | 137 | 79 | 69 | 9 | 71 | 3 | 5 | 114 | 9 | 4.11 |
| Parsons, 14 T-15 D | 29 | 14 | 2 | 1 | 3 | 5 | 1 | .375 | 118 | 137 | 69 | 58 | 6 | 42 | 8 | 2 | 57 | 3 | 4.42 |
| Payne, Ind ...... | 26 | 25 | 4 | 2 | 9 | 12 | 0 | .429 | 154 | 136 | 67 | 54 | 13 | 64 | 4 | 5 | 105 | 2 | 3.16 |
| Pentz, Evansville. | 16 | 0 | 0 | 0 | 2 | 3 | 4 | .400 | 21 | 22 | 8 | 7 | 0 | 15 | 4 | 0 | 17 | 1 | 3.00 |
| Pitlock, Denver* .. | 13 | 4 | 2 | 0 | 4 | 1 | 0 | .800 | 46 | 55 | 24 | 20 | 5 | 21 | 1 | 5 | 32 | 0 | 3.91 |
| Prall, Wichita* ... | 29 | 27 | 4 | 2 | 11 | 7 | 1 | .611 | 188 | 191 | 105 | 78 | 16 | 74 | 1 | 2 | 54 | 4 | 3.73 |
| Proly, Tulsa ..... | 55 | 0 | 0 | 0 | 7 | 10 | 17 | .412 | 86 | 101 | 42 | 37 | 7 | 43 | 11 | 3 | 51 | 6 | 3.87 |
| Raich, Okla City.. | 7 | 7 | 3 | 0 | 1 | 4 | 0 | .200 | 47 | 53 | 24 | 16 | 0 | 18 | 2 | 0 | 23 | 0 | 3.06 |
| Rasmussen, Tulsa | 18 | 18 | 5 | 1 | 10 | 5 | 0 | .667 | 129 | 133 | 56 | 53 | 7 | 36 | 4 | 2 | 89 | 3 | 3.70 |
| Ray, Denver ..... | 2 | 0 | 0 | 0 | 0 | 0 | 1 | .000 | 1 | 0 | 0 | 0 | 0 | 3 | 0 | 0 | 0 | 0 | 0.00 |
| Reuschel, Wichita | 35 | 0 | 0 | 0 | 6 | 4 | 2 | .600 | 57 | 63 | 35 | 31 | 3 | 28 | 8 | 2 | 32 | 3 | 4.89 |

| Pitcher—Club | G | GS | CG | ShO | W | L | Sv | Pct. | IP | H | R | ER | HR | BB | Int. BB | HB | SO | WP | ERA |
|---|---|---|---|---|---|---|---|---|---|---|---|---|---|---|---|---|---|---|---|
| Reynolds, Tulsa* | 19 | 19 | 7 | 1 | 10 | 4 | 0 | .714 | 138 | 106 | 59 | 56 | 16 | 79 | 3 | 3 | 103 | 13 | 3.65 |
| Rothermel, Iowa* | 48 | 0 | 0 | 0 | 4 | 2 | 6 | .667 | 64 | 57 | 28 | 26 | 4 | 30 | 6 | 3 | 29 | 1 | 3.66 |
| Roznovsky, Iowa.. | 35 | 19 | 2 | 0 | 4 | 8 | 1 | .333 | 122 | 120 | 71 | 59 | 8 | 51 | 2 | 4 | 72 | 5 | 4.35 |
| Scarce, Ind* | 60 | 2 | 0 | 0 | 5 | 3 | 3 | .625 | 80 | 91 | 52 | 58 | 1 | 42 | 4 | 3 | 58 | 7 | 4.28 |
| Schultz, Wichita* | 47 | 1 | 0 | 0 | 2 | 8 | 9 | .200 | 60 | 62 | 38 | 27 | 1 | 21 | 2 | 0 | 48 | 3 | 4.05 |
| Selak, Iowa | 16 | 16 | 5 | 2 | 4 | 4 | 0 | .333 | 96 | 97 | 43 | 36 | 8 | 45 | 1 | 4 | 76 | 0 | 3.38 |
| Shaffer, Denver | 27 | 0 | 0 | 0 | 6 | 1 | 4 | .857 | 59 | 59 | 27 | 20 | 5 | 21 | 4 | 2 | 38 | 3 | 3.05 |
| Siebert, Iowa* | 30 | 28 | 12 | 5 | 12 | 12 | 1 | .500 | 194 | 200 | 90 | 84 | 13 | 55 | 4 | 4 | 115 | 9 | 3.90 |
| Skok, Evansville* | 13 | 12 | 4 | 2 | 7 | 3 | 0 | .700 | 84 | 83 | 38 | 35 | 6 | 22 | 4 | 0 | 49 | 2 | 3.75 |
| Slayback, Evans .. | 27 | 26 | 9 | 1 | 9 | 11 | 0 | .450 | 188 | 179 | 79 | 70 | 9 | 66 | 6 | 2 | 114 | 5 | 3.35 |
| Solomon, 8 Wich-<br>7 Tulsa | 15 | 14 | 4 | 0 | 8 | 5 | 0 | .615 | 90 | 96 | 64 | 50 | 9 | 42 | 0 | 0 | 60 | 3 | 5.00 |
| Spinks, Iowa | 3 | 3 | 0 | 0 | 3 | 3 | 0 | .000 | 10 | 9 | 10 | 3 | 0 | 14 | 0 | 1 | 5 | 1 | 2.70 |
| Sprinkle, Iowa | 28 | 0 | 0 | 0 | 1 | 4 | 4 | .200 | 53 | 49 | 18 | 18 | 2 | 26 | 6 | 2 | 27 | 4 | 3.06 |
| Staniland, Tulsa .. | 4 | 4 | 0 | 0 | 2 | 0 | 0 | .000 | 19 | 19 | 19 | 18 | 2 | 20 | 0 | 0 | 11 | 4 | 8.53 |
| Stanton, Iowa | 18 | 18 | 3 | 1 | 5 | 11 | 0 | .313 | 107 | 95 | 56 | 49 | 8 | 66 | 3 | 7 | 105 | 5 | 4.12 |
| Strahler, Okla City | 10 | 0 | 0 | 0 | 0 | 2 | 0 | .000 | 21 | 23 | 13 | 10 | 0 | 23 | 1 | 0 | 10 | 3 | 4.29 |
| Strickland, Okla C* | 50 | 3 | 0 | 0 | 7 | 4 | 12 | .636 | 110 | 98 | 51 | 40 | 2 | 73 | 10 | 4 | 114 | 12 | 3.27 |
| Swanson, Evans .. | 25 | 24 | 3 | 1 | 9 | 6 | 0 | .600 | 136 | 147 | 91 | 85 | 16 | 60 | 2 | 1 | 58 | 7 | 5.63 |
| Taylor, Ind | 51 | 0 | 0 | 0 | 8 | 1 | 5 | .889 | 81 | 65 | 22 | 20 | 5 | 61 | 10 | 5 | 61 | 5 | 2.22 |
| Temple, Wichita | 18 | 1 | 0 | 0 | 0 | 2 | 0 | .000 | 39 | 51 | 24 | 18 | 2 | 14 | 2 | 1 | 23 | 2 | 4.15 |
| Terlecky, Tulsa .. | 14 | 11 | 2 | 0 | 3 | 4 | 0 | .429 | 82 | 102 | 48 | 47 | 5 | 28 | 3 | 1 | 32 | 1 | 5.16 |
| Throop, Omaha .. | 26 | 26 | 10 | 3 | 12 | 9 | 0 | .571 | 186 | 173 | 73 | 61 | 11 | 49 | 6 | 6 | 115 | 1 | 2.95 |
| Turner, Wichita .. | 5 | 5 | 0 | 0 | 1 | 1 | 0 | .500 | 25 | 39 | 23 | 18 | 0 | 11 | 0 | 1 | 8 | 1 | 6.48 |
| Vuckovich, . Denver | 19 | 18 | 4 | 0 | 11 | 4 | 0 | .733 | 116 | 103 | 63 | 56 | 12 | 54 | 1 | 1 | 86 | 2 | 4.34 |
| Waits, Okla City* | 9 | 6 | 4 | 0 | 1 | 5 | 0 | .167 | 53 | 55 | 29 | 26 | 4 | 27 | 0 | 1 | 31 | 2 | 4.42 |
| Walker, Iowa* | 20 | 18 | 2 | 0 | 7 | 7 | 0 | .500 | 106 | 124 | 60 | 51 | 4 | 65 | 3 | 1 | 84 | 6 | 4.33 |
| Wallace, Tulsa* .. | 21 | 8 | 1 | 0 | 5 | 6 | 2 | .455 | 75 | 80 | 41 | 37 | 5 | 43 | 4 | 0 | 62 | 3 | 4.44 |
| Waterbury, Tulsa | 11 | 11 | 4 | 1 | 4 | 2 | 0 | .667 | 75 | 68 | 36 | 33 | 1 | 45 | 0 | 3 | 41 | 6 | 3.96 |
| Watt, Wichita | 44 | 0 | 0 | 0 | 4 | 5 | 7 | .444 | 81 | 94 | 41 | 35 | 3 | 23 | 3 | 3 | 46 | 4 | 3.89 |
| Weiss, Wichita | 2 | 0 | 0 | 0 | 0 | 0 | 0 | .000 | 3 | 4 | 2 | 2 | 0 | 2 | 0 | 0 | 2 | 0 | 6.00 |
| Wilcox, Wichita | 8 | 8 | 3 | 0 | 4 | 3 | 0 | .571 | 48 | 56 | 31 | 23 | 3 | 15 | 2 | 3 | 18 | 2 | 4.31 |
| Wiles, Tulsa* | 11 | 5 | 0 | 0 | 3 | 3 | 0 | .500 | 38 | 45 | 26 | 25 | 3 | 21 | 1 | 0 | 30 | 0 | 5.92 |
| Williams, Iowa | 4 | 0 | 0 | 0 | 1 | 0 | 0 | 1.000 | 7 | 15 | 14 | 11 | 2 | 6 | 0 | 1 | 2 | 0 | 14.14 |
| Willoughby, Tulsa | 15 | 15 | 7 | 3 | 8 | 6 | 0 | .571 | 114 | 112 | 43 | 41 | 4 | 28 | 7 | 3 | 62 | 2 | 3.24 |
| York, Iowa | 31 | 0 | 0 | 0 | 2 | 2 | 7 | .500 | 45 | 44 | 20 | 16 | 2 | 16 | 3 | 4 | 33 | 2 | 3.20 |
| Zachry, Indpls .... | 27 | 22 | 6 | 4 | 10 | 7 | 0 | .588 | 159 | 120 | 52 | 43 | 3 | 70 | 6 | 3 | 100 | 5 | 2.43 |

BALKS—Andersen, 4; Alfonso, de los Santos, Grow, McCutchin, Selak, Strickland, Swanson, Vuckovich, 2 each; Alcala, Allen, Baird, Bass, Bernard, Fidrych, Glynn, Grossman, Henninger, Holdsworth, Lance, Larson, Littell, McGough, Moran, Otten, Payne, Pentz, Schultz, Sprinkle, Staniland, Stanton, Taylor, 1 each.

COMBINATION SHUTOUTS—DeBarr-Grilli, MacCormack-Brookens, Evansville; Alcala-Taylor, Payne-Scarce-Taylor, Payne-Scarce, Carroll-Henderson, Grow-Eastwick, Zachry-Taylor, Indianapolis; Walker-Sprinkle, Iowa; Throop-Angelini, Littell-Angelini, Bruno-Angelini, Omaha; Rasmussen-Foor, Wallace-Proly, Waterbury-Terlecky, Tulsa; Solomon-Schultz-Reuschel, Solomon-Watt, Dettore-Schultz, Copeland-Schultz, Wichita.

NO-HIT GAMES—None.

# International League

## CLASS AAA

**Leading Batter**
**MIKE VAIL**
Tidewater

**League President**
**GEORGE SISLER, JR.**

**Leading Pitcher**
**PABLO TORREALBA**
Richmond

### CHAMPIONSHIP WINNERS IN PREVIOUS YEARS

| | | |
|---|---|---|
| 1884—Trenton .520 | 1924—Baltimore .709 | 1953—Rochester .630 |
| 1885—Syracuse .584 | 1925—Baltimore .633 | Montreal (2nd)† .586 |
| 1886—Utica .646 | 1926—Toronto .657 | 1954—Toronto .630 |
| 1887—Toronto .644 | 1927—Buffalo .667 | Syracuse (4th)§ .510 |
| 1888—Syracuse .723 | 1928—Rochester .549 | 1955—Montreal .617 |
| 1889—Detroit .649 | 1929—Rochester .613 | Rochester (4th)† .497 |
| 1890—Detroit .617 | 1930—Rochester .629 | 1956—Toronto .566 |
| 1891—Buffalo (reg. season) .727 | 1931—Rochester .601 | Rochester (2nd)† .553 |
| Binghamton* (supplem'l) .680 | 1932—Newark .649 | 1957—Toronto .575 |
| 1892—Providence .615 | 1933—Newark .622 | Buffalo (2nd)† .571 |
| Binghamton* .667 | Buffalo (4th)† .494 | 1958—Montreal‡ .588 |
| 1893—Erie .606 | Toronto (3rd)† .559 | 1959—Buffalo .582 |
| 1894—Providence .696 | 1934—Newark .608 | Havana (3rd)† .523 |
| 1895—Springfield .687 | Montreal (2nd)† .597 | 1960—Toronto‡ .649 |
| 1896—Providence .602 | 1935—Montreal .597 | 1961—Columbus .597 |
| 1897—Syracuse .682 | Syracuse (2nd)† .565 | Buffalo (3rd)† .559 |
| 1898—Montreal .586 | 1936—Buffalo‡ .610 | 1962—Jacksonville .610 |
| 1899—Rochester .624 | 1937—Newark‡ .717 | Atlanta (3rd)† .539 |
| 1900—Providence .616 | 1938—Newark‡ .684 | 1963—Syracuse x .533 |
| 1901—Rochester .642 | 1939—Jersey City .582 | Indianapolis† .562 |
| 1902—Toronto .669 | Rochester (2nd)† .556 | 1964—Jacksonville .589 |
| 1903—Jersey City .642 | 1940—Rochester .611 | Rochester (4th)† .532 |
| 1904—Buffalo .657 | Newark (2nd)† .594 | 1965—Columbus .582 |
| 1905—Providence .638 | 1941—Newark .649 | Toronto (3rd)† .556 |
| 1906—Buffalo .607 | Montreal (2nd)† .584 | 1966—Rochester .565 |
| 1907—Toronto .619 | 1942—Newark .601 | Toronto (2nd-tied)† .559 |
| 1908—Baltimore .593 | Syracuse (3rd)† .513 | 1967—Richmond .574 |
| 1909—Rochester .596 | 1943—Toronto .625 | Toledo (3rd)† .525 |
| 1910—Rochester .601 | Syracuse (3rd)† .536 | 1968—Toledo .565 |
| 1911—Rochester .645 | 1944—Baltimore‡ .553 | Jacksonville (4th)† .514 |
| 1912—Toronto .595 | 1945—Montreal .621 | 1969—Tidewater .563 |
| 1913—Newark .625 | Newark (2nd)† .582 | Syracuse (3rd)† .536 |
| 1914—Providence .617 | 1946—Montreal‡ .649 | 1970—Syracuse‡ .600 |
| 1915—Buffalo .632 | 1947—Jersey City .610 | 1971—Rochester‡ .614 |
| 1916—Buffalo .586 | Syracuse (3rd)† .575 | 1972—Louisville .563 |
| 1917—Toronto .604 | 1948—Montreal‡ .614 | Tidewater (3rd)† .545 |
| 1918—Toronto .693 | 1949—Buffalo .584 | 1973—Charleston .586 |
| 1919—Baltimore .671 | Montreal (3rd)† .545 | Pawtucket y† .534 |
| 1920—Baltimore .719 | 1950—Rochester .609 | 1974—Memphis .613 |
| 1921—Baltimore .717 | Baltimore (3rd)† .556 | Rochester x‡ .611 |
| 1922—Baltimore .689 | 1951—Montreal‡ .617 | |
| 1923—Baltimore .677 | 1952—Montreal .629 | |
| | Rochester (3rd)† .619 | |

*Won split-season playoff. †Won four-team playoff. ‡Won championship and four-team playoff.
§Defeated Havana in game to decide fourth place, then won four-team playoff. xLeague was divided into Northern, Southern divisions. yLeague divided into American, National divisions. (NOTE—Known as Eastern League in 1884, New York State League in 1885, International League in 1886-87, International Association in 1888, International League in 1889-90, Eastern Association in 1891, and Eastern League from 1892 until 1912.)

## STANDING OF CLUBS AT CLOSE OF SEASON, SEPTEMBER 2

| Club | Tide. | Roch. | Syr. | Char. | Mem. | Rich. | Tol. | Paw. | W. | L. | T. | Pct. | G.B. |
|---|---|---|---|---|---|---|---|---|---|---|---|---|---|
| Tidewater (Mets) ....... | .. | 9 | 15 | 14 | 9 | 13 | 14 | 12 | 86 | 55 | 0 | .610 | .. |
| Rochester (Orioles) .... | 12 | .. | 10 | 9 | 12 | 13 | 12 | 17 | 85 | 56 | 0 | .603 | 1 |
| Syracuse (Yankees) .. | 5 | 10 | .. | 10 | 13 | 9 | 11 | 14 | 72 | 64 | 0 | .529 | 11½ |
| Charleston (Pirates) .. | 6 | 11 | 9 | .. | 12 | 11 | 10 | 13 | 72 | 67 | 0 | .518 | 13 |
| Memphis (Expos) .... | 11 | 8 | 7 | 8 | .. | 9 | 10 | 12 | 65 | 75 | 0 | .464 | 20½ |
| Richmond (Braves) .... | 7 | 7 | 8 | 9 | 11 | .. | 12 | 8 | 62 | 75 | 0 | .453 | 22 |
| Toledo (Phillies) .... | 6 | 8 | 9 | 10 | 10 | 8 | .. | 11 | 62 | 78 | 0 | .443 | 23½ |
| Pawtucket (Red Sox) .. | 8 | 3 | 6 | 7 | 8 | 12 | 9 | .. | 53 | 87 | 0 | .379 | 32½ |

Tidewater defeated Rochester, one game to none, in playoff for championship.
Protested game—Richmond-Toledo game of June 14, replayed from point of protest on August 5.
Tidewater club represented Norfolk and Portsmouth, Va.
Major league affiliations in parentheses.
Playoffs—Tidewater defeated Charleston, three games to none; Syracuse defeated Rochester, three games to one; Tidewater defeated Syracuse, three games to one (for Governor's Cup).
Regular-Season Attendance—Charleston, 79,119; Memphis, 75,462; Pawtucket, 118,289; Richmond, 68,348; Rochester, 326,072; Syracuse, 193,467; Tidewater, 117,446; Toledo, 103,189. Total, 1,081,392. All-Star Game, 5,167. Playoffs, 24,555.
Managers: Charleston—Steve Demeter; Memphis—Karl Kuehl; Pawtucket—Joe Morgan; Richmond—Clint Courtney, Bob Lemon; Rochester—Joe Altobelli; Syracuse—Bobby Cox; Tidewater—Joe Frazier; Toledo—Jim Bunning.
All-Star Team: 1B—Pemberton, Tidewater; 2B—Randolph, Charleston; 3B—Staiger, Tidewater; SS—Bailor, Rochester; OF—Vail, Tidewater; Valentine, Memphis; Stillman, Rochester; C—Nahorodny, Toledo; Nolan, Richmond; P— Swan, Tidewater; Flanagan, Rochester; Manager—Frazier, Tidewater.
(Compiled by Ed Williams, League Statistician, Shawnee, Okla.)

## CLUB BATTING

| Club | G. | AB. | R. | OR. | H. | TB. | 2B. | 3B. | HR. | RBI. | SH. | SF. | Int. BB. | BB. | HP. | SO. | SB. | CS. | LOB. | Pct. |
|---|---|---|---|---|---|---|---|---|---|---|---|---|---|---|---|---|---|---|---|---|
| Charleston | 139 | 4512 | 553 | 535 | 1191 | 1650 | 179 | 35 | 70 | 521 | 34 | 40 | 471 | 43 | 23 | 767 | 144 | 54 | 1014 | .264 |
| Tidewater | 141 | 4493 | 547 | 425 | 1165 | 1541 | 1:7 | 29 | 47 | 492 | 71 | 38 | 465 | 64 | 29 | 794 | 67 | 36 | 1026 | .259 |
| Rochester | 141 | 4530 | 579 | 496 | 1171 | 1686 | 171 | 37 | 90 | 532 | 56 | 34 | 510 | 44 | 28 | 800 | 59 | 33 | 1009 | .258 |
| Richmond | 137 | 4273 | 489 | 534 | 1065 | 1524 | 168 | 21 | 83 | 456 | 51 | 28 | 439 | 29 | 19 | 715 | 62 | 49 | 922 | .249 |
| Memphis | 140 | 4571 | 524 | 509 | 1104 | 1588 | 159 | 41 | 81 | 470 | 107 | 31 | 498 | 63 | 23 | 791 | 78 | 46 | 1004 | .242 |
| Syracuse | 136 | 4282 | 544 | 568 | 1025 | 1405 | 178 | 32 | 46 | 475 | 84 | 40 | 578 | 41 | 28 | 676 | 43 | 41 | 1006 | .239 |
| Pawtucket | 140 | 4534 | 434 | 542 | 1075 | 1427 | 142 | 15 | 60 | 409 | 53 | 20 | 468 | 42 | 26 | 763 | 61 | 40 | 1019 | .237 |
| Toledo | 140 | 4406 | 507 | 568 | 1007 | 1491 | 163 | 27 | 89 | 436 | 75 | 34 | 516 | 37 | 22 | 776 | 98 | 41 | 946 | .229 |

NOTE—Championship playoff game included in both club and individual averages.

## INDIVIDUAL BATTING
### (Leading Qualifiers for Batting Championship—378 or More Plate Appearances)
*Bats lefthanded.    †Switch-hitter.

| Player and Club | G. | AB. | R. | H. | TB. | 2B. | 3B. | HR. | RBI. | SH. | SF. | BB. | HP. | SO. | SB. | CS. | Pct. |
|---|---|---|---|---|---|---|---|---|---|---|---|---|---|---|---|---|---|
| Vail, Michael, Tidewater...115 | 409 | 53 | 140 | 202 | 23 | 9 | 7 | 79 | 1 | 3 | 34 | 3 | 74 | 3 | 5 | .342 |
| Stillman, Royle, Rochester*.126 | 444 | 65 | 139 | 215 | 30 | 2 | 14 | 75 | 1 | 1 | 49 | 1 | 51 | 2 | 3 | .313 |
| Reynolds, G. Craig, Charl*..108 | 425 | 51 | 131 | 177 | 22 | 3 | 6 | 42 | 1 | 0 | 21 | 1 | 32 | 5 | 9 | .308 |
| Valentine, Ellis, Memphis..139 | 494 | 87 | 151 | 226 | 30 | 3 | 13 | 66 | 9 | 5 | 59 | 4 | 106 | 18 | 10 | .306 |
| Moore, Alvin, Richmond ....128 | 460 | 60 | 138 | 208 | 18 | 5 | 14 | 65 | 3 | 3 | 42 | 3 | 34 | 4 | 5 | .300 |
| Armas, Antonio, Charleston.128 | 450 | 65 | 135 | 207 | 28 | 4 | 12 | 72 | 1 | 5 | 36 | 0 | 84 | 6 | 3 | .300 |
| Pemberton, Brock, Tide†....137 | 474 | 68 | 141 | 169 | 24 | 2 | 0 | 56 | 4 | 5 | 49 | 0 | 42 | 4 | 5 | .297 |
| White, Jerome, Memphis*... | 98 | 354 | 44 | 105 | 161 | 16 | 5 | 10 | 45 | 11 | 2 | 18 | 5 | 31 | 13 | 8 | .297 |
| Bailor, Robert, Rochester....129 | 501 | 68 | 147 | 193 | 19 | 6 | 5 | 39 | 4 | 4 | 43 | 4 | 28 | 21 | 8 | .293 |
| Reinbach, Michael, Roch*..127 | 435 | 76 | 126 | 191 | 24 | 4 | 11 | 62 | 2 | 3 | 58 | 3 | 64 | 4 | 1 | .290 |

Departmental Leaders: G—E. Valentine, 139; AB—Bailor, 501; R—E. Valentine, 87; H—E. Valentine, 151; TB—E. Valentine, 226; 2B—Stillman, E. Valentine, 30; 3B—Vail, 9; HR— Nahorodny, 19; RBI—Staiger, 81; SH—Sterling, 12; SF—Diggle, 10; BB—Velez, 87; HP—Fuller, 7; SO—Fuller, 133; SB—Dilone, 48; CS—Asselstine, 16.

### (All Players—Listed Alphabetically)

| Player and Club | G. | AB. | R. | H. | TB. | 2B. | 3B. | HR. | RBI. | SH. | SF. | BB. | HP. | SO. | SB. | CS. | Pct. |
|---|---|---|---|---|---|---|---|---|---|---|---|---|---|---|---|---|---|
| Aase, Donald V., Pawtucket | 29 | 49 | 6 | 8 | 16 | 2 | 0 | 2 | 3 | 9 | 0 | 4 | 0 | 26 | 0 | 0 | .163 |
| Abraham, Brian A., Mem*.. | 12 | 8 | 0 | 0 | 0 | 0 | 0 | 0 | 0 | 0 | 0 | 0 | 0 | 6 | 0 | 0 | .000 |
| Albin, Donald J., Memphis.. | 27 | 36 | 7 | 11 | 12 | 1 | 0 | 0 | 4 | 0 | 0 | 0 | 0 | 8 | 0 | 0 | .306 |
| Alexander, Roger G., Rich... | 1 | 0 | 0 | 0 | 0 | 0 | 0 | 0 | 0 | 0 | 0 | 0 | 0 | 0 | 0 | 0 | .000 |
| Anderson, Richard E., Char.. | 8 | 11 | 0 | 1 | 1 | 0 | 0 | 0 | 0 | 0 | 0 | 0 | 0 | 7 | 0 | 0 | .091 |
| Andrew, Kim D., Pawtucket | 79 | 292 | 34 | 89 | 106 | 10 | 2 | 1 | 20 | 0 | 0 | 26 | 1 | 25 | 4 | 1 | .305 |
| Andrews, Freddie, Toledo ...119 | 430 | 44 | 111 | 157 | 23 | 4 | 5 | 36 | 16 | 1 | 47 | 1 | 48 | 13 | 7 | .258 |
| Armas M., Antonio, Char...128 | 450 | 65 | 135 | 207 | 28 | 4 | 12 | 72 | 1 | 5 | 36 | 0 | 84 | 6 | 3 | .300 |
| Asselstine, Brian H., Rich*..122 | 444 | 66 | 126 | 154 | 21 | 2 | 1 | 22 | 4 | 1 | 51 | 3 | 53 | 25 | 16 | .284 |
| Atkinson, William, Memphis* | 50 | 25 | 1 | 2 | 2 | 0 | 0 | 0 | 0 | 0 | 0 | 0 | 0 | 12 | 0 | 0 | .080 |
| Augustine, David, Charleston | 75 | 191 | 12 | 45 | 54 | 2 | 2 | 1 | 19 | 0 | 3 | 15 | 0 | 34 | 5 | 2 | .236 |
| Aviles M., Ramon, Paw ...123 | 287 | 20 | 63 | 74 | 6 | 1 | 1 | 22 | 8 | 1 | 39 | 0 | 29 | 1 | 2 | .220 |
| Ayala F., Benigno, Tidewater | 65 | 177 | 24 | 49 | 80 | 13 | 0 | 6 | 28 | 0 | 2 | 16 | 2 | 33 | 3 | 0 | .277 |

| Player and Club | G. | AB. | R. | H. | TB. | 2B. | 3B. | HR. | RBI. | SH. | SF. | BB. | HP. | SO. | SB. | CS. | Pct. |
|---|---|---|---|---|---|---|---|---|---|---|---|---|---|---|---|---|---|
| Babcock, Robert, Rochester.. | 10 | 7 | 0 | 0 | 0 | 0 | 0 | 0 | 0 | 1 | 0 | 0 | 0 | 7 | 0 | 0 | .000 |
| Bailor, Robert M., Rochester | 129 | 501 | 68 | 147 | 193 | 19 | 6 | 5 | 39 | 4 | 4 | 43 | 4 | 28 | 21 | 8 | .293 |
| Bair, C. Douglas, Charleston | 26 | 54 | 1 | 9 | 12 | 3 | 0 | 0 | 5 | 3 | 0 | 5 | 0 | 23 | 0 | 0 | .167 |
| Baker, Jack E., Pawtucket.. | 132 | 456 | 42 | 115 | 195 | 20 | 3 | 18 | 63 | 0 | 3 | 40 | 4 | 111 | 0 | 1 | .252 |
| Bannister Alan, Toledo ..... | 101 | 335 | 50 | 74 | 102 | 7 | 3 | 5 | 27 | 3 | 5 | 74 | 3 | 48 | 23 | 14 | .221 |
| Barr, Mark, Pawtucket....... | 70 | 14 | 0 | 1 | 1 | 0 | 0 | 0 | 1 | 0 | 0 | 2 | 0 | 5 | 0 | 0 | .071 |
| Barr, Steven, Pawtucket*... | 24 | 49 | 4 | 8 | 8 | 0 | 0 | 0 | 1 | 2 | 0 | 0 | 0 | 17 | 0 | 0 | .163 |
| Bartlett, Robert, Tidewater* | 4 | 4 | 0 | 1 | 1 | 0 | 0 | 0 | 0 | 0 | 0 | 0 | 0 | 3 | 0 | 0 | .250 |
| Beall, Robert B., Richmond† | 78 | 238 | 30 | 56 | 86 | 11 | 2 | 5 | 27 | 2 | 1 | 60 | 0 | 53 | 7 | 5 | .235 |
| Beard, Michael R., Rich*... | 13 | 4 | 0 | 1 | 2 | 0 | 0 | 1 | 0 | 0 | 2 | 0 | 2 | 0 | 0 | .250 |
| Beattie, James, Syracuse ... | 5 | 10 | 0 | 1 | 1 | 0 | 0 | 0 | 1 | 1 | 1 | 0 | 0 | 3 | 0 | 0 | .100 |
| Belloir, Robert, Richmond.... | 36 | 122 | 16 | 31 | 41 | 5 | 1 | 1 | 8 | 1 | 2 | 16 | 0 | 11 | 3 | 1 | .254 |
| Beltran G., Miguel, Toledo.. | 8 | 4 | 0 | 2 | 2 | 0 | 0 | 0 | 0 | 0 | 0 | 0 | 0 | 2 | 0 | 0 | .500 |
| Bernard, Dwight V., Tide.. | 27 | 38 | 3 | 4 | 5 | 1 | 0 | 0 | 1 | 4 | 0 | 2 | 0 | 16 | 0 | 0 | .105 |
| Bernhardt C., Juan, Syracuse | 79 | 297 | 22 | 90 | 123 | 19 | 1 | 4 | 44 | 4 | 6 | 11 | 2 | 16 | 0 | 3 | .303 |
| Bladt, Richard A., Syracuse | 79 | 259 | 43 | 69 | 112 | 10 | 6 | 7 | 49 | 4 | 0 | 42 | 2 | 14 | 1 | 6 | .266 |
| Boisclair, Bruce A., Tide*.. | 127 | 453 | 62 | 126 | 164 | 16 | 5 | 4 | 37 | 5 | 2 | 54 | 2 | 94 | 20 | 7 | .278 |
| Bomback, Mark, Pawtucket.. | 7 | 11 | 0 | 2 | 2 | 0 | 0 | 0 | 1 | 0 | 0 | 2 | 0 | 2 | 0 | 0 | .182 |
| Breazeale, James, Richmond* | 91 | 234 | 25 | 50 | 85 | 8 | 0 | 9 | 31 | 0 | 2 | 28 | 2 | 31 | 0 | 2 | .214 |
| Breeden, Harold, Memphis.. | 64 | 224 | 32 | 57 | 110 | 8 | 0 | 15 | 43 | 1 | 3 | 31 | 1 | 43 | 0 | 0 | .254 |
| Browne, Byron E., Toledo... | 18 | 44 | 7 | 13 | 23 | 4 | 0 | 2 | 13 | 0 | 1 | 3 | 0 | 8 | 0 | 0 | .295 |
| Burton, James, Pawtucket.. | 14 | 33 | 3 | 5 | 6 | 1 | 0 | 0 | 2 | 2 | 0 | 1 | 0 | 10 | 0 | 0 | .152 |
| Candelaria, John, Charleston* | 10 | 18 | 3 | 5 | 6 | 1 | 0 | 0 | 4 | 2 | 1 | 2 | 0 | 4 | 0 | 0 | .278 |
| Carrion M., Leonel, Memphis | 14 | 38 | 2 | 9 | 9 | 0 | 0 | 0 | 3 | 1 | 0 | 5 | 1 | 5 | 0 | 0 | .237 |
| Carrithers, Donald, Memphis | 12 | 25 | 2 | 4 | 4 | 0 | 0 | 0 | 1 | 0 | 0 | 0 | 0 | 5 | 0 | 0 | .160 |
| Caskey, Craig, Charleston*.. | 31 | 5 | 0 | 0 | 0 | 0 | 0 | 0 | 0 | 2 | 0 | 1 | 0 | 2 | 0 | 0 | .000 |
| Castle, Donald H., Syr*... | 102 | 311 | 29 | 58 | 87 | 12 | 1 | 5 | 41 | 5 | 9 | 29 | 0 | 65 | 0 | 1 | .186 |
| Chavez B., J. Guadalupe, Tol* | 23 | 70 | 4 | 11 | 13 | 2 | 0 | 0 | 2 | 2 | 0 | 8 | 0 | 11 | 0 | 0 | .157 |
| Cheadle, David B., Syracuse* | 33 | 22 | 1 | 5 | 5 | 0 | 0 | 0 | 1 | 0 | 0 | 4 | 0 | 8 | 0 | 0 | .227 |
| Childers, Terry O., Memphis.. | 10 | 32 | 3 | 9 | 10 | 1 | 0 | 0 | 2 | 1 | 1 | 1 | 0 | 7 | 0 | 0 | .281 |
| Christenson, Larry R., Toledo | 2 | 5 | 0 | 0 | 0 | 0 | 0 | 0 | 0 | 0 | 0 | 0 | 0 | 3 | 0 | 0 | .000 |
| Clark, Ronald B., Toledo.... | 114 | 330 | 31 | 87 | 107 | 14 | 0 | 2 | 23 | 6 | 6 | 41 | 3 | 44 | 0 | 2 | .264 |
| Clay, Kenneth P., Syracuse.. | 9 | 16 | 0 | 5 | 5 | 0 | 0 | 0 | 2 | 2 | 0 | 0 | 0 | 8 | 0 | 0 | .313 |
| Clemons, Lance, Pawtucket*. | 66 | 13 | 1 | 3 | 3 | 0 | 0 | 0 | 1 | 0 | 0 | 3 | 0 | 6 | 0 | 0 | .231 |
| Closter, Alan E., Richmond* | 38 | 15 | 1 | 1 | 1 | 0 | 0 | 0 | 0 | 0 | 0 | 2 | 0 | 6 | 0 | 0 | .067 |
| Coleman, David L., Paw.... | 70 | 164 | 21 | 29 | 46 | 8 | 0 | 3 | 11 | 1 | 0 | 31 | 2 | 45 | 0 | 1 | .177 |
| Coletta, Christopher, Paw*.. | 108 | 321 | 29 | 87 | 106 | 13 | 0 | 2 | 35 | 1 | 3 | 32 | 1 | 32 | 4 | 3 | .271 |
| Conigliaro, Anthony, Paw.... | 37 | 123 | 11 | 25 | 36 | 2 | 0 | 3 | 12 | 0 | 1 | 8 | 2 | 17 | 1 | 1 | .203 |
| Contreras, Arnaldo J., Tide† | 36 | 8 | 2 | 2 | 3 | 1 | 0 | 0 | 1 | 0 | 2 | 0 | 3 | 0 | 0 | .250 |
| Cox, James C., Memphis.... | 135 | 497 | 45 | 131 | 199 | 27 | 4 | 11 | 67 | 9 | 2 | 48 | 3 | 93 | 7 | 4 | .264 |
| Cox, Larry E., Toledo...... | 32 | 80 | 5 | 10 | 12 | 2 | 0 | 0 | 1 | 0 | 0 | 10 | 0 | 8 | 0 | 0 | .125 |
| Cram, Gerald A., Tidewater.. | 31 | 7 | 0 | 2 | 2 | 0 | 0 | 0 | 2 | 1 | 0 | 0 | 0 | 4 | 0 | 0 | .286 |
| Crane, Mark G., Toledo..... | 2 | 2 | 0 | 0 | 0 | 0 | 0 | 0 | 0 | 0 | 0 | 2 | 0 | 0 | 0 | 0 | .000 |
| Creech, T. Edwin, Memphis.. | 28 | 81 | 7 | 12 | 15 | 0 | 0 | 1 | 2 | 1 | 0 | 4 | 0 | 12 | 0 | 1 | .148 |
| Cromartie, Warren, Mem*... | 119 | 400 | 42 | 107 | 144 | 16 | 6 | 3 | 38 | 2 | 9 | 30 | 1 | 45 | 5 | 2 | .268 |
| Culver, George R., Toledo... | 17 | 11 | 0 | 2 | 2 | 0 | 0 | 0 | 0 | 2 | 0 | 0 | 0 | 4 | 0 | 0 | .182 |
| Cummings, Michael L., Rich | 13 | 18 | 5 | 6 | 7 | 1 | 0 | 0 | 2 | 0 | 0 | 4 | 0 | 2 | 1 | 0 | .333 |
| Dancy, William W., Toledo† | 77 | 240 | 22 | 60 | 73 | 11 | 1 | 0 | 16 | 4 | 1 | 16 | 0 | 35 | 1 | 1 | .250 |
| Dauer, Richard, Rochester... | 18 | 47 | 2 | 8 | 9 | 1 | 0 | 0 | 0 | 0 | 0 | 3 | 0 | 3 | 0 | 1 | .170 |
| Deidel, James L., Syracuse.. | 110 | 349 | 27 | 64 | 81 | 11 | 0 | 2 | 27 | 0 | 3 | 28 | 3 | 61 | 0 | 1 | .183 |
| DeJohn, Mark S., Tide†..... | 122 | 386 | 31 | 93 | 109 | 13 | 0 | 1 | 25 | 6 | 1 | 36 | 3 | 64 | 1 | 3 | .241 |
| Devine, P. Adrian, Richmond | 28 | 55 | 2 | 4 | 6 | 2 | 0 | 0 | 1 | 5 | 0 | 0 | 0 | 27 | 0 | 0 | .073 |
| Diehl, Gregory D., Syracuse | 7 | 3 | 0 | 0 | 0 | 0 | 0 | 0 | 0 | 0 | 0 | 1 | 0 | 3 | 0 | 0 | .000 |
| Diggle, Ronnie J., Tide*.... | 113 | 338 | 59 | 89 | 122 | 12 | 3 | 5 | 33 | 3 | 10 | 35 | 1 | 55 | 5 | 4 | .263 |
| Dillard, Stephen, Pawtucket | 57 | 155 | 20 | 30 | 34 | 4 | 0 | 0 | 4 | 0 | 0 | 19 | 0 | 28 | 12 | 2 | .194 |
| Dilone R., Miguel, Char†.... | 125 | 471 | 61 | 102 | 127 | 12 | 5 | 1 | 26 | 4 | 1 | 48 | 2 | 71 | 48 | 14 | .217 |
| Dineen, Kerry M., Syracuse* | 104 | 348 | 56 | 84 | 97 | 9 | 2 | 0 | 30 | 11 | 3 | 46 | 1 | 41 | 12 | 3 | .241 |
| Diorio, Ronald M., Memphis | 31 | 5 | 0 | 0 | 0 | 0 | 0 | 0 | 0 | 0 | 0 | 0 | 0 | 3 | 0 | 0 | .000 |
| Down, Richard J., Memphis | 112 | 290 | 29 | 62 | 83 | 7 | 4 | 2 | 20 | 5 | 1 | 41 | 2 | 60 | 0 | 4 | .214 |
| Duncan, Taylor M., Roch | 119 | 384 | 43 | 109 | 149 | 16 | 3 | 6 | 54 | 6 | 5 | 37 | 1 | 51 | 1 | 1 | .284 |
| Easterly, James M., Rich†... | 2 | 3 | 0 | 1 | 1 | 0 | 0 | 0 | 2 | 0 | 0 | 0 | 0 | 1 | 0 | 0 | .333 |
| Edwards, Michael, Charleston | 31 | 132 | 11 | 37 | 48 | 6 | 1 | 1 | 15 | 1 | 1 | 8 | 0 | 22 | 3 | 2 | .280 |
| Enyart, Terry G., Memphis.. | 29 | 7 | 1 | 2 | 2 | 0 | 0 | 0 | 0 | 1 | 0 | 0 | 0 | 4 | 0 | 0 | .286 |
| Erickson, G. Charles, Paw... | 53 | 109 | 11 | 22 | 32 | 4 | 0 | 2 | 14 | 0 | 1 | 17 | 1 | 25 | 0 | 1 | .202 |
| Espinosa, Arnulfo A., Tide†.. | 26 | 53 | 5 | 8 | 10 | 2 | 0 | 0 | 1 | 0 | 0 | 17 | 0 | 6 | 0 | 0 | .151 |
| Farias, Thomas, Pawtucket.. | 6 | 12 | 0 | 2 | 2 | 0 | 0 | 0 | 0 | 0 | 0 | 2 | 0 | 6 | 0 | 0 | .167 |
| Figueroa R., Domingo, Rich* | 29 | 39 | 3 | 5 | 6 | 1 | 0 | 0 | 0 | 2 | 0 | 0 | 0 | 19 | 0 | 0 | .128 |
| Fiore, Michael G., Roch*.... | 79 | 194 | 36 | 52 | 72 | 3 | 1 | 5 | 40 | 1 | 5 | 49 | 0 | 23 | 1 | 0 | .268 |
| Flanagan, Michael K., Roch* | 34 | 67 | 5 | 13 | 21 | 5 | 0 | 1 | 6 | 3 | 0 | 4 | 0 | 16 | 0 | 0 | .194 |
| Flowers, Burnel, Cha 2-<br>Paw 123* | 125 | 463 | 54 | 109 | 136 | 14 | 2 | 3 | 29 | 3 | 1 | 45 | 3 | 75 | 21 | 14 | .235 |
| Foster, Leonard N., Tide.... | 94 | 304 | 42 | 75 | 94 | 7 | 3 | 2 | 25 | 6 | 1 | 47 | 4 | 47 | 11 | 4 | .247 |
| Freeman, Jimmy, Rich 1-<br>Roch 38* | 39 | 32 | 8 | 9 | 12 | 3 | 0 | 0 | 2 | 0 | 0 | 7 | 0 | 11 | 0 | 0 | .281 |
| Fritz, Laurence J., Toledo*.. | 92 | 296 | 39 | 65 | 117 | 8 | 1 | 14 | 45 | 0 | 3 | 62 | 2 | 76 | 2 | 0 | .220 |
| Fuller, James H., Rochester | 113 | 362 | 51 | 77 | 145 | 7 | 5 | 17 | 50 | 0 | 3 | 54 | 7 | 133 | 1 | 0 | .213 |
| Galasso, Robert J., Roch*... | 36 | 65 | 5 | 15 | 26 | 0 | 1 | 3 | 8 | 0 | 0 | 1 | 0 | 20 | 0 | 0 | .231 |
| Gallagher, Alan M., Rich.... | 78 | 219 | 23 | 57 | 67 | 7 | 0 | 1 | 16 | 3 | 0 | 24 | 2 | 26 | 0 | 1 | .260 |
| Gallagher, Robert C., Tide* | 12 | 40 | 5 | 6 | 12 | 1 | 1 | 1 | 3 | 0 | 0 | 8 | 0 | 9 | 0 | 1 | .150 |
| Garcia, Alfonso, Roch ...... | 122 | 405 | 34 | 99 | 121 | 11 | 1 | 3 | 32 | 6 | 3 | 27 | 1 | 56 | 5 | 2 | .244 |

| Player and Club | G. | AB. | R. | H. | TB. | 2B. | 3B. | HR. | RBI. | SH. | SF. | BB. | HP. | SO. | SB. | CS. | Pct. |
|---|---|---|---|---|---|---|---|---|---|---|---|---|---|---|---|---|---|
| Gardner, Richard F., Syr | 10 | 2 | 1 | 1 | 2 | 1 | 0 | 0 | 0 | 0 | 0 | 0 | 0 | 0 | 0 | 0 | .500 |
| Geach, Jeffrey A., Richmond | 129 | 406 | 48 | 97 | 152 | 20 | 1 | 11 | 43 | 3 | 5 | 32 | 1 | 39 | 0 | 2 | .239 |
| Gebhard, Robert H., Mem | 44 | 8 | 1 | 1 | 1 | 0 | 0 | 0 | 0 | 2 | 0 | 1 | 0 | 6 | 0 | 0 | .125 |
| Godby, Danny, Pawtucket | 124 | 368 | 35 | 89 | 112 | 8 | 3 | 3 | 28 | 4 | 3 | 37 | 2 | 66 | 4 | 7 | .242 |
| Gonzalez, J. Fernando, Char | 45 | 154 | 21 | 43 | 61 | 9 | 3 | 1 | 21 | 0 | 2 | 19 | 0 | 19 | 0 | 2 | .279 |
| Guidry, Ronald A., Syracuse | 43 | 13 | 1 | 3 | 3 | 0 | 0 | 0 | 1 | 1 | 0 | 0 | 0 | 3 | 0 | 0 | .231 |
| Hanna, Preston L., Richmond | 35 | 54 | 2 | 8 | 9 | 1 | 0 | 0 | 2 | 2 | 0 | 3 | 0 | 18 | 0 | 0 | .148 |
| Harlow, Larry D., Roch* | 132 | 424 | 65 | 108 | 133 | 11 | 4 | 2 | 31 | 4 | 3 | 45 | 3 | 84 | 16 | 15 | .255 |
| Heinold, Douglas W., Syr | 1 | 2 | 0 | 0 | 0 | 0 | 0 | 0 | 0 | 0 | 0 | 0 | 0 | 2 | 0 | 0 | .000 |
| Hernaiz R., Jesus, Toledo | 60 | 14 | 2 | 2 | 2 | 0 | 0 | 0 | 3 | 0 | 0 | 4 | 0 | 4 | 0 | 0 | .143 |
| Hernandez, Guillermo, Tol* | 13 | 27 | 3 | 4 | 6 | 2 | 0 | 0 | 1 | 4 | 0 | 2 | 0 | 7 | 0 | 0 | .148 |
| Hickey, Donald P., Rochester | 50 | 121 | 10 | 28 | 42 | 3 | 1 | 3 | 17 | 0 | 2 | 6 | 2 | 17 | 2 | 1 | .231 |
| Hill, R. Quency, Toledo* | 22 | 46 | 2 | 8 | 10 | 2 | 0 | 0 | 7 | 0 | 4 | 0 | 5 | 12 | 0 | 1 | .174 |
| Hodges, Ronald W., Tide* | 95 | 278 | 27 | 74 | 88 | 8 | 0 | 2 | 33 | 5 | 2 | 45 | 3 | 34 | 2 | 0 | .266 |
| Holdsworth, Fredrick, Roch | 20 | 31 | 2 | 4 | 4 | 0 | 0 | 0 | 1 | 1 | 0 | 4 | 0 | 19 | 0 | 0 | .129 |
| Hopkins, Randolph, Char* | 13 | 1 | 0 | 0 | 0 | 0 | 0 | 0 | 0 | 0 | 0 | 0 | 0 | 1 | 0 | 0 | .000 |
| Howard, James C., Tidewater | 4 | 6 | 0 | 0 | 0 | 0 | 0 | 0 | 0 | 0 | 0 | 0 | 0 | 3 | 0 | 0 | .000 |
| Howe, Arthur, Charleston | 11 | 42 | 4 | 15 | 22 | 1 | 3 | 0 | 3 | 1 | 1 | 2 | 0 | 4 | 0 | 0 | .357 |
| Hughes, Terry W., Paw | 135 | 415 | 33 | 105 | 135 | 10 | 1 | 6 | 38 | 3 | 3 | 33 | 2 | 53 | 2 | 1 | .253 |
| Hunter, Harold, Pawtucket | 70 | 222 | 18 | 52 | 71 | 9 | 2 | 2 | 27 | 2 | 0 | 24 | 0 | 27 | 0 | 0 | .234 |
| Hutto, James, Rochester | 110 | 347 | 48 | 83 | 137 | 16 | 1 | 12 | 42 | 3 | 0 | 54 | 1 | 77 | 1 | 0 | .239 |
| Iorg, Dane Charles, Toledo* | 13 | 36 | 7 | 7 | 9 | 2 | 0 | 0 | 2 | 1 | 0 | 4 | 0 | 4 | 0 | 0 | .194 |
| Jiminez M., Juan, Charleston | 40 | 27 | 4 | 7 | 7 | 0 | 0 | 0 | 2 | 0 | 0 | 1 | 0 | 7 | 0 | 0 | .259 |
| Johnson, David C., Rochester | 28 | 8 | 0 | 1 | 1 | 0 | 0 | 0 | 1 | 0 | 0 | 0 | 0 | 3 | 0 | 0 | .125 |
| Johnson, Larry D., Memphis | 108 | 320 | 33 | 76 | 108 | 10 | 5 | 4 | 33 | 7 | 2 | 36 | 0 | 39 | 6 | 5 | .238 |
| Johnson, Robert D., Syracuse* | 25 | 13 | 2 | 0 | 0 | 0 | 0 | 0 | 0 | 0 | 1 | 2 | 0 | 9 | 0 | 0 | .000 |
| Jones, Odell, Charleston | 28 | 67 | 3 | 4 | 4 | 0 | 0 | 0 | 1 | 2 | 0 | 4 | 1 | 38 | 0 | 0 | .060 |
| Juran, Timothy A., Tide* | 3 | 1 | 0 | 0 | 0 | 0 | 0 | 0 | 0 | 0 | 0 | 0 | 0 | 1 | 0 | 0 | .000 |
| Kammeyer, Robert L., Syr | 27 | 43 | 3 | 6 | 7 | 1 | 0 | 0 | 8 | 6 | 0 | 3 | 0 | 20 | 0 | 0 | .140 |
| Kavanagh, Michael, Char | 9 | 10 | 2 | 2 | 4 | 0 | 1 | 0 | 1 | 0 | 0 | 3 | 0 | 4 | 0 | 0 | .200 |
| Keener, Joseph D., Memphis | 19 | 31 | 0 | 4 | 4 | 0 | 0 | 0 | 1 | 4 | 0 | 4 | 0 | 23 | 0 | 0 | .129 |
| Kelley, Thomas H., Richmond | 29 | 16 | 0 | 0 | 0 | 0 | 0 | 0 | 0 | 0 | 0 | 0 | 0 | 6 | 0 | 0 | .000 |
| Kenney, Gerald T., Syracuse* | 99 | 283 | 50 | 70 | 84 | 8 | 3 | 0 | 19 | 9 | 2 | 58 | 0 | 24 | 4 | 8 | .247 |
| Kinard, Rudolph R., Mem | 55 | 140 | 8 | 21 | 27 | 4 | 1 | 0 | 8 | 5 | 1 | 9 | 0 | 21 | 3 | 1 | .150 |
| Kirkpatrick, William, Mem | 27 | 50 | 6 | 3 | 3 | 0 | 0 | 0 | 1 | 8 | 0 | 7 | 0 | 19 | 0 | 0 | .060 |
| Kiser, Larry G., Toledo | 17 | 34 | 2 | 1 | 1 | 0 | 0 | 0 | 0 | 2 | 0 | 1 | 0 | 14 | 0 | 0 | .029 |
| Kleven, Jay A., Tidewater | 72 | 208 | 21 | 53 | 68 | 7 | 1 | 2 | 22 | 0 | 1 | 18 | 2 | 39 | 0 | 0 | .255 |
| Koegel, Peter, Charleston | 69 | 149 | 13 | 33 | 43 | 1 | 0 | 3 | 20 | 1 | 3 | 30 | 0 | 35 | 0 | 0 | .221 |
| Koritko, Michael, Pawtucket | 79 | 117 | 19 | 25 | 40 | 4 | 1 | 3 | 6 | 1 | 0 | 11 | 0 | 20 | 5 | 0 | .214 |
| Kosco, Andrew J., Toledo | 48 | 149 | 19 | 35 | 62 | 5 | 2 | 6 | 22 | 0 | 2 | 18 | 1 | 31 | 0 | 0 | .235 |
| Kouns, William, Pawtucket | 27 | 15 | 2 | 4 | 5 | 1 | 0 | 0 | 1 | 0 | 0 | 1 | 0 | 4 | 0 | 0 | .267 |
| Kreuger, Richard, Pawtucket | 33 | 46 | 2 | 4 | 4 | 0 | 0 | 0 | 2 | 2 | 0 | 8 | 0 | 23 | 0 | 0 | .087 |
| Kurpiel, Edward A., Mem* | 29 | 80 | 12 | 14 | 17 | 1 | 1 | 0 | 9 | 0 | 2 | 13 | 0 | 15 | 1 | 0 | .175 |
| LaCorte, Frank J., Richmond | 28 | 43 | 3 | 11 | 13 | 2 | 0 | 0 | 3 | 0 | 0 | 1 | 0 | 12 | 0 | 0 | .256 |
| Lang, Robert D., Memphis | 31 | 56 | 1 | 9 | 11 | 2 | 0 | 0 | 7 | 8 | 0 | 0 | 1 | 26 | 0 | 0 | .161 |
| Langford, J. Rick, Charleston | 20 | 34 | 3 | 8 | 14 | 3 | 0 | 1 | 9 | 0 | 0 | 0 | 0 | 12 | 0 | 0 | .235 |
| Laxton, William H., Tide* | 24 | 48 | 4 | 9 | 9 | 0 | 0 | 0 | 3 | 0 | 1 | 0 | 0 | 15 | 0 | 0 | .188 |
| Leshnock, Donald, Char* | 2 | 2 | 0 | 0 | 0 | 0 | 0 | 0 | 0 | 0 | 0 | 0 | 0 | 2 | 0 | 0 | .000 |
| Lockwood, Claude E., Tide | 3 | 1 | 1 | 1 | 4 | 0 | 0 | 1 | 1 | 0 | 0 | 0 | 0 | 0 | 0 | 0 | 1.000 |
| Macha, Kenneth, Charleston | 138 | 478 | 63 | 128 | 193 | 21 | 1 | 14 | 63 | 2 | 3 | 65 | 3 | 76 | 11 | 7 | .268 |
| Mahler, Michael J., Rich* | 27 | 54 | 2 | 5 | 5 | 0 | 0 | 0 | 0 | 2 | 0 | 7 | 0 | 19 | 0 | 0 | .093 |
| Manderbach, Gary M., Tide | 23 | 44 | 2 | 3 | 3 | 0 | 0 | 0 | 0 | 0 | 0 | 4 | 0 | 19 | 0 | 0 | .068 |
| Manz, George W., Rochester | 36 | 4 | 0 | 0 | 0 | 0 | 0 | 0 | 0 | 2 | 0 | 1 | 0 | 4 | 0 | 0 | .000 |
| Martin, Jerry L., Toledo | 94 | 342 | 64 | 89 | 151 | 12 | 4 | 14 | 40 | 1 | 2 | 48 | 3 | 49 | 24 | 5 | .260 |
| Martinez, Felix A., Syracuse* | 15 | 34 | 3 | 1 | 1 | 0 | 0 | 0 | 0 | 0 | 5 | 0 | 6 | 0 | 18 | 0 | .029 |
| Martinez, J. Dennis, Roch | 2 | 0 | 0 | 0 | 0 | 0 | 0 | 0 | 0 | 0 | 0 | 0 | 0 | 0 | 0 | 0 | .000 |
| Matchick, J. Thomas, Roch* | 84 | 254 | 32 | 70 | 95 | 11 | 4 | 2 | 33 | 8 | 2 | 26 | 2 | 35 | 1 | 1 | .276 |
| McCartney, Stephen L., Tol | 10 | 22 | 3 | 3 | 6 | 3 | 0 | 0 | 1 | 0 | 0 | 4 | 0 | 9 | 0 | 0 | .136 |
| McGregor, Scott H., Syr† | 46 | 65 | 8 | 18 | 20 | 2 | 0 | 0 | 6 | 5 | 0 | 9 | 0 | 5 | 0 | 0 | .277 |
| McGrew, Alvin, Ro 63-Tol 23 | 86 | 214 | 29 | 55 | 85 | 4 | 4 | 6 | 25 | 0 | 2 | 27 | 1 | 48 | 3 | 2 | .257 |
| Mendoza A., Mario, Char | 31 | 106 | 14 | 29 | 36 | 7 | 0 | 0 | 8 | 1 | 0 | 13 | 3 | 20 | 2 | 2 | .274 |
| Merchant, J. Anderson, Paw* | 119 | 375 | 31 | 105 | 132 | 15 | 0 | 4 | 31 | 10 | 2 | 54 | 4 | 47 | 3 | 4 | .280 |
| Miller, Dyar K., Rochester | 19 | 8 | 0 | 1 | 1 | 0 | 0 | 0 | 0 | 1 | 0 | 1 | 1 | 5 | 0 | 0 | .125 |
| Minshall, James E., Char | 45 | 8 | 0 | 2 | 2 | 0 | 0 | 0 | 0 | 2 | 0 | 0 | 0 | 2 | 0 | 0 | .250 |
| Mitchell, Paul M., Rochester | 14 | 34 | 0 | 4 | 4 | 0 | 0 | 0 | 2 | 1 | 0 | 1 | 0 | 10 | 0 | 0 | .118 |
| Molush, Edward N., Toledo | 20 | 1 | 0 | 1 | 1 | 0 | 0 | 0 | 0 | 0 | 0 | 0 | 0 | 0 | 0 | 0 | 1.000 |
| Montague, John E., Memphis | 20 | 45 | 2 | 7 | 7 | 0 | 0 | 0 | 3 | 4 | 0 | 1 | 0 | 13 | 0 | 0 | .156 |
| Monzon, Daniel F., Memphis | 130 | 421 | 60 | 100 | 140 | 15 | 2 | 7 | 40 | 10 | 3 | 82 | 2 | 59 | 11 | 4 | .238 |
| Moore, Alvin E., Richmond | 128 | 460 | 60 | 138 | 208 | 18 | 5 | 14 | 65 | 3 | 3 | 42 | 3 | 34 | 4 | 5 | .300 |
| Moore, Balor L., Memphis* | 14 | 4 | 0 | 0 | 0 | 0 | 0 | 0 | 0 | 0 | 0 | 0 | 0 | 2 | 0 | 0 | .000 |
| Moose, Robert, Charleston | 5 | 12 | 2 | 2 | 5 | 0 | 0 | 1 | 2 | 1 | 0 | 0 | 0 | 1 | 0 | 0 | .167 |
| Moreno Q., Omar, Char* | 130 | 447 | 73 | 127 | 178 | 20 | 2 | 9 | 51 | 1 | 6 | 51 | 9 | 77 | 39 | 8 | .284 |
| Morlan, John, Charleston | 32 | 45 | 7 | 7 | 7 | 0 | 0 | 0 | 4 | 3 | 0 | 1 | 0 | 17 | 0 | 0 | .156 |
| Murphy, Marlan T., Rich | 74 | 182 | 20 | 44 | 66 | 3 | 2 | 5 | 29 | 3 | 0 | 23 | 0 | 51 | 2 | 1 | .242 |
| Murrell, Ivan A., Richmond | 98 | 297 | 41 | 79 | 127 | 10 | 1 | 12 | 26 | 3 | 1 | 12 | 0 | 63 | 4 | 4 | .266 |
| Myrick, Robert H., Tidewater | 7 | 2 | 0 | 1 | 1 | 0 | 0 | 0 | 0 | 0 | 0 | 0 | 0 | 0 | 0 | 0 | .500 |
| Nahorodny, William G., Tol | 125 | 411 | 51 | 105 | 187 | 17 | 4 | 19 | 64 | 2 | 3 | 29 | 2 | 55 | 0 | 0 | .255 |
| Navarrete S., Juan, Mem* | 119 | 346 | 34 | 80 | 96 | 1 | 6 | 1 | 25 | 6 | 3 | 34 | 2 | 21 | 8 | 5 | .231 |
| Nelson, Roger A., Pawtucket | 27 | 60 | 3 | 11 | 15 | 1 | 0 | 1 | 4 | 0 | 0 | 7 | 1 | 10 | 0 | 0 | .183 |
| Newhauser, Donald, Paw | 66 | 10 | 0 | 2 | 2 | 0 | 0 | 0 | 1 | 0 | 0 | 1 | 0 | 5 | 0 | 0 | .200 |

| Player and Club | G. | AB. | R. | H. | TB. | 2B. | 3B. | HR. | RBI. | SH. | SF. | BB. | HP. | SO. | SB. | CS. | Pct. |
|---|---|---|---|---|---|---|---|---|---|---|---|---|---|---|---|---|---|
| Newman, Jeffrey L., Toledo.. | 32 | 64 | 7 | 12 | 22 | 4 | 0 | 2 | 5 | 1 | 0 | 4 | 0 | 14 | 0 | 0 | .188 |
| Nolan, Joseph William, Rich* | 111 | 342 | 41 | 92 | 123 | 13 | 0 | 6 | 53 | 1 | 4 | 47 | 2 | 49 | 1 | 4 | .269 |
| Nordhagen, Wayne O., Rich. | 34 | 90 | 8 | 23 | 32 | 3 | 0 | 2 | 8 | 0 | 1 | 7 | 0 | 16 | 0 | 0 | .256 |
| Ott, N. Edward, Charleston* | 121 | 425 | 66 | 121 | 182 | 21 | 5 | 10 | 55 | 0 | 3 | 49 | 4 | 54 | 1 | 3 | .285 |
| Pagan, David P., Syracuse | 15 | 8 | 0 | 1 | 1 | 0 | 0 | 0 | 0 | 0 | 0 | 0 | 0 | 5 | 0 | 0 | .125 |
| Parker, William D., Syracuse | 39 | 83 | 10 | 26 | 32 | 6 | 0 | 0 | 16 | 0 | 0 | 10 | 0 | 19 | 1 | 0 | .313 |
| Parrott, Michael E., Roch.. | 2 | 0 | 0 | 0 | 0 | 0 | 0 | 0 | 0 | 0 | 0 | 0 | 0 | 0 | 0 | 0 | .000 |
| Patterson, Daryl, Char*..... | 10 | 2 | 0 | 0 | 0 | 0 | 0 | 0 | 0 | 0 | 0 | 0 | 0 | 1 | 0 | 0 | .000 |
| Paul, Michael G., Toledo*.. | 45 | 10 | 0 | 1 | 1 | 0 | 0 | 0 | 1 | 4 | 0 | 0 | 0 | 6 | 0 | 0 | .100 |
| Peguero, Felix A., Memphis* | 8 | 19 | 3 | 6 | 9 | 1 | 1 | 0 | 1 | 0 | 0 | 4 | 0 | 4 | 2 | 0 | .316 |
| Pemberton, Brock, Tide†.... | 137 | 474 | 68 | 141 | 169 | 24 | 2 | 0 | 56 | 4 | 5 | 49 | 0 | 42 | 4 | 5 | .297 |
| Pichardo, Nelson, Syracuse. | 102 | 335 | 53 | 77 | 87 | 10 | 0 | 0 | 21 | 9 | 1 | 16 | 6 | 40 | 12 | 3 | .230 |
| Pirtle, Gerald E., Syracuse. | 61 | 16 | 1 | 3 | 4 | 1 | 0 | 0 | 0 | 1 | 0 | 0 | 0 | 5 | 0 | 0 | .188 |
| Puig, Richard G., Tidewater* | 13 | 44 | 5 | 8 | 8 | 0 | 0 | 0 | 3 | 0 | 0 | 7 | 0 | 9 | 0 | 0 | .182 |
| Rahe, Gary D., Charleston*. | 18 | 32 | 1 | 7 | 7 | 0 | 0 | 0 | 1 | 0 | 4 | 0 | 0 | 6 | 0 | 0 | .219 |
| Rajsich, David, Syracuse*.. | 4 | 11 | 0 | 0 | 0 | 0 | 0 | 0 | 0 | 0 | 0 | 0 | 0 | 4 | 0 | 0 | .000 |
| Randolph, Willie L., Char... | 91 | 313 | 41 | 106 | 150 | 13 | 5 | 7 | 42 | 2 | 6 | 37 | 2 | 29 | 14 | 0 | .339 |
| Reece, Robert S., Memphis.. | 81 | 258 | 24 | 56 | 71 | 7 | 1 | 2 | 26 | 4 | 2 | 11 | 1 | 25 | 0 | 1 | .217 |
| Reinbach, Michael W., Roch* | 127 | 435 | 76 | 126 | 191 | 24 | 4 | 11 | 62 | 2 | 3 | 58 | 3 | 64 | 4 | 1 | .290 |
| Reynolds, G. Craig, Char* | 108 | 425 | 51 | 131 | 177 | 22 | 3 | 6 | 42 | 1 | 0 | 21 | 1 | 32 | 5 | 9 | .308 |
| Ricks, Edward L., Syracuse. | 35 | 55 | 9 | 6 | 10 | 1 | 0 | 1 | 6 | 3 | 0 | 3 | 1 | 22 | 0 | 0 | .109 |
| Riley, Edward P., Memphis. | 21 | 6 | 0 | 1 | 1 | 0 | 0 | 0 | 0 | 0 | 0 | 0 | 0 | 2 | 0 | 0 | .167 |
| Rivera T., Jesus, Memphis.. | 40 | 140 | 22 | 41 | 75 | 5 | 1 | 9 | 22 | 0 | 1 | 23 | 0 | 31 | 3 | 1 | .293 |
| Robson, Gary T., Rochester. | 13 | 2 | 0 | 0 | 0 | 0 | 0 | 0 | 0 | 0 | 0 | 0 | 0 | 0 | 0 | 0 | .000 |
| Rogodzinski, Michael G., Tol* | 49 | 155 | 11 | 36 | 48 | 6 | 0 | 2 | 18 | 0 | 1 | 22 | 3 | 36 | 1 | 0 | .232 |
| Ross, Charles, Pawtucket*.. | 16 | 27 | 3 | 6 | 8 | 2 | 0 | 0 | 1 | 0 | 1 | 0 | 1 | 7 | 0 | 0 | .222 |
| Ruthven, Richard D., Toledo | 24 | 48 | 3 | 6 | 6 | 0 | 0 | 0 | 1 | 3 | 0 | 4 | 0 | 16 | 0 | 0 | .125 |
| Sadowski, James M., Charl.. | 34 | 41 | 3 | 4 | 4 | 0 | 0 | 0 | 0 | 1 | 0 | 2 | 0 | 11 | 0 | 0 | .098 |
| Sandate, Richard, Toledo*.. | 7 | 10 | 0 | 1 | 1 | 0 | 0 | 0 | 1 | 0 | 0 | 0 | 0 | 4 | 0 | 0 | .100 |
| Sanders, Kenneth T., Tide... | 28 | 8 | 1 | 1 | 1 | 0 | 0 | 0 | 1 | 2 | 1 | 1 | 0 | 0 | 0 | 0 | .125 |
| Sanders, Reginald J., Rich.. | 117 | 408 | 50 | 108 | 173 | 15 | 4 | 14 | 76 | 0 | 6 | 31 | 2 | 69 | 6 | 4 | .265 |
| Sanserino, Gary, Charleston. | 83 | 166 | 11 | 40 | 51 | 5 | 0 | 2 | 32 | 0 | 1 | 20 | 0 | 24 | 2 | 1 | .241 |
| Santana, Blas S., Toledo..... | 108 | 347 | 34 | 85 | 117 | 10 | 2 | 6 | 34 | 4 | 2 | 12 | 3 | 43 | 1 | 1 | .245 |
| Sawyer, Richard C., Syracuse | 25 | 52 | 1 | 5 | 5 | 0 | 0 | 0 | 2 | 5 | 0 | 7 | 0 | 14 | 0 | 0 | .096 |
| Scanlon, J. Patrick, Mem*.. | 29 | 85 | 14 | 15 | 30 | 4 | 1 | 3 | 14 | 1 | 1 | 25 | 0 | 24 | 1 | 0 | .176 |
| Schneck, David Lee, Toledo* | 93 | 240 | 28 | 52 | 85 | 11 | 2 | 6 | 25 | 3 | 3 | 30 | 0 | 38 | 4 | 3 | .217 |
| Sekel, Robert E., Rochester. | 29 | 12 | 2 | 3 | 3 | 0 | 0 | 0 | 0 | 0 | 0 | 0 | 0 | 2 | 0 | 0 | .250 |
| Senn, Terrence J., Tidewater | 51 | 148 | 25 | 37 | 52 | 9 | 0 | 2 | 14 | 1 | 1 | 23 | 1 | 26 | 4 | 1 | .250 |
| Shupe, John A., Syracuse*.. | 88 | 217 | 27 | 56 | 78 | 6 | 5 | 2 | 20 | 0 | 0 | 48 | 4 | 46 | 0 | 3 | .258 |
| Simpson, Wayne K., Toledo. | 29 | 59 | 6 | 7 | 14 | 2 | 1 | 1 | 4 | 5 | 0 | 2 | 0 | 31 | 0 | 0 | .119 |
| Skaggs, David L., Rochester | 41 | 99 | 4 | 22 | 30 | 8 | 0 | 0 | 10 | 1 | 1 | 18 | 0 | 19 | 2 | 0 | .222 |
| Skidmore, R. Roe, Pawtucket | 12 | 16 | 1 | 2 | 2 | 0 | 0 | 0 | 1 | 0 | 0 | 1 | 0 | 4 | 0 | 0 | .125 |
| Smith, Myrl, Rochester ..... | 2 | 0 | 0 | 0 | 0 | 0 | 0 | 0 | 0 | 0 | 0 | 0 | 0 | 0 | 0 | 0 | .000 |
| Snyder, Robert, Rochester†.. | 10 | 5 | 0 | 2 | 2 | 0 | 0 | 0 | 0 | 0 | 0 | 0 | 0 | 2 | 0 | 0 | .400 |
| Soderholm, Dale R., Rich.... | 80 | 232 | 15 | 49 | 64 | 11 | 2 | 0 | 16 | 2 | 0 | 19 | 4 | 65 | 6 | 2 | .211 |
| Spencer, Gerald W., Paw.... | 8 | 13 | 1 | 1 | 1 | 0 | 0 | 0 | 1 | 2 | 0 | 0 | 0 | 3 | 0 | 0 | .077 |
| Staiger, Roy J., Tidewater... | 137 | 471 | 52 | 133 | 197 | 29 | 4 | 9 | 81 | 4 | 9 | 36 | 3 | 56 | 2 | 3 | .282 |
| Stanhouse, Donald J., Mem. | 17 | 33 | 2 | 7 | 10 | 3 | 0 | 0 | 1 | 0 | 0 | 1 | 0 | 13 | 0 | 0 | .212 |
| Stearns, William A., Syracuse | 95 | 266 | 35 | 66 | 87 | 12 | 3 | 1 | 25 | 4 | 3 | 47 | 3 | 32 | 4 | 2 | .248 |
| Stein, W. Randolph, Roch... | 22 | 36 | 0 | 2 | 2 | 0 | 0 | 0 | 3 | 1 | 0 | 2 | 0 | 18 | 0 | 0 | .056 |
| Stephenson, C. Earl, Rich*.. | 24 | 8 | 1 | 1 | 1 | 0 | 0 | 0 | 1 | 1 | 0 | 0 | 0 | 2 | 0 | 0 | .125 |
| Sterling, Randall, Tidewater† | 29 | 54 | 3 | 3 | 4 | 1 | 0 | 0 | 2 | 12 | 0 | 5 | 2 | 28 | 0 | 0 | .056 |
| Stillman, Royle E., Roch*... | 126 | 444 | 65 | 139 | 215 | 30 | 2 | 14 | 75 | 1 | 1 | 49 | 1 | 51 | 2 | 3 | .313 |
| Swan, Craig S., Tidewater... | 26 | 62 | 1 | 8 | 8 | 0 | 0 | 0 | 2 | 3 | 0 | 1 | 0 | 24 | 0 | 0 | .129 |
| Tekulve, Kenton, Charleston | 24 | 18 | 0 | 0 | 0 | 0 | 0 | 0 | 0 | 1 | 0 | 4 | 0 | 11 | 0 | 0 | .000 |
| Tepedino, Francis R., Rich*. | 90 | 259 | 27 | 70 | 93 | 15 | 1 | 2 | 22 | 2 | 2 | 26 | 0 | 33 | 3 | 2 | .270 |
| Theodore, George B., Tide. | 106 | 285 | 39 | 72 | 90 | 3 | 0 | 5 | 25 | 4 | 0 | 29 | 3 | 35 | 9 | 3 | .253 |
| Thomas, Reginald A., Toledo | 85 | 218 | 39 | 53 | 76 | 5 | 3 | 4 | 22 | 0 | 2 | 36 | 1 | 48 | 27 | 4 | .243 |
| Thomas, Roy J., Toledo..... | 20 | 39 | 1 | 5 | 6 | 1 | 0 | 0 | 7 | 3 | 1 | 2 | 0 | 15 | 0 | 0 | .128 |
| Thomason, M. Erskine, Tol.. | 39 | 16 | 1 | 1 | 2 | 1 | 0 | 0 | 3 | 0 | 0 | 0 | 0 | 10 | 0 | 0 | .063 |
| Torrealba, Pablo A., Rich*.. | 64 | 29 | 0 | 2 | 2 | 0 | 0 | 0 | 2 | 2 | 0 | 2 | 0 | 9 | 0 | 0 | .069 |
| Trapp, Randolph A., Tide... | 47 | 123 | 11 | 25 | 33 | 6 | 1 | 0 | 12 | 0 | 0 | 13 | 0 | 40 | 1 | 0 | .203 |
| Tyler, Thomas C., Tidewater | 2 | 0 | 0 | 0 | 0 | 0 | 0 | 0 | 0 | 0 | 0 | 0 | 0 | 2 | 0 | 0 | .000 |
| Vail, Michael L., Tidewater.. | 115 | 409 | 53 | 140 | 202 | 23 | 9 | 7 | 79 | 1 | 3 | 34 | 3 | 74 | 3 | 5 | .342 |
| Valentine, Ellis C., Memphis | 139 | 494 | 87 | 151 | 226 | 30 | 3 | 13 | 66 | 9 | 5 | 59 | 4 | 106 | 18 | 10 | .306 |
| Valentine, Robert J., Char.. | 56 | 175 | 27 | 41 | 48 | 4 | 0 | 1 | 17 | 0 | 2 | 30 | 4 | 16 | 8 | 2 | .234 |
| Vazquez M., Efrain, Paw†... | 112 | 273 | 27 | 69 | 95 | 8 | 0 | 6 | 29 | 1 | 2 | 20 | 4 | 27 | 4 | 2 | .253 |
| Velez F., Otoniel, Syracuse.. | 81 | 244 | 56 | 61 | 113 | 18 | 2 | 10 | 35 | 0 | 4 | 87 | 2 | 54 | 1 | 1 | .250 |
| Vukovich, John C., Toledo.. | 26 | 97 | 6 | 22 | 27 | 5 | 0 | 0 | 10 | 3 | 0 | 13 | 0 | 12 | 1 | 0 | .227 |
| Wallace, David, Toledo..... | 13 | 1 | 0 | 0 | 0 | 0 | 0 | 0 | 0 | 0 | 0 | 0 | 0 | 1 | 0 | 0 | .000 |
| Warthen, Daniel D., Mem†.. | 8 | 13 | 0 | 1 | 1 | 0 | 0 | 0 | 1 | 1 | 0 | 1 | 0 | 6 | 0 | 0 | .077 |
| Webb, Henry M., Tidewater. | 3 | 4 | 0 | 1 | 1 | 0 | 0 | 0 | 0 | 1 | 0 | 1 | 0 | 0 | 0 | 0 | .250 |
| Wegener, Michael D., Tide.. | 41 | 17 | 3 | 3 | 4 | 1 | 0 | 0 | 1 | 2 | 0 | 0 | 0 | 4 | 0 | 1 | .176 |
| White, Jerome C., Memphis† | 99 | 354 | 44 | 105 | 161 | 16 | 5 | 10 | 45 | 11 | 2 | 18 | 5 | 31 | 13 | 8 | .297 |
| Whitfield, Terry B., Syr*... | 111 | 390 | 47 | 106 | 171 | 24 | 4 | 11 | 69 | 1 | 5 | 45 | 2 | 74 | 3 | 6 | .272 |
| Willis, Michael H., Roch*... | 32 | 49 | 0 | 8 | 8 | 0 | 0 | 0 | 4 | 6 | 0 | 2 | 1 | 15 | 0 | 0 | .163 |
| Wissel, Richard J., Toledo*. | 41 | 116 | 8 | 22 | 28 | 3 | 0 | 1 | 13 | 2 | 1 | 8 | 0 | 12 | 0 | 1 | .190 |
| Woodson, Richard Lee, Rich. | 21 | 2 | 0 | 0 | 0 | 0 | 0 | 0 | 0 | 0 | 0 | 0 | 0 | 0 | 0 | 0 | .000 |
| Wright, James C., Paw ..... | 19 | 31 | 4 | 4 | 4 | 0 | 0 | 0 | 2 | 1 | 0 | 3 | 0 | 13 | 1 | 0 | .129 |
| Yancy, Hugh, Syracuse ..... | 60 | 198 | 26 | 56 | 73 | 11 | 3 | 0 | 16 | 2 | 1 | 28 | 1 | 16 | 3 | 2 | .283 |
| Zeber, George W., Syracuse† | 110 | 347 | 33 | 87 | 116 | 16 | 2 | 3 | 36 | 6 | 1 | 47 | 1 | 49 | 2 | 2 | .251 |

GRAND-SLAM HOME RUNS—R. Sanders 2; Armas, Baker, Beall, Breeden, Diggle, Duncan, Harlow, Langford, Murphy, Nahorodny, Navarrete, Nolan, Rivera, Stillman, 1 each.

AWARDED FIRST BASE ON INTERFERENCE—Navarrete 4 (Hutto 2, Merchant, Nolan); Aviles 2 (Breazeale, Cox), Kammeyer 2 (Hutto, Merchant); Bernhardt (Kleven), Diggle (Johnson), L. Johnson (Hickey), Merchant (Reece), Randolph (Reece).

## CLUB FIELDING

| Club | G. | PO. | A. | E. | DP. | PB. | Pct. | Club | G. | PO. | A. | E. | DP. | PB. | Pct. |
|------|----|-----|----|----|----|----|-----|------|----|-----|----|----|----|----|-----|
| Tidewater | 141 | 3565 | 1525 | 113 | 127 | 13 | .978 | Syracuse | 136 | 3475 | 1415 | 161 | 123 | 19 | .968 |
| Charleston | 139 | 3520 | 1394 | 150 | 108 | 25 | .970 | Pawtucket | 140 | 3613 | 1637 | 175 | 137 | 14 | .968 |
| Rochester | 141 | 3601 | 1531 | 168 | 137 | 11 | .968 | Richmond | 127 | 3388 | 1267 | 157 | 113 | 16 | .967 |
| Toledo | 140 | 3568 | 1543 | 168 | 118 | 14 | .968 | Memphis | 140 | 3700 | 1720 | 197 | 145 | 16 | .965 |

TRIPLE PLAYS—Richmond, Toledo, 1 each.

## INDIVIDUAL FIELDING

### FIRST BASEMEN

*Throws lefthanded.

| Player and Club | G. | PO. | A. | E. | DP. | Pct. | Player and Club | G. | PO. | A. | E. | DP. | Pct. |
|-----------------|----|-----|----|----|----|-----|-----------------|----|-----|----|----|----|-----|
| Iorg, Toledo | 10 | 76 | 2 | 0 | 5 | 1.000 | Hutto, Rochester | 21 | 169 | 10 | 3 | 17 | .984 |
| Stillman, Rochester* | 62 | 508 | 26 | 1 | 48 | .998 | Macha, Charleston | 135 | 1049 | 86 | 20 | 93 | .983 |
| PEMBERTON, Tid* | 134 | 1184 | 66 | 8 | 98 | .994 | Velez, Syracuse | 31 | 274 | 16 | 5 | 20 | .983 |
| Hughes, Pawtucket | 33 | 163 | 9 | 1 | 16 | .994 | Kosco, Toledo | 27 | 222 | 16 | 4 | 20 | .983 |
| Reece, Memphis | 13 | 100 | 5 | 1 | 14 | .991 | Baker, Pawtucket | 130 | 1080 | 75 | 20 | 102 | .983 |
| Shupe, Syracuse* | 82 | 564 | 51 | 6 | 57 | .990 | Down, Memphis | 20 | 163 | 11 | 3 | 16 | .983 |
| Fiore, Rochester* | 59 | 467 | 32 | 5 | 45 | .990 | Sanders, Richmond | 87 | 684 | 37 | 14 | 69 | .981 |
| Breazeale, Richmond | 26 | 190 | 18 | 2 | 18 | .990 | Breeden, Memphis* | 62 | 571 | 60 | 16 | 54 | .975 |
| Kurpiel, Memphis* | 21 | 169 | 18 | 2 | 12 | .989 | Bernhardt, Syracuse | 16 | 108 | 8 | 3 | 8 | .975 |
| Fritz, Toledo* | 87 | 732 | 53 | 11 | 57 | .986 | Nahorodny, Toledo | 14 | 107 | 9 | 3 | 13 | .975 |
| Beall, Richmond* | 19 | 134 | 8 | 2 | 8 | .986 | Castle, Syracuse* | 36 | 160 | 23 | 6 | 15 | .968 |
| Cromartie, Memphis* | 47 | 364 | 31 | 6 | 37 | .985 | Theodore, Tidewater | 11 | 97 | 6 | 5 | 13 | .954 |

Triple Plays—Kosco, Breazeale, 1 each.

#### (Fewer Than Ten Games)

| Player and Club | G. | PO. | A. | E. | DP. | Pct. | Player and Club | G. | PO. | A. | E. | DP. | Pct. |
|-----------------|----|-----|----|----|----|-----|-----------------|----|-----|----|----|----|-----|
| Matchick, Rochester | 7 | 45 | 3 | 0 | 2 | 1.000 | Erickson, Pawtucket | 5 | 8 | 0 | 0 | 1 | 1.000 |
| Fuller, Rochester | 7 | 31 | 6 | 0 | 4 | 1.000 | Skidmore, Pawtucket | 3 | 6 | 0 | 0 | 0 | 1.000 |
| Clark, Toledo | 4 | 24 | 2 | 0 | 4 | 1.000 | Nordhagen, Richmond | 2 | 6 | 0 | 0 | 0 | 1.000 |
| Vazquez, Pawtucket | 7 | 22 | 1 | 0 | 0 | 1.000 | Conigliaro, Pawtucket | 1 | 2 | 0 | 0 | 1 | 1.000 |
| Wissel, Toledo | 3 | 20 | 2 | 0 | 4 | 1.000 | McGrew, Rochester | 1 | 2 | 0 | 0 | 0 | 1.000 |
| Koegel, Charleston | 5 | 20 | 1 | 0 | 2 | 1.000 | Valentine, Memphis | 1 | 1 | 0 | 0 | 0 | 1.000 |
| Tepedino, Richmond* | 6 | 17 | 1 | 0 | 1 | 1.000 | Gallagher, Richmond | 9 | 54 | 2 | 1 | 5 | .982 |
| Schneck, Toledo* | 2 | 16 | 2 | 0 | 2 | 1.000 | Coleman, Pawtucket | 8 | 15 | 0 | 1 | 0 | .938 |
| Scanlon, Memphis | 4 | 10 | 0 | 0 | 1 | 1.000 | Sanserino, Charleston | 2 | 7 | 0 | 1 | 1 | .875 |
| Santana, Toledo | 1 | 9 | 0 | 0 | 0 | 1.000 | Johnson, Memphis | 4 | 25 | 1 | 4 | 1 | .867 |

### SECOND BASEMEN

| Player and Club | G. | PO. | A. | E. | DP. | Pct. | Player and Club | G. | PO. | A. | E. | DP. | Pct. |
|-----------------|----|-----|----|----|----|-----|-----------------|----|-----|----|----|----|-----|
| Staiger, Tidewater | 15 | 26 | 41 | 0 | 10 | 1.000 | Matchick, Rochester | 34 | 62 | 100 | 5 | 21 | .970 |
| Hughes, Pawtucket | 19 | 28 | 36 | 0 | 4 | 1.000 | Garcia, Rochester | 119 | 233 | 293 | 17 | 71 | .969 |
| Puig, Tidewater | 13 | 33 | 34 | 1 | 7 | .985 | Andrews, Toledo | 117 | 287 | 328 | 21 | 65 | .967 |
| Hunter, Pawtucket | 55 | 121 | 167 | 6 | 35 | .980 | Foster, Tidewater | 73 | 138 | 188 | 11 | 41 | .967 |
| Dauer, Rochester | 10 | 15 | 29 | 1 | 5 | .978 | Pichardo, Syracuse | 25 | 46 | 43 | 3 | 7 | .967 |
| MOORE, Richmond | 94 | 219 | 223 | 11 | 59 | .976 | Randolph, Charleston | 90 | 189 | 250 | 16 | 63 | .965 |
| Clark, Toledo | 27 | 51 | 66 | 3 | 14 | .975 | Navarrete, Memphis | 28 | 65 | 78 | 6 | 15 | .960 |
| Senn, Tidewater | 41 | 99 | 110 | 6 | 21 | .972 | Cox, Memphis | 109 | 211 | 341 | 25 | 64 | .957 |
| Sanserino, Charleston | 14 | 31 | 38 | 2 | 4 | .972 | Geach, Richmond | 43 | 99 | 77 | 8 | 23 | .957 |
| Zober, Syracuse | 99 | 197 | 280 | 14 | 61 | .971 | Parker, Syracuse | 13 | 29 | 27 | 3 | 10 | .949 |
| Edwards, Charleston | 31 | 48 | 84 | 4 | 12 | .971 | Andrew, Pawtucket | 78 | 169 | 198 | 21 | 39 | .946 |

Triple Play—Andrews.

#### (Fewer Than Ten Games)

| Player and Club | G. | PO. | A. | E. | DP. | Pct. | Player and Club | G. | PO. | A. | E. | DP. | Pct. |
|-----------------|----|-----|----|----|----|-----|-----------------|----|-----|----|----|----|-----|
| Kinard, Memphis | 6 | 15 | 26 | 0 | 7 | 1.000 | Vazquez, Pawtucket | 2 | 0 | 1 | 0 | 0 | 1.000 |
| Peguero, Memphis | 5 | 11 | 17 | 0 | 6 | 1.000 | Cummings, Richmond | 1 | 0 | 1 | 0 | 1 | 1.000 |
| Gallagher, Richmond | 5 | 6 | 3 | 0 | 1 | 1.000 | Trapp, Tidewater | 8 | 6 | 13 | 1 | 3 | .950 |
| Murrell, Richmond | 3 | 3 | 4 | 0 | 1 | 1.000 | Howe, Charleston | 4 | 9 | 10 | 1 | 4 | .950 |
| Aviles, Pawtucket | 2 | 3 | 4 | 0 | 1 | 1.000 | Yancy, Syracuse | 3 | 16 | 20 | 3 | 4 | .923 |
| Monzon, Memphis | 1 | 0 | 2 | 0 | 0 | 1.000 | Gonzalez, Charleston | 3 | 4 | 5 | 1 | 1 | .900 |

### THIRD BASEMEN

| Player and Club | G. | PO. | A. | E. | DP. | Pct. | Player and Club | G. | PO. | A. | E. | DP. | Pct. |
|-----------------|----|-----|----|----|----|-----|-----------------|----|-----|----|----|----|-----|
| STAIGER, Tidewater | 113 | 112 | 258 | 5 | 22 | .987 | Clark, Toledo | 27 | 23 | 40 | 3 | 6 | .955 |
| Vukovich, Toledo | 25 | 24 | 49 | 2 | 4 | .973 | Vazquez, Pawtucket | 110 | 61 | 146 | 10 | 15 | .954 |
| Bernhardt, Syracuse | 33 | 23 | 62 | 3 | 1 | .966 | Santana, Toledo | 90 | 84 | 195 | 14 | 8 | .952 |
| Geach, Richmond | 63 | 45 | 116 | 6 | 12 | .964 | Valentine, Charleston | 54 | 44 | 74 | 6 | 10 | .952 |
| Matchick, Rochester | 37 | 24 | 78 | 4 | 8 | .962 | Yancy, Syracuse | 48 | 42 | 92 | 7 | 6 | .950 |
| Gonzalez, Charleston | 38 | 27 | 67 | 4 | 4 | .959 | Hughes, Pawtucket | 86 | 56 | 150 | 11 | 20 | .949 |
| Gallagher, Richmond | 44 | 29 | 57 | 4 | 10 | .956 | | | | | | | |

## THIRD BASEMEN—Continued

| Player and Club | G. | PO. | A. | E. | DP. | Pct. |
|---|---|---|---|---|---|---|
| Sanserino, Charleston | 32 | 21 | 53 | 4 | 7 | .949 |
| Duncan, Rochester | 108 | 94 | 222 | 19 | 28 | .943 |
| Monzon, Memphis | 99 | 72 | 182 | 17 | 15 | .937 |
| Moore, Richmond | 35 | 28 | 60 | 7 | 6 | .926 |
| Trapp, Tidewater | 31 | 22 | 55 | 8 | 8 | .906 |
| Augustine, Charleston | 17 | 20 | 28 | 5 | 2 | .906 |
| Scanlon, Memphis | 26 | 22 | 53 | 8 | 2 | .904 |
| Velez, Syracuse | 50 | 28 | 74 | 14 | 12 | .879 |
| Cox, Memphis | 17 | 13 | 38 | 7 | 3 | .879 |
| Navarrete, Memphis | 11 | 3 | 13 | 3 | 0 | .842 |

Triple Play—Santana.

### (Fewer Than Ten Games)

| Player and Club | G. | PO. | A. | E. | DP. | Pct. |
|---|---|---|---|---|---|---|
| Howe, Charleston | 7 | 6 | 13 | 0 | 0 | 1.000 |
| Kinard, Memphis | 2 | 6 | 3 | 0 | 0 | 1.000 |
| Koritko, Pawtucket | 5 | 2 | 2 | 0 | 0 | 1.000 |
| Coleman, Pawtucket | 4 | 1 | 1 | 0 | 0 | 1.000 |
| Parker, Syracuse | 1 | 1 | 0 | 0 | 0 | 1.000 |
| Bladt Syracuse | 1 | 0 | 1 | 0 | 0 | 1.000 |
| Kosco, Toledo | 8 | 6 | 12 | 1 | 1 | .947 |
| Hunter, Pawtucket | 7 | 4 | 10 | 1 | 3 | .933 |
| Kenney, Syracuse | 7 | 4 | 10 | 1 | 1 | .933 |
| Murrell, Richmond | 4 | 4 | 4 | 1 | 0 | .889 |
| Nolan, Richmond | 3 | 1 | 5 | 2 | 0 | .750 |
| Dauer, Rochester | 2 | 2 | 1 | 1 | 0 | .750 |
| Zeber, Syracuse | 4 | 1 | 5 | 4 | 1 | .600 |
| Macha, Charleston | 2 | 1 | 2 | 2 | 2 | .600 |
| Down, Memphis | 1 | 0 | 1 | 1 | 0 | .500 |

## SHORTSTOPS

| Player and Club | G. | PO. | A. | E. | DP. | Pct. |
|---|---|---|---|---|---|---|
| Navarrete, Memphis | 71 | 122 | 227 | 14 | 54 | .961 |
| DeJOHN, Tidewater | 121 | 203 | 347 | 24 | 63 | .958 |
| Aviles, Pawtucket | 115 | 176 | 333 | 23 | 62 | .957 |
| Belloir, Richmond | 35 | 40 | 114 | 7 | 27 | .957 |
| Creech, Memphis | 26 | 48 | 86 | 6 | 13 | .957 |
| Kenney, Syracuse | 82 | 124 | 201 | 16 | 41 | .953 |
| Gallagher, Richmond | 11 | 13 | 25 | 2 | 4 | .950 |
| Bailor, Rochester | 128 | 198 | 386 | 32 | 64 | .948 |
| Mendoza, Charleston | 31 | 54 | 68 | 7 | 12 | .946 |
| Reynolds, Charleston | 108 | 151 | 287 | 26 | 64 | .944 |
| Pichardo, Syracuse | 71 | 112 | 193 | 19 | 40 | .941 |
| Dancy, Toledo | 74 | 88 | 243 | 23 | 35 | .935 |
| Kinard, Memphis | 40 | 58 | 100 | 11 | 20 | .935 |
| Geach, Richmond | 24 | 30 | 56 | 6 | 10 | .935 |
| Foster, Tidewater | 27 | 32 | 59 | 7 | 14 | .929 |
| Chavez, Toledo | 21 | 43 | 74 | 9 | 10 | .929 |
| Clark, Toledo | 49 | 61 | 115 | 14 | 21 | .926 |
| Garcia, Rochester | 17 | 27 | 62 | 8 | 15 | .918 |
| Soderholm, Richmond | 72 | 103 | 200 | 29 | 27 | .913 |
| Dillard, Pawtucket | 41 | 53 | 100 | 19 | 17 | .890 |
| Monzon, Memphis | 21 | 35 | 59 | 12 | 16 | .887 |
| Hughes, Pawtucket | 30 | 11 | 24 | 6 | 3 | .854 |

Triple Play—Geach.

### (Fewer Than Ten Games)

| Player and Club | G. | PO. | A. | E. | DP. | Pct. |
|---|---|---|---|---|---|---|
| Senn, Tidewater | 6 | 7 | 6 | 0 | 1 | 1.000 |
| Crane, Toledo | 2 | 4 | 3 | 0 | 0 | 1.000 |
| Vazquez, Pawtucket | 1 | 2 | 3 | 0 | 0 | 1.000 |
| Asselstine, Richmond | 1 | 1 | 1 | 0 | 0 | 1.000 |
| Staiger, Tidewater | 7 | 6 | 24 | 1 | 2 | .968 |
| Santana, Toledo | 8 | 14 | 24 | 2 | 3 | .950 |

## OUTFIELDERS

| Player and Club | G. | PO. | A. | E. | DP. | Pct. |
|---|---|---|---|---|---|---|
| Tepedino, Richmond* | 77 | 103 | 8 | 0 | 2 | 1.000 |
| Theodore, Tidewater | 64 | 83 | 5 | 0 | 1 | 1.000 |
| Stearns, Syracuse | 41 | 74 | 5 | 0 | 1 | 1.000 |
| Augustine, Charleston | 38 | 49 | 4 | 0 | 1 | 1.000 |
| Nordhagen, Richmond | 25 | 44 | 2 | 0 | 0 | 1.000 |
| Koegel, Charleston | 13 | 28 | 0 | 0 | 0 | 1.000 |
| Gallagher, Tidewater* | 12 | 20 | 3 | 0 | 0 | 1.000 |
| Rahe, Charleston* | 11 | 12 | 0 | 0 | 0 | 1.000 |
| Monzon, Memphis | 11 | 8 | 0 | 0 | 0 | 1.000 |
| DINEEN, Syracuse* | 97 | 230 | 8 | 2 | 2 | .992 |
| Vail, Tidewater | 108 | 182 | 9 | 2 | 3 | .990 |
| Coleman, Pawtucket | 50 | 79 | 5 | 1 | 2 | .988 |
| Beall, Richmond* | 55 | 74 | 6 | 1 | 0 | .988 |
| Armas, Charleston | 123 | 220 | 14 | 3 | 0 | .987 |
| Boisclair, Tidewater | 120 | 264 | 9 | 4 | 0 | .986 |
| Martin, Toledo | 94 | 205 | 7 | 3 | 1 | .986 |
| Koritko, Pawtucket | 63 | 59 | 3 | 1 | 0 | .984 |
| Bernhardt, Syracuse | 33 | 59 | 3 | 1 | 0 | .984 |
| Moreno, Charleston* | 127 | 328 | 10 | 6 | 2 | .983 |
| McGrew, Roch-Tol | 60 | 105 | 4 | 2 | 3 | .982 |
| Conigliaro, Pawtucket | 35 | 55 | 0 | 1 | 0 | .982 |
| Diggle, Tidewater | 93 | 148 | 9 | 3 | 1 | .981 |
| Dilone, Charleston | 120 | 275 | 11 | 6 | 0 | .979 |
| Valentine, Memphis | 136 | 265 | 12 | 6 | 3 | .979 |
| Murrell, Richmond | 76 | 135 | 4 | 3 | 1 | .979 |
| White, Memphis | 94 | 223 | 6 | 6 | 0 | .974 |
| Harlow, Richmond* | 122 | 280 | 10 | 8 | 5 | .973 |
| Bannister, Toledo | 98 | 209 | 3 | 6 | 0 | .972 |
| Down, Memphis | 75 | 101 | 1 | 3 | 0 | .971 |
| Godby, Pawtucket | 114 | 149 | 12 | 5 | 1 | .970 |
| Wissel, Toledo | 30 | 30 | 1 | 1 | 0 | .969 |
| Fuller, Rochester | 100 | 172 | 8 | 6 | 1 | .968 |
| Murphy, Richmond | 60 | 86 | 3 | 3 | 1 | .967 |
| Bladt, Syracuse | 79 | 151 | 6 | 6 | 2 | .963 |
| Reinbach, Rochester | 125 | 276 | 5 | 11 | 1 | .962 |
| Asselstine, Richmond | 117 | 283 | 5 | 12 | 0 | .960 |
| Flowers, Pawtucket* | 123 | 256 | 14 | 12 | 1 | .957 |
| Schneck, Toledo* | 73 | 103 | 7 | 5 | 1 | .957 |
| Whitfield, Syracuse | 109 | 208 | 10 | 10 | 2 | .956 |
| Reg. Thomas, Toledo | 64 | 83 | 4 | 4 | 0 | .956 |
| Stillman, Rochester* | 57 | 90 | 12 | 5 | 1 | .953 |
| Castle, Syracuse* | 66 | 91 | 5 | 5 | 2 | .950 |
| Browne, Toledo | 15 | 16 | 2 | 1 | 1 | .947 |
| Carrion, Memphis | 11 | 17 | 1 | 1 | 0 | .947 |
| Ayala, Tidewater | 50 | 66 | 1 | 4 | 1 | .944 |
| Rivera, Memphis | 39 | 57 | 7 | 4 | 1 | .941 |
| Coletta Pawtucket* | 96 | 99 | 7 | 7 | 1 | .938 |
| Sanders, Richmond | 31 | 39 | 2 | 3 | 0 | .932 |
| Cromartie, Memphis | 79 | 114 | 4 | 9 | 1 | .929 |
| Rogodzinski, Toledo | 47 | 71 | 3 | 6 | 0 | .925 |
| Nelson, Pawtucket | 23 | 23 | 1 | 2 | 0 | .923 |

### (Fewer Than Ten Games)

| Player and Club | G. | PO. | A. | E. | DP. | Pct. |
|---|---|---|---|---|---|---|
| McCartney, Toledo | 8 | 12 | 0 | 0 | 0 | 1.000 |
| Kosco, Toledo | 8 | 9 | 0 | 0 | 0 | 1.000 |
| Hickey, Rochester | 9 | 8 | 1 | 0 | 0 | 1.000 |
| Vazquez, Pawtucket | 7 | 8 | 1 | 0 | 1 | 1.000 |
| Yancy, Syracuse | 1 | 4 | 0 | 0 | 0 | 1.000 |
| Parker, Syracuse | 7 | 1 | 1 | 0 | 0 | 1.000 |
| Yukovich, Toledo | 1 | 2 | 0 | 0 | 0 | 1.000 |
| Clark, Toledo | 1 | 2 | 0 | 0 | 0 | 1.000 |
| Macha, Charleston | 1 | 1 | 0 | 0 | 0 | 1.000 |
| Cox, Memphis | 5 | 1 | 0 | 0 | 0 | 1.000 |
| Aviles, Pawtucket | 1 | 1 | 0 | 0 | 0 | 1.000 |
| Ott, Charleston | 6 | 9 | 0 | 1 | 0 | .900 |
| Johnson, Memphis | 7 | 4 | 0 | 1 | 0 | .800 |
| Howard Tidewater | 2 | 3 | 0 | 1 | 0 | .750 |
| Cummings, Richmond | 4 | 2 | 0 | 2 | 0 | .500 |
| Kenney, Syracuse | 5 | 0 | 0 | 1 | 0 | .000 |
| Hanna, Richmond | 1 | 0 | 0 | 1 | 0 | .000 |

## CATCHERS

| Player and Club | G. | PO. | A. | E. | DP. | PB. | Pct. |
|---|---|---|---|---|---|---|---|
| Childers, Memphis | 8 | 32 | 4 | 0 | 1 | 1 | 1.000 |
| Murphy, Richmond | 2 | 19 | 0 | 0 | 1 | | 1.000 |
| Erickson, Paw | 44 | 188 | 15 | 1 | 6 | 2 | .995 |
| Koegel, Charleston | 28 | 168 | 15 | 1 | 2 | 2 | .995 |
| NAHO'DNY, Tol | 103 | 584 | 62 | 4 | 11 | 7 | .994 |
| Merchant, Paw | 116 | 655 | 76 | 6 | 16 | 12 | .992 |
| Nolan, Richmond | 102 | 571 | 46 | 5 | 8 | 9 | .992 |
| Deidel, Syracuse | 102 | 588 | 54 | 6 | 12 | 14 | .991 |
| Kleven, Tidewater | 64 | 332 | 30 | 4 | 8 | 9 | .989 |
| D. Johnson, Mem | 84 | 379 | 40 | 5 | 7 | 8 | .988 |
| Hodges, Tidewater | 82 | 431 | 45 | 7 | 9 | 4 | .986 |
| Reece, Memphis | 56 | 288 | 14 | 6 | 1 | 7 | .981 |
| Breazeale, Rich | 44 | 223 | 16 | 5 | 3 | 6 | .980 |
| Skaggs, Rochester | 40 | 177 | 18 | 4 | 3 | 0 | .980 |
| Cox, Toledo | 30 | 168 | 19 | 4 | 3 | 3 | .979 |
| Newman, Toledo | 20 | 87 | 6 | 2 | 2 | 4 | .979 |
| Hutto, Rochester | 88 | 487 | 47 | 13 | 6 | 9 | .976 |
| Ott, Charleston | 114 | 688 | 59 | 20 | 3 | 23 | .974 |
| Hickey, Rochester | 30 | 176 | 15 | 5 | 0 | 2 | .974 |
| Stearns, Syracuse | 50 | 253 | 23 | 8 | 5 | 5 | .972 |

Triple Play—Nahorodny.

## PITCHERS

| Player and Club | G. | PO. | A. | E. | DP. | Pct. |
|---|---|---|---|---|---|---|
| ESPINOSA, Tide | 24 | 9 | 30 | 0 | 3 | 1.000 |
| Simpson, Toledo | 26 | 20 | 18 | 0 | 1 | 1.000 |
| Kreuger, Pawtucket | 33 | 1 | 37 | 0 | 1 | 1.000 |
| Kammeyer, Syracuse | 27 | 14 | 24 | 0 | 5 | 1.000 |
| Hill, Toledo* | 29 | 6 | 29 | 0 | 2 | 1.000 |
| Atkinson, Memphis | 49 | 10 | 21 | 0 | 1 | 1.000 |
| Swan, Tidewater | 26 | 9 | 19 | 0 | 0 | 1.000 |
| Carrithers, Memphis | 12 | 6 | 21 | 0 | 3 | 1.000 |
| Tekulve, Charleston | 24 | 8 | 16 | 0 | 1 | 1.000 |
| Sanders, Tidewater | 28 | 6 | 16 | 0 | 1 | 1.000 |
| Langford, Charleston | 13 | 9 | 11 | 0 | 0 | 1.000 |
| Gebhard, Memphis | 44 | 8 | 11 | 0 | 1 | 1.000 |
| Mitchell, Rochester | 14 | 7 | 12 | 0 | 2 | 1.000 |
| Cram, Tidewater | 31 | 5 | 11 | 0 | 1 | 1.000 |
| Laxton, Tidewater* | 24 | 3 | 11 | 0 | 1 | 1.000 |
| Stephenson, Rich* | 23 | 4 | 10 | 0 | 2 | 1.000 |
| Wegener, Tidewater | 41 | 0 | 12 | 0 | 0 | 1.000 |
| Sekel, Rochester | 29 | 3 | 8 | 0 | 0 | 1.000 |
| Moore, Memphis* | 14 | 0 | 11 | 0 | 1 | 1.000 |
| Johnson, Rochester | 28 | 3 | 7 | 0 | 0 | 1.000 |
| Kouns, Pawtucket | 27 | 1 | 8 | 0 | 2 | 1.000 |
| Candelaria, Char* | 10 | 2 | 6 | 0 | 0 | 1.000 |
| Enyart, Memphis* | 29 | 1 | 6 | 0 | 0 | 1.000 |
| Miller, Rochester | 19 | 1 | 5 | 0 | 2 | 1.000 |
| Babcock, Rochester | 10 | 2 | 4 | 0 | 0 | 1.000 |
| Pagan, Syracuse | 15 | 1 | 2 | 0 | 0 | 1.000 |
| Hopkins, Charleston* | 13 | 2 | 1 | 0 | 0 | 1.000 |
| Robson, Rochester | 13 | 0 | 2 | 0 | 0 | 1.000 |
| Gardner, Syracuse* | 10 | 0 | 2 | 0 | 0 | 1.000 |
| Wallace, Toledo | 13 | 0 | 1 | 0 | 0 | 1.000 |
| Albin, Memphis | 25 | 25 | 24 | 1 | 2 | .980 |
| Aase, Pawtucket | 29 | 17 | 31 | 1 | 2 | .980 |
| Flanagan, Rochester | 27 | 5 | 33 | 1 | 2 | .974 |
| Figueroa, Richmond* | 26 | 12 | 23 | 1 | 1 | .972 |
| Jimenez, Charleston | 40 | 3 | 32 | 1 | 1 | .972 |
| Hernaiz, Toledo | 59 | 12 | 22 | 1 | 3 | .971 |
| Stein, Rochester | 21 | 18 | 14 | 1 | 1 | .970 |
| Sadowski, Charleston | 27 | 9 | 19 | 1 | 1 | .966 |
| Devine, Richmond | 27 | 8 | 19 | 1 | 0 | .964 |
| Sawyer, Syracuse | 25 | 12 | 40 | 2 | 2 | .963 |
| Thomason, Toledo | 39 | 7 | 19 | 1 | 3 | .963 |
| Pirtle, Syracuse | 61 | 6 | 17 | 1 | 2 | .958 |
| Sterling, Tidewater | 29 | 14 | 29 | 2 | 4 | .956 |
| Burton, Pawtucket* | 12 | 1 | 20 | 1 | 2 | .955 |
| Kirkpatrick, Memphis | 27 | 11 | 30 | 2 | 4 | .953 |
| Paul, Toledo* | 45 | 3 | 16 | 1 | 1 | .950 |
| Bernard, Tidewater | 27 | 12 | 25 | 2 | 3 | .949 |
| Roy Thomas, Toledo | 19 | 8 | 28 | 2 | 1 | .947 |
| Montague, Memphis | 18 | 15 | 21 | 2 | 2 | .947 |
| Caskey, Charleston* | 31 | 3 | 15 | 1 | 0 | .947 |
| Manderbach, Tide* | 23 | 4 | 31 | 2 | 3 | .946 |
| M. Barr, Pawtucket | 70 | 9 | 24 | 2 | 1 | .943 |
| Hernandez, Toledo* | 13 | 2 | 13 | 1 | 0 | .938 |
| McGregor, Syracuse* | 21 | 6 | 37 | 3 | 2 | .935 |
| Ricks, Syracuse | 26 | 6 | 22 | 2 | 1 | .933 |
| Holdsworth, Rochester | 19 | 3 | 11 | 1 | 0 | .933 |
| Minshall, Charleston | 45 | 6 | 7 | 1 | 0 | .929 |
| Lang, Memphis | 31 | 13 | 38 | 4 | 4 | .927 |
| Bair, Charleston | 26 | 15 | 23 | 3 | 1 | .927 |
| Guidry, Syracuse* | 42 | 5 | 7 | 1 | 0 | .923 |
| S. Barr, Paw* | 23 | 7 | 28 | 3 | 2 | .921 |
| LaCorte, Richmond | 24 | 12 | 11 | 2 | 1 | .920 |
| Stanhouse, Memphis | 13 | 9 | 14 | 2 | 3 | .920 |
| Ross, Pawtucket* | 13 | 3 | 20 | 2 | 0 | .920 |
| Clemons, Pawtucket* | 66 | 6 | 16 | 2 | 2 | .917 |
| Diorio, Memphis | 31 | 3 | 8 | 1 | 1 | .917 |
| Torrealba, Richmond* | 64 | 8 | 24 | 3 | 1 | .914 |
| Mahler, Richmond* | 27 | 5 | 16 | 2 | 1 | .913 |
| Morlan, Charleston | 22 | 7 | 13 | 2 | 0 | .909 |
| Newhauser, Pawtucket | 66 | 3 | 7 | 1 | 0 | .909 |
| Willis, Rochester* | 32 | 4 | 23 | 3 | 2 | .900 |
| Keener, Memphis | 19 | 8 | 19 | 3 | 0 | .900 |
| Ruthven, Toledo | 23 | 6 | 29 | 4 | 3 | .897 |
| Galasso, Rochester | 30 | 10 | 24 | 4 | 1 | .895 |
| Hanna, Richmond | 26 | 3 | 30 | 4 | 0 | .892 |
| Jones, Charleston | 26 | 19 | 22 | 5 | 1 | .891 |
| Beard, Richmond* | 13 | 3 | 5 | 1 | 0 | .889 |
| Abraham, Memphis* | 12 | 4 | 4 | 1 | 0 | .889 |
| Patterson, Charleston | 10 | 4 | 4 | 1 | 0 | .889 |
| Martinez, Syracuse* | 14 | 13 | 10 | 3 | 0 | .885 |
| Freeman, Rich-Roc* | 34 | 5 | 10 | 2 | 1 | .882 |
| Contreras, Tidewater | 36 | 3 | 11 | 2 | 0 | .875 |
| Closter, Richmond* | 37 | 1 | 6 | 1 | 0 | .875 |
| Culver, Toledo | 17 | 4 | 3 | 1 | 1 | .875 |
| Wright, Pawtucket | 17 | 5 | 15 | 3 | 2 | .870 |
| Kiser, Toledo* | 31 | 3 | 15 | 3 | 0 | .857 |
| Cheadle, Syracuse* | 31 | 4 | 8 | 2 | 1 | .857 |
| Manz, Rochester | 36 | 2 | 4 | 1 | 1 | .857 |
| Kelley, Richmond | 29 | 3 | 12 | 4 | 1 | .789 |
| Woodson, Richmond | 21 | 1 | 8 | 3 | 0 | .750 |
| Johnson, Syracuse | 25 | 1 | 3 | 2 | 0 | .667 |
| Molush, Toledo | 20 | 0 | 2 | 1 | 0 | .667 |
| Riley, Memphis | 21 | 0 | 1 | 1 | 0 | .500 |

### (Fewer Than Ten Games)

| Player and Club | G. | PO. | A. | E. | DP. | Pct. |
|---|---|---|---|---|---|---|
| Farias, Pawtucket | 6 | 4 | 10 | 0 | 1 | 1.000 |
| Clay, Syracuse | 9 | 4 | 8 | 0 | 0 | 1.000 |
| Snyder, Rochester* | 9 | 1 | 7 | 0 | 0 | 1.000 |
| Bartlett, Tidewater | 4 | 1 | 4 | 0 | 1 | 1.000 |
| Christenson, Toledo | 2 | 0 | 4 | 0 | 0 | 1.000 |
| Diehl, Syracuse | 7 | 1 | 2 | 0 | 0 | 1.000 |
| Myrick, Tidewater* | 7 | 2 | 1 | 0 | 0 | 1.000 |
| Heinold, Syracuse | 1 | 1 | 1 | 0 | 0 | 1.000 |
| Beltran, Toledo | 8 | 1 | 0 | 0 | 0 | 1.000 |
| Juran, Tidewater* | 3 | 0 | 1 | 0 | 0 | 1.000 |
| Tyler, Tidewater | 2 | 0 | 1 | 0 | 0 | 1.000 |
| Parrott, Rochester | 2 | 0 | 1 | 0 | 0 | 1.000 |
| Alexander, Richmond | 1 | 0 | 1 | 0 | 0 | 1.000 |
| Warthen, Memphis* | 8 | 4 | 11 | 1 | 2 | .938 |
| Kavanagh, Charleston | 9 | 2 | 8 | 1 | 0 | .909 |
| Spencer, Pawtucket | 8 | 2 | 7 | 1 | 1 | .900 |
| Anderson, Charleston | 8 | 0 | 8 | 1 | 0 | .889 |
| Webb, Tidewater | 5 | 3 | 7 | 1 | 0 | .875 |
| Beattie, Syracuse | 5 | 0 | 5 | 1 | 0 | .833 |
| Moose, Charleston | 5 | 3 | 7 | 2 | 1 | .833 |
| Bomback, Pawtucket | 7 | 5 | 2 | 2 | 0 | .778 |
| Sandate, Toledo* | 7 | 1 | 1 | 1 | 0 | .667 |
| Lockwood, Tidewater | 3 | 0 | 1 | 1 | 0 | .000 |
| Fiore, Rochester* | 2 | 0 | 0 | 1 | 0 | .000 |

The following players do not have any recorded accepted chances at the positions indicated; therefore, are not listed in the fielding averages for those particular positions: Beall*, p; Castle*, p; Easterly*, p; Erickson, of; Hodges, 1b-of; Hughes, of; Hunter, ss; Iorg, 3b; Kenney, p; Kinard, of-p; Kleven, of; Koegel, p; Leshnock*, p; J. Martinez, p; McCartney, 3b; Navarrete, of; Nolan, 2b-of; Nordhagen, 3b; Pemberton*, p; Rajsich*, p; Sanserino, ss-of; Santana, p; Schneck*, p; Senn, of; Skaggs, 1b; Skidmore,, of; Smith*, p; Soderholm, 2b.

## CLUB PITCHING

| Club | G. | CG. | ShO. | Sv. | IP. | H. | R. | ER. | HR. | BB. | Int. BB. | HB. | SO. | WP. | Bk. | ERA. |
|------|-----|-----|------|-----|------|------|-----|-----|-----|-----|-----|-----|-----|-----|-----|------|
| Tidewater | 141 | 47 | 21 | 21 | 1188 | 1005 | 425 | 370 | 62 | 452 | 36 | 26 | 678 | 34 | 3 | 2.80 |
| Memphis | 140 | 35 | 13 | 24 | 1233 | 1129 | 509 | 404 | 71 | 447 | 40 | 21 | 683 | 46 | 5 | 2.95 |
| Rochester | 141 | 38 | 12 | 30 | 1200 | 1068 | 496 | 394 | 65 | 520 | 42 | 19 | 787 | 57 | 2 | 2.96 |
| Charleston | 139 | 39 | 13 | 22 | 1173 | 1053 | 535 | 436 | 70 | 498 | 29 | 31 | 786 | 68 | 2 | 3.35 |
| Pawtucket | 140 | 31 | 8 | 14 | 1204 | 1125 | 542 | 455 | 75 | 533 | 79 | 26 | 798 | 48 | 6 | 3.40 |
| Toledo | 140 | 36 | 9 | 23 | 1189 | 1173 | 568 | 460 | 83 | 463 | 63 | 23 | 788 | 55 | 4 | 3.48 |
| Richmond | 137 | 26 | 12 | 20 | 1129 | 1090 | 534 | 458 | 73 | 431 | 31 | 26 | 767 | 59 | 7 | 3.65 |
| Syracuse | 136 | 27 | 11 | 30 | 1158 | 1160 | 568 | 488 | 67 | 498 | 43 | 26 | 795 | 65 | 5 | 3.79 |

## PITCHERS' RECORDS

(Leading Qualifiers for Earned-Run Average Leadership—112 or More Innings)
*Throws lefthanded.

| Pitcher—Club | G. | GS. | CG. | ShO. | W. | L. | Sv. | Pct. | IP. | H. | R. | ER. | HR. | BB. | Int. BB. | HB. | SO. | WP. | ERA. |
|------|-----|-----|-----|------|-----|-----|-----|------|-----|-----|-----|-----|-----|-----|-----|-----|-----|-----|------|
| Torrealba, Rich* | 64 | 0 | 0 | 0 | 12 | 9 | 15 | .571 | 137 | 97 | 30 | 22 | 5 | 48 | 11 | 1 | 114 | 5 | 1.45 |
| Montague, Mem | 18 | 17 | 8 | 2 | 7 | 8 | 1 | .467 | 135 | 114 | 36 | 26 | 6 | 27 | 1 | 1 | 68 | 6 | 1.73 |
| Simpson, Toledo | 26 | 23 | 11 | 4 | 12 | 7 | 1 | .632 | 170 | 131 | 58 | 41 | 7 | 56 | 7 | 7 | 110 | 9 | 2.17 |
| Swan, Tidewater | 26 | 24 | 13 | 4 | 13 | 7 | 2 | .650 | 177 | 136 | 48 | 44 | 9 | 38 | 1 | 1 | 111 | 1 | 2.24 |
| Sawyer, Syracuse | 25 | 24 | 10 | 4 | 13 | 9 | 0 | .591 | 175 | 131 | 53 | 48 | 9 | 47 | 3 | 5 | 96 | 7 | 2.47 |
| Laxton, Tidewater* | 24 | 18 | 5 | 2 | 11 | 4 | 1 | .733 | 130 | 91 | 37 | 36 | 14 | 56 | 1 | 3 | 113 | 3 | 2.49 |
| Flanagan, Roch* | 27 | 25 | 10 | 4 | 13 | 4 | 0 | .765 | 173 | 155 | 58 | 48 | 8 | 56 | 3 | 1 | 135 | 5 | 2.50 |
| Willis, Rochester* | 32 | 25 | 7 | 3 | 14 | 8 | 2 | .636 | 175 | 151 | 71 | 50 | 12 | 54 | 2 | 2 | 84 | 6 | 2.57 |
| Espinosa, Tidewater | 24 | 21 | 8 | 2 | 8 | 5 | 2 | .615 | 141 | 127 | 48 | 41 | 6 | 38 | 5 | 2 | 83 | 3 | 2.62 |
| Jones, Charleston | 26 | 26 | 8 | 3 | 14 | 9 | 0 | .609 | 188 | 133 | 67 | 56 | 10 | 88 | 1 | 4 | 157 | 9 | 2.68 |

Departmental Leaders: G—M. Barr, 70; GS—Aase, 29; CG—Swan, 13; ShO—Flanagan, Sawyer, Simpson, Swan, 4; W—Jones, Willis, 14; L—Kreuger, 15; Sv—Torrealba, 15; Pct.—Flanagan, .765; IP—Jones, 188; H—Kirkpatrick, 183; R—Sterling, 86; ER—Figueroa, 76; HR—Mahler, Sterling, 15; BB—Hanna, 92; IBB—M. Barr, 18; HB—Simpson, 8; SO—Jones, 157; WP—S. Barr, Lang, 16.

(All Pitchers—Listed Alphabetically)

| Pitcher—Club | G. | GS. | CG. | ShO. | W. | L. | Sv. | Pct. | IP. | H. | R. | ER. | HR. | BB. | Int. BB. | HB. | SO. | WP. | ERA. |
|------|-----|-----|-----|------|-----|-----|-----|------|-----|-----|-----|-----|-----|-----|-----|-----|-----|-----|------|
| Aase, Pawtucket | 29 | 29 | 7 | 3 | 8 | 13 | 0 | .381 | 186 | 173 | 85 | 75 | 9 | 88 | 6 | 3 | 125 | 5 | 3.63 |
| Abraham, Mem* | 12 | 4 | 0 | 0 | 0 | 2 | 1 | .000 | 25 | 29 | 28 | 26 | 5 | 22 | 1 | 1 | 21 | 1 | 9.36 |
| Albin, Memphis | 25 | 14 | 4 | 2 | 8 | 3 | 1 | .727 | 107 | 107 | 35 | 28 | 4 | 23 | 2 | 1 | 38 | 4 | 2.36 |
| Alexander, Rich | 1 | 1 | 0 | 0 | 0 | 0 | 0 | .000 | 4 | 6 | 1 | 1 | 0 | 5 | 0 | 0 | 0 | 1 | 2.25 |
| Anderson, Char | 8 | 5 | 1 | 0 | 1 | 4 | 0 | .200 | 37 | 40 | 29 | 24 | 4 | 21 | 1 | 0 | 19 | 1 | 5.84 |
| Atkinson, Memphis | 49 | 3 | 1 | 1 | 3 | 4 | 5 | .429 | 106 | 94 | 38 | 33 | 9 | 36 | 6 | 1 | 72 | 1 | 2.80 |
| Babcock, Roch | 10 | 1 | 0 | 0 | 2 | 2 | 1 | .500 | 26 | 27 | 16 | 14 | 1 | 13 | 0 | 2 | 11 | 0 | 4.85 |
| Bair, Charleston | 26 | 26 | 7 | 3 | 9 | 12 | 0 | .429 | 167 | 157 | 72 | 56 | 5 | 58 | 3 | 2 | 113 | 13 | 3.02 |
| M. Barr, Paw | 70 | 1 | 0 | 0 | 6 | 9 | 4 | .400 | 120 | 107 | 45 | 37 | 9 | 41 | 18 | 4 | 59 | 2 | 2.78 |
| S. Barr, Paw* | 23 | 22 | 7 | 1 | 6 | 12 | 0 | .333 | 148 | 128 | 65 | 48 | 6 | 80 | 7 | 4 | 110 | 16 | 2.92 |
| Bartlett, Tide | 4 | 2 | 1 | 0 | 1 | 1 | 0 | .000 | 12 | 12 | 5 | 4 | 0 | 7 | 0 | 0 | 4 | 0 | 3.00 |
| Beall, Roch* | 1 | 0 | 0 | 0 | 0 | 0 | 0 | .000 | ¼ | 0 | 0 | 0 | 0 | 0 | 0 | 0 | 0 | 0 | 0.00 |
| Beard, Rich* | 13 | 0 | 0 | 0 | 2 | 1 | 0 | .667 | 23 | 20 | 9 | 8 | 0 | 9 | 0 | 0 | 16 | 0 | 2.88 |
| Beattie, Syr | 5 | 5 | 0 | 0 | 2 | 2 | 0 | .500 | 33 | 25 | 14 | 12 | 3 | 21 | 1 | 1 | 30 | 3 | 3.27 |
| Beltran, Toledo | 8 | 0 | 0 | 0 | 1 | 0 | 0 | .000 | 13 | 17 | 9 | 9 | 0 | 4 | 1 | 0 | 8 | 0 | 6.23 |
| Bernard, Tide | 27 | 22 | 6 | 3 | 9 | 9 | 0 | .500 | 126 | 96 | 51 | 46 | 5 | 77 | 4 | 3 | 70 | 2 | 3.29 |
| Bomback, Paw | 7 | 7 | 0 | 0 | 0 | 4 | 0 | .000 | 39 | 43 | 29 | 29 | 7 | 21 | 2 | 0 | 37 | 0 | 6.69 |
| Burton, Paw* | 12 | 12 | 8 | 2 | 8 | 2 | 0 | .800 | 94 | 51 | 20 | 16 | 5 | 32 | 2 | 1 | 73 | 1 | 1.53 |
| Candelaria, Char* | 10 | 9 | 4 | 3 | 7 | 1 | 1 | .875 | 61 | 53 | 15 | 12 | 5 | 17 | 0 | 1 | 48 | 1 | 1.77 |
| Carrithers, Mem | 12 | 9 | 4 | 2 | 3 | 5 | 0 | .375 | 70 | 62 | 28 | 18 | 2 | 17 | 1 | 3 | 34 | 2 | 2.31 |
| Caskey, Char* | 31 | 1 | 0 | 0 | 2 | 1 | 2 | .667 | 43 | 49 | 36 | 29 | 2 | 24 | 2 | 4 | 26 | 2 | 6.07 |
| Castle, Syracuse | 1 | 0 | 0 | 0 | 0 | 0 | 0 | .000 | 1 | 6 | 7 | 6 | 0 | 3 | 0 | 0 | 1 | 1 | 54.00 |
| Cheadle, Syracuse* | 31 | 10 | 0 | 0 | 2 | 6 | 0 | .250 | 81 | 96 | 54 | 52 | 6 | 53 | 4 | 5 | 64 | 6 | 5.78 |
| Christenson, Tol | 2 | 2 | 0 | 0 | 2 | 0 | 0 | 1.000 | 12 | 5 | 0 | 0 | 0 | 3 | 0 | 0 | 10 | 0 | 0.00 |
| Clay, Syracuse | 2 | 2 | 0 | 0 | 0 | 2 | 0 | .375 | 48 | 60 | 34 | 32 | 6 | 27 | 1 | 2 | 32 | 4 | 6.00 |
| Clemons, Paw* | 66 | 0 | 0 | 0 | 6 | 4 | 3 | .600 | 70 | 65 | 35 | 29 | 2 | 31 | 12 | 2 | 39 | 4 | 3.73 |
| Closter, Rich* | 37 | 4 | 1 | 0 | 2 | 4 | 3 | .333 | 83 | 73 | 33 | 29 | 4 | 32 | 2 | 6 | 57 | 7 | 3.14 |
| Contreras, Tide | 36 | 1 | 0 | 0 | 3 | 4 | 1 | .429 | 60 | 49 | 18 | 13 | 2 | 35 | 6 | 4 | 40 | 2 | 1.95 |
| Cram, Tidewater | 31 | 0 | 0 | 0 | 8 | 1 | 3 | .889 | 50 | 43 | 20 | 16 | 2 | 16 | 5 | 1 | 24 | 2 | 2.88 |
| Culver, Toledo | 17 | 6 | 0 | 0 | 1 | 5 | 0 | .167 | 51 | 66 | 35 | 22 | 1 | 23 | 2 | 3 | 19 | 1 | 3.88 |
| Devine, Richmond | 27 | 24 | 6 | 1 | 10 | 6 | 0 | .625 | 148 | 148 | 55 | 49 | 6 | 51 | 2 | 2 | 82 | 4 | 2.98 |
| Diehl, Syracuse | 7 | 0 | 0 | 0 | 0 | 0 | 0 | .000 | 15 | 15 | 7 | 7 | 1 | 5 | 1 | 0 | 7 | 1 | 4.20 |
| Diorio, Memphis | 31 | 0 | 0 | 0 | 2 | 5 | 3 | .286 | 48 | 45 | 22 | 13 | 0 | 17 | 8 | 1 | 28 | 0 | 2.44 |
| Easterly, Rich* | 2 | 2 | 0 | 0 | 1 | 1 | 0 | .500 | 10 | 11 | 3 | 2 | 0 | 6 | 0 | 4 | 1 | 0 | 1.80 |
| Enyart, Memphis* | 29 | 0 | 0 | 0 | 2 | 2 | 5 | .500 | 40 | 43 | 26 | 23 | 8 | 21 | 2 | 1 | 34 | 2 | 5.18 |
| Espinosa, Tide | 24 | 21 | 8 | 2 | 8 | 5 | 2 | .615 | 141 | 127 | 48 | 41 | 6 | 38 | 5 | 2 | 83 | 3 | 2.62 |
| Farias, Paw | 6 | 6 | 0 | 0 | 2 | 2 | 0 | .500 | 39 | 34 | 18 | 17 | 5 | 23 | 4 | 1 | 30 | 0 | 3.92 |
| Figueroa, Rich* | 26 | 23 | 2 | 0 | 7 | 12 | 0 | .368 | 120 | 144 | 82 | 76 | 12 | 72 | 6 | 3 | 59 | 11 | 5.70 |

| Pitcher—Club | G. | GS. | CG. | ShO. | W. | L. | Sv. | Pct. | IP. | H. | R. | ER. | HR. | BB. | Int. BB. | HB. | SO. | WP. | ERA. |
|---|---|---|---|---|---|---|---|---|---|---|---|---|---|---|---|---|---|---|---|
| Fiore, Roch* | 2 | 0 | 0 | 0 | 0 | 0 | 0 | .000 | 4 | 2 | 1 | 1 | 0 | 0 | 0 | 0 | 0 | 0 | 2.25 |
| Flanagan, Roch* | 27 | 25 | 10 | 4 | 13 | 4 | 0 | .765 | 173 | 155 | 58 | 48 | 8 | 56 | 3 | 1 | 135 | 5 | 2.50 |
| Freeman, 1 Rich-33 Roch* | 34 | 15 | 2 | 0 | 7 | 6 | 1 | .538 | 115 | 109 | 61 | 40 | 6 | 77 | 7 | 2 | 95 | 8 | 3.13 |
| Galasso, Roch | 30 | 22 | 5 | 0 | 9 | 7 | 0 | .563 | 155 | 135 | 55 | 49 | 5 | 88 | 3 | 4 | 68 | 13 | 2.85 |
| Gardner, Sy* | 10 | 0 | 0 | 0 | 0 | 1 | 2 | .000 | 13 | 8 | 3 | 3 | 1 | 10 | 0 | 0 | 2 | 0 | 2.08 |
| Gebhard, Memphis | 44 | 0 | 0 | 0 | 4 | 3 | 4 | .571 | 64 | 55 | 21 | 19 | 6 | 21 | 7 | 1 | 41 | 2 | 2.67 |
| Guidry, Syracuse* | 42 | 0 | 0 | 0 | 6 | 5 | 14 | .545 | 62 | 46 | 24 | 20 | 0 | 37 | 5 | 0 | 76 | 3 | 2.90 |
| Hanna, Richmond | 26 | 25 | 5 | 3 | 10 | 10 | 0 | .500 | 141 | 125 | 73 | 62 | 6 | 92 | 1 | 4 | 101 | 2 | 3.96 |
| Heinold, Syracuse | 1 | 1 | 0 | 0 | 0 | 1 | 0 | .000 | 6 | 8 | 3 | 3 | 0 | 1 | 0 | 0 | 0 | 0 | 4.50 |
| Hernaiz, Toledo | 59 | 1 | 0 | 0 | 5 | 8 | 6 | .385 | 106 | 117 | 57 | 46 | 9 | 47 | 15 | 1 | 61 | 4 | 3.91 |
| Hernandez, Toledo* | 13 | 13 | 4 | 0 | 6 | 4 | 0 | .600 | 80 | 86 | 43 | 29 | 3 | 26 | 4 | 0 | 46 | 4 | 3.26 |
| Hill, Toledo* | 29 | 23 | 4 | 0 | 10 | 11 | 0 | .476 | 149 | 147 | 71 | 68 | 9 | 64 | 5 | 3 | 89 | 8 | 4.11 |
| Holdsworth, Roch | 19 | 18 | 4 | 0 | 4 | 9 | 0 | .308 | 111 | 99 | 49 | 40 | 8 | 43 | 2 | 4 | 99 | 4 | 3.24 |
| Hopkins, Char* | 13 | 0 | 0 | 0 | 0 | 0 | 1 | .000 | 17 | 21 | 15 | 9 | 2 | 6 | 1 | 2 | 13 | 1 | 4.76 |
| Jimenez, Char | 40 | 8 | 2 | 1 | 7 | 3 | 3 | .700 | 104 | 105 | 37 | 35 | 4 | 26 | 7 | 2 | 51 | 2 | 3.03 |
| Johnson, Rochester | 28 | 0 | 0 | 0 | 3 | 1 | 5 | .750 | 46 | 54 | 35 | 29 | 9 | 25 | 2 | 0 | 39 | 1 | 5.67 |
| Johnson, Syracuse | 25 | 3 | 0 | 0 | 3 | 3 | 1 | .500 | 57 | 65 | 34 | 33 | 10 | 17 | 2 | 3 | 41 | 6 | 5.21 |
| Jones, Charleston | 26 | 26 | 8 | 3 | 14 | 9 | 0 | .609 | 188 | 133 | 67 | 56 | 10 | 98 | 1 | 4 | 157 | 9 | 2.68 |
| Juran, Tidewater* | 3 | 0 | 0 | 0 | 0 | 0 | 0 | .000 | 5 | 6 | 5 | 4 | 1 | 3 | 0 | 0 | 5 | 0 | 7.20 |
| Kammeyer, Syr | 27 | 24 | 5 | 1 | 9 | 10 | 0 | .474 | 144 | 175 | 89 | 70 | 9 | 42 | 4 | 2 | 52 | 8 | 4.38 |
| Kavanagh, Char | 9 | 4 | 0 | 0 | 1 | 1 | 1 | .500 | 36 | 42 | 27 | 24 | 8 | 22 | 1 | 0 | 25 | 3 | 6.00 |
| Keener, Memphis | 19 | 18 | 2 | 1 | 7 | 5 | 0 | .583 | 101 | 106 | 51 | 41 | 6 | 25 | 0 | 0 | 49 | 4 | 3.65 |
| Kelley, Richmond | 29 | 8 | 1 | 1 | 1 | 7 | 0 | .125 | 86 | 82 | 43 | 36 | 7 | 41 | 1 | 0 | 58 | 6 | 3.77 |
| Kenney, Syracuse | 1 | 0 | 0 | 0 | 0 | 0 | 0 | .000 | 2 | 0 | 0 | 0 | 0 | 0 | 0 | 0 | 0 | 0 | 0.00 |
| Kinard, Memphis | 1 | 0 | 0 | 0 | 0 | 0 | 0 | .000 | 1 | 0 | 0 | 0 | 0 | 0 | 0 | 0 | 0 | 0 | 0.00 |
| Kirkpatrick, Mem | 27 | 25 | 3 | 0 | 11 | 8 | 1 | .579 | 166 | 183 | 77 | 61 | 11 | 29 | 3 | 4 | 67 | 0 | 3.31 |
| Kiser, Toledo* | 16 | 15 | 3 | 0 | 3 | 7 | 0 | .300 | 99 | 99 | 41 | 31 | 7 | 41 | 5 | 1 | 73 | 9 | 2.82 |
| Koegel, Charleston | 3 | 0 | 0 | 0 | 0 | 0 | 0 | .000 | 5 | 5 | 3 | 3 | 0 | 3 | 0 | 0 | 4 | 1 | 5.40 |
| Kouns, Pawtucket | 27 | 4 | 0 | 0 | 3 | 2 | 1 | .600 | 59 | 58 | 23 | 23 | 2 | 32 | 3 | 0 | 27 | 1 | 3.51 |
| Kreuger, Paw* | 33 | 23 | 5 | 1 | 6 | 15 | 1 | .286 | 165 | 177 | 71 | 62 | 13 | 50 | 6 | 2 | 107 | 7 | 3.38 |
| LaCorte, Rich | 24 | 24 | 3 | 0 | 9 | 7 | 0 | .563 | 128 | 121 | 65 | 61 | 11 | 71 | 2 | 2 | 108 | 16 | 4.29 |
| Lang, Memphis | 31 | 27 | 6 | 1 | 8 | 13 | 0 | .381 | 181 | 151 | 75 | 60 | 6 | 81 | 6 | 3 | 98 | 16 | 2.93 |
| Langford, Char | 13 | 8 | 3 | 0 | 7 | 2 | 0 | .778 | 65 | 55 | 26 | 24 | 3 | 20 | 0 | 0 | 41 | 3 | 3.32 |
| Laxton, Tide* | 24 | 18 | 5 | 2 | 11 | 4 | 1 | .733 | 130 | 91 | 37 | 36 | 14 | 56 | 1 | 3 | 113 | 3 | 2.49 |
| Leshnock, Char* | 2 | 0 | 0 | 0 | 0 | 0 | 0 | .000 | 5 | 8 | 4 | 4 | 0 | 1 | 0 | 0 | 3 | 1 | 10.80 |
| Lockwood, Tide | 3 | 0 | 0 | 0 | 1 | 0 | 0 | 1.000 | 5 | 4 | 0 | 0 | 0 | 1 | 1 | 0 | 5 | 0 | 0.00 |
| Mahler, Rich* | 27 | 26 | 8 | 2 | 6 | 14 | 0 | .300 | 166 | 167 | 82 | 71 | 15 | 70 | 6 | 6 | 129 | 9 | 3.85 |
| Manderbach, Tide* | 23 | 22 | 5 | 1 | 8 | 9 | 0 | .471 | 135 | 124 | 59 | 51 | 5 | 57 | 2 | 1 | 65 | 9 | 3.40 |
| Manz, Roch | 36 | 1 | 0 | 0 | 6 | 5 | 8 | .545 | 49 | 56 | 26 | 26 | 4 | 18 | 5 | 0 | 19 | 2 | 4.78 |
| Martinez, Syr* | 14 | 14 | 4 | 1 | 8 | 2 | 0 | .800 | 110 | 91 | 39 | 25 | 3 | 35 | 3 | 0 | 105 | 5 | 2.05 |
| Martinez, Roch | 2 | 0 | 0 | 0 | 0 | 0 | 0 | .000 | 5 | 7 | 4 | 3 | 0 | 2 | 0 | 0 | 4 | 1 | 5.40 |
| McGregor, Syr* | 21 | 20 | 5 | 2 | 6 | 9 | 0 | .400 | 124 | 134 | 73 | 55 | 2 | 60 | 3 | 2 | 72 | 6 | 3.99 |
| Miller, Roch | 19 | 1 | 0 | 0 | 5 | 0 | 7 | 1.000 | 41 | 24 | 10 | 10 | 0 | 25 | 3 | 0 | 38 | 1 | 2.20 |
| Minshall, Char | 45 | 0 | 0 | 0 | 3 | 4 | 10 | .429 | 65 | 35 | 12 | 10 | 3 | 39 | 4 | 5 | 64 | 8 | 1.38 |
| Mitchell, Roch | 14 | 14 | 5 | 3 | 10 | 1 | 0 | .909 | 96 | 73 | 31 | 22 | 6 | 19 | 0 | 1 | 78 | 4 | 2.06 |
| Molush, Toledo | 20 | 0 | 0 | 0 | 2 | 2 | 2 | .500 | 22 | 16 | 9 | 7 | 1 | 10 | 3 | 0 | 20 | 1 | 2.86 |
| Montague, Mem | 18 | 17 | 8 | 2 | 7 | 8 | 1 | .467 | 135 | 114 | 36 | 26 | 6 | 27 | 1 | 1 | 68 | 6 | 1.73 |
| Moore, Mem* | 14 | 3 | 0 | 0 | 1 | 3 | 0 | .250 | 27 | 17 | 14 | 12 | 0 | 45 | 0 | 0 | 19 | 4 | 4.00 |
| Moose, Paw | 5 | 5 | 2 | 0 | 2 | 2 | 0 | .500 | 36 | 41 | 16 | 13 | 1 | 6 | 0 | 0 | 15 | 0 | 3.25 |
| Morlan, Char | 22 | 21 | 6 | 0 | 8 | 12 | 0 | .400 | 134 | 127 | 68 | 51 | 11 | 65 | 5 | 2 | 85 | 8 | 3.43 |
| Myrick, Tide* | 7 | 0 | 0 | 0 | 3 | 0 | 0 | 1.000 | 11 | 7 | 0 | 0 | 0 | 2 | 2 | 1 | 9 | 0 | 0.00 |
| Newhauser, Paw | 66 | 0 | 0 | 0 | 4 | 7 | 5 | .364 | 80 | 74 | 34 | 31 | 4 | 52 | 6 | 4 | 79 | 9 | 3.49 |
| Pagan, Syra | 15 | 2 | 0 | 0 | 5 | 1 | 5 | .833 | 32 | 31 | 8 | 8 | 0 | 15 | 3 | 0 | 32 | 0 | 2.25 |
| Parrott, Roch | 2 | 0 | 0 | 0 | 1 | 0 | 0 | 1.000 | 2 | 1 | 0 | 0 | 0 | 2 | 0 | 1 | 2 | 0 | 0.00 |
| Patterson, Char | 1 | 0 | 0 | 0 | 0 | 0 | 0 | .000 | 6 | 18 | 13 | 12 | 1 | 8 | 1 | 0 | 8 | 1 | 6.00 |
| Paul, Toledo* | 45 | 6 | 0 | 0 | 3 | 4 | 0 | .429 | 79 | 95 | 45 | 41 | 8 | 16 | 6 | 3 | 60 | 3 | 4.67 |
| Pemberton, Tide* | 1 | 0 | 0 | 0 | 0 | 0 | 0 | .000 | 1 | 3 | 1 | 1 | 0 | 0 | 0 | 0 | 1 | 0 | 9.00 |
| Pirtle, Syr | 61 | 0 | 0 | 0 | 7 | 3 | 8 | .700 | 100 | 93 | 38 | 30 | 4 | 39 | 5 | 5 | 83 | 2 | 2.70 |
| Rajsich, Syr* | 4 | 0 | 0 | 0 | 0 | 0 | 0 | .000 | 8 | 22 | 15 | 12 | 1 | 3 | 1 | 2 | 6 | 0 | 13.50 |
| Ricks, Syracuse | 26 | 24 | 1 | 1 | 8 | 7 | 0 | .533 | 149 | 148 | 82 | 72 | 12 | 83 | 7 | 6 | 98 | 12 | 4.35 |
| Riley, Mem | 21 | 0 | 0 | 0 | 1 | 4 | 3 | .200 | 28 | 24 | 15 | 13 | 3 | 23 | 1 | 1 | 19 | 2 | 4.18 |
| Robson, Roch | 13 | 0 | 0 | 0 | 1 | 2 | 0 | .333 | 25 | 21 | 7 | 6 | 1 | 7 | 1 | 0 | 15 | 0 | 2.16 |
| Ross, Paw* | 13 | 13 | 2 | 1 | 2 | 6 | 0 | .250 | 74 | 75 | 44 | 32 | 5 | 23 | 1 | 1 | 32 | 0 | 3.89 |
| Ruthven, Toledo | 23 | 23 | 10 | 3 | 10 | 12 | 0 | .455 | 153 | 148 | 72 | 54 | 9 | 69 | 5 | 1 | 144 | 2 | 3.18 |
| Sadowski, Char | 27 | 21 | 4 | 3 | 6 | 12 | 0 | .333 | 126 | 124 | 70 | 58 | 9 | 76 | 1 | 6 | 70 | 9 | 4.14 |
| Sandate, Tol* | 7 | 5 | 0 | 0 | 1 | 3 | 1 | .250 | 30 | 38 | 19 | 14 | 5 | 8 | 0 | 0 | 22 | 2 | 4.20 |
| Sanders, Tide | 27 | 0 | 0 | 0 | 6 | 1 | 9 | .857 | 47 | 39 | 9 | 7 | 1 | 8 | 2 | 2 | 29 | 2 | 1.34 |
| Santana, Tol | 3 | 0 | 0 | 0 | 0 | 0 | 0 | .000 | 7 | 3 | 1 | 1 | 1 | 3 | 0 | 0 | 3 | 0 | 1.29 |
| Sawyer, Syr | 25 | 24 | 10 | 4 | 13 | 9 | 0 | .591 | 175 | 134 | 53 | 48 | 9 | 47 | 3 | 3 | 96 | 7 | 2.47 |
| Schneck, Toledo* | 1 | 0 | 0 | 0 | 0 | 0 | 0 | .000 | 2 | 2 | 2 | 2 | 0 | 3 | 0 | 0 | 1 | 0 | 9.00 |
| Sekel, Roch | 29 | 0 | 0 | 0 | 1 | 6 | 4 | .143 | 55 | 47 | 21 | 14 | 0 | 18 | 4 | 1 | 32 | 3 | 2.29 |
| Simpson, Tol | 26 | 23 | 11 | 4 | 12 | 7 | 1 | .632 | 170 | 131 | 58 | 41 | 7 | 56 | 7 | 8 | 110 | 9 | 2.17 |
| Smith, Roch* | 2 | 0 | 0 | 0 | 0 | 2 | 0 | .000 | 3 | 6 | 3 | 3 | 0 | 1 | 1 | 0 | 2 | 0 | 9.00 |
| Snyder, Roch* | 9 | 0 | 0 | 0 | 1 | 1 | 1 | .500 | 21 | 18 | 9 | 8 | 1 | 19 | 2 | 0 | 14 | 3 | 3.43 |
| Spencer, Paw | 8 | 6 | 0 | 0 | 1 | 1 | 0 | .500 | 39 | 39 | 18 | 15 | 2 | 15 | 3 | 1 | 19 | 0 | 3.46 |
| Stanhouse, Mem | 13 | 12 | 5 | 2 | 6 | 5 | 0 | .545 | 80 | 67 | 27 | 17 | 1 | 30 | 1 | 1 | 47 | 2 | 1.91 |
| Stein, Roch | 21 | 19 | 5 | 0 | 8 | 2 | 1 | .800 | 110 | 91 | 47 | 38 | 3 | 62 | 5 | 2 | 59 | 6 | 3.11 |
| Stephenson, Rich* | 23 | 0 | 0 | 0 | 2 | 1 | 1 | .667 | 47 | 52 | 28 | 16 | 1 | 20 | 3 | 2 | 21 | 5 | 3.06 |

| Pitcher—Club | G. | GS. | CG. | ShO. | W. | L. | Sv. | Pct. | IP. | H. | R. | ER. | HR. | BB. | Int. BB. | HB. | SO. | WP. | ERA. |
|---|---|---|---|---|---|---|---|---|---|---|---|---|---|---|---|---|---|---|---|
| Sterling, Tide ... | 29 | 28 | 7 | 2 | 10 | 11 | 1 | .476 | 179 | 178 | 86 | 71 | 15 | 50 | 4 | 4 | 64 | 2 | 3.57 |
| Swan, Tide ...... | 26 | 24 | 13 | 4 | 13 | 7 | 2 | .650 | 177 | 136 | 48 | 44 | 9 | 38 | 1 | 1 | 111 | 1 | 2.24 |
| Tekulve, Char.... | 24 | 5 | 2 | 0 | 5 | 4 | 4 | .556 | 71 | 47 | 23 | 14 | 2 | 19 | 2 | 3 | 46 | 5 | 1.77 |
| Roy Thomas, Tol.. | 19 | 18 | 4 | 0 | 4 | 9 | 0 | .308 | 119 | 112 | 63 | 53 | 13 | 49 | 6 | 3 | 95 | 8 | 4.01 |
| Thomason, Tol ... | 39 | 5 | 0 | 0 | 1 | 5 | 10 | .167 | 82 | 78 | 39 | 34 | 5 | 35 | 4 | 0 | 47 | 3 | 3.73 |
| Torrealba, Rich*.. | 64 | 0 | 0 | 0 | 12 | 9 | 15 | .571 | 137 | 97 | 30 | 22 | 5 | 48 | 11 | 1 | 114 | 5 | 1.45 |
| Tyler, Tide ...... | 2 | 1 | 1 | 0 | 0 | 2 | 0 | .000 | 6 | 7 | 5 | 5 | 0 | 3 | 1 | 0 | 2 | 0 | 7.50 |
| Wallace, Tol ... | 13 | 0 | 0 | 0 | 2 | 0 | 3 | 1.000 | 18 | 15 | 8 | 8 | 5 | 7 | 0 | 0 | 12 | 1 | 4.00 |
| Warthen, Mem*.. | 8 | 8 | 2 | 0 | 2 | 5 | 0 | .286 | 54 | 32 | 16 | 14 | 4 | 30 | 1 | 2 | 48 | 0 | 2.33 |
| Webb, Tide ...... | 3 | 2 | 1 | 1 | 1 | 0 | 0 | 1.000 | 15 | 9 | 1 | 1 | 0 | 6 | 0 | 0 | 6 | 1 | 0.60 |
| Wegener, Tide | 41 | 0 | 0 | 0 | 5 | 1 | 1 | .833 | 88 | 78 | 32 | 30 | 2 | 55 | 2 | 4 | 47 | 7 | 3.07 |
| Willis, Roch* .... | 32 | 25 | 7 | 3 | 14 | 8 | 2 | .636 | 175 | 151 | 71 | 50 | 12 | 54 | 2 | 2 | 84 | 6 | 2.57 |
| Woodson, Rich ... | 21 | 0 | 0 | 0 | 0 | 3 | 0 | .000 | 32 | 42 | 24 | 20 | 6 | 10 | 1 | 0 | 15 | 2 | 5.63 |
| Wright, Paw ...... | 17 | 17 | 1 | 0 | 1 | 10 | 0 | .091 | 102 | 105 | 51 | 40 | 6 | 46 | 9 | 3 | 69 | 3 | 3.53 |

BALKS—Abraham, M. Barr, Devine, 3 each; McGregor, 2; Aase, Bair, S. Barr, Beard, Beattie, Contreras, Espinosa, Figueroa, Freeman, Hernaiz, Hill, Holdsworth, Jones, Kammeyer, Kiser, LaCorte, Manderbach, Montague, Pirtle, Riley, Simpson, Woodson, Wright, 1 each.

COMBINATION SHUTOUTS—Warthen-Gebhard, Lang-Enyart, Memphis; LaCorte-Torrealba 2, Devine-Closter, Figueroa-Torrealba, Hanna-Torrealba, Richmond; Flanagan-Johnson, Holdsworth-Johnson, Rochester; Martinez-Guidry, Kammeyer-Guidry, Syracuse; Laxton-Cram 3, Bernard-Sanders 2, Espinosa-Bernard-Sanders, Tidewater; Paul-Wallace, Christenson-Wallace, Toledo.

NO-HIT GAMES—Burton, Pawtucket, defeated Tidewater, 2-0, June 8; Simpson, Toledo, defeated Syracuse, 3-0, June 20 (seven innings).

# INTERNATIONAL LEAGUE HALL OF FAME

◆◆◆

| | | |
|---|---|---|
| John Berly | Rube Parnham | Herb Pennock |
| Jack Bentley | Charley Keller | Dick Porter |
| Bruno Betzel | Billy Kelly | Pat Powers |
| Joe Boley | Ernest J. Lanigan | Jimmy Ripple |
| Ike Boone | Fritz Maisel | Jackie Robinson |
| Joe Brown | Al Mamaux | Dick Rudolph |
| Ollie Carnegie | William J. Manley | Ben Sankey |
| Rip Collins | Joe McCarthy | George Selkirk |
| Estel Crabtree | Frank McGowan | Frank Shaughnessy |
| Jack Dunn | Fred Merkle | Harry Smythe |
| George Earnshaw | Bill Meyer | Billy Southworth |
| Jewel Ens | Howard Moss | George Stallings |
| Luke Hamlin | William J. Murray | Tommy Thomas |
| Ed Holly | Glenn Nelson | George Toporcer |
| Dan Howley | Jack Ogden | Dixie Walker |
| Fred Hutchinson | Steve O'Neill | Jimmy Walsh |
| Merwin Jacobson | Ed Onslow | George Wiltse |

# Mexican League

## CLASS AAA

| Leading Batter | League President | Leading Pitcher |
|---|---|---|
| PAT BOURQUE | ANTONIO RAMIREZ M. | RICARDO SANDATE |
| Mexico City Reds | | Poza Rica |

### CHAMPIONSHIP WINNERS IN PREVIOUS YEARS

| | | |
|---|---|---|
| 1955—Mexico City Tigers* .539 | 1962—Monterrey ......... .592 | Mexico City Reds ... .607 |
| 1956—Mexico City Reds .. .692 | 1963—Puebla ........... .606 | 1971—Jalisco§ .......... .558 |
| 1957—Yucatan .......... .567 | 1964—Mexico City Reds .. .586 | Saltillo ............ .593 |
| Mex. C. Reds (2nd)† .550 | 1965—Mexico City Tigers . .590 | 1972—Saltillo ........... .636 |
| 1958—Nuevo Laredo ...... .625 | 1966—Mexico City Tigers‡ .614 | Cordoba§ .......... .541 |
| 1959—Poza Rica ........ .575 | Mexico City Reds .. .571 | 1973—Saltillo ........... .656 |
| Mex. C. Reds (3rd)† .507 | 1967—Jalisco ........... .607 | Mexico City Reds x .590 |
| 1960—Mexico City Tigers . .538 | 1968—Mexico City Reds .. .586 | 1974—Jalisco ........... .627 |
| 1961—Veracruz .......... .575 | 1969—Reynosa .......... .591 | Mexico City Reds x .551 |
| | 1970—Aguila§ .......... .580 | |

*Defeated Nuevo Laredo, two games to none, in playoff for pennant.  †Won four-team playoff
†Won split-season playoff.  §League divided into Northern, Southern divisions: won two-team playoff.
xLeague divided into Northern, Southern Zones; sub-divided into Eastern, Western Divisions; won
eight-team playoff.

### STANDING OF CLUBS AT CLOSE OF SEASON, AUGUST 3

#### SOUTHERN ZONE

#### EASTERN DIVISION

| Club | Cor. | MR. | PR. | Vil. | Pue. | Jal. | MT. | Ags. | Tam. | Mon. | Rey. | Coa. | Sal. | UL. | Chi. | Jua. | W. | L. | T. | Pct. | G.B. |
|---|---|---|---|---|---|---|---|---|---|---|---|---|---|---|---|---|---|---|---|---|---|
| Cordoba ... | .. | 7 | 10 | 8 | 6 | 5 | 5 | 6 | 4 | 4 | 5 | 6 | 3 | 7 | 6 | | 87 | 47 | 3 | .649 | .. |
| Mexico Reds | 6 | .. | 8 | 8 | 2 | 5 | 5 | 5 | 3 | 5 | 6 | 5 | 4 | 7 | 6 | 5 | 80 | 57 | 2 | .584 | 8½ |
| Poza Rica .. | 4 | 6 | .. | 8 | 6 | 5 | 4 | 3 | 4 | 5 | 4 | 3 | 4 | 2 | 5 | | 68 | 67 | 3 | .504 | 19½ |
| Villahermosa | 6 | 6 | 4 | .. | 3 | 3 | 6 | 3 | 1 | 3 | 3 | 5 | 5 | 1 | 4 | 3 | 56 | 76 | 2 | .424 | 30 |

#### WESTERN DIVISION

| Club | Cor. | MR. | PR. | Vil. | Pue. | Jal. | MT. | Ags. | Tam. | Mon. | Rey. | Coa. | Sal. | UL. | Chi. | Jua. | W. | L. | T. | Pct. | G.B. |
|---|---|---|---|---|---|---|---|---|---|---|---|---|---|---|---|---|---|---|---|---|---|
| Puebla .... | 2 | 6 | 2 | 5 | .. | 5 | 5 | 8 | 5 | 8 | 6 | 4 | 5 | 5 | 6 | 8 | 80 | 58 | 0 | .580 | .... |
| Jalisco .... | 3 | 3 | 3 | 5 | 9 | .. | 10 | 9 | 2 | 5 | 4 | 5 | 4 | 5 | 2 | 4 | 73 | 61 | 2 | .545 | 5 |
| Mex. Tigers | 2 | 3 | 4 | 2 | 9 | 3 | .. | 12 | 5 | 1 | 5 | 2 | 2 | 5 | 4 | 5 | 64 | 72 | 0 | .471 | 15 |
| Aguascalien. | 2 | 3 | 3 | 4 | 6 | 5 | 2 | .. | 4 | 1 | 4 | 6 | 1 | 3 | 2 | 5 | 51 | 85 | 1 | .375 | 28 |

## NORTHERN ZONE

### EASTERN DIVISION

| Club | Cor. | MR. | PR. | Vil. | Pue. | Jal. | MT. | Ags. | Tam. | Mon. | Rey. | Coa. | Sal. | UL. | Chi. | Jua. | W. | L. | T. | Pct. | G.B. |
|---|---|---|---|---|---|---|---|---|---|---|---|---|---|---|---|---|---|---|---|---|---|
| Tampico ... | 3 | 5 | 4 | 7 | 3 | 6 | 4 | .. | 10 | 6 | 7 | 3 | 3 | 5 | 4 | 73 | 62 | 3 | .541 | .... |
| Monterrey .. | 4 | 3 | 4 | 5 | 0 | 3 | 7 | 6 | 4 | .. | 7 | 7 | 2 | 4 | 3 | 5 | 64 | 73 | 1 | .467 | 10 |
| Reynosa .... | 3 | 2 | 3 | 2 | 2 | 4 | 3 | 4 | 8 | 7 | .. | 7 | 1 | 6 | 3 | 3 | 58 | 75 | 0 | .436 | 14 |
| Coahuila ... | 2 | 3 | 4 | 3 | 4 | 2 | 6 | 2 | 6 | 7 | 5 | .. | 2 | 2 | 4 | 5 | 57 | 77 | 1 | .425 | 15½ |

### WESTERN DIVISION

| Saltillo .... | 2 | 4 | 5 | 3 | 3 | 4 | 6 | 7 | 5 | 6 | 7 | 6 | .. | 8 | 7 | 8 | 81 | 55 | 1 | .596 | .... |
|---|---|---|---|---|---|---|---|---|---|---|---|---|---|---|---|---|---|---|---|---|---|
| Union Lag. | 5 | 1 | 4 | 7 | 3 | 3 | 5 | 5 | 4 | 2 | 6 | 6 | .. | 7 | 7 | 68 | 70 | 1 | .493 | 14 |
| Chihuahua | 1 | 2 | 6 | 4 | 2 | 4 | 4 | 6 | 3 | 5 | 4 | 6 | 7 | .. | 7 | 66 | 69 | 2 | .489 | 14½ |
| Juarez ..... | 2 | 3 | 3 | 5 | 0 | 3 | 4 | 3 | 4 | 3 | 5 | 3 | 6 | 7 | 7 | .. | 58 | 80 | 0 | .420 | 24 |

Jalisco club represented Guadalajara, Jalisco.
Tampico club represented Tampico and Ciudad Madero.
Coahuila club represented Monclova and Sabinas.
Union Laguna club represented Gomez Palacio and Torreon.

Playoffs—Monterrey defeated Saltillo, four games to three; Tampico defeated Union Laguna, four games to two; Mexico City Reds defeated Puebla, four games to two; Cordoba defeated Jalisco, four games to three. Cordoba defeated Mexico City Reds, four games to three; Tampico defeated Monterrey, four games to three. Tampico defeated Cordoba, four games to one for league championship.

Regular-Season Attendance—Aguascalientes, 274,643; Chihuahua, 229,195; Coahuila, 186,139; Cordoba, 311,809; Jalisco, 165,784; Juarez, 136,912; Mexico City Reds, 380,528; Mexico City Tigers, 179,162; Monterrey, 242,000; Poza Rica, 206,772; Puebla, 188,092; Reynosa, 72,067; Saltillo, 193,912; Tampico, 370,506; Union Laguna, 259,511; Villahermosa, 162,251. Total, 3,559,283. Playoffs, 436,944. No All-Star Game.

Managers: Aguascalientes—Ronaldo Camacho; Chihuahua—Miguel Gaspar; Coahuila—Tomas Herrera; Cordoba—Napoleon Reyes; Jalisco—Vinicio Garcia; Juarez—C. Rigoberto Mendoza; Mexico City Reds—Benjamin Reyes; Mexico City Tigers—Jose Luis Garcia; Monterrey—Miguel Sotelo; Poza Rica—Moises Camacho; Puebla—Antonio Castano; Reynosa—Jorge Fitch; Saltillo—David Garcia; Tampico—Benjamin Valenzuela; Union Laguna—Jose Guerrero, Manolo Fortes; Villahermosa—J. Francisco Herrera, Pedro Ramos.

All-Star Team: 1B—Bourque, Mexico City Reds; Espino, Tampico; 2B—Hernandez Z., Mexico City Reds; 3B—Torres, Tampico; SS—Villaescusa, Mexico City Reds; Utility—Alvarez, Cordoba; OF—Mora, Saltillo; Davalillo, Cordoba; Canada, Union Laguna; C—Estrada, Puebla; DH—Dugan, Jalisco; P—Pena, Villahermosa; Sandate, Poza Rica; Manager—Valenzuela, Tampico.

(Compiled by Antonio Silva Vidaurry, League Statistician, Mexico, D. F.)

## CLUB BATTING

| Club | G. | AB. | R. | OR. | H. | TB. | 2B. | 3B. | HR. | RBI | SH. | SF. | Int. BB. | BB. | HP. | SO. | SB. | CS. | LOB. | Pct. |
|---|---|---|---|---|---|---|---|---|---|---|---|---|---|---|---|---|---|---|---|---|
| Mexico Reds | 139 | 4653 | 683 | 554 | 1391 | 1790 | 187 | 43 | 42 | 624 | 68 | 55 | 488 | 61 | 31 | 546 | 103 | 72 | 1031 | .299 |
| Jalisco .... | 136 | 4510 | 642 | 590 | 1317 | 1858 | 183 | 38 | 94 | 604 | 59 | 33 | 467 | 47 | 31 | 711 | 43 | 74 | 1020 | .290 |
| Cordoba ... | 137 | 4533 | 646 | 448 | 1300 | 1755 | 166 | 44 | 67 | 606 | 88 | 58 | 460 | 68 | 53 | 613 | 61 | 63 | 1063 | .287 |
| Saltillo ... | 137 | 4489 | 589 | 512 | 1282 | 1772 | 169 | 39 | 81 | 535 | 89 | 35 | 344 | 52 | 42 | 525 | 35 | 41 | 960 | .286 |
| Juarez .... | 138 | 4412 | 497 | 560 | 1235 | 1515 | 145 | 24 | 29 | 436 | 76 | 29 | 333 | 37 | 32 | 448 | 103 | 77 | 944 | .280 |
| Aguascal .. | 137 | 4592 | 529 | 549 | 1254 | 1626 | 158 | 44 | 42 | 447 | 91 | 38 | 374 | 47 | 31 | 606 | 59 | 72 | 1007 | .273 |
| Puebla .... | 138 | 4443 | 547 | 503 | 1208 | 1583 | 182 | 35 | 41 | 503 | 89 | 37 | 427 | 47 | 33 | 610 | 58 | 52 | 997 | .272 |
| Union Lag. | 139 | 4547 | 618 | 608 | 1233 | 1713 | 198 | 48 | 62 | 556 | 57 | 47 | 482 | 57 | 32 | 691 | 84 | 64 | 991 | .271 |
| Mexico Tig | 136 | 4216 | 518 | 560 | 1131 | 1442 | 146 | 39 | 29 | 469 | 96 | 34 | 426 | 44 | 34 | 715 | 58 | 67 | 910 | .268 |
| Chihuahua | 137 | 4567 | 543 | 541 | 1223 | 1592 | 154 | 49 | 39 | 460 | 67 | 37 | 452 | 53 | 36 | 630 | 29 | 42 | 1071 | .268 |
| Tampico .. | 138 | 4492 | 569 | 517 | 1196 | 1619 | 161 | 8 | 81 | 516 | 84 | 28 | 491 | 74 | 42 | 664 | 29 | 29 | 1035 | .266 |
| Coahuila .. | 135 | 4352 | 441 | 549 | 1157 | 1488 | 141 | 26 | 46 | 399 | 69 | 21 | 379 | 46 | 37 | 660 | 47 | 51 | 987 | .266 |
| Reynosa .. | 133 | 4166 | 447 | 522 | 1101 | 1434 | 143 | 44 | 34 | 382 | 90 | 40 | 415 | 55 | 32 | 607 | 55 | 80 | 908 | .264 |
| Monterrey .. | 138 | 4447 | 491 | 521 | 1158 | 1578 | 152 | 38 | 64 | 449 | 82 | 32 | 380 | 39 | 28 | 774 | 54 | 48 | 930 | .260 |
| Villaherm | 134 | 4333 | 391 | 498 | 1110 | 1362 | 129 | 42 | 13 | 352 | 67 | 23 | 322 | 57 | 27 | 650 | 97 | 82 | 866 | .256 |
| Poza Rica. | 138 | 4543 | 484 | 507 | 1138 | 1514 | 144 | 56 | 40 | 432 | 98 | 32 | 429 | 67 | 49 | 557 | 50 | 78 | 1018 | .250 |

## INDIVIDUAL BATTING

(Leading Qualifiers for Batting Championship—373 or More Plate Appearances)
*Bats lefthanded.  †Switch-hitter.

| Player and Club | G. | AB. | R. | H. | TB. | 2B. | 3B. | HR. | RBI. | SH. | SF. | BB. | HP. | SO. | SB. | CS. | Pct. |
|---|---|---|---|---|---|---|---|---|---|---|---|---|---|---|---|---|---|
| Bourque, Patrick, Mex Reds* | 99 | 339 | 56 | 126 | 183 | 22 | 7 | 7 | 74 | 0 | 5 | 66 | 2 | 32 | 6 | 1 | .372 |
| Dugan, James H., Jalisco... | 136 | 492 | 81 | 178 | 265 | 28 | 7 | 15 | 86 | 0 | 3 | 63 | 1 | 89 | 0 | 7 | .362 |
| Clark, James, Mexico Reds. | 134 | 485 | 89 | 175 | 223 | 21 | 6 | 5 | 93 | 0 | 6 | 68 | 2 | 45 | 12 | 10 | .361 |
| Suarez, Miguel, Mex Reds* | 134 | 514 | 74 | 185 | 215 | 18 | 3 | 2 | 59 | 3 | 4 | 42 | 4 | 34 | 4 | 7 | .360 |
| Espino, Hector, Tampico.... | 119 | 428 | 73 | 153 | 222 | 18 | 0 | 17 | 75 | 0 | 4 | 55 | 9 | 31 | 3 | 2 | .357 |
| Davalillo, Victor, Cordoba* | 114 | 408 | 70 | 145 | 199 | 21 | 3 | 9 | 70 | 2 | 7 | 49 | 1 | 37 | 7 | 2 | .355 |
| Bravo, Angel, 25 Monterrey- | | | | | | | | | | | | | | | | | |
| 101 Cordoba* | 126 | 480 | 91 | 162 | 190 | 15 | 5 | 1 | 35 | 3 | 0 | 73 | 3 | 40 | 27 | 24 | .338 |
| Anderson, Donald R., Sal* | 101 | 356 | 52 | 119 | 159 | 18 | 2 | 6 | 49 | 12 | 4 | 49 | 5 | 34 | 0 | 0 | .334 |
| Ford, Theodore, Jalisco.... | 130 | 449 | 80 | 149 | 218 | 29 | 5 | 10 | 74 | 0 | 4 | 75 | 4 | 57 | 4 | 6 | .332 |
| Canada, Romel, Union Lag* | 136 | 492 | 91 | 163 | 258 | 34 | 5 | 17 | 72 | 0 | 4 | 70 | 6 | 48 | 24 | 9 | .331 |

Departmental Leaders: G—Lamboy, V. M. Lopez, Matias, 138; AB—G. Villalobos, 583; R—Bravo, Canada, Silverio, 91; H—G. Villalobos, 187; TB—A. Mora, 288; 2B—Canada, 34; 3B—A. Diaz, 19; HR—A. Mora, 35; RBI—A. Mora, 109; SH—S. Mendoza, 24; SF—Blanco, Vidal, 10; BB—Silverio, 92; HP—C. Sanchez, 12; SO—Jac. Hernandez, 126; SB—A. Briones, 42; CS—Bravo, 24.

(All Players—Listed Alphabetically)

| Player and Club | G. | AB. | R. | H. | TB. | 2B. | 3B. | HR. | RBI. | SH. | SF. | BB. | HP. | SO. | SB. | CS. | Pct |
|---|---|---|---|---|---|---|---|---|---|---|---|---|---|---|---|---|---|
| Abarca, David, Jalisco | 2 | 1 | 0 | 0 | 0 | 0 | 0 | 0 | 0 | 0 | 0 | 0 | 0 | 0 | 0 | 0 | .000 |
| Acosta, Cecilio, Puebla | 1 | 1 | 0 | 0 | 0 | 0 | 0 | 0 | 0 | 0 | 0 | 0 | 0 | 0 | 0 | 0 | .000 |
| Acosta, Teolindo, Villaherm* | 109 | 416 | 43 | 133 | 158 | 9 | 8 | 0 | 30 | 5 | 1 | 36 | 2 | 19 | 19 | 19 | .320 |
| Agramon, Oscar, Reynosa | 14 | 42 | 2 | 6 | 8 | 2 | 0 | 0 | 1 | 2 | 0 | 3 | 1 | 9 | 0 | 0 | .143 |
| Aguilar, Enrique, Aguas | 10 | 4 | 4 | 1 | 1 | 0 | 0 | 0 | 1 | 0 | 0 | 0 | 0 | 1 | 0 | 1 | .250 |
| Aguilar, Jose L., Mex T† | 104 | 288 | 32 | 86 | 100 | 9 | 1 | 1 | 35 | 8 | 2 | 41 | 1 | 38 | 2 | 5 | .299 |
| Aguilera, Jorge, Villaherm | 16 | 45 | 3 | 10 | 14 | 1 | 0 | 1 | 3 | 0 | 0 | 0 | 0 | 12 | 0 | 0 | .222 |
| Aguirre, Trinidad, Mex R. | 76 | 235 | 27 | 59 | 76 | 7 | 2 | 2 | 33 | 2 | 3 | 17 | 0 | 49 | 1 | 4 | .251 |
| Alanis, Hector, Chihuahua | 46 | 46 | 10 | 8 | 8 | 0 | 0 | 0 | 2 | 4 | 1 | 6 | 0 | 16 | 0 | 2 | .174 |
| Alcaide, Jose, 23 Cordoba- | | | | | | | | | | | | | | | | | |
| 68 Coahuila* | 91 | 284 | 43 | 72 | 128 | 9 | 1 | 15 | 49 | 2 | 4 | 52 | 3 | 45 | 3 | 2 | .254 |
| Alcaraz, A. Luis, Cordoba | 113 | 405 | 49 | 119 | 177 | 18 | 2 | 12 | 85 | 4 | 7 | 57 | 1 | 74 | 3 | 2 | .294 |
| Almaraz, Jose, Tampico | 22 | 55 | 4 | 13 | 15 | 2 | 0 | 0 | 2 | 2 | 0 | 1 | 2 | 9 | 1 | 0 | .236 |
| Alvarado, Alejandro, Rey* | 118 | 377 | 44 | 99 | 114 | 9 | 3 | 0 | 17 | 5 | 2 | 45 | 3 | 28 | 4 | 19 | .263 |
| Alvarado, Natanael, | | | | | | | | | | | | | | | | | |
| 27 Coahuila-17 Puebla | 44 | 53 | 11 | 9 | 9 | 0 | 0 | 0 | 1 | 2 | 0 | 9 | 0 | 11 | 1 | 2 | .170 |
| Alvarez, Juan C., Tampico | 5 | 15 | 1 | 2 | 2 | 0 | 0 | 0 | 0 | 0 | 0 | 0 | 0 | 4 | 0 | 0 | .133 |
| Alvarez, Manuel, Cordoba* | 124 | 454 | 78 | 146 | 218 | 22 | 7 | 12 | 85 | 8 | 8 | 32 | 5 | 55 | 7 | 7 | .322 |
| Amador, Jose Luis, Puebla | 2 | 4 | 0 | 1 | 1 | 0 | 0 | 0 | 0 | 0 | 0 | 0 | 0 | 0 | 0 | 0 | .250 |
| Anderson, Donald R., Sal* | 101 | 356 | 52 | 119 | 159 | 18 | 2 | 6 | 49 | 12 | 4 | 49 | 5 | 34 | 0 | 0 | .334 |
| Arano, Antonio, Cordoba | 4 | 9 | 1 | 4 | 4 | 0 | 0 | 0 | 3 | 0 | 0 | 0 | 0 | 1 | 0 | 0 | .444 |
| Arano, Wilfredo, | | | | | | | | | | | | | | | | | |
| 12 Cordoba-83 Poa Rica. | 95 | 287 | 38 | 71 | 80 | 4 | 1 | 1 | 17 | 9 | 1 | 24 | 6 | 39 | 2 | 9 | .247 |
| Arevalo, Angel, Villaherm | 43 | 96 | 10 | 23 | 27 | 4 | 0 | 0 | 11 | 1 | 3 | 3 | 0 | 13 | 3 | 1 | .240 |
| Arvizu, Juan, 88 Mex T- | | | | | | | | | | | | | | | | | |
| 38 Puebla | 126 | 354 | 38 | 83 | 111 | 15 | 2 | 3 | 38 | 13 | 2 | 65 | 0 | 104 | 3 | 6 | .234 |
| Azcarraga, Ernesto, Puebla.. | 2 | 0 | 1 | 0 | 0 | 0 | 0 | 0 | 0 | 0 | 0 | 0 | 0 | 0 | 0 | 0 | .000 |
| Barandica, Jesus, Puebla | 4 | 1 | 0 | 0 | 0 | 0 | 0 | 0 | 0 | 0 | 0 | 0 | 0 | 0 | 0 | 0 | .000 |
| Barrientos, Virgilio, U L. | 4 | 3 | 0 | 0 | 0 | 0 | 0 | 0 | 0 | 0 | 0 | 0 | 0 | 0 | 0 | 0 | .000 |
| Barron, Rafael, Mex Reds | 117 | 369 | 42 | 97 | 117 | 11 | 3 | 1 | 33 | 8 | 2 | 14 | 1 | 45 | 4 | 5 | .263 |
| Beal, James, Reynosa | 39 | 156 | 24 | 52 | 64 | 3 | 3 | 1 | 12 | 7 | 0 | 9 | 0 | 9 | 7 | 5 | .333 |
| Beltran, Alfredo, Mex T* | 55 | 137 | 13 | 30 | 38 | 4 | 2 | 0 | 9 | 0 | 1 | 8 | 2 | 16 | 0 | 0 | .219 |
| Benitez, Jose Luis, Aguas | 71 | 207 | 15 | 48 | 59 | 7 | 2 | 0 | 27 | 4 | 3 | 11 | 0 | 44 | 1 | 3 | .232 |
| Bernal, Arturo, Monterrey* | 107 | 316 | 27 | 95 | 125 | 14 | 2 | 4 | 39 | 2 | 6 | 19 | 1 | 55 | 2 | 1 | .301 |
| Berzunza, William, Villa* | 81 | 231 | 11 | 51 | 57 | 6 | 0 | 0 | 21 | 2 | 0 | 18 | 4 | 28 | 1 | 1 | .221 |
| Blanco, C. Oswaldo, | | | | | | | | | | | | | | | | | |
| 77 Cordoba-47 Puebla | 124 | 439 | 66 | 131 | 206 | 31 | 4 | 12 | 78 | 1 | 10 | 55 | 3 | 78 | 1 | 2 | .298 |
| Bojorquez, Jose, 1 Villa- | | | | | | | | | | | | | | | | | |
| 65 Cordoba | 66 | 180 | 15 | 54 | 67 | 7 | 0 | 2 | 28 | 1 | 3 | 20 | 1 | 35 | 1 | 2 | .300 |
| Bonilla, Antelmo, | | | | | | | | | | | | | | | | | |
| 56 Tampico-17 Chihua.. | 73 | 235 | 15 | 53 | 60 | 7 | 0 | 0 | 16 | 6 | 0 | 11 | 1 | 32 | 0 | 5 | .226 |
| Bonilla, Clemente, Puebla.. | 1 | 3 | 0 | 0 | 0 | 0 | 0 | 0 | 0 | 0 | 0 | 0 | 0 | 2 | 0 | 0 | .000 |
| Bourque, Patrick, Mex Reds* | 99 | 339 | 56 | 126 | 183 | 22 | 7 | 7 | 74 | 0 | 5 | 66 | 2 | 32 | 6 | 1 | .372 |
| Bravo, Angel, 25 Monterrey- | | | | | | | | | | | | | | | | | |
| 101 Cordoba* | 126 | 480 | 91 | 162 | 190 | 15 | 5 | 1 | 35 | 3 | 0 | 73 | 3 | 40 | 27 | 24 | .338 |
| Briones, Antonio, Juarez.... | 130 | 469 | 58 | 131 | 148 | 9 | 4 | 0 | 31 | 17 | 0 | 41 | 5 | 32 | 42 | 18 | .279 |
| Briones, Eleazar, Mon | 82 | 220 | 13 | 32 | 36 | 2 | 1 | 0 | 11 | 12 | 0 | 18 | 2 | 47 | 0 | 0 | .145 |
| Brookins, Lendon, Chihua.. | 111 | 402 | 53 | 121 | 169 | 26 | 5 | 4 | 65 | 7 | 6 | 36 | 5 | 46 | 3 | 4 | .301 |
| Brooks, Robert, | | | | | | | | | | | | | | | | | |
| 19 Aguas-20 Chihuahua.. | 39 | 128 | 14 | 24 | 35 | 3 | 1 | 2 | 15 | 1 | 1 | 21 | 0 | 31 | 1 | 0 | .188 |
| Brown, Curtis, Union Laguna | 135 | 507 | 64 | 163 | 212 | 30 | 5 | 3 | 61 | 6 | 7 | 45 | 5 | 33 | 14 | 11 | .321 |
| Browne, Byron, Coahuila.. | 113 | 369 | 54 | 114 | 191 | 19 | 2 | 18 | 66 | 0 | 1 | 63 | 2 | 62 | 4 | 6 | .309 |
| Calero, Jose, Chihuahua.... | 24 | 87 | 10 | 26 | 37 | 4 | 2 | 1 | 10 | 1 | 2 | 7 | 1 | 11 | 0 | 0 | .299 |
| Calvo Bernardo, Aguas.... | 129 | 510 | 50 | 164 | 181 | 30 | 3 | 1 | 45 | 13 | 3 | 32 | 0 | 36 | 5 | 6 | .322 |
| Camacho, Moises, Poza Rica | 4 | 6 | 0 | 0 | 0 | 0 | 0 | 0 | 1 | 0 | 0 | 1 | 0 | 0 | 0 | 0 | .000 |
| Camacho, Ronaldo, Aguas... | 35 | 72 | 6 | 15 | 20 | 2 | 0 | 1 | 8 | 0 | 0 | 12 | 1 | 22 | 0 | 0 | .208 |
| Camarero, Rolando, | | | | | | | | | | | | | | | | | |
| 87 Aguas-51 Tampico | 138 | 456 | 33 | 105 | 152 | 22 | 2 | 7 | 69 | 8 | 3 | 40 | 0 | 76 | 2 | 3 | .230 |
| Camargo, Fernando, Mon | 15 | 27 | 2 | 9 | 11 | 2 | 0 | 0 | 3 | 1 | 0 | 1 | 1 | 13 | 1 | 1 | .333 |
| Cambero, Alberto, Poza Rica | 10 | 39 | 2 | 9 | 11 | 2 | 0 | 0 | 4 | 1 | 0 | 2 | 0 | 4 | 0 | 0 | .231 |
| Canada, Romel, Union Lag* | 136 | 492 | 91 | 163 | 258 | 34 | 5 | 17 | 72 | 0 | 4 | 70 | 6 | 48 | 24 | 9 | .331 |
| Castellon, Roberto, Tampico. | 23 | 80 | 6 | 14 | 16 | 2 | 0 | 0 | 6 | 2 | 0 | 2 | 2 | 8 | 0 | 1 | .175 |
| Castro, Arnoldo, Coahuila ..| 106 | 400 | 39 | 118 | 146 | 18 | 2 | 2 | 34 | 14 | 2 | 19 | 3 | 45 | 9 | 5 | .295 |
| Cedeno, Rosendo, Chihua*.. | 137 | 465 | 66 | 129 | 170 | 16 | 2 | 7 | 38 | 4 | 0 | 86 | 4 | 56 | 3 | 8 | .277 |
| Cerda, Benjamin, Jalisco ...| 128 | 474 | 49 | 130 | 176 | 22 | 0 | 8 | 49 | 8 | 3 | 48 | 5 | 42 | 1 | 6 | .274 |
| Cervantes, Refugio, Mex T†.. | 70 | 184 | 15 | 45 | 63 | 9 | 0 | 3 | 26 | 5 | 0 | 8 | 4 | 38 | 1 | 1 | .245 |
| Chavez, Francisco, Union L. | 128 | 457 | 57 | 102 | 121 | 12 | 2 | 1 | 42 | 6 | 5 | 52 | 2 | 79 | 7 | 6 | .223 |
| Chavez, J. Guadalupe, Salt* | 66 | 244 | 30 | 65 | 82 | 7 | 2 | 2 | 22 | 5 | 4 | 23 | 4 | 28 | 3 | 3 | .266 |
| Chavez, Juan de Dios, Pue.. | 119 | 276 | 25 | 47 | 57 | 8 | 1 | 0 | 21 | 14 | 3 | 24 | 3 | 53 | 2 | 3 | .170 |
| Clark, James, Mexico Reds* | 134 | 485 | 89 | 175 | 223 | 21 | 6 | 5 | 93 | 0 | 6 | 68 | 2 | 45 | 12 | 10 | .361 |
| Colon, Raul, Poza Rica* | 106 | 378 | 53 | 124 | 173 | 24 | 8 | 3 | 49 | 2 | 2 | 54 | 3 | 44 | 4 | 6 | .328 |
| Conkle, Francisco, Villa | 67 | 215 | 13 | 58 | 64 | 6 | 0 | 0 | 21 | 1 | 3 | 18 | 0 | 20 | 2 | 1 | .270 |
| Cornejo, Francisco, Villa | 1 | 4 | 0 | 1 | 1 | 0 | 0 | 0 | 0 | 0 | 0 | 0 | 0 | 0 | 0 | 0 | .250 |
| Cota, Sergio, Reynosa | 9 | 7 | 0 | 0 | 0 | 0 | 0 | 0 | 0 | 1 | 0 | 0 | 0 | 2 | 0 | 0 | .000 |
| Crane, Mark, 18 Salt-7 P R.. | 25 | 78 | 13 | 17 | 19 | 0 | 1 | 0 | 8 | 1 | 0 | 11 | 0 | 12 | 0 | 0 | .218 |
| Crawford, Alfred, | | | | | | | | | | | | | | | | | |
| 51 Puebla-28 Aguas | 79 | 302 | 50 | 97 | 125 | 11 | 7 | 1 | 27 | 5 | 0 | 15 | 5 | 41 | 15 | 9 | .321 |

| Player and Club | G. | AB. | R. | H. | TB. | 2B. | 3B. | HR. | RBI. | SH. | SF. | BB. | HP. | SO. | SB. | CS. | Pct. |
|---|---|---|---|---|---|---|---|---|---|---|---|---|---|---|---|---|---|
| Crespo, Manuel, Villaherm.. | 50 | 199 | 14 | 55 | 69 | 6 | 4 | 0 | 20 | 5 | 2 | 9 | 0 | 17 | 2 | 3 | .276 |
| Cruz, Domingo, Saltillo..... | 137 | 502 | 66 | 142 | 192 | 19 | 5 | 7 | 44 | 9 | 3 | 40 | 9 | 38 | 9 | 7 | .283 |
| Davalillo, Victor, Cordoba*.. | 114 | 408 | 70 | 145 | 199 | 21 | 3 | 9 | 70 | 2 | 7 | 49 | 1 | 37 | 7 | 2 | .355 |
| Davila, Angel, Juarez* ...... | 1 | 0 | 0 | 0 | 0 | 0 | 0 | 0 | 0 | 0 | 0 | 0 | 0 | 0 | 0 | 0 | .000 |
| Davila, L. Alberto, Juarez | 120 | 393 | 41 | 113 | 130 | 13 | 2 | 0 | 28 | 5 | 2 | 26 | 5 | 39 | 2 | 5 | .288 |
| De Hoyos, Arnoldo, Coa*....119 | 119 | 416 | 53 | 127 | 141 | 7 | 2 | 1 | 20 | 4 | 1 | 39 | 2 | 57 | 4 | 9 | .305 |
| Delgado, Julio, Mex Tig*.... | 1 | 2 | 0 | 0 | 0 | 0 | 0 | 0 | 0 | 0 | 0 | 0 | 0 | 1 | 0 | 0 | .000 |
| Del Moral, Jose, Monterrey.. | 98 | 374 | 54 | 112 | 145 | 20 | 5 | 1 | 35 | 10 | 5 | 16 | 6 | 33 | 10 | 5 | .299 |
| Del Toro, Francisco, Jua*.. | 56 | 167 | 19 | 46 | 53 | 3 | 2 | 0 | 11 | 0 | 2 | 10 | 1 | 37 | 1 | 1 | .275 |
| Diaz, Albino, Poza Rica.. | 130 | 485 | 58 | 130 | 187 | 13 | 19 | 2 | 40 | 15 | 2 | 37 | 5 | 53 | 8 | 10 | .268 |
| Diaz Rdz., Arsenio, U L... | 134 | 498 | 57 | 144 | 198 | 17 | 8 | 7 | 74 | 6 | 5 | 36 | 3 | 40 | 14 | 10 | .289 |
| Diaz, Cesar, Aguascalientes.. | 19 | 0 | 5 | 0 | 0 | 0 | 0 | 0 | 1 | 0 | 1 | 0 | 1 | 0 | 1 | 1 | .000 |
| Diaz, Hector M., Mex Tigers | 88 | 260 | 27 | 62 | 84 | 11 | 1 | 3 | 29 | 7 | 5 | 23 | 0 | 60 | 3 | 4 | .238 |
| Dugan, James H., Jalisco..136 | 136 | 492 | 81 | 178 | 265 | 28 | 7 | 15 | 86 | 0 | 3 | 63 | 1 | 89 | 0 | 7 | .362 |
| Duran, Roberto, Cordoba*.. | 9 | 19 | 3 | 6 | 6 | 0 | 0 | 0 | 4 | 0 | 0 | 2 | 1 | 0 | 2 | 0 | .316 |
| Elguezabal, Jose A., Puebla.101 | 101 | 253 | 28 | 67 | 91 | 6 | 6 | 2 | 28 | 7 | 1 | 11 | 2 | 31 | 6 | 4 | .265 |
| Enriquez, Graciano, Mont.. | 124 | 460 | 48 | 127 | 154 | 12 | 3 | 3 | 36 | 9 | 2 | 23 | 1 | 74 | 5 | 6 | .276 |
| Escalante, Victor M., M T.. | 82 | 171 | 23 | 36 | 43 | 5 | 1 | 0 | 17 | 7 | 2 | 30 | 2 | 43 | 2 | 4 | .211 |
| Esparza, Julio, Poza Rica... | 43 | 99 | 11 | 25 | 32 | 3 | 2 | 0 | 7 | 4 | 1 | 7 | 0 | 20 | 0 | 3 | .253 |
| Espino, Hector, Tampico...119 | 119 | 428 | 73 | 153 | 222 | 18 | 0 | 17 | 75 | 0 | 4 | 55 | 9 | 31 | 3 | 2 | .357 |
| Espinosa, Cruz, 7 Mex Reds- | | | | | | | | | | | | | | | | | |
| 90 Villahermosa ....... | 97 | 301 | 28 | 68 | 88 | 11 | 3 | 1 | 19 | 6 | 2 | 24 | 4 | 64 | 4 | 5 | .226 |
| Espinosa, Ernesto, Mont ...119 | 119 | 416 | 45 | 98 | 124 | 11 | 6 | 1 | 19 | 8 | 0 | 37 | 3 | 66 | 4 | 3 | .236 |
| Espinosa, Nestor, Mexico T... | 1 | 2 | 1 | 1 | 2 | 1 | 0 | 0 | 0 | 0 | 0 | 0 | 1 | 0 | 0 | 0 | .500 |
| Esquivel, Ramiro, Tampico.. | 46 | 126 | 11 | 24 | 32 | 2 | 0 | 2 | 10 | 2 | 0 | 9 | 1 | 24 | 0 | 0 | .190 |
| Estrada, Francisco, Puebla..122 | 122 | 442 | 50 | 139 | 173 | 17 | 1 | 5 | 64 | 7 | 6 | 35 | 4 | 22 | 4 | 3 | .314 |
| Fabela, Victor, Coahuila ...115 | 115 | 339 | 42 | 89 | 112 | 11 | 3 | 2 | 33 | 1 | 2 | 55 | 9 | 46 | 6 | 6 | .263 |
| Faudoa, Victor, Chihuahua*.. | 71 | 156 | 15 | 34 | 43 | 3 | 3 | 0 | 8 | 3 | 0 | 14 | 0 | 38 | 1 | 2 | .218 |
| Felix, Fernando, 27 Union | | | | | | | | | | | | | | | | | |
| Laguna-79 Villahermosa .106 | 106 | 302 | 38 | 79 | 106 | 14 | 5 | 1 | 28 | 3 | 3 | 21 | 1 | 67 | 10 | 7 | .262 |
| Felix, Victor, Union Lag... | 124 | 415 | 71 | 122 | 165 | 20 | 7 | 3 | 43 | 10 | 7 | 47 | 5 | 82 | 5 | 10 | .294 |
| Figueroa, Baldemar, Villa .. | 81 | 209 | 30 | 48 | 55 | 5 | 1 | 0 | 9 | 5 | 0 | 10 | 1 | 41 | 9 | 6 | .230 |
| Figueroa, Leobardo, Tampico | 61 | 185 | 25 | 47 | 56 | 4 | 1 | 1 | 12 | 5 | 2 | 7 | 1 | 21 | 2 | 1 | .254 |
| Fitch, Jorge, Reynosa ........ | 5 | 12 | 1 | 2 | 3 | 1 | 0 | 0 | 2 | 0 | 0 | 1 | 0 | 0 | 0 | 0 | .167 |
| Ford, Lambert, Reynosa*.... | 93 | 299 | 40 | 90 | 123 | 7 | 10 | 2 | 26 | 5 | 1 | 55 | 1 | 39 | 1 | 7 | .301 |
| Ford, Theodore, Jalisco...... | 130 | 449 | 80 | 149 | 218 | 29 | 5 | 10 | 74 | 0 | 4 | 75 | 4 | 57 | 4 | 6 | .332 |
| Foster, Roy, Chihuahua ... | 71 | 253 | 25 | 66 | 85 | 8 | 1 | 3 | 34 | 1 | 2 | 36 | 1 | 45 | 1 | 1 | .261 |
| Freed, Roger, Monterrey ...103 | 103 | 330 | 56 | 94 | 165 | 12 | 1 | 19 | 58 | 1 | 2 | 72 | 4 | 77 | 1 | 0 | .285 |
| Fuentes, Antonio, Poza R...101 | 101 | 327 | 29 | 77 | 93 | 9 | 2 | 1 | 26 | 13 | 2 | 32 | 6 | 24 | 5 | 7 | .235 |
| Gallegos, Narciso, Reynosa.. | 4 | 3 | 0 | 0 | 0 | 0 | 0 | 0 | 0 | 0 | 0 | 0 | 0 | 1 | 0 | 0 | .000 |
| Garcia, Alonso, Coahuila ... | 54 | 175 | 18 | 36 | 47 | 11 | 0 | 0 | 6 | 3 | 0 | 17 | 1 | 41 | 2 | 2 | .206 |
| Garcia, Bulmaro, Tampico ...110 | 110 | 410 | 49 | 100 | 112 | 9 | 0 | 1 | 30 | 16 | 3 | 19 | 3 | 40 | 6 | 2 | .244 |
| Garcia, Eden, Juarez........ | 12 | 20 | 1 | 5 | 5 | 0 | 0 | 0 | 1 | 0 | 0 | 2 | 0 | 6 | 0 | 0 | .250 |
| Garcia, Humberto, Reynosa.131 | 131 | 460 | 61 | 116 | 199 | 25 | 2 | 18 | 73 | 1 | 5 | 52 | 1 | 88 | 11 | 12 | .252 |
| Garcia, Victor, Tampico..... | 3 | 0 | 1 | 0 | 0 | 0 | 0 | 0 | 0 | 0 | 0 | 0 | 0 | 0 | 0 | 0 | .000 |
| Garza, Carlos, Mex Tigers*..120 | 120 | 355 | 57 | 86 | 123 | 11 | 4 | 6 | 41 | 0 | 2 | 75 | 1 | 79 | 3 | 5 | .242 |
| Garza, Gustavo, Coahuila*.. | 81 | 198 | 13 | 56 | 63 | 7 | 0 | 0 | 14 | 8 | 2 | 22 | 2 | 21 | 1 | 2 | .283 |
| Garzon, Felix, Mex Tigers.. | 14 | 23 | 4 | 11 | 12 | 1 | 0 | 0 | 3 | 0 | 3 | 0 | 3 | 1 | 0 | 0 | .478 |
| Gonzalez, Arturo, Mont ....111 | 111 | 313 | 21 | 74 | 104 | 11 | 5 | 3 | 39 | 7 | 2 | 12 | 1 | 73 | 5 | 5 | .236 |
| Gonzalez, Efrain, Union L... | 34 | 44 | 5 | 7 | 9 | 0 | 1 | 0 | 3 | 0 | 1 | 3 | 0 | 20 | 0 | 0 | .159 |
| Gonzalez, Jose A., Villa*... | 16 | 60 | 3 | 11 | 16 | 0 | 1 | 1 | 3 | 0 | 0 | 4 | 0 | 8 | 0 | 0 | .183 |
| Gonzalez, J. Fernando, P R.. | 95 | 370 | 38 | 101 | 142 | 20 | 6 | 3 | 40 | 2 | 3 | 19 | 1 | 30 | 9 | 7 | .273 |
| Gonzalez, Wenceslao, P R....104 | 104 | 345 | 37 | 80 | 136 | 13 | 2 | 13 | 46 | 4 | 1 | 32 | 9 | 76 | 1 | 1 | .232 |
| Goodwin, Donnell, Saltillo... | 1 | 1 | 0 | 0 | 0 | 0 | 0 | 0 | 0 | 0 | 0 | 0 | 0 | 0 | 0 | 0 | .000 |
| Greene, Steven, Reynosa† ... | 2 | 8 | 0 | 1 | 1 | 0 | 0 | 0 | 0 | 0 | 0 | 1 | 0 | 4 | 0 | 0 | .125 |
| Guerrero, J. Encarn', Tam*.. | 7 | 12 | 1 | 1 | 2 | 1 | 0 | 0 | 2 | 0 | 1 | 1 | 0 | 7 | 0 | 0 | .083 |
| Guerrero, Leobardo, Jalisco.. | 96 | 311 | 41 | 80 | 91 | 7 | 2 | 0 | 23 | 6 | 1 | 25 | 1 | 50 | 10 | 15 | .257 |
| Guillen, Norberto, | | | | | | | | | | | | | | | | | |
| 2 Mex Tig-55 Coahuila...57 | 57 | 118 | 5 | 25 | 29 | 2 | 1 | 0 | 6 | 2 | 0 | 7 | 0 | 26 | 0 | 0 | .212 |
| Gutierrez, Eduardo, Reynosa.. | 1 | 1 | 0 | 0 | 0 | 0 | 0 | 0 | 0 | 0 | 0 | 0 | 0 | 0 | 0 | 0 | .000 |
| Gutierrez, Gerardo, Coahuila. | 93 | 264 | 16 | 57 | 66 | 7 | 1 | 0 | 22 | 4 | 0 | 17 | 0 | 51 | 2 | 0 | .216 |
| Hart, James, Aguascalientes.. | 22 | 63 | 9 | 17 | 28 | 2 | 0 | 3 | 16 | 0 | 2 | 20 | 1 | 17 | 0 | 0 | .270 |
| Hermoso, Angel, Villaherm .. | 63 | 238 | 24 | 64 | 74 | 8 | 1 | 0 | 19 | 6 | 0 | 18 | 0 | 16 | 10 | 4 | .269 |
| Hernandez, Jacinto, Villa..131 | 131 | 491 | 53 | 121 | 173 | 18 | 11 | 4 | 35 | 8 | 1 | 35 | 5 | 126 | 9 | 5 | .246 |
| Hernandez, Javier, Poza R.... | 8 | 22 | 1 | 5 | 6 | 1 | 0 | 0 | 1 | 0 | 0 | 2 | 0 | 2 | 0 | 0 | .227 |
| Hernandez, Pedro, Puebla... | 10 | 26 | 3 | 6 | 12 | 3 | 0 | 1 | 4 | 0 | 0 | 2 | 0 | 2 | 1 | 0 | .231 |
| Hernandez, S., Rafael, Aguas.. | 1 | 0 | 0 | 0 | 0 | 0 | 0 | 0 | 0 | 0 | 0 | 0 | 0 | 0 | 0 | 0 | .000 |
| Hernandez Z., Ramon, M R..133 | 133 | 524 | 88 | 166 | 193 | 19 | 4 | 0 | 58 | 14 | 6 | 52 | 1 | 33 | 17 | 9 | .317 |
| Hernandez, Rodolfo, Jalisco.. | 99 | 322 | 42 | 94 | 129 | 16 | 2 | 5 | 46 | 7 | 4 | 20 | 1 | 42 | 1 | 2 | .292 |
| Hernandez, Salvador, M T... | 24 | 56 | 6 | 14 | 16 | 2 | 0 | 3 | 1 | 0 | 6 | 1 | 9 | 3 | 4 | .250 |
| Herrera, Jose, Coahuila ... | 66 | 261 | 20 | 77 | 94 | 9 | 1 | 2 | 28 | 1 | 1 | 9 | 2 | 16 | 2 | 2 | .295 |
| Herrera, Roberto, Coahuila.. | 25 | 76 | 5 | 22 | 26 | 1 | 0 | 1 | 7 | 1 | 0 | 7 | 1 | 13 | 2 | 1 | .289 |
| Herrera, Ruben, Villaherm.. | 4 | 9 | 0 | 2 | 2 | 0 | 0 | 0 | 0 | 0 | 0 | 0 | 0 | 4 | 0 | 0 | .222 |
| Hottman, Kenneth, Juarez... | 10 | 29 | 0 | 5 | 5 | 0 | 0 | 0 | 2 | 0 | 0 | 2 | 0 | 9 | 0 | 0 | .172 |
| Howard, Charles, Tampico† .113 | 113 | 378 | 60 | 109 | 162 | 18 | 1 | 11 | 48 | 3 | 1 | 75 | 8 | 64 | 9 | 3 | .288 |
| Ibarra, Humberto, Union L*.119 | 119 | 393 | 43 | 90 | 104 | 12 | 1 | 0 | 33 | 8 | 3 | 44 | 2 | 51 | 0 | 4 | .229 |
| Iglesias, Domingo, Aguas... | 32 | 75 | 5 | 12 | 13 | 1 | 0 | 0 | 3 | 6 | 0 | 12 | 0 | 26 | 1 | 0 | .160 |
| Jackson, Alfonso, Union L...107 | 107 | 331 | 28 | 65 | 93 | 7 | 0 | 7 | 35 | 3 | 2 | 17 | 3 | 72 | 0 | 0 | .196 |
| James, Cleo, Puebla ........ | 20 | 78 | 11 | 25 | 33 | 3 | 1 | 1 | 7 | 3 | 0 | 13 | 1 | 12 | 2 | 3 | .321 |
| James, Willie, Poza Rica..... | 51 | 166 | 18 | 43 | 57 | 7 | 2 | 1 | 25 | 2 | 2 | 16 | 0 | 37 | 6 | 2 | .259 |

# The Sporting News
# SPORTS PUBLICATIONS
## authored and researched by nationally-known sports experts and statisticians

### OFFICIAL BASEBALL GUIDE
Contains complete official major and minor league averages, directory of major league club officials, photographs of all major league clubs and stories on pennant races. Also Review of the Year, All-Star Game, Hall of Fame and farm systems. Published annually in April.          Price $3.00.
Plus 50c postage and handling.

### OFFICIAL BASEBALL REGISTER
Complete season-by-season records and personal data of more than 1,000 active major league players, managers, coaches and former umpires. The Register will be published and delivered in June after player changes have been made, bringing player personnel up to date.          Price $5.00.
Plus 50c postage and handling.

### OFFICIAL WORLD SERIES RECORDS
Box scores, summary and composite batting and pitching averages of all World Series games played from 1903 through current Series. Includes all Series individual and club batting, fielding and pitching records. Also lists all player and manager participants in over 400 pages. Annually in December.          Price $3.00.
Plus 50c postage and handling.

### THE SPORTING NEWS
### OFFICIAL BASEBALL RECORD BOOK
All-time major league baseball club and individual performance records. Completely indexed for easy reference. Used by sports writers and broadcasters. Published annually in March. (Former title: One For The Book.)          Price $2.50
Plus 50c postage and handling.

### OFFICIAL BASEBALL DOPE BOOK
Rosters of all major league clubs, diagrams of ball parks, All-Star Game records and player averages and many more important facts in handy pocket-size form. Published annually in May.          Price $1.50.
Plus 50c postage and handling.

## HOCKEY REGISTER

More than 450 pages . . . the complete career playing record of players in the NHL, WHA, AHL, CHL, WHL and amateur leagues . . . Lists all outstanding records and achievements of each player, also personal data . . . The only book of its kind published . . . A MUST for all hockey fans. Annually in Dec.

Price $5.00.

Plus 50c postage and handling.

## PRO AND AMATEUR HOCKEY GUIDE

More than 200 pages . . . Official Statistics of Professional and Amateur Leagues, Club Directories, All-Star Teams, All-Time Records for all Pro Leagues, Draft Lists, Stanley Cup Records . . . includes teams and colleges in both the United States and Canada and international teams . . . Photos. Annually in December.

Price $3.00.

Plus 50c postage and handling.

## THE SPORTING NEWS' NATIONAL FOOTBALL GUIDE

Club directories of all NFL and WFL teams, complete NFL statistics. Diagrams of NFL stadia. All-time records and many other features, plus photos. Annually in July.

Price $3.00.

Plus 50c postage and handling.

## OFFICIAL AMERICAN FOOTBALL LEAGUE HISTORY

Complete statistics and review of 1969 season, team records, 1960-69; all-time AFL records, records of championship, All-Star and Super-Bowl Games.    Price $4.00.

Plus 50c postage and handling.

## FOOTBALL REGISTER

Complete season-by-season records of active National Football League players and coaches. Annually in August.

Price $5.00.

Plus 50c postage and handling.

| Player and Club | G. | AB. | R. | H. | TB. | 2B. | 3B. | HR. | RBI. | SH. | SF. | BB. | HP. | SO. | SB. | CS. | Pct. |
|---|---|---|---|---|---|---|---|---|---|---|---|---|---|---|---|---|---|
| Jimenez, F. Elvio, Coahuila.. | 33 | 118 | 7 | 29 | 38 | 7 | 1 | 0 | 14 | 1 | 1 | 5 | 0 | 12 | 0 | 0 | .246 |
| Jimenez, Rogelio,. | | | | | | | | | | | | | | | | | .238 |
| 22 Coahuila-73 Villaherm | 95 | 324 | 24 | 77 | 88 | 9 | 1 | 0 | 24 | 1 | 0 | 26 | 0 | 42 | 7 | 8 | .238 |
| Juarez, Clemente, Poza R*.. | 4 | 14 | 0 | 2 | 2 | 0 | 0 | 0 | 1 | 0 | 0 | 2 | 0 | 4 | 0 | 0 | .143 |
| Juarez, Marcelo, Saltillo .... | 79 | 309 | 42 | 90 | 123 | 15 | 6 | 2 | 28 | 2 | 3 | 14 | 2 | 26 | 5 | 9 | .291 |
| Kelly, Robert, Poza Rica* .. | 17 | 64 | 10 | 12 | 17 | 3 | 1 | 0 | 3 | 4 | 2 | 3 | 1 | 5 | 0 | 1 | .188 |
| King, Harold, 50 Puebla- | | | | | | | | | | | | | | | | | |
| 48 Cordoba* ........... | 98 | 330 | 39 | 100 | 142 | 15 | 3 | 7 | 49 | 0 | 5 | 61 | 4 | 38 | 4 | 1 | .303 |
| Kokor, Steven, Aguas ........ | 1 | 0 | 1 | 0 | 0 | 0 | 0 | 0 | 0 | 0 | 0 | 0 | 0 | 0 | 0 | 0 | .000 |
| Lara, Armando, Mexico Tig. | 133 | 494 | 66 | 153 | 211 | 28 | 6 | 6 | 63 | 11 | 1 | 23 | 7 | 57 | 5 | 6 | .310 |
| Lara, Francisco, Puebla..... | 109 | 367 | 46 | 100 | 114 | 10 | 2 | 0 | 31 | 7 | 5 | 12 | 4 | 21 | 1 | 6 | .272 |
| Lara, Hdz., Jose, Coahuila.. | 23 | 38 | 3 | 8 | 9 | 1 | 0 | 0 | 4 | 2 | 1 | 1 | 0 | 9 | 1 | 1 | .211 |
| Lara, Santos, Poza Rica..... | 39 | 109 | 10 | 20 | 24 | 1 | 0 | 1 | 7 | 1 | 0 | 19 | 1 | 20 | 2 | 1 | .183 |
| Lazaro, Alfredo, Union Lag.. | 98 | 258 | 42 | 54 | 82 | 12 | 2 | 4 | 36 | 7 | 1 | 45 | 3 | 74 | 0 | 3 | .209 |
| Leal, Felipe, Chihuahua..... | 26 | 21 | 5 | 5 | 5 | 0 | 0 | 0 | 2 | 0 | 0 | 6 | 0 | 3 | 0 | 0 | .238 |
| Leon, Eduardo, Tampico...... | 72 | 253 | 23 | 56 | 70 | 5 | 0 | 3 | 22 | 8 | 2 | 26 | 0 | 70 | 3 | 1 | .221 |
| Lizarraga, Miguel, Saltillo.. | 62 | 185 | 18 | 43 | 58 | 5 | 2 | 2 | 19 | 2 | 2 | 9 | 4 | 43 | 0 | 0 | .232 |
| Lopez, Armando, Juarez ..... | 39 | 107 | 5 | 21 | 23 | 2 | 0 | 0 | 8 | 2 | 0 | 7 | 1 | 21 | 1 | 1 | .196 |
| Lopez, Aurelio, Mexico Reds. | 1 | 1 | 0 | 0 | 0 | 0 | 0 | 0 | 0 | 0 | 0 | 0 | 0 | 0 | 0 | 0 | .000 |
| Lopez, Baudel, Mexico Reds* | 18 | 50 | 6 | 11 | 13 | 0 | 1 | 0 | 3 | 0 | 0 | 9 | 0 | 7 | 0 | 0 | .220 |
| Lopez, Jaime, Chihuahua*.... | 137 | 551 | 70 | 181 | 219 | 24 | 7 | 0 | 60 | 10 | 4 | 32 | 0 | 33 | 1 | 3 | .328 |
| Lopez, Lorenzo, Tampico..... | 120 | 402 | 39 | 90 | 114 | 16 | 1 | 2 | 45 | 5 | 4 | 50 | 1 | 67 | 1 | 1 | .224 |
| Lopez, Victor Manuel, U L.. | 138 | 540 | 73 | 162 | 240 | 27 | 12 | 9 | 58 | 6 | 2 | 44 | 2 | 80 | 11 | 5 | .300 |
| Lugo, Donaldo, Saltillo ..... | 10 | 23 | 6 | 4 | 5 | 1 | 0 | 0 | 4 | 1 | 0 | 2 | 0 | 2 | 0 | 0 | .174 |
| Lugo, Gabriel, Saltillo...... | 131 | 495 | 75 | 146 | 210 | 28 | 0 | 12 | 65 | 4 | 4 | 32 | 5 | 36 | 7 | 2 | .295 |
| Lugo, Pedro, Poza Rica..... | 49 | 144 | 6 | 32 | 34 | 2 | 0 | 0 | 9 | 2 | 0 | 2 | 0 | 15 | 0 | 1 | .222 |
| Luque, Gregorio, Saltillo... | 101 | 320 | 27 | 88 | 98 | 8 | 1 | 0 | 29 | 13 | 3 | 8 | 1 | 19 | 0 | 2 | .275 |
| Mariscal, Alfredo, Saltillo*.. | 1 | 1 | 1 | 1 | 1 | 0 | 0 | 0 | 1 | 0 | 0 | 0 | 0 | 0 | 0 | 0 | 1.000 |
| Marquez, Francisco, Aguas.. | 123 | 427 | 52 | 109 | 165 | 20 | 3 | 10 | 40 | 2 | 5 | 22 | 10 | 70 | 4 | 8 | .255 |
| Marquez, Gonzalo, Puebla*.. | 24 | 86 | 14 | 27 | 36 | 2 | 2 | 1 | 14 | 0 | 1 | 14 | 0 | 11 | 0 | 1 | .314 |
| Marquez, Roberto, Reynosa.. | 27 | 65 | 4 | 12 | 16 | 0 | 2 | 0 | 4 | 2 | 1 | 5 | 2 | 14 | 1 | 0 | .185 |
| Martinez, Antonio, Reynosa† | 86 | 243 | 22 | 55 | 71 | 8 | 1 | 2 | 19 | 12 | 4 | 17 | 1 | 27 | 1 | 1 | .226 |
| Martinez, Bernardo, Mex T.. | 2 | 0 | 0 | 0 | 0 | 0 | 0 | 0 | 0 | 0 | 0 | 0 | 0 | 0 | 1 | 0 | .000 |
| Martinez, Humberto, Reynosa | 21 | 52 | 4 | 10 | 12 | 0 | 1 | 0 | 3 | 0 | 4 | 0 | 0 | 19 | 0 | 2 | .192 |
| Martinez, C., Juan, Mont... | 98 | 317 | 35 | 79 | 128 | 10 | 3 | 11 | 50 | 4 | 3 | 30 | 1 | 93 | 1 | 1 | .249 |
| Matias, John, Juarez*........ | 138 | 499 | 70 | 164 | 216 | 28 | 3 | 6 | 69 | 5 | 7 | 47 | 2 | 29 | 10 | 5 | .329 |
| Maytorena, Francisco, Tamp. | 3 | 1 | 0 | 0 | 0 | 0 | 0 | 0 | 0 | 1 | 0 | 1 | 0 | 0 | 0 | 0 | .000 |
| McFadden, Leon, Reynosa... | 29 | 108 | 16 | 25 | 36 | 2 | 3 | 1 | 12 | 1 | 0 | 7 | 3 | 19 | 2 | 2 | .231 |
| McGuffin, James, Reynosa .. | 1 | 3 | 1 | 1 | 1 | 0 | 0 | 0 | 0 | 0 | 0 | 2 | 0 | 1 | 0 | 0 | .333 |
| Mena, Rigoberto, Saltillo ..131 | 131 | 471 | 50 | 146 | 179 | 14 | 5 | 3 | 47 | 15 | 5 | 24 | 0 | 10 | 0 | 1 | .310 |
| Menchaca, J. Francisco, | | | | | | | | | | | | | | | | | |
| 6 Union Laguna-76 Salt | 82 | 269 | 32 | 80 | 99 | 11 | 1 | 2 | 32 | 2 | 3 | 15 | 1 | 41 | 3 | 1 | .297 |
| Mendez, Roberto, Jalisco... | 127 | 443 | 72 | 125 | 149 | 17 | 2 | 1 | 35 | 15 | 3 | 46 | 9 | 61 | 8 | 5 | .282 |
| Mendoza, Porfirio, Juarez... | 83 | 240 | 32 | 57 | 75 | 6 | 3 | 2 | 27 | 12 | 1 | 22 | 0 | 42 | 4 | 7 | .238 |
| Mendoza, Saul, | | | | | | | | | | | | | | | | | |
| 16 Poza Rico-101 Puebla | 117 | 391 | 35 | 85 | 107 | 17 | 1 | 1 | 26 | 24 | 0 | 38 | 3 | 50 | 2 | 2 | .217 |
| Mercado, Raul, Coahuila ... | 2 | 0 | 0 | 0 | 0 | 0 | 0 | 0 | 0 | 0 | 0 | 0 | 0 | 0 | 0 | 0 | .000 |
| Mere, Luis, Mexico Reds.... | 5 | 1 | 0 | 0 | 0 | 0 | 0 | 0 | 0 | 0 | 0 | 0 | 0 | 0 | 0 | 0 | .000 |
| Mojica, Bartolo, Tampico.... | 2 | 1 | 0 | 0 | 0 | 0 | 0 | 0 | 0 | 0 | 0 | 0 | 0 | 0 | 0 | 0 | .000 |
| Montes Correa, Jose, Rey.... | 5 | 14 | 1 | 4 | 4 | 0 | 0 | 0 | 0 | 0 | 0 | 1 | 0 | 2 | 0 | 0 | .286 |
| Montoya, Ramon, Mex Reds.. | 82 | 260 | 24 | 70 | 80 | 6 | 2 | 0 | 29 | 5 | 4 | 19 | 2 | 22 | 2 | 2 | .269 |
| Montoya, Raul, Juarez...... | 134 | 523 | 72 | 159 | 175 | 8 | 4 | 0 | 38 | 11 | 2 | 30 | 3 | 26 | 28 | 16 | .304 |
| Montoya, Raul, Aguas* ..... | 5 | 5 | 2 | 3 | 0 | 0 | 0 | 0 | 1 | 0 | 0 | 0 | 0 | 1 | 0 | 0 | .600 |
| Moore, Curtis, Jalisco*..... | 88 | 285 | 65 | 84 | 161 | 12 | 4 | 19 | 62 | 0 | 3 | 60 | 3 | 67 | 2 | 3 | .295 |
| Mora, Andres, Saltillo ......133 | 133 | 492 | 82 | 151 | 288 | 18 | 7 | 35 | 109 | 0 | 1 | 43 | 3 | 86 | 2 | 2 | .307 |
| Mora, Jesus, 53 Reynosa- | | | | | | | | | | | | | | | | | |
| 59 Aguascalientes ......112 | 112 | 365 | 28 | 85 | 103 | 14 | 2 | 0 | 34 | 5 | 6 | 29 | 1 | 19 | 4 | 7 | .233 |
| Morales, Alfredo, Chihuahua | 34 | 112 | 16 | 21 | 25 | 2 | 1 | 0 | 7 | 1 | 0 | 13 | 1 | 18 | 1 | 1 | .188 |
| Morales, Carlos, Juarez† ... | 35 | 74 | 6 | 13 | 17 | 4 | 0 | 0 | 8 | 0 | 0 | 7 | 0 | 20 | 0 | 0 | .176 |
| Mota, Francisco, Puebla..... | 3 | 0 | 1 | 0 | 0 | 0 | 0 | 0 | 0 | 0 | 0 | 0 | 0 | 0 | 0 | 0 | .000 |
| Naranjo, Jose Luis, Mex T*.. | 16 | 21 | 3 | 2 | 2 | 0 | 0 | 0 | 1 | 2 | 0 | 5 | 1 | 6 | 0 | 0 | .095 |
| Nieto, Rodolfo, Tampico*.... | 1 | 0 | 0 | 0 | 0 | 0 | 0 | 0 | 0 | 0 | 0 | 0 | 0 | 0 | 0 | 0 | .000 |
| Noriega, Fco. Javier, Aguas | 124 | 435 | 58 | 128 | 172 | 18 | 7 | 4 | 46 | 14 | 4 | 35 | 9 | 33 | 9 | 9 | .294 |
| Ochoa, Angel, Villahermosa.. | 6 | 14 | 0 | 2 | 2 | 0 | 0 | 0 | 0 | 1 | 0 | 1 | 0 | 5 | 0 | 0 | .143 |
| Ochoa, David, Aguas........ | 35 | 129 | 13 | 28 | 34 | 3 | 0 | 1 | 11 | 0 | 3 | 5 | 0 | 27 | 2 | 2 | .217 |
| Orea, Diacono, Juarez ...... | 1 | 0 | 1 | 0 | 0 | 0 | 0 | 0 | 0 | 0 | 0 | 0 | 0 | 0 | 0 | 0 | .000 |
| Ornelas, Rafael, Saltillo....109 | 109 | 317 | 48 | 85 | 121 | 9 | 3 | 7 | 30 | 10 | 0 | 55 | 3 | 88 | 5 | 5 | .268 |
| Orozco, Arturo, 11 Mex R- | | | | | | | | | | | | | | | | | |
| 46 Villa-22 Mex Tigers. | 79 | 230 | 28 | 46 | 64 | 6 | 3 | 2 | 21 | 1 | 3 | 27 | 4 | 68 | 4 | 1 | .200 |
| Orozco, Victor, Monterrey... | 72 | 188 | 11 | 47 | 54 | 7 | 0 | 0 | 16 | 4 | 0 | 9 | 2 | 28 | 2 | 0 | .250 |
| Ortiz, U., Alfredo, Mex R*... | 23 | 22 | 2 | 6 | 7 | 1 | 0 | 0 | 5 | 1 | 0 | 3 | 0 | 4 | 1 | 0 | .273 |
| Ortiz, Jose Luis, Villa ..... | 5 | 11 | 1 | 0 | 0 | 0 | 0 | 0 | 0 | 0 | 0 | 0 | 0 | 4 | 1 | 0 | .000 |
| Ortiz, Jose Manuel, Mont... | 125 | 438 | 42 | 110 | 134 | 12 | 3 | 2 | 31 | 6 | 1 | 30 | 2 | 53 | 6 | 8 | .251 |
| Ortiz, Reyes, Juarez ........ | 132 | 470 | 57 | 143 | 199 | 26 | 3 | 8 | 70 | 6 | 2 | 32 | 6 | 36 | 7 | 6 | .304 |
| Osuna, Carlos, 7 Sal-78 Coa. | 85 | 226 | 24 | 47 | 57 | 5 | 1 | 1 | 13 | 5 | 1 | 11 | 1 | 49 | 0 | 2 | .208 |
| Osuna, Elpidio, Juarez......122 | 122 | 408 | 40 | 100 | 127 | 13 | 1 | 4 | 45 | 3 | 4 | 25 | 3 | 52 | 2 | 3 | .245 |
| Pactwa, Joseph, Tampico*....73 | 73 | 184 | 38 | 55 | 104 | 8 | 1 | 13 | 38 | 0 | 0 | 66 | 3 | 70 | 0 | 1 | .299 |
| Paredes, Jesus, Cordoba....117 | 117 | 397 | 62 | 114 | 140 | 8 | 6 | 2 | 34 | 10 | 2 | 23 | 10 | 66 | 9 | 5 | .287 |
| Parra, Manuel, Cordoba...... | 13 | 25 | 3 | 5 | 8 | 1 | 1 | 0 | 0 | 0 | 0 | 1 | 0 | 8 | 0 | 0 | .200 |
| Paz, Carlos, Villahermosa... | 8 | 3 | 1 | 0 | 0 | 0 | 0 | 0 | 0 | 0 | 0 | 0 | 0 | 0 | 0 | 0 | .000 |
| Pena, Jose, Villahermosa..... | 4 | 1 | 0 | 0 | 0 | 0 | 0 | 0 | 0 | 0 | 0 | 0 | 0 | 1 | 0 | 0 | .000 |

| Player and Club | G. | AB. | R. | H. | TB. | 2B. | 3B. | HR. | RBI. | SH. | SF. | BB. | HP. | SO. | SB. | CS. | Pct. |
|---|---|---|---|---|---|---|---|---|---|---|---|---|---|---|---|---|---|
| Peralta, Luis, Juarez........102 | 338 | 38 | 96 | 132 | 15 | 0 | 7 | 39 | 4 | 4 | 34 | 2 | 43 | 0 | 4 | .284 |
| Peralta, Vicente, Poza R....108 | 350 | 24 | 88 | 101 | 6 | 2 | 1 | 40 | 11 | 2 | 20 | 5 | 38 | 4 | 5 | .251 |
| Perea, Tomas, Villaherm... 28 | 58 | 3 | 11 | 12 | 1 | 0 | 0 | 5 | 1 | 0 | 3 | 0 | 10 | 2 | 2 | .190 |
| Perez, Jorge Victor, Tamp†.. 11 | 18 | 1 | 1 | 1 | 0 | 0 | 0 | 0 | 0 | 0 | 1 | 0 | 1 | 0 | 0 | .056 |
| Perez, Jose Luis, Aguas*... 12 | 27 | 2 | 5 | 6 | 1 | 0 | 0 | 2 | 1 | 0 | 0 | 0 | 6 | 0 | 1 | .185 |
| Perez Torres, Miguel, PR*.. 81 | 235 | 28 | 54 | 64 | 8 | 1 | 0 | 20 | 11 | 5 | 25 | 0 | 14 | 2 | 5 | .230 |
| Pettaway, Nathaniel, Jal*..132 | 454 | 74 | 118 | 218 | 17 | 4 | 25 | 83 | 1 | 2 | 59 | 4 | 122 | 4 | 7 | .260 |
| Phillips, Adolfo, Mex Reds..101 | 350 | 62 | 86 | 141 | 17 | 4 | 10 | 45 | 5 | 3 | 44 | 4 | 57 | 22 | 5 | .246 |
| Pina, Francisco, Saltillo.... 19 | 68 | 8 | 16 | 23 | 2 | 1 | 1 | 8 | 1 | 0 | 2 | 2 | 6 | 0 | 1 | .235 |
| Pizarro, Juan, Cordoba* .... 1 | 1 | 0 | 0 | 0 | 0 | 0 | 0 | 0 | 0 | 0 | 0 | 0 | 0 | 0 | 0 | .000 |
| Plascencia, Obed, Mex Tig... 95 | 289 | 36 | 80 | 109 | 13 | 2 | 4 | 49 | 1 | 7 | 29 | 2 | 31 | 1 | 1 | .277 |
| Plascencia, Rigoberto, Coa... 98 | 305 | 18 | 81 | 98 | 9 | 4 | 0 | 31 | 3 | 2 | 18 | 1 | 40 | 1 | 1 | .266 |
| Pollorena, Antonio, U L.... 6 | 2 | 2 | 0 | 0 | 0 | 0 | 0 | 0 | 0 | 0 | 0 | 0 | 2 | 0 | 0 | .000 |
| Ponce, Manuel, Mex Tigers..120 | 353 | 42 | 107 | 118 | 6 | 1 | 1 | 38 | 20 | 5 | 34 | 2 | 31 | 6 | 8 | .303 |
| Prieto, Juvencio, Cordoba... 13 | 12 | 4 | 3 | 3 | 0 | 0 | 0 | 0 | 0 | 0 | 3 | 0 | 2 | 0 | 1 | .250 |
| Ramirez, Alfredo, Union L... 1 | 4 | 0 | 1 | 1 | 0 | 0 | 0 | 1 | 0 | 0 | 0 | 0 | 0 | 0 | 0 | .250 |
| Ramirez, Gustavo, Chihua..123 | 486 | 57 | 129 | 150 | 15 | 3 | 0 | 31 | 13 | 4 | 50 | 1 | 49 | 3 | 5 | .265 |
| Ramirez, Milton, Reynosa.... 6 | 18 | 1 | 4 | 4 | 0 | 0 | 0 | 0 | 0 | 0 | 2 | 0 | 2 | 0 | 0 | .222 |
| Rey, Arturo, Tampico ......110 | 350 | 30 | 79 | 110 | 13 | 0 | 6 | 49 | 12 | 1 | 30 | 3 | 51 | 0 | 3 | .226 |
| Reyes, Jose, Tampico ....... 28 | 68 | 4 | 13 | 15 | 2 | 0 | 0 | 3 | 4 | 0 | 2 | 2 | 13 | 0 | 0 | .191 |
| Reyes, Orlando, Reynosa*..115 | 369 | 48 | 109 | 146 | 26 | 1 | 3 | 52 | 6 | 4 | 41 | 5 | 82 | 4 | 3 | .275 |
| Reyes, Pablo, Jalisco....... 35 | 75 | 8 | 27 | 34 | 2 | 1 | 1 | 15 | 1 | 2 | 8 | 0 | 10 | 2 | 0 | .360 |
| Rios, Federico, Juarez ...... 18 | 38 | 2 | 5 | 6 | 1 | 0 | 0 | 3 | 0 | 0 | 3 | 0 | 7 | 0 | 0 | .132 |
| Rios, Juan, Reynosa........112 | 401 | 34 | 118 | 136 | 11 | 2 | 1 | 36 | 0 | 9 | 18 | 5 | 17 | 4 | 3 | .294 |
| Rivas, F. Rolando, Coahuila*. 1 | 0 | 1 | 0 | 0 | 0 | 0 | 0 | 0 | 0 | 0 | 0 | 0 | 0 | 0 | 0 | .000 |
| Rivera, Carlos, Mex Tigers... 80 | 248 | 29 | 72 | 86 | 8 | 3 | 0 | 27 | 5 | 3 | 11 | 0 | 48 | 4 | 3 | .290 |
| Rivera, Eduardo, Villaherm.111 | 331 | 28 | 83 | 96 | 8 | 1 | 1 | 25 | 5 | 0 | 33 | 2 | 66 | 6 | 7 | .251 |
| Rivero, Gener, Cordoba.....126 | 385 | 52 | 97 | 110 | 5 | 4 | 0 | 19 | 23 | 0 | 28 | 2 | 33 | 5 | 5 | .252 |
| Robles, Alejandro, Aguas*..127 | 407 | 52 | 107 | 129 | 9 | 2 | 3 | 39 | 13 | 2 | 38 | 2 | 30 | 9 | 6 | .263 |
| Rodriguez, Francisco, Ags...137 | 533 | 68 | 158 | 218 | 20 | 5 | 10 | 69 | 9 | 3 | 37 | 3 | 84 | 2 | 7 | .296 |
| Rodriguez, Jose, Villa......107 | 387 | 36 | 99 | 121 | 7 | 3 | 3 | 32 | 8 | 4 | 19 | 1 | 39 | 2 | 11 | .256 |
| Rodriguez, Leonardo, Mont† 88 | 181 | 24 | 41 | 43 | 2 | 0 | 0 | 7 | 10 | 0 | 23 | 0 | 25 | 1 | 3 | .227 |
| Romero, Esteban, Reynosa... 4 | 9 | 2 | 2 | 2 | 0 | 0 | 0 | 1 | 0 | 0 | 1 | 0 | 3 | 0 | 1 | .222 |
| Romo, Enrique, Mexico R.... 3 | 1 | 0 | 0 | 0 | 0 | 0 | 0 | 0 | 0 | 1 | 0 | 0 | 0 | 0 | 0 | .000 |
| Romo, Walter, Aguas....... 11 | 18 | 1 | 1 | 2 | 1 | 0 | 0 | 0 | 0 | 0 | 5 | 0 | 11 | 0 | 0 | .056 |
| Roque, Jorge, Puebla........ 93 | 327 | 39 | 84 | 123 | 15 | 3 | 6 | 41 | 1 | 3 | 30 | 3 | 83 | 8 | 5 | .257 |
| Rosario, Santiago, | | | | | | | | | | | | | | | | | |
| 63 Aguas-60 Villaherm*..123 | 436 | 72 | 138 | 180 | 23 | 5 | 3 | 52 | 2 | 4 | 65 | 3 | 51 | 8 | 6 | .317 |
| Rosas, Clemente, Jalisco...100 | 343 | 28 | 92 | 113 | 9 | 0 | 4 | 45 | 5 | 5 | 16 | 0 | 47 | 1 | 2 | .268 |
| Rubio, Arturo, Puebla .... 99 | 366 | 43 | 90 | 98 | 6 | 1 | 0 | 24 | 5 | 1 | 25 | 1 | 35 | 11 | 7 | .246 |
| Ruiz, Miguel Angel, Coah... 20 | 40 | 3 | 7 | 11 | 1 | 0 | 1 | 3 | 1 | 0 | 4 | 0 | 6 | 2 | 2 | .175 |
| Ruiz, Porfirio, Cordoba.....116 | 349 | 30 | 76 | 98 | 12 | 5 | 0 | 31 | 11 | 1 | 23 | 3 | 47 | 1 | 1 | .218 |
| Saiz, Francisco, Poza R*.... 92 | 269 | 38 | 70 | 89 | 7 | 6 | 0 | 19 | 8 | 0 | 41 | 3 | 30 | 3 | 5 | .260 |
| Salazar, Mario, Jalisco...... 78 | 233 | 42 | 62 | 76 | 3 | 4 | 1 | 20 | 1 | 1 | 20 | 0 | 25 | 9 | 4 | .266 |
| Saldana, Ruben, Monterrey.. 47 | 166 | 11 | 32 | 43 | 6 | 1 | 1 | 12 | 4 | 0 | 10 | 2 | 16 | 1 | 0 | .193 |
| Saldivar, Arturo, Mex Tex .. 1 | 1 | 0 | 0 | 0 | 0 | 0 | 0 | 0 | 0 | 0 | 0 | 0 | 0 | 0 | 0 | .000 |
| Salgado, Octavio, Reynosa... 3 | 10 | 2 | 1 | 2 | 1 | 0 | 0 | 1 | 0 | 0 | 1 | 0 | 4 | 0 | 0 | .100 |
| Salinas, Hilario, Cordoba.... 40 | 100 | 7 | 22 | 26 | 1 | 0 | 1 | 4 | 1 | 2 | 5 | 1 | 11 | 0 | 0 | .220 |
| Salinas, Juan Manuel, | | | | | | | | | | | | | | | | | |
| 32 Aguascalientes-34 Rey 66 | 173 | 16 | 32 | 34 | 2 | 0 | 0 | 7 | 7 | 0 | 28 | 1 | 34 | 1 | 1 | .185 |
| Salinas, Merced, Chihuahua. 72 | 189 | 16 | 46 | 51 | 3 | 1 | 0 | 28 | 6 | 1 | 13 | 3 | 27 | 2 | 0 | .243 |
| Sanchez, Celerino, Cordoba..110 | 400 | 65 | 115 | 162 | 18 | 4 | 7 | 64 | 8 | 8 | 33 | 12 | 45 | 0 | 2 | .288 |
| Sanchez, Leonides, Poza R... 82 | 209 | 16 | 43 | 44 | 1 | 0 | 0 | 11 | 4 | 3 | 9 | 1 | 16 | 0 | 5 | .206 |
| Sanchez, Raul, Union Lag*.. 46 | 90 | 9 | 22 | 27 | 1 | 2 | 6 | 1 | 0 | 0 | 9 | 0 | 19 | 3 | 0 | .244 |
| Sanders, Clement, Monterrey 116 | 400 | 62 | 117 | 198 | 20 | 8 | 15 | 62 | 3 | 6 | 59 | 2 | 87 | 8 | 7 | .293 |
| Sandoval, Rodolfo, Chihua..101 | 311 | 16 | 75 | 90 | 10 | 1 | 1 | 31 | 0 | 2 | 37 | 2 | 45 | 0 | 1 | .241 |
| Sauceda, Victor, Chihuahua.133 | 468 | 50 | 116 | 178 | 15 | 10 | 9 | 68 | 2 | 9 | 31 | 7 | 104 | 3 | 5 | .248 |
| Serna, Joel, Villaherm..... 129 | 448 | 41 | 116 | 169 | 18 | 10 | 5 | 42 | 9 | 3 | 38 | 2 | 79 | 5 | 9 | .259 |
| Serrato, Ramon, Reynosa....100 | 333 | 50 | 93 | 110 | 6 | 4 | 1 | 21 | 5 | 2 | 23 | 1 | 60 | 14 | 9 | .279 |
| Sifuentes, Francisco, Cord*.. 2 | 4 | 0 | 1 | 1 | 0 | 0 | 0 | 0 | 0 | 0 | 0 | 0 | 1 | 0 | 0 | .250 |
| Silicato, Thomas, Poza R.... 8 | 29 | 2 | 6 | 8 | 2 | 0 | 0 | 2 | 1 | 0 | 4 | 0 | 10 | 0 | 1 | .207 |
| Silverio, Tomas, Tampico*..133 | 505 | 91 | 144 | 210 | 21 | 3 | 13 | 43 | 1 | 3 | 92 | 2 | 87 | 11 | 7 | .285 |
| Silvey, Dennis, Saltillo*..... 23 | 86 | 9 | 20 | 28 | 5 | 0 | 1 | 12 | 2 | 1 | 3 | 0 | 10 | 0 | 0 | .233 |
| Solis, Francisco, Coahuila... 3 | 0 | 1 | 0 | 0 | 0 | 0 | 0 | 0 | 0 | 0 | 0 | 0 | 0 | 0 | 0 | .000 |
| Solis, Miguel, Saltillo....... 1 | 1 | 0 | 0 | 0 | 0 | 0 | 0 | 0 | 0 | 0 | 0 | 0 | 0 | 0 | 0 | .000 |
| Sommers, Jesus, Puebla..... 91 | 318 | 38 | 92 | 139 | 17 | 2 | 8 | 32 | 3 | 3 | 38 | 1 | 52 | 4 | 2 | .289 |
| Sosa, Emilio, Poza Rica ..... 28 | 78 | 7 | 32 | 36 | 2 | 1 | 0 | 8 | 2 | 0 | 4 | 1 | 8 | 0 | 2 | .410 |
| Soto, Carlos, Mexico Reds... 48 | 116 | 11 | 28 | 35 | 5 | 1 | 0 | 18 | 2 | 2 | 9 | 2 | 22 | 0 | 0 | .241 |
| Soto, Jose, Juarez*......... 1 | 1 | 0 | 1 | 1 | 0 | 0 | 0 | 0 | 0 | 0 | 0 | 0 | 0 | 0 | 0 | 1.000 |
| Sposito, Gustavo, Chihua..116 | 481 | 59 | 137 | 175 | 8 | 9 | 4 | 42 | 8 | 4 | 28 | 3 | 49 | 7 | 6 | .285 |
| Staton, Joseph, Mex Reds*.. 31 | 110 | 12 | 28 | 36 | 3 | 1 | 1 | 15 | 0 | 2 | 7 | 1 | 16 | 6 | 2 | .255 |
| Suarez, Miguel, Mex Reds*..134 | 514 | 74 | 185 | 215 | 18 | 4 | 2 | 59 | 3 | 4 | 42 | 4 | 34 | 4 | 7 | .360 |
| Talley, Joseph, Puebla*..... 73 | 253 | 41 | 71 | 104 | 12 | 3 | 5 | 30 | 3 | 1 | 46 | 0 | 52 | 5 | 4 | .281 |
| Tapia, Miguel, Mex Tigers..100 | 231 | 22 | 44 | 50 | 4 | 1 | 0 | 17 | 10 | 0 | 26 | 6 | 53 | 2 | 1 | .190 |
| Terrazas, Martin, Mex Tig.. 1 | 3 | 0 | 0 | 0 | 0 | 0 | 0 | 0 | 0 | 0 | 0 | 0 | 3 | 0 | 0 | .000 |
| Teixidor, Esteban, Reynosa.. 6 | 1 | 1 | 0 | 0 | 0 | 0 | 0 | 0 | 0 | 0 | 1 | 0 | 0 | 0 | 0 | .000 |
| Thompson, Albert, Chihua... 94 | 162 | 27 | 40 | 71 | 5 | 1 | 8 | 29 | 0 | 1 | 22 | 1 | 29 | 2 | 0 | .247 |
| Thompson, Narciso, Cordoba. 5 | 7 | 1 | 0 | 0 | 0 | 0 | 0 | 0 | 0 | 0 | 2 | 0 | 4 | 0 | 0 | .000 |
| Tiburcio, Edgar, Mex. Tig*..108 | 336 | 35 | 96 | 121 | 8 | 7 | 1 | 32 | 7 | 2 | 25 | 1 | 52 | 4 | 4 | .286 |
| Torres, Reyes, Chihuahua... 77 | 253 | 36 | 64 | 81 | 10 | 2 | 1 | 23 | 6 | 0 | 21 | 6 | 39 | 1 | 3 | .253 |

| Player and Club | G. | AB. | R. | H. | TB. | 2B. | 3B. | HR. | RBI. | SH. | SF. | BB. | HP. | SO. | SB. | CS. | Pct. |
|---|---|---|---|---|---|---|---|---|---|---|---|---|---|---|---|---|---|
| Torres, Victor, Tampico.....128 | 514 | 65 | 163 | 207 | 23 | 0 | 7 | 77 | 10 | 7 | 19 | 3 | 20 | 1 | 2 | .317 |
| Tovar, J. Jesus, | | | | | | | | | | | | | | | | | |
| 36 Puebla-77 Coahuila ..113 | 369 | 43 | 93 | 112 | 10 | 3 | 1 | 33 | 13 | 0 | 10 | 4 | 64 | 3 | 8 | .252 |
| Trevino, Carlos, Union Lag...128 | 440 | 66 | 125 | 187 | 25 | 2 | 11 | 85 | 3 | 9 | 63 | 1 | 76 | 4 | 3 | .284 |
| Trevino, Juan, Reynosa.... 11 | 25 | 0 | 6 | 6 | 0 | 0 | 1 | 0 | 0 | 0 | 9 | 0 | 0 | 0 | 0 | .240 |
| Trujillo, Hipolito, Juarez .. 4 | 13 | 3 | 6 | 7 | 1 | 0 | 0 | 2 | 0 | 0 | 0 | 0 | 5 | 0 | 0 | .462 |
| Tucker, Bobby, Mex Reds.... 94 | 318 | 47 | 88 | 137 | 21 | 2 | 8 | 42 | 3 | 3 | 31 | 1 | 33 | 1 | 1 | .277 |
| Urias, Eladio, | | | | | | | | | | | | | | | | | |
| 55 Villahermosa-38 Tam. 93 | 313 | 30 | 90 | 106 | 9 | 2 | 1 | 22 | 11 | 1 | 19 | 4 | 25 | 5 | 3 | .288 |
| Valadez, Steve, Tampico..... 1 | 2 | 0 | 0 | 0 | 0 | 0 | 0 | 0 | 0 | 0 | 0 | 0 | 1 | 0 | 0 | .000 |
| Valenzuela, Carlos, Rey .. 131 | 401 | 29 | 117 | 137 | 16 | 2 | 0 | 43 | 8 | 1 | 58 | 6 | 59 | 1 | 2 | .292 |
| Valenzuela, Felipe, Mont*.... 23 | 78 | 10 | 17 | 18 | 1 | 0 | 0 | 5 | 1 | 0 | 3 | 0 | 11 | 1 | 1 | .218 |
| Valenzuela, Humberto, M R.. 3 | 0 | 1 | 0 | 0 | 0 | 0 | 0 | 0 | 0 | 0 | 0 | 0 | 0 | 0 | 0 | .000 |
| Valenzuela, Jose M., Jal ... 99 | 264 | 26 | 83 | 117 | 12 | 5 | 4 | 35 | 1 | 0 | 20 | 3 | 69 | 0 | 5 | .314 |
| Valle, Hector, Juarez.....135 | 454 | 35 | 135 | 160 | 17 | 1 | 2 | 48 | 2 | 3 | 40 | 2 | 43 | 2 | 6 | .297 |
| Vazquez, Jesus, Coahuila... 20 | 43 | 5 | 7 | 12 | 1 | 0 | 2 | 0 | 0 | 1 | 2 | 0 | 8 | 0 | 1 | .163 |
| Vazquez, Nicolas, Coahuila..122 | 434 | 43 | 121 | 158 | 13 | 3 | 6 | 58 | 5 | 4 | 27 | 6 | 65 | 6 | 2 | .279 |
| Vega, Abelardo, Mex Reds..118 | 424 | 51 | 103 | 153 | 17 | 2 | 3 | 60 | 8 | 6 | 45 | 6 | 76 | 3 | 6 | .243 |
| Vega, Valenciano, Juarez ... 83 | 243 | 22 | 48 | 53 | 3 | 1 | 0 | 14 | 5 | 1 | 12 | 2 | 21 | 4 | 5 | .198 |
| Vidal, Jose, Poza Rica.......131 | 454 | 62 | 117 | 189 | 21 | 3 | 15 | 71 | 3 | 10 | 73 | 4 | 73 | 5 | 5 | .258 |
| Villaescusa, Antonio, M R...133 | 483 | 79 | 148 | 174 | 18 | 4 | 0 | 49 | 17 | 7 | 55 | 5 | 59 | 24 | 20 | .306 |
| Villalobos, Gonzalo, Aguas..137 | 583 | 63 | 187 | 239 | 21 | 11 | 3 | 46 | 11 | 2 | 33 | 0 | 53 | 3 | 11 | .321 |
| Villalobos, Lauro, Jalisco...123 | 394 | 34 | 95 | 111 | 9 | 2 | 1 | 31 | 14 | 2 | 7 | 0 | 30 | 1 | 12 | .241 |
| Walseth, Michael, Puebla*...135 | 481 | 63 | 157 | 221 | 29 | 4 | 9 | 86 | 3 | 9 | 47 | 5 | 55 | 0 | 2 | .326 |
| Wissel, Richard, Cordoba*.. 24 | 81 | 10 | 24 | 35 | 5 | 0 | 2 | 14 | 0 | 2 | 6 | 1 | 11 | 0 | 2 | .296 |
| Yepes, Francisco, Poza R.... 73 | 179 | 15 | 33 | 36 | 1 | 1 | 0 | 6 | 3 | 0 | 16 | 3 | 32 | 4 | 5 | .184 |
| Zabala, Faustino, Mont..... 37 | 134 | 17 | 38 | 57 | 7 | 0 | 4 | 20 | 0 | 5 | 13 | 0 | 19 | 0 | 1 | .284 |
| Zamudio, Hector, Mex Tig..114 | 443 | 69 | 133 | 162 | 11 | 6 | 2 | 43 | 2 | 2 | 37 | 3 | 36 | 20 | 16 | .300 |
| Zavala, Alfredo, | | | | | | | | | | | | | | | | | |
| 6 Cordoba-83 Saltillo.... 89 | 309 | 30 | 80 | 101 | 10 | 4 | 1 | 33 | 9 | 2 | 17 | 3 | 53 | 1 | 9 | .259 |
| Zuniga, Faustino, Cordoba...116 | 345 | 36 | 83 | 101 | 6 | 3 | 2 | 39 | 13 | 5 | 22 | 2 | 61 | 2 | 10 | .241 |

The following pitchers had no plate appearances primarily through use of designated-hitters, listed alphabetically by club, games in parentheses:

AGUASCALIENTES—Beltran, Julio (4); Brito, Hector (9); Byron Quiroz, Ricardo (49); Escalante, Sergio (4); Moncayo, Bernardo (3); Moreno, Angel (3); Pina, Horacio (26); President, Larry (32); Ramirez, Guillermo (6); Sierra, Pedro (3); Valdez R., Mario (1); Valle, Urbano (7); Yard, Dennis (8).

CHIHUAHUA—Chavez, Rene (34); Guzman, Ramon (52); McRae, Norman (33); Reyes, Javier (29); Reynosa, Ramon (13); Sandoval, Rodrigo (25); Soto, J. Francisco (17); Tafoya, Daniel (4); Travis, John (28).

COAHUILA—Ballinger, Mark (6); Barbosa, Antonio (30); Brandon, Darrell (12); Cisneros, Alfonso (29); Dominguez, Hector (2); Lee, Won Kuk (33); Miali, Thomas (14); Morales, Mario (11); Raygoza, German (18); Valencia, Alfonso (2).

CORDOBA—Arano, Ramon (26); Armas, Abel (19); Ayon, Andres (10); Buentello, Israel (36); Delfin, Justino (15); Gutierrez, Pablo (35); Munoz, Adan (25); Romo, Vicente (22); Salomon, Porfirio (22).

JALISCO—Barrios, Francisco (31); Bustamante, Gilardo (2); Cazares, Sergio (27); Colorado, Salvador (2); Cordova, Ernesto (36); Dillon, Russell (8); Gutierrez, Guillermo (24); Guzman, Luis Fdo. (41); Holly, Jeffrey (10); Kealey, Steven (4); Lugo, Manuel (6); Martinez, Raul (3); Newson, Michael (10); Rabouin, Andre (5); Saucedo, Oscar (7); Uresti, Crisanto (6); Velo, Waldo (40).

JUAREZ—Almonte, Secundino (8); Beltran, Miguel (34); Fajardo, Ignacio (56); Hambright, Roger (28); Lozano, Francisco (25); Moreno, Carlos Alberto (32); Puente, Miguel A. (30).

MEXICO CITY REDS—Acosta L., Eduardo (31); Bellacetin, Adolfo (8); Gamez, Raul (19); Rodriguez,. Manuel (34)

MEXICO CITY TIGERS—Agundez, Victor (52); Azcarraga, Paz (3); Castro, Adolfo (8); Garcia, Ruben (42); Lopez, Fernando (33); Lopez, Hector (1); Meza, Alfredo (45); Rubio, Jorge (5); Valdez, Jose Humberto (14); Villanueva, Luis (12).

MONTERREY—Bernal, Othon (17); Carrasco, Carlos (30); Cruz, Concepcion (37); Garcia, Jose Luis (4); Luna Domingo (21); Martinez H. Francisco (33); Morales Raul (3); Moreno, Cesar (24); Penalver, Luis (36); Rodriguez, Pilar (33); Tatum, Kenneth (9); Volkening, Larry (32).

POZA RICA—Brunet, George (34); Carrillo, Lucio (1); Cavanaugh, Carl (36); Cruz, Eleuterio (24); Fernandez, Victor M. (2); Franco, David (16); Garduza, Jose M. (2); Hernandez, Angel (33); Lagunes, Jorge (3); Lara, Gilberto (9); Madrigal, Hector (34); Rodriquez, Roberto (14); Sandate, Ricardo (28).

PUEBLA—Bracamontes, Ignacio (31); Diorio, Ronald (17); Garcia, Nicolas (31); Gowell, Lawrence (5); Lugo, Luis (1); Martinez A., Francisco (30); Monteagudo, Aurelio (27); Pereira, Miguel (32).

REYNOSA—Aponte, Bonifacio (33); Arauz, Lorenzo (8); Campoy, Alejandro (15); Diaz, Justino (4); Hernandez, J. Guadalupe (3); Lanfranco, Guadalupe (8); Leon, Roberto (2); Montero, Hernan (22); Ochoa, Roberto (16); Olivo, Milciades (1); Orea, Ignacio (6); Salinas, Guadalupe (33); Santos, Victor (5); Thompson, Richard (1).

SALTILLO—Ahumada, Alejo (31); Armas, Tomas (27); Gage-Cole, Murray (45); Hernandez, David (26); Snyder, Robert (11); Soto, Alvaro (5); Verdugo, Roberto (28).

TAMPICO—Chavez, Carlos (5); Collazo, Alfonso (15); Cruz, Julio (27); Garcia, Rogelio (3); Isom, Curtis (8); Lefevre, Keith (21); Lopez, Ricardo (2); O'Toole, Dennis (5); Valle, Reynaldo (1); Valiejano, Rodolfo (33).

UNION LAGUNA—Beltran, Eleazar (2); Britton, Jimmy (24); Burns, Timothy (2); Cabrales, Carlos (8); Castillo, Enrique (36); DeLaTorre, Adolfo (35); Deutsch, John (2); Farmer, Edward (2); Gonzalez, Guillermo (29); Mena, Jorge (2); Pate, Edgar (4); Pena, Manuel (24); Plodinec, Timothy (7); Rodriguez, Rafael (11); Tovar, Pedro (30).

VILLAHERMOSA——Cordeiro, Raymond (23); Fabela, Wilfredo (31); Gallegos, Miguel (5); Johnson, Tomas (6); Lagunas, Crescencio (25); Martinez, Javier (34); Mellado, Oscar (21); Montane, Alfredo (1); Ochoa, Domingo (1); Valencia, Ignacio (3).

TWO CLUBS—Acosta M., Eduardo (13 Union Laguna, 22 Villahermosa); Adame, Arnulfo (7 Saltillo, 21 Aguascalientes); Boyd, T. Randy (10 Saltillo, 14 Puebla); Figueroa, Agustin (7 Coahuila, 17 Poza Rica); Mondragon, Manuel (1 Cordoba, 1 Puebla); Puig, Arturo (6 Chihuahua, 7 Reynosa); Ramos, Pedro, (2 Mexico City Reds, 8 Villahermosa); Stephenson, C. Earl (5 Monterrey, 4 Juarez); Suby, Juan (34 Mexico City Tigers, 11 Tampico); Valenzuela, Hector (4 Saltillo, 20 Coahuila).

GRAND-SLAM HOME RUNS—Pettaway, 3; Canada, 0. Plascencia, C. Trevino, 2 each; Alcaide, Alcaraz, Browne, Camarero, Crawford, Diaz Rdz., Enriquez, Estrada, V. Felix, H. Garcia, Jackson, A. Lara, L. Lopez, R. Ortiz, Rey, Roque, Sanders, Silverio, Zamudio, 1 each.

AWARDED FIRST BASE ON INTERFERENCE—Luque 2 (Esquivel, Estrada), O. Plascencia 2 (G. Gutierrez 2), Tucker 2 (Esquivel, Luque); Barron (Jackson) Berzunza (M. Salinas), F. Chavez (Lizarraga), Crawford (Trevino), Guillen (Lugo), M. Juarez (Rosas), F. Marquez (Diaz Rdz.), Matias (Soto), Mendez (M. Salinas), P. Mendoza (Marquez), Rosario (Tiburcio), P. Ruiz (Esquivel), Serna (Barron), J. Vazquez (Rey), 1 each.

## CLUB FIELDING

| CLUB | G. | PO. | A. | E. | DP. | PB. | Pct. | CLUB | G. | PO. | A. | E. | DP. | PB. | Pct. |
|---|---|---|---|---|---|---|---|---|---|---|---|---|---|---|---|
| Cordoba | 137 | 3543 | 1426 | 116 | 133 | 24 | .9771 | Puebla | 138 | 3513 | 1481 | 155 | 116 | 16 | .970 |
| Mexico Tigers | 136 | 3381 | 1504 | 116 | 143 | 30 | .9768 | Saltillo | 137 | 3486 | 1621 | 159 | 136 | 13 | .970 |
| Mexico Reds | 139 | 3606 | 1563 | 143 | 153 | 27 | .973 | Chihuahua | 137 | 3543 | 1430 | 168 | 120 | 19 | .967 |
| Juarez | 138 | 3411 | 1542 | 138 | 125 | 20 | .973 | Villahermosa | 134 | 3498 | 1566 | 178 | 138 | 23 | .966 |
| Monterrey | 138 | 3528 | 1599 | 152 | 132 | 32 | .971 | Union Laguna | 139 | 3555 | 1512 | 179 | 162 | 7 | .966 |
| Jalisco | 136 | 3483 | 1490 | 151 | 108 | 34 | .971 | Poza Rica | 138 | 3651 | 1488 | 190 | 112 | 23 | .964 |
| Tampico | 138 | 3546 | 1483 | 153 | 126 | 18 | .970 | Aguascalientes | 137 | 3549 | 1750 | 197 | 145 | 52 | .964 |
| Reynosa | 133 | 3342 | 1415 | 146 | 112 | 17 | .970 | Coahuila | 135 | 3402 | 1399 | 181 | 111 | 25 | .964 |

Triple Play—Puebla.

## INDIVIDUAL FIELDING

### FIRST BASEMEN

*Throws lefthanded.

| Player and Club | G. | PO. | A. | E. | DP. | Pct. | Player and Club | G. | PO. | A. | E. | DP. | Pct. |
|---|---|---|---|---|---|---|---|---|---|---|---|---|---|
| Garcia, Reynosa | 32 | 269 | 18 | 0 | 18 | 1.000 | Menchaca, Saltillo | 16 | 156 | 5 | 2 | 13 | .988 |
| Plascencia, M Tig. | 15 | 125 | 8 | 0 | 16 | 1.000 | Wissell, Cordoba | 20 | 151 | 8 | 2 | 13 | .988 |
| Boiorquez, Cordoba | 12 | 74 | 4 | 0 | 5 | 1.000 | Marquez, Puebla* | 18 | 144 | 9 | 2 | 11 | .987 |
| Diaz Rdz., U Laguna | 13 | 65 | 3 | 0 | 5 | 1.000 | Lopez, Chihuahua* | 137 | 1143 | 76 | 16 | 106 | .987 |
| ESPINO, Tampico | 105 | 900 | 73 | 3 | 89 | .997 | Espino, M R-Vil | 47 | 433 | 20 | 6 | 46 | .987 |
| Staton, Mex Reds* | 24 | 199 | 16 | 1 | 16 | .995 | Silvey, Saltillo* | 23 | 213 | 5 | 3 | 21 | .986 |
| Cervantes, M Tig | 32 | 203 | 11 | 1 | 26 | .995 | Trevino, U Laguna | 63 | 487 | 21 | 7 | 64 | .986 |
| Perez Torres, PR* | 58 | 446 | 23 | 3 | 40 | .994 | Rosario, Aguas-Vil* | 112 | 958 | 71 | 16 | 88 | .985 |
| Bourque, Mex Reds* | 97 | 807 | 46 | 6 | 101 | .993 | Colon, Poza Rica* | 79 | 616 | 45 | 11 | 54 | .983 |
| Garza, Mex Tigers | 101 | 773 | 46 | 6 | 86 | .993 | Sanders, Monterrey | 112 | 1059 | 38 | 19 | 84 | .983 |
| Blanco, Cord-Pue | 117 | 985 | 53 | 8 | 105 | .992 | Morales, Puebla | 16 | 104 | 10 | 2 | 4 | .983 |
| Anderson, Saltillo* | 95 | 856 | 47 | 7 | 79 | .992 | Fabela, Coahuila | 108 | 845 | 53 | 16 | 82 | .982 |
| Bravo, Mont-Cord* | 14 | 120 | 5 | 1 | 15 | .992 | Zabala, Monterrey | 12 | 105 | 6 | 2 | 12 | .982 |
| Robles, Aguas* | 64 | 548 | 53 | 5 | 49 | .992 | Sanchez, Cordoba | 29 | 255 | 14 | 5 | 26 | .982 |
| Berzunza, Villa* | 29 | 226 | 8 | 2 | 30 | .992 | Hernandez, Jalisco | 15 | 99 | 4 | 2 | 7 | .981 |
| Reyes, Reynosa* | 103 | 857 | 55 | 8 | 78 | .991 | Osuna, Juarez | 23 | 177 | 17 | 4 | 20 | .980 |
| Pettaway, Jalisco* | 126 | 1014 | 58 | 10 | 89 | .991 | Alcaide, Cord-Coah* | 24 | 174 | 8 | 4 | 14 | .978 |
| L. Lopez, Tampico | 12 | 100 | 7 | 1 | 14 | .991 | Camarero, Ags-Tamp | 26 | 217 | 10 | 6 | 24 | .974 |
| Ortiz, Juarez | 34 | 288 | 24 | 3 | 27 | .990 | Camacho, Aguas | 13 | 77 | 5 | 3 | 10 | .965 |
| Ibarra, U Laguna* | 77 | 647 | 38 | 7 | 86 | .990 | J. Herrera, Coah | 10 | 68 | 6 | 3 | 5 | .961 |
| Clark, Mexico Reds. | 11 | 93 | 2 | 1 | 11 | .990 | Rivera, Villa | 10 | 66 | 8 | 4 | 4 | .949 |
| Walseth, Puebla | 70 | 624 | 49 | 8 | 49 | .988 | W. Gonzalez, PR | 15 | 62 | 1 | 4 | 4 | .940 |
| Matias, Juarez* | 88 | 690 | 64 | 9 | 65 | .988 | | | | | | | |

Triple Play—Blanco.

### (Fewer Than Ten Games)

| Player and Club | G. | PO. | A. | E. | DP. | Pct. | Player and Club | G. | PO. | A. | E. | DP. | Pct. |
|---|---|---|---|---|---|---|---|---|---|---|---|---|---|
| Jimenez, Villa | 8 | 58 | 1 | 0 | 6 | 1.000 | Parra, Cordoba | 2 | 5 | 0 | 0 | 1 | 1.000 |
| Howard, Tampico | 7 | 41 | 3 | 0 | 1 | 1.000 | Valenzuela, Jalisco | 1 | 5 | 0 | 0 | 0 | 1.000 |
| Browne, Coahuila | 5 | 40 | 1 | 0 | 1 | 1.000 | Iglesias, Aguas | 1 | 5 | 0 | 0 | 0 | 1.000 |
| Freed, Monterrey | 6 | 37 | 1 | 0 | 6 | 1.000 | King, Cordoba | 1 | 4 | 0 | 0 | 0 | 1.000 |
| A. Bernal, Mont* | 4 | 32 | 1 | 0 | 3 | 1.000 | Ornelas, Saltillo | 1 | 4 | 0 | 0 | 0 | 1.000 |
| Tucker, Mexico Reds | 3 | 23 | 1 | 0 | 1 | 1.000 | Delgado, M Tigers* | 1 | 3 | 0 | 0 | 1 | 1.000 |
| Gonzalez, Villa* | 6 | 20 | 1 | 0 | 1 | 1.000 | Paz, Villahermosa* | 1 | 3 | 0 | 0 | 1 | 1.000 |
| Dugan, Jalisco | 3 | 19 | 0 | 0 | 1 | 1.000 | Crespo, Villa | 1 | 2 | 1 | 0 | 1 | 1.000 |
| Ortiz, U. Mex Reds* | 4 | 18 | 0 | 0 | 1 | 1.000 | Yepes, Poza Rica | 1 | 2 | 1 | 0 | 0 | 1.000 |
| Calvo, Aguas | 2 | 17 | 1 | 0 | 0 | 1.000 | Diaz, Poza Rica | 1 | 2 | 1 | 0 | 1 | 1.000 |
| Alvarez, Tampico | 2 | 16 | 0 | 0 | 0 | 1.000 | Saldana, Monterrey | 1 | 2 | 0 | 0 | 0 | 1.000 |
| Reyes, Jalisco | 2 | 13 | 0 | 0 | 2 | 1.000 | Esquivel, Tampico | 1 | 1 | 0 | 0 | 0 | 1.000 |
| Vidal, Poza Rica | 1 | 11 | 0 | 0 | 0 | 1.000 | Figueroa, Tampico | 1 | 1 | 0 | 0 | 0 | 1.000 |
| Canada, U Laguna | 3 | 10 | 1 | 0 | 0 | 1.000 | H. Martinez, Rey | 1 | 1 | 0 | 0 | 0 | 1.000 |
| Guerrero, Tampico* | 2 | 9 | 0 | 0 | 1 | 1.000 | Pina, Saltillo | 8 | 82 | 7 | 1 | 11 | .989 |
| Camacho, Poza Rica | 2 | 7 | 0 | 0 | 0 | 1.000 | J. Hernandez, P R | 3 | 26 | 2 | 1 | 3 | .966 |
| Torres, Tampico | 1 | 7 | 0 | 0 | 0 | 1.000 | Sosa, Poza Rica | 4 | 21 | 3 | 1 | 3 | .962 |
| Mora, Aguascalientes | 1 | 6 | 1 | 0 | 1 | 1.000 | Davalillo, Cordoba* | 7 | 49 | 0 | 3 | 3 | .942 |
| Soto, Mexico Reds | 1 | 5 | 1 | 0 | 0 | 1.000 | McFadden, Reynosa | 2 | 9 | 2 | 1 | 0 | .917 |
| Jackson, U Laguna | 1 | 5 | 0 | 0 | 0 | 1.000 | Naranjo, M Tigers* | 3 | 7 | 0 | 1 | 1 | .875 |

## SECOND BASEMEN

| Player and Club | G. | PO. | A. | E. | DP. | Pct. |
|---|---|---|---|---|---|---|
| MENDEZ, Jalisco .. | 101 | 232 | 218 | 4 | 51 | .991 |
| Aguirre, Mex Reds .. | 20 | 39 | 50 | 1 | 14 | .989 |
| Hernandez, Z., M R. | 125 | 330 | 360 | 9 | 92 | .987 |
| Espinosa, Monterrey .. | 15 | 37 | 31 | 1 | 11 | .986 |
| Castro, Coahuila .. | 77 | 185 | 206 | 6 | 51 | .985 |
| Diaz, Mex Tigers... | 36 | 85 | 81 | 3 | 19 | .982 |
| Arvizu, M Tig-Pue.. | 15 | 27 | 25 | 1 | 7 | .981 |
| Serrato, Reynosa .. | 71 | 180 | 170 | 7 | 37 | .980 |
| Hermoso, Villa .... | 60 | 161 | 161 | 7 | 33 | .979 |
| B. Garcia, Tampico . | 97 | 237 | 214 | 10 | 54 | .978 |
| Serna, Reynosa .. | 52 | 154 | 133 | 7 | 31 | .976 |
| R. Torres, Chihua .. | 77 | 196 | 183 | 10 | 60 | .974 |
| Lazaro, U Laguna .. | 17 | 42 | 33 | 2 | 8 | .974 |
| Ortiz, Monterrey .. | 123 | 341 | 328 | 18 | 77 | .974 |
| Hernandez, Jalisco . | 50 | 87 | 97 | 5 | 9 | .974 |
| Tapia, Mex Tigers . | 91 | 212 | 225 | 12 | 63 | .973 |
| Briones, Juarez .. | 128 | 371 | 352 | 21 | 75 | .972 |
| G. Lugo, Saltillo... | 127 | 332 | 391 | 21 | 93 | .972 |
| Morales, Chihuahua.. | 34 | 68 | 69 | 4 | 14 | .972 |
| Alcaraz, Cordoba .... | 110 | 250 | 259 | 15 | 73 | .971 |
| Chavez, U Laguna . | 127 | 360 | 371 | 22 | 102 | .971 |
| Crespo, Villa ..... | 49 | 139 | 115 | 8 | 40 | .969 |
| J. Chavez, Puebla .. | 115 | 247 | 224 | 15 | 53 | .969 |
| Elguezabal, Puebla... | 59 | 88 | 99 | 6 | 14 | .969 |
| Hernandez, M Tigers | 21 | 47 | 44 | 3 | 9 | .968 |
| Sanchez, Poza Rico.. | 73 | 151 | 178 | 12 | 41 | .965 |
| Castellon, Tampico.. | 23 | 40 | 40 | 3 | 11 | .964 |
| Camarero, Aguas-Tam | 11 | 21 | 30 | 2 | 8 | .962 |
| Garcia, Coahuila .. | 52 | 116 | 109 | 9 | 24 | .962 |
| Reyes, Jalisco ...... | 23 | 44 | 31 | 3 | 6 | .962 |
| Calvo, Aguas ...... | 120 | 305 | 313 | 27 | 81 | .958 |
| Alvarez, Cordoba .. | 31 | 63 | 74 | 6 | 19 | .958 |
| Marquez, Reynosa .. | 10 | 22 | 20 | 2 | 1 | .955 |
| Alaniz, Chihuahua .. | 11 | 25 | 14 | 2 | 5 | .951 |
| J. F. Gonzalez, PR.. | 83 | 228 | 190 | 23 | 46 | .948 |
| Figueroa, Villa .... | 31 | 64 | 63 | 9 | 15 | .934 |
| Rios, Juarez ........ | 14 | 36 | 23 | 6 | 8 | .908 |
| Bonilla, Tamp-Chih.. | 17 | 29 | 27 | 8 | 4 | .875 |

Triple Play—J. Chavez.

### (Fewer Than Ten Games)

| Player and Club | G. | PO. | A. | E. | DP. | Pct. |
|---|---|---|---|---|---|---|
| Osuna, Coahuila .... | 8 | 29 | 35 | 0 | 7 | 1.000 |
| Iglesias, Aguas .... | 9 | 15 | 22 | 0 | 0 | 1.000 |
| Howard, Tampico .. | 8 | 8 | 14 | 0 | 3 | 1.000 |
| Sposito, Chihuahua .. | 8 | 9 | 12 | 0 | 3 | 1.000 |
| Zavala, Saltillo .... | 4 | 10 | 8 | 0 | 1 | 1.000 |
| Paz, Villahermosa .. | 4 | 5 | 3 | 0 | 2 | 1.000 |
| Silicato, Poza R .... | 1 | 2 | 6 | 0 | 2 | 1.000 |
| Mora, Saltillo ...... | 2 | 4 | 3 | 0 | 1 | 1.000 |
| Zamudio, Mex Tig .. | 3 | 2 | 5 | 0 | 0 | 1.000 |
| Arano, Poza Rica .... | 2 | 6 | 0 | 0 | 0 | 1.000 |
| Montes Correa, Rey. | 1 | 3 | 3 | 0 | 0 | 1.000 |
| J. Herrera, Coahuila | 2 | 2 | 4 | 0 | 1 | 1.000 |
| Noriega, Aguas .... | 2 | 2 | 4 | 0 | 0 | 1.000 |
| Rivera, Mex Tigers.. | 1 | 4 | 1 | 0 | 0 | 1.000 |
| Aguilar, Aguas .... | 1 | 2 | 2 | 0 | 2 | 1.000 |
| Plascencia, Coahuila | 1 | 2 | 0 | 0 | 0 | 1.000 |
| V. Escalante, M Tig | 3 | 1 | 1 | 0 | 0 | 1.000 |
| Romo, Aguascalientes | 1 | 0 | 2 | 0 | 0 | 1.000 |
| Guerrero, Jalisco ... | 2 | 1 | 0 | 0 | 1 | 1.000 |
| Vega, Juarez ........ | 2 | 1 | 0 | 0 | 1 | 1.000 |
| Ruiz, Coahuila ...... | 1 | 1 | 0 | 0 | 0 | 1.000 |
| Sauceda, Chihuahua.. | 1 | 0 | 1 | 0 | 0 | 1.000 |
| Prieto, Cordoba .... | 1 | 0 | 1 | 0 | 0 | 1.000 |
| Salinas, Aguas .... | 9 | 17 | 18 | 1 | 5 | .972 |
| Del Moral, Monterrey | 4 | 11 | 23 | 1 | 2 | .971 |
| Rodriguez, Mont .... | 4 | 9 | 5 | 1 | 4 | .933 |
| Reyes, Tampico .... | 6 | 6 | 6 | 1 | 2 | .923 |
| D. Lugo, Saltillo.... | 7 | 10 | 11 | 2 | 3 | .913 |
| Sommers, Puebla .... | 5 | 10 | 7 | 2 | 4 | .895 |
| Agramon, Reynosa .. | 4 | 8 | 6 | 3 | 1 | .824 |
| Tovar, Puebla ...... | 2 | 1 | 2 | 1 | 0 | .750 |
| Fitch, Reynosa ..... | 1 | 1 | 3 | 2 | 0 | .667 |
| Rubio, Puebla ...... | 2 | 1 | 1 | 1 | 0 | .667 |

## THIRD BASEMEN

| Player and Club | G. | PO. | A. | E. | DP. | Pct. |
|---|---|---|---|---|---|---|
| Plascencia, M Tig .. | 18 | 19 | 36 | 1 | 4 | .982 |
| MENA, Saltillo .... | 105 | 79 | 255 | 7 | 28 | .979 |
| Rivera, Mex Tigers . | 21 | 7 | 38 | 1 | 5 | .978 |
| Saldana, Monterrey . | 45 | 25 | 101 | 4 | 6 | .969 |
| J. Herrera, Coah .. | 57 | 45 | 113 | 6 | 7 | .963 |
| Montoya, Juarez .. | 128 | 109 | 222 | 13 | 23 | .962 |
| Garza, Mex Tigers .. | 18 | 19 | 31 | 2 | 5 | .962 |
| Arvizu, M Tig-Pue. | 114 | 112 | 211 | 13 | 29 | .961 |
| Fuentes, Poza Rica.. | 100 | 80 | 198 | 12 | 13 | .959 |
| Torres, Tampico .. | 122 | 123 | 243 | 17 | 24 | .956 |
| Alvarez, Cordoba .. | 69 | 47 | 146 | 9 | 17 | .955 |
| Vega, Mexico Reds .. | 117 | 102 | 216 | 16 | 20 | .952 |
| Rios, Reynosa .... | 112 | 122 | 233 | 18 | 21 | .952 |
| Jimenez, Coah-Villa.. | 75 | 72 | 137 | 11 | 18 | .950 |
| Cerda, Jalisco ...... | 128 | 121 | 287 | 22 | 19 | .949 |
| Diaz Rdz., U Laguna | 77 | 73 | 164 | 15 | 22 | .940 |
| Serna, Reynosa .. | 14 | 17 | 30 | 3 | 1 | .940 |
| Conkle, Villa ...... | 47 | 40 | 96 | 9 | 9 | .938 |
| Espinosa, Monterrey . | 20 | 11 | 34 | 3 | 5 | .938 |
| Castro, Coahuila ... | 26 | 15 | 43 | 4 | 1 | .935 |
| Sposito, Chihuahua .. | 105 | 110 | 249 | 27 | 20 | .930 |
| Lazaro, U Laguna .. | 64 | 51 | 114 | 14 | 15 | .922 |
| Sanchez, Cordoba .. | 67 | 36 | 116 | 13 | 10 | .921 |
| Sommers, Puebla .. | 89 | 87 | 179 | 23 | 15 | .920 |
| S. Lara, Poza Rica.. | 36 | 28 | 84 | 10 | 11 | .918 |
| Noriega, Aguas ... | 124 | 108 | 251 | 33 | 23 | .916 |
| Mora, Saltillo ..... | 34 | 23 | 74 | 9 | 8 | .915 |
| Del Moral, Monterrey | 73 | 55 | 152 | 20 | 5 | .912 |
| Almaraz, Tampico .. | 10 | 8 | 11 | 2 | 1 | .905 |
| Aguirre, Mex Reds... | 30 | 14 | 52 | 7 | 5 | .904 |
| Osuna, Coahuila ... | 31 | 20 | 52 | 8 | 3 | .900 |
| Elguezabal, Puebla .. | 23 | 15 | 29 | 5 | 0 | .898 |
| Martinez, C., Mont .. | 11 | 7 | 10 | 2 | 0 | .895 |
| Brookins, Chihuahua. | 39 | 28 | 72 | 12 | 4 | .893 |
| Figueroa, Villa .... | 38 | 25 | 75 | 12 | 4 | .893 |
| Lara, Coahuila ...... | 13 | 10 | 9 | 9 | 0 | .679 |

Triple Play—Arvizu.

### (Fewer Than Ten Games)

| Player and Club | G. | PO. | A. | E. | DP. | Pct. |
|---|---|---|---|---|---|---|
| Bojorquez, Cordoba .. | 5 | 1 | 8 | 0 | 1 | 1.000 |
| Brown, Union Laguna | 4 | 1 | 8 | 0 | 0 | 1.000 |
| J. M. Salinas, Rey .. | 3 | 5 | 2 | 0 | 0 | 1.000 |
| Rodriguez, Aguas .... | 3 | 3 | 4 | 0 | 0 | 1.000 |
| Silicato, Poza Rica .. | 3 | 1 | 5 | 0 | 0 | 1.000 |
| Alaniz, Chihuahua .. | 2 | 2 | 3 | 0 | 0 | 1.000 |
| Bonilla, Tampico .... | 2 | 1 | 4 | 0 | 2 | 1.000 |
| Camarero, Tampico .. | 1 | 2 | 1 | 0 | 0 | 1.000 |
| Estrada, Puebla .... | 2 | 1 | 2 | 0 | 0 | 1.000 |
| Sanchez, Poza Rica.. | 1 | 1 | 1 | 0 | 0 | 1.000 |
| Villalobos, Aguas .. | 1 | 0 | 1 | 0 | 0 | 1.000 |
| Lara, Mexico Tigers.. | 1 | 0 | 1 | 0 | 0 | 1.000 |
| Yepes, Poza Rica .. | 1 | 0 | 1 | 0 | 0 | 1.000 |
| Ramirez, Union Lag.. | 1 | 0 | 1 | 0 | 1 | 1.000 |
| Ramirez, Chihuahua.. | 2 | 0 | 1 | 0 | 0 | 1.000 |
| Ortiz, Monterrey ..... | 1 | 0 | 1 | 0 | 0 | 1.000 |
| Reyes, Jalisco ...... | 9 | 5 | 19 | 1 | 1 | .960 |
| Iglesias, Aguas .... | 9 | 4 | 17 | 1 | 2 | .955 |
| Hernandez, Jalisco .. | 6 | 6 | 13 | 1 | 1 | .950 |
| Garcia, Reynosa .... | 3 | 7 | 7 | 1 | 0 | .933 |
| Cambero, Poza Rica.. | 5 | 5 | 6 | 1 | 0 | .917 |
| Zavala, Cord-Salt ... | 9 | 3 | 15 | 2 | 1 | .900 |
| Vega, Juarez ....... | 8 | 5 | 13 | 2 | 1 | .900 |
| Garzon, Mex Tigers . | 3 | 6 | 2 | 1 | 3 | .889 |
| Romo, Aguascalientes | 7 | 5 | 5 | 2 | 3 | .833 |
| Plascencia, Coahuila | 6 | 2 | 2 | 1 | 0 | .800 |

### THIRD BASEMEN—Continued

| Player and Club | G. | PO. | A. | E. | DP. | Pct. |
|---|---|---|---|---|---|---|
| Howard, Tampico .. | 7 | 6 | 8 | 4 | 1 | .778 |
| Romero, Reynosa .... | 2 | 1 | 2 | 1 | 0 | .750 |
| Cervantes, Mex Tig .. | 1 | 0 | 2 | 1 | 0 | .667 |
| Trujillo, Juarez ..... | 3 | 0 | 3 | 2 | 0 | .600 |
| A. Arano, Cordoba ... | 2 | 0 | 1 | 1 | 0 | .500 |

### SHORTSTOPS

| Player and Club | G. | PO. | A. | E. | DP. | Pct. |
|---|---|---|---|---|---|---|
| J. F. Gonzalez, PR .. | 23 | 28 | 37 | 0 | 6 | 1.000 |
| Reyes, Tampico ...... | 21 | 31 | 55 | 1 | 5 | .989 |
| B. Garcia, Tampico.. | 14 | 28 | 32 | 1 | 6 | .984 |
| L. Rodriguez, Mont.. | 67 | 110 | 215 | 6 | 38 | .982 |
| RIVERO, Cordoba ... | 125 | 227 | 379 | 12 | 78 | .981 |
| Mendoza, P R-Pue.. | 115 | 236 | 376 | 14 | 68 | .978 |
| Salinas, Aguas-Rey.. | 31 | 63 | 94 | 4 | 21 | .975 |
| Mendez, Jalisco .... | 49 | 54 | 121 | 5 | 14 | .972 |
| V. Escalante, M Tig.. | 68 | 108 | 212 | 10 | 36 | .970 |
| Vega, Juarez ...... | 71 | 111 | 243 | 12 | 44 | .967 |
| Hernandez Z., M R.. | 10 | 12 | 15 | 1 | 5 | .964 |
| Rodriguez, Aguas ... | 135 | 279 | 542 | 34 | 87 | .960 |
| Espinosa, Monterrey.. | 66 | 137 | 309 | 22 | 48 | .953 |
| Mendoza, Juarez .... | 71 | 139 | 251 | 20 | 32 | .951 |
| Osuna, Coahuila .... | 29 | 43 | 72 | 6 | 10 | .950 |
| Villaescusa, M R ... | 133 | 252 | 457 | 37 | 89 | .949 |
| Rivera, Mex Tigers.. | 57 | 77 | 145 | 12 | 30 | .949 |
| Hernandez, Villa ... | 129 | 304 | 483 | 46 | 89 | .945 |
| Villalobos, Jalisco .. | 112 | 181 | 329 | 30 | 61 | .944 |
| Ramirez, Chihuahua | 123 | 212 | 348 | 33 | 65 | .944 |
| Serna, Reynosa...... | 66 | 107 | 218 | 20 | 36 | .942 |
| Diaz, Mex Tigers ... | 40 | 55 | 107 | 10 | 17 | .942 |
| Jimenez, Coah-Villa. | 11 | 18 | 31 | 3 | 9 | .940 |
| Crane, Salt-P R .... | 25 | 37 | 87 | 8 | 8 | .939 |
| Leon, Tampico ...... | 72 | 119 | 246 | 24 | 40 | .938 |
| Yepes, Poza Rica ... | 70 | 91 | 186 | 19 | 33 | .936 |
| Lopez, U Laguna ... | 138 | 228 | 454 | 48 | 85 | .934 |
| Chavez, Saltillo .... | 65 | 117 | 238 | 25 | 41 | .934 |
| Mena, Saltillo ...... | 14 | 22 | 34 | 4 | 8 | .933 |
| Tovar, Puebla-Coah. | 111 | 185 | 329 | 37 | 44 | .933 |
| Bonila, Tamp-Chih.. | 48 | 81 | 152 | 18 | 30 | .928 |
| Sposito, Chihuahua .. | 12 | 15 | 23 | 3 | 1 | .927 |
| Esparza, Poza Rica.. | 41 | 46 | 98 | 12 | 13 | .923 |
| Alvarez, Cordoba ... | 21 | 29 | 53 | 7 | 7 | .921 |
| J. Vazquez, Coah ... | 20 | 16 | 37 | 5 | 5 | .914 |
| McFadden, Reynosa . | 29 | 42 | 78 | 12 | 10 | .909 |
| Zava'a, Saltillo ..... | 42 | 62 | 140 | 21 | 14 | .906 |
| Marquez, Reynosa ... | 10 | 14 | 23 | 4 | 4 | .902 |
| Ruiz, Coahuila ..... | 18 | 33 | 33 | 5 | 8 | .895 |
| Alaniz, Chihuahua .. | 16 | 14 | 26 | 5 | 5 | .889 |

#### (Fewer Than Ten Games)

| Player and Club | G. | PO. | A. | E. | DP. | Pct. |
|---|---|---|---|---|---|---|
| Lazaro, U Laguna ... | 1 | 4 | 6 | 0 | 3 | 1.000 |
| A. Arano, Cordoba... | 3 | 3 | 5 | 0 | 1 | 1.000 |
| Del Moral, Monterrey | 5 | 3 | 4 | 0 | 0 | 1.000 |
| Crespo, Villahermosa | 3 | 3 | 3 | 0 | 0 | 1.000 |
| Sanchez, Poza Rica.. | 2 | 2 | 3 | 0 | 1 | 1.000 |
| S. Lara, Poza Rica.. | 2 | 1 | 4 | 0 | 1 | 1.000 |
| Sanchez, Cordoba ... | 2 | 1 | 3 | 0 | 0 | 1.000 |
| Montes Correa, Rey .. | 2 | 1 | 2 | 0 | 0 | 1.000 |
| Calvo, Aguas ....... | 1 | 1 | 1 | 0 | 0 | 1.000 |
| Guerrero, Jalisco .... | 1 | 1 | 0 | 0 | 0 | 1.000 |
| Tapia, Mex Tigers .. | 3 | 0 | 1 | 0 | 0 | 1.000 |
| Chavez, Puebla ..... | 5 | 9 | 12 | 1 | 4 | .955 |
| Montoya, Juarez .... | 5 | 6 | 21 | 2 | 1 | .931 |
| Silicato, Poza Rica .. | 6 | 7 | 19 | 2 | 2 | .929 |
| Alvarado, Coahuila .. | 7 | 10 | 19 | 3 | 5 | .906 |
| Cambero, Poza Rica.. | 5 | 13 | 22 | 4 | 8 | .897 |
| Sommers, Puebla .... | 2 | 5 | 3 | 2 | 0 | .800 |
| Hernandez, Jalisco .. | 4 | 4 | 3 | 2 | 0 | .778 |
| Greene, Reynosa .... | 2 | 2 | 5 | 2 | 0 | .778 |
| Ramirez, Reynosa ... | 6 | 7 | 5 | 5 | 1 | .706 |
| Fitch, Reynosa ...... | 1 | 2 | 1 | 2 | 0 | .600 |

### OUTFIELDERS

| Player and Club | G. | PO. | A. | E. | DP. | Pct. |
|---|---|---|---|---|---|---|
| MORA, Saltillo ..... | 99 | 156 | 7 | 0 | 1 | 1.000 |
| Tucker, Mexico Reds | 51 | 93 | 3 | 0 | 0 | 1.000 |
| Lopez, Juarez ...... | 33 | 50 | 1 | 0 | 0 | 1.000 |
| Perea, Villahermosa.. | 25 | 40 | 2 | 0 | 0 | 1.000 |
| Garza, Coahuila .... | 28 | 32 | 1 | 0 | 0 | 1.000 |
| Aguirre, Mexico Reds | 21 | 32 | 1 | 0 | 0 | 1.000 |
| H. Martinez, Reynosa | 17 | 28 | 4 | 0 | 1 | 1.000 |
| Diaz Rdz., U Laguna | 17 | 25 | 4 | 0 | 0 | 1.000 |
| B. Lopez, Mex Reds. | 16 | 25 | 2 | 0 | 0 | 1.000 |
| Del Moral, Monterrey. | 22 | 23 | 3 | 0 | 0 | 1.000 |
| Rosario, Aguas-Vil*.. | 17 | 21 | 3 | 0 | 0 | 1.000 |
| Osuna, Juarez ...... | 15 | 21 | 0 | 0 | 0 | 1.000 |
| Prieto, Cordoba ..... | 10 | 8 | 0 | 0 | 0 | 1.000 |
| Zamudio, Mex Tigers | 114 | 285 | 11 | 1 | 3 | .997 |
| Ford, Reynosa ...... | 93 | 212 | 10 | 1 | 1 | .996 |
| L. A. Davila, Juarez | 120 | 284 | 11 | 2 | 3 | .993 |
| Zuniga, Cordoba .... | 106 | 227 | 8 | 2 | 0 | .992 |
| Faudoa, Chihuahua*.. | 58 | 94 | 3 | 1 | 1 | .990 |
| Browne, Coahuila ... | 84 | 155 | 12 | 2 | 4 | .988 |
| Juarez, Saltillo .... | 75 | 158 | 7 | 2 | 1 | .988 |
| Enriquez, Monterrey | 123 | 254 | 9 | 4 | 2 | .985 |
| Menchaca, UL-Salt . | 31 | 54 | 5 | 1 | 2 | .983 |
| Ponce, Mex Tigers .. | 116 | 269 | 12 | 5 | 2 | .983 |
| Aguilar, Mex Tigers | 41 | 51 | 5 | 1 | 2 | .982 |
| Paredes, Cordoba ... | 113 | 210 | 5 | 4 | 1 | .982 |
| Suarez, Mex Reds*.. | 134 | 245 | 18 | 5 | 3 | .981 |
| Talley, Puebla ..... | 72 | 141 | 8 | 3 | 1 | .980 |
| Crawford, Pue-Aguas | 68 | 134 | 6 | 3 | 1 | .979 |
| T. Acosta, Villa*... | 106 | 172 | 14 | 4 | 3 | .979 |
| Brooks, Aguas-Chihua | 29 | 43 | 3 | 1 | 0 | .979 |
| Freed, Monterrey ... | 73 | 130 | 6 | 3 | 1 | .978 |
| Beltran, Mex Tig*... | 34 | 40 | 3 | 1 | 0 | .977 |
| Lara, Mexico Tigers. | 133 | 280 | 20 | 7 | 2 | .977 |
| Ford, Jalisco ...... | 93 | 198 | 15 | 5 | 0 | .977 |
| V. M. Felix, U Lag | 123 | 237 | 14 | 6 | 2 | .977 |
| Real, Reynosa ...... | 30 | 70 | 3 | 2 | 1 | .970 |
| Davalil'o, Cordoba*.. | 82 | 197 | 7 | 5 | 1 | .976 |
| James, Puebla ...... | 20 | 38 | 2 | 1 | 0 | .976 |
| Cedeno, Chihuahua* | 136 | 230 | 8 | 6 | 1 | .975 |
| Guerrero, Jalisco ... | 87 | 156 | 2 | 4 | 0 | .975 |
| Lara, Puebla ...... | 95 | 191 | 5 | 5 | 0 | .975 |
| Valenzuela, Mont*... | 21 | 34 | 5 | 1 | 1 | .975 |
| Urias, Villa-Tamp ... | 73 | 109 | 3 | 3 | 0 | .974 |
| Mora, Reynosa-Aguas | 61 | 70 | 2 | 2 | 1 | .973 |
| Martinez C., Mont .. | 85 | 132 | 10 | 4 | 0 | .973 |
| Valenzuela, Jalisco . | 40 | 64 | 7 | 2 | 0 | .973 |
| Silverio, Tampico*.. | 133 | 301 | 18 | 9 | 2 | .973 |
| Thompson, Chihua*.. | 23 | 30 | 5 | 1 | 2 | .972 |
| Matias, Juarez* .... | 49 | 97 | 7 | 3 | 1 | .972 |
| Rodriguez, Villa .... | 103 | 222 | 15 | 7 | 4 | .971 |
| Diaz, Poza Rica .... | 130 | 288 | 13 | 9 | 0 | .971 |
| Brookins, Chihuahua | 69 | 121 | 11 | 4 | 2 | .971 |
| Cruz, Saltillo ...... | 137 | 278 | 14 | 9 | 3 | .970 |
| Bojorquez, Vil-Cor .. | 13 | 31 | 0 | 1 | 0 | .969 |
| Phillips, Mex Reds .. | 99 | 232 | 14 | 8 | 4 | .969 |
| Ortiz, Juarez ...... | 81 | 141 | 11 | 5 | 3 | .968 |
| A. Martinez, Reynosa | 51 | 87 | 4 | 3 | 0 | .968 |
| Brown, Union Laguna | 128 | 312 | 12 | 11 | 3 | .967 |
| Villalobos, Jalisco .. | 17 | 26 | 2 | 1 | 0 | .966 |
| Canada, U Laguna .. | 133 | 313 | 20 | 12 | 1 | .965 |
| Clark, Mexico Reds.. | 82 | 159 | 7 | 6 | 1 | .965 |
| Robles, Aguas* ..... | 57 | 78 | 5 | 3 | 0 | .965 |
| Bravo, Mont-Cord*.. | 113 | 183 | 9 | 7 | 0 | .965 |
| Peralta, Juarez .... | 96 | 204 | 8 | 8 | 0 | .964 |
| N. Vazquez, Coahuila | 102 | 177 | 8 | 7 | 2 | .964 |
| Arano, Cord-Poza R.. | 85 | 175 | 9 | 7 | 2 | .963 |
| Figueroa, Tampico .. | 54 | 101 | 4 | 4 | 0 | .963 |
| Rubio, Puebla ...... | 92 | 147 | 6 | 6 | 1 | .962 |
| Salazar, Jalisco .... | 60 | 148 | 2 | 6 | 0 | .962 |
| L. Lopez, Tampico .. | 96 | 164 | 9 | 7 | 2 | .961 |
| Serrato, Reynosa ... | 17 | 19 | 5 | 1 | 1 | .960 |

## OUTFIELDERS—Continued

| Player and Club | G. | PO. | A. | E. | DP. | Pct. |
|---|---|---|---|---|---|---|
| Gonzalez, Monterrey.. | 99 | 178 | 12 | 8 | 4 | .960 |
| James, Aguascalientes | 44 | 64 | 7 | 3 | 0 | .959 |
| Plascencia, Coahuila | 83 | 133 | 6 | 6 | 0 | .959 |
| Ornelas, Saltillo .... | 78 | 105 | 9 | 5 | 0 | .958 |
| Sauceda, Chihuahua | 133 | 319 | 10 | 15 | 2 | .956 |
| Roque, Puebla ...... | 91 | 208 | 4 | 10 | 0 | .955 |
| Villalobos, Aguas .. | 137 | 279 | 31 | 15 | 5 | .954 |
| De Hoyos, Coahuila* | 110 | 232 | 7 | 12 | 2 | .952 |
| Vidal, Poza Rica .... | 114 | 202 | 9 | 11 | 3 | .950 |
| Kelly, Poza Rica .... | 13 | 18 | 1 | 1 | 0 | .950 |
| F. Felix, UL-Villa .. | 93 | 194 | 13 | 11 | 3 | .950 |
| Alvarado, Reynosa* .. | 98 | 112 | 7 | 7 | 2 | .944 |
| Alcaide, Cord-Coah* | 18 | 33 | 1 | 2 | 0 | .944 |
| Howard, Tampico .... | 93 | 152 | 13 | 10 | 2 | .943 |
| Gonzalez, Villa* .... | 14 | 24 | 6 | 2 | 1 | .938 |
| Moore, Jalisco ...... | 86 | 154 | 8 | 11 | 3 | .936 |
| Ochoa, Aguascalientes | 35 | 61 | 9 | 5 | 2 | .933 |
| Garcia, Reynosa .... | 82 | 138 | 13 | 11 | 2 | .932 |
| Dugan, Jalisco ...... | 25 | 35 | 3 | 3 | 0 | .927 |
| Del Toro, Juarez* .... | 30 | 54 | 3 | 5 | 0 | .919 |
| Colon, Poza Rica* .. | 35 | 59 | 3 | 6 | 0 | .912 |
| Saiz, Poza Rica* .... | 62 | 108 | 4 | 11 | 0 | .911 |
| Camarero, Aguas-Tam | 42 | 56 | 1 | 6 | 0 | .905 |
| Espinosa, Villa...... | 35 | 62 | 2 | 7 | 0 | .901 |
| Montoya, Mex Reds... | 27 | 33 | 2 | 4 | 0 | .897 |
| Marquez, Aguas .... | 27 | 35 | 4 | 5 | 0 | .886 |
| Sanchez, U Laguna*.. | 23 | 22 | 1 | 3 | 1 | .885 |

### (Fewer Than Ten Games)

| Player and Club | G. | PO. | A. | E. | DP. | Pct. |
|---|---|---|---|---|---|---|
| F. E. Jimenez, Coah | 9 | 14 | 0 | 0 | 0 | 1.000 |
| Sosa, Poza Rica .... | 7 | 11 | 1 | 0 | 0 | 1.000 |
| Aguilera, Villa ..... | 6 | 7 | 1 | 0 | 0 | 1.000 |
| Perez, Tampico ...... | 6 | 7 | 1 | 0 | 0 | 1.000 |
| Duran, Cordoba ..... | 8 | 7 | 0 | 0 | 0 | 1.000 |
| Almaraz, Tampico .. | 7 | 7 | 0 | 0 | 0 | 1.000 |
| Pina, Saltillo ...... | 5 | 7 | 0 | 0 | 0 | 1.000 |
| McFadden, Reynosa.. | 4 | 7 | 0 | 0 | 0 | 1.000 |
| Orozco, Monterrey .. | 7 | 6 | 0 | 0 | 0 | 1.000 |
| A. Ochoa, Villa ..... | 5 | 6 | 0 | 0 | 0 | 1.000 |
| Herrera, Villa ...... | 4 | 5 | 1 | 0 | 0 | 1.000 |
| Juarez, Poza Rica* .. | 2 | 5 | 0 | 0 | 0 | 1.000 |
| Elguezabal, Puebla .. | 4 | 4 | 0 | 0 | 0 | 1.000 |
| Ortiz, Villahermosa.. | 3 | 4 | 0 | 0 | 0 | 1.000 |
| Perez, Aguascalientes | 4 | 3 | 0 | 0 | 0 | 1.000 |
| Sanchez, Cordoba ... | 1 | 3 | 0 | 0 | 0 | 1.000 |
| McGuffin, Reynosa .. | 1 | 3 | 0 | 0 | 0 | 1.000 |
| Wissel, Cordoba ..... | 6 | 2 | 0 | 0 | 0 | 1.000 |
| Calvo, Aguascalientes | 4 | 2 | 0 | 0 | 0 | 1.000 |
| Diaz, Mexico Tigers.. | 3 | 2 | 0 | 0 | 0 | 1.000 |
| W. Gonzalez, PR .... | 3 | 2 | 0 | 0 | 0 | 1.000 |
| Thompson, Cordoba .. | 2 | 2 | 0 | 0 | 0 | 1.000 |
| Espinosa, Monterrey | 1 | 2 | 0 | 0 | 0 | 1.000 |
| Leal, Chihuahua .... | 5 | 1 | 0 | 0 | 0 | 1.000 |
| Trevino, U Laguna .. | 3 | 1 | 0 | 0 | 0 | 1.000 |
| Martinez, Mex Tig .. | 2 | 1 | 0 | 0 | 0 | 1.000 |
| Romo, Mexico Reds.. | 2 | 1 | 0 | 0 | 0 | 1.000 |
| Bourque, Mex Reds* | 2 | 1 | 0 | 0 | 0 | 1.000 |
| Ibarra, U Laguna*.. | 2 | 1 | 0 | 0 | 0 | 1.000 |
| Lizarraga, Saltillo .. | 2 | 1 | 0 | 0 | 0 | 1.000 |
| Pollorena, U Laguna | 1 | 1 | 0 | 0 | 0 | 1.000 |
| Reyes, Tampico ..... | 1 | 1 | 0 | 0 | 0 | 1.000 |
| Alvarado, Coahuila.. | 1 | 1 | 0 | 0 | 0 | 1.000 |
| Hottman, Juarez .... | 9 | 15 | 0 | 1 | 0 | .938 |
| Arevalo, Villa ...... | 7 | 12 | 2 | 1 | 0 | .933 |
| Barron, Mexico Reds | 7 | 12 | 0 | 1 | 0 | .923 |
| Pettaway, Jalisco* .. | 8 | 16 | 0 | 3 | 0 | .812 |
| Lara, Coahuila ...... | 3 | 3 | 1 | 1 | 0 | .800 |
| Walseth, Puebla .... | 7 | 6 | 0 | 2 | 0 | .750 |
| Morales, Puebla ..... | 1 | 3 | 0 | 1 | 0 | .750 |
| Foster, Chihuahua .. | 3 | 2 | 0 | 1 | 0 | .667 |

## CATCHERS

| Player and Club | G. | PO. | A. | E. | DP. | PB. | Pct. |
|---|---|---|---|---|---|---|---|
| Camargo, Mont .. | 10 | 22 | 5 | 0 | 1 | 1 | 1.000 |
| TIBURCIO, M Tig | 98 | 389 | 75 | 2 | 6 | 17 | .996 |
| Ruiz, Cordoba .. | 116 | 551 | 46 | 4 | 4 | 17 | .993 |
| Rodo, Sandoval, Chi | 87 | 467 | 58 | 4 | 3 | 9 | .992 |
| R. Herrera, Coah.. | 18 | 97 | 5 | 1 | 1 | 3 | .990 |
| Rey, Tampico ... | 107 | 592 | 67 | 7 | 10 | 10 | .989 |
| Orozco,MR-Vi-MT | 49 | 220 | 42 | 3 | 4 | 14 | .989 |
| Valenzuela, Jal .. | 45 | 223 | 27 | 3 | 1 | 11 | .988 |
| Peralta, Poza R .. | 104 | 596 | 56 | 8 | 5 | 17 | .988 |
| Valle, Juarez .... | 134 | 537 | 69 | 8 | 6 | 13 | .987 |
| Lugo, Poza Rica.. | 45 | 208 | 17 | 3 | 1 | 5 | .987 |
| Alvarado, Coa-Pue | 26 | 69 | 5 | 1 | 1 | 2 | .987 |
| Briones, Monterrey | 72 | 309 | 32 | 5 | 7 | 11 | .986 |
| Valenzuela, Rey .. | 126 | 654 | 90 | 11 | 11 | 16 | .985 |
| Guillen, MT-Coah | 52 | 240 | 25 | 4 | 2 | 11 | .985 |
| Rivera, Villa .... | 98 | 453 | 69 | 9 | 5 | 12 | .983 |
| Gutierrez, Coah .. | 86 | 413 | 46 | 8 | 6 | 10 | .983 |
| Luque, Saltillo ... | 99 | 446 | 69 | 9 | 6 | 8 | .983 |
| Jackson, U Lag .. | 104 | 403 | 53 | 8 | 5 | 2 | .983 |
| Salinas, Chihuahua | 71 | 338 | 49 | 7 | 1 | 10 | .982 |
| Estrada, Puebla .. | 117 | 524 | 83 | 11 | 8 | 9 | .982 |
| Salinas, Cordoba .. | 39 | 140 | 7 | 3 | 0 | 5 | .980 |
| Barron, Mex Reds | 110 | 551 | 85 | 13 | 12 | 17 | .980 |
| Arevalo, Villa.... | 23 | 79 | 16 | 2 | 4 | 2 | .979 |
| Rosas, Jalisco .... | 99 | 537 | 75 | 13 | 6 | 23 | .979 |
| Marquez, Aguas .. | 83 | 465 | 68 | 12 | 7 | 25 | .978 |
| Esquivel, Tampico | 42 | 223 | 31 | 6 | 4 | 8 | .977 |
| King, Puebla-Cord | 12 | 37 | 5 | 1 | 0 | 3 | .977 |
| Orozco, Monterrey. | 49 | 175 | 15 | 5 | 2 | 15 | .974 |
| Diaz Rdz., U Lag | 40 | 164 | 22 | 5 | 5 | 3 | .974 |
| E. Gonzalez, U L | 25 | 31 | 5 | 1 | 2 | 2 | .973 |
| Soto, Mexico Reds | 41 | 164 | 13 | 5 | 1 | 9 | .973 |
| Zabala, Monterrey | 26 | 114 | 18 | 4 | 4 | 4 | .971 |
| Trevino, Reynosa.. | 10 | 28 | 5 | 1 | 1 | 1 | .971 |
| Benites, Aguas .. | 67 | 320 | 38 | 11 | 8 | 27 | .970 |
| Garcia, Juarez .... | 12 | 27 | 3 | 1 | 0 | 7 | .968 |
| Lizarraga, Salt ... | 50 | 220 | 20 | 9 | 1 | 5 | .964 |
| Hernandez, Puebla | 10 | 38 | 8 | 2 | 1 | 2 | .958 |
| Aguilar, M Tigers | 37 | 127 | 12 | 9 | 3 | 8 | .939 |

### (Fewer Than Ten Games)

| Player and Club | G. | PO. | A. | E. | DP. | PB. | Pct. |
|---|---|---|---|---|---|---|---|
| Cota, Reynosa .. | 8 | 17 | 0 | 0 | 1 | 0 | 1.000 |
| Sosa, Poza Rica .. | 3 | 11 | 0 | 0 | 0 | 0 | 1.000 |
| Clark, Mex Reds .. | 1 | 5 | 0 | 0 | 0 | 1 | 1.000 |
| Gallegos, Reynosa.. | 4 | 4 | 0 | 0 | 0 | 0 | 1.000 |
| Bojorquez, Cord .. | 4 | 3 | 0 | 0 | 0 | 0 | 1.000 |
| Terrazas, Mex T .. | 1 | 2 | 0 | 0 | 0 | 0 | 1.000 |
| Alaniz, Chihuahua | 1 | 2 | 0 | 0 | 0 | 0 | 1.000 |
| Saldana, Mont.... | 1 | 0 | 2 | 0 | 0 | 0 | 1.000 |
| Amador, Puebla .. | 2 | 1 | 0 | 0 | 0 | 0 | 1.000 |
| Elguezabal, Pue .. | 7 | 16 | 0 | 1 | 0 | 2 | .941 |
| Freed, Monterrey.. | 2 | 9 | 2 | 1 | 0 | 0 | .917 |
| Gutierrez, Rey ... | 1 | 0 | 0 | 1 | 0 | 0 | .000 |

## PITCHERS

| Player and Club | G. | PO. | A. | E. | DP. | Pct. |
|---|---|---|---|---|---|---|
| G. SALINAS, Rey.... | 33 | 15 | 52 | 0 | 3 | 1.000 |
| KOKOR, Aguas .... | 28 | 10 | 57 | 0 | 6 | 1.000 |
| Gutierrez, Cordoba .. | 35 | 18 | 45 | 0 | 3 | 1.000 |
| Ahumada, Saltillo .. | 31 | 14 | 34 | 0 | 3 | 1.000 |
| Aponte, Reynosa .... | 33 | 12 | 30 | 0 | 3 | 1.000 |
| A. Hernandez, P R .. | 33 | 8 | 34 | 0 | 1 | 1.000 |
| Bracamontes, Puebla* | 31 | 10 | 27 | 0 | 1 | 1.000 |
| R. Amaro, Cordoba... | 26 | 8 | 29 | 0 | 2 | 1.000 |
| Leal, Chihuahua .... | 27 | 8 | 27 | 0 | 2 | 1.000 |
| V. Garcia, Tampico.. | 31 | 3 | 32 | 0 | 1 | 1.000 |

### PITCHERS—Continued

| Player and Club | G. | PO. | A. | E. | DP. | Pct. |
|---|---|---|---|---|---|---|
| Hambright, Juarez .. | 28 | 7 | 25 | 0 | 0 | 1.000 |
| Agundez, Mex Tigers | 52 | 3 | 27 | 0 | 1 | 1.000 |
| Reyes, Chihuahua* .. | 29 | 4 | 22 | 0 | 2 | 1.000 |
| Rodr. Sandoval, Chih | 25 | 2 | 19 | 0 | 1 | 1.000 |
| Britton, U Laguna*.. | 24 | 3 | 16 | 0 | 0 | 1.000 |
| Tovar, Union Laguna. | 30 | 1 | 18 | 0 | 1 | 1.000 |
| Cruz, Poza Rica .... | 24 | 7 | 10 | 0 | 0 | 1.000 |
| Ayon, Cordoba ..... | 10 | 7 | 10 | 0 | 0 | 1.000 |
| Campoy, Reynosa ... | 15 | 5 | 12 | 0 | 1 | 1.000 |
| Collazo, Tampico ... | 15 | 5 | 14 | 0 | 1 | 1.000 |
| Solis, Coahuila .... | 31 | 3 | 12 | 0 | 2 | 1.000 |
| Gutierrez, Reynosa .. | 26 | 4 | 10 | 0 | 1 | 1.000 |
| Moreno, Monterrey .. | 24 | 1 | 13 | 0 | 0 | 1.000 |
| Reynoso, Chihuahua.. | 13 | 4 | 9 | 0 | 0 | 1.000 |
| Rodriquez, Poza R .. | 14 | 2 | 11 | 0 | 0 | 1.000 |
| Fabela, Villahermosa | 31 | 3 | 8 | 0 | 0 | 1.000 |
| Villanueva, M Tig*.. | 12 | 2 | 9 | 0 | 0 | 1.000 |
| Cazares, Jalisco* ... | 27 | 1 | 10 | 0 | 1 | 1.000 |
| Nieto, Tampico .... | 15 | 4 | 6 | 0 | 0 | 1.000 |
| Cisneros, Coahuila .. | 29 | 3 | 7 | 0 | 3 | 1.000 |
| Barandica, Puebla .. | 14 | 3 | 7 | 0 | 0 | 1.000 |
| Martinez H., Mont* . | 33 | 2 | 8 | 0 | 1 | 1.000 |
| Lozano, Juarez* .... | 25 | 2 | 8 | 0 | 0 | 1.000 |
| Holly, Jalisco* ...... | 10 | 1 | 9 | 0 | 0 | 1.000 |
| Mellado, Villa ..... | 21 | 3 | 5 | 0 | 1 | 1.000 |
| Ochoa, Reynosa .... | 16 | 3 | 5 | 0 | 2 | 1.000 |
| Valenzuela, M Reds.. | 17 | 2 | 5 | 0 | 1 | 1.000 |
| Franco, Poza Rica .. | 16 | 2 | 5 | 0 | 0 | 1.000 |
| Buentello, Cordoba .. | 36 | 0 | 6 | 0 | 1 | 1.000 |
| O. Bernal, Mont .... | 17 | 3 | 2 | 0 | 0 | 1.000 |
| Hernandez S., Aguas | 30 | 2 | 3 | 0 | 0 | 1.000 |
| Delfin, Cordoba .... | 15 | 1 | 4 | 0 | 0 | 1.000 |
| Ramos, M Reds-Villa | 10 | 1 | 4 | 0 | 0 | 1.000 |
| Montero, Reynosa ... | 22 | 2 | 2 | 0 | 0 | 1.000 |
| Gamez, Mex Reds* .. | 19 | 1 | 3 | 0 | 0 | 1.000 |
| Morales, Coahuila ... | 11 | 0 | 3 | 0 | 0 | 1.000 |
| Rodriguez, U Laguna | 11 | 0 | 1 | 0 | 0 | 1.000 |
| Romo, Cordoba ..... | 22 | 12 | 34 | 1 | 1 | .979 |
| Meza, Mex Tigers* .. | 45 | 5 | 39 | 1 | 3 | .978 |
| Monteagudo, Puebla.. | 27 | 10 | 33 | 1 | 3 | .977 |
| Pizarro, Cordoba* .. | 23 | 6 | 34 | 1 | 1 | .976 |
| Penalver, Monterrey . | 36 | 12 | 25 | 1 | 1 | .974 |
| Garcia, Puebla ...... | 31 | 4 | 33 | 1 | 2 | .974 |
| Barrios, Jalisco .... | 31 | 9 | 26 | 1 | 1 | .972 |
| McRae, Chihuahua .. | 33 | 25 | 35 | 2 | 2 | .968 |
| Lagunas, Villa ..... | 25 | 5 | 25 | 1 | 1 | .968 |
| Orea, Juarez ........ | 46 | 4 | 25 | 1 | 0 | .967 |
| Beltran, Juarez ..... | 34 | 8 | 20 | 1 | 2 | .966 |
| Ortiz, U.. Mex Reds* | 30 | 4 | 47 | 2 | 1 | .962 |
| Chavez, Chihuahua .. | 34 | 14 | 35 | 2 | 4 | .961 |
| Martinez, Villa .... | 34 | 10 | 39 | 2 | 3 | .961 |
| President, Aguas* ... | 32 | 10 | 38 | 2 | 0 | .960 |
| Fajardo, Juarez ..... | 56 | 4 | 19 | 1 | 2 | .958 |
| Armas, Saltillo* .... | 27 | 3 | 20 | 1 | 0 | .958 |
| Guzman Jalisco .... | 41 | 2 | 20 | 1 | 0 | .957 |
| Madrigal, Poza Rica. | 34 | 6 | 16 | 1 | 0 | .957 |
| Saldivar, M Tigers.. | 41 | 7 | 36 | 2 | 2 | .956 |
| Texidor, Reynosa ... | 34 | 10 | 30 | 2 | 2 | .952 |
| Suby, M Tig-Tampico | 45 | 7 | 13 | 1 | 1 | .952 |
| F. Lopez, M Tigers .. | 33 | 2 | 18 | 1 | 1 | .952 |
| Castillo, U Laguna .. | 36 | 4 | 16 | 1 | 2 | .952 |
| DeLaTorre, U Laguna | 33 | 7 | 31 | 2 | 7 | .950 |
| Soto, Juarez* ...... | 32 | 6 | 32 | 2 | 1 | .950 |
| P. Rodriguez, Mont.. | 33 | 3 | 16 | 1 | 0 | .950 |
| Romo, Mexico Reds.. | 30 | 19 | 37 | 3 | 3 | .949 |
| Luna, Monterrey .... | 21 | 7 | 30 | 2 | 1 | .949 |
| Pactwa, Tampico* .. | 26 | 12 | 42 | 3 | 3 | .947 |
| Gage-Cole, Saltillo .. | 45 | 4 | 32 | 2 | 1 | .947 |
| Hernandez, Saltillo .. | 26 | 8 | 28 | 2 | 3 | .947 |
| Pena, Villahermosa . | 42 | 17 | 53 | 4 | 8 | .946 |
| Barbosa, Coahuila* .. | 30 | 9 | 60 | 4 | 3 | .945 |
| Sandate, Poza Rica* . | 28 | 8 | 26 | 2 | 2 | .944 |
| Paz, Villahermosa .. | 13 | 2 | 15 | 1 | 1 | .944 |
| Azcarraga, Puebla .. | 33 | 16 | 50 | 4 | 7 | .943 |
| Brunet, Poza Rica* . | 34 | 3 | 30 | 2 | 2 | .943 |
| G. Gonzalez, U L* .. | 29 | 2 | 14 | 1 | 1 | .941 |
| Mercado, Coahuila .. | 28 | 3 | 13 | 1 | 1 | .941 |
| Rodriguez, Mex Reds | 34 | 4 | 43 | 3 | 4 | .940 |
| Pina, Aguascalientes . | 26 | 16 | 43 | 4 | 2 | .937 |
| Vallejano, Tampico .. | 33 | 8 | 35 | 3 | 3 | .935 |
| Maytorena, Tampico . | 53 | 5 | 23 | 2 | 2 | .933 |
| Barrientos, U Laguna | 39 | 4 | 10 | 1 | 0 | .933 |
| Abarca, Jalisco ..... | 19 | 3 | 11 | 1 | 1 | .933 |
| Rivas, Coahuila* ... | 15 | 1 | 13 | 1 | 0 | .933 |
| Volkening, Mont .... | 32 | 21 | 62 | 6 | 5 | .933 |
| Adame, Salt-Aguas .. | 28 | 7 | 34 | 3 | 2 | .932 |
| Diaz, Aguascalientes . | 37 | 13 | 55 | 5 | 2 | .932 |
| Munoz, Cordoba .... | 25 | 2 | 25 | 2 | 5 | .931 |
| Moreno, Juarez .... | 32 | 11 | 29 | 3 | 1 | .930 |
| Lee, Coahuila ...... | 33 | 11 | 42 | 4 | 1 | .930 |
| Puente, Juarez ..... | 30 | 6 | 33 | 3 | 2 | .929 |
| Salomon, Cordoba .. | 22 | 8 | 31 | 3 | 5 | .929 |
| Mota, Puebla ...... | 32 | 4 | 22 | 2 | 0 | .929 |
| Travis, Chihuahua .. | 28 | 7 | 19 | 2 | 0 | .929 |
| Brandon, Coahuila .. | 12 | 6 | 20 | 2 | 0 | .929 |
| Pereira, Puebla ..... | 32 | 4 | 9 | 1 | 0 | .929 |
| Carrasco, Monterrey . | 30 | 5 | 32 | 3 | 1 | .925 |
| Acosta L., Mex Reds | 31 | 17 | 31 | 4 | 1 | .923 |
| Miali, Coahuila* ... | 14 | 0 | 12 | 1 | 0 | .923 |
| Cavanaugh, Poza R .. | 36 | 19 | 51 | 6 | 0 | .921 |
| Lefevre, Tampico ... | 21 | 10 | 13 | 2 | 0 | .920 |
| Cordova, Jalisco .... | 36 | 9 | 25 | 3 | 1 | .919 |
| Boyd, Salt-Puebla*.. | 24 | 3 | 8 | 1 | 0 | .917 |
| Solis, Saltillo ...... | 28 | 13 | 19 | 3 | 3 | .914 |
| Acosta M., U L-Vill | 35 | 7 | 46 | 5 | 1 | .914 |
| Espinosa, Mex Tigers | 33 | 2 | 19 | 2 | 0 | .913 |
| Salgado, Reynosa ... | 35 | 3 | 20 | 2 | 0 | .913 |
| Cordeiro, Villa* .... | 32 | 6 | 25 | 3 | 0 | .912 |
| Cruz, Monterrey .... | 37 | 0 | 10 | 1 | 1 | .909 |
| Verdugo, Saltillo ... | 28 | 2 | 8 | 1 | 0 | .909 |
| Montoya, Tam-Agua* | 27 | 5 | 5 | 1 | 0 | .909 |
| Pollorena, U Laguna | 35 | 8 | 31 | 4 | 2 | .907 |
| Raygoza, Coahuila .. | 18 | 9 | 10 | 2 | 1 | .905 |
| Valenzuela, Sal-Coa | 24 | 3 | 15 | 2 | 1 | .900 |
| A. Lopez, Mex Reds.. | 71 | 6 | 20 | 3 | 2 | .897 |
| Byron Quiros, Aguas | 49 | 6 | 20 | 3 | 2 | .897 |
| Goodwin, Saltillo ... | 30 | 7 | 19 | 3 | 0 | .897 |
| Velo, Jalisco ....... | 40 | 4 | 21 | 3 | 0 | .893 |
| Guzman, Chihuahua.. | 52 | 3 | 13 | 2 | 0 | .889 |
| Garcia, Mex Tigers.. | 42 | 0 | 16 | 2 | 0 | .889 |
| Puig, Chihua-Rey* .. | 13 | 4 | 4 | 1 | 0 | .889 |
| Cruz, Tampico ..... | 27 | 5 | 17 | 3 | 1 | .880 |
| Mere, Mexico Reds.. | 36 | 8 | 21 | 4 | 2 | .879 |
| Snyder, Saltillo .... | 11 | 4 | 16 | 3 | 1 | .870 |
| Gutierrez, Jalisco* .. | 24 | 6 | 12 | 3 | 1 | .857 |
| Martinez A., Puebla* | 30 | 0 | 6 | 1 | 0 | .857 |
| Pena, U Laguna* ... | 24 | 1 | 4 | 1 | 0 | .833 |
| Acosta, Puebla ..... | 26 | 2 | 12 | 3 | 1 | .824 |
| Newson, Jalisco .... | 10 | 1 | 13 | 3 | 2 | .824 |
| Figueroa, Coa-P R .. | 24 | 1 | 8 | 2 | 0 | .818 |
| Valdez, Mex Tigers.. | 14 | 2 | 2 | 1 | 0 | .800 |
| Diorio, Puebla ..... | 17 | 1 | 6 | 2 | 1 | .778 |
| Diaz, Mexico Tigers | 17 | 1 | 8 | 3 | 0 | .750 |
| Armas, Cordoba* ... | 19 | 1 | 2 | 1 | 0 | .750 |
| Soto, Chihuahua .... | 17 | 2 | 1 | 1 | 0 | .750 |
| Delgado, M Tigers*.. | 19 | 0 | 4 | 2 | 0 | .667 |

(Fewer Than Ten Games)

| Player and Club | G. | PO. | A. | E. | DP. | Pct. |
|---|---|---|---|---|---|---|
| Valadez, Tampico ... | 9 | 6 | 9 | 0 | 0 | 1.000 |
| Brito, Aguas ........ | 9 | 5 | 7 | 0 | 1 | 1.000 |
| Yard, Aguascalientes . | 8 | 2 | 5 | 0 | 0 | 1.000 |
| Dillon, Jalisco* ..... | 8 | 1 | 6 | 0 | 1 | 1.000 |
| Santos, Reynosa .... | 5 | 1 | 5 | 0 | 1 | 1.000 |
| Valle, Aguas* ...... | 7 | 2 | 2 | 0 | 0 | 1.000 |
| Saucedo, Jalisco .... | 7 | 1 | 3 | 0 | 0 | 1.000 |
| A. Davila, Juarez*.. | 9 | 0 | 4 | 0 | 1 | 1.000 |
| Castro, Mex Tigers .. | 8 | 0 | 4 | 0 | 1 | 1.000 |
| Rabouin, Jalisco .... | 5 | 0 | 4 | 0 | 0 | 1.000 |
| Kealey, Jalisco ..... | 4 | 0 | 4 | 0 | 0 | 1.000 |
| Cabrales, U Laguna . | 8 | 1 | 2 | 0 | 0 | 1.000 |
| Sifuentes, Cordoba*. | 4 | 1 | 2 | 0 | 0 | 1.000 |
| Valencia, Villa ..... | 3 | 1 | 2 | 0 | 0 | 1.000 |

## PITCHERS—Continued

| Player and Club | G. | PO. | A. | E. | DP. | Pct. |
|---|---|---|---|---|---|---|
| G. Lara, Poza Rica*. | 9 | 0 | 3 | 0 | 0 | 1.000 |
| Almonte, Juarez .... | 8 | 0 | 3 | 0 | 0 | 1.000 |
| Thompson, Reynosa*.. | 1 | 0 | 3 | 0 | 0 | 1.000 |
| Lugo, Puebla ....... | 1 | 2 | 0 | 0 | 0 | 1.000 |
| Lugo, Jalisco ...... | 6 | 1 | 1 | 0 | 0 | 1.000 |
| Chavez, Tampico .... | 5 | 1 | 1 | 0 | 0 | 1.000 |
| Gowell, Puebla ..... | 5 | 1 | 1 | 0 | 0 | 1.000 |
| Pate, Union Laguna . | 4 | 1 | 1 | 0 | 0 | 1.000 |
| Beltran, Aguas* .... | 4 | 1 | 1 | 0 | 0 | 1.000 |
| Escalante, Aguas* .. | 4 | 1 | 1 | 0 | 0 | 1.000 |
| Lagunes, Poza Rica.. | 3 | 1 | 1 | 0 | 0 | 1.000 |
| Colorado, Jalisco .. | 2 | 1 | 1 | 0 | 1 | 1.000 |
| Beltran, U Laguna .. | 2 | 0 | 2 | 0 | 0 | 1.000 |
| Fernandez, Poz R .. | 2 | 0 | 2 | 0 | 0 | 1.000 |
| Mondragon, Cor-Pue . | 2 | 0 | 2 | 0 | 0 | 1.000 |
| R. Garcia, Tampico .. | 3 | 0 | 2 | 0 | 0 | 1.000 |
| Morales, Monterrey .. | 3 | 0 | 2 | 0 | 1 | 1.000 |
| Azcarraga, Mex Tig.. | 3 | 0 | 2 | 0 | 0 | 1.000 |
| Uresti, Jalisco .... | 6 | 0 | 2 | 0 | 0 | 1.000 |
| Arauz, Reynosa* .... | 8 | 1 | 0 | 0 | 0 | 1.000 |
| Orea, Reynosa ...... | 6 | 1 | 0 | 0 | 0 | 1.000 |
| Dominguez, Coahuila . | 2 | 1 | 0 | 0 | 0 | 1.000 |
| Diaz, Reynosa ...... | 4 | 0 | 1 | 0 | 0 | 1.000 |
| Gallegos, Villa ..... | 5 | 0 | 1 | 0 | 1 | 1.000 |
| Moncayo, Aguas ..... | 3 | 0 | 1 | 0 | 0 | 1.000 |
| Sierra, Aguas ....... | 3 | 0 | 1 | 0 | 0 | 1.000 |
| Martinez, Jalisco ... | 3 | 0 | 1 | 0 | 0 | 1.000 |
| Burns, Union Laguna . | 2 | 0 | 1 | 0 | 0 | 1.000 |
| Garduza, Poza Rica.. | 2 | 0 | 1 | 0 | 0 | 1.000 |
| Valle, Tampico* .... | 1 | 0 | 1 | 0 | 0 | 1.000 |
| Valdez, Aguas*...... | 1 | 0 | 1 | 0 | 0 | 1.000 |
| Carrillo, Poza R .... | 1 | 0 | 1 | 0 | 0 | 1.000 |
| Tatum, Monterrey .. | 9 | 6 | 10 | 1 | 2 | .941 |
| Plodinec, U Laguna . | 7 | 2 | 8 | 1 | 0 | .909 |
| Stephenson, Mon-Jua* | 9 | 2 | 6 | 1 | 2 | .889 |
| Soto, Saltillo ...... | 5 | 2 | 6 | 1 | 0 | .889 |
| Bellacetin, Mex Reds | 8 | 1 | 5 | 1 | 0 | .857 |
| Isom, Tampico* ..... | 8 | 4 | 11 | 3 | 1 | .833 |
| Lanfranco, Reynosa . | 8 | 1 | 3 | 1 | 1 | .800 |
| Ballinger, Coahuila.. | 6 | 2 | 5 | 2 | 1 | .778 |
| Mena, Union Laguna . | 2 | 1 | 2 | 1 | 0 | .750 |
| O'Toole, Tampico .... | 5 | 1 | 1 | 1 | 0 | .667 |
| Mariscal, Saltillo* .. | 5 | 1 | 2 | 2 | 0 | .600 |
| Johnson, Villa ...... | 6 | 1 | 0 | 1 | 0 | .500 |
| Deutsch, U Laguna.. | 2 | 0 | 0 | 1 | 0 | .000 |

NOTE: No compilation made of fielders who had no chances.

## CLUB PITCHING

| Club | G. | CG. | ShO. | Sv. | IP. | H. | R. | ER. | HR. | BB. | Int. BB. | HB. | SO. | WP. | Bk | ERA. |
|---|---|---|---|---|---|---|---|---|---|---|---|---|---|---|---|---|
| Cordoba ................ | 137 | 73 | 22 | 19 | 1181 | 1141 | 448 | 349 | 38 | 378 | 51 | 19 | 657 | 36 | 0 | 2.66 |
| Poza Rica .............. | 138 | 67 | 24 | 11 | 1217 | 1219 | 507 | 365 | 49 | 338 | 64 | 29 | 735 | 45 | 2 | 2.70 |
| Villahermosa .......... | 134 | 66 | 13 | 15 | 1166 | 1140 | 498 | 354 | 35 | 424 | 93 | 51 | 545 | 44 | 2 | 2.73 |
| Puebla ................. | 138 | 49 | 18 | 23 | 1171 | 1186 | 503 | 391 | 49 | 365 | 48 | 42 | 553 | 28 | 1 | 3.01 |
| Chihuahua ............. | 137 | 54 | 15 | 13 | 1181 | 1147 | 541 | 407 | 43 | 546 | 60 | 48 | 733 | 42 | 2 | 3.10 |
| Mexico Reds ........... | 139 | 50 | 12 | 29 | 1202 | 1259 | 554 | 422 | 36 | 457 | 40 | 39 | 675 | 59 | 2 | 3.16 |
| Saltillo ................ | 137 | 59 | 13 | 16 | 1162 | 1175 | 512 | 408 | 52 | 392 | 40 | 35 | 609 | 38 | 3 | 3.16 |
| Monterrey ............. | 138 | 61 | 15 | 7 | 1176 | 1236 | 521 | 413 | 64 | 419 | 68 | 40 | 543 | 46 | 2 | 3.16 |
| Reynosa ............... | 133 | 66 | 16 | 13 | 1114 | 1131 | 522 | 396 | 49 | 404 | 48 | 31 | 639 | 30 | 1 | 3.20 |
| Jalisco ................ | 136 | 52 | 13 | 25 | 1161 | 1249 | 597 | 413 | 51 | 442 | 30 | 27 | 719 | 57 | 2 | 3.20 |
| Tampico ............... | 138 | 49 | 13 | 21 | 1182 | 1164 | 517 | 422 | 68 | 395 | 40 | 38 | 722 | 40 | 0 | 3.21 |
| Juarez ................ | 138 | 53 | 15 | 9 | 1137 | 1280 | 560 | 414 | 47 | 409 | 56 | 31 | 487 | 48 | 0 | 3.28 |
| Coahuila .............. | 135 | 52 | 19 | 6 | 1134 | 1168 | 549 | 413 | 49 | 365 | 52 | 31 | 684 | 37 | 4 | 3.28 |
| Aguascalientes ........ | 137 | 53 | 10 | 9 | 1183 | 1316 | 638 | 448 | 48 | 457 | 40 | 50 | 698 | 43 | 1 | 3.41 |
| Union Laguna ......... | 139 | 46 | 7 | 15 | 1185 | 1363 | 608 | 448 | 70 | 380 | 55 | 31 | 523 | 50 | 4 | 3.55 |
| Mexico Tigers ......... | 136 | 29 | 5 | 21 | 1127 | 1260 | 560 | 453 | 56 | 498 | 66 | 28 | 485 | 44 | 2 | 3.62 |

## PITCHERS' RECORDS

(Leading Qualifiers for Earned-Run Average Leadership—110 or More Innings)
*Throws lefthanded.

| Pitcher—Club | G. | GS. | CG. | ShO. | W. | L. | Sv. | Pct. | IP. | H. | R. | ER. | HR. | BB. | Int. BB. | HB. | SO. | WP. | ERA. |
|---|---|---|---|---|---|---|---|---|---|---|---|---|---|---|---|---|---|---|---|
| Sandate, Poza R*.. | 28 | 22 | 14 | 6 | 13 | 6 | 1 | .684 | 177 | 140 | 46 | 28 | 3 | 47 | 5 | 1 | 161 | 9 | 1.42 |
| J. Pena, Villa..... | 42 | 30 | 25 | 6 | 21 | 12 | 4 | .636 | 287 | 216 | 76 | 59 | 7 | 102 | 17 | 17 | 199 | 11 | 1.85 |
| Pizarro, Cordoba*.. | 23 | 23 | 17 | 6 | 14 | 7 | 0 | .667 | 191 | 169 | 56 | 42 | 3 | 85 | 7 | 1 | 157 | 7 | 1.98 |
| Gage-Cole, Saltillo | 45 | 0 | 0 | 0 | 7 | 3 | 12 | .700 | 112 | 108 | 32 | 25 | 3 | 29 | 9 | 3 | 74 | 4 | 2.01 |
| Pina, Aguas ..... | 26 | 22 | 14 | 3 | 10 | 13 | 1 | .435 | 180 | 162 | 62 | 43 | 3 | 40 | 7 | 14 | 135 | 5 | 2.15 |
| Goodwin, Saltillo . | 30 | 15 | 8 | 2 | 11 | 7 | 2 | .611 | 158 | 122 | 53 | 38 | 3 | 56 | 4 | 1 | 111 | 6 | 2.16 |
| Moreno, Juarez ... | 32 | 25 | 11 | 2 | 12 | 12 | 0 | .500 | 164 | 152 | 66 | 40 | 6 | 69 | 6 | 9 | 72 | 10 | 2.20 |
| Salomon, Cordoba.. | 22 | 22 | 14 | 4 | 15 | 3 | 0 | .833 | 172 | 142 | 49 | 43 | 5 | 58 | 5 | 3 | 87 | 2 | 2.25 |
| Cordeiro, Villa* ... | 23 | 20 | 6 | 1 | 7 | 11 | 0 | .389 | 136 | 125 | 54 | 34 | 2 | 68 | 11 | 5 | 73 | 6 | 2.25 |
| Texidor, Reynosa.. | 34 | 21 | 15 | 3 | 9 | 14 | 5 | .391 | 187 | 175 | 66 | 48 | 9 | 60 | 13 | 2 | 120 | 6 | 2.31 |

Departmental Leaders: G—A. Lopez, 71; GS—Volkening, 32; CG—J. Pena, 25; ShO—Brunet, 8; W—J. Pena, 21; L—Lee, 20; Sv—A. Lopez, 23; Pct.—Salomon, .833; IP—J. Pena, 287; H—Cavanaugh, 267; R—President, 114; ER—M. Rodriguez, 82; HR—Pollorena, 15; BB—Saldivar, 126; IBB—J. Martinez, 21; HB—J. Pena, 17; SO—J. Pena, 199; WP—A. Lopez, 18.

(All Pitchers—Listed Alphabetically)

| Pitcher—Club | G. | GS. | CG. | ShO. | W. | L. | Sv. | Pct. | IP. | H. | R. | ER. | HR. | BB. | Int. BB. | HB. | SO. | WP. | ERA. |
|---|---|---|---|---|---|---|---|---|---|---|---|---|---|---|---|---|---|---|---|
| Abarca, Jalisco ... | 19 | 14 | 1 |  | 6 | 3 | 0 | .667 | 77 | 90 | 45 | 36 | 6 | 39 | 1 | 1 | 41 | 1 | 4.21 |
| Acosta, Puebla ... | 28 | 23 | 5 | 3 | 7 | 8 | 6 | .467 | 111 | 101 | 44 | 32 | 3 | 34 | 7 | 4 | 59 | 1 | 2.59 |
| Acosta L, M Reds | 31 | 31 | 11 | 1 | 14 | 9 | 0 | .609 | 208 | 207 | 97 | 71 | 6 | 82 | 1 | 7 | 110 | 10 | 3.07 |
| Acosta M., 13 U L-22 Villa ... | 35 | 29 | 15 | 1 | 12 | 14 | 2 | .462 | 221 | 232 | 96 | 68 | 5 | 55 | 15 | 6 | 86 | 10 | 2.77 |
| Adame, 7 Sal-21 Ags | 28 | 20 | 7 | 1 | 5 | 17 | 0 | .227 | 131 | 168 | 79 | 55 | 8 | 36 | 2 | 2 | 52 | 2 | 3.78 |
| Agundez, M Tigers | 52 | 12 | 11 | 0 | 15 | 11 | 7 | .577 | 191 | 194 | 77 | 66 | 12 | 37 | 13 | 2 | 43 | 6 | 3.11 |
| Ahumada, Saltillo | 31 | 28 | 14 | 3 | 15 | 8 | 0 | .652 | 188 | 170 | 83 | 77 | 9 | 96 | 10 | 10 | 110 | 4 | 3.69 |

| Pitcher—Club | G | GS | CG | ShO | W | L | Sv | Pct. | IP | H | R | ER | HR | BB | Int. BB | HB | SO | WP | ERA |
|---|---|---|---|---|---|---|---|---|---|---|---|---|---|---|---|---|---|---|---|
| Alcaide, Coahuila* | 1 | 0 | 0 | 0 | 0 | 0 | 0 | .000 | 5 | 7 | 4 | 2 | 1 | 3 | 0 | 0 | 4 | 1 | 3.60 |
| Almonte, Juarez | 8 | 6 | 1 | 0 | 1 | 3 | 0 | .250 | 23 | 31 | 17 | 13 | 2 | 14 | 1 | 0 | 7 | 1 | 5.09 |
| Aponte, Reynosa | 33 | 31 | 15 | 4 | 12 | 15 | 1 | .444 | 220 | 208 | 95 | 72 | 4 | 102 | 2 | 7 | 189 | 2 | 2.95 |
| R. Arano, Cordoba | 26 | 26 | 14 | 1 | 15 | 8 | 0 | .652 | 175 | 187 | 74 | 61 | 6 | 38 | 3 | 0 | 66 | 1 | 3.14 |
| Arauz, Reynosa* | 8 | 0 | 0 | 0 | 0 | 1 | 0 | .000 | 10 | 14 | 13 | 10 | 0 | 7 | 1 | 1 | 5 | 3 | 9.00 |
| Armas, Cordoba* | 19 | 0 | 0 | 0 | 1 | 1 | 0 | .833 | 33 | 25 | 19 | 14 | 4 | 18 | 4 | 0 | 13 | 0 | 3.82 |
| Armas, Saltillo* | 27 | 13 | 7 | 1 | 10 | 4 | 1 | .714 | 102 | 100 | 36 | 30 | 9 | 12 | 2 | 2 | 53 | 2 | 2.65 |
| Ayon, Cordoba | 10 | 9 | 2 | 0 | 2 | 5 | 0 | .286 | 51 | 55 | 28 | 22 | 3 | 18 | 4 | 0 | 24 | 0 | 3.88 |
| Azcarraga, Puebla | 33 | 29 | 16 | 2 | 16 | 9 | 2 | .640 | 213 | 226 | 80 | 58 | 6 | 38 | 6 | 6 | 93 | 4 | 2.45 |
| Azcarraga, M Tig | 3 | 2 | 0 | 0 | 0 | 1 | 0 | .000 | 7 | 10 | 3 | 3 | 0 | 4 | 1 | 0 | 3 | 0 | 3.86 |
| Ballinger, Coah | 6 | 6 | 0 | 0 | 0 | 3 | 0 | .000 | 30 | 37 | 24 | 18 | 1 | 18 | 3 | 1 | 27 | 5 | 5.40 |
| Barandica, Puebla | 14 | 3 | 0 | 0 | 1 | 2 | 0 | .333 | 43 | 49 | 23 | 20 | 3 | 14 | 0 | 1 | 12 | 0 | 4.19 |
| Barbosa, Coahuila* | 30 | 28 | 16 | 5 | 9 | 15 | 0 | .375 | 200 | 199 | 78 | 60 | 4 | 60 | 8 | 3 | 136 | 3 | 2.70 |
| Barrientos, U Lag | 39 | 8 | 3 | 0 | 8 | 4 | 5 | .667 | 117 | 140 | 54 | 38 | 5 | 42 | 5 | 4 | 104 | 10 | 2.92 |
| Barrios, Jalisco | 31 | 23 | 15 | 4 | 10 | 12 | 2 | .455 | 183 | 169 | 77 | 55 | 6 | 85 | 3 | 7 | 138 | 7 | 2.70 |
| Bellacetin, M R | 8 | 1 | 0 | 0 | 1 | 0 | 0 | 1.000 | 21 | 25 | 5 | 4 | 1 | 3 | 0 | 0 | 2 | 0 | 1.71 |
| Beltran, U Laguna | 2 | 0 | 0 | 0 | 0 | 0 | 0 | .000 | 3 | 4 | 2 | 1 | 0 | 3 | 0 | 0 | 0 | 1 | 3.00 |
| Beltran, Aguas* | 4 | 0 | 0 | 0 | 0 | 0 | 0 | .000 | 6 | 2 | 0 | 0 | 0 | 3 | 0 | 0 | 4 | 0 | 0.00 |
| Beltran, Juarez | 34 | 23 | 8 | 3 | 9 | 9 | 0 | .500 | 154 | 170 | 66 | 52 | 8 | 54 | 6 | 2 | 64 | 4 | 3.04 |
| O. Bernal, Mont | 17 | 0 | 0 | 0 | 0 | 2 | 0 | .000 | 34 | 40 | 30 | 20 | 4 | 16 | 3 | 0 | 16 | 3 | 5.29 |
| Boyd, 10 S-14 Pue* | 24 | 7 | 0 | 0 | 3 | 6 | 5 | .333 | 79 | 76 | 41 | 33 | 3 | 19 | 4 | 1 | 44 | 2 | 5.03 |
| Bracamontes, Pue* | 31 | 27 | 7 | 5 | 12 | 7 | 0 | .632 | 184 | 169 | 64 | 52 | 7 | 63 | 7 | 3 | 108 | 7 | 2.54 |
| Brandon, Coahuila | 12 | 12 | 6 | 1 | 6 | 4 | 0 | .600 | 92 | 73 | 28 | 20 | 2 | 33 | 4 | 2 | 73 | 4 | 1.96 |
| Brito, Aguas | 9 | 8 | 1 | 0 | 1 | 5 | 1 | .167 | 37 | 52 | 34 | 29 | 8 | 26 | 1 | 4 | 16 | 0 | 7.05 |
| Britton, U Laguna* | 24 | 17 | 8 | 1 | 11 | 5 | 0 | .688 | 140 | 173 | 67 | 54 | 8 | 41 | 3 | 1 | 52 | 3 | 3.47 |
| Brunet, Poza Rica* | 34 | 30 | 15 | 8 | 17 | 9 | 0 | .654 | 230 | 190 | 82 | 67 | 6 | 71 | 9 | 5 | 147 | 12 | 2.62 |
| Buentello, Cordoba | 36 | 1 | 1 | 0 | 3 | 3 | 6 | .500 | 64 | 66 | 28 | 18 | 2 | 36 | 9 | 0 | 29 | 7 | 2.53 |
| Burns, U Laguna | 2 | 0 | 0 | 0 | 0 | 0 | 0 | .000 | 3 | 4 | 6 | 6 | 0 | 3 | 2 | 0 | 4 | 0 | 18.00 |
| Bustamante, Jal | 2 | 0 | 0 | 0 | 0 | 0 | 0 | .000 | 1 | 5 | 7 | 3 | 0 | 2 | 1 | 0 | 1 | 0 | 27.00 |
| Byron Quiroz, Ags | 49 | 2 | 0 | 0 | 6 | 6 | | .500 | 119 | 130 | 73 | 52 | 4 | 63 | 5 | 5 | 79 | 5 | 3.93 |
| Cabrales, U Lag. | 8 | 1 | 0 | 0 | 1 | 0 | 0 | .000 | 22 | 22 | 13 | 10 | 1 | 11 | 2 | 2 | 6 | 6 | 4.09 |
| Campoy, Reynosa | 15 | 12 | 6 | 1 | 5 | 5 | 1 | .500 | 92 | 91 | 34 | 24 | 3 | 29 | 5 | 3 | 45 | 1 | 2.35 |
| Carrasco, Mont | 30 | 25 | 9 | 4 | 9 | 10 | 0 | .474 | 148 | 192 | 81 | 62 | 7 | 48 | 8 | 9 | 51 | 4 | 3.77 |
| Carrillo, Poza R | 1 | 0 | 0 | 0 | 0 | 0 | 0 | .000 | 1 | 2 | 1 | 0 | 0 | 2 | 1 | 0 | 0 | 0 | 0.00 |
| Castillo, U Lag | 36 | 14 | 4 | 0 | 8 | 12 | 3 | .400 | 122 | 150 | 68 | 51 | 9 | 44 | 17 | 8 | 49 | 5 | 3.76 |
| Castro, M Tigers | 8 | 4 | 0 | 0 | 0 | 1 | 0 | .000 | 17 | 26 | 19 | 19 | 3 | 5 | 1 | 3 | 0 | 10 | 06 |
| Cavanaugh, Poza R | 36 | 30 | 18 | 4 | 12 | 16 | 2 | .429 | 249 | 267 | 104 | 75 | 11 | 52 | 14 | 4 | 111 | 4 | 2.71 |
| Cazares, Jalisco* | 27 | 1 | 0 | 0 | 1 | 2 | 0 | .333 | 59 | 66 | 33 | 24 | 1 | 21 | 1 | 1 | 25 | 3 | 3.66 |
| Chavez, Tampico | 5 | 0 | 0 | 0 | 1 | 0 | 0 | 1.000 | 9 | 12 | 11 | 7 | 1 | 7 | 0 | 2 | 5 | 3 | 7.00 |
| R. Chavez, Chih | 34 | 31 | 17 | 5 | 18 | 10 | 0 | .643 | 234 | 204 | 88 | 61 | 6 | 104 | 14 | 7 | 187 | 4 | 2.35 |
| Cisneros, Coah | 29 | 1 | 1 | 0 | 5 | 4 | 2 | .556 | 82 | 79 | 35 | 28 | 4 | 22 | 6 | 3 | 59 | 1 | 3.07 |
| Collazo, Tampico | 15 | 10 | 1 | 0 | 5 | 3 | 0 | .625 | 56 | 71 | 36 | 37 | 6 | 20 | 1 | 0 | 34 | 2 | 4.34 |
| Colorado, Jalisco | 2 | 0 | 0 | 0 | 1 | 0 | 0 | 1.000 | 6 | 1 | 0 | 0 | 0 | 0 | 0 | 0 | 6 | 0 | 0.00 |
| Cordeiro, Villa* | 23 | 20 | 0 | 1 | 7 | 11 | 0 | .389 | 136 | 125 | 54 | 34 | 2 | 68 | 11 | 5 | 73 | 6 | 2.25 |
| Cordova, Jalisco | 36 | 29 | 14 | 2 | 16 | 10 | 3 | .615 | 222 | 241 | 102 | 72 | 7 | 55 | 4 | 5 | 120 | 4 | 2.92 |
| Cruz, Monterrey | 37 | 0 | 0 | 0 | 3 | 7 | 3 | .300 | 81 | 72 | 26 | 20 | 3 | 42 | 12 | 1 | 50 | 2 | 2.22 |
| Cruz, Poza Rica | 24 | 3 | 0 | 0 | 3 | 4 | 0 | .429 | 69 | 62 | 31 | 23 | 3 | 23 | 5 | 2 | 40 | 2 | 3.00 |
| Cruz, Tampico | 27 | 18 | 4 | 0 | 5 | 9 | 0 | .357 | 105 | 133 | 68 | 58 | 11 | 25 | 3 | 2 | 53 | 1 | 4.97 |
| A. Davila, Juarez* | 9 | 0 | 0 | 0 | 1 | 0 | 0 | 1.000 | 16 | 7 | 3 | 2 | 0 | 13 | 0 | 1 | 5 | 2 | 1.13 |
| DeLaTorre, U Lag | 35 | 23 | 5 | 0 | 7 | 9 | 1 | .438 | 163 | 185 | 75 | 60 | 7 | 37 | 7 | 2 | 32 | 5 | 3.31 |
| Delfin, Cordoba | 15 | 0 | 0 | 0 | 1 | 1 | 0 | .500 | 30 | 29 | 8 | 7 | 1 | 7 | 2 | 1 | 10 | 1 | 2.10 |
| Delgado, M Tig* | 19 | 11 | 0 | 0 | 0 | 1 | 0 | .000 | 40 | 39 | 19 | 15 | 2 | 26 | 1 | 1 | 17 | 0 | 3.38 |
| Deutsch, U Laguna | 2 | 2 | 0 | 0 | 1 | 0 | 0 | .000 | 2 | 4 | 5 | 3 | 0 | 2 | 0 | 0 | 1 | 1 | 13.50 |
| C. Diaz, Aguas | 37 | 30 | 14 | 3 | 11 | 18 | 1 | .379 | 230 | 232 | 110 | 71 | 2 | 62 | 9 | 14 | 170 | 7 | 2.78 |
| H. Diaz, M Tigers | 17 | 5 | 0 | 0 | 2 | 5 | 1 | .286 | 46 | 63 | 29 | 22 | 2 | 22 | 4 | 4 | 20 | 3 | 4.30 |
| Diaz, Reynosa | 4 | 0 | 0 | 0 | 0 | 0 | 0 | .000 | 6 | 7 | 9 | 8 | 2 | 4 | 1 | 0 | 4 | 0 | 12.00 |
| Dillon, Jalisco* | 8 | 7 | 2 | 0 | 3 | 2 | 0 | .600 | 43 | 50 | 20 | 11 | 1 | 10 | 1 | 0 | 14 | 3 | 2.30 |
| Diorio, Puebla | 17 | 0 | 0 | 0 | 5 | 0 | 4 | 1.000 | 24 | 24 | 12 | 8 | 3 | 12 | 4 | 1 | 4 | 0 | 3.00 |
| Dominguez, Coah. | 2 | 0 | 0 | 0 | 0 | 0 | 0 | .000 | 6 | 5 | 2 | 2 | 0 | 3 | 0 | 0 | 4 | 0 | 3.00 |
| Escalante, Aguas* | 4 | 0 | 0 | 0 | 2 | 0 | 0 | .009 | 7 | 14 | 10 | 10 | 2 | 3 | 1 | 0 | 1 | 2 | 12.86 |
| Espinosa, M Tigers | 33 | 21 | 3 | 0 | 9 | 6 | 1 | .600 | 126 | 109 | 46 | 39 | 4 | 56 | 5 | 3 | 84 | 3 | 2.79 |
| Fabela, Villa | 31 | 4 | 1 | 0 | 4 | 7 | 4 | .364 | 82 | 80 | 42 | 32 | 3 | 37 | 7 | 7 | 65 | 5 | 3.51 |
| Fajardo, Juarez | 56 | 0 | 0 | 0 | 3 | 4 | 3 | .429 | 129 | 152 | 54 | 40 | 5 | 31 | 12 | 2 | 36 | 2 | 2.79 |
| Farmer, U Laguna | 2 | 2 | 0 | 0 | 1 | 0 | 0 | .000 | 1 | 1 | 4 | 3 | 0 | 4 | 0 | 0 | 0 | 1 | 27.00 |
| Faudoa, Chihua*.. | 1 | 0 | 0 | 0 | 0 | 0 | 0 | .000 | 1 | 0 | 0 | 0 | 0 | 1 | 0 | 0 | 0 | 0 | 0.00 |
| Fernandez, P Rica | 2 | 0 | 0 | 0 | 0 | 0 | 0 | .000 | 1 | 3 | 4 | 3 | 0 | 3 | 2 | 0 | 0 | 0 | 27.00 |
| Figueroa, 7 Coah- 17 Poza Rica | 24 | 2 | 0 | 0 | 2 | 3 | 1 | .400 | 69 | 100 | 46 | 34 | 7 | 21 | 10 | 2 | 30 | 4 | 4.43 |
| Franco, Poza Rice | 16 | 3 | 1 | 0 | 2 | 1 | 0 | .667 | 39 | 36 | 18 | 14 | 5 | 15 | 1 | 4 | 11 | 4 | 3.23 |
| Gage-Cole, Saltillo | 45 | 0 | 0 | 0 | 7 | 3 | 12 | .700 | 112 | 108 | 32 | 25 | 3 | 29 | 9 | 3 | 74 | 4 | 2.01 |
| Gallegos, Villa | 5 | 1 | 0 | 0 | 0 | 1 | 0 | .000 | 10 | 18 | 6 | 5 | 0 | 5 | 0 | 0 | 2 | 2 | 4.50 |
| Gamez, M Reds* | 19 | 0 | 0 | 0 | 0 | 1 | 0 | .000 | 20 | 26 | 15 | 10 | 0 | 10 | 1 | 1 | 10 | 2 | 4.50 |
| Garcia, Monterrey | 4 | 0 | 0 | 0 | 0 | 0 | 0 | .000 | 6 | 8 | 3 | 3 | 0 | 3 | 1 | 0 | 3 | 1 | 4.50 |
| Garcia, Puebla | 31 | 21 | 0 | 0 | 8 | 8 | 1 | .500 | 134 | 164 | 73 | 57 | 7 | 38 | 5 | 5 | 47 | 4 | 3.83 |
| Rog. Garcia, Tamp | 3 | 1 | 0 | 0 | 0 | 1 | 0 | .000 | 12 | 19 | 9 | 5 | 0 | 4 | | 2 | 7 | 2 | 3.75 |
| Garcia, M Tigers.. | 42 | 8 | 2 | 0 | 6 | 5 | 1 | .545 | 125 | 131 | 59 | 51 | 7 | 45 | 9 | 3 | 47 | 2 | 3.67 |
| V. Garcia, Tampico | 31 | 25 | 7 | 1 | 10 | 9 | 3 | .526 | 173 | 165 | 64 | 55 | 9 | 40 | 5 | 1 | 92 | 3 | 2.80 |
| Garduza, P Rica.. | 2 | 0 | 0 | 0 | 0 | 0 | 0 | .000 | 1 | 2 | 1 | 0 | 0 | 3 | 0 | 0 | 0 | 0 | 0.00 |
| G. Gonzalez, U L* | 29 | 3 | 0 | 0 | 1 | 4 | 0 | .200 | 60 | 64 | 25 | 20 | 4 | 32 | 1 | 4 | 34 | 1 | 3.00 |

| Pitcher—Club | G. | GS. | CG. | ShO. | W. | L. | Sv. | Pct. | IP. | H. | R. | ER. | HR. | BB. | Int. BB. | HB. | SO. | WP. | ERA. |
|---|---|---|---|---|---|---|---|---|---|---|---|---|---|---|---|---|---|---|---|
| Goodwin, Saltillo.. | 30 | 15 | 8 | 2 | 11 | 7 | 2 | .611 | 158 | 122 | 53 | 38 | 3 | 56 | 4 | 1 | 111 | 6 | 2.16 |
| Gowell, Puebla ... | 5 | 4 | 1 | 1 | 1 | 0 | 0 | 1.000 | 16 | 17 | 13 | 10 | 1 | 15 | 0 | 3 | 8 | 2 | 5.63 |
| Gutierrez, Rey ... | 26 | 10 | 1 | 1 | 3 | 5 | 2 | .375 | 72 | 78 | 34 | 25 | 3 | 34 | 1 | 2 | 35 | 2 | 3.13 |
| Gutierrez, Jalisco* | 24 | 14 | 4 | 0 | 7 | 2 | 1 | .778 | 102 | 123 | 65 | 34 | 4 | 46 | 1 | 3 | 75 | 9 | 3.00 |
| Gutierrez, Cordoba | 35 | 18 | 11 | 4 | 10 | 9 | 8 | .526 | 179 | 177 | 70 | 55 | 4 | 36 | 9 | 11 | 80 | 4 | 2.77 |
| Guzman, Jalisco ... | 41 | 4 | 1 | 0 | 7 | 6 | 9 | .538 | 109 | 102 | 57 | 40 | 1 | 38 | 3 | 2 | 79 | 9 | 3.30 |
| Guzman, Chihuahua | 52 | 1 | 0 | 0 | 8 | 8 | 10 | .500 | 108 | 100 | 32 | 26 | 1 | 49 | 9 | 8 | 95 | 2 | 2.17 |
| Hambright, Juarez | 28 | 22 | 14 | 2 | 8 | 13 | 1 | .381 | 170 | 166 | 63 | 44 | 3 | 63 | 9 | 6 | 126 | 4 | 2.33 |
| A. Hernandez, P R | 33 | 25 | 7 | 1 | 6 | 11 | 1 | .353 | 181 | 187 | 91 | 62 | 10 | 43 | 6 | 3 | 114 | 2 | 3.08 |
| Hernandez, Salt .. | 26 | 26 | 11 | 4 | 13 | 11 | 0 | .542 | 173 | 165 | 64 | 48 | 11 | 47 | 3 | 4 | 85 | 3 | 2.50 |
| Hernandez, Reynosa | 3 | 0 | 0 | 0 | 0 | 0 | 0 | .000 | 1 | 5 | 6 | 6 | 0 | 1 | 0 | 1 | 0 | 1 | 54.00 |
| Hernandez S., Ags | 30 | 0 | 0 | 0 | 1 | 2 | 0 | .333 | 52 | 80 | 37 | 25 | 1 | 20 | 3 | 1 | 32 | 3 | 4.33 |
| Holly, Jalisco* .... | 10 | 6 | 1 | 0 | 3 | 2 | 1 | .600 | 49 | 51 | 18 | 13 | 1 | 15 | 1 | 1 | 38 | 2 | 2.39 |
| Ibarra, U Laguna* | 1 | 0 | 0 | 0 | 0 | 0 | 0 | .000 | 1 | 0 | 0 | 0 | 0 | 0 | 0 | 0 | 0 | 0 | 0.00 |
| Isom, Tampico* .. | 8 | 8 | 1 | 0 | 1 | 4 | 0 | .200 | 46 | 37 | 23 | 14 | 1 | 37 | 1 | 1 | 33 | 7 | 2.74 |
| Johnson, Villa .... | 6 | 2 | 1 | 0 | 1 | 1 | 0 | .500 | 29 | 26 | 12 | 6 | 1 | 13 | 2 | 5 | 19 | 3 | 1.86 |
| Kealey, Jalisco .. | 4 | 3 | 0 | 0 | 1 | 0 | 0 | .000 | 10 | 20 | 11 | 10 | 2 | 6 | 1 | 0 | 2 | 0 | 9.00 |
| Kokor, Aguas ... | 28 | 27 | 9 | 1 | 8 | 8 | 0 | .500 | 179 | 200 | 89 | 66 | 11 | 44 | 1 | 10 | 92 | 5 | 3.32 |
| Lagunas, Villa ... | 25 | 21 | 8 | 1 | 7 | 11 | 0 | .389 | 136 | 152 | 68 | 51 | 5 | 41 | 13 | 1 | 35 | 0 | 3.88 |
| Lagunes, P Rica.. | 3 | 0 | 0 | 0 | 0 | 0 | 0 | .000 | 7 | 10 | 1 | 1 | 0 | 1 | 0 | 2 | 4 | 0 | 1.29 |
| Lanfranco, Rey*... | 8 | 2 | 0 | 0 | 0 | 1 | 0 | .000 | 21 | 22 | 9 | 6 | 2 | 9 | 0 | 1 | 9 | 0 | 2.57 |
| G. Lara, P Rica*.. | 9 | 0 | 0 | 0 | 0 | 0 | 0 | .000 | 9 | 17 | 11 | 10 | 0 | 9 | 2 | 0 | 5 | 1 | 10.00 |
| Leal, Chihuahua .. | 27 | 21 | 5 | 1 | 7 | 7 | 1 | .500 | 135 | 119 | 62 | 50 | 5 | 77 | 7 | 7 | 69 | 6 | 3.33 |
| Lee, Coahuila ... | 33 | 30 | 12 | 4 | 7 | 20 | 1 | .259 | 200 | 210 | 98 | 74 | 8 | 53 | 6 | 5 | 96 | 8 | 3.33 |
| Lefevre, Tampico.. | 21 | 20 | 12 | 1 | 10 | 9 | 0 | .526 | 160 | 146 | 60 | 50 | 10 | 41 | 3 | 5 | 100 | 1 | 2.81 |
| Leon, Reynosa ... | 2 | 0 | 0 | 0 | 0 | 0 | 0 | .000 | 2 | 5 | 3 | 2 | 0 | 0 | 0 | 1 | 0 | | 9.00 |
| A. Lopez, M Reds | 71 | 0 | 0 | 0 | 10 | 8 | 23 | .556 | 114 | 97 | 46 | 36 | 3 | 68 | 8 | 2 | 114 | 18 | 2.84 |
| F. Lopez, M Tig . | 33 | 14 | 1 | 0 | 4 | 8 | 0 | .333 | 99 | 129 | 69 | 51 | 6 | 62 | 6 | 3 | 47 | 6 | 4.64 |
| H. Lopez, M Tig . | 1 | 0 | 0 | 0 | 0 | 0 | 0 | .000 | 0 | 3 | 3 | 3 | 0 | 1 | 0 | 0 | 0 | 0 | .. |
| R. Lopez, Tampico | 2 | 0 | 0 | 0 | 0 | 0 | 0 | .000 | 3 | 1 | 0 | 0 | 0 | 2 | 0 | 0 | 4 | 0 | 0.00 |
| Lozano, Juarez* .. | 25 | 0 | 0 | 0 | 1 | 1 | 0 | .500 | 26 | 38 | 18 | 14 | 3 | 7 | 3 | 2 | 11 | 3 | 4.85 |
| Lugo, Puebla ... | 1 | 0 | 0 | 0 | 0 | 0 | 0 | .000 | 3 | 5 | 4 | 4 | 0 | 1 | 0 | 0 | 0 | | 9.00 |
| Lugo, Jalisco ... | 6 | 0 | 0 | 0 | 2 | 1 | 0 | .667 | 12 | 8 | 6 | 4 | 0 | 10 | 1 | 0 | 4 | 0 | 3.00 |
| Luna, Monterrey . | 21 | 20 | 9 | 3 | 8 | 7 | 0 | .533 | 131 | 137 | 52 | 40 | 5 | 56 | 6 | 3 | 44 | 3 | 2.75 |
| Madrigal, Poza R.. | 34 | 22 | 12 | 4 | 11 | 13 | 4 | .458 | 176 | 185 | 68 | 49 | 8 | 46 | 9 | 6 | 102 | 6 | 2.51 |
| Mariscal, Saltillo* | 5 | 4 | 1 | 0 | 1 | 2 | 0 | .333 | 21 | 26 | 12 | 7 | 1 | 6 | 0 | 1 | 8 | 0 | 3.00 |
| A. Martinez, Rey.. | 2 | 0 | 0 | 0 | 0 | 0 | 0 | .000 | 2 | 7 | 4 | 4 | 2 | 2 | 0 | 1 | 0 | | 18.00 |
| Martinez A., Pue* | 30 | 3 | 0 | 0 | 1 | 3 | 1 | .250 | 55 | 59 | 25 | 18 | 4 | 33 | 5 | 2 | 25 | 2 | 2.95 |
| Martinez H., Mon* | 33 | 6 | 0 | 0 | 4 | 3 | 2 | .571 | 67 | 76 | 40 | 30 | 2 | 34 | 2 | 1 | 42 | 5 | 4.03 |
| J. Martinez, Villa | 34 | 23 | 9 | 1 | 5 | 14 | 3 | .263 | 186 | 190 | 86 | 60 | 4 | 56 | 21 | 3 | 41 | 7 | 2.90 |
| Martinez, Jalisco.. | 3 | 0 | 0 | 0 | 1 | 0 | 0 | 1.000 | 7 | 11 | 5 | 4 | 0 | 0 | 0 | 0 | 2 | 0 | 5.14 |
| Maytorena, Tam .. | 33 | 1 | 1 | 0 | 10 | 4 | 17 | .714 | 106 | 72 | 24 | 20 | 4 | 41 | 14 | 8 | 84 | 3 | 1.70 |
| McRae, Chihuahua | 33 | 30 | 17 | 2 | 10 | 18 | 0 | .357 | 231 | 218 | 98 | 65 | 7 | 104 | 13 | 3 | 149 | 10 | 2.53 |
| Mellado, Villa.... | 21 | 2 | 1 | 0 | 1 | 2 | 1 | .333 | 43 | 48 | 27 | 15 | 1 | 18 | 4 | 1 | 12 | 1 | 3.14 |
| Mena, U Laguna*.. | 2 | 1 | 0 | 0 | 0 | 0 | 0 | .000 | 6 | 8 | 4 | 2 | 0 | 5 | 0 | 1 | 0 | | 3.00 |
| Mercado, Coahuila | 28 | 8 | 1 | 0 | 3 | 7 | 0 | .300 | 81 | 105 | 54 | 40 | 5 | 19 | 4 | 3 | 28 | 3 | 4.44 |
| Mere, Mexico Reds | 36 | 17 | 4 | 1 | 11 | 7 | 3 | .611 | 156 | 162 | 90 | 60 | 1 | 86 | 10 | 6 | 78 | 11 | 3.46 |
| Meza, Mex Tigers* | 45 | 18 | 5 | 0 | 13 | 10 | 6 | .565 | 155 | 180 | 73 | 62 | 5 | 74 | 6 | 3 | 66 | 6 | 3.60 |
| Miall, Coahuila*.. | 14 | 14 | 7 | 3 | 5 | 7 | 0 | .545 | 88 | 64 | 34 | 22 | 1 | 48 | 2 | 2 | 89 | 6 | 2.25 |
| Moncayo, Aguas... | 3 | 0 | 0 | 0 | 0 | 0 | 0 | .000 | 8 | 10 | 5 | 4 | 1 | 4 | 0 | 0 | 4 | 2 | 4.50 |
| Mondragon, 1 Cord-1 Pue.. | 2 | 1 | 0 | 0 | 0 | 0 | 0 | .000 | 8 | 8 | 0 | 0 | 0 | 1 | 0 | 0 | 3 | 1 | 0.00 |
| Montane, Villa.... | 1 | 0 | 0 | 0 | 0 | 0 | 0 | .000 | 3 | 2 | 2 | 2 | 0 | 0 | 0 | 0 | 0 | 0 | 18.00 |
| Monteagudo, Pue | 27 | 26 | 13 | 3 | 15 | 9 | 1 | .625 | 185 | 171 | 73 | 62 | 6 | 43 | 5 | 9 | 115 | 3 | 3.02 |
| Montero, Reynosa | 22 | 1 | 0 | 0 | 1 | 4 | 0 | .200 | 38 | 44 | 30 | 24 | 2 | 18 | 0 | 2 | 27 | 0 | 5.68 |
| Montoya, 17 Tam- 10 Aguas* .... | 27 | 6 | 1 | 0 | 1 | 4 | 0 | .200 | 66 | 87 | 48 | 40 | 4 | 28 | 1 | 3 | 21 | 3 | 5.45 |
| Morales, Coahuila | 11 | 0 | 0 | 0 | 0 | 0 | 0 | .000 | 20 | 35 | 21 | 18 | 3 | 10 | 0 | 1 | 9 | 1 | 8.10 |
| Morales, Mont ... | 3 | 0 | 0 | 0 | 0 | 0 | 0 | .000 | 4 | 10 | 6 | 6 | 3 | 1 | 0 | 0 | 2 | 0 | 13.50 |
| Moreno, Aguas ... | 3 | 3 | 0 | 0 | 0 | 1 | 0 | .000 | 3 | 2 | 4 | 4 | 1 | 5 | 1 | 0 | 0 | 1 | 12.00 |
| Moreno, Juarez | 32 | 25 | 11 | 2 | 12 | 12 | 0 | .500 | 164 | 152 | 66 | 40 | 6 | 69 | 6 | 9 | 72 | 10 | 2.20 |
| Moreno, Monterrey | 24 | 4 | 0 | 0 | 1 | 3 | 0 | .250 | 77 | 82 | 38 | 30 | 4 | 43 | 5 | 5 | 50 | 5 | 3.51 |
| Mota, Puebla .... | 32 | 8 | 0 | 0 | 5 | 10 | 2 | .333 | 90 | 93 | 48 | 38 | 5 | 31 | 6 | 2 | 42 | 1 | 3.80 |
| Munoz, Cordoba .. | 25 | 15 | 3 | 2 | 8 | 4 | 0 | .667 | 114 | 126 | 45 | 31 | 6 | 43 | 3 | 3 | 83 | 7 | 2.45 |
| Newson, Jalisco .. | 10 | 10 | 5 | 0 | 3 | 7 | 0 | .300 | 64 | 72 | 42 | 27 | 6 | 33 | 1 | 2 | 27 | 4 | 3.80 |
| Nieto, Tampico* .. | 15 | 1 | 0 | 0 | 0 | 0 | 0 | .000 | 34 | 38 | 21 | 18 | 1 | 18 | 0 | 0 | 13 | 2 | 4.76 |
| D. Ochoa, Villa.. | 1 | 0 | 0 | 0 | 0 | 0 | 0 | .000 | 2 | 5 | 3 | 2 | 0 | 1 | 0 | 0 | 3 | 1 | 9.00 |
| Ochoa, Reynosa .. | 16 | 0 | 0 | 0 | 1 | 2 | 1 | .333 | 29 | 34 | 22 | 18 | 1 | 25 | 2 | 4 | 20 | 2 | 5.59 |
| Olivo, Reynosa .. | 3 | 2 | 0 | 0 | 0 | 0 | 0 | .000 | 4 | 11 | 13 | 11 | 2 | 8 | 1 | 0 | 5 | 2 | 24.75 |
| Orea, Juarez ... | 46 | 8 | 1 | 0 | 5 | 13 | 4 | .278 | 120 | 172 | 91 | 70 | 5 | 41 | 7 | 4 | 59 | 10 | 5.25 |
| Orea, Reynosa ... | 6 | 0 | 0 | 0 | 0 | 1 | 0 | .000 | 5 | 9 | 8 | 5 | 1 | 6 | 1 | 2 | 3 | 0 | 9.00 |
| Ortiz U., Mex R*.. | 30 | 28 | 12 | 4 | 15 | 11 | 0 | .577 | 211 | 240 | 98 | 80 | 9 | 53 | 4 | 7 | 94 | 7 | 3.41 |
| O'Toole, Tampico.. | 5 | 0 | 0 | 0 | 2 | 2 | 0 | .500 | 9 | 10 | 8 | 7 | 1 | 3 | 0 | 2 | 5 | 1 | 7.00 |
| Pactwa, Tampico* | 26 | 26 | 18 | 7 | 17 | 6 | 0 | .739 | 201 | 181 | 66 | 56 | 4 | 76 | 6 | 3 | 169 | 9 | 2.51 |
| Pate, U Laguna*.. | 4 | 4 | 1 | 0 | 2 | 0 | 0 | 1.000 | 16 | 19 | 10 | 8 | 2 | 12 | 0 | 0 | 5 | 1 | 4.00 |
| Paz, Villahermosa | 13 | 10 | 4 | 1 | 2 | 7 | 0 | .222 | 72 | 82 | 39 | 31 | 3 | 34 | 4 | 5 | 23 | 0 | 3.88 |
| J. Pena, Villa.... | 42 | 30 | 25 | 6 | 21 | 12 | 4 | .636 | 287 | 216 | 76 | 59 | 7 | 102 | 17 | 17 | 199 | 11 | 1.85 |
| Pena, U Laguna.. | 24 | 1 | 0 | 0 | 1 | 4 | 0 | .200 | 46 | 64 | 41 | 30 | 4 | 30 | 3 | 0 | 19 | 4 | 5.87 |
| Penalver, Mont ... | 36 | 25 | 13 | 2 | 13 | 15 | 1 | .464 | 206 | 218 | 84 | 68 | 11 | 32 | 10 | 5 | 88 | 2 | 2.97 |

|  |  |  |  |  |  |  |  |  |  |  |  |  |  | Int. |  |  |  |  |
|---|---|---|---|---|---|---|---|---|---|---|---|---|---|---|---|---|---|---|
| Pitcher—Club | G. | GS. | CG. | ShO. | W. | L. | Sv. | Pct. | IP. | H. | R. | ER. | HR. | BB. | BB. | HB. | SO. | WP. | ERA |
| Pereira, Puebla ... | 32 | 0 | 0 | 0 | 8 | 0 | 2 | 1.000 | 74 | 71 | 30 | 23 | 2 | 33 | 3 | 6 | 11 | 2 | 2.80 |
| Pina, Aguas ..... | 26 | 22 | 14 | 3 | 10 | 13 | 1 | .435 | 180 | 162 | 62 | 43 | 3 | 60 | 7 | 14 | 135 | 5 | 2.15 |
| Pizarro, Cordoba* | 23 | 23 | 17 | 6 | 14 | 7 | 0 | .667 | 191 | 169 | 56 | 42 | 3 | 85 | 7 | 1 | 157 | 7 | 1.98 |
| Plodinec, U Lag .. | 7 | 1 | 0 | 1 | 0 | 4 | 0 | .200 | 26 | 40 | 25 | 18 | 1 | 15 | 0 | 1 | 10 | 6 | 6.23 |
| Pollorena, U Lag.. | 35 | 30 | 23 | 5 | 20 | 11 | 1 | .645 | 254 | 236 | 79 | 67 | 15 | 50 | 7 | 2 | 136 | 3 | 2.37 |
| President, Aguas* | 32 | 29 | 8 | 0 | 9 | 13 | 0 | .409 | 178 | 212 | 114 | 75 | 5 | 96 | 5 | 1 | 88 | 4 | 3.79 |
| Puente, Juarez .... | 30 | 29 | 12 | 2 | 10 | 15 | 1 | .400 | 188 | 221 | 103 | 80 | 8 | 52 | 2 | 5 | 62 | 4 | 3.83 |
| Puig, 6 Ch-7 Rey* | 13 | 0 | 0 | 0 | 0 | 0 | 0 | .000 | 20 | 22 | 10 | 8 | 1 | 8 | 0 | 0 | 9 | 1 | 3.60 |
| Rabouin, Jalisco.. | 5 | 4 | 1 | 0 | 0 | 3 | 0 | .000 | 19 | 23 | 19 | 10 | 2 | 13 | 0 | 0 | 11 | 1 | 4.74 |
| Ramirez, Aguas ... | 6 | 0 | 0 | 0 | 0 | 0 | 0 | .000 | 11 | 10 | 3 | 3 | 1 | 3 | 0 | 0 | 2 | 0 | 2.45 |
| Ramos, 2 MR-8 Vil | 10 | 7 | 0 | 0 | 1 | 5 | 1 | .167 | 38 | 51 | 28 | 21 | 6 | 14 | 2 | 2 | 20 | 0 | 4.97 |
| Raygoza, Coahuila | 18 | 8 | 1 | 1 | 3 | 2 | 0 | .600 | 71 | 79 | 34 | 28 | 7 | 17 | 2 | 4 | 35 | 1 | 3.55 |
| Reyes, Chihuahua* | 29 | 18 | 4 | 2 | 7 | 9 | 0 | .438 | 112 | 118 | 57 | 48 | 7 | 41 | 4 | 2 | 44 | 1 | 3.86 |
| Reynoso, Chihua ... | 13 | 0 | 0 | 0 | 0 | 1 | 0 | .000 | 40 | 40 | 21 | 16 | 0 | 27 | 6 | 2 | 16 | 3 | 3.60 |
| Rivas, Coahuila* .. | 15 | 11 | 2 | 1 | 4 | 5 | 0 | .444 | 71 | 72 | 42 | 30 | 6 | 26 | 0 | 1 | 46 | 2 | 3.80 |
| M. Rodriguez, MR | 34 | 29 | 8 | 1 | 16 | 9 | 1 | .640 | 200 | 243 | 98 | 82 | 10 | 78 | 8 | 12 | 81 | 4 | 3.69 |
| P. Rodriguez, Mon | 33 | 13 | 2 | 0 | 6 | 7 | 1 | .462 | 103 | 74 | 43 | 36 | 5 | 60 | 11 | 4 | 67 | 3 | 3.15 |
| Rodriguez, U Lag | 11 | 0 | 0 | 0 | 0 | 0 | 0 | .000 | 18 | 30 | 15 | 12 | 2 | 5 | 0 | 0 | 8 | 2 | 6.00 |
| Rodriquez, P Rica | 14 | 0 | 0 | 0 | 2 | 4 | 2 | .333 | 28 | 44 | 20 | 14 | 0 | 8 | 1 | 0 | 19 | 2 | 4.50 |
| Romo, Mexico Reds | 30 | 29 | 15 | 3 | 13 | 8 | 0 | .619 | 219 | 194 | 71 | 57 | 5 | 52 | 6 | 4 | 146 | 5 | 2.34 |
| Romo, Cordoba .. | 22 | 22 | 11 | 4 | 13 | 6 | 0 | .684 | 161 | 149 | 60 | 47 | 3 | 32 | 4 | 0 | 101 | 6 | 2.63 |
| Rubio, M Tigers .. | 5 | 0 | 0 | 0 | 0 | 0 | 0 | .000 | 9 | 5 | 0 | 0 | 0 | 4 | 1 | 0 | 6 | 0 | 0.00 |
| Saldivar, Mex T.. | 41 | 27 | 5 | 0 | 6 | 16 | 2 | .273 | 170 | 192 | 102 | 68 | 4 | 126 | 11 | 6 | 88 | 12 | 3.60 |
| Salgado, Reynosa.. | 35 | 25 | 11 | 1 | 11 | 14 | 1 | .440 | 164 | 159 | 72 | 50 | 8 | 40 | 7 | 3 | 55 | 5 | 2.74 |
| G. Salinas, Rey... | 33 | 28 | 18 | 2 | 16 | 12 | 1 | .571 | 227 | 213 | 78 | 63 | 9 | 57 | 14 | 2 | 108 | 4 | 2.50 |
| Salomon, Cordoba.. | 22 | 22 | 14 | 4 | 15 | 3 | 0 | .833 | 172 | 142 | 49 | 43 | 5 | 58 | 5 | 3 | 87 | 2 | 2.25 |
| Sandate, Poza R* | 28 | 22 | 14 | 6 | 13 | 6 | 1 | .684 | 177 | 140 | 46 | 28 | 3 | 47 | 5 | 1 | 161 | 9 | 1.42 |
| Rodr. Sandoval, Ch | 25 | 19 | 5 | 2 | 8 | 9 | 0 | .471 | 131 | 150 | 70 | 56 | 6 | 53 | 2 | 6 | 56 | 5 | 3.85 |
| Santos, Reynosa ... | 5 | 0 | 0 | 0 | 0 | 0 | 0 | .000 | 16 | 27 | 15 | 13 | 0 | 2 | 0 | 1 | 5 | 2 | 7.31 |
| Saucedo, Jalisco .. | 7 | 0 | 0 | 0 | 1 | 0 | 1 | 1.000 | 17 | 26 | 6 | 5 | 3 | 5 | 0 | 1 | 9 | 0 | 2.65 |
| Serna, Reynosa ... | 1 | 0 | 0 | 0 | 0 | 0 | 0 | .000 | 3 | 6 | 4 | 2 | 1 | 0 | 0 | 0 | 2 | 0 | 6.00 |
| Sierra, Aguas.... | 3 | 0 | 0 | 0 | 0 | 0 | 0 | .000 | 3 | 5 | 4 | 3 | 1 | 3 | 0 | 0 | 1 | 0 | 9.00 |
| Sifuentes, Cord* ... | 4 | 1 | 0 | 0 | 1 | 0 | 1 | 1.000 | 9 | 13 | 11 | 9 | 1 | 6 | 1 | 0 | 6 | 1 | 9.00 |
| Snyder, Saltillo* .. | 11 | 3 | 1 | 0 | 4 | 2 | 0 | .667 | 59 | 72 | 41 | 30 | 2 | 30 | 1 | 4 | 31 | 7 | 4.58 |
| Solis, Coahuila .. | 31 | 0 | 0 | 0 | 6 | 3 | 3 | .667 | 64 | 71 | 28 | 20 | 3 | 28 | 10 | 1 | 32 | 1 | 2.81 |
| Solis, Saltillo .... | 28 | 25 | 13 | 1 | 16 | 7 | 0 | .696 | 184 | 179 | 70 | 54 | 8 | 48 | 4 | 5 | 70 | 4 | 2.64 |
| Soto, Saltillo ...... | 5 | 4 | 1 | 0 | 0 | 2 | 0 | .000 | 22 | 30 | 13 | 8 | 0 | 6 | 2 | 0 | 7 | 0 | 3.27 |
| Soto, Juarez,* .... | 32 | 22 | 6 | 3 | 8 | 7 | 0 | .533 | 134 | 150 | 62 | 47 | 6 | 53 | 8 | 0 | 37 | 5 | 3.16 |
| Soto, Chihuahua.. | 17 | 1 | 1 | 0 | 1 | 0 | 1 | 1.000 | 31 | 39 | 25 | 14 | 1 | 14 | 0 | 4 | 7 | 4 | 4.06 |
| Stephenson, | | | | | | | | | | | | | | | | | | | |
| 5 Mont-4 Jua* | 9 | 7 | 0 | 0 | 1 | 4 | 0 | .200 | 34 | 45 | 31 | 24 | 2 | 28 | 3 | 5 | 15 | 8 | 6.35 |
| Suarez, Mex Reds* | 2 | 0 | 0 | 0 | 0 | 0 | 0 | .000 | 2 | 4 | 4 | 2 | 1 | 5 | 0 | 0 | 2 | 0 | 9.00 |
| Suby, 34 Mex Tig- | | | | | | | | | | | | | | | | | | | |
| 11 Tampico | 45 | 4 | 2 | 0 | 6 | 7 | 3 | .462 | 115 | 151 | 53 | 44 | 13 | 18 | 9 | 3 | 43 | 3 | 3.44 |
| Tafoya, Chihuahua | 4 | 0 | 0 | 0 | 0 | 2 | 0 | .000 | 12 | 14 | 7 | 7 | 2 | 7 | 0 | 2 | 3 | 1 | 5.25 |
| Tatum, Monterrey | 9 | 9 | 6 | 0 | 4 | 4 | 0 | .500 | 70 | 65 | 26 | 20 | 7 | 22 | 5 | 4 | 27 | 4 | 2.57 |
| Texidor, Reynosa.. | 34 | 21 | 15 | 3 | 9 | 14 | 5 | .391 | 187 | 175 | 66 | 48 | 9 | 60 | 13 | 2 | 120 | 6 | 2.31 |
| Thompson, Reynosa* | 1 | 1 | 0 | 0 | 0 | 0 | 0 | .000 | 3 | 2 | 3 | 3 | 0 | 5 | 0 | 0 | 2 | 0 | 9.00 |
| Tovar, U Laguna.. | 30 | 13 | 1 | 0 | 4 | 8 | 5 | .333 | 107 | 128 | 69 | 50 | 9 | 25 | 5 | 6 | 36 | 2 | 4.21 |
| Travis, Chihuahua | 28 | 16 | 5 | 1 | 7 | 7 | 2 | .500 | 138 | 137 | 75 | 58 | 9 | 63 | 5 | 7 | 104 | 6 | 3.78 |
| Uresti, Jalisco .... | 6 | 0 | 0 | 0 | 1 | 1 | 0 | .500 | 11 | 10 | 6 | 5 | 0 | 5 | 1 | 1 | 7 | 3 | 4.09 |
| Valadez, Tampico.. | 9 | 8 | 1 | 0 | 1 | 4 | 0 | .200 | 48 | 37 | 18 | 14 | 3 | 13 | 1 | 1 | 14 | 0 | 2.63 |
| Valdez, Mex Tig .. | 14 | 6 | 0 | 0 | 3 | 1 | 0 | .750 | 34 | 40 | 15 | 14 | 2 | 13 | 2 | 0 | 20 | 3 | 3.71 |
| Valdez, Aguas* .. | 1 | 0 | 0 | 0 | 0 | 0 | 0 | .000 | 1 | 1 | 1 | 0 | 0 | 1 | 0 | 0 | 0 | 0 | 0.00 |
| Valencia, Coahuila | 2 | 0 | 0 | 0 | 0 | 0 | 0 | .000 | 2 | 5 | 6 | 5 | 0 | 2 | 0 | 0 | 0 | 0 | 22.50 |
| Valencia, Villa .. | 3 | 0 | 0 | 0 | 0 | 0 | 0 | .000 | 9 | 16 | 11 | 8 | 2 | 3 | 0 | 0 | 3 | 3 | 8.00 |
| Valenzuela, | | | | | | | | | | | | | | | | | | | |
| 4 Salt-20 Coah | 24 | 18 | 6 | 3 | 8 | 9 | 0 | .471 | 112 | 122 | 55 | 40 | 0 | 20 | 7 | 5 | 39 | 2 | 3.21 |
| Valenzuela, M R.. | 17 | 2 | 0 | 0 | 2 | 1 | 0 | .000 | 41 | 48 | 24 | 15 | 0 | 14 | 2 | 0 | 28 | 2 | 3.29 |
| Valle, Tampico* .. | 1 | 0 | 0 | 0 | 0 | 0 | 0 | .000 | 2 | 4 | 3 | 3 | 0 | 2 | 0 | 0 | 2 | 0 | 13.50 |
| Valle, Aguas* .... | 7 | 0 | 0 | 0 | 0 | 0 | 0 | .000 | 9 | 12 | 5 | 5 | 0 | 6 | 1 | 0 | 6 | 1 | 5.00 |
| Vallejano, Tampico | 33 | 15 | 3 | 0 | 9 | 5 | 2 | .643 | 139 | 137 | 55 | 43 | 9 | 36 | 3 | 7 | 72 | 3 | 2.79 |
| Velo, Jalisco ...... | 40 | 21 | 8 | 3 | 11 | 8 | 7 | .579 | 170 | 177 | 78 | 60 | 11 | 59 | 10 | 3 | 120 | 11 | 3.18 |
| Verdugo, Saltillo.. | 28 | 0 | 0 | 0 | 1 | 0 | 1 | 1.000 | 83 | 95 | 46 | 40 | 2 | 38 | 3 | 3 | 34 | 5 | 4.34 |
| Villanueva, M Tig* | 12 | 4 | 0 | 0 | 1 | 1 | 0 | .500 | 25 | 25 | 8 | 8 | 0 | 5 | 1 | 1 | 15 | 1 | 2.88 |
| Volkening, Mont .. | 32 | 32 | 22 | 6 | 15 | 14 | 0 | .517 | 232 | 238 | 78 | 66 | 12 | 47 | 4 | 3 | 96 | 7 | 2.56 |
| Yard, Aguas ..... | 8 | 5 | 0 | 0 | 2 | 4 | 0 | .333 | 34 | 44 | 20 | 14 | 2 | 22 | 3 | 0 | 27 | 3 | 3.71 |

**BALKS**—Acosta M., Ahumada, Barbosa, Tovar, 2 each; Acosta L., Barrios, Cavanaugh, R. Chavez, DeLaTorre, C. Diaz, H. Diaz, Espinosa, Goodwin, Lee, Luna, Miali, Mota, J. Pena, M. Rodriguez, P. Rodriguez, G. Salinas, Sandate, Tafoya, Velo, 1 each.

**COMBINATION SHUTOUTS**—C. Diaz-Byron Quiroz, President-Byron Quiroz, Aguascalientes; Rodr. Sandoval-Guzman, Reyes-Guzman, Chihuahua; Valenzuela-Solis, Coahuila; Romo-Gutierrez, Cordoba; Abarca-Velo, Gutierrez-Guzman, Cordova-Colorado, Jalisco; Soto-Fajardo, Beltran-A. Davila, Moreno-Orea, Juarez; Bellacetin-A. Lopez, Romo-A. Lopez-M. Rodriguez, Mexico Reds; Delgado-Saldivar-Agundez, Espinosa-Agundez, Espinosa-Garcia, Delgado-F. Lopez-Agundez, Villanueva-Valdez-Delgado-Agundez, Mexico Tigers; Brunet-Rodriguez, Poza Rica; Azcarraga-Diorio-Pereira-Martinez A., Acosta-Bracamontes, Acosta-Boyd, Barandica-Bracamontes-Boyd, Puebla; G. Salinas-Texidor 2, Salgado-Texidor, Aponte-Texidor, Reynosa; Hernandez-Goodwin, Saltillo; V. Garcia-

Maytorena, Collazo-Vallejano-Maytorena, Vallejano-Maytorena, Collazo-Vallejano, Tampico; Acosta M.-G. Gonzalez-Tovar, Union Laguna; Cordeiro-Fabela, Lagunas-Acosta M., Villahermosa.

NO-HIT GAMES— Pina, Aguascalientes, defeated Juarez, 1-0, May 10 (seven innings); Hambright, Juarez, defeated Tampico, 4-0, May 20 (seven innings); Miali, Coahuila, defeated Chihuahua, 1-0, June 8 (seven innings); Espinosa (three innings), Garcia (two innings), Mexico Tigers, defeated Puebla, 1-0, July 17 (five innings); Valenzuela, Coahuila defeated Tampico, 3-0, July 21.

## MAJORS PICK FIVE IN DRAFT

Only five players were selected for the $25,000 price in the major league draft at the winter meetings at the Diplomat Hotel in Hollywood, Fla. in 1975.

In a draft which took only 13 minutes to complete, the Detroit Tigers made the first selection, choosing Bruce Taylor, a righthanded pitcher from the Cincinnati Reds' organization.

The Houston Astros also opted for a righthanded hurler, Gil Rondon, who was the property of the California Angels.

Another California farmhand, Luis Quintana, was picked up by the Atlanta Braves. A lefthanded relief pitcher, Quintana worked in four games for the Angels in 1975, with an 0-2 record and 6.43 ERA.

California made the fourth pick with the selection of first baseman Ed Kurpiel from the Detroit Tigers' chain.

In a delayed phase of the major league draft, the New York Yankees selected first baseman-outfielder Tom Robson from the Texas Rangers. This announcement was made some 12 hours after the regular draft had been completed.

# *Pacific Coast League*

## CLASS AAA

**Leading Batter
JERRY ROYSTER**
Albuquerque

**League President
ROY JACKSON**

**Leading Pitcher
STEVE LUEBBER**
Tacoma

### CHAMPIONSHIP WINNERS IN PREVIOUS YEARS

| | | |
|---|---|---|
| 1903—Los Angeles ...... .630 | 1930—Los Angeles ...... .576 | 1953—Hollywood ........ .589 |
| 1904—Tacoma§ ......... .589 | Hollywood* ...... .650 | 1954—San Diego y ...... .604 |
| Tacoma§ ......... .571 | 1931—Hollywood ........ .626 | 1955—Seattle .......... .552 |
| Los Angeles§ .... .571 | San Francisco* ... .608 | 1956—Los Angeles ...... .637 |
| 1905—Tacoma .......... .583 | 1932—Portland ......... .587 | 1957—San Francisco .... .601 |
| Los Angeles* .... .604 | 1933—Los Angeles ...... .610 | 1958—Phoenix .......... .578 |
| 1906—Portland ......... .657 | 1934—Los Angeles z .... .786 | 1959—Salt Lake City ... .552 |
| 1907—Los Angeles ...... .608 | Los Angeles z .... .689 | 1960—Spokane .......... .601 |
| 1908—Los Angeles ...... .585 | 1935—Los Angeles ...... .648 | 1961—Tacoma .......... .630 |
| 1909—San Francisco .... .623 | San Francisco* ... .608 | 1962—San Diego ....... .604 |
| 1910—Portland ......... .567 | 1936—Portland‡ ........ .549 | 1963—Spokane .......... .620 |
| 1913—Portland ......... .559 | 1937—Sacramento ....... .573 | Oklahoma City a .. .532 |
| 1911—Portland ......... .589 | San Diego (3rd)† .. .545 | 1964—Arkansas ........ .609 |
| 1912—Oakland ......... .591 | 1938—Los Angeles ...... .590 | San Diego a ...... .576 |
| 1914—Portland ......... .574 | Sacramento (3rd)† . .537 | 1965—Oklahoma City a .. .628 |
| 1916—Los Angeles ...... .601 | 1939—Seattle .......... .580 | Portland .......... .547 |
| 1917—San Francisco .... .561 | Sacramento (4th)† . .500 | 1966—Seattle a ........ .561 |
| 1915—San Francisco .... .570 | 1940—Seattle‡ ......... .629 | Tulsa ............ .578 |
| 1918—Vernon .......... .569 | 1941—Seattle‡ ......... .598 | 1967—San Diego a ...... .574 |
| Los Angeles (2nd)x .548 | 1942—Sacramento ....... .590 | Spokane .......... .541 |
| 1919—Vernon .......... .613 | Seattle (3rd)† .... .539 | 1968—Tulsa a .......... .642 |
| 1920—Vernon .......... .556 | 1943—Los Angeles ...... .710 | Spokane .......... .586 |
| 1921—Los Angeles ...... .574 | S. Francisco (2nd)† .574 | 1969—Tacoma a ........ .589 |
| 1922—San Francisco .... .638 | 1944—Los Angeles ...... .586 | Eugene .......... .603 |
| 1923—San Francisco .... .617 | S. Francisco (3rd)† .509 | 1970—Spokane a ........ .644 |
| 1924—Seattle .......... .545 | 1945—Portland ......... .622 | Hawaii .......... .671 |
| 1925—San Francisco .... .643 | S. Francisco (4th)† .525 | 1971—Salt Lake City a.. .534 |
| 1926—Los Angeles ...... .599 | 1946—San Francisco‡ ... .628 | Tacoma .......... .545 |
| 1927—Oakland ......... .615 | 1947—Los Angeles†† .... .567 | 1972—Albuquerque a .... .622 |
| 1928—San Francisco* ... .630 | 1948—Oakland‡ ........ .606 | Eugene .......... .534 |
| Sacramento§§ ..... .626 | 1949—Hollywood‡ ....... .583 | 1973—Tucson a ........ .583 |
| San Francisco§§ .. .626 | 1950—Oakland ......... .590 | Spokane a ........ .563 |
| 1929—Mission ......... .643 | 1951—Seattle‡ ......... .593 | 1974—Spokane a ........ .549 |
| Hollywood* ....... .592 | 1952—Los Angeles ...... .606 | Albuquerque ...... .535 |

*Won split-season playoff. †Won four-team playoff. ‡Won pennant and four-team playoff.
§Tied for second-half title with Tacoma winning playoff. §§Tied for second-half title, with Sacramento winning playoff. ††Ended regular season in tie with San Francisco and won one-game

playoff for pennant, then won four-club playoff. xWon playoff from first-place Vernon and awarded championship. yDefeated Hollywood in one-game playoff for pennant. zWon both halves, no playoff. aLeague was divided into Northern, Southen divisions in 1963, 1969-70-71, and Eastern, Western divisions in 1964-65-66-67-68-72-73; won two-team playoff. NOTE—Championship awarded to playoff winner. 1936-37.

## STANDING OF CLUBS AT CLOSE OF SEASON, SEPTEMBER 1

### EASTERN DIVISION

| Club | S.L.C. | Tuc. | Alb. | Phx. | Haw. | Tac. | Spo. | Sac. | W. | L. | T. | Pct. | G.B. |
|---|---|---|---|---|---|---|---|---|---|---|---|---|---|
| Salt Lake City (Angels).... | .. | 16 | 17 | 24 | 5 | 5 | 6 | 7 | 80 | 64 | 0 | .556 | .... |
| Tucson (Athletics) .... | 16 | .. | 13 | 15 | 3 | 8 | 8 | 9 | 72 | 71 | 0 | .503 | 7½ |
| Albuquerque (Dodgers) .... | 15 | 19 | .. | 17 | 6 | 4 | 6 | 4 | 71 | 73 | 0 | .493 | 9 |
| Phoenix (Giants) .... | 8 | 16 | 15 | .. | 4 | 7 | 8 | 8 | 66 | 77 | 0 | .462 | 13½ |

### WESTERN DIVISION

| Club | S.L.C. | Tuc. | Alb. | Phx. | Haw. | Tac. | Spo. | Sac. | W. | L. | T. | Pct. | G.B. |
|---|---|---|---|---|---|---|---|---|---|---|---|---|---|
| Hawaii (Padres) ......... | 7 | 9 | 6 | 8 | .. | 17 | 22 | 19 | 88 | 56 | 0 | .611 | .... |
| Tacoma (Twins) ......... | 7 | 4 | 8 | 5 | 15 | .. | 15 | 19 | 73 | 69 | 0 | .514 | 14 |
| Spokane (Rangers) ....... | 6 | 4 | 6 | 4 | 10 | 15 | .. | 19 | 64 | 78 | 0 | .451 | 23 |
| Sacramento (Brewers) ..... | 5 | 3 | 8 | 4 | 13 | 13 | 13 | .. | 59 | 85 | 0 | .410 | 29 |

Hawaii club represented Honolulu, Hawaii.
Major league affiliations in parentheses.
Playoff—Hawaii defeated Salt Lake City, four games to two.
Regular-Season Attendance—Albuquerque, 157,863; Hawaii, 213,432; Phoenix, 160,897; Sacramento, 252,201; Salt Lake City, 122,251; Spokane, 103,803; Tacoma, 197,583; Tucson, 170,521. Total, 1,378,551. All-Star Game, 3,200. Playoffs, 40,281.
Managers: Albuquerque—Stan Wasiak; Hawaii—Roy Hartsfield; Phoenix—Everett (Rocky) Bridges; Sacramento—Harry Bright; Salt Lake City—Norm Sherry; Spokane—Del Wilber; Tacoma—Cal Ermer; Tucson—Hank Aguirre.
All-Star Team: 1B—Robson, Spokane; 2B—Sheldon, Sacramento; 3B—Royster, Albuquerque; SS—LeMaster, Phoenix; OF—Moates, Spokane; Cruz, Spokane; Turner, Hawaii; C—Davis, Hawaii; DH—Manuel, Albuquerque; P—Ross, Hawaii; Bane, Tacoma; Manager—Hartsfield, Hawaii.

(Compiled by William J. Weiss, League Statistician, San Mateo, Calif.)

## CLUB BATTING

| Club | G. | AB. | R. | OR. | H. | TB. | 2B. | 3B. | HR. | RBI. | SH. | SF. | Int. BB. | BB. | HP. | SO. | SB. | CS. | LOB. | Pct. |
|---|---|---|---|---|---|---|---|---|---|---|---|---|---|---|---|---|---|---|---|---|
| Albuq'que | 144 | 4701 | 694 | 720 | 1330 | 1923 | 234 | 46 | 89 | 632 | 51 | 40 | 479 | 53 | 33 | 646 | 122 | 67 | 927 | .283 |
| Sacramento | 144 | 4851 | 773 | 880 | 1354 | 2155 | 177 | 18 | 196 | 713 | 20 | 31 | 547 | 23 | 24 | 753 | 40 | 24 | 1015 | .279 |
| Tucson | 144 | 4672 | 710 | 728 | 1298 | 1877 | 229 | 46 | 86 | 625 | 19 | 55 | 613 | 34 | 21 | 684 | 135 | 58 | 1030 | .278 |
| Salt L. C. | 144 | 4488 | 726 | 670 | 1236 | 1765 | 197 | 64 | 68 | 657 | 63 | 48 | 525 | 36 | 29 | 677 | 184 | 93 | 912 | .275 |
| Hawaii | 144 | 4663 | 766 | 579 | 1284 | 1819 | 223 | 24 | 88 | 678 | 56 | 49 | 689 | 31 | 29 | 655 | 105 | 43 | 1123 | .275 |
| Phoenix | 143 | 4747 | 647 | 641 | 1287 | 1779 | 186 | 72 | 54 | 576 | 41 | 39 | 482 | 22 | 30 | 662 | 126 | 58 | 1028 | .271 |
| Spokane | 142 | 4646 | 665 | 758 | 1255 | 1798 | 196 | 37 | 91 | 611 | 41 | 40 | 546 | 28 | 36 | 646 | 78 | 42 | 1025 | .270 |
| Tacoma | 142 | 4637 | 663 | 658 | 1205 | 1788 | 164 | 25 | 123 | 592 | 52 | 31 | 555 | 28 | 38 | 840 | 71 | 27 | 1048 | .260 |

## INDIVIDUAL BATTING

(Leading Qualifiers for Batting Championship—389 or More Plate Appearances)

*Bats lefthanded. †Switch-hitter.

| Player and Club | G. | AB. | R. | H. | TB. | 2B. | 3B. | HR. | RBI. | SH. | SF. | BB. | HP. | SO. | SB. | CS. | Pct. |
|---|---|---|---|---|---|---|---|---|---|---|---|---|---|---|---|---|---|
| Royster, Jeron, Alb | 133 | 487 | 91 | 162 | 237 | 31 | 7 | 10 | 65 | 5 | 5 | 53 | 2 | 46 | 33 | 11 | .333 |
| Turner, John, Hawaii* | 142 | 535 | 88 | 176 | 242 | 27 | 3 | 11 | 91 | 5 | 5 | 56 | 4 | 36 | 15 | 7 | .329 |
| Eden, E. Michael, Phoenix† | 121 | 450 | 64 | 144 | 189 | 24 | 9 | 1 | 49 | 6 | 3 | 61 | 0 | 33 | 13 | 9 | .320 |
| Sandt, Thomas, Tucson | 116 | 391 | 62 | 121 | 147 | 20 | 0 | 2 | 49 | 1 | 5 | 34 | 2 | 39 | 16 | 6 | .309 |
| Torres, Rosendo, SLC† | 107 | 369 | 59 | 113 | 173 | 18 | 9 | 8 | 64 | 5 | 6 | 60 | 1 | 66 | 6 | 11 | .306 |
| Reynolds, Tommie, Sac | 131 | 477 | 82 | 145 | 241 | 13 | 4 | 25 | 89 | 0 | 5 | 52 | 5 | 55 | 3 | 1 | .304 |
| Alvarez, J. Orlando, Alb | 138 | 515 | 68 | 156 | 222 | 26 | 5 | 10 | 79 | 1 | 3 | 41 | 4 | 69 | 10 | 3 | .303 |
| McKinney, C. Richard, Tuc | 110 | 394 | 57 | 117 | 188 | 26 | 3 | 13 | 74 | 0 | 6 | 54 | 0 | 48 | 9 | 2 | .297 |
| LeMaster, Johnnie, Phoenix | 143 | 520 | 75 | 152 | 206 | 26 | 8 | 4 | 58 | 4 | 3 | 34 | 2 | 98 | 17 | 7 | .292 |
| Randall, Robert, Alb | 107 | 391 | 62 | 114 | 149 | 23 | 3 | 2 | 43 | 7 | 3 | 37 | 5 | 36 | 2 | 4 | .292 |

Departmental Leaders: G—Almon, Gaspar, Ron Jackson, 144; AB—J. Lopez, 542; R—Royster, 91; H—Turner, 176; TB—Hansen, 247; 2B—C. Cruz, 35; 3B—Darrow, Eden, Torres, 9; HR—Hansen, 29; RBI—Hansen, 102; SH—Darrow, 15; SF—Criscione, 10; BB—Gaspar, 102; HP—Bass, 8; SO—Poepping, 132; SB—Almon, Royster, 33; CS—Simpson, 9.

(All Players—Listed Alphabetically)

| Player and Club | G. | AB. | R. | H. | TB. | 2B. | 3B. | HR. | RBI. | SH. | SF. | BB. | HP. | SO. | SB. | CS. | Pct. |
|---|---|---|---|---|---|---|---|---|---|---|---|---|---|---|---|---|---|
| Adams, Glenn, Phoenix* | 19 | 67 | 9 | 20 | 29 | 4 | 1 | 1 | 8 | 0 | 0 | 9 | 1 | 7 | 1 | 0 | .299 |
| Alexander, Gary, Phoenix | 7 | 14 | 2 | 2 | 3 | 1 | 0 | 0 | 1 | 0 | 0 | 5 | 0 | 6 | 0 | 0 | .143 |
| Allietta, Robert, SLC | 42 | 144 | 18 | 43 | 56 | 9 | 2 | 0 | 18 | 1 | 3 | 17 | 4 | 18 | 2 | 0 | .299 |
| Almon, William, Hawaii | 144 | 496 | 76 | 113 | 138 | 22 | 0 | 1 | 47 | 11 | 4 | 56 | 3 | 106 | 33 | 6 | .228 |
| Alvarez, J. Orlando, Alb | 138 | 515 | 68 | 156 | 222 | 26 | 5 | 10 | 79 | 1 | 3 | 41 | 4 | 69 | 10 | 3 | .303 |
| Anderson, Lawrence, Sac | 19 | 1 | 0 | 0 | 0 | 0 | 0 | 0 | 0 | 0 | 0 | 0 | 0 | 0 | 0 | 0 | .000 |
| Arnold, Christopher, Phoenix | 35 | 127 | 24 | 43 | 54 | 6 | 1 | 1 | 15 | 1 | 0 | 12 | 0 | 15 | 1 | 0 | .339 |
| Ashford, Samuel, SLC* | 3 | 7 | 1 | 2 | 5 | 1 | 1 | 0 | 1 | 0 | 0 | 1 | 0 | 3 | 0 | 0 | .286 |
| Astroth, Jonathan, Spo* | 56 | 168 | 19 | 41 | 62 | 9 | 0 | 4 | 22 | 2 | 1 | 39 | 1 | 28 | 2 | 1 | .244 |
| Augustine, Gerald, Sac* | 15 | 3 | 0 | 0 | 0 | 0 | 0 | 0 | 0 | 0 | 0 | 0 | 0 | 2 | 0 | 0 | .000 |
| Ault, Douglas, Spokane | 48 | 175 | 23 | 60 | 93 | 8 | 2 | 7 | 37 | 0 | 2 | 15 | 3 | 27 | 0 | 1 | .343 |
| Balaz, John, Salt Lake City | 59 | 208 | 28 | 57 | 88 | 8 | 4 | 5 | 33 | 0 | 1 | 12 | 4 | 46 | 4 | 2 | .274 |

| Player and Club | G | AB | R | H | TB | 2B | 3B | HR | RBI | SH | SF | BB | HP | SO | SB | CS | Pct. |
|---|---|---|---|---|---|---|---|---|---|---|---|---|---|---|---|---|---|
| Baldwin, Michael, Sac* | 10 | 2 | 0 | 0 | 0 | 0 | 0 | 0 | 0 | 0 | 0 | 0 | 0 | 1 | 0 | 0 | .000 |
| Bass, Randy, Tacoma* | 120 | 397 | 64 | 102 | 180 | 14 | 5 | 18 | 80 | 0 | 4 | 73 | 8 | 89 | 0 | 0 | .257 |
| Beach, Randolph, Tacoma | 45 | 144 | 21 | 37 | 40 | 1 | 1 | 0 | 8 | 2 | 0 | 15 | 0 | 18 | 5 | 3 | .257 |
| Beasley, Lewis, Spokane* | 28 | 99 | 13 | 31 | 46 | 7 | 1 | 2 | 16 | 0 | 2 | 10 | 2 | 7 | 5 | 0 | .313 |
| Bianco, Thomas, Sac† | 96 | 350 | 53 | 102 | 161 | 11 | 0 | 16 | 58 | 0 | 1 | 32 | 0 | 50 | 2 | 0 | .291 |
| Blessitt, Isaiah, Tucson | 84 | 227 | 46 | 65 | 105 | 13 | 6 | 5 | 27 | 0 | 3 | 31 | 2 | 39 | 10 | 4 | .286 |
| Bordes, Charles, Spokane | 75 | 238 | 29 | 63 | 71 | 5 | 0 | 1 | 17 | 7 | 1 | 32 | 2 | 34 | 2 | 7 | .265 |
| Bostock, Lyman, Tacoma* | 22 | 92 | 16 | 36 | 41 | 5 | 0 | 0 | 13 | 1 | 0 | 6 | 1 | 12 | 3 | 2 | .391 |
| Bowling, Stephen, Sac | 139 | 447 | 70 | 106 | 180 | 12 | 1 | 20 | 61 | 4 | 3 | 68 | 4 | 128 | 3 | 4 | .237 |
| Bradley, J. Richard, Phoe. | 65 | 221 | 22 | 56 | 71 | 5 | 2 | 2 | 26 | 2 | 3 | 18 | 2 | 44 | 0 | 1 | .253 |
| Breitzman, Robert, Tucson* | 6 | 19 | 3 | 4 | 4 | 0 | 0 | 0 | 1 | 0 | 0 | 8 | 0 | 3 | 1 | 1 | .211 |
| Briggs, Dan, Salt Lake C* | 80 | 260 | 45 | 84 | 103 | 12 | 2 | 1 | 37 | 1 | 3 | 34 | 2 | 32 | 5 | 5 | .323 |
| Brown, Leon, Phoenix | 92 | 256 | 38 | 84 | 110 | 10 | 5 | 2 | 36 | 2 | 4 | 19 | 1 | 19 | 17 | 4 | .328 |
| Burney, O. Wayne, Alb* | 61 | 165 | 11 | 37 | 46 | 2 | 2 | 1 | 19 | 5 | 0 | 18 | 1 | 23 | 0 | 4 | .224 |
| Butera, Salvatore, Tacoma | 73 | 215 | 21 | 52 | 67 | 9 | 0 | 2 | 26 | 4 | 0 | 15 | 0 | 23 | 0 | 0 | .242 |
| Cannizzaro, Christopher, Haw | 4 | 5 | 0 | 0 | 0 | 0 | 0 | 0 | 0 | 1 | 0 | 1 | 0 | 3 | 0 | 0 | .000 |
| Chant, Charles, Tucson | 135 | 505 | 75 | 145 | 197 | 27 | 5 | 5 | 69 | 2 | 6 | 43 | 5 | 60 | 21 | 7 | .287 |
| Christensen, Bruce, 23 Phoenix-38 Sac* | 61 | 199 | 28 | 58 | 70 | 4 | 1 | 2 | 17 | 3 | 0 | 29 | 1 | 12 | 3 | 2 | .291 |
| Collins, David, Salt Lake C† | 51 | 193 | 41 | 60 | 79 | 7 | 6 | 0 | 24 | 0 | 0 | 23 | 1 | 26 | 32 | 7 | .311 |
| Collins, Terry, Alb* | 64 | 153 | 24 | 48 | 61 | 5 | 4 | 0 | 10 | 2 | 0 | 18 | 1 | 19 | 2 | 3 | .314 |
| Criscione, David, Spokane | 118 | 391 | 41 | 91 | 132 | 12 | 4 | 7 | 52 | 3 | 10 | 38 | 1 | 54 | 3 | 5 | .233 |
| Cruz, Cirilo, Spokane* | 138 | 524 | 72 | 151 | 218 | 35 | 4 | 8 | 87 | 2 | 3 | 51 | 3 | 62 | 6 | 1 | .288 |
| Cruz, Henry, Albuquerque* | 71 | 255 | 44 | 79 | 119 | 13 | 3 | 7 | 41 | 4 | 3 | 30 | 1 | 20 | 5 | 5 | .310 |
| Cubbage, Michael, Spokane* | 56 | 217 | 50 | 68 | 120 | 18 | 2 | 10 | 34 | 0 | 0 | 33 | 1 | 33 | 0 | 0 | .313 |
| Dade, L. Paul, Salt Lake C | 9 | 33 | 12 | 18 | 34 | 5 | 1 | 3 | 14 | 2 | 0 | 4 | 1 | 5 | 2 | 0 | .545 |
| Darrow, Darrell, Salt La C | 141 | 434 | 65 | 106 | 137 | 10 | 9 | 1 | 36 | 15 | 1 | 34 | 0 | 66 | 12 | 6 | .244 |
| Davis, Robert, Hawaii | 94 | 331 | 45 | 109 | 154 | 19 | 4 | 6 | 69 | 4 | 3 | 32 | 2 | 67 | 2 | 1 | .329 |
| DeFilippis, Arthur, Spokane* | 33 | 6 | 0 | 2 | 2 | 0 | 0 | 0 | 0 | 0 | 0 | 0 | 0 | 0 | 0 | 0 | .333 |
| de Jesus, Ivan, Albuquerque | 62 | 221 | 24 | 60 | 77 | 10 | 2 | 1 | 21 | 4 | 1 | 19 | 1 | 38 | 9 | 1 | .271 |
| Doherty, John, Salt Lake C* | 75 | 257 | 37 | 77 | 115 | 18 | 7 | 2 | 47 | 0 | 5 | 25 | 0 | 30 | 5 | 4 | .300 |
| Dressler, Robert, Phoenix | 28 | 0 | 1 | 0 | 0 | 0 | 0 | 0 | 0 | 0 | 0 | 0 | 0 | 0 | 0 | 0 | .000 |
| Eden, E. Michael, Phoenix | 121 | 450 | 64 | 144 | 189 | 24 | 9 | 1 | 49 | 6 | 3 | 61 | 0 | 33 | 13 | 9 | .320 |
| Elliott, Randy, Hawaii | 95 | 338 | 63 | 93 | 157 | 22 | 3 | 12 | 60 | 3 | 6 | 44 | 3 | 53 | 10 | 2 | .275 |
| Ellis, Robert, Sacramento | 54 | 168 | 23 | 43 | 60 | 10 | 2 | 1 | 20 | 0 | 2 | 21 | 1 | 34 | 1 | 1 | .256 |
| Englert, Reuben, Phoenix* | 24 | 80 | 12 | 20 | 25 | 3 | 1 | 0 | 10 | 0 | 0 | 8 | 1 | 9 | 3 | 3 | .250 |
| Epperly, Thomas, Tacoma | 75 | 182 | 36 | 52 | 84 | 10 | 2 | 6 | 29 | 0 | 3 | 27 | 1 | 39 | 2 | 2 | .286 |
| Espy, Duane, Sacramento | 50 | 150 | 19 | 32 | 47 | 4 | 1 | 3 | 11 | 0 | 0 | 15 | 0 | 23 | 4 | 2 | .213 |
| Essian, James, Hawaii | 40 | 129 | 14 | 27 | 35 | 2 | 0 | 2 | 9 | 0 | 1 | 21 | 2 | 16 | 1 | 0 | .209 |
| Fairey, James, Hawaii* | 104 | 324 | 68 | 95 | 167 | 17 | 5 | 15 | 54 | 2 | 6 | 44 | 3 | 47 | 4 | 1 | .293 |
| Fanzone, Carmen, Hawaii | 54 | 157 | 32 | 34 | 50 | 5 | 1 | 3 | 18 | 2 | 0 | 50 | 3 | 27 | 3 | 0 | .217 |
| Ferrer, Sergio, Tacoma† | 47 | 154 | 28 | 33 | 43 | 3 | 2 | 1 | 6 | 1 | 1 | 17 | 3 | 16 | 6 | 2 | .214 |
| Flores, Gilberto, SLC | 44 | 170 | 34 | 56 | 73 | 5 | 3 | 2 | 23 | 7 | 0 | 18 | 0 | 19 | 14 | 7 | .329 |
| Friedman, Martin, SLC* | 28 | 95 | 22 | 26 | 37 | 2 | 3 | 1 | 20 | 0 | 1 | 14 | 1 | 7 | 4 | 0 | .274 |
| Galliher, Marvin, Hawaii | 63 | 209 | 34 | 64 | 79 | 9 | 0 | 2 | 31 | 1 | 4 | 28 | 1 | 24 | 1 | 0 | .306 |
| Gaspar, Rodney, Hawaii† | 144 | 531 | 90 | 140 | 162 | 15 | 2 | 1 | 58 | 5 | 4 | 102 | 0 | 48 | 11 | 11 | .264 |
| Gatlin, Michael, Tacoma | 14 | 40 | 3 | 10 | 13 | 3 | 0 | 0 | 2 | 0 | 0 | 8 | 1 | 2 | 1 | 2 | .250 |
| George, Frankie, SLC | 105 | 331 | 61 | 84 | 123 | 13 | 1 | 8 | 47 | 6 | 2 | 52 | 0 | 48 | 28 | 10 | .254 |
| Gil, T. Gustavo, 23 Alb-77 Hawaii | 100 | 337 | 54 | 96 | 122 | 18 | 1 | 2 | 49 | 7 | 3 | 58 | 0 | 32 | 1 | 1 | .285 |
| Goddard, Joseph, Hawaii | 30 | 84 | 9 | 21 | 32 | 5 | 0 | 2 | 13 | 2 | 2 | 14 | 0 | 12 | 1 | 0 | .250 |
| Gomez, Juan, Tucson | 15 | 25 | 4 | 7 | 9 | 0 | 1 | 0 | 2 | 0 | 0 | 2 | 0 | 6 | 2 | 0 | .280 |
| Gorinski, Robert, Tacoma | 89 | 304 | 44 | 71 | 121 | 7 | 2 | 13 | 38 | 2 | 1 | 18 | 1 | 79 | 3 | 1 | .234 |
| Grabarkewitz, Billy, Tuc | 94 | 308 | 57 | 86 | 145 | 19 | 8 | 8 | 40 | 0 | 5 | 63 | 1 | 56 | 5 | 1 | .279 |
| Guarnaccia, John, Sac* | 7 | 10 | 2 | 0 | 0 | 0 | 0 | 0 | 0 | 0 | 0 | 3 | 0 | 4 | 0 | 0 | .000 |
| Guarnera, Richard, Spokane | 64 | 207 | 17 | 43 | 48 | 5 | 0 | 0 | 16 | 3 | 0 | 23 | 1 | 22 | 2 | 2 | .208 |
| Haines, Dennis, Tucson* | 1 | 1 | 1 | 1 | 1 | 0 | 0 | 0 | 0 | 0 | 0 | 0 | 0 | 0 | 0 | 0 | 1.000 |
| Hale, John, Albuquerque* | 67 | 244 | 38 | 69 | 126 | 14 | 5 | 11 | 45 | 1 | 0 | 24 | 3 | 43 | 6 | 2 | .283 |
| Hampton, Isaac, SLC† | 76 | 251 | 43 | 65 | 112 | 15 | 1 | 10 | 51 | 5 | 3 | 28 | 1 | 56 | 6 | 5 | .259 |
| Hansen, Robert, Sac* | 135 | 488 | 86 | 136 | 247 | 22 | 1 | 29 | 102 | 1 | 7 | 61 | 2 | 64 | 0 | 1 | .279 |
| Heintzelman, Thomas, Phoe | 123 | 453 | 71 | 111 | 161 | 19 | 8 | 5 | 50 | 6 | 3 | 47 | 2 | 73 | 10 | 6 | .245 |
| Herndon, Larry, Phoenix | 115 | 427 | 49 | 115 | 135 | 6 | 4 | 2 | 44 | 1 | 3 | 30 | 1 | 44 | 17 | 9 | .269 |
| Hilton, J. David, Hawaii | 9 | 35 | 7 | 10 | 17 | 4 | 0 | 1 | 5 | 1 | 1 | 1 | 0 | 2 | 1 | 0 | .286 |
| Holt, James, Tucson* | 8 | 31 | 5 | 7 | 7 | 0 | 0 | 0 | 2 | 0 | 0 | 1 | 0 | 2 | 1 | 0 | .226 |
| Hooten, M. Leon, Tucson | 43 | 0 | 1 | 0 | 0 | 0 | 0 | 0 | 0 | 0 | 0 | 0 | 0 | 0 | 0 | 0 | .000 |
| Hopkins, Donald, Tucson* | 24 | 81 | 15 | 21 | 27 | 1 | 1 | 1 | 4 | 0 | 0 | 5 | 0 | 9 | 15 | 2 | .259 |
| Huntz, Stephen, Hawaii† | 101 | 332 | 57 | 91 | 145 | 16 | 1 | 12 | 72 | 4 | 2 | 84 | 2 | 43 | 3 | 2 | .274 |
| Jackson, Roland, Hawaii* | 94 | 294 | 41 | 75 | 85 | 10 | 0 | 0 | 19 | 0 | 0 | 33 | 0 | 18 | 8 | 6 | .255 |
| Jackson, Ronnie, Salt Lake C | 144 | 513 | 67 | 144 | 205 | 24 | 5 | 9 | 85 | 5 | 7 | 44 | 3 | 46 | 20 | 12 | .281 |
| James, Philip, Phoenix* | 105 | 317 | 48 | 76 | 122 | 9 | 8 | 7 | 51 | 3 | 4 | 48 | 1 | 58 | 12 | 0 | .240 |
| Johnson, Frank, 4 Phoe-31 Ha | 35 | 93 | 10 | 24 | 37 | 7 | 0 | 2 | 15 | 1 | 2 | 12 | 0 | 12 | 0 | 3 | .258 |
| Jones, Robert O., Spokane* | 109 | 404 | 69 | 112 | 187 | 12 | 6 | 17 | 67 | 1 | 2 | 37 | 5 | 95 | 6 | 4 | .277 |
| Jordan, Edward, SLC | 55 | 145 | 24 | 35 | 57 | 7 | 0 | 5 | 21 | 3 | 3 | 14 | 3 | 20 | 2 | 1 | .241 |
| Kaaihue, Kala, Hawaii | 5 | 11 | 0 | 2 | 3 | 1 | 0 | 0 | 1 | 0 | 0 | 3 | 0 | 2 | 0 | 0 | .182 |
| Kelly, J. Thomas, Tacoma* | 62 | 202 | 38 | 51 | 83 | 5 | 0 | 9 | 29 | 0 | 2 | 47 | 1 | 36 | 6 | 1 | .252 |
| Kemp, Richard, Spokane* | 25 | 1 | 0 | 0 | 0 | 0 | 0 | 0 | 0 | 0 | 0 | 0 | 0 | 0 | 0 | 0 | .000 |
| Kimm, Bruce, Tucson | 5 | 15 | 3 | 2 | 2 | 0 | 0 | 0 | 1 | 0 | 0 | 2 | 0 | 0 | 0 | 0 | .133 |
| Kinard, Rudolph, Spokane | 45 | 137 | 14 | 22 | 26 | 2 | 1 | 0 | 9 | 2 | 1 | 9 | 0 | 24 | 1 | 4 | .161 |
| Krausse, Lewis, Tucson | 45 | 6 | 0 | 2 | 2 | 0 | 0 | 0 | 1 | 0 | 0 | 1 | 0 | 1 | 0 | 0 | .333 |
| Kusick, Craig, Tacoma | 56 | 177 | 20 | 46 | 56 | 4 | 0 | 2 | 16 | 1 | 1 | 40 | 1 | 41 | 1 | 1 | .260 |

| Player and Club | G | AB | R | H | TB | 2B | 3B | HR | RBI | SH | SF | BB | HP | SO | SB | CS | Pct. |
|---|---|---|---|---|---|---|---|---|---|---|---|---|---|---|---|---|---|
| Kusnyer, Arthur, Sac | 128 | 448 | 62 | 118 | 207 | 10 | 2 | 25 | 76 | 2 | 2 | 28 | 2 | 79 | 1 | 0 | .263 |
| LeMaster, Johnnie, Phoenix | 143 | 520 | 75 | 152 | 206 | 26 | 8 | 4 | 58 | 4 | 3 | 34 | 2 | 98 | 17 | 7 | .292 |
| Lemon, Chester, Tucson | 65 | 243 | 43 | 68 | 94 | 7 | 2 | 5 | 33 | 0 | 2 | 37 | 3 | 37 | 17 | 4 | .280 |
| Lieppman, Keith, Tucson | 110 | 336 | 43 | 86 | 141 | 18 | 8 | 7 | 44 | 1 | 3 | 41 | 0 | 51 | 3 | 3 | .256 |
| Lind, Jackson, Sacramento† | 62 | 220 | 41 | 57 | 85 | 19 | 0 | 3 | 16 | 0 | 1 | 38 | 0 | 38 | 0 | 0 | .259 |
| Lindsey, David, Sacramento* | 98 | 315 | 51 | 88 | 165 | 12 | 1 | 21 | 58 | 2 | 0 | 35 | 1 | 48 | 1 | 0 | .279 |
| Llenas, Winston, Salt Lake C | 16 | 63 | 8 | 16 | 23 | 5 | 1 | 0 | 9 | 0 | 1 | 9 | 0 | 8 | 0 | 0 | .254 |
| Locklear, Gene, Hawaii* | 18 | 64 | 17 | 24 | 38 | 0 | 1 | 4 | 11 | 0 | 2 | 12 | 0 | 12 | 1 | 1 | .375 |
| Lollis, Ronald, Spokane | 8 | 11 | 1 | 1 | 1 | 0 | 0 | 0 | 1 | 0 | 0 | 3 | 0 | 4 | 0 | 0 | .091 |
| Lopez, Carlos A., SLC | 15 | 48 | 3 | 12 | 17 | 2 | 0 | 1 | 5 | 0 | 0 | 1 | 1 | 1 | 2 | 1 | .250 |
| Lopez, Juan, Sacramento | 131 | 542 | 73 | 154 | 204 | 19 | 2 | 9 | 59 | 6 | 3 | 29 | 4 | 65 | 4 | 4 | .284 |
| Lundstedt, Thomas, Tacoma† | 42 | 148 | 12 | 39 | 59 | 5 | 0 | 5 | 22 | 0 | 1 | 10 | 0 | 26 | 0 | 0 | .264 |
| Manuel, Charles, Alb* | 81 | 243 | 40 | 79 | 146 | 17 | 1 | 16 | 64 | 0 | 6 | 39 | 2 | 32 | 3 | 1 | .325 |
| Martin, Joseph M., Phoenix* | 9 | 28 | 1 | 6 | 8 | 2 | 0 | 0 | 1 | 0 | 0 | 3 | 0 | 2 | 0 | 0 | .214 |
| McCartney, Stephen, Sac | 47 | 169 | 31 | 49 | 83 | 5 | 1 | 9 | 28 | 0 | 1 | 13 | 3 | 59 | 5 | 3 | .290 |
| McDermott, Terrence, Alb | 69 | 223 | 32 | 49 | 81 | 7 | 2 | 7 | 27 | 3 | 1 | 22 | 6 | 63 | 10 | 2 | .220 |
| McKay, David L., Tacoma | 109 | 370 | 56 | 95 | 132 | 12 | 2 | 7 | 39 | 0 | 2 | 6 | 54 | 0 | 48 | 0 | 2 | .257 |
| McKinney, C. Richard, Tuc. | 110 | 394 | 57 | 117 | 188 | 26 | 3 | 13 | 74 | 0 | 0 | 21 | 0 | 21 | 0 | 0 | .297 |
| McNulty, William, Sac | 40 | 154 | 30 | 47 | 88 | 8 | 0 | 11 | 36 | 0 | 0 | 21 | 2 | 50 | 7 | 7 | .305 |
| Miley, Michael, SLC† | 81 | 263 | 31 | 55 | 82 | 8 | 5 | 3 | 34 | 3 | 2 | 41 | 2 | 50 | 7 | 7 | .209 |
| Miller, Roger, Sacramento | 24 | 1 | 0 | 0 | 0 | 0 | 0 | 0 | 0 | 0 | 0 | 0 | 0 | 0 | 0 | 0 | .000 |
| Moates, David, Spokane* | 90 | 363 | 58 | 100 | 126 | 13 | 2 | 3 | 32 | 7 | 2 | 35 | 4 | 38 | 27 | 7 | .275 |
| Moharter, David, Spokane*· | 49 | 6 | 0 | 2 | 2 | 0 | 0 | 0 | 0 | 0 | 0 | 0 | 0 | 0 | 0 | 0 | .333 |
| Mull, Jack, Phoenix | 27 | 60 | 5 | 11 | 14 | 0 | 0 | 1 | 7 | 1 | 0 | 7 | 1 | 10 | 1 | 0 | .183 |
| Nettles, Morris, Salt Lake C* | 13 | 47 | 9 | 9 | 11 | 0 | 1 | 0 | 1 | 3 | 0 | 5 | 2 | 12 | 4 | 1 | .191 |
| Newman, Jeffrey, Salt Lake C | 58 | 176 | 24 | 40 | 65 | 10 | 0 | 5 | 25 | 5 | 2 | 19 | 0 | 30 | 4 | 0 | .227 |
| Nitschke, David, Tucson | 133 | 389 | 37 | 95 | 110 | 12 | 0 | 1 | 35 | 5 | 2 | 43 | 0 | 42 | 11 | 4 | .244 |
| Norman, Donald, Spokane· | 26 | 2 | 0 | 0 | 0 | 0 | 0 | 0 | 0 | 0 | 0 | 1 | 0 | 1 | 0 | 0 | .000 |
| Osburn, L. Patrick, Sac* | 29 | 1 | 0 | 0 | 0 | 0 | 0 | 0 | 0 | 0 | 0 | 0 | 0 | 0 | 0 | 0 | .000 |
| Palat, Edward, Tacoma | 120 | 423 | 49 | 106 | 162 | 18 | 4 | 10 | 61 | 4 | 3 | 38 | 2 | 76 | 4 | 2 | .251 |
| Palmer, Lowell, Sacramento· | 39 | 19 | 1 | 2 | 2 | 0 | 0 | 0 | 2 | 1 | 1 | 0 | 0 | 10 | 0 | 0 | .105 |
| Pape, Kenneth, Spokane | 46 | 162 | 27 | 47 | 58 | 4 | 2 | 1 | 16 | 1 | 2 | 19 | 0 | 17 | 6 | 1 | .290 |
| Pasley, Kevin, Albuquerque· | 98 | 337 | 37 | 84 | 97 | 7 | 0 | 2 | 34 | 3 | 6 | 8 | 2 | 15 | 3 | 3 | .249 |
| Peguero, Pablo, Alb | 21 | 58 | 6 | 10 | 11 | 0 | 0 | 0 | 3 | 4 | 0 | 3 | 1 | 4 | 0 | 0 | .172 |
| Pena, George, Tacoma· | 2 | 7 | 0 | 0 | 0 | 0 | 0 | 0 | 1 | 0 | 0 | 1 | 0 | 4 | 0 | 0 | .000 |
| Pepper, C. Anthony, Phoe· | 134 | 478 | 60 | 121 | 169 | 14 | 5 | 8 | 65 | 1 | 1 | 6 | 57 | 1 | 74 | 6 | 4 | .253 |
| Pinkerton, C. Wayne, Spot· | 17 | 30 | 0 | 3 | 3 | 0 | 0 | 0 | 1 | 1 | 0 | 9 | 0 | 9 | 1 | 0 | .100 |
| Pitts, Gaylen, Tucson | 135 | 482 | 74 | 129 | 189 | 23 | 2 | 11 | 58 | 2 | 2 | 6 | 74 | 1 | 76 | 11 | 5 | .268 |
| Poepping, Michael, Tacoma | 129 | 441 | 55 | 109 | 189 | 17 | 3 | 19 | 75 | 8 | 5 | 47 | 6 | 132 | 2 | 0 | .247 |
| Powell, Paul, Albuquerque· | 21 | 70 | 10 | 18 | 29 | 9 | 1 | 0 | 9 | 1 | 1 | 13 | 1 | 10 | 1 | 0 | .257 |
| Pruitt, Ronald, Spokane | 77 | 271 | 51 | 75 | 118 | 10 | 3 | 9 | 42 | 1 | 3 | 50 | 2 | 29 | 0 | 1 | .277 |
| Pryor, Gregory, Spokane | 135 | 481 | 59 | 117 | 167 | 21 | 2 | 5 | 53 | 6 | 6 | 41 | 7 | 49 | 7 | 4 | .243 |
| Ralston, William, Tacoma | 119 | 445 | 52 | 105 | 134 | 15 | 5 | 1 | 4 | 43 | 4 | 3 | 46 | 1 | 46 | 3 | 3 | .236 |
| Ramirez, Orlando, SLC | 28 | 76 | 9 | 15 | 19 | 0 | 1 | 1 | 8 | 0 | 1 | 8 | 0 | 11 | 5 | 1 | .197 |
| Randall, Robert, Alb | 107 | 391 | 62 | 114 | 149 | 23 | 3 | 2 | 43 | 7 | 3 | 37 | 5 | 36 | 2 | 4 | .292 |
| Redmon, Glenn, Phoenix | 106 | 393 | 39 | 103 | 136 | 16 | 4 | 3 | 54 | 4 | 7 | 24 | 2 | 32 | 6 | 4 | .262 |
| Renick, W. Richard, Tacoma | 76 | 259 | 42 | 70 | 119 | 9 | 2 | 12 | 38 | 2 | 0 | 48 | 2 | 57 | 2 | 1 | .270 |
| Reynolds, Tommie, Sac | 131 | 477 | 82 | 125 | 241 | 13 | 4 | 25 | 89 | 0 | 5 | 52 | 5 | 55 | 3 | 1 | .304 |
| Roberts, David W., Hawaii· | 121 | 442 | 60 | 116 | 189 | 31 | 3 | 12 | 71 | 3 | 5 | 48 | 5 | 101 | 11 | 4 | .262 |
| Robinson, Lee, Albuquerque· | 90 | 277 | 42 | 76 | 106 | 16 | 1 | 4 | 38 | 3 | 5 | 24 | 3 | 54 | 6 | 2 | .274 |
| Robson, Thomas, Spokane | 87 | 322 | 58 | 103 | 160 | 12 | 3 | 13 | 57 | 0 | 3 | 48 | 1 | 44 | 1 | 0 | .320 |
| Rosario, Angel, Sacramento† | 88 | 328 | 70 | 106 | 171 | 17 | 3 | 14 | 55 | 3 | 4 | 46 | 3 | 33 | 8 | 3 | .323 |
| Royster, Jeron, Alb | 133 | 487 | 91 | 162 | 237 | 31 | 7 | 10 | 65 | 5 | 5 | 53 | 2 | 46 | 33 | 11 | .333 |
| Sadek, Michael, Phoenix | 50 | 160 | 29 | 43 | 69 | 8 | 6 | 2 | 28 | 4 | 0 | 11 | 3 | 19 | 1 | 2 | .269 |
| Sands, Charles, Tucson*· | 105 | 287 | 56 | 81 | 150 | 10 | 1 | 19 | 66 | 0 | 5 | 91 | 4 | 70 | 3 | 1 | .282 |
| Sandt, Thomas, Tucson | 116 | 391 | 62 | 121 | 147 | 20 | 0 | 2 | 49 | 1 | 5 | 34 | 2 | 39 | 16 | 6 | .309 |
| Sanner, Dale, Tucson* | 129 | 359 | 53 | 102 | 141 | 26 | 2 | 3 | 41 | 5 | 4 | 30 | 1 | 65 | 10 | 6 | .284 |
| Selma, Richard, Albuquerque | 31 | 0 | 0 | 0 | 0 | 0 | 0 | 0 | 0 | 0 | 0 | 0 | 0 | 0 | 0 | 0 | .000 |
| Sheldon, Bob, Sacramento*· | 82 | 327 | 44 | 102 | 127 | 10 | 0 | 5 | 23 | 1 | 1 | 49 | 0 | 28 | 6 | 5 | .312 |
| Simpson, Joe, Alb* | 133 | 514 | 84 | 142 | 184 | 24 | 6 | 2 | 49 | 4 | 2 | 70 | 0 | 69 | 30 | 20 | .276 |
| Smalley, Roy, Spokane†· | 43 | 162 | 26 | 55 | 71 | 8 | 1 | 2 | 19 | 2 | 0 | 23 | 1 | 24 | 0 | 0 | .340 |
| Smith, Billy E., Salt Lake C† | 64 | 226 | 37 | 67 | 89 | 11 | 1 | 3 | 34 | 1 | 2 | 22 | 3 | 28 | 9 | 7 | .296 |
| Smith, Cleophclus, Alb | 138 | 472 | 73 | 122 | 201 | 23 | 4 | 16 | 70 | 3 | 3 | 59 | 3 | 98 | 6 | 5 | .258 |
| Speed, Horace, Phoenix | 92 | 305 | 54 | 83 | 145 | 16 | 5 | 12 | 38 | 1 | 1 | 43 | 7 | 85 | 17 | 5 | .272 |
| Summers, John, Tucson* | 17 | 54 | 5 | 17 | 21 | 0 | 2 | 0 | 7 | 0 | 0 | 7 | 0 | 9 | 1 | 2 | .315 |
| Terpko, Jeffrey, Spokane | 43 | 2 | 0 | 0 | 0 | 0 | 0 | 0 | 0 | 0 | 0 | 0 | 0 | 0 | 0 | 0 | .000 |
| Terrell, Jerry, Tacoma | 45 | 178 | 35 | 57 | 78 | 13 | 1 | 2 | 14 | 6 | 2 | 14 | 1 | 7 | 19 | 4 | .320 |
| Timberlake, Gary, Tucson | 10 | 1 | 0 | 0 | 0 | 0 | 0 | 0 | 0 | 0 | 0 | 0 | 0 | 0 | 0 | 0 | .000 |
| Torres, Rosendo, SLC† | 107 | 369 | 59 | 113 | 173 | 18 | 9 | 8 | 64 | 5 | 6 | 60 | 1 | 66 | 6 | 11 | .306 |
| Turner, John, Hawaii· | 142 | 535 | 88 | 176 | 242 | 27 | 3 | 11 | 91 | 5 | 5 | 56 | 4 | 36 | 15 | 7 | .329 |
| Valentine, Robert, SLC | 46 | 147 | 29 | 45 | 53 | 6 | 1 | 0 | 17 | 2 | 0 | 15 | 1 | 13 | 4 | 2 | .306 |
| Van Wyck, James, Tacoma·· | 89 | 312 | 44 | 86 | 94 | 8 | 0 | 0 | 14 | 8 | 1 | 36 | 1 | 32 | 4 | 2 | .276 |
| Vasquez, George, Sac† | 22 | 64 | 11 | 16 | 27 | 2 | 0 | 3 | 8 | 0 | 0 | 11 | 1 | 16 | 0 | 0 | .250 |
| Velazquez, Carlos, Sac | 51 | 1 | 0 | 0 | 0 | 0 | 0 | 0 | 0 | 0 | 0 | 0 | 0 | 0 | 0 | 0 | .000 |
| Walton, Daniel, Tacoma† | 49 | 157 | 27 | 48 | 93 | 6 | 0 | 13 | 38 | 0 | 1 | 32 | 0 | 30 | 0 | 0 | .306 |
| Weathers, S. Michael, Tuc. | 106 | 297 | 36 | 75 | 97 | 17 | 1 | 1 | 35 | 1 | 5 | 23 | 2 | 55 | 3 | 6 | .253 |
| Webster, Ramon, Tucson*· | 76 | 219 | 31 | 67 | 100 | 10 | 4 | 5 | 39 | 1 | 3 | 23 | 0 | 16 | 4 | 2 | .306 |
| Wheelock, Gary, Salt Lake C | 32 | 3 | 0 | 0 | 0 | 0 | 0 | 0 | 0 | 0 | 0 | 0 | 0 | 5 | 0 | 0 | .000 |
| Widmar, A. Thomas, Sac | 9 | 11 | 1 | 2 | 2 | 0 | 0 | 0 | 0 | 0 | 0 | 0 | 0 | 0 | 0 | 0 | .182 |
| Wilkins, Vernon, Spokane·· | 78 | 263 | 38 | 68 | 97 | 15 | 4 | 2 | 34 | 0 | 2 | 39 | 2 | 37 | 9 | 5 | .259 |

| Player and Club | G. | AB. | R. | H. | TB. | 2B. | 3B. | HR. | RBI. | SH. | SF. | BB. | HP. | SO. | SB. | CS. | Pct. |
|---|---|---|---|---|---|---|---|---|---|---|---|---|---|---|---|---|---|
| Williams, James O., Phoe† | 98 | 341 | 38 | 87 | 119 | 15 | 4 | 3 | 29 | 2 | 2 | 35 | 5 | 50 | 5 | 0 | .255 |
| Wilson, Randolph, SLC* | 12 | 29 | 4 | 7 | 8 | 1 | 0 | 0 | 2 | 0 | 0 | 5 | 0 | 12 | 0 | 1 | .241 |
| Woodson, Richard, Spokane | 5 | 1 | 0 | 0 | 0 | 0 | 0 | 0 | 0 | 0 | 0 | 0 | 0 | 1 | 0 | 0 | .000 |

The following pitchers had no plate appearances primarily through use of designated-hitters, listed alphabetically by club, games in parentheses:

ALBUQUERQUE—Allen, James (40); Donovan, John (2); Haller, James (40); Hudson, Rex (30); Lewallyn, Dennis (29); Miller, Wayne (26); Nitz, Rick (28); Shanahan, P. Gregory (30); Solomon, Eddie (4); Wall, Stanley (23).

HAWAII—Gerhardt, A. Russell (6); Hardy, H. Lawrence (37); Hartenstein, Charles (27); Johnson, Jerry M. (16); Linzy, Frank (37); Metzger, Clarence (36); Miller, Robert (15); Ross, Gary (27); Shellenback, James (32); Strampe, Robert (30); Strom, Brent (12); Wehrmeister, David (10).

PHOENIX—Bradley, Thomas (9); Gonzalez, L. Antonio (23); Halicki, Edward (8); Hypes, Kyle (17); Knepper, Robert (26); Minton, Gregory (44); Nolan, Robert (13); Rose, Donald (34); Sielicki, John (7); Sukla, Edward (36); Toms, Thomas (40).

SACRAMENTO—Austerman, Carl (29); Austin, Rick (29); Barker, Jeffrey (8); Crane, Gordon (5); Farmer, Edward (14); Kobel, Kevin (7); O'Toole, Dennis (3); Robson, Gary (14); Travers, William (12).

SALT LAKE CITY—Blateric, Stephen (29); Dobson, Charles (19); Figueroa, Eduardo (2); Hockenbery, Charles (15); Hudson, Charles (21); Kenyon, Frank (4); Lange, Richard (3); Monge, Isidro (27); Quintana, Luis (37); Raziano, Barry (39); Ryerson, Gary (27); Verhoeven, John (18).

SPOKANE—Bacsik, Michael (19); Bostic, Jerry (27); Gideon, James (11); Harper, David (20); Kekich, Michael (14); Moore, Tommy (6); Perzanowski, Stanley (20); Waits, M. Richard (11).

TACOMA—Bane, Edward (33); Bemis, Gregg (11); Cutler, Bradley (38); Johnson, Thomas (33); Lerner, Lewis (22); Luebber, Stephen (24); Myers, Dennis (2); Norton, Thomas (20); Pazik, Michael (20); Smith, W. Coleman (15); Stone, Gail (30); Thayer, Gregory (14); Veintidos, Juan (28); Wiley, Mark (17).

TUCSON—Abbott, W. Glenn (4); Barlow, Michael (16); Copeland, Howell (5); Griffin, Alan (21); Lacey, Robert (10); Lockwood, Claude (30); Mazzone, Leo (39); Mitchell, Craig (18); Nelson, Roger E. (20); Pena, Orlando (21); Pitlock, Lee (17); Rauch, Robert (7); Scarbery, Randy (12); Strahler, Michael (5); Taylor, Randall (2); Todd, James (2); Van Bommel, William (13).

TWO CLUBS—Sells, David (13 Salt Lake City—9 Albuquerque).

GRAND-SLAM HOME RUNS—C. Cruz, 3; Hampton, McNulty, 2 each; Bowling, Epperly, Flores, Grabarkewitz, Hale, Heintzelman, Huntz, Kelly, Kusnyer, Lemon, Lindsey, Palat, Roberts, Robson, Smalley, Walton, 1 each.

AWARDED FIRST BASE ON INTERFERENCE—Pryor (Kusnyer).

## CLUB FIELDING

| Club | G. | PO. | A. | E. | DP. | PB. | Pct. |
|---|---|---|---|---|---|---|---|
| Phoenix | 143 | 3651 | 1721 | 164 | 165 | 16 | .9703 |
| Sacramento | 144 | 3648 | 1489 | 160 | 173 | 24 | .9697 |
| Hawaii | 144 | 3657 | 1571 | 175 | 153 | 17 | .968 |
| Spokane | 142 | 3607 | 1655 | 177 | 148 | 22 | .967 |

| Club | G. | PO. | A. | E. | DP. | PB. | Pct. |
|---|---|---|---|---|---|---|---|
| Tucson | 143 | 3630 | 1420 | 174 | 125 | 28 | .967 |
| Tacoma | 144 | 3611 | 1496 | 177 | 129 | 23 | .967 |
| Salt Lake City | 144 | 3536 | 1553 | 193 | 150 | 24 | .963 |
| Albuquerque | 144 | 3678 | 1693 | 215 | 153 | 14 | .962 |

Triple Plays—Tacoma, Albuquerque, 1 each.

## INDIVIDUAL FIELDING

*Throws lefthanded.

### FIRST BASEMEN

| Player and Club | G. | PO. | A. | E. | DP. | Pct. |
|---|---|---|---|---|---|---|
| Kusick, Tacoma | 29 | 212 | 21 | 0 | 29 | 1.000 |
| Fairey, Hawaii* | 14 | 98 | 9 | 0 | 5 | 1.000 |
| James, Phoenix* | 13 | 91 | 14 | 0 | 9 | 1.000 |
| Burney, Alb* | 60 | 408 | 41 | 2 | 39 | .996 |
| LIEPPMAN, Tucson | 100 | 754 | 52 | 4 | 67 | .995 |
| Robson, Spokane | 86 | 823 | 55 | 5 | 77 | .994 |
| Bass, Tacoma | 100 | 795 | 74 | 6 | 74 | .993 |
| McDermott, Alb | 13 | 120 | 7 | 1 | 9 | .992 |
| Newman, SLC | 11 | 105 | 5 | 1 | 11 | .991 |
| Doherty, SLC* | 67 | 564 | 40 | 6 | 58 | .990 |
| Gil, Hawaii | 53 | 469 | 36 | 5 | 68 | .990 |
| Hansen, Sacramento* | 86 | 653 | 46 | 8 | 91 | .989 |
| Pitts, Tucson | 12 | 89 | 5 | 1 | 5 | .989 |

Triple Plays—Bass, Smith.

| Player and Club | G. | PO. | A. | E. | DP. | Pct. |
|---|---|---|---|---|---|---|
| Jackson, Salt Lake C | 13 | 79 | 7 | 1 | 15 | .989 |
| Webster, Tucson* | 49 | 300 | 23 | 4 | 39 | .988 |
| Wilson, Salt Lake C* | 10 | 77 | 4 | 1 | 4 | .988 |
| Galliher, Hawaii | 37 | 327 | 22 | 5 | 34 | .986 |
| Briggs, Salt Lake C* | 34 | 301 | 33 | 5 | 35 | .985 |
| Fanzone, Hawaii | 42 | 370 | 30 | 6 | 29 | .985 |
| Smith, Albuquerque | 86 | 743 | 44 | 16 | 85 | .980 |
| Lindsey, Sacramento* | 28 | 221 | 11 | 5 | 34 | .979 |
| Pepper, Phoenix* | 132 | 1286 | 83 | 33 | 140 | .976 |
| McNulty, Sacramento | 27 | 228 | 16 | 6 | 29 | .976 |
| Valentine, SLC | 10 | 71 | 3 | 2 | 4 | .974 |
| Ault, Spokane* | 48 | 403 | 41 | 13 | 45 | .972 |
| Kelly, Tacoma* | 17 | 91 | 11 | 3 | 12 | .971 |

#### (Fewer Than Ten Games)

| Player and Club | G. | PO. | A. | E. | DP. | Pct. |
|---|---|---|---|---|---|---|
| Johnson, Phoe-Hawaii | 7 | 50 | 2 | 0 | 1 | 1.000 |
| Poepping, Tacoma | 7 | 31 | 4 | 0 | 3 | 1.000 |
| Holt, Tucson | 3 | 18 | 4 | 0 | 3 | 1.000 |
| Cubbage, Spokane | 2 | 16 | 4 | 0 | 1 | 1.000 |
| Llenas, Salt Lake C. | 2 | 17 | 1 | 0 | 0 | 1.000 |
| Reynolds, Sacramento | 2 | 10 | 0 | 0 | 1 | 1.000 |
| Guarnera, Spokane | 2 | 8 | 1 | 0 | 1 | 1.000 |

| Player and Club | G. | PO. | A. | E. | DP. | Pct. |
|---|---|---|---|---|---|---|
| Jones, Spokane* | 1 | 3 | 0 | 0 | 1 | 1.000 |
| George, Salt Lake City | 1 | 2 | 0 | 0 | 0 | 1.000 |
| Renick, Tacoma | 1 | 1 | 0 | 0 | 0 | 1.000 |
| Wilkins, Spokane* | 6 | 57 | 1 | 1 | 11 | .983 |
| Bianco, Sacramento | 8 | 66 | 5 | 2 | 2 | .973 |
| Smith, Salt Lake City | 4 | 31 | 0 | 1 | 4 | .969 |
| Sands, Tucson | 1 | 11 | 1 | 1 | 0 | .923 |

## SECOND BASEMEN

| Player and Club | G. | PO. | A. | E. | DP. | Pct. |
|---|---|---|---|---|---|---|
| Lind, Sacramento ... | 22 | 46 | 47 | 0 | 15 | 1.000 |
| McKinney, Tucson .. | 10 | 17 | 16 | 0 | 4 | 1.000 |
| REDMON, Phoenix . | 96 | 234 | 282 | 6 | 73 | .989 |
| Bordes, Spokane .... | 12 | 28 | 34 | 1 | 10 | .984 |
| Van Wyck, Tacoma.. | 12 | 27 | 30 | 1 | 7 | .983 |
| Christensen, Pho-Sac | 58 | 120 | 118 | 5 | 38 | .979 |
| Cubbage, Spokane ... | 45 | 96 | 115 | 5 | 29 | .977 |
| Kinard, Spokane .... | 37 | 85 | 83 | 4 | 24 | .977 |
| Sheldon, Sacramento | 82 | 193 | 245 | 12 | 68 | .973 |
| Roberts, Hawaii .... | 81 | 176 | 235 | 12 | 59 | .972 |
| Randall, Albuquerque | 107 | 273 | 323 | 19 | 85 | .968 |
| Ralston, Tacoma .... | 73 | 196 | 203 | 13 | 44 | .968 |
| Collins, Albuquerque | 32 | 60 | 82 | 5 | 16 | .966 |
| Guarnera, Spokane .. | 44 | 105 | 129 | 9 | 29 | .963 |
| Heintzelman, Phoenix | 42 | 92 | 111 | 8 | 34 | .962 |
| Weathers, Tucson .. | 84 | 154 | 186 | 14 | 41 | .960 |
| Terrell, Tacoma .... | 43 | 86 | 107 | 8 | 23 | .960 |
| Grabarkewitz, Tucson | 48 | 101 | 110 | 9 | 23 | .959 |
| Darrow, Salt Lake C | 141 | 303 | 389 | 30 | 104 | .958 |
| Jackson, Hawaii .... | 47 | 115 | 130 | 13 | 25 | .950 |
| Gil, Alb-Hawaii .... | 20 | 32 | 12 | 5 | 8 | .944 |
| Ferrer, Tacoma .... | 21 | 41 | 59 | 6 | 12 | .943 |
| Pitts, Tucson ...... | 20 | 51 | 38 | 6 | 13 | .937 |

(Fewer Than Ten Games)

| Player and Club | G. | PO. | A. | E. | DP. | Pct. |
|---|---|---|---|---|---|---|
| Hilton, Hawaii ...... | 9 | 22 | 31 | 0 | 14 | 1.000 |
| Pryor, Spokane ..... | 4 | 14 | 10 | 0 | 1 | 1.000 |
| Sandt, Tucson ...... | 4 | 9 | 4 | 0 | 2 | 1.000 |
| Powell, Albuquerque | 2 | 4 | 6 | 0 | 2 | 1.000 |
| Smith, Salt Lake City | 3 | 3 | 7 | 0 | 1 | 1.000 |
| Espy, Sacramento ... | 7 | 2 | 8 | 0 | 2 | 1.000 |
| Hampton, Salt Lake C | 5 | 13 | 11 | 1 | 1 | .960 |
| Smalley, Spokane .... | 6 | 20 | 17 | 2 | 8 | .919 |
| Reynolds, Sacramento | 9 | 20 | 23 | 3 | 5 | .935 |
| Pape, Spokane ...... | 3 | 7 | 10 | 2 | 3 | .895 |
| Rosario, Sacramento. | 1 | 4 | 1 | 1 | 0 | .833 |

## THIRD BASEMEN

| Player and Club | G. | PO. | A. | E. | DP. | Pct. |
|---|---|---|---|---|---|---|
| Collins, Albuquerque | 10 | 5 | 10 | 0 | 1 | 1.000 |
| Bordes, Spokane ..... | 34 | 18 | 91 | 3 | 11 | .973 |
| Galliher, Hawaii ... | 12 | 4 | 28 | 1 | 1 | .970 |
| Lind, Sacramento.... | 20 | 26 | 35 | 2 | 6 | .968 |
| Pitts, Tucson ...... | 56 | 45 | 118 | 6 | 10 | .964 |
| McCartney, Sac .... | 16 | 20 | 31 | 2 | 2 | .962 |
| Pryor, Spokane .... | 44 | 34 | 76 | 5 | 9 | .957 |
| Hunt, Hawaii ...... | 88 | 68 | 175 | 12 | 18 | .953 |
| Heintzelman, Phoenix | 79 | 63 | 176 | 12 | 19 | .952 |
| Renick, Tacoma .... | 46 | 36 | 89 | 8 | 10 | .940 |
| Eden, Phoenix ...... | 64 | 40 | 138 | 12 | 10 | .937 |
| JACKSON, SLC .... | 117 | 89 | 260 | 25 | 31 | .933 |
| Ralston, Tacoma .... | 40 | 33 | 79 | 8 | 11 | .933 |
| Cubbage, Tacoma... | 12 | 8 | 33 | 3 | 8 | .932 |
| Roberts, Hawaii ..... | 36 | 28 | 79 | 8 | 8 | .930 |
| Gil, Albuquerque ... | 12 | 7 | 17 | 2 | 0 | .923 |
| Smith, Salt Lake C.. | 18 | 5 | 41 | 4 | 3 | .920 |
| Bianco, Sacramento.. | 84 | 71 | 178 | 22 | 17 | .919 |
| Smith, Albuquerque.. | 14 | 9 | 25 | 3 | 1 | .919 |
| Royster, Albuquerque | 67 | 55 | 121 | 17 | 13 | .912 |
| Pape, Spokane ...... | 38 | 22 | 91 | 11 | 10 | .911 |
| McKay, Tacoma .... | 39 | 35 | 67 | 12 | 5 | .895 |
| Van Wyck, Tacoma.. | 19 | 11 | 39 | 6 | 5 | .893 |
| McDermott, Alb .... | 42 | 29 | 62 | 12 | 8 | .883 |
| Reynolds, Sacramento | 15 | 9 | 26 | 5 | 3 | .875 |
| Grabarkewitz, Tucson | 24 | 23 | 32 | 8 | 3 | .873 |
| Lemon, Tucson ..... | 57 | 45 | 70 | 19 | 6 | .858 |
| Powell, Albuquerque | 15 | 7 | 20 | 5 | 1 | .844 |
| Pruitt, Spokane .... | 25 | 14 | 45 | 13 | 6 | .819 |
| Fanzone, Hawaii .... | 12 | 8 | 19 | 8 | 3 | .771 |

(Fewer Than Ten Games)

| Player and Club | G. | PO. | A. | E. | DP. | Pct. |
|---|---|---|---|---|---|---|
| McNulty, Sacramento. | 9 | 4 | 21 | 0 | 1 | 1.000 |
| Valentine, SLC ..... | 7 | 6 | 10 | 0 | 1 | 1.000 |
| Llenas, Salt Lake City | 4 | 3 | 6 | 0 | 1 | 1.000 |
| Redmon, Phoenix ... | 3 | 3 | 4 | 0 | 2 | 1.000 |
| Epperly, Tacoma ..... | 1 | 2 | 3 | 0 | 1 | 1.000 |
| Weathers, Tucson ... | 2 | 0 | 2 | 0 | 1 | 1.000 |
| Robinson, Albuquerque | 1 | 1 | 0 | 0 | 0 | 1.000 |
| Christensen, Sac ..... | 1 | 0 | 1 | 0 | 0 | 1.000 |
| Breitzman, Tucson .. | 6 | 2 | 13 | 1 | 0 | .938 |
| Ellis, Sacramento .... | 5 | 5 | 8 | 1 | 0 | .929 |
| Terrell, Tacoma ..... | 2 | 2 | 5 | 1 | 1 | .875 |
| Dade, Salt Lake City. | 3 | 3 | 5 | 2 | 1 | .800 |
| Jackson, Hawaii ..... | 1 | 1 | 3 | 1 | 0 | .800 |
| Lieppman, Tucson ... | 3 | 1 | 2 | 4 | 0 | .429 |

## SHORTSTOPS

| Player and Club | G. | PO. | A. | E. | DP. | Pct. |
|---|---|---|---|---|---|---|
| Smalley, Spokane... | 38 | 68 | 134 | 8 | 20 | .962 |
| Ramirez, SLC ...... | 27 | 32 | 63 | 4 | 19 | .960 |
| Van Wyck, Tacoma | 58 | 91 | 143 | 10 | 24 | .959 |
| SANDT, Tucson.... | 102 | 183 | 283 | 22 | 58 | .9549 |
| LeMaster, Phoenix .. | 143 | 207 | 489 | 33 | 107 | .9547 |
| Weathers, Tucson .. | 18 | 18 | 45 | 3 | 5 | .9545 |
| Pitts, Tucson ....... | 31 | 55 | 76 | 7 | 23 | .949 |
| McKay, Tacoma... | 69 | 139 | 197 | 19 | 40 | .946 |
| Lopez, Sacramento | 129 | 209 | 392 | 35 | 98 | .945 |
| Royster, Alb ........ | 67 | 128 | 228 | 21 | 56 | .944 |
| Pryor, Spokane ..... | 88 | 136 | 325 | 28 | 58 | .943 |
| Smith, Salt Lake City | 39 | 64 | 108 | 11 | 26 | .940 |
| Almon, Hawaii .... | 114 | 288 | 456 | 48 | 102 | .939 |
| de Jesus, Alb........ | 62 | 97 | 265 | 24 | 44 | .938 |
| Ferrer, Tacoma .... | 24 | 46 | 72 | 8 | 16 | .937 |
| Miley, Salt Lake City | 81 | 154 | 232 | 29 | 61 | .930 |
| Collins, Albuquerque | 18 | 22 | 43 | 6 | 8 | .915 |
| Lind, Sacramento.... | 10 | 13 | 21 | 4 | 9 | .895 |
| Pinkerton, Spokane . | 13 | 17 | 30 | 6 | 9 | .887 |

Triple Play—McKay.

(Fewer Than Ten Games)

| Player and Club | G. | PO. | A. | E. | DP. | Pct. |
|---|---|---|---|---|---|---|
| Christensen, Pho-Sac. | 6 | 8 | 23 | 0 | 0 | 1.000 |
| Gil, Albuquerque .... | 2 | 1 | 12 | 0 | 0 | 1.000 |
| Eden, Phoenix ....... | 1 | 3 | 2 | 0 | 2 | 1.000 |
| Grabarkewitz, Tucson | 1 | 3 | 0 | 0 | 1 | 1.000 |
| Dade, Salt Lake City | 1 | 0 | 3 | 0 | 0 | 1.000 |
| Huntz, Hawaii ...... | 1 | 1 | 1 | 0 | 0 | 1.000 |
| Bianco, Sacramento.. | 1 | 1 | 0 | 0 | 0 | 1.000 |
| Bordes, Spokane .... | 1 | 1 | 0 | 0 | 0 | 1.000 |
| Roberts, Hawaii ..... | 1 | 1 | 0 | 0 | 0 | 1.000 |
| Darrow, Salt Lake C | 1 | 0 | 1 | 0 | 0 | 1.000 |
| Redmon, Phoenix .. | 1 | 0 | 1 | 0 | 0 | 1.000 |
| Kinard, Spokane .... | 7 | 13 | 24 | 2 | 6 | .949 |
| Pape, Spokane ...... | 3 | 3 | 6 | 2 | 1 | .818 |
| McCartney, Sac ..... | 3 | 4 | 4 | 3 | 1 | .727 |
| Jackson, Hawaii ..... | 1 | 1 | 1 | 1 | 0 | .667 |

## OUTFIELDERS

| Player and Club | G | PO | A | E | DP | Pct. |
|---|---|---|---|---|---|---|
| Balaz, Salt Lake City | 54 | 85 | 4 | 0 | 0 | 1.000 |
| McCartney, Sac | 28 | 59 | 2 | 0 | 1 | 1.000 |
| Jackson, Hawaii | 37 | 45 | 4 | 0 | 1 | 1.000 |
| Wilkins, Spokane* | 11 | 27 | 0 | 0 | 0 | 1.000 |
| Hampton, SLC | 15 | 23 | 3 | 0 | 0 | 1.000 |
| Jackson, SLC | 16 | 21 | 2 | 0 | 0 | 1.000 |
| Summers, Tucson | 15 | 21 | 0 | 0 | 0 | 1.000 |
| Pruitt, Spokane | 11 | 14 | 0 | 0 | 0 | 1.000 |
| Ellis, Sacramento | 13 | 12 | 0 | 0 | 0 | 1.000 |
| Grabarkewitz, Tucson | 15 | 5 | 3 | 0 | 0 | 1.000 |
| GASPAR, Hawaii* | 144 | 340 | 14 | 4 | 5 | .989 |
| Jones, Spokane* | 108 | 207 | 4 | 3 | 1 | .986 |
| Bowling, Sacramento | 139 | 298 | 13 | 5 | 2 | .984 |
| Torres, Salt Lake C. | 107 | 290 | 10 | 5 | 4 | .984 |
| Friedman SLC* | 28 | 54 | 7 | 1 | 0 | .984 |
| Collins, Salt Lake C* | 36 | 58 | 2 | 1 | 0 | .984 |
| Simpson, Alb* | 130 | 289 | 8 | 5 | 1 | .983 |
| Robinson, Alb | 25 | 50 | 1 | 1 | 0 | .981 |
| Palat, Tacoma | 107 | 225 | 15 | 5 | 3 | .980 |
| James, Phoenix | 85 | 135 | 10 | 3 | 0 | .980 |
| Bordes, Spokane | 34 | 48 | 2 | 1 | 0 | .980 |
| Moates, Spokane* | 90 | 227 | 4 | 5 | 2 | .979 |
| Sanner, Tucson | 120 | 243 | 10 | 6 | 2 | .977 |
| Espy, Sacramento | 41 | 75 | 8 | 2 | 2 | .976 |
| Beasley, Spokane | 28 | 76 | 3 | 2 | 1 | .975 |
| Criscione, Spokane | 16 | 32 | 5 | 1 | 0 | .974 |
| Brown, Phoenix | 84 | 130 | 11 | 4 | 3 | .972 |
| Chant, Tucson | 134 | 279 | 18 | 9 | 3 | .971 |
| Cruz, Spokane* | 138 | 250 | 14 | 8 | 3 | .971 |
| Kelly, Tacoma* | 47 | 94 | 1 | 3 | 0 | .969 |
| Speed, Phoenix | 91 | 143 | 10 | 5 | 2 | .968 |
| Herndon, Phoenix | 115 | 287 | 10 | 10 | 1 | .967 |
| Bostock, Tacoma | 22 | 55 | 0 | 2 | 0 | .965 |
| Briggs, Salt Lake C* | 34 | 51 | 3 | 2 | 0 | .964 |
| Nettles, Salt Lake C* | 13 | 25 | 1 | 1 | 0 | .963 |
| Englert, Phoenix* | 21 | 48 | 2 | 2 | 1 | .962 |
| McKinney, Tucson | 95 | 137 | 9 | 6 | 0 | .961 |
| Williams, Phoenix | 67 | 92 | 3 | 4 | 0 | .960 |
| Goddard, Hawaii | 17 | 21 | 3 | 1 | 0 | .960 |
| Rosario, Sacramento | 86 | 169 | 9 | 8 | 1 | .957 |
| Hale, Albuquerque | 67 | 130 | 4 | 6 | 2 | .957 |
| Beach, Tacoma | 44 | 108 | 4 | 5 | 1 | .957 |
| Reynolds, Sacramento | 86 | 147 | 6 | 7 | 2 | .956 |
| Elliott, Hawaii | 94 | 140 | 9 | 7 | 1 | .955 |
| Alvarez, Albuquerque | 138 | 246 | 2 | 12 | 0 | .954 |
| Cruz, Albuquerque* | 71 | 160 | 3 | 8 | 1 | .953 |
| Blessitt, Tucson | 64 | 138 | 4 | 7 | 0 | .953 |
| Gorinski, Tacoma | 72 | 131 | 7 | 7 | 0 | .952 |
| Flores, Salt Lake C. | 42 | 79 | 0 | 4 | 0 | .952 |
| Hopkins, Tucson | 22 | 37 | 3 | 2 | 0 | .952 |
| Poepping, Tacoma | 116 | 238 | 10 | 15 | 2 | .943 |
| Valentine, SLC. | 10 | 15 | 1 | 1 | 0 | .941 |
| Lindsey, Sacramento* | 49 | 68 | 7 | 5 | 1 | .938 |
| Epperly, Tacoma | 19 | 27 | 3 | 2 | 0 | .938 |
| George, Salt Lake C | 76 | 138 | 7 | 10 | 1 | .935 |
| Gatlin, Tacoma | 12 | 14 | 0 | 1 | 0 | .933 |
| Turner, Hawaii* | 142 | 195 | 8 | 16 | 1 | .927 |
| Lopez, Salt Lake City | 14 | 27 | 3 | 4 | 1 | .882 |

### (Fewer Than Ten Games)

| Player and Club | G | PO | A | E | DP | Pct. |
|---|---|---|---|---|---|---|
| Lemon, Tucson | 5 | 15 | 0 | 0 | 0 | 1.000 |
| Holt, Tucson | 5 | 9 | 1 | 0 | 0 | 1.000 |
| Fairey, Hawaii* | 9 | 8 | 0 | 0 | 0 | 1.000 |
| Webster, Tucson* | 4 | 7 | 1 | 0 | 0 | 1.000 |
| Ashford, Salt Lake C | 2 | 5 | 0 | 0 | 0 | 1.000 |
| Guarnaccia, Sac* | 5 | 4 | 0 | 0 | 0 | 1.000 |
| Astroth, Spokane | 2 | 2 | 1 | 0 | 1 | 1.000 |
| Smith, Albuquerque | 3 | 2 | 0 | 0 | 0 | 1.000 |
| Galliher, Hawaii | 2 | 2 | 0 | 0 | 0 | 1.000 |
| Krausse, Tucson | 1 | 2 | 0 | 0 | 0 | 1.000 |
| Sandt, Tucson | 2 | 1 | 0 | 0 | 0 | 1.000 |
| DeFilippis, Spokane* | 1 | 1 | 0 | 0 | 0 | 1.000 |
| Lind, Sacramento | 1 | 1 | 0 | 0 | 0 | 1.000 |
| Manuel, Albuquerque | 1 | 1 | 0 | 0 | 0 | 1.000 |
| Palmer, Sacramento | 5 | 13 | 0 | 2 | 0 | .867 |
| Kusick, Tacoma | 9 | 11 | 1 | 2 | 0 | .857 |
| Locklear, Hawaii | 3 | 3 | 0 | 1 | 0 | .750 |
| Johnson, Hawaii | 1 | 0 | 0 | 1 | 0 | .000 |
| Kinard, Spokane | 1 | 0 | 0 | 1 | 0 | .000 |

## CATCHERS

| Player and Club | G | PO | A | E | DP | PB | Pct. |
|---|---|---|---|---|---|---|---|
| Jordan, SLC | 37 | 148 | 13 | 0 | 2 | 7 | 1.000 |
| Pruitt, Spokane | 15 | 155 | 17 | 1 | 3 | 2 | .994 |
| KUSNYER, Sac | 128 | 720 | 55 | 6 | 11 | 19 | .992 |
| Essian, Hawaii | 40 | 228 | 22 | 2 | 4 | 5 | .992 |
| Sadek, Phoenix | 50 | 293 | 48 | 3 | 3 | 5 | .991 |
| Lundstedt, Tacoma | 42 | 212 | 20 | 2 | 3 | 4 | .991 |
| Robinson, Alb | 33 | 190 | 18 | 2 | 3 | 7 | .990 |
| Butera, Tacoma | 73 | 376 | 36 | 6 | 6 | 7 | .986 |
| Davis, Hawaii | 92 | 499 | 54 | 9 | 9 | 6 | .984 |
| Sands, Tucson | 13 | 54 | 0 | 1 | 1 | 6 | .982 |
| Nitschke, Tucson | 132 | 675 | 109 | 15 | 7 | 21 | .981 |
| Gomez, Tucson | 13 | 39 | 5 | 1 | 0 | 1 | .978 |
| Criscione, Spokane | 83 | 348 | 40 | 9 | 4 | 14 | .977 |
| Hampton, SLC | 50 | 204 | 26 | 6 | 4 | 5 | .975 |
| Mull, Phoenix | 27 | 104 | 12 | 3 | 0 | 3 | .975 |
| Epperly, Tacoma | 44 | 155 | 29 | 5 | 2 | 12 | .974 |
| Goddard, Hawaii | 11 | 34 | 3 | 1 | 0 | 3 | .974 |
| Alietta, SLC | 33 | 159 | 18 | 5 | 3 | 7 | .973 |
| Pasley, Alb | 96 | 492 | 66 | 16 | 8 | 5 | .972 |
| J. Bradley, Phoenix | 65 | 272 | 45 | 9 | 5 | 8 | .972 |
| Peguero, Alb | 16 | 55 | 17 | 3 | 1 | 2 | .960 |
| Vasquez, Sac | 19 | 97 | 12 | 5 | 1 | 5 | .956 |
| Astroth, Spokane | 32 | 142 | 18 | 8 | 2 | 5 | .952 |
| Newman, SLC | 35 | 162 | 17 | 11 | 4 | 5 | .942 |

Triple Play—Robinson.

### (Fewer Than Ten Games)

| Player and Club | G | PO | A | E | DP | PB | Pct. |
|---|---|---|---|---|---|---|---|
| Ellis, Sacramento | 6 | 21 | 2 | 0 | 0 | 2 | 2.000 |
| Cannizzaro, Hawaii | 3 | 10 | 0 | 0 | 0 | 2 | 1.000 |
| Walton, Tacoma | 2 | 8 | 2 | 0 | 0 | | 1.000 |
| Lollis, Spokane | 1 | 2 | 0 | 0 | 0 | | 1.000 |
| Huntz, Hawaii | 1 | 1 | 0 | 0 | 0 | | 1.000 |
| McDermott, Alb | 1 | 1 | 0 | 0 | 0 | | 1.000 |
| Martin, Phoenix | 9 | 41 | 3 | 1 | 0 | 0 | .978 |
| Kimm, Tucson | 5 | 25 | 1 | 1 | 0 | 0 | .963 |
| Powell, Alb | 7 | 23 | 1 | 1 | 0 | 0 | .960 |
| Pena, Tacoma | 2 | 14 | 1 | 1 | 0 | 0 | .938 |
| Kaaihue, Hawaii | 4 | 16 | 0 | 2 | 0 | 0 | .889 |

## PITCHERS

| Player and Club | G | PO | A | E | DP | Pct. |
|---|---|---|---|---|---|---|
| MINTON, Phoenix | 42 | 14 | 38 | 0 | 2 | 1.000 |
| Miller, Sacramento | 23 | 11 | 33 | 0 | 6 | 1.000 |
| Hudson, Salt Lake C* | 24 | 10 | 22 | 0 | 2 | 1.000 |
| Sukla, Phoenix | 36 | 6 | 22 | 0 | 1 | 1.000 |
| Strampe, Hawaii | 30 | 10 | 17 | 0 | 0 | 1.000 |
| Wiley, Tacoma | 17 | 14 | 12 | 0 | 1 | 1.000 |
| Pitlock, Tucson* | 17 | 5 | 19 | 0 | 1 | 1.000 |
| Johnson, Tacoma | 33 | 4 | 19 | 0 | 0 | 1.000 |
| Hartenstein, Hawaii | 27 | 3 | 19 | 0 | 3 | 1.000 |
| Veintidos, Tacoma | 28 | 8 | 13 | 0 | 2 | 1.000 |
| Pazik, Tacoma* | 20 | 2 | 19 | 0 | 1 | 1.000 |
| Blateric, SLC | 29 | 6 | 13 | 0 | 0 | 1.000 |

PITCHERS—Continued

| Player and Club | G. | PO. | A. | E. | DP. | Pct. |
|---|---|---|---|---|---|---|
| Gonzalez, Phoenix* .. | 23 | 3 | 16 | 0 | 0 | 1.000 |
| Travers, Sacramento* | 12 | 4 | 14 | 0 | 1 | 1.000 |
| Haller, Albuquerque | 40 | 0 | 17 | 0 | 0 | 1.000 |
| Verhoeven, SLC .... | 18 | 4 | 11 | 0 | 1 | 1.000 |
| Palmer, Sacramento.. | 34 | 5 | 9 | 0 | 2 | 1.000 |
| Griffin, Tucson ..... | 21 | 3 | 11 | 0 | 1 | 1.000 |
| Augustine, Sac* ..... | 15 | 1 | 13 | 0 | 0 | 1.000 |
| Robson, Sacramento | 14 | 7 | 6 | 0 | 1 | 1.000 |
| Norton, Tacoma .... | 20 | 6 | 7 | 0 | 0 | 1.000 |
| Velazquez, Sac ..... | 51 | 3 | 10 | 0 | 0 | 1.000 |
| Lacey, Tucson* ..... | 10 | 3 | 8 | 0 | 0 | 1.000 |
| Austin, Sacramento*.. | 29 | 3 | 7 | 0 | 0 | 1.000 |
| Barlow, Tucson .... | 16 | 2 | 5 | 0 | 1 | 1.000 |
| Wehrmeister, Hawaii | 10 | 2 | 5 | 0 | 0 | 1.000 |
| Pena, Tucson....... | 21 | 2 | 4 | 0 | 0 | 1.000 |
| Scarbery, Tucson .... | 12 | 2 | 4 | 0 | 0 | 1.000 |
| Terpko, Spokane .... | 43 | 1 | 5 | 0 | 0 | 1.000 |
| Baldwin, Sacramento | 10 | 1 | 5 | 0 | 1 | 1.000 |
| Mazzone, Tucson* .... | 39 | 0 | 6 | 0 | 0 | 1.000 |
| Lerner, Tacoma .... | 22 | 1 | 4 | 0 | 0 | 1.000 |
| Bemis, Tacoma* .... | 11 | 1 | 2 | 0 | 0 | 1.000 |
| Timberlake, Tucson* | 10 | 0 | 2 | 0 | 0 | 1.000 |
| Ross, Hawaii ...... | 27 | 19 | 33 | 1 | 3 | .981 |
| Rose, Phoenix ..... | 34 | 12 | 37 | 1 | 2 | .980 |
| Hudson, Albuquerque | 30 | 14 | 33 | 1 | 3 | .979 |
| Shanahan, Alb ..... | 29 | 13 | 27 | 1 | 3 | .976 |
| Metzger, Hawaii .... | 36 | 9 | 20 | 1 | 1 | .967 |
| Hypes, Phoenix* .... | 17 | 5 | 24 | 1 | 3 | .967 |
| DeFilippis, Spokane* | 31 | 12 | 16 | 1 | 0 | .966 |
| Waits, Spokane* .... | 11 | 9 | 19 | 1 | 0 | .966 |
| Wheelock, SLC ..... | 31 | 6 | 22 | 1 | 1 | .966 |
| Ryerson, SLC* ..... | 27 | 10 | 40 | 2 | 2 | .962 |
| Stone, Tacoma ..... | 30 | 10 | 15 | 1 | 4 | .962 |
| Austerman, Sac .... | 29 | 7 | 16 | 1 | 1 | .958 |
| Nitz, Albuquerque .. | 28 | 9 | 34 | 2 | 3 | .956 |
| Shellenback, Hawaii* | 32 | 5 | 16 | 1 | 0 | .955 |
| Perzanowski, Spokane | 20 | 1 | 20 | 1 | 0 | .955 |
| Lewallyn, Alb ..... | 29 | 17 | 50 | 4 | 2 | .944 |
| Dressler, Phoenix .. | 25 | 13 | 38 | 3 | 2 | .944 |
| Moharter, Spokane*.. | 48 | 6 | 28 | 2 | 2 | .944 |

| Player and Club | G. | PO. | A. | E. | DP. | Pct. |
|---|---|---|---|---|---|---|
| Harper, Spokane ... | 20 | 9 | 8 | 1 | 0 | .944 |
| Gideon, Spokane ... | 11 | 1 | 16 | 1 | 1 | .944 |
| J. Johnson, Hawaii .. | 16 | 5 | 11 | 1 | 0 | .941 |
| Dobson, Salt Lake C | 18 | 10 | 20 | 2 | 2 | .938 |
| Bostic, Spokane* ... | 27 | 3 | 11 | 1 | 0 | .933 |
| Hooten, Tucson .... | 34 | 14 | 40 | 4 | 2 | .931 |
| Kemp, Spokane* ... | 25 | 6 | 20 | 2 | 1 | .929 |
| Mitchell, Tucson ... | 18 | 4 | 9 | 1 | 0 | .929 |
| Norman, Spokane* .. | 26 | 9 | 16 | 2 | 0 | .926 |
| Osburn, Sacramento* | 28 | 8 | 17 | 2 | 1 | .926 |
| Monge, Salt Lake C* | 27 | 4 | 21 | 2 | 2 | .926 |
| Knepper, Phoenix*.. | 26 | 9 | 25 | 3 | 2 | .919 |
| Bacsik, Spokane .... | 19 | 12 | 10 | 2 | 0 | .917 |
| Anderson, Sacramento | 19 | 6 | 5 | 1 | 0 | .917 |
| Linzy, Hawaii ..... | 37 | 3 | 8 | 1 | 1 | .917 |
| Kekich, Spokane* ... | 14 | 3 | 8 | 1 | 3 | .917 |
| Toms, Phoenix ..... | 40 | 6 | 15 | 2 | 1 | .913 |
| Strom, Hawaii* .... | 12 | 5 | 16 | 2 | 1 | .913 |
| Miller, Alb* ....... | 26 | 4 | 17 | 2 | 2 | .913 |
| Wall, Albuquerque* | 23 | 2 | 19 | 2 | 0 | .913 |
| Raziano, Salt Lake C | 39 | 5 | 5 | 1 | 0 | .909 |
| Van Bommel, Tucson | 13 | 4 | 6 | 1 | 1 | .909 |
| Thayer, Tacoma ... | 14 | 3 | 6 | 1 | 0 | .900 |
| Bane, Tacoma* ..... | 32 | 6 | 28 | 4 | 2 | .895 |
| Krausse, Tucson ... | 44 | 4 | 12 | 2 | 3 | .889 |
| Selma, Albuquerque | 31 | 3 | 20 | 3 | 1 | .885 |
| Sells, SLC-Alb .... | 22 | 13 | 31 | 6 | 2 | .880 |
| Luebber, Tacoma... | 24 | 9 | 20 | 4 | 5 | .879 |
| Nelson, Tucson .... | 20 | 7 | 19 | 4 | 1 | .867 |
| Hardy, Hawaii ..... | 37 | 6 | 7 | 2 | 0 | .867 |
| Lockwood, Tucson .. | 30 | 4 | 9 | 2 | 0 | .867 |
| Cutler, Tacoma* ... | 38 | 2 | 9 | 2 | 0 | .846 |
| Quintana, SLC* .... | 37 | 1 | 9 | 2 | 2 | .833 |
| Smith, Tacoma* .... | 15 | 0 | 10 | 2 | 0 | .833 |
| Miller, Hawaii .... | 15 | 2 | 3 | 1 | 0 | .833 |
| Allen, Albuquerque* | 40 | 6 | 22 | 6 | 3 | .824 |
| Farmer, Sacramento | 14 | 6 | 3 | 2 | 1 | .818 |
| Hockenbery, SLC ... | 15 | 2 | 18 | 5 | 1 | .800 |
| Nolan, Phoenix* .... | 13 | 0 | 4 | 1 | 1 | .800 |

(Fewer Than Ten Games)

| Player and Club | G. | PO. | A. | E. | DP. | Pct. |
|---|---|---|---|---|---|---|
| Moore, Spokane .... | 6 | 5 | 4 | 0 | 1 | 1.000 |
| Barker, Sacramento .. | 8 | 5 | 2 | 0 | 0 | 1.000 |
| Copeland, Tucson ... | 5 | 4 | 3 | 0 | 0 | 1.000 |
| Solomon, Albuquerque | 3 | 3 | 4 | 0 | 0 | 1.000 |
| Sielicki, Phoenix* .... | 7 | 0 | 7 | 0 | 1 | 1.000 |
| Lange, Salt Lake C.. | 3 | 3 | 3 | 0 | 0 | 1.000 |
| Abbott, Tucson ..... | 4 | 2 | 4 | 0 | 2 | 1.000 |
| Widmar, Sacramento. | 6 | 1 | 4 | 0 | 1 | 1.000 |
| Rauch, Tucson ..... | 7 | 0 | 5 | 0 | 1 | 1.000 |
| Gerhardt, Hawaii* .. | 6 | 0 | 5 | 0 | 0 | 1.000 |

| Player and Club | G. | PO. | A. | E. | DP. | Pct. |
|---|---|---|---|---|---|---|
| Kenyon, Salt Lake C* | 4 | 4 | 4 | 0 | 0 | 1.000 |
| Woodson, Spokane .. | 5 | 1 | 2 | 0 | 0 | 1.000 |
| Kobel, Sacramento* .. | 7 | 3 | 0 | 0 | 0 | 1.000 |
| O'Toole, Sacramento.. | 3 | 0 | 1 | 0 | 1 | 1.000 |
| Myers, Tacoma ..... | 2 | 1 | 0 | 0 | 0 | 1.000 |
| T. Bradley, Phoenix.. | 9 | 9 | 6 | 1 | 2 | .938 |
| Halicki, Phoenix .... | 8 | 7 | 4 | 2 | 0 | .846 |
| Figueroa, Salt Lake C | 2 | 3 | 2 | 1 | 0 | .833 |
| Strahler, Tucson .... | 5 | 3 | 1 | 1 | 1 | .800 |
| Todd, Tucson ....... | 2 | 2 | 1 | 1 | 0 | .750 |

The following players do not have any recorded accepted chances at the positions indicated; therefore, are not listed in the fielding averages for those particular positions: Alexander, of; Ault*, of; Breitzman, 2b; Burney*, of; Crane, p; Donovan, p; Hansen*, of; Lindsey*, p; Llenas, 2b-of; Lollis, of; Powell, of; Renick, p; Robinson, 1b; C. Smith, ss; Taylor, p; Valentine, 2b; Van Wyck, of.

The following appeared as designated-hitters/pinch-hitters only: Adams, Arnold, Haines.

## CLUB PITCHING

| Club | G. | CG. | ShO. | Sv. | IP. | H. | R. | ER. | HR. | BB. | Int. BB. | HB. | SO. | WP. | Bk. | ERA. |
|---|---|---|---|---|---|---|---|---|---|---|---|---|---|---|---|---|
| Hawaii ............... | 144 | 52 | 13 | 29 | 1219 | 1190 | 579 | 496 | 107 | 435 | 18 | 29 | 763 | 53 | 2 | 3.66 |
| Phoenix ............. | 143 | 45 | 11 | 22 | 1217 | 1264 | 641 | 522 | 76 | 534 | 56 | 29 | 648 | 50 | 14 | 3.86 |
| Tacoma ............. | 142 | 51 | 16 | 20 | 1204 | 1192 | 658 | 531 | 89 | 574 | 26 | 31 | 727 | 70 | 10 | 3.97 |
| Salt Lake City ........ | 144 | 49 | 10 | 21 | 1179 | 1238 | 670 | 547 | 77 | 502 | 22 | 18 | 625 | 53 | 4 | 4.18 |
| Albuquerque ......... | 144 | 63 | 7 | 11 | 1226 | 1341 | 720 | 585 | 85 | 509 | 36 | 25 | 688 | 53 | 13 | 4.29 |
| Tucson ............. | 143 | 45 | 6 | 27 | 1210 | 1318 | 728 | 626 | 66 | 557 | 63 | 29 | 745 | 81 | 7 | 4.66 |
| Spokane ............. | 142 | 42 | 2 | 19 | 1202 | 1321 | 758 | 655 | 97 | 603 | 31 | 32 | 583 | 57 | 3 | 4.90 |
| Sacramento ........... | 144 | 36 | 9 | 12 | 1216 | 1385 | 880 | 772 | 196 | 722 | 10 | 44 | 788 | 99 | 11 | 5.71 |

## PITCHERS' RECORDS

### (Leading Qualifiers for Earned-Run Average Leadership—115 or More Innings)

| Pitcher—Club | G. | GS. | CG. | ShO. | W. | L. | Sv. | Pct. | IP. | H. | R. | ER. | HR. | BB. | Int. BB. | HB. | SO. | WP. | ERA. |
|---|---|---|---|---|---|---|---|---|---|---|---|---|---|---|---|---|---|---|---|
| Luebber, Tacoma ..24 | 23 | 15 | 3 | 14 | 7 | 6 | 0 | .667 | 177 | 145 | 62 | 47 | 6 | 79 | 4 | 3 | 123 | 12 | 2.39 |
| Ross, Hawaii ... 27 | 27 | 11 | 3 | 16 | 8 | 0 | .667 | 188 | 170 | 70 | 52 | 12 | 44 | 3 | 8 | 123 | 12 | 2.49 | |
| Minton, Phoenix ..42 | 12 | 7 | 2 | 10 | 6 | 4 | .625 | 177 | 178 | 73 | 51 | 6 | 76 | 11 | 4 | 76 | 7 | 2.59 | |
| Wheelock, SLC ...31 | 12 | 5 | 1 | 7 | 6 | 0 | .538 | 120 | 113 | 56 | 41 | 9 | 47 | 2 | 0 | 68 | 10 | 3.08 | |
| Pazik, Tacoma* .. 20 | 19 | 11 | 3 | 9 | 9 | 1 | .500 | 140 | 117 | 61 | 49 | 11 | 46 | 0 | 5 | 99 | 4 | 3.15 | |
| Sells, 13 SLC- | | | | | | | | | | | | | | | | | | | |
| 9 Albuquerque ..22 | 19 | 10 | 1 | 11 | 8 | 0 | .579 | 146 | 134 | 69 | 56 | 10 | 51 | 2 | 3 | 68 | 8 | 3.45 |
| Dressler, Phoenix .25 | 23 | 9 | 3 | 8 | 14 | 0 | .364 | 169 | 174 | 81 | 65 | 10 | 58 | 7 | 5 | 91 | 8 | 3.46 |
| Moharter, Spo* ..48 | 1 | 0 | 0 | 4 | 4 | 4 | .500 | 130 | 142 | 63 | 52 | 8 | 48 | 10 | 5 | 57 | 6 | 3.60 |
| Metzger, Hawaii ..36 | 20 | 9 | 2 | 15 | 7 | 5 | .682 | 169 | 163 | 86 | 68 | 16 | 78 | 3 | 5 | 114 | 3 | 3.62 |
| DeFilippis, Spo* ..31 | 10 | 5 | 0 | 6 | 7 | 0 | .462 | 135 | 112 | 62 | 55 | 10 | 84 | 6 | 2 | 88 | 5 | 3.67 |

Departmental Leaders: G—Velazquez, 51; GS—Bane, 31; CG—Luebber, 15; ShO—Dressler, C. Hudson, Lewallyn, Luebber, Pazik, Ross, Travers, 3; W—Ross, 16; L—Austerman, R. Hudson, Rose, 16; Sv—T. Johnson, Terpko, 13; Pct.—Metzger, .682; IP—Hooten, 207; H—Austerman, 226; R—Austerman, 157; ER—Austerman, 131; HR—Austerman, 38; BB—Palmer, 109; IBB—Hooten, Krausse, 13; HB—Anderson, 9; SO—Shanahan, 147; WP—Anderson, 27.

### (All Pitchers—Listed Alphabetically)

| Pitcher—Club | G. | GS. | CG. | ShO. | W. | L. | Sv. | Pct. | IP. | H. | R. | ER. | HR. | BB. | Int. BB. | HB. | SO. | WP. | ERA. |
|---|---|---|---|---|---|---|---|---|---|---|---|---|---|---|---|---|---|---|---|
| Abbott, Tucson .... 4 | 4 | 3 | 0 | 2 | 2 | 0 | .500 | 30 | 30 | 14 | 12 | 3 | 11 | 1 | 2 | 18 | 4 | 3.60 |
| Allen, Alb* ....40 | 0 | 0 | 0 | 2 | 3 | 0 | .400 | 84 | 85 | 50 | 43 | 9 | 45 | 1 | 0 | 35 | 3 | 4.61 |
| Anderson, Sac ... 19 | 19 | 7 | 1 | 7 | 9 | 0 | .438 | 110 | 107 | 70 | 67 | 9 | 95 | 0 | 9 | 87 | 27 | 5.48 |
| Augustine, Sac* ..15 | 11 | 3 | 0 | 4 | 3 | 0 | .571 | 79 | 90 | 49 | 42 | 6 | 40 | 0 | 3 | 27 | 2 | 4.78 |
| Austerman, Sac .. 29 | 25 | 6 | 0 | 3 | 16 | 0 | .158 | 155 | 226 | 157 | 131 | 38 | 72 | 0 | 6 | 90 | 10 | 7.61 |
| Austin, Sac* .... 29 | 1 | 0 | 0 | 3 | 2 | 5 | .600 | 61 | 54 | 51 | 25 | 7 | 40 | 0 | 1 | 53 | 5 | 3.69 |
| Bacsik, Spokane .. 19 | 19 | 5 | 0 | 6 | 10 | 0 | .375 | 110 | 135 | 82 | 67 | 12 | 38 | 1 | 4 | 48 | 3 | 5.48 |
| Baldwin, Sac.* ..10 | 2 | 0 | 0 | 0 | 2 | 0 | .500 | 26 | 36 | 21 | 20 | 4 | 17 | 1 | 0 | 10 | 2 | 6.92 |
| Bane, Tacoma* ..32 | 31 | 12 | 1 | 15 | 11 | 0 | .577 | 199 | 200 | 118 | 89 | 21 | 83 | 2 | 4 | 106 | 6 | 4.03 |
| Barker, Sac ... 8 | 7 | 0 | 0 | 2 | 2 | 0 | .500 | 35 | 43 | 35 | 30 | 12 | 13 | 0 | 0 | 21 | 1 | 7.71 |
| Barlow, Tucson ..16 | 2 | 2 | 1 | 4 | 1 | 2 | .800 | 45 | 20 | 16 | 13 | 3 | 26 | 2 | 1 | 43 | 5 | 2.60 |
| Bemis, Tacoma* ..11 | 2 | 1 | 0 | 1 | 1 | 0 | .750 | 29 | 34 | 16 | 12 | 2 | 16 | 3 | 0 | 21 | 2 | 3.72 |
| Blateric, SLC .. 29 | 5 | 2 | 0 | 5 | 5 | 5 | .375 | 70 | 79 | 46 | 41 | 6 | 26 | 3 | 1 | 41 | 5 | 5.27 |
| Bostic, Spokane* ..27 | 17 | 4 | 0 | 5 | 8 | 0 | .385 | 119 | 145 | 81 | 67 | 7 | 56 | 0 | 1 | 57 | 1 | 5.07 |
| T. Bradley, Phoe . 9 | 8 | 7 | 0 | 5 | 3 | 0 | .625 | 66 | 68 | 32 | 31 | 6 | 18 | 5 | 2 | 36 | 1 | 4.23 |
| Copeland, Tucson . 5 | 4 | 0 | 0 | 0 | 4 | 0 | .000 | 19 | 25 | 19 | 18 | 1 | 12 | 1 | 3 | 6 | 0 | 8.53 |
| Crane, Sacramento. 5 | 0 | 0 | 0 | 0 | 6 | 0 | .000 | 6 | 20 | 17 | 17 | 4 | 11 | 0 | 0 | 3 | 0 | 25.50 |
| Cutler, Tacoma* ..38 | 2 | 0 | 0 | 4 | 4 | 1 | .500 | 74 | 85 | 42 | 32 | 3 | 22 | 1 | 1 | 23 | 0 | 3.89 |
| DeFilippis, Spo* ..31 | 10 | 5 | 0 | 6 | 7 | 0 | .462 | 135 | 112 | 62 | 55 | 10 | 84 | 6 | 2 | 88 | 5 | 3.67 |
| Dobson, SLC ....18 | 18 | 10 | 1 | 9 | 7 | 0 | .462 | 133 | 132 | 62 | 55 | 10 | 84 | 6 | 2 | 88 | 5 | 3.67 |
| Donovan, Alb ... 2 | 0 | 0 | 0 | 0 | 0 | 0 | .000 | 2 | 7 | 7 | 7 | 4 | 2 | 0 | 0 | 0 | 0 | 31.50 |
| Dressler, Phoenix . 25 | 23 | 9 | 3 | 8 | 14 | 0 | .364 | 169 | 174 | 81 | 65 | 10 | 58 | 7 | 5 | 91 | 2 | 3.46 |
| Farmer, Sac ....14 | 13 | 1 | 0 | 2 | 8 | 0 | .200 | 61 | 69 | 59 | 53 | 9 | 67 | 0 | 3 | 53 | 7 | 7.82 |
| Figueroa, SLC ... 2 | 2 | 1 | 0 | 2 | 0 | 1 | 1.000 | 15 | 15 | 5 | 3 | 0 | 3 | 0 | 0 | 6 | 1 | 1.80 |
| Gerhardt, Hawaii* . 6 | 6 | 0 | 0 | 1 | 3 | 0 | .250 | 27 | 26 | 25 | 22 | 4 | 20 | 0 | 1 | 13 | 1 | 7.33 |
| Gideon, Spokane ..11 | 3 | 0 | 0 | 4 | 5 | 0 | .444 | 58 | 58 | 47 | 43 | 6 | 42 | 0 | 2 | 28 | 7 | 6.67 |
| Gonzalez, Phoe* ..23 | 22 | 3 | 0 | 5 | 9 | 0 | .357 | 122 | 107 | 64 | 55 | 8 | 74 | 1 | 1 | 49 | 4 | 4.06 |
| Griffin, Tucson ..21 | 19 | 6 | 0 | 6 | 6 | 0 | .500 | 119 | 129 | 67 | 54 | 11 | 48 | 1 | 0 | 59 | 8 | 4.08 |
| Halkl, Phoenix ... 8 | 7 | 5 | 1 | 5 | 3 | 0 | .675 | 56 | 46 | 26 | 24 | 1 | 21 | 4 | 1 | 55 | 3 | 3.86 |
| Haller, Alb .....40 | 0 | 0 | 0 | 2 | 4 | 2 | .500 | 63 | 64 | 36 | 24 | 1 | 40 | 5 | 5 | 35 | 5 | 3.43 |
| Hardy, Hawaii ..37 | 1 | 0 | 0 | 6 | 4 | 5 | .600 | 87 | 84 | 39 | 35 | 8 | 30 | 2 | 3 | 66 | 4 | 3.62 |
| Harper, Spokane . 20 | 14 | 1 | 1 | 2 | 5 | 0 | .286 | 93 | 114 | 71 | 59 | 11 | 38 | 1 | 3 | 35 | 5 | 5.71 |
| Hartenstein, Haw .27 | 1 | 0 | 0 | 6 | 2 | 5 | .750 | 76 | 76 | 26 | 25 | 5 | 12 | 0 | 2 | 32 | 1 | 2.96 |
| Hockenbery, SLC . 15 | 13 | 4 | 1 | 4 | 5 | 0 | .444 | 92 | 112 | 63 | 48 | 5 | 44 | 3 | 2 | 31 | 4 | 4.70 |
| Hooten, Tucson ..34 | 30 | 12 | 1 | 15 | 11 | 0 | .577 | 207 | 216 | 110 | 101 | 11 | 97 | 13 | 5 | 122 | 12 | 4.39 |
| C. Hudson, SLC* .24 | 24 | 8 | 3 | 13 | 7 | 0 | .650 | 160 | 152 | 89 | 76 | 10 | 92 | 2 | 3 | 60 | 2 | 4.28 |
| R. Hudson, Alb ..30 | 30 | 11 | 1 | 10 | 16 | 0 | .385 | 191 | 208 | 129 | 115 | 15 | 77 | 2 | 5 | 122 | 5 | 5.42 |
| Hypes, Phoenix* ..17 | 17 | 2 | 1 | 1 | 8 | 4 | .667 | 105 | 106 | 51 | 42 | 4 | 53 | 3 | 5 | 34 | 3 | 3.60 |
| J. Johnson, Haw .16 | 15 | 2 | 0 | 10 | 3 | 0 | .761 | 104 | 83 | 41 | 34 | 6 | 50 | 0 | 0 | 61 | 8 | 2.94 |
| T. Johnson, Tac . 33 | 0 | 0 | 0 | 4 | 4 | 13 | .667 | 68 | 66 | 23 | 22 | 3 | 20 | 0 | 3 | 53 | 4 | 2.91 |
| Kekich, Spokane* ..14 | 4 | 1 | 0 | 7 | 4 | 1 | .636 | 45 | 40 | 20 | 17 | 4 | 25 | 0 | 1 | 30 | 4 | 3.40 |
| Kemp, Spokane* .25 | 12 | 3 | 0 | 3 | 9 | 0 | .250 | 95 | 127 | 73 | 66 | 10 | 48 | 1 | 0 | 37 | 5 | 6.25 |
| Kenyon, SLC* .... 3 | 3 | 0 | 0 | 1 | 2 | 0 | .333 | 11 | 15 | 17 | 16 | 2 | 19 | 0 | 1 | 6 | 2 | 13.09 |
| Knepper, Phoenix*.26 | 26 | 8 | 1 | 11 | 11 | 0 | .500 | 155 | 169 | 101 | 79 | 14 | 78 | 4 | 3 | 94 | 16 | 4.59 |
| Kobel, Sac* .... 7 | 5 | 0 | 0 | 3 | 2 | 0 | .600 | 30 | 29 | 11 | 8 | 0 | 7 | 0 | 1 | 9 | 0 | 2.40 |
| Krausse, Tucson ..44 | 4 | 0 | 0 | 3 | 4 | 6 | .667 | 105 | 123 | 68 | 63 | 4 | 60 | 13 | 2 | 59 | 6 | 5.40 |
| Lacey, Tucson* ..10 | 4 | 2 | 1 | 3 | 1 | 0 | .750 | 35 | 35 | 14 | 12 | 1 | 19 | 1 | 1 | 17 | 1 | 3.09 |
| Lange, SLC ..... 3 | 3 | 1 | 0 | 0 | 1 | 0 | .000 | 18 | 18 | 14 | 14 | 1 | 9 | 1 | 0 | 11 | 1 | 4.50 |
| Lerner, Tacoma ..29 | 3 | 0 | 0 | 2 | 2 | 2 | .500 | 46 | 41 | 20 | 15 | 6 | 29 | 0 | 0 | 38 | 2 | 2.93 |
| Lewallyn, Alb ..29 | 28 | 12 | 3 | 13 | 10 | 0 | .565 | 180 | 207 | 102 | 78 | 9 | 49 | 5 | 0 | 81 | 3 | 3.90 |
| Lindsey, Sac* .... 1 | 0 | 0 | 0 | 0 | 0 | 0 | .000 | 3 | 2 | 4 | 4 | 0 | 1 | 1 | 9 | 1.00 | | |
| Linzy, Hawaii ..37 | 0 | 0 | 0 | 1 | 4 | 8 | .200 | 56 | 59 | 24 | 19 | 4 | 15 | 5 | 2 | 18 | 2 | 3.05 |
| Lockwood, Tucson .30 | 9 | 2 | 0 | 6 | 2 | 10 | .750 | 84 | 99 | 49 | 41 | 2 | 32 | 3 | 3 | 84 | 5 | 4.39 |
| Luebber, Tacoma .24 | 23 | 15 | 3 | 14 | 7 | 0 | .667 | 177 | 145 | 62 | 47 | 6 | 79 | 4 | 3 | 123 | 12 | 2.39 |
| Mazzone, Tucson* .39 | 0 | 0 | 0 | 4 | 5 | 4 | .444 | 56 | 64 | 29 | 26 | 4 | 32 | 7 | 1 | 38 | 2 | 4.18 |
| Metzger, Hawaii .36 | 20 | 9 | 2 | 15 | 7 | 5 | .682 | 169 | 163 | 86 | 68 | 16 | 78 | 3 | 5 | 114 | 3 | 3.62 |

| Pitcher—Club | G | GS | CG | ShO | W | L | Sv | Pct. | IP | H | R | ER | HR | BB | Int. BB | HB | SO | WP | ERA |
|---|---|---|---|---|---|---|---|---|---|---|---|---|---|---|---|---|---|---|---|
| Miller, Hawaii ...15 | 1 | 0 | 0 | 0 | 1 | 3 | .000 | 25 | 32 | 17 | 16 | 3 | 8 | 0 | 0 | 9 | 3 | 5.76 |
| Miller, Sac ......23 | 21 | 6 | 2 | 7 | 12 | 0 | .368 | 149 | 186 | 111 | 102 | 28 | 57 | 2 | 1 | 73 | 4 | 6.16 |
| Miller, Alb* ......26 | 6 | 2 | 0 | 1 | 7 | 2 | .125 | 65 | 84 | 50 | 44 | 4 | 33 | 7 | 0 | 31 | 2 | 6.09 |
| Minton, Phoenix .42 | 12 | 7 | 2 | 10 | 6 | 4 | .625 | 177 | 178 | 73 | 51 | 6 | 76 | 11 | 4 | 76 | 7 | 2.59 |
| Mitchell, Tucson .18 | 17 | 0 | 1 | 7 | 4 | 0 | .636 | 90 | 90 | 59 | 48 | 3 | 43 | 2 | 0 | 49 | 8 | 4.80 |
| Moharter, Spo* ..48 | 1 | 0 | 0 | 4 | 4 | 4 | .500 | 130 | 142 | 63 | 52 | 8 | 48 | 10 | 5 | 57 | 5 | 3.60 |
| Monge, SLC* .....27 | 27 | 7 | 0 | 14 | 9 | 0 | .609 | 167 | 175 | 98 | 86 | 9 | 93 | 1 | 1 | 106 | 8 | 4.63 |
| Moore, Spokane .. 6 | 4 | 2 | 0 | 1 | 3 | 0 | .250 | 32 | 23 | 17 | 15 | 2 | 24 | 0 | 1 | 14 | 1 | 4.22 |
| Myers, Tacoma .. 2 | 2 | 0 | 0 | 1 | 0 | 0 | 1.000 | 8 | 2 | 2 | 2 | 0 | 7 | 0 | 0 | 10 | 1 | 2.25 |
| Nelson, Tucson ..20 | 20 | 6 | 0 | 7 | 8 | 0 | .467 | 123 | 125 | 64 | 51 | 5 | 41 | 1 | 3 | 78 | 11 | 3.73 |
| Nitz, Albuquerque .28 | 28 | 10 | 2 | 9 | 12 | 0 | .429 | 168 | 209 | 114 | 91 | 17 | 69 | 3 | 1 | 67 | 5 | 4.88 |
| Nolan, Phoenix* .13 | 0 | 0 | 0 | 0 | 1 | 0 | .000 | 28 | 28 | 20 | 16 | 4 | 14 | 1 | 1 | 26 | 2 | 5.14 |
| Norman, Spokane* .26 | 24 | 4 | 0 | 7 | 9 | 0 | .438 | 125 | 152 | 94 | 86 | 13 | 83 | 0 | 3 | 49 | 3 | 6.19 |
| Norton, Tacoma ..20 | 12 | 2 | 1 | 5 | 6 | 1 | .455 | 79 | 74 | 44 | 37 | 9 | 55 | 1 | 2 | 38 | 10 | 4.22 |
| Osburn, Sac* .....28 | 15 | 3 | 1 | 7 | 7 | 1 | .500 | 113 | 119 | 61 | 58 | 22 | 67 | 0 | 3 | 85 | 9 | 4.62 |
| O'Toole, Sac ..... 3 | 0 | 0 | 0 | 0 | 0 | 0 | .000 | 2 | 1 | 6 | 3 | 0 | 9 | 0 | 1 | 0 | 1 | 13.50 |
| Palmer, Sac ......34 | 3 | 1 | 0 | 0 | 2 | 0 | .200 | 102 | 88 | 75 | 67 | 14 | 109 | 3 | 8 | 85 | 18 | 5.91 |
| Pazik, Tacoma* ..20 | 19 | 11 | 3 | 9 | 9 | 1 | .500 | 140 | 117 | 61 | 49 | 11 | 61 | 4 | 0 | 99 | 4 | 3.15 |
| Pena, Tucson .....21 | 0 | 0 | 0 | 2 | 6 | 1 | .571 | 113 | 104 | 57 | 48 | 5 | 40 | 5 | 7 | 48 | 6 | 3.82 |
| Perzanowski, Spo .20 | 15 | 8 | 0 | 8 | 6 | 1 | .308 | 101 | 102 | 60 | 49 | 42 | 1 | 46 | 3 | 4 | 56 | 3 | 3.74 |
| Pitlock, Tucson* .17 | 14 | 4 | 1 | 4 | 9 | 0 | .600 | 45 | 58 | 32 | 26 | 4 | 16 | 0 | 2 | 35 | 2 | 5.20 |
| Quintana, SLC* ..37 | 0 | 0 | 0 | 3 | 1 | 0 | .667 | 22 | 22 | 10 | 10 | 1 | 9 | 2 | 1 | 17 | 3 | 4.09 |
| Rauch, Tucson ... 7 | 1 | 0 | 0 | 2 | 1 | 0 | .667 | 76 | 70 | 30 | 20 | 5 | 33 | 4 | 1 | 67 | 5 | 2.37 |
| Raziano, SLC ....39 | 0 | 0 | 0 | 6 | 1 | 11 | .857 | 0 | 0 | 0 | ½ | 0 | 0 | 0 | 0 | 0 | 0 | 0.00 |
| Renick, Tacoma .. 1 | 0 | 0 | 0 | 0 | 0 | 0 | .000 | 5 | 2 | 5 | 2 | 0 | 1 | 4 | 0 | 5 | 2 | 5.26 |
| Robson, Sac .....14 | 14 | 5 | 0 | 6 | 5 | 0 | .545 | 101 | 108 | 69 | 59 | 22 | 50 | 1 | 4 | 81 | 2 | 6.30 |
| Rose, Phoenix ...34 | 21 | 4 | 0 | 7 | 16 | 3 | .304 | 140 | 174 | 110 | 98 | 12 | 66 | 7 | 2 | 86 | 9 | 6.30 |
| Ross, Hawaii ....27 | 27 | 11 | 3 | 16 | 8 | 0 | .667 | 188 | 170 | 70 | 52 | 12 | 44 | 3 | 8 | 123 | 8 | 2.49 |
| Ryerson, SLC* ...27 | 27 | 7 | 1 | 9 | 14 | 0 | .391 | 180 | 222 | 105 | 95 | 83 | 8 | 38 | 1 | 4 | 88 | 4 | 4.15 |
| Scarbery, Tucson .12 | 5 | 1 | 0 | 1 | 1 | 0 | .500 | 44 | 56 | 39 | 29 | 2 | 17 | 2 | 0 | 18 | 3 | 5.73 |
| Sells, 13 SLC- | | | | | | | | | | | | | | | | | | |
| 9 Albuquerque ..22 | 19 | 10 | 1 | 11 | 8 | 0 | .579 | 146 | 134 | 69 | 56 | 10 | 51 | 2 | 3 | 68 | 8 | 3.45 |
| Selma, Alb .......31 | 0 | 0 | 0 | 8 | 1 | 7 | .889 | 70 | 59 | 29 | 22 | 6 | 40 | 5 | 0 | 49 | 3 | 2.83 |
| Shanahan, Alb ...29 | 29 | 12 | 0 | 9 | 13 | 0 | .409 | 203 | 219 | 118 | 95 | 12 | 73 | 2 | 8 | 147 | 17 | 4.21 |
| Shellenback, Haw* .32 | 23 | 6 | 0 | 10 | 6 | 3 | .625 | 160 | 184 | 8 | 80 | 15 | 49 | 1 | 0 | 91 | 8 | 4.50 |
| Sielicki, Phoe* ... 7 | 6 | 0 | 0 | 1 | 1 | 0 | .500 | 31 | 41 | 21 | 18 | 3 | 16 | 0 | 2 | 16 | 1 | 5.23 |
| Smith, Tacoma* ..15 | 9 | 1 | 0 | 0 | 7 | 0 | .000 | 57 | 87 | 51 | 45 | 5 | 17 | 2 | 0 | 26 | 2 | 7.11 |
| Solomon, Alb ..... 3 | 3 | 2 | 0 | 3 | 0 | 0 | 1.000 | 27 | 33 | 13 | 12 | 2 | 16 | 1 | 3 | 21 | 2 | 4.00 |
| Stone, Tacoma ...30 | 1 | 0 | 0 | 1 | 5 | 0 | .167 | 63 | 75 | 51 | 36 | 4 | 40 | 4 | 7 | 38 | 8 | 5.14 |
| Strahler, Tucson . 5 | 1 | 0 | 0 | 0 | 1 | 0 | .000 | 10 | 10 | 9 | 8 | 1 | 9 | 0 | 4 | 3 | 7 | 7.20 |
| Strampe, Hawaii .30 | 28 | 13 | 1 | 12 | 10 | 0 | .545 | 186 | 179 | 103 | 93 | 20 | 83 | 1 | 3 | 120 | 6 | 4.50 |
| Strom, Hawaii* ..12 | 12 | 8 | 1 | 8 | 3 | 0 | .727 | 90 | 70 | 22 | 15 | 7 | 22 | 1 | 1 | 85 | 7 | 1.50 |
| Sukla, Phoenix ..36 | 1 | 0 | 0 | 5 | 5 | 4 | .500 | 94 | 110 | 35 | 33 | 3 | 32 | 7 | 1 | 40 | 1 | 3.16 |
| Taylor, Tucson ... 2 | 0 | 0 | 0 | 0 | 0 | 0 | .000 | 1 | 5 | 5 | 5 | 0 | 2 | 1 | 0 | 0 | 0 | 45.00 |
| Terpko, Spokane .43 | 0 | 0 | 0 | 6 | 4 | 13 | .600 | 70 | 76 | 39 | 32 | 4 | 33 | 4 | 3 | 46 | 10 | 4.11 |
| Thayer, Tacoma ..14 | 8 | 0 | 0 | 1 | 3 | 0 | .250 | 39 | 46 | 36 | 32 | 1 | 39 | 3 | 0 | 26 | 5 | 7.38 |
| Timberlake, Tuc* .10 | 1 | 0 | 0 | 0 | 1 | 1 | .000 | 17 | 23 | 17 | 15 | 0 | 7 | 1 | 0 | 10 | 3 | 7.94 |
| Todd, Tucson .... 2 | 0 | 0 | 0 | 1 | 0 | 0 | 1.000 | 13 | 11 | 3 | 3 | 0 | 4 | 0 | 1 | 9 | 0 | 2.08 |
| Toms, Phoenix ...40 | 0 | 0 | 0 | 1 | 4 | 11 | .200 | 74 | 63 | 27 | 17 | 5 | 28 | 6 | 2 | 45 | 1 | 2.07 |
| Travers, Sac* ....12 | 7 | 4 | 3 | 3 | 3 | 0 | .500 | 61 | 55 | 24 | 20 | 1 | 21 | 1 | 1 | 46 | 3 | 2.95 |
| Van Bommel, Tuc .13 | 6 | 1 | 0 | 0 | 4 | 0 | .000 | 35 | 51 | 39 | 35 | 2 | 33 | 3 | 3 | 15 | 4 | 9.00 |
| Veintidos, Tacoma. 28 | 24 | 3 | 1 | 5 | 11 | 0 | .313 | 132 | 148 | 104 | 91 | 15 | 97 | 0 | 5 | 82 | 7 | 6.20 |
| Velazquez, Sac ...51 | 0 | 0 | 0 | 9 | 9 | 4 | .500 | 104 | 127 | 60 | 52 | 16 | 28 | 0 | 2 | 62 | 5 | 4.50 |
| Verhoeven, SLC ..18 | 0 | 0 | 0 | 3 | 1 | 2 | .750 | 26 | 24 | 15 | 13 | 0 | 18 | 3 | 0 | 9 | 3 | 4.50 |
| Waits, Spokane* ..11 | 11 | 6 | 0 | 5 | 4 | 0 | .556 | 67 | 76 | 46 | 36 | 3 | 37 | 2 | 0 | 38 | 1 | 4.84 |
| Wall, Alb* ......23 | 11 | 8 | 0 | 9 | 5 | 0 | .643 | 106 | 105 | 44 | 28 | 2 | 42 | 4 | 1 | 66 | 4 | 2.38 |
| Wehrmeister, Haw .10 | 10 | 2 | 1 | 3 | 5 | 0 | .375 | 52 | 63 | 37 | 37 | 7 | 24 | 2 | 4 | 31 | 2 | 6.40 |
| Wheelock, SLC ...31 | 12 | 5 | 1 | 7 | 6 | 0 | .538 | 120 | 113 | 56 | 41 | 9 | 47 | 2 | 0 | 68 | 10 | 3.08 |
| Widmar, Sac ..... 6 | 1 | 0 | 0 | 0 | 1 | 0 | .000 | 18 | 25 | 17 | 15 | 2 | 8 | 2 | 0 | 3 | 2 | 7.50 |
| Wiley, Tacoma ...17 | 9 | 6 | 1 | 9 | 1 | 1 | .900 | 92 | 72 | 28 | 22 | 3 | 24 | 0 | 0 | 47 | 4 | 2.15 |
| Woodson, Spokane . 5 | 0 | 0 | 0 | 0 | 0 | 0 | .000 | 9 | 17 | 12 | 12 | 2 | 7 | 1 | 0 | 8 | 2 | 12.00 |

BALKS—Minton, 6; Bane, 5; Augustine, Miller (Sac), 4 each; Haller, Hooten, Shanahan, Wall, 3 each; Gonzalez, Knepper, Robson, Sells, 2 each; Austerman, Bostic, Cutler, Griffin, Halicki, Hockenbery, Hypes, Kemp, Lacey, Metzger, Mitchell, Monge, Myers, Nitz, Nolan, Norman, Pazik, Selma, Sielicki, Solomon, Strampe, Thayer, Van Bommel, Veintidos, Verhoeven, 1 each.

COMBINATION SHUTOUTS—Lewallyn-Wall-Haller, Albuquerque; Ross-Metzger 2, Johnson-Linzy-Hartenstein, Strampe-Linzy, Strom-Metzger, Hawaii; Rose-Minton 2, Dressler-Toms, Phoenix; Barker-Velazquez, Osburn-Velazquez, Sacramento; Blateric-Quintana-Verhoeven, Ryerson-Wheelock, Salt Lake City; Perzanowski-Moharter, Spokane; Luebber-Johnson, Myers-Johnson, Norton-Pazik, Pazik-Lerner, Thayer-Johnson, Wiley-Johnson, Tacoma; Nelson-Barlow, Tucson.

NO-HIT GAMES—Ross, Hawaii, defeated Salt Lake City, 19-0, May 19 (five innings—PERFECT); Norton, Tacoma, defeated Hawaii, 1-0, June 21; Dobson, Salt Lake City, defeated Hawaii, 5-0, July 17 (seven innings).

# *Eastern League*

## CLASS AA

**Leading Batter**
**DAVE BERGMAN**
**West Haven**

**League President**
**PAT McKERNAN**

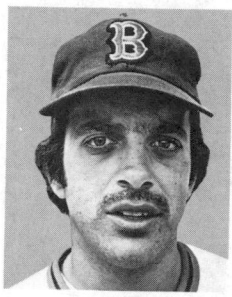

**Leading Pitcher**
**TOM FARIAS**
**Bristol**

### CHAMPIONSHIP WINNERS IN PREVIOUS YEARS

1923—Williamsport ...... .661
1924—Williamsport ...... .654
1925—York§ ............. .583
   Williamsport§ ...... .583
1926—Scranton .......... .627
1927—Harrisburg ....... .630
1928—Harrisburg ....... .603
1929—Binghamton ....... .597
1930—Wilkes-Barre ..... .572
1931—Harrisburg ....... .597
1932—Wilkes-Barre ..... .561
1933—Binghamton ...... .690
1934—Binghamton ...... .694
   Williamsport* ...... .603
1935—Scranton ......... .657
   Binghamton* ....... .580
1936—Scranton* ........ .609
   Elmira ............ .629
1937—Elmira† .......... .622
1938—Binghamton ...... .622
   Elmira (3rd) ‡ ..... .522
1939—Scranton† ........ .571
1940—Scranton ......... .568
   Binghamton (2nd)‡. .554
1942—Albany ........... .600
   Scranton (2nd) ‡ ... .593
1943—Scranton ......... .630
   Elmira (2nd)‡ ..... .568

1944—Hartford ......... .723
   Binghamton (4th)‡. .474
1945—Utica ............ .615
   Albany (3rd)‡ ..... .564
1946—Scranton† ........ .691
1947—Utica† ........... .652
1948—Scranton† ........ .636
1949—Albany ........... .664
   Binghamton (4th)‡. .500
1950—Wilkes-Barre‡ .... .652
1951—Wikles-Barre ..... .612
   Scranton (2nd)† ... .562
1952—Albany ........... .603
   Binghamton (2nd)‡. .562
1953—Reading .......... .682
   Binghamton (2nd)‡. .636
1954—Wilkes-Barre ..... .576
   Albany (3rd)‡ ..... .540
1955—Reading .......... .613
   Allentown (2nd)‡ .. .565
1941—Wilkes-Barre ..... .630
   Elmira (3rd)‡ ..... .514
1956—Schenectady† ..... .609
1957—Binghamton ...... .607
   Reading (3rd)‡ .... .529
1958—Lancaster x ...... .568
   Binghamton (6th)‡. .493

1959—Springfield† ....... .607
1960—Williamsport y .... .551
   Springfield (3rd)y . .496
1961—Springfield ....... .612
1962—Williamsport ...... .593
   Elmira (2nd)‡ ..... .514
1963—Charleston ....... .593
1964—Elmira ........... .586
1965—Pittsfield ........ .607
1966—Elmira ........... .633
1967—Binghamton z ..... .586
   Elmira ............ .532
1968—Pittsfield ....... .604
   Reading (2nd)‡ .... .579
1969—York ............. .640
1970—Waterbury a ...... .560
   Reading a ......... .553
1971—Three Rivers ..... .569
   Elmira b .......... .561
1972—West Haven b ..... .600
   Three Rivers ..... .559
1973—Reading b ........ .551
   Pittsfield ........ .551
1974—Thetford Mines
   (2nd) c .......... .536
   Pittsfield (2nd) ... .496

*Won split-season playoff. †Won championship and four-team playoff. ‡Won four-team playoff. §Tied for pennant, York winning play ff. xLeague was divided into Northern, Southern divisions and played a split season; Lancaster over-all season leader. yPlayoff finals canceled after one game because of rain with Williamsport and Springfield declared playoff co-champions. zLeague was divided into Eastern, Western divisions; Binghamton won playoff. aTied for pennant, Waterbury winning playoff. bLeague was divided into American, National divisions; won playoff. (NOTE—Known as New York-Pennsylvania League prior to 1938.)

   c League was divided into American and National Divisions; won four-team playoff.

## STANDING OF CLUBS AT CLOSE OF FIRST HALF, JUNE 26

| Club | W. | L. | T. | Pct. | G.B. | Club | W. | L. | T. | Pct. | G.B. |
|---|---|---|---|---|---|---|---|---|---|---|---|
| Reading (Phillies) ..... | 41 | 20 | 0 | .672 | .... | Thetford M. (Brewers) . | 28 | 35 | 0 | .444 | 14 |
| Waterbury (Dodgers) .. | 42 | 26 | 0 | .618 | 2½ | Quebec City (Expos) .... | 28 | 36 | 0 | .438 | 14½ |
| Bristol (Red Sox) .... | 35 | 30 | 0 | .538 | 8 | West Haven (Yankees) .. | 27 | 37 | 0 | .422 | 15½ |
| Pittsfield (Rangers) ... | 27 | 32 | 0 | .458 | 13 | Three Rivers (Reds) ... | 25 | 37 | 0 | .403 | 16½ |

## STANDING OF CLUBS AT CLOSE OF SECOND HALF, SEPTEMBER 1

| Club | W. | L. | T. | Pct. | G.B. | Club | W. | L. | T. | Pct. | G.B. |
|---|---|---|---|---|---|---|---|---|---|---|---|
| Bristol (Red Sox) ..... | 46 | 27 | 0 | .630 | .... | Quebec City (Expos) .... | 35 | 37 | 0 | .486 | 10½ |
| Reading (Phillies) .... | 43 | 33 | 0 | .566 | 4½ | Pittsfield (Rangers) ... | 32 | 41 | 0 | .438 | 14 |
| West Haven (Yankees) .. | 39 | 34 | 0 | .534 | 7 | Three Rivers (Reds) ... | 32 | 43 | 0 | .427 | 15 |
| Waterbury (Dodgers) ... | 35 | 33 | 0 | .515 | 8½ | Thetford M. (Brewers) . | 31 | 45 | 0 | .408 | 16½ |

## COMPOSITE STANDING OF CLUBS AT CLOSE OF SEASON, SEPTEMBER 1

| Club | Read. | Bris. | Wat. | W.H. | Q.C. | Pitt. | T.M. | T.R. | W. | L. | T. | Pct. | G.B. |
|---|---|---|---|---|---|---|---|---|---|---|---|---|---|
| Reading (Phillies) ........ | .. | 11 | 9 | 12 | 12 | 12 | 14 | 13 | 84 | 53 | 0 | .613 | .. |
| Bristol (Red Sox) ....... | 9 | .. | 9 | 10 | 12 | 12 | 16 | 13 | 81 | 57 | 0 | .587 | 3½ |
| Waterbury (Dodgers) ... | 9 | 9 | .. | 11 | 12 | 14 | 9 | 13 | 77 | 59 | 0 | .566 | 6½ |
| West Haven (Yankees) .. | 8 | 10 | 9 | .. | 13 | 8 | 8 | 10 | 66 | 71 | 0 | .482 | 18 |
| Quebec City (Expos) ... | 6 | 8 | 8 | 7 | .. | 7 | 15 | 10 | 63 | 73 | 0 | .463 | 20½ |
| Pittsfield (Rangers) ..... | 6 | 8 | 6 | 9 | 9 | .. | 13 | 8 | 59 | 73 | 0 | .447 | 22½ |
| Thetford Mines (Brewers).. | 7 | 4 | 11 | 12 | 5 | 7 | .. | 13 | 59 | 80 | 0 | .424 | 26 |
| Three Rivers (Reds) ...... | 6 | 7 | 7 | 10 | 10 | 11 | 6 | .. | 57 | 80 | 0 | .416 | 27 |

FORFEITED GAME—Reading at Waterbury, August 26 (1st game). Reading forfeited with the score 3-3. There were no winning or losing pitchers.

Major league affiliations in parentheses.

Playoff—Bristol defeated Reading three games to none for league championship.

Regular-Season Attendance—Bristol, 42,238; Pittsfield, 34,878; Quebec City, 55,509; Reading, 85,257; Thetford Mines, 16,360; Three Rivers, 54,436; Waterbury, 63,847; West Haven, 26,549. Total, 379,074. Playoffs, 4,046. No All-Star Game.

Managers: Bristol—Dick McAuliffe, Bill Slack; Pittsfield—Jackie Moore, Orlando Martinez; Quebec City—Lance Nichols; Reading—Bob Wellman; Thetford Mines—John Felske; Three Rivers—Jim Snyder, Ron Plaza; Waterbury—Don LeJohn; West Haven—Pete Ward.

All-Star Team: 1B—Bergman, West Haven; 2B—Sakata, Thetford Mines; 3B—Hobson, Bristol; SS—Landestoy, Waterbury; OF—Roenicke, Quebec City; Bosetti, Reading; Alston, West Haven; C—Bastable, Reading; Util—Wills, Pittsfield; P—Lerch, Reading; Farias, Bristol; Heinold, West Haven. Manager—Bob Wellman, Reading.

(Compiled by Elias Sports Bureau, New York, N. Y.)

## CLUB BATTING

| Club | G. | AB. | R. | OR. | H. | TB. | 2B. | 3B. | HR. | RBI. | SH. | Int. SF.BB. | | HP.SO.SB. | | | CS.LOB. | | Pct. |
|---|---|---|---|---|---|---|---|---|---|---|---|---|---|---|---|---|---|---|---|
| Waterbury | .136 | 4295 | 552 | 485 | 1130 | 1559 | 157 | 46 | 60 | 474 | 53 | 41 | 470 | 51 | 21 | 634 | 201 | 88 | 944 | .263 |
| W. Haven | 137 | 4527 | 556 | 538 | 1125 | 1518 | 174 | 39 | 47 | 483 | 59 | 46 | 424 | 22 | 22 | 555 | 134 | 50 | 899 | .260 |
| Reading | 137 | 4286 | 576 | 476 | 1097 | 1537 | 165 | 40 | 65 | 511 | 42 | 40 | 474 | 32 | 38 | 590 | 138 | 49 | 970 | .256 |
| Bristol | .138 | 4282 | 511 | 440 | 1079 | 1448 | 162 | 24 | 53 | 442 | 32 | 37 | 453 | 20 | 27 | 524 | 51 | 39 | 939 | .252 |
| Pittsfield | .132 | 4073 | 500 | 537 | 1007 | 1358 | 133 | 25 | 56 | 434 | 49 | 35 | 463 | 15 | 40 | 594 | 85 | 37 | 945 | .247 |
| Quebec City | 136 | 431) | 504 | 535 | 1041 | 1427 | 163 | 14 | 65 | 441 | 55 | 34 | 463 | 15 | 67 | 783 | 125 | 42 | 977 | .241 |
| Thetford M | 139 | 4272 | 501 | 590 | 1004 | 1522 | 170 | 15 | 106 | 449 | 33 | 27 | 426 | 22 | 36 | 805 | 110 | 38 | 903 | .235 |
| Three R | ...137 | 4192 | 389 | 488 | 920 | 1135 | 129 | 19 | 16 | 326 | 88 | 28 | 498 | 29 | 25 | 745 | 90 | 53 | 977 | .219 |

## INDIVIDUAL BATTING

### (Leading Qualifiers for Batting Championship—378 or More Plate Appearances)

*Bats lefthanded. †Switch-hitter.

| Player and Club | G. | AB. | R. | H. | TB. | 2B. | 3B. | HR. | RBI. | SH. | SF. | BB. | HP. | SO. | SB. | CS. | Pct. |
|---|---|---|---|---|---|---|---|---|---|---|---|---|---|---|---|---|---|
| Bergman, David, W H* | .124 | 399 | 76 | 124 | 184 | 15 | 6 | 11 | 60 | 3 | 6 | 83 | 1 | 60 | 15 | 3 | .311 |
| Alston, Wendell, W H* | .119 | 452 | 77 | 139 | 189 | 18 | 7 | 6 | 47 | 3 | 3 | 41 | 1 | 31 | 33 | 12 | .308 |
| Wills, Elliott, Pitt† | .122 | 456 | 72 | 140 | 194 | 23 | 2 | 9 | 49 | 2 | 3 | 46 | 7 | 52 | 13 | 5 | .307 |
| Patchin, Steven, Waterbury | .127 | 435 | 48 | 128 | 186 | 24 | 0 | 10 | 67 | 2 | 2 | 66 | 0 | 34 | 6 | 7 | .294 |
| Stitzel, Glenn, Reading* | .109 | 341 | 49 | 99 | 139 | 17 | 1 | 7 | 56 | 3 | 4 | 56 | 0 | 25 | 3 | 1 | .290 |
| Phillips, Lanny, Bristol | ...123 | 445 | 37 | 129 | 148 | 12 | 2 | 1 | 56 | 2 | 3 | 39 | 0 | 43 | 26 | 9 | .288 |
| Baez, Jose, Waterbury | ...114 | 441 | 64 | 127 | 171 | 20 | 9 | 2 | 37 | 3 | 1 | 39 | 0 | 33 | 67 | 5 | .285 |
| Roenicke, Gary, Quebec C. | .131 | 466 | 67 | 133 | 198 | 22 | 0 | 14 | 74 | 0 | 5 | 58 | 12 | 73 | 6 | 5 | .285 |
| Landestoy, Rafael, Wat | ...130 | 439 | 61 | 123 | 147 | 10 | 7 | 0 | 31 | 9 | 2 | 31 | 1 | 61 | 41 | 13 | .280 |
| Hart, J. Michael, Q C† | ...129 | 446 | 68 | 124 | 166 | 17 | 2 | 7 | 44 | 1 | 5 | 70 | 7 | 90 | 24 | 6 | .278 |

Departmental Leaders: G—Gantner, Hobson, 138; AB—McLaughlin, 502; R—Alston, 77; H—Wills, 140; TB—Hobson, 201; 2B—Ward, 26; 3B—Baez, 9; HR—R. Davis, 16; RBI—Roenicke, 74; SH—Sherrill, 16; SF—Coulson, T. Jones, 10; BB—Cooper, 86; HP—Gates, Roenicke, 12; SO—Biagini, 106; SB—Burke, 48; CS—Burke, 19.

### (All Players—Listed Alphabetically)

| Player and Club | G. | AB. | R. | H. | TB. | 2B. | 3B | HR. | RBI. | SH. | SF. | BB. | HP. | SO. | SB. | CS. | Pct. |
|---|---|---|---|---|---|---|---|---|---|---|---|---|---|---|---|---|---|
| Alexander, Robert, T.M. | .26 | 4 | 0 | 1 | 1 | 0 | 0 | 0 | 1 | 0 | 0 | 0 | 0 | 2 | 0 | 0 | .250 |
| Alston, Wendell, W.H.* | .119 | 452 | 77 | 139 | 189 | 18 | 7 | 6 | 47 | 3 | 3 | 41 | 1 | 31 | 33 | 12 | .308 |
| Andrew, Kim, Bris. | .17 | 67 | 8 | 25 | 31 | 4 | 1 | 0 | 8 | 0 | 1 | 2 | 0 | 10 | 0 | 0 | .373 |
| Andujar, Joaquin, T.R. | .18 | 19 | 1 | 2 | 5 | 1 | 1 | 0 | 2 | 0 | 0 | 1 | 0 | 19 | 0 | 0 | .105 |
| Armstrong, Michael, T.R. | .25 | 47 | 3 | 7 | 7 | 0 | 0 | 0 | 2 | 6 | 0 | 4 | 0 | 19 | 0 | 0 | .149 |

| Player and Club | G. | AB. | R. | H. | TB. | 2B. | 3B. | HR. | RBI. | SH. | SF. | BB. | HP. | SO. | SB. | CS. | Pct. |
|---|---|---|---|---|---|---|---|---|---|---|---|---|---|---|---|---|---|
| Arnett, G. Curt, Pitt.* | 19 | 74 | 4 | 20 | 21 | 1 | 0 | 0 | 6 | 0 | 0 | 7 | 0 | 12 | 1 | 2 | .270 |
| Astroth, Jonathan, Pitt.* | 49 | 145 | 21 | 35 | 59 | 6 | 0 | 6 | 23 | 0 | 4 | 37 | 0 | 17 | 0 | 0 | .241 |
| Ault, Douglas, Pitt. | 75 | 277 | 42 | 78 | 130 | 13 | 3 | 11 | 56 | 2 | 5 | 18 | 4 | 28 | 4 | 2 | .282 |
| Baez, Jose, Wat. | 114 | 441 | 64 | 127 | 171 | 20 | 9 | 2 | 37 | 3 | 1 | 39 | 0 | 43 | 26 | 9 | .288 |
| Barker, Leonard, Pitt. | 24 | 4 | 0 | 0 | 0 | 0 | 0 | 0 | 0 | 0 | 0 | 0 | 0 | 2 | 0 | 0 | .000 |
| Bastable, John, Read.† | 135 | 457 | 56 | 107 | 152 | 23 | 5 | 4 | 50 | 3 | 5 | 57 | 5 | 72 | 7 | 12 | .234 |
| Beasley, Lewis, Pitt.* | 81 | 306 | 42 | 89 | 135 | 15 | 2 | 9 | 49 | 3 | 4 | 20 | 2 | 28 | 15 | 5 | .291 |
| Benedetti, Ludwig, Bris. | 91 | 263 | 29 | 61 | 73 | 6 | 3 | 0 | 23 | 3 | 3 | 32 | 1 | 39 | 4 | 1 | .232 |
| Bennett, Michael, Bris.* | 102 | 305 | 45 | 71 | 107 | 13 | 4 | 5 | 26 | 1 | 3 | 53 | 1 | 28 | 7 | 2 | .233 |
| Benson, Wayne, W.H. | 94 | 321 | 35 | 92 | 125 | 19 | 4 | 2 | 35 | 2 | 3 | 25 | 2 | 20 | 4 | 1 | .287 |
| Bergman, David, W.H.* | 124 | 399 | 76 | 124 | 184 | 15 | 6 | 11 | 60 | 3 | 6 | 83 | 1 | 60 | 15 | 3 | .311 |
| Bernhardt, Juan, W.H | 41 | 160 | 16 | 51 | 66 | 10 | 1 | 1 | 28 | 0 | 3 | 3 | 0 | 11 | 0 | 0 | .319 |
| Biagini, Gregory, Q.C.† | 128 | 451 | 56 | 112 | 174 | 17 | 3 | 13 | 63 | 2 | 4 | 44 | 1 | 106 | 2 | 1 | .248 |
| Boggs, Thomas, Pitt. | 25 | 11 | 0 | 3 | 3 | 0 | 0 | 0 | 1 | 1 | 0 | 0 | 0 | 3 | 0 | 0 | .273 |
| Bohne, William, Q.C.† | 7 | 21 | 4 | 2 | 5 | 0 | 0 | 1 | 1 | 0 | 0 | 0 | 1 | 0 | 0 | 0 | .095 |
| Boitano, Danny, Read. | 40 | 2 | 0 | 0 | 0 | 0 | 0 | 0 | 1 | 1 | 0 | 3 | 0 | 3 | 1 | 0 | .000 |
| Bolick, Frank, Pitt. | 31 | 2 | 0 | 1 | 1 | 0 | 0 | 0 | 0 | 0 | 0 | 0 | 0 | 0 | 0 | 0 | .500 |
| Bordes, Charles, Pitt. | 43 | 146 | 17 | 37 | 41 | 4 | 0 | 0 | 11 | 3 | 2 | 16 | 1 | 11 | 4 | 0 | .253 |
| Bosetti, Richard, Read. | 110 | 432 | 73 | 118 | 167 | 21 | 5 | 6 | 34 | 1 | 3 | 34 | 1 | 47 | 47 | 15 | .273 |
| Bowen, Samuel, Bris. | 44 | 143 | 18 | 28 | 46 | 4 | 1 | 4 | 13 | 2 | 1 | 23 | 0 | 39 | 3 | 5 | .196 |
| Bucci, Michael, Pitt. | 12 | 41 | 4 | 10 | 14 | 2 | 1 | 0 | 5 | 1 | 0 | 5 | 0 | 11 | 1 | 0 | .244 |
| Burke, Glenn, Wat. | 119 | 478 | 66 | 129 | 183 | 14 | 2 | 12 | 49 | 2 | 2 | 29 | 2 | 56 | 48 | 19 | .270 |
| Carrion, Leonel, Q.C. | 127 | 436 | 53 | 113 | 145 | 18 | 1 | 4 | 45 | 9 | 4 | 48 | 10 | 63 | 27 | 3 | .259 |
| Childers, Terry, Q.C. | 51 | 145 | 15 | 23 | 33 | 7 | 0 | 1 | 14 | 1 | 3 | 11 | 1 | 28 | 0 | 1 | .159 |
| Clark, Robert, T.M.* | 109 | 317 | 30 | 70 | 102 | 14 | 0 | 6 | 32 | 0 | 3 | 56 | 3 | 63 | 0 | 1 | .221 |
| Clyde, David, Pitt.* | 22 | 0 | 0 | 0 | 0 | 0 | 0 | 0 | 0 | 0 | 0 | 0 | 0 | 0 | 0 | 0 | .000 |
| Coleman, David, Bris | 64 | 210 | 32 | 53 | 88 | 11 | 3 | 6 | 28 | 1 | 2 | 32 | 5 | 49 | 3 | 1 | .252 |
| Collins, Terry, Wat.* | 4 | 9 | 2 | 1 | 1 | 0 | 0 | 0 | 1 | 2 | 0 | 3 | 0 | 2 | 0 | 0 | .111 |
| Colzie, Richard, T.R. | 23 | 73 | 14 | 15 | 17 | 2 | 0 | 0 | 6 | 4 | 1 | 16 | 2 | 12 | 4 | 4 | .205 |
| Cooper, Gary M., Pitt.* | 100 | 331 | 62 | 79 | 99 | 7 | 5 | 1 | 23 | 6 | 2 | 86 | 5 | 26 | 11 | 3 | .239 |
| Coulson, Steven, W.H.* | 126 | 468 | 59 | 121 | 147 | 14 | 3 | 2 | 52 | 7 | 10 | 50 | 0 | 49 | 13 | 7 | .259 |
| Crane, Mark, Read. | 24 | 63 | 9 | 12 | 13 | 1 | 0 | 0 | 7 | 3 | 0 | 5 | 0 | 7 | 0 | 0 | .190 |
| Creech, T. Edwin, Q.C. | 84 | 313 | 35 | 68 | 83 | 11 | 2 | 0 | 21 | 5 | 2 | 20 | 1 | 53 | 15 | 5 | .217 |
| Crowley, Raymond, Q.C.* | 21 | 75 | 10 | 24 | 41 | 1 | 2 | 4 | 13 | 1 | 1 | 15 | 0 | 16 | 1 | 0 | .320 |
| Cunningham, Mark, Q.C. | 117 | 369 | 39 | 82 | 104 | 12 | 2 | 2 | 23 | 5 | 1 | 49 | 7 | 58 | 11 | 5 | .222 |
| Dancy, William, Read.† | 37 | 122 | 12 | 34 | 43 | 9 | 0 | 0 | 11 | 2 | 0 | 12 | 0 | 18 | 1 | 0 | .279 |
| Danforth, Perry, T.M.† | 105 | 400 | 46 | 102 | 147 | 11 | 2 | 10 | 49 | 4 | 2 | 10 | 0 | 36 | 11 | 4 | .255 |
| Daniels, David, Pitt.† | 105 | 368 | 41 | 75 | 100 | 6 | 2 | 5 | 27 | 8 | 1 | 46 | 4 | 82 | 12 | 9 | .204 |
| Danson, J. Roger, T.M. | 117 | 376 | 39 | 78 | 119 | 15 | 1 | 8 | 26 | 4 | 3 | 45 | 3 | 103 | 15 | 7 | .207 |
| Davis, Richard, T.M. | 132 | 455 | 66 | 115 | 188 | 23 | 1 | 16 | 67 | 2 | 6 | 43 | 3 | 77 | 14 | 8 | .253 |
| Davis, William N., T.R.† | 41 | 71 | 4 | 13 | 14 | 1 | 0 | 0 | 4 | 3 | 1 | 4 | 0 | 26 | 1 | 1 | .183 |
| de Armas, Ronaldo, Read. | 20 | 64 | 6 | 17 | 20 | 1 | 1 | 0 | 10 | 1 | 0 | 4 | 0 | 5 | 0 | 0 | .266 |
| Deidel, Thomas, T.M.* | 28 | 4 | 0 | 0 | 0 | 0 | 0 | 0 | 0 | 0 | 0 | 0 | 0 | 0 | 0 | 0 | .000 |
| Del Busto, Oscar, T.R. | 85 | 237 | 9 | 59 | 60 | 6 | 1 | 0 | 16 | 2 | 2 | 24 | 0 | 42 | 2 | 3 | .219 |
| Detherage, Robert, Wat. | 127 | 433 | 53 | 109 | 144 | 21 | 1 | 4 | 35 | 6 | 4 | 46 | 4 | 84 | 31 | 8 | .252 |
| Dillard, Stephen, Bris. | 68 | 261 | 34 | 73 | 85 | 5 | 2 | 1 | 20 | 4 | 2 | 29 | 2 | 32 | 8 | 4 | .280 |
| Dimmel, Michael, Wat. | 135 | 476 | 69 | 131 | 193 | 17 | 6 | 11 | 59 | 7 | 5 | 64 | 4 | 68 | 26 | 17 | .275 |
| Doerr, Timothy, T.R. | 90 | 263 | 21 | 51 | 72 | 5 | 2 | 4 | 25 | 2 | 3 | 19 | 0 | 66 | 2 | 1 | .194 |
| Dollar, E. Blaine, T.R. | 51 | 14 | 2 | 4 | 5 | 1 | 0 | 0 | 2 | 2 | 0 | 3 | 0 | 4 | 1 | 0 | .286 |
| Driscoll, James, T.R.* | 8 | 25 | 0 | 4 | 6 | 2 | 0 | 0 | 2 | 0 | 0 | 8 | 0 | 8 | 0 | 0 | .160 |
| Duran, Daniel, Pitt.* | 53 | 178 | 17 | 39 | 54 | 6 | 0 | 3 | 17 | 0 | 2 | 20 | 3 | 24 | 0 | 1 | .219 |
| Espy, Duane, T.M. | 55 | 182 | 22 | 44 | 57 | 7 | 0 | 2 | 14 | 1 | 0 | 16 | 5 | 33 | 3 | 3 | .242 |
| Essian, James, Read. | 12 | 36 | 5 | 7 | 12 | 2 | 0 | 1 | 2 | 0 | 0 | 11 | 0 | 7 | 0 | 0 | .194 |
| Fischetti, Arthur, Wat.† | 9 | 15 | 2 | 2 | 4 | 2 | 0 | 0 | 3 | 0 | 0 | 3 | 0 | 6 | 0 | 1 | .133 |
| Fitzgerald, Daniel, Read. | 103 | 321 | 39 | 74 | 130 | 13 | 5 | 11 | 37 | 2 | 3 | 39 | 2 | 105 | 15 | 6 | .231 |
| Ford, Edward, Bris.† | 110 | 354 | 47 | 89 | 118 | 14 | 0 | 5 | 31 | 6 | 4 | 17 | 1 | 35 | 10 | 4 | .251 |
| Fritz, Laurence, Read.* | 15 | 51 | 12 | 14 | 40 | 2 | 0 | 8 | 19 | 0 | 1 | 10 | 3 | 8 | 1 | 0 | .275 |
| Gantner, James, T.M.* | 138 | 456 | 61 | 117 | 170 | 17 | 0 | 12 | 48 | 2 | 4 | 49 | 4 | 96 | 20 | 2 | .257 |
| Gates, Eddie, Q.C. | 101 | 327 | 40 | 76 | 120 | 20 | 0 | 8 | 45 | 2 | 1 | 43 | 12 | 78 | 6 | 3 | .232 |
| Geigel, German, Read.† | 6 | 20 | 3 | 3 | 3 | 0 | 0 | 0 | 0 | 0 | 0 | 1 | 0 | 2 | 1 | 0 | .150 |
| Gingrich, Gary, Q.C.† | 41 | 115 | 7 | 20 | 23 | 1 | 1 | 0 | 5 | 4 | 2 | 11 | 3 | 13 | 4 | 2 | .174 |
| Goodman, Bobbie, Q.C. | 79 | 244 | 19 | 47 | 69 | 8 | 1 | 4 | 24 | 2 | 2 | 27 | 3 | 79 | 0 | 1 | .193 |
| Gronlund, David, Q.C. | 23 | 0 | 1 | 0 | 0 | 0 | 0 | 0 | 0 | 0 | 0 | 0 | 0 | 0 | 0 | 0 | .000 |
| Harper, David, Pitt. | 6 | 2 | 0 | 1 | 1 | 0 | 0 | 0 | 0 | 0 | 0 | 1 | 0 | 0 | 0 | 0 | .500 |
| Harrison, John, T.R.† | 4 | 11 | 0 | 2 | 2 | 0 | 0 | 0 | 0 | 1 | 0 | 1 | 0 | 4 | 0 | 0 | .182 |
| Hart, J. Michael, Q.C.† | 129 | 446 | 68 | 124 | 166 | 17 | 2 | 7 | 44 | 5 | 1 | 70 | 7 | 90 | 24 | 6 | .278 |
| Heintz, Michael, T.R. | 44 | 8 | 1 | 1 | 1 | 0 | 0 | 0 | 1 | 0 | 0 | 0 | 0 | 3 | 0 | 0 | .125 |
| Hobson, Clell, Bris. | 138 | 471 | 68 | 125 | 201 | 25 | 3 | 15 | 73 | 1 | 3 | 48 | 0 | 90 | 6 | 3 | .265 |
| Huizenga, Kenneth, Bris. | 7 | 25 | 4 | 4 | 8 | 1 | 0 | 1 | 5 | 0 | 0 | 2 | 1 | 4 | 0 | 0 | .160 |
| Hume, Thomas, T.R. | 9 | 16 | 2 | 4 | 6 | 0 | 1 | 0 | 0 | 0 | 0 | 3 | 0 | 3 | 0 | 0 | .250 |
| Husband, Paul, T.R. | 67 | 217 | 15 | 51 | 66 | 7 | 1 | 2 | 27 | 0 | 2 | 30 | 2 | 36 | 0 | 0 | .235 |
| Iorg, Dane, Read.* | 97 | 319 | 47 | 88 | 135 | 19 | 5 | 6 | 59 | 1 | 5 | 57 | 1 | 53 | 1 | 1 | .276 |
| Iorg, Garth, W.H.† | 76 | 236 | 19 | 59 | 69 | 6 | 2 | 0 | 21 | 5 | 1 | 22 | 0 | 30 | 8 | 2 | .250 |
| Ireland, Timothy, 7 Q.C.35-T.R. | 42 | 118 | 14 | 23 | 30 | 5 | 1 | 0 | 7 | 2 | 0 | 23 | 0 | 31 | 2 | 2 | .195 |
| Irwin, Dennis, W.H. | 107 | 351 | 37 | 73 | 101 | 10 | 0 | 6 | 44 | 7 | 3 | 27 | 2 | 58 | 9 | 5 | .208 |
| Jacobson, Kent, T.M.* | 47 | 140 | 9 | 33 | 56 | 12 | 4 | 1 | 17 | 0 | 2 | 16 | 3 | 34 | 0 | 2 | .236 |
| Jaramillo, Rudolpho, Pitt. | 87 | 278 | 26 | 69 | 89 | 9 | 1 | 3 | 30 | 3 | 1 | 25 | 3 | 54 | 1 | 1 | .248 |
| Jefferson, Milton, Bris. | 61 | 180 | 22 | 41 | 69 | 10 | 0 | 6 | 17 | 0 | 1 | 32 | 2 | 36 | 0 | 1 | .228 |
| Jensen, R. Lawrence, T.R.* | 20 | 15 | 3 | 2 | 2 | 0 | 0 | 0 | 1 | 3 | 0 | 2 | 0 | 2 | 0 | 0 | .133 |
| Jones, Darryl, W.H | 127 | 460 | 52 | 123 | 164 | 18 | 4 | 5 | 58 | 5 | 6 | 30 | 3 | 31 | 11 | 6 | .267 |

| Player and Club | G. | AB. | R. | H. | TB. | 2B. | 3B. | HR. | RBI. | SH. | SF. | BB. | HP. | SO. | SB. | CS. | Pct. |
|---|---|---|---|---|---|---|---|---|---|---|---|---|---|---|---|---|---|
| Jones, Lynn, T.R. | 53 | 141 | 12 | 29 | 37 | 3 | 1 | 1 | 14 | 5 | 0 | 12 | 0 | 16 | 5 | 2 | .206 |
| Jones, Robert C., T.R. | 76 | 261 | 40 | 62 | 72 | 8 | 1 | 0 | 15 | 5 | 1 | 43 | 1 | 38 | 10 | 4 | .238 |
| Jones, Terrence, Read. | 122 | 442 | 55 | 114 | 161 | 10 | 5 | 9 | 67 | 9 | 10 | 35 | 8 | 48 | 26 | 3 | .258 |
| Kelly, Van, Q.C.* | 32 | 105 | 11 | 32 | 42 | 7 | 0 | 1 | 11 | 2 | 0 | 15 | 0 | 19 | 0 | 0 | .305 |
| Klobas, Russell, Read. | 133 | 452 | 69 | 110 | 149 | 15 | 6 | 4 | 44 | 2 | 3 | 57 | 5 | 72 | 20 | 3 | .243 |
| Klutts, Gene, W.H. | 69 | 221 | 26 | 48 | 66 | 10 | 1 | 2 | 23 | 3 | 3 | 21 | 5 | 36 | 1 | 3 | .217 |
| Landestoy, Rafael, Wat. | 130 | 439 | 61 | 123 | 147 | 10 | 7 | 0 | 31 | 9 | 2 | 31 | 1 | 61 | 41 | 13 | .280 |
| Landreth, Larry, Q.C. | 26 | 0 | 1 | 0 | 0 | 0 | 0 | 0 | 0 | 0 | 0 | 0 | 0 | 0 | 0 | 0 | .000 |
| LaRocque, Gary, T.M.* | 6 | 16 | 0 | 2 | 2 | 0 | 0 | 0 | 2 | 0 | 0 | 2 | 0 | 1 | 0 | 0 | .125 |
| Lett, James, T.R. | 128 | 432 | 27 | 111 | 136 | 18 | 2 | 1 | 49 | 13 | 7 | 43 | 6 | 38 | 6 | 5 | .257 |
| Lindsey, Stephen, W.H. | 86 | 267 | 25 | 65 | 94 | 13 | 2 | 4 | 25 | 1 | 2 | 29 | 2 | 61 | 3 | 0 | .243 |
| Magner, Richard, Wat. | 97 | 296 | 41 | 83 | 97 | 8 | 3 | 0 | 30 | 7 | 2 | 25 | 3 | 41 | 5 | 0 | .280 |
| Mahlberg, Gregory, Pitt.* | 111 | 324 | 41 | 61 | 79 | 9 | 0 | 3 | 27 | 7 | 2 | 53 | 4 | 39 | 1 | 1 | .188 |
| Mannerino, Frank, Bris. | 132 | 439 | 50 | 106 | 147 | 20 | 3 | 5 | 46 | 3 | 2 | 52 | 3 | 34 | 2 | 5 | .241 |
| Mantlo, Gerald, T.M. | 95 | 279 | 29 | 72 | 106 | 13 | 0 | 7 | 27 | 7 | 1 | 12 | 2 | 47 | 2 | 0 | .258 |
| Martinez, Orlando, Pitt.† | 20 | 27 | 2 | 11 | 11 | 0 | 0 | 0 | 3 | 2 | 0 | 3 | 0 | 4 | 0 | 0 | .407 |
| Martinez, Sebastian, Bris. | 60 | 194 | 15 | 44 | 46 | 2 | 0 | 0 | 13 | 0 | 2 | 3 | 0 | 13 | 0 | 2 | .227 |
| McLaughlin, Alan, Read. | 129 | 502 | 72 | 139 | 155 | 12 | 2 | 0 | 36 | 8 | 1 | 33 | 1 | 26 | 11 | 3 | .277 |
| McLaurine, W. Lee, T.M.* | 49 | 1 | 0 | 0 | 0 | 0 | 0 | 0 | 0 | 0 | 0 | 0 | 0 | 0 | 0 | 0 | .000 |
| McLin, Anthony, Bris. | 83 | 289 | 31 | 69 | 80 | 11 | 0 | 0 | 28 | 4 | 4 | 26 | 2 | 39 | 1 | 2 | .239 |
| McPherson, George, T.R.* | 38 | 84 | 10 | 13 | 18 | 2 | 0 | 1 | 2 | 0 | 0 | 15 | 1 | 13 | 4 | 3 | .155 |
| Meier, George, T.R. | 6 | 10 | 0 | 0 | 0 | 0 | 0 | 0 | 1 | 0 | 0 | 0 | 0 | 3 | 0 | 0 | .000 |
| Mejias, Samuel, T.M. | 134 | 455 | 56 | 103 | 154 | 18 | 3 | 9 | 50 | 2 | 1 | 44 | 1 | 67 | 18 | 4 | .226 |
| Meltz, Richard, W.H. | 1 | 4 | 1 | 0 | 0 | 0 | 0 | 0 | 0 | 0 | 0 | 0 | 0 | 2 | 0 | 0 | .000 |
| Mersch, Neal, W.H. | 38 | 1 | 0 | 0 | 0 | 0 | 0 | 0 | 0 | 0 | 0 | 0 | 0 | 1 | 0 | 0 | .000 |
| Meyers, Charles, Bris.* | 90 | 305 | 40 | 85 | 105 | 12 | 1 | 2 | 27 | 1 | 4 | 23 | 1 | 15 | 2 | 2 | .279 |
| Moore, David, T.R. | 27 | 59 | 1 | 5 | 5 | 0 | 0 | 0 | 0 | 4 | 0 | 0 | 0 | 33 | 0 | 0 | .085 |
| Munoz, J. Edward, T.R. | 122 | 383 | 43 | 86 | 108 | 11 | 4 | 1 | 22 | 5 | 2 | 47 | 2 | 60 | 19 | 3 | .225 |
| Murray, Larry, W.H.† | 105 | 396 | 60 | 99 | 139 | 14 | 4 | 6 | 32 | 4 | 2 | 41 | 1 | 60 | 28 | 8 | .250 |
| Mutz, Thomas, T.R.* | 71 | 202 | 20 | 48 | 59 | 5 | 0 | 2 | 18 | 1 | 2 | 39 | 0 | 21 | 3 | 3 | .238 |
| Newell, Stephen, Q.C.† | 117 | 424 | 42 | 101 | 124 | 8 | 0 | 5 | 31 | 4 | 2 | 31 | 2 | 47 | 14 | 2 | .238 |
| Nina, Rafael, T.R.† | 113 | 317 | 24 | 69 | 81 | 8 | 2 | 0 | 24 | 5 | 3 | 31 | 0 | 38 | 12 | 12 | .218 |
| Overstreet, David, T.R. | 41 | 48 | 10 | 11 | 13 | 2 | 0 | 0 | 3 | 7 | 0 | 1 | 2 | 14 | 0 | 0 | .229 |
| Pacheco, Edwin, W.H. | 53 | 168 | 11 | 35 | 45 | 10 | 0 | 0 | 11 | 2 | 2 | 6 | 0 | 17 | 0 | 0 | .208 |
| Pagnotta, Michael, T.M. | 49 | 152 | 12 | 27 | 40 | 4 | 0 | 3 | 10 | 3 | 0 | 6 | 0 | 27 | 0 | 0 | .178 |
| Patchin, Steven, Wat. | 127 | 435 | 48 | 128 | 186 | 24 | 2 | 10 | 67 | 2 | 2 | 66 | 0 | 34 | 6 | 7 | .294 |
| Peguero, Felix, Q.C.† | 84 | 279 | 28 | 66 | 78 | 9 | 0 | 1 | 22 | 9 | 4 | 13 | 6 | 41 | 14 | 8 | .237 |
| Phillips, Lanny, Bris. | 123 | 445 | 37 | 129 | 148 | 12 | 2 | 1 | 56 | 2 | 3 | 38 | 7 | 31 | 2 | 3 | .290 |
| Philyaw, Thaddeus, Wat.* | 57 | 185 | 13 | 36 | 50 | 7 | 2 | 1 | 20 | 0 | 4 | 21 | 1 | 34 | 0 | 1 | .195 |
| Polaski, Robert 4ST R-13Wat | 61 | 173 | 22 | 37 | 46 | 6 | 0 | 1 | 18 | 2 | 1 | 29 | 1 | 30 | 1 | 3 | .214 |
| Polinsky, Robert, W.H. | 24 | 2 | 0 | 0 | 0 | 0 | 0 | 0 | 0 | 0 | 0 | 0 | 0 | 0 | 0 | 0 | .000 |
| Poloni, John, Pitt.* | 7 | 3 | 1 | 1 | 1 | 0 | 0 | 0 | 0 | 0 | 0 | 1 | 0 | 1 | 0 | 0 | .333 |
| Pyka, Terry, Pitt. | 130 | 439 | 46 | 99 | 122 | 10 | 2 | 3 | 45 | 6 | 4 | 47 | 2 | 82 | 10 | 3 | .226 |
| Quintana, Willibaldo, Read. | 91 | 280 | 25 | 75 | 93 | 10 | 4 | 0 | 28 | 2 | 4 | 16 | 4 | 19 | 2 | 3 | .268 |
| Reece, Robert, Q.C. | 24 | 83 | 6 | 13 | 15 | 2 | 0 | 0 | 2 | 0 | 2 | 2 | 0 | 10 | 0 | 0 | .157 |
| Richardson, James, T.M. | 57 | 166 | 20 | 31 | 59 | 4 | 0 | 8 | 15 | 0 | 0 | 27 | 1 | 41 | 0 | 0 | .187 |
| Riggleman, James, Wat. | 129 | 439 | 61 | 113 | 174 | 14 | 7 | 11 | 57 | 5 | 2 | 54 | 3 | 86 | 14 | 7 | .257 |
| Roatche, J. Daniel, Bris. | 30 | 79 | 12 | 12 | 15 | 3 | 0 | 0 | 9 | 1 | 1 | 8 | 1 | 18 | 1 | 0 | .152 |
| Roenicke, Gary, Q.C. | 131 | 466 | 67 | 133 | 198 | 23 | 0 | 14 | 74 | 0 | 5 | 58 | 12 | 73 | 6 | 5 | .285 |
| Rogodzinski, Michael, Read.* | 42 | 137 | 16 | 29 | 48 | 2 | 1 | 5 | 23 | 0 | 3 | 22 | 3 | 35 | 1 | 0 | .212 |
| Ruddell, Michael, T.R. | 13 | 13 | 0 | 1 | 1 | 0 | 0 | 0 | 0 | 0 | 0 | 0 | 0 | 3 | 0 | 0 | .077 |
| Ruling, Stephen, T.M. | 29 | 1 | 0 | 0 | 0 | 0 | 0 | 0 | 0 | 0 | 0 | 0 | 0 | 0 | 0 | 0 | .000 |
| Sakata, Lenn, T.M. | 121 | 421 | 63 | 108 | 150 | 9 | 3 | 9 | 43 | 6 | 4 | 52 | 3 | 67 | 16 | 5 | .257 |
| Salter, Robert, Read. | 14 | 40 | 4 | 10 | 10 | 0 | 0 | 0 | 1 | 0 | 1 | 6 | 0 | 6 | 0 | 0 | .250 |
| Santo Domingo, Rafael, TR† | 110 | 341 | 29 | 69 | 76 | 5 | 1 | 0 | 13 | 6 | 1 | 27 | 1 | 79 | 8 | 6 | .202 |
| Sarmiento, Manuel, T.R. | 64 | 33 | 0 | 6 | 7 | 1 | 0 | 0 | 1 | 0 | 0 | 1 | 0 | 11 | 0 | 0 | .182 |
| Sherrill, Dennis, W.H. | 113 | 335 | 47 | 74 | 97 | 10 | 1 | 1 | 34 | 16 | 2 | 23 | 2 | 73 | 8 | 3 | .221 |
| Shubert, Richard, Pitt.* | 22 | 1 | 0 | 0 | 0 | 0 | 0 | 0 | 0 | 0 | 0 | 1 | 0 | 1 | 0 | 0 | .000 |
| Shupe, John, W.H.* | 30 | 86 | 15 | 22 | 32 | 7 | 0 | 1 | 13 | 0 | 0 | 23 | 3 | 15 | 1 | 0 | .256 |
| Silicato, Thomas, T.R. | 64 | 207 | 23 | 47 | 53 | 6 | 0 | 0 | 17 | 6 | 2 | 26 | 1 | 25 | 6 | 1 | .227 |
| Skalisky, Roger, Read.* | 41 | 130 | 11 | 30 | 41 | 5 | 0 | 2 | 16 | 2 | 1 | 5 | 1 | 22 | 0 | 0 | .231 |
| Smith, Keith, Pitt. | 101 | 338 | 31 | 84 | 114 | 10 | 7 | 2 | 30 | 2 | 3 | 14 | 3 | 29 | 5 | 3 | .249 |
| Stafford, Gil, T.M. | 26 | 65 | 4 | 8 | 12 | 1 | 0 | 1 | 5 | 2 | 1 | 2 | 0 | 20 | 1 | 0 | .123 |
| Steele, J. Timothy, Wat.* | 92 | 282 | 34 | 60 | 91 | 9 | 2 | 6 | 36 | 2 | 8 | 52 | 2 | 70 | 1 | 1 | .213 |
| Steen, Michael, Pitt. | 23 | 1 | 0 | 0 | 0 | 0 | 0 | 0 | 0 | 0 | 0 | 0 | 0 | 0 | 0 | 0 | .000 |
| Stitzel, Glenn, Read.* | 109 | 341 | 49 | 99 | 139 | 17 | 1 | 7 | 56 | 3 | 4 | 56 | 0 | 25 | 3 | 1 | .290 |
| Stouffer, Blair, Pitt.† | 61 | 181 | 24 | 48 | 59 | 8 | 0 | 1 | 18 | 1 | 0 | 38 | 2 | 52 | 7 | 2 | .265 |
| Sutton, Johnny, Pitt. | 51 | 2 | 0 | 0 | 0 | 0 | 0 | 0 | 0 | 0 | 0 | 0 | 0 | 1 | 0 | 0 | .000 |
| Thomas, Danny, T.M. | 53 | 191 | 25 | 48 | 85 | 11 | 1 | 8 | 23 | 0 | 0 | 15 | 3 | 42 | 9 | 2 | .251 |
| Thomas, James, Pitt. | 47 | 135 | 7 | 27 | 31 | 4 | 0 | 0 | 11 | 2 | 2 | 9 | 0 | 34 | 0 | 0 | .200 |
| Thomas, Roy, Read. | 10 | 2 | 0 | 0 | 0 | 0 | 0 | 0 | 1 | 0 | 0 | 0 | 0 | 1 | 0 | 0 | .000 |
| Vasquez, George, T.M.† | 64 | 191 | 19 | 45 | 74 | 11 | 0 | 6 | 20 | 0 | 0 | 31 | 5 | 45 | 1 | 0 | .236 |
| Ward, Edgar, T.R.* | 122 | 411 | 44 | 106 | 143 | 26 | 1 | 3 | 45 | 2 | 0 | 56 | 6 | 71 | 4 | 1 | .258 |
| Webb, Marvin, Wat. | 98 | 330 | 35 | 82 | 112 | 11 | 5 | 3 | 46 | 8 | 7 | 23 | 1 | 36 | 3 | 4 | .248 |
| Whitt, Ernest, Bris.* | 82 | 252 | 29 | 64 | 81 | 9 | 1 | 2 | 19 | 3 | 1 | 33 | 0 | 19 | 2 | 3 | .254 |
| Wills, Elliott, Pitt.† | 122 | 456 | 72 | 140 | 194 | 23 | 2 | 9 | 49 | 2 | 3 | 46 | 7 | 52 | 13 | 5 | .307 |
| Wissell, Richard, Read.* | 22 | 73 | 13 | 17 | 26 | 3 | 0 | 2 | 11 | 0 | 0 | 13 | 0 | 8 | 1 | 0 | .233 |

The following pitchers had no plate appearances primarily through use of designated-hitters, listed alphabetically by club, games in parentheses:

BRISTOL—Bomback, Mark (22); Brayton, Roswell (20); Farias, Thomas (19); Foran, Stephen

(23); Jones, T. Frederick (13); Kouns, William (8); LaRose, H. John (20); Percival, Curran (11); Ripley, Allen (1); Ross, Charles (6); Sbragia, Barry (10); Scruggs, E. Keith (19); Spencer, Gerald (14); Watkins, Kenneth (31); Wright, James C. (11).

PITTSFIELD—Brown, John M. (9); Fairbanks, Randal (28); Szado, Edward (2).

QUEBEC CITY—Abraham, Brian (19); Albin, Donald (15); Drumright, David (25); Dues, Hal (3); Fierbaugh, N. Randolph (23); Hannahs, Gerald (19); Keener, Joseph (7); Kerrigan, Joseph (27); Leonhard, David (20); Murphy, Timothy (1); O'Neill, Gerard (9); Riley, Edward (6); Rushing, Kenneth (19).

READING—Brenizer, Todd (12); Cates, Steve (8); Chamberlain, James (25); Greenhalgh, Daniel (14); Hernandez, Guillermo (13); Kiser, Larry (12); Kniffin, Charles (18); Kreke, Donald (14); Lerch, Randy (25); McCoy, Patrick (19); Molush, Edward (9); Seoane, Manuel (17); Thomason, M. Erskine (6).

THETFORD MINES—Anderson, Lawrence (8); Beare, Gary (36); Currence, D. Lafayette (19); Erardi, J. Gregory (11); Hinds, Samuel (25); Morris, John (5); Widmar, A. Thomas (26); Yount, Lawrence (22).

WATERBURY—Badcock, W. Thomas (28); Corrigan, Lawrence (10); Donovan, John (7); Forry, Dewey (53); Lanfair, David (17); Lesslie, Robert (28); Mestek, Robert (27); Rautzhan, Clarence (28); Standley, Donald (30); Todd, Guy (2); Van Der Beek, James (27).

WEST HAVEN—Anderson, Richard L. (21); Arnold, Robert L. (35); Clay, Kenneth (15); Heinold, Douglas (23); Hoyt, D. LaMarr (6); Lawson, David (24); McElwain, Eugene (33); Norris, Jody (6); Olivo, Milciades (4); Spinks, Scipio (7).

GRAND-SLAM HOME RUNS—Astroth, Bastable, Rosetti, R. Davis, Gantner, Gates, D. Iorg, Irwin, Klobas, Steele, Stitzel, Wills, 1 each.

AWARDED FIRST BASE ON INTERFERENCE—Espy (Pacheco), Polaski (Mahlberg), Smith (Bastable).

## CLUB FIELDING

| Club | G. | PO. | A. | E. | DP. | PB. | Pct. | Club | G. | PO. | A. | E. | DP. | PB. | Pct. |
|------|----|----|----|----|----|----|----|------|----|----|----|----|----|----|----|
| Three Rivers | 137 | 3438 | 1256 | 159 | 85 | 22 | .9672 | West Haven | 137 | 3416 | 1475 | 205 | 89 | 14 | .960 |
| Reading | 137 | 3384 | 1417 | 166 | 114 | 25 | .9665 | Quebec City | 136 | 3432 | 1411 | 203 | 102 | 18 | .960 |
| Bristol | 138 | 3416 | 1451 | 179 | 97 | 19 | .965 | Thetford Mines | 139 | 3367 | 1430 | 205 | 120 | 21 | .959 |
| Pittsfield | 132 | 3206 | 1389 | 180 | 123 | 23 | .962 | Waterbury | 136 | 3422 | 1480 | 228 | 135 | 17 | .956 |

Triple Play—Waterbury.

## INDIVIDUAL FIELDING

*Throws lefthanded.

### FIRST BASEMEN

| Player and Club | G. | PO. | A. | E. | DP. | Pct. | Player and Club | G. | PO. | A. | E. | DP. | Pct. |
|------|----|----|----|----|----|----|------|----|----|----|----|----|----|
| Ward, T.R.* | 92 | 712 | 32 | 3 | 52 | .996 | Biagini, Q.C. | 59 | 480 | 29 | 7 | 42 | .986 |
| Steele, Wat.* | 92 | 812 | 44 | 4 | 69 | .995 | Ault, Pitt.* | 75 | 596 | 43 | 10 | 65 | .985 |
| Bergman, W.H.* | 64 | 539 | 58 | 3 | 38 | .995 | Shupe, W.H.* | 12 | 109 | 12 | 2 | 9 | .984 |
| Lindsey, W.H. | 38 | 360 | 20 | 2 | 23 | .995 | Clark, T.M. | 45 | 343 | 14 | 6 | 34 | .983 |
| Duran, Pitt.* | 53 | 457 | 33 | 3 | 42 | .994 | Newell, Q.C. | 76 | 616 | 46 | 12 | 46 | .982 |
| Stitzel, Read. | 22 | 145 | 11 | 1 | 11 | .994 | Manto, T.M. | 30 | 284 | 13 | 6 | 20 | .980 |
| Fritz, Read.* | 15 | 138 | 7 | 1 | 8 | .993 | Jefferson, Bris. | 40 | 340 | 28 | 8 | 26 | .979 |
| Coleman, Bris. | 64 | 567 | 25 | 5 | 42 | .992 | Bernhardt, W.H. | 27 | 260 | 19 | 6 | 12 | .979 |
| Lett, T.R. | 38 | 302 | 22 | 3 | 19 | .991 | Espy, T.M. | 16 | 130 | 2 | 3 | 8 | .978 |
| IORG, Read. | 97 | 827 | 44 | 9 | 78 | .990 | Richardson, T.M. | 52 | 424 | 22 | 12 | 49 | .974 |
| Bennett, Bris. | 29 | 246 | 14 | 3 | 13 | .989 | Patchin, Wat. | 48 | 420 | 20 | 13 | 53 | .971 |

#### (Fewer Than Ten Games)

| Player and Club | G. | PO. | A. | E. | DP. | Pct. | Player and Club | G. | PO. | A. | E. | DP. | Pct. |
|------|----|----|----|----|----|----|------|----|----|----|----|----|----|
| Doerr, T.R. | 9 | 43 | 3 | 0 | 4 | 1.000 | Jaramillo, Pitt. | 3 | 2 | 0 | 0 | 0 | 1.000 |
| DeArmas, Read | 6 | 36 | 0 | 0 | 4 | 1.000 | Polaski, T.R. | 1 | 2 | 0 | 0 | 1 | 1.000 |
| Pyka, Pitt. | 4 | 28 | 0 | 0 | 3 | 1.000 | Husband, T.R. | 6 | 32 | 2 | 1 | 1 | .971 |
| Crowley, Q.C.* | 3 | 16 | 0 | 0 | 2 | 1.000 | Goodman, Q.C. | 5 | 30 | 4 | 1 | 0 | .971 |
| Driscoll, T.R. | 1 | 8 | 2 | 0 | 0 | 1.000 | Jacobson, T.M. | 3 | 19 | 3 | 1 | 2 | .957 |
| Bastable, Read. | 2 | 6 | 2 | 0 | 0 | 1.000 | Roatche, Bris. | 8 | 69 | 4 | 4 | 5 | .948 |
| Whitt, Bris. | 1 | 6 | 1 | 0 | 1 | 1.000 | Magner, Wat. | 1 | 3 | 0 | 1 | 0 | .750 |

Triple Play—Steele.

### SECOND BASEMEN

| Player and Club | G. | PO. | A. | E. | DP. | Pct. | Player and Club | G. | PO. | A. | E. | DP. | Pct. |
|------|----|----|----|----|----|----|------|----|----|----|----|----|----|
| Silicato, T.R. | 59 | 127 | 138 | 2 | 16 | .993 | Andrew, Bris. | 17 | 44 | 35 | 3 | 6 | .963 |
| Meyers, Bris. | 61 | 116 | 152 | 5 | 33 | .982 | Creech, Q.C. | 12 | 21 | 31 | 2 | 4 | .963 |
| Nina, T.R. | 50 | 115 | 121 | 5 | 23 | .979 | Coulson, W.H. | 126 | 220 | 306 | 24 | 49 | .956 |
| Ireland, QT-T.R. | 36 | 88 | 102 | 4 | 17 | .979 | Peguero, Q.C. | 72 | 130 | 152 | 13 | 33 | .956 |
| McLAUGHLIN, Re. | 129 | 309 | 296 | 15 | 65 | .976 | Bordes, Pitt. | 23 | 56 | 70 | 6 | 15 | .955 |
| Wills, Pitt. | 60 | 138 | 149 | 7 | 39 | .976 | Dillard, Bris. | 15 | 30 | 33 | 3 | 8 | .955 |
| Sakata, T.M. | 117 | 243 | 304 | 16 | 77 | .972 | Webb, Wat. | 26 | 51 | 73 | 6 | 13 | .954 |
| Daniels, Pitt. | 54 | 128 | 141 | 9 | 35 | .968 | Cunningham, Q.C. | 58 | 119 | 132 | 20 | 25 | .926 |
| Baez, Wat | 114 | 289 | 337 | 22 | 83 | .966 | Clark, T.M. | 15 | 29 | 37 | 6 | 7 | .917 |
| Benedetti, Bris. | 53 | 106 | 142 | 9 | 21 | .965 | | | | | | | |

### (Fewer Than Ten Games)

| Player and Club | G. | PO. | A. | E. | DP. | Pct. |
|---|---|---|---|---|---|---|
| Larocque, T.M. | 6 | 13 | 24 | 0 | 3 | 1.000 |
| Espy, T.M. | 2 | 0 | 3 | 0 | 0 | 1.000 |
| Cooper, Pitt. | 1 | 3 | 0 | 0 | 0 | 1.000 |
| Klobas, Read. | 9 | 25 | 30 | 1 | 9 | .982 |
| Pacheco, W.H. | 7 | 12 | 15 | 2 | 2 | .931 |
| Danforth, T.M. | 4 | 4 | 9 | 1 | 1 | .929 |
| Iorg, W.H. | 5 | 10 | 10 | 2 | 3 | .909 |
| Pagnotta, T.M. | 2 | 5 | 4 | 1 | 2 | .900 |
| Polaski, Wat. | 2 | 0 | 7 | 1 | 2 | .875 |
| Doerr, T.R. | 2 | 1 | 3 | 1 | 0 | .800 |

Triple Play—Baez.

### THIRD BASEMEN

| Player and Club | G. | PO. | A. | E. | DP. | Pct. |
|---|---|---|---|---|---|---|
| Bucci, Pitt. | 12 | 13 | 21 | 0 | 0 | 1.000 |
| COOPER, Pitt. | 97 | 77 | 204 | 11 | 12 | .962 |
| Cunningham, Q.C. | 26 | 17 | 34 | 2 | 2 | .962 |
| Lett, T.R. | 90 | 77 | 144 | 9 | 12 | .961 |
| Klobas, Read. | 40 | 34 | 89 | 8 | 10 | .939 |
| Kelly, Q.C. | 28 | 31 | 44 | 5 | 3 | .938 |
| Gantner, T.M. | 135 | 118 | 310 | 29 | 18 | .937 |
| Daniels, Pitt. | 20 | 15 | 44 | 4 | 3 | .937 |
| Hobson, Bris. | 137 | 102 | 309 | 28 | 29 | .936 |
| Bastable, Read. | 21 | 37 | 4 | 3 |  | .935 |
| Stitzel, Read. | 78 | 54 | 172 | 16 | 16 | .934 |
| Doerr, T.R. | 53 | 40 | 104 | 11 | 9 | .929 |
| Klutts, W.H. | 68 | 50 | 168 | 17 | 14 | .928 |
| Gates, Q.C. | 87 | 83 | 179 | 26 | 16 | .910 |
| Iorg, W.H. | 51 | 31 | 128 | 20 | 5 | .888 |
| Lindsey, W.H. | 10 | 6 | 17 | 3 | 1 | .885 |
| Riggleman, Wat. | 129 | 106 | 267 | 53 | 30 | .876 |
| Bernhardt, W.H. | 13 | 7 | 23 | 5 | 1 | .857 |

### (Fewer Than Ten Games)

| Player and Club | G. | PO. | A. | E. | DP. | Pct. |
|---|---|---|---|---|---|---|
| Fischetti, Wat. | 5 | 4 | 8 | 0 | 0 | 1.000 |
| Danforth, T.M. | 3 | 3 | 6 | 0 | 1 | 1.000 |
| Bordes, Pitt. | 2 | 4 | 3 | 0 | 1 | 1.000 |
| Webb, Wat. | 1 | 0 | 6 | 0 | 0 | 1.000 |
| Pyka, Pitt. | 2 | 3 | 2 | 0 | 0 | 1.000 |
| Pacheco, W.H. | 3 | 1 | 3 | 0 | 0 | 1.000 |
| Mahlberg, Pitt. | 1 | 1 | 1 | 0 | 0 | 1.000 |
| Meyers, Bris. | 1 | 1 | 0 | 0 | 0 | 1.000 |
| Bosetti, Read. | 4 | 1 | 6 | 1 | 2 | .875 |
| Essian, Read. | 3 | 2 | 5 | 1 | 1 | .875 |
| Clark, T.M. | 4 | 2 | 3 | 1 | 1 | .833 |
| Creech, Q.C. | 2 | 2 | 1 | 1 | 1 | .750 |
| Polaski, Wat. | 3 | 3 | 2 | 3 | 1 | .625 |
| Jefferson, Bris. | 1 | 0 | 1 | 1 | 0 | .500 |

### SHORTSTOPS

| Player and Club | G. | PO. | A. | E. | DP. | Pct. |
|---|---|---|---|---|---|---|
| Bordes, Pitt. | 17 | 29 | 41 | 2 | 12 | .972 |
| Dancy, Read. | 37 | 60 | 126 | 6 | 24 | .969 |
| Iorg, W.H. | 22 | 38 | 64 | 4 | 9 | .962 |
| Gingrich, Q.C. | 40 | 62 | 102 | 7 | 17 | .959 |
| Creech, Q.C. | 72 | 142 | 204 | 16 | 40 | .956 |
| Espy, T.M. | 19 | 28 | 49 | 4 | 10 | .951 |
| Doerr, T.R. | 15 | 22 | 31 | 3 | 9 | .946 |
| DANFORTH, T.M. | 97 | 141 | 298 | 29 | 58 | .938 |
| Santo Domingo, T.R. | 110 | 157 | 228 | 27 | 37 | .934 |
| Crane, Read. | 23 | 34 | 59 | 7 | 9 | .930 |
| Wills, Pitt. | 52 | 85 | 155 | 19 | 38 | .927 |
| Sherrill, W.H. | 112 | 159 | 332 | 39 | 38 | .926 |
| Stouffer, Pitt. | 60 | 98 | 163 | 21 | 32 | .926 |
| Klobas, Read. | 76 | 131 | 201 | 27 | 30 | .925 |
| Cunningham, Q.C. | 32 | 35 | 76 | 9 | 8 | .925 |
| Benedetti, Bris. | 40 | 58 | 104 | 15 | 11 | .915 |
| Ford, Bris. | 108 | 154 | 267 | 40 | 42 | .913 |
| Landestoy, Wat. | 126 | 199 | 387 | 60 | 73 | .907 |
| Clark, T.M. | 24 | 29 | 58 | 10 | 8 | .897 |

Triple Play—Landestoy.

### (Fewer Than Ten Games)

| Player and Club | G. | PO. | A. | E. | DP. | Pct. |
|---|---|---|---|---|---|---|
| Ireland, T.R. | 1 | 0 | 1 | 0 | 0 | 1.000 |
| Stitzel, Read. | 5 | 7 | 12 | 1 | 1 | .950 |
| Daniels, Pitt. | 6 | 7 | 16 | 3 | 3 | .885 |
| Klutts, W.H. | 3 | 3 | 12 | 2 | 0 | .882 |
| Webb, Wat. | 7 | 12 | 15 | 4 | 3 | .871 |
| L. Jones, T.R. | 7 | 13 | 19 | 5 | 0 | .865 |
| Collins, Wat. | 4 | 3 | 9 | 2 | 0 | .857 |
| Driscoll, T.R. | 7 | 13 | 13 | 5 | 2 | .839 |
| Pacheco, W.H. | 7 | 5 | 10 | 3 | 0 | .833 |
| Gantner, T.M. | 5 | 11 | 7 | 4 | 1 | .818 |
| Harrison, T.R. | 4 | 10 | 10 | 6 | 2 | .769 |
| Lindsey, W.H. | 1 | 0 | 0 | 1 | 0 | .000 |
| Polaski, Wat. | 1 | 0 | 0 | 1 | 0 | .000 |

### OUTFIELDERS

| Player and Club | G. | PO. | A. | E. | DP. | Pct. |
|---|---|---|---|---|---|---|
| Arnett, Pitt.* | 19 | 47 | 2 | 0 | 0 | 1.000 |
| Espy, T.M. | 21 | 33 | 6 | 0 | 0 | 1.000 |
| Jacobson, T.M. | 25 | 32 | 0 | 0 | 0 | 1.000 |
| Klobas, Read. | 14 | 24 | 1 | 0 | 0 | 1.000 |
| Bastable, Read. | 11 | 21 | 3 | 0 | 0 | 1.000 |
| Mahlberg, Pitt. | 10 | 13 | 1 | 0 | 0 | 1.000 |
| MUNOZ, T.R. | 112 | 236 | 9 | 3 | 1 | .988 |
| Bowen, Bris. | 42 | 78 | 7 | 1 | 1 | .988 |
| L. Jones, T.R. | 40 | 76 | 6 | 1 | 0 | .988 |
| Polaski, TR-Wat. | 42 | 71 | 3 | 1 | 2 | .987 |
| Burke, Wat. | 119 | 211 | 7 | 4 | 0 | .982 |
| Bosetti, Read. | 108 | 232 | 12 | 5 | 1 | .980 |
| McLin, Bris. | 58 | 142 | 4 | 3 | 0 | .980 |
| Beasley, Pitt. | 79 | 169 | 5 | 4 | 1 | .978 |
| Mannerino, Bris. | 125 | 211 | 6 | 5 | 0 | .977 |
| Fitzgerald, Read. | 97 | 187 | 4 | 5 | 0 | .974 |
| Bergman, W.H.* | 51 | 71 | 3 | 2 | 0 | .974 |
| Carrion, Q.C. | 127 | 343 | 17 | 10 | 3 | .973 |
| Mejias, T.M. | 134 | 280 | 11 | 8 | 2 | .973 |
| Murray, W.H. | 105 | 245 | 6 | 7 | 1 | .973 |
| Bennett, Bris. | 65 | 131 | 8 | 4 | 1 | .972 |
| Detherage, Wat. | 127 | 313 | 11 | 11 | 3 | .967 |
| Jaramillo, Pitt. | 82 | 136 | 4 | 5 | 1 | .966 |
| Pyka, Pitt. | 125 | 258 | 16 | 10 | 5 | .965 |
| Phillips, Bris. | 114 | 180 | 14 | 7 | 2 | .965 |
| Jones, Read. | 113 | 201 | 14 | 8 | 2 | .964 |
| Quintana, Read. | 42 | 73 | 5 | 3 | 1 | .963 |
| Roenicke, Q.C. | 122 | 223 | 22 | 10 | 4 | .961 |
| Benson, W.H. | 72 | 116 | 7 | 5 | 3 | .961 |
| Alston, W.H. | 96 | 181 | 12 | 8 | 2 | .960 |
| Jones, W.H. | 95 | 155 | 12 | 7 | 5 | .960 |
| Webb, Wat. | 50 | 20 | 4 | 1 | 1 | .960 |
| R. Jones, T.R. | 76 | 209 | 3 | 9 | 0 | .959 |
| Husband, T.R. | 59 | 85 | 7 | 4 | 1 | .958 |
| Dimmel, Wat. | 125 | 212 | 12 | 11 | 0 | .953 |
| Hart, Q.C. | 114 | 181 | 12 | 10 | 0 | .951 |
| Nina, T.R. | 40 | 76 | 2 | 4 | 0 | .951 |
| Thomas, T.M. | 35 | 55 | 3 | 3 | 1 | .951 |
| McPherson, T.R.* | 30 | 53 | 5 | 3 | 1 | .951 |
| Biagini, Q.C. | 42 | 68 | 2 | 4 | 2 | .946 |
| Danson, T.M. | 116 | 209 | 13 | 13 | 1 | .945 |
| Colzie, T.R. | 23 | 45 | 0 | 3 | 0 | .938 |
| Davis, T.M. | 67 | 124 | 4 | 10 | 1 | .928 |
| Skalisky, Read. | 30 | 46 | 3 | 4 | 0 | .925 |
| Smith, Pitt. | 86 | 145 | 7 | 15 | 3 | .910 |
| Ward, T.R.* | 27 | 27 | 1 | 3 | 0 | .903 |
| Pagnotta, T.M. | 31 | 59 | 3 | 7 | 1 | .899 |
| Philyaw, Wat.* | 18 | 17 | 0 | 3 | 0 | .850 |

### (Fewer Than Ten Games)

| Player and Club | G. | PO. | A. | E. | DP. | Pct. | Player and Club | G. | PO. | A. | E. | DP. | Pct. |
|---|---|---|---|---|---|---|---|---|---|---|---|---|---|
| Newell, Q.C. ...... | 7 | 14 | 2 | 0 | 1 | 1.000 | Geigel, Bris.* .... | 1 | 2 | 0 | 0 | 0 | 1.000 |
| Rogodzinski, Read. | 3 | 7 | 0 | 0 | 0 | 1.000 | Stitzel, Read. .... | 1 | 2 | 0 | 0 | 0 | 1.000 |
| Thomas, Pitt. .... | 3 | 7 | 0 | 0 | 0 | 1.000 | Wissel, Read. .... | 1 | 1 | 0 | 0 | 1 | 1.000 |
| Astroth, Pitt. .... | 7 | 5 | 0 | 0 | 0 | 1.000 | Huizenga, Bris. ... | 7 | 11 | 2 | 1 | 0 | .929 |
| Landestoy, Wat. ... | 4 | 4 | 1 | 0 | 0 | 1.000 | Bohne, Q.C. ...... | 5 | 15 | 2 | 2 | 0 | .882 |
| Benedetti, Bris. ... | 1 | 4 | 0 | 0 | 0 | 1.000 | Patchin, Wat. .... | 5 | 5 | 0 | 1 | 0 | .833 |
| Lett, T.R. ...... | 2 | 3 | 0 | 0 | 0 | 1.000 | Jefferson, Bris. ... | 8 | 6 | 1 | 2 | 0 | .778 |
| Silicato, T.R. ...... | 2 | 2 | 0 | 0 | 0 | 1.000 | Whitt, Bris. ...... | 6 | 8 | 0 | 3 | 0 | .727 |

### CATCHERS

| Player and Club | G. | PO. | A. | E. | PB. | DP. | Pct. | Player and Club | G. | PO. | A. | E. | PB. | DP. | Pct. |
|---|---|---|---|---|---|---|---|---|---|---|---|---|---|---|---|
| Whitt, Bris. ..... | 69 | 349 | 36 | 4 | 10 | 3 | .990 | Goodman, Q.C. .. | 72 | 380 | 42 | 13 | 11 | 2 | .970 |
| Patchin, Wat. .. | 44 | 206 | 31 | 3 | 8 | 3 | .988 | Astroth, Pitt. ... | 29 | 144 | 19 | 5 | 15 | 3 | .970 |
| Mantlo, T.M. .. | 62 | 298 | 11 | 4 | 8 | 3 | .987 | Bastable, Read. | .102 | 492 | 79 | 18 | 17 | 14 | .969 |
| DEL BUSTO, TR | 81 | 405 | 57 | 8 | 12 | 6 | .983 | Vasquez, T.M. .. | 63 | 291 | 29 | 12 | 5 | 2 | .964 |
| Roatche, Bris. .. | 21 | 105 | 6 | 2 | 1 | 1 | .982 | Mahlberg, Pitt. .. | 88 | 413 | 60 | 18 | 7 | 3 | .963 |
| Magner, Wat. .. | 97 | 473 | 45 | 10 | 9 | 4 | .981 | Thomas, Pitt. ... | 20 | 69 | 7 | 3 | 1 | 0 | .962 |
| Martinez, Bris. .. | 57 | 296 | 41 | 8 | 8 | 5 | .977 | Salter, Read. .. | 14 | 83 | 8 | 4 | 5 | 1 | .958 |
| Childers, Q.C. .. | 48 | 211 | 37 | 6 | 3 | 5 | .976 | Pacheco, W.H. .. | 35 | 151 | 19 | 8 | 1 | 5 | .955 |
| Reece, Q.C. .... | 24 | 131 | 25 | 4 | 2 | 1 | .975 | Stafford, T.M. .. | 25 | 119 | 7 | 6 | 6 | 0 | .955 |
| Mutz, T.R. .... | 66 | 330 | 34 | 10 | 10 | 1 | .973 | DeArmas, Read.. | 14 | 69 | 2 | 4 | 1 | 1 | .947 |
| Irwin, W.H. .. | 106 | 594 | 45 | 19 | 12 | 5 | .971 | | | | | | | | |

### (Fewer Than Ten Games)

| Player and Club | G. | PO. | A. | E. | PB. | DP. | Pct. | Player and Club | G. | PO. | A. | E. | PB. | DP. | Pct. |
|---|---|---|---|---|---|---|---|---|---|---|---|---|---|---|---|
| Essian, Read. ... | 9 | 59 | 7 | 0 | 1 | 0 | 1.000 | Meier, T.R. ..... | 6 | 18 | 2 | 1 | 0 | 0 | .952 |
| Rogoczinski, Read. | 2 | 2 | 0 | 0 | 2 | 0 | 1.000 | Meltz, W.H. ..... | 1 | 3 | 0 | 1 | 1 | 0 | .750 |
| Newell, Q.C. ... | 1 | 1 | 0 | 0 | 2 | 0 | 1.000 | Clark, T.M. .... | 1 | 0 | 0 | 0 | 2 | 0 | .000 |
| Nina, T.R. ..... | 1 | 1 | 0 | 0 | 0 | 0 | 1.000 | | | | | | | | |

### PITCHERS

| Player and Club | G. | PO. | A. | E. | DP. | Pct. | Player and Club | G. | PO. | A. | E. | DP. | Pct. |
|---|---|---|---|---|---|---|---|---|---|---|---|---|---|
| CURRENCE, T.M.* | 19 | 5 | 25 | 0 | 2 | 1.000 | Polinsky, W.H. .... | 24 | 8 | 25 | 2 | 0 | .943 |
| Clay, W.H. ...... | 15 | 6 | 20 | 0 | 1 | 1.000 | Deidel, T.M.* .... | 28 | 1 | 15 | 1 | 0 | .941 |
| Badcock, Wat.* ... | 28 | 8 | 17 | 0 | 1 | 1.000 | Clyde, Pitt.* .... | 22 | 9 | 33 | 3 | 3 | .933 |
| Forry, Wat. ...... | 33 | 9 | 13 | 0 | 2 | 1.000 | Foran, Bris.* .... | 23 | 4 | 24 | 2 | 0 | .933 |
| LaRose, Bris.* .... | 20 | 4 | 17 | 0 | 1 | 1.000 | Gronlund, Q.C. ... | 21 | 10 | 18 | 2 | 3 | .933 |
| McElwain, W.H.* | 33 | 6 | 14 | 0 | 1 | 1.000 | Heintz, T.R.* .... | 44 | 5 | 9 | 1 | 1 | .933 |
| Sarmiento, T.R. .. | 64 | 6 | 13 | 0 | 1 | 1.000 | Mestek, Wat. .... | 27 | 9 | 18 | 2 | 1 | .931 |
| Widmar, T.M. .. | 26 | 4 | 15 | 0 | 2 | 1.000 | Spencer, Bris. ... | 14 | 11 | 28 | 3 | 1 | .929 |
| Kniffin, Read.* .. | 18 | 4 | 10 | 0 | 1 | 1.000 | Jensen, T.R.* .... | 20 | 3 | 10 | 1 | 1 | .929 |
| Kreke, Read. .... | 18 | 8 | 6 | 0 | 0 | 1.000 | Lanfair, Wat. .... | 17 | 2 | 11 | 1 | 1 | .929 |
| Dollar, T.R. .... | 51 | 3 | 9 | 0 | 0 | 1.000 | Percival, Bris. ... | 11 | 1 | 12 | 1 | 0 | .929 |
| McCoy, Read. .. | 19 | 2 | 10 | 0 | 0 | 1.000 | Landreth, Q.C. ... | 25 | 7 | 31 | 3 | 1 | .927 |
| Jones, Bris.* .... | 13 | 2 | 10 | 0 | 0 | 1.000 | Boggs, Pitt. .... | 24 | 14 | 24 | 3 | 1 | .927 |
| Leonhard, Q.C. .. | 20 | 2 | 9 | 0 | 1 | 1.000 | Armstrong, T.R. .. | 25 | 7 | 18 | 2 | 0 | .926 |
| McLaurine, T.M.* | 49 | 1 | 7 | 0 | 0 | 1.000 | Steen, Pitt.* .... | 21 | 5 | 19 | 2 | 0 | .923 |
| Albin, Q.C. .... | 15 | 0 | 8 | 0 | 0 | 1.000 | Arnold, W.H. .... | 35 | 7 | 5 | 1 | 0 | .923 |
| Brayton, Bris.* .. | 20 | 1 | 6 | 0 | 1 | 1.000 | Lesslie, Wat. .... | 28 | 7 | 28 | 3 | 1 | .921 |
| Brenizer, Read.* .. | 12 | 1 | 4 | 0 | 0 | 1.000 | Scruggs, Bris. ... | 19 | 3 | 8 | 1 | 1 | .917 |
| Ruling, T.M. .... | 29 | 0 | 4 | 0 | 0 | 1.000 | Davis, T.R. ..... | 29 | 11 | 42 | 5 | 4 | .914 |
| Sbragia, Bris. ... | 10 | 2 | 1 | 0 | 1 | 1.000 | Beare, T.M. ..... | 36 | 3 | 18 | 2 | 0 | .913 |
| Erardi, T.M. .... | 11 | 0 | 2 | 0 | 1 | 1.000 | Van Der Beek, Wat. | 27 | 7 | 23 | 3 | 1 | .909 |
| Bomback, Bris. ... | 21 | 7 | 27 | 1 | 0 | .971 | Shubert, Pitt.* .. | 22 | 7 | 23 | 3 | 1 | .909 |
| Rautzhan, Wat.* .. | 28 | 13 | 52 | 2 | 3 | .970 | Wright, Bris. .... | 10 | 7 | 13 | 2 | 0 | .909 |
| Alexander, T.M. .. | 26 | 5 | 25 | 1 | 2 | .968 | Seoane, Read. .... | 17 | 8 | 19 | 3 | 1 | .900 |
| Farias, Bris. .... | 19 | 5 | 25 | 1 | 2 | .968 | Chamberlain, Rea.* | 25 | 4 | 21 | 3 | 0 | .893 |
| Reinold, W.H. .. | 23 | 18 | 37 | 2 | 2 | .965 | Greenhalgh, Read. | 14 | 4 | 4 | 1 | 0 | .889 |
| Standley, Wat. .. | 30 | 4 | 23 | 1 | 1 | .964 | Sutton, Pitt. .... | 49 | 2 | 21 | 3 | 2 | .885 |
| Kiser, Read.* .... | 12 | 2 | 25 | 1 | 1 | .964 | Drumright, Q.C. .. | 23 | 9 | 27 | 5 | 3 | .878 |
| Anderson, W.H. .. | 21 | 10 | 16 | 1 | 0 | .963 | Barker, Pitt. .... | 24 | 8 | 20 | 4 | 1 | .875 |
| Abraham, Q.C.* .. | 19 | 5 | 21 | 1 | 2 | .963 | Hernandez, Read.* | 13 | 5 | 16 | 3 | 0 | .875 |
| Thomas, Read. .. | 10 | 8 | 16 | 1 | 1 | .960 | Moore, T.R. .... | 26 | 7 | 27 | 5 | 0 | .872 |
| Hannahs, Q.C.* .. | 19 | 3 | 18 | 1 | 0 | .955 | Boltano, Read. ... | 40 | 2 | 12 | 2 | 0 | .867 |
| Lerch, Read.* .... | 25 | 3 | 35 | 2 | 0 | .950 | Fierbaugh, Q.C. .. | 23 | 11 | 21 | 5 | 2 | .865 |
| Rushing, Q.C.* .. | 29 | 3 | 16 | 1 | 1 | .950 | Overstreet, T.R. .. | 27 | 4 | 21 | 4 | 3 | .862 |
| Kerrigan, Q.C. ... | 27 | 5 | 14 | 1 | 1 | .950 | Watkins, Bris. ... | 31 | 2 | 15 | 3 | 1 | .850 |
| Hinds, T.M. .... | 25 | 8 | 27 | 2 | 0 | .946 | Fairbanks, Pitt.* .. | 28 | 3 | 7 | 2 | 0 | .833 |
| Lawson, W.H. .... | 24 | 11 | 23 | 2 | 2 | .944 | Yount, T.M. ..... | 22 | 7 | 25 | 7 | 2 | .821 |
| Bolick, Pitt. .... | 30 | 3 | 14 | 1 | 1 | .944 | Corrigan, Wat. ... | 10 | 0 | 9 | 2 | 0 | .818 |
| Mersch, W.H. .... | 38 | 12 | 21 | 2 | 2 | .943 | Andujar, T.R. ... | 18 | 4 | 12 | 4 | 1 | .800 |

### (Fewer Than Ten Games)

| Player and Club | G. | PO. | A. | E. | DP. | Pct. | Player and Club | G. | PO. | A. | E. | DP. | Pct. |
|---|---|---|---|---|---|---|---|---|---|---|---|---|---|
| Anderson, T.M. ... | 8 | 4 | 10 | 0 | 0 | 1.000 | Dues, Q.C. ...... | 3 | 2 | 2 | 0 | 0 | 1.000 |
| Harper, Pitt. .... | 6 | 2 | 9 | 0 | 1 | 1.000 | Martinez, Pitt. ... | 6 | 2 | 1 | 0 | 0 | 1.000 |
| Ross, Bris.* ...... | 6 | 1 | 10 | 0 | 0 | 1.000 | Olivo, W.H. ..... | 4 | 2 | 1 | 0 | 0 | 1.000 |
| Morris, T.M. ...... | 5 | 3 | 4 | 0 | 0 | 1.000 | Norris, W.H. .... | 6 | 0 | 2 | 0 | 0 | 1.000 |

## PITCHERS—Continued
### (Fewer Than Ten Games)

| Player and Club | G. | PO. | A. | E. | DP. | Pct. |
|---|---|---|---|---|---|---|
| Murphy, Q.C.* | 1 | 0 | 2 | 0 | 0 | 1.000 |
| Ripley, Bris. | 1 | 1 | 1 | 0 | 0 | 1.000 |
| Molush, Read. | 9 | 0 | 1 | 0 | 0 | 1.000 |
| Riley, Q.C. | 6 | 1 | 0 | 0 | 0 | 1.000 |
| Thomason, Read. | 6 | 1 | 0 | 0 | 0 | 1.000 |
| Skalisky, Read. | 1 | 0 | 1 | 0 | 1 | 1.000 |
| Stitzel, Read. | 1 | 1 | 0 | 0 | 0 | 1.000 |
| Kouns, Bris. | 8 | 5 | 14 | 1 | 0 | .950 |
| Hume, T.R. | 7 | 5 | 8 | 1 | 0 | .929 |
| Hoyt, W.H. | 8 | 7 | 7 | 2 | 2 | .875 |
| Keener, Q.C. | 7 | 4 | 10 | 2 | 1 | .875 |
| O'Neill, Q.C.* | 9 | 2 | 4 | 1 | 0 | .857 |
| Spinks, W.H. | 7 | 3 | 3 | 1 | 0 | .857 |
| Poloni, Pitt.* | 7 | 2 | 8 | 2 | 1 | .833 |
| Brown, Pitt. | 9 | 3 | 3 | 2 | 1 | .750 |
| Cates, Read.* | 8 | 0 | 2 | 1 | 0 | .667 |
| Ruddell, T.R. | 7 | 1 | 0 | 2 | 0 | .333 |

The following players do not have any recorded accepted chances to the positions indicated; therefore, are not listed in the fielding averages for those particular positions: Bolick, of; Donovan, p; Gingrich, 1b; Jacobson, p; R. Jones, 1b; Klutts, 1b; Lett, p; Lindsey, of; O. Martinez, 3b; Munoz, p; Nina, p; Phillips, 2b; Stafford, p; Sutton, p; Szado*, p; Todd, p.

## CLUB PITCHING

| Club | G. | CG. | ShO. | Sv. | IP. | H. | R. | ER. | HR. | BB. | Int. BB. | HB. | SO. | WP. | Bk. | ERA. |
|---|---|---|---|---|---|---|---|---|---|---|---|---|---|---|---|---|
| Waterbury | 136 | 65 | 20 | 20 | 1141 | 1072 | 485 | 341 | 53 | 404 | 25 | 29 | 621 | 46 | 1 | 2.69 |
| Bristol | 138 | 77 | 21 | 19 | 1139 | 972 | 440 | 358 | 50 | 435 | 15 | 42 | 689 | 58 | 3 | 2.83 |
| Three Rivers | 137 | 27 | 14 | 20 | 1146 | 1039 | 488 | 402 | 41 | 466 | 43 | 43 | 687 | 37 | 12 | 3.16 |
| Reading | 137 | 64 | 15 | 24 | 1128 | 1098 | 476 | 404 | 51 | 332 | 29 | 24 | 656 | 51 | 6 | 3.22 |
| West Haven | 137 | 58 | 11 | 21 | 1139 | 1037 | 538 | 416 | 68 | 445 | 30 | 40 | 691 | 57 | 2 | 3.29 |
| Quebec City | 136 | 57 | 11 | 16 | 1144 | 1081 | 535 | 422 | 67 | 489 | 17 | 27 | 654 | 66 | 3 | 3.32 |
| Pittsfield | 132 | 54 | 9 | 15 | 1069 | 1020 | 537 | 434 | 45 | 567 | 33 | 33 | 599 | 76 | 6 | 3.65 |
| Thetford Mines | 139 | 56 | 9 | 17 | 1122 | 1084 | 590 | 474 | 93 | 562 | 12 | 38 | 633 | 88 | 3 | 3.80 |

## PITCHERS' RECORDS
### (Leading Qualifiers for Earned Run Average Leadership—112 or More Innings)
*Throws lefthanded.

| Pitcher—Club | G. | GS. | CG. | ShO. | W. | L. | Sv. | Pct. | IP. | H. | R. | ER. | HR. | BB. | Int. BB. | HB. | SO. | WP. | ERA. |
|---|---|---|---|---|---|---|---|---|---|---|---|---|---|---|---|---|---|---|---|
| Farias, Bristol | 19 | 18 | 14 | 3 | 7 | 11 | 0 | .389 | 145 | 103 | 42 | 25 | 4 | 46 | 5 | 4 | 87 | 7 | 1.55 |
| Rautzhan, Wat* | 28 | 28 | 21 | 4 | 14 | 10 | 0 | .583 | 218 | 200 | 73 | 50 | 6 | 62 | 4 | 6 | 115 | 8 | 2.06 |
| Lesslie, Wat | 28 | 28 | 16 | 3 | 15 | 8 | 0 | .652 | 193 | 166 | 94 | 47 | 10 | 63 | 5 | 5 | 114 | 5 | 2.19 |
| Davis, Three R | 29 | 24 | 8 | 2 | 11 | 12 | 0 | .478 | 178 | 159 | 66 | 44 | 4 | 62 | 8 | 8 | 105 | 5 | 2.22 |
| Heinold, West H | 23 | 23 | 12 | 2 | 10 | 7 | 0 | .588 | 169 | 139 | 60 | 43 | 4 | 36 | 0 | 9 | 74 | 6 | 2.29 |
| Bombach, Bristol | 21 | 21 | 14 | 2 | 12 | 6 | 0 | .667 | 163 | 130 | 49 | 42 | 13 | 59 | 0 | 0 | 118 | 5 | 2.32 |
| Seoane, Reading | 17 | 17 | 6 | 3 | 9 | 4 | 0 | .692 | 128 | 120 | 49 | 35 | 3 | 28 | 1 | 3 | 64 | 3 | 2.46 |
| Sarmiento, T R | 64 | 1 | 0 | 0 | 6 | 8 | 15 | .429 | 129 | 104 | 41 | 37 | 8 | 51 | 9 | 2 | 114 | 0 | 2.58 |
| Landreth, Que C | 25 | 25 | 17 | 4 | 10 | 12 | 0 | .455 | 181 | 143 | 78 | 54 | 8 | 85 | 3 | 1 | 133 | 13 | 2.69 |
| Lerch, Reading* | 25 | 25 | 14 | 1 | 16 | 6 | 0 | .727 | 177 | 173 | 66 | 53 | 4 | 45 | 2 | 8 | 108 | 7 | 2.69 |

Departmental Leaders: G—Sarmiento, 64; GS—Deidel, Lesslie, Rautzhan, 28; CG—Rautzhan, 21; ShO—Mestek, 5; W—Lerch, 16; L—Deidel, 14; Sv—Sarmiento, 15; Pct.—Lerch, .727; IP—Rautzhan, 218; H—Rautzhan, 200; R—Deidel, 95; ER—Deidel, 80; HR—Deidel, 24; BB—Deidel, 123; IBB—Sutton, 10; HB—Armstrong, Heinold, 9; SO—Anderson, 138; WP—Alexander, 16.

### (All Pitchers—Listed Alphabetically)

| Pitcher—Club | G. | GS. | CG. | ShO. | W. | L. | Sv. | Pct. | IP. | H. | R. | ER. | HR. | BB. | Int. BB. | HB. | SO. | WP. | ERA. |
|---|---|---|---|---|---|---|---|---|---|---|---|---|---|---|---|---|---|---|---|
| Abraham, Que C* | .19 | 18 | 7 | 0 | 5 | 12 | 1 | .294 | 118 | 137 | 65 | 50 | 9 | 46 | 2 | 3 | 44 | 9 | 3.81 |
| Albin, Que C | .15 | 0 | 0 | 0 | 5 | 0 | 5 | 1.000 | 29 | 27 | 7 | 7 | 2 | 8 | 1 | 0 | 21 | 2 | 2.17 |
| Alexander, Thet M | 26 | 16 | 7 | 2 | 8 | 7 | 1 | .533 | 122 | 119 | 71 | 51 | 7 | 55 | 0 | 4 | 46 | 16 | 3.76 |
| Anderson, Thet M | 8 | 8 | 3 | 0 | 4 | 0 | 0 | .429 | 56 | 43 | 23 | 21 | 1 | 23 | 1 | 2 | 38 | 10 | 3.38 |
| Anderson, West H. | 21 | 19 | 5 | 1 | 11 | 9 | 0 | .550 | 143 | 115 | 70 | 57 | 12 | 81 | 5 | 6 | 138 | 9 | 3.59 |
| Andujar, Three R. | 18 | 11 | 1 | 1 | 4 | 8 | 0 | .333 | 62 | 57 | 36 | 28 | 1 | 40 | 1 | 5 | 44 | 0 | 4.06 |
| Armstrong, T R | .25 | 24 | 5 | 1 | 5 | 10 | 0 | .333 | 150 | 116 | 55 | 45 | 6 | 44 | 4 | 9 | 86 | 3 | 2.70 |
| Arnold, West H. | 35 | 2 | 1 | 0 | 3 | 3 | 9 | .500 | 71 | 75 | 31 | 26 | 5 | 20 | 3 | 2 | 55 | 7 | 3.30 |
| Badcock, Wat* | .28 | 8 | 0 | 0 | 8 | 3 | 4 | .727 | 79 | 75 | 39 | 29 | 3 | 40 | 4 | 0 | 52 | 4 | 3.30 |
| Barker, Pittsfield | .24 | 24 | 10 | 3 | 7 | 12 | 0 | .368 | 159 | 117 | 72 | 51 | 5 | 109 | 2 | 6 | 133 | 15 | 2.89 |
| Beare, Thetford M. | 36 | 9 | 2 | 0 | 3 | 9 | 7 | .250 | 92 | 95 | 49 | 35 | 5 | 57 | 4 | 2 | 61 | 6 | 3.42 |
| Boggs, Pittsfield. | .24 | 24 | 12 | 2 | 10 | 11 | 0 | .476 | 162 | 153 | 84 | 63 | 10 | 73 | 4 | 4 | 100 | 11 | 3.50 |
| Boitano, Reading | 40 | 0 | 0 | 0 | 3 | 10 | .769 | 78 | 59 | 31 | 29 | 3 | 32 | 5 | 0 | 63 | 7 | 3.35 |
| Bolick, Pittsfield | .30 | 2 | 1 | 0 | 3 | 4 | 1 | .429 | 78 | 79 | 35 | 32 | 7 | 20 | 4 | 2 | 21 | 1 | 3.69 |
| Bombach, Bristol | 21 | 21 | 14 | 2 | 12 | 6 | 0 | .667 | 163 | 130 | 49 | 42 | 13 | 59 | 0 | 0 | 118 | 5 | 2.32 |
| Brayton, Bristol* | .20 | 2 | 1 | 0 | 2 | 6 | .500 | 50 | 43 | 14 | 12 | 1 | 21 | 1 | 1 | 26 | 1 | 2.16 |
| Brenizer, Reading* | 12 | 2 | 0 | 0 | 5 | 1 | .000 | 23 | 20 | 14 | 7 | 1 | 17 | 1 | 0 | 10 | 4 | 2.74 |
| Brown, Pittsfield | 9 | 2 | 0 | 0 | 1 | 0 | .000 | 18 | 17 | 10 | 7 | 0 | 10 | 0 | 1 | 5 | 1 | 3.50 |
| Cates, Reading* | 8 | 6 | 0 | 0 | 1 | 1 | 0 | .000 | 13 | 15 | 13 | 13 | 2 | 6 | 2 | 0 | 14 | 1 | 9.00 |
| Chamberlain, Read* | 25 | 25 | 10 | 3 | 11 | 10 | 0 | .524 | 172 | 179 | 79 | 69 | 18 | 33 | 4 | 6 | 90 | 8 | 3.61 |
| Clay, West Haven. | 15 | 6 | 2 | 0 | 2 | 4 | 0 | .833 | 106 | 83 | 39 | 31 | 5 | 44 | 1 | 4 | 77 | 3 | 2.63 |
| Clyde, Pitts* | .22 | 22 | 14 | 1 | 12 | 8 | 0 | .600 | 161 | 145 | 68 | 55 | 4 | 94 | 2 | 3 | 131 | 13 | 3.07 |
| Corrigan, Wat | .10 | 10 | 3 | 1 | 4 | 4 | 0 | .500 | 63 | 62 | 29 | 23 | 3 | 24 | 0 | 1 | 44 | 2 | 3.29 |
| Currence, Thet M*.19 | 19 | 14 | 3 | 1 | 10 | 6 | 0 | .625 | 146 | 114 | 52 | 44 | 9 | 70 | 1 | 0 | 92 | 7 | 2.71 |

| Pitcher—Club | G. | GS. | CG. | ShO. | W. | L. | Sv. | Pct. | IP. | H. | R. | ER. | HR. | BB. | Int.BB. | HB. | SO. | WP. | ERA. |
|---|---|---|---|---|---|---|---|---|---|---|---|---|---|---|---|---|---|---|---|
| Davis, Three R. | 29 | 24 | 8 | 2 | 11 | 12 | 0 | .478 | 178 | 159 | 66 | 44 | 4 | 62 | 8 | 8 | 105 | 5 | 2.22 |
| Deidel, Thet M* | 28 | 28 | 10 | 1 | 9 | 14 | 0 | .391 | 155 | 139 | 95 | 80 | 24 | 123 | 0 | 6 | 101 | 6 | 4.65 |
| Dollar, Three R. | 51 | 2 | 1 | 0 | 6 | 7 | 3 | .462 | 89 | 100 | 44 | 42 | 1 | 35 | 7 | 4 | 36 | 4 | 4.25 |
| Donovan, Wat | 7 | 0 | 0 | 0 | 0 | 0 | 1 | .000 | 15 | 24 | 12 | 9 | 1 | 5 | 0 | 0 | 5 | 2 | 5.40 |
| Drumright, Que C. | 23 | 16 | 5 | 1 | 6 | 10 | 0 | .375 | 107 | 106 | 60 | 48 | 9 | 47 | 1 | 8 | 43 | 2 | 4.04 |
| Dues, Quebec City | 3 | 3 | 0 | 0 | 0 | 2 | 0 | .000 | 14 | 23 | 19 | 12 | 2 | 10 | 0 | 0 | 2 | 3 | 7.71 |
| Erardi, Thet M. | 11 | 0 | 0 | 0 | 0 | 0 | 0 | .000 | 29 | 34 | 21 | 21 | 2 | 14 | 0 | 1 | 20 | 3 | 6.52 |
| Fairbanks, Pitt* | 28 | 6 | 2 | 0 | 4 | 8 | 0 | .333 | 78 | 86 | 56 | 42 | 3 | 32 | 4 | 6 | 51 | 3 | 4.85 |
| Farias, Bristol | 19 | 18 | 14 | 3 | 7 | 11 | 0 | .389 | 145 | 103 | 42 | 25 | 4 | 46 | 5 | 4 | 87 | 7 | 1.55 |
| Fierbaugh, Que C. | 23 | 23 | 8 | 2 | 8 | 10 | 0 | .444 | 152 | 143 | 79 | 60 | 9 | 72 | 0 | 7 | 94 | 12 | 3.55 |
| Foran, Bristol* | 23 | 12 | 6 | 2 | 6 | 7 | 2 | .462 | 98 | 88 | 41 | 29 | 4 | 33 | 2 | 1 | 67 | 5 | 2.66 |
| Forry, Waterbury | 33 | 0 | 0 | 0 | 5 | 5 | 10 | .500 | 80 | 70 | 19 | 14 | 0 | 28 | 9 | 2 | 53 | 5 | 1.58 |
| Greenhalgh, Read | 14 | 13 | 8 | 2 | 5 | 4 | 0 | .556 | 92 | 71 | 28 | 25 | 2 | 11 | 1 | 2 | 38 | 0 | 2.45 |
| Gronlund, Que C. | 21 | 18 | 6 | 1 | 5 | 10 | 1 | .333 | 129 | 136 | 73 | 60 | 8 | 57 | 3 | 1 | 71 | 8 | 4.19 |
| Hannahs, Que C* | 19 | 16 | 7 | 2 | 8 | 3 | 0 | .727 | 121 | 94 | 43 | 38 | 4 | 66 | 1 | 0 | 86 | 7 | 2.83 |
| Harper, Pittsfield | 6 | 6 | 3 | 0 | 4 | 0 | 0 | .000 | 46 | 48 | 23 | 21 | 4 | 15 | 2 | 2 | 12 | 4 | 4.11 |
| Heinold, West H. | 22 | 22 | 12 | 2 | 10 | 7 | 0 | .588 | 169 | 139 | 60 | 43 | 4 | 36 | 0 | 9 | 74 | 6 | 2.29 |
| Heintz, Three R* | 44 | 2 | 0 | 0 | 2 | 1 | 2 | .667 | 57 | 58 | 29 | 26 | 1 | 26 | 8 | 2 | 33 | 1 | 4.11 |
| Hernandez, Read* | 13 | 11 | 7 | 1 | 8 | 2 | 0 | .800 | 91 | 79 | 32 | 30 | 5 | 25 | 3 | 1 | 48 | 0 | 2.97 |
| Hinds, Thet M. | 25 | 25 | 7 | 0 | 6 | 13 | 0 | .316 | 167 | 153 | 86 | 65 | 15 | 73 | 1 | 7 | 98 | 14 | 3.50 |
| Hoyt, West Haven | 8 | 3 | 0 | 0 | 2 | 4 | 0 | .333 | 44 | 45 | 25 | 15 | 0 | 13 | 3 | 3 | 22 | 2 | 3.07 |
| Hume, Three R. | 7 | 6 | 2 | 1 | 3 | 2 | 0 | .600 | 45 | 43 | 20 | 15 | 0 | 15 | 2 | 1 | 19 | 0 | 3.00 |
| Jacobson, Thet M. | 1 | 0 | 0 | 0 | 0 | 0 | 0 | .000 | 2 | 3 | 2 | 1 | 0 | 1 | 0 | 0 | 0 | 1 | 4.50 |
| Jensen, Three R* | 20 | 11 | 1 | 1 | 4 | 7 | 0 | .364 | 72 | 79 | 42 | 38 | 5 | 47 | 0 | 3 | 35 | 4 | 4.75 |
| Jones, Bristol* | 13 | 12 | 9 | 3 | 7 | 4 | 0 | .636 | 81 | 67 | 35 | 33 | 3 | 33 | 0 | 2 | 59 | 2 | 3.67 |
| Keener, Quebec C. | 7 | 7 | 2 | 1 | 4 | 1 | 0 | .800 | 47 | 40 | 14 | 13 | 3 | 13 | 0 | 2 | 24 | 1 | 2.49 |
| Kerrigan, Que C* | 27 | 0 | 0 | 0 | 6 | 2 | 4 | .750 | 53 | 38 | 11 | 4 | 0 | 15 | 1 | 3 | 28 | 3 | 0.68 |
| Kiser, Reading | 12 | 12 | 5 | 1 | 6 | 5 | 0 | .545 | 83 | 82 | 45 | 35 | 6 | 37 | 0 | 1 | 61 | 9 | 3.80 |
| Kniffin, Reading* | 18 | 7 | 2 | 0 | 5 | 2 | 1 | .714 | 59 | 75 | 21 | 19 | 1 | 11 | 0 | 0 | 34 | 1 | 2.90 |
| Kouns, Bristol | 8 | 3 | 0 | 0 | 4 | 2 | 0 | .667 | 56 | 53 | 27 | 21 | 3 | 24 | 0 | 1 | 24 | 5 | 3.38 |
| Kreke, Reading | 14 | 12 | 5 | 0 | 5 | 4 | 1 | .556 | 77 | 100 | 45 | 41 | 5 | 19 | 5 | 0 | 37 | 2 | 4.79 |
| Landreth, Que C. | 25 | 25 | 17 | 4 | 10 | 12 | 0 | .455 | 181 | 143 | 78 | 54 | 8 | 85 | 3 | 1 | 133 | 13 | 2.69 |
| Lanfair, Wat | 17 | 7 | 1 | 0 | 1 | 6 | 1 | .143 | 57 | 75 | 59 | 36 | 4 | 39 | 2 | 4 | 25 | 2 | 5.68 |
| LaRose, Bristol* | 20 | 11 | 6 | 1 | 8 | 1 | 0 | .889 | 104 | 93 | 40 | 28 | 2 | 45 | 1 | 2 | 47 | 6 | 2.42 |
| Lawson, West H. | 24 | 9 | 1 | 1 | 9 | 10 | 0 | .474 | 102 | 161 | 93 | 62 | 8 | 78 | 4 | 3 | 74 | 14 | 5.42 |
| Leonhard, Que C. | 20 | 1 | 1 | 0 | 3 | 2 | 3 | .600 | 52 | 64 | 35 | 29 | 5 | 26 | 2 | 1 | 25 | 5 | 5.02 |
| Lerch, Reading* | 25 | 25 | 14 | 1 | 16 | 6 | 0 | .727 | 177 | 173 | 66 | 53 | 4 | 45 | 2 | 8 | 108 | 7 | 2.69 |
| Lesslie, Wat | 28 | 28 | 16 | 3 | 15 | 8 | 0 | .652 | 193 | 166 | 69 | 47 | 10 | 63 | 5 | 5 | 114 | 5 | 2.19 |
| Lett, Three Rivers | 1 | 0 | 0 | 0 | 0 | 0 | 0 | .000 | 1 | 0 | 0 | 0 | 0 | 1 | 0 | 1 | 0 | 0 | 0.00 |
| Martinez, Pitt | 6 | 0 | 0 | 0 | 1 | 0 | 0 | 1.000 | 21 | 20 | 7 | 5 | 1 | 8 | 1 | 1 | 7 | 0 | 2.14 |
| McCoy, Reading | 19 | 3 | 2 | 0 | 1 | 3 | 4 | .259 | 44 | 56 | 25 | 19 | 1 | 23 | 1 | 0 | 18 | 1 | 3.89 |
| McElwain, W H* | 33 | 0 | 0 | 0 | 3 | 6 | 2 | .333 | 64 | 66 | 29 | 20 | 4 | 29 | 2 | 1 | 43 | 5 | 2.81 |
| McLaurine, T M* | 49 | 0 | 0 | 0 | 1 | 3 | 4 | .250 | 52 | 54 | 21 | 17 | 3 | 24 | 1 | 2 | 25 | 3 | 2.94 |
| Mersch, West H. | 38 | 6 | 5 | 0 | 6 | 8 | 10 | .429 | 103 | 97 | 56 | 43 | 8 | 40 | 5 | 5 | 50 | 2 | 3.76 |
| Mestek, Waterbury | 27 | 27 | 12 | 5 | 13 | 8 | 0 | .619 | 188 | 178 | 80 | 58 | 10 | 57 | 5 | 5 | 107 | 7 | 2.78 |
| Molush, Reading | 9 | 0 | 0 | 0 | 1 | 0 | 4 | 1.000 | 10 | 7 | 3 | 3 | 0 | 6 | 1 | 0 | 8 | 0 | 2.70 |
| Moore, Three R. | 26 | 26 | 4 | 1 | 8 | 12 | 0 | .400 | 184 | 153 | 67 | 56 | 9 | 63 | 2 | 7 | 116 | 10 | 2.74 |
| Morris, Thet M. | 5 | 5 | 2 | 1 | 2 | 1 | 0 | .667 | 28 | 29 | 12 | 12 | 2 | 6 | 1 | 0 | 18 | 1 | 3.86 |
| Munoz, Three R. | 1 | 0 | 0 | 0 | 0 | 0 | 0 | .000 | 1 | 0 | 0 | 0 | 0 | 0 | 0 | 0 | 0 | 0 | 0.00 |
| Murphy, Que C* | 1 | 0 | 0 | 0 | 0 | 0 | 0 | .000 | 2 | 3 | 0 | 0 | 0 | 3 | 0 | 0 | 0 | 0 | 0.00 |
| Nina, Three Rivers | 1 | 0 | 0 | 0 | 0 | 0 | 0 | .000 | ½ | 2 | 2 | 2 | 0 | 0 | 0 | 0 | 0 | 0 | 54.00 |
| Norris, West Haven | 6 | 6 | 1 | 0 | 2 | 4 | 0 | .333 | 33 | 42 | 24 | 23 | 7 | 19 | 0 | 0 | 13 | 1 | 6.27 |
| Olivo, West Haven | 4 | 3 | 1 | 1 | 1 | 2 | 0 | .333 | 22 | 22 | 12 | 7 | 1 | 6 | 0 | 0 | 10 | 1 | 2.86 |
| O'Neill, Que C* | 9 | 5 | 2 | 0 | 0 | 3 | 1 | .000 | 40 | 32 | 11 | 9 | 2 | 17 | 1 | 0 | 20 | 0 | 2.03 |
| Overstreet, T R | 27 | 25 | 5 | 2 | 8 | 9 | 0 | .471 | 149 | 137 | 64 | 53 | 5 | 60 | 2 | 1 | 84 | 4 | 3.20 |
| Percival, Bristol | 11 | 10 | 2 | 0 | 4 | 4 | 0 | .500 | 50 | 50 | 33 | 31 | 5 | 22 | 0 | 3 | 26 | 2 | 5.58 |
| Polinsky, West H. | 24 | 24 | 12 | 2 | 8 | 13 | 0 | .381 | 184 | 155 | 84 | 65 | 13 | 60 | 7 | 5 | 121 | 4 | 3.18 |
| Poloni, Pitt* | 7 | 5 | 1 | 0 | 2 | 3 | 0 | .400 | 33 | 37 | 25 | 24 | 1 | 12 | 2 | 1 | 16 | 1 | 6.55 |
| Rautzhan, Wat* | 28 | 28 | 21 | 4 | 14 | 10 | 0 | .583 | 218 | 200 | 73 | 50 | 6 | 62 | 4 | 6 | 115 | 8 | 2.06 |
| Riley, Quebec C. | 6 | 0 | 0 | 0 | 0 | 0 | 1 | .000 | 8 | 5 | 5 | 3 | 0 | 5 | 1 | 0 | 3 | 0 | 3.38 |
| Ripley, Bristol | 1 | 1 | 0 | 0 | 1 | 0 | 0 | 1.000 | 5 | 7 | 2 | 1 | 0 | 1 | 0 | 1 | 3 | 0 | 1.80 |
| Ross, Bristol* | 6 | 6 | 3 | 2 | 4 | 1 | 0 | .800 | 46 | 38 | 14 | 12 | 2 | 17 | 0 | 3 | 28 | 0 | 2.35 |
| Ruddell, Three R. | 7 | 5 | 0 | 0 | 0 | 4 | 0 | .000 | 27 | 31 | 22 | 16 | 1 | 23 | 0 | 0 | 15 | 6 | 5.33 |
| Ruling, Thet M. | 29 | 1 | 0 | 0 | 5 | 5 | 3 | .500 | 43 | 46 | 27 | 21 | 1 | 29 | 2 | 5 | 39 | 6 | 4.40 |
| Rushing, Que C* | 29 | 4 | 2 | 0 | 5 | 6 | 0 | .455 | 90 | 94 | 35 | 35 | 6 | 19 | 1 | 1 | 60 | 1 | 3.50 |
| Sarmiento, T R | 64 | 1 | 0 | 0 | 6 | 8 | 15 | .429 | 129 | 104 | 41 | 37 | 8 | 51 | 9 | 2 | 114 | 0 | 2.58 |
| Sbragia, Bristol | 10 | 1 | 0 | 0 | 2 | 0 | 0 | 1.000 | 20 | 15 | 9 | 7 | 1 | 12 | 0 | 1 | 11 | 4 | 3.15 |
| Scruggs, Bristol | 19 | 10 | 4 | 2 | 6 | 5 | 3 | .545 | 91 | 79 | 41 | 34 | 4 | 36 | 0 | 7 | 38 | 4 | 3.36 |
| Seoane, Reading | 17 | 6 | 3 | 9 | 4 | 0 | 0 | .692 | 128 | 120 | 43 | 35 | 3 | 28 | 1 | 3 | 64 | 3 | 2.46 |
| Shubert, Pitt* | 22 | 5 | 0 | 6 | 9 | 0 | 0 | .400 | 128 | 122 | 69 | 60 | 3 | 100 | 1 | 3 | 52 | 6 | 4.22 |
| Skalisky, Reading | 1 | 0 | 0 | 0 | 0 | 0 | 0 | .000 | 2 | 3 | 2 | 2 | 0 | 0 | 0 | 0 | 1 | 0 | 9.00 |
| Spencer, Bristol | 14 | 13 | 7 | 1 | 8 | 6 | 0 | .571 | 99 | 86 | 33 | 26 | 4 | 28 | 1 | 4 | 42 | 6 | 2.36 |
| Spinks, West Haven | 7 | 3 | 1 | 1 | 3 | 0 | 0 | .250 | 35 | 37 | 25 | 24 | 1 | 19 | 0 | 2 | 14 | 3 | 6.17 |
| Stafford, Thet M. | 1 | 0 | 0 | 0 | 0 | 0 | 0 | .000 | 2 | 2 | 1 | 0 | 0 | 0 | 0 | 0 | 0 | 0 | 0.00 |
| Standley, Wat | 30 | 1 | 0 | 0 | 4 | 2 | 4 | .667 | 70 | 64 | 25 | 14 | 0 | 21 | 4 | 0 | 24 | 1 | 1.80 |
| Steen, Pittsfield* | 21 | 18 | 6 | 2 | 7 | 9 | 0 | .438 | 102 | 129 | 60 | 50 | 5 | 48 | 1 | 3 | 39 | 15 | 4.41 |
| Stitzel, Reading | 1 | 0 | 0 | 0 | 0 | 0 | 0 | .000 | 2 | 1 | 1 | 0 | 1 | 0 | 0 | 0 | 2 | 0 | 4.50 |
| Sutton, Pittsfield | 40 | 0 | 0 | 0 | 7 | 4 | 14 | .636 | 81 | 63 | 26 | 22 | 2 | 44 | 10 | 1 | 32 | 6 | 2.44 |
| Szado, Pittsfield* | 2 | 1 | 0 | 0 | 0 | 0 | 0 | .000 | 2 | 2 | 2 | 2 | 0 | 2 | 0 | 0 | 0 | 0 | 9.00 |

| Pitcher—Club | G. | GS. | CG. | ShO. | W. | L. | Sv. | Pct. | IP. | H. | R. | ER. | HR. | BB. | Int. BB. | HB. | SO. | WP. | ERA. |
|---|---|---|---|---|---|---|---|---|---|---|---|---|---|---|---|---|---|---|---|
| Thomas, Reading ..| 10 | 10 | 5 | 1 | 6 | 3 | 0 | .667 | 67 | 50 | 22 | 19 | 0 | 29 | 3 | 3 | 53 | 3 | 2.55 |
| Thomason, Read .. | 6 | 0 | 0 | 0 | 1 | 0 | 2 | 1.000 | 10 | 7 | 6 | 4 | 0 | 7 | 0 | 0 | 9 | 2 | 3.60 |
| Todd, Waterbury .. | 2 | 0 | 0 | 0 | 0 | 0 | 0 | .000 | 1 | 1 | 2 | 2 | 0 | 3 | 0 | 0 | 0 | 0 | 18.00 |
| Van Der Beek, Wat | 27 | 27 | 12 | 4 | 12 | 13 | 0 | .480 | 178 | 157 | 78 | 59 | 16 | 62 | 2 | 6 | 82 | 10 | 2.98 |
| Watkins, Bristol .| 31 | 3 | 2 | 0 | 4 | 7 | 6 | .364 | 61 | 59 | 32 | 30 | 0 | 28 | 2 | 6 | 47 | 7 | 4.43 |
| Widmar, Thet M..| 26 | 6 | 4 | 0 | 4 | 6 | 2 | .400 | 96 | 100 | 46 | 37 | 6 | 18 | 1 | 4 | 46 | 5 | 3.47 |
| Wright, Bristol ...| 10 | 10 | 6 | 1 | 7 | 1 | 0 | .875 | 69 | 61 | 28 | 27 | 4 | 30 | 2 | 6 | 66 | 4 | 3.52 |
| Yount, Thet M....| 22 | 22 | 5 | 1 | 8 | 12 | 0 | .400 | 131 | 153 | 84 | 69 | 18 | 67 | 0 | 5 | 49 | 10 | 4.74 |

BALKS—Dollar, 3; Andujar, Boitano, Chamberlain, Jensen. Poloni, Sarmiento, Spencer, 2 each; Alexander, Anderson (WH), Armstrong, Boggs, Brayton, Clyde, Forry, Gronlund, Hannahs, Heintz, Hinds, Kiser, Kreke, McLaurine, Mersch, Overstreet, Rushing, Shubert, Steen, 1 each.

COMBINATION SHUTOUTS—Farias-Brayton, LaRose-Scruggs, Ross-Sbragia. Sbragia-Foran-Watkins, Bristol; Szado-Bolick, Pittsfield; Greenhalgh-Kniffin, Hernandez-Molush, Seoane-Thomason, Reading; Yount-McLaurine, Thetford Mines; Davis-Sarmiento 2, Andujar-Sarmiento, Hume-Dollar, Jensen-Sarmiento, Three Rivers; Badcock-Forry, Corrigan-Forry, Lesslie-Badcock, Waterbury; Anderson-Arnold, West Haven.

NO-HIT GAME—Farias, Bristol, defeated Thetford Mines, 2-0, June 14 (seven innings).

# *Southern League*

## CLASS AA

League President
**BILLY HITCHCOCK**

Leading Pitcher
**DANIEL LARSON**
Columbus

### CHAMPIONSHIP WINNERS IN PREVIOUS YEARS

1904—Macon ............. .598
1905—Macon ............. .625
1906—Savannah ........... .637
1907—Charleston .......... .620
1908—Jacksonville ........ .694
1909—Chattanooga* ...... .738
　　　Augusta ........... .702
1910—Columbus .......... .588
1911—Columbus* ........ .681
　　　Columbia .......... .710
1912—Jacksonville* ...... .679
　　　Columbus ......... .632
1913—Savannah ......... .754
　　　Savannah ......... .593
1914—Savannah* ........ .667
　　　Albany ........... .650
1915—Macon ............ .588
　　　Columbus* ....... .686
1916—Augusta* ......... .617
　　　Columbia ......... .631
1917—Charleston ........ .741
　　　Columbia* ........ .667
1918—Did not operate.
1919—Columbia ......... .585
1920—Columbia ......... .633
1921—Columbia ......... .642
1922—Charleston ........ .625
1923—Charlotte* ........ .653
　　　Macon ........... .580
1924—Augusta .......... .612
1925—Spartanburg ...... .620
1926—Greenville ........ .662
1927—Greenville ........ .622

1928—Asheville .......... .664
1929—Asheville .......... .605
　　　Knoxville* ........ .634
1930—Greenville* ....... .620
　　　Macon ........... .643
1931-32-33-34-35—Did not
　　　operate.
1936—Jacksonville ...... .652
　　　Columbus* ....... .650
1937—Columbus ........ .572
　　　Savannah (3rd)† .. .565
1938—Savannah ........ .574
　　　Macon (2nd)† .... .570
1939—Columbus ........ .601
　　　Augusta (2nd)† ... .597
1940—Savannah ........ .627
　　　Columbus (2nd)† .. .583
1941—Macon ........... .643
　　　Columbia (2nd)† .. .636
1942—Charleston ....... .620
　　　Macon (2nd)† .... .585
1943-44-45—Did not operate.
1946—Columbus ........ .568
　　　Augusta (4th)† ... .547
1947—Columbus ........ .575
　　　Savannah (2nd)† .. .563
1948—Charleston ....... .572
　　　Greenville (3rd)† .. .549
1949—Macon‡ .......... .623
1950—Macon‡ .......... .588
1951—Montgomery ...... .607
1952—Columbia ........ .649
　　　Montgomery (3rd)† .558

1953—Jacksonville ....... .679
　　　Savannah (2nd)† .. .571
1954—Jacksonville ...... .593
　　　Savannah (2nd)† .. .571
1955—Columbia ........ .636
　　　Augusta (3rd)† ... .543
1956—Jacksonville‡ ...... .621
1957—Augusta .......... .636
　　　Charlotte (2nd)† .. .562
1958—Augusta .......... .550
　　　Macon (3rd)† .... .500
1959—Knoxville ........ .557
　　　Gastonia (4th)† .. .504
1960—Columbia ........ .597
　　　Savannah (3rd)† .. .561
1961—Asheville ........ .635
1962—Savannah ........ .662
　　　Macon (3rd)† .... .576
1963—Augusta* ........ 661
　　　Lynchburg ....... .662
1964—Lynchburg ....... .579
1965—Columbus ........ .572
1966—Mobile .......... .629
1967—Birmingham ..... .604
1968—Asheville ........ .614
1969—Charlotte ........ .579
1970—Columbus ........ .569
1971—Did not operate as league
　—clubs were members of Dixie
Association.
1972—Asheville ........ .583
　　　Montgomery§ .... .561
1973—Montgomery§ .... .580
　　　Jacksonville ..... .559
1974—Columbus ....... .565
　　　Knoxville§ ....... .533

*Won split-season playoff. †Won four-club playoff. ‡Won championship and four-club playoff.
§League was divided into Eastern and Western Divisions: won playoff.

### STANDING OF CLUBS AT CLOSE OF SEASON, SEPTEMBER 5
#### WESTERN DIVISION

| Club | Mon. | Bir. | Knx. | Ash. | Orl. | Sav. | Col. | Jax. | Won | Lost | Tied | Pct. | G.B. |
|---|---|---|---|---|---|---|---|---|---|---|---|---|---|
| Montgomery (Tigers) | .. | 10 | 11 | 11 | 10 | 11 | 6 | 14 | 73 | 61 | 0 | .545 | ... |
| Birmingham (Athletics) | 10 | .. | 11 | 8 | 8 | 5 | 11 | 12 | 65 | 69 | 0 | .485 | 8 |
| Knoxville (White Sox) | 9 | 9 | .. | 9 | 11 | 7 | 8 | 10 | 63 | 75 | 0 | .457 | 12 |
| Asheville (Orioles) | 9 | 12 | 11 | .. | 8 | 6 | 9 | 8 | 63 | 75 | 0 | .457 | 12 |

#### EASTERN DIVISION

| Club | Mon. | Bir. | Knx. | Ash. | Orl. | Sav. | Col. | Jax. | Won | Lost | Tied | Pct. | G.B. |
|---|---|---|---|---|---|---|---|---|---|---|---|---|---|
| Orlando (Twins) | 10 | 11 | 8 | 12 | .. | 14 | 14 | 12 | 81 | 57 | 0 | .587 | ... |
| Savannah (Braves) | 8 | 11 | 12 | 14 | 6 | .. | 9 | 10 | 70 | 64 | 0 | .522 | 9 |
| Columbus (Astros) | 9 | 9 | 12 | 10 | 6 | 11 | .. | 13 | 70 | 64 | 0 | .522 | 9 |
| Jacksonville (Royals) | 6 | 7 | 10 | 11 | 8 | 10 | 7 | .. | 59 | 79 | 0 | .428 | 22 |

Major league affiliations in parentheses.

Playoff—Montgomery defeated Orlando, three games to none.

Regular-Season Attendance—Asheville, 48,928; Birmingham, 30,483; Columbus, 74,797; Jacksonville, 52,737; Knoxville, 43,730; Montgomery, 35,751; Orlando, 44,405; Savannah, 67,971. Total. 398,802. All-Star Game, 1,910. Playoffs, 1,337.

Managers: Asheville—Jim Schaffer; Birmingham—Harry Malmberg; Columbus—Jim Beauchamp; Jacksonville—E. William (Billy) Scripture; Knoxville—Jim Napier; Montgomery—Les Moss; Orlando—Dick Phillips; Savannah—Tommie Aaron.

All-Star Team: 1B—Squires, Knoxville; 2B—Stodgel, Knoxville; 3B—Mankowski, Montgomery; SS—Rockett, Savannah; Utility—Picciolo, Birmingham; OF—Javier, Columbus; Valle, Montgomery; Bryant, Birmingham; Heil, Asheville; C—Velazquez, Savannah; DH—Obradovich, Orlando; P—Kravec, Knoxville; Maneely, Orlando; Manager—Phillips, Orlando.

(Compiled by Howe News Bureau, Chicago, Ill.)

### CLUB BATTING

| Club | G. | AB. | R. | OR. | H. | TB. | 2B | 3B. | HR. | RBI. | SH. | SF. | Int. BB. | BB. | HP. | SO. | CS. | LOB. | Pct. |
|---|---|---|---|---|---|---|---|---|---|---|---|---|---|---|---|---|---|---|---|
| Asheville | .138 | 4540 | 584 | 620 | 1201 | 1656 | 181 | 23 | 76 | 512 | 37 | 31 | 425 | 32 | 24 | 590 | 57 | 44 | 974 | .265 |
| M'tgomery | .134 | 4244 | 523 | 508 | 1117 | 1612 | 161 | 29 | 92 | 473 | 45 | 37 | 474 | 49 | 27 | 550 | 73 | 59 | 962 | .263 |
| Knoxville | .138 | 4348 | 540 | 571 | 1129 | 1506 | 164 | 21 | 57 | 481 | 53 | 39 | 522 | 26 | 22 | 625 | 83 | 78 | 918 | .260 |
| Birm'gham | .134 | 4204 | 553 | 502 | 1091 | 1459 | 163 | 35 | 45 | 486 | 84 | 41 | 540 | 25 | 28 | 572 | 62 | 36 | 1009 | .260 |
| Savannah | .134 | 4237 | 490 | 480 | 1074 | 1391 | 115 | 23 | 52 | 426 | 59 | 40 | 426 | 39 | 43 | 694 | 122 | 59 | 926 | .253 |
| Orlando | .138 | 4143 | 512 | 462 | 1019 | 1398 | 115 | 27 | 70 | 463 | 45 | 41 | 611 | 36 | 15 | 652 | 94 | 48 | 1023 | .246 |
| Columbus | .134 | 4210 | 481 | 475 | 1016 | 1371 | 152 | 28 | 49 | 412 | 54 | 26 | 478 | 36 | 46 | 672 | 77 | 41 | 933 | .241 |
| Jacksonville | 138 | 4254 | 473 | 538 | 1017 | 1392 | 162 | 21 | 57 | 413 | 44 | 38 | 505 | 24 | 34 | 731 | 127 | 71 | 931 | .239 |

### INDIVIDUAL BATTING

(Leading Qualifiers for Batting Championship—378 or More Plate Appearances)

*Bats lefthanded.  †Switch-hitter.

| Player and Club | G. | AB. | R. | H. | TB. | 2B. | 3B. | HR. | RBI. | SH. | SF. | BB. | HP. | SO. | SB. | CS. | Pct. |
|---|---|---|---|---|---|---|---|---|---|---|---|---|---|---|---|---|---|
| Heil, Charles, Asheville*...115 | 423 | 60 | 136 | 189 | 15 | 4 | 10 | 57 | 2 | 4 | 28 | 1 | 35 | 3 | 4 | .322 |
| Maloof, Jack, Orlando*......119 | 385 | 62 | 122 | 140 | 11 | 2 | 1 | 40 | 1 | 2 | 105 | 4 | 35 | 16 | 8 | .317 |
| Squires, Michael, Knoxville*.129 | 448 | 68 | 136 | 178 | 23 | 5 | 3 | 50 | 6 | 3 | 67 | 1 | 31 | 24 | 13 | .304 |
| Javier, I. Alfredo, Columbus*.117 | 448 | 51 | 135 | 188 | 14 | 6 | 9 | 72 | 1 | 6 | 23 | 15 | 42 | 18 | 11 | .301 |
| Tevlin, Creighton, Asheville* 116 | 439 | 54 | 130 | 153 | 18 | 1 | 1 | 34 | 7 | 2 | 54 | 4 | 41 | 6 | 7 | .296 |
| Collins, Jimmie, Savannah*..131 | 470 | 55 | 139 | 171 | 16 | 5 | 2 | 43 | 4 | 4 | 36 | 5 | 85 | 16 | 11 | .296 |
| Bryant, Derek, Birmingham..134 | 509 | 64 | 147 | 183 | 25 | 4 | 1 | 58 | 4 | 6 | 48 | 1 | 26 | 8 | 4 | .289 |
| Valle, John, Montgomery ...134 | 460 | 76 | 130 | 218 | 15 | 2 | 23 | 72 | 2 | 6 | 75 | 3 | 71 | 3 | 4 | .283 |
| Mankowski, Philip, Mon*...124 | 407 | 44 | 115 | 164 | 18 | 2 | 9 | 49 | 3 | 1 | 33 | 4 | 31 | 1 | 3 | .283 |
| Kilpatrick, Cleo, Knoxville*..133 | 471 | 64 | 133 | 190 | 30 | 3 | 7 | 65 | 2 | 3 | 47 | 1 | 57 | 10 | 11 | .282 |

Departmental Leaders: G—Wolfe, 138; AB—Bryant, 509; R—Portley, 82; H—Bryant, 147; TB—Valle, 218; 2B—Kilpatrick, 30; 3B—Gonzales, 11; HR—Obradovich, 27; RBI—Obradovich, 74; SH—Ingalls, 20; SF—Velazquez, 9; BB—Maloof, 105; HP—Javier, 15; SO—Shipley, 92; SB—Mallory, 42; CS—Eschen, 16.

(All Players—Listed Alphabetically)

| Player and Club | G. | AB. | R. | H. | TB. | 2B. | 3B. | HR. | RBI. | SH. | SF. | BB. | HP. | SO. | SB. | CS. | Pct. |
|---|---|---|---|---|---|---|---|---|---|---|---|---|---|---|---|---|---|
| Adams, Robert Melvin, Mon | 89 | 297 | 30 | 84 | 104 | 11 | 0 | 3 | 26 | 2 | 1 | 30 | 2 | 35 | 1 | 1 | .283 |
| Albert, Richard, Savannah... | 31 | 102 | 9 | 25 | 30 | 3 | 1 | 0 | 11 | 2 | 1 | 12 | 1 | 25 | 0 | 2 | .245 |
| Arcia, Jose, Jacksonville ... | 46 | 149 | 9 | 34 | 47 | 1 | 0 | 4 | 19 | 3 | 3 | 5 | 0 | 26 | 1 | 1 | .228 |
| Argenti, Robert, Bir† | .134 | 472 | 62 | 117 | 134 | 9 | 1 | 2 | 36 | 19 | 2 | 46 | 3 | 65 | 8 | 11 | .248 |
| Arline, James, Savannah*... | 70 | 211 | 21 | 48 | 60 | 5 | 2 | 1 | 17 | 5 | 1 | 20 | 1 | 77 | 8 | 5 | .227 |
| Baldwin, Robert, Mon† | 78 | 322 | 45 | 97 | 159 | 9 | 4 | 15 | 48 | 1 | 4 | 23 | 2 | 33 | 9 | 5 | .301 |
| Bates, Charles, Mon† | 46 | 160 | 18 | 35 | 52 | 7 | 2 | 2 | 18 | 2 | 1 | 20 | 0 | 34 | 0 | 0 | .219 |
| Beaurivage, Ronald, Birm*..133 | 439 | 60 | 103 | 149 | 19 | 3 | 7 | 65 | 3 | 8 | 73 | 1 | 62 | 3 | 2 | .235 |
| Bell, Kevin, Knoxville ..... | 66 | 224 | 31 | 68 | 118 | 15 | 1 | 11 | 41 | 2 | 5 | 29 | 0 | 55 | 4 | 3 | .304 |
| Best, Kurt, Knoxville ..... | 1 | 1 | 0 | 1 | 2 | 1 | 0 | 0 | 0 | 0 | 0 | 0 | 0 | 0 | 0 | 0 | 1.000 |
| Blessitt, Isaiah, Birmingham | 13 | 44 | 6 | 9 | 15 | 2 | 2 | 0 | 9 | 0 | 0 | 10 | 0 | 8 | 1 | 0 | .205 |
| Blomberg, Steven, Jacksonville | 9 | 16 | 2 | 1 | 1 | 0 | 0 | 0 | 0 | 0 | 0 | 2 | 0 | 4 | 1 | 0 | .063 |
| Boone, Rodney, Columbus ... | 68 | 217 | 19 | 54 | 73 | 12 | 2 | 1 | 16 | 2 | 1 | 24 | 2 | 42 | 0 | 1 | .249 |
| Brandenburg, Gary, Asheville | 58 | 186 | 22 | 45 | 64 | 10 | 0 | 3 | 21 | 0 | 3 | 18 | 2 | 37 | 0 | 2 | .242 |
| Brazell, Ted, Montgomery .. | 92 | 288 | 29 | 80 | 102 | 11 | 1 | 3 | 31 | 1 | 4 | 37 | 4 | 47 | 1 | 2 | .278 |
| Breitzman, Robert, Bir* ... | 31 | 73 | 12 | 18 | 28 | 1 | 3 | 1 | 13 | 4 | 1 | 15 | 0 | 12 | 0 | 4 | .247 |
| Bridges, Keith, Jacksonville | 35 | 95 | 8 | 20 | 23 | 3 | 0 | 0 | 4 | 2 | 0 | 7 | 1 | 23 | 3 | 1 | .211 |
| Brookens, Thomas, Mon.....100 | 329 | 37 | 73 | 109 | 11 | 2 | 7 | 36 | 1 | 5 | 29 | 0 | 69 | 4 | 5 | .222 |
| Brown, Rogers, Asheville† | .. 6 | 27 | 5 | 7 | 7 | 0 | 0 | 0 | 2 | 0 | 0 | 1 | 0 | 7 | 0 | 1 | .259 |
| Bryant, Derek, Birmingham..134 | 509 | 64 | 147 | 183 | 25 | 4 | 1 | 58 | 4 | 6 | 48 | 1 | 26 | 8 | 4 | .289 |

| Player and Club | G. | AB. | R. | H. | TB. | 2B. | 3B. | HR. | RBI. | SH. | SF. | BB. | HP. | SO. | SB. | CS. | Pct |
|---|---|---|---|---|---|---|---|---|---|---|---|---|---|---|---|---|---|
| Buckner, James, Asheville* | 124 | 481 | 56 | 130 | 191 | 23 | 1 | 12 | 58 | 1 | 3 | 30 | 4 | 53 | 17 | 8 | .270 |
| Butera, Salvatore, Orlando | 20 | 51 | 8 | 9 | 11 | 2 | 0 | 0 | 4 | 0 | 1 | 15 | 0 | 5 | 1 | 0 | .176 |
| Butler, Thomas, Montgomery | 15 | 47 | 4 | 8 | 9 | 1 | 0 | 0 | 1 | 0 | 1 | 3 | 0 | 9 | 0 | 0 | .170 |
| Cador, Roger, Savannah* | 129 | 468 | 53 | 110 | 163 | 12 | 1 | 13 | 63 | 5 | 8 | 37 | 5 | 70 | 20 | 4 | .235 |
| Capehart, James, Bir* | 113 | 353 | 51 | 98 | 134 | 14 | 5 | 4 | 43 | 1 | 2 | 60 | 1 | 60 | 7 | 3 | .278 |
| Cariel, Rafael, Orlando | 28 | 70 | 4 | 14 | 20 | 0 | 0 | 2 | 11 | 2 | 5 | 4 | 1 | 5 | 1 | 1 | .200 |
| Clark, Douglas, Jacksonville | 132 | 457 | 41 | 105 | 169 | 24 | 2 | 12 | 52 | 2 | 4 | 40 | 1 | 78 | 5 | 2 | .230 |
| Collins, Donald E., Savannah | 1 | 1 | 0 | 0 | 0 | 0 | 0 | 0 | 0 | 0 | 0 | 0 | 0 | 0 | 0 | 0 | .000 |
| Collins, Jimmie, Savannah* | 131 | 470 | 55 | 139 | 171 | 16 | 5 | 2 | 43 | 4 | 4 | 36 | 5 | 85 | 16 | 11 | .296 |
| Colon, Raul, Montgomery* | 29 | 82 | 10 | 17 | 26 | 3 | 0 | 2 | 7 | 0 | 1 | 10 | 0 | 12 | 0 | 0 | .207 |
| Connolly, Kevin, Savannah* | 40 | 113 | 8 | 29 | 39 | 2 | 1 | 2 | 13 | 5 | 0 | 9 | 1 | 14 | 0 | 0 | .257 |
| Corcoran, Timothy, Mon* | 122 | 388 | 42 | 95 | 130 | 20 | 3 | 3 | 36 | 4 | 2 | 46 | 5 | 35 | 7 | 5 | .245 |
| Coughlan, Kip, Montgomery | 22 | 63 | 10 | 15 | 23 | 2 | 0 | 2 | 7 | 3 | 0 | 6 | 0 | 10 | 0 | 0 | .238 |
| Cripe, David, Jacksonville | 98 | 354 | 40 | 93 | 119 | 14 | 3 | 2 | 33 | 3 | 1 | 43 | 1 | 45 | 4 | 2 | .263 |
| Crosta, James, Knoxville | 8 | 23 | 3 | 6 | 6 | 0 | 0 | 0 | 1 | 0 | 0 | 1 | 0 | 2 | 0 | 1 | .261 |
| Cummings, Michael, Savannah | 95 | 334 | 39 | 87 | 103 | 6 | 5 | 0 | 26 | 3 | 3 | 29 | 1 | 25 | 13 | 8 | .260 |
| Dauer, Richard, Asheville | 106 | 374 | 51 | 94 | 125 | 13 | 0 | 6 | 44 | 2 | 2 | 51 | 0 | 24 | 5 | 3 | .251 |
| Davey, Michael, Savannah | 2 | 4 | 0 | 1 | 1 | 0 | 0 | 0 | 1 | 1 | 0 | 0 | 1 | 0 | 0 | | .250 |
| Davis, Kenzie, Jacksonville | 68 | 177 | 26 | 39 | 53 | 6 | 1 | 2 | 10 | 2 | 0 | 26 | 1 | 55 | 16 | 7 | .220 |
| DeBarr, Dennis, Montgomery | 1 | 0 | 0 | 0 | 0 | 0 | 0 | 0 | 0 | 0 | 0 | 0 | 0 | 0 | 0 | 0 | .000 |
| de la Rosa, Jesus, Columbus | 29 | 102 | 11 | 20 | 26 | 6 | 0 | 0 | 9 | 1 | 1 | 4 | 0 | 25 | 5 | 1 | .196 |
| Dlugach, Michael, Knoxville | 63 | 202 | 28 | 50 | 62 | 7 | 1 | 1 | 29 | 3 | 2 | 27 | 1 | 36 | 2 | 1 | .248 |
| Doyle, Blake, Asheville* | 108 | 354 | 41 | 92 | 112 | 9 | 4 | 1 | 31 | 7 | 1 | 30 | 1 | 25 | 4 | 2 | .260 |
| Drake, Kevin, Columbus | 39 | 121 | 12 | 20 | 27 | 4 | 0 | 1 | 10 | 2 | 0 | 6 | 2 | 42 | 1 | 0 | .165 |
| Englert, Reuben, Columbus* | 82 | 296 | 34 | 74 | 96 | 13 | 3 | 1 | 25 | 2 | 0 | 33 | 1 | 27 | 9 | 2 | .250 |
| Englishbey, Stephen, Col* | 120 | 341 | 46 | 69 | 126 | 8 | 2 | 15 | 60 | 1 | 6 | 103 | 5 | 81 | 8 | 5 | .202 |
| Enright, George, Knoxville | 118 | 370 | 36 | 94 | 104 | 5 | 1 | 1 | 32 | 2 | 2 | 31 | 4 | 37 | 4 | 1 | .254 |
| Epperly, Thomas, Orlando | 6 | 14 | 3 | 2 | 2 | 0 | 0 | 0 | 2 | 0 | 0 | 3 | 0 | 1 | 0 | 1 | .143 |
| Eschen, James, Montgomery† | 119 | 385 | 54 | 96 | 108 | 9 | 0 | 1 | 22 | 9 | 2 | 88 | 1 | 32 | 31 | 16 | .249 |
| Fife, Danny, Orlando | 7 | 12 | 0 | 2 | 2 | 0 | 0 | 0 | 2 | 0 | 1 | 1 | 0 | 1 | 0 | 0 | .167 |
| Fleming, John, Jacksonville | 107 | 338 | 26 | 76 | 118 | 16 | 4 | 6 | 36 | 4 | 4 | 20 | 4 | 52 | 1 | 1 | .225 |
| Floyd, G. Michael, Columbus | 31 | 104 | 14 | 26 | 46 | 6 | 1 | 4 | 18 | 0 | 1 | 8 | 3 | 24 | 1 | 0 | .250 |
| Foley, Marvis, Knoxville* | 51 | 150 | 22 | 44 | 56 | 9 | 0 | 1 | 27 | 4 | 3 | 24 | 0 | 27 | 1 | 3 | .293 |
| Foster, Larry, Knoxville | 67 | 213 | 35 | 60 | 93 | 9 | 3 | 6 | 40 | 1 | 5 | 47 | 1 | 45 | 5 | 4 | .282 |
| Giegler, Mark, Montgomery | 52 | 138 | 17 | 34 | 39 | 5 | 0 | 0 | 12 | 2 | 1 | 7 | 0 | 21 | 3 | 5 | .246 |
| Gomez, Juan, Birmingham | 1 | 4 | 0 | 1 | 1 | 0 | 0 | 0 | 0 | 0 | 0 | 0 | 0 | 1 | 0 | 0 | .250 |
| Gonzales, Daniel, Mon* | 123 | 467 | 45 | 123 | 194 | 19 | 11 | 10 | 54 | 5 | 3 | 21 | 6 | 48 | 8 | 8 | .263 |
| Gonzalez, Luis, Jacksonville | 14 | 38 | 2 | 1 | 1 | 0 | 0 | 0 | 0 | 1 | 0 | 1 | 0 | 10 | 1 | 0 | .026 |
| Gross, Wayne, Birmingham* | 130 | 435 | 69 | 121 | 205 | 23 | 2 | 19 | 71 | 1 | 2 | 84 | 6 | 68 | 3 | 1 | .278 |
| Hacker, Jimmie, Birmingham | 105 | 323 | 36 | 73 | 93 | 12 | 1 | 2 | 40 | 8 | 2 | 53 | 5 | 55 | 0 | 2 | .226 |
| Haines, Dennis, Bir* | 115 | 366 | 47 | 97 | 125 | 15 | 2 | 3 | 48 | 2 | 6 | 72 | 3 | 72 | 4 | 2 | .265 |
| Heil, Charles, Asheville† | 115 | 423 | 60 | 136 | 189 | 15 | 4 | 10 | 57 | 2 | 4 | 28 | 1 | 35 | 3 | 4 | .322 |
| Howard, Larry, Savannah | 42 | 136 | 15 | 30 | 39 | 6 | 0 | 1 | 15 | 0 | 3 | 24 | 2 | 23 | 0 | 0 | .221 |
| Ingalls, Richard, Bir* | 87 | 277 | 24 | 69 | 80 | 5 | 0 | 2 | 23 | 20 | 2 | 19 | 1 | 17 | 2 | 4 | .249 |
| Javier, I. Alfredo, Columbus | 117 | 448 | 51 | 135 | 188 | 14 | 6 | 9 | 72 | 1 | 6 | 23 | 15 | 42 | 18 | 11 | .301 |
| Johnson, James L., Columbus | 52 | 171 | 20 | 44 | 56 | 6 | 0 | 2 | 11 | 1 | 2 | 16 | 0 | 19 | 0 | 1 | .257 |
| Johnson, John C., Columbus | 99 | 301 | 20 | 63 | 67 | 4 | 0 | 0 | 16 | 8 | 2 | 20 | 5 | 37 | 2 | 1 | .209 |
| Jones, Bryan, Jacksonville | 42 | 124 | 16 | 24 | 38 | 5 | 0 | 3 | 11 | 1 | 2 | 16 | 1 | 31 | 1 | 3 | .194 |
| Kilpatrick, Cleo, Knoxville* | 133 | 471 | 64 | 133 | 190 | 30 | 3 | 7 | 65 | 2 | 3 | 47 | 1 | 57 | 10 | 11 | .282 |
| Kravec, Kenneth, Knoxville* | 1 | 1 | 0 | 0 | 0 | 0 | 0 | 0 | 0 | 0 | 0 | 0 | 0 | 0 | 0 | 0 | .000 |
| Lacey, John, Savannah* | 118 | 382 | 29 | 89 | 112 | 12 | 1 | 3 | 33 | 4 | 4 | 25 | 1 | 69 | 6 | 3 | .233 |
| Lantigua, Manuel, Columbus | 18 | 54 | 5 | 11 | 15 | 2 | 1 | 0 | 6 | 0 | 2 | 2 | 0 | 11 | 0 | 0 | .204 |
| Larkin, Michael, Jacksonville* | 1 | 1 | 0 | 0 | 0 | 0 | 0 | 0 | 0 | 0 | 0 | 0 | 0 | 0 | 0 | 0 | .000 |
| Liranzo, Rafael, Asheville | 81 | 279 | 30 | 71 | 103 | 18 | 1 | 4 | 29 | 1 | 3 | 16 | 0 | 59 | 3 | 1 | .254 |
| Lonchar, John, Orlando | 106 | 332 | 35 | 78 | 99 | 10 | 1 | 3 | 19 | 2 | 0 | 35 | 0 | 51 | 3 | 1 | .235 |
| Mallory, Sheldon, Jack* | 123 | 432 | 68 | 103 | 161 | 18 | 2 | 12 | 56 | 6 | 3 | 69 | 4 | 71 | 42 | 13 | .238 |
| Maloof, Jack, Orlando* | 119 | 385 | 62 | 122 | 140 | 11 | 2 | 1 | 40 | 1 | 2 | 105 | 4 | 35 | 16 | 8 | .317 |
| Mankowski, Philip, Mon* | 124 | 407 | 44 | 115 | 164 | 18 | 2 | 9 | 49 | 3 | 1 | 33 | 4 | 31 | 1 | 3 | .283 |
| McCord, G. Toy, Knoxville | 50 | 162 | 10 | 37 | 48 | 2 | 0 | 3 | 19 | 2 | 1 | 16 | 0 | 20 | 3 | 2 | .228 |
| McKinney, Lynn, Jack* | 1 | 0 | 0 | 0 | 0 | 0 | 0 | 0 | 0 | 0 | 0 | 0 | 0 | 0 | 0 | 0 | .000 |
| McLaughlin, Donnie E., Col | 87 | 302 | 28 | 80 | 101 | 12 | 3 | 1 | 24 | 2 | 2 | 20 | 2 | 39 | 0 | 1 | .265 |
| Medeiros, Gary, Birmingham | 14 | 24 | 1 | 2 | 2 | 0 | 0 | 0 | 0 | 0 | 0 | 2 | 0 | 1 | 0 | 0 | .143 |
| Meier, F. Calvin, Columbus | 42 | 142 | 27 | 41 | 52 | 7 | 2 | 0 | 13 | 1 | 0 | 23 | 0 | 19 | 1 | 1 | .289 |
| Melendez, William, Col | 58 | 187 | 14 | 46 | 59 | 8 | 1 | 1 | 21 | 3 | 0 | 22 | 0 | 22 | 1 | 0 | .246 |
| Murphy, Brian, Jacksonville | 121 | 358 | 33 | 92 | 100 | 6 | 1 | 0 | 23 | 1 | 2 | 53 | 2 | 45 | 0 | 3 | .257 |
| Murphy, Marlan, Savannah | 20 | 59 | 8 | 14 | 21 | 4 | 0 | 1 | 1 | 0 | 9 | 0 | 15 | 3 | 1 | | .237 |
| Murphy, Scott, Asheville | 75 | 244 | 28 | 55 | 62 | 7 | 0 | 0 | 21 | 3 | 1 | 30 | 0 | 28 | 2 | 0 | .225 |
| Muray, Eddie, Asheville | 124 | 436 | 66 | 115 | 189 | 13 | 5 | 17 | 68 | 2 | 2 | 53 | 4 | 79 | 7 | 4 | .264 |
| Nasif, Ralph, Montgomery | 53 | 164 | 16 | 41 | 54 | 8 | 1 | 1 | 13 | 4 | 0 | 7 | 0 | 30 | 3 | 3 | .250 |
| Noah, Russell, Orlando* | 67 | 179 | 21 | 35 | 50 | 7 | 1 | 2 | 17 | 3 | 2 | 26 | 0 | 50 | 2 | 1 | .196 |
| Norton, Fred, Knoxville | 39 | 145 | 9 | 25 | 29 | 1 | 0 | 1 | 9 | 5 | 0 | 11 | 0 | 33 | 2 | 3 | .172 |
| Norton, Thomas, Orlando | 1 | 3 | 1 | 0 | 0 | 0 | 0 | 0 | 0 | 0 | 0 | 1 | 0 | 2 | 0 | 0 | .000 |
| Norwood, Willie, Orlando | 128 | 443 | 55 | 115 | 171 | 13 | 5 | 11 | 55 | 3 | 5 | 40 | 4 | 83 | 15 | 7 | .260 |
| Obradovich, James, Orlando* | 134 | 424 | 61 | 97 | 188 | 10 | 0 | 27 | 74 | 2 | 7 | 75 | 0 | 87 | 3 | 2 | .229 |
| Ondina, Mike, Knoxville* | 128 | 418 | 54 | 105 | 155 | 14 | 0 | 12 | 42 | 6 | 4 | 63 | 1 | 85 | 7 | 7 | .251 |
| Oquendo, Ismael, Asheville* | 115 | 404 | 57 | 105 | 166 | 23 | 4 | 10 | 56 | 3 | 2 | 35 | 3 | 59 | 5 | 2 | .260 |
| O'Rear, John, Asheville | 115 | 428 | 57 | 101 | 142 | 12 | 1 | 9 | 46 | 7 | 4 | 23 | 3 | 68 | 3 | 3 | .236 |
| Pacplxo, Dennis, Jacksonville | 63 | 169 | 7 | 32 | 39 | 4 | 0 | 1 | 12 | 1 | 1 | 22 | 1 | 36 | 0 | 3 | .189 |
| Palmer, Robert, Knoxville | 15 | 40 | 3 | 6 | 8 | 2 | 0 | 0 | 4 | 0 | 0 | 4 | 0 | 15 | 0 | 0 | .150 |
| Patterson, Paul, Knoxville* | 2 | 1 | 0 | 1 | 1 | 0 | 0 | 0 | 0 | 0 | 0 | 0 | 1 | 0 | 0 | 0 | 1.000 |

| Player and Club | G. | AB. | R. | H. | TB. | 2B. | 3B. | HR. | RBI. | SH. | SF. | BB. | HP. | SO. | SB. | CS. | Pct. |
|---|---|---|---|---|---|---|---|---|---|---|---|---|---|---|---|---|---|
| Picciolo, Robert, Bir...... | 133 | 488 | 55 | 135 | 179 | 23 | 6 | 3 | 62 | 13 | 7 | 15 | 1 | 67 | 7 | 1 | .277 |
| Pittman, Joseph, Columbus.. | 21 | 71 | 8 | 19 | 41 | 2 | 0 | 0 | 1 | 1 | 0 | 11 | | 2 | 2 | | .268 |
| Poquette, Thomas, Jack*... | 105 | 355 | 50 | 91 | 122 | 16 | 0 | 5 | 40 | 3 | 4 | 47 | 10 | 38 | 8 | 3 | .256 |
| Portley, Calvin, Columbus.. | 133 | 464 | 82 | 111 | 126 | 11 | 2 | 0 | 24 | 15 | 0 | 99 | 5 | 73 | 22 | 9 | .239 |
| Puig, Richard, Knoxville*.. | 83 | 245 | 29 | 53 | 72 | 11 | 1 | 2 | 25 | 2 | 1 | 36 | 0 | 35 | 6 | 4 | .216 |
| Rahe, Gary, Jacksonville*.. | 25 | 80 | 11 | 25 | 35 | 6 | 2 | 0 | 8 | 1 | 1 | 10 | 0 | 13 | 1 | 2 | .313 |
| Reed, Kenneth, Columbus ... | 23 | 84 | 6 | 13 | 14 | 1 | 0 | 0 | 1 | 0 | 0 | 10 | 0 | 10 | 1 | 1 | .155 |
| Rockett, Patrick, Savannah. | 130 | 453 | 50 | 115 | 131 | 8 | 1 | 2 | 35 | 8 | 4 | 60 | 8 | 59 | 8 | 4 | .254 |
| Roderick, Barry, Orlando*.. | 68 | 176 | 8 | 31 | 35 | 4 | 0 | 0 | 8 | 8 | 0 | 12 | 1 | 22 | 5 | 0 | .176 |
| Royster, Willie, Asheville .. | 61 | 201 | 22 | 51 | 72 | 10 | 1 | 3 | 21 | 2 | 0 | 17 | 1 | 53 | 2 | 4 | .254 |
| Rubertino, Joseph, Mon* ... | 1 | 1 | 0 | 0 | 0 | 0 | 0 | 0 | 0 | 0 | 0 | 0 | 0 | 0 | 0 | 0 | .000 |
| Ruiz, Manuel, Savannah .... | 107 | 355 | 52 | 96 | 123 | 10 | 4 | 3 | 41 | 5 | 1 | 47 | 3 | 48 | 11 | 2 | .270 |
| Ryan, Terry, Orlando ....... | 3 | 1 | 0 | 0 | 0 | 0 | 0 | 0 | 0 | 0 | 0 | 0 | 0 | 0 | 0 | 0 | .000 |
| Safrit, Cass, Asheville ..... | 18 | 65 | 8 | 16 | 18 | 2 | 0 | 0 | 6 | 0 | 0 | 7 | 0 | 6 | 0 | 0 | .246 |
| Schlueter, Jay, Columbus†.. | 14 | 43 | 2 | 3 | 6 | 0 | 0 | 1 | 3 | 1 | 0 | 4 | 0 | 14 | 0 | 0 | .070 |
| Schultz, Theodore, Knoxville† | 20 | 43 | 4 | 9 | 12 | 3 | 0 | 0 | 4 | 2 | 0 | 8 | 0 | 8 | 0 | 0 | .209 |
| Scott, Rodney, Jacksonville.. | 20 | 77 | 19 | 26 | 28 | 2 | 0 | 0 | 8 | 1 | 2 | 14 | 0 | 9 | 12 | 2 | .338 |
| Seidholz, Donn, Knoxville .. | 64 | 211 | 13 | 52 | 66 | 9 | 1 | 1 | 19 | 3 | 3 | 8 | 2 | 36 | 2 | 3 | .246 |
| Sevillano, Jose, Savannah ... | 1 | 1 | 0 | 1 | 1 | 0 | 0 | 0 | 0 | 0 | 0 | 0 | 0 | 0 | 0 | 0 | 1.000 |
| Shaffer, Duane, Knoxville ... | 1 | 1 | 0 | 0 | 0 | 0 | 0 | 0 | 0 | 0 | 0 | 0 | 0 | 1 | 0 | 0 | .000 |
| Shipley, Ted, Orlando ...... | 116 | 363 | 54 | 81 | 112 | 9 | 8 | 2 | 31 | 6 | 4 | 55 | 2 | 92 | 12 | 6 | .223 |
| Shippy, Gregory, Mon ...... | 9 | 24 | 1 | 2 | 5 | 0 | 0 | 1 | 3 | 3 | 0 | 1 | 0 | 9 | 0 | 1 | .083 |
| Sinovich, Mark, Bir ........ | 42 | 114 | 9 | 22 | 36 | 8 | 1 | 1 | 9 | 0 | 2 | 10 | 0 | 24 | 0 | 1 | .193 |
| Skaggs, David, Asheville ... | 59 | 199 | 26 | 53 | 63 | 8 | 1 | 0 | 24 | 0 | 4 | 32 | 1 | 16 | 0 | 3 | .266 |
| Smith, Calvin, Savannah*.. | 94 | 342 | 45 | 88 | 95 | 4 | 0 | 1 | 16 | 5 | 0 | 30 | 6 | 50 | 29 | 13 | .257 |
| Smith, Charles W., Jack†... | 98 | 285 | 24 | 68 | 101 | 16 | 1 | 5 | 36 | 4 | 5 | 40 | 1 | 63 | 2 | 7 | .239 |
| Spare, Donald, Birmingham.. | 57 | 132 | 17 | 26 | 32 | 3 | 0 | 1 | 6 | 4 | 1 | 25 | 2 | 18 | 2 | 1 | .197 |
| Squires, Michael, Knoxville* | 129 | 448 | 68 | 136 | 178 | 23 | 5 | 3 | 50 | 6 | 3 | 67 | 1 | 31 | 24 | 13 | .304 |
| Stanton, Michael, Columbus | 1 | 3 | 0 | 0 | 0 | 0 | 0 | 0 | 0 | 0 | 0 | 0 | 0 | 1 | 0 | 0 | .000 |
| Stinson, Homer, Knoxville*.. | 5 | 5 | 2 | 0 | 0 | 0 | 0 | 0 | 0 | 0 | 1 | 0 | 0 | 3 | 0 | 0 | .000 |
| Stodgel, Douglas, Knoxville | 131 | 491 | 78 | 126 | 167 | 13 | 2 | 8 | 32 | 7 | 4 | 48 | 3 | 36 | 7 | 10 | .257 |
| Stone, Steven A., Savannah.. | 3 | 4 | 1 | 3 | 4 | 1 | 0 | 0 | 1 | 0 | 0 | 4 | 0 | 0 | 0 | 0 | .750 |
| Tatis, Fernando, Columbus.. | 86 | 314 | 41 | 81 | 119 | 18 | 4 | 4 | 38 | 6 | 2 | 24 | 2 | 50 | 5 | 3 | .258 |
| Tevlin, Creighton, Asheville* | 116 | 439 | 54 | 130 | 153 | 18 | 1 | 1 | 34 | 7 | 2 | 54 | 4 | 41 | 6 | 7 | .296 |
| Thayer, Gregory, Orlando ... | 1 | 2 | 0 | 0 | 0 | 0 | 0 | 0 | 0 | 0 | 0 | 0 | 0 | 0 | 0 | 0 | .000 |
| Thomasson, Harold, Jack.... | 21 | 44 | 8 | 10 | 11 | 1 | 0 | 0 | 2 | 1 | 0 | 5 | 0 | 14 | 0 | 0 | .227 |
| Thompson, Jason, Mon* .... | 75 | 222 | 42 | 72 | 116 | 12 | 1 | 10 | 38 | 2 | 5 | 38 | 0 | 22 | 2 | 1 | .324 |
| Tobik, David, Montgomery ... | 1 | 0 | 1 | 0 | 0 | 0 | 0 | 0 | 0 | 0 | 0 | 0 | 0 | 0 | 0 | 0 | .000 |
| Valle, John, Montgomery... | 134 | 460 | 76 | 130 | 218 | 15 | 2 | 23 | 72 | 2 | 6 | 75 | 3 | 71 | 3 | 4 | .283 |
| Velazquez, Federico, Sav ... | 129 | 477 | 59 | 126 | 205 | 14 | 1 | 21 | 69 | 3 | 9 | 31 | 4 | 78 | 8 | 4 | .264 |
| Ward, Gary, Orlando ...... | 124 | 438 | 45 | 117 | 169 | 18 | 5 | 8 | 71 | 0 | 8 | 51 | 0 | 85 | 4 | 1 | .267 |
| Washington, Ronald, Jack... | 26 | 267 | 32 | 61 | 70 | 7 | 1 | 0 | 20 | 7 | 2 | 21 | 2 | 39 | 18 | 9 | .228 |
| Wheeler, Edward, Knoxville.. | 45 | 144 | 28 | 48 | 55 | 5 | 1 | 0 | 12 | 1 | 2 | 32 | 1 | 24 | 5 | 8 | .333 |
| Wilfong, Robert, Orlando*.. | 125 | 403 | 54 | 99 | 127 | 14 | 1 | 4 | 37 | 6 | 2 | 64 | 1 | 63 | 21 | 11 | .246 |
| Willis, James, Columbus..... | 125 | 445 | 41 | 106 | 153 | 18 | 1 | 9 | 44 | 7 | 1 | 35 | 4 | 82 | 1 | 2 | .238 |
| Wolf, Michael, Knoxville..... | 112 | 338 | 23 | 75 | 84 | 5 | 2 | 0 | 30 | 4 | 1 | 23 | 6 | 39 | 1 | 4 | .222 |
| Wolfe, Lawrence, Orlando.... | 138 | 436 | 46 | 109 | 127 | 6 | 0 | 4 | 42 | 6 | 2 | 63 | 0 | 39 | 5 | 5 | .250 |
| Woods, Alvis, Orlando*..... | 123 | 411 | 55 | 108 | 145 | 11 | 4 | 6 | 50 | 6 | 2 | 62 | 2 | 32 | 6 | 4 | .263 |
| Woods, Gary, Birmingham ... | 134 | 484 | 76 | 126 | 156 | 15 | 6 | 1 | 43 | 13 | 2 | 63 | 7 | 70 | 17 | 12 | .260 |
| Zdeb, Joseph, Jacksonville .. | 129 | 438 | 60 | 116 | 156 | 17 | 5 | 5 | 43 | 1 | 4 | 63 | 4 | 80 | 11 | 12 | .265 |

The following pitchers had no plate appearances primarily through use of designated hitters, listed alphabetically by club, games in parentheses.

ASHEVILLE—Babcock, Robert (28); Dierker, Richard (6); Flinn, John (20); Hayden, William (6); Hile, Michael* (27); Martinez, J. Dennis (6); McCall, Larry* (19); Moore, Henry* (5); Parrott, Michael (25); Peach, Russell* (22); Robson, Gary (4); Smith, Myrl (35); Smith, Wilbur* (25); Wessel, Douglas (24).

BIRMINGHAM—Batton, Christopher (29); Bockewitz, Stanley (28); Griffin, Alan (8); Harrell, Clarence (6); Lacey, Robert (33); Lysander, Richard (8); Mazzone, Leo* (8); Mitchell, Craig, (12); Sapp, Carl (2); Scarbery, Randy (17); Stegman, Dennis (27); Taylor, Randall, (33); Tronerud, Ricky (28); Van Bommel, William (16); Wibberley, Christopher (3).

COLUMBUS—Aloi, David (8); Culpepper, David (25); de los Santos, Ramon* (40); Elenes, Larry (13); Larson, Daniel (17); Lauzerique, George (8); McLaughlin, Michael (15); Sambito, Joseph* (30); Sanchez, Luis (21); Selak, Ronald (6); Sosa, Jose (29); Taylor, Charles L. (15); Williams, Richard A. (22).

JACKSONVILLE—Balderson, Richard (20); Ballinger, Mark (18); Barr, Robert* (7); Bernard, Edward (33); Branch, Roy (18); Bruno, Thomas (4); Falcon, Robert* (10); Garcia, Ruben (29); Hammon, Randal (27); Hasbach, David (24); Hrovat, Dale (9); Leshnock, Donald* (16); McClure, Robert (9); Olsen, Lewis (16); Pelz, Paul (6); Quisenberry, Daniel (6); Wright, Gary Evan* (15).

KNOXVILLE—Bock, Paul (3); Frost, C. David (28); Holly, Jeffrey* (17); Kucek, John (21); Lehman, William (8); Lukevics, Mitchell (4); Smith, Barry (30); Stoddard, Timothy (31); Williams, Leo (26).

MONTGOMERY—Alonso, Julio* (2); Cappuzzello, George (8); Christenson, Gary (15); Fidrych, M. Steven (7); Glynn, Edward (21); Ibarguen, Michael (11); Ignasiak, Gary (15); Kuhl, Gregory (7); Lantz, Thomas† (9); Lemongello, Mark (15); MacCormack, Frank (22); Madden, William (2); Meyerrose, Michael (3); Motil, John (25); Murphy, Patrick (4); Pentz, Eugene (22); Sykes, Robert* (27); Trella, Stephen (2).

ORLANDO—Bethke, Rick* (14); Lerner, Lewis (20); Luebber, Stephen (6); Maier, John (25); Maneely, Robert (23); Schultz, Kenneth (4); Schuster, Frank* (4); Seberger, Michael (30); Smith, W. Coleman† (16); Stiegemeier, William (11); Stone, Gail (10); Van DeCasteele, Michael (20).

SAVANNAH—Alexander, Roger G. (20); Box, Robert* (25); Camp, Rick (25); Campbell, David A. (22); Ford, P. Wentworth (6); Johnson, Jerome (8); Lusic, George (32); McLaughlin, Joey (8); Rios, Wilfredo* (31).

GRAND-SLAM HOME RUNS: Cador, 3; Clark, 2; Arcia, Bates, Englishbey, Gross, Melendez, Murray, O'Rear, Seidholz, Willis, 1 each.

AWARDED FIRST BASE ON INTERFERENCE: Cador 2 (Haines, Melendez), Giegler (Boone), Haines (Lantigua), Ruiz (Adams), Seidholz (Paepke).

## CLUB FIELDING

| Club | G. | PO. | A. | E. | DP. | PB. | Pct. | Club | G. | PO. | A. | E. | DP. | PB. | Pct. |
|---|---|---|---|---|---|---|---|---|---|---|---|---|---|---|---|
| Orlando | 138 | 3358 | 1521 | 124 | 129 | 10 | .9752 | Asheville | 138 | 3482 | 1572 | 153 | 146 | 8 | .971 |
| Montgomery | 134 | 3354 | 1515 | 126 | 120 | 24 | .9747 | Savannah | 134 | 3398 | 1406 | 157 | 101 | 12 | .968 |
| Birmingham | 134 | 3337 | 1417 | 131 | 133 | 25 | .973 | Columbus | 134 | 3411 | 1464 | 178 | 99 | 26 | .965 |
| Knoxville | 138 | 3453 | 1480 | 143 | 127 | 70 | .972 | Jacksonville | 138 | 3442 | 1361 | 181 | 101 | 19 | .964 |

## INDIVIDUAL FIELDING
### FIRST BASEMEN

*Throws lefthanded.

| Player and Club | G. | PO. | A. | E. | DP. | Pct. | Player and Club | G. | PO. | A. | E. | DP. | Pct. |
|---|---|---|---|---|---|---|---|---|---|---|---|---|---|
| Corcoran, Montgomery | 22 | 173 | 19 | 0 | 13 | 1.000 | Willis, Columbus | 124 | 1104 | 107 | 9 | 79 | .993 |
| Velazquez, Savannah | 15 | 140 | 6 | 0 | 9 | 1.000 | Maloof, Orlando* | 104 | 896 | 75 | 7 | 86 | .993 |
| D. McLaughlin, Col. | 7 | 54 | 3 | 0 | 1 | 1.000 | Beaurivage, Bir* | 133 | 1132 | 91 | 12 | 116 | .990 |
| Colon, Montgomery* | 5 | 30 | 1 | 0 | 2 | 1.000 | Lacey, Savannah* | 118 | 966 | 48 | 12 | 78 | .989 |
| Washington, Jackson. | 3 | 21 | 0 | 0 | 2 | 1.000 | Murray, Asheville | 65 | 629 | 33 | 9 | 73 | .987 |
| Arcia, Jacksonville. | 3 | 15 | 1 | 0 | 1 | 1.000 | Wheeler, Knoxville | 10 | 72 | 3 | 1 | 7 | .987 |
| Rahe, Jacksonville* | 1 | 8 | 0 | 0 | 1 | 1.000 | Thompson, Mon* | 71 | 633 | 47 | 10 | 56 | .986 |
| Gross, Birmingham | 1 | 5 | 0 | 0 | 1 | 1.000 | Obradovich, Orlando* | 37 | 332 | 21 | 5 | 30 | .986 |
| Skaggs, Asheville | 1 | 3 | 0 | 0 | 1 | 1.000 | Clark, Jacksonville | 130 | 1105 | 56 | 18 | 83 | .985 |
| Enright, Knoxville | 1 | 3 | 0 | 0 | 0 | 1.000 | Cador, Savannah* | 6 | 54 | 4 | 1 | 5 | .983 |
| Seidholz, Knoxville | 1 | 2 | 0 | 0 | 1 | 1.000 | Oquendo, Asheville | 74 | 669 | 41 | 13 | 54 | .982 |
| Paepke, Jacksonville | 1 | 2 | 0 | 0 | 0 | 1.000 | Bates, Montgomery | 43 | 410 | 40 | 12 | 33 | .974 |
| Breitzman, Birmingham | 1 | 1 | 0 | 0 | 1 | 1.000 | Mallory, Jacksonville. | 7 | 30 | 4 | 1 | 3 | .971 |
| Murphy, Asheville | 1 | 1 | 0 | 0 | 1 | 1.000 | Foley, Knoxville | 5 | 43 | 3 | 3 | 2 | .944 |
| Fleming, Jacksonville | 1 | 0 | 1 | 0 | 0 | 1.000 | Tatis, Columbus | 4 | 29 | 3 | 2 | 6 | .941 |
| SQUIRES, Knx* | 128 | 1085 | 78 | 6 | 100 | .995 | Boone, Columbus | 1 | 3 | 2 | 2 | 0 | .714 |

### SECOND BASEMEN

| Player and Club | G. | PO. | A. | E. | DP. | Pct. | Player and Club | G. | PO. | A. | E. | DP. | Pct. |
|---|---|---|---|---|---|---|---|---|---|---|---|---|---|
| Giegler, Montgomery | 11 | 26 | 29 | 0 | 11 | 1.000 | Wilfong, Orlando | 122 | 274 | 347 | 16 | 80 | .975 |
| Nasif, Montgomery | 8 | 18 | 17 | 0 | 2 | 1.000 | Argenti, Birmingham | 134 | 310 | 395 | 21 | 91 | .971 |
| McCord, Knoxville | 4 | 5 | 8 | 0 | 2 | 1.000 | Murphy, Asheville | 38 | 71 | 122 | 6 | 16 | .970 |
| Albert, Savannah | 1 | 4 | 0 | 0 | 1 | 1.000 | Roderick, Orlando | 25 | 51 | 80 | 4 | 20 | .970 |
| D. McLaughlin, Col. | 2 | 3 | 1 | 0 | 0 | 1.000 | Doyle, Asheville | 106 | 238 | 344 | 22 | 81 | .964 |
| Ingalls, Birmingham. | 3 | 1 | 3 | 0 | 1 | 1.000 | Washington, Jackson | 51 | 76 | 129 | 8 | 21 | .962 |
| Wolf, Knoxville | 1 | 1 | 1 | 0 | 1 | 1.000 | Murphy, Jacksonville | 55 | 95 | 153 | 10 | 19 | .961 |
| Dauer, Asheville | 2 | 1 | 1 | 0 | 1 | 1.000 | Smith, Savannah | 93 | 224 | 271 | 21 | 49 | .959 |
| Breitzman, Birm | 1 | 0 | 1 | 0 | 0 | 1.000 | Portley, Columbus | 132 | 221 | 219 | 22 | 70 | .952 |
| Cummings, Savannah | 1 | 0 | 0 | 0 | 0 | 1.000 | Gonzalez, Jacksonville | 11 | 16 | 24 | 2 | 6 | .952 |
| STODGEL, Knoxville | 98 | 201 | 269 | 4 | 63 | .992 | Jones, Jacksonville | 37 | 59 | 93 | 8 | 16 | .950 |
| Puig, Knoxville | 46 | 88 | 148 | 2 | 25 | .992 | Butler, Montgomery | 8 | 15 | 23 | 2 | 4 | .950 |
| Eschen, Montgomery | 113 | 287 | 345 | 11 | 72 | .983 | Crosta, Knoxville | 2 | 5 | 6 | 1 | 3 | .917 |
| Ruiz, Savannah | 46 | 109 | 148 | 6 | 26 | .977 | | | | | | | |

### THIRD BASEMEN

| Player and Club | G. | PO. | A. | E. | DP. | Pct. | Player and Club | G. | PO. | A. | E. | DP. | Pct. |
|---|---|---|---|---|---|---|---|---|---|---|---|---|---|
| Willis, Columbus | 1 | 3 | 3 | 0 | 0 | 1.000 | Safrit, Asheville | 17 | 13 | 35 | 4 | 3 | .923 |
| Roderick, Orlando | 3 | 0 | 6 | 0 | 0 | 1.000 | Spare, Birmingham | 51 | 40 | 63 | 9 | 2 | .920 |
| Nasif, Montgomery | 4 | 1 | 5 | 0 | 1 | 1.000 | D. McLaughlin, Col. | 78 | 61 | 130 | 17 | 7 | .918 |
| Murphy, Jacksonville | 2 | 2 | 2 | 0 | 0 | 1.000 | Coughlan, Montgomery | 17 | 9 | 36 | 4 | 6 | .918 |
| Crosta, Knoxville | 3 | 1 | 2 | 0 | 0 | 1.000 | Seidolz, Knoxville | 57 | 45 | 98 | 14 | 10 | .911 |
| McCord, Knoxville | 1 | 1 | 0 | 0 | 0 | 1.000 | Arcia, Jacksonville | 2 | 2 | 8 | 1 | 1 | .909 |
| Tatis, Columbus | 1 | 1 | 1 | 0 | 0 | 1.000 | Hacker, Savannah | 52 | 49 | 99 | 15 | 10 | .908 |
| DAUER, Asheville | 103 | 97 | 194 | 6 | 28 | .980 | Murphy, Asheville | 4 | 3 | 6 | 1 | 0 | .900 |
| Reed, Columbus | 13 | 6 | 25 | 1 | 1 | .969 | Pittman, Columbus | 12 | 13 | 22 | 4 | 2 | .897 |
| Cripe, Jacksonville | 98 | 87 | 159 | 9 | 9 | .965 | Jim Johnson, Columbus | 17 | 14 | 32 | 7 | 0 | .868 |
| Bell, Knoxville | 66 | 68 | 117 | 7 | 11 | .964 | Thomasson, Jack | 19 | 16 | 23 | 7 | 3 | .848 |
| Mankowski, Mont | 118 | 81 | 257 | 13 | 22 | .963 | Murray, Asheville | 14 | 8 | 25 | 6 | 1 | .846 |
| Wolfe, Orlando | 138 | 101 | 266 | 15 | 18 | .961 | Washington, Jackson | 26 | 20 | 39 | 12 | 0 | .831 |
| Puig, Knoxville | 19 | 19 | 29 | 2 | 1 | .960 | Giegler, Montgomery | 3 | 3 | 5 | 2 | 1 | .800 |
| Ruiz, Savannah | 58 | 53 | 124 | 9 | 5 | .952 | Breitzman, Bir | 12 | 10 | 12 | 6 | 1 | .786 |
| Albert, Savannah | 27 | 15 | 55 | 4 | 6 | .946 | Velazquez, Savannah | 1 | 1 | 1 | 1 | 0 | .667 |
| Meier, Columbus | 13 | 15 | 28 | 3 | 3 | .935 | Cummings, Savannah | 1 | 0 | 1 | 2 | 0 | .333 |
| Ingalls, Birmingham | 84 | 64 | 147 | 16 | 20 | .930 | Smith, Jacksonville | 1 | 0 | 0 | 2 | 0 | .000 |

## SHORTSTOPS

| Player and Club | G. | PO. | A. | E. | DP. | Pct. |
|---|---|---|---|---|---|---|
| Albert, Savannah ... | 4 | 4 | 12 | 0 | 2 | 1.000 |
| Giegler, Montgomery .4 | 3 | 7 | 0 | 1 | 1.000 | |
| Gonzalez, Jacksonville | 3 | 7 | 2 | 0 | 2 | 1.000 |
| Spare, Birmingham.. | 3 | 3 | 2 | 0 | 0 | 1.000 |
| PICCIOLO, Birm .. | 133 | 278 | 404 | 18 | 91 | .974 |
| Nasif, Montgomery... | 33 | 45 | 104 | 5 | 17 | .968 |
| O'Rear, Asheville .. | 115 | 197 | 357 | 21 | 77 | .963 |
| Shipley, Orlando .. | 114 | 144 | 331 | 19 | 66 | .962 |
| Murphy, Jackson .. | 63 | 99 | 183 | 11 | 37 | .962 |
| Meier, Columbus .. | 29 | 57 | 91 | 6 | 17 | .961 |
| Washington, Jackson | 18 | 16 | 31 | 2 | 8 | .959 |
| Stodgel, Knoxville .. | 41 | 53 | 106 | 7 | 21 | .958 |
| Roderick, Orlando .. | 35 | 52 | 77 | 6 | 14 | .956 |
| Rockett, Savannah .. | 130 | 215 | 391 | 36 | 66 | .944 |
| John Johnson, Col... | 99 | 181 | 243 | 27 | 45 | .940 |
| Brookens, Montgomery | 99 | 139 | 298 | 31 | 40 | .934 |
| Butler, Montgomery .. | 7 | 10 | 17 | 2 | 7 | .931 |
| Jim Johnson, Col ... | 10 | 14 | 23 | 3 | 5 | .925 |
| Wolf, Knoxville .... | 110 | 191 | 309 | 41 | 56 | .924 |
| Scott, Jacksonville .. | 20 | 34 | 49 | 7 | 5 | .922 |
| Murphy, Asheville .. | 23 | 34 | 70 | 9 | 11 | .920 |
| Arcia, Jacksonville .. | 42 | 79 | 106 | 17 | 18 | .916 |
| Pittman, Columbus.. | 5 | 7 | 7 | 2 | 2 | .875 |
| Ruiz, Savannah ..... | 13 | 1 | 2 | 1 | 0 | .750 |

## OUTFIELDERS

| Player and Club | G. | PO. | A. | E. | DP. | Pct. |
|---|---|---|---|---|---|---|
| Brown, Asheville .. | 6 | 13 | 2 | 0 | 1 | 1.000 |
| Blessitt, Birmingham | 3 | 7 | 0 | 0 | 0 | 1.000 |
| Capehart, Birmingham | 3 | 6 | 0 | 0 | 0 | 1.000 |
| Colon, Montgomery*.. | 3 | 5 | 0 | 0 | 0 | 1.000 |
| Dlugach, Knoxville..... | 2 | 3 | 0 | 0 | 0 | 1.000 |
| Murphy, Asheville .. | 5 | 3 | 0 | 0 | 0 | 1.000 |
| Fleming, Jacksonville | 1 | 1 | 0 | 0 | 0 | 1.000 |
| McCord, Knoxville.. | 1 | 1 | 0 | 0 | 0 | 1.000 |
| Jones, Jacksonville... | 3 | 1 | 0 | 0 | 0 | 1.000 |
| Foster, Knoxville .. | 67 | 102 | 4 | 1 | 0 | .991 |
| GONZALES, Mont .. | 122 | 181 | 11 | 2 | 1 | .990 |
| Zdeb, Jacksonville .. | 124 | 246 | 11 | 3 | 4 | .988 |
| Woods, Orlando* .. | 120 | 248 | 9 | 4 | 2 | .985 |
| Poquette, Jackson .. | 105 | 179 | 16 | 3 | 4 | .985 |
| Bryant, Birmingham | 134 | 235 | 10 | 4 | 3 | .984 |
| Woods, Birmingham .. | 134 | 366 | 20 | 7 | 3 | .982 |
| Valle, Montgomery .. | 124 | 208 | 6 | 4 | 0 | .982 |
| Ward, Orlando .. | 122 | 201 | 10 | 4 | 3 | .981 |
| Baldwin, Mont*..... | 77 | 154 | 5 | 3 | 1 | .981 |
| Englert, Columbus*.. | 82 | 183 | 2 | 4 | 0 | .979 |
| Giegler, Montgomery | 24 | 46 | 1 | 1 | 1 | .979 |
| Mallory, Jacksonville* | 94 | 212 | 6 | 5 | 0 | .978 |
| Buckner, Asheville .. | 111 | 155 | 16 | 4 | 3 | .977 |
| Cador, Savannah* .. | 125 | 238 | 10 | 6 | 0 | .976 |
| Murphy, Savannah .. | 19 | 39 | 1 | 1 | 0 | .976 |
| Tevlin, Asheville* .. | 108 | 216 | 18 | 6 | 3 | .975 |
| Ondina, Knoxville .. | 127 | 249 | 9 | 7 | 0 | .974 |
| Heil, Asheville* .... | 112 | 204 | 19 | 6 | 6 | .974 |
| J. Collins, Savannah .. | 130 | 263 | 14 | 8 | 2 | .972 |
| Davis, Orlando .. | 57 | 118 | 6 | 4 | 0 | .969 |
| Cummings, Savannah | 76 | 117 | 7 | 4 | 1 | .969 |
| Liranzo, Asheville .. | 79 | 187 | 15 | 7 | 3 | .967 |
| Corcoran, Montgomery | 59 | 110 | 2 | 4 | 1 | .966 |
| Norwood, Orlando .. | 125 | 262 | 8 | 10 | 1 | .964 |
| Schlueter, Columbus | 13 | 27 | 0 | 1 | 0 | .964 |
| de la Rosa, Columbus | 20 | 25 | 1 | 1 | 0 | .963 |
| Jim Johnson, Col .. | 21 | 23 | 2 | 1 | 0 | .962 |
| Noah, Orlando* .. | 53 | 74 | 0 | 3 | 0 | .961 |
| Schultz, Knoxville.. | 19 | 20 | 4 | 1 | 1 | .960 |
| Kilpatrick, Knx*... | 132 | 241 | 14 | 11 | 5 | .959 |
| Norton, Knoxville .. | 39 | 101 | 4 | 5 | 1 | .955 |
| Javier, Columbus .. | 117 | 202 | 7 | 11 | 0 | .950 |
| Wheeler, Knoxville .. | 34 | 54 | 2 | 3 | 1 | .949 |
| Arline, Savannah* .. | 64 | 132 | 7 | 8 | 0 | .946 |
| Drake, Columbus .. | 39 | 83 | 1 | 5 | 0 | .944 |
| Gross, Birmingham .. | 129 | 188 | 16 | 13 | 4 | .940 |
| Bridges, Jacksonville | 24 | 35 | 2 | 3 | 1 | .925 |
| Englishbey, Col* .... | 107 | 166 | 5 | 14 | 0 | .924 |
| Enright, Knoxville.. | 5 | 10 | 2 | 1 | 0 | .923 |
| Rahe, Jacksonville* .. | 13 | 22 | 0 | 2 | 0 | .917 |
| Roderick, Orlando .. | 5 | 11 | 3 | 2 | 0 | .875 |
| Reed, Columbus ..... | 10 | 14 | 0 | 2 | 0 | .875 |
| Blomberg, Jacksonville | 6 | 7 | 0 | 1 | 0 | .875 |
| Smith, Jacksonville .. | 12 | 12 | 0 | 2 | 0 | .857 |
| Floyd, Columbus .. | 9 | 14 | 1 | 4 | 0 | .789 |
| Seidholz, Knoxville.. | 8 | 6 | 1 | 2 | 0 | .778 |

## CATCHERS

| Player and Club | G. | PO. | A. | E. | DP. | PB. | Pct. |
|---|---|---|---|---|---|---|---|
| Cariel, Orlando.. | 26 | 105 | 13 | 0 | 3 | 2 | 1.000 |
| Dlugach, Knx.. | 36 | 79 | 5 | 0 | 1 | 0 | 1.000 |
| Butera, Orlando | 16 | 61 | 14 | 0 | 4 | 0 | 1.000 |
| Epperly, Orlando | 3 | 14 | 4 | 0 | 1 | 0 | 1.000 |
| Medeiros, Bir... | 6 | 14 | 3 | 0 | 0 | 0 | 1.000 |
| Arline, Sav* .. | 1 | 8 | 0 | 0 | 0 | 0 | 1.000 |
| Gomez, Bir ..... | 1 | 7 | 0 | 0 | 0 | 0 | 1.000 |
| Ward, Orlando .. | 1 | 3 | 0 | 0 | 0 | 0 | 1.000 |
| Stone, Savannah | 1 | 1 | 0 | 0 | 0 | 0 | 1.000 |
| Melendez, Col .. | 55 | 309 | 32 | 2 | 6 | 10 | .994 |
| Brazell, Mont .. | 56 | 272 | 25 | 2 | 5 | 11 | .993 |
| ENRIGHT, Knx | 118 | 446 | 73 | 4 | 13 | 19 | .992 |
| Lantigua, Col ... | 17 | 95 | 11 | 1 | 1 | 3 | .991 |
| Haines, Bir .... | 106 | 488 | 72 | 7 | 7 | 19 | .988 |
| Palmer, Knx .. | 14 | 71 | 5 | 1 | 1 | 0 | .987 |
| Velazquez, Sav.. | 84 | 443 | 58 | 7 | 3 | 5 | .986 |
| Brandenburg, Ash | 30 | 118 | 20 | 2 | 0 | 3 | .986 |
| Lonchar, Orlando | 99 | 454 | 73 | 8 | 6 | 8 | .985 |
| Skaggs, Asheville | 56 | 294 | 40 | 5 | 4 | 3 | .985 |
| Adams, Mon .. | 75 | 370 | 43 | 7 | 5 | 9 | .983 |
| Howard, Sav... | 32 | 152 | 20 | 3 | 1 | 4 | .983 |
| Royster, Asheville | 57 | 283 | 41 | 6 | 5 | 2 | .982 |
| Connolly, Sav .. | 24 | 84 | 11 | 2 | 0 | 3 | .979 |
| Fleming, Jackson | 95 | 511 | 74 | 14 | 13 | 14 | .978 |
| Boone, Columbus | 65 | 359 | 41 | 12 | 3 | 13 | .971 |
| Paepke, Jackson | 48 | 218 | 20 | 7 | 2 | 5 | .971 |
| Sinovich, Bir ... | 27 | 108 | 18 | 4 | 2 | 5 | .969 |
| Foley, Knoxville | 11 | 26 | 3 | 1 | 0 | 0 | .967 |
| Shippy, Mon .... | 9 | 40 | 4 | 2 | 0 | 4 | .957 |

## PITCHERS

| Player and Club | G. | PO. | A. | E. | DP. | Pct. |
|---|---|---|---|---|---|---|
| CULPEPPER, Col.. | 25 | 13 | 19 | 0 | 1 | 1.000 |
| M. McLaughlin, Col.. | 15 | 8 | 17 | 0 | 1 | 1.000 |
| Christenson, Mon*.. | 15 | 12 | 10 | 0 | 1 | 1.000 |
| MacCormack, Mon .. | 22 | 7 | 15 | 0 | 0 | 1.000 |
| Lusic, Savannah ... | 32 | 5 | 16 | 0 | 1 | 1.000 |
| Flinn, Asheville ... | 20 | 4 | 15 | 0 | 1 | 1.000 |
| Lacey, Birmingham* | 33 | 6 | 13 | 0 | 0 | 1.000 |
| Aloi, Columbus ..... | 8 | 10 | 7 | 0 | 0 | 1.000 |
| Stiegemeier, Orlando | 11 | 7 | 8 | 0 | 0 | 1.000 |
| DeBarr, Montgomery* | 18 | 3 | 12 | 0 | 0 | 1.000 |
| Tronerud, Bir ...... | 28 | 5 | 10 | 0 | 0 | 1.000 |
| Ibarguen, Montgomery | 11 | 5 | 9 | 0 | 0 | 1.000 |
| Ignasiak, Mon* ..... | 14 | 1 | 13 | 0 | 0 | 1.000 |
| Taylor, Columbus ... | 15 | 7 | 7 | 0 | 1 | 1.000 |
| Tobik, Montgomery.. | 20 | 8 | 6 | 0 | 0 | 1.000 |
| Sevillano, Savannah.. | 29 | 7 | 6 | 0 | 1 | 1.000 |
| Holly, Knoxville* ... | 17 | 2 | 10 | 0 | 0 | 1.000 |
| Taylor, Birmingham | 33 | 3 | 9 | 0 | 0 | 1.000 |
| Robson, Asheville ... | 4 | 4 | 7 | 0 | 0 | 1.000 |
| Martinez, Asheville.. | 6 | 2 | 8 | 0 | 0 | 1.000 |
| Harrell, Birmingham | 6 | 4 | 5 | 0 | 1 | 1.000 |
| Hayden, Asheville .. | 6 | 4 | 5 | 0 | 0 | 1.000 |
| McLaughlin, Sav .. | 8 | 4 | 5 | 0 | 1 | 1.000 |
| Meyerrose, Mon .... | 18 | 2 | 6 | 0 | 1 | 1.000 |
| Motil, Mon* ....... | 25 | 1 | 7 | 0 | 0 | 1.000 |
| Rios, Savannah* .... | 31 | 3 | 5 | 0 | 0 | 1.000 |
| M. Smith, Asheville* | 35 | 0 | 8 | 0 | 1 | 1.000 |
| Lysander, Birmingham | 8 | 2 | 2 | 0 | 0 | 1.000 |

## PITCHERS—Continued

| Player and Club | G. | PO. | A. | E. | DP. | Pct. |
|---|---|---|---|---|---|---|
| Lantz, Montgomery .. | 9 | 6 | 1 | 0 | 1 | 1.000 |
| McClure, Jackson* .. | 9 | 1 | 6 | 0 | 0 | 1.000 |
| Ryan, Orlando* .. | 17 | 1 | 6 | 0 | 1 | 1.000 |
| Bruno, Jacksonville.. | 4 | 3 | 3 | 0 | 0 | 1.000 |
| Wibberley, Bir .... | 3 | 1 | 4 | 0 | 0 | 1.000 |
| Lauzerique, Columbus | 8 | 3 | 2 | 0 | 0 | 1.000 |
| Stone, Orlando .... | 10 | 1 | 4 | 0 | 0 | 1.000 |
| Balderson, Jackson .. | 20 | 4 | 1 | 0 | 0 | 1.000 |
| Pentz, Montgomery .. | 22 | 2 | 3 | 0 | 0 | 1.000 |
| Bernard, Jacksonville | 33 | 2 | 3 | 0 | 1 | 1.000 |
| Bock, Knoxville* ... | 3 | 0 | 4 | 0 | 0 | 1.000 |
| Fidrych, Montgomery | 7 | 1 | 3 | 0 | 1 | 1.000 |
| Lehman, Knoxville .. | 8 | 2 | 2 | 0 | 1 | 1.000 |
| Falcon, Jacksonville* | 9 | 1 | 3 | 0 | 0 | 1.000 |
| Leshnock, Jack*..... | 16 | 1 | 3 | 0 | 0 | 1.000 |
| Moore, Asheville .. | 5 | 0 | 3 | 0 | 0 | 1.000 |
| Dierker, Asheville .. | 6 | 0 | 3 | 0 | 0 | 1.000 |
| Kuhl, Montgomery .. | 7 | 3 | 0 | 0 | 0 | 1.000 |
| Johnson, Savannah .. | 8 | 2 | 1 | 0 | 1 | 1.000 |
| Hrovat, Jacksonville | 9 | 2 | 1 | 0 | 0 | 1.000 |
| Campbell, Savannah | 22 | 0 | 3 | 0 | 0 | 1.000 |
| Oquendo, Asheville*.. | 1 | 2 | 0 | 0 | 0 | 1.000 |
| Trella, Montgomery .. | 2 | 0 | 2 | 0 | 0 | 1.000 |
| Lukevics, Knoxville.. | 4 | 0 | 2 | 0 | 0 | 1.000 |
| Murphy, Montgomery* | 4 | 1 | 1 | 0 | 0 | 1.000 |
| Schuster, Jack* .... | 4 | 0 | 2 | 0 | 0 | 1.000 |
| Pelz, Jacksonville.... | 6 | 1 | 1 | 0 | 1 | 1.000 |
| Barr, Jacksonville*.. | 7 | 2 | 0 | 0 | 0 | 1.000 |
| Shaffer, Knoxville .. | 14 | 0 | 2 | 0 | 0 | 1.000 |
| Larson, Columbus... | 17 | 12 | 35 | 1 | 1 | .979 |
| Batton, Birmingham | 29 | 13 | 21 | 1 | 2 | .971 |
| Williams, Columbus.. | 22 | 10 | 22 | 1 | 1 | .970 |
| Seberger, Orlando .. | 30 | 12 | 18 | 1 | 1 | .968 |
| Hasbach, Jackson .. | 24 | 9 | 18 | 1 | 1 | .964 |
| Babcock, Asheville .. | 28 | 3 | 20 | 1 | 3 | .958 |
| Sambito, Columbus* | 30 | 17 | 50 | 3 | 0 | .957 |
| Sykes, Montgomery | 27 | 10 | 34 | 2 | 1 | .957 |
| Glynn, Montgomery* | 19 | 14 | 27 | 2 | 1 | .953 |
| Scarbery, Birmingham | 17 | 5 | 15 | 1 | 0 | .952 |
| Stinson, Knoxville*.. | 31 | 5 | 28 | 2 | 4 | .944 |
| Maneely, Orlando .. | 23 | 7 | 27 | 2 | 2 | .944 |
| Sanchez, Columbus.. | 21 | 11 | 22 | 2 | 0 | .943 |
| Stegman, Birmingham | 25 | 7 | 26 | 2 | 0 | .943 |
| Patterson, Knoxville | 33 | 7 | 25 | 2 | 0 | .941 |
| Norton, Orlando .... | 10 | 7 | 9 | 1 | 3 | .941 |
| Thayer, Orlando .... | 15 | 2 | 14 | 1 | 1 | .941 |

| Player and Club | G. | PO. | A. | E. | DP. | Pct. |
|---|---|---|---|---|---|---|
| Wright, Jacksonville* | 15 | 1 | 15 | 1 | 1 | .941 |
| Alexander, Savannah | 20 | 5 | 11 | 1 | 0 | .941 |
| Selak, Columbus .... | 6 | 5 | 10 | 1 | 0 | .938 |
| Fife, Orlando ...... | 8 | 7 | 8 | 1 | 2 | .938 |
| Mitchell, Birmingham | 12 | 5 | 10 | 1 | 3 | .938 |
| Box, Savannah* .... | 25 | 9 | 19 | 2 | 1 | .933 |
| Davey, Savannah* ... | 25 | 11 | 17 | 2 | 1 | .933 |
| Maier, Orlando .... | 25 | 12 | 28 | 3 | 5 | .930 |
| Frost, Knoxville .... | 28 | 10 | 30 | 3 | 1 | .930 |
| Griffin, Birmingham.. | 7 | 5 | 8 | 1 | 2 | .929 |
| Kucek, Knoxville.... | 21 | 10 | 15 | 2 | 1 | .926 |
| Smith, Knoxville ... | 30 | 8 | 17 | 2 | 2 | .926 |
| Parrott, Asheville .. | 25 | 7 | 28 | 3 | 1 | .921 |
| McCall, Asheville .. | 19 | 5 | 17 | 2 | 0 | .917 |
| D. Collins, Savannah* | 24 | 8 | 14 | 2 | 1 | .917 |
| Luebber, Orlando .. | 6 | 1 | 10 | 1 | 1 | .917 |
| Garcia, Jacksonville* | 29 | 6 | 37 | 4 | 0 | .915 |
| Hile, Asheville* .... | 27 | 7 | 25 | 3 | 0 | .914 |
| Bethke, Orlando* ... | 14 | 3 | 27 | 3 | 2 | .909 |
| Stanton, Columbus .. | 10 | 6 | 4 | 1 | 1 | .909 |
| Ballinger, Jacksonville | 18 | 3 | 7 | 1 | 1 | .909 |
| de los Santos, Col*.. | 40 | 4 | 6 | 1 | 0 | .909 |
| Camp, Savannah ... | 25 | 4 | 25 | 3 | 1 | .906 |
| Smith, Orlando* .... | 16 | 4 | 5 | 1 | 0 | .900 |
| Branch, Jacksonville | 17 | 4 | 5 | 1 | 0 | .900 |
| Best, Knoxville .... | 36 | 3 | 6 | 1 | 0 | .900 |
| Kravec, Knoxville*.. | 28 | 7 | 19 | 3 | 1 | .897 |
| Stoddard, Knoxville | 31 | 0 | 8 | 1 | 2 | .889 |
| Lemongello, Mon .... | 14 | 8 | 15 | 3 | 0 | .885 |
| McKinney, Jackson.. | 15 | 7 | 8 | 2 | 0 | .882 |
| Hammon, Jacksonville | 27 | 9 | 25 | 5 | 0 | .872 |
| Bockewitz, Bir* .... | 28 | 7 | 20 | 4 | 2 | .871 |
| Sosa, Columbus .... | 29 | 2 | 11 | 2 | 0 | .867 |
| Van Bommel, Bir .. | 16 | 5 | 14 | 3 | 0 | .864 |
| Peach, Asheville* .. | 22 | 5 | 18 | 4 | 0 | .852 |
| Williams, Knoxville.. | 26 | 4 | 6 | 2 | 0 | .833 |
| Quisenberry, Jackson | 6 | 1 | 4 | 1 | 0 | .833 |
| Mazzone, Bir* ...... | 8 | 2 | 3 | 1 | 0 | .833 |
| Olsen, Jacksonville .. | 16 | 6 | 18 | 5 | 2 | .828 |
| Van DeCasteele, Orl.. | 20 | 9 | 18 | 6 | 0 | .818 |
| Larkin, Jacksonville | 14 | 0 | 4 | 1 | 0 | .800 |
| Wessel, Asheville.... | 24 | 4 | 11 | 4 | 0 | .789 |
| Elenes, Columbus ... | 13 | 3 | 6 | 3 | 0 | .750 |
| Cappuzzello, Mon*.. | 8 | 1 | 4 | 2 | 0 | .714 |
| W. Smith, Asheville* | 25 | 1 | 5 | 3 | 1 | .667 |
| Lerner, Orlando .... | 20 | 2 | 0 | 1 | 0 | .667 |

The following pitchers did not have any recorded accepted chances; therefore are not listed in the fielding averages for that position: Alonso*, Ford, Madden, Sapp, Schultz.

Rubertino appeared as a pinch-runner only.

## CLUB PITCHING

| Club | G. | CG. | ShO. | Sv. | IP. | H. | R. | ER. | HR. | BB. | Int. E.B. | HB. | SO. | WP. | Bk. | ERA. |
|---|---|---|---|---|---|---|---|---|---|---|---|---|---|---|---|---|
| Columbus | 134 | 51 | 14 | 25 | 1137 | 1076 | 475 | 389 | 62 | 449 | 41 | 25 | 702 | 59 | 7 | 3.079 |
| Birmingham | 134 | 63 | 9 | 15 | 1112 | 1088 | 502 | 381 | 53 | 538 | 63 | 23 | 559 | 71 | 5 | 3.083 |
| Savannah | 134 | 53 | 10 | 16 | 1133 | 1046 | 480 | 393 | 47 | 450 | 18 | 33 | 619 | 53 | 4 | 3.12 |
| Jacksonville | 134 | 49 | 9 | 14 | 1147 | 1066 | 538 | 405 | 60 | 496 | 52 | 30 | 678 | 62 | 7 | 3.18 |
| Orlando | 138 | 71 | 20 | 18 | 1119 | 1049 | 462 | 397 | 57 | 473 | 18 | 28 | 594 | 69 | 0 | 3.19 |
| Montgomery | 134 | 45 | 14 | 23 | 1118 | 997 | 508 | 410 | 50 | 550 | 34 | 30 | 640 | 71 | 7 | 3.30 |
| Knoxville | 138 | 29 | 12 | 30 | 1151 | 1108 | 571 | 476 | 59 | 537 | 26 | 37 | 661 | 53 | 8 | 3 72 |
| Asheville | 138 | 56 | 13 | 11 | 1161 | 1234 | 620 | 522 | 110 | 488 | 25 | 33 | 633 | 40 | 6 | 4.05 |

## PITCHERS' RECORDS

(Leading Qualifiers for Earned-Run Average Leadership—112 or More Innings)

*Throws lefthanded.

| Pitcher—Club | G. | GS. | CG. | ShO. | W. | L. | Sv. | Pct. | IP. | H. | R. | ER. | HR. | BB. | Int. BB. | HB. | SO. | WP. | ERA. |
|---|---|---|---|---|---|---|---|---|---|---|---|---|---|---|---|---|---|---|---|
| Larson, Columbus.17 | 17 | 12 | 1 | | 7 | 8 | 0 | .467 | 132 | 118 | 42 | 32 | 7 | 46 | 1 | 4 | 76 | 8 | 2.18 |
| Stegman, Bir ..25 | 18 | 11 | 1 | | 8 | 10 | 0 | .444 | 157 | 140 | 59 | 42 | 9 | 65 | 11 | 1 | 66 | 8 | 2.41 |
| Kravec, Knoxville* 28 | 22 | 7 | 2 | | 14 | 7 | 1 | .667 | 168 | 139 | 52 | 45 | 6 | 79 | 7 | 2 | 119 | 10 | 2.41 |
| Patterson, Knox ..33 | 8 | 2 | 0 | | 8 | 5 | 2 | .615 | 118 | 87 | 42 | 32 | 6 | 48 | 4 | 3 | 54 | 4 | 2.44 |
| Seberger, Orlando..30 | 16 | 11 | 2 | | 13 | 7 | 3 | .650 | 144 | 116 | 53 | 41 | 8 | 55 | 8 | 10 | 65 | 11 | 2.56 |
| Williams, Col ..22 | 15 | 6 | 2 | | 8 | 7 | 2 | .533 | 118 | 111 | 46 | 35 | 0 | 35 | 5 | 2 | 46 | 3 | 2.67 |
| Garcia, Jackson..29 | 23 | 7 | 0 | | 6 | 12 | 0 | .333 | 167 | 135 | 70 | 50 | 7 | 66 | 5 | 4 | 106 | 5 | 2.69 |
| Lusie, Savannah ..32 | 9 | 7 | 2 | | 9 | 8 | 4 | .529 | 118 | 106 | 42 | 36 | 6 | 35 | 5 | 2 | 74 | 5 | 2.75 |
| Kucek, Knoxville..21 | 16 | 4 | 2 | | 10 | 4 | 0 | .714 | 114 | 03 | 38 | 35 | 4 | 48 | 0 | 3 | 77 | 5 | 2.76 |
| Maneely, Orlando.. 23 | 23 | 12 | 4 | | 14 | 8 | 0 | .636 | 149 | 142 | 52 | 46 | 4 | 59 | 3 | 0 | 91 | 9 | 2.78 |

Departmental Leaders: G—de los Santos, 40; GS—Batton, Sambito, 28; CG—Parrott, 14; ShO—Batton, Hasbach, Maneely, 4; W—Kravec, Maneely, Sykes, 14; L—Frost, Hile, Stinson, 14; Sv—Lerner, Shaffer, 9; Pct.—Kucek, .714; IP—Sambito, 209; H—Sambito, 200; R—Wessel, 101; ER—Wessel, 84; HR—Wessel, 18; BB—Batton, 109; IBB—Batton, Stegman, 11; HB— Alexander, 12; SO—Sambito, 140; WP—Sambito, 14.

### (All Pitchers—Listed Alphabetically)

| Pitcher—Club | G. | GS. | CG. | ShO. | W. | L. | Sv. | Pct. | IP. | H. | R. | ER. | HR. | BB. | Int. BB. | HB. | SO. | WP. | ERA. |
|---|---|---|---|---|---|---|---|---|---|---|---|---|---|---|---|---|---|---|---|
| Alexander, Sav | 20 | 18 | 4 | 1 | 4 | 9 | 0 | .308 | 109 | 94 | 53 | 42 | 7 | 55 | 1 | 12 | 53 | 5 | 3.47 |
| Aloi, Columbus | 8 | 8 | 2 | 0 | 2 | 5 | 0 | .286 | 45 | 45 | 24 | 22 | 4 | 15 | 0 | 1 | 33 | 0 | 4.40 |
| Alonso, Mon* | 2 | 0 | 0 | 0 | 1 | 0 | 0 | 1.000 | 5 | 2 | 1 | 1 | 0 | 4 | 0 | 0 | 2 | 0 | 1.80 |
| Babcock, Asheville | 28 | 7 | 3 | 2 | 9 | 5 | 3 | .643 | 92 | 73 | 29 | 25 | 3 | 36 | 3 | 6 | 49 | 2 | 2.45 |
| Balderson, Jackson | 20 | 0 | 0 | 0 | 0 | 3 | 0 | .000 | 29 | 34 | 19 | 12 | 3 | 17 | 3 | 0 | 8 | 1 | 3.72 |
| Ballinger, Jackson | 18 | 3 | 2 | 0 | 4 | 3 | 0 | .571 | 48 | 39 | 18 | 16 | 3 | 24 | 4 | 5 | 20 | 4 | 3.00 |
| Barr, Jacksonville* | 7 | 1 | 0 | 0 | 0 | 2 | 1 | .000 | 17 | 17 | 7 | 7 | 0 | 6 | 1 | 0 | 8 | 0 | 3.71 |
| Batton, Birm | 29 | 28 | 12 | 4 | 13 | 10 | 0 | .565 | 190 | 192 | 89 | 77 | 9 | 109 | 11 | 0 | 96 | 9 | 3.65 |
| Bernard, Jackson | 33 | 0 | 0 | 0 | 5 | 1 | 7 | .833 | 45 | 38 | 16 | 9 | 0 | 24 | 5 | 0 | 45 | 6 | 1.80 |
| Best, Knoxville | 36 | 1 | 1 | 0 | 2 | 3 | 7 | .400 | 54 | 43 | 38 | 29 | 4 | 20 | 1 | 5 | 43 | 3 | 4.83 |
| Bethke, Orlando* | 14 | 14 | 8 | 0 | 8 | 4 | 0 | .667 | 93 | 97 | 43 | 31 | 4 | 46 | 0 | 4 | 41 | 8 | 3.00 |
| Bock, Knoxville* | 3 | 1 | 0 | 0 | 0 | 0 | 0 | .000 | 9 | 7 | 6 | 5 | 0 | 9 | 0 | 0 | 8 | 1 | 5.00 |
| Bockewitz, Birm* | 28 | 16 | 4 | 1 | 4 | 9 | 0 | .308 | 122 | 142 | 63 | 40 | 5 | 77 | 10 | 7 | 59 | 5 | 2.95 |
| Box, Savannah* | 25 | 25 | 7 | 2 | 9 | 12 | 0 | .429 | 151 | 151 | 71 | 55 | 6 | 64 | 0 | 1 | 62 | 6 | 3.28 |
| Branch, Jack | 17 | 14 | 8 | 0 | 7 | 6 | 0 | .538 | 92 | 91 | 50 | 39 | 4 | 50 | 2 | 5 | 75 | 5 | 3.82 |
| Bruno, Jacksonville | 4 | 4 | 2 | 0 | 1 | 3 | 0 | .250 | 31 | 24 | 10 | 7 | 1 | 15 | 2 | 0 | 12 | 2 | 2.03 |
| Camp, Savannah | 25 | 25 | 13 | 1 | 12 | 10 | 0 | .545 | 176 | 161 | 68 | 56 | 2 | 62 | 2 | 2 | 100 | 9 | 2.86 |
| Campbell, Savannah | 22 | 0 | 0 | 0 | 3 | 1 | 4 | .750 | 28 | 24 | 11 | 9 | 0 | 21 | 3 | 0 | 24 | 1 | 2.89 |
| Cappuzzello, Mon* | 8 | 4 | 1 | 0 | 0 | 3 | 0 | .000 | 32 | 27 | 17 | 13 | 1 | 20 | 3 | 2 | 22 | 0 | 3.66 |
| Christenson, Mon* | 15 | 15 | 8 | 2 | 8 | 4 | 0 | .667 | 93 | 77 | 38 | 34 | 6 | 46 | 0 | 2 | 67 | 3 | 3.29 |
| D. Collins, Sav* | 24 | 24 | 8 | 0 | 8 | 7 | 0 | .533 | 157 | 153 | 66 | 55 | 6 | 69 | 0 | 3 | 79 | 10 | 3.15 |
| Culpepper, Col | 25 | 11 | 2 | 0 | 6 | 5 | 4 | .545 | 102 | 112 | 59 | 51 | 11 | 32 | 2 | 2 | 37 | 0 | 4.50 |
| Davey, Savannah* | 25 | 25 | 10 | 2 | 12 | 10 | 0 | .545 | 174 | 164 | 78 | 66 | 9 | 54 | 1 | 5 | 114 | 7 | 3.41 |
| DeBarr, Mon* | 18 | 3 | 1 | 0 | 4 | 3 | 1 | .571 | 55 | 45 | 17 | 13 | 1 | 22 | 6 | 0 | 28 | 0 | 2.13 |
| de los Santos, Col* | 40 | 1 | 1 | 0 | 4 | 3 | 7 | .571 | 52 | 59 | 20 | 20 | 3 | 32 | 7 | 5 | 44 | 4 | 3.46 |
| Dierker, Asheville | 6 | 0 | 0 | 0 | 2 | 0 | 0 | 1.000 | 15 | 13 | 5 | 3 | 0 | 8 | 0 | 0 | 3 | 0 | 1.80 |
| Elenes, Columbus | 13 | 8 | 0 | 0 | 4 | 2 | 1 | .667 | 58 | 54 | 24 | 18 | 0 | 33 | 4 | 1 | 39 | 10 | 2.79 |
| Falcon, Jacksonville* | 9 | 1 | 0 | 0 | 0 | 3 | 0 | .000 | 15 | 19 | 17 | 12 | 2 | 15 | 2 | 0 | 5 | 1 | 7.20 |
| Fidrych, Mon | 7 | 0 | 0 | 0 | 2 | 0 | 4 | 1.000 | 14 | 15 | 5 | 5 | 1 | 3 | 1 | 0 | 11 | 2 | 3.21 |
| Fife, Orlando | 8 | 6 | 0 | 0 | 3 | 1 | 0 | .750 | 43 | 39 | 17 | 17 | 1 | 31 | 0 | 0 | 21 | 2 | 3.56 |
| Flinn, Asheville | 20 | 10 | 2 | 0 | 0 | 9 | 0 | .000 | 85 | 99 | 58 | 50 | 8 | 37 | 3 | 6 | 53 | 1 | 5.29 |
| Ford, Savannah | 5 | 0 | 0 | 0 | 1 | 0 | 0 | 1.000 | 15 | 14 | 8 | 7 | 2 | 7 | 0 | 0 | 4 | 1 | 4.20 |
| Frost, Knoxville | 28 | 25 | 7 | 1 | 5 | 14 | 0 | .263 | 171 | 157 | 73 | 61 | 6 | 68 | 0 | 7 | 100 | 8 | 3.21 |
| Garcia, Jackson* | 29 | 23 | 7 | 0 | 6 | 12 | 0 | .333 | 167 | 135 | 70 | 50 | 7 | 66 | 5 | 4 | 106 | 5 | 2.69 |
| Glynn, Mon* | 19 | 19 | 6 | 0 | 10 | 5 | 0 | .667 | 127 | 116 | 50 | 44 | 3 | 72 | 3 | 0 | 66 | 8 | 3.12 |
| Griffin, Birmingham | 7 | 7 | 5 | 0 | 5 | 1 | 0 | .833 | 53 | 43 | 18 | 12 | 2 | 11 | 0 | 0 | 34 | 5 | 2.04 |
| Hammon, Jackson | 27 | 27 | 9 | 1 | 10 | 11 | 0 | .476 | 181 | 182 | 96 | 64 | 13 | 76 | 7 | 6 | 112 | 6 | 3.18 |
| Harrell, Bir | 6 | 4 | 0 | 0 | 1 | 1 | 0 | .500 | 24 | 26 | 11 | 12 | 2 | 20 | 0 | 2 | 14 | 4 | 4.50 |
| Hasbach, Jackson | 24 | 24 | 11 | 4 | 9 | 10 | 0 | .474 | 164 | 139 | 66 | 57 | 7 | 58 | 1 | 4 | 92 | 12 | 3.13 |
| Hayden, Asheville | 6 | 5 | 1 | 0 | 2 | 2 | 0 | .500 | 39 | 48 | 24 | 21 | 4 | 9 | 0 | 0 | 8 | 4 | 4.85 |
| Hile, Asheville* | 27 | 27 | 5 | 1 | 6 | 14 | 0 | .300 | 159 | 186 | 96 | 79 | 9 | 82 | 2 | 2 | 59 | 10 | 4.47 |
| Holly, Knoxville* | 17 | 2 | 0 | 0 | 1 | 2 | 0 | .333 | 38 | 45 | 29 | 22 | 2 | 23 | 4 | 0 | 26 | 3 | 5.21 |
| Hrovat, Jacksonville | 9 | 0 | 0 | 0 | 1 | 0 | 0 | 1.000 | 12 | 14 | 10 | 9 | 0 | 6 | 2 | 1 | 4 | 1 | 6.75 |
| Ibarguen, Mon | 11 | 4 | 1 | 0 | 1 | 0 | 0 | .857 | 69 | 48 | 23 | 20 | 3 | 32 | 1 | 0 | 40 | 4 | 2.61 |
| Ignasiak, Mon* | 14 | 6 | 1 | 0 | 4 | 10 | 0 | .286 | 86 | 83 | 55 | 52 | 5 | 50 | 0 | 7 | 35 | 9 | 5.44 |
| Johnson, Savannah | 8 | 0 | 0 | 0 | 1 | 0 | 0 | .000 | 18 | 26 | 19 | 16 | 1 | 19 | 2 | 2 | 11 | 2 | 8.00 |
| Kravec, Knoxville* | 28 | 22 | 7 | 2 | 14 | 7 | 1 | .667 | 168 | 138 | 52 | 45 | 6 | 78 | 2 | 7 | 119 | 10 | 2.41 |
| Kucek, Knoxville | 21 | 16 | 4 | 2 | 10 | 4 | 0 | .714 | 114 | 93 | 38 | 35 | 4 | 48 | 0 | 3 | 77 | 5 | 2.76 |
| Kuhl, Montgomery | 7 | 0 | 0 | 0 | 0 | 0 | 0 | .000 | 14 | 14 | 12 | 9 | 0 | 8 | 1 | 0 | 6 | 1 | 5.79 |
| Lacey, Bir* | 33 | 5 | 2 | 1 | 3 | 6 | 4 | .333 | 68 | 81 | 34 | 28 | 5 | 39 | 8 | 0 | 47 | 3 | 3.71 |
| Lantz, Montgomery | 9 | 4 | 0 | 0 | 1 | 3 | 0 | .250 | 24 | 27 | 14 | 14 | 1 | 18 | 3 | 0 | 7 | 2 | 5.25 |
| Larkin, Jackson | 14 | 0 | 0 | 0 | 1 | 2 | 1 | .333 | 19 | 19 | 10 | 4 | 1 | 5 | 1 | 1 | 14 | 3 | 1.89 |
| Larson, Columbus | 17 | 17 | 12 | 1 | 7 | 8 | 0 | .467 | 132 | 118 | 42 | 32 | 7 | 46 | 1 | 4 | 76 | 8 | 2.18 |
| Lauzerique, Col | 3 | 2 | 0 | 0 | 1 | 1 | 0 | .500 | 20 | 17 | 6 | 4 | 2 | 14 | 1 | 1 | 17 | 1 | 1.80 |
| Lehman, Knoxville | 8 | 0 | 0 | 0 | 0 | 2 | 1 | .000 | 17 | 20 | 10 | 10 | 0 | 6 | 0 | 0 | 10 | 2 | 5.29 |
| Lemongello, Mon | 14 | 14 | 5 | 1 | 6 | 3 | 0 | .667 | 93 | 90 | 43 | 26 | 4 | 26 | 4 | 4 | 44 | 5 | 2.52 |
| Lerner, Orlando | 20 | 0 | 0 | 0 | 2 | 2 | 9 | .500 | 28 | 17 | 12 | 10 | 1 | 24 | 0 | 2 | 31 | 1 | 3.21 |
| Leshnock, Jackson* | 16 | 0 | 0 | 0 | 1 | 1 | 2 | .500 | 18 | 23 | 8 | 8 | 2 | 14 | 6 | 0 | 11 | 3 | 4.00 |
| Luebber, Orlando | 6 | 6 | 3 | 0 | 2 | 2 | 0 | .500 | 47 | 43 | 16 | 16 | 3 | 15 | 1 | 1 | 26 | 1 | 3.06 |
| Lukevics, Knoxville | 4 | 0 | 0 | 0 | 1 | 1 | 0 | .500 | 11 | 16 | 8 | 7 | 1 | 4 | 0 | 0 | 7 | 2 | 5.73 |
| Lusic, Savannah | 32 | 9 | 7 | 2 | 9 | 8 | 4 | .529 | 118 | 106 | 62 | 36 | 6 | 35 | 5 | 2 | 74 | 2 | 2.75 |
| Lysander, Bir | 8 | 8 | 5 | 0 | 5 | 2 | 0 | .714 | 57 | 58 | 24 | 21 | 2 | 20 | 1 | 1 | 25 | 3 | 3.32 |
| MacCormack, Mon | 22 | 4 | 0 | 0 | 3 | 4 | 2 | .429 | 67 | 44 | 27 | 17 | 5 | 33 | 3 | 2 | 52 | 8 | 2.28 |
| Madden, Mon | 2 | 0 | 0 | 0 | 0 | 0 | 0 | .000 | 3 | 3 | 2 | 2 | 0 | 2 | 1 | 2 | 0 | 0 | 6.00 |
| Maier, Orlando | 25 | 14 | 9 | 2 | 10 | 5 | 0 | .667 | 157 | 163 | 68 | 63 | 11 | 48 | 2 | 0 | 54 | 8 | 3.61 |
| Maneely, Orlando | 23 | 23 | 12 | 4 | 14 | 8 | 0 | .636 | 149 | 142 | 52 | 46 | 4 | 59 | 3 | 0 | 91 | 9 | 2.78 |
| Martinez, Asheville | 6 | 4 | 1 | 1 | 0 | 4 | 0 | .800 | 45 | 45 | 16 | 13 | 4 | 12 | 1 | 0 | 18 | 0 | 2.60 |
| Mazzone, Bir* | 8 | 0 | 0 | 0 | 0 | 1 | 1 | .000 | 12 | 9 | 5 | 5 | 1 | 6 | 1 | 0 | 5 | 0 | 3.75 |
| McCall, Asheville | 19 | 15 | 13 | 0 | 8 | 7 | 0 | .533 | 130 | 123 | 52 | 46 | 15 | 33 | 7 | 1 | 40 | 3 | 3.45 |
| McClure, Jackson* | 9 | 4 | 2 | 1 | 3 | 2 | 0 | .600 | 42 | 31 | 18 | 11 | 3 | 23 | 2 | 2 | 39 | 3 | 2.36 |
| McKinney, Jackson | 15 | 14 | 2 | 0 | 4 | 5 | 1 | .444 | 86 | 91 | 42 | 34 | 3 | 38 | 0 | 1 | 57 | 0 | 3.56 |

| Pitcher—Club | G | GS | CG | ShO | W | L | Sv | Pct. | IP | H | R | ER | HR | BB | Int. BB | HB | SO | WP | ERA |
|---|---|---|---|---|---|---|---|---|---|---|---|---|---|---|---|---|---|---|---|
| McLaughlin, Sav.. | 8 | 8 | 4 | 0 | 4 | 3 | 0 | .571 | 53 | 41 | 21 | 20 | 3 | 16 | 0 | 2 | 29 | 4 | 3.40 |
| M. McLaughlin, Col | 15 | 12 | 5 | 2 | 5 | 4 | 0 | .556 | 95 | 73 | 40 | 35 | 9 | 27 | 1 | 0 | 77 | 3 | 3.32 |
| Meyerrose, Mon ... | 18 | 0 | 0 | 0 | 1 | 0 | 0 | 1.000 | 45 | 39 | 22 | 11 | 1 | 29 | 0 | 2 | 22 | 4 | 2.20 |
| Mitchell, Bir .... | 12 | 12 | 5 | 1 | 6 | 3 | 0 | .667 | 76 | 61 | 31 | 24 | 4 | 42 | 4 | 1 | 39 | 5 | 2.84 |
| Moore, Asheville*.. | 5 | 0 | 0 | 0 | 1 | 2 | 0 | .333 | 19 | 25 | 17 | 16 | 7 | 4 | 0 | 0 | 11 | 0 | 7.58 |
| Motil, Montgomery* | 25 | 0 | 0 | 0 | 2 | 3 | 7 | .400 | 38 | 40 | 19 | 15 | 1 | 15 | 1 | 0 | 28 | 4 | 3.55 |
| Murphy, Mon* .... | 4 | 1 | 0 | 0 | 0 | 1 | 0 | .000 | 9 | 7 | 8 | 8 | 0 | 9 | 0 | 2 | 10 | 2 | 8.00 |
| Norton, Orlando ... | 10 | 5 | 3 | 6 | 4 | 4 | 0 | .600 | 63 | 42 | 28 | 23 | 5 | 38 | 1 | 1 | 23 | 2 | 3.29 |
| Olsen, Jacksonville | 16 | 16 | 3 | 0 | 2 | 10 | 0 | .167 | 100 | 95 | 51 | 41 | 7 | 27 | 4 | 1 | 34 | 6 | 3.69 |
| Oquendo, Asheville* | 1 | 0 | 0 | 0 | 0 | 0 | 0 | .000 | 1 | 1 | 0 | 0 | 0 | 1 | 0 | 0 | 1 | 0 | 0.00 |
| Parrott, Asheville | 25 | 25 | 14 | 2 | 12 | 10 | 0 | .545 | 177 | 168 | 79 | 67 | 15 | 70 | 1 | 5 | 107 | 4 | 3.41 |
| Patterson, Knx.... | 33 | 8 | 2 | 0 | 8 | 5 | 2 | .615 | 118 | 87 | 42 | 32 | 6 | 48 | 4 | 3 | 54 | 4 | 2.44 |
| Peach, Asheville | 22 | 21 | 9 | 3 | 5 | 10 | 1 | .333 | 135 | 139 | 65 | 49 | 7 | 62 | 3 | 3 | 85 | 3 | 3.27 |
| Pelz, Jacksonville.. | 6 | 0 | 0 | 0 | 1 | 1 | 0 | .500 | 11 | 11 | 5 | 5 | 1 | 9 | 2 | 0 | 3 | 0 | 4.09 |
| Pentz, Montgomery | 22 | 0 | 0 | 0 | 4 | 2 | 7 | .667 | 44 | 23 | 10 | 8 | 2 | 23 | 4 | 0 | 43 | 4 | 1.64 |
| Quisenberry, Jack.. | 6 | 0 | 0 | 0 | 1 | 1 | 0 | .000 | 8 | 5 | 3 | 2 | 0 | 4 | 1 | 0 | 2 | 0 | 2.25 |
| Rios, Savannah* .. | 31 | 0 | 0 | 0 | 4 | 1 | 4 | .800 | 45 | 41 | 15 | 9 | 2 | 20 | 2 | 0 | 23 | 0 | 1.80 |
| Robson, Asheville.. | 4 | 2 | 0 | 0 | 3 | 0 | 0 | .000 | 29 | 27 | 19 | 17 | 6 | 8 | 0 | 2 | 17 | 0 | 5.28 |
| Ryan, Orlando* ... | 17 | 1 | 0 | 0 | 2 | 1 | 0 | .667 | 28 | 30 | 10 | 10 | 1 | 18 | 1 | 4 | 18 | 0 | 3.21 |
| Sambito, Col* ... | 30 | 28 | 10 | 2 | 12 | 9 | 0 | .571 | 209 | 200 | 85 | 70 | 7 | 85 | 5 | 3 | 140 | 14 | 3.01 |
| Sanchez, Columbus | 21 | 21 | 6 | 3 | 6 | 12 | 0 | .333 | 132 | 137 | 76 | 59 | 9 | 64 | 4 | 4 | 60 | 8 | 4.02 |
| Sapp, Birmingham | 1 | 0 | 0 | 0 | 0 | 0 | 0 | .000 | 2 | 2 | 1 | 1 | 0 | 2 | 0 | 0 | 1 | 1 | 4.50 |
| Scarbery, Birm.... | 17 | 10 | 1 | | 6 | 10 | 0 | .375 | 116 | 121 | 66 | 50 | 7 | 42 | 3 | 3 | 51 | 10 | 3.88 |
| Schultz, Orlando .. | 4 | 0 | 0 | 0 | 0 | 0 | 0 | .000 | 10 | 11 | 7 | 7 | 3 | 4 | 0 | 0 | 4 | 1 | 6.30 |
| Schuster, Orlando* | 4 | 0 | 0 | 0 | 0 | 1 | 1 | .000 | 4 | 6 | 2 | 2 | 0 | 0 | 0 | 0 | 2 | 0 | 4.50 |
| Seberger, Orlando.. | 30 | 16 | 11 | 2 | 13 | 7 | 3 | .650 | 144 | 116 | 53 | 41 | 8 | 55 | 8 | 10 | 65 | 11 | 2.56 |
| Selak, Columbus .. | 6 | 4 | 1 | | 4 | 2 | 0 | .667 | 49 | 44 | 13 | 12 | 5 | 7 | 1 | 0 | 30 | 1 | 2.20 |
| Sevillano, Savannah | 20 | 0 | 0 | 0 | 4 | 4 | 0 | .667 | 88 | 71 | 28 | 22 | 3 | 28 | 2 | 4 | 46 | 3 | 2.25 |
| Shaffer, Knoxville | 14 | 0 | 0 | 0 | 1 | 0 | 9 | 1.000 | 16 | 13 | 5 | 5 | 0 | 5 | 0 | 0 | 8 | 2 | 2.81 |
| Smith, Knoxville .. | 30 | 26 | 2 | 0 | 6 | 13 | 0 | .316 | 142 | 189 | 91 | 75 | 12 | 61 | 4 | 2 | 50 | 2 | 4.75 |
| M. Smith, Ash* ... | 35 | 0 | 0 | 0 | 7 | 1 | 6 | .875 | 74 | 58 | 14 | 12 | 4 | 22 | 4 | 0 | 66 | 3 | 1.46 |
| W. Smith, Ash* .. | 25 | 3 | 1 | 1 | 3 | 3 | 1 | .500 | 74 | 90 | 45 | 41 | 10 | 43 | 1 | 0 | 61 | 7 | 4.99 |
| Smith, Orlando* .. | 16 | 4 | 4 | 1 | 4 | 2 | 0 | .667 | 43 | 60 | 16 | 17 | 3 | 5 | 0 | 0 | 14 | 1 | 1.26 |
| Sosa, Columbus ... | 29 | 0 | 0 | 0 | 6 | 2 | 8 | .750 | 49 | 33 | 8 | 6 | 1 | 26 | 7 | 1 | 46 | 4 | 1.10 |
| Stanton, Columbus | 10 | 4 | 3 | 1 | 2 | 3 | 2 | .400 | 39 | 31 | 13 | 10 | 9 | 10 | 1 | 1 | 41 | 2 | 2.31 |
| Stegman, Bir ...... | 25 | 18 | 11 | 1 | 8 | 10 | 0 | .444 | 157 | 140 | 59 | 42 | 9 | 65 | 11 | 1 | 66 | 9 | 2.41 |
| Stiegemeier, Orl ... | 11 | 11 | 2 | 2 | 4 | 4 | 0 | .500 | 66 | 70 | 35 | 32 | 4 | 34 | 0 | 0 | 46 | 6 | 4.36 |
| Stinson, Knoxville* | 31 | 25 | 4 | 0 | 8 | 14 | 3 | .364 | 156 | 158 | 95 | 80 | 14 | 78 | 1 | 8 | 86 | 3 | 4.62 |
| Stoddard, Knoxville | 31 | 6 | 2 | 1 | 3 | 4 | 7 | .429 | 66 | 66 | 40 | 31 | 1 | 43 | 5 | 0 | 37 | 5 | 4.23 |
| Stone, Orlando ... | 10 | 2 | 2 | 1 | 1 | 1 | 2 | .500 | 34 | 34 | 15 | 13 | 1 | 15 | 1 | 3 | 24 | 2 | 3.44 |
| Sykes, Montgomery* | 27 | 27 | 11 | 2 | 14 | 10 | 0 | .583 | 191 | 180 | 83 | 67 | 9 | 87 | 2 | 7 | 88 | 10 | 3.16 |
| Taylor, Columbus . | 15 | 1 | 0 | 0 | 3 | 1 | 1 | .750 | 36 | 42 | 19 | 15 | 4 | 14 | 3 | 0 | 16 | 1 | 3.75 |
| Taylor, Birmingham | 33 | 0 | 0 | 0 | 3 | 3 | 5 | .500 | 44 | 45 | 15 | 12 | 2 | 22 | 4 | 2 | 17 | 3 | 2.45 |
| Thayer, Orlando .. | 15 | 13 | 9 | 3 | 6 | 6 | 0 | .500 | 91 | 78 | 33 | 33 | 2 | 44 | 6 | 0 | 72 | 9 | 3.26 |
| Tobik, Montgomery | 20 | 17 | 3 | 3 | 6 | 9 | 1 | .400 | 99 | 107 | 57 | 48 | 5 | 44 | 3 | 1 | 62 | 5 | 4.36 |
| Trella, Montgomery | 2 | 1 | 0 | 0 | 1 | 0 | 0 | .000 | 10 | 10 | 3 | 3 | 1 | 7 | 0 | 0 | 4 | 0 | 2.70 |
| Tronerud, Bir .... | 28 | 1 | 0 | 0 | 4 | 5 | 4 | .429 | 59 | 55 | 27 | 19 | 2 | 22 | 4 | 2 | 29 | 5 | 2.90 |
| Van Bommel, Bir | 16 | 16 | 9 | 0 | 7 | 9 | 0 | .438 | 118 | 103 | 52 | 38 | 3 | 53 | 5 | 4 | 74 | 8 | 2.90 |
| Van DeCasteele, Or | 20 | 18 | 6 | 2 | 6 | 9 | 0 | .400 | 120 | 121 | 61 | 47 | 4 | 35 | 1 | 2 | 62 | 8 | 3.53 |
| Wessel, Asheville | 24 | 13 | 2 | 1 | 4 | 8 | 0 | .333 | 97 | 139 | 101 | 84 | 18 | 61 | 0 | 8 | 55 | 7 | 7.79 |
| Wibberley, Bir ... | 3 | 2 | 0 | 0 | 1 | 0 | 0 | 1.000 | 10 | 10 | 4 | 2 | 0 | 8 | 1 | 0 | 2 | 1 | 1.29 |
| Williams, Knoxville | 26 | 6 | 0 | 0 | 4 | 6 | 0 | .400 | 70 | 76 | 44 | 39 | 3 | 46 | 5 | 2 | 36 | 3 | 5.01 |
| Williams, Col ... | 22 | 15 | 6 | 2 | 8 | 7 | 2 | .533 | 118 | 111 | 46 | 35 | 0 | 35 | 5 | 2 | 46 | 3 | 2.67 |
| Wright, Jackson* .. | 11 | 8 | 5 | 2 | 5 | 3 | 0 | .625 | 63 | 59 | 22 | 18 | 3 | 19 | 2 | 0 | 31 | 2 | 2.57 |

BALKS—Smith (Knoxville), Sykes, 3 each; Bockewitz, Camp, Garcia, Hile, Larson, McClure, Peach, Sanchez, Stinson, Van Bommel, 2 each; Alexander, Best, Branch, Christenson, Culpepper, Davey, Frost, Glynn, Hammon, Lacey, Lukevics, McCall, M. McLaughlin, Olsen, Pentz, Sosa, Tobik, Wessel, 1 each.

COMBINATION SHUTOUTS—Babcock-M. Smith (2), Asheville; Williams-Culpepper, Elenes-Sosa, Columbus; Wright-Bernard, Garcia-Bernard, McKinney-Bernard-Quisenberry, Jacksonville; Kravec-Smith-Best, Smith-Kravec, Stinson-Stoddard, Kucek-Stoddard, Kravec-Best, Kucek-Stoddard-Best, Knoxville; Sykes-MacCormack, Lemongello-Pentz, MacCormack-Motil, Tobik-Alonso, Montgomery; Davey-Campbell, Alexander-Rios, Savannah.

NO-HIT GAMES—None.

# Texts League

## CLASS AA

**League President
BOBBY BRAGAN**

**Leading Pitcher
MICHAEL BRUHERT
Jackson**

### CHAMPIONSHIP WINNERS IN PREVIOUS YEARS

| | | |
|---|---|---|
| 1868—Dallas ............ .671 | Fort Worth ....... .662 | 1951—Houston‡ ......... .619 |
| 1889—Houston .......... .551 | Fort Worth ....... .694 | 1952—Dallas ............ .571 |
| 1890—Galveston ........ .705 | Fort Worth ....... .711 | Shreveport (3rd)§ . .522 |
| 1892—Houston .......... .741 | 1923—Fort Worth ....... .632 | 1953—Dallas‡ ........... .571 |
| Houston ........... .613 | 1924—Fort Worth ....... .689 | 1954—Shreveport ........ .559 |
| 1895—Dallas ............ .754 | Fort Worth ....... .763 | Houston (2nd)§ ... .553 |
| Fort Worth* ....... .750 | 1925—Fort Worth ....... .711 | 1955—Dallas ............ .581 |
| 1896—Fort Worth ....... .757 | Fort Worth y ..... .653 | Shreveport (3rd)§ . .540 |
| Houston* .......... .679 | 1926—Dallas ........... .574 | 1956—Houston‡ ......... .623 |
| Galveston† ........ .548 | 1927—Wichita Falls .... .654 | 1957—Dallas ............ .662 |
| 1897—San Antonio† ..... .657 | 1928—Houston* ......... .679 | Houston (2nd)§ ... .630 |
| Galveston† ........ .717 | Wichita Falls .... .731 | 1958—Fort Worth ....... .582 |
| 1898—League disbanded. | 1929—Dallas* .......... .588 | Cor. Christi (3rd)§ .507 |
| 1899—Galveston ........ .632 | Wichita Falls .... .620 | 1959—Victoria .......... .589 |
| Galveston ......... .762 | 1930—Wichita Falls .... .697 | Austin (2nd)§ .... .548 |
| 1900-01—Did not operate. | Fort Worth* ...... .632 | 1960—Rio Grande Valley .590 |
| 1902—Corsicana ........ .866 | 1931—Houston** ........ .625 | Tulsa (3rd)§ ...... .528 |
| Corsicana ......... .682 | Houston ........... .734 | 1961—Amarillo ......... .643 |
| 1903—Paris-Waco ....... .615 | 1932—Beaumont* ....... .640 | San Antonio (3rd)§ .532 |
| Dallas* ........... .648 | Dallas ............ .727 | 1962—El Paso .......... .571 |
| 1904—Corsicana* ....... .615 | 1933—Houston ......... .623 | Tulsa (2nd)§ ..... .550 |
| Fort Worth ....... .800 | San Antonio (4th)§ .523 | 1963—San Antonio ...... .564 |
| 1905—Fort Worth ....... .545 | 1934—Galveston‡ ....... .579 | Tulsa (3rd)§ ...... .529 |
| 1906—Fort Worth ....... .677 | 1935—Oklahoma City‡ ... .590 | 1964—San Antonio‡ ..... .607 |
| Cleburne x ........ .609 | 1936—Dallas ........... .604 | 1965—Tulsa ............ .574 |
| 1907—Austin ........... .629 | Tulsa (3rd)§ ...... .519 | Albuquerque xx ... .550 |
| 1908—San Antonio ...... .664 | 1937—Oklahoma City .... .635 | 1966—Arkansas ......... .579 |
| 1909—Houston .......... .601 | Fort Worth (3rd)§ .535 | 1967—Albuquerque ...... .557 |
| 1910—Dallas† .......... .586 | 1938—Beaumont ........ .635 | 1968—Arkansas ......... .586 |
| Houston† .......... .586 | 1939—Houston ......... .606 | El Paso xx ........ .562 |
| 1911—Austin ........... .575 | Fort Worth (4th)§ .540 | 1969—Amarillo ......... .593 |
| 1912—Houston .......... .626 | 1940—Houston‡ ......... .652 | Memphis xx ....... .504 |
| 1913—Houston .......... .620 | 1941—Houston ......... .673 | 1970—Albuquerque** ... .615 |
| 1914—Houston† ......... .671 | Dallas (4th)§ ..... .519 | Memphis ........... .507 |
| Waco† ............ .671 | 1942—Beaumont ........ .605 | 1971—Did not operate as league |
| 1915—Waco ............ .592 | Shreveport (2nd)§ . .576 | —clubs were members of |
| 1916—Waco ............ .587 | 1943-44-45—Did not operate. | Dixie Association. |
| 1917—Dallas ........... .600 | 1946—Fort Worth ...... .656 | 1972—Alexandria ....... .600 |
| 1918—Dallas ........... .584 | Dallas (2nd)§ ..... .591 | El Paso xx ........ .557 |
| 1919—Shreveport* ...... .677 | 1947—Houston‡ ......... .623 | 1973—San Antonio ...... .590 |
| Fort Worth ....... .651 | 1948—Fort Worth‡ ...... .601 | Memphis xx ....... .558 |
| 1920—Fort Worth ....... .703 | Tulsa (2nd)§ ...... .584 | 1974—Victoria xx ....... .581 |
| Fort Worth ....... .750 | 1949—Fort Worth ...... .649 | El Paso .......... .555 |
| 1921—Fort Worth ....... .691 | 1950—Beaumont ........ .595 | |
| | San Antonio (4th)§ .513 | |

*Won split-season playoff     †No playoff for title.     ‡Finished first and won four-club playoff.

— 427 —

§Won four-club playoff. xTitle to Cleburne by default . yTied with Dallas in second half and won playoff for championship. zFort Worth disbanded. **Tied with Beaumont at end of first half and won title in best-of-five series played as part of second half schedule. xxLeague divided into Eastern, Western divisions; won two-team playoff. NOTE—Championship awarded to winner of four-team play-off, 1933-51; first-place team and playoff winner co-champions, 1952-64.

## STANDING OF CLUBS AT CLOSE OF SEASON, SEPTEMBER 1

### EASTERN DIVISION

| Club | Laf. | Jack. | Ark. | Alex. | Mid. | Shreve. | ElP. | S.A. | W. | L. | T. | Pct. | G.B. |
|---|---|---|---|---|---|---|---|---|---|---|---|---|---|
| Lafayette (Giants) ........ | .. | 20 | 18 | 17 | 3 | 5 | 4 | 5 | 72 | 57 | 0 | .558 | .... |
| Jackson (Mets) .......... | 10 | .. | 16 | 18 | 2 | 5 | 7 | 7 | 65 | 65 | 0 | .500 | 7½ |
| Arkansas (Cardinals) ..... | 13 | 16 | .. | 16 | 5 | 2 | 3 | 8 | 63 | 72 | 0 | .467 | 12 |
| Alexandria (Padres) ..... | 12 | 14 | 16 | .. | 6 | 1 | 6 | 3 | 58 | 72 | 1 | .446 | 14½ |

### WESTERN DIVISION

| Club | Laf. | Jack. | Ark. | Alex. | Mid. | Shreve. | ElP. | S.A. | W. | L. | T. | Pct. | G.B. |
|---|---|---|---|---|---|---|---|---|---|---|---|---|---|
| Midland (Cubs) ........ | 7 | 7 | 5 | 4 | .. | 19 | 18 | 21 | 81 | 53 | 2 | .604 | .... |
| Shreveport (Pirates) ..... | 4 | 3 | 8 | 6 | 13 | .. | 20 | 22 | 76 | 52 | 0 | .594 | 2 |
| El Paso (Angels) ........ | 6 | 3 | 7 | 4 | 13 | 10 | .. | 19 | 62 | 71 | 0 | .466 | 18½ |
| San Antonio (Indians) ... | 5 | 2 | 2 | 7 | 11 | 10 | 13 | .. | 50 | 85 | 1 | .370 | 31½ |

Arkansas Club represented Little Rock, Ark.
Major league affiliations in parentheses.
FORFEITED GAME—August 27 (second game), Alexandria forfeited to Arkansas in first inning. No statistics compiled for this game.
Playoff—Midland and Lafayette each won two games; rain prevented completion of series, and Midland and Lafayette were declared co-champions by league president.
Regular-Season Attendance—Alexandria, 47,874; Arkansas, 67,473; El Paso, 162,399; Jackson, 77,046; Lafayette, 72,549; Midland, 69,678; San Antonio, 138,517; Shreveport, 39,088. Total, 674,624. Playoffs, 5,388. All-Star Game, 2,317.
Managers: Alexandria—Pat Corrales; Arkansas—Roy Majtyka; El Paso—James F. Williams; Jackson—John Antonelli; Lafayette—Dennis Sommers; Midland—Howard (Doc) Edwards; San Antonio—Forrest (Woody) Smith; Shreveport—Tim Murtaugh.
All-Star Team: 1B—Young, Arkansas; 2B—Montreuil, Midland; 3B—Clark, Lafayette; SS—Templeton, Arkansas; OF—Potter, Arkansas; Thomas, Shreveport; Lopez, El Paso; C—Nicosia, Shreveport; Stone, Alexandria; DH—Alexander, Lafayette; P—Butkus, Arkansas; Riccelli, Lafayette; Manager—Sommers, Lafayette.

(Compiled by Ed Williams, League Statistician, Shawnee, Okla.)

## CLUB BATTING

| Club | G. | AB. | R. | OR. | H. | TB. | 2B. | 3B. | HR. | RBI. | SH. | SF. | Int. BB. | BB. | HP. | SO. | SB. | CS. | LOB. | Pct. |
|---|---|---|---|---|---|---|---|---|---|---|---|---|---|---|---|---|---|---|---|---|
| El Paso ... | 133 | 4380 | 742 | 710 | 1228 | 1819 | 205 | 47 | 94 | 641 | 39 | 44 | 528 | 40 | 35 | 792 | 148 | 80 | 922 | .283 |
| Midland ... | 136 | 4396 | 714 | 540 | 1220 | 1776 | 213 | 44 | 85 | 627 | 53 | 38 | 621 | 44 | 34 | 728 | 140 | 100 | 1038 | .278 |
| Lafayette .. | 129 | 4192 | 630 | 567 | 1140 | 1636 | 188 | 22 | 88 | 551 | 41 | 50 | 526 | 33 | 14 | 542 | 68 | 22 | 971 | .272 |
| Shreveport . | 128 | 4031 | 660 | 562 | 1091 | 1735 | 217 | 44 | 113 | 596 | 24 | 41 | 495 | 32 | 46 | 687 | 155 | 52 | 860 | .271 |
| Alexandria .. | 130 | 4185 | 552 | 605 | 1125 | 1488 | 186 | 24 | 43 | 473 | 57 | 42 | 436 | 34 | 16 | 568 | 88 | 45 | 958 | .269 |
| Arkansas .. | 134 | 4282 | 534 | 605 | 1097 | 1500 | 184 | 27 | 55 | 488 | 39 | 34 | 437 | 33 | 32 | 561 | 66 | 37 | 933 | .256 |
| San Antonio | 136 | 4456 | 494 | 743 | 1120 | 1510 | 179 | 35 | 44 | 417 | 44 | 30 | 462 | 49 | 23 | 621 | 66 | 49 | 996 | .251 |
| Jackson ... | 130 | 4159 | 560 | 554 | 1024 | 1412 | 181 | 42 | 41 | 499 | 52 | 36 | 507 | 33 | 26 | 598 | 28 | 5 | 962 | .246 |

## INDIVIDUAL BATTING

(Leading Qualifiers for Batting Championship—367 or More Plate Appearances)
*Bats lefthanded. †Switch-hitter.

| Player and Club | G. | AB. | R. | H. | TB. | 2B. | 3B. | HR. | RBI. | SH. | SF. | BB. | HP. | SO. | SB. | CS. | Pct. |
|---|---|---|---|---|---|---|---|---|---|---|---|---|---|---|---|---|---|
| Alberts, Francis, El Paso .. | 88 | 325 | 66 | 111 | 191 | 19 | 8 | 15 | 51 | 1 | 0 | 33 | 3 | 52 | 7 | 6 | .342 |
| Dade, L. Paul, El Paso .... | 100 | 343 | 81 | 114 | 195 | 23 | 5 | 16 | 84 | 0 | 13 | 66 | 5 | 62 | 17 | 4 | .332 |
| Young, John, Arkansas* ... | 125 | 433 | 83 | 143 | 220 | 23 | 3 | 16 | 65 | 3 | 3 | 63 | 2 | 54 | 5 | 8 | .330 |
| Alexander, Gary, Lafayette | 103 | 346 | 80 | 114 | 209 | 24 | 1 | 23 | 81 | 0 | 2 | 76 | 4 | 90 | 5 | 1 | .329 |
| Lopez, Carlos A., El Paso | 112 | 428 | 77 | 140 | 209 | 22 | 10 | 9 | 78 | 0 | 7 | 30 | 3 | 67 | 11 | 16 | .327 |
| Montreuil, Allan, Midland.. | 117 | 404 | 71 | 131 | 189 | 21 | 5 | 9 | 62 | 4 | 5 | 60 | 5 | 39 | 5 | 0 | .324 |
| Ortiz, Jose L., Midland ... | 107 | 399 | 80 | 129 | 167 | 17 | 3 | 5 | 51 | 1 | 3 | 73 | 6 | 46 | 45 | 4 | .323 |
| Cacek, Craig, Jackson .... | 129 | 432 | 63 | 135 | 181 | 20 | 7 | 4 | 57 | 3 | 6 | 80 | 3 | 51 | 0 | 0 | .313 |
| Walton, Reginald, Laf .... | 124 | 452 | 77 | 140 | 197 | 23 | 5 | 8 | 78 | 3 | 7 | 52 | 1 | 60 | 12 | 7 | .310 |
| Rhea, Marc, Alexandria .. | 125 | 455 | 92 | 140 | 205 | 24 | 7 | 9 | 64 | 1 | 6 | 52 | 2 | 69 | 27 | 9 | .308 |

Alberts did not have the required number of plate appearances but when charged with five official at bats to reach the qualification plateau he thus became the leader with .336 average. Under the provisions of scoring rule 10.23a, Alberts, El Paso, qualified for the batting championship.
Departmental Leaders: G—Guerra, Machemer, 133; AB—Biasas, 513; R—Machemer, 101; H—Machemer, 153; TB—J. Clark, 239; 2B—Potter, 32; 3B—Lopez, 10; HR—Alexander, J. Clark, Page, 23; RBI—Page, 90; SH—Champion, Stedman, Wilhelm, 11; SF—Dade, 13; BB—Guerra, 92; HP—Sexton, 11; SO—Tyrone, 105; SB—Sexton, 48; CS—Machemer, 20.

(All Players—Listed Alphabetically)

| Player and Club | G. | AB. | R. | H. | TB. | 2B. | 3B. | HR. | RBI. | SH. | SF. | BB. | HP. | SO. | SB. | CS. | Pct. |
|---|---|---|---|---|---|---|---|---|---|---|---|---|---|---|---|---|---|
| Aaron, Wilmer, San Ant† | 132 | 503 | 65 | 135 | 171 | 21 | 6 | 1 | 45 | 6 | 4 | 36 | 6 | 55 | 12 | 8 | .268 |
| Agosto, Michael, Jackson*.. | 104 | 336 | 40 | 76 | 119 | 12 | 2 | 9 | 50 | 1 | 4 | 54 | 2 | 76 | 0 | 0 | .226 |
| Ahu, Aran, Alexandria ... | 51 | 142 | 13 | 32 | 51 | 6 | 2 | 3 | 14 | 1 | 1 | 25 | 2 | 37 | 1 | 2 | .225 |
| Alberts, Francis, El Paso .. | 88 | 325 | 66 | 111 | 191 | 19 | 8 | 15 | 51 | 1 | 0 | 33 | 3 | 52 | 7 | 6 | .342 |
| Alexander, Gary, Lafayette | 103 | 346 | 80 | 114 | 209 | 24 | 1 | 23 | 81 | 0 | 2 | 76 | 4 | 90 | 5 | 1 | .329 |
| Alfano, Donnie, Alex* ...... | 96 | 95 | 7 | 20 | 24 | 4 | 0 | 0 | 5 | 0 | 1 | 6 | 0 | 16 | 1 | 0 | .211 |

| Player and Club | G. | AB. | R. | H. | TB. | 2B. | 3B. | HR. | RBI. | SH. | SF. | BB. | HP. | SO. | SB. | CS. | Pct. |
|---|---|---|---|---|---|---|---|---|---|---|---|---|---|---|---|---|---|
| Allen, Michael, Alexandria . | 21 | 0 | 1 | 0 | 0 | 0 | 0 | 0 | 0 | 0 | 0 | 0 | 0 | 0 | 0 | 0 | .000 |
| Ashford, Samuel, El Paso* . | 100 | 357 | 52 | 92 | 143 | 15 | 3 | 10 | 59 | 5 | 5 | 29 | 2 | 80 | 5 | 3 | .258 |
| Ashford, Thomas, Alex .... | 120 | 376 | 33 | 89 | 112 | 12 | 1 | 3 | 38 | 6 | 3 | 25 | 0 | 39 | 3 | 1 | .237 |
| Atwell, Gary, Lafayette .. | 87 | 314 | 52 | 87 | 114 | 16 | 1 | 3 | 23 | 2 | 4 | 44 | 1 | 26 | 14 | 1 | .277 |
| Barnes, Craig, Lafayette* . | 96 | 302 | 37 | 79 | 126 | 11 | 0 | 12 | 51 | 0 | 5 | 32 | 1 | 54 | 2 | 0 | .262 |
| Beerbower, Dan, El Paso . | 74 | 244 | 33 | 66 | 79 | 9 | 2 | 0 | 28 | 4 | 2 | 25 | 0 | 19 | 1 | 3 | .270 |
| Belloir, Robert, San An .. | 58 | 221 | 16 | 48 | 70 | 15 | 2 | 1 | 27 | 2 | 1 | 11 | 1 | 18 | 0 | 2 | .217 |
| Bialas, David, Arkansas .. | 132 | 513 | 50 | 141 | 165 | 11 | 5 | 1 | 54 | 3 | 1 | 33 | 3 | 48 | 6 | 2 | .275 |
| Bolinger, Monte, Arkansas. | 58 | 178 | 20 | 44 | 57 | 10 | 0 | 1 | 17 | 1 | 0 | 26 | 1 | 24 | 1 | 1 | .247 |
| Bonfiis, Peter, El Paso .. | 28 | 12 | 2 | 2 | 2 | 0 | 0 | 0 | 0 | 0 | 0 | 0 | 0 | 5 | 0 | 0 | .167 |
| Bowman, Edwin, Arkansas . | 99 | 331 | 24 | 80 | 104 | 11 | 2 | 3 | 34 | 2 | 3 | 15 | 1 | 25 | 2 | 0 | .242 |
| Boyne, Bryan, Lafayette .. | 15 | 35 | 4 | 6 | 6 | 0 | 0 | 0 | 6 | 0 | 1 | 4 | 0 | 4 | 0 | 0 | .171 |
| Bright, William, Midland*. | 121 | 416 | 67 | 127 | 184 | 31 | 4 | 6 | 69 | 5 | 8 | 43 | 0 | 52 | 4 | 2 | .305 |
| Brooks, Michael, San An .. | 50 | 190 | 13 | 41 | 62 | 11 | 2 | 2 | 24 | 3 | 1 | 25 | 0 | 38 | 0 | 1 | .216 |
| Brown, Jerald, Lafayette .. | 19 | 75 | 13 | 23 | 34 | 5 | 0 | 2 | 14 | 0 | 2 | 6 | 0 | 7 | 2 | 0 | .307 |
| Brown, Scott A., Alex*.... | 107 | 299 | 44 | 81 | 91 | 10 | 0 | 0 | 22 | 9 | 2 | 40 | 4 | 37 | 12 | 6 | .271 |
| Bynum, R. Rex, San An*.. | 53 | 164 | 9 | 30 | 37 | 3 | 2 | 0 | 11 | 0 | 0 | 21 | 1 | 46 | 2 | 3 | .183 |
| Cacek, Craig, Jackson .... | 129 | 432 | 63 | 135 | 181 | 20 | 7 | 4 | 57 | 3 | 6 | 80 | 3 | 51 | 0 | 0 | .313 |
| Cage, Wayne, San Antonio*. | 41 | 153 | 15 | 32 | 55 | 8 | 3 | 3 | 12 | 0 | 1 | 12 | 0 | 42 | 1 | 0 | .209 |
| Calufetti, Lawrence, Jack.. | 54 | 159 | 14 | 38 | 51 | 7 | 0 | 2 | 18 | 3 | 0 | 15 | 1 | 21 | 0 | 0 | .239 |
| Cantres, Angel, Jackson .. | 115 | 386 | 59 | 93 | 137 | 19 | 5 | 5 | 60 | 4 | 5 | 46 | 3 | 42 | 1 | 0 | .241 |
| Champion, R. Michael, Alex | 125 | 403 | 54 | 117 | 160 | 23 | 4 | 4 | 36 | 11 | 6 | 15 | 2 | 56 | 4 | 4 | .290 |
| Chew, Earle, Midland .... | 16 | 40 | 8 | 18 | 28 | 1 | 3 | 1 | 14 | 0 | 0 | 6 | 0 | 9 | 1 | 0 | .450 |
| Christiansen, David, El P.. | 47 | 153 | 23 | 37 | 58 | 7 | 1 | 4 | 21 | 1 | 1 | 21 | 1 | 34 | 5 | 1 | .242 |
| Clancy, Stephen, Midland.. | 86 | 244 | 34 | 52 | 83 | 9 | 0 | 7 | 42 | 6 | 1 | 38 | 2 | 36 | 1 | 2 | .217 |
| Clarey, Douglas, Arkansas. | 130 | 433 | 51 | 89 | 119 | 17 | 2 | 3 | 44 | 4 | 6 | 38 | 8 | 56 | 1 | 2 | .206 |
| Clark, Craig, Jackson .... | 104 | 369 | 39 | 90 | 109 | 13 | 0 | 2 | 41 | 5 | 5 | 29 | 3 | 53 | 5 | 0 | .244 |
| Clark, Jack, Lafayette .... | 126 | 466 | 94 | 141 | 239 | 25 | 2 | 23 | 77 | 0 | 4 | 65 | 0 | 59 | 9 | 0 | .303 |
| Cleverly, Gary, San An* .. | 92 | 295 | 33 | 65 | 75 | 6 | 2 | 0 | 13 | 2 | 2 | 42 | 2 | 50 | 12 | 4 | .220 |
| Coe, Roger, Alexandria* ... | 8 | 1 | 0 | 0 | 0 | 0 | 0 | 0 | 0 | 0 | 0 | 0 | 0 | 1 | 0 | 0 | .000 |
| Collins, Gregory, Midland. | 46 | 122 | 14 | 29 | 39 | 4 | 0 | 2 | 16 | 1 | 0 | 18 | 1 | 25 | 1 | 0 | .238 |
| Cornejo, N. Mardie, Jackson. | 26 | 0 | 0 | 0 | 0 | 0 | 0 | 0 | 0 | 3 | 0 | 0 | 0 | 0 | 0 | 0 | .000 |
| Corrales, Patrick, Alex .... | 2 | 0 | 0 | 0 | 0 | 0 | 0 | 0 | 0 | 0 | 0 | 0 | 0 | 1 | 0 | 0 | .000 |
| Cristelli, Patrick, El P*... | 27 | 2 | 2 | 2 | 2 | 0 | 0 | 0 | 0 | 0 | 0 | 0 | 0 | 0 | 0 | 0 | 1.000 |
| Croswell, Robert, Jackson†.. | 72 | 247 | 32 | 55 | 64 | 9 | 0 | 0 | 28 | 1 | 2 | 29 | 2 | 26 | 0 | 0 | .223 |
| Dade, L. Paul, El Paso .. | 100 | 343 | 81 | 114 | 195 | 23 | 5 | 16 | 84 | 0 | 13 | 66 | 5 | 62 | 17 | 4 | .332 |
| Daves, William, Arkansas .. | 7 | 17 | 1 | 1 | 1 | 0 | 0 | 0 | 0 | 0 | 0 | 3 | 0 | 1 | 0 | 0 | .059 |
| Davis, Bryshear, San An* .. | 43 | 149 | 24 | 40 | 48 | 5 | 0 | 1 | 16 | 2 | 2 | 26 | 1 | 18 | 5 | 4 | .268 |
| Davis, Kenzie, Arkansas ... | 36 | 122 | 16 | 29 | 39 | 4 | 0 | 2 | 18 | 1 | 0 | 8 | 2 | 21 | 11 | 4 | .238 |
| Del Orbe, Lazaro, Laf .... | 8 | 16 | 1 | 1 | 1 | 0 | 0 | 0 | 1 | 0 | 0 | 0 | 0 | 2 | 0 | 0 | .063 |
| Delyon, Eugene, Alex .... | 95 | 329 | 42 | 100 | 133 | 21 | 0 | 4 | 62 | 3 | 2 | 45 | 0 | 52 | 3 | 0 | .304 |
| Dillard, Jay, Lafayette .... | 20 | 1 | 0 | 0 | 0 | 0 | 0 | 0 | 0 | 0 | 0 | 0 | 0 | 1 | 0 | 0 | .000 |
| D'Innocenzio, Richard, Laf. | 30 | 79 | 9 | 23 | 29 | 1 | 1 | 1 | 13 | 0 | 1 | 14 | 1 | 12 | 2 | 1 | .291 |
| Djakanow, Paul, Shreveport. | 111 | 369 | 66 | 86 | 160 | 20 | 3 | 16 | 58 | 0 | 2 | 47 | 4 | 65 | 7 | 3 | .233 |
| Donohue, Thomas, El Paso. | 100 | 338 | 46 | 91 | 146 | 15 | 2 | 12 | 59 | 6 | 1 | 13 | 5 | 98 | 7 | 5 | .269 |
| Droege, William, Midland . | 109 | 426 | 76 | 124 | 168 | 24 | 1 | 6 | 57 | 2 | 4 | 50 | 5 | 62 | 16 | 5 | .291 |
| Dupree, Michael, Alex .... | 124 | 417 | 47 | 111 | 129 | 12 | 3 | 0 | 34 | 3 | 2 | 42 | 1 | 41 | 4 | 4 | .266 |
| Edelen, Benny, Arkansas .. | 69 | 193 | 18 | 36 | 51 | 8 | 0 | 5 | 22 | 3 | 5 | 18 | 2 | 50 | 1 | 1 | .187 |
| Edwards, Michael, Shrev .. | 93 | 368 | 57 | 112 | 153 | 26 | 3 | 3 | 41 | 6 | 1 | 31 | 2 | 39 | 27 | 9 | .304 |
| Flores, Gilberto, El Paso .. | 62 | 238 | 51 | 73 | 102 | 11 | 6 | 2 | 31 | 1 | 2 | 21 | 5 | 28 | 32 | 7 | .307 |
| Friedman, Martin, El P* .. | 95 | 341 | 59 | 92 | 127 | 20 | 3 | 3 | 54 | 4 | 4 | 68 | 3 | 55 | 10 | 5 | .270 |
| Froede, Kent, El Paso .... | 33 | 104 | 10 | 18 | 20 | 2 | 0 | 0 | 9 | 1 | 2 | 13 | 0 | 21 | 2 | 1 | .173 |
| Gerhardt, Allen, Alex† .... | 16 | 1 | 0 | 1 | 1 | 0 | 0 | 0 | 0 | 0 | 0 | 0 | 0 | 0 | 0 | 0 | 1.000 |
| Gibbon, Charles, El Paso† . | 18 | 1 | 0 | 0 | 0 | 0 | 0 | 0 | 0 | 0 | 0 | 0 | 0 | 0 | 0 | 0 | .000 |
| Goddard, Joseph, Alex .... | 39 | 97 | 7 | 11 | 13 | 2 | 0 | 0 | 9 | 2 | 4 | 15 | 0 | 10 | 0 | 1 | .113 |
| Gonzalez, Julio, Midland .. | 81 | 324 | 37 | 88 | 111 | 13 | 2 | 2 | 27 | 4 | 3 | 17 | 3 | 33 | 9 | 0 | .272 |
| Gonzalez, Orlando, San An* | 54 | 210 | 38 | 66 | 86 | 11 | 3 | 1 | 22 | 2 | 3 | 22 | 1 | 19 | 10 | 3 | .314 |
| Goodwin, Danny, El Paso* . | 46 | 138 | 10 | 38 | 50 | 6 | 0 | 2 | 18 | 1 | 3 | 21 | 0 | 23 | 0 | 1 | .275 |
| Green, Joel, Midland .... | 38 | 117 | 18 | 26 | 35 | 5 | 2 | 0 | 6 | 2 | 0 | 16 | 0 | 17 | 6 | 1 | .222 |
| Grundler, Frank, Shrev ... | 110 | 368 | 67 | 104 | 174 | 21 | 2 | 15 | 59 | 1 | 0 | 52 | 5 | 43 | 12 | 3 | .283 |
| Guerra, Richard, San An .. | 133 | 450 | 73 | 138 | 228 | 30 | 3 | 18 | 69 | 0 | 9 | 92 | 3 | 67 | 3 | 1 | .307 |
| Hall, Clifford, Midland*... | 9 | 17 | 3 | 2 | 4 | 0 | 1 | 0 | 2 | 0 | 0 | 3 | 0 | 6 | 0 | 0 | .118 |
| Hamilton, William, Alex†.. | 49 | 151 | 16 | 46 | 68 | 11 | 1 | 3 | 23 | 0 | 4 | 15 | 2 | 17 | 1 | 1 | .305 |
| Hannah, James, San An .. | 74 | 237 | 20 | 62 | 79 | 8 | 3 | 0 | 35 | 3 | 4 | 33 | 1 | 37 | 2 | 3 | .262 |
| Harmon, Thomas, Arkansas*. | 60 | 177 | 17 | 37 | 45 | 5 | 0 | 1 | 18 | 2 | 2 | 16 | 1 | 11 | 0 | 0 | .209 |
| Harris, Richard, Jackson . | 87 | 306 | 37 | 78 | 112 | 21 | 5 | 1 | 29 | 1 | 2 | 30 | 1 | 42 | 1 | 1 | .255 |
| Heise, Benjamin, San An . | 36 | 97 | 10 | 33 | 41 | 6 | 1 | 0 | 7 | 2 | 3 | 14 | 0 | 10 | 0 | 1 | .340 |
| Hickey, Robert, San An†... | 38 | 104 | 12 | 26 | 26 | 0 | 0 | 0 | 4 | 1 | 0 | 9 | 1 | 11 | 2 | 3 | .250 |
| Hilton, J. David, Alex .... | 44 | 151 | 30 | 45 | 77 | 14 | 0 | 6 | 27 | 1 | 4 | 21 | 1 | 14 | 2 | 1 | .298 |
| Hiss, William, San An .... | 60 | 163 | 12 | 37 | 42 | 5 | 0 | 0 | 8 | 4 | 0 | 26 | 1 | 34 | 0 | 1 | .227 |
| Hrapman, Robert, Arkansas† | 471 | 56 | 112 | 132 | 12 | 4 | 0 | 36 | 6 | 2 | 33 | 2 | 64 | 9 | 5 | .238 |
| Huisman, William, Midland. | 61 | 206 | 41 | 56 | 87 | 8 | 4 | 5 | 27 | 6 | 1 | 35 | 1 | 27 | 9 | 1 | .272 |
| Hund, John, El Paso .... | 6 | 15 | 0 | 2 | 2 | 0 | 0 | 0 | 0 | 0 | 0 | 0 | 0 | 3 | 0 | 0 | .133 |
| Husband, Paul, Arkansas .. | 21 | 76 | 7 | 14 | 21 | 4 | 0 | 1 | 3 | 0 | 0 | 9 | 0 | 9 | 0 | 0 | .184 |
| Johnson, John C., Ark .... | 2 | 5 | 0 | 0 | 0 | 0 | 0 | 0 | 0 | 0 | 0 | 0 | 0 | 1 | 0 | 0 | .000 |
| Jordan, Edward, El Paso .. | 8 | 22 | 2 | 4 | 5 | 1 | 0 | 0 | 2 | 0 | 0 | 1 | 0 | 7 | 0 | 1 | .182 |
| Kidder, James, Jackson ... | 88 | 345 | 50 | 91 | 118 | 15 | 3 | 2 | 33 | 7 | 3 | 30 | 2 | 36 | 0 | 1 | .264 |
| Kim, Wendell, Lafayette ... | 87 | 302 | 44 | 72 | 85 | 9 | 2 | 0 | 19 | 5 | 3 | 37 | 1 | 29 | 3 | 0 | .238 |
| Krizmanich, Mike, 57 San Antonio-22 Shrev . | 79 | 249 | 36 | 63 | 79 | 10 | 0 | 2 | 26 | 4 | 1 | 25 | 3 | 28 | 11 | 2 | .253 |
| Langerhans, John, San An.. | 12 | 9 | 2 | 2 | 2 | 0 | 0 | 0 | 1 | 0 | 0 | 1 | 0 | 0 | 0 | 0 | .222 |

| Player and Club | G. | AB. | R. | H. | TB. | 2B. | 3B. | HR. | RBI. | SH. | SF. | BB. | HP. | SO. | SB. | CS. | Pct. |
|---|---|---|---|---|---|---|---|---|---|---|---|---|---|---|---|---|---|
| Lanthorn, Eugene, Laf .... | 20 | 1 | 0 | 1 | 1 | 0 | 0 | 0 | 1 | 1 | 0 | 0 | 0 | 0 | 0 | 0 | 1.000 |
| Lantigua, Manuel, San An. | 76 | 274 | 19 | 68 | 84 | 5 | 4 | 1 | 22 | 2 | 2 | 9 | 1 | 35 | 1 | 1 | .248 |
| Lee, Leon, Arkansas ...... | 44 | 152 | 24 | 51 | 71 | 12 | 1 | 2 | 29 | 0 | 1 | 16 | 1 | 15 | 0 | 0 | .336 |
| Lopez, Carlos A., El Paso ..| 112 | 428 | 77 | 140 | 209 | 22 | 10 | 9 | 78 | 0 | 7 | 30 | 3 | 67 | 11 | 16 | .327 |
| Lora, Luis, Jackson* ...... | 20 | 74 | 10 | 18 | 25 | 5 | 1 | 0 | 5 | 0 | 0 | 6 | 0 | 8 | 3 | 0 | .243 |
| Machemer, David, El Paso.| 110 | 509 | 101 | 153 | 185 | 17 | 6 | 1 | 46 | 5 | 2 | 89 | 4 | 45 | 45 | 20 | .301 |
| Mann, Stanley, Jackson ...| 30 | 102 | 16 | 26 | 32 | 3 | 0 | 1 | 12 | 0 | 3 | 8 | 1 | 15 | 1 | 0 | .255 |
| Manning, Anthony, San An.| 71 | 231 | 24 | 46 | 73 | 9 | 3 | 4 | 18 | 2 | 1 | 19 | 1 | 25 | 2 | 4 | .199 |
| Martin, Joseph W., Laf*...| 73 | 213 | 19 | 56 | 69 | 4 | 0 | 3 | 25 | 1 | 4 | 31 | 0 | 13 | 1 | 2 | .263 |
| Maxwell, J. Rodney, El P*..| 13 | 1 | 0 | 0 | 0 | 0 | 0 | 0 | 0 | 0 | 0 | 0 | 0 | 1 | 0 | 0 | .000 |
| Melvin, Kenneth, Shrev. | 110 | 350 | 53 | 94 | 153 | 16 | 2 | 13 | 55 | 3 | 3 | 54 | 2 | 96 | 4 | 4 | .269 |
| Miller, Richard E., Jack*.| 110 | 382 | 48 | 88 | 124 | 18 | 6 | 2 | 35 | 9 | 1 | 33 | 0 | 70 | 2 | 1 | .230 |
| Milner, Timothy, Jackson | 7 | 5 | 1 | 1 | 1 | 0 | 0 | 0 | 0 | 0 | 0 | 0 | 0 | 0 | 0 | 0 | .200 |
| Mitchell, Ronald, Shrev | 124 | 446 | 64 | 116 | 185 | 25 | 7 | 10 | 72 | 3 | 8 | 40 | 5 | 78 | 5 | 5 | .260 |
| Montreuil, Allan, Midland.| 117 | 404 | 71 | 131 | 189 | 21 | 5 | 9 | 62 | 4 | 5 | 60 | 5 | 39 | 5 | 0 | .324 |
| Moore, Donnie, Midland* ..| 37 | 1 | 3 | 1 | 1 | 0 | 0 | 0 | 2 | 0 | 0 | 0 | 0 | 0 | 0 | 0 | 1.000 |
| Newsome, Alan, El Paso ..| 17 | 46 | 5 | 9 | 12 | 3 | 0 | 0 | 2 | 0 | 0 | 4 | 1 | 12 | 0 | 0 | .196 |
| Nicosia, Steven, Shrev ...| 119 | 370 | 52 | 99 | 144 | 15 | 6 | 6 | 39 | 3 | 1 | 38 | 6 | 44 | 12 | 3 | .268 |
| Oliver, David J., San An*.| 75 | 289 | 34 | 82 | 92 | 10 | 0 | 0 | 17 | 7 | 1 | 21 | 0 | 22 | 4 | 6 | .284 |
| Oliveras, Max, Shreveport.| 78 | 234 | 27 | 59 | 72 | 6 | 2 | 1 | 22 | 4 | 5 | 17 | 2 | 34 | 5 | 4 | .252 |
| Ortiz, Jose L., Midland ...| 107 | 399 | 80 | 129 | 167 | 17 | 3 | 5 | 51 | 1 | 3 | 73 | 6 | 46 | 45 | 4 | .323 |
| Page, Mitchell, Shrev* ....| 122 | 413 | 73 | 120 | 219 | 24 | 3 | 23 | 90 | 1 | 8 | 56 | 5 | 87 | 23 | 6 | .291 |
| Panick, Francis, El Paso..| 32 | 1 | 0 | 0 | 0 | 0 | 0 | 0 | 0 | 0 | 0 | 0 | 0 | 0 | 0 | 0 | .000 |
| Pavlick, Gregory, Jackson | 36 | 1 | 1 | 0 | 0 | 0 | 0 | 0 | 0 | 0 | 0 | 0 | 0 | 0 | 0 | 0 | .000 |
| Perry, Kenneth, Jackson | 33 | 114 | 18 | 26 | 34 | 3 | 1 | 1 | 8 | 3 | 0 | 12 | 1 | 13 | 2 | 0 | .228 |
| Person, Carl, El Paso ...| 11 | 34 | 7 | 9 | 10 | 1 | 0 | 0 | 3 | 0 | 0 | 1 | 0 | 4 | 1 | 0 | .265 |
| Potter, Michael, Arkansas | 131 | 464 | 62 | 140 | 217 | 32 | 3 | 13 | 76 | 1 | 8 | 60 | 3 | 65 | 3 | 1 | .302 |
| Putman, Eddy, Midland ...| 24 | 68 | 8 | 14 | 21 | 1 | 0 | 2 | 6 | 1 | 0 | 13 | 0 | 24 | 1 | 0 | .206 |
| Raco, Gary, Arkansas ....| 51 | 107 | 9 | 17 | 22 | 2 | 0 | 1 | 7 | 4 | 1 | 11 | 1 | 27 | 4 | 3 | .159 |
| Rametta, Steven, San An | 75 | 265 | 23 | 60 | 93 | 14 | 2 | 5 | 32 | 2 | 3 | 5 | 1 | 29 | 1 | 1 | .226 |
| Randall, Aaron, Midland† ..| 54 | 181 | 16 | 41 | 59 | 5 | 2 | 3 | 17 | 4 | 2 | 6 | 0 | 37 | 3 | 1 | .227 |
| Rhea, Marc, Alexandria ..| 125 | 455 | 92 | 140 | 205 | 24 | 7 | 9 | 64 | 1 | 6 | 59 | 2 | 69 | 27 | 9 | .308 |
| Richardson, Richard, El P.| 17 | 53 | 7 | 10 | 16 | 6 | 0 | 0 | 7 | 0 | 0 | 8 | 0 | 8 | 0 | 0 | .189 |
| Rodriguez, Adriano, San An.| 91 | 268 | 28 | 68 | 95 | 8 | 2 | 5 | 24 | 1 | 2 | 24 | 1 | 45 | 3 | 0 | .254 |
| Rosado, Luis, Jackson ....| 24 | 82 | 7 | 19 | 21 | 2 | 0 | 0 | 13 | 1 | 2 | 6 | 0 | 8 | 0 | 0 | .232 |
| Rothan, William, El Paso | 27 | 2 | 0 | 0 | 0 | 0 | 0 | 0 | 0 | 0 | 0 | 0 | 0 | 0 | 0 | 0 | .000 |
| Rush, Lawrence, El Paso | 83 | 296 | 51 | 78 | 108 | 13 | 1 | 5 | 39 | 5 | 1 | 29 | 1 | 70 | 3 | 3 | .264 |
| Saferight, Harry, Shreve*..| 86 | 280 | 35 | 67 | 110 | 15 | 5 | 6 | 42 | 1 | 3 | 29 | 0 | 36 | 2 | 0 | .239 |
| Sagredo, Carlos, Jackson*| 85 | 262 | 47 | 64 | 95 | 8 | 7 | 3 | 32 | 1 | 1 | 50 | 3 | 55 | 8 | 1 | .244 |
| Sallinger, Robert, Jack†..| 44 | 134 | 10 | 30 | 42 | 7 | 1 | 1 | 20 | 5 | 1 | 15 | 2 | 19 | 0 | 0 | .224 |
| Schlueter, Jay, Arkansas..| 54 | 168 | 23 | 30 | 52 | 9 | 2 | 3 | 15 | 4 | 1 | 25 | 2 | 39 | 5 | 1 | .179 |
| Scott, John, Alexandria ...| 61 | 239 | 40 | 64 | 86 | 11 | 1 | 3 | 37 | 0 | 4 | 10 | 1 | 25 | 15 | 5 | .268 |
| Sember, Michael, Midland.| 125 | 402 | 64 | 101 | 151 | 13 | 5 | 9 | 59 | 2 | 2 | 69 | 6 | 104 | 13 | 4 | .251 |
| Senn, Terrence, Jackson | 19 | 78 | 12 | 17 | 25 | 3 | 1 | 1 | 7 | 0 | 0 | 8 | 0 | 10 | 0 | 1 | .218 |
| Sexton, Jimmy, Shreveport.| 103 | 383 | 82 | 105 | 147 | 23 | 5 | 3 | 28 | 1 | 4 | 53 | 11 | 64 | 48 | 12 | .274 |
| Smith, Thomas J., Laf†....| 108 | 379 | 55 | 91 | 141 | 17 | 6 | 7 | 56 | 6 | 3 | 38 | 0 | 56 | 10 | 5 | .240 |
| Stedman, Thomas, Laf ...| 104 | 384 | 57 | 102 | 119 | 14 | 0 | 1 | 31 | 11 | 5 | 36 | 1 | 19 | 2 | 2 | .266 |
| Stone, Gerard, Alex† .....| 120 | 389 | 34 | 111 | 148 | 21 | 2 | 4 | 58 | 2 | 2 | 74 | 0 | 53 | 2 | 4 | .285 |
| Stumpp, Richard, El Paso*.| 15 | 1 | 1 | 1 | 1 | 0 | 0 | 0 | 1 | 0 | 0 | 0 | 0 | 0 | 0 | 0 | 1.000 |
| Tamargo, John, Arkansas†.| 39 | 120 | 20 | 31 | 43 | 7 | 1 | 1 | 12 | 2 | 1 | 41 | 2 | 16 | 0 | 0 | .258 |
| Taylor, Robert, Alex .....| 88 | 227 | 31 | 51 | 61 | 3 | 2 | 1 | 10 | 7 | 0 | 19 | 1 | 45 | 7 | 3 | .225 |
| Templeton, Garry, Ark†...| 42 | 177 | 36 | 71 | 94 | 9 | 4 | 2 | 20 | 0 | 0 | 6 | 1 | 22 | 16 | 9 | .401 |
| Thomas, T. William, Shrev.| 109 | 377 | 71 | 107 | 190 | 20 | 6 | 17 | 77 | 0 | 4 | 71 | 3 | 92 | 5 | 3 | .284 |
| Todd, Jackson, Jackson ...| 15 | 0 | 1 | 0 | 0 | 0 | 0 | 0 | 0 | 0 | 0 | 0 | 0 | 0 | 0 | 0 | .000 |
| Trapp, Randolph, Jackson | 77 | 261 | 50 | 67 | 108 | 16 | 2 | 7 | 38 | 2 | 1 | 46 | 2 | 32 | 5 | 0 | .257 |
| Tyrone, O. Wayne, Midland.| 131 | 470 | 79 | 119 | 217 | 27 | 4 | 21 | 82 | 2 | 5 | 83 | 2 | 105 | 9 | 5 | .253 |
| Umfleet, R. Michael, Mid*.| 47 | 168 | 33 | 50 | 63 | 9 | 2 | 0 | 22 | 2 | 0 | 30 | 1 | 27 | 1 | 0 | .298 |
| Verban, Steve, Midland*...| 19 | 51 | 9 | 13 | 18 | 3 | 1 | 0 | 7 | 3 | 2 | 8 | 0 | 10 | 4 | 1 | .255 |
| Verhoeven, John, El Paso .| 31 | 1 | 0 | 0 | 0 | 0 | 0 | 0 | 0 | 0 | 0 | 0 | 0 | 0 | 0 | 0 | .000 |
| Wallis, H. Joseph, Mid†...| 102 | 348 | 53 | 93 | 153 | 23 | 5 | 7 | 59 | 6 | 2 | 53 | 2 | 80 | 13 | 4 | .384 |
| Walton, Reginald, Laf ....| 124 | 452 | 77 | 140 | 197 | 23 | 5 | 8 | 78 | 3 | 7 | 52 | 1 | 60 | 12 | 7 | .310 |
| Wilhelm, James, Alex ....| 119 | 415 | 61 | 108 | 131 | 12 | 1 | 3 | 37 | 11 | 1 | 25 | 1 | 56 | 6 | 1 | .260 |
| Williams, James F., El P. .| 6 | 17 | 3 | 2 | 2 | 0 | 0 | 0 | 2 | 0 | 0 | 2 | 0 | 2 | 0 | 0 | .118 |
| Wilson, Randolph, El P*...| 106 | 360 | 48 | 94 | 154 | 15 | 0 | 15 | 49 | 1 | 2 | 53 | 2 | 96 | 3 | 3 | .261 |
| Wilson, Ward, Jackson ...| 26 | 57 | 5 | 9 | 12 | 1 | 1 | 0 | 10 | 3 | 0 | 7 | 0 | 8 | 0 | 0 | .158 |
| Wolfe, W. Scott, Lafayette.| 121 | 389 | 35 | 87 | 143 | 13 | 2 | 3 | 35 | 9 | 5 | 27 | 1 | 50 | 1 | 0 | .224 |
| Wrenn, Luther, Shreveport .| 2 | 6 | 2 | 2 | 2 | 0 | 0 | 0 | 2 | 0 | 1 | 2 | 0 | 1 | 0 | 0 | .333 |
| Yeglinski, John, Laf* .....| 101 | 335 | 48 | 96 | 129 | 23 | 2 | 2 | 38 | 3 | 2 | 60 | 2 | 27 | 5 | 3 | .287 |
| Young, Ernest, Lafayette†.| 30 | 102 | 4 | 19 | 22 | 3 | 0 | 0 | 5 | 3 | 2 | 4 | 0 | 21 | 0 | 0 | .186 |
| Young, John, Arkansas*...| 125 | 433 | 83 | 143 | 220 | 23 | 3 | 16 | 65 | 3 | 3 | 63 | 2 | 54 | 5 | 8 | .330 |
| Young, Richard, El Paso* .| 5 | 1 | 0 | 0 | 0 | 0 | 0 | 0 | 0 | 0 | 0 | 0 | 0 | 0 | 0 | 0 | .000 |
| Zimmer, Thomas, Arkansas.| 51 | 148 | 17 | 31 | 39 | 8 | 0 | 0 | 18 | 3 | 1 | 9 | 1 | 8 | 2 | 0 | .209 |

The following pitchers had no plate appearances primarily through use of designated-hitters, listed alphabetically by club, games in parentheses:

ALEXANDRIA—Butcher, Clifton (37); Eichelberger, Juan (8); Franklin, John (21); Garcia, Ralph (16); Hefftner, Michael (19); McAllen, John (43); Snook, Frank (26); Troedson, Richard (30); Wehrmeister, David (17); Yard, Dennis (28); Zail, Gregory (5).

ARKANSAS—Benson, V. Randall (26); Butkus, Stanley (55); Camper, Cardell (13); Camuso, Michael (9); Capilla, Douglas (16); Covert, Mark (28); Gonzalez, L. Antonio (4); Ibarguen,

Michael (12); Kurosaki, Ryan (34); Sorensen, Kristian (8); Staniland, Stephen (13); Stewart, Robert (10); Torres, Angel (31); Waterbury, Steven (11); Wiles, Randall (12).

EL PASO—Kenyon, Frank (24); Officer, James (7); Overy, H. Michael (36); Rondon, Gilbert (9); Smith, Randy (11); Texidor, Esteban (5); Whiteley, Thomas (12); Wright, G. Lamar (18).

JACKSON—Bruhert, Michael (24); Gentry, Gary (1); Grose, Jeffrey (24); Klenda, David (47); Litle, R. Gene (4); Myrick, Robert (22); Perez, Gregorio (30); Solari, Dennis (21); Tyler, Thomas (14); Wojcik, Stephen (3).

LAFAYETTE—Cornutt, Terry (42); Division, Julio (25); Dressler, Robert (6); Fuqua, David (27); Greenough, D. Steven (10); Hypes, Kyle (10); Little. D. Jeffrey (26); Quezada, Silvano (45); Riccelli, Frank (26); Sielicki, John (3).

MIDLAND—Beckman, Bernhard (17); Corder, Daniel (19); Crosby, Kenneth (1); Geisel, John (35); Hamrick, Stephen (13); Junge, Gary (29); Krulow, Michael (29); Lamp, Dennis (37); Schroeder, Donald (7); Sutter, H. Bruce (41); Ware, Richard (14); Weiss, Michael (21).

SAN ANTONIO—Alvarez, Miguel (4); Arsenault, Edward (15); Bell, Jerry (19); Flanagan, Donald (8); Crossman, Robert (17); Kinney, Dennis (52); Linnert, Thomas (24); McCutchin, James (13); McGough, Thomas (7); Rosiek, Matthew (12); Salyer, Ronald (28); Starkovich, Paul (6); Weese, Gary (54); Werd, Norman (13).

SHREVEPORT—Anderson, Richard E. (10); Caskey, Craig (5); Geddes, James (7); Gonzalez, Michael (27); Hopkins, Randolph (25); Jones, Timothy (24); Kavanagh, Michael (17); Langford, J. Rick (16); Leshnock, Donald (6); Nelson, David (22); Nelson, J. Douglas (26); Price, Raymond (6); Sealy, Randall (23); Standart, Richard (5); Williams, Steven (27).

GRAND-SLAM HOME RUNS — Agosto, Clancy, Dade, Delyon, Donohue, Edelen, Sember, Thomas, Trapp. 1 each.

AWARDED FIRST BASE ON INTERFERENCE—J. Young 4 (Calufetti 2, Collins, Rosado); Green 3 (Rodriguez 2, Tamargo); Lopez 3 (Clancy, Putman, Young); Barnes (Zimmer); Droege (Martin); Montreuil (Rodriguez); Thomas (Clancy).

## CLUB FIELDING

| Club | G. | PO. | A. | E. | DP. | PB. | Pct. | Club | G. | PO. | A. | E. | DP. | PB. | Pct. |
|------|----|----|----|----|----|----|----|------|----|----|----|----|----|----|----|
| Alexandria | 130 | 3201 | 1261 | 168 | 116 | 10 | .964 | Shreveport | 128 | 3151 | 1238 | 130 | 95 | 17 | .959 |
| Midland | 136 | 3453 | 1540 | 190 | 120 | 19 | .963 | Arkansas | 134 | 3355 | 1391 | 218 | 117 | 14 | .956 |
| San Antonio | 136 | 3472 | 1618 | 213 | 138 | 20 | .960 | Lafayette | 129 | 3244 | 1370 | 217 | 120 | 19 | .955 |
| El Paso | 133 | 3355 | 1361 | 202 | 136 | 47 | .959 | Jackson | 130 | 3249 | 1363 | 230 | 84 | 13 | .952 |

Triple Play—Midland.

## INDIVIDUAL FIELDING

*Throws lefthanded.

### FIRST BASEMEN

| Player and Club | G. | PO. | A. | E. | DP. | Pct. | Player and Club | G. | PO. | A. | E. | DP. | Pct. |
|------|----|----|----|----|----|----|------|----|----|----|----|----|----|
| Tyrone, Midland | 87 | 770 | 49 | 5 | 79 | .994 | Rodriguez, San An.. | 32 | 208 | 16 | 3 | 14 | .987 |
| Richardson, El Paso. | 16 | 131 | 4 | 1 | 17 | .993 | Cacek, Jackson | 120 | 1085 | 70 | 16 | 69 | .986 |
| Delyon, Alexandria | 38 | 230 | 23 | 2 | 24 | .992 | Gonzalez, San An* | 54 | 517 | 37 | 8 | 51 | .986 |
| BROWN, Alexandria* | 98 | 749 | 34 | 7 | 74 | .991 | Wilson, El Paso* | 42 | 314 | 14 | 5 | 26 | .985 |
| Barnes, Lafayette* | 85 | 771 | 30 | 9 | 67 | .989 | Walton, Lafayette | 44 | 350 | 15 | 6 | 29 | .984 |
| Rush, El Paso | 71 | 634 | 24 | 7 | 58 | .989 | Mitchell, Shrev | 120 | 981 | 68 | 18 | 77 | .983 |
| Lee, Arkansas | 20 | 164 | 12 | 2 | 16 | .989 | Randall, Midland* | 50 | 472 | 33 | 11 | 38 | .979 |
| Cage, San Antonio* | 41 | 390 | 27 | 5 | 39 | .988 | Hamilton, Alex | 12 | 45 | 2 | 1 | 0 | .979 |
| Young, Arkansas* | 94 | 767 | 44 | 11 | 63 | .987 | Bolinger, Arkansas | 20 | 150 | 9 | 5 | 14 | .970 |

Triple Play—Randall.

### (Fewer Than Ten Games)

| Player and Club | G. | PO. | A. | E. | DP. | Pct. | Player and Club | G. | PO. | A. | E. | DP. | Pct. |
|------|----|----|----|----|----|----|------|----|----|----|----|----|----|
| Lantigua, San An | 9 | 58 | 2 | 0 | 7 | 1.000 | Calufetti, Jackson | 1 | 8 | 0 | 0 | 0 | 1.000 |
| Bynum, San Antonio* | 7 | 57 | 2 | 0 | 10 | 1.000 | Cleverly, San An | 1 | 3 | 0 | 0 | 0 | 1.000 |
| Grundler, Shrev | 6 | 34 | 1 | 0 | 4 | 1.000 | Corrales, Alex | 1 | 3 | 0 | 0 | 0 | 1.000 |
| Newsome, El Paso | 5 | 32 | 1 | 0 | 3 | 1.000 | Sagredo, Jackson* | 9 | 70 | 9 | 1 | 6 | .988 |
| Hannah, San Antonio | 4 | 21 | 2 | 0 | 0 | 1.000 | Bowman, Arkansas | 6 | 51 | 3 | 1 | 6 | .982 |
| Goodwin, El Paso | 2 | 19 | 1 | 0 | 1 | 1.000 | Goddard, Alex | 9 | 50 | 1 | 1 | 4 | .981 |
| Langerhans. San An* | 2 | 13 | 1 | 0 | 1 | 1.000 | Brown, Lafayette | 4 | 34 | 0 | 1 | 5 | .971 |
| Verban, Midland* | 2 | 10 | 2 | 0 | 0 | 1.000 | Alberts, El Paso | 3 | 28 | 1 | 1 | 4 | .967 |
| Alfano, Alexandria*. | 2 | 9 | 0 | 0 | 1 | 1.000 | Saferight, Shrev | 3 | 29 | 3 | 2 | 3 | .941 |
| Djakanow, Shrev | 2 | 9 | 0 | 0 | 1 | 1.000 | Martin, Lafayette | 2 | 5 | 0 | 1 | 1 | .833 |

### SECOND BASEMEN

| Player and Club | G. | PO. | A. | E. | DP. | Pct. | Player and Club | G. | PO. | A. | E. | DP. | Pct. |
|------|----|----|----|----|----|----|------|----|----|----|----|----|----|
| Montreuil, Midland.. | 76 | 166 | 210 | 5 | 61 | .987 | Champion, Alex | 124 | 303 | 262 | 25 | 69 | .958 |
| Huisman, Midland | 43 | 94 | 110 | 4 | 28 | .981 | Kidder, Jackson | 84 | 196 | 239 | 19 | 42 | .958 |
| Aaron, San Antonio | 49 | 130 | 114 | 5 | 22 | .980 | Clarey, Arkansas | 122 | 280 | 320 | 29 | 74 | .954 |
| Kim, Lafayette | 57 | 126 | 117 | 7 | 34 | .972 | Dade, El Paso | 56 | 126 | 159 | 16 | 34 | .947 |
| Ashford, El Paso | 44 | 66 | 107 | 5 | 29 | .972 | Perry, Jackson | 33 | 71 | 68 | 8 | 12 | .946 |
| EDWARDS, Shrev | 91 | 189 | 212 | 13 | 45 | .969 | Beerbower, El Paso. | 32 | 63 | 70 | 8 | 23 | .943 |
| Oliveras, Shrev | 38 | 77 | 80 | 5 | 25 | .969 | Hrapman, Arkansas | 14 | 25 | 29 | 4 | 9 | .931 |
| Stedman, Lafayette | 65 | 168 | 180 | 12 | 39 | .967 | Rhea, Alexandria | 10 | 12 | 10 | 2 | 4 | .917 |
| Oliver, San An | 72 | 178 | 187 | 14 | 52 | .963 | Green, Midland | 17 | 28 | 41 | 9 | 6 | .885 |

Triple Play—Montreuil.

## SECOND BASEMEN—Continued
### (Fewer Than Ten Games)

| Player and Club | G. | PO. | A. | E. | DP. | Pct. |
|---|---|---|---|---|---|---|
| Rodriguez, San An .. | 8 | 14 | 17 | 0 | 0 | 1.000 |
| Trapp, Jackson ..... | 3 | 7 | 9 | 0 | 0 | 1.000 |
| Senn, Jackson ...... | 3 | 6 | 9 | 0 | 1 | 1.000 |
| Hilton, Alexandria . | 2 | 7 | 5 | 0 | 1 | 1.000 |
| Froede, El Paso ... | 3 | 5 | 6 | 0 | 0 | 1.000 |
| Bowman, Arkansas . | 1 | 4 | 1 | 0 | 0 | 1.000 |
| Clark, Jackson ..... | 1 | 1 | 3 | 0 | 1 | 1.000 |
| Taylor, Alexandria . | 3 | 1 | 2 | 0 | 1 | 1.000 |
| Djakanow, Shrev ... | 1 | 1 | 2 | 0 | 1 | 1.000 |
| Krizmanich, S A-Sh. | 2 | 1 | 1 | 0 | 0 | 1.000 |
| Heise, San Antonio. | 4 | 1 | 0 | 0 | 1 | 1.000 |
| Croswell, Jackson .. | 9 | 19 | 9 | 1 | 3 | .966 |
| Wolfe, Lafayette ... | 9 | 20 | 22 | 2 | 6 | .955 |
| Gonzalez, Midland . | 3 | 7 | 7 | 1 | 1 | .933 |
| Brooks, San Antonio. | 9 | 23 | 18 | 3 | 5 | .932 |
| Hund, El Paso ..... | 6 | 12 | 9 | 2 | 2 | .913 |
| Del Orbe, Lafayette . | 3 | 3 | 2 | 1 | 1 | .833 |
| Harris, Jackson ..... | 3 | 2 | 2 | 1 | 0 | .800 |

## THIRD BASEMEN

| Player and Club | G. | PO. | A. | E. | DP. | Pct. |
|---|---|---|---|---|---|---|
| Delyon, Alexandria . | 24 | 21 | 32 | 2 | 4 | .964 |
| Hilton, Alexandria . | 41 | 38 | 94 | 5 | 9 | .964 |
| Huisman, Midland .. | 10 | 7 | 16 | 1 | 2 | .958 |
| Rametta, San An .. | 73 | 72 | 208 | 18 | 23 | .940 |
| Trapp, Jackson ..... | 76 | 57 | 145 | 14 | 8 | .935 |
| Umfleet, Midland ... | 47 | 35 | 105 | 10 | 12 | .933 |
| Dade, El Paso ..... | 46 | 29 | 109 | 10 | 11 | .932 |
| Clark, Jackson ...... | 45 | 27 | 93 | 9 | 5 | .930 |
| Guerra, San Antonio. | 28 | 37 | 80 | 10 | 10 | .921 |
| Ashford, Alexandria . | 80 | 67 | 162 | 20 | 18 | .920 |
| Gonzalez, Midland ... | 71 | 80 | 141 | 20 | 19 | .917 |
| Djakanow, Shrev ... | 42 | 32 | 84 | 11 | 7 | .913 |
| Edelen, Arkansas ... | 68 | 57 | 138 | 20 | 10 | .907 |
| Alberts, El Paso .... | 71 | 50 | 122 | 18 | 8 | .905 |
| Hrapman, Arkansas . | 20 | 52 | 39 | 10 | 4 | .901 |
| Bowman, Arkansas . | 51 | 36 | 75 | 13 | 10 | .895 |
| Grundler, Shrev .... | 84 | 45 | 173 | 30 | 12 | .888 |
| Heise, San Antonio . | 32 | 27 | 51 | 10 | 3 | .886 |
| CLARK, Lafayette .121 | 102 | 278 | 56 | 29 | .872 |
| Ashford, El Paso ... | 16 | 8 | 34 | 8 | 3 | .840 |

### (Fewer Than Ten Games)

| Player and Club | G. | PO. | A. | E. | DP. | Pct. |
|---|---|---|---|---|---|---|
| Senn, Jackson ...... | 3 | 4 | 8 | 0 | 1 | 1.000 |
| Green, Midland .... | 4 | 2 | 7 | 0 | 1 | 1.000 |
| Sember, Midland ... | 2 | 2 | 5 | 0 | 1 | 1.000 |
| Croswell, Jackson .. | 2 | 3 | 3 | 0 | 0 | 1.000 |
| Oliveras, Shrev .... | 2 | 0 | 4 | 0 | 2 | 1.000 |
| Rodriguez, San An.. | 2 | 0 | 3 | 0 | 0 | 1.000 |
| Raco, Arkansas .... | 1 | 3 | 0 | 0 | 0 | 1.000 |
| Aaron, San Antonio . | 1 | 0 | 1 | 0 | 1 | 1.000 |
| Brooks, San Antonio. | 4 | 1 | 13 | 1 | 1 | .933 |
| Stedman, Lafayette . | 6 | 5 | 18 | 2 | 0 | .920 |
| Bolinger, Arkansas . | 3 | 2 | 7 | 1 | 0 | .900 |
| Del Orbe, Lafayette . | 2 | 3 | 5 | 1 | 0 | .889 |
| Cleverly, San An ... | 3 | 0 | 7 | 1 | 0 | .875 |
| Oliver, San Antonio . | 2 | 1 | 6 | 1 | 0 | .875 |
| Clarey, Arkansas ... | 7 | 4 | 14 | 3 | 1 | .857 |
| Rhea, Alexandria ... | 2 | 2 | 4 | 1 | 0 | .857 |
| Tyrone, Midland .... | 7 | 5 | 7 | 3 | 0 | .800 |
| Rush, El Paso ..... | 2 | 1 | 6 | 2 | 1 | .778 |
| Melvin, Shreveport . | 2 | 0 | 2 | 1 | 0 | .667 |
| Kidder, Jackson .... | 2 | 0 | 1 | 1 | 0 | .500 |
| Harris, Jackson .... | 2 | 1 | 1 | 3 | 0 | .400 |
| Johnson, Arkansas .. | 2 | 0 | 0 | 2 | 0 | .000 |
| Person, El Paso .... | 1 | 0 | 0 | 2 | 0 | .000 |

## SHORTSTOPS

| Player and Club | G. | PO. | A. | E. | DP. | Pct. |
|---|---|---|---|---|---|---|
| Brooks, San Antonio | 16 | 31 | 58 | 2 | 15 | .978 |
| Belloir, San An .. | 58 | 87 | 215 | 17 | 41 | .947 |
| Taylor, Alexandria . | 79 | 109 | 223 | 21 | 45 | .941 |
| SEMBER, Midland .121 | 218 | 405 | 42 | 62 | .937 |
| Wolfe, Lafayette ...111 | 160 | 334 | 38 | 65 | .929 |
| Machemer, El Paso .132 | 197 | 414 | 48 | 77 | .927 |
| Sexton, Shreveport .103 | 148 | 279 | 34 | 43 | .926 |
| Templeton, Arkansas. | 42 | 60 | 131 | 18 | 24 | .914 |
| Rhea, Alexandria . | 33 | 44 | 81 | 13 | 11 | .906 |
| Ashford, Alexandria . | 39 | 58 | 92 | 16 | 12 | .904 |
| Hiss, San Antonio .. | 60 | 91 | 174 | 29 | 16 | .901 |
| Senn, Jackson ..... | 13 | 20 | 43 | 7 | 8 | .900 |
| Hrapman, Arkansas . | 91 | 133 | 267 | 45 | 55 | .899 |
| Croswell, Jackson .. | 49 | 61 | 130 | 22 | 23 | .897 |
| Cleverly, San An .. | 11 | 11 | 22 | 4 | 3 | .892 |
| Djakanow, Shrev .. | 19 | 17 | 44 | 8 | 6 | .884 |
| Mann, Jackson .... | 30 | 38 | 77 | 17 | 12 | .871 |
| Clark, Jackson ..... | 41 | 63 | 135 | 30 | 13 | .868 |
| Boyne, Lafayette .. | 10 | 8 | 22 | 5 | 1 | .857 |

Triple Play—Sember.

### (Fewer Than Ten Games)

| Player and Club | G. | PO. | A. | E. | DP. | Pct. |
|---|---|---|---|---|---|---|
| Edwards, Shreveport. | 2 | 5 | 9 | 0 | 1 | 1.000 |
| Beerbower, El Paso.. | 1 | 4 | 6 | 0 | 0 | 1.000 |
| Heise, San Antonio . | 1 | 4 | 5 | 0 | 2 | 1.000 |
| Green, Midland .... | 1 | 1 | 3 | 0 | 1 | 1.000 |
| Kim, Lafayette .... | 5 | 10 | 18 | 2 | 3 | .933 |
| Gonzalez, Midland .. | 7 | 8 | 26 | 3 | 4 | .919 |
| Huisman, Midland .. | 8 | 12 | 30 | 4 | 3 | .913 |
| Raco, Arkansas .... | 4 | 6 | 4 | 1 | 1 | .909 |
| Stedman, Lafayette . | 9 | 7 | 14 | 4 | 6 | .840 |
| Oliveras, Shrev .... | 7 | 12 | 11 | 7 | 2 | .767 |

## OUTFIELDERS

| Player and Club | G. | PO. | A. | E. | DP. | Pct. |
|---|---|---|---|---|---|---|
| Ortiz, Midland ..... | 62 | 116 | 5 | 0 | 1 | 1.000 |
| Schlueter, Arkansas . | 53 | 119 | 2 | 0 | 0 | 1.000 |
| Delyon, Alexandria . | 46 | 64 | 8 | 0 | 1 | 1.000 |
| Alfano, Alexandria*. | 25 | 41 | 1 | 0 | 1 | 1.000 |
| Oliveras, Shrev ... | 25 | 37 | 2 | 0 | 0 | 1.000 |
| Rhea, Alexandria .. | 22 | 30 | 5 | 0 | 2 | 1.000 |
| Stedman, Lafayette . | 14 | 27 | 2 | 0 | 0 | 1.000 |
| Verban, Midland* .. | 13 | 28 | 1 | 0 | 0 | 1.000 |
| Bowman, Arkansas.. | 13 | 17 | 1 | 0 | 0 | 1.000 |
| Bolinger, Arkansas . | 11 | 18 | 0 | 0 | 0 | 1.000 |
| Brown, Alexandria*. | 10 | 8 | 0 | 0 | 0 | 1.000 |
| DUPREE, Alex ...117 | 209 | 20 | 3 | 4 | .987 |
| Yeglinski, Laf* .... | 81 | 139 | 8 | 2 | 1 | .987 |
| Hickey, San Antonio. | 32 | 67 | 4 | 1 | 1 | .986 |
| Krizmanich, SH-SA . | 68 | 116 | 4 | 2 | 1 | .984 |
| Raco, Arkansas .... | 40 | 96 | 4 | 2 | 0 | .980 |
| Bright, Midland ...111 | 176 | 10 | 4 | 3 | .979 |
| Brooks, San Antonio .121 | 45 | 2 | 1 | 0 | .979 |
| Bialas, Arkansas ...120 | 250 | 11 | 6 | 1 | .978 |
| Friedman, El Paso*. 95 | 226 | 13 | 6 | 3 | .976 |
| Husband, Arkansas . 19 | 41 | 0 | 1 | 0 | .976 |
| Wilhelm, Alex ....117 | 289 | 10 | 8 | 0 | .974 |
| Lora, Jackson* .... 20 | 36 | 2 | 1 | 0 | .974 |
| Melvin, Shreveport .107 | 205 | 14 | 6 | 4 | .973 |
| Cleverly, San An .. 78 | 126 | 8 | 4 | 3 | .971 |
| Davis, Arkansas ... 35 | 62 | 2 | 2 | 2 | .969 |
| Cantres, Jackson ...103 | 146 | 12 | 5 | 0 | .969 |
| Wallis, Midland ...102 | 108 | 14 | 7 | 3 | .968 |
| D'Innocenzio, Laf .. 18 | 27 | 2 | 1 | 0 | .967 |
| Droege, Midland ...103 | 154 | 6 | 6 | 2 | .964 |
| Saferight, Shrev .. 12 | 22 | 4 | 1 | 1 | .963 |
| Smith, Lafayette .. 96 | 217 | 11 | 9 | 2 | .962 |

## OUTFIELDERS—Continued

| Player and Club | G. | PO. | A. | E. | DP. | Pct | Player and Club | G. | PO. | A. | E. | DP. | Pct. |
|---|---|---|---|---|---|---|---|---|---|---|---|---|---|
| Potter, Arkansas | 130 | 211 | 15 | 9 | 3 | .962 | Agosto, Jackson* | 78 | 131 | 7 | 8 | 0 | .945 |
| Harris, Jackson | 71 | 144 | 6 | 6 | 0 | .962 | Manning, San An. | 56 | 100 | 3 | 6 | 0 | .945 |
| Thomas, Shreveport | 96 | 211 | 8 | 9 | 2 | .961 | Walton, Lafayette | 71 | 99 | 9 | 7 | 4 | .939 |
| Lopez, El Paso | 112 | 198 | 9 | 9 | 2 | .958 | Scott, Alexandria | 58 | 114 | 9 | 8 | 1 | .939 |
| Bynum, San Antonio* | 44 | 80 | 8 | 4 | 2 | .957 | Kim, Lafayette | 13 | 13 | 2 | 1 | 1 | .938 |
| Atwell, Lafayette | 81 | 155 | 6 | 8 | 0 | .953 | Page, Shreveport | 121 | 191 | 8 | 14 | 2 | .934 |
| Flores, El Paso | 61 | 115 | 6 | 6 | 0 | .953 | Ahu, Alexandria | 41 | 62 | 5 | 5 | 2 | .931 |
| Beerbower, Jackson | 28 | 38 | 3 | 2 | 0 | .953 | Donohue, El Paso | 32 | 36 | 3 | 3 | 1 | .929 |
| Guerra, San Antonio | 103 | 164 | 13 | 9 | 2 | .952 | Ashford, El Paso | 39 | 55 | 3 | 5 | 0 | .921 |
| Miller, Jackson | 109 | 256 | 14 | 14 | 0 | .951 | Sagredo, Jackson* | 12 | 18 | 1 | 2 | 0 | .905 |
| Froede, El Paso | 28 | 34 | 4 | 2 | 0 | .950 | Chew, Midland | 15 | 28 | 0 | 3 | 0 | .903 |
| Davis, San Antonio* | 39 | 94 | 0 | 5 | 0 | .949 | Alexander, Lafayette | 24 | 34 | 3 | 4 | 0 | .902 |
| Djakanow, Shrev | 15 | 18 | 0 | 1 | 0 | .947 | | | | | | | |

### (Fewer Than Ten Games)

| Player and Club | G. | PO. | A. | E. | DP. | Pct. | Player and Club | G. | PO. | A. | E. | DP. | Pct. |
|---|---|---|---|---|---|---|---|---|---|---|---|---|---|
| Green, Midland | 6 | 9 | 2 | 0 | 0 | 1.000 | Hall, Midland* | 2 | 2 | 0 | 0 | 0 | 1.000 |
| Newsome, El Paso | 5 | 8 | 0 | 0 | 0 | 1.000 | Milner, Jackson | 1 | 2 | 0 | 0 | 0 | 1.000 |
| Clark, Lafayette | 3 | 5 | 1 | 0 | 0 | 1.000 | Goddard, Alexandria | 1 | 1 | 0 | 0 | 0 | 1.000 |
| Aaron, San Antonio | 3 | 5 | 0 | 0 | 0 | 1.000 | Langerhans, San An* | 1 | 1 | 0 | 0 | 0 | 1.000 |
| Bonfils, El Paso* | 2 | 4 | 0 | 0 | 0 | 1.000 | Wrenn, Shreveport | 1 | 1 | 0 | 0 | 0 | 1.000 |
| Nicosia, Shreveport | 2 | 2 | 1 | 0 | 0 | 1.000 | Person, El Paso | 9 | 16 | 1 | 2 | 0 | .895 |
| Randall, Midland* | 1 | 2 | 1 | 0 | 0 | 1.000 | Rodriguez, San An | 5 | 5 | 0 | 2 | 0 | .714 |
| Hannah, San Antonio | 3 | 2 | 0 | 0 | 0 | 1.000 | | | | | | | |

## CATCHERS

| Player and Club | G. | PO. | A. | E. | DP. | PB. | Pct. | Player and Club | G. | PO. | A. | E. | DP. | PB. | Pct. |
|---|---|---|---|---|---|---|---|---|---|---|---|---|---|---|---|
| Hamilton, Alex | 21 | 105 | 12 | 0 | 2 | 0 | 1.000 | Harmon, Arkansas | 58 | 296 | 33 | 7 | 6 | 5 | .979 |
| Collins, Midland | 44 | 203 | 25 | 2 | 2 | 6 | .991 | Martin, Lafayette | 58 | 255 | 22 | 6 | 5 | 6 | .979 |
| Donohue, El Paso | 54 | 304 | 33 | 4 | 4 | 24 | .988 | Putman, Midland | 24 | 114 | 23 | 3 | 2 | 3 | .979 |
| Christiansen, ElP | 46 | 310 | 19 | 4 | 2 | 13 | .988 | Tamargo, Arkansas | 33 | 167 | 20 | 4 | 3 | 3 | .979 |
| Young, Laf | 28 | 146 | 9 | 2 | 2 | 3 | .987 | Rodriguez, San An | 56 | 225 | 45 | 7 | 3 | 8 | .975 |
| NICOSIA, Shrev | 84 | 525 | 44 | 8 | 7 | 14 | .9861 | Alexander, Laf | 48 | 241 | 19 | 7 | 5 | 10 | .974 |
| Stone, Alexandria | 93 | 385 | 37 | 6 | 8 | 10 | .9859 | Goddard, Alex | 28 | 91 | 14 | 3 | 1 | 0 | .972 |
| Goodwin, El Paso | 35 | 205 | 9 | 3 | 2 | 7 | .986 | Zimmer, Arkansas | 45 | 211 | 18 | 7 | 2 | 5 | .970 |
| Sallinger, Jack | 44 | 189 | 14 | 3 | 2 | 3 | .985 | Rosado, Jackson | 20 | 105 | 16 | 4 | 0 | 1 | .968 |
| Calufetti, Jack | 48 | 217 | 13 | 4 | 1 | 3 | .983 | Lantigua, San An | 66 | 302 | 48 | 13 | 6 | 6 | .964 |
| Clancy, Midla: d | 86 | 441 | 51 | 10 | 4 | 10 | .980 | Wilson, Jackson | 26 | 98 | 9 | 4 | 2 | 6 | .964 |
| Saferight, Shrev | 47 | 237 | 14 | 5 | 1 | 3 | .980 | Hannah, San An. | 25 | 112 | 19 | 7 | 2 | 6 | .949 |

Triple Play—Putman.

### (Fewer Than Ten Games)

| Player and Club | G. | PO. | A. | E. | DP. | PB. | Pct. | Player and Club | G. | PO. | A. | E. | DP. | PB. | Pct. |
|---|---|---|---|---|---|---|---|---|---|---|---|---|---|---|---|
| Jordan, El Paso | 7 | 37 | 4 | 0 | 0 | 3 | 1.000 | Milner, Jackson | 7 | 5 | 0 | 0 | 0 | 0 | 1.000 |
| Daves, Arkansas | 7 | 27 | 3 | 0 | 0 | 1 | 1.000 | Corrales, Alex | 1 | 1 | 0 | 0 | 0 | 0 | 1.000 |

## PITCHERS

| Player and Club | G. | PO. | A. | E. | DP. | Pct | Player and Club | G. | PO. | A. | E. | DP. | Pct. |
|---|---|---|---|---|---|---|---|---|---|---|---|---|---|
| GROSE, Jackson* | 24 | 7 | 25 | 0 | 3 | 1.000 | Kinney, San An* | 52 | 7 | 10 | 1 | 1 | .944 |
| Rothan, El Paso | 25 | 6 | 24 | 0 | 0 | 1.000 | Corder, Midland | 19 | 7 | 25 | 2 | 0 | .941 |
| Torres, Arkansas* | 30 | 6 | 22 | 0 | 1 | 1.000 | Tyler, Jackson | 14 | 8 | 8 | 1 | 0 | .941 |
| Geisel, Midland* | 35 | 8 | 19 | 0 | 3 | 1.000 | Anderson, Shreveport | 10 | 3 | 12 | 1 | 0 | .938 |
| Troedson, Alex* | 30 | 7 | 19 | 0 | 2 | 1.000 | Divison, Lafayette | 25 | 7 | 36 | 3 | 2 | .935 |
| Kurosaki, Arkansas | 34 | 3 | 18 | 0 | 1 | 1.000 | Riccelli, Lafayette* | 26 | 2 | 36 | 3 | 4 | .927 |
| Covert, Arkansas | 28 | 6 | 13 | 0 | 0 | 1.000 | Linnert, San An* | 24 | 7 | 31 | 3 | 4 | .927 |
| Camper, Arkansas | 13 | 5 | 7 | 0 | 0 | 1.000 | Cornutt, Lafayette | 42 | 4 | 20 | 2 | 4 | .923 |
| Todd, Jackson | 13 | 1 | 6 | 0 | 0 | 1.000 | Sutter, Midland | 41 | 7 | 5 | 1 | 0 | .923 |
| Verhoeven, El Paso | 31 | 1 | 5 | 0 | 0 | 1.000 | Solari, Jackson | 21 | 9 | 15 | 2 | 1 | .923 |
| Hefftner, Alex* | 19 | 0 | 6 | 0 | 0 | 1.000 | Kavanagh, Shreveport | 17 | 6 | 17 | 2 | 1 | .920 |
| Dupree, Alexandria | 14 | 2 | 4 | 0 | 0 | 1.000 | Bell, San Antonio | 19 | 9 | 25 | 3 | 1 | .919 |
| Ibarguen, Arkansas | 12 | 2 | 4 | 0 | 0 | 1.000 | Butkus, Arkansas | 55 | 6 | 16 | 2 | 3 | .917 |
| Werd, San Antonio* | 13 | 2 | 2 | 0 | 0 | 1.000 | Langford, Shreveport | 16 | 2 | 9 | 1 | 0 | .917 |
| Gerhardt, Alex* | 15 | 2 | 1 | 0 | 0 | 1.000 | Staniland, Arkansas | 13 | 3 | 8 | 1 | 0 | .917 |
| Ware, Midland* | 14 | 0 | 3 | 0 | 0 | 1.000 | Stewart, Arkansas | 10 | 1 | 10 | 1 | 0 | .917 |
| Stump, El Paso | 15 | 0 | 2 | 0 | 0 | 1.000 | McCutchin, San An | 13 | 5 | 15 | 2 | 0 | .909 |
| Myrick, Jackson* | 22 | 11 | 26 | 1 | 2 | .974 | Rosiek, San Antonio | 12 | 4 | 6 | 1 | 0 | .909 |
| Salyer, San An* | 28 | 7 | 27 | 1 | 1 | .971 | Hypes, Lafayette* | 10 | 0 | 10 | 1 | 0 | .909 |
| Benson, Arkansas* | 26 | 8 | 26 | 1 | 3 | .971 | Jones, Shreveport | 24 | 12 | 27 | 4 | 2 | .907 |
| J. Nelson, Shrev* | 26 | 5 | 24 | 1 | 1 | .967 | Garcia, Alexandria | 16 | 3 | 16 | 2 | 3 | .905 |
| Snook, Alexandria | 25 | 7 | 18 | 1 | 0 | .962 | Krukow, Midland | 24 | 10 | 18 | 3 | 3 | .903 |
| Weese, San Antonio | 54 | 6 | 17 | 1 | 3 | .958 | Williams, Shrev* | 27 | 2 | 7 | 1 | 1 | .900 |
| Pavlick, Jackson | 34 | 5 | 17 | 1 | 3 | .957 | Franklin, Alex | 21 | 12 | 15 | 3 | 0 | .900 |
| Hamrick, Midland* | 13 | 8 | 14 | 1 | 2 | .957 | Bonfils, El Paso* | 21 | 8 | 19 | 3 | 0 | .900 |
| Panick, El Paso | 32 | 5 | 15 | 1 | 1 | .952 | Wright, El Paso* | 18 | 3 | 6 | 1 | 1 | .900 |
| Gonzalez, Shrev | 27 | 9 | 11 | 1 | 1 | .952 | Lamp, Midland | 37 | 4 | 31 | 4 | 6 | .897 |
| Little, Lafayette* | 26 | 3 | 16 | 1 | 0 | .950 | Arsenault, San An | 15 | 10 | 7 | 2 | 1 | .895 |
| Quezada, Lafayette | 45 | 1 | 17 | 1 | 1 | .947 | Butcher, Alexandria | 37 | 3 | 5 | 1 | 1 | .889 |
| Capilla, Arkansas* | 16 | 3 | 15 | 1 | 0 | .947 | Dillard, Lafayette | 20 | 9 | 15 | 3 | 2 | .889 |

## PITCHERS—Continued

| Player and Club | G. | PO. | A. | E. | DP. | Pct. |
|---|---|---|---|---|---|---|
| Cornejo, Jackson | 26 | 9 | 27 | 5 | 0 | .878 |
| Overy, El Paso | 36 | 4 | 10 | 2 | 1 | .875 |
| Cristelli, El Paso | 24 | 5 | 30 | 5 | 1 | .875 |
| Lanthorn, Lafayette | 20 | 3 | 4 | 1 | 0 | .875 |
| Sealy, Shreveport | 23 | 10 | 16 | 4 | 0 | .867 |
| Allen, Alexandria | 19 | 5 | 8 | 2 | 0 | .867 |
| McAllen, Alexandria* | 42 | 0 | 6 | 1 | 1 | .857 |
| Perez, Jackson* | 30 | 1 | 5 | 1 | 0 | .857 |
| D. Nelson, Shrev | 22 | 5 | 13 | 3 | 1 | .857 |
| Fuqua, Lafayette | 27 | 3 | 20 | 4 | 1 | .852 |
| Klenda, Jackson | 47 | 4 | 18 | 4 | 0 | .846 |
| Bruhert, Jackson | 24 | 12 | 29 | 8 | 2 | .837 |
| Hopkins, Shreveport* | 25 | 0 | 5 | 1 | 0 | .833 |
| Wehrmeister, Alex | 17 | 6 | 9 | 3 | 1 | .833 |

| Player and Club | G. | PO. | A. | E. | DP. | Pct. |
|---|---|---|---|---|---|---|
| Grossman, San An | 17 | 6 | 9 | 3 | 0 | .833 |
| Smith, El Paso* | 11 | 3 | 11 | 3 | 1 | .824 |
| Moore, Midland | 28 | 10 | 41 | 11 | 0 | .823 |
| Maxwell, El Paso* | 13 | 1 | 8 | 2 | 0 | .818 |
| Junge, Midland | 29 | 0 | 4 | 1 | 0 | .800 |
| Yard, Alexandria | 24 | 2 | 2 | 1 | 0 | .800 |
| Kenyon, El Paso* | 24 | 0 | 8 | 2 | 0 | .800 |
| Whiteley, El Paso | 12 | 2 | 6 | 2 | 0 | .800 |
| Wiles, Arkansas* | 12 | 1 | 10 | 3 | 0 | .786 |
| Beckman, Midland* | 17 | 1 | 9 | 3 | 0 | .769 |
| Weiss, Midland | 21 | 6 | 7 | 4 | 1 | .765 |
| Gibbon, El Paso* | 18 | 0 | 9 | 3 | 1 | .750 |
| Waterbury, Arkansas | 11 | 2 | 7 | 3 | 1 | .750 |
| Greenough, Laf* | 10 | 0 | 0 | 2 | 0 | .000 |

### (Fewer Than Ten Games)

| Player and Club | G. | PO. | A. | E. | DP. | Pct. |
|---|---|---|---|---|---|---|
| Dressler, Lafayette | 6 | 3 | 14 | 0 | 2 | 1.000 |
| Langerhans, San An* | 9 | 1 | 11 | 0 | 1 | 1.000 |
| Geddes, Shreveport | 7 | 1 | 8 | 0 | 0 | 1.000 |
| Schroeder, Midland | 7 | 4 | 4 | 0 | 2 | 1.000 |
| Flanagan, San An | 8 | 2 | 3 | 0 | 1 | 1.000 |
| Starkovich, San An | 6 | 2 | 3 | 0 | 0 | 1.000 |
| Price, Shreveport | 6 | 1 | 4 | 0 | 0 | 1.000 |
| Young, El Paso* | 5 | 1 | 4 | 0 | 1 | 1.000 |
| Alvarez, San An | 4 | 1 | 4 | 0 | 0 | 1.000 |
| Brooks, San Antonio | 4 | 0 | 4 | 0 | 0 | 1.000 |
| Sorensen, Arkansas | 8 | 1 | 2 | 0 | 0 | 1.000 |
| Leshnock, Shrev* | 6 | 0 | 3 | 0 | 0 | 1.000 |
| Little, Jackson | 4 | 2 | 1 | 0 | 0 | 1.000 |

| Player and Club | G. | PO. | A. | E. | DP. | Pct. |
|---|---|---|---|---|---|---|
| Officer, El Paso* | 7 | 0 | 2 | 0 | 1 | 1.000 |
| Texidor, El Paso | 5 | 1 | 1 | 0 | 1 | 1.000 |
| Caskey, Shreveport* | 5 | 1 | 1 | 0 | 0 | 1.000 |
| Milner, Jackson | 5 | 1 | 1 | 0 | 0 | 1.000 |
| Coe, Alexandria* | 7 | 0 | 1 | 0 | 0 | 1.000 |
| Sielicki, Laf* | 3 | 1 | 0 | 0 | 0 | 1.000 |
| Wojcik, Jackson* | 3 | 0 | 1 | 0 | 0 | 1.000 |
| Eichelberger, Alex | 8 | 8 | 4 | 1 | 0 | .923 |
| Camuso, Arkansas | 9 | 2 | 7 | 1 | 2 | .900 |
| Zail, Alexandria | 5 | 0 | 7 | 1 | 2 | .875 |
| Gonzalez, Ark* | 4 | 1 | 6 | 1 | 1 | .875 |
| Rondon, El Paso | 9 | 2 | 4 | 1 | 1 | .857 |
| McGough, San An | 7 | 0 | 2 | 1 | 0 | .667 |

The following players do not have any recorded accepted chances at the positions indicated; therefore, are not listed in the fielding averages for their particular positions: T. Ashford, of; Boyne, 3b; Butcher, of; Crosby, p; Del Orbe, of-p; Gentry, p; Goodwin, of; Hannah, 3b; Hickey, ss; Krizmanich, 3b; Mitchell, p; Rametta, of; Rush, of; Standart, p; Stone, 3b; Taylor, of; Trapp, of; Tyrone, of; Wolfe, 3b. J. Williams appeared as a designated-hitter only.

## CLUB PITCHING

| Club | G. | CG. | ShO. | Sv. | IP. | H. | R. | ER. | HR. | BB. | Int. BB. | HB. | SO. | WP. | Bk. | ERA |
|---|---|---|---|---|---|---|---|---|---|---|---|---|---|---|---|---|
| Jackson | 130 | 37 | 8 | 16 | 1083 | 1060 | 554 | 472 | 42 | 472 | 43 | 22 | 569 | 34 | 2 | 3.42 |
| Midland | 136 | 41 | 15 | 36 | 1151 | 1138 | 540 | 439 | 74 | 507 | 43 | 36 | 700 | 64 | 5 | 3.43 |
| Lafayette | 129 | 36 | 7 | 25 | 1081 | 1052 | 567 | 425 | 67 | 445 | 23 | 21 | 599 | 42 | 8 | 3.54 |
| Arkansas | 134 | 37 | 12 | 22 | 1118 | 1128 | 605 | 443 | 63 | 493 | 29 | 16 | 647 | 37 | 0 | 3.57 |
| Shreveport | 128 | 43 | 11 | 23 | 1050 | 991 | 562 | 423 | 71 | 521 | 31 | 26 | 718 | 71 | 6 | 3.63 |
| Alexandria | 130 | 31 | 7 | 13 | 1067 | 1130 | 605 | 499 | 80 | 442 | 44 | 38 | 501 | 51 | 2 | 4.21 |
| El Paso | 133 | 27 | 5 | 19 | 1118 | 1218 | 710 | 572 | 84 | 608 | 45 | 33 | 792 | 60 | 4 | 4.60 |
| San Antonio | 136 | 37 | 3 | 17 | 1157 | 1338 | 743 | 601 | 85 | 524 | 40 | 35 | 571 | 77 | 6 | 4.68 |

## PITCHERS' RECORDS

### (Leading Qualifiers for Earned-Run Average Leadership—109 or More Innings)

| Pitcher—Club | G. | GS. | CG. | ShO. | W. | L. | Sv. | Pct. | IP. | H. | R. | ER. | HR. | BB. | Int. BB. | HB. | SO. | WP. | ERA |
|---|---|---|---|---|---|---|---|---|---|---|---|---|---|---|---|---|---|---|---|
| Bruhert, Jackson | 24 | 19 | 7 | 3 | 5 | 8 | 0 | .385 | 130 | 99 | 62 | 38 | 3 | 66 | 1 | 3 | 63 | 8 | 2.63 |
| Cornutt, Lafayette | 42 | 1 | 0 | 0 | 6 | 4 | 6 | .600 | 111 | 92 | 44 | 35 | 4 | 44 | 4 | 1 | 77 | 9 | 2.84 |
| Moore, Midland | 28 | 27 | 7 | 3 | 14 | 8 | 0 | .636 | 185 | 191 | 79 | 61 | 16 | 67 | 4 | 5 | 123 | 6 | 2.97 |
| Jones, Shreveport | 24 | 23 | 14 | 2 | 16 | 6 | 0 | .727 | 172 | 158 | 73 | 58 | 11 | 62 | 4 | 6 | 108 | 7 | 3.03 |
| Cornejo, Jackson | 26 | 24 | 5 | 1 | 6 | 8 | 0 | .429 | 158 | 161 | 80 | 55 | 3 | 40 | 4 | 3 | 70 | 5 | 3.13 |
| Torres, Arkansas* | 30 | 13 | 4 | 1 | 5 | 7 | 1 | .417 | 134 | 126 | 64 | 48 | 5 | 61 | 3 | 1 | 62 | 6 | 3.22 |
| Riccelli, Laf* | 26 | 26 | 10 | 0 | 14 | 6 | 0 | .700 | 185 | 176 | 87 | 67 | 13 | 87 | 0 | 2 | 120 | 3 | 3.26 |
| Myrick, Jackson* | 22 | 12 | 4 | 1 | 7 | 4 | 0 | .636 | 116 | 98 | 54 | 42 | 6 | 49 | 5 | 0 | 70 | 3 | 3.26 |
| Divison, Lafayette | 25 | 25 | 13 | 2 | 15 | 6 | 0 | .714 | 174 | 175 | 84 | 64 | 9 | 58 | 3 | 4 | 76 | 6 | 3.31 |
| Lamp, Midland | 37 | 5 | 5 | 7 | 6 | 4 | 8 | .583 | 127 | 112 | 52 | 47 | 7 | 54 | 7 | 5 | 71 | 8 | 3.33 |

Departmental Leaders: G—Butkus, 55; GS—Moore, 27; CG—Jones, 14; ShO—Anderson, Bruhert, Moore, 3; W—Jones, 16; L—Benson, Salyer, 13; Sv—Quezada, Sutter, 13; Pct.—Jones, .727; IP—Moore, Riccelli, 185; H—Salyer, 196; R—Salyer, 104; ER—Salyer, 85; HR—Moore, J. Nelson, 16; BB—Covert, 95; IBB—Klenda, 12; HB—Cristelli, 9; SO—Panick, 126; WP—Corder, 16.

### (All Pitchers—Listed Alphabetically)

| Pitcher—Club | G. | GS. | CG. | ShO. | W. | L. | Sv. | Pct. | IP. | H. | R. | ER. | HR. | BB. | Int. BB. | HB. | SO. | WP. | ERA |
|---|---|---|---|---|---|---|---|---|---|---|---|---|---|---|---|---|---|---|---|
| Allen, Alexandria | 19 | 17 | 5 | 0 | 4 | 8 | 0 | .333 | 112 | 125 | 55 | 44 | 8 | 31 | 1 | 5 | 47 | 5 | 3.57 |
| Alvarez, San An | 4 | 4 | 1 | 0 | 1 | 2 | 0 | .333 | 21 | 27 | 18 | 14 | 2 | 13 | 0 | 0 | 7 | 1 | 6.00 |
| Anderson, Shrev | 10 | 9 | 4 | 3 | 7 | 2 | 0 | .778 | 64 | 58 | 25 | 22 | 4 | 16 | 0 | 2 | 46 | 4 | 3.09 |
| Arsenault, San An | 15 | 0 | 0 | 0 | 0 | 4 | 0 | .000 | 47 | 54 | 29 | 21 | 6 | 18 | 2 | 0 | 24 | 3 | 4.02 |
| Beckman, Mid* | 17 | 8 | 0 | 0 | 9 | 2 | 1 | .818 | 86 | 73 | 35 | 28 | 3 | 44 | 2 | 4 | 60 | 8 | 2.93 |
| Bell, San Antonio | 19 | 10 | 8 | 0 | 6 | 10 | 0 | .375 | 123 | 141 | 71 | 52 | 10 | 39 | 5 | 2 | 46 | 7 | 3.80 |

| Pitcher—Club | G. | GS. | CG. | ShO. | W. | L. | Sv. | Pct. | IP. | H. | R. | ER. | HR. | BB. | Int. BB. | HB. | SO. | WP. | ERA. |
|---|---|---|---|---|---|---|---|---|---|---|---|---|---|---|---|---|---|---|---|
| Benson, Arkansas* | 26 | 23 | 6 | 1 | 8 | 13 | 0 | .381 | 148 | 174 | 90 | 67 | 9 | 22 | 1 | 2 | 79 | 2 | 4.07 |
| Bonfils, El Paso* | 21 | 13 | 1 | 0 | 3 | 9 | 0 | .250 | 105 | 118 | 68 | 56 | 10 | 46 | 5 | 1 | 50 | 5 | 4.80 |
| Brooks, San An .. | 4 | 0 | 0 | 0 | 1 | 0 | 0 | 1.000 | 11 | 9 | 6 | 2 | 0 | 7 | 1 | 1 | 7 | 1 | 1.64 |
| Bruhert, Jackson | 24 | 19 | 7 | 3 | 5 | 8 | 1 | .385 | 130 | 99 | 62 | 38 | 3 | 66 | 1 | 3 | 63 | 8 | 2.63 |
| Butcher, Alex ... | 37 | 0 | 0 | 0 | 2 | 5 | 5 | .286 | 48 | 53 | 28 | 27 | 5 | 34 | 10 | 4 | 10 | 3 | 5.06 |
| Butkus, Arkansas | 55 | 1 | 0 | 0 | 5 | 5 | 12 | .500 | 106 | 112 | 55 | 30 | 2 | 40 | 10 | 2 | 75 | 4 | 2.55 |
| Camper, Arkansas. | 13 | 12 | 6 | 1 | 6 | 6 | 0 | .500 | 75 | 79 | 34 | 23 | 5 | 41 | 1 | 0 | 43 | 1 | 2.76 |
| Camuso, Arkansas. | 9 | 5 | 1 | 0 | 1 | 4 | 0 | .200 | 34 | 48 | 35 | 25 | 3 | 18 | 0 | 0 | 14 | 3 | 6.62 |
| Capilla, Arkansas* | 16 | 12 | 4 | 0 | 3 | 5 | 1 | .375 | 80 | 91 | 51 | 41 | 9 | 34 | 0 | 4 | 48 | 4 | 4.61 |
| Caskey, Shrev* .. | 5 | 0 | 0 | 0 | 0 | 0 | 0 | .000 | 8 | 15 | 9 | 9 | 0 | 7 | 1 | 1 | 6 | 2 | 10.13 |
| Coe, Alexandria* . | 7 | 0 | 0 | 0 | 2 | 0 | 0 | 1.000 | 10 | 10 | 5 | 3 | 0 | 10 | 0 | 0 | 6 | 1 | 2.70 |
| Corder, Midland | 19 | 19 | 2 | 0 | 8 | 2 | 0 | .727 | 110 | 98 | 58 | 47 | 7 | 76 | 5 | 7 | 57 | 16 | 3.85 |
| Cornejo, Jackson | 28 | 24 | 6 | 1 | 6 | 8 | 0 | .429 | 158 | 161 | 80 | 55 | 3 | 40 | 4 | 3 | 70 | 5 | 3.13 |
| Cornutt, Lafayette | 42 | 1 | 0 | 0 | 6 | 4 | 0 | .600 | 111 | 92 | 44 | 35 | 4 | 44 | 4 | 1 | 77 | 9 | 2.84 |
| Covert, Arkansas | 28 | 17 | 4 | 0 | 3 | 12 | 0 | .200 | 111 | 102 | 76 | 56 | 7 | 95 | 4 | 0 | 80 | 6 | 4.54 |
| Cristelli, El P .. | 24 | 23 | 9 | 0 | 11 | 10 | 0 | .524 | 148 | 148 | 87 | 65 | 11 | 76 | 7 | 9 | 123 | 5 | 3.95 |
| Crosby, Midland . | 1 | 1 | 0 | 0 | 1 | 0 | 0 | 1.000 | 6 | 7 | 2 | 1 | 0 | 1 | 0 | 0 | 9 | 0 | 1.50 |
| Del Orbe, Laf .. | 1 | 0 | 0 | 0 | 0 | 0 | 0 | .000 | 3 | 1 | 0 | 0 | 0 | 0 | 0 | 0 | 0 | 0 | 0.00 |
| Dillard, Lafayette | 26 | 15 | 2 | 1 | 7 | 4 | 0 | .636 | 98 | 90 | 58 | 43 | 5 | 68 | 1 | 4 | 57 | 4 | 3.95 |
| Divison, Lafayette | 25 | 25 | 13 | 2 | 15 | 6 | 0 | .714 | 174 | 175 | 84 | 64 | 9 | 58 | 3 | 4 | 76 | 6 | 3.31 |
| Dressler, Laf ... | 6 | 6 | 3 | 1 | 5 | 1 | 0 | .833 | 46 | 32 | 11 | 10 | 1 | 9 | 0 | 0 | 5 | 0 | 1.96 |
| Dupree, Alexandria | 14 | 0 | 0 | 0 | 5 | 0 | 3 | 1.000 | 33 | 30 | 8 | 8 | 3 | 3 | 2 | 0 | 31 | 1 | 2.18 |
| Eichelberger, Alex | 8 | 8 | 4 | 1 | 3 | 4 | 0 | .429 | 50 | 52 | 31 | 24 | 6 | 21 | 0 | 1 | 31 | 10 | 4.32 |
| Flanagan, San An | 8 | 3 | 1 | 0 | 1 | 2 | 0 | .333 | 40 | 38 | 22 | 14 | 3 | 20 | 0 | 2 | 13 | 2 | 3.15 |
| Franklin, Alex ... | 21 | 21 | 5 | 1 | 6 | 9 | 0 | .400 | 121 | 131 | 85 | 69 | 9 | 48 | 4 | 4 | 34 | 4 | 5.13 |
| Fuqua, Lafayette. | 27 | 19 | 2 | 0 | 4 | 11 | 2 | .267 | 125 | 143 | 83 | 64 | 7 | 50 | 4 | 2 | 68 | 1 | 4.61 |
| Garcia, Alexandria | 16 | 16 | 5 | 1 | 7 | 6 | 0 | .538 | 116 | 102 | 58 | 47 | 6 | 58 | 1 | 4 | 79 | 3 | 3.65 |
| Geddes, Shreveport | 7 | 7 | 3 | 0 | 2 | 3 | 0 | .400 | 37 | 50 | 27 | 19 | 3 | 22 | 1 | 1 | 19 | 2 | 4.62 |
| Geisel, Midland* . | 35 | 14 | 4 | 1 | 3 | 5 | 5 | .615 | 132 | 149 | 67 | 59 | 8 | 44 | 5 | 4 | 75 | 2 | 4.02 |
| Gentry, Jackson . | 1 | 1 | 0 | 0 | 0 | 0 | 0 | .000 | 0 | 1 | 1 | 1 | 0 | 1 | 0 | 0 | 0 | 0 | .... |
| Gerhardt, Alex* | 15 | 6 | 0 | 0 | 2 | 3 | 0 | .400 | 49 | 57 | 42 | 35 | 10 | 22 | 2 | 2 | 23 | 2 | 6.43 |
| Gibbon, El Paso* | 18 | 1 | 0 | 0 | 3 | 1 | 0 | .500 | 49 | 61 | 39 | 36 | 0 | 44 | 3 | 0 | 41 | 5 | 6.61 |
| Gonzalez, Shrev .. | 27 | 5 | 2 | 1 | 4 | 3 | 0 | .571 | 88 | 73 | 42 | 38 | 9 | 51 | 1 | 5 | 37 | 9 | 3.89 |
| Gonzalez, Ark* .. | 4 | 4 | 0 | 0 | 1 | 0 | 0 | 1.000 | 29 | 31 | 15 | 11 | 3 | 17 | 0 | 0 | 13 | 0 | 3.41 |
| Greenough, Laf* | 10 | 0 | 0 | 0 | 1 | 0 | 0 | 1.000 | 16 | 15 | 13 | 3 | 1 | 8 | 0 | 0 | 12 | 1 | 1.69 |
| Grose, Jackson* . | 24 | 24 | 7 | 0 | 13 | 8 | 0 | .619 | 145 | 149 | 74 | 57 | 2 | 85 | 3 | 8 | 87 | 6 | 3.54 |
| Grossman, San An | 17 | 17 | 3 | 0 | 6 | 6 | 0 | .500 | 105 | 118 | 75 | 65 | 7 | 79 | 1 | 5 | 57 | 10 | 5.57 |
| Hamrick, Midland* | 13 | 13 | 5 | 2 | 7 | 2 | 0 | .778 | 84 | 75 | 39 | 30 | 4 | 48 | 1 | 0 | 52 | 5 | 3.21 |
| Hefftner, Alex* | 19 | 2 | 1 | 0 | 0 | 3 | 0 | .000 | 48 | 56 | 30 | 25 | 1 | 22 | 2 | 0 | 28 | 4 | 4.69 |
| Hopkins, Shrev* | 25 | 0 | 0 | 0 | 4 | 1 | 10 | .800 | 35 | 24 | 12 | 11 | 0 | 30 | 2 | 1 | 30 | 2 | 2.83 |
| Hypes, Lafayette* | 10 | 10 | 4 | 0 | 2 | 1 | 0 | .667 | 70 | 75 | 40 | 27 | 10 | 25 | 1 | 0 | 28 | 2 | 3.47 |
| Ibarguen, Arkansas | 12 | 2 | 0 | 0 | 2 | 2 | 1 | .500 | 31 | 27 | 18 | 14 | 3 | 14 | 0 | 2 | 21 | 3 | 4.06 |
| Jones, Shreveport | 24 | 23 | 14 | 2 | 16 | 6 | 0 | .727 | 172 | 158 | 73 | 58 | 11 | 62 | 4 | 6 | 108 | 7 | 3.03 |
| Junge, Midland .. | 29 | 0 | 0 | 0 | 4 | 3 | 8 | .571 | 52 | 50 | 16 | 13 | 3 | 13 | 3 | 2 | 23 | 4 | 2.25 |
| Kavanagh, Shrev . | 17 | 17 | 7 | 2 | 9 | 6 | 0 | .600 | 115 | 94 | 59 | 47 | 8 | 72 | 3 | 3 | 79 | 6 | 3.68 |
| Kenyon, El Paso* | 24 | 3 | 0 | 0 | 3 | 2 | 0 | .600 | 43 | 44 | 31 | 26 | 1 | 43 | 5 | 7 | 37 | 4 | 5.44 |
| Kinney, San An* | 52 | 6 | 1 | 0 | 5 | 8 | 8 | .385 | 104 | 133 | 75 | 64 | 8 | 39 | 7 | 5 | 68 | 6 | 5.54 |
| Klenda, Jackson | 47 | 1 | 1 | 0 | 9 | 7 | 1 | .563 | 104 | 105 | 42 | 31 | 4 | 57 | 12 | 1 | 62 | 5 | 2.68 |
| Krukow, Midland | 24 | 23 | 9 | 2 | 13 | 6 | 0 | .684 | 153 | 143 | 65 | 58 | 7 | 66 | 3 | 3 | 100 | 7 | 3.41 |
| Kurosaki, Arkansas | 34 | 1 | 0 | 0 | 7 | 2 | 7 | .778 | 80 | 72 | 28 | 18 | 1 | 21 | 6 | 1 | 43 | 3 | 2.03 |
| Lamp, Midland .. | 37 | 9 | 5 | 2 | 7 | 5 | 5 | .583 | 127 | 112 | 52 | 47 | 7 | 54 | 7 | 5 | 71 | 3 | 3.33 |
| Langerhans, SanA* | 9 | 8 | 2 | 0 | 2 | 4 | 0 | .333 | 45 | 50 | 29 | 28 | 3 | 19 | 2 | 1 | 32 | 5 | 5.60 |
| Langford, Shrev | 16 | 5 | 1 | 0 | 5 | 2 | 1 | .714 | 42 | 40 | 25 | 17 | 1 | 22 | 4 | 1 | 39 | 6 | 3.64 |
| Lanthorn, Laf .. | 20 | 1 | 0 | 0 | 5 | 4 | 0 | .556 | 48 | 41 | 19 | 17 | 3 | 15 | 4 | 1 | 21 | 0 | 3.19 |
| Leshnock, Shrev* | 6 | 2 | 0 | 0 | 0 | 2 | 0 | .000 | 20 | 15 | 17 | 14 | 2 | 10 | 1 | 0 | 14 | 3 | 6.30 |
| Linnert, San An* | 24 | 20 | 6 | 0 | 3 | 11 | 0 | .214 | 134 | 143 | 82 | 66 | 9 | 73 | 4 | 7 | 64 | 10 | 4.43 |
| Litle, Jackson ... | 4 | 2 | 1 | 0 | 1 | 1 | 0 | .500 | 18 | 12 | 7 | 5 | 1 | 10 | 0 | 0 | 9 | 0 | 2.50 |
| Little, Lafayette* | 26 | 24 | 0 | 0 | 5 | 12 | 0 | .294 | 115 | 143 | 84 | 69 | 8 | 53 | 1 | 3 | 59 | 14 | 5.40 |
| Maxwell, El Paso* | 13 | 13 | 4 | 0 | 5 | 7 | 0 | .417 | 75 | 101 | 48 | 41 | 4 | 25 | 2 | 0 | 32 | 1 | 4.92 |
| McAllen, Alex* .. | 42 | 1 | 0 | 0 | 5 | 3 | 2 | .625 | 57 | 69 | 37 | 28 | 4 | 31 | 4 | 2 | 31 | 3 | 4.42 |
| McCutchin, San A. | 13 | 10 | 2 | 0 | 4 | 4 | 0 | .500 | 65 | 76 | 37 | 28 | 1 | 27 | 0 | 2 | 25 | 5 | 3.88 |
| McGough, San An | 7 | 7 | 1 | 1 | 2 | 2 | 0 | .500 | 42 | 43 | 22 | 20 | 3 | 11 | 0 | 1 | 23 | 1 | 4.29 |
| Milner, Jackson . | 5 | 0 | 0 | 0 | 1 | 1 | 1 | .500 | 7 | 8 | 5 | 5 | 2 | 8 | 0 | 0 | 6 | 0 | 6.43 |
| Mitchell, Shrev . | 2 | 0 | 0 | 0 | 0 | 0 | 0 | .000 | 1 | 1 | 2 | 2 | 0 | 1 | 0 | 0 | 1 | 0 | 18.00 |
| Moore, Midland . | 28 | 27 | 7 | 3 | 14 | 8 | 0 | .636 | 185 | 191 | 79 | 61 | 16 | 67 | 4 | 5 | 123 | 6 | 2.97 |
| Myrick, Jackson* | 22 | 12 | 4 | 1 | 7 | 4 | 0 | .636 | 116 | 98 | 54 | 42 | 6 | 49 | 5 | 0 | 70 | 3 | 3.26 |
| D. Nelson, Shrev* | 22 | 3 | 1 | 1 | 5 | 3 | 2 | .625 | 62 | 79 | 45 | 29 | 3 | 17 | 3 | 2 | 41 | 5 | 4.21 |
| J. Nelson, Shrev* | 26 | 24 | 3 | 0 | 8 | 10 | 0 | .444 | 161 | 140 | 96 | 69 | 16 | 91 | 1 | 2 | 100 | 8 | 3.86 |
| Officer, El Paso* | 7 | 2 | 0 | 0 | 0 | 2 | 0 | .000 | 14 | 22 | 21 | 16 | 4 | 11 | 0 | 0 | 12 | 2 | 10.29 |
| Overy, El Paso .. | 36 | 0 | 0 | 0 | 4 | 4 | 8 | .500 | 78 | 68 | 35 | 23 | 8 | 32 | 2 | 1 | 78 | 2 | 2.65 |
| Panick, El Paso . | 32 | 19 | 2 | 0 | 5 | 9 | 2 | .357 | 137 | 144 | 90 | 70 | 12 | 71 | 3 | 4 | 126 | 5 | 4.60 |
| Pavlick, Jackson . | 34 | 7 | 1 | 0 | 3 | 6 | 2 | .333 | 103 | 98 | 54 | 42 | 5 | 47 | 6 | 2 | 42 | 4 | 3.67 |
| Perez, Jackson* | 30 | 1 | 1 | 0 | 5 | 5 | 0 | .500 | 38 | 46 | 21 | 17 | 0 | 17 | 3 | 1 | 27 | 2 | 4.03 |
| Price, Shreveport | 6 | 6 | 4 | 0 | 3 | 0 | 0 | 1.000 | 41 | 32 | 13 | 9 | 3 | 12 | 2 | 0 | 19 | 0 | 1.98 |
| Quezada, Laf ... | 45 | 2 | 1 | 0 | 4 | 6 | 13 | .400 | 84 | 65 | 38 | 24 | 6 | 23 | 5 | 3 | 47 | 0 | 2.57 |
| Riccelli, Laf* ... | 26 | 26 | 10 | 0 | 14 | 6 | 0 | .700 | 185 | 176 | 87 | 67 | 13 | 87 | 0 | 2 | 120 | 3 | 3.26 |
| Rondon, El Paso | 9 | 5 | 1 | 0 | 4 | 1 | 0 | .800 | 31 | 32 | 20 | 20 | 2 | 25 | 0 | 2 | 24 | 1 | 5.81 |
| Rosiek, San An .. | 12 | 2 | 0 | 0 | 4 | 1 | 0 | 1.000 | 50 | 69 | 46 | 38 | 6 | 17 | 0 | 1 | 22 | 5 | 6.84 |
| Rothan, El Paso . | 25 | 24 | 9 | 1 | 11 | 8 | 0 | .579 | 143 | 165 | 88 | 71 | 8 | 76 | 5 | 3 | 58 | 7 | 4.47 |

| Pitcher—Club | G | GS | CG | ShO | W | L | Sv | Pct. | IP | H | R | ER | HR | BB | Int. BB | HB | SO | WP | ERA |
|---|---|---|---|---|---|---|---|---|---|---|---|---|---|---|---|---|---|---|---|
| Salyer, San An* | 28 | 25 | 5 | 0 | 6 | 13 | 0 | .316 | 152 | 196 | 104 | 85 | 5 | 51 | 4 | 4 | 51 | 5 | 5.03 |
| Schroeder, Midland | 7 | 7 | 0 | 0 | 2 | 4 | 0 | .333 | 38 | 44 | 20 | 12 | 2 | 12 | 1 | 0 | 20 | 2 | 2.84 |
| Sealy, Shreveport | 23 | 22 | 4 | 1 | 10 | 5 | 0 | .667 | 139 | 152 | 85 | 67 | 8 | 66 | 2 | 2 | 84 | 13 | 4.34 |
| Sielicki, Laf* | 3 | 0 | 0 | 0 | 0 | 0 | 0 | .000 | 4 | 6 | 4 | 4 | 0 | 5 | 0 | 0 | 3 | 0 | 9.00 |
| Smith, El Paso* | 11 | 11 | 1 | 0 | 4 | 3 | 0 | .571 | 60 | 78 | 48 | 35 | 9 | 24 | 1 | 2 | 25 | 4 | 5.25 |
| Snook, Alexandria | 25 | 14 | 4 | 1 | 4 | 6 | 0 | .400 | 109 | 114 | 62 | 59 | 9 | 45 | 7 | 8 | 48 | 4 | 4.87 |
| Solari, Jackson | 21 | 18 | 6 | 2 | 7 | 7 | 0 | .500 | 115 | 126 | 68 | 52 | 5 | 40 | 2 | 3 | 69 | 1 | 4.07 |
| Sorensen, Arkansas | 8 | 0 | 0 | 0 | 1 | 0 | 1 | 1.000 | 19 | 21 | 15 | 12 | 0 | 9 | 1 | 0 | 7 | 0 | 5.68 |
| Standart, Shrev | 5 | 2 | 0 | 0 | 0 | 2 | 0 | .000 | 7 | 6 | 4 | 3 | 0 | 3 | 0 | 0 | 7 | 0 | 3.86 |
| Staniland, Ark | 13 | 13 | 4 | 1 | 6 | 4 | 0 | .600 | 77 | 68 | 39 | 28 | 7 | 40 | 1 | 0 | 60 | 2 | 3.27 |
| Starkovich, San An | 6 | 5 | 1 | 0 | 0 | 5 | 0 | .000 | 22 | 42 | 33 | 26 | 5 | 11 | 2 | 0 | 10 | 6 | 10.64 |
| Stewart, Arkansas | 10 | 8 | 2 | 1 | 3 | 3 | 0 | .500 | 48 | 47 | 25 | 16 | 1 | 15 | 1 | 1 | 25 | 1 | 3.00 |
| Stumpp, El Paso | 15 | 1 | 0 | 0 | 2 | 2 | 2 | .500 | 30 | 34 | 18 | 16 | 2 | 16 | 2 | 0 | 13 | 3 | 4.80 |
| Sutter, Midland | 41 | 0 | 0 | 0 | 5 | 7 | 13 | .417 | 67 | 64 | 26 | 16 | 6 | 21 | 3 | 1 | 50 | 3 | 2.15 |
| Texidor, El Paso | 5 | 0 | 0 | 0 | 0 | 0 | 0 | .000 | 13 | 17 | 6 | 5 | 2 | 4 | 0 | 0 | 12 | 2 | 3.46 |
| Todd, Jackson | 13 | 4 | 1 | 0 | 3 | 4 | 0 | .429 | 54 | 52 | 29 | 19 | 3 | 20 | 3 | 0 | 31 | 0 | 3.17 |
| Torres, Arkansas* | 30 | 13 | 4 | 1 | 5 | 7 | 1 | .417 | 134 | 126 | 64 | 48 | 5 | 61 | 3 | 1 | 62 | 6 | 3.22 |
| Troedson, Alex* | 30 | 21 | 3 | 1 | 8 | 9 | 2 | .471 | 134 | 170 | 79 | 59 | 8 | 44 | 6 | 3 | 24 | 0 | 3.96 |
| Tyler, Jackson | 14 | 14 | 3 | 1 | 4 | 5 | 0 | .444 | 85 | 93 | 47 | 39 | 5 | 31 | 3 | 1 | 43 | 2 | 4.13 |
| Verhoeven, El Paso | 31 | 0 | 0 | 0 | 4 | 0 | 4 | 1.000 | 56 | 45 | 18 | 10 | 2 | 26 | 4 | 0 | 46 | 2 | 1.61 |
| Ware, Midland* | 14 | 0 | 0 | 0 | 0 | 1 | 0 | .000 | 21 | 23 | 17 | 13 | 2 | 16 | 3 | 0 | 13 | 1 | 5.57 |
| Waterbury, Ark | 11 | 11 | 4 | 1 | 7 | 4 | 0 | .636 | 69 | 50 | 31 | 29 | 5 | 32 | 0 | 3 | 32 | 2 | 3.78 |
| Weese, San An | 54 | 0 | 0 | 0 | 8 | 6 | 8 | .571 | 97 | 102 | 48 | 40 | 7 | 69 | 8 | 3 | 80 | 13 | 3.71 |
| Wehrmeister, Alex | 17 | 17 | 4 | 0 | 5 | 8 | 0 | .385 | 105 | 103 | 54 | 40 | 7 | 36 | 2 | 5 | 58 | 4 | 3.43 |
| Weiss, Midland | 21 | 15 | 3 | 0 | 3 | 7 | 1 | .300 | 94 | 112 | 64 | 51 | 9 | 45 | 6 | 5 | 41 | 2 | 4.88 |
| Werd, San An* | 13 | 13 | 6 | 0 | 5 | 4 | 0 | .556 | 101 | 100 | 47 | 39 | 10 | 35 | 5 | 1 | 43 | 0 | 3.48 |
| Whiteley, El Paso | 12 | 12 | 0 | 0 | 2 | 6 | 0 | .250 | 67 | 78 | 57 | 50 | 5 | 46 | 1 | 3 | 45 | 6 | 6.72 |
| Wiles, Arkansas* | 12 | 12 | 2 | 2 | 4 | 5 | 0 | .444 | 73 | 81 | 34 | 28 | 3 | 31 | 1 | 0 | 45 | 0 | 3.45 |
| Williams, Shrev* | 27 | 3 | 0 | 0 | 3 | 4 | 3 | .429 | 57 | 54 | 23 | 19 | 2 | 39 | 6 | 0 | 46 | 4 | 3.00 |
| Wojcik, Jackson* | 3 | 3 | 0 | 0 | 1 | 1 | 0 | .500 | 9 | 13 | 10 | 8 | 2 | 4 | 0 | 0 | 1 | 0 | 8.00 |
| Wright, El Paso* | 18 | 1 | 0 | 0 | 0 | 2 | 2 | .000 | 47 | 38 | 19 | 16 | 3 | 26 | 3 | 0 | 47 | 6 | 3.06 |
| Yard, Alexandria | 28 | 2 | 0 | 0 | 4 | 4 | 1 | .500 | 46 | 45 | 29 | 21 | 3 | 26 | 4 | 0 | 17 | 2 | 4.11 |
| Young, El Paso* | 5 | 5 | 0 | 0 | 1 | 3 | 0 | .250 | 20 | 25 | 17 | 15 | 1 | 17 | 2 | 1 | 8 | 0 | 6.75 |
| Zail, Alexandria | 5 | 5 | 0 | 0 | 3 | 0 | 0 | .250 | 24 | 34 | 12 | 9 | 1 | 11 | 0 | 0 | 11 | 0 | 3.38 |

BALKS—Cornutt, 3; Bonfils, Dillard, Gonzalez (Shrev), Kavanagh, Moore, Quezada, 2 each; Alvarez, Arsenault, Bell, Corder, Cornejo, Fuqua, Gibbon, Hamrick, Krukow, McGough, Price, Salyer, Sealy, Snook, Solari, Starkovich, Texidor, Troedson, 1 each.

COMBINATION SHUTOUTS—Troedson-Butcher, Allen-Butcher, Alexandria; Benson-Kurosaki, Torres-Butkus, Staniland-Butkus, Waterbury-Butkus, Arkansas; Panick-Overy Rothan-Officer, Whiteley-Verhoeven, Kenyon-Panick, El Paso; Dressler-Quezada, Divison-Quezada, Little-Greenough-Quezada, Lafayette; Krukow-Lamp, Moore-Junge, Moore-Sutter-Junge, Beckman-Junge, Corder-Sutter-Geisel, Midland; McGough-Weese, Langerhans-Weese, San Antonio; Williams-Langford, Shreveport. Midland; McGough-Weese, Langerhans-Weese, San Antonio; Williams-Langford, Shreveport.

NO-HIT GAMES—McGough, San Antonio, defeated Shreveport, 1-0, May 11; Little (five innings), Greenough (one inning), Quezada (one inning), Lafayette, defeated Jackson, 1-0, September 1 (2nd game) (seven innings).

# California League

## CLASS A

### CHAMPIONSHIP WINNERS IN PREVIOUS YEARS

| | | |
|---|---|---|
| 1914—Fresno ............ .571 | 1955—Stockton .......... .733 | 1965—San Jose .......... .586 |
| 1915—Modesto ......... .857 |      Fresno§ .......... .718 |      Stockton§ .......... .614 |
| 1916-40—Did not operate. | 1956—Fresno‡ .......... .650 | 1966—Modesto ......... .577 |
| 1941—Fresno ........... .643 | 1957—Visalia x ........ .622 |      Modesto ........... .671 |
|      S. Barbara (2nd)* .597 |      Salinas (4th)* ... .504 | 1967—San Jose§ ....... .676 |
| 1942—Santa Barbara† ... .642 | 1958—Fresno* ......... .639 |      Modesto ........... .586 |
| 1943-44-45—Did not operate. |      Bakersfield ........ .672 | 1968—San Jose ........ .629 |
| 1946—Stockton‡ ........ .600 | 1959—Bakersfield ....... .592 |      Fresno§ ........... .623 |
| 1947—Stockton‡ ........ .679 |      Modesto§ .......... .643 | 1969—Stockton‡ ........ .600 |
| 1948—Fresno ........... .607 | 1960—Reno ............ .614 |      Visalia ........... .614 |
|      S. Barbara (3rd)* .529 |      Reno ............ .657 | 1970—Bakersfield ...... .667 |
| 1949—Bakersfield ........ .612 | 1961—Reno ............ .743 |      Bakersfield ........ .671 |
|      San Jose (4th*)* .543 |      Reno ............ .643 | 1971—Visalia§ ......... .583 |
| 1950—Ventura ......... .607 | 1962—San Jose§ ....... .686 |      Fresno ............ .500 |
|      Modesto (2nd)* .586 |      Reno ............ .587 | 1972—Modesto§ ........ .547 |
| 1951—Santa Barbara‡ ... .599 | 1963—Modesto ......... .589 |      Bakersfield ........ .629 |
| 1952—Fresno‡ .......... .629 |      Stockton§ ......... .687 | 1973—Lodi§ ........... .657 |
| 1953—San Jose‡ ........ .664 | 1964—Fresno .......... .638 |      Bakersfield ........ .571 |
| 1954—Modesto‡ ........ .623 |      Fresno .......... .600 | 1974—Fresno§ ......... .607 |
| | |      San Jose .......... .579 |

*Won four-club playoff. †League disbanded June 28. ‡Won championship and four-club playoff. §Won split-season playoff. xWon both halves of split-season.

### STANDING OF CLUBS AT CLOSE OF FIRST HALF, JUNE 22

| Club | W. | L. | T. | Pct. | G.B. | Club | W. | L. | T. | Pct. | G.B. |
|---|---|---|---|---|---|---|---|---|---|---|---|
| Reno (Twins/Padres) ... | 43 | 27 | 0 | .614 | .... | Salinas (Angels) ........ | 35 | 35 | 0 | .500 | 8 |
| Fresno (Giants) ........ | 37 | 33 | 0 | .529 | 6 | Modesto (Athletics) ...... | 33 | 37 | 0 | .471 | 10 |
| San Jose (Indians) ..... | 37 | 33 | 0 | .529 | 6 | Bakersfield (Dodgers) .... | 32 | 38 | 0 | .457 | 11 |
| Lodi (Orioles) .......... | 35 | 35 | 0 | .500 | 8 | Visalia (Mets) .......... | 28 | 42 | 0 | .400 | 15 |

### STANDING OF CLUBS AT CLOSE OF SECOND HALF, AUGUST 31

| Club | W. | L. | T. | Pct. | G.B. | Club | W. | L. | T. | Pct. | G.B. |
|---|---|---|---|---|---|---|---|---|---|---|---|
| Reno (Twins/Padres) .. | 43 | 27 | 0 | .614 | .... | Modesto (Athletics) ...... | 35 | 35 | 0 | .500 | 8 |
| Visalia (Mets) ......... | 39 | 31 | 0 | .557 | 4 | Salinas (Angels) ........ | 32 | 38 | 0 | .457 | 11 |
| Fresno (Giants) ........ | 37 | 33 | 0 | .529 | 6 | San Jose (Indians) ...... | 30 | 40 | 0 | .429 | 13 |
| Lodi (Orioles) .......... | 36 | 34 | 0 | .514 | 7 | Bakersfield (Dodgers) .. | 28 | 42 | 0 | .400 | 15 |

### COMPOSITE STANDING OF CLUBS AT CLOSE OF SEASON, AUGUST 31

| Club | Reno | Fr. | Lodi. | Mod. | Sal. | Vis. | S.J. | Bak. | W. | L. | T. | Pct. | G.B. |
|---|---|---|---|---|---|---|---|---|---|---|---|---|---|
| Reno (Twins/Padres) .... | | 13 | 13 | 13 | 14 | 14 | 8 | 11 | 86 | 54 | 0 | .614 | ... |
| Fresno (Giants) .......... | 7 | .. | 12 | 10 | 11 | 11 | 11 | 12 | 74 | 66 | 0 | .529 | 12 |
| Lodi (Orioles) ........... | 7 | 8 | .. | 13 | 7 | 10 | 10 | 16 | 71 | 69 | 0 | .507 | 15 |
| Modesto (Athletics) ....... | 7 | 10 | 7 | .. | 9 | 11 | 11 | 13 | 68 | 72 | 0 | .486 | 18 |
| Salinas (Angels) ......... | 6 | 9 | 13 | 11 | .. | 10 | 11 | 7 | 67 | 73 | 0 | .479 | 19 |
| Visalia (Mets) ........... | 6 | 9 | 10 | 9 | 10 | .. | 11 | 12 | 67 | 73 | 0 | .479 | 19 |
| San Jose (Indians) ....... | 12 | 9 | 10 | 9 | 9 | 9 | .. | 9 | 67 | 73 | 0 | .479 | 19 |
| Bakersfield (Dodgers) .... | 9 | 8 | 4 | 7 | 13 | 8 | 11 | .. | 60 | 80 | 0 | .429 | 26 |

Major League affiliations in parentheses.

Playoff—None.

Regular-Season Attendance—Bakersfield, 34,987; Fresno, 57,005; Lodi, 33,813; Modesto, 59,145; Reno, 48,314; Salinas, 44,725; San Jose, 88,995; Visalia, 51,169. Total, 418,153. No Playoff. No All-Star Game.

Managers: Bakersfield—Ronald Brand; Fresno—John Van Ornum; Lodi—Bobby Malkmus; Modesto—Rene Lachemann; Reno—Harry Warner; Salinas—Robert Rodgers; San Jose—Del Youngblood; Visalia—Jack Aker.

All-Star Team: 1B—Ryan, Lodi; 2B—Perry, Visalia; 3B—Hance, Bakersfield; SS—Villaran, Bakersfield; OF—Richards, Reno; Edwards, Reno; Lora, Visalia; C—Wynegar, Reno; Utility—Garcia, Visalia; P—Garvin, Reno; Ausman, Reno; Plank, Fresno; Ward, Lodi; Manager—Warner, Reno.

(Compiled by William J. Weiss, League Statistician, San Mateo, Calif.)

## CLUB BATTING

| Club | G. | AB. | R. | OR. | H. | TB. | 2B. | 3B. | HR. | RBI. | SH. | SF. | BB. | Int. BB. | HP. | SO. | SB. | CS. | LOB. | Pct. |
|------|----|----|----|----|----|----|----|----|----|----|----|----|----|----|----|----|----|----|----|----|
| Reno ....|140|4640|881|655|1364|1986|199|66|97|754|45|58|675|54|48|739|178|52|1122|.294|
| Visalia ..|140|4654|794|773|1319|1949|203|41|115|698|31|53|541|30|32|740|131|51|1038|.283|
| Lodi ....|140|4464|669|670|1189|1603|167|35|59|588|40|51|532|37|32|802|166|68|977|.266|
| Bakers'ld .|140|4570|680|777|1211|1674|190|24|75|571|52|44|533|23|35|720|181|56|987|.265|
| San Jose .|140|4450|622|683|1170|1560|163|46|45|518|38|45|535|28|39|894|153|65|1000|.263|
| Fresno ..|140|4511|636|655|1181|1620|162|26|75|562|43|44|577|22|33|800|93|36|1083|.262|
| Modesto .|140|4426|660|734|1151|1603|190|23|72|577|35|49|611|20|38|850|148|49|1008|.260|
| Salinas ..|140|4385|548|542|1067|1439|160|31|50|459|37|32|599|27|26|749|169|78|1023|.243|

## INDIVIDUAL BATTING

**(Leading Qualifiers for Batting Championship—378 or More Plate Appearances)**

*Bats lefthanded.   †Switch-hitter.

| Player and Club | G. | AB. | R. | H. | TB. | 2B. | 3B. | HR. | RBI. | SH. | SF. | BB. | HP. | SO. | SB. | CS. | Pct. |
|------|----|----|----|----|----|----|----|----|----|----|----|----|----|----|----|----|----|
| Richards, Eugene, Reno* ..|.134|501|148|191|276|29|10|12|58|3|5|116|7|75|85|14|.381|
| Wynegar, Harold, Reno†...|.139|468|106|147|234|18|6|19|112|0|7|142|5|55|1|2|.314|
| Alfano, Donnie, Reno* ....|92|347|47|109|167|23|4|9|74|2|8|20|0|60|1|0|.314|
| Perry, Kenneth, Visalia ..|.104|384|81|119|192|16|6|15|64|0|2|58|4|63|12|4|.310|
| Garcia, Luis, Visalia ....|.115|285|78|119|202|30|3|19|84|2|5|55|4|85|3|2|.309|
| Ryan, Craig, Lodi* ......|.138|484|81|149|226|22|2|17|105|1|9|70|2|99|6|6|.308|
| Duncan, Richard, Reno ..|96|345|74|106|150|19|2|7|58|2|4|33|2|46|9|3|.307|
| Kubski Gilbert, Salinas* ..|.118|433|64|133|175|15|6|5|47|8|3|32|1|66|31|10|.307|
| Edwards, David, Reno ....|.137|481|103|147|207|21|9|7|75|1|5|96|11|75|23|11|.306|
| Villaran, Miguel, Bak ....|.120|450|68|137|193|32|0|8|55|10|9|18|4|62|8|5|.304|
| Bauers, Wayne, Visalia ..|.106|375|64|114|146|11|6|3|34|3|2|30|1|54|8|5|.304|

Departmental Leaders: G—Bryan, Wynegar, 139; AB—Perlozzo, 531; R—E. Richards, 148; H—E. Richards, 191; TB—E. Richards, 276; 2B—Keough, 34; 3B—Gardner, 13; HR—Westmoreland, 20; RBI—Wynegar, 112; SH—Perlozzo, 15; SF—Andrews, Keough, Ryan, Villaran, 9; BB—Wynegar, 142; HP—Edwards, 11; SO—Stroughter, 119; SB—E. Richards, 85; CS—Mazzilli, 16.

### (All Players—Listed Alphabetically)

| Player and Club | G. | AB. | R. | H. | TB. | 2B. | 3B. | HR. | RBI. | SH. | SF. | BB. | HP. | SO. | SB. | CS. | Pct. |
|------|----|----|----|----|----|----|----|----|----|----|----|----|----|----|----|----|----|
| Ahu, Aran, Reno ... ..|43|152|32|45|79|6|2|8|38|1|2|14|3|48|0|0|.296|
| Alberts, Francis, Salinas ..|30|113|12|33|55|7|3|3|21|1|1|11|2|14|5|3|.292|
| Alfano, Donnie, Reno* ..|92|347|47|109|167|23|4|9|74|2|8|20|0|60|1|0|.314|
| Amenita, Thomas, San Jose.|21|1|0|0|0|0|0|0|0|0|0|0|0|1|0|0|.000|
| Andrews, John M., Fresno..|.128|430|67|118|161|23|1|6|52|7|9|69|2|71|7|1|.274|
| Baker, Charles, Reno ....|81|305|44|75|124|14|4|9|47|3|4|14|4|56|2|0|.246|
| Bauers, Wayne, Visalia ..|.106|375|64|114|146|11|6|3|34|3|2|30|1|54|8|5|.304|
| Bell, Riccardo, San Jose ..|48|100|8|24|32|6|1|0|7|2|0|10|0|14|4|2|.240|
| Benedetti, Donald, Lodi* ..|8|19|0|0|0|0|0|0|1|0|1|2|0|9|0|0|.000|
| Bengston, Richard, Visalia.|.113|378|48|101|163|18|1|14|71|4|4|40|1|69|3|2|.267|
| Beras, Hermogenes, San Jose|13|24|3|5|8|0|1|0|2|0|0|6|0|8|1|0|.208|
| Blaylock, Gary, Visalia* ..|.116|432|58|129|210|18|3|19|98|0|3|23|6|70|3|3|.299|
| Boyne, Bryan, Fresno ....|24|68|8|13|15|0|1|0|6|2|0|12|0|7|1|1|.191|
| Brand, Ronald, Bakersfield.|31|64|15|13|16|3|0|0|5|1|0|10|1|6|4|2|.203|
| Bratsen, James, San Jose*.|48|131|15|33|41|2|3|0|20|0|3|21|0|36|1|0|.252|
| Bridges, Keith, San Jose ..|72|250|45|69|89|6|4|2|18|2|1|21|1|37|11|5|.276|
| Brown, Rogers, Lodi† ....|.133|491|77|146|195|15|8|6|64|4|5|50|1|94|23|7|.297|
| Bryan, James, Lodi* ......|.139|500|102|141|179|21|4|3|67|3|7|75|3|72|27|8|.282|
| Budaska, Mark, Modesto†..|.120|400|69|111|173|27|1|11|68|1|5|77|6|89|13|2|.278|
| Cage, Wayne, San Jose* ..|92|308|44|86|112|11|3|3|48|1|4|28|2|87|11|4|.279|
| Califano, Kenneth, Lodi ..|.25|1|0|0|0|0|0|0|0|0|0|0|0|0|0|0|.000|
| Camilo, Luis, Fresno ....|80|262|39|64|79|5|2|2|25|4|2|16|2|30|6|0|.244|
| Cardoza, Donald, Bak* ....|.129|439|51|116|149|17|2|4|48|3|1|37|1|29|6|2|.264|
| Cariel, Rafael, Reno ....|61|225|29|65|82|6|4|1|31|2|2|13|1|28|5|1|.289|
| Chapados, James, Bak* ....|26|62|3|9|11|2|0|0|8|3|0|5|0|10|0|2|.145|
| Christiansen, David, Sal ..|53|172|20|49|73|9|0|5|39|1|6|29|3|25|7|4|.285|
| Clark, Daniel, San Jose ..|9|27|1|1|1|0|0|0|0|0|0|0|0|6|0|0|.037|
| Clarke, William, Lodi ....|6|18|0|3|3|0|0|0|0|0|1|0|1|4|1|1|.167|
| Cosey, D. Ray, Modesto* ..|.106|397|69|108|168|17|2|13|49|3|5|27|2|82|16|5|.272|
| Cruz, Ponciano, Salinas ..|42|117|10|14|16|2|0|0|4|1|0|6|0|27|1|5|.120|
| Cuoco, Richard, Lodi† ....|.132|498|77|127|180|20|3|9|51|4|6|41|3|79|21|9|.255|
| Daly, William, Visalia* ..|62|187|28|42|55|8|1|1|22|5|2|32|1|39|3|1|.225|
| Daniel, Daniel, Visalia† ..|14|35|2|3|5|2|0|0|1|0|0|2|1|10|0|0|.086|
| Delyon, Eugene, Reno ....|34|125|19|38|63|9|2|4|19|1|2|14|1|14|0|0|.304|
| DiStasi, Ernest, Visalia ..|18|36|2|9|10|1|0|0|2|0|0|10|0|5|0|1|.250|
| Dolf, Michael, San Jose ..|79|214|28|58|82|15|0|3|20|1|0|19|0|53|3|0|.271|
| Donohue, Thomas, Salinas..|8|20|3|6|11|2|0|1|6|0|0|6|0|3|0|1|.300|
| Drevnak, David, Salinas* ..|.128|379|44|83|124|19|2|6|47|4|3|86|1|70|12|6|.219|
| Duncan, Richard, Reno ..|96|345|74|106|150|19|2|7|58|2|4|33|2|46|9|3|.307|
| Edwards, David, Reno ....|.137|481|103|147|207|21|9|7|75|1|5|96|11|75|23|11|.306|
| Eichelberger, Juan, Reno ..|17|0|1|0|0|0|0|0|0|0|0|0|0|0|0|0|.000|
| Elrod, James, Fresno ....|21|61|6|13|22|4|1|1|8|0|0|5|0|11|4|0|.213|
| Farkas, Ronald, Reno ....|.135|422|57|99|147|10|10|6|63|5|3|65|1|83|2|3|.235|
| Farr, Theodore, Bakersfield.|37|97|10|21|37|4|0|4|12|2|0|10|2|28|2|0|.216|
| Frazier, Dyain, Salinas†...|28|0|2|0|0|0|0|0|0|0|0|0|0|0|0|0|.000|
| Frazier, Frederic, Salinas.|6|24|3|10|11|1|0|0|2|0|0|2|1|2|3|1|.417|
| Froehlich, Denis, Fresno ...|65|192|24|45|54|7|1|0|18|6|3|24|1|41|5|1|.234|

| Player and Club | G. | AB. | R. | H. | TB. | 2B. | 3B. | HR. | RBI. | SH. | SF. | BB. | HP. | SO. | SB. | CS. | Pct. |
|---|---|---|---|---|---|---|---|---|---|---|---|---|---|---|---|---|---|
| Garcia, Luis, Visalia | 115 | 385 | 78 | 119 | 202 | 20 | 3 | 19 | 84 | 2 | 5 | 55 | 4 | 85 | 3 | 2 | .309 |
| Gardner, Vassie, San Jose. | 134 | 506 | 74 | 140 | 190 | 15 | 13 | 3 | 75 | 1 | 8 | 52 | 3 | 98 | 26 | 11 | .277 |
| Gatlin, Michael, Reno | 65 | 239 | 36 | 70 | 91 | 5 | 3 | 4 | 34 | 5 | 2 | 14 | 1 | 49 | 6 | 2 | .293 |
| George, Larry, Modesto | 91 | 300 | 40 | 72 | 87 | 12 | 3 | 0 | 28 | 2 | 2 | 22 | 3 | 62 | 11 | 6 | .240 |
| Gibbon, Charles, Salinas† | 13 | 2 | 0 | 0 | 0 | 0 | 0 | 0 | 0 | 0 | 0 | 1 | 0 | 0 | 0 | 0 | .000 |
| Gifford, William, Visalia* | 108 | 344 | 70 | 101 | 135 | 23 | 1 | 3 | 48 | 3 | 2 | 32 | 0 | 59 | 7 | 1 | .294 |
| Glass, Robert, Bakersfield† | 124 | 394 | 51 | 115 | 168 | 19 | 2 | 10 | 70 | 2 | 7 | 67 | 2 | 35 | 8 | 4 | .292 |
| Greene, Steven, Salinas† | 19 | 43 | 5 | 6 | 7 | 1 | 0 | 0 | 1 | 0 | 1 | 6 | 1 | 7 | 4 | 2 | .140 |
| Griffin, Alfredo, San Jose | 124 | 358 | 42 | 82 | 92 | 4 | 3 | 0 | 25 | 13 | 1 | 20 | 10 | 82 | 11 | 9 | .229 |
| Hamilton, William, Reno† | 38 | 132 | 20 | 49 | 76 | 13 | 1 | 4 | 24 | 1 | 3 | 17 | 1 | 21 | 1 | 0 | .371 |
| Hance, Mark, Bakersfield | 125 | 419 | 70 | 123 | 172 | 19 | 3 | 8 | 70 | 5 | 6 | 78 | 4 | 68 | 11 | 5 | .294 |
| Harrison, Mack, Modesto† | 14 | 37 | 9 | 8 | 9 | 1 | 0 | 0 | 4 | 0 | 0 | 4 | 0 | 10 | 4 | 0 | .216 |
| Hickey, Robert, San Jose† | 66 | 192 | 38 | 48 | 57 | 7 | 1 | 0 | 15 | 2 | 2 | 39 | 2 | 30 | 20 | 8 | .250 |
| Hill, Gary, Visalia | 40 | 97 | 14 | 22 | 32 | 4 | 0 | 2 | 10 | 1 | 0 | 15 | 1 | 14 | 2 | 0 | .227 |
| Hinshaw, Gary, Salinas | 15 | 37 | 5 | 15 | 16 | 1 | 0 | 0 | 5 | 0 | 0 | 6 | 0 | 5 | 1 | 3 | .405 |
| Hobbs, William, Modesto* | 106 | 339 | 44 | 82 | 128 | 17 | 1 | 9 | 60 | 3 | 2 | 68 | 5 | 86 | 9 | 4 | .242 |
| Hodge, Harold, San Jose† | 16 | 40 | 2 | 17 | 21 | 4 | 0 | 0 | 6 | 0 | 1 | 1 | 1 | 7 | 0 | 1 | .425 |
| Hough, Stanley, Visalia | 18 | 54 | 9 | 11 | 17 | 1 | 1 | 1 | 6 | 1 | 0 | 3 | 0 | 5 | 0 | 0 | .204 |
| Howerton, Ricky, San Jose | 86 | 245 | 27 | 63 | 85 | 14 | 1 | 2 | 29 | 2 | 2 | 22 | 3 | 58 | 0 | 0 | .257 |
| Hund, John, Salinas | 56 | 161 | 12 | 32 | 39 | 7 | 0 | 0 | 13 | 0 | 1 | 18 | 2 | 26 | 2 | 1 | .199 |
| Iorg, Lee, Visalia | 129 | 467 | 82 | 139 | 196 | 28 | 4 | 7 | 59 | 3 | 3 | 56 | 1 | 41 | 6 | 2 | .298 |
| Isaac, Luis, San Jose | 40 | 132 | 15 | 38 | 53 | 4 | 1 | 3 | 19 | 1 | 0 | 7 | 1 | 21 | 0 | 0 | .288 |
| Jackson, Erskine, Lodi | 70 | 197 | 26 | 54 | 79 | 9 | 2 | 4 | 22 | 3 | 3 | 30 | 1 | 57 | 3 | 2 | .274 |
| Jackson, Noah, Visalia | 5 | 11 | 1 | 1 | 4 | 0 | 0 | 1 | 3 | 0 | 1 | 0 | 0 | 2 | 0 | 0 | .091 |
| James, Charles, Lodi | 7 | 20 | 6 | 7 | 14 | 0 | 2 | 1 | 3 | 1 | 0 | 2 | 0 | 2 | 1 | 0 | .350 |
| Jarquin, Gersan, Lodi | 119 | 414 | 50 | 105 | 121 | 11 | 1 | 1 | 31 | 3 | 3 | 42 | 6 | 48 | 19 | 5 | .254 |
| Jones, Doak, Modesto | 78 | 232 | 29 | 47 | 68 | 9 | 0 | 4 | 30 | 1 | 3 | 47 | 1 | 54 | 4 | 2 | .203 |
| Jones, Henry, Bakersfield | 88 | 281 | 47 | 65 | 72 | 7 | 0 | 0 | 16 | 6 | 1 | 51 | 0 | 57 | 39 | 6 | .229 |
| Judge, S. Franklin, Sal | 67 | 209 | 24 | 40 | 49 | 6 | 0 | 1 | 11 | 3 | 0 | 30 | 1 | 37 | 3 | 5 | .191 |
| Kelly, D. Patrick, Salinas | 13 | 36 | 4 | 8 | 9 | 1 | 0 | 0 | 0 | 0 | 0 | 5 | 0 | 9 | 0 | 0 | .222 |
| Keough, Matthew, Modesto | 123 | 445 | 73 | 135 | 212 | 34 | 2 | 13 | 81 | 4 | 9 | 50 | 2 | 106 | 7 | 5 | .303 |
| Kubski, Gilbert, Salinas* | 118 | 433 | 64 | 133 | 175 | 15 | 6 | 5 | 47 | 8 | 3 | 32 | 1 | 66 | 31 | 10 | .307 |
| Larson, Duane, Reno† | 34 | 120 | 22 | 33 | 37 | 2 | 1 | 0 | 22 | 0 | 0 | 21 | 1 | 3 | 2 | 1 | .275 |
| Laubert, Richard, Fresno* | 22 | 63 | 7 | 14 | 17 | 1 | 1 | 0 | 6 | 0 | 1 | 14 | 1 | 18 | 2 | 1 | .222 |
| Leavitt, Raymond, Modesto | .105 | 377 | 47 | 98 | 108 | 10 | 0 | 0 | 41 | 0 | 3 | 41 | 2 | 44 | 5 | 6 | .260 |
| Lee, Michael, Fresno† | 61 | 162 | 21 | 44 | 45 | 1 | 0 | 0 | 22 | 6 | 1 | 26 | 2 | 14 | 2 | 2 | .272 |
| Lee, Rodney, Lodi† | 98 | 283 | 54 | 79 | 125 | 15 | 2 | 9 | 54 | 1 | 1 | 46 | 2 | 83 | 14 | 4 | .279 |
| Leisle, Rodney, Reno | 34 | 95 | 18 | 19 | 42 | 7 | 2 | 4 | 14 | 0 | 0 | 9 | 0 | 31 | 0 | 1 | .200 |
| Leonard, Jeffrey, Bak | 106 | 320 | 44 | 89 | 118 | 11 | 3 | 4 | 37 | 1 | 1 | 51 | 4 | 64 | 20 | 3 | .278 |
| Lora, Luis, Visalia* | 90 | 334 | 68 | 113 | 164 | 18 | 9 | 5 | 44 | 2 | 1 | 23 | 1 | 31 | 24 | 6 | .338 |
| Lozano, David, Visalia | 2 | 8 | 1 | 2 | 2 | 0 | 0 | 0 | 1 | 0 | 0 | 1 | 0 | 3 | 0 | 0 | .250 |
| Malinoff, Jeffrey, Salinas* | 44 | 128 | 16 | 30 | 37 | 4 | 0 | 1 | 12 | 1 | 0 | 26 | 0 | 24 | 1 | 0 | .234 |
| Manderino, Michael, S J | 19 | 39 | 5 | 8 | 8 | 0 | 0 | 0 | 4 | 0 | 0 | 3 | 1 | 3 | 1 | 0 | .205 |
| Manning, Anthony, San Jose | 31 | 91 | 19 | 25 | 28 | 3 | 0 | 0 | 7 | 0 | 1 | 10 | 1 | 8 | 14 | 1 | .275 |
| Marin, Arturo, Fresno | 107 | 353 | 39 | 80 | 87 | 5 | 1 | 0 | 34 | 4 | 2 | 44 | 2 | 33 | 3 | 1 | .227 |
| Marple, M. Daniel, Lodi* | 107 | 374 | 65 | 100 | 126 | 14 | 6 | 0 | 37 | 2 | 2 | 73 | 0 | 54 | 26 | 9 | .267 |
| Martinson, Michael, Salinas | 61 | 193 | 11 | 33 | 35 | 2 | 0 | 0 | 18 | 3 | 0 | 11 | 1 | 23 | 3 | 1 | .171 |
| Mazzilli, Lee, Visalia† | 125 | 430 | 103 | 121 | 178 | 10 | 4 | 13 | 52 | 4 | 3 | 88 | 7 | 72 | 49 | 16 | .281 |
| McBride, John, Visalia | 55 | 150 | 18 | 27 | 29 | 2 | 0 | 0 | 8 | 1 | 0 | 14 | 1 | 26 | 1 | 0 | .180 |
| McCatty, Steven, Modesto | 37 | 2 | 0 | 0 | 0 | 0 | 0 | 0 | 0 | 0 | 0 | 0 | 0 | 1 | 0 | 0 | .000 |
| McCoy, Stuart, Reno | 33 | 80 | 13 | 11 | 17 | 1 | 1 | 1 | 11 | 2 | 3 | 17 | 3 | 42 | 2 | 2 | .138 |
| McQueen, Russell, Salinas. | 54 | 2 | 0 | 0 | 0 | 0 | 0 | 0 | 0 | 0 | 0 | 0 | 0 | 1 | 0 | 0 | .000 |
| Miller, Danny, Salinas† | 54 | 204 | 20 | 47 | 48 | 1 | 0 | 0 | 3 | 0 | 0 | 24 | 1 | 43 | 26 | 8 | .230 |
| Minaya, Felix, Visalia | 19 | 83 | 8 | 22 | 32 | 2 | 1 | 2 | 10 | 1 | 2 | 1 | 1 | 11 | 4 | 1 | .265 |
| Moldenhauer, James, Mod* | 39 | 137 | 9 | 25 | 78 | 6 | 2 | 1 | 30 | 8 | 2 | 35 | 3 | 53 | 5 | 2 | .234 |
| Mollenhauer, Robert, Mod | .125 | 455 | 64 | 132 | 162 | 17 | 5 | 1 | 33 | 6 | 5 | 66 | 2 | 49 | 20 | 5 | .290 |
| Moran, E. Michael, S J | .114 | 276 | 51 | 67 | 78 | 7 | 2 | 0 | 15 | 5 | 2 | 52 | 4 | 55 | 16 | 4 | .243 |
| Mulliniks, S. Rance, Sal* | 59 | 209 | 38 | 54 | 62 | 8 | 0 | 0 | 10 | 3 | 2 | 32 | 1 | 30 | 13 | 6 | .258 |
| Murphy, Dwayne, Modesto* | 126 | 429 | 81 | 125 | 183 | 20 | 7 | 8 | 71 | 3 | 4 | 74 | 6 | 82 | 37 | 4 | .291 |
| Newsome, Alan, Salinas | 58 | 182 | 31 | 43 | 83 | 9 | 5 | 7 | 23 | 0 | 0 | 26 | 0 | 37 | 4 | 0 | .236 |
| Nickeson, Robert, Modesto | 30 | 76 | 11 | 17 | 19 | 2 | 0 | 0 | 5 | 0 | 2 | 8 | 0 | 8 | 0 | 0 | .224 |
| Norrid, Timothy, San Jose* | 91 | 253 | 28 | 64 | 81 | 10 | 2 | 1 | 23 | 1 | 3 | 33 | 2 | 47 | 5 | 6 | .253 |
| Olivares, Oswaldo, Vis* | 17 | 64 | 9 | 15 | 15 | 0 | 0 | 0 | 6 | 1 | 0 | 5 | 0 | 10 | 5 | 1 | .234 |
| Ollar, C. Richard, Bak* | 114 | 405 | 77 | 109 | 126 | 11 | 0 | 2 | 31 | 6 | 1 | 66 | 2 | 43 | 16 | 8 | .269 |
| Orr, David, Fresno* | 102 | 329 | 45 | 82 | 114 | 8 | 3 | 6 | 37 | 1 | 4 | 30 | 1 | 68 | 3 | 3 | .249 |
| Pebley, Edward, Lodi* | 91 | 278 | 34 | 71 | 89 | 14 | 2 | 0 | 39 | 2 | 3 | 30 | 3 | 35 | 7 | 5 | .255 |
| Peregud, Michael, Modesto | 17 | 10 | 0 | 0 | 0 | 0 | 0 | 0 | 0 | 0 | 0 | 0 | 0 | 1 | 0 | 0 | .000 |
| Perlozzo, Samuel, Reno | .125 | 531 | 99 | 139 | 172 | 17 | 5 | 2 | 63 | 15 | 6 | 63 | 6 | 42 | 40 | 10 | .262 |
| Perry, Kenneth, Visalia | .104 | 384 | 81 | 119 | 192 | 16 | 6 | 15 | 64 | 0 | 2 | 58 | 4 | 63 | 12 | 4 | .310 |
| Person, Carl, Salinas | 41 | 126 | 15 | 35 | 42 | 2 | 1 | 1 | 17 | 2 | 3 | 10 | 4 | 9 | 7 | 1 | .278 |
| Peters, James, Salinas* | 131 | 447 | 62 | 107 | 158 | 17 | 8 | 6 | 47 | 7 | 1 | 69 | 1 | 98 | 11 | 10 | .239 |
| Peterson, Randolph, Vis | 45 | 119 | 16 | 22 | 32 | 4 | 0 | 2 | 14 | 0 | 0 | 21 | 0 | 25 | 1 | 1 | .185 |
| Picone, John, Salinas | 53 | 172 | 13 | 40 | 58 | 7 | 1 | 3 | 26 | 1 | 1 | 18 | 0 | 30 | 1 | 2 | .233 |
| Polock, Robert, Reno | 28 | 67 | 11 | 17 | 18 | 1 | 0 | 0 | 5 | 2 | 2 | 6 | 1 | 11 | 0 | 1 | .254 |
| Rametta, Steven, San Jose | 55 | 186 | 25 | 56 | 79 | 10 | 2 | 3 | 31 | 0 | 1 | 15 | 1 | 14 | 4 | 1 | .301 |
| Ramirez, Nolan, Modesto | 80 | 225 | 33 | 56 | 70 | 8 | 0 | 2 | 19 | 3 | 0 | 42 | 2 | 38 | 9 | 5 | .249 |
| Rich, James, Salinas | 82 | 240 | 28 | 52 | 78 | 8 | 0 | 6 | 28 | 0 | 4 | 31 | 1 | 72 | 3 | 2 | .217 |
| Richards, David, Bak | 55 | 145 | 16 | 32 | 36 | 2 | 1 | 0 | 14 | 5 | 0 | 7 | 3 | 24 | 4 | 0 | .221 |
| Richards, Eugene, Reno* | 134 | 501 | 148 | 191 | 276 | 29 | 10 | 12 | 58 | 3 | 5 | 116 | 7 | 75 | 85 | 14 | .381 |
| Rickman, Richard, Lodi* | 134 | 406 | 46 | 95 | 109 | 7 | 2 | 6 | 48 | 13 | 7 | 28 | 8 | 65 | 10 | 9 | .234 |
| Robinson, Bruce, Modesto | 24 | 84 | 11 | 21 | 40 | 4 | 0 | 5 | 19 | 2 | 0 | 8 | 2 | 18 | 0 | 2 | .250 |

| Player and Club | G. | AB. | R. | H. | TB. | 2B. | 3B. | HR. | RBI. | SH. | SF. | BB. | HP. | SO. | SB. | CS. | Pct |
|---|---|---|---|---|---|---|---|---|---|---|---|---|---|---|---|---|---|
| Rodgers, Robert, Salinas† .. | 4 | 3 | 1 | 1 | 1 | 0 | 0 | 0 | 0 | 0 | 0 | 3 | 0 | 1 | 0 | 1 | .333 |
| Rodriguez, Michael, Mod .. | 10 | 18 | 2 | 3 | 8 | 0 | 1 | 1 | 3 | 0 | 0 | 7 | 0 | 9 | 1 | 0 | .167 |
| Rosado, Luis, Visalia ... | 80 | 267 | 31 | 78 | 112 | 13 | 0 | 7 | 50 | 1 | 3 | 23 | 1 | 42 | 0 | 4 | .292 |
| Royster, Willie, Lodi .... | 53 | 192 | 19 | 42 | 64 | 11 | 1 | 3 | 20 | 0 | 2 | 13 | 1 | 54 | 5 | 0 | .219 |
| Ryan, Craig, Lodi* ...... | 138 | 484 | 81 | 149 | 226 | 22 | 2 | 17 | 105 | 1 | 9 | 70 | 2 | 99 | 6 | 6 | .308 |
| Safrit, Cass, Lodi ..... | 1 | 4 | 1 | 1 | 2 | 1 | 0 | 0 | 0 | 0 | 0 | 0 | 0 | 0 | 0 | 0 | .250 |
| Sanderlin, Richard, Fresno | 134 | 497 | 68 | 128 | 141 | 8 | 1 | 1 | 48 | 8 | 7 | 70 | 4 | 74 | 27 | 11 | .258 |
| Sauer, Henry, Fresno ..... | 122 | 399 | 64 | 106 | 168 | 18 | 4 | 12 | 61 | 2 | 2 | 72 | 4 | 82 | 14 | 5 | .266 |
| Segrest, Walter, Reno .. | 2 | 5 | 2 | 4 | 4 | 0 | 0 | 0 | 6 | 0 | 1 | 0 | 0 | 0 | 0 | 0 | .800 |
| Senn, Terrence, Visalia .. | 15 | 34 | 4 | 9 | 18 | 4 | 1 | 1 | 11 | 1 | 0 | 8 | 1 | 4 | 0 | 0 | .265 |
| Servoss, Robert, San Jose*.. | 127 | 423 | 66 | 113 | 150 | 17 | 4 | 4 | 47 | 4 | 6 | 61 | 1 | 55 | 23 | 9 | .267 |
| Shirley, Steven, Bak*..... | 24 | 0 | 0 | 0 | 0 | 0 | 0 | 0 | 1 | 0 | 0 | 0 | 0 | 0 | 0 | 0 | .000 |
| Sinovich, Mark, Modesto .. | 8 | 29 | 3 | 4 | 7 | 0 | 0 | 1 | 3 | 0 | 0 | 1 | 0 | 14 | 1 | 0 | .138 |
| Smith, Randy, Salinas .. | 13 | 2 | 0 | 0 | 0 | 0 | 0 | 0 | 0 | 0 | 0 | 0 | 0 | 0 | 0 | 0 | .000 |
| Snider, John, Bakersfield* .. | 55 | 106 | 15 | 22 | 23 | 1 | 0 | 0 | 9 | 1 | 2 | 3 | 0 | 5 | 4 | 2 | .208 |
| Stabelfeldt, David, Fresno .. | 121 | 445 | 53 | 117 | 180 | 21 | 3 | 12 | 73 | 0 | 3 | 36 | 3 | 99 | 0 | 0 | .263 |
| Stajduhar, Martin, Modesto. | 82 | 239 | 30 | 58 | 72 | 6 | 1 | 2 | 28 | 1 | 5 | 27 | 2 | 34 | 0 | 0 | .243 |
| Strougher, Stephen, Fr*.. | 131 | 472 | 70 | 142 | 217 | 24 | 3 | 15 | 74 | 1 | 2 | 56 | 5 | 119 | 14 | 3 | .301 |
| Stupy, Terry, Salinas .... | 128 | 455 | 68 | 126 | 166 | 24 | 2 | 4 | 56 | 1 | 5 | 58 | 3 | 23 | 13 | 1 | .277 |
| Sularz, Guy, Fresno ..... | 92 | 293 | 46 | 83 | 106 | 16 | 2 | 1 | 28 | 2 | 1 | 47 | 3 | 42 | 5 | 3 | .283 |
| Sutcliffe, Richard, Bak* .. | 29 | 2 | 0 | 0 | 0 | 0 | 0 | 0 | 0 | 0 | 0 | 0 | 0 | 1 | 0 | 0 | .000 |
| Tisdale, Freddie, Bak*.... | 126 | 462 | 66 | 131 | 178 | 24 | 4 | 5 | 57 | 2 | 2 | 37 | 3 | 55 | 13 | 6 | .284 |
| Tufts, Glenn, San Jose ... | 102 | 252 | 31 | 68 | 105 | 8 | 1 | 9 | 43 | 0 | 4 | 49 | 2 | 76 | 2 | 1 | .270 |
| Vanderhook, H. Randolph, Lo | 74 | 248 | 28 | 67 | 87 | 8 | 0 | 4 | 45 | 3 | 2 | 27 | 2 | 30 | 3 | 3 | .270 |
| Villaran, Miguel, Bak .... | 120 | 450 | 68 | 137 | 193 | 32 | 0 | 8 | 55 | 10 | 9 | 18 | 4 | 62 | 8 | 5 | .304 |
| Volk, Daniel, Bakersfield .. | 120 | 362 | 48 | 93 | 140 | 13 | 2 | 10 | 45 | 7 | 2 | 46 | 2 | 97 | 6 | 4 | .257 |
| Wallace, Rhoderick, Sal*... | 113 | 276 | 37 | 70 | 86 | 7 | 3 | 1 | 23 | 1 | 1 | 53 | 2 | 67 | 18 | 3 | .254 |
| Washko, Patrick, San Jose† | 108 | 314 | 43 | 77 | 136 | 18 | 4 | 11 | 49 | 1 | 4 | 46 | 3 | 83 | 3 | 1 | .245 |
| Webb, Marvin, Bakersfield. | 9 | 20 | 4 | 7 | 10 | 3 | 0 | 0 | 4 | 0 | 0 | 1 | 0 | 3 | 0 | 0 | .350 |
| Weirum, Ronald, Bak* .... | 17 | 51 | 5 | 8 | 11 | 3 | 0 | 0 | 1 | 0 | 1 | 5 | 2 | 16 | 0 | 0 | .157 |
| Westmoreland, Claude, Bak. | 136 | 485 | 90 | 121 | 214 | 19 | 7 | 20 | 81 | 1 | 7 | 61 | 5 | 117 | 40 | 7 | .249 |
| Witte, Vincent, Lodi .... | 16 | 37 | 3 | 2 | 5 | 0 | 0 | 1 | 0 | 0 | 0 | 2 | 0 | 17 | 0 | 0 | .054 |
| Whiteley, Thomas, Salinas . | 15 | 3 | 0 | 0 | 0 | 0 | 0 | 0 | 0 | 0 | 0 | 0 | 0 | 0 | 0 | 0 | .000 |
| Woodard, Darrell, Modesto . | 27 | 63 | 13 | 9 | 11 | 0 | 1 | 0 | 6 | 2 | 0 | 7 | 0 | 10 | 7 | 1 | .143 |
| Woodruff, Bary, San Jose*. | 43 | 2 | 0 | 0 | 0 | 0 | 0 | 0 | 0 | 0 | 0 | 0 | 0 | 0 | 0 | 0 | .000 |
| Wynegar, Harold, Reno† ... | 139 | 468 | 106 | 147 | 234 | 18 | 6 | 19 | 112 | 0 | 7 | 142 | 5 | 55 | 1 | 2 | .314 |
| Yoder, Kris, San Jose ... | 31 | 85 | 11 | 28 | 32 | 2 | 1 | 0 | 15 | 1 | 2 | 19 | 1 | 16 | 1 | 1 | .329 |
| Zagarino, Joe, Fresno .... | 137 | 485 | 79 | 132 | 214 | 21 | 2 | 19 | 80 | 0 | 7 | 56 | 3 | 91 | 0 | 1 | .272 |

The following pitchers had no plate appearances primarily through use of designated-hitters, listed alphabetically by club, games in parentheses:

BAKERSFIELD—Carroll, Edgar (18); Cody, James (31); Heydeman, Gregory (22); Mattison, Vandon (20); McNulty, Steven (28); O'Brien, Steven (29); Slocum, W. Douglas (40); Todd, Guy (38); Wouters, Leonard (24).

FRESNO—Barnicle, Theodore (5); Browning, James (20); Davidson, James (39); Flores, Martin (11); Greenfield, Monroe (19); Lanthorn, Eugene (16); McKay, Jeff (21); Muhlstock, Andrew (13); O'Donnell, Thomas (14); Plank, Edward (28); Roberts, Kenneth (25); Rowland, Michael (9); Scarcella, Jerome (25); Sielicki, John (10); Tallman, William (19).

LODI—Bird, William D. (29); Darr, Michael (7); Garcia, David A. (18); Hayden, William (21); Johnson, Duane (15); McLaughlin, Byron (12); Neimeyer, Jack (3); Nevarez, Larry (6); Pagnozzi, Michael (25); Peach, Russell (6); Quiros, Gustavo (49); Reimann, Richard (6); Walker, Robert (21); Ward, Gregory (13); Weimers, Larry (37).

MODESTO—Bell, Ronald (5); Brownlee, John (3); Cochran, Gregory (12); Lysander, Richard (21); Oldham, James (28); Owens, Maddison (2); Salas, Bobby (27); Sapp, Carl (33); Staniland, Stephen (6); Tuttle, James (8); Wibberley, Christopher (56); Williams, Gary D. (11); Zoss, Richard (23).

RENO—Ausman, Paul (47); Bovee, Rodney (17); Buehner, Lynn (4); Burns, Byron (11); Coe, Roger (10); Duncan, Bradley (25); Garcia, David (9); Garvin, T. Jared (25); Gill, Ronald (12); Hefftner, Michael (3); Lockwood, Mark (15); McSpadden, Galen (22); Messman, Michael (24); Rehn, Bradley (46); Wells, James (13); Zail, Gregory (15).

SALINAS—Bonfils, Peter (3); Caneira, John (9); Castillo, Andrew (11); Corkins, Michael (4); Kukaulua, Fred (33); Lacki, Stephen (27); Maxwell, J. Rodney (14); Moore, Balor (5); Oliva, Ernest (6); Prichard, Glenn (6); Rondon, Gilbert (29); Stumpp, Richard (15); Wright, Lamar (24).

SAN JOSE—Arnold, John (26); Arsenault, Edward (20); Flanagan, Donald (20); Fox, Timothy (3); Harvey, M. Craig (3); Jones, Michael E. (29); Klein, Stephen (36); Melson, Gary (15); Reid, James (6); Saulnier, Donald (12); Sorensen, Kristian (5); Vaughn, Michael (2); Werd, Norman (13); Widner, Steven (24); Wihtol, Alexander (15).

VISALIA—Anderson, Michael L. (36); Aronson, Michael (11); Bishop, Robert (2); Bolden, Billy (8); Burley, C. Frederick (12); Butler, David (38); Dyer, Paul (5); Gonzalez, Francisco (6); Gorgie, Alex (5); Harts, Gregory (19); Hughes, Stephen R. (7); Jacobsen, Lowell (12); Johnson, Jimmie (20); Kanas, Joseph (6); Lea, Frederick (11); Litle, R. Gene (18); Milke, George (17); Milner, Timothy (12); Neringer, Gary (2); Prewitt, Larry (17); Sander, Richard (9); Wojcik, Stephen (23).

GRAND-SLAM HOME RUNS—Ryan, 3; Lora, Westmoreland, 2 each; Cage, Drevnak, R. Duncan, Glass, Hance, D. Jones, Kubski, R. Lee, Murphy, Perlozzo, Rosado, Sauer, Stabelfeldt, Washko, Wynegar, 1 each.

AWARDED FIRST BASE ON INTERFERENCE—Cuoco 4 (Farr, Howerton, D. Richards, Rosado); Bryan 3 (Peterson, D. Richards, Wynegar); Alfano 2 (Isaac, Stabelfeldt); H. Jones 2 (Stabelfeldt, Vanderhook); Bridges (Stupy), R. Duncan (Peterson), Study (Peterson).

## CLUB FIELDING

| Club | G. | PO. | A. | E. | DP. | PB. | Pct. | Club | G. | PO. | A. | E. | DP. | PB. | Pct. |
|------|----|----|----|----|----|----|----|------|----|----|----|----|----|----|----|
| Reno | 140 | 3506 | 1561 | 196 | 128 | 28 | .963 | Salinas | 140 | 3496 | 1428 | 222 | 99 | 30 | .957 |
| Lodi | 140 | 3490 | 1599 | 214 | 115 | 37 | .960 | Bakersfield | 140 | 3533 | 1459 | 228 | 119 | 70 | .956 |
| Fresno | 140 | 3491 | 1594 | 220 | 124 | 34 | .959 | Modesto | 140 | 3481 | 1395 | 230 | 114 | 18 | .955 |
| San Jose | 140 | 3478 | 1361 | 217 | 107 | 20 | .957 | Visalia | 140 | 3480 | 1387 | 247 | 113 | 38 | .952 |

Triple Plays—Reno, 2; Modesto, 1.

## INDIVIDUAL FIELDING

*Throws lefthanded.

### FIRST BASEMEN

| Player and Club | G. | PO. | A. | E. | DP. | Pct | Player and Club | G. | PO. | A. | E. | DP. | Pct. |
|-----------------|----|----|----|----|----|----|-----------------|----|----|----|----|----|----|
| Malinoff, Salinas* | 25 | 171 | 21 | 1 | 15 | .995 | Jones, Modesto | 32 | 247 | 21 | 5 | 18 | .982 |
| ZAGARINO, Fresno | 135 | 1253 | 93 | 14 | 100 | .990 | Rich, Salinas | 53 | 412 | 22 | 9 | 31 | .980 |
| R. Duncan, Reno | 13 | 97 | 3 | 1 | 8 | .990 | Cardoza, Bak* | 123 | 1013 | 71 | 23 | 80 | .979 |
| Garcia, Visalia | 13 | 90 | 5 | 1 | 7 | .990 | Cage, San Jose* | 92 | 708 | 68 | 18 | 58 | .977 |
| Ryan, Lodi | 120 | 1106 | 68 | 13 | 96 | .989 | Tufts, San Jose | 29 | 158 | 7 | 4 | 17 | .976 |
| Alfano, Reno* | 91 | 796 | 44 | 11 | 69 | .987 | Blaylock, Visalia | 54 | 386 | 31 | 11 | 39 | .974 |
| Pebley, Lodi | 26 | 194 | 13 | 3 | 10 | .986 | Bratsen, San Jose*. | 42 | 269 | 25 | 8 | 18 | .974 |
| Hobbs, Modesto* | 91 | 776 | 49 | 13 | 66 | .984 | Tisdale, Bakersfield | 11 | 66 | 7 | 2 | 6 | .973 |
| Delyon, Reno | 29 | 290 | 13 | 5 | 30 | .984 | Polock, Reno | 12 | 64 | 5 | 2 | 7 | .972 |
| Hence, Bakersfield | 18 | 117 | 7 | 2 | 12 | .984 | Moldenhauer, Mod | 11 | 84 | 7 | 4 | 8 | .958 |
| Bengston, Visalia | 79 | 616 | 62 | 12 | 45 | .983 | Budaska, Modesto*.. | 11 | 79 | 6 | 4 | 7 | .955 |
| Wallace, Salinas* | 85 | 549 | 43 | 10 | 41 | .983 | | | | | | | |

Triple Plays—Alfano, 2; Hobbs.

### (Fewer Than Ten Games)

| Player and Club | G. | PO. | A. | E. | DP. | Pct. | Player and Club | G. | PO. | A. | E. | DP. | Pct. |
|-----------------|----|----|----|----|----|----|-----------------|----|----|----|----|----|----|
| Hamilton, Reno | 6 | 50 | 2 | 0 | 1 | 1.000 | Nickeson, Modesto | 1 | 2 | 0 | 0 | 0 | 1.000 |
| Orr, Fresno | 4 | 31 | 3 | 0 | 3 | 1.000 | Robinson, Modesto | 1 | 2 | 0 | 0 | 1 | 1.000 |
| Ramirez, Modesto | 2 | 21 | 5 | 0 | 1 | 1.000 | Washko, San Jose | 1 | 2 | 0 | 0 | 0 | 1.000 |
| Stroughter, Fresno | 3 | 19 | 1 | 0 | 2 | 1.000 | Chapados, Bak* | 1 | 1 | 0 | 0 | 0 | 1.000 |
| Brown, Lodi | 4 | 16 | 0 | 0 | 1 | 1.000 | Farr, Bakersfield | 1 | 1 | 0 | 0 | 0 | 1.000 |
| Andrews, Fresno | 1 | 8 | 1 | 0 | 0 | 1.000 | Newsome, Salinas | 4 | 34 | 3 | 1 | 2 | .974 |
| Iorg, Visalia* | 4 | 7 | 1 | 0 | 0 | 1.000 | Rosado, Visalia | 4 | 35 | 1 | 2 | 3 | .947 |
| Norrid, San Jose | 1 | 6 | 0 | 0 | 0 | 1.000 | Westmoreland, Bak | 5 | 24 | 0 | 3 | 3 | .889 |
| Christiansen, Sal | 2 | 5 | 0 | 0 | 0 | 1.000 | Ollar, Bakersfield* | 1 | 8 | 0 | 1 | 0 | .889 |
| Cariel, Reno | 1 | 3 | 0 | 0 | 0 | 1.000 | | | | | | | |

### SECOND BASEMEN

| Player and Club | G. | PO. | A. | E. | DP. | Pct | Player and Club | G. | PO. | A. | E. | DP. | Pct. |
|-----------------|----|----|----|----|----|----|-----------------|----|----|----|----|----|----|
| Leavitt, Modesto | 11 | 12 | 24 | 0 | 3 | 1.000 | Minaya, Fresno | 19 | 36 | 48 | 4 | 6 | .955 |
| Manderino, San Jose. | 19 | 29 | 33 | 1 | 8 | .984 | Marin, Fresno | 107 | 211 | 343 | 30 | 64 | .949 |
| Garcia, Visalia | 13 | 18 | 44 | 1 | 7 | .984 | Perry, Visalia | 104 | 205 | 288 | 27 | 61 | .948 |
| PERLOZZO, Reno | 134 | 262 | 444 | 19 | 82 | .974 | Villaran, Bak | 64 | 136 | 164 | 17 | 34 | .946 |
| Mollenhauer, Mod | 124 | 242 | 370 | 21 | 72 | .967 | Sularz, Fresno | 30 | 48 | 87 | 8 | 15 | .944 |
| Cruz, Salinas | 37 | 77 | 99 | 7 | 14 | .962 | Bellini, San Jose | 36 | 58 | 71 | 8 | 8 | .942 |
| Hund, Salinas | 49 | 99 | 121 | 9 | 25 | .961 | Tisdale, Bakersfield | 71 | 91 | 162 | 17 | 42 | .937 |
| Lee, Fresno | 16 | 18 | 29 | 2 | 8 | .959 | Judge, Salinas | 40 | 72 | 104 | 12 | 22 | .936 |
| Moran, San Jose | 77 | 153 | 177 | 15 | 38 | .957 | Hickey, San Jose | 38 | 71 | 75 | 11 | 9 | .930 |
| Cueco, Lodi | 131 | 233 | 401 | 29 | 69 | .956 | Harrison, Modesto | 14 | 22 | 28 | 7 | 7 | .877 |

Triple Plays—Perlozzo, 2; Mollenhauer.

### (Fewer Than Ten Games)

| Player and Club | G. | PO. | A. | E. | DP. | Pct | Player and Club | G. | PO. | A. | E. | DP. | Pct. |
|-----------------|----|----|----|----|----|----|-----------------|----|----|----|----|----|----|
| Farkas, Reno | 8 | 20 | 23 | 0 | 5 | 1.000 | Mulliniks, Salinas.. | 1 | 1 | 0 | 0 | 0 | 1.000 |
| Jarquin, Lodi | 6 | 15 | 16 | 0 | 4 | 1.000 | Leisle, Reno | 1 | 0 | 1 | 0 | 1 | 1.000 |
| Snider, Bakersfield | 9 | 13 | 18 | 0 | 1 | 1.000 | Rich, Salinas | 1 | 0 | 1 | 0 | 0 | 1.000 |
| Brand, Bakersfield | 8 | 5 | 10 | 0 | 2 | 1.000 | F. Frazier, Salinas | 6 | 15 | 13 | 1 | 1 | .966 |
| Senn, Visalia | 3 | 6 | 4 | 0 | 1 | 1.000 | Person, Salinas | 7 | 9 | 12 | 1 | 3 | .955 |
| Lozano, Visalia | 2 | 3 | 5 | 0 | 0 | 1.000 | Hinshaw, Salinas | 7 | 7 | 13 | 1 | 1 | .952 |
| Ramirez, Modesto | 1 | 2 | 5 | 0 | 1 | 1.000 | Pebley, Lodi | 3 | 10 | 18 | 2 | 4 | .933 |
| Jones, Bakersfield | 3 | 1 | 3 | 0 | 0 | 1.000 | Webb, Bakersfield | 3 | 6 | 8 | 1 | 1 | .933 |
| Daniel, Visalia | 2 | 1 | 1 | 0 | 1 | 1.000 | Greene, Salinas | 9 | 18 | 16 | 3 | 6 | .919 |
| Stupy, Salinas | 1 | 1 | 1 | 0 | 0 | 1.000 | Richards, Bak | 1 | 0 | 1 | 1 | 0 | .500 |
| Norrid, San Jose | 1 | 0 | 2 | 0 | 0 | 1.000 | Boyne, Fresno | 1 | 1 | 0 | 2 | 0 | .333 |

### THIRD BASEMEN

| Player and Club | G. | PO. | A. | E. | DP. | Pct. | Player and Club | G. | PO. | A. | E. | DP. | Pct. |
|-----------------|----|----|----|----|----|----|-----------------|----|----|----|----|----|----|
| Weirum, Bakersfield | 10 | 6 | 18 | 1 | 1 | .960 | Andrews, Fresno | 123 | 103 | 246 | 33 | 22 | .914 |
| Rametta, San Jose | 51 | 47 | 111 | 7 | 11 | .958 | Picone, Salinas | 40 | 44 | 77 | 12 | 7 | .910 |
| HANCE, Bakersfield | 108 | 82 | 169 | 14 | 18 | .947 | Stupy, Salinas | 38 | 34 | 57 | 9 | 4 | .910 |
| Glass, Modesto | 11 | 15 | 14 | 2 | 1 | .935 | Alberts, Salinas | 30 | 26 | 69 | 10 | 3 | .905 |
| Judge, Salinas | 16 | 9 | 30 | 3 | 2 | .929 | Gatlin, Reno | 33 | 27 | 55 | 9 | 1 | .901 |
| Farkas, Reno | 68 | 47 | 121 | 13 | 11 | .928 | Daly, Visalia | 61 | 37 | 96 | 15 | 9 | .899 |
| Ramirez, Modesto | 54 | 41 | 81 | 11 | 4 | .917 | Dolf, San Jose | 27 | 18 | 38 | 7 | 3 | .889 |
| Leavitt, Modesto | 92 | 85 | 145 | 21 | 21 | .916 | Leisle, Reno | 12 | 9 | 15 | 3 | 3 | .889 |
| Jarquin, Lodi | 105 | 64 | 214 | 26 | 19 | .914 | Larson, Reno | 34 | 25 | 55 | 11 | 4 | .879 |

## THIRD BASEMEN—Continued

| Player and Club | G. | PO. | A. | E. | DP. | Pct. |
|---|---|---|---|---|---|---|
| Person, Salinas | 19 | 19 | 24 | 6 | 2 | .878 |
| Pebley, Lodi | 43 | 23 | 69 | 13 | 3 | .876 |
| Garcia, Visalia | 69 | 53 | 92 | 23 | 8 | .863 |
| Norrid, San Jose | 68 | 48 | 79 | 23 | 7 | .847 |
| Elrod, Fresno | 10 | 7 | 19 | 5 | 3 | .839 |
| Villaran, Bak | 14 | 13 | 24 | 8 | 1 | .822 |

Triple Play—Gatlin.

### (Fewer Than Ten Games)

| Player and Club | G. | PO. | A. | E. | DP. | Pct |
|---|---|---|---|---|---|---|
| Clark, San Jose | 5 | 3 | 7 | 0 | 1 | 1.000 |
| Vanderhook, Lodi | 6 | 1 | 8 | 0 | 0 | 1.000 |
| Brand, Bakersfield | 7 | 2 | 2 | 0 | 0 | 1.000 |
| Safrit, Lodi | 1 | 0 | 4 | 0 | 0 | 1.000 |
| Bengston, Visalia | 3 | 1 | 2 | 0 | 0 | 1.000 |
| McBride, Visalia | 4 | 0 | 3 | 0 | 0 | 1.000 |
| Boyne, Fresno | 3 | 0 | 3 | 0 | 0 | 1.000 |
| Polock, Reno | 1 | 1 | 1 | 0 | 0 | 1.000 |
| Westmoreland, Bak | 1 | 1 | 1 | 0 | 0 | 1.000 |
| Senn, Visalia | 3 | 1 | 0 | 0 | 0 | 1.000 |
| Daniel, Visalia | 2 | 0 | 1 | 0 | 0 | 1.000 |
| Bauers, Visalia | 1 | 0 | 1 | 0 | 0 | 1.000 |
| Brown, Lodi | 1 | 0 | 1 | 0 | 0 | 1.000 |
| Stajduhar, Modesto | 1 | 0 | 1 | 0 | 0 | 1.000 |
| Gifford, Visalia | 7 | 5 | 8 | 1 | 0 | .929 |
| Keough, Modesto | 4 | 4 | 9 | 1 | 0 | .929 |
| Rich, Salinas | 4 | 2 | 11 | 1 | 2 | .929 |
| Hough, Visalia | 5 | 4 | 8 | 1 | 1 | .923 |
| Hamilton, Reno | 4 | 3 | 8 | 1 | 1 | .917 |
| Lee, Fresno | 7 | 4 | 10 | 3 | 0 | .824 |
| Snider, Bakersfield | 8 | 6 | 7 | 3 | 0 | .813 |
| Bellini, San Jose | 4 | 2 | 1 | 1 | 0 | .750 |
| Delyon, Reno | 3 | 3 | 5 | 4 | 0 | .667 |
| Camilo, Fresno | 1 | 1 | 1 | 1 | 0 | .667 |

## SHORTSTOPS

| Player and Club | G. | PO. | A. | E. | DP. | Pct. |
|---|---|---|---|---|---|---|
| McBride, Visalia | 50 | 88 | 128 | 7 | 32 | .969 |
| Judge, Salinas | 13 | 14 | 28 | 2 | 3 | .955 |
| Lee, Fresno | 15 | 28 | 34 | 3 | 8 | .954 |
| Jones, Bakersfield | 85 | 151 | 256 | 21 | 57 | .951 |
| Villaran, Bak | 47 | 73 | 112 | 10 | 18 | .949 |
| Jarquin, Lodi | 18 | 20 | 31 | 3 | 7 | .944 |
| Mulliniks, Salinas | 59 | 87 | 146 | 14 | 21 | .943 |
| RICKMAN, Lodi | 134 | 208 | 440 | 40 | 78 | .942 |
| Froehlich, Fresno | 65 | 39 | 168 | 17 | 31 | .940 |
| Boyne, Fresno | 19 | 32 | 51 | 6 | 7 | .933 |
| Farkas, Reno | 59 | 102 | 190 | 26 | 41 | .918 |
| Woodard, Modesto | 11 | 18 | 25 | 4 | 9 | .915 |
| Snider, Bakersfield | 18 | 30 | 34 | 6 | 4 | .914 |
| Griffin, San Jose | 121 | 189 | 281 | 47 | 51 | .909 |
| Nickeson, Modesto | 26 | 23 | 66 | 9 | 10 | .908 |
| Baker, Reno | 81 | 126 | 247 | 39 | 46 | .905 |
| Moran, San Jose | 33 | 31 | 54 | 9 | 5 | .904 |
| Miller, Salinas | 53 | 81 | 133 | 24 | 23 | .899 |
| Keough, Salinas | 110 | 187 | 303 | 56 | 55 | .897 |
| Sularz, Fresno | 44 | 65 | 115 | 24 | 19 | .882 |
| Gifford, Visalia | 93 | 142 | 197 | 49 | 39 | .874 |

Triple Play—Keough.

### (Fewer Than Ten Games)

| Player and Club | G. | PO. | A. | E. | DP. | Pct. |
|---|---|---|---|---|---|---|
| Tisdale, Bakersfield | 2 | 1 | 6 | 0 | 1 | 1.000 |
| Ramirez, Modesto | 1 | 2 | 2 | 0 | 1 | 1.000 |
| Polock, Reno | 2 | 1 | 3 | 0 | 1 | 1.000 |
| Bellini, San Jose | 2 | 0 | 4 | 0 | 0 | 1.000 |
| Dolf, San Jose | 2 | 1 | 2 | 0 | 0 | 1.000 |
| Glass, Bakersfield | 1 | 1 | 1 | 0 | 1 | 1.000 |
| Norrid, San Jose | 2 | 0 | 2 | 0 | 0 | 1.000 |
| Cruz, Salinas | 1 | 1 | 0 | 0 | 0 | 1.000 |
| Hund, Salinas | 6 | 12 | 16 | 1 | 4 | .966 |
| Brand, Bakersfield | 4 | 10 | 10 | 1 | 2 | .952 |
| Hinshaw, Salinas | 7 | 9 | 26 | 2 | 3 | .946 |
| Senn, Visalia | 9 | 8 | 17 | 3 | 1 | .893 |
| Daniel, Visalia | 8 | 11 | 15 | 4 | 1 | .867 |
| Andrews, Fresno | 2 | 5 | 5 | 2 | 2 | .833 |
| Greene, Salinas | 6 | 8 | 11 | 8 | 2 | .704 |
| Hill, Visalia | 1 | 0 | 0 | 2 | 0 | .000 |

## OUTFIELDERS

| Player and Club | G. | PO. | A. | E. | DP. | Pct. |
|---|---|---|---|---|---|---|
| SERVOSS, San Jose | 103 | 198 | 11 | 0 | 2 | 1.000 |
| Jackson, Lodi | 23 | 26 | 0 | 0 | 1 | 1.000 |
| Hill, Visalia | 17 | 22 | 2 | 0 | 2 | 1.000 |
| Wallace, Salinas* | 11 | 14 | 0 | 0 | 1 | 1.000 |
| Rye, Lodi | 11 | 12 | 0 | 0 | 0 | 1.000 |
| Lora, Visalia* | 82 | 185 | 6 | 3 | 1 | .985 |
| Cosey, Modesto* | 98 | 177 | 9 | 3 | 2 | .984 |
| Gardner, San Jose | 133 | 209 | 10 | 4 | 3 | .982 |
| Orr, Fresno | 77 | 101 | 10 | 2 | 2 | .982 |
| Ollar, Bakersfield* | 110 | 182 | 13 | 4 | 0 | .980 |
| Edwards, Reno | 137 | 320 | 13 | 7 | 4 | .979 |
| R. Duncan, Reno | 83 | 98 | 6 | 3 | 1 | .972 |
| George, Modesto | 88 | 157 | 9 | 5 | 0 | .971 |
| Washko, San Jose | 77 | 129 | 6 | 4 | 0 | .971 |
| Hickey, San Jose | 26 | 31 | 2 | 1 | 0 | .971 |
| Sanderlin, Fresno | 134 | 299 | 14 | 10 | 4 | .969 |
| Murphy, Modesto | 122 | 250 | 7 | 9 | 2 | .966 |
| Budaska, Modesto* | 101 | 192 | 6 | 7 | 0 | .966 |
| Bryan, Lodi* | 130 | 212 | 10 | 8 | 4 | .965 |
| Bridges, Reno | 70 | 153 | 12 | 6 | 2 | .965 |
| Drevnak, Salinas* | 122 | 148 | 15 | 6 | 2 | .964 |
| Manning, San Jose | 13 | 26 | 1 | 1 | 1 | .964 |
| Richards, Reno* | 128 | 203 | 6 | 8 | 1 | .963 |
| Iorg, Visalia* | 125 | 222 | 18 | 10 | 6 | .960 |
| Volk, Bakersfield* | 114 | 219 | 10 | 10 | 3 | .958 |
| Stroughter, Fresno | 101 | 166 | 6 | 8 | 2 | .957 |
| Mazzilli, Visalia | 109 | 185 | 9 | 9 | 2 | .956 |
| Gatlin, Reno | 42 | 63 | 2 | 3 | 1 | .956 |
| Kubski, Salinas | 117 | 200 | 6 | 10 | 2 | .954 |
| Leonard, Bak | 73 | 137 | 5 | 7 | 1 | .953 |
| Marple, Lodi | 90 | 146 | 14 | 8 | 3 | .952 |
| Person, Salinas | 14 | 17 | 0 | 1 | 0 | .944 |
| Tisdale, Bakersfield | 12 | 17 | 0 | 1 | 0 | .944 |
| Lee, Lodi* | 57 | 91 | 7 | 6 | 1 | .942 |
| White, Lodi | 16 | 27 | 3 | 2 | 1 | .938 |
| Peters, Salinas* | 131 | 218 | 17 | 16 | 3 | .936 |
| Westmoreland, Bak | 132 | 195 | 20 | 15 | 4 | .935 |
| Bauers, Visalia | 90 | 120 | 10 | 9 | 1 | .935 |
| Brown, Lodi | 104 | 162 | 9 | 12 | 3 | .934 |
| Sauer, Fresno | 116 | 147 | 12 | 13 | 3 | .924 |
| Dolf, San Jose | 31 | 31 | 4 | 3 | 0 | .921 |
| Newsome, Salinas | 27 | 32 | 2 | 3 | 0 | .919 |
| Jones, Modesto | 30 | 31 | 2 | 3 | 0 | .917 |
| McCoy, Reno | 28 | 32 | 1 | 4 | 0 | .892 |
| Olivares, Visalia* | 17 | 23 | 1 | 3 | 1 | .889 |
| Ahu, Reno | 13 | 8 | 0 | 1 | 0 | .889 |

### (Fewer Than Ten Games)

| Player and Club | G. | PO. | A. | E. | DP. | Pct. |
|---|---|---|---|---|---|---|
| James, Lodi | 5 | 10 | 0 | 0 | 0 | 1.000 |
| Beras, San Jose | 7 | 8 | 1 | 0 | 1 | 1.000 |
| Polock, Reno | 9 | 4 | 0 | 0 | 0 | 1.000 |
| Andrews, Fresno | 3 | 4 | 0 | 0 | 0 | 1.000 |
| Picone, Salinas | 2 | 4 | 0 | 0 | 0 | 1.000 |
| Chapados, Bak* | 3 | 3 | 0 | 0 | 0 | 1.000 |
| Laubert, Fresno | 3 | 3 | 0 | 0 | 0 | 1.000 |
| Sularz, Fresno | 3 | 3 | 0 | 0 | 0 | 1.000 |
| Cardoza, Bak* | 1 | 3 | 0 | 0 | 0 | 1.000 |
| Bengston, Visalia | 1 | 2 | 0 | 0 | 0 | 1.000 |

### OUTFIELDERS—Continued
#### (Fewer Than Ten Games)

| Player and Club | G. | PO. | A. | E. | DP. | Pct. |
|---|---|---|---|---|---|---|
| Snider, Bakersfield . | 1 | 1 | 1 | 0 | 0 | 1.000 |
| Elrod, Fresno ... | 4 | 1 | 0 | 0 | 0 | 1.000 |
| Brand, Bakersfield . | 1 | 1 | 0 | 0 | 0 | 1.000 |
| Lee, Fresno .... | 1 | 1 | 0 | 0 | 0 | 1.000 |
| Stabelfeldt, Fresno . | 4 | 9 | 0 | 1 | 0 | .900 |
| Donohue, Salinas ... | 6 | 8 | 1 | 1 | 0 | .900 |
| Stupy, Salinas ..... | 5 | 5 | 0 | 2 | 0 | .714 |
| Rich, Salinas ...... | 2 | 1 | 0 | 0 | 0 | .500 |

### CATCHERS

| Player and Club | G. | PO. | A. | E. | DP. | PB. | Pct. |
|---|---|---|---|---|---|---|---|
| Servoss, San Jose . | 19 | 87 | 7 | 0 | 0 | 3 | 1.000 |
| Jackson, Lodi.... | 29 | 163 | 12 | 1 | 0 | 11 | .994 |
| Christiansen, Sal. | 35 | 241 | 26 | 2 | 2 | 5 | .993 |
| Isaac, San Jose .. | 40 | 265 | 28 | 3 | 2 | 1 | .989 |
| WYNEGAR, Re .1 | 27 | 734 | 99 | 9 | 5 | 26 | .989 |
| Brand, Bak ... | 12 | 73 | 14 | 1 | 2 | 4 | .989 |
| Rosado, Visalia . | 72 | 478 | 74 | 8 | 4 | 16 | .986 |
| Kelly, Salinas .. | 11 | 60 | 7 | 1 | 0 | 1 | .985 |
| Robinson, Modesto | 21 | 104 | 11 | 2 | 0 | 3 | .983 |
| Stabelfeldt, Fr .. | 80 | 389 | 74 | 9 | 2 | 22 | .981 |
| Stupy, Salinas .. | 38 | 230 | 32 | 5 | 2 | 5 | .981 |
| Hough, Visalia .. | 11 | 47 | 5 | 1 | 0 | 1 | .981 |
| Vanderhook, Lodi. | 66 | 389 | 27 | 9 | 1 | 5 | .979 |
| Stajduhar, Mod .. | 75 | 345 | 28 | 9 | 2 | 6 | .976 |
| Martinson, Salinas | 60 | 233 | 50 | 7 | 11 | 18 | .976 |
| Camilo, Fresno .. | 62 | 350 | 57 | 11 | 7 | 12 | .974 |
| Howerton, S J .. | 70 | 348 | 29 | 10 | 4 | 11 | .974 |
| Glass, Bakersfield | 76 | 387 | 46 | 13 | 2 | 37 | .971 |
| DiStasi, Salinas . | 16 | 57 | 10 | 2 | 0 | 7 | .971 |
| Cariel, Reno .... | 11 | 59 | 7 | 2 | 0 | 2 | .971 |
| Yoder, San Jose . | 31 | 140 | 23 | 5 | 3 | 5 | .970 |
| Moldenhauer, Mod | 48 | 280 | 28 | 11 | 6 | 8 | .966 |
| Richards, Bak ... | 53 | 269 | 32 | 12 | 4 | 18 | .962 |
| Peterson, Visalia . | 45 | 260 | 22 | 12 | 3 | 11 | .959 |
| Royster, Lodi ... | 47 | 273 | 46 | 14 | 3 | 19 | .958 |
| Farr, Bak ...... | 12 | 61 | 7 | 4 | 0 | 4 | .944 |
| Bengston, Visalia | 10 | 52 | 2 | 4 | 2 | 3 | .931 |

Triple Play—Moldenhauer.

#### (Fewer Than Ten Games)

| Player and Club | G. | PO. | A. | E. | DP. | PB. | Pct. |
|---|---|---|---|---|---|---|---|
| Benedetti, Lodi . | 6 | 20 | 2 | 0 | 0 | 2 | 1.000 |
| Rodriguez, Mod . | 5 | 13 | 2 | 0 | 0 | 1 | 1.000 |
| Hamilton, Reno .. | 1 | 8 | 1 | 0 | 0 | 0 | 1.000 |
| Segrest, Reno ... | 1 | 1 | 0 | 0 | 0 | 0 | 1.000 |
| Senn, Visalia ... | 1 | 1 | 0 | 0 | 0 | 0 | 1.000 |
| Picone, Salinas .. | 8 | 50 | 7 | 4 | 1 | 1 | .934 |
| Jackson Visalia . | 5 | 15 | 4 | 2 | 2 | 0 | .905 |
| Hance, Bakersfield | 9 | 26 | 2 | 3 | 1 | 7 | .903 |
| Sinovich, Mod ... | 1 | 2 | 3 | 1 | 0 | | .833 |

### PITCHERS

| Player and Club | G. | PO. | A. | E. | DP. | Pct. |
|---|---|---|---|---|---|---|
| DAVIDSON, Fresno | 39 | 14 | 23 | 0 | 1 | 1.000 |
| Califano, Lodi* .. | 24 | 2 | 28 | 0 | 0 | 1.000 |
| D. Frazier, Sal* .. | 25 | 5 | 19 | 0 | 0 | 1.000 |
| Rondon, Salinas .. | 29 | 4 | 13 | 0 | 0 | 1.000 |
| Lanthorn, Fresno | 16 | 2 | 13 | 0 | 1 | 1.000 |
| McQueen, Salinas | 54 | 1 | 13 | 0 | 0 | 1.000 |
| Williams, Modesto | 11 | 7 | 6 | 0 | 0 | 1.000 |
| Zoss, Modesto* .. | 23 | 4 | 9 | 0 | 0 | 1.000 |
| Rehn, Reno ...... | 46 | 1 | 12 | 0 | 0 | 1.000 |
| McKay, Fresno .. | 21 | 3 | 9 | 0 | 0 | 1.000 |
| Wright, Salinas* . | 24 | 4 | 7 | 0 | 1 | 1.000 |
| Whiteley, Salinas | 15 | 1 | 9 | 0 | 0 | 1.000 |
| Cochran, Modesto . | 12 | 3 | 6 | 0 | 0 | 1.000 |
| McLaughlin, Lodi . | 12 | 3 | 6 | 0 | 0 | 1.000 |
| Saulnier, San Jose* | 12 | 3 | 6 | 0 | 1 | 1.000 |
| Burley, Visalia* . | 12 | 1 | 8 | 0 | 0 | 1.000 |
| Litle, Visalia ... | 18 | 1 | 6 | 0 | 1 | 1.000 |
| Walker, Lodi .... | 21 | 1 | 5 | 0 | 0 | 1.000 |
| Gill, Reno ...... | 12 | 1 | 3 | 0 | 0 | 1.000 |
| Bovee, Reno* .... | 17 | 1 | 3 | 0 | 0 | 1.000 |
| Mattison, Bak* .. | 20 | 1 | 2 | 0 | 0 | 1.000 |
| Harts, Visalia* .. | 19 | 1 | 2 | 0 | 1 | 1.000 |
| Lea, Visalia .... | 11 | 1 | 1 | 0 | 0 | 1.000 |
| Stelicki, Fresno* . | 10 | 0 | 1 | 0 | 0 | 1.000 |
| Plank, Fresno ... | 28 | 16 | 37 | 1 | 3 | .981 |
| Garvin, Reno* ... | 25 | 9 | 37 | 1 | 3 | .979 |
| Oldham, Modesto . | 28 | 11 | 20 | 1 | 1 | .969 |
| Milke, Visalia ... | 17 | 17 | 13 | 1 | 0 | .968 |
| Arnold, San Jose* . | 26 | 3 | 27 | 1 | 0 | .968 |
| Sutcliffe, Bak .... | 28 | 18 | 40 | 2 | 0 | .967 |
| McSpadden, Reno* | 22 | 5 | 21 | 1 | 1 | .963 |
| Quiros, Lodi .... | 49 | 6 | 19 | 1 | 1 | .962 |
| Messman, Reno .. | 24 | 6 | 19 | 1 | 2 | .960 |
| McCatty, Modesto . | 37 | 4 | 20 | 1 | 1 | .960 |
| Woodruff, San Jose* | 43 | 5 | 21 | 1 | 2 | .958 |
| Werd, San Jose* . | 13 | 6 | 17 | 1 | 1 | .958 |
| Ausman, Reno* ... | 47 | 3 | 20 | 1 | 0 | .958 |
| Stumpp, Salinas .. | 15 | 10 | 12 | 1 | 0 | .957 |
| Maxwell, Salinas* | 14 | 4 | 18 | 1 | 1 | .957 |
| Greenfield, Fresno | 19 | 11 | 10 | 1 | 1 | .955 |
| Scarcella, Fresno . | 25 | 5 | 16 | 1 | 0 | .955 |
| Roberts, Fresno .. | 25 | 14 | 26 | 2 | 1 | .952 |
| Ward, Lodi ...... | 13 | 8 | 12 | 1 | 0 | .952 |
| Flanagan, San Jose. | 19 | 5 | 13 | 1 | 2 | .947 |
| Eichelberger, Reno.. | 16 | 9 | 25 | 2 | 0 | .944 |
| Widner, San Jose* . | 24 | 4 | 13 | 1 | 0 | .944 |
| Wihtol, San Jose* . | 15 | 5 | 11 | 1 | 1 | .941 |
| O'Brien, Bakersfield | 29 | 14 | 15 | 2 | 2 | .935 |
| Milner, Visalia ... | 12 | 6 | 8 | 1 | 0 | .933 |
| Smith, Salinas* .. | 13 | 3 | 11 | 1 | 3 | .933 |
| Kuhaulua, Salinas* | 33 | 5 | 9 | 1 | 0 | .933 |
| Klein, San Jose .. | 36 | 9 | 17 | 2 | 2 | .929 |
| Johnson, Lodi .... | 15 | 6 | 7 | 1 | 1 | .929 |
| Lysander, Modesto | 21 | 9 | 16 | 2 | 0 | .926 |
| Prewitt, Visalia .. | 17 | 7 | 18 | 2 | 1 | .926 |
| Bird, Lodi ....... | 29 | 11 | 25 | 3 | 2 | .923 |
| Gibbon, Salinas* .. | 13 | 8 | 14 | 2 | 2 | .917 |
| Todd, Bakersfield . | 38 | 1 | 10 | 1 | 0 | .917 |
| Butler, Visalia ... | 38 | 10 | 10 | 2 | 0 | .909 |
| Muhlstock, Fresno . | 13 | 5 | 15 | 2 | 2 | .909 |
| Arsenault, San Jose. | 20 | 2 | 8 | 1 | 0 | .909 |
| Snider, Bakersfield . | 20 | 1 | 9 | 1 | 1 | .909 |
| Wojcik, Visalia* .. | 23 | 10 | 29 | 4 | 3 | .907 |
| B. Duncan, Reno .. | 25 | 7 | 30 | 4 | 1 | .902 |
| Garcia, Lodi ..... | 18 | 8 | 10 | 2 | 0 | .900 |
| Wibberley, Modesto | 56 | 6 | 12 | 2 | 0 | .900 |
| Cody, Bakersfield . | 31 | 3 | 6 | 1 | 0 | .900 |
| Lacki, Salinas* ... | 27 | 5 | 21 | 3 | 1 | .897 |
| McNulty, Bakersfield | 28 | 5 | 19 | 3 | 1 | .889 |
| Shirley, Bak* .... | 24 | 2 | 22 | 3 | 2 | .889 |
| Tallman, Fresno .. | 19 | 4 | 19 | 3 | 0 | .885 |
| Jones, San Jose .. | 29 | 8 | 7 | 2 | 1 | .882 |
| Salas, Modesto ... | 26 | 15 | 13 | 4 | 0 | .875 |
| Hayden, Lodi ..... | 21 | 6 | 15 | 3 | 4 | .875 |
| Jacobsen, Visalia . | 12 | 2 | 5 | 1 | 1 | .875 |
| Coe, Reno* ....... | 10 | 1 | 6 | 1 | 0 | .875 |
| Johnson, Visalia .. | 20 | 7 | 11 | 3 | 1 | .857 |
| Wouters, Bakersfield | 24 | 5 | 7 | 2 | 1 | .857 |
| Flores, Fresno* ... | 11 | 3 | 3 | 1 | 0 | .857 |
| Carroll, Bak* .... | 18 | 0 | 6 | 1 | 0 | .857 |
| Anderson, Visalia* | 36 | 5 | 18 | 4 | 1 | .852 |
| Browning, Fresno . | 20 | 3 | 7 | 2 | 0 | .833 |
| Castillo, Salinas .. | 11 | 4 | 1 | 1 | 0 | .833 |
| Zail, Reno ....... | 15 | 1 | 4 | 1 | 0 | .833 |
| Peregud, Modestc . | 17 | 7 | 11 | 4 | 1 | .818 |
| Amenita, San Jose . | 21 | 3 | 6 | 2 | 0 | .818 |
| Pagnozzi, Lodi* ... | 25 | 9 | 31 | 9 | 2 | .816 |
| Heydeman, Bak ... | 22 | 3 | 10 | 3 | 1 | .813 |
| Sapp, Modesto .... | 33 | 2 | 11 | 3 | 1 | .813 |
| Melson, San Jose .. | 15 | 5 | 16 | 5 | 0 | .808 |
| Lockwood, Reno* .. | 15 | 2 | 2 | 1 | 0 | .800 |
| Aronson, Visalia .. | 11 | 1 | 3 | 1 | 1 | .800 |
| Slocum, Bakersfield | 35 | 7 | 13 | 8 | 1 | .714 |
| Weimers, Lodi .... | 37 | 1 | 5 | 4 | 0 | .600 |
| Burns, Reno ...... | 11 | 2 | 1 | 2 | 0 | .600 |

Triple Play—B. Duncan.

## PITCHERS—Continued
### (Fewer Than Ten Games)

| Player and Club | G. | PO. | A. | E. | DP. | Pct. | Player and Club | G. | PO. | A. | E. | DP. | Pct. |
|---|---|---|---|---|---|---|---|---|---|---|---|---|---|
| Rowland, Fresno | 9 | 3 | 14 | 0 | 0 | 1.000 | Washko, San Jose | 1 | 1 | 0 | 0 | 0 | 1.000 |
| Sander, Visalia | 9 | 7 | 8 | 0 | 0 | 1.000 | Hefftner, Reno* | 3 | 0 | 1 | 0 | 0 | 1.000 |
| Peach, Lodi* | 6 | 4 | 9 | 0 | 0 | 1.000 | Neimeyer, Lodi | 3 | 0 | 1 | 0 | 0 | 1.000 |
| Gorgie, Visalia | 5 | 4 | 5 | 0 | 0 | 1.000 | Bishop, Visalia | 2 | 0 | 1 | 0 | 0 | 1.000 |
| Bolden, Visalia* | 8 | 3 | 5 | 0 | 0 | 1.000 | Caneira, Salinas | 9 | 4 | 8 | 1 | 0 | .923 |
| Hughes, Visalia | 7 | 1 | 4 | 0 | 0 | 1.000 | O'Donnell, Fresno* | 9 | 1 | 11 | 1 | 0 | .923 |
| Reid, San Jose* | 6 | 0 | 5 | 0 | 0 | 1.000 | Moore, Salinas* | 5 | 3 | 5 | 1 | 0 | .889 |
| Owens, Modesto | 2 | 2 | 2 | 0 | 0 | 1.000 | Bell, Modesto | 5 | 4 | 2 | 1 | 0 | .857 |
| Tuttle, Modesto | 8 | 1 | 3 | 0 | 0 | 1.000 | Gonzalez, Visalia | 6 | 1 | 5 | 1 | 0 | .857 |
| Garcia, Reno | 8 | 0 | 4 | 0 | 1 | 1.000 | Staniland, Modesto | 6 | 2 | 8 | 2 | 0 | .833 |
| Oliva, Salinas | 6 | 1 | 2 | 0 | 0 | 1.000 | Darr, Lodi | 7 | 2 | 7 | 2 | 0 | .818 |
| Buehner, Reno* | 4 | 1 | 2 | 0 | 0 | 1.000 | Kanas, Visalia | 6 | 1 | 3 | 1 | 0 | .800 |
| Nevarez, Lodi | 6 | 0 | 3 | 0 | 0 | 1.000 | Sorensen, San Jose | 5 | 0 | 4 | 2 | 0 | .667 |
| Barnicle, Fresno | 5 | 0 | 3 | 0 | 0 | 1.000 | Brownlee, Modesto | 3 | 2 | 4 | 4 | 0 | .600 |
| Dyer, Visalia* | 5 | 0 | 3 | 0 | 0 | 1.000 | Corkins, Salinas | 4 | 1 | 1 | 2 | 0 | .500 |
| Prichard, Salinas | 6 | 0 | 2 | 0 | 0 | 1.000 | Reimann, Lodi | 6 | 0 | 0 | 1 | 0 | .000 |
| Bonfils, Salinas* | 3 | 1 | 0 | 0 | 1 | 1.000 | | | | | | | |

The following players do not have any recorded accepted chances at the positions indicated; therefore, are not listed in the fielding averages for those particular positions: Brand, p; Cardoza*, p; Clark, of; Daniel, of; Fox, p; Greene, 3b; Harvey, p; Hill, p; Hinshaw, 3b; Hund, 3b; E. Jackson, 3b; H. Jones, 3b; Mazzilli, 1b; Mollenhauer, 3b; Nevinger, p; Pebley, of-c; Picone, 2b; Segrest, of; Tisdale, 3b; Vaughn, p; Wells*, p.

Clarke, Hodge, Rodgers, were used as designated-hitters/pinch-hitters only.

## CLUB PITCHING

| Club | G. | CG. | ShO. | Sv. | IP. | H. | R. | ER. | HR. | BB. | Int. BB. | HB. | SO. | WP. | Bk. | ERA. |
|---|---|---|---|---|---|---|---|---|---|---|---|---|---|---|---|---|
| Salinas | 140 | 31 | 18 | 20 | 1165 | 1142 | 542 | 416 | 41 | 457 | 24 | 41 | 912 | 51 | 8 | 3.21 |
| Fresno | 140 | 50 | 10 | 11 | 1164 | 1137 | 656 | 507 | 66 | 534 | 13 | 36 | 713 | 88 | 9 | 3.92 |
| Reno | 140 | 44 | 9 | 24 | 1169 | 1219 | 655 | 513 | 78 | 550 | 38 | 24 | 759 | 72 | 9 | 3.95 |
| San Jose | 140 | 39 | 7 | 18 | 1159 | 1157 | 683 | 539 | 74 | 640 | 27 | 28 | 776 | 71 | 17 | 4.19 |
| Lodi | 146 | 41 | 9 | 18 | 1163 | 1212 | 670 | 541 | 78 | 529 | 40 | 41 | 798 | 56 | 22 | 4.19 |
| Modesto | 140 | 38 | 9 | 15 | 1160 | 1245 | 734 | 565 | 87 | 517 | 45 | 21 | 699 | 78 | 15 | 4.38 |
| Bakersfield | 140 | 28 | 4 | 20 | 1178 | 1263 | 777 | 580 | 57 | 675 | 29 | 59 | 782 | 94 | 11 | 4.43 |
| Visalia | 140 | 45 | 11 | 20 | 1160 | 1277 | 773 | 601 | 92 | 701 | 23 | 31 | 857 | 73 | 15 | 4.66 |

## PITCHERS' RECORDS
### (Leading Qualifiers for Earned-Run Average Leadership—112 or More Innings)
*Throws lefthanded.

| Pitcher—Club | G. | GS. | CG. | ShO. | W. | L. | Sv. | Pct. | IP. | H. | R. | ER. | HR. | BB. | Int. BB. | HB. | SO. | WP. | ERA. |
|---|---|---|---|---|---|---|---|---|---|---|---|---|---|---|---|---|---|---|---|
| Plank, Fresno | 28 | 26 | 15 | 3 | 17 | 7 | 0 | .708 | 195 | 185 | 70 | 49 | 5 | 42 | 1 | 3 | 97 | 4 | 2.26 |
| Garvin, Reno* | 25 | 25 | 17 | 3 | 17 | 5 | 0 | .773 | 201 | 188 | 77 | 57 | 12 | 56 | 9 | 5 | 129 | 4 | 2.55 |
| Eichelberger, Reno | 16 | 16 | 7 | 1 | 10 | 4 | 0 | .714 | 117 | 105 | 52 | 36 | 4 | 54 | 0 | 1 | 92 | 8 | 2.77 |
| Oldham, Modesto | 28 | 19 | 8 | 3 | 12 | 5 | 0 | .706 | 154 | 155 | 70 | 53 | 10 | 58 | 3 | 2 | 74 | 6 | 3.10 |
| Arnold, San Jose* | 26 | 25 | 11 | 2 | 12 | 7 | 1 | .632 | 177 | 151 | 67 | 62 | 11 | 80 | 2 | 1 | 109 | 4 | 3.15 |
| Lacki, Salinas* | 27 | 27 | 8 | 2 | 11 | 11 | 0 | .500 | 173 | 178 | 81 | 61 | 5 | 49 | 2 | 5 | 121 | 8 | 3.17 |
| Wojcik, Visalia* | 23 | 23 | 11 | 2 | 11 | 7 | 0 | .611 | 157 | 181 | 71 | 56 | 10 | 41 | 1 | 0 | 114 | 2 | 3.21 |
| Hayden, Lodi | 21 | 16 | 5 | 1 | 7 | 6 | 1 | .538 | 128 | 150 | 61 | 47 | 8 | 40 | 4 | 3 | 69 | 3 | 3.30 |
| Woodruff, S J* | 43 | 9 | 3 | 1 | 6 | 7 | 8 | .462 | 130 | 139 | 71 | 49 | 9 | 60 | 3 | 1 | 104 | 7 | 3.39 |
| Bird, Lodi | 29 | 17 | 9 | 2 | 9 | 10 | 1 | .474 | 157 | 157 | 75 | 64 | 11 | 54 | 10 | 4 | 102 | 7 | 3.67 |

Departmental Leaders: G—Wibberley, 56; GS—Sutcliffe, 28; CG—Garvin, 17; ShO—Garvin. Gibbon, Milke, Oldham, Plank, 3; W—Garvin, Plank, 17; L—Sutcliffe, 16; Sv—Ausman, 12; Pct.—Garvin, .773; IP—Garvin, 201; H—Sutcliffe, 214; R—Sutcliffe, 115; ER—Sutcliffe, 89; HR—B. Duncan, 14; BB—McNulty, 100; IBB—Wibberley, 15; HB—Heydeman, 12; SO—Garvin, 129; WP—Tallman, 17.

### (All Pitchers—Listed Alphabetically)

| Pitcher—Club | G. | GS. | CG. | ShO. | W. | L. | Sv. | Pct. | IP. | H. | R. | ER. | HR. | BB. | Int. BB. | HB. | SO. | WP. | ERA. |
|---|---|---|---|---|---|---|---|---|---|---|---|---|---|---|---|---|---|---|---|
| Amenita, San Jose | 21 | 1 | 1 | 0 | 3 | 2 | 0 | .600 | 49 | 40 | 42 | 28 | 2 | 42 | 3 | 1 | 59 | 6 | 5.14 |
| Anderson, Vis* | 36 | 1 | 0 | 0 | 2 | 7 | 7 | .222 | 72 | 71 | 44 | 36 | 5 | 56 | 4 | 1 | 52 | 5 | 4.50 |
| Arnold, San Jose* | 26 | 25 | 11 | 2 | 12 | 7 | 1 | .632 | 177 | 151 | 67 | 62 | 11 | 80 | 2 | 1 | 109 | 4 | 3.15 |
| Aronson, Visalia | 11 | 11 | 1 | 0 | 2 | 4 | 0 | .333 | 53 | 60 | 46 | 32 | 3 | 49 | 1 | 5 | 39 | 4 | 5.43 |
| Arsenault, S J | 20 | 0 | 0 | 0 | 4 | 5 | 3 | .444 | 35 | 35 | 14 | 13 | 1 | 14 | 4 | 2 | 18 | 2 | 3.34 |
| Ausman, Reno* | 47 | 0 | 0 | 0 | 6 | 3 | 12 | .667 | 90 | 88 | 39 | 25 | 5 | 42 | 7 | 1 | 92 | 4 | 2.50 |
| Barnicle, Fresno* | 5 | 5 | 2 | 0 | 0 | 4 | 0 | .000 | 27 | 24 | 28 | 25 | 3 | 28 | 0 | 3 | 20 | 4 | 8.33 |
| Bell, Modesto | 5 | 5 | 3 | 1 | 4 | 1 | 0 | .806 | 38 | 29 | 15 | 13 | 2 | 12 | 1 | 1 | 18 | 0 | 3.08 |
| Bird, Lodi | 29 | 17 | 9 | 2 | 9 | 10 | 1 | .474 | 157 | 157 | 75 | 64 | 11 | 54 | 10 | 4 | 102 | 7 | 3.67 |
| Bishop, Visalia | 2 | 1 | 0 | 0 | 0 | 1 | 0 | 1.000 | 2 | 1 | 3 | 1 | 0 | 4 | 0 | 0 | 3 | 2 | 4.50 |
| Bolden, Visalia* | 8 | 7 | 2 | 0 | 2 | 3 | 0 | .400 | 41 | 46 | 29 | 26 | 6 | 29 | 0 | 0 | 24 | 6 | 5.71 |
| Bonfils, Salinas* | 3 | 0 | 0 | 0 | 1 | 0 | 0 | 1.000 | 4 | 1 | 1 | 1 | 0 | 3 | 0 | 0 | 4 | 0 | 2.25 |
| Bovee, Reno* | 17 | 1 | 0 | 0 | 2 | 3 | 2 | .400 | 32 | 34 | 26 | 17 | 2 | 18 | 0 | 4 | 24 | 4 | 4.78 |
| Brand, Bakersfield | 3 | 0 | 0 | 0 | 0 | 0 | 0 | .000 | 6 | 5 | 4 | 4 | 1 | 2 | 0 | 0 | 2 | 1 | 6.00 |
| Browning, Fresno | 20 | 0 | 0 | 0 | 4 | 3 | 2 | .571 | 34 | 22 | 17 | 10 | 2 | 33 | 2 | 1 | 19 | 5 | 2.65 |
| Brownlee, Modesto | 3 | 3 | 0 | 0 | 0 | 2 | 0 | .000 | 18 | 18 | 14 | 7 | 0 | 11 | 0 | 0 | 14 | 3 | 3.50 |
| Buehner, Reno* | 4 | 0 | 0 | 0 | 0 | 0 | 0 | .000 | 4 | 7 | 8 | 8 | 1 | 6 | 0 | 0 | 2 | 0 | 18.00 |
| Hurley, Visalia* | 12 | 0 | 0 | 0 | 0 | 1 | 0 | .000 | 38 | 43 | 28 | 22 | 2 | 26 | 2 | 1 | 20 | 0 | 5.21 |

| Pitcher—Club | G | GS | CG | ShO | W | L | Sv | Pct. | IP | H | R | ER | HR | BB | Int. BB | HB | SO | WP | ERA |
|---|---|---|---|---|---|---|---|---|---|---|---|---|---|---|---|---|---|---|---|
| Burns, Reno | 11 | 8 | 1 | 0 | 4 | 3 | 0 | .571 | 39 | 39 | 25 | 23 | 6 | 10 | 0 | 1 | 23 | 1 | 5.31 |
| Butler, Visalia | 38 | 1 | 0 | 0 | 5 | 5 | 3 | .500 | 68 | 71 | 43 | 28 | 3 | 34 | 1 | 2 | 59 | 7 | 3.71 |
| Califano, Lodi* | 24 | 23 | 7 | 2 | 10 | 7 | 0 | .588 | 128 | 128 | 72 | 62 | 12 | 72 | 4 | 7 | 70 | 7 | 4.36 |
| Caneira, Salinas | 9 | 9 | 1 | 0 | 0 | 4 | 0 | .000 | 51 | 51 | 25 | 18 | 3 | 12 | 2 | 0 | 33 | 2 | 3.18 |
| Cardoza, Bak* | 1 | 0 | 0 | 0 | 0 | 0 | 0 | .000 | 1 | 1 | 0 | 0 | 0 | 1 | 0 | 0 | 1 | 0 | 0.00 |
| Carroll, Bak* | 18 | 6 | 0 | 0 | 0 | 0 | 4 | .000 | 44 | 40 | 35 | 23 | 1 | 50 | 1 | 1 | 35 | 6 | 4.70 |
| Castillo, Salinas | 11 | 5 | 0 | 0 | 1 | 2 | 0 | .333 | 37 | 33 | 11 | 8 | 1 | 14 | 0 | 2 | 23 | 0 | 1.95 |
| Cochran, Modesto | 12 | 12 | 2 | 1 | 3 | 7 | 0 | .300 | 70 | 78 | 49 | 40 | 7 | 39 | 1 | 0 | 51 | 10 | 5.14 |
| Cody, Bakersfield | 31 | 0 | 0 | 0 | 2 | 2 | 8 | .500 | 55 | 63 | 29 | 17 | 4 | 20 | 4 | 5 | 32 | 0 | 2.78 |
| Coe, Reno* | 10 | 8 | 1 | 0 | 3 | 3 | 0 | .500 | 40 | 50 | 29 | 24 | 2 | 16 | 0 | 0 | 15 | 3 | 5.40 |
| Corkins, Salinas | 4 | 1 | 0 | 0 | 0 | 1 | 0 | .000 | 6 | 6 | 6 | 4 | 0 | 5 | 0 | 0 | 7 | 2 | 6.00 |
| Darr, Lodi | 7 | 1 | 0 | 0 | 2 | 2 | 0 | .500 | 35 | 30 | 21 | 20 | 0 | 27 | 1 | 1 | 35 | 4 | 5.14 |
| Davidson, Fresno | 39 | 10 | 3 | 0 | 6 | 6 | 2 | .500 | 110 | 132 | 74 | 58 | 6 | 42 | 3 | 8 | 46 | 10 | 4.75 |
| B. Duncan, Reno | 25 | 25 | 4 | 1 | 8 | 8 | 0 | .500 | 143 | 174 | 99 | 76 | 14 | 60 | 3 | 0 | 44 | 2 | 4.78 |
| Dyer, Visalia* | 5 | 5 | 0 | 0 | 0 | 3 | 0 | .000 | 17 | 27 | 27 | 18 | 3 | 20 | 1 | 1 | 5 | 5 | 9.53 |
| Eichelberger, Reno | 16 | 16 | 7 | 1 | 10 | 4 | 0 | .714 | 117 | 105 | 52 | 36 | 4 | 54 | 0 | 1 | 92 | 8 | 2.77 |
| Flanagan, San Jose | 19 | 13 | 3 | 0 | 6 | 3 | 0 | .667 | 89 | 107 | 62 | 47 | 10 | 38 | 1 | 2 | 31 | 4 | 4.75 |
| Flores, Fresno* | 11 | 8 | 1 | 0 | 2 | 4 | 0 | .333 | 38 | 46 | 36 | 29 | 6 | 23 | 0 | 0 | 28 | 4 | 6.87 |
| Fox, San Jose | 3 | 2 | 0 | 0 | 0 | 3 | 0 | .000 | 8 | 10 | 9 | 7 | 0 | 10 | 1 | 0 | 2 | 0 | 7.88 |
| D. Frazier, Sal* | 25 | 22 | 2 | 1 | 7 | 9 | 0 | .438 | 134 | 131 | 75 | 56 | 4 | 85 | 1 | 3 | 110 | 11 | 3.76 |
| Garcia, Reno | 8 | 8 | 2 | 0 | 0 | 4 | 0 | .000 | 34 | 47 | 52 | 28 | 3 | 22 | 0 | 1 | 31 | 3 | 7.41 |
| Garcia, Lodi | 18 | 11 | 1 | 0 | 3 | 6 | 0 | .333 | 85 | 111 | 85 | 57 | 10 | 40 | 1 | 4 | 50 | 7 | 4.98 |
| Garvin, Reno* | 25 | 25 | 17 | 3 | 17 | 5 | 0 | .773 | 201 | 189 | 77 | 57 | 12 | 56 | 9 | 5 | 129 | 4 | 2.55 |
| Gibbon, Salinas* | 13 | 13 | 6 | 5 | 7 | 0 | 0 | .417 | 90 | 93 | 40 | 26 | 2 | 36 | 3 | 4 | 72 | 2 | 2.60 |
| Gill, Reno | 12 | 0 | 0 | 0 | 1 | 0 | 0 | .000 | 16 | 20 | 12 | 10 | 2 | 10 | 0 | 1 | 9 | 4 | 5.63 |
| Gonzalez, Visalia | 6 | 5 | 0 | 0 | 0 | 3 | 0 | .000 | 25 | 39 | 30 | 22 | 3 | 27 | 0 | 0 | 18 | 0 | 7.92 |
| Gorgie, Visalia | 5 | 4 | 2 | 0 | 1 | 2 | 1 | .333 | 31 | 30 | 17 | 14 | 1 | 13 | 1 | 1 | 21 | 1 | 4.06 |
| Greenfield, Fresno | 19 | 18 | 5 | 2 | 6 | 8 | 0 | .429 | 106 | 97 | 57 | 44 | 5 | 58 | 1 | 6 | 64 | 3 | 3.74 |
| Harts, Visalia* | 19 | 0 | 0 | 0 | 2 | 4 | 0 | .000 | 29 | 31 | 22 | 19 | 4 | 31 | 0 | 1 | 32 | 4 | 5.90 |
| Harvey, San Jose | 3 | 1 | 0 | 0 | 0 | 1 | 0 | .000 | 6 | 8 | 5 | 5 | 0 | 6 | 0 | 0 | 9 | 2 | 7.50 |
| Hayden, Lodi | 21 | 16 | 5 | 1 | 7 | 6 | 1 | .538 | 128 | 150 | 61 | 47 | 8 | 40 | 4 | 3 | 69 | 3 | 3.30 |
| Hefftner, Reno* | 3 | 0 | 0 | 0 | 0 | 1 | 0 | .000 | 6 | 13 | 8 | 8 | 2 | 6 | 1 | 0 | 7 | 1 | 12.00 |
| Heydeman, Bak | 12 | 13 | 0 | 0 | 1 | 11 | 0 | .083 | 76 | 82 | 81 | 58 | 5 | 73 | 2 | 12 | 57 | 16 | 6.87 |
| Hill, Visalia | 1 | 0 | 0 | 0 | 0 | 0 | 0 | .000 | 2 | 6 | 5 | 4 | 1 | 2 | 0 | 1 | 2 | 0 | 18.00 |
| Hughes, Visalia | 7 | 7 | 1 | 0 | 1 | 4 | 0 | .200 | 38 | 42 | 36 | 24 | 3 | 32 | 0 | 2 | 25 | 4 | 5.68 |
| Jacobsen, Visalia | 12 | 1 | 0 | 0 | 3 | 2 | 0 | .600 | 36 | 45 | 35 | 26 | 4 | 27 | 0 | 1 | 34 | 2 | 6.50 |
| Johnson, Lodi | 15 | 15 | 3 | 0 | 4 | 5 | 0 | .444 | 70 | 86 | 50 | 41 | 6 | 37 | 1 | 1 | 38 | 3 | 5.27 |
| Johnson, Visalia | 20 | 13 | 5 | 0 | 7 | 8 | 0 | .467 | 85 | 101 | 67 | 50 | 5 | 51 | 0 | 3 | 44 | 9 | 5.29 |
| Jones, San Jose | 29 | 11 | 2 | 0 | 5 | 6 | 1 | .455 | 107 | 113 | 82 | 73 | 12 | 64 | 2 | 3 | 65 | 5 | 6.14 |
| Kanas, Visalia | 6 | 3 | 0 | 0 | 0 | 2 | 0 | .000 | 22 | 30 | 22 | 21 | 3 | 18 | 0 | 0 | 11 | 2 | 8.59 |
| Klein, San Jose | 36 | 18 | 3 | 1 | 8 | 8 | 4 | .500 | 131 | 130 | 76 | 68 | 9 | 90 | 2 | 6 | 74 | 8 | 4.67 |
| Kuhaulua, Salinas* | 33 | 4 | 1 | 0 | 3 | 4 | 5 | .429 | 85 | 88 | 40 | 33 | 1 | 39 | 0 | 2 | 59 | 7 | 3.49 |
| Lacki, Salinas* | 27 | 27 | 8 | 2 | 11 | 11 | 0 | .500 | 173 | 178 | 81 | 61 | 5 | 49 | 2 | 5 | 121 | 8 | 3.17 |
| Lanthorn, Fresno | 16 | 1 | 0 | 0 | 8 | 0 | 3 | 1.000 | 52 | 46 | 23 | 19 | 3 | 16 | 1 | 1 | 26 | 0 | 3.29 |
| Lea, Visalia | 11 | 2 | 0 | 0 | 2 | 1 | 1 | .667 | 27 | 46 | 26 | 25 | 6 | 11 | 1 | 2 | 21 | 2 | 8.33 |
| Litle, Visalia | 18 | 5 | 4 | 2 | 5 | 4 | 2 | .556 | 69 | 57 | 29 | 18 | 3 | 32 | 2 | 1 | 40 | 0 | 2.35 |
| Lockwood, Reno* | 15 | 0 | 0 | 0 | 2 | 1 | 1 | .637 | 26 | 26 | 22 | 14 | 2 | 23 | 1 | 1 | 19 | 1 | 4.85 |
| Lysander, Mod | 21 | 20 | 7 | 0 | 8 | 8 | 0 | .500 | 131 | 152 | 92 | 70 | 10 | 38 | 2 | 1 | 82 | 4 | 4.81 |
| Mattison, Bak* | 20 | 0 | 0 | 0 | 1 | 0 | 1 | 1.000 | 30 | 24 | 10 | | 1 | 22 | 1 | 0 | 16 | 2 | 3.60 |
| Maxwell, Salinas* | 14 | 13 | 4 | 2 | 5 | 5 | 1 | .500 | 86 | 80 | 35 | 28 | 3 | 18 | 1 | 5 | 65 | 1 | 2.93 |
| McCatty, Modesto | 37 | 11 | 2 | 0 | 4 | 8 | 0 | .333 | 126 | 138 | 80 | 64 | 11 | 54 | 5 | 4 | 75 | 12 | 4.57 |
| McKay, Fresno | 21 | 1 | 0 | 0 | 1 | 1 | 0 | .500 | 59 | 65 | 51 | 41 | 9 | 39 | 1 | 2 | 32 | 4 | 6.25 |
| McLaughlin, Lodi | 12 | 0 | 0 | 0 | 0 | 0 | 0 | .000 | 27 | 29 | 17 | 14 | 0 | 17 | 3 | 2 | 12 | 1 | 4.67 |
| McNulty, Bak | 28 | 27 | 6 | 1 | 11 | 10 | 0 | .524 | 158 | 169 | 96 | 75 | 8 | 100 | 3 | 6 | 97 | 10 | 4.27 |
| McQueen, Salinas | 54 | 0 | 0 | 0 | 6 | 5 | 8 | .545 | 91 | 96 | 37 | 32 | 4 | 21 | 6 | 3 | 74 | 1 | 3.16 |
| McSpadden, Reno* | 22 | 15 | 2 | 0 | 10 | 2 | 0 | .833 | 94 | 121 | 53 | 41 | 5 | 33 | 3 | 3 | 57 | 8 | 3.93 |
| Melson, San Jose | 15 | 15 | 6 | 2 | 7 | 8 | 0 | .467 | 94 | 84 | 47 | 36 | 2 | 51 | 2 | 4 | 92 | 10 | 3.45 |
| Messman, Reno | 24 | 24 | 5 | 2 | 10 | 8 | 0 | .556 | 153 | 140 | 85 | 71 | 7 | 98 | 1 | 3 | 87 | 14 | 4.18 |
| Milke, Visalia | 17 | 16 | 8 | 3 | 8 | 3 | 0 | .727 | 119 | 115 | 58 | 49 | 11 | 56 | 1 | 5 | 117 | 5 | 3.71 |
| Milner, Visalia | 12 | 8 | 1 | 0 | 3 | 2 | 0 | .600 | 50 | 60 | 35 | 28 | 8 | 26 | 2 | 0 | 27 | 1 | 5.04 |
| Moore, Salinas* | 5 | 4 | 2 | 2 | 2 | 2 | 0 | .500 | 28 | 24 | 8 | 3 | 1 | 10 | 0 | 2 | 15 | 0 | 0.96 |
| Muhlstock, Fresno | 13 | 8 | 5 | 1 | 7 | 3 | 0 | .700 | 74 | 67 | 22 | 22 | 1 | 13 | 1 | 1 | 71 | 5 | 2.68 |
| Neimeyer, Lodi | 3 | 0 | 0 | 0 | 0 | 0 | 0 | .000 | 5 | 9 | 6 | 6 | 0 | 6 | 1 | 1 | 3 | 0 | 10.80 |
| Nevarez, Lodi | 6 | 3 | 1 | 0 | 2 | 1 | 0 | .667 | 27 | 28 | 16 | 10 | 2 | 13 | 0 | 1 | 31 | 2 | 3.33 |
| Nevinger, Visalia | 2 | 2 | 0 | 0 | 0 | 2 | 0 | .000 | 7 | 14 | 13 | 12 | 1 | 11 | 0 | 0 | 7 | 0 | 15.43 |
| O'Brien, Bak | 29 | 15 | 3 | 0 | 8 | 9 | 0 | .471 | 134 | 139 | 73 | 62 | 3 | 48 | 2 | 5 | 75 | 16 | 4.16 |
| O'Donnell, Fr* | 9 | 8 | 0 | 0 | 2 | 4 | 0 | .333 | 38 | 47 | 26 | 18 | 4 | 17 | 0 | 0 | 8 | 0 | 4.26 |
| Oldham, Modesto | 28 | 19 | 8 | 3 | 12 | 5 | 0 | .706 | 154 | 155 | 79 | 53 | 10 | 58 | 3 | 2 | 74 | 6 | 3.10 |
| Oliva, Salinas | 6 | 6 | 0 | 0 | 1 | 0 | 0 | 1.000 | 13 | 18 | 12 | 9 | 1 | 16 | 0 | 1 | 15 | 2 | 6.23 |
| Owens, Modesto | 2 | 2 | 0 | 0 | 1 | 1 | 0 | .500 | 12 | 14 | 12 | 12 | 1 | 12 | 0 | 0 | 8 | 1 | 9.00 |
| Pagnozzi, Lodi* | 25 | 25 | 4 | 0 | 7 | 12 | 0 | .368 | 153 | 133 | 90 | 75 | 8 | 95 | 1 | 6 | 111 | 10 | 4.41 |
| Peach, Lodi* | 6 | 6 | 3 | 1 | 4 | 0 | 0 | 1.000 | 47 | 30 | 15 | 13 | 5 | 15 | 0 | 1 | 47 | 0 | 2.49 |
| Peregud, Modesto | 17 | 12 | 2 | 0 | 4 | 6 | 0 | .400 | 82 | 90 | 57 | 46 | 8 | 37 | 2 | 1 | 53 | 6 | 5.05 |
| Plank, Fresno | 28 | 26 | 15 | 3 | 17 | 7 | 0 | .708 | 195 | 185 | 70 | 49 | 5 | 42 | 1 | 3 | 97 | 4 | 2.26 |
| Prewitt, Visalia | 17 | 16 | 7 | 1 | 9 | 6 | 0 | .600 | 111 | 99 | 59 | 45 | 4 | 80 | 6 | 2 | 110 | 11 | 3.65 |
| Prichard, Salinas | 6 | 3 | 0 | 0 | 2 | 1 | 0 | .667 | 18 | 16 | 9 | 8 | 1 | 11 | 0 | 0 | 15 | 2 | 4.00 |
| Quiros, Lodi | 49 | 0 | 0 | 0 | 6 | 8 | 6 | .429 | 88 | 96 | 51 | 38 | 5 | 40 | 3 | 2 | 63 | 4 | 3.89 |
| Rehn, Reno | 46 | 0 | 0 | 0 | 7 | 7 | 9 | .500 | 76 | 64 | 34 | 24 | 3 | 36 | 9 | 2 | 55 | 4 | 2.84 |
| Reid, San Jose* | 6 | 0 | 0 | 0 | 1 | 1 | 0 | .500 | 8 | 17 | 9 | 8 | 0 | 9 | 1 | 0 | 3 | 3 | 9.00 |
| Reimann, Lodi | 6 | 1 | 0 | 0 | 1 | 0 | 0 | 1.000 | 11 | 15 | 14 | 8 | 0 | 8 | 1 | 1 | 8 | 2 | 6.55 |

| Pitcher—Club | G. | GS. | CG. | ShO. | W. | L. | Sv. | Pct. | IP. | H. | R. | ER. | HR. | BB. | Int. BB. | HB. | SO. | WP. | ERA. |
|---|---|---|---|---|---|---|---|---|---|---|---|---|---|---|---|---|---|---|---|
| Roberts, Fresno .25 | 18 | 7 | 0 | | 5 | 13 | 0 | .278 | 142 | 123 | 77 | 62 | 8 | 55 | 2 | 6 | 111 | 13 | 3.93 |
| Rondon, Salinas .29 | 3 | 1 | 0 | | 6 | 1 | 1 | .857 | 82 | 63 | 28 | 24 | 2 | 40 | 0 | 3 | 84 | 5 | 2.63 |
| Rowland, Fresno . 9 | 8 | 2 | 1 | | 3 | 1 | 0 | .750 | 57 | 46 | 26 | 16 | 4 | 21 | 0 | 0 | 50 | 2 | 2.53 |
| Salas, Modesto ..26 | 18 | 6 | 0 | | 7 | 10 | 0 | .412 | 123 | 136 | 93 | 68 | 12 | 51 | 5 | 0 | 77 | 7 | 4.98 |
| Sander, Visalia . 9 | 9 | 3 | 1 | | 6 | 1 | 0 | .857 | 60 | 63 | 28 | 26 | 3 | 25 | 1 | 2 | 32 | 1 | 3.90 |
| Sapp, Modesto ...33 | 5 | 0 | 0 | | 7 | 3 | 3 | .700 | 75 | 92 | 51 | 44 | 9 | 38 | 3 | 2 | 35 | 3 | 5.28 |
| Saulnier, S J* ...12 | 5 | 0 | 0 | | 0 | 2 | 0 | .000 | 31 | 36 | 34 | 19 | 3 | 28 | 1 | 1 | 14 | 2 | 5.52 |
| Scarcella, Fresno .25 | 13 | 3 | 0 | | 3 | 4 | 0 | .429 | 104 | 115 | 78 | 61 | 6 | 89 | 1 | 5 | 56 | 14 | 5.28 |
| Shirley, Bak* ...24 | 24 | 6 | 1 | | 8 | 9 | 0 | .471 | 154 | 162 | 95 | 67 | 9 | 84 | 1 | 4 | 107 | 14 | 3.92 |
| Sielicki, Fresno* .10 | 0 | 0 | 0 | | 2 | 1 | 3 | .667 | 18 | 14 | 6 | 6 | 4 | 0 | 0 | 0 | 17 | 3 | 3.00 |
| Slocum, Bak ....35 | 12 | 3 | 1 | | 7 | 7 | 3 | .500 | 111 | 120 | 86 | 63 | 3 | 83 | 1 | 5 | 108 | 7 | 5.11 |
| Smith, Salinas* .13 | 12 | 1 | 0 | | 3 | 8 | 0 | .273 | 67 | 76 | 45 | 33 | 7 | 21 | 3 | 7 | 29 | 4 | 4.43 |
| Snider, Bak ....20 | 0 | 0 | 0 | | 5 | 4 | 2 | .556 | 35 | 35 | 12 | 10 | 1 | 13 | 2 | 2 | 13 | 1 | 2.57 |
| Sorensen, S J .... 5 | 4 | 0 | 0 | | 1 | 2 | 0 | .333 | 21 | 30 | 18 | 16 | 2 | 20 | 0 | 0 | 13 | 2 | 6.86 |
| Staniland, Mod . 6 | 6 | 1 | 1 | | 2 | 2 | 0 | .500 | 41 | 29 | 25 | 15 | 1 | 25 | 1 | 1 | 35 | 6 | 3.29 |
| Stumpp, Salinas .15 | 14 | 3 | 2 | | 5 | 6 | 0 | .455 | 96 | 89 | 45 | 37 | 2 | 37 | 2 | 1 | 65 | 1 | 3.47 |
| Sutcliffe, Bak ...28 | 28 | 10 | 0 | | 8 | 16 | 0 | .333 | 193 | 214 | 115 | 89 | 9 | 68 | 8 | 6 | 91 | 6 | 4.15 |
| Tallman, Fresno .19 | 16 | 6 | 2 | | 8 | 7 | 0 | .533 | 109 | 108 | 65 | 47 | 4 | 54 | 0 | 0 | 68 | 17 | 3.88 |
| Todd, Bakersfield .38 | 2 | 0 | 0 | | 8 | 2 | 5 | .800 | 87 | 79 | 35 | 33 | 5 | 35 | 4 | 8 | 68 | 5 | 3.41 |
| Tuttle, Modesto . 8 | 1 | 0 | 0 | | 1 | 1 | 0 | .500 | 20 | 26 | 16 | 13 | 1 | 16 | 0 | 0 | 12 | 3 | 5.85 |
| Vaughn, San Jose . 2 | 0 | 0 | 0 | | 0 | 0 | 0 | .000 | 3 | 5 | 3 | 3 | 1 | 0 | | 0 | 1 | 2 | 9.00 |
| Walker, Lodi ....21 | 0 | 0 | 0 | | 4 | 2 | 6 | .667 | 30 | 27 | 15 | 12 | 2 | 16 | 4 | 0 | 26 | 1 | 3.60 |
| Ward, Lodi .....13 | 13 | 7 | 2 | | 8 | 3 | 0 | .727 | 92 | 84 | 36 | 32 | 4 | 16 | 1 | 3 | 81 | 2 | 3.13 |
| Washko, San Jose 1 | 0 | 0 | 0 | | 0 | 0 | 0 | .000 | 5 | 5 | 4 | 0 | 0 | 0 | | 1 | 7 | 0 | 0.00 |
| Weimers, Lodi ...37 | 3 | 0 | 0 | | 4 | 6 | 4 | .400 | 83 | 99 | 65 | 52 | 5 | 33 | 5 | 4 | 52 | 3 | 5.64 |
| Wells, Reno* ....13 | 0 | 0 | 0 | | 0 | 0 | 0 | .000 | 23 | 25 | 12 | 12 | 1 | 15 | 0 | 0 | 13 | 2 | 4.70 |
| Werd, San Jose* .13 | 7 | 0 | 0 | | 7 | 3 | 0 | .700 | 104 | 85 | 35 | 25 | 3 | 25 | 3 | 2 | 75 | 1 | 2.16 |
| Whiteley, Salinas. 15 | 9 | 2 | 1 | | 5 | 4 | 1 | .556 | 66 | 65 | 30 | 25 | 3 | 23 | 4 | 3 | 84 | 2 | 3.41 |
| Wibberley, Mod .56 | 0 | 0 | 0 | | 7 | 9 | 10 | .438 | 99 | 101 | 48 | 33 | 3 | 46 | 15 | 1 | 65 | 6 | 3.00 |
| Widner, San Jose* .24 | 17 | 3 | 1 | | 6 | 8 | 1 | .429 | 102 | 90 | 56 | 42 | 1 | 73 | 1 | 1 | 57 | 10 | 3.71 |
| Wihtol, San Jose .15 | 6 | 0 | 0 | | 1 | 7 | 0 | .125 | 58 | 74 | 46 | 38 | 8 | 30 | 2 | 2 | 43 | 3 | 5.90 |
| Williams, Modesto 11 | 11 | 3 | 1 | | 2 | 3 | 0 | .400 | 67 | 76 | 40 | 26 | 2 | 22 | 3 | 2 | 37 | 0 | 3.49 |
| Wojcik, Visalia* .23 | 23 | 11 | 2 | | 11 | 7 | 0 | .611 | 157 | 181 | 71 | 56 | 10 | 41 | 1 | 0 | 114 | 2 | 3.21 |
| Woodruff, S J* ..43 | 9 | 3 | 1 | | 6 | 7 | 8 | .462 | 130 | 139 | 71 | 49 | 9 | 60 | 3 | 1 | 104 | 7 | 3.39 |
| Wouters, Bak ...24 | 13 | 0 | 0 | | 1 | 8 | 1 | .111 | 100 | 124 | 92 | 69 | 7 | 76 | 0 | 5 | 80 | 10 | 6.21 |
| Wright, Salinas* .24 | 0 | 0 | 0 | | 4 | 3 | 4 | .571 | 39 | 34 | 14 | 10 | 1 | 13 | 0 | 0 | 37 | 1 | 2.31 |
| Zail, Reno ......15 | 10 | 5 | 1 | | 7 | 1 | 0 | .875 | 74 | 78 | 42 | 39 | 7 | 45 | 4 | 1 | 60 | 9 | 4.74 |
| Zoss, Modesto* .23 | 10 | 4 | 1 | | 6 | 6 | 0 | .500 | 106 | 111 | 72 | 64 | 10 | 72 | 4 | 6 | 63 | 11 | 5.43 |

BALKS—Melson, 6; Anderson, Pagnozzi, 5 each; Darr, 4; Davidson, Garvin, Gibbon, Litle, Peregud, Sutcliffe, Walker, Widner, Woodruff, Zoss, 3 each; Bell, Flores, Garcia (Lodi), Greenfield, Klein, Lacki, Lysander, O'Brien, Sander, Wibberley, 2 each; Arnold, Ausman, Bolden, Bovee, Butler, Califano, Cochran, Cody, Duncan, Eichelberger, Harts, Harvey, Hayden, Heydeman, Johnson (Lodi), McLaughlin, McNulty, McQueen, Messman, Milke, Neimeyer, Nevarez, Oldham, Oliva, Sapp, Scarcella, Shirley, Stumpp, Tallman, Todd, Ward, Weimers, Wihtol, Wojcik, Wouters, Zail, 1 each.

COMBINATION SHUTOUTS — Carroll-O'Brien, Bakersfield; Plank-McKay, Fresno; Darr-Quiros, Lodi; Cochran-Sapp, Modesto; Burns-Bovee, Reno; Frazier-McQueen 2, Frazier-Whiteley, Oliva-Kuhaulua, Smith-Rondon, Salinas; Aronson-Anderson, Prewitt-Butler, Visalia.

NO-HIT GAME—Frazier, Salinas, defeated San Jose, 8-0, July 4 (seven innings).

# *Carolina League*

## CLASS A

### CHAMPIONSHIP WINNERS IN PREVIOUS YEARS

1945—Danville* ......... .681
1946—Greensboro .599
    Raleigh (2nd)† .... .563
1947—Burlington .613
    Raleigh (3rd)† ... .574
1948—Raleigh .592
    Martinsville (2nd)† .570
1949—Danville .601
    Burlington (4th)† .. .500
1950—Winston-Salem* .693
    Wins-Salem (2nd)† .583
1951—Durham .600
    Raleigh .581
    Reidsville (4th)† ... .536
1953—Raleigh .593
    Danville (2nd)† ... .572
1954—Fayetteville* .628
1955—HP-Thomasville .580
    Danville (2nd)† ... .533
1956—HP-Thomasville .591
    Fayetteville (4th)†.. .523

1957—Durham ........... .632
    HP-Thomasville ... .622
1958—Danville .576
    Burlington (4th)† .. .511
1959—Raleigh .600
    Wilson (2nd)† ... .590
1960—Greensboro‡ .636
    Burlington .586
1961—Wilson .594
1962—Durham .636
    Wilson .600
    Kinston (2nd)† ... .593
1963—Kinston§ .538
    Greensboro§ .590
    Wilson (2nd)† .... .535
1964—Kinston§ .572
    Winston-Salem§† .590
1965—Peninsula§ .597
    Durham§ .580
    Tidewater† .528

1966—Kinston§ .......... .547
    Winston-Salem§ ... .586
    Rocky Mount† ..... .533
1967—Durham x (West.) ... .536
    Raleigh (East.) .... .542
1968—Salem (West.) .... .607
    Ral-Dur (East.) ... .597
    H P-Thom. y (W.) .493
1969—Rocky M (East.) ... .569
    Salem (West.) .... .542
    Ral-Dur z (East.) ... .560
1970—Winston-Salem‡ ... .586
    Burlington .597
1971—Peninsula‡ ........ .647
    Kinston .623
1972—Salem‡ ........... .657
    Burlington .632
1973—Lynchburg .588
    Winston-Salem .557
1974—Salem .671
    Salem ............. .582

*Won championship and four-club playoff. †Won four-club playoff. ‡Won split-season playoff. §League was divided into Eastern. Western divisions. xWon eight-club, two-division playoff. yWon eight-club, two-division playoff against Raleigh-Durham. zWon eight-club, two-division playoff against Burlington.

### STANDING OF CLUBS AT CLOSE OF FIRST HALF, JUNE 19

| Club | W. | L. | T. | Pct. | G.B. | Club | W. | L. | T. | Pct. | G.B. |
|---|---|---|---|---|---|---|---|---|---|---|---|
| Rocky Mount (Phillies) .. | 48 | 24 | 0 | .667 | .... | Salem (Pirates) ........ | 33 | 36 | 1 | .478 | 13½ |
| Winston-Salem (Red Sox) | 44 | 27 | 1 | .620 | 3½ | Lynchburg (Rangers) ... | 30 | 36 | 0 | .455 | 15 |

### STANDING OF CLUBS AT CLOSE OF SECOND HALF, AUGUST 28

| Club | W. | L. | T. | Pct. | G.B. | Club | W. | L. | T. | Pct. | G.B. |
|---|---|---|---|---|---|---|---|---|---|---|---|
| Rocky Mount (Phillies) .. | 43 | 27 | 0 | .614 | .... | Winston-Salem (Red Sox) | 37 | 35 | 0 | .514 | 7 |
| Salem (Pirates) ........ | 41 | 30 | 0 | .577 | 2½ | Lynchburg (Rangers) ... | 30 | 42 | 0 | .417 | 14 |

### FINAL STANDING OF CAROLINA LEAGUE VS. WESTERN CAROLINAS LEAGUE

| Club | W. | L. | T. | Pct. | G.B. | Club | W. | L. | T. | Pct. | G.B. |
|---|---|---|---|---|---|---|---|---|---|---|---|
| Rocky Mount (Phillies) .. | 38 | 8 | 0 | .826 | .... | Lynchburg (Rangers) .... | 19 | 24 | 0 | .442 | 17½ |
| Winston-Salem (Red Sox) | 31 | 16 | 0 | .660 | 7½ | Anderson (Rangers) W/C.. | 18 | 26 | 0 | .409 | 19 |
| Salem (Pirates) ......... | 27 | 18 | 0 | .600 | 10½ | Greenwood (Braves) W/C | 16 | 29 | 0 | .356 | 21½ |
| Spartanburg (Phillies) W/C | 21 | 25 | 0 | .457 | 17 | Charleston (Pirates) W/C | 11 | 35 | 0 | .239 | 27 |

### COMPOSITE STANDINGS OF CLUBS AT CLOSE OF SEASON, AUGUST 28

| Club | R.M. | W.-S. | Sal. | Lyn. | Spa. | And. | Gwd. | Cha. | W. | L. | T. | Pct. | G.B. |
|---|---|---|---|---|---|---|---|---|---|---|---|---|---|
| Rocky Mount (Phillies) .... | .. | 17 | 20 | 16 | 10 | 9 | 9 | 10 | 91 | 51 | 0 | .641 | .... |
| Winston-Salem (Red Sox) .. | 15 | .. | 17 | 18 | 5 | 7 | 9 | 10 | 81 | 62 | 1 | .566 | 10½ |
| Salem (Pirates) ........... | 12 | 15 | .. | 20 | 6 | 7 | 4 | 10 | 74 | 66 | 1 | .529 | 16 |
| Lynchburg (Rangers) ...... | 16 | 14 | 11 | .. | 4 | 3 | 7 | 5 | 60 | 78 | 0 | .435 | 29 |
| Spartanburg (Phillies) ..... | 2 | 7 | 5 | 7 | .. | 19 | 18 | 23 | 81 | 59 | 0 | .579 | .. |
| Anderson (Rangers) ....... | 3 | 4 | 4 | 7 | 11 | .. | 17 | 21 | 67 | 70 | 0 | .489 | 12½ |
| Greenwood (Braves) ...... | 1 | 3 | .7 | 5 | 14 | 15 | .. | 17 | 62 | 79 | 0 | .440 | 19½ |
| Charleston (Pirates) ...... | 2 | 2 | 2 | 5 | 9 | 10 | 15 | .. | 45 | 96 | 0 | .319 | 36½ |

Major league affiliations in parentheses.

NOTE: Forfeited Game—Spartanburg (WCL) forfeited to Winston-Salem, June 12 at Winston-Salem.

Managers: Lynchburg—Wayne Terwilliger; Rocky Mount—Cal Emery; Salem—John Lipon; Winston-Salem—John Kennedy.

Regular-Season Attendance—Lynchburg, 28,527; Rocky Mount, 24,345; Salem, 39,007; Winston-Salem, 38,226. Total, 130,105. All-Star Game, 459. No playoff.

All-Star Team: 1B—Poff, Rocky Mount; 2B—Doyle, Lynchburg; Gerlecz, Salem; 3B—Morrison, Rocky Mount; SS—Albert, Lynchburg; OF—Wrenn, Salem; Thompson, Lynchburg; Berg, Winston-Salem; Louis, Salem; C—Tarbell, Winston-Salem; P—Bradford, Lynchburg; Jones, Winston-Salem; Brusstar, Rocky Mount; Manager—Emery, Rocky Mount.

(Compiled by Howe News Bureau, Chicago, Ill.)

## CLUB BATTING

| Club | G. | AB. | R. | OR. | H. | TR. | 2B. | 3B. | HR. | RBI. | SH. | SF. | Int. BB. | BB. | HP. | SO. | SB. | CS. | LOB. | Pct. |
|------|----|----|----|----|----|----|----|----|----|----|----|----|----|----|----|----|----|----|----|----|
| Win-Salem | 144 | 4595 | 681 | 563 | 1189 | 1582 | 168 | 48 | 43 | 563 | 126 | 46 | 647 | 30 | 23 | 571 | 136 | 62 | 1082 | .259 |
| Salem | 141 | 4406 | 651 | 592 | 1131 | 1604 | 169 | 38 | 76 | 555 | 79 | 49 | 589 | 37 | 32 | 649 | 127 | 62 | 998 | .257 |
| Rocky Mt | 142 | 4476 | 677 | 5?8 | 1123 | 1635 | 192 | 49 | 74 | 578 | 35 | 52 | 605 | 45 | 38 | 807 | 134 | 44 | 939 | .251 |
| Lynchburg | 138 | 4322 | 579 | 686 | 1045 | 1381 | 161 | 29 | 39 | 496 | 37 | 46 | 719 | 42 | 43 | 746 | 162 | 63 | 1072 | .242 |

## INDIVIDUAL BATTING

### (Leading Qualifiers for Batting Championship—389 or More Plate Appearances)

*Bats lefthanded.　†Switch-hitter.

| Player and Club | G. | AB. | R. | H. | TB. | 2B. | 3B. | HR. | RBI. | SH. | SF. | BB. | HP. | SO. | SB. | CS. | Pct. |
|------|----|----|----|----|----|----|----|----|----|----|----|----|----|----|----|----|----|
| Cox, W. Ted, W. S. .....137 | 137 | 505 | 63 | 154 | 217 | 23 | 5 | 10 | 80 | 5 | 4 | 62 | 2 | 63 | 4 | 7 | .305 |
| Thompson, Bobby, Lynch† | 119 | 429 | 87 | 128 | 173 | 19 | 10 | 2 | 43 | 7 | 4 | 91 | 4 | 67 | 65 | 15 | .298 |
| Wrenn, Luther, Salem ....133 | 133 | 454 | 76 | 133 | 203 | 22 | 6 | 12 | 97 | 0 | 5 | 86 | 1 | 49 | 11 | 3 | .293 |
| Berg, Richard, Win-Salem* | 111 | 342 | 72 | 99 | 124 | 14 | 4 | 1 | 40 | 15 | 1 | 69 | 1 | 33 | 17 | 8 | .289 |
| Morrison, James, Rocky Mt | 140 | 497 | 98 | 143 | 239 | 24 | 6 | 20 | 88 | 5 | 6 | 65 | 6 | 80 | 22 | 6 | .288 |
| Hughes, John D., Rocky Mt | 115 | 398 | 58 | 113 | 176 | 30 | 3 | 9 | 67 | 5 | 7 | 52 | 0 | 63 | 6 | 3 | .284 |
| Albert, Richard, Lynchburg | 105 | 349 | 62 | 98 | 127 | 23 | 0 | 2 | 53 | 5 | 7 | 78 | 6 | 53 | 11 | 3 | .281 |
| Gerlecz, Steven, Salem ....109 | 109 | 340 | 54 | 95 | 139 | 11 | 0 | 11 | 47 | 13 | 4 | 52 | 5 | 52 | 10 | 8 | .279 |
| McClure, Paul, Win-Salem* | 110 | 346 | 54 | 93 | 123 | 14 | 5 | 2 | 41 | 6 | 1 | 55 | 2 | 53 | 2 | 5 | .269 |
| Hargis, Gary, Salem ......134 | 134 | 485 | 66 | 130 | 165 | 27 | 1 | 2 | 53 | 11 | 6 | 20 | 4 | 44 | 17 | 6 | .268 |

**DEPARTMENTAL LEADERS:** G—Harer, Reilly, 144; AB—Harer, 527; R—Morrison, 98; H—Cox, 154; TB—Morrison, 239; 2B—Hughes, 30; 3B—Louis, Thompson, 10; HR—Morrison, 20; RBI—Wrenn, 97; SH—Reilly, 19; SF—Krsnich, Thomas, 8; BB—Barrow, 97; HB—Marshall, Reilly, 9; SO—Peltier, 112; SB—Thompson, 65; CS—Barrow, 19.

### (All Players—Listed Alphabetically)

| Player and Club | G. | AB. | R. | H. | TB. | 2B. | 3B. | HR. | RBI. | SH. | SF. | BB. | HP. | SO. | SB. | CS. | Pct. |
|------|----|----|----|----|----|----|----|----|----|----|----|----|----|----|----|----|----|
| Albert, Richard, Lynchburg | 105 | 349 | 62 | 98 | 127 | 23 | 0 | 2 | 53 | 5 | 7 | 78 | 6 | 53 | 11 | 3 | .281 |
| Anderson, Billy, Rocky Mt .42 | 42 | 100 | 13 | 22 | 30 | 3 | 1 | 1 | 13 | 2 | 1 | 22 | 0 | 21 | 1 | 0 | .220 |
| Angell, Larry, Salem ....... | 2 | 3 | 0 | 0 | 0 | 0 | 0 | 0 | 0 | 0 | 0 | 0 | 0 | 2 | 0 | 0 | .000 |
| Arnett, G. Curtiss, Lynch*.. | 90 | 252 | 30 | 53 | 60 | 3 | 2 | 0 | 14 | 3 | 2 | 29 | 3 | 44 | 13 | 5 | .210 |
| Baker, Henry, Winston-Salem | 89 | 276 | 42 | 74 | 104 | 12 | 6 | 2 | 31 | 6 | 2 | 32 | 0 | 35 | 12 | 3 | .268 |
| Ban, George, Lynchburg ... | 88 | 235 | 20 | 48 | 65 | 11 | 0 | 2 | 34 | 1 | 2 | 44 | 4 | 63 | 2 | 1 | .204 |
| Barrow, Melvin, Lynchburg | 120 | 396 | 67 | 100 | 134 | 19 | 3 | 3 | 40 | 5 | 3 | 97 | 4 | 56 | 31 | 19 | .253 |
| Berg, Richard, Win-Salem* | 111 | 342 | 72 | 99 | 124 | 14 | 4 | 1 | 40 | 15 | 1 | 69 | 1 | 33 | 17 | 8 | .289 |
| Blomberg, Steven R., Salem | 93 | 337 | 52 | 86 | 140 | 11 | 5 | 11 | 34 | 4 | 3 | 16 | 2 | 63 | 18 | 5 | .255 |
| Burgoon, Richard, Salem ... | 1 | 1 | 0 | 0 | 0 | 0 | 0 | 0 | 0 | 0 | 0 | 0 | 0 | 0 | 0 | 0 | .000 |
| Byrd, Leland, Lynchburg .. | 18 | 53 | 2 | 4 | 4 | 0 | 0 | 0 | 1 | 0 | 0 | 5 | 1 | 10 | 0 | 0 | .075 |
| Carey, Paul, Rocky Mount.. | 9 | 22 | 2 | 4 | 4 | 0 | 0 | 0 | 1 | 1 | 0 | 5 | 1 | 10 | 0 | 0 | .182 |
| Cole, Winston, Salem* ....105 | 105 | 333 | 55 | 81 | 111 | 17 | 2 | 3 | 30 | 4 | 2 | 69 | 1 | 27 | 9 | 10 | .243 |
| Cox, W. Ted, Win-Salem. .137 | 137 | 505 | 63 | 154 | 217 | 23 | 5 | 10 | 80 | 5 | 4 | 62 | 2 | 63 | 4 | 7 | .305 |
| Cruz, Pablo, Salem ........ | 96 | 346 | 45 | 98 | 109 | 7 | 2 | 0 | 34 | 9 | 3 | 28 | 2 | 21 | 4 | 3 | .283 |
| Cruz, Todd, Rocky Mount .134 | 134 | 453 | 57 | 92 | 150 | 23 | 1 | 11 | 67 | 2 | 5 | 35 | 8 | 101 | 9 | 4 | .203 |
| de Armas, Rolando, Rocky Mt | 29 | 79 | 10 | 22 | 26 | 4 | 0 | 0 | 5 | 0 | 1 | 10 | 1 | 6 | 1 | 0 | .278 |
| Delgado, Luis, Win-Salem* | 104 | 389 | 63 | 100 | 122 | 11 | 4 | 1 | 31 | 11 | 2 | 33 | 2 | 53 | 40 | 12 | .257 |
| Diaz, Baudilio, Win-Salem | 59 | 179 | 22 | 47 | 75 | 8 | 1 | 6 | 29 | 3 | 2 | 18 | 0 | 16 | 0 | 1 | .263 |
| Dinzey, Amado, Lynchburg | 79 | 264 | 24 | 63 | 77 | 10 | 2 | 0 | 19 | 0 | 0 | 18 | 2 | 58 | 8 | 1 | .239 |
| Doyle, Brian, Lynchburg*..107 | 107 | 369 | 41 | 88 | 101 | 4 | 3 | 1 | 37 | 3 | 4 | 42 | 1 | 20 | 6 | 2 | .238 |
| Duran, Daniel, Lynchburg*.. | 68 | 258 | 36 | 63 | 88 | 9 | 2 | 4 | 41 | 0 | 2 | 26 | 1 | 59 | 3 | 4 | .244 |
| Dusenbury, John, Salem ... | 73 | 219 | 19 | 50 | 64 | 8 | 0 | 2 | 25 | 3 | 1 | 13 | 0 | 19 | 4 | 0 | .228 |
| Erardi, J. Gregory, Salem ... | 1 | 0 | 0 | 0 | 0 | 0 | 0 | 0 | 0 | 0 | 0 | 0 | 0 | 0 | 0 | 0 | .000 |
| Fahey, William J., W-Salem | 89 | 252 | 48 | 69 | 92 | 6 | 1 | 5 | 31 | 5 | 4 | 57 | 0 | 39 | 7 | 0 | .274 |
| Gardner, Gerald, Rocky Mt | 84 | 294 | 51 | 81 | 114 | 13 | 4 | 4 | 30 | 5 | 4 | 39 | 3 | 51 | 11 | 4 | .276 |
| Geigel, German, Rocky Mt* | 70 | 181 | 21 | 40 | 50 | 4 | 3 | 0 | 18 | 2 | 2 | 22 | 1 | 44 | 8 | 5 | .221 |
| Gerlecz, Steven, Salem .....109 | 109 | 340 | 54 | 95 | 139 | 11 | 0 | 11 | 47 | 13 | 4 | 52 | 5 | 52 | 10 | 8 | .279 |
| Gonzalez, Ernest, Rocky Mt | 122 | 456 | 54 | 114 | 150 | 14 | 8 | 2 | 39 | 3 | 7 | 48 | 2 | 57 | 23 | 4 | .250 |
| Guarnaccia, John, R Mt* .119 | 119 | 344 | 70 | 81 | 130 | 17 | 4 | 8 | 55 | 0 | 6 | 86 | 7 | 97 | 13 | 5 | .235 |
| Gunter, Chester, Salem ..... | 4 | 0 | 1 | 0 | 0 | 0 | 0 | 0 | 0 | 0 | 0 | 0 | 0 | 0 | 0 | 0 | .000 |
| Hall, John, Salem ......... | 1 | 0 | 0 | 0 | 0 | 0 | 0 | 0 | 0 | 0 | 0 | 0 | 0 | 0 | 0 | 0 | .000 |
| Hammond, Charles, Lynch.† | 2 | 6 | 0 | 0 | 0 | 0 | 0 | 0 | 0 | 0 | 0 | 0 | 0 | 1 | 0 | 0 | .000 |
| Harer, Wayne, Win-Salem† | 144 | 527 | 86 | 137 | 166 | 13 | 8 | 0 | 53 | 18 | 7 | 92 | 0 | 46 | 23 | 8 | .260 |
| Hargis, Gary, Salem ......134 | 134 | 485 | 66 | 130 | 165 | 27 | 1 | 2 | 53 | 11 | 6 | 20 | 4 | 44 | 17 | 6 | .268 |
| Hicks, Lawrence, Rocky Mt* | 29 | 39 | 5 | 4 | 5 | 1 | 0 | 0 | 3 | 1 | 0 | 2 | 0 | 10 | 2 | 0 | .103 |
| Hughes, John D., Rocky Mt | 115 | 398 | 58 | 113 | 176 | 30 | 3 | 9 | 67 | 5 | 7 | 52 | 0 | 63 | 6 | 3 | .284 |
| Jefferson, Milton, Win-Salem | 37 | 113 | 13 | 33 | 48 | 5 | 2 | 2 | 23 | 1 | 2 | 9 | 0 | 13 | 0 | 1 | .292 |
| Johnson, Jerome, Lynchburg | 1 | 0 | 0 | 0 | 0 | 0 | 0 | 0 | 0 | 0 | 0 | 1 | 0 | 0 | 0 | 0 | .000 |
| Johnson, William M., Lynch | 83 | 239 | 26 | 50 | 55 | 3 | 0 | 0 | 16 | 0 | 0 | 41 | 4 | 27 | 1 | 3 | .209 |
| Klass, Robert, Win.-Salem.. | 1 | 0 | 0 | 0 | 0 | 0 | 0 | 0 | 0 | 0 | 0 | 0 | 0 | 0 | 0 | 0 | .000 |
| Krsnich, Joseph, Win-Salem* | 114 | 372 | 53 | 87 | 128 | 20 | 3 | 5 | 52 | 12 | 8 | 73 | 3 | 40 | 5 | 5 | .234 |
| Long, Robert, Lynchburg* .. | 45 | 126 | 17 | 23 | 36 | 5 | 1 | 2 | 14 | 3 | 2 | 9 | 1 | 23 | 1 | 0 | .183 |
| Louis, Alberto, Salem ....... | 83 | 295 | 51 | 89 | 137 | 7 | 10 | 7 | 33 | 7 | 3 | 40 | 2 | 70 | 24 | 9 | .302 |
| Marshall, David, Salem ...107 | 107 | 301 | 35 | 75 | 90 | 10 | 1 | 1 | 30 | 10 | 7 | 52 | 9 | 19 | 1 | 2 | .249 |
| Martin, J. Michael, Rocky Mt* | 8 | 21 | 1 | 3 | 3 | 0 | 0 | 0 | 0 | 0 | 0 | 0 | 0 | 10 | 0 | 1 | .143 |
| McClure, Paul, Win-Salem* | 110 | 346 | 54 | 93 | 123 | 14 | 5 | 2 | 41 | 6 | 1 | 55 | 2 | 53 | 2 | 5 | .269 |
| McMahon, Edward, Win-Sal | 94 | 284 | 42 | 61 | 74 | 8 | 1 | 1 | 32 | 5 | 6 | 34 | 2 | 48 | 7 | 2 | .215 |
| Medick, Jack, Win-Salem .. | 15 | 38 | 2 | 4 | 6 | 0 | 1 | 0 | 4 | 2 | 0 | 1 | 0 | 14 | 1 | 1 | .105 |
| Miller, Kenneth, Lynchburg. | 1 | 1 | 0 | 0 | 0 | 0 | 0 | 0 | 0 | 0 | 0 | 0 | 0 | 0 | 0 | 0 | .000 |

| Player and Club | G. | AB. | R. | H. | TB. | 2B. | 3B. | HR. | RBI. | SH. | SF. | BB. | HP. | SO. | SB. | CS. | Pct. |
|---|---|---|---|---|---|---|---|---|---|---|---|---|---|---|---|---|---|
| Morrison, James, Rocky Mt.. | 140 | 497 | 98 | 143 | 239 | 24 | 6 | 20 | 88 | 5 | 6 | 65 | 6 | 80 | 22 | 6 | .288 |
| Nakamoto, Brian, Lynchburg | 120 | 370 | 47 | 89 | 136 | 15 | 1 | 10 | 53 | 1 | 7 | 93 | 3 | 97 | 5 | 2 | .241 |
| Neal, Joseph, Salem* .... | 1 | 0 | 0 | 0 | 0 | 0 | 0 | 0 | 0 | 0 | 0 | 0 | 0 | 0 | 0 | 0 | .000 |
| Nelson, Paul, Salem* ..... | 115 | 367 | 61 | 85 | 120 | 14 | 3 | 5 | 42 | 5 | 4 | 51 | 2 | 63 | 7 | 7 | .232 |
| Oliveros, Eudaldo, Rocky Mt | 94 | 286 | 40 | 75 | 102 | 14 | 5 | 1 | 31 | 3 | 4 | 41 | 0 | 55 | 6 | 2 | .262 |
| Olson, Terry, Lynchburg* .. | 8 | 25 | 1 | 7 | 7 | 0 | 0 | 0 | 4 | 0 | 0 | 3 | 0 | 4 | 1 | 0 | .280 |
| Peltier, Dwayne, Sal ..... | 127 | 413 | 68 | 101 | 169 | 20 | 3 | 14 | 68 | 4 | 6 | 88 | 2 | 112 | 11 | 4 | .245 |
| Poff, John, Rocky Mount*.. | 127 | 445 | 76 | 119 | 175 | 20 | 6 | 8 | 62 | 1 | 6 | 83 | 4 | 77 | 9 | 4 | .267 |
| Prazych, Thomas, Salem ... | 81 | 199 | 25 | 43 | 63 | 5 | 0 | 5 | 24 | 1 | 1 | 20 | 1 | 50 | 2 | 1 | .216 |
| Putnam, Patrick, Lynch* .. | 44 | 158 | 15 | 35 | 57 | 7 | 0 | 5 | 22 | 2 | 2 | 10 | 1 | 20 | 0 | 0 | .222 |
| Ramer, Stephen, Rocky Mount | 8 | 17 | 3 | 2 | 6 | 0 | 2 | 0 | 1 | 0 | 0 | 2 | 0 | 7 | 0 | 0 | .118 |
| Reilly, Charles W-Salem .. | 144 | 429 | 61 | 105 | 136 | 13 | 3 | 4 | 58 | 19 | 5 | 67 | 9 | 60 | 11 | 5 | .245 |
| Robinson, Stephen, Rocky Mt | 1 | 0 | 0 | 0 | 0 | 0 | 0 | 0 | 0 | 0 | 0 | 0 | 0 | 0 | 0 | 0 | .000 |
| Rockhill, Ronald, Lynchburg | 15 | 39 | 2 | 6 | 8 | 2 | 0 | 0 | 5 | 1 | 1 | 5 | 0 | 14 | 0 | 0 | .154 |
| Rodriguez, Felix, Salem* .. | 87 | 250 | 33 | 56 | 78 | 8 | 4 | 2 | 25 | 5 | 3 | 42 | 0 | 36 | 6 | 3 | .224 |
| Rodriguez, Gerardo, Salem.. | 16 | 44 | 4 | 7 | 12 | 2 | 0 | 1 | 4 | 1 | 1 | 7 | 1 | 12 | 0 | 1 | .159 |
| Salter, Robert, Rocky Mt... | 17 | 46 | 7 | 17 | 20 | 3 | 0 | 0 | 7 | 0 | 2 | 3 | 0 | 2 | 1 | 0 | .370 |
| Scurry, Rodney, Salem* .... | 1 | 1 | 0 | 0 | 0 | 0 | 0 | 0 | 0 | 0 | 0 | 0 | 0 | 0 | 0 | 0 | .000 |
| Silveira, Larry, Rocky Mt... | 91 | 259 | 28 | 55 | 72 | 10 | 2 | 1 | 23 | 3 | 0 | 28 | 6 | 55 | 4 | 0 | .212 |
| Skalisky, Roger, Rocky Mt... | 82 | 272 | 43 | 73 | 114 | 10 | 2 | 9 | 39 | 2 | 0 | 30 | 0 | 32 | 5 | 2 | .268 |
| Smith, Glenn, Lynchburg.. | 67 | 174 | 21 | 44 | 47 | 1 | 1 | 0 | 11 | 4 | 1 | 28 | 3 | 26 | 1 | 2 | .253 |
| Sosa, Fausto, Salem ...... | 12 | 20 | 5 | 3 | 5 | 0 | 1 | 0 | 4 | 0 | 1 | 0 | 0 | 5 | 2 | 0 | .150 |
| Tarbell, Steven, Win-Salem | 102 | 318 | 34 | 79 | 112 | 17 | 2 | 4 | 40 | 13 | 2 | 35 | 1 | 28 | 2 | 0 | .248 |
| Thomas, Donald, Lyuchburg | 135 | 489 | 70 | 124 | 176 | 27 | 2 | 7 | 80 | 0 | 8 | 80 | 4 | 90 | 14 | 6 | .254 |
| Thompson, Bobby, Lynch† | 119 | 429 | 87 | 128 | 173 | 19 | 10 | 2 | 43 | 7 | 4 | 91 | 4 | 67 | 65 | 15 | .298 |
| Townsend, Marvin, W-Salem | 75 | 225 | 25 | 47 | 55 | 4 | 2 | 0 | 17 | 5 | 0 | 9 | 1 | 30 | 5 | 4 | .209 |
| Westlake, Thomas, Lynch*... | 37 | 90 | 10 | 22 | 30 | 1 | 2 | 1 | 11 | 1 | 1 | 19 | 1 | 16 | 0 | 0 | .244 |
| Williams, Wayne, Rocky Mt | .90 | 266 | 39 | 63 | 69 | 2 | 2 | 0 | 24 | 1 | 0 | 34 | 0 | 32 | 13 | 5 | .237 |
| Wrenn, Luther, Salem ...... | 133 | 454 | 76 | 133 | 203 | 22 | 6 | 12 | 97 | 0 | 5 | 86 | 1 | 49 | 11 | 3 | .293 |

The following pitchers had no plate appearances primarily through use of designated hitters, listed alphabetically by club, games in parentheses:

LYNCHBURG—Bradford, Larry (24); Buford, Bobby (24); Cuellar, Robert (49); Holman, C. Edward (28); Jones, Lamar (16); Mohme, Larry* (3); Rainbolt, Rayburn (25); Scott, Jeffrey (23); Tanner, Mark* (20).

ROCKY MOUNT—Bell, Oliver* (27); Brenizer, Todd (13); Brusstar, Warren (25); Cates, Steven* (29); Clammachilli, Frank (10); Gregson, Glenn (52); Kirkpatrick, Michael (12); Klein, Mark (13); Kreke, Donald (13); McCoy, Patrick (16); Quiroga, Roger (19); White, Thomas* (26).

SALEM—Brandt, Randy* (7); Burman, Timothy* (3); Davis, Rodney (40); Hagins, William* (49); Martinez, Silvio, (4); Price, Raymond (12); Thomas, Gerard* (26).

WINSTON-SALEM—Aponte, Luis (40); Brayton, Roswell (16); Caldera, V. Jose† (24); Cross, Wilfred (6); Jones, T. Frederick* (17); Newcomer, F. Breen (12); Paxton, Michael (8); Percival, Curran (5); Rainey, Charles (20); Ripley, Allen (25); Suter, W. Burke (25); Vosk, James (20).

GRAND-SLAM HOME RUNS (9): T. Cruz 2; Delgado, Dusenbury, Morrison, Peltier, Poff, Prazych, Skalisky, 1 each.

AWARDED FIRST BASE ON INTEREFENCE (9): Harer 2 (Silveira 2); McClure 2 (Marshall, Stone); Reilly 2 (de Armas, Silveira); Cole (Silveira); Peltier (Hughes); Williams (Ban).

### CLUB FIELDING

| Club | G. | PO. | A. | E. | DP. | PB. | Pct. | Club | G. | PO. | A. | E. | DP. | PB. | Pct. |
|---|---|---|---|---|---|---|---|---|---|---|---|---|---|---|---|
| Lynchburg .... | 138 | 3484 | 1505 | 181 | 124 | 33 | .96499 | Win-Salem ... | 144 | 3699 | 1500 | 192 | 111 | 31 | .96438 |
| Salem ....... | 141 | 3519 | 1469 | 181 | 114 | 17 | .96498 | Rocky Mount.. | 142 | 3595 | 1640 | 215 | 144 | 19 | .961 |

Triple Play—Salem.

### INDIVIDUAL FIELDING

*Throws lefthanded.
#### FIRST BASEMEN

| Player and Club | G. | PO. | A. | E. | DP. | Pct. | Player and Club | G. | PO. | A. | E. | DP. | Pct. |
|---|---|---|---|---|---|---|---|---|---|---|---|---|---|
| F. Rodriguez, Salem* | 19 | 162 | 10 | 0 | 13 | 1.000 | Anderson, Rocky Mt | 23 | 154 | 12 | 2 | 18 | .988 |
| Hughes, Rocky Mount | 1 | 7 | 0 | 0 | 0 | 1.000 | Poff, Rocky Mount* | 124 | 1154 | 72 | 16 | 104 | .987 |
| Nakamoto, Lynchburg | 1 | 1 | 0 | 0 | 0 | 1.000 | Prazych, Salem ... | 8 | 69 | 3 | 1 | 6 | .986 |
| Oliveros, Rocky Mount | 1 | 3 | 0 | 0 | 0 | 1.000 | Arnett, Lynchburg* . | 25 | 210 | 13 | 4 | 14 | .982 |
| Olson, Lynchburg* .. | 1 | 3 | 0 | 0 | 0 | 1.000 | Cruz, Salem ...... | 26 | 169 | 6 | 4 | 13 | .978 |
| Duran, Lynchburg* .. | 67 | 552 | 42 | 4 | 44 | .993 | Thomas, Lynchburg .. | 11 | 76 | 4 | 2 | 10 | .976 |
| COLE, Salem* ....... | 101 | 867 | 45 | 7 | 68 | .992 | Guarnaccia, Rocky Mt* | 3 | 29 | 0 | 1 | 2 | .967 |
| Putnam, Lynchburg .. | 38 | 346 | 22 | 3 | 31 | .992 | de Armas, Rocky Mt | 3 | 16 | 0 | 1 | 2 | .941 |
| Harer, Win-Salem* | 144 | 1282 | 92 | 14 | 87 | .990 | | | | | | | |

Triple Play—F. Rodriguez.

#### SECOND BASEMEN

| Player and Club | G. | PO. | A. | E. | DP. | Pct. | Player and Club | G. | PO. | A. | E. | DP. | Pct. |
|---|---|---|---|---|---|---|---|---|---|---|---|---|---|
| Sosa, Salem ........ | 5 | 2 | 8 | 0 | 0 | 1.000 | W. Johnson, Lynch .. | 15 | 35 | 36 | 2 | 9 | .973 |
| Thomas, Salem .. | 1 | 2 | 1 | 0 | 0 | 1.000 | Cruz, Salem ...... | 48 | 99 | 122 | 7 | 26 | .969 |
| Gonzalez, Rocky Mount | 1 | 1 | 1 | 0 | 1 | 1.000 | Reilly, Win-Salem .. | 144 | 296 | 373 | 27 | 66 | .961 |
| Nakamoto, Lynchburg | 1 | 2 | 0 | 0 | 0 | 1.000 | Williams, Rocky Mt | 83 | 167 | 185 | 16 | 44 | .957 |
| Marshall, Salem .... | 19 | 23 | 54 | 1 | 7 | .987 | Oliveros, Rocky Mount | 69 | 166 | 204 | 18 | 46 | .954 |
| DOYLE, Lynchburg | 101 | 262 | 258 | 14 | 65 | .974 | Smith, Lynchburg .. | 26 | 58 | 62 | 6 | 7 | .952 |

## SECOND BASEMEN—Continued

| Player and Club | G. | PO. | A. | E. | DP. | Pct. | Player and Club | G. | PO. | A. | E. | DP. | Pct. |
|---|---|---|---|---|---|---|---|---|---|---|---|---|---|
| Gerlecz, Salem | 84 | 163 | 184 | 24 | 40 | .935 | Anderson, Rocky Mt | 7 | 9 | 15 | 2 | 5 | .923 |
| McMahon, Win-Salem | 7 | 3 | 10 | 1 | 2 | .929 | McClure, Win-Salem* | 1 | 0 | 0 | 1 | 0 | .000 |
| Triple Play—Cruz. | | | | | | | | | | | | | |

## THIRD BASEMEN

| Player and Club | G. | PO. | A. | E. | DP. | Pct. | Player and Club | G. | PO. | A. | E. | DP. | Pct. |
|---|---|---|---|---|---|---|---|---|---|---|---|---|---|
| Marshall, Salem | 2 | 3 | 4 | 0 | 1 | 1.000 | Peltier, Salem | 127 | 86 | 256 | 23 | 22 | .937 |
| Blomberg, Salem | 1 | 0 | 2 | 0 | 0 | 1.000 | Smith, Lynchburg | 4 | 4 | 10 | 1 | 4 | .933 |
| Nakamoto, Lynchburg | 1 | 0 | 2 | 0 | 0 | 1.000 | Morrison, Rocky Mt | 129 | 119 | 311 | 32 | 35 | .931 |
| Gonzalez, Rocky Mt | 1 | 0 | 1 | 0 | 0 | 1.000 | Oliveros, Rocky Mount | 13 | 12 | 17 | 5 | 3 | .853 |
| THOMAS, Lynchburg | 116 | 118 | 263 | 13 | 27 | .967 | Fahey, Winston-Salem | 7 | 1 | 7 | 3 | 2 | .727 |
| Anderson, Rocky Mt | 9 | 4 | 18 | 1 | 0 | .957 | Townsend, Win-Salem | 2 | 1 | 2 | 2 | 0 | .600 |
| W. Johnson, Lynch | 20 | 10 | 33 | 2 | 5 | .956 | Hargis, Salem | 1 | 0 | 1 | 1 | 0 | .500 |
| Cruz, Salem | 14 | 16 | 26 | 2 | 2 | .955 | Hughes, Rocky Mount | 1 | 0 | 0 | 1 | 0 | .000 |
| Cox, Winston-Salem | 137 | 125 | 287 | 25 | 27 | .943 | | | | | | | |

## SHORTSTOPS

| Player and Club | G. | PO. | A. | E. | DP. | Pct. | Player and Club | G. | PO. | A. | E. | DP. | Pct. |
|---|---|---|---|---|---|---|---|---|---|---|---|---|---|
| Williams, Rocky Mt. | 3 | 5 | 4 | 0 | 1 | 1.000 | Hargis, Salem | 134 | 178 | 395 | 45 | 37 | .927 |
| Anderson, Rocky Mt | 1 | 1 | 6 | 0 | 0 | 1.000 | Morrison, Rocky Mt | 12 | 16 | 20 | 3 | 7 | .923 |
| W. Johnson, Lynch... | 2 | 2 | 5 | 0 | 0 | 1.000 | Albert, Lynchburg.. | 102 | 143 | 308 | 38 | 49 | .922 |
| Oliveros, Rocky Mt.. | 3 | 3 | 4 | 0 | 0 | 1.000 | Townsend, Win-Salem | 68 | 84 | 154 | 21 | 26 | .919 |
| Marshall, Salem | 2 | 2 | 4 | 0 | 0 | 1.000 | McMahon, Win-Salem | 89 | 109 | 238 | 31 | 34 | .918 |
| Doyle, Lynchburg | 1 | 2 | 2 | 0 | 1 | 1.000 | Byrd, Lynchburg | 18 | 17 | 56 | 7 | 12 | .913 |
| Thomas, Lynchburg | 1 | 0 | 3 | 0 | 0 | 1.000 | Cruz, Salem | 5 | 7 | 10 | 2 | 1 | .895 |
| CRUZ, Rocky Mount | 133 | 218 | 457 | 41 | 74 | .943 | Peltier, Salem | 2 | 3 | 5 | 1 | 1 | .889 |
| Sosa, Salem | 5 | 6 | 10 | 1 | 2 | .941 | Smith, Lynchburg | 20 | 15 | 43 | 8 | 4 | .879 |

## OUTFIELDERS

| Player and Club | G. | PO. | A. | E. | DP. | Pct. | Player and Club | G. | PO. | A. | E. | DP. | Pct. |
|---|---|---|---|---|---|---|---|---|---|---|---|---|---|
| Fahey, Winston-Salem | 19 | 32 | 2 | 0 | 2 | 1.000 | Gardner, Rocky Mt.. | 79 | 158 | 7 | 6 | 5 | .965 |
| Jefferson, Win-Salem | 4 | 9 | 0 | 0 | 1 | 1.000 | Geigel, Rocky Mount* | 65 | 103 | 2 | 4 | 0 | .963 |
| Putnam, Lynchburg | 3 | 6 | 0 | 0 | 0 | 1.000 | F. Rodriguez, Salem* | 59 | 77 | 5 | 3 | 2 | .963 |
| Hicks, Rocky Mount* | 3 | 5 | 0 | 0 | 0 | 1.000 | Dinzey, Lynchburg .. | 77 | 138 | 10 | 6 | 4 | .961 |
| Olson, Lynchburg* .. | 3 | 4 | 0 | 0 | 0 | 1.000 | Louis, Salem | 79 | 183 | 10 | 8 | 1 | .960 |
| Poff, Rocky Mount* | 11 | 4 | 0 | 0 | 0 | 1.000 | Gonzalez, Rocky Mt | 101 | 160 | 10 | 9 | 2 | .950 |
| Gerlecz, Salem | 2 | 0 | 1 | 0 | 0 | 1.000 | Guarnaccia, R Mt* | 113 | 199 | 22 | 12 | 5 | .948 |
| Skalisky, Rocky Mt | 78 | 130 | 7 | 2 | 3 | .986 | Baker, Win-Salem | 76 | 126 | 2 | 7 | 1 | .948 |
| BERG, Win-Salem* | 109 | 175 | 3 | 3 | 1 | .9834 | Thompson, Lynch | 117 | 269 | 26 | 18 | 6 | .942 |
| Krsnich, Win-Salem | 99 | 164 | 11 | 3 | 5 | .9831 | Long, Lynchburg* .. | 41 | 51 | 7 | 4 | 1 | .935 |
| Nelson, Salem* | 103 | 160 | 7 | 4 | 1 | .977 | Oliveros, Rocky Mt.. | 13 | 14 | 0 | 1 | 0 | .933 |
| Nakamoto, Lynchburg | 23 | 32 | 6 | 1 | 2 | .974 | Westlake, Lynchburg | 7 | 10 | 1 | 1 | 0 | .917 |
| Barrow, Lynchburg | 118 | 223 | 16 | 7 | 1 | .972 | Arnett, Lynchburg*.. | 60 | 64 | 6 | 8 | 0 | .897 |
| Blomberg, Salem | 45 | 156 | 6 | 5 | 2 | .970 | Cole, Salem* | 5 | 7 | 0 | 1 | 0 | .875 |
| Delgado, Win-Salem* | 100 | 234 | 9 | 8 | 4 | .968 | Hammond, Lynchburg* | 1 | 2 | 1 | 1 | 0 | .750 |
| Wrenn, Salem | 117 | 190 | 9 | 7 | 4 | .966 | Ramer, Rocky Mount | 6 | 7 | 0 | 3 | 0 | .700 |
| McClure, Win-Salem* | 49 | 84 | 2 | 3 | 1 | .966 | | | | | | | |

## CATCHERS

| Player and Club | G. | PO. | A. | E. | DP. | PB. | Pct. | Player and Club | G. | PO. | A. | E. | DP. | PB. | Pct. |
|---|---|---|---|---|---|---|---|---|---|---|---|---|---|---|---|
| Salter, Rocky Mt.. | 16 | 63 | 9 | 0 | 0 | 3 | 1.000 | Hughes, Rocky Mt | 25 | 147 | 15 | 2 | 4 | 0 | .988 |
| Carey, Rocky Mt .. | 9 | 27 | 3 | 0 | 0 | 1 | 1.000 | TARBELL, Wi-Sal | 95 | 591 | 53 | 10 | 10 | 18 | .985 |
| Putnam, Lynchburg | 4 | 14 | 1 | 0 | 1 | 1 | 1.000 | Nakamoto, Lynch | 56 | 265 | 43 | 6 | 4 | 16 | .981 |
| Thomas, Lynchburg | 2 | 6 | 0 | 0 | 0 | 0 | 1.000 | de Armas, Roc Mt | 23 | 81 | 14 | 2 | 1 | 4 | .979 |
| Gerlecz, Salem .. | 1 | 4 | 0 | 0 | 0 | 0 | 1.000 | Ban, Lynchburg .. | 80 | 379 | 56 | 10 | 8 | 15 | .978 |
| Oliveros, Rocky Mt | 1 | 2 | 0 | 0 | 0 | 1 | 1.000 | Marshall, Salem.. | 85 | 448 | 65 | 13 | 5 | 12 | .975 |
| G. Rodriguez, Sal | 16 | 91 | 11 | 1 | 1 | 1 | .990 | Diaz, Win-Salem | 52 | 271 | 45 | 9 | 5 | 12 | .972 |
| Rockhill, Lynch... | 14 | 78 | 12 | 1 | 1 | 1 | .989 | Silveira, Rocky Mt | 88 | 356 | 50 | 18 | 6 | 11 | .958 |
| Dusenbury, Salem | 54 | 292 | 32 | 4 | 5 | 4 | .988 | Medick, W-Salem | 12 | 58 | 6 | 3 | 1 | 1 | .955 |
| Triple Play—Marshall. | | | | | | | | | | | | | | | |

## PITCHERS

| Player and Club | G. | PO. | A. | E. | DP. | Pct. | Player and Club | G. | PO. | A. | E. | DP. | Pct. |
|---|---|---|---|---|---|---|---|---|---|---|---|---|---|
| SCOTT, Lynchburg.... | 23 | 16 | 38 | 0 | 3 | 1.000 | Martinez, Salem | 4 | 0 | 2 | 0 | 0 | 1.000 |
| Rainbolt, Lynchburg.. | 25 | 8 | 15 | 0 | 2 | 1.000 | Vosk, Winston-Salem | 20 | 8 | 21 | 1 | 3 | .967 |
| Tanner, Lynchburg .. | 20 | 9 | 12 | 0 | 1 | 1.000 | Bradford, Lynchburg* | 24 | 7 | 22 | 1 | 1 | .967 |
| Kreke, Rocky Mount .. | 13 | 8 | 11 | 0 | 1 | 1.000 | Jones, Winston-Salem* | 17 | 4 | 21 | 1 | 0 | .962 |
| Newcomer, Win-Salem* | 12 | 3 | 14 | 0 | 0 | 1.000 | Buford, Lynchburg ... | 24 | 9 | 16 | 1 | 2 | .962 |
| Davis, Salem | 40 | 6 | 11 | 0 | 0 | 1.000 | Gunter, Salem | 32 | 7 | 17 | 1 | 1 | .960 |
| Brayton, Win-Salem | 16 | 1 | 11 | 0 | 0 | 1.000 | Martin, Rocky Mt* | 13 | 2 | 18 | 1 | 0 | .952 |
| Hagins, Salem* | 49 | 5 | 5 | 0 | 1 | 1.000 | McCoy, Rocky Mt.... | 16 | 0 | 19 | 1 | 0 | .950 |
| Mohme, Lynchburg .. | 3 | 3 | 6 | 0 | 0 | 1.000 | Cuellar, Lynchburg .. | 49 | 6 | 12 | 1 | 1 | .947 |
| Erardi, Salem | 15 | 1 | 8 | 0 | 0 | 1.000 | Brusstar, Rocky Mt... | 25 | 6 | 29 | 2 | 1 | .946 |
| Benizer, Rocky Mount* | 13 | 1 | 6 | 0 | 0 | 1.000 | Ripley, Winston-Salem | 25 | 11 | 35 | 3 | 4 | .939 |
| Paxton, Win-Salem .. | 8 | 2 | 4 | 0 | 0 | 1.000 | Klein, Rocky Mount | 13 | 4 | 11 | 1 | 1 | .938 |
| Brandt, Salem* | 7 | 0 | 5 | 0 | 0 | 1.000 | Price, Salem | 12 | 5 | 9 | 1 | 0 | .933 |
| Jones, Lynchburg | 16 | 0 | 4 | 0 | 0 | 1.000 | Cates, Rocky Mount* | 29 | 4 | 10 | 1 | 0 | .933 |
| Cross, Winston-Salem | 6 | 1 | 2 | 0 | 0 | 1.000 | White, Rocky Mount*.. | 26 | 1 | 26 | 2 | 0 | .931 |
| Ciammachilli, Rock Mt | 10 | 3 | 0 | 0 | 0 | 1.000 | Thomas, Salem* | 25 | 6 | 20 | 2 | 3 | .929 |

## PITCHERS—Continued

| Player and Club | G. | PO. | A. | E. | DP. | Pct. |
|---|---|---|---|---|---|---|
| Neal, Salem* | 13 | 2 | 11 | 1 | 0 | .929 |
| Prazych, Salem | 22 | 5 | 20 | 2 | 3 | .926 |
| Quiroga, Rocky Mount | 19 | 10 | 14 | 2 | 2 | .923 |
| Robinson, Rocky Mt | 24 | 4 | 8 | 1 | 0 | .923 |
| Caldera, Win-Salem* | 24 | 1 | 22 | 2 | 0 | .920 |
| Angell, Salem | 24 | 4 | 30 | 3 | 0 | .919 |
| Percival, Win-Salem | 5 | 1 | 9 | 1 | 0 | .909 |
| Rainey, Winston-Salem | 20 | 9 | 20 | 3 | 1 | .906 |
| Hall, Salem | 19 | 4 | 15 | 2 | 0 | .905 |
| Suter, Winston-Salem | 25 | 20 | 27 | 5 | 2 | .904 |
| Gregson, Rocky Mount | 52 | 4 | 21 | 3 | 0 | .893 |
| Bell, Rocky Mount* | 27 | 7 | 24 | 4 | 3 | .886 |
| Holman, Lynchburg* | 27 | 4 | 23 | 4 | 0 | .871 |
| Scurry, Salem* | 26 | 2 | 18 | 3 | 1 | .870 |
| Hammond, Lynchburg* | 38 | 4 | 9 | 2 | 0 | .867 |
| Burgoon, Salem | 27 | 2 | 4 | 1 | 1 | .857 |
| Aponte, Winston-Salem | 40 | 2 | 13 | 3 | 0 | .833 |
| Miller, Lynchburg | 30 | 2 | 10 | 3 | 0 | .800 |
| J. Johnson, Lynch | 18 | 3 | 3 | 2 | 1 | .750 |
| Klass, Winston-Salem | 9 | 0 | 3 | 2 | 0 | .600 |

The following pitchers do not have any recorded accepted chances; therefore, are not listed in the fielding averages: Anderson, Burman*, Hicks, Kirkpatrick, Oliveros, Skalisy.

## CLUB PITCHING

| Club | G. | CG. | ShO. | Sv. | IP. | H. | R. | ER. | HR. | Tot. BB. | Int BB. | HB. | SO. | WP. | Bk. | ERA. |
|---|---|---|---|---|---|---|---|---|---|---|---|---|---|---|---|---|
| Rocky Mount | 142 | 48 | 19 | 26 | 1198 | 1039 | 508 | 389 | 32 | 557 | 31 | 33 | 642 | 83 | 4 | 2.92 |
| Winston-Salem | 144 | 81 | 15 | 11 | 1233 | 1086 | 563 | 450 | 47 | 584 | 54 | 33 | 880 | 77 | 7 | 3.28 |
| Salem | 141 | 20 | 10 | 31 | 1173 | 1053 | 592 | 472 | 66 | 648 | 27 | 37 | 797 | 79 | 14 | 3.62 |
| Lynchburg | 138 | 35 | 6 | 18 | 1161 | 1133 | 686 | 565 | 60 | 688 | 37 | 34 | 685 | 102 | 10 | 4.38 |

### (Leading Qualifiers for Earned-Run Average Leadership—115 or More Innings)

*Throws lefthanded.

| Pitcher—Club | G. | GS. | CG. | ShO. | W. | L. | Sv. | Pct. | IP. | H. | R. | ER. | HR. | BB. | Int BB. | HB. | SO. | WP. | ERA. |
|---|---|---|---|---|---|---|---|---|---|---|---|---|---|---|---|---|---|---|---|
| Jones, Win-Salem* | 17 | 17 | 14 | 1 | 13 | 3 | 0 | .813 | 145 | 107 | 36 | 34 | 3 | 35 | 3 | 4 | 118 | 3 | 2.11 |
| Brusstar, Rocky Mt | 25 | 24 | 12 | 2 | 14 | 8 | 0 | .636 | 162 | 117 | 61 | 40 | 3 | 94 | 1 | 2 | 123 | 23 | 2.22 |
| Angell, Salem | 24 | 18 | 5 | 3 | 13 | 1 | 0 | .929 | 139 | 136 | 58 | 38 | 4 | 39 | 2 | 2 | 68 | 6 | 2.46 |
| Bell, Rocky Mt* | 27 | 24 | 11 | 4 | 14 | 11 | 0 | .560 | 170 | 153 | 70 | 48 | 3 | 57 | 3 | 0 | 67 | 11 | 2.54 |
| Bradford, Lynch* | 24 | 24 | 10 | 3 | 13 | 9 | 0 | .591 | 159 | 145 | 61 | 46 | 5 | 64 | 2 | 2 | 84 | 7 | 2.60 |
| Quiroga, Rocky Mt | 19 | 18 | 6 | 2 | 10 | 4 | 0 | .714 | 128 | 111 | 43 | 38 | 4 | 39 | 2 | 0 | 52 | 3 | 2.67 |
| Ripley, Wins-Salem | 25 | 25 | 14 | 3 | 14 | 7 | 0 | .667 | 186 | 150 | 70 | 57 | 5 | 75 | 4 | 6 | 120 | 8 | 2.76 |
| Vosk, Wins-Salem | 20 | 15 | 7 | 1 | 5 | 6 | 0 | .455 | 124 | 145 | 68 | 48 | 5 | 59 | 7 | 7 | 69 | 11 | 3.48 |
| Suter, Win-Salem | 25 | 24 | 11 | 3 | 10 | 13 | 0 | .435 | 182 | 152 | 81 | 71 | 13 | 101 | 7 | 2 | 150 | 7 | 3.51 |
| Scurry, Salem* | 26 | 26 | 5 | 0 | 9 | 12 | 0 | .429 | 150 | 128 | 79 | 61 | 9 | 118 | 5 | 7 | 143 | 11 | 3.66 |

Departmental Leaders: G—Gregson, 52; GS—Scurry, 26; CG—Jones (W-S), 14; ShO—Bell, Kreke, 4; W—Bell, Brusstar, Ripley, 14; L—Scott, Suter, Thomas, 15; Sv—Cuellar, 17; Pct.—Angell, .929; IP—Ripley, 186; H—Bell, 153; R—Buford, 97; ER—Buford, 90; HR—Suter, 13; BB—Buford, 121; IBB—Aponte, 10; HB—White, 9; SO—Suter, 150; WP—Brusstar, 23.

### (All Pitchers—Listed Alphabetically)

| Pitcher—Club | G. | GS. | CG. | ShO. | W. | L. | Sv. | Pct. | IP. | H. | R. | ER. | HR. | BB. | Int BB. | HB. | SO. | WP. | ERA. |
|---|---|---|---|---|---|---|---|---|---|---|---|---|---|---|---|---|---|---|---|
| Anderson, Rocky Mt | 2 | 0 | 0 | 0 | 0 | 0 | 0 | .000 | 2 | 2 | 0 | 0 | 0 | 0 | 0 | 0 | 1 | 0 | 0.00 |
| Angell, Salem | 24 | 18 | 5 | 3 | 13 | 1 | 0 | .929 | 139 | 136 | 58 | 38 | 4 | 39 | 2 | 2 | 68 | 6 | 2.46 |
| Aponte, Win-Salem | 40 | 0 | 0 | 0 | 9 | 3 | 9 | 1.000 | 62 | 52 | 20 | 19 | 3 | 37 | 10 | 1 | 38 | 4 | 2.76 |
| Bell, Rocky Mt* | 27 | 24 | 11 | 4 | 14 | 11 | 0 | .560 | 170 | 153 | 70 | 48 | 3 | 57 | 3 | 0 | 67 | 11 | 2.54 |
| Bradford, Lynch* | 24 | 24 | 10 | 3 | 13 | 9 | 0 | .591 | 159 | 145 | 61 | 46 | 5 | 64 | 2 | 2 | 84 | 7 | 2.60 |
| Brandt, Salem* | 7 | 7 | 0 | 0 | 5 | 1 | 0 | .833 | 42 | 43 | 12 | 11 | 3 | 19 | 0 | 3 | 28 | 3 | 2.36 |
| Brayton, Wi-Salem* | 16 | 1 | 1 | 0 | 5 | 1 | 1 | .833 | 41 | 46 | 22 | 17 | 0 | 16 | 2 | 1 | 33 | 7 | 3.73 |
| Brenizer, Rock Mt | 13 | 5 | 1 | 1 | 2 | 3 | 1 | .400 | 28 | 22 | 18 | 13 | 2 | 20 | 0 | 2 | 14 | 2 | 4.18 |
| Brusstar, Rock Mt | 25 | 24 | 12 | 2 | 14 | 8 | 0 | .636 | 162 | 117 | 61 | 40 | 3 | 94 | 1 | 2 | 123 | 23 | 2.22 |
| Buford, Lynchburg | 24 | 23 | 2 | 0 | 5 | 10 | 0 | .333 | 129 | 133 | 97 | 90 | 8 | 121 | 1 | 2 | 76 | 14 | 6.28 |
| Burgoon, Salem | 27 | 0 | 0 | 0 | 0 | 3 | 4 | .000 | 63 | 73 | 64 | 53 | 10 | 56 | 2 | 6 | 27 | 14 | 7.57 |
| Burman, Salem* | 3 | 0 | 0 | 0 | 0 | 1 | 0 | .000 | 3 | 4 | 1 | 0 | 0 | 0 | 0 | 0 | 2 | 0 | 0.00 |
| Caldera, W-Salem* | 24 | 20 | 7 | 2 | 9 | 8 | 0 | .529 | 138 | 130 | 71 | 57 | 6 | 70 | 3 | 7 | 104 | 8 | 3.72 |
| Cates, Rocky Mt* | 29 | 1 | 0 | 0 | 3 | 1 | 11 | .750 | 48 | 40 | 14 | 11 | 0 | 24 | 5 | 2 | 27 | 4 | 2.06 |
| Ciammachilli, R Mt | 10 | 4 | 0 | 0 | 2 | 0 | 0 | 1.000 | 20 | 32 | 28 | 25 | 3 | 14 | 3 | 0 | 15 | 0 | 11.25 |
| Cross, Win-Salem | 6 | 4 | 0 | 0 | 0 | 3 | 0 | .000 | 20 |  |  |  |  |  |  |  |  |  |  |
| Cuellar, Lynchburg | 49 | 0 | 0 | 0 | 9 | 4 | 17 | .692 | 91 | 70 | 32 | 26 | 3 | 55 | 7 | 2 | 73 | 6 | 2.57 |
| Davis, Salem | 40 | 1 | 0 | 0 | 6 | 7 | 2 | .462 | 84 | 66 | 43 | 39 | 4 | 37 | 2 | 2 | 73 | 7 | 4.18 |
| Erardi, Salem | 15 | 0 | 0 | 0 | 3 | 2 | 2 | .600 | 32 | 26 | 16 | 14 | 3 | 21 | 1 | 5 | 24 | 4 | 3.94 |
| Gregson, Rocky Mt | 52 | 0 | 0 | 0 | 4 | 3 | 6 | .571 | 83 | 56 | 26 | 20 | 1 | 46 | 1 | 2 | 44 | 2 | 2.17 |
| Gunter, Salem | 32 | 3 | 0 | 0 | 4 | 5 | 15 | .444 | 74 | 67 | 34 | 25 | 6 | 31 | 6 | 1 | 59 | 0 | 3.04 |
| Hagins, Salem* | 49 | 0 | 0 | 0 | 5 | 4 | 2 | .556 | 93 | 73 | 44 | 38 | 9 | 55 | 3 | 0 | 57 | 1 | 3.68 |
| Hall, Salem | 19 | 16 | 0 | 0 | 5 | 4 | 2 | .250 | 70 | 70 | 47 | 35 | 2 | 50 | 5 | 0 | 41 | 5 | 4.50 |
| Hammond, Lynch* | 38 | 1 | 0 | 0 | 1 | 0 | 0 | 1.000 | 13 | 8 | 5 | 5 | 1 | 11 | 0 | 2 | 13 | 2 | 3.46 |
| Hicks, Rocky Mount* | 8 | 1 | 0 | 0 | 1 | 0 | 0 | 1.000 |  |  |  |  |  |  |  |  |  |  |  |
| Holman, Lynch* | 27 | 19 | 5 | 0 | 6 | 8 | 0 | .429 | 138 | 104 | 52 | 44 | 9 | 55 | 0 | 2 | 61 | 17 | 2.87 |
| J. Johnson, Lynch | 18 | 6 | 1 | 0 | 5 | 3 | 0 | .625 | 61 | 52 | 40 | 25 | 2 | 55 | 0 | 2 | 61 | 17 | 3.69 |
| Jones, Lynchburg | 16 | 0 | 0 | 0 | 0 | 0 | 0 | .000 | 23 | 24 | 23 | 17 | 5 | 15 | 1 | 5 | 8 | 3 | 6.63 |
| Jones, Win-Salem* | 17 | 17 | 14 | 1 | 13 | 3 | 0 | .813 | 145 | 107 | 36 | 34 | 3 | 35 | 3 | 4 | 118 | 3 | 2.11 |
| Kirkpatrick, R Mt | 2 | 0 | 0 | 0 | 0 | 0 | 0 | 1.000 | 10 | 18 | 23 | 20 |  |  |  |  |  |  | 8.63 |
| Klass, Win-Salem | 9 | 1 | 1 | 0 | 1 | 3 | 0 | .250 | 34 | 34 | 24 | 21 | 3 | 28 | 4 | 1 | 21 | 6 | 5.56 |
| Klein, Rocky Mount | 13 | 11 | 3 | 1 | 7 | 2 | 0 | .778 | 71 | 62 | 29 | 24 | 3 | 34 | 0 | 3 | 41 | 3 | 3.04 |
| Kreke, Rocky Mt. | 13 | 13 | 7 | 4 | 9 | 2 | 0 | .818 | 94 | 73 | 27 | 24 | 3 | 21 | 0 | 1 | 41 | 3 | 2.30 |

| Pitcher—Club | G. | GS. | CG. | ShO. | W. | L. | Sv. | Pct. | IP. | H. | R. | ER. | HR. | BB. | Int. BB. | HB. | SO. | WP. | ERA. |
|---|---|---|---|---|---|---|---|---|---|---|---|---|---|---|---|---|---|---|---|
| Martin, Rocky Mt* | 13 | 12 | 2 | 1 | 5 | 3 | 0 | .625 | 71 | 80 | 37 | 30 | 2 | 23 | 2 | 1 | 43 | 8 | 3.80 |
| Martinez, Salem | 4 | 4 | 2 | 0 | 2 | 1 | 0 | .667 | 29 | 25 | 10 | 10 | 4 | 10 | 0 | 0 | 28 | 1 | 3.10 |
| McCoy, Rocky Mt.. | 16 | 6 | 2 | 1 | 4 | 2 | 3 | .667 | 59 | 42 | 18 | 15 | 1 | 22 | 2 | 4 | 33 | 4 | 2.29 |
| Miller, Lynchburg | 30 | 3 | 0 | 0 | 2 | 7 | 1 | .222 | 83 | 72 | 47 | 42 | 7 | 62 | 3 | 6 | 43 | 9 | 4.55 |
| Mohme, Lynchburg | 3 | 3 | 0 | 0 | 0 | 2 | 0 | .000 | 15 | 14 | 10 | 7 | 0 | 8 | 0 | 0 | 10 | 2 | 4.20 |
| Neal, Salem* .... | 13 | 8 | 1 | 1 | 4 | 1 | 0 | .800 | 53 | 34 | 20 | 16 | 0 | 42 | 1 | 1 | 47 | 7 | 2.72 |
| Newcomer, W-S*.. | 12 | 10 | 9 | 1 | 9 | 3 | 0 | .750 | 91 | 81 | 36 | 26 | 0 | 44 | 2 | 0 | 50 | 2 | 2.57 |
| Oliveros, Rocky Mt | 1 | 0 | 0 | 0 | 0 | 0 | 0 | .000 | 1 | 1 | 0 | 0 | 0 | 0 | 0 | 0 | 0 | 0 | 0.00 |
| Paxton, Win-Salem | 8 | 7 | 1 | 5 | 3 | 0 | 0 | .625 | 64 | 46 | 16 | 10 | 0 | 24 | 2 | 1 | 55 | 1 | 1.41 |
| Percival, Win-Salem | 5 | 5 | 4 | 0 | 2 | 3 | 0 | .400 | 36 | 25 | 16 | 12 | 2 | 15 | 3 | 0 | 30 | 1 | 3.00 |
| Prazych, Salem ... | 22 | 18 | 2 | 0 | 6 | 8 | 0 | .429 | 108 | 116 | 77 | 58 | 2 | 79 | 1 | 5 | 61 | 10 | 4.83 |
| Price, Salem ...... | 12 | 12 | 0 | 5 | 4 | 4 | 0 | .556 | 73 | 65 | 31 | 26 | 2 | 31 | 2 | 0 | 49 | 3 | 3.21 |
| Quiroga, Rocky Mt | 19 | 18 | 6 | 2 | 10 | 4 | 0 | .714 | 128 | 111 | 43 | 38 | 4 | 39 | 2 | 0 | 52 | 3 | 2.67 |
| Rainbolt, Lynchburg | 25 | 25 | 7 | 2 | 8 | 11 | 0 | .421 | 160 | 136 | 85 | 71 | 7 | 90 | 3 | 7 | 96 | 18 | 3.99 |
| Rainey, Win-Salem | 20 | 15 | 6 | 0 | 4 | 9 | 1 | .3˙8 | 109 | 110 | 75 | 53 | 4 | 66 | 4 | 3 | 77 | 19 | 4.38 |
| Ripley, Win-Salem | 25 | 25 | 14 | 3 | 14 | 7 | 0 | .667 | 186 | 150 | 70 | 57 | 5 | 75 | 4 | 6 | 120 | 8 | 2.76 |
| Robinson, Rocky Mt | 24 | 1 | 0 | 0 | 3 | 4 | 3 | .429 | 76 | 65 | 40 | 33 | 3 | 41 | 5 | 3 | 39 | 6 | 3.91 |
| Scott, Lynchburg.. | 23 | 22 | 7 | 0 | 8 | 13 | 0 | .381 | 141 | 144 | 82 | 72 | 10 | 55 | 3 | 5 | 69 | 8 | 4.60 |
| Scurry, Salem* ... | 26 | 26 | 5 | 0 | 9 | 12 | 0 | .429 | 150 | 128 | 79 | 61 | 9 | 118 | 5 | 7 | 143 | 11 | 3.66 |
| Skalisky, Rocky Mt | 3 | 0 | 0 | 0 | 0 | 0 | 0 | .000 | 2 | 2 | 1 | 1 | 0 | 4 | 0 | 0 | 1 | 0 | 4.50 |
| Suter, Win-Salem | 25 | 24 | 11 | 3 | 10 | 13 | 0 | .435 | 182 | 152 | 81 | 71 | 13 | 101 | 7 | 2 | 150 | 7 | 3.51 |
| Tanner, Lynchburg | 20 | 12 | 3 | 0 | 3 | 8 | 0 | .273 | 92 | 120 | 83 | 68 | 3 | 44 | 3 | 4 | 42 | 5 | 6.65 |
| Thomas, Salem* .. | 25 | 25 | 3 | 2 | 8 | 13 | 0 | .381 | 147 | 151 | 77 | 63 | 9 | 64 | 3 | 8 | 87 | 10 | 3.86 |
| Vosk, Win-Salem.. | 20 | 15 | 7 | 1 | 5 | 6 | 0 | .455 | 124 | 116 | 68 | 48 | 5 | 59 | 7 | 7 | 69 | 11 | 3.48 |
| White, Rocky Mt* | 26 | 22 | 4 | 0 | 7 | 9 | 1 | .438 | 145 | 147 | 86 | 65 | 5 | 85 | 3 | 9 | 79 | 5 | 4.03 |

BALKS—Thomas, 5; Scurry, 4; Caldera, Scott, 3 each; Bradford, Hammond, Holman, Neal, 2 each; Angell, Bell, Brusstar, Burgoon, Jones (W-S), McCoy, Newcomer, Price, Robinson, Suter, Tanner, Vosk, 1 each.

COMBINATION SHUTOUTS—Bradford-Cuellar, Lynchburg; White-Hicks, Kreke-Cates-Gregson, Kreke-Cates, Rocky Mount; Brandt-Hagins 2, Angell-Hagins, Thomas-Hagins, Salem; Ripley-Aponte 2, Rainey-Aponte, Winston-Salem.

NO-HIT GAMES—Neal, Salem, defeated Anderson (Western Carolinas League), 1-0, May 27; Scurry (7 innings) and Gunter (1 inning), Salem, lost to Lynchburg, 2-1, August 11.

# MAJOR LEAGUE PLAYERS WITH 50 OR MORE HOME RUNS IN ONE SEASON

## NATIONAL LEAGUE

| | | | |
|---|---|---|---|
| Hack Wilson, Chicago, 1930 | 56 | Ralph Kiner, Pittsburgh, 1947 | 51 |
| Ralph Kiner, Pittsburgh, 1949 | 54 | Johnny Mize, New York, 1947 | 51 |
| Willie Mays, San Fran., 1965 | 52 | Willie Mays, New York, 1955 | 51 |

## AMERICAN LEAGUE

| | | | |
|---|---|---|---|
| Roger Maris, New York, 1961 | 61 | Babe Ruth, New York, 1920 | 54 |
| Babe Ruth, New York, 1927 | 60 | Babe Ruth, New York, 1928 | 54 |
| Babe Ruth, New York, 1921 | 59 | Mickey Mantle, New York, 1961 | 54 |
| Hank Greenberg, Detroit, 1938 | 58 | Mickey Mantle, New York, 1956 | 52 |
| Jimmy Foxx, Phila., 1932 | 58 | Jimmy Foxx, Boston, 1938 | 50 |

# *Florida State League*

## CLASS A

### CHAMPIONSHIP WINNERS IN PREVIOUS YEARS

1919—Sanford* .......... .605
    Orlando* .......... .703
1920—Tampa .......... .654
    Tampa .......... .722
1921—Orlando .......... .635
1922—St. Petersburg .... .503
    St. Petersburg .... .618
1923—Orlando .......... .667
    Orlando .......... .678
1924—Lakeland .......... .695
    Lakeland .......... .683
1925—St. Petersburg ..... .667
    Tampa† .......... .696
1926—Sanford .......... .647
    Sanford .......... .623
1927—Orlando† .......... .600
    Miami .......... .661
1928-35—Did not operate.
1936—Gainesville .......... .542
    St. Augustine (4th)† .492
1937—Gainesville§ ........ .616
1938—Leesburg .......... .626
    Gainesville (2nd)‡ .615
1939—Sanford§ .......... .787
1940—Daytona Beach .... .619
    Orlando (4th)‡ .... .507
1941—St. Augustine .... .659
    Leesburg (4th)‡ .... .488
1942-45—Did not operate.

1946—Orlando§ .......... .681
1947—St. Augustine .... .625
    Gainesville (2nd)‡ . .584
1948—Orlando .......... .643
    Daytona B'ch (2nd)‡ .616
1949—Gainesville .......... .635
    St. Augustine (3rd)‡ .556
1950—Orlando .......... .629
    DeLand (3rd)‡ .... .590
1951—DeLand§ .......... .643
1952—DeLand x .......... .704
    Palatka (3rd)‡ .... .569
1953—Daytona Beach† .... .657
    DeLand .......... .703
1954—Jacksonville Beach .629
    Lakeland† .......... .594
1955—Orlando .......... .671
    Orlando .......... .643
1956—Cocoa .......... .614
    Cocoa .......... .671
1957—Palatka .......... .629
    Tampa† .......... .681
1958—St. Petersburg .... .732
    St. Petersburg .... .681
1959—Tampa .......... .591
    St. Petersburg† .... .612
1960—Lakeland .......... .731
    Palatka† .......... .614

1961—Tampa† .......... .710
    Sarasota .......... .696
1962—Sarasota .......... .689
    Fort Lauderdale† .. .623
1963—Sarasota .......... .645
    Sarasota .......... .667
1964—Fort Lauderdale† ... .629
    St. Petersburg .... .594
1965—Fort Lauderdale .... .627
    Fort Lauderdale .... .634
1966—Leesburg z .......... .781
    St. Petersburg .... .700
1967—St. Petersburg y .... .691
    Orlando .......... .638
1968—Miami .......... .613
    Orlando z .......... .579
1969—Miami a .......... .606
    Orlando .......... .606
1970—Miami b .......... .662
    St. Petersburg .... .600
1971—Miami b .......... .667
    Daytona Beach .... .586
1972—Miami c .......... .562
    Daytona Beach .... .606
1973—St. Petersburg d.... .575
    West Palm Beach .. .580
1974—West Palm Beach d.. .598
    Ft. Lauderdale .... .626

*Split-season playoff abandoned after each team won three games. †Won split-season playoff.
‡Won four-club playoff. §Won championship and four-club playoff. xWon both halves of split-season. St. Petersburg and
yLeague divided into Eastern and Western divisions with split-season. St. Petersburg won playoff.
Orlando won both halves of split season; St. Petersburg won playoff.
zLeague divided into Eastern and Western divisions. Miami won regular-season pennant on
basis of highest won-lost percentage. Orlando won four-club playoff involving first two teams
in each division.
aLeague divided into Southern and Central divisions. Miami won playoff between division leaders.
(NOTE—Pennant awarded to playoff winner in 1936.)
bLeague divided into Eastern and Western Divisions. Miami won regular-season pennant on basis
of highest won-loss percentage, and also won four-club playoff involving first two teams in each division.
cLeague divided into Eastern and Western Divisions. Won four-club playoff involving first two
teams in each division.
dLeague divided into Northern and Southern Divisions. Won four-club playoff involving first
two teams in each division.

### COMPOSITE STANDING OF CLUBS AT CLOSE OF SEASON, AUGUST 30

#### NORTHERN DIVISION

| Club | StP. | Tam. | W.H. | Lak. | Mia. | K.W. | FtL. | WPB. | W. | L. | T. | Pct. | G.B. |
|---|---|---|---|---|---|---|---|---|---|---|---|---|---|
| St. Petersburg (Cardinals).. | .. | 24 | 25 | 27 | 3 | 4 | 2 | 3 | 88 | 47 | 0 | .652 | .... |
| Tampa (Reds) ............ | 16 | .. | 21 | 24 | 2 | 3 | 3 | 1 | 72 | 59 | 0 | .550 | 14 |
| Winter Haven (Red Sox).... | 14 | 16 | .. | 21 | 3 | 1 | 1 | 1 | 57 | 70 | 0 | .449 | 27 |
| Lakeland (Tigers) ......... | 13 | 14 | 17 | .. | 1 | 1 | 3 | 4 | 53 | 79 | 1 | .402 | 33½ |

#### SOUTHERN DIVISION

| Club | StP. | Tam. | W.H. | Lak. | Mia. | K.W. | FtL. | WPB. | W. | L. | T. | Pct. | G.B. |
|---|---|---|---|---|---|---|---|---|---|---|---|---|---|
| Miami (Orioles) ........... | 1 | 2 | 1 | 3 | .. | 22 | 26 | 24 | 79 | 57 | 0 | .581 | .... |
| Key West (Cubs) .......... | 0 | 1 | 1 | 3 | 18 | .. | 23 | 19 | 65 | 69 | 0 | .485 | 13 |
| Ft. Lauderdale (Yankees)... | 2 | 1 | 3 | 1 | 14 | 17 | .. | 23 | 61 | 75 | 1 | .449 | 18 |
| West Palm Beach (Expos).. | 1 | 1 | 2 | 0 | 16 | 21 | 17 | .. | 58 | 77 | 2 | .430 | 20½ |

Major league affiliations in parentheses.
Playoffs—St. Petersburg defeated Key West, two games to one; Tampa defeated Miami two games
to none. St. Petersburg defeated Tampa three games to two.

Managers: Ft. Lauderdale—Leo Posada; Key West—Walt Dixon; Lakeland—Frank Overmire; Miami—George Farson; St. Petersburg—Jack Krol; Tampa—Russ Nixon; West Palm Beach—Gordon MacKenzie; Winter Haven—Rac Slider.

Regular-Season Attendance—Ft. Lauderdale, 43,600; Key West, 18,088; Lakeland, 22,281; Miami, 52,106; St. Petersburg, 132,666; Tampa, 71,433; West Palm Beach, 125,568; Winter Haven, 9,844. Total, 475,586. Playoffs, 7,137. No All-Star Game.

All-Star Team: 1B—Chism, Miami; 2B—Bernazard, West Palm Beach; 3B—Parrill, Miami; SS—Templeton, St. Petersburg; Utility—K. Gordon, Key West; OF—Whiting, Miami; Chew, Key West; Norman, Tampa; Rosseau, St. Petersburg; C—Unsoeld, Tampa; M. Gordon, Key West; P—Caudill, St. Petersburg; Viebrock, Tampa; Manager—Krol, St. Petersburg.

(Compiled by Howe News Bureau, Chicago, Ill.

## CLUB BATTING

| Club | G. | AB. | R. | OR. | H. | TB. | 2B. | 3B.HR.RBI. | SH. | SF.BB. | Int. BB. | HP.SO. | SB. | CS. | LOB. | Pct. |
|---|---|---|---|---|---|---|---|---|---|---|---|---|---|---|---|---|
| St. Peters. .135 | 4283 | 561 | 403 | 1100 | 1472 | 163 | 43 | 41 487 | 55 | 47 521 | 23 | 41 611 | 123 | 43 | 1008 | .257 |
| Miami | 136 | 4401 | 566 | 488 | 10 9 | 1388 | 148 | 24 | 31 488 | 81 | 39 568 | 28 | 53 683 | 110 | 58 | 1045 | .250 |
| Tampa | 131 | 4118 | 464 | 366 | 994 | 1274 | 95 | 61 | 21 391 | 100 | 24 452 | 27 | 41 681 | 114 | 49 | 952 | .241 |
| Key West .134 | 4410 | 533 | 538 | 1040 | 1353 | 137 | 28 | 40 454 | 57 | 34 583 | 11 | 22 675 | 109 | 48 | 1038 | .236 |
| Ft. Lauder .137 | 4286 | 478 | 533 | 988 | 1254 | 122 | 24 | 32 398 | 44 | 34 494 | 14 | 50 649 | 140 | 67 | 941 | .231 |
| W Palm B .137 | 4308 | 485 | 551 | 990 | 1284 | 116 | 17 | 48 432 | 54 | 35 538 | 15 | 50 802 | 113 | 61 | 985 | .230 |
| Win Haven | 127 | 3921 | 400 | 490 | 897 | 1168 | 133 | 33 | 24 337 | 57 | 23 445 | 8 | 29 652 | 50 | 22 | 888 | .229 |
| Lakeland .133 | 4087 | 396 | 514 | 885 | 1144 | 116 | 25 | 31 358 | 82 | 42 458 | 14 | 25 642 | 62 | 12 | 887 | .217 |

## INDIVIDUAL BATTING

(Leading Qualifiers for Batting Championship—367 or More Plate Appearances)

*Bats lefthanded. †Switch-hitter.

| Player and Club | G. | AB. | R. | H. | TB. | 2B. | 3B.HR.RBI. | SH. | SF.BB. | HP.SO. | SB. | CS. | Pct. |
|---|---|---|---|---|---|---|---|---|---|---|---|---|---|
| Chism, Thomas, Miami* | 117 | 395 | 54 | 124 | 167 | 16 | 0 9 64 | 2 | 2 48 | 6 45 | 2 | 3 | .314 |
| Rosseau, Ernest, St. Peter* | 133 | 501 | 79 | 151 | 164 | 5 | 4 0 43 | 9 | 2 68 | 4 43 | 55 | 15 | .301 |
| Chew, Earle, Key West | 106 | 379 | 47 | 112 | 165 | 15 | 7 8 54 | 2 | 0 47 | 1 91 | 12 | 6 | .296 |
| Parrill, Martin, Miami* | 116 | 431 | 62 | 125 | 182 | 24 | 6 7 75 | 3 | 6 58 | 6 37 | 4 | 1 | .290 |
| Thompson, Marvin, Ft Lau | 105 | 329 | 53 | 95 | 126 | 12 | 5 3 43 | 3 | 6 66 | 2 39 | 12 | 3 | .289 |
| Edwards, Marshall, Miami* | 124 | 459 | 62 | 128 | 142 | 8 | 3 0 31 | 13 | 3 32 | 8 38 | 38 | 19 | .279 |
| Whiting, Don, Miami* | 126 | 456 | 66 | 127 | 171 | 20 | 3 6 62 | 2 | 3 64 | 4 62 | 6 | 6 | .279 |
| Henderson, Stephen, Tampa | 123 | 413 | 59 | 115 | 156 | 9 | 16 0 54 | 5 | 4 53 | 6 82 | 31 | 9 | .278 |
| Boras, Scott, St. Pete | 99 | 300 | 39 | 83 | 112 | 15 | 4 2 36 | 5 | 0 60 | 3 24 | 1 | 1 | .277 |
| Gordon, Karl, Key West | 130 | 479 | 58 | 131 | 148 | 13 | 2 0 49 | 4 | 3 47 | 1 25 | 28 | 7 | .273 |
| Norman, Daniel, Tampa | 129 | 461 | 71 | 126 | 181 | 14 | 10 7 52 | 7 | 4 69 | 4 61 | 18 | 10 | .273 |

Departmental Leaders: G—Bernazard, 134; AB—Bernazard, 509; R—Rosseau, 79; H—Rosseau, 151; TB—Parrill, 182; 2B—Parrill, 24; 3B—Henderson, 16; HR—Fry, 14; RBI—Parrill, 75; SH—Rosseau, 55; CS—Edwards, 19.

Jackson, 17; SF—Blackwell, 12; BB—Jimenez, 105; HP—Ford, Narron, 10; SO—Sorey, 137; SB—

## (All Players—Listed Alphabetically)

| Player and Club | G. | AB. | R. | H. | TB. | 2B. | 3B.HR.RBI. | SH. | SF.BB. | HP.SO. | SB. | CS. | Pct. |
|---|---|---|---|---|---|---|---|---|---|---|---|---|---|
| Adams, R. Lee, Tampa | 1 | 1 | 0 | 0 | 0 | 0 | 0 0 0 | 0 | 0 0 | 0 0 | 0 | 0 | .000 |
| Alvarez, Jose R., Ft. Laud. | 35 | 86 | 8 | 15 | 15 | 0 | 0 0 9 | 2 | 1 18 | 0 15 | 2 | 0 | .174 |
| Alvarez, Manuel, Lakeland* | 7 | 21 | 1 | 5 | 6 | 1 | 0 0 3 | 0 | 1 1 | 0 3 | 0 | 0 | .238 |
| Anderson, Michael D., Key W | 16 | 40 | 5 | 4 | 6 | 0 | 1 0 3 | 0 | 1 3 | 0 10 | 1 | 0 | .100 |
| Antonetty, Jose, Ft Laud. | 28 | 61 | 8 | 6 | 6 | 0 | 0 0 5 | 0 | 0 9 | 3 18 | 1 | 0 | .098 |
| Austin, Frederick, Lakeland | 4 | 13 | 1 | 3 | 3 | 0 | 0 0 3 | 0 | 0 1 | 1 0 | 0 | 0 | .231 |
| Bendick, James, Ft Laud* | 19 | 68 | 6 | 11 | 13 | 2 | 0 0 9 | 0 | 0 9 | 1 1 | 0 | 0 | .162 |
| Bernazard, Antonio, WPB† | 134 | 509 | 65 | 121 | 159 | 16 | 2 6 50 | 10 | 6 63 | 3 71 | 27 | 15 | .238 |
| Bird, William R., St Peter† | 2 | 0 | 0 | 0 | 0 | 0 | 0 0 0 | 0 | 0 0 | 0 0 | 0 | 0 | .000 |
| Blackwell, Gary, St Peter | 101 | 345 | 40 | 88 | 111 | 17 | 0 2 56 | 5 | 12 46 | 4 41 | 4 | 3 | .255 |
| Boras, Scott, St Peter* | 99 | 300 | 39 | 83 | 112 | 15 | 4 2 36 | 5 | 0 60 | 3 24 | 1 | 1 | .277 |
| Bombard, Marc, Tampa | 26 | 33 | 1 | 5 | 6 | 1 | 0 0 2 | 5 | 0 3 | 0 5 | 0 | 0 | .152 |
| Bowden, David, Lakeland | 63 | 196 | 12 | 36 | 44 | 5 | 0 1 19 | 8 | 1 31 | 0 17 | 0 | 0 | .184 |
| Bowen, Samuel, Winter Haven | 12 | 38 | 3 | 7 | 14 | 1 | 0 2 9 | 0 | 0 1 | 0 11 | 1 | 0 | .184 |
| Brockway, Ricky, Key West. | 33 | 77 | 9 | 9 | 10 | 1 | 0 0 7 | 0 | 2 5 | 0 12 | 1 | 2 | .117 |
| Buba, Mark, Winter Haven. | 88 | 285 | 27 | 60 | 88 | 12 | 3 2 24 | 6 | 3 33 | 3 42 | 19 | 3 | .211 |
| Butler, Thomas, Lakeland | 74 | 280 | 34 | 64 | 88 | 12 | 1 4 29 | 1 | 1 42 | 5 30 | 0 | 0 | .229 |
| Cacciatore, Frank, Lakeland* | 72 | 202 | 23 | 45 | 60 | 10 | 1 0 14 | 6 | 1 42 | 5 30 | 0 | 0 | .223 |
| Chandler, Jeff, Tampa† | 28 | 39 | 7 | 13 | 13 | 0 | 0 0 5 | 10 | 0 11 | 0 10 | 0 | 0 | .333 |
| Chew, Earle, Key West | 106 | 379 | 47 | 112 | 165 | 15 | 7 8 54 | 2 | 0 47 | 1 91 | 12 | 6 | .296 |
| Chism, Thomas, Miami* | 117 | 395 | 54 | 124 | 167 | 16 | 0 9 64 | 2 | 2 48 | 6 45 | 2 | 3 | .314 |
| Clancy, Stephen, Key West. | 26 | 73 | 10 | 13 | 17 | 1 | 0 1 7 | 0 | 1 15 | 1 11 | 0 | 0 | .178 |
| Cline, John, Miami* | 67 | 193 | 20 | 37 | 43 | 4 | 1 0 24 | 7 | 1 18 | 2 15 | 1 | 2 | .192 |
| Colzie, Richard, Tampa | 43 | 113 | 12 | 25 | 26 | 1 | 0 0 4 | 2 | 0 16 | 0 13 | 5 | 4 | .221 |
| Coombs, Michael, Lakeland* | 32 | 95 | 10 | 24 | 25 | 1 | 0 0 4 | 1 | 4 14 | 1 5 | 1 | 0 | .253 |
| Cooper, Michael, W Palm Bea | 17 | 50 | 0 | 11 | 12 | 1 | 0 0 7 | 1 | 1 2 | 0 8 | 0 | 0 | .220 |
| Corbett, Douglas, Tampa | 27 | 10 | 0 | 0 | 0 | 0 | 0 0 0 | 0 | 0 0 | 0 3 | 0 | 0 | .000 |
| Costantine, Robert, Tampa | 67 | 183 | 5 | 43 | 50 | 4 | 1 0 16 | 2 | 1 11 | 2 26 | 0 | 0 | .235 |
| Coughlan, Kip, Lakeland | 55 | 182 | 16 | 39 | 53 | 6 | 1 2 14 | 3 | 2 16 | 1 33 | 2 | 0 | .214 |
| Cowens, William, St Peter. | 28 | 74 | 6 | 16 | 22 | 4 | 1 0 12 | 0 | 1 11 | 0 17 | 2 | 2 | .216 |
| Crockett, Claude, St Peter. | 115 | 385 | 45 | 100 | 145 | 11 | 8 6 41 | 5 | 2 40 | 6 87 | 9 | 4 | .260 |
| 27 Lak | 82 | 280 | 29 | 54 | 67 | 7 | 0 2 27 | 2 | 1 33 | 0 38 | 6 | 5 | .193 |

## FLORIDA STATE LEAGUE—CLASS A

| Player and Club | G. | AB. | R. | H. | TB. | 2B. | 3B. | HR. | RBI. | SH. | SF. | BB. | HP. | SO. | SB. | CS. | Pct. |
|---|---|---|---|---|---|---|---|---|---|---|---|---|---|---|---|---|---|
| Daves, William, St Peter | 31 | 94 | 11 | 19 | 25 | 4 | 1 | 0 | 15 | 1 | 4 | 15 | 2 | 14 | 0 | 1 | .202 |
| DeLeon, Luis, Winter Haven | 73 | 219 | 17 | 47 | 54 | 5 | 1 | 0 | 18 | 5 | 1 | 8 | 1 | 38 | 7 | 2 | .215 |
| DiPietro, Alfred, Lakeland | 24 | 81 | 7 | 21 | 28 | 1 | 0 | 2 | 10 | 0 | 1 | 3 | 2 | 20 | 0 | 0 | .259 |
| Doland, Wayne, Key West | 1 | 2 | 0 | 1 | 0 | 0 | 0 | 0 | 0 | 0 | 0 | 0 | 0 | 0 | 0 | 0 | .500 |
| Draimin, Sheldon, Miami† | 2 | 5 | 0 | 1 | 1 | 0 | 0 | 0 | 0 | 0 | 0 | 0 | 0 | 0 | 0 | 0 | .200 |
| Drury, Kevin, Key West | 122 | 474 | 55 | 105 | 122 | 11 | 0 | 2 | 36 | 12 | 5 | 30 | 4 | 67 | 9 | 3 | .222 |
| Dumoulin, Daniel, Tampa | 45 | 13 | 0 | 2 | 2 | 0 | 0 | 0 | 1 | 0 | 0 | 0 | 0 | 5 | 0 | 0 | .154 |
| Edelen, Benny, St Peter | 24 | 31 | 5 | 8 | 11 | 1 | 1 | 0 | 7 | 0 | 0 | 3 | 0 | 9 | 0 | 0 | .258 |
| Edwards, Marshall, Miami* | 124 | 459 | 62 | 128 | 142 | 8 | 3 | 0 | 31 | 13 | 3 | 32 | 8 | 38 | 38 | 19 | .279 |
| Ehrig, Robert, Miami | 18 | 21 | 2 | 3 | 3 | 0 | 0 | 0 | 1 | 1 | 0 | 7 | 0 | 8 | 0 | 0 | .143 |
| Evans, Godfrey, WPB | 50 | 147 | 17 | 38 | 39 | 1 | 0 | 0 | 14 | 1 | 0 | 17 | 2 | 23 | 0 | 2 | .259 |
| Evans, Ronald, Winter Haven | 59 | 182 | 22 | 45 | 58 | 5 | 1 | 2 | 14 | 7 | 1 | 29 | 1 | 25 | 2 | 0 | .247 |
| Feramisco, Jeffrey, Miami | 3 | 4 | 1 | 0 | 0 | 0 | 0 | 0 | 0 | 4 | 0 | 0 | 0 | 7 | 0 | 0 | .000 |
| Ferreyra, Raul, Tampa | 45 | 11 | 0 | 0 | 0 | 0 | 0 | 0 | 0 | 0 | 0 | 4 | 0 | 0 | 0 | 0 | .000 |
| Figueroa, Jesus, Ft Lauder* | 94 | 343 | 49 | 86 | 93 | 7 | 0 | 0 | 12 | 5 | 0 | 33 | 5 | 22 | 15 | 8 | .251 |
| Fischlin, Michael, Ft Lauder | 29 | 104 | 7 | 19 | 23 | 4 | 0 | 0 | 7 | 1 | 0 | 10 | 1 | 16 | 1 | 2 | .183 |
| Flesh, Henry, Miami* | 121 | 403 | 69 | 93 | 123 | 21 | 3 | 1 | 34 | 7 | 3 | 76 | 0 | 108 | 21 | 7 | .231 |
| Floyd, Stanley, Winter Haven | 26 | 85 | 8 | 20 | 27 | 4 | 0 | 1 | 8 | 0 | 0 | 14 | 0 | 15 | 0 | 5 | .235 |
| Ford, Ricky, Miami | 126 | 396 | 47 | 99 | 122 | 17 | 0 | 2 | 53 | 8 | 7 | 85 | 10 | 46 | 4 | 5 | .250 |
| Foster, Otis, Winter Haven | 67 | 215 | 26 | 53 | 72 | 9 | 2 | 2 | 20 | 1 | 3 | 35 | 4 | 74 | 2 | 2 | .247 |
| Fry, Jerry, West Palm Beach | 129 | 484 | 43 | 107 | 160 | 11 | 0 | 14 | 67 | 3 | 5 | 43 | 4 | 57 | 0 | 0 | .221 |
| Garboza, T. Antonio, W H* | 83 | 264 | 23 | 69 | 93 | 7 | 4 | 3 | 25 | 3 | 0 | 3 | 0 | 5 | 0 | 1 | .261 |
| Garvey, Patrick, Tampa | 18 | 22 | 0 | 4 | 5 | 1 | 0 | 0 | 0 | 4 | 0 | 3 | 0 | 5 | 0 | 0 | .182 |
| Gill, Sheldon, Ft Lauder* | 72 | 218 | 8 | 41 | 46 | 5 | 0 | 0 | 13 | 3 | 1 | 21 | 2 | 37 | 4 | 1 | .188 |
| Gingrich, Gary, WPB† | 58 | 218 | 28 | 55 | 60 | 5 | 0 | 0 | 8 | 6 | 0 | 30 | 2 | 48 | 14 | 5 | .252 |
| Gonzalez, Joseph, WPB | 4 | 16 | 2 | 3 | 3 | 0 | 0 | 0 | 0 | 0 | 0 | 1 | 0 | 3 | 0 | 0 | .188 |
| Gordon, Karl, Key West | 130 | 479 | 58 | 131 | 148 | 13 | 2 | 0 | 49 | 4 | 3 | 47 | 1 | 25 | 28 | 7 | .273 |
| Gordon, Michael, Key West† | 109 | 340 | 37 | 82 | 113 | 10 | 5 | 0 | 40 | 2 | 3 | 54 | 1 | 59 | 1 | 0 | .241 |
| Grace, Michael, Tampa | 118 | 380 | 29 | 87 | 110 | 5 | 6 | 2 | 41 | 6 | 1 | 36 | 2 | 90 | 10 | 2 | .229 |
| Grandy, Eric, Key West | 42 | 92 | 12 | 15 | 21 | 0 | 0 | 2 | 8 | 0 | 0 | 20 | 1 | 33 | 4 | 2 | .163 |
| Graumann, A. Dean, Tampa | 124 | 486 | 50 | 107 | 120 | 9 | 2 | 0 | 30 | 14 | 2 | 25 | 2 | 36 | 17 | 6 | .220 |
| Halgerson, Keith, Tampa | 8 | 1 | 0 | 0 | 0 | 0 | 0 | 0 | 0 | 0 | 0 | 0 | 0 | 0 | 0 | 0 | .000 |
| Hall, Clifford, Key West* | 92 | 316 | 43 | 78 | 109 | 14 | 1 | 5 | 39 | 2 | 1 | 32 | 3 | 55 | 6 | 4 | .247 |
| Hampton, Robert, Win Haven | 56 | 174 | 12 | 35 | 48 | 6 | 2 | 1 | 13 | 4 | 1 | 14 | 1 | 28 | 1 | 1 | .201 |
| Harrison, Robert, St Peter* | 15 | 43 | 2 | 9 | 10 | 1 | 0 | 0 | 1 | 0 | 0 | 3 | 0 | 5 | 0 | 0 | .209 |
| Heath, Michael, Ft Lauder | 98 | 376 | 43 | 87 | 103 | 7 | 3 | 1 | 23 | 7 | 2 | 25 | 1 | 50 | 13 | 4 | .231 |
| Helget, Dale, 1 Tam-56 WH* | 57 | 163 | 14 | 27 | 40 | 6 | 2 | 1 | 16 | 6 | 4 | 22 | 1 | 39 | 1 | 1 | .166 |
| Henderson, Stephen, Tampa | 123 | 413 | 59 | 115 | 156 | 9 | 16 | 0 | 54 | 5 | 4 | 53 | 8 | 82 | 31 | 9 | .278 |
| Hendcn, Michael, Win Haven | 32 | 70 | 14 | 16 | 18 | 0 | 0 | 0 | 3 | 1 | 0 | 9 | 2 | 27 | 4 | 1 | .229 |
| Hernandez, Gary, St Peter* | 131 | 462 | 61 | 120 | 164 | 23 | 3 | 5 | 53 | 3 | 6 | 54 | 4 | 58 | 1 | 3 | .260 |
| Hernandez, Joseph, Key West | 48 | 178 | 31 | 51 | 60 | 7 | 1 | 0 | 17 | 1 | 3 | 27 | 0 | 12 | 9 | 4 | .287 |
| Hill, Ronald, Key West | 17 | 38 | 2 | 8 | 10 | 2 | 0 | 0 | 0 | 0 | 0 | 6 | 0 | 9 | 0 | 0 | .211 |
| Hoyles, Timothy, Miami | 3 | 0 | 0 | 0 | 0 | 0 | 0 | 0 | 0 | 0 | 0 | 0 | 0 | 0 | 0 | 0 | .000 |
| Huizenga, Kenneth, W Haven | 98 | 339 | 39 | 84 | 111 | 19 | 1 | 2 | 32 | 2 | 1 | 42 | 1 | 49 | 9 | 1 | .248 |
| Iorg, Garth, Ft Lauder† | 50 | 186 | 10 | 47 | 55 | 4 | 2 | 0 | 16 | 3 | 0 | 27 | 1 | 19 | 7 | 2 | .253 |
| Ireland, Timothy, Miami | 41 | 139 | 28 | 33 | 40 | 5 | 1 | 0 | 13 | 6 | 0 | 27 | 1 | 19 | 7 | 2 | .237 |
| Jackson, Melvin, Lakeland | 113 | 350 | 34 | 74 | 83 | 3 | 3 | 0 | 33 | 2 | 5 | 14 | 0 | 25 | 5 | 2 | .211 |
| James, Charles, Miami | 68 | 219 | 24 | 61 | 72 | 7 | 2 | 0 | 34 | 2 | 4 | 16 | 1 | 39 | 5 | 5 | .279 |
| Jimenez, Alfonso, Key West | 132 | 446 | 63 | 96 | 129 | 17 | 5 | 2 | 34 | 12 | 4 | 105 | 3 | 63 | 5 | 5 | .215 |
| Johnson, Jerry D., St Peter | 4 | 11 | 1 | 0 | 0 | 0 | 0 | 0 | 0 | 1 | 0 | 1 | 0 | 9 | 4 | 0 | .000 |
| Jones, Robert C., Tampa | 59 | 202 | 33 | 56 | 77 | 6 | 3 | 3 | 21 | 0 | 1 | 33 | 9 | 15 | 14 | 5 | .277 |
| Kane, Gregory, Winter Haven | 25 | 75 | 7 | 19 | 26 | 1 | 0 | 2 | 7 | 0 | 0 | 15 | 0 | 20 | 0 | 0 | .253 |
| Koza, David, Winter Haven | 110 | 368 | 40 | 95 | 133 | 15 | 4 | 5 | 36 | 3 | 4 | 31 | 6 | 60 | 4 | 2 | .258 |
| Krause, Guy, W Palm Bea† | 118 | 375 | 62 | 89 | 135 | 9 | 2 | 11 | 51 | 4 | 4 | 91 | 8 | 81 | 4 | 3 | .237 |
| Kwasny, Joseph, Ft Lauder | 1 | 1 | 0 | 0 | 0 | 0 | 0 | 0 | 0 | 0 | 0 | 0 | 1 | 0 | 0 | 0 | .000 |
| LaCoss, Michael, Tampa | 24 | 46 | 2 | 4 | 6 | 2 | 0 | 0 | 4 | 0 | 0 | 5 | 0 | 18 | 0 | 0 | .087 |
| Landrum, Terry, St Peter | 132 | 435 | 76 | 96 | 158 | 21 | 4 | 11 | 45 | 3 | 5 | 36 | 4 | 95 | 29 | 6 | .221 |
| Lentine, James, St Peter | 12 | 42 | 3 | 10 | 15 | 2 | 0 | 1 | 5 | 0 | 0 | 6 | 0 | 11 | 0 | 0 | .238 |
| Leyva, Nicolas, St Peter | 47 | 157 | 16 | 42 | 54 | 8 | 2 | 0 | 21 | 4 | 4 | 23 | 2 | 18 | 1 | 0 | .268 |
| Litras, Stephen, Lakeland | 34 | 117 | 15 | 30 | 31 | 1 | 0 | 0 | 10 | 1 | 3 | 17 | 0 | 24 | 0 | 2 | .256 |
| Loomans, Byron, Key West | 35 | 121 | 14 | 26 | 38 | 1 | 1 | 3 | 17 | 0 | 2 | 23 | 0 | 24 | 1 | 2 | .215 |
| Lyle, Donald, Tampa | 96 | 280 | 34 | 71 | 89 | 6 | 3 | 2 | 30 | 3 | 0 | 14 | 1 | 18 | 1 | 2 | .254 |
| Maier, Martin, Ft Lauder | 33 | 92 | 8 | 20 | 23 | 4 | 0 | 0 | 9 | 1 | 0 | 14 | 0 | 17 | 2 | 1 | .217 |
| Marshall, J. Blake, Key West† | 36 | 117 | 9 | 32 | 40 | 6 | 1 | 0 | 9 | 0 | 1 | 14 | 0 | 11 | 7 | 0 | .274 |
| Martinez, Juan J., Miami | 18 | 35 | 3 | 8 | 8 | 0 | 0 | 0 | 3 | 1 | 0 | 7 | 0 | 7 | 2 | 0 | .229 |
| Martinez, Ronald, Lakeland | 101 | 333 | 32 | 75 | 100 | 12 | 3 | 0 | 27 | 4 | 4 | 15 | 4 | 77 | 5 | 5 | .225 |
| Marvelle, Michael, WPB | 44 | 140 | 10 | 25 | 28 | 3 | 0 | 0 | 10 | 1 | 3 | 11 | 0 | 24 | 0 | 0 | .179 |
| Massee, M. Lee, Key West* | 14 | 26 | 3 | 4 | 5 | 1 | 0 | 0 | 2 | 0 | 0 | 0 | 0 | 11 | 0 | 0 | .154 |
| Matthews, James, WPB* | 5 | 13 | 1 | 1 | 1 | 0 | 0 | 0 | 0 | 0 | 0 | 1 | 0 | 0 | 0 | 0 | .077 |
| McAlister, Richard, WH* | 45 | 136 | 8 | 43 | 56 | 7 | 3 | 0 | 18 | 1 | 1 | 13 | 1 | 25 | 0 | 1 | .316 |
| McCarthy, Richard, Miami | 16 | 6 | 4 | 3 | 3 | 0 | 0 | 0 | 0 | 0 | 0 | 2 | 0 | 1 | 0 | 0 | .500 |
| McMillan, Kevin, Miami | 15 | 42 | 6 | 10 | 11 | 1 | 0 | 0 | 3 | 0 | 0 | 2 | 0 | 15 | 0 | 0 | .238 |
| Meek, Richard, Ker West* | 97 | 314 | 29 | 63 | 86 | 7 | 2 | 4 | 24 | 1 | 1 | 30 | 5 | 123 | 6 | 3 | .201 |
| Meltz, Richard, Ft Lauder | 1 | 0 | 0 | 0 | 0 | 0 | 0 | 0 | 0 | 0 | 0 | 0 | 0 | 0 | 0 | 0 | .000 |
| Melvin, Douglas, Ft Lauder | 1 | 0 | 0 | 0 | 0 | 0 | 0 | 0 | 0 | 0 | 0 | 0 | 0 | 0 | 0 | 0 | .000 |
| Merenda, Henry, Lakeland | 37 | 115 | 11 | 25 | 30 | 2 | 0 | 1 | 7 | 0 | 0 | 23 | 0 | 11 | 9 | 1 | .217 |
| Moore, Steven, Tampa | 1 | 2 | 1 | 1 | 1 | 0 | 0 | 0 | 0 | 0 | 0 | 0 | 0 | 0 | 0 | 0 | .500 |
| Morello, Lawrence, W Haven | 107 | 364 | 43 | 95 | 125 | 16 | 2 | 0 | 31 | 3 | 0 | 52 | 2 | 36 | 2 | 2 | .261 |
| Moretto, Tony, Tampa* | 7 | 17 | 0 | 2 | 2 | 0 | 0 | 0 | 0 | 0 | 0 | 0 | 0 | 0 | 0 | 0 | .118 |
| Morgan, Curtis, Lakeland* | 91 | 296 | 27 | 64 | 93 | 9 | 7 | 2 | 25 | 13 | 2 | 30 | 3 | 34 | 0 | 1 | **.216** |

| Player and Club | G. | AB. | R. | H. | TB. | 2B. | 3B. | HR. | RBI. | SH. | SF. | BB. | HP. | SO. | SB. | CS. | Pct. |
|---|---|---|---|---|---|---|---|---|---|---|---|---|---|---|---|---|---|
| Narron, Jerry, Ft Lauder*.. | 113 | 360 | 39 | 76 | 94 | 12 | 0 | 2 | 34 | 2 | 5 | 30 | 10 | 38 | 6 | 4 | .211 |
| Natchez, Jeffrey, Lakeland.. | 62 | 203 | 20 | 37 | 49 | 4 | 1 | 2 | 20 | 2 | 4 | 16 | 1 | 41 | 3 | 0 | .182 |
| Norman, Daniel, Tampa..... | 129 | 461 | 71 | 126 | 181 | 14 | 1 | 13 | 52 | 7 | 4 | 49 | 4 | 61 | 18 | 10 | .273 |
| Norris, D. Scott, Ft Lauder.. | 64 | 207 | 31 | 48 | 63 | 6 | 0 | 3 | 17 | 4 | 0 | 29 | 6 | 29 | 14 | 8 | .232 |
| Oberkfell, Kenneth, St Peter* | 41 | 134 | 14 | 47 | 55 | 6 | 1 | 0 | 22 | 2 | 1 | 21 | 1 | 12 | 1 | 0 | .351 |
| O'Berry, P. Michael, WH.... | 39 | 96 | 5 | 8 | 12 | 2 | 1 | 0 | 5 | 4 | 0 | 13 | 0 | 28 | 0 | 0 | .083 |
| Oester, Ronald, Tampa‡..... | 117 | 375 | 40 | 82 | 93 | 3 | 4 | 0 | 25 | 5 | 0 | 38 | 2 | 56 | 3 | 1 | .219 |
| Parrill, Martin, Miami*..... | 116 | 431 | 62 | 125 | 182 | 24 | 6 | 7 | 75 | 3 | 6 | 58 | 6 | 37 | 4 | 1 | .290 |
| Parrish, Lance, Lakeland .. | 100 | 341 | 30 | 75 | 109 | 15 | 2 | 5 | 37 | 1 | 3 | 30 | 1 | 85 | 0 | 0 | .220 |
| Pastore, Alex, St Peter ..... | 29 | 88 | 21 | 21 | 29 | 3 | 1 | 1 | 8 | 0 | 0 | 14 | 1 | 17 | 1 | 0 | .239 |
| Perez, Benjamin, Ft Lauder | 118 | 358 | 28 | 87 | 98 | 9 | 1 | 0 | 20 | 2 | 2 | 27 | 4 | 53 | 10 | 5 | .243 |
| Perez, Julio, W Palm Beach† | 98 | 337 | 33 | 87 | 95 | 6 | 1 | 0 | 20 | 4 | 1 | 41 | 2 | 22 | 5 | 7 | .258 |
| Peterson, Patrick, Ft Lauder | 118 | 418 | 35 | 96 | 119 | 12 | 1 | 3 | 41 | 3 | 2 | 26 | 0 | 46 | 6 | 5 | .230 |
| Plunkett, L. Wilson, FtL*.. | 121 | 383 | 44 | 90 | 135 | 14 | 5 | 7 | 60 | 2 | 7 | 57 | 6 | 51 | 16 | 7 | .235 |
| Pritchett, Dennis, St. Peter.. | 3 | 3 | 0 | 0 | 0 | 0 | 0 | 0 | 0 | 0 | 0 | 0 | 0 | 0 | 0 | 0 | .000 |
| Putman, Eddy, Key West..... | 92 | 293 | 39 | 65 | 90 | 15 | 2 | 2 | 32 | 4 | 6 | 55 | 2 | 57 | 0 | 0 | .222 |
| Ramos, Roberto, WPB..... | 73 | 204 | 16 | 39 | 53 | 7 | 2 | 1 | 12 | 7 | 0 | 38 | 6 | 57 | 0 | 3 | .191 |
| Randall, Aaron, Key West† | 55 | 195 | 23 | 40 | 62 | 4 | 0 | 6 | 30 | 2 | 1 | 13 | 1 | 25 | 5 | 1 | .205 |
| Redoglia, Donald, St. Peter.. | 28 | 80 | 6 | 18 | 26 | 5 | 0 | 1 | 7 | 1 | 0 | 11 | 0 | 12 | 0 | 0 | .225 |
| Reed, Kenneth, Miami..... | 82 | 263 | 38 | 62 | 70 | 4 | 2 | 0 | 13 | 5 | 1 | 44 | 6 | 24 | 9 | 5 | .236 |
| Reed, Steven, Tampa ..... | 23 | 54 | 4 | 7 | 8 | 1 | 0 | 0 | 4 | 0 | 0 | 2 | 1 | 28 | 0 | 0 | .130 |
| Register, Jerome, W Haven.. | 30 | 107 | 13 | 26 | 32 | 1 | 1 | 1 | 7 | 0 | 0 | 12 | 0 | 20 | 1 | 1 | .243 |
| Rinden, Ronnie, Miami*..... | 8 | 10 | 3 | 1 | 1 | 0 | 0 | 0 | 0 | 1 | 0 | 2 | 0 | 3 | 0 | 0 | .100 |
| Rosseau, Ernest, St Peter.. | 133 | 501 | 79 | 151 | 164 | 5 | 4 | 0 | 43 | 9 | 2 | 68 | 4 | 43 | 55 | 15 | .301 |
| Rubertino, Joseph, Lakeland* | 85 | 259 | 24 | 57 | 75 | 7 | 4 | 1 | 20 | 5 | 4 | 22 | 0 | 41 | 4 | 2 | .220 |
| Rump, Kenneth, Win Haven | 24 | 77 | 6 | 10 | 10 | 0 | 0 | 0 | 6 | 3 | 2 | 10 | 0 | 22 | 0 | 0 | .130 |
| Russo, Ralph, Win Haven*.. | 58 | 203 | 18 | 44 | 59 | 8 | 2 | 1 | 22 | 2 | 1 | 23 | 0 | 28 | 0 | 1 | .217 |
| Sansosti, Francis, St Peter.. | 3 | 7 | 0 | 1 | 1 | 0 | 0 | 0 | 0 | 0 | 0 | 0 | 0 | 0 | 0 | 0 | .143 |
| Santo Domingo, Rafael, Tam† | 15 | 48 | 7 | 13 | 14 | 1 | 0 | 0 | 10 | 0 | 1 | 5 | 1 | 14 | 0 | 0 | .271 |
| Schafer, Randall, WPB..... | 51 | 171 | 21 | 38 | 56 | 5 | 2 | 3 | 26 | 0 | 4 | 21 | 0 | 34 | 0 | 0 | .222 |
| Signan, S. Lee, Miami†..... | 127 | 391 | 31 | 88 | 93 | 5 | 0 | 0 | 35 | 13 | 0 | 42 | 0 | 80 | 2 | 2 | .225 |
| Simonton, Kenneth, W Haven | 27 | 60 | 7 | 7 | 7 | 0 | 0 | 0 | 3 | 1 | 1 | 4 | 1 | 15 | 2 | 0 | .117 |
| Snyder, Vernon, Miami..... | 1 | 1 | 0 | 0 | 0 | 0 | 0 | 0 | 0 | 0 | 0 | 1 | 0 | 0 | 0 | 0 | .000 |
| Sorey, Ronald, WPB....... | 124 | 407 | 56 | 92 | 131 | 10 | 4 | 7 | 49 | 2 | 4 | 60 | 9 | 137 | 28 | 10 | .226 |
| Spilman, W. Harry, Tampa* | 115 | 348 | 33 | 90 | 108 | 13 | 1 | 1 | 38 | 4 | 5 | 61 | 2 | 43 | 6 | 4 | .259 |
| Staggs, Ronald, WPB*..... | 74 | 260 | 23 | 62 | 84 | 11 | 1 | 3 | 38 | 3 | 3 | 29 | 2 | 35 | 0 | 0 | .238 |
| Stapleton, David, Win Haven | 56 | 199 | 23 | 48 | 61 | 8 | 1 | 1 | 14 | 2 | 0 | 11 | 1 | 13 | 5 | 3 | .241 |
| Stephenson, Kevin, WH..... | 65 | 202 | 25 | 39 | 47 | 6 | 1 | 0 | 15 | 5 | 1 | 24 | 3 | 34 | 2 | 1 | .193 |
| Stone, Michael, St Peter.. | 88 | 288 | 30 | 65 | 88 | 12 | 1 | 3 | 32 | 6 | 2 | 28 | 6 | 53 | 1 | 0 | .226 |
| Styles, Marlon, Tampa*..... | 3 | 3 | 0 | 0 | 0 | 0 | 0 | 0 | 0 | 0 | 0 | 0 | 0 | 1 | 0 | 0 | .000 |
| Sullivan, James, Ft Lauder.. | 1 | 1 | 0 | 0 | 0 | 0 | 0 | 0 | 0 | 0 | 0 | 0 | 0 | 0 | 0 | 0 | .000 |
| Swanson, Fred, Lakeland*.. | 124 | 469 | 39 | 105 | 116 | 8 | 0 | 1 | 35 | 6 | 3 | 24 | 2 | 54 | 0 | 0 | .224 |
| Temple, V. James, Key West | 1 | 1 | 0 | 0 | 0 | 0 | 0 | 0 | 0 | 0 | 0 | 0 | 0 | 0 | 0 | 0 | .000 |
| Templeton, Garry, St Peter†.. | 82 | 349 | 50 | 92 | 118 | 7 | 8 | 1 | 32 | 1 | 3 | 10 | 1 | 40 | 18 | 6 | .264 |
| Thompson, Lloyd, WPB..... | 40 | 118 | 9 | 27 | 30 | 3 | 0 | 0 | 7 | 7 | 0 | 12 | 0 | 42 | 18 | 6 | .229 |
| Thompson, Marvin, Ft Laud | 105 | 329 | 53 | 95 | 126 | 12 | 5 | 3 | 43 | 3 | 6 | 19 | 1 | 20 | 2 | 1 | .289 |
| Thompson, Thomas Neil, Lak | 4 | 9 | 1 | 1 | 1 | 0 | 0 | 0 | 0 | 0 | 0 | 2 | 2 | 39 | 12 | 3 | .111 |
| Thompson, V. Scott, K W* | 123 | 424 | 40 | 95 | 116 | 6 | 3 | 3 | 41 | 7 | 0 | 34 | 2 | 53 | 10 | 1 | .224 |
| Treuel, Ralph, Lakeland.. | 1 | 1 | 0 | 0 | 0 | 0 | 0 | 0 | 0 | 0 | 0 | 0 | 0 | 0 | 0 | 0 | .000 |
| Turner, Darrell, Key West.. | 1 | 1 | 0 | 0 | 0 | 0 | 0 | 0 | 0 | 0 | 0 | 1 | 0 | 0 | 0 | 0 | .000 |
| Tyler, Gerald, Lakeland*.. | 1 | 2 | 0 | 0 | 0 | 0 | 0 | 0 | 0 | 0 | 0 | 0 | 0 | 0 | 0 | 0 | .000 |
| Uhey, Jackie, Key West*.. | 1 | 1 | 0 | 0 | 0 | 0 | 0 | 0 | 0 | 0 | 0 | 0 | 0 | 1 | 0 | 0 | .000 |
| Umfleet, R. Michael, K W* | 8 | 27 | 4 | 10 | 15 | 2 | 0 | 1 | 9 | 1 | 0 | 4 | 0 | 3 | 1 | 0 | .370 |
| Underwood, John, Tampa..... | 4 | 12 | 1 | 2 | 2 | 0 | 0 | 0 | 2 | 0 | 0 | 3 | 1 | 0 | 0 | 0 | .167 |
| Unsoeld, Mark, Tampa..... | 87 | 265 | 45 | 80 | 123 | 11 | 10 | 4 | 33 | 3 | 0 | 36 | 5 | 45 | 2 | 0 | .302 |
| Urena, Jacobo, Miami ..... | 94 | 276 | 26 | 41 | 59 | 4 | 1 | 4 | 24 | 4 | 2 | 24 | 0 | 58 | 7 | 3 | .149 |
| Vazquez, Esteban, St Peter.. | 126 | 454 | 57 | 114 | 164 | 18 | 4 | 8 | 59 | 5 | 4 | 60 | 4 | 53 | 0 | 1 | .251 |
| Verban, Steve, Key West*.. | 72 | 260 | 28 | 63 | 76 | 10 | 0 | 1 | 24 | 2 | 2 | 40 | 2 | 34 | 14 | 8 | .237 |
| Viebrock, Alan, Tampa*..... | 23 | 44 | 8 | 5 | 6 | 1 | 0 | 0 | 4 | 4 | 10 | 1 | 8 | 17 | 0 | 0 | .114 |
| Viefhaus, Stephen, Lakeland | 130 | 430 | 47 | 88 | 126 | 18 | 1 | 6 | 59 | 7 | 5 | 78 | 1 | 85 | 3 | 0 | .205 |
| Villa, Joseph, Miami..... | 84 | 256 | 20 | 55 | 77 | 12 | 2 | 2 | 21 | 5 | 4 | 18 | 4 | 87 | 1 | 1 | .215 |
| Ware, Richard, Key West*.. | 1 | 2 | 0 | 0 | 0 | 0 | 0 | 0 | 0 | 0 | 0 | 0 | 0 | 0 | 0 | 0 | .000 |
| Welsh, William, WPB....... | 70 | 202 | 24 | 49 | 50 | 1 | 0 | 0 | 17 | 1 | 1 | 41 | 5 | 30 | 5 | 1 | .243 |
| Werth, Dennis, Ft Lauder.. | 121 | 381 | 63 | 101 | 156 | 18 | 5 | 9 | 54 | 3 | 4 | 78 | 3 | 69 | 18 | 9 | .265 |
| Westerman, Michal, Tampa† | 5 | 6 | 0 | 0 | 0 | 0 | 0 | 0 | 0 | 0 | 0 | 0 | 0 | 0 | 0 | 0 | .000 |
| Whiteaker, David, WPB..... | 3 | 11 | 0 | 2 | 3 | 1 | 0 | 0 | 0 | 0 | 0 | 0 | 0 | 4 | 0 | 0 | .182 |
| Whiting, Don, Miami*..... | 196 | 456 | 66 | 127 | 171 | 20 | 3 | 6 | 62 | 2 | 3 | 64 | 4 | 62 | 6 | 6 | .279 |
| Wood, W. Christopher, WPB | 53 | 205 | 21 | 56 | 65 | 7 | 1 | 0 | 18 | 1 | 3 | 0 | 2 | 38 | 3 | 2 | .273 |
| Woodland, Robert, WPB*... | 85 | 253 | 31 | 51 | 77 | 13 | 2 | 3 | 20 | 2 | 2 | 7 | 6 | 68 | 18 | 4 | .202 |
| Woolley, David, Tampa..... | 79 | 250 | 22 | 54 | 76 | 10 | 3 | 2 | 31 | 4 | 3 | 22 | 5 | 52 | 2 | 2 | .216 |

The following players had no plate appearances primarily through use of designated hitters; listed alphabetically, games in parentheses:

FT. LAUDERDALE—Alcantara, Jose (12), Bierman, James* (23), Carp, Steven (16), Delgatti, Scott (17), Diehl, Gregory (23), Fleshman, Richard (27), Hoyt, D. LaMarr (7), Kruppa, Kenneth* (32), Mendez, Sabah (10), Paz, Carlos (2), Rajsich, David* (23), Robles, Julio (13), Rusk, Michael, (5), Trotter, Joseph (8), Wright, Dave (18).

KEY WEST—Bickerton, Brien* (3), Groover, Lawrence† (2), Hamrick, Stephen (15), Moore, Michael (6), Riley, George* (28), Rogers, Charles* (11), Tufts, William* (16), Vernoy, Brian* (22), Vogel, Rick* (5), Wilkerson, Byron (19), Wood, David (29).

LAKELAND—Alonso, Julio* (13), Cappuzzello, George (16), Daniels, William (7), Dwyer, Michael (11), Farrow, Willie† (3), Fidrych, M. Steven (17), Harris, Frank (7), Irwin, C. Lou (14). Madden, William (28), Mercier, Ronald (26), Meyerrose, Michael (8), Motil, John (6), Murphy, Patrick* (18), Tobik, David (5).

MIAMI—Broomis, Gregory (5), Chevez, Antonio (33), Darr, Michael (15), Flinn, John (4), Ford, David (2), Kibbee, Thomas (32), Martinez, J. Dennis (22), Mayo, Ricky (25), Miller, Randall (55), Moore, Henry* (27), Rineer, Jeffrey* (11), Smith, Bryn (26), Vallejos, Juan (5).

ST. PETERSBURG—Bashaw, Lawrence (34), Camper, Cardell (13), Capilla, Douglas* (8), Caudill, William (25), Kennedy, Robert (23), Lopez, Jose A. (7), Meek, Stanley* (23), Murphy, Michael (43), Redmon, Charles (1), Replogle, Andrew (5), Rieger, Karl* (8), Sorensen, Kristian (18), Staniland, Stephen (2), Stewart, Robert (14), Trumbauer, Gary* (6), Urrea, John (23).

WEST PALM BEACH—Baby, James* (5), Baltz, W. Nicholas (10), Bastian, Jose (23), Dues, Hal (18), Ewell, Mark (23), Finlayson, Michael (13), Gingrich, Jeffrey (16). Grabowski, Michael (8), Hannahs, Gerald† (8), Horn, Larry (16), Horstmann, Gary (21), Kerrigan, Joseph (22), Knose, Mark (5), MacQuarrie, David (21), O'Neil, Gerard* (2), Rawley, Shane (24), Riley, Edward (11), Swanson, Richard (9).

WINTER HAVEN—Agosto, Juan* (6), Antor, Gregory (22), Burke, Steven (26), Cross, Wilfred (14), Finch, Joel (26), Hardeman, W. Gary (20), Kleibl, Craig (16), Polonio, Ivan (19), Proctor, John (35), Remmerswaal, Wilhelmus (37), Stanley, Robert (27).

GRAND-SLAM HOME RUNS—Bernazard, Fry, Peterson, Plunkett, Vazquez, Werth, 1 each.

AWARDED FIRST BASE ON INTERFERENCE—R. Ford (Schafer), LaCoss (O'Berry), Natchez (Helget), Pastore (O'Berry), Simonton (Parrish).

OBSTRUCTION: Marvelle on Figueroa.

## CLUB FIELDING

| Club | G. | PO. | A. | E. | DP. | PB. | Pct. | Club | G. | PO. | A. | E. | DP. | PB. | Pct. |
|---|---|---|---|---|---|---|---|---|---|---|---|---|---|---|---|
| St. Petersburg | 135 | 3445 | 1286 | 137 | 112 | 18 | .972 | Miami | 136 | 3561 | 1586 | 183 | 136 | 37 | .966 |
| Tampa | 131 | 3323 | 1440 | 156 | 121 | 28 | .968 | W. Palm Beach | 137 | 3486 | 1459 | 188 | 112 | 47 | .963 |
| Lakeland | 133 | 3364 | 1338 | 157 | 115 | 42 | .968 | Winter Haven | 127 | 3198 | 1420 | 194 | 108 | 22 | .960 |
| Key West | 134 | 3526 | 1601 | 181 | 115 | 28 | .966 | Ft. Lauderdale | 137 | 3473 | 1396 | 206 | 101 | 37 | .959 |

Triple Plays—None.

## INDIVIDUAL FIELDING
### FIRST BASEMEN

*Throws lefthanded.

| Player and Club | G. | PO. | A. | E. | DP. | Pct. | Player and Club | G. | PO. | A. | E. | DP. | Pct. |
|---|---|---|---|---|---|---|---|---|---|---|---|---|---|
| Narron, Ft Lauder | 36 | 234 | 16 | 0 | 19 | 1.000 | Werth, Ft Lauder | 69 | 557 | 40 | 9 | 40 | .985 |
| Unsoeld, Tampa | 14 | 110 | 7 | 0 | 12 | 1.000 | Krause, WPB | 14 | 119 | 10 | 2 | 14 | .985 |
| Natchez, Lakeland | 4 | 24 | 3 | 0 | 2 | 1.000 | Russo, Winter Haven* | 56 | 519 | 45 | 9 | 41 | .984 |
| Alvarez, Lakeland* | 3 | 23 | 0 | 0 | 2 | 1.000 | Spilman, Tampa | 106 | 946 | 56 | 17 | 82 | .983 |
| James, Miami | 3 | 12 | 1 | 0 | 2 | 1.000 | Staggs, WPB* | 73 | 655 | 53 | 12 | 49 | .983 |
| Rump, Winter Haven | 1 | 2 | 0 | 0 | 0 | 1.000 | Loomans, Key West | 35 | 304 | 26 | 6 | 27 | .982 |
| Register, Winter Haven | 1 | 0 | 1 | 0 | 0 | 1.000 | Pastore, St Peter | 7 | 54 | 2 | 1 | 5 | .982 |
| Foster, Winter Haven | 60 | 551 | 58 | 4 | 42 | .993 | M. Gordon, Key West | 16 | 148 | 5 | 3 | 9 | .981 |
| Morgan, Lakeland | 84 | 783 | 47 | 7 | 66 | .992 | Chism, Miami* | 38 | 325 | 17 | 7 | 35 | .980 |
| Marvelle, WPB | 40 | 321 | 28 | 3 | 19 | .991 | Plunkett, Ft Lauder* | 43 | 331 | 29 | 9 | 24 | .976 |
| HERNANDEZ, StP* | 131 | 1126 | 53 | 13 | 97 | .989 | Garboza, Winter Haven | 15 | 117 | 6 | 3 | 19 | .976 |
| Randall, Key West* | 55 | 508 | 40 | 6 | 40 | .989 | Thompson, WPB | 5 | 32 | 1 | 1 | 1 | .971 |
| Costantine, Tampa | 19 | 175 | 8 | 2 | 14 | .989 | Curran, WPB | 7 | 59 | 6 | 2 | 8 | .970 |
| Coughlan, Lakeland | 47 | 414 | 27 | 6 | 32 | .987 | Schafer, WPB | 3 | 28 | 3 | 1 | 2 | .969 |
| Hall, Key West* | 34 | 336 | 11 | 5 | 25 | .986 | Sansosti, St Peter | 2 | 14 | 2 | 1 | 1 | .941 |
| R. Ford, Miami | 109 | 1042 | 50 | 17 | 89 | .985 | Thompson, Key West* | 1 | 5 | 0 | 1 | 0 | .833 |

### SECOND BASEMEN

| Player and Club | G. | PO. | A. | E. | DP. | Pct. | Player and Club | G. | PO. | A. | E. | DP. | Pct. |
|---|---|---|---|---|---|---|---|---|---|---|---|---|---|
| McMillan, Miami | 14 | 18 | 34 | 0 | 4 | 1.000 | Drury, Key West | 119 | 303 | 367 | 25 | 58 | .964 |
| Massee, Key West | 9 | 17 | 12 | 0 | 1 | 1.000 | Boras, St Peter | 92 | 158 | 201 | 14 | 46 | .962 |
| Perez, W Palm Beach | 3 | 9 | 13 | 0 | 2 | 1.000 | Austin, Lakeland | 4 | 9 | 16 | 1 | 4 | .962 |
| Jimenez, Key West | 2 | 8 | 8 | 0 | 3 | 1.000 | Bernazard, WPB | 132 | 280 | 386 | 28 | 62 | .960 |
| Sigman, Miami | 2 | 6 | 7 | 0 | 2 | 1.000 | Reed, Miami | 45 | 72 | 114 | 8 | 21 | .959 |
| Matthews, WPB | 2 | 6 | 4 | 0 | 1 | 1.000 | Stapleton, Win Haven | 33 | 83 | 99 | 8 | 19 | .958 |
| Thompson, Ft Lauder | 1 | 3 | 3 | 0 | 0 | 1.000 | Alvarez, Ft Laud | 16 | 31 | 34 | 3 | 6 | .956 |
| Thompson, WPB | 1 | 3 | 0 | 0 | 0 | 1.000 | Buba, Winter Haven | 87 | 198 | 265 | 23 | 43 | .953 |
| K. Gordon, Key West | 2 | 2 | 1 | 0 | 1 | 1.000 | Maier, Ft Lauder | 11 | 18 | 23 | 2 | 3 | .953 |
| Draimin, Miami | 1 | 1 | 1 | 0 | 1 | 1.000 | J. J. Martinez, Miami | 10 | 13 | 27 | 2 | 5 | .952 |
| R. Ford, Miami | 1 | 0 | 0 | 0 | 1 | 1.000 | Ireland, Miami | 38 | 80 | 123 | 11 | 30 | .949 |
| Stephenson, W Haven | 1 | 0 | 1 | 0 | 0 | 1.000 | Perez, Ft Lauder | 112 | 230 | 304 | 30 | 56 | .947 |
| GRAUMANN, Tam. | 124 | 262 | 369 | 13 | 87 | .980 | Litras, Lakeland | 18 | 34 | 54 | 5 | 8 | .946 |
| Bowden, Lakeland | 58 | 126 | 124 | 6 | 38 | .977 | Costantine, Tampa | 5 | 6 | 9 | 1 | 1 | .938 |
| Butler, Lakeland | 55 | 133 | 139 | 7 | 39 | .975 | Iorg, Ft Lauder | 11 | 25 | 28 | 4 | 3 | .930 |
| Urena, Miami | 47 | 95 | 98 | 6 | 26 | .970 | Cowens, St Peter | 26 | 52 | 56 | 9 | 10 | .923 |
| Rump, Winter Haven | 12 | 29 | 31 | 2 | 3 | .968 | Santo Domingo, Tam | 5 | 7 | 14 | 2 | 1 | .913 |
| Redoglia, St Peter | 28 | 50 | 60 | 4 | 12 | .965 | Brockway, Key West | 11 | 18 | 26 | 5 | 3 | .898 |

## THIRD BASEMEN

| Player and Club | G. | PO. | A. | E. | DP. | Pct. |
|---|---|---|---|---|---|---|
| Brockway, Key West | 15 | 12 | 21 | 0 | 1 | 1.000 |
| Evans, WPB | 3 | 3 | 5 | 0 | 2 | 1.000 |
| Merenda, Lakeland | 2 | 5 | 2 | 0 | 1 | 1.000 |
| Butler, Lakeland | 2 | 1 | 5 | 0 | 1 | 1.000 |
| Bowden, Lakeland | 2 | 1 | 2 | 0 | 0 | 1.000 |
| Draimin, Miami | 1 | 1 | 1 | 0 | 0 | 1.000 |
| Massee, Key West | 1 | 0 | 2 | 0 | 0 | 1.000 |
| Matthews, WPB | 1 | 0 | 1 | 0 | 0 | 1.000 |
| McCarthy, Miami | 1 | 0 | 1 | 0 | 0 | 1.000 |
| R. Ford, Miami | 18 | 10 | 25 | 1 | 3 | .972 |
| Umfleet, Key West | 8 | 7 | 24 | 1 | 1 | .969 |
| Reed, Miami | 15 | 12 | 18 | 1 | 0 | .968 |
| Leyva, St Peter | 30 | 26 | 53 | 3 | 1 | .963 |
| Edelen, St Peter | 18 | 5 | 21 | 1 | 2 | .963 |
| VAZQUEZ, St Peter | 94 | 92 | 165 | 11 | 17 | .959 |
| Evans, Winter Haven | 58 | 45 | 110 | 8 | 9 | .951 |
| Stephenson, W Haven | 13 | 9 | 29 | 2 | 3 | .950 |
| Coughlan, Lakeland | 6 | 3 | 16 | 1 | 0 | .950 |
| Grace, Tampa | 113 | 107 | 276 | 21 | 27 | .948 |
| Fry, W Palm Beach | 125 | 118 | 236 | 21 | 10 | .944 |
| Peterson, Ft Lauder | 105 | 100 | 182 | 19 | 13 | .937 |
| Parrill, Miami | 105 | 69 | 222 | 20 | 14 | .936 |
| Costantine, Tampa | 27 | 11 | 44 | 4 | 7 | .932 |
| K. Gordon, Key West | 119 | 113 | 230 | 27 | 9 | .927 |
| Iorg, Ft Lauder | 31 | 26 | 45 | 6 | 3 | .922 |
| Viefhaus, Lakeland | 121 | 86 | 282 | 33 | 23 | .918 |
| Curran, WPB-Lake. | 6 | 4 | 6 | 1 | 0 | .909 |
| Garboza, Win Haven | 51 | 40 | 85 | 13 | 6 | .906 |
| Rump, Winter Haven | 9 | 8 | 3 | 1 | 1 | .842 |
| Thompson, WPB | 3 | 6 | 4 | 2 | 0 | .833 |
| Boras, St Peter | 4 | 2 | 3 | 1 | 0 | .833 |
| Ireland, Miami | 4 | 3 | 6 | 2 | 1 | .818 |
| Urena, Miami | 2 | 2 | 2 | 1 | 0 | .800 |
| Litras, Lakeland | 1 | 2 | 1 | 1 | 0 | .750 |
| Alvarez, Ft Lauder | 4 | 2 | 1 | 1 | 0 | .750 |
| Maier, Ft Lauder | 2 | 2 | 0 | 1 | 0 | .667 |

## SHORTSTOPS

| Player and Club | G. | PO. | A. | E. | DP. | Pct. |
|---|---|---|---|---|---|---|
| Drury, Key West | 5 | 9 | 13 | 0 | 1 | 1.000 |
| Grace, Tampa | 5 | 4 | 10 | 0 | 1 | 1.000 |
| Bernazard, WPB | 1 | 2 | 3 | 0 | 0 | 1.000 |
| Perez, Ft Lauder | 1 | 0 | 5 | 0 | 0 | 1.000 |
| Peterson, Ft Lauder | 1 | 2 | 2 | 0 | 0 | 1.000 |
| Henderson, Tampa | 2 | 1 | 0 | 0 | 0 | 1.000 |
| Butler, Lakeland | 14 | 33 | 43 | 2 | 8 | .974 |
| Oberkfell, St Peter | 39 | 71 | 107 | 6 | 17 | .967 |
| G. Gingrich, WPB. | 44 | 75 | 142 | 8 | 25 | .964 |
| Reed, Miami | 22 | 33 | 61 | 4 | 9 | .959 |
| JIMENEZ, Key West | 129 | 232 | 444 | 35 | 73 | .951 |
| Sigman, Miami | 126 | 181 | 431 | 33 | 73 | .949 |
| Leyva, St Peter | 17 | 22 | 52 | 4 | 9 | .949 |
| Brockway, Key West | 8 | 5 | 13 | 1 | 3 | .947 |
| Merenda, Lakeland | 7 | 7 | 9 | 1 | 1 | .941 |
| Oester, Tampa | 117 | 174 | 358 | 34 | 69 | .940 |
| Costantine, Tampa | 4 | 7 | 8 | 1 | 2 | .938 |
| Perez, W Palm Beach | 23 | 38 | 50 | 6 | 11 | .936 |
| Fischlin, Ft Lauder | 29 | 54 | 90 | 10 | 19 | .935 |
| Heath, Ft Lauder | 97 | 184 | 256 | 31 | 42 | .934 |
| Templeton, St Peter | 82 | 130 | 253 | 29 | 53 | .930 |
| Stephenson, W Haven | 52 | 108 | 170 | 21 | 29 | .930 |
| Jackson, Lakeland | 113 | 190 | 323 | 39 | 66 | .929 |
| Maier, Ft Lauder | 10 | 14 | 22 | 3 | 4 | .923 |
| Rump, Win Haven | 2 | 3 | 8 | 1 | 1 | .917 |
| Evans, W Palm Beach | 41 | 63 | 99 | 15 | 13 | .915 |
| Stapleton, W Haven | 13 | 16 | 44 | 6 | 5 | .909 |
| DeLeon, Win Haven. | 67 | 102 | 215 | 33 | 43 | .906 |
| Thompson, WPB | 32 | 57 | 72 | 15 | 16 | .896 |
| Iorg, Ft Lauder | 2 | 3 | 5 | 1 | 0 | .889 |
| Urena, Miami | 5 | 10 | 13 | 3 | 4 | .885 |
| Santo Domingo, Tam | 8 | 4 | 26 | 4 | 0 | .882 |
| Thompson, Lakeland | 3 | 5 | 6 | 2 | 0 | .846 |
| Matthews, WPB | 1 | 1 | 4 | 1 | 1 | .833 |
| McCarthy, Miami | 4 | 2 | 3 | 1 | 1 | .833 |
| Cowens, St Peter | 1 | 1 | 3 | 1 | 0 | .800 |
| Westerman, Tampa | 3 | 3 | 8 | 4 | 2 | .733 |

## OUTFIELDERS

| Player and Club | G. | PO. | A. | E. | DP. | Pct. |
|---|---|---|---|---|---|---|
| Hernandez, Key West | 48 | 94 | 5 | 0 | 1 | 1.000 |
| Natchez, Lakeland | 34 | 51 | 0 | 0 | 0 | 1.000 |
| Colzie, Tampa | 27 | 41 | 1 | 0 | 0 | 1.000 |
| Grandy, Key West | 30 | 41 | 1 | 0 | 0 | 1.000 |
| Narron, Ft Lauder | 26 | 34 | 3 | 0 | 0 | 1.000 |
| K. Gordon, Key West | 17 | 22 | 1 | 0 | 0 | 1.000 |
| Lentine, St Peter | 7 | 16 | 2 | 0 | 0 | 1.000 |
| Werth, Ft Lauder | 10 | 14 | 2 | 0 | 0 | 1.000 |
| Alvarez, Ft Lauder | 6 | 11 | 2 | 0 | 0 | 1.000 |
| Iorg, Ft Lauder | 8 | 13 | 0 | 0 | 0 | 1.000 |
| Maier, Ft Lauder | 11 | 9 | 1 | 0 | 0 | 1.000 |
| Stapleton, W Haven. | 3 | 7 | 0 | 0 | 0 | 1.000 |
| Reed, Miami | 2 | 5 | 1 | 0 | 0 | 1.000 |
| Moretto, Tampa | 5 | 4 | 2 | 0 | 1 | 1.000 |
| Rinden, Miami | 6 | 5 | 1 | 0 | 0 | 1.000 |
| G. Gingrich, WPB | 9 | 6 | 0 | 0 | 0 | 1.000 |
| Costantine, Tampa | 2 | 4 | 1 | 0 | 0 | 1.000 |
| Viefhaus, Lakeland. | 2 | 5 | 0 | 0 | 0 | 1.000 |
| Gonzalez, WPB | 4 | 5 | 0 | 0 | 0 | 1.000 |
| Drury, Key West | 1 | 2 | 2 | 0 | 0 | 1.000 |
| Feramisco, Miami | 1 | 3 | 0 | 0 | 0 | 1.000 |
| Meek, Key West* | 3 | 2 | 1 | 0 | 1 | 1.000 |
| Jimenez, Key West | 1 | 2 | 0 | 0 | 0 | 1.000 |
| Marshall, Key West. | 1 | 1 | 1 | 0 | 0 | 1.000 |
| Boras, St Peter | 2 | 2 | 0 | 0 | 0 | 1.000 |
| Pastore, St Peter. | 2 | 2 | 0 | 0 | 0 | 1.000 |
| Draimin, Miami | 1 | 1 | 0 | 0 | 0 | 1.000 |
| Unsoeld, Tampa | 1 | 1 | 0 | 0 | 0 | 1.000 |
| Putman, Key West | 2 | 1 | 0 | 0 | 0 | 1.000 |
| HUIZENGA, WH. | 91 | 207 | 6 | 1 | 1 | .995 |
| Welsh, WPB | 68 | 149 | 5 | 1 | 2 | .994 |
| Jones, Tampa | 55 | 130 | 4 | 1 | 0 | .993 |
| Martinez, Lakeland. | 99 | 219 | 4 | 2 | 1 | .991 |
| Flesh, Miami* | 120 | 172 | 17 | 2 | 3 | .990 |
| Thompson, Ft Lauder | 101 | 195 | 16 | 3 | 0 | .986 |
| Lyle, Tampa | 69 | 121 | 7 | 2 | 0 | .985 |
| Whiting, Miami* | 120 | 192 | 10 | 4 | 1 | .981 |
| Morello, W Haven | 79 | 140 | 5 | 3 | 1 | .980 |
| Landrum, St Peter | 132 | 313 | 5 | 7 | 1 | .978 |
| Chew, Key West | 100 | 216 | 8 | 5 | 0 | .978 |
| Norris, Ft Lauder | 47 | 86 | 2 | 2 | 1 | .978 |
| Sorey, WPB | 117 | 241 | 5 | 6 | 4 | .976 |
| Edwards, Miami* | 124 | 234 | 12 | 6 | 2 | .976 |
| Norman, Tampa | 123 | 192 | 9 | 5 | 4 | .976 |
| Verban, Key West | 67 | 72 | 11 | 2 | 1 | .976 |
| Wood, WPB | 46 | 76 | 5 | 2 | 1 | .976 |
| Koza, W Haven* | 104 | 151 | 8 | 4 | 0 | .975 |
| Blackwell, St. Peter. | 100 | 178 | 6 | 5 | 0 | .974 |
| Hampton, W Haven. | 51 | 103 | 6 | 3 | 0 | .973 |
| Henderson, Tampa | 116 | 262 | 7 | 8 | 1 | .971 |
| Figueroa, Ft Lauder* | 90 | 215 | 13 | 7 | 4 | .970 |
| Meltz, Ft Lauder | 59 | 93 | 3 | 3 | 0 | .970 |
| Crockett, St Peter | 112 | 209 | 6 | 8 | 2 | .964 |
| Cacciatore, Lakeland* | 72 | 105 | 2 | 4 | 1 | .964 |
| Bowen, W Haven | 12 | 26 | 0 | 1 | 0 | .963 |
| Krause, Miami | 100 | 190 | 11 | 8 | 2 | .962 |
| Bendick, Ft Lauder. | 19 | 48 | 1 | 2 | 1 | .961 |
| James, Miami | 31 | 48 | 1 | 2 | 0 | .961 |
| Register, W Haven | 14 | 22 | 1 | 1 | 0 | .958 |
| Rosseau, St Peter | 54 | 84 | 3 | 4 | 0 | .956 |
| Swanson, Lakeland* | 106 | 166 | 4 | 8 | 0 | .955 |
| Plunkett, Ft L* | 44 | 72 | 4 | 4 | 1 | .950 |
| Woodland, WPB | 73 | 106 | 4 | 6 | 1 | .948 |
| Urena, Miami | 34 | 51 | 4 | 3 | 1 | .948 |
| Thompson, K West* | 119 | 181 | 10 | 11 | 1 | .946 |
| Rubertino, Lakeland* | 81 | 107 | 4 | 7 | 1 | .941 |
| Curran, WPB-Lake. | 22 | 38 | 1 | 3 | 0 | .929 |
| Anderson, Key West. | 15 | 34 | 3 | 3 | 0 | .925 |
| Hall, Key West* | 34 | 47 | 0 | 4 | 0 | .922 |
| Hendon, W. Haven. | 26 | 36 | 1 | 4 | 0 | .902 |
| Simonton, W. Haven. | 19 | 25 | 1 | 3 | 0 | .897 |
| Antonetty, Ft Lauder | 25 | 23 | 2 | 7 | 0 | .781 |

## CATCHERS

| Player and Club | G. | PO. | A. | E. | DP. | PB. | Pct. |
|---|---|---|---|---|---|---|---|
| Curran, WPB-Lak | 28 | 143 | 11 | 0 | 3 | 10 | 1.000 |
| Ehrig, Miami...... | 9 | 28 | 0 | 0 | 0 | 1 | 1.000 |
| Johnson, St Peter.. | 4 | 23 | 1 | 0 | 1 | 0 | 1.000 |
| Whiteaker, WPB .. | 3 | 16 | 2 | 0 | 1 | 0 | 1.000 |
| Styles, Tampa .... | 1 | 1 | 0 | 0 | 0 | 1 | 1.000 |
| Daves, St Peter.. | 38 | 493 | 35 | 2 | 6 | 8 | .996 |
| STONE. St Peter..31 | 191 | 10 | 1 | 1 | 4 | | .995 |
| DiPietro, Lakeland | 14 | 80 | 8 | 1 | 1 | 3 | .989 |
| Narron, Ft Lauder | 34 | 157 | 14 | 2 | 2 | 5 | .988 |
| Harrison, St Peter | 14 | 80 | 4 | 1 | 0 | 5 | .988 |
| Parrish, Lakeland | 84 | 460 | 50 | 7 | 8 | 31 | .986 |
| Werth, Ft Lauder | 15 | 93 | 6 | 2 | 1 | 7 | .980 |
| Putman, K West | 54 | 283 | 42 | 7 | 6 | 11 | .979 |
| Coombs, Lakeland | 32 | 169 | 16 | 4 | 4 | 5 | .979 |
| Cline, Miami ....64 | 348 | 39 | 9 | 2 | 23 | | .977 |
| Woolley, Tampa ..75 | 370 | 43 | 10 | 4 | 18 | | .976 |
| Gill, Ft Lauder ..60 | 326 | 38 | 9 | 4 | 11 | | .976 |
| Unsoeld, Tampa ..64 | 329 | 20 | 9 | 2 | 9 | | .975 |
| Kane, W Haven ..21 | 108 | 10 | 3 | 2 | 7 | | .975 |
| Clancy, Key West..26 | 180 | 20 | 6 | 2 | 3 | | .971 |
| Villa, Miami ....81 | 424 | 57 | 15 | 3 | 13 | | .970 |
| Ramos, WPB .....61 | 374 | 49 | 13 | 5 | 24 | | .970 |
| Floyd, W Haven ..15 | 55 | 10 | 2 | 0 | 4 | | .970 |
| Helget, Tam-WH ..53 | 232 | 21 | 8 | 0 | 7 | | .969 |
| Meltz, Ft Lauder..42 | 193 | 28 | 7 | 2 | 14 | | .969 |
| Schafer, WPB ....37 | 170 | 20 | 6 | 2 | 12 | | .969 |
| M. Gordon, KW...65 | 245 | 30 | 9 | 0 | 12 | | .968 |
| Cooper, WPB .... | 17 | 75 | 7 | 3 | 1 | 4 | .965 |
| McAlister, WH ...11 | 49 | 3 | 3 | 1 | 1 | | .945 |
| Fry, WPB ....... | 3 | 12 | 2 | 1 | 0 | 0 | .933 |
| O'Berry, W Haven | 39 | 120 | 24 | 11 | 1 | 3 | .929 |
| Hill, Key West .. | 3 | 8 | 3 | 1 | 0 | 2 | .917 |
| Pritchett, St Peter | 3 | 10 | 1 | 1 | 0 | 0 | .917 |

## PITCHERS

| Player and Club | G. | PO. | A. | E. | DP. | Pct. |
|---|---|---|---|---|---|---|
| Turner, Key West ... | 24 | 10 | 28 | 0 | 0 | 1.000 |
| Uhey, Key West .. | 31 | 4 | 24 | 0 | 1 | 1.000 |
| Bashaw, St Peter ... | 34 | 4 | 23 | 0 | 2 | 1.000 |
| Cappuzzello, Lake*.. | 16 | 3 | 22 | 0 | 1 | 1.000 |
| Fidrych, Lakeland . | 17 | 8 | 16 | 0 | 0 | 1.000 |
| Viebrock, Tampa* .. | 23 | 8 | 16 | 0 | 1 | 1.000 |
| Reed, Tampa ........ | 23 | 4 | 17 | 0 | 1 | 1.000 |
| Madden, Lakeland .. | 28 | 8 | 10 | 0 | 1 | 1.000 |
| Capilla, St. Peter*.. | 8 | 1 | 15 | 0 | 0 | 1.000 |
| Harris, Lakeland ... | 7 | 2 | 13 | 0 | 1 | 1.000 |
| Murphy, St Peter .. | 43 | 2 | 13 | 0 | 1 | 1.000 |
| Dumoulin, Tampa .. | 45 | 1 | 14 | 0 | 1 | 1.000 |
| Trotter, Ft Lauder . | 8 | 3 | 11 | 0 | 1 | 1.000 |
| Hannahs, WPB*.... | 8 | 4 | 9 | 0 | 0 | 1.000 |
| Kleibl, W Haven .. | 16 | 7 | 6 | 0 | 0 | 1.000 |
| Polonio, W Haven . | 19 | 6 | 6 | 0 | 2 | 1.000 |
| Meek, St Peter* ... | 23 | 3 | 9 | 0 | 2 | 1.000 |
| Proctor, W Haven . | 35 | 5 | 7 | 0 | 2 | 1.000 |
| Finlayson, WPB ... | 13 | 3 | 8 | 0 | 0 | 1.000 |
| Ware, Key West* ... | 27 | 2 | 9 | 0 | 1 | 1.000 |
| Kerrigan, WPB .... | 22 | 3 | 7 | 0 | 2 | 1.000 |
| Ewell, WPB ........ | 23 | 3 | 7 | 0 | 0 | 1.000 |
| Replogle, St Peter . | 5 | 1 | 8 | 0 | 0 | 1.000 |
| Agosto, W Haven* . | 6 | 2 | 6 | 0 | 0 | 1.000 |
| Riley, WPB .........11 | 0 | 8 | 0 | 2 | | 1.000 |
| Murphy, Lakeland*.. | 18 | 1 | 7 | 0 | 1 | 1.000 |
| Mendez, Ft Lauder .10 | 4 | 3 | 0 | 0 | | 1.000 |
| Kwasny, Ft Lauder .12 | 1 | 6 | 0 | 0 | | 1.000 |
| Sullivan, Ft Lauder* | 6 | 1 | 5 | 0 | 0 | 1.000 |
| Rieger, St Peter*.... | 8 | 1 | 4 | 0 | 0 | 1.000 |
| Vogel, Key West*... | 5 | 1 | 3 | 0 | 0 | 1.000 |
| Dwyer, Lakeland ...11 | 0 | 4 | 0 | 0 | | 1.000 |
| Flinn, Miami ....... | 4 | 1 | 2 | 0 | 0 | 1.000 |
| Broomis, Miami ... | 5 | 0 | 3 | 0 | 1 | 1.000 |
| Staniland, St Peter . | 2 | 2 | 0 | 0 | 0 | 1.000 |
| Edelen, St. Peter ... | 5 | 0 | 2 | 0 | 0 | 1.000 |
| Motil, Lakeland* ... | 6 | 1 | 1 | 0 | 0 | 1.000 |
| Trumbauer, St Peter* | 6 | 0 | 2 | 0 | 0 | 1.000 |
| Daniels, Lakeland ... | 7 | 0 | 2 | 0 | 0 | 1.000 |
| Baltz, WPB .........10 | 1 | 1 | 0 | 0 | | 1.000 |
| Tufts, Key West* ...13 | 1 | 1 | 0 | 0 | | 1.000 |
| D. Ford, Miami ... | 2 | 1 | 0 | 0 | 0 | 1.000 |
| Paz, Ft Lauder .... | 2 | 0 | 1 | 0 | 0 | 1.000 |
| Urrea, St Peter ...23 | 15 | 30 | 1 | 1 | | .978 |
| Doland, Key West...28 | 16 | 29 | 1 | 2 | | .978 |
| Burke, Winter Haven | 26 | 18 | 26 | 1 | 0 | .978 |
| Stanley, W Haven... | 27 | 12 | 30 | 1 | 2 | .977 |
| J. D. Martinez, Miami | 20 | 9 | 29 | 1 | 2 | .974 |
| Hamrick, Key West* | 15 | 6 | 21 | 1 | 2 | .964 |
| Mercier, Lakeland ..26 | 12 | 13 | 1 | 2 | | .962 |
| Bombard, Tampa*...21 | 5 | 19 | 1 | 1 | | .960 |
| Caudill, St. Peter ..25 | 3 | 21 | 1 | 2 | | .960 |
| Remmerswaal, W Hav | 27 | 6 | 18 | 1 | 0 | .960 |
| Temple, Key West....39 | 7 | 15 | 1 | 2 | | .957 |
| Finch, Winter Haven | 26 | 17 | 26 | 2 | 3 | .956 |
| Diehl, Ft Lauder....23 | 18 | 36 | 3 | 3 | | .947 |
| Smith, Miami ......26 | 7 | 29 | 2 | 0 | | .947 |
| Vernoy, Key West* ..22 | 5 | 12 | 1 | 1 | | .944 |
| Chevez, Miami .....33 | 17 | 30 | 3 | 3 | | .940 |
| Treuel, Lakeland ...26 | 14 | 16 | 2 | 0 | | .938 |
| MacQuarrie, WPB ..21 | 4 | 25 | 2 | 1 | | .935 |
| Stewart, St Peter ...14 | 8 | 20 | 2 | 5 | | .933 |
| Tyler, Lakeland* ...27 | 11 | 17 | 2 | 2 | | .933 |
| Irwin, Lakeland ....14 | 2 | 12 | 1 | 2 | | .933 |
| Moore, Miami* .....17 | 4 | 10 | 1 | 1 | | .933 |
| Riley, Key West*...28 | 5 | 9 | 1 | 1 | | .932 |
| Delgatti, Ft Lauder..16 | 13 | 13 | 2 | 0 | | .930 |
| Antor, Winter Haven | 22 | 5 | 8 | 1 | 1 | .929 |
| Ferreyra, Tampa ...45 | 4 | 9 | 1 | 1 | | .929 |
| Rogers, Key West ...11 | 8 | 17 | 2 | 0 | | .926 |
| Snyder, Miami .....25 | 3 | 9 | 1 | 0 | | .923 |
| Rawley, WPB*......24 | 1 | 34 | 3 | 1 | | .921 |
| Rajsich, Ft Lauder*..23 | 3 | 20 | 2 | 2 | | .920 |
| LaCoss. Tampa ....23 | 8 | 25 | 3 | 2 | | .917 |
| Hoyt, Ft Lauder .... | 7 | 5 | 6 | 1 | 0 | .917 |
| Rineer, Miami* .....11 | 0 | 10 | 1 | 1 | | .909 |
| Kruppa, Ft Lauder*..32 | 3 | 7 | 1 | 0 | | .909 |
| Dues, WPB .........18 | 5 | 33 | 4 | 1 | | .905 |
| Horn, WPB ........ | 16 | 7 | 21 | 3 | 1 | .903 |
| Kennedy, St Peter ..23 | 6 | 12 | 2 | 2 | | .900 |
| Hoyles, Miami ..... | 7 | 4 | 5 | 1 | 1 | .900 |
| Woodland, WPB ... | 7 | 5 | 4 | 1 | 0 | .900 |
| Bierman, Ft Lauder* | 23 | 2 | 7 | 1 | 0 | .900 |
| J. Gingrich, WPB ..16 | 5 | 12 | 2 | 3 | | .895 |
| Alonso, Lakeland* ..13 | 2 | 6 | 1 | 2 | | .889 |
| Corbett, Tampa ....27 | 2 | 6 | 1 | 0 | | .889 |
| Melvin, Ft Lauder ..28 | 5 | 16 | 3 | 1 | | .875 |
| Robles, Ft Lauder ..13 | 5 | 2 | 1 | 0 | | .875 |
| Sorensen, St Peter ..18 | 0 | 7 | 1 | 1 | | .875 |
| Mayo, Miami ......25 | 9 | 18 | 4 | 5 | | .871 |
| Cross, Winter Haven.14 | 8 | 5 | 2 | 0 | | .867 |
| Bastian, WPB ......23 | 12 | 24 | 6 | 3 | | .857 |
| Camper, St Peter ...13 | 3 | 15 | 3 | 0 | | .857 |
| Swanson, WPB ..... | 9 | 4 | 2 | 1 | 1 | .857 |
| Wright, Ft Lauder ..18 | 1 | 5 | 1 | 0 | | .857 |
| Kibbee, Miami .....32 | 4 | 13 | 3 | 3 | | .850 |
| Miller, Miami ......55 | 1 | 21 | 4 | 0 | | .846 |
| Wood, Key West ...29 | 9 | 17 | 5 | 1 | | .839 |
| Carp, Ft Lauder ...16 | 1 | 9 | 2 | 0 | | .833 |
| Underwood, Tampa . | 4 | 2 | 3 | 1 | 1 | .833 |
| Chandler, Tampa* ..24 | 4 | 23 | 6 | 1 | | .818 |
| Garvey, Tampa .....18 | 4 | 9 | 3 | 0 | | .813 |
| Fleshman, Ft Lauder | 27 | 10 | 19 | 7 | 2 | .806 |
| Hardeman, W Haven.20 | 4 | 8 | 3 | 0 | | .800 |
| Knose, WPB ....... | 5 | 3 | 1 | 1 | 0 | .800 |
| Tobik, Lakeland ... | 5 | 0 | 7 | 2 | 0 | .778 |
| Wilkerson, Key West | 19 | 1 | 8 | 3 | 2 | .750 |
| Rusk, Ft Lauder .... | 4 | 0 | 3 | 1 | 0 | .750 |
| Grabowski, WPB ... | 8 | 1 | 2 | 1 | 0 | .750 |
| Halgerson, Tampa .. | 8 | 0 | 3 | 1 | 0 | .750 |
| Alcantara, Ft Lauder.12 | 4 | 6 | 4 | 0 | | .714 |
| Darr, Miami ........14 | 2 | 7 | 4 | 0 | | .692 |
| Moore, Key West ... | 6 | 1 | 1 | 1 | 0 | .667 |
| Moore, Tampa ..... | 6 | 0 | 2 | 1 | 0 | .667 |
| Meyerrose, Lakeland. | 8 | 1 | 1 | 2 | 0 | .500 |
| Baby, WPB* ........ | 5 | 0 | 1 | 1 | 0 | .500 |

The following players do not have any recorded accepted chances at the positions indicated; therefore, are not listed in the fielding averages for those particular positions: Adams, p; Bickerton*, p; Colzie, p; Ehrig, p; Farrow*, p; Groover*, p; Lopez, p; O'Neill*, p; Plunkett*, p; Redmon, c; Vallejos, p. Bird appeared as a pinch-runner only.

## CLUB PITCHING

| Club | G. | CG. | ShO. | Sv. | IP. | H. | R. | ER. | HR. | BB. | Int. BB. | HB. | SO. | WP. | Bk. | ERA. |
|------|-----|-----|------|-----|------|------|-----|-----|-----|-----|-----|-----|-----|-----|-----|------|
| Tampa | 131 | 39 | 25 | 14 | 1108 | 879 | 366 | 289 | 29 | 384 | 17 | 25 | 659 | 47 | 7 | 2.35 |
| St. Petersburg | 135 | 52 | 20 | 25 | 1148 | 917 | 403 | 326 | 27 | 500 | 24 | 33 | 731 | 58 | 11 | 2.56 |
| Miami | 136 | 33 | 11 | 26 | 1187 | 1031 | 488 | 362 | 41 | 475 | 11 | 41 | 739 | 54 | 13 | 2.74 |
| Winter Haven | 127 | 45 | 9 | 14 | 1066 | 995 | 490 | 368 | 24 | 434 | 13 | 38 | 504 | 40 | 12 | 3.11 |
| Ft. Lauderdale | 137 | 46 | 21 | 15 | 1158 | 1005 | 533 | 420 | 36 | 578 | 18 | 44 | 709 | 55 | 15 | 3.26 |
| West Palm Beach | 137 | 48 | 5 | 13 | 1162 | 1035 | 551 | 428 | 30 | 587 | 15 | 35 | 727 | 85 | 14 | 3.31 |
| Lakeland | 133 | 60 | 8 | 10 | 1121 | 1037 | 514 | 422 | 32 | 531 | 10 | 46 | 679 | 58 | 10 | 3.39 |
| Key West | 134 | 31 | 10 | 23 | 1175 | 1094 | 538 | 455 | 49 | 570 | 32 | 49 | 647 | 48 | 7 | 3.49 |

(Leading Qualifiers for Earned-Run Average Leadership—109 or More Innings)
*Throws lefthanded.

| Pitcher—Club | G. | GS. | CG. | ShO. | W. | L. | Sv. | Pct. | IP. | H. | R. | ER. | HR. | BB. | Int. BB. | HB. | SO. | WP. | ERA. |
|------|-----|-----|-----|------|-----|-----|-----|------|-----|-----|-----|-----|-----|-----|-----|-----|-----|-----|------|
| Bashaw, St Peter. | 34 | 0 | 0 | 0 | 6 | 3 | 3 | .667 | 117 | 103 | 30 | 22 | 1 | 34 | 5 | 3 | 52 | 4 | 1.69 |
| Stewart, St Peter | 14 | 14 | 9 | 5 | 11 | 2 | 0 | .846 | 113 | 72 | 24 | 22 | 0 | 34 | 3 | 2 | 56 | 3 | 1.75 |
| Hamrick, K West* | 15 | 15 | 4 | 2 | 5 | 6 | 0 | .455 | 111 | 81 | 29 | 24 | 1 | 53 | 3 | 1 | 97 | 5 | 1.95 |
| Chandler, Tam* | 24 | 22 | 8 | 6 | 10 | 8 | 1 | .556 | 157 | 102 | 43 | 34 | 3 | 55 | 2 | 7 | 83 | 3 | 1.95 |
| Reed, Tampa | 23 | 22 | 7 | 3 | 12 | 8 | 0 | .600 | 157 | 123 | 48 | 35 | 4 | 52 | 1 | 0 | 98 | 2 | 2.01 |
| Chevez, Miami | 33 | 18 | 8 | 2 | 14 | 6 | 3 | .700 | 156 | 136 | 52 | 36 | 6 | 30 | 1 | 8 | 70 | 1 | 2.08 |
| Urrea, St Peter | 23 | 22 | 11 | 2 | 14 | 8 | 0 | .636 | 153 | 138 | 61 | 41 | 1 | 60 | 1 | 4 | 108 | 7 | 2.11 |
| Smith, Miami | 26 | 20 | 5 | 2 | 11 | 7 | 1 | .611 | 139 | 117 | 48 | 33 | 4 | 59 | 1 | 5 | 93 | 8 | 2.14 |
| Diehl, Ft Lauder. | 23 | 23 | 10 | 3 | 11 | 10 | 0 | .524 | 167 | 149 | 63 | 45 | 6 | 42 | 1 | 4 | 93 | 1 | 2.43 |
| Rajsich, Ft Laud* | 23 | 15 | 10 | 4 | 5 | 9 | 0 | .357 | 125 | 88 | 45 | 34 | 3 | 48 | 0 | 4 | 79 | 5 | 2.45 |
| Bombard, Tampa* | 21 | 19 | 2 | 2 | 6 | 5 | 0 | .545 | 110 | 80 | 38 | 30 | 6 | 46 | 2 | 2 | 72 | 1 | 2.45 |

Departmental Leaders: G—Miller, 55; GS—Finch, Riley (KW), Stanley, Tyler, 26; CG—Caudill, 12; ShO—Chandler, 6; W—Caudill, Chevez, Urrea, 14; L—Stanley, 17; Sv—Murphy (StP), 16; Pct.—Stewart, .846; IP—Finch, 184; H—Tyler, 174; R—Tyler, 88; ER—Tyler, 78; HR—Uhey, 10; BB—MacQuarrie, 94; IBB—Uhey, 7; HB—Riley (KW), 16; SO—Caudill, 153; WP—MacQuarrie, 20.

(All Pitchers—Listed Alphabetically)

| Pitcher—Club | G. | GS. | CG. | ShO. | W. | L. | Sv. | Pct. | IP. | H. | R. | ER. | HR. | BB. | Int. BB. | HB. | SO. | WP. | ERA. |
|------|-----|-----|-----|------|-----|-----|-----|------|-----|-----|-----|-----|-----|-----|-----|-----|-----|-----|------|
| Adams, Tampa | 1 | 1 | 0 | 0 | 0 | 1 | 0 | .000 | 5 | 5 | 5 | 5 | 0 | 3 | 0 | 0 | 6 | 5 | 9.00 |
| Agosto, W Haven* | 6 | 0 | 0 | 0 | 0 | 4 | 0 | .000 | 28 | 35 | 23 | 18 | 2 | 24 | 0 | 3 | 19 | 3 | 5.79 |
| Alcantara, Ft Laud | 12 | 12 | 2 | 0 | 2 | 8 | 0 | .200 | 66 | 70 | 35 | 27 | 3 | 25 | 0 | 5 | 40 | 3 | 3.68 |
| Alonso, Lakeland* | 13 | 4 | 2 | 0 | 3 | 5 | 1 | .375 | 62 | 46 | 22 | 19 | 0 | 26 | 0 | 1 | 41 | 3 | 2.76 |
| Antor, W Haven | 22 | 3 | 0 | 0 | 4 | 3 | 0 | .571 | 53 | 65 | 28 | 26 | 3 | 17 | 0 | 3 | 15 | 1 | 4.42 |
| Baby, WPB* | 5 | 0 | 0 | 0 | 1 | 3 | 0 | .250 | 7 | 16 | 9 | 9 | 1 | 4 | 1 | 0 | 4 | 0 | 11.57 |
| Baltz, WPB | 10 | 1 | 0 | 0 | 1 | 1 | 1 | .500 | 18 | 21 | 14 | 12 | 1 | 8 | 0 | 1 | 13 | 3 | 6.00 |
| Bashaw, St Peter | 34 | 0 | 0 | 0 | 6 | 3 | 3 | .667 | 117 | 103 | 30 | 22 | 1 | 34 | 5 | 3 | 52 | 4 | 1.69 |
| Bastian, WPB | 23 | 22 | 8 | 0 | 8 | 11 | 0 | .421 | 143 | 136 | 70 | 57 | 5 | 72 | 3 | 7 | 112 | 6 | 3.59 |
| Bickerton, K West* | 3 | 1 | 0 | 0 | 0 | 0 | 0 | .000 | 6 | 8 | 6 | 6 | 0 | 8 | 0 | 2 | 1 | 9 | 9.00 |
| Bierman, Ft Laud | 23 | 2 | 0 | 0 | 1 | 3 | 4 | .250 | 41 | 37 | 17 | 15 | 1 | 24 | 3 | 1 | 30 | 2 | 3.29 |
| Bombard, Tampa* | 21 | 19 | 2 | 2 | 6 | 5 | 0 | .545 | 110 | 80 | 38 | 30 | 6 | 46 | 2 | 2 | 72 | 1 | 2.45 |
| Broomis, Miami | 5 | 0 | 0 | 0 | 0 | 0 | 4 | .000 | 11 | 7 | 1 | 0 | 0 | 2 | 0 | 0 | 8 | 0 | 0.00 |
| Burke, W Haven | 26 | 22 | 11 | 1 | 12 | 9 | 1 | .571 | 166 | 117 | 78 | 69 | 4 | 59 | 2 | 5 | 73 | 11 | 3.74 |
| Camper, St Peter | 13 | 13 | 4 | 3 | 8 | 2 | 0 | .800 | 88 | 77 | 30 | 25 | 4 | 34 | 0 | 2 | 46 | 3 | 2.56 |
| Capilla, St Peter* | 8 | 8 | 2 | 1 | 3 | 4 | 0 | .429 | 51 | 38 | 20 | 12 | 0 | 39 | 0 | 1 | 45 | 3 | 2.12 |
| Cappuzzello, Lake* | 16 | 16 | 7 | 0 | 5 | 8 | 0 | .385 | 110 | 92 | 46 | 31 | 1 | 64 | 0 | 3 | 89 | 10 | 2.54 |
| Carp, Ft Lauder. | 16 | 5 | 0 | 0 | 1 | 5 | 0 | .167 | 45 | 39 | 31 | 27 | 2 | 49 | 3 | 2 | 27 | 3 | 5.40 |
| Caudill, St Peter | 25 | 25 | 12 | 5 | 14 | 8 | 0 | .636 | 163 | 123 | 63 | 57 | 6 | 87 | 0 | 5 | 153 | 12 | 3.15 |
| Chandler, Tampa* | 24 | 22 | 8 | 6 | 10 | 8 | 1 | .556 | 157 | 102 | 43 | 34 | 3 | 55 | 2 | 7 | 83 | 3 | 1.95 |
| Chevez, Miami | 33 | 18 | 8 | 2 | 14 | 6 | 3 | .700 | 156 | 136 | 52 | 36 | 6 | 30 | 1 | 8 | 70 | 1 | 2.08 |
| Colzie, Tampa | 1 | 0 | 0 | 0 | 0 | 0 | 0 | .000 | 1 | 4 | 3 | 3 | 0 | 0 | 0 | 0 | 2 | 1 | 27.00 |
| Corbett, Tampa | 27 | 3 | 1 | 1 | 2 | 3 | 1 | .400 | 61 | 42 | 11 | 10 | 1 | 21 | 1 | 2 | 48 | 0 | 1.48 |
| Cross, W Haven | 14 | 6 | 1 | 0 | 1 | 8 | 1 | .111 | 47 | 58 | 36 | 25 | 0 | 27 | 1 | 0 | 27 | 0 | 4.79 |
| Daniels, Lakeland | 7 | 0 | 0 | 0 | 0 | 0 | 0 | .000 | 14 | 16 | 16 | 15 | 1 | 13 | 0 | 0 | 9 | 4 | 9.64 |
| Darr, Miami | 14 | 13 | 0 | 0 | 2 | 6 | 0 | .250 | 78 | 69 | 43 | 39 | 4 | 48 | 1 | 9 | 62 | 16 | 4.50 |
| Delgatti, Ft Lauder | 16 | 15 | 3 | 1 | 7 | 4 | 0 | .636 | 91 | 80 | 37 | 34 | 2 | 29 | 0 | 5 | 59 | 2 | 2.47 |
| Doland, Key West. | 28 | 25 | 5 | 1 | 11 | 9 | 0 | .524 | 167 | 149 | 63 | 45 | 6 | 42 | 1 | 4 | 93 | 1 | 2.43 |
| Dues, WPB | 18 | 18 | 8 | 1 | 6 | 7 | 0 | .462 | 118 | 99 | 49 | 39 | 3 | 61 | 0 | 1 | 65 | 4 | 2.97 |
| Dumoulin, Tampa | 45 | 0 | 0 | 0 | 7 | 3 | 8 | .700 | 84 | 55 | 22 | 19 | 0 | 46 | 4 | 1 | 64 | 8 | 2.04 |
| Dwyer, Lakeland | 11 | 0 | 0 | 0 | 2 | 1 | 1 | .667 | 15 | 12 | 5 | 1 | 1 | 10 | 0 | 1 | 13 | 0 | 0.60 |
| Edelen, St Peter | 5 | 0 | 0 | 0 | 1 | 0 | 0 | .000 | 10 | 5 | 4 | 0 | 0 | 5 | 0 | 0 | 7 | 1 | 0.00 |
| Ehrig, Miami | 1 | 0 | 0 | 0 | 0 | 0 | 0 | .000 | 4 | 4 | 0 | 0 | 0 | 6 | 0 | 0 | 0 | 0 | 0.00 |
| Ewell, WPB | 23 | 0 | 0 | 0 | 3 | 6 | 3 | .333 | 51 | 48 | 30 | 27 | 3 | 32 | 4 | 1 | 25 | 6 | 4.76 |
| Farrow, Lakeland* | 3 | 0 | 0 | 0 | 1 | 1 | 0 | .500 | 13 | 15 | 12 | 10 | 0 | 13 | 0 | 0 | 12 | 1 | 6.92 |
| Ferreyra, Tampa | 45 | 0 | 0 | 0 | 7 | 4 | 4 | .636 | 89 | 69 | 15 | 11 | 1 | 34 | 4 | 0 | 55 | 5 | 1.11 |
| Fidrych, Lakeland | 17 | 16 | 10 | 0 | 5 | 9 | 0 | .357 | 117 | 111 | 58 | 49 | 2 | 50 | 1 | 0 | 73 | 5 | 3.77 |
| Finch, W Haven | 26 | 26 | 9 | 3 | 11 | 11 | 0 | .500 | 184 | 154 | 72 | 51 | 0 | 71 | 3 | 5 | 88 | 4 | 2.49 |
| Finlayson, WPB | 13 | 4 | 2 | 0 | 1 | 4 | 0 | .250 | 40 | 40 | 17 | 12 | 3 | 14 | 0 | 1 | 15 | 2 | 2.70 |

| Pitcher—Club | G. | GS. | CG. | ShO. | W. | L. | Sv. | Pct. | IP. | H. | R. | ER. | HR. | BB. | Int.BB. | HB. | SO. | WP. | ERA. |
|---|---|---|---|---|---|---|---|---|---|---|---|---|---|---|---|---|---|---|---|
| Fleshman, Ft Laud | 27 | 22 | 10 | 4 | 10 | 10 | 0 | .500 | 170 | 123 | 66 | 48 | 2 | 88 | 1 | 6 | 113 | 4 | 2.54 |
| Flinn, Miami | 4 | 2 | 0 | 0 | 1 | 2 | 0 | .333 | 13 | 15 | 8 | 8 | 1 | 9 | 0 | 1 | 14 | 2 | 5.54 |
| D. Ford, Miami | 2 | 2 | 1 | 1 | 0 | 0 | 0 | 1.000 | 12 | 8 | 3 | 3 | 1 | 4 | 0 | 0 | 7 | 0 | 2.25 |
| Garvey, Tampa | 18 | 15 | 2 | 1 | 4 | 7 | 0 | .364 | 88 | 80 | 38 | 30 | 2 | 32 | 0 | 2 | 54 | 3 | 3.07 |
| J. Gingrich, WPB | 16 | 7 | 2 | 1 | 5 | 2 | 0 | .714 | 73 | 57 | 24 | 20 | 1 | 36 | 2 | 2 | 40 | 3 | 2.47 |
| Grabowski, WPB | 8 | 0 | 0 | 0 | 1 | 1 | 0 | .500 | 21 | 15 | 6 | 5 | 1 | 7 | 0 | 1 | 16 | 1 | 2.14 |
| Groover, Key West* | 2 | 1 | 0 | 0 | 0 | 1 | 0 | .000 | 4 | 8 | 5 | 5 | 1 | 2 | 0 | 0 | 3 | 0 | 11.25 |
| Halgerson, Tampa | 8 | 0 | 0 | 0 | 1 | 2 | 0 | .333 | 11 | 17 | 15 | 10 | 1 | 5 | 3 | 0 | 8 | 1 | 8.18 |
| Hamrick, K West* | 15 | 15 | 4 | 2 | 5 | 6 | 0 | .455 | 111 | 81 | 29 | 24 | 1 | 53 | 3 | 1 | 97 | 5 | 1.95 |
| Hannahs, WPB* | 8 | 1 | 1 | 2 | 3 | 0 | 0 | .400 | 55 | 38 | 17 | 12 | 0 | 27 | 0 | 1 | 46 | 5 | 1.96 |
| Hardeman, W Hav | 20 | 5 | 2 | 0 | 2 | 4 | 0 | .333 | 68 | 58 | 34 | 24 | 2 | 45 | 1 | 4 | 38 | 8 | 3.18 |
| Harris, Lakeland | 7 | 7 | 6 | 1 | 3 | 4 | 0 | .429 | 54 | 48 | 17 | 14 | 1 | 17 | 0 | 5 | 36 | 2 | 2.33 |
| Horn, WPB | 16 | 16 | 4 | 0 | 6 | 9 | 0 | .400 | 105 | 104 | 61 | 40 | 1 | 52 | 0 | 3 | 48 | 7 | 3.33 |
| Horstmann, WPB | 9 | 3 | 0 | 3 | 4 | 0 | 0 | .429 | 88 | 90 | 44 | 33 | 0 | 34 | 0 | 2 | 40 | 4 | 3.38 |
| Hoyles, Miami | 7 | 7 | 0 | 0 | 2 | 4 | 0 | .333 | 39 | 40 | 20 | 14 | 4 | 23 | 0 | 2 | 30 | 5 | 3.23 |
| Hoyt, Ft Lauder | 7 | 3 | 1 | 1 | 2 | 1 | 0 | .667 | 26 | 24 | 14 | 13 | 2 | 8 | 0 | 1 | 12 | 1 | 4.50 |
| Irwin, Lakeland | 14 | 9 | 3 | 0 | 2 | 6 | 0 | .250 | 72 | 62 | 39 | 29 | 3 | 36 | 0 | 3 | 34 | 2 | 3.63 |
| Kennedy, St Peter | 23 | 23 | 5 | 1 | 12 | 7 | 0 | .632 | 131 | 129 | 66 | 56 | 9 | 65 | 4 | 6 | 52 | 7 | 3.85 |
| Kerrigan, WPB | 22 | 0 | 0 | 0 | 2 | 3 | 0 | .000 | 23 | 24 | 7 | 7 | 0 | 11 | 1 | 0 | 24 | 1 | 2.74 |
| Kibbee, Miami | 32 | 4 | 0 | 0 | 5 | 5 | 1 | .500 | 74 | 68 | 49 | 26 | 2 | 41 | 0 | 1 | 48 | 5 | 3.16 |
| Kleibl, W Haven | 16 | 12 | 5 | 1 | 6 | 4 | 0 | .600 | 80 | 68 | 28 | 24 | 4 | 30 | 2 | 4 | 30 | 0 | 2.70 |
| Knose, WPB | 5 | 4 | 1 | 1 | 1 | 2 | 0 | .333 | 17 | 16 | 11 | 11 | 1 | 15 | 0 | 0 | 8 | 2 | 5.82 |
| Kruppa, Ft Laud* | 32 | 8 | 5 | 3 | 8 | 4 | 4 | .667 | 101 | 71 | 22 | 17 | 2 | 27 | 0 | 3 | 52 | 3 | 1.51 |
| Kwasny, Ft Lauder | 12 | 0 | 0 | 0 | 0 | 0 | 0 | .000 | 28 | 23 | 16 | 13 | 0 | 24 | 0 | 2 | 19 | 4 | 4.18 |
| LaCoss, Tampa | 23 | 22 | 9 | 4 | 7 | 10 | 0 | .412 | 151 | 131 | 61 | 48 | 2 | 41 | 0 | 7 | 72 | 11 | 2.86 |
| Lopez, St Peter | 7 | 1 | 0 | 0 | 0 | 0 | 0 | .000 | 22 | 24 | 15 | 15 | 2 | 3 | 0 | 0 | 8 | 0 | 6.14 |
| MacQuarrie, WPB | 21 | 21 | 7 | 0 | 5 | 7 | 0 | .417 | 138 | 108 | 77 | 62 | 4 | 94 | 1 | 9 | 84 | 20 | 4.04 |
| Madden, Lakeland | 28 | 5 | 1 | 0 | 4 | 5 | 4 | .444 | 89 | 94 | 39 | 38 | 5 | 29 | 3 | 1 | 43 | 3 | 3.84 |
| J. D. Martinez, Mia | 20 | 20 | 9 | 3 | 12 | 4 | 0 | .750 | 145 | 125 | 54 | 42 | 1 | 35 | 0 | 5 | 114 | 3 | 2.61 |
| Mayo, Miami | 25 | 23 | 3 | 0 | 7 | 7 | 0 | .500 | 165 | 134 | 66 | 52 | 2 | 86 | 3 | 6 | 97 | 7 | 2.84 |
| Meek, St. Peter* | 23 | 6 | 3 | 1 | 6 | 2 | 2 | .750 | 68 | 44 | 12 | 8 | 0 | 21 | 1 | 1 | 63 | 4 | 1.06 |
| Melvin, Ft Lauder | 28 | 8 | 2 | 0 | 6 | 4 | 1 | .600 | 84 | 83 | 49 | 32 | 0 | 55 | 1 | 2 | 58 | 5 | 3.43 |
| Mendez, Ft Lauder | 3 | 0 | 0 | 1 | 1 | 4 | 0 | .200 | 35 | 32 | 22 | 18 | 1 | 29 | 1 | 3 | 20 | 4 | 4.63 |
| Mercier, Lakeland | 26 | 11 | 9 | 1 | 5 | 1 | 1 | .455 | 116 | 97 | 43 | 37 | 4 | 47 | 2 | 8 | 88 | 3 | 2.87 |
| Meyerrose, Lakeland | 8 | 0 | 0 | 0 | 3 | 1 | 0 | .750 | 17 | 22 | 12 | 12 | 0 | 10 | 0 | 0 | 8 | 0 | 5.29 |
| Miller, Miami | 55 | 0 | 0 | 0 | 8 | 5 | 15 | .615 | 98 | 68 | 26 | 20 | 2 | 35 | 4 | 3 | 64 | 2 | 1.84 |
| Moore, Miami* | 27 | 17 | 5 | 2 | 9 | 5 | 1 | .643 | 133 | 112 | 49 | 39 | 8 | 44 | 0 | 1 | 72 | 0 | 2.64 |
| Moore, Key West | 6 | 0 | 0 | 0 | 0 | 0 | 0 | .000 | 19 | 23 | 13 | 9 | 0 | 9 | 0 | 0 | 5 | 1 | 4.26 |
| Moore, Tampa | 6 | 0 | 0 | 1 | 2 | 0 | 0 | .333 | 9 | 6 | 9 | 5 | 1 | 6 | 0 | 0 | 8 | 2 | 5.00 |
| Wotil, Lakeland* | 6 | 0 | 0 | 1 | 0 | 2 | 1 | 1.000 | 5 | 5 | 1 | 1 | 0 | 1 | 0 | 0 | 18 | 0 | 0.60 |
| Murphy, St Peter | 43 | 0 | 0 | 0 | 5 | 1 | 16 | .833 | 63 | 43 | 12 | 10 | 0 | 27 | 3 | 1 | 49 | 3 | 1.43 |
| Murphy, Lakeland* | 18 | 7 | 0 | 0 | 3 | 5 | 1 | .375 | 62 | 71 | 34 | 23 | 3 | 49 | 0 | 2 | 30 | 4 | 3.34 |
| O'Neill, WPB* | 2 | 0 | 0 | 0 | 2 | 0 | 0 | 1.000 | 4 | 1 | 1 | 1 | 0 | 3 | 0 | 0 | 5 | 0 | 2.25 |
| Paz, Ft Lauder | 2 | 0 | 0 | 0 | 0 | 0 | 0 | .000 | 5 | 3 | 1 | 1 | 1 | 1 | 0 | 0 | 1 | 0 | 1.80 |
| Plunkett, Ft Laud* | 2 | 0 | 0 | 0 | 1 | 1 | 0 | .500 | 9 | 8 | 6 | 6 | 0 | 7 | 0 | 0 | 2 | 1 | 6.00 |
| Polonio, W Haven | 19 | 0 | 0 | 0 | 1 | 1 | 1 | .500 | 48 | 36 | 20 | 13 | 1 | 34 | 1 | 1 | 22 | 3 | 2.44 |
| Proctor, W Haven. | 35 | 4 | 1 | 1 | 7 | 2 | 8 | .778 | 95 | 78 | 35 | 25 | 0 | 20 | 2 | 1 | 54 | 1 | 2.37 |
| Rajsich, WPB | 23 | 15 | 10 | 4 | 5 | 9 | 2 | .357 | 125 | 88 | 45 | 34 | 3 | 48 | 0 | 4 | 79 | 5 | 2.45 |
| Rawley, WPB* | 24 | 24 | 9 | 1 | 12 | 8 | 0 | .400 | 165 | 148 | 80 | 56 | 5 | 73 | 0 | 3 | 113 | 13 | 3.05 |
| Reed, Tampa | 23 | 22 | 7 | 3 | 12 | 8 | 0 | .600 | 157 | 123 | 48 | 35 | 4 | 52 | 1 | 0 | 98 | 2 | 2.01 |
| Remmerswaal, WH | 27 | 16 | 8 | 0 | 8 | 7 | 3 | .533 | 127 | 136 | 60 | 38 | 6 | 33 | 1 | 5 | 65 | 2 | 2.69 |
| Replogle, St Peter | 5 | 2 | 0 | 2 | 2 | 2 | 0 | .500 | 32 | 19 | 13 | 12 | 0 | 11 | 0 | 3 | 18 | 0 | 3.38 |
| Rieger, St Peter* | 8 | 8 | 1 | 0 | 4 | 1 | 0 | .800 | 49 | 40 | 19 | 17 | 1 | 34 | 0 | 1 | 21 | 2 | 3.33 |
| Riley, WPB | 11 | 0 | 0 | 0 | 2 | 1 | 6 | .667 | 28 | 17 | 6 | 4 | 0 | 13 | 3 | 1 | 18 | 4 | 1.29 |
| Riley, Key West* | 28 | 4 | 0 | 10 | 10 | 0 | 0 | .500 | 155 | 141 | 75 | 62 | 7 | 81 | 0 | 16 | 84 | 5 | 3.60 |
| Rineer, Miami* | 11 | 7 | 2 | 0 | 3 | 3 | 0 | .500 | 48 | 69 | 36 | 30 | 2 | 20 | 0 | 0 | 25 | 0 | 5.63 |
| Robles, Ft Lauder | 13 | 6 | 1 | 0 | 0 | 4 | 0 | .000 | 40 | 52 | 47 | 33 | 2 | 30 | 4 | 2 | 12 | 3 | 7.43 |
| Rogers, Key West | 11 | 8 | 2 | 6 | 3 | 0 | 0 | .667 | 90 | 70 | 16 | 15 | 2 | 15 | 3 | 1 | 33 | 1 | 1.50 |
| Rusk, Ft Lauder | 4 | 2 | 0 | 0 | 0 | 1 | 0 | .000 | 17 | 12 | 10 | 10 | 1 | 19 | 0 | 0 | 12 | 6 | 5.29 |
| Smith, Miami | 26 | 20 | 5 | 2 | 11 | 7 | 1 | .611 | 139 | 117 | 48 | 33 | 4 | 59 | 1 | 5 | 93 | 8 | 2.14 |
| Snyder, Miami | 25 | 2 | 0 | 0 | 4 | 2 | 1 | .667 | 61 | 44 | 22 | 15 | 4 | 25 | 1 | 0 | 25 | 4 | 2.21 |
| Sorensen, St Peter | 18 | 2 | 1 | 0 | 2 | 2 | 4 | .500 | 46 | 42 | 13 | 10 | 1 | 16 | 5 | 0 | 30 | 4 | 1 96 |
| Staniland, St Peter | 2 | 2 | 1 | 1 | 1 | 0 | 0 | .500 | 15 | 12 | 4 | 2 | 1 | 2 | 0 | 0 | 15 | 1 | 1.20 |
| Stanley, W Haven. | 27 | 26 | 10 | 0 | 5 | 17 | 0 | .227 | 169 | 136 | 76 | 55 | 2 | 74 | 0 | 7 | 73 | 7 | 2 93 |
| Stewart, St Peter. | 14 | 14 | 9 | 5 | 11 | 2 | 0 | .846 | 113 | 72 | 24 | 22 | 0 | 34 | 3 | 2 | 56 | 3 | 1.75 |
| Sullivan, Ft Laud* | 6 | 4 | 0 | 0 | 0 | 2 | 0 | .000 | 21 | 23 | 20 | 17 | 2 | 20 | 0 | 0 | 19 | 1 | 7.29 |
| Swanson, WPB | 9 | 0 | 0 | 0 | 1 | 0 | 0 | 1.000 | 25 | 23 | 11 | 11 | 3 | 14 | 0 | 2 | 18 | 3 | 3.96 |
| Temple, Key West. | 39 | 0 | 0 | 0 | 5 | 3 | 11 | .625 | 69 | 54 | 19 | 17 | 2 | 20 | 2 | 3 | 49 | 3 | 2.22 |
| Tobik, Lakeland | 5 | 2 | 0 | 1 | 4 | 0 | 0 | .200 | 36 | 29 | 14 | 10 | 0 | 19 | 2 | 0 | 22 | 4 | 2.50 |
| Treuel, Lakeland | 26 | 24 | 4 | 9 | 9 | 9 | 0 | .500 | 160 | 143 | 68 | 57 | 4 | 67 | 0 | 14 | 87 | 6 | 3 21 |
| Trotter, Ft Lauder* | 8 | 7 | 2 | 0 | 3 | 3 | 0 | .500 | 58 | 48 | 20 | 15 | 0 | 32 | 3 | 1 | 30 | 0 | 2 33 |
| Trumbauer, StP*... | 6 | 0 | 0 | 0 | 0 | 3 | 0 | .000 | 9 | 8 | 17 | 17 | 0 | 32 | 0 | 4 | 8 | 4 | 17.00 |
| Tufts, Key West* | 3 | 0 | 0 | 2 | 1 | 1 | 0 | .667 | 11 | 6 | 7 | 6 | 1 | 7 | 1 | 0 | 11 | 0 | 4.91 |
| Turner, Key West. | 24 | 17 | 4 | 0 | 8 | 9 | 0 | .471 | 127 | 123 | 66 | 59 | 7 | 65 | 6 | 4 | 47 | 6 | 4.18 |
| Tyler, Lakeland* | 27 | 26 | 11 | 1 | 6 | 15 | 0 | .286 | 168 | 174 | 88 | 78 | 8 | 86 | 2 | 6 | 76 | 11 | 4.18 |
| Uhey, Key West | 31 | 9 | 1 | 0 | 5 | 6 | 2 | .333 | 102 | 108 | 51 | 39 | 10 | 39 | 7 | 4 | 51 | 2 | 3.44 |
| Underwood, Tampa | 4 | 1 | 0 | 2 | 1 | 0 | 0 | .667 | 30 | 27 | 10 | 6 | 1 | 8 | 0 | 1 | 18 | 1 | 1.80 |
| Urrea, St Peter | 23 | 22 | 11 | 2 | 14 | 8 | 0 | .636 | 175 | 138 | 61 | 41 | 1 | 60 | 1 | 4 | 108 | 7 | 2.11 |
| Vallejos, Miami | 5 | 1 | 0 | 0 | 1 | 0 | 0 | .000 | 11 | 15 | 11 | 5 | 0 | 8 | 0 | 0 | 10 | 1 | 4.09 |

| Pitcher—Club | G. | GS. | CG. | ShO. | W. | L. | Sv. | Pct. | IP. | H. | R. | ER. | HR. | BB. | Int. BB. | HB. | SO. | WP. | ERA. |
|---|---|---|---|---|---|---|---|---|---|---|---|---|---|---|---|---|---|---|---|
| Vernoy, Key West* | 22 | 5 | 1 | 0 | 5 | 3 | 0 | .625 | 73 | 56 | 35 | 33 | 2 | 61 | 0 | 7 | 37 | 7 | 4.07 |
| Viebrock, Tampa* | 23 | 23 | 9 | 3 | 13 | 5 | 0 | .722 | 155 | 138 | 48 | 43 | 7 | 35 | 0 | 3 | 71 | 4 | 2.50 |
| Vogel, Key West* | 5 | 4 | 1 | 0 | 1 | 2 | 0 | .333 | 21 | 26 | 18 | 16 | 2 | 17 | 1 | 0 | 12 | 2 | 6.86 |
| Ware, Key West* | 27 | 0 | 0 | 1 | 3 | 4 | | .250 | 40 | 40 | 20 | 19 | 1 | 28 | 4 | 0 | 35 | 0 | 4.28 |
| Wilkerson, K West | 19 | 3 | 0 | 2 | 1 | 4 | | .667 | 55 | 61 | 40 | 28 | 0 | 34 | 0 | 4 | 46 | 4 | 4.58 |
| Wood, Key West | 29 | 17 | 3 | 0 | 6 | 12 | 1 | .333 | 133 | 117 | 65 | 55 | 7 | 73 | 5 | 4 | 45 | 6 | 3.72 |
| Woodland, WPB | 7 | 3 | 3 | 0 | 2 | 3 | 0 | .400 | 39 | 34 | 15 | 10 | 0 | 17 | 0 | 0 | 33 | 1 | 2.31 |
| Wright, Ft Lauder | 18 | 0 | 0 | 0 | 3 | 2 | 3 | .600 | 29 | 40 | 24 | 24 | 6 | 21 | 1 | 2 | 32 | 7 | 7.45 |

BALKS—Bastian, 6; Mayo, 5; Mendez, 4; Agosto, Delgatti, Rawley, Reed, Remmerswaal, Treuel, Urrea, 3 each; Doland, Dues, Fidrych, Finch, LaCoss, Rieger, Snyder, Wilkinson, 2 each; Alonso, Bashaw, Bierman, Burke, Cappuzzello, Carp, Chevez, Diehl, Garvey, Hardeman, Horn, Horstmann, Hoyles, Irwin, Kennedy, Kruppa, Kwasny, MacQuarrie, Madden, Meek, Melvin, Miller, Moore (Miami), Murphy (StP), Proctor, Rajsich, Rineer, Rusk, Smith, Staniland, Stanley, Stewart, Temple, Tyler, Vernoy, Viebrock, Ware, 1 each.

COMBINATION SHUTOUTS—Delgatti-Wright, Delgatti-Kruppa-Wright, Diehl-Rajsich, Kruppa-Fleshman, Trotter-Kruppa, Ft. Lauderdale; Hamrick-Temple, Doland-Temple, Riley-Temple-Tufts-Wilkerson, Riley-Uhey, Riley-Uhey-Ware, Key West; Cappuzzello-Dwyer, Lakeland; Smith-Miller, Miami; Kennedy-Murphy, St. Petersburg; Viebrock-Dumoulin; Bombard-Chandler, Garvey-Ferreyra, Bombard-Dumoulin, Bombard-Ferreyra-Dumoulin, Tampa; Rawley-Ewell, West Palm Beach; Agosto-Antor, Remmerswaal-Proctor, Hardeman-Polonio, Winter Haven.

NO-HIT GAMES—Caudill, St. Petersburg, defeated Winter Haven, 4-0, May 14 (six innings); Bombard, Tampa, defeated Lakeland, 1-0, June 6 (PERFECT).

# Mexican Center League

## CLASS A
### CHAMPIONSHIP WINNERS IN PREVIOUS YEARS

| | | |
|---|---|---|
| 1960—Salamanca ......... .582 | 1967—Leon ............. .604 | 1972—Ebano ............. .692 |
| 1961—Aguascalientes ... .567 | 1968—Saltillo ........... .648 | Aguascalientes* ..... .703 |
| 1962—Fresnillo .......... .588 | 1969—San Luis Potosi* . .705 | 1973—Zacatecas† ......... .721 |
| 1963—Guanajuato ....... .627 | Zacatecas .......... .667 | Ebano ............. .657 |
| 1964—Leon ............. .630 | 1970—Ciudad Madero ... .632 | 1974—Durango† .......... .693 |
| 1965—San Luis Potosi .. .633 | Ciudad Madero ... .655 | Ciudad Valles ..... .513 |
| 1966—Guanajuato* ...... .701 | 1971—Ebano† ........... .704 | |
| San Luis Potosi .. .750 | San Luis Potosi .... .625 | |

*Won split-season playoff.
†League divided into Gulf and Center Divisions; won playoff.

### STANDING OF CLUBS AT CLOSE OF SEASON, JUNE 23

| Club | Ur. | Cor. | Cel. | Gto. | L.M. | Leon | Acam. | Sal. | W. | L. | T. | Pct. | G.B. |
|---|---|---|---|---|---|---|---|---|---|---|---|---|---|
| Uriangato (Mexico Tigers) ...... | | 7 | 8 | 9 | 3 | 6 | 10 | 55 | 14 | 2 | .797 | |
| Cortazar (Saltillo) .......--.... | 3 | | 4 | 6 | 5 | 6 | 8 | 8 | 40 | 28 | 2 | .588 | 14½ |
| Celaya (Union Laguna) ........ | 2 | 6 | | 7 | 2 | 7 | 7 | 5 | 36 | 33 | 1 | .522 | 19 |
| Guanajuato (Poza Rica) ....... | 1 | 3 | 3 | | 6 | 8 | 3 | 8 | 32 | 34 | 6 | .485 | 21½ |
| Lagos de Moreno (Mexico Reds) | 2 | 5 | 7 | 2 | .. | 5 | 6 | 4 | 31 | 35 | 4 | .470 | 22½ |
| Leon (Jalisco) .............. | 2 | 3 | 3 | 2 | 5 | .. | 8 | 5 | 28 | 39 | 3 | .418 | 26 |
| Acambaro (Tampico) .......... | 4 | 2 | 3 | 6 | 4 | 2 | .. | 5 | 26 | 43 | 2 | .377 | 29 |
| Salamanca (Monterrey) ........ | 0 | 2 | 5 | 2 | 5 | 4 | 5 | .. | 23 | 45 | 2 | .338 | 31½ |

Farm clubs of Mexican League teams as shown in parentheses.
Uriangato represented Moreleon.
Playoffs—Cortazar defeated Guanajuato, three games to none; Uriangato defeated Celaya, three games to none. Uriangato and Cortazar each won two games in the final playoff when rain cancelled the playoff; Uriangato was declared league champion with the highest won-lost percentage in the regular season.
Regular-Season Attendance—Acambaro, 15,431; Celaya, 4,972; Cortazar, 7,591; Guanajuato, 12,481; Lagos de Moreno, 10,391; Leon, 5,754; Salamanca, 7,638; Uriangato, 10,254. Total, 74,512. Playoffs, 5,299.
Managers: Acambaro—Roberto Castellon; Celaya—Felipe Hernandez; Cortazar—Hector Villalobos; Guanajuato—Juan Hernandez; Lagos de Moreno—Arturo Cacheux; Leon—Orestes Minoso; Salamanca—Jose (Bimbo) Villegas; Uriangato—Domingo Rivera.
All-Star Team: 1B—Hermida, Guanajuato; 2B—J. M. Hernandez, Leon; 3B—Ibarra, Acambaro; SS—Elizondo, Cortazar; OF—Juarez, Guanajuato; Arvallo, Uriangato; Quiroz, Leon; C—Camargo, Salamanca; Terrazas, Uriangato; P—Soto, Cortazar; Garcia, Acambaro; Manager—Rivera, Uriangato.
(Compiled by Antonio Silva Vidaurry, League Statistician, Mexico, D. F.)

### CLUB BATTING

| Club | G. | AB. | R. | OR. | H. | TB. | 2B. | 3B. | HR. | RBI. | SH. | SF. | Int. BB. | BB. | HP. | SO. | SB. | CS. | LOB. | Pct. |
|---|---|---|---|---|---|---|---|---|---|---|---|---|---|---|---|---|---|---|---|---|
| Guanajuato ..72 | 2316 | 356 | 355 | 690 | 965 | 110 | 27 | 37 | 329 | 28 | 21 | 241 | 23 | 41 | 331 | 81 | 44 | 501 | .298 |
| Cortazar ......70 | 2388 | 333 | 292 | 691 | 908 | 103 | 18 | 26 | 321 | 58 | 26 | 192 | 15 | 37 | 279 | 61 | 37 | 525 | .289 |
| Celaya .........70 | 2282 | 321 | 272 | 627 | 857 | 92 | 36 | 22 | 295 | 29 | 18 | 170 | 14 | 10 | 273 | 71 | 34 | 447 | .275 |
| Uriangato ......71 | 2229 | 354 | 160 | 600 | 844 | 93 | 35 | 27 | 325 | 48 | 22 | 261 | 27 | 22 | 325 | 73 | 50 | 474 | .269 |
| Lagos de Moreno 70 | 2252 | 328 | 382 | 603 | 817 | 85 | 18 | 31 | 305 | 37 | 14 | 275 | 21 | 35 | 306 | 43 | 21 | 513 | .268 |
| Leon .........70 | 2303 | 288 | 334 | 611 | 869 | 114 | 30 | 28 | 267 | 43 | 18 | 170 | 11 | 25 | 302 | 72 | 56 | 457 | .265 |
| Salamanca ....70 | 2257 | 276 | 344 | 584 | 770 | 91 | 22 | 17 | 245 | 40 | 16 | 195 | 13 | 24 | 319 | 70 | 42 | 457 | .259 |
| Acambaro ......71 | 2240 | 272 | 389 | 563 | 739 | 82 | 23 | 16 | 260 | 32 | 21 | 242 | 18 | 22 | 316 | 33 | 14 | 469 | .251 |

### INDIVIDUAL BATTING
(Leading Qualifiers for Batting Championship—189 or More Plate Appearances)
*Bats lefthanded.   †Switch-hitter.

| Player and Club | G. | AB. | R. | H. | TB. | 2B. | 3B. | HR. | RBI. | SH. | SF. | BB. | HP. | SO. | SB. | CS. | Pct. |
|---|---|---|---|---|---|---|---|---|---|---|---|---|---|---|---|---|---|
| Hernandez, Jose Maria, Leon | 49 | 191 | 25 | 71 | 98 | 12 | 6 | 1 | 26 | 1 | 4 | 12 | 0 | 21 | 6 | 6 | .372 |
| Ibarra, Jeronimo, Acambaro | 71 | 276 | 52 | 101 | 121 | 14 | 3 | 0 | 36 | 3 | 1 | 9 | 4 | 11 | 12 | 2 | .366 |
| Juarez, Clemente, Guan* | 69 | 270 | 46 | 96 | 146 | 20 | 6 | 6 | 51 | 0 | 2 | 10 | 4 | 23 | 10 | 6 | .356 |
| Arballo, Mario Uriangato | 52 | 175 | 27 | 62 | 81 | 11 | 4 | 0 | 31 | 2 | 0 | 18 | 3 | 10 | 7 | 4 | .354 |
| Garzon, Felix, Uriangato | 69 | 233 | 37 | 82 | 101 | 7 | 6 | 0 | 46 | 2 | 4 | 39 | 2 | 21 | 10 | 6 | .352 |
| Lugo, Donaldo, Cortazar | 69 | 294 | 51 | 102 | 125 | 15 | 1 | 2 | 37 | 4 | 2 | 16 | 3 | 16 | 15 | 6 | .347 |
| Villagomez, David, L. M. | 70 | 252 | 39 | 83 | 106 | 12 | 4 | 1 | 48 | 1 | 5 | 25 | 4 | 26 | 8 | 2 | .329 |
| Ortiz, Armando, L. M. | 67 | 244 | 49 | 80 | 129 | 15 | 2 | 10 | 44 | 1 | 0 | 39 | 6 | 37 | 3 | 2 | .328 |
| Sanudo, Ismael, Cortazar | 64 | 237 | 31 | 77 | 102 | 6 | 2 | 5 | 49 | 7 | 5 | 30 | 5 | 23 | 6 | 6 | .325 |
| Elizondo, Fernando, Cor. | 69 | 278 | 36 | 90 | 112 | 20 | 1 | 0 | 43 | 7 | 5 | 17 | 2 | 13 | 6 | 2 | .324 |

Departmental Leaders: G—Ibarra, 71; AB—Lugo, 294; R—Cardona, 59; H—Lugo, 102; TB—Juarez, 146; 2B—Elizondo, Juarez, 20; 3B—Manuel Ramirez, 9; HR—Quiroz, 12; RBI—Barrera, Juarez, 51; SH—A. Espinosa, Gaytan, 9; SF—Elizondo, Lara M., Sanudo, Villagomez, 5; BB—Navarrete, 40; HP—Navarrete, 9; SO—Valle, 56; SB—Lugo, Morales P., 15; CS—Clayton, 10.

(All Players—Listed Alphabetically)

| Player and Club | G. | AB. | R. | H. | TB. | 2B. | 3B. | HR. | RBI. | SH. | SF. | BB. | HP. | SO. | SB. | CS. | Pct |
|---|---|---|---|---|---|---|---|---|---|---|---|---|---|---|---|---|---|
| Aguilar, Rafael, Celaya | 5 | 6 | 1 | 1 | 1 | 0 | 0 | 0 | 0 | 0 | 0 | 0 | 0 | 1 | 0 | 0 | .167 |
| Alfonso, Julio, Cortazar | 33 | 88 | 8 | 22 | 25 | 1 | 1 | 0 | 3 | 0 | 5 | 1 | 12 | 1 | 2 | | .250 |
| Alvarez, Jesus M., Urian | 12 | 7 | 0 | 1 | 1 | 0 | 0 | 0 | 0 | 2 | 0 | 1 | 0 | 6 | 0 | 0 | .143 |
| Alvarez, Juan C., Acambaro | 69 | 228 | 26 | 59 | 84 | 14 | 1 | 3 | 26 | 1 | 1 | 32 | 4 | 35 | 3 | 2 | .259 |
| Amador, Jesus, Lagos de M. | 13 | 40 | 5 | 12 | 16 | 1 | 0 | 1 | 9 | 0 | 0 | 2 | 0 | 6 | 0 | 0 | .300 |
| Arballo, Mario, Uriangato | 52 | 175 | 27 | 62 | 81 | 11 | 4 | 0 | 31 | 2 | 0 | 18 | 3 | 10 | 7 | 4 | .354 |
| Arce, Juan, Lagos de Moreno | 15 | 20 | 1 | 2 | 2 | 0 | 0 | 0 | 1 | 0 | 0 | 1 | 0 | 2 | 0 | 0 | .100 |
| Arellano, Gerardo, Cor | 43 | 150 | 11 | 41 | 49 | 6 | 1 | 0 | 21 | 6 | 3 | 6 | 0 | 16 | 3 | 0 | .273 |
| Avalos, Santiago, Leon | 21 | 70 | 6 | 11 | 16 | 5 | 0 | 0 | 6 | 1 | 0 | 2 | 2 | 15 | 0 | 2 | .157 |
| Avila, Luis J., Acambaro | 45 | 118 | 17 | 26 | 35 | 4 | 1 | 1 | 18 | 2 | 3 | 13 | 3 | 31 | 0 | 0 | .220 |
| Azcarraga, Paz, Uriangato | 14 | 29 | 3 | 4 | 5 | 1 | 0 | 0 | 2 | 3 | 0 | 3 | 1 | 4 | 0 | 1 | .138 |
| Ballesteros, Jesus, L. M. | 54 | 160 | 18 | 43 | 60 | 7 | 2 | 2 | 22 | 2 | 1 | 21 | 1 | 24 | 2 | 2 | .269 |
| Barrera, Nelson, L. M. | 69 | 267 | 56 | 85 | 124 | 11 | 2 | 8 | 51 | 2 | 0 | 24 | 1 | 38 | 5 | 8 | .318 |
| Beltran, Eleazar, Celaya | 11 | 24 | 1 | 9 | 12 | 3 | 0 | 0 | 4 | 1 | 1 | 2 | 0 | 6 | 0 | 1 | .375 |
| Beltran, Margarito, Celaya | 28 | 24 | 2 | 2 | 2 | 0 | 0 | 0 | 1 | 0 | 1 | 0 | 1 | 7 | 0 | 0 | .083 |
| Briseno, Homobono, Acambaro | 4 | 5 | 0 | 0 | 0 | 0 | 0 | 0 | 0 | 0 | 0 | 0 | 0 | 1 | 0 | 0 | .000 |
| Cabrales, Carlos Celaya | 15 | 26 | 6 | 9 | 12 | 1 | 1 | 0 | 2 | 1 | 1 | 1 | 0 | 6 | 0 | 0 | .346 |
| Camargo, Fernando, Sal | 69 | 256 | 42 | 80 | 123 | 17 | 4 | 6 | 39 | 0 | 2 | 18 | 2 | 29 | 6 | 4 | .313 |
| Cardona, Candelario, Cor | 70 | 282 | 59 | 88 | 132 | 18 | 4 | 6 | 39 | 3 | 2 | 28 | 6 | 46 | 6 | 9 | .312 |
| Carrillo, Lucio, Guanaj | 39 | 19 | 4 | 5 | 7 | 0 | 1 | 0 | 3 | 0 | 0 | 2 | 1 | 1 | 0 | 0 | .263 |
| Castellon, Roberto, Acam | 43 | 131 | 20 | 42 | 67 | 10 | 3 | 3 | 18 | 0 | 1 | 13 | 1 | 14 | 3 | 2 | .321 |
| Castro, Adolfo, Uriangato | 9 | 21 | 4 | 4 | 7 | 0 | 0 | 1 | 2 | 1 | 0 | 4 | 1 | 5 | 1 | 0 | .190 |
| Castro, Alberto, Celaya | 60 | 212 | 38 | 63 | 86 | 7 | 2 | 4 | 30 | 1 | 1 | 9 | 1 | 8 | 5 | 1 | .297 |
| Castro, Rafael, Acambaro | 53 | 153 | 9 | 19 | 19 | 0 | 0 | 0 | 10 | 5 | 4 | 15 | 3 | 25 | 0 | 1 | .124 |
| Cervantes, Refugio, Urian† | 12 | 29 | 5 | 8 | 10 | 2 | 0 | 0 | 3 | 0 | 0 | 10 | 0 | 5 | 2 | 0 | .276 |
| Chavez, Ramon, Cortazar | 65 | 198 | 28 | 44 | 63 | 6 | 2 | 3 | 20 | 3 | 2 | 27 | 2 | 28 | 6 | 5 | .222 |
| Clayton, Leonardo, Sal† | 70 | 263 | 30 | 66 | 84 | 11 | 2 | 1 | 27 | 3 | 2 | 21 | 3 | 41 | 13 | 10 | .251 |
| Contreras, Juan V., Celaya | 61 | 202 | 26 | 56 | 89 | 11 | 5 | 4 | 27 | 1 | 0 | 6 | 0 | 18 | 8 | 3 | .277 |
| Contreras, Patricio, Urian | 16 | 32 | 4 | 8 | 11 | 2 | 0 | 0 | 4 | 2 | 1 | 2 | 1 | 15 | 0 | 1 | .250 |
| Cota, Jorge, Cortazar | 4 | 3 | 0 | 1 | 1 | 0 | 0 | 0 | 1 | 1 | 0 | 0 | 0 | 0 | 0 | 0 | .333 |
| Cota, Leoncio, Lagos de M. | 3 | 3 | 0 | 2 | 2 | 0 | 0 | 0 | 0 | 0 | 0 | 0 | 0 | 0 | 0 | 0 | .667 |
| Cruz, Nicolas, Acambaro | 65 | 220 | 17 | 50 | 59 | 3 | 3 | 0 | 15 | 0 | 3 | 16 | 3 | 31 | 2 | 0 | .227 |
| Cruz, Pedro, Acambaro | 62 | 195 | 18 | 53 | 65 | 8 | 2 | 0 | 25 | 4 | 0 | 27 | 1 | 19 | 2 | 3 | .272 |
| Delgado, Julio, Uriangato | 10 | 9 | 3 | 3 | 3 | 0 | 0 | 0 | 1 | 2 | 0 | 3 | 0 | 1 | 0 | 0 | .333 |
| Diaz, Francisco, Leon | 23 | 47 | 7 | 15 | 17 | 2 | 0 | 0 | 3 | 0 | 0 | 7 | 2 | 10 | 1 | 0 | .319 |
| Dominguez, Angel, L. M. | 17 | 12 | 0 | 0 | 0 | 0 | 0 | 0 | 1 | 0 | 0 | 2 | 0 | 3 | 0 | 0 | .000 |
| Dominguez, Guillermo, Leon | 12 | 17 | 1 | 2 | 2 | 0 | 0 | 0 | 1 | 0 | 0 | 0 | 0 | 4 | 0 | 0 | .118 |
| Duarte, Florentino, Leon | 14 | 24 | 1 | 2 | 3 | 1 | 0 | 0 | 0 | 3 | 0 | 0 | 1 | 3 | 0 | 1 | .083 |
| Elizondo, Fernando, Cor | 69 | 278 | 36 | 90 | 112 | 20 | 1 | 0 | 43 | 7 | 5 | 17 | 2 | 13 | 6 | 2 | .324 |
| Enriquez, Jose M., Urian | 7 | 8 | 1 | 2 | 3 | 1 | 0 | 0 | 0 | 0 | 0 | 0 | 0 | 1 | 0 | 0 | .250 |
| Esparza, Julio, Guanaj | 35 | 132 | 23 | 49 | 60 | 4 | 2 | 1 | 19 | 1 | 2 | 11 | 2 | 3 | 8 | 4 | .371 |
| Espinosa, Alejo, Leon | 70 | 242 | 32 | 64 | 94 | 18 | 0 | 4 | 26 | 9 | 1 | 23 | 1 | 40 | 6 | 9 | .264 |
| Espinosa, Ricardo, Guanaj | 23 | 6 | 0 | 0 | 0 | 0 | 0 | 0 | 0 | 3 | 0 | 1 | 0 | 2 | 0 | 0 | .000 |
| Felix, Concepcion, Leon | 46 | 151 | 23 | 35 | 45 | 4 | 3 | 0 | 13 | 0 | 1 | 11 | 3 | 14 | 5 | 5 | .232 |
| Fernandez, Victor M., Gua | 26 | 23 | 3 | 5 | 6 | 1 | 0 | 0 | 1 | 0 | 2 | 0 | 4 | 0 | 1 | | .217 |
| Figueroa, Roman, Uriangato | 63 | 218 | 44 | 54 | 85 | 13 | 6 | 2 | 24 | 6 | 0 | 20 | 5 | 42 | 11 | 4 | .248 |
| Flores, Fernando, Acambaro | 15 | 8 | 0 | 0 | 0 | 0 | 0 | 0 | 0 | 0 | 0 | 1 | 0 | 0 | 0 | 0 | .000 |
| Flores, Florencio, Cor | 21 | 43 | 1 | 5 | 6 | 1 | 0 | 0 | 3 | 0 | 1 | 0 | 0 | 11 | 1 | 0 | .116 |
| Flores, Ignacio, Salamanca | 68 | 252 | 26 | 69 | 85 | 8 | 4 | 0 | 25 | 7 | 2 | 17 | 3 | 32 | 11 | 5 | .274 |
| Flores, Leonel, Acambaro | 41 | 130 | 23 | 36 | 67 | 8 | 4 | 5 | 29 | 1 | 3 | 27 | 0 | 29 | 0 | 1 | .277 |
| Flores, Miguel A., L. M. | 31 | 57 | 6 | 17 | 24 | 5 | 1 | 0 | 10 | 1 | 0 | 5 | 0 | 3 | 2 | 0 | .298 |
| Flores, Ramiro, Guanajuato | 63 | 214 | 24 | 62 | 80 | 10 | 1 | 2 | 34 | 0 | 2 | 22 | 1 | 14 | 2 | 6 | .290 |
| Flores, Teodoro, Uriangato | 9 | 18 | 2 | 7 | 7 | 0 | 0 | 0 | 1 | 0 | 0 | 2 | 0 | 1 | 0 | 0 | .389 |
| Fraigo, David, Salamanca | 21 | 28 | 5 | 6 | 12 | 3 | 0 | 1 | 2 | 0 | 0 | 3 | 0 | 9 | 0 | 0 | .214 |
| Fuentes, Antonio, Guanaj | 10 | 37 | 9 | 16 | 31 | 3 | 0 | 4 | 14 | 0 | 0 | 5 | 0 | 3 | 1 | 1 | .432 |
| Garate, Fernando, Leon | 17 | 15 | 2 | 5 | 6 | 1 | 0 | 0 | 1 | 1 | 0 | 1 | 0 | 2 | 0 | 0 | .333 |
| Garcia, Jesus, Salamanca | 1 | 3 | 0 | 0 | 0 | 0 | 0 | 0 | 0 | 0 | 0 | 0 | 0 | 0 | 0 | 0 | .000 |
| Garcia, Jose Luis, Sal | 14 | 18 | 0 | 2 | 2 | 0 | 0 | 0 | 1 | 0 | 0 | 0 | 0 | 2 | 0 | 0 | .111 |
| Garcia, Rogelio, Acambaro | 34 | 58 | 6 | 11 | 12 | 1 | 0 | 0 | 2 | 1 | 0 | 4 | 0 | 15 | 0 | 0 | .190 |
| Garcia, Ruben, Guanajuato | 12 | 2 | 0 | 0 | 0 | 0 | 0 | 0 | 0 | 0 | 0 | 1 | 0 | 0 | 0 | 0 | .000 |
| Garduza, Jose M., Guanaj | 20 | 28 | 3 | 7 | 8 | 1 | 0 | 0 | 1 | 1 | 0 | 0 | 0 | 8 | 0 | 0 | .250 |
| Garzon, Fernando, Uriangato | 69 | 233 | 37 | 82 | 101 | 7 | 6 | 0 | 46 | 2 | 4 | 39 | 2 | 21 | 10 | 6 | .352 |
| Gaytan, Ricardo, Cortazar | 65 | 220 | 25 | 56 | 78 | 8 | 1 | 4 | 27 | 9 | 1 | 29 | 6 | 45 | 6 | 3 | .255 |
| Gil, Joel, Celaya | 1 | 2 | 0 | 0 | 0 | 0 | 0 | 0 | 0 | 0 | 0 | 0 | 1 | 0 | 0 | | .000 |
| Gomez, Graciano, Leon | 18 | 42 | 3 | 7 | 10 | 1 | 0 | 0 | 6 | 2 | 1 | 2 | 1 | 15 | 2 | 0 | .167 |
| Gonzalez, Jose Luis, Acam | 19 | 46 | 5 | 12 | 12 | 0 | 0 | 0 | 1 | 0 | 0 | 3 | 0 | 6 | 2 | 0 | .261 |
| Gonzalez, Marcos, Sal | 34 | 56 | 6 | 13 | 21 | 1 | 2 | 1 | 7 | 1 | 0 | 5 | 1 | 10 | 0 | 0 | .232 |
| Gonzalez, Rene, Lagos de M. | 5 | 4 | 0 | 1 | 1 | 0 | 0 | 0 | 1 | 0 | 0 | 0 | 0 | 2 | 0 | 0 | .250 |
| Granados, Felipe, Guanaj | 6 | 8 | 1 | 2 | 2 | 0 | 0 | 0 | 0 | 0 | 0 | 0 | 0 | 3 | 0 | 0 | .250 |
| Guerrero, J. Encarn', Acam* | 43 | 134 | 22 | 38 | 52 | 5 | 0 | 3 | 21 | 0 | 2 | 22 | 2 | 17 | 0 | 2 | .284 |
| Guevara, Marcos, Acambaro | 4 | 5 | 0 | 2 | 2 | 0 | 0 | 0 | 1 | 0 | 0 | 0 | 1 | 0 | 0 | 0 | .400 |
| Guzman, Guadalupe, Celaya | 2 | 0 | 0 | 0 | 0 | 0 | 0 | 0 | 0 | 0 | 0 | 0 | 0 | 0 | 0 | 0 | .000 |
| Guzman, Horacio, Acambaro | 16 | 61 | 8 | 12 | 13 | 1 | 0 | 0 | 4 | 0 | 1 | 3 | 0 | 11 | 3 | 0 | .197 |
| Guzman, Ramiro, Acambaro* | 67 | 237 | 29 | 58 | 74 | 7 | 3 | 1 | 22 | 6 | 2 | 34 | 1 | 28 | 9 | 0 | .245 |
| Guzman, Ubaldo, Uriangato | 57 | 176 | 32 | 45 | 59 | 7 | 2 | 1 | 21 | 3 | 2 | 20 | 2 | 37 | 8 | 4 | .256 |
| Hermida, Ignacio, Guanaj | 61 | 190 | 28 | 58 | 85 | 10 | 4 | 3 | 39 | 1 | 2 | 20 | 1 | 24 | 8 | 3 | .305 |
| Hernandez, Francisco, Leon | 4 | 4 | 1 | 0 | 0 | 0 | 0 | 0 | 0 | 0 | 0 | 0 | 0 | 2 | 0 | 0 | .000 |
| Hernandez, Jesus, Acambaro | 19 | 26 | 1 | 6 | 6 | 0 | 0 | 0 | 1 | 0 | 0 | 0 | 0 | 10 | 0 | 0 | .231 |
| Hernandez, Jose Maria, Leon | 49 | 191 | 25 | 71 | 98 | 12 | 6 | 1 | 26 | 1 | 4 | 12 | 0 | 21 | 6 | 6 | .372 |

| Player and Club | G. | AB. | R. | H. | TB. | 2B. | 3B. | HR. | RBI. | SH. | SF. | BB. | HP. | SO. | SB. | CS. | Pct. |
|---|---|---|---|---|---|---|---|---|---|---|---|---|---|---|---|---|---|
| Hernandez, Reyes, Cortazar ..18 | 15 | 1 | 4 | 5 | 1 | 0 | 0 | 1 | 2 | 0 | 2 | 1 | 3 | 0 | 0 | .267 |
| Hernandez, Salvador, Urian ..58 | 215 | 38 | 55 | 82 | 9 | 3 | 4 | 33 | 5 | 2 | 23 | 2 | 14 | 7 | 8 | .256 |
| Herrera, Manuel, | | | | | | | | | | | | | | | | | |
| 11 Celaya-16 Lagos de M 27 | 25 | 1 | 5 | 6 | 1 | 0 | 0 | 3 | 3 | 0 | 2 | 0 | 7 | 0 | 0 | .200 |
| Hinostrosa, Emiliano, Guan...22 | 41 | 5 | 8 | 8 | 0 | 0 | 0 | 2 | 4 | 0 | 8 | 0 | 20 | 0 | 1 | .195 |
| Hurtado, Antonio, Leon .....39 | 93 | 5 | 16 | 18 | 2 | 0 | 0 | 5 | 1 | 1 | 8 | 1 | 10 | 3 | 2 | .172 |
| Ibarra, Jeronimo, Acambaro ..71 | 276 | 52 | 101 | 121 | 14 | 3 | 0 | 36 | 3 | 1 | 9 | 4 | 11 | 12 | 2 | .366 |
| Jara, Leonel, Celaya ........ 7 | 9 | 0 | 2 | 4 | 0 | 1 | 0 | 0 | 0 | 0 | 0 | 0 | 4 | 0 | 0 | .222 |
| Jimenez, Fco. Javier, Acam..19 | 52 | 3 | 8 | 10 | 0 | 1 | 0 | 2 | 0 | 0 | 8 | 0 | 6 | 1 | 0 | .154 |
| Juarez, Clemente, Guan* ...69 | 270 | 46 | 96 | 146 | 20 | 6 | 6 | 51 | 0 | 2 | 10 | 4 | 23 | 10 | 6 | .356 |
| Lara M., Francisco, Urian...61 | 207 | 31 | 55 | 89 | 7 | 3 | 7 | 41 | 4 | 5 | 11 | 1 | 17 | 4 | 5 | .266 |
| Lara, Gilberto, Guanaj ......13 | 13 | 5 | 4 | 5 | 1 | 0 | 0 | 0 | 1 | 0 | 6 | 0 | 1 | 1 | 0 | .308 |
| Lara, Santos, Guanajuato ...36 | 104 | 27 | 43 | 78 | 8 | 0 | 9 | 28 | 0 | 1 | 31 | 5 | 12 | 8 | 1 | .413 |
| Lazaro, Manuel, Celaya .....67 | 264 | 47 | 80 | 108 | 12 | 5 | 2 | 42 | 6 | 3 | 20 | 2 | 16 | 14 | 3 | .303 |
| Ledezma, Humberto, L. M...50 | 133 | 13 | 26 | 29 | 1 | 1 | 0 | 8 | 5 | 0 | 16 | 2 | 17 | 2 | 2 | .195 |
| Leon, Clemente, Cortazar ...15 | 28 | 5 | 6 | 9 | 1 | 1 | 0 | 1 | 1 | 0 | 3 | 2 | 9 | 0 | 0 | .214 |
| Leyva, Ramon, Leon ........17 | 29 | 0 | 8 | 9 | 1 | 0 | 0 | 2 | 2 | 0 | 1 | 9 | 0 | 1 | .276 |
| Lopez, Baudel, Lagos de M*..44 | 159 | 32 | 44 | 58 | 6 | 1 | 2 | 16 | 2 | 0 | 31 | 3 | 11 | 6 | 4 | .277 |
| Lopez, Hector, Uriangato ...11 | 30 | 2 | 4 | 5 | 1 | 0 | 0 | 3 | 1 | 0 | 3 | 0 | 4 | 0 | 0 | .133 |
| Lopez, Juan Manuel, L. M...35 | 106 | 10 | 31 | 39 | 5 | 0 | 1 | 15 | 0 | 0 | 12 | 0 | 11 | 1 | 2 | .292 |
| Lopez, Norberto, Acambaro .. 9 | 12 | 0 | 1 | 2 | 1 | 0 | 0 | 0 | 0 | 0 | 1 | 0 | 5 | 0 | 0 | .083 |
| Loza, Salvador, Lagos de M... 7 | 15 | 1 | 5 | 6 | 1 | 0 | 0 | 1 | 0 | 0 | 0 | 0 | 2 | 0 | 0 | .333 |
| Lugo, Donaldo, Cortazar ...69 | 294 | 51 | 102 | 159 | 15 | 1 | 2 | 37 | 4 | 2 | 16 | 3 | 16 | 15 | 6 | .347 |
| Martinez, Guadalupe, Sal ...13 | 11 | 0 | 1 | 1 | 0 | 0 | 0 | 0 | 0 | 0 | 0 | 0 | 1 | 0 | 0 | .091 |
| Martinez, Juan, Salamanca ..70 | 252 | 41 | 75 | 110 | 18 | 1 | 5 | 34 | 2 | 2 | 19 | 3 | 48 | 3 | 4 | .298 |
| Martinez, Raul, Leon ....... 4 | 7 | 1 | 2 | 3 | 1 | 0 | 0 | 0 | 0 | 0 | 2 | 0 | 1 | 0 | 0 | .286 |
| Mena, Jorge, Celaya ........25 | 40 | 3 | 9 | 14 | 2 | 0 | 1 | 3 | 1 | 0 | 2 | 0 | 13 | 0 | 0 | .225 |
| Mendez, Juan, Celaya*......32 | 88 | 10 | 12 | 16 | 1 | 0 | 1 | 6 | 2 | 0 | 7 | 0 | 25 | 4 | 3 | .136 |
| Mendoza, Juan Jose, Sal.....61 | 224 | 29 | 60 | 69 | 3 | 3 | 0 | 12 | 3 | 0 | 32 | 2 | 21 | 10 | 4 | .268 |
| Menendez, Rolando, Cor......26 | 58 | 7 | 16 | 21 | 2 | 0 | 1 | 7 | 0 | 2 | 2 | 0 | 8 | 0 | 0 | .276 |
| Mercado, Juan, Cortazar .... 1 | 2 | 1 | 1 | 2 | 1 | 0 | 0 | 0 | 0 | 0 | 0 | 0 | 0 | 0 | 0 | .500 |
| Mercado, Ruben, Cortazar ...20 | 42 | 2 | 7 | 7 | 0 | 0 | 0 | 3 | 2 | 0 | 4 | 2 | 7 | 0 | 0 | .167 |
| Meza, Juan Luis, L. M......10 | 27 | 5 | 6 | 11 | 0 | 1 | 1 | 7 | 0 | 1 | 5 | 3 | 7 | 0 | 0 | .222 |
| Miranda, Carlos, L. M. ...... 8 | 11 | 0 | 2 | 2 | 0 | 0 | 0 | 0 | 1 | 0 | 1 | 0 | 2 | 0 | 0 | .182 |
| Molina, Eduardo, Cortazar... 1 | 0 | 0 | 0 | 0 | 0 | 0 | 0 | 0 | 0 | 0 | 0 | 0 | 0 | 0 | 0 | .000 |
| Monreal, Moises, Celaya.....24 | 67 | 7 | 16 | 19 | 3 | 0 | 0 | 4 | 0 | 0 | 3 | 1 | 13 | 1 | 1 | .239 |
| Monsivais, Hector, Sal ......21 | 64 | 12 | 20 | 22 | 2 | 0 | 0 | 6 | 1 | 1 | 10 | 2 | 6 | 4 | 6 | .313 |
| Montijo, Roberto, L. M..... 3 | 1 | 0 | 0 | 0 | 0 | 0 | 0 | 0 | 0 | 0 | 1 | 0 | 1 | 0 | 0 | .000 |
| Morales P., Alfredo, Sal.....70 | 224 | 27 | 59 | 75 | 6 | 5 | 0 | 27 | 8 | 2 | 30 | 4 | 20 | 15 | 4 | .263 |
| Morales R., Alfredo, Sal....58 | 187 | 14 | 40 | 57 | 6 | 1 | 3 | 27 | 3 | 2 | 7 | 0 | 38 | 3 | 0 | .214 |
| Moreno, Antonio, Acambaro..13 | 5 | 0 | 0 | 0 | 0 | 0 | 0 | 0 | 1 | 0 | 0 | 0 | 0 | 0 | 0 | .000 |
| Moroyoqui, Antonio, Guana... 9 | 12 | 1 | 2 | 2 | 0 | 0 | 0 | 1 | 0 | 0 | 3 | 0 | 4 | 0 | 0 | .167 |
| Nava, Mario, Celaya .......60 | 199 | 27 | 50 | 65 | 7 | 4 | 0 | 23 | 4 | 2 | 19 | 3 | 22 | 4 | 4 | .251 |
| Navarrete, Carlos, L. M. ...69 | 231 | 42 | 61 | 88 | 9 | 3 | 4 | 28 | 4 | 4 | 40 | 9 | 21 | 3 | 1 | .264 |
| Nieblas, Armando, Sal ......23 | 42 | 4 | 5 | 7 | 0 | 0 | 0 | 4 | 3 | 2 | 3 | 0 | 11 | 0 | 0 | .119 |
| Nunez, Jorge, Leon ........19 | 36 | 3 | 10 | 11 | 1 | 0 | 0 | 4 | 2 | 0 | 2 | 0 | 4 | 1 | 2 | .278 |
| Ochoa, Julio, Leon ......... 2 | 6 | 1 | 0 | 0 | 0 | 0 | 0 | 1 | 1 | 0 | 0 | 0 | 2 | 0 | 0 | .000 |
| Ornelas, Rolando, Celaya ..68 | 257 | 46 | 76 | 100 | 12 | 3 | 2 | 42 | 3 | 4 | 20 | 3 | 28 | 8 | 7 | .296 |
| Orozco, Juan Manuel, Acam..21 | 30 | 1 | 6 | 7 | 1 | 0 | 0 | 2 | 3 | 0 | 1 | 0 | 1 | 0 | 0 | .200 |
| Ortega, Francisco, Acam ....14 | 32 | 0 | 4 | 4 | 0 | 0 | 0 | 1 | 2 | 0 | 2 | 0 | 6 | 0 | 0 | .125 |
| Ortega, Jose Luis, Leon ....16 | 42 | 9 | 8 | 10 | 2 | 0 | 0 | 4 | 1 | 0 | 5 | 1 | 6 | 2 | 0 | .190 |
| Ortiz, Armando, L. M......67 | 244 | 49 | 80 | 129 | 15 | 2 | 10 | 44 | 1 | 0 | 39 | 6 | 37 | 3 | 2 | .328 |
| Paredes, Raul, Cortazar ....49 | 160 | 32 | 44 | 56 | 7 | 1 | 1 | 24 | 5 | 1 | 4 | 3 | 15 | 7 | 2 | .275 |
| Paz, Marcos, Acambaro ..... 9 | 6 | 1 | 1 | 1 | 0 | 0 | 0 | 1 | 0 | 0 | 0 | 4 | 0 | 0 | .167 |
| Pena, Ramiro, Salamanca .... 5 | 14 | 1 | 3 | 5 | 2 | 0 | 0 | 0 | 0 | 0 | 1 | 0 | 2 | 0 | 0 | .214 |
| Pereda, Pablo, Lagos de M..14 | 36 | 4 | 5 | 5 | 0 | 0 | 0 | 4 | 3 | 0 | 1 | 0 | 10 | 1 | 0 | .139 |
| Perez, Alfredo, Celaya .....64 | 237 | 31 | 67 | 103 | 14 | 5 | 4 | 42 | 1 | 2 | 19 | 0 | 30 | 5 | 2 | .283 |
| Perez, Candelario, Sal......18 | 28 | 3 | 6 | 6 | 0 | 0 | 0 | 2 | 3 | 0 | 2 | 1 | 7 | 0 | 0 | .214 |
| Perez, Gabino, Leon .......21 | 13 | 1 | 1 | 1 | 0 | 0 | 0 | 0 | 1 | 0 | 1 | 0 | 5 | 0 | 0 | .077 |
| Pina, Francisco, Cortazar ...13 | 35 | 3 | 12 | 19 | 2 | 1 | 1 | 6 | 0 | 1 | 3 | 1 | 4 | 0 | 1 | .343 |
| Pina, Javier R., Urian ......10 | 11 | 3 | 2 | 2 | 0 | 0 | 0 | 0 | 1 | 0 | 2 | 0 | 2 | 0 | 0 | .182 |
| Pineda, Juan Jose, Cor .....51 | 176 | 24 | 56 | 73 | 7 | 2 | 2 | 28 | 2 | 2 | 10 | 3 | 10 | 3 | 0 | .318 |
| Quinones, Jorge Luis, Urian..26 | 55 | 3 | 10 | 13 | 3 | 0 | 0 | 3 | 2 | 0 | 13 | 0 | 10 | 1 | 0 | .182 |
| Quiroz, Jose Luis, Leon ...70 | 260 | 37 | 78 | 139 | 13 | 6 | 12 | 46 | 1 | 1 | 21 | 2 | 28 | 13 | 7 | .300 |
| Ramirez, Manuel, Leon .....69 | 271 | 40 | 84 | 126 | 15 | 9 | 3 | 45 | 1 | 2 | 23 | 1 | 20 | 5 | 9 | .310 |
| Ramirez, Mario, Leon ......14 | 37 | 3 | 7 | 8 | 1 | 0 | 0 | 3 | 1 | 0 | 5 | 0 | 9 | 0 | 0 | .189 |
| Rangel, Jose, Cortazar .....22 | 42 | 4 | 10 | 13 | 0 | 0 | 1 | 5 | 0 | 0 | 3 | 0 | 9 | 0 | 0 | .238 |
| Reynoso, Jesus, Lagos de M..16 | 32 | 1 | 8 | 8 | 0 | 0 | 0 | 3 | 4 | 0 | 0 | 0 | 4 | 1 | 0 | .250 |
| Rios, Carlos, Leon ........65 | 234 | 20 | 58 | 76 | 13 | 1 | 1 | 23 | 3 | 2 | 9 | 2 | 22 | 7 | 5 | .248 |
| Robles, Jesus, Guanajuato ..20 | 50 | 5 | 9 | 11 | 2 | 0 | 0 | 1 | 0 | 0 | 5 | 2 | 19 | 2 | 0 | .180 |
| Rodriguez, Gilberto, Celaya..20 | 77 | 8 | 26 | 33 | 0 | 0 | 1 | 9 | 0 | 1 | 4 | 0 | 9 | 1 | 0 | .338 |
| Rodriguez, Guadalupe, Urian 5 | 3 | 1 | 1 | 1 | 0 | 0 | 0 | 0 | 0 | 0 | 3 | 0 | 2 | 0 | 1 | .333 |
| Rodriguez, Jesus, Leon .....45 | 128 | 14 | 37 | 42 | 2 | 0 | 1 | 8 | 1 | 0 | 9 | 3 | 19 | 8 | 3 | .289 |
| Rodriguez, Ricardo, Cor.....17 | 14 | 1 | 3 | 3 | 0 | 0 | 0 | 0 | 1 | 0 | 3 | 0 | 3 | 1 | 1 | .214 |
| Rodriguez, Roberto, Celaya..15 | 51 | 5 | 12 | 15 | 3 | 0 | 0 | 8 | 1 | 0 | 6 | 0 | 7 | 2 | 0 | .235 |
| Rojas, Olegario, Celaya ....16 | 47 | 4 | 9 | 10 | 1 | 0 | 0 | 2 | 0 | 2 | 0 | 6 | 0 | 0 | .191 |
| Romo, Jesus, Lagos de M ...37 | 83 | 10 | 20 | 24 | 4 | 0 | 0 | 8 | 3 | 0 | 11 | 1 | 13 | 1 | 0 | .241 |
| Ruiz, Miguel Angel, Leon ... 5 | 15 | 4 | 5 | 7 | 2 | 0 | 0 | 3 | 0 | 1 | 3 | 1 | 2 | 1 | 0 | .333 |
| Salas, Roberto, Guanajuato ..57 | 139 | 17 | 34 | 46 | 8 | 2 | 0 | 14 | 1 | 3 | 17 | 6 | 20 | 3 | 2 | .245 |
| Salas, Wilber, Guanajuato ...13 | 32 | 3 | 3 | 4 | 1 | 0 | 0 | 2 | 1 | 0 | 4 | 0 | 7 | 0 | 0 | .094 |

| Player and Club | G. | AB. | R. | H. | TB. | 2B. | 3B. | HR. | RBI. | SH. | SF. | BB. | HP. | SO. | SB. | CS. | Pct. |
|---|---|---|---|---|---|---|---|---|---|---|---|---|---|---|---|---|---|
| Salcido, Ernesto, Uriangato | 12 | 15 | 1 | 4 | 5 | 1 | 0 | 0 | 1 | 1 | 0 | 2 | 0 | 8 | 0 | 0 | .267 |
| Saldana, Eulogio, Guanajuato | 24 | 34 | 4 | 4 | 11 | 0 | 2 | 1 | 3 | 3 | 0 | 1 | 1 | 8 | 0 | 0 | .118 |
| Saldana, Mario, Uriangato | 27 | 91 | 7 | 16 | 21 | 2 | 0 | 1 | 8 | 3 | 0 | 5 | 0 | 13 | 4 | 1 | .176 |
| Salomon, Felix, Guanajuato | 11 | 5 | 0 | 0 | 0 | 0 | 0 | 0 | 0 | 0 | 0 | 2 | 0 | 0 | 0 | 0 | .000 |
| Sanchez, Jorge, Salamanca | 24 | 34 | 3 | 3 | 3 | 0 | 0 | 0 | 1 | 1 | 0 | 3 | 1 | 8 | 0 | 0 | .088 |
| Sanchez, Jose, Salamanca | 1 | 3 | 3 | 1 | 1 | 0 | 0 | 0 | 0 | 0 | 0 | 0 | 0 | 0 | 0 | 0 | .333 |
| Sanchez, Juan, Guanajuato | 47 | 120 | 28 | 32 | 41 | 5 | 2 | 0 | 13 | 4 | 0 | 26 | 2 | 21 | 4 | 3 | .267 |
| Sanchez, Raul, Celaya | 40 | 140 | 31 | 47 | 60 | 2 | 4 | 1 | 17 | 3 | 3 | 26 | 0 | 13 | 13 | 2 | .336 |
| San Roman, Alejandro, Guan. | 51 | 176 | 29 | 48 | 57 | 5 | 2 | 0 | 12 | 2 | 1 | 20 | 5 | 25 | 9 | 9 | .273 |
| Santos, Guadalupe, L. M. | 23 | 66 | 7 | 15 | 21 | 3 | 0 | 1 | 12 | 0 | 0 | 8 | 0 | 25 | 2 | 1 | .227 |
| Santos, Tobias, Guanajuato | 66 | 209 | 18 | 55 | 77 | 10 | 0 | 4 | 31 | 2 | 1 | 11 | 5 | 29 | 0 | 2 | .263 |
| Sanudo, Ismael, Cortazar | 64 | 237 | 31 | 77 | 102 | 6 | 2 | 5 | 49 | 7 | 5 | 30 | 5 | 23 | 6 | 6 | .325 |
| Sauceda, Hector, Celaya | 70 | 255 | 27 | 77 | 103 | 12 | 4 | 2 | 32 | 2 | 0 | 18 | 0 | 26 | 5 | 7 | .302 |
| Sauceda, Ramiro, Salamanca | 16 | 27 | 3 | 10 | 11 | 1 | 0 | 0 | 4 | 0 | 0 | 0 | 0 | 2 | 0 | 0 | .370 |
| Saucedo, Salvador, Sal | 67 | 251 | 24 | 56 | 65 | 9 | 0 | 0 | 23 | 4 | 0 | 21 | 2 | 26 | 4 | 3 | .223 |
| Solis, Guillermo, Acambaro | 30 | 68 | 13 | 17 | 24 | 3 | 2 | 0 | 16 | 1 | 1 | 11 | 0 | 7 | 0 | 1 | .250 |
| Solis, Victor, Celaya | 17 | 20 | 0 | 0 | 0 | 0 | 0 | 0 | 1 | 0 | 0 | 5 | 0 | 5 | 0 | 0 | .000 |
| Soto, Alvaro, Cortazar | 11 | 23 | 3 | 6 | 7 | 1 | 0 | 0 | 3 | 0 | 0 | 1 | 0 | 1 | 0 | 0 | .261 |
| Soto, Rosendo, Guanajuato | 52 | 114 | 14 | 29 | 35 | 3 | 0 | 1 | 7 | 2 | 1 | 5 | 1 | 27 | 1 | 1 | .254 |
| Terrazas, Martin, Urian | 189 | 34 | 52 | 78 | 8 | 3 | 4 | 30 | 2 | 3 | 30 | 1 | 19 | 3 | 3 | .275 |
| Thomas, Pablo, Leon | 39 | 151 | 24 | 46 | 75 | 11 | 3 | 4 | 26 | 1 | 3 | 7 | 3 | 12 | 5 | 2 | .305 |
| Tiburcio, Ceferino, Guan | 61 | 185 | 26 | 56 | 85 | 9 | 1 | 6 | 34 | 0 | 4 | 17 | 1 | 39 | 2 | 3 | .303 |
| Torres A., Jesus, L. M. | 18 | 26 | 3 | 7 | 8 | 1 | 0 | 0 | 1 | 0 | 1 | 2 | 0 | 3 | 1 | 0 | .269 |
| Torres B., Jesus, Celaya | 18 | 25 | 1 | 2 | 2 | 0 | 0 | 0 | 1 | 1 | 0 | 2 | 0 | 6 | 0 | 0 | .080 |
| Torres, Nemesio, Salamanca | 7 | 20 | 3 | 9 | 11 | 2 | 0 | 0 | 4 | 1 | 1 | 3 | 0 | 4 | 1 | 2 | .450 |
| Uresti, Crisanto, Leon | 15 | 15 | 3 | 2 | 2 | 0 | 0 | 0 | 0 | 2 | 0 | 0 | 0 | 3 | 0 | 0 | .133 |
| Urias, Juan, Acambaro | 7 | 4 | 1 | 1 | 1 | 0 | 0 | 0 | 0 | 0 | 0 | 0 | 0 | 3 | 0 | 0 | .250 |
| Valdez, Jose Humberto, Urian | 19 | 17 | 2 | 5 | 5 | 0 | 0 | 0 | 4 | 0 | 0 | 0 | 0 | 4 | 0 | 0 | .294 |
| Valenzuela, Agustin, L. M. | 69 | 252 | 27 | 45 | 51 | 4 | 1 | 0 | 15 | 5 | 2 | 28 | 4 | 34 | 5 | 4 | .179 |
| Valle, Jose Guadalupe, Uri | 59 | 185 | 24 | 42 | 65 | 6 | 1 | 5 | 30 | 3 | 3 | 30 | 2 | 56 | 6 | 5 | .227 |
| Valles, Miguel Angel, Guan. | 11 | 3 | 0 | 0 | 0 | 0 | 0 | 0 | 0 | 0 | 0 | 0 | 0 | 2 | 0 | 0 | .000 |
| Vallin, Rosendo, Leon | 51 | 160 | 22 | 37 | 51 | 6 | 1 | 2 | 6 | 7 | 1 | 17 | 0 | 23 | 7 | 1 | .231 |
| Vargas, Fidel, Leon | 12 | 3 | 0 | 0 | 0 | 0 | 0 | 0 | 0 | 0 | 0 | 0 | 0 | 1 | 0 | 0 | .000 |
| Villagomez, David, L. M. | 70 | 252 | 39 | 83 | 106 | 12 | 4 | 1 | 48 | 1 | 5 | 24 | 4 | 26 | 8 | 2 | .329 |
| Villanueva, Luis, Urian* | 6 | 18 | 6 | 6 | 6 | 0 | 0 | 0 | 1 | 0 | 0 | 0 | 0 | 4 | 0 | 0 | .333 |
| Wilfer, Carlos, Guanajuato | 2 | 3 | 1 | 1 | 2 | 1 | 0 | 0 | 0 | 0 | 0 | 0 | 0 | 0 | 0 | 0 | .333 |
| Yepes, Francisco, Guanajuato | 36 | 147 | 32 | 62 | 78 | 8 | 4 | 0 | 18 | 1 | 2 | 9 | 4 | 11 | 14 | 1 | .422 |
| Zamora, Roberto, Uriangato | 67 | 232 | 36 | 66 | 95 | 11 | 6 | 2 | 35 | 3 | 2 | 17 | 1 | 24 | 9 | 7 | .284 |

GRAND-SLAM HOME RUNS—J. V. Contreras, Hermida, S. Hernandez, Lazaro, B. Lopez, Oritz, Tiburcio, 1 each.

AWARDED FIRST BASE ON INTERFERENCE—Chavez, Esparza, S. Hernandez, Ledezma, Mario Ramirez, M. Saldana, San Roman, 1 each (catchers not listed).

## CLUB FIELDING

| Club | G. | PO. | A. | E. | DP. | PB. | Pct. | Club | G. | PO. | A. | E. | DP. | PB. | Pct. |
|---|---|---|---|---|---|---|---|---|---|---|---|---|---|---|---|
| Uriangato | 71 | 1815 | 886 | 75 | 82 | 21 | .973 | Salamanca | 70 | 1773 | 777 | 123 | 75 | 41 | .954 |
| Cortazar | 70 | 1854 | 906 | 86 | 71 | 38 | .970 | Lagos de Moreno | 70 | 1752 | 876 | 138 | 65 | 33 | .950 |
| Celaya | 70 | 1770 | 825 | 102 | 65 | 30 | .962 | Leon | 70 | 1800 | 782 | 136 | 71 | 27 | .950 |
| Guanajuato | 72 | 1791 | 647 | 116 | 72 | 26 | .955 | Acambaro | 71 | 1782 | 947 | 163 | 96 | 40 | .944 |

Triple Plays—Leon, Acambaro, 1 each.

## INDIVIDUAL FIELDING

*Throws lefthanded.

### FIRST BASEMEN

| Player and Club | G. | PO. | A. | E. | DP. | Pct. | Player and Club | G. | PO. | A. | E. | DP. | Pct. |
|---|---|---|---|---|---|---|---|---|---|---|---|---|---|
| Lara, Uriangato | 30 | 268 | 10 | 0 | 27 | 1.000 | Chavez, Cortazar | 43 | 396 | 21 | 7 | 36 | .983 |
| Montiel, Cortazar | 15 | 143 | 8 | 0 | 12 | 1.000 | PEREZ, Celaya | 52 | 513 | 20 | 9 | 43 | .983 |
| G. Rodriguez, Celaya* | 10 | 108 | 5 | 0 | 6 | 1.000 | Santos, Lagos de M. | 13 | 101 | 6 | 2 | 12 | .982 |
| Castellon, Acambaro | 16 | 135 | 9 | 1 | 9 | .993 | Ortiz, Lagos de M. | 12 | 105 | 2 | 2 | 12 | .982 |
| Cervantes, Uriangato | 11 | 121 | 4 | 1 | 8 | .992 | Espinosa, Leon | 34 | 285 | 17 | 7 | 25 | .977 |
| N. Cruz, Acambaro | 15 | 115 | 2 | 1 | 10 | .992 | Clayton, Salamanca* | 67 | 525 | 32 | 13 | 55 | .977 |
| Tiburcio, Guanajuato | 33 | 297 | 4 | 3 | 27 | .990 | Barrera, Lagos de M. | 20 | 158 | 5 | 4 | 10 | .976 |
| J. M. Lopez, L M | 32 | 271 | 11 | 3 | 24 | .989 | Guerrero, Acambaro* | 40 | 374 | 24 | 10 | 28 | .975 |
| Zamora, Uriangato | 15 | 155 | 7 | 2 | 16 | .988 | Thomas, Leon | 39 | 301 | 8 | 10 | 22 | .969 |

Triple Plays—Espinosa, Guerrero, 1 each.

### (Fewer Than Ten Games)

| Player and Club | G. | PO. | A. | E. | DP. | Pct. | Player and Club | G. | PO. | A. | E. | DP. | Pct. |
|---|---|---|---|---|---|---|---|---|---|---|---|---|---|
| Pina, Cortazar | 9 | 108 | 3 | 0 | 6 | 1.000 | Ornelas, Celaya | 1 | 7 | 0 | 0 | 1 | 1.000 |
| Quinones, Uriangato | 8 | 65 | 4 | 0 | 6 | 1.000 | Garzon, Uriangato | 2 | 7 | 0 | 0 | 0 | 1.000 |
| Castro, Celaya | 6 | 41 | 2 | 0 | 2 | 1.000 | Mendez, Celaya | 1 | 6 | 0 | 0 | 0 | 1.000 |
| Pineda, Cortazar | 4 | 38 | 2 | 0 | 4 | 1.000 | Gomez, Leon | 8 | 62 | 1 | 1 | 4 | .984 |
| Flores, Uriangato | 3 | 30 | 3 | 0 | 2 | 1.000 | Terrazas, Uriangato | 4 | 36 | 1 | 1 | 3 | .974 |
| Camargo, Salamanca | 6 | 26 | 3 | 0 | 4 | 1.000 | R. Salas, Guanajuato | 6 | 53 | 2 | 2 | 5 | .965 |
| Guzman, Uriangato | 4 | 21 | 1 | 0 | 1 | 1.000 | Gaytan, Cortazar | 3 | 17 | 1 | 1 | 2 | .947 |
| Enriquez, Urlangato | 3 | 15 | 1 | 0 | 1 | 1.000 | Alvarez, Acambaro | 8 | 54 | 3 | 4 | 5 | .934 |
| Felix, Leon | 1 | 14 | 1 | 0 | 0 | 1.000 | | | | | | | |

## SECOND BASEMEN

| Player and Club | G. | PO. | A. | E. | DP. | Pct. | Player and Club | G. | PO. | A. | E. | DP. | Pct. |
|---|---|---|---|---|---|---|---|---|---|---|---|---|---|
| HERNANDEZ, Urian | 53 | 138 | 118 | 7 | 40 | .973 | San Roman, Guanaj. | 48 | 107 | 106 | 11 | 25 | .950 |
| Lugo, Cortazar | 69 | 207 | 190 | 12 | 55 | .971 | P. Cruz, Acambaro.. | 12 | 30 | 23 | 3 | 3 | .946 |
| Castro, Acambaro | 46 | 103 | 92 | 6 | 28 | .970 | J. M. Hernandez, Leon | 26 | 70 | 68 | 8 | 16 | .945 |
| Saucedo, Salamanca | 65 | 176 | 148 | 11 | 44 | .967 | Lazaro, Celaya | 18 | 47 | 42 | 6 | 9 | .937 |
| Castellon, Acambaro | 25 | 50 | 50 | 4 | 16 | .962 | Soto, Guanajuato | 18 | 41 | 43 | 6 | 16 | .933 |
| Barrera, Lagos de M | 17 | 36 | 30 | 3 | 14 | .957 | Vallin, Leon | 39 | 96 | 106 | 15 | 24 | .931 |
| Nava, Celaya | 39 | 83 | 105 | 9 | 18 | .954 | Ortiz, Lagos de M... | 55 | 152 | 120 | 22 | 30 | .925 |
| Rojas, Celaya | 13 | 21 | 19 | 2 | 2 | .952 | | | | | | | |

### (Fewer Than Ten Games)

| Player and Club | G. | PO. | A. | E. | DP. | Pct. | Player and Club | G. | PO. | A. | E. | DP. | Pct. |
|---|---|---|---|---|---|---|---|---|---|---|---|---|---|
| Hermida, Guanajuato | 5 | 10 | 3 | 0 | 1 | 1.000 | W. Salas, Guanaj ... | 5 | 14 | 9 | 1 | 1 | .958 |
| Montiel, Cortazar | 2 | 2 | 4 | 0 | 1 | 1.000 | Saldana, Uriangato | 9 | 17 | 28 | 2 | 6 | .957 |
| Pineda, Cortazar | 2 | 4 | 2 | 0 | 1 | 1.000 | Gonzalez, Salamanca | 7 | 12 | 8 | 1 | 4 | .952 |
| Gonzalez, Acambaro | 2 | 3 | 2 | 0 | 1 | 1.000 | Garzon, Uriangato .... | 3 | 7 | 8 | 1 | 3 | .938 |
| N. Cruz, Acambaro | 2 | 3 | 1 | 0 | 0 | 1.000 | Monsivais, Salamanca | 2 | 5 | 4 | 1 | 1 | .900 |
| Flores, Uriangato | 4 | 1 | 3 | 0 | 1 | 1.000 | Ruiz, Leon | 5 | 9 | 8 | 2 | 5 | .895 |
| S. Lara, Guanajuato | 5 | 15 | 11 | 1 | 2 | .963 | | | | | | | |

## THIRD BASEMEN

| Player and Club | G. | PO. | A. | E. | DP. | Pct. | Player and Club | G. | PO. | A. | E. | DP. | Pct. |
|---|---|---|---|---|---|---|---|---|---|---|---|---|---|
| Fuentes, Guanajuato | 10 | 13 | 25 | 1 | 3 | .974 | Manuel Ramirez, Leon | 69 | 75 | 166 | 20 | 12 | .923 |
| GARZON, Uriangato | 64 | 66 | 228 | 14 | 26 | .955 | Nava, Celaya | 15 | 13 | 34 | 4 | 3 | .922 |
| Soto, Guanajuato .... | 11 | 10 | 32 | 2 | 2 | .955 | Contreras, Celaya.... | 56 | 40 | 140 | 18 | 11 | .909 |
| Sanudo, Cortazar | 64 | 88 | 178 | 15 | 14 | .947 | Ibarra, Acambaro... | 71 | 65 | 241 | 34 | 18 | .900 |
| Morales P., Salaman | 66 | 86 | 161 | 15 | 20 | .943 | Valenzuela, L M ... | 68 | 83 | 180 | 30 | 11 | .898 |
| S. Lara, Guanajuato | 30 | 32 | 90 | 8 | 8 | .938 | Tiburcio, Guanajuato | 20 | 16 | 46 | 13 | 3 | .827 |

### (Fewer Than Ten Games)

| Player and Club | G. | PO. | A. | E. | DP. | Pct. | Player and Club | G. | PO. | A. | E. | DP. | Pct. |
|---|---|---|---|---|---|---|---|---|---|---|---|---|---|
| Barrera, Lagos de M.. | 3 | 6 | 12 | 0 | 5 | 1.000 | Thomas, Leon | 1 | 0 | 3 | 0 | 0 | 1.000 |
| Rodriguez, Uriangato.. | 4 | 2 | 11 | 0 | 2 | 1.000 | Zamora, Uriangato | 6 | 3 | 18 | 1 | 1 | .955 |
| Pineda, Cortazar | 2 | 3 | 8 | 0 | 0 | 1.000 | Montiel, Cortazar .... | 5 | 2 | 9 | 2 | 0 | .846 |
| Hermida, Guanajuato | 3 | 2 | 8 | 0 | 0 | 1.000 | Flores, Salamanca ... | 5 | 1 | 7 | 2 | 0 | .800 |
| P. Cruz, Acambaro .. | 2 | 1 | 3 | 0 | 0 | 1.000 | | | | | | | |

## SHORTSTOPS

| Player and Club | G. | PO. | A. | E. | DP. | Pct. | Player and Club | G. | PO. | A. | E. | DP. | Pct. |
|---|---|---|---|---|---|---|---|---|---|---|---|---|---|
| Saldana, Uriangato | 18 | 24 | 56 | 3 | 7 | .964 | R. Rodriguez, Celaya | 14 | 23 | 39 | 6 | 6 | .912 |
| Romo, Lagos de M.. | 28 | 38 | 83 | 5 | 11 | .960 | Flores, Salamanca.. | 59 | 93 | 184 | 29 | 31 | .905 |
| ELIZONDO, Cortazar | 69 | 107 | 289 | 22 | 42 | .947 | P. Cruz, Acambaro.. | 44 | 63 | 142 | 24 | 22 | .895 |
| Lazaro, Celaya | 50 | 74 | 187 | 16 | 31 | .942 | Rios, Leon | 64 | 103 | 216 | 38 | 42 | .894 |
| Valle, Uriangato | 58 | 81 | 203 | 18 | 35 | .940 | Jimenez, Acambaro.. | 13 | 26 | 42 | 12 | 10 | .850 |
| Yepes, Guanajuato | 29 | 34 | 106 | 9 | 12 | .940 | Barrera, Lagos de M | 11 | 10 | 29 | 7 | 5 | .848 |
| Ledezma, Lagos de M | 43 | 52 | 130 | 12 | 18 | .938 | Solis, Acambaro .... | 12 | 19 | 30 | 9 | 6 | .845 |
| Esparza, Guanajuato | 34 | 38 | 126 | 11 | 21 | .937 | | | | | | | |

Triple Plays—Rios, Jimenez, 1 each.

### (Fewer Than Ten Games)

| Player and Club | G. | PO. | A. | E. | DP. | Pct. | Player and Club | G. | PO. | A. | E. | DP. | Pct. |
|---|---|---|---|---|---|---|---|---|---|---|---|---|---|
| S. Lara, Guanajuato | 2 | 3 | 9 | 0 | 2 | 1.000 | W. Salas, Guanajuato | 1 | 3 | 5 | 1 | 0 | .889 |
| Saucedo, Salamanca .. | 2 | 3 | 5 | 0 | 2 | 1.000 | Castro, Acambaro ... | 6 | 12 | 23 | 6 | 2 | .854 |
| J. M. Hernandez, Leon | 2 | 3 | 5 | 0 | 1 | 1.000 | Garzon, Uriangato ... | 1 | 2 | 3 | 1 | 0 | .833 |
| Ortiz, Lagos de M... | 1 | 2 | 2 | 0 | 1 | 1.000 | Vallin, Leon | 4 | 3 | 6 | 2 | 1 | .818 |
| Torres, Salamanca ... | 7 | 12 | 21 | 1 | 4 | .971 | Ballesteros, L M ... | 2 | 3 | 1 | 1 | 0 | .800 |
| Nava, Celaya | 7 | 10 | 18 | 2 | 4 | .933 | Morales P., Salaman | 6 | 8 | 17 | 7 | 3 | .781 |
| Soto, Guanajuato .... | 5 | 9 | 14 | 2 | 1 | .920 | Granados, Guanajuato | 1 | 1 | 4 | 2 | 0 | .714 |

## OUTFIELDERS

| Player and Club | G. | PO. | A. | E. | DP. | Pct. | Player and Club | G. | PO. | A. | E. | DP. | Pct. |
|---|---|---|---|---|---|---|---|---|---|---|---|---|---|
| Paredes, Cortazar | 43 | 85 | 4 | 0 | 1 | 1.000 | Hurtado, Leon | 30 | 46 | 7 | 2 | 2 | .964 |
| Chavez, Cortazar | 17 | 24 | 4 | 0 | 1 | 1.000 | Sanchez, Guanajuato | 35 | 72 | 4 | 3 | 1 | .962 |
| Diaz, Leon | 13 | 27 | 1 | 0 | 0 | 1.000 | Barrera, Lagos de M | 24 | 48 | 2 | 2 | 1 | .962 |
| Thomas, Leon | 10 | 19 | 0 | 0 | 0 | 1.000 | Arballo, Uriangato*.. | 52 | 70 | 3 | 3 | 2 | .961 |
| Felix, Leon | 39 | 73 | 9 | 1 | 2 | .988 | N. Cruz, Acambaro.. | 50 | 92 | 4 | 4 | 2 | .960 |
| Arellano, Cortazar... | 29 | 59 | 3 | 1 | 1 | .984 | Rodriguez, Leon | 35 | 67 | 4 | 3 | 1 | .959 |
| Avalos, Leon | 21 | 56 | 5 | 1 | 1 | .984 | B. Lopez, Lagos de M | 44 | 97 | 10 | 5 | 3 | .955 |
| FIGUEROA, Urianga | 57 | 94 | 8 | 2 | 3 | .981 | Monsivais, Salaman | 16 | 39 | 3 | 2 | 1 | .955 |
| Mendez, Celaya | 27 | 45 | 1 | 1 | 1 | .979 | Juarez, Guanajuato.. | 68 | 124 | 12 | 7 | 4 | .951 |
| Guzman, Uriangato.. | 52 | 77 | 4 | 2 | 3 | .976 | L. Flores, Acambaro | 40 | 85 | 7 | 5 | 2 | .948 |
| R. Guzman, Acambaro | 67 | 110 | 10 | 3 | 4 | .976 | Ornelas, Celaya | 66 | 105 | 5 | 6 | 1 | .948 |
| Cardona, Cortazar ... | 70 | 189 | 8 | 5 | 2 | .975 | Avila, Acambaro | 38 | 50 | 4 | 3 | 2 | .947 |
| Mendoza, Salamanca | 61 | 166 | 16 | 5 | 2 | .973 | Zamora, Uriangato .. | 46 | 76 | 10 | 5 | 2 | .945 |
| Amador, Lagos de M | 12 | 29 | 5 | 1 | 1 | .971 | Quiroz, Leon | 70 | 127 | 6 | 8 | 2 | .943 |
| Sauceda, Celaya ... | 70 | 128 | 7 | 4 | 2 | .971 | Perez, Celaya | 12 | 16 | 0 | 1 | 0 | .941 |
| Flores, Salamanca .. | 61 | 88 | 8 | 3 | 2 | .970 | Juan Martinez, Salam | 70 | 117 | 10 | 8 | 2 | .941 |
| Morales R., Salaman | 55 | 119 | 4 | 4 | 1 | .969 | Pineda, Cortazar | 39 | 59 | 3 | 4 | 1 | .939 |
| R. Salas, Guanajuato | 37 | 52 | 4 | 2 | 1 | .966 | Villagomez, L M... | 70 | 130 | 12 | 10 | 2 | .934 |

## OUTFIELDER—Continued

| Player and Club | G. | PO. | A. | E. | DP. | Pct. |
|---|---|---|---|---|---|---|
| Ballesteros, L M | 45 | 70 | 9 | 6 | 2 | .929 |
| H. Guzman, Acambaro | 16 | 24 | 2 | 2 | 0 | .929 |
| Lara, Uriangato | 10 | 11 | 2 | 1 | 0 | .929 |
| Rangel, Cortazar | 12 | 10 | 1 | 1 | 0 | .917 |
| Sanchez, Celaya | 39 | 50 | 3 | 5 | 0 | .914 |
| Hermida, Guanajuato | 12 | 19 | 2 | 2 | 0 | .913 |

### (Fewer Than Ten Games)

| Player and Club | G. | PO. | A. | E. | DP. | Pct. |
|---|---|---|---|---|---|---|
| Flores, Salamanca | 6 | 11 | 3 | 0 | 0 | 1.000 |
| Santos, Lagos de M | 8 | 11 | 1 | 0 | 0 | 1.000 |
| Gomez, Leon | 5 | 10 | 1 | 0 | 0 | 1.000 |
| W. Salas, Guanajuato | 5 | 6 | 1 | 0 | 0 | 1.000 |
| Hernandez, Uriangato | 4 | 6 | 0 | 0 | 0 | 1.000 |
| Clayton, Salamanca* | 6 | 5 | 0 | 0 | 0 | 1.000 |
| Montiel, Cortazar | 5 | 5 | 0 | 0 | 0 | 1.000 |
| Castro, Uriangato | 3 | 3 | 0 | 0 | 0 | 1.000 |
| Alvarez, Acambaro | 1 | 3 | 0 | 0 | 0 | 1.000 |
| Yepes, Guanajuato | 7 | 22 | 1 | 1 | 0 | .958 |
| Solis, Acambaro | 6 | 12 | 1 | 1 | 0 | .929 |
| Meza, Lagos de M | 9 | 8 | 4 | 1 | 3 | .923 |

## CATCHERS

| Player and Club | G. | PO. | A. | E. | DP. | PB. | Pct. |
|---|---|---|---|---|---|---|---|
| Ortega, Leon | 16 | 65 | 11 | 0 | 1 | 6 | 1.000 |
| Robles, Guanaj. | 13 | 61 | 9 | 0 | 1 | 5 | 1.000 |
| TERRAZAS, Uri | 51 | 271 | 34 | 2 | 3 | 18 | .993 |
| Lara, Uriangato | 22 | 133 | 15 | 1 | 2 | 3 | .993 |
| Monreal, Celaya | 21 | 112 | 15 | 1 | 2 | 9 | .992 |
| J. M. Hern'dez, L | 20 | 103 | 14 | 1 | 1 | 9 | .992 |
| Espinosa, Leon | 34 | 148 | 26 | 2 | 3 | 12 | .989 |
| Castro, Celaya | 53 | 312 | 43 | 6 | 9 | 21 | .983 |
| Gonzalez, Acam | 14 | 55 | 3 | 1 | 1 | 7 | .983 |
| Gaytan, Cortaz | 62 | 238 | 52 | 6 | 3 | 34 | .980 |
| Camargo, Sala | 67 | 325 | 59 | 8 | 8 | 39 | .980 |
| Santos, Guanaj. | 61 | 305 | 44 | 8 | 4 | 21 | .978 |
| Navarrete, L M | 68 | 297 | 80 | 13 | 7 | 33 | .967 |
| Alvarez, Acam | 63 | 292 | 44 | 14 | 2 | 33 | .960 |
| Fraigo, Salaman | 11 | 23 | 4 | 3 | 0 | 2 | .900 |

### (Fewer Than Ten Games)

| Player and Club | G. | PO. | A. | E. | DP. | PB. | Pct. |
|---|---|---|---|---|---|---|---|
| Arellano, Cortazar | 9 | 33 | 7 | 0 | 1 | 4 | 1.000 |
| Ballesteros, L M | 3 | 17 | 2 | 0 | 0 | 1 | 1.000 |
| Gomez, Leon | 2 | 18 | 3 | 0 | 0 | 0 | 1.000 |

## PITCHERS

| Player and Club | G. | PO. | A. | E. | DP. | Pct. |
|---|---|---|---|---|---|---|
| M. BELTRAN, Celaya | 28 | 2 | 25 | 0 | 2 | 1.000 |
| Fernandez, Guanaj | 24 | 4 | 16 | 0 | 1 | 1.000 |
| Solis, Celaya | 17 | 1 | 19 | 0 | 1 | 1.000 |
| Contreras, Uriangato | 12 | 3 | 16 | 0 | 2 | 1.000 |
| Torres B., Celaya | 17 | 1 | 18 | 0 | 2 | 1.000 |
| Herrera, Celaya-L M | 26 | 1 | 14 | 0 | 1 | 1.000 |
| Arce, Lagos de M | 15 | 2 | 12 | 0 | 0 | 1.000 |
| Rodriguez, Cortazar | 15 | 5 | 8 | 0 | 1 | 1.000 |
| Quinones, Uriangato | 13 | 1 | 9 | 0 | 1 | 1.000 |
| E. Beltran, Celaya | 11 | 0 | 10 | 0 | 0 | 1.000 |
| Garate, Leon | 16 | 1 | 8 | 0 | 1 | 1.000 |
| Dominguez, Leon | 12 | 1 | 7 | 0 | 0 | 1.000 |
| Pina, Uriangato | 10 | 1 | 7 | 0 | 1 | 1.000 |
| Salcido, Uriangato | 12 | 0 | 8 | 0 | 0 | 1.000 |
| Salomon, Guanajuato | 11 | 0 | 7 | 0 | 0 | 1.000 |
| Garcia, Guanajuato | 12 | 1 | 5 | 0 | 1 | 1.000 |
| Moreno, Acambaro | 12 | 2 | 4 | 0 | 1 | 1.000 |
| Alvarez, Uriangato | 12 | 1 | 4 | 0 | 0 | 1.000 |
| Dominguez, L M | 17 | 0 | 5 | 0 | 0 | 1.000 |
| Uresti, Leon | 15 | 0 | 5 | 0 | 0 | 1.000 |
| Delgado, Uriangato* | 10 | 0 | 5 | 0 | 1 | 1.000 |
| Valles, Guanajuato | 11 | 1 | 3 | 0 | 0 | 1.000 |
| Flores, Lagos de M | 22 | 8 | 33 | 1 | 2 | .976 |
| Menendez, Cortazar | 19 | 2 | 29 | 1 | 1 | .969 |
| Cabrales, Celaya | 14 | 3 | 20 | 1 | 1 | .958 |
| Mena, Celaya | 19 | 4 | 18 | 1 | 1 | .957 |
| Reynoso, Lagos de M | 16 | 4 | 18 | 1 | 1 | .957 |
| Carrillo, Guanajuato | 39 | 3 | 17 | 1 | 2 | .952 |
| Mar. Ramirez, Leon | 14 | 4 | 16 | 1 | 1 | .952 |
| Hernandez, Cortazar | 18 | 4 | 16 | 1 | 1 | .952 |
| Gonzalez, Salamanca | 21 | 9 | 10 | 1 | 2 | .950 |
| Flores, Cortazar | 21 | 3 | 16 | 1 | 2 | .950 |
| R. Mercado, Cortazar | 19 | 8 | 24 | 2 | 2 | .941 |
| Espinosa, Guanajuato | 21 | 5 | 11 | 1 | 1 | .941 |
| Nieblas, Salamanca | 23 | 3 | 22 | 2 | 2 | .926 |
| G. Rodriguez, Celaya | 15 | 5 | 18 | 2 | 1 | .920 |
| Pereda, Lagos de M | 14 | 4 | 26 | 3 | 2 | .917 |
| G. Lara, Guanajuato | 13 | 0 | 11 | 1 | 1 | .917 |
| Azcarraga, Uriangato | 14 | 1 | 19 | 2 | 1 | .909 |
| Torres A., L M | 14 | 3 | 15 | 2 | 1 | .900 |
| Valdez, Uriangato | 19 | 1 | 8 | 1 | 0 | .900 |
| Ortega, Acambaro | 14 | 1 | 23 | 3 | 1 | .889 |
| Soto, Cortazar | 11 | 8 | 14 | 3 | 2 | .880 |
| Rog. Garcia, Acam. | 34 | 5 | 24 | 4 | 1 | .879 |
| Leon, Cortazar | 14 | 3 | 11 | 2 | 1 | .875 |
| Nunez, Leon | 13 | 5 | 22 | 4 | 1 | .871 |
| Perez, Salamanca | 18 | 2 | 17 | 3 | 1 | .864 |
| Jorge Sanchez, Salam | 21 | 2 | 17 | 3 | 1 | .864 |
| Sauceda, Salamanca | 13 | 4 | 8 | 2 | 0 | .857 |
| J. L. Garcia, Salaman | 14 | 1 | 5 | 1 | 0 | .857 |
| Leyva, Leon | 17 | 1 | 8 | 2 | 2 | .818 |
| Hinostroza, Guanaj. | 22 | 4 | 18 | 5 | 2 | .815 |
| Lopez, Uriangato | 11 | 4 | 9 | 3 | 1 | .813 |
| Perez, Leon | 21 | 3 | 10 | 3 | 1 | .813 |
| Orozco, Acambaro | 20 | 2 | 15 | 4 | 1 | .810 |
| Garduza, Guanajuato | 19 | 4 | 4 | 2 | 0 | .800 |
| Solis, Acambaro | 10 | 0 | 8 | 2 | 1 | .800 |
| Hernandez, Acambaro | 19 | 1 | 10 | 3 | 1 | .786 |
| Saldana, Guanajuato | 20 | 4 | 10 | 4 | 1 | .778 |
| Duarte, Leon | 12 | 4 | 10 | 5 | 1 | .737 |
| G. Martinez, Salam. | 13 | 0 | 2 | 1 | 0 | .667 |

Triple Play—Rog. Garcia.

### (Fewer Than Ten Games)

| Player and Club | G. | PO. | A. | E. | DP. | Pct. |
|---|---|---|---|---|---|---|
| Lopez, Acambaro | 9 | 2 | 8 | 0 | 1 | 1.000 |
| Pena, Salamanca | 5 | 0 | 7 | 0 | 0 | 1.000 |
| Paz, Acambaro | 8 | 3 | 3 | 0 | 0 | 1.000 |
| Martinez, Leon | 4 | 2 | 4 | 0 | 0 | 1.000 |
| Cota, Cortazar | 4 | 4 | 1 | 0 | 0 | 1.000 |
| Loza, Lagos de M | 5 | 0 | 5 | 0 | 0 | 1.000 |
| Cota, Lagos de M | 3 | 0 | 4 | 0 | 0 | 1.000 |
| Gonzalez, Lagos de M | 5 | 1 | 1 | 0 | 0 | 1.000 |
| Castro, Uriangato | 6 | 3 | 11 | 1 | 0 | .933 |
| Miranda, Lagos de M | 8 | 3 | 10 | 1 | 1 | .929 |
| Villanueva, Urian* | 6 | 0 | 7 | 1 | 0 | .875 |
| Moroyoqui, Guanaj | 8 | 1 | 5 | 1 | 1 | .857 |
| Jara, Celaya | 7 | 0 | 5 | 1 | 0 | .833 |
| Aguilar, Celaya | 5 | 0 | 3 | 1 | 0 | .750 |
| Montijo, Lagos de M | 2 | 0 | 3 | 1 | 1 | .750 |

NOTE: No compilation made of fielders who had no chances.

## CLUB PITCHING

| Club | G. | CG. | ShO. | Sv. | IP. | H. | R. | ER. | HR. | BB. | Int. BB. | HB. | SO. | WP. | Bk. | ERA. |
|---|---|---|---|---|---|---|---|---|---|---|---|---|---|---|---|---|
| Uriangato | 71 | 33 | 14 | 15 | 605 | 469 | 160 | 104 | 12 | 176 | 7 | 23 | 370 | 18 | 0 | 1.55 |
| Cortazar | 70 | 39 | 7 | 5 | 618 | 615 | 292 | 169 | 41 | 200 | 12 | 26 | 246 | 37 | 5 | 2.46 |
| Celaya | 70 | 20 | 9 | 7 | 590 | 527 | 272 | 175 | 17 | 197 | 4 | 19 | 367 | 34 | 1 | 2.67 |
| Leon | 70 | 33 | 5 | 2 | 600 | 651 | 334 | 198 | 16 | 212 | 26 | 31 | 285 | 24 | 5 | 2.97 |
| Acambaro | 71 | 17 | 3 | 8 | 594 | 628 | 389 | 217 | 20 | 239 | 17 | 40 | 285 | 50 | 3 | 3.29 |
| Salamanca | 70 | 30 | 4 | 4 | 591 | 693 | 344 | 225 | 23 | 269 | 14 | 27 | 288 | 36 | 3 | 3.43 |
| Lagos de Moreno | 70 | 22 | 2 | 11 | 584 | 700 | 382 | 229 | 50 | 230 | 18 | 25 | 279 | 36 | 3 | 3.53 |
| Guanajuato | 72 | 17 | 4 | 9 | 597 | 686 | 355 | 236 | 25 | 223 | 44 | 25 | 333 | 30 | 5 | 3.56 |

## PITCHERS' RECORDS

(Leading Qualifiers for Earned-Run Average Leadership—56 or More Innings)
*Throws lefthanded.

| Pitcher—Club | G. | GS. | CG. | ShO. | W. | L. | Sv. | Pct. | IP. | H. | R. | ER. | HR. | BB. | Int. BB. | HB. | SO. | WP. | ERA. |
|---|---|---|---|---|---|---|---|---|---|---|---|---|---|---|---|---|---|---|---|
| A. Soto, Cortazar | 11 | 7 | 7 | 2 | 8 | 1 | 1 | .889 | 72 | 47 | 14 | 5 | 1 | 12 | 1 | 2 | 38 | 2 | 0.63 |
| Azcarraga, Urian | 14 | 12 | 7 | 3 | 8 | 2 | 2 | .800 | 95 | 66 | 13 | 9 | 3 | 16 | 1 | 0 | 59 | 0 | 0.85 |
| H. Lopez, Urian | 11 | 11 | 8 | 3 | 8 | 1 | 0 | .889 | 87 | 61 | 20 | 10 | 0 | 21 | 0 | 2 | 66 | 2 | 1.03 |
| Contreras, Urian | 12 | 9 | 2 | 1 | 5 | 3 | 0 | .625 | 63 | 43 | 16 | 10 | 0 | 26 | 1 | 5 | 42 | 4 | 1.43 |
| Torres B., Celaya | 17 | 9 | 4 | 1 | 6 | 3 | 0 | .667 | 76 | 63 | 19 | 14 | 1 | 20 | 0 | 1 | 31 | 1 | 1.66 |
| Mar. Ramirez, Urian | 14 | 13 | 9 | 1 | 9 | 3 | 0 | .750 | 108 | 101 | 37 | 21 | 1 | 32 | 3 | 7 | 56 | 2 | 1.75 |
| Menendez, Cortazar | 19 | 13 | 10 | 3 | 9 | 6 | 2 | .600 | 138 | 127 | 48 | 28 | 7 | 32 | 1 | 4 | 41 | 4 | 1.85 |
| Mena, Celaya | 19 | 11 | 5 | 2 | 8 | 4 | 1 | .667 | 96 | 76 | 34 | 20 | 0 | 34 | 0 | 3 | 87 | 4 | 1.88 |
| G. Rodriguez, Cel. | 15 | 14 | 4 | 2 | 8 | 3 | 0 | .727 | 81 | 70 | 30 | 17 | 1 | 20 | 0 | 2 | 63 | 2 | 1.89 |
| Rog. Garcia, Acam | 34 | 16 | 9 | 0 | 11 | 14 | 5 | .440 | 158 | 149 | 74 | 36 | 5 | 52 | 5 | 13 | 100 | 14 | 2.05 |

Departmental Leaders: G—Carrillo, 39; GS—Nieblas, 19; CG—Menendez, 10; ShO—Azcarraga, Leyva, H. Lopez, Menendez, 3; W—Rog. Garcia, 14; L—Rog. Garcia, 14; Sv—Carrillo, 8; Pct.—Delgado, 1.000; IP—Rog. Garcia, 158; H.—Rog. Garcia, 149; R—Rog. Garcia, 74; ER—M. Flores, Nieblas, 44; HR—Mercado, Torres A., 11; BB—Jorge Sanchez, 58; IBB—Carrillo, 12; HB—Rog. Garcia, 13; SO—Rog. Garcia, 100; WP—Rog. Garcia, 14.

## (All Pitchers—Listed Alphabetically)

| Pitcher—Club | G. | GS. | CG. | ShO. | W. | L. | Sv. | Pct. | IP. | H. | R. | ER. | HR. | BB. | Int. BB. | HB. | SO. | WP. | ERA. |
|---|---|---|---|---|---|---|---|---|---|---|---|---|---|---|---|---|---|---|---|
| Aguilar, Celaya | 5 | 2 | 0 | 0 | 1 | 0 | 0 | 1.000 | 13 | 15 | 13 | 9 | 0 | 7 | 0 | 1 | 8 | 3 | 6.23 |
| Alvarez, Urian | 12 | 2 | 0 | 0 | 2 | 0 | 0 | 1.000 | 29 | 44 | 20 | 14 | 3 | 10 | 0 | 1 | 14 | 2 | 4.34 |
| Amador, L. M. | 2 | 0 | 0 | 0 | 0 | 0 | 0 | .000 | 5 | 8 | 3 | 1 | 0 | 3 | 1 | 1 | 3 | 3 | 1.80 |
| Arce, Lagos de M. | 15 | 4 | 0 | 0 | 6 | 2 | 3 | .750 | 54 | 72 | 36 | 19 | 5 | 10 | 1 | 1 | 17 | 1 | 3.17 |
| Avila, Acambaro | 2 | 1 | 0 | 0 | 0 | 0 | 0 | .000 | 3 | 2 | 1 | 1 | 1 | 0 | 0 | 0 | 1 | 1 | 9.00 |
| Azcarraga, Urian | 14 | 12 | 7 | 3 | 8 | 2 | 2 | .800 | 95 | 66 | 13 | 9 | 3 | 16 | 1 | 0 | 59 | 0 | 0.85 |
| Ballesteros, L. M. | 1 | 0 | 0 | 0 | 0 | 0 | 0 | .000 | 1 | 2 | 1 | 1 | 0 | 2 | 0 | 0 | 1 | 1 | 9.00 |
| E. Beltran, Urian | 11 | 8 | 3 | 1 | 2 | 4 | 0 | .333 | 66 | 61 | 34 | 22 | 2 | 28 | 1 | 2 | 47 | 3 | 3.00 |
| M. Beltran, Celaya | 28 | 5 | 0 | 0 | 5 | 5 | 0 | .500 | 82 | 75 | 45 | 28 | 6 | 22 | 0 | 5 | 52 | 5 | 3.07 |
| Briseno, Acambaro | 4 | 3 | 0 | 0 | 1 | 1 | 0 | .500 | 23 | 23 | 10 | 5 | 0 | 9 | 2 | 1 | 13 | 0 | 1.96 |
| Cabrales, Celaya | 14 | 10 | 2 | 1 | 4 | 3 | 0 | .571 | 76 | 70 | 43 | 27 | 2 | 20 | 0 | 1 | 30 | 7 | 3.20 |
| Carrillo, Guanaj | 39 | 4 | 2 | 0 | 4 | 6 | 8 | .400 | 75 | 77 | 40 | 24 | 1 | 26 | 12 | 2 | 41 | 2 | 2.88 |
| Castro, Uriangato | 6 | 3 | 2 | 4 | 1 | 1 | 0 | .800 | 47 | 34 | 4 | 4 | 0 | 6 | 0 | 2 | 29 | 2 | 0.77 |
| Contreras, Urian | 12 | 9 | 2 | 1 | 5 | 3 | 0 | .625 | 63 | 43 | 16 | 10 | 0 | 26 | 1 | 5 | 42 | 4 | 1.43 |
| Cota, Cortazar | 4 | 4 | 0 | 0 | 1 | 1 | 0 | .500 | 10 | 12 | 8 | 3 | 0 | 9 | 0 | 1 | 5 | 0 | 2.70 |
| Cota, Lagos de M. | 3 | 0 | 0 | 0 | 0 | 1 | 0 | .000 | 9 | 13 | 6 | 3 | 1 | 3 | 1 | 1 | 4 | 0 | 3.00 |
| Delgado, Urian | 10 | 6 | 1 | 0 | 7 | 0 | 0 | 1.000 | 46 | 34 | 14 | 11 | 1 | 15 | 0 | 3 | 32 | 2 | 2.15 |
| A. Dominguez, L M | 17 | 1 | 0 | 0 | 2 | 0 | 0 | 1.000 | 36 | 40 | 22 | 10 | 0 | 21 | 2 | 2 | 18 | 4 | 2.50 |
| G. Dominguez, Leon | 12 | 6 | 1 | 0 | 1 | 3 | 0 | .250 | 46 | 48 | 39 | 23 | 1 | 28 | 3 | 0 | 27 | 2 | 4.50 |
| Duarte, Leon | 12 | 10 | 4 | 0 | 3 | 8 | 0 | .273 | 70 | 79 | 45 | 31 | 2 | 28 | 6 | 7 | 30 | 3 | 3.99 |
| Espinosa, Guanaj. | 21 | 1 | 0 | 0 | 0 | 2 | 0 | .000 | 42 | 56 | 26 | 18 | 4 | 12 | 3 | 2 | 6 | 1 | 3.86 |
| Fernandez, Guanaj | 24 | 8 | 2 | 1 | 7 | 5 | 1 | .583 | 61 | 89 | 50 | 28 | 3 | 21 | 5 | 1 | 35 | 2 | 4.13 |
| Fdo. Flores, Acam. | 15 | 0 | 0 | 0 | 0 | 1 | 0 | .000 | 25 | 29 | 24 | 16 | 1 | 15 | 0 | 2 | 9 | 3 | 5.76 |
| Flor. Flores, Cor. | 21 | 9 | 3 | 1 | 9 | 4 | 1 | .692 | 102 | 104 | 51 | 32 | 3 | 36 | 1 | 6 | 41 | 6 | 2.82 |
| Flores, Salamanca | 1 | 0 | 0 | 0 | 0 | 0 | 0 | .000 | 1 | 2 | 2 | 2 | 0 | 3 | 0 | 0 | 1 | 0 | 18.00 |
| M. Flores, L. M. | 22 | 14 | 6 | 0 | 4 | 7 | 3 | .364 | 110 | 128 | 67 | 44 | 9 | 54 | 4 | 5 | 67 | 10 | 3.60 |
| Garate, Leon | 16 | 0 | 0 | 0 | 2 | 0 | 1 | 1.000 | 39 | 47 | 20 | 10 | 2 | 16 | 3 | 3 | 15 | 2 | 2.31 |
| J. Garcia, Sal. | 1 | 1 | 0 | 0 | 1 | 0 | 0 | .000 | 8 | 7 | 3 | 2 | 0 | 1 | 0 | 0 | 1 | 0 | 2.25 |
| J. L. Garcia, Sal* | 14 | 3 | 1 | 0 | 2 | 2 | 1 | .500 | 53 | 48 | 20 | 14 | 1 | 19 | 0 | 1 | 38 | 2 | 2.38 |
| Rog. Garcia, Acam | 34 | 16 | 9 | 0 | 11 | 14 | 5 | .440 | 158 | 149 | 74 | 36 | 5 | 52 | 5 | 13 | 100 | 14 | 2.05 |
| Garcia, Guanaj | 11 | 2 | 0 | 0 | 0 | 0 | 0 | .000 | 17 | 23 | 12 | 8 | 0 | 8 | 1 | 1 | 10 | 2 | 4.24 |
| Garduza, Guanaj | 19 | 10 | 2 | 0 | 6 | 3 | 1 | .667 | 77 | 86 | 44 | 29 | 3 | 20 | 5 | 2 | 58 | 4 | 3.39 |
| Gonzalez, Sal | 21 | 2 | 0 | 4 | 3 | 1 | 7 | .571 | 78 | 92 | 40 | 27 | 7 | 27 | 0 | 5 | 41 | 3 | 3.12 |
| Gonzalez, L. M. | 5 | 0 | 0 | 0 | 0 | 0 | 0 | .000 | 16 | 29 | 19 | 12 | 1 | 11 | 1 | 0 | 5 | 1 | 6.75 |
| Guerrero, Acam* | 1 | 0 | 0 | 0 | 0 | 0 | 0 | .000 | ⅓ | 0 | 3 | 2 | 0 | 2 | 0 | 1 | 0 | 0 | 54.00 |
| Guevara, Acambaro | 4 | 0 | 0 | 0 | 0 | 1 | 0 | .000 | 11 | 15 | 15 | 12 | 1 | 5 | 2 | 0 | 4 | 2 | 9.82 |
| Guzman, Celaya | 2 | 1 | 0 | 0 | 0 | 0 | 0 | .000 | 4 | 3 | 2 | 2 | 0 | 3 | 0 | 0 | 4 | 0 | 4.50 |
| F. Hernandez, Leon | 3 | 0 | 0 | 0 | 0 | 0 | 0 | .000 | 7 | 10 | 7 | 3 | 0 | 1 | 0 | 2 | 0 | 0 | 3.86 |
| J. Hernandez, Ac.. | 19 | 7 | 1 | 1 | 4 | 3 | 0 | .571 | 72 | 71 | 40 | 18 | 2 | 27 | 2 | 8 | 27 | 7 | 2.25 |
| Hernandez, Cor | 18 | 7 | 1 | 0 | 1 | 2 | 0 | .333 | 49 | 69 | 49 | 26 | 8 | 20 | 4 | 2 | 15 | 3 | 4.78 |
| Herrera, 11 Celaya-15 LM | 26 | 2 | 1 | 0 | 2 | 6 | 5 | .250 | 75 | 102 | 48 | 31 | 5 | 22 | 1 | 4 | 37 | 2 | 3.72 |
| Hinostrosa, Guan | 22 | 16 | 5 | 1 | 7 | 6 | 0 | .538 | 120 | 123 | 57 | 38 | 5 | 32 | 3 | 7 | 54 | 4 | 2.85 |

| Pitcher—Club | G. | GS. | CG. | ShO. | W. | L. | Sv. | Pct. | IP. | H. | R. | ER. | HR. | BB. | Int. BB. | HB. | SO. | WP. | ERA. |
|---|---|---|---|---|---|---|---|---|---|---|---|---|---|---|---|---|---|---|---|
| Jara, Celaya ...... | 7 | 5 | 1 | 1 | 2 | 1 | 0 | .667 | 23 | 13 | 16 | 10 | 1 | 18 | 1 | 2 | 18 | 6 | 3.91 |
| G. Lara, Guanaj .. | 13 | 7 | 2 | 1 | 1 | 3 | 0 | .250 | 58 | 57 | 37 | 26 | 2 | 34 | 4 | 2 | 41 | 3 | 4.03 |
| Leon, Cortazar .... | 14 | 12 | 8 | 1 | 6 | 4 | 0 | .600 | 90 | 87 | 45 | 25 | 6 | 30 | 0 | 5 | 33 | 7 | 2.50 |
| Leyva, Leon ...... | 17 | 15 | 6 | 3 | 5 | 10 | 0 | .333 | 91 | 104 | 48 | 25 | 1 | 33 | 4 | 3 | 39 | 5 | 2.47 |
| H. Lopez, Urian .. | 11 | 11 | 8 | 3 | 8 | 1 | 0 | .889 | 87 | 61 | 20 | 10 | 0 | 21 | 0 | 2 | 66 | 2 | 1.03 |
| Lopez, Acambaro .. | 9 | 3 | 0 | 0 | 1 | 2 | 0 | .333 | 31 | 24 | 16 | 13 | 1 | 13 | 0 | 2 | 15 | 1 | 3.77 |
| Loza, Lagos de M. | 5 | 5 | 1 | 0 | 2 | 1 | 0 | .667 | 28 | 32 | 17 | 12 | 4 | 11 | 0 | 0 | 8 | 1 | 3.86 |
| G. Martinez, Leon | 13 | 0 | 0 | 0 | 1 | 2 | 1 | .333 | 29 | 36 | 17 | 9 | 0 | 9 | 0 | 1 | 14 | 3 | 2.79 |
| Martinez, Leon ... | 4 | 3 | 2 | 0 | 1 | 0 | 0 | 1.000 | 27 | 24 | 8 | 3 | 1 | 10 | 1 | 0 | 18 | 2 | 1.00 |
| Mena, Celaya ...... | 19 | 11 | 5 | 2 | 8 | 4 | 1 | .667 | 96 | 76 | 34 | 20 | 0 | 34 | 0 | 3 | 87 | 4 | 1.88 |
| Menendez, Cortazar | 19 | 13 | 10 | 3 | 9 | 6 | 2 | .600 | 136 | 127 | 48 | 28 | 7 | 32 | 1 | 4 | 41 | 4 | 1.85 |
| R. Mercado, Cor ... | 19 | 15 | 9 | 0 | 6 | 8 | 1 | .429 | 119 | 113 | 50 | 33 | 11 | 40 | 5 | 4 | 60 | 9 | 2.50 |
| Miranda, L. M.... | 8 | 6 | 0 | 0 | 0 | 5 | 0 | .000 | 22 | 30 | 22 | 13 | 4 | 13 | 0 | 1 | 7 | 1 | 5.32 |
| Molina, Cortazar .. | 1 | 1 | 0 | 0 | 0 | 0 | 0 | .000 | 2 | 0 | 0 | 0 | 0 | 4 | 0 | 0 | 0 | 0 | 0.00 |
| Montijo, L. M..... | 2 | 1 | 0 | 0 | 0 | 1 | 0 | .000 | 6 | 7 | 9 | 5 | 1 | 5 | 2 | 0 | 5 | 0 | 7.50 |
| Moreno, Acambaro. | 12 | 2 | 0 | 0 | 1 | 1 | 0 | .500 | 25 | 38 | 35 | 16 | 3 | 11 | 0 | 2 | 9 | 1 | 5.76 |
| Moroyoqui, Guanaj | 8 | 6 | 0 | 0 | 1 | 2 | 0 | .333 | 25 | 26 | 11 | 8 | 0 | 14 | 2 | 1 | 21 | 4 | 2.88 |
| Nieblas, Sal ...... | 23 | 19 | 9 | 0 | 6 | 10 | 0 | .375 | 129 | 138 | 68 | 44 | 5 | 56 | 3 | 6 | 65 | 10 | 3.07 |
| Nunez, Leon ...... | 13 | 10 | 6 | 1 | 4 | 5 | 1 | .444 | 77 | 79 | 31 | 19 | 3 | 19 | 1 | 7 | 28 | 4 | 2.22 |
| Ochoa, Leon ...... | 2 | 2 | 2 | 0 | 1 | 1 | 0 | .500 | 17 | 22 | 10 | 6 | 0 | 4 | 1 | 1 | 6 | 1 | 3.18 |
| Orozco, Acambaro. | 20 | 13 | 3 | 1 | 4 | 8 | 1 | .333 | 92 | 92 | 58 | 28 | 1 | 40 | 1 | 4 | 32 | 7 | 2.74 |
| Ortega, Acambaro .. | 14 | 13 | 3 | 0 | 4 | 6 | 0 | .400 | 85 | 95 | 47 | 28 | 2 | 33 | 3 | 2 | 47 | 10 | 2.96 |
| Paredes, Cortazar | 1 | 0 | 0 | 0 | 0 | 0 | 0 | .000 | 2 | 4 | 1 | 1 | 0 | 2 | 0 | 0 | 0 | 0 | 4.50 |
| Paz, Acambaro ... | 8 | 3 | 0 | 0 | 0 | 1 | 0 | .000 | 20 | 26 | 17 | 12 | 2 | 12 | 0 | 0 | 7 | 2 | 5.40 |
| Pena, Salamanca .. | 5 | 5 | 3 | 0 | 0 | 3 | 0 | .000 | 39 | 46 | 23 | 14 | 1 | 18 | 1 | 1 | 22 | 3 | 3.23 |
| Pereda, Lagos de M | 14 | 13 | 5 | 1 | 6 | 5 | 0 | .545 | 88 | 80 | 47 | 23 | 7 | 48 | 2 | 9 | 31 | 6 | 2.35 |
| C. Perez, Sal ..... | 18 | 10 | 3 | 0 | 3 | 6 | 0 | .333 | 79 | 100 | 60 | 37 | 4 | 57 | 6 | 7 | 33 | 7 | 4.22 |
| G. Perez, Leon... | 21 | 4 | 1 | 0 | 0 | 5 | 0 | .000 | 46 | 57 | 36 | 19 | 1 | 13 | 1 | 2 | 30 | 1 | 3.72 |
| Pina, Uriangato .. | 10 | 7 | 2 | 1 | 3 | 1 | 1 | .750 | 33 | 34 | 13 | 8 | 2 | 11 | 0 | 3 | 17 | 0 | 2.18 |
| Quinones, Urian .. | 13 | 10 | 4 | 1 | 5 | 2 | 2 | .714 | 74 | 70 | 30 | 21 | 2 | 20 | 3 | 2 | 25 | 2 | 2.55 |
| Mar. Ramirez, Leon | 14 | 13 | 9 | 1 | 9 | 3 | 0 | .750 | 108 | 101 | 37 | 21 | 1 | 32 | 3 | 7 | 56 | 1 | 1.75 |
| Reynoso, L. M.... | 16 | 14 | 6 | 1 | 5 | 7 | 1 | .417 | 97 | 103 | 55 | 33 | 6 | 21 | 3 | 1 | 57 | 4 | 3.06 |
| G. Rodriguez, Cel. | 15 | 14 | 4 | 2 | 8 | 3 | 0 | .727 | 81 | 70 | 30 | 17 | 1 | 20 | 0 | 2 | 63 | 2 | 1.89 |
| J. Rodriguez, Leon | 1 | 0 | 0 | 0 | 0 | 0 | 0 | .000 | 1 | 2 | 4 | 4 | 0 | 1 | 1 | 0 | 0 | 0 | 36.00 |
| R. Rodriguez, Cor. | 5 | 2 | 1 | 0 | 0 | 2 | 0 | .000 | 38 | 49 | 26 | 16 | 5 | 15 | 0 | 2 | 13 | 6 | 3.79 |
| Salcido, Urian .... | 12 | 4 | 1 | 0 | 2 | 3 | 0 | .400 | 46 | 34 | 13 | 10 | 1 | 23 | 0 | 3 | 24 | 2 | 1.96 |
| Saldana, Guanaj .. | 20 | 15 | 4 | 0 | 6 | 6 | 0 | .500 | 95 | 111 | 58 | 42 | 6 | 33 | 7 | 2 | 55 | 4 | 3.98 |
| Salomon, Guanaj .. | 11 | 3 | 0 | 0 | 0 | 1 | 0 | .000 | 13 | 15 | 12 | 9 | 0 | 12 | 0 | 1 | 4 | 4 | 6.23 |
| Jorge Sanchez, Sal. | 21 | 17 | 8 | 1 | 3 | 12 | 1 | .200 | 101 | 122 | 62 | 42 | 3 | 58 | 2 | 3 | 46 | 7 | 3.74 |
| Jose Sanchez, Sal.. | 1 | 1 | 0 | 0 | 1 | 0 | 0 | 1.000 | 6 | 8 | 3 | 3 | 0 | 1 | 0 | 0 | 0 | 0 | 4.50 |
| Sauceda, Salamanca | 13 | 12 | 3 | 0 | 3 | 6 | 0 | .333 | 67 | 94 | 46 | 31 | 2 | 20 | 2 | 3 | 27 | 1 | 4.16 |
| Solis, Acambaro .. | 10 | 10 | 1 | 0 | 1 | 6 | 0 | .143 | 39 | 50 | 38 | 23 | 1 | 19 | 2 | 5 | 17 | 3 | 5.31 |
| Solis, Celaya ...... | 17 | 5 | 1 | 1 | 5 | 4 | 0 | .556 | 47 | 45 | 16 | 15 | 1 | 13 | 2 | 1 | 23 | 3 | 2.87 |
| A. Soto, Cortazar.. | 11 | 7 | 2 | 2 | 8 | 1 | 1 | .889 | 72 | 47 | 14 | 5 | 1 | 12 | 1 | 2 | 38 | 2 | 0.63 |
| R. Soto, Guanaj .. | 2 | 0 | 0 | 0 | 0 | 0 | 0 | .000 | 1 | 7 | 2 | 2 | 0 | 1 | 0 | 0 | 0 | 0 | 18.00 |
| Torres A., L. M. .. | 14 | 10 | 3 | 0 | 4 | 4 | 1 | .500 | 63 | 90 | 50 | 33 | 11 | 18 | 0 | 1 | 27 | 2 | 4.71 |
| Torres B., Celaya .. | 17 | 9 | 4 | 1 | 6 | 3 | 0 | .667 | 76 | 63 | 19 | 14 | 1 | 20 | 0 | 1 | 31 | 1 | 1.66 |
| Uresti, Leon ...... | 15 | 5 | 2 | 0 | 2 | 2 | 0 | .500 | 50 | 51 | 31 | 22 | 1 | 15 | 1 | 0 | 29 | 2 | 3.96 |
| Urias, Acambaro .. | 5 | 0 | 0 | 0 | 0 | 0 | 0 | .000 | 8 | 8 | 4 | 3 | 1 | 1 | 0 | 0 | 2 | 0 | 3.38 |
| Valdez, Uriangato. | 19 | 0 | 0 | 0 | 8 | 1 | 7 | .889 | 44 | 16 | 3 | 0 | 0 | 14 | 1 | 2 | 36 | 1 | 0.00 |
| Valles, Guanaj .. | 11 | 1 | 0 | 0 | 0 | 0 | 0 | .000 | 13 | 16 | 6 | 4 | 1 | 10 | 2 | 4 | 8 | 2 | 2.77 |
| Vargas, Leon ...... | 12 | 2 | 0 | 0 | 2 | 0 | 0 | .000 | 20 | 25 | 18 | 12 | 3 | 10 | 1 | 0 | 5 | 0 | 5.40 |
| Villanueva, Uri* .. | 6 | 5 | 3 | 0 | 3 | 0 | 1 | 1.000 | 41 | 33 | 14 | 7 | 0 | 14 | 0 | 0 | 26 | 1 | 1.54 |

BALKS—Garduza, Leon, Jorge Sanchez, 2 each; Aguilar, Carrillo, A. Dominguez, G. Dominguez, Fdo. Flores, Flor. Flores, M. Flores, Garate, J. Hernandez, Lara, Mercado, Moreno, Pereda, G. Perez, Mar. Ramirez, R. Rodriguez, Sauceda, Uresti, Valles, 1 each.

COMBINATION SHUTOUTS—Ortega-Rog. Garcia, Acambaro; Saldana-Carrillo, Guanajuato; Contreras-Valdez, Azcarraga-Valdez, Pina-Valdez, Uriangato.

NO-HIT GAME—None.

---

**MAJOR LEAGUE CENTRAL SCOUTING BUREAU**

1200 Quail Street, Suite 270

Newport Beach, California 92660

Phone: 752-0712 (Area Code 714)

# *Midwest League*

## CLASS A

### CHAMPIONSHIP WINNERS IN PREVIOUS YEARS

| | | |
|---|---|---|
| 1947—Belleville ........ .667 | 1958—Michigan City ... .623 | 1967—Wisconsin Rapids .. .685 |
| Belleville ......... .672 | Waterloo z ......... .613 | Appleton z ........ .587 |
| 1948—West Frankfort* .. .708 | 1959—Waterloo .......... .613 | 1968—Decatur ........... .656 |
| 1949—Centralia ........ .627 | Waterloo .......... .613 | Quad Cities z ... .648 |
| Paducah (4th)† .. .454 | 1960—Waterloo .......... .629 | 1969—Appleton .......... .648 |
| 1950—Centralia‡ ....... .675 | Waterloo .......... .677 | Appleton .......... .690 |
| 1951—Paris§ ........... .700 | 1961—Waterloo .......... .613 | 1970—Quincy z .......... .691 |
| Danville (4th)† .. .432 | Quincy z .......... .594 | Quad Cities ....... .581 |
| 1952—Danville x ....... .685 | 1962—Dubuque z ........ .667 | 1971—Appleton .......... .642 |
| Decatur (3rd)† .. .584 | Waterloo .......... .625 | Quad Cities a ... .548 |
| 1953—Decatur* ........ .576 | 1963—Clinton .......... .710 | 1972—Appleton .......... .598 |
| 1954—Decatur ......... .587 | Clinton .......... .629 | Danville a ........ .584 |
| Danville (2nd)‡ .. .528 | 1964—Clinton .......... .667 | 1973—Wisconsin Rapids a. .562 |
| 1955—Dubuque* ........ .587 | Fox Cities z ...... .667 | Danville .......... .537 |
| 1956—Paris y ......... .656 | 1965—Burlington ....... .667 | 1974—Appleton .......... .593 |
| Dubuque .......... .603 | Burlington ....... .677 | Danville a ........ .517 |
| 1957—Decatur y ....... .683 | 1966—Fox Cities z ..... .689 | |
| Clinton .......... .623 | Cedar Rapids ..... .762 | |

*Won championship and four-club playoff. †Won four-club playoff. ‡Playoff finals cancelled because of bad weather. xWon first half of split-season and tied Paris for second-half title. yWon first-half title and four-team playoff. zWon split-season playoff. (NOTE—Known as Illinois State League in 1947-48 and Mississippi-Ohio Valley League from 1949 through 1955.)

aLeague divided into Northern and Southern Divisions and played split-season. Playoff winner.

### STANDING OF CLUBS AT CLOSE OF FIRST HALF, JUNE 22

#### NORTHERN DIVISION

| Club | W. | L. | T. | Pct. | G.B. |
|---|---|---|---|---|---|
| Waterloo (Royals) ......49 | 13 | 1 | .790 | .... |
| Dubuque (Astros) ......29 | 30 | 0 | .492 | 18½ |
| Wisconsin Rap (Twins) .25 | 33 | 0 | .431 | 22 |
| Appleton (White Sox) ..22 | 37 | 0 | .373 | 25½ |
| Wausau (Mets) .........21 | 37 | 0 | .362 | 26 |

#### SOUTHERN DIVISION

| Club | W. | L. | T. | Pct. | G.B. |
|---|---|---|---|---|---|
| Quad Cities (Angels) ....35 | 25 | 0 | .583 | .... |
| Danville (Dodgers) .....35 | 27 | 0 | .565 | 1 |
| Burlington (Brewers) ....31 | 31 | 0 | .500 | 5 |
| Clinton (Tigers) ........29 | 31 | 1 | .483 | 6 |
| Cedar Rapids (Giants)...23 | 35 | 0 | .397 | 11 |

### STANDING OF CLUBS AT CLOSE OF SECOND HALF, AUGUST 29

#### NORTHERN DIVISION

| Club | W. | L. | T. | Pct. | G.B. |
|---|---|---|---|---|---|
| Waterloo (Royals) ......44 | 22 | 1 | .667 | .... |
| Wisconsin Rap (Twins) .46 | 25 | 0 | .648 | ½ |
| Dubuque (Astros) ......29 | 37 | 1 | .439 | 15 |
| Wausau (Mets) .........30 | 40 | 0 | .429 | 16 |
| Appleton (White Sox) ..28 | 40 | 0 | .412 | 17 |

#### SOUTHERN DIVISION

| Club | W. | L. | T. | Pct. | G.B. |
|---|---|---|---|---|---|
| Quad Cities (Angels) ....43 | 22 | 0 | .662 | .... |
| Clinton (Tigers) ........38 | 30 | 0 | .559 | 6½ |
| Burlington (Brewers) ...33 | 35 | 0 | .485 | 11½ |
| Danville (Dodgers) .....30 | 36 | 0 | .455 | 13½ |
| Cedar Rapids (Giants) ..18 | 52 | 0 | .257 | 27½ |

### COMPOSITE STANDING OF CLUBS AT CLOSE OF SEASON, AUGUST 29

#### NORTHERN DIVISION

| Club | Wat. | W.R. | Dub. | Wau. | Apl. | Q.C. | Cln. | Dan. | Bur. | C.R. | W. | L. | T. | Pct. | G.B. |
|---|---|---|---|---|---|---|---|---|---|---|---|---|---|---|---|
| Waterloo (Royals) ...... | .. | 9 | 12 | 12 | 10 | 9 | 9 | 9 | 8 | 15 | 93 | 35 | 2 | .727 | .... |
| Wisconsin Rapids (Twins) | 5 | .. | 5 | 11 | 10 | 5 | 9 | 8 | 7 | 11 | 71 | 58 | 0 | .550 | 22½ |
| Dubuque (Astros) ...... | 1 | 9 | .. | 7 | 7 | 1 | 11 | 8 | 6 | 8 | 58 | 67 | 1 | .464 | 33½ |
| Wausau (Mets) ........ | 2 | 5 | 6 | .. | 8 | 5 | 3 | 4 | 7 | 11 | 51 | 77 | 0 | .398 | 42 |
| Appleton (White Sox) . | 4 | 5 | 7 | 7 | .. | 4 | 4 | 5 | 5 | 9 | 50 | 77 | 0 | .394 | 42½ |

#### SOUTHERN DIVISION

| Club | Wat. | W.R. | Dub. | Wau. | Apl. | Q.C. | Cln. | Dan. | Bur. | C.R. | W. | L. | T. | Pct. | G.B. |
|---|---|---|---|---|---|---|---|---|---|---|---|---|---|---|---|
| Quad Cities (Angels) ... | 5 | 9 | 13 | 9 | 10 | .. | 8 | 6 | 7 | 11 | 78 | 47 | 0 | .624 | .... |
| Clinton (Tigers) ........ | 5 | 5 | 5 | 11 | 10 | 6 | .. | 9 | 9 | 7 | 67 | 61 | 1 | .523 | 12½ |
| Danville (Dodgers) ..... | 4 | 6 | 5 | 10 | 9 | 8 | 5 | .. | 11 | 7 | 65 | 63 | 0 | .508 | 14½ |
| Burlington (Brewers) ... | 6 | 7 | 8 | 7 | 9 | 7 | 5 | 7 | .. | 8 | 64 | 66 | 0 | .492 | 16½ |
| Cedar Rapids (Giants).. | 3 | 3 | 6 | 3 | 4 | 2 | 7 | 7 | 6 | .. | 41 | 87 | 0 | .320 | 38½ |

Quad Cities represented Davenport and Bettendorf, Ia., and Moline and Rock Island, Ill.

Major league affiliations in parentheses.

Playoffs—Waterloo (Northern Division Champion) defeated Quad Cities (Southern Division Champion), two games to none for League Championship.

Regular-Season Attendance—Appleton, 45,838; Burlington, 46,948; Cedar Rapids, 47,251; Clinton, 41,555; Danville, 54,057; Dubuque, 54,371; Quad Cities, 60,840; Waterloo, 91,625; Wausau, 63,461; Wisconsin Rapids, 58,422. Total, 564,368. All-Star Game, 1,647. Playoffs, 5,407.

Managers: Appleton—Gordon Lund; Burlington—Matt Galante; Cedar Rapids—Robert Hartsfield; Clinton—Jim Leyland; Danville—Bart Shirley; Dubuque—Robert Cluck; Quad Cities—Bobby Knoop; Waterloo—John Sullivan; Wausau—Owen Friend; Wisconsin Rapids—John Goryl.

All-Star Team: 1B—Aikens, Quad Cities; Beamon, Waterloo; 2B—Gates, Waterloo; 3B—Guerrero, Danville; SS—Wagner, Clinton; OF—Wilson, Waterloo; Bosley, Quad Cities; Puhl, Dubuque; C—Bulling, Wisconsin Rapids; P—Bobinger, Danville; Dorsey, Quad Cities; Manager—John Sullivan, Waterloo.

(Compiled by Howe News Bureau, Chicago, Ill.)

## CLUB BATTING

| Club | G. | AB. | R. | OR. | H. | TB. | 2B. | 3B. | HR. | RBI. | SH. | SF. | BB. | Int. BB. | HP. | SO. | SB. | CS. | LOB. | Pct. |
|---|---|---|---|---|---|---|---|---|---|---|---|---|---|---|---|---|---|---|---|---|
| Dan. | 128 | 4100 | 615 | 553 | 1045 | 1415 | 168 | 38 | 42 | 525 | 61 | 35 | 478 | 16 | 26 | 732 | 115 | 44 | 903 | .255 |
| Q.C. | 125 | 3903 | 611 | 432 | 984 | 1287 | 115 | 31 | 42 | 514 | 45 | 48 | 534 | 25 | 29 | 657 | 182 | 31 | 865 | .252 |
| W.R. | 129 | 4069 | 569 | 505 | 1004 | 1454 | 164 | 17 | 84 | 487 | 77 | 26 | 537 | 35 | 25 | 732 | 78 | 34 | 938 | .250 |
| Wat. | 130 | 4053 | 681 | 437 | 1003 | 1403 | 145 | 27 | 67 | 571 | 73 | 35 | 521 | 30 | 49 | 860 | 188 | 59 | 876 | .247 |
| Wau. | 128 | 3973 | 482 | 609 | 976 | 1331 | 147 | 23 | 54 | 419 | 50 | 21 | 418 | 15 | 25 | 714 | 114 | 41 | 879 | .246 |
| Dub. | 126 | 4030 | 475 | 545 | 962 | 1263 | 131 | 28 | 38 | 385 | 82 | 28 | 429 | 29 | 26 | 815 | 154 | 47 | 917 | .239 |
| Apl. | 127 | 3864 | 458 | 587 | 894 | 1207 | 110 | 43 | 39 | 380 | 54 | 33 | 468 | 23 | 21 | 830 | 89 | 41 | 840 | .231 |
| Bur. | 130 | 4169 | 494 | 571 | 951 | 1395 | 166 | 34 | 70 | 425 | 58 | 23 | 465 | 23 | 32 | 1001 | 89 | 39 | 885 | .228 |
| Cin. | 129 | 4057 | 470 | 445 | 901 | 1218 | 133 | 23 | 46 | 400 | 77 | 22 | 483 | 20 | 27 | 820 | 81 | 37 | 917 | .222 |
| C.R. | 128 | 4028 | 433 | 604 | 876 | 1160 | 129 | 19 | 39 | 367 | 32 | 30 | 454 | 20 | 26 | 670 | 54 | 30 | 872 | .217 |

## INDIVIDUAL BATTING

### (Leading Qualifiers for Batting Championship—351 or More Plate Appearances)

*Bats lefthanded. †Switch-hitter.

| Player and Club | G. | AB. | R. | H. | TB. | 2B. | 3B. | HR. | RBI. | SH. | SF. | BB. | HP. | SO. | SB. | CS. | Pct. |
|---|---|---|---|---|---|---|---|---|---|---|---|---|---|---|---|---|---|
| Guerrero, Pedro, Dan | 104 | 351 | 81 | 121 | 186 | 25 | 5 | 10 | 76 | 1 | 5 | 63 | 3 | 57 | 10 | 4 | .345 |
| Puhl, Terry, Dub | 104 | 346 | 57 | 115 | 129 | 10 | 2 | 0 | 28 | 5 | 3 | 41 | 1 | 30 | 30 | 4 | .332 |
| Beamon, Charles, Wat* | 109 | 370 | 57 | 113 | 140 | 16 | 4 | 1 | 63 | 4 | 2 | 44 | 5 | 45 | 14 | 5 | .305 |
| Parker, Darrell, Wat† | 108 | 411 | 66 | 125 | 176 | 21 | 3 | 8 | 59 | 4 | 4 | 36 | 4 | 69 | 13 | 6 | .304 |
| Rushde, Michael, Dan* | 109 | 361 | 65 | 109 | 149 | 13 | 6 | 5 | 63 | 4 | 3 | 34 | 1 | 48 | 11 | 1 | .302 |
| Beck, Michael, WR* | 117 | 368 | 52 | 110 | 182 | 29 | 2 | 13 | 63 | 3 | 0 | 45 | 3 | 79 | 2 | 2 | .299 |
| Bosley, Thaddis, QC* | 108 | 379 | 67 | 113 | 134 | 12 | 3 | 1 | 50 | 4 | 6 | 73 | 3 | 46 | 37 | 6 | .298 |
| Contreras, Rafael, Wau | 120 | 386 | 55 | 113 | 166 | 24 | 1 | 9 | 58 | 3 | 2 | 51 | 6 | 52 | 18 | 4 | .293 |
| Rolle, Shadrach, Wau† | 99 | 376 | 56 | 109 | 162 | 14 | 3 | 11 | 47 | 1 | 0 | 20 | 1 | 58 | 25 | 5 | .290 |
| Aikens, Willie, QC* | 125 | 443 | 69 | 126 | 196 | 17 | 1 | 17 | 91 | 0 | 9 | 58 | 5 | 64 | 6 | 2 | .284 |
| Meyer, William, Cln* | 111 | 398 | 69 | 113 | 156 | 19 | 6 | 4 | 50 | 1 | 5 | 51 | 0 | 44 | 9 | 3 | .284 |

Departmental Leaders: G—Holmberg, Rasmussen, 130; AB—Rasmussen, 498; R—Gates, 115; H—W. Wilson, 132; TB—Hill, 219; 2B—Beck, 29; 3B—Olszta, 12; HR—Hill, 31; RBI—Aikens, 91; SH—Caughey, Cruz, 11; SF—Aikens, 9; BB—Gates, 122; HP—W. Wilson, 13; SO—Ervin, 107; SB—W. Wilson, 76; CS—Gates, 14.

### (All Players—Listed Alphabetically)

| Player and Club | G. | AB. | R. | H. | TB. | 2B. | 3B. | HR. | RBI. | SH. | SF. | BB. | HP. | SO. | SB. | CS. | Pct. |
|---|---|---|---|---|---|---|---|---|---|---|---|---|---|---|---|---|---|
| Aikens, Willie, QC* | 125 | 443 | 69 | 126 | 196 | 17 | 1 | 17 | 91 | 0 | 9 | 58 | 5 | 64 | 6 | 2 | .284 |
| Alfaro, Jose, Dub | 46 | 37 | 3 | 13 | 17 | 0 | 2 | 0 | 5 | 0 | 0 | 2 | 0 | 7 | 0 | 0 | .351 |
| Allen, Kim, QC | 49 | 138 | 33 | 37 | 51 | 11 | 0 | 1 | 11 | 1 | 0 | 29 | 2 | 14 | 26 | 3 | .268 |
| Aloi, David, Dub | 22 | 39 | 2 | 6 | 6 | 0 | 0 | 0 | 2 | 2 | 0 | 0 | 0 | 16 | 0 | 1 | .154 |
| Alvarado, Arnaldo, Dub | 80 | 171 | 37 | 35 | 50 | 2 | 5 | 1 | 17 | 6 | 0 | 14 | 2 | 49 | 6 | 5 | .205 |
| Amerson, Archie, WR | 109 | 348 | 51 | 86 | 141 | 14 | 1 | 13 | 48 | 0 | 3 | 37 | 2 | 66 | 4 | 3 | .247 |
| Anyzeski, Fred, Apl* | 30 | 27 | 1 | 2 | 2 | 0 | 0 | 0 | 1 | 1 | 0 | 0 | 0 | 8 | 1 | 0 | .074 |
| Arthur, Albert, WR | 24 | 11 | 0 | 3 | 4 | 1 | 0 | 0 | 0 | 1 | 0 | 2 | 0 | 8 | 0 | 0 | .273 |
| Atilano, Luis, Cln | 64 | 201 | 19 | 42 | 62 | 10 | 2 | 2 | 22 | 0 | 0 | 16 | 3 | 49 | 0 | 0 | .209 |
| Attardi, Gerald, Apl* | 42 | 49 | 4 | 14 | 19 | 1 | 2 | 0 | 8 | 0 | 0 | 2 | 0 | 15 | 0 | 0 | .286 |
| Ayers, James, CR | 31 | 89 | 6 | 13 | 17 | 1 | 0 | 1 | 5 | 0 | 0 | 7 | 0 | 17 | 0 | 0 | .146 |
| Baker, Alvin, Cln | 9 | 6 | 0 | 1 | 1 | 0 | 0 | 0 | 0 | 1 | 0 | 1 | 0 | 3 | 0 | 0 | .167 |
| Barger, Robert, Wau* | 34 | 6 | 1 | 0 | 0 | 0 | 0 | 0 | 0 | 0 | 0 | 1 | 0 | 2 | 0 | 0 | .000 |
| Barranca, German, Wat* | 65 | 190 | 26 | 43 | 54 | 5 | 3 | 0 | 22 | 3 | 1 | 33 | 4 | 23 | 6 | 2 | .226 |
| Barrett, Charles, Dan | 30 | 38 | 1 | 6 | 6 | 0 | 0 | 0 | 4 | 6 | 1 | 3 | 0 | 12 | 0 | 0 | .158 |
| Bartell, Michael, Cln† | 56 | 187 | 13 | 43 | 49 | 4 | 1 | 0 | 18 | 4 | 2 | 21 | 0 | 28 | 0 | 2 | .230 |
| Bass, John, Wat* | 10 | 16 | 2 | 4 | 9 | 2 | 0 | 1 | 4 | 0 | 0 | 0 | 0 | 9 | 0 | 0 | .250 |
| Bates, Charles, Cln† | 55 | 202 | 29 | 65 | 104 | 12 | 3 | 7 | 37 | 1 | 0 | 22 | 0 | 41 | 2 | 1 | .322 |
| Beamon, Charles, Wat* | 109 | 370 | 57 | 113 | 140 | 16 | 4 | 1 | 63 | 4 | 2 | 44 | 5 | 45 | 14 | 5 | .305 |
| Beck, Michael, WR* | 117 | 368 | 52 | 110 | 182 | 29 | 2 | 13 | 63 | 3 | 0 | 45 | 3 | 79 | 2 | 2 | .299 |
| Beitey, Daniel, CR | 27 | 33 | 1 | 6 | 7 | 1 | 0 | 0 | 3 | 0 | 0 | 4 | 0 | 10 | 1 | 0 | .182 |
| Bell, Kevin, Apl | 67 | 239 | 32 | 68 | 116 | 16 | 4 | 8 | 42 | 0 | 2 | 22 | 1 | 66 | 3 | 1 | .285 |
| Bemis, Gregg, WR* | 15 | 1 | 0 | 0 | 0 | 0 | 0 | 0 | 0 | 0 | 0 | 0 | 0 | 0 | 0 | 0 | .000 |
| Benedetti, Donald, CR* | 56 | 149 | 8 | 32 | 42 | 5 | 1 | 1 | 13 | 0 | 1 | 25 | 0 | 18 | 0 | 0 | .215 |
| Berenguer, Juan, Wau | 18 | 28 | 3 | 4 | 6 | 0 | 1 | 0 | 2 | 4 | 0 | 0 | 0 | 5 | 0 | 0 | .143 |
| Best, Kurt, Apl | 2 | 2 | 1 | 1 | 1 | 0 | 0 | 0 | 0 | 0 | 0 | 0 | 0 | 1 | 0 | 0 | .500 |
| Bhagwat, Thomas, CR | 28 | 103 | 7 | 24 | 29 | 1 | 2 | 0 | 7 | 0 | 0 | 11 | 1 | 10 | 1 | 0 | .233 |
| Bianco, Robert, Apl | 16 | 39 | 4 | 8 | 9 | 1 | 0 | 0 | 3 | 0 | 0 | 2 | 0 | 7 | 0 | 0 | .205 |
| Bigusiak, Michael, Dan | 11 | 0 | 0 | 0 | 0 | 0 | 0 | 0 | 0 | 0 | 0 | 0 | 0 | 0 | 0 | 0 | .000 |
| Blanco, Romualdo, Dub | 9 | 4 | 0 | 2 | 3 | 1 | 0 | 0 | 0 | 0 | 0 | 1 | 0 | 0 | 0 | 0 | .500 |

| Player and Club | G | AB | R | H | TB | 2B | 3B | HR | RBI | SH | SF | BB | HP | SO | SB | CS | Pct. |
|---|---|---|---|---|---|---|---|---|---|---|---|---|---|---|---|---|---|
| Blood, Steven, WR | 11 | 10 | 1 | 0 | 0 | 0 | 0 | 1 | 2 | 0 | 2 | 2 | 0 | 7 | 0 | 0 | .000 |
| Bobinger, Mitchell, Dan | 30 | 78 | 5 | 6 | 6 | 0 | 0 | 0 | 2 | 7 | 0 | 3 | 0 | 30 | 0 | 0 | .077 |
| Bock, Paul, Apl | 29 | 13 | 0 | 1 | 1 | 0 | 0 | 0 | 1 | 3 | 0 | 1 | 0 | 4 | 0 | 0 | .077 |
| Bosley, Thaddis, QC* | 108 | 379 | 67 | 113 | 134 | 12 | 3 | 1 | 50 | 4 | 6 | 73 | 3 | 46 | 37 | 6 | .298 |
| Botting, Ralph, QC* | 20 | 38 | 1 | 1 | 1 | 0 | 0 | 0 | 0 | 3 | 0 | 3 | 0 | 13 | 0 | 0 | .026 |
| Bradbury, George, Wau | 20 | 59 | 7 | 11 | 11 | 0 | 0 | 0 | 1 | 0 | 4 | 1 | 0 | 16 | 0 | 0 | .186 |
| Bradley, Wayne, CR* | 48 | 31 | 10 | 6 | 8 | 2 | 0 | 0 | 2 | 3 | 0 | 5 | 0 | 7 | 1 | 0 | .194 |
| Branch, Roy, Wat | 10 | 26 | 1 | 3 | 3 | 0 | 0 | 0 | 0 | 1 | 0 | 1 | 0 | 8 | 0 | 0 | .115 |
| Brisbin, Steve, QC | 19 | 36 | 5 | 11 | 16 | 0 | 1 | 1 | 4 | 2 | 0 | 1 | 0 | 5 | 0 | 0 | .306 |
| Buffamoyer, John, Bur | 95 | 295 | 14 | 56 | 77 | 10 | 1 | 3 | 23 | 4 | 1 | 35 | 1 | 92 | 0 | 0 | .190 |
| Bulling, Terry, WR | 104 | 296 | 31 | 71 | 109 | 11 | 0 | 9 | 40 | 1 | 1 | 77 | 0 | 48 | 1 | 1 | .240 |
| Callis, Alfred, Cln | 28 | 5 | 0 | 1 | 1 | 0 | 0 | 0 | 0 | 1 | 0 | 1 | 0 | 3 | 0 | 0 | .200 |
| Caneira, John, QC | 9 | 22 | 0 | 1 | 1 | 0 | 0 | 0 | 3 | 2 | 1 | 1 | 0 | 8 | 0 | 0 | .045 |
| Cannon, Joseph, Dub* | 119 | 346 | 47 | 72 | 108 | 8 | 5 | 6 | 37 | 5 | 0 | 23 | 2 | 97 | 28 | 6 | .208 |
| Carroll, Edward, Cln* | 10 | 26 | 4 | 5 | 5 | 0 | 0 | 0 | 1 | 1 | 0 | 3 | 0 | 4 | 0 | 0 | .192 |
| Carter, Dwight, Cln | 119 | 367 | 61 | 87 | 142 | 12 | 5 | 11 | 39 | 3 | 2 | 76 | 8 | 77 | 9 | 4 | .237 |
| Carter, Jeffrey, Wau | 6 | 10 | 1 | 1 | 2 | 1 | 0 | 0 | 1 | 1 | 0 | 0 | 0 | 4 | 0 | 0 | .100 |
| Cash, Michael, CR | 108 | 322 | 32 | 88 | 124 | 13 | 4 | 5 | 45 | 1 | 2 | 29 | 3 | 29 | 1 | 2 | .273 |
| Castillo, Andrew, QC | 9 | 14 | 3 | 2 | 2 | 0 | 0 | 0 | 1 | 4 | 0 | 2 | 0 | 7 | 1 | 0 | .143 |
| Castillo, Arthur, WR | 25 | 28 | 1 | 10 | 10 | 0 | 0 | 0 | 3 | 1 | 0 | 1 | 0 | 6 | 0 | 0 | .357 |
| Castillo, E. Manuel, Wau† | 68 | 212 | 28 | 69 | 89 | 9 | 4 | 1 | 34 | 1 | 4 | 1 | 0 | 16 | 2 | 2 | .325 |
| Caughey, Wayne, WR* | 127 | 461 | 70 | 113 | 143 | 13 | 1 | 5 | 38 | 11 | 5 | 57 | 2 | 48 | 20 | 5 | .245 |
| Centeno, Jose, Cln* | 90 | 310 | 30 | 71 | 90 | 9 | 2 | 2 | 26 | 5 | 4 | 17 | 0 | 40 | 2 | 1 | .229 |
| Channel, Thomas, WR | 33 | 25 | 10 | 3 | 3 | 0 | 0 | 0 | 0 | 0 | 0 | 2 | 0 | 12 | 2 | 2 | .120 |
| Cipot, Edwin, Wau* | 119 | 402 | 47 | 90 | 118 | 13 | 0 | 5 | 42 | 3 | 2 | 51 | 2 | 68 | 8 | 2 | .224 |
| Clark, Willie, Wat | 23 | 48 | 3 | 2 | 5 | 0 | 0 | 1 | 4 | 4 | 0 | 4 | 1 | 29 | 0 | 0 | .042 |
| Cliburn, Stanley, QC | 27 | 80 | 9 | 16 | 18 | 2 | 0 | 0 | 7 | 0 | 1 | 14 | 1 | 17 | 0 | 0 | .200 |
| Cline, Steven, CR | 56 | 51 | 14 | 7 | 7 | 0 | 0 | 0 | 4 | 2 | 0 | 1 | 0 | 13 | 0 | 0 | .137 |
| Cluck, Robert, Dub* | 1 | 0 | 0 | 0 | 0 | 0 | 0 | 0 | 0 | 0 | 0 | 0 | 0 | 0 | 0 | 0 | .000 |
| Combs, Robert, Apl | 42 | 24 | 1 | 5 | 6 | 1 | 0 | 0 | 2 | 1 | 1 | 2 | 0 | 8 | 0 | 0 | .208 |
| Conn, Garry, Bur | 50 | 19 | 1 | 2 | 2 | 0 | 0 | 0 | 0 | 0 | 0 | 2 | 1 | 6 | 0 | 0 | .105 |
| Contreras, Rafael, Wau | 120 | 386 | 55 | 113 | 166 | 24 | 1 | 9 | 58 | 3 | 2 | 51 | 6 | 52 | 18 | 4 | .293 |
| Cort, Barry, Bur | 30 | 80 | 8 | 19 | 33 | 0 | 1 | 4 | 13 | 3 | 0 | 3 | 2 | 27 | 0 | 0 | .238 |
| Costell, Arnold, Dub | 8 | 6 | 0 | 1 | 1 | 0 | 0 | 0 | 0 | 1 | 0 | 0 | 0 | 4 | 0 | 0 | .167 |
| Coulter, E. Roy, Apl* | 32 | 30 | 1 | 3 | 6 | 1 | 1 | 0 | 2 | 0 | 0 | 0 | 0 | 12 | 0 | 1 | .100 |
| Crosta, James, Apl | 19 | 53 | 9 | 15 | 17 | 0 | 1 | 0 | 1 | 2 | 0 | 12 | 0 | 3 | 0 | 2 | .283 |
| Cruz, Julio L., QC | 108 | 368 | 79 | 96 | 114 | 6 | 6 | 0 | 35 | 11 | 0 | 70 | 3 | 61 | 60 | 8 | .261 |
| Cuen, Eleno, Dub | 13 | 22 | 0 | 2 | 2 | 0 | 0 | 0 | 0 | 0 | 0 | 2 | 0 | 8 | 0 | 0 | .091 |
| Cummings, Charles, Wau* | 19 | 43 | 3 | 10 | 15 | 2 | 0 | 1 | 5 | 5 | 0 | 1 | 0 | 11 | 0 | 0 | .233 |
| Curran, Patrick, Wat | 93 | 275 | 44 | 71 | 118 | 10 | 2 | 11 | 56 | 4 | 4 | 34 | 2 | 46 | 4 | 2 | .258 |
| Daniels, Robert, WR | 32 | 88 | 12 | 17 | 19 | 2 | 0 | 0 | 3 | 2 | 0 | 12 | 1 | 14 | 2 | 1 | .193 |
| Davis, George H., Cln* | 11 | 37 | 4 | 5 | 6 | 1 | 0 | 0 | 2 | 0 | 0 | 4 | 0 | 13 | 2 | 1 | .135 |
| Dean, Robert, Dub | 29 | 33 | 3 | 5 | 11 | 0 | 0 | 2 | 3 | 5 | 0 | 3 | 0 | 15 | 0 | 0 | .152 |
| de la Cruz, Gerardo, Dan | 72 | 170 | 20 | 46 | 57 | 5 | 0 | 2 | 19 | 3 | 2 | 10 | 5 | 22 | 4 | 0 | .271 |
| deLeeuw, Karel, Wat | 74 | 171 | 33 | 48 | 89 | 4 | 2 | 11 | 42 | 0 | 2 | 33 | 7 | 48 | 1 | 2 | .281 |
| deLeon, Paulo, Dub | 32 | 28 | 2 | 6 | 7 | 1 | 0 | 0 | 2 | 3 | 0 | 2 | 0 | 4 | 1 | 0 | .214 |
| de los Santos, German, CR | 114 | 384 | 34 | 73 | 113 | 16 | 0 | 8 | 33 | 0 | 5 | 33 | 0 | 95 | 0 | 2 | .190 |
| DelVecchio, James, Dan | 83 | 155 | 32 | 30 | 32 | 2 | 0 | 0 | 14 | 1 | 0 | 33 | 0 | 26 | 14 | 6 | .194 |
| DeMerritt, Martin, Bur | 25 | 48 | 3 | 6 | 6 | 0 | 0 | 0 | 1 | 4 | 0 | 5 | 0 | 18 | 0 | 0 | .125 |
| Dinkelmeyer, John, Cln | 33 | 16 | 0 | 2 | 2 | 0 | 0 | 0 | 1 | 1 | 0 | 0 | 0 | 10 | 0 | 0 | .125 |
| Ditto, Julian, Dan | 99 | 309 | 46 | 75 | 99 | 14 | 2 | 2 | 29 | 4 | 2 | 31 | 1 | 70 | 5 | 3 | .243 |
| Dixon, Thomas, Dub | 32 | 25 | 0 | 3 | 3 | 0 | 0 | 0 | 0 | 1 | 0 | 0 | 0 | 8 | 0 | 0 | .120 |
| Dodd, Michael, CR | 47 | 155 | 15 | 33 | 46 | 6 | 2 | 1 | 13 | 0 | 2 | 9 | 0 | 23 | 0 | 0 | .213 |
| Dorsey, James, QC | 25 | 56 | 2 | 5 | 8 | 1 | 1 | 0 | 6 | 1 | 1 | 4 | 1 | 29 | 0 | 0 | .089 |
| Drake, Kevin, Dub | 51 | 150 | 22 | 33 | 46 | 4 | 0 | 3 | 11 | 1 | 1 | 9 | 0 | 47 | 9 | 2 | .220 |
| Driskill, Donald, Wau | 35 | 14 | 1 | 2 | 2 | 0 | 0 | 0 | 1 | 1 | 0 | 1 | 0 | 1 | 0 | 0 | .143 |
| Edge, Claude, Bur | 43 | 35 | 11 | 6 | 6 | 0 | 0 | 0 | 2 | 0 | 0 | 1 | 0 | 11 | 0 | 1 | .171 |
| Edmondson, Robert, Wat | 89 | 300 | 16 | 51 | 89 | 11 | 0 | 9 | 44 | 2 | 3 | 32 | 0 | 67 | 1 | 1 | .170 |
| Ervin, Terrence, Wau | 98 | 359 | 61 | 93 | 139 | 14 | 4 | 8 | 28 | 2 | 1 | 37 | 2 | 107 | 35 | 7 | .259 |
| Estes, Frank, WR* | 64 | 228 | 38 | 72 | 83 | 8 | 0 | 1 | 26 | 3 | 2 | 18 | 0 | 27 | 8 | 3 | .316 |
| Fahrow, Bryant, QC | 115 | 390 | 47 | 89 | 127 | 13 | 2 | 7 | 66 | 1 | 5 | 43 | 2 | 40 | 7 | 5 | .228 |
| Falcon, Robert, Wat* | 32 | 0 | 15 | 0 | 0 | 0 | 0 | 0 | 1 | 0 | 0 | 1 | 0 | 0 | 0 | 0 | .000 |
| Felda, Brian, CR | 83 | 231 | 21 | 57 | 73 | 7 | 3 | 1 | 16 | 0 | 2 | 26 | 1 | 22 | 2 | 2 | .247 |
| Feola, Lawrence, 9Cln-15Wau | 24 | 28 | 3 | 3 | 5 | 2 | 0 | 0 | 1 | 0 | 0 | 3 | 0 | 10 | 0 | 0 | .107 |
| Ferrell, Frank, CR | 44 | 145 | 18 | 28 | 32 | 4 | 0 | 0 | 14 | 0 | 3 | 16 | 1 | 15 | 3 | 0 | .193 |
| Ferrer, Luis, Wau | 55 | 159 | 16 | 40 | 45 | 5 | 0 | 0 | 16 | 0 | 0 | 11 | 1 | 13 | 2 | 1 | .252 |
| Filkins, Leslie, Cln* | 26 | 98 | 15 | 19 | 30 | 3 | 1 | 2 | 7 | 1 | 0 | 7 | 1 | 10 | 1 | 3 | .194 |
| Fischetti, Arthur, Dan† | 24 | 75 | 15 | 15 | 24 | 1 | 1 | 2 | 7 | 0 | 0 | 14 | 1 | 8 | 5 | 1 | .200 |
| Flanders, Craig, Wat | 11 | 1 | 0 | 0 | 0 | 0 | 0 | 0 | 0 | 0 | 0 | 0 | 0 | 1 | 0 | 0 | .000 |
| Floyd, Samuel, WR | 88 | 34 | 43 | 7 | 8 | 1 | 0 | 0 | 3 | 2 | 0 | 4 | 0 | 8 | 10 | 7 | .206 |
| Floyd, Stanley, WR | 1 | 2 | 0 | 0 | 0 | 0 | 0 | 0 | 0 | 0 | 0 | 2 | 0 | 0 | 0 | 0 | .000 |
| Foley, Marvis, Apl* | 6 | 13 | 1 | 4 | 4 | 0 | 0 | 0 | 1 | 0 | 0 | 1 | 0 | 1 | 0 | 0 | .308 |
| Frankum, Randall, Wau | 18 | 34 | 3 | 6 | 7 | 1 | 0 | 0 | 3 | 0 | 0 | 1 | 0 | 7 | 0 | 0 | .176 |
| Galvez, Jose, Apl | 8 | 23 | 1 | 4 | 5 | 1 | 0 | 0 | 1 | 0 | 0 | 2 | 0 | 12 | 0 | 1 | .174 |
| Gamby, Stephen, Cln | 21 | 24 | 1 | 2 | 2 | 0 | 0 | 0 | 1 | 4 | 1 | 0 | 0 | 9 | 0 | 0 | .083 |
| Garcia, David, WR† | 22 | 34 | 1 | 2 | 5 | 0 | 0 | 1 | 1 | 6 | 0 | 3 | 0 | 14 | 0 | 0 | .059 |
| Garcia, Miguel, Bur | 2 | 0 | 0 | 0 | 0 | 0 | 0 | 0 | 0 | 0 | 0 | 0 | 0 | 0 | 0 | 0 | .000 |
| Garrison, Venoy, Cln | 47 | 107 | 11 | 31 | 42 | 4 | 2 | 1 | 14 | 0 | 1 | 13 | 1 | 10 | 1 | 1 | .290 |
| Gates, Joseph, Wat* | 123 | 411-115 | 111 | 143 | 15 | 4 | 3 | 44 | 10 | 1 | 122 | 6 | 101 | 55 | 14 | .270 |
| Gaton, Francisco, Bur | 36 | 13 | 0 | 2 | 3 | 1 | 0 | 0 | 2 | 1 | 0 | 0 | 0 | 5 | 0 | 0 | .154 |

| Player and Club | G. | AB. | R. | H. | TB. | 2B. | 3B. | HR. | RBI. | SH. | SF. | BB. | HP. | SO. | SB. | CS. | Pct |
|---|---|---|---|---|---|---|---|---|---|---|---|---|---|---|---|---|---|
| Geddes, James, Apl | 8 | 4 | 0 | 0 | 0 | 0 | 0 | 0 | 0 | 1 | 0 | 0 | 0 | 0 | 0 | 1 | .000 |
| Gimenez, Isaac, Cln | 14 | 46 | 9 | 9 | 18 | 6 | 0 | 1 | 5 | 0 | 0 | 11 | 0 | 11 | 0 | 0 | .196 |
| Gimenez, Ramon, Cln | 91 | 270 | 44 | 53 | 72 | 7 | 0 | 4 | 36 | 4 | 3 | 65 | 2 | 43 | 6 | 3 | .196 |
| Goetz, John, Dub | 23 | 43 | 2 | 9 | 10 | 1 | 0 | 0 | 1 | 2 | 0 | 1 | 0 | 7 | 0 | 1 | .209 |
| Gonzalez, Luis, Wat | 65 | 195 | 20 | 42 | 48 | 4 | 1 | 0 | 18 | 2 | 2 | 14 | 1 | 25 | 0 | 4 | .215 |
| Goulding, Richard, Dan | 1 | 0 | 0 | 0 | 0 | 0 | 0 | 0 | 0 | 0 | 0 | 0 | 0 | 0 | 0 | 0 | .000 |
| Grady, C. Edward, Wau* | 75 | 151 | 27 | 36 | 53 | 8 | 0 | 3 | 13 | 1 | 0 | 43 | 1 | 45 | 6 | 6 | .238 |
| Graham, Daniel, WR* | 54 | 154 | 12 | 42 | 66 | 8 | 2 | 4 | 27 | 1 | 1 | 19 | 0 | 43 | 0 | 0 | .273 |
| Groff, Theodore, WR | 14 | 3 | 0 | 1 | 2 | 1 | 0 | 0 | 1 | 0 | 0 | 0 | 0 | 1 | 0 | 0 | .333 |
| Guerrero, Alexis, QC | 106 | 371 | 57 | 94 | 127 | 16 | 4 | 3 | 51 | 3 | 7 | 36 | 0 | 79 | 6 | 3 | .253 |
| Guerrero, Pedro, Dan | 104 | 351 | 81 | 121 | 186 | 25 | 5 | 10 | 76 | 1 | 5 | 63 | 3 | 57 | 10 | 4 | .345 |
| Haas, Bryan, Bur | 53 | 60 | 16 | 15 | 27 | 3 | 0 | 3 | 4 | 6 | 0 | 0 | 16 | 1 | 1 | | .250 |
| Haas, Randy, Cln | 36 | 98 | 7 | 24 | 28 | 1 | 0 | 1 | 5 | 2 | 0 | 5 | 1 | 28 | 1 | 2 | .245 |
| Harper, Glenn, Wau | 25 | 19 | 4 | 4 | 8 | 1 | 0 | 1 | 2 | 0 | 0 | 2 | 0 | 3 | 0 | 0 | .211 |
| Hart, John, Wat | 14 | 15 | 3 | 2 | 2 | 0 | 0 | 0 | 0 | 2 | 0 | 1 | 0 | 5 | 0 | 0 | .133 |
| Hartzell, Paul, QC | 24 | 9 | 0 | 2 | 3 | 1 | 0 | 0 | 2 | 0 | 0 | 0 | 0 | 4 | 0 | 0 | .222 |
| Hasley, Michael, Dub* | 17 | 10 | 1 | 2 | 3 | 1 | 0 | 0 | 1 | 1 | 0 | 1 | 0 | 3 | 0 | 0 | .200 |
| Haynes, Richard, Dub | 35 | 110 | 10 | 22 | 26 | 2 | 1 | 0 | 6 | 0 | 2 | 12 | 0 | 28 | 1 | 0 | .200 |
| Heenan, John, Dub | 6 | 10 | 0 | 1 | 1 | 0 | 0 | 0 | 0 | 0 | 0 | 0 | 0 | 3 | 0 | 0 | .100 |
| Heinen, Joseph, CR | 55 | 14 | 0 | 3 | 4 | 1 | 0 | 0 | 1 | 0 | 0 | 2 | 0 | 8 | 0 | 0 | .214 |
| Heredia, Ubaldo, Dan | 26 | 57 | 3 | 13 | 16 | 3 | 0 | 0 | 8 | 3 | 0 | 0 | 0 | 15 | 0 | 0 | .228 |
| Hill, Elmore, WR | 126 | 404 | 71 | 111 | 219 | 13 | 1 | 31 | 86 | 2 | 6 | 64 | 2 | 78 | 2 | 1 | .275 |
| Hodges, Ronald A., CR | 33 | 23 | 9 | 3 | 3 | 0 | 0 | 0 | 3 | 0 | 2 | 0 | 5 | 1 | 0 | | .130 |
| Holland, Clifton, Apl* | 10 | 35 | 4 | 7 | 8 | 1 | 0 | 0 | 0 | 0 | 0 | 7 | 0 | 5 | 0 | 1 | .200 |
| Holm, David, Cln | 24 | 34 | 1 | 7 | 7 | 0 | 0 | 0 | 3 | 0 | 0 | 0 | 0 | 12 | 0 | 0 | .206 |
| Holmberg, Dennis, Bur* | 130 | 430 | 51 | 95 | 167 | 23 | 2 | 15 | 65 | 5 | 7 | 93 | 8 | 92 | 4 | 3 | .221 |
| Holmgren, Mark, WR | 21 | 28 | 5 | 5 | 5 | 0 | 0 | 0 | 0 | 0 | 0 | 3 | 0 | 4 | 0 | 0 | .179 |
| Hough, Stanley, Wau | 39 | 133 | 11 | 39 | 55 | 5 | 1 | 3 | 14 | 2 | 0 | 10 | 0 | 13 | 4 | 1 | .293 |
| Howard, Michael, QC* | 5 | 8 | 0 | 2 | 2 | 0 | 0 | 0 | 0 | 0 | 0 | 0 | 0 | 5 | 0 | 0 | .250 |
| Hrovat, Dale, Wat | 25 | 7 | 0 | 1 | 2 | 1 | 0 | 0 | 0 | 1 | 0 | 0 | 0 | 4 | 0 | 0 | .143 |
| Hughes, Timothy, CR | 19 | 45 | 5 | 9 | 12 | 0 | 0 | 1 | 6 | 0 | 0 | 11 | 0 | 8 | 0 | 0 | .200 |
| Hunt, Benjamin, Cln† | 112 | 394 | 45 | 85 | 104 | 13 | 0 | 2 | 33 | 7 | 1 | 53 | 2 | 78 | 6 | 8 | .216 |
| Jackson, K. Mark, Apl | 8 | 19 | 0 | 0 | 0 | 0 | 0 | 0 | 0 | 1 | 0 | 2 | 0 | 6 | 0 | 0 | .000 |
| Jackson, Roy, Wau | 5 | 13 | 2 | 4 | 4 | 0 | 0 | 0 | 0 | 0 | 0 | 2 | 0 | 1 | 0 | 0 | .308 |
| Jimenez, Manuel, QC | 12 | 4 | 0 | 0 | 0 | 0 | 0 | 0 | 0 | 0 | 0 | 0 | 0 | 3 | 0 | 0 | .000 |
| Johnson, Jimmie, Wau | 2 | 5 | 1 | 0 | 0 | 0 | 0 | 0 | 0 | 0 | 0 | 0 | 0 | 0 | 0 | 0 | .000 |
| Johnson, John H., CR* | 25 | 37 | 2 | 5 | 6 | 1 | 0 | 0 | 2 | 1 | 0 | 5 | 0 | 12 | 0 | 0 | .135 |
| Johnson, Steven, WR | 24 | 6 | 1 | 2 | 3 | 1 | 0 | 0 | 3 | 0 | 0 | 0 | 0 | 3 | 0 | 0 | .333 |
| Jones, Ronald, WR | 17 | 8 | 0 | 0 | 0 | 0 | 0 | 0 | 0 | 0 | 0 | 0 | 0 | 3 | 0 | 0 | .000 |
| Jones, Sammie, Bur | 49 | 157 | 14 | 31 | 49 | 4 | 1 | 4 | 14 | 1 | 0 | 16 | 0 | 46 | 3 | 4 | .197 |
| Kautzer, William, Apl | 35 | 42 | 2 | 6 | 7 | 1 | 0 | 0 | 4 | 1 | 1 | 0 | 14 | 0 | 0 | | .143 |
| Keefe, Kevin, Dan | 45 | 8 | 0 | 0 | 0 | 0 | 0 | 0 | 0 | 0 | 0 | 2 | 0 | 7 | 0 | 0 | .000 |
| Keller, Joseph, Dan | 31 | 25 | 3 | 3 | 3 | 0 | 0 | 0 | 2 | 0 | 1 | 0 | 8 | 0 | 0 | | .120 |
| Kelley, Steven, QC | 17 | 15 | 3 | 3 | 8 | 0 | 1 | 1 | 4 | 1 | 0 | 1 | 0 | 5 | 0 | 0 | .200 |
| Kelly, Brian, Cln | 63 | 87 | 20 | 14 | 19 | 5 | 0 | 0 | 6 | 1 | 1 | 9 | 1 | 35 | 3 | 0 | .161 |
| Kelly, D. Patrick, QC | 40 | 115 | 14 | 38 | 42 | 1 | 0 | 1 | 8 | 1 | 1 | 7 | 0 | 22 | 2 | 1 | .330 |
| Kelly, Rafael, QC | 9 | 27 | 2 | 2 | 5 | 0 | 0 | 1 | 1 | 1 | 0 | 2 | 0 | 5 | 1 | 0 | .074 |
| Kenny, Terrance, CR* | 17 | 14 | 0 | 0 | 0 | 0 | 0 | 0 | 0 | 0 | 0 | 1 | 0 | 6 | 0 | 0 | .000 |
| Killingsworth, Samuel, Bur | 118 | 369 | 49 | 92 | 143 | 18 | 3 | 9 | 53 | 0 | 3 | 53 | 6 | 85 | 6 | 4 | .249 |
| Kiner, Michael, Wau | 25 | 69 | 7 | 19 | 21 | 2 | 0 | 0 | 6 | 0 | 0 | 15 | 1 | 15 | 0 | 0 | .275 |
| King, Thomas F., Apl* | 21 | 14 | 0 | 4 | 7 | 1 | 1 | 0 | 2 | 0 | 0 | 0 | 0 | 2 | 0 | 0 | .286 |
| Klein, Robert, Apl | 20 | 5 | 1 | 1 | 4 | 0 | 0 | 1 | 2 | 0 | 0 | 0 | 0 | 2 | 0 | 0 | .200 |
| Kline, Gregory, Cln* | 56 | 68 | 18 | 9 | 9 | 0 | 0 | 0 | 1 | 2 | 0 | 4 | 0 | 23 | 5 | 4 | .132 |
| Knapp, R. Christian, Apl | 14 | 29 | 2 | 7 | 7 | 0 | 0 | 0 | 1 | 4 | 0 | 3 | 0 | 12 | 0 | 0 | .241 |
| Knicely, Alan, Dub | 27 | 35 | 5 | 11 | 15 | 1 | 0 | 1 | 9 | 3 | 0 | 3 | 0 | 7 | 0 | 0 | .314 |
| Komadina, Tony, Apl* | 20 | 30 | 3 | 6 | 6 | 0 | 0 | 0 | 1 | 0 | 0 | 3 | 0 | 13 | 0 | 0 | .200 |
| Kordosky, Joseph, WR | 71 | 224 | 22 | 40 | 51 | 11 | 0 | 0 | 23 | 6 | 0 | 37 | 2 | 46 | 5 | 0 | .179 |
| Lacy, Steven, Wat* | 46 | 138 | 27 | 24 | 37 | 5 | 1 | 2 | 16 | 3 | 1 | 24 | 0 | 22 | 1 | 1 | .174 |
| Lahey, Kevin, Wat | 3 | 7 | 0 | 0 | 0 | 0 | 0 | 0 | 0 | 0 | 0 | 0 | 0 | 3 | 0 | 0 | .000 |
| Lantz, Thomas, Cln* | 13 | 29 | 0 | 1 | 1 | 0 | 0 | 0 | 1 | 1 | 1 | 3 | 0 | 11 | 0 | 0 | .034 |
| Larkin, Michael, Wat* | 17 | 16 | 0 | 2 | 2 | 0 | 0 | 0 | 0 | 0 | 1 | 0 | 4 | 0 | 0 | | .125 |
| Laseter, Thomas, Wat | 32 | 34 | 16 | 4 | 4 | 0 | 0 | 0 | 0 | 2 | 0 | 6 | 0 | 9 | 4 | 3 | .118 |
| Laurent, Michael, Dan | 30 | 6 | 0 | 0 | 0 | 0 | 0 | 0 | 0 | 1 | 0 | 2 | 0 | 5 | 0 | 0 | .000 |
| Lauzerique, George, Dub | 16 | 10 | 0 | 2 | 3 | 1 | 0 | 0 | 3 | 0 | 0 | 1 | 1 | 3 | 0 | 0 | .200 |
| Lea, Frederick, Wau | 2 | 0 | 0 | 0 | 0 | 0 | 0 | 0 | 0 | 0 | 0 | 1 | 0 | 0 | 0 | 0 | .000 |
| Lee, Randall, WR | 8 | 0 | 0 | 0 | 0 | 0 | 0 | 0 | 0 | 0 | 0 | 1 | 0 | 0 | 0 | 0 | .000 |
| Lee, Terry, CR* | 111 | 379 | 48 | 78 | 115 | 19 | 3 | 4 | 34 | 2 | 1 | 54 | 6 | 87 | 3 | 2 | .206 |
| Lehman, William, Apl | 14 | 3 | 0 | 0 | 0 | 0 | 0 | 0 | 0 | 0 | 0 | 0 | 0 | 2 | 0 | 0 | .000 |
| Leonard, Robert P., Wau* | 11 | 12 | 0 | 1 | 1 | 0 | 0 | 0 | 1 | 1 | 1 | 1 | 0 | 5 | 0 | 0 | .083 |
| Leonardo, Juan, Apl* | 16 | 28 | 4 | 5 | 6 | 1 | 0 | 0 | 3 | 0 | 0 | 4 | 0 | 2 | 0 | 0 | .179 |
| Loehr, C. Theodore, Apl | 17 | 5 | 1 | 0 | 0 | 0 | 0 | 0 | 0 | 0 | 0 | 0 | 0 | 0 | 0 | 0 | .000 |
| Madden, William, Cln | 2 | 0 | 0 | 0 | 0 | 0 | 0 | 0 | 0 | 0 | 0 | 0 | 0 | 0 | 0 | 0 | .000 |
| Mann, Stanley, Wau | 85 | 269 | 19 | 50 | 68 | 5 | 2 | 3 | 31 | 1 | 3 | 36 | 3 | 63 | 3 | 4 | .186 |
| Maria, Esteban, Bur | 17 | 33 | 6 | 6 | 8 | 2 | 0 | 0 | 1 | 0 | 3 | 0 | 18 | 1 | 0 | | .182 |
| Marichal, Victor, Bur | 76 | 243 | 17 | 54 | 75 | 12 | 3 | 1 | 22 | 4 | 0 | 17 | 1 | 46 | 2 | 2 | .222 |
| Maropis, Peter, Apl | 19 | 46 | 3 | 8 | 8 | 0 | 0 | 0 | 4 | 1 | 2 | 4 | 0 | 12 | 1 | 0 | .174 |
| Martinson, Michael, QC | 40 | 126 | 21 | 34 | 37 | 3 | 0 | 0 | 18 | 1 | 2 | 18 | 0 | 10 | 0 | 0 | .270 |
| Massimini, Kenneth, WR* | 11 | 10 | 0 | 1 | 1 | 0 | 0 | 0 | 0 | 2 | 0 | 3 | 0 | 1 | 0 | 0 | .100 |
| May, Davis, WR | 24 | 27 | 2 | 6 | 7 | 1 | 0 | 0 | 5 | 0 | 4 | 0 | 7 | 0 | 0 | | .222 |
| McClellan, Robert, Apl* | 9 | 21 | 1 | 6 | 9 | 3 | 0 | 0 | 1 | 1 | 0 | 1 | 0 | 7 | 0 | 0 | .286 |
| McKinney, Lynn, Wat | 11 | 25 | 1 | 4 | 4 | 0 | 0 | 0 | 2 | 5 | 0 | 0 | 9 | 0 | 0 | | .160 |

| Player and Club | G. | AB. | R. | H. | TB. | 2B. | 3B. | HR. | RBI. | SH. | SF. | BB. | HP. | SO. | SB. | CS. | Pct |
|---|---|---|---|---|---|---|---|---|---|---|---|---|---|---|---|---|---|
| McLaren, John, Dub | 102 | 297 | 19 | 78 | 131 | 17 | 0 | 12 | 55 | 5 | 5 | 48 | 6 | 44 | 5 | 2 | .263 |
| McManus, Dana, Cln | 10 | 24 | 2 | 7 | 10 | 0 | 0 | 1 | 2 | 3 | 0 | 0 | 0 | 4 | 0 | 0 | .292 |
| Meche, Carl, QC | 27 | 21 | 3 | 6 | 10 | 1 | 0 | 1 | 7 | 1 | 0 | 2 | 0 | 8 | 0 | 0 | .286 |
| Mejias, Marcos, Bur | 68 | 192 | 19 | 47 | 61 | 9 | 1 | 1 | 17 | 1 | 0 | 22 | 1 | 49 | 5 | 1 | .245 |
| Mendoza, Michael, Dub | 16 | 19 | 0 | 2 | 2 | 0 | 0 | 0 | 0 | 4 | 0 | 2 | 1 | 12 | 0 | 0 | .105 |
| Mercado, Candido, Apl | 5 | 16 | 2 | 2 | 2 | 0 | 0 | 0 | 1 | 0 | 2 | 0 | 3 | 1 | 0 | | .125 |
| Meyer, William, Dan | 111 | 398 | 69 | 113 | 156 | 19 | 6 | 4 | 50 | 1 | 5 | 51 | 0 | 44 | 9 | 3 | .284 |
| Michael, William, Cln* | 110 | 357 | 43 | 90 | 112 | 9 | 2 | 3 | 33 | 3 | 2 | 40 | 1 | 68 | 29 | 6 | .252 |
| Miller, Danny, QC† | 58 | 162 | 22 | 33 | 37 | 2 | 1 | 0 | 23 | 3 | 4 | 30 | 5 | 29 | 7 | 0 | .204 |
| Minaya, Felix, Wau | 101 | 356 | 43 | 87 | 112 | 9 | 2 | 4 | 32 | 4 | 2 | 36 | 3 | 53 | 27 | 3 | .244 |
| Monroe, Lawrence, Apl | 23 | 36 | 2 | 0 | 0 | 0 | 0 | 0 | 1 | 3 | 1 | 4 | 0 | 21 | 0 | 0 | .000 |
| Monteau, R. Samuel, Bur† | 30 | 75 | 4 | 13 | 14 | 1 | 0 | 0 | 10 | 0 | 0 | 10 | 0 | 22 | 0 | 0 | .173 |
| Moore, Calvin, CR | 25 | 89 | 11 | 13 | 18 | 2 | 0 | 1 | 8 | 1 | 3 | 8 | 1 | 20 | 2 | 3 | .146 |
| Moore, S. Wesley, Dan | 13 | 6 | 0 | 0 | 0 | 0 | 0 | 0 | 0 | 0 | 0 | 0 | 0 | 5 | 0 | 0 | .000 |
| Moreno, Jorge, Dub | 85 | 127 | 31 | 33 | 43 | 3 | 2 | 1 | 13 | 2 | 1 | 8 | 0 | 32 | 10 | 4 | .260 |
| Moreta, Manuel, Wat | 39 | 40 | 13 | 10 | 10 | 0 | 0 | 0 | 2 | 2 | 0 | 3 | 0 | 8 | 1 | 1 | .250 |
| Mueller, Willard, Bur | 25 | 31 | 0 | 6 | 9 | 3 | 0 | 0 | 2 | 0 | 0 | 1 | 0 | 7 | 0 | 0 | .194 |
| Mulliniks, S. Rance, QC* | 52 | 186 | 34 | 50 | 63 | 6 | 2 | 1 | 21 | 2 | 4 | 30 | 1 | 25 | 7 | 0 | .269 |
| Murray, James, Cln* | 31 | 25 | 0 | 2 | 2 | 0 | 0 | 0 | 1 | 2 | 0 | 1 | 0 | 9 | 0 | 0 | .080 |
| Narron, John, Apl* | 108 | 359 | 24 | 82 | 109 | 7 | 1 | 6 | 57 | 4 | 4 | 25 | 0 | 61 | 4 | 1 | .228 |
| Nerone, Philip, Apl | 90 | 268 | 39 | 53 | 76 | 11 | 3 | 2 | 26 | 3 | 2 | 48 | 1 | 67 | 3 | 1 | .198 |
| Nix, John, CR | 14 | 11 | 0 | 0 | 0 | 0 | 0 | 0 | 1 | 0 | 0 | 0 | 0 | 4 | 0 | 0 | .000 |
| Olsen, Lewis, Wat | 9 | 25 | 2 | 6 | 9 | 0 | 0 | 1 | 3 | 1 | 0 | 1 | 0 | 10 | 0 | 0 | .240 |
| Olson, Dean, WR* | 26 | 60 | 0 | 10 | 12 | 2 | 0 | 0 | 6 | 2 | 1 | 5 | 0 | 10 | 0 | 0 | .167 |
| Olszta, Edwin, Apl | 124 | 411 | 58 | 113 | 177 | 19 | 12 | 7 | 55 | 0 | 4 | 57 | 1 | 98 | 5 | 4 | .275 |
| Osofsky, Alvin, Dub† | 34 | 68 | 7 | 15 | 18 | 1 | 1 | 0 | 8 | 3 | 0 | 9 | 0 | 14 | 4 | 0 | .221 |
| Pacella, John, Wau | 19 | 42 | 5 | 5 | 6 | 1 | 0 | 0 | 4 | 5 | 0 | 2 | 0 | 19 | 0 | 0 | .119 |
| Paciorek, Michael, Dan | 97 | 279 | 37 | 64 | 94 | 14 | 2 | 4 | 37 | 3 | 4 | 41 | 3 | 58 | 2 | 5 | .229 |
| Palmer, Robert, Apl | 65 | 217 | 22 | 47 | 80 | 7 | 4 | 6 | 23 | 2 | 1 | 16 | 2 | 56 | 0 | 0 | .217 |
| Parish, Jacky, Dan | 41 | 124 | 22 | 29 | 38 | 6 | 0 | 1 | 26 | 5 | 1 | 19 | 3 | 15 | 4 | 2 | .234 |
| Parker, Darrell, Wat† | 108 | 411 | 66 | 125 | 176 | 21 | 3 | 8 | 59 | 4 | 4 | 36 | 4 | 69 | 13 | 6 | .304 |
| Patterson, W.O. Ricky, Wau | 10 | 23 | 2 | 6 | 7 | 1 | 0 | 0 | 2 | 1 | 0 | 2 | 3 | 4 | 0 | 0 | .261 |
| Peguero, Pablo, Dan | 46 | 143 | 9 | 42 | 52 | 7 | 0 | 1 | 20 | 0 | 1 | 13 | 1 | 14 | 3 | 0 | .294 |
| Pena, Abelino, Bur* | 19 | 22 | 1 | 2 | 3 | 1 | 0 | 0 | 1 | 3 | 0 | 0 | 0 | 15 | 0 | 0 | .091 |
| Perez, Carlos J., QC | 18 | 2 | 1 | 1 | 1 | 0 | 0 | 0 | 2 | 0 | 0 | 0 | 0 | 1 | 0 | 0 | .500 |
| Perkins, Thomas, Cln | 56 | 14 | 0 | 3 | 5 | 2 | 0 | 0 | 3 | 2 | 0 | 2 | 0 | 5 | 0 | 0 | .214 |
| Person, Carl, QC | 65 | 226 | 45 | 63 | 78 | 8 | 2 | 1 | 33 | 0 | 3 | 19 | 3 | 15 | 4 | 1 | .279 |
| Peterson, Jerry, Wat | 34 | 7 | 2 | 2 | 2 | 0 | 0 | 0 | 2 | 1 | 0 | 1 | 0 | 2 | 0 | 0 | .286 |
| Pladson, Gordon, Dub | 17 | 7 | 0 | 1 | 1 | 0 | 0 | 0 | 1 | 1 | 0 | 0 | 0 | 5 | 0 | 0 | .143 |
| Plut, Stephen, Dan* | 91 | 290 | 51 | 86 | 126 | 15 | 2 | 7 | 44 | 3 | 2 | 32 | 3 | 38 | 16 | 4 | .297 |
| Polanco, Roger, Dub | 99 | 138 | 41 | 25 | 27 | 0 | 1 | 0 | 7 | 1 | 1 | 11 | 1 | 28 | 13 | 5 | .181 |
| Powers, Steve, QC | 19 | 15 | 2 | 3 | 4 | 1 | 0 | 0 | 2 | 1 | 0 | 1 | 0 | 10 | 0 | 0 | .200 |
| Price, Harris, Apl* | 66 | 167 | 6 | 32 | 37 | 5 | 0 | 0 | 15 | 3 | 1 | 18 | 1 | 22 | 0 | 0 | .192 |
| Puhl, Terry, Dub* | 104 | 346 | 57 | 115 | 129 | 10 | 2 | 0 | 28 | .5 | 3 | 41 | 1 | 30 | 30 | 4 | .332 |
| Pujols, Luis, Dub | 102 | 341 | 23 | 75 | 90 | 13 | 1 | 0 | 31 | 4 | 4 | 18 | 4 | 54 | 5 | 1 | .220 |
| Quintero, Frank, WR | 25 | 45 | 1 | 10 | 12 | 2 | 0 | 0 | 3 | 6 | 0 | 1 | 1 | 10 | 0 | 0 | .222 |
| Quirk, Eugene, Wau* | 92 | 270 | 55 | 77 | 110 | 13 | 7 | 2 | 21 | 5 | 1 | 40 | 0 | 33 | 10 | 8 | .285 |
| Quisenberry, Daniel, Wat | 20 | 9 | 1 | 2 | 2 | 0 | 0 | 0 | 1 | 0 | 0 | 2 | 0 | 2 | 0 | 0 | .222 |
| Rasmussen, Neil, Bur | 130 | 498 | 68 | 128 | 191 | 16 | 7 | 11 | 62 | 2 | 2 | 37 | 3 | 95 | 7 | 2 | .257 |
| Ray, James A., CR* | 81 | 280 | 43 | 66 | 74 | 6 | 1 | 0 | 17 | 3 | 2 | 38 | 0 | 32 | 15 | 4 | .236 |
| Reinke, Jeffrey, Cln* | 13 | 19 | 2 | 6 | 10 | 2 | 1 | 0 | 5 | 3 | 0 | 0 | 0 | 5 | 0 | 0 | .316 |
| Repke, Frederick, Dan | 24 | 20 | 2 | 4 | 4 | 0 | 0 | 0 | 1 | 3 | 0 | 2 | 0 | 2 | 0 | 0 | .200 |
| Richards, David, Dan | 21 | 60 | 6 | 17 | 22 | 3 | 1 | 0 | 11 | 1 | 2 | 6 | 1 | 8 | 3 | 1 | .283 |
| Richardson, David, Wau | 23 | 36 | 3 | 8 | 10 | 2 | 0 | 0 | 3 | 1 | 0 | 2 | 0 | 10 | 0 | 0 | .222 |
| Richartz, Scott, Apl | 110 | 384 | 56 | 97 | 122 | 14 | 1 | 3 | 33 | 4 | 5 | 42 | 2 | 73 | 8 | 6 | .253 |
| Richmond, Glenn, WR | 11 | 27 | 0 | 4 | 5 | 1 | 0 | 0 | 2 | 0 | 0 | 5 | 0 | 9 | 1 | 0 | .148 |
| Riddle, John, CR* | 14 | 2 | 0 | 0 | 0 | 0 | 0 | 0 | 0 | 0 | 0 | 0 | 0 | 2 | 0 | 0 | .000 |
| Rima, Thomas, Dub* | 84 | 282 | 38 | 77 | 93 | 13 | 0 | 1 | 21 | 3 | 3 | 43 | 3 | 27 | 15 | 8 | .273 |
| Robles, Silvano, Apl | 93 | 310 | 39 | 82 | 95 | 7 | 3 | 0 | 11 | 3 | 2 | 15 | 2 | 44 | 13 | 7 | .265 |
| Roche, Timothy, Dan* | 76 | 170 | 10 | 35 | 42 | 5 | 0 | 1 | 21 | 1 | 1 | 25 | 0 | 48 | 1 | 0 | .206 |
| Rodriguez, Alejandro, Bur | 126 | 456 | 67 | 119 | 175 | 21 | 4 | 9 | 43 | 6 | 3 | 63 | 4 | 76 | 17 | 6 | .261 |
| Rogers, Randell, Dan | 124 | 443 | 72 | 102 | 125 | 19 | 2 | 0 | 27 | 4 | 1 | 66 | 2 | 71 | 15 | 7 | .230 |
| Rolle, Shadrach, Wau† | 99 | 376 | 56 | 109 | 162 | 14 | 3 | 11 | 47 | 1 | 0 | 20 | 1 | 58 | 25 | 5 | .290 |
| Roof, David, WR | 20 | 45 | 0 | 10 | 10 | 0 | 0 | 0 | 1 | 5 | 0 | 4 | 0 | 16 | 0 | 0 | .222 |
| Rosario, Salvador, Bur | 117 | 337 | 44 | 72 | 97 | 16 | 3 | 1 | 24 | 6 | 3 | 23 | 4 | 57 | 3 | 5 | .214 |
| Roslund, John, QC | 38 | 18 | 0 | 0 | 0 | 0 | 0 | 0 | 1 | 0 | 0 | 1 | 0 | 12 | 0 | 0 | .000 |
| Royal, Gary, Wau | 16 | 47 | 4 | 12 | 14 | 0 | 1 | 0 | 5 | 0 | 0 | 5 | 0 | 8 | 0 | 1 | .255 |
| Rozema, David, Cln | 27 | 54 | 2 | 5 | 6 | 1 | 0 | 0 | 2 | 5 | 0 | 1 | 0 | 29 | 0 | 0 | .093 |
| Rushde, Michael, Dan* | 109 | 361 | 65 | 109 | 149 | 13 | 6 | 5 | 63 | 4 | 3 | 34 | 1 | 48 | 11 | 1 | .302 |
| Ryals, Bruce, Wau | 15 | 27 | 4 | 5 | 5 | 0 | 0 | 0 | 0 | 0 | 0 | 4 | 0 | 8 | 0 | 0 | .185 |
| Sain, Thomas, WR | 66 | 250 | 41 | 84 | 115 | 12 | 8 | 1 | 37 | 4 | 0 | 19 | 5 | 18 | 11 | 2 | .336 |
| Sanchez, Luis M., Dub | 7 | 9 | 1 | 2 | 2 | 0 | 0 | 0 | 1 | 2 | 0 | 0 | 0 | 6 | 0 | 0 | .222 |
| Sanchez, Pedro, Bur | 37 | 65 | 3 | 12 | 12 | 0 | 0 | 0 | 6 | 0 | 0 | 2 | 0 | 11 | 0 | 0 | .185 |
| Sander, Richard, Wau | 12 | 23 | 1 | 5 | 5 | 0 | 0 | 0 | 2 | 0 | 0 | 2 | 0 | 7 | 0 | 0 | .217 |
| Santos, Edgardo, Dan | 99 | 345 | 45 | 85 | 122 | 13 | 9 | 2 | 43 | 0 | 4 | 17 | 2 | 65 | 13 | 7 | .246 |
| Sasser, Donald, CR | 128 | 476 | 51 | 117 | 158 | 21 | 1 | 6 | 68 | 2 | 4 | 35 | 4 | 54 | 10 | 2 | .246 |
| Scarborough, R. Carey, Bur* | 31 | 14 | 7 | 1 | 1 | 0 | 0 | 0 | 1 | 1 | 0 | 1 | 0 | 3 | 0 | 0 | .071 |
| Schoenhaus, Edward, CR | 17 | 56 | 4 | 17 | 20 | 3 | 0 | 0 | 4 | 1 | 0 | 9 | 0 | 3 | 0 | 1 | .304 |
| Schultz, Theodore, Apl† | 18 | 61 | 7 | 16 | 18 | 2 | 0 | 0 | 5 | 0 | 0 | 10 | 0 | 14 | 0 | 1 | .262 |
| Seidholz, Donn, Apl | 50 | 169 | 14 | 38 | 50 | 2 | 2 | 2 | 18 | 2 | 2 | 6 | 0 | 33 | 2 | 1 | .225 |
| Sempsrott, Edward, Wat* | 23 | 38 | 1 | 9 | 9 | 0 | 0 | 1 | 4 | 0 | 1 | 0 | 0 | 16 | 1 | 0 | .237 |

| Player and Club | G. | AB. | R. | H. | TB. | 2B. | 3B. | HR. | RBI. | SH. | SF. | BB. | HP. | SO. | SB. | CS. | Pct. |
|---|---|---|---|---|---|---|---|---|---|---|---|---|---|---|---|---|---|
| Shippy, Gregory, Cln | 76 | 253 | 20 | 58 | 88 | 15 | 0 | 5 | 26 | 1 | 1 | 26 | 2 | 38 | 3 | 0 | .229 |
| Silverio, Luis, Wat | 12 | 26 | 2 | 3 | 6 | 1 | 1 | 0 | 3 | 0 | 0 | 2 | 0 | 14 | 0 | 0 | .115 |
| Skoglund, Craig, Wau | 101 | 303 | 31 | 69 | 101 | 15 | 1 | 5 | 29 | 1 | 1 | 28 | 1 | 61 | 6 | 0 | .228 |
| Slattery, Kevin, Cln | 55 | 143 | 15 | 30 | 41 | 5 | 0 | 2 | 16 | 0 | 2 | 30 | 3 | 39 | 1 | 0 | .210 |
| Slaymaker, Joe, Bur* | 26 | 21 | 4 | 1 | 3 | 0 | 1 | 0 | 0 | 0 | 0 | 3 | 0 | 15 | 0 | 1 | .048 |
| Slettvet, Douglas, QC | 31 | 67 | 9 | 17 | 26 | 1 | 1 | 2 | 10 | 0 | 0 | 8 | 0 | 12 | 0 | 1 | .254 |
| Smith, Charles D., WR | 32 | 24 | 2 | 2 | 2 | 0 | 0 | 0 | 0 | 2 | 0 | 4 | 0 | 8 | 0 | 0 | .083 |
| Smith, Daniel J., CR* | 3 | 5 | 0 | 0 | 0 | 0 | 0 | 0 | 0 | 1 | 0 | 0 | 0 | 1 | 0 | 0 | .000 |
| Smith, Daniel R., Dan | 41 | 13 | 1 | 3 | 3 | 0 | 0 | 0 | 1 | 0 | 0 | 2 | 0 | 3 | 0 | 0 | .231 |
| Smith, Jeffrey, Dub* | 105 | 325 | 24 | 80 | 104 | 14 | 2 | 2 | 36 | 4 | 2 | 28 | 1 | 48 | 1 | 1 | .246 |
| Smith, Ronald W., Bur | 54 | 182 | 20 | 50 | 64 | 8 | 3 | 0 | 21 | 3 | 3 | 32 | 0 | 43 | 5 | 2 | .275 |
| Smotherman, Richard, Wat† | 82 | 253 | 52 | 73 | 110 | 15 | 2 | 6 | 51 | 0 | 6 | 24 | 0 | 68 | 5 | 1 | .289 |
| Soriano, Hilario, Dan | 38 | 123 | 10 | 32 | 43 | 3 | 1 | 2 | 17 | 1 | 1 | 4 | 0 | 30 | 0 | 0 | .260 |
| Souza, K. Mark, Wat* | 33 | 9 | 4 | 2 | 3 | 1 | 0 | 0 | 0 | 0 | 0 | 1 | 0 | 3 | 0 | 0 | .222 |
| Speck, R. Clifford, Wau | 8 | 8 | 0 | 0 | 0 | 0 | 0 | 0 | 1 | 0 | 0 | 4 | 0 | 7 | 0 | 0 | .000 |
| Srock, William, WR | 11 | 5 | 0 | 0 | 0 | 0 | 0 | 0 | 0 | 0 | 0 | 0 | 0 | 5 | 0 | 0 | .000 |
| Stafford, Gil, Bur | 39 | 118 | 7 | 23 | 30 | 4 | 0 | 1 | 11 | 3 | 0 | 4 | 1 | 28 | 0 | 0 | .195 |
| Stamps, Jerry, CR* | 50 | 88 | 5 | 23 | 26 | 0 | 0 | 1 | 9 | 0 | 1 | 12 | 1 | 15 | 1 | 2 | .261 |
| Stipetich, Mark, QC | 23 | 61 | 6 | 11 | 11 | 0 | 0 | 0 | 3 | 0 | 0 | 6 | 0 | 9 | 0 | 0 | .180 |
| Storti, Larry, WR | 48 | 156 | 18 | 30 | 34 | 4 | 0 | 0 | 9 | 3 | 0 | 27 | 1 | 37 | 1 | 2 | .192 |
| Strong, Garret, CR* | 62 | 212 | 29 | 49 | 76 | 6 | 0 | 7 | 22 | 0 | 0 | 32 | 2 | 26 | 2 | 1 | .231 |
| Sylvia, David, Bur | 10 | 3 | 0 | 0 | 0 | 0 | 0 | 0 | 0 | 0 | 0 | 0 | 0 | 3 | 0 | 0 | .000 |
| Tanner, Roy, Wat† | 55 | 139 | 16 | 35 | 37 | 2 | 0 | 0 | 15 | 2 | 1 | 8 | 5 | 19 | 0 | 1 | .252 |
| Tatis, Rafael, Dub | 103 | 317 | 37 | 71 | 95 | 13 | 4 | 1 | 27 | 4 | 0 | 43 | 1 | 75 | 17 | 5 | .224 |
| Taylor, William, QC* | 83 | 262 | 39 | 67 | 92 | 11 | 4 | 2 | 27 | 0 | 3 | 38 | 2 | 37 | 2 | 2 | .256 |
| Thomas, Eric, Apl† | 88 | 200 | 35 | 39 | 47 | 2 | 3 | 0 | 8 | 6 | 1 | 15 | 0 | 47 | 9 | 0 | .195 |
| Thomas, Lawrence, WR* | 33 | 84 | 10 | 18 | 26 | 2 | 0 | 2 | 12 | 1 | 2 | 10 | 0 | 16 | 0 | 1 | .214 |
| Thomasson, Harold, Wat | 86 | 283 | 39 | 66 | 91 | 10 | 0 | 5 | 42 | 5 | 3 | 51 | 1 | 71 | 5 | 4 | .233 |
| Thompson, Fay, Dub* | 103 | 265 | 26 | 62 | 98 | 8 | 2 | 8 | 28 | 3 | 4 | 51 | 1 | 89 | 2 | 0 | .234 |
| Thompson, Robert E., CR | 40 | 37 | 1 | 1 | 1 | 0 | 0 | 0 | 1 | 3 | 0 | 2 | 0 | 23 | 0 | 0 | .027 |
| Toman, Thomas, Apl* | 114 | 345 | 60 | 89 | 103 | 3 | 4 | 1 | 28 | 2 | 4 | 111 | 7 | 50 | 29 | 11 | .258 |
| Torreano, John, WR* | 1 | 0 | 0 | 0 | 0 | 0 | 0 | 0 | 0 | 0 | 0 | 0 | 0 | 0 | 0 | 0 | .000 |
| Trella, Stephen, Cln | 24 | 47 | 2 | 5 | 5 | 0 | 0 | 0 | 1 | 9 | 0 | 4 | 0 | 21 | 0 | 0 | .106 |
| Trucks, Phil, Apl | 11 | 29 | 2 | 6 | 10 | 1 | 0 | 1 | 2 | 0 | 0 | 3 | 1 | 14 | 0 | 0 | .207 |
| Turner, Robert, WR | 32 | 89 | 15 | 22 | 34 | 7 | 1 | 1 | 10 | 0 | 0 | 22 | 2 | 22 | 0 | 0 | .247 |
| Twellman, Thomas, Dub | 119 | 397 | 37 | 99 | 115 | 16 | 0 | 0 | 30 | 10 | 2 | 53 | 2 | 40 | 7 | 2 | .249 |
| Uremovich, Michael, Cln* | 37 | 71 | 1 | 8 | 12 | 1 | 0 | 1 | 6 | 2 | 1 | 7 | 2 | 11 | 0 | 0 | .113 |
| Wagner, Mark, Cln | 119 | 436 | 52 | 111 | 133 | 11 | 4 | 1 | 50 | 5 | 5 | 0 | 40 | 53 | 10 | 1 | .255 |
| Wallace, W. Edward, Wau | 49 | 148 | 14 | 40 | 47 | 7 | 0 | 0 | 20 | 2 | 3 | 4 | 1 | 23 | 3 | 1 | .270 |
| Washington, Malvin, QC† | 78 | 226 | 38 | 59 | 71 | 2 | 2 | 2 | 28 | 0 | 1 | 34 | 1 | 47 | 16 | 0 | .261 |
| Weeber, Mike, Dub | 17 | 14 | 0 | 2 | 2 | 0 | 0 | 0 | 2 | 0 | 0 | 1 | 0 | 6 | 0 | 0 | .143 |
| Wheeler, Edward, Apl | 44 | 96 | 17 | 23 | 33 | 2 | 1 | 2 | 17 | 2 | 0 | 27 | 3 | 11 | 6 | 2 | .240 |
| Whiting, John, Bur | 15 | 7 | 0 | 0 | 0 | 0 | 0 | 0 | 0 | 0 | 0 | 1 | 0 | 7 | 0 | 0 | .000 |
| Wilbins, Michael, CR | 49 | 161 | 15 | 34 | 39 | 2 | 0 | 1 | 12 | 3 | 1 | 21 | 0 | 28 | 7 | 5 | .211 |
| Williams, Gary G., Wat* | 21 | 48 | 6 | 9 | 12 | 3 | 0 | 0 | 5 | 0 | 1 | 2 | 0 | 6 | 0 | 0 | .188 |
| Williams, Leo, Apl | 8 | 4 | 0 | 0 | 0 | 0 | 0 | 0 | 0 | 0 | 0 | 0 | 0 | 3 | 0 | 0 | .000 |
| Williams, Michael W., Wat | 27 | 34 | 6 | 4 | 5 | 1 | 0 | 0 | 6 | 0 | 0 | 10 | 0 | 14 | 1 | 0 | .118 |
| Wilson, Barney, CR | 36 | 13 | 0 | 1 | 1 | 0 | 0 | 0 | 0 | 0 | 0 | 1 | 0 | 7 | 0 | 0 | .077 |
| Wilson, Billy, Dan | 31 | 55 | 5 | 9 | 10 | 1 | 0 | 0 | 5 | 7 | 0 | 4 | 0 | 23 | 0 | 0 | .164 |
| Wilson, Mark, WR | 79 | 253 | 33 | 70 | 94 | 13 | 1 | 3 | 35 | 1 | 3 | 20 | 2 | 31 | 7 | 1 | .277 |
| Wilson, Willie, Wat | 127 | 486 | 92 | 132 | 182 | 18 | 4 | 8 | 73 | 3 | 4 | 26 | 13 | 99 | 76 | 12 | .272 |
| Woodbrey, Mark, CR* | 53 | 135 | 12 | 31 | 37 | 4 | 1 | 0 | 9 | 0 | 2 | 23 | 2 | 31 | 4 | 4 | .230 |
| Wulfemeyer, Mark, QC | 1 | 1 | 0 | 0 | 0 | 0 | 0 | 0 | 0 | 0 | 0 | 0 | 0 | 1 | 0 | 0 | .000 |
| Yost, Edgar, Wau | 79 | 265 | 26 | 51 | 76 | 7 | 0 | 6 | 27 | 2 | 2 | 34 | 1 | 69 | 0 | 3 | .192 |
| Young, Ernest, CR† | 27 | 84 | 5 | 13 | 14 | 1 | 0 | 0 | 5 | 0 | 1 | 11 | 0 | 18 | 0 | 0 | .155 |
| Young, Richard, QC* | 11 | 17 | 1 | 2 | 2 | 1 | 0 | 0 | 0 | 0 | 1 | 2 | 0 | 6 | 0 | 0 | .118 |
| Youngbauer, Jeffrey, WR* | 56 | 172 | 25 | 42 | 49 | 7 | 0 | 0 | 7 | 3 | 2 | 27 | 2 | 26 | 3 | 2 | .244 |
| Yount, Lawrence, Bur | 4 | 6 | 0 | 0 | 0 | 0 | 0 | 0 | 0 | 0 | 0 | 1 | 0 | 1 | 0 | 0 | .000 |
| Yurak, Jeffrey, CR† | 58 | 175 | 26 | 46 | 58 | 7 | 1 | 1 | 15 | 0 | 0 | 19 | 4 | 22 | 2 | 0 | .263 |

GRAND SLAM HOME RUNS (20): Curran 2, Sasser 2, Aikens, deLeeuw, Edmondson, Fahrow, Hill, Holmberg, Kelley, Killingsworth, Knicely, Meche, Palmer, Parish, Parker, Thomasson, F. Thompson, Wagner, 1 each.

AWARDED FIRST BASE ON INTERFERENCE (7): Mayer 2 (Tanner, Washington), Galvez (Yost), Michael (McLaren), Price (Hough), Rushde (Dodd), Stafford (Graham).

## CLUB FIELDING

| Club | G. | PO. | A. | E. | DP. | PB. | Pct. | Club | G. | PO. | A. | E. | DP. | PB. | Pct. |
|---|---|---|---|---|---|---|---|---|---|---|---|---|---|---|---|
| Quad Cities | 125 | 3120 | 1140 | 168 | 54 | 16 | .9620 | Dubuque | 126 | 3180 | 1259 | 219 | 88 | 28 | .953 |
| Wisconsin Rap | 129 | 3182 | 1415 | 182 | 109 | 30 | .9619 | Danville | 128 | 3187 | 1376 | 229 | 94 | 28 | .952 |
| Waterloo | 130 | 3255 | 1430 | 207 | 93 | 41 | .958 | Wausau | 128 | 3096 | 1356 | 226 | 113 | 26 | .952 |
| Clinton | 129 | 3280 | 1424 | 213 | 78 | 17 | .957 | Burlington | 130 | 3368 | 1345 | 249 | 94 | 16 | .950 |
| Cedar Rapids | 128 | 3204 | 1380 | 210 | 92 | 46 | .956 | Appleton | 127 | 3120 | 1326 | 243 | 90 | 30 | .948 |

Triple Plays: Waterloo, Clinton, Danville, 1 each.

## INDIVIDUAL FIELDING

*Throws lefthanded.

### FIRST BASEMEN

| Player and Club | G. | PO. | A. | E. | DP. | Pct. | Player and Club | G. | PO. | A. | E. | DP. | Pct. |
|---|---|---|---|---|---|---|---|---|---|---|---|---|---|
| Royal, Wau | 14 | 112 | 10 | 0 | 11 | 1.000 | deLeeuw, Wat | 3 | 19 | 3 | 0 | 0 | 1.000 |
| Plut, Dan | 11 | 116 | 3 | 0 | 3 | 1.000 | Foley, Apl | 2 | 14 | 1 | 0 | 1 | 1.000 |
| Pujols, Dub | 6 | 26 | 3 | 0 | 1 | 1.000 | Shippy, Cln | 1 | 10 | 0 | 0 | 1 | 1.000 |

## FIRST BASEMEN—Continued

| Player and Club | G. | PO. | A. | E. | DP. | Pct. |
|---|---|---|---|---|---|---|
| Tatis, Dub | 3 | 10 | 0 | 0 | 0 | 1.000 |
| Haas, Cln | 1 | 7 | 0 | 0 | 0 | 1.000 |
| Holland, Apl* | 1 | 6 | 0 | 0 | 0 | 1.000 |
| Meyer, Dan | 31 | 227 | 19 | 2 | 16 | .992 |
| Wilson, WR | 14 | 108 | 14 | 1 | 9 | .992 |
| Puhl, Dub | 13 | 81 | 6 | 1 | 4 | .989 |
| Bates, Cln | 53 | 539 | 44 | 7 | 31 | .988 |
| Holmberg, Bur | 9 | 79 | 4 | 1 | 6 | .988 |
| CIPOT, WAU* | 116 | 994 | 54 | 15 | 90 | .986 |
| Beamon, Wat* | 86 | 775 | 60 | 12 | 48 | .986 |
| Wheeler, Apl | 17 | 134 | 7 | 2 | 10 | .986 |
| Paciorek, Dan | 84 | 694 | 52 | 11 | 55 | .985 |
| Schultz, Apl | 6 | 60 | 6 | 1 | 3 | .985 |
| Monteau, Bur | 18 | 169 | 12 | 3 | 13 | .984 |
| Ditto, Dan | 13 | 113 | 7 | 2 | 8 | .984 |
| Sasser, CR | 128 | 1187 | 69 | 22 | 83 | .983 |
| Beck, WR | 103 | 902 | 48 | 16 | 74 | .983 |
| Centeno, Cln* | 25 | 219 | 11 | 4 | 19 | .983 |
| Thompson, Dub^b | 94 | 624 | 45 | 13 | 49 | .981 |
| McLaren, Dub | 37 | 248 | 14 | 5 | 17 | .981 |
| Narron, Apl | 98 | 786 | 41 | 17 | 62 | .980 |
| Smotherman, Wat | 48 | 423 | 24 | 9 | 28 | .980 |
| Killingsworth, Bur | 104 | 914 | 47 | 21 | 61 | .978 |
| Hill, WR | 16 | 126 | 9 | 3 | 7 | .978 |
| Aikens, QC | 125 | 1038 | 53 | 26 | 49 | .977 |
| McClellan, Apl | 4 | 36 | 3 | 1 | 2 | .975 |
| Atilano, Cln | 54 | 464 | 19 | 21 | 23 | .958 |
| Galvez, Apl | 2 | 18 | 0 | 2 | 3 | .900 |
| Moreno, Dub | 1 | 5 | 0 | 1 | 0 | .833 |

Triple Play: Beamon, Paciorek, Atilano.

## SECOND BASEMEN

| Player and Club | G. | PO. | A. | E. | DP. | Pct. |
|---|---|---|---|---|---|---|
| de los Santos, CR | 5 | 9 | 23 | 0 | 4 | 1.000 |
| Haynes, Dub | 4 | 11 | 15 | 0 | 2 | 1.000 |
| Wheeler, Apl | 4 | 17 | 8 | 0 | 3 | 1.000 |
| Gonzalez, Wat | 4 | 7 | 4 | 0 | 0 | 1.000 |
| Parish, Dan | 1 | 1 | 3 | 0 | 3 | 1.000 |
| Mann, Wau | 1 | 1 | 3 | 0 | 1 | 1.000 |
| Storti, WR | 1 | 1 | 0 | 0 | 0 | 1.000 |
| Crosta, Apl | 14 | 23 | 41 | 1 | 8 | .985 |
| Bianco, Apl | 11 | 28 | 20 | 1 | 5 | .980 |
| Caughey, WR | 71 | 172 | 225 | 9 | 52 | .978 |
| Bradbury, Wau | 20 | 39 | 51 | 2 | 14 | .978 |
| Fischetti, Dan | 21 | 37 | 50 | 2 | 6 | .978 |
| TWELLMAN, DUB | 117 | 246 | 309 | 13 | 52 | .977 |
| Sain, WR | 6 | 18 | 18 | 1 | 2 | .973 |
| Cruz, QC | 105 | 228 | 259 | 14 | 27 | .972 |
| Minaya, Wau | 101 | 270 | 302 | 17 | 60 | .971 |
| Gates, Wat | 122 | 227 | 332 | 17 | 53 | .970 |
| Thomas, Apl | 30 | 66 | 89 | 5 | 14 | .969 |
| Bartell, Cln | 7 | 14 | 17 | 1 | 3 | .969 |
| I. Gimenez, Cln | 12 | 35 | 23 | 2 | 2 | .967 |
| Richartz, Apl | 18 | 44 | 42 | 3 | 6 | .966 |
| Fahrow, QC | 21 | 59 | 44 | 4 | 5 | .963 |
| Meyer, Dan | 65 | 111 | 163 | 12 | 28 | .958 |
| Rosario, Bur | 63 | 132 | 160 | 13 | 32 | .957 |
| Tanner, Wat | 5 | 9 | 13 | 1 | 1 | .957 |
| Hunt, Cln | 100 | 188 | 327 | 24 | 46 | .955 |
| Marichal, Bur | 68 | 149 | 163 | 17 | 21 | .948 |
| Wilbins, CR | 45 | 96 | 104 | 11 | 16 | .948 |
| Wallace, Wau | 2 | 10 | 7 | 1 | 3 | .944 |
| Cash, CR | 40 | 82 | 112 | 12 | 25 | .942 |
| Turner, WR | 29 | 66 | 77 | 9 | 11 | .941 |
| Roche, Dan | 3 | 4 | 10 | 1 | 0 | .933 |
| DelVecchio, Dan | 51 | 107 | 112 | 16 | 20 | .932 |
| Woodbrey, CR | 39 | 96 | 108 | 15 | 22 | .932 |
| Jones, Bur | 4 | 4 | 8 | 1 | 0 | .923 |
| Kelly, Cln | 14 | 24 | 32 | 5 | 3 | .918 |
| Polanco, Dub | 18 | 17 | 33 | 5 | 3 | .909 |
| Daniels, WR | 29 | 62 | 50 | 12 | 11 | .903 |
| Alvardo, Dub | 3 | 5 | 4 | 1 | 0 | .900 |
| Robles, Apl | 56 | 130 | 135 | 33 | 27 | .889 |
| Lee, CR | 2 | 4 | 4 | 1 | 1 | .889 |
| Scarborough, Bur | 3 | 4 | 4 | 1 | 2 | .889 |
| Schultz, Apl | 2 | 3 | 4 | 1 | 0 | .875 |
| Rolle, Wau | 6 | 20 | 18 | 6 | 4 | .864 |
| Samuel Floyd, WR | 1 | 1 | 1 | 1 | 0 | .667 |

Triple Play—Gates, I. Gimenez.

## THIRD BASEMEN

| Player and Club | G. | PO. | A. | E. | DP. | Pct. |
|---|---|---|---|---|---|---|
| Samuel Floyd, WR | 5 | 8 | 7 | 0 | 0 | 1.000 |
| McLaren, Dub | 3 | 1 | 7 | 0 | 0 | 1.000 |
| Twellman, Dub | 2 | 1 | 4 | 0 | 0 | 1.000 |
| Polanco, Dub | 1 | 1 | 3 | 0 | 0 | 1.000 |
| Wallace, Wau | 2 | 1 | 3 | 0 | 0 | 1.000 |
| Turner, WR | 1 | 1 | 2 | 0 | 0 | 1.000 |
| Slattery, Cln | 2 | 0 | 1 | 0 | 0 | 1.000 |
| Stipetich, QC | 19 | 10 | 26 | 1 | 3 | .973 |
| Cash, CR | 20 | 15 | 43 | 3 | 2 | .951 |
| Graham, WR | 18 | 6 | 41 | 3 | 5 | .940 |
| Thomasson, Wat | 86 | 62 | 182 | 18 | 14 | .931 |
| Fahrow, QC | 69 | 46 | 100 | 11 | 2 | .930 |
| Sain, WR | 59 | 33 | 121 | 13 | 14 | .922 |
| Rolle, Wau | 79 | 62 | 150 | 19 | 13 | .918 |
| Bartell, Cln | 45 | 28 | 96 | 12 | 8 | .912 |
| Roche, Dan | 40 | 37 | 72 | 11 | 2 | .908 |
| SMITH, DUB | 98 | 85 | 139 | 22 | 17 | .907 |
| Lee, CR | 104 | 79 | 230 | 34 | 16 | .901 |
| Storti, WR | 47 | 28 | 108 | 15 | 7 | .901 |
| Rasmussen, Bur | 30 | 20 | 61 | 9 | 3 | .900 |
| Meyer, Dan | 11 | 6 | 21 | 3 | 1 | .900 |
| Thomas, Apl | 9 | 7 | 27 | 4 | 1 | .895 |
| Guerrero, Dan | 84 | 83 | 165 | 30 | 11 | .892 |
| Seidholz, Apl | 48 | 49 | 92 | 17 | 6 | .892 |
| Carter, Cln | 80 | 65 | 138 | 25 | 10 | .890 |
| Crosta, Apl | 3 | 2 | 6 | 1 | 1 | .889 |
| Bell, Apl | 07 | 57 | 137 | 25 | 12 | .888 |
| Castillo, Wau | 55 | 39 | 109 | 19 | 6 | .886 |
| Gonzalez, Wat | 42 | 31 | 69 | 13 | 7 | .885 |
| Holmberg, Bur | 103 | 97 | 183 | 38 | 17 | .881 |
| Schoenhaus, CR | 6 | 9 | 13 | 3 | 2 | .880 |
| Alvarado, Dub | 17 | 6 | 14 | 3 | 1 | .870 |
| Person, QC | 45 | 41 | 57 | 16 | 0 | .860 |
| Hunt, Cln | 3 | 1 | 5 | 1 | 0 | .857 |
| Tatis, Dub | 23 | 21 | 25 | 8 | 2 | .852 |
| Bates, Cln | 3 | 2 | 6 | 2 | 1 | .800 |
| Nerone, Apl | 2 | 0 | 4 | 1 | 0 | .800 |
| Palmer, Apl | 2 | 1 | 3 | 1 | 0 | .800 |
| Ferrer, Wau | 2 | 0 | 3 | 1 | 0 | .750 |
| Wilson, WR | 2 | 1 | 5 | 3 | 2 | .667 |
| Mann, Wau | 1 | 1 | 1 | 1 | 0 | .667 |
| Tanner, Wat | 2 | 0 | 2 | 1 | 0 | .667 |
| Caughey, WR | 1 | 0 | 3 | 2 | 1 | .600 |
| Schultz, Apl | 3 | 1 | 1 | 2 | 0 | .500 |

Triple Play—Guerrero.

## SHORTSTOPS

| Player and Club | G. | PO. | A. | E. | DP. | Pct. |
|---|---|---|---|---|---|---|
| Woodbrey, CR | 1 | 2 | 5 | 0 | 0 | 1.000 |
| Hunt, Cln | 1 | 2 | 0 | 0 | 0 | 1.000 |
| Rolle, Wau | 1 | 2 | 0 | 0 | 0 | 1.000 |
| Fahrow, QC | 19 | 32 | 49 | 2 | 6 | .976 |
| Cash, CR | 22 | 36 | 67 | 6 | 8 | .945 |
| Thomas, Apl | 19 | 33 | 52 | 5 | 11 | .944 |
| WAGNER, CLN | 118 | 175 | 339 | 31 | 40 | .943 |
| Moreta, Wat | 16 | 17 | 31 | 3 | 5 | .941 |
| Meyer, Dan | 9 | 3 | 26 | 2 | 1 | .935 |
| Kordosky, WR | 71 | 114 | 195 | 22 | 38 | .934 |
| Rasmussen, Bur | 103 | 148 | 307 | 34 | 46 | .930 |
| Caughey, WR | 55 | 74 | 157 | 18 | 18 | .928 |

## SHORTSTOPS—Continued

| Player and Club | G. | PO. | A. | E. | DP. | Pct. |
|---|---|---|---|---|---|---|
| Mulliniks, QC | 52 | 82 | 136 | 17 | 18 | .928 |
| Ferrer, Wau | 42 | 50 | 119 | 14 | 26 | .923 |
| Mann, Wau | 80 | 98 | 249 | 30 | 40 | .920 |
| Rogers, Dan | 124 | 166 | 356 | 47 | 50 | .917 |
| Maropis, Apl | 15 | 18 | 37 | 5 | 5 | .917 |
| Wallace, Wau | 9 | 11 | 22 | 3 | 2 | .917 |
| Alvarado, Dub | 29 | 44 | 65 | 10 | 10 | .916 |
| Haynes, Dub | 29 | 34 | 63 | 9 | 11 | .915 |
| Rosario, Bur | 32 | 48 | 106 | 15 | 12 | .911 |
| de los Santos, CR | 107 | 160 | 295 | 45 | 43 | .910 |
| Barranca, Wat | 64 | 74 | 197 | 27 | 28 | .909 |
| Tatis, Dub | 53 | 68 | 101 | 17 | 22 | .909 |
| Samuel Floyd, WR | 5 | 8 | 12 | 2 | 1 | .909 |
| Lacy, Wat | 45 | 71 | 158 | 25 | 17 | .902 |
| Miller, QC | 56 | 63 | 128 | 21 | 13 | .901 |
| Kelly, Cln | 25 | 16 | 33 | 6 | 3 | .891 |
| Richartz, Apl | 92 | 120 | 220 | 42 | 36 | .890 |
| Gonzalez, Wat | 12 | 14 | 25 | 8 | 3 | .830 |
| Polanco, Dub | 30 | 34 | 76 | 23 | 8 | .827 |
| Mercado, Apl | 5 | 4 | 11 | 5 | 0 | .750 |
| Bianco, Apl | 1 | 0 | 0 | 1 | 0 | .000 |

Triple Play—Wagner.

## OUTFIELDERS

| Player and Club | G. | PO. | A. | E. | DP. | Pct. |
|---|---|---|---|---|---|---|
| Filkins, Cln* | 25 | 45 | 3 | 0 | 1 | 1.000 |
| Ayers, CR | 28 | 37 | 2 | 0 | 0 | 1.000 |
| Beamon, Wat* | 24 | 33 | 5 | 0 | 2 | 1.000 |
| Holmberg, Bur | 20 | 30 | 1 | 0 | 1 | 1.000 |
| Schoenhaus, CR | 11 | 16 | 2 | 0 | 1 | 1.000 |
| Alvarado, Dub | 12 | 17 | 0 | 0 | 0 | 1.000 |
| Silverio, Wat | 11 | 15 | 0 | 0 | 0 | 1.000 |
| R. Kelly, QC | 9 | 12 | 1 | 0 | 0 | 1.000 |
| Holland, Apl* | 9 | 12 | 0 | 0 | 0 | 1.000 |
| Carroll, Cln* | 6 | 10 | 0 | 0 | 0 | 1.000 |
| Wheeler, Apl | 10 | 8 | 1 | 0 | 0 | 1.000 |
| Leonardo, Apl* | 8 | 7 | 1 | 0 | 0 | 1.000 |
| Laseter, Wat | 10 | 7 | 1 | 0 | 0 | 1.000 |
| Carter, Wau | 4 | 5 | 1 | 0 | 0 | 1.000 |
| Shippy, Cln | 3 | 5 | 0 | 0 | 0 | 1.000 |
| Channel, WR | 13 | 5 | 0 | 0 | 0 | 1.000 |
| Price, Apl | 2 | 2 | 1 | 0 | 0 | 1.000 |
| Foley, Apl | 1 | 2 | 0 | 0 | 0 | 1.000 |
| Stipetich, QC | 1 | 2 | 0 | 0 | 0 | 1.000 |
| Fahrow, QC | 2 | 1 | 1 | 0 | 0 | 1.000 |
| Fischetti, Dan | 2 | 2 | 0 | 0 | 0 | 1.000 |
| Holmgren, WR | 6 | 2 | 0 | 0 | 0 | 1.000 |
| Castillo, WR | 1 | 0 | 1 | 0 | 0 | 1.000 |
| Uremovich, Cln | 1 | 0 | 1 | 0 | 0 | 1.000 |
| Killingsworth, Bur | 2 | 1 | 0 | 0 | 0 | 1.000 |
| Taylor, QC | 77 | 117 | 3 | 1 | 0 | .992 |
| Ditto, Dan | 71 | 113 | 5 | 1 | 1 | .992 |
| Estes, WR* | 55 | 94 | 7 | 1 | 2 | .990 |
| Ray, CR | 77 | 155 | 5 | 2 | 0 | .988 |
| Nerone, Apl | 82 | 124 | 10 | 2 | 1 | .985 |
| R. Gimenez, Cln | 80 | 125 | 6 | 2 | 1 | .985 |
| BOSLEY, QC* | 105 | 206 | 2 | 4 | 0 | .981 |
| Ferrell, CR | 36 | 44 | 4 | 1 | 2 | .980 |
| Youngbauer, WR | 50 | 86 | 7 | 2 | 1 | .979 |
| Garrison, Cln | 30 | 42 | 4 | 1 | 1 | .979 |
| Curran, Wat | 77 | 131 | 4 | 3 | 2 | .978 |
| Hill, WR | 104 | 123 | 8 | 3 | 0 | .978 |
| Felda, CR | 65 | 88 | 3 | 2 | 0 | .978 |
| Rodriguez, Bur | 126 | 287 | 8 | 7 | 1 | .977 |
| Washington, QC | 34 | 43 | 0 | 1 | 0 | .977 |
| Toman, Apl* | 112 | 209 | 11 | 7 | 1 | .969 |
| Guerrero, Dan | 20 | 28 | 3 | 1 | 0 | .969 |
| Robles, Apl | 31 | 29 | 2 | 1 | 0 | .969 |
| Rushde, Dan* | 98 | 137 | 16 | 5 | 8 | .968 |
| Allen, QC | 43 | 54 | 6 | 2 | 0 | .968 |
| Centeno, Cln* | 59 | 82 | 5 | 3 | 1 | .967 |
| Amerson, WR | 104 | 149 | 9 | 6 | 4 | .963 |
| Puhl, Dub | 87 | 149 | 5 | 6 | 1 | .963 |
| Quirk, Wau* | 78 | 128 | 1 | 5 | 0 | .963 |
| Tatis, Dub | 26 | 21 | 5 | 1 | 0 | .963 |
| Wilson, WR | 58 | 93 | 9 | 4 | 2 | .962 |
| Marla, Bur | 13 | 21 | 1 | 1 | 0 | .957 |
| Wallace, Wau | 29 | 41 | 2 | 2 | 0 | .956 |
| Rima, Dub | 83 | 121 | 6 | 6 | 0 | .955 |
| Guerrero, QC | 100 | 137 | 9 | 7 | 2 | .954 |
| Michael, Cln* | 102 | 171 | 8 | 9 | 1 | .952 |
| Haas, Cln | 27 | 38 | 2 | 2 | 1 | .952 |
| Kline, Cln* | 22 | 38 | 1 | 2 | 0 | .951 |
| Skoglund, Wau | 96 | 146 | 5 | 8 | 0 | .950 |
| Davis, Cln | 10 | 17 | 2 | 1 | 0 | .950 |
| Mejias, Bur | 55 | 104 | 8 | 6 | 0 | .949 |
| Yurak, CR | 47 | 70 | 2 | 4 | 1 | .947 |
| Rolle, Wau | 13 | 16 | 2 | 1 | 1 | .947 |
| Strong, CR* | 60 | 83 | 5 | 5 | 0 | .946 |
| Bhagwat, CR | 27 | 49 | 4 | 3 | 0 | .946 |
| Contreras, Wau | 117 | 161 | 9 | 10 | 2 | .944 |
| Person, QC | 18 | 32 | 0 | 2 | 0 | .941 |
| Wilson, Wat | 126 | 249 | 17 | 17 | 5 | .940 |
| Thomas, WR* | 23 | 27 | 4 | 2 | 1 | .939 |
| Olszta, Apl | 123 | 194 | 4 | 13 | 1 | .938 |
| Plut, Dan | 64 | 100 | 6 | 7 | 1 | .938 |
| Cannon, Dub | 97 | 160 | 17 | 12 | 8 | .937 |
| Smith, Bur | 54 | 81 | 5 | 6 | 1 | .935 |
| Grady, Wau | 49 | 81 | 2 | 6 | 1 | .933 |
| Kiner, Wau | 19 | 13 | 1 | 1 | 0 | .933 |
| Parker, Wat | 106 | 119 | 5 | 9 | 0 | .932 |
| Moore, CR | 23 | 40 | 0 | 3 | 0 | .930 |
| Goetz, Dub | 10 | 13 | 0 | 1 | 0 | .929 |
| Ervin, Bur | 93 | 142 | 9 | 12 | 2 | .926 |
| Drake, Dub | 41 | 58 | 3 | 5 | 0 | .924 |
| deLeeuw, Wat | 46 | 54 | 4 | 5 | 1 | .921 |
| Santos, Dan | 96 | 134 | 8 | 14 | 1 | .910 |
| Carter, Cln | 35 | 56 | 4 | 6 | 1 | .909 |
| de la Cruz, Dan | 50 | 57 | 10 | 7 | 1 | .905 |
| Cash, CR | 7 | 9 | 0 | 1 | 0 | .900 |
| Rvals, Wau | 8 | 8 | 1 | 1 | 0 | .900 |
| Pujols, Dub | 17 | 14 | 3 | 2 | 1 | .895 |
| Roche, Dan | 4 | 8 | 0 | 1 | 0 | .889 |
| Moreno, Dub | 35 | 37 | 2 | 6 | 0 | .867 |
| Schultz, Apl | 8 | 13 | 0 | 2 | 0 | .867 |
| Osofsky, Dub | 21 | 18 | 1 | 3 | 0 | .864 |
| Jones, Bur | 38 | 58 | 3 | 10 | 0 | .859 |
| Stafford, Bur | 6 | 4 | 2 | 1 | 0 | .857 |
| Tanner, Wat | 8 | 3 | 2 | 1 | 0 | .833 |
| Stamps, CR | 21 | 18 | 0 | 5 | 0 | .783 |
| Galvez, CR | 4 | 4 | 0 | 2 | 0 | .667 |
| Smotherman, Wat | 4 | 2 | 0 | 1 | 0 | .667 |
| Parish, Dan | 1 | 1 | 0 | 1 | 0 | .500 |

## CATCHERS

| Player and Club | G. | PO. | A. | E. | DP. | PB. | Pct. |
|---|---|---|---|---|---|---|---|
| Kiner, Wau | 2 | 13 | 1 | 0 | 0 | 1 | 1.000 |
| Stanley, Floyd, WR | 1 | 7 | 0 | 0 | 0 | 1 | 1.000 |
| Garrison, Cln | 1 | 4 | 0 | 0 | 0 | 0 | 1.000 |
| Holmberg, Bur | 1 | 4 | 0 | 0 | 0 | 0 | 1.000 |
| McClellan, Apl | 1 | 4 | 0 | 0 | 0 | 0 | 1.000 |
| Martinson, QC | 38 | 247 | 28 | 2 | 1 | 4 | .993 |
| Young, CR | 23 | 121 | 8 | 1 | 0 | 7 | .992 |
| EDMONDSON, W | 88 | 568 | 59 | 7 | 10 | 26 | .9889 |
| Pujols, Dub | 78 | 558 | 56 | 7 | 5 | 16 | .9887 |
| Price, Apl | 54 | 325 | 46 | 5 | 2 | 7 | .987 |
| Palmer, Apl | 69 | 379 | 40 | 6 | 4 | 19 | .986 |
| Graham, WR | 29 | 169 | 26 | 3 | 5 | 9 | .985 |
| Richmond, WR | 11 | 58 | 9 | 1 | 0 | 1 | .985 |
| Washington, QC | 36 | 256 | 24 | 5 | 2 | 6 | .982 |
| Slattery, Cln | 48 | 247 | 29 | 5 | 1 | 7 | .982 |
| D. P. Kelly, QC | 33 | 239 | 22 | 5 | 2 | 6 | .981 |
| Hughes, CR | 14 | 95 | 11 | 2 | 0 | 3 | .981 |
| Patterson, Wau | 9 | 48 | 4 | 1 | 0 | 0 | .981 |
| Bulling, WR | 95 | 596 | 51 | 13 | 10 | 19 | .980 |
| Shippy, Cln | 67 | 443 | 41 | 10 | 4 | 9 | .980 |
| McLaren, Dub | 61 | 375 | 36 | 9 | 7 | 12 | .979 |
| Dodd, CR | 43 | 288 | 23 | 7 | 6 | 14 | .978 |
| Parish, Dan | 35 | 199 | 20 | 5 | 4 | 8 | .978 |
| Richards, Dan | 20 | 130 | 19 | 4 | 1 | 2 | .974 |

## CATCHERS—Continued

| Player and Club | G. | PO. | A. | E. | DP. | PB. | Pct. |
|---|---|---|---|---|---|---|---|
| Buffamoyer, Bur | 93 | 573 | 58 | 19 | 4 | 8 | .971 |
| Trucks, Apl | 11 | 59 | 9 | 2 | 0 | 3 | .971 |
| Soriano, Dan | 36 | 243 | 20 | 8 | 3 | 13 | .970 |
| Benedetti, CR | 50 | 271 | 44 | 10 | 2 | 22 | .969 |
| Sanchez, Bur | 17 | 90 | 3 | 3 | 0 | 5 | .969 |
| Uremovich, Cln | 18 | 108 | 10 | 4 | 0 | 1 | .967 |
| Tanner, Wat | 25 | 129 | 10 | 5 | 0 | 7 | .965 |
| Yost, Wau | 79 | 450 | 42 | 19 | 7 | 20 | .963 |
| Jackson, Apl | 7 | 46 | 4 | 2 | 0 | 1 | .962 |
| Hough, Wau | 39 | 214 | 24 | 10 | 1 | 5 | .960 |
| Stafford, Bur | 26 | 146 | 15 | 7 | 5 | 3 | .958 |
| Cliburn, QC | 24 | 149 | 11 | 7 | 0 | 0 | .958 |
| Smotherman, Wat | 21 | 136 | 1 | 6 | 0 | 8 | .958 |
| Peguero, Dan | 42 | 254 | 29 | 13 | 3 | 5 | .956 |
| Goetz, Dub | 9 | 17 | 1 | 1 | 0 | 0 | .947 |
| Tatis, Dub | 1 | 0 | 0 | 1 | 0 | 0 | .000 |

Triple Play—Edmondson.

## PITCHERS

| Player and Club | G. | PO. | A. | E. | DP. | Pct. |
|---|---|---|---|---|---|---|
| CLINE, CR | 23 | 11 | 28 | 0 | 1 | 1.000 |
| Thompson, CR* | 40 | 4 | 26 | 0 | 0 | 1.000 |
| Berenguer, Wau | 18 | 5 | 20 | 0 | 1 | 1.000 |
| Perkins, Cln | 56 | 2 | 23 | 0 | 0 | 1.000 |
| May, WR | 17 | 5 | 16 | 0 | 1 | 1.000 |
| Meche, QC | 27 | 2 | 19 | 0 | 3 | 1.000 |
| Wilson, CR | 36 | 4 | 17 | 0 | 0 | 1.000 |
| Bock, Apl* | 29 | 2 | 19 | 0 | 1 | 1.000 |
| Castillo, WR | 23 | 2 | 18 | 0 | 2 | 1.000 |
| Heinen, CR | 55 | 7 | 12 | 0 | 0 | 1.000 |
| Attardi, Apl* | 24 | 2 | 16 | 0 | 0 | 1.000 |
| Cuen, Dub | 13 | 7 | 10 | 0 | 0 | 1.000 |
| Frola, Cln-Wau* | 24 | 1 | 15 | 0 | 0 | 1.000 |
| Leonard, Wau | 11 | 1 | 16 | 0 | 0 | 1.000 |
| Hasley, Dub* | 17 | 0 | 15 | 0 | 0 | 1.000 |
| Weeber, Dub | 15 | 3 | 10 | 0 | 0 | 1.000 |
| Repke, Dan* | 24 | 3 | 10 | 0 | 0 | 1.000 |
| Dinkelmeyer, Cln | 33 | 2 | 10 | 0 | 1 | 1.000 |
| Bass, Wat | 10 | 7 | 4 | 0 | 0 | 1.000 |
| Hart, Wat | 14 | 1 | 10 | 0 | 1 | 1.000 |
| Powers, QC | 19 | 3 | 8 | 0 | 2 | 1.000 |
| Quisenberry, Wat | 20 | 4 | 7 | 0 | 0 | 1.000 |
| Massimini, WR* | 11 | 1 | 9 | 0 | 0 | 1.000 |
| Moore, Dan | 13 | 2 | 7 | 0 | 0 | 1.000 |
| Kelley, QC | 17 | 3 | 6 | 0 | 0 | 1.000 |
| Peterson, Wat | 34 | 4 | 5 | 0 | 0 | 1.000 |
| Speck, Wau | 8 | 2 | 6 | 0 | 0 | 1.000 |
| Caneira, QC | 9 | 3 | 5 | 0 | 0 | 1.000 |
| Sylvia, Bur | 10 | 3 | 3 | 0 | 0 | 1.000 |
| Bemis, WR* | 15 | 2 | 4 | 0 | 0 | 1.000 |
| Smith, CR* | 3 | 0 | 5 | 0 | 1 | 1.000 |
| Lauzerique, Dub | 16 | 0 | 5 | 0 | 0 | 1.000 |
| Lahey, Wau | 3 | 1 | 3 | 0 | 0 | 1.000 |
| Blood, WR | 11 | 0 | 4 | 0 | 0 | 1.000 |
| Lehman, Apl | 14 | 0 | 4 | 0 | 0 | 1.000 |
| Riddle, CR* | 14 | 0 | 4 | 0 | 0 | 1.000 |
| Johnson, Wau | 2 | 1 | 0 | 0 | 0 | 1.000 |
| Blanco, Dub | 9 | 1 | 2 | 0 | 0 | 1.000 |
| Flanders, Wat | 11 | 1 | 2 | 0 | 0 | 1.000 |
| Srock, WR* | 11 | 1 | 2 | 0 | 0 | 1.000 |
| Costell, Dub* | 8 | 0 | 2 | 0 | 0 | 1.000 |
| Jimenez, QC | 12 | 0 | 2 | 0 | 0 | 1.000 |
| Perez, QC | 18 | 1 | 1 | 0 | 0 | 1.000 |
| Goulding, Dan | 1 | 0 | 1 | 0 | 0 | 1.000 |
| Best, Apl | 2 | 0 | 1 | 0 | 0 | 1.000 |
| Madden, Cln | 2 | 1 | 0 | 0 | 0 | 1.000 |
| Clark, Wat | 23 | 10 | 40 | 1 | 0 | .980 |
| Sempscrott, Wat* | 23 | 6 | 28 | 1 | 2 | .971 |
| Lantz, Cln | 12 | 7 | 26 | 1 | 0 | .971 |
| Edge, Bur | 17 | 3 | 27 | 1 | 2 | .968 |
| Branch, Wat | 10 | 9 | 18 | 1 | 1 | .964 |
| Knicely, Dub | 26 | 11 | 15 | 1 | 1 | .963 |
| McManus, Cln | 10 | 7 | 18 | 1 | 1 | .962 |
| Johnson, CR* | 22 | 4 | 21 | 1 | 1 | .962 |
| Murray, Cln* | 31 | 3 | 22 | 1 | 0 | .962 |
| Conn, Bur | 50 | 9 | 16 | 1 | 1 | .962 |
| Coulter, Apl* | 31 | 4 | 20 | 1 | 0 | .960 |
| Monroe, Apl | 23 | 14 | 27 | 2 | 0 | .953 |
| Trella, Cln | 24 | 8 | 32 | 2 | 1 | .952 |
| Dixon, Dub | 32 | 2 | 18 | 1 | 0 | .952 |
| M. Williams, Wat* | 21 | 9 | 30 | 2 | 0 | .951 |
| Gaton, Bur | 36 | 4 | 15 | 1 | 0 | .950 |
| Heredia, Dan | 26 | 10 | 26 | 2 | 1 | .947 |
| Larkin, Wat | 17 | 4 | 14 | 1 | 2 | .947 |
| Laurent, Dan | 30 | 6 | 12 | 1 | 0 | .947 |
| DeMerritt, Bur | 25 | 10 | 25 | 2 | 1 | .946 |
| Roof, WR | 29 | 8 | 27 | 2 | 0 | .946 |
| Komadina, Apl* | 19 | 1 | 16 | 1 | 0 | .944 |
| Haas, Bur | 25 | 6 | 27 | 2 | 2 | .943 |
| Knapp, Apl | 14 | 1 | 15 | 1 | 0 | .941 |
| Roslund, QC* | 38 | 4 | 12 | 1 | 0 | .941 |
| Olson, WR* | 25 | 12 | 50 | 4 | 2 | .939 |
| Beitey, CR | 26 | 4 | 27 | 2 | 1 | .939 |
| Wilson, Dan | 29 | 22 | 35 | 4 | 0 | .934 |
| Keller, Dan | 30 | 6 | 22 | 2 | 0 | .933 |
| Smith, WR | 26 | 2 | 12 | 1 | 0 | .933 |
| G. Williams, Wat* | 19 | 4 | 23 | 2 | 3 | .931 |
| Slettvet, QC | 23 | 7 | 46 | 4 | 3 | .930 |
| Bobinger, Dan* | 30 | 11 | 29 | 3 | 4 | .930 |
| Harper, Wau | 25 | 4 | 9 | 1 | 2 | .929 |
| Quintero, WR | 23 | 11 | 27 | 3 | 1 | .927 |
| Kautzer, Apl | 28 | 7 | 30 | 3 | 4 | .925 |
| Pena, Bur* | 19 | 2 | 10 | 1 | 0 | .923 |
| Slaymaker, Bur* | 21 | 1 | 11 | 1 | 0 | .923 |
| Keefe, Dan | 45 | 3 | 9 | 1 | 1 | .923 |
| Young, QC* | 19 | 1 | 22 | 2 | 1 | .920 |
| Hodges, CR | 14 | 7 | 15 | 2 | 0 | .917 |
| Hartzell, QC | 24 | 1 | 10 | 1 | 0 | .917 |
| Bradley, CR | 30 | 2 | 19 | 2 | 0 | .913 |
| Heenan, Dub | 6 | 3 | 7 | 1 | 0 | .909 |
| Botting, QC* | 20 | 0 | 10 | 1 | 0 | .909 |
| Kenny, CR* | 17 | 1 | 18 | 2 | 2 | .905 |
| Alfaro, Dub | 45 | 9 | 28 | 4 | 2 | .902 |
| Rozema, Cln | 27 | 8 | 28 | 4 | 1 | .900 |
| Mendoza, Dub | 15 | 4 | 14 | 2 | 0 | .900 |
| Brisbin, QC | 17 | 4 | 14 | 2 | 0 | .900 |
| Cummings, Wau* | 19 | 11 | 13 | 3 | 1 | .889 |
| Garcia, WR | 22 | 2 | 6 | 1 | 0 | .889 |
| McKinney, Wat | 11 | 12 | 18 | 4 | 1 | .882 |
| Dean, Dub | 28 | 5 | 24 | 4 | 2 | .879 |
| Baker, Cln | 9 | 0 | 7 | 1 | 1 | .875 |
| King, Apl* | 21 | 1 | 6 | 1 | 0 | .875 |
| Barger, Wau* | 34 | 0 | 7 | 1 | 0 | .875 |
| Barrett, Dan | 21 | 11 | 23 | 5 | 2 | .872 |
| Dorsey, QC | 25 | 7 | 13 | 3 | 0 | .870 |
| deLeon, Dub | 29 | 2 | 18 | 3 | 2 | .870 |
| Olsen, Wat | 9 | 4 | 9 | 2 | 0 | .867 |
| Driskill, Wau | 35 | 6 | 7 | 2 | 2 | .867 |
| Combs, Anl | 42 | 6 | 18 | 4 | 0 | .857 |
| Jackson, Wau | 5 | 2 | 4 | 1 | 1 | .857 |
| Klein, Anl | 20 | 1 | 5 | 1 | 0 | .857 |
| Reinke, Cln* | 13 | 8 | 14 | 4 | 1 | .846 |
| Gomby, Cln | 21 | 6 | 15 | 4 | 1 | .840 |
| Williams, Anl | 6 | 1 | 4 | 1 | 0 | .833 |
| Johnson, WR | 24 | 0 | 5 | 1 | 0 | .833 |
| Aloi, Dub | 22 | 6 | 21 | 6 | 1 | .818 |
| Sander, Wau | 12 | 6 | 12 | 4 | 1 | .818 |
| Pacella, Wau | 19 | 8 | 22 | 7 | 3 | .811 |
| Cort, Bur | 24 | 7 | 22 | 7 | 1 | .806 |
| Richardson, Wau | 23 | 8 | 17 | 6 | 1 | .806 |
| Whiting, Bur* | 14 | 3 | 5 | 2 | 0 | .800 |
| Geddes, Apl | 5 | 1 | 3 | 1 | 0 | .800 |
| Biguslak, Dan | 11 | 0 | 4 | 1 | 0 | .800 |
| Mueller, Bur | 25 | 3 | 12 | 4 | 1 | .789 |
| Anvzeski, Apl* | 27 | 5 | 21 | 7 | 0 | .788 |
| Arthur, WR | 24 | 3 | 8 | 3 | 0 | .786 |
| Yount, Bur | 4 | 2 | 5 | 2 | 0 | .778 |
| Castillo, QC | 9 | 0 | 10 | 3 | 1 | .769 |
| Callis, Cln* | 28 | 5 | 11 | 5 | 0 | .762 |
| Holm, Cln | 24 | 4 | 8 | 4 | 0 | .750 |

## PITCHERS—Continued

| Player and Club | G. | PO. | A. | E. | DP. | Pct. | Player and Club | G. | PO. | A. | E. | DP. | Pct. |
|---|---|---|---|---|---|---|---|---|---|---|---|---|---|
| Souza, Wat* | 32 | 3 | 6 | 3 | 1 | .750 | Jones, WR | 17 | 0 | 2 | 1 | 0 | .667 |
| Sanchez, Dub | 6 | 0 | 3 | 1 | 0 | .750 | Smith, Dan | 41 | 2 | 5 | 4 | 1 | .636 |
| Groff, WR* | 14 | 1 | 2 | 1 | 0 | .750 | Pladson, Dub | 17 | 0 | 6 | 4 | 0 | .600 |
| Frankum, Wau | 18 | 7 | 15 | 8 | 2 | .733 | Howard, QC* | 4 | 1 | 3 | 3 | 0 | .571 |
| Hrovat, Wat | 25 | 1 | 4 | 2 | 0 | .714 | Loehr, Apl | 17 | 0 | 2 | 2 | 0 | .500 |
| Nix, CR | 14 | 0 | 7 | 3 | 0 | .700 | Lea, Wau | 2 | 0 | 1 | 0 | 0 | .000 |

The following pitchers do not have any recorded accepted chances at that position; therefore, are not listed in the fielding averages: Cluck*, Falcon*, M. Garcia, R. Lee*, Torreano*, Wulfemeyer appeared as a pinch-hitter only.

## CLUB PITCHING

| Club | G. | CG. | ShO. | Sv. | IP. | H. | R. | ER. | HR. | BB. | Int. BB. | HB. | SO. | WP. | Bk. | ERA. |
|---|---|---|---|---|---|---|---|---|---|---|---|---|---|---|---|---|
| Waterloo | 130 | 41 | 12 | 29 | 1085 | 910 | 437 | 315 | 52 | 405 | 20 | 24 | 797 | 60 | 14 | 2.61 |
| Clinton | 129 | 39 | 18 | 16 | 1093 | 915 | 445 | 328 | 26 | 478 | 34 | 23 | 757 | 49 | 9 | 2.70 |
| Quad Cities | 125 | 38 | 13 | 18 | 1040 | 840 | 432 | 321 | 43 | 409 | 5 | 15 | 841 | 29 | 11 | 2.78 |
| Danville | 128 | 36 | 6 | 14 | 1062 | 986 | 553 | 382 | 54 | 498 | 12 | 28 | 787 | 55 | 15 | 3.24 |
| Wisconsin Rapids | 129 | 35 | 15 | 23 | 1061 | 951 | 505 | 386 | 56 | 472 | 30 | 23 | 798 | 54 | 13 | 3.27 |
| Burlington | 130 | 46 | 10 | 13 | 1123 | 1021 | 571 | 424 | 59 | 475 | 22 | 27 | 762 | 55 | 9 | 3.40 |
| Dubuque | 126 | 29 | 12 | 11 | 1060 | 955 | 545 | 423 | 52 | 552 | 43 | 33 | 887 | 81 | 9 | 3.59 |
| Appleton | 127 | 25 | 6 | 16 | 1049 | 1005 | 587 | 417 | 39 | 516 | 20 | 35 | 786 | 72 | 9 | 3.61 |
| Cedar Rapids | 128 | 33 | 5 | 13 | 1068 | 1061 | 604 | 439 | 70 | 460 | 37 | 33 | 726 | 61 | 9 | 3.70 |
| Wausau | 128 | 41 | 10 | 16 | 1032 | 952 | 609 | 450 | 70 | 522 | 13 | 45 | 690 | 83 | 8 | 3.92 |

## PITCHERS' RECORDS

(Leading Qualifiers for Earned-Run Average Leadership—104 or More Innings)
*Throws lefthanded.

| Pitcher—Club | G. | GS. | CG. | ShO. | W. | L. | Sv. | Pct. | IP. | H. | R. | ER. | HR. | BB. | Int. BB. | HB. | SO. | WP. | ERA. |
|---|---|---|---|---|---|---|---|---|---|---|---|---|---|---|---|---|---|---|---|
| Aloi, Dub | 22 | 13 | 8 | 4 | 8 | 4 | 0 | .667 | 117 | 106 | 36 | 22 | 3 | 32 | 3 | 2 | 101 | 1 | 1.69 |
| Trella, Cin | 24 | 24 | 11 | 5 | 11 | 9 | 0 | .550 | 164 | 116 | 46 | 32 | 1 | 77 | 2 | 3 | 136 | 9 | 1.76 |
| Sempsrott, Wat* | 23 | 15 | 4 | 3 | 8 | 5 | 1 | .615 | 111 | 89 | 32 | 24 | 0 | 25 | 2 | 3 | 70 | 5 | 1.95 |
| Haas, Bur | 25 | 24 | 12 | 3 | 11 | 8 | 0 | .579 | 117 | 149 | 66 | 39 | 6 | 49 | 3 | 0 | 146 | 8 | 2.05 |
| Rozema, Cln | 27 | 19 | 9 | 5 | 14 | 5 | 0 | .737 | 164 | 128 | 50 | 38 | 1 | 32 | 2 | 2 | 123 | 3 | 2.09 |
| Dorsey, QC | 25 | 24 | 4 | 15 | 3 | 4 | 0 | .833 | 161 | 114 | 49 | 38 | 6 | 56 | 0 | 2 | 161 | 4 | 2.12 |
| G. Williams, Wat* | 19 | 17 | 4 | 1 | 12 | 2 | 0 | .857 | 116 | 75 | 40 | 28 | 2 | 47 | 0 | 2 | 112 | 9 | 2.17 |
| Roof, WR | 19 | 19 | 5 | 2 | 8 | 9 | 1 | .471 | 152 | 133 | 58 | 38 | 7 | 37 | 3 | 3 | 104 | 1 | 2.25 |
| Botting, QC* | 20 | 19 | 7 | 2 | 8 | 9 | 0 | .471 | 115 | 91 | 48 | 33 | 9 | 55 | 0 | 2 | 125 | 2 | 2.58 |
| Clark, Wat | 23 | 23 | 7 | 0 | 10 | 6 | 0 | .625 | 146 | 120 | 61 | 42 | 6 | 68 | 1 | 3 | 78 | 11 | 2.59 |

Departmental Leaders: G—Perkins, 56; GS—Bobinger, 29; CG—Bobinger, 15; ShO—Rozema, Trella, 5; W—Bobinger, 17; L—Heredia, Wilson (Danville), 13; SV—Perkins, 13; Pct.—G. Williams, .857; IP—Bobinger, 213; H—Wilson (Danville), 177; R—Bradley, Cline, 92; ER—Bradley, 74; HR—Cline, 14; BB—Olson, 97; IBB—Perkins, 11; HB—Berenguer, Bobinger, Richardson, 8; SO—Bobinger, 201; WP—Feola, 16.

(All Pitchers—Listed Alphabetically)

| Pitcher—Club | G. | GS. | CG. | ShO. | W. | L. | Sv. | Pct. | IP. | H. | R. | ER. | HR. | BB. | Int. BB. | HB. | SO. | WP. | ERA. |
|---|---|---|---|---|---|---|---|---|---|---|---|---|---|---|---|---|---|---|---|
| Alfaro, Dub | 45 | 7 | 4 | 2 | 13 | 8 | 5 | .619 | 126 | 93 | 47 | 39 | 6 | 51 | 7 | 7 | 111 | 6 | 2.79 |
| Aloi, Dub | 22 | 13 | 8 | 4 | 8 | 4 | 0 | .667 | 117 | 106 | 36 | 22 | 3 | 32 | 3 | 2 | 101 | 1 | 1.69 |
| Anyzeski, Apl* | 27 | 13 | 3 | 0 | 5 | 3 | 0 | .625 | 92 | 82 | 43 | 25 | 1 | 34 | 0 | 1 | 61 | 5 | 2.45 |
| Arthur, WR | 24 | 4 | 0 | 0 | 4 | 4 | 0 | .500 | 52 | 46 | 25 | 18 | 0 | 14 | 3 | 1 | 54 | 1 | 3.12 |
| Attardi, Apl* | 24 | 7 | 1 | 0 | 4 | 2 | 1 | .667 | 73 | 78 | 39 | 28 | 1 | 28 | 4 | 3 | 42 | 3 | 3.45 |
| Baker, Cln | 9 | 6 | 0 | 0 | 0 | 4 | 0 | .000 | 35 | 36 | 27 | 19 | 0 | 33 | 2 | 1 | 23 | 2 | 4.89 |
| Barger, Wau* | 34 | 1 | 1 | 0 | 3 | 5 | 7 | .375 | 58 | 48 | 30 | 18 | 2 | 27 | 2 | 2 | 36 | 2 | 2.79 |
| Barrett, Dan | 21 | 20 | 4 | 1 | 8 | 2 | 1 | .800 | 131 | 123 | 63 | 49 | 7 | 44 | 0 | 3 | 94 | 3 | 3.37 |
| Bass, Wat | 10 | 8 | 2 | 0 | 4 | 2 | 0 | .667 | 46 | 39 | 20 | 15 | 1 | 21 | 0 | 1 | 23 | 4 | 2.93 |
| Beitey, CR | 26 | 16 | 8 | 2 | 7 | 8 | 0 | .467 | 123 | 125 | 64 | 44 | 6 | 57 | 2 | 1 | 75 | 11 | 3.22 |
| Bemis, WR* | 15 | 0 | 0 | 0 | 0 | 4 | 0 | .000 | 18 | 10 | 2 | 2 | 0 | 4 | 0 | 0 | 21 | 0 | 1.00 |
| Berenguer, Wau | 18 | 12 | 4 | 1 | 5 | 4 | 1 | .556 | 95 | 83 | 41 | 31 | 4 | 50 | 1 | 8 | 58 | 9 | 2.94 |
| Best, Apl | 2 | 0 | 0 | 0 | 0 | 0 | 0 | .000 | 6 | 6 | 3 | 3 | 0 | 0 | 0 | 0 | 7 | 0 | 4.50 |
| Bigusiak, Dan | 11 | 0 | 0 | 0 | 0 | 0 | 0 | .000 | 11 | 13 | 12 | 7 | 0 | 14 | 0 | 1 | 7 | 1 | 5.73 |
| Blanco, Dub | 9 | 3 | 0 | 0 | 2 | 1 | 0 | .667 | 18 | 17 | 8 | 7 | 1 | 14 | 1 | 1 | 13 | 3 | 3.50 |
| Blood, WR | 11 | 7 | 2 | 0 | 0 | 8 | 0 | .250 | 37 | 46 | 35 | 22 | 5 | 18 | 0 | 0 | 25 | 3 | 5.35 |
| Bobinger, Dan* | 30 | 29 | 15 | 2 | 17 | 7 | 0 | .708 | 213 | 171 | 80 | 62 | 11 | 61 | 2 | 8 | 201 | 10 | 2.62 |
| Bock, Apl* | 29 | 5 | 0 | 0 | 3 | 3 | 4 | .500 | 65 | 63 | 35 | 24 | 2 | 30 | 2 | 1 | 58 | 4 | 3.32 |
| Botting, QC* | 20 | 19 | 7 | 2 | 8 | 9 | 0 | .471 | 115 | 91 | 48 | 33 | 9 | 55 | 0 | 2 | 125 | 2 | 2.58 |
| Bradley, CR | 39 | 17 | 4 | 0 | 4 | 11 | 0 | .267 | 120 | 133 | 92 | 74 | 11 | 60 | 2 | 6 | 68 | 6 | 5.55 |
| Branch, Wat | 10 | 4 | 0 | 0 | 6 | 1 | 0 | .857 | 70 | 56 | 24 | 15 | 3 | 33 | 0 | 3 | 51 | 1 | 1.93 |
| Brisbin, QC | 17 | 15 | 3 | 0 | 5 | 4 | 0 | .556 | 84 | 66 | 35 | 29 | 5 | 48 | 1 | 2 | 72 | 2 | 3.11 |
| Callis, Cln* | 28 | 1 | 0 | 0 | 2 | 3 | 0 | .400 | 47 | 47 | 31 | 16 | 0 | 22 | 2 | 0 | 29 | 3 | 3.06 |
| Caneira, QC | 9 | 9 | 2 | 1 | 7 | 1 | 0 | .875 | 58 | 46 | 19 | 17 | 1 | 18 | 0 | 0 | 49 | 1 | 2.64 |
| Castillo, QC | 9 | 8 | 2 | 0 | 4 | 3 | 0 | .571 | 50 | 47 | 28 | 19 | 2 | 15 | 0 | 0 | 43 | 1 | 3.42 |
| Castillo, WR | 23 | 8 | 2 | 0 | 5 | 2 | 0 | .714 | 75 | 72 | 39 | 26 | 4 | 32 | 2 | 1 | 44 | 7 | 3.12 |
| Clark, Wat | 23 | 23 | 7 | 0 | 10 | 6 | 0 | .625 | 146 | 120 | 61 | 42 | 6 | 68 | 1 | 3 | 78 | 11 | 2.59 |
| Cline, CR | 23 | 23 | 4 | 1 | 5 | 12 | 0 | .294 | 152 | 166 | 92 | 65 | 14 | 52 | 4 | 3 | 108 | 6 | 3.85 |
| Cluck, Dub* | 1 | 0 | 0 | 0 | 0 | 0 | 0 | .000 | 1 | 0 | 0 | 0 | 0 | 0 | 0 | 0 | 3 | 0 | 0.00 |

| Pitcher—Club | G | GS | CG | ShO | W | L | Sv | Pct. | IP | H | R | ER | HR | BB | Int. BB | HB | SO | WP | ERA. |
|---|---|---|---|---|---|---|---|---|---|---|---|---|---|---|---|---|---|---|---|
| Combs, Apl | 42 | 2 | 1 | 0 | 6 | 8 | 4 | .429 | 91 | 88 | 49 | 29 | 3 | 31 | 2 | 4 | 73 | 3 | 2.87 |
| Conn, Bur | 50 | 0 | 0 | 0 | 6 | 7 | 11 | .462 | 89 | 84 | 37 | 31 | 2 | 31 | 7 | 7 | 51 | 0 | 3.13 |
| Cort, Bur | 24 | 24 | 12 | 3 | 14 | 9 | 0 | .609 | 188 | 161 | 85 | 67 | 10 | 75 | 0 | 1 | 152 | 3 | 3.21 |
| Costell, Dub* | 8 | 3 | 0 | 0 | 0 | 0 | 0 | .000 | 20 | 15 | 11 | 11 | 2 | 26 | 1 | 0 | 17 | 4 | 4.95 |
| Coulter, Apl* | 31 | 11 | 2 | 0 | 3 | 7 | 1 | .300 | 105 | 81 | 50 | 35 | 2 | 58 | 1 | 4 | 82 | 7 | 3.00 |
| Cuen, Dub | 13 | 8 | 3 | 2 | 4 | 1 | 0 | .800 | 61 | 52 | 21 | 20 | 4 | 27 | 1 | 3 | 43 | 3 | 2.95 |
| Cummings, Wau* | 19 | 19 | 7 | 1 | 9 | 5 | 0 | .643 | 125 | 117 | 71 | 47 | 9 | 47 | 0 | 1 | 112 | 6 | 3.38 |
| Dean, Dub | 28 | 13 | 3 | 1 | 6 | 9 | 1 | .400 | 126 | 130 | 67 | 53 | 5 | 62 | 7 | 3 | 133 | 8 | 3.79 |
| deLeon, Dub | 12 | 3 | 1 | 8 | 7 | 0 | 0 | .533 | 103 | 87 | 46 | 37 | 6 | 63 | 5 | 4 | 86 | 8 | 3.23 |
| DeMerritt, Bur | 25 | 24 | 6 | 0 | 7 | 11 | 0 | .389 | 153 | 143 | 87 | 66 | 10 | 53 | 4 | 3 | 97 | 6 | 3.88 |
| Dinkelmeyer, Cln | 33 | 2 | 1 | 1 | 5 | 2 | 0 | .714 | 67 | 49 | 22 | 16 | 4 | 16 | 3 | 2 | 49 | 3 | 2.15 |
| Dixon, Dub | 32 | 5 | 0 | 0 | 2 | 4 | 3 | .333 | 80 | 66 | 35 | 26 | 2 | 40 | 4 | 0 | 63 | 4 | 2.93 |
| Dorsey, QC | 25 | 24 | 7 | 4 | 15 | 3 | 0 | .833 | 161 | 114 | 49 | 38 | 6 | 56 | 0 | 2 | 161 | 4 | 2.12 |
| Driskill, Wau | 35 | 4 | 1 | 0 | 0 | 5 | 5 | .000 | 79 | 85 | 50 | 34 | 6 | 24 | 4 | 3 | 50 | 4 | 3.87 |
| Edge, Bur | 17 | 16 | 5 | 0 | 4 | 7 | 0 | .364 | 105 | 87 | 50 | 39 | 0 | 54 | 0 | 3 | 82 | 6 | 3.34 |
| Falcon, Wat* | 3 | 0 | 0 | 0 | 0 | 0 | 0 | .000 | 6 | 7 | 5 | 5 | 1 | 9 | 1 | 0 | 6 | 1 | 7.50 |
| Feola, 9Cln-15Wau* | 24 | 17 | 4 | 1 | 4 | 10 | 0 | .286 | 95 | 100 | 76 | 51 | 7 | 78 | 0 | 3 | 59 | 16 | 4.83 |
| Flanders, Wat | 11 | 0 | 0 | 0 | 1 | 0 | 0 | 1.000 | 14 | 11 | 6 | 1 | 0 | 7 | 1 | 1 | 9 | 0 | 0.64 |
| Frankum, Wau | 18 | 15 | 3 | 2 | 4 | 8 | 0 | .333 | 92 | 90 | 68 | 54 | 12 | 50 | 1 | 1 | 36 | 5 | 5.28 |
| Gamby, Cln | 21 | 15 | 2 | 0 | 3 | 8 | 0 | .273 | 88 | 81 | 50 | 41 | 4 | 63 | 4 | 4 | 51 | 8 | 4.19 |
| Garcia, WR | 22 | 17 | 8 | 4 | 10 | 6 | 2 | .625 | 114 | 107 | 43 | 38 | 6 | 38 | 5 | 1 | 103 | 7 | 3.00 |
| Garcia, Bur | 2 | 0 | 0 | 0 | 0 | 0 | 0 | .000 | 1 | 9 | 10 | 10 | 0 | 3 | 0 | 1 | 0 | 0 | 90.00 |
| Gaton, Bur | 36 | 1 | 1 | 0 | 6 | 4 | 1 | .600 | 74 | 84 | 47 | 35 | 8 | 34 | 2 | 5 | 49 | 5 | 4.26 |
| Geddes, Apl | 5 | 2 | 0 | 0 | 1 | 2 | 0 | .333 | 10 | 15 | 20 | 15 | 1 | 19 | 0 | 1 | 10 | 2 | 13.50 |
| Goulding, Dan | 1 | 0 | 0 | 0 | 0 | 0 | 0 | .000 | 2 | 2 | 3 | 2 | 0 | 5 | 0 | 0 | 1 | 0 | 9.00 |
| Groff, WR* | 14 | 0 | 0 | 0 | 0 | 0 | 5 | .000 | 18 | 21 | 19 | 17 | 4 | 8 | 1 | 1 | 19 | 1 | 8.50 |
| Haas, Bur | 25 | 24 | 12 | 3 | 11 | 8 | 0 | .579 | 171 | 149 | 66 | 39 | 6 | 49 | 3 | 0 | 146 | 8 | 2.05 |
| Harper, Wau | 25 | 0 | 0 | 0 | 3 | 3 | 1 | .500 | 55 | 62 | 44 | 38 | 5 | 49 | 2 | 2 | 49 | 12 | 6.22 |
| Hart, Wat | 14 | 6 | 2 | 1 | 3 | 4 | 1 | .429 | 48 | 38 | 20 | 16 | 5 | 24 | 1 | 0 | 28 | 3 | 3.00 |
| Hartzell, QC | 24 | 1 | 0 | 0 | 2 | 1 | 5 | .667 | 46 | 48 | 28 | 14 | 7 | 12 | 0 | 1 | 37 | 3 | 1.37 |
| Hasley, Dub* | 17 | 5 | 0 | 0 | 1 | 0 | 0 | .000 | 42 | 38 | 25 | 18 | 1 | 25 | 3 | 0 | 27 | 3 | 3.86 |
| Heenan, Dub | 6 | 5 | 0 | 0 | 0 | 2 | 0 | .000 | 29 | 33 | 22 | 14 | 2 | 16 | 3 | 1 | 29 | 4 | 4.34 |
| Heinen, CR | 55 | 2 | 1 | 0 | 5 | 6 | 11 | .455 | 99 | 79 | 45 | 31 | 4 | 47 | 7 | 4 | 95 | 5 | 2.82 |
| Heredia, Dan | 26 | 25 | 8 | 2 | 11 | 13 | 0 | .458 | 154 | 158 | 87 | 57 | 11 | 75 | 0 | 4 | 99 | 7 | 3.33 |
| Hodges, CR | 14 | 12 | 3 | 0 | 2 | 8 | 0 | .200 | 83 | 68 | 43 | 26 | 2 | 42 | 5 | 1 | 63 | 6 | 2.82 |
| Holm, Cln | 24 | 16 | 4 | 3 | 7 | 8 | 0 | .467 | 113 | 100 | 48 | 38 | 6 | 43 | 0 | 1 | 68 | 1 | 3.03 |
| Howard, QC* | 4 | 2 | 0 | 0 | 0 | 0 | 0 | .000 | 15 | 21 | 12 | 9 | 1 | 10 | 0 | 2 | 6 | 0 | 5.40 |
| Hrovat, Wat | 25 | 0 | 0 | 0 | 6 | 0 | 9 | 1.000 | 55 | 37 | 7 | 2 | 2 | 13 | 3 | 2 | 30 | 2 | 0.51 |
| Jackson, Wau | 5 | 5 | 2 | 1 | 1 | 3 | 0 | .250 | 38 | 29 | 12 | 10 | 1 | 7 | 0 | 0 | 35 | 2 | 2.37 |
| Jimenez, QC | 12 | 0 | 0 | 0 | 1 | 2 | 0 | .333 | 21 | 24 | 13 | 9 | 0 | 6 | 2 | 0 | 19 | 0 | 3.86 |
| Johnson, Wau | 2 | 1 | 1 | 0 | 1 | 0 | 1 | 1.000 | 12 | 10 | 3 | 3 | 1 | 11 | 0 | 1 | 11 | 0 | 2.25 |
| Johnson, CR* | 22 | 21 | 3 | 0 | 4 | 12 | 0 | .250 | 127 | 127 | 72 | 53 | 9 | 49 | 1 | 3 | 89 | 3 | 3.76 |
| Johnson, WR | 24 | 0 | 0 | 0 | 3 | 2 | 0 | .600 | 28 | 20 | 8 | 7 | 1 | 10 | 2 | 2 | 10 | 1 | 2.25 |
| Jones, WR | 17 | 2 | 0 | 0 | 1 | 2 | 2 | .333 | 35 | 44 | 29 | 27 | 3 | 24 | 3 | 2 | 18 | 1 | 6.94 |
| Kautzer, Apl | 28 | 22 | 7 | 2 | 7 | 11 | 0 | .389 | 139 | 131 | 78 | 57 | 6 | 68 | 0 | 7 | 82 | 13 | 3.69 |
| Keefe, Dan | 45 | 1 | 0 | 0 | 1 | 1 | 10 | .083 | 58 | 54 | 33 | 22 | 1 | 32 | 1 | 3 | 63 | 4 | 3.41 |
| Keller, Dan | 30 | 12 | 0 | 0 | 1 | 5 | 0 | .167 | 94 | 88 | 60 | 36 | 3 | 55 | 3 | 4 | 56 | 7 | 3.45 |
| Kelley, QC | 17 | 4 | 1 | 0 | 4 | 2 | 1 | .667 | 46 | 37 | 19 | 14 | 1 | 20 | 1 | 2 | 32 | 1 | 2.74 |
| Kenny, CR* | 17 | 8 | 2 | 0 | 2 | 6 | 0 | .250 | 58 | 56 | 37 | 26 | 3 | 37 | 1 | 1 | 27 | 9 | 4.03 |
| King, Apl* | 21 | 9 | 0 | 0 | 6 | 1 | 0 | .000 | 60 | 81 | 54 | 42 | 8 | 26 | 0 | 1 | 30 | 0 | 6.30 |
| Klein, Apl | 20 | 3 | 0 | 0 | 1 | 3 | 0 | .250 | 29 | 39 | 36 | 29 | 5 | 30 | 1 | 3 | 20 | 3 | 9.00 |
| Knapp, Apl | 14 | 13 | 5 | 1 | 6 | 6 | 0 | .500 | 87 | 49 | 23 | 19 | 0 | 45 | 2 | 5 | 99 | 4 | 1.97 |
| Knicely, Dub | 26 | 20 | 4 | 1 | 4 | 10 | 1 | .286 | 122 | 113 | 59 | 49 | 5 | 62 | 2 | 4 | 87 | 7 | 3.61 |
| Komadina, Apl* | 19 | 13 | 3 | 1 | 5 | 5 | 1 | .500 | 88 | 83 | 36 | 26 | 3 | 41 | 1 | 0 | 52 | 9 | 2.66 |
| Lahey, Wat | 3 | 3 | 0 | 0 | 2 | 1 | 0 | .667 | 18 | 14 | 9 | 5 | 2 | 5 | 1 | 0 | 13 | 0 | 2.50 |
| Lantz, Cln | 12 | 12 | 6 | 1 | 6 | 2 | 0 | .750 | 89 | 69 | 29 | 25 | 3 | 25 | 0 | 1 | 54 | 0 | 2.53 |
| Larkin, Wat | 17 | 3 | 1 | 0 | 6 | 0 | 3 | 1.000 | 43 | 34 | 14 | 10 | 3 | 8 | 0 | 1 | 31 | 4 | 2.09 |
| Laurent, Dan | 30 | 2 | 1 | 0 | 1 | 1 | 1 | .500 | 54 | 45 | 30 | 21 | 1 | 38 | 0 | 0 | 38 | 5 | 3.50 |
| Lauzerique, Dub | 16 | 1 | 0 | 0 | 4 | 2 | 1 | .667 | 36 | 25 | 12 | 9 | 4 | 19 | 1 | 1 | 22 | 5 | 2.25 |
| Lea, Wau | 2 | 0 | 0 | 0 | 0 | 0 | 0 | .000 | 6 | 3 | 0 | 0 | 0 | 0 | 0 | 0 | 7 | 0 | 0.00 |
| Lee, WR* | 8 | 0 | 0 | 0 | 0 | 0 | 0 | .000 | 11 | 11 | 8 | 6 | 2 | 7 | 1 | 0 | 12 | 0 | 4.91 |
| Lehman, Apl | 14 | 0 | 0 | 0 | 3 | 2 | 2 | .600 | 27 | 25 | 13 | 6 | 0 | 19 | 0 | 1 | 34 | 4 | 2.00 |
| Leonard, Wau | 11 | 7 | 0 | 0 | 0 | 8 | 0 | .000 | 50 | 57 | 38 | 31 | 3 | 27 | 0 | 5 | 26 | 4 | 5.58 |
| Loehr, Apl | 17 | 2 | 0 | 0 | 1 | 4 | 0 | .200 | 24 | 33 | 25 | 19 | 1 | 19 | 2 | 2 | 30 | 2 | 7.13 |
| Madden, Cln | 2 | 0 | 0 | 0 | 0 | 1 | 0 | .000 | 3 | 1 | 2 | 0 | 0 | 3 | 0 | 0 | 4 | 1 | 0.00 |
| Massimini, WR* | 11 | 8 | 1 | 0 | 2 | 2 | 0 | .500 | 40 | 43 | 30 | 20 | 4 | 13 | 0 | 0 | 34 | 4 | 4.50 |
| May, WR | 17 | 14 | 5 | 2 | 9 | 2 | 0 | .818 | 93 | 68 | 33 | 28 | 4 | 43 | 0 | 3 | 82 | 5 | 2.71 |
| McManus, Cln | 10 | 10 | 5 | 1 | 5 | 3 | 0 | .625 | 70 | 47 | 19 | 16 | 2 | 25 | 1 | 3 | 34 | 2 | 2.06 |
| McKinney, Wat | 11 | 11 | 7 | 3 | 8 | 2 | 0 | .800 | 84 | 61 | 22 | 19 | 0 | 22 | 0 | 1 | 65 | 1 | 2.04 |
| Meche, QC | 27 | 4 | 1 | 1 | 6 | 0 | 7 | 1.000 | 71 | 45 | 16 | 10 | 2 | 14 | 0 | 3 | 47 | 2 | 1.27 |
| Mendoza, Dub | 15 | 15 | 1 | 0 | 1 | 6 | 0 | .143 | 65 | 60 | 61 | 48 | 1 | 48 | 1 | 2 | 64 | 15 | 6.65 |
| Monroe, Apl | 23 | 19 | 3 | 1 | 5 | 11 | 2 | .313 | 121 | 118 | 66 | 48 | 4 | 48 | 4 | 2 | 59 | 12 | 3.57 |
| Moore, Dan | 15 | 3 | 0 | 0 | 3 | 1 | 1 | .750 | 26 | 26 | 15 | 10 | 2 | 11 | 1 | 0 | 25 | 0 | 3.46 |
| Mueller, Bur | 25 | 10 | 5 | 0 | 5 | 4 | 1 | .556 | 98 | 89 | 44 | 34 | 5 | 42 | 3 | 1 | 41 | 6 | 3.12 |
| Murray, Cln* | 31 | 11 | 1 | 0 | 6 | 5 | 2 | .545 | 77 | 75 | 35 | 24 | 1 | 38 | 6 | 1 | 41 | 5 | 2.81 |
| Nix, CR | 14 | 5 | 1 | 0 | 2 | 4 | 1 | .333 | 41 | 34 | 24 | 17 | 3 | 26 | 2 | 0 | 38 | 3 | 3.73 |
| Olsen, Wat | 9 | 9 | 3 | 1 | 5 | 1 | 0 | .833 | 65 | 66 | 28 | 24 | 5 | 14 | 0 | 1 | 43 | 4 | 3.32 |
| Olson, WR* | 25 | 23 | 6 | 4 | 11 | 8 | 1 | .579 | 162 | 130 | 64 | 52 | 8 | 97 | 3 | 3 | 107 | 6 | 2.89 |
| Pacella, Wau | 19 | 18 | 8 | 0 | 9 | 8 | 0 | .529 | 132 | 124 | 71 | 56 | 8 | 58 | 2 | 7 | 73 | 7 | 3.82 |

| Pitcher—Club | G. | GS. | CG. | ShO. | W. | L. | Sv. | Pct. | IP. | H. | R. | ER. | HR. | BB. | Int.BB. | HB. | SO. | WP. | ERA. |
|---|---|---|---|---|---|---|---|---|---|---|---|---|---|---|---|---|---|---|---|
| Pena, Bur* | 19 | 10 | 4 | 2 | 6 | 2 | 0 | .750 | 84 | 59 | 26 | 20 | 5 | 20 | 1 | 1 | 31 | 1 | 2.14 |
| Perez, QC | 18 | 0 | 0 | 0 | 3 | 2 | 2 | .600 | 26 | 22 | 12 | 10 | 2 | 11 | 1 | 0 | 22 | 1 | 3.46 |
| Perkins, Cln | 56 | 0 | 0 | 0 | 6 | 6 | 13 | .500 | 99 | 78 | 32 | 29 | 4 | 45 | 11 | 2 | 92 | 6 | 2.64 |
| Peterson, Wat | 34 | 2 | 0 | 0 | 5 | 2 | 6 | .714 | 51 | 47 | 24 | 21 | 4 | 25 | 2 | 1 | 59 | 2 | 3.71 |
| Pladson, Dub | 17 | 4 | 0 | 0 | 1 | 5 | 0 | .167 | 33 | 37 | 33 | 26 | 4 | 24 | 2 | 1 | 28 | 5 | 7.09 |
| Powers, QC | 19 | 6 | 1 | 1 | 3 | 2 | 1 | .600 | 61 | 47 | 30 | 28 | 1 | 36 | 0 | 0 | 46 | 4 | 4.13 |
| Quintero, WR | 23 | 21 | 5 | 0 | 8 | 8 | 1 | .500 | 130 | 118 | 66 | 50 | 4 | 72 | 3 | 3 | 92 | 10 | 3.46 |
| Quisenberry, Wat | 20 | 1 | 1 | 0 | 3 | 2 | 4 | .600 | 44 | 40 | 16 | 12 | 4 | 6 | 1 | 2 | 31 | 0 | 2.45 |
| Reinke, Cln* | 13 | 10 | 0 | 0 | 4 | 8 | 0 | .333 | 61 | 64 | 25 | 22 | 0 | 35 | 1 | 3 | 39 | 4 | 3.25 |
| Repke, Dan* | 24 | 11 | 1 | 0 | 5 | 5 | 1 | .500 | 71 | 73 | 51 | 33 | 10 | 41 | 0 | 1 | 47 | 4 | 4.18 |
| Richardson, Wau | 23 | 15 | 4 | 2 | 5 | 9 | 1 | .357 | 105 | 81 | 67 | 45 | 5 | 62 | 0 | 8 | 76 | 13 | 3.86 |
| Riddle, CR* | 14 | 0 | 0 | 0 | 0 | 1 | 0 | .000 | 23 | 23 | 14 | 9 | 1 | 5 | 1 | 0 | 22 | 0 | 3.52 |
| Roof, WR | 29 | 19 | 5 | 2 | 8 | 9 | 1 | .471 | 152 | 133 | 58 | 38 | 7 | 37 | 3 | 3 | 104 | 1 | 2.25 |
| Roslund, QC* | 38 | 2 | 1 | 1 | 6 | 4 | 2 | .600 | 69 | 55 | 28 | 25 | 4 | 25 | 0 | 0 | 65 | 0 | 3.26 |
| Rozema, Cln | 27 | 19 | 9 | 5 | 14 | 5 | 0 | .737 | 164 | 128 | 50 | 38 | 1 | 32 | 2 | 2 | 123 | 3 | 2.09 |
| Sanchez, Dub | 6 | 5 | 2 | 0 | 2 | 3 | 0 | .400 | 31 | 25 | 19 | 12 | 2 | 10 | 2 | 3 | 19 | 2 | 3.48 |
| Sander, Wau | 12 | 9 | 4 | 2 | 5 | 5 | 0 | .500 | 69 | 51 | 25 | 16 | 4 | 16 | 1 | 0 | 48 | 2 | 2.09 |
| Sempsrott, Wat* | 23 | 15 | 4 | 3 | 8 | 5 | 1 | .615 | 111 | 89 | 32 | 24 | 0 | 25 | 2 | 3 | 70 | 5 | 1.95 |
| Slaymaker, Bur* | 21 | 14 | 0 | 0 | 4 | 5 | 0 | .444 | 81 | 75 | 53 | 41 | 7 | 56 | 1 | 1 | 51 | 9 | 4.56 |
| Slettvet, QC | 23 | 22 | 12 | 1 | 12 | 8 | 0 | .600 | 159 | 151 | 80 | 53 | 5 | 53 | 0 | 0 | 83 | 4 | 3.00 |
| Smith, WR | 26 | 6 | 1 | 0 | 7 | 2 | 3 | .778 | 80 | 68 | 39 | 28 | 2 | 43 | 4 | 3 | 59 | 3 | 3.15 |
| Smith, CR* | 3 | 3 | 0 | 0 | 0 | 2 | 0 | .000 | 17 | 16 | 10 | 7 | 1 | 5 | 0 | 2 | 13 | 1 | 3.71 |
| Smith, Dan | 41 | 2 | 1 | 0 | 8 | 5 | 0 | .615 | 69 | 56 | 34 | 24 | 2 | 55 | 3 | 4 | 60 | 7 | 3.13 |
| Souza, Wat* | 32 | 1 | 1 | 0 | 3 | 1 | 5 | .750 | 58 | 61 | 35 | 30 | 7 | 25 | 1 | 1 | 64 | 2 | 4.66 |
| Speck, Wau | 8 | 8 | 1 | 0 | 2 | 6 | 0 | .250 | 38 | 36 | 33 | 28 | 3 | 37 | 0 | 4 | 28 | 3 | 6.63 |
| Srock, WR* | 11 | 0 | 0 | 0 | 1 | 0 | | 1.000 | 16 | 14 | 7 | 7 | 2 | 11 | 0 | 0 | 14 | 2 | 3.94 |
| Sylvia, Bur | 10 | 0 | 0 | 0 | 1 | 0 | | 1.000 | 20 | 23 | 16 | 14 | 3 | 6 | 0 | 0 | 12 | 0 | 6.30 |
| Thompson, CR* | 40 | 17 | 4 | 0 | 7 | 12 | 1 | .368 | 152 | 163 | 74 | 59 | 11 | 49 | 7 | 5 | 90 | 9 | 3.49 |
| Torreano, WR* | 1 | 0 | 0 | 0 | 0 | 0 | 0 | .000 | 0 | 0 | 0 | 0 | 0 | 1 | 0 | 0 | 0 | 0 | 0.00 |
| Trella, Cln | 24 | 24 | 11 | 5 | 11 | 9 | 0 | .550 | 164 | 116 | 46 | 32 | 1 | 77 | 2 | 3 | 136 | 9 | 1.76 |
| Weeber, Dub | 15 | 7 | 1 | 0 | 3 | 4 | 0 | .429 | 48 | 68 | 43 | 32 | 4 | 15 | 0 | 1 | 41 | 1 | 6.00 |
| Whiting, Bur* | 14 | 3 | 0 | 0 | 0 | 5 | 0 | .000 | 37 | 31 | 25 | 15 | 3 | 36 | 1 | 2 | 37 | 7 | 3.65 |
| G. Williams, Wat* | 19 | 17 | 4 | 1 | 12 | 2 | 0 | .857 | 116 | 75 | 40 | 28 | 2 | 47 | 0 | 2 | 112 | 9 | 2.17 |
| Williams, Apl | 6 | 6 | 0 | 0 | 0 | 3 | 0 | .000 | 23 | 17 | 12 | 12 | 2 | 11 | 1 | 0 | 17 | 1 | 4.70 |
| M. Williams, Wat* | 21 | 21 | 5 | 1 | 11 | 6 | 0 | .647 | 130 | 132 | 74 | 46 | 7 | 53 | 2 | 2 | 84 | 11 | 3.18 |
| Wilson, C.R | 36 | 4 | 3 | 1 | 3 | 5 | 0 | .375 | 74 | 69 | 37 | 28 | 5 | 31 | 5 | 7 | 38 | 2 | 3.41 |
| Wilson, Dan | 29 | 25 | 8 | 1 | 10 | 13 | 0 | .435 | 178 | 177 | 85 | 59 | 6 | 67 | 2 | 1 | 96 | 7 | 2.98 |
| Young, QC* | 10 | 9 | 1 | 1 | 2 | 4 | 0 | .333 | 57 | 46 | 29 | 20 | 3 | 30 | 0 | 1 | 34 | 4 | 3.16 |
| Yount, Bur | 4 | 4 | 1 | 0 | 0 | 4 | 0 | .000 | 22 | 27 | 25 | 13 | 0 | 16 | 0 | 2 | 13 | 4 | 5.32 |

BALKS—Souza, 6; Botting, Garcia (WR), Slaymaker, 4 each; Heredia, Holm, Repke, 3 each; Alfaro, Attardi, Barger, Blanco, Bobinger, Bock, Brisbin, Gamby, Hodges, Keller, Lantz, Mueller, Pacella, Slettvet, G. Williams, 2 each; Anyzeski, Arthur, Barrett, Bass, Beitey, Bradley, Callis, Caneira, Castillo (WR), Clark, Cline, Cort, Coulter, Cuen, deLeon, Driskill, Edge, Feola, Hart, Hasley, Heenan, Keefe, Klein, Laurent, Lee, Loehr, Massimini, May, Meche, Monroe, Nix, Olsen, Olson, Peterson, Pladson, Powers, Quintero, Richardson, Roof, Sempsrott, Smith (CR), Smith (Dan), Speck, Srock, Thompson, Trella, Whiting, Wilson (CR), Wilson (Dan), 1 each.

COMBINATION SHUTOUTS—Knapp-Coulter, Appleton; Slaymaker-Haas-Gaton, Edge-Conn, Burlington; Thompson-Heinen, Cedar Rapids; Gamby-Perkins, Reinke-Perkins-Murray, Clinton; Blanco-Lauzerique, Dubuque; Dorsey-Meche, Quad Cities; G. Williams-Peterson, Bass-Hrovat, Waterloo; Olson-Costello, Massimini-Johnson, May-Jones, Wisconsin Rapids.

NO-HIT GAMES—Dorsey, Quad Cities, defeated Clinton, 4-0, May 20 (seven innings); Olson, Wisconsin Rapids defeated Clinton, 6-0, June 30; Pena, Burlington, defeated Cedar Rapids, 2-0, July 20 (PERFECT) (seven innings); Alfaro, Dubuque, defeated Cedar Rapids, 5-0, August 16; Monroe, Appleton, defeated Cedar Rapids, 1-0, August 22 (seven innings).

# New York-Pennsylvania League

## CLASS A

### CHAMPIONSHIP WINNERS IN PREVIOUS YEARS

| | | |
|---|---|---|
| 1939—Olean* ............ .631 | 1951—Olean ............. .622 | 1962—Jamestown ........ .580 |
| 1940—Olean* ............ .625 | Hornell (3rd)† ..... .568 | Auburn (3rd)† ..... .521 |
| 1941—Jamestown ........ .618 | 1952—Hamilton ......... .659 | 1963—Auburn ........... .585 |
| Bradford (2nd)† ... .549 | Jamestown (2nd)† .. .643 | Batavia (3rd)† .... .485 |
| 1942—Jamestown* ....... .672 | 1953—Jamestown* ....... .704 | 1964—Auburn§ .......... .622 |
| 1943—Lockport ........ .591 | 1954—Corning* ......... .621 | 1965—Binghamton ...... .677 |
| Wellsville (3rd)† .. .532 | 1955—Hamilton* ........ .656 | Binghamton ...... .607 |
| 1944—Lockport ........ .608 | 1956—Wellsville* ...... .617 | 1966—Auburn x ........ .620 |
| Jamestown (2nd)† .. .565 | 1957—Wellsville ....... .632 | Binghamton ...... .646 |
| 1945—Batavia* ......... .677 | Erie (2nd)† ....... .598 | 1967—Auburn .......... .667 |
| 1946—Jamestown‡ ....... .672 | 1958—Wellsville ....... .556 | 1968—Auburn .......... .645 |
| Batavia‡ ........ .672 | Geneva (2nd)† ..... .548 | Oneonta (2nd)* ... .558 |
| 1947—Jamestown* ....... .690 | 1959—Wellsville† ...... .635 | 1969—Oneonta ......... .662 |
| 1948—Lockport* ........ .603 | 1960—Erie ............. .623 | 1970—Auburn .......... .623 |
| 1949—Bradford* ........ .635 | Wellsville (2nd)† .. .535 | 1971—Oneonta ......... .662 |
| 1950—Hornell .......... .653 | 1961—Geneva ........... .616 | 1972—Niagara Falls ... .686 |
| Olean (2nd)† ...... .568 | Olean (4th)† ...... .512 | 1973—Auburn .......... .667 |
| | | 1974—Oneonta ......... .768 |

*Won championship and four-club playoff. †Won four-club playoff. ‡Jamestown and Batavia declared co-champions; Batavia defeated Jamestown in final of four-club playoff. §Won championship and two-club playoff. xWon split-season playoff. (NOTE—Known as Pennsylvania-Ontario-New York League from 1929 through 1956.)

### STANDING OF CLUBS AT CLOSE OF FIRST HALF, JULY 26

| Club | W. | L. | T. | Pct. | G.B. | Club | W. | L. | T. | Pct. | G.B. |
|---|---|---|---|---|---|---|---|---|---|---|---|
| Newark ........ | 22 | 10 | 0 | .688 | .... | Auburn ........ | 16 | 17 | 0 | .485 | 6½ |
| Elmira ........ | 18 | 15 | 0 | .545 | 4½ | Oneonta ...... | 15 | 19 | 0 | .441 | 8 |
| Niagara Falls .. | 17 | 17 | 0 | .500 | 6 | Batavia ....... | 12 | 22 | 0 | .353 | 11 |

### STANDING OF CLUBS AT CLOSE OF SECOND HALF, AUGUST 30

| Club | W. | L. | T. | Pct. | G.B. | Club | W. | L. | T. | Pct. | G.B. |
|---|---|---|---|---|---|---|---|---|---|---|---|
| Newark ........ | 25 | 10 | 0 | .714 | .... | Auburn ........ | 15 | 20 | 0 | .429 | 10 |
| Elmira ........ | 20 | 15 | 0 | .571 | 5 | Batavia ....... | 12 | 21 | 0 | .364 | 12 |
| Oneonta ....... | 20 | 15 | 0 | .571 | 5 | Niagara Falls .. | 12 | 23 | 0 | .343 | 13 |

### COMPOSITE STANDING OF CLUBS AT CLOSE OF SEASON, AUGUST 30

| Club | New. | Elm. | Ont. | Aub. | N.F. | Bat. | Won | Lost | Tied | Pct. | G.B. |
|---|---|---|---|---|---|---|---|---|---|---|---|
| Newark (Brewers) ...... | — | 8 | 10 | 10 | 10 | 9 | 47 | 20 | 0 | .701 | .... |
| Elmira (Red Sox) ....... | 5 | — | 7 | 7 | 10 | 9 | 38 | 30 | 0 | .559 | 9½ |
| Oneonta (Yankees) ..... | 4 | 7 | — | 7 | 6 | 11 | 35 | 34 | 0 | .507 | 13 |
| Auburn (Phillies) ...... | 4 | 6 | 7 | — | 8 | 6 | 31 | 37 | 0 | .456 | 16½ |
| Niagara Falls (Pirates).. | 4 | 4 | 8 | 5 | — | 8 | 29 | 40 | 0 | .420 | 19 |
| Batavia (Co-op) ....... | 3 | 5 | 2 | 8 | 6 | — | 24 | 43 | 0 | .358 | 23 |

Major league affiliations in parentheses.
Playoff—None.
Forfeited Game—Batavia forfeited to Niagara Falls, July 4.
Regular-Season Attendance—Auburn, 43,765; Batavia, 32,650; Elmira, 42,546; Newark, 18,430; Niagara Falls, 37,145; Oneonta, 33,732. Total, 208,268. No playoff. No All-Star Game.

MANAGERS: Auburn—June Raines; Batavia—Hal White; Elmira—Richard (Dick) Berardino; Newark—Anton (Tony) Roig; Niagara Falls—Glenn Ezell; Oneonta—Michael Ferraro.

All-Star Team: 1B—Robbins, Niagara Falls; 2B—LaRocque, Newark; 3B—Berra, Niagara Falls; SS—Hall, Newark; Utility—Saber, Niagara Falls; OF—Severns, Newark; Anderson, Newark; Chapman, Oneonta; Pinkney, Batavia; DH—DeBattista, Niagara Falls; C—Bevington, Oneonta; Schmidt, Elmira; P—Dick, Newark; Patterson, Oneonta; Waller, Elmira; Schneider, Auburn; Manager—Roig, Newark.

### (Compiled by Howe News Bureau, Chicago, Ill.)

### CLUB BATTING

| Club | G. | AB. | R. | OR. | H. | TB. | 2B. | 3B. | HR. | RBI. | SH. | SF. | Int. BB. | BB. | HP. | SO. | SB. | CS. | LOB. | Pct. |
|---|---|---|---|---|---|---|---|---|---|---|---|---|---|---|---|---|---|---|---|---|
| Newark ........ | 67 | 2231 | 372 | 242 | 586 | 761 | 78 | 8 | 27 | 305 | 17 | 22 | 367 | 30 | 21 | 358 | 87 | 30 | 575 | .263 |
| Elmira ........ | 68 | 2184 | 323 | 302 | 547 | 718 | 88 | 16 | 17 | 260 | 48 | 24 | 401 | 23 | 11 | 606 | 50 | 26 | 542 | .250 |
| Auburn ........ | 68 | 2250 | 306 | 348 | 557 | 730 | 82 | 20 | 17 | 248 | 13 | 20 | 272 | 18 | 9 | 376 | 115 | 26 | 499 | .248 |
| Niagara Falls.. | 69 | 2275 | 314 | 334 | 561 | 735 | 89 | 20 | 15 | 259 | 22 | 16 | 278 | 18 | 22 | 420 | 72 | 26 | 542 | .247 |
| Batavia ....... | 67 | 2139 | 292 | 382 | 518 | 683 | 62 | 17 | 23 | 231 | 38 | 17 | 249 | 8 | 15 | 422 | 130 | 40 | 444 | .242 |
| Oneonta ...... | 69 | 2246 | 304 | 303 | 524 | 687 | 59 | 31 | 14 | 247 | 13 | 23 | 304 | 35 | 18 | 421 | 69 | 16 | 512 | .233 |

## INDIVIDUAL BATTING

(Leading Qualifiers for Batting Championship—189 or More Plate Appearances)

*Bats lefthanded. †Switch-hitter.

| Player and Club | G. | AB. | R. | H. | TB. | 2B. | 3B. | HR. | RBI. | SH. | SF. | BB. | HP. | SO. | SB. | CS. | Pct. |
|---|---|---|---|---|---|---|---|---|---|---|---|---|---|---|---|---|---|
| Pinkney, Charles, Batavia... | 64 | 246 | 48 | 76 | 100 | 6 | 3 | 4 | 24 | 3 | 0 | 31 | 4 | 33 | 24 | 11 | .3089 |
| Vega, Jesus, Newark... | 52 | 188 | 26 | 58 | 76 | 7 | 4 | 1 | 27 | 0 | 2 | 20 | 3 | 12 | 2 | 1 | .3085 |
| Anderson, Gregory, Newark.. | 50 | 212 | 34 | 62 | 98 | 9 | 0 | 9 | 33 | 0 | 3 | 26 | 1 | 30 | 5 | 2 | .292 |
| Coletta, Matthew, Elmira.... | 65 | 229 | 22 | 66 | 90 | 15 | 0 | 3 | 35 | 3 | 3 | 26 | 1 | 52 | 26 | 5 | .292 |
| DeBattista, Daniel, Niagara F | 66 | 240 | 37 | 69 | 84 | 11 | 2 | 0 | 23 | 3 | 0 | 30 | 1 | 25 | 3 | 4 | .288 |
| McDonald, James, Oneonta*.. | 69 | 261 | 22 | 74 | 97 | 11 | 3 | 2 | 37 | 1 | 2 | 37 | 1 | 30 | 2 | 1 | .284 |
| Jones, Sammie, Batavia | 62 | 234 | 42 | 66 | 112 | 9 | 5 | 9 | 43 | 3 | 2 | 20 | 4 | 43 | 15 | 1 | .282 |
| Kruzelock, Steven, Auburn.. | 52 | 196 | 23 | 55 | 79 | 10 | 1 | 4 | 38 | 0 | 4 | 17 | 0 | 22 | 3 | 1 | .282 |
| Saber, Mark, Niagara Falls.. | 68 | 268 | 43 | 75 | 88 | 6 | 2 | 1 | 23 | 2 | 1 | 38 | 4 | 48 | 11 | 5 | .281 |
| Franklin, Elliott, Newark*.. | 58 | 222 | 31 | 62 | 76 | 6 | 2 | 2 | 25 | 1 | 3 | 18 | 2 | 37 | 3 | 2 | .279 |

Departmental Leaders: G—James McDonald, 69; AB—Berra, 269; R—Pinkney, 48; H—Pinkney, 76; TB—S. Jones, 112; 2B—Robbins, 19; 3B—Chapman, 6; HR—Anderson, S. Jones, 9; RBI—Berra, 49; SH—Purcell, 13; SF—Berra, 8; BB—LaRocque, 67; HP—Coletta, Hall, Marino, 5; SO—Espino, 61; SB—Hiller, 34; CS—Pinkney, 11.

## (All Players—Listed Alphabetically)

| Player and Club | G. | AB. | R. | H. | TB. | 2B. | 3B. | HR. | RBI. | SH. | SF. | BB. | HP. | SO. | SB. | CS. | Pct. |
|---|---|---|---|---|---|---|---|---|---|---|---|---|---|---|---|---|---|
| Alvarez, Jose R., Oneonta.... | 62 | 187 | 33 | 29 | 39 | 3 | 2 | 1 | 17 | 1 | 3 | 56 | 1 | 30 | 5 | 2 | .155 |
| Anderson, Gregory, Newark... | 50 | 212 | 34 | 62 | 98 | 9 | 0 | 9 | 33 | 0 | 3 | 26 | 1 | 30 | 5 | 2 | .292 |
| Avila, Carlos, Batavia ..... | 38 | 101 | 7 | 17 | 22 | 2 | 0 | 1 | 7 | 1 | 0 | 9 | 3 | 31 | 2 | 0 | .168 |
| Barnes, J. Kenneth, Niag F. | 37 | 133 | 14 | 23 | 27 | 4 | 0 | 0 | 6 | 2 | 0 | 6 | 0 | 14 | 2 | 0 | .173 |
| Bendick, James, Oneonta*... | 38 | 132 | 16 | 33 | 49 | 3 | 2 | 3 | 31 | 1 | 2 | 17 | 1 | 11 | 4 | 1 | .250 |
| Berra, Dale, Niagara Falls.. | 67 | 269 | 36 | 69 | 92 | 6 | 4 | 3 | 49 | 0 | 8 | 19 | 1 | 47 | 9 | 2 | .257 |
| Berriatua, Joseph, Auburn* | 52 | 185 | 22 | 44 | 58 | 8 | 3 | 0 | 16 | 1 | 2 | 17 | 2 | 33 | 7 | 1 | .238 |
| Bevington, Terry, Oneonta... | 60 | 193 | 24 | 51 | 70 | 11 | 1 | 2 | 23 | 0 | 1 | 25 | 3 | 19 | 3 | 0 | .264 |
| Bonito, Arturo, Batavia ..... | 54 | 176 | 25 | 47 | 61 | 4 | 2 | 2 | 16 | 1 | 0 | 12 | 0 | 52 | 18 | 3 | .267 |
| Carty, Jorge, Niagara Falls. | 18 | 58 | 11 | 13 | 16 | 1 | 1 | 0 | 4 | 1 | 0 | 6 | 3 | 9 | 2 | 2 | .224 |
| Castillo, Neldy, Batavia†.... | 21 | 61 | 5 | 8 | 9 | 1 | 0 | 0 | 5 | 1 | 1 | 9 | 0 | 22 | 4 | 2 | .131 |
| Chapman, Nathan, Oneonta*. | 58 | 237 | 40 | 64 | 81 | 2 | 6 | 1 | 23 | 1 | 2 | 24 | 1 | 29 | 22 | 5 | .270 |
| Clemmons, Timothy, Elmira.. | 52 | 129 | 21 | 28 | 43 | 2 | 2 | 3 | 19 | 0 | 1 | 32 | 0 | 49 | 5 | 0 | .217 |
| Coletta, Matthew, Elmira.... | 65 | 229 | 22 | 66 | 90 | 15 | 0 | 3 | 35 | 3 | 3 | 29 | 5 | 31 | 4 | 1 | .288 |
| Corona, Louis, Batavia*...... | 16 | 44 | 4 | 12 | 17 | 0 | 1 | 1 | 5 | 0 | 0 | 3 | 1 | 9 | 2 | 0 | .273 |
| Cronk, Jeffrey, Auburn ..... | 40 | 134 | 18 | 34 | 47 | 5 | 1 | 2 | 17 | 0 | 1 | 21 | 1 | 40 | 3 | 0 | .254 |
| Cruz, Orlando, Oneonta ..... | 49 | 174 | 16 | 39 | 46 | 4 | 0 | 1 | 16 | 1 | 2 | 9 | 0 | 34 | 1 | 1 | .224 |
| Daniels, Joseph, Auburn...... | 10 | 20 | 3 | 3 | 3 | 0 | 0 | 0 | 0 | 0 | 0 | 5 | 0 | 8 | 0 | 0 | .150 |
| DeBattista, Daniel, NiagaraF | 66 | 240 | 37 | 69 | 84 | 11 | 2 | 0 | 23 | 3 | 0 | 30 | 1 | 25 | 3 | 4 | .288 |
| DeLaCruz, Heriberto, Auburn | 34 | 120 | 14 | 28 | 39 | 5 | 0 | 2 | 14 | 0 | 2 | 2 | 2 | 29 | 1 | 1 | .233 |
| de la Rosa, Jorge, Batavia F | 58 | 193 | 21 | 50 | 61 | 7 | 0 | 2 | 21 | 3 | 1 | 21 | 2 | 44 | 4 | 4 | .259 |
| DelCarmen, Manuel, Batavia. | 57 | 133 | 30 | 53 | 61 | 8 | 0 | 0 | 13 | 4 | 1 | 14 | 0 | 38 | 14 | 7 | .248 |
| Ejarque, Luis, Batavia ..... | 29 | 89 | 5 | 13 | 20 | 4 | 0 | 1 | 4 | 2 | 0 | 8 | 0 | 29 | 1 | 1 | .146 |
| Erardi, J. Gregory, Newark.. | 2 | 1 | 2 | 0 | 0 | 0 | 0 | 0 | 0 | 0 | 0 | 0 | 0 | 0 | 0 | 0 | .000 |
| Espino, Juan, Oneonta ..... | 48 | 157 | 24 | 36 | 57 | 5 | 5 | 2 | 23 | 1 | 1 | 26 | 4 | 61 | 1 | 0 | .229 |
| Faust, Alvin, Elmira ...... | 1 | 1 | 0 | 0 | 0 | 0 | 0 | 0 | 0 | 0 | 0 | 0 | 0 | 1 | 0 | 0 | .000 |
| Fermin, Pompilio, Elmira..... | 53 | 144 | 11 | 29 | 33 | 4 | 0 | 0 | 6 | 9 | 0 | 17 | 0 | 19 | 1 | 0 | .201 |
| Fischlin, Michael, Oneonta... | 35 | 135 | 22 | 31 | 41 | 4 | 3 | 0 | 6 | 1 | 2 | 15 | 2 | 37 | 3 | 0 | .230 |
| Flores, Adalberto, Newark... | 40 | 136 | 21 | 33 | 49 | 6 | 2 | 2 | 22 | 2 | 2 | 12 | 0 | 27 | 6 | 1 | .243 |
| Franklin, E. Alan, Batavia... | 62 | 226 | 25 | 58 | 69 | 4 | 2 | 1 | 30 | 3 | 3 | 25 | 0 | 35 | 10 | 5 | .257 |
| Franklin, Elliott, Newark*... | 58 | 222 | 31 | 62 | 76 | 8 | 2 | 2 | 25 | 1 | 3 | 18 | 2 | 37 | 3 | 2 | .279 |
| Frias, Gerardo, Batavia ..... | 15 | 31 | 2 | 3 | 3 | 0 | 0 | 0 | 0 | 0 | 1 | 2 | 1 | 13 | 0 | 0 | .097 |
| Garcia, Damaso, Oneonta .... | 50 | 157 | 28 | 42 | 50 | 4 | 2 | 0 | 17 | 1 | 2 | 20 | 1 | 37 | 8 | 2 | .268 |
| Gomez, Esteban, Newark.... | 38 | 139 | 13 | 42 | 48 | 3 | 0 | 1 | 20 | 1 | 1 | 8 | 0 | 24 | 3 | 1 | .302 |
| Hall, Raymond, Newark...... | 67 | 238 | 42 | 64 | 73 | 6 | 0 | 1 | 27 | 1 | 1 | 62 | 5 | 28 | 17 | 4 | .269 |
| Hawkins, Dennis, Auburn .... | 53 | 169 | 23 | 41 | 49 | 8 | 0 | 0 | 13 | 3 | 2 | 15 | 0 | 24 | 15 | 2 | .243 |
| Hiller, Mark, Batavia†....... | 26 | 43 | 4 | 3 | 51 | 60 | 7 | 1 | 0 | 22 | 10 | 2 | 55 | 0 | 32 | 34 | 5 | .222 |
| Holliday, Thomas, Niagara F. | 33 | 126 | 15 | 29 | 38 | 2 | 2 | 1 | 20 | 1 | 0 | 7 | 0 | 32 | 0 | 0 | .230 |
| Hyman, Larry, Elmira ..... | 48 | 142 | 23 | 38 | 53 | 4 | 1 | 3 | 22 | 1 | 0 | 42 | 1 | 25 | 3 | 2 | .268 |
| Isales, Orlando, Auburn ..... | 43 | 111 | 17 | 23 | 28 | 1 | 2 | 0 | 9 | 1 | 0 | 10 | 0 | 16 | 7 | 1 | .207 |
| Jones, Joe Louis, Auburn.... | 49 | 184 | 17 | 49 | 67 | 8 | 5 | 0 | 22 | 1 | 0 | 6 | 0 | 23 | 3 | 1 | .266 |
| Jones, Sammie, Batavia .... | 62 | 234 | 42 | 66 | 112 | 9 | 5 | 9 | 43 | 3 | 2 | 20 | 4 | 43 | 15 | 1 | .282 |
| Jurak, Edward, Elmira...... | 68 | 250 | 41 | 63 | 78 | 9 | 3 | 0 | 25 | 2 | 3 | 34 | 1 | 28 | 5 | 1 | .252 |
| Kalmus, L. Joseph, Auburn.. | 1 | 0 | 0 | 0 | 0 | 0 | 0 | 0 | 0 | 0 | 0 | 0 | 0 | 0 | 0 | 0 | .000 |
| Kane, Gregory, Elmira ..... | 53 | 148 | 22 | 36 | 54 | 10 | 1 | 2 | 25 | 3 | 2 | 35 | 3 | 39 | 8 | 0 | .243 |
| Kettering, Wilbur, Batavia.. | 35 | 99 | 11 | 19 | 23 | 1 | 0 | 1 | 13 | 2 | 2 | 14 | 0 | 16 | 0 | 1 | .192 |
| Kruzelock, Steven, Auburn.. | 52 | 196 | 23 | 55 | 79 | 10 | 1 | 4 | 38 | 0 | 4 | 17 | 0 | 22 | 3 | 1 | .281 |
| Kwasny, Joseph, Oneonta.... | 2 | 2 | 0 | 1 | 1 | 0 | 0 | 0 | 0 | 0 | 0 | 0 | 0 | 1 | 0 | 0 | .500 |
| LaRocque, Gary, Newark*.... | 65 | 236 | 45 | 49 | 54 | 2 | 0 | 1 | 27 | 1 | 3 | 67 | 1 | 29 | 11 | 7 | .208 |
| LaTorre, Gary, Elmira....... | 65 | 213 | 30 | 56 | 73 | 9 | 1 | 2 | 34 | 2 | 6 | 35 | 0 | 21 | 2 | 2 | .263 |
| Lloyd, Benny, Oneonta ..... | 48 | 182 | 19 | 39 | 45 | 4 | 1 | 0 | 13 | 1 | 2 | 20 | 1 | 56 | 8 | 0 | .214 |
| Luis, Beban, Oneonta........ | 48 | 159 | 21 | 38 | 57 | 3 | 5 | 0 | 14 | 4 | 1 | 10 | 1 | 36 | 3 | 2 | .239 |
| Maldonado, Santiago, Batavia | 25 | 85 | 7 | 14 | 18 | 2 | 1 | 0 | 6 | 3 | 2 | 8 | 0 | 22 | 3 | 1 | .165 |
| Maria, Esteban, Newark..... | 53 | 181 | 23 | 49 | 69 | 11 | 0 | 3 | 28 | 1 | 4 | 17 | 0 | 51 | 3 | 1 | .271 |
| Marino, David, Newark...... | 46 | 148 | 32 | 31 | 36 | 5 | 0 | 0 | 14 | 3 | 0 | 33 | 5 | 24 | 3 | 1 | .209 |
| McCormack, Donald, 42 Bat-4 Auburn ............. | 46 | 161 | 21 | 36 | 54 | 10 | 1 | 2 | 25 | 1 | 2 | 18 | 1 | 27 | 2 | 3 | .224 |

| Player and Club | G. | AB. | R. | H. | TB. | 2B. | 3B. | HR. | RBI. | SH. | SF. | BB. | HP. | SO. | SB. | CS. | Pct. |
|---|---|---|---|---|---|---|---|---|---|---|---|---|---|---|---|---|---|
| McDonald, James, Oneonta*.. | 69 | 261 | 22 | 74 | 97 | 11 | 3 | 2 | 37 | 1 | 3 | 27 | 1 | 30 | 2 | 1 | .284 |
| McDonald, Jerry, Niagara F* | 61 | 233 | 36 | 56 | 00 | 2 | 1 | 0 | 13 | 5 | 0 | 32 | 3 | 25 | 26 | 4 | .240 |
| Moreno, Jose, Auburn...... | 58 | 231 | 40 | 62 | 84 | 11 | 1 | 3 | 22 | 1 | 2 | 22 | 2 | 25 | 23 | 3 | .268 |
| Muriel, Arnaldo, Auburn.... | 31 | 115 | 6 | 27 | 31 | 2 | 1 | 0 | 9 | 0 | 0 | 7 | 1 | 11 | 0 | 0 | .235 |
| Nichols, Gary, Baiavia..... | 3 | 5 | 0 | 1 | 1 | 0 | 0 | 0 | 0 | 0 | 0 | 0 | 0 | 3 | 0 | 0 | .200 |
| Noles, Dickie, Auburn ..... | 1 | 3 | 0 | 1 | 1 | 0 | 0 | 0 | 0 | 0 | 0 | 0 | 0 | 1 | 0 | 0 | .333 |
| Nuss, Edward, Elmira...... | 1 | 0 | 0 | 0 | 0 | 0 | 0 | 0 | 0 | 0 | 0 | 1 | 0 | 0 | 0 | 0 | .000 |
| O'Brien, Kenneth, Auburn.. | 67 | 234 | 30 | 58 | 75 | 7 | 2 | 2 | 30 | 1 | 3 | 49 | 1 | 49 | 9 | 7 | .248 |
| O'Keeffe, Richard, Newark*.. | 4 | 14 | 2 | 4 | 4 | 0 | 0 | 0 | 1 | 0 | 0 | 0 | 0 | 4 | 0 | 0 | .286 |
| Pagnozzi, Timothy, Auburn† | 48 | 145 | 20 | 27 | 31 | 4 | 0 | 0 | 9 | 1 | 0 | 18 | 0 | 26 | 8 | 2 | .186 |
| Pinkney, Charles, Batavia .. | 64 | 246 | 48 | 76 | 100 | 6 | 3 | 4 | 24 | 3 | 0 | 31 | 4 | 33 | 24 | 11 | .309 |
| Presser, Donald, Niagara F . | 2 | 3 | 0 | 0 | 0 | 0 | 0 | 0 | 0 | 0 | 0 | 0 | 0 | 0 | 0 | 0 | .000 |
| Purcell, Gary, Elmira....... | 39 | 128 | 23 | 36 | 49 | 9 | 2 | 0 | 12 | 13 | 1 | 20 | 1 | 13 | 3 | 0 | .281 |
| Ramer, Stephen, Auburn .... | 2 | 7 | 1 | 1 | 1 | 0 | 0 | 0 | 0 | 0 | 0 | 1 | 0 | 1 | 0 | 0 | .143 |
| Ramos, Domingo, Oneonta.. | 49 | 166 | 29 | 39 | 45 | 4 | 1 | 0 | 21 | 0 | 2 | 34 | 1 | 30 | 5 | 0 | .235 |
| Rein, Frederick, Niagara F.. | 26 | 94 | 13 | 25 | 39 | 6 | 1 | 2 | 12 | 0 | 0 | 14 | 0 | 35 | 1 | 0 | .266 |
| Reyes, Rafael, Newark ..... | 1 | 1 | 0 | 1 | 1 | 0 | 0 | 0 | 0 | 0 | 0 | 0 | 0 | 0 | 0 | 0 | 1.000 |
| Rivera, Ivan, Elmira* ..... | 49 | 163 | 29 | 39 | 41 | 2 | 0 | 0 | 12 | 2 | 1 | 30 | 0 | 30 | 3 | 2 | .239 |
| Robbins, W. Vaughn, NF*.. | 67 | 224 | 37 | 62 | 95 | 19 | 1 | 4 | 37 | 1 | 1 | 58 | 2 | 37 | 0 | 0 | .277 |
| Rodriguez, Nelson, Newark.. | 1 | 0 | 1 | 0 | 0 | 0 | 0 | 0 | 0 | 0 | 0 | 0 | 0 | 0 | 0 | 0 | .000 |
| Rogers, Mark, Auburn...... | 60 | 200 | 43 | 49 | 67 | 6 | 3 | 2 | 22 | 2 | 4 | 60 | 0 | 42 | 18 | 3 | .245 |
| Ross, R. Charles, Newark*.. | 46 | 133 | 25 | 36 | 45 | 6 | 0 | 1 | 18 | 1 | 0 | 30 | 3 | 13 | 2 | 3 | .271 |
| Saber, Mark, Niagara Falls.. | 68 | 268 | 43 | 75 | 88 | 6 | 2 | 1 | 23 | 2 | 1 | 38 | 4 | 48 | 11 | 5 | .280 |
| Sanchez, Arsenio, Niagara F. | 48 | 137 | 16 | 26 | 32 | 4 | 1 | 0 | 8 | 2 | 2 | 21 | 2 | 23 | 13 | 2 | .190 |
| Schmidt, David, Elmira .... | 59 | 181 | 32 | 45 | 69 | 11 | 2 | 3 | 20 | 3 | 0 | 56 | 2 | 41 | 13 | 0 | .249 |
| Schneider, Jeffery, Auburn†.. | 1 | 2 | 1 | 1 | 1 | 0 | 0 | 0 | 0 | 0 | 0 | 0 | 0 | 0 | 0 | 0 | .500 |
| Schoppee, David Elmira .... | 1 | 1 | 0 | 0 | 0 | 0 | 0 | 0 | 0 | 0 | 0 | 0 | 0 | 1 | 0 | 0 | .000 |
| Severns, Billy, Newark*.... | 60 | 209 | 41 | 56 | 79 | 10 | 2 | 3 | 35 | 3 | 3 | 48 | 0 | 10 | 7 | 1 | .268 |
| Shankle, James, Elmria.... | 55 | 194 | 25 | 54 | 69 | 8 | 2 | 1 | 30 | 1 | 5 | 22 | 2 | 23 | 2 | 0 | .278 |
| Smith, David A., Newark.... | 1 | 0 | 1 | 0 | 0 | 0 | 0 | 0 | 0 | 0 | 0 | 0 | 0 | 0 | 0 | 0 | .000 |
| Smith, David R., Auburn†.. | 37 | 109 | 14 | 22 | 26 | 4 | 0 | 0 | 8 | 6 | 2 | 16 | 0 | 17 | 9 | 3 | .202 |
| Smith, Robert P., 6 On- | | | | | | | | | | | | | | | | | |
| 48 Bat* | 54 | 166 | 21 | 46 | 55 | 4 | 1 | 2 | 22 | 3 | 2 | 27 | 1 | 21 | 4 | 0 | .277 |
| Smoak, James, Auburn...... | 16 | 69 | 11 | 30 | 41 | 3 | 1 | 2 | 19 | 0 | 0 | 6 | 0 | 8 | 8 | 1 | .435 |
| Soliday, Raymond, Niagara F | 28 | 100 | 6 | 21 | 39 | 7 | 1 | 3 | 11 | 0 | 9 | 9 | 0 | 36 | 0 | 2 | .210 |
| Steele, Carlton, Elmira.... | 49 | 166 | 27 | 42 | 50 | 4 | 2 | 0 | 13 | 5 | 1 | 26 | 1 | 21 | 27 | 1 | .253 |
| Streightiff, Thomas, Elmira . | 3 | 9 | 5 | 3 | 3 | 0 | 0 | 0 | 1 | 2 | 0 | 3 | 0 | 0 | 0 | 0 | .333 |
| Summers, Harry, Niagara F. | 30 | 77 | 2 | 15 | 21 | 6 | 0 | 0 | 13 | 1 | 1 | 7 | 2 | 19 | 1 | 1 | .195 |
| Sylvia, David, Newark ..... | 1 | 1 | 0 | 0 | 0 | 0 | 0 | 0 | 0 | 0 | 0 | 0 | 0 | 1 | 0 | 0 | .000 |
| Tanks, Talmadge, Newark ... | 52 | 172 | 32 | 40 | 54 | 5 | 0 | 3 | 26 | 3 | 0 | 25 | 1 | 46 | 9 | 2 | .233 |
| Upshaw, Willie, Oneonta*... | 29 | 91 | 8 | 8 | 9 | 1 | 0 | 0 | 4 | 0 | 0 | 15 | 0 | 19 | 1 | 1 | .088 |
| Vega, Jesus, Newark....... | 52 | 188 | 26 | 58 | 76 | 7 | 4 | 1 | 27 | 0 | 2 | 20 | 3 | 12 | 2 | 1 | .309 |
| Vincent, Happy, Elmira..... | 39 | 86 | 11 | 12 | 13 | 1 | 0 | 0 | 6 | 2 | 1 | 19 | 0 | 31 | 3 | 1 | .140 |
| Welch, Phillip, Elmira ..... | 1 | 0 | 1 | 0 | 0 | 0 | 0 | 0 | 0 | 0 | 0 | 0 | 0 | 0 | 0 | 0 | .000 |
| Wick, R. Michael, Niagara F | 36 | 120 | 18 | 28 | 43 | 8 | 2 | 1 | 19 | 0 | 2 | 10 | 2 | 26 | 0 | 0 | .233 |

The following pitchers had no plate appearances primarily through use of designated hitters, listed alphabetically by club, games in parentheses):

AUBURN—Bradford, Gregory (13); Cooper, M. Neal (14); Day, David* (1); Fowler, Don (12); Herring, G. Stephen (7); Kirkpatrick, Michael (4); McDaniel, Leo (14); Nickerson, James (1); Welborn, Sammye (10); Williams, Roger* (6); Wilson, Robert C.* (14).

BATAVIA—Bohr, Robert (14); Boulter, James (15); Dalton, James (14); Fox, Jimmy L. (28); Gonzalez, Juan (15); Medina, Freddy (4); Mendez, Adolfo (6); Santana, Dionicio, 2 Elmira-11 Batavia (13); Tagliarino, John (12).

ELMIRA—Agosto, Juan* (9); Bigos, Walter (14); Howard, Michael S. (13); Lopez, Carlos (15); Paxton, Michael (15); Roman, Leovigildo* (16); Waller, Richard (12).

NEWARK—Dick, William* (13); Edge, Alvin (11); Garcia, Miguel (10); Hannon, John (13); Meagher, Bradley* (9); Minier, Patricio* (8); Morris, John (9); Quinones, Felipe (1); Rodriguez, Jose A.* (2); Ruling, Stephen (2); Whiting, John (1).

NIAGARA FALLS—Bolden, Dennis (15); Burman, Timothy* (16); Cieply, Walter (20); Clark, Bryan* (13); Hall, Robert (14); Holland, Alfred (6); Isaac, Joseph (13); May, Gerald* (8); Pinkus, Jeffrey (14); Robles, Victor (10); Seabol, Russell (6); Tapia, Mark (2).

ONEONTA—Alcantara, Jose (10); Beattie, James (5); Caffrey, Martin (23); Carp, Steven (1); Francisco, Enrique (7); Houston, Jerry, 1 Auburn-9 Oneonta (10); Laurent, Leonce (11); Mendez, Sabah (7); Niemann, Randy (8); Patterson, Gilbert (14); Santana, Rafael (7); Trotter, Joseph* (11); Wright, Dave (17).

GRAND-SLAM HOME RUNS (7), Anderson, Bonito, Flores, Holliday, Maria, McCormack, Rogers, 1 each.

AWARDED FIRST BASE ON INTERFERENCE (6): Bendick (Avila), Carty (Avila), Hall (Avila), Hawkins (Flores), Shankle (Kettering), R. Smith (Schmidt).

## CLUB FIELDING

| Club | G. | PO. | A. | E. | DP. | PB. | Pct. | Club | G. | PO. | A. | E. | DP. | PB. | Pct. |
|---|---|---|---|---|---|---|---|---|---|---|---|---|---|---|---|
| Newark ........ | 69 | 1752 | 673 | 112 | 55 | 21 | .956 | Elmira ........ | 68 | 1758 | 728 | 135 | 47 | 14 | .948 |
| Niagara Falls.. | 69 | 1748 | 790 | 132 | 52 | 22 | .951 | Auburn ........ | 68 | 1750 | 712 | 145 | 56 | 13 | .944 |
| Oneonta ........ | 69 | 1787 | 837 | 138 | 62 | 19 | .950 | Batavia ........ | 67 | 1698 | 734 | 167 | 58 | 22 | .936 |

Triple Plays—None.

## INDIVIDUAL FIELDING

### FIRST BASEMEN

*Throws lefthanded.

| Player and Club | G. | PO. | A. | E. | DP. | Pct. |
|---|---|---|---|---|---|---|
| Barnes, Niagara Falls | 3 | 17 | 0 | 0 | 1 | 1.000 |
| Presser, Niagara Falls | 1 | 3 | 1 | 0 | 0 | 1.000 |
| McCormack, Batavia | 1 | 1 | 0 | 0 | 0 | 1.000 |
| LaTORRE, Elmira | 55 | 463 | 22 | 7 | 30 | .986 |
| McDonald, Oneonta* | 69 | 683 | 28 | 11 | 53 | .985 |
| Franklin, Batavia | 26 | 229 | 11 | 4 | 26 | .984 |
| Smith, Batavia* | 44 | 379 | 24 | 7 | 25 | .983 |
| Tanks, Newark* | 52 | 459 | 10 | 9 | 40 | .981 |
| Robbins, Niagara Falls | 67 | 610 | 38 | 14 | 40 | .979 |
| Vega, Newark | 17 | 128 | 7 | 3 | 8 | .978 |
| Berriatua, Auburn* | 50 | 425 | 24 | 11 | 31 | .976 |
| Muriel, Auburn | 19 | 159 | 5 | 4 | 12 | .976 |
| Kane, Elmira | 24 | 148 | 5 | 7 | 7 | .956 |

### SECOND BASEMEN

| Player and Club | G. | PO. | A. | E. | DP. | Pct. |
|---|---|---|---|---|---|---|
| LaROCQUE, Newark | 65 | 160 | 162 | 8 | 30 | .976 |
| Alvarez, Oneonta | 22 | 54 | 74 | 4 | 13 | .970 |
| Coletta, Elmira | 30 | 53 | 55 | 4 | 8 | .964 |
| Barnes, Niagara Falls | 14 | 38 | 39 | 3 | 9 | .963 |
| Moreno, Auburn | 57 | 132 | 162 | 12 | 31 | .961 |
| Saber, Niagara Falls | 31 | 75 | 93 | 7 | 20 | .960 |
| Hiller, Batavia | 60 | 138 | 159 | 15 | 33 | .952 |
| Fermin, Elmira | 49 | 93 | 123 | 12 | 21 | .947 |
| DeBattista, Niagara F. | 9 | 19 | 22 | 3 | 3 | .932 |
| Garcia, Oneonta | 49 | 103 | 118 | 17 | 33 | .929 |
| de la Rosa, N Falls | 15 | 33 | 42 | 6 | 7 | .926 |
| Smith, Auburn | 14 | 39 | 25 | 6 | 6 | .914 |
| Jones, Batavia | 7 | 19 | 14 | 4 | 4 | .892 |
| Franklin, Newark | 2 | 5 | 3 | 1 | 2 | .889 |

### THIRD BASEMEN

| Player and Club | G. | PO. | A. | E. | DP. | Pct. |
|---|---|---|---|---|---|---|
| Jones, Batavia | 3 | 1 | 7 | 0 | 1 | 1.000 |
| DeBattista, N Falls | 1 | 1 | 4 | 0 | 1 | 1.000 |
| McCormack, Batavia | 1 | 2 | 2 | 0 | 1 | 1.000 |
| Franklin, Batavia | 26 | 32 | 61 | 5 | 5 | .949 |
| Cruz, Oneonta | 21 | 22 | 49 | 5 | 5 | .934 |
| Muriel, Auburn | 4 | 5 | 9 | 1 | 2 | .933 |
| Coletta, Elmira | 46 | 43 | 90 | 10 | 7 | .930 |
| O'BRIEN, Auburn | 63 | 68 | 123 | 16 | 13 | .923 |
| DelCarmen, Batavia | 41 | 38 | 118 | 13 | 11 | .923 |
| Marino, Newark | 40 | 28 | 75 | 9 | 7 | .920 |
| Vincent, Elmira | 36 | 35 | 52 | 8 | 3 | .916 |
| Ramos, Oneonta | 13 | 8 | 27 | 4 | 3 | .897 |
| Berra, Niagara Falls | 67 | 67 | 137 | 24 | 13 | .895 |
| Alvarez, Oneonta | 38 | 32 | 94 | 15 | 8 | .894 |
| Franklin, Newark | 28 | 21 | 45 | 11 | 3 | .857 |
| Pagnozzi, Auburn | 1 | 1 | 3 | 1 | 1 | .800 |
| Maria, Newark | 2 | 2 | 2 | 3 | 1 | .571 |

### SHORTSTOPS

| Player and Club | G. | PO. | A. | E. | DP. | Pct. |
|---|---|---|---|---|---|---|
| Hiller, Batavia | 7 | 5 | 21 | 0 | 3 | 1.000 |
| Jones, Batavia | 1 | 1 | 0 | 0 | 0 | 1.000 |
| Saber, Niagara Falls | 37 | 55 | 138 | 9 | 13 | .955 |
| Daniels, Auburn | 8 | 8 | 13 | 1 | 2 | .955 |
| Ramos, Oneonta | 34 | 52 | 116 | 10 | 14 | .944 |
| HALL, Newark | 64 | 110 | 193 | 23 | 28 | .929 |
| Barnes, Niagara Falls | 21 | 31 | 76 | 9 | 11 | .922 |
| DeBattista, N Falls | 11 | 8 | 39 | 4 | 6 | .922 |
| Fischlin, Oneonta | 35 | 34 | 128 | 15 | 16 | .915 |
| Maldonado, Batavia | 25 | 37 | 76 | 12 | 14 | .904 |
| Smith, Auburn | 20 | 34 | 58 | 10 | 7 | .902 |
| Pagnozzi, Auburn | 46 | 52 | 117 | 19 | 16 | .899 |
| Jurak, Elmira | 67 | 104 | 192 | 43 | 24 | .873 |
| Castillo, Batavia | 21 | 31 | 52 | 16 | 13 | .838 |
| Alvarez, Oneonta | 3 | 4 | 11 | 3 | 3 | .833 |
| LaTorre, Elmira | 1 | 0 | 4 | 1 | 0 | .800 |
| DelCarmen, Batavia | 16 | 18 | 43 | 17 | 5 | .782 |
| Marino, Newark | 3 | 4 | 3 | 2 | 1 | .778 |
| Fermin, Elmira | 2 | 1 | 2 | 1 | 0 | .750 |

### OUTFIELDERS

| Player and Club | G. | PO. | A. | E. | DP. | Pct. |
|---|---|---|---|---|---|---|
| Purcell, Elmira | 37 | 71 | 5 | 0 | 2 | 1.000 |
| Cronk, Auburn | 23 | 23 | 0 | 0 | 0 | 1.000 |
| Corona, Batavia | 8 | 10 | 0 | 0 | 0 | 1.000 |
| Summers, N Falls | 4 | 8 | 0 | 0 | 1 | 1.000 |
| Smith, Ont-Bat* | 6 | 5 | 3 | 0 | 1 | 1.000 |
| Upshaw, Oneonta* | 6 | 7 | 1 | 0 | 1 | 1.000 |
| Holliday, Niagara Falls | 1 | 4 | 0 | 0 | 1 | 1.000 |
| O'Brien, Auburn | 4 | 4 | 0 | 0 | 0 | 1.000 |
| Kwasny, Oneonta | 2 | 2 | 0 | 0 | 0 | 1.000 |
| Gomez, Newark | 25 | 37 | 1 | 1 | 0 | .974 |
| Rein, Niagara Falls | 26 | 37 | 0 | 1 | 0 | .974 |
| Vega, Newark | 28 | 32 | 3 | 1 | 1 | .972 |
| Luis, Oneonta | 46 | 64 | 4 | 2 | 2 | .971 |
| HAWKINS, Auburn | 51 | 108 | 5 | 4 | 1 | .966 |
| McDonald, N Falls | 60 | 106 | 3 | 4 | 0 | .965 |
| Clemmons, Elmira | 51 | 47 | 6 | 2 | 0 | .964 |
| Bonito, Batavia | 31 | 45 | 3 | 2 | 0 | .960 |
| Severns, Newark* | 60 | 132 | 13 | 7 | 4 | .954 |
| Hyman, Elmira | 42 | 56 | 2 | 3 | 1 | .951 |
| Carty, Niagara Falls | 18 | 38 | 1 | 2 | 0 | .951 |
| Jones, Batavia | 54 | 93 | 3 | 5 | 0 | .950 |
| DeBattista, N Falls | 15 | 16 | 2 | 1 | 1 | .947 |
| Lloyd, Oneonta | 48 | 83 | 3 | 5 | 0 | .945 |
| Maria, Newark | 49 | 97 | 4 | 6 | 1 | .944 |
| Steele, Elmira | 47 | 90 | 7 | 6 | 1 | .942 |
| Smoak, Auburn | 16 | 32 | 0 | 2 | 0 | .941 |
| Chapman, Oneonta* | 58 | 122 | 13 | 10 | 4 | .931 |
| Bendick, Oneonta | 37 | 38 | 1 | 3 | 0 | .929 |
| Franklin, Batavia | 17 | 24 | 2 | 2 | 0 | .929 |
| Rivera, Elmira* | 44 | 92 | 7 | 8 | 0 | .925 |
| Rogers, Auburn* | 57 | 112 | 8 | 10 | 4 | .923 |
| Ejarque, Batavia | 12 | 10 | 1 | 1 | 0 | .917 |
| Sanchez, N Falls | 47 | 61 | 4 | 6 | 1 | .915 |
| de la Rosa, N Falls | 22 | 23 | 5 | 3 | 2 | .903 |
| Soliday, Niagara Falls | 22 | 31 | 3 | 4 | 0 | .895 |
| McCormack, Batavia | 19 | 23 | 2 | 3 | 1 | .893 |
| Anderson, Newark | 47 | 62 | 5 | 9 | 1 | .882 |
| Pinkney, Batavia | 63 | 131 | 7 | 20 | 1 | .873 |
| LaTorre, Elmira | 9 | 18 | 0 | 3 | 0 | .857 |
| Frias, Batavia | 7 | 8 | 3 | 2 | 0 | .846 |
| Isales, Auburn | 38 | 49 | 5 | 10 | 2 | .844 |
| Cruz, Oneonta | 16 | 17 | 4 | 4 | 1 | .840 |
| DeLaCruz, Auburn | 30 | 40 | 6 | 9 | 1 | .836 |
| Streightiff, Elmira | 3 | 3 | 0 | 1 | 0 | .750 |
| Espino, Oneonta | 1 | 1 | 0 | 1 | 0 | .500 |

### CATCHERS

| Player and Club | G. | PO. | A. | E. | DP. | PB. | Pct. |
|---|---|---|---|---|---|---|---|
| Nichols, Batavia | 2 | 5 | 0 | 0 | 0 | 0 | 1.000 |
| ROSS, Newark | 42 | 275 | 30 | 4 | 12 | | .987 |
| Bevington, Ont | 58 | 359 | 46 | 8 | 5 | 12 | .981 |
| Holliday, N Falls | 24 | 135 | 8 | 3 | 1 | 10 | .979 |
| Schmidt, Elmira | 53 | 303 | 48 | 8 | 1 | 10 | .978 |
| Wick, N Falls | 31 | 219 | 11 | 6 | 0 | 8 | .975 |

## CATCHERS—Continued

| Player and Club | G. | PO. | A. | E. | DP. | PB. | Pct. |
|---|---|---|---|---|---|---|---|
| McCormack, Ba-Au | 24 | 137 | 14 | 4 | 3 | 8 | .974 |
| Kruzelock, Auburn | 32 | 195 | 24 | 6 | 4 | 6 | .973 |
| Kane, Elmira | 13 | 63 | 6 | 2 | 1 | 3 | .972 |
| Jones, Auburn | 36 | 229 | 38 | 9 | 6 | 6 | .967 |
| Flores, Newark | 31 | 185 | 14 | 7 | 1 | 9 | .966 |
| Espino, Oneonta | 6 | 25 | 3 | 1 | 1 | 3 | .966 |
| Shankle, Elmira | 11 | 34 | 6 | 2 | 1 | 1 | .952 |
| Kettering, Batavia | 28 | 161 | 21 | 11 | 2 | 8 | .943 |
| Cruz, Oneonta | 12 | 55 | 10 | 4 | 3 | 4 | .942 |
| Avila, Batavia | 25 | 113 | 13 | 9 | 1 | 7 | .933 |
| Summers, N Falls | 15 | 69 | 6 | 6 | 2 | 4 | .926 |

## PITCHERS

| Player and Club | G. | PO. | A. | E. | DP. | Pct. |
|---|---|---|---|---|---|---|
| WELCH, Elmira* | 9 | 9 | 12 | 0 | 2 | 1.000 |
| Boulter, Batavia* | 14 | 5 | 13 | 0 | 2 | 1.000 |
| Niemann, Oneonta* | 8 | 2 | 13 | 0 | 1 | 1.000 |
| Bohr, Batavia | 14 | 2 | 13 | 0 | 0 | 1.000 |
| Dick, Newark* | 13 | 0 | 13 | 0 | 2 | 1.000 |
| Bolden, Niagara Falls | 15 | 3 | 9 | 0 | 1 | 1.000 |
| Garcia, Newark | 10 | 2 | 9 | 0 | 0 | 1.000 |
| Holland, Niagara F* | 6 | 1 | 9 | 0 | 1 | 1.000 |
| Roman, Elmira* | 16 | 1 | 9 | 0 | 1 | 1.000 |
| Wright, Oneonta | 17 | 0 | 10 | 0 | 0 | 1.000 |
| Minier, Newark* | 8 | 1 | 8 | 0 | 1 | 1.000 |
| Agosto, Elmira* | 9 | 2 | 7 | 0 | 0 | 1.000 |
| Noles, Auburn | 9 | 1 | 8 | 0 | 1 | 1.000 |
| Schoppee, Elmira | 14 | 4 | 3 | 0 | 1 | 1.000 |
| Sylvia, Newark | 20 | 1 | 6 | 0 | 1 | 1.000 |
| Tapia, Niagara Falls | 2 | 2 | 4 | 0 | 0 | 1.000 |
| Medina, Batavia | 4 | 2 | 4 | 0 | 1 | 1.000 |
| Paxton, Elmira | 5 | 1 | 5 | 0 | 1 | 1.000 |
| Nuss, Elmira | 13 | 2 | 4 | 0 | 0 | 1.000 |
| Santana, Oneonta | 7 | 1 | 4 | 0 | 0 | 1.000 |
| Reyes, Newark | 10 | 1 | 4 | 0 | 0 | 1.000 |
| Smith, Batavia | 2 | 0 | 4 | 0 | 0 | 1.000 |
| Williams, Auburn | 6 | 0 | 4 | 0 | 0 | 1.000 |
| Erardi, Newark | 13 | 0 | 4 | 0 | 0 | 1.000 |
| Kalmus, Auburn | 13 | 0 | 4 | 0 | 0 | 1.000 |
| Ruling, Newark | 2 | 0 | 3 | 0 | 0 | 1.000 |
| Smith, Newark | 7 | 1 | 2 | 0 | 0 | 1.000 |
| Day, Auburn* | 1 | 0 | 2 | 0 | 1 | 1.000 |
| Carp, Oneonta | 1 | 1 | 1 | 0 | 0 | 1.000 |
| Summers, N Falls | 4 | 0 | 2 | 0 | 0 | 1.000 |
| Cieply, Niagara Falls | 20 | 0 | 2 | 0 | 0 | 1.000 |
| Kirkpatrick, Auburn | 4 | 0 | 1 | 0 | 0 | 1.000 |
| Robles, Niagara Falls | 10 | 1 | 0 | 0 | 0 | 1.000 |
| Waller, Elmira | 12 | 6 | 14 | 1 | 0 | .952 |
| Caffrey, Oneonta | 23 | 5 | 14 | 1 | 0 | .950 |
| Pinkus, Niagara Falls | 14 | 11 | 21 | 2 | 0 | .941 |
| Alcantara, Oneonta | 10 | 2 | 14 | 1 | 1 | .941 |
| Edge, Newark | 11 | 1 | 15 | 1 | 2 | .941 |
| Bigos, Elmira | 14 | 8 | 23 | 2 | 0 | .939 |
| Isaac, Niagara Falls | 13 | 5 | 9 | 1 | 0 | .933 |
| Fowler, Auburn | 12 | 6 | 20 | 2 | 1 | .929 |
| Presser, Niagara Falls | 14 | 9 | 25 | 3 | 1 | .919 |
| Faust, Elmira | 12 | 0 | 10 | 1 | 0 | .909 |
| Dalton, Batavia | 14 | 5 | 13 | 2 | 0 | .900 |
| Welborn, Auburn | 10 | 4 | 5 | 1 | 1 | .900 |
| Morris, Newark | 9 | 2 | 15 | 2 | 1 | .895 |
| Clark, Niagara Falls* | 13 | 3 | 21 | 3 | 0 | .889 |
| Trotter, Oneonta* | 11 | 1 | 7 | 1 | 0 | .889 |
| O'Keeffe, Newark* | 11 | 3 | 11 | 2 | 1 | .875 |
| May, Niagara Falls* | 8 | 2 | 5 | 1 | 0 | .875 |
| Lopez, Elmira | 15 | 3 | 4 | 1 | 1 | .875 |
| Burman, N Falls* | 16 | 2 | 5 | 1 | 0 | .875 |
| Hannon, Newark | 13 | 1 | 11 | 2 | 0 | .857 |
| Cooper, Auburn | 14 | 4 | 8 | 2 | 1 | .857 |
| Beattie, Oneonta | 5 | 1 | 5 | 1 | 0 | .857 |
| Houston, Aub-Ont | 10 | 2 | 4 | 1 | 1 | .857 |
| Schneider, Auburn* | 21 | 0 | 6 | 1 | 0 | .857 |
| Bradford, Auburn* | 13 | 0 | 10 | 2 | 0 | .833 |
| Mendez, Batavia | 6 | 1 | 4 | 1 | 0 | .833 |
| Gonzalez, Batavia | 15 | 5 | 4 | 2 | 0 | .818 |
| Patterson, Oneonta | 14 | 3 | 17 | 5 | 2 | .800 |
| Tagliarino, Batavia | 12 | 2 | 6 | 2 | 0 | .800 |
| Herring, Auburn* | 7 | 0 | 4 | 1 | 0 | .800 |
| Wilson, Auburn | 14 | 1 | 3 | 1 | 1 | .800 |
| Kwasny, Oneonta | 13 | 1 | 10 | 3 | 1 | .786 |
| McDaniel, Auburn* | 14 | 2 | 12 | 4 | 0 | .778 |
| Seabol, Niagara Falls | 6 | 3 | 4 | 2 | 0 | .778 |
| Fox, Batavia | 28 | 0 | 15 | 5 | 2 | .750 |
| Francisco, Oneonta | 7 | 0 | 3 | 1 | 0 | .750 |
| Meagher, Newark | 9 | 1 | 2 | 1 | 0 | .750 |
| Laurent, Oneonta | 11 | 1 | 2 | 1 | 0 | .750 |
| Howard, Elmira | 13 | 1 | 3 | 2 | 1 | .667 |
| Mendez, Oneonta | 7 | 1 | 1 | 1 | 0 | .667 |
| Hall, Niagara Falls | 14 | 1 | 2 | 3 | 0 | .571 |
| Santana, Elm-Bat | 13 | 1 | 0 | 2 | 0 | .333 |

The following pitchers do not have any recorded accepted chances; therefore, are not listed in the fielding averages at that position: Kane, LaTorre, Nickerson, Quinones, J. Rodriguez*, Whiting*. Ramer and N. Rodriguez appeared as pinch-hitters and/or pinch-runners only.

## CLUB PITCHING

| Club | G. | CG. | ShO. | Sv. | IP. | H. | R. | ER. | HR. | BB. | Int. BB. | HB. | SO. | WP. | Bk. | ERA. |
|---|---|---|---|---|---|---|---|---|---|---|---|---|---|---|---|---|
| Newark | 67 | 20 | 10 | 13 | 584 | 496 | 242 | 188 | 18 | 260 | 13 | 9 | 440 | 27 | 4 | 2.90 |
| Elmira | 68 | 19 | 7 | 6 | 586 | 574 | 302 | 201 | 14 | 275 | 28 | 19 | 378 | 29 | 4 | 3.09 |
| Oneonta | 69 | 17 | 6 | 7 | 596 | 553 | 303 | 206 | 11 | 272 | 15 | 24 | 400 | 38 | 2 | 3.11 |
| Niagara Falls | 69 | 18 | 3 | 5 | 583 | 534 | 334 | 246 | 16 | 350 | 15 | 20 | 399 | 72 | 9 | 3.80 |
| Auburn | 68 | 24 | 5 | 6 | 583 | 544 | 348 | 260 | 25 | 366 | 6 | 16 | 407 | 48 | 3 | 4.01 |
| Batavia | 67 | 21 | 1 | 8 | 586 | 592 | 382 | 255 | 29 | 348 | 55 | 13 | 364 | 38 | 3 | 4.05 |

## PITCHERS' RECORDS

(Leading Qualifiers for Earned-Run Average Leadership—56 or More Innings)

*Throws lefthanded.

| Pitcher—Club | G. | GS. | CG. | ShO. | W. | L. | Sv. | Pct. | IP. | H. | R. | ER. | HR. | BB. | Int. BB. | HB. | SO. | WP. | ERA. |
|---|---|---|---|---|---|---|---|---|---|---|---|---|---|---|---|---|---|---|---|
| Waller, Elmira | 12 | 11 | 1 | 0 | 6 | 1 | 0 | .857 | 79 | 57 | 22 | 12 | 2 | 23 | 3 | 6 | 73 | 1 | 1.37 |
| Caffrey, Oneonta | 23 | 1 | 0 | 0 | 3 | 3 | 4 | .500 | 62 | 60 | 20 | 10 | 1 | 21 | 5 | 1 | 40 | 0 | 1.45 |
| Morris, Newark | 9 | 8 | 4 | 1 | 6 | 1 | 0 | .857 | 72 | 61 | 22 | 15 | 0 | 17 | 3 | 0 | 48 | 1 | 1.88 |
| Patterson, Oneonta | 14 | 13 | 6 | 1 | 8 | 4 | 0 | .667 | 106 | 79 | 32 | 23 | 2 | 33 | 0 | 4 | 97 | 5 | 1.95 |
| Bigos, Elmira | 14 | 13 | 7 | 2 | 9 | 1 | 0 | .900 | 107 | 104 | 36 | 31 | 4 | 29 | 5 | 2 | 41 | 2 | 2.61 |
| Dick, Newark* | 13 | 9 | 3 | 1 | 9 | 1 | 0 | .900 | 80 | 66 | 27 | 24 | 4 | 18 | 0 | 1 | 51 | 0 | 2.70 |
| Cooper, Auburn | 14 | 14 | 10 | 1 | 8 | 5 | 0 | .615 | 109 | 90 | 47 | 33 | 2 | 50 | 0 | 2 | 54 | 3 | 2.72 |
| O'Keeffe, Newark* | 11 | 11 | 3 | 2 | 7 | 3 | 0 | .700 | 67 | 43 | 28 | 21 | 0 | 54 | 1 | 0 | 59 | 2 | 2.82 |
| Kwasny, Oneonta | 13 | 13 | 4 | 0 | 4 | 6 | 0 | .400 | 87 | 90 | 51 | 28 | 0 | 26 | 1 | 7 | 41 | 2 | 2.90 |
| Alcantara, Oneonta | 10 | 10 | 3 | 2 | 6 | 3 | 0 | .667 | 73 | 79 | 29 | 24 | 1 | 23 | 0 | 4 | 57 | 1 | 2.96 |

Departmental Leaders: G—Fox, 28; GS—Cooper, Pinkus, Presser, 14; CG—Cooper, 10; ShO—Alcantara, Bigos, Holland, O'Keeffe, Paxton, Smith (Newark), 2; W—Bigos, Dick, 9; L—Clark, 10; Sv—Sylvia, 7; Pct.—Bigos, Dick, .900; IP—Cooper, 109; H—Bigos, 104; R—Dalton, 65; ER—Dalton, 44; HR—Hannon, 7; BB—Clark, 71; IBB—Fox, 18; HB—Kwasny, 7; SO—Patterson, 97; WP—Clark, 24.

# OFFICIAL BASEBALL GUIDE

(All Pitchers—Listed Alphabetically)

| Pitcher—Club | G. | GS. | CG. | ShO. | W. | L. | Sv. | Pct. | IP. | H. | R. | ER. | HR. | BB. | Int.BB. | HB. | SO. | WP. | ERA. |
|---|---|---|---|---|---|---|---|---|---|---|---|---|---|---|---|---|---|---|---|
| Agosto, Elmira* .. | 9 | 5 | 0 | 0 | 1 | 4 | 0 | .200 | 23 | 27 | 37 | 22 | 2 | 34 | 1 | 1 | 22 | 2 | 8.61 |
| Alcantara, Oneonta | 10 | 10 | 3 | 2 | 6 | 3 | 0 | .667 | 73 | 79 | 29 | 24 | 1 | 23 | 0 | 4 | 57 | 1 | 2.96 |
| Beattie, Oneonta.. | 5 | 4 | 0 | 0 | 2 | 0 | 0 | 1.000 | 24 | 15 | 11 | 5 | 1 | 7 | 0 | 2 | 22 | 3 | 1.88 |
| Bigos, Elmira .... | 14 | 13 | 7 | 2 | 9 | 1 | 0 | .900 | 107 | 104 | 36 | 31 | 4 | 29 | 5 | 2 | 41 | 2 | 2.61 |
| Bohr, Batavia .... | 14 | 8 | 3 | 0 | 4 | 5 | 0 | .444 | 67 | 76 | 48 | 27 | 2 | 40 | 7 | 1 | 44 | 6 | 3.63 |
| Bolden, N Falls... | 15 | 0 | 0 | 0 | 2 | 1 | 2 | .667 | 36 | 39 | 18 | 14 | 1 | 6 | 1 | 0 | 19 | 1 | 3.50 |
| Boulter, Batavia*.. | 14 | 13 | 5 | 0 | 4 | 9 | 0 | .308 | 93 | 97 | 60 | 36 | 3 | 56 | 9 | 2 | 48 | 2 | 3.48 |
| Bradford, Auburn* | 13 | 13 | 5 | 0 | 6 | 5 | 0 | .545 | 79 | 79 | 51 | 40 | 2 | 48 | 0 | 4 | 64 | 10 | 4.56 |
| Burman, N Falls*. | 16 | 0 | 0 | 0 | 2 | 4 | 2 | .333 | 37 | 37 | 16 | 12 | 1 | 13 | 3 | 3 | 30 | 0 | 2.92 |
| Caffrey, Oneonta .. | 23 | 1 | 0 | 0 | 3 | 3 | 4 | .500 | 62 | 60 | 20 | 10 | 1 | 21 | 5 | 1 | 40 | 0 | 1.45 |
| Carp, Oneonta .... | 1 | 1 | 0 | 0 | 0 | 1 | 0 | .000 | 3 | 4 | 6 | 6 | 0 | 8 | 1 | 1 | 2 | 1 | 18.00 |
| Cieply, N Falls... | 20 | 3 | 0 | 0 | 1 | 3 | 0 | .250 | 50 | 38 | 24 | 20 | 1 | 29 | 2 | 4 | 45 | 6 | 3.60 |
| Clark, N Falls*... | 13 | 13 | 3 | 0 | 3 | 10 | 0 | .231 | 74 | 47 | 49 | 37 | 0 | 71 | 2 | 2 | 59 | 24 | 4.50 |
| Cooper, Auburn .. | 14 | 14 | 10 | 1 | 8 | 5 | 0 | .615 | 109 | 90 | 47 | 33 | 2 | 50 | 0 | 2 | 54 | 3 | 2.72 |
| Dalton, Batavia .. | 14 | 11 | 4 | 1 | 5 | 8 | 0 | .385 | 93 | 102 | 65 | 44 | 6 | 48 | 7 | 0 | 71 | 7 | 4.26 |
| Day, Auburn* .... | 1 | 1 | 0 | 0 | 0 | 1 | 0 | .000 | 7 | 4 | 1 | 0 | 0 | 2 | 0 | 0 | 4 | 0 | 0.00 |
| Dick, Newark* ... | 13 | 9 | 3 | 1 | 9 | 1 | 0 | .900 | 80 | 66 | 27 | 24 | 4 | 18 | 0 | 1 | 51 | 0 | 2.70 |
| Edge, Newark .... | 11 | 10 | 3 | 1 | 4 | 4 | 0 | .500 | 68 | 66 | 33 | 24 | 1 | 31 | 1 | 1 | 46 | 5 | 3.18 |
| Erardi, Newark ... | 13 | 0 | 0 | 0 | 2 | 1 | 4 | .667 | 28 | 21 | 5 | 4 | 0 | 14 | 3 | 1 | 42 | 3 | 1.29 |
| Faust, Elmira .... | 12 | 7 | 0 | 0 | 3 | 2 | 0 | .600 | 49 | 57 | 33 | 25 | 0 | 33 | 3 | 0 | 20 | 3 | 4.59 |
| Fowler, Auburn ... | 12 | 10 | 4 | 1 | 5 | 4 | 0 | .556 | 82 | 73 | 41 | 29 | 2 | 32 | 2 | 3 | 59 | 3 | 3.18 |
| Fox, Batavia ..... | 28 | 5 | 1 | 0 | 3 | 5 | 6 | .375 | 84 | 83 | 47 | 38 | 3 | 58 | 18 | 1 | 67 | 6 | 4.07 |
| Francisco, Oneonta | 7 | 0 | 0 | 0 | 0 | 0 | 0 | .000 | 17 | 18 | 12 | 9 | 0 | 11 | 1 | 2 | 5 | 1 | 4.76 |
| Garcia, Newark .. | 10 | 5 | 1 | 0 | 3 | 2 | 0 | .600 | 45 | 42 | 25 | 21 | 4 | 25 | 1 | 3 | 24 | 4 | 4.20 |
| Gonzalez, Batavia | 15 | 12 | 1 | 0 | 2 | 5 | 0 | .286 | 55 | 73 | 49 | 40 | 4 | 54 | 5 | 5 | 40 | 7 | 6.55 |
| Hall, Niagara Falls | 14 | 0 | 0 | 0 | 1 | 0 | 1 | 1.000 | 23 | 26 | 27 | 23 | 1 | 21 | 0 | 1 | 24 | 7 | 9.00 |
| Hannon, Newark .. | 13 | 13 | 4 | 1 | 6 | 2 | 0 | .750 | 76 | 75 | 43 | 35 | 7 | 29 | 1 | 0 | 52 | 3 | 4.14 |
| Herring, Auburn*. | 7 | 0 | 0 | 0 | 1 | 1 | 0 | .500 | 16 | 11 | 11 | 9 | 1 | 22 | 0 | 1 | 8 | 4 | 5.06 |
| Holland, N Falls* | 6 | 6 | 5 | 2 | 4 | 2 | 0 | .667 | 49 | 44 | 20 | 14 | 1 | 14 | 1 | 1 | 50 | 4 | 2.57 |
| Houston, 1 Au-9 On.. | 10 | 5 | 0 | 0 | 1 | 2 | 1 | .333 | 25 | 23 | 29 | 19 | 1 | 24 | 1 | 0 | 22 | 4 | 6.84 |
| Howard, Elmira .. | 13 | 2 | 0 | 0 | 1 | 2 | 1 | .333 | 33 | 39 | 19 | 13 | 0 | 18 | 0 | 0 | 19 | 3 | 3.55 |
| Isaac, N Falls .... | 13 | 1 | 0 | 0 | 1 | 1 | 1 | .500 | 34 | 33 | 13 | 12 | 0 | 19 | 3 | 1 | 26 | 4 | 3.18 |
| Kalmus, Auburn .. | 13 | 1 | 0 | 0 | 2 | 3 | 0 | .400 | 30 | 33 | 22 | 17 | 3 | 28 | 0 | 0 | 31 | 2 | 5.10 |
| Kane, Elmira .... | 1 | 0 | 0 | 0 | 0 | 0 | 0 | .000 | 4 | 4 | 0 | 0 | 0 | 3 | 0 | 0 | 4 | 0 | 0.00 |
| Kirkpatrick, Aub.. | 4 | 0 | 0 | 0 | 0 | 1 | 0 | .000 | 8 | 5 | 2 | 2 | 0 | 4 | 0 | 1 | 4 | 3 | 2.25 |
| Kwasny, Oneonta.. | 13 | 13 | 4 | 0 | 4 | 6 | 0 | .400 | 87 | 90 | 51 | 28 | 0 | 26 | 1 | 7 | 41 | 2 | 2.90 |
| LaTorre, Elmira .. | 1 | 0 | 0 | 0 | 0 | 0 | 0 | .000 | 1 | 0 | 0 | 0 | 0 | 1 | 0 | 0 | 2 | 0 | 0.00 |
| Laurent, Oneonta.. | 11 | 11 | 1 | 0 | 3 | 5 | 0 | .375 | 46 | 50 | 41 | 34 | 1 | 40 | 0 | 0 | 21 | 8 | 6.65 |
| Lopez, Elmira .... | 15 | 1 | 0 | 0 | 4 | 3 | 2 | .571 | 42 | 46 | 19 | 14 | 0 | 19 | 4 | 3 | 20 | 2 | 3.00 |
| May, N Falls* ... | 8 | 8 | 0 | 0 | 1 | 3 | 0 | .250 | 32 | 45 | 34 | 26 | 2 | 27 | 0 | 0 | 21 | 3 | 7.31 |
| McDaniel, Auburn* | 14 | 9 | 2 | 1 | 1 | 5 | 1 | .167 | 62 | 66 | 45 | 40 | 4 | 41 | 3 | 1 | 41 | 6 | 5.81 |
| Meagher, Newark.. | 9 | 2 | 0 | 0 | 0 | 0 | 0 | .000 | 18 | 21 | 16 | 11 | 0 | 13 | 2 | 1 | 10 | 4 | 5.50 |
| Medina, Batavia .. | 4 | 4 | 3 | 0 | 1 | 3 | 0 | .250 | 31 | 24 | 12 | 11 | 3 | 20 | 2 | 0 | 13 | 3 | 3.19 |
| Mendez, Batavia .. | 6 | 0 | 0 | 0 | 0 | 1 | 0 | .000 | 16 | 21 | 20 | 15 | 3 | 11 | 3 | 1 | 5 | 2 | 8.44 |
| Mendez, Oneonta .. | 7 | 0 | 0 | 0 | 0 | 0 | 0 | .000 | 16 | 11 | 5 | 2 | 1 | 14 | 1 | 0 | 6 | 1 | 1.13 |
| Minier, Newark* .. | 8 | 2 | 0 | 0 | 2 | 0 | 1 | 1.000 | 21 | 13 | 4 | 3 | 0 | 8 | 0 | 1 | 10 | 0 | 1.29 |
| Morris, Newark ... | 9 | 8 | 4 | 1 | 6 | 1 | 0 | .857 | 72 | 61 | 22 | 15 | 0 | 17 | 3 | 0 | 48 | 1 | 1.88 |
| Nickerson, Auburn. | 1 | 1 | 0 | 0 | 0 | 1 | 0 | .000 | 2 | 2 | 6 | 4 | 0 | 6 | 0 | 2 | 0 | 1 | 18.00 |
| Niemann, Oneonta* | 8 | 8 | 3 | 1 | 3 | 3 | 0 | .500 | 55 | 53 | 26 | 15 | 1 | 20 | 0 | 1 | 23 | 2 | 2.45 |
| Noles, Auburn .... | 9 | 9 | 2 | 0 | 2 | 2 | 0 | .500 | 50 | 49 | 30 | 20 | 2 | 27 | 0 | 0 | 31 | 1 | 3.60 |
| Nuss, Elmira ..... | 13 | 12 | 4 | 0 | 4 | 6 | 0 | .400 | 79 | 80 | 54 | 30 | 1 | 44 | 3 | 1 | 63 | 8 | 3.42 |
| O'Keeffe, Newark* | 11 | 11 | 3 | 2 | 7 | 3 | 0 | .700 | 67 | 43 | 28 | 21 | 0 | 54 | 1 | 0 | 59 | 2 | 2.82 |
| Patterson, Elmira | 14 | 13 | 6 | 1 | 8 | 4 | 0 | .667 | 106 | 79 | 32 | 23 | 2 | 33 | 0 | 4 | 97 | 5 | 1.95 |
| Paxton, Elmira ... | 5 | 5 | 5 | 2 | 5 | 0 | 0 | 1.000 | 43 | 26 | 7 | 3 | 0 | 5 | 1 | 1 | 43 | 2 | 0.63 |
| Pinkus, N Falls .. | 14 | 14 | 3 | 0 | 5 | 5 | 0 | .500 | 90 | 87 | 44 | 33 | 4 | 36 | 1 | 3 | 38 | 6 | 3.30 |
| Presser, N Falls .. | 14 | 14 | 5 | 1 | 4 | 7 | 0 | .364 | 88 | 70 | 46 | 31 | 1 | 56 | 0 | 3 | 35 | 12 | 3.17 |
| Quinones, Newark | 1 | 0 | 0 | 0 | 0 | 0 | 0 | .000 | 2 | 7 | 5 | 5 | 0 | 0 | 0 | 1 | 0 | 2 | 22.50 |
| Reyes Newark .... | 10 | 0 | 0 | 0 | 3 | 1 | 1 | .750 | 22 | 27 | 16 | 14 | 1 | 13 | 0 | 0 | 19 | 2 | 5.73 |
| Robles, N Falls ... | 10 | 0 | 0 | 0 | 0 | 1 | 0 | .000 | 13 | 15 | 6 | 5 | 2 | 8 | 1 | 0 | 9 | 3 | 3.46 |
| J. Rodriguez, New* | 2 | 0 | 0 | 0 | 0 | 0 | 0 | .000 | 6 | 4 | 1 | 1 | 0 | 0 | 0 | 0 | 3 | 0 | 1.50 |
| Roman, Elmira* .. | 16 | 1 | 0 | 0 | 1 | 2 | 1 | .333 | 26 | 27 | 22 | 17 | 1 | 22 | 1 | 1 | 12 | 2 | 5.88 |
| Ruling, Newark ... | 2 | 1 | 0 | 0 | 0 | 1 | 0 | .000 | 12 | 10 | 2 | 2 | 0 | 5 | 1 | 0 | 10 | 1 | 1.50 |
| Santana, 2 Elmira-11 Batavia ....13 | 13 | 0 | 0 | 0 | 1 | 2 | | .500 | 38 | 26 | 15 | 10 | 1 | 22 | 3 | 2 | 24 | 1 | 2.37 |
| Santana, Oneonta.. | 7 | 2 | 0 | 0 | 0 | 2 | 0 | .000 | 22 | 20 | 13 | 10 | 2 | 15 | 0 | 2 | 6 | 3 | 4.09 |
| Schneider, Auburn* | 21 | 0 | 0 | 0 | 3 | 2 | | .600 | 51 | 45 | 25 | 16 | 3 | 24 | 1 | 0 | 37 | 4 | 2.82 |
| Schoppee, Elmira.. | 14 | 5 | 0 | 0 | 1 | 7 | 1 | .125 | 46 | 59 | 39 | 23 | 4 | 32 | 6 | 2 | 28 | 2 | 4.50 |
| Seabol, N Falls .... | 6 | 6 | 0 | 0 | 1 | 2 | 0 | .333 | 24 | 27 | 31 | 15 | 2 | 35 | 1 | 2 | 14 | 3 | 5.63 |
| Smith, Newark ... | 7 | 6 | 2 | 2 | 3 | 3 | 0 | .500 | 38 | 19 | 10 | 5 | 5 | 18 | 0 | 1 | 47 | 1 | 1.18 |
| Smith, Batavia* .. | 2 | 1 | 0 | 0 | 0 | 1 | 0 | .000 | 9 | 9 | 5 | 2 | 0 | 3 | 0 | 1 | 4 | 2 | 2.00 |
| Summers, N Falls | 4 | 1 | 0 | 0 | 1 | 1 | 0 | .500 | 13 | 12 | 3 | 2 | 0 | 6 | 0 | 0 | 18 | 2 | 1.38 |
| Sylvia, Newark ... | 20 | 0 | 0 | 0 | 2 | 2 | | .500 | 28 | 21 | 5 | 3 | 0 | 13 | 0 | 0 | 18 | 1 | 0.96 |
| Tagliarino, Batavia | 12 | 12 | 4 | 0 | 4 | 5 | 0 | .444 | 83 | 83 | 52 | 32 | 4 | 36 | 1 | 3 | 52 | 4 | 3.47 |
| Tapia, N Falls.... | 2 | 2 | 0 | 0 | 2 | 0 | 1 | 1.000 | 18 | 14 | 3 | 2 | 0 | 9 | 0 | 0 | 11 | 0 | 1.00 |
| Trotter, Oneonta* | 11 | 0 | 0 | 0 | 1 | 3 | 0 | .250 | 24 | 24 | 14 | 11 | 0 | 14 | 0 | 0 | 27 | 4 | 4.13 |
| Waller, Elmira .... | 12 | 11 | 1 | 0 | 6 | 1 | 0 | .857 | 79 | 57 | 22 | 12 | 2 | 23 | 3 | 6 | 73 | 3 | 1.37 |
| Welborn, Auburn.. | 10 | 10 | 1 | 1 | 2 | 5 | 0 | .286 | 45 | 42 | 45 | 31 | 3 | 50 | 0 | 1 | 45 | 9 | 6.20 |

|                      |     |     |      |      |    |    |    | Int. |      |     |    |    |     |    |      |     |     |    |      |
| Pitcher—Club         | G.  | GS. | CG. | ShO. | W. | L. | Sv. | Pct. | IP. | H. | R. | ER. | HR. | BB. | BB. | HB. | SO. | WP. | ERA. |
| Welch, Elmira*....   | 9   | 6   | 2    | 0    | 3  | 2  | 1  | .600 | 51   | 46  | 14 | 11  | 0   | 12  | 1   | 0   | 27  | 0   | 1.94 |
| Whiting, Newark*     | 1   | 0   | 0    | 0    | 0  | 0  | 0  | .000 | ⅓    | 0   | 0  | 0   | 0   | 2   | 0   | 0   | 0   | 0   | 0.00 |
| Williams, Auburn..   | 6   | 0   | 0    | 0    | 1  | 0  | 0  | 1.000 | 14  | 17  | 10 | 9   | 1   | 9   | 0   | 0   | 10  | 0   | 5.79 |
| Wilson, Auburn ..    | 14  | 0   | 0    | 0    | 2  | 2  | 0  | .000 | 28   | 28  | 12 | 10  | 2   | 23  | 0   | 1   | 19  | 2   | 3.21 |
| Wright, Oneonta ..   | 17  | 1   | 0    | 0    | 4  | 2  | 2  | .667 | 35   | 27  | 14 | 10  | 0   | 16  | 2   | 0   | 31  | 3   | 2.57 |

BALKS—Holland, 5; Agosto, Bigos, Cieply, Trotter, 2 each; Bradford, Dick, Fox, Garcia, Gonzalez, Hall, Herring, Minier, Presser, Smith (Newark), Tagliarino, Williams, 1 each.

COMBINATION SHUTOUTS—Fowler-Wilson, Auburn; Bigos-Agosto, Waller-Roman, Welch-Lopez, Elmira; Dick-Reyes, Edge-Erardi, Newark; Beattie-Wright, Kwasny-Wright, Oneonta.

NO-HIT GAME—Morris, Newark, defeated Oneonta, 10-0, July 6.

# Northwest League

## CLASS A

### CHAMPIONSHIP WINNERS IN PREVIOUS YEARS

| | | | | |
|---|---|---|---|---|
| 1901—Portland | .675 | 1938—Yakima | .583 | 1958—Lewiston ...... .621 |
| 1902—Butte ............ .608 | | Bellingham (2nd)† .511 | | Yakima* ............ .594 |
| 1903—Butte ............ .578 | | 1939—Wenatchee ...... .601 | | 1959—Salem ......... .623 |
| 1904—Boise ............ .625 | | Tacoma (2nd)† .... .533 | | Yakima* ............ .563 |
| 1905—Vancouver ...... .586 | | 1940—Spokane ........ .587 | | 1960—Yakima‡ ....... .638 |
| Everett* ........ .667 | | Tacoma (4th)† .... .500 | | Yakima ............ .562 |
| 1906—Tacoma ......... .600 | | 1941—Spokane ........ .669 | | 1961—Lewiston* ...... .621 |
| 1907—Aberdeen ....... .625 | | 1942—Vancouver ...... .594 | | Yakima ............ .600 |
| 1908—Vancouver ...... .578 | | 1943-44-45—Did not operate. | | 1962—Wenatchee* ... .574 |
| 1909—Seattle ......... .653 | | 1946—Wenatchee ...... .622 | | Tri-City ........... .580 |
| 1910—Spokane ........ .598 | | 1947—Vancouver ...... .566 | | 1963—Lewiston ...... .594 |
| 1911—Vancouver ...... .628 | | 1948—Spokane ........ .614 | | Yakima* ........... .613 |
| 1912—Seattle ......... .600 | | 1949—Yakima ........ .660 | | 1964—Eugene ........ .636 |
| 1913—Vancouver ...... .600 | | Vancouver (2nd)† .615 | | Yakima* ........... .611 |
| 1914—Vancouver ...... .632 | | 1950—Yakima ........ .613 | | 1965—Lewiston ...... .667 |
| 1915—Seattle ......... .564 | | 1951—Spokane ........ .655 | | Tri-City* .......... .681 |
| 1916—Spokane ........ .622 | | 1952—Victoria ....... .631 | | 1966—Tri-City ...... .679 |
| 1917—Great Falls ...... .593 | | 1953—Salem ......... .635 | | 1967—Medford ...... .607 |
| 1918—Seattle ......... .588 | | Spokane* ........ .590 | | 1968—Tri-City ...... .600 |
| 1919—Seattle ......... .590 | | 1954—Vancouver* ..... .636 | | 1969—Rogue Valley .. .633 |
| 1920—Victoria ........ .600 | | Lewiston ......... .629 | | 1970—Lewiston a .... .538 |
| 1921—Yakima ......... .710 | | 1955—Salem ......... .646 | | Coos Bay-No. Bend .563 |
| Yakima§ ......... .660 | | Eugene* .......... .639 | | 1971—Tri-City a ..... .625 |
| 1922—Calgary§ ....... .600 | | 1956—Yakima ........ .691 | | Bend .............. .538 |
| 1923-36—Did not operate. | | Yakima ............ .619 | | 1972—Lewiston a ..... .675 |
| 1937—Wenatchee ...... .603 | | 1957—Eugene ........ .576 | | Walla Walla ....... .513 |
| Tacoma* ......... .627 | | Wenatchee* ....... .647 | | 1973—Walla Walla b .. .638 |
| | | | | Portland .......... .563 |
| | | | | 1974—Bellingham .... .619 |
| | | | | Eugene c ......... .571 |

*Won split-season playoff. †Won four-club playoff. §League disbanded June 18. aLeague divided into Northern and Southern Divisions, declared champion under league rules. (NOTE—Known as Pacific Northwest League 1901-02. Pacific National League 1903-04. Northwestern League 1905-18. Pacific Coast International League 1919-22 and Western International League 1937-54.) bLeague divided into Eastern and Western Divisions, declared champion under league rules. cLeague divided into Eastern and Western Divisions; won two-team playoff.

### STANDING OF CLUBS AT CLOSE OF SEASON, AUGUST 30

#### NORTHERN DIVISION

| Club | Port. | Sea. | Bell. | Eug. | W.W. | Boise | W. | L. | T. | Pct. | G.B. |
|---|---|---|---|---|---|---|---|---|---|---|---|
| Portland (Independent) ............... | .. | 9 | 13 | 6 | 9 | 5 | 42 | 35 | 0 | .545 | ... |
| Seattle (Independent) .............. | 6 | .. | 9 | 5 | 7 | 8 | 35 | 44 | 0 | .443 | 8 |
| Bellingham (Dodgers) .............. | 2 | 7 | .. | 2 | 1 | 5 | 17 | 61 | 0 | .218 | 25½ |

#### SOUTHERN DIVISION

| Club | Port. | Sea. | Bell. | Eug. | W.W. | Boise | W. | L. | T. | Pct. | G.B. |
|---|---|---|---|---|---|---|---|---|---|---|---|
| Eugene (Reds) ..................... | 10 | 11 | 14 | .. | 11 | 8 | 54 | 25 | 0 | .684 | .... |
| Walla Walla (Padres) ............. | 7 | 9 | 14 | 5 | .. | 13 | 48 | 31 | 0 | .608 | 6 |
| Boise (Athletics) .................. | 10 | 8 | 11 | 7 | 3 | .. | 39 | 39 | 0 | .500 | 14½ |

Major league affiliations in parentheses.
Forfeited Game—Portland forfeited to Boise, July 23.
Playoff—Eugene defeated Portland, two games to none.
Regular-Season Attendance—Bellingham, 21,357; Boise, 29,286; Eugene, 64,864; Portland, 119,253; Seattle, 22,686; Walla Walla, 25,662. Total, 283,108. Playoffs—13,326. No All-Star Game.
Managers: Bellingham—Bill Berrier; Boise—Thomas Trebelhorn; Eugene—Gregory Riddoch; Portland—Frank Peters; Seattle—Ronald Gibson, Douglas Peterson, William Tsoukalas; Walla Walla—Cliff Ditto.
All-Star Team: 1B—Lucich, Eugene; 2B—Watkins, Eugene; 3B—Helfrick, Portland; SS—Woodard, Boise; OF—Reynolds, Walla Walla; McPherson, Eugene; Jones, Eugene; C—Sweet, Walla Walla; Utility—Collette, Portland; DH—Rodriguez, Boise; Gilmartin, Seattle; P—Benson, Seattle; Moskau, Eugene; Hicks, Portland; Gill, Walla Walla; Manager—Riddoch, Eugene.

(Compiled by William J. Weiss, League Statistician, San Mateo, Calif.)

## CLUB BATTING

| Club | G. | AB. | R. | OR. | H. | TB. | 2B. | 3B. | HR. | RBI. | SH. | SF. | BB. | Int. BB. | HP. | SO. | SB. | CS. | LOB. | Pct. |
|------|----|-----|----|-----|----|----|-----|-----|-----|------|-----|-----|-----|-----|-----|-----|-----|-----|------|------|
| Eugene | 79 | 2543 | 540 | 378 | 717 | 1074 | 106 | 31 | 63 | 455 | 36 | 37 | 484 | 13 | 23 | 404 | 100 | 25 | 657 | .282 |
| Boise | 78 | 2442 | 471 | 440 | 675 | 917 | 87 | 19 | 39 | 377 | 50 | 31 | 426 | 1 | 32 | 430 | 150 | 44 | 594 | .276 |
| Portland | 77 | 2333 | 430 | 401 | 633 | 905 | 138 | 19 | 32 | 352 | 29 | 29 | 384 | 13 | 18 | 326 | 115 | 42 | 539 | .271 |
| Seattle | 79 | 2369 | 371 | 423 | 616 | 792 | 76 | 11 | 26 | 290 | 39 | 30 | 410 | 12 | 27 | 320 | 96 | 40 | 587 | .260 |
| Walla Walla | 79 | 2454 | 445 | 341 | 628 | 923 | 85 | 24 | 54 | 386 | 19 | 25 | 423 | 12 | 27 | 420 | 82 | 24 | 623 | .256 |
| Bellingham | 78 | 2354 | 281 | 555 | 508 | 677 | 86 | 13 | 19 | 231 | 11 | 9 | 373 | 3 | 27 | 579 | 92 | 23 | 600 | .216 |

## INDIVIDUAL BATTING

(Leading Qualifiers for Batting Championship—216 or More Plate Appearances)

*Bats lefthanded. †Switch-hitter.

| Player and Club | G. | AB. | R. | H. | TB. | 2B. | 3B. | HR. | RBI. | SH. | SF. | BB. | HP. | SO. | SB. | CS. | Pct. |
|-----------------|----|-----|----|----|----|-----|-----|-----|------|-----|-----|-----|-----|-----|-----|-----|------|
| Sweet, Richard, Walla W†.. | 75 | 260 | 48 | 91 | 149 | 21 | 2 | 11 | 66 | 0 | 4 | 44 | 3 | 18 | 8 | 2 | .350 |
| Collette, Steven, Portland .. | 77 | 260 | 51 | 90 | 135 | 24 | 0 | 7 | 43 | 3 | 2 | 41 | 2 | 24 | 22 | 5 | .346 |
| Medeiros, Gary, Boise | 64 | 210 | 35 | 71 | 78 | 7 | 0 | 0 | 41 | 6 | 5 | 30 | 4 | 14 | 4 | 1 | .338 |
| Jones, Lynn, Eugene | 62 | 211 | 53 | 71 | 129 | 13 | 3 | 13 | 63 | 1 | 3 | 36 | 2 | 25 | 12 | 5 | .336 |
| Watkins, Thomas, Eugene .. | 76 | 296 | 67 | 98 | 149 | 14 | 2 | 11 | 61 | 1 | 1 | 31 | 1 | 39 | 5 | 1 | .331 |
| Reynolds, Donald, Walla W. | 78 | 263 | 79 | 84 | 148 | 11 | 4 | 15 | 61 | 1 | 5 | 62 | 6 | 37 | 11 | 0 | .319 |
| Bothwell, Monte, Boise* .... | 64 | 186 | 46 | 59 | 95 | 10 | 1 | 8 | 43 | 1 | 3 | 34 | 4 | 44 | 10 | 4 | .317 |
| Gilmartin, Paul, Seattle† .. | 78 | 282 | 43 | 89 | 116 | 11 | 2 | 4 | 57 | 2 | 3 | 31 | 2 | 32 | 12 | 2 | .316 |
| Woodard, Darrell, Boise .... | 64 | 246 | 46 | 77 | 87 | 5 | 1 | 1 | 23 | 4 | 1 | 39 | 1 | 26 | 22 | 8 | .313 |
| McPherson, George, Eugene* | 75 | 288 | 71 | 89 | 124 | 11 | 6 | 4 | 38 | 5 | 0 | 64 | 3 | 43 | 28 | 8 | .309 |

Departmental Leaders: G—Gibson, 79; AB—Watkins, 296; R—Reynolds, 79; H—Watkins, 98; TB—Sweet, Watkins, 149; 2B—Collette, 24; 3B—McPherson, 6; HR—Reynolds, 15; RBI—Sweet, 66; SH—M. Harrison, May, 13; SF—Lucich, 76; HP—Moss, 8; SO—M. Jones, 58; SB—McPherson, 28; CS—Dixson, McPherson, Woodard, 8.

### (All Players—Listed Alphabetically)

| Player and Club | G. | AB. | R. | H. | TB. | 2B. | 3B. | HR. | RBI. | SH. | SF. | BB. | HP. | SO. | SB. | CS. | Pct. |
|-----------------|----|-----|----|----|----|-----|-----|-----|------|-----|-----|-----|-----|-----|-----|-----|------|
| Adams, A. Dwight, W W†.. | 54 | 204 | 25 | 50 | 63 | 7 | 0 | 2 | 16 | 1 | 1 | 10 | 1 | 40 | 7 | 5 | .245 |
| Adams, Robert W., Bell† | 51 | 128 | 10 | 23 | 28 | 0 | 0 | 0 | 3 | 2 | 0 | 25 | 2 | 41 | 5 | 0 | .180 |
| Argee, Daniel, Boise* | 54 | 162 | 29 | 50 | 65 | 6 | 0 | 3 | 34 | 7 | 2 | 21 | 4 | 25 | 7 | 2 | .309 |
| Bird, William, Eugene† | 75 | 272 | 63 | 75 | 116 | 12 | 4 | 7 | 43 | 3 | 6 | 43 | 3 | 37 | 7 | 2 | .276 |
| Bothwell, Monte, Boise* | 64 | 186 | 46 | 59 | 95 | 10 | 1 | 8 | 43 | 1 | 3 | 34 | 4 | 44 | 10 | 4 | .317 |
| Bradley, Mark, Bellingham | 76 | 239 | 27 | 61 | 78 | 7 | 2 | 2 | 33 | 0 | 0 | 51 | 2 | 82 | 6 | 7 | .255 |
| Brinkley, Gregory, Port | 21 | 44 | 5 | 8 | 8 | 0 | 0 | 0 | 1 | 1 | 0 | 5 | 0 | 9 | 2 | 0 | .182 |
| Brumfield, Alan, W W*.... | 28 | 75 | 12 | 18 | 19 | 1 | 0 | 0 | 4 | 0 | 0 | 8 | 0 | 18 | 1 | 2 | .240 |
| Carreno, Luis, Bell* | 21 | 35 | 2 | 3 | 3 | 0 | 0 | 0 | 2 | 1 | 0 | 5 | 1 | 14 | 4 | 0 | .086 |
| Castillo, Anthony, W W .... | 45 | 140 | 15 | 32 | 35 | 0 | 0 | 1 | 16 | 2 | 0 | 20 | 0 | 25 | 0 | 1 | .229 |
| Cervantes, Edward, Portland | 67 | 232 | 48 | 71 | 102 | 20 | 1 | 3 | 38 | 2 | 7 | 37 | 3 | 32 | 5 | 4 | .306 |
| Chapados, James, Bell* | 3 | 4 | 0 | 0 | 0 | 0 | 0 | 0 | 0 | 0 | 0 | 1 | 0 | 3 | 0 | 0 | .000 |
| Cheek, Jeffrey, Portland* | 3 | 4 | 2 | 1 | 1 | 0 | 0 | 0 | 0 | 0 | 0 | 2 | 0 | 0 | 0 | 0 | .250 |
| Collette, Steven, Portland | 77 | 260 | 51 | 90 | 135 | 24 | 0 | 7 | 43 | 3 | 2 | 41 | 2 | 24 | 22 | 5 | .346 |
| Colon, Victor, Bellingham* | 26 | 65 | 10 | 14 | 19 | 2 | 0 | 1 | 9 | 0 | 1 | 18 | 0 | 15 | 1 | 0 | .215 |
| Colton, Lawrence, Port* | 11 | 20 | 2 | 6 | 12 | 3 | 0 | 1 | 7 | 0 | 1 | 3 | 0 | 3 | 0 | 0 | .300 |
| Combe, Geoffrey, Eugene | 19 | 42 | 4 | 3 | 3 | 0 | 0 | 0 | 2 | 0 | 1 | 0 | 0 | 16 | 0 | 0 | .071 |
| Cox, Jeffrey, Boise | 54 | 161 | 33 | 38 | 45 | 7 | 0 | 0 | 12 | 3 | 2 | 34 | 2 | 15 | 15 | 1 | .236 |
| Craft, Gerry, Portland | 44 | 124 | 26 | 36 | 47 | 8 | 0 | 1 | 15 | 1 | 0 | 25 | 1 | 29 | 5 | 3 | .290 |
| Crissman, William, Port | 7 | 1 | 0 | 0 | 0 | 0 | 0 | 0 | 0 | 0 | 0 | 0 | 0 | 0 | 0 | 0 | .000 |
| Derryberry, Timothy, W W*. | 31 | 96 | 17 | 17 | 33 | 2 | 1 | 4 | 18 | 0 | 2 | 12 | 2 | 27 | 2 | 0 | .177 |
| Dixson, Xavier, Seattle* | 77 | 281 | 59 | 84 | 107 | 12 | 1 | 3 | 29 | 2 | 1 | 51 | 5 | 34 | 17 | 8 | .299 |
| Drake, Harold, Walla W | 60 | 217 | 28 | 54 | 76 | 8 | 1 | 4 | 39 | 2 | 2 | 15 | 1 | 48 | 4 | 1 | .249 |
| Duval, Michael, Eugene* | 70 | 230 | 38 | 67 | 85 | 10 | 4 | 0 | 47 | 5 | 8 | 33 | 0 | 39 | 16 | 4 | .291 |
| Edge, Evan, Eugene* | 9 | 17 | 4 | 3 | 3 | 0 | 0 | 0 | 1 | 0 | 0 | 7 | 1 | 4 | 0 | 0 | .176 |
| Elston, James, Portland* | 31 | 48 | 6 | 8 | 13 | 2 | 0 | 1 | 6 | 1 | 0 | 9 | 2 | 10 | 1 | 0 | .167 |
| Emery, James, Portland | 18 | 1 | 1 | 1 | 1 | 3 | 0 | 1 | 1 | 0 | 0 | 0 | 0 | 0 | 0 | 0 | 1.000 |
| Fajardo, Eddie, Bellingham. | 53 | 167 | 31 | 41 | 57 | 7 | 3 | 1 | 14 | 1 | 0 | 26 | 1 | 43 | 4 | 1 | .246 |
| Farr, Theodore, Bellingham. | 27 | 79 | 9 | 15 | 20 | 2 | 0 | 1 | 14 | 0 | 2 | 18 | 1 | 13 | 0 | 1 | .190 |
| Frias, Gerardo, Bellingham . | 4 | 9 | 1 | 2 | 2 | 0 | 0 | 0 | 0 | 0 | 0 | 3 | 0 | 1 | 0 | 0 | .222 |
| Gallino, David, Boise | 63 | 184 | 40 | 54 | 68 | 8 | 3 | 0 | 25 | 3 | 3 | 37 | 3 | 18 | 11 | 4 | .293 |
| Garrison, Marvin, Bell | 59 | 189 | 18 | 38 | 48 | 5 | 1 | 1 | 13 | 2 | 2 | 21 | 3 | 55 | 10 | 3 | .201 |
| Getz, R. William, Port* | 57 | 162 | 30 | 38 | 43 | 3 | 1 | 0 | 13 | 2 | 2 | 25 | 1 | 12 | 11 | 6 | .235 |
| Gibson, Ronald, Seattle | 79 | 261 | 37 | 70 | 103 | 7 | 1 | 8 | 41 | 2 | 5 | 36 | 5 | 43 | 8 | 2 | .268 |
| Gilmartin, Paul, Seattle† | 78 | 282 | 43 | 89 | 116 | 11 | 2 | 4 | 57 | 2 | 3 | 31 | 2 | 32 | 12 | 2 | .316 |
| Givler, Robert, Bell† | 45 | 140 | 24 | 41 | 59 | 8 | 2 | 2 | 15 | 1 | 0 | 32 | 0 | 20 | 3 | 3 | .293 |
| Gonzalez, Ramon, Seattle*.. | 72 | 240 | 45 | 64 | 86 | 9 | 2 | 3 | 23 | 3 | 2 | 50 | 4 | 15 | 12 | 3 | .267 |
| Goulding, Richard, Bell .... | 23 | 2 | 0 | 1 | 1 | 0 | 0 | 0 | 0 | 0 | 0 | 0 | 0 | 0 | 0 | 0 | .500 |
| Gulden, Bradley, Bell* | 66 | 203 | 25 | 33 | 43 | 4 | 0 | 2 | 15 | 1 | 0 | 35 | 4 | 39 | 6 | 2 | .163 |
| Harrison, John, Eugene† | 34 | 85 | 11 | 21 | 23 | 2 | 0 | 0 | 8 | 2 | 0 | 25 | 0 | 15 | 7 | 2 | .247 |
| Harrison, Mack, Boise* | 73 | 253 | 38 | 56 | 67 | 5 | 3 | 0 | 22 | 13 | 3 | 51 | 3 | 43 | 20 | 4 | .221 |
| Helfrick, John, Portland | 73 | 235 | 40 | 72 | 94 | 13 | 3 | 1 | 45 | 5 | 1 | 35 | 1 | 21 | 2 | 0 | .306 |
| Heuberger, Donald, Portland | 32 | 75 | 13 | 15 | 17 | 2 | 0 | 0 | 8 | 4 | 1 | 9 | 1 | 21 | 2 | 0 | .200 |
| Hicks, Joseph, Walla W.... | 67 | 225 | 28 | 54 | 79 | 5 | 1 | 6 | 37 | 2 | 0 | 30 | 1 | 40 | 8 | 2 | .240 |
| Hicks, Rick, Portland | 27 | 1 | 0 | 0 | 0 | 0 | 0 | 0 | 0 | 0 | 0 | 1 | 0 | 0 | 0 | 0 | .000 |
| Holland, Clifton, Portland*. | 65 | 244 | 32 | 65 | 95 | 23 | 2 | 1 | 39 | 3 | 4 | 10 | 1 | 31 | 5 | 3 | .266 |
| Hunter, Kenneth, Boise | 22 | 54 | 6 | 10 | 13 | 1 | 1 | 0 | 4 | 1 | 1 | 5 | 1 | 20 | 6 | 0 | .185 |
| Jackson, Rogerald, Sea† | 22 | 36 | 5 | 9 | 10 | 1 | 0 | 0 | 5 | 2 | 1 | 6 | 0 | 3 | 3 | 2 | .250 |

| Player and Club | G. | AB. | R. | H. | TB. | 2B. | 3B. | HR. | RBI. | SH. | SF. | BB. | HP. | SO. | SB. | CS. | Pct. |
|---|---|---|---|---|---|---|---|---|---|---|---|---|---|---|---|---|---|
| Jones, Lynn, Eugene | 62 | 211 | 53 | 71 | 129 | 13 | 3 | 13 | 63 | 1 | 3 | 36 | 2 | 25 | 12 | 5 | .336 |
| Jones, Michael L., Boise† | 66 | 198 | 46 | 54 | 93 | 7 | 1 | 10 | 47 | 4 | 3 | 35 | 2 | 58 | 10 | 3 | .273 |
| Kessler, C. Bradford, Eug. | 11 | 18 | 2 | 4 | 4 | 0 | 0 | 0 | 0 | 0 | 0 | 3 | 0 | 5 | 0 | 0 | .222 |
| King, Robert, Seattle | 76 | 244 | 40 | 54 | 69 | 10 | 1 | 1 | 30 | 4 | 2 | 51 | 3 | 28 | 7 | 5 | .221 |
| Lackey, Steven, Portland | 24 | 92 | 30 | 33 | 54 | 5 | 2 | 4 | 23 | 0 | 2 | 13 | 1 | 9 | 15 | 3 | .359 |
| Larson, Duane, Walla W†.. | 2 | 5 | 0 | 0 | 0 | 0 | 0 | 0 | 0 | 0 | 0 | 1 | 0 | 3 | 2 | 0 | .000 |
| Lowman, Robert, Bellingham | 15 | 2 | 0 | 0 | 0 | 0 | 0 | 0 | 0 | 0 | 0 | 0 | 0 | 1 | 0 | 0 | .000 |
| Lucich, Mark, Eugene* | 78 | 264 | 75 | 80 | 140 | 18 | 3 | 12 | 61 | 1 | 7 | 76 | 2 | 31 | 3 | 0 | .303 |
| Maglio, Carl, Walla Walla.. | 31 | 70 | 11 | 8 | 11 | 1 | 1 | 0 | 4 | 0 | 0 | 17 | 0 | 15 | 0 | 0 | .114 |
| Maldonado, Santiago, Bell.. | 21 | 59 | 7 | 10 | 12 | 0 | 1 | 0 | 4 | 0 | 0 | 8 | 1 | 16 | 0 | 0 | .169 |
| Malito, Steven, Boise† | 67 | 241 | 38 | 63 | 83 | 12 | 4 | 0 | 37 | 4 | 2 | 37 | 0 | 50 | 25 | 4 | .261 |
| Martin, Charles, Bellingham | 48 | 145 | 10 | 29 | 36 | 5 | 1 | 0 | 8 | 1 | 0 | 10 | 1 | 39 | 3 | 2 | .200 |
| May, Kenneth, Seattle* | 71 | 212 | 40 | 54 | 56 | 2 | 0 | 0 | 12 | 13 | 1 | 45 | 2 | 23 | 13 | 5 | .255 |
| Mayberry, Carl, Walla W... | 26 | 57 | 10 | 11 | 14 | 1 | 1 | 0 | 10 | 0 | 3 | 9 | 0 | 17 | 2 | 0 | .193 |
| McCoy, Stuart, Walla Walla | 46 | 122 | 29 | 19 | 35 | 2 | 4 | 2 | 17 | 1 | 1 | 35 | 5 | 50 | 7 | 2 | .156 |
| McGuffin, James, Walla W. | 1 | 4 | 0 | 0 | 0 | 0 | 0 | 0 | 0 | 0 | 0 | 0 | 0 | 2 | 0 | 0 | .000 |
| McPherson, George, Eugene | 75 | 288 | 71 | 89 | 124 | 11 | 6 | 4 | 38 | 5 | 0 | 64 | 3 | 43 | 28 | 8 | .309 |
| Medeiros, Gary, Boise | 64 | 210 | 35 | 71 | 78 | 7 | 0 | 0 | 41 | 6 | 5 | 30 | 4 | 14 | 4 | 1 | .338 |
| Meier, George, Eugene | 29 | 79 | 16 | 15 | 20 | 2 | 0 | 1 | 8 | 1 | 2 | 25 | 1 | 15 | 1 | 0 | .190 |
| Meily, Richard, Portland*.. | 72 | 218 | 47 | 55 | 91 | 11 | 2 | 7 | 44 | 0 | 1 | 67 | 1 | 27 | 5 | 6 | .252 |
| Mendoza, Luis, Bellingham* | 20 | 47 | 5 | 13 | 15 | 2 | 0 | 0 | 4 | 0 | 0 | 8 | 0 | 15 | 0 | 0 | .277 |
| Menes, H. Eugene, W W | 25 | 225 | 62 | 62 | 87 | 9 | 2 | 4 | 27 | 3 | 0 | 70 | 6 | 26 | 14 | 5 | .276 |
| Meyer, Douglas, Portland* | 47 | 140 | 20 | 27 | 38 | 6 | 1 | 1 | 21 | 1 | 0 | 35 | 0 | 27 | 12 | 4 | .193 |
| Mitchell, Robert D., W W* | 65 | 218 | 37 | 62 | 90 | 6 | 5 | 4 | 37 | 4 | 2 | 34 | 1 | 24 | 14 | 3 | .284 |
| Moore, Steven, Eugene | 14 | 29 | 3 | 3 | 3 | 0 | 0 | 0 | 2 | 1 | 0 | 2 | 0 | 9 | 0 | 0 | .103 |
| Moskau, Paul, Eugene | 22 | 45 | 10 | 14 | 25 | 2 | 0 | 3 | 11 | 0 | 1 | 4 | 0 | 9 | 0 | 0 | .311 |
| Mosley, Ronald, Portland | 48 | 136 | 21 | 34 | 48 | 6 | 1 | 2 | 16 | 1 | 3 | 23 | 3 | 16 | 6 | 3 | .250 |
| Moss, Barry, Eugene† | 74 | 256 | 62 | 71 | 110 | 12 | 3 | 7 | 55 | 3 | 6 | 67 | 8 | 30 | 11 | 0 | .277 |
| Neal, Charles, Eugene* | 26 | 21 | 3 | 4 | 4 | 0 | 0 | 0 | 0 | 3 | 2 | 4 | 0 | 7 | 0 | 0 | .190 |
| Ogle, Robin, Walla Walla* | 34 | 92 | 10 | 23 | 32 | 6 | 0 | 1 | 14 | 0 | 3 | 14 | 0 | 16 | 0 | 0 | .250 |
| Owens, Maddison, Boise† | 22 | 0 | 1 | 0 | 0 | 0 | 0 | 0 | 0 | 0 | 0 | 1 | 0 | 0 | 0 | 0 | .000 |
| Patterson, Michael, Boise* | 35 | 74 | 8 | 20 | 21 | 1 | 0 | 0 | 9 | 2 | 0 | 5 | 0 | 22 | 1 | 1 | .270 |
| Peterson, Dennis, Seattle† | 32 | 76 | 2 | 12 | 13 | 1 | 0 | 0 | 9 | 0 | 1 | 8 | 0 | 24 | 0 | 0 | .158 |
| Peterson, Douglas, Seattle† | 76 | 262 | 46 | 69 | 96 | 11 | 2 | 4 | 32 | 5 | 5 | 46 | 2 | 46 | 8 | 3 | .263 |
| Rasmussen, Robert, Port†.. | 20 | 31 | 8 | 6 | 6 | 0 | 0 | 0 | 4 | 0 | 1 | 5 | 0 | 10 | 2 | 1 | .194 |
| Reichle, Richard, Portland† | 2 | 3 | 0 | 0 | 0 | 0 | 0 | 0 | 0 | 0 | 0 | 2 | 0 | 1 | 0 | 0 | .000 |
| Renneau, Charles, Eugene*. | 16 | 27 | 4 | 9 | 12 | 3 | 0 | 0 | 2 | 0 | 0 | 4 | 0 | 2 | 0 | 0 | .333 |
| Reynolds, Donald, Walla W. | 78 | 263 | 79 | 84 | 148 | 11 | 4 | 15 | 61 | 1 | 5 | 62 | 6 | 27 | 11 | 0 | .319 |
| Rodrigues, Kenneth, Boise | 39 | 87 | 19 | 18 | 28 | 2 | 1 | 2 | 17 | 2 | 2 | 25 | 2 | 22 | 7 | 4 | .207 |
| Rodriguez, Gabriel, Eugene | 26 | 53 | 5 | 9 | 12 | 1 | 1 | 0 | 6 | 0 | 1 | 7 | 0 | 19 | 1 | 0 | .170 |
| Rodriguez, Michael, Boise | 65 | 211 | 62 | 64 | 118 | 11 | 2 | 13 | 37 | 0 | 2 | 45 | 5 | 38 | 7 | 3 | .303 |
| Rothschild, Lawrence, Eug*. | 21 | 6 | 1 | 0 | 0 | 0 | 0 | 0 | 0 | 0 | 0 | 0 | 0 | 3 | 0 | 0 | .000 |
| Sander, Clinton, Seattle | 68 | 183 | 18 | 39 | 43 | 2 | 1 | 0 | 20 | 3 | 4 | 27 | 1 | 41 | 11 | 6 | .213 |
| Scott, Ronald, Portland | 41 | 102 | 17 | 23 | 32 | 3 | 3 | 0 | 16 | 1 | 2 | 22 | 0 | 21 | 4 | 0 | .225 |
| Segrest, Walter, Walla W | 8 | 13 | 3 | 1 | 1 | 0 | 0 | 0 | 2 | 0 | 0 | 1 | 4 | 0 | 0 | 0 | .077 |
| Soto, Mario, Eugene | 7 | 11 | 1 | 2 | 2 | 0 | 0 | 0 | 0 | 0 | 0 | 2 | 0 | 4 | 0 | 0 | .182 |
| Styles, Marlon, Eugene* | 54 | 148 | 30 | 40 | 67 | 4 | 4 | 5 | 35 | 3 | 2 | 34 | 2 | 31 | 9 | 2 | .270 |
| Sucarichi, George, Eugene | 25 | 76 | 7 | 19 | 20 | 1 | 0 | 0 | 3 | 2 | 0 | 4 | 0 | 13 | 0 | 1 | .250 |
| Sufrin, D. Scott, Port* | 5 | 10 | 2 | 1 | 1 | 0 | 0 | 0 | 1 | 0 | 1 | 1 | 0 | 0 | 0 | 0 | .100 |
| Swanson, James, Portland* | 12 | 15 | 0 | 0 | 0 | 0 | 0 | 0 | 0 | 2 | 0 | 1 | 0 | 4 | 0 | 0 | .000 |
| Sweet, Richard, Walla W†.. | 75 | 260 | 48 | 91 | 149 | 21 | 2 | 11 | 66 | 0 | 4 | 44 | 3 | 18 | 8 | 2 | .350 |
| Thomas, Reginald, Portland | 22 | 79 | 19 | 28 | 46 | 7 | 1 | 3 | 12 | 0 | 0 | 12 | 0 | 10 | 11 | 3 | .354 |
| Thompson, Narciso, Bell | 40 | 134 | 14 | 36 | 59 | 14 | 0 | 3 | 23 | 0 | 1 | 12 | 1 | 25 | 2 | 0 | .269 |
| Trezona, Thomas, Seattle | 33 | 116 | 9 | 25 | 36 | 5 | 0 | 2 | 13 | 1 | 2 | 5 | 0 | 16 | 2 | 2 | .216 |
| Tsoukalas, William, Sea* | 13 | 5 | 1 | 2 | 2 | 0 | 0 | 0 | 0 | 0 | 0 | 1 | 0 | 0 | 0 | 0 | .400 |
| Tuttle, James, Boise | 53 | 165 | 23 | 39 | 54 | 5 | 2 | 2 | 24 | 1 | 2 | 26 | 1 | 32 | 4 | 5 | .236 |
| Underwood, John, Eugene | 12 | 27 | 5 | 7 | 10 | 1 | 1 | 0 | 4 | 1 | 0 | 1 | 0 | 4 | 0 | 0 | .259 |
| Uremovich, Michael, Port* | 23 | 60 | 10 | 15 | 19 | 2 | 1 | 0 | 8 | 2 | 1 | 2 | 0 | 9 | 2 | 1 | .250 |
| Waite, Kenneth, Seattle | 64 | 171 | 26 | 45 | 55 | 5 | 1 | 1 | 19 | 2 | 3 | 53 | 3 | 15 | 3 | 2 | .263 |
| Walker, Donald, Boise | 11 | 10 | 1 | 2 | 5 | 0 | 0 | 1 | 0 | 0 | 0 | 0 | 0 | 3 | 1 | 0 | .200 |
| Walraven, Randy, Eugene | 20 | 28 | 2 | 8 | 8 | 0 | 0 | 0 | 0 | 0 | 0 | 5 | 0 | 3 | 0 | 0 | .286 |
| Washington, Donald, Bell | 46 | 114 | 17 | 12 | 17 | 2 | 0 | 1 | 3 | 0 | 0 | 14 | 5 | 55 | 5 | 4 | .105 |
| Watkins, Thomas, Eugene | 76 | 296 | 67 | 98 | 149 | 14 | 2 | 11 | 61 | 1 | 1 | 31 | 1 | 39 | 5 | 1 | .331 |
| Weirum, Ronald, Belling* | 77 | 246 | 38 | 58 | 82 | 16 | 1 | 2 | 35 | 1 | 2 | 62 | 1 | 48 | 4 | 2 | .236 |
| White, Myron, Bellingham* | 26 | 193 | 25 | 49 | 62 | 8 | 1 | 1 | 25 | 1 | 0 | 9 | 3 | 45 | 10 | 3 | .254 |
| Williams, Robert, Eugene | 26 | 14 | 4 | 5 | 5 | 0 | 0 | 0 | 3 | 1 | 0 | 5 | 0 | 1 | 0 | 0 | .357 |
| Winkelbauer, Thomas, Port. | 15 | 1 | 0 | 0 | 0 | 0 | 0 | 0 | 0 | 0 | 0 | 0 | 0 | 1 | 0 | 0 | .000 |
| Wittmayer, Kurt, Walla W. | 49 | 165 | 30 | 40 | 47 | 5 | 1 | 0 | 18 | 2 | 2 | 38 | 0 | 20 | 1 | 1 | .242 |
| Woodard, Darrell, Boise | 64 | 246 | 46 | 77 | 87 | 5 | 1 | 2 | 23 | 4 | 1 | 39 | 1 | 26 | 22 | 8 | .313 |
| Zepponi, Kenneth, Bell | 49 | 150 | 10 | 29 | 41 | 4 | 1 | 2 | 9 | 0 | 1 | 14 | 1 | 52 | 8 | 0 | .193 |

The following pitchers had no plate appearances primarily through use of designated-hitters, listed alphabetically by club, games in parentheses:

BELLINGHAM—Carlson, Thomas (19); Evans, James (13); Gonzalez, Juan (1); Lake, Michael (22); Medina, Freddy (12); Scheller, Rodney (13); Stewart, David (22); Stoffle, Robert (17); Tennant, Michael (13); Townsend, Kenneth (16).

BOISE—Bell, Ronald (9); Bowman, Kenneth (16); Hagman, David (16); Joyce, Kevin (21); Kingman, Brian (16); Murphy, Guy (10); Voelkel, Ransom (6); Walsh, Timothy (22); Zedalis, W. Patrick (19).

EUGENE—Halgerson, Keith (3).

PORTLAND—Alexander, James (2); Benedetti, Jeffrey (8); Bouton, James (5); Guischer, Michael (15); Gullotti, Steven (2); Nelson, Robert (2); Olson, Daniel (5); Readdick, L. Harold (5); Rusteck, Richard (11); Shortell, Robert (6).

SEATTLE—Allan, Lynn (9); Benson, George (14); Herman, Lawrence (5); Meyring, George (19); Morris, Dale (14); Stillwell, Stephen (13); Strong, Darnell (24); Tener, Stephen (14); Williams, Jimmie (13).

WALLA WALLA—Bernal, Victor (10); Bovee, Rodney (11); Burns, Byron (2); French, Martin (15); Gill, Ronald (23); Hollingsworth, Guy (15); Jett, Rodney (7); Joseph, William (12); Lentz, Michael (11); Owen, Gregory (1); Roak, Steven (11); Silvestri, Pardo (4); Wilkes, Gregory (14).

TWO CLUBS—Sloan, David (3 Walla Walla—8 Seattle).

GRAND-SLAM HOME RUNS—Bird, 2; A. Adams, J. Hicks, McPherson, Douglas Peterson, Sweet, Thomas, Weirum, 1 each.

AWARDED FIRST BASE ON INTERFERENCE—R. Adams (Den. Peterson), Meyer (Gulden).

## CLUB FIELDING

| Club | G. | PO. | A. | E. | DP. | PB. | Pct. | Club | G. | PO. | A. | E. | DP. | PB. | Pct. |
|------|----|----|----|----|-----|-----|------|------|----|----|----|----|-----|-----|------|
| Portland | 77 | 1845 | 860 | 118 | 70 | 19 | .958 | Seattle | 79 | 1901 | 813 | 157 | 50 | 31 | .945 |
| Eugene | 79 | 1959 | 837 | 141 | 74 | 25 | .952 | Boise | 78 | 1912 | 804 | 163 | 68 | 38 | .943 |
| Walla Walla | 79 | 1908 | 841 | 153 | 70 | 23 | .947 | Bellingham | 78 | 1836 | 784 | 228 | 62 | 38 | .920 |

Triple Play—Boise.

## INDIVIDUAL FIELDING

*Throws lefthanded.

### FIRST BASEMEN

| Player and Club | G. | PO. | A. | E. | DP. | Pct. | Player and Club | G. | PO. | A. | E. | DP. | Pct. |
|------|----|----|----|----|-----|------|------|----|----|----|----|-----|------|
| GILMARTIN, Seat* | 77 | 667 | 48 | 9 | 41 | .988 | Elston, Portland* | 15 | 124 | 13 | 4 | 9 | .972 |
| Lucich, Eugene* | 78 | 684 | 57 | 12 | 61 | .984 | Ogle, Walla Walla | 32 | 202 | 9 | 7 | 22 | .968 |
| Meyer, Portland* | 43 | 347 | 23 | 7 | 35 | .981 | Helfrick, Portland | 12 | 81 | 6 | 3 | 7 | .967 |
| Brumfield, W W | 23 | 172 | 14 | 4 | 11 | .979 | Zepponi, Bell* | 29 | 234 | 17 | 10 | 19 | .962 |
| Argee, Boise* | 50 | 370 | 34 | 9 | 30 | .978 | Farr, Bellingham | 27 | 185 | 8 | 8 | 22 | .960 |
| Rodrigues, Boise | 30 | 192 | 28 | 5 | 19 | .978 | Colon, Bellingham* | 22 | 138 | 16 | 8 | 5 | .951 |
| Sweet, Walla Walla | 31 | 228 | 24 | 6 | 28 | .977 | | | | | | | |

Triple Play—Rodrigues.

#### (Fewer Than Ten Games)

| Player and Club | G. | PO. | A. | E. | DP. | Pct. | Player and Club | G. | PO. | A. | E. | DP. | Pct. |
|------|----|----|----|----|-----|------|------|----|----|----|----|-----|------|
| Martin, Bellingham | 9 | 46 | 3 | 0 | 3 | 1.000 | Gibson, Seattle | 1 | 1 | 0 | 0 | 1 | 1.000 |
| Collette, Portland | 3 | 20 | 6 | 0 | 4 | 1.000 | Holland, Portland* | 7 | 42 | 10 | 1 | 3 | .981 |
| Derryberry, W W | 2 | 15 | 1 | 0 | 2 | 1.000 | Cox, Boise | 6 | 46 | 2 | 1 | 6 | .980 |
| Medeiros, Boise | 2 | 14 | 0 | 0 | 3 | 1.000 | Getz, Portland* | 6 | 44 | 3 | 1 | 5 | .979 |
| King, Seattle | 2 | 13 | 1 | 0 | 1 | 1.000 | Drake, Walla Walla | 3 | 23 | 2 | 2 | 2 | .926 |
| Sander, Seattle | 1 | 8 | 0 | 0 | 1 | 1.000 | Thomas, Portland | 4 | 21 | 4 | 2 | 4 | .926 |
| Kessler, Eugene | 1 | 2 | 1 | 0 | 1 | 1.000 | Bothwell, Boise* | 2 | 11 | 2 | 4 | 1 | .765 |

### SECOND BASEMEN

| Player and Club | G. | PO. | A. | E. | DP. | Pct. | Player and Club | G. | PO. | A. | E. | DP. | Pct. |
|------|----|----|----|----|-----|------|------|----|----|----|----|-----|------|
| Cox, Boise | 10 | 17 | 18 | 0 | 5 | 1.000 | Harrison, Eugene | 22 | 48 | 53 | 6 | 17 | .944 |
| MENEES, Walla W | 65 | 141 | 182 | 12 | 41 | .964 | Maldonado, Bell | 14 | 34 | 40 | 5 | 5 | .937 |
| Watkins, Eugene | 52 | 97 | 126 | 10 | 26 | .957 | Wittmayer, W W | 13 | 31 | 40 | 5 | 8 | .934 |
| Bird, Eugene | 14 | 27 | 32 | 3 | 5 | .952 | Mav, Seattle | 67 | 135 | 156 | 23 | 26 | .927 |
| Collette, Portland | 35 | 77 | 78 | 8 | 13 | .951 | Fajardo, Bell | 24 | 50 | 64 | 10 | 17 | .919 |
| Harrison, Boise | 72 | 159 | 194 | 19 | 34 | .949 | Adams, Bellingham | 47 | 87 | 102 | 25 | 15 | .883 |
| Cervantes, Portland | 42 | 97 | 134 | 13 | 36 | .947 | Jackson, Seattle | 10 | 15 | 22 | 5 | 3 | .881 |

Triple Play—Cox.

#### (Fewer Than Ten Games)

| Player and Club | G. | PO. | A. | E. | DP. | Pct. | Player and Club | G. | PO. | A. | E. | DP. | Pct. |
|------|----|----|----|----|-----|------|------|----|----|----|----|-----|------|
| Mitchell, Walla W | 3 | 6 | 6 | 0 | 1 | 1.000 | Walker, Boise | 2 | 1 | 2 | 1 | 1 | .750 |
| Rasmussen, Portland | 2 | 4 | 3 | 1 | 2 | .875 | Trezona, Seattle | 1 | 1 | 1 | 1 | 0 | .667 |
| Waite, Seattle | 3 | 4 | 9 | 3 | 0 | .813 | Bradley, Bellingham | 1 | 1 | 1 | 2 | 0 | .500 |

### THIRD BASEMEN

| Player and Club | G. | PO. | A. | E. | DP. | Pct. | Player and Club | G. | PO. | A. | E. | DP. | Pct. |
|------|----|----|----|----|-----|------|------|----|----|----|----|-----|------|
| MOSS, Eugene | 73 | 76 | 138 | 9 | 9 | .960 | Weirum, Bellingham | 77 | 63 | 147 | 20 | 16 | .913 |
| Helfrick, Portland | 63 | 52 | 135 | 11 | 11 | .944 | Gallino, Boise | 51 | 34 | 81 | 12 | 5 | .906 |
| Mitchell, Walla W | 58 | 52 | 99 | 9 | 14 | .944 | Maglio, Walla Walla | 23 | 15 | 35 | 11 | 3 | .820 |
| Collette, Portland | 15 | 9 | 21 | 2 | 1 | .938 | Cox, Boise | 36 | 20 | 46 | 15 | 7 | .815 |
| King, Seattle | 72 | 60 | 156 | 20 | 9 | .915 | | | | | | | |

#### (Fewer Than Ten Games)

| Player and Club | G. | PO. | A. | E. | DP. | Pct. | Player and Club | G. | PO. | A. | E. | DP. | Pct. |
|------|----|----|----|----|-----|------|------|----|----|----|----|-----|------|
| Maldonado, Bell | 4 | 5 | 1 | 0 | 0 | 1.000 | Wittmayer, W W | 1 | 0 | 4 | 1 | 0 | .800 |
| Uremovich, Portland | 1 | 4 | 1 | 0 | 0 | 1.000 | Trezona, Seattle | 5 | 4 | 14 | 5 | 0 | .783 |
| Gibson, Seattle | 2 | 1 | 4 | 0 | 0 | 1.000 | Bird, Eugene | 4 | 1 | 6 | 2 | 3 | .778 |
| Jackson, Seattle | 2 | 0 | 4 | 0 | 0 | 1.000 | Jones, Eugene | 4 | 2 | 4 | 2 | 0 | .750 |
| Craft, Portland | 2 | 1 | 0 | 0 | 0 | 1.000 | Medeiros, Boise | 1 | 0 | 1 | 1 | 0 | .500 |
| Sander, Seattle | 1 | 1 | 0 | 0 | 0 | 1.000 | Reichle, Portland | 2 | 0 | 0 | 2 | 0 | .000 |
| Adams, Bellingham | 2 | 0 | 1 | 0 | 0 | 1.000 | Fajardo, Bell | 1 | 0 | 0 | 1 | 0 | .000 |
| Menees, Walla W | 1 | 0 | 1 | 0 | 0 | 1.000 | Walker, Boise | 2 | 0 | 0 | 0 | 0 | .000 |

## SHORTSTOPS

| Player and Club | G. | PO. | A. | E. | DP. | Pct. |
|---|---|---|---|---|---|---|
| Mosley, Portland ... | 47 | 89 | 153 | 13 | 32 | .949 |
| WOODARD, Boise . | 63 | 116 | 179 | 18 | 38 | .942 |
| Rasmussen, Portland | 14 | 16 | 23 | 3 | 3 | .929 |
| Cervantes, Portland | 23 | 34 | 50 | 7 | 7 | .923 |
| Bird, Eugene ..... | 55 | 87 | 139 | 22 | 24 | .911 |
| Doug. Peterson, Seat. | 76 | 119 | 202 | 34 | 30 | .904 |
| Wittmayer, W W .. | 35 | 42 | 100 | 15 | 16 | .904 |
| Gallino, Boise ...... | 13 | 28 | 19 | 5 | 2 | .904 |
| Bradley, Bellingham | 61 | 112 | 137 | 28 | 24 | .899 |
| Drake, Walla Walla | 44 | 73 | 126 | 26 | 28 | .884 |
| Fajardo, Bellingham. | 20 | 38 | 49 | 14 | 5 | .861 |
| Sucarichi, Eugene .. | 24 | 15 | 56 | 15 | 9 | .826 |

### (Fewer Than Ten Games)

| Player and Club | G. | PO. | A. | E. | DP. | Pct. |
|---|---|---|---|---|---|---|
| Collette, Portland . | 4 | 7 | 12 | 1 | 1 | .950 |
| Cox, Boise ........ | 4 | 5 | 9 | 1 | 2 | .933 |
| Walker, Boise .... | 5 | 7 | 6 | 1 | 2 | .929 |
| Den. Peterson, Sea.. | 3 | 7 | 10 | 2 | 3 | .895 |
| Harrison, Eugene .. | 8 | 12 | 23 | 5 | 4 | .875 |
| Brumfield, W W ... | 1 | 3 | 1 | 1 | 0 | .800 |
| Lackey, Portland ... | 3 | 2 | 3 | 2 | 1 | .714 |
| Adams, Bellingham . | 1 | 1 | 0 | 2 | 0 | .333 |

Triple Play—Walker.

## OUTFIELDERS

| Player and Club | G. | PO. | A. | E. | DP. | Pct. |
|---|---|---|---|---|---|---|
| Lackey, Portland .. | 15 | 20 | 1 | 0 | 0 | 1.000 |
| Collette, Portland . | 14 | 16 | 0 | 0 | 0 | 1.000 |
| Martin, Bellingham | 18 | 13 | 0 | 0 | 0 | 1.000 |
| Mayberry, Walla W . | 10 | 6 | 1 | 0 | 0 | 1.000 |
| REYNOLDS, W W . | 77 | 106 | 8 | 1 | 1 | .991 |
| Holland, Portland* . | 60 | 110 | 3 | 2 | 0 | .983 |
| Sander, Seattle .... | 60 | 96 | 6 | 3 | 0 | .971 |
| Malito, Boise* .... | 66 | 135 | 6 | 5 | 2 | .966 |
| Dixson, Seattle* ... | 75 | 149 | 9 | 6 | 2 | .963 |
| Duval, Eugene .... | 68 | 118 | 8 | 5 | 1 | .962 |
| Givler, Bellingham . | 42 | 62 | 10 | 3 | 2 | .960 |
| Getz, Portland* ... | 41 | 44 | 4 | 2 | 0 | .960 |
| Jones, Eugene .... | 56 | 88 | 5 | 4 | 1 | .959 |
| Craft, Portland .... | 35 | 39 | 6 | 2 | 0 | .957 |
| McCoy, Walla Walla | 44 | 64 | 1 | 3 | 0 | .956 |
| Gonzalez, Seattle* . | 69 | 118 | 7 | 6 | 1 | .954 |
| Bothwell, Boise* ... | 60 | 71 | 6 | 4 | 1 | .951 |
| Hicks, Walla Walla. | 67 | 124 | 6 | 7 | 1 | .949 |
| Washington, Bell .. | 42 | 62 | 3 | 4 | 1 | .942 |
| Rodriguez, Eugene . | 21 | 30 | 2 | 2 | 1 | .941 |
| White, Bellingham* . | 53 | 104 | 5 | 7 | 1 | .940 |
| McPherson, Eugene* | 75 | 119 | 14 | 10 | 3 | .930 |
| Adams, Walla Walla | 18 | 12 | 1 | 1 | 0 | .929 |
| Jones, Boise ...... | 61 | 113 | 2 | 9 | 1 | .927 |
| Meily, Portland .... | 59 | 74 | 5 | 8 | 2 | .908 |
| Watkins, Eugene .. | 27 | 42 | 6 | 5 | 1 | .906 |
| Garrison, Bell .... | 54 | 71 | 4 | 8 | 0 | .904 |
| Zepponi, Bell* .... | 14 | 25 | 0 | 3 | 0 | .893 |
| Trezona, Seattle ... | 25 | 20 | 1 | 4 | 1 | .882 |
| Brinkley, Portland . | 19 | 15 | 0 | 2 | 0 | .882 |
| Derryberry, W W .. | 25 | 36 | 1 | 5 | 0 | .881 |
| Bradley, Bellingham | 15 | 25 | 2 | 4 | 1 | .871 |
| Thompson, Bell .... | 14 | 16 | 4 | 3 | 1 | .870 |
| Tuttle, Boise ..... | 44 | 49 | 6 | 9 | 1 | .859 |
| Patterson, Boise ... | 23 | 24 | 0 | 5 | 0 | .828 |
| Carreno, Bellingham | 14 | 14 | 1 | 5 | 0 | .750 |

### (Fewer Than Ten Games)

| Player and Club | G. | PO. | A. | E. | DP. | Pct. |
|---|---|---|---|---|---|---|
| Waite, Seattle .... | 6 | 6 | 1 | 0 | 0 | 1.000 |
| May, Seattle ...... | 3 | 1 | 0 | 0 | 0 | 1.000 |
| Swanson, Portland* . | 6 | 2 | 1 | 0 | 0 | 1.000 |
| Meyer, Portland* .. | 3 | 3 | 0 | 0 | 0 | 1.000 |
| Argee, Boise* ..... | 3 | 2 | 0 | 0 | 0 | 1.000 |
| Gilmartin, Seattle* . | 3 | 2 | 0 | 0 | 0 | 1.000 |
| Den. Peterson, Sea . | 3 | 2 | 0 | 0 | 0 | 1.000 |
| Scott, Portland .... | 1 | 2 | 0 | 0 | 0 | 1.000 |
| Kessler, Eugene ... | 3 | 1 | 0 | 0 | 0 | 1.000 |
| Thomas, Portland .. | 9 | 6 | 0 | 1 | 0 | .857 |
| Segrest, Walla W .. | 7 | 5 | 0 | 1 | 0 | .833 |
| Drake, Walla Walla | 4 | 6 | 0 | 2 | 0 | .750 |

## CATCHERS

| Player and Club | G. | PO. | A. | E. | DP. | PB. | Pct. |
|---|---|---|---|---|---|---|---|
| Mendoza, Bell ... | 20 | 90 | 10 | 1 | 4 | 11 | .990 |
| Scott, Portland .. | 37 | 175 | 29 | 3 | 4 | 8 | .986 |
| SWEET, Walla W . | 43 | 243 | 29 | 5 | 1 | 6 | .982 |
| Waite, Seattle .. | 52 | 261 | 37 | 7 | 5 | 9 | .977 |
| He-berger, Port . | 31 | 109 | 19 | 3 | 1 | 6 | .977 |
| Medeiros, Boise . | 47 | 244 | 41 | 7 | | 18 | .976 |
| Styles, Eugene .. | 50 | 266 | 34 | 9 | 4 | 15 | .971 |
| Meier, Eugene .. | 28 | 149 | 16 | 5 | 1 | 8 | .971 |
| Castillo, W W .. | 44 | 256 | 41 | 11 | 3 | 17 | .964 |
| Gibson, Seattle . | 21 | 102 | 19 | 5 | 0 | 11 | .960 |
| Rodriguez, Boise | 29 | 145 | 20 | 8 | 0 | 14 | .954 |
| Hunter, Boise .. | 14 | 62 | 3 | 4 | 0 | 6 | .942 |
| Uremovich, Port . | 21 | 93 | 15 | 7 | 1 | 5 | .939 |
| Gulden, Bell .... | 63 | 319 | 70 | 33 | 9 | 23 | .922 |
| Den. Peterson, Sea | 14 | 53 | 3 | 7 | 0 | 11 | .889 |

### (Fewer Than Ten Games)

| Player and Club | G. | PO. | A. | E. | DP. | PB. | Pct. |
|---|---|---|---|---|---|---|---|
| Swanson, Port* . | 3 | 8 | 1 | 0 | 0 | 0 | 1.000 |
| Sufrin, Portland . | 1 | 6 | 0 | 0 | 0 | 0 | 1.000 |
| Edge, Eugene ... | 7 | 34 | 3 | 1 | 1 | 2 | .974 |
| Givler, Bell ..... | 2 | 3 | 4 | 2 | 1 | 4 | .778 |

## PITCHERS

| Player and Club | G. | PO | A. | E. | DP. | Pct. |
|---|---|---|---|---|---|---|
| COMBE, Eugene .. | 19 | 9 | 18 | 0 | 1 | 1.000 |
| Winkelbauer, Port . | 15 | 8 | 15 | 0 | 1 | 1.000 |
| Goulding, Bell ... | 23 | 8 | 11 | 0 | 4 | 1.000 |
| Rusteck, Portland* . | 13 | 3 | 15 | 0 | 3 | 1.000 |
| Joseph, Walla W* .. | 12 | 2 | 13 | 0 | 1 | 1.000 |
| Hagman, Boise ... | 16 | 6 | 7 | 0 | 0 | 1.000 |
| Sloan, W W-Seattle | 11 | 6 | 5 | 0 | 1 | 1.000 |
| Strong, Seattle* .. | 21 | 1 | 10 | 0 | 0 | 1.000 |
| Medina, Bellingham | 12 | 7 | 2 | 0 | 0 | 1.000 |
| Elston, Portland* .. | 11 | 0 | 9 | 0 | 1 | 1.000 |
| Hicks, Portland ... | 27 | 5 | 3 | 0 | 0 | 1.000 |
| Rothschild, Eugene | 21 | 3 | 5 | 0 | 0 | 1.000 |
| Roak, Walla Walla . | 11 | 2 | 5 | 0 | 0 | 1.000 |
| Lowman, Bellingham | 15 | 1 | 1 | 0 | 0 | 1.000 |
| Morris, Seattle .... | 14 | 0 | 1 | 0 | 0 | 1.000 |
| Guischer, Portland . | 15 | 19 | 11 | 1 | 0 | .968 |
| Benson, Seattle ... | 14 | 3 | 23 | 1 | 0 | .963 |
| Williams, Seattle .. | 13 | 11 | 11 | 1 | 0 | .957 |
| Bernal, Walla W ... | 10 | 8 | 8 | 1 | 0 | .941 |
| Neal, Eugene ..... | 26 | 4 | 10 | 1 | 2 | .933 |
| Moore, Eugene .... | 14 | 4 | 22 | 2 | 1 | .929 |
| Gill, Walla Walla .. | 23 | 6 | 7 | 1 | 1 | .929 |
| Stillwell, Seattle* . | 13 | 2 | 11 | 1 | 0 | .929 |
| Kingman, Boise ... | 16 | 6 | 5 | 1 | 1 | .917 |
| French, Walla W .. | 15 | 7 | 25 | 3 | 2 | .914 |
| Wilkins, Eugene ... | 24 | 5 | 15 | 2 | 1 | .909 |
| Reineau, Eugene .. | 14 | 8 | 11 | 2 | 2 | .905 |
| Tener, Seattle .... | 14 | 8 | 10 | 2 | 1 | .900 |

### PITCHERS—Continued

| Player and Club | G. | PO. | A. | E. | DP. | Pct. | Player and Club | G. | PO. | A. | E. | DP. | Pct. |
|---|---|---|---|---|---|---|---|---|---|---|---|---|---|
| Walsh, Boise | 22 | 6 | 11 | 2 | 0 | .895 | Stoffle, Bellingham | 17 | 2 | 15 | 3 | 0 | .850 |
| Murphy, Boise | 10 | 3 | 14 | 2 | 1 | .895 | Townsend, Bell | 16 | 2 | 9 | 2 | 0 | .846 |
| Wilkes, Walla W. | 14 | 10 | 14 | 3 | 1 | .889 | Owens, Boise | 21 | 9 | 16 | 5 | 1 | .833 |
| Moskau, Eugene | 13 | 6 | 10 | 2 | 1 | .889 | Joyce, Boise* | 21 | 5 | 18 | 5 | 0 | .821 |
| Walraven, Eugene* | 15 | 5 | 11 | 2 | 0 | .889 | Tsoukalas, Seattle* | 10 | 3 | 18 | 5 | 2 | .808 |
| Hollingsworth, W W* | 15 | 2 | 14 | 2 | 1 | .889 | Bovee, Walla W* | 11 | 1 | 3 | 1 | 0 | .800 |
| Tennant, Bellingham | 13 | 4 | 10 | 2 | 1 | .875 | Stewart, Bellingham | 22 | 4 | 8 | 4 | 1 | .750 |
| Scheller, Bell | 13 | 1 | 13 | 2 | 0 | .875 | Meyring, Seattle | 19 | 3 | 9 | 5 | 0 | .706 |
| Zedalis, Boise | 19 | 4 | 3 | 1 | 0 | .875 | Emery, Portland* | 17 | 3 | 9 | 5 | 1 | .706 |
| Lake, Bellingham* | 22 | 3 | 9 | 2 | 0 | .857 | Lentz, Walla W* | 11 | 1 | 6 | 3 | 0 | .700 |
| Bowman, Boise | 16 | 6 | 17 | 4 | 2 | .852 | Carlson, Bell* | 19 | 1 | 2 | 2 | 1 | .600 |
| Underwood, Eugene | 11 | 11 | 6 | 3 | 1 | .850 | Evans, Bellingham* | 13 | 0 | 4 | 4 | 0 | .500 |

### (Fewer Than Ten Games)

| Player and Club | G. | PO. | A. | E. | DP. | Pct. | Player and Club | G. | PO. | A. | E. | DP. | Pct. |
|---|---|---|---|---|---|---|---|---|---|---|---|---|---|
| Bouton, Portland | 5 | 3 | 8 | 0 | 1 | 1.000 | Holland, Portland* | 9 | 0 | 2 | 0 | 0 | 1.000 |
| Soto, Eugene | 5 | 4 | 6 | 0 | 0 | 1.000 | Voelkel, Boise* | 6 | 0 | 1 | 0 | 0 | 1.000 |
| Shortell, Portland | 6 | 4 | 5 | 0 | 0 | 1.000 | Getz, Portland* | 5 | 0 | 1 | 0 | 0 | 1.000 |
| Bell, Boise | 9 | 2 | 7 | 0 | 0 | 1.000 | Nelson, Portland* | 2 | 0 | 1 | 0 | 0 | 1.000 |
| Benedetti, Portland | 8 | 2 | 5 | 0 | 0 | 1.000 | Thomas, Portland | 2 | 0 | 1 | 0 | 0 | 1.000 |
| Allan, Seattle* | 9 | 0 | 4 | 0 | 0 | 1.000 | Jett, Walla Walla* | 7 | 3 | 8 | 2 | 0 | .846 |
| Colton, Portland | 3 | 0 | 4 | 0 | 0 | 1.000 | Crissman, Portland | 7 | 1 | 3 | 1 | 0 | .800 |
| Readdick, Portland | 5 | 1 | 2 | 0 | 0 | 1.000 | Silvestri, W W* | 4 | 1 | 1 | 1 | 0 | .667 |
| Burns, Walla Walla. | 2 | 1 | 2 | 0 | 0 | 1.000 | Herman, Seattle | 5 | 2 | 1 | 2 | 1 | .600 |
| Alexander, Portland | 2 | 0 | 3 | 0 | 0 | 1.000 | Zepponi, Bell* | 1 | 0 | 1 | 1 | 0 | .500 |
| Jackson, Seattle | 3 | 2 | 0 | 0 | 0 | 1.000 | Owen, Walla Walla | 1 | 0 | 0 | 1 | 0 | .000 |

The following players do not have any recorded accepted chances at the positions indicated; therefore, are not listed in the fielding averages for those particular positions: Brumfield, 3b; Cheek*, of; Elston*, of; Gilmartin*, p; J. Gonzalez, p; Gullotti, p; Halgerson, p; M. Harrison. p; Helfrick, ss, Jackson, ss; Lackey, 3b-p; Moss, of; Olson, p; Douglas Peterson, 1b; Rodrigues. p; Sander, 2b; Styles, 3b; Sufrin, of; Tuttle, p; Uremovich, p; Walker, p; Chapados, Frias, Larson and McGuffin appeared as designated-hitters/pinch-hitters only.

### CLUB PITCHING

| Club | G. | CG. | ShO. | Sv. | IP. | H. | R. | ER. | HR. | BB. | Int. BB. | HB. | SO. | WP. | Bk. | ERA. |
|---|---|---|---|---|---|---|---|---|---|---|---|---|---|---|---|---|
| Walla Walla | 79 | 36 | 9 | 10 | 636 | 571 | 341 | 260 | 41 | 366 | 9 | 22 | 487 | 58 | 6 | 3.68 |
| Eugene | 79 | 21 | 7 | 18 | 653 | 617 | 378 | 308 | 30 | 389 | 2 | 37 | 416 | 55 | 1 | 4.25 |
| Portland | 77 | 29 | 4 | 6 | 615 | 621 | 401 | 313 | 31 | 382 | 10 | 24 | 362 | 46 | 4 | 4.58 |
| Seattle | 79 | 40 | 5 | 4 | 634 | 637 | 423 | 325 | 45 | 399 | 4 | 33 | 397 | 51 | 5 | 4.61 |
| Boise | 78 | 23 | 6 | 6 | 637 | 666 | 440 | 333 | 47 | 434 | 20 | 18 | 428 | 62 | 4 | 4.70 |
| Bellingham | 78 | 13 | 3 | 8 | 612 | 666 | 555 | 371 | 36 | 530 | 9 | 18 | 387 | 77 | 5 | 5.46 |

### PITCHERS' RECORDS

(Leading Qualifiers for Earned-Run Average Leadership—67 or More Innings)

*Throws lefthanded.

| Pitcher—Club | G. | GS. | CG. | ShO. | W. | L. | Sv. | Pct. | IP. | H. | R. | ER. | HR. | BB. | Int. BB. | HB. | SO. | WP. | ERA. |
|---|---|---|---|---|---|---|---|---|---|---|---|---|---|---|---|---|---|---|---|
| Moskau, Eugene | 13 | 12 | 7 | 2 | 10 | 1 | 0 | .909 | 84 | 52 | 22 | 14 | 0 | 41 | 0 | 1 | 92 | 5 | 1.50 |
| Gill, Walla Walla | 23 | 2 | 1 | 0 | 7 | 4 | 5 | .636 | 64 | 43 | 27 | 14 | 3 | 33 | 5 | 0 | 63 | 4 | 1.97 |
| Benson, Seattle | 14 | 11 | 11 | 3 | 9 | 2 | 0 | .818 | 88 | 75 | 26 | 20 | 3 | 29 | 1 | 4 | 50 | 2 | 2.05 |
| Tsoukalas, Seattle* | 10 | 10 | 9 | 0 | 7 | 3 | 0 | .700 | 79 | 63 | 74 | 20 | 5 | 6 | 0 | 3 | 49 | 5 | 2.28 |
| Combe, Eugene | 19 | 11 | 3 | 0 | 9 | 3 | 1 | .750 | 102 | 99 | 40 | 31 | 2 | 41 | 1 | 2 | 40 | 2 | 2.74 |
| Evans, Belling* | 13 | 10 | 1 | 0 | 4 | 5 | 0 | .444 | 67 | 59 | 44 | 21 | 3 | 69 | 0 | 1 | 39 | 2 | 2.82 |
| Lentz, Walla W* | 11 | 11 | 6 | 2 | 5 | 3 | 0 | .625 | 67 | 45 | 26 | 22 | 5 | 46 | 1 | 1 | 74 | 5 | 2.96 |
| Winkelbauer, Port | 15 | 14 | 6 | 1 | 6 | 6 | 0 | .500 | 97 | 90 | 49 | 33 | 2 | 47 | 1 | 0 | 72 | 4 | 3.06 |
| Underwood, Eug | 11 | 10 | 5 | 1 | 6 | 3 | 0 | .667 | 69 | 63 | 27 | 24 | 1 | 26 | 0 | 7 | 46 | 2 | 3.13 |
| Hollingsw'th, WW* | 15 | 11 | 6 | 1 | 6 | 3 | 1 | .667 | 83 | 85 | 40 | 32 | 7 | 57 | 1 | 2 | 51 | 6 | 3.47 |

Departmental Leaders: G—Hicks, 27; GS—French, Moore, Renneau, Wilkes, Winkelbauer, 14; CG—Benson, 11; ShO—Benson, 3; W—Moskau, 10; L—Goulding, Townsend, 10; Sv—Neal, Roth-schild, 6; Pct.—Moskau, .909; IP—Combe, 102; H—Bowman, 117; R—Renneau, 74; ER—Renneau, 68; HR—Renneau, 11; BB—Owens, 85; IBB—Gill, Hicks, 5; HB—Emery, 9; SO—Moskau, 92; WP—Carlson, Owens, Renneau, 14.

### (All Pitchers—Listed Alphabetically)

| Pitcher—Club | G. | GS. | CG. | ShO. | W. | L. | Sv. | Pct. | IP. | H. | R. | ER. | HR. | BB. | Int. BB. | HB. | SO. | WP. | ERA. |
|---|---|---|---|---|---|---|---|---|---|---|---|---|---|---|---|---|---|---|---|
| Alexander, Port | 2 | 0 | 0 | 0 | 1 | 0 | 0 | 1.000 | 8 | 3 | 3 | 3 | 0 | 3 | 0 | 0 | 4 | 0 | 4.50 |
| Allan, Seattle* | 9 | 0 | 0 | 0 | 1 | 3 | 0 | .250 | 18 | 30 | 35 | 24 | 3 | 17 | 1 | 1 | 17 | 3 | 12.00 |
| Bell, Boise | 9 | 3 | 1 | 0 | 6 | 2 | 0 | .750 | 63 | 61 | 38 | 25 | 3 | 25 | 3 | 1 | 33 | 1 | 3.57 |
| Benedetti, Port | 8 | 2 | 1 | 0 | 1 | 1 | 0 | .500 | 18 | 19 | 11 | 11 | 1 | 9 | 1 | 2 | 6 | 2 | 5.50 |
| Benson, Seattle | 14 | 11 | 11 | 3 | 9 | 2 | 0 | .818 | 88 | 75 | 26 | 20 | 3 | 29 | 1 | 4 | 50 | 2 | 2.05 |
| Bernal, Walla W | 10 | 6 | 3 | 0 | 4 | 3 | 1 | .571 | 53 | 55 | 21 | 19 | 2 | 13 | 1 | 4 | 59 | 8 | 3.23 |
| Bouton, Portland | 5 | 5 | 4 | 0 | 4 | 1 | 0 | .800 | 41 | 32 | 13 | 10 | 2 | 16 | 0 | 0 | 17 | 0 | 2.20 |
| Bovee, Walla W* | 11 | 2 | 1 | 0 | 3 | 0 | 2 | 1.000 | 23 | 11 | 2 | 2 | 0 | 16 | 0 | 0 | 25 | 1 | 0.78 |
| Bowman, Boise | 16 | 13 | 6 | 1 | 7 | 5 | 0 | .583 | 99 | 117 | 59 | 47 | 5 | 42 | 4 | 2 | 50 | 7 | 4.27 |
| Burns, Walla W. | 2 | 1 | 0 | 0 | 1 | 0 | 0 | .000 | 9 | 13 | 9 | 7 | 1 | 4 | 0 | 0 | 4 | 1 | 7.00 |
| Carlson, Bell* | 19 | 1 | 0 | 0 | 0 | 0 | 0 | .000 | 26 | 19 | 33 | 24 | 0 | 67 | 0 | 2 | 26 | 14 | 8.31 |
| Colton, Portland | 3 | 3 | 1 | 0 | 0 | 0 | 0 | .000 | 11 | 18 | 16 | 13 | 3 | 5 | 0 | 0 | 2 | 0 | 10.64 |
| Combe, Eugene | 19 | 11 | 3 | 0 | 9 | 3 | 1 | .750 | 102 | 99 | 40 | 31 | 2 | 41 | 1 | 2 | 40 | 2 | 2.74 |
| Crissman, Port | 7 | 1 | 0 | 0 | 1 | 0 | 0 | .000 | 22 | 39 | 26 | 23 | 4 | 11 | 1 | 2 | 11 | 2 | 9.41 |
| Elston, Portland* | 11 | 2 | 0 | 0 | 1 | 1 | 0 | .500 | 37 | 46 | 36 | 28 | 2 | 39 | 0 | 2 | 12 | 1 | 6.81 |

| Pitcher—Club | G | GS | CG | ShO | W | L | Sv | Pct. | IP | H | R | ER | HR | BB | Int. BB | HB | SO | WP | ERA |
|---|---|---|---|---|---|---|---|---|---|---|---|---|---|---|---|---|---|---|---|
| Emery, Portland* .17 | 13 | 5 | 0 | 4 | 6 | 0 | .400 | 77 | 80 | 62 | 50 | 6 | 67 | 0 | 9 | 48 | 13 | 5.84 |
| Evans, Bellingham* | 13 | 10 | 1 | 0 | 4 | 5 | 0 | .444 | 67 | 59 | 44 | 21 | 3 | 69 | 0 | 1 | 39 | 2 | 2.82 |
| French, Walla W..15 | 14 | 7 | 2 | 7 | 3 | 0 | .700 | 101 | 98 | 56 | 45 | 7 | 52 | 1 | 1 | 64 | 7 | 4.01 |
| Getz, Portland* .. 5 | 1 | 0 | 0 | 0 | 0 | 0 | .000 | 13 | 9 | 4 | 4 | 0 | 10 | 0 | 0 | 4 | 0 | 2.77 |
| Gill, Walla Walla | 23 | 2 | 1 | 0 | 7 | 4 | 5 | .636 | 64 | 43 | 27 | 14 | 3 | 33 | 5 | 0 | 63 | 4 | 1.97 |
| Gilmartin, Sea* .. | 1 | 0 | 0 | 0 | 0 | 0 | 0 | .000 | ½ | 4 | 3 | 3 | 0 | 2 | 0 | 0 | 0 | 0 | 81.00 |
| Gonzalez, Bell .. | 1 | 0 | 0 | 0 | 0 | 0 | 0 | .000 | 0 | 1 | 3 | 1 | 0 | 2 | 0 | 0 | 0 | 2 | .... |
| Goulding, Portland .23 | 10 | 5 | 1 | 3 | 10 | 1 | .231 | 79 | 86 | 67 | 51 | 8 | 64 | 3 | 2 | 54 | 8 | 5.81 |
| Guischer, Portland | 15 | 12 | 3 | 2 | 8 | 3 | 0 | .727 | 85 | 86 | 52 | 41 | 3 | 25 | 0 | 4 | 68 | 5 | 4.34 |
| Gullotti, Portland .. | 2 | 0 | 0 | 0 | 0 | 0 | 0 | .000 | 6 | 6 | 3 | 3 | 0 | 7 | 0 | 1 | 2 | 1 | 4.50 |
| Hagman, Boise ...16 | 7 | 2 | 0 | 4 | 3 | 1 | .571 | 59 | 59 | 42 | 33 | 4 | 42 | 1 | 5 | 46 | 3 | 5.03 |
| Halgerson, Boise | 3 | 0 | 0 | 0 | 0 | 0 | 0 | .000 | 5 | 8 | 6 | 6 | 1 | 4 | 0 | 0 | 2 | 1 | 10.80 |
| Harrison, Boise .. | 1 | 0 | 0 | 0 | 0 | 0 | 0 | .000 | 2 | 2 | 0 | 0 | 0 | 2 | 1 | 1 | 0 | 1 | 0.00 |
| Herman, Seattle .. 5 | 4 | 2 | 0 | 2 | 0 | 0 | 1.000 | 26 | 30 | 19 | 16 | 5 | 17 | 0 | 0 | 23 | 2 | 5.54 |
| Hicks, Portland .27 | 1 | 0 | 0 | 8 | 1 | 5 | .889 | 61 | 40 | 16 | 12 | 0 | 36 | 5 | 1 | 27 | 2 | 1.77 |
| Holland, Portland* | 9 | 0 | 0 | 0 | 1 | 0 | .000 | 10 | 18 | 12 | 7 | 0 | 6 | 0 | 1 | 10 | 3 | 6.30 |
| Hollinsworth, WW* | 15 | 11 | 4 | 0 | 6 | 3 | 1 | .667 | 83 | 85 | 40 | 32 | 7 | 57 | 1 | 2 | 51 | 6 | 3.47 |
| Jackson, Seattle .. | 3 | 0 | 0 | 0 | 0 | 0 | 0 | .000 | 3 | 2 | 1 | 0 | 1 | 0 | 1 | 0 | 0 | 1 | 0.00 |
| Jett, Walla Walla* | 7 | 4 | 1 | 0 | 1 | 2 | 0 | .333 | 26 | 27 | 27 | 21 | 1 | 32 | 0 | 1 | 13 | 3 | 7.27 |
| Joseph, Walla W* .12 | 9 | 5 | 1 | 4 | 5 | 0 | .444 | 63 | 54 | 33 | 23 | 6 | 33 | 0 | 6 | 43 | 5 | 3.29 |
| Joyce, Boise* ...12 | 7 | 1 | 0 | 2 | 6 | 2 | .250 | 58 | 70 | 44 | 34 | 6 | 47 | 2 | 0 | 43 | 10 | 5.28 |
| Kingman, Boise ..16 | 11 | 5 | 1 | 4 | 6 | 0 | .400 | 74 | 73 | 46 | 32 | 6 | 32 | 0 | 0 | 70 | 2 | 3.89 |
| Lackey, Portland .. 2 | 0 | 0 | 0 | 1 | 0 | 0 | 1.000 | 4 | 4 | 2 | 2 | 0 | 3 | 1 | 0 | 1 | 1 | 4.50 |
| Lake, Bellingham* | 22 | 3 | 1 | 1 | 3 | 4 | 2 | .429 | 55 | 60 | 43 | 25 | 2 | 44 | 1 | 1 | 45 | 12 | 4.09 |
| Lentz, Walla W* .11 | 11 | 6 | 2 | 5 | 3 | 0 | .625 | 67 | 45 | 26 | 22 | 5 | 46 | 1 | 1 | 74 | 5 | 2.96 |
| Lowman, Belling .15 | 0 | 0 | 0 | 0 | 0 | 2 | .000 | 25 | 26 | 17 | 11 | 1 | 9 | 0 | 1 | 14 | 2 | 3.96 |
| Medina, Bell ...12 | 1 | 0 | 0 | 0 | 2 | 0 | .000 | 23 | 31 | 29 | 18 | 3 | 27 | 1 | 1 | 14 | 5 | 7.04 |
| Meyring, Seattle .19 | 4 | 1 | 0 | 2 | 7 | 1 | .222 | 55 | 55 | 51 | 40 | 1 | 51 | 1 | 4 | 45 | 11 | 6.55 |
| Moore, Eugene ...14 | 14 | 1 | 0 | 5 | 4 | 0 | .556 | 78 | 79 | 54 | 43 | 1 | 47 | 0 | 8 | 47 | 6 | 4.96 |
| Morris, Seattle ...14 | 0 | 0 | 0 | 0 | 1 | 0 | .000 | 22 | 31 | 19 | 16 | 2 | 22 | 0 | 1 | 9 | 2 | 6.55 |
| Moskau, Eugene ..13 | 12 | 7 | Σ | 10 | 1 | 0 | .909 | 84 | 52 | 22 | 14 | 0 | 41 | 0 | 1 | 92 | 5 | 1.50 |
| Murphy, Boise ...10 | 8 | 2 | 0 | 3 | 3 | 0 | .400 | 42 | 39 | 26 | 19 | 4 | 27 | 1 | 2 | 21 | 5 | 4.07 |
| Neal, Eugene ...26 | 0 | 0 | 0 | 2 | 6 | 2 | .750 | 66 | 62 | 33 | 27 | 5 | 22 | 0 | 7 | 24 | 2 | 3.68 |
| Nelson, Portland* . 2 | 1 | 0 | 0 | 0 | 0 | 0 | .000 | 6 | 5 | 8 | 8 | 0 | 11 | 0 | 1 | 3 | 0 | 12.00 |
| Olson, Portland .. 5 | 0 | 0 | 0 | 0 | 1 | 0 | .000 | 2 | 4 | 5 | 4 | 1 | 8 | 0 | 0 | 3 | 0 | 18.00 |
| Owen, Walla Walla | 1 | 0 | 0 | 0 | 0 | 0 | 0 | .000 | 2 | 1 | 1 | 0 | 0 | 5 | 0 | 0 | 0 | 0 | 0.00 |
| Owens, Boise ...21 | 9 | 2 | 0 | 6 | 5 | 1 | .545 | 80 | 62 | 51 | 35 | 3 | 85 | 3 | 3 | 72 | 14 | 3.94 |
| Readdick, Portland . 5 | 2 | 0 | 0 | 1 | 1 | 0 | .500 | 21 | 22 | 13 | 9 | 0 | 8 | 0 | 0 | 17 | 3 | 3.86 |
| Renneau, Eugene ..14 | 14 | 2 | 0 | 3 | 4 | 0 | .429 | 66 | 82 | 74 | 68 | 11 | 57 | 0 | 4 | 51 | 14 | 9.27 |
| Roak, Walla Walla | 11 | 2 | 0 | 0 | 1 | 1 | .500 | 32 | 38 | 28 | 25 | 4 | 18 | 0 | 1 | 18 | 4 | 7.03 |
| Rodrigues, Boise . 2 | 0 | 0 | 0 | 0 | 0 | 0 | .000 | 6 | 9 | 7 | 5 | 1 | 5 | 0 | 0 | 1 | 1 | 7.50 |
| Rothschild, Eugene | 21 | 0 | 0 | 3 | 0 | 6 | 11.000 | 33 | 17 | 11 | 10 | 1 | 21 | 0 | 2 | 36 | 4 | 2.73 |
| Rusteck, Portland* | 11 | 11 | 6 | 0 | 4 | 5 | 0 | .444 | 72 | 68 | 52 | 36 | 5 | 47 | 1 | 1 | 42 | 5 | 4.50 |
| Scheller, Bell ...13 | 12 | 0 | 0 | 2 | 8 | 0 | .200 | 64 | 75 | 70 | 49 | 2 | 48 | 0 | 4 | 28 | 3 | 6.89 |
| Shortell, Portland . 6 | 5 | 1 | 1 | 2 | 3 | 0 | .400 | 24 | 25 | 18 | 16 | 2 | 23 | 0 | 0 | 12 | 1 | 6.00 |
| Silvestri, W W* .. 4 | 3 | 0 | 0 | 2 | 1 | 0 | .667 | 19 | 14 | 8 | 6 | 0 | 6 | 0 | 0 | 12 | 1 | 2.84 |
| Sloan, 3 Walla Walla-8 Seattle .11 | 8 | 2 | 0 | 3 | 3 | 0 | .500 | 50 | 50 | 29 | 19 | 2 | 51 | 0 | 5 | 30 | 4 | 3.42 |
| Soto, Eugene ... 5 | 5 | 2 | 0 | 3 | 3 | 0 | .500 | 30 | 33 | 21 | 14 | 4 | 18 | 0 | 1 | 11 | 4 | 4.20 |
| Stewart, Bell ...22 | 5 | 1 | 0 | 0 | 5 | 2 | .000 | 49 | 59 | 46 | 30 | 2 | 49 | 1 | 3 | 37 | 10 | 5.51 |
| Stillwell, Sea* ...13 | 10 | 2 | 0 | 2 | 7 | 0 | .222 | 70 | 85 | 61 | 49 | 8 | 68 | 0 | 0 | 26 | 9 | 6.30 |
| Stoffle, Bell ...17 | 12 | 2 | 0 | 2 | 8 | 1 | .200 | 89 | 103 | 71 | 54 | 4 | 44 | 1 | 1 | 53 | 7 | 5.46 |
| Strong, Seattle* ..21 | 6 | 3 | 0 | 3 | 7 | 3 | .500 | 58 | 62 | 45 | 41 | 4 | 41 | 0 | 3 | 42 | 2 | 6.36 |
| Tener, Seattle ...14 | 11 | 3 | 0 | 4 | 4 | 0 | .500 | 76 | 79 | 60 | 43 | 5 | 47 | 0 | 7 | 37 | 8 | 5.09 |
| Tennant, Bell ...13 | 12 | 0 | 0 | 2 | 8 | 0 | .200 | 63 | 67 | 52 | 41 | 3 | 58 | 2 | 1 | 40 | 7 | 5.86 |
| Thomas, Portland . 2 | 0 | 0 | 0 | 0 | 0 | 0 | .000 | 2 | 0 | 0 | 0 | 0 | 1 | 0 | 0 | 1 | 0 | 0.00 |
| Townsend, Bell ..16 | 12 | 0 | 0 | 1 | 10 | 0 | .091 | 71 | 80 | 69 | 46 | 8 | 42 | 0 | 1 | 36 | 5 | 5.83 |
| Tsoukalas, Seattle* | 10 | 10 | 9 | 0 | 7 | 3 | 0 | .700 | 79 | 63 | 24 | 20 | 5 | 6 | 0 | 3 | 49 | 5 | 2.28 |
| Tuttle, Boise ... 1 | 0 | 0 | 0 | 0 | 0 | 0 | .000 | 3 | 1 | 0 | 0 | 0 | 1 | 0 | 0 | 2 | 0 | 0.00 |
| Underwood, Eugene | 11 | 10 | 5 | 1 | 6 | 3 | 0 | .667 | 69 | 63 | 27 | 24 | 1 | 26 | 0 | 7 | 46 | 2 | 3.13 |
| Uremovich, Port .. | 1 | 0 | 0 | 0 | 0 | 0 | 0 | .000 | 2 | 2 | 0 | 0 | 0 | 0 | 0 | 0 | 0 | 0 | 0.00 |
| Voelkel, Boise* ... 6 | 3 | 0 | 0 | 0 | 1 | 0 | .000 | 17 | 17 | 15 | 11 | 1 | 18 | 2 | 1 | 8 | 4 | 5.82 |
| Walker, Boise ... 1 | 0 | 0 | 0 | 0 | 0 | 0 | .000 | 2 | 0 | 0 | 0 | 1 | 0 | 0 | 1 | 0 | 0.00 |
| Walraven, Eugene* | 15 | 13 | 1 | 1 | 6 | 4 | 0 | .600 | 66 | 60 | 56 | 41 | 2 | 76 | 0 | 2 | 32 | 9 | 5.59 |
| Walsh, Boise ...22 | 6 | 2 | 0 | 5 | 4 | 2 | .556 | 70 | 67 | 50 | 45 | 9 | 52 | 1 | 2 | 45 | 2 | 5.79 |
| Wilkes, Walla W .14 | 14 | 8 | 1 | 8 | 5 | 0 | .615 | 91 | 85 | 57 | 39 | 5 | 42 | 0 | 6 | 57 | 11 | 3.86 |
| J. Williams, Sea .13 | 12 | 7 | 1 | 2 | 7 | 0 | .222 | 92 | 83 | 56 | 37 | 7 | 56 | 1 | 5 | 72 | 5 | 3.62 |
| Williams, Eugene .24 | 0 | 0 | 0 | 4 | 1 | 5 | .800 | 55 | 62 | 34 | 29 | 2 | 36 | 1 | 3 | 35 | 6 | 4.75 |
| Winkelbauer, Port .15 | 14 | 6 | 1 | 6 | 6 | 0 | .500 | 97 | 90 | 49 | 33 | 2 | 47 | 1 | 0 | 72 | 4 | 3.06 |
| Zedalis, Boise ...19 | 6 | 0 | 0 | 3 | 4 | 0 | .429 | 61 | 89 | 60 | 49 | 5 | 55 | 2 | 1 | 36 | 12 | 7.23 |
| Zepponi, Bell* | 1 | 0 | 0 | 0 | 0 | 0 | 0 | .000 | 3 | 7 | 1 | 0 | 7 | 0 | 0 | 1 | 0 | 9.00 |

BALKS—Hollingsworth, Stewart, Walsh, 2 each; Allan, Bell, Benson, Bernal, Elston, Emery, Evans, Gill, Goulding, Lake, Lentz, Neal, Roak, Rusteck, Stillwell, Tener, J. Williams, Winkelbauer, Zedalis, 1 each.

COMBINATION SHUTOUTS—Scheller-Stoffle, Bellingham; Walsh-Kingman, Boise; Combe-Rothschild, Moskau-Neal, Walraven-Williams, Eugene; Strong-Morris-Meyring, Seattle; Bovee-Bernal, Hollingsworth-Gill, Lentz-Gill, Walla Walla.

NO-HIT GAMES—None.

# Western Carolinas League

## CLASS A

### CHAMPIONSHIP WINNERS IN PREVIOUS YEARS

| | | |
|---|---|---|
| 1948—Lincolnton* ........ .627 | Shelby (4th)† ...... .481 | Greenwood‡ ........ .597 |
| 1949—Newton-Conover ... .667 | 1962—Statesville ......... .563 | 1969—Greenwood‡ ........ .587 |
| Ruth'ford Co. (2nd)† .627 | Statesville ......... .700 | Shelby ............. .565 |
| 1950—Newton-Conover ... .627 | 1963—Greenville† ........ .576 | 1970—Greenville ......... .576 |
| Lenoir (2nd)† .. .626 | Salisbury .......... .631 | Greenville ......... .619 |
| 1951—Morganton ....... .645 | 1964—Rock Hill ........ .672 | 1971—Greenwood ......... .631 |
| Shelby (2nd)† ..... .604 | Salisbury‡ ......... .631 | Greenwood ......... .759 |
| 1952—Lincolnton ....... .649 | 1965—Salisbury ......... .641 | 1972—Spartanburg‡ ....... .788 |
| Shelby (2nd)† .... .645 | Rock Hill‡ ......... .603 | Greenville ......... .652 |
| 1953-59—League inactive. | 1966—Spartanburg ....... .682 | 1973—Spartanburg‡ ....... .646 |
| 1960—Lexington ....... .707 | Spartanburg ....... .767 | Gastonia ........... .619 |
| Salisbury (2nd)† .. .650 | 1967—Spartanburg ....... .730 | 1974—Gastonia ........... .606 |
| 1961—Salisbury ........ .627 | Spartanburg ....... .567 | Gastonia ........... .672 |
| | 1968—Spartanburg ........ .597 | |

*Won championship and four-club playoff. †Won four-club playoff. ‡Won split-season playoff.
(NOTE—Known as Western Carolina League from 1948 through 1962.)

### STANDING OF CLUBS AT CLOSE OF FIRST HALF, JUNE 19

| Club | W. | L. | T. | Pct. | G.B. | Club | W. | L. | T. | Pct. | G.B. |
|---|---|---|---|---|---|---|---|---|---|---|---|
| Spartanburg (Phillies) ....38 | 38 | 32 | 0 | .543 | .... | Charleston (Pirates) ......29 | 29 | 40 | 0 | .420 | 8½ |
| Anderson (Rangers) ......30 | 30 | 36 | 0 | .455 | 6 | Greenwood (Braves) ......25 | 25 | 46 | 0 | .352 | 13½ |

### STANDING OF CLUBS AT CLOSE OF SECOND HALF, AUGUST 28

| Club | W. | L. | T. | Pct. | G.B. | Club | W. | L. | T. | Pct. | G.B. |
|---|---|---|---|---|---|---|---|---|---|---|---|
| Spartanburg (Phillies) ....43 | 43 | 27 | 0 | .614 | .... | Anderson (Rangers) .......37 | 37 | 34 | 0 | .521 | 6½ |
| Greenwood (Braves) ......37 | 37 | 33 | 0 | .529 | 6 | Charleston (Pirates) ......16 | 16 | 56 | 0 | .222 | 28 |

### FINAL STANDINGS OF WESTERN CAROLINAS LEAGUE VS. CAROLINA LEAGUE

| Club | W. | L. | T. | Pct. | G.B. | Club | W. | L. | T. | Pct. | G.B. |
|---|---|---|---|---|---|---|---|---|---|---|---|
| Rocky Mount (Phillies) ..38 | 38 | 8 | 0 | .826 | .... | Lynchburg (Rangers) .....19 | 19 | 24 | 0 | .442 | 17½ |
| Winston-Salem (Red Sox) ..31 | 31 | 16 | 0 | .660 | 7½ | Anderson (Rangers) ......18 | 18 | 26 | 0 | .409 | 19 |
| Salem (Pirates) ..........27 | 27 | 18 | 0 | .600 | 10½ | Greenwood (Braves) ......16 | 16 | 29 | 0 | .356 | 21½ |
| Spartanburg (Phillies) ....21 | 21 | 25 | 0 | .457 | 17 | Charleston (Pirates) ......11 | 11 | 35 | 0 | .239 | 27 |

### COMPOSITE STANDINGS OF CLUBS AT CLOSE OF SEASON, AUGUST 28

| Club | Spa. | And. | Gwd. | Cha. | R.M. | W.S. | Sal. | Lyn. | W. | L. | T. | Pct. | G.B. |
|---|---|---|---|---|---|---|---|---|---|---|---|---|---|
| Spartanburg (Phillies) ...... | .. | 19 | 18 | 23 | 2 | 7 | 5 | 7 | 81 | 59 | 0 | .579 | .... |
| Anderson (Rangers) ........ | 11 | .. | 17 | 21 | 3 | 4 | 4 | 7 | 67 | 70 | 0 | .489 | 12½ |
| Greenwood (Braves) ........ | 14 | 15 | .. | 17 | 1 | 3 | 7 | 5 | 62 | 79 | 0 | .440 | 19½ |
| Charleston (Pirates) ....... | 9 | 10 | 15 | .. | 2 | 2 | 5 | 2 | 45 | 96 | 0 | .319 | 36½ |
| Rocky Mount (Phillies) ..... | 10 | 9 | 9 | 10 | .. | 17 | 20 | 16 | 91 | 51 | 0 | .641 | .... |
| Winston-Salem (Red Sox) ... | 5 | 7 | 9 | 10 | 15 | .. | 17 | 18 | 81 | 62 | 1 | .566 | 10½ |
| Salem (Pirates) ............ | 6 | 7 | 4 | 10 | 12 | 15 | .. | 20 | 74 | 66 | 1 | .529 | 16 |
| Lynchburg (Rangers) ........ | 4 | 3 | 7 | 5 | 16 | 14 | 11 | .. | 60 | 78 | 0 | .435 | 29 |

Major League affiliations in parentheses.
NOTE: Forfeited Game—Spartanburg forfeited to Winston-Salem (CL), June 12, at Winston-Salem.

Regular-Season Attendance—Anderson, 25,591; Charleston, 21,693; Greenwood, 23,195; Spartanburg, 27,336. Total, 97,815. All-Star Game, 607. No playoff.

All-Star Team: 1B—Begnaud, Spartanburg; 2B—Ryan, Greenwood; 3B—Maddox, Greenwood; SS—Brookens, Anderson; OF—O'Bonnell, Greenwood; Smith, Spartanburg; Bernazard, Charleston; C—Murphy, Greenwood; P—Bright, Anderson; Gibson, Spartanburg; Manager—Elia, Spartanburg.

Managers: Anderson—Rich Donnelly; Charleston—Michael Ryan; Greenwood—Bobby Dews; Spartanburg—Lee Elia.

(Compiled by Howe News Bureau, Chicago, Ill.)

### CLUB BATTING

| Club | G. | AB. | R. | OR. | H. | TB. | 2B. | 3B. | HR. | RBI. | SH. | SF. | Int. BB. | BB. | HP. | SO. | SB. | CS. | LOB. | Pct. |
|---|---|---|---|---|---|---|---|---|---|---|---|---|---|---|---|---|---|---|---|---|
| Spartanburg | 140 | 4436 | 645 | 546 | 1112 | 1524 | 185 | 22 | 61 | 561 | 54 | 50 | 604 | 17 | 50 | 718 | 125 | 50 | 1049 | .251 |
| Charleston | 141 | 4423 | 474 | 694 | 1099 | 1367 | 143 | 19 | 29 | 400 | 64 | 40 | 525 | 13 | 22 | 742 | 70 | 55 | 1082 | .248 |
| Greenwood | 141 | 4469 | 580 | 648 | 1065 | 1482 | 170 | 32 | 61 | 495 | 75 | 37 | 599 | 19 | 23 | 913 | 123 | 51 | 1049 | .238 |
| Anderson | 137 | 4221 | 573 | 623 | 952 | 1303 | 137 | 20 | 58 | 473 | 62 | 36 | 645 | 16 | 51 | 981 | 121 | 74 | 986 | .226 |

## INDIVIDUAL BATTING
(Leading Qualifiers for Batting Championship—389 or More Plate Appearances)

*Bats lefthanded. †Switch-hitter.

| Player and Club | G. | AB. | R. | H. | TB. | 2B. | 3B. | HR. | RBI. | SH. | SF. | BB. | HP. | SO. | SB. | CS. | Pct. |
|---|---|---|---|---|---|---|---|---|---|---|---|---|---|---|---|---|---|
| Bonnell, Robert, 23 Spa- 101 Greenwood | 124 | 457 | 86 | 148 | 216 | 20 | 6 | 12 | 80 | 0 | 5 | 51 | 5 | 38 | 15 | 4 | .324 |
| Smith, Lonnie, Spartanburg | 131 | 465 | 114 | 150 | 202 | 23 | 4 | 7 | 40 | 4 | 3 | 96 | 9 | 63 | 56 | 14 | .323 |
| Begnaud, Gary, Spartanburg | 137 | 465 | 99 | 143 | 251 | 37 | 3 | 25 | 100 | 0 | 10 | 92 | 9 | 68 | 2 | 0 | .308 |
| Gray, Gary, Anderson | 135 | 487 | 79 | 147 | 230 | 27 | 1 | 18 | 95 | 1 | 7 | 55 | 6 | 79 | 6 | 5 | .302 |
| Lebron, Juan, Charleston | 136 | 499 | 36 | 139 | 167 | 21 | 2 | 1 | 59 | 6 | 12 | 36 | 1 | 41 | 3 | 5 | .279 |
| Yearby, Melvin, Spartanburg | 129 | 442 | 76 | 123 | 174 | 21 | 6 | 6 | 82 | 8 | 4 | 66 | 5 | 82 | 8 | 6 | .278 |
| DeLiza, Juan, Charleston | 126 | 475 | 54 | 132 | 146 | 10 | 2 | 0 | 36 | 6 | 1 | 19 | 1 | 59 | 9 | 6 | .278 |
| Bernazard, Oscar, Charles* | 131 | 434 | 55 | 119 | 155 | 23 | 2 | 3 | 46 | 5 | 4 | 105 | 3 | 81 | 6 | 3 | .274 |
| Reedy, Jerome, Spartanburg | 131 | 463 | 73 | 124 | 146 | 19 | 0 | 1 | 37 | 5 | 3 | 59 | 0 | 54 | 19 | 6 | .268 |
| Jones, Alvin, Greenwood*.. | 135 | 488 | 59 | 127 | 169 | 27 | 3 | 3 | 48 | 5 | 1 | 67 | 1 | 117 | 16 | 10 | .260 |

DEPARTMENTAL LEADERS: G—Brady, 139; AB—Lebron, 499; R—L. Smith, 114; H—L. Smith, 150; TB—Begnaud, 251; 2B—Begnaud, Gray, Jones, 27; 3B—Bonnell, Evans, Sosa, Yearby, 6; HR—Begnaud 25; RBI—Begnaud, 100; SH—Richard, 20; SF—Lebron, 12; BB—Bernazard, 105; HP—Lisi, 13; SO—Purvis, 174; SB—L. Smith, 56; CS—Ryan, L. Smith, 14.

### (All Players—Listed Alphabetically)

| Player and Club | G. | AB. | R. | H. | TB. | 2B. | 3B. | HR. | RBI. | SH. | SF. | BB. | HP. | SO. | SB. | CS. | Pct. |
|---|---|---|---|---|---|---|---|---|---|---|---|---|---|---|---|---|---|
| Ammons, Mark, Charleston | 55 | 176 | 15 | 42 | 46 | 4 | 0 | 0 | 16 | 1 | 5 | 8 | 1 | 28 | 3 | 0 | .239 |
| Andino, Javier, Charleston*.. | 86 | 266 | 21 | 77 | 98 | 9 | 0 | 4 | 40 | 2 | 4 | 17 | 1 | 22 | 2 | 2 | .289 |
| Aristimuno, Jesus, Charleston | 54 | 192 | 28 | 51 | 63 | 6 | 0 | 2 | 16 | 3 | 0 | 29 | 0 | 14 | 0 | 1 | .266 |
| Baker, David, Spartanburg.. | 35 | 99 | 14 | 28 | 36 | 8 | 0 | 0 | 15 | 2 | 1 | 7 | 0 | 10 | 0 | 1 | .283 |
| Begnaud, Gary, Spartanburg | 137 | 465 | 99 | 143 | 251 | 37 | 3 | 25 | 100 | 0 | 10 | 92 | 9 | 68 | 2 | 0 | .308 |
| Bernazard, Oscar, Charles* | 131 | 434 | 55 | 119 | 155 | 23 | 2 | 3 | 46 | 5 | 4 | 105 | 3 | 81 | 6 | 3 | .274 |
| Bonnell, Robert, 23 Spar 101 Greenwood | 124 | 457 | 86 | 148 | 216 | 20 | 6 | 12 | 80 | 0 | 5 | 51 | 5 | 38 | 15 | 4 | .324 |
| Brady, James, Charleston | 139 | 455 | 63 | 97 | 120 | 12 | 1 | 3 | 21 | 7 | 1 | 94 | 2 | 128 | 8 | 4 | .213 |
| Brandt, Randy, Charleston*.. | 1 | 1 | 0 | 0 | 0 | 0 | 0 | 0 | 0 | 0 | 0 | 0 | 0 | 0 | 0 | 0 | .000 |
| Bright G. Donald, Anderson | 2 | 1 | 0 | 0 | 0 | 0 | 0 | 0 | 0 | 0 | 0 | 0 | 0 | 1 | 0 | 0 | .000 |
| Brookens, Timothy, Anderson | 127 | 453 | 73 | 109 | 173 | 22 | 3 | 12 | 56 | 5 | 3 | 47 | 2 | 118 | 19 | 9 | .241 |
| Buckner, Richard, Charleston | 21 | 58 | 2 | 10 | 14 | 1 | 0 | 1 | 6 | 1 | 1 | 6 | 1 | 14 | 0 | 1 | .172 |
| Busby, James, Charleston*.. | 70 | 267 | 32 | 64 | 78 | 10 | 2 | 0 | 21 | 3 | 5 | 26 | 3 | 33 | 4 | 6 | .240 |
| Byrd, Jeffrey, Anderson | 2 | 2 | 0 | 0 | 0 | 0 | 0 | 0 | 0 | 0 | 0 | 0 | 0 | 0 | 0 | 0 | .000 |
| Byrd, Leland, Greenwood | 87 | 225 | 29 | 38 | 42 | 1 | 0 | 1 | 13 | 5 | 1 | 30 | 3 | 66 | 9 | 4 | .182 |
| Carey, Paul, Spartanburg.. | 22 | 55 | 2 | 7 | 7 | 0 | 0 | 0 | 0 | 0 | 0 | 1 | 1 | 18 | 0 | 0 | .127 |
| Chauncey, Keathel, And*... | 134 | 471 | 61 | 122 | 138 | 11 | 1 | 1 | 48 | 5 | 3 | 77 | 2 | 77 | 27 | 13 | .259 |
| Crall, James, Anderson | 55 | 130 | 9 | 15 | 15 | 0 | 0 | 0 | 4 | 4 | 0 | 12 | 2 | 38 | 0 | 1 | .115 |
| Dean, John, Charleston* | 65 | 203 | 22 | 57 | 73 | 11 | 1 | 1 | 19 | 3 | 1 | 27 | 1 | 38 | 2 | 3 | .281 |
| de la Rosa, Jorge, Char. | 30 | 90 | 8 | 19 | 22 | 3 | 0 | 0 | 5 | 2 | 1 | 7 | 0 | 20 | 1 | 2 | .211 |
| DeLiza, Juan, Charleston | 126 | 475 | 54 | 132 | 146 | 10 | 2 | 0 | 36 | 6 | 1 | 19 | 1 | 59 | 9 | 6 | .278 |
| DeMeo, Robert, Spartanburg | 78 | 238 | 19 | 44 | 50 | 4 | 1 | 0 | 16 | 6 | 0 | 27 | 2 | 35 | 1 | 2 | .185 |
| Evans, Freeman, Anderson† | 130 | 447 | 77 | 109 | 127 | 6 | 6 | 0 | 31 | 8 | 2 | 92 | 6 | 59 | 25 | 5 | .244 |
| Fletcher, Donald, Greenwood† | 83 | 229 | 24 | 34 | 53 | 12 | 2 | 1 | 25 | 0 | 5 | 42 | 1 | 92 | 3 | 3 | .148 |
| Gaines, Gary, Anderson | 7 | 8 | 0 | 0 | 0 | 0 | 0 | 0 | 0 | 0 | 0 | 0 | 0 | 5 | 1 | 0 | .000 |
| Gambrell, John, Spartanburg | 99 | 321 | 29 | 77 | 97 | 12 | 1 | 2 | 38 | 6 | 4 | 32 | 6 | 49 | 8 | 3 | .240 |
| Getter, R. Kerry, Anderson* | 1 | 1 | 1 | 1 | 1 | 0 | 0 | 0 | 0 | 0 | 0 | 0 | 0 | 0 | 0 | 0 | 1.000 |
| Gibson, John, Spartanburg*.. | 6 | 14 | 0 | 0 | 0 | 0 | 0 | 0 | 0 | 1 | 0 | 5 | 0 | 8 | 0 | 0 | .000 |
| Goodale Wesley, Anderson*.. | 102 | 316 | 27 | 68 | 101 | 17 | 2 | 4 | 34 | 0 | 1 | 46 | 2 | 89 | 1 | 3 | .215 |
| Gray, Gary, Anderson | 135 | 487 | 79 | 147 | 230 | 27 | 1 | 18 | 95 | 1 | 7 | 55 | 6 | 79 | 6 | 5 | .302 |
| Green, Richard B., Gwd†... | 53 | 164 | 20 | 28 | 48 | 6 | 1 | 4 | 25 | 0 | 3 | 20 | 0 | 45 | 1 | 3 | .171 |
| Hicks, Lawrence, Spar* | 2 | 2 | 0 | 0 | 0 | 0 | 0 | 0 | 0 | 0 | 0 | 0 | 0 | 0 | 0 | 0 | .000 |
| Hughes, Stephen A., Char... | 101 | 308 | 36 | 72 | 81 | 6 | 0 | 1 | 19 | 8 | 2 | 38 | 4 | 49 | 6 | 5 | .234 |
| Jackson, Ronald, Spar | 105 | 325 | 37 | 69 | 97 | 9 | 2 | 5 | 46 | 6 | 3 | 40 | 5 | 48 | 9 | 3 | .212 |
| Jones, Alvin, Greenwood*.. | 135 | 488 | 59 | 127 | 169 | 27 | 3 | 3 | 48 | 5 | 1 | 67 | 1 | 117 | 16 | 10 | .260 |
| Lebron, Juan, Charleston | 136 | 499 | 36 | 139 | 167 | 21 | 2 | 1 | 59 | 6 | 12 | 36 | 1 | 41 | 3 | 5 | .279 |
| Linares, Rufino, Greenwood | 106 | 302 | 36 | 77 | 99 | 12 | 2 | 2 | 35 | 2 | 5 | 43 | 0 | 62 | 5 | 2 | .255 |
| Lisi, Riccardo, Anderson | 135 | 436 | 74 | 102 | 165 | 21 | 3 | 12 | 67 | 4 | 3 | 81 | 13 | 109 | 7 | 3 | .234 |
| Long, Robert, Greenwood*.. | 69 | 231 | 31 | 64 | 86 | 10 | 3 | 2 | 21 | 8 | 1 | 18 | 0 | 31 | 3 | 3 | .277 |
| Lora, Ramon, Spartanburg. | 11 | 37 | 5 | 6 | 8 | 2 | 0 | 0 | 2 | 0 | 0 | 3 | 2 | 13 | 0 | 0 | .162 |
| Maddox, Jerry, Greenwood.. | 65 | 221 | 40 | 62 | 104 | 11 | 2 | 9 | 35 | 2 | 2 | 44 | 1 | 25 | 1 | 2 | .281 |
| McCormack, Donald Spa.. | 24 | 79 | 13 | 16 | 23 | 4 | 0 | 1 | 11 | 1 | 2 | 11 | 0 | 20 | 1 | 0 | .203 |
| Meily, Richard D., Spa*.. | 33 | 86 | 12 | 14 | 20 | 3 | 0 | 1 | 8 | 0 | 0 | 29 | 1 | 16 | 3 | 0 | .163 |
| Miller, Mark, Anderson†.. | 106 | 329 | 32 | 61 | 72 | 8 | 0 | 1 | 31 | 4 | 5 | 52 | 2 | 71 | 3 | 6 | .185 |
| Moreland, Bobby, Spartanburg | 69 | 246 | 28 | 68 | 86 | 13 | 1 | 1 | 41 | 2 | 11 | 21 | 3 | 18 | 2 | 2 | .276 |
| Mosley, Ronald, Spartanburg | 56 | 186 | 21 | 41 | 51 | 10 | 0 | 0 | 22 | 1 | 3 | 26 | 2 | 26 | 3 | 1 | .220 |
| Murphy, Dale, Greenwood... | 131 | 443 | 48 | 101 | 138 | 20 | 1 | 5 | 48 | 8 | 3 | 36 | 1 | 63 | 5 | 1 | .228 |
| Newell, Daniel, Greenwood.. | 82 | 239 | 20 | 48 | 61 | 7 | 0 | 2 | 22 | 2 | 3 | 26 | 2 | 85 | 11 | 2 | .201 |
| Nieves, Raul, Spartanburg . | 15 | 41 | 3 | 8 | 12 | 1 | 0 | 1 | 7 | 1 | 2 | 4 | 0 | 9 | 0 | 1 | .195 |
| Nottle, Edward, Anderson.. | 1 | 3 | 0 | 1 | 1 | 0 | 0 | 0 | 0 | 0 | 0 | 0 | 0 | 1 | 0 | 0 | .333 |
| Olson, Richard, Charleston | 66 | 186 | 10 | 24 | 27 | 3 | 0 | 0 | 10 | 5 | 0 | 26 | 1 | 58 | 3 | 4 | .129 |
| Olson, Terry, Anderson*.. | 31 | 73 | 10 | 15 | 22 | 2 | 1 | 1 | 5 | 1 | 0 | 8 | 1 | 27 | 1 | 3 | .205 |
| Patten, William, Anderson*. | 1 | 1 | 0 | 0 | 0 | 0 | 0 | 0 | 0 | 0 | 0 | 0 | 0 | 0 | 0 | 0 | .000 |
| Purvis, Glenn, Anderson... | 135 | 434 | 54 | 92 | 128 | 11 | 2 | 7 | 44 | 9 | 4 | 61 | 7 | 174 | 15 | 11 | .212 |
| Ramer, Stephen, Spartanburg | 15 | 41 | 6 | 11 | 12 | 1 | 0 | 0 | 1 | 0 | 0 | 7 | 0 | 7 | 0 | 2 | .268 |

| Player and Club | G. | AB. | R. | H. | TB. | 2B. | 3B. | HR. | RBI. | SH. | SF. | BB. | HP. | SO. | SB. | CS. | Pct. |
|---|---|---|---|---|---|---|---|---|---|---|---|---|---|---|---|---|---|
| Reedy, Jerome, Spartanburg..131 | 463 | 73 | 124 | 146 | 19 | 0 | 1 | 37 | 5 | 3 | 59 | 0 | 54 | 19 | 6 | .268 |
| Richard, Jose, Greenwood.... 97 | 254 | 23 | 50 | 57 | 5 | 1 | 0 | 25 | 20 | 1 | 16 | 3 | 39 | 0 | 1 | .197 |
| Roberts, Melvin, Spartanburg 1 | 4 | 0 | 0 | 0 | 0 | 0 | 0 | 1 | 0 | 0 | 0 | 0 | 3 | 0 | 0 | .000 |
| Robinson, Charles, Chart.. 25 | 80 | 10 | 14 | 15 | 1 | 0 | 0 | 5 | 0 | 1 | 10 | 0 | 16 | 1 | 0 | .175 |
| Rockhill, Ronald, Greenwood 16 | 33 | 6 | 7 | 15 | 3 | 1 | 1 | 4 | 1 | 0 | 7 | 0 | 13 | 0 | 0 | .212 |
| Rodriguez, Felix, Charleston* 35 | 132 | 19 | 39 | 56 | 4 | 2 | 3 | 16 | 1 | 0 | 15 | 0 | 11 | 2 | 4 | .295 |
| Runyon, R. Curtis, Anderson 11 | 31 | 3 | 2 | 2 | 0 | 0 | 0 | 1 | 0 | 0 | 4 | 0 | 11 | 1 | 0 | .065 |
| Russell, Joseph, Anderson....130 | 371 | 45 | 72 | 89 | 11 | 0 | 2 | 40 | 12 | 6 | 72 | 8 | 73 | 6 | 11 | .194 |
| Russo, Andrew, Spartanburg 9 | 25 | 1 | 8 | 10 | 2 | 0 | 0 | 5 | 0 | 0 | 4 | 0 | 7 | 0 | 0 | .320 |
| Ryan, Albert, Greenwood....138 | 469 | 89 | 118 | 143 | 17 | 4 | 0 | 23 | 13 | 1 | 102 | 5 | 72 | 50 | 14 | .252 |
| Ryczek, Martin, Spartanburg 34 | 101 | 10 | 26 | 35 | 4 | 1 | 1 | 10 | 6 | 1 | 11 | 1 | 17 | 2 | 1 | .257 |
| Sanchez, Arsenio, Charleston 15 | 43 | 3 | 6 | 6 | 0 | 0 | 0 | 1 | 2 | 0 | 4 | 0 | 12 | 2 | 0 | .140 |
| Small, George H., Greenwood 58 | 215 | 25 | 53 | 85 | 5 | 3 | 7 | 29 | 1 | 1 | 20 | 2 | 30 | 0 | 0 | .247 |
| Smith, Cannon, Greenwood* 121 | 469 | 48 | 97 | 154 | 17 | 2 | 12 | 61 | 0 | 2 | 67 | 0 | 109 | 4 | 2 | .207 |
| Smith, Lonnie, Spartanburg..131 | 465 | 114 | 150 | 202 | 23 | 4 | 7 | 40 | 4 | 3 | 96 | 9 | 63 | 56 | 14 | .323 |
| Smith, Thomas G., Anderson 90 | 222 | 28 | 36 | 39 | 1 | 1 | 0 | 16 | 9 | 2 | 37 | 0 | 40 | 9 | 3 | .162 |
| Smoak, James, Spartanburg 33 | 106 | 20 | 23 | 33 | 3 | 2 | 1 | 9 | 3 | 0 | 23 | 2 | 31 | 7 | 2 | .217 |
| Sosa, Fausto, Charleston .... 76 | 220 | 29 | 57 | 85 | 10 | 6 | 2 | 20 | 4 | 0 | 39 | 1 | 24 | 5 | 4 | .259 |
| Stone, Gregory, Spartanburg 2 | 1 | 0 | 0 | 0 | 0 | 0 | 0 | 0 | 0 | 0 | 0 | 0 | 0 | 0 | 0 | .000 |
| Stone, Steven A., Greenwood 28 | 43 | 3 | 11 | 12 | 1 | 0 | 0 | 1 | 2 | 0 | 10 | 0 | 6 | 0 | 0 | .256 |
| Tidwell, Danny, Anderson .. 1 | 2 | 0 | 0 | 0 | 0 | 0 | 0 | 0 | 0 | 0 | 0 | 0 | 1 | 0 | 0 | .000 |
| Vargas, Angel, Spartanburg.. 45 | 108 | 6 | 15 | 17 | 2 | 0 | 0 | 7 | 0 | 1 | 5 | 0 | 45 | 2 | 1 | .139 |
| Westlake, Thomas, Gwd*.... 52 | 154 | 9 | 27 | 39 | 2 | 2 | 2 | 19 | 6 | 5 | 13 | 0 | 27 | 2 | 2 | .175 |
| Whitehurst, Marvin, Char* 102 | 339 | 31 | 80 | 115 | 9 | 1 | 8 | 45 | 3 | 2 | 21 | 2 | 94 | 13 | 5 | .236 |
| Yearby, Melvin, Spartanburg 129 | 442 | 76 | 123 | 174 | 21 | 6 | 6 | 82 | 8 | 4 | 66 | 5 | 82 | 8 | 6 | .278 |
| Ysursa, Nicolas, Spartanburg 102 | 368 | 39 | 86 | 118 | 11 | 0 | 7 | 42 | 3 | 0 | 18 | 1 | 59 | 4 | 4 | .234 |

The following pitchers had no plate appearances primarily through use of designated hitters, listed alphabetically by club, games in parentheses:

ANDERSON—Carroll, Robert (25) ; Clancy, James (23) ; Frolin, Darrel (24) ; McCarthy, David* (10) ; Nickerson, Drew (26) ; Smith, Ward* (25).

CHARLESTON—Breining, Fred (35) ; Clark, Bryan* (12) ; Clites, Robert (8) ; Davis, Dennis (21) ; Frye, Vincent* (21) ; Galante, Joseph (29) ; Isaac, Joseph (4) ; Johnston, James* (11) ; Martinez, Silvio (19) ; Mazur, Robert (15) ; Mercer, Mark* (14) ; Presser, Donald (2) ; Robles, Victor (6) ; Ryan, Michael (21) ; Whitson, Edward (24) ; Williams, Albert (29).

GREENWOOD—Campbell, David A. (33) ; Costello, Timothy* (25) ; Cranford, William* (5) ; Harlee, William* (11) ; Harper, Terry (14) ; Jones, Lamar (25) ; Kerns, Steven* (9) ; McLaughlin, Joey (20) ; McLean, John (35) ; McWilliams, Larry* (17) ; Meistickle, Kevin (8) ; Peeples, Jeffrey (9) ; Phillips, G. William (33) ; Stein, Gary (22) ; Theiss, Duane (21) ; Titus, Vincent* (29) ; Waclawczyk, Timothy (8).

SPARTANBURG—Ciammachilli, Frank (17) ; Cooper, M. Neal (13) ; Hernandez, Angel (20) ; Houston, Jerry (18) ; Keller, Robert (10) ; Klein, Mark (12) ; LaPointe, Raymond (15) ; Manos, Peter (23) ; McDaniel, Leo* (18) ; Saucier, Kevin (25) ; Wertz, Larry (24) ; Wright, James L. (26).

GRAND SLAM HOME RUNS (7) : Lisi 2; Begnaud, Brookens, Gray, Maddox, Whitehurst, Ysursa, 1 each.

AWARDED FIRST BASE ON INTERFERENCE: None.

## CLUB FIELDING

| Club | G. | PO. | A. | E. | DP. | PB. | Pct. | Club | G. | PO. | A. | E. | DP. | PB. | Pct. |
|---|---|---|---|---|---|---|---|---|---|---|---|---|---|---|---|
| Spartanburg | 140 | 3526 | 1382 | 192 | 102 | 21 | .962 | Greenwood | 141 | 3548 | 1390 | 221 | 127 | 20 | .957 |
| Anderson | 137 | 3469 | 1421 | 217 | 120 | 25 | .958 | Charleston | 141 | 3459 | 1357 | 234 | 95 | 43 | .954 |

Triple Play—Charleston.

## INDIVIDUAL FIELDING

*Throws lefthanded.

### FIRST BASEMEN

| Player and Club | G. | PO. | A. | E. | DP. | Pct. | Player and Club | G. | PO. | A. | E. | DP. | Pct. |
|---|---|---|---|---|---|---|---|---|---|---|---|---|---|
| Rockhill, Gwd ...... | 3 | 15 | 1 | 0 | 2 | 1 000 | Smith, Greenwood*.. | 43 | 350 | 22 | 8 | 35 | .979 |
| McCormack, Spa .. | 1 | 11 | 0 | 0 | 1 | 1 000 | Gray, Anderson .....134 | 1138 | 71 | 27 | 96 | .978 |
| Lebron, Charleston .. | 1 | 8 | 1 | 0 | 1 | 1 000 | DeLiza, Charleston..104 | 729 | 55 | 18 | 51 | .978 |
| Meily, Spartanburg .. | 1 | 6 | 0 | 0 | 0 | 1 000 | Andino, Charleston*.. | 34 | 239 | 18 | 6 | 24 | .977 |
| Roberts, Spartanburg. | 1 | 5 | 0 | 0 | 1 | 1 000 | Goodale, Anderson .. | 5 | 36 | 2 | 1 | 3 | .974 |
| Murphy, Greenwood.. | 1 | 1 | 0 | 0 | 1 | 1 000 | Green, Greenwood.... | 42 | 320 | 14 | 11 | 28 | .968 |
| Ammons, Charleston.. | 13 | 86 | 9 | 1 | 8 | .990 | Newell, Greenwood .. | 5 | 22 | 2 | 3 | 4 | .889 |
| BEGNAUD, Spartan | 137 | 1141 | 83 | 17 | 88 | .986 | Carey, Spartanburg .. | 1 | 2 | 0 | 1 | 0 | .667 |
| Small, Greenwood .. | 58 | 455 | 31 | 7 | 38 | .986 | | | | | | | |

Triple Play—DeLiza.

### SECOND BASEMEN

| Player and Club | G. | PO. | A. | E. | DP. | Pct. | Player and Club | G. | PO. | A. | E. | DP. | Pct. |
|---|---|---|---|---|---|---|---|---|---|---|---|---|---|
| Nottle, Anderson .... | 1 | 3 | 2 | 0 | 0 | 1 000 | Vargas, Spartanburg.. | 12 | 21 | 19 | 2 | 3 | .952 |
| Nieves, Spartanburg.. | 1 | 1 | 2 | 0 | 0 | 1 000 | Brady, Charleston ... | 29 | 80 | 68 | 8 | 16 | .949 |
| Evans, Anderson .... | 3 | 1 | 1 | 0 | 1 | 1 000 | Reedy, Spartanburg..131 | 314 | 325 | 36 | 62 | .947 |
| Richard, Charleston.. | 13 | 27 | 30 | 1 | 4 | .983 | Hughes, Charleston .. | 22 | 39 | 31 | 4 | 7 | .946 |
| Aristmuno, Char ... | 35 | 78 | 71 | 4 | 15 | .974 | Brookens, Anderson.. | 21 | 35 | 55 | 8 | 4 | .918 |
| Miller, Anderson .... | 70 | 136 | 186 | 9 | 37 | .973 | de la Rosa, Charleston | 22 | 37 | 40 | 7 | 5 | .917 |
| RYAN, Greenwood ..134 | 314 | 332 | 28 | 74 | .958 | Sosa, Charleston .... | 46 | 66 | 81 | 15 | 16 | .907 |
| T. Smith, Anderson .. | 59 | 103 | 119 | 11 | 29 | .953 | | | | | | | |

Triple Play—Sosa.

## THIRD BASEMEN

| Player and Club | G. | PO. | A. | E. | DP. | Pct. |
|---|---|---|---|---|---|---|
| Sosa, Charleston .... | 1 | 1 | 2 | 0 | 0 | 1.000 |
| McCormack, Spar .. | 1 | 0 | 2 | 0 | 0 | 1.000 |
| Buckner, Charleston . | 1 | 1 | 0 | 0 | 0 | 1.000 |
| Hughes, Charleston.. | 77 | 51 | 150 | 14 | 15 | .935 |
| Dean, Charleston .... | 62 | 46 | 118 | 12 | 9 | .932 |
| Maddox, Greenwood.. | 65 | 55 | 137 | 16 | 13 | .923 |
| Richard, Greenwood.. | 10 | 3 | 21 | 2 | 4 | .923 |
| Mosley, Spartanburg.. | 50 | 42 | 90 | 12 | 9 | .917 |
| Moreland, Spartanburg | 69 | 52 | 128 | 17 | 11 | .914 |
| LISI, Anderson...... | 135 | 123 | 274 | 42 | 26 | .904 |
| Newell, Greenwood... | 57 | 37 | 86 | 13 | 10 | .904 |
| Byrd, Greenwood..... | 5 | 2 | 5 | 1 | 1 | .875 |
| Miller, Anderson .... | 3 | 3 | 10 | 2 | 0 | .867 |
| Vargas, Spartanburg.. | 17 | 8 | 24 | 5 | 4 | .865 |
| Nieves, Spartanburg.. | 7 | 6 | 15 | 5 | 1 | .808 |
| Ammos, Charleston... | 4 | 3 | 3 | 2 | 0 | .750 |
| Aristimuno, Charleston | 4 | 1 | 6 | 3 | 0 | .700 |
| Fletcher, Greenwood . | 18 | 14 | 10 | 16 | 3 | .600 |

## SHORTSTOPS

| Player and Club | G. | PO. | A. | E. | DP. | Pct. |
|---|---|---|---|---|---|---|
| Maddox, Greenwood.. | 4 | 0 | 10 | 0 | 1 | 1.000 |
| Gaines, Anderson .... | 4 | 0 | 2 | 0 | 1 | 1.000 |
| Miller, Anderson .... | 22 | 25 | 59 | 2 | 5 | .977 |
| Vargas, Spartanburg.. | 8 | 15 | 17 | 1 | 7 | .970 |
| Richard, Greenwood.. | 80 | 92 | 179 | 9 | 32 | .968 |
| Ryczek, Spartanburg.. | 34 | 50 | 105 | 6 | 13 | .963 |
| Mosley, Spartanburg.. | 6 | 8 | 12 | 1 | 3 | .952 |
| BRADY, Charleston.. | 117 | 184 | 297 | 32 | 42 | .938 |
| Ysursa, Spartanburg.. | 99 | 157 | 296 | 33 | 37 | .932 |
| T. Smith, Anderson.. | 18 | 23 | 42 | 5 | 4 | .929 |
| Brookens, Anderson... | 104 | 195 | 300 | 40 | 52 | .925 |
| DeLiza, Charleston .. | 31 | 39 | 100 | 14 | 18 | .908 |
| Byrd, Greenwood .... | 81 | 121 | 200 | 33 | 41 | .907 |
| Hughes, Charleston... | 1 | 0 | 0 | 1 | 0 | .000 |

## OUTFIELDERS

| Player and Club | G. | PO. | A. | E. | DP. | Pct. |
|---|---|---|---|---|---|---|
| Smoak, Spartanburg.. | 33 | 48 | 3 | 0 | 2 | 1.000 |
| Olson, Anderson*.... | 20 | 17 | 1 | 0 | 0 | 1.000 |
| Ramer, Spartanburg.. | 9 | 8 | 0 | 0 | 0 | 1.000 |
| Russell, Anderson.... | 5 | 3 | 0 | 0 | 0 | 1.000 |
| Byrd, Greenwood..... | 1 | 0 | 1 | 0 | 1 | 1.000 |
| Goodale, Anderson.... | 1 | 1 | 0 | 0 | 0 | 1.000 |
| Rodriguez, Char* .... | 35 | 56 | 4 | 1 | 0 | .984 |
| Busby, Charleston*.. | 70 | 163 | 8 | 3 | 2 | .983 |
| YEARBY, Spar...... | 125 | 211 | 3 | 4 | 0 | .982 |
| Buckner, Charleston .. | 19 | 32 | 0 | 1 | 0 | .970 |
| Newell, Greenwood... | 15 | 30 | 1 | 1 | 0 | .969 |
| Purvis, Anderson.... | 133 | 249 | 23 | 9 | 9 | .968 |
| Smith, Spartanburg.. | 129 | 317 | 9 | 11 | 1 | .967 |
| Jones, Greenwood.... | 135 | 226 | 10 | 8 | 3 | .967 |
| Whitehurst, Char* .. | 101 | 153 | 5 | 6 | 1 | .963 |
| Gambrell, Spartan .. | 74 | 117 | 9 | 5 | 0 | .962 |
| Westlake, Greenwood | 43 | 72 | 3 | 3 | 0 | .962 |
| Lebron, Charleston .. | 13 | 24 | 1 | 1 | 0 | .962 |
| Bonnell, Spar-Gwd .. | 123 | 276 | 19 | 12 | 6 | .961 |
| Evans, Anderson .... | 127 | 211 | 12 | 10 | 1 | .957 |
| Ammons, Charleston . | 29 | 42 | 1 | 2 | 0 | .956 |
| Linares, Greenwood .. | 88 | 178 | 6 | 10 | 3 | .948 |
| Long, Greenwood*... | 66 | 114 | 8 | 7 | 3 | .946 |
| Bernazard, Charleston | 131 | 202 | 13 | 15 | 0 | .935 |
| Meily, Spartanburg.. | 15 | 26 | 2 | 2 | 0 | .933 |
| Sosa, Charleston .... | 31 | 40 | 7 | 4 | 0 | .922 |
| Sanchez, Charleston.. | 15 | 22 | 1 | 2 | 0 | .920 |
| Jackson, Spartanburg | 24 | 39 | 3 | 4 | 1 | .913 |
| Runyon, Anderson ... | 10 | 9 | 0 | 1 | 0 | .900 |
| Brooken, Anderson... | 7 | 7 | 0 | 1 | 0 | .875 |
| Fletcher, Greenwood . | 5 | 2 | 1 | 1 | 0 | .750 |

## CATCHERS

| Player and Club | G. | PO. | A. | E. | DP. | PB. | Pct. |
|---|---|---|---|---|---|---|---|
| McCormack, Spar | 9 | 43 | 2 | 0 | 0 | 1 | 1.000 |
| Baker, Spartan .. | 31 | 137 | 20 | 2 | 2 | 1 | .987 |
| Crall, Anderson.. | 25 | 60 | 4 | 1 | 0 | 4 | .985 |
| DeMEO, Spartan | 78 | 436 | 36 | 8 | 4 | 8 | .983 |
| Olson, Charleston | 66 | 445 | 43 | 9 | 4 | 18 | .982 |
| Carey, Spartan .. | 20 | 84 | 14 | 2 | 0 | 4 | .980 |
| Murphy, Green.. | 129 | 722 | 81 | 18 | 13 | 18 | .978 |
| Russo, Spar .... | 9 | 76 | 8 | 2 | 1 | 2 | .977 |
| Lebron, Charleston | 51 | 365 | 44 | 10 | 8 | 17 | .976 |
| Russell, Anderson | 126 | 728 | 85 | 22 | 16 | 21 | .974 |
| Stone, Greenwood | 18 | 53 | 5 | 2 | 2 | 1 | .967 |
| Robinson, Char.. | 25 | 170 | 15 | 8 | 2 | 8 | .959 |
| Rockhill, Gwd .. | 6 | 25 | 1 | 2 | 0 | 1 | .929 |
| Lora, Spartanburg | 4 | 26 | 2 | 3 | 0 | 1 | .903 |

## PITCHERS

| Player and Club | G. | PO. | A. | E. | DP. | Pct. |
|---|---|---|---|---|---|---|
| COSTELLO, Gwd*.. | 25 | 2 | 24 | 0 | 0 | 1.000 |
| Hernandez, Spa ... | 20 | 9 | 15 | 0 | 1 | 1.000 |
| Harper, Greenwood... | 14 | 6 | 17 | 0 | 0 | 1.000 |
| Theiss, Greenwood .. | 22 | 5 | 15 | 0 | 1 | 1.000 |
| Kerns, Greenwood .... | 9 | 1 | 15 | 0 | 1 | 1.000 |
| Galante, Charleston.. | 29 | 6 | 7 | 0 | 1 | 1.000 |
| Frolin, Anderson .... | 24 | 4 | 8 | 0 | 0 | 1.000 |
| Clark, Charleston*.. | 12 | 1 | 9 | 0 | 0 | 1.000 |
| Keller, Spartanburg.. | 10 | 2 | 6 | 0 | 1 | 1.000 |
| Harlee, Greenwood*.. | 11 | 2 | 6 | 0 | 0 | 1.000 |
| Houston, Spartanburg | 18 | 2 | 6 | 0 | 0 | 1.000 |
| Jones, Greenwood .... | 25 | 1 | 7 | 0 | 1 | 1.000 |
| Ciammachilli, Spa .. | 17 | 2 | 5 | 0 | 0 | 1.000 |
| Peeples, Greenwood .. | 9 | 1 | 5 | 0 | 1 | 1.000 |
| McCarthy, Anderson* | 10 | 1 | 5 | 0 | 0 | 1.000 |
| LaPointe, Spartanburg | 15 | 0 | 5 | 0 | 0 | 1.000 |
| Manos, Spartanburg.. | 23 | 2 | 4 | 0 | 0 | 1.000 |
| Cooper, Spartanburg.. | 13 | 2 | 3 | 0 | 0 | 1.000 |
| Presser, Charleston... | 2 | 1 | 0 | 0 | 0 | 1.000 |
| Cranford, Greenwood* | 5 | 0 | 2 | 0 | 0 | 1.000 |
| Hicks, Spartanburg.. | 6 | 0 | 2 | 0 | 0 | 1.000 |
| Waclawczyk, Gwd .. | 8 | 1 | 1 | 0 | 0 | 1.000 |
| McDaniel, Spa* .... | 18 | 2 | 0 | 0 | 0 | 1.000 |
| Nottle, Anderson ... | 2 | 1 | 0 | 0 | 0 | 1.000 |
| Roberts, Spartanburg | 2 | 0 | 1 | 0 | 0 | 1.000 |
| Saucier, Spartanburg* | 25 | 7 | 24 | 1 | 2 | .969 |
| Stein, Greenwood ... | 22 | 4 | 22 | 1 | 1 | .963 |
| Bright, Anderson.... | 46 | 10 | 16 | 1 | 0 | .963 |
| Williams, Charleston | 29 | 6 | 18 | 1 | 1 | .960 |
| Gibson, Spartanburg* | 27 | 14 | 33 | 2 | 2 | .959 |
| Titus, Greenwood*... | 29 | 9 | 13 | 1 | 0 | .957 |
| Tidwell, Anderson .. | 26 | 14 | 25 | 2 | 1 | .951 |
| Wertz, Spartanburg*. | 24 | 7 | 12 | 1 | 1 | .950 |
| Nickerson, Anderson.. | 25 | 17 | 12 | 1 | 1 | .950 |
| Breining, Charleston.. | 35 | 4 | 14 | 1 | 1 | .947 |
| McWilliams, Gwd*.. | 17 | 5 | 11 | 1 | 0 | .941 |
| Brandt, Charleston*.. | 22 | 3 | 13 | 1 | 0 | .941 |
| Byrd, Anderson .... | 22 | 4 | 22 | 2 | 1 | .929 |
| Mazur, Charleston ... | 15 | 6 | 7 | 1 | 0 | .929 |
| Phillips, Greenwood.. | 33 | 5 | 8 | 1 | 0 | .929 |
| Carroll, Anderson ... | 24 | 9 | 16 | 2 | 1 | .926 |
| W. Smith, Anderson* | 25 | 3 | 22 | 2 | 3 | .926 |
| Klein, Spartanburg... | 12 | 5 | 7 | 1 | 0 | .923 |
| Patten, Anderson* .. | 26 | 5 | 7 | 1 | 0 | .923 |
| Wright, Spartanburg. | 26 | 14 | 32 | 4 | 1 | .920 |
| Whitson, Charleston.. | 24 | 7 | 27 | 4 | 0 | .895 |
| Clancy, Anderson .... | 23 | 7 | 26 | 4 | 1 | .892 |
| McLean, Greenwood.. | 35 | 5 | 11 | 2 | 1 | .889 |
| Clites, Charleston .... | 8 | 1 | 7 | 1 | 0 | .889 |
| McLaughlin, Gwd ... | 20 | 7 | 16 | 3 | 2 | .885 |
| Frye, Charleston* ... | 21 | 2 | 12 | 2 | 0 | .875 |
| Campbell, Greenwood | 33 | 3 | 4 | 1 | 1 | .875 |

### PITCHERS—Continued

| Player and Club | G. | PO. | A. | E. | DP. | Pct. |
|---|---|---|---|---|---|---|
| Martinez, Charleston.. | 19 | 9 | 18 | 4 | 0 | .871 |
| Stone, Spartanburg.. | 21 | 1 | 5 | 1 | 0 | .857 |
| Robles, Charleston .. | 6 | 2 | 2 | 1 | 0 | .800 |
| Davis, Charleston ..... | 21 | 6 | 14 | 6 | 0 | .769 |
| Getter, Anderson .... | 36 | 4 | 2 | 2 | 0 | .750 |

| Player and Club | G. | PO. | A. | E. | DP. | Pct. |
|---|---|---|---|---|---|---|
| Johnston, Charleston.. | 11 | 2 | 3 | 2 | 0 | .714 |
| Isaac, Charleston .... | 4 | 1 | 1 | 1 | 0 | .667 |
| Mercer, Charleston*.. | 14 | 0 | 8 | 5 | 2 | .615 |
| Meistickle, Gwd | 8 | 0 | 1 | 1 | 0 | .500 |
| Ryan, Charleston .... | 2 | 0 | 0 | 0 | 0 | .000 |

### CLUB PITCHING

| Club | G. | GS. | ShO. | Sv. | IP. | H. | R. | ER. | HR. | Tot. BB. | Int. BB. | HB. | SO. | WP. | Bk. | ERA. |
|---|---|---|---|---|---|---|---|---|---|---|---|---|---|---|---|---|
| Spartanburg | 140 | 61 | 15 | 10 | 1175 | 1051 | 546 | 421 | 48 | 572 | 33 | 35 | 766 | 69 | 8 | 3.22 |
| Anderson | 137 | 44 | 10 | 16 | 1156 | 1117 | 623 | 481 | 67 | 567 | 6 | 19 | 720 | 68 | 11 | 3.743 |
| Greenwood | 141 | 23 | 10 | 20 | 1183 | 1169 | 648 | 492 | 50 | 580 | 24 | 29 | 724 | 67 | 6 | 3.744 |
| Charleston | 141 | 42 | 9 | 13 | 1153 | 1068 | 694 | 536 | 71 | 737 | 7 | 62 | 913 | 117 | 10 | 4.18 |

(Leading Qualifiers for Earned-Run Average Leadership—115 or More Innings)

*Throws lefthanded.

| Pitcher—Club | G. | GS. | CG. | ShO. | W. | L. | Sv. | Pct. | IP. | H. | R. | ER. | HR. | BB. | Int. BB. | HB. | SO. | WP. | ERA. |
|---|---|---|---|---|---|---|---|---|---|---|---|---|---|---|---|---|---|---|---|
| McLaughlin, Gwd.. | 20 | 16 | 6 | 3 | 12 | 5 | 0 | .706 | 122 | 112 | 47 | 35 | 5 | 49 | 2 | 0 | 59 | 1 | 2.58 |
| Wright, Spa | 26 | 26 | 15 | 4 | 14 | 7 | 0 | .667 | 181 | 166 | 83 | 55 | 7 | 56 | 3 | 8 | 127 | 6 | 2.73 |
| Wertz, Spartanburg* | 24 | 17 | 6 | 4 | 12 | 3 | 0 | .800 | 135 | 113 | 58 | 43 | 3 | 68 | 1 | 2 | 82 | 3 | 2.87 |
| Tidwell, Anderson.. | 26 | 26 | 9 | 1 | 7 | 11 | 0 | .389 | 174 | 160 | 88 | 61 | 9 | 71 | 1 | 2 | 76 | 3 | 3.16 |
| Gibson, Spa* | 27 | 27 | 14 | 2 | 13 | 10 | 0 | .565 | 189 | 167 | 84 | 69 | 8 | 100 | 2 | 4 | 143 | 16 | 3.29 |
| Saucier, Spa* | 25 | 25 | 12 | 4 | 12 | 9 | 0 | .571 | 159 | 138 | 72 | 59 | 6 | 61 | 3 | 7 | 90 | 5 | 3.34 |
| Martinez, Char | 19 | 19 | 12 | 1 | 6 | 9 | 0 | .400 | 133 | 115 | 63 | 53 | 13 | 55 | 2 | 3 | 113 | 6 | 3.59 |
| Williams, Char | 29 | 18 | 8 | 1 | 4 | 12 | 1 | .250 | 148 | 148 | 94 | 63 | 12 | 65 | 0 | 3 | 115 | 7 | 3.83 |
| Clancy, Anderson.. | 23 | 23 | 11 | 3 | 6 | 13 | 0 | .316 | 148 | 139 | 85 | 63 | 7 | 91 | 1 | 0 | 109 | 9 | 3.83 |
| Byrd, Anderson | 22 | 22 | 5 | 1 | 7 | 11 | 0 | .389 | 141 | 115 | 78 | 62 | 5 | 104 | 1 | 6 | 82 | 22 | 3.96 |

Departmental Leaders: G—Bright, 46; GS—Gibson, 27; CG—Wright, 15; ShO—Saucier, Wertz, Wright, 4; W—Wright, 14; L—Whitson, 15; Sv—Bright, 14; Pct.—Wertz, .800; IP—Gibson, 189; H—Gibson, 167; R—Whitson, 96; ER—Whitson, 80; HR—Martinez, 13; BB—Byrd, 104; IBB—La-Pointe, Manos, McLean, 5; HB—Whitson, 15; SO—Gibson, 143; WP—Byrd, 22.

### (All Pitchers—Listed Alphabetically)

| Pitcher—Club | G. | GS. | CG. | ShO. | W. | L. | Sv. | Pct. | IP. | H. | R. | ER. | HR. | BB. | Int. BB. | HB. | SO. | WP. | ERA. |
|---|---|---|---|---|---|---|---|---|---|---|---|---|---|---|---|---|---|---|---|
| Brandt, Char* | 22 | 4 | 1 | 0 | 4 | 4 | 5 | .500 | 69 | 63 | 25 | 20 | 2 | 29 | 1 | 1 | 61 | 2 | 2.61 |
| Breining, Char | 35 | 4 | 0 | 0 | 3 | 8 | 3 | .273 | 92 | 75 | 57 | 46 | 3 | 60 | 0 | 11 | 82 | 14 | 4.50 |
| Bright, Anderson. | 46 | 0 | 0 | 0 | 12 | 4 | 14 | .750 | 95 | 74 | 24 | 16 | 2 | 29 | 1 | 2 | 81 | 3 | 1.52 |
| Byrd, Anderson | 22 | 22 | 5 | 1 | 7 | 11 | 0 | .389 | 141 | 115 | 78 | 62 | 5 | 104 | 1 | 6 | 82 | 22 | 3.96 |
| Campbell, Gwd... | 33 | 0 | 0 | 0 | 4 | 3 | 6 | .571 | 65 | 41 | 31 | 17 | 0 | 35 | 2 | 3 | 64 | 3 | 2.35 |
| Carroll, Anderson | 24 | 19 | 4 | 0 | 7 | 10 | 0 | .412 | 122 | 137 | 78 | 61 | 10 | 35 | 1 | 2 | 49 | 3 | 4.50 |
| Ciammachilli, Spa | 17 | 5 | 0 | 0 | 3 | 4 | 0 | .429 | 56 | 57 | 28 | 24 | 5 | 29 | 2 | 1 | 30 | 5 | 3.86 |
| Clancy, Anderson. | 23 | 23 | 11 | 3 | 6 | 13 | 0 | .316 | 148 | 139 | 85 | 63 | 7 | 91 | 1 | 0 | 109 | 9 | 3.83 |
| Clark, Charleston* | 12 | 12 | 2 | 0 | 4 | 7 | 0 | .364 | 57 | 56 | 48 | 34 | 1 | 67 | 0 | 3 | 38 | 13 | 5.37 |
| Clites, Charleston | 8 | 8 | 4 | 1 | 3 | 5 | 0 | .375 | 57 | 53 | 26 | 19 | 4 | 29 | 1 | 0 | 49 | 5 | 3.00 |
| Cooper, Spartanburg | 13 | 1 | 0 | 0 | 0 | 1 | 0 | .000 | 27 | 17 | 10 | 4 | 0 | 17 | 0 | 1 | 20 | 5 | 1.33 |
| Costello, Gwd* | 25 | 25 | 1 | 0 | 5 | 10 | 0 | .333 | 134 | 135 | 88 | 73 | 6 | 92 | 1 | 2 | 76 | 10 | 4.90 |
| Cranford, Gwd* | 5 | 1 | 0 | 0 | 0 | 0 | 0 | .000 | 12 | 15 | 10 | 5 | 1 | 7 | 0 | 1 | 8 | 1 | 3.75 |
| Davis, Charleston. | 21 | 19 | 4 | 1 | 6 | 11 | 0 | .353 | 112 | 108 | 76 | 62 | 7 | 98 | 0 | 11 | 91 | 20 | 4.98 |
| Frolin, Anderson . | 24 | 10 | 5 | 1 | 8 | 6 | 0 | .571 | 108 | 104 | 45 | 35 | 10 | 38 | 0 | 7 | 77 | 4 | 2.92 |
| Frye, Charleston*.. | 21 | 15 | 4 | 1 | 3 | 10 | 1 | .231 | 100 | 89 | 55 | 43 | 7 | 66 | 0 | 4 | 66 | 8 | 3.87 |
| Galante, Charleston | 29 | 0 | 0 | 0 | 0 | 3 | 0 | .000 | 64 | 57 | 39 | 30 | 3 | 42 | 1 | 4 | 57 | 13 | 4.22 |
| Getter, Anderson . | 36 | 0 | 0 | 0 | 1 | 1 | 0 | .500 | 55 | 55 | 39 | 31 | 1 | 42 | 0 | 2 | 47 | 6 | 5.07 |
| Gibson, Spa* | 27 | 27 | 14 | 2 | 13 | 10 | 0 | .565 | 189 | 167 | 84 | 69 | 8 | 100 | 2 | 4 | 143 | 16 | 3.29 |
| Harlee, Greenwood* | 11 | 6 | 0 | 0 | 1 | 4 | 0 | .200 | 38 | 32 | 26 | 13 | 2 | 13 | 1 | 1 | 19 | 3 | 3.08 |
| Harper, Greenwood. | 14 | 13 | 0 | 0 | 1 | 5 | 0 | .167 | 69 | 95 | 48 | 40 | 4 | 39 | 1 | 3 | 27 | 8 | 5.22 |
| Hernandez, Spa | 20 | 13 | 6 | 0 | 7 | 7 | 0 | .500 | 102 | 91 | 46 | 38 | 8 | 30 | 3 | 3 | 49 | 0 | 3.35 |
| Hicks, Spartanburg | 6 | 0 | 0 | 0 | 0 | 0 | 0 | .000 | 12 | 7 | 1 | 1 | 0 | 10 | 0 | 1 | 9 | 2 | 0.75 |
| Houston, Spa | 18 | 0 | 0 | 0 | 2 | 0 | 1 | 1.000 | 28 | 27 | 15 | 9 | 0 | 27 | 2 | 0 | 21 | 6 | 2.89 |
| Isaac, Charleston | 4 | 4 | 0 | 0 | 0 | 3 | 0 | .000 | 22 | 26 | 16 | 14 | 0 | 17 | 1 | 0 | 12 | 4 | 5.73 |
| Johnston, Char | 11 | 7 | 1 | 1 | 1 | 4 | 1 | .200 | 34 | 26 | 21 | 17 | 1 | 17 | 0 | 3 | 22 | 5 | 4.50 |
| L. Jones, Gwd | 25 | 0 | 0 | 0 | 4 | 3 | 8 | .571 | 49 | 38 | 13 | 10 | 0 | 16 | 1 | 0 | 44 | 2 | 1.84 |
| Keller, Spartanburg | 10 | 8 | 1 | 0 | 3 | 3 | 0 | .500 | 46 | 43 | 31 | 24 | 2 | 41 | 0 | 0 | 29 | 5 | 4.70 |
| Kerns, Greenwood. | 9 | 6 | 1 | 1 | 2 | 3 | 0 | .400 | 40 | 56 | 30 | 26 | 2 | 18 | 1 | 0 | 23 | 0 | 5.85 |
| Klein, Spartanburg | 12 | 9 | 4 | 1 | 6 | 6 | 0 | .500 | 81 | 70 | 33 | 23 | 3 | 31 | 2 | 2 | 55 | 2 | 2.56 |
| LaPointe, Spa | 15 | 8 | 3 | 0 | 2 | 4 | 0 | .333 | 59 | 67 | 38 | 31 | 3 | 36 | 5 | 3 | 34 | 1 | 4.73 |
| Manos, Spartanburg | 23 | 0 | 0 | 0 | 4 | 1 | 0 | .800 | 36 | 30 | 9 | 9 | 0 | 17 | 5 | 0 | 22 | 1 | 2.25 |
| Martinez, Char | 19 | 19 | 12 | 1 | 6 | 9 | 0 | .400 | 133 | 115 | 63 | 53 | 13 | 55 | 2 | 3 | 113 | 6 | 3.59 |
| Mazur, Charleston. | 15 | 0 | 0 | 0 | 1 | 0 | 2 | 1.000 | 32 | 27 | 19 | 11 | 8 | 3 | 23 | 0 | 1 | 24 | 5 | 2.25 |
| McCarthy, And* | 10 | 6 | 1 | 0 | 1 | 3 | 0 | .250 | 26 | 41 | 31 | 30 | 3 | 17 | 0 | 0 | 27 | 0 | 10.38 |
| McDaniel, Spa* | 18 | 0 | 0 | 0 | 0 | 2 | 0 | .000 | 21 | 27 | 16 | 14 | 2 | 22 | 4 | 1 | 18 | 8 | 6.00 |
| McLaughlin, Gwd.. | 20 | 16 | 6 | 3 | 12 | 5 | 0 | .706 | 122 | 112 | 47 | 35 | 5 | 49 | 2 | 0 | 59 | 1 | 2.58 |
| McLean, Greenwood | 35 | 4 | 0 | 0 | 3 | 6 | 1 | .333 | 107 | 99 | 54 | 40 | 1 | 43 | 5 | 1 | 82 | 8 | 3.36 |
| McWilliams, Gwd*. | 17 | 13 | 4 | 2 | 8 | 4 | 0 | .667 | 93 | 83 | 36 | 29 | 0 | 18 | 0 | 5 | 71 | 2 | 2.81 |
| Meistickle, Gwd | 8 | 1 | 0 | 0 | 1 | 1 | 0 | .500 | 12 | 11 | 3 | 3 | 0 | 6 | 0 | 0 | 6 | 0 | 2.25 |
| Mercer, Char* | 14 | 7 | 1 | 0 | 2 | 5 | 0 | .286 | 60 | 55 | 49 | 32 | 6 | 48 | 0 | 1 | 48 | 3 | 4.80 |

| Pitcher—Club | G. | GS. | CG. | ShO. | W. | L. | Sv. | Pct. | IP. | H. | R. | ER. | HR. | BB. | Int. BB. | HB. | SO. | WP. | ERA. |
|---|---|---|---|---|---|---|---|---|---|---|---|---|---|---|---|---|---|---|---|
| Nickerson, And ... | 25 | 6 | 4 | 1 | 4 | 5 | 0 | .444 | 93 | 99 | 53 | 36 | 8 | 26 | 1 | 5 | 50 | 6 | 3.48 |
| Nottle, Anderson .. | 2 | 0 | 0 | 0 | 0 | 1 | 0 | .000 | 3 | 1 | 0 | 0 | 0 | 0 | 0 | 0 | 3 | 0 | 0.00 |
| Patten, Anderson*.. | 26 | 0 | 0 | 0 | 1 | 0 | 1 | 1.000 | 38 | 40 | 18 | 12 | 0 | 22 | 0 | 0 | 23 | 2 | 2.84 |
| Peeples, Greenwood | 9 | 0 | 0 | 0 | 0 | 1 | 0 | .000 | 29 | 28 | 20 | 16 | 5 | 8 | 0 | 0 | 18 | 3 | 4.97 |
| Phillips, Gwd .... | 33 | 9 | 4 | 0 | 5 | 6 | 1 | .455 | 97 | 111 | 57 | 42 | 8 | 20 | 3 | 5 | 52 | 7 | 3.90 |
| Presser, Charleston | 2 | 0 | 0 | 0 | 0 | 0 | 0 | .000 | 4 | 4 | 5 | 5 | 0 | 5 | 0 | 0 | 4 | 1 | 0.00 |
| Roberts, Spa ...... | 2 | 0 | 0 | 0 | 0 | 0 | 0 | .000 | 2 | 2 | 0 | 0 | 0 | 1 | 0 | 0 | 1 | 0 | 11.25 |
| Robles, Charleston. | 6 | 0 | 0 | 0 | 0 | 0 | 0 | .000 | 21 | 26 | 10 | 7 | 1 | 14 | 1 | 1 | 11 | 1 | 3.00 |
| Ryan, Charleston.. | 2 | 0 | 0 | 0 | 0 | 0 | 0 | .000 | 5 | 7 | 3 | 3 | 1 | 3 | 0 | 1 | 0 | 0 | 5.40 |
| Saucier, Spa* .... | 25 | 25 | 12 | 4 | 12 | 9 | 0 | .571 | 159 | 138 | 72 | 59 | 6 | 61 | 3 | 7 | 90 | 5 | 3.34 |
| W. Smith, And* .. | 25 | 25 | 5 | 2 | 13 | 6 | 0 | .684 | 155 | 148 | 84 | 74 | 12 | 92 | 0 | 0 | 96 | 10 | 4.30 |
| Stein, Greenwood .. | 22 | 21 | 3 | 2 | 5 | 11 | 0 | .313 | 109 | 108 | 67 | 50 | 3 | 73 | 1 | 3 | 71 | 8 | 4.13 |
| Stone, Spartanburg | 21 | 1 | 0 | 0 | 3 | 1 | 1 | .750 | 41 | 34 | 19 | 18 | 2 | 26 | 1 | 2 | 36 | 4 | 3.95 |
| Theiss, Greenwood.. | 22 | 1 | 0 | 0 | 2 | 5 | 2 | .286 | 58 | 40 | 18 | 14 | 1 | 32 | 4 | 4 | 35 | 1 | 2.17 |
| Tidwell, Anderson | 26 | 26 | 9 | 1 | 7 | 11 | 0 | .389 | 174 | 160 | 88 | 61 | 9 | 71 | 1 | 2 | 76 | 3 | 3.16 |
| Titus, Greenwood* | 29 | 20 | 4 | 0 | 8 | 10 | 0 | .444 | 122 | 141 | 78 | 64 | 10 | 59 | 1 | 1 | 54 | 8 | 4.72 |
| Waclawczyk, Gwd.. | 8 | 6 | 0 | 0 | 1 | 2 | 0 | .333 | 28 | 24 | 22 | 15 | 3 | 23 | 0 | 0 | 15 | 2 | 4.82 |
| Wertz, Spar* .... | 24 | 17 | 6 | 4 | 12 | 3 | 0 | .800 | 135 | 113 | 58 | 43 | 3 | 68 | 1 | 2 | 82 | 3 | 2.87 |
| Whitson, Charleston | 24 | 24 | 5 | 1 | 8 | 15 | 0 | .348 | 142 | 140 | 96 | 80 | 7 | 99 | 0 | 15 | 120 | 10 | 5.07 |
| Williams, Char ... | 29 | 18 | 8 | 1 | 4 | 12 | 1 | .250 | 148 | 148 | 94 | 63 | 12 | 65 | 0 | 3 | 115 | 7 | 3.83 |
| Wright, Spa...... | 26 | 26 | 15 | 4 | 14 | 7 | 0 | .667 | 181 | 166 | 83 | 55 | 7 | 56 | 3 | 8 | 127 | 6 | 2.73 |

BALKS—McCarthy, 4; Williams, 3; Byrd, Clark, Gibson, Nickerson, Phillips, W. Smith, Wertz, 2 each; Breining, Carroll, Davis, Harlee, Hernandez, Johnston, L. Jones, LaPointe, Martinez, McLaughlin, McWilliams, Saucier, Whitson, Wright, 1 each.

COMBINATION SHUTOUTS—W. Smith-Getter, Anderson; Davis-Brandt, Mercer-Breining-Mazur, Charleston; Stein-Campbell, Titus-Campbell, Greenwood.

NO-HIT GAMES—None.

# *Appalachian League*

## ROOKIE CLASSIFICATION

### CHAMPIONSHIP WINNERS IN PREVIOUS YEARS

| | | |
|---|---|---|
| 1921—Greenville ........ .608 | Bristol y ......... .617 | 1959—Morristown ........ .603 |
| Johnson City* ..... .627 | 1944—Kingsport‡ ........ .575 | 1960—Wytheville ........ .614 |
| 1922—Bristol ........ .557 | 1945—Kingsport‡ ........ .670 | 1961—Middlesboro ........ .591 |
| 1923—Knoxville ........ .635 | 1946—New River‡ ........ .675 | 1962—Bluefield ........ .671 |
| 1924—Knoxville* ........ .642 | 1947—Pulaski ........ .648 | 1963—Bluefield ........ .652 |
| Bristol ........ .607 | New River (3rd)† .. .516 | 1964—Johnson City ...... .614 |
| 1925—Greenville ........ .667 | 1948—Pulaski‡ ........ .680 | 1965—Salem ........ .623 |
| 1926-36—Did not operate. | 1949—Bluefield‡ ........ .721 | 1966—Marion ........ .623 |
| 1937—Elizabethton ...... .559 | 1950—Bluefield ........ .600 | 1967—Bluefield ........ .583 |
| Pennington Gap* .. .580 | Bluefield z ........ .745 | 1968—Marion ........ .576 |
| 1938—Elizabethton ...... .664 | 1951—Kingsport‡ ........ .659 | 1969—Pulaski a ........ .544 |
| Greenville (3rd)† .. .571 | 1952—Johnson City ...... .559 | Johnson City ...... .638 |
| 1939—Elizabethton† ...... .597 | Welch (3rd)† ...... .509 | 1970—Bluefield ........ .638 |
| 1940—Johnson City§ ...... .726 | 1953—Welch ........ .705 | 1971—Bluefield a ........ .609 |
| Elizabethton ...... .750 | Johnson City ...... .672 | Kingsport ........ .559 |
| 1941—Johnson City ...... .614 | 1954—Bluefield‡ ........ .619 | 1972—Bristol a ........ .588 |
| Elizabethton* ..... .661 | 1955—Salem** ........ .689 | Covington ........ .586 |
| 1942—Bristol ........ .667 | 1956—Did not operate. | 1973—Kingsport ........ .757 |
| Bristol x ........ .660 | 1957—Bluefield ........ .701 | 1974—Bristol a ........ .754 |
| 1943—Bristol ........ .755 | 1958—Johnson City ...... .662 | Bluefield ........ .536 |

*Won split-season playoff. †Won four-team playoff. ‡Won championship and four-team playoff.
§Johnson City, first-half winner, won playoff involving six clubs. xWon both halves and defeated
second-place Elizabethton in playoff. yWon both halves, but Erwin won four-team playoff. zWon
both halves, but Bristol won two-club playoff. **Salem and Johnson City declared playoff co-champions
when weather forced cancellation of final series. aLeague was divided into Northern, Southern divisions
in 1969, 1971, 1972; declared league champion, based on highest won-lost percentage.

### STANDING OF CLUBS AT CLOSE OF SEASON, AUGUST 28

#### SOUTHERN DIVISION

| Club | J.C. | Eliz. | Bri. | Kpt. | Mar. | Cov. | Pul. | Blu. | W. | L. | T. | Pct. | G.B. |
|---|---|---|---|---|---|---|---|---|---|---|---|---|---|
| Johnson City (Cardinals)...... | | 7 | 5 | 5 | 6 | 6 | 7 | 41 | 27 | 0 | .603 | .... |
| Elizabethton (Twins)........ | 3 | | 3 | 5 | 7 | 7 | 6 | 7 | 38 | 30 | 0 | .559 | 3 |
| Bristol (Tigers)............. | 3 | 7 | | 4 | 5 | 7 | 5 | 6 | 37 | 31 | 0 | .544 | 4 |
| Kingsport (Braves)........... | 5 | 5 | 6 | | 4 | 4 | 3 | 6 | 33 | 33 | 0 | .500 | 7 |

#### NORTHERN DIVISION

| Club | J.C. | Eliz. | Bri. | Kpt. | Mar. | Cov. | Pul. | Blu. | W. | L. | T. | Pct. | G.B. |
|---|---|---|---|---|---|---|---|---|---|---|---|---|---|
| Marion (Mets)............... | 5 | 1 | 5 | 6 | | 5 | 8 | 5 | 35 | 33 | 0 | .515 | .... |
| Covington (Astros)........... | 4 | 4 | 3 | 5 | 5 | | | 8 | 7 | 35 | 34 | 0 | .507 | ½ |
| Pulaski (Phillies)........... | 4 | 4 | 5 | 3 | 2 | | | 5 | 27 | 41 | 0 | .397 | 8 |
| Bluefield (Orioles)........... | 3 | 3 | 4 | 3 | 5 | 3 | 5 | | 26 | 43 | 0 | .377 | 9½ |

Johnson City declared league champion on basis of highest won-lost percentage.

Major league affiliations in parentheses.

Playoffs—None.

Managers: Bluefield—Paul Flesner; Bristol—Joe Lewis; Covington—Billy Smith; Elizabethton—
Fred Waters; Johnson City—Tom Burgess; Kingsport—Gene Hassell; Marion—Chuck Hiller, Billy
Connors; Pulaski—Bob Wren.

Regular-Season Attendance—Bluefield, 17,153; Bristol, 9,999; Covington, 18,376; Elizabethton,
18,193; Johnson City, 41,896; Kingsport, 19,672; Marion, 10,258; Pulaski, 15,385; Total, 150,932.
No playoff. No All-Star Game.

All-Star Team: 1B—Green, Kingsport; 2B—Draper, Bristol; 3B—Draimin, Bluefield; SS—
Ramsey, Johnson City; OF—Powell, Elizabethton; Mays, Johnson City; Smith, Bluefield; C—Bochy,
Covington; P—Lee, Elizabethton; Strelitz, Johnson City; Jackson, Marion; Ford, Bluefield; Simon,
Marion. Manager—Burgess, Johnson City.

(Compiled by Howe News Bureau, Chicago, Ill.)

### CLUB BATTING

| Club | G. | AB. | R. | OR. | H. | TB. | 2B. | 3B. | HR. | RBI. | SH. | SF. | BB. | BB.HP. | SO. | SB. | CS. | LOB. | Pct. |
|---|---|---|---|---|---|---|---|---|---|---|---|---|---|---|---|---|---|---|---|
| Johnson City ...68 | 2336 | 409 | 276 | 633 | 935 | 118 | 20 | 48 | 334 | 53 | 21 | 305 | 15 | 11 | 355 | 68 | 16 | 562 | .271 |
| Kingsport .....66 | 2087 | 376 | 360 | 562 | 807 | 97 | 23 | 34 | 326 | 14 | 27 | 306 | 11 | 24 | 371 | 51 | 21 | 473 | .269 |
| Pulaski .......68 | 2270 | 380 | 432 | 597 | 835 | 107 | 19 | 31 | 296 | 26 | 17 | 236 | 3 | 14 | 393 | 35 | 12 | 464 | .263 |
| Bluefield .....69 | 2288 | 312 | 463 | 596 | 778 | 93 | 13 | 21 | 263 | 20 | 12 | 250 | 9 | 13 | 443 | 54 | 24 | 514 | .260 |
| Marion .......68 | 2276 | 375 | 351 | 374 | 872 | 80 | 25 | 56 | 309 | 26 | 14 | 284 | 5 | 37 | 476 | 82 | 26 | 590 | .252 |
| Elizabethton ..68 | 2254 | 375 | 330 | 564 | 808 | 117 | 23 | 27 | 315 | 13 | 17 | 341 | 5 | 19 | 488 | 70 | 9 | 545 | .250 |
| Covington .....69 | 2231 | 345 | 360 | 556 | 763 | 101 | 14 | 26 | 279 | 31 | 20 | 261 | 7 | 24 | 464 | 40 | 22 | 492 | .249 |
| Bristol .......68 | 2116 | 324 | 304 | 514 | 719 | 96 | 17 | 25 | 273 | 22 | 17 | 307 | 4 | 29 | 353 | 74 | 21 | 506 | .243 |

### INDIVIDUAL BATTING

(Leading Qualifiers for Batting Championship—189 or More Plate Appearances)

*Bats lefthanded.  †Switch-hitter.

| Player and Club | G | AB | R | H | TB | 2B | 3B | HR | RBI | SH | SF | BB | HP | SO | SB | CS | Pct. |
|---|---|---|---|---|---|---|---|---|---|---|---|---|---|---|---|---|---|
| Smith, Bobby G., Bluefield*..68 | 259 | 36 | 94 | 117 | 10 | 5 | 1 | 41 | 0 | 0 | 22 | 1 | 25 | 8 | 5 | .363 |
| Doherty, James, Kingsport...62 | 226 | 48 | 77 | 92 | 13 | 1 | 0 | 30 | 2 | 4 | 31 | 0 | 23 | 9 | 0 | .341 |
| Berger, Kenneth, Pulaski*...66 | 264 | 58 | 89 | 119 | 15 | 6 | 1 | 22 | 3 | 1 | 30 | 3 | 26 | 21 | 2 | .337 |
| Powell, Hosken, Elizabeth*...64 | 249 | 45 | 82 | 126 | 23 | 6 | 3 | 58 | 0 | 0 | 37 | 7 | 22 | 20 | 0 | .329 |
| Brant, Marshall, Marion ....64 | 245 | 49 | 80 | 144 | 15 | 5 | 13 | 45 | 0 | 1 | 27 | 4 | 44 | 3 | 1 | .327 |
| Martinez, Juan J., Bluefield..56 | 194 | 26 | 63 | 68 | 5 | 0 | 0 | 15 | 0 | 0 | 11 | 2 | 19 | 7 | 6 | .325 |
| Drainin, Sheldon, Bluefield†  51 | 188 | 37 | 61 | 81 | 8 | 0 | 4 | 24 | 0 | 2 | 17 | 0 | 28 | 8 | 4 | .324 |
| Mays, Henry, Johnson City..64 | 250 | 58 | 81 | 125 | 15 | 4 | 7 | 48 | 4 | 4 | 51 | 1 | 20 | 12 | 3 | .324 |
| Farnish, Eugene, Pulaski ...46 | 173 | 32 | 55 | 66 | 6 | 1 | 1 | 24 | 0 | 0 | 17 | 0 | 23 | 3 | 1 | .318 |
| Pisarkiewicz, Michael, J C*..63 | 231 | 43 | 70 | 134 | 16 | 6 | 12 | 49 | 0 | 3 | 44 | 0 | 41 | 3 | 1 | .303 |

Departmental Leaders: G—Smith, Witt, 68; AB—Ramsey, 277; R—Berger, Mays, 58; H—Smith, 94; TB—Brant, 144; 2B—Powell, 23; 3B—Pisker, 7; HR—Brant, 13; RBI—Powell, 58; SH—Ramsey, 12; SF—Reynolds, 6; BB—Mays, Witt, 51; HP—Hicks, 8; SO—Channel, 83; SB—Hicks, 40; CS—Cooper, Reynolds, 7.

### (All Players—Listed Alphabetically)

| Player and Club | G | AB | R | H | TB | 2B | 3B | HR | RBI | SH | SF | BB | HP | SO | SB | CS | Pct. |
|---|---|---|---|---|---|---|---|---|---|---|---|---|---|---|---|---|---|
| Alvarez, Manuel, Bristol*...38 | 92 | 14 | 22 | 40 | 6 | 0 | 4 | 24 | 0 | 3 | 14 | 4 | 12 | 1 | 0 | .239 |
| Amancio, Ramon, Pulaski ...14 | 4 | 1 | 0 | 0 | 0 | 0 | 0 | 0 | 0 | 0 | 0 | 0 | 0 | 0 | 0 | .000 |
| Andersen, Edward, Covington† 14 | 27 | 3 | 5 | 6 | 1 | 0 | 0 | 0 | 3 | 0 | 0 | 0 | 5 | 0 | 0 | .185 |
| Anderson, Jeff C., Bluefield..11 | 4 | 0 | 0 | 0 | 0 | 0 | 0 | 1 | 1 | 0 | 0 | 0 | 0 | 0 | 0 | .000 |
| Antone, Michael, Eliz*  ...42 | 132 | 24 | 37 | 49 | 7 | 1 | 1 | 18 | 1 | 3 | 35 | 0 | 24 | 6 | 0 | .280 |
| Armstrong, Louis, Bluefield..27 | 79 | 13 | 18 | 26 | 3 | 1 | 1 | 7 | 0 | 0 | 11 | 0 | 27 | 4 | 0 | .228 |
| Arroyo, Carlos, Pulaski*....12 | 17 | 1 | 6 | 9 | 3 | 0 | 0 | 2 | 0 | 0 | 1 | 0 | 4 | 0 | 0 | .353 |
| Arthur, Dallas, Marion......14 | 0 | 0 | 0 | 0 | 0 | 0 | 0 | 0 | 0 | 0 | 0 | 0 | 0 | 0 | 0 | .000 |
| Bacon, Michael, Elizabethton 32 | 90 | 12 | 25 | 29 | 4 | 0 | 0 | 10 | 1 | 2 | 12 | 1 | 21 | 1 | 0 | .278 |
| Bardot, Gene, Marion.......25 | 8 | 0 | 0 | 0 | 0 | 0 | 0 | 0 | 0 | 0 | 0 | 0 | 5 | 0 | 0 | .000 |
| Barr, Calvin, Johnson City*..30 | 96 | 14 | 27 | 36 | 4 | 1 | 1 | 11 | 0 | 0 | 8 | 1 | 15 | 3 | 0 | .281 |
| Batista, Juan, Johnson City.. 1 | 3 | 0 | 1 | 1 | 0 | 0 | 0 | 0 | 0 | 0 | 0 | 1 | 0 | 0 | 0 | .333 |
| Benton, Alfred, Marion. ... 45 | 145 | 25 | 36 | 55 | 11 | 1 | 2 | 18 | 0 | 0 | 18 | 4 | 38 | 1 | 0 | .248 |
| Berger, Kenneth, Pulaski*...66 | 264 | 58 | 89 | 119 | 15 | 6 | 1 | 22 | 3 | 1 | 30 | 3 | 26 | 21 | 2 | .337 |
| Berry, Richard, Covington... 2 | 2 | 0 | 0 | 0 | 0 | 0 | 0 | 0 | 0 | 0 | 0 | 0 | 0 | 0 | 0 | .000 |
| Black, Gregory, Bristol...... 6 | 5 | 1 | 1 | 1 | 0 | 0 | 0 | 0 | 0 | 0 | 0 | 0 | 0 | 0 | 0 | .200 |
| Blank, Robert, Covington..14 | 7 | 0 | 1 | 1 | 0 | 0 | 0 | 1 | 0 | 0 | 1 | 0 | 5 | 0 | 0 | .143 |
| Bochy, Bruce, Covington....37 | 145 | 31 | 49 | 70 | 9 | 0 | 4 | 34 | 0 | 1 | 10 | 0 | 18 | 0 | 0 | .338 |
| Bodie, Keith, Marion........42 | 144 | 31 | 45 | 73 | 3 | 2 | 7 | 27 | 0 | 2 | 25 | 2 | 32 | 9 | 3 | .313 |
| Bowman, William, Kingsport* 27 | 38 | 6 | 9 | 13 | 4 | 0 | 0 | 2 | 0 | 0 | 7 | 0 | 12 | 3 | 0 | .237 |
| Boyer, David, Johnson City...52 | 207 | 33 | 54 | 73 | 11 | 1 | 2 | 28 | 2 | 3 | 14 | 1 | 22 | 1 | 2 | .261 |
| Bradbury, George, Marion ...21 | 57 | 9 | 10 | 16 | 3 | 0 | 1 | 4 | 1 | 0 | 10 | 6 | 12 | 0 | 3 | .175 |
| Brant, Marshall, Marion ....64 | 245 | 49 | 80 | 144 | 15 | 5 | 13 | 45 | 0 | 1 | 27 | 4 | 44 | 3 | 1 | .327 |
| Broomis, Gregory, Bluefield..19 | 16 | 2 | 4 | 7 | 3 | 0 | 0 | 4 | 0 | 0 | 3 | 0 | 6 | 0 | 0 | .250 |
| Brown, Michael T., Bluefield 10 | 11 | 1 | 0 | 0 | 0 | 0 | 0 | 0 | 0 | 0 | 1 | 0 | 6 | 0 | 0 | .000 |
| Brown, Randall S., Marion...10 | 18 | 4 | 6 | 6 | 0 | 0 | 0 | 2 | 0 | 0 | 0 | 0 | 2 | 0 | 0 | .333 |
| Bruchanski, Kenneth, Bristol.10 | 21 | 2 | 8 | 10 | 2 | 0 | 0 | 5 | 1 | 0 | 2 | 0 | 4 | 0 | 0 | .381 |
| Brummer, Glenn, Johnson C 50 | 183 | 27 | 47 | 71 | 7 | 1 | 5 | 28 | 2 | 2 | 11 | 1 | 19 | 7 | 2 | .257 |
| Bruno, Fernando, Kingsport.13 | 10 | 0 | 1 | 1 | 0 | 0 | 0 | 0 | 1 | 0 | 1 | 0 | 6 | 0 | 0 | .100 |
| Buckley, David, Covington†..15 | 26 | 2 | 2 | 3 | 1 | 0 | 0 | 1 | 0 | 0 | 2 | 0 | 12 | 0 | 0 | .077 |
| Bugden, Gerald, Johnson City* 19 | 8 | 0 | 1 | 1 | 0 | 0 | 0 | 0 | 0 | 0 | 1 | 0 | 4 | 0 | 0 | .125 |
| Burnside, Sheldon, Bristol..21 | 25 | 2 | 4 | 4 | 0 | 0 | 0 | 0 | 2 | 0 | 3 | 0 | 7 | 0 | 0 | .160 |
| Burton, Daniel, Bristol.....43 | 121 | 25 | 27 | 45 | 10 | 1 | 2 | 14 | 0 | 1 | 9 | 1 | 21 | 7 | 1 | .223 |
| Cacciatore, Paul, Marion....11 | 11 | 0 | 0 | 0 | 0 | 0 | 0 | 0 | 1 | 1 | 0 | 0 | 0 | 0 | 0 | .000 |
| Capra, Robert, Kingsport*...16 | 2 | 2 | 1 | 2 | 1 | 0 | 0 | 2 | 0 | 0 | 2 | 0 | 0 | 0 | 0 | .500 |
| Carbis, Charles, Elizabethton. 5 | 3 | 0 | 0 | 0 | 0 | 0 | 0 | 0 | 0 | 0 | 0 | 0 | 0 | 0 | 0 | .000 |
| Carriger, Ricky, Kingsport... 5 | 2 | 0 | 0 | 0 | 0 | 0 | 0 | 0 | 0 | 0 | 0 | 0 | 0 | 0 | 0 | .000 |
| Carroll, Edward, Bristol*... 22 | 51 | 4 | 11 | 13 | 2 | 0 | 0 | 7 | 0 | 0 | 6 | 1 | 11 | 1 | 1 | .216 |
| Carter, Jeffrey, Marion......11 | 26 | 6 | 8 | 11 | 1 | 1 | 0 | 4 | 0 | 0 | 5 | 1 | 10 | 1 | 0 | .308 |
| Carty, Landre, Kingsport.. 14 | 35 | 5 | 10 | 14 | 4 | 0 | 0 | 3 | 0 | 0 | 2 | 0 | 4 | 0 | 1 | .286 |
| Castro, Anthony, Pulaski*...63 | 226 | 41 | 62 | 108 | 18 | 2 | 8 | 35 | 1 | 1 | 23 | 0 | 30 | 1 | 0 | .274 |
| Cavaletto, Gary, Kingsport.. 5 | 11 | 3 | 0 | 0 | 0 | 0 | 0 | 1 | 0 | 1 | 3 | 2 | 5 | 1 | 0 | .000 |
| Cervantes, Eric, Kingsport*..51 | 85 | 13 | 23 | 32 | 3 | 3 | 0 | 24 | 0 | 0 | 14 | 1 | 5 | 1 | 0 | .271 |
| Channel, Thomas, Eliz......67 | 257 | 55 | 68 | 96 | 15 | 2 | 3 | 28 | 0 | 1 | 38 | 0 | 83 | 10 | 1 | .265 |
| Checko, Randy, Bluefield.. 10 | 4 | 1 | 1 | 1 | 0 | 0 | 0 | 0 | 0 | 0 | 0 | 0 | 0 | 0 | 0 | .250 |
| Cias, Darryll, Bluefield ...48 | 164 | 15 | 37 | 45 | 6 | 1 | 0 | 17 | 1 | 4 | 2 | 0 | 25 | 2 | 1 | .226 |
| Clark, LeRoy, Covington.....13 | 18 | 0 | 1 | 1 | 0 | 0 | 0 | 0 | 0 | 0 | 3 | 0 | 10 | 0 | 0 | .056 |
| Clark, Russell, Marion......14 | 36 | 8 | 7 | 12 | 2 | 0 | 1 | 5 | 0 | 1 | 0 | 1 | 9 | 0 | 0 | .194 |
| Cloherty, John, Covington*..23 | 63 | 13 | 13 | 22 | 4 | 0 | 1 | 5 | 1 | 0 | 3 | 0 | 10 | 0 | 0 | .206 |
| Cooper, Gary N., Kingsport*..51 | 163 | 26 | 39 | 52 | 8 | 1 | 1 | 12 | 0 | 1 | 8 | 0 | 14 | 0 | 0 | .239 |
| Cordero, Pedro, Covington...58 | 230 | 35 | 59 | 71 | 12 | 0 | 0 | 29 | 2 | 1 | 12 | 2 | 41 | 13 | 7 | .257 |
| Corness, D. Wayne, Covington 8 | 5 | 0 | 1 | 1 | 0 | 0 | 0 | 2 | 0 | 1 | 2 | 2 | 43 | 4 | 0 | .200 |
| Cornwell, Alan, Covington...12 | 6 | 0 | 0 | 0 | 0 | 0 | 0 | 0 | 0 | 0 | 3 | 0 | 3 | 0 | 0 | .000 |
| Coury, William, Bristol......48 | 139 | 21 | 28 | 46 | 11 | 2 | 1 | 18 | 0 | 2 | 15 | 1 | 24 | 5 | 0 | .201 |
| Cranford, William, Kingsport 9 | 12 | 0 | 3 | 3 | 0 | 0 | 0 | 0 | 0 | 0 | 0 | 1 | 0 | 0 | 0 | .250 |
| Crisp, H. Dean, Elizabethton.34 | 98 | 10 | 16 | 25 | 5 | 2 | 0 | 11 | 0 | 3 | 18 | 0 | 25 | 3 | 0 | .163 |
| Curbelo, George, Elizabethton 23 | 62 | 5 | 12 | 15 | 3 | 0 | 0 | 11 | 0 | 0 | 8 | 0 | 8 | 0 | 0 | .194 |
| Darichuk, Greg, Bristol*....24 | 21 | 2 | 3 | 4 | 1 | 0 | 0 | 0 | 0 | 0 | 5 | 1 | 4 | 1 | 0 | .143 |
| Darnell, R. Steven, Marion*..28 | 6 | 1 | 0 | 0 | 0 | 0 | 0 | 0 | 0 | 0 | 1 | 0 | 4 | 0 | 0 | .000 |

| Player and Club | G. | AB. | R. | H. | TB. | 2B. | 3B. | HR. | RBI. | SH. | SF. | BB. | HP. | SO. | SB. | CS. | Pct. |
|---|---|---|---|---|---|---|---|---|---|---|---|---|---|---|---|---|---|
| Davis, George, Bristol* ......32 | 49 | 3 | 9 | 10 | 1 | 0 | 0 | 1 | 0 | 0 | 6 | 0 | 13 | 0 | 0 | .184 |
| Dearstone, Mickey, Kingsport 22 | 52 | 9 | 11 | 16 | 3 | 1 | 0 | 10 | 0 | 2 | 14 | 1 | 10 | 0 | 0 | .212 |
| DeGrande, Ronald, Bluefield. 4 | 4 | 0 | 0 | 0 | 0 | 0 | 0 | 0 | 0 | 0 | 0 | 0 | 2 | 0 | 0 | .000 |
| DeJesus, Julian M., Covington 10 | 15 | 2 | 3 | 5 | 2 | 0 | 0 | 3 | 0 | 0 | 1 | 0 | 7 | 0 | 0 | .200 |
| DiPietro, Alfred, Bristol..... 50 | 165 | 29 | 46 | 67 | 7 | 1 | 4 | 27 | 1 | 0 | 16 | 1 | 27 | 0 | 1 | .279 |
| Dockins, Rodney, Pulaski.....25 | 9 | 0 | 2 | 2 | 0 | 0 | 0 | 2 | 0 | 0 | 0 | 0 | 4 | 0 | 0 | .222 |
| Doherty, James, Kingsport....62 | 226 | 48 | 77 | 92 | 13 | 1 | 0 | 30 | 2 | 4 | 31 | 0 | 23 | 9 | 0 | .341 |
| Doktor, Phillip, Bristol† ....43 | 122 | 31 | 32 | 50 | 3 | 6 | 1 | 18 | 0 | 0 | 32 | 1 | 15 | 7 | 1 | .262 |
| Dolan, John, Bristol..........38 | 100 | 17 | 27 | 33 | 4 | 1 | 0 | 10 | 1 | 3 | 15 | 2 | 22 | 4 | 1 | .270 |
| Donaghu, Raymond, Johnson C 14 | 27 | 2 | 4 | 5 | 1 | 0 | 0 | 1 | 5 | 0 | 3 | 0 | 15 | 0 | 0 | .148 |
| Douglas, Stephen, Eliz.......62 | 246 | 42 | 74 | 109 | 11 | 6 | 4 | 31 | 2 | 0 | 17 | 4 | 30 | 7 | 1 | .301 |
| Draimin, Sheldon, Bluefield† 51 | 188 | 37 | 61 | 81 | 8 | 0 | 4 | 24 | 0 | 2 | 17 | 0 | 28 | 8 | 4 | .324 |
| Draper, James, Bristol .......58 | 194 | 35 | 56 | 68 | 10 | 1 | 0 | 11 | 2 | 0 | 38 | 2 | 12 | 10 | 4 | .289 |
| Drysdale, Bradford, Pulaski..12 | 7 | 1 | 2 | 2 | 0 | 0 | 0 | 0 | 0 | 0 | 2 | 0 | 3 | 0 | 0 | .286 |
| Dyer, James, Marion* ........50 | 168 | 26 | 42 | 59 | 5 | 0 | 4 | 20 | 1 | 0 | 10 | 1 | 34 | 1 | 0 | .250 |
| Dyer, John, Bluefield* .......12 | 8 | 0 | 1 | 1 | 0 | 0 | 0 | 0 | 0 | 0 | 1 | 2 | 0 | 0 | 0 | .125 |
| Echols, Tony, Marion.........44 | 150 | 28 | 40 | 59 | 4 | 3 | 3 | 16 | 0 | 0 | 9 | 2 | 39 | 5 | 3 | .267 |
| Eicher, Charles, Elizabethton 3 | 3 | 0 | 0 | 0 | 0 | 0 | 0 | 0 | 0 | 0 | 0 | 0 | 1 | 0 | 0 | .000 |
| Elders, Michael, Bristol.....19 | 7 | 1 | 1 | 1 | 0 | 0 | 0 | 0 | 0 | 0 | 2 | 0 | 2 | 0 | 0 | .143 |
| Farnish, Eugene, Pulaski.....46 | 173 | 32 | 55 | 66 | 6 | 1 | 1 | 24 | 0 | 0 | 17 | 0 | 23 | 3 | 1 | .318 |
| Felt, William, Pulaski*......49 | 146 | 32 | 46 | 80 | 17 | 1 | 5 | 24 | 0 | 0 | 27 | 0 | 25 | 0 | 0 | .315 |
| Fernandez, Rolando, Blu.....13 | 3 | 0 | 0 | 0 | 0 | 0 | 0 | 0 | 0 | 0 | 0 | 0 | 1 | 0 | 0 | .000 |
| Field, Gregory, Elizabethton .13 | 25 | 1 | 4 | 4 | 0 | 0 | 0 | 1 | 3 | 0 | 2 | 0 | 13 | 0 | 0 | .160 |
| Filkins, Leslie, Bristol*....32 | 108 | 19 | 32 | 52 | 5 | 0 | 5 | 26 | 1 | 1 | 17 | 4 | 6 | 16 | 2 | .296 |
| Fletcher, C. Scott, Bluefield*.12 | 7 | 1 | 1 | 1 | 0 | 0 | 0 | 1 | 0 | 0 | 0 | 0 | 1 | 0 | 0 | .143 |
| Flores, Steven, Pulaski.......20 | 9 | 2 | 4 | 5 | 1 | 0 | 0 | 0 | 1 | 0 | 4 | 0 | 1 | 0 | 0 | .444 |
| Ford, David A., Bluefield.... 7 | 17 | 1 | 3 | 3 | 0 | 0 | 0 | 2 | 0 | 0 | 5 | 0 | 6 | 0 | 0 | .176 |
| Franz, Robert, Elizabethton*.15 | 19 | 4 | 1 | 1 | 0 | 0 | 0 | 1 | 0 | 0 | 5 | 0 | 6 | 0 | 0 | .053 |
| Garrison, Steven, Pulaski....45 | 123 | 13 | 28 | 34 | 6 | 0 | 0 | 12 | 1 | 0 | 9 | 0 | 19 | 1 | 2 | .228 |
| Gaughran, Gregg, Eliz*.......33 | 96 | 12 | 22 | 32 | 2 | 1 | 2 | 11 | 0 | 1 | 10 | 0 | 18 | 0 | 0 | .229 |
| Gesquiere, Mark, Pulaski..... 6 | 4 | 2 | 1 | 1 | 0 | 0 | 0 | 1 | 0 | 0 | 1 | 0 | 1 | 0 | 0 | .250 |
| Gierhan, Samuel, Bluefield... 9 | 18 | 1 | 1 | 1 | 0 | 0 | 0 | 1 | 2 | 0 | 1 | 0 | 7 | 0 | 0 | .056 |
| Gomez, Hector M., Kingsport 12 | 22 | 6 | 6 | 14 | 0 | 1 | 2 | 8 | 1 | 0 | 5 | 0 | 6 | 0 | 2 | .273 |
| Grant, Robert, Marion†.......12 | 24 | 3 | 0 | 0 | 0 | 0 | 0 | 0 | 0 | 0 | 7 | 1 | 7 | 1 | 0 | .000 |
| Graves, Lary, Bristol........14 | 21 | 2 | 4 | 5 | 1 | 0 | 0 | 1 | 0 | 0 | 1 | 0 | 4 | 0 | 1 | .190 |
| Green, Larry, Covington......17 | 17 | 6 | 3 | 3 | 0 | 0 | 0 | 1 | 1 | 0 | 5 | 0 | 9 | 0 | 0 | .176 |
| Green, Richard B., Kingsport† 64 | 220 | 48 | 60 | 110 | 12 | 1 | 12 | 51 | 0 | 2 | 38 | 5 | 40 | 1 | 0 | .273 |
| Groff, Theodore, Elizabethton 15 | 20 | 3 | 2 | 2 | 0 | 0 | 0 | 0 | 2 | 0 | 8 | 0 | 0 | 0 | 0 | .100 |
| Grunsky, Gary, Elizabethton* 4 | 2 | 0 | 0 | 0 | 0 | 0 | 0 | 0 | 0 | 0 | 1 | 0 | 0 | 0 | 0 | .000 |
| Hallgren, Robert, Covington* 50 | 154 | 31 | 40 | 64 | 9 | 0 | 5 | 19 | 1 | 1 | 42 | 2 | 34 | 3 | 2 | .260 |
| Hamner, James P., Marion..26 | 70 | 9 | 14 | 24 | 2 | 1 | 2 | 10 | 0 | 0 | 14 | 1 | 13 | 0 | 0 | .200 |
| Hannah, Raymond, Marion..10 | 9 | 0 | 1 | 1 | 0 | 0 | 0 | 2 | 1 | 0 | 1 | 0 | 4 | 0 | 0 | .111 |
| Harris, Frank, Bristol......7 | 16 | 0 | 2 | 3 | 1 | 0 | 0 | 1 | 2 | 0 | 0 | 0 | 5 | 0 | 0 | .125 |
| Hasley, Michael, Covington*..3 | 8 | 1 | 2 | 5 | 0 | 0 | 1 | 1 | 0 | 0 | 0 | 0 | 0 | 0 | 0 | .250 |
| Hayes, Melvin, Bristol......36 | 104 | 12 | 22 | 28 | 3 | 0 | 1 | 11 | 0 | 0 | 13 | 0 | 36 | 0 | 1 | .212 |
| Herman, Gregory, Johnson C*.14 | 37 | 1 | 5 | 7 | 2 | 0 | 0 | 4 | 0 | 2 | 0 | 0 | 4 | 0 | 0 | .135 |
| Herr, Thomas, Johnson City† .42 | 133 | 29 | 41 | 51 | 8 | 1 | 0 | 15 | 7 | 2 | 16 | 0 | 11 | 10 | 0 | .308 |
| Herrera, Jose F., Covington..23 | 65 | 5 | 11 | 12 | 1 | 0 | 0 | 3 | 3 | 0 | 9 | 0 | 10 | 0 | 1 | .169 |
| Hicks, Edward, Marion........65 | 242 | 52 | 58 | 85 | 9 | 3 | 4 | 33 | 0 | 3 | 38 | 8 | 54 | 40 | 6 | .240 |
| Holmgren, Mark, Elizabethton 8 | 25 | 2 | 3 | 4 | 1 | 0 | 0 | 2 | 0 | 0 | 2 | 0 | 6 | 0 | 0 | .120 |
| Houser, Brett, Johnson City..24 | 6 | 1 | 1 | 1 | 0 | 0 | 0 | 0 | 0 | 0 | 2 | 0 | 1 | 0 | 0 | .167 |
| Howard, James, Marion.......55 | 212 | 34 | 55 | 93 | 6 | 4 | 8 | 36 | 0 | 3 | 30 | 0 | 35 | 5 | 6 | .259 |
| Hubbard, Glenn, Kingsport...53 | 136 | 31 | 39 | 59 | 6 | 4 | 2 | 21 | 1 | 2 | 27 | 6 | 24 | 2 | 0 | .287 |
| Jackson, Roy, Marion.........9 | 15 | 0 | 0 | 0 | 0 | 0 | 0 | 1 | 1 | 1 | 1 | 0 | 5 | 0 | 0 | .000 |
| James, Jaime, Kingsport......29 | 42 | 6 | 8 | 15 | 1 | 0 | 2 | 7 | 0 | 0 | 3 | 0 | 16 | 1 | 0 | .190 |
| Janney, Barry, Pulaski........11 | 30 | 4 | 12 | 16 | 2 | 1 | 0 | 6 | 0 | 0 | 1 | 0 | 7 | 0 | 0 | .400 |
| Johnson, David M., Johnson C 5 | 9 | 1 | 4 | 7 | 1 | 1 | 0 | 0 | 0 | 0 | 1 | 0 | 4 | 0 | 0 | .444 |
| Johnson, Jeffrey, Pulaski.....25 | 56 | 3 | 5 | 5 | 0 | 0 | 0 | 1 | 2 | 0 | 6 | 0 | 16 | 0 | 1 | .089 |
| Johnson, Steven A., Eliz.... 3 | 2 | 0 | 0 | 0 | 0 | 0 | 0 | 0 | 0 | 0 | 0 | 0 | 0 | 0 | 0 | .000 |
| Joyce, Timothy, Covington.... 4 | 2 | 0 | 0 | 0 | 0 | 0 | 0 | 0 | 0 | 0 | 0 | 0 | 0 | 0 | 0 | .000 |
| Kettering, Wilbur, Marion... 1 | 1 | 0 | 1 | 1 | 0 | 0 | 0 | 0 | 0 | 0 | 0 | 0 | 0 | 0 | 0 | 1.000 |
| King, William, Kingsport*.. 12 | 25 | 3 | 6 | 10 | 1 | 0 | 1 | 7 | 1 | 1 | 2 | 0 | 7 | 0 | 0 | .240 |
| Kline, Gregory, Bristol*.....21 | 38 | 5 | 7 | 7 | 0 | 0 | 0 | 4 | 0 | 0 | 11 | 1 | 9 | 1 | 0 | .184 |
| Koppens, Kirk, Kingsport*...12 | 1 | 0 | 0 | 0 | 0 | 0 | 0 | 1 | 0 | 0 | 0 | 0 | 0 | 0 | 0 | .000 |
| Kuhnhoff, Donald, Bluefield 46 | 122 | 17 | 32 | 33 | 1 | 0 | 0 | 12 | 3 | 0 | 24 | 0 | 13 | 3 | 1 | .262 |
| LaFerrara, Stephen, Kingsport 18 | 32 | 2 | 6 | 12 | 1 | 1 | 1 | 2 | 0 | 0 | 1 | 0 | 7 | 0 | 0 | .188 |
| LaHonta, Kenneth, Cov*......60 | 191 | 40 | 56 | 69 | 10 | 0 | 1 | 18 | 2 | 1 | 33 | 3 | 43 | 13 | 5 | .293 |
| Lake, Steven, Bluefield......49 | 162 | 17 | 45 | 66 | 12 | 0 | 3 | 24 | 1 | 1 | 12 | 1 | 21 | 3 | 0 | .278 |
| Lally, Michael, Covington.....15 | 38 | 7 | 12 | 15 | 3 | 0 | 0 | 4 | 1 | 1 | 6 | 0 | 6 | 0 | 0 | .316 |
| LaLonde, Robert, Bristol.....13 | 1 | 0 | 0 | 0 | 0 | 0 | 0 | 0 | 0 | 0 | 0 | 0 | 0 | 0 | 0 | .000 |
| Lane, Frederick, Covington .. 8 | 19 | 1 | 4 | 5 | 1 | 0 | 0 | 2 | 0 | 0 | 3 | 0 | 3 | 0 | 0 | .211 |
| Lasek, James, Pulaski*.......12 | 20 | 5 | 6 | 9 | 0 | 0 | 1 | 1 | 0 | 0 | 1 | 0 | 6 | 0 | 0 | .300 |
| Lashley, Edwin, Bluefield....25 | 46 | 4 | 8 | 10 | 2 | 0 | 0 | 3 | 0 | 0 | 7 | 0 | 19 | 1 | 1 | .174 |
| Leader, Ramon, Covington*...19 | 26 | 3 | 5 | 8 | 1 | 1 | 0 | 2 | 1 | 0 | 1 | 0 | 9 | 1 | 1 | .192 |
| Lebron, Jorge, Pulaski.......33 | 91 | 8 | 23 | 26 | 3 | 0 | 0 | 9 | 1 | 2 | 13 | 1 | 19 | 0 | 0 | .253 |
| Lee, Randall, Elizabethton*..17 | 19 | 1 | 4 | 5 | 1 | 0 | 0 | 3 | 2 | 0 | 6 | 0 | 9 | 0 | 0 | .211 |
| Lentine, James, Johnson City.29 | 91 | 25 | 31 | 44 | 5 | 1 | 2 | 15 | 1 | 1 | 22 | 2 | 14 | 1 | 2 | .341 |
| Leonard, Robert, Marion*.... 8 | 8 | 2 | 3 | 3 | 0 | 0 | 0 | 3 | 0 | 0 | 0 | 0 | 2 | 0 | 0 | .375 |
| Lobdell, William, Johnson C 17 | 9 | 1 | 0 | 0 | 0 | 0 | 0 | 0 | 2 | 0 | 2 | 0 | 2 | 0 | 0 | .000 |
| Lockwood, Mark, Eliz*........12 | 20 | 3 | 5 | 10 | 2 | 0 | 1 | 4 | 0 | 0 | 2 | 0 | 4 | 0 | 0 | .250 |

| Player and Club | G | AB | R | H | TB | 2B | 3B | HR | RBI | SH | SF | BB | HP | SO | SB | CS | Pct. |
|---|---|---|---|---|---|---|---|---|---|---|---|---|---|---|---|---|---|
| Lott, Stephen, Marion | 4 | 8 | 3 | 5 | 8 | 0 | 1 | 0 | 6 | 0 | 0 | 2 | 0 | 3 | 2 | 0 | .625 |
| Luna, Darwin, Bluefield | 4 | 7 | 1 | 3 | 4 | 1 | 0 | 0 | 1 | 0 | 0 | 2 | 0 | 2 | 0 | 0 | .429 |
| Lunar, Luis, Marion | 18 | 25 | 1 | 4 | 4 | 0 | 0 | 0 | 0 | 0 | 4 | 3 | 0 | 11 | 0 | 0 | .160 |
| Mahler, Richard, Kingsport | 26 | 21 | 1 | 5 | 9 | 4 | 0 | 0 | 3 | 1 | 0 | 0 | 3 | 0 | 0 | 0 | .238 |
| Makela, Scott, Covington* | 67 | 214 | 19 | 52 | 64 | 10 | 1 | 0 | 17 | 3 | 2 | 28 | 1 | 43 | 2 | 1 | .243 |
| Marietta, Dean, Kingsport | 13 | 23 | 2 | 4 | 5 | 1 | 0 | 0 | 1 | 2 | 0 | 2 | 0 | 6 | 0 | 0 | .174 |
| Mariska, Kent, Pulaski | 22 | 22 | 6 | 5 | 6 | 1 | 0 | 0 | 4 | 0 | 0 | 2 | 1 | 9 | 0 | 0 | .227 |
| Marshall, J. Blake, Covington† | 3 | 12 | 1 | 1 | 1 | 0 | 0 | 0 | 1 | 0 | 0 | 0 | 0 | 1 | 0 | 0 | .083 |
| Martinez, Juan J., Bluefield | 56 | 194 | 26 | 63 | 68 | 5 | 0 | 0 | 15 | 0 | 0 | 11 | 2 | 19 | 7 | 6 | .325 |
| Martinez, Nicolas, Johnson C | 2 | 1 | 0 | 0 | 0 | 0 | 0 | 0 | 0 | 0 | 0 | 0 | 0 | 0 | 0 | 0 | .000 |
| Mays, Henry, Johnson City | 64 | 250 | 58 | 81 | 125 | 15 | 4 | 7 | 48 | 4 | 4 | 51 | 1 | 20 | 12 | 3 | .324 |
| McCarthy, Richard, Bluefield | 19 | 47 | 8 | 7 | 10 | 1 | 1 | 0 | 1 | 1 | 0 | 8 | 1 | 14 | 2 | 0 | .149 |
| McGinnis, William, Eliz | 12 | 38 | 8 | 8 | 10 | 2 | 0 | 0 | 3 | 0 | 0 | 5 | 0 | 5 | 0 | 0 | .211 |
| McIver, Jeryl, Marion | 36 | 110 | 12 | 30 | 51 | 3 | 3 | 4 | 18 | 1 | 1 | 6 | 1 | 25 | 6 | 1 | .273 |
| McLaughlin, Byron, Blu | 15 | 7 | 1 | 1 | 1 | 0 | 0 | 0 | 1 | 1 | 0 | 3 | 1 | 1 | 0 | 0 | .143 |
| McManus, Dana, Bristol | 4 | 12 | 1 | 0 | 0 | 0 | 0 | 0 | 0 | 0 | 0 | 1 | 0 | 3 | 0 | 0 | .000 |
| Mendenhall, Hugh, Johnson C | 27 | 51 | 9 | 10 | 10 | 0 | 0 | 0 | 3 | 0 | 0 | 2 | 0 | 16 | 2 | 0 | .196 |
| Meyer, A. Theis, Johnson C | 22 | 22 | 5 | 6 | 8 | 2 | 0 | 0 | 4 | 1 | 0 | 4 | 0 | 3 | 0 | 0 | .273 |
| Meyers, Kenneth, Eliz | 12 | 6 | 2 | 0 | 0 | 0 | 0 | 0 | 0 | 0 | 0 | 2 | 0 | 4 | 0 | 0 | .000 |
| Miller, Richard L., Covington† | 17 | 24 | 3 | 4 | 4 | 0 | 0 | 0 | 0 | 0 | 1 | 2 | 0 | 5 | 0 | 0 | .167 |
| Mitchell, G. Hunt, Blu† | 51 | 160 | 28 | 41 | 50 | 6 | 0 | 1 | 14 | 1 | 0 | 36 | 1 | 32 | 5 | 1 | .256 |
| Moloney, James, Kingsport* | 11 | 6 | 1 | 1 | 1 | 0 | 0 | 0 | 0 | 0 | 0 | 2 | 0 | 2 | 0 | 0 | .167 |
| Morrissey, Kevin, Johnson C | 14 | 30 | 2 | 2 | 2 | 0 | 0 | 0 | 1 | 0 | 0 | 2 | 0 | 2 | 0 | 0 | .067 |
| Mota, Jose, Covington | 32 | 74 | 13 | 20 | 21 | 1 | 0 | 0 | 5 | 0 | 0 | 9 | 0 | 17 | 9 | 3 | .270 |
| Murphy, John, Bristol* | 10 | 13 | 3 | 0 | 0 | 0 | 0 | 0 | 0 | 1 | 2 | 0 | 0 | 6 | 0 | 0 | .000 |
| Murray, E. Leon, Bluefield† | 47 | 154 | 23 | 44 | 65 | 8 | 2 | 3 | 22 | 0 | 0 | 33 | 2 | 22 | 6 | 2 | .286 |
| Nedelak, Gary, Johnson City* | 40 | 104 | 12 | 25 | 35 | 6 | 2 | 0 | 11 | 4 | 1 | 13 | 0 | 8 | 2 | 1 | .240 |
| Neimeyer, Jack, Bluefield | 9 | 8 | 3 | 2 | 3 | 1 | 0 | 0 | 0 | 0 | 0 | 1 | 0 | 2 | 0 | 0 | .250 |
| Nickerson, James, Pulaski | 11 | 26 | 3 | 1 | 1 | 0 | 0 | 0 | 4 | 0 | 1 | 0 | 0 | 5 | 0 | 0 | .038 |
| Oberkfell, Kenneth, John C* | 17 | 54 | 15 | 19 | 25 | 3 | 0 | 1 | 8 | 0 | 0 | 15 | 1 | 7 | 3 | 1 | .352 |
| Oliva, Steve, Kingsport† | 25 | 63 | 12 | 20 | 20 | 0 | 0 | 0 | 5 | 1 | 0 | 5 | 1 | 9 | 3 | 2 | .317 |
| Ornest, Michael, Bluefield | 20 | 57 | 3 | 11 | 13 | 2 | 0 | 0 | 8 | 0 | 0 | 12 | 0 | 13 | 1 | 0 | .193 |
| Ortiz, Leonardo, Bluefield | 32 | 106 | 10 | 24 | 27 | 3 | 0 | 0 | 12 | 0 | 1 | 7 | 0 | 15 | 1 | 0 | .226 |
| Osofsky, Alvin, Covington† | 15 | 54 | 7 | 10 | 17 | 2 | 1 | 1 | 11 | 0 | 2 | 5 | 0 | 10 | 0 | 0 | .185 |
| Park, Michael, Kingsport | 14 | 26 | 6 | 4 | 7 | 0 | 0 | 1 | 2 | 3 | 0 | 3 | 0 | 7 | 0 | 0 | .154 |
| Parrott, Stephen, Eliz | 11 | 15 | 0 | 2 | 2 | 0 | 0 | 0 | 0 | 0 | 0 | 3 | 0 | 0 | 0 | 0 | .133 |
| Pastore, Alex, Johnson City | 9 | 30 | 4 | 8 | 17 | 1 | 1 | 2 | 9 | 0 | 1 | 5 | 0 | 11 | 0 | 0 | .267 |
| Paulino, Jose, Marion | 22 | 64 | 10 | 14 | 22 | 2 | 0 | 2 | 8 | 0 | 0 | 9 | 2 | 17 | 0 | 0 | .219 |
| Perez, Francisco, Marion | 64 | 253 | 27 | 61 | 77 | 10 | 0 | 2 | 31 | 2 | 0 | 33 | 2 | 26 | 5 | 1 | .241 |
| Perez, Jose M., Covington | 1 | 3 | 1 | 1 | 1 | 0 | 0 | 0 | 0 | 0 | 0 | 0 | 0 | 0 | 0 | 0 | .333 |
| Perez, Martin, Covington | 18 | 24 | 1 | 3 | 4 | 1 | 0 | 0 | 2 | 0 | 1 | 1 | 0 | 11 | 0 | 0 | .125 |
| Perez, Valentin, Covington | 8 | 2 | 0 | 0 | 0 | 0 | 0 | 0 | 0 | 0 | 0 | 0 | 1 | 0 | 0 | 0 | .000 |
| Petrowitz, Daniel, Eliz* | 21 | 11 | 2 | 2 | 2 | 0 | 0 | 0 | 1 | 0 | 0 | 1 | 0 | 3 | 0 | 0 | .182 |
| Pisarkiewicz, Michael, J C* | 63 | 231 | 43 | 70 | 134 | 16 | 6 | 12 | 49 | 0 | 3 | 44 | 0 | 41 | 3 | 1 | .303 |
| Pisker, Donald, Covington* | 46 | 169 | 25 | 51 | 96 | 13 | 7 | 6 | 31 | 0 | 3 | 11 | 2 | 51 | 0 | 3 | .302 |
| Pittman, John, Elizabethton | 66 | 236 | 43 | 60 | 100 | 14 | 1 | 8 | 40 | 0 | 3 | 46 | 4 | 55 | 5 | 3 | .254 |
| Plante, Gerald, Pulaski | 13 | 36 | 6 | 5 | 7 | 1 | 0 | 1 | 0 | 4 | 1 | 1 | 0 | 14 | 0 | 0 | .139 |
| Popovich, Nicholas, Pulaski | 60 | 199 | 36 | 51 | 66 | 6 | 3 | 1 | 28 | 1 | 1 | 23 | 3 | 28 | 3 | 0 | .256 |
| Powell, Hosken, Elizabethton* | 64 | 249 | 45 | 82 | 126 | 23 | 4 | 3 | 58 | 0 | 0 | 37 | 7 | 22 | 20 | 0 | .329 |
| Proud, John, Elizabethton | 2 | 5 | 3 | 1 | 1 | 0 | 0 | 0 | 1 | 0 | 0 | 4 | 0 | 1 | 0 | 0 | .200 |
| Raines, Levi, Elizabethton* | 59 | 172 | 34 | 50 | 62 | 7 | 1 | 1 | 28 | 0 | 0 | 24 | 0 | 27 | 10 | 1 | .291 |
| Ramsey, Michael, Johnson C† | 65 | 277 | 43 | 79 | 95 | 14 | 1 | 0 | 25 | 12 | 1 | 14 | 0 | 20 | 14 | 0 | .285 |
| Raymond, Charles, Bristol | 19 | 38 | 2 | 8 | 10 | 2 | 0 | 0 | 5 | 0 | 1 | 6 | 0 | 11 | 1 | 0 | .211 |
| Redd, Dexter, Bristol* | 42 | 90 | 4 | 27 | 34 | 3 | 2 | 0 | 13 | 1 | 0 | 11 | 3 | 12 | 4 | 2 | .300 |
| Reimann, Richard, Bluefield | 12 | 18 | 1 | 1 | 1 | 0 | 0 | 0 | 0 | 0 | 0 | 3 | 0 | 4 | 0 | 0 | .056 |
| Replogle, Andrew, Johnson C | 7 | 20 | 2 | 1 | 1 | 0 | 0 | 0 | 1 | 3 | 0 | 4 | 0 | 10 | 0 | 1 | .050 |
| Reynolds, Michael, Kpt* | 55 | 174 | 33 | 50 | 70 | 6 | 4 | 2 | 22 | 0 | 6 | 33 | 0 | 19 | 9 | 7 | .287 |
| Rhodes, Richard, Kingsport | 12 | 24 | 4 | 4 | 4 | 0 | 0 | 0 | 2 | 0 | 0 | 6 | 0 | 4 | 0 | 0 | .167 |
| Rineer, Jeffrey, Bluefield* | 4 | 7 | 1 | 3 | 3 | 0 | 0 | 0 | 5 | 1 | 0 | 6 | 0 | 4 | 0 | 0 | .429 |
| Robinson, Martin, Pulaski | 15 | 23 | 1 | 3 | 4 | 1 | 0 | 0 | 1 | 0 | 0 | 1 | 0 | 0 | 0 | 0 | .130 |
| Rockhill, Ronald, Kingsport | 6 | 17 | 2 | 3 | 4 | 1 | 0 | 0 | 4 | 1 | 0 | 4 | 0 | 11 | 0 | 0 | .176 |
| Rodriguez, Luis R., Pulaski | 50 | 188 | 27 | 46 | 52 | 4 | 1 | 0 | 15 | 3 | 1 | 4 | 0 | 2 | 1 | 0 | .245 |
| Rogers, Sherwin, Bristol | 24 | 69 | 9 | 16 | 18 | 2 | 0 | 0 | 6 | 0 | 0 | 11 | 0 | 6 | 2 | 1 | .232 |
| Roman, Roberto, Pulaski† | 42 | 89 | 10 | 19 | 26 | 4 | 0 | 1 | 17 | 0 | 4 | 14 | 1 | 20 | 0 | 2 | .213 |
| Romero, John, Bristol | 61 | 227 | 39 | 63 | 81 | 11 | 2 | 1 | 36 | 2 | 4 | 28 | 1 | 31 | 9 | 3 | .278 |
| Rondon, Alberto, Covington† | 27 | 73 | 10 | 13 | 16 | 0 | 0 | 1 | 6 | 2 | 0 | 11 | 2 | 27 | 0 | 1 | .178 |
| Roper, David, Pulaski | 51 | 158 | 26 | 40 | 52 | 2 | 2 | 2 | 18 | 1 | 1 | 15 | 0 | 32 | 1 | 3 | .253 |
| Rosario, Jose N., Pulaski* | 10 | 2 | 0 | 0 | 0 | 0 | 0 | 0 | 0 | 0 | 0 | 0 | 1 | 0 | 0 | 0 | .000 |
| Rosario, Simon, Covington | 35 | 120 | 18 | 31 | 45 | 4 | 2 | 2 | 21 | 0 | 0 | 6 | 0 | 19 | 2 | 0 | .258 |
| Rothrock, Brian, Eliz* | 19 | 11 | 2 | 3 | 4 | 1 | 0 | 0 | 1 | 1 | 0 | 2 | 0 | 2 | 0 | 0 | .273 |
| Ryals, Bruce, Marion | 23 | 72 | 11 | 18 | 28 | 2 | 1 | 2 | 8 | 0 | 1 | 10 | 0 | 17 | 1 | 0 | .250 |
| Sanchez, Orlando, Pulaski* | 52 | 167 | 34 | 44 | 76 | 11 | 0 | 7 | 46 | 1 | 4 | 9 | 3 | 30 | 3 | 0 | .263 |
| Schmidt, Raymond, Pulaski | 20 | 47 | 5 | 10 | 10 | 0 | 0 | 0 | 6 | 0 | 1 | 4 | 0 | 3 | 0 | 0 | .213 |
| Serum, Gary, Elizabethton* | 7 | 2 | 0 | 0 | 0 | 0 | 0 | 0 | 0 | 0 | 0 | 0 | 0 | 3 | 0 | 0 | .000 |
| Shaffer, Jack, Bristol | 13 | 1 | 0 | 0 | 0 | 0 | 0 | 0 | 0 | 0 | 0 | 0 | 0 | 0 | 0 | 0 | .000 |
| Shambaugh, Dennis, Kpt | 12 | 6 | 0 | 0 | 0 | 0 | 0 | 0 | 0 | 0 | 0 | 0 | 0 | 1 | 0 | 0 | .000 |
| Shanks, James, Kpt* | 5 | 1 | 0 | 0 | 0 | 0 | 0 | 0 | 0 | 0 | 0 | 0 | 0 | 4 | 0 | 0 | .000 |
| Shartzer, Steven, Johnson C | 50 | 201 | 33 | 57 | 74 | 5 | 0 | 4 | 29 | 4 | 2 | 13 | 2 | 24 | 6 | 2 | .284 |
| Sherman, Wynn, Bristol | 35 | 109 | 20 | 28 | 48 | 5 | 0 | 5 | 11 | 0 | 0 | 10 | 1 | 19 | 4 | 0 | .257 |
| Simon, Willie, Marion | 16 | 34 | 5 | 10 | 11 | 1 | 0 | 0 | 4 | 0 | 0 | 2 | 0 | 9 | 0 | 0 | .294 |

| Player and Club | G | AB | R | H | TB | 2B | 3B | HR | RBI | SH | SF | BB | HP | SO | SB | CS | Pct. |
|---|---|---|---|---|---|---|---|---|---|---|---|---|---|---|---|---|---|
| Smith, Bobby G., Bluefield* | 68 | 259 | 36 | 94 | 117 | 10 | 5 | 1 | 41 | 0 | 0 | 22 | 1 | 25 | 8 | 5 | .363 |
| Sofield, Richard, Eliz* | 61 | 208 | 37 | 43 | 64 | 9 | 3 | 2 | 29 | 0 | 1 | 38 | 0 | 62 | 4 | 2 | .207 |
| Stevens, David, Kingsport | 47 | 160 | 22 | 55 | 70 | 7 | 1 | 2 | 25 | 0 | 2 | 12 | 0 | 8 | 1 | 0 | .344 |
| Stewart, Samuel, Bluefield | 18 | 12 | 1 | 3 | 5 | 2 | 0 | 0 | 1 | 0 | 0 | 1 | 0 | 6 | 0 | 0 | .250 |
| Stewart, William, Kingsport | 19 | 49 | 4 | 7 | 8 | 1 | 0 | 0 | 4 | 0 | 1 | 6 | 1 | 22 | 0 | 0 | .143 |
| Strelitz, Leonard, Johnson C. | 13 | 30 | 6 | 3 | 6 | 0 | 0 | 1 | 8 | 2 | 0 | 11 | 1 | 9 | 0 | 0 | .100 |
| Switzer, William, Bristol | 2 | 2 | 0 | 0 | 0 | 0 | 0 | 0 | 0 | 0 | 0 | 0 | 0 | 2 | 0 | 0 | .000 |
| Taylor, Gerald, Covington | 20 | 54 | 11 | 12 | 20 | 2 | 0 | 2 | 10 | 0 | 0 | 16 | 1 | 13 | 0 | 2 | .222 |
| Taylor, James M., Bristol* | 13 | 2 | 0 | 0 | 0 | 0 | 0 | 0 | 0 | 0 | 0 | 0 | 1 | 1 | 0 | 0 | .000 |
| Tenge, Gerald, Marion | 9 | 6 | 0 | 1 | 1 | 0 | 0 | 0 | 1 | 0 | 0 | 0 | 0 | 3 | 0 | 0 | .167 |
| Thiel, Douglas, Bluefield | 41 | 110 | 14 | 27 | 34 | 4 | 0 | 1 | 6 | 1 | 2 | 19 | 1 | 15 | 2 | 1 | .245 |
| Thomas, Donald E., Bristol | 12 | 8 | 0 | 1 | 1 | 0 | 0 | 0 | 0 | 3 | 0 | 0 | 0 | 3 | 0 | 0 | .125 |
| Thomas, Lynd, Bluefield* | 21 | 63 | 11 | 14 | 22 | 1 | 2 | 1 | 8 | 0 | 0 | 16 | 0 | 16 | 0 | 0 | .222 |
| Thomas, Vernon, Bluefield | 60 | 215 | 33 | 45 | 79 | 14 | 1 | 6 | 35 | 0 | 3 | 25 | 1 | 75 | 5 | 2 | .209 |
| Torreano, John, Elizabethton* | 9 | 0 | 0 | 0 | 0 | 0 | 0 | 0 | 0 | 0 | 0 | 0 | 0 | 0 | 0 | 0 | .000 |
| Trevino, Alejandro, Marion | 22 | 60 | 10 | 12 | 13 | 1 | 0 | 0 | 3 | 0 | 1 | 8 | 1 | 7 | 0 | 0 | .200 |
| Turner, Robert E., Eliz | 31 | 76 | 13 | 12 | 14 | 2 | 0 | 0 | 6 | 0 | 1 | 17 | 2 | 12 | 1 | 1 | .158 |
| Tyler, Michael, Covington* | 42 | 140 | 18 | 42 | 53 | 6 | 1 | 1 | 21 | 0 | 2 | 12 | 3 | 15 | 2 | 2 | .300 |
| Vallejos, Juan, Bluefield | 11 | 8 | 2 | 1 | 1 | 0 | 0 | 0 | 0 | 2 | 0 | 1 | 0 | 3 | 0 | 0 | .125 |
| Vavruska, Paul, Bristol | 16 | 31 | 4 | 2 | 2 | 0 | 0 | 0 | 2 | 3 | 0 | 3 | 0 | 11 | 0 | 0 | .065 |
| Wagner, Steven, Elizabethton | 14 | 24 | 1 | 5 | 6 | 0 | 0 | 0 | 0 | 0 | 0 | 2 | 0 | 0 | 0 | 0 | .208 |
| Walker, Robert H., Bluefield | 9 | 1 | 0 | 0 | 0 | 0 | 0 | 0 | 0 | 1 | 0 | 0 | 0 | 0 | 0 | 0 | .000 |
| Walker, Thomas E., Pulaski | 39 | 103 | 19 | 28 | 47 | 8 | 1 | 3 | 17 | 1 | 1 | 14 | 1 | 24 | 1 | 1 | .272 |
| Whisenton, Larry, Kingsport* | 65 | 218 | 42 | 65 | 90 | 11 | 1 | 4 | 35 | 0 | 4 | 41 | 4 | 29 | 3 | 0 | .298 |
| Whitaker, Louis, Bristol* | 42 | 114 | 17 | 27 | 38 | 6 | 1 | 1 | 17 | 0 | 2 | 25 | 0 | 13 | 1 | 1 | .237 |
| Williams, Roger, Pulaski* | 10 | 21 | 2 | 4 | 7 | 0 | 0 | 1 | 4 | 1 | 0 | 0 | 0 | 6 | 0 | 0 | .190 |
| Wilson, Ward, Marion | 11 | 34 | 4 | 9 | 11 | 0 | 1 | 0 | 4 | 1 | 0 | 10 | 1 | 1 | 2 | 2 | .265 |
| Witt, Harold, Johnson City | 68 | 227 | 43 | 56 | 106 | 17 | 0 | 11 | 41 | 4 | 0 | 51 | 1 | 64 | 6 | 1 | .247 |
| Wolff, Chris, Pulaski | 22 | 8 | 1 | 0 | 0 | 0 | 0 | 0 | 0 | 0 | 0 | 1 | 0 | 3 | 0 | 1 | .000 |
| Woltman, Brian, Covington* | 1 | 0 | 1 | 0 | 0 | 0 | 0 | 0 | 0 | 0 | 0 | 0 | 0 | 0 | 0 | 0 | .000 |
| Wood, Robert, Covington | 58 | 204 | 37 | 49 | 60 | 8 | 0 | 1 | 21 | 5 | 2 | 24 | 5 | 14 | 4 | 1 | .240 |
| Wylie, Anthony, Marion | 11 | 16 | 3 | 4 | 4 | 0 | 0 | 0 | 0 | 1 | 0 | 0 | 0 | 4 | 0 | 0 | .250 |
| Yarborough, Donald, Eliz | 32 | 80 | 11 | 23 | 36 | 7 | 0 | 2 | 12 | 0 | 2 | 6 | 1 | 22 | 3 | 0 | .288 |
| Young, Donald, Kingsport | 53 | 186 | 39 | 46 | 75 | 9 | 4 | 4 | 31 | 0 | 0 | 25 | 1 | 48 | 3 | 2 | .247 |

GRAND SLAM-HOME RUNS—Sanchez 2; Echols, R. Green, James, King, Mays, Pisarkiewicz, Strelitz, 1 each.

AWARDED FIRST BASE ON INTERFERENCE—Burton (Stevens).

## CLUB FIELDING

| Club | G | PO | A | E | DP | PB | Pct. |
|---|---|---|---|---|---|---|---|
| Johnson City | 68 | 1772 | 766 | 129 | 53 | 9 | .952 |
| Bristol | 68 | 1677 | 755 | 126 | 61 | 15 | .951 |
| Kingsport | 66 | 1613 | 669 | 132 | 36 | 15 | .945 |
| Covington | 69 | 1731 | 765 | 154 | 70 | 24 | .942 |
| Marion | 68 | 1703 | | 155 | 45 | 17 | .941 |
| Elizabethton | 68 | 1735 | 678 | 157 | 45 | 24 | .939 |
| Bluefield | 69 | 1723 | 678 | 168 | 39 | 22 | .935 |
| Pulaski | 68 | 1697 | 548 | 179 | 32 | 20 | .926 |

Triple Plays—None.

## INDIVIDUAL FIELDING
### FIRST BASEMEN

*Throws lefthanded.

| Player and Club | G | PO | A | E | DP | Pct. |
|---|---|---|---|---|---|---|
| Hamner, Marion | 6 | 39 | 5 | 0 | 0 | 1.000 |
| Gaughran, Eliz | 2 | 20 | 2 | 0 | 1 | 1.000 |
| Cias, Bluefield | 11 | 78 | 8 | 1 | 8 | .989 |
| Rodriguez, Pulaski | 45 | 331 | 17 | 6 | 17 | .983 |
| Coury, Bristol | 38 | 340 | 23 | 7 | 31 | .981 |
| L. Thomas, Bluefield* | 20 | 147 | 8 | 3 | 7 | .981 |
| BRANT, Marion | 62 | 516 | 50 | 11 | 38 | .9809 |
| Boyer, Johnson City | 48 | 481 | 28 | 10 | 31 | .9807 |
| Tyler, Covington | 18 | 135 | 10 | 3 | 12 | .980 |
| Green, Kingsport | 63 | 531 | 36 | 12 | 29 | .979 |
| Taylor, Covington | 18 | 162 | 19 | 4 | 22 | .978 |
| Darichuk, Bristol* | 21 | 79 | 6 | 2 | 6 | .977 |
| Alvarez, Bristol* | 27 | 228 | 14 | 6 | 18 | .976 |
| Pittman, Elizabethton | 66 | 535 | 24 | 17 | 38 | .970 |
| Clotherty, Covington | 10 | 52 | 7 | 2 | 6 | .967 |
| Thiel, Bluefield | 40 | 270 | 15 | 10 | 15 | .966 |
| Rondon, Covington | 26 | 209 | 18 | 8 | 13 | .966 |
| Pisarkiewicz, J C* | 20 | 189 | 11 | 7 | 14 | .966 |
| Cavaletto, Kingsport | 3 | 20 | 4 | 1 | 1 | .960 |
| Carter, Marion | 2 | 18 | 2 | 1 | 0 | .952 |
| V. Thomas, Bluefield | 2 | 20 | 0 | 1 | 0 | .952 |
| Sanchez, Pulaski | 23 | 167 | 3 | 9 | 9 | .950 |
| Dearstone, Kingsport | 3 | 14 | 1 | 1 | 3 | .938 |
| Rosario, Covington | 6 | 46 | 8 | 4 | 6 | .931 |
| Shartzer, Johnson City | 4 | 9 | 1 | 1 | 1 | .909 |
| Lashley, Bluefield | 7 | 46 | 3 | 5 | 4 | .907 |

### SECOND BASEMEN

| Player and Club | G | PO | A | E | DP | Pct. |
|---|---|---|---|---|---|---|
| Carty, Kingsport | 5 | 3 | 7 | 0 | 1 | 1.000 |
| Marshall, Covington | 3 | 6 | 8 | 0 | 0 | 1.000 |
| Raines, Elizabethton | 1 | 1 | 2 | 0 | 1 | 1.000 |
| Hubbard, Kingsport | 2 | 0 | 3 | 0 | 0 | 1.000 |
| Herr, Johnson City | 33 | 71 | 121 | 5 | 19 | .975 |
| Rogers, Bristol | 21 | 35 | 38 | 2 | 13 | .973 |
| Dyer, Marion | 20 | 41 | 59 | 3 | 11 | .971 |
| Turner, Elizabethton | 21 | 55 | 58 | 4 | 16 | .966 |
| DRAPER, Bristol | 50 | 114 | 155 | 10 | 30 | .964 |
| Ramsey, Johnson City | 14 | 33 | 39 | 3 | 6 | .960 |
| Martinez, Bluefield | 50 | 101 | 97 | 9 | 17 | .957 |
| Wood, Covington | 51 | 116 | 144 | 13 | 32 | .952 |
| Reynolds, Kingsport | 48 | 122 | 111 | 13 | 20 | .947 |
| Douglas, Elizabethton | 50 | 104 | 132 | 16 | 15 | .937 |
| Farnish, Pulaski | 44 | 88 | 103 | 13 | 12 | .936 |
| Witt, Johnson City | 4 | 4 | 10 | 1 | 1 | .933 |
| Mitchell, Bluefield | 11 | 20 | 27 | 4 | 1 | .922 |
| Herrera, Covington | 17 | 33 | 36 | 6 | 6 | .920 |
| Kuhnhoff, Bluefield | 13 | 20 | 26 | 4 | 3 | .920 |
| Bradbury, Marion | 17 | 37 | 42 | 7 | 8 | .919 |
| Nedelak, Johnson City | 18 | 36 | 63 | 9 | 9 | .917 |
| Roper, Pulaski | 12 | 22 | 24 | 5 | 5 | .902 |
| Schmidt, Pulaski | 16 | 32 | 22 | 6 | 5 | .900 |
| McIver, Marion | 32 | 65 | 73 | 17 | 16 | .890 |
| Oliva, Kingsport | 19 | 38 | 38 | 11 | 5 | .874 |
| Draimin, Bluefield | 6 | 3 | 8 | 2 | 0 | .846 |
| Trevino, Marion | 2 | 4 | 1 | 2 | 0 | .714 |
| Doherty, Kingsport | 1 | 0 | 0 | 1 | 0 | .000 |

## THIRD BASEMEN

| Player and Club | G. | PO. | A. | E. | DP. | Pct. |
|---|---|---|---|---|---|---|
| Kuhnhoff, Bluefield .... 5 | | 8 | 16 | 0 | 1 | 1.000 |
| Herrera, Covington ....7 | | 2 | 9 | 0 | 1 | 1.000 |
| Roman, Pulaski ..... 1 | | 2 | 1 | 0 | 0 | 1.000 |
| Armstrong, Bluefield 1 | | 2 | 0 | 0 | 0 | 1.000 |
| LaFerrera, Kingsport 1 | | 0 | 1 | 0 | 0 | 1.000 |
| Romero, Bristol ..... 1 | | 0 | 1 | 0 | 0 | 1.000 |
| Popovich, Pulaski .... 6 | | 8 | 9 | 1 | 1 | .944 |
| Doktor, Bristol ....33 | | 23 | 88 | 7 | 9 | .941 |
| Draimin, Bluefield ..37 | | 40 | 57 | 7 | 3 | .933 |
| HUBBARD, King.... 47 | | 44 | 79 | 9 | 7 | .932 |
| Witt, Johnson City ..63 | | 60 | 151 | 17 | 7 | .925 |
| Whitaker, Bristol ...35 | | 34 | 67 | 9 | 3 | .918 |
| Janney, Pulaski ...... 8 | | 12 | 10 | 2 | 0 | .917 |
| Makela, Covington ..67 | | 57 | 120 | 17 | 18 | .912 |
| Lebron, Pulaski .....28 | | 25 | 36 | 7 | 3 | .897 |
| Bacon, Elizabethton ..25 | | 23 | 42 | 8 | 5 | .890 |
| Raines, Elizabethton ..43 | | 35 | 92 | 17 | 7 | .882 |
| Bodie, Marion ......40 | | 33 | 70 | 14 | 3 | .880 |
| Hamner, Marion ....15 | | 22 | 20 | 6 | 3 | .875 |
| Ornest, Bluefield ...16 | | 12 | 20 | 5 | 1 | .865 |
| Roper, Pulaski .....30 | | 34 | 34 | 11 | 2 | .861 |
| Cias, Bluefield .....17 | | 13 | 36 | 8 | 2 | .860 |
| Stewart, Kingsport ...19 | | 22 | 27 | 8 | 2 | .860 |
| Boyer, Johnson City .. 3 | | 3 | 9 | 2 | 1 | .857 |
| Rodriguez, Pulaski .. 2 | | 3 | 3 | 1 | 0 | .857 |
| Reynolds, Kingsport.. 3 | | 1 | 5 | 1 | 0 | .857 |
| Dyer, Marion .......17 | | 19 | 23 | 8 | 2 | .840 |
| Oliva, Kingsport .... 1 | | 0 | 3 | 1 | 1 | .750 |
| Turner, Elizabethton 1 | | 1 | 2 | 1 | 1 | .750 |
| Shartzer, Johnson City 2 | | 2 | 1 | 1 | 0 | .750 |
| Douglas, Elizabethton 2 | | 1 | 5 | 3 | 0 | .667 |
| Rockhill, Kingsport .. 2 | | 3 | 1 | 2 | 0 | .667 |
| Cavaletto, Kingsport.. 2 | | 2 | 1 | 2 | 0 | .600 |

## SHORTSTOPS

| Player and Club | G. | PO. | A. | E. | DP. | Pct. |
|---|---|---|---|---|---|---|
| Herr, Johnson City... 2 | | 3 | 4 | 0 | 1 | 1.000 |
| Hubbard, Kingsport... 5 | | 0 | 6 | 0 | 1 | 1.000 |
| Trevino, Marion ...... 1 | | 0 | 1 | 0 | 0 | 1.000 |
| Oberkfell, Johnson C 17 | | 21 | 58 | 4 | 6 | .952 |
| Wood, Covington .... 7 | | 12 | 33 | 3 | 3 | .938 |
| RAMSEY, Johnson C 50 | | 65 | 144 | 14 | 30 | .937 |
| Carty, Kingsport ..... 9 | | 9 | 18 | 2 | 3 | .931 |
| Perez, Marion .......63 | | 96 | 186 | 26 | 31 | .916 |
| Doherty, Kingsport ..62 | | 89 | 171 | 24 | 18 | .915 |
| Draimin, Bluefield .. 4 | | 8 | 13 | 2 | 0 | .913 |
| Mitchell, Bluefield ..34 | | 70 | 93 | 16 | 13 | .911 |
| Romero, Bristol .....60 | | 86 | 178 | 26 | 35 | .910 |
| Dyer, Marion ....... 7 | | 14 | 14 | 3 | 4 | .903 |
| Douglas, Elizabethton 8 | | 11 | 17 | 3 | 3 | .903 |
| Sofield, Elizabethton 59 | | 103 | 154 | 28 | 22 | .902 |
| Kuhnhoff, Bluefield ..19 | | 38 | 46 | 10 | 5 | .894 |
| Doktor, Bristol ..... 3 | | 3 | 11 | 2 | 2 | .875 |
| Codero, Covington ...58 | | 100 | 169 | 41 | 35 | .868 |
| Popovich, Pulaski ...52 | | 78 | 142 | 37 | 14 | .856 |
| McCarthy, Bluefield ..16 | | 25 | 40 | 12 | 7 | .844 |
| Draper, Bristol ..... 3 | | 2 | 6 | 2 | 0 | .800 |
| Johnson, Pulaski ....21 | | 33 | 31 | 19 | 3 | .771 |
| Proud, Elizabethton .. 2 | | 2 | 1 | 1 | 0 | .750 |
| Whitaker, Bristol ... 6 | | 4 | 15 | 7 | 0 | .731 |
| Lane, Covington .... 7 | | 1 | 18 | 7 | 1 | .731 |
| Martinez, Bluefield... 2 | | 1 | 1 | 3 | 0 | .400 |

## OUTFIELDERS

| Player and Club | G. | PO. | A. | E. | DP. | Pct. |
|---|---|---|---|---|---|---|
| Mota, Covington ....21 | | 33 | 0 | 0 | 0 | 1.000 |
| Redd, Bristol* ......34 | | 26 | 2 | 0 | 0 | 1.000 |
| Sherman, Bristol ....18 | | 20 | 3 | 0 | 2 | 1.000 |
| Pastore, Johnson City 8 | | 17 | 0 | 0 | 0 | 1.000 |
| Kline, Bristol* ......17 | | 15 | 0 | 0 | 0 | 1.000 |
| Bowman, Kingsport*..15 | | 14 | 0 | 0 | 0 | 1.000 |
| Cias, Bluefield .....11 | | 12 | 1 | 0 | 0 | 1.000 |
| Carroll, Bristol* ....17 | | 11 | 1 | 0 | 0 | 1.000 |
| Holmgren, Elizabethton 7 | | 11 | 0 | 0 | 0 | 1.000 |
| DeJesus, Covington ... 4 | | 8 | 0 | 0 | 0 | 1.000 |
| Franz, Elizabethton .. 4 | | 7 | 0 | 0 | 0 | 1.000 |
| Mariska, Pulaski .... 3 | | 4 | 1 | 0 | 0 | 1.000 |
| Raines, Elizabethton 1 | | 3 | 0 | 0 | 0 | 1.000 |
| Trevino, Marion .... 2 | | 3 | 0 | 0 | 0 | 1.000 |
| Wylie, Marion ...... 5 | | 3 | 0 | 0 | 0 | 1.000 |
| Leader, Covington* ... 8 | | 3 | 0 | 0 | 0 | 1.000 |
| Batista, Johnson City 1 | | 1 | 0 | 0 | 0 | 1.000 |
| Gaughran, Elizabethton 1 | | 1 | 0 | 0 | 0 | 1.000 |
| Witt, Johnson City .. 1 | | 1 | 0 | 0 | 0 | 1.000 |
| Lott, Marion ....... 2 | | 1 | 0 | 0 | 0 | 1.000 |
| SMITH, Bluefield* ...64 | | 113 | 3 | 2 | 0 | .983 |
| LaHonta, Covington* ..53 | | 93 | 6 | 2 | 2 | .980 |
| Young, Kingsport ...53 | | 94 | 3 | 2 | 2 | .980 |
| Cervantes, Kingsport* 30 | | 37 | 0 | 1 | 0 | .974 |
| Plante, Pulaski ....12 | | 25 | 1 | 1 | 0 | .963 |
| Hicks, Marion .....63 | | 114 | 7 | 5 | 2 | .960 |
| Mays, Johnson City..63 | | 106 | 4 | 5 | 0 | .957 |
| Shartzer, Johnson City 43 | | 66 | 0 | 3 | 0 | .957 |
| Paulino, Marion ....20 | | 22 | 0 | 1 | 0 | .957 |
| Sanchez, Pulaski ....20 | | 21 | 1 | 1 | 0 | .957 |
| V. Thomas, Bluefield 58 | | 122 | 4 | 6 | 0 | .955 |
| Garrison, Pulaski ...35 | | 61 | 1 | 3 | 0 | .954 |
| Lentine, Johnson City 26 | | 35 | 2 | 2 | 0 | .949 |
| Draimin, Bluefield .. 5 | | 17 | 1 | 1 | 1 | .947 |
| Berger, Pulaski* ....66 | | 151 | 3 | 9 | 0 | .945 |
| Castro, Pulaski ....61 | | 98 | 3 | 6 | 1 | .944 |
| Howard, Marion ....55 | | 92 | 7 | 6 | 2 | .943 |
| Echols, Marion ....41 | | 76 | 5 | 5 | 1 | .942 |
| Hallgren, Covington ..45 | | 61 | 1 | 4 | 0 | .939 |
| Dolan, Bristol .....33 | | 29 | 1 | 2 | 0 | .938 |
| Lally, Covington .... 9 | | 15 | 0 | 1 | 0 | .938 |
| Cooper, Kingsport ...49 | | 76 | 10 | 6 | 1 | .935 |
| Powell, Elizabethton* 64 | | 98 | 9 | 8 | 0 | .930 |
| Filkins, Bristol* ....32 | | 52 | 1 | 4 | 0 | .930 |
| Pisarkiewicz, J C*....43 | | 61 | 2 | 5 | 0 | .926 |
| Channel, Elizabethton 66 | | 137 | 7 | 12 | 2 | .923 |
| Davis, Bristol .....29 | | 23 | 1 | 2 | 0 | .923 |
| Hayes, Bristol .....34 | | 44 | 2 | 4 | 0 | .920 |
| Roman, Pulaski ....18 | | 23 | 0 | 2 | 0 | .920 |
| Whisenton, Kpt* ....65 | | 74 | 5 | 7 | 0 | .919 |
| Crisp, Elizabethton ..30 | | 32 | 2 | 3 | 0 | .919 |
| Pisker, Covington* ..44 | | 71 | 6 | 7 | 3 | .917 |
| Gomez, Kingsport ...11 | | 11 | 0 | 1 | 0 | .917 |
| Mendenhall, J C ....19 | | 18 | 3 | 2 | 0 | .913 |
| Burton, Bristol .... 33 | | 39 | 1 | 4 | 1 | .909 |
| Nedelak, Johnson City 8 | | 8 | 2 | 1 | 2 | .909 |
| Rosario, Covington ..24 | | 27 | 1 | 3 | 1 | .903 |
| Antone, Elizabethton* 39 | | 52 | 6 | 7 | 0 | .892 |
| Lashley, Bluefield .. 5 | | 8 | 0 | 1 | 0 | .889 |
| Armstrong, Bluefield 19 | | 30 | 2 | 5 | 0 | .865 |
| Ryals, Marion .....21 | | 19 | 0 | 3 | 0 | .864 |
| Osofsky, Covington ..13 | | 22 | 2 | 4 | 0 | .857 |
| Ortiz, Bluefield ....10 | | 11 | 0 | 2 | 0 | .846 |
| Murray, Bluefield ...41 | | 65 | 5 | 13 | 1 | .843 |
| James, Kingsport ...12 | | 9 | 1 | 2 | 0 | .833 |
| Carter, Marion .... 9 | | 8 | 1 | 4 | 0 | .692 |
| Kuhnhoff, Bluefield .. 1 | | 0 | 0 | 1 | 0 | .000 |

## CATCHERS

| Player and Club | G. | PO. | A. | E. | DP. | PB. | Pct. |
|---|---|---|---|---|---|---|---|
| Kline, Bristol* ..... 1 | | 1 | 0 | 0 | 0 | 0 | 1.000 |
| STEVENS, Kpt ....44 | | 224 | 23 | 1 | 1 | 9 | .996 |
| Wilson, Marion ...10 | | 76 | 8 | 1 | 1 | 3 | .988 |
| Tyler, Covington ..24 | | 138 | 17 | 2 | 2 | 5 | .987 |
| Bochy, Covington ..37 | | 231 | 36 | 4 | 5 | 8 | .985 |
| Raymond, Bristol ..15 | | 60 | 7 | 1 | 0 | 2 | .985 |
| McGinnis, Eliz ....11 | | 86 | 3 | 2 | 0 | 2 | .978 |
| Curbelo, Eliz ....20 | | 120 | 7 | 3 | 0 | 9 | .977 |

## CATCHERS—Continued

| Player and Club | G. | PO. | A. | E. | DP. | PB. | Pct. |
|---|---|---|---|---|---|---|---|
| Dearstone, Kpt ...19 | | 106 | 15 | 3 | 0 | 5 | .976 |
| Sherman, Bristol ..18 | | 68 | 10 | 2 | 0 | 5 | .975 |
| Grant, Marion .... 7 | | 36 | 3 | 1 | 1 | 2 | .975 |
| Cias, Bluefield ... 7 | | 34 | 4 | 1 | 0 | 3 | .974 |
| Ortiz, Bluefield ..20 | | 118 | 19 | 4 | 1 | 4 | .972 |
| Brummer, J C ...48 | | 278 | 23 | 9 | 1 | 4 | .971 |
| Lake, Bluefield...47 | | 254 | 39 | 9 | 4 | 15 | .970 |
| Gaughran, Eliz ...23 | | 145 | 8 | 5 | 0 | 8 | .968 |
| Roman, Pulaski.. 4 | | 29 | 1 | 1 | 0 | 0 | .968 |
| Felt, Pulaski ....44 | | 257 | 18 | 10 | 3 | 9 | .965 |
| Benton, Marion ..40 | | 284 | 27 | 12 | 2 | 10 | .963 |
| Walker, Pulaski ..26 | | 174 | 9 | 7 | 0 | 11 | .963 |
| Trevino, Marion ..15 | | 89 | 7 | 4 | 0 | 2 | .960 |
| DiPietro, Bristol ..46 | | 301 | 28 | 14 | 0 | 8 | .959 |
| Cloherty, Covington 10 | | 63 | 1 | 3 | 2 | 11 | .955 |
| Yarborough, Eliz..19 | | 126 | 11 | 8 | 1 | 5 | .945 |
| Barr, Johnson City 24 | | 163 | 9 | 12 | 1 | 5 | .935 |
| LaFerrara, Kpt ... 8 | | 20 | 3 | 2 | 0 | 1 | .920 |
| Brant, Marion .... 1 | | 9 | 1 | 1 | 0 | 0 | .909 |
| Coury, Bristol .... 1 | | 9 | 0 | 1 | 0 | 0 | .900 |
| Rockhill, Kpt .... 4 | | 18 | 3 | 3 | 0 | 0 | .875 |
| J. Perez,Covington.. 1 | | 7 | 0 | 1 | 0 | 0 | .875 |

## PITCHERS

| Pitcher and Club | G. | PO. | A. | E. | DP. | Pct. |
|---|---|---|---|---|---|---|
| PARK, Kingsport ..14 | 8 | 21 | 0 | 1 | 1.000 |
| Herman, Johnson C*..14 | 6 | 12 | 0 | 1 | 1.000 |
| Bruchanski, Bristol ..10 | 5 | 12 | 0 | 2 | 1.000 |
| King, Kingsport .....12 | 6 | 11 | 0 | 0 | 1.000 |
| Jackson, Marion..... 8 | 3 | 13 | 0 | 1 | 1.000 |
| Meyer, Johnson City..22 | 3 | 12 | 0 | 0 | 1.000 |
| Lee, Elizabethton*...17 | 1 | 11 | 0 | 0 | 1.000 |
| Petrowitz, Eliz* .....20 | 1 | 10 | 0 | 3 | 1.000 |
| Corness, Covington .. 8 | 0 | 10 | 0 | 2 | 1.000 |
| Parrott, Elizabethton 11 | 2 | 8 | 0 | 0 | 1.000 |
| Elders, Bristol .......19 | 1 | 9 | 0 | 1 | 1.000 |
| McManus, Bristol ... 4 | 2 | 7 | 0 | 0 | 1.000 |
| Lockwood, Elizabeth* 12 | 0 | 9 | 0 | 0 | 1.000 |
| Broomis, Bristol ...19 | 2 | 6 | 0 | 0 | 1.000 |
| Bugden, Johnson City* 19 | 0 | 8 | 0 | 0 | 1.000 |
| Rothrock, Elizabethton 19 | 2 | 6 | 0 | 0 | 1.000 |
| Hasley, Covington* ... 3 | 0 | 7 | 0 | 1 | 1.000 |
| Leonard, Marion ..... 8 | 3 | 4 | 0 | 1 | 1.000 |
| Brown, Marion .....10 | 3 | 4 | 0 | 0 | 1.000 |
| Serum, Elizabethton .. 7 | 1 | 5 | 0 | 0 | 1.000 |
| Arroyo, Pulaski* ....10 | 0 | 6 | 0 | 1 | 1.000 |
| McLaughlin, Bluefield 14 | 0 | 6 | 0 | 0 | 1.000 |
| LaLonde, Bristol .....13 | 1 | 4 | 0 | 0 | 1.000 |
| Blank, Covington ....14 | 0 | 5 | 0 | 0 | 1.000 |
| Neimeyer, Bluefield .. 8 | 0 | 4 | 0 | 0 | 1.000 |
| Walker, Bluefield .... 9 | 0 | 4 | 0 | 0 | 1.000 |
| Hannah, Marion ......10 | 1 | 3 | 0 | 0 | 1.000 |
| Vallejos, Bluefield ..11 | 1 | 3 | 0 | 0 | 1.000 |
| Wolff, Pulaski .......22 | 0 | 4 | 0 | 0 | 1.000 |
| Houser, Johnson City 24 | 2 | 2 | 0 | 0 | 1.000 |
| V. Perez, Covington .. 8 | 0 | 3 | 0 | 0 | 1.000 |
| Shaffer, Bristol .......13 | 0 | 3 | 0 | 0 | 1.000 |
| Amancio, Pulaski ....14 | 1 | 2 | 0 | 0 | 1.000 |
| Arthur, Marion* ....14 | 0 | 3 | 0 | 0 | 1.000 |
| Mariska, Pulaski ....16 | 2 | 1 | 0 | 0 | 1.000 |
| Shanks, Kingsport ... 5 | 0 | 2 | 0 | 1 | 1.000 |
| Black, Bristol ....... 6 | 0 | 2 | 0 | 0 | 1.000 |
| Fernandez, Bluefield..13 | 0 | 2 | 0 | 0 | 1.000 |
| Taylor, Bristol* ......13 | 0 | 2 | 0 | 0 | 1.000 |
| Martinez, Johnson C...2 | 0 | 1 | 0 | 0 | 1.000 |
| Grunsky, Eliz* ....... 4 | 1 | 0 | 0 | 0 | 1.000 |
| Thomas, Bristol .......12 | 0 | 1 | 0 | 0 | 1.000 |
| Strelitz, Johnson City 13 | 5 | 11 | 1 | 1 | .941 |
| Andersen, Covington ..14 | 8 | 8 | 1 | 0 | .941 |
| Gierhan, Bluefield .. 9 | 2 | 12 | 1 | 0 | .933 |
| Bruno, Kingsport ....13 | 4 | 9 | 1 | 0 | .929 |
| Mahler, Kingsport ...26 | 1 | 12 | 1 | 0 | .929 |
| Simon, Marion .....14 | 4 | 21 | 2 | 0 | .926 |
| Harris, Bristol ...... 7 | 4 | 8 | 1 | 3 | .923 |
| Clark, Marion .......14 | 7 | 15 | 2 | 0 | .917 |
| Wagner, Elizabethton 14 | 6 | 16 | 2 | 0 | .917 |
| Dockins, Pulaski ....25 | 2 | 9 | 1 | 0 | .917 |
| Buckley, Covington*..15 | 7 | 23 | 3 | 2 | .909 |
| Clark, Covington ......13 | 0 | 10 | 1 | 0 | .909 |
| Burnside, Bristol* ...21 | 5 | 14 | 2 | 0 | .905 |
| Groff, Elizabethton* ..15 | 6 | 12 | 2 | 3 | .900 |
| Darnell, Marion* ...28 | 5 | 4 | 1 | 0 | .900 |
| Williams, Pulaski ....10 | 4 | 12 | 2 | 1 | .889 |
| Miller, Covington* ...17 | 2 | 14 | 2 | 0 | .889 |
| Cornwell, Covington ..12 | 2 | 6 | 1 | 0 | .889 |
| Shambaugh, Kpt .....12 | 2 | 6 | 1 | 0 | .889 |
| Marietta, Kingsport ..13 | 4 | 11 | 2 | 0 | .882 |
| Vavruska, Bristol ...16 | 8 | 14 | 3 | 1 | .880 |
| Stewart, Bluefield ...18 | 4 | 10 | 2 | 2 | .875 |
| Cacciatore, Marion ...11 | 4 | 3 | 1 | 0 | .875 |
| Green, Covington ....17 | 3 | 10 | 2 | 0 | .867 |
| Replogle, Johnson City 7 | 7 | 12 | 3 | 1 | .864 |
| Lobdell, Johnson City 17 | 3 | 9 | 2 | 0 | .857 |
| Nickerson, Pulaski ...11 | 2 | 15 | 3 | 0 | .850 |
| Graves, Bristol ......14 | 4 | 13 | 3 | 0 | .850 |
| Lasek, Pulaski .......12 | 7 | 9 | 3 | 0 | .842 |
| Anderson, Bluefield ..11 | 2 | 3 | 1 | 0 | .833 |
| Lunar, Marion ......18 | 7 | 12 | 4 | 0 | .826 |
| Ford, Bluefield ...... 7 | 0 | 9 | 2 | 0 | .818 |
| Brown, Bluefield .....10 | 1 | 8 | 2 | 0 | .818 |
| Tenge, Marion ...... 9 | 1 | 3 | 1 | 0 | .800 |
| Cranford, Kpt* ...... 9 | 2 | 8 | 3 | 0 | .769 |
| Rhodes, Kingsport* ..12 | 3 | 7 | 3 | 1 | .769 |
| Morrissey, Johnson C 14 | 3 | 7 | 3 | 1 | .769 |
| Bardot, Marion ......25 | 4 | 6 | 3 | 0 | .769 |
| Murphy, Bristol* ....10 | 1 | 8 | 3 | 0 | .750 |
| Reimann, Bluefield ..12 | 4 | 5 | 3 | 0 | .750 |
| Field, Elizabethton ..13 | 0 | 9 | 3 | 0 | .750 |
| Fletcher, Bluefield ...12 | 2 | 4 | 2 | 1 | .750 |
| Johnson, Elizabethton 3 | 1 | 2 | 1 | 0 | .750 |
| Luna, Bluefield...... 4 | 2 | 1 | 1 | 0 | .750 |
| Carriger, Kingsport .. 9 | 0 | 3 | 1 | 0 | .750 |
| Franz, Elizabethton* 11 | 0 | 3 | 1 | 0 | .750 |
| Capra, Kingsport* ...16 | 0 | 3 | 1 | 0 | .750 |
| Koppens, Kingsport.. 12 | 1 | 4 | 2 | 0 | .714 |
| Flores, Pulaski ......20 | 0 | 5 | 2 | 0 | .714 |
| Donaghu, Johnson C...14 | 7 | 7 | 6 | 0 | .700 |
| M. Perez, Covington..18 | 4 | 5 | 4 | 0 | .692 |
| Dyer, Bluefield* ....11 | 0 | 4 | 2 | 0 | .667 |
| Gesquiere, Pulaski ... 6 | 0 | 2 | 1 | 0 | .667 |
| Meyers, Elizabethton..12 | 0 | 2 | 1 | 1 | .667 |
| Checkos, Bluefield ...10 | 0 | 3 | 2 | 0 | .600 |
| Rosario, Pulaski* ....10 | 0 | 3 | 2 | 0 | .600 |
| Drysdale, Pulaski ....12 | 0 | 3 | 2 | 0 | .600 |
| Rineer, Bluefield*.. 4 | 4 | 0 | 3 | 0 | .571 |
| Robinson, Pulaski ...15 | 1 | 4 | 5 | 1 | .500 |
| Torreano, Eliz* ..... 9 | 1 | 1 | 1 | 0 | .500 |
| Moloney, Kingsport*..11 | 1 | 0 | 1 | 0 | .500 |
| Sanchez, Pulaski ..... 1 | 0 | 0 | 1 | 0 | .000 |
| Joyce, Covington* ... 4 | 0 | 0 | 1 | 0 | .000 |
| Johnson, Johnson City* 5 | 0 | 0 | 1 | 0 | .000 |

The following players do not have any recorded accepted chances at the positions indicated; therefore, are not listed in the fielding averages for those particular positions: Carbis, p; Eicher, p; Nedelak, p; Rondon, p; Switzer, 3b. Berry, DeGrande, Kettering and Woltman appeared as pinch-hitters and/or pinch-runners only.

## CLUB PITCHING

| Club | G. | CG. | ShO. | Sv. | IP. | H. | R. | ER. | HR. | BB. | Int. BB. | HB. | SO. | WP. | Bk. | ERA. |
|---|---|---|---|---|---|---|---|---|---|---|---|---|---|---|---|---|
| Johnson City | 68 | 19 | 6 | 16 | 591 | 518 | 276 | 210 | 32 | 224 | 4 | 23 | 415 | 25 | 3 | 3.20 |
| Bristol | 68 | 24 | 5 | 4 | 559 | 515 | 304 | 226 | 20 | 278 | 20 | 23 | 423 | 39 | 12 | 3.64 |
| Elizabethton | 68 | 7 | 6 | 10 | 578 | 570 | 330 | 237 | 27 | 269 | 13 | 12 | 452 | 43 | 12 | 3.69 |
| Marion | 68 | 14 | 3 | 11 | 590 | 580 | 351 | 284 | 35 | 325 | 6 | 11 | 458 | 36 | 5 | 4.33 |
| Covington | 69 | 20 | 2 | 8 | 577 | 588 | 360 | 287 | 34 | 279 | 1 | 16 | 422 | 29 | 7 | 4.48 |
| Kingsport | 66 | 13 | 5 | 9 | 538 | 567 | 360 | 283 | 42 | 250 | 3 | 24 | 346 | 45 | 7 | 4.73 |
| Bluefield | 69 | 14 | 1 | 8 | 574 | 644 | 463 | 373 | 41 | 327 | 10 | 30 | 390 | 50 | 21 | 5.85 |
| Pulaski | 68 | 13 | 4 | 8 | 566 | 614 | 452 | 377 | 37 | 338 | 2 | 32 | 438 | 58 | 8 | 5.99 |

## PITCHERS' RECORDS
### (Leading Qualifiers for Earned-Run Average Leadership—56 or More Innings)
*Throws lefthanded.

| Pitcher—Club | G. | GS. | CG. | ShO. | W. | L. | Sv. | Pct. | IP. | H. | R. | ER. | HR. | BB. | Int. BB. | HB. | SO. | WP. | ERA. |
|---|---|---|---|---|---|---|---|---|---|---|---|---|---|---|---|---|---|---|---|
| Lee, Elizabethton* | .17 | 7 | 2 | 1 | 7 | 2 | 1 | .778 | 69 | 50 | 31 | 18 | 2 | 46 | 2 | 1 | 58 | 10 | 2.35 |
| Strelitz, Johnson C | 13 | 13 | 7 | 3 | 9 | 4 | 0 | .692 | 95 | 80 | 31 | 25 | 5 | 21 | 0 | 2 | 65 | 2 | 2.37 |
| Bruchanski, Bri | .10 | 9 | 4 | 2 | 6 | 3 | 0 | .667 | 64 | 49 | 23 | 19 | 1 | 26 | 1 | 0 | 53 | 1 | 2.67 |
| Miller, Covington* | .17 | 8 | 5 | 1 | 6 | 2 | 1 | .750 | 79 | 63 | 39 | 24 | 3 | 27 | 0 | 0 | 88 | 2 | 2.73 |
| Herman, J C* | .14 | 13 | 3 | 1 | 6 | 1 | 1 | .857 | 93 | 82 | 40 | 30 | 6 | 22 | 0 | 0 | 57 | 0 | 2.90 |
| Mahler, Kingsport | .26 | 1 | 0 | 0 | 2 | 2 | 5 | .500 | 64 | 52 | 33 | 21 | 2 | 26 | 0 | 1 | 58 | 3 | 2.95 |
| Nickerson, Pulaski | 11 | 11 | 6 | 2 | 4 | 2 | 0 | .667 | 79 | 65 | 37 | 27 | 6 | 40 | 0 | 3 | 69 | 5 | 3.08 |
| Vavruska, Bristol | 16 | 14 | 6 | 0 | 6 | 6 | 0 | .500 | 94 | 82 | 46 | 33 | 5 | 29 | 0 | 1 | 62 | 4 | 3.16 |
| King, Kingsport | .12 | 12 | 3 | 1 | 5 | 2 | 0 | .714 | 73 | 60 | 34 | 27 | 6 | 39 | 0 | 4 | 46 | 4 | 3.33 |
| R. Clark, Marion | 14 | 14 | 5 | 0 | 6 | 4 | 0 | .600 | 99 | 92 | 53 | 37 | 8 | 41 | 0 | 1 | 68 | 7 | 3.36 |

Departmental Leaders: G—Darnell, 28; GS—R. Clark, Robinson, Simon, Vavruska, 14; CG—Strelitz, 7; ShO—Strelitz 3; W—Strelitz, 9; L—Park, M. Perez, Reimann, 7; Sv—Houser, 8; Pct.—Herman, .857; IP—R. Clark, 99; H—Simon, 96; R—Robinson, 70; ER—Robinson, 62; HR—M. Brown, R. Clark, Morrissey, Park, Robinson, 8; BB—Simon, 54; IBB—Wagner, 4; HB—Burnside, 8; SO—Miller, 88; WP—M. Brown, 11.

### (All Pitchers—Listed Alphabetically)

| Pitcher—Club | G. | GS. | CG. | ShO. | W. | L. | Sv. | Pct. | IP. | H. | R. | ER. | HR. | BB. | Int. BB. | HB. | SO. | WP. | ERA. |
|---|---|---|---|---|---|---|---|---|---|---|---|---|---|---|---|---|---|---|---|
| Amancio, Pulaski | .14 | 0 | 0 | 0 | 0 | 0 | 0 | .000 | 26 | 35 | 34 | 29 | 2 | 18 | 0 | 2 | 22 | 9 | 10.04 |
| Andersen, Covington | 14 | 13 | 4 | 0 | 4 | 6 | 0 | .400 | 78 | 78 | 51 | 38 | 7 | 33 | 0 | 3 | 48 | 3 | 4.38 |
| Anderson, Bluefield | 11 | 0 | 0 | 0 | 1 | 0 | 1 | 1.000 | 16 | 17 | 17 | 14 | 2 | 12 | 0 | 3 | 8 | 0 | 7.88 |
| Arroyo, Pulaski* | .10 | 9 | 1 | 0 | 3 | 5 | 0 | .375 | 46 | 61 | 36 | 30 | 3 | 11 | 0 | 2 | 20 | 1 | 5.87 |
| Arthur, Marion* | .14 | 0 | 0 | 0 | 1 | 1 | 0 | .500 | 16 | 22 | 17 | 15 | 1 | 15 | 3 | 1 | 12 | 0 | 8.44 |
| Bardot, Marion | .25 | 2 | 0 | 0 | 0 | 6 | 2 | .000 | 47 | 36 | 27 | 23 | 4 | 23 | 1 | 2 | 43 | 2 | 4.40 |
| Black, Bristol | 6 | 1 | 0 | 1 | 1 | 0 | 0 | .500 | 17 | 16 | 6 | 6 | 2 | 6 | 2 | 0 | 13 | 1 | 3.18 |
| Blank, Covington | 14 | 4 | 1 | 0 | 3 | 3 | 2 | .500 | 45 | 51 | 30 | 27 | 3 | 22 | 0 | 1 | 39 | 2 | 5.40 |
| Broomis, Bluefield | 19 | 2 | 1 | 1 | 5 | 2 | 3 | .714 | 56 | 46 | 28 | 21 | 4 | 10 | 0 | 0 | 42 | 0 | 3.38 |
| M. Brown, Bluefield | 10 | 10 | 0 | 0 | 1 | 4 | 0 | .200 | 36 | 49 | 49 | 44 | 8 | 38 | 0 | 4 | 20 | 11 | 11.00 |
| Brown, Marion | 10 | 9 | 0 | 0 | 2 | 3 | 0 | .400 | 43 | 44 | 32 | 23 | 4 | 34 | 0 | 0 | 25 | 2 | 4.81 |
| Bruchanski, Bristol | 10 | 9 | 4 | 2 | 6 | 3 | 0 | .667 | 64 | 49 | 23 | 19 | 1 | 26 | 1 | 0 | 53 | 1 | 2.67 |
| Bruno, Kingsport | .13 | 5 | 0 | 0 | 2 | 4 | 2 | .333 | 43 | 47 | 30 | 27 | 6 | 11 | 0 | 1 | 31 | 4 | 5.65 |
| Buckley, Covington* | 15 | 10 | 3 | 0 | 5 | 3 | 0 | .625 | 79 | 76 | 51 | 38 | 3 | 36 | 1 | 1 | 43 | 3 | 4.33 |
| Bugden, Johnson C* | 19 | 3 | 0 | 0 | 1 | 5 | 3 | .167 | 41 | 26 | 19 | 17 | 2 | 20 | 0 | 1 | 36 | 1 | 3.73 |
| Burnside, Bristol* | 21 | 9 | 4 | 0 | 4 | 6 | 1 | .400 | 78 | 66 | 49 | 33 | 0 | 48 | 3 | 8 | 65 | 4 | 3.81 |
| Cacciatore, Marion | 11 | 5 | 0 | 0 | 3 | 3 | 0 | .500 | 40 | 40 | 34 | 28 | 1 | 39 | 0 | 1 | 41 | 8 | 6.30 |
| Capra, Kingsport* | 16 | 0 | 0 | 0 | 3 | 1 | 0 | .750 | 20 | 17 | 11 | 6 | 1 | 12 | 0 | 2 | 8 | 2 | 2.70 |
| Carbis, Elizabethton | 5 | 2 | 0 | 0 | 0 | 0 | 0 | .000 | 11 | 11 | 9 | 7 | 0 | 9 | 1 | 0 | 5 | 0 | 5.73 |
| Carriger, Kingsport | 9 | 0 | 0 | 0 | 0 | 0 | 0 | .000 | 12 | 20 | 18 | 8 | 2 | 9 | 0 | 0 | 4 | 3 | 6.00 |
| Checkos, Bluefield | 9 | 0 | 0 | 0 | 1 | 0 | 1 | 1.000 | 19 | 26 | 22 | 18 | 0 | 12 | 0 | 1 | 14 | 1 | 8.53 |
| Clark, Covington | .13 | 6 | 2 | 0 | 4 | 3 | 1 | .571 | 60 | 54 | 30 | 26 | 4 | 26 | 0 | 0 | 46 | 0 | 3.90 |
| R. Clark, Marion | .14 | 14 | 5 | 0 | 6 | 4 | 0 | .600 | 99 | 92 | 53 | 37 | 8 | 41 | 0 | 1 | 68 | 7 | 3.36 |
| Corness, Covington | 8 | 3 | 0 | 0 | 0 | 2 | 0 | .000 | 27 | 23 | 11 | 9 | 0 | 16 | 0 | 3 | 16 | 5 | 3.00 |
| Cornwell, Covington | 12 | 3 | 0 | 0 | 2 | 3 | 0 | .400 | 27 | 23 | 11 | 9 | 0 | 16 | 0 | 3 | 16 | 5 | 3.00 |
| Cranford, Kingsport* | 9 | 0 | 0 | 0 | 3 | 5 | 0 | .375 | 37 | 42 | 34 | 28 | 3 | 33 | 0 | 1 | 36 | 5 | 5.23 |
| Darnell, Marion* | .28 | 0 | 0 | 0 | 2 | 3 | 7 | .400 | 41 | 41 | 18 | 12 | 2 | 15 | 2 | 0 | 33 | 2 | 2.63 |
| Dockins, Pulaski | .25 | 0 | 0 | 0 | 5 | 3 | 6 | .625 | 48 | 43 | 25 | 18 | 1 | 22 | 0 | 2 | 39 | 5 | 3.52 |
| Donaghu, Johnson C | 14 | 13 | 3 | 0 | 5 | 4 | 0 | .556 | 76 | 70 | 48 | 31 | 4 | 39 | 0 | 5 | 45 | 6 | 3.67 |
| Drysdale, Pulaski | .12 | 5 | 0 | 0 | 1 | 3 | 0 | .250 | 27 | 40 | 44 | 37 | 1 | 36 | 0 | 3 | 29 | 4 | 12.33 |
| Dyer, Bluefield* | .11 | 11 | 0 | 0 | 0 | 4 | 0 | .000 | 41 | 40 | 46 | 38 | 4 | 48 | 0 | 0 | 21 | 7 | 11.03 |
| Eicher, Elizabethton | 3 | 2 | 0 | 0 | 0 | 0 | 0 | .000 | 9 | 7 | 8 | 7 | 0 | 9 | 0 | 1 | 5 | 3 | 7.00 |
| Elders, Bristol | .19 | 0 | 0 | 0 | 5 | 2 | 0 | .714 | 36 | 36 | 17 | 12 | 1 | 12 | 2 | 2 | 38 | 2 | 3.00 |
| Fernandez, Bluefield | 13 | 0 | 0 | 0 | 0 | 0 | 0 | .000 | 19 | 29 | 18 | 16 | 2 | 8 | 2 | 0 | 10 | 1 | 7.58 |
| Field, Elzabethton | .13 | 11 | 2 | 1 | 5 | 5 | 0 | .500 | 69 | 86 | 48 | 37 | 2 | 15 | 0 | 1 | 53 | 1 | 4.83 |
| Fletcher, Bluefield | 12 | 0 | 0 | 0 | 1 | 0 | 0 | .000 | 21 | 31 | 22 | 18 | 1 | 24 | 1 | 4 | 7 | 1 | 7.71 |
| Flores, Pulaski | .20 | 3 | 1 | 0 | 2 | 6 | 2 | .250 | 45 | 51 | 36 | 28 | 4 | 22 | 1 | 3 | 32 | 3 | 5.60 |
| Ford, Bluefield | 7 | 7 | 4 | 0 | 3 | 3 | 0 | .500 | 52 | 50 | 23 | 18 | 2 | 16 | 0 | 2 | 33 | 1 | 3.12 |
| Franz, Eliz* | .11 | 4 | 0 | 0 | 1 | 0 | 1 | 1.000 | 30 | 36 | 20 | 15 | 1 | 15 | 0 | 1 | 22 | 5 | 4.50 |
| Gesquiere, Pulaski | 6 | 1 | 0 | 0 | 0 | 2 | 0 | .000 | 14 | 13 | 9 | 8 | 3 | 11 | 0 | 0 | 9 | 0 | 5.14 |
| Gierhan, Bluefield | 9 | 2 | 0 | 0 | 2 | 5 | 0 | .286 | 54 | 57 | 48 | 42 | 6 | 41 | 0 | 3 | 31 | 5 | 7.00 |
| Graves, Bristol | .14 | 12 | 3 | 0 | 1 | 6 | 0 | .143 | 67 | 70 | 49 | 39 | 3 | 53 | 2 | 3 | 34 | 10 | 5.24 |
| Green, Covington | .17 | 10 | 1 | 0 | 3 | 6 | 1 | .333 | 66 | 77 | 48 | 36 | 5 | 31 | 0 | 2 | 45 | 3 | 4.91 |

| Pitcher—Club | G | GS | CG | ShO | W | L | Sv | Pct. | IP | H | R | ER | HR | BB | Int. BB | HB | SO | WP | ERA |
|---|---|---|---|---|---|---|---|---|---|---|---|---|---|---|---|---|---|---|---|
| Groff, Eliz* ......15 | 10 | 0 | 0 | 3 | 3 | 0 | .500 | 72 | 68 | 45 | 27 | 2 | 19 | 0 | 0 | 57 | 2 | 3.38 |
| Grunsky, Eliz*.... 4 | 0 | 0 | 0 | 1 | 0 | 0 | 1.000 | 7 | 7 | 6 | 5 | 0 | 3 | 0 | 0 | 3 | 1 | 6.43 |
| Hannah, Marion ...10 | 6 | 0 | 0 | 1 | 3 | 1 | .250 | 31 | 43 | 32 | 26 | 4 | 24 | 0 | 0 | 19 | 2 | 7.55 |
| Harris, Bristol ... 7 | 5 | 3 | 1 | 3 | 2 | 0 | .600 | 45 | 30 | 13 | 11 | 4 | 9 | 1 | 4 | 41 | 1 | 2.20 |
| Hasley, Covington*.. 3 | 3 | 1 | 0 | 2 | 0 | 0 | 1.000 | 20 | 19 | 13 | 11 | 2 | 10 | 0 | 0 | 14 | 0 | 4.95 |
| Herman, Johnson C* 14 | 13 | 3 | 1 | 6 | 1 | 1 | .857 | 93 | 86 | 40 | 30 | 6 | 22 | 0 | 0 | 57 | 0 | 2.90 |
| Houser, Johnson C 24 | 0 | 0 | 0 | 3 | 2 | 8 | .600 | 33 | 25 | 12 | 8 | 0 | 14 | 0 | 4 | 48 | 4 | 2.18 |
| Jackson, Marion .. 8 | 5 | 3 | 1 | 4 | 2 | 0 | .667 | 50 | 35 | 10 | 8 | 1 | 14 | 0 | 1 | 35 | 0 | 1.44 |
| Johnson, Johnson C* 5 | 4 | 1 | 1 | 2 | 2 | 0 | .500 | 25 | 20 | 11 | 9 | 1 | 5 | 0 | 1 | 23 | 0 | 3.24 |
| Johnson, Eliz .... 3 | 1 | 0 | 0 | 0 | 0 | 0 | .000 | 6 | 8 | 4 | 4 | 1 | 4 | 1 | 1 | 3 | 0 | 6.00 |
| Joyce, Covington*... 4 | 0 | 0 | 0 | 0 | 0 | 0 | .000 | 8 | 9 | 4 | 4 | 0 | 10 | 0 | 0 | 4 | 1 | 4.50 |
| King, Kingsport ..12 | 12 | 3 | 1 | 5 | 2 | 0 | .714 | 73 | 60 | 34 | 27 | 6 | 39 | 0 | 4 | 46 | 4 | 3.33 |
| Koppens, Kingsport 12 | 0 | 0 | 0 | 0 | 0 | 1 | .000 | 22 | 21 | 9 | 9 | 3 | 4 | 0 | 0 | 16 | 3 | 3.68 |
| LaLonde, Bristol ..13 | 0 | 0 | 0 | 0 | 0 | 0 | .000 | 11 | 13 | 11 | 9 | 0 | 11 | 3 | 1 | 3 | 4 | 7.36 |
| Lasek, Pulaski ...12 | 12 | 2 | 1 | 5 | 1 | 0 | .833 | 73 | 77 | 34 | 29 | 2 | 23 | 0 | 0 | 65 | 6 | 3.58 |
| Lee, Elizabethton* 17 | 7 | 2 | 1 | 7 | 2 | 1 | .778 | 69 | 50 | 31 | 18 | 2 | 46 | 2 | 1 | 58 | 10 | 2.35 |
| Leonard, Marion .. 8 | 5 | 0 | 0 | 1 | 2 | 0 | .333 | 31 | 46 | 28 | 23 | 3 | 9 | 0 | 2 | 19 | 1 | 6.68 |
| Lobdell, Johnson C 17 | 2 | 0 | 0 | 1 | 2 | 1 | .333 | 42 | 44 | 24 | 15 | 2 | 10 | 2 | 5 | 25 | 2 | 3.21 |
| Lockwood, Eliz* ...12 | 9 | 2 | 1 | 4 | 2 | 0 | .667 | 54 | 47 | 27 | 16 | 3 | 31 | 0 | 0 | 48 | 3 | 2.67 |
| Luna, Bluefield .. 4 | 3 | 2 | 0 | 2 | 2 | 0 | .500 | 22 | 16 | 9 | 6 | 3 | 6 | 0 | 1 | 18 | 0 | 2.45 |
| Lunar, Marion ...18 | 8 | 4 | 1 | 6 | 3 | 0 | .667 | 78 | 63 | 37 | 32 | 4 | 26 | 0 | 1 | 64 | 6 | 3.69 |
| Mahler, Kingsport .26 | 1 | 0 | 0 | 2 | 3 | 5 | .500 | 64 | 52 | 33 | 21 | 2 | 26 | 0 | 1 | 58 | 3 | 2.95 |
| Marietta, Kingsport 13 | 13 | 0 | 0 | 2 | 6 | 0 | .250 | 71 | 76 | 59 | 42 | 2 | 35 | 0 | 5 | 28 | 6 | 6.20 |
| Mariska, Pulaski ..16 | 0 | 0 | 0 | 0 | 0 | 0 | .000 | 27 | 33 | 23 | 22 | 1 | 29 | 0 | 4 | 17 | 5 | 7.33 |
| Martinez, Johnson C 2 | 0 | 0 | 0 | 0 | 0 | 0 | .000 | 5 | 0 | 0 | 0 | 0 | 4 | 0 | 0 | 4 | 0 | 0.00 |
| McLaughlin, Blu ..14 | 2 | 0 | 0 | 1 | 2 | 1 | .333 | 35 | 45 | 31 | 29 | 3 | 15 | 1 | 2 | 32 | 2 | 7.46 |
| McManus, Bristol.. 4 | 4 | 1 | 0 | 2 | 0 | 0 | .000 | 28 | 32 | 17 | 10 | 0 | 7 | 1 | 2 | 28 | 2 | 3.21 |
| Meyer, Johnson C..22 | 1 | 0 | 0 | 2 | 2 | 2 | .500 | 55 | 48 | 20 | 15 | 3 | 25 | 2 | 1 | 38 | 2 | 2.45 |
| Meyers, Eliz ...12 | 0 | 0 | 0 | 3 | 1 | 0 | .750 | 27 | 26 | 13 | 9 | 2 | 7 | 2 | 0 | 16 | 1 | 3.00 |
| Miller, Covington* 17 | 8 | 5 | 1 | 6 | 2 | 1 | .750 | 79 | 63 | 39 | 24 | 3 | 27 | 0 | 0 | 88 | 2 | 2.73 |
| Moloney, Kings* ..11 | 2 | 1 | 1 | 3 | 0 | 1 | 1.000 | 20 | 19 | 12 | 9 | 1 | 7 | 0 | 0 | 11 | 1 | 4.05 |
| Morrissey, J C ...14 | 12 | 3 | 0 | 6 | 3 | 1 | .667 | 75 | 78 | 53 | 47 | 8 | 48 | 0 | 4 | 44 | 6 | 5.64 |
| Murphy, Bristol* ..10 | 1 | 1 | 1 | 5 | 3 | 0 | .625 | 58 | 59 | 30 | 23 | 1 | 20 | 1 | 1 | 46 | 0 | 3.57 |
| Nedelak, Johnson C 1 | 0 | 0 | 0 | 0 | 0 | 0 | .000 | 1/3 | 2 | 1 | 1 | 0 | 0 | 0 | 0 | 0 | 0 | 27.00 |
| Neimeyer, Bluefield 8 | 2 | 1 | 0 | 1 | 1 | 0 | .500 | 26 | 28 | 16 | 13 | 2 | 8 | 0 | 1 | 17 | 2 | 4.50 |
| Nickerson, Pulaski 11 | 11 | 6 | 2 | 6 | 3 | 0 | .667 | 79 | 65 | 37 | 27 | 6 | 40 | 0 | 3 | 69 | 5 | 3.08 |
| Park, Kingsport ..14 | 11 | 4 | 1 | 5 | 7 | 0 | .417 | 83 | 93 | 49 | 46 | 8 | 21 | 0 | 6 | 61 | 5 | 4.99 |
| Parrott, Eliz ...11 | 9 | 0 | 0 | 3 | 4 | 0 | .429 | 44 | 44 | 32 | 28 | 1 | 32 | 0 | 1 | 35 | 3 | 5.73 |
| M. Perez, Covington 18 | 9 | 3 | 1 | 6 | 7 | 2 | .462 | 72 | 83 | 48 | 43 | 6 | 38 | 0 | 3 | 55 | 6 | 5.38 |
| V. Perez, Covington 8 | 0 | 0 | 0 | 0 | 1 | 0 | .000 | 11 | 14 | 14 | 13 | 0 | 13 | 0 | 1 | 5 | 0 | 10.64 |
| Petrowitz, Eliz* .. 20 | 2 | 0 | 0 | 3 | 3 | 3 | .500 | 45 | 52 | 24 | 15 | 4 | 24 | 3 | 1 | 36 | 4 | 3.00 |
| Reimann, Bluefield 12 | 11 | 1 | 0 | 2 | 7 | 0 | .222 | 70 | 72 | 41 | 30 | 1 | 33 | 2 | 2 | 40 | 7 | 3.86 |
| Replogle, Johnson C 7 | 2 | 0 | 0 | 4 | 2 | 0 | .667 | 50 | 39 | 16 | 12 | 1 | 16 | 0 | 0 | 30 | 2 | 2.16 |
| Rhodes, Kingsport* 12 | 12 | 5 | 1 | 6 | 4 | 0 | .600 | 71 | 80 | 51 | 37 | 5 | 34 | 1 | 1 | 35 | 4 | 4.69 |
| Rhner, Bluefield* 4 | 3 | 2 | 0 | 1 | 2 | 0 | .333 | 23 | 23 | 12 | 8 | 0 | 6 | 0 | 0 | 13 | 2 | 3.13 |
| Robinson, Pulaski ..15 | 14 | 1 | 1 | 3 | 6 | 0 | .333 | 64 | 73 | 70 | 62 | 8 | 49 | 0 | 5 | 58 | 9 | 8.72 |
| Rondon, Covington .. 1 | 0 | 0 | 0 | 0 | 0 | 0 | .000 | 2 | 2 | 0 | 0 | 0 | 0 | 0 | 0 | 1 | 0 | 0.00 |
| Rosario, Pulaski* ..10 | 0 | 0 | 0 | 2 | 0 | 0 | .000 | 16 | 17 | 22 | 18 | 0 | 13 | 0 | 2 | 8 | 2 | 10.13 |
| Rothrock, Eliz ...19 | 1 | 0 | 0 | 3 | 2 | 4 | .600 | 42 | 30 | 11 | 7 | 1 | 20 | 1 | 0 | 27 | 0 | 1.50 |
| Sanchez, Pulaski .. 1 | 0 | 0 | 0 | 0 | 0 | 0 | .000 | 2 | 3 | 6 | 5 | 1 | 4 | 0 | 1 | 0 | 2 | 22.50 |
| Serum, Elizabethton 7 | 0 | 0 | 0 | 0 | 0 | 0 | .000 | 10 | 17 | 10 | 9 | 3 | 5 | 0 | 0 | 2 | 1 | 8.10 |
| Shaffer, Bristol .. 13 | 0 | 0 | 0 | 1 | 1 | 0 | .500 | 16 | 16 | 12 | 8 | 1 | 14 | 3 | 0 | 11 | 1 | 4.50 |
| Shambaugh, Kpt ..12 | 0 | 0 | 0 | 2 | 1 | 0 | .667 | 22 | 32 | 25 | 19 | 3 | 15 | 2 | 3 | 7 | 4 | 7.77 |
| Shanks, Kingsport 5 | 1 | 0 | 0 | 0 | 1 | 0 | .000 | 8 | 5 | 4 | 0 | 4 | 0 | 0 | 0 | 5 | 1 | 4.00 |
| Simon, Marion ...14 | 14 | 2 | 1 | 8 | 3 | 0 | .727 | 93 | 96 | 51 | 47 | 3 | 54 | 0 | 2 | 82 | 2 | 4.55 |
| Stewart, Bluefield .. 18 | 4 | 0 | 0 | 3 | 3 | 1 | .500 | 43 | 62 | 44 | 29 | 1 | 26 | 3 | 4 | 29 | 6 | 6.07 |
| Strelitz, Johnson C 13 | 13 | 7 | 3 | 9 | 4 | 0 | .692 | 95 | 80 | 31 | 25 | 5 | 21 | 0 | 2 | 65 | 2 | 2.37 |
| Taylor, Bristol* ...13 | 0 | 0 | 0 | 1 | 0 | 0 | .000 | 22 | 20 | 11 | 9 | 0 | 27 | 1 | 1 | 13 | 6 | 3.68 |
| Tenge, Marion ... 9 | 0 | 0 | 0 | 1 | 0 | 0 | 1.000 | 22 | 22 | 12 | 10 | 0 | 21 | 0 | 0 | 17 | 4 | 4.29 |
| Thomas, Bristol ...12 | 4 | 2 | 1 | 2 | 1 | 1 | .667 | 23 | 26 | 20 | 14 | 2 | 16 | 0 | 0 | 16 | 3 | 5.48 |
| Torreano, Eliz* ... 9 | 0 | 0 | 0 | 0 | 2 | 1 | .000 | 12 | 13 | 8 | 5 | 0 | 11 | 0 | 2 | 7 | 1 | 3.75 |
| Vallejos, Bluefield..11 | 5 | 1 | 0 | 3 | 2 | 0 | .600 | 38 | 31 | 21 | 16 | 1 | 17 | 0 | 3 | 42 | 4 | 3.79 |
| Vavruska, Bluefield 16 | 14 | 6 | 0 | 6 | 6 | 0 | .500 | 94 | 82 | 46 | 33 | 5 | 29 | 0 | 1 | 62 | 4 | 3.16 |
| Wagner, Eliz ...14 | 10 | 1 | 0 | 5 | 6 | 0 | .455 | 72 | 68 | 34 | 28 | 5 | 19 | 4 | 2 | 75 | 8 | 3.50 |
| Walker, Bluefield 9 | 0 | 0 | 0 | 1 | 2 | 0 | .000 | 11 | 22 | 16 | 13 | 1 | 7 | 1 | 0 | 13 | 0 | 8.36 |
| Williams, Pulaski 10 | 9 | 0 | 0 | 2 | 6 | 0 | .250 | 58 | 64 | 39 | 30 | 1 | 28 | 0 | 2 | 39 | 2 | 4.66 |
| Wolff, Pulaski ...22 | 2 | 0 | 0 | 4 | 4 | 0 | .000 | 40 | 40 | 37 | 34 | 4 | 32 | 0 | 3 | 31 | 5 | 7.12 |

BALKS—Checkos, 7; Vallejos, 4; Burnside, Cranford, Field, Stewart, Vavruska, Wolff, 3 each; Andersen, Harris, Lee, McLaughlin, M. Perez, Simon, Torreano, 2 each; Arroyo, Broomis, Bruno, Cacciatore, Corness, Drysdale, Eicher, Elders, Ford, Franz, Graves, Grunsky, Herman, Houser, Koppens, Lasek, Leonard, Lockwood, Luna, Lunar, Mariska, McManus, Miller, Morrissey, Park, Reimann, Rhodes, Robinson, Rondon, Shaffer, Wagner, Walker, 1 each.

COMBINATION SHUTOUTS—Groff-Rothrock, Lee-Lockwood-Torreano, Wagner-Rothrock, Elizabethton; Replogle-Houser, Johnson City; Cranford-Mahler, Kingsport.

NO-HIT GAMES—None.

# Gulf Coast League

## ROOKIE CLASSIFICATION
### CHAMPIONSHIP WINNERS IN PREVIOUS YEARS

1964—Sarasota Braves .... .610
1965—Bradenton Astros .. .632
1966—New York AL ...... .667
1967—Kansas City ....... .614
1968—Oakland ........... .650
1969—Montreal .......... .585
1970—Chicago AL ........ .600
1971—Kansas City ....... .755
1972—Chicago NL a...... .651
　　　 Kansas City a...... .651
1973—Texas ............. .732
1974—Chicago NL ....... .702

(Note—Known as Sarasota Rookie League in 1964 and Florida Rookie League in 1965.)
aDeclared co-champions; no playoff.

### STANDING OF CLUBS AT CLOSE OF SEASON, AUGUST 29

| Club | Tex. | K.C. | Chi. NL | Pitt. | Chi. AL | Clev. | St.L. | W. | L. | T. | Pct. | G.B. |
|---|---|---|---|---|---|---|---|---|---|---|---|---|
| Texas ............ | .. | 5 | 6 | 7 | 8 | 7 | 8 | 41 | 12 | 0 | .774 | .... |
| Kansas City ...... | 3 | .. | 5 | 6 | 6 | 5 | 6 | 31 | 18 | 0 | .633 | 8 |
| Chicago-NL ....... | 3 | 4 | .. | 5 | 6 | 6 | 6 | 30 | 24 | 0 | .556 | 11½ |
| Pittsburgh ........ | 2 | 3 | 4 | .. | 6 | 5 | 3 | 23 | 31 | 0 | .426 | 18½ |
| Chicago-AL ....... | 1 | 3 | 3 | 3 | .. | 6 | 7 | 23 | 31 | 0 | .426 | 18½ |
| Cleveland ........ | 2 | 2 | 3 | 4 | 3 | .. | 5 | 19 | 33 | 0 | .365 | 21½ |
| St. Louis ........ | 1 | 1 | 3 | 6 | 2 | 4 | .. | 17 | 35 | 0 | .327 | 23½ |

Texas declared league champion on basis of highest won-lost percentage.
Club names indicate major league connections.
Playoff—None. Games played at Bradenton and Sarasota, Fla.
Regular Season Attendance—No paid attendance.

Managers: Chicago NL—Joe Jones; Chicago NL—Jack Hiatt; Cleveland—Tony Pacheco; Kansas City—Gary Blaylock; Pittsburgh—Elwood (Woody) Huyke; St. Louis—Fred Koenig; Texas—Joe Klein.

All-Star Team: 1B—Chapman, Texas; 2B—Denevi, Kansas City; 3B—Alessio, Chicago-NL; SS—Ithier, Cleveland; OF—Rosinski, Chicago-NL; Hurdle, Kansas City; Silverio, Kansas City; C—Hill, Chicago-NL; P—McMurray, Texas; Soroko, Texas; Manager—Klein, Texas.

(Compiled by Howe News Bureau, Chicago, Ill.)

### CLUB BATTING

| Club | G. | AB. | R. | OR. | H. | TB. | 2B. | 3B. | HR. | RBI. | SH. | Int. SF. | BB. | HP. | SO. | SB. | CS. | LOB. | Pct. |
|---|---|---|---|---|---|---|---|---|---|---|---|---|---|---|---|---|---|---|---|
| Kansas City ...49 | 1563 | 250 | 136 | 383 | 501 | 47 | 25 | 7 | 204 | 8 | 11 | 249 | 6 | 21 | 252 | 62 | 18 | 392 | .245 |
| Texas .........53 | 1754 | 303 | 145 | 428 | 568 | 54 | 25 | 12 | 244 | 21 | 21 | 298 | 7 | 16 | 355 | 98 | 23 | 427 | .244 |
| Chicago-NL ....54 | 1672 | 216 | 205 | 398 | 526 | 64 | 17 | 10 | 172 | 28 | 18 | 240 | 5 | 20 | 301 | 35 | 24 | 408 | .238 |
| Cleveland .....52 | 1631 | 209 | 288 | 382 | 485 | 57 | 17 | 4 | 151 | 21 | 9 | 264 | 5 | 17 | 329 | 43 | 23 | 415 | .234 |
| Pittsburgh ....54 | 1733 | 172 | 215 | 388 | 474 | 44 | 12 | 6 | 141 | 8 | 10 | 192 | 5 | 16 | 297 | 107 | 49 | 346 | .224 |
| St. Louis .....52 | 1630 | 167 | 299 | 347 | 415 | 39 | 10 | 3 | 138 | 24 | 12 | 205 | 4 | 20 | 316 | 47 | 28 | 378 | .213 |
| Chicago-AL ....54 | 1668 | 184 | 213 | 345 | 452 | 67 | 11 | 6 | 152 | 13 | 15 | 238 | 5 | 12 | 348 | 57 | 31 | 393 | .207 |

Departmental Leaders: G—Harper, Tejada, 54; AB—Norman, 202; R—Miller, 47; H—Norman, 53; TB—Brown, 70; 2B—Etchandy, 11; 3B—Brown, 6; HR—Silverio, 5; RBI—Hurdle, 31; SH—Burgess, Travis, 6; SF—Rodriguez, J. Stewart, 4; BB—Miller, 51; HP—Hurdle, Tejada, 6; SO—Miller, 58; SB—Miller, 30; CS—Fleming, 8.

### INDIVIDUAL BATTING
(Leading Qualifiers for Batting Championship—146 or More Plate Appearances)
*Bats lefthanded. †Switch-hitter.

| Player and Club | G. | AB. | R. | H. | TB. | 2B. | 3B. | HR. | RBI. | SH. | SF. | BB. | HP. | SO. | SB. | CS. | Pct. |
|---|---|---|---|---|---|---|---|---|---|---|---|---|---|---|---|---|---|
| Alessio, James, Chicago-NL...35 | 130 | 16 | 43 | 51 | 6 | 1 | 0 | 13 | 0 | 1 | 16 | 0 | 25 | 1 | 5 | .331 |
| Rosinski, Brian, Chi-NL......40 | 140 | 20 | 43 | 56 | 5 | 4 | 0 | 23 | 0 | 3 | 29 | 2 | 20 | 4 | 4 | .307 |
| Laseter, Thomas, Kansas City 44 | 170 | 33 | 50 | 63 | 5 | 4 | 0 | 18 | 0 | 3 | 16 | 1 | 13 | 11 | 1 | .294 |
| Pettinger, Ronald, Chi-NL....44 | 126 | 18 | 37 | 54 | 9 | 4 | 0 | 17 | 4 | 3 | 14 | 2 | 26 | 1 | 1 | .294 |
| Denevi, Michael, Kansas City 47 | 151 | 24 | 43 | 53 | 7 | 0 | 1 | 20 | 1 | 2 | 22 | 2 | 15 | 5 | 2 | .285 |
| Rivera, David B., Texas......37 | 137 | 20 | 39 | 65 | 6 | 4 | 4 | 23 | 1 | 1 | 6 | 1 | 38 | 1 | 2 | .285 |
| Brown, John E., Cleveland*...52 | 177 | 34 | 50 | 70 | 5 | 6 | 1 | 10 | 2 | 0 | 41 | 1 | 39 | 7 | 4 | .282 |
| Ithier, Pedro, Cleveland ....46 | 171 | 26 | 48 | 57 | 9 | 0 | 0 | 10 | 3 | 0 | 19 | 1 | 12 | 7 | 2 | .281 |
| Hurdle, Clinton, Kansas City* 49 | 175 | 34 | 48 | 63 | 4 | 4 | 1 | 31 | 0 | 1 | 24 | 6 | 23 | 1 | 1 | .274 |
| Pinkerton, Chester, Texas†...35 | 139 | 24 | 38 | 45 | 3 | 2 | 0 | 17 | 1 | 1 | 18 | 4 | 26 | 12 | 2 | .273 |
| Moreta, Manuel, Kansas City 43 | 154 | 26 | 42 | 51 | 7 | 1 | 0 | 17 | 2 | 1 | 13 | 1 | 22 | 14 | 1 | .273 |

(All Players—Listed Alphabetically)

| Player and Club | G. | AB. | R. | H. | TB. | 2B. | 3B. | HR. | RBI. | SH. | SF. | BB. | HP. | SO. | SB. | CS. | Pct. |
|---|---|---|---|---|---|---|---|---|---|---|---|---|---|---|---|---|---|
| Alessio, James, Chicago-NL..35 | 130 | 16 | 43 | 51 | 6 | 1 | 0 | 13 | 0 | 1 | 16 | 0 | 25 | 1 | 5 | .331 |
| Anderson, Michael D., Chi-NL 39 | 147 | 18 | 37 | 53 | 5 | 1 | 3 | 14 | 4 | 1 | 13 | 1 | 20 | 1 | 4 | .252 |
| Angulo, Aquiles, Cleveland ..23 | 57 | 3 | 10 | 11 | 1 | 0 | 0 | 8 | 1 | 0 | 1 | 0 | 20 | 0 | 0 | .175 |
| Baez, Ramon, St. Louis ......30 | 86 | 9 | 18 | 18 | 0 | 0 | 0 | 4 | 1 | 2 | 4 | 0 | 18 | 3 | 0 | .209 |
| Baker, Phillip, Kansas City*..24 | 57 | 9 | 11 | 18 | 1 | 3 | 0 | 4 | 1 | 0 | 13 | 0 | 8 | 1 | 0 | .193 |
| Barranca, German, Kan City* 22 | 64 | 14 | 17 | 19 | 2 | 0 | 0 | 4 | 0 | 0 | 20 | 0 | 11 | 7 | 3 | .260 |
| Batista, Juan, St. Louis......36 | 123 | 11 | 28 | 34 | 4 | 1 | 0 | 10 | 2 | 0 | 7 | 4 | 23 | 8 | 1 | .228 |

| Player and Club | G. | AB. | R. | H. | TB. | 2B. | 3B. | HR. | RBI. | SH. | SF. | BB. | HP. | SO. | SB. | CS. | Pct. |
|---|---|---|---|---|---|---|---|---|---|---|---|---|---|---|---|---|---|
| Bauer, Phillip, Chicago-AL | 48 | 150 | 14 | 27 | 34 | 7 | 0 | 0 | 8 | 1 | 2 | 34 | 1 | 24 | 5 | 2 | .180 |
| Bellini, Riccardo, Cleveland | 4 | 13 | 2 | 2 | 5 | 1 | 1 | 0 | 1 | 0 | 0 | 2 | 0 | 4 | 0 | 0 | .154 |
| Borges, Jeffrey, St. Louis | 35 | 112 | 19 | 27 | 28 | 1 | 0 | 0 | 8 | 5 | 2 | 18 | 1 | 13 | 5 | 1 | .241 |
| Bright, Thomas, Chicago-AL | 48 | 164 | 14 | 28 | 44 | 8 | 1 | 2 | 18 | 0 | 0 | 16 | 1 | 56 | 3 | 2 | .171 |
| Brockway, Ricky, Chicago-NL | 4 | 14 | 1 | 3 | 3 | 0 | 0 | 0 | 3 | 1 | 0 | 1 | 0 | 2 | 1 | 0 | .214 |
| Brooks, Carlos, Cleveland* | 13 | 21 | 2 | 2 | 2 | 0 | 0 | 0 | 0 | 0 | 0 | 2 | 0 | 5 | 0 | 0 | .095 |
| Brown, John E., Cleveland* | 52 | 177 | 34 | 50 | 70 | 5 | 6 | 1 | 10 | 2 | 0 | 41 | 1 | 39 | 7 | 4 | .282 |
| Bryant, Dwight, Chicago-NL | 29 | 44 | 5 | 7 | 7 | 0 | 0 | 0 | 1 | 0 | 8 | 0 | 11 | 3 | 2 | .159 |
| Bucci, Michael, Texas | 40 | 100 | 24 | 25 | 35 | 3 | 2 | 1 | 12 | 1 | 3 | 19 | 0 | 11 | 2 | 0 | .250 |
| Burgess, Thomas, St. Louis† | 43 | 125 | 14 | 32 | 36 | 2 | 1 | 0 | 13 | 6 | 1 | 19 | 2 | 31 | 3 | 2 | .256 |
| Chapman, David, Texas | 36 | 117 | 19 | 31 | 43 | 4 | 1 | 2 | 12 | 2 | 1 | 22 | 1 | 21 | 3 | 0 | .265 |
| Christensen, Kenneth, Chi-NL | 21 | 33 | 4 | 5 | 5 | 0 | 0 | 0 | 2 | 0 | 0 | 8 | 0 | 8 | 0 | 0 | .152 |
| Cooper, Marco, Pittsburgh* | 26 | 55 | 10 | 11 | 14 | 1 | 1 | 0 | 2 | 0 | 0 | 15 | 0 | 15 | 4 | 1 | .200 |
| Costanzo, Ralph, St. Louis | 38 | 130 | 12 | 35 | 40 | 1 | 1 | 1 | 15 | 0 | 1 | 15 | 0 | 16 | 3 | 3 | .269 |
| Davis, Albert, Kansas City | 15 | 35 | 3 | 4 | 4 | 0 | 0 | 0 | 0 | 0 | 0 | 6 | 1 | 17 | 0 | 1 | .114 |
| Delph, Randall, Texas† | 24 | 71 | 15 | 21 | 27 | 2 | 2 | 0 | 14 | 1 | 1 | 13 | 0 | 8 | 3 | 0 | .296 |
| Denevi, Michael, Kansas City | 47 | 151 | 24 | 43 | 53 | 7 | 0 | 1 | 20 | 1 | 2 | 22 | 2 | 15 | 5 | 2 | .285 |
| Deskins, Thomas, Chicago-NL | 37 | 93 | 12 | 26 | 31 | 3 | 1 | 0 | 9 | 1 | 0 | 10 | 2 | 16 | 0 | 0 | .280 |
| Docen, Moises, Cleveland | 25 | 47 | 6 | 5 | 5 | 0 | 0 | 0 | 1 | 4 | 0 | 5 | 0 | 13 | 1 | 2 | .106 |
| Duran, Hector, Pittsburgh | 31 | 108 | 13 | 25 | 26 | 1 | 0 | 0 | 7 | 3 | 2 | 6 | 1 | 5 | 9 | 1 | .231 |
| Eagle, Gary, Chicago-AL | 35 | 100 | 19 | 22 | 29 | 4 | 0 | 1 | 8 | 0 | 1 | 30 | 1 | 18 | 8 | 3 | .220 |
| Easley, Marland, Chicago-AL | 14 | 29 | 1 | 2 | 2 | 0 | 0 | 0 | 1 | 0 | 0 | 4 | 0 | 7 | 1 | 1 | .069 |
| Edrington, Heyward, Pitt. | 21 | 51 | 7 | 6 | 6 | 0 | 0 | 0 | 2 | 1 | 0 | 9 | 0 | 19 | 8 | 2 | .118 |
| Elter, Leo, Chicago-AL | 24 | 67 | 7 | 11 | 15 | 4 | 0 | 0 | 5 | 0 | 1 | 10 | 0 | 20 | 0 | 0 | .164 |
| Etchandy, Curtis, Chicago-AL | 49 | 153 | 22 | 30 | 47 | 11 | 0 | 2 | 18 | 2 | 3 | 32 | 4 | 32 | 1 | 1 | .196 |
| Ezell, Richard, Cleveland | 46 | 155 | 18 | 37 | 44 | 4 | 0 | 1 | 14 | 1 | 2 | 25 | 1 | 24 | 6 | 1 | .239 |
| Fleming, Steven, Pittsburgh† | 43 | 129 | 15 | 24 | 39 | 3 | 3 | 2 | 10 | 0 | 0 | 29 | 1 | 41 | 9 | 8 | .186 |
| Ford, Stephen, Pittsburgh | 3 | 10 | 0 | 0 | 0 | 0 | 0 | 0 | 0 | 0 | 0 | 1 | 0 | 3 | 0 | 0 | .000 |
| Frazier, Michael, St. Louis | 37 | 125 | 16 | 25 | 31 | 4 | 1 | 0 | 13 | 1 | 2 | 21 | 2 | 18 | 4 | 4 | .200 |
| Fuentes, Frank, St. Louis | 11 | 28 | 2 | 2 | 2 | 0 | 0 | 0 | 0 | 0 | 0 | 2 | 0 | 15 | 0 | 0 | .071 |
| Garcia, Daniel R., Kan City* | 48 | 171 | 25 | 43 | 51 | 4 | 2 | 0 | 24 | 0 | 1 | 33 | 2 | 20 | 11 | 2 | .251 |
| Garcia, Manuel A., Chi-NL | 24 | 39 | 4 | 5 | 5 | 0 | 0 | 0 | 2 | 1 | 0 | 4 | 0 | 6 | 1 | 0 | .128 |
| Garcia, Pedro, Cleveland† | 41 | 74 | 8 | 11 | 13 | 0 | 1 | 0 | 4 | 2 | 2 | 4 | 0 | 3 | 1 | 1 | .149 |
| Gillen, Kevin, Kansas City* | 43 | 121 | 17 | 22 | 36 | 4 | 5 | 0 | 21 | 1 | 2 | 25 | 1 | 24 | 1 | 1 | .182 |
| Glabman, Barry, Cleveland | 11 | 20 | 2 | 1 | 1 | 0 | 0 | 0 | 1 | 0 | 0 | 3 | 1 | 8 | 0 | 0 | .050 |
| Grandy, Eric, Chicago-NL | 50 | 153 | 29 | 35 | 59 | 6 | 3 | 4 | 23 | 4 | 1 | 31 | 4 | 39 | 8 | 0 | .229 |
| Guess, Thomas, Cleveland* | 52 | 157 | 17 | 40 | 58 | 7 | 4 | 1 | 28 | 0 | 1 | 37 | 0 | 27 | 3 | 1 | .255 |
| Harmon, Larry, Cleveland | 26 | 80 | 7 | 23 | 25 | 0 | 1 | 0 | 8 | 1 | 0 | 7 | 1 | 13 | 0 | 1 | .288 |
| Harper, Marshall, Chi-AL | 54 | 200 | 26 | 50 | 62 | 4 | 4 | 0 | 14 | 3 | 3 | 22 | 0 | 19 | 21 | 7 | .250 |
| Henry, Isidro, Cleveland* | 9 | 9 | 0 | 0 | 0 | 0 | 0 | 0 | 0 | 0 | 1 | 0 | 6 | 0 | 0 | .000 |
| Hernandez, Joseph, Chicago-NL | 4 | 13 | 4 | 5 | 6 | 1 | 0 | 0 | 0 | 0 | 0 | 2 | 1 | 0 | 1 | 0 | .385 |
| Higgins, Marion, Pittsburgh* | 2 | 8 | 0 | 1 | 1 | 0 | 0 | 0 | 0 | 0 | 0 | 0 | 0 | 0 | 0 | 0 | .125 |
| Hill, Ronald, Chicago-NL | 44 | 131 | 18 | 28 | 46 | 9 | 0 | 3 | 14 | 1 | 2 | 23 | 0 | 31 | 0 | 0 | .214 |
| Hudson, Jack, Kansas City | 18 | 49 | 2 | 7 | 7 | 0 | 0 | 0 | 5 | 0 | 0 | 4 | 1 | 13 | 0 | 3 | .143 |
| Hurdle, Clinton, Kansas City* | 49 | 175 | 34 | 48 | 63 | 9 | 0 | 1 | 31 | 0 | 1 | 24 | 6 | 23 | 1 | 1 | .274 |
| Ihler, Pdero, Cleveland | 46 | 171 | 26 | 48 | 57 | 9 | 0 | 0 | 10 | 3 | 0 | 19 | 1 | 12 | 7 | 2 | .281 |
| Johnson, Jerry D., St. Louis | 24 | 81 | 9 | 15 | 17 | 2 | 0 | 0 | 4 | 2 | 0 | 9 | 0 | 23 | 0 | 0 | .185 |
| Jordan, Earl, Cleveland | 36 | 92 | 12 | 23 | 29 | 4 | 1 | 0 | 10 | 2 | 1 | 25 | 0 | 14 | 6 | 3 | .250 |
| Joyner, David, Pittsburgh | 18 | 58 | 5 | 15 | 20 | 3 | 1 | 0 | 9 | 0 | 0 | 7 | 2 | 12 | 6 | 2 | .259 |
| Katts, Raymond, Chicago-AL | 39 | 124 | 10 | 26 | 27 | 1 | 0 | 0 | 14 | 0 | 1 | 14 | 1 | 20 | 2 | 2 | .210 |
| Lacy, Steven, Kansas City* | 10 | 31 | 5 | 9 | 10 | 1 | 0 | 0 | 5 | 1 | 0 | 8 | 1 | 5 | 2 | 0 | .290 |
| Laseter, Thomas, Kansas City | 44 | 170 | 33 | 50 | 63 | 5 | 4 | 0 | 18 | 0 | 3 | 16 | 1 | 13 | 11 | 1 | .294 |
| Lentine, James, St. Louis | 4 | 15 | 2 | 7 | 13 | 2 | 2 | 0 | 4 | 0 | 3 | 0 | 0 | 0 | 0 | .467 |
| Leonardo, Juan, Chicago-AL* | 32 | 103 | 17 | 26 | 32 | 4 | 1 | 0 | 8 | 1 | 0 | 13 | 0 | 10 | 6 | 2 | .252 |
| Leyva, Nicolas, St. Louis | 4 | 18 | 3 | 5 | 7 | 2 | 0 | 0 | 0 | 0 | 0 | 2 | 1 | 0 | .278 |
| Llodrat, Fernando, Kan City | 32 | 106 | 17 | 26 | 32 | 4 | 1 | 0 | 10 | 1 | 0 | 9 | 0 | 17 | 3 | 3 | .245 |
| LoGrande, Angelo, Cleveland | 45 | 170 | 19 | 45 | 61 | 9 | 2 | 1 | 19 | 1 | 0 | 10 | 4 | 30 | 3 | 2 | .265 |
| Lundsford, David, St. Louis* | 41 | 92 | 8 | 18 | 21 | 3 | 0 | 0 | 7 | 1 | 1 | 17 | 0 | 15 | 1 | 2 | .196 |
| Lundstedt, David, St. Louis | 43 | 125 | 10 | 30 | 35 | 5 | 0 | 0 | 11 | 2 | 1 | 21 | 3 | 24 | 1 | 2 | .240 |
| Mabee, Victor, Texas | 36 | 117 | 15 | 24 | 38 | 2 | 3 | 2 | 14 | 2 | 2 | 20 | 0 | 25 | 5 | 0 | .205 |
| Maffey, Stanley, 14 Cleveland-30 St. Louis | 44 | 136 | 13 | 26 | 33 | 5 | 1 | 0 | 14 | 1 | 0 | 22 | 3 | 40 | 4 | 2 | .191 |
| Marichal, Santiago, Kan City | 1 | 9 | 1 | 0 | 0 | 0 | 0 | 0 | 0 | 0 | 0 | 0 | 0 | 0 | 0 | 0 | .000 |
| Massee, M. Lee, Chicago-NL* | 29 | 85 | 6 | 20 | 25 | 5 | 0 | 0 | 10 | 0 | 1 | 7 | 0 | 14 | 0 | 1 | .235 |
| Mathias, Jack, Cleveland | 18 | 49 | 6 | 7 | 7 | 0 | 0 | 0 | 0 | 0 | 0 | 9 | 0 | 15 | 2 | 0 | .143 |
| McClellan, Robert, Chi-AL* | 27 | 83 | 6 | 15 | 17 | 2 | 0 | 0 | 5 | 1 | 0 | 13 | 2 | 17 | 1 | 1 | .181 |
| McGlade, Michael, Cleveland | 24 | 77 | 15 | 17 | 23 | 6 | 0 | 0 | 10 | 0 | 1 | 11 | 1 | 23 | 0 | 0 | .221 |
| Mercado, Candido, Chi-AL | 27 | 73 | 6 | 19 | 21 | 2 | 0 | 0 | 9 | 1 | 0 | 11 | 0 | 15 | 1 | 5 | .260 |
| Miller, Edward, Texas* | 51 | 180 | 47 | 46 | 57 | 5 | 3 | 0 | 21 | 2 | 1 | 51 | 4 | 58 | 30 | 7 | .256 |
| Moreta, Manuel, Kansas City | 43 | 154 | 26 | 42 | 51 | 7 | 1 | 0 | 17 | 2 | 1 | 13 | 1 | 22 | 14 | 1 | .273 |
| Mota, Cornelio, Pittsburgh | 25 | 69 | 4 | 13 | 13 | 0 | 0 | 0 | 1 | 0 | 1 | 13 | 0 | 20 | 2 | 2 | .188 |
| Mullins, John, Chi-NL* | 39 | 95 | 9 | 22 | 28 | 4 | 1 | 0 | 8 | 0 | 0 | 9 | 2 | 16 | 0 | 1 | .232 |
| Negron, Raymond, Pittsburgh | 2 | 7 | 0 | 1 | 1 | 0 | 0 | 0 | 1 | 0 | 0 | 0 | 0 | 0 | 0 | 0 | .143 |
| Norman, Nelson, Pittsburgh | 51 | 202 | 19 | 53 | 58 | 5 | 0 | 0 | 13 | 8 | 0 | 4 | 11 | 12 | 7 | 2 | .262 |
| Olson, Terry, Texas* | 41 | 134 | 21 | 29 | 36 | 5 | 1 | 0 | 23 | 3 | 2 | 18 | 0 | 30 | 12 | 4 | .216 |
| Pacheco, Antonio H., Clev. | 39 | 129 | 12 | 31 | 35 | 4 | 0 | 0 | 13 | 3 | 2 | 14 | 4 | 27 | 0 | 5 | .240 |
| Paris, Kelly, St. Louis† | 34 | 123 | 14 | 29 | 37 | 2 | 0 | 2 | 13 | 0 | 0 | 15 | 0 | 18 | 7 | 2 | .236 |
| Peoples, Charles, Chicago-NL | 24 | 61 | 7 | 9 | 10 | 1 | 0 | 0 | 1 | 4 | 0 | 8 | 1 | 14 | 0 | 0 | .148 |
| Pettinger, Ronald, Chicago-NL | 44 | 126 | 18 | 37 | 54 | 9 | 4 | 0 | 17 | 4 | 3 | 14 | 2 | 26 | 1 | 1 | .294 |

| Player and Club | G. | AB. | R. | H. | TB. | 2B. | 3B. | HR. | RBI. | SH. | SF. | BB. | HP. | SO. | SB. | CS. | Pct. |
|---|---|---|---|---|---|---|---|---|---|---|---|---|---|---|---|---|---|
| Pinkerton, C. Wayne, Texas† | .35 | 139 | 24 | 38 | 45 | 3 | 2 | 0 | 17 | 1 | 1 | 18 | 4 | 26 | 12 | 2 | .273 |
| Pritchett, Dennis, St. Louis | 20 | 49 | 0 | 12 | 14 | 2 | 0 | 0 | 8 | 1 | 0 | 7 | 0 | 2 | 1 | 4 | .245 |
| Putnam, Patrick, Texas* | .18 | 73 | 13 | 21 | 33 | 4 | 1 | 2 | 17 | 2 | 1 | 6 | 1 | 4 | 1 | 0 | .288 |
| Ramirez, Manuel V., Chi-AL | 27 | 82 | 13 | 17 | 31 | 3 | 4 | 1 | 11 | 1 | 1 | 17 | 3 | 3 | .207 |
| Redoglia, Donald, St. Louis | 4 | 4 | 4 | 7 | 3 | 0 | 0 | 5 | 0 | 0 | 3 | 0 | 2 | 1 | 0 | .250 |
| Rein, Frederick, Pittsburgh | .25 | 78 | 10 | 20 | 27 | 4 | 0 | 1 | 12 | 0 | 1 | 16 | 0 | 13 | 8 | 1 | .256 |
| Reynolds, Randall, Texas | .37 | 128 | 15 | 27 | 34 | 4 | 0 | 1 | 19 | 1 | 1 | 7 | 1 | 31 | 9 | 0 | .211 |
| Rivera, David B., Texas | .37 | 137 | 20 | 39 | 65 | 6 | 4 | 4 | 23 | 1 | 1 | 6 | 1 | 38 | 1 | 2 | .285 |
| Robinson, Charles, St. Louis | .70 | 30 | 1 | 6 | 8 | 2 | 0 | 0 | 1 | 0 | 0 | 6 | 1 | 8 | 2 | 0 | .200 |
| Rodriguez, Eduardo M., Chicago-NL | .42 | 137 | 17 | 31 | 39 | 4 | 2 | 0 | 15 | 1 | 4 | 16 | 2 | 18 | 9 | 0 | .226 |
| Rosinski, Brian, Chicago-NL | .40 | 140 | 20 | 43 | 56 | 5 | 4 | 0 | 23 | 0 | 3 | 29 | 2 | 20 | 4 | 4 | .307 |
| Rothwell, Donald, Kansas City | 26 | 71 | 10 | 16 | 20 | 2 | 1 | 0 | 12 | 0 | 0 | 13 | 1 | 9 | 2 | 1 | .225 |
| Ryan, John, St Louis | .33 | 96 | 5 | 15 | 16 | 1 | 0 | 0 | 1 | 1 | 2 | 3 | 23 | 1 | 1 | .156 |
| Sansosti, Francis, St. Louis | .9 | 24 | 1 | 5 | 6 | 1 | 0 | 0 | 2 | 0 | 0 | 1 | 0 | 8 | 0 | 0 | .208 |
| Sarmiento, Victor, Pitt* | .45 | 138 | 13 | 29 | 36 | 3 | 2 | 0 | 13 | 3 | 0 | 21 | 1 | 20 | 14 | 6 | .210 |
| Schuller, Gregory, Kan City† | 9 | 16 | 3 | 2 | 2 | 0 | 0 | 0 | 2 | 0 | 0 | 1 | 0 | 5 | 0 | 0 | .125 |
| Schultz, Theodore, Chi-AL† | .2 | 5 | 0 | 1 | 1 | 0 | 0 | 0 | 0 | 0 | 0 | 0 | 1 | 0 | 1 | 0 | .200 |
| Selbo, Ronald, Pittsburgh | .12 | 25 | 3 | 4 | 4 | 0 | 0 | 0 | 2 | 0 | 0 | 1 | 0 | 5 | 1 | 0 | .160 |
| Selby, Donnie, Texas | .27 | 36 | 7 | 4 | 8 | 0 | 2 | 0 | 2 | 0 | 0 | 8 | 0 | 18 | 0 | 0 | .111 |
| Shuford, George, St. Louis* | .38 | 98 | 11 | 14 | 19 | 1 | 2 | 0 | 5 | 2 | 0 | 24 | 2 | 23 | 6 | 3 | .143 |
| Silverio, Luis, Kansas City | .44 | 150 | 20 | 35 | 61 | 5 | 3 | 5 | 29 | 0 | 0 | 26 | 0 | 38 | 2 | 2 | .233 |
| Smith, Michael, Chicago-AL* | 47 | 158 | 17 | 35 | 42 | 5 | 1 | 0 | 15 | 1 | 2 | 9 | 1 | 38 | 3 | 0 | .222 |
| Stewart, Joseph, Texas | .47 | 152 | 27 | 38 | 47 | 7 | 1 | 0 | 25 | 0 | 4 | 44 | 0 | 36 | 5 | 1 | .250 |
| Stewart, Willis, Chicago-NL | .48 | 144 | 18 | 28 | 31 | 3 | 0 | 0 | 10 | 2 | 1 | 23 | 0 | 24 | 3 | 3 | .194 |
| Stone, William, Texas | .44 | 133 | 17 | 27 | 30 | 3 | 0 | 0 | 17 | 5 | 1 | 24 | 2 | 8 | 1 | 2 | .203 |
| Takacs, John, Texas* | .28 | 63 | 9 | 10 | 14 | 2 | 1 | 0 | 5 | 0 | 1 | 16 | 1 | 9 | 2 | 3 | .159 |
| Tejada, Manuel, Pittsburgh | .54 | 197 | 14 | 46 | 55 | 5 | 2 | 0 | 20 | 0 | 2 | 10 | 6 | 41 | 2 | 4 | .234 |
| Tena, Roberto, 1 StL-42 Pitt | 43 | 140 | 15 | 29 | 37 | 3 | 1 | 9 | 0 | 1 | 8 | 0 | 18 | 4 | 3 | .207 |
| Thomas, James L., Texas | .1 | 3 | 1 | 0 | 0 | 0 | 0 | 0 | 0 | 0 | 0 | 1 | 0 | 0 | 0 | 0 | .000 |
| Tomski, Jeffrey, Cleveland | .36 | 91 | 16 | 22 | 30 | 6 | 1 | 0 | 16 | 0 | 0 | 39 | 2 | 16 | 2 | 1 | .242 |
| Torbush, Carl, Kansas City | .20 | 43 | 7 | 8 | 11 | 1 | 1 | 0 | 2 | 0 | 1 | 9 | 4 | 10 | 2 | 0 | .186 |
| Torres, Nelson, Pittsburgh | .24 | 71 | 5 | 15 | 20 | 5 | 0 | 0 | 5 | 0 | 0 | 7 | 0 | 20 | 0 | 1 | .211 |
| Travis, James, Chicago-NL | .28 | 57 | 5 | 9 | 12 | 3 | 0 | 0 | 5 | 6 | 1 | 16 | 3 | 9 | 2 | 3 | .158 |
| Trucks, Phil, Chicago-AL | .37 | 103 | 6 | 18 | 24 | 6 | 0 | 0 | 9 | 1 | 1 | 14 | 0 | 33 | 0 | 2 | .175 |
| Tufts, William, Chicago-NL* | 13 | 25 | 4 | 2 | 2 | 0 | 0 | 0 | 2 | 0 | 0 | 2 | 0 | 1 | 0 | 0 | .080 |
| Umfleet, R Michael, Chi-NL* | 4 | 16 | 1 | 4 | 4 | 0 | 0 | 0 | 1 | 0 | 0 | 1 | 0 | 4 | 0 | 0 | .250 |
| Valdez, Radhames, St. Louis | 23 | 66 | 6 | 8 | 10 | 0 | 1 | 0 | 3 | 1 | 0 | 4 | 0 | 18 | 1 | 1 | .121 |
| Vargas, Freddy, Pittsburgh | .3 | 6 | 1 | 2 | 2 | 0 | 0 | 0 | 1 | 0 | 1 | 1 | 0 | 1 | 0 | 0 | .333 |
| Varner, John, Texas* | .32 | 79 | 8 | 19 | 20 | 1 | 0 | 0 | 6 | 0 | 1 | 12 | 0 | 22 | 0 | 0 | .241 |
| Ventura, Candido, Pittsburgh | 34 | 115 | 13 | 33 | 43 | 3 | 2 | 1 | 14 | 0 | 0 | 8 | 0 | 33 | 3 | 6 | .287 |
| Ventura, Nelson, Pittsburgh | .15 | 39 | 3 | 6 | 8 | 2 | 0 | 0 | 4 | 0 | 0 | 4 | 0 | 10 | 2 | 0 | .154 |
| Von Ahnen, William, Chi-NL* | 1 | 0 | 0 | 0 | 0 | 0 | 0 | 0 | 0 | 0 | 0 | 1 | 0 | 0 | 0 | 0 | .000 |
| Washington, Larue, Texas | .24 | 91 | 21 | 29 | 36 | 3 | 2 | 0 | 16 | 0 | 0 | 13 | 1 | 9 | 12 | 2 | .319 |
| Woods, Jeffrey, Pittsburgh* | .52 | 200 | 21 | 49 | 56 | 4 | 0 | 1 | 12 | 1 | 2 | 12 | 0 | 29 | 17 | 5 | .245 |
| Yesenchak, Edward, Chi-AL | .24 | 74 | 6 | 18 | 24 | 6 | 0 | 0 | 9 | 1 | 0 | 6 | 0 | 21 | 1 | 0 | .243 |

The following pitchers had no plate appearances primarily through use of designated hitters, listed alphabetically, games in parentheses:

CHICAGO-AL—Attardi, Gerald* (6); Farrell, Michael (14); Gottleber, Wayne (6); Handley, James (14); Hunziker, Kent (14); Joyce, Thomas (14); Loehr, C. Theodore (12); Lukevics, Mitchell (8); Madden, Robert (14); Muckenthaler, Richard (11); Seltzer, Randall* (5).

CHICAGO-NL—Barreto, Miguel (18); Cameron, Michael (14); Ledbetter, Charles (12); Lucchesi, Jeffrey* (10); Moore, Michael (4); Rogers, Charles* (2); Smith, Lee (10); Taylor, Michael (12); Vogel, Rick* (6); Weber, James* (20); Yopp, Robert (10).

CLEVELAND—Alvarez, Miguel (5); Amenita, Thomas (2); Arp, Ronald (6); Bullard, Larkin (13); Hanson, Steven (6); Harvey, M. Craig (10); Huusfeldt, Steven (10); Pedroza, Alberto (16); Saulnier, Donald* (4); Skiba, Daniel (12); Vaughn, Michael (12); Wihtol, Alexander (8); Yraguen, David (6).

KANSAS CITY—Barr, Robert* (7); Cvejdlik, Kent (9); Gale, Richard (9); Greene, Henry (10); Hart, John (2); Lahey, Kevin (2); Martinez, Oscar (10); Passalacqua, Francisco (15); Rosario, Luis* (6); Sebastian, John (6); Smith, Ronald (10); Wilson, William D* (11); Winters, David (11).

PITTSBURGH—Anthony, Paul* (4); Burkett, J. Mark* (9); Hogle, Timothy* (4); Holland, Alfred* (5); Johnson, Alejandro* (10); Losasso, Robert* (9); Marcial (Lira), Nelo 8 Cleveland—3 Pittsburgh (11); Martin, Ricky* (11); Ney, James (2); Peterson, Darnley* (11); Rivas, Martin (13); Robinson, Don (10); Robles, Victor (2); Seabol, Russell (2); Semerano, Robert (2); Tapia, Mark (7); Valera, Salvador (3); Viera, Jose (11).

ST. LOUIS—Arthur, James† (16); Dennard, Anthony (14); Grassano, Kenneth (11); Gray, Terry (12); Guerrero, Federico (15); Guillermo, Felix, (2); Johnson, David M. (7); Martinez, Nicolas (19); Oliver, David A. (11); Propst, James (5); Rieger, Karl* (11); Wright, Robert (11).

TEXAS—Arrington, Michael (15); Burgess, Lawrence* (9); Couch, Richard* (10); Gideon, James (2); Kelly, Harold (11); McCarthy, David* (11); McMurray, Randall (10); Moock, Patrick, (19); Patten, William* (6); Poloni, John* (4); Soroko, Mark (14).

GRAND-SLAM HOME RUN—Mabee 1.

AWARDED FIRST BASE ON INTERFERENCE—Eagle 2 (Mota, Peoples), Olson 2 (Christensen 2), Rivera (Trucks), Travis (Putnam), Tufts (Yesenchak), Woods (Trucks).

### CLUB FIELDING

| Club | G. | PO. | A. | E. | DP. | PB. | Pct. |
|---|---|---|---|---|---|---|---|
| Kansas City | 49 | 1230 | 454 | 55 | 38 | 17 | .968 |
| Texas | 53 | 1428 | 626 | 98 | 37 | 10 | .954 |
| Chicago-NL | 54 | 1379 | 600 | 96 | 31 | 15 | .954 |
| Pittsburgh | 54 | 1432 | 585 | 109 | 39 | 20 | .949 |
| St. Louis | 52 | 1319 | 596 | 110 | 47 | 7 | .946 |
| Cleveland | 52 | 1296 | 518 | 122 | 32 | 29 | .937 |
| Chicago-AL | 54 | 1350 | 580 | 140 | 39 | 15 | .932 |

Triple Play—None.

### INDIVIDUAL FIELDING
#### FIRST BASEMEN

*Throws lefthanded.

| Player and Club | G. | PO. | A. | E. | DP. | Pct |
|---|---|---|---|---|---|---|
| Lundstedt, St Louis | 5 | 22 | 0 | 0 | 3 | 1.000 |
| Sansosti, St.Louis | 2 | 21 | 0 | 0 | 2 | 1.000 |
| Hill, Chicago-NL | 3 | 17 | 0 | 0 | 1 | 1.000 |
| Tena, Pittsburgh | 1 | 7 | 0 | 0 | 1 | 1.000 |
| Delph, Texas | 1 | 5 | 0 | 0 | 0 | 1.000 |
| Alessio, Chicago-NL | 1 | 2 | 0 | 0 | 1 | 1.000 |
| Denevi, Kansas City | 1 | 2 | 0 | 0 | 0 | 1.000 |
| Pettinger, Chi-NL | 17 | 125 | 8 | 1 | 3 | .993 |
| Putnam, Texas | 13 | 111 | 7 | 1 | 6 | .992 |
| McClellan, Chi-AL | 14 | 98 | 7 | 1 | 9 | .991 |
| MULLINS, Chi-NL* | 38 | 246 | 17 | 3 | 14 | .989 |
| Lundsford, St Louis* | 14 | 112 | 8 | 2 | 8 | .984 |
| Burgess, St Louis* | 34 | 267 | 18 | 5 | 22 | .983 |
| Chapman, Texas | 28 | 233 | 8 | 5 | 14 | .980 |
| Garcia, Kansas City* | 41 | 308 | 15 | 7 | 32 | .979 |
| Torbush, Kansas City | 14 | 91 | 3 | 2 | 1 | .979 |
| Christensen, Chi-NL | 9 | 34 | 4 | 1 | 4 | .974 |
| Tejada, Pittsburgh | 54 | 446 | 24 | 14 | 32 | .971 |
| Olson, Texas* | 19 | 158 | 10 | 5 | 10 | .971 |
| Stewart, Chi-NL | 5 | 30 | 3 | 1 | 1 | .971 |
| Guess, Cleveland* | 5 | 26 | 6 | 1 | 2 | .970 |
| LoGrande, Cleveland | 42 | 324 | 18 | 14 | 21 | .961 |
| Smith, Chicago-AL | 45 | 345 | 29 | 17 | 22 | .957 |
| Pacheco, Cleveland | 7 | 42 | 0 | 2 | 4 | .955 |
| Maffey, Clev-StL | 8 | 33 | 0 | 3 | 2 | .917 |
| Tufts, Chicago-NL* | 2 | 9 | 0 | 1 | 1 | .900 |
| Sarmiento, Pitt* | 4 | 4 | 0 | 2 | 0 | .667 |

#### SECOND BASEMEN

| Player and Club | G. | PO. | A. | E. | DP. | Pct. |
|---|---|---|---|---|---|---|
| Duran, Pittsburgh | 7 | 17 | 15 | 0 | 6 | 1.000 |
| Garcia, Chicago-NL | 12 | 10 | 13 | 0 | 0 | 1.000 |
| Brockway, Chicago-NL | 4 | 11 | 8 | 0 | 2 | 1.000 |
| Lundstedt, St Louis | 4 | 6 | 5 | 0 | 0 | 1.000 |
| Rodriguez, Chi-NL | 3 | 4 | 3 | 0 | 0 | 1.000 |
| Alessio, Chicago-NL | 1 | 3 | 3 | 0 | 1 | 1.000 |
| Davis, Kansas City | 1 | 0 | 3 | 0 | 0 | 1.000 |
| STONE, Texas | 42 | 84 | 85 | 4 | 24 | .977 |
| Borges, St Louis | 35 | 86 | 82 | 4 | 20 | .977 |
| Denevi, Kansas City | 29 | 60 | 61 | 3 | 13 | .976 |
| Deskins, Chicago-NL | 32 | 56 | 49 | 3 | 7 | .972 |
| Docen, Cleveland | 22 | 38 | 42 | 3 | 6 | .964 |
| Bauer, Chicago-AL | 31 | 74 | 76 | 6 | 12 | .962 |
| Woods, Pittsburgh | 45 | 133 | 114 | 11 | 17 | .957 |
| Llodrat, Kansas City | 24 | 41 | 35 | 4 | 10 | .950 |
| Massee, Chicago-NL | 23 | 48 | 42 | 5 | 6 | .947 |
| Harmon, Cleveland | 23 | 57 | 49 | 6 | 9 | .946 |
| Costanzo, St Louis | 3 | 9 | 8 | 1 | 4 | .944 |
| Mahee, Texas | 14 | 23 | 18 | 3 | 3 | .932 |
| Eagle, Chicago-AL | 24 | 49 | 46 | 8 | 9 | .922 |
| Ryan, St Louis | 14 | 25 | 22 | 4 | 4 | .922 |
| Garcia, Cleveland | 16 | 27 | 30 | 5 | 3 | .919 |
| Takacs, Texas | 6 | 7 | 4 | 1 | 2 | .917 |
| N. Ventura, Pittsburgh | 6 | 10 | 8 | 2 | 3 | .900 |
| Schultz, Chicago-AL | 2 | 5 | 4 | 1 | 1 | .900 |
| Glabman, Cleveland | 3 | 3 | 5 | 1 | 0 | .889 |
| Redoglia, St Louis | 4 | 14 | 12 | 4 | 2 | .867 |
| Ithier, Cleveland | 1 | 2 | 2 | 1 | 0 | .800 |
| Stewart, Chi-NL | 1 | 0 | 2 | 2 | 0 | .500 |

#### THIRD BASEMEN

| Player and Club | G. | PO. | A. | E. | DP. | Pct. |
|---|---|---|---|---|---|---|
| Garcia, Cleveland | 4 | 5 | 6 | 0 | 0 | 1.000 |
| Denevi, Kansas City | 7 | 4 | 3 | 0 | 0 | 1.000 |
| Baker, Kansas City | 1 | 0 | 2 | 0 | 0 | 1.000 |
| J. Johnson, St Louis | 1 | 0 | 2 | 0 | 0 | 1.000 |
| Pettinger, Chicago-NL | 1 | 0 | 1 | 0 | 0 | 1.000 |
| Pritchett, St. Louis | 1 | 0 | 1 | 0 | 0 | 1.000 |
| Garcia, Chicago-NL | 2 | 0 | 1 | 0 | 0 | 1.000 |
| MORETA, Kan City | 38 | 42 | 62 | 6 | 3 | .945 |
| Lundstedt, St Louis | 14 | 7 | 24 | 2 | 1 | .939 |
| Washington, Texas | 24 | 20 | 74 | 7 | 4 | .931 |
| Umfleet, Chi-NL | 4 | 2 | 11 | 1 | 0 | .929 |
| Massee, Chicago-NL | 6 | 5 | 8 | 1 | 0 | .929 |
| Stewart, Chi-NL | 41 | 30 | 83 | 9 | 3 | .926 |
| Tena, St Louis-Pitt | 27 | 34 | 52 | 7 | 5 | .925 |
| Alessio, Chicago-NL | 9 | 9 | 21 | 3 | 2 | .909 |
| Joyner, Pittsburgh | 16 | 17 | 31 | 5 | 2 | .906 |
| Stone, Texas | 2 | 2 | 7 | 1 | 0 | .900 |
| Davis, Kansas City | 13 | 12 | 30 | 5 | 5 | .894 |
| N. Ventura, Pitt | 5 | 4 | 20 | 3 | 2 | .889 |
| Etchandy, Chi-AL | 43 | 31 | 91 | 16 | 8 | .884 |
| Costanzo, St Louis | 33 | 32 | 75 | 14 | 9 | .884 |
| Elter, Chicago-AL | 15 | 14 | 31 | 6 | 2 | .882 |
| Bucci, Texas | 20 | 17 | 40 | 8 | 5 | .877 |
| Ezell, Cleveland | 32 | 24 | 67 | 13 | 3 | .875 |
| Duran, Pittsburgh | 7 | 12 | 13 | 4 | 0 | .862 |
| Fuentes, St Louis | 4 | 1 | 5 | 1 | 0 | .857 |
| Takacs, Texas | 17 | 9 | 32 | 7 | 2 | .854 |
| C. Ventura, Pittsburgh | 3 | 3 | 2 | 1 | 0 | .833 |
| Deskins, Chicago-NL | 4 | 1 | 4 | 1 | 0 | .833 |
| McGlade, Cleveland | 18 | 12 | 33 | 10 | 2 | .818 |
| Tomski, Cleveland | 2 | 3 | 1 | 1 | 0 | .800 |
| Leyva, St Louis | 3 | 5 | 8 | 4 | 1 | .765 |
| Travis, Chicago-NL | 3 | 0 | 3 | 1 | 0 | .750 |
| Valdez, St. Louis | 5 | 0 | 5 | 2 | 0 | .714 |

#### SHORTSTOPS

| Player and Club | G. | PO. | A. | E. | DP. | Pct. |
|---|---|---|---|---|---|---|
| Denevi, Kansas City | 5 | 10 | 15 | 0 | 3 | 1.000 |
| Duran, Pittsburgh | 2 | 4 | 7 | 0 | 1 | 1.000 |
| Leyva, St. Louis | 1 | 3 | 3 | 0 | 1 | 1.000 |
| Elter, Chicago-AL | 2 | 1 | 2 | 0 | 0 | 1.000 |
| C. Ventura, Pittsburgh | 1 | 0 | 2 | 0 | 0 | 1.000 |
| Borges, St. Louis | 1 | 1 | 0 | 0 | 0 | 1.000 |
| Baker, Kansas City | 17 | 27 | 34 | 2 | 6 | .968 |
| Pinkerton, Texas | 35 | 55 | 135 | 8 | 12 | .960 |
| Barranca, Kansas City | 20 | 21 | 47 | 3 | 8 | .958 |
| Glabman, Cleveland | 7 | 10 | 11 | 1 | 2 | .955 |
| Lacy, Kansas City | 10 | 11 | 26 | 2 | 2 | .949 |
| Lundstedt, St Louis | 22 | 29 | 69 | 6 | 10 | .942 |
| Moreta, Kansas City | 8 | 7 | 8 | 1 | 2 | .938 |
| Bauer, Chicago-AL | 16 | 35 | 37 | 5 | 6 | .935 |
| Travis, Chicago-NL | 24 | 39 | 69 | 8 | 11 | .931 |
| NORMAN, Pittsburgh | 51 | 101 | 137 | 22 | 22 | .915 |
| Paris, St Louis | 32 | 59 | 92 | 14 | 11 | .915 |
| Ithier, Cleveland | 41 | 69 | 80 | 14 | 7 | .914 |
| Bellini, Cleveland | 3 | 6 | 14 | 2 | 0 | .909 |
| Alessio, Chicago-NL | 28 | 34 | 66 | 11 | 5 | .901 |
| Ramirez, Chicago-AL | 17 | 27 | 37 | 7 | 8 | .901 |
| Mercado, Chicago-AL | 27 | 36 | 71 | 12 | 5 | .899 |

## SHORTSTOPS—Continued

| Player and Club | G. | PO. | A. | E. | DP. | Pct. |
|---|---|---|---|---|---|---|
| Garcia, Chicago-NL | 12 | 10 | 16 | 3 | 2 | .897 |
| Mabee, Texas | 16 | 19 | 65 | 14 | 9 | .857 |
| Garcia, Cleveland | 10 | 11 | 17 | 5 | 3 | .848 |
| Harmon, Cleveland | 1 | 1 | 2 | 1 | 0 | .750 |
| Negron, Pittsburgh | 2 | 1 | 3 | 2 | 0 | .667 |
| Takacs, Texas | 4 | 0 | 1 | 2 | 0 | .333 |

## OUTFIELDERS

| Player and Club | G. | PO. | A. | E. | DP. | Pct. |
|---|---|---|---|---|---|---|
| ROSINSKI, Chi-NL | 40 | 55 | 4 | 0 | 1 | 1.000 |
| Rein, Pittsburgh | 25 | 42 | 2 | 0 | 1 | 1.000 |
| Rivera, Texas | 29 | 43 | 1 | 0 | 0 | 1.000 |
| Bucci, Texas | 23 | 25 | 2 | 0 | 0 | 1.000 |
| Gillen, Kansas City | 7 | 12 | 0 | 0 | 0 | 1.000 |
| Hernandez, Chi-NL | 4 | 10 | 0 | 0 | 0 | 1.000 |
| Lentine, St Louis | 4 | 6 | 1 | 0 | 1 | 1.000 |
| Tena, Pittsburgh | 2 | 6 | 0 | 0 | 0 | 1.000 |
| Selbo, Pittsburgh | 5 | 6 | 0 | 0 | 0 | 1.000 |
| Garcia, Cleveland | 4 | 4 | 0 | 0 | 0 | 1.000 |
| Maffey, Cleveland | 1 | 2 | 0 | 0 | 0 | 1.000 |
| Denevi, Kansas City | 1 | 2 | 0 | 0 | 0 | 1.000 |
| Tufts, Chicago-NL* | 1 | 2 | 0 | 0 | 0 | 1.000 |
| Christensen, Chi-NL | 1 | 1 | 0 | 0 | 0 | 1.000 |
| Easley, Chicago-AL | 1 | 1 | 0 | 0 | 0 | 1.000 |
| Hill, Chicago-NL | 1 | 1 | 0 | 0 | 0 | 1.000 |
| Ithier, Cleveland | 1 | 1 | 0 | 0 | 0 | 1.000 |
| Torbush, Kansas City | 1 | 1 | 0 | 0 | 0 | 1.000 |
| Costanzo, St Louis | 2 | 1 | 0 | 0 | 0 | 1.000 |
| Elter, Chicago-AL | 2 | 1 | 0 | 0 | 0 | 1.000 |
| Deskins, Chicago-NL | 5 | 0 | 1 | 0 | 0 | 1.000 |
| Laseter, Kansas City | 42 | 77 | 2 | 1 | 2 | .988 |
| Fleming, Pittsburgh | 40 | 70 | 4 | 1 | 1 | .987 |
| Stewart, Texas | 45 | 65 | 5 | 1 | 1 | .986 |
| Anderson, Chicago-NL | 39 | 90 | 9 | 2 | 1 | .980 |
| Hurdle, Kansas City | 49 | 94 | 5 | 2 | 1 | .980 |
| Guess, Cleveland* | 31 | 31 | 4 | 1 | 1 | .972 |
| Silverio, Kan City | 43 | 61 | 6 | 2 | 2 | .971 |
| Torres, Pittsburgh | 16 | 28 | 3 | 1 | 0 | .969 |
| Miller, Texas | 51 | 125 | 2 | 5 | 1 | .962 |
| Brown, Cleveland* | 51 | 91 | 10 | 4 | 1 | .962 |
| Cooper, Pittsburgh* | 18 | 24 | 1 | 1 | 0 | .962 |
| Baez, St Louis | 29 | 43 | 6 | 2 | 2 | .961 |
| Valdez, St Louis | 19 | 23 | 0 | 1 | 0 | .958 |
| Rodriguez, Chi-NL | 23 | 43 | 2 | 2 | 1 | .957 |
| Garcia, Kansas City* | 12 | 22 | 0 | 1 | 0 | .957 |
| Varner, Texas | 24 | 22 | 0 | 1 | 0 | .957 |
| Grandy, Chicago-NL | 47 | 78 | 4 | 4 | 1 | .953 |
| Bryant, Chicago-NL | 22 | 17 | 2 | 1 | 0 | .950 |
| Pacheco, Cleveland | 19 | 33 | 3 | 2 | 0 | .947 |
| Shuford, St Louis* | 36 | 47 | 4 | 3 | 1 | .944 |
| Sarmiento, Pitt* | 43 | 74 | 8 | 5 | 2 | .943 |
| Bright, Chicago-AL | 46 | 46 | 4 | 3 | 1 | .943 |
| Batista, St Louis | 35 | 58 | 7 | 4 | 2 | .942 |
| Katts, Chicago-AL | 39 | 46 | 3 | 3 | 1 | .942 |
| Harper, Chicago-AL | 54 | 100 | 9 | 7 | 3 | .940 |
| Frazier, St Louis | 37 | 79 | 5 | 6 | 1 | .933 |
| Selby, Texas | 23 | 11 | 2 | 1 | 0 | .929 |
| C. Ventura, Pittsburgh | 26 | 43 | 2 | 4 | 0 | .918 |
| Olson, Texas* | 8 | 11 | 0 | 1 | 0 | .917 |
| Jordan, Cleveland | 32 | 46 | 5 | 5 | 1 | .911 |
| Ezell, Cleveland | 6 | 8 | 1 | 1 | 0 | .900 |
| Leonardo, Chi-AL* | 31 | 28 | 4 | 5 | 0 | .865 |
| Henry, Cleveland* | 8 | 5 | 1 | 1 | 1 | .857 |
| Angulo, Cleveland | 22 | 21 | 2 | 4 | 0 | .852 |
| Ford, Pittsburgh | 2 | 2 | 2 | 1 | 0 | .800 |
| Lundsford, St Louis* | 11 | 10 | 0 | 3 | 0 | .769 |
| Vargas, Pittsburgh | 3 | 1 | 0 | 2 | 0 | .333 |

## CATCHERS

| Player and Club | G. | PO. | A. | E. | DP. | PB. | Pct. |
|---|---|---|---|---|---|---|---|
| Rothwell, Kan C | 16 | 77 | 3 | 0 | 0 | 1 | 1.000 |
| Higgins, Pitt. | 2 | 15 | 1 | 0 | 0 | 1 | 1.000 |
| McGlade, Clev. | 3 | 11 | 2 | 0 | 1 | 1 | 1.000 |
| Torbush, Kan C. | 2 | 12 | 0 | 0 | 0 | 0 | 1.000 |
| Torres, Pittsburgh | 1 | 6 | 0 | 0 | 0 | 2 | 1.000 |
| Ryan, St Louis | 18 | 84 | 12 | 1 | 3 | 1 | .990 |
| Hill, Chicago-NL | 26 | 130 | 21 | 2 | 1 | 3 | .987 |
| REYNOLDS, Tex | 37 | 224 | 29 | 4 | 3 | 7 | .984 |
| Delph, Texas | 20 | 101 | 12 | 2 | 1 | 1 | .983 |
| Tomski, Cleveland | 36 | 215 | 30 | 5 | 2 | 14 | .980 |
| Mathias, Cleveland | 9 | 71 | 10 | 2 | 0 | 5 | .976 |
| Maffey, Clev-StL. | 6 | 38 | 1 | 0 | 0 | 5 | .975 |
| Gillen, Kan City | 25 | 125 | 24 | 4 | 1 | 8 | .974 |
| Putnam, Texas | 5 | 33 | 2 | 1 | 0 | 2 | .972 |
| J. Johnson, StL | 23 | 125 | 21 | 5 | 2 | 3 | .967 |
| Pritchett, StL | 14 | 70 | 13 | 3 | 0 | 2 | .965 |
| C. Robinson, Pitt | 10 | 72 | 10 | 3 | 1 | 5 | .965 |
| Hudson, Kan City | 16 | 73 | 9 | 3 | 0 | 6 | .965 |
| Yesenchak, Chi-A | 23 | 136 | 26 | 6 | 5 | 7 | .964 |
| Mota, Pittsburgh | 25 | 148 | 29 | 7 | 1 | 4 | .962 |
| Edrington, Pitt | 20 | 90 | 24 | 5 | 2 | 8 | .958 |
| Pettinger, Chi-NL | 14 | 54 | 5 | 3 | 1 | 1 | .952 |
| Brooks, Cleveland | 11 | 41 | 11 | 3 | 0 | 5 | .945 |
| Peoples, Chi-NL | 24 | 123 | 24 | 9 | 2 | 9 | .942 |
| Trucks, Chi-AL | 37 | 243 | 32 | 20 | 3 | 8 | .932 |
| Schuller, Kan City | 6 | 22 | 2 | 2 | 1 | 2 | .923 |
| Christensen, Chi-N | 8 | 26 | 5 | 4 | 1 | 2 | .886 |

## PITCHERS

| Player and Club | G. | PO. | A. | E. | DP. | Pct. |
|---|---|---|---|---|---|---|
| ARRINGTON, Texas | 15 | 5 | 13 | 0 | 1 | 1.000 |
| Skiba, Cleveland | 12 | 4 | 12 | 0 | 1 | 1.000 |
| D. Johnson, St Louis* | 7 | 0 | 14 | 0 | 1 | 1.000 |
| McCarthy, Texas* | 11 | 2 | 11 | 0 | 1 | 1.000 |
| Viera, Pittsburgh* | 11 | 1 | 10 | 0 | 1 | 1.000 |
| Moock, Texas | 19 | 2 | 9 | 0 | 0 | 1.000 |
| Gale, Kansas City | 9 | 4 | 5 | 0 | 1 | 1.000 |
| Winters, Kansas City | 11 | 2 | 7 | 0 | 0 | 1.000 |
| Guerrero, St Louis | 15 | 0 | 9 | 0 | 0 | 1.000 |
| Rosario, Kansas City* | 6 | 2 | 6 | 0 | 1 | 1.000 |
| Cvejdlik, Kansas City | 9 | 1 | 7 | 0 | 0 | 1.000 |
| D. Robinson, Pitt | 10 | 2 | 6 | 0 | 0 | 1.000 |
| Sebastian, Kansas City | 6 | 0 | 7 | 0 | 1 | 1.000 |
| Vogel, Chicago-NL* | 6 | 2 | 5 | 0 | 0 | 1.000 |
| Vaughn, Cleveland | 11 | 3 | 4 | 0 | 0 | 1.000 |
| Passalacqua, Kan City | 15 | 2 | 5 | 0 | 0 | 1.000 |
| Seabol, Pittsburgh | 2 | 1 | 5 | 0 | 2 | 1.000 |
| Von Ahnen, Chi-NL* | 14 | 0 | 6 | 0 | 2 | 1.000 |
| Pedroza, Cleveland | 16 | 2 | 4 | 0 | 0 | 1.000 |
| Rogers, Chicago-NL | 2 | 1 | 4 | 0 | 1 | 1.000 |
| Attardi, Chicago-AL* | 6 | 1 | 4 | 0 | 0 | 1.000 |
| Hanson, Cleveland | 6 | 1 | 4 | 0 | 0 | 1.000 |
| Rivas, Pittsburgh | 13 | 0 | 5 | 0 | 0 | 1.000 |
| Arp, Cleveland | 6 | 0 | 4 | 0 | 0 | 1.000 |
| Losasso, Pittsburgh* | 9 | 0 | 3 | 0 | 0 | 1.000 |
| Amenita, Cleveland | 2 | 1 | 1 | 0 | 0 | 1.000 |
| Robles, Pittsburgh | 2 | 0 | 2 | 0 | 0 | 1.000 |
| Anthony, Pittsburgh* | 4 | 1 | 1 | 0 | 0 | 1.000 |
| Seltzer, Chicago-AL* | 5 | 0 | 2 | 0 | 0 | 1.000 |
| Gottleber, Chicago-AL | 6 | 1 | 1 | 0 | 0 | 1.000 |
| Lundsford, St Louis* | 6 | 2 | 0 | 0 | 0 | 1.000 |
| Martinez, Kansas City | 10 | 1 | 1 | 0 | 0 | 1.000 |
| Rieger, St Louis* | 1 | 0 | 1 | 0 | 1 | 1.000 |
| Ney, Pittsburgh | 2 | 0 | 1 | 0 | 0 | 1.000 |
| Semerano, Pittsburgh | 2 | 1 | 0 | 0 | 0 | 1.000 |
| Saulnier, Cleveland* | 4 | 0 | 1 | 0 | 0 | 1.000 |
| Peterson, Pittsburgh* | 11 | 0 | 1 | 0 | 0 | 1.000 |
| Smith, Chicago-NL. | 10 | 4 | 14 | 1 | 2 | .947 |
| Ledbetter, Chi-NL | 12 | 4 | 13 | 1 | 1 | .944 |
| Lukevics, Chicago-AL | 8 | 6 | 10 | 1 | 1 | .941 |
| Joyce, Chicago-AL* | 14 | 4 | 12 | 1 | 1 | .941 |
| Tapia, Pittsburgh | 7 | 3 | 11 | 1 | 2 | .933 |
| Taylor, Chicago-NL | 12 | 5 | 9 | 1 | 1 | .933 |
| Hunziker, Chicago-AL | 14 | 3 | 11 | 1 | 2 | .933 |

PITCHERS—Continued

| Player and Club | G. | PO. | A. | E. | DP. | Pct. |
|---|---|---|---|---|---|---|
| Couch, Texas* | 10 | 3 | 7 | 1 | 0 | .909 |
| Grassano, St Louis | 11 | 3 | 7 | 1 | 0 | .909 |
| Oliver, St Louis | 11 | 4 | 14 | 2 | 1 | .900 |
| McMurray, Texas | 10 | 5 | 4 | 1 | 0 | .900 |
| Smith, Kansas City | 10 | 1 | 8 | 1 | 0 | .900 |
| Huusfeldt, Cleveland | 14 | 5 | 4 | 1 | 0 | .900 |
| Gray, St Louis | 12 | 2 | 14 | 2 | 1 | .889 |
| Burkett, Pittsburgh | 9 | 3 | 5 | 1 | 1 | .889 |
| Lucchesi, Chi-NL* | 10 | 3 | 5 | 1 | 0 | .889 |
| Cameron, Chicago-NL | 14 | 1 | 7 | 1 | 0 | .889 |
| Martinez, St Louis | 19 | 0 | 8 | 1 | 1 | .889 |
| Harvey, Cleveland | 10 | 1 | 13 | 2 | 1 | .875 |
| Holland, Pittsburgh* | 5 | 1 | 6 | 1 | 0 | .875 |
| Dennard, St Louis | 14 | 3 | 10 | 2 | 0 | .867 |
| Soroko, Texas | 14 | 3 | 16 | 3 | 0 | .864 |
| Wilson, Kansas City* | 10 | 1 | 5 | 1 | 0 | .857 |
| Marcial (Lira), Cleveland-Pittsburgh | 11 | 2 | 4 | 1 | 0 | .857 |
| Martin, Pittsburgh* | 11 | 0 | 6 | 1 | 0 | .857 |
| Kelly, Texas | 11 | 3 | 8 | 2 | 0 | .846 |
| Barreto, Chicago-NL | 18 | 1 | 10 | 2 | 0 | .846 |
| Farrell, Chicago-AL | 12 | 5 | 10 | 3 | 1 | .833 |
| Barr, Kansas City* | 7 | 2 | 3 | 1 | 0 | .833 |

| Player and Club | G. | PO. | A. | E. | DP. | Pct. |
|---|---|---|---|---|---|---|
| Wright, St Louis* | 11 | 6 | 8 | 3 | 1 | .824 |
| Handley, Chicago-AL | 14 | 5 | 7 | 3 | 0 | .800 |
| Moore, Chicago-NL | 4 | 1 | 3 | 1 | 1 | .800 |
| Marichal, Kan City | 11 | 2 | 2 | 1 | 0 | .800 |
| Madden, Chicago-AL | 14 | 7 | 7 | 4 | 1 | .778 |
| Poloni, Texas* | 4 | 1 | 6 | 2 | 0 | .778 |
| Johnson, Pittsburgh* | 10 | 1 | 5 | 2 | 0 | .750 |
| Gideon, Texas | 2 | 1 | 2 | 1 | 0 | .750 |
| Alvarez, Cleveland | 5 | 1 | 2 | 1 | 2 | .750 |
| Greene, Kansas City* | 10 | 3 | 3 | 1 | 0 | .750 |
| Yopp, Chicago-NL | 10 | 2 | 3 | 2 | 0 | .714 |
| Muckenthaler, Chi-AL | 11 | 1 | 6 | 3 | 0 | .700 |
| Bullard, Cleveland | 13 | 2 | 7 | 4 | 0 | .692 |
| Weber, Chicago-NL* | 20 | 0 | 9 | 4 | 0 | .692 |
| Patton, Texas* | 6 | 0 | 4 | 2 | 0 | .667 |
| Yraguen, Cleveland | 6 | 1 | 1 | 1 | 0 | .667 |
| Loehr, Chicago-AL | 12 | 1 | 1 | 1 | 0 | .667 |
| Burgess, Texas* | 9 | 0 | 5 | 4 | 0 | .556 |
| Hogle, Pittsburgh* | 4 | 0 | 1 | 1 | 0 | .500 |
| Propst, St Louis | 5 | 0 | 1 | 1 | 0 | .500 |
| Wihtol, Cleveland | 7 | 0 | 2 | 3 | 0 | .400 |
| Arthur, St Louis* | 16 | 0 | 1 | 2 | 0 | .333 |

The following pitchers had no recorded accepted chances; therefore are not listed in the fielding averages for that position: Guillermo, p; Hart, p; Lahey, p; Sansosti, p; Selbo, p; Torres, p; Valera, p. Thomas appeared as a designated hitter only.

CLUB PITCHING

| Club | G. | CG. | ShO. | Sv. | IP. | H. | R. | ER. | HR. | BB. | Int. BB. | HB. | SO. | WP. | Bk. | ERA. |
|---|---|---|---|---|---|---|---|---|---|---|---|---|---|---|---|---|
| Texas | 53 | 10 | 11 | 13 | 476 | 348 | 145 | 96 | 3 | 150 | 1 | 11 | 343 | 22 | 7 | 1.82 |
| Kansas City | 49 | 4 | 7 | 10 | 410 | 292 | 136 | 108 | 8 | 200 | 1 | 17 | 277 | 23 | 4 | 2.37 |
| Chicago-AL | 54 | 7 | 5 | 9 | 450 | 389 | 213 | 147 | 8 | 207 | 6 | 14 | 366 | 30 | 2 | 2.94 |
| Chicago-NL | 54 | 10 | 7 | 7 | 460 | 389 | 205 | 155 | 6 | 249 | 9 | 15 | 305 | 31 | 5 | 3.03 |
| Pittsburgh | 54 | 10 | 6 | 10 | 477 | 390 | 215 | 165 | 13 | 292 | 4 | 20 | 308 | 34 | 7 | 3.11 |
| Cleveland | 52 | 4 | 2 | 7 | 432 | 425 | 288 | 200 | 4 | 280 | 8 | 22 | 326 | 58 | 6 | 4.17 |
| St. Louis | 52 | 8 | 2 | 6 | 440 | 448 | 299 | 221 | 6 | 308 | 8 | 23 | 273 | 47 | 6 | 4.52 |

(Leading Qualifiers for Earned-Run Average Leadership—43 or More Innings)
*Throws lefthanded.

| Pitcher—Club | G. | GS. | CG. | ShO. | W. | L. | Sv. | Pct. | IP. | H. | R. | ER. | HR. | BB. | Int. BB. | HB. | SO. | WP. | ERA. |
|---|---|---|---|---|---|---|---|---|---|---|---|---|---|---|---|---|---|---|---|
| Kelly, Texas | 11 | 5 | 1 | 1 | 5 | 1 | 0 | .833 | 51 | 33 | 14 | 5 | 0 | 9 | 0 | 2 | 40 | 4 | 0.88 |
| Soroko, Texas | 14 | 4 | 3 | 0 | 6 | 0 | 3 | 1.000 | 55 | 39 | 7 | 6 | 0 | 9 | 0 | 3 | 46 | 1 | 0.98 |
| McMurray, Texas | 10 | 6 | 3 | 2 | 6 | 0 | 2 | 1.000 | 59 | 38 | 8 | 7 | 0 | 11 | 0 | 2 | 41 | 1 | 1.07 |
| Lukevics, Chi-AL | 8 | 6 | 2 | 0 | 4 | 1 | 0 | .800 | 43 | 36 | 10 | 6 | 1 | 6 | 0 | 1 | 31 | 4 | 1.26 |
| Joyce, Chi-AL* | 14 | 9 | 0 | 0 | 3 | 5 | 1 | .375 | 67 | 42 | 24 | 12 | 3 | 28 | 0 | 1 | 48 | 6 | 1.61 |
| Barreto, Chi-AL | 18 | 3 | 1 | 5 | 4 | 0 | 5 | .556 | 44 | 43 | 13 | 8 | 0 | 12 | 2 | 0 | 25 | 1 | 1.64 |
| Tapia, Pittsburgh | 7 | 6 | 4 | 1 | 4 | 2 | 0 | .667 | 56 | 43 | 19 | 11 | 1 | 22 | 0 | 1 | 31 | 7 | 1.77 |
| Skiba, Cleveland | 12 | 10 | 2 | 1 | 3 | 5 | 1 | .375 | 70 | 44 | 21 | 15 | 0 | 30 | 1 | 1 | 48 | 1 | 1.93 |
| Couch, Texas* | 10 | 9 | 0 | 0 | 3 | 1 | 0 | .750 | 43 | 31 | 16 | 10 | 0 | 27 | 0 | 1 | 27 | 1 | 2.09 |
| Smith, Chi-NL | 10 | 8 | 1 | 0 | 3 | 5 | 0 | .375 | 62 | 35 | 23 | 16 | 0 | 49 | 0 | 2 | 35 | 4 | 2.32 |

Departmental Leaders: G—Weber, 20; GS—Handley, 12; CG—Ledbetter, Tapia, 4; ShO—McMurray, 2; W—Barr, McCarthy, McMurray, Soroko, 6; L—Gray, Handley, 8; Sv—Arrington, Moock, Passalacqua, Weber, 4; Pct.—McMurray, Soroko, 1.000; IP—Handley, 77; H—Martin, 71; R—Oliver, 49; ER—Oliver, 40; HR—A. Johnson, 4; BB—L. Smith, 49; IBB—Ledbetter, N. Martinez, Yopp, 3; HB—Hunziker, D. Robinson, 4; SO—D. Robinson, 70; WP—Vaughn, 15.

(All Pitchers—Listed Alphabetically)

| Pitcher—Club | G. | GS. | CG. | ShO. | W. | L. | Sv. | Pct. | IP. | H. | R. | ER. | HR. | BB. | Int. BB. | HB. | SO. | WP. | ERA. |
|---|---|---|---|---|---|---|---|---|---|---|---|---|---|---|---|---|---|---|---|
| Alvarez, Cleveland | 5 | 3 | 0 | 1 | 0 | 1 | 0 | .500 | 22 | 21 | 13 | 6 | 0 | 14 | 0 | 1 | 13 | 3 | 2.45 |
| Amenita, Cleveland | 2 | 0 | 0 | 0 | 0 | 1 | 0 | .000 | 9 | 8 | 5 | 3 | 0 | 7 | 1 | 0 | 8 | 1 | 3.00 |
| Anthony, Pitt* | 4 | 0 | 0 | 0 | 0 | 1 | 2 | .000 | 3 | 1 | 2 | 1 | 0 | 3 | 0 | 0 | 4 | 0 | 3.00 |
| Arp, Cleveland | 6 | 3 | 0 | 0 | 0 | 2 | 0 | .000 | 14 | 13 | 14 | 7 | 0 | 14 | 0 | 2 | 10 | 3 | 4.50 |
| Arrington, Texas | 15 | 2 | 1 | 1 | 3 | 2 | 4 | .600 | 51 | 34 | 16 | 15 | 2 | 7 | 0 | 0 | 41 | 2 | 2.65 |
| Arthur, StL* | 16 | 1 | 0 | 0 | 0 | 2 | 0 | .000 | 27 | 31 | 23 | 13 | 1 | 24 | 1 | 1 | 24 | 3 | 4.33 |
| Attardi, Chi-AL* | 6 | 2 | 0 | 0 | 1 | 1 | 0 | .500 | 21 | 21 | 13 | 7 | 0 | 8 | 0 | 0 | 17 | 1 | 3.00 |
| Barr, Kansas City* | 7 | 7 | 1 | 1 | 6 | 1 | 0 | .857 | 40 | 24 | 4 | 3 | 1 | 16 | 0 | 2 | 39 | 2 | 0.68 |
| Barreto, Chi-NL | 18 | 3 | 1 | 5 | 4 | 0 | 5 | .556 | 44 | 43 | 13 | 8 | 0 | 12 | 2 | 0 | 25 | 1 | 1.64 |
| Bullard, Cleveland | 13 | 11 | 1 | 0 | 3 | 4 | 0 | .429 | 56 | 57 | 35 | 29 | 1 | 33 | 0 | 3 | 33 | 5 | 4.66 |
| Burkett, Pittsburgh | 9 | 8 | 1 | 1 | 3 | 2 | 1 | .800 | 38 | 27 | 18 | 8 | 0 | 15 | 1 | 1 | 32 | 2 | 1.89 |
| Burgess, Texas* | 9 | 5 | 0 | 0 | 4 | 1 | 0 | .800 | 38 | 27 | 18 | 13 | 1 | 32 | 0 | 3 | 21 | 3 | 1.76 |
| Cameron, Chi-NL | 14 | 1 | 0 | 0 | 0 | 0 | 0 | .000 | 31 | 33 | 23 | 19 | 1 | 22 | 0 | 3 | 21 | 1 | 5.52 |
| Couch, Texas* | 10 | 9 | 0 | 0 | 3 | 1 | 0 | .750 | 43 | 31 | 16 | 10 | 0 | 27 | 0 | 1 | 27 | 1 | 2.09 |
| Cvejdlik, Kan City | 9 | 8 | 1 | 1 | 4 | 3 | 1 | .571 | 50 | 40 | 19 | 17 | 0 | 16 | 1 | 0 | 46 | 0 | 3.06 |
| Dennard, StL | 14 | 6 | 1 | 0 | 2 | 4 | 1 | .333 | 49 | 42 | 36 | 20 | 0 | 39 | 0 | 4 | 31 | 7 | 3.67 |
| Farrell, Chi-AL | 12 | 7 | 2 | 0 | 1 | 6 | 2 | .143 | 56 | 56 | 29 | 20 | 1 | 19 | 0 | 1 | 36 | 4 | 3.21 |
| Gale, Kansas City | 9 | 4 | 0 | 0 | 3 | 1 | 0 | .750 | 33 | 23 | 11 | 10 | 0 | 16 | 1 | 2 | 18 | 2 | 2.73 |

| Pitcher—Club | G. | GS. | CG. | ShO. | W. | L. | Sv. | Pct. | IP. | H. | R. | ER. | HR. | BB. | Int. BB. | HB. | SO. | WP. | ERA. |
|---|---|---|---|---|---|---|---|---|---|---|---|---|---|---|---|---|---|---|---|
| Gideon, Texas .... | 2 | 2 | 1 | 1 | 2 | 0 | 1.000 | 16 | 3 | 0 | 0 | 0 | 1 | 0 | 1 | 14 | 0 | 0.00 |
| Gottleber, Chi-AL | 6 | 0 | 0 | 0 | 0 | 0 | 0 | .000 | 10 | 10 | 6 | 5 | 0 | 10 | 2 | 0 | 8 | 1 | 4.50 |
| Grassano, St Louis | 11 | 1 | 0 | 0 | 1 | 2 | 1 | .333 | 25 | 17 | 20 | 11 | 0 | 19 | 0 | 2 | 16 | 4 | 3.96 |
| Gray, St Louis ... | 12 | 11 | 1 | 0 | 1 | 8 | 0 | .111 | 69 | 69 | 44 | 36 | 0 | 41 | 1 | 3 | 46 | 4 | 4.70 |
| Greene, Kan City* | 10 | 2 | 0 | 0 | 2 | 2 | 0 | .500 | 26 | 20 | 10 | 6 | 1 | 16 | 0 | 0 | 30 | 3 | 2.08 |
| Guerrero, St Louis | 15 | 1 | 1 | 0 | 3 | 0 | 0 | .000 | 29 | 39 | 33 | 22 | 1 | 31 | 1 | 2 | 13 | 6 | 7.14 |
| Guillermo, St Louis | 2 | 0 | 0 | 0 | 0 | 0 | 0 | .000 | 2 | 5 | 7 | 4 | 0 | 5 | 0 | 1 | 1 | 0 | 18.00 |
| Handley, Chi-AL.. | 14 | 12 | 2 | 1 | 4 | 8 | 1 | .333 | 77 | 68 | 35 | 25 | 0 | 38 | 2 | 3 | 63 | 3 | 2.92 |
| Hanson, Cleveland.. | 6 | 0 | 0 | 1 | 2 | 0 | .333 | 15 | 19 | 6 | 6 | 0 | 6 | 0 | 0 | 13 | 0 | 3.86 |
| Hart, Kansas City | 2 | 1 | 0 | 0 | 1 | 0 | 0 | 1.000 | 8 | 3 | 1 | 0 | 0 | 5 | 0 | 0 | 10 | 0 | 0.00 |
| Harvey, Cleveland ..10 | 8 | 0 | 0 | 3 | 4 | 1 | .429 | 54 | 43 | 26 | 21 | 0 | 38 | 0 | 3 | 47 | 10 | 3.50 |
| Hogle, Pittsburgh* | 4 | 1 | 0 | 0 | 1 | 0 | .000 | 9 | 7 | 5 | 5 | 1 | 6 | 0 | 1 | 6 | 1 | 5.00 |
| Holland, Pitt* .... | 5 | 5 | 1 | 0 | 2 | 2 | 0 | .500 | 40 | 24 | 6 | 5 | 0 | 20 | 0 | 1 | 39 | 0 | 1.13 |
| Hunziker, Chi-AL | 14 | 6 | 1 | 0 | 2 | 4 | 0 | .333 | 55 | 57 | 31 | 24 | 0 | 19 | 0 | 6 | 40 | 3 | 3.93 |
| Huusfeldt, Clev ... | 14 | 2 | 0 | 0 | 1 | 4 | 1 | .200 | 35 | 35 | 21 | 13 | 0 | 23 | 1 | 1 | 17 | 2 | 3.34 |
| A. Johnson, Pitt*.. | 10 | 1 | 1 | 0 | 3 | 2 | 1 | .600 | 42 | 39 | 25 | 16 | 4 | 16 | 2 | 1 | 21 | 2 | 3.43 |
| D. Johnson, StL* | 7 | 7 | 1 | 0 | 3 | 2 | 0 | .600 | 41 | 33 | 9 | 9 | 0 | 30 | 1 | 2 | 22 | 2 | 1.98 |
| Joyce, Chicago-AL* | 14 | 9 | 0 | 0 | 3 | 5 | 1 | .375 | 67 | 42 | 24 | 12 | 3 | 28 | 0 | 1 | 48 | 6 | 1.61 |
| Kelly, Texas ...... | 11 | 5 | 1 | 1 | 5 | 1 | 0 | .833 | 51 | 33 | 14 | 5 | 0 | 9 | 0 | 2 | 40 | 4 | 0.88 |
| Lahey, Kansas City | 2 | 0 | 0 | 0 | 0 | 0 | 0 | .000 | 2 | 3 | 1 | 1 | 0 | 2 | 0 | 0 | 3 | 0 | 4.50 |
| Ledbetter, Chi-NL | 12 | 9 | 4 | 0 | 4 | 4 | 0 | .500 | 70 | 60 | 33 | 25 | 1 | 26 | 3 | 3 | 51 | 1 | 3.21 |
| Loehr, Chicago-AL | 12 | 5 | 0 | 0 | 2 | 1 | 3 | .667 | 27 | 17 | 9 | 5 | 0 | 9 | 0 | 0 | 29 | 0 | 1.67 |
| Losasso, Pitt* .... | 9 | 3 | 0 | 0 | 0 | 2 | 1 | .000 | 24 | 27 | 18 | 17 | 1 | 15 | 0 | 4 | 13 | 1 | 6.38 |
| Lucchesi, Chi-NL* | 10 | 6 | 1 | 1 | 1 | 3 | 0 | .250 | 39 | 42 | 23 | 20 | 0 | 23 | 0 | 0 | 30 | 3 | 4.62 |
| Lukevics, Chi-AL. | 8 | 6 | 2 | 0 | 4 | 1 | 0 | .800 | 43 | 36 | 10 | 6 | 1 | 6 | 0 | 1 | 31 | 4 | 1.26 |
| Lundsford, StL* .. | 6 | 0 | 0 | 0 | 1 | 0 | .000 | 13 | 14 | 8 | 6 | 0 | 7 | 0 | 1 | 6 | 1 | 4.15 |
| Madden, Chi-AL .. | 14 | 8 | 0 | 0 | 5 | 2 | 0 | .714 | 54 | 49 | 32 | 25 | 1 | 47 | 0 | 1 | 64 | 6 | 4.17 |
| Marcial (Lira), 8 Clev-3 Pitt.. | 11 | 2 | 0 | 0 | 1 | 1 | 0 | .000 | 28 | 21 | 24 | 17 | 1 | 29 | 0 | 1 | 23 | 4 | 5.46 |
| Marichal, Kan City | 11 | 2 | 0 | 0 | 1 | 1 | 0 | .500 | 33 | 27 | 10 | 6 | 1 | 7 | 0 | 1 | 11 | 1 | 1.64 |
| Martin, Pittsburgh* | 11 | 10 | 0 | 0 | 3 | 7 | 0 | .300 | 61 | 71 | 37 | 29 | 2 | 27 | 0 | 1 | 36 | 3 | 4.28 |
| N. Martinez, StL.. | 19 | 3 | 1 | 0 | 4 | 3 | 2 | .571 | 48 | 39 | 21 | 19 | 0 | 34 | 3 | 1 | 39 | 8 | 3.56 |
| O. Martinez, KC.. | 10 | 4 | 1 | 0 | 2 | 3 | 2 | .400 | 34 | 28 | 15 | 14 | 2 | 14 | 0 | 2 | 14 | 4 | 3.71 |
| McCarthy, Texas*.. | 11 | 11 | 1 | 1 | 6 | 2 | 0 | .750 | 67 | 47 | 25 | 21 | 1 | 34 | 0 | 1 | 44 | 4 | 2.82 |
| McMurray, Texas.. | 10 | 6 | 3 | 2 | 6 | 0 | 2 | 1.000 | 59 | 38 | 8 | 7 | 0 | 11 | 0 | 2 | 41 | 1 | 1.07 |
| Moock, Texas .... | 19 | 0 | 0 | 0 | 3 | 3 | 4 | .500 | 40 | 39 | 15 | 6 | 0 | 12 | 0 | 0 | 30 | 3 | 1.35 |
| Moore, Chi-NL .. | 4 | 1 | 0 | 0 | 0 | 2 | 0 | .000 | 15 | 17 | 15 | 9 | 0 | 5 | 0 | 1 | 12 | 1 | 5.40 |
| Muckenthaler, Chi-AL ...... | 11 | 1 | 0 | 0 | 0 | 2 | 0 | .000 | 25 | 24 | 22 | 16 | 1 | 17 | 1 | 1 | 20 | 2 | 5.76 |
| Ney, Pittsburgh .. | 2 | 0 | 0 | 0 | 0 | 0 | 0 | .000 | 1 | 1 | 0 | 0 | 0 | 2 | 0 | 0 | 0 | 0 | 0.00 |
| Oliver, St Louis .. | 11 | 8 | 1 | 0 | 2 | 5 | 0 | .286 | 55 | 60 | 49 | 40 | 1 | 37 | 1 | 4 | 18 | 3 | 6.55 |
| Passalacqua, KC .. | 15 | 0 | 0 | 0 | 3 | 2 | 4 | .600 | 30 | 19 | 8 | 8 | 0 | 10 | 0 | 3 | 18 | 2 | 2.40 |
| Patten, Texas* ... | 6 | 5 | 0 | 0 | 1 | 1 | 0 | .500 | 26 | 34 | 19 | 11 | 0 | 13 | 0 | 0 | 11 | 2 | 3.81 |
| Pedroza, Cleveland | 16 | 0 | 0 | 0 | 2 | 3 | 0 | .000 | 25 | 29 | 33 | 21 | 0 | 21 | 0 | 1 | 24 | 6 | 7.56 |
| Peterson, Pitt* ... | 11 | 2 | 0 | 0 | 0 | 0 | 0 | .000 | 24 | 11 | 11 | 9 | 1 | 30 | 0 | 0 | 16 | 4 | 3.38 |
| Poloni, Texas* ... | 4 | 4 | 0 | 0 | 2 | 1 | 0 | .667 | 30 | 23 | 12 | 7 | 0 | 12 | 0 | 0 | 17 | 2 | 2.10 |
| Propst, St Louis .. | 5 | 3 | 0 | 0 | 2 | 1 | 0 | .667 | 20 | 18 | 9 | 6 | 0 | 10 | 0 | 1 | 17 | 3 | 2.70 |
| Rieger, St Louis* | 1 | 1 | 1 | 1 | 1 | 0 | 0 | 1.000 | 9 | 4 | 0 | 0 | 0 | 0 | 0 | 1 | 5 | 1 | 0.00 |
| Rivas, Pittsburgh.. | 13 | 0 | 0 | 0 | 2 | 1 | 2 | .667 | 27 | 27 | 15 | 12 | 0 | 15 | 0 | 1 | 12 | 1 | 4.00 |
| D. Robinson, Pitt.. | 10 | 10 | 2 | 1 | 2 | 3 | 0 | .400 | 66 | 51 | 23 | 18 | 0 | 31 | 0 | 6 | 70 | 3 | 2.45 |
| Robles, Pittsburgh | 2 | 0 | 0 | 0 | 1 | 0 | .000 | 3 | 0 | 1 | 0 | 0 | 1 | 1 | 0 | 1 | 0 | 0.00 |
| Rogers, Chi-NL .. | 2 | 2 | 0 | 0 | 2 | 0 | 0 | 1.000 | 12 | 7 | 0 | 0 | 0 | 2 | 1 | 0 | 7 | 0 | 0.00 |
| Rosario, Kan City* | 6 | 3 | 0 | 0 | 3 | 1 | 2 | .750 | 23 | 13 | 6 | 2 | 0 | 17 | 0 | 2 | 9 | 3 | 0.78 |
| Sansosti, St Louis | 1 | 0 | 0 | 0 | 0 | 0 | 0 | .000 | 2 | 1 | 0 | 0 | 0 | 3 | 0 | 1 | 2 | 0 | 0.00 |
| Saulnier, Clev* ... | 4 | 2 | 0 | 0 | 1 | 1 | 0 | .500 | 16 | 15 | 10 | 10 | 1 | 13 | 1 | 1 | 15 | 0 | 5.63 |
| Seabol, Pittsburgh | 2 | 1 | 0 | 0 | 1 | 1 | 0 | .500 | 13 | 10 | 6 | 5 | 1 | 9 | 0 | 1 | 3 | 3 | 3.46 |
| Sebastian, Kan C | 4 | 1 | 0 | 0 | 0 | 1 | 0 | .000 | 10 | 6 | 1 | 1 | 0 | 4 | 0 | 2 | 6 | 0 | 0.90 |
| Selbo, Pittsburgh | 4 | 1 | 0 | 0 | 1 | 0 | 0 | 1.000 | 9 | 5 | 6 | 6 | 1 | 12 | 0 | 1 | 5 | 4 | 5.40 |
| Seltzer, Chi-AL*.. | 3 | 1 | 0 | 0 | 1 | 1 | 0 | .500 | 15 | 9 | 2 | 2 | 1 | 6 | 1 | 0 | 10 | 0 | 1.20 |
| Semerano, Pitt.... | 2 | 1 | 0 | 0 | 0 | 1 | 0 | .000 | 7 | 11 | 6 | 5 | 0 | 6 | 0 | 0 | 4 | 1 | 6.43 |
| Skiba, Cleveland .. | 12 | 10 | 2 | 1 | 3 | 5 | 1 | .375 | 70 | 44 | 21 | 15 | 0 | 30 | 1 | 1 | 48 | 1 | 1.93 |
| L. Smith,Chi-NL.. | 10 | 10 | 2 | 1 | 3 | 5 | 0 | .375 | 62 | 35 | 23 | 16 | 0 | 49 | 0 | 2 | 35 | 4 | 2.32 |
| Smith, Kan City.. | 10 | 5 | 0 | 0 | 1 | 0 | 0 | 1.000 | 37 | 28 | 9 | 5 | 1 | 14 | 0 | 1 | 21 | 0 | 1.22 |
| Soroko, Texas .... | 14 | 4 | 3 | 0 | 6 | 0 | 3 | 1.000 | 55 | 39 | 7 | 6 | 0 | 9 | 0 | 3 | 46 | 1 | 0.98 |
| Tapia, Pittsburgh.. | 7 | 6 | 4 | 1 | 4 | 2 | 0 | .667 | 56 | 43 | 11 | 11 | 1 | 22 | 0 | 1 | 31 | 7 | 1.77 |
| Taylor, Chicago-NL | 12 | 10 | 1 | 0 | 3 | 2 | 0 | .600 | 51 | 48 | 29 | 24 | 2 | 34 | 0 | 3 | 33 | 2 | 4.24 |
| Torres, Pittsburgh | 1 | 0 | 0 | 0 | 0 | 0 | 0 | .000 | 1 | 0 | 0 | 0 | 0 | 0 | 0 | 0 | 0 | 0 | 0.00 |
| Valera, Pittsburgh | 3 | 1 | 0 | 0 | 0 | 1 | 0 | .000 | 5 | 5 | 8 | 6 | 0 | 7 | 0 | 1 | 0 | 1 | 10.80 |
| Vaughn, Cleveland | 11 | 7 | 0 | 0 | 3 | 3 | 0 | .500 | 45 | 56 | 44 | 25 | 0 | 36 | 1 | 3 | 31 | 15 | 5.00 |
| Viera, Pittsburgh* | 11 | 0 | 0 | 0 | 2 | 3 | 2 | .400 | 32 | 23 | 10 | 8 | 1 | 29 | 1 | 1 | 19 | 0 | 2.25 |
| Vogel, Chicago-NL* | 6 | 5 | 1 | 0 | 3 | 2 | 0 | .600 | 37 | 19 | 8 | 3 | 0 | 20 | 0 | 0 | 19 | 3 | 0.73 |
| Von Ahnen, Chi-N* | 14 | 4 | 0 | 0 | 4 | 1 | 3 | .800 | 37 | 33 | 14 | 13 | 0 | 21 | 0 | 1 | 28 | 7 | 3.16 |
| Weber, Chi-NL*.. | 20 | 0 | 0 | 0 | 2 | 0 | 4 | 1.000 | 32 | 32 | 12 | 10 | 1 | 12 | 0 | 0 | 26 | 0 | 2.81 |
| Wilson, Kan City | 10 | 4 | 0 | 0 | 2 | 1 | 1 | .667 | 36 | 24 | 18 | 15 | 1 | 28 | 0 | 1 | 29 | 1 | 3.75 |
| Winters, Kan City | 11 | 8 | 1 | 0 | 2 | 3 | 0 | .400 | 47 | 34 | 23 | 20 | 1 | 35 | 0 | 2 | 23 | 5 | 3.83 |
| Wihtol, Cleveland.. | 7 | 4 | 1 | 0 | 3 | 1 | 0 | .750 | 38 | 44 | 26 | 18 | 1 | 18 | 2 | 2 | 44 | 5 | 4.26 |
| Wright, St Louis* | 11 | 10 | 1 | 0 | 1 | 6 | 0 | .143 | 50 | 66 | 40 | 34 | 3 | 28 | 0 | 0 | 33 | 5 | 6.12 |
| Yopp, Chi-NL .... | 10 | 3 | 0 | 0 | 3 | 1 | 0 | .750 | 31 | 20 | 12 | 8 | 1 | 23 | 0 | 3 | 18 | 2 | 2.32 |
| Yraguen, Cleveland | 6 | 0 | 0 | 0 | 3 | 0 | .000 | 15 | 24 | 14 | 13 | 0 | 9 | 1 | 3 | 7 | 3 | 7.80 |

BALKS—McCarthy, 4; Holland, Huusfeldt, 3 each; Arthur, Greene, L. Smith, 2 each; Arrington, Attardi, Dennard, Farrell, Grassano, Hanson, Harvey, Lucchesi, Martin, N. Martinez, O. Martinez, Peterson, Poloni, Propst, Rosario, Semerano, Soroko, Valera, Vogel, Von Ahnen, Yraguen, 1 each.

COMBINATION SHUTOUTS — Loehr-Joyce-Handley, Joyce-Gottleber-Muckenthaler, Lukevics-Hunziker, Madden-Loehr, Chicago AL; Rogers-Weber-Ledbetter, Rogers-Moore, Ledbetter-Cameron, Vogel-Barreto, Chicago NL; Vaughn-Pedroza, Cleveland; Martinez-Hart-Smith, Gale-Passalacqua, Barr-Sebastian, Cvejdlik-Smith-Passalacqua, Sebastian-Gale-Marichal-Passalacqua, Kansas City; Holland-Losasso, Burkett-Johnson-Robles, Burkett-Viera, Pittsburgh; Propst-Dennard, St. Louis; McCarthy-Moock, Couch-Arrington-McMurray; Gideon-Kelly, Couch-Arrington, Patten-Kelly-McMurray-Arrington-Moock-Soroko, Texas.

NO-HIT GAMES—McCarthy, Texas, defeated Chicago-AL, 5-0, July 24; Patten (4 innings), Kelly (1 inning), McMurray (1 inning), Arrington (1 inning), Moock (1 inning), Soroko (1 inning), Texas, defeated Chicago-AL, 1-0, August 29.

# *Pioneer League*

## ROOKIE CLASSIFICATION

### CHAMPIONSHIP WINNERS IN PREVIOUS YEARS

| | | |
|---|---|---|
| 1939—Twin Falls* ....... .581 | Great Falls (3rd)* . .559 | 1961—Boise ............. .638 |
| 1940—Salt Lake City .... .608 | 1952—Pocatello ......... .595 | Great Falls* ...... .571 |
| Ogden (4th)* .... .492 | Idaho Falls (2nd)* . .573 | 1962—Boise§ ........... .565 |
| 1941—Boise ............. .623 | 1953—Ogden ........... .679 | Billings† ......... .706 |
| Ogden (2nd)* .... .598 | Salt Lake C. (4th)* . .527 | 1963—Idaho Falls ....... .702 |
| 1942—Pocatello† ........ .690 | 1954—Salt Lake City .... .595 | Magic Valley† .... .643 |
| Boise ........... .683 | Great Falls (4th)* ... .530 | 1964—Treasure Valley ... .615 |
| 1943-44-45—Did not operate | 1955—Boise ............ .588 | 1965—Treasure Valley ... .530 |
| 1946—Twin Falls* ...... .585 | Magic Valley (4th)* . .489 | 1966—Ogden ........... .591 |
| Salt Lake City† ... .585 | 1956—Boise ............ .561 | 1967—Ogden ........... .521 |
| 1947—Salt Lake City .... .618 | 1957—Salt Lake City .... .650 | 1968—Ogden ........... .609 |
| Twin Falls† ...... .600 | Billings† ......... .582 | 1969—Ogden ........... .620 |
| 1948—Pocatello ........ .611 | 1958—Great Falls ....... .582 | 1970—Idaho Falls ....... .629 |
| Twin Falls (2nd)* . .595 | Boise† ............ .615 | 1971—Great Falls ....... .643 |
| 1949—Twin Falls ....... .624 | 1959—Boise ............ .633 | 1972—Billings ......... .694 |
| Pocatello (3rd)* .. .595 | Billings (2nd)* ... .523 | 1973—Billings ......... .629 |
| 1950—Pocatello ........ .635 | 1960—Boise† ........... .686 | 1974—Idaho Falls ....... .569 |
| Billings (3rd)* ... .571 | Idaho Falls ....... .650 | |
| 1951—Salt Lake City .... .618 | | |

*Won four-club playoff. †Won split-season playoff. ‡Ended first half in tie with Salt Lake City and won one-game playoff. §Ended first-half in tie with Billings and Great Falls and won playoff.

### STANDING OF CLUBS AT CLOSE OF SEASON, AUGUST 31

| Club | G.F. | I.F. | Leth. | Bil. | W. | L. | T. | Pct. | G.B. |
|---|---|---|---|---|---|---|---|---|---|
| Great Falls (Giants) ............... .. | 12 | 12 | 17 | 41 | 30 | 1 | .577 | .... |
| Idaho Falls (Angels) ...... | 12 | | 14 | 15 | 41 | 31 | 0 | .569 | ½ |
| Lethbridge (Expos) ...... | 12 | 10 | .. | 13 | 35 | 37 | 0 | .486 | 6½ |
| Billings (Reds) .................. | 6 | 9 | 11 | .. | 26 | 45 | 1 | .366 | 15 |

Major league affiliations in parentheses.

Playoff—None.

Regular-Season Attendance—Billings, 30,488; Great Falls, 30,892; Idaho Falls, 27,430; Lethbridge, 31,719. Total, 120,529. No playoff. No All-Star Game.

All-Star Team: 1B—Weicker, Billings; 2B—Brewster, Idaho Falls; 3B—Grimes, Great Falls; SS—Anderson, Idaho Falls; OF—Dawson, Lethbridge; Dyes, Lethbridge; Elrod, Great Falls; C—Cato, Great Falls; P—Perez, Idaho Falls; Schmidt, Great Falls.

Managers: Billings—James Hoff; Great Falls—Ernest Rodriguez; Idaho Falls—Larry Himes; Lethbridge—Van Kelly.

(Compiled by William J. Weiss, League Statistician, San Mateo, Calif.)

### CLUB BATTING

| Club | G. | AB. | R. | OR. | H. | TB. | 2B. | 3B. | HR. | RBI. | SH. | SF. | BB. | Int. BB. | HP. | SO. | SB. | CS. | LOB. | Pct. |
|---|---|---|---|---|---|---|---|---|---|---|---|---|---|---|---|---|---|---|---|---|
| Great Falls | ....72 | 2380 | 371 | 309 | 656 | 876 | 119 | 16 | 23 | 312 | 35 | 20 | 287 | 9 | 23 | 401 | 72 | 21 | 594 | .276 |
| Idaho Falls | ....72 | 2331 | 387 | 350 | 633 | 827 | 76 | 32 | 18 | 299 | 45 | 15 | 346 | 17 | 13 | 452 | 155 | 56 | 554 | .272 |
| Lethbridge | .....72 | 2449 | 403 | 437 | 659 | 950 | 115 | 28 | 40 | 338 | 26 | 23 | 329 | 17 | 25 | 553 | 97 | 38 | 588 | .269 |
| Billings | ........72 | 2318 | 324 | 389 | 599 | 768 | 88 | 12 | 19 | 276 | 31 | 21 | 252 | 7 | 15 | 396 | 110 | 26 | 533 | .258 |

### INDIVIDUAL BATTING
(Leading Qualifiers for Batting Championship—194 or More Plate Appearances)
*Bats lefthanded. †Switch-hitter.

| Player and Club | G. | AB. | R. | H. | TB. | 2B. | 3B. | HR. | RBI. | SH. | SF. | BB. | HP. | SO. | SB. | CS. | Pct. |
|---|---|---|---|---|---|---|---|---|---|---|---|---|---|---|---|---|---|
| Brewester, Richard, Idaho F* | 72 | 274 | 61 | 95 | 107 | 8 | 2 | 0 | 24 | 7 | 0 | 49 | 1 | 15 | 34 | 18 | .347 |
| Crowley, Raymond, Leth* | .....46 | 151 | 31 | 51 | 82 | 15 | 2 | 4 | 32 | 0 | 1 | 47 | 0 | 16 | 7 | 4 | .338 |
| Dawson, Andre, Lethbridge | ...72 | 300 | 52 | 99 | 166 | 14 | 7 | 13 | 50 | 2 | 5 | 23 | 6 | 59 | 11 | 10 | .330 |
| Elrod, James, Great Falls | ...68 | 265 | 37 | 87 | 118 | 26 | 1 | 1 | 47 | 1 | 4 | 20 | 3 | 23 | 2 | 0 | .328 |
| Dyes, Andrew, Lethbridge | ...71 | 290 | 44 | 94 | 118 | 7 | 1 | 5 | 58 | 2 | 1 | 30 | 1 | 61 | 40 | 5 | .324 |
| Waller, Reginald, Billings | ...68 | 234 | 40 | 74 | 89 | 7 | 1 | 2 | 24 | 3 | 3 | 22 | 3 | 27 | 10 | 3 | .316 |
| Weicker, George, Billings | ...72 | 244 | 49 | 76 | 124 | 23 | 2 | 7 | 50 | 0 | 1 | 55 | 1 | 28 | 6 | 0 | .311 |
| Wright, Kenneth F., I F | ....66 | 219 | 45 | 65 | 90 | 8 | 4 | 3 | 30 | 0 | 3 | 32 | 1 | 37 | 17 | 11 | .297 |
| Knox, John T., Idaho F* | .....61 | 164 | 26 | 48 | 60 | 6 | 3 | 0 | 22 | 3 | 1 | 34 | 2 | 34 | 12 | 7 | .293 |
| Anderson, James L., I F | ....71 | 253 | 42 | 73 | 88 | 3 | 6 | 0 | 27 | 6 | 2 | 53 | 0 | 34 | 20 | 9 | .289 |

Departmental Leaders: G—Brewster, Clark, Dawson, Paris, Rayford, Weicker, 72; AB—Dawson, 300; R—Brewster, 61; H—Dawson, 99; TB—Dawson, 166; 2B—Elrod, 26; 3B—Clark, 9; HR—Dawson, 13; RBI—Dyes, 58; SH—Brewster, Paris, 7; SF—Dawson, Hopper, 5; BB—Paris, Weicker, 55; HP—Dawson, 6; SO—Dyes, 61; SB—Dyes, 40; CS—Brewster, 18.

(All Players—Listed Alphabetically)

| Player and Club | G. | AB. | R. | H. | TB. | 2B. | 3B. | HR. | RBI. | SH. | SF. | BB. | HP. | SO. | SB. | CS. | Pct. |
|---|---|---|---|---|---|---|---|---|---|---|---|---|---|---|---|---|---|
| Anderson, David, Great F...19 | 10 | 2 | 1 | 1 | 0 | 0 | 0 | 1 | 2 | 0 | 0 | 0 | 4 | 0 | 0 | | .100 |
| Anderson, James L., I F.....71 | 253 | 42 | 73 | 88 | 3 | 6 | 0 | 27 | 6 | 2 | 53 | 0 | 34 | 20 | 9 | .289 |
| Ayers, James, Great Falls ...10 | 25 | 3 | 6 | 8 | 2 | 0 | 0 | 2 | 0 | 0 | 0 | 0 | 6 | 1 | 0 | .240 |
| Baby, James, Lethbridge*...12 | 20 | 4 | 3 | 3 | 0 | 0 | 0 | 0 | 2 | 0 | 0 | 0 | 11 | 0 | 0 | .150 |
| Baggett, William, Billings ...23 | 46 | 7 | 9 | 11 | 0 | 1 | 0 | 6 | 0 | 0 | 2 | 0 | 11 | 2 | 0 | .196 |
| Barnicle, Theodore, G F†...8 | 14 | 0 | 3 | 4 | 1 | 0 | 0 | 1 | 2 | 0 | 0 | 0 | 7 | 0 | 0 | .214 |
| Barrios, Jose, Great Falls ...47 | 166 | 21 | 46 | 63 | 7 | 2 | 2 | 26 | 1 | 2 | 15 | 1 | 48 | 5 | 0 | .277 |
| Berthiaume, Gerald, Bil*...24 | 75 | 10 | 22 | 24 | 2 | 0 | 0 | 2 | 0 | 1 | 3 | 0 | 10 | 1 | 1 | .293 |
| Bhagwat, Thomas, Great F..32 | 116 | 23 | 37 | 50 | 6 | 2 | 1 | 27 | 0 | 3 | 16 | 2 | 5 | 0 | 1 | .319 |
| Bohr, Robert, Lethbridge ....1 | 2 | 1 | 1 | 1 | 0 | 0 | 0 | 0 | 0 | 0 | 1 | 0 | 1 | 0 | 0 | .500 |
| Boyle, Gary, Idaho Falls ...13 | 18 | 6 | 5 | 7 | 2 | 0 | 0 | 6 | 4 | 0 | 2 | 0 | 2 | 0 | 0 | .278 |
| Brewster, Richard, Idaho F*..72 | 274 | 61 | 95 | 107 | 8 | 2 | 0 | 24 | 7 | 0 | 49 | 1 | 15 | 34 | 18 | .347 |
| Brown, Jimmy, Idaho Falls ...10 | 13 | 3 | 3 | 3 | 0 | 0 | 0 | 2 | 0 | 0 | 0 | 0 | 7 | 0 | 0 | .231 |
| Brown, Scott E., Billings ...10 | 2 | 0 | 0 | 0 | 0 | 0 | 0 | 0 | 0 | 0 | 0 | 0 | 2 | 0 | 0 | .000 |
| Calderon, Eduardo, Great F..11 | 11 | 2 | 2 | 2 | 0 | 0 | 0 | 1 | 1 | 0 | 1 | 0 | 5 | 0 | 0 | .182 |
| Case, William, Idaho Falls... 3 | 1 | 0 | 0 | 0 | 0 | 0 | 0 | 0 | 0 | 0 | 0 | 0 | 1 | 0 | 0 | .000 |
| Cato, Wayne, Great Falls ...50 | 164 | 26 | 61 | 82 | 10 | 1 | 3 | 26 | 1 | 3 | 13 | 1 | 12 | 3 | 0 | .372 |
| Chapman, Bert, Great Falls..4 | 0 | 1 | 0 | 0 | 0 | 0 | 0 | 0 | 0 | 0 | 0 | 0 | 0 | 0 | 0 | .000 |
| Chaus, Michael, Idaho F.....6 | 7 | 0 | 0 | 0 | 0 | 0 | 0 | 0 | 0 | 0 | 1 | 0 | 7 | 0 | 0 | .000 |
| Cipolla, Mitchell, Leth......50 | 161 | 26 | 46 | 81 | 7 | 2 | 8 | 32 | 0 | 3 | 31 | 2 | 31 | 1 | 0 | .286 |
| Clark, Robert, Idaho Falls ...72 | 253 | 43 | 64 | 101 | 7 | 9 | 4 | 38 | 2 | 2 | 34 | 1 | 58 | 22 | 2 | .253 |
| Clear, Mark, Idaho Falls ....13 | 5 | 0 | 0 | 0 | 0 | 0 | 0 | 0 | 0 | 0 | 0 | 0 | 2 | 0 | 0 | .000 |
| Cliburn, Stanley, Idaho F....57 | 179 | 33 | 45 | 55 | 10 | 0 | 0 | 25 | 3 | 2 | 41 | 2 | 23 | 8 | 1 | .251 |
| Connors, Stephen, Idaho F...35 | 80 | 12 | 19 | 22 | 3 | 0 | 0 | 4 | 1 | 0 | 9 | 2 | 9 | 2 | 0 | .238 |
| Cooper, Michael, Leth ...... 9 | 26 | 5 | 7 | 7 | 0 | 0 | 0 | 4 | 0 | 0 | 3 | 0 | 5 | 0 | 0 | .269 |
| Crowley, Raymond, Leth*...46 | 151 | 31 | 51 | 82 | 15 | 2 | 4 | 32 | 0 | 1 | 47 | 0 | 16 | 7 | 4 | .338 |
| Dahl, Gregory, Billings ....63 | 206 | 29 | 52 | 85 | 15 | 0 | 6 | 40 | 2 | 1 | 24 | 4 | 58 | 1 | 1 | .252 |
| Daughtry, Mark, Great F ...11 | 23 | 1 | 4 | 5 | 1 | 0 | 0 | 1 | 0 | 0 | 2 | 0 | 2 | 1 | 0 | .174 |
| Davidson, Randall, Billings..19 | 51 | 11 | 12 | 17 | 3 | 1 | 0 | 5 | 1 | 1 | 5 | 0 | 1 | 2 | 0 | .235 |
| Davis, George E., Great F....33 | 84 | 8 | 18 | 20 | 2 | 0 | 0 | 8 | 0 | 1 | 1 | 1 | 14 | 1 | 0 | .214 |
| Dawson, Andre, Lethbridge ..72 | 300 | 52 | 99 | 166 | 14 | 7 | 13 | 50 | 2 | 5 | 23 | 6 | 59 | 11 | 10 | .330 |
| D'Innocenzio, Richard, G F..4 | 7 | 2 | 2 | 3 | 1 | 0 | 0 | 1 | 0 | 0 | 0 | 0 | 1 | 0 | 0 | .286 |
| Dyes, Andrew, Lethbridge...71 | 290 | 44 | 94 | 118 | 7 | 1 | 5 | 58 | 2 | 1 | 30 | 1 | 61 | 40 | 5 | .324 |
| Eddy, Steven, Idaho Falls ...11 | 20 | 1 | 3 | 3 | 0 | 0 | 0 | 1 | 0 | 0 | 0 | 0 | 13 | 0 | 0 | .150 |
| Edge, Evan, Billings*......21 | 61 | 7 | 17 | 21 | 4 | 0 | 0 | 8 | 3 | 0 | 7 | 0 | 11 | 1 | 0 | .279 |
| Eickenhorst, Randall, Leth ...71 | 293 | 49 | 81 | 107 | 10 | 5 | 2 | 33 | 1 | 2 | 15 | 0 | 44 | 10 | 3 | .276 |
| Elrod, James, Great Falls*...68 | 265 | 37 | 87 | 118 | 26 | 1 | 1 | 47 | 1 | 4 | 20 | 3 | 23 | 2 | 0 | .328 |
| Ferrara, Salvatore, Billings ...11 | 9 | 2 | 2 | 2 | 0 | 0 | 0 | 1 | 1 | 0 | 2 | 1 | 1 | 0 | 0 | .222 |
| Finlayson, Michael, Leth...10 | 15 | 3 | 3 | 4 | 1 | 0 | 0 | 2 | 1 | 0 | 2 | 0 | 4 | 0 | 0 | .200 |
| Fleury, Denis, Lethbridge...37 | 85 | 8 | 23 | 27 | 0 | 2 | 0 | 4 | 0 | 0 | 3 | 0 | 23 | 0 | 0 | .271 |
| Flores, Martin, Great F*... 2 | 5 | 0 | 0 | 0 | 0 | 0 | 0 | 0 | 0 | 0 | 0 | 0 | 2 | 0 | 0 | .000 |
| Fredrickson, David, Leth ...18 | 13 | 4 | 2 | 2 | 0 | 0 | 0 | 4 | 2 | 0 | 2 | 1 | 6 | 0 | 0 | .154 |
| Gerdes, Robert, Lethbridge ...13 | 19 | 1 | 1 | 1 | 0 | 0 | 0 | 0 | 0 | 0 | 2 | 0 | 1 | 1 | 0 | .053 |
| Goldetsky, Lawrence, Leth ...44 | 134 | 24 | 30 | 40 | 8 | 1 | 0 | 13 | 0 | 1 | 25 | 3 | 28 | 5 | 3 | .224 |
| Gonzalez, Joseph, Leth ..... 5 | 14 | 2 | 3 | 3 | 0 | 0 | 0 | 1 | 0 | 0 | 1 | 0 | 4 | 0 | 0 | .214 |
| Grabowski, Michael, Leth ...12 | 22 | 0 | 1 | 1 | 0 | 0 | 0 | 0 | 0 | 1 | 0 | 0 | 14 | 0 | 0 | .045 |
| Grana, Anthony, Billings ...15 | 7 | 0 | 0 | 0 | 0 | 0 | 0 | 0 | 0 | 0 | 2 | 0 | 1 | 0 | 0 | .000 |
| Grimes, Steven, Great F.....60 | 175 | 34 | 50 | 78 | 10 | 3 | 4 | 28 | 2 | 4 | 29 | 3 | 38 | 4 | 1 | .286 |
| Groves, Lawrence, Billings*...10 | 11 | 0 | 2 | 2 | 0 | 0 | 0 | 0 | 0 | 0 | 2 | 0 | 1 | 1 | 0 | .182 |
| Halvarson, Dale, Leth ...... 6 | 10 | 1 | 3 | 4 | 1 | 0 | 0 | 0 | 1 | 0 | 1 | 0 | 5 | 0 | 0 | .300 |
| Harshey, Chris, Lethbridge ..30 | 8 | 0 | 2 | 2 | 0 | 0 | 0 | 0 | 0 | 0 | 0 | 0 | 2 | 0 | 0 | .250 |
| Herron, Donald, Lethbridge ..10 | 1 | 0 | 0 | 0 | 0 | 0 | 0 | 0 | 0 | 0 | 0 | 0 | 0 | 0 | 0 | .000 |
| Hill, Rickey, Lethbridge...39 | 106 | 7 | 23 | 32 | 4 | 1 | 1 | 11 | 0 | 1 | 7 | 0 | 25 | 1 | 1 | .217 |
| Hopper, Mark, Billings ....70 | 254 | 29 | 69 | 75 | 6 | 0 | 0 | 25 | 1 | 5 | 14 | 1 | 15 | 8 | 2 | .272 |
| Howard, Garry, Great Falls†... 4 | 19 | 4 | 5 | 5 | 0 | 0 | 0 | 2 | 0 | 0 | 1 | 1 | 6 | 0 | 1 | .263 |
| Hughes, Timothy, Great Falls 7 | 11 | 3 | 3 | 5 | 2 | 0 | 0 | 3 | 0 | 0 | 0 | 0 | 3 | 1 | 0 | .273 |
| Huntington, John, Billings*..34 | 25 | 4 | 7 | 11 | 1 | 0 | 1 | 4 | 0 | 0 | 3 | 0 | 7 | 2 | 1 | .280 |
| Ingraham, Patrick, Billings...52 | 112 | 13 | 25 | 26 | 1 | 0 | 0 | 10 | 1 | 0 | 11 | 0 | 35 | 5 | 3 | .223 |
| Jensen, Kelly, Billings ....23 | 32 | 2 | 11 | 13 | 0 | 1 | 0 | 7 | 0 | 0 | 3 | 0 | 8 | 1 | 1 | .344 |
| Johnson, Walter, Leth*....23 | 62 | 15 | 13 | 18 | 5 | 0 | 0 | 5 | 0 | 1 | 14 | 2 | 25 | 2 | 1 | .210 |
| Kay, Jeffrey, Lethbridge*...14 | 5 | 2 | 0 | 0 | 0 | 0 | 0 | 0 | 0 | 0 | 0 | 2 | 0 | 0 | 0 | .000 |
| Kelly, Rafael, Idaho Falls...58 | 158 | 25 | 53 | 58 | 1 | 2 | 0 | 23 | 0 | 0 | 28 | 2 | 33 | 14 | 1 | .335 |
| Knose, Mark, Lethbridge ...14 | 19 | 8 | 7 | 12 | 3 | 1 | 0 | 6 | 2 | 0 | 1 | 0 | 5 | 0 | 0 | .368 |
| Knox, John T., Idaho Falls*.61 | 164 | 26 | 48 | 60 | 6 | 3 | 0 | 22 | 3 | 1 | 34 | 2 | 34 | 12 | 7 | .293 |
| Kulesza, Gregory, Idaho F...10 | 0 | 2 | 2 | 0 | 0 | 0 | 0 | 0 | 0 | 0 | 0 | 0 | 0 | 0 | 0 | .200 |
| LaFave, Robert, Idaho Falls..23 | 23 | 3 | 4 | 5 | 1 | 0 | 0 | 2 | 0 | 0 | 3 | 0 | 8 | 0 | 0 | .174 |
| Lansford, Carney, Idaho F.. 8 | 27 | 5 | 6 | 11 | 2 | 0 | 1 | 1 | 1 | 0 | 2 | 0 | 6 | 2 | 0 | .222 |
| Lee, Dennis E., Great Falls..30 | 65 | 16 | 17 | 22 | 1 | 2 | 0 | 10 | 1 | 1 | 17 | 0 | 12 | 4 | 1 | .262 |
| Lorick, Arthur, Idaho Falls..36 | 83 | 6 | 18 | 27 | 3 | 0 | 2 | 18 | 0 | 2 | 2 | 1 | 24 | 3 | 0 | .217 |
| McMullen, Dale, Lethbridge..45 | 131 | 17 | 32 | 55 | 11 | 0 | 4 | 22 | 0 | 1 | 24 | 1 | 52 | 5 | 1 | .244 |
| McNally, Patrick, Idaho F*..42 | 136 | 21 | 36 | 62 | 9 | 1 | 5 | 24 | 1 | 1 | 22 | 1 | 19 | 1 | 2 | .265 |
| Merritt, Michael, Idaho Falls 14 | 30 | 5 | 3 | 3 | 1 | 0 | 1 | 3 | 3 | 0 | 5 | 0 | 12 | 0 | 0 | .100 |
| Miles, Arthur, Lethbridge*..64 | 226 | 39 | 52 | 80 | 15 | 2 | 3 | 22 | 1 | 0 | 48 | 2 | 57 | 7 | 6 | .230 |
| Miller, Mark J., Billings ...53 | 100 | 7 | 23 | 28 | 5 | 0 | 0 | 9 | 1 | 2 | 5 | 1 | 28 | 1 | 0 | .230 |
| Mills, Alan, Great Falls ...47 | 152 | 22 | 47 | 65 | 6 | 0 | 4 | 24 | 1 | 2 | 25 | 2 | 22 | 0 | 1 | .309 |
| Mitchell, Howard, Great F..66 | 235 | 48 | 67 | 92 | 14 | 1 | 3 | 31 | 5 | 4 | 38 | 2 | 33 | 8 | 5 | .285 |
| Moline, Stanley, Great Falls.18 | 14 | 0 | 2 | 2 | 0 | 0 | 0 | 0 | 0 | 0 | 0 | 0 | 10 | 0 | 0 | .143 |
| Moore, Calvin, Great Falls.. 9 | 36 | 10 | 17 | 21 | 2 | 1 | 0 | 55 | 0 | 1 | 5 | 0 | 3 | 5 | 1 | .472 |

| Player and Club | G. | AB. | R. | H. | TB. | 2B. | 3B. | HR. | RBI. | SH. | SF. | BB. | HP. | SO. | SB. | CS. | Pct. |
|---|---|---|---|---|---|---|---|---|---|---|---|---|---|---|---|---|---|
| Moore, Charles A., Billings | 18 | 20 | 0 | 5 | 6 | 1 | 0 | 0 | 4 | 3 | 0 | 1 | 0 | 3 | 2 | 0 | .250 |
| Moretto, Tony, Billings* | 46 | 154 | 15 | 36 | 50 | 2 | 3 | 2 | 24 | 1 | 1 | 20 | 1 | 22 | 6 | 3 | .234 |
| Morrow, Stacy, Billings | 42 | 137 | 23 | 37 | 46 | 6 | 0 | 1 | 9 | 0 | 0 | 21 | 2 | 23 | 14 | 5 | .270 |
| Moskau, Paul, Billings | 2 | 3 | 0 | 1 | 1 | 0 | 0 | 0 | 0 | 0 | 0 | 0 | 0 | 1 | 0 | 0 | .333 |
| Mraz, Donald, Idaho Falls | 13 | 29 | 1 | 2 | 2 | 0 | 0 | 0 | 3 | 0 | 1 | 0 |  | 18 | 0 | 1 | .069 |
| Muhlstock, Andrew, Great F. | 3 | 1 | 0 | 0 | 0 | 0 | 0 | 0 | 0 | 0 | 0 | 1 | 0 | 0 | 0 | 0 | .000 |
| Murray, Richard, Great Falls | 25 | 85 | 8 | 23 | 30 | 2 | 1 | 1 | 14 | 0 | 1 | 4 | 1 | 12 | 1 | 0 | .271 |
| Nelms, A. Chris, Billings | 49 | 169 | 34 | 47 | 52 | 3 | 1 | 0 | 15 | 2 | 0 | 20 | 1 | 22 | 21 | 3 | .278 |
| Newby, Kevin, Lethbridge* | 43 | 67 | 12 | 15 | 19 | 2 | 1 | 0 | 2 | 0 | 0 | 4 | 0 | 17 | 5 | 1 | .224 |
| Osborne, Steven, Great Falls | 34 | 72 | 7 | 11 | 15 | 1 | 0 | 1 | 7 | 1 | 1 | 1 | 1 | 16 | 2 | 0 | .153 |
| Paris, Bret, Great Falls† | 72 | 260 | 49 | 62 | 74 | 7 | 1 | 1 | 11 | 7 | 0 | 55 | 1 | 55 | 32 | 8 | .238 |
| Pastore, Frank, Billings | 15 | 28 | 0 | 1 | 1 | 0 | 0 | 0 | 1 | 0 | 0 | 3 | 0 | 17 | 0 | 0 | .036 |
| Pekarcik, Lawrence, Billings | 17 | 27 | 1 | 5 | 6 | 1 | 0 | 0 | 1 | 2 | 0 | 0 |  | 4 | 1 | 0 | .185 |
| Perez, Carlos, Idaho Falls | 13 | 35 | 5 | 6 | 6 | 0 | 0 | 0 | 1 | 0 | 0 | 0 |  | 4 | 1 | 0 | .171 |
| Peterson, Timothy, Great F. | 4 | 2 | 0 | 0 | 0 | 0 | 0 | 0 | 4 | 1 | 0 | 3 | 0 | 11 | 0 | 0 | .000 |
| Plent, Bernard, Billings | 24 | 20 | 2 | 6 | 7 | 1 | 0 | 0 | 0 | 0 | 0 | 0 |  | 1 | 0 | 0 | .300 |
| Quigley, Jerry, Idaho Falls | 18 | 11 | 1 | 2 | 2 | 0 | 0 | 0 | 0 | 0 | 0 | 3 | 0 | 6 | 0 | 0 | .182 |
| Ratzer, Stephen, Lethbridge | 30 | 24 | 5 | 6 | 6 | 0 | 0 | 0 | 5 | 3 | 0 | 0 |  | 3 | 0 | 0 | .250 |
| Rayford, Floyd, Idaho Falls | 72 | 272 | 43 | 77 | 105 | 12 | 5 | 2 | 43 | 5 | 2 | 23 | 2 | 56 | 24 | 5 | .283 |
| Richter, Gary, Billings | 65 | 215 | 31 | 50 | 60 | 6 | 2 | 0 | 24 | 5 | 4 | 17 | 0 | 27 | 22 | 1 | .233 |
| Rothschild, Lawrence, Billings | 6 | 1 | 0 | 0 | 0 | 0 | 0 | 0 | 0 | 0 | 0 | 0 | 0 | 0 | 0 | 0 | .000 |
| Rowland, Michael, Great F. | 5 | 10 | 2 | 1 | 1 | 0 | 0 | 0 | 0 | 0 | 0 | 1 | 0 | 3 | 0 | 0 | .100 |
| Ryan, Patrick, Great Falls | 31 | 90 | 7 | 20 | 24 | 4 | 0 | 0 | 10 | 3 | 2 | 13 | 0 | 4 | 5 | 1 | .222 |
| Ryan, Timothy, Idaho Falls* | 20 | 5 | 0 | 1 | 1 | 0 | 0 | 0 | 1 | 0 | 0 | 0 |  | 2 | 0 | 0 | .200 |
| Schaefer, Douglas, Great F. | 14 | 32 | 4 | 8 | 13 | 2 | 0 | 1 | 2 | 2 | 0 | 4 | 0 | 7 | 0 | 0 | .250 |
| Schmidt, E. Eugene, Great F | 14 | 33 | 5 | 1 | 1 | 0 | 0 | 0 | 1 | 0 | 0 | 7 | 0 | 10 | 0 | 0 | .030 |
| Schoenhaus, Edward, Great F | 16 | 60 | 12 | 19 | 22 | 1 | 1 | 0 | 4 | 0 | 0 | 7 | 0 | 10 | 0 | 0 | .317 |
| Steck, David, Idaho Falls | 13 | 26 | 0 | 2 | 2 | 0 | 0 | 0 | 1 | 1 | 0 | 6 | 0 | 5 | 2 | 1 | .077 |
| Steen, Rick, Great Falls | 21 | 10 | 0 | 2 | 3 | 1 | 0 | 0 | 1 | 0 | 1 | 0 |  | 15 | 0 | 0 | .200 |
| Stuthard, Timothy, Leth. | 1 | 1 | 0 | 0 | 0 | 0 | 0 | 0 | 0 | 0 | 0 |  |  | 5 | 0 | 0 | .000 |
| Sucarichi, George, Billings | 20 | 48 | 7 | 9 | 10 | 1 | 0 | 0 | 6 | 2 | 2 | 4 | 0 | 1 | 0 | 0 | .188 |
| Trickey, Brad, Lethbridge | 53 | 166 | 23 | 37 | 50 | 7 | 3 | 0 | 15 | 3 | 2 | 36 | 2 | 27 | 2 | 3 | .223 |
| Uebbing, Michael, Lethbridge | 15 | 7 | 0 | 0 | 0 | 0 | 0 | 0 | 0 | 1 | 0 | 0 |  | 4 | 0 | 0 | .000 |
| Waller, Reginald, Billings | 68 | 234 | 40 | 74 | 89 | 7 | 1 | 2 | 24 | 3 | 3 | 22 | 3 | 27 | 10 | 3 | .316 |
| Warren, Frederick, Billings | 15 | 26 | 1 | 1 | 1 | 0 | 0 | 0 | 0 | 0 | 0 | 2 | 0 | 9 | 1 | 3 | .038 |
| Watson, Steven E., Great F. | 13 | 16 | 1 | 4 | 5 | 1 | 0 | 0 | 2 | 0 | 1 | 0 |  | 4 | 0 | 0 | .250 |
| Weatherford, Robert, Leth. | 5 | 4 | 0 | 0 | 0 | 0 | 0 | 0 | 0 | 0 | 0 | 0 |  | 3 | 0 | 0 | .000 |
| Weicker, George, Billings | 72 | 244 | 49 | 76 | 124 | 23 | 2 | 7 | 50 | 0 | 1 | 55 | 1 | 28 | 6 | 0 | .311 |
| Williams, Wayne A., Idaho F | 2 | 1 | 0 | 1 | 1 | 0 | 0 | 0 | 0 | 0 | 0 | 0 | 0 | 0 | 0 | 0 | 1.000 |
| Wirth, Alan, Great Falls | 14 | 39 | 4 | 10 | 13 | 3 | 0 | 0 | 3 | 0 | 2 | 0 |  | 11 | 0 | 0 | .256 |
| Wood, W. Christopher, Leth. | 20 | 66 | 17 | 25 | 31 | 6 | 0 | 0 | 15 | 0 | 1 | 8 | 0 | 5 | 1 | 0 | .379 |
| Wright, Kenneth F., Idaho F | 66 | 219 | 45 | 65 | 90 | 8 | 4 | 3 | 30 | 0 | 3 | 32 | 1 | 37 | 17 | 11 | .297 |
| Wulfemeyer, Mark, Idaho F. | 4 | 1 | 0 | 0 | 0 | 0 | 0 | 0 | 0 | 0 | 0 | 1 | 0 | 0 | 0 | 0 | .000 |
| Yurak, Jeffrey, Great F† | 34 | 73 | 9 | 20 | 29 | 6 | 1 | 0 | 13 | 0 | 0 | 5 | 2 | 9 | 0 | 0 | .274 |

GRAND-SLAM HOME RUNS—Barrios, Dahl, Dawson, Murray, 1 each.

AWARDED FIRST BASE ON INTERFERENCE—Cliburn (Dahl), Crowley (Dahl), Goldetsky (Dahl), Hopper (Cliburn), Nelms (Cato).

## CLUB FIELDING

| Club | G. | P.O. | A. | E. | DP. | PB. | Pct. |
|---|---|---|---|---|---|---|---|
| Great Falls | 72 | 1816 | 799 | 114 | 57 | 15 | .958 |
| Billings | 72 | 1752 | 731 | 155 | 43 | 25 | .941 |
| Idaho Falls | 72 | 1829 | 789 | 165 | 54 | 17 | .941 |
| Lethbridge | 72 | 1861 | 854 | 192 | 53 | 23 | .934 |

Triple Plays—None.

## INDIVIDUAL FIELDING

*Throws lefthanded.

### FIRST BASEMEN

| Player and Club | G. | PO. | A. | E. | DP. | Pct. |
|---|---|---|---|---|---|---|
| Mills, Great Falls | 45 | 385 | 18 | 4 | 36 | .990 |
| McNally, Idaho Falls* | 38 | 328 | 20 | 4 | 24 | .989 |
| Connors, Idaho Falls | 28 | 180 | 9 | 3 | 13 | .984 |
| Crowley, Lethbridge* | 44 | 401 | 24 | 9 | 26 | .979 |
| WEICKER, Billings | 70 | 542 | 34 | 13 | 32 | .978 |
| Barrios, Great Falls | 11 | 98 | 7 | 3 | 12 | .972 |
| Murray, Great Falls | 16 | 122 | 2 | 4 | 5 | .969 |
| Fleury, Lethbridge* | 16 | 122 | 6 | 5 | 6 | .962 |
| McMullen, Lethbridge | 14 | 121 | 6 | 6 | 6 | .955 |

#### (Fewer Than Ten Games)

| Player and Club | G. | PO. | A. | E. | DP. | Pct. |
|---|---|---|---|---|---|---|
| Cliburn, Idaho Falls | 5 | 48 | 2 | 0 | 6 | 1.000 |
| Clark, Idaho Falls | 4 | 26 | 2 | 0 | 2 | 1.000 |
| Davidson, Billings | 2 | 12 | 1 | 0 | 2 | 1.000 |
| Elrod, Great Falls | 2 | 10 | 1 | 0 | 0 | 1.000 |
| Miller, Billings | 3 | 7 | 0 | 0 | 1 | 1.000 |
| Dahl, Billings | 3 | 5 | 2 | 0 | 0 | 1.000 |
| Baggett, Billings | 2 | 6 | 0 | 0 | 0 | 1.000 |
| Pekarcik, Billings | 1 | 1 | 0 | 0 | 0 | 1.000 |
| Brown, Idaho Falls | 1 | 1 | 0 | 0 | 0 | 1.000 |
| Rayford, Idaho Falls | 7 | 39 | 3 | 1 | 1 | .977 |
| Yurak, Great Falls | 5 | 58 | 3 | 2 | 2 | .953 |
| Knox, Idaho Falls* | 2 | 20 | 1 | 2 | 1 | .913 |

## SECOND BASEMEN

| Player and Club | G. | PO. | A. | E. | DP. | Pct. |
|---|---|---|---|---|---|---|
| MITCHELL, Great F | 66 | 156 | 176 | 9 | 38 | .974 |
| Trickey, Lethbridge | 44 | 97 | 123 | 9 | 22 | .961 |
| Brewster, Idaho Falls | 72 | 170 | 198 | 21 | 37 | .946 |
| Richter, Billings | 50 | 129 | 102 | 14 | 18 | .943 |
| Goldetsky, Lethbridge | 30 | 78 | 74 | 11 | 14 | .933 |
| Davidson, Billings | 12 | 31 | 26 | 5 | 6 | .919 |
| Lee, Great Falls | 16 | 17 | 26 | 4 | 5 | .915 |
| Sucarichi, Billings | 12 | 19 | 29 | 6 | 3 | .889 |

### (Fewer Than Ten Games)

| Player and Club | G. | PO. | A. | E. | DP. | Pct. |
|---|---|---|---|---|---|---|
| Grimes, Great Falls | 1 | 4 | 3 | 0 | 0 | 1.000 |
| Lorick, Idaho Falls | 1 | 0 | 1 | 0 | 0 | 1.000 |

## THIRD BASEMEN

| Player and Club | G. | PO. | A. | E. | DP. | Pct. |
|---|---|---|---|---|---|---|
| Lee, Great Falls | 12 | 5 | 18 | 1 | 2 | .958 |
| GRIMES, Great Falls | 54 | 34 | 110 | 11 | 4 | .929 |
| Daughtry, Great F | 10 | 7 | 18 | 2 | 0 | .926 |
| Elrod, Great Falls | 10 | 10 | 19 | 3 | 4 | .906 |
| Nelms, Billings | 46 | 31 | 112 | 16 | 4 | .899 |
| Rayford, Idaho Falls | 38 | 39 | 76 | 14 | 4 | .891 |
| Eickenhorst, Leth | 60 | 62 | 140 | 29 | 11 | .874 |
| Goldetsky, Leth | 11 | 12 | 20 | 6 | 3 | .842 |
| Dahl, Billings | 21 | 20 | 43 | 12 | 5 | .840 |
| Kelly, Idaho Falls | 19 | 16 | 37 | 13 | 1 | .803 |

### (Fewer Than Ten Games)

| Player and Club | G. | PO. | A. | E. | DP. | Pct. |
|---|---|---|---|---|---|---|
| Cliburn, Idaho Falls | 1 | 1 | 0 | 0 | 0 | 1.000 |
| Jensen, Billings | 1 | 1 | 0 | 0 | 0 | 1.000 |
| Groves, Billings | 5 | 0 | 1 | 0 | 0 | 1.000 |
| Trickey, Lethbridge | 4 | 4 | 9 | 1 | 0 | .929 |
| Richter, Billings | 8 | 3 | 12 | 2 | 2 | .882 |
| Weicker, Billings | 4 | 2 | 3 | 1 | 0 | .833 |
| Sucarichi, Billings | 2 | 2 | 2 | 1 | 0 | .800 |
| Lorick, Idaho Falls | 6 | 5 | 9 | 5 | 1 | .737 |
| Lansford, Idaho Falls | 8 | 8 | 14 | 9 | 0 | .710 |
| Clark, Idaho Falls | 2 | 2 | 3 | 3 | 1 | .625 |
| Baggett, Billings | 1 | 1 | 0 | 1 | 0 | .500 |
| Newby, Lethbridge | 1 | 0 | 0 | 1 | 0 | .000 |

## SHORTSTOPS

| Player and Club | G. | PO. | A. | E. | DP. | Pct. |
|---|---|---|---|---|---|---|
| ANDERSON, Idaho F | 71 | 94 | 239 | 27 | 32 | .925 |
| Paris, Great Falls | 72 | 83 | 213 | 26 | 34 | .919 |
| Hopper, Billings | 70 | 81 | 180 | 26 | 24 | .909 |
| Miles, Lethbridge | 64 | 94 | 197 | 42 | 27 | .874 |

### (Fewer Than Ten Games)

| Player and Club | G. | PO. | A. | E. | DP. | Pct. |
|---|---|---|---|---|---|---|
| Groves, Billings | 3 | 2 | 4 | 0 | 0 | 1.000 |
| Mitchell, Great Falls | 2 | 3 | 0 | 0 | 0 | 1.000 |
| Trickey, Lethbridge | 1 | 2 | 1 | 0 | 0 | 1.000 |
| Grimes, Great Falls | 3 | 2 | 0 | 0 | 0 | 1.000 |
| Rayford, Idaho Falls | 1 | 0 | 2 | 0 | 0 | 1.000 |
| Baggett, Billings | 1 | 0 | 1 | 0 | 0 | 1.000 |
| Nelms, Billings | 1 | 0 | 1 | 0 | 0 | 1.000 |
| Plent, Billings | 1 | 0 | 1 | 0 | 0 | 1.000 |
| Eickenhorst, Leth | 9 | 21 | 32 | 7 | 3 | .883 |
| Kelly, Idaho Falls | 2 | 3 | 9 | 2 | 1 | .857 |
| Sucarichi, Billings | 3 | 4 | 4 | 3 | 0 | .727 |

## OUTFIELDERS

| Player and Club | G. | PO. | A. | E. | DP. | Pct. |
|---|---|---|---|---|---|---|
| Osborne, Great Falls | 21 | 24 | 2 | 0 | 0 | 1.000 |
| Schoenhaus, Great F | 15 | 24 | 2 | 0 | 1 | 1.000 |
| Dahl, Billings | 12 | 17 | 1 | 0 | 0 | 1.000 |
| Bhagwat, Great Falls | 32 | 50 | 1 | 1 | 0 | .981 |
| CLARK, Idaho Falls | 65 | 126 | 5 | 3 | 0 | .978 |
| Moretto, Billings | 45 | 77 | 5 | 2 | 0 | .976 |
| Wood, Lethbridge | 15 | 28 | 0 | 1 | 0 | .966 |
| Morrow, Billings | 37 | 49 | 3 | 2 | 0 | .963 |
| Berthiaume, Billings* | 18 | 24 | 1 | 1 | 0 | .962 |
| McMullen, Lethbridge | 25 | 23 | 2 | 1 | 0 | .962 |
| Kelly, Idaho Falls | 25 | 44 | 3 | 2 | 0 | .959 |
| Dyes, Lethbridge | 70 | 127 | 19 | 8 | 4 | .948 |
| Waller, Billings | 68 | 120 | 8 | 7 | 3 | .948 |
| Yurak, Great Falls | 12 | 15 | 3 | 1 | 0 | .947 |
| Dawson, Lethbridge | 70 | 142 | 7 | 10 | 1 | .937 |
| Elrod, Great Falls | 59 | 42 | 1 | 3 | 0 | .935 |
| Baggett, Billings | 16 | 11 | 1 | 1 | 1 | .923 |
| Barrios, Great Falls | 37 | 43 | 4 | 4 | 0 | .922 |
| Davis, Great Falls | 32 | 31 | 1 | 3 | 0 | .914 |
| Wright, Idaho Falls | 64 | 61 | 5 | 7 | 1 | .904 |
| Hill, Lethbridge | 25 | 22 | 5 | 3 | 1 | .900 |
| Ingraham, Billings | 41 | 39 | 5 | 5 | 0 | .898 |
| Knox, Idaho Falls* | 51 | 57 | 2 | 9 | 1 | .868 |
| Newby, Lethbridge | 22 | 25 | 2 | 5 | 0 | .844 |
| Lorick, Idaho Falls | 18 | 20 | 0 | 4 | 0 | .833 |
| LaFave, Idaho Falls | 17 | 9 | 1 | 2 | 0 | .833 |

### (Fewer Than Ten Games)

| Player and Club | G. | PO. | A. | E. | DP. | Pct. |
|---|---|---|---|---|---|---|
| Moore, Great Falls | 9 | 13 | 0 | 0 | 0 | 1.000 |
| Richter, Billings | 7 | 10 | 0 | 0 | 0 | 1.000 |
| Rayford, Idaho Falls | 4 | 5 | 0 | 0 | 0 | 1.000 |
| Grimes, Great Falls | 3 | 5 | 0 | 0 | 0 | 1.000 |
| Grana, Billings | 1 | 2 | 0 | 0 | 0 | 1.000 |
| Cato, Great Falls | 1 | 1 | 0 | 0 | 0 | 1.000 |
| Crowley, Lethbridge* | 1 | 1 | 0 | 0 | 0 | 1.000 |
| D'Innocenzio, Great F | 1 | 1 | 0 | 0 | 0 | 1.000 |
| Howard, Great Falls | 4 | 6 | 1 | 1 | 0 | .875 |
| Ayers, Great Falls | 5 | 4 | 0 | 1 | 0 | .800 |
| Gonzalez, Lethbridge | 3 | 4 | 0 | 1 | 0 | .800 |
| Huntington, Billings* | 2 | 4 | 0 | 1 | 0 | .800 |
| Murray, Great Falls | 6 | 6 | 1 | 3 | 0 | .700 |

## CATCHERS

| Player and Club | G. | PO. | A. | E. | DP. | PB. | Pct. |
|---|---|---|---|---|---|---|---|
| Edge, Billings | 18 | 114 | 10 | 0 | 0 | 2 | 1.000 |
| CLIBURN, Ida F | 48 | 318 | 32 | 3 | 3 | 8 | .992 |
| Cato, Great Falls | 45 | 323 | 37 | 7 | 1 | 7 | .981 |
| Ryan, Great Falls | 27 | 190 | 26 | 6 | 0 | 7 | .973 |
| Miller, Billings | 29 | 191 | 14 | 6 | 2 | 13 | .972 |
| Rayford, Idaho F | 25 | 161 | 19 | 6 | 2 | 7 | .968 |
| Cipolla, Leth | 47 | 255 | 41 | 10 | 1 | 11 | .967 |
| Johnson, Leth | 22 | 138 | 16 | 6 | 2 | 8 | .963 |
| Dahl, Billings | 32 | 164 | 27 | 12 | 2 | 10 | .941 |

## CATCHERS—Continued
### (Fewer Than Ten Games)

| Player and Club | G. | PO. | A. | E. | DP. | PB. | Pct. | | Player and Club | G. | PO. | A. | E. | DP. | PB. | Pct. |
|---|---|---|---|---|---|---|---|---|---|---|---|---|---|---|---|---|
| Cooper, Leth | 8 | 41 | 14 | 0 | 1 | 4 | 1.000 | | Hughes, Great Falls | 6 | 23 | 0 | 1 | 1 | 0 | .958 |
| Yurak, Great Falls | 1 | 2 | 0 | 0 | 0 | 1 | 1.000 | | Chaus, Iaho Falls | 3 | 21 | 0 | 3 | 0 | 2 | .875 |
| Lorick, Idaho Falls | 1 | 1 | 0 | 0 | 0 | 0 | 1.000 | | | | | | | | | |

## PITCHERS

| Player and Club | G. | PO. | A. | E. | DP. | Pct. | | Player and Club | G. | PO. | A. | E. | DP. | Pct. |
|---|---|---|---|---|---|---|---|---|---|---|---|---|---|---|
| WATSON, Great F. | 12 | 6 | 16 | 0 | 2 | 1.000 | | Wirth, Great Falls | 14 | 7 | 23 | 3 | 0 | .909 |
| Pekarcik, Billings | 14 | 3 | 15 | 0 | 0 | 1.000 | | Gerdes, Lethbridge | 13 | 6 | 12 | 2 | 1 | .900 |
| Boyle, Idaho Falls | 13 | 4 | 11 | 0 | 0 | 1.000 | | Quigley, Idaho Falls | 18 | 2 | 7 | 1 | 0 | .900 |
| Kulesza, Idaho Falls | 14 | 2 | 10 | 0 | 0 | 1.000 | | Anderson, Great Falls | 19 | 0 | 7 | 1 | 0 | .875 |
| Huntington, Billings* | 22 | 4 | 6 | 0 | 1 | 1.000 | | Ferrara, Billings | 10 | 0 | 7 | 1 | 1 | .875 |
| Steen, Great Falls | 21 | 4 | 5 | 0 | 0 | 1.000 | | Perez, Idaho Falls | 13 | 2 | 17 | 3 | 1 | .864 |
| Calderon, Great Falls | 11 | 2 | 6 | 0 | 0 | 1.000 | | Merritt, Idaho Falls | 14 | 7 | 11 | 3 | 0 | .857 |
| Moline, Great Falls | 18 | 2 | 5 | 0 | 0 | 1.000 | | Baby, Lethbridge* | 12 | 0 | 17 | 3 | 1 | .857 |
| Ryan, Idaho Falls* | 20 | 1 | 5 | 0 | 0 | 1.000 | | Grana, Billings | 14 | 1 | 5 | 1 | 0 | .857 |
| Kay, Lethbridge* | 14 | 0 | 5 | 0 | 0 | 1.000 | | Brown, Billings | 10 | 1 | 5 | 1 | 0 | .857 |
| Herron, Lethbridge | 10 | 3 | 1 | 0 | 0 | 1.000 | | Clear, Idaho Falls | 13 | 2 | 9 | 2 | 0 | .846 |
| Pastore, Billings | 15 | 7 | 17 | 1 | 0 | .960 | | Eddy, Idaho Falls | 11 | 2 | 10 | 3 | 1 | .800 |
| Moore, Billings | 16 | 6 | 9 | 1 | 0 | .938 | | Uebbing, Lethbridge | 15 | 4 | 4 | 2 | 0 | .800 |
| Finlayson, Lethbridge | 10 | 2 | 13 | 1 | 0 | .938 | | Grabowski, Leth | 12 | 2 | 11 | 4 | 0 | .765 |
| Ratzer, Lethbridge | 30 | 7 | 21 | 2 | 4 | .933 | | Schaefer, Great Falls | 14 | 4 | 11 | 5 | 1 | .750 |
| Schmidt, Great Falls | 14 | 12 | 12 | 2 | 2 | .923 | | Plent, Billings | 23 | 5 | 11 | 6 | 1 | .727 |
| Harshey, Lethbridge | 30 | 7 | 5 | 1 | 0 | .923 | | Mraz, Idaho Falls | 13 | 2 | 7 | 4 | 0 | .692 |
| Warren, Billings | 15 | 9 | 14 | 2 | 0 | .920 | | Stek, Idaho Falls | 13 | 2 | 6 | 4 | 0 | .667 |
| Fredrickson, Leth | 18 | 2 | 9 | 1 | 0 | .917 | | Jensen, Billings | 19 | 3 | 6 | 5 | 0 | .643 |

### (Fewer Than Ten Games)

| Player and Club | G. | PO. | A. | E. | DP. | Pct. | | Player and Club | G. | PO. | A. | E. | DP. | Pct. |
|---|---|---|---|---|---|---|---|---|---|---|---|---|---|---|
| Weatherford, Leth | 5 | 2 | 7 | 0 | 1 | 1.000 | | Rothschild, Billings | 6 | 0 | 1 | 0 | 1 | 1.000 |
| Rowland, Great Falls | 5 | 1 | 7 | 0 | 1 | 1.000 | | Morrow, Billings | 3 | 0 | 1 | 0 | 1 | 1.000 |
| Barnicle, Great F*. | 8 | 1 | 6 | 0 | 1 | 1.000 | | Bohr, Lethbridge | 1 | 0 | 1 | 0 | 0 | 1.000 |
| Halvarson, Leth | 6 | 0 | 4 | 0 | 0 | 1.000 | | Brown, Idaho Falls | 7 | 2 | 2 | 1 | 0 | .800 |
| Stuthard, Lethbridge | 1 | 1 | 2 | 0 | 0 | 1.000 | | Chapman, Great Falls | 3 | 0 | 2 | 1 | 0 | .667 |
| Muhlstock, Great F | 3 | 0 | 3 | 0 | 1 | 1.000 | | Knose, Lethbridge | 9 | 4 | 4 | 5 | 1 | .615 |
| Wulfemeyer, Idaho F | 4 | 1 | 0 | 0 | 0 | 1.000 | | Flores, Great Falls* | 2 | 0 | 3 | 2 | 0 | .600 |

The following players do not have any recorded accepted chances at the positions indicated; therefore, are not listed in the fielding averages for those particular positions: J. Anderson, 2b; Baggett, p; Berthiaume*, p; Case, p; Cliburn, of; Ferrara, of; Lansford, ss; Chas. Moore, of; Moskau, p; Nelms, of; Peterson, p. Williams appeared as a pinch-hitter only.

## CLUB PITCHING

| Club | G. | CG. | ShO. | Sv. | IP. | H. | R. | ER. | HR. | BB. | Int. BB. | HB. | SO. | WP. | Bk. | ERA. |
|---|---|---|---|---|---|---|---|---|---|---|---|---|---|---|---|---|
| Idaho Falls | 72 | 19 | 5 | 12 | 610 | 639 | 350 | 232 | 17 | 280 | 15 | 21 | 465 | 47 | 7 | 3.42 |
| Great Falls | 72 | 19 | 4 | 6 | 605 | 578 | 309 | 246 | 24 | 276 | 5 | 14 | 512 | 36 | 13 | 3.66 |
| Billings | 72 | 16 | 5 | 6 | 584 | 616 | 389 | 281 | 26 | 347 | 20 | 22 | 426 | 35 | 12 | 4.33 |
| Lethbridge | 72 | 7 | 2 | 12 | 620 | 714 | 437 | 305 | 31 | 311 | 10 | 19 | 398 | 65 | 11 | 4.43 |

## PITCHERS' RECORDS
### (Leading Qualifiers for Earned-Run Average Leadership—58 or More Innings)
*Throws lefthanded.

| Pitcher—Club | G. | GS. | CG. | ShO. | W. | L. | Sv. | Pct. | IP. | H. | R. | ER. | HR. | BB. | Int. BB. | HB. | SO. | WP. | ERA. |
|---|---|---|---|---|---|---|---|---|---|---|---|---|---|---|---|---|---|---|---|
| Perez, Idaho Falls | 13 | 13 | 7 | 1 | 9 | 3 | 0 | .750 | 95 | 88 | 26 | 20 | 4 | 29 | 1 | 3 | 80 | 9 | 1.89 |
| Schmidt, Great F. | 14 | 13 | 6 | 1 | 10 | 0 | 0 | 1.000 | 94 | 77 | 29 | 24 | 0 | 32 | 0 | 5 | 81 | 1 | 2.30 |
| Ratzer, Lethbridge | 30 | 6 | 0 | 0 | 3 | 4 | 5 | .429 | 85 | 85 | 42 | 22 | 4 | 16 | 2 | 1 | 58 | 0 | 2.33 |
| Mraz, Idaho Falls | 13 | 11 | 3 | 0 | 4 | 3 | 0 | .571 | 80 | 82 | 50 | 21 | 0 | 24 | 1 | 2 | 70 | 6 | 2.36 |
| Pastore, Billings | 15 | 13 | 3 | 1 | 5 | 7 | 1 | .417 | 88 | 89 | 47 | 25 | 5 | 27 | 3 | 3 | 69 | 2 | 2.56 |
| Plent, Billings | 23 | 6 | 3 | 0 | 4 | 4 | 4 | .500 | 68 | 58 | 35 | 23 | 0 | 32 | 2 | 3 | 46 | 1 | 3.04 |
| Wirth, Great Falls | 14 | 14 | 7 | 0 | 8 | 5 | 0 | .615 | 105 | 96 | 44 | 36 | 4 | 39 | 1 | 1 | 90 | 5 | 3.09 |
| Merritt, Idaho F. | 14 | 14 | 6 | 3 | 6 | 5 | 0 | .545 | 93 | 86 | 48 | 32 | 2 | 33 | 1 | 2 | 60 | 5 | 3.10 |
| Grabowski, Leth | 12 | 12 | 2 | 1 | 3 | 6 | 0 | .333 | 72 | 68 | 44 | 27 | 0 | 43 | 1 | 3 | 51 | 9 | 3.38 |
| Gerdes, Lethbridge | 13 | 11 | 2 | 1 | 4 | 6 | 0 | .400 | 67 | 75 | 42 | 28 | 2 | 34 | 1 | 0 | 67 | 8 | 3.76 |

Departmental Leaders: G—Harshey, Ratzer, 30; GS—Merritt, Wirth, 14; CG—Perez, Wirth, 7; ShO—Merritt, 3; W—Schmidt, 10; L—Pastore, Steck, 7; Sv—Harshey, 6; Pct.—Schmidt, 1.000; IP—Wirth, 105; H—Wirth, 96; R—Mraz, Schaefer, Steck, 50; ER—Jensen, 38; HR—Harshey, Pekarcik, 6; BB—Schaefer, 47; IBB—Pekarcik, 5; HB—Steck, 7; SO—Wirth, 90; WP—Warren, 11.

### (All Pitchers—Listed Alphabetically)

| Pitcher—Club | G. | GS. | CG. | ShO. | W. | L. | Sv. | Pct. | IP. | H. | R. | ER. | HR. | BB. | Int. BB. | HB. | SO. | WP. | ERA. |
|---|---|---|---|---|---|---|---|---|---|---|---|---|---|---|---|---|---|---|---|
| Anderson, Great F. | 19 | 4 | 0 | 0 | 3 | 4 | 1 | .429 | 43 | 46 | 23 | 16 | 2 | 29 | 2 | 0 | 35 | 2 | 3.35 |
| Baby Lethbridge* | 12 | 8 | 2 | 0 | 3 | 5 | 0 | .375 | 56 | 75 | 35 | 28 | 1 | 23 | 2 | 0 | 36 | 9 | 4.50 |
| Baggett, Billings | 1 | 0 | 0 | 0 | 0 | 0 | 0 | .000 | 2 | 0 | 0 | 0 | 0 | 1 | 0 | 0 | 0 | 0 | 0.00 |
| Barnicle, Great F*. | 8 | 8 | 1 | 0 | 2 | 5 | 0 | .286 | 47 | 46 | 27 | 24 | 1 | 38 | 0 | 1 | 60 | 8 | 4.60 |
| Berthiaume, Bil* | 1 | 0 | 0 | 0 | 0 | 0 | 0 | .000 | 2 | 3 | 1 | 1 | 0 | 0 | 0 | 1 | 0 | 0 | 4.50 |

| Pitcher—Club | G. | GS. | CG. | ShO. | W. | L. | Sv. | Pct. | IP. | H. | R. | ER. | HR. | BB. | Int. BB. | HB. | SO. | WP. | ERA. |
|---|---|---|---|---|---|---|---|---|---|---|---|---|---|---|---|---|---|---|---|
| Bohr, Lethbridge .. 1 | 1 | 0 | 0 | 1 | 0 | 0 | 1.000 | 6 | 9 | 5 | 5 | 0 | 2 | 0 | 0 | 5 | 1 | 7.50 |
| Boyle, Idaho Falls 13 | 4 | 1 | 1 | 6 | 1 | 2 | .857 | 51 | 53 | 23 | 15 | 2 | 21 | 2 | 0 | 20 | 1 | 2.65 |
| Brown, Idaho Falls 7 | 2 | 0 | 0 | 2 | 1 | 1 | .667 | 19 | 32 | 15 | 8 | 0 | 9 | 1 | 0 | 14 | 2 | 3.79 |
| S. Brown, Billings 10 | 2 | 0 | 0 | 1 | 0 | 0 | .000 | 18 | 25 | 25 | 13 | 0 | 21 | 0 | 2 | 13 | 2 | 6.50 |
| Calderon, Great F. .11 | 4 | 0 | 0 | 1 | 1 | 0 | .500 | 37 | 47 | 29 | 23 | 4 | 10 | 0 | 0 | 23 | 1 | 5.59 |
| Case, Idaho Falls... 3 | 0 | 0 | 0 | 0 | 1 | 0 | .000 | 4 | 7 | 12 | 5 | 0 | 10 | 0 | 0 | 3 | 1 | 11.25 |
| Chapman, Great F 3 | 0 | 0 | 0 | 0 | 0 | 0 | .000 | 5 | 9 | 12 | 10 | 2 | 6 | 0 | 1 | 5 | 3 | 18.00 |
| Clear, Idaho Falls 13 | 1 | 0 | 0 | 1 | 2 | 1 | .333 | 28 | 24 | 14 | 6 | 0 | 30 | 1 | 0 | 29 | 1 | 1.93 |
| Eddy, Idaho Falls 11 | 10 | 0 | 0 | 3 | 3 | 0 | .500 | 49 | 58 | 39 | 31 | 4 | 35 | 1 | 4 | 36 | 6 | 5.69 |
| Ferrara, Billings ..10 | 9 | 1 | 1 | 2 | 6 | 0 | .250 | 36 | 33 | 34 | 27 | 1 | 44 | 0 | 2 | 24 | 8 | 6.75 |
| Finlayson, Leth ....10 | 8 | 1 | 0 | 4 | 5 | 0 | .444 | 52 | 66 | 36 | 29 | 4 | 16 | 0 | 2 | 28 | 6 | 5.02 |
| Flores, Great F*... 2 | 2 | 1 | 1 | 1 | 0 | 0 | 1.000 | 14 | 7 | 1 | 1 | 0 | 8 | 0 | 1 | 11 | 0 | 0.64 |
| Fredrickson, Leth ..13 | 4 | 0 | 0 | 4 | 0 | 1 | 1.000 | 51 | 71 | 43 | 35 | 5 | 25 | 0 | 4 | 20 | 2 | 6.18 |
| Gerdes, Lethbridge 13 | 11 | 2 | 1 | 4 | 6 | 0 | .400 | 67 | 75 | 42 | 28 | 2 | 34 | 1 | 0 | 67 | 8 | 3.76 |
| Grabowski, Leth ..12 | 12 | 2 | 1 | 3 | 6 | 0 | .333 | 72 | 68 | 44 | 27 | 0 | 43 | 1 | 3 | 51 | 9 | 3.38 |
| Grana, Billings ....14 | 3 | 0 | 0 | 1 | 1 | 0 | .500 | 32 | 57 | 42 | 30 | 1 | 20 | 4 | 2 | 12 | 1 | 8.44 |
| Halverson, Leth.... 6 | 6 | 0 | 0 | 1 | 2 | 0 | .333 | 29 | 37 | 22 | 16 | 0 | 15 | 0 | 2 | 16 | 4 | 4.97 |
| Harshey, Leth .... 30 | 1 | 0 | 0 | 5 | 2 | 6 | .714 | 55 | 58 | 39 | 27 | 6 | 24 | 1 | 0 | 42 | 7 | 4.42 |
| Herron, Lethbridge 10 | 0 | 0 | 0 | 1 | 1 | 0 | .500 | 18 | 16 | 9 | 7 | 1 | 14 | 3 | 0 | 12 | 3 | 3.50 |
| Huntington, Bill* ..22 | 3 | 1 | 0 | 0 | 3 | 0 | .000 | 43 | 50 | 32 | 23 | 5 | 32 | 3 | 1 | 37 | 4 | 4.81 |
| Jensen, Billings ...19 | 8 | 2 | 0 | 4 | 5 | 0 | .444 | 71 | 74 | 47 | 38 | 5 | 43 | 2 | 2 | 69 | 1 | 4.82 |
| Kay, Lethbridge* ..14 | 0 | 0 | 0 | 0 | 0 | 0 | .000 | 24 | 38 | 29 | 18 | 0 | 19 | 0 | 0 | 15 | 2 | 6.75 |
| Knose, Lethbridge.. 9 | 9 | 0 | 0 | 3 | 2 | 0 | .600 | 46 | 62 | 45 | 32 | 4 | 27 | 0 | 2 | 17 | 5 | 6.26 |
| Kulesza, Idaho F..14 | 3 | 1 | 0 | 2 | 2 | 0 | .500 | 39 | 49 | 24 | 20 | 2 | 8 | 1 | 0 | 21 | 3 | 4.62 |
| Merritt, Idaho F..14 | 14 | 6 | 3 | 6 | 5 | 0 | .545 | 93 | 86 | 48 | 32 | 2 | 33 | 1 | 2 | 60 | 5 | 3.10 |
| Moline, Great F...18 | 2 | 1 | 0 | 3 | 5 | 1 | .375 | 42 | 51 | 29 | 25 | 3 | 12 | 0 | 2 | 28 | 2 | 5.36 |
| Moore, Billings ...16 | 6 | 2 | 1 | 5 | 3 | 0 | .625 | 57 | 54 | 22 | 19 | 0 | 30 | 1 | 0 | 28 | 2 | 3.00 |
| Morrow, Billings... 3 | 0 | 0 | 0 | 1 | 0 | 0 | 1.000 | 6 | 7 | 4 | 1 | 7 | 0 | 1 | 7 | 1 | 7.20 |
| Moskau, Billings .. 1 | 0 | 0 | 0 | 0 | 1 | 0 | .000 | 4 | 3 | 5 | 1 | 0 | 3 | 0 | 0 | 6 | 0 | 2.25 |
| Mraz, Idaho Falls.13 | 11 | 3 | 0 | 4 | 3 | 0 | .571 | 80 | 82 | 50 | 21 | 0 | 24 | 1 | 2 | 70 | 6 | 2.35 |
| Muhlstock, Great F 3 | 0 | 0 | 0 | 0 | 0 | 0 | .000 | 5 | 3 | 2 | 2 | 1 | 1 | 0 | 0 | 9 | 0 | 3.60 |
| Pastore, Billings ..15 | 13 | 1 | 5 | 7 | 1 | .417 | 86 | 89 | 47 | 25 | 5 | 27 | 3 | 3 | 69 | 2 | 2.56 |
| Pekarcik, Billings..14 | 12 | 3 | 1 | 2 | 6 | 0 | .250 | 80 | 75 | 37 | 35 | 6 | 37 | 5 | 2 | 55 | 2 | 3.94 |
| Perez, Idaho Falls 13 | 13 | 7 | 1 | 3 | 6 | 0 | .750 | 95 | 88 | 26 | 20 | 4 | 29 | 1 | 3 | 80 | 9 | 1.89 |
| Peterson, Great F 4 | 0 | 0 | 0 | 0 | 0 | 0 | .000 | 8 | 8 | 8 | 6 | 0 | 9 | 0 | 0 | 5 | 0 | 9.00 |
| Plent, Billings .....23 | 6 | 3 | 0 | 4 | 4 | 4 | .500 | 68 | 58 | 35 | 23 | 0 | 32 | 2 | 3 | 46 | 1 | 3.04 |
| Quigley, Idaho F...18 | 1 | 0 | 0 | 4 | 2 | 4 | .667 | 44 | 44 | 15 | 11 | 1 | 15 | 2 | 2 | 41 | 4 | 2.25 |
| Ratzer, Lethbridge 30 | 6 | 0 | 0 | 3 | 4 | 5 | .429 | 85 | 85 | 42 | 22 | 4 | 16 | 2 | 1 | 58 | 0 | 2.33 |
| Rothschild, Bil .... 6 | 0 | 0 | 0 | 0 | 2 | 1 | .000 | 8 | 14 | 11 | 7 | 0 | 7 | 0 | 0 | 12 | 0 | 7.88 |
| Rowland, Great F.. 5 | 5 | 1 | 0 | 2 | 2 | 0 | .500 | 32 | 19 | 9 | 8 | 2 | 10 | 0 | 1 | 26 | 0 | 2.25 |
| Ryan, Idaho Falls* 20 | 0 | 0 | 0 | 2 | 1 | 4 | .667 | 30 | 43 | 32 | 26 | 1 | 19 | 4 | 1 | 27 | 4 | 7.80 |
| Schaefer, Great F..14 | 13 | 0 | 0 | 5 | 4 | 0 | .556 | 80 | 80 | 50 | 35 | 1 | 47 | 0 | 1 | 64 | 7 | 3.94 |
| Schmidt, Great F...14 | 13 | 6 | 1 | 10 | 0 | 0 | 1.000 | 94 | 77 | 29 | 24 | 0 | 32 | 0 | 5 | 81 | 1 | 2.30 |
| Steck, Idaho Falls 13 | 13 | 1 | 0 | 2 | 7 | 0 | .222 | 75 | 71 | 50 | 36 | 1 | 41 | 0 | 7 | 62 | 5 | 4.32 |
| Steen, Great Falls 21 | 2 | 1 | 1 | 3 | 2 | 3 | .400 | 45 | 41 | 21 | 15 | 3 | 11 | 0 | 1 | 30 | 4 | 3.00 |
| Stuthard, Leth .... 1 | 1 | 0 | 0 | 1 | 0 | 0 | .000 | 5 | 5 | 7 | 4 | 0 | 4 | 2 | 0 | 2 | 7 | 7.20 |
| Uebbing, Leth ....15 | 0 | 0 | 0 | 2 | 0 | 0 | 1.000 | 33 | 31 | 26 | 17 | 4 | 30 | 0 | 3 | 22 | 0 | 4.64 |
| Warren, Billings ...15 | 11 | 1 | 0 | 2 | 6 | 0 | .250 | 70 | 75 | 44 | 35 | 2 | 43 | 0 | 4 | 47 | 11 | 4.50 |
| Watson, Great F...12 | 5 | 1 | 1 | 4 | 1 | 0 | .800 | 51 | 48 | 25 | 21 | 1 | 24 | 2 | 0 | 45 | 3 | 3.71 |
| Weatherford, Leth.. 5 | 5 | 0 | 0 | 1 | 3 | 0 | .250 | 21 | 18 | 13 | 10 | 0 | 19 | 0 | 0 | 9 | 5 | 4.29 |
| Wirth, Great Falls 14 | 14 | 7 | 0 | 8 | 5 | 0 | .615 | 105 | 96 | 44 | 36 | 4 | 39 | 1 | 1 | 90 | 5 | 3.09 |
| Wulfemeyer, Ida F 4 | 0 | 0 | 0 | 0 | 0 | 0 | .000 | 4 | 2 | 1 | 1 | 0 | 6 | 0 | 0 | 3 | 2 | 2.25 |

BALKS—Wirth, 5; Ratzer, 4; Kulesza, Schaefer, Watson, 3 each; Baby, Moore, Pastore, Steck, 2 each; Anderson, Baggett, S. Brown, Calderon, Ferrara, Fredrickson, Herron, Huntington, Jensen, Kay, Knose, Pekarcik, Perez, Plent, Quigley, Warren, Weatherford, 1 each.

COMBINATION SHUTOUT—Plent-Moore, Billings.

NO-HIT GAMES—Ferrara, Billings, defeated Lethbridge, 9-0, July 14; Plent (six innings), Moore (1 inning), Billings, defeated Great Falls, 11-0, July 27 (seven innings).

# Attendance Records

## AMERICAN LEAGUE

| Club | Single Day Game | (a) Doubleheader | Night Game |
|---|---|---|---|
| Balt. | 46,534 (April 15, 1954) | 46,796 (May  16, 1954) | 48,042 (May  17, 1975) |
| Boston | 36,350 (Aug.  7, 1956) | 41,766 (Aug. 12, 1934) | 36,228 (June 28, 1949) |
| Calif. | 42,655 (May  14, 1966) | 30,760 (May  30, 1966) | 53,591 (July 13, 1962) |
| Chicago | 44,444 (Aug.  5, 1962) | 55,555 (May  20, 1973) | 53,940 (June  8, 1951) |
| Cleve. | 74,420 (April  7, 1973) | 84,587 (Sept. 12, 1954) | 78,382 (Aug. 20, 1948) |
| Detroit | 57,888 (Sept. 26, 1948) | 58,369 (July  20, 1947) | 56,586 (Aug.  9, 1948) |
| ●K. City | 30,035 (May  24, 1970) | 31,872 (April 20, 1969) | 39,464 (April 10, 1973) |
| ‡K. City | 34,065 (Aug. 27, 1961) | 35,295 (June 20, 1971) | 39,474 (June 29, 1974) |
| Milw. | 48,160 (April 11, 1975) | 41,655 (May  20, 1973) | 33,747 (July 13, 1973) |
| Minn. | 44,184 (May  4, 1969) | 43,419 (July 16, 1967) | 45,890 (July  4, 1973) |
| N. York | 73,205 (April 19, 1931) | 81,841 (May  30, 1938) | 74,747 (May  26, 1947) |
| Oakland | 48,758 (June  6, 1970) | 33,477 (June 27, 1971) | 47,741 (June 12, 1972) |
| Phila. | 37,534 (May  16, 1937) | 38,800 (July 13, 1931) | 37,383 (June 27, 1947) |
| St. Louis | 34,625 (Oct.  1, 1944) | 31,932 (June 27, 1928) | 22,847 (May  24, 1940) |
| Seattle | 21,900 (Aug.  3, 1969) | 18,147 (June 20, 1969) | 20,490 (May  28, 1969) |
| Texas | 20,598 (April 12, 1975) | 16,207 (May  29, 1972) | 39,269 (June  1, 1974) |
| §Wash. | 31,728 (April 19, 1948) | 35,563 (July  4, 1936) | 30,701 (June 17, 1947) |
| †Wash. | 45,125 (April  7, 1969) | 40,359 (June 14, 1964) | 30,421 (July 31, 1962) |

(a) two day games.

Largest all-time twilight-night doubleheader attendance, 62,355 (New York at Cleveland), Tuesday, July 15, 1947. Twilight game, Sunday, July 4, 1971, attendance 44,631, Oakland at California.

Twilight-night doubleheader attendance, 18,147 (Kansas City at Seattle), Friday, June 20, 1969.

Twilight-night doubleheader attendance, 25,610, California at Texas, Thursday, July 27, 1973.

Twilight-night doubleheader attendance, 26,169, California at Texas, Friday, June 21, 1974.

†Washington second club. §Washington original club (now Minnesota). ‡Former Kansas City club (now Oakland). ●Present Kansas City club.

## NATIONAL LEAGUE

| Club | Single Day Game | (a) Doubleheader | Night Game |
|---|---|---|---|
| Atlanta | 51,275 (June 26, 1966) | 46,489 (July  18, 1971) | 53,775 (April  8, 1974) |
| Boston | 41,527 (Aug.  8, 1948) | 47,123 (May  22, 1932) | 39,549 (Aug.  5, 1946) |
| Br'klyn | 37,512 (Aug. 30, 1947) | 41,209 (May  30, 1934) | 35,583 (Sept. 24, 1949) |
| Chicago | 46,572 (May  18, 1947) | 46,965 (May  31, 1948) | No lights |
| Cinn. | 52,526 (April  7, 1975) | 52,147 (June 23, 1974) | 52,315 (Sept. 15, 1973) |
| Houston | 49,442 (Sept.  5, 1965) | 42,648 (June 20, 1965) | 50,908 (June 22, 1966) |
| Los Ang. | 78,672 (April 18, 1958) | 53,856 (July  7, 1963) | 67,550 (April 12, 1960) |
| Milw. | 48,642 (Sept. 27, 1959) | 47,604 (Sept.  3, 1956) | 46,944 (Aug. 27, 1954) |
| Mont. | 34,331 (Sept. 15, 1973) | 30,416 (July  7, 1974) | 28,536 (Aug. 20, 1969) |
| ‡N. York | 54,922 (April 20, 1941) | 60,747 (May  31, 1937) | 51,790 (May  27, 1947) |
| §N. York | 56,738 (June 23, 1968) | 57,175 (June 13, 1965) | 56,658 (May  13, 1966) |
| Phila. | 60,120 (May  6, 1973) | 40,720 (May  11, 1947) | 58,294 (July  6, 1973) |
| Pitts. | 50,469 (Sept. 27, 1970) | 48,230 (July 18, 1971) | 48,846 (July  16, 1970) |
| St. Louis | 50,548 (Sept. 14, 1975) | 49,743 (June 23, 1968) | 49,093 (Aug. 12, 1967) |
| S. Diego | 32,176 (June 22, 1975) | 25,995 (April 27, 1975) | 49,618 (July  5, 1975) |
| S. Fran. | 44,256 (Sept.  1, 1973) | 42,787 (July  7, 1963) | 42,647 (Aug. 26, 1970) |

(a) two day games.

Largest all-time twilight-night doubleheader attendance, 72,140 (Cincinnati at Los Angeles), Wednesday, August 16, 1961. Twilight-night doubleheader attendance, St. Louis at Montreal, 28,819, June 25, 1969.

Twilight-night doubleheader attendance, Thursday, July 27, 1972, New York at Pittsburgh, 49,886. Twilight-night doubleheader attendance, Friday, August 3, 1973, Houston at Cincinnati, 52,285.

‡Former New York club (now San Francisco). §Present New York club.

## AMERICAN LEAGUE ALL-TIME CLUB SEASON RECORD

| Club | Home | Year | Finished | Road | Year | Finished |
|---|---|---|---|---|---|---|
| Baltimore | 1,203,366 | 1966 | First | 1,312,337 | 1970 | First(E) |
| Boston | 1,940,788 | 1968 | Fourth | 1,779,936 | 1946 | First |
| California | 1,400,321 | 1966 | Sixth | 976,786 | 1970 | Third(W) |
| Chicago | 1,644,460 | 1960 | Third | 1,280,554 | 1955 | Third |
| Cleveland | 2,620,627 | 1948 | First | 1,762,564 | 1948 | First |
| Detroit | 2,031,847 | 1968 | First | 1,414,126 | 1950 | Second |
| Kansas City‡ | 1,345,341 | 1973 | Second(W) | 1,005,823 | 1973 | Second(W) |
| Kansas City§ | 1,393,054 | 1955 | Sixth | 938,214 | 1967 | Tenth |
| Milwaukee | 1,213,357 | 1975 | Fifth(E) | 1,136,428 | 1975 | Fifth(E) |
| Minnesota | 1,483,547 | 1967 | Second | 1,325,806 | 1967 | Second |
| New York | 2,373,901 | 1948 | Third | 2,216,159 | 1962 | First |
| Oakland | 1,075,518 | 1975 | First(W) | 1,526,630 | 1974 | First(W) |
| Philadelphia | 945,076 | 1948 | Fourth | 1,562,360 | 1948 | Fourth |
| St. Louis | 712,918 | 1922 | Second | 1,170,349 | 1948 | Sixth |
| Seattle | 677,944 | 1969 | Sixth(W) | 889,578 | 1969 | Sixth(W) |
| Texas | 1,193,902 | 1974 | Second(W) | 921,396 | 1974 | Second(W) |
| Washington* | 1,027,216 | 1946 | Fourth | 1,055,171 | 1948 | Fourth |
| Washington† | 918,106 | 1969 | Fourth(E) | 1,042,638 | 1968 | Tenth |

American League Attendance, Season ......................................................... 11,150,099 in 1948  ( 8-club league)
        11,336,923 in 1967  (10-club league)
        13,433,604 in 1973  (12-club league)

*Original Washington club (now Minnesota). †Second Washington club (now Texas). ‡Present Kansas City club. §Former Kansas City club (now Oakland).

## NATIONAL LEAGUE ALL-TIME CLUB SEASON RECORD

| Club | Home | Year | Finished | Road | Year | Finished |
|---|---|---|---|---|---|---|
| Atlanta | 1,539,801 | 1966 | Fifth | 1,688,970 | 1974 | Third(W) |
| Boston | 1,455,439 | 1948 | First | 1,308,175 | 1947 | Third |
| Brooklyn | 1,807,526 | 1947 | First | 1,863,542 | 1947 | First |
| Chicago | 1,674,993 | 1969 | Second(E) | 1,484,057 | 1970 | Second(E) |
| Cincinnati | 2,315,603 | 1975 | First(W) | 1,694,160 | 1975 | First(W) |
| Houston | 2,151,470 | 1965 | Ninth | 1,261,515 | 1972 | Second(W) |
| Los Angeles | 2,755,184 | 1962 | Second | 2,141,212 | 1966 | First |
| Milwaukee | 2,215,404 | 1957 | First | 1,633,569 | 1959 | Second |
| Montreal | 1,424,683 | 1970 | Sixth(E) | 1,269,163 | 1974 | Fourth(E) |
| New York* | 1,600,793 | 1947 | Fourth | 1,526,727 | 1971 | Third(E)§ |
| New York† | 2,697,479 | 1970 | Third(E) | 1,673,050 | 1970 | Third(E) |
| Philadelphia | 1,909,233 | 1975 | Second(E) | 1,459,482 | 1966 | Fourth |
| Pittsburgh | 1,705,828 | 1960 | First | 1,682,182 | 1975 | First(E) |
| St. Louis | 2,090,145 | 1967 | First | 1,532,595 | 1968 | First |
| San Diego | 1,281,747 | 1975 | Fourth(W) | 1,211,545 | 1971 | Sixth(W) |
| San Francisco | 1,795,356 | 1960 | Fifth | 2,207,530 | 1966 | Second |

National League Attendance, Season ......................................................... 10,684,963 in 1960  ( 8-club league)
        15,015,471 in 1966  (10-club league)
        17,324,857 in 1971  (12-club league)

*Former New York club (now San Francisco). †Present New York club.
§Tied for position.

## OPENING DAY AT HOME

| American League | | | National League | | |
|---|---|---|---|---|---|
| Club | Attendance | Year | Club | Attendance | Year |
| Baltimore | 46,354 | 1954 | Atlanta | *53,775 | 1974 |
| Boston | 35,343 | 1969 | Boston | 25,000 | 1935 |
| California | *31,284 | 1966 | Brooklyn | 34,530 | 1949 |
| Chicago | 43,253 | 1971 | Chicago | 43,824 | 1929 |
| Cleveland | 74,420 | 1973 | Cincinnati | 52,526 | 1975 |
| Detroit | 54,089 | 1971 | Houston | *42,652 | 1965 |
| Kansas City† | 31,895 | 1955 | Los Angeles | 78,672 | 1958 |
| Kansas City‡ | *39,464 | 1973 | Milwaukee | 43,640 | 1955 |
| Milwaukee | 48,160 | 1975 | Montreal | 31,769 | 1975 |
| Minnesota | 24,606 | 1961 | New York† | 54,393 | 1936 |
| New York | 54,826 | 1946 | New York‡ | 52,812 | 1966 |
| Oakland | *47,233 | 1968 | Philadelphia | 55,352 | 1971 |
| Philadelphia | 32,825 | 1927 | Pittsburgh | 51,695 | 1973 |
| St. Louis | 19,561 | 1923 | San Diego | *39,083 | 1974 |
| Seattle | 14,993 | 1969 | St. Louis | *47,568 | 1970 |
| Texas | *28,787 | 1975 | San Francisco | 42,894 | 1965 |
| Washington x | 31,728 | 1948 | | | |
| Washington y | 45,125 | 1969 | | | |

*Night game. †Former club (now Oakland). ‡Present club. xOriginal Washington club (now Minnesota, yWashington second club (now Texas).

# AMERICAN LEAGUE SCHEDULE—EAST

Bold figures denote Sundays
Asterisks * denote night games

Major League All-Star Game at Philadelphia, July 13th
Hall of Fame Game at Cooperstown, N. Y., August 9—New York Mets vs. Milwaukee

| | AT MILWAUKEE | AT DETROIT | AT CLEVELAND | AT BALTIMORE | AT NEW YORK | AT BOSTON |
|---|---|---|---|---|---|---|
| **OAKLAND** | June 11°, 12°, **13** Aug. 16°, 17°, 18° | April 27, 28 July 15°, 16°, 17°, **18** | April 23°, 24, **25** July 19°, 19°, 20° | April 30°, May 1, **2, 2** Aug. 23°, 24° | June 4°. 5. **6, 6** July 21°, 22 | June 8°, 9°, **10**°, Aug. 20°, 21, **22** |
| **CALIFORNIA** | April 23°, 24, **25**, 26 July 19°, 20° | June 11°, 12, **13** Aug. 17°, 18°, 19° | April 30°, May 1, **2, 2** July 21°, 22° | April 27°, 28° July 15°, 16°, 17°, **18** | June 8°, 9°, 10° Aug. 20°, 21°, **22** | June 4°, 5, **6** Aug. 23°, 24°, 25 |
| **TEXAS** | May 4°, 5° July 9°, 10, **11,** 11 | April 23, 24, **25** Aug. 9°, 10°, 11° | April 20, 21 Aug. 13°, 14, **15, 15** | June 7°, 8°, **9** Aug. 27°, 28°, **29** | June 11°, 12°, **13** Aug. 16°, 17°, 18° | May 7°, 8, **9** Aug. 30°, 31°, Sept. 1 |
| **KANSAS CITY** | April 20, 21 Aug. 19°, 20°, 21, **22** | June 14°, 15°, 16° July 9°, 10, 11 | June 18°, 19°, **20** July 9°, 10, 11 Aug. 23°, 24°, 25° | May 7°, 8°, **9** Aug. 30°, 31°, Sept. 1° | April 23°, 24, **25** July 5°, 6°, 7° | May 4°, 5° Aug. 26°, 27°, 28, **29** |
| **MINNESOTA** | May 7°, 8, **9** July 5°, 6°, 7° | May 4°, 5°, 6° Aug. 20°, 21, 22, **22** | June 7°, 8°, 9° Aug. 27°, 28°, **29** | June 4°, 5, **6, 6** Aug. 10°, 11° | April 15, 17, **18** Aug. 23°, 24°, 25° | April 19, 20 July 8°, 9°, 10, **11** |
| **CHICAGO** | June 8°, 9°, 10 Aug. 27°, 28°, **29** | May 7°, 8, **9** Aug. 23°, 24°, 25° | June 11°, 12, **13, 13** Aug. 9°, 11° | May 4°, 5° Aug. 13°, 14°, 14°, **15** | April 20, 21 July 8°, 9°, 10°, **11** | April 15, 17, **18** July 5, 6°, 7 |
| **MILWAUKEE** | | April 13 May 31° June 1°, 1°, 2°, 3° Sept. 3°, 4, **5** | May 21°, 22, **23, 23** June 28°, 29° Sept. 24°, 25°, 26 | May 17°, 18°, 19° July 23°, 24°, 24°, **25** Sept. 28°, 29° | May 24°, 25° June 25°, 26, **27, 27** Sept. 8°, 9°, 10° | May 14°, 15, **16** Aug. 6°, 7, **8** Sept. 21°, 22°, 23 |
| **DETROIT** | June 21°, 22°, 23° July 26°, 27°, 28° Oct. 1°, 2, **3** | | April 10, **11** July 23°, 24, **25, 25** Sept. 27°, 29°, 30° | May 21°, 22°, **23** July 1°, 2° July 31°, Aug. **1** Sept. 14°, 15° | May 11°, 12°, 13° April 2°, 3° Sept. 11, **12, 12,** 13° | May 24°, 25° June 24°, 25°, 26, **27** Sept. 8°, 9°, 10° |
| **CLEVELAND** | May 28°, 29, **30** July 30°, 31°, Aug. **1** Sept. 6, 6, 7° | May 14°, 15, **16** Aug. 6°, 7, 8, **8** Sept. 21°, 22 | | May 24°, 25° June 25°, 26, **27, 27** Sept. 8°, 9°, 10° | May 26°, 27° June 21°, 22°, 23°, 24° Oct. 1°, 2, **3** | April 12, 14 July 26°, 27°, 28°, 29 Sept. 11°, **12,** 13° |
| **BALTIMORE** | May 11°, 12°, 13 Aug. 2°, 2°, 3° Sept. 11°, **12,** 13° | May 26°, 26°, 27° July 3°, **4** July 29°, 30° Sept. 6°, 7° | May 31°, 31°, June 2° Aug. 4°, 5° Sept. 17°, 18, **19, 19** | | May 14°, 15, **16** Aug. 6°, 7, **8** Sept. 21°, 22°, 23° | May 28°, 29°, **30** June 28°, 29°, 30 Oct. 1°, 2, **3** |
| **NEW YORK** | April 8, 10, **11** Aug. 4°, 5 Sept. 17°, 18, **19,** 20° | May 28°, 29, **30** June 28°, 29°, 30° Sept. 24°, 25, **26** | May 17°, 18°, 19° July 1°, 2°, 3°, **4°** Sept. 14°, 15° | April 12°, 13° July 26°, 27°, 28° Sept. 3°, 4°, 4°, **5** | | May 31°, June 1°, 2°, 3° July 30°, 31, Aug. 1 Sept. 28°, 29° |
| **BOSTON** | May 26°, 27 July 1°, 2°, 3°, **4** Sept. 14°, 15°, 16° | May 17°, 18°, 19° Aug. 4°, 5° Sept. 17°, 18, **19,** 20° | May 11°, 12°, 13° Aug. 2°, 3° Sept. 3°, 4°, 4°, **5** | April 9, 10, **11** June 21°, 22°, 23° Sept. 24°, 25°, **26** | May 20°, 21°, 22°, **23** July 23°, 24, **25** Sept. 6°, 7° | |

# AMERICAN LEAGUE SCHEDULE—WEST

Bold figures denote Sundays
Asterisks * denote night games

Major League All-Star Game at Philadelphia, July 13th
Hall of Fame Game at Cooperstown, N. Y., August 9—New York Mets vs. Milwaukee

| | AT OAKLAND | AT CALIFORNIA | AT TEXAS | AT KANSAS CITY | AT MINNESOTA | AT CHICAGO |
|---|---|---|---|---|---|---|
| **OAKLAND** | | April 9*, 10, **11** June 23*, 24* Sept. 3*, 4*, **5,** 6 | April 12*, 13*, 14 June 28*, 29*, 30* Sept. 10*, 11*, **12** | May 19*, 20* July 1*, 2*, 3*, **4** Sept. 21*, 22*, 23* | May 17*, 18* July 30*, 31, Aug. **1, 1,** 2* Sept. 13*, 14 | May 21*, 22, **23, 23** Aug. 3*, 4* Sept. 24*, 25* **26** |
| **CALIFORNIA** | May 10*, 11* Aug. 6*, 7, **8, 8** Oct. 1*, 2, **3** | | May 20*, 21*, 22*, **23** Aug. 3*, 4*, 5* Sept. 13*, 14* | April 13*, 14*, 15* June 25*, 26*, **27** Sept. 7*, 8*, 9* | May 31* June 1*, 2* July 2*, 3, **4, 4** Sept. 25, **26** | May 17*, 18* June 29*, 30*, July 1* Sept. 10*, 11, **12, 12** |
| **TEXAS** | May 14*, 15, **16** June 21*, 22 Sept. 17*, 18, **19, 19** | May 12*, 13* July 24*, 24*, **25** Sept. 20*, 21*, 22*, 23* | | May 17*, 18* July 30*, 31*, Aug. **1*** Sept. 3*, 4*, **5,** 6* | May 28*, 29, **30** July 26*, 27* 28*, 29 Sept. 28, 29 | May 31* June 1*, 2* July 2*, 3, **4, 4** Sept. 15*, 16 |
| **KANSAS CITY** | May 31 June 1*, 2* July 23*, 24, **25** Sept. 27*, 28*, 29* | May 28*, 29*, 29*, **30** July 26*, 27* 28* Sept. 15*, 16* | May 24*, 25*, 26*, 27* June 23*, 24* Sept. 24*, 25* **26** | | May 21*, 22, **23** June 28*, 29*, 30* Sept. 10*, 11, **12** | April 9, **11, 11** Aug. 6*, 7, **8, 8** Sept. 13*, 14 |
| **MINNESOTA** | May 24*, 25*, 26*, 27 June 25*, 26, **27** Sept. 15*, 16* | May 14*, 15*, **15, 16** June 21*, 22 Sept. 17*, 18*, **19** | April 9*, 10*, **11** Aug. 6*, 7*, **8*** Sept. 7*, 8*, 9* | May 10*, 11*, 12* Aug. 3*, 4*, 5* Oct. 1*, 2*, **3** | | May 19*, 20* July 23*, 24, **25, 25** Sept. 21*, 22*, 23* |
| **CHICAGO** | May 28*, 29, **30** July 26*, 27*, 28* Sept. 7*, 8*, 9 | May 24*, 25*, 26*, 27* July 30*, 31*, Aug. **1** Sept. 29*, 30* | May 10*, 11* June 25*, 25*, 26*, **27*** Oct. 1*, 2*, **3** | May 13*, 14*, **15, 16** June 21*, 22* Sept. 17*, 18*, **19** | April 13, 14 June 23*, 23* 24 Sept. 3*, 4, **5,** 6 | |
| **MILWAUKEE** | June 18*, 19, **20** Aug. 10*, 11*, 12* | June 15*, 16*, 17* Aug. 13*, 14*, **15** | April 16*, 17*, **18** Aug. 23*, 24*, 25* | June 4*, 5*, 5*, **6** July 21*, 22* | May 1, **2** Aug. 30*, 31*, Sept. 1*, 2 | April 27*, 28* July 15*, 16*, 17*, **18** |
| **DETROIT** | April 19*, 20*, 21* Aug. 27*, 28, **29** | April 16*, 17, **18** Aug. 30*, 31*, Sept. 1* | June 4*, 5*, **6*** July 5*, 6*, 7* | June 7*, 8*, 9* Aug. 13*, 14*, **15** | June 17*, 18*, 19, **20** July 19*, 20* | April 30*, May 1, **2, 2** July 21*, 22* |
| **CLEVELAND** | May 3*, 4*, 5* July 9*, 10, **11** | May 7*, 8*, **9** July 5*, 6*, 7* | June 15*, 16* Aug. 19*, 20*, 21*, **22*** | April 16*, 17*, **18** Aug. 16*, 17*, 18* | April 27, 28 July 15*, 16*, 17*, **18** | June 4*, 5, **6, 6** Aug. 31*, Sept. 1* |
| **BALTIMORE** | April 17, **18** July 5*, 6*, 7*, 8* | April 19*, 20*, 21* July 9*, 10*, **11** | June 17*, 18*, 19*, **20*** July 21*, 22* | June 10*, 11*, **12, 13** July 19*, 20* | April 24, **25** Aug. 16*, 17*, 18*, 19 | June 15*, 16* Aug. 20*, 21*, **22, 22** |
| **NEW YORK** | May 7*, 8, **9** Aug. 30*, 31*, Sept. 1* | May 4*, 5*, 6* Aug. 27*, 28*, **29** | April 27*, 28* July 15*, 16*, 17*, **18*** | April 30*, May 1*, **2** Aug. 9*, 10*, 11* | June 15*, 16* Aug. 12*, 13*, 14, **15** | June 17* 18*, **19, 20** July 19*, 20* |
| **BOSTON** | June 15*, 16*, 17* Aug. 13*, 14, **15** | June 18*, 19*, **20** Aug. 10*, 11*, 12* | April 29*, 30*, May 1, **2** July 19*, 20* | April 27*, 28* July 15*, 16*, 17*, **18** | June 11*, 12, **13, 14*** July 21*, 22* | April 23*, 24*, **25** Aug. 16*, 17*, 18* |

# NATIONAL LEAGUE SCHEDULE—EAST

Bold figures denote Sundays    Major League All-Star Game at Philadelphia, July 13
Asterisks * denote night games    Hall of Fame Game at Cooperstown, N. Y., August 9—Mets vs. Brewers

| | AT CHICAGO | AT MONTREAL | AT NEW YORK | AT PHILADELPHIA | AT PITTSBURGH | AT ST. LOUIS |
|---|---|---|---|---|---|---|
| **CHICAGO** | | May 18*, 19*, 20* Aug. 5*, 6*, 7*, **8** Sept. 15*, 16 | June 2*, 3 July 2*, 3, **4, 4** Sept. 24*, 25, **26** | May 31, 31 June 1* July 28*, 29 Sept. 9*, 10*, 11*, **12** | May 21*, 22, **23, 23** June 28*, 29*, 30* Sept. 28*, 29* | April 9*, 10, **11** July 22*, 23*, 24*, **25** Sept. 13*, 14* |
| **MONTREAL** | April 19, 20, 21, 22 July 26, 27 Oct. 1, 2, **3** | | April 9, 10, **11** Aug. 2*, 3*, 4 Sept. 27*, 28*, 29* | May 28*, 29*, **30** June 21*, 22* Aug. 17*, 18* Sept. 13*, 14* | May 24*, 25*, 26* July 30*, 31* Aug. 1 Sept. 10*, 11*, **12** | April 17, **18** July 2*, 3*, **4,** 28*, 28*, Sept. 8*, 9* |
| **NEW YORK** | April 13, 14, 15 June 25, 26, **27** Sept. 6, 7, 8 | May 21*, 22*, **23** July 23*, 24*, **25** Sept. 21*, 22*, 23* | | May 24*, 25*, 26*, 27* July 26*, 27* Oct. 1*, 2*, **3** | April 16*, 17, **18** Aug. 5*, 6*, 7*, **8** Sept. 13*, 14* | April 19*, 20*, 21 June 21*, 22*, **23** Sept. 10*, 11, **12** |
| **PHILADELPHIA** | April 17, **18** Aug. 2, 3, 3, 4 Sept. 17, 18, **19** | April 14, 15 June 28*, 29*, 30* July 1* Sept. 24*, 25, **26** | May 18*, 19*, 20 July 30*, 31 Aug. 1 Sept. 3*, 4, **5** | | April 20, 21 July 2*, 3, **4, 4** Sept. 6, 6, 8* | June 2*, 3* Aug. 5*, 6*, 7, **8** Sept. 27*, 28*, 29* |
| **PITTSBURGH** | May 28, 29, **30** June 22, 23, 24 Sept. 21, 22, 23 | June 2*, 3*, 25*, 26*, **27** Sept. 3*, 3*, 4*, **5** | May 31, 31 June 1* July 28*, 29 Sept. 17*, 18, **19,** 20 | April 10, **11** July 22*, 23*, 24*, **24*, 25** Sept. 15*, 16* | | May 17*, 18*, 19*, 20 July 26*, 27* Sept. 24*, 25, **26** |
| **ST. LOUIS** | May 25, 26, 27 July 30, 31 Aug. **1** Sept. 3, 4, **5** | May 31*, 31* June 1* Sept. 6*, 7*, 17*, 18, **19, 19** | May 28*, 29*, **30** June 28*, 29*, 30* July 1 Sept. 15*, 16* | May 21*, 22*, **23** June 25*, 26*, **27** Sept. 21*, 22*, 23* | April 13, 15 Aug. 2*, 3*, 3*, 4* Oct. 1, 2, **3** | |
| **ATLANTA** | June 8, 9, 10 Aug. 27, 28, **29** | June 4*, 5*, **6** July 20*, 21*, 22* | April 26, 27, 28, 29 July **18,** 19* | April 23*, 24* **25** Aug. 10*, 11*, 12* | May 7*, 8, **9** July 15*, 16*, 17 | June 14*, 15*, 16* Aug. 20*, 21*, **22** |
| **CINCINNATI** | May 7, 8, **9** Aug. 10, 11, 12 | April 23, 24, **25** July 5*, 6*, 7* | May 4*, 5*, 6 Aug. 13*, 14, **15** | April 26*, 27*, 28* June 18*, 19*, 20 | June 7*, 8*, 9*, 10* July **18,** 19* | June 4*, 5*, **6** Aug. 30*, 31* Sept. 1* |
| **HOUSTON** | June 11, 12, **13** Aug. 24, 25, 26 | April 26, 27, 28, 29 July **18*,** 19* | April 30* May 1, **2** July 15*, 16*, 17 | May 4*, **5** Aug. 19*, 20*, 21*, **22** | June 18*, 19, **20, 20** July 20*, 21* | May 7*, 8*, **9** Aug. 9*, 10*, 11* |
| **LOS ANGELES** | May 4, 5, 6 Aug. 13, 14, **15** | June 18*, 19, **20** Aug. 31* Sept. 1*, 2* | June 15*, 16*, 17* Aug. 27*, 28, **29** | May 7*, 8*, **9** July 5*, 6*, 7* | May 14*, 15, **16** Aug. 9*, 10*, 11* | May 10*, 11*, 12 July 9*, 10*, **11** |
| **SAN DIEGO** | May 14, 15, **16** July 5, 6, 7 | May 4*, 5*, 6* Aug. 13*, 14,* **15** | May 7*, 8, **9** Aug. 10*, 11*, 12 | May 11*, 12* July 9*, 10*, 10*, **11** | June 4*, 5*, **6** Aug. 31* Sept. 1*, 2* | June 18*, 19*, **20** Aug. 16*, 17*, 18* |
| **SAN FRANCISCO** | May 11, 12, **13** July 9, 10, **11** | May 7*, 8, **9** Aug. 9*, 10*, 11* | June 18*, 19, **20** Aug. 31* Sept. 1*, 2 | June 15*, 16*, 17* Aug. 13*, 14*, **15** | May 4*, 5*, 6* Aug. 27*, 28*, **29** | May 14*, 15*, **16** July 5, 6*, 7* |

# NATIONAL LEAGUE SCHEDULE—WEST

Bold figures denote Sundays
Asterisks * denote night games

Major League All-Star Game at Philadelphia, July 13
Hall of Fame Game at Cooperstown, N. Y., August 9—Mets vs. Brewers

| | AT ATLANTA | AT CINCINNATI | AT HOUSTON | AT LOS ANGELES | AT SAN DIEGO | AT SAN FRANCISCO |
|---|---|---|---|---|---|---|
| **CHICAGO** | June 18*, 19*, 19*, **20** Aug. 31* Sept. 1 * | June 14*, 15*, 16 Aug. 20*, 21*, **22** | June 4*, 5*, **6, 6** Aug. 16*, 17* | April 23*, 24*, **25** July 15*, 16*, 17 | April 26*, 27*, 28*, 29 July **18**, 19* | Aoril 30* May 1, **2, 2** July 20*, 21 |
| **MONTREAL** | May14 *, 15*, 15*, **16** June 23*, 24* | April 30* May 1*, **2** July 15*, 16*, 17* | May 11*, 12* July 8*, 9*, 10*, **11** | June 11*, 12*, **13** Aug. 23*, 24*, **25*** | June 14*, 15*, 16 Aug. 27*, 28*, **29** | June 8*, 9, 10 Aug. 20*, 21, **22** |
| **NEW YORK** | May 11*, 12* July 8*, 9*, 10* **11** | May 14*, 15*, **16, 16** July 20*, 21* | April 23*, 24*, **25** July 5*, 6*, 7* | June 4*, 5*, **6** Aug. 17*, 18*, 19* | June 7*, 8*, 9*, 10* Aug. 20*, **22** | June 11*, 12, **13, 13** Aug. 24*, 25 |
| **PHILADELPHIA** | April 30* May 1*, **2** Aug. 23*, 24*, **25*** | June 23*, 24* Aug. 26*, 27*, 28, **29** | May 14*, 15*, **16** Aug. 30*, 31* Sept. 1* | June 7*, 8*, 9*, 10* July **18**, 19* | June 11*, 12*, **13, 13** July 20*, 21 | June 4*, 5, **6** July 15, 16*, 17 |
| **PITTSBURGH** | June 11*, 12*, **13** July 5*, 6*, 7* | May 11*, 12* July 9*, 9*, 10, **11** | June 14*, 15*, 16* Aug. 13*, 14, **15** | April 26*, 27*, 28* Aug. 20*, 21*, **22** | April 30* May 1*, **2** Aug. 23*, 24*, **25*** | April 23*, 24, **25** Aug. 17*, 18, 19 |
| **ST. LOUIS** | May 4*, 5*, **6** Aug. 13*, 14*, **15** | June 11*, 12*, **13, 13** Aug. 23*, 24* | June 7* ,8*, 9* Aug. 27*, 28, **29** | April 29*, 30* May 1*, **2** July 20*, 21 | April 23*, 24*, **25** July 15*, 16*, 17 | April 26*, 27*, 28 July **18, 18**, 19 |
| **ATLANTA** | | May 25*, 26 Aug. 16*, 17*, 18*, 19* Oct. 1*, 2, **3** | May 17*, 17*, 18* July 30*, 31*, 31* Aug. **1** Sept. 21*, 22* | May 19*, 20* June 28*, 29*, 30* Sept. 10*, 11*, 11*, **12** | April 9*, 10* **11** June 25*, 26,* 26*, **27** Sept. 8* 9* | May 21*, 22, **23, 23** July 2*, 3, **4** Sept. 6, 7* |
| **CINCINNATI** | April 13*, 15* July 23*, 24,* 24*, **25** Sept. 3*, 4*, **5** | | May 31* June 1*, 2*, 3*, 25*, 26*, **27** Sept. 8*, 9* | May 17*, 18* Aug. 5*, 6*, 7*, **8** Sept. 24*, 25, **26** | May 21*, 22*, **23** June 28*, 29*, 30* Sept. 27*, 28*, 29* | May 19*, 20 Aug. 2*, 3*, 4 Sept. 10*, 11, **12, 12** |
| **HOUSTON** | May 28*, 29*, **30, 30** June 21*, 22* Sept. 14*, 15*, 16* | April 8, 10, **11** July 2*, 2*, 3*, **4** Sept. 6*, 7* | | May 21*, 22*, **23** Aug 2*, 3*, 4* Sept. 27*, 28*, 29* | May 19*, 20 Aug. 5*, 6*, 7*, **8** Sept. 10*, 10*, 11* | May 24*, 25*, 26 June 28, 29*, 30 Sept. 24*, 25, **26** |
| **LOS ANGELES** | April 16*, 17*, **18** July 26*, 27*, 28* Sept. 17*, 18*, **19** | May 28*, 29, **30, 30** June 21*, 22* Sept. 14*, 15*, 16* | April 19*, 20*, 21*, 22* June 23*, 24* Sept. 3*, 4*, **5** | | May 24*, 25*, 26* July 1*, 2*, 24*, **25** Sept. 6*, 7* | April 9, 10, **11** July 30*, 31 Aug. **1** Sept. 21*, 22*, 23* |
| **SAN DIEGO** | May 31* June 1*, 2* Aug. 2*, 3*, 4 Sept. 24*, 25,* **26** | April 20*, 21 July 29*, 30*, 30*, 31* Aug. **1** Sept. 21*, 22* | April 16*, 17*, **18, 18** July 26*, 27*, 28* Sept. 18*, **19** | April 12*, 13*, **14** July 3*, **4,** 22*, **23** Oct. 1*, **3** | | May 17*, 18 June 23*, 23*, 24 Sept. 3*, 4, **5, 5** |
| **SAN FRANCISCO** | April 20*, 21* Aug. 5*, 6*, 7*, **8, 8** Sept. 28*, 29* | April 16*, 17, 18 July 26*, 27*, 28* Sept. 17*, 18*, **19** | April 12*, 13,* **14** July 23*, 24*, 24*, **25** Oct. 1* 2 | May 31* June 1*, 2*, 3*, 25*, 26*, **27** Sept. 8*, 9* | May 27*, 28*, 29* **30** June 21*, 22* Sept. 13*, 14*, 15* | |

## Major League Baseball Players Association

375 Park Avenue, New York, N. Y. 10022
Telephone—752-0940 (area code 212)

Marvin J. Miller—Executive Director
Richard M. Moss—General Counsel
Secretarial Staff—Sue Carr and Marlene Widrow

### EXECUTIVE BOARD

Brooks Robinson—American League Representative
Joe Torre—National League Representative
Tom Seaver—Pension Committee
Plus all remaining player representatives

### NATIONAL LEAGUE PLAYER REPRESENTATIVES

Carl Morton—Atlanta Braves
Rick Monday—Chicago Cubs
Bill Plummer—Cincinnati Reds
Bob Watson—Houston Astros
Mike Marshall—Los Angeles Dodgers
Steve Renko—Montreal Expos
Tom Seaver—New York Mets
Bob Boone—Philadelphia Phillies
Jerry Reuss—Pittsburgh Pirates
Lou Brock—St. Louis Cardinals
Willie McCovey—San Diego Padres
Jim Barr—San Francisco Giants

### AMERICAN LEAGUE PLAYER REPRESENTATIVES

Brooks Robinson—Baltimore Orioles
Bill Lee—Boston Red Sox
Andy Etchebarren—California Angels
Pete Varney—Chicago White Sox
Tom Buskey—Cleveland Indians
Joe Coleman—Detroit Tigers
Steve Busby—Kansas City Royals
Mike Hegan—Milwaukee Brewers
Bert Blyleven—Minnesota Twins
Larry Gura, New York Yankees
Sal Bando—Oakland Athletics
Bill Singer—Texas Rangers

# Index to Minor League Clubs, Cities

# Index to Contents

## AMERICAN LEAGUE

## NATIONAL LEAGUE

### 1975 Game Scores

### 1975 Game Scores

## NATIONAL ASSOCIATION (MINOR LEAGUE) AVERAGES

# NOTES

# NOTES